1968	1970	1972	1974	1975	1976	1977	1978	1979	1980	1981	1982	1983	1984
132.0	137.1	144.1	150.1	153.2	156.2	159.0	161.9	164.9	167.7	170.1	172.3	174.2	176.4
78.7	82.8	87.0	91.9	93.8	96.2	99.0	102.3	105.0	106.9	108.7	110.2	111.6	113.5
59.6	60.4	60.4	61.3	61.2	61.6	62.3	63.2	63.7	63.8	63.9	64.0	64.0	64.4
80.1	79.7	78.9	78.7	77.9	77.5	77.7	77.9	77.8	77.4	77.0	76.6	76.4	76.4
41.6	43.3	43.9	45.7	46.3	47.3	48.4	50.0	50.9	51.5	52.1	52.6	52.9	53.6
59.3	60.2	60.4	61.4	61.5	61.8	62.5	63.3	63.9	64.1	64.3	64.3	64.3	64.6
62.2	61.8	60.2	60.3	59.6	59.8	60.4	62.2	62.2	61.7	61.3	61.6	62.1	62.6
75.9	78.7	82.2	86.8	85.8	88.8	92.0	96.0	98.8	99.3	100.4	99.5	100.8	105.0
2.8	4.1	4.9	5.2	7.9	7.4	7.0	6.2	6.1	7.6	8.3	10.7	10.7	8.5
3.6	4.9	5.6	5.6	8.5	7.7	7.1	6.1	5.8	7.1	7.6	9.7	9.6	7.5
2.9	4.4	5.0	4.9	7.9	7.1	6.3	5.3	5.1	6.9	7.4	9.9	9.9	7.4
4.8	5.9	6.6	6.7	9.3	8.6	8.2	7.2	6.8	7.4	7.9	9.4	9.2	7.6
3.2	4.5	5.1	5.0	7.8	7.0	6.2	5.2	5.1	6.3	6.7	8.6	8.4	6.5
6.7	8.2	10.0	9.9	13.8	13.1	13.1	11.9	11.3	13.1	14.2	17.3	17.8	14.4
12.7	15.3	16.2	16.0	19.9	19.0	17.8	16.4	16.1	17.8	19.6	23.2	122.4	18.9
3.02	3.4	3.9	4.43	4.73	5.06	5.44	5.88	6.34	6.85	7.44	7.87	8.2	8.49
37.7	37	36.9	36.4	36	36.1	35.9	35.8	35.6	35.2	35.2	34.7	34.9	35.1
315	313	332	315	305	310	311	311	299	282	278	273	278	280
1.3	−1.3	4.3	−5.0	−3.1	1.5	0.4	0.0	−3.7	−5.9	−1.4	−1.7	1.7	0.6
1.60	1.60	1.60	2.00	2.10	2.30	2.30	2.65	2.90	3.10	3.35	3.35	3.35	3.35
3.4	2.0	3.2	−1.6	3.5	3.1	1.7	1.1	0.0	−0.2	2.1	−0.8	3.6	2.7
3.7	1.9	3.0	−1.3	1.0	2.7	1.4	1.7	0.3	−0.2	0.2	1.2	0.0	0.4
4.5	5.6	3	11.4	6.5	5.3	6.2	7.5	9.8	11	7.4	8.1	0.6	1.7
18.9	21.2	21.7	22.8	22.4	22.7	22.5	22.8	22.6	22.4	na	19.8	17.7	17.3
26.9	26.1	25.5	24.9	24.6	23.9	23.1	22.6	23.4	22.2	21.4	20.7	19.7	18.4
392	381	250	424	235	231	298	219	235	187	145	96	81	62
.20	.29	.09	.16	.09	.12	.10	.11	.09	.09	.07	.04	.08	.04
63.7	66.3	65.3	66.4	65.6	65.7	65.6	65.9	66.7	67.7	66.6	67.2	66.2	64.8

eDays idle in strikes involving 1,000 or more workers divided by total estimated working time

Contemporary Labor Economics

Eighth Edition

Campbell R. McConnell
University of Nebraska

Stanley L. Brue
Pacific Lutheran University

David A. Macpherson
Florida State University

McGraw-Hill
Higher Education

Boston   Burr Ridge, IL   Dubuque, IA   New York   San Francisco   St. Louis
Bangkok   Bogotá   Caracas   Kuala Lumpur   Lisbon   London   Madrid   Mexico City
Milan   Montreal   New Delhi   Santiago   Seoul   Singapore   Sydney   Taipei   Toronto

McGraw-Hill
Higher Education

CONTEMPORARY LABOR ECONOMICS
Published by McGraw-Hill/Irwin, a business unit of The McGraw-Hill Companies, Inc., 1221
Avenue of the Americas, New York, NY, 10020. Copyright © 2009 by The McGraw-Hill
Companies, Inc. All rights reserved. No part of this publication may be reproduced or distributed
in any form or by any means, or stored in a database or retrieval system, without the prior written
consent of The McGraw-Hill Companies, Inc., including, but not limited to, in any network or
other electronic storage of transmission, or broadcast for distance learning.

Some ancillaries, including electronic and print components, may not be available to customers
outside the United States.

This book is printed on acid-free paper.

1 2 3 4 5 6 7 8 9 0 DOC/DOC 0 9 8 7

ISBN   978-0-07-351132-0
MHID   0-07-351132-3

Executive editor: *Douglas Reiner*
Editorial coordinator: *Elizabeth Clevenger*
Associate marketing manager: *Kelly Odom*
Project manager: *Bruce Gin*
Production supervisor: *Gina Hangos*
Lead designer: *Matthew Baldwin*
Lead media project manager: *Cathy L. Tepper*
Cover design: *Matthew Baldwin*
Cover image: *© Getty Images*
Typeface: *10/12 Times New Roman*
Compositor: *Aptara, Inc.*
Printer: *R. R. Donnelley*

Library of Congress Cataloging-in-Publication Data

McConnell, Campbell R.
    Contemporary labor economics / Campbell R. McConnell, Stanley L. Brue,
David A. Macpherson. — 8th ed.
        p. cm.
    Includes index.
    ISBN-13: 978-0-07-351132-0 (alk. paper)
    ISBN-10: 0-07-351132-3 (alk. paper)
    1. Labor economics. I. Brue, Stanley L., 1945- II. Macpherson, David A., 1960-
III. Title.
HD4901.M15 2008
331—dc22

                                                                            2007026353

www.mhhe.com

About the Authors

Campbell R. McConnell earned his PhD from the University of Iowa after receiving degrees from Cornell College and the University of Illinois. He taught at the University of Nebraska–Lincoln from 1953 until his retirement in 1990. He is also the coauthor of *Economics* (McGraw-Hill/Irwin), currently in its 17th edition and the leading introductory economics textbook. He has also edited readers for the principles and labor economics courses. He is a recipient of both the University of Nebraska Distinguished Teaching Award and the James A. Lake Academic Freedom Award and is past president of the Midwest Economics Association. His primary areas of interest are labor economics and economic education. He has an impressive collection of jazz recordings and enjoys reading jazz history.

Stanley L. Brue did his undergraduate work at Augustana College (SD) and received its Distinguished Achievement Award in 1991. He received his PhD from the University of Nebraska–Lincoln. He is a professor at Pacific Lutheran University, where he has been honored as recipient of the Burlington Northern Faculty Achievement Award. He has also received the national Leavey Award for excellence in economic education. Professor Brue has served as national president and chair of the Board of Trustees of Omicron Delta Epsilon International Economics Honorary. He is coauthor of *Economic Scenes,* 5/e (Prentice-Hall), *Economics,* 17/e (McGraw-Hill/Irwin), *The Evolution of Economic Thought,* 7/e (South-Western), and *Essentials of Economics,* 1/e (McGraw-Hill/Irwin). For relaxation, he enjoys international travel, attending sporting events, and skiing with family and friends.

David A. Macpherson received his undergraduate degree and PhD from The Pennsylvania State University. He is the Rod and Hope Brim Eminent Scholar of Economics and director of the Pepper Institute on Aging and Public Policy at Florida State University, where he has received two universitywide awards for teaching excellence. Professor Macpherson is the author of many articles in leading labor economics and industrial relations journals, including the *Journal of Labor Economics, Industrial and Labor Relations Review,* and the *Journal of Human Resources.* He is coauthor of the annual *Union Membership and Earnings Data Book: Compilations from the Current Population Survey,* published by the Bureau of National Affairs. He is also coauthor of *Pensions and Productivity* and *Economics: Private and Public Choice,* 11/e. His specialty is applied labor economics. His current research interests include pensions, discrimination, industry deregulation, labor unions, and the minimum wage. He enjoys listening to classic rock, seeing movies and plays, playing sports with his sons, and going to the seashore with his family.

Preface

BACKGROUND AND PURPOSE

One benefit of authoring a text that has met the test of the market is the opportunity to revise. Revision provides for improvement—to delete the archaic and install the novel, to rectify errors of omission or commission, to rewrite misleading or obscure statements, to introduce more relevant illustrations, to bring more recent data to bear, to upgrade organizational structure, and to enhance pedagogical aids—in short, to build on an accepted framework of ideas. We feel that those who examine this new eighth edition of *Contemporary Labor Economics* will agree that we have fully exploited this opportunity.

Our basic purpose remains that of presenting the content of the "new" labor economics in a logical and readable fashion. While such traditional topics as labor law, the structure of unions, and collective bargaining have not been entirely crowded out, our focus is clearly on labor economics as an applied field of micro and macro theory. This volume is based on the assumption that labor economics is no longer an area tangential to the core of analytical economics but rather a critical component of that core.

The level of analysis is tailored for the undergraduate student who has completed a standard sequence on macro and micro principles. The book is designed for a one-semester or one-quarter course, although appropriate supplementation can make it usable as the focal point of a two-semester course.

THE EIGHTH EDITION

This new edition incorporates many significant changes, several of which were motivated by the comments of colleagues and students. We are especially grateful to the scholars cited in the acknowledgments who provided reviews of the various editions or commented on drafts of the new edition.

The most visible and significant modifications and additions to *Contemporary Labor Economics* are these:

- **Public policy issues:** This edition includes a number of new discussions of public policy issues, including illegal aliens, human trafficking, union bargaining power, private military companies, the gender wage gap, unemployment benefits, and participant direction in pension plans.

- **Continuing and expanded emphasis on global aspects of U.S. labor markets:** The text's integrated focus on global aspects of U.S. labor markets has continued and been expanded with this edition. For example, this edition includes new World of Work boxes on human trafficking (Chapter 9), illegal aliens (Chapter 9), and the Danish flexicurity labor market model (Chapter 18). These new World of Work boxes join existing discussions of comparative advantage and international trade (Chapter 5), outsourcing (Chapter 5), trade liberalization and labor standards (Chapter 6), NAFTA (Chapter 6), international pay differences (Chapter 8), international differences in the gender pay gap (Chapter 14), and cross-country differences in intergenerational earnings mobility (Chapter 16). Also, each chapter includes Global Perspectives boxes that provide international comparison in various topics.

- **New World of Work sections:** Fourteen of the World of Work boxes are new to this edition. The new titles to this edition are More Flexible Work Schedules; The Power of the Pill; Time Stress; Reversal of the College Gender Gap; Do Medical Students Know How Much Doctors Earn?; Participant Direction in Pension Plans; Do Former College Athletes Earn More Than Nonathletes?; Human Trafficking; What Jobs Do Illegal Aliens Hold?; A Divorce in the Union Movement; The Highest-Paid Blue-Collar Workers; Private Military Companies; The Gender Pay Gap: Slowing Convergence; and the Danish Flexicurity Model.

ORGANIZATION AND CONTENT

The subject matter in this book generally proceeds from micro to macro topics. Figure 1.1 and the "Overview" section of Chapter 1 outline the organizational framework in some detail. Thus we simply call your attention to the figure here; we trust that Figure 1.1 and its accompanying discussion will clearly express our organizational approach. We recognize that other chapter orderings are possible and in fact may be optimal for many professors. Also, our bias has been to be inclusive in our presentation of topics. Professors can easily overcome this bias by selecting chapters for their own classes.

DISTINGUISHING FEATURES

At the hazard of immodesty, we feel that this volume embodies a number of features that distinguish it from other books in the field.

Content

In the area of subject matter, the emphasis in Chapter 6 and elsewhere on allocative efficiency is both unique and desirable. The efficiency emphasis makes students realize that *society* has an interest in how labor markets function. Chapter 7 brings together the literature on the principal–agent problem and the "new economics of personnel" in a single, focused chapter. Chapter 8 on the wage structure has been consistently praised by instructors for providing a thorough, systematic treatment of wage differentials and a simplified presentation of the hedonic wage theory. The comprehensive analysis of the impacts of unions and government on labor markets found in Chapters 10–13 also sets this book apart.

Chapter 14 provides extensive analysis of labor market discrimination and antidiscrimination policies. Chapter 15 discusses job search within and outside the firm. Chapter 16 confines its focus almost entirely to the distribution of personal *earnings,* rather than the usual discussion of the distribution of *income* and the poverty problem. We believe this approach is more relevant for a textbook on *labor* economics. The critical topic of labor productivity has been largely ignored or treated in a piecemeal fashion in other books. We have upgraded this topic by according it extensive treatment in Chapter 17. Chapter 18 looks at employment and unemployment through a stock–flow perspective and uses the aggregate demand–aggregate supply model to examine natural versus cyclic unemployment. Finally, the appendix provides a comprehensive discussion of information sources that can be used to widen and deepen the reader's understanding of the field.

Organization and Presentation

We have put great stress on the logical organization of subject matter, not only chapter by chapter but within each chapter. We have sought to develop the subject matter logically from micro to macro, from simple theory to real-world complications, and from analysis to policy. Similarly, considerable time has been spent in seeking the optimal arrangement of topics within each chapter. Chapter subheadings have been used liberally; our feeling is that the student should always be aware of the organizational structure and directional flow of the subject matter.

Many key topics of labor economics will be intellectually challenging for most students. We have tried not to impair student understanding with clumsy or oblique exposition. Our purpose is to communicate effectively with students. To this end we have taken great care that our writing be clear, direct, and uncluttered. It is our goal that the material contained herein be highly accessible to the typical college undergraduate who has limited training in economics.

Pedagogical Features

We have included a variety of pedagogical devices that instructors tell us significantly contribute to student understanding. First, the introduction of each chapter states the goals of the chapter and, in many cases, relates the chapter to prior or future chapters. Second, end-of-chapter summaries provide a concise, point-by-point recapitulation of each chapter. Third, key terms and concepts are highlighted at the end of each chapter, and a comprehensive glossary of these and other terms is located at the end of the book. Fourth, ample lists of questions are provided at the end of each chapter. These range from open-ended discussion questions to numerical problems that let students test their understanding of basic analytical concepts. Fifth, each chapter includes one or two Internet exercises and links that help students increase their understanding of the material as well as obtain the most current data available. Sixth, we have used the inside covers of the book to present relevant historical statistics that are valuable to both students and instructors. Seventh, the within-chapter "Quick Review" summaries and "Your Turn" questions should help students identify key points and study for exams. Furthermore, as indicated previously, the appendix of the book lists and discusses ways the interested reader can update statistical materials found in the book and continue the learning process beyond the course. Finally, we have included 72 short "World of Work" minireadings in this edition.

Instructor's Manual

Contemporary Labor Economics is accompanied by a comprehensive Instructor's Manual by Norris Peterson of Pacific Lutheran University. Among other features, it contains chapter outlines and learning objectives, and answers to end-of-chapter text questions.

Test Bank

The eighth edition is accompanied by a Test Bank, also written by Norris Peterson. The Test Bank is available in Word format and through EZ Test Online, McGraw-Hill's computerized test bank program.

PowerPoint Slides

An extensive set of PowerPoint slides is available for each chapter. These slides, which highlight the main points of each chapter using animation, are available at the text's Online Learning Center.

Web Site

A new Web site, **www.mhhe.com/mcconnellCLE8e.com,** contains the entire supplementary package for instructors and students. Instructors can access the Test Bank and Instructor's Manual in the password-protected portion of the site while the PowerPoint presentations, interactive quizzes, updated data, links to relevant Web sites, and a Digital Image Library containing all of the text's table and graphs, can be viewed by students and instructors alike.

Acknowledgments

We would like to express our thanks for the many useful comments and suggestions provided by colleagues who reviewed previous editions of this text during the development stage:

Neil Alper
Northeastern University

John Antel
University of Houston

Martin Asher
Villanova University

Peter S. Barth
University of Connecticut–Storrs

Clive Bull
New York University

Don Bruce
University of Tennessee

Robert Catlett
Emporia State University

David H. Ciscel
Memphis State University

Vito Colapietro
William Jewell College

John Conant
Indiana State

Michael J. Dinoto
University of Idaho

Arthur Dobbelaere
Loyola University

Peter B. Doeringer
Boston University

Roger Frantz
San Diego State University

Scott Fuess, Jr.
University of Nebraska–Lincoln

Robert Gitter
Ohio Wesleyan University

Lonnie M. Golden
University of Wisconsin

Daphne Greenwood
University of Colorado at Colorado Springs

Richard Hansen
Southeast Missouri State University

Michael D. Harsh
Randolph–Macon College

Julia Heath
Memphis State University

Jack Hou
California State University–Long Beach

David Huffman
Bridgewater College

Ronald S. Warren, Jr.
University of Georgia

Carl P. Kaiser
Washington and Lee University

Douglas Kruse
Rutgers University

Julia Lane
University of Louisville

Kevin Lang
Boston University

Laura Leete
Case Western Reserve University

Robert I. Lerman
The Urban Institute

Eng Seng Loh
Kent State University

John Marcis
Virginia Commonwealth University

J. Peter Mattila
Iowa State University

Eric Nilsson
California State University–San Bernardino

John F. O'Connell
Holy Cross

Norris Peterson
Pacific Lutheran University

Jerry Petr
University of Nebraska–Lincoln

Bruce Pietrykowski
University of Michigan–Dearborn

Douglas Romrell
Utah State University

Blair Ruble
Social Sciences Research Council

Timothy Schibik
University of Southern Indiana

Robert Simonson
Mankato State University

Patricia Simpson
Loyola University

Larry Singell
University of Oregon

Russell Snyder
Eastern Washington University

Steven Stern
University of Virginia

Chris Swann
SUNY–Stoney Brook

Wade Thomas
Ithaca College

William Torrence
University of Nebraska–Lincoln

Thomas A. Webb
South-Western College

Bill Wilkes
Athens State University

The eighth edition has benefited from the critiques and suggestions of

Greg Delemeester
Marietta College

William D. Ferguson
Grinnell College

Melanie Fox Kean
Austin College

Mark Pernecky
St. Olaf College

Bill Wilkes
Athens State University

We are also greatly indebted to the many professionals at Irwin/McGraw-Hill—in particular, Beth Clevenger, Bruce Gin, Gina Hargos, Matt Baldwin, Kelly Odom, Douglas Reiner, and Cathy Tepper—for their expertise in the production and marketing of this book.

Campbell R. McConnell

Stanley L. Brue

David A. Macpherson

Contents

Chapter 9
Mobility, Migration, and Efficiency   275

Chapter 10
Labor Unions and Collective Bargaining   305

Chapter 11
The Economic Impact of Unions   335

Chapter 12
Government and the Labor Market: Employment, Expenditures, and Taxation   368

Labor Economics: Introduction and Overview

The core problem of economics permeates all of its specialized branches or subdivisions. This problem is that productive resources are relatively scarce or limited. Society's material wants—the desires of consumers, businesses, and governmental units for goods and services—exceed our productive capacity. That is, our economic system is incapable of providing all the products and services that individuals and institutions would like to have. Because absolute material abundance is impossible, society must choose what goods and services should be produced, how they should be produced, and who should receive them. *Economics* is concerned with the discovery of rules or principles that indicate how such choices can be rationally and efficiently rendered. Because resources are scarce and wants are virtually unlimited, society needs to manage its resources as efficiently as possible to achieve the maximum fulfillment of its wants. Labor, of course, is one of society's scarce productive resources, and this book centers on the problem of its efficient use. *Labor economics examines the organization, functioning, and outcomes of labor markets; the decisions of prospective and present labor market participants; and the public policies relating to the employment and payment of labor resources.*

LABOR ECONOMICS AS A DISCIPLINE

How can a special field of economics concerned solely with labor be justified? What makes labor economics important as an area of inquiry? There are several answers to these questions.

Socioeconomic Issues

First, evidence of the importance of labor economics is all around us. We need simply glance at the newspaper headlines: "Senator calls for increase in minimum wage"; "General Motors cuts workforce"; "Labor productivity surges"; "Teamsters gain wage hike"; "Growing wage inequality"; "Jobless recovery"; "Free-trade agreement: Boon or bane for employment?"; "Workplace safety improves"; "Gender discrimination charged"; "More single parents in labor force"; "Illegal immigration continues"; "High executive salaries questioned"; "Jobs shipped out to foreigners."

Moreover, labor economics helps us understand causes and outcomes of major socio-economic "megatrends" occurring over the past several decades: the rapid rise in employment in the service industries; the surge in the number of female workers; the precipitous drop in union membership as a percentage of the workforce; the recent increase in immigration to the United States; and the expanding globalization of labor markets.

Quantitative Importance

A second justification for labor economics is quantitative. About 70 percent of the nation's income flows to workers as wages and salaries. Ironically, in the capitalistic economies of the world, the bulk of income is received not as capitalist income (profit, rent, interest) but as wages! The primary source of income for the vast majority of households in the United States is from providing labor services. Quantitatively, labor is our most important economic resource.

Unique Characteristics

Finally, the markets in which labor services are "bought" and "sold" embody special characteristics and peculiarities calling for separate study. Labor market transactions are a far cry from product market transactions. As succinctly stated by the famous British economist Alfred Marshall,

> It matters nothing to the seller of bricks whether they are to be used in building a palace or a sewer: but it matters a great deal to the seller of labor, who undertakes to perform a task of given difficulty, whether or not the place in which it is to be done is a wholesome and pleasant one, and whether or not his associates will be such as he cares to have.[1]

Or as explained by a more recent observer,

> The labor market is a rich and complicated place. When a worker takes a job he expects to earn a wage, but will also care about rates of wage growth, fringe benefits, levels of risk, retirement practices, pensions, promotion and layoff rules, seniority rights, and grievance procedures. In return the worker must give up some time, but he is also asked to upgrade his skills, train other workers, provide effort and ideas, and defer to authority in questions of how his time is spent.[2]

---

[1] Alfred Marshall, *Principles of Economics,* 8th ed. (London: Macmillan and Co., Limited, 1938), p. 566.
[2] H. Lorne Carmichael, "Self-Enforcing Contracts, Shirking, and Life Cycle Incentives," *Journal of Economic Perspectives,* Fall 1989, p. 65.

The complexity of labor markets means that the concepts of supply and demand must be substantially revised and reoriented when applied to labor markets. On the supply side, the labor services a worker "rents" to an employer are inseparable from the worker. Because a worker must spend 40 or so hours per week on the job delivering labor services, the nonmonetary facets of a job become extremely significant. Aside from remuneration, the worker is interested in a job's health and safety features, the arduousness of the work, stability of employment, and opportunities for training and advancement. These nonmonetary characteristics may well be as important as the direct pay. Indeed a worker's social status, self-esteem, and independence may all depend on the availability of labor market work. Thus the supply decisions of workers are more complex than the supply concept that applies to product markets.

Similarly, whereas the demand for a product is based on the satisfaction or utility it yields, labor is demanded because of its contribution—its productivity—in creating goods and services. The demands for particular kinds of labor are derived from the demands for the products they produce. Society has a demand for automobile workers because there is a demand for automobiles. We have a demand for accountants because we value accounting services. The demand for labor is therefore an indirect or "derived" demand.

The point to be underscored is that an understanding of labor markets presumes an appreciation of the special attributes of labor supply and demand. Unique institutional considerations—such as labor unions and collective bargaining, the minimum wage, occupational licensing, and discrimination—all affect the functioning of labor markets and require special attention.

THE "OLD" AND THE "NEW"

The field of labor economics has long been recognized as an important area of study. But the content or subject matter of the field has changed rather dramatically in the past two decades or so. If you were to go to the library and examine a labor text published 25 or 30 years ago, you would find its orientation to be highly descriptive and historical. Its emphasis would be on the history of the labor movement, a recitation of labor law and salient court cases, the institutional structure of labor unions, and the scope and composition of collective bargaining agreements. In short, the "old" study of labor was highly descriptive, emphasizing historical developments, facts, institutions, and legal considerations. A primary reason for this approach was that the complexities of labor markets seemed to make them more or less immune to economic analysis. To be sure, labor markets and unemployment were accorded some attention, but the analysis was typically minimal and superficial.

This state of affairs has changed significantly in recent decades. Economists have achieved important analytical breakthroughs in studying labor markets and labor problems. As a result, economic analysis has crowded out historical, institutional, legal, and anecdotal material. Labor economics increasingly has become applied micro and macro theory. The present volume focuses on the techniques and understandings associated with the "new" labor economics. This is not to say, however, that all descriptive aspects of the field have been discarded. As noted earlier, the unique institutional features of labor markets are part of the justification for a special field of economics devoted to labor. Yet the focal point of our approach is the application of economic reasoning to labor markets and labor issues.

ECONOMIC PERSPECTIVE

Contemporary labor economics employs theories of *choice* to analyze and predict the behavior of labor market participants and the economic consequences of labor market activity. It attempts to answer such questions as these. Why do some people decide to work while others do not? Why do some prospective labor market participants choose to delay their labor force entry to attend college? Why do some employers employ few workers and much capital while others use many workers and little capital? Why do firms lay off some workers during recessions but retain others? Labor economists also examine the *outcomes* of the choices made in the labor market. Why do some workers earn $8.00 an hour while others are paid $20 or $50 per hour? Why have women entered the labor force in record numbers during the past few decades? What impact, if any, does immigration have on the wages of native workers?

In short, contemporary labor economics focuses on choices—why they are made and how they generate particular outcomes. It therefore is important to be aware of three implicit assumptions underlying this *economic perspective.*

Relative Scarcity

We know that land, labor, capital, and entrepreneurial resources are scarce, or limited, relative to the many individual and collective wants of society. This relative scarcity dictates that society must choose how and for what purpose labor and other resources should be allocated. Similarly, individuals face a relative scarcity of time and spendable income. They must choose, for example, how much time to devote to jobs, to work in the home, and to leisure. They must choose how much present income (goods and services) to forgo for the prospect of obtaining higher future earnings. They must decide which goods and services to buy and, consequently, which to forgo. Relative scarcity—of time, personal income, and societal resources—is a basic element of the economic perspective.

Purposeful Behavior

Because relative scarcity keeps us from having everything we want, we are forced to choose among alternatives. For every choice, say to work longer hours or to institute a national service program, something is gained and something else is sacrificed. This sacrifice—forgone leisure, forgone private sector output—is an *opportunity cost.*

The economic perspective assumes that people compare costs with expected benefits. A worker will compare the extra utility (income) gained from an added hour of work with the value of the lost leisure. A firm will compare the added revenue from hiring a worker with the extra wage cost, and so forth. Thus contemporary labor economics looks for purpose, or rationality, in labor market behavior and, for that matter, in many labor market institutions. Relative scarcity necessitates that choices be made; the economic perspective assumes that these choices will be made purposefully rather than randomly or in a chaotic way.

To say that labor market participants behave rationally, however, is not to say that they always achieve their intended goals. Information is imperfect or imperfectly processed; unforeseen events occur; choices made by others positively or adversely affect the outcomes of our own choices. But even those choices that in retrospect were "poor" choices are assumed to have been made with the *expectation* of net gain.

Adaptability

Because relative scarcity forces people to make choices, and because choices are made purposefully, labor market participants respond to changes in perceived costs and benefits. Some workers will adjust the number of hours they desire to work when the wage rate they receive changes. Fewer people will decide to obtain a specific skill when the training cost rises or when the wage paid to those already possessing the skill falls. Firms will adjust their hiring when the demand for their product changes. Some workers will migrate from lower-paid regions to areas experiencing a significant rise in labor demand and therefore in wage rates. Union officials will lower their wage demands when the economy encounters recession and unemployment among union workers is high. Restated, the economic perspective assumes that workers, employers, and other labor market participants *adapt, adjust,* or *alter* their behaviors in response to changes in expected costs and expected gains. Contemporary labor economics sorts out these responses, finds predictable patterns, and, by so doing, adds to our understanding of the economy.

These three assumptions of the economic perspective—the scarcity of resources relative to wants, purposeful behavior based on comparisons of benefits and costs, and the adaptability of behavior to changing circumstances—underlie all that follows in this text.

1.1
Quick Review

- Labor economics examines the organization, functioning, and outcomes of labor markets; the decisions of prospective and present labor market participants; and the public policies relating to the employment and payment of labor resources.
- The new labor economics employs the economic perspective, which assumes that resources are scarce relative to wants, individuals make choices by comparing costs and benefits, and people respond to incentives and disincentives.

Your Turn

Which of these two statements best reflects the economic perspective? "Most workers in America would retire at age 65 even without pensions because this age has long been the customary retirement age." "Most workers in America retire at age 65 because at this age they become eligible for private pensions and full Social Security benefits." (*Answer:* See page 596.)

1.1

	World of Work	Gary Becker: Nobel Laureate
1.1		

Few economists were surprised when the University of Chicago's Gary Becker was named the winner of the 1992 Nobel Prize in economics. More than any other recent economist, Becker has extended the boundaries of economic analysis.

Becker's theories presume that individuals or households make purposeful choices in attempting to maximize their utility and that these choices depend heavily on incentives. His basic contribution has been to apply this perspective to aspects of human behavior that traditionally were believed to be noneconomic.

Becker's theory of marriage is illustrative. People allegedly seek marriage partners much as they search for jobs or decide which products to buy. Couples stop far short of obtaining complete information about each other before marriage. At some point the costs of obtaining additional information—the main cost being the benefits of marriage forgone—exceed the extra benefits of more information. After being married for months or years, however, a person learns additional information about his or her spouse's personality and attributes. This new information in some cases places the spouse in a less favorable light, ending the optimality of the original match and causing divorce.

Becker views the household as a little factory, allocating its time between labor market work, household production, and household consumption in producing utility-providing "commodities" (Chapter 3). Households have fewer children—time-intensive "durable goods"—as the "price" of children rises. A major component of this "price" is the forgone earnings associated with having and caring for children.

Becker's theory of human capital (Chapter 4) holds that decisions to invest in education and training are analogous to decisions by firms to purchase physical capital. Applying his approach to crime, Becker concludes that criminals rationally choose between crime and normal labor market work. Also, they respond to changes in costs and benefits, just as do noncriminals. Becker analyzes labor market discrimination (Chapter 14) as a preference or "taste" for which the discriminator is willing to pay.

Because Becker has invaded the traditional territories of sociology, anthropology, demography, and law, he has been called an "intellectual imperialist" (by both supporters and detractors). But as stated by Summers, there can be no doubt that Becker "has profoundly influenced the future of economics by demonstrating the breadth, range, and power of economic reasoning in a context that seemed unimagined a generation ago."*

* Lawrence Summers, as quoted in "An Economist for the Common Man," *BusinessWeek*, October 26, 1992. For a more thorough review of Becker's contributions, see Stanley L. Brue and Randy R. Grant, *The Evolution of Economic Thought*, 6th ed. (Mason OH: Thomson-South-Western, 2007), pp. 508–16.

OVERVIEW

Before plunging into the details of specific topics, let's pause for a brief overview of our field of study. This overview is useful for two closely related reasons. First, it provides a sense of direction. More specifically, it reveals the logic underlying the sequence of topics constituting each chapter. Second, the overview yields insights about how the subject matter of any particular chapter relates to other chapters.[3]

[3] This text covers more topics in economics than most instructors will choose to cover in a single course. Also note that chapters and topics can be logically sequenced in numerous ways.

FIGURE 1.1   An Overview of Labor Economics

This diagram shows how the chapters of this volume are divided between microeconomic and macroeconomic topics. Microeconomics focuses on the determinants of labor supply and demand and the ways supply and demand interact to determine wage rates and employment in various labor markets. In these labor markets, the types and composition of pay are determined, as is the wage structure. Some wage differences persist; others are eroded by mobility and migration. Labor unions, government, and discrimination all affect labor markets through either supply or demand. Macroeconomics stresses the aggregative aspects of labor markets and, in particular, the distribution of earnings, labor productivity, and the overall level of employment.

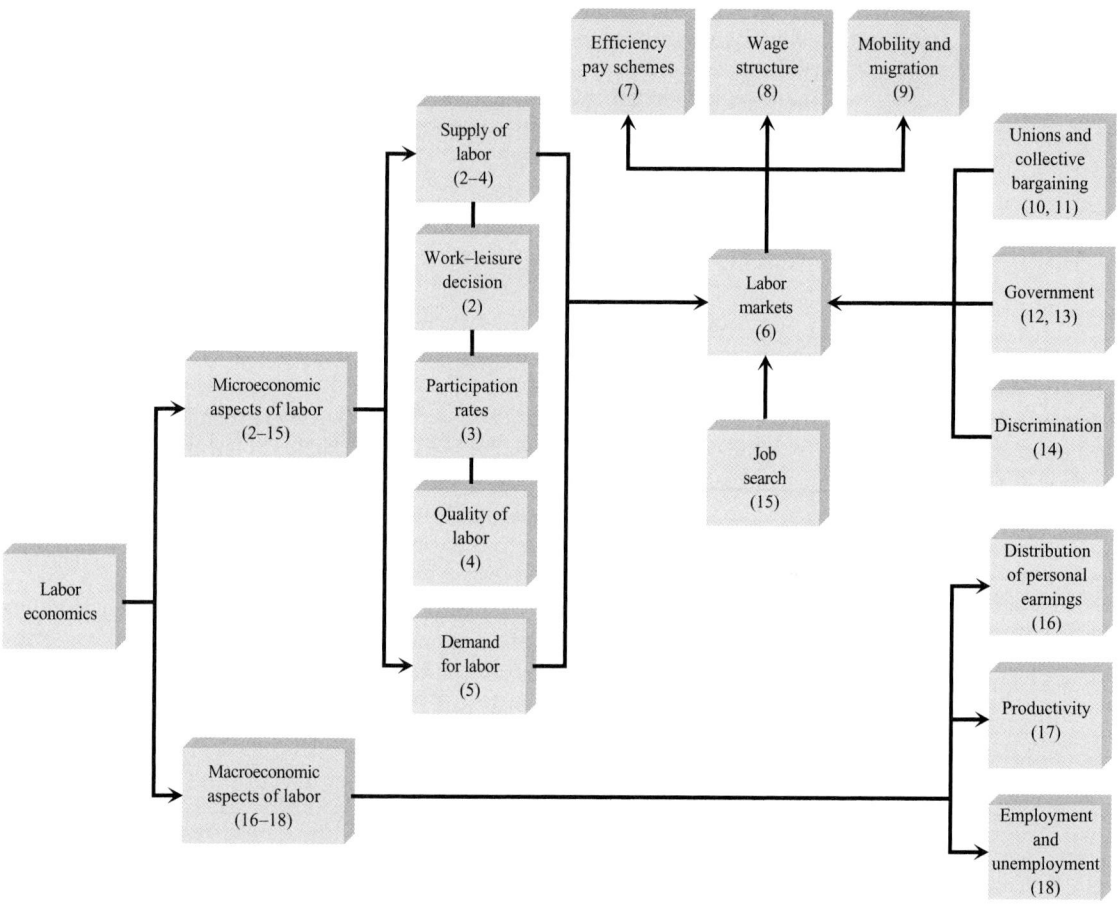

Figure 1.1 is helpful in presenting the overview. Reading from left to right, we note that most aspects of labor economics can be fitted without too much arbitrariness under the headings of "microeconomics" or "macroeconomics." ***Microeconomics*** is concerned with the decisions of individual economic units and the functioning of specific markets. On the other hand, ***macroeconomics*** is concerned with the economy as a whole or with basic aggregates that constitute the economy. The determination of the wage rate and the level of employment in a particular market—carpenters in Oshkosh or

retail clerks in Okoboji—are clearly microeconomic matters. In contrast, the average level of real wages, the aggregate levels of employment and unemployment, and the overall price level are issues in macroeconomics. Because some topics straddle micro- and macroeconomics, the subject matter of individual chapters will sometimes pertain to both aspects of economics. However, it is fair to say that Chapters 2 to 15 address topics that are "mainly micro." Similarly, Chapters 16 to 18 are "mainly macro."

Figure 1.1 reemphasizes that microeconomics stresses the working of individual markets. The goal of Chapters 2 to 6 is to develop and bring together the concepts that underlie labor supply and demand. Specifically, in Chapter 2 we examine the simple theory of labor supply. Here we analyze the basic factors that determine whether a person will participate in the labor force and, if so, the number of hours that the individual would prefer to work. We also consider how various pay schemes and income mainte- nance programs might affect the person's decision to supply labor services.

In Chapter 3 we consider the major determinants of the aggregate amount of labor sup- plied: population, the labor force participation rates of various demographic groups, and hours of work. In particular, we examine labor supply from a household perspective and explore reasons for the rapid increase in the labor force participation of married women.

Chapter 4 introduces a qualitative dimension to labor supply. Workers can provide more productive effort if they have training. Thus in Chapter 4 we examine the decision to invest in human capital—that is, in education and training—and explain why it is rational for different individuals to invest in different quantities of human capital.

We turn to the demand side of the labor market in Chapter 5. Here we systematically derive the short-run labor demand curve, explaining how the curve varies between a firm that is selling its product competitively and one that is not. The notion of a long- run demand curve is also explored, as is the concept of wage elasticity of demand. Sev- eral short applications of demand and elasticity then follow.

Chapter 6 combines labor supply and labor demand to explain how the equilibrium wage rate and level of employment are determined. An array of market models is pre- sented, ranging from a basic perfectly competitive model to relatively complex bilateral monopoly and "cobweb" models. Because of the importance of using scarce resources prudently, the emphasis in Chapter 6 is on the efficiency with which labor is allocated. Is the socially desirable or "right" amount of labor employed in a particular labor mar- ket? If not, what is the efficiency loss to society?

Chapters 7 to 9 are important elaborations and modifications of Chapter 6's discus- sion of the working conditions and outcomes of labor markets. In Chapter 6 worker compensation is treated as a standard hourly wage rate, such as $10 per hour. In Chapter 7 we recognize that worker compensation also involves a whole range of fringe benefits, including health insurance, paid vacations, sick leave, contributions to pensions, and so forth. We attempt to explain why different compensation packages might appeal to dif- ferent workers. More important, Chapter 7 explains how pay schemes might be designed to promote worker efficiency and productivity.

In Chapter 8 we confront the complex topic of the wage structure. Why do different workers receive different wages? We find that wage differences are traceable to such factors as the varying working conditions and skill requirements of jobs, differences in the human capital and job preferences of workers, and imperfections in labor mobility and the flow of job information.

Chapter 9 continues our elaboration of the labor market, explaining how the movement of labor—from employer to employer, occupation to occupation, and place to place—can contribute to economic efficiency. This mobility is analyzed as an investment in human capital and has a variety of economic ramifications.

As Figure 1.1 suggests, Chapters 10 to 15 focus on a variety of real-world considerations that have a pervasive and profound impact on how wages are determined and how labor markets operate. Specifically, in these chapters we examine in some depth how labor unions, government, and discrimination affect labor markets. Using the unionized models of labor markets in Chapter 6 as a springboard, Chapters 10 and 11 are concerned with unions and collective bargaining. In Chapter 10 we explore the demographics of trade union membership, discuss the size and institutional structure of the labor movement, and present models of the wage bargaining process and strike activity. Chapter 11 is devoted to the effects of unions and collective bargaining on the operation of labor markets. The discussion focuses on the impact of unions on wage rates, efficiency and productivity, firm profitability, and the distribution of earnings.

The direct and subtle ways in which government influences labor markets are the subject matter of Chapters 12 and 13. Chapter 12 considers government as a direct employer of labor and explores how government's fiscal functions affect labor markets. More specifically, we seek to determine how government expenditures and taxes alter wages and employment. In Chapter 13 our attention shifts to the impact of the legislative and regulatory functions of government on labor markets. What are the implications, for example, of minimum wage legislation and regulations concerning worker health and safety?

In addition to labor unions and government, the "institution" of discrimination greatly affects labor markets. Thus Chapter 14 presents facts and figures about differences in pay by race and gender, introduces several models of race and gender discrimination, and discusses how much of the observed gender and racial wage differences results from discrimination. This chapter also examines antidiscrimination policies and issues in some detail.

Job search behavior has important implications for issues such as unemployment and economic efficiency. Thus Chapter 15 is devoted to job search within as well as outside a firm.

The next three chapters deal primarily with macroeconomic aspects and outcomes of labor markets. The personal distribution of earnings is the subject of Chapter 16. Here we discuss alternative ways of portraying the overall earnings distribution and measuring the degree of observed inequality. We then offer explanations for the pattern of earnings and discuss related topics such as the degree of mobility within the earnings distribution and the recent trend toward greater earnings inequality.

In Chapter 17 we consider productivity for the important reason that the average levels of real wages—and thus living levels—are intimately related to it. The factors that contribute to the growth of productivity are examined, as are the systematic changes in productivity that occur during the business cycle. The relationship of changes in productivity to the price level and the level of employment is also explained.

Chapter 18 is devoted to the problem of unemployment. Among other things, distinctions are made between frictional, structural, and cyclic unemployment. The distribution

1.2 **World of Work**	Lotto Winners: Who Quit?

Of the many reasons people work, monetary compensation usually is the leading incentive. Indeed the word *compensation* implies that workers require reimbursement or indemnification—in this case, for the loss of utility associated with forgone leisure.

Although most of us profess to like our work, the economic perspective suggests that many of us would quit our jobs if we were assured of a substantial amount of nonlabor income each year. Quite simply, nonlabor income reduces our incentive to work. The greater the amount of nonlabor income, the greater the likelihood of our quitting our jobs.

A *Seattle Times* survey of lottery winners in the state of Washington supports this perspective. Three-quarters of the Lotto winners surveyed were employed when they won.

Observe in the accompanying figure that winners of "small" jackpots tended to continue to work. Only 7 percent of those winning jackpots of $1 million or less quit. Bear in mind that a $1 million jackpot is paid as 20 annual payments of $40,000, with $10,000 more a year being withheld for taxes. Conversely, those who won large jackpots were much more likely to quit. Seventy-seven percent of the winners of jackpots of $4 million or more chose to quit. Note from the charts that the larger the jackpot winnings, the greater was the percentage of workers who opted out of the workforce.*

Source: Data from *Seattle Times* survey, Jack Broom "Lotto Winners—Unlike Fantasy. Most Jackpot Winners Don't Say, 'Take This Job and Shove It'," 1999.

* A more extensive survey of lottery winners also supports this generalization. See Guido W. Imbens, Donald B. Rubin, and Bruce Sacerdote, "Estimating the Effects of Unearned Income on Labor Supply, Earnings, Savings, and Consumption: Evidence from a Survey of Lottery Players," *American Economic Review*, September 2001, pp. 778–94.

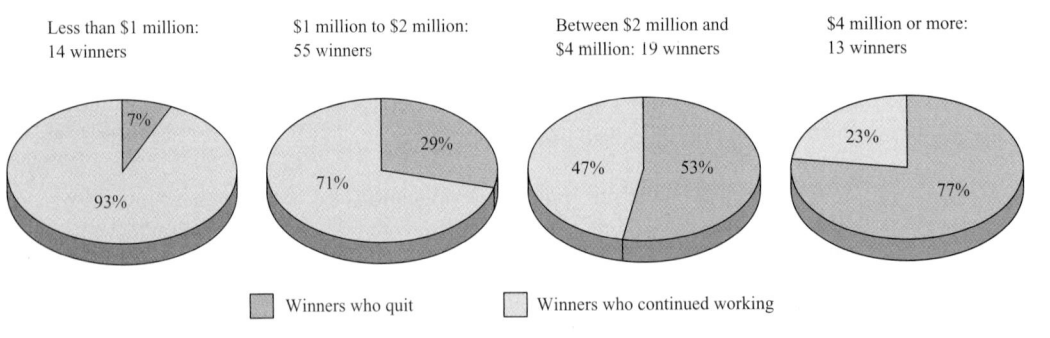

Less than $1 million: 14 winners | $1 million to $2 million: 55 winners | Between $2 million and $4 million: 19 winners | $4 million or more: 13 winners

■ Winners who quit   □ Winners who continued working

of unemployment by occupations and by demographic groups is considered, as are a variety of public policies designed to alleviate unemployment.

The appendix falls outside Figure 1.1's overview, but it is important for staying aware of future developments in labor economics and continuing the study of the field. It lists and discusses sources of labor-related statistics; discusses bibliographic, technical, and nontechnical journals in the field; and cites advanced textbooks in labor economics along with books in the closely related fields of labor relations, collective bargaining,

| 1.2 |

and labor law. Students doing term papers or other written assignments in labor economics will want to read this appendix at the outset. Appendix Table 1 lists numerous potential term paper topics that may be of interest.

PAYOFFS

What benefits might you derive from studying labor economics? The payoffs from a basic understanding of the field may be both personal and social. Labor economics yields information and develops analytical tools that may be useful in making personal and managerial decisions relevant to labor markets. Also, a grasp of the field puts you in a better position as a citizen and voter to develop informed positions on labor market issues and policies.

Personal Perspective

At the personal level, the vast majority of readers have already been labor market participants. You have worked summers, in part-time jobs, on your family farm, or perhaps in a school-related internship. Most of you will receive the bulk of your future incomes from the labor market. Thus many of the topics addressed in this book will have immediate relevance to you. Such topics as job search, unemployment, migration, discrimination, unionism, and labor productivity, to enumerate only a few, will take on new meaning and relevance. For example, if you become a public schoolteacher or a state employee, what might you personally expect to gain in terms of salary and fringe benefits by unionization? To what extent does a college education contribute to higher earnings? That is, what rate of return can you expect from investing in higher education? What are the peculiarities of labor markets for college-trained workers? If you are a woman or member of a minority group, how might discrimination affect your access to specific occupations and your earnings? Similarly, some of you will find yourselves in managerial positions with responsibilities for personnel and labor relations. The background and analytical perspective provided by an understanding of labor economics should be useful in making rational managerial decisions concerning the hiring, firing, promotion, training, and remuneration of workers.

Social Perspective

From a societal viewpoint, a knowledge of labor economics should help make you a more informed citizen and more intelligent voter. The issues here are broad in scope and impact. Should unionization be encouraged or discouraged? Are unions on balance positive or negative forces in our society? Should government place limits on the salaries of executives, athletes, and entertainers? How might a given change in the tax structure—for example, to a more progressive federal income tax—affect incentives to work? Should government restrict outsourcing of American jobs to firms or subsidiaries abroad? Should U.S. immigration policies be liberalized or made more restrictive? Should industrially advanced countries use international trade agreements to force developing countries to increase minimum wages, improve working conditions, and meet other labor standards?

Should formal education and vocational training be given more or less public support? Is it desirable for employers to pay teenagers wage rates that are lower than the legislated minimum wage? Although detailed and definitive answers to such questions cannot be guaranteed, an understanding of labor economics will provide valuable insights that should help you formulate opinions on these and similar issues.

Chapter Summary

1. The relative scarcity of labor and other productive resources provides an incentive for society to use such resources efficiently.
2. The importance of labor economics is reflected in *(a)* current socioeconomic issues and problems, *(b)* the quantitative dominance of labor as a resource, and *(c)* the unique characteristics of labor supply and demand.
3. In the past two decades the field of labor economics has put greater emphasis on economic analysis and has deemphasized historical, institutional, and legal aspects.
4. The economic perspective assumes that *(a)* labor and other resources are relatively scarce, *(b)* individuals and institutions make rational or purposeful decisions, and *(c)* decisions are altered or adapted in the light of changing economic circumstances.
5. This volume examines a series of pertinent microeconomic and macroeconomic topics, as outlined in Figure 1.1.
6. An understanding of the content and analytical tools of labor economics contributes to more intelligent personal and social decisions.

Terms and Concepts

labor economics, 1　　　　microeconomics, 7　　　　macroeconomics, 7
economic perspective, 4

Note: To aid you with terminology, we have included an extensive glossary at the end of this book.

Questions and Study Suggestions

1. Why is economics a science of choices? Explain the kinds of choices confronting workers and employers in labor markets. Distinguish between microeconomics and macroeconomics.
2. In 2006, 151.4 million workers were in the U.S. labor force, of which 7.0 million were unemployed. In view of these facts, how can economists say that labor is a scarce resource?
3. Indicate whether each of the following statements pertains to microeconomics or macroeconomics:
   a. The unemployment rate in the United States was 4.6 percent in 2006.
   b. Workers at the Sleepy Eye grain elevator are paid $8 per hour.
   c. The productivity of American workers as a whole increased by more than 2 percent per year in the last decade.

    d. The money or nominal wages of nursing aides increased by 3 percent in 2006.

    e. The Alpo dog food plant in Bowser, Indiana, laid off 15 workers last month.

4. Why must the concepts of supply and demand as they pertain to product markets be modified when applied to labor markets?

5. What is the relative importance of labor as an economic resource?

6. Briefly compare the "old" and "new" labor economics.

7. What are the major features or assumptions of the economic perspective?

8. Briefly state and justify your position on each of the following proposals:

    a. Women and minorities should be paid the same wage as white males, provided the work is comparable.

    b. The United States should close its boundaries to all immigration.

    c. The federal government should take measures to achieve the 4 percent unemployment rate specified by the Humphrey–Hawkins Act of 1978.

    d. So-called right-to-work laws, which specify that workers who refuse to join unions cannot thereby be deprived of their jobs, should be repealed.

    e. Conditions of worker health and safety should be determined by the labor market, not by governmental regulation.

9. What benefits might accrue to you from studying labor economics?

Internet Exercise

Gary Becker

Go to the Web site for 1992 Economics Nobel Prize winner Gary Becker (**http://home.uchicago.edu/~gbecker/**). In sequence select "Articles" and "Business Week column articles." Locate and cite an article that covers a labor economics issue. In which chapter of this book is the issue discussed?

    (Addresses for Internet Web sites sometimes change. If you encounter dead links or outdated directions in any end-of-chapter Internet Exercises, check the text's Web site (**http://www.contemporarylabor.com**) for posted updates.)

Internet Links

The Nobel e-Museum Web site provides information about the Nobel Prize winners in economics (**http://nobelprize.org/nobel_prizes/economics/**).

The Web site for the Open Directory Project supplies many labor economics–related links (**http://dmoz.org/Science/Social_Sciences/Economics/Labor_Economics/**).

Chapter 2

The Theory of Individual Labor Supply

In supplying labor, human beings are a curious and diverse lot. Adams moonlights at a second job, while Anderson takes numerous unpaid absences from his only job. College student Brown works full-time while attending school; roommate Bailey works part-time; and classmate Brinkman doesn't work at all. Conway quit her job to raise her young children; Cohen, also with young children, continues to work full-time in the workplace. Downy quickly grabs an opportunity for early retirement; Wong plans to work until she can no longer do so because of old age. Evans welcomes overtime work; Ebert, given an option, routinely rejects it. Fleming supplies more hours of labor when her wage rate rises; Hernandez cuts back on his work hours.

How are these diverse labor supply decisions made? How do individuals decide on the number of hours of labor, if any, to supply in the labor market? Our main goal in this chapter is to develop and apply a basic theory of individual labor supply that will help answer these questions.

THE WORK–LEISURE DECISION: BASIC MODEL

Imagine an individual with a certain amount of education and labor force experience and, therefore, a given level of skills. That individual, having a fixed amount of time available, must decide how that time should be allocated among *work* (labor market activity) and *leisure* (non–labor market activity). In the present context, *work* is time devoted to a paying job. The term *leisure* is used here in a broad sense to include all kinds of activities for which a person does not get paid: work within the

Global Perspective   **2.1**   Annual Hours of Work per Employee

Average hours worked per year differ substantially across countries. For example, the average Czech employee works 567 more hours per year than the average German worker.

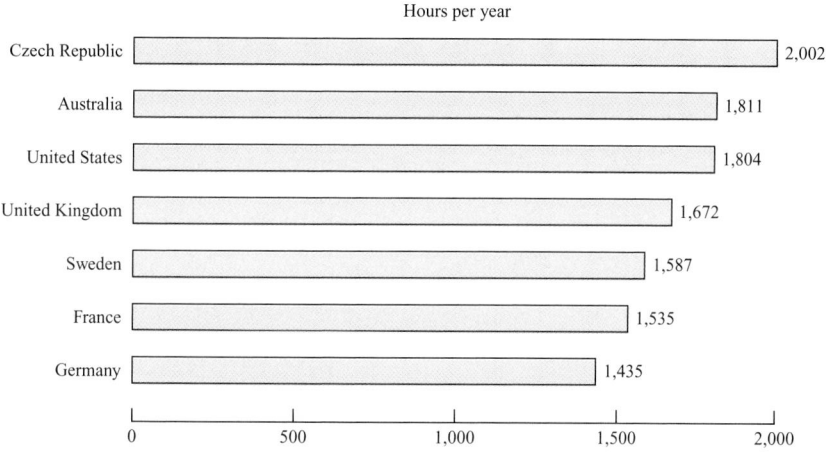

Hours per year

Country	Hours
Czech Republic	2,002
Australia	1,811
United States	1,804
United Kingdom	1,672
Sweden	1,587
France	1,535
Germany	1,435

Source: Organization for Economic Cooperation and Development, *Employment Outlook,* July 2006, Table F.

household and time spent on consumption, education, commuting, rest, relaxation, and so forth.

   Two sets of information are necessary to determine the optimal distribution of an individual's time between work and leisure. First, we require *subjective,* psychological information concerning the individual's work–leisure preferences. This information is embodied in *indifference curves.* Second, we need the *objective* market information that is reflected in a *budget constraint.*

Indifference Curves

As applied to the work–leisure decision, an *indifference curve shows the various combinations of real income and leisure time that will yield some specific level of utility or satisfaction to the individual.* Curve I_1 in Figure 2.1 is illustrative. Note that we measure daily income on the vertical axis and hours of leisure, or non–labor market activities, from left to right on the horizontal axis. The second horizontal axis reminds us that, given the fixed 24 hours available each day, we may measure the number of hours of work from right to left. According to the definition of indifference curves, each

FIGURE 2.1 An Income–Leisure Indifference Curve

The indifference curve shows the various combinations of income (goods) and leisure that yield some given level of total utility. The curve slopes downward because the additional utility associated with more leisure must be offset by less income so that total utility remains unchanged. The convexity of the curve reflects a diminishing marginal rate of substitution of leisure for income.

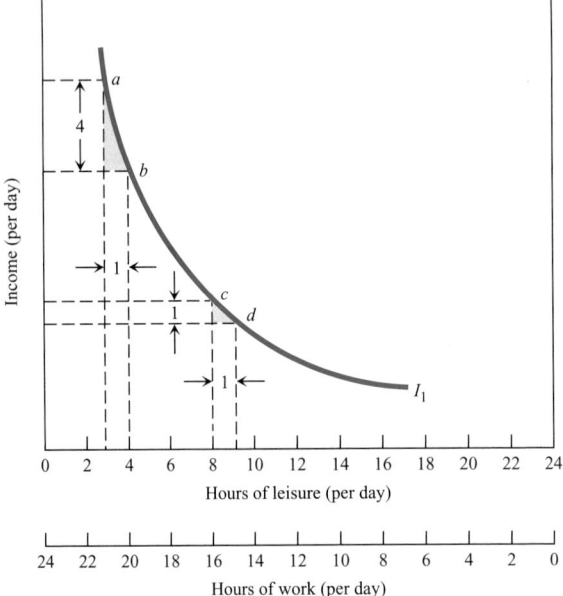

combination of income and leisure designated by any point on I_1 is equally satisfactory; each point on the curve yields the same level of utility to the individual.

Indifference curves embody several salient properties.

1 Negative Slope

The indifference curve slopes downward because real income from work and leisure are both sources of utility or satisfaction. In moving southeast down the curve, some amount of real income—of goods and services—must be given up to compensate for the acquisition of more leisure if total utility is to remain constant. Stated differently, the indifference curve is downward-sloping because as an individual gets more of one good (leisure), some of the other good (real income) must be surrendered to maintain the same level of utility.

2 Convex to Origin

A downward-sloping curve can be concave, convex, or linear. We note in Figure 2.1 that our indifference curve is *convex* (bowed inward) to the origin; alternatively stated, the absolute value of the curve's slope *diminishes* as we move down the curve to the southeast.

Why are indifference curves convex to the origin? We will explain this characteristic in intuitive terms and then more technically. Both explanations are rooted in two considerations. First, the slope of the curve reflects an individual's subjective willingness to substitute between leisure and income. And second, the individual's willingness to substitute leisure for income, or vice versa, varies with the amounts of leisure and income initially possessed.

The convexity of an indifference curve reflects the idea that an individual becomes increasingly reluctant to give up any good (in this case income) as it becomes increasingly scarce. Consider the *ab* range of our indifference curve, where the individual has a relatively large amount of income and very little leisure. Here the individual would be willing to give up a relatively large amount of abundant income (four units) in exchange for an additional unit, say an hour, of scarce leisure. The extra utility from the added hour of leisure will perfectly offset the loss of utility from having four fewer units of income. But as we move down the curve to the *cd* range, we find that the individual's circumstances are different in that income is now relatively scarcer and leisure is more abundant. The individual is now willing to trade only a small amount of scarce income (one unit) for an extra hour of leisure. As the individual obtains more leisure, the amount of income the person is willing to give up to gain still more units of leisure becomes smaller and smaller. Thus the indifference curve becomes flatter and flatter. By definition, a curve that flattens out as we move to the southeast is convex to the origin.

In more technical terms, the slope of the indifference curve is measured by the *marginal rate of substitution of leisure for income* (MRS *L, Y*). *The MRS L, Y is the amount of income one must give up to compensate for the gain of 1 more unit (hour) of leisure.* Although the slope of the indifference curve shown in Figure 2.1 is negative, it is convenient to think of the MRS *L, Y* as an absolute value. In these terms, MRS *L, Y* is large—that is, the slope of the indifference curve is steep—in the northwest or upper range of the curve. You can see this by penciling in a straight line tangent to I_1 at point *a* in Figure 2.1. The slope of your line measures the slope of I_1 at *a*. Observe the steep slope—the high MRS *L, Y*. This high MRS *L, Y* occurs because the person has much income and little leisure. The subjective relative valuation of income is low at the margin, and the subjective relative valuation of leisure is high at the margin. The individual therefore is willing to forgo many units of income (four) for an additional unit of leisure.

In moving down the indifference curve to the southeast, the quantities of income and leisure change at each point so that the individual now has less income and more leisure. Relatively more abundant leisure therefore has less value at the margin, and increasingly scarce income has more value at the margin. This is seen by penciling in a straight line tangent to *d* on I_1 in Figure 2.1 and comparing the slope to point *a*. This slope (at *d*) is smaller than the slope of the curve at *a*. The basic point is that MRS *L, Y*—the slope of the indifference curve—declines as one moves down the curve. Any curve whose slope or MRS *L, Y* declines as one moves southeast along it is, by definition, convex to the origin.

3 Indifference Map

It is useful to consider an indifference map, which is a whole family or field of indifference curves, as shown in Figure 2.2. Each curve reflects some different level of total utility, much as each contour line on a topographical map reflects a different elevation. Figure 2.2

FIGURE 2.2
An Indifference Map for Income and Leisure
An indifference map comprises a number of indifference curves. Each successive curve to the northeast reflects a higher level of total utility.

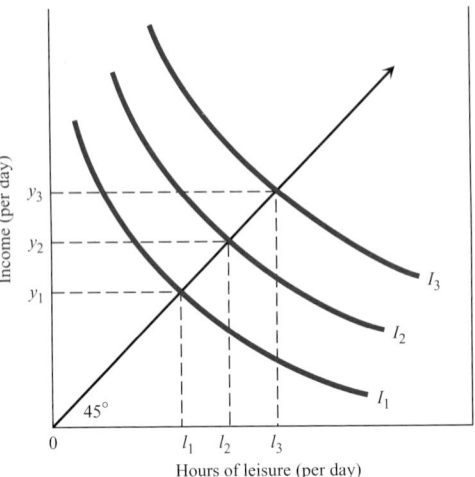

illustrates only three of a potentially unlimited number of indifference curves. Every possible combination of income and leisure will lie on some indifference curve. Curves farther from the origin indicate higher levels of utility. This can be demonstrated by drawing a 45° diagonal from the origin and noting that its intersection with each successive curve denotes larger amounts of *both* income and leisure. The $y_2 l_2$ combination of income and leisure is preferred to the $y_1 l_1$ combination because the former indicates larger amounts of *both* income and leisure. Similarly, the $y_3 l_3$ combination entails greater total utility than $y_2 l_2$, and so on.[1] It is evident that an individual will maximize total utility by achieving a position on the highest *attainable* indifference curve.

4 Different Work–Leisure Preferences

Just as the tastes of various consumers for specific goods and services vary greatly, so do individual preferences for work and leisure. Different preferences for the relative desirability of work and leisure are reflected in the shape of one's indifference curves. In Figure 2.3(a) we present the indifference curves of a "workaholic" who places a low value on leisure and a high value on work (income). Note that the workaholic's curves are relatively flat, indicating that this individual would give up an hour of leisure for a relatively small increase in income. Figure 2.3(b) shows the indifference curves of a "leisure lover" who puts a high value on leisure and a low value on work (income). Observe that this individual's indifference curves are steep, which means that a relatively large increase in income must be realized to sacrifice an hour of leisure. In each case the indifference curves are convex to the origin, but the rate of decline of MRS *L, Y* is far greater for the leisure lover than for the workaholic.

---

[1] Indifference curves cannot intersect. We know that all points on any one curve reflect the same amount of utility, whereas any point above (below) that curve represents a larger (smaller) level of utility. If two indifference curves intersected, the level of utility would be the same at the point of intersection. However, at all other points the levels of utility would differ. Given the definition of an indifference curve, this is logically impossible.

FIGURE 2.3   **Different Preferences for Work (Income) and Leisure**

The shape of one's indifference curves depends on one's relative preferences for work (income) and leisure. In (a) we portray a "workaholic" who is willing to give up an hour of leisure for only a small increase in income. In comparison the "leisure lover" shown in (b) requires a large increase in income to sacrifice an hour of leisure or non–labor market time.

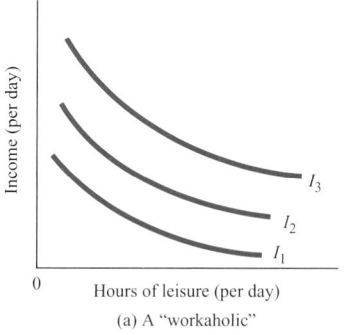

(a) A "workaholic"

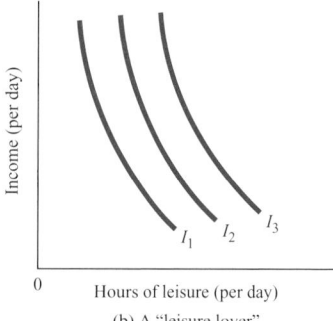

(b) A "leisure lover"

Why the differences? In the first place, it may be purely a matter of tastes or preferences rooted in personality. A second and related point is that the occupations of individuals differ. The flat curves of Figure 2.3(a) may pertain to a person who has a creative and challenging occupation—for example, a painter, ceramist, or musician. Work entails very little disutility, and hence it takes only a small increase in income to induce the artist to sacrifice an hour of leisure. Conversely, an unpleasant job in a coal mine or on an assembly line may elicit steep indifference curves. Such work involves substantial disutility, and a large increase in income is required to induce one to give up an hour of leisure. Finally, an individual's personal circumstances may affect his or her relative evaluations of labor market work and leisure. For example, a young mother with two or three preschool children or a college student may have relatively steep indifference curves because "leisure" (non–labor market time) is valuable for child care and studying. Similarly, José may be married and therefore may have substantial financial obligations. Consequently, his indifference curves are relatively flat: He is quite willing to give up leisure for income. On the other hand, John is single and his financial responsibilities are less compelling. He is less willing to give up leisure for income, and his indifference curves are therefore relatively steep. In short, personality, the type of work under consideration, and personal circumstances may influence the shape of a person's indifference curves.

Budget Constraint

Our assertion that the individual maximizes utility by achieving a position on the highest *attainable* indifference curve implies that the choice of curves is constrained. Specifically, the individual is constrained by the amount of monetary income that is available. Let's assume for the moment that an individual's only source of monetary income is from work. In other words, we are assuming that the individual has no nonlabor income, no accumulated savings to draw on, and no possibility of borrowing funds.

FIGURE 2.4

Budget Constraints

A budget constraint (line) can be drawn for each possible wage rate. The wage rate determines the slope of each budget line. Specifically, budget lines fan out clockwise from the right origin as the wage rate increases.

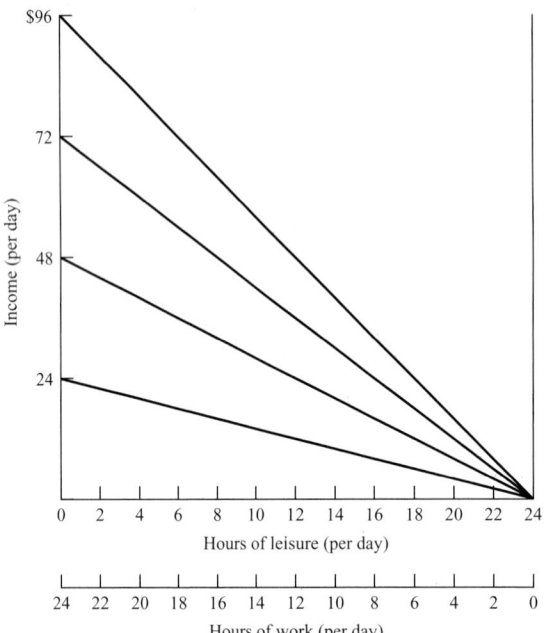

Let's also suppose that the wage rate confronting this person in the labor market is given in that the individual cannot alter the hourly wage paid for his or her services by varying the number of hours worked.[2] Thus we can draw a *budget (wage) constraint line, which shows all the various combinations of income (goods) and leisure that a worker might realize or obtain, given the wage rate*. If the going wage rate is $1, we can draw a budget line from 24 hours on the horizontal leisure axis to $24 on the vertical income axis in Figure 2.4. Given the $1 wage rate, at the extremes an individual could obtain (1) 24 hours of leisure and no income or (2) $24 of income and no leisure. The line connecting these two points reveals all other attainable options: $8 of income and 16 hours of leisure, $12 of income and 12 hours of leisure, and so forth. Observe that the absolute value of the slope of this budget line is 1, reflecting the $1 wage rate. In moving northwest along the line, one hour of leisure must be sacrificed to obtain each $1 of income. This is true because the wage rate is $1.

Similarly, if the wage rate is $2, the appropriate budget line would be anchored at 24 hours of leisure and $48 of real income. The slope of this line is 2, again reflecting the wage rate. The budget constraints for wage rates of $3 and $4 are also shown in Figure 2.4. We observe that the budget lines fan out clockwise from the right origin as the wage rate goes up. In each case the wage rate—the slope of the budget line—reflects the objective or market rate of exchange between income and leisure. If the wage rate is $1, an individual can exchange one hour of leisure (by working) and obtain $1 worth

[2] This assumption permits us to use a linear budget constraint.

FIGURE 2.5
Utility Maximization: The Optimal Choice between Leisure and Income
The optimal or utility-maximizing combination of leisure and income for the worker is at point u_1, where the budget constraint is tangent to the highest attainable indifference curve I_2.

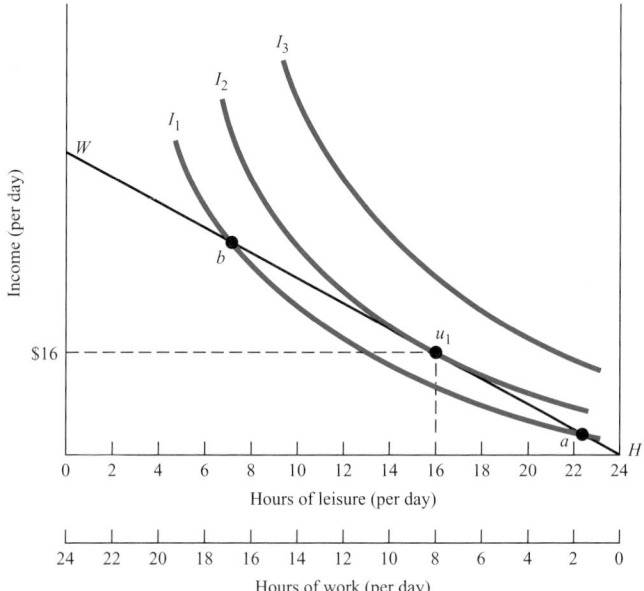

of income. If the wage rate is $2, one hour of leisure can be exchanged in the labor market for $2 of income, and so forth.[3]

Utility Maximization

The individual's optimal or utility-maximizing position can be determined by bringing together the subjective preferences embodied in the indifference curves and the objective market information contained in each budget line. This is shown in Figure 2.5, where we assume that the wage rate is $2.

Recall that the farther the indifference curve is from the origin, the greater the person's total utility. Therefore, an individual will maximize total utility by attaining the highest possible indifference curve. Given the $2 wage rate, no leisure–income combination is attainable outside—to the northeast—of the resulting HW budget constraint. This particular budget constraint allows the individual to realize the highest attainable level of utility at point u_1, where the budget line just touches (is tangent to) indifference curve I_2. Of all the attainable positions on the various indifference curves, point u_1 is clearly on the curve that is farthest from the origin and therefore yields the highest achievable level of total utility. We observe that the individual will choose to work 8 hours, earning a daily income of $16 and enjoying 16 hours of leisure.

It is important to recognize that at this optimal position, the individual and the market agree about the relative worth of leisure and income at the margin. At u_1 the slope of

---

[3] In equation form, the budget constraint is $Y = WH$, where Y = income, W = wage rate, and H = number of hours of work. Hence $Y = W(24 - L) = 24W - WL$, where L = number of hours of leisure and the slope of the budget line is $-W$.

indifference curve I_2 and the slope of the budget line are equal. The individual's preferences are such that he or she is subjectively willing to substitute leisure for income at
precisely the same exchange rate as the objective information of the labor market
requires. The **optimal work–leisure position** *is achieved where MRS L, Y (the slope of
the indifference curve) is equal to the wage rate (the slope of the budget line).* By definition,
these slopes are equal only at the point of tangency.

We can reinforce our understanding of the optimal work–leisure position by considering
briefly why points *a* and *b* are *not* optimal. Let's start with point *b,* where we note that
indifference curve I_1 is steeper than the budget line or, more technically, MRS *L, Y* is
greater than the wage rate. For example, the MRS *L, Y* might be 4 while the wage rate
is $2. What does this mean? It indicates that an additional hour of leisure is worth $4 to
this individual but that she will have to sacrifice only $2 of income to obtain that extra
hour of leisure. Acquiring something worth $4 at the cost of something worth only $2 is
clearly a beneficial exchange. Thus "trading" income (by working fewer hours) for
leisure will benefit her. These trades in effect move her down budget line *HW* and on to
successively higher indifference curves. At point u_1 all such trades are exhausted, and
this individual and the market agree about the value of work (income) and leisure at the
margin. As noted earlier, at u_1 the MRS *L, Y* equals the wage rate. At this point the individual and the market agree that the marginal hour of leisure is worth $2. Later we will
note that at point *b* the individual will feel "overemployed" in that she can increase her
total utility by working fewer hours—that is, by moving to a point such as u_1 where she
has more leisure and less income.

The situation is just the opposite at point *a.* Here the slope of indifference curve I_1 is
less than the budget line; in other words, MRS *L, Y* is less than the wage rate. To illustrate, the wage rate is $2 and the MRS *L, Y* might be only $1. This indicates that an hour
of leisure is worth only $1 at the margin but that the individual can actually get $2 worth
of income by sacrificing an hour of leisure. Getting something worth $2 by giving up
something worth only $1 is obviously a beneficial trade. In trading leisure for income
(by working more hours) the individual moves up the *HW* budget line to preferred positions on higher indifference curves. Again, all such beneficial exchanges of leisure for
income will be completed when point u_1 is achieved because here the MRS *L, Y* and the
wage rate are equal. At u_1 leisure and income are of equal value at the margin. At point *a*
the individual would feel "underemployed." She could increase her total utility by
working more hours—that is, by moving to a point such as u_1 where she has less leisure
and more income.

2.1
*Quick
Review*

- An income–leisure indifference curve represents all combinations of income and leisure that provide equal total utility; its slope is called the marginal rate of substitution (MRS).
- Each successive curve to the northeast in an indifference map indicates a greater level of total utility.
- An income–leisure budget line reveals all combinations of income and leisure that a worker can achieve at a specific hourly wage rate.

- The utility-maximizing combination of income and leisure occurs at the point of tangency between the budget line and the highest attainable indifference curve; there MRS *L, Y* (the slope of the indifference curve) equals the wage rate (the slope of the budget line).

Your Turn

Suppose that at a particular combination of income and leisure, the slope of the budget line is steeper than the slope of the indifference curve it intersects. How should the worker adjust work hours? (*Answer:* See page 596.)

Wage Rate Changes: Income and Substitution Effects

Will an individual choose to work more or fewer hours as the wage rate changes? It depends. Figure 2.6(a) repeats the u_1 utility-maximizing position of Figure 2.5 but adds four more budget lines and indicates the relevant optimal positions associated with each.

FIGURE 2.6   Derivation of the Backward-Bending Labor Supply Curve

In (a) higher wage rates result in a series of increasingly steep budget lines whose tangencies with indifference curves locate a series of utility-maximizing positions. The movement from u_1 to u_2 and u_3 reveals that for a time higher wage rates are associated with longer hours of work, whereas the shifts from u_3 to u_4 and u_5 indicate that still higher wage rates entail fewer hours of work. The overall result is a backward-bending labor supply curve as shown in (b).

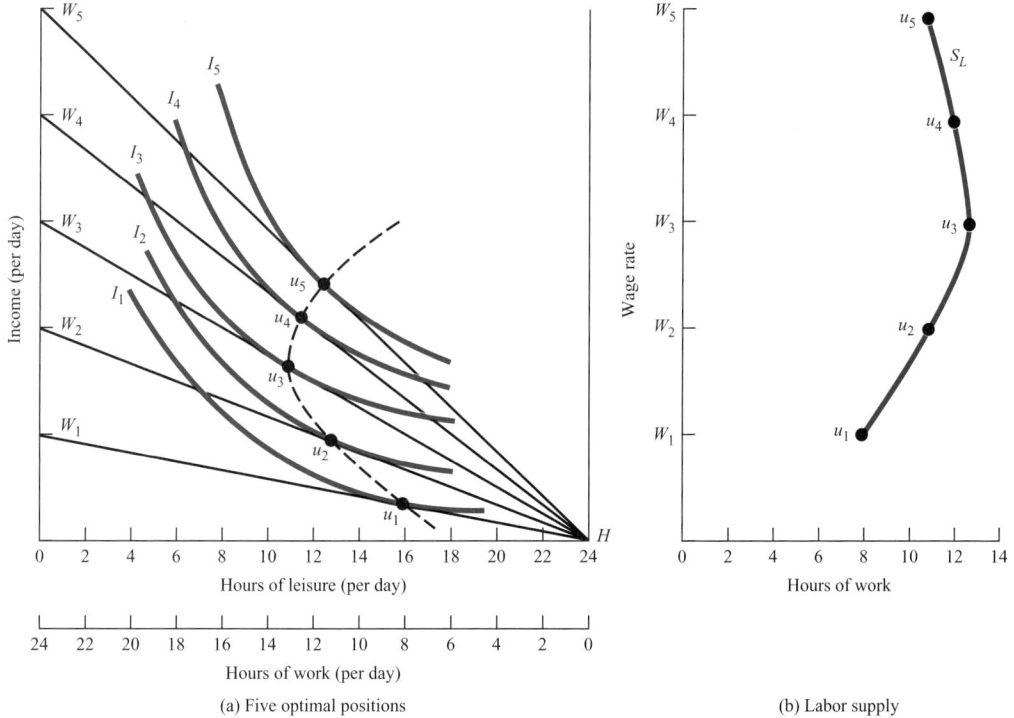

(a) Five optimal positions

(b) Labor supply

We observe that for the wage rate increase that moves the budget line from W_1 to W_2, the optimal position moves from u_1 to u_2. On the horizontal axis we find that the individual chooses fewer hours of leisure and more hours of work. Similarly, the wage rate increase that shifts the budget constraint from W_2 to W_3 also entails more hours of work and fewer hours of leisure at u_3 than is the case at u_2. But the further wage rate boost reflected by the shift of the budget line from W_3 to W_4 produces an optimum at u_4 that involves less work and more leisure than the prior optimum u_3. Similarly, the wage increase depicted by the increase in the budget line from W_4 to W_5 causes a further reduction in hours of work at u_5.

This analysis suggests that *for a specific person, hours of work may for a time increase as wage rates rise; but beyond some point, further wage increases may reduce the hours of labor supplied.* Indeed, we can translate the hours of work–wage rate combinations associated with the five optimal positions of Figure 2.6(a) into a diagram such as that shown in Figure 2.6(b), which has traditional axes measuring wage rates on the vertical axis and hours of labor supplied left to right on the horizontal axis. In so doing we find that this individual's labor supply curve is forward-rising for a time and then backward-bending. This curve is known as a *backward-bending labor supply curve,* the forward-rising portion being expected or taken for granted. We can envision an individual labor supply curve for each person in the economy. But keep in mind that each individual's preferences for work versus leisure are unique, so the exact location, shape, and point of the backward bend of the curve vary from person to person.

Why is a backward-bending labor supply curve a realistic possibility? This can be explained in terms of the income and substitution effects. When the wage rate changes, these two effects tend to alter one's utility-maximizing position.

Income Effect

The income effect refers to the change in the desired hours of work resulting from a change in income, holding the wage rate constant.[4] We will discover that the income effect of a wage *increase* is found by isolating the increase in work hours resulting solely from the increase in potential income per hour of work, *as if the price of leisure (the wage rate) did not change.* A wage rate increase means that a larger money income is obtainable from a given number of hours of work. We would expect an individual to use a part of this enhanced income to buy goods and services: a new TV, movie tickets, and so on. But if we make the reasonable assumption that leisure is a *normal good*—a good of which more is consumed as income rises—then we can expect that a part of one's expanded income might be used to "purchase" leisure. Consumers derive utility not from goods alone but from combinations of goods and nonmarket time (leisure). Movie tickets yield satisfaction only if one has the time to enjoy them. How does one purchase leisure or nonmarket time? In a unique way: by working fewer hours. This means that when wage rates *rise,* and leisure is a normal good, the income effect reduces the desired number of hours of work.

[4] In mathematical terms, income effect $= \dfrac{\Delta H}{\Delta Y}\Big|\ \overline{W} < 0$, where H = hours of work, Y = income, and $\overline{W}$ = constant wage.

Substitution Effect

The substitution effect indicates the change in the desired hours of work resulting from a change in the wage rate, keeping income constant.[5] In the context of a wage rate increase, it evidences itself in an increase in the desired number of hours of work. When the wage rate increases, the relative price of leisure is altered. Specifically, an increase in the wage rate raises the "price" or opportunity cost of leisure. Because of the higher wage rate, one must now forgo more income (goods) for each hour of leisure consumed (not worked). The basic theory of economic choice implies that an individual will purchase less of any normal good when it becomes relatively more expensive. In brief, the higher price of leisure prompts one to consume less leisure or, in other words, to work more. The substitution effect merely tells us that when wage rates rise and leisure becomes more expensive, it is sensible to substitute work for leisure. For a wage *increase,* the substitution effect makes the person want to work more hours.[6]

Net Effect

The overall effect of an increase in the wage rate on the number of hours an individual wants to work depends on the relative magnitudes of these two effects. Economic theory does not predict the outcome. *If the substitution effect dominates the income effect, the individual will choose to work more hours when the wage rate rises.* Dominance of the substitution effect is reflected in shifts from u_1 to u_2 to u_3 in Figure 2.6(a) and the upward-sloping portion of the labor supply curve in Figure 2.6(b). *But if the income effect is larger than the substitution effect, a wage increase will prompt the individual to work fewer hours.* The movements from u_3 to u_4 and u_5 in Figure 2.6(a) and the backward-bending portion of the labor supply curve in Figure 2.6(b) are relevant in this case.

Table 2.1 provides a useful summary and extension of our discussion of the implications of the relative sizes of the substitution and income effects for the desired hours of work. Columns 1, 2a, and 3 summarize the discussion we have just completed. Note from column 2a that this discussion was couched in terms of a wage rate *increase.* Columns 1, 2b, and 3 are important because they reveal that the impact of the substitution and income effects on hours of work is reversed if we assume a wage *decrease.* The income effect associated with a wage decline is that the desired hours of work increase. That is, a decline in the wage rate will reduce an individual's income from a given number of hours of work, and we can expect the individual to purchase less leisure and therefore choose to work more hours. Similarly, in terms of a wage decline, the substitution effect evidences itself as a decline in work hours. A reduction in the wage rate makes leisure

---

[5] In mathematical terms, substitution effect $= \dfrac{\Delta H}{\Delta W}\bigg|\, \bar{Y} > 0$, where H = hours of work, W = wage, and $\bar{Y}$ = constant wage.

[6] An alternative way to express the substitution effect is to say that a higher wage rate reduces the "price of income" because it now takes a smaller amount of work time to obtain $1 worth of goods. When the wage rate is $2 per hour, the "price" of $1 of income is half an hour of work time. But if the wage rate increases to $4 per hour, the "price" of $1 of income falls to one-quarter of an hour. Now that income is cheaper, it makes sense to purchase more of it. This purchase is made by working more hours and taking less leisure. The classic article is Lionel Robbins, "On the Elasticity of Demand for Income in Terms of Effort," *Economica,* June 1930, pp. 123–29.

TABLE 2.1

Wage Changes and Hours of Work: Substitution and Income Effects

(1) Size of Effects	(2) Impact on Hours of Work		(3) Slope of Labor Supply Curve
	(a) Wage Rate Increase	(b) Wage Rate Decrease	
Substitution effect exceeds income effect.	Increase	Decrease	Positive
Income effect equals substitution effect.	No change	No change	Vertical
Income effect exceeds substitution effect.	Decrease	Increase	Negative

cheaper, prompting one to consume more of it. Once again, the final outcome depends on the relative strength of the two effects. You should study Table 2.1 carefully to be certain that you fully understand it.

Graphic Portrayal of Income and Substitution Effects

Figure 2.7 permits us to isolate graphically the income and substitution effects associated with a wage rate increase for a specific person. Remember that the substitution effect reflects the change in desired hours of work arising solely because an increase in the wage rate alters the relative prices of income and leisure. Therefore, to isolate the substitution effect, we must control for the increase in income created by the increase in the wage rate. Recall, too, that the income effect indicates the change in the hours of work occurring solely because the higher wage rate means a larger total income from any number of hours of work. In portraying the income effect, we must hold constant the relative prices of income and leisure—in other words, the wage rate.

Consider Figure 2.7. As the wage rate increases and shifts the budget line from HW_1 to HW_2, the resulting movement of the utility-maximizing position from u_1 on I_1 to u_2 on I_2 is the consequence of the combined income and substitution effects. The *income effect* is isolated by drawing the budget line nW', which is parallel to HW_1 and tangent to I_2 at point u_2'. The vertical distance Hn measures the amount of *nonlabor* income that would be required to make the individual just as well off (that is, attain the same total utility) at u_2' as at u_2. But by moving the individual from curve I_1 to curve I_2 with *nonlabor* income, we have left the wage rate (that is, the relative prices of leisure and goods) unchanged.[7] No substitution effect is involved here. The movement from u_1 to u_2' therefore measures or isolates the income effect. As noted earlier, this effect results in fewer work hours when analyzed from the vantage point of an increase in wage rates and hence an increase in income. Specifically, the income effect would result in the individual wanting to work $h_1 h_2'$ fewer hours.

The *substitution effect* is isolated as follows. The substitution effect occurs solely because the slope of the budget line—the relative prices of income and leisure—has been altered by the assumed increase in the wage rate. We are concerned with budget lines

[7] Note that the slopes of HW_1 and nW' are the same; the lines are parallel, meaning the wage rate embodied in both budget lines is the same.

FIGURE 2.7   **The Income and Substitution Effects of a Wage Rate Increase**
Assuming leisure is a normal good, the income effect associated with a wage increase will always reduce hours of work. It is shown here as a reduction in work time of h_1h_2' hours. The substitution effect, stemming from a rise in the wage rate, evidences itself in an increase in the hours of work. The increase in hours of work of $h_2'h_2$ hours shows the substitution effect. In this instance the substitution effect outweighs the income effect, and the worker chooses to work h_1h_2 additional hours as a result of the higher wage.

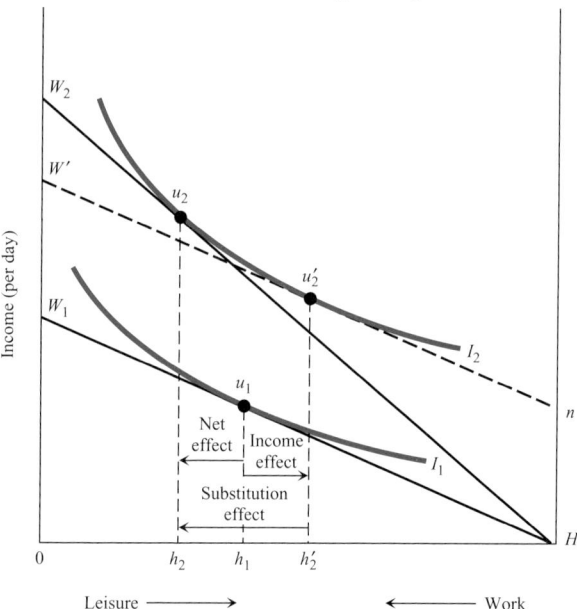

nW' and HW_2 because their comparison involves no change in the individual's well-being; they pertain to the same indifference curve I_2. Line nW', however, reflects the original wage rate (also embodied in HW_1), whereas HW_2 mirrors the new higher wage rate. The movement from u_2' to u_2 on curve I_2 is the substitution effect. It is solely the result of a change in the relative prices of leisure and goods or, specifically, the fact that goods have become cheaper and leisure more expensive. It is no surprise that this prompts a substitution of work (goods) for leisure. For a wage rate increase, the hours of work rise (the substitution effect). In this case, the individual wishes to work $h_2'h_2$ more hours.

Keep in mind that the individual does not actually "move" to a new optimal position in two distinct steps, but rather goes directly from u_1 to u_2. We have conceptually isolated the income and substitution effects to stress that there are two opposing ways in which a wage increase affects the worker: by increasing monetary income *and* by increasing the relative price of leisure. Both effects are at work, but one effect may dominate the other.[8]

---

[8] We have presented the Hicks decomposition of income and substitution effects, which holds the utility constant, when deriving the substitution effect. An alternative approach is the Slutsky decomposition, which holds income level constant, when calculating the substitution effect. The decompositions don't differ in the ultimate impact of a wage change on labor supply—just in the intermediate steps.

In Figure 2.7, the income and substitution effects can be thought of in terms of a boating analogy. Assume a boat is drifting on the ocean. Suppose the tide moves the boat eastward while the surface wind blows it westward. Both forces are present, but whether the boat actually moves east or west depends on which of these forces is strongest. So it is also with the income and substitution effects of a wage change.

To summarize: In this instance the income effect is represented by the rightward horizontal movement from u_1 to u_2'—that is, from Hh_1 to Hh_2' hours of work. The substitution effect is shown by the leftward horizontal movement from u_2' to u_2—that is, from Hh_2' to Hh_2 hours of work. In this case, the substitution effect (increased work hours) is larger than the income effect (reduced work hours). The net effect is an increase in hours of work from Hh_1 to Hh_2; at the higher wage rate, the individual wants to work h_1h_2 additional hours. This individual is clearly on the upward-sloping segment of his or her labor supply curve; the wage rate and the desired hours of work are directly related.

It is a worthwhile exercise for you to diagram and explain the case in which the income effect is larger than the substitution effect, causing the labor supply curve to be backward-bending. Questions 2 and 3 at the end of this chapter also are relevant.

Rationale for Backward-Bending Supply Curve

From Figure 2.6 we remember that wage rate increases are initially associated with the desire to work more hours. Specifically, for the wage increases that shift the budget line from W_1 through W_3 the absolute value of the substitution effects must be greater than that of the income effects, yielding the forward-rising segment of the labor supply curve. But further increases in the wage rate that shift the budget line from W_3 through W_5 are associated with the choice to work fewer hours. The income effects of these wage rate increases are greater than the substitution effects, yielding the backward-bending segment of the labor supply curve.

What is the rationale for this reversal? The answer is that points u_1 and u_2 are at positions on indifference curves where the amount of leisure is large relative to the amount of income (goods). That is, u_1 and u_2 are located on relatively flat portions of indifference curves, where MRS L, Y is small because the individual is willing to give up substantial amounts of leisure for an additional unit of income or goods. This means that the substitution effect is large—so large that it dominates the income effect. The individual's labor supply curve is forward-rising: Higher wage rates induce more hours of work. But points u_3, u_4, and u_5 are reached only after much leisure has been exchanged in the labor market for income. At these points, the individual has a relatively large amount of income and relatively little leisure. This is reflected in the relative steepness of the indifference curves. In other words, MRS L, Y is large, indicating that the individual is willing to give up only a small amount of leisure for an additional unit of income. This means that the substitution effect is small and in this case is dominated by the income effect. Consequently, the labor supply curve of the individual becomes backward-bending: Rising wage rates are associated with fewer hours of work.

Empirical Evidence

What do empirical studies reveal about labor supply curves? The evidence differs rather sharply between males and females. Specifically, most studies indicate that male labor supply is quite insensitive to changes in wage rates, whereas female labor supply is fairly responsive to changes in wage rates. In a survey of 18 to 20 studies, Blundell and McCurdy report that a 10 percent increase in male wage rates would increase the amount of labor supplied by 1 percent in the median study.[9] However, the corresponding figure for married women was 8 percent.[10] Apparently for men the substitution effect very slightly dominates the income effect when wage rates rise. For women, the substitution effect seems to substantially dominate the income effect.

How might we explain the apparent differences in the labor supply responses of males and females to a wage change? The answer hinges on existing differences in the allocation of time. A high percentage of prime-age adult males—over 90 percent—work full-time. Furthermore, men on the average do relatively little housework. Thus increased hours of work in response to a wage rate increase would have to come at the expense of pure leisure—that is, nonproductive activities or rest and relaxation. Apparently pure leisure and labor market work are not highly substitutable. The result is a small substitution effect for men and a nearly vertical labor supply curve. In comparison, the labor market participation rate for women is significantly less than that for men; many women work part-time, and women assume major responsibility for work within the home. At the risk of oversimplification, this means that while men use their time in basically two ways (market work and pure leisure), women use their time in three ways (market work, work in the home, and pure leisure). For many married women, work in the home and work in the labor market are highly substitutable. That is, household work may be accomplished by doing it oneself *or* by working in the labor market and using a portion of one's earnings for hiring housecleaning and child care help and purchasing prepared meals. Thus when wage rates increase, many women substitute labor market work for work in the home. They enter the labor force, switch from part-time to full-time jobs, or increase their hours on full-time jobs.[11] In other words, a strong substitution effect occurs, which implies an upward-sloping labor supply curve for married women.

It is important to note that the sensitivity of married women to wage rates appears to be diminishing over time, and their responsiveness is becoming more like that of men. Blau and Kahn report that the responsiveness of married women to changes in wage rates fell by half between 1980 and 2000.[12] They argue that this finding is the result of women's greater labor market attachment and men and women more equally sharing home and market responsibilities.

---

[9] Richard E. Blundell and Thomas E. McCurdy, "Labor Supply: A Review of Alternative Approaches," in Orley Ashenfelter and David Card (eds.), *Handbook of Labor Economics Volume 3A* (Amsterdam: North-Holland, 1999), pp. 1559–1695.

[10] For a similar finding for women, see Joyce P. Jacobsen, *The Economics of Gender*, 2nd Edition (Oxford, UK: Blackwell, 1998).

[11] Most of the gender differences in the labor supply result from differences in labor force participation between men and women, not from differences in the hours of work supplied by those working. See James J. Heckman, "What Has Been Learned about Labor Supply in the Past Twenty Years?" *American Economic Review,* May 1993, pp. 116–21.

[12] Francine D. Blau and Lawrence M. Kahn, "Changes in the Labor Supply of Married Women: 1980–2000," *Journal of Labor Economics*, 2007.

2.1	**World of Work**	Sleep Time Linked to Earnings*

The horizontal axis in our graphs in this chapter measures leisure, which includes hours spent sleeping. If sleep time is biologically determined, then a worker has a fixed amount of nonsleep time to allocate between work and waking leisure. But a novel study by Jeff Biddle and Daniel Hamermesh suggests that sleep time itself may be a matter of economic discretion.

Biddle and Hamermesh analyzed minute-to-minute diaries kept by 706 people between the ages of 23 and 65. They found that a 25 percent increase in wages reduced sleep time for the average worker by about 1 percent. A doubling of wages resulted, on average, in 20 fewer minutes of sleep time each night.

The researchers observed interesting differences in work–sleep choices between men and women. Higher wages reduced sleep time among men but did not increase hours worked. Instead men substi-

tuted waking leisure for sleep time. Men apparently responded to the income effect of the wage increase by sleeping less as a way of freeing more time to enjoy the products made available by their increased income. Alternatively, women responded to wage increases by working more hours but not reducing their sleep time. Working women took their added work time from hours of waking leisure. Why didn't women reduce their sleep time? The answer may lie in the fact that women, on average, slept 5 percent fewer hours than working men. Women may simply have been operating too close to their biological limits to reduce their sleep time further.

* Based on Jeff Biddle and Daniel Hamermesh, "Sleep and the Allocation of Time," *Journal of Political Economy*, October 1990, pp. 922–43.

Elasticity versus Changes in Labor Supply

To this point, we have been discussing the direction in which wage changes cause an individual to alter the hours of work supplied. Implicitly, our discussion has focused on the wage elasticity of individual labor supply. More precisely, **wage elasticity of labor supply** is defined as follows:

$$E_s = \frac{\text{percentage change in quantity of labor supplied}}{\text{percentage change in the wage rate}} \qquad \textbf{(2.1)}$$

Over specific ranges of an individual's labor supply curve, the elasticity coefficient given in Equation (2.1) may be zero (perfectly inelastic), infinite (perfectly elastic), less than 1 (relatively inelastic), greater than 1 (relatively elastic), or negative (backward-bending). The elasticity will depend on the relative strengths of the income and substitution effects generated by a wage rate change. But these movements *along* an existing individual labor supply curve [as in Figure 2.6(b)] should not be confused with *shifts* in the entire supply curve. These shifts—increases or decreases in labor supply—occur in response to changes in either of two factors that we have heretofore held constant. First, changes in *nonlabor income* may shift an individual's labor supply curve. Receiving a large inheritance, winning a lottery, qualifying for a pension, or becoming eligible for welfare benefits may shift one's labor supply curve leftward—that is, cause a decrease in labor supply. Or conversely, the layoff of one's spouse or a significant decline in dividend income may produce an increase (rightward shift) in labor supply.

Second, a change in a person's indifference map—that is, in work–leisure preferences—may shift the labor supply curve. An improvement in working conditions, availability of child care, or large medical bills may change a person's indifference map in ways that increase his or her labor supply. Working in the opposite direction, purchasing a product requiring leisure to enjoy or reading a culturally acceptable retirement age may alter one's indifference map so that labor supply declines. A more detailed treatment of factors that shift the labor supply curve is found in Chapter 6.

To summarize: As Figure 2.6 suggests, given work–leisure preferences and nonlabor income, a change in wage rates traces out or locates the individual's labor supply curve. The elasticity of this curve for any particular wage change—that is, the sensitivity of hours one wants to work to a change in wages—depends on the relative sizes of the income and substitution effects. In contrast, changes in work–leisure preferences or in nonlabor income shift the location of one's labor supply curve.

<table>
<tr>
<td>

2.2

Quick Review

</td>
<td>

- A change in the wage rate produces two simultaneous effects: *(a)* an income effect that, taken alone, changes a worker's desired hours of work in the opposite direction as the wage rate change, and *(b)* a substitution effect that, taken alone, changes a worker's desired hours of work in the same direction as the wage rate change.

- As the wage rate rises, the labor supply curve for a typical person first is positively sloped as the substitution effect swamps the income effect; eventually the curve becomes negatively sloped (turns backward) as the income effect of further wage rate hikes exceeds the substitution effect.

- The wage elasticity of supply is the percentage change in the quantity of labor supplied divided by the percentage change in the wage rate.

Your Turn

Suppose an individual's wage rate decreases and the income effect dominates the substitution effect. What will be the impact on the desired hours of work? What is the relevant segment of the person's labor supply curve? (*Answers:* See page 596.)

</td>
</tr>
</table>

APPLYING AND EXTENDING THE MODEL

The basic model just developed outlines the logic of the work–leisure decision, provides a rationale for an individual's backward-bending labor supply curve, and helps us understand changes in individual labor supply. Our goal now is to extend, embellish, and apply the basic work–leisure model. Specifically, we want to show that the work–leisure model is useful in delineating reasons for nonparticipation in the labor force, in explaining how a standard workweek might cause certain workers to feel overemployed or underemployed, and in comparing the impact that various pay schemes and income maintenance programs might have on work incentives.

Nonparticipants and the Reservation Wage

Figure 2.8 portrays the case of a nonparticipant: an individual who decides *not* to be in the labor force. Note the following characteristics in Figure 2.8. First, the person's indifference curves are steep, indicating that leisure (nonmarket time) is valued very highly relative to income. The marginal rates of substitution of leisure for income are high, meaning that the individual is very willing to forgo income for leisure or nonmarket time. This might reflect the preferences of, say, a 20-year-old who deems it important to devote time and effort to attending college. Second, we note the availability of nonlabor income *HN*. (Ignore all other budget lines but *HNW* for the moment.) Perhaps this nonlabor income takes the form of an intrahousehold transfer to the young student from the earned income of parents. Finally, the relative flatness of the *NW* budget line indicates that the wage rate that this individual can earn in the labor market is relatively low. For example, the student may have modest skills and little or no labor market experience and therefore is not yet able to command a high wage rate by working.

The optimal position in Figure 2.8 is based on the same principle employed in Figure 2.5: Given budget line *HNW*, choose the position that puts one on the highest attainable indifference curve. In this case, the highest level of utility is achieved at point *N*. Here the budget constraint *HNW* touches I_3. At this point the individual is *not* participating in the labor market; all of this person's time is devoted to nonmarket activities. The technical reason is that at all points within the axes of the diagram, the person's indifference curves are more steeply sloped than the budget constraint. In other words, at all points within the diagram, the individual values leisure (nonmarket time) more highly at the margin than does the market. Note that in contrast to

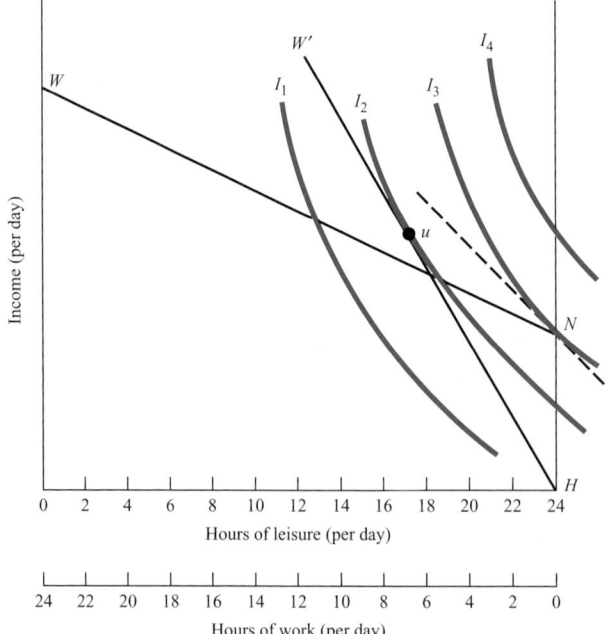

FIGURE 2.8

Nonparticipation: The College Student

A high subjective evaluation of nonwork time (reflected in steep indifference curves), the availability of nonlabor income (*HN*), and low earning ability (*NW* is relatively flat) are all factors conducive to not participating in the labor force.

Figure 2.5, the optimal outcome at *N* is *not* a tangency position but rather a "corner" solution. At *N* the wage rate is less than MRS *L, Y,* which means the individual values nonmarket time more highly than does the market. But given the fact that the individual is a nonparticipant, no further substitution of leisure for work is possible.

The importance of low earning capacity in the labor market and the availability of nonlabor income can be understood if we replace the original budget line *HNW* in Figure 2.8 with *HuW'*. This new budget line reduces nonlabor income to zero *and* assumes that a much higher wage rate can be garnered in the labor market. Suppose, for example, that our student is a highly skilled computer programmer who has immediate employment opportunities at a high wage. Or to make the point even more graphic, suppose the student is a premier college basketball player who is sought by the National Basketball Association. We find that under these new conditions the individual would prefer to participate in the labor force. The optimal position will now be at *u,* where the person will want to work six or seven hours per day.

Figure 2.8 also allows us to introduce the concept of the reservation wage, which is useful in understanding why some individuals participate in the labor force and others do not. In simple terms, the *reservation wage is the highest wage rate at which an individual chooses* not *to work or, if you prefer, the lowest wage rate at which one would decide to work.* When nonlabor income is *HN,* as in Figure 2.8, the reservation wage is the market wage rate implicit in the broken budget line that is equal to the slope of indifference curve I_3 at zero hours of work. At this particular wage rate, the value of work and the value of nonmarket time (leisure) are equal. If the market wage is below the reservation wage, the individual will clearly choose to be a nonparticipant. The relatively low market wage rate embodied in the *NW* segment of the *HNW* budget line demonstrates this decision *not* to be in the labor force. In nontechnical terms, at point *N* the value of nonmarket time to this individual exceeds the value of work, and therefore this person's well-being would be reduced by working. Conversely, if the market wage rate were above the reservation wage, the individual would be induced to become a labor market participant. You can demonstrate this by drawing a steeper budget line from point *N* that is tangent to I_4 at some point. With this steeper (higher market wage) budget line, we would find at point *N* that the value of work would be greater than the value of nonmarket time and that the individual's economic welfare would be enhanced by working.

Figure 2.9 illustrates another common instance of nonparticipation in the labor force. Here we assume that an elderly worker is initially participating in the labor force, working about nine hours per day at optimal position *u* on indifference curve I_1. Suppose now that when the worker reaches age 65 a private or public pension of *HN* becomes available, *provided* the individual retires fully from work. In other words, the choice is between budget line *HW* and the associated optimal position at *u* or budget line *NN'* and the corner solution at point *N*. We find that *N* is preferable to *u* because it is associated with the higher indifference curve I_2. In this case, the availability of a pension—for example, Social Security benefits—induces the individual to become a nonparticipant. Stated differently, it shifts the person's labor supply curve [Figure 2.6(b)] leftward so that no labor is supplied at the market wage. Note that the decision to be a nonparticipant entails a *reduction* in money income but a more than compensating *increase* in leisure. The individual is better off at *N* than at *u,* even though income is reduced.

FIGURE 2.9

Nonparticipation: Pensions and the Elderly

An elderly worker whose wage rate yields the budget line *HW* will be a labor force participant at *u*. However, when a pension of *HN* becomes available at, say, age 65, the individual will prefer to become a nonparticipant at point *N*.

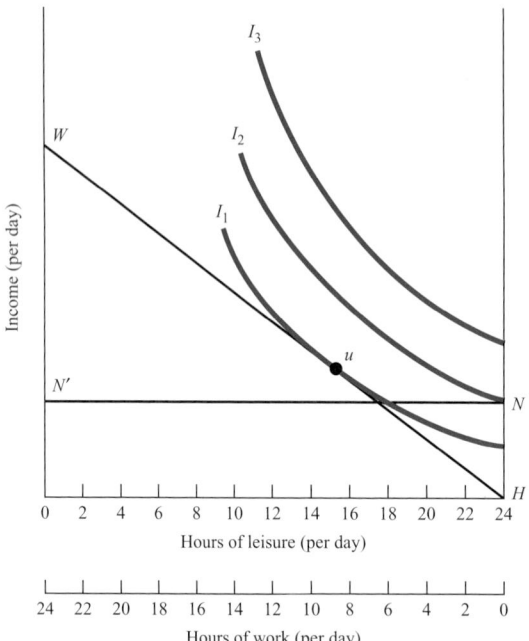

Empirical research confirms several generalizations arising from our discussion of Figures 2.8 and 2.9. First, other things being equal, full-time college attendance *is* a deterrent to labor force participation. This is also true of such things as the desire to care for one's preschool children. Stated alternatively, those who attach great marginal utility to nonmarket time (college attendance, child care) are more likely to be nonparticipants in the labor force. Second, other things being the same, the higher the nonlabor income available to a person from parents, spouses, Social Security benefits, private pensions, welfare, and other sources, the less likely it is that the person will be a labor force participant. Finally, all else being equal, the greater the opportunity cost of not working—that is, the higher the wage obtainable in the labor market—the more likely it is that a person will be a labor force participant.[13]

2.2

Standard Workday

Our discussion thus far has implicitly assumed that workers can individually determine the number of hours they work. This is typically not the case. In the United States a standard

---

[13] Numerous studies confirm these conclusions. For example, for a discussion of the impact of Social Security (nonlabor income) on the participation decision, see Michel J. Vanderhart, "Labor Supply of Older Men: Does Social Security Matter?" *Economic Inquiry,* April 2003, pp. 250–63. For an analysis of the effect of child care costs on the labor force participation decision, see Rachel Connelly and Jean Kimmel, "The Effect of Child Care Costs on the Employment and Welfare Recipiency of Single Mothers," *Southern Economic Journal,* March 2002, pp. 498–519. For an investigation of the impact of tax changes, see Richard Blundell, Alan Duncan, and Costas Meghir, "Estimating Labor Supply Responses Using Tax Reforms," *Econometrica,* July 1998, pp. 827–61.

2.2	World of Work	The Carnegie Conjecture*

In 1891 Andrew Carnegie, the well-known philanthropist and baron of U.S. Steel, asserted that "parents who leave their children enormous wealth generally deaden their children's talents and energies and tempt them to lead less productive lives." In the language of the work–leisure model, Carnegie was suggesting that large inheritances have a significant pure income effect. We know that if leisure is a normal good, this effect may cause some workers to reduce their work hours or possibly withdraw from the labor force. Graphically, inheritances will produce an upward parallel shift in the wage rate line facing an individual. The result will be a decline in the optimal number of work hours.

In 1992 Holtz-Eakin, Joulfaian, and Rosen examined three years of data from tax returns for 4,300 people receiving inheritances. Their findings lend general support to Carnegie's conjecture. For example, a single person receiving an inheritance of more than $150,000 was about four times more likely to leave the labor force as a single person inheriting $25,000. Specifically, 4.6 percent of people receiving inheritances of less than $25,000 exited the labor force; 10 percent of the people getting inheritances between $25,000 and $150,000 left; and 18.2 percent of those inheriting $150,000 or more quit their jobs.

Also, for families receiving large inheritances whose members continued to work, the growth of labor earnings slowed compared to families receiving lesser inheritances. This suggests that large inheritances may reduce work hours or the supply of effort, even when people receiving inheritances continue to work.

Two other findings of this study are of interest. First, people not working when they received large inheritances were less likely than those receiving smaller inheritances to enter the labor force in subsequent years. Second, people receiving larger inheritances were less likely to be working during the years immediately preceding the inheritance. Perhaps people *anticipating* large inheritances have lower incentives to work. An alternative explanation is that those expecting large inheritances can better afford to quit their jobs to attend to the needs of their dying parents.

Although inheritances reduce labor force participation, they permit the children to attain higher indifference curves—to achieve greater total utility. Moreover, those taking extra "leisure" may use it for socially beneficial activities such as volunteer work and educational pursuits. The point is simply that nonlabor income—be it from lottery winnings, pensions, intrahousehold transfers, or inheritance—is an important factor in understanding labor supply behavior.

* Based on Douglas Holtz-Eakin, David Joulfaian, and Harvey S. Rosen, "The Carnegie Conjecture: Some Empirical Evidence," *Quarterly Journal of Economics,* May 1993, pp. 413–36.

workday of 8 hours (40 hours per week) has evolved. This is partly due to federal legislation that obligates employers to pay time and a half for hours worked in excess of 40 per week. Furthermore, industries whose technologies involve the continuous processing of goods or components are able to divide the workday into three 8-hour shifts.

Overemployment

What may happen when a worker confronts a standard workday of HD hours, as illustrated in Figure 2.10? Consider first the solid indifference curves for Smith shown in the lower right portion of the diagram. Smith's optimal position is at u_s, where he prefers to work only Hh_s hours per day. But this is not a relevant choice; Smith can either work HD hours or not at all. That is, the relevant choice is between working the standard workday at P or

FIGURE 2.10

Overemployment and Underemployment

When confronted with a standard workday of *HD*, Smith (solid indifference curves) will feel overemployed while Jones (broken indifference curves) will feel underemployed.

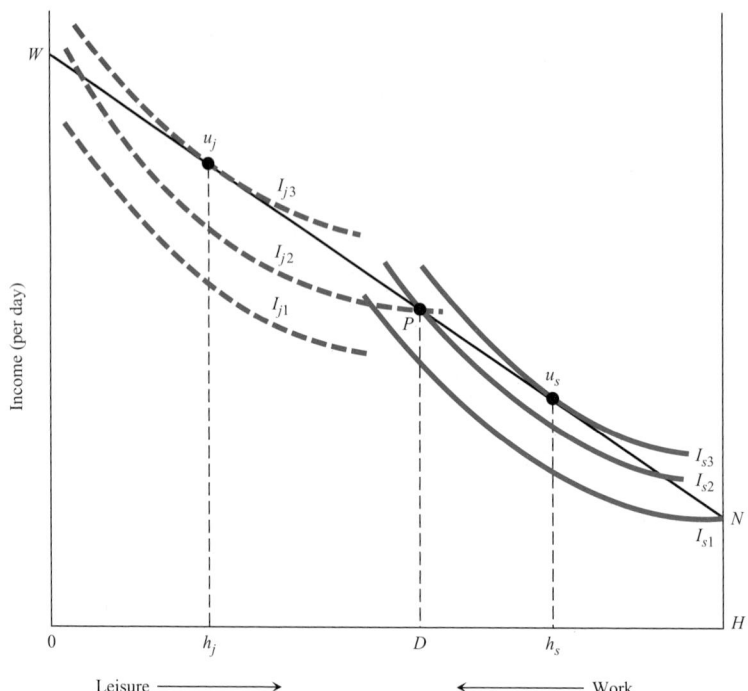

being a nonparticipant at *N*. What to do? In this instance, it is preferable to work the standard workday because it entails a higher indifference curve I_{s2} as opposed to I_{s1}. Note once again that this is not a tangency position. At *P* the slope of I_{s2} is greater than the slope of the budget line *NW*. The marginal rate of substitution of leisure for income exceeds the wage rate, which means that the worker values leisure more highly at the margin than does the market. Clearly Smith would be better off at u_s with more leisure and less work per day.

Simply put, at point *P* in Figure 2.10 Smith will feel **overemployed.** Faced with a standard workday denying him added leisure, Smith may compensate by engaging in absenteeism; he may more or less habitually miss a day of work every week or so. In fact, the absence rate—the ratio of full-time workers with absences in a typical week to total full-time employment—was 3.2 percent in 2006. In that year lost work time from absences was 1.8 percent of total hours usually worked. Many of these absent workers are absent without pay. Also, the overemployed worker described in Figure 2.10 may have a relatively high rate of job turnover. The worker obtains more leisure by frequently being "between jobs." Of course, we have purposely ruled out the possibility of part-time employment, which would appeal to this overemployed worker.

Underemployment

The broken indifference curves in the upper left portion of Figure 2.10 portray the position of Jones, an **underemployed** worker. Jones would prefer to be at u_j, where she would work the long workday of Hh_j hours as opposed to the shorter standard workday of *HD* hours. Note again that *P* is not a tangency position. At *P* the slope of Jones's indifference curve

2.3 World of Work

More Flexible Work Schedules*

Wal-Mart, the largest private employer in the United States, is radically changing how it sets the schedules of its workers. In 2007 Wal-Mart started switching from traditional worker shifts to flexible worker shifts that start at nonstandard times and vary from week to week. Wal-Mart uses computer software to determine the work schedules based on the numbers of customers in their stores at different times. Other stores, such as Payless Shoes and Radio Shack, have also adopted this approach to setting work schedules.

This new scheduling approach has advantages to both stores and customers. Customers have shorter checkout times because stores have enough personnel to meet customer demand. Stores can reduce labor costs by scaling back work hours if a worker is approaching full-time status or will receive overtime pay. Managers spend less time on setting work schedules, which lets them devote their attention to other issues.

There are some disadvantages to flexible scheduling for workers. It can lead to some unusual work shifts. For example, instead of three 8-hour days a week, a person may work four 6-hour shifts, which may be mornings one week and evenings the next week. In addition, the number of hours worked may vary from week to week. These unpredictable work schedules lead to unpredictable paychecks as well as difficulty in scheduling child care.

* Based on Kris Maher, "Wal-Mart Seeks New Flexibility in Worker Shifts," *The Wall Street Journal*, January 3, 2007, p. A1.

I_{j2} is less than the budget line. Jones's marginal rate of substitution of leisure for income is less than the wage rate. Simply stated, at the margin Jones values leisure less highly than does the market. This means that Jones will feel *underemployed* at P. Jones may realize her desire for more work and less leisure by moonlighting, or taking a second job. You should use Figure 2.10 to demonstrate that Jones might be willing to take a second job even if the wage rate were less than that paid on the primary job. In fact, in 2005 some 7.5 million workers—approximately 5.3 percent of all employees—held multiple jobs.

Survey data suggest that the majority of workers are satisfied with the number of hours they work. In 1985 the Bureau of Labor Statistics surveyed some 84,000 workers, and almost two-thirds indicated that they would prefer to work their current number of hours at their present rate of pay, rather than work more or fewer hours at proportionately higher or lower earnings. Only 8 percent expressed a preference for shorter hours, with a proportionate decline in earnings. Approximately one-fourth of all surveyed workers wanted to work more hours, with a proportionate increase in earnings. Not surprisingly, this latter group was dominated by young workers and low-wage earners.[14]

Premium Pay versus Straight Time

Although we ordinarily think of a worker receiving the same wage rate regardless of the number of hours worked, this is not always the case. Indeed, the Fair Labor Standards Act of 1938 specifies that workers covered by the legislation must be paid a premium

[14] Susan E. Shank, "Preferred Hours of Work and Corresponding Earnings," *Monthly Labor Review*, November 1986, pp. 40–44. For an analysis of racial differences in preferred work hours, see Linda A. Bell, "Differences in Work Hours and Hours Preferences by Race in the U.S." *Review of Social Economy*, Winter 1998, pp. 481–500.

2.4	**World of Work**	New Overtime Rules*

In March 2003 the U.S. Department of Labor proposed new rules for determining which workers are eligible for overtime pay under the Fair Labor Standards Act (FLSA). The FLSA requires that covered workers receive time and a half for every hour worked past 40 hours during a workweek. Prior to the rule changes, about 80 percent of workers were eligible to receive overtime pay.

The rule changes were strongly supported by business groups and fiercely opposed by labor unions and other worker associations. Bills were introduced in Congress to stop implementation of the rule changes. However, no bill passed both houses of Congress. As a result, the changes were finalized in April 2004. The controversy continued after the rule changes were implemented, and additional attempts were made to overturn them.

To be exempt from overtime pay regulations, a worker has to meet three tests. First, the worker must earn more than a certain level. Second, the employee has to be paid a fixed salary and not by the hour. Third, the worker's duties have to be primarily administrative, professional, or executive in nature.

One of the rule changes increased the number of workers eligible for overtime pay. The minimum salary level to be exempt from overtime pay was raised from $155 ($170 for professionals) to $455 per week. The minimum salary level had not been raised since 1975. The U.S. Department of Labor estimated that 1.3 million workers would be covered as a result of this change.

Other rule changes decreased the number of white-collar workers eligible for overtime pay. For example, salaried workers who do nonmanual labor and earn more than $100,000 per year would be exempt from overtime provisions. The definitions of which workers could be classified as professional, administrative, or executive were expanded. Debate exists on how many additional workers would be exempt due to these changes. Supporters of the rule changes claimed only 107,000 more workers would lose the right to overtime pay. Critics argued many more workers would be exempt from overtime pay.

* Based on wire reports, **www.dol.gov**, and Ross Eisenbrey and Jared Bernstein, "Eliminating the Right to Overtime Pay," Economic Policy Institute Briefing Paper, June 2003.

wage—specifically, time and a half—for hours worked in excess of 40 per week. What impact does this premium pay provision have on the work–leisure decision? And how does it compare with a straight-time equivalent wage rate that provides an identical daily or weekly income from the same number of hours of work? Suppose, for example, that in a given industry a 10-hour workday (50-hour workweek) becomes commonplace. Does it make any difference with respect to work incentives to pay $6 per hour for the first 8 hours of work and $9 per hour for an additional 2 hours of overtime *or* to pay $6.60 per hour for each 10 hours of work? Both payment plans yield the same daily income of $66, so one is inclined to conclude that it makes no difference. But with the aid of Figure 2.11, we find that it *does* make a difference.

We assume in Figure 2.11 that a worker is initially at the optimal point u_1, where HW is tangent to indifference curve I_1. At u_1 the individual chooses to work Hh_1 hours, which we will presume to be the standard workday. Let us now suppose that the employer offers additional hours of overtime work at premium pay. This renders the u_1W segment of HW irrelevant, and the budget constraint now becomes Hu_1P. We observe that the optimal position will move to u_2 on the higher indifference curve I_2 and that the worker will choose to work h_1h_2 additional hours. Daily earnings will be u_2h_2.

FIGURE 2.11
Premium Wages and Straight-Time Equivalent
Premium wage rates for overtime work will be more conducive to more hours of work (Hh_2) than a straight-time wage rate that would yield an equivalent daily income (Hh_3).

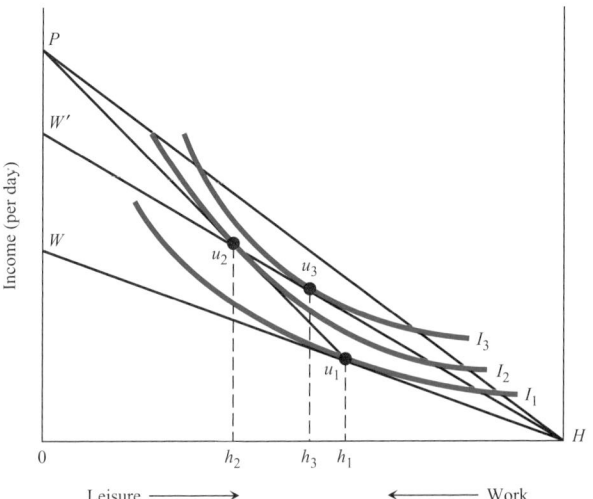

Consider now the alternative of a straight-line equivalent wage—that is, a standard hourly wage rate that will yield the same daily income of u_2h_2 for the Hh_2 hours of work. We can show the straight-time equivalent wage by drawing a new budget line HW' through u_2. The budget lines Hu_1P and HW' will both yield the same monetary income of u_2h_2 for Hh_2 hours of work. The important point is that if confronted with HW', the worker will want to move from u_2 to a new optimal position at u_3, where fewer hours than Hh_2 are worked. Stated differently, at u_2 indifference curve I_2 cuts HW' from above; that is, MRS L, Y is greater than the wage rate. This means that the worker subjectively values leisure more highly at the margin than does the market, and thus u_2 is no longer the optimal position under a straight-time pay arrangement. Our worker will feel over-employed when working Hh_2 hours on a straight-time pay plan (recall Figure 2.10).

Here is the conclusion: Premium wage rates for overtime work will call forth more hours of work than a straight-time wage rate that yields the same income at the same number of hours as that actually chosen by an individual paid the overtime premium. Why the difference? The use of premium pay will have a relatively small income effect because it applies only to hours worked in excess of Hh_1. In comparison, the straight-time equivalent wage will have a much larger income effect because it applies to *all* hours of work.[15] Figure 2.11 is essentially the labor market analog of price discrimination in the product market. Sellers of some products can obtain more revenue by charging different prices for different quantities of output. In the present analysis, we are observing that an employer can obtain a greater amount of labor for a given outlay by paying different wage rates for different hours of work.[16]

2.4

[15] Figure 2.11 is drawn so that for the straight-time equivalent wage the substitution effect dominates the income effect, and therefore the individual is on the forward-rising portion of her or his labor supply curve. This is why u_3 entails more hours of work than u_1. Such an outcome is not necessary. The diagram could have been drawn so that u_3 was to the right of u_1, in which case our basic conclusion would be even more evident.
[16] Kenneth E. Boulding, *Economic Analysis,* vol. 1, 4th ed. (New York: Harper and Row, 1966), p. 616. Our conclusion holds only if we restrict the employer from hiring additional workers.

2.3
Quick Review

- Steep indifference curves, the availability of nonlabor income, and low earning ability all contribute to nonparticipation in the labor force.
- The reservation wage is the lowest acceptable wage rate; below this wage a person would decide not to participate in the labor force.
- The standard eight-hour workday may leave some workers wanting additional hours of work (underemployed) and others wishing to work fewer hours (overemployed), depending on their indifference maps and earning abilities.
- Premium wage rates for overtime work provide a greater incentive for additional hours of work than a straight-time wage rate yielding an equivalent daily income.

Your Turn

Suppose you have a choice between two otherwise identical jobs, including hourly pay. In one job the employer sets the hours of work each week and in the other you select the number of hours. Which job would you prefer? Why? (*Answer:* See page 596.)

Income Maintenance Programs

The United States has a variety of *income maintenance programs*—also dubbed welfare or public assistance programs—whose purpose is to provide some minimum level of income to all families and individuals.[17] These programs include Supplemental Security Income, Temporary Assistance for Needy Families, food stamps, and Medicaid. Our objective is to examine the possible effects of such programs on work incentives.

Three Basic Features

Although details vary greatly, income maintenance programs have three basic features.

1 The **Income Guarantee or Basic Benefit**, *B*   This is the amount of public subsidy an individual or family would be paid if no earned income were received.[18]

2 The **Benefit Reduction Rate**, *t*   This refers to the rate at which a family's basic benefit is reduced as earned income increases. For example, if *t* is .50, then a family's basic benefit will be reduced by $.50 for every $1.00 of wage income earned. This means that

---

[17] Income maintenance programs are not to be confused with various social insurance programs. Income maintenance programs are designed to assist families and individuals who have more or less permanent disabilities or dependent children. These programs are financed out of general tax revenues and are regarded as public charity. To qualify for aid, one must demonstrate economic need. In contrast, social insurance programs (such as Old Age and Survivors Insurance and unemployment compensation) are tailored to replace a portion of the earnings lost due to retirement or temporary unemployment. They are financed by earmarked payroll taxes, and benefits are viewed as earned rights as a consequence of prior financial contributions. For a discussion of a variety of means-tested transfer programs, see Robert A. Moffitt (ed.), *Means-Tested Transfer Programs in the United States* (Chicago, IL: University of Chicago Press, 2003).

[18] We simplify by assuming that no nonwage income in the form of, say, interest or dividends is received.

if the market wage rate is $5.00, the family's *net* wage rate will be just $2.50 when the benefit reduction provision is taken into account. The critical point is that the benefit reduction rate reduces one's net gain from work. Economists often refer to the benefit reduction rate as an "implicit tax rate" because t has the same impact on the net income of a person participating in an income maintenance program as income tax rates have on the earnings of individuals not in the program.

3 The Break-Even Level of Income, Y_b   The basic benefit and the benefit reduction rate permit the calculation of the *break-even income*. This is the level of earned income at which the actual subsidy payment received by an individual or family becomes zero. It is the level of earned income at which an individual is dropped from an income maintenance program. As we will see in a moment, the break-even income depends on the sizes of the basic benefit and the benefit reduction rate.

Illustration

A simple numerical illustration might help relate these concepts to one another. The *actual subsidy payment S* received by an individual can be determined by the following formula:

$$S = B - tY \qquad\qquad \textbf{(2.2)}$$

where B = basic benefit.

t = benefit reduction rate.

Y = level of earned income.

Thus, for example, if B is $2,000, t is .50, and Y is $2,000, the actual subsidy payment received will be $1,000:

$$\$1,000 = \$2,000 - .50(\$2,000)$$

Furthermore, the break-even level of income can be calculated readily. A glance back at Equation (2.2) suggests that S will become zero—that is, the break-even income will be reached—when earned income Y is equal to B/t.[19] For our illustrative numbers, B is $2,000 and t is .50, so B/t—the break-even level of income—is therefore $2,000/.50, or $4,000. We verify this by substituting the relevant numbers into Equation (2.2):

$$\$0 = \$2,000 - .50(\$4,000)$$

Let's incorporate these concepts into Figure 2.12 to examine the impact of an income maintenance program on work incentives. The *HW* line shows us the budget constraint confronting the individual in the absence of an income maintenance program. The resulting optimal position is at u_1. For simplicity's sake, let's assume that the wage rate is $1.00 per hour and that the individual chooses to work 40 hours per week. Over the 50-week workyear earned income would be $2,000, as shown on the left vertical axis.

---

[19] The algebra is simple. By setting $S = 0$ in Equation (2.2) we get $0 = B - tY$. Therefore, $tY = B$ and $Y = B/t$.

FIGURE 2.12
Income Maintenance and Incentives to Work
An income maintenance program that incorporates both a basic benefit and a benefit reduction rate will change the budget constraint from *HW* to *HBY$_b$W*. This alteration moves the utility-maximizing position from u_1 to u_2 and reduces hours of work.

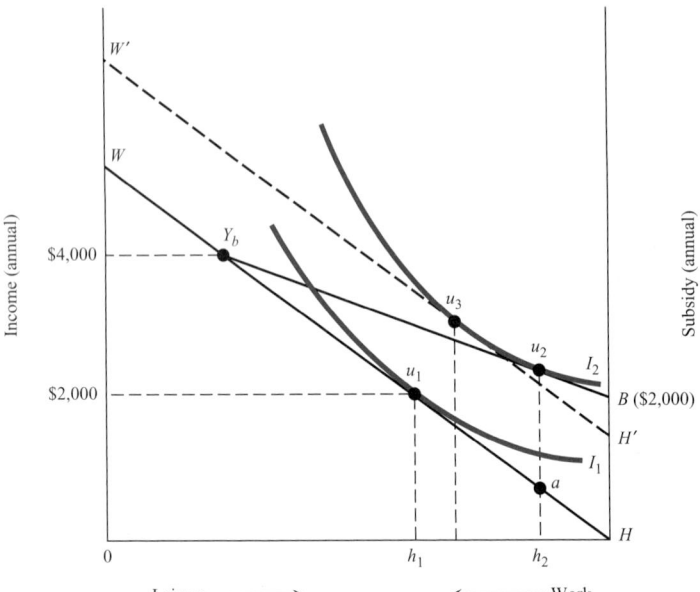

Now suppose an income maintenance program with the characteristics just described is enacted. The impact of this program is to change the budget constraint from *HW* to *HBY$_b$W*. Note that *HB* on the right vertical axis is the basic benefit; it is the amount of income subsidy the individual would receive if he or she had no earned income. The *BY$_b$* segment of the new budget constraint reflects the influence of the benefit reduction rate. Specifically, the slope of the *BY$_b$* segment is measured by the *net* wage rate—that is, the market wage rate as it is reduced by the benefit reduction rate. Thus while the absolute value of the slope of *HW* is 1.00 (reflecting the $1.00 wage rate), the slope of *BY$_b$* is only .50 (reflecting the $.50 *net* wage rate).[20] The vertical distance between *HW* and *BY$_b$* is equal to *S*, the actual subsidy received. Point *Y$_b$* indicates the break-even level of income because at this point the individual's earned income is sufficiently large ($4,000 in this case) so that the application of the .50 benefit reduction rate causes the actual subsidy payment *S* to become zero [see Equation (2.2)].

We observe in Figure 2.12 that the new optimal position is at u_2, where *HBY$_b$W* is tangent to indifference curve I_2. Although the individual's total money income has increased (from h_1u_1 to h_2u_2), *earned* income and the number of hours worked have both declined (from h_1u_1 to h_2a and from Hh_1 to Hh_2, respectively). In our earlier

[20] As noted, the slope of *BY$_b$* reflects the net wage rate w_n, which is the wage rate w multiplied by $(1-t)$; that is, $w_n = (1-t)w$. In our example the slope of *BY$_b$* is .50 = $(1-.5)1$. If the benefit reduction rate were .25, the net wage rate and slope of *BY$_b$* would be .75 = $(1-.25)1$. If the benefit reduction rate were 1.00, *BY$_b$* would be horizontal.

analysis of a wage *increase* (Figure 2.7), we found that the net effect on hours of work (work incentives) depended on the relative sizes of the income effect (reduction in hours of work) and the substitution effect (increase in hours of work). *In the present case, the income and substitution effects both reduce hours of work.* The tendency for the income effect to reduce hours of work is no surprise. The income maintenance program increases monetary income; and assuming leisure is a normal good, some of that income is "spent" on leisure and therefore fewer hours are worked. But curiously, the substitution effect also reduces hours of work. The presence of the benefit reduction rate *reduces* the *net* wage rate; it makes BY_b flatter than HW. Even though the basic benefit raises total monetary income, the benefit reduction feature means there has been an effective decrease in wage rates. Leisure is now cheaper—one sacrifices only \$.50 by not working an hour rather than \$1.00—so leisure is substituted for work.

Recalling our earlier diagrammatic separation of the income and substitution effects (Figure 2.7), we can draw the broken line $H'W'$ parallel to HW and tangent to I_2 at u_3. The horizontal distance between u_1 and u_3 is the income effect, and the horizontal distance between u_3 and u_2 is the substitution effect. We observe that both reduce the amount of work supplied.

Controversy

The various income maintenance programs have long been surrounded by controversy. This stems in part from fundamental ideological differences among policy makers. But it also reflects the fact that the accepted goals of income maintenance programs are in conflict with one another and that it is easy to disagree over the proper or optimal trade-offs. In particular, it is generally agreed that income maintenance programs should (1) effectively get poor people out of poverty, (2) maintain incentives to work, and (3) achieve goals 1 and 2 at a reasonable cost.

Figure 2.12 is a useful point of reference in explaining these goal conflicts. The imposition of an income maintenance program triggers income and substitution effects, both of which are negative with respect to work. Furthermore, we might improve the effectiveness of the program in eliminating poverty by increasing the basic benefit—that is, by shifting the BY_b line upward in Figure 2.12. But this will clearly make the program more costly. On one hand, a larger basic benefit would relocate point Y_b to the northwest on line HW and cause additional families to be eligible for subsidies. On the other hand, with a higher basic benefit, people already in the income maintenance program will each receive larger subsidy payments. Goal 1 conflicts with goal 3.

Finally, given the basic benefit, one might want to reduce the benefit reduction rate (increase the slope of the BY_b line) to preserve incentives to work. A reduction in the benefit reduction rate increases the net wage rate, boosting the price of leisure and inducing the substitution of work for leisure. The higher net wage rate may also prompt individuals who are currently not in the labor force to become participants (see Figure 2.8). However, the resulting increase in the slope of the BY_b line will extend point Y_b to the northwest along HW, making more families eligible for subsidies and therefore increasing program costs. An increase in the slope of the BY_b line will also boost costs by increasing the actual subsidy received for any given number of hours worked. Goal 2 conflicts with goal 3.[21]

The End of Welfare as an Entitlement

In August 1996 President Clinton signed the Personal Responsibility and Work Opportunity Reconciliation Act (PRWORA), which fundamentally changed the welfare system in the United States. In prior years the welfare system had been criticized for its inherent work disincentives as well as accused of encouraging dependence among welfare recipients. The welfare reform attempted to correct these perceived deficiencies in several ways and shift more control over welfare to state governments.

A major goal of the law is to make receiving welfare a transition period before returning to work. The law replaced the existing Aid to Families with Dependent Children (AFDC) program with the **Temporary Assistance for Needy Families (TANF)** program. In contrast to AFDC, TANF requires welfare recipients to work after two years of receiving assistance with few exceptions.[22] Welfare recipients may meet the work provision by being employed, attending vocational training, or performing community service. The act also mandates a five year lifetime limit on the receipt of cash welfare payments (though states may exempt up to 20 percent of their recipients).[23] It also provides child care and health insurance for families entering the job market. Finally, most forms of public assistance are denied to legal immigrants for five years or until they become citizens.

The PRWORA also tries to encourage responsibility regarding parenthood. It includes provisions to help enforce the collection of child support payments. Teen pregnancy is discouraged with measures such as requiring that unmarried minor parents must live with an adult and stay in school to receive assistance.

As Figure 2.13 shows, since the enactment of welfare reform, there has been a large drop in the number of families receiving welfare. In 1996, 4.6 million families were receiving welfare. By 2006, this figure had fallen by 61 percent to 1.8 million families.

Several factors account for this dramatic drop in caseloads. First, the economic boom during the 1990s improved the labor market conditions facing welfare recipients. The unemployment rate fell over the decade, while inflation-adjusted wages of less skilled workers rose. Wallace and Blank found that the strong economy can explain about one-fifth of the decline in caseloads.[24] Second, the substantial expansion in the early

---

[21] In fact, the effect of a reduction in the benefit reduction rate on work incentives is more complex than our discussion suggests. On one hand, a decline in the benefit reduction rate will reduce the size of the negative income and substitution effects for those currently receiving benefits. Therefore, the hours of work for this group will increase. On the other hand, the lower benefit reduction rate will extend program benefits to additional families that originally had not received benefits. The resultant income and substitution effects will both be negative for this group, causing them to work fewer hours. The overall impact on work incentives will depend on the average response of each group and their relative sizes. See Gary Burtless, "The Economist's Lament: Public Assistance in America," *Journal of Economic Perspectives,* Winter 1990, pp. 68–70.

[22] For an overview of the differences between TANF and AFDC, see Rebecca M. Blank and David T. Ellwood, "The Clinton Legacy for America's Poor," in Jeffrey A. Frankel and Peter R. Orszag (eds.), *American Economic Policy in the 1990s* (Cambridge, MA: MIT Press, 2002).

[23] States are permitted to impose stricter limits if they so choose.

[24] Geoffrey Wallace and Rebecca M. Blank, "What Goes Up Must Come Down? Explaining the Recent Changes in Public Assistance Caseloads," in Sheldon Danziger (ed.), *Economic Conditions and Welfare Reform* (Kalamazoo, MI: Upjohn Institute, 1999).

FIGURE 2.13 **Welfare Caseloads**

Between 1970 and 1994, welfare caseloads under the Aid to Families with Dependent Children (AFDC) program generally expanded. Following enactment of the Temporary Assistance for Needy Families (TANF) program in 1996, welfare caseloads declined by roughly 60 percent.

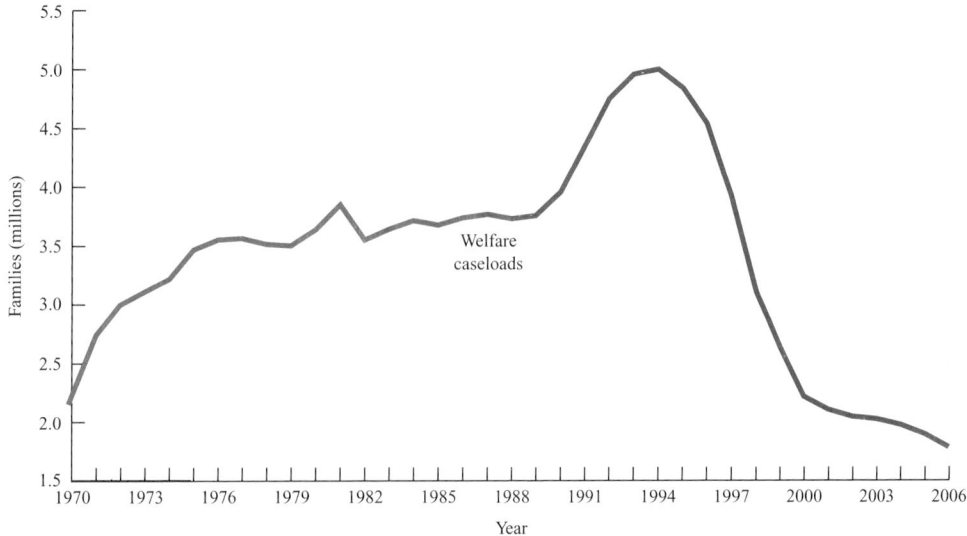

2.5

1990s of the earned income tax credit (EITC) program, which provides a tax subsidy to working low-income families, increased the incentive of welfare recipients to enter the labor market and thus lowered the number of recipients.[25] Third, policy changes such as benefit time limits, welfare benefit reductions, child care expansions, and changes in training programs appear to account for a significant portion of the decline in welfare caseloads. The importance of each factor has yet to be precisely determined.[26] The long-run consequences of welfare reform, including its success in reducing poverty rates, remain to be evaluated.[27]

---

[25] One study suggests that the expansion of the EITC is the most important factor in the reduction of the welfare caseload. See Bruce D. Meyer and Dan T. Rosenbaum, "Welfare, the Earned Income Tax Credit, and the Labor Supply of Single Mothers," *Quarterly Journal of Economics,* August 2001, pp. 1063–133. For another study showing a large effect of the EITC, see David T. Ellwood, "The Impact of the Earned Income Tax Credit and Social Policy Reforms on Work, Marriage, and Living Arrangements," *National Tax Journal,* December 2000, pp. 1063–105.

[26] For a review of the early evidence on the impact of welfare reform, see Rebecca M. Blank, "Evaluating Welfare Reform in the United States," *Journal of Economic Literature,* December 2002, pp. 1105–66. Also see Jeffrey Grogger and Lynn A. Karoly, *Welfare Reform: Effects of a Decade of Change* (Cambridge, MA: Harvard University Press, 2005).

[27] For some speculation on the long-run consequences, see David T. Ellwood, "Anti-Poverty Policy for Families in the Next Century: From Welfare to Work—and Worries," *Journal of Economic Perspectives,* Winter 2000, pp. 187–206. It is important to note that the reduction in welfare caseloads has increased caseloads in other public assistance programs such as Supplemental Security Income. See Lucie Schmidt and Purvi Sevak, "AFDC, SSI, and Welfare Reform Aggressiveness: Caseload Reductions versus Caseload Shifting," *Journal of Human Resources,* Summer 2004, pp. 792–812.

2.5	**World of Work**	The Labor Supply Impact of the Earned Income Tax Credit*

Since its initiation in 1975, the earned income tax credit (EITC) has grown rapidly and is now the largest antipoverty program in the United States. Currently over 19 million people participate in the program. Spending on EITC is nearly as much as the combined spending on Temporary Assistance for Needy Families and food stamps.

The EITC supplements the wages of low-income working families by providing a tax credit that reduces their income tax liability. If the tax credit is larger than the amount of income taxes owed, the family receives a check for the difference. The tax credit increases with the number of children and adults in the family, as well as the amount earned, until a plateau is achieved. For example, in 2006 the maximum tax credit was $4,536 for a married couple with two children who earned $13,000. The EITC is phased out as family income level increases. In 2006, families could participate in the program if their income was less than $38,348.

The EITC has two effects on labor supply. First, labor force participation should rise because only employed people may participate in the program. Second, it has an uncertain effect on the hours worked by employed people. Below the plateau level the EITC is the equivalent to a wage increase, and in the phase-out range above the plateau it acts as a wage decrease. Because wage changes have income and substitution effects that work in opposing directions on hours worked, the labor supply effects among those currently working cannot be determined in theory.

There are many studies of the labor supply effects of the EITC. Hotz and Scholz conclude that the EITC has increased the labor force participation rate, particularly for single parents. In fact, another study has found that the EITC could account for nearly two-thirds of the rise in the participation rate of single mothers between 1984 and 1996. Also, though the program appears to slightly reduce the hours of those currently working, the overall impact on hours worked is positive once the EITC's hours-increasing effect on participation is accounted for.

* Based on V. Joseph Hotz and John Karl Scholz, "The Earned Income Tax Credit," in Robert A. Moffitt (ed.), *Means-Tested Transfer Programs in the United States* (Chicago, IL: University of Chicago Press, 2003).

Chapter Summary

1. In the work–leisure choice model, an indifference curve shows the various combinations of income and leisure that will yield a given level of utility to an individual. Indifference curves are convex to the origin, reflecting a diminishing marginal rate of substitution of leisure for income. Curves farther from the origin indicate higher levels of utility.

2. The budget (wage) constraint line shows the various combinations of income and leisure that are obtainable at a given wage rate. The absolute value of the slope of the budget line reflects the wage rate.

3. The individual achieves an optimal or utility-maximizing position by selecting the point that puts him or her on the highest attainable indifference curve.

4. Changing the wage rate and observing predicted changes in one's optimal position suggest the possibility of a backward-bending individual labor supply curve.

5. The impact of a wage change on hours of work depends on the sizes of the income and substitution effects. The income effect measures the portion of a total change in desired hours of work that is due solely to the change in income caused by the wage change. The substitution effect is the portion of a total change in desired hours of work that is due solely to the wage rate change, the level of income or utility being held constant. For a wage increase (decrease), the income effect decreases (increases) while the substitution effect increases (decreases) desired hours of work.

6. Empirical evidence suggests that women are significantly more responsive to a wage change in their labor supply decisions than are men.

7. The responsiveness of the quantity of labor supplied to a given change in wage rates is measured by the elasticity of labor supply. This is calculated as the percentage change in quantity of labor supplied divided by the percentage change in the wage rate. In contrast, changes in nonlabor income or work–leisure preferences alter the location of an individual's labor supply curve.

8. The case of nonparticipants—individuals who choose not to do labor market work—is portrayed by a corner solution on the right vertical axis of the work–leisure model.

9. The reservation wage is the lowest wage rate at which a person would decide to work.

10. A worker may be overemployed or underemployed when forced to conform to a standard workday. A worker is overemployed (underemployed) when for the standard workday his or her marginal rate of substitution of leisure for income is greater (less) than the wage rate.

11. A system of premium pay—such as time and a half for overtime work—has a more positive effect on work incentives than the straight-time wage rate that would yield an equivalent income for the same hours of work.

12. Most income maintenance programs entail a basic benefit and a benefit reduction rate from which the break-even level of income can be calculated. Because *(a)* the basic benefit causes only an income effect and *(b)* the benefit reduction rate *reduces* the net wage rate, the income and substitution effects both contribute to a decline in desired hours of work.

13. Welfare is no longer an entitlement, but rather is a temporary assistance program. Between 1996 and 2006, the number of welfare recipients declined by about 60 percent.

| **Terms and Concepts** | indifference curve, 15
marginal rate of substitution of leisure for income, 17
budget (wage) constraint, 20
optimal work–leisure position, 22
backward-bending labor supply curve, 24
income effect, 24 | substitution effect, 25
wage elasticity of labor supply, 30
reservation wage, 33
overemployed, 36
underemployed, 36
income maintenance program, 40
income guarantee or basic benefit, 40
benefit reduction rate, 40 | break-even level of income, 41
actual subsidy payment, 41
Temporary Assistance for Needy Families (TANF), 44 |

Questions and Study Suggestions

1. What information is embodied in *(a)* an indifference curve and *(b)* the budget line in the work–leisure model? Why are indifference curves *(a)* downward-sloping and *(b)* convex to the origin? Draw an indifference map and budget line and locate a worker's optimal position.

2. Indicate in each of the following instances whether the specified circumstances will cause a worker to want to work more or fewer hours:

   a. The wage rate increases and the substitution effect is greater than the income effect.

   b. The wage rate decreases and the income effect is greater than the substitution effect.

   c. The wage rate decreases and the substitution effect is greater than the income effect.

   d. The wage rate increases and the income effect is greater than the substitution effect.

3. Employ a diagram similar to Figure 2.5 to show an individual's leisure–income choices before and after a wage rate *decrease*. Isolate the income and substitution effects, indicate whether each increases or decreases hours of work, and use the two effects to explain the overall impact of the wage decline on hours of work. Is your worker on the forward-rising or backward-bending portion of the labor supply curve?

4. The "supply-side" economics of the Reagan administration (1981–1988) presumed that income tax cuts would stimulate incentives to work and thereby increase economic growth. Demonstrate this outcome with a work–leisure diagram. What does this outcome assume about the relative sizes of the income and substitution effects? Explain: "The predicted increase in work incentives associated with supply-side tax cuts might in fact be more relevant for women than for men."

5. Suppose Lauren is given two options by her employer. *First option:* She may choose her own hours of work and will be paid the relatively low wage rate implied by budget line HW_1 shown in the accompanying diagram. *Second option:* She can work exactly HR hours and will be paid the relatively high wage rate implied by budget line HW_2. Which option will she choose? Justify your answer.

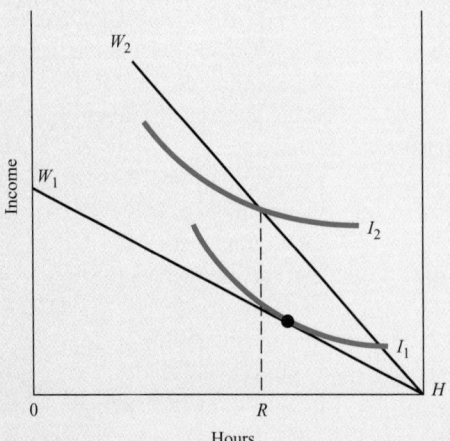

6. Use a work–leisure diagram that includes nonlabor income to portray an individual who is maximizing utility by working, say, eight hours per day. Now compare the labor supply effects of imposing *(a)* a lump-sum tax (a tax that is the same absolute amount at all levels of earned income); and *(b)* a proportional tax of, say, 30 percent on earned income. Do hours of work rise or fall in each case? Can you generalize these outcomes to *all* individuals in the economy? Explain.

7. What set of circumstances will tend to cause an individual to choose not to participate in the labor force? What generalizations can you formulate on the basis of *(a)* education, *(b)* the presence of preschool children, *(c)* level of spouse's income, *(d)* race, *(e)* location of a household (urban or rural) on the one hand and the probability that a married woman will be a labor force participant on the other?

8. What is the reservation wage? "Other things being equal, one's reservation wage increases as larger amounts of nonlabor income are realized." Do you agree? Explain. Redraw the indifference curves of Figure 2.8 to demonstrate that anything that lowers (raises) the value of nonmarket time will increase (reduce) the probability of labor force participation.

9. Using Figure 2.10, demonstrate that Smith has a stronger "taste" for leisure and a weaker "taste" for work than Jones. What factor(s) might underlie this difference in tastes? Redraw Smith's indifference curves to show the case where she would rather be a nonparticipant than work the standard *HD* workweek.

10. Use Figure 2.11 to explain the following statement: "Although premium wage rates for overtime work will induce workers to work more hours than would a straight-time equivalent wage rate, the latter will entail a higher level of well-being."

11. If an income maintenance program entails a $3,000 basic benefit and a benefit reduction rate of .30, what will be the size of the subsidy received by a family that earns $2,000 per year? What will be the family's total income? What break-even level of income does this program imply?

12. In the accompanying diagram *WH* is the budget line resulting from labor market work. Describe the characteristics of the income maintenance programs implicit in budget lines *HBW'*, *HBYW*, and *HBW*. Given an individual's work–leisure preferences, which program will entail the strongest disincentives to work? Why? Which entails the weakest disincentives to work? Why? "The higher the basic benefit and the higher the benefit reduction rate, the weaker the work incentive." Do you agree?

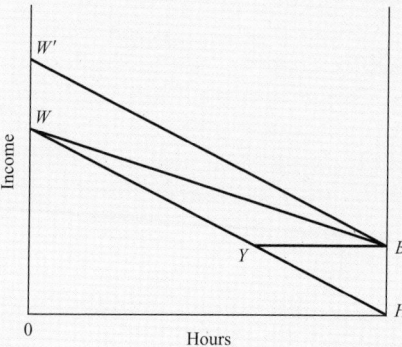

13. In the United States payments to disabled workers on the average replace about half of their former earnings. In some other countries such as Sweden and the Netherlands disabled workers receive as much as 70 to 90 percent of their average earnings. We also observe that the proportion of workers receiving disability benefits is much lower in the United States than in the latter two nations. Are these findings consistent with the work–leisure model? Explain.

14. Suppose Congress changed our Social Security law to allow recipients to earn as much as they wanted with no reduction in benefits. Use a work–leisure diagram to show the predicted effects on labor supply.

15. One way of aiding low-income families is to increase the minimum wage. An alternative is to provide a direct grant of nonlabor income. Compare the impact of these two options on work incentives.

16. Evaluate the following statements:

    a. "An employer might reduce worker absenteeism by changing from a standard wage rate to premium pay for hours that exceed a fixed minimum."

    b. "A worker who feels underemployed may moonlight even though the wage rate is somewhat lower than the one paid in the worker's first job."

    c. "Given the wage rate, an individual will always prefer a job in which the worker, as opposed to the employer, selects the number of hours worked."

    d. "If at all points within the work–leisure diagram a person's indifference curves are flatter than the budget constraint, then that individual will choose to be a nonparticipant."

    e. "The income effect of any given wage increase is larger for individuals who are currently working many hours than it is for those who are currently working few or no hours."

17. Steve Slacker is age 25, has an MBA degree, but is not working. Instead he is living at a major ski area, using the $2,000 per week he gets from his wealthy family. The family, however, seeing that Steve is becoming a permanent slacker, ends this weekly payment. As a result, Steve chooses to take a job that pays $1,000 a week for 40 hours of work. Construct a single income–leisure choice graph to show Steve's situation before and after his parents' decision. Briefly summarize the outcome for hours of work, total weekly income, and Steve's total utility.

Internet Exercise

What Has Happened to Welfare Caseloads?

Go to the Administration for Children and Families U.S. Welfare Caseloads statistics Web site **(http://www.acf.hhs.gov/programs/ofa/caseload/caseloadindex.htm)**. Click on the link with the most recent caseload figures.

What was the percentage change in the number of TANF families between 1996 and 2006? What are some possible explanations for this change?

What was the number of TANF families in 2006? For the most recent year shown? What is the percentage change over this period? What are the corresponding numbers for your state?

Internet Links

The Office of Family Assistance in the U.S. Department of Health and Human Services publishes detailed information about the Temporary Assistance for Needy Families program **(http://www.acf.dhhs.gov/programs/ofa/)**.

The Joint Center for Poverty Research Web site provides academic research, research summaries, and policy briefs on issues related to poverty **(http://www.jcpr.org/)**.

Chapter

3

Population, Participation Rates, and Hours of Work

"The times they are a changin'."[1] The 1946–1964 baby boom that added about 76 million people to the labor force gave way to a "baby bust" that will mean much smaller increases in the labor force in the immediate future. During the past decade immigration added over 8 million people to the U.S. population. Disadvantaged groups such as African-Americans and Hispanics constitute a growing percentage of our labor force. Dual-worker families were 9 percent of all families in 1940; today they are 39 percent.

The hustle-bustle of our lives has greatly increased as we juggle education, market work, household activities, and leisure. Divorces are much more common than in earlier periods. The percentage of families with children maintained by single mothers has nearly doubled from 12 percent in 1970 to 23 percent today. Since 1950 women have increasingly participated in the labor force; meanwhile the participation rates of older working-age men have declined. The workweek decreased by 20 percent during the first half of the 20th century, but since then it has remained relatively constant.

These facts all relate to the supply of labor, examined more broadly here than in the previous chapter. For the economy as a whole, the concept of labor supply has many dimensions. As Figure 3.1 indicates, the aggregate of labor services available to a society depends on (1) the size and demographic composition of the population, which in turn depend on births, deaths, and net immigration; (2) the labor force participation rate—that is, the percentage of the working-age population that is actually working or seeking work; (3) the number of hours worked per week or year; and (4) the quality of

---

[1] Bob Dylan lyrics.

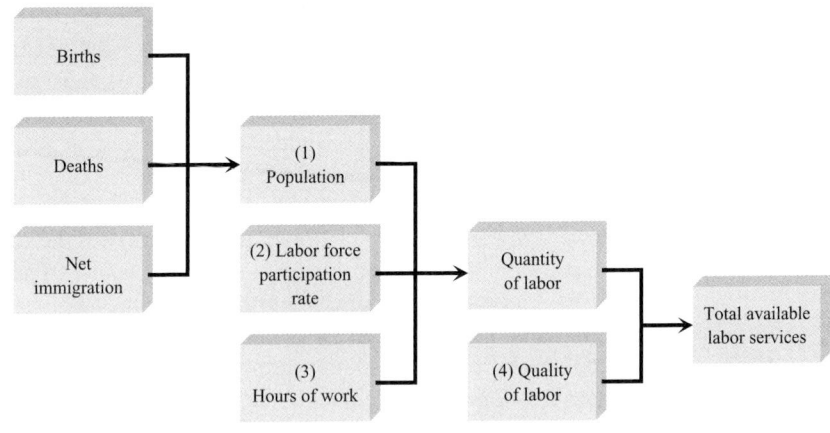

FIGURE 3.1
Determinants of the Total Labor Services Available
The total amount of labor services available in an economy depends on population size, the labor force participation rate, the length of the workweek and workyear, and the quality of the labor force.

the labor force. In this chapter we consider the first three of these aspects of labor supply: population, participation rates, and hours of work. Labor quality will be analyzed in Chapter 4.

THE POPULATION BASE

As a broad generalization, the size of a nation's labor force depends on the size of its population and the fraction of its population participating in the labor market. Figure 3.2 portrays the growth of the U.S. population and labor force over the 1950–2006 period.

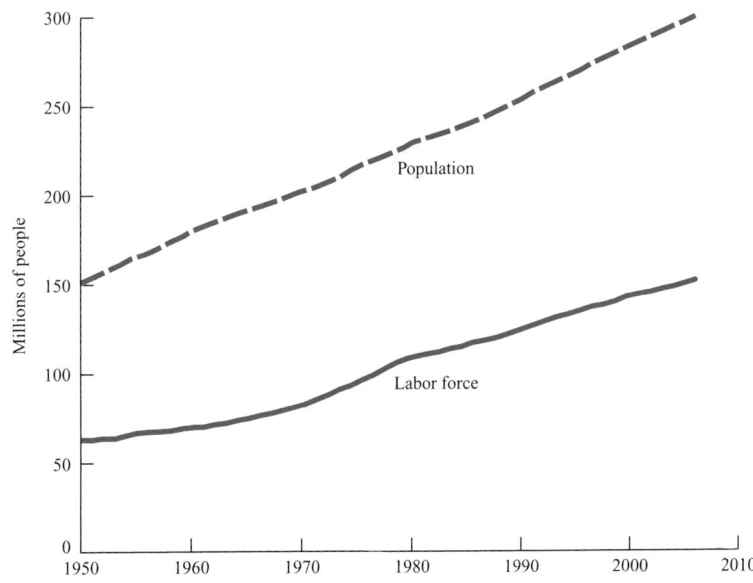

FIGURE 3.2
Population and Labor Force Growth
Population and labor force have both grown significantly in the United States, but rates of growth have varied from one period to another.

Recalling Figure 3.1, we know that population grows partly as a result of natural increases—that is, the excess of births over deaths—and net immigration. Because death rates are less variable (declining slowly over time), most of the variations in U.S. population growth have resulted from changes in birthrates and net immigration. For example, the 1946–1964 baby boom added almost 76 million people to the U.S. population who, some 20 years later, entered the labor force in extraordinarily large numbers. Birthrates declined sharply following the baby boom, and this decline has resulted in slightly lower growth of the population in recent years. But the U.S. population continues to expand. Immigration (considered in detail in Chapter 9) has also fluctuated over time, largely as a consequence of changes in U.S. immigration policies. In some recent years immigration has accounted for as much as 20–25 percent of population growth.

3.1 With this backdrop of population growth in mind, let's now turn to an economic theory that sheds light on participation rates.

BECKER'S MODEL: THE ALLOCATION OF TIME

In Chapter 2 we introduced a model in which an *individual* was making a choice between labor market work and leisure. While this model proved useful in generating an understanding of the work–leisure decision and a number of its implications, the model has been generalized and expanded by Becker (World of Work 1.1) and others.[2] This generalized *model of the allocation of time* is particularly useful in understanding the main topic at hand, labor force participation.

Two Fundamental Changes

The basic work–leisure choice model can be extended in two fundamental ways.

1 Household Perspective

The first change is that it is frequently more informative to think of the household as the basic decision-making unit rather than the individual. Most people are members of households, and decisions about how they spend their time are strongly influenced by the decisions of other household members. Decision making is interrelated; for example, a wife's decision about whether she should seek labor market work may depend on whether her husband is currently employed, and vice versa.

2 Multiple Uses of Time

In Becker's model of household allocation of time, the traditional work–leisure dichotomy is replaced by a more complex categorization of the uses of time. As Becker sees it, a household should be regarded as an economic unit that is *producing* utility-yielding "commodities." These utility-yielding *commodities* are produced by the household by

[2] The landmark article is Gary Becker, "A Theory of the Allocation of Time," *Economic Journal,* September 1965, pp. 493–517. See also Staffan B. Linder, *The Harried Leisure Class* (New York: Columbia University Press, 1970).

3.1	**World of Work**	The Changing Face of America*

In 1996 the Census Bureau issued a revised population forecast that suggests greater long-term growth of the U.S. population than did earlier estimates. The report also predicts even more diversity in the population than was projected earlier. By 2050 the U.S. population is expected to rise to 420 million from 299 million in 2006. This new projection for 2050 is up 26 million from earlier projections.

How will the composition of the population be different in 2050 compared to 2000? As shown in the accompanying pie charts, the population in 2050 is expected to be much more diverse. Asians, Hispanics, African–Americans, and other nonwhite groups will comprise nearly half of the population in 2050.

Although population growth will slow in the next decade or so, several factors will drive rapid increases in population in subsequent decades. Legislation in 1990 increased the number of legal immigrants to the United States. The Census Bureau now estimates that 1,450,000 immigrants will arrive each year, up from earlier estimates of 824,000. The number of Asians and Pacific Islanders will increase by 210 percent, to about 8 percent of the total population. Hispanics will overtake African-Americans as the nation's largest minority group, comprising an expected 24.4 percent of the population in 2050. The increase in Hispanics and Asians will also boost the nation's fertility rate—from 2.05 children per average woman today to 2.22 children.

If the Census Bureau's predictions are accurate, they have several important implications for the labor force. First, the projected slowdown in labor force growth in recent years—and the potential for labor shortages—should be only a short-term problem. Second, the higher immigration and greater fertility rates will slow and eventually reverse the present aging of the American population. This means, for example, that the ratio of receivers of Social Security benefits to the number of people paying into the system will not rise as fast as once expected. Third, a renewed emphasis on education and training will be necessary to prepare the growing number of racially diverse youth for high-quality jobs. Finally, workplaces will be transformed, with owners, managers, and workers increasingly being nonwhite. Greater tolerance for racial and ethnic differences will be an absolute necessity if the United States is to retain its high labor productivity and standard of living.

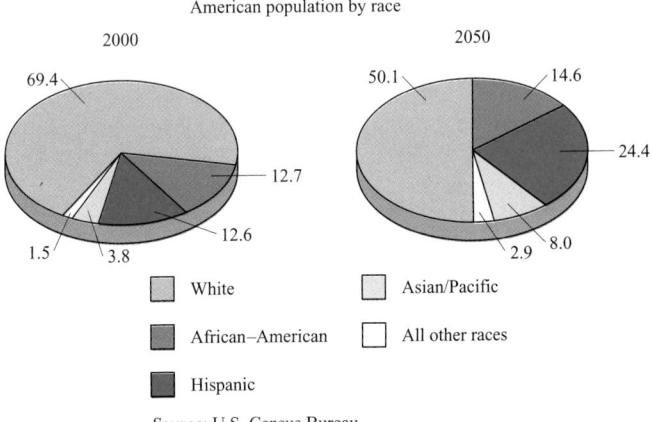

American population by race

Source: U.S. Census Bureau.

* Based partly on U.S. Census Bureau, *U.S. Interim Projections by Age, Sex, Race, and Hispanic Origin,* March 2004, and "A Spicier Stew in the Melting Pot," *BusinessWeek,* December 1992, pp. 29–30. Updated.

combining *goods* (goods and services) with *time*. More generally, a household can use the time available to it in at least three basic ways. Time can be (1) sold in the labor market to obtain the monetary income required to purchase goods and services (labor market time), (2) used in household production (household production time), and (3) used in actual consumption of goods and services (consumption time).

Thus, for the typical household, the commodity we call a *meal* is produced by combining certain goods acquired through the provision of labor market time (food bought at the supermarket) with household production time (the time it takes to prepare these goods as a meal) and consumption time (the time it takes to eat the meal). Because the total amount of time available to the household is limited, the alternative uses of time compete with one another. For example, other things being equal, a family in which both spouses engage in labor market work will have less time available for household production and consumption than a family with one nonworking spouse.

Commodity Characteristics

Commodities have two characteristics of considerable significance for any discussion of how a household might allocate its time in general and how it might make labor market participation decisions in particular. First, some commodities are relatively time-intensive, whereas others are relatively goods-intensive. *Time-intensive commodities* are composed of a large amount of time and a small amount of goods. Examples include such "pure" leisure activities as watching the sunset at the beach or dozing in a hammock.[3] *Goods-intensive commodities* require quite large amounts of goods and little time, such as a meal at a fast-food restaurant. One implication of this distinction is that as time becomes more valuable in the labor market (if wage rates increase), a household may sacrifice time-intensive commodities in favor of goods-intensive commodities to devote more time to labor market work.

The second characteristic of commodities is that, within limits, time and goods are usually substitutable in producing them. Thus a specific commodity can be produced by the household with much time and a small amount of goods or vice versa. At one extreme a household can produce a meal with home-grown, home-prepared food. At the other extreme it can purchase a meal at a restaurant. The former is a highly time-intensive commodity; the latter is a goods-intensive commodity.

Household Choices

In the Becker model, the household has a number of questions to answer as it seeks to maximize its utility. First, what commodities does it want to consume? Second, how does it want to produce these commodities? That is, to what extent should commodities be provided through labor market work as opposed to production in the home? Third, how should individual family members allocate their time among labor market work, home production, consumption, and other possible uses?

---

[3] In the Becker model we can think of leisure as the pleasurable consumption of time per se wherein the amount of goods required is zero.

The third question is most relevant for the topic at hand.[4] The general principle employed in deciding how each household member should allocate his or her time is that of comparative advantage. The principle of comparative advantage says that an individual should specialize in the productive endeavor that can be performed with the greatest relative efficiency, or in other words, with the least opportunity cost. In apportioning its available time, a household should compare the productivity for each family member in all of the various market and nonmarket activities needing to be performed in producing commodities. The basic rule is that the more productive or proficient one is in a certain activity as compared to other family members, the greater the amount of one's time that should be devoted to that activity. Because family members normally have different characteristics with respect to age, sex, educational attainment, and previous labor market and nonlabor market experience, at any point in time they will differ substantially in the relative efficiency of producing commodities (utility) from market and nonmarket activities. Obviously the wife has a biologically determined comparative advantage in childbearing. Also, through socialization (role definition by society) or because of preferences, or both, many females develop a comparative advantage in other aspects of household production, such as homemaking activities like cleaning, food preparation, and caring for children. Furthermore, we will find evidence in Chapter 14 suggesting that women are often discriminated against in the labor market. Because of such discrimination and assuming that other things (such as education, job training, and labor market experience) are equal, many husbands can obtain more income and therefore more goods for the household from a given amount of labor market work than their wives. Historically, for many households the principle of comparative advantage led husbands to devote much of their time to labor market work while their wives engaged in nonmarket work within the home. Similarly, we will find in Chapter 4 that children have a comparative advantage in acquiring education. Education is an investment in human capital, and other things being equal, the rate of return on that investment varies directly with the length of time a person will be in the labor market after his or her education is completed.[5]

[4] The second question will be treated in the ensuing discussion of the participation rates of the various subaggregates of the population. With regard to the first question, we will assume that the household's preferences for commodities are given, noting that in Becker's model the theory of consumer behavior must be modified to account for the economic value of time. More precisely, a household will be purchasing the utility-maximizing combination of goods (*a, b, . . . , n*) when the marginal utility of the last dollar spent on each is the same. Algebraically stated, utility is maximized when $MUa/Pa = MUb/Pb = \cdots = MUn/Pn$, where MU is marginal utility and P is product price. Becker contends that the appropriate prices to be used are *not* simply the market prices of each good but rather the "full price": the market price of a good *plus* the market value of the time used in its consumption. Thus if good *a* is a two-hour concert whose price is $8 and your time is worth $10 per hour in the labor market, then the full price of the concert is $28 = $8 + (2 × $10). Taking the value of time into account, the full prices of highly time-intensive goods will rise relatively and those of less time-intensive goods will fall relatively, generating a different utility-maximizing combination of goods than if only market prices were used.

[5] For an interesting discussion of the *disadvantages* of intrahousehold specialization, see Francine D. Blau, Marianne A. Ferber, and Anne E. Winkler, *The Economics of Women, Men, and Work,* 5th ed. (Englewood Cliffs, NJ: Prentice-Hall, 2006), pp. 43–49.

Income and Substitution Effects Revisited

It is helpful in understanding Becker's model to reexamine the income and substitution effects within its more general framework.

Becker Income Effect

Assume there is an increase in wage rates. The *income effect* indicates that the household now realizes a larger income for any number of hours of labor market work, and therefore the consumption of most goods will increase.[6] But the consumption of additional goods requires more time. Remember that goods must be combined with time to produce utility-yielding commodities. Therefore, with consumption time increasing, hours of work will tend to fall. Although the rationale is different, the income effect reduces hours of work as it did in the simpler model of Chapter 2.

Becker Substitution Effect

There is also a more complex *substitution effect.* A higher market wage rate means that time is more valuable not only in the labor market but also in both the production and consumption activities occurring within the household. On one hand, the household will substitute goods for time in the *production* of commodities as the wage rate rises. This implies that the household will produce commodities in less time-intensive ways. For example, the family may patronize fast-food restaurants with greater frequency and therefore spend less time in meal preparation within the home. On the other hand, with respect to *consumption,* the household will alter the mix of commodities it consumes, shifting from time-intensive to goods-intensive commodities as wage rates increase. Such time-intensive activities as vacations and playing golf may give way to the purchase of a work of art or racquetball. Or alternatively, a week's skiing in Colorado can be made less time-intensive for a Chicagoan by flying to the resort rather than driving. These adjustments in both the production and consumption of commodities release time for paid work in the labor market. Therefore, as in our simpler model, this more complex substitution effect increases hours of work when wage rates rise.

As in our simpler model, the net impact of the income and substitution effects on the hours of labor market work could be either positive or negative, depending on their relative magnitudes. But the alleged superiority of Becker's model is that it embodies a more comprehensive and more realistic portrayal of the uses of time. People do not merely divide their time between the assembly line and the hammock, as a narrow interpretation of Chapter 2's simpler model might imply. As noted earlier, the Becker model is a useful tool for understanding labor force participation rates, the topic to which we now turn.

---

[6] The exception, of course, is *inferior goods,* which are goods for which purchases decline as incomes increase.

3.1

*Quick
Review*

- The population base underlying the total supply of labor depends on the birthrate, the death rate, and the rate of net immigration.
- The Becker model of the allocation of time regards households as economic units deciding how best to allocate their time among work, household production, and household consumption to obtain utility-yielding commodities.
- In the Becker income effect, a rise in the wage rate raises income, allowing the household to buy more goods; hours of work fall because these goods require more time to consume.
- In the Becker substitution effect, a rise in the wage rate increases hours of work because households substitute *(a)* goods for time in the production of commodities and *(b)* goods-intensive commodities for time-intensive commodities in consumption.

Your Turn

In general, women's educational levels and real wage rates have increased greatly over the past several decades. Also, women are increasingly participating in the workplace. What do these facts imply about the relative strengths of the Becker income and substitution effects? (*Answer:* See page 596.)

PARTICIPATION RATES: DEFINED AND MEASURED

The labor force participation rate is determined by comparing the actual labor force with the potential labor force or what is sometimes called the "age-eligible population."

In the United States we consider the *potential labor force* or age-eligible population to be the entire population *less* (1) young people under 16 years of age and (2) people who are institutionalized. Children under 16 are excluded on the assumption that schooling and child labor laws keep most of them out of the labor force.[7] Furthermore, the segment of the population that is institutionalized—in penal or mental institutions, nursing homes, and so on—is also not available for labor market activities.[8] The *actual labor force* consists of those people who are either (1) employed or (2) unemployed but actively seeking a job.[9] Thus in percentage form we can say that the *labor force participation rate* (LFPR) is

$$\text{LFPR} = \frac{\text{actual labor force}}{\text{potential labor force}} \times 100 \qquad \textbf{(3.1)}$$

[7] Although excluded from the official definition of the labor force, many peoples under 16 years of age do engage in labor market activities.

[8] Since 1983 all armed forces personnel stationed in the United States have been considered to be members of the labor force, the rationale being that joining the military is a voluntary decision and therefore represents a viable labor market alternative. Prior to 1983 members of the military were not counted as part of the labor force. The Bureau of Labor Statistics now reports data for both the total labor force and the civilian labor force.

[9] More precise definitions will be introduced in Chapter 18. Note that all part-time workers are included in the labor force.

or

$$\text{LFPR} = \frac{\begin{array}{c}\text{noninstitutional population}\\\text{16 years or over in the labor force}\end{array}}{\text{noninstitutional population}} \times 100 \qquad \textbf{(3.2)}$$

In February 2007, for example,

$$\frac{152{,}784{,}000}{230{,}834{,}000} \times 100 = 66.2\%$$

Participation rates can be similarly determined for various subaggregates of the population, such as married women, African–American teenage females, and so forth.

SECULAR TREND OF PARTICIPATION RATES

3.2 Let's now turn to the long-run or secular trend of participation rates in the United States as portrayed in Figure 3.3. You should be forewarned that the factors affecting participation rates are varied and complex; some are economic variables, while others are of an institutional, legal, or attitudinal nature. Thus, although the Becker model is useful in explaining many important changes in participation rates, it cannot be realistically expected to provide a complete understanding of all the forces at work.

Figure 3.3 reveals that the aggregate participation rate has gradually drifted upward since World War II. In 1950 about 60 percent of the age-eligible population were labor force participants. By 2006 that figure had increased to about 66 percent, with most of the rise occurring in the 1970s and 1980s. In Figure 3.3 we also observe that the participation rate of males has declined steadily. Specifically, male participation rates declined from about 86 percent in 1950 to approximately 74 percent in 2006. But concomitant increases in female participation rates have more than offset this

FIGURE 3.3 Total, Male, and Female Participation Rates
The total or aggregate participation rate has slowly drifted upward over time. This is the net consequence of the rapidly rising female participation rate more than compensating for a declining male rate.

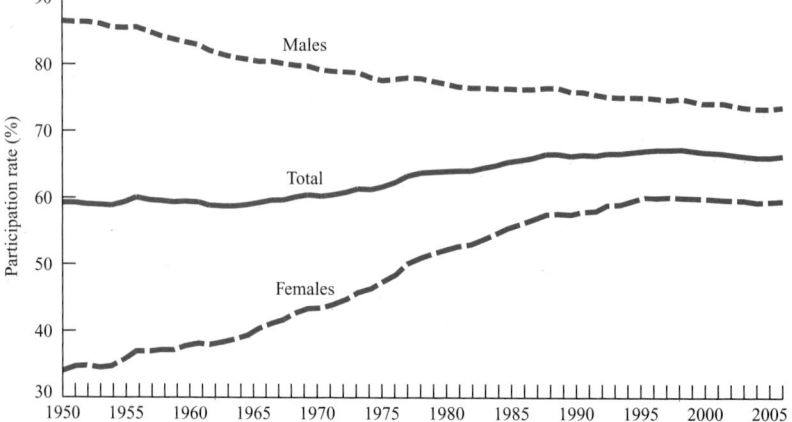

3.2	World of Work	Fewer Teens Have Summer Jobs*

Over the past decade, the proportion of teens holding a summer job has significantly declined. In July 1994 the labor force participation rate of 16- to 19-year-olds was 65.4 percent. By July 2006 this figure had fallen to 53.5 percent. The July labor force participation rate for teens was lower in 2006 than in 1994 for both sexes and all racial and ethnic groups.

There are two main reasons for the decline in the teen labor force participation rate. One cause is the steady rise in summer school enrollment since 1994. The percentage of teens enrolled in school in July rose from 20 percent in 1994 to 44 percent in 2005. This helps explain the decline because teens enrolled in school are much less likely to participate in the labor force.

The reasons for enrolling in summer courses are varied. A relatively small portion of students are required to take summer classes to get promoted to the next grade. Most students who attend summer school do so for academic enrichment. For example, some students are preparing to take a more advanced course during the regular school year. Others take review courses for college entrance exams and specialty summer camps.

Another related cause of the participation decline is higher wealth of families with teenage students due to increased financial aid. Since 1993, 16 states have initiated statewide merit college scholarships that provide free or substantially reduced tuition to students attending state universities or colleges. This subsidy will increase the number of students attending college and reduce the percentage of teens working due to time constraints. It will also reduce the need to work to pay for college. Aaronson, Park, and Sullivan find that between 2000 and 2005 the labor force participation rate of 16- to 17-year-olds fell by 1.7 percentage points more in states with statewide merit college scholarships than in states without such programs.

The reduced employment of teens in the summer may have some negative short-run effects but little long-run impact. A study based on teenagers randomly assigned to get assistance for summer job placement concluded that such jobs have only a short-lived effect. The main benefit of summer jobs for teens seems to be the money received. There appears to be no impact of summer employment on academic outcomes or educational goals one year later. In contrast, increased summer school enrollment that is related to academic enrichment is likely to yield long-run benefits.

* Based on Daniel Aaronson, Kyung-Hong Park, and Daniel Sullivan, "The Decline in Teen Labor Force Participation," Federal Reserve Bank of Chicago *Economic Perspectives*, Quarter 1, 2006, pp. 2–18; Tiffany Stringer, "Summertime, Summer Teens: What Do Teens Do in the Summer?" *Occupational Outlook Quarterly*, Winter 2002–2003, pp. 36–41; and Alan B. Krueger, "There Are Fewer Summer Jobs for Teenagers, but That Might Not Hurt Long Term," *The New York Times*, July 19, 2001.

decline. Female participation rates rose from about 34 percent in 1950 to about 59 percent in 2006. In short, male and female participation rates are tending to converge. It is important that we understand the major causal factors underlying these trends.

Declining Participation Rates of Older Males

Figure 3.4 shows male participation rates by age groups. The message here is that the participation rates of older males have declined markedly. We find a large reduction in the participation rates for males 65 and older over the 1950–2006 period.[10] We also observe a sharp 17 percentage point decline for males aged 55 to 64 over the past four decades.

[10] Economic incentives don't fully explain the spike in retirement at age 65. See Robin L. Lumsdaine, James H. Stock, and David A. Wise, "Why Are Retirement Rates So High at Age 65?" in David A. Wise (ed.), *Advances in the Economics of Aging* (Chicago, IL: University of Chicago Press, 1996).

FIGURE 3.4

Male Participation Rates by Age Group

While the participation rates of males in the 20–24 and 25–54 age groups have remained quite constant, the rates for older males have fallen significantly over the past 56 years.

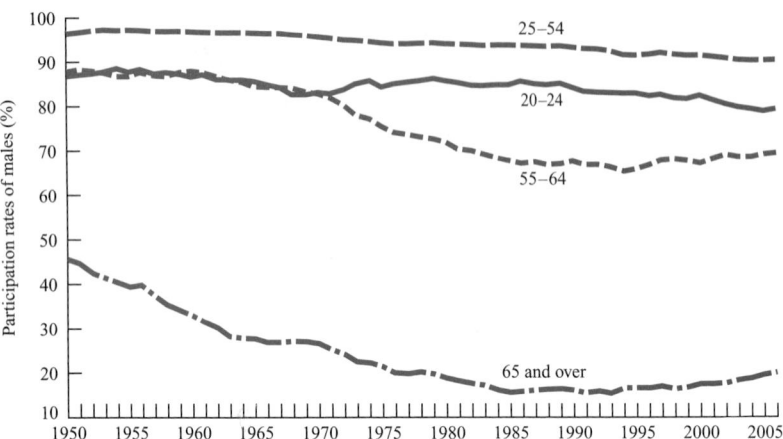

A variety of factors have been cited to explain these declines. These include (1) rising real wages and earnings, (2) the increasing availability of public and private pensions, (3) increasing access to disability benefits, and (4) the allocation of time over one's life cycle.

1 Rising Real Wages and Earnings

Economic growth has been accompanied by rising real wages and earnings. For example, real gross domestic product per capita has increased about threefold since 1940. We know that rising real wages entail both income and substitution effects. In the case of older men, the income effect has dominated the substitution effect and, consequently, many have chosen more leisure in the form of retirement. In many instances, the deteriorating health of older males may also have induced retirement by increasing their preferences for leisure or, in terms of Chapter 2, by making their indifference curves steeper.[11] Put in simpler language, as our society has become more affluent over time, the secular increase in real wages and earnings has allowed more workers to accumulate sufficient wealth to retire at an earlier age. The average age of final retirement has fallen by between four and five years for both men and women since 1950.[12]

2 Social Security and Private Pensions

An additional factor in explaining the declining participation rates of older males is the availability of Social Security and private pensions. Established in 1935, the Social Security program now provides retirement benefits for older workers and their survivors in addition to income support in the case of disability or illness. Social Security retirement benefits have been characterized by both expanding coverage and increasingly generous levels, thereby providing an important source of nonlabor income that has induced large

---

[11] Health status played a more important role in the labor force participation decisions of older men early in the 20th century. See Dora L. Costa, "Health and Labor Force Participation of Older Men, 1900–1991," *Journal of Economic History,* March 1996, pp. 62–89.

[12] Murray Gendell, "Retirement Age Declines in 1990s," *Monthly Labor Review,* October 2001, pp. 12–21.

numbers of elderly male workers to withdraw from the labor force (see Figure 2.9). In recent years Social Security benefits have been rising faster than wages in real terms, which enhances the relative attractiveness of retirement. Furthermore, retirement benefits prior to age 65 are subject to a substantial benefit reduction rate—that is, an implicit tax on earned income—which further enhances the incentive for older workers to withdraw from the labor force.[13] Thus both the income *and* substitution effects associated with Social Security generate disincentives to work.

Although federal legislation prohibits mandatory retirement, the availability of private pensions has been an inducement to early retirement. In 1950 only 16 percent of the labor force was covered by private pension plans; by 2003, 45 percent of all workers were covered. Declining participation rates for the 55–64 age group undoubtedly reflect that many pension plans allow retirement with full or partial benefits on completion of a specified number of years—say, 20 or 30—of employment.

Research by Ippolito[14] suggests that approximately half of the decline in the participation rates of men aged 55 to 64 in the 1970–1986 period is attributable to two factors: (1) changes in the Social Security system that increased retirement benefits by about 50 percent and (2) the alteration of private pension rules that encouraged early retirement.

Ruhm, however, finds that pensions have offsetting effects on the labor supply of older men.[15] He reports that pensions increase the participation of men in their late fifties and early sixties, but decrease the participation of men aged 65 to 69. He argues that this finding is the result of incentives included in pensions to retire in certain age ranges.

3 Disability Benefits

Evidence also exists to suggest that the disability component of the Social Security program has become increasingly generous and is progressive in the sense that low-wage workers receive relatively larger benefits than high-wage workers. As a result, low-wage workers are more inclined to seek disability benefits as an alternative to labor market participation.[16] Because African–American workers are generally lower-income workers, this consideration may explain the larger decline in the participation rates of older African–American workers compared to older white workers.[17]

[13] Prior to 2000, the benefit reduction also applied to workers aged 65 to 69. For an analysis of the labor supply impact of this implicit tax, see Jonathan Gruber and Peter Orszag, "Does the Social Security Earnings Test Affect Labor Supply and Benefits Receipt?" *National Tax Journal*, December 2003, pp. 755–73.
[14] Richard A. Ippolito, "Toward Explaining Earlier Retirement after 1970," *Industrial and Labor Relations Review*, July 1990, pp. 556–69. From a public policy perspective, however, it may be difficult to reverse the increase in early retirement by reducing Social Security benefits. See Alan B. Krueger and Jorn-Steffen Pischke, "The Effect of Social Security on Labor Supply: A Cohort Analysis of the Notch Generation," *Journal of Labor Economics*, October 1992, pp. 412–37.
[15] Christopher J. Ruhm, "Do Pensions Increase the Labor Supply of Older Men?" *Journal of Public Economics*, February 1996, pp. 157–75. See also Andrew A. Samwick, "New Evidence on Pensions, Social Security, and the Timing of Retirement," *Journal of Public Economics*, November 1998, pp. 207–36.
[16] One obvious solution to the problem of able individuals receiving disability benefits is to deny the benefit applications from such people. Some evidence exists that program officials can fairly effectively screen out claims from able individuals. See Jonathan Gruber and Jeffrey D. Kubik, "Disability Insurance Rejection Rates and the Labor Supply of Older Workers," *Journal of Public Economics*, April 1997, pp. 1–23.
[17] See Donald O. Parsons, "Racial Trends in Male Labor Force Participation," *American Economic Review*, December 1980, pp. 911–20.

4 Life Cycle Considerations

Let's consider a fourth and final factor that may account for the declining participation rates of older males. You may have recognized that the factors discussed thus far have centered on the income effect. The availability of nonlabor income in the form of public or private pensions, disability payments, or income from accumulated wealth generates a pure income effect that is sufficient to induce many older males to become nonparticipants. Some economists feel that a kind of substitution effect is also at work over time in encouraging older workers to withdraw from the labor force. In particular, they observe that the real earnings of many workers rise quite significantly until they reach, say, their mid-fifties; then earnings grow slowly or gradually decline. A glance ahead at Figure 4.1 seems to confirm this trend of earnings. The alleged reason for the decline in the earnings of older workers is that, on average, their formal education and on-the-job training become obsolete and their mental and physical capabilities diminish. This means that in allocating time over one's lifetime, it is rational to work continuously and for long hours during one's younger years because one's earning potential is high and therefore leisure is expensive. Conversely, as a person grows older, the earning potential becomes smaller and leisure becomes relatively cheaper, meaning that one is inclined to substitute leisure for work. In the extreme, this substitution is complete, and retirement is chosen.

3.3

Rising Female Participation Rates

Figure 3.5 portrays the participation rates of females by age groups. Excepting women aged 65 and over, the participation rates of all female age groups have increased over the 56 years shown. We observe particularly pronounced increases for the two younger age groups.

FIGURE 3.5

Female Participation Rates by Age Group

Aside from the 65 and older group, the participation rates of all women have risen over the past 56 years. The sharpest increases have been for younger women in the 20–24 and 25–54 age groups.

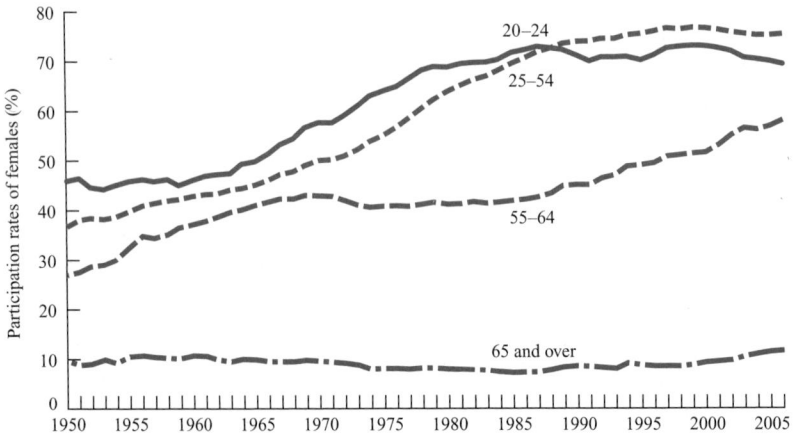

| 3.3 | World of Work | The Later Male Retirement Puzzle* |

Though the labor force participation rate has been falling overall for males aged 55 and older over the past several decades, it has been rising for a subset of older males in recent years—specifically men between the ages of 60 and 69. The participation rate of men aged 60 to 64 increased from 55.5 percent in 1990 to 58.6 percent in 2006. Likewise, the participation rate for men aged 65 to 69 rose from 26.0 percent in 1990 to 34.4 percent in 2006.

Richard Johnson has examined three possible explanations for this rise in labor force participation among older males. First, Social Security reforms have increased the incentive for older males to work more. In 1993 Congress increased the proportion of Social Security benefits that are subject to income tax for higher-income individuals. This decrease in the after-tax value of Social Security benefits may have induced higher-income men to work longer. However, Johnson concluded the tax increase can't explain the rise in the participation rate because it rose by a similar amount for those who were less likely as well as those who were more likely to be affected by the income tax change.

Another possible Social Security–related cause is that the reductions in benefits instituted in 1983 and 1993 may have caused fear that there will be more such benefit reductions in the future, which encouraged older men to work longer. This is not likely to be a factor because any future decrease in benefits is probably not going to affect males in their 60s. Furthermore, the participation rate has continued to decline for males aged 55 to 59, who have a greater chance to be affected by a Social Security benefit reduction. Also, the Social Security penalty for working past age 65 was reduced in 1990 and eliminated altogether in 2000. Johnson's analysis indicates this change can account for only 6 percent of the rise in the participation rate.

Second, there has been a switch away from defined benefit toward defined contribution pension plans, which has permitted older males to work longer. Defined benefit plans penalize workers who work past the normal retirement age; defined contribution plans contain no such provisions. However, the timing of the change in the proportion of workers with defined benefit pension plans does not correspond well with the change in the labor force participation rate.

Third, the slowdown in the growth of the labor force may have increased the labor market opportunities for older men. The reduced labor supply may have increased wages for older males in the short run and thus encouraged them to remain in the workforce. However, there appears to be only a weak relationship between the labor force growth rate and the participation rate of older males.

Johnson argues that the rise in labor force participation among men in their 60s remains a puzzle. He suggests that noneconomic factors such as tastes for work are playing a role, and he points to survey data indicating that 56 percent of those who worked for pay since retirement did so because they "enjoyed working and wanted to stay involved." Only about 1 in 10 stated they worked because they needed the money.

* Based on Richard Johnson, "The Puzzle of Later Male Retirement," *Federal Reserve Bank of Kansas City Economic Review*, 3rd Quarter 2002, pp. 5–26.

Most of the increase in female participation rates shown in Figure 3.5 has been accounted for by married women. For example, the total number of females in the labor force increased by approximately 50 million over the 1950–2006 period. Of this total increase, about two-thirds were married women. In one sense, this is a surprising phenomenon. From the perspective of a household, one might have expected that the participation rate of married women would have declined since World War II as a

| Global Perspective 3.1 | Labor Force Participation for Women Aged 25 to 54 |

Large variations exist in women's labor force participation rates across industrialized countries.

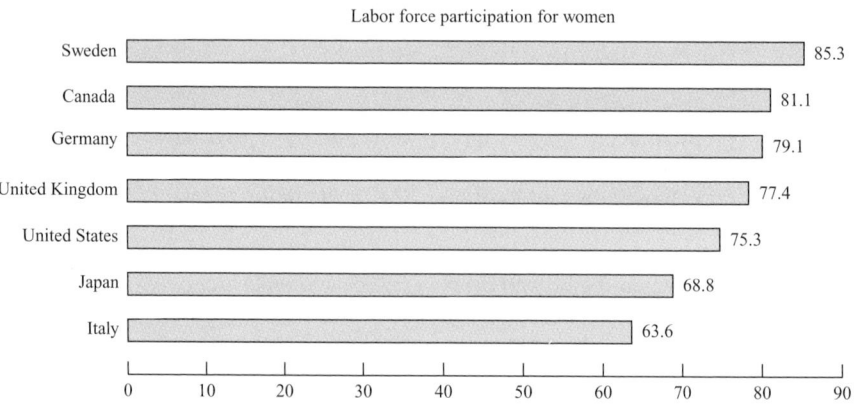

Labor force participation for women

Sweden	85.3
Canada	81.1
Germany	79.1
United Kingdom	77.4
United States	75.3
Japan	68.8
Italy	63.6

Source: Organization for Economic Cooperation and Development, *Employment Outlook,* July 2006, Table C.

consequence of the generally rising real wage rates and incomes of married males. And indeed, cross-sectional (point-in-time) studies reveal that the participation rates of married women do in fact vary inversely with their husbands' income. Our analysis in Chapter 2 suggests the reason: If leisure is a normal good, then a household will purchase more leisure as its income rises. Historically, this purchase of leisure was likely to be in the form of the wife's nonparticipation in the labor market. In terms of Figure 2.8, as the husband's income rises, an expanding intrahousehold transfer of income is available to the wife, and the consequent income effect induces her to be a nonparticipant. This line of reasoning suggests that wives in lower-income families are likely to work in the labor market because of economic necessity; but as the husband's income increases, more families will enjoy the luxury of having the wife produce commodities at home.

How can this reasoning be reconciled with the evidence that the participation rates of married women have actually increased over time? The answer lies partly in the fact that cross-sectional studies do not have a time dimension and therefore ignore or hold constant certain variables other than the husband's income that might have an impact on a wife's decision to participate in the labor force. That is, a number of factors besides husbands' rising incomes have been influencing the participation rates of married women over time. These other factors have so strongly influenced women to enter the labor market that they

World of Work   3.4

Many Wives Outearn Their Husbands*

The number of married couples with two earners has been steadily increasing over time. Between 1967 and 2003, the percentage of two-earner couples rose from 44 to 58 percent of all married couples. By 2003, there were nearly 33 million dual-earner couples.

As a result, the share of family earnings contributed by women has been rising as well. Currently women contribute about 35 percent of family earnings in dual-earner families. In fact, in 25 percent of dual-earner families, the wife outearns her husband. This figure is up from 16 percent in 1981.

It is important to recognize that men and women do not randomly marry each other. Instead individuals tend to marry others with similar education and earnings. Half of dual-earner couples have the same level of education. Likewise, high wage–earning males tend to be married to high wage–earning females.

Not surprisingly, wives tend to earn more than their husbands when the husbands' earnings are low. When the husband's wage is in the lowest earnings quintile, then nearly 60 percent of wives have earnings that exceed those of their husbands. The corresponding figure is 6 percent when the husband's wage is in the top quintile.

* Based on Anne Winkler, "Earnings of Husbands and Wives in Dual-Earner Families," *Monthly Labor Review*, April 1998, pp. 42–48. Updated.

have overwhelmed the negative effect on labor market work of the generally rising incomes of husbands. Also, during the past two decades, the real income growth of many husbands has slowed or even ceased.

3.4

Economists have cited several possible reasons for the rapid rise in women's labor force participation.[18]

1 Rising Real Wage Rates for Women

There has been a long-run increase in the real wage rates that women can earn in the labor market. This is primarily a consequence of women having acquired more skills through education. As already noted, higher wage rates generate both income and substitution effects within the framework of Becker's model. While the income effect reduces hours of work, the substitution effects related to both production- and consumption-related activities within the home tend to increase them. Goods will be substituted for time in the production of commodities *and* goods-intensive commodities will be substituted for time-intensive goods in the household's mix of consumer commodities. Both adjustments will free the wife's time from household activities so she may spend more time in the labor market. Presumably the substitution effect has dominated the income effect for many women, causing their participation rates to

[18] See James P. Smith and Michael P. Ward, "Time Series Growth in the Female Labor Force," *Journal of Labor Economics, Supplement,* January 1985, pp. S59–90; Barbara Bergmann, *The Economic Emergence of Women* (New York: Basic Books, 1986), chaps. 2–3; Claudia Goldin, *Understanding the Gender Gap* (New York: Oxford University Press, 1990); and Francine D. Blau, "Trends in the Well-Being of American Women, 1970–1995," *Journal of Economic Literature,* March 1998, pp. 112–65.

rise. The income effect for married women may be small because its size will vary directly with the amount of time they are already devoting to labor market work. In the extreme, the income effect of a rise in wage rates will be zero for a married woman who is not currently participating in labor market work. A wage rate increase will increase a person's income only if the individual is currently providing hours of labor market work.

2 Changing Preferences and Attitudes

Rising female participation rates may also result from a fundamental change in female preferences in favor of labor market work. First, the feminist movement of the 1960s may have altered the career objectives of women toward labor market participation. Similarly, antidiscrimination legislation of the 1960s—which specifies equal pay for equal work and presumably has made "men's jobs" more accessible—also may have made labor market work more attractive compared to work in the home. Furthermore, aside from its positive impact on wage rates, greater education for women may have enhanced their tastes or preferences for labor market careers. More generally, society's attitudes about work have changed greatly. In the 1920s and 1930s there was general disapproval of married women working outside the home. A man would lose status and be regarded as a "poor provider" if his wife was "forced" to take a job. But in the post–World War II period an attitudinal turnabout emerged: Labor force participation by married women is now widely condoned and encouraged.

Reference to Figure 2.8 is helpful in distinguishing between how higher wage rates on the one hand and changing preferences on the other affect female participation rates. The availability of higher wage rates increases the slope of the budget line, which—given preferences—encourages labor market participation. Similarly, given the wage rates, a change in preferences favorable to market work makes the indifference curves flatter, which is also conducive to participation.

3 Rising Productivity in the Household

The use of more and technologically superior capital goods by businesses over time has been an important factor in increasing the productivity of work time and therefore in raising real wage rates. Larger amounts of improved machinery and equipment permit workers to produce a unit of output with less time. Similarly, the availability of more and better capital goods for household use has permitted households to reduce the amount of time needed to accomplish both production and consumption within the home. For example, supermarkets and the availability of home refrigerators and freezers greatly reduce the amount of time devoted to grocery shopping. The supermarket permits one-stop shopping, and refrigerators and freezers further reduce the number of shopping trips needed per week. Similarly, microwave ovens, vacuum cleaners, automatic clothes washers and dryers, and dishwashers have reduced the amount of time involved in food preparation and housework. Fast-food restaurants circumvent the time-intensive activity of food preparation in the home. By providing direct and convenient transportation, the automobile has reduced the time required to attend a concert, movie, or football game. In terms of Becker's model, the increased availability of such household capital goods has increased productivity in the home, thereby freeing time from household production and consumption and allowing many women to engage in part- and full-time employment in the labor market.[19] Also, the increasing availability of child care centers has facilitated the transition of married women from work in the home to labor market work.

4 Declining Birthrates

The presence of children (particularly preschool children) is associated with low participation rates for wives. Child care is a highly time-intensive household productive activity that keeps many wives out of the labor force. Although babysitters, nurseries, husbands, and child care centers can substitute for wives in caring for children, the expense and opportunity cost involved often discourage such substitutions. Over time, the widespread availability and use of birth control techniques, coupled with changing lifestyles, have reduced birthrates *and* compacted the span of time over which a family's children are born. Whereas there were about 3.8 lifetime births per women in 1957 at the peak of the baby boom, that figure has declined to only 1.8 over the past decade. Fewer children reduce associated homemaking responsibilities and free married women for labor market work. Moreover, the compression of the time span over which children are born reduces the amount of time during which many women are absent from the labor force for child care responsibilities and is therefore more conducive to their pursuit of a labor market career.

Two points must be added. First, higher wage rates are associated with lower fertility rates. More educated women who can command relatively high wage rates in the labor market tend to have fewer children than less educated women for whom wages are low. Becker's model provides one explanation for this relationship. Child rearing is a highly time-intensive activity, and thus the opportunity cost of children—the income sacrificed by not being in the labor market—is higher for more educated women than for those who are less educated.

The second point is that the presence of young children is currently less of an inhibitor to labor market participation than it has been in the recent past. In fact, the largest increases in labor force participation have been for wives with very young children. In 2004, 59 percent of wives with preschool children participated in the labor force, compared to only 30 percent in 1970. Currently more than half of all mothers return to work before their youngest child is 2 years old.

5 Rising Divorce Rates

Marital instability as evidenced in rising divorce rates has undoubtedly motivated many women to establish and maintain labor market ties. Divorce rates rose rapidly in the 1970s and 1980s; and although they have declined slightly since then, they remain much higher than in earlier periods. The economic impact of divorce on women is often disastrous because relatively few women receive substantial alimony or child support payments from their former husbands. All too often the options are poverty, welfare support,

---

[19] For a detailed discussion of rising productivity in the home, see Bergmann, op. cit., chap. 12.

3.5	World of Work	The Power of the Pill*

The first birth control pill was released to the public in 1960. The pill has allowed women to have nearly certain prevention of pregnancy. This invention has caused far-reaching changes to society, including permitting women to plan their careers and childbearing to a much greater degree than before.

The pill was adopted at different rates depending on marital status. Married women quickly adopted the pill as their preferred method of birth control. Within five years, 41 percent of married women under the age of 30 who employed contraception were using it. However, due to legal and social factors, the pill was more slowly adopted by unmarried single women. The age of legal access to the pill was 21 for all but nine states in 1969. The age of legal access was lowered for nearly all states between 1969 and 1974. Thus by 1976 nearly three-quarters of all single women aged 18 and 19 and using contraception had tried the pill.

Goldin and Katz exploit these interstate differences in the timing of legal access to the pill to examine its impact on the age of first marriage and the proportion of women in professional occupations. Their analysis indicates that access to the pill can account for about one-third of the rise in the female percentage in professional occupations between 1970 and 1990. Legalized pill access to minors can account for 24–37 percent of the 8.7 percentage point decrease in the proportion of women married before age 23 between the cohorts of women born in the 1940s compared to those born in the early 1950s.

Bailey also utilized interstate differences in timing of legal access to the pill to examine the effects of the pill on female labor supply. Her results show that early access to the pill can account for 3 of the 20 percentage points of increase in labor force participation rates between 1970 and 1990. It can also account for 67 of the 450 additional annual hours worked on average by women aged 16–30 over that period.

* Based on Claudia Goldin and Lawrence F. Katz, "The Power of the Pill: Oral Contraceptives and Women's Career and Marriage Decisions," *Journal of Political Economy*, August 2002, pp. 730–70; and Martha J. Bailey, "More Power of the Pill: The Impact of Contraceptive Freedom on Women's Life Cycle Labor Supply," *Quarterly Journal of Economics*, February 2006, pp. 289–320.

or labor market work. In short, more and more married women, not to mention women contemplating marriage, may participate in the labor force as a means of protecting themselves against the financial exigencies of potential divorce. In terms of Figure 2.8, divorced women find themselves with substantially less nonlabor income, and this reduction is an inducement to labor market work.

A word of caution: The cause-and-effect relationships among fertility, divorce rates, and labor force participation are complex and unclear. For example, declines in fertility resulting from more efficient and less costly birth control techniques undoubtedly encourage labor force participation. On the other hand, the initial choice of a woman to pursue a labor market career may precipitate the decision to have fewer children. Similarly, the increased likelihood of divorce will tend to reduce fertility because child care is more difficult after a marriage dissolves. Conversely, the presence of few or no children makes divorce less painful and less costly.[20]

[20] For further discussion, you might consult Blau, Ferber, and Winkler, op. cit., pp. 294–97.

6 Expanding Job Accessibility

In addition to a decline in gender discrimination, a variety of other factors have made jobs more accessible to women. First, since World War II there has been a great expansion both absolutely and relatively in the kinds of employment that have traditionally been "women's jobs," such as clerical and secretarial work, retail sales, teaching, and nursing. Second, there has been a long-run shift of the population from farms and rural regions to urban areas, where jobs for women are more abundant and more geographically accessible. Third, the availability of part-time jobs has increased. This development has made it easier for women to reconcile labor market employment with housekeeping tasks.

7 Attempts to Maintain Living Standards

The growth of male earnings during the past two decades has been quite stagnant compared to earlier decades. In fact, for some men—particularly low-wage workers and those in industries hurt by imports—*real* weekly earnings are lower today than a decade, or even two decades, ago. Many households have adjusted to these realities by having both spouses work. That is, they have substituted labor market time for household production time to preserve the family's standard of living (defined either absolutely or relative to other households).[21]

In this view, part of the more recent rise in the female labor force participation rate has been necessitated by the family's desire to make ends meet. In some cases, making ends meet implies paying for basic food, clothing, and shelter. In other instances, it means preserving middle- or upper-class lifestyles, including living in comfortable homes, driving nice cars, enjoying household electronic equipment, and taking family trips. Understandably families look for ways to maintain their standards of living, whatever those levels might be. If spouses had not entered the labor force in record numbers during the past two decades, many households would have suffered absolute or relative declines in real income. Undoubtedly many wives entered the labor force to prevent this from happening. In addition, couples may be concerned about their family income compared to other families; as the entry of some women into the labor market may encourage other women to enter in order to maintain their families' relative income levels.[22]

Relative Importance

Fuchs has analyzed the various factors that may have contributed to rising female participation rates, with a view to discerning their comparative significance.[23] He discounts

---

[21] Some doubt has been cast on the hypothesis that married women are increasing work effort in response to declining wages of husbands. See Chinhui Juhn and Kevin M. Murphy, "Wage Inequality and Family Labor Supply," *Journal of Labor Economics,* January 1997, pp. 72–97.

[22] For some evidence consistent with this hypothesis, see David Neumark and Andrew Postlewaite, "Relative Income Concerns and the Rise in Married Women's Employment," *Journal of Public Economics,* October 1998, pp. 157–83.

[23] Victor R. Fuchs, *How We Live* (Cambridge: Harvard University Press, 1983), pp. 127–33.

the importance of such considerations as antidiscrimination legislation and the feminist movement, largely on the basis that their timing is bad. That is, the growth of female participation rates predates both the feminist movement and the passage of antidiscrimination laws (Chapter 14). It also predates the stagnant growth of real earnings experienced by many husbands during the past two decades. The problem with attributing rising participation rates for women to the availability of time-saving household goods and related innovations is that cause and effect are unclear. Did innovations such as clothes washers, freezers, fast-food restaurants, and supermarkets simply appear and thereby free up time that married women could devote to labor market work? Or were these innovations made largely in response to needs that arose when women decided for other reasons to enter the labor force? Fuchs believes that their spread in the United States is the *result* of the rising value of time and the rising female participation rates, rather than a causal factor.

More positively, Fuchs feels that rising real wage rates and the expansion of "women's jobs" in the service industries are the most important reasons for rising female participation rates. Better control of fertility is also deemed significant, but once again cause and effect are difficult to unravel. Do women first decide on labor force participation and, as a consequence of this decision, choose to have fewer children? Or does the decision to have smaller families precede the decision to enter the labor force? Fuchs also contends that the growing probability of divorce compels women to achieve and maintain their ties to the labor market. Smith and Ward are in substantial agreement with Fuchs. Their research leads them to conclude that rising real wage rates directly (by creating incentives to work) and indirectly (by inducing lower birthrates) have accounted for almost 60 percent of the increase in the female labor force that has occurred since World War II.[24]

Racial Differences

Important gender differences mark the effect of race on labor force participation rates.

Females

The participation rates of African–American and white women are nearly identical. This situation was not always the case. In the past, the participation rate of African–American women exceeded that of white women. For example, in the mid-1950s, the difference between the participation rates of African–American and white women was 12 to 15 percentage points. The gap has been closed because the rise in the participation rate of women (discussed in the previous section) has been concentrated among white women. Relatively little change has occurred in the participation of African–American women because their participation traditionally has been high.[25]

The decline in the racial gap in participation may be a critical factor in explaining why the ratio of African–American incomes to white incomes has increased only modestly in

[24] Smith and Ward, op. cit., pp. S59–90.
[25] For a discussion of the reasons for the historical racial gap in participation, see Glen Cain, *Married Women in the Labor Force* (Chicago: University of Chicago Press, 1966), pp. 77–83.

Global Perspective	Maximum Duration of Statutory Parental Leave in Weeks

Countries differ greatly in the duration of leave that firms are required to give new parents.

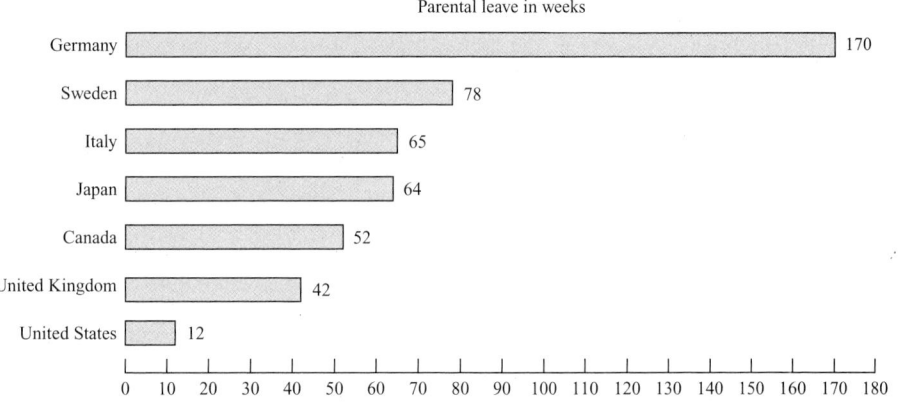

Parental leave in weeks

Germany	170
Sweden	78
Italy	65
Japan	64
Canada	52
United Kingdom	42
United States	12

Source: Clearinghouse on International Developments in Child, Youth, and Family Policies, Columbia University, "Mother's Day: More Than Candy and Flowers, Working Parents Need Paid Time Off," Issue Brief, Spring 2002. Data are for the 1998–2002 period. Maternity and parental leave have been combined.

the past two decades or so. The income gains for African–American families, which may have resulted from antidiscrimination legislation and more enlightened attitudes toward minorities, may have been largely offset by the relatively larger numbers of white married women entering the labor force.[26]

Males

Since the 1950s a gap has evolved between the participation rates of African–American males and white males. Thus, for example, in 1955 the participation rates of both groups were approximately 85 percent. But by 2000 the participation rate of white males was 75 percent compared to only 69 percent for African–American males. The gap has stabilized at about 6–7 percent since the mid-1990s.

Why the significantly lower participation rates for African–American men? There is no consensus on this question, but several hypotheses have been offered. First,

[26] In this section we have focused on the factors that explain the rise in female labor market employment. For an interesting discussion of the effects of women's labor force participation on marriage, fertility, divorce, and the general well-being of family members, see Blau, Ferber, and Winkler, op. cit., chap. 9.

| 3.6 | World of Work | Family and Medical Leave Act of 1993 |

After eight years of debate, in 1993 Congress passed the Family and Medical Leave Act (FMLA). Passage of this act relates directly to the growing labor force participation of women. Increased participation in labor market work has left women with less time to care for newborn children, temporarily disabled spouses, and aging parents. Before passage of this law, many workers—both female and male—faced the prospect of permanent loss of their jobs if they had to leave work temporarily to care for loved ones.

The FMLA permits workers to take up to 12 weeks a year of unpaid leave to care for (1) a spouse, a parent, or a child with a serious medical condition; (2) a newborn or newly adopted child; or (3) the worker's own serious health problem. Employees must provide 30 days' advance notice for foreseeable leaves. They retain their health insurance during their leaves and are guaranteed their original jobs or equivalent positions when they return to work.

FMLA covers employers with 50 or more workers within a 75-mile radius of the firm. Part-time employees and those who have been on the job for less than one year are excluded from eligibility. Also, firms can deny leaves to the highest-paid 10 percent of their salaried workers if allowing the leaves would create "substantial and grievous" injury to the business operation. The idea here is to exclude key management from the provisions of the act.

Debate has been considerable on the merits and impacts of the FMLA. Critics claim that it raises costs to firms and discourages the hiring of women (the group predicted to make the heaviest use of the leave provisions). Proponents argue that the law is a way for employees to mesh work and nonwork responsibilities and decrease career interruptions for women. The result, they say, will be increased worker and family well-being.

The evidence so far indicates that the FMLA has had little impact. According to Ruhm, neither the benefits to workers nor the costs imposed by the law are large.* This is partly the result of few workers getting additional leave time due to the law's many exemptions. In addition, workers often had other ways to get leave time before the law's passage. Relatedly, research by Ruhm and Teague, using cross-country data on mandated family leaves, indicates such leaves have little impact on productivity.†

* Christopher J. Ruhm, "Policy Watch: The Family Medical Leave Act," *Journal of Economic Perspectives,* Summer 1997, pp. 175–86.

† Christopher J. Ruhm and Jacqueline L. Teague, "Parental Leave Policies in Europe and North America," in Francine Blau and Ronald Ehrenberg (eds.), *Gender and Family Issues in the Workplace* (New York: Russell Sage Foundation Press, 1997). For evidence that the medical leave laws increase the number of mothers who eventually return to their prechildbirth jobs, see Charles L. Baum, "The Effects of Maternity Leave Legislation on Mothers' Labor Supply after Childbirth," *Southern Economic Journal,* April 2003, pp. 772–99.

"a demand-side" hypothesis suggests that the difference may be largely attributable to poorer labor market opportunities for African–American males in general, as reflected in relatively lower wages and weaker prospects for finding jobs. African–American males have lower average levels of educational attainment than white males. Also, on average, the quality of education (as measured by test scores) received by African–American males is lower than that for white males. In this demand-side view, discrimination as embodied in poorer education, lower wages, less desirable jobs, and the tendency to be the "last hired and first fired" explains why some African–American males remain outside the labor force. A spatial mismatch also may exist between African–American workers and employment opportunities because jobs have moved out of the central cities, where substantial African-American populations are concentrated.[27]

A second view explains the high labor market inactivity of African–Americans as residing primarily on the supply side of the market. Welch[28] has argued that nonlabor market opportunities may have improved for African–Americans, affording them more attractive alternatives to labor market work. What are those nonlabor market opportunities? One is the receipt of Social Security or public assistance. Indeed, we found in Chapter 2 that the increased availability and enhanced generosity of public income maintenance programs encourage income receivers of all races to withdraw from the labor force (see Figure 2.9 in particular). Because African–Americans are disproportionately represented among the lowest-income groups in our society, we would expect the participation rates of African–Americans to be less than those of whites. Welch notes that in 1980 over 30 percent of African–American men aged 20–24 and almost 22 percent of African–American men aged 35–44 either received Social Security or public assistance or lived with someone who did. Comparable figures for white males were only 13 and 10 percent, respectively. Welch also ponders whether illegal activities are more attractive than labor market work for many African–American men. He points out that young African–American males are six to seven times as likely to be in jail as are whites. Thus in 1980 some 4.6 percent of African–Americans aged 20–24 were incarcerated as compared to only 0.7 percent for whites. Since 1980, the incarceration rate has risen particularly for African–American males. By 1999, 3 percent of white males and 20 percent of African–American males had served some time in jail by their early thirties.[29]

Third, differences in health status may play a role in the differences in the participation rates of older African–American and white males. Bound, Schoenbaum, and Waidmann conclude that racial differences in age, education, and health status can account for 44 percent of the African–American–white difference in participation of males aged 51–61.[30] Evidence exists that some of these health differences may partly be the result of African–American males holding more physically demanding and stressful jobs.

Finally, the relatively lower participation rate for African–American married males may also reflect the relatively high participation rate of African–American wives noted earlier. In terms of Becker's model, African–American women may incur less discrimination in the labor market than African–American men, making it rational for relatively more African–American women and relatively fewer African–American men to participate in labor market work.

---

[27] For a review of studies examining the spatial mismatch hypothesis, see John F. Kain, "The Spatial Mismatch Hypothesis: Three Decades Later," *Housing Policy Debate,* no. 2 (1992), pp. 371–460; and Keith R. Ihlanfeldt and David L. Sjoquist, "The Spatial Mismatch: A Review of Recent Studies and Their Implications for Welfare Reform," *Housing Policy Debate,* no. 4 (1998), pp. 849–92.

[28] Finis Welch, "The Employment of Black Men," *Journal of Labor Economics,* January 1990, pp. S26–74.

[29] Becky Pettit and Bruce Western, "Mass Imprisonment and the Life Course: Race and Class Inequality in U.S. Incarceration," *American Sociological Review,* April 2004, pp. 151–69.

[30] John Bound, Michael Schoenbaum, and Timothy Waidmann, "Race and Education Differences in Disability Status and Labor Force Attachment in the Health and Retirement Survey," *Journal of Human Resources,* Suppl. 1995, pp. S227–67.

CYCLIC CHANGES IN PARTICIPATION RATES

Our discussion has concentrated on long-term or secular changes in participation rates. We must now recognize that cyclic changes also occur. Let's consider how cyclic fluctuations might affect a family in which one spouse engages in labor market work while the other performs productive activities within the home. Assume that a recession occurs, causing the employed spouse to lose her or his job. The net effect on overall participation rates depends on the size of the added-worker effect and the discouraged-worker effect.

Added-Worker Effect

The *added-worker effect* is the idea that when the primary breadwinner in a family loses his or her job, other family members will temporarily enter the labor force in the hope of finding employment to offset the decline in the family's income. The rationale involved is reminiscent of Chapter 2's income effect. Specifically, one spouse's earned income may be treated as nonlabor income from the standpoint of the other spouse. In our illustration, the nonemployed family member receives an intrahousehold transfer of some portion of the employed spouse's earnings. From the perspective of the person working in the home, this transfer is nonlabor income. In terms of Figure 2.8, the spouse's job loss will reduce nonlabor income as measured on the right vertical axis. Other things being equal, a decrease in nonlabor (transfer) income tends to cause one to become a labor force participant. This is the underlying rationale of the added-worker effect.[31]

Discouraged-Worker Effect

The *discouraged-worker effect* works in the opposite direction. The discouraged-worker effect suggests that during a recession some unemployed workers (for example, the unemployed spouse in our illustration) become so pessimistic about finding a job with an acceptable wage rate that they cease to actively seek employment and thereby temporarily become nonparticipants. This phenomenon can be explained in terms of Chapter 2's substitution effect. Recessions generally entail declines in the real wages available to unemployed workers and new job seekers, increasing the price of income (that is, increasing the amount of work time that must be expended to earn $1 of goods) and decreasing the price of leisure. This causes some workers to substitute leisure (nonparticipation) for job search. Other things being equal, a decrease in the wage rate will cause some individuals to withdraw from the labor force now that the wage rate available to them is lower. Remember that the substitution effect suggests that a decline in the wage rate available to a worker will decrease the incentive to engage in labor market work.[32]

---

[31] For an examination of the added worker effect, see J. Melvin Stephens, "Worker Displacement and the Added Worker Effect," *Journal of Labor Economics,* July 2002, pp. 504–37.

[32] For an evaluation of the discouraged-worker effect, see Yolanda K. Kodrzycki, "Discouraged and Other Marginally Attached Workers: Evidence on Their Role in the Labor Market," *New England Economic Review,* May/June 2000, pp. 35–40. Also see Luca Benati, "Some Empirical Evidence on the 'Discouraged Worker' Effect," *Economics Letters,* March 2001, pp. 387–95.

Procyclic Labor Force Changes

These two effects influence participation rates and labor force size in opposite ways. The added-worker effect increases and the discouraged-worker effect decreases participation rates and labor force size during an economic downturn. Which effect is dominant? What actually happens to participation rates over the business cycle? Empirical research generally indicates that the discouraged-worker effect is dominant, as is evidenced by the fact that the aggregate labor force participation rate varies inversely with the unemployment rate. When the unemployment rate increases, the participation rate falls and vice versa.

Why does the discouraged-worker effect apparently outweigh the added-worker effect? Why does the size of the labor force vary in a procyclic fashion? The conventional wisdom is that the discouraged-worker effect applies to many more households than the added-worker effect. For example, if the nation's unemployment rate rises from, say, 5 to 8 percent, only the 3 percent or so of all families that now contain an additional unemployed member will be subject to the added-worker effect. On the other hand, worsening labor market conditions evidenced by the increase in the unemployment rate and decline in real wages may discourage actual and potential labor force participants in *all* households. Thus, as the economy moves into a recession, young people who are deciding whether to continue school or drop out to seek employment will take note that wage rates are less attractive and jobs more difficult to find. Many of them will decide to stay in school rather than participate in the labor force.

Procyclic changes in the labor force size also have been explained in terms of the *timing* of labor force participation by some individuals. For example, many married women are marginally attached to the labor force in that they plan to engage in labor market work for, say, only half of their adult years. The other half of their time will be spent in household production. Given this planned overall division of time, it is only rational for such women to participate in the labor force in prosperous times when jobs are readily available and real wages are relatively high and, conversely, to be nonparticipants when unemployment is high and available wage rates are low.[33]

The procyclic changes in labor force size are of more than idle academic interest. Such changes have a significant bearing on the magnitude of the official unemployment rate and hence an indirect bearing on macroeconomic policy (Chapter 18). The apparent dominance of the discouraged-worker effect over the added-worker effect means that the labor force shrinks (or at least grows at a below-normal rate) during recession, and the official unemployment rate understates unemployment. During economic expansions, the discouraged-worker effect becomes an "encouraged-worker" effect, and the added-worker effect becomes a "subtracted-worker" effect. The former dominates the latter, and the labor force expands as a result. This means there is a larger-than-normal increase in the labor force during an economic expansion that keeps the official unemployment rate higher than would otherwise be the case. In short, cyclic changes in participation rates cause the official unemployment rate to understate unemployment during a cyclic downswing and to overstate it during an upswing.

---

[33] See Jacob Mincer, "Labor-Force Participation and Unemployment: A Review of Recent Evidence," in R. A. Gordon and M. S. Gordon (eds.), *Prosperity and Unemployment* (New York: John Wiley & Sons, Inc., 1966), pp. 73–112.

HOURS OF WORK: TWO TRENDS

Observe in Figure 3.1 that the total amount of labor supplied in the economy depends not only on the number of labor force participants but also on the average number of hours worked per week and per year by those participants. Therefore, let's now consider what has happened to hours of work over time.

Figure 3.6 provides an overview of secular changes in the average workweek. The figure shows decade averages of the workweek for production workers in U.S. manufacturing industries. Two important observations are apparent. First, hours of work declined steadily from 1910 to World War II. The average workweek fell by almost 16 percent [(49.4 − 41.5)/49.4] over the 1910–1919 to 1940–1949 period.[34] Second, the average workweek has changed little since the 1940s. Although there is no universally accepted explanation of these trends, interesting and plausible theories have been put forth.

Workweek Decline, 1900–1940

The pre–World War II decline in the workweek is explainable in terms of the basic work–leisure model described in Chapter 2. The essential contention is that the declining workweek is simply a supply response to historically rising real wages and earnings. More precisely, given (1) worker income–leisure preferences, (2) nonwage incomes, and (3) the assumption that leisure is a normal good, rising wage rates over time will reduce the number of hours individuals want to work, provided the income effect exceeds the

---

[34] The shorter hours of the 1930s are largely explainable in terms of the Great Depression; the shorter workweek was widely instituted to spread the smaller demand for labor among more workers.

FIGURE 3.6

The average workweek declined between 1910 and 1940. It has changed little since then.

Source: John Brack and Keith Cowling, "Advertising and Labour Supply: Workweek and Workyear in U.S. Manufacturing Industries 1919–1976," *Kyklos*, no. 2 (1983), pp. 285–303. Workweek data for 1970–1999 are from *Employment and Earnings*.

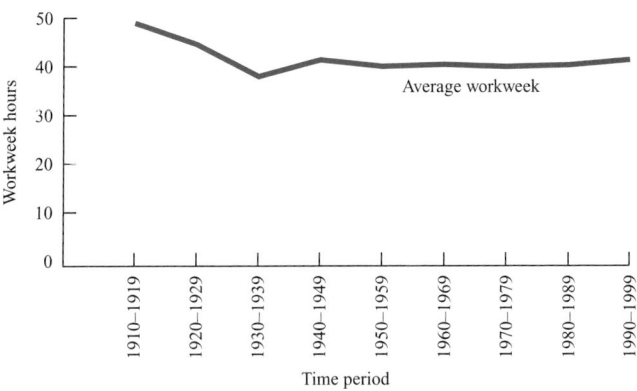

substitution effect. And, in fact, a substantial amount of empirical evidence indicates that the net effect of wage increases on hours of work has been negative.[35]

Post–World War II: Workweek Stability

But how does one explain the relative constancy of the workweek in the postwar era? Real wages have continued to rise; but either the substitution effect has somehow offset the income effect, or perhaps some additional factors have been at work in recent decades to offset the tendency of higher wage rates to reduce the workweek.[36]

Kniesner argues that educational attainment has played an important role in the constancy of the workweek since World War II.[37] He hypothesizes that the supply of labor is positively related to education. Furthermore, he notes that increases in educational attainment have been much greater in the postwar period than the prewar period; in the 1910–1940 period the increase in the median years of schooling completed was only about 6 percent compared to a 34 percent increase in the 1940–1970 period. Kniesner argues that these differences in educational attainment account for the two trends evidenced in Figure 3.6.

Why might more education increase or sustain hours of work? First, a change in preferences may be involved. Education is a means of enhancing one's earning power in the labor market. Decisions to acquire more education may therefore reflect a change in

[35] For a good discussion of these studies, see John T. Addison and W. Stanley Siebert, *The Market for Labor: An Analytical Treatment* (Santa Monica, CA: Goodyear Publishing Company, Inc., 1979), pp. 85–90.
[36] Though the average workweek has changed little in the past 50 years, the demographic composition of the workforce has changed dramatically. For more on this point, see Ellen R. McGrattan and Richard Rogerson, "Changes in Hours Worked since 1950," *Quarterly Review* (Federal Reserve Bank of Minneapolis), Winter 1998, pp. 2–19.
[37] Thomas J. Kniesner, "The Full-Time Workweek in the United States, 1900–1970," *Industrial and Labor Relations Review*, October 1976, pp. 3–5. See also Ethel B. Jones, "Comment," and Kniesner, "Reply," *Industrial and Labor Relations Review*, April 1980, pp. 379–89.

3.7	World of Work	Time Stress*

Surveys show that many workers face *time stress:* a lack of time to do their desired activities. Among U.S. married couples in which at least one spouse works, 44 percent of men and 55 percent of women say that they are always or often time stressed. Surveys in other countries also indicate that many married couples are time stressed. Australians report a similar amount of time stress as Americans. About one-third of Germans report they are stressed for time, while 70 percent of South Koreans report they suffer this condition.

Using data from these four countries, Hamermesh and Lee examine the factors causing time stress among married couples. Not surprisingly, increases in hours devoted to market work or household production intensify time stress. Holding constant market and household hours worked, they find that increases in earnings lead to greater time stress. They assert that people feel that they are in a time crunch because they have don't have enough time to consume the goods they can purchase with their higher income. This does not mean higher-income people would be happy if they earned less. They are assumed to be maximizing their utility, but they are unhappy about the time limits they face. Consistent with that assumption, higher-income individuals indicate that they are happier with their income and life in general than their lower-income counterparts.

Some interesting patterns related to household production also appeared in these data. Household production work appears to generate less time stress than an equivalent amount of market work. Increased efficiency in household production should reduce the amount of time stress. Consistent with that conjecture, an improvement in health status from fair or poor to at least good reduced time stress by the equivalent of at least 10 hours of market work per week.

* Based on Daniel S. Hamermesh and Jungmin Lee, "Stressed Out on Four Continents: Time Crunch or Yuppie Kvetch?" *Review of Economics and Statistics*, May 2007, pp. 374–83.

---

tastes favoring a stronger commitment to labor market work. Second, more educated workers generally acquire more pleasant jobs—that is, jobs that are less physically demanding, less structured, more challenging, and so forth. Other things being equal, such job characteristics would make workers less willing to reduce the workweek. Finally, a more educated workforce may increase employer resistance to a declining workweek. The reason for this is that employers incur more fixed-cost expenditures in recruiting more educated workers and in training them over their job tenures compared to less educated workers. A shorter workweek will increase these fixed costs per worker hour and thus will increase the overall hourly cost of any given quantity of labor. As their labor forces have become more educated, employers have stiffened their resistance to a shorter workweek.[38]

---

[38] Employer resistance to a shrinking workweek may be reinforced by the growth of fringe benefits that has occurred in the postwar period (Chapter 7). Employer expenditures for such benefits as worker life and health insurance are also fixed costs on a per worker basis, and as with recruitment and training costs, a shortened workweek would entail higher hourly labor costs.

Three explanations in addition to changes in educational attainment have been suggested for the constancy of the workweek. First, the *Fair Labor Standards Act of 1938* (FLSA) requires employers to pay a wage premium for all hours worked in excess of 40 per week. This legislation tended not only to reduce the length of the workweek but also to standardize it at 40 hours.[39] Second, the rise in the marginal income tax rates since the start of World War II has translated into smaller increases in net (aftertax) wage rates. Thus the negative supply, or hours of work, response has been much smaller in the postwar era than in earlier decades. Finally, advertising has increased quantitatively and in effectiveness in the post–World War II period. This may have increased the desires of workers for more goods and services and therefore induced them to work more hours than otherwise would be the case.

Chapter Summary

1. The aggregate quantity of labor supplied depends on population size, the labor force participation rate, and the number of hours worked weekly and annually.
2. It is fruitful to examine and explain participation rates in terms of Becker's time allocation model. This model views households as producing utility-yielding commodities by combining goods and time. In this context, household members allocate their time to labor market work, household production, and consumption on the basis of comparative advantage.
3. The labor force participation rate is the actual labor force as a percentage of the potential or age-eligible population.
4. In the post–World War II period the aggregate participation rate has drifted upward from about 59 percent in 1950 to about 66 percent in 2006. This is basically the result of greater participation rates of women (particularly married women), which have more than offset the declining participation rates of males.
5. Older males account for most of the decline in male participation rates. The declining participation rates of older men are attributed to *(a)* rising real wages and earnings, *(b)* the availability of public and private pensions, *(c)* greater access to disability benefits, and *(d)* age–earnings profiles that suggest that the cost of leisure may decline for older workers.
6. Rising participation rates for women have been caused by *(a)* rising relative wage rates for women, *(b)* stronger female preferences for labor market work, *(c)* rising productivity within the household, *(d)* declining birthrates, *(e)* greater marital instability, *(f)* the greater accessibility of jobs, and *(g)* attempts to maintain family standards of living.
7. The participation rates of African–American women and white women are nearly identical today. In the past, the rates of African–American women exceeded those of white women.

[39] For contrary evidence suggesting the FLSA has had little impact on overtime hours, see Stephen J. Trejo, "Does the Statutory Overtime Premium Discourage Long Workweeks?" *Industrial and Labor Relations Review,* April 2003, pp. 530–51.

8. The participation rates of African–American males have declined over time and are currently 6–7 percentage points lower than for white males. Some analysts stress such demand-side factors as labor market discrimination, inferior educational opportunities, and the geographic inaccessibility of jobs in explaining lower African-American rates. Others focus on such supply-side factors as the availability of public assistance and illegal activities.

9. Cyclic changes in participation rates reflect the net impact of the added-worker and discouraged-worker effects. The added-worker effect suggests that when a family's primary breadwinner loses his or her job, other family members will become labor market participants to sustain the family's income. The discouraged-worker effect indicates that during recession, some unemployed workers will become pessimistic about their prospects for reemployment and will therefore withdraw from the labor force. Most empirical studies suggest that the discouraged-worker effect is dominant, with the result that the aggregate labor force participation rate varies inversely with the unemployment rate.

10. The average workweek and workyear declined during the 1910–1940 period, but since World War II both have been quite stable. The earlier workweek and workyear declines have been explained in terms of the income effect's domination of the substitution effect as real wage rates have risen historically. The post–World War II stability of the workweek and workyear has been attributed to increases in education as well as other factors.

Terms and Concepts

Becker's model of the allocation of time, *54*

time-intensive and goods-intensive commodities, *56*

potential and actual labor forces, *59*

labor force participation rate, *59*

added-worker and discouraged-worker effects, *76*

Fair Labor Standards Act of 1938, *81*

Questions and Study Suggestions

1. Briefly discuss the major components of aggregate labor supply.

2. In what specific ways does Becker's model of the allocation of time differ from the simple work–leisure choice model? Compare the functioning of the income and substitution effects in each of the two models. Do the two effects have the same impact on labor market work in both models?

3. In 2006 the United States had a population of 299 million, of which 70 million were either under 16 years of age or institutionalized. Approximately 151 million people were either employed or unemployed but actively seeking work. What was the participation rate in 2006?

4. What has happened to the aggregate labor force participation rate in the post–World War II period? To the participation rates of males and females?

5. What factors account for the declining participation rates of older males?

6. What factors account for the increase in the participation rates of married women? Use a work–leisure diagram (similar, for example, to Figure 2.8) to explain how

each of these factors might individually alter either the indifference curves or the budget lines of women and make labor force participation more likely.

7. Compare the participation rates of *(a)* white and African–American women and *(b)* white and African–American men. In each case explain any differences.

8. "The ratio of the incomes of African–American families to the incomes of white families has increased quite slowly in the past two or three decades, despite legislation and a variety of public policies to ameliorate discrimination. One may therefore conclude that government programs have failed to lessen racial discrimination." Discuss critically.

9. Use a work–leisure diagram to demonstrate that *(a)* if African–Americans have labor market opportunities that are inferior to those of whites and *(b)* nonlabor income is available in the form of, say, disability benefits, African–Americans will have lower participation rates even though the work–leisure preferences (indifference curves) of African–Americans and whites are identical.

10. "Empirical evidence for the United States suggests that labor force participation varies directly with unemployment." Do you agree? Explain in terms of the discouraged-worker and added-worker effects.

11. "The added-worker effect can be explained in terms of the income effect, while the discouraged-worker effect is based on the substitution effect." Do you agree?

12. What has happened to the length of the workweek and workyear during the past hundred years? Explain any significant trends.

13. The accompanying diagram restates the basic work–leisure choice model as presented in Chapter 2. Use this diagram to explain the declining workweek occurring in the pre–World War II period, making explicit the assumptions underlying your analysis. We noted in the present chapter that the stability of the workweek in the post–World War II era has been attributed by various scholars to such considerations as *(a)* higher taxes on earnings, *(b)* acquisition of more education, and *(c)* advertising. Make alterations in the indifference curves or budget line of the diagram to indicate how *each* of these three factors might contribute to a relatively stable workweek despite rising before-tax real wages.

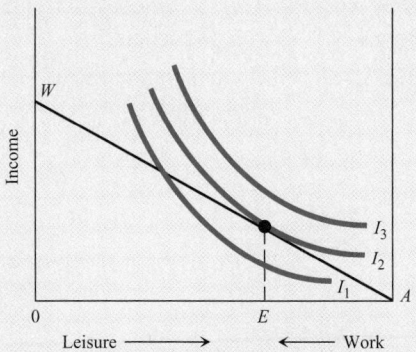

Internet Exercise

Who Is Participating More in the Labor Force? Who Less?

Go to the Bureau of Labor Statistics Web site for the current population survey **(http://www.bls.gov/cps/home.htm)** and select "Historical Data for Series in the Monthly Employment Situation News Release" to find information about civilian labor force participation rates (LFPRs) and civilian employment–population ratios (EPRs).

1. What were the LFPRs for men and women in January 1950 and for the most recent month shown? Which rate has increased over this period? Which has declined? What are some possible explanations for these changes?

2. What has been the combined effect of these two trends on the overall labor force participation rate, 1950 to the present? (In your answer, provide the specific overall LFPRs for January 1950 and the most recent month shown.)

3. What were the LFPRs for white women and African–American women in January 1955 and for the most recent month shown? What was the gap in these rates at the beginning of the period and the end of the period? What are some possible explanations for this change?

4. What was the overall civilian employment–population ratio for the most recent month shown? Why are overall EPRs lower than overall LFPRs? (Use this book's glossary definitions for help with this question.)

Internet Links

The Bureau of Labor Statistics Web site provides many detailed statistics for labor force participation and hours of work **(http://www.bls.gov/)**.

The Wage and Hour Division of the U.S. Department of Labor Web site has detailed information about the Family and Medical Leave Act **(http://www.dol.gov/esa/whd/fmla/index.htm)**.

Chapter 4

Labor Quality: Investing in Human Capital

Education and training are much in the current news. Today's challenge is being able to compete effectively in the rapidly emerging global marketplace. Experts agree that to maintain our relative standard of living, we must upgrade the education and skill levels of our workforce. They also agree that the dynamic aspects of global technological innovation and product competition have rendered many of our jobs less secure. Continuous education, training, and retraining will be crucial to keeping our workforce fully employed.

In Chapters 2 and 3 we looked primarily at the decisions of whether and to what degree to participate in the labor market. Our emphasis there was on the work–leisure decision and the various participation rates. In this chapter we turn from the quantitative to the qualitative aspects of labor supply. Workers bring differing levels of formal educational attainment and skills to the labor market. They also acquire substantially different amounts of on-the-job training. A more educated, better-trained person is capable of supplying a larger amount of useful productive effort than one with less education and training.

Any activity that increases the quality (productivity) of labor may be considered an investment in human capital. Human capital investments include expenditures not only on formal education and on-the-job training but also on health, migration, job search, and the preschool nurturing of children. Workers can become more productive by improving their physical or mental health and also by moving from locations and jobs where their productivity is relatively low to other locations and jobs where their productivity is relatively high. In fact, in Chapter 9 human capital theory will be the core concept used to analyze labor migration.

INVESTMENT IN HUMAN CAPITAL: CONCEPT AND DATA

When a firm invests in physical capital, it is acquiring some asset that is expected to enhance the firm's flow of net profits over a period of time. For example, a company might purchase new machinery designed to increase output and therefore sales revenues over, say, the 10-year projected useful life of the machinery. The unique characteristic of investment is that *current* expenditures or costs are incurred with the intent that these costs will be more than compensated for by enhanced *future* revenues or returns. Analogously, investments are made in human capital. When a person (or a person's parents or society at large) makes a current expenditure on education or training, it is anticipated that the individual's knowledge and skills and therefore future earnings will be enhanced.[1] The important point is that expenditures on education and training can be fruitfully treated as **investment in human capital** just as expenditures on capital equipment can be understood as investment in physical capital.

Relevant data reveal three things. First, expenditures on education and training are substantial. In the school year 2003–2004 Americans spent some $827 billion on elementary, secondary, and higher education. In addition, an estimated 2 percent of payroll is spent each year by employers for on-the-job training.

Second, the educational attainment of the labor force has increased dramatically over time. For example, in 1970 over 36 percent of the civilian labor force had achieved less than a high school education, while a mere 14 percent had completed four or more years of college. Similar figures for 2006 were 12 and 29 percent, respectively.

Third, investments in education result in an enlarged flow of earnings. This tendency is reflected in the *age–earnings profiles* of Figure 4.1, which show the lifetime earning patterns of male workers who have attained various educational levels. Observe that the average earnings of more educated workers exceed those of less educated workers. Also, the earnings profiles of more educated workers rise more rapidly than those of less educated workers. Differences in the earnings of more and less educated workers tend to widen during workers' prime earning years.

Not shown, the age–earnings profiles of females display similar overall characteristics to those in Figure 4.1 but lie significantly below those of men. Also, the profiles for women are much flatter than those for men. We discuss these gender differences in earnings in detail in Chapter 14.[2]

---

[1] As will be noted later, the payoff from an investment in education may also take nonmonetary forms, such as obtaining a more pleasant job or a greater appreciation of literature and art.

[2] The fact that the age–earnings profiles ultimately decline must be interpreted with some care. Although it is tempting to attribute the declining incomes of older workers to diminished physical vigor and mental alertness, the obsolescence of education and skills, or the decision to work shorter hours, the decline may be largely due to the character of the data. In particular, these data do *not* track the earnings of specific individuals through their lifetimes. Rather, these cross-sectional data show the earnings of different individuals of different ages in some particular year. Longitudinal data that trace the earnings of specific people over time indicate that earnings continue to increase until retirement. The declining segments of the age–earnings profiles in Figure 4.1 may occur because the U.S. economy has been growing, and therefore each succeeding generation has earned more than the preceding one. Thus the average 45-year-old college-educated worker has higher earnings as shown in the age–earnings profiles simply because he or she is a member of a more recent generation than a 65-year-old college-educated worker.

FIGURE 4.1

Age–Earnings Profiles by Years of Education

Age–earnings profiles (in this case for males in 2005) indicate that education "pays" in that more–educated workers obtain higher average annual earnings than less–educated workers of the same age group.

Source: Derived from U.S. Bureau of the Census, Educational *Attainment in the United States: March 2006*, Table 9.

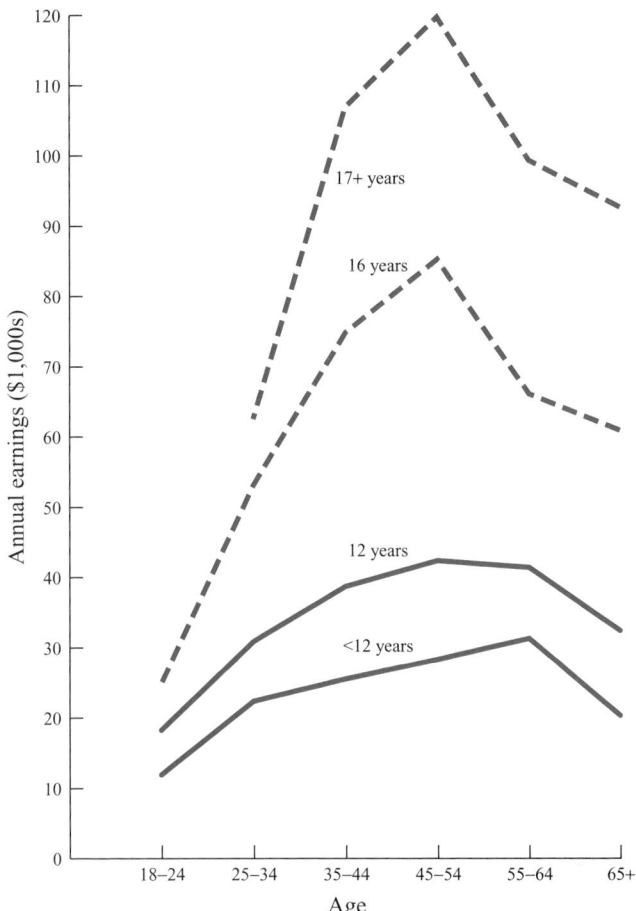

THE HUMAN CAPITAL MODEL

Let's introduce a simple model to analyze the decision to invest in, say, a college education. Assume you have just graduated from high school and are deciding whether to go to college. From a purely economic standpoint, a rational decision will involve a comparison of the associated costs and benefits. The monetary costs incurred in the purchase of a college education are of two general types. On one hand, there are *direct* or *out-of-pocket costs* in the form of expenditures for tuition, special fees, and books and supplies. Expenditures for room and board are *not* included as a part of direct costs because you would need food and shelter regardless of whether you attended college or entered the labor market. On the other hand, the *indirect* or *opportunity cost* of going to college is the earnings you give up by not entering the labor market after completing high school. For example, estimates suggest that indirect costs may account for as much as 60–70 percent of the total cost of a college education, at least at public universities.

The economic *benefit* of investing in a college education, as we know from Figure 4.1, is an enlarged future flow of earnings.

This conception of a human capital investment decision is portrayed graphically in Figure 4.2. Curve *HH* represents your earnings profile if you decide not to attend college, but rather enter the labor market immediately on the completion of high school at age 18. The *CC* curve is your cost–earnings profile if you decide to undertake a four-year college degree before entering the labor market. We note that area 1 below the horizontal axis represents the direct or out-of-pocket costs (the negative income) incurred in attending college. Area 2 reflects the indirect or opportunity costs—that is, the earnings you forgo while attending college. The sum of areas 1 and 2 shows the total cost (your total investment) in a college education. Area 3—the difference between the *CC* and *HH* curves over ages 22 to 65—shows the gross *incremental* earnings that you will realize by obtaining a college degree; it shows how much *additional* income you will obtain as a college graduate over your work life compared to what you would have earned with just a high school diploma. Your work life in this case is presumed to extend over the 43-year period from age 22 to age 65.

Discounting and Net Present Value

We know that to make a rational decision you will want to compare costs (areas 1 and 2) with benefits (area 3). But a complication arises at this point. The costs and benefits associated with investing in a college education accrue at different points in

FIGURE 4.2 Age–Earnings Profiles with and without a College Education

If an individual decides to enter the labor market after graduation from high school at age 18, the age–earnings profile will be *HH* in comparison with the *CC* profile if she or he had gone to college. Attending college entails both direct costs (tuition, fees, books) and indirect costs (forgone earnings). But on entering the labor market at age 22, the college graduate will enjoy a higher level of annual earnings over her or his working life. To determine whether it is economically rational to invest in a college education, its net present value must be found by discounting costs and benefits back to the present (age 18).

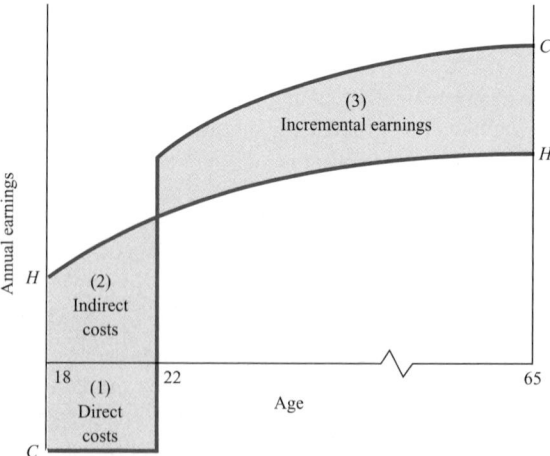

College Graduates Worldwide

The percentage of adults aged 25–64 who have a college degree in major industrial countries ranges from 11 percent in Italy to 30 percent in the United States.

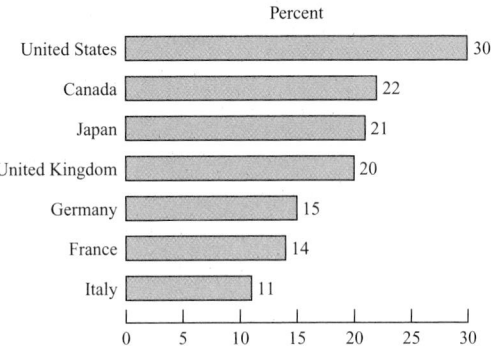

Source: Organization for Economic Cooperation and Development, *Education at a Glance, 2006* (Paris: OECD, 2006). Data are for 2006.

time. This is important because dollars expended and received at different points in time have different value. A meaningful comparison of the costs and benefits associated with a college education requires that these costs and benefits be compared in terms of a common point in time, such as the present. What we seek to determine from the vantage point of an 18-year-old youth is the net present discounted value, or simply the *net present value,* of the present and future costs *and* present and future benefits of a college education.

Time Preference

Why do dollars earned (or expended) have a different value a year, or two or three years, from now than they have today? The immediate answer is that a positive interest rate is paid for borrowing or "renting" money. But this raises an additional question: *Why* is interest paid for the use of money? The answer lies in the notion of *time preference:* the idea that, given the choice, most people prefer the pleasure of indulgence today to the promise of indulgence tomorrow. Most individuals prefer present consumption to future consumption because, given the uncertainties and vagaries of life, the former seems more tangible and therefore more valuable. Time preference, in short, is the idea that people are impatient and subjectively prefer goods in the present over the same goods in the future. It follows that an individual must be compensated by an interest payment to defer present consumption or, alternatively stated, to save a portion of her or his income. If an individual equates $100 worth of goods today with $110 worth of goods a year from now, we can say that his or her time preference rate is 10 percent. The individual must be paid $10 or 10 percent as an inducement to forgo $100 worth of present consumption.

Present Value Formula

Because the preference for present consumption necessitates payment of a positive interest rate, a dollar received a year from now is worth less than a dollar obtained today. A dollar received today can be lent or invested at some positive interest rate and thereby can be worth more than a dollar a year from now. If the interest rate is 10 percent, one can lend $1 today and receive $1.10 at the end of the year; the $1.10 comprises the original $1 plus $.10 of interest. This can be shown algebraically as follows:

$$V_p(1 + i) = V_1 \tag{4.1}$$

where V_p = present or current value—for example, $1.00 today.

V_1 = value (of the $1.00) one year from now.

i = interest rate.

The $(1 + i)$ term indicates that one receives back the original or present value ($1.00) *plus* the interest. Substituting our illustrative numbers, we have

$$\$1.00(1.10) = \$1.10$$

This formulation tells us that, given a 10 percent interest rate, $1.10 received next year is the equivalent of $1.00 in hand today.

Equation (4.1) focuses on determining the *future* value of the $1.00 one has today. As indicated earlier, our goal is to determine the *present* (today's) value of expenditures and revenues incurred and received in the future. We can get at this by restating our original question. Instead of asking how much $1.00 obtained today will be worth a year from now, let's inquire how much $1.10 received a year from now would be worth today. In general terms, the answer is found by solving Equation (4.1) for V_p. Thus

$$V_p = \frac{V_1}{(1 + i)} \tag{4.2}$$

Equation (4.2) is a **discount formula** for a one-year period. Inserting our illustrative numbers,

$$\$1.00 = \frac{\$1.10}{1.10}$$

That is, $1.10 received a year from now is worth only $1.00 today if the interest rate is 10 percent.

Observing in Figure 4.2 that both costs and benefits are incurred over a number of years, we can extend the discounting formula of Equation (4.2) as follows:

$$V_p = E_0 + \frac{E_1}{(1+i)^1} + \frac{E_2}{(1+i)^2} + \frac{E_3}{(1+i)^3} + \cdots + \frac{E_n}{(1+i)^n} \qquad \textbf{(4.3)}$$

where the E values represent a stream of incremental earnings (E_0 being any additional income received immediately, E_1 the additional income received next year, E_2 the incremental earnings received two years from now, and so forth); n is the duration of the earnings stream or, in other words, the individual's expected working life; and i is the interest rate.[3] Observe that incremental earnings (or costs), E_0, incurred immediately need not be discounted. But the incremental earnings received next year, or one year hence, E_1, must be discounted one year. Note further that the denominator of the third term is squared, the fourth is cubed, and so forth. This is so because the values of E_2 and E_3 must be discounted two and three years, respectively, to determine their present value. Dividing E_2—the incremental earnings to be received two years hence—by $(1 + i)$ discounts the value of those earnings for the time elapsed in the first year; but *that* value must be again divided by $(1 + i)$ to find its present value because the time between the first and second year further diminishes the value.

Restating the formula for our high school graduate who enters the labor force at age 18, we have

$$V_p = E_{18} + \frac{E_{19}}{(1+i)} + \frac{E_{20}}{(1+i)^2} + \frac{E_{21}}{(1+i)^3} + \cdots + \frac{E_{64}}{(1+i)^{46}} \qquad \textbf{(4.4)}$$

which can be more compactly stated as

$$V_p = \sum_{n=18}^{64} \frac{E_n}{(1+i)^{n-18}} \qquad \textbf{(4.5)}$$

This formulation tells us that we are calculating the present value (V_p) of the sum (Σ) of the discounted incremental earnings (E_n) over the individual's working life, which runs from age 18 through age 64, after which time he or she retires when attaining age 65. Because n is 64 years of age, the $n = 18$ notation indicates that we are discounting future earnings over $46\ (= 64 - 18)$ years of working life.

Figure 4.2 reminds us that the decision to invest in a college education entails both costs and benefits (enhanced earnings). How can both be accounted for in Equation (4.3) or (4.4)? The answer is to treat costs as negative earnings. Thus the "earnings" for the four years the individual is in college (E_0, E_1, E_2, and E_3) will be the negative sum of the direct and indirect costs incurred in each of those years. For each succeeding year until retirement, incremental earnings will be positive. We therefore are actually calculating the *net* present value of a college education in these two equations.

---

[3] We are sidestepping the troublesome problem of deciding which interest rate is appropriate. A small difference in the rate used can have a substantial impact on the calculation of present value.

Decision Rule: $V_p < 0$

The relevant investment criterion or decision rule based on this calculation is that *the individual should make the investment if its net present value is greater than zero.* A positive value tells us that the present discounted value of the benefits exceeds the present discounted value of the costs, and when this is so—when benefits exceed costs—the decision to invest is economically rational. If the net present value is negative, then costs exceed benefits and the investment is not economically justifiable.

Illustration

A truncated example may be helpful at this point. Assume that after graduating from high school Carl Carlson contemplates enrolling in a one-year intensive course in data processing. The direct costs of the course are $1,000, and the opportunity cost is $5,000. Upon completion of the course, he has been promised employment with the Computex Corporation. Expecting to receive a large inheritance, he plans to work only three years and then retire permanently from the labor force. The incremental income he anticipates earning because of his data processing training is $2,500, $3,000, and $3,500 for the three years he intends to work. The relevant interest rate at this time is 10 percent. Is the decision to enroll in the data processing course rational? Substituting these figures in Equation (4.3), we have

$$V_p = E_0 + \frac{E_1}{(1 + i)} + \frac{E_2}{(1 + i)^2} + \frac{E_3}{(1 + i)^3}$$

$$V_p = -\$6,000 + \frac{\$2,500}{(1.10)} + \frac{\$3,000}{(1.10)^2} + \frac{\$3,500}{(1.10)^3}$$

$$V_p = -\$6,000 + \$2,273 + \$2,479 + \$2,630$$

$$V_p = \$1,382$$

Our formula shows that the present value of the benefits (the incremental earnings) totals $7,382 (= $2,273 + $2,479 + $2,630) and exceeds the present value of the costs of $6,000 by $1,382. This positive net present value indicates that it *is* economically rational for Carlson to make this investment in human capital.

Internal Rate of Return

An alternative means of making an investment decision involves calculating the *internal rate of return, r,* on a prospective investment and comparing it with the interest rate *i. By definition, the internal rate of return is the rate of discount at which the net present value of a human capital investment will be zero.*

Formula

Instead of using the interest rate *i* in Equation (4.3) to calculate whether the net present value is positive or negative, one determines what particular rate of discount *r* will equate the present values of future costs and benefits so that the net present value is zero. We must modify Equation (4.3) as follows:

$$V_P = E_0 + \frac{E_1}{(1 + r)} + \frac{E_2}{(1 + r)^2} + \cdots + \frac{E_n}{(1 + r)^n} = 0 \quad \textbf{(4.6)}$$

Instead of solving for V_p as in Equation (4.3), we solve for r, given the E values and assuming V_p is zero. A moment's reflection makes clear that r indicates the maximum rate of interest that one could pay on borrowed funds to finance a human capital investment and still break even.

Decision Rule: r = i

The investment criterion or decision rule appropriate to this approach involves a comparison of the internal rate of return r with the interest rate i. *If r exceeds the market i, the investment is profitable and should be undertaken.* For example, if one can borrow funds at a 10 percent interest rate and make an investment that yields 15 percent, it is profitable to do so. But *if r is less than i, the investment is unprofitable and should not be undertaken.* If one can borrow money at a 10 percent rate and the prospective investment yields only 5 percent, it is not profitable to invest. As we will discover momentarily, investing in human capital is subject to diminishing returns, so r generally declines as the number of years of schooling increases (look ahead to Figure 4.4). In this case, given i, it will be profitable to invest in all human capital investment opportunities up to the point where $r = i$.

Generalizations and Implications

The explanatory power of the human capital model is considerable. Let's pause at this point to consider several generalizations that stem from the basic model presented in Figure 4.2 and Equations (4.3) and (4.6).

1 Length of Income Stream

Other things being equal, the longer the stream of postinvestment incremental earnings, the more likely the net present value of an investment in human capital will be positive. Alternatively, the longer the earnings stream, the higher the internal rate of return. A human capital investment made later in life will have a lower net present value (and a lower r) simply because fewer years of work life and, hence, of positive incremental earnings will remain after completion of the investment. This generalization helps explain why it is primarily young people who go to college[4] and why younger people are more likely to migrate (invest in geographic mobility) than older people. It also explains a portion of the earnings differential that has traditionally existed between women and men. In many cases, the participation of women in the labor force has been discontinuous. That is, many women work for a few years after the completion of formal schooling, then marry and stay out of the labor force for a time to bear and raise children. They then reenter the labor force sometime after the last child begins school. In Equations (4.3)

---

[4] Although perhaps not rational on investment grounds, the decision of older people to return to college may be justified in terms of consumption (utility) criteria.

and (4.6), this means an abbreviated stream of earnings. This dampens the economic incentive of these particular women to invest in their own human capital by lowering the net present value or the rate of return. Furthermore, their discontinuous labor force participation inhibits employers from investing in their on-the-job training.

2 Costs

Other things being equal, the lower the cost of a human capital investment, the larger the number of people who will find that investment to be profitable. If the direct or indirect costs of attending college were to fall, we would expect enrollment to rise. For example, the guaranteeing of student loans by the government eliminates the risk to the lender and lowers the interest rate charged for borrowing funds to attend college. By reducing the private direct cost[5] of a college education, such loan guarantees increase college enrollment.[6] Lower direct or indirect costs increase the net present value of a college education, making the investment in education profitable for some who previously found it to be unprofitable.[7]

> 4.1

A more subtle point ties in with our previous generalization that older individuals are less likely to invest in human capital. Our age–earnings profiles (Figure 4.1) reveal that earnings rise with age. Thus the opportunity cost of attending college will be greater for older worker; and other things being equal, the net present value and the internal rate of return associated with human capital investments will be lower. In other words, there are two reasons older people are less likely to invest in a college education: (1) The length of their future earnings stream will be relatively short, and (2) their opportunity costs of attending college will be high.

3 Earnings Differentials

Not only is the *length* of the incremental earnings stream critical in making a human capital investment decision, but so is the *size* of that differential. The generalization is that *other things being equal, the larger the college–high school earnings differential, the larger the number of people who will invest in a college education*. Empirical evidence confirms this generalization. Freeman has argued that in 1970 the labor market for college graduates changed from one characterized by shortages to one of surpluses. One manifestation of this change was that the incremental earnings associated with a college education declined sharply.[8] As a result, the proportion of young people enrolling

---

[5] Of course there is no free lunch. Taxpayers (society as a whole) pay the costs associated with loan guarantees. But in calculating the cost of a college education from a *private* (as opposed to *social*) perspective, loan guarantees reduce the costs to the individual enrollee and increase the private net present value associated with a college education.

[6] Public subsidies appear to have large enrollment effects, particularly for low-income students and those attending community colleges. See Thomas J. Kane and Cecilia Elena Rouse, "The Community College: Educating Students at the Margin between College and Work," *Journal of Economic Perspectives,* Winter 1999, pp. 63–84.

[7] For a series of papers examining the impact of college costs and other factors on college choices, see Caroline M. Hoxby (ed.), *College Choices: The Economics of Where to Go, When to Go, and How to Pay for It* (Chicago, IL: University of Chicago Press, 2004).

[8] Richard B. Freeman, *The Overeducated American* (New York: Academic Press, 1976).

4.1	World of Work	Recessions and the College Enrollment Rate*

Do recessions increase or decrease the number of college students? The answer, in theory, is uncertain because business downturns yield conflicting effects on college enrollment rates.

Three factors related to the ability to pay for a college education tend to reduce the number of college students during recessions. First, the availability of part-time jobs that may help finance college expenses usually decreases in downturns. Second, the ability of parents to borrow money for college educations (perhaps due to a reduction in income and asset values) may decline. Finally, state and private spending for financial aid may decrease during recessions.

In contrast, recessions tend to lower the cost of attending college because they reduce the earnings of high school graduates or lower the probability of obtaining a job. As a result, the opportunity cost of

attending college will fall, and enrollment rates will therefore rise.

The empirical evidence indicates that the decreased opportunity cost of college in recessions dominates the reduced ability to pay because college enrollment rates tend to rise significantly during recessions. Dellas and Sakellaris find that a 1 percentage point increase in the unemployment rate increases the college enrollment rate of 18- to 22-year-olds by .8 percentage points. Their models indicate that some recessions may have added more than 400,000 college students. Men and women do not appear to respond differently to recessions. However, the college enrollment rate of nonwhites is less sensitive than that of whites to business downturns.

* Based on Harris Dellas and Plutarchos Sakellaris, "On the Cyclicality of Schooling: Theory and Evidence," *Oxford Economic Papers,* January 2003, pp. 148–72.

in colleges declined significantly in the early 1970s. In the 1980s the earnings advantage for college graduates rebounded. Kane finds that part of the sharp rise in the rate of college attendance that occurred over the 1979–1988 period was due to the rise in the college premium.[9]

Empirical Data

Numerous empirical studies have estimated the returns of human capital investments at all educational levels. Here we concentrate on those showing private rates of return on investments in a college education.

Rate-of-Return Studies

Speaking very generally, most rate-of-return studies have estimated such rates to be on the order of 10–15 percent.[10] For example in his classic work Becker estimated the

[9] Thomas J. Kane, "College Entry by Blacks since 1970: The Role of College Costs, Family Background, and the Returns to Education," *Journal of Political Economy,* October 1994, pp. 878–911. For an analysis finding that the college–high school earnings premium has a larger impact on the decision to attend college for men than women, see Susan L. Averett and Mark L. Burton, "College Attendance and the College Wage Premium: Differences by Gender," *Economics of Education Review,* February 1996, pp. 37–49.
[10] For a survey of recent studies, see David Card, "Causal Effect of Education on Earnings," in Orley Ashenfelter and David Card (eds.), *Handbook of Labor Economics,* Volume 3A (Amsterdam: North-Holland, 1999).

4.2	Global Perspective	Rate of Return per Year of College Education

The rate of return per year of college education for males ranges from 8.3 percent in Denmark to 16.7 percent in Finland.

Rate of return

Country	Rate of return
Finland	16.7
United States	14.3
Norway	12.1
Belgium	10.7
Switzerland	10
Sweden	8.9
Denmark	8.3

Source: Organization for Economic Cooperation and Development, *Education at a Glance, 2006,* Table A9.6. All data are for males in 2003.

internal rate of return to be 14.5, 13.0, and 14.8 in 1939, 1949, and 1958, respectively.[11] Estimates by Freeman indicate that the private rate of return ranged from 8.5 to 11.0 percent over the 1959–1974 period.[12] The social rate of return for the corresponding period was estimated to range from 7.5 to 11.1 percent. Card finds a return of 10 percent in 1976.[13] Kane and Rouse report a rate of return of 9 percent to higher education for 1986.[14] In a more recent study Jaeger finds a private rate of return of 11 percent for 1998.[15]

The College Wage Premium

Readers might have a special interest in the trend of the college wage premium in recent decades. We define the **college wage premium** as *the ratio of the earnings of college*

---

[11] Gary Becker, *Human Capital,* 2nd ed. (New York: National Bureau of Economic Research, 1975).

[12] Richard B. Freeman, "Overinvestment in College Training?" *Journal of Human Resources,* Summer 1975, p. 296.

[13] David Card, "Using Geographic Variation in College Proximity to Estimate the Return to Schooling," in Louis N. Christofides, E. Kenneth Grant, and Robert Swindisky (eds.), *Labour Market Behavior: Essays in Honour of John Vanderkamp* (Toronto, University of Toronto Press: 1995).

[14] Thomas J. Kane and Cecilia Rouse, "Labor Market Returns to Two- and Four-Year Colleges," *American Economic Review,* June 1995, pp. 600–13.

[15] David A. Jaeger, "Estimating the Returns to Education Using the Newest Current Population Survey Education Questions," *Economics Letters,* March 2003, pp. 385–94.

| 4.2 | World of Work | Twins, Education, and Earnings* |

In August 1991 the 16th annual Twins Day Festival was held in Twinsburg, Ohio. The festival (the largest gathering of twins in the world) attracted more than 3,000 sets of twins, triplets, and quadruplets. It also attracted two labor economists, Ashenfelter and Krueger, who wanted to study the relationship between educational attainment and earnings.

Monozygotic (identical) twins result from the division of a single fertilized egg and are considered genetically identical. Studying identical twins who grow up together thus allows researchers to control for genetic endowments and family background. Such differences, of course, complicate comparisons of unrelated individuals.

Ashenfelter and Krueger interviewed about 500 twins over the age of 18, looking especially for identical twins with different levels of education. During the interviews the twins were separated and, as a cross-check, the questioners asked each twin to report on his or her own schooling level and that of the twin. About half the pairs of identical twins had the same schooling levels.

The authors discovered a relatively high variability of earnings among identical twins with the same education levels. Despite this fact, better-educated pairs of twins tended to have higher earnings levels than less educated pairs. Also, individual twins having more education tended to have higher earnings than their twin brothers or sisters. On average, an additional year of schooling increased wages by 16 percent. This is a considerably higher estimate of the economic returns to education than found in previous studies, including those involving twins. Thus this study lends support to the basic investment in human capital model.

*Based on Orley C. Ashenfelter and Alan B. Krueger, "Estimates of the Return to Schooling from a New Sample of Twins," *American Economic Review*, December 1994, pp. 1157–73.

graduates to the earnings of high school graduates. Figure 4.3 presents this wage premium over the 1973–2006 period for women and men. Data are for workers with exactly a high school or college degree. We observe that in 1973 the ratio was 1.48 for women and 1.38 for men, meaning that college-educated women earned 48 percent and men 38 percent more than high school graduates of the same gender. During the 1970s, the premium dropped moderately for women and fell modestly for men. But since the late 1970s, the wage premiums for women and men have increased sharply, rising from 36 percent to 73 percent for women and from 34 percent to 76 percent for men. Studies have found that the most rapid rise in the wage premium has been for young college graduates with one to five years of experience.[16]

Explanations of changes in the college wage premium center on labor supply and demand. It is generally agreed that the declining premium in the 1970s resulted from the large influx of baby boomers completing college, coupled with a relatively stagnant demand for college graduates. There is less consensus about why the college premium soared in the 1980s. Murphy and Welch[17] explain the rapid increase in the wage premium

[16] Kevin Murphy and Finis Welch, "Wage Premiums for College Graduates: Recent Growth and Possible Explanations," *Educational Researcher*, May 1989, pp. 17–26.
[17] Ibid., pp. 13–26.

FIGURE 4.3   **Recent Trends in College Wage Premiums**

The college wage premium—measured here as the ratio of earnings of college graduates to the earnings of high school graduates—has varied substantially over time. The premium for women fell moderately in the 1970s. The premium for men drifted downward from 1974 to 1979. Since 1979 the wage premiums for both groups have increased dramatically. Changes in the college premium are generally explained by changes in the supply of and the demand for college - and high school–educated workers.

Source: Author calculations from 1973–1978 *May Current Population Survey* and the monthly *Outgoing Rotation Group Current Population Survey* files from 1979 to 2006.

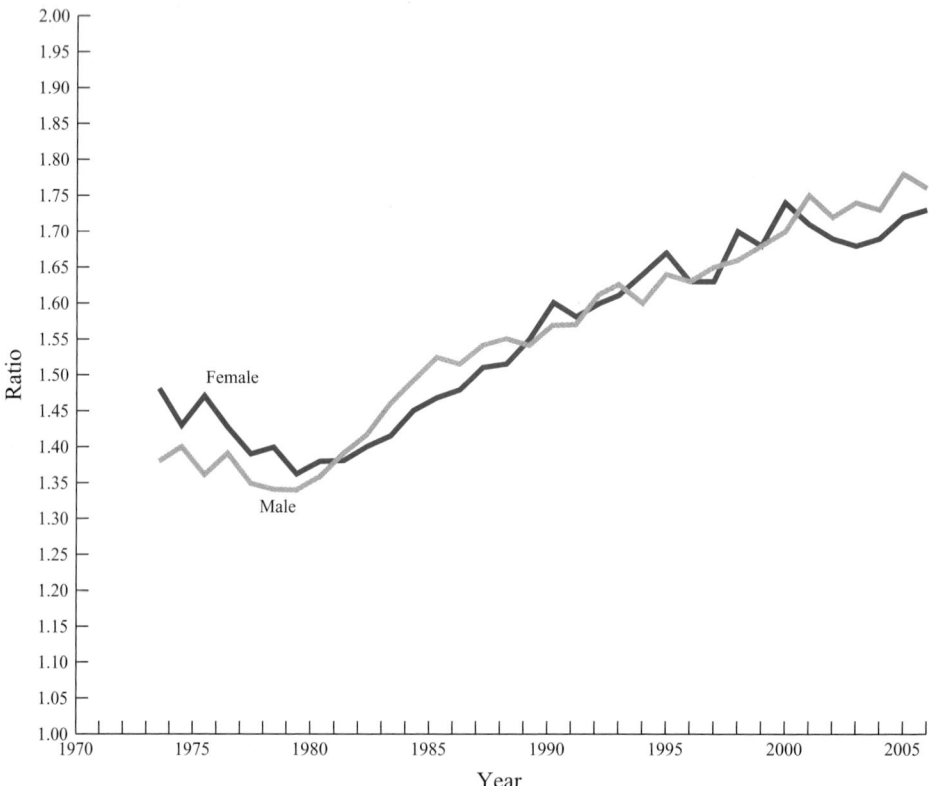

in terms of huge increases in the demand for college-trained workers. In particular, changes in the structure of domestic industry (for example, the shift of employment to high-technology industries) and changes in production techniques (for example, the greater use of computer-aided technologies) may have greatly increased the demand for college-trained workers.[18] Coupled with a slowdown in the growth of the college-educated workforce, the college premium has risen sharply.

[18] See Steven G. Allen, "Technology and the Wage Structure," *Journal of Labor Economics,* April 2001, pp. 440–83.

Although the Murphy–Welch interpretation is generally accepted, some economists have pointed out that a growing number of college graduates are working in occupations where college degrees have not traditionally been required. This fact seems to contradict the idea of a growing demand for college graduates relative to their supply. Hecker[19] contends that the increasing college wage premium has resulted not from increased demand for college-educated workers but from declining demand for high school graduates, particularly males. In this view, a decline in the wages of high school graduates has pushed up the college wage premium.

Gottschalk and Hansen disagree that an increasing portion of college graduates are taking jobs requiring only a high school degree.[20] They report that Hecker's assertion does not hold when one uses a rigorous definition of noncollege jobs rather than the perceptions of survey respondents. In fact, they find that as the college wage premium increased between the mid-1980s and the mid-1990s, the proportion of college workers in noncollege jobs declined.

Caveats

But all such empirical data must be interpreted with some care. First, we have no way of accurately predicting the future. Economists cannot accurately estimate what the future earnings of a new college graduate will be. Data used in research studies to calculate rates of return on human capital investments or the college wage premium are *historical* data. They represent the age–earnings profiles of *past* college graduates who obtained their education as far back as, say, 1970 or even earlier. The observation that college graduates in the labor market in 2005 received on average $25,200 more per year than the typical high school graduate is no guarantee that this difference will persist into the future. By 2015 the amount of incremental income might have widened or diminished.

Also, while incremental earnings affect the decision to invest in a college education, the decision to invest in a college education affects incremental earnings. If college graduates have enjoyed a high earnings differential compared with high school graduates in the recent *past,* an increasing proportion of new high school graduates will invest in a college education. But this investment will increase the supply of college as opposed to high school graduates and will reduce the *future* earnings differential or college premium. A high rate of return in the recent past could contribute to a decreasing rate of return in the future.

Second, the historical data used in human capital studies are in the form of *average* (median) earnings, and the distribution of earnings by educational level around the average is wide. Although a given study may calculate that the average rate of return on a college education is 10 percent, some individuals may earn 30 or 50 percent, whereas the return may be negative for others. A significant percentage of those with only high school educations earn more than the median income of college

[19] Daniel E. Hecker, "Reconciling Conflicting Data on Jobs for College Graduates," *Monthly Labor Review,* July 1992, pp. 3–21.
[20] Peter Gottschalk and Michael Hansen, "Is the Proportion of College Workers in Noncollege Jobs Increasing?" *Journal of Labor Economics,* April 2003, pp. 449–71.

graduates. And some college graduates earn less than the median income of high school graduates.

Third, the discussion so far has focused on amount of schooling rather than quality of schooling. We have implicitly assumed that the only relevant factor was the number of years students spend in school. However, schooling quality will likely affect the rate of return to schooling. For example, higher-quality teachers, better classroom resources, and greater studying by students should increase the rate of return to schooling.

Some evidence exists on how schooling inputs affect the rate of return.[21] A study by Card and Krueger indicates that higher teacher salaries and lower student–teacher ratios raise the return to schooling.[22] They also find that relative improvements in schooling quality among African–Americans account for 20 percent of the decline in the male African–American–white wage gap between 1960 and 1980.[23] However, Heckman, Layne-Farrar, and Todd conclude that schooling inputs have a more modest impact on the return to schooling than estimated by Card and Krueger.[24]

Strayer examines the ways in which school quality affects earnings. He reports that greater high school quality increases the likelihood that a student will attend either a four-year or a two-year college. This increased rate of college attendance in turn raises future earnings. He finds weaker evidence for direct effects of school quality on earnings.[25]

Private versus Social Perspective

To this point we have viewed the human capital investment decision from a *personal* or **private perspective.** That is, we have viewed benefits and costs strictly from the standpoint of an individual who is contemplating a human capital investment. The investment decision also can be viewed from a *public* or **social perspective.** In changing perspectives we can retain Equations (4.3) and (4.6); however, we must alter our conceptions of costs and benefits. The private approach includes only costs and benefits accruing to the individual. But from the social perspective the scope of relevant costs and benefits must be broadened. In particular, the private perspective excludes any public subsidies to education in calculating costs simply because such subsidies are *not*

---

[21] For a survey, see David Card and Alan B. Krueger, "School Resources and Student Outcomes: An Overview of the Literature and New Evidence from North and South Carolina," *Journal of Economic Perspectives,* Fall 1996, pp. 31–50.

[22] David Card and Alan B. Krueger, "Does School Quality Matter? Returns to Education and the Characteristics of Public Schools in the United States," *Journal of Political Economy,* February 1992, pp. 1–40.

[23] See David Card and Alan B. Krueger, "School Quality and Black/White Relative Earnings: A Direct Assessment," *Quarterly Journal of Economics,* February 1992, pp. 151–200.

[24] James J. Heckman, Anne Layne-Farrar, and Petra Todd, "Does Measured School Quality Really Matter? An Examination of the Earnings–Quality Relationship," in Gary Burtless (ed.), *Does Money Matter? The Effect of School Resources on Student Achievement and Adult Success* (Washington, DC: Brookings Institution, 1996). For a similar conclusion, see Iida Hakkinen, Tanja Kirjavainen, and Roope Uusitalo, "School Resources and Student Achievement Revisited: New Evidence from Panel Data," *Economics of Education Review,* June 2003, pp. 329–35.

[25] Wayne Strayer, "The Returns to School Quality: College Choice and Earnings," *Journal of Labor Economics,* July 2002, pp. 475–503.

| 4.3 | **World of Work** | Higher Education: Making the Right Choices |

The accompanying table shows the annual salaries of 2006–2007 college graduates by major. Clearly which major one chooses affects one's earnings. These data raise the question of whether other decisions impact a college graduate's earnings. For example, does it matter which college or university one attends?

Dale and Krueger shed light on this and related questions by examining the 1995 earnings of 6,355 individuals who were accepted and rejected by 30 colleges or universities in 1976.* An innovative feature of this study is that the researchers were able to compare the earnings of (1) those who were accepted by a more selective college but decided to attend a less selective college with (2) those who actually attended a more selective college. This technique enables them to control for the ability problem that plagued previous studies of the impact of college quality on earnings. That is, earlier studies did not sort out whether students who attended elite universities gained higher earnings because they went to a selective school or because the students were smart and ambitious.

The study's results indicate that it does *not* pay to attend a more selective college as measured by the average SAT score of entering freshmen. For example, a student who attended a highly selective school such as Princeton University did not earn more than one who attended a less selective school such as the Pennsylvania State University. An exception to this finding is that students from disadvantaged backgrounds do tend to benefit from attending a highly selective school. This may be the result of these students getting connections they would not be otherwise able to obtain.

However, earnings *are* positively related to the average SAT score of the schools a student applied to but did not attend. The authors note the example of the acclaimed movie producer and director Steven Spielberg, who applied to the film schools at USC and UCLA and was rejected at both places. He instead attended Cal State Long Beach. This suggests that ambition and a willingness to work hard are more important determinants of earnings than the selectivity of the school one attends.

One school characteristic *does* appear to be related to subsequent earnings. Students who attended schools with higher tuition earned significantly higher incomes. This may be the result of schools with higher tuition fees being able to provide more or better resources to students. The study notes that the rapid rise in tuition in the last two decades probably has diminished this effect.

* Stacy Berg Dale and Alan B. Krueger, "Estimating the Payoff to Attending a More Selective College: An Application of Selection on Observables and Unobservables," *Quarterly Journal of Economics,* November 2002, pp. 1491–528.

Estimated Starting Salaries For New College Graduates 2006–2007

Academic Major	Estimated Starting Salary	Academic Major	Estimated Starting Salary
Chemical engineering	$56,269	Computer science	50,744
Electrical engineering	53,300	Information science and systems	47,182
Computer engineering	53,096	Civil engineering	46,084
Mechanical engineering	51,808	Management information systems	45,391

Nursing	45,347	Secondary education	33,089
Accounting	44,928	History	33,071
Logistics/supply chain management	44,810	Hospitality services management	32,213
Mathematics	44,672	Elementary education	32,110
Economics/finance	44,588	Communications	31,749
Business administration/management	41,155	English	31,385
Chemistry	39,804	Sociology	31,096
Marketing/marketing management	37,191	Criminal justice	30,764
Environmental science	35,696	Psychology	30,369
Political science	33,094	Social work	28,190

Source: National Association of Colleges and Employers, *Fall 2006 Salary Survey* (Bethlehem, PA: National Association of Colleges and Employers, 2006).

Global Perspective   4.3

Schooling Quality

Schooling quality based on scores on standardized tests varies widely across the world.

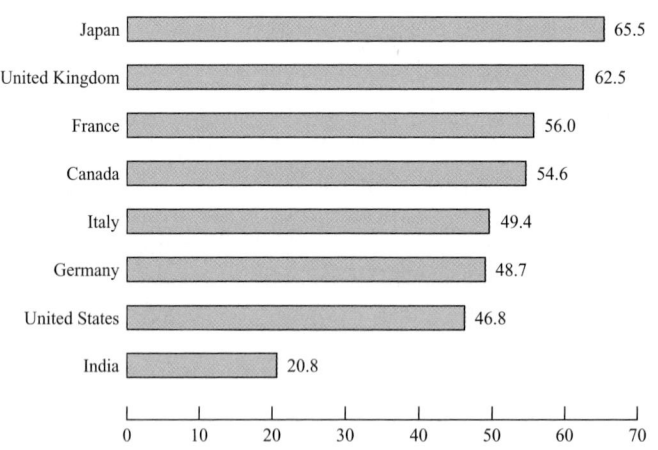

Japan	65.5
United Kingdom	62.5
France	56.0
Canada	54.6
Italy	49.4
Germany	48.7
United States	46.8
India	20.8

Source: Eric A. Hanushek and Dennis D. Kimko, "Schooling, Labor Force Quality, and Economic Growth," *American Economic Review,* December 2000, pp. 1184–1208. The scores are normalized to make the world average across 39 countries to be 50.

paid by the individual. Similarly, benefits (incremental earnings) should be calculated on an *after-tax* basis from the personal point of view. From the standpoint of society, costs should include any public subsidies to education, and benefits should be in terms of *before-tax* incremental earnings. Presumably the part of incremental earnings taxed away by government will be used to finance public goods and services beneficial to society as a whole.

Furthermore, most economists believe that education entails substantial *external* or *social benefits*—that is, benefits accruing to parties other than the individual acquiring the education. From a social perspective, these benefits should clearly be included in estimating the rate of return on human capital investments. What are these social benefits? First, it is well known that more educated workers have lower unemployment rates than less educated workers. Having high unemployment rates, poorly educated workers receive unemployment compensation and welfare benefits with greater frequency and may also find crime a relatively attractive alternative source of income. This means that society might benefit from investing in education by having to pay less in taxes for social welfare programs, crime prevention, and law enforcement. Second, political participation and, presumably, the quality of political decisions might improve with increased literacy and education. More education might mean that society's political processes would function more effectively to the benefit of society at large. Third, there may be intergenerational benefits: The children of better-educated parents may grow up in a more desirable home environment and receive better care, guidance, and informal preschool education. Fourth, the research discoveries of highly educated people might yield large and widely disbursed benefits to society. Jonas Salk's discovery of an effective and economic polio vaccine is illustrative.[26]

Why is our distinction between private and social rates of return on human capital investments significant? First, the difference between the private and the social perspectives is of potential importance because efficiency demands that the economy's total investment outlay be allocated so that rates of return on human and physical capital should be equal at the margin. If a given amount of investment spending is currently being allocated so that the rate of return on human capital investment is, say, 12 percent, while that on physical capital is only 8 percent, society would benefit by relocating investment from physical to human capital. In making this comparison it is correct to use the social, rather than the private, rate of return. Thus if we were to find that the *private* rate of return on human capital was in fact equal to the rate of return on physical capital, it would not necessarily be correct to conclude that investment resources were being efficiently divided between human and real capital. If the *social* rate of return was higher (lower) than the private rate, resources would have been underallocated (overallocated) to human capital investments. Incidentally, most studies of social rates of return yield rates that are quite comparable to those found in studies estimating private rates of return.

---

[26] For more detailed discussions of the social and nonmarket benefits from education, see Burton A. Weisbrod, "Investing in Human Capital," *Journal of Human Resources,* Summer 1966, pp. 1–21; and Robert H. Haveman and Barbara W. Wolfe, "Schooling and Economic Well-Being: The Role of Nonmarket Effects," *Journal of Human Resources,* Summer 1984, pp. 377–406. Also see Thomas S. Dee, "Are There Civic Returns to Education?" *Journal of Public Economics,* August 2004, pp. 1697–1720.

A second reason that the distinction between the private and social perspectives is important has to do with policy. The social or external benefits associated with education provide the rationale for subsidizing education with public funds. In the interest of allocative efficiency, the size of these public subsidies to education should be determined on the basis of the magnitude of the associated social benefits.

4.1

Quick Review

- Human capital consists of the accumulation of prior investments in education, on-the-job training, health, and other factors that increase productivity.
- The net present value method of computing the return on a human capital investment uses a market interest rate to discount the net earnings of the investment to its present value. If the net present value is positive, the investment should be undertaken.
- The internal rate of return method discovers the unique rate of discount that equates the present value of future earnings and the investment costs. If this internal rate of return exceeds the interest cost of borrowing, the investment should be undertaken.
- Private rates of return on investments in education are on the order of 10 to 15 percent and seem to be rising; social rates of return are thought to be similar.

Your Turn

Suppose the net present value of an educational investment is highly positive. What can you infer about the investment's internal rate of return relative to the interest cost of borrowing? (*Answer:* See page 596.)

HUMAN CAPITAL INVESTMENT AND THE DISTRIBUTION OF EARNINGS

Why do people vary significantly in the amounts of human capital that they acquire? Why is Nguyen a high school dropout, Brooks a high school graduate, and Hassan a PhD? The reasons are many and complex; but by presenting a simple model of the demand for and the supply of human capital, we can gain valuable insights pertinent to this question. In so doing we will also achieve some understanding or why earnings are quite unequally distributed.

Diminishing Rates of Return

In Figure 4.4 we plot the marginal internal rate of return—the extra return from additional education—for a specific individual for successive years of education. For simplicity we have assumed that the rate of return falls continuously. In reality, the rate of return on the fourth year of college—the year a student graduates—may yield a higher marginal return than the third year. But in general, it is reasonable to assume that rates

FIGURE 4.4
Rates of Return from Successive Years of Schooling The rate of return from investing in successive years of schooling diminishes because (1) such investment is subject to the law of diminishing returns and (2) costs rise and benefits fall as more education is obtained.

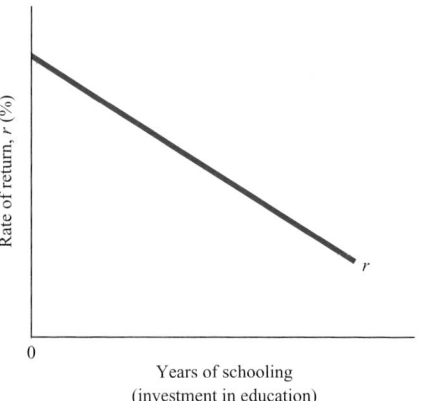

of return fall as more investment takes place. Why do these rates of return diminish? The answer is essentially twofold. On one hand, investment in human capital (education) is subject to the law of diminishing returns. On the other hand, as additional education is undertaken, the attendant benefits fall and the associated costs rise so as to reduce the internal rate of return.

1 Diminishing Returns

Investment in education is subject to the law of diminishing returns. The extra knowledge and skills produced by education or schooling become smaller and smaller as the amount of schooling is increased. This means that the incremental earnings from each additional year of schooling will diminish, and therefore so will the rate of return. Think of the individual as analogous to a firm that combines fixed resources with variable inputs to generate a certain output. An individual combines certain physical and mental characteristics with inputs of education or schooling to generate outputs of labor market skills. The individual's physical and mental characteristics—IQ, motor coordination, and so forth—are essentially fixed resources determined by genes and the home environment. To these fixed resources we add variable inputs in the form of years of schooling. As with any other situation where a variable input is added to some fixed input, the resulting increases in the amount of human capital produced—the new knowledge and skills acquired by the individual—will ultimately decline. And diminishing returns mean that the rate of return on successive human capital investments will also diminish.

2 Falling Benefits, Rising Costs

We have already touched on the second reason the internal rate of return will decline as additional education is acquired. Costs tend to rise and benefits tend to fall for successive years of schooling. In addition to having essentially fixed mental and physical characteristics, the individual also possesses a fixed amount of time—that is, a finite work life. It follows that the more years one invests in education, the fewer one has during which to realize the benefits of incremental income from that investment; hence the lower rate of return. The rate of return also declines because the costs of successive years of schooling tend to rise. On one hand, the opportunity cost of one's time increases as more education is acquired. That is, an additional year of school has a greater opportunity cost for the holder of a bachelor's degree than for someone who has only a high school diploma. Similarly, the private direct costs of schooling increase. Public subsidies make elementary and high school education essentially free, but a substantial portion of the cost of college and graduate school is borne by the individual student. Studies confirm that the rate of return on schooling diminishes as the amount of schooling increases.

Demand, Supply, and Equilibrium

Why have we identified the curve labeled r in Figure 4.5 as a *demand for human capital curve* (D_{hc})? This identification is the result of applying the previously discussed decision rule, which says that investment is profitable if $r > i$ and unprofitable if $r < i$. Or, in the context of Figure 4.5, it is profitable to invest in human capital or schooling up to the point where the marginal rate of return equals the interest rate or, in short, where $r = i$. Thus in Figure 4.5 we assume that the individual is a "price taker" in borrowing funds for educational purposes and that needed amounts of money capital can be borrowed at a given interest rate. The horizontal line drawn at, say, i_2 indicates that the individual faces a perfectly elastic *supply of investment funds* S_2 at this interest rate. Our $r = i$ rule indicates that e_2 is the most profitable number of years of schooling in which to invest. Similarly, if the market rate of interest were higher at i_3,

FIGURE 4.5   Deriving the Demand for Human Capital Curve
Application of the $r = i$ rule reveals that the marginal internal rate of return curve is also the demand for human capital curve. Each of the equilibrium points (1, 2, 3) indicates the financial price of investing (i) on the vertical axis and the quantity of human capital demanded on the horizontal axis. This information about price and quantity demanded constitutes the demand curve for human capital.

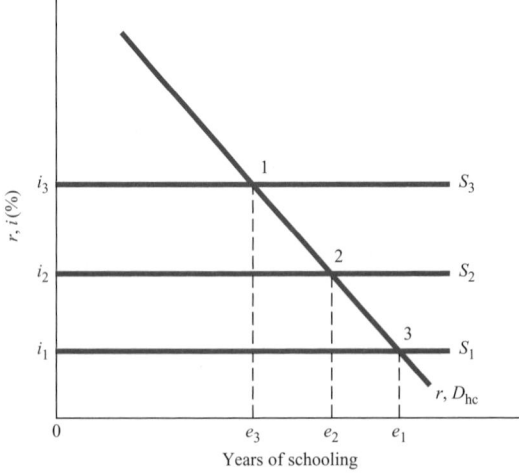

the application of the $r = i$ rule would make only e_3 years of schooling profitable. If the interest rate were lower at i_1, it would be profitable to invest in e_1 years of schooling. By applying a selection of possible interest rates or money capital prices to the marginal rate of return curve, we locate a number of equilibrium points (1, 2, 3) that indicate the financial price of investing (various possible interest rates) on the vertical axis *and* the corresponding quantities of human capital demanded on the horizontal axis. Any curve containing such information about price and quantity demanded is, by definition, a demand curve—in this case the demand curve for human capital or schooling.

Differences in Human Capital Investment

The demand and supply curves of Figure 4.5 can explain why different people invest in different amounts of human capital *and,* therefore, realize substantially different earnings. Our emphasis is on three considerations: (1) differences in ability, (2) differing degrees of uncertainty concerning the capacity to transform skills and knowledge into enhanced earnings due to discrimination, and (3) differing access to borrowed funds for human capital investment. The first two factors work through the demand side of the human capital market; the third works through the supply side.

1 Ability Differences

Figure 4.6 embodies two different demand curves for human capital—D_A and D_B for Adams and Bowen, respectively—and a common supply curve. The common supply curve shows that money capital for investment in schooling is available to Adams and Bowen on identical terms. The key question is why Bowen's demand curve for human capital (D_B) is to the right of Adams's (D_A). The answer may be that Bowen has greater abilities—better mental and physical talents and perhaps greater motivation and self-discipline—which cause any given input of schooling to be translated into a larger increase in labor market productivity and earning ability. That is, Bowen is more able than Adams to obtain enhanced earnings for each year of schooling; Bowen is capable of getting more out of education that is useful in the labor market than Adams. Thus the rate of return on each year of schooling is higher, and Bowen's demand curve for human capital is therefore farther to the right. Given the interest rate and the perfectly elastic supply of financial capital, this means that Bowen will invest in e_B years of schooling, whereas Adams will choose to invest in only e_A years.[27]

Note that because it is rational for more able people to obtain more education than less able people, earnings differentials are compounded. Given the same amount of schooling, we would expect Bowen to earn more than Adams because of the former's greater innate ability. Because it is rational for Bowen to obtain more education than Adams, we would anticipate a further widening of the earnings differential.

---

[27] Some evidence indicates that less educated people obtain less education mainly because they have a higher discount rate (perhaps they come from a poorer family or have a distaste for education) rather than because they lack ability. See David Card, "Earnings, Schooling, and Ability Revisited," *Research in Labor Economics* 16 (1995), pp. 23–48.

FIGURE 4.6 Ability, Discrimination, and Investment in Human Capital
If Bowen has greater ability to translate schooling into increased labor market productivity
and higher earnings than Adams, then Bowen's demand curve for human capital (D_B) will lie
farther to the right than Adams's (D_A). Given the interest rate, it will be rational for Bowen to
invest in more education than Adams. Similarly, if Adams and Bowen have equal ability but
discrimination reduces the amount of incremental income Adams can obtain from additional
education, it will be rational for Adams to invest in less education than Bowen.

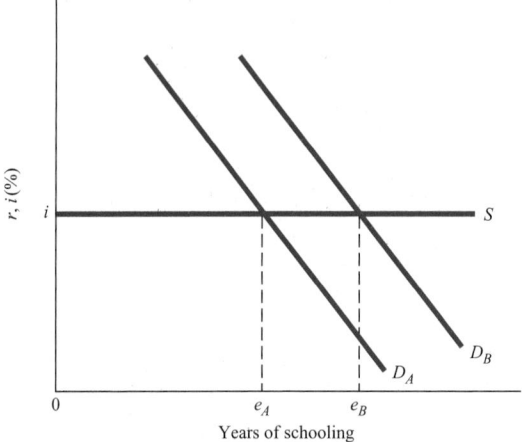

2 Discrimination: Uncertainty of Earnings

Let's now assume that Adams and Bowen are identical in terms of ability. But let's suppose that Adams is African–American or female and therefore is more likely to encounter discriminatory barriers to selling in the labor market the higher productivity acquired through education. In other words, Adams may encounter various forms of discrimination that reduce the likelihood of transforming the labor market skills acquired through education into incremental earnings. In Equations (4.3) and (4.6), discrimination creates the probability that the flow of earnings to African–American (female) Adams will be smaller than those accruing to white (male) Bowen from the same amount of education. This means rates of return on each level of education are lower to Adams than to Bowen. In Figure 4.6, Adams's demand for human capital is less than Bowen's. Given equal access to funds for the financing of education, (the iS curve in Figure 4.6), Bowen will again find it rational to invest in more human capital than Adams. Discrimination, which reduces wages and earnings, also has the perverse impact of reducing the incentive for those discriminated against to invest in human capital.

3 Access to Funds

This brings us to a final consideration. Figure 4.7 portrays the situation where the demand for human capital curves for Adams and Bowen are identical, but Bowen can acquire money capital on more favorable terms than Adams. Why the difference? Bowen may be from a wealthier family that is in a position to pledge certain financial or real

FIGURE 4.7

Access to Funds and Human Capital Investment

If Bowen has access to financial resources on more favorable terms than Adams, it will be rational for Bowen to invest in a larger amount of education.

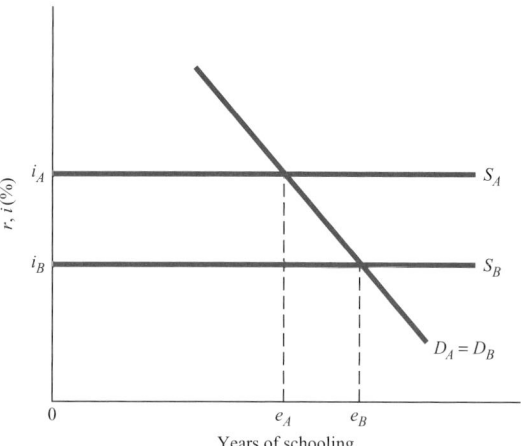

Years of schooling

assets as collateral and therefore obtain a lower interest rate. Under these conditions it is rational for Bowen to invest in more years of schooling than Adams.[28]

Interactions

The basic point is that differences in ability, the impact of discrimination, and varying access to financial resources are all reasons various individuals find it rational to obtain different amounts of education. As shown in the age–earnings profiles in Figure 4.1, we note that these differences in educational attainment are important in generating inequality in the distribution of earnings. In fact, the factors that explain educational inequality may interact to generate greater earnings inequality than our discussion would suggest. For example, discrimination may not only influence the demand side of the human capital market to reduce the demands of African–Americans and females for education but may also appear on the supply side. If a lender reasons that discrimination makes it less likely that an African–American or a female will be able to achieve employment in the occupation for which he or she is training, the lender will compensate for this greater risk by charging a higher rate of interest. This causes the supply of investment funds curve for African–Americans and women to shift upward as in Figure 4.7, and the amount of education

[28] A more elusive factor, one's *time preference,* also affects human capital investment. For example, Curt may be highly present-oriented in that he is relatively reluctant to sacrifice current consumption for future benefits. In terms of Equation (4.3), Curt would in effect use a high interest rate in discounting the future flow of earnings. Other things being equal, this would reduce the present value of a human capital investment and decrease the likelihood that it would be undertaken. Conversely, Beth may be highly future-oriented in that she is quite willing to forgo current consumption for future benefits. She would use a low interest rate in discounting Equation (4.3)'s future flow of earnings, tending to increase the present value of a human capital investment and enhancing the likelihood that it will be undertaken. The notion of time preference is helpful in explaining why individuals who are quite homogeneous with respect to ability and access to funds acquire much different amounts of human capital. This matter will be considered further in Chapter 8. For an analysis showing that more educated individuals are more future-oriented, see John T. Warner and Saul Pleeter, "The Personal Discount Rate: Evidence from Military Downsizing Programs," *American Economic Review,* March 2001, pp. 33–53.

4.4	**World of Work**	Reversal of the College Gender Gap*

In 1960 there were 0.63 female graduates for every male graduating from college. This ratio has steadily risen over time. There are now more women than men who graduate from college. By 2004 there were 1.35 females for every male graduating from college.

From the late 1950s to the early 1970s, many female students attended college to pursue traditionally female occupations such as teaching and intended to be in the labor force for a limited extent. Starting in the late 1960s and early 1970s, the career expectations of young women started to change: They expected to have much more attachment to the labor market. Many factors played a role in this change, including the women's movement, birth control (see World of Work 3.5), reduced gender discrimination, and an increased labor force participation rate among female college graduates of the previous generation.

As a result of their increased future work expectations, high school girls started to prepare for college in a different manner. They started to take more math and science classes. In 1972 high school boys took 24 percent more math classes and 20 percent more science classes than high school girls. By 1992 virtual parity was achieved between high school boys and girls in math and science class enrollment. High school girls also increased their achievement scores compared to boys. In fact, by 1992 high school girls had an advantage in combined math and reading achievement scores. Goldin, Katz, and Kuziemko find that the increased proportion of high school girls taking math and science classes as well as the rise in the achievement scores of girls relative to boys can account for between 37 and 63 percent of the rise in the female to male ratio of college graduates between the 1970s and the 1990s.

Why have women gone past parity to become a majority of college students? Goldin, Katz, and Kuziemko argue that noncognitive factors may play an important role. In particular, boys have more behavioral problems than girls. Boys are two to three times more likely to suffer from attention deficit hyperactivity disorder (ADHD) than are girls. They are much more likely than girls to engage in criminal activity, get suspended from school, or be in a special education program.

* Based on Claudia Goldin, Lawrence Katz, and Ilyana Kuziemko, "The Homecoming of American College Women: The Reversal of the College Gender Gap," *National Bureau of Economic Research Working Paper Number 12139*, April 2006; and National Center for Education Statistics (**http://nces.ed.gov**).

acquired will be further diminished. Similarly, individuals with greater ability may also enjoy lower financial costs. Greater ability may stem not simply from one's genetic inheritance but also from the quality of one's home environment. The child fortunate to be born into a high-income family may enjoy more and better preschool education, have greater motivation and self-discipline, and place a higher value on education in general. These considerations mean that the child may have greater ability to absorb education and to increase his or her labor market productivity and earnings. Being born into a high-income family also means a greater ability to finance education on favorable terms.[29]

The comments here correctly imply that public policy may also play a significant role in determining the amounts of human capital various individuals acquire and the

---

[29] For an interesting discussion of how parents affect the earnings of their children, see Paul Taubman, *Income Distribution and Redistribution* (Reading, MA: Addison-Wesley Publishing Company, 1978), chap. 5.

consequent distribution of earnings. For example, to the extent that antidiscrimination policies have been effective, variations in individual demand curves for education have been reduced, and so has earnings inequality. Scholarships based on student ability mean that students with the strongest demand curves for human capital would also have the greatest access to funds—a combination that would increase inequality in the distribution of human capital and earnings. Conversely, scholarships on the basis of need or targeted education programs for children from disadvantaged or minority families would reduce inequality in the dispersion of human capital and earnings.

Capital Market Imperfections

The capital market may include certain biases or imperfections causing it to favor investment in physical, rather than human, capital. Such biases are termed *capital market imperfections*. Specifically, funds may be less readily available, or accessible only on less favorable terms, for investment in human capital as compared to real capital or the purchase of consumer durables. Perhaps the primary reason for this is that human capital is embodied in the borrower and therefore is not available as collateral on a loan. If one defaults on a house mortgage or an automobile loan, there is a tangible asset the lender can repossess and sell to recover losses. But in a nation that rejects slavery and indentured servitude, there is no designated asset for the lender to seize if the borrower fails to repay an educational loan. This increases risk to the lender and prompts the inclusion of a risk premium in the interest rate charged. Furthermore, we have noted that other things being equal, it is more rational for young people to make human capital investments than for old people. But young people are less likely to have established credit ratings or collateral assets to allow them to borrow on reasonable terms. Finally, the variation in returns on human capital investments is large. Recall that although college graduates *on the average* earn substantially more than high school graduates, many college graduates earn less than the average high school graduate. This uncertainty of return may inflate the risk premium charged for human capital loans.[30]

The relative unsuitability of the capital market for educational loans has one or two important consequences. First, because of the problems and uncertainties just noted, financial institutions may choose *not* to make human capital loans. This means the amount of human capital investment individuals can undertake will depend on their, or their families', income and wealth. Thus well-to-do families can finance the college educations of their children by the relatively painless process of reducing their volume of saving. But poor families cannot save, and therefore the financing of a college education implies a possibly severe cut in living standards.[31] These circumstances may perpetuate a

[30] For a further discussion of capital market imperfections, see Lester Thurow, *Investment in Human Capital* (Belmont, CA: Wadsworth Publishing Company, 1970), pp. 77–83.

[31] Even publicly supported colleges and universities that feature relatively low tuition and fees may attract few students from low-income families simply because their families may not be able to afford the opportunity costs (see Figure 4.2). A very poor family may not be able to forgo the income that a son or daughter can earn by entering the labor market immediately upon graduating from high school. Federal education loan programs have mitigated this problem in recent years. For an analysis of the impact of family finances on college enrollment, see Bhashkar Mazumder, "Family Resources and College Enrollment," *Economic Perspectives* (Federal Reserve Bank of Chicago), 4th Quarter 2003, pp. 30–41.

vicious cycle. Individuals and families with little human capital (education) may be poor; being poor, it is extremely difficult for them to finance the acquisition of additional human capital.

Capital market imperfections have a second important implication. If it is in the social interest to achieve a balance or equilibrium between investment in real capital and human capital, then the government may have to offset the imperfections by subsidizing or providing human capital loans. Ideally, an equilibrium between investment in real and human capital would occur when the last dollar spent on human capital contributes the same amount to the domestic output as the last dollar expended on real capital. But the higher interest rates charged for educational loans will restrict expenditures on human capital so that the relative contribution of the last unit to the national output will exceed that of the last unit of real capital. This indicates that investment resources are being underallocated to human capital. This rationale in part lies behind the loan guarantees and financial resources that government has provided to stimulate educational loans.

4.2

Quick Review

- The rate of return from investing in successive units of human capital declines—that is, the investment demand curve is down-sloping—because opportunity costs rise and marginal benefits fall as more investment occurs.
- The optimal level of investment in human capital occurs when the marginal rate of return, *r*, equals the interest rate, *i* (the price of investing).
- It is rational for people having greater ability to obtain more education than others; conversely, those who are discriminated against in the labor market have less incentive to invest in human capital.
- People who have greater access to financial funding for investment on more favorable interest terms will rationally invest more in education than others.
- Imperfections in the capital market may bias investment toward physical capital rather than human capital.

Your Turn

In equilibrium, the marginal rates of return, *r*, for those with more ability to extract earnings from formal education and those with less ability are equal (see Figure 4.6). So why do people with greater ability get more formal education? (*Answer:* See page 596.)

ON-THE-JOB TRAINING

Many of the usable labor market skills that workers possess are acquired not through formal schooling but rather through *on-the-job training.* Such training may be somewhat formal; that is, workers may undertake a structured trainee program or an apprenticeship program. On the other hand, on-the-job training is often highly informal and therefore difficult to measure or even detect. Less experienced workers often engage in "learning by doing"; they acquire new skills by simply observing more skilled workers, filling in for them when they are ill or on vacation, or engaging in informal conversation during coffee breaks.

Costs and Benefits

Like formal education, on-the-job training entails present sacrifices and future benefits. It thus is an investment in human capital and can be analyzed through the net present value and internal rate of return frameworks [Equations (4.3) and (4.6)]. In deciding whether to provide on-the-job training, a firm will weigh the expected added revenues generated by the training against the costs of providing it. If the net present value of the training investment is positive, the firm will invest; if it is negative, it won't. Alternatively, the firm will invest if the internal rate of return of the investment exceeds the interest cost of borrowing.

For employers, providing training may involve such direct costs as classroom instruction or increased worker supervision, along with such indirect costs as reduced worker output during the training period. Workers may have to accept the cost of lower wages during the training period. The potential benefit to firms is that a trained workforce will be more productive and will therefore make greater contributions to the firm's total revenue. Similarly, trained workers can expect higher wages because of their enhanced productivity.

General and Specific Training

To understand how the associated costs and benefits are distributed among workers and employers, we must distinguish between two polar types of on-the-job training. At one extreme, *general training refers to the creation of skills or characteristics that are equally usable in* all *firms and industries*. Stated differently, general training enhances the productivity of workers to all firms. At the other end of the continuum, *specific training is training that can be used* only *in the particular firm that provides that training*. Specific training increases the worker's productivity only in the firm providing that training. In practice, most on-the-job training contains elements of both general and specific training, and it is therefore difficult to offer unequivocal examples. Nevertheless, we might venture that the abilities to concentrate on a task for a reasonable period of time, to show up for work regularly and be punctual, to read, to perform simple mathematical manipulations, and to follow instructions all constitute general training. Similarly, gaining word processing, carpentry, or accounting skills would be considered general training. Alternatively, the ability to perform an assembly procedure unique to a firm's product exemplifies specific training. The training of personnel to answer toll-free telephone questions about a firm's products is another example of specific training.

The distinction between general and specific training is important for at least two reasons. First, it is helpful in explaining whether the worker or the employer is more likely to pay for on-the-job training. Second, it is useful in understanding why employers might be particularly anxious to retain certain of their trained workers.

Distributing Training Costs

Analyzing whether workers or firms pay the costs of on-the-job training gets a bit complex. Let's start by looking at pure cases and then modify our analysis to account for real-world observations. We begin with two broad generalizations, each based on the assumptions that markets are competitive and that workers are perfectly mobile. First, *the worker will pay for general training through lower wages during the training period.* Second, *the firm must bear the cost of specific training.*

General training gives a worker skills and understanding that are transferable; they can be sold to other firms at a higher wage rate. If the employer were to bear the cost, the worker might leave the firm's employment after completion of the training and thus deprive the employer of any return (benefit) on the training investment. Alternatively, in the posttraining period the employer would have to pay a wage rate commensurate with the worker's higher productivity, eliminating any possible return on the training investment to the employer. Therefore, if general on-the-job training is undertaken, it is paid for by the worker in the form of a reduced wage rate during the training period.

On the other hand, a specific skill is not transferable or salable by a worker. Thus the worker will not pay for such training. If a worker is fired or laid off at the end of a period of specific training, the worker has gained nothing of value to sell in the labor market. The cost is borne by the employer. This typically means that the employer will pay a wage rate in excess of the worker's contribution to the firm's revenue during the training period. Figure 4.8 is useful in elaborating these generalizations.

General Training

Figure 4.8(a) shows the case of general training. Here W_u and MRP_u indicate what wage rate and marginal revenue product would be for an untrained worker. **Marginal revenue product** *is the increase in a firm's total revenue associated with the employment of a given worker.*[32] The employment of an additional worker will add to a firm's total output and therefore to its revenue. This addition to its revenue is the MRP.

In Figure 4.8(a) the wage rate and marginal revenue product *during* training are represented by W_t and MRP_t while W_p and MRP_p are the posttraining wage rate and marginal revenue product. MRP_t is below that for an untrained worker because during the training period the worker is diverting time from production to learning. It is important to stress that the higher posttraining marginal revenue product (MRP_p) is relevant *to all firms* because the training is general. Competing firms will therefore bid up the wage rate of this trained worker until it is equal to MRP_p. It is precisely for this reason—that competition will force the posttraining wage rate upward into equality with the posttraining marginal revenue product—that the employer will normally *not* be willing to pay for general training. The employer has no opportunity to obtain a return on its training investment by paying a wage rate less than the worker's marginal revenue product. Why should the employer bear general training costs when the benefits accrue solely to the trained employee in the form of higher wages? To repeat: The worker pays for general training costs by accepting a wage below that of the untrained worker (W_t as compared to W_u) during the training period. Incidentally, the fact that competition will bid a worker's wage rate up into equality with his or her higher posttraining marginal revenue product (MRP_p), and thereby preclude a return to the employer, explains why general education typically occurs in schools and not on the job.

---

[32] This concept will be explored in more detail in Chapter 5.

FIGURE 4.8 **Wage Rates and Marginal Revenue Products for General and
Specific Training**

(a) *General training*. Because general training is salable to other firms and industries ($W_p = \text{MRP}_p$),
workers normally must pay for such training that a firm provides. This payment is in the form of
a reduced wage ($W_t < W_u$) during the training period. A possible exception is where the firm
faces a legal minimum wage and needs to provide remedial basic education to have a qualified
workforce. The firm may conclude that it can pay a wage rate above W_t in the training period
and recoup its investment by paying a wage rate slightly below W_p in the posttraining period.
Workers facing high costs of job search and relocation may not leave for jobs paying W_p.
(b) *Specific training*. Specific training is not transferable to other firms; therefore, the employer
must pay for such training. During the training period the employer pays a wage rate in excess of
the worker's marginal revenue product ($W_u > \text{MRP}_t$). In the posttraining period the employer
receives a return on specific training because the worker's marginal revenue product will exceed
his or her wage rate ($\text{MRP}_p > W_u$). Because the employer's return on specific training varies
directly with the length of the posttraining period, the employer might voluntarily pay an
above-competitive wage (W'_p as compared to W_u) to reduce worker turnover.

Source: Adapted from John T. Addison and W. Stanley Siebert, *The Market for Labor: An Analytical Treatment* (Santa Monica, CA:
Goodyear Publishing Company, 1979), p. 114.

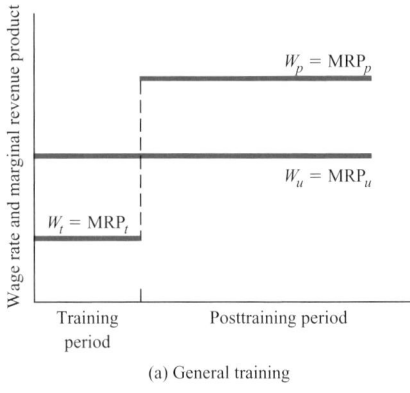

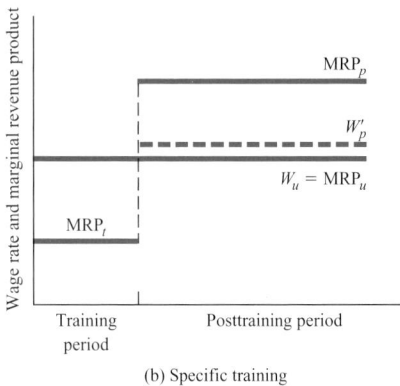

(a) General training

(b) Specific training

Specific Training

Figure 4.8(b) pertains to specific training. Again, W_u and MRP_u are the wage rate and
marginal revenue product of an untrained worker, and MRP_t and MRP_p, respectively,
show marginal revenue productivity during and after specific training. In contrast to
Figure 4.8(a), the posttraining marginal revenue product applies *only to this firm*. The
worker has acquired specific training that will increase productivity in *this* firm; but by
definition, specific training is *not* transferable or useful to other firms. Because specific
training is not transferable—that is, it will not allow the worker to obtain a higher wage
rate as the consequence of labor market competition for his or her services—the worker
will refuse to pay for such training and will not accept a lower wage during the training
period. Note that during the training period the wage rate will remain at W_u, which
means that the employer must bear the cost of the training by paying a wage rate that is
in excess of the worker's marginal revenue product (MRP_t). However, because specific

Global Perspective 4.4 — Percentage of Workers Receiving Employer-Provided Education and Training

The percentage of workers who receive employer-provided job-related education and training ranges from 12 percent in Ireland to 46 percent in Norway.

Employer-provided education and training

Country	Percentage
Norway	46.0
Finland	42.0
United States	35.0
Canada	31.0
Australia	27.0
Czech Republic	20.0
Italy	14.0
Ireland	12.0

Source: Organization for Economic Cooperation and Development, *Employment Outlook,* July 2003, Table 5.1.

The statistics are based on samples of workers aged 25 to 64 from the middle to late 1990s.

training is not transferable—that is, it does not increase the worker's marginal revenue product to other firms—the employer need not increase the wage rate above W_u in the posttraining period. Thus, from the employer's standpoint, training imposes a flow of costs (W_u exceeds MRP_t) in the training period that is followed by a flow of benefits or incremental revenues (MRP_p exceeds W_u) in the posttraining period. As shown in Equation (4.3), if the net present value of these flows is positive, the firm will find it profitable to undertake specific training for its workers. Indeed, you have undoubtedly noticed that Figure 4.8(b) resembles Figure 4.2.

Modifications

Our discussion of general and specific training merits modifications in some important ways. First, let's look again at general training [Figure 4.8(a)]. Recently some firms have begun providing new employees with general training—remedial reading, writing, and mathematics—to compensate for a decline in the quality of primary and secondary education. These firms have been forced to provide this general training to ensure themselves a sufficient number of qualified workers. Usually these firms reduce the wage during the training period, as suggested in Figure 4.8. But in other instances, the legal minimum wage (Chapter 13) precludes this strategy. Thus some firms may have to pay part of the training costs themselves.

In Figure 4.8(a), we are suggesting that the minimum wage may force some firms offering general training to pay more than W_t during the training period. How is it possible for these firms to recoup these general training expenses? Won't employees take their services elsewhere if they are paid less than W_p after completion of the training? The answer is that, in the real world, workers are not perfectly mobile; it is costly to change jobs and to relocate geographically. Thus these firms may be able to recoup their investments in general training through paying less than the workers' marginal productivity during part or all of the posttraining period. The extra pay the worker could get by changing jobs may not be sufficient to cover the worker's job search and relocation costs.

We also need to modify our discussion of Figure 4.8(b). We have observed that in the posttraining period the employer realizes a return from specific training by paying a wage (W_u) that is less than each worker's contribution to the firm's total revenue (MRP_p). The total amount of revenue or profit derived from this discrepancy will vary directly with the length of time the worker remains employed by the firm. In short, the employer has a financial interest in lowering the turnover or quit rates of workers with specific training. The employer might accomplish this by voluntarily paying a wage rate somewhat higher than the worker could obtain elsewhere—for example, W'_p rather than W_u. Stated differently, the wage in the posttraining period is likely to be set so as to divide the gains from specific training between employer and employee. Specific training is one of a number of considerations that changes labor from a variable input to a *quasi-fixed* factor of production.[33]

A final comment: On the average, individuals who receive the largest amount of formal education also receive more on-the-job specific training. This is not surprising. A person who has demonstrated his or her trainability by completing, say, a college degree is more likely to be selected by an employer for specific on-the-job training than someone with only a high school diploma. Why? Because that individual will be trainable at a lower cost. Indeed, Figure 4.8(b) implies that on-the-job training will have a higher rate of return to employers when workers can absorb training in a short time. A college degree is evidence of the capacity to absorb training quickly. The fact that people with more formal education on the average receive more on-the-job training helps explain why age–earnings profiles of more highly educated workers rise faster than those of less educated workers (see Figure 4.1).

4.3

Quick Review

- Because general training is salable to other firms, workers must normally pay for it indirectly through reduced pay during the training period.

- Specific training is not transferable to other firms; therefore, the employer normally must pay for it, recouping the investment cost later by paying these workers less than their MRPs.

---

[33] The classic study is Walter Oi, "Labor as a Quasi-Fixed Factor," *Journal of Political Economy,* December 1962, pp. 538–55.

- Faced with a legal minimum wage, some firms needing qualified workers may pay for general training, recouping their expenses by paying workers less than their MRPs during the posttraining period. Because of high job search and relocation costs, many workers will stay at their jobs even though they might be able to earn more elsewhere.

- The employer's return on specific training varies directly with the length of the post-training period; thus the employer may pay a higher-than-competitive wage to reduce worker turnover and increase its return on its investment.

Your Turn

Suppose that after graduation you take a job with an employer that offers to pay full tuition for employees wishing to return to school to get an MBA degree during non-work hours. You are not required to continue working for the firm after getting your MBA. What type of training is this? Who do you think actually pays for it? (*Answer:* See page 596.)

Empirical Evidence

In 1995, 70 percent of employees in establishments with 50 or more workers reported participating in formal training to improve their job skills in the last year. Nearly 90 percent of college-educated workers received training, while 60 percent of those with a high school degree or less obtained training. An equal percentage of white and African–American workers received training at work. In 1995, two-thirds of men received training, while 73 percent of women participated in training.[34]

There has been a kaleidoscope of new research on training. Here are a few recent findings:

- Workers with postsecondary education receive more training than those with less education.[35]

- Positive productivity effects have been found for general but not specific training.[36]

- The likelihood of participating in employer-provided training is greater in larger firms than in smaller ones.[37]

- Most training appears to be general in nature rather than firm-specific.[38]

---

[34] Harley Frazis, Maury Gittleman, Michael Horrigan, and Mary Joyce, "Results from the 1995 Survey of Employer-Provided Training," *Monthly Labor Review,* June 1998, pp. 3–13.

[35] Harley Frazis, Maury Gittleman, and Mary Joyce, "Correlates of Training: An Analysis Using Both Employer and Employee Characteristics," *Industrial and Labor Relations Review,* April 2000, pp. 443–62.

[36] Alan Barrett and Philip J. O'Connell, "Does Training Generally Work? The Returns to In-Company Training," *Industrial and Labor Relations Review,* April 2001, pp. 647–62.

[37] Dan A. Black, Brett J. Noel, and Zheng Wang, "On-the-Job Training, Establishment Size, and Firm Size: Evidence for Economies of Scale in the Production of Human Capital," *Southern Economic Journal,* July 1999, pp. 82–100.

[38] Mark A. Loewenstein and James R. Spletzer, "General and Specific Training: Evidence and Implications," *Journal of Human Resources,* Fall 1999, pp. 710–33.

- The accumulation of on-the-job training raises a worker's real wages. Each year of training with the current employer, among younger workers, raises earnings by 13 percent.[39]

- Firms offering training appear to attract higher-ability workers.[40]

- Training lowers the starting wages of workers by a modest amount. The impact of training on productivity growth is much larger.[41]

- Formal training lengthens employment durations.[42]

- Gender differences in the amount of on-the-job training play only a small role in the gender wage gap.[43]

CRITICISMS OF HUMAN CAPITAL THEORY

A number of criticisms have been made of the human capital model and its applications. The first two criticisms discussed here are concerned with measurement problems and suggest that estimates of the rates of return for investments in education are likely to be biased. Two other criticisms also have implications for measuring the rate of return on human capital investments but are more profound in that they challenge the very concept or theory of investing in human capital.

Investment or Consumption?

One criticism of measuring the rate of return on human capital investment is that it is *not* correct to treat all expenditures for education as investment because, in fact, a portion of such outlays are consumption expenditures. The decision to attend college, for example, is based on broader and more complex considerations than expected increases in labor productivity and enhanced earnings. Some substantial portion of one's expenditures on a college education yields consumption benefits either immediately or in the long run.[44] Expenditures for courses on Shakespeare, ceramics, music appreciation, and

---

[39] Daniel Parent, "Wages and Mobility: The Impact of Employer-Provided Training," *Journal of Labor Economics,* April 1999, pp. 298–317.

[40] David H. Autor, "Why Do Temporary Help Firms Provide Free General Skills Training?" *Quarterly Journal of Economics,* November 2001, pp. 1409–48.

[41] John M. Barron, Mark C. Berger, and Dan A. Black, "Do Workers Pay for On-the-Job Training?" *Journal of Human Resources,* Spring 1999, pp. 235–52.

[42] Adam Grossberg, "The Effect of Formal Training on Employment Duration," *Industrial Relations,* October 2000, pp. 578–99. See also Federico Garcia, Jeremy Arkes, and Robert Trost, "Does Employer-Financed General Training Pay? Evidence from the U.S. Navy," *Economics of Education Review,* February 2002, pp. 19–27.

[43] Paul Sicilian and Adam J. Grossberg, "Investment in Human Capital and Gender Wage Differences: Evidence from the NLSY," *Applied Economics* 33, no. 4 (March 2001), pp. 463–71.

[44] Interestingly, a recent study indicates that light to moderate employment during high school has positive effects on later economic outcomes and does not just provide resources for current consumption. See Christopher J. Ruhm. "Is High School Employment Consumption or Investment?" *Journal of Labor Economics,* October 1997, pp. 735–76.

so forth yield both immediate and long-run consumption benefits by enlarging an individual's range of interests, tastes, and activities. It is true, of course, that a course in 19th century English literature not only yields consumption benefits but also enhances the capacity of oral and written expression. And this ability has value in the labor market; it increases productivity and earnings. The problem, however, is that there is no reasonable way to determine what portion of the expense for a literature course is investment and what part is consumption. The main point is that by ignoring the consumption component of educational expenditures and considering *all* such outlays as investment, empirical researchers *understate* the rate of return on educational investments. In other words, by overstating the investment costs we understate the return on that investment.

Nonwage Benefits

In calculating the internal rate of return, most researchers simply compare the differences in the earnings of high school and college graduates. But the jobs of high school and college graduates differ in other respects. First, the fringe benefits associated with the jobs obtained by college graduates are more generous—both absolutely and as a percentage of earnings—than those received by high school graduates. By ignoring fringe benefits, empirical studies *understate* the rate of return on a college education. Second, the jobs acquired by college graduates are generally more pleasant and interesting than those of high school graduates. This means that a calculated rate of return based on incremental earnings *understates* the total benefits accruing from a college education.

The Ability Problem

Two other related criticisms, labeled the *ability problem* and the *screening hypothesis,* question the very concept of human capital investment. We first consider the **ability problem.**

It is widely recognized that average incomes vary directly with the level of education. But it is less well accepted that a strong, clear-cut cause–effect relationship exists between the two. Critics of human capital theory doubt that the observed income differential is solely—or even primarily—the result of the additional education. To state the problem somewhat differently, the "other things being equal" assumption underlies the simple model of Figure 4.2 and the conclusions derived from it. Critics of human capital theory contend that other things in fact are not likely to be equal. It is widely acknowledged that those who have more intelligence, more self-discipline, and greater motivation—not to mention more family wealth and better job market connections—are more likely to go to college. If we could somehow blot out all of the knowledge and understanding that college graduates acquired in college, we would still expect this group to earn larger incomes than those who decided *not* to attend college. Thus one can argue that although college graduates earn higher incomes than high school graduates, a substantial portion of that incremental income is *not* traceable to the investment in a college education. In other words, people with high abilities tend to do well in the labor market; the fact that they also attend college may be somewhat incidental to this success. "The only reason that education is correlated with income is that the combination of ability, motivation, and personal habits that it takes to succeed in education happens to be the same combination that it takes to be a productive worker."[45] This criticism implies that if a substantial portion of the incremental earnings enjoyed by college graduates is attributable to their *ability* and not to their *schooling,* then estimated rates of return on investing in a college education will be *overstated.*

Accepting the validity of this criticism, a number of researchers have tried to determine what portion of incremental earnings derives from human capital investment as opposed to differences in ability and other personal characteristics. For example, a study of identical twins concludes that ability bias plays a small role in the measurement of the rate of return to schooling.[46] Other studies using other approaches reach a similar conclusion.[47]

It is also worth observing that the causal relationship between education and earnings has important implications for public policy. *If* human capital theorists are correct in arguing that education is the sole or primary cause of higher earnings, then it makes sense to provide more education and training to low-income workers if society chooses to reduce poverty and the degree of income inequality. On the other hand, *if* high incomes are caused primarily by ability, independent of education and training, then a policy of increased spending on the education and training of low-income groups may be of limited success in increasing their incomes and alleviating income inequality.

The Screening Hypothesis

The *screening hypothesis* (or *signaling hypothesis*) is closely related to the ability problem. This hypothesis suggests that education affects earnings not primarily by altering the labor market productivity of students but by grading and labeling students in such a way as to determine their job placement and thereby their earnings.[48] It is argued that employers use educational attainment—for example, the possession of a college degree—as an inexpensive means of identifying workers who are likely to be of high quality. A college degree or other credential thus signals trainability and competence and becomes a ticket of admission to higher-level, higher-paying jobs where opportunities for further training and promotion are good. Less educated workers are screened from these positions, not necessarily because of their inability to perform the jobs but simply because they do not have the college degrees to give them access to the positions. The incremental income enjoyed by college graduates might be a payment for being credentialed rather than a reward for being more productive.

[45] Alice M. Rivlin, "Income Distribution—Can Economics Help?" *American Economic Review,* May 1975, p. 10.
[46] Orley Ashenfelter and Alan Krueger, "Estimates of the Economic Returns to Schooling from a New Sample of Twins," *American Economic Review,* December 1994, pp. 1157–73. For similar results using identical twins, see Orley Ashenfelter and Cecilia Rouse, "Income, Schooling, and Ability: Evidence from a New Sample of Identical Twins," *Quarterly Journal of Economics,* February 1998, pp. 253–84.
[47] For example, see McKinley Blackburn and David Neumark, "Omitted-Ability Bias and the Increase in the Return to Schooling," *Journal of Labor Economics,* July 1993, pp. 521–44.
[48] Michael Spence, "Job Market Signaling," *Quarterly Journal of Economics,* August 1973, pp. 355–74. For a survey of the screening literature, see Andrew Weiss, "Human Capital vs. Signaling Explanations of Wages," *Journal of Economic Perspectives,* Fall 1996, pp. 133–54.

Viewed from a private perspective, screening should have no effect on the internal rate of return. Whether one is admitted to a higher-paying position because of the knowledge and skills acquired in college or because one possesses the necessary credential (a college degree), the fact remains that having attended college typically results in higher earnings. But from a social perspective, the screening hypothesis, if valid, is very important. One might well question the expenditure of $745 billion (in 2002) on elementary, secondary, and higher education if the payoff is merely to signal employers that certain workers are above average in terms of intelligence, motivation, and self-discipline. To the extent that a college graduate's incremental earnings stem from screening, the social rate of return of investing in a college education will be *overstated*.

To what extent are the higher earnings of more educated workers due to education augmenting the productivity of workers, as the human capital view suggests? Similarly, to what degree are the higher earnings of such individuals attributable to the screening hypothesis, which indicates that schooling merely flags more productive workers? Does schooling produce skills or merely identify preexistent skills? Empirical evidence is mixed. For example, research by Chatterji and colleagues suggests that as much as 30 percent of the effect of education on earnings might result from screening.[49]

On the other hand, studies by Altonji and Pierret, Wolpin, and Wise question the importance of screening. Altonji and Pierret argue that signaling is likely to be an important part of the return to schooling only to the extent that firms lack good information about the productivity of new workers and that they learn slowly over time.[50] They find evidence that firms do screen young workers on the basis of education, but that employers learn quickly about worker productivity. Altonji and Pierret's calculations suggest that the screening component of the return to schooling is probably only a small part of the difference in wages associated with education. Wolpin has reasoned that if education is a screening device, workers who are to be screened in the process of job acquisition will be prone to purchase more schooling than workers who are not screened. He notes that while salaried workers are screened, self-employed workers are not. Therefore, if schooling is a screening device, salaried workers will tend to purchase more schooling than the self-employed. But he finds that in fact the two groups of workers acquire about the same amount of education, which Wolpin regards as "evidence against a predominant screening interpretation" of the positive association between schooling and earnings.[51] Similarly, Wise has argued that if education does affect worker productivity as the human capital theory suggests, then college degrees of differing quality *and* student performance while attending college should be reflected in salary differentials. That is, if human capital theory is correct, workers with bachelor degrees from high-quality institutions *and* workers who achieved higher grade point

---

[49] Monojit Chatterji, Paul T. Seaman, Larry D. Singell, Jr., "A Test of the Signaling Hypothesis," *Oxford Economic Papers,* April 2003, pp. 191–215. For further support of the signaling hypothesis, see Harley Frazis, "Human Capital, Signaling, and the Pattern of Returns to Education," *Oxford Economic Papers,* April 2002, pp. 298–320.

[50] Joseph G. Altonji and Charles R. Pierret, "Employer Learning and the Signaling Value of Education," in I. Ohashi and T. Tachibanaki (eds.), *Internal Labour Markets, Incentives, and Employment* (New York: MacMillan Publishing, 1998).

[51] Kenneth Wolpin, "Education and Screening," *American Economic Review,* December 1977, pp. 949–58.

4.5	**World of Work**	How Much Is a Standardized Test Point Worth?*

A four-hour standardized test, the Law School Admissions Test (LSAT), plays a very important role in the law school admissions process. Typically law schools give roughly equal weight to an applicant's LSAT score and her undergraduate grade point average. As a result, the LSAT test preparation services industry has become a big business. The industry, which is dominated by two firms, has annual revenues of $30 million.

Berkowitz examines the economic value of this signal of ability. Using data from 50 top law schools, her study examines the impact of the average LSAT score on the average starting salary. She reports that one LSAT point is worth $2,600 in the first year after law school. However, this result includes the effect of two factors. First, a higher LSAT score increases the chance of being admitted to a higher-quality law school. Second, students with higher LSAT scores have more ability, controlling for school quality.

To eliminate the influence of school quality, the study examines the impact of the LSAT score on starting salary among graduates of one law school. The analysis reveals that the potency of the LSAT score is greatly diminished. In fact, an LSAT point is worth only one-seventh of what the cross-school model indicates. Thus most of the impact of the LSAT score is captured in its effect on which school a student attends.

* Based on Ruth Berkowitz, "One Point on the LSAT: How Much Is It Worth? Standardized Tests as a Determinant of Earnings," *American Economist*, Fall 1998, pp. 80–89.

averages should be more productive and therefore earn higher salaries. Examining data for some 1,300 college graduates employed by Ford Motor Company, Wise found a "consistent positive relationship between commonly used measures of academic achievement [institutional quality and grade point average] and rates of salary increase." Wise concludes that a "college education is not only a signal of productive ability, but in fact enhances this ability."[52]

Recapitulation

There is no question that human capital theory has been the basis for important insights and the cornerstone for myriad revealing empirical studies. But as the ability problem and the screening hypothesis suggest, human capital theory is not universally accepted, and some who accept it do so only with reservations. While there is almost universal agreement about the positive association between education and earnings, there is disagreement over the *reasons* for this association. Empirical testing is usually indirect in that it is first determined that those with more education and training have higher earnings, and then it is *inferred* that the additional education and training increase worker productivity and thereby cause the enhanced earnings. But the issue remains: Does

[52] David A. Wise, "Academic Achievement and Job Performance," *American Economic Review*, June 1975, pp. 350–66. For evidence that education per se, as opposed to ability or screening, enhances earnings in two less developed nations (Kenya and Tanzania), see M. Boissiere, J. B. Knight, and R. H. Sabot, "Earnings, Schooling, and Cognitive Skills," *American Economic Review*, December 1985, pp. 1016–30.

education increase one's productivity? Or do those who acquire more education earn more simply because they are more able and more motivated? Do educational degrees simply identify productive workers?[53]

Most economists reject the various criticisms of human capital theory, believing that education and training directly increase productivity and earnings. But they also recognize that not all investments in education and training have a positive net present value; some investments are poor ones, and others have sharply diminishing returns. Thus human capital theory cannot be used uncritically as a basis for public policy. For example, taken alone, massive government investments in human capital to increase economic growth may yield disappointing results. Such policies need to be balanced against alternative policies promoting new technology and greater investment in physical capital.

Chapter Summary

1. Expenditures on education and training that increase one's productivity and future earnings in the labor market can be treated as a human capital investment decision.

2. The decision to invest in a college education entails both direct (out-of-pocket) and indirect (forgone earnings) costs. Benefits take the form of future incremental earnings.

3. There are two basic methods of comparing the benefits and costs associated with a human capital investment. The net present value approach uses a discounting formula to compare the present value of costs and benefits. If net present value is positive, it is rational to invest. The internal rate of return is the rate of discount at which the net present value of the investment is zero. If the internal rate of return exceeds the interest rate, it is rational to invest.

4. Most empirical studies suggest that the rate of return on investing in a college education has ranged from 10 to 15 percent.

5. The college wage premium—the percentage differential in the earnings of college and high school graduates—has varied significantly over time, rising rapidly since 1979. Changes in the supply of and the demand for college and high school graduates can be used to explain changes in the college wage premium.

6. From a private perspective, the human capital decision excludes public subsidies to education, considers after-tax earnings, and ignores any social or external benefits associated with education. The social perspective includes public subsidies and external benefits and considers before-tax earnings.

7. The demand for human capital curve and the supply of investment funds curve can be combined to explain why various people invest in different amounts of human capital. Ability differences, discrimination, and varying access to financial resources all help explain differences in education and earnings among individuals.

[53] For excellent elaborations of the criticisms of human capital theory, see Bobbie McCrackin, "Education's Contribution to Productivity and Economic Growth," *Economic Review* (Federal Reserve Bank of Atlanta), November 1984, pp. 8–23; and Gian Singh Sahota, "Theories of Personal Income Distribution: A Survey," *Journal of Economic Literature,* March 1978, pp. 11–19.

8. The money market may provide funds for human capital investment on less favorable terms than for investment in physical capital, providing some justification for public subsidization of human capital investments.

9. It is useful to distinguish between general and specific on-the-job training. General training generates worker skills that are useful in all firms and industries. Specific training is useful only in the specific firm providing that training. Given competitive markets, workers will normally pay for general training provided by a firm by accepting lower wages during the training period. An exception may occur where firms must pay a legal minimum wage. Employers pay for specific training. Seeking to retain trained workers, employers may share with workers the increases in total revenue resulting from specific training.

10. Criticisms of human capital theory include the following: *(a)* By failing to recognize that a part of education expenditures is consumption rather than investment, empirical studies understate the rate of return on education; *(b)* empirical studies understate the rate of return on a college education by not taking into account that the jobs of college graduates are more pleasant and entail better fringe benefits than the jobs of high school graduates; *(c)* to the extent that the incremental earnings of college graduates are due to their greater ability and not to schooling per se, the rate of return on a college education will be overstated; *(d)* if a portion of the incremental earnings of college graduates is attributable to screening, the social rate of return on a college education will be overstated.

Terms and Concepts

investment in
  human capital, *86*
age-earnings profiles, *86*
net present value, *89*
time preference, *89*
discount formula, *90*
internal rate of return, *92*
college wage premium, *96*

private and social
  perspectives, *100*
demand for human
  capital curve, *106*
supply of investment
  funds, *106*
capital market
  imperfections, *111*

on-the-job training, *112*
general versus specific
  training, *113*
marginal revenue
  product, *114*
ability problem, *120*
screening hypothesis, *121*

Questions and Study Suggestions

1. Why might the decision to undertake an educational program be treated as an investment? From a private perspective, what costs and benefits are associated with obtaining a college education? What are the costs and benefits from a social perspective? Explain why it is necessary to determine the present value of costs and benefits in making a rational human capital investment decision.

2. What is the internal rate of return on a human capital investment? Given the internal rate of return, what is the appropriate investment criterion? Compare this to the criterion relevant to the present value approach.

3. Floyd is now working on a job that pays $8,000 per year. He is contemplating a one-year automobile mechanics course that entails costs of $1,000 for books and tuition. Floyd estimates that the course will increase his income to $13,000 in each of the

three years following completion of the course. At the end of those three years, Floyd plans to retire to a commune in Boulder, Colorado. The current interest rate is 10 percent. Is it economically rational for Floyd to enroll in the course?

4. Comment on each of the following statements:

   a. Given the work life cycle of the "traditional" woman, it may be rational for women to invest in less human capital than men.

   b. Older workers are less mobile geographically than younger workers.

   c. An economic recession tends to stimulate college enrollments.

   d. One of the disadvantages of Social Security's benefit reduction rate (reducing benefits when earnings exceed a certain level during retirement years) is that it biases investment away from human capital and toward bonds and stocks.

   e. The age–earnings profiles of Figure 4.1 clearly indicate that people with more education earn more than people with less education; therefore, personal spending on education is always a good investment.

5. What is the college wage premium? Can you explain why the premium *(a)* declined in the 1970s and *(b)* increased in the 1980s and 1990s?

6. Assume that a recent high school graduate reads in a magazine that the rate of return on a college education has been estimated to be 15 percent. What advice would you give the graduate in using this information as he or she decides whether to attend college?

7. Why is the internal rate of return from human capital investment subject to diminishing returns? Explain the rationale for identifying the "diminishing rate of returns to education curve" as the "demand for human capital curve." Combine the demand for human capital curve with a "supply of investment funds curve" to explain why various individuals find it rational to invest in different amounts of human capital. What are the implications of your answer for the personal distribution of income? Do you think that the educational system in the United States contributes to more or less equality in the distribution of earnings? Explain. If you wanted to reduce inequality in the distribution of earnings, what policy recommendations would you make?

8. Why might funds be available on less favorable terms for human capital investments than for physical capital investments? In your judgment, does this difference justify public subsidy in the form, say, of federal guarantees of loans to college students? What are some external benefits associated with education? Do you feel that these benefits justify public subsidies to education? Can you provide a rationale for the argument that public subsidies should diminish as students advance to higher and higher educational levels?

9. Describe the expected effects that college scholarships based on *(a)* student ability and *(b)* student need are likely to have on the distribution of earnings.

10. Distinguish between general and specific on-the-job training. Who normally pays for general training? Specific training? Why the difference? Are there any exceptions to these generalizations? Explain.

11. As this diagram indicates, the distribution of "ability" (here measured by IQ scores) is normal or bell-shaped, but the distribution of earnings is skewed to the right. Can you use human capital theory to reconcile these two distributions?

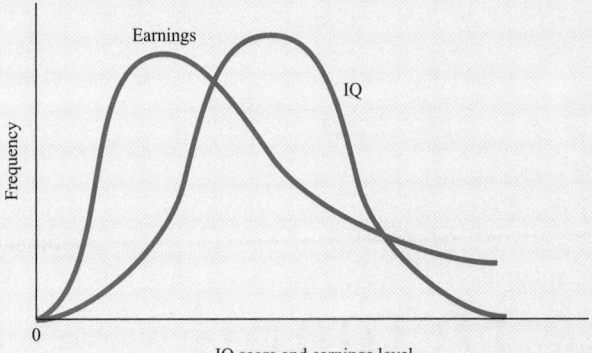

12. Data show that the age–earnings profiles of women are considerably lower and flatter than those for men. Can you explain these differences?

13. Indicate the implications of each of the following for estimates of the rate of return on a college education: *(a)* the screening hypothesis, *(b)* the possibility that a portion of one's expenditures on college should be considered as consumption rather than investment, *(c)* the fact that people who go to college are generally more able than those who do not, and *(d)* the fact that jobs acquired by college graduates generally entail larger fringe benefits than the jobs of high school graduates. What implications do the ability problem and the screening hypothesis have for public policy toward education?

Internet Exercise

What Is a College Degree Worth?

Go to the Census Bureau Web site **(http://www.census.gov)** and in sequence select "E" in the Subjects area, "Educational Attainment," and "Table A.3" under Historical Tables to find information about earnings of workers by education.

What were the annual earnings for high school and college graduates in 1975? For the most recent year shown? What was the ratio of the earnings of college graduates to high school graduates in 1975? In the most recent year? Has the ratio increased or decreased over this period? What factors might help explain this change?

Internet Links

The National Center for Education Statistics Web site has extensive statistics on primary, secondary, and college education in the United States **(http://nces.ed.gov/)**.

The U.S. Department of Education Web site gives information regarding the U.S. education system **(http://www.ed.gov/)**.

Chapter 5

The Demand for Labor

The previous three chapters have examined the supply of labor. In the present chapter our attention shifts to the demand side of the labor market. Why do Microsoft, Micron, and Motorola wish to employ those willing to supply their particular labor services? How is Mattel's demand for labor affected by increases in the demand for the toys it produces? What factors alter Maytag's and McDonald's demand for labor? Why might Monsanto adjust its level of employment more than Merck when wage rates change for a particular type of labor?

Answers to these and related questions motivate our discussion of labor demand. Then, in Chapter 6, we will combine our understanding of labor demand and labor supply to explain how wage rates are determined.

DERIVED DEMAND FOR LABOR

We should note at the outset that the demand for labor, or for any other productive resource, is a *derived demand*. This means that the demand for labor depends on, or is derived from, the demand for the product or service it is helping to produce or provide. In manufacturing, labor is demanded for the contribution it makes to the production of such products as automobiles, television sets, or loaves of bread. Thus a decrease in the demand for automobiles will reduce the demand for automobile workers. In the service sector, labor is demanded by firms because it directly provides benefits to consumers. An increase in the demand for child care services, for example, will increase the derived demand for child care workers.

The fact that the demand for labor is a derived demand means that the strength of the demand for any particular type of labor will depend on (1) how productive that labor is in helping to create some product or service and (2) the market value of that item. If type A labor is highly productive in turning out product X, and if product X is highly

Global Perspective | Annual Net Employment Change as a Percentage of Total Employment

The United States had a relatively high rate of employment growth between 1995 and 2005.

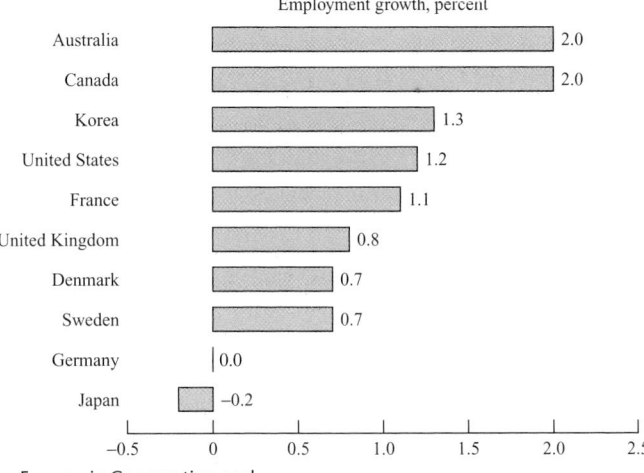

Employment growth, percent

Australia	2.0
Canada	2.0
Korea	1.3
United States	1.2
France	1.1
United Kingdom	0.8
Denmark	0.7
Sweden	0.7
Germany	0.0
Japan	−0.2

Source: Organization for Economic Cooperation and Development (http://www.oecd.org).

valued by society, then a strong demand for type A labor will exist. Conversely, the demand will be weak for some kind of labor that is relatively unproductive in producing a good or service that is not of great value to society.

These observations point the way for our discussion. We will find that the immediate determinants of the demand for labor are labor's marginal productivity and the value (price) of its output. Let's begin by examining the short-run production function for a typical firm and then introduce the role of product price. Although our discussion will be cast in terms of a firm producing a particular good, the concepts developed apply equally to firms hiring workers to produce services.

A FIRM'S SHORT-RUN PRODUCTION FUNCTION

A *production function* is a relationship between quantities of resources (inputs) and the corresponding production outcomes (output). We will assume that the production process entails just two inputs—labor L and capital K. To simplify further, let's suppose that a single type of labor is being employed or, in other words, that the firm is hiring homogeneous inputs of labor. Furthermore, initially we examine the firm as it operates in the short run, *a period in which at least one resource is fixed*. In this case the fixed resource is the firm's stock of capital—its plant, machinery, and other equipment. As shown in Equation (5.1),

$$TP_{SR} = f(L, \overline{K}) \qquad \textbf{(5.1)}$$

the firm's total product in the short run (TP_{SR}) is a function of a variable input L (labor) and a fixed input K (capital).

Total, Marginal, and Average Product

What happens to the total product (output) as successive inputs of labor are added to a fixed plant? The answer is provided in Figure 5.1, where the upper graph (a) shows

FIGURE 5.1 A Firm's Short-Run Production Function
As labor is added to a fixed amount of capital, total product will eventually increase by diminishing amounts, reach a maximum, and then decline as shown in (a). Marginal products in (b) reflect the changes in total product associated with each additional input of labor. The relationship between marginal product and average product is such that MP intersects AP where AP is at its maximum. The *yz* segment of the MP curve in stage II is the basis for the short-run labor demand curve.

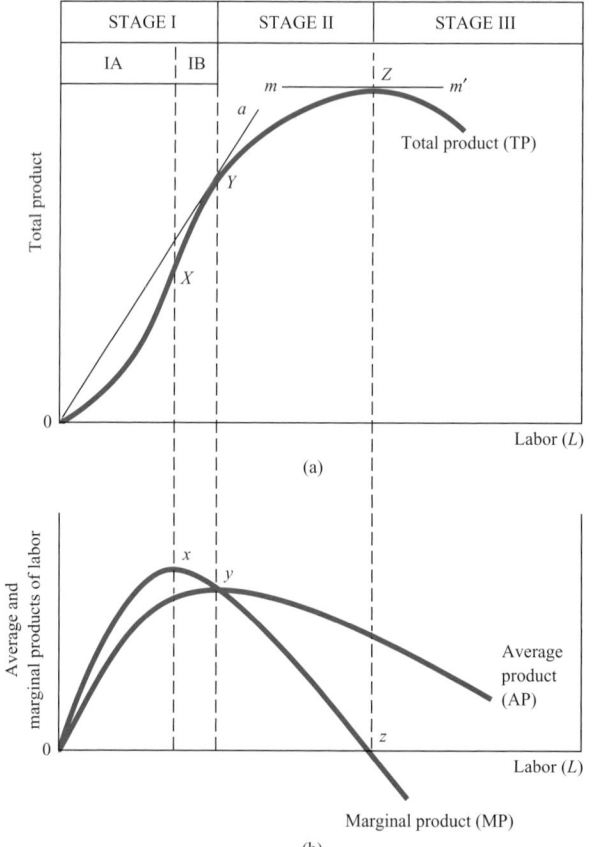

a short-run production function or total product (TP) curve and the lower graph (b) displays the corresponding curves for the marginal product of labor (MP) and the average product of labor (AP).

In the short run, the ***total product*** (TP) shown in (a) is *the total output produced by each combination of the variable resource (labor) and the fixed amount of capital.* The ***marginal product*** (MP) of labor is *the change in total product associated with the addition of one more unit of labor.* It is the absolute change in TP and can be found by drawing a line tangent to the TP curve at any point and then determining the slope of that line. For example, notice line *mm'*, which is drawn tangent to point Z on the TP curve. The slope of *mm'* is zero, and this is the marginal product MP as shown at point z on the MP curve in the lower graph. The ***average product*** (AP) of labor is *the total product divided by the number of labor units.* Geometrically, it is measured as the slope of any straight line drawn from the origin to or through any particular point on the TP curve. For example, observe line 0a, which radiates from the origin through point Y on TP. The slope (ΔTP/ΔL) of 0a tells us the AP associated with this particular combination of TP and labor input L. For example, if TP were 20 at point Y, and L were 4, then AP would be 5 (= 20/4). This is the value of the slope of line 0a, which as measured from the origin is the *vertical* rise (= 20) divided by the *horizontal* run (= 4). If we assume that labor units are labor hours, rather than workers, then this slope measures output per worker hour.

Stages of Production

The relationships between total, marginal, and average products are important. To show these relationships *and* to permit us later to isolate the region in which the firm will operate if it decides to do so, we have divided the total product curve (TP) into three stages, but we have also subdivided stage I into two parts. Over segment 0X of the TP curve—or stated alternatively, within part IA of stage I—the total product curve is increasing at an *increasing* rate. As observed in the lower graph, this implies that MP (= ΔTP/ΔL) necessarily is rising. For example, suppose the TPs associated with the first three workers were 3, 8, and 15, respectively. The corresponding MPs would be 3 (= 3 − 0), 5 (= 8 − 3), and 7 (= 15 − 8). Note, too, from the lower graph that because MP exceeds average product (AP), the latter also is rising. This is a matter of arithmetic necessity: Whenever a number that is greater than the average of some total is added to that total, the average must rise. In the present context, marginal product is the addition to total product while average product is the average of total product. Hence, when MP exceeds AP, AP must rise.[1]

Next observe segment *XY*—or stage IB—of the production function in Figure 5.1(a). The total product curve is now such that TP is still increasing as more workers are hired, but at a *decreasing* rate, and therefore MP (graph b) is declining. Notice that MP reached its maximum at point x in the lower graph and that this point corresponds to point X on the production function. But beyond points X and x, MP falls. We see, however, that

---

[1] You raise your cumulative grade point average by earning grades in the most recent (marginal) semester that are higher than your current average.

even though MP is now falling, it still is above AP, and hence AP continues to rise. Finally, observe that the end of range IB of stage I is marked by the point at which AP is at its maximum and just equals MP (point *y*). The fact that AP is at a maximum at point *Y* on the TP curve is confirmed by ray 0*a*. The slope of 0*a*—which, remember, measures AP—is greater than would be the slope of any other straight line drawn between the origin and a specific point on the TP curve.

In stage II, later referred to as the *zone of production,* total product continues to rise at a diminishing rate. Consequently, MP continues to decline. But now AP also falls because MP finally is less than AP. Again, simple arithmetic tells us that when a number (MP) that is less than the current average of a total is added to that total (TP), the average (AP) must fall.

At the dividing line between stages II and III, TP reaches its maximum point *Z* and MP becomes zero (point *z*), indicating that beyond this point additional workers detract from total product. In stage III, TP falls and MP is therefore negative, the latter causing AP to continue to decline.

Law of Diminishing Marginal Returns

Why do TP, MP, and AP behave in the manner shown in Figure 5.1? Let's focus on marginal product, keeping in mind that changes in MP are related to changes in TP and AP. Why does MP rise, then fall, and eventually become negative? It is *not* because the quality of labor declines as more of it is hired; remember that all workers are assumed to be identical. Rather, the reason is that the fixed capital at first gets used increasingly productively as more workers are employed but eventually becomes more and more burdened. Imagine a firm that possesses a fixed amount of machinery and equipment. As this firm hires its initial workers, each worker will contribute more to output than the previous worker because the firm will be better able to use its machinery and equipment. Time will be saved because each worker can specialize in a task and will no longer have to scramble from one job operation to another. Successively greater increases in output will occur because the new workers will permit capital equipment to be used more intensively during the day. Thus, for a time the added, or marginal, product of extra workers will rise.

These increases in marginal product cannot be realized indefinitely. As still more labor is added to the fixed machinery and equipment, the *law of diminishing marginal returns* will take hold. This law states that *as successive units of a variable resource (labor) are added to a fixed resource (capital), beyond some point the marginal product attributable to each additional unit of the variable resource will decline.* At some point labor will become so abundant relative to the fixed capital that additional workers cannot add as much to output as did previous workers. For example, an added worker may have to wait in line to use the machines. At the extreme, the continuous addition of labor will so overcrowd the plant that the marginal product of still more labor will become negative, reducing total product (stage III).

Zone of Production

The characteristics of TP, MP, and AP discussed in Figure 5.1 are summarized in Table 5.1. In reviewing this table, notice that stage II of the production function is designated

TABLE 5.1   **Production Function Variables: A Summary**

			Total Product, TP_L	Marginal Product, MP_L	Average Product, AP_L
	STAGE I	IA	Increasing at an increasing rate	Increasing and greater than AP	Increasing
		IB	Increasing at a decreasing rate	Declining but greater than AP	Increasing
Zone of Production	STAGE II		Increasing at a decreasing rate	Declining and less than AP	Declining
	STAGE III		Declining	Negative and less than AP	Declining

as the *zone of production.* To see why, let's establish that the left boundary of stage II in Figure 5.1 is where the efficiency of labor—as measured by its average product—is at a maximum. Similarly, the right boundary is where the efficiency of the fixed resource capital is maximized. Notice first that at point Y on TP and y on AP and MP, total product *per unit of labor* is at its maximum. This is shown both by ray $0a$, which is the steepest line that can be drawn from the origin to any point on TP, and by the AP curve, because AP *is* TP/L. Next, note that at point Z on TP and z on MP, total product is at a maximum. Because capital (K) is fixed, this implies that the average product of K is also at a maximum. That is, total product *per unit of capital* is greater at the right boundary of stage II than at any other point. The generalization here is that if a firm chooses to operate, *it will want to produce at a level of output where changes in labor contribute to increasing efficiency of either labor or capital.*[2]

This is *not* the case in either stage I or III. In stage I, additions to labor *increase* both the efficiency of labor *and* the efficiency of capital. The former can easily be seen by the rising AP curve; the latter is true because capital is constant and TP is rising, thereby increasing the average product of capital ($= TP/K$). The firm therefore will desire to move at least to the left boundary of stage II.

What about stage III? Inspection of Figure 5.1(a) and (b) shows that the addition of labor *reduces* the efficiency of *both* labor and capital. Notice that the average product of labor is falling. Also, because there is less total product than before, the TP/K ratio is declining. Stated differently, the firm will not operate in stage III because it can *add* to the efficiency of labor and capital and to its total product by *reducing* employment.

[2] This generalization applies only to a competitive firm. For an imperfectly competitive firm such as a monopoly, *only* stage III is necessarily a nonprofit maximizing area. In maximizing profits, a monopolist may restrict output and therefore employment to some point in stage I.

Conclusion? The profit-maximizing or loss-minimizing firm that chooses to operate will face a marginal product curve indicated by line segment *yz* in Figure 5.1(b). *This MP curve is the underlying basis for the firm's short-run demand for labor curve.*

SHORT-RUN DEMAND FOR LABOR: THE PERFECTLY COMPETITIVE SELLER

To see how segment *yz* in Figure 5.1(b) relates to labor demand, let's next (1) transform the TP and MP information in that figure to hypothetical numbers via a table and (2) convert our analysis from output to monetary terms. Employers, after all, decide how many workers to hire in terms of *revenues* and *costs* rather than in output terms.

Consider Table 5.2. Columns 1 to 3 are merely numerical illustrations of the relationships within the zone of production, showing total and marginal product but omitting average product. To simplify, we have identified only the range of labor inputs over which diminishing marginal productivity sets in. Recalling our earlier discussion of the demand for labor as a derived demand, note that column 4 shows the price of the product that is being produced. The fact that this $2 price does not decline as more output is produced and sold indicates that the firm is selling its output in a perfectly competitive market. In technical terms, the firm's *product* demand curve is perfectly elastic; the firm is a "price taker." For example, this firm may be selling standardized products such as grain or fresh fish.

Multiplying column 2 by column 4, we obtain total revenue (sometimes called *total revenue product*) in column 5. From these total revenue data we can easily compute *marginal revenue product* (MRP), which is *the increase (change) in total revenue resulting from the employment of each additional labor unit.* These figures are shown in column 6. The MRP schedule shown by columns 1 and 6 is strictly proportionate to the MP schedule, shown by columns 1 and 3. In this case, MRP is *twice* as large as MP because price is $2.

Columns 1 and 6—the MRP schedule—constitute the firm's *short-run labor demand curve.* To justify and explain this assertion we must first understand the rule that a profit-maximizing firm will apply in determining the number of workers to employ.

TABLE 5.2
Demand for Labor: Firm Selling in a Perfectly Competitive Product Market (Hypothetical Data)

(1) Units of Labor, L	(2) TP	(3) MP	(4) Product Price, P	(5) Total Revenue, TR	(6) MRP ($\Delta TR/\Delta L$)	(7) VMP (MP × P)
4	15		$2	$30		
5	27	12	2	54	$24	$24
6	36	9	2	72	18	18
7	42	6	2	84	12	12
8	45	3	2	90	6	6
9	46	1	2	92	2	2

A profit-maximizing employer should hire workers so long as each successive worker adds more to the firm's total revenue than to its total cost. We have just noted that the amount that each successive unit of labor adds to total revenue is measured by MRP. The amount that a worker adds to total costs is measured by *marginal wage cost* (MWC), defined as *the change in total wage cost resulting from the employment of one more labor unit.* Thus we can abbreviate our rule by saying that the profit-maximizing firm should hire units of labor up to the point at which MRP = MWC.[3] If at some level of employment MRP exceeds MWC, it will be profitable to employ more labor. If for some level of employment MWC exceeds MRP, the firm will increase its profits by hiring less labor.

Let's now assume that the employer for whom Table 5.2 is relevant is hiring labor under purely competitive conditions. This means the firm is a "wage taker" in that it employs a negligible portion of the total labor supply and therefore exerts no perceptible influence on the wage rate. Perhaps this is a fish-processing firm that is hiring people to clean fish. The market wage rate is "given" to the employer, and it follows that total wage cost (the wage bill) increases by the amount of the wage rate W for each additional unit of labor hired. In other words, the wage rate and marginal wage cost are equal. We can thus modify our MRP = MWC rule for the firm hiring competitively and restate it as the MRP = W rule. The profit-maximizing firm that is a perfectly competitive employer of labor should employ units of labor up to the point at which marginal revenue product MRP equals the wage rate W.

We now can apply the MRP = W rule to demonstrate our earlier assertion: The MRP schedule shown in columns 1 and 6, derived directly from the MRP data from the zone of production, *is* the firm's short-run labor demand curve. The MRP data from columns 1 and 6 are graphed in Figure 5.2 to demonstrate this point. This schedule and curve indicate the amount of labor this firm would demand at several separate competitively determined wage rates. First let's suppose that the wage rate is $23.99, an amount infinitesimally less than $24. This firm will decide to employ five units of labor because it either adds to profits or subtracts from losses by hiring these units of labor. But the firm will not employ the sixth, seventh, and further units because MRP < W for each of them.

Next suppose that the wage rate falls to $11.99. The MRP = W rule indicates that the firm will now also hire the sixth and seventh units of labor. If the wage rate falls further to, say, $1.99, it will employ nine units of labor. We conclude then that *the MRP curve in Figure 5.2 is the firm's short-run labor demand curve* because each point on it indicates the quantity of labor that a firm will demand at each possible wage rate that might exist. Any curve that embodies this information on wage rate and quantity of labor demanded is, by definition, the firm's labor demand curve.

One further point needs to be made: Where there is perfect competition in the product market, a firm's marginal revenue product or labor demand curve is also the *value of marginal product* (VMP) curve. *The value of marginal product is the extra output*

---

[3] The rationale for this rule is the same as that for the marginal revenue equals marginal cost (MR = MC) rule, which identifies the profit-maximizing output in the product market. The difference is that the MRP = MWC rule is in terms of *inputs* of labor, whereas the MR = MC rule is in terms of *outputs* of product.

FIGURE 5.2 **The Labor Demand Curve of a Perfectly Competitive Seller**

Application of the MRP = *W* rule reveals that the MRP curve is the firm's short-run labor demand curve. Under perfect competition in the product market, MRP = VMP and the labor demand curve slopes downward solely because of diminishing marginal productivity.

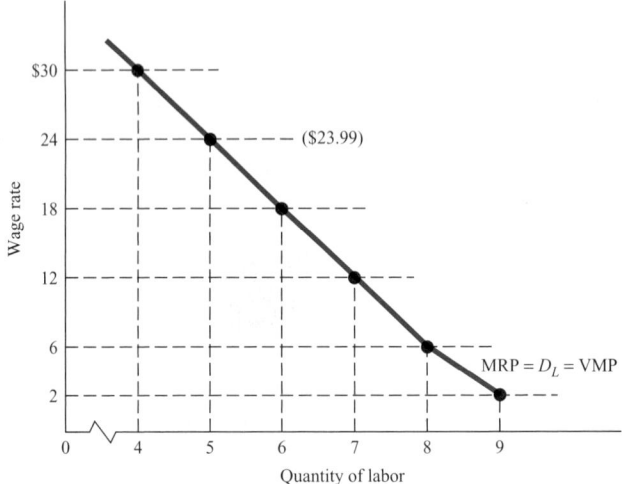

in dollar terms that accrues to society when an extra unit of labor is employed. Columns 1 and 7 in Table 5.2 show the VMP schedule in our example. Notice that VMP is determined by multiplying marginal product MP (column 3) by the product price (column 4). We observe in this case that VMP, the value of the marginal product, is identical to MRP, the extra revenue accruing to the firm when it adds a unit of labor (column 6). For this reason we label the demand for labor curve in Figure 5.2 as VMP, as well as MRP.

What is the logic underlying the equality of VMP and MRP when perfect competition prevails in the product market? Because the competitive firm is a price taker, it can sell as many units of output as it desires at the market price (= $2). The sale of *each* additional unit of the product adds the product price (= $2) to the firm's total revenue; therefore, the seller's *marginal revenue* (MR) is constant and is equal to the product price. In this situation, the extra *revenue* to the firm from employing an additional labor unit (= MR × MP) equals the social *value* of the extra output (= *P* × MP) contributed by that unit of labor.

SHORT-RUN DEMAND FOR LABOR: THE IMPERFECTLY COMPETITIVE SELLER

Most firms in our economy do *not* sell their products in purely competitive markets; rather, they sell under imperfectly competitive conditions. That is, the firms are monopolies, oligopolies, or monopolistically competitive sellers. When a firm can set its price—rather than being forced to accept a market-determined price—it has some monopoly power.

The change in assumptions about product market conditions from pure competition to imperfect competition alters our analysis in an important way. Because of product uniqueness or differentiation, the imperfectly competitive seller's product demand curve is downward-sloping rather than perfectly elastic. This means the firm must lower its price to sell the output contributed by each successive worker. Furthermore, because we assume that the firm cannot engage in price discrimination, it must lower the price not only on the last unit produced but also on all other units, which otherwise would have commanded a higher price. The sale of an extra unit of output therefore does *not* add its full price to the firm's marginal revenue, as it does in perfect competition. To obtain the marginal revenue for the imperfectly competitive seller, one must subtract the potential revenue lost on the other units from the new revenue gained from the last unit. Because marginal revenue is less than the product price, the imperfectly competitive seller's marginal revenue product ($= MR \times MP$) is less than that of the perfectly competitive seller ($= P \times MP$). Recall that the perfectly competitive firm suffers no decline in marginal revenue as it sells the extra output of added workers.

Thus the MRP or labor demand curve of the purely competitive seller falls for a *single* reason—marginal product diminishes as more units of labor are employed. But the MRP or labor demand curve of the imperfectly competitive seller declines for *two* reasons—marginal product falls as more units of labor are employed *and* product price declines as output increases. Table 5.3 takes this second consideration into account. The production data of columns 1 to 3 are precisely the same as in Table 5.2, but in column 4 we recognize that product price must drop to sell the marginal product of each successive worker.

It is worth reemphasizing that the lower price accompanying each increase in output applies not only to the output produced by each additional worker but also to all prior units that otherwise could have been sold at a higher price. For example, the fifth worker's marginal product is 12 units, and these 12 units can be sold for $2.40 each or, as a group, for $28.80. This is the value of the marginal product (VMP) of labor—that is, the value of the added output from society's perspective (column 7). But the MRP of the fifth worker is only $25.80. Why the $3.00 difference? To sell the 12 units

TABLE 5.3   Demand for Labor: Firm Selling in an Imperfectly Competitive Product Market (Hypothetical Data)

(1) Units of Labor, L	(2) TP	(3) MP	(4) Product Price, P	(5) Total Revenue, TR	(6) MRP ($\Delta TR/\Delta L$)	(7) VMP ($MP \times P$)
4	15		$2.60	$39.00		
5	27	12	2.40	64.80	$25.80	$28.80
6	36	9	2.20	79.20	14.40	19.80
7	42	6	2.10	88.20	9.00	12.60
8	45	3	2.00	90.00	1.80	6.00
9	46	1	1.90	87.40	−2.60	1.80

associated with the fifth worker, the firm must accept a $.20 price cut on *each* of the 15 units produced by the previous workers—units that could have been sold for $2.60 each. Thus the MRP of the fifth worker is only $25.80 [= $28.80 − (15 × $.20)]. Similarly, the sixth worker's MRP is only $14.40. Although the 9 units produced are worth $2.20 each in the market and therefore their VMP is $19.80, the worker does *not* add $19.80 to the firm's total revenue when account is taken of the $.20 price cut that must be taken on the 27 units produced by the previous workers. Specifically, the sixth worker's MRP is $14.40 [= $19.80 − (27 × $.20)]. The other MRP figures in column 6 of Table 5.3 are similarly explained. Comparison of columns 6 and 7 reveals that at each level of employment, VMP (the value of the extra product to buyers) exceeds MRP (the extra revenue to the firm). The efficiency implications of this difference will be examined in Chapter 6.

As in the case of the purely competitive seller, application of the MRP = *W* rule to the MRP curve will yield the conclusion that the MRP curve *is* the firm's labor demand curve. However, by plotting the imperfectly competitive seller's MRP or labor demand curve D_L in Figure 5.3 and comparing it with the demand curve in Figure 5.2, we find visual support for an important generalization: *All else being equal, the imperfectly competitive seller's labor demand curve is less elastic than that of the purely competitive seller.* It is not surprising that a firm that possesses monopoly power is less

FIGURE 5.3 The Labor Demand for an Imperfectly Competitive Seller

Under imperfect competition in the product market, the firm's demand curve will slope downward because marginal product diminishes as more units of labor are employed *and* because the firm must reduce the product price on all units of output as more output is produced. Also, the MRP (= MR × MP) for the imperfect competitor is less than the VMP (= *P* × MP) at all levels of employment beyond the first unit.

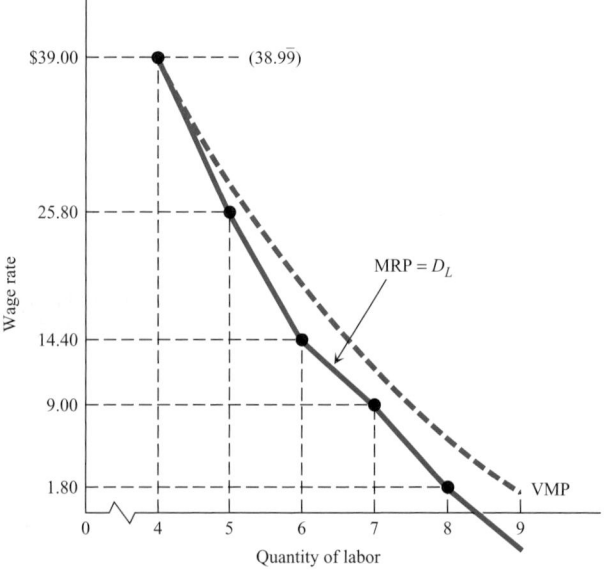

responsive to wage rate changes than a purely competitive seller. The tendency for the imperfectly competitive seller to add fewer workers as the wage rate declines is merely the labor market reflection of the firm's restriction of output in the product market. Other things being equal, the seller possessing monopoly power will find it profitable to produce less output than it would in a purely competitive industry. In producing this smaller output, the seller with monopoly power will employ fewer workers.

Finally, notice that the VMP schedule that is also plotted in Figure 5.3 lies to the right of the firm's D_L = MRP curve. This visually depicts our previous conclusion: The marginal revenue accruing to an imperfectly competitive seller from hiring an additional unit of labor is less than the market value of the extra output the unit of labor helps produce [(MRP = MR × MP) < (VMP = P × MP)].

5.1

Quick Review

- The demand for labor is derived from the demand for the product or service that it helps produce.
- As labor is added to a fixed amount of capital, the total product of labor first increases at an increasing rate, then increases at a diminishing rate, and then declines; this implies that the marginal product of labor first rises, then falls, and finally becomes negative.
- Because a perfectly competitive firm will hire employees up to where WR = MRP, the MRP curve is the firm's labor demand curve.
- The labor demand curve for an imperfectly competitive seller will not be as strong as for a perfectly competitive seller because the former must lower its product price on all units of output as more output is produced (MR < P).

Your Turn

Assume labor is the only variable input and that an additional unit of labor increases total output from 65 to 73 units. If the product sells for $4 per unit in a perfectly competitive market, what is the MRP of this additional worker? Would the MRP be higher or lower than this amount if the firm were a monopolist and had to lower its price to sell all 73 units? (*Answers:* See page 597.)

THE LONG-RUN DEMAND FOR LABOR[4]

Thus far we have derived and discussed the firm's short-run production function [Equation (5.1)] and demand for labor, which presuppose that labor is a variable input and that the amount of capital is fixed. We now turn to the long-run production

---

[4] We provide a more advanced derivation of the long-run demand for labor curve in the appendix of this chapter. There, and in the discussion that follows, we ignore the long-run "profit-maximizing effect" of a wage rate change. For simplicity, we focus on the short-run output effect and the long-run substitution effect.

relationship shown in Equation (5.2), where we find that *both* labor and capital are variable. Once again we assume that L and K are the only two inputs and that labor is homogeneous.

$$TP_{LR} = f(L, K) \qquad\qquad \textbf{(5.2)}$$

The *long-run demand for labor* is *a schedule or curve indicating the amount of labor that firms will employ at each possible wage rate when both labor and capital are variable.* The long-run labor demand curve declines because a wage change produces a short-run output effect and a long-run substitution effect, which together alter the firm's optimal level of employment.

Output Effect

As it relates to labor demand, the *output effect* (also called the *scale effect*) is *the change in employment resulting solely from the effect of the wage change on the employer's costs of production.* This effect is present in the short run and is demonstrated in Figure 5.4. Under normal circumstances, a decline in the wage rate shifts a firm's marginal cost curve downward, as from MC_1 to MC_2. That is, the firm can produce any additional unit of output at less cost than before. The reduced marginal cost (MC_2) relative to the firm's marginal revenue (MR) means that marginal revenue now exceeds marginal costs for each of the Q_1 to Q_2 units. Adhering to the MR = MC profit-maximizing rule, the firm will now find it profitable to increase its output from Q_1 to Q_2. To accomplish this, it will wish to expand its employment of labor.

FIGURE 5.4   **The Output Effect of a Wage Rate Decline**
All else being equal, a decline in the wage rate will reduce marginal cost (from MC_1 to MC_2) and increase the profit-maximizing level (MR = MC) of output (from Q_1 to Q_2). To produce the extra output, the firm will wish to employ more labor.

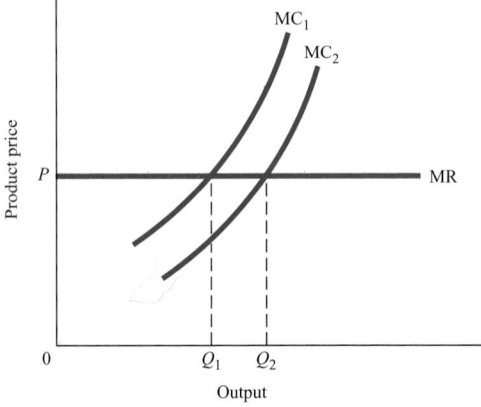

Substitution Effect

As it relates to long-run labor demand, the **substitution effect** is *the change in employment resulting solely from a change in the relative price of labor, output being held constant.* In the short run, capital is fixed, and therefore substitution in production between labor and capital *cannot* occur. In the long run, however, the firm can respond to a wage reduction by substituting the relatively less expensive labor in the production process for some types of capital. This fact means that the long-run response to a wage change will be greater than the short-run response. In other words, the long-run demand for labor will be more elastic than the short-run demand curve.

The Combined Effects

In Figure 5.5 we use these ideas to depict a long-run labor demand curve D_{LR}. Initially, suppose that the firm faces the short-run labor demand curve D_{SR} and also that the initial equilibrium wage rate and equilibrium quantity of labor are W_1 and Q as shown by point *a*. Now suppose that the wage rate declines from W_1 to W_2 resulting in an *output effect* that increases employment to Q_1 at *b*. In the long run, however, capital is variable, and therefore, a *substitution effect* also occurs that further increases the quantity of

FIGURE 5.5   **The Long-Run Labor Demand Curve**
A wage reduction from W_1 to W_2 increases the equilibrium short-run quantity of labor from Q to Q_1 *(output effect)*. In the long run, however, the firm also substitutes labor for capital, resulting in a *substitution effect* of Q_1 Q_2. The long-run labor demand curve therefore results from both effects and is found by connecting points such as *a* and *c*.

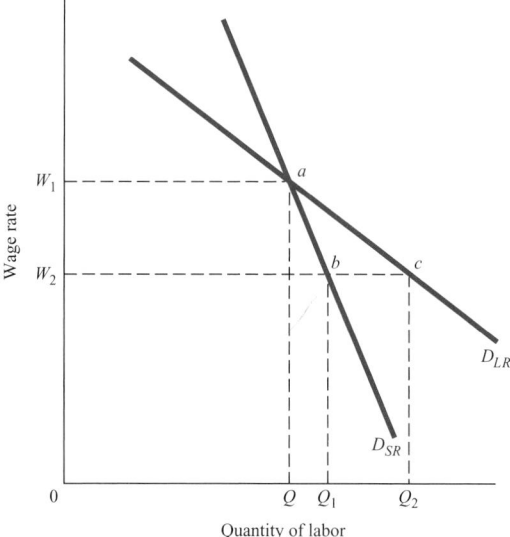

labor employed to Q_2 at point *c*. Although the short-run adjustment is from *a* to *b*, the additional long-run adjustment is from *b* to *c*. The locus of the long-run adjustment points *a* and *c* determines the location of the *long-run* demand for labor curve. As observed in Figure 5.5, the long-run curve D_{LR} is more elastic than the short-run labor demand curve.

Other Factors

Several other factors tend to make a firm's long-run labor demand curve more elastic than its short-run curve. Three such factors in particular deserve mention.

1 Product Demand

As we will explain shortly in our discussion of the determinants of the elasticity of labor demand, *product demand* is more elastic in the long run than in the short run, making the demand for labor more elastic over longer periods. Other things being equal, the greater the consumer response to a product price change, the greater the firm's employment response to a wage rate change.

2 Labor–Capital Interactions

Under production conditions described as "normal," a change in the quantity of one factor causes the marginal product of another factor to change in the same direction. This idea relates to the demand for labor as follows. Let's again assume that the wage rate for a particular type of labor falls, causing the quantity of labor demanded in the short run to rise. This increase in the quantity of labor itself becomes important to the long-run adjustment process: It increases the marginal product and hence the MRP of capital. Just as the MRP of labor *is* the firm's short-run demand for labor, the MRP of capital *is* the firm's short-run demand for capital (labor being constant). Given the price of capital, we would therefore expect more capital to be employed, which in turn will increase the marginal product and demand for labor. Thus the long-run employment response resulting from the wage decrease will be greater than the short-run response.

3 Technology

In the long run, the technology implicitly assumed constant when we constructed our short-run production function can be expected to change in response to major, permanent movements in relative factor prices. Investors and entrepreneurs direct their greatest effort toward discovering and implementing new technologies that reduce the need for relatively higher-priced inputs. When the price of labor falls relative to the price of capital, these efforts get channeled toward technologies that economize on the use of capital and that increase the use of labor. The long-run response to the wage rate decline therefore exceeds the short-run response.

Here's an important point: We have cast our entire discussion of the downward-sloping long-run labor demand curve in terms of a wage *decline.* You are urged to reinforce the conclusion that labor demand is more elastic in the long run than in the short run by analyzing the short- versus long-run effects of an *increase* in the wage rate.

5.1

5.1	**World of Work**	Why Has Manufacturing Employment Fallen?*

Recently there has been increasing concern about the dramatic drop in U.S. manufacturing employment. In 2006, 11 percent of workers were employed in manufacturing, down from 31 percent in 1950. The number of manufacturing workers has declined from 18.7 million in 1980 to 14.2 million in 2006.

There are four reasons for the decrease in manufacturing employment. First, consumer spending, in the United States as well as other industrialized countries, has shifted away from manufactured goods. In 2006, 43 percent of U.S. consumer spending was on goods. The corresponding figures for 1979 and 1950 were 53 percent and 67 percent. The likely reasons behind this shift are the rise in real wages and labor force participation of married women, which caused households to substitute purchased services for tasks previously done at home.

Second, U.S. manufacturing firms have been investing in more and higher-quality capital equipment to keep competitive in global markets. This investment has permitted them to increase their output and at the same time use fewer workers. Since 1979, the productivity of manufacturing workers has been rising at an annual rate of 3.3 percent, which is much greater than the 2 percent annual increase for overall nonfarm labor productivity.

Third, the expansion of international trade has changed the mix of goods produced in the United States. Gains from trade occur when countries specialize in goods they can produce more efficiently relative to other nations. The United States has specialized in goods that are produced using relatively more capital and skilled workers than other countries. As a result, employment has fallen in industries, such as apparel, that are labor-intensive and use less skilled workers.

Finally, U.S. manufacturers have increasingly used workers from temporary help agencies to handle short-term fluctuations in demand rather than hire permanent workers. These temporary workers are counted as service workers, not manufacturing workers. Also, manufacturing firms have hired service companies to provide support functions such as janitorial and payroll processing. The Congressional Budget Office estimates that 500,000 to 1 million of the 2.2 million decline in manufacturing employment between 1979 and 2000 resulted from the expansion of the use of temporary help workers.

* Based on Congressional Budget Office, "What Accounts for the Decline in Manufacturing Employment?" Economic and Budget Issue Brief, February 18, 2004. Updated statistics from **www.bls.gov** and **www.bea.gov.**

THE MARKET DEMAND FOR LABOR

We have now demonstrated that the MRP curve derives from the MP curve in the firm's zone of production and *is* the firm's short-run demand curve for labor. We also have established that a firm's long-run demand for labor is more elastic than its short-run demand. Let's next turn our attention to the market demand for labor. At first thought, we might reason that the total or *market demand for labor* of a particular type can be determined by simply summing (horizontally on a graph) the labor demand curves of all firms that employ this kind of labor. Thus if there were, say, 200 firms with labor demand curves identical to the firm portrayed in Table 5.2, we would simply multiply the amounts of labor demanded at the various wage rates by 200 and thereby determine the market demand curve. However, this simple process ignores an important aggregation problem. The problem arises because certain magnitudes (such as product price), which are correctly viewed as constant from the vantage point of the *individual firm,* must be treated as variable from the standpoint of the *entire market.*

To illustrate, let's suppose there are, say, 200 competitive firms, each with a labor demand curve identical to that shown earlier in Figure 5.2. Assume also that these firms are all producing a given product that they are selling in competition with one another. From the perspective of the *individual firm,* when the wage rate declines, the use of more labor will result in a *negligible* increase in the market supply of the product and, therefore, no change in product price. But because *all firms* experience the lower wage rate and respond by hiring more workers and increasing their outputs, there will be a *substantial* increase in the supply of the product. This change in supply will reduce the product price. This point is critical because, as we showed earlier in Table 5.2, product price is a determinant of each firm's labor demand curve. Specifically, a lower product price will reduce MRP and shift the labor demand curve of each firm to the left. This implies that the market demand for labor is in fact *less elastic* than that yielded by a simple summation of each firm's labor demand curve.[5]

Consider Figure 5.6, in which the diagram on the left (a) shows labor demand for one of the 200 firms and the diagram on the right (b) shows the market demand for labor. The individual firm is initially in equilibrium at point *c,* where the wage rate is W_1 and employment is Q_1. The labor demand curve D_{L1} is based on a product price of $2.00, as shown in column 4 of Table 5.2. If the wage rate falls to W_2, ceteris paribus (other things being equal), the firm would now find it profitable to move to a new equilibrium at e', where it would hire Q'_2, workers. But our ceteris paribus assumption does *not* hold in the context of a number of firms that are hiring this kind of labor to produce the same product. The lower wage induces *all* of the firms to hire more labor. This increases output or product supply, which then reduces product price. This lower price—say $1.60 as compared to the original $2.00—feeds back to the labor demand curve for each firm, shifting those curves leftward as indicated by the move from D_{L1} to D_{L2} in Figure 5.6(a). In effect, each firm then recalculates its MRP or labor demand using the new lower price. Thus each firm achieves equilibrium at point *e* by hiring only Q_2, as opposed to Q'_2, workers at the wage rate W_2. The market labor demand curve in Figure 5.6(b) is therefore *not* curve CE', the simple horizontal summation of the demand for labor curves for all 200 firms. Rather, it is the horizontal summation of all quantities, such as Q_1 at wage rate W_1 on D_{L1}, *and* the summation of all quantities, such as Q_2 at wage rate W_2, that fall on the "price-adjusted" market demand curve that cuts through points CE in Figure 5.6(b). As shown there, the correct price-adjusted market demand curve CE is less elastic than the incorrect "simple summation" CE' curve.

---

[5] If *all* employers are monopolists in their distinct product markets, our conclusion does not hold. As pointed out in the discussion of Figure 5.3, the monopolist's labor demand curve already incorporates the declines in product price that accompany output increases. Thus to get the market labor demand curve, one can sum the labor demand curves of the monopolists.

FIGURE 5.6   **The Market Demand Curve for Labor**

The market demand curve for labor is less elastic than the simple horizontal summation of the labor demand curves of the individual employers. A lower wage induces all firms to hire more labor and produce more output, causing the supply of the product to increase. The resulting decline in product price shifts the firms' labor demand curves to the left. Consequently, total employment rises from C to E in graph (b), rather than from C to E'.

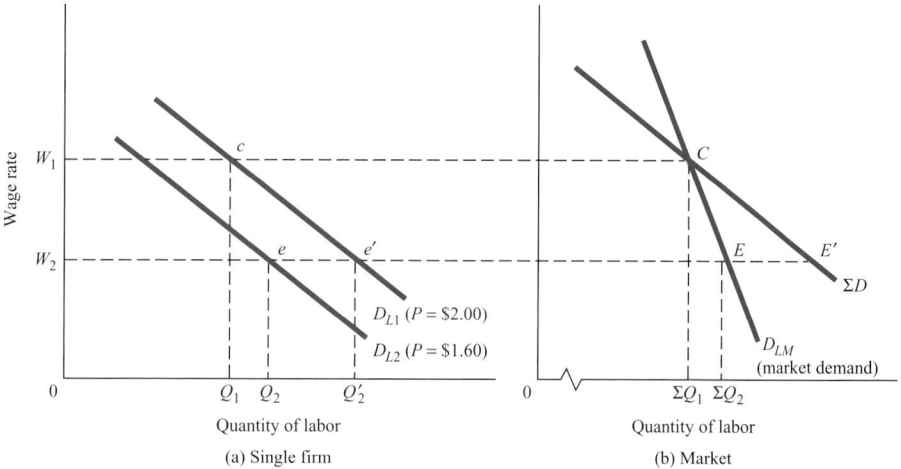

(a) Single firm

(b) Market

5.2

Quick Review

- The long-run demand curve for labor is more elastic than the short-run curve because in the long run there are both output and substitution effects; only an output effect occurs in the short run.

- The output effect of a wage rate change is the change in employment resulting from a change in the employer's costs of production; the substitution effect is the employment change caused by the altered price of labor relative to the price of capital.

- The market demand curve for labor is less elastic than the simple summation of the labor demand curves of individual employers; by inducing all firms to hire more labor and produce more output, the lower wage increases product supply, reduces product price, and lowers each firm's MRP.

Your Turn

In the 1970s, the United Automobile Workers greatly increased wage rates in the American auto industry. Referring to the output and substitution effects, explain how these high wages might have contributed to the decline in auto employment experienced by General Motors, Ford, and Chrysler in the 1980s. (*Answer:* See page 597.)

5.2

| 5.2 | **World of Work** | Comparative Advantage and the Demand for Labor |

As it applies to international trade, the principle of comparative advantage states that total output will be greatest when each good is produced by the nation with the lower opportunity cost. For example, suppose that in the United States 15 units of chemicals must be sacrificed to produce 1 unit of raincoats, whereas in South Korea 10 units of chemicals must be sacrificed for each unit of raincoats. The opportunity cost of a unit of raincoats in South Korea thus is lower (= 10 units of chemicals) than it is in the United States (= 15 units of chemicals). South Korea, therefore, should specialize in raincoats. Similarly, the United States should specialize in producing chemicals because it has lower opportunity costs (= 1/15 raincoats) than South Korea (= 1/10 raincoats). South Korea will specialize in raincoats and trade them for chemicals; the United States will specialize in chemicals and trade them for raincoats.

How will this specialization and trade affect labor demand in the United States and South Korea? Most obviously, the demand for workers employed in chemical production will rise in the United States, and the demand for workers who produce raincoats will fall. The opposite outcomes will occur in South Korea. Because international trade causes both positive and negative shifts in the demand for labor, the impact on the total demand for labor in each country is uncertain. It is clear, however, that specialization will increase the total output available in the two nations. Specialization promotes the expansion of relatively efficient industries that have a comparative advantage and indirectly causes the contraction of relatively inefficient industries. This means that specialization shifts resources—including labor—toward more productive uses. If the total number of workers remains constant in each nation, each worker on average will be able to buy more output. That is, either wages will rise or the prices of goods will fall so that real earnings (= nominal earnings/price level) will increase.

It is important to note that comparative advantage, not differences in wage rates between two nations, drives international trade. Low wage rates in South Korea do *not* give it a special international advantage. High American wage rates do *not* condemn the United States to be a net importer of goods. Even if low wages in South Korea would have permitted it to produce chemicals more cheaply in dollar terms than the United States, South Korea would still benefit by specializing in raincoats and buying chemicals from the United States. By so doing, South Korea could reduce its true costs of obtaining chemicals (raincoats forgone), just as trade permits the United States to get raincoats at a lower true cost (chemicals forgone) than if it had to use domestic resources for this purpose.

ELASTICITY OF LABOR DEMAND

We have concluded that the long-run demand curve is more elastic than the short-run curve and that the market demand for labor is less elastic than a curve derived by a simple summation of labor demand curves of individual firms. These references to elasticity raise an important unanswered question: What determines the *sensitivity* of employment to a change in the wage rate? That is, what determines the ***elasticity of labor demand?*** Let's examine this topic in more detail.

The Elasticity Coefficient

The sensitivity of the quantity of labor demanded to wage rate changes is measured by the *wage elasticity coefficient E_d*, as shown in Equation (5.3).

$$E_d = \frac{\text{percentage change in quantity of labor demanded}}{\text{percentage change in the wage rate}} \quad \textbf{(5.3)}$$

Because the wage rate and the quantity of labor demanded are inversely related, the elasticity coefficient will always be negative. By convention, the minus sign is taken as understood and therefore is ignored. Also, you should be aware that percentage calculations present a "reversibility" problem. For example, a wage rate increase from $5 to $10 is a *100 percent* increase, whereas a wage decrease from $10 to $5 is only a *50 percent* decline. Economists therefore use the *averages* of the two wages and the *averages* of the two quantities as the bases when computing wage elasticity coefficients. In terms of our previous example, a wage change from $10 to $5 and one from $5 to $10 are each considered to be 67 percent changes {= 5/[($10 + $5)/2]}.

The equation that incorporates the averaging technique when computing wage elasticity is known as a *midpoints formula* and is shown as Equation (5.4).

$$E_d = \frac{\text{change in quantity}}{\text{sum of quantities}/2} \div \frac{\text{change in wage}}{\text{sum of wages}/2} \quad \textbf{(5.4)}$$

Demand is *elastic*—meaning that employers are quite responsive to a change in wage rates—if a given percentage change in the wage rate results in a larger percentage change in the quantity of labor demanded. In this case the absolute value of the elasticity coefficient will be greater than 1. Conversely, demand is *inelastic* when a given percentage change in the wage rate causes a smaller percentage change in the amount of labor demanded. In this instance E_d will be less than 1, indicating that employers are relatively insensitive to changes in wage rates. Finally, demand is *unit elastic*—meaning that the coefficient is 1—when a given percentage in the wage rate causes an equal percentage change in the amount of labor demanded.

The Total Wage Bill Rules

You may recall from basic economics that we can determine the price elasticity of demand for a product by observing what happens to total revenue when product price changes. Similar rules, called the *total wage bill rules*, are used to assess the wage elasticity of demand.

Consider Figure 5.7, which displays two separate labor demand curves D_{L1} and D_{L2}. Suppose initially that the wage rate is $8, at which the firm hires five units of labor. The *total wage bill,* defined as $W \times Q$, in this case is $40 (= $8 × 5). This amount also happens to be the *total wage income* as viewed by the five workers. Now let's suppose the wage rate rises to $12. This increase produces two opposing effects on the wage bill. The higher wage rate increases the wage bill, but the decrease in employment reduces it. With D_{L1}, the firm responds to the $4 higher wage rate by reducing the amount of labor employed from five to two units. The wage increase boosts the wage bill by $8 (= $4 × 2), while the decline in employment lowers it by

FIGURE 5.7 **The Total Wage Bill Rules**

If a change in the wage rate causes the total wage bill ($W \times Q$) to change in the opposite direction, then labor demand is elastic. This is the case along the $8 to $12 segment of D_{L1}, where the total wage bill falls from $40 (= 8×5) to $24 (= 12×2) when the wage rate rises from $8 to $12. In the case of labor demand D_{L2}, however, this same wage increase causes the total wage bill to rise from $40 to $48 (= 12×4). This second situation supports the generalization that when demand is inelastic, the wage rate and the total wage bill change in the same direction.

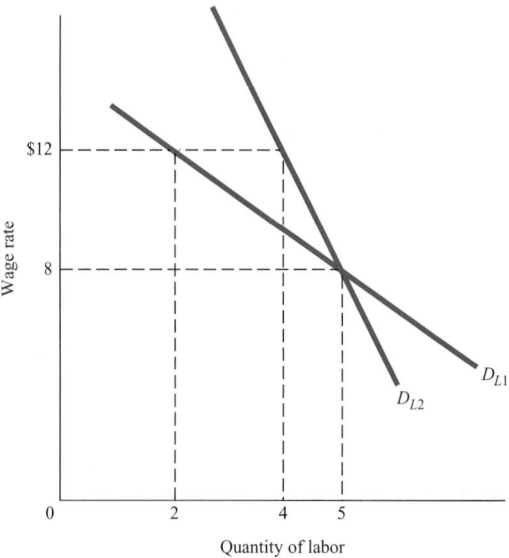

Quantity of labor

$24 (= 8×3). The net effect is that the wage bill falls by $16 from $40 (= 8×5) to $24 (= 12×2). *When labor demand is elastic, a change in the wage rate causes the total wage bill to move in the opposite direction.*

On the other hand, notice that for labor demand D_{L2}, the $4 higher wage adds more to the wage bill ($4 \times 4 = 16) than the one-unit decline in employment subtracts ($8 \times 1 = 8), causing the total wage bill to rise from $40 (= 8×5) to $48 (= 12×4). *When labor demand is inelastic, a change in the wage rate causes the total wage bill to move in the same direction.* Finally, *where labor demand is unit elastic (= 1), a change in the wage rate leaves the total wage bill unchanged.*

We can confirm the results of the total wage bill tests by using the midpoints formula [Equation (5.4)] to compute elasticity coefficients for the appropriate segments of D_{L1} and D_{L2} in Figure 5.7. The $8 to $12 wage change is a 40 percent increase {$= $4/[($8 + $12)/2]$}, whereas we see from D_{L1} that the three-unit change in quantity is an 86 percent decline {$= 4/[(5 + 2)/2]$}. Because the percentage decrease in quantity exceeds the percentage increase in the wage, labor demand is elastic (the wage bill falls as the wage increases). In the case of D_{L2}, the same 40 percent rise in the wage produces only a 22 percent employment decline {$= 1/[(5 + 4)/2]$}; hence demand is inelastic (the wage bill increases as the wage rises).

Determinants of Elasticity

What determines the elasticity of the market demand for labor? The theoretical generalizations are as follows.[6]

1 Elasticity of Product Demand

Because the demand for labor is a derived demand, the elasticity of demand for labor's output will influence the elasticity of demand for labor. Other things being equal, *the greater the price elasticity of product demand, the greater the elasticity of labor demand.* It is simple to see why this is so. If the wage rate falls, the cost of producing the product will decline. This cuts the price of the product and increases the quantity demanded. If the elasticity of product demand is great, that increase in the quantity of the product demanded will be large and thus necessitate a large increase in the quantity of labor to produce that additional output. This implies an elastic demand for labor. But if the demand for the product is inelastic, the increase in the amount of the product demanded will be small, as will be the increase in the quantity of labor demanded. This suggests that the demand for labor would be inelastic.

This generalization has two noteworthy implications. First, other things being equal, the greater the monopoly power an individual firm possesses in the product market, the less elastic is its demand for labor. This is confirmed by Figures 5.2 and 5.3, discussed previously. Recall that in Figure 5.2 the firm is selling its product in a perfectly competitive market, implying that it is a price taker facing a perfectly elastic product demand curve. The resulting demand for labor curve slopes downward solely because of diminishing returns. Contrast that curve to the one for the imperfectly competitive seller shown in Figure 5.3. This firm's product demand curve is less elastic, as evidenced by marginal revenue being less than price (Table 5.3). Thus the labor demand curve in Figure 5.3 also is less elastic; it slopes downward not only because of diminishing marginal productivity but also because of the less than perfectly elastic product demand, meaning that product price falls with increased output.

A second implication is that labor demand will be more elastic in the long run than in the short run. Wage elasticity tends to be greater in the long run because price elasticity of product demand is greater in the long run. Consumers are often creatures of habit and only slowly change their buying behavior in response to a price change. Coffee drinkers may not immediately reduce their consumption when the price of coffee rises; but given sufficient time, some may acquire a taste for tea. Another factor at work here is that some products are used mainly in conjunction with costly durable goods. For example, when the price of electricity rises, people who have electric furnaces and other appliances do not respond by greatly reducing their consumption of electricity. But as time transpires, the elasticity of the demand for electricity—*and the elasticity of the derived demand for workers in that industry*—become greater. People eventually replace their electric furnaces and water heaters with devices that use natural gas, solar energy, wood, or even coal.

---

[6] These generalizations were developed in 1890 by Alfred Marshall in his *Principles of Economics* (London: Macmillan Publishing Company, 1890) and refined by John R. Hicks, *The Theory of Wages,* 2nd ed. (New York: St. Martin's Press, 1966), pp. 241–47. For this reason they are often referred to as the "Hicks–Marshall rules of derived demand."

2 Ratio of Labor Costs to Total Costs

In general, all other things being the same, *the larger the proportion of total production costs accounted for by labor, the greater will be the elasticity of demand for labor.*[7] The rationale here is straightforward. Compare these two cases. *Case one:* If labor costs were the only production cost—that is, if the ratio of labor to total costs were 100 percent—then a 20 percent increase in the wage rate would increase unit costs by 20 percent. Given product demand, this large cost increase eventually would cause a considerable increase in product price, a sizable reduction in sales of output, and therefore a large decline in the employment of labor. *Case two:* If labor costs were only 10 percent of total cost, then the same 20 percent increase in the wage rate would increase total unit costs by only 2 percent. Assuming the same product demand as in case one, this relatively small cost increase will generate a more modest decline in employment. Case one implies a more elastic demand for labor than case two. The same 20 percent wage increase caused a larger percentage decline in employment in case one than in case two.

Service industries such as education, temporary workers, and building maintenance exemplify situations in which firms' labor costs are a large percentage of total costs. In these industries wage increases translate into large cost increases, resulting in relatively elastic labor demand curves. Conversely, highly capital-intensive industries such as electricity generation and brewing are examples of markets in which labor costs are small relative to total costs. Labor demand curves in these industries are relatively inelastic.

3 Substitutability of Other Inputs

Other things being equal, *the greater the substitutability of other inputs for labor, the greater will be the elasticity of demand for labor.* If technology is such that capital is readily substitutable for labor, then a small increase in the wage rate will elicit a substantial increase in the amount of machinery used and a large decline in the amount of labor employed. Conversely, a small drop in the wage rate will induce a large substitution of labor for capital. The demand for labor will tend to be elastic in this case. In other instances, technology may dictate that a certain amount of labor is more or less indispensable to the production process; that is, the substitution of capital for labor is highly constrained. In the extreme, the production process may involve fixed proportions; for example, two airline pilots—no more and no less—may be required to fly a commercial airliner. In this case, a change in the wage rate will have little short-run effect on the number of pilots employed, and this implies an inelastic demand for labor.

It is worth noting that *time* plays an important role in the input substitution process, just as it does in the previously discussed process through which consumer goods are substituted for one another. The longer the period of elapsed time since a wage rate was changed, the more elastic are labor demand curves. For example, a firm's truck drivers may obtain a substantial wage increase with little or no immediate decline in employment. But over time, as the firm's trucks wear out and are replaced, the company may purchase larger trucks and thereby be able to deliver the same total output with significantly fewer drivers. Alternatively, as the firm's trucks depreciate, it might turn to entirely different means of transportation for delivery.

[7] *Technical note:* This proposition assumes that the product demand elasticity is greater than the elasticity of substitution between capital and labor. See Hicks, op. cit., pp. 241–47.

4 Supply Elasticity of Other Inputs

The fourth determinant of the elasticity of demand for labor is simply an extension of the third determinant. The generalization is that other things being equal, *the greater the elasticity of the supply of other inputs, the greater the elasticity of demand for labor.* In discussing our third generalization, we implicitly assumed that the prices of nonlabor inputs—such as capital—are unaffected by a change in the demand for them. But this may not be realistic.

To illustrate, assume once again that an increase in the wage rate prompts the firm to substitute capital for labor. This increase in the demand for capital will leave the price of capital unchanged only in the special case where the supply of capital is perfectly elastic. But let's suppose the supply of capital curve slopes upward, so that an increase in demand would increase its price. Furthermore, the less elastic the supply of capital, the greater the increase in the price of capital in response to any given increase in demand. Any resulting change in the price of capital is important because it will retard or dampen the substitution of capital for labor and reduce the elasticity of demand for labor. More specifically, if the supply of capital is inelastic, a given increase in the demand for capital will cause a large increase in the price of capital, greatly retarding the substitution process. This implies that the demand for labor will be inelastic. Conversely, if the supply of capital is highly elastic, the same increase in demand will cause only a small increase in the price of capital, dampening the substitution process only slightly. This suggests that the demand for labor will be elastic.

Estimates of Wage Elasticity

Hamermesh has summarized and compared more than 100 studies of labor demand and has concluded that the overall long-run labor demand elasticity in the United States is 1.0.[8] This coefficient implies a unitary elastic labor demand curve, which means that for every 10 percent change in the wage rate, employment changes in the opposite direction by 10 percent. Hamermesh concludes that about two-thirds of the long-run elasticity response takes the form of the output effect, with the other third consisting of the substitution effect. Other studies generally support Hamermesh's estimates, although problems of statistical design and incomplete data make research in this area difficult.

Studies also reveal that labor demand elasticities vary greatly by industry, type of labor, and occupational group. For example, Clark and Freeman estimate that the wage elasticity for all U.S. manufacturing is about 1.[9] Ashenfelter and Ehrenberg find that the wage elasticity in public education is 1.06.[10] Other studies show that the elasticity of labor demand is higher for teenagers than for adults, is greater for production workers than for nonproduction workers, is higher for low-skilled workers than for high-skilled workers, and is larger in nondurable goods industries than in durable goods industries.

[8] Daniel S. Hamermesh, *Labor Demand* (Princeton, NJ: Princeton University Press, 1993), chap. 3.
[9] Kim B. Clark and Richard B. Freeman, "How Elastic Is the Demand for Labor?" *Review of Economics and Statistics,* November 1980, pp. 509–20.
[10] Orley Ashenfelter and Ronald G. Ehrenberg, "The Demand for Labor in the Public Sector," in Daniel Hamermesh (ed.), *Labor in the Public and Nonprofit Sectors* (Princeton, NJ: Princeton University Press, 1975), p. 71.

Significance of Wage Elasticity

Of what practical significance are such estimates of labor demand elasticity? The answer is that private and public policies might be greatly affected by the size of the wage rate–employment trade-off suggested by the elasticity estimates.

In the private sphere, a union's bargaining strategy might be influenced by the elasticity of labor demand for its workers. We might expect a union of higher-skilled engineers in the aerospace industry (where the demand for labor is inelastic) to bargain more aggressively for higher wages than a union of restaurant workers (where the demand for labor is elastic). The reason? A given percentage increase in wage rates will generate a smaller decline in employment for the higher-skilled engineers than for the lower-skilled restaurant workers.

Similarly, a union will wish to know something about its employer's wage elasticity before agreeing to a wage reduction purportedly necessary to save jobs threatened by intense import competition. The more elastic the employer's demand for labor, the greater the likelihood that the union will agree to a wage concession. Under conditions of elastic labor demand, the wage cut will be more effective in preserving jobs than when demand is inelastic.

The effectiveness and impact of government policies often depend on the elasticity of labor demand. The employment consequences of a rise in the minimum wage rate, for example, will depend on the elasticity of demand for workers affected by the change. Similarly, the effectiveness of a program providing wage subsidies to employers who hire disadvantaged workers will depend on the elasticity of labor demand in the industries employing low-skilled labor. The more elastic the labor demand, the greater will be the increase in employment resulting from the wage subsidies.

DETERMINANTS OF DEMAND FOR LABOR

The movement along a labor demand curve implied by the concept of elasticity is quite distinct from an increase or decrease in labor demand. The latter imply shifts of the demand for labor curve either rightward or leftward. What factors cause such shifts? The major ***determinants of labor demand*** are product demand, productivity, the number of employers, and the prices of other resources.

Product Demand

A change in the demand for the product that a particular type of labor is producing, all else being equal, will shift the labor demand curve in the same direction. For example, suppose that in Table 5.2 and Figure 5.2 an increase in product demand occurs, causing the product price to rise from $2 to $3. If we plotted the *new* MRP data onto Figure 5.2, we would observe that the demand for labor curve shifted rightward. A decline in the demand for the product would likewise shift the labor demand curve leftward.

Productivity

Assuming that it does not cause a fully offsetting change in product price, a change in the marginal product of labor (MP) will shift the labor demand curve in the same direction.

Again return to Table 5.2 and Figure 5.2. Suppose technology improves, shifting the entire production function (column 2 in relationship to column 1 in Table 5.2) upward. More concretely, let's assume a doubling of the total product produced by each worker in combination with the fixed capital. Clearly MP in column 3 and consequently MRP in column 6 would increase. If the new MRP data were plotted in Figure 5.2, we would observe that labor demand had shifted rightward. Conversely, a decline in productivity would shift the labor demand curve leftward.

Number of Employers

Recall that we found the market demand for labor in Figure 5.6 by summing horizontally the "price-adjusted" labor demand curves of individual employers. *Assuming no change in employment by other firms, a change in the number of firms employing a particular type of labor will change the demand for labor in the same direction.* In terms of Figure 5.6, D_{LR} will shift rightward if additional firms enter this labor market to hire workers; it will shift leftward if firms leave, all else being equal.

Prices of Other Resources

Changes in the prices of other inputs such as capital, land, and raw materials can shift the demand curve for labor. To illustrate this idea, we focus solely on changes in the price of capital. Normally labor and capital are *substitutes in production,* meaning that a given quantity of output can be produced with much capital and little labor *or* much labor and little capital. Now suppose the price of capital falls. Our task is to determine the impact of this price decline on the demand for labor.

Gross Substitutes[11]

If labor and capital are **gross substitutes,** the decline in the price of capital will *decrease* the demand for labor. *Gross substitutes are inputs such that when the price of one changes, the demand for the other changes in the same direction.* This correctly implies that here the substitution effect outweighs the output effect. The decline in the price of capital lowers the marginal cost of producing the output, which taken alone would result in an expansion of output and an *increase* in the demand for labor (the output effect). But the lower-priced capital is substituted for labor, which taken alone would *reduce* the demand for labor (the substitution effect). Where labor and capital are gross substitutes, this latter substitution effect swamps the output effect, and labor demand falls. For example, the decline in the price of security equipment used by businesses to protect against illegal entries has reduced the demand for night guards.

Gross Complements

If, on the other hand, labor and capital are **gross complements,** a decline in the price of capital will *increase* the demand for labor. *Gross complements are inputs such that when the price of one changes, the demand for the other changes in the opposite direction,*

---

[11] The term *gross* as a modifier of *substitutes* and *complements* in this discussion is in keeping with terminology used in advanced economics. As used here, the concepts are *gross* because they encompass both substitution and output effects. So-called *net* substitutes and complements, on the other hand, focus only on substitution effects, holding output constant.

In this case of a decline in the price of capital, the output effect, outweighs the substitution effect, and the demand for labor increases. Restated, the fall in the price of capital reduces production costs and increases sales so much that the resulting increased demand for labor overwhelms the substitution of capital for labor occurring in the production process. When labor and capital are gross complements, a decrease (increase) in the price of capital increases (decreases) the demand for labor. For example, the decline in the price of computers over the past three decades increased the demand for computer programmers.

Thus far we have assumed that labor and capital are substitutes in production. What can we conclude about the impact of a change in the price of capital on the demand for labor in the extreme case in which labor and capital are *not* substitutable in the production process? Suppose instead that labor and capital are *pure complements in production,* meaning they are used in direct proportion to one another in producing the output. An example would be crane operators and cranes; more cranes require more operators on a one-for-one basis. The decline in the price of capital in this instance will unambiguously increase the demand for labor. Pure complements in production are always gross complements because there is no substitution effect. The lower price of capital will reduce the firm's marginal cost and cause it to increase its output, bolstering its demand for labor.

Remember these generalizations: *(1) A change in the price of a resource that is a substitute in production for labor may change the demand for labor either in the same or in the opposite direction, depending on whether the resources are gross substitutes or gross complements, respectively; (2) a change in the price of a resource that is a pure complement in production (used in a fixed proportion with labor) will change the demand for labor in the opposite direction—it will always be a gross complement.*

5.3

Quick Review

- Wage elasticity measures the sensitivity of the amount of labor demanded to wage rate changes; it is the percentage change in quantity of labor demanded divided by the percentage change in price.

- When changes in the wage rate cause the wage bill ($W \times Q$) to move in the opposite direction, labor demand is elastic; when the wage bill remains constant, labor demand is unit elastic; and when the wage bill moves in the same direction, labor demand is inelastic.

- The major determinants of wage elasticity are the *(a)* elasticity of product demand, *(b)* ratio of labor costs to total costs, *(c)* substitutability of other inputs, and *(d)* supply elasticity of other inputs.

- The factors that shift the labor demand curve include *(a)* changes in product demand, *(b)* changes in labor productivity, *(c)* changes in the number of employers, and *(d)* changes in the prices of other inputs.

Your Turn

Suppose the price of capital falls relative to the wage rate and, as a result, the demand for labor increases. Are these inputs gross substitutes, or are they gross complements? What can you infer about the relative strengths of the output and substitution effects? (*Answers:* See page 597.)

5.2 Global Perspective

Self-Employment as a Percentage of Total Employment

The percentage of workers who are self-employed in the United States is the lowest among the major industrialized countries.

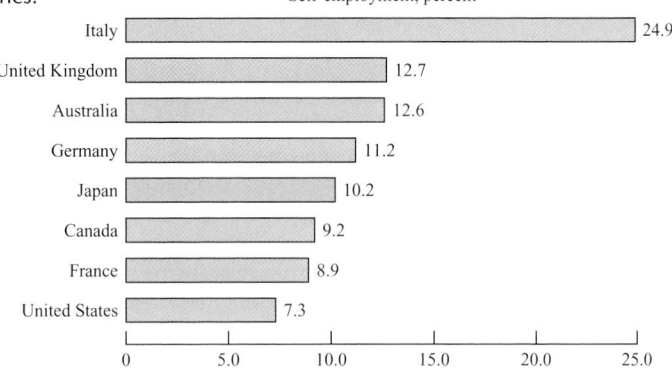

Self-employment, percent

Country	Percent
Italy	24.9
United Kingdom	12.7
Australia	12.6
Germany	11.2
Japan	10.2
Canada	9.2
France	8.9
United States	7.3

Source: Organization for Economic Cooperation and Development, *OECD in Figures, 2006–2007 Edition.*

All data are for 2005.

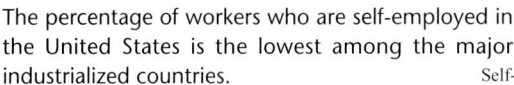

5.3 Global Perspective

Temporary Employment as a Percentage of Total Employment

The United States has a low rate of employment in jobs with time-limited contracts relative to other countries.

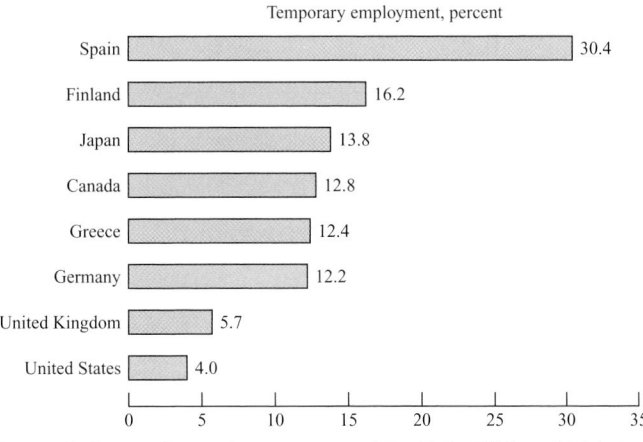

Temporary employment, percent

Country	Percent
Spain	30.4
Finland	16.2
Japan	13.8
Canada	12.8
Greece	12.4
Germany	12.2
United Kingdom	5.7
United States	4.0

Source: Organization for Economic Cooperation and Development (http://www.oecd.org). Data are for 2005, except the United States, which is for 2001, and Germany and Japan, which are for 2003.

5.3 World of Work

Offshore Outsourcing of White-Collar Jobs*

In recent years, there has been increasing anxiety about foreign outsourcing: work done for a company by foreigners instead of its original workers. One well-publicized study concluded that 11 percent of U.S. jobs are at risk of being sent abroad. These jobs are mainly service jobs such as data entry clerks, call center operators, and computer programmers and operators. Another analysis projects that 3.3 million jobs will leave the United States by 2015. In 2004, concern about outsourcing became an election issue and led to a federal law banning the outsourcing of federal contracts overseas.

Academic researchers argue that the concern about overseas outsourcing is exaggerated—and perhaps totally unwarranted. They point out that the potential loss of 3.3 million jobs is small relative to the size of the U.S. labor market. About 8 million U.S. jobs are eliminated on average in any three-month period. But over the long term, more jobs are created than destroyed. Between 1995 and 2005, the number of U.S. workers rose by 17 million, even though many jobs disappeared and some were outsourced abroad.

Second, the jobs threatened with elimination usually are low-skilled ones that pay less than the average U.S. wage. These less skilled jobs may face elimination through technological change, regardless of whether they are outsourced overseas or not. For example, call center operators are increasingly being replaced with sophisticated automated phone responses.

Third, Catherine Mann argues that outsourcing may increase employment in the United States. She points out that outsourcing reduces production costs, which helps spread new technology and encourages job-creating investment. She estimates that trade and globalized production lowered the costs of manufacturing computer hardware by 10 to 30 percent. These lower prices raised productivity growth and increased GDP by $230 billion between 1995 and 2002.

* Based on "The Great Hollowing-Out Myth," *The Economist,* February 21, 2004, pp. 27–29; Jacob F. Kirkegaard, "Outsourcing Stains on the White-Collar?" Institute for International Economics Working Paper, June 2003; and Catherine L. Mann, "Globalization of IT Services and White Collar Jobs: The Next Wave of Productivity Growth," Institute for International Economics Policy Brief 03-11, December 2003. Updated in **www.bls.gov.**

REAL-WORLD APPLICATIONS

The concepts of labor demand and the elasticity of labor demand have great practical significance, as seen in the following examples.

Textile and Apparel Industries

In 1973 there were 2.4 million textile and apparel workers; by 2004, this figure had dropped to 700,000 workers. An additional 320,000 workers are expected to lose their job by 2014. Several factors help explain this dramatic decline in jobs. First, foreign competition, due to decreased trade barriers, has reduced the demand for American textiles and apparel. The share of total American textile and apparel sales accounted for by domestic producers has fallen from 95 percent in 1970 to less than 60 percent today.

Another factor has been the spread of automation in textile and apparel manufacturing. Industrial robots and assembly-line labor are gross substitutes, meaning that lower prices for robots have produced substitution effects exceeding output effects. The net effect has been a decline in the demand for textile and apparel workers. Coupled with the reduced demand for the product, the substitution of robots for workers has sharply reduced employment in these industries.[12]

Fast-Food Workers

In the past several years, McDonald's and other fast-food establishments have undertaken advertising campaigns to attract homemakers and older people to work in their restaurants. One important reason for these efforts has been the rapid increase in the demand for fast-food workers. The labor force participation rate of women and the number of two-worker families has increased, raising the opportunity cost of time (recall the Becker model in Chapter 3). In Becker's terms, people have substituted goods (restaurant meals) for time (home-prepared meals). The growing demand for restaurant meals has increased the demand for fast-food workers. Because the labor supply of traditional fast-food workers—teenagers—has not kept pace, many restaurants are now recruiting homemakers and semiretired workers.

Personal Computers

The last decade has seen a remarkable drop in the average price of personal computers and an equally amazing rise in the computing power of the typical machine. The effects of these developments on labor demand have been pervasive. For example, the demand for workers in some segments of the computer industry has significantly increased. Between 1990 and 2005, employment in the computer systems design industry (programming and software) expanded at an annual 8 percent growth rate. Dell Corporation, which was founded in 1984, boasted 75,100 workers in 2006. Microsoft, a major producer of software, employed 71,000 people in 2006, up from 476 workers in 1983.

In some offices, personal computers have been gross substitutes for labor, thus reducing the demand for labor and allowing these firms to use fewer workers to produce their outputs. But in other instances, computers and labor have proven to be gross complements. The decline in computer prices has reduced production costs to the extent that product prices have dropped, product sales have increased, and the derived demand for workers has risen. Also, keyboard personnel and computers are pure complements. Thus there is no substitution effect; a keyboard worker is needed for each computer.

Today 77 million people work with personal computers at least sometime during the day. Krueger has estimated that workers who use computers earn 10 to 15 percent more than otherwise similar workers who do not use this technology.[13]

---

[12] For more about employment trends in the textile and apparel industries, see Mark Mittelhauser, "Employment Trends in Textiles and Apparel, 1973–2005," *Monthly Labor Review,* August 1997, pp. 24–35.

[13] Alan B. Krueger, "How Computers Have Changed the Wage Structure: Evidence from Microdata, 1984–1989," *Quarterly Journal of Economics,* February 1993, pp. 33–60. For additional evidence regarding the impact of computers on wages, see David H. Autor, Lawrence F. Katz, and Alan B. Krueger, "Computing Inequality: Have Computers Changed the Labor Market?" *Quarterly Journal of Economics,* November 1998, pp. 1169–1213.

<table>
<tr><td>**5.4**</td><td>**World of Work**</td><td>Occupational Employment Trends</td></tr>
</table>

Labor demand shifts are important because they alter wage rates and employment in specific occupations. An increase in labor demand for a particular occupation will raise employment in the occupation, and declines in labor demand will lower it. For example, let's examine occupations that are facing increases in labor demand (wage rates are discussed in the next chapter).

The table below lists the 10 fastest-growing occupations, in percentage terms, for 2004–2014. Not surprisingly, service occupations dominate the list. Overall, the demand for service workers is growing faster than the demand for manufacturing, construction, and mining workers.

Seven of the top 10 fastest-growing occupations are related to health care. The rising demand for home health aides, medical assistants, physician assistants, physical therapy assistants, dental hygienists, dental

assistants, and personal and home care aides comes from several factors: (a) the aging of the U.S. population with increased extended illnesses; (b) rising income, which has led to greater spending on health care; (c) the rising rate of private and public insurance, which enables more people to buy health care.

Three of the fastest-growing occupations are related to computers. The increase in demand for network systems and data communications analysts, computer software applications engineers, and computer systems software engineers is related to expanding demand for computers and the Internet. The demand increase is also due to the substantial rise in the productivity of computers that these workers use on their jobs. In addition, the falling prices of computers have created an output effect that outweighs the substitution effect, which also increases the demand for these workers.

The 10 Fastest-Growing Occupations in Percentage Terms, 2004–2014

Occupation	Employment (Thousands of Jobs)		Percentage Increase
	2004	2014	
Home health aides	624	974	56%
Network systems and data communications analysts	231	357	55
Medical assistants	387	589	52
Physician assistants	62	93	50
Computer applications software engineers	460	682	48
Physical therapy assistants	59	85	44
Dental hygienists	158	226	43
Computer systems software engineers	340	486	43
Dental assistants	267	382	43
Personal and home care aides	701	988	41

Source: Bureau of Labor Statistics, "Employment Projections" (stats.bls.gov).

Minimum Wage

As we detail in Chapter 13, federal law requires that covered workers earn an hourly wage rate of at least $5.15 until July 2007, when it became $5.85, and rising in steps in 2008 and 2009 until it reaches $7.25. Critics contend that an above-equilibrium minimum wage moves employers upward along their downsloping labor demand curves and causes unemployment, particularly among teenage workers. Workers who remain employed at the minimum wage will receive higher incomes than otherwise. The amount of income lost by job losers and the income gained by those who keep their jobs will depend on the elasticity of demand for minimum-wage labor. Studies have generally found that a 10 percent increase in the minimum wage reduces employment from 1 to 3 percent, meaning that demand is inelastic. Thus the minimum wage increases the wage income to minimum-wage workers as a group (increases the wage bill). The case made by critics of the minimum wage would be stronger if the demand for low-wage labor were elastic.

Bank Tellers

Between 1989 and 2000, 81,000 bank tellers lost their jobs, and 28,000 of the remaining bank tellers could lose their jobs by 2008. Three factors have been causing this employment decline. First, banks have been replacing tellers with automated teller machines (ATMs) because ATMs serve customers more cost-effectively than tellers. Between 1980 and 2005, the number of ATMs rose from 18,500 to 396,000. This trend is projected to continue. Second, new technology is letting customers bank by telephone and personal computer; thus banks can further substitute electronic machinery for bank tellers. Third, the direct deposit of paychecks and benefit checks is increasing and will further reduce the demand for bank tellers.

Contingent Workers

A dramatic labor market change of recent years has been that many employers have reduced the size of their core workforce. Simultaneously, they have increased the use of contingent workers (temporary help, independent contractors, and on-call workers). Between 1990 and 2005, employment in the temporary help industry grew at the rapid rate of 5.4 percent per year, which was more than four times the growth rate of nonfarm employment. The number of workers in the industry rose from 1,156,000 to 2,539,000 over this period.

Why has the demand for contingent workers increased so rapidly? Several factors have been at work. These workers are usually paid less than permanent workers. Also, increasingly expensive fringe benefits are minimal or nonexistent for many contingent workers.

A second and closely related reason for the growing demand for contingent workers is that these workers give firms more flexibility in responding to changing economic conditions. As product demand shifts, firms can readily increase or decrease the sizes of their workforces through altering their temporary, on-call, and subcontracted employment. This flexibility enhances the competitive positions of firms and improves their ability to succeed in international markets.

September 11, 2001

The terrorist attacks on the United States on September 11, 2001, and the U.S. war on terrorism that followed significantly altered labor demand in various industries. For example, the sharp decline in air travel directly reduced the demand for pilots and flight attendants and indirectly reduced the demand for workers at travel-related firms such as hotels, restaurants, and car rental agencies. The number of airline workers fell from 581,000 in September 2001 to 464,000 in September 2003. The corresponding figures for the hotel and motel industry were 1,508,000 and 1,426,000. By 2006 the hotel and motel industry had recovered somewhat. However, airline industry employment continued to decline. The decline in air travel also reduced the resource demand for new jetliners and thus the demand for workers who assemble them. Boeing, in fact, laid off 30,000 workers at its assembly plants. The attacks also dampened consumer confidence and reduced consumer spending. As a result, labor demand fell in numerous industries across the economy.

In contrast, the terrorist attacks and the war on terrorism increased the demand for some workers, such as security workers, defense industry workers, and Arabic-speaking interpreters.

Chapter Summary

1. The demand for labor is a derived demand and therefore depends on the marginal productivity of labor and the price or market value of the product.

2. The segment of the marginal product curve that is positive and lies below the average product curve is the basis for the short-run labor demand curve. More specifically, the short-run demand curve for labor is determined by applying the MRP = W rule to the firm's marginal revenue product data.

3. Other things being equal, the demand for labor curve of a perfectly competitive seller is more elastic than that of an imperfectly competitive seller. This difference occurs because the imperfectly competitive seller needs to reduce product price to sell additional units of output, whereas the purely competitive seller does not. This also means that the imperfectly competitive seller's marginal revenue product curve lies to the left of the corresponding value of marginal product curve, whereas marginal revenue product and the value of the marginal product are identical for the perfectly competitive seller.

4. A firm's long-run labor demand curve is more elastic than its short-run curve because in the long run the firm has sufficient time to adjust nonlabor inputs such as capital. In the short run a wage change produces only an output effect; in the long run it also creates a substitution effect. Additionally, such factors as product demand elasticity, labor–capital interactions, and technology contribute to the greater long-run wage elasticity.

5. The market demand for a given type of labor is less elastic than a simple horizontal summation of the short- or long-run demand curves of individual employers. The reason for this is that as employers as a group hire more workers and produce more output, product supply will increase significantly and product price will therefore decline.

6. The elasticity of labor demand is measured by comparing the percentage change in the quantity of labor demanded with a given percentage change in the wage rate. If the elasticity coefficient is greater than 1, demand is relatively elastic. If it is less than 1, demand is relatively inelastic. When demand is elastic, changes in the wage rate cause the total wage bill to change in the *opposite* direction. When demand is inelastic, changes in the wage rate cause the total wage bill to move in the *same* direction.

7. The demand for labor generally is more elastic *(a)* the greater the elasticity of product demand, *(b)* the larger the ratio of labor cost to total cost, *(c)* the greater the substitutability of other inputs for labor, and *(d)* the greater the elasticity of supply of other inputs.

8. The location of the labor demand curve depends on *(a)* product demand, *(b)* the marginal productivity of labor, *(c)* the number of employers, and *(d)* the prices of other inputs. When any of these determinants of demand change, the labor demand curve shifts to a new location.

9. Labor and capital can be either substitutes or pure complements in production. If they are substitutes in production, they can be either gross substitutes or gross complements. When the price of a gross substitute changes, the demand for the other resource changes in the same direction. When the price of gross complement changes, the demand for the other resource changes in the opposite direction.

10. The concepts of labor demand, changes in labor demand, and the elasticity of labor demand have great applicability to real-world situations.

Terms and Concepts

derived demand, *128*
production function, *129*
total product, *131*
marginal product, *131*
average product, *131*
law of diminishing marginal returns, *132*
zone of production, *133*
marginal revenue product, *134*
short-run labor demand curve, *134*

marginal wage cost, *135*
value of marginal product, *135*
long-run demand for labor, *140*
output effect, *140*
substitution effect, *141*
market demand for labor, *143*
elasticity of labor demand, *146*

wage elasticity coefficient, *147*
total wage bill rules, *147*
determinants of labor demand, *152*
gross substitutes, *153*
gross complements, *153*

Questions and Study Suggestions

1. Graph a short-run production function (one variable resource) showing the correct relationships between total product, average product, and marginal product.

2. "Only that portion of the MP curve that lies below AP constitutes the basis for the firm's short-run demand curve for labor." Explain.

3. Explain how marginal revenue product is derived. Why is the MRP curve the firm's short-run labor demand curve? Explain how and why the labor demand curves of a perfectly competitive seller and an imperfectly competitive seller differ.

4. Given the data in Table A, complete the labor demand schedule shown in Table B. Contrast this schedule to the value of marginal product schedule that would exist given these data. Explain why the labor demand and VMP schedules differ.

Table A

Inputs of Labor	Total Product	Product Price
0	0	$1.10
1	17	1.00
2	32	.90
3	45	.80
4	55	.70
5	62	.65
6	68	.60

Table B

Labor Demand Schedule	
Wage Rate	Quantity Demanded
$18	
14	
11	
6	
2	
1	

5. Explain how each of the following would affect the demand schedule you derived in Question 4: *(a)* an increase in the price of a gross substitute for labor, *(b)* a decrease in the price of a pure complement in production with labor, *(c)* a decrease in the demand for the product that the labor helps produce.

6. Referring to the output and substitution effects, explain why an increase in the wage rate for autoworkers will generate more of a negative employment response in the long run than in the short run. Assume there is no productivity increase and no change in the price of nonlabor resources.

7. "It would be incorrect to say that an industry's labor demand curve is simply the horizontal sum of the demand curves of the individual firms." Do you agree? Explain.

8. Suppose marginal productivity tripled while product price fell by half in Table 5.2. What would be the net impact on the location of the short-run labor demand curve in Figure 5.2?

9. Use the concepts of *(a)* substitutes in production versus pure complements in production and *(b)* gross substitutes versus gross complements to assess the likely impact of the rapid decline in the price of computers and related office equipment on the labor demand for secretaries.

10. Use the total wage bill rules and the labor demand schedule in Question 4 to determine whether demand is elastic or inelastic over the $6 to $11 wage rate range. Compute the elasticity coefficient using Equation (5.4).

11. The productivity of farm labor has increased substantially since World War II. How can this be reconciled with the fact that labor has moved from agricultural to nonagricultural occupations over this period?

12. Contrast and explain changes in the demand for textile workers and fast-food workers over the past two decades. Why is the elasticity of labor demand crucial to the debate on the effects of increasing the minimum wage?

Internet Exercise

Which Industries Are Growing and Which Are Declining?

Go to the Bureau of Labor Statistics Current Employment Statistics Web site (**http://www.bls.gov/ces/home.htm**) and in sequence select "Get Detailed Statistics" and "Most Requested Statistics" to find information about employment by industry. Click on "reformat" to change the years of data extracted.

What was the amount for total nonfarm employment in January 1980 and for the most recent month shown? What is the percentage change in employment over this period?

What was the employment level for manufacturing and services in January 1980 and for the most recent month shown? In which industry has employment increased over this period? In which has it declined? What has been the percentage change in employment for both sectors? Suggest a possible explanation for the difference in employment growth between these sectors.

Provide *one* other specific statistic of your choice from the data on employment levels. For example, "In January 2007, the employment level for the mining industry was *xxx.x* thousand workers."

Internet Links

The Bureau of Labor Statistics Employment and Unemployment Web site provides information about layoffs and job turnover, as well as employment by state, occupation, and industry (**http://www.bls.gov/bls/employment.htm**).

Appendix

Isoquant–Isocost Analysis of the Long-Run Demand for Labor

A more advanced derivation of the firm's long-run downward-sloping labor demand curve is based on (1) isoquant and (2) isocost curves.

ISOQUANT CURVES

An *isoquant curve shows the various possible combinations of two inputs that are capable of producing a specific quantity of physical output.* By definition, then, output is the same at all points on a *single* isoquant. For example, total output is 100 units of some product or service on curve Q_{100} in Figure 5.8 when 20 units of capital are combined with 7 units of labor *or* when 10 units of capital and 15 units of labor are employed.[14] Isoquants—or equal output curves—possess several other characteristics.

1 DOWNWARD SLOPE

Assuming that capital and labor are substitutes in production, if a firm employs less capital (K), then to maintain a specific level of output, it must employ more labor (L). Conversely, to hold total output constant, using less of L will require it to employ more of K. There is thus an *inverse* relationship between K and L at each output level, implying a downward-sloping isoquant curve.

2 CONVEXITY TO THE ORIGIN

Isoquants are convex to the origin because capital and labor are not perfect substitutes for one another. For example, an excavating company can substitute labor and capital to produce a specific level of output—perhaps clearing 1,000 acres of wooded land in a fixed amount of time. But labor and capital are not perfectly substitutable for this purpose. To understand this and see why the firm's isoquant curve is convex to the origin, compare the following circumstances. First suppose the firm is using a single bulldozer and hundreds of workers. Clearly an extra bulldozer would compensate, or substitute, for many workers in producing this output. Contrast that to a second situation in which the firm has 100 bulldozers but relatively few workers. The addition of still another machine would have a relatively low substitution value; for example, it might compensate for only one or two workers. Why? The firm already has numerous bulldozers; it

---

[14] For simplicity we will assume that the only two resources are capital and labor, disregarding all combinations of capital and labor that are not within a firm's zone of production.

FIGURE 5.8 Isoquant Curves

Every point on a specific isoquant represents some combination of inputs (in this case, capital and labor) that produces a given level of total output. Isoquants, or "equal output curves," farther to the northeast indicate higher levels of total output.

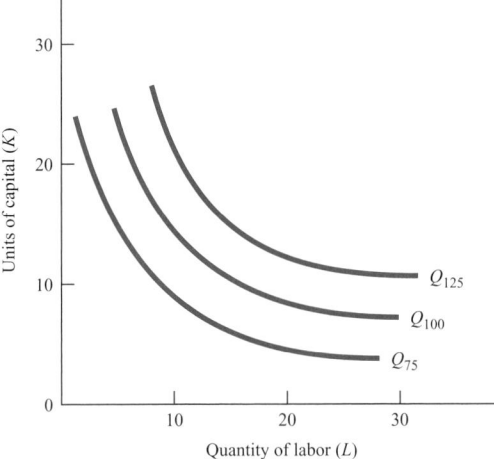

needs people to operate them, supervise the operation, and cut down the trees that cannot be bulldozed.

This same concept can be viewed in the opposite way. When the firm is employing only a small amount of labor and a large amount of equipment, an extra worker will possess a relatively high substitution value—that is, compensate for the reduction of a large amount of capital. As more labor is added, however, the decrease in capital permitted by an added unit of labor will decline. Stated in technical terms, the absolute value of the *marginal rate of technical substitution* of labor for capital will fall as more labor is added. This MRTS *L, K,* shown symbolically in Equation (5.5), is the absolute value of the slope of the isoquant at a given point.

$$\text{MRTS } L, K = \frac{\Delta K}{\Delta L} \qquad\qquad (5.5)$$

Returning to Figure 5.8, we see that each isoquant is convex to the origin. As one moves along Q_{75} from left to right, the absolute value of the slope of the curve declines; in other words, the curve gets flatter. A curve that gets flatter (whose absolute slope declines) as one moves southeast is convex to the origin.

3 HIGHER OUTPUT TO THE NORTHEAST

Each isoquant farther to the northeast reflects combinations of K and L that produce a greater level of total output than the previous curve. Isoquant Q_{125} represents greater output than Q_{100}, which in turn reflects more output than Q_{75}. Two other points are relevant here. First, we have drawn only three of the many possible isoquant curves.

Second, just as equal elevation lines on a contour map never intersect, neither do these equal output lines.

ISOCOST CURVES

A profit-maximizing firm will seek to minimize the costs of producing a given output. To accomplish this task, it will need to know the prices of K and L. These prices let the firm determine the various combinations of K and L that are available to it for a specific expenditure. For example, if the prices of K and L are \$6 and \$4 per unit, respectively, the input combinations that can be obtained from a given outlay, say \$120, would be \$6 times the quantity of K plus \$4 times the quantity of L. One possibility would be to use 20 units of K ($= \$120 = \$6 \times 20$) and no labor. At the other extreme, this firm could use zero units of capital and 30 units of labor ($= \$120 = 30 \times \$4$). Another such combination would be $10K$ and $15L$. In Figure 5.9 we plot these three points and connect them with a straight line. This line is an *isocost curve; it shows all the various combinations of capital and labor that can be purchased by a particular outlay, given the prices of K and L.* Note that the absolute value of the slope of this "equal expenditure" line is the ratio of the price of labor to the price of capital; that is, the slope is $\frac{2}{3}$ ($= \$4/\$6$).

The location of a particular isocost curve depends on (1) the total expenditure and (2) the relative prices of L and K. Given the prices of K and L, the greater the total

FIGURE 5.9 **An Isocost Curve**
An isocost (equal expenditure) curve shows the various combinations of two inputs—in this case, capital and labor—that can be purchased with a specific dollar outlay, given the prices of the two inputs. The slope of an isocost line measures the price of one input divided by the price of the other.

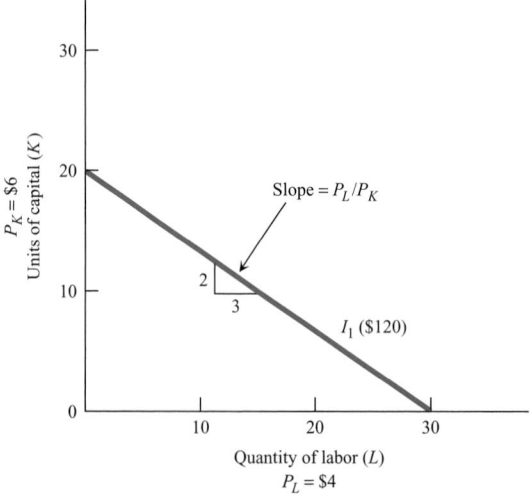

expenditure, the farther the isocost curve will lie outward from the origin. If the total outlay were enlarged from $120 to $150, and the prices of K and L remained unchanged, the isocost curve shown in Figure 5.9 would shift outward in a parallel fashion. Similarly, a smaller outlay would shift it inward. Second, the location of an isocost curve depends on the relative prices of L and K. Given the total expenditure, the higher the price of L relative to the price of K, the *steeper* the isocost curve; the lower the price of L relative to the price of K, the *flatter* the curve.

LEAST-COST COMBINATION OF CAPITAL AND LABOR

By overlaying the isocost curve in Figure 5.9 onto Figure 5.8's isoquant map, we can determine the firm's cost-minimizing combination of K and L for a given quantity of total output. Stated somewhat differently, this allows us to determine the lowest cost *per unit of output.* This *least-cost combination of resources* occurs at the *tangency point* of the isoquant curve Q_{100} and the isocost curve I_1 (point *a*) in Figure 5.10. At point *a* the slope of the isoquant, the MRTS $L, K,$ just equals the ratio of the prices of labor and capital—the slope of the isocost curve. The firm will use 10 units of capital and employ 15 units of labor. This expenditure of $120 is the minimum outlay possible in achieving this level of output. To reinforce this proposition, you should determine why combinations of K and L represented by other points on Q_{100} are *not* optimal.

FIGURE 5.10   The Least-Cost Combination of Capital and Labor
The least-cost combination of capital and labor used to produce 100 units of output is at point *a*, where the isocost line is tangent to isoquant Q_{100}. At *a*, the marginal rate of technical substitution of labor for capital (MRTS L, K) equals the ratio of the price of labor to the price of capital. In this case, the firm will use 10 units of capital, employ 15 units of labor, and in the process expend $120.

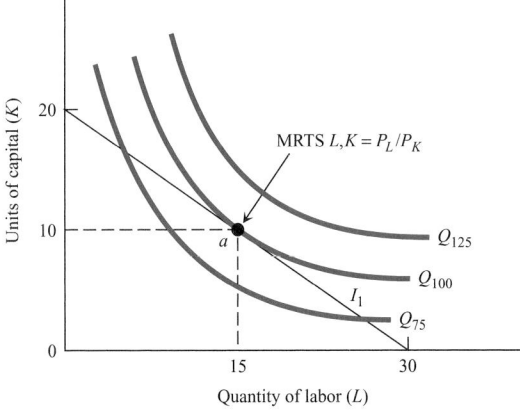

DERIVING THE LONG-RUN LABOR DEMAND CURVE

Earlier in this chapter we derived a *short-run* labor demand curve by holding capital constant, adding units of labor to generate a marginal product schedule, multiplying MP times the extra revenue gained from the sale of additional product, and graphing the resulting marginal revenue product schedule. By applying the $W = \text{MRP}$ rule, we demonstrated that the MRP curve *is* the short-run labor demand curve. Now we derive a *long-run* labor demand curve directly from our isoquant–isocost analysis. In Figure 5.11(a) we reproduce our $120 isocost line I_1 and the isoquant Q_{100}, which is tangent to it at point *a*. We

FIGURE 5.11 Deriving the Long-Run Labor Demand Curve
When the price of labor rises from $4 to $12, the substitution effect causes the firm to use more capital and less labor, while the output effect reduces the use of both. The labor demand curve is determined in (b) by plotting the quantity of labor demanded before and after the increase in the wage rate from $4 to $12.

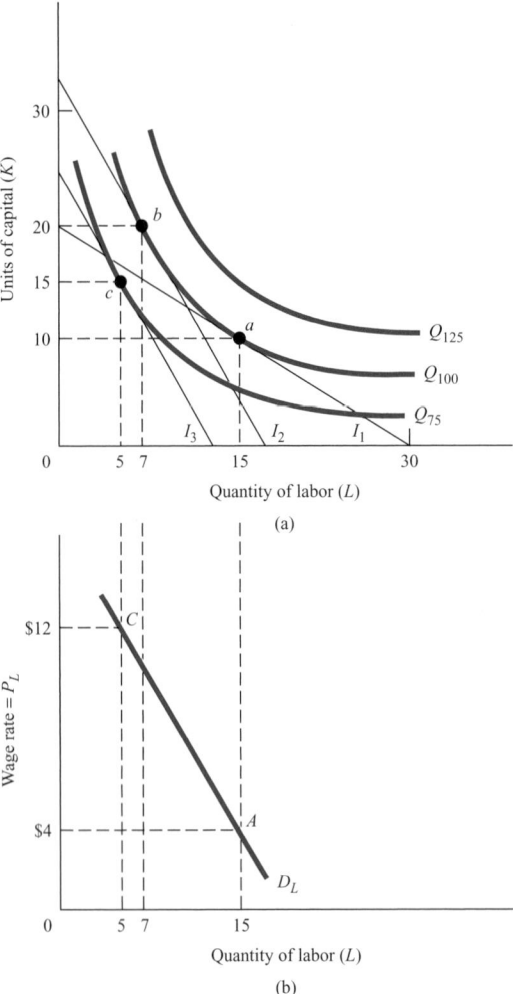

then drop a perpendicular dashed line down to the horizontal axis of graph (b), which also measures units of labor, but measures the price of labor, or wage rate, vertically. Recall that the price of *L* is assumed to be $4, at which the optimal level of employment is 15 units of labor. This gives us point *A* in the lower graph.

Now suppose some factor (perhaps emigration) reduces labor supply and increases the price of labor from $4 to $12. We need to ascertain graphically the effect of this increase of the wage rate on the quantity of labor demanded. To accomplish this, let's proceed in several steps. First we must draw a new isocost curve, reflecting the new ratio of the price of *L* to *K*. Inasmuch as the price of labor is now $12 while the price of *K* is assumed to remain constant at $6, the new isocost curve will have a slope of 2 (= $12/$6). Because we wish initially to hold the level of output constant at Q_{100}, we construct isocost curve I_2, which has a slope of 2 and is tangent to Q_{100} at point *b* in Figure 5.11(a).

Our next step is to determine the new combination of *K* and *L* that would be used *if* output were to be held constant. This is shown at point *b*, where the marginal rate of technical substitution on isoquant curve Q_{100} equals the slope of isocost curve I_2 (20*K* and 7*L*). Notice what has happened thus far: In response to the higher wage rate, the firm has substituted more capital (+10) for less labor (−8). This is the **substitution effect** of the wage increase. It is defined as *the change in the quantity of an input demanded resulting from a change in the price of the input, with the output remaining constant.*

The final step is to acknowledge that the increase of the price of labor from $4 to $12 will cause the firm to reassess its profit-maximizing level of output. In particular, production costs are now higher and, given product demand, the firm will find it profitable to produce less output. Let's assume that this reevaluation results in the firm's decision to reduce its output from Q_{100} to Q_{75}. Given the new $12 to $6 price ratio of *L* and *K*, we simply push the I_2 line inward in a parallel fashion until it is tangent with this lower isoquant. The new tangency position is at *c*, where the firm is using 15*K* and 5*L*. This **output effect** further reduces the cost-minimizing quantity of labor: Not as much labor is needed to produce the smaller quantity of output. This effect is defined as *the change in employment of an input resulting from the cost change associated with the change in the input's price.* Dropping a dashed perpendicular line downward from point *c*, we derive point *C* in the lower graph. At the new wage rate of $12, the firm desires to hire only 5 units of labor. By finding a series of points such as *a* and *c* in the upper graph and *A* and *C* in the lower one, and then by determining the locus of these latter points, we derive a long-run labor demand curve such as D_L in graph (b). This curve slopes downward because of both a *substitution effect* (−8 labor units) and an *output effect* (−2 units).

Appendix Summary

1. An isoquant curve shows the various possible combinations of two inputs that are capable of producing a specific quantity of physical output.

2. An isocost curve shows the various combinations of two inputs that a firm can purchase with a given outlay or expenditure.

3. The firm's cost-minimizing combination of inputs in achieving a given output is found at the tangency point between the isocost and isoquant curves, where the marginal rate of technical substitution of labor for capital (slope of the isoquant curve) equals the ratio of the input prices (slope of the isocost curve).

4. Changing the price of either input while holding the price of the other resource and the level of output constant produces a new isocost curve that has a new tangency position on the given isoquant curve. This generates a *substitution effect* that results in the use of less of the resource that rose in price and more of the resource that did not experience a price change.

5. An increase in the price of a resource also increases the cost per unit of the product. This creates an *output effect* tending to reduce the employment of both labor and capital.

6. A downward-sloping long-run labor demand curve can be derived by plotting the wage rate–quantity combinations associated with changing the price of labor (wage rate).

Appendix Terms and Concepts

isoquant curve, *164*
marginal rate of technical
  substitution, *165*

isocost curve, *166*
least-cost combination of
  resources, *167*

substitution effect, *169*
output effect, *169*

Appendix Questions and Study Suggestions

1. Explain why isoquant curves for inputs that are substitutes in production *(a)* are negatively sloped, *(b)* are convex to the origin, and *(c)* never intersect.

2. Suppose the quantity of capital is fixed at 10 units in Figure 5.8. Explain, by drawing a horizontal line rightward from $10K$, the short-run law of diminishing marginal returns discussed in the body of this chapter. *Hint:* Observe the distance between the isoquants along your horizontal line.

3. Explain how each of the following, other things being equal, would shift the isocost curve shown in Figure 5.9: *(a)* a decrease in the price of L, *(b)* a simultaneous and proportionate increase in the prices of both K and L, and *(c)* an increase in the total outlay, or expenditure, from $120 to $150.

4. Explain graphically how isoquant–isocost analysis can be used to derive a long-run labor demand curve. Distinguish between the substitution and output effects.

5. By referring to Figure 5.11(a), explain the impact of the increase of the price of labor on the cost-minimizing quantity of capital. What can you conclude about the relative strengths of the substitution and output effects as they relate to the demand for capital in this specific situation?

6. Is labor demand *(a)* elastic, *(b)* unit elastic, or *(c)* inelastic over the $4 to $12 wage rate range of D_L in Figure 5.11(b)? Explain by referring to the total wage bill rules (Figure 5.7) and the midpoint formula for elasticity [Equation (5.4)].

Chapter 6

Wage Determination and the Allocation of Labor

Something quite remarkable happens in the United States every workday. Over 146 million of us go to work sometime, somewhere, during the day. We work at an amazing array of jobs: We are carpenters, secretaries, executives, professional athletes, lawyers, dockworkers, farmhands, geologists, hairstylists, nurses, managers, truck drivers, and professors. And the list goes on. Equally remarkable are the pay differences among us. Professional baseball players make, on average, $1,433 an hour; restaurant employees, $10 per hour.

Who or what determines the occupational composition of the total jobs in the economy? What mechanisms allocate us to our various occupations and specific workplaces? How are occupational and individual wage rates determined? In this chapter we combine labor supply (Chapters 2–4) and labor demand (Chapter 5) into basic models that help us answer these important questions.

In reading this chapter beware: We are assuming for simplicity that all compensation is paid in the form of the wage rate. In Chapter 7 we will relax this assumption, specifically looking at the composition of pay and the economics of fringe benefits.

THEORY OF A PERFECTLY COMPETITIVE LABOR MARKET

A *perfectly competitive labor market* has the following characteristics that contrast it with other labor markets: (1) a large number of firms competing with one another to hire a specific type of labor to fill identical jobs; (2) numerous qualified people who have identical skills and independently supply their labor services; (3) "wage-taking" behavior—that is, neither workers nor firms exert control over the market wage; and (4) perfect, costless information and labor mobility.

Let's examine the components, operation, and outcomes of this stylized labor market in some detail. Specifically, we will divide our discussion into three subsections: the labor market, the hiring decision by an individual firm, and allocative efficiency.

The Labor Market

The competitive market for a specific type of labor can best be analyzed by separating it into two parts: labor demand, which reflects the behavior of employers; and labor supply, deriving from the decisions of workers.

Labor Demand and Supply

Recall from the previous chapter (Figure 5.6) that the market demand for a particular type of labor is found by summing over a range of wage rates the price-adjusted amounts of labor that employers desire to hire at each of the various wage rates. Also remember, specifically from Chapter 2, that *individual* labor supply curves are normally backward-bending. Can we then conclude that the *market* supply of a particular grade of labor is also backward-bending? In most labor markets this is not the case; market supply curves generally slope upward and to the right, indicating that collectively workers will offer more labor hours at higher relative wage rates. Why is this so?

Figure 6.1 helps explain the positive relationship between the wage rate and the quantity of labor hours supplied in most labor markets. Graph (a) displays five separate

FIGURE 6.1 **The Market Supply of Labor**
Even though specific individuals normally have backward-bending labor supply curves, market labor supply curves generally are positively sloped over realistic wage ranges. Higher relative wages attract workers away from household production, leisure, or their previous jobs. The height of the market labor supply measures the opportunity cost of using the marginal labor hour in this employment. The shorter the time period, the less elastic this curve.

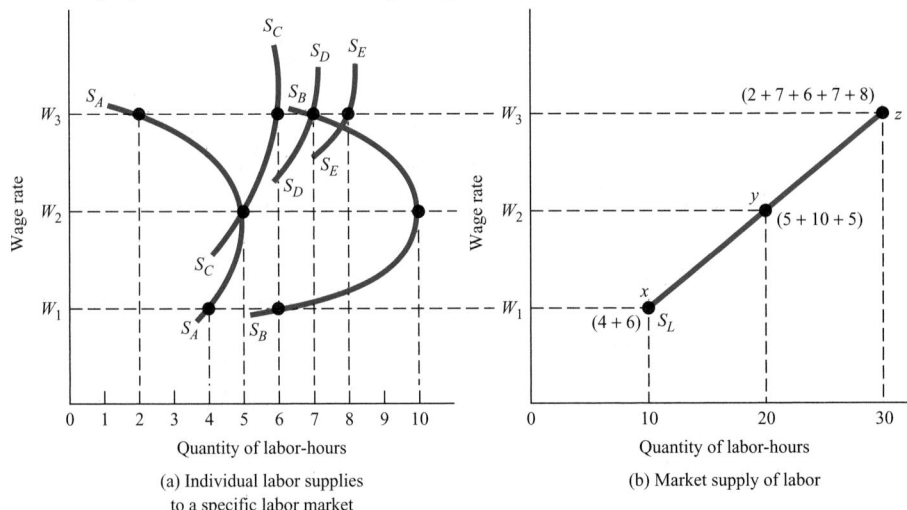

(a) Individual labor supplies
to a specific labor market

(b) Market supply of labor

backward-bending *individual* labor supply curves in a specific labor market, while graph (b) sums the curves horizontally to produce a *market* labor supply curve.[1] Notice from their respective labor supply curves S_A and S_B that at wage W_1, Adams will offer 4 hours of labor and Bates 6 hours. We simply sum these outcomes (4 + 6) to get point x at wage W_1 on the market labor supply curve shown in graph (b). Now let's suppose the wage rate rises from W_1 to W_2 in this labor market while all other wage rates remain constant. Adams will increase her hours from 4 to 5 and Bates will work 10 hours rather than 6. We know from previous analysis that this implies that for these two workers, substitution effects exceed income effects over the W_1 to W_2 wage range. But also notice that at W_2, a third worker—Choy (S_C)—chooses to participate in this labor market, deciding to offer 5 hours of labor. Presumably he is attracted away from another labor market, household production, or leisure by the W_2 wage rate. Thus the total quantity of hours supplied is 20 (= 5 + 10 + 5), as shown by point y in the right graph. Finally, observe wage rate W_3, at which Adams and Bates choose to work fewer hours than previously, but Choy decides to offer 6 hours, and two new workers—Davis (S_D) and Egan (S_E)—now enter this labor market. The total number of hours, as observed at point z on the market labor supply curve, is now 30 (= 2 + 7 + 6 + 7 + 8).

Conclusion? Even though specific people may reduce their hours of work as the market wage rises, labor supply curves of specific labor markets generally are positively sloped over realistic wage ranges. *Higher relative wages attract workers away from household production, leisure, or other labor markets and toward the labor market in which the wage increased.*

The vertical height of the market labor supply curve *xyz* measures the opportunity cost of employing the last labor hour in this occupation. For example, point y on S_L in Figure 6.1(b) indicates that wage rate W_2 is necessary to entice the 20th hour of labor. Where there is competition in product and labor markets, perfect information, and costless migration, the value of the alternative activity which that hour previously produced—either as utility from leisure or output from work in a different occupation—is equivalent to W_2. To attract 30 hours of labor compared to 20, the wage must rise to W_3 (point z) because the 21st through 30th hours generate more than W_2 worth of value to workers and society in their alternative uses. To attract these hours to this labor market, these opportunity costs must be compensated for via a higher wage rate. *In perfectly competitive product and labor markets, labor supply curves measure marginal opportunity costs.*

One final point needs to be emphasized concerning market labor supply. The shorter the time period and the more specialized the variety of labor, the less elastic the labor supply curve. In the short run increases in the wage may not result in significant increases in the number of workers in a market, but in the long run human capital investments can be undertaken that will allow greater responsiveness to the higher relative wage (Chapter 4).

---

[1] We are assuming that while all these workers have identical skills, they have differing preferences for leisure, differing levels of nonwage income, and so forth. Thus their reservation wages and individual labor supply curves differ.

FIGURE 6.2 Wage and Employment Determination

The equilibrium wage rate W_0 and level of employment Q_0 occur at the intersection of labor supply and demand. A surplus, or excess supply, of *ba* would occur at wage rate W_{es}; a shortage, or excess demand, of *ec* would result if the wage were W_{ed}.

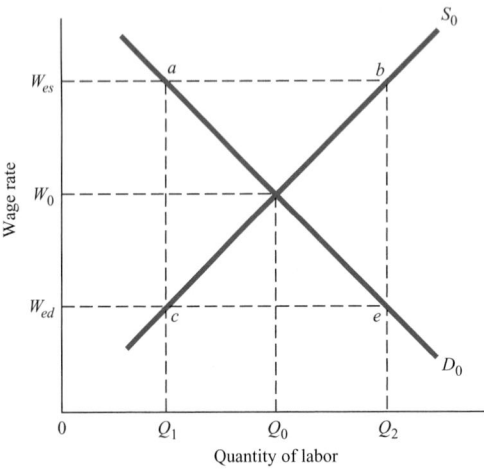

Equilibrium

Figure 6.2 combines the market labor demand and supply curves for a specific type of labor and shows the equilibrium wage W_0 and the equilibrium quantity of labor Q_0. If the wage were W_{es}, an *excess supply* or surplus of labor ($b - a$) would occur, driving the wage down to W_0. If instead the wage rate were W_{ed}, an *excess demand* or shortage ($e - c$) of workers would develop, and the wage would increase to W_0. Wage W_0 and employment level Q_0 are the only wage–employment combination at which the market clears. At W_0 the number of hours offered by labor suppliers just matches the number of hours that firms desire to employ.

Determinants

The supply and demand curves in Figure 6.2 are drawn holding all factors other than the wage rate for this variety of labor constant. But a number of other factors—or *determinants of labor supply and demand*—can change and cause either rightward or leftward shifts in the curves. We discussed many of these factors in Chapters 2 and 5; they are simply formalized here in Table 6.1. The distinction between "changes in demand" versus "changes in quantity demanded" *and* "changes in supply" versus "changes in quantity supplied" apply to the labor market as well as the product market. Changes in the determinants of labor demand and supply shown in the table shift the entire curves; these curve shifts are designated as "changes in labor demand" and "changes in labor supply." Changes in the wage rate, on the other hand, cause movements *along* demand and supply curves; that is, the quantity of labor demanded or supplied changes. But in the short run changes in the wage rate normally do not cause shifts of the curves themselves.

TABLE 6.1
**The Determinants
of Labor Supply
and Demand**

Determinants of Labor Supply

1. Other wage rates
An increase (decrease) in the wages paid in other occupations for which workers in a particular labor market are qualified will decrease (increase) labor supply.

2. Nonwage income
An increase (decrease) in income other than from employment will decrease (increase) labor supply.

3. Preferences for work versus leisure
A net increase (decrease) in people's preferences for work relative to leisure will increase (decrease) labor supply.

4. Nonwage aspects of the job
An improvement (worsening) of the nonwage aspects of the job will increase (reduce) labor supply.

5. Number of qualified suppliers
An increase (decrease) in the number of qualified suppliers of a specific grade of labor will increase (decrease) labor supply.

Determinants of Labor Demand

1. Product demand
Changes in product demand that increase (decrease) the product price will raise (lower) the marginal revenue product (MRP) of labor and therefore increase (decrease) the demand for labor.

2. Productivity
Assuming that it does not cause an offsetting decline in product price, an increase (decrease) in productivity will increase (decrease) the demand for labor.

3. Prices of other resources
Where resources are *gross complements* (output effect > substitution effect), an increase (decrease) in the price of a substitute in production will decrease (increase) the demand for labor; where resources are *gross substitutes* (substitution effect > output effect), an increase (decrease) in the price of a substitute in production will increase (decrease) the demand for labor. An increase (decrease) in the price of a pure complement in production will decrease (increase) labor demand (no substitution effect; therefore a gross complement).

4. Number of employers
Assuming no change in employment by other firms hiring a specific grade of labor, an increase (decrease) in the number of employers will increase (decrease) the demand for labor.

To demonstrate how a competitive market for a particular type of labor operates and to emphasize the role of the determinants of supply and demand, let's suppose that the labor market in Figure 6.3 is characterized by labor demand D_0 and labor supply S_0, which together produce equilibrium wage and employment levels W_0 and Q_0 (point c). Next assume that demand declines for the product produced by firms hiring this labor,

FIGURE 6.3 **Changes in Demand, Supply, and Market Equilibrium**

Changes in labor supply and demand create initial shortages or surpluses in labor markets, followed by adjustments to new equilibrium wage rates and employment. Here the decline in demand from D_0 to D_1 and increase in supply from S_0 to S_1 produce an initial excess supply of ab at wage W_0. Consequently the wage rate falls to W_1, and because the decline in demand is large relative to the increase in supply, the equilibrium quantity falls from Q_0 to Q_1.

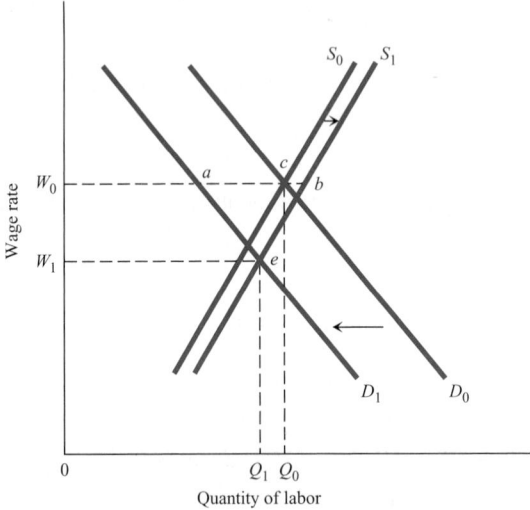

reducing the price of the product and thus the *marginal revenue product* (MRP) of labor (demand determinant 1, Table 6.1). Also, let's suppose that simultaneously the federal government releases findings of a definitive research study that concludes that the considerable health and safety risks that were heretofore associated with this occupation are in fact minimal. Taken alone, this information will increase the relative nonwage attractiveness of this labor and shift the labor supply curve rightward—say, from S_0 to S_1 (supply determinant 4, Table 6.1).

Now observe that at the initial wage rate W_0 the number of workers seeking jobs in this occupation (point b) exceeds the number of workers that firms wish to hire (point a). How will the market adjust to this surplus? Because wages are assumed to be perfectly flexible, the wage rate will drop to W_1, where the labor market will once again clear (point e). Figure 6.3 illustrates two generalizations. First, taken alone, a decline in labor demand reduces *both* the wage rate and quantity of labor employed. Second, an increase in labor supply—also viewed separately—reduces the wage rate and increases equilibrium quantity. In this case the net outcome of the simultaneous changes in supply and demand is a decline in the wage rate from W_0 to W_1 and a fall in the quantity of labor offered and employed from Q_0 to Q_1. The latter occurred because the decrease in demand was greater than the increase in labor supply. At W_1 the Q_1Q_0 workers formerly employed in this market were not sufficiently compensated for their opportunity costs, and they left this occupation for leisure, household production, or other jobs.

6.1

The Hiring Decision by an Individual Firm

Given the presence of market wage W_0 or W_1 in Figure 6.3, how will a firm operating in a perfectly competitive labor and product market decide on the quantity of labor to employ? The answer can be found in Figure 6.4. Graph (a) portrays the labor market for a specific occupational group, and graph (b) shows the labor supply and demand curves for an individual firm hiring this labor. Because this particular employer is just one of many firms in this labor market, its decision on how many workers to employ will not affect the market wage. Instead this firm is a wage taker in the same sense that a perfectly competitive seller is a price taker in the product market. The single employer in (b) has no incentive to pay more than the equilibrium wage W_0 because at the W_0 wage, it can attract as many labor units as it wants. On the other hand, if it offers a wage below W_0 it will attract *no* units of labor. All workers who possess this skill have marginal opportunity costs of at least W_0; they can get a minimum of W_0 in alternative employment. Consequently, the horizontal wage line W_0 in Figure 6.4(b) *is* this firm's labor supply curve (S_L). You will observe that it is perfectly elastic.

FIGURE 6.4   Perfect Competition: The Labor Market (a) and the Individual Firm (b)
In a perfectly competitive labor market, the equilibrium wage rate W_0 and quantity of labor Q_0
are determined by supply and demand, as shown in (a). The individual firm (b) hiring in this
market is a wage taker; its labor supply curve, S_L = MWC = AWC, is perfectly elastic at
W_0. The firm maximizes its profits by hiring Q_0 units of labor (MRP = MWC). Assuming
competition in the product market, this employment level constitutes an efficient allocation
of resources (VMP = P_L).

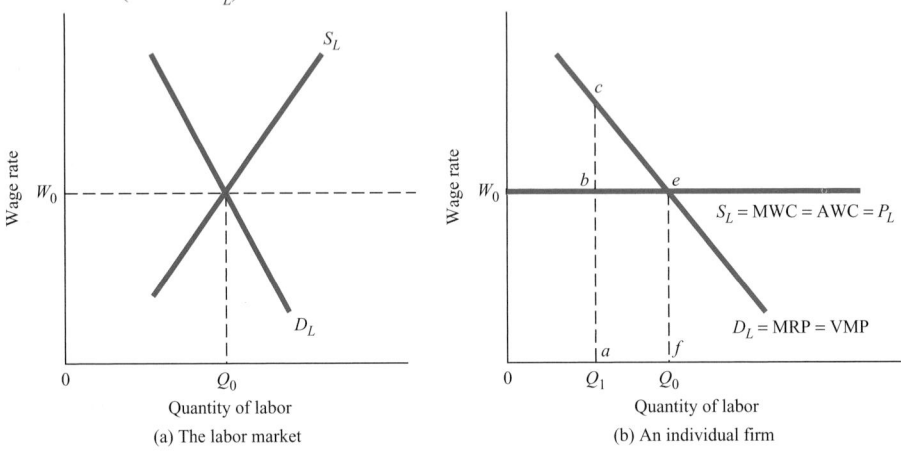

(a) The labor market

(b) An individual firm

Curve S_L in graph (b) also indicates this firm's average wage cost and marginal wage
cost. *Average wage cost* (AWC) is *the total wage cost divided by the number of units
of labor employed. Marginal wage cost* (MWC), on the other hand, is *the absolute
change in total wage cost resulting from the employment of an additional unit of labor.*
To see why average and marginal wage costs are equal in this case, suppose that the
firm hires 100 labor hours at $8 per hour. The total hourly wage bill will be
$800 (= $8 × 100). What will be the average wage cost and marginal wage cost?
Answers: AWC = $8 (= $800/100); MWC (extra cost of the last worker hour) =
$8 (= $800 − $792). And if the firm hires 200 labor hours? Answers: total wage
cost = $1,600; AWC = $8 (= $1,600/200); MWC = $8 (= $1,600 − $1,592). For
all levels of employment, W = $8 = MWC = AWC = S_L in this labor market.

Recall from Chapter 5 that in the short run a firm's demand for labor curve *is* its
marginal revenue product curve. Thus this firm can compare the additional revenue
(MRP) obtained by hiring one more unit of labor with the added cost (MWC) or, in this
case, the wage rate (W = MWC). If MRP > W, it will employ the particular hour of
labor; on the other hand, if MRP < W, it will not. To generalize: *The profit-maximizing
employer will obtain its optimal level of employment where MRP = MWC.* We label this
equality the **MRP = MWC rule.**

The profit-maximizing quantity is Q_0 in Figure 6.4(b). To confirm this, observe level
Q_1, where MRP, as shown by the vertical distance *ac,* exceeds MWC (distance *ab*).
Clearly this firm will gain profits if it hires this unit of labor because it can sell the
added product produced by this worker for more than the wage W_0 (= MWC). This is
true for all units of labor up to Q_0, where MRP and MWC are equal (distance *fe*).
Beyond Q_0 diminishing returns finally reduce marginal product (MP) to the extent that

MRP (= MP × P) lies below the market wage W_0 (= MWC). Thus this firm's total profit will fall if it hires more than Q_0 worker hours.

Allocative Efficiency

We stressed at the outset of Chapter 1 that labor is a scarce resource and it therefore behooves society to use it efficiently. How do we define an efficient allocation of labor? Is labor efficiently allocated in the perfectly competitive labor market just discussed? And what about the noncompetitive labor market models to follow?

Labor Market Efficiency

Let's first bring the notion of allocative efficiency into focus. An **efficient allocation of labor** is realized when workers are being directed to their highest-valued uses. Labor is being allocated efficiently when society obtains the largest amount of domestic output from the given amount of labor available. Stated technically, available labor is efficiently allocated when its value of marginal product or VMP—the dollar value to society of its marginal product—is the same in all alternative employments.

This assertion can be demonstrated through a simple example. Suppose that type A labor (for example, assembly-line labor) is capable of producing both product x (autos) and product y (refrigerators). Suppose the available amount of type A labor is currently allocated so that the value of marginal product of labor in producing autos is \$12 and its value of marginal product in producing refrigerators is \$8. In short, VMP_{Ax} (= \$12) > VMP_{Ay} (= \$8). This is *not* an efficient allocation of type A labor because it is not making the maximum contribution to domestic output. It is clear that by shifting a worker from producing y (refrigerators) to making x (autos), the domestic output can be increased by \$4 (= \$12 − \$8). This reallocation will cause a movement down the VMP curve for x and up the VMP curve for y. That is, VMP_{Ax} will fall and VMP_{Ay} will rise. The indicated reallocation from y to x should continue until the VMP of type A labor is the same for both products, or $VMP_{Ax} = VMP_{Ay}$. In our example, this might occur where, say, $VMP_{Ax} = VMP_{Ay} = \$10$. When this equality is achieved, no further reallocation of labor will cause a net increase in the domestic output.

If we expand our example from just two products to any number of products (that is, n products), we can state the condition for allocative efficiency for any given type of labor by the following equation:

$$VMP_{Ax} = VMP_{Ay} = \cdots = VMP_{An} = P_{LA} \qquad \textbf{(6.1)}$$

where A is the given type of labor; $x, y, \ldots, n$ represent all possible products that labor might produce; and VMP is the value of labor's marginal product in producing the various products.

Observe that in Equation (6.1) we have made the VMPs of labor equal not only to one another but also to the **price of labor** P_L. Why so? The reason is that we take into consideration that type A labor will be made available in this labor market only if the price of labor is sufficiently high to cover the opportunity costs of those supplying their labor services. Type A labor may be used in nontype A work, household production (child care, meal preparation, and the like), or pure leisure. Indeed, the optimal position in Chapter 2's work–leisure model (specifically point u_1 in Figure 2.5) defines an efficient allocation of labor (time) between labor market and nonlabor market activities. In

Figure 6.1 we found that such individual work–leisure allocations—along with wage opportunities in other labor markets—are reflected in the labor supply curve within a competitive labor market. Thus Equation (6.1) tells us that human resources are efficiently allocated when the value of the last units of labor in various labor market uses (producing goods $x, y, \ldots , n$) are all equal and these values in turn are equal to the opportunity cost of labor P_L (the marginal value of alternative work, non–labor market production, and leisure). Alternatively, an *underallocation* of a particular type of labor to labor market production occurs when its VMP in any employment exceeds P_L; an *overallocation* occurs when its VMP in any labor market employment is less than P_L.

Perfect Competition and Allocative Efficiency

Having defined allocative efficiency, let's consider our second question: Do perfectly competitive labor markets result in an efficient allocation of labor? Figure 6.5 is simply an expansion of Figure 6.4 to show the equilibrium positions of representative firms from several competitive industries—that is, industries producing $x, y,$ and n with type A labor. Note that equilibrium for the three representative firms occurs at employment levels $Q_{Ax}, Q_{Ay},$ and $Q_{An},$ respectively. The equilibrium positions are the result of each firm's desire to maximize profits by equating the MRPs of A with the MWC of A. But perfect competition in the hiring of labor means that P_{LA} equals the MWC of A. Similarly, perfect competition in the sale of the three products means that the MRP of A equals its VMP for all three products. Thus each firm maximizes profits where MWC = MRP. But because P_{LA} = MWC *and* MRP = VMP for all competitive firms using type A labor, we find that Equation (6.1) is fulfilled. In short, competitive labor markets *do* result in an efficient allocation of labor. This is an example of Adam Smith's famous concept of the "invisible hand." In competitive labor and product markets, pursuit of private self-interest (profit maximization) furthers society's interest

FIGURE 6.5 **Perfect Competition and an Efficient Allocation of Labor**
Representative firms producing goods such as $x, y,$ and n maximize profits by employing type A labor where the marginal revenue product of labor (MRP) equals the marginal wage cost (MWC). Perfect competition in the product market ensures that MRP equals the value of marginal product (VMP), and perfect competition in the labor market means that MWC equals the price of labor (P_L). Thus VMP matches P_L in each use, satisfying the condition for efficiency in the allocation of type A labor: $\text{VMP}_{Ax} = \text{VMP}_{Ay} = \cdots = \text{VMP}_{An} = P_L.$

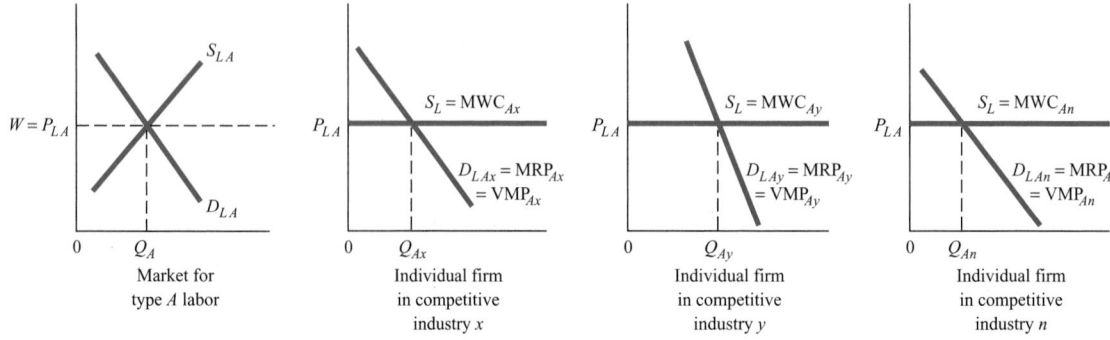

(an efficient allocation of scarce resources). It is as if there is an unseen coordinator moving resources to where they are most beneficial to society.

With this understanding of allocative efficiency and its realization when perfect competition prevails, let's now seek to determine whether noncompetitive labor markets are consistent with an efficient allocation of labor.

WAGE AND EMPLOYMENT DETERMINATION: MONOPOLY IN THE PRODUCT MARKET

To this point we have assumed that the employers hiring labor in a perfectly competitive labor market are price takers in the product market; that is, they do not possess monopoly power. But recall from Chapter 5, specifically Table 5.3 and Figure 5.3, that if a firm is a monopolist in the sale of its product, it will face a downward-sloping product demand curve. This means that increases in its output will require price reductions, and because the lower prices will apply to all the firm's output, its marginal revenue (MR) will be less than its price. Consequently, MRP_L ($= MP \times MR$) will fall for two reasons: (1) MP will decline because of diminishing returns (also true for perfect product market competition), *and* (2) MR will decline more rapidly than price as more workers are hired (in perfect competition, MR is constant and equals product price P).

The labor market consequences of product market monopoly are shown in Figure 6.6. Here we assume that the labor market is perfectly competitive but that one particular

FIGURE 6.6   Wage Rate and Employment Determination: Monopoly in the Product Market

Because a product market monopolist faces a downward-sloping demand curve, increased hiring of labor and the resulting larger output force the firm to lower its price. And because it must lower its price on all units, its marginal revenue (MR) is less than the price. Thus the firm's MRP curve (MP × MR) lies below the VMP curve (MP × P), and this employer hires Q_m rather than Q_c units of labor. An efficiency loss to society of *bce* results.

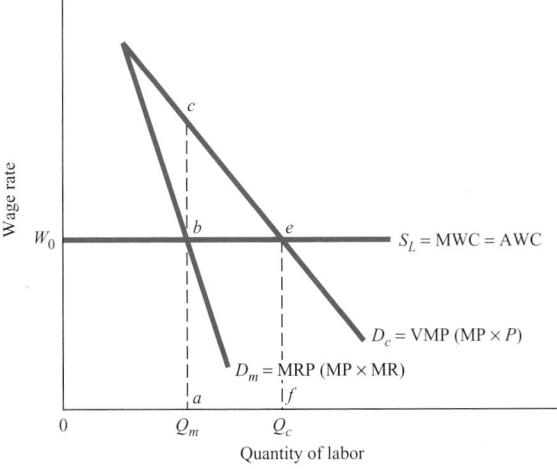

firm hiring this type of labor is a monopolist in the sale of its product. Restated, this type of labor is used by thousands of firms, not just this monopolist, and thus there is competition in the labor market.

Figure 6.6 indicates that this monopolist is a wage taker and therefore faces the perfectly elastic labor supply curve shown as S_L. This supply curve coincides with the firm's marginal wage cost (MWC) and its average wage cost (AWC), just as it did in our previous model.

Labor demand curve D_c is the MRP curve that would have existed had there been competition rather than monopoly and therefore no decline in marginal revenue as the firm increased its employment and output. This MRP curve would be equal to VMP; the firm's revenue gain from hiring one more worker would equal society's gain in output. On the other hand, demand curve D_m is the *monopolist's* MRP curve. In this case, MRP *does not equal* VMP. The value of the extra output of each worker to the monopolist is less than the value to society. The reason again: The monopolist's sale of an additional unit of output does not add the full amount of the product's price to its marginal revenue. Thus MRP ($=$ MR $\times$ MP)—the value to the firm—is less than VMP ($= P \times$ MP)—the value to society.[2]

Several noteworthy outcomes of monopoly in the product market are evident in Figure 6.6. First, the monopolist's labor demand curve D_m is *less elastic* than the competitive curve D_c. Second, the monopolist behaves in the same way as the competitor by determining its profit-maximizing level of employment where MRP $=$ MWC. Nevertheless, this equality produces a lower level of employment—Q_m in this case—than would occur under competitive product market conditions (Q_c). Third, the wage paid by the monopolist is the same as that paid by competitive firms. Without unions, both are wage takers.[3] Fourth, labor resources are misallocated. To understand why, recall that in a perfectly competitive labor market the price of labor ($P_L = W$) reflects the marginal opportunity cost to society of using a resource in a particular employment. Also remember that the VMP of labor is a measure of the added contribution to output of a worker in a specific employment. Notice in the figure VMP $> P_L (W_0)$ for the Q_m through Q_c workers. This implies that too few labor resources are being allocated to this employment and therefore too many are allocated somewhere else. An efficiency loss of area *bec* occurs. Assuming costless labor mobility, if $Q_m Q_c$ (or *be*) workers were reallocated from alternative activities to work in this industry, the *net* value of society's output would rise by area *bce*. These workers would contribute output valued at *acef* in this employment—the value of the total product added—

[2] If you are not clear on this point, review Table 5.3 and Figure 5.3.

[3] For evidence supporting this theoretical prediction, see Leonard W. Weiss, "Concentration and Labor Earnings," *American Economic Review,* March 1966, pp. 96–117.

The less elastic labor demand curve possessed by the monopolist, however, may increase the collective bargaining power of unions and result in a higher wage for workers in monopolized product markets. For evidence of a positive impact of monopoly power on wages, see Stephen Nickell, "Product Markets and Labour Markets," *Labour Economics,* March 1999, pp. 1–20.

whereas they previously contributed output valued at area *abef*—the opportunity cost to society of using them here.[4]

MONOPSONY

Thus far, we have assumed that the labor market is perfectly competitive. Now we wish to analyze a labor market where either a single firm is the sole hirer of a particular type of labor or two or more employers collude to fix a below-competitive wage. These market circumstances are called *pure monopsony* and *joint monopsony*, respectively. For simplicity, our discussion will be confined to pure forms of monopsony; but keep in mind that monopsony power, much the same as monopoly power, extends beyond the *pure* model to include weaker forms of market power.

We will again assume that (1) there are numerous qualified, homogeneous workers who act independently to secure employment in the monopsonized labor market, and (2) information is perfect and mobility is costless. But unlike the perfect competitor, the monopsonist is a wage setter; it can control the wage rate it pays by adjusting the amount of labor it hires, much as a product market monopolist can control its price by adjusting its output.

---

[4] We are assuming that the monopoly firm cannot "price discriminate." If it could charge purchasers the exact price they would be willing to pay rather than do without the product, MRP would coincide with VMP in Figure 6.6. The firm would now find it profitable to hire Q_c (rather than Q_m) workers, and labor resources would be allocated efficiently (Q_c).

TABLE 6.2
Wage and
Employment
Determination:
Monopsony
(Hypothetical
Data)

(1) Units of Labor	(2) (AWC) Wage	(3) TWC	(4) MWC	(5) (VMP) MRP
1	$1	$1	$1	$7
2	2	4	3	6
3	3	9	5	5
4	4	16	7	4
5	5	25	9	3
6	6	36	11	2

Table 6.2 contains the elements needed to examine labor supply and demand, wage and employment determination, and allocative outcomes in the monopsony model. Comprehension of the table will greatly clarify the graphic analysis that follows.

Notice in Table 6.2 that columns 1 and 2 indicate that the firm must increase the wage rate it pays to attract more units of labor toward this market and away from alternative employment opportunities. We assume that this firm cannot "wage discriminate" when hiring additional workers; it must pay the higher wage *to all workers,* including those who could have been attracted at a lower wage. This fact is reflected in column 3, where total wage cost (TWC) is shown. The values for TWC are found by multiplying the units of labor times the wage rate, rather than by summing the wage column. For example, if the monopsonist hires five units of labor, it will have to pay $5 for each, for a total of $25. Next notice the marginal wage cost (MWC) shown in column 4. The extra cost of hiring, say, the fifth unit of labor ($9) is more than the wage paid for that unit ($5). Each of the four labor units that could have been attracted at $4 must now also be paid $5. The $1 extra wage paid for each of these workers (= $4 total) plus the $5 paid for the fifth worker yields the $9 MWC in column 4. To generalize: *The monopsonist's marginal wage cost exceeds the wage rate because it must pay a higher wage to attract more workers, and it must pay this higher wage to all workers.*

Finally, note column 5 in Table 6.2, which shows the marginal revenue product (MRP) of labor. We know that the MRP schedule is the firm's short-run demand for labor curve. In this case we can avoid unnecessary complexity by assuming that the monopsonist is selling its product in a perfectly competitive market, and therefore MRP = VMP. We will soon discover, however, that the monopsonist will disregard this MRP schedule once it selects its profit-maximizing level of employment.

Figure 6.7 shows the monopsony model graphically. The labor supply curve slopes upward because the monopsonist is the only firm hiring this labor and hence faces the market labor supply curve. Notice that S_L is also the firm's average wage cost (AWC) curve (total wage cost/quantity of labor). Marginal wage cost (MWC) lies above and rises more rapidly than S_L because the higher wage rate paid to attract an additional worker must also be paid to all workers already employed. As we previously indicated,

FIGURE 6.7   Wage Rate and Employment Determination Monopsony
The firm's MWC lies above the S_L = AWC curve in a monopsonistic labor market. The monopsonist equates MRP with its MWC at point a and chooses to hire Q_1 units of labor. To attract these workers it need only pay W_1 an hour, as shown by point e. The firm thus pays a lower wage rate (W_1 rather than W_c) and hires fewer units of labor (Q_1 as compared to Q_c) than firms in a competitive labor market. Society loses area eac because of allocative inefficiency.

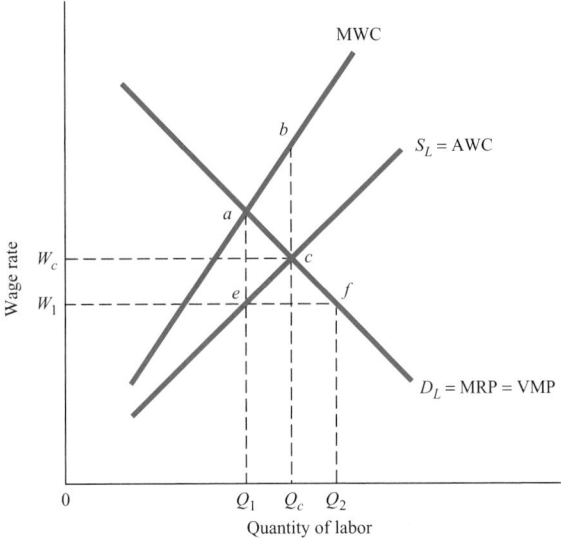

the marginal revenue curve MRP is the competitive labor demand curve and also measures the value of the marginal product of labor, VMP.

What quantity of labor will this monopsonistic firm hire, and what wage will it pay? To maximize profits, the firm will equate MWC with MRP, as shown at point $a,$ and employ Q_1 units of labor. To understand this, suppose the firm employed Q_c units of labor rather than Q_1. The MWC of the Q_c unit is shown by point b on the MWC curve, but the MRP of the extra labor is only c. Thus the firm would lose profits equal to area abc by its action. To repeat: *The monopsonist, like the perfect competitor, finds its profit-maximizing employment level where MRP equals MWC.*

Having decided to hire Q_1 units of labor, the monopsonist's effective labor demand becomes a single point e rather than the entire curve D_L. This point lies along the market labor supply curve $S_L,$ allowing the firm to set the wage at W_1. The market clears at this wage; the quantity of labor demanded by the firm, $Q_1,$ equals the amount of labor that suppliers are willing to offer. This equilibrium wage corresponds to that in Table 6.2 (circled row of data). Notice from point f on the MRP = VMP curve in Figure 6.7, however, that this monopsonist would prefer to hire Q_2 units of labor *if* it could hire each unit at a W_1 wage. Thus the monopsonist may perceive a shortage of this type of labor. It would like more units of labor at the W_1 wage than it can get, but its self-interest keeps it from raising the wage above W_1. This may explain why monopsony markets, such as the one for nurses, are characterized by chronically unfilled job vacancies.[5] If we transformed this labor market into a perfectly competitive one, the equilibrium wage and quantity of labor would be W_c and Q_c units, respectively (point c). But as previously indicated, it simply is not profitable for this monopsonist to hire the Q_c units of labor and pay W_c to all Q_c workers. Instead it restricts the quantity of labor hired and pays (1) a lower-than-competitive wage (W_1 compared to W_c) and (2) a wage below the MRP of the last unit of labor employed (e as opposed to a).

It is easy to see the basic divergence between the monopsonist's profit-maximizing goal and society's desire to maximize the total value of its output. Indeed, MRP equals MWC at Q_1 units of labor, but VMP is greater than the supply price of labor, W_1 ($= Q_1e$). Remember that the market labor supply curve reflects the price of labor in terms of the value of the output that the labor can produce in the next best employment opportunity. We observe that along segment ac of the VMP curve, the value of the marginal product of the Q_1Q_c labor units exceeds the opportunity cost to society of using that labor in this specific employment (shown by ec on the supply of labor curve). Therefore, if society reallocated this labor from alternative employments to this market, it would gain output of more value than it would forgo. The labor would contribute total output shown by area Q_1acQ_c in Figure 6.7. Society would forgo area Q_1ecQ_c of domestic product elsewhere, and thus the net gain would be area eac. This latter triangle identifies the allocative cost to society of the monopsonized labor market. Labor is underallocated to the goods and services produced in monopsonized industries.

Several attempts have been made to identify and measure monopsony power in real-world labor markets. Monopsony outcomes are not widespread in the U.S. economy.[6] Many potential employers exist for most workers, particularly when these workers are occupationally and geographically mobile (Chapter 9). Also, strong labor unions counteract monopsony power in many labor markets (Chapters 10 and 11).

Table 6.3 provides a matrix showing the wage outcomes of the three labor market models discussed thus far. The outcome in the bottom right corner of the matrix simply extends the monopsony outcome to a market where the monopsonist is an imperfect competitor in the sale of the product. You are urged to study each part of this table carefully.

6.2

---

[5] The traditional view is that the labor market for nurses is monopsonistic. Hospitals are relatively few, particularly in small- and medium-size cities. See Richard Hurd, "Equilibrium Vacancies in a Labor Market Dominated by Non-Profit Firms: The 'Shortage' of Nurses," *Review of Economics and Statistics,* May 1973, pp. 234–40. More recent research, however, questions whether monopsony exists in the market for nurses. See Barry T. Hirsch and Edward J. Schumacher, "Monopsony Power and Relative Wages in the Labor Market for Nurses," *Journal of Health Economics,* October 1995, pp. 443–76.

[6] For a survey of theoretical and empirical studies of monopsony, see William M. Boal and Michael R. Ransom, "Monopsony in the Labor Market," *Journal of Economic Literature,* March 1997, pp. 86–112. See also Alan Manning, *Monopsony in Motion: Imperfect Competition in Labor Markets* (Princeton, NJ: Princeton University Press, 2003).

TABLE 6.3
Wage Outcomes of Labor Markets without Unions

		Product Market Structure (Firm)	
		Perfect competitor in sale of product $(MR = P)$	Monopolist in sale of product $(MR < P)$
Labor Market Structure (Firm)	Perfect competitor in hire of labor $(MWC = W)$	$W = MRP = VMP$ (Figure 6.4)	$W = MRP$ $W < VMP$ (Figure 6.6)
	Monopsonist in hire of labor $(MWC > W)$	$W < MRP (= VMP)$ (Figure 6.7)	$W < MRP (< VMP)$

UNIONS AND WAGE DETERMINATION

We assumed throughout the previous discussion that workers *independently* supplied their labor services and therefore competed for available jobs. But in some labor markets workers have organized into unions to sell their labor services *collectively.* These unions can increase the wage rate paid to their members who have jobs by (1) increasing the demand for labor, (2) restricting the supply of labor, and (3) bargaining for an above-equilibrium wage.

Increasing the Demand for Labor

To the limited extent that a union can increase the demand for labor, it can raise *both* the market wage rate and the quantity of labor hired. This is shown in Figure 6.8, where an increase in labor demand from D_0 to D_1 results in a rise in the wage rate from W_0 to W_1 and an increase in employment from Q_0 to Q_1. The more elastic the supply of labor, the less the increase in the wage rate relative to the rise in employment.

Is the Q_1 level of employment an overallocation of labor to this use? It depends. If Q_0 is indeed the efficient level of employment, then triangle *abc* represents an efficiency loss resulting from the union's actions. The opportunity cost of the Q_0Q_1 units of labor (shown by segment *ab* of S) exceeds the VMP of labor (shown by segment *ac* of D_0). But Q_0 need not be the efficient allocation of labor in all instances to which this model applies. We will highlight one such circumstance in the following discussion.

A union can increase labor demand through actions that alter one or more of the determinants of labor demand (Table 6.1). Specifically, it can try to (1) increase product demand, (2) enhance labor productivity, (3) influence the price of related resources, and (4) increase the number of buyers of its specific labor services. Let's analyze these actions and cite examples of each.

| 6.2 | World of Work | Pay and Performance in Professional Baseball |

Professional baseball has provided an interesting laboratory in which the predictions of orthodox wage theory have been empirically tested. Until 1976 professional baseball players were bound to a single team through the so-called reserve clause that prevented players from selling their talents on the open (competitive) market. Stated differently, the reserve clause conferred monopsony power on the team that originally drafted the player. Labor market theory (Figure 6.7) would lead us to predict that this monopsony power would let teams pay wages less than a player's marginal revenue product (MRP). However, since 1976 major league players have been able to become "free agents" at the end of their sixth season of play; at that time they can sell their services to any team. Theory suggests that free agents should be able to increase their salaries and bring them more closely into accord with their MRPs. Research tends to confirm both predictions.

Scully* found that before baseball players could become free agents their salaries were substantially below their MRPs. He estimated a player's MRP as follows. First he determined the relationship between a team's winning percentage and its revenue. Then he estimated the relationship between various possible measures of player productivity and a team's winning percentage. He found the ratio of strikeouts to walks for pitchers and the slugging averages for hitters (all nonpitchers) to be the best indicators of a player's contribution to the winning percentage. These two estimates were combined to calculate the contribution of a player to a team's total revenue.

Scully discovered that prior to free agency the estimated MRPs of both pitchers and hitters were substantially greater than player salaries. Even the lowest-quality pitchers received on the average salaries amounting to only about 54 percent of their MRPs. "Star" players were exploited more than other players. The best pitchers received salaries that were only about 21 percent of their MRPs, according to Scully. The same general results applied to hitters. For example, the least productive hitters on the average received a salary equal to about 37 percent of their MRPs.

Several researchers have examined the impact of free agency on baseball players' salaries.[†] In accordance with the predictions of labor market theory, their studies indicate that the competitive bidding of free agency brought the salaries of free agents more closely into accord with their MRPs. The overturning of the monopsonistic reserve clause forced owners to pay players more closely in relation to their contribution to team revenues.

Thanks largely to free agency, the average salary in major league baseball had soared to $2,866,544 for the 2006 season.

* Gerald W. Scully, "Pay and Performance in Major League Baseball," *American Economic Review,* December 1974, pp. 915–30.

[†] For surveys of such studies, see Andrew Zimbalist, *Baseball and Billions* (New York: Basic Books, 1992); and Lawrence M. Kahn, "The Sports Business as a Labor Market Laboratory," *Journal of Economic Perspectives,* Summer 2000, pp. 75–94.

1 Increasing Product Demand

Unions do not have direct control over the demand for the product they help produce, but they can influence it through political lobbying. For example, unions often actively support proposed legislation that would increase government purchases of the products they make. It is not surprising to see the construction union lobbying for new highway projects, urban mass transit proposals, plans to revitalize urban areas, or flood control

Global Perspective 6.1 — Percentage of Union Wage Differential, Controlling for Worker Characteristics

Japan has the highest union wage differential (the percentage by which union pay exceeds nonunion pay) among major industrial countries.

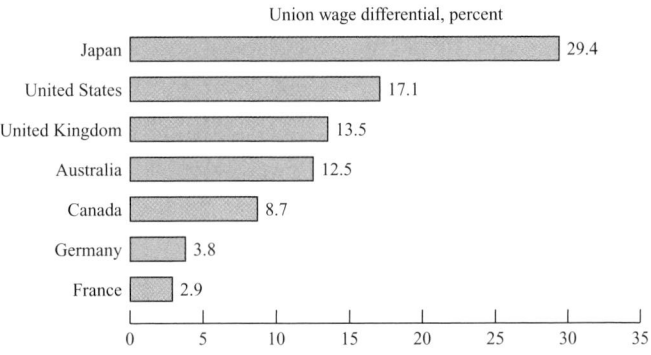

Union wage differential, percent

Japan	29.4
United States	17.1
United Kingdom	13.5
Australia	12.5
Canada	8.7
Germany	3.8
France	2.9

Source: David G. Blachflower and Alex Bryson, "Changes over Time in Union Relative Wage Effects in the UK and US Revisited," in John T. Addison and Claus Schnabel (eds.), *International Handbook of Trade Unions* (Cheltenham, England and Northhampton, MA: Edward Elgar 2003), chap. 7. The wage differential estimates cover the period 1994–1999.

FIGURE 6.8

Union Techniques: Increasing the Demand for Labor

To the extent that unions can increase the demand for union labor (D_0 to D_1), they can realize higher wage rates (W_0 to W_1) and increased employment (Q_0 to Q_1).

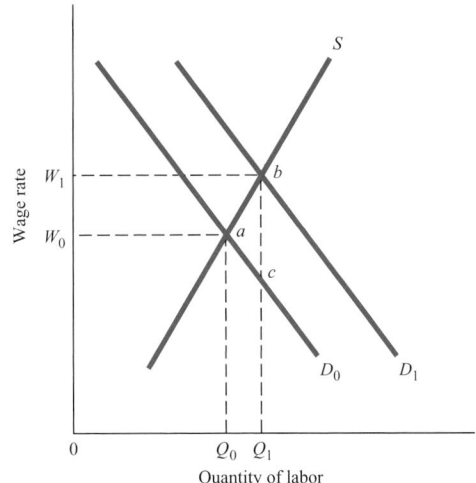

and related water projects. Nor is it unusual to discover teachers' organizations pushing for legislation to increase government spending on education.

For similar reasons, unions also lobby for legislation that bolsters private sector demand for union-made products. For example, unions in the aerospace industry strongly supported legislation granting interest rate subsidies to foreign purchasers of commercial airplanes produced in the United States.

Still another way unions may increase product demand is through political support for laws that increase the price of goods that are close substitutes for those made by union members. For instance, in 2002 the United Steel Workers of America (USWA) joined with major U.S. steel companies to obtain U.S. tariffs on imported steel. These tariffs increased the price of a substitute good (imported steel), raising the demand for domestic steel and strengthening the demand for USWA members.

Finally, some unions recognize that they can enhance the demand for their own labor by lobbying successfully for legislation that *reduces* the price of goods or services that are *complements* to the services they render. For example, unions representing restaurant employees often resist attempts to increase city excise taxes levied on hotels and motels. The lower lodging prices help attract convention business, which increases the demand for restaurant meals and the derived demand for restaurant workers.

6.3

2 Enhancing Productivity

We know that the strength of labor demand in a specific occupation depends partly on productivity (MP). Firms control most factors that determine worker productivity. But two possible ways unions might be able to influence output per worker-hour are participation in joint labor–management committees on productivity (sometimes called *quality circles*) and *codetermination,* which consists of direct worker participation in the decision processes of the firms. The latter also is sometimes called *worker democracy.* The purpose of both approaches is to improve internal communication within the firm and increase productivity through more emphasis on teamwork and profit incentives.

In many cases, unions have resisted participation in quality circles and codetermination, contending that these programs circumvent the collective bargaining process and undermine union authority. In other instances, unions have agreed to participate on an experimental basis. To the extent that either approach raises the marginal product of labor, the demand for labor will increase, improving the union's prospect for negotiating a wage increase.[7] This rightward shift in the labor demand curve does not produce the efficiency loss *abc* in Figure 6.8. The higher level of employment results from the increased productivity of labor, not from an artificial distortion of the allocation of society's resources.

3 Influencing the Prices of Related Inputs

Where labor and some other resource are gross substitutes (substitution effect > output effect), unions can bolster the demand for their own labor by raising the relative price of

---

[7] For one study that finds a positive impact on productivity from cooperative union–management programs, see Michael Schuster, "The Impact of Union–Management Cooperation on Productivity and Employment," *Industrial and Labor Relations Review,* April 1983, pp. 415–30.

6.3	**World of Work**	**The WTO, Trade Liberalization, and Labor Standards***

In November 1999, tens of thousands of people took part in sometimes violent demonstrations in Seattle. The protestors were expressing their opposition to the policies of the World Trade Organization (WTO), which was meeting to reach an agreement on a plan for trade liberalization. The WTO has continued to face protestors at its more recent meetings. The activists are concerned that the nearly 150-nation WTO is not addressing issues involving worker rights and the environment.

The objective of the WTO, which was formed in 1995, is to lessen trade barriers. Its main principle is that each country must treat all other member countries equally with regard to trade barriers. For example, if the United States decides to lower the tariff on foreign cars, then it must lower this tariff for *all* imported cars. There are exceptions for regional trade pacts and developing countries. If a country violates the rules, the WTO may levy sanctions against it.

Labor unions, which were heavily involved in the Seattle protests, want the WTO to have labor and environmental standards. For example, they want the WTO to include in international trade rules a minimum age for child labor, the right to organize and collectively bargain wages, a minimum wage, and working condition standards.

Union members would clearly benefit if these labor standards were adopted. The cost of manufacturing foreign goods would rise and increase the relative price of foreign goods. As a result, the demand for the products that unions help produce would shift rightward. This in turn would raise the demand for union workers.

However, most WTO member nations believe that making such labor and environmental standards part of international trade agreements would simply benefit union workers in the highly developed nations at the broader expense of consumers in the industrially advanced nations as well as consumers and workers in the developing nations. By increasing labor and production costs in the developing nations, such standards would give an advantage to industrially advanced nations that already meet the standards. That would reduce imports and raise prices to consumers worldwide. It would also do great harm to the developing nations by impeding their economic growth. Such growth enables them eventually to afford and implement stricter labor and environmental standards.

* Compiled from news reports.

the other resource. Unions do not have direct control over prices of alternative resources, but there are examples of political actions by unions that might influence such prices. First, unions—generally being populated by higher-paid, skilled workers—may support increases in the minimum wage as a way to raise the relative price of substitutable less skilled, non-unionized labor. As a simple example, suppose two less skilled workers can produce the same amount of output in an hour as one skilled union laborer, but that the hourly pay for the unskilled workers is $2 while the union scale is $5. Obviously firms would hire unskilled workers (per unit wage cost of output = $4). Now assume that unions successfully lobby for a $3 per hour minimum wage for all workers. Assuming that skilled and unskilled workers are substitutes in production and also gross substitutes, this increase in the price of unskilled workers will increase the demand for skilled, union workers. The reason is that now each unit of the product can be produced at less cost by hiring one union worker at $5 an hour rather than employing two unskilled workers at $6 (= 2 × $3).

The *Davis–Bacon Act* (1931) and its amendments provide another example of how unions might be able to increase the price of a resource that is a substitute in production with labor—in this case the price of *skilled nonunion* labor. The act, which has strong union support, requires contractors engaged in federally financed projects to pay "prevailing wages." The latter, in effect, are union wages because the formula for determining prevailing wages mandates that the wage rate that occurs with the greatest frequency be observed. Because nonunion firms normally pay their workers less than the union scale, the act has the effect of raising the price of nonunion labor. Where union and nonunion labor are gross substitutes, the demand for union labor rises, enabling unions to bargain for higher wages without fear of losing federal work to nonunion firms.[8]

Unions also can increase the demand for their labor through support of government actions that reduce the price of resources that are complements in production with labor. As one example, affected unions occasionally argue against rate increases proposed by electric or natural gas utilities, particularly when the industries where they work use substantial amounts of these energy sources. Where labor and energy inputs are pure complements in production and thus gross complements, these price increases will reduce the demand for labor through a significant output effect (higher production costs).

4 Increasing the Number of Employers

Unions can increase the demand for their labor by lobbying for government programs that encourage new employers to establish operations in a local area. For example, unions might favor the issuing of industrial revenue bonds to build industrial parks and property tax breaks to attract domestic or foreign manufacturers.

As a more specific example, the United Auto Workers unsuccessfully lobbied Congress to pass "domestic content" legislation that would have required that substantial portions of automobiles sold in the United States be produced here. This restricted U.S. auto firms from moving the manufacture of major auto components abroad and encouraged foreign firms to locate operations in the United States. In both cases, the domestic demand for U.S. unionized autoworkers would be strengthened.

Restricting the Supply of Labor

Unions also can boost wages by reducing the supply of labor. By referring back to Figure 6.2, you will observe that a union can obtain a higher wage rate if it can shift the labor supply curve leftward. However, the union must accept a decrease in employment in achieving this wage hike. Fortunately for the union, the restriction of labor supply is more likely to occur in a dynamic context wherein the effect is merely to restrict the growth of job opportunities.

In Figure 6.9 we depict a dynamic labor market in which both labor demand and supply are increasing. Let's suppose that demand is rising because of increases in product demand and productivity; supply is increasing because of population growth, which is expanding

---

[8] For empirical evidence in support of the hypothesis that the Davis–Bacon Act increases union wages by increasing union bargaining power, the reader should consult Daniel P. Kessler and Lawrence F. Katz, "Prevailing Wage Laws and Construction Labor Markets," *Industrial and Labor Relations Review,* January 2001, pp. 259–74.

FIGURE 6.9   Union Techniques: Restricting the Supply of Labor

In a dynamic labor market characterized by normal expansions of labor demand and supply, such as D_0 to D_1 and S_0 to S_1, a union or professional organization may be able to increase wage rates (W_1 to W_u) through actions that restrict normal increases in labor supply (S_0 rather than S_1). However, these actions also slow the rate of growth of union employment [$(Q_u - Q_0)/Q_0$ compared to $(Q_1 - Q_0)/Q_0$].

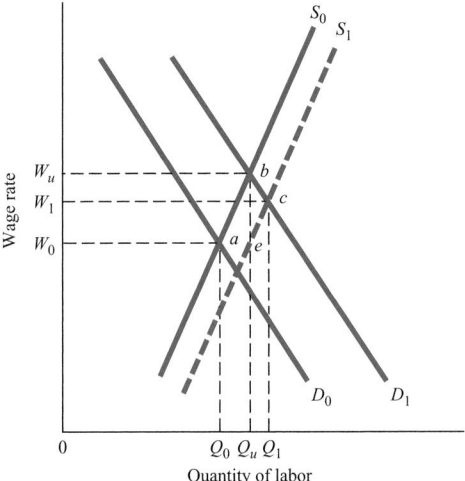

the number of people qualified to supply this labor. In the absence of the union, the increases in demand (D_0 to D_1) and supply (S_0 to the broken line S_1) would raise the wage rate and level of employment from W_0 to W_1 and Q_0 to Q_1, respectively (point *a* to *c*).

Now let's introduce the union and suppose that it takes actions that keep labor supply from expanding to S_1. The result? The market wage will rise to W_u, not W_1, and the quantity of labor hired will be Q_u, as opposed to Q_1. This union has increased the wage rate by restricting the growth of labor supply. In this case, the action also slows the growth rate of employment: $(Q_u - Q_0)/Q_0$ compared to $(Q_1 - Q_0)/Q_0$. The greater the elasticity of labor demand, of course, the greater the negative employment impact of a given supply restriction. Finally, the union action causes an efficiency loss of triangle *ebc*. If the $Q_u Q_1$ workers had been employed here, they would have contributed more to the value of society's output (segment *bc* of D_1 than they would have added in their best alternative employment (segment *ec* of S_1).

Unions can restrict labor supply by taking actions or supporting government policies that alter one or more determinants of labor supply (Table 6.1). One of these factors in particular (reducing the number of qualified suppliers) is most easily influenced by unions. One other (influencing nonwage income) is also of some significance.

1 Reducing the Number of Qualified Suppliers of Labor

One way that unions in general can limit the supply of qualified workers in a specific labor market is to restrict the overall "stock" of qualified workers in the nation. This partially explains why organized labor has strongly supported (a) limited immigration, (b) child labor laws, (c) compulsory retirement, and (d) shorter workweeks.

Unions also can restrict labor supply for particular jobs by limiting entry into the occupation itself. For example, craft unions composed of workers of a specific skill—such as plumbers, carpenters, or bricklayers—and some professional groups such as the American Medical Association allegedly have controlled access to training and established extraordinarily long apprenticeship programs to limit labor supply. Thus this type of unionism is sometimes referred to as *exclusive unionism;* the supply restriction derives from actions that exclude potential workers from participating in the trade or profession.

Of perhaps greater importance, unions and professional groups have been able to limit entry to certain jobs through **occupational licensure,** *which is the enactment of laws by government to force practitioners of a trade to meet certain requirements.* These requirements may specify the level of educational attainment or amount of work experience needed and may also include the passing of an examination to obtain a license. State licensing boards have wide discretion in establishing the tests and standards needed to qualify for a license. In fact, there is evidence suggesting that some boards adjust the "pass rate" as a way to control the rate of entry into the licensed occupation.[9] Furthermore, the licensing requirements may include a minimum residency stipulation that inhibits the flow of qualified workers between states. Hence occupational licensure restricts labor supply and increases the wage rate as shown in Figure 6.9.[10]

A final means by which unions may limit labor supply to an occupation is through discrimination by race or gender. Some predominantly male craft unions and professional organizations have explicitly or implicitly argued that their particular type of work is "too physical" or "too stressful" to be performed by females and then have taken such actions as instituting overly rigorous physical requirements to make it difficult for women to enter the trade or occupation. Some craft unions also have engaged in racial segregation, perhaps resulting from the direct economic self-interest evident in Figure 6.9.[11]

2 Influencing Nonwage Income

Unions and professional organizations may also improve their wages by affecting the nonwage income determinant of labor supply. They may be able to accomplish this through legislation that provides income to unemployed workers, partially disabled workers, and older citizens. Stated differently, among the several reasons why labor unions generally support increased unemployment compensation, workers' compensation, and Social Security retirement benefits is the fact that these sources of nonwage income reduce labor force participation (Chapter 2) and therefore raise the before-tax

[9] Alex Maurizi, "Occupational Licensing and the Public Interest," *Journal of Political Economy,* March/April 1974, pp. 399–413.

[10] For evidence consistent with this point, see Morris Kliener, "Occupational Licensing," *Journal of Economic Perspectives,* Fall 2000, pp. 189–202. Also see Morris M. Kleiner, *Licensing Occupations: Ensuring Quality or Restricting Competition?* (Kalamazoo, MI: W.E. Upjohn Institute, 2006).

[11] For evidence of discrimination by unions, see Orley Ashenfelter, "Discrimination and Trade Unions," in Orley Ashenfelter and Albert Rees (eds.), *Discrimination in Labor Markets* (Princeton, NJ: Princeton University Press, 1973). See also Larry D. Singell, Jr., "Racial Differences in the Employment Policy of State and Local Governments: The Case of Male Workers," *Southern Economic Journal,* October 1991, pp. 430–44. The economic aspects of labor market discrimination will be examined in detail in Chapters 14 and 15.

wages to those employed. This is *not* to suggest that this is a primary reason for such support; after all, union members must join others in paying for government transfers through higher taxes (lower after-tax wages). Rather, such support is consistent with Figure 6.9.

Bargaining for an Above-Equilibrium Wage

In addition to restricting the supply of labor to an occupation (shifting the labor supply curve leftward), some unions succeed in enlisting as union members a large percentage of the available workers in an industry or occupation. Through recruitment of union members, an *industrial union* can gain control over a firm's labor supply. During negotiations the union therefore can credibly threaten to withhold labor—to strike—unless the employer increases its wage offer. Because these unions attempt to attract or "include" all potential industry workers into the union, this form of unionism is called *inclusive unionism.* Examples of industrial unions that control high percentages of industry labor supply within the domestic economy include the United Auto Workers and the United Steelworkers of America (USA).

The impact of control over labor supply by a union is shown graphically in Figure 6.10. Suppose employers in this labor market act independently, and in the absence of the union the competitive equilibrium wage rate and level of employment are W_c and Q_c. Now suppose a union forms and successfully bargains for the higher, above-equilibrium wage rate W_u. This in effect makes the labor supply curve perfectly elastic

FIGURE 6.10   Union Techniques: Bargaining for a Higher Wage
By organizing all available workers and securing union shops, inclusive unions may successfully bargain for a wage rate, such as W_u, that is above the competitive wage rate W_c. The effects are to make the labor supply curve perfectly elastic between W_u and point e (MWC = AWC = S_L), to reduce employment from Q_c to Q_u, and to create an efficiency loss of area *fba.* The more elastic the labor demand, the greater the employment and allocative impacts.

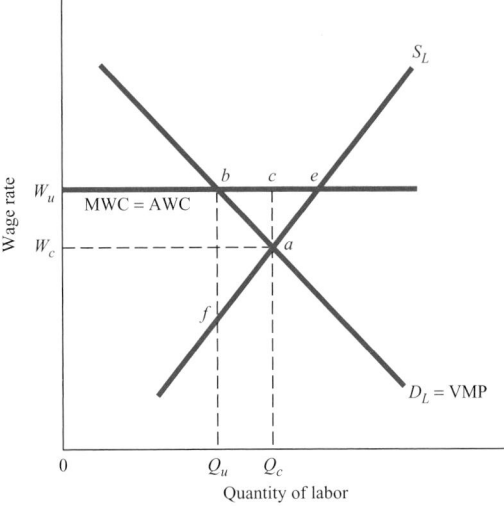

over the $W_u e$ range. If employers hire any number of workers within this range, they must pay the union scale W_u or the union will withdraw *all* labor via a strike. If the employers desire more than e workers, however, say because of a major expansion of labor demand during the life of the union contract, they will need to pay wages above the union's scale to attract workers away from alternative jobs paying more than W_u.

Notice the *postunion* employment outcome in Figure 6.10. Employers respond to the union-imposed wage rate W_u by discharging cb workers ($Q_c Q_u$). Furthermore, the higher wage attracts ce additional job seekers to the occupation. Thus excess labor supply be exists at the union-imposed wage. The greater the elasticity of demand, the wider the range cb. The more elastic the preunion supply of labor, the greater the gap ce.

This model enables us to understand several observed labor market phenomena and union actions. First, it explains why some unionized labor markets are characterized by chronic waiting lists for jobs. Second, and closely related, it clarifies why labor organizations place great emphasis on gaining *union security* provisions in labor contracts. The union's bargaining power relies to a great extent on the credibility of its threat to call for a strike and on its ability to withhold the firm's entire labor supply once a work stoppage occurs. A **union shop clause** permits the firm to hire nonunion workers but requires that workers join the union following a probationary period. These clauses typically increase the percentage of workers who are union members. Thus a strike occurring when the existing contract expires is likely to deprive the firm of such a substantial portion of its labor supply that the firm will be forced to curtail or cease production. The potential or actual loss of profit from a threatened or actual strike increases the union's bargaining power and improves the union's chances of getting an above-equilibrium wage, such as W_u in Figure 6.10.

Third, the distance bc in Figure 6.10 sheds light on why unions are interested in securing contract provisions that reduce the elasticity of labor demand. The lower this elasticity, the smaller the number of displaced workers from any given wage increase. Recall that one major determinant of the elasticity of labor demand is the substitutability of other inputs. What contract provisions might reduce the substitution of capital for union labor? What provisions might limit the substitution of nonunion labor for union workers? Examples of the first include provisions limiting new technology, requiring redundant labor ("featherbedding"), and providing supplementary unemployment benefits (SUBs). By dictating the pace of the introduction of new technology and engaging in featherbedding, the union can temporarily reduce the elasticity of labor demand—that is, slow the substitution of capital for labor in response to wage increases. SUBs and severance pay provisions perform a similar function; if high enough, they raise the effective price of any capital used to replace union labor. Examples of contract provisions that reduce the substitutability of nonunion and union labor include clauses preventing subcontracting and plant relocation. Both are sometimes used to economize on the use of union labor following union-imposed wage increases. But by preventing such actions, the union at least temporarily reduces the elasticity of labor demand.

The employment impact of the union-imposed above-equilibrium wage in Figure 6.10 will be greater as time transpires. For example, the firm may resist continuing

World of Work

6.4

Has Deunionization Increased Earnings Inequality?*

A major economic trend of the past two decades has been the sharp rise in earnings inequality. One measure of inequality is the 90–10 wage ratio, which is the hourly wage at the 90th percentile divided by the hourly wage at the 10th percentile. That ratio rose from 3.7 in 1974 to 4.5 in 2005. Over the same period unionization declined rapidly. In 1974, 23.6 percent of wage and salary workers were union members; by 2005, union membership had dropped to 12.5 percent.

In theory, unionism has ambiguous effects on income inequality. On one hand, unions increase income inequality because they raise the wages of union workers relative to their nonunion counterparts and because they are made up largely of higher-paid blue-collar workers. On the other hand, unions lower income inequality because they equalize wages within and across firms with unionized workers. In addition, unions tend to lower the wage gap between white-collar and blue-collar workers because they raise the relative wages of their mainly blue-collar members. Though unions have uncertain effects in theory on income inequality, the evidence generally indicates they tend to reduce income inequality.

How much has the decline in unionization contributed to the increased income inequality? Card concludes that 15–20 percent of the rise in earnings inequality among male workers and little of the rise in inequality among female workers are due to declining unionism. Other factors, such as greater demand for skilled workers due to improvements in technology as well as an increased supply of low-skilled workers because of growth in immigration, also contributed to the rise in inequality.

* Based on David Card, "The Effect of Unions on Wage Inequality in the U.S. Labor Market," *Industrial and Labor Relations Review*, January 2001, pp. 296–315; and Barry T. Hirsch and David A. Macpherson, *Union Membership and Earnings Databook: Compilations from the Current Population Survey* (Washington, DC: Bureau of National Affairs, 2006). Updated.

the contract provisions that keep the short-run demand curve inelastic. Alternatively, foreign or nonunion competition may arise in response to the high product prices in unionized industries. On the other hand, in a growing economy the demand curves for most types of labor gradually shift rightward over time. Instead of an absolute decline in the number of jobs in the unionized labor market, the outcome may simply be slower growth of job opportunities. In this respect, no specific layoff of existing union workers is observed. This may explain why some union leaders have in the past erroneously concluded that demand for labor curves are highly inelastic.

A final observation from Figure 6.10 is that given homogeneous workers, a union-imposed above-equilibrium wage creates a misallocation of labor resources. Notice that the value of the marginal product b exceeds the marginal opportunity cost of labor f at wage W_u and quantity Q_u. If $Q_u Q_c$ workers were transferred from competitive labor markets to this one, society would experience a net gain in the value of its output equal to area fba.[12]

6.4

[12] A more complete analysis of the efficiency losses created by unions is provided in Chapter 11.

BILATERAL MONOPOLY

In the previous section we assumed that a union had gained control over the supply of labor in an otherwise competitive labor market. But what if a monopsonist and a strong industrial union coexist in a labor market? This situation is characteristic of some U.S. labor markets. For example, in the eastern coal industry the United Mine Workers (UMW) union confronts a multiemployer bargaining unit in negotiating a standard labor contract. In the labor market for automobile workers, the UAW bargains individually with the "Big Three" U.S. auto manufacturers. Similarly, the Communication Workers union negotiates with regional telephone service monopsonists, and the players' associations of various professional sports bargain against unified team owners. Will the wage be below or above the competitive equilibrium wage in these *bilateral monopoly* situations?[13] The answer is that the wage outcome is *indeterminate:* The negotiated wage rate may be either above, below, or equal to the competitive wage rate. Let's explore why.

In Figure 6.11 we combine the monopsony model (Figure 6.7) and the union model (Figure 6.10) to illustrate bilateral monopoly. For simplicity, we once again assume that the product is sold in a perfectly competitive market (MRP = VMP). If monopsony alone existed in this market, the wage rate would be W_m and the level of employment

FIGURE 6.11   Bilateral Monopoly in the Labor Market

When a monopsonistic employer must buy labor services from a monopolistic union, the wage rate and employment outcomes are indeterminate. However, if the union negotiates a wage above W_m but below W_u employment will increase and allocative efficiency will improve relative to the situation under monopsony alone (W_m, Q_1).

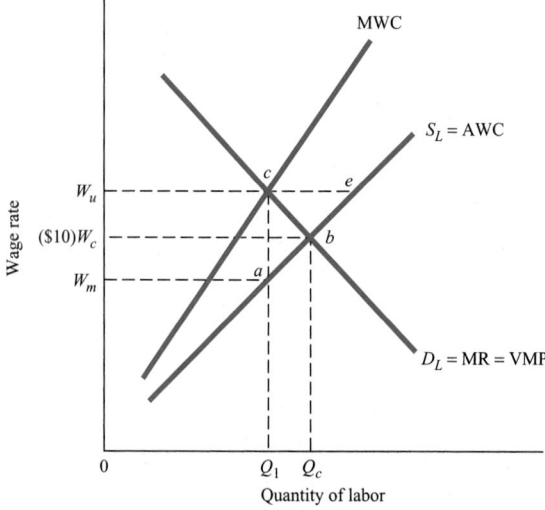

[13] It is important to note that we are using the term *monopoly* conceptually here. Legally, labor unions are not monopolies and are not subject to antitrust laws when engaged in their normal activities. Congress and the courts have declared that "labor is not an article of commerce."

would be Q_1. On the other hand, if the union could set any wage rate it desired, it might select W_u.[14] Neither the employer nor the union, however, can impose its desired wage on the other in this situation. If the monopsonist offers W_m, the union may threaten to withhold the supply of labor via a strike. If the union demands W_u, the monopsonist may resist, believing that it is too costly to pay the wage rate relative to the expected costs associated with either allowing the strike or locking out workers. Thus we are left with a *range* of possible wage outcomes—W_m to W_u—and the mutual interest of the two parties will normally result in a negotiated wage rate acceptable to each. The final wage will depend on the relative bargaining strength and prowess of each party (Chapter 10).

Careful scrutiny of the bilateral monopoly situation shown in Figure 6.11 reveals several interesting points. First, it is possible that the negotiated wage will be at or near the wage rate W_c, which would have occurred if *neither* monopsony nor union power existed in the market. In that case the quantity of labor hired would be Q_c (point b). The perfectly elastic segment of S_L would now be $W_c b$, which means that the coincident MWC intersects MRP at the Q_c level of employment. And because perfect competition is assumed to exist in the product market, labor resources would be efficiently allocated.

Second, the union may be able simultaneously to increase (1) the wage rate, (2) the level of employment, and (3) allocative efficiency. Notice that any increase in the wage above W_m but below W_u causes the firm to increase its employment beyond Q_1. Why? Once the firm agrees to one of these wage rates, its incentive to restrict employment disappears; at the negotiated wage, its marginal wage cost (MWC) and average wage cost (AWC) become perfectly horizontal overlaying lines. Therefore, the firm equates the negotiated wage (MWC) with the marginal revenue product (MRP) and hires more workers than it would if its MWC exceeded its AWC. For example, if the negotiated wage is W_c, and this happens to be $10 an hour, then from the firm's perspective, the MWC and AWC are also $10 per hour. The firm will operate where MRP and this wage rate are equal and hire b rather than a units of labor. Notice also that area abc portrays the efficiency loss associated with either wage rate W_m or W_u. If the union negotiates a wage above W_m but below W_u, this area will diminish. In the case of W_c, it disappears! Hence the presence of unions in monopsonized labor markets may enhance allocative efficiency. Galbraith has called this tendency ***countervailing power,*** or offsetting power.

A caution: Some economists reject the proposition that countervailing power is the actual outcome in circumstances of bilateral monopoly. Adams and Brock, for example, argue that where firms possessing monopsony power also dominate their product markets, countervailing power gives way to ***coalescing power.*** This coalescing power results from tacit vertical collusion between the union and the firm to suppress competition in the firm's product market. More concretely, the union and firm may jointly use their political power to secure government regulation of entry into the industry, tariff protection, domestic content legislation, and so on, which increase both product prices *and* wages.[15]

A final observation from Figure 6.11 is that even though the low monopsony wage W_m and the high union wage W_u result in the same employment level (Q_1), at wages W_m through W_c the labor market clears (although there may be a perceived shortage). But

---

[14] In Chapter 10 we will analyze the criteria that a union might use to determine this wage rate.

[15] Walter Adams and James W. Brock, "Tacit Collusion and the Labor-Industrial Complex," *Nebraska Law Review,* 1983, pp. 623–707.

for wages above W_c unemployment occurs. For example, at wage W_u the firm hires only *c* units of labor, but *e* units are supplied. Some of the *ce* suppliers may be willing to wait for job turnover to enable them to gain employment in this market. Because they are in the labor force and seeking work, they are officially unemployed.

Table 6.4 summarizes the wage and employment outcomes under unionism where both competitive hiring and monopsony exist. This table merits careful review.

6.2
Quick Review

- A monopsonist pays a lower wage rate and employs fewer workers than firms hiring in a competitive labor market; this outcome is allocatively inefficient.
- Unions can raise the wage rate by increasing labor demand through actions that *(a)* increase product demand, *(b)* enhance productivity, *(c)* alter the prices of related inputs, and *(d)* increase the number of employees.
- Unions can increase the wage rate by restricting labor supply; actions include *(a)* reducing the number of qualified labor suppliers and *(b)* influencing nonwage income.
- Unions can raise the wage rate by gaining control over a firm's potential labor supply and threatening to withhold labor unless an acceptable negotiated wage rate is obtained.
- When a monopsonistic employer faces a monopolistic union, the wage rate and employment outcomes are indeterminate; they are set through collective bargaining.

Your Turn

 Why does the monopsonist's MWC curve lie above the market labor supply curve? Isn't this a disadvantage to the monopsonist? (*Answers:* See page 597.)

TABLE 6.4
Wage (*W*) and Employment (*Q*) Outcomes of Labor Markets with Unions

		Labor Market Structure (Firms)	
		Perfect competition in hire of labor	Monopsonist
Labor Market Structure (Workers)	No union	Competitive *W* and *Q* (Figure 6.4)	Less than competitive *W*; reduced *Q* (Figure 6.7)
	Union	Higher than competitive *W*; reduced *Q* (Figures 6.9 and 6.10); increased *Q* (Figure 6.8)	Indeterminate *W* and *Q* (Figure 6.11)

6.5	World of Work	NAFTA and American Labor

After much national and congressional debate, in late 1993 Congress passed the North American Free Trade Agreement (NAFTA). This agreement will eliminate tariffs and other trade barriers among the United States, Canada, and Mexico over a 15-year period. NAFTA will constitute the world's largest free-trade zone, covering 440 million people. Economists generally agree that this trade pact will raise the standard of living of U.S. citizens and Mexicans, mainly through increased output and lower product prices.

Some preliminary analysis has been done on NAFTA's impact on international trade. Trade among the United States, Canada, and Mexico has expanded. The largest increase has been between the United States and Mexico. For example, Mexico's share of U.S. imports rose from 6.6 percent in 1993 to 10.4 percent in 2004, while Mexico's share of U.S. exports rose from 8.9 percent to 13.5 percent over this period.* Gould finds that imports and exports between the United States and Mexico are 16 percent higher with NAFTA than without it.†

The effect of NAFTA on employment appears to have been modest. Thorbecke and Eigen-Zucchi conclude that there has been little net employment change in the United States due to NAFTA.‡ They note that in the first 65 months of NAFTA, about 3,000 people per month have received unemployment benefits as a result of a government-certified job loss due to NAFTA. They also point out that NAFTA-certified layoffs were about 1.5 percent of the monthly employment growth during this period.

So NAFTA won't be fully implemented until 2009, so it will take several more years to make a more definite conclusion about its effects.

* http://www.wto.org and http://www.stlouisfed.org.

† David M. Gould, "Has NAFTA Changed North American Trade?" *Federal Reserve Bank of Dallas Economic Review,* 1st Quarter 1998, pp. 12–23.

‡ Willem Thorbecke and Christian Eigen-Zucchi, "Did NAFTA Cause a Giant 'Sucking Sound'?" *Journal of Labor Research,* Fall 2002, pp. 647–58.

WAGE DETERMINATION: DELAYED SUPPLY RESPONSES

The standard supply and demand model of the labor market (Figures 6.2 and 6.3) assumes that suppliers of labor respond quickly to changes in the market wage rate brought about by changes in labor demand. When the market wage rate rises in relative terms, more workers offer their labor services in that market. When the market wage falls, fewer workers supply their labor services there. Movements of this sort along a market supply of labor curve bring the quantity of labor supplied into equality with the quantity of labor demanded at the equilibrium wage rate. In brief, the labor market immediately clears.

Although rapid supply responses are indeed characteristic of some labor markets, in other situations labor supply adjustments are less rapid than the standard model suggests. In fact, in some cases supply adjustments may take several years. Our attention now turns to a model of one of these slowly adjusting labor markets.

Cobweb Model

Consider Figure 6.12, where we depict the market for new engineers who are recent college graduates. Suppose labor demand and supply initially are *D* and *S*, respectively.

FIGURE 6.12 Cobweb Model

The market for highly trained professionals such as engineers is characterized by delayed supply responses to changes in demand and wage rates. Because the quantity of labor supplied is temporarily fixed at Q_0, the wage rate rises to W_1 when demand changes from D to D_1. At wage rate W_1, Q_1 engineers eventually are attracted to this profession. With supply fixed at Q_1, however, the wage rate falls to W_2. Given this wage rate, the quantity of engineers available eventually falls to Q_2. This cycle repeats until equilibrium is achieved—in this case at the intersection of S and D_1.

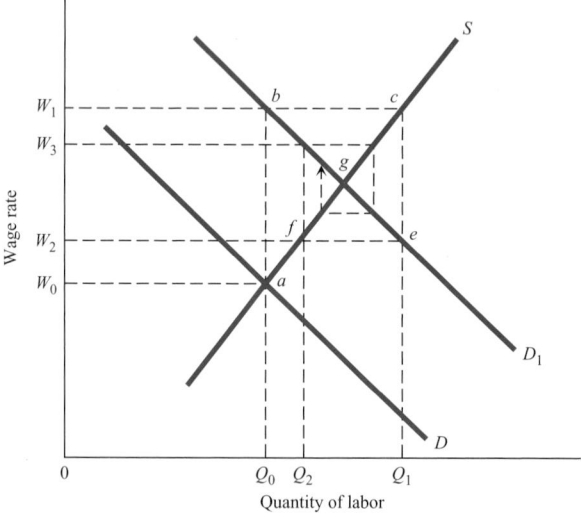

Also assume that the market is presently in equilibrium at *a,* where the wage rate is W_0 and the level of employment is Q_0.

Now suppose an unexpected increase in the demand for engineers occurs, perhaps because of the emergence of new technologies. In the standard labor market model the market would quickly clear at the intersection of supply S and demand D_1. But the market for new engineers and other highly trained professionals is atypical. It is not unusual in these markets to observe four- or five-year delays in the supply response to the new labor market conditions. Students currently enrolling in engineering schools will not graduate and enter the labor force for several years.

In the immediate market period the number of new engineers available remains temporarily fixed at Q_0. The immediate market period is so short that there is no quantity-supplied response to a change in the wage rate. We might therefore envision a vertical *immediate-market-period labor supply curve* emanating upward from Q_0 through *a* and *b.* Supply curve *S,* on the other hand, may be thought of as the *long-run supply curve;* it indicates the *eventual* response of labor suppliers to changes in wage rates. Here the long run entails a four- to five-year period.

Given that Q_0 engineers are now in the labor force and that demand now is D_1, a *shortage* of workers will occur at W_0 and the market wage rate will shoot upward to W_1. This wage rate will eliminate the shortage because at point *b,* demand curve D_1 intersects the vertical immediate-market-period labor supply curve comprised of Q_0ab.

This is only the beginning of the story. Because of the high wage rate W_1, numerous new students will flock to the field of engineering. When they graduate some five years hence, Q_1 engineers will be available in the labor market. This supply response is determined at c on the long-run supply curve S and results from the previous wage rate W_1. In effect, the vertical immediate-market-period labor supply curve shifts rightward in a parallel fashion from Q_0 to Q_1.

Now that the quantity of labor supplied is again temporarily fixed—this time at Q_1— a *surplus* of bc engineers occurs at W_1. The wage rate consequently drops to W_2 (point e on D_1. Here the new immediate-market-period labor supply curve going upward from Q_1 through e and c cuts the demand curve D_1 at e, and the surplus is eliminated.

This scenario continues. Although the new starting wage rate W_2 is considerably lower than W_1, it will not immediately elicit a decline in the number of new engineers offering their labor services. Recent graduates holding engineering degrees are not likely to abandon their careers in response to lower relative salaries. Moreover, wage rate W_2 in all likelihood is higher than wage rates available to engineers in nonengineering jobs. The relatively low wage rate W_2, however, *does* affect the decisions of beginning college students who are planning their academic programs. The poor starting pay will discourage these students from opting to become engineers. In four or five years colleges will confer fewer engineering diplomas during their graduation ceremonies. The number of new engineers in this labor market will fall from Q_1 to Q_2, the latter being determined at f on long-run supply curve S. Given demand D_1, a shortage of fe engineers occurs, and the wage rate responds by rising from W_2 to W_3.

The cycle just described repeats itself. The quantity of labor *demanded* in each period depends on the wage rate at that time; the quantity of labor *supplied* in each period results from the wage rate during the previous period when education and career decisions were originally made. In this instance, equilibrium eventually is achieved at the intersection of the long-run labor supply curve S and demand curve D_1. You are urged to carry the analysis forward through another cycle to test your understanding of this unusual model. The adjustment path toward equilibrium at g results in a cobweb pattern; for that reason this model is called a **cobweb model.**

Two further observations merit comment. It is entirely possible for still another shift in labor demand to occur before the cobweb path is completed to g. Thus a new set of cobweb adjustments may be necessitated. Also, the elasticities of the demand and supply curves might be such that the market does not move to the ultimate equilibrium at g, but rather continues to oscillate between periodic shortages and surpluses.[16]

Evidence and Controversy

Cobweb models help explain adjustments in several labor markets having long training periods and highly specialized labor. For example, historical cobweb adjustments have been found in the markets for new engineers, lawyers, and physicists.[17]

---

[16] For the cobweb model to converge toward equilibrium, the supply curve must be steeper than the demand curve.

[17] Richard B. Freeman, "A Cobweb Model of the Starting Salary of New Engineers," *Industrial and Labor Relations Review,* January 1976, pp. 236–48; Freeman, "Legal Cobwebs: A Recursive Model of the Market for New Lawyers," *Review of Economics and Statistics,* May 1975, pp. 171–80; Freeman, "Supply and Salary Adjustments to the Changing Science Manpower Markets: Physics, 1948–1973," *American Economic Review,* March 1975, pp. 27–39.

World of Work 6.6

Do Medical Students Know How Much Doctors Earn?*

Usually labor economists assume that individuals make unbiased predictions about their future income prospects. That is, people make income forecasts that are not systematically high or low. Economists also assume that people have access to the same information and use this information in the same manner to generate their income forecasts.

Nicholson tested these assumptions by examining how much medical students know about the current earnings of physicians. To conduct his study, Nicholson used data from an annual survey, conducted between 1974 and 1998, of medical students at a large medical school in Philadelphia. The survey asks first- and fourth-year medical school students how much physicians currently receive in six specialties and which specialty they prefer.

The results indicate that medical students have a significant amount of error in their estimates of current earnings of physicians. The average medical student overestimated physician earnings in the 1970s, but now she underestimates earnings by 25 percent. Though the average error rate is substantial, students are more accurate in estimating earnings for their preferred specialties. Also, students learn over time: Their forecast error is 35 percent lower for students in the fourth year than those in the first year. The error rate varies by demographic group: Students who are female, older, or have a higher medical entrance exam score tend to underestimate earnings more than their peers.

* Based on Sean Nicholson, "How Much Do Medical Students Know about Physician Income?" *Journal of Human Resources*, Winter 2005, pp. 100–14.

But not all economists find the cobweb model persuasive. Some critics question the relevance of the model to the majority of today's labor markets for the college-trained workforce. You will note that in the model labor market participants are assumed to adjust their career decisions to changes in *starting salaries.* Some economists suggest that the more likely scenario is that college students look to the present value of *lifetime earnings streams* (Chapter 4) in making education and career decisions.[18] Other critics assert that today's students are highly attuned to the possible boom–bust potential in some labor markets. Therefore, they form *rational expectations* about the end result of any sudden change in the demand for labor and adjust their supply responses accordingly. If either of these two related criticisms is correct, the abrupt changes in immediate-market-period labor supply in the cobweb model and the resulting oscillating path to equilibrium are less likely to occur. That is, equilibrium is more likely to be achieved without the cobweb effects.

In any event, the cobweb model is important because it reminds us that labor supply adjustments are not always as immediate or as certain as our basic labor market model predicts. The upshot is that many labor markets may better be characterized as moving toward allocative efficiency ($VMP = P_L$) than as having actually achieved it.

[18] See Joel W. Hay, "Physicians' Specialty Choice and Specialty Income," in G. Duru and J. H. P. Paelinck (eds.), *Econometrics of Health Care* (Netherlands: Kluwer Academic, 1991); and Sean Nicholson, "Physician Specialty Choice under Uncertainty," *Journal of Labor Economics,* October 2002, pp. 816–47.

Chapter Summary

1. In a competitive labor market, the demand for labor is a price-adjusted summation of labor demand by independently acting individual employers, and the supply of labor is a summation of the responses of individual workers to various wage rates. Market supply and demand determine an equilibrium wage rate and level of employment.

2. The vertical height of the market labor supply curve measures the opportunity cost to society of employing the last worker in some specific use (P_L). The vertical height of the labor demand curve indicates the extra revenue the employer gains by hiring that unit of labor (MRP) and, given perfectly competitive markets, the value of that output to society (VMP).

3. The locations of the supply and demand curves in the labor market depend on the determinants of each (Table 6.1). When one of these determinants changes, the affected curve shifts either rightward or leftward, altering the equilibrium wage and employment levels.

4. The individual firm operating in a perfectly competitive labor market is a wage taker. This implies that its MWC equals the wage rate W; that is, the supply of labor is perfectly elastic. This firm maximizes its profits by hiring the quantity of labor at which MRP = MWC, or MRP = W.

5. An efficient allocation of labor occurs when the VMPs of a particular type of labor are equal in various uses and these VMPs also equal the opportunity cost P_L of that labor. Perfectly competitive product and resource markets result in allocative efficiency. By maximizing profits where MRP = MWC, firms also equate VMP and P_L because MRP = VMP and MWC = P_L.

6. Monopoly in the product market causes marginal revenue to fall faster than product price as more workers are hired and output is expanded. Because product price P exceeds marginal revenue MR, it follows that MRP (= MP × MR) is less than VMP (= MP × P). The result is less employment and an underallocation of labor resources relative to the case of perfect competition in the product market.

7. Under monopsony MWC > S_L (or P_L) because the employer must bid up wages to attract a greater quantity of labor and pay the higher wage to all workers. Consequently, it will employ fewer workers than under competitive conditions and pay a wage rate below the MRP of labor. This underallocation of labor resources (VMP > P_L) reduces the total value of output in the economy.

8. Unions can increase the wage rate paid to members who are employed by *(a)* increasing the demand for labor, *(b)* restricting the supply of labor, and *(c)* bargaining for an above-equilibrium wage. To increase the demand for labor, unions try to increase product demand, enhance productivity, influence the price of related inputs, and increase the number of employers. To restrict labor supply, unions attempt to affect the number of qualified suppliers, nonwage income, and alternative wages. To control labor supply, unions organize inclusively and bargain for union shops.

9. Bilateral monopoly is a labor market situation in which a union that controls labor supply faces a monopsonistic employer or coalition of employers. Although the wage rate and employment outcomes are indeterminate, the possibility arises that

through collective bargaining a union may be able to enhance simultaneously *(a)* its wage rate, *(b)* the level of employment, and *(c)* allocative efficiency.

10. The cobweb model traces labor supply adjustments to changes in labor demand and wage rates in markets characterized by long training periods. The equilibrium wage rate is achieved only after a period of oscillating wage rate changes caused by recurring labor shortages and surpluses.

Terms and Concepts

perfectly competitive labor market, *171*
determinants of labor supply and demand, *174*
marginal revenue product, *176*
average wage cost, *178*
marginal wage cost, *178*

MRP = MWC rule, *178*
efficient allocation of labor, *179*
price of labor, *179*
pure monopsony, *183*
joint monopsony, *183*
Davis–Bacon Act, *192*
exclusive unionism, *194*

occupational licensure, *194*
inclusive unionism, *195*
union shop clause, *196*
bilateral monopoly, *198*
countervailing power, *199*
coalescing power, *199*
cobweb model, *203*

Questions and Study Suggestions

1. List the distinct characteristics of a perfectly competitive labor market and compare them to the characteristics of monopsony.

2. Explain why most market labor supply curves slope upward and to the right, even though individual labor supply curves are presumed to be backward-bending. How does the height of a market labor supply curve relate to the concept of opportunity costs?

3. What effect will each of the following have on the market labor demand for a specific type of labor?

   a. An increase in product demand that increases product price.
   b. A decline in the productivity of this type of labor.
   c. An increase in the price of a gross substitute for labor.
   d. A decline in the price of a gross complement for labor.
   e. The demise of several firms that hire this labor.
   f. A decline in the market wage rate for this labor.
   g. A series of mergers that transforms the product market into a monopoly.

4. Predict the impact of each of the following on the equilibrium wage rate and level of employment in labor market *A*:

   a. An increase in labor demand and supply in labor market *A*.
   b. The transformation of labor market *A* from a competitive to a monopsonistic market.

5. Assume a surplus of doctors exists. Use labor market supply and demand graphics to depict this outcome. How would the market remedy this situation in the short run and the long run?

Q_B	VMP_{Bx}	VMP_{By}
1	$18	$23
2	15	19
3	12	15
4	9	11
5	6	9
6	3	5

6. Answer the following questions on the basis of the table shown here. Q_B is type B labor, and VMP_{Bx} and VMP_{By} are the industry values of the marginal products of this labor in producing x and y, the only two goods in the economy.
   a. Explain why the VMPs in the table decline as more units of labor are employed.
   b. If the supply price or opportunity cost of labor P_L is $9, how many units of type B labor need to be used in producing x and y to achieve an efficient allocation of labor? What will be the combined total value of the two outputs?
   c. Suppose P_L is $15 and that presently five units of labor are being allocated to producing x while two units are being allocated to y. Is this an efficient allocation of labor? Why or why not? If not, what is the efficient allocation of type B labor?
   d. Suppose P_L is $25 and three units of labor are being allocated to producing x, while six units are being allocated to producing y. Explain why this is not an efficient allocation of labor. What *is* the efficient allocation of this type of labor? What gain in the total value of leisure, alternative outputs, or home production results from this reallocation of labor?
   e. Suppose product x is sold in a perfectly competitive product market. Also ignore the VMP_{By} column and assume that the VMP_{Bx} schedule is representative of each firm hiring workers in a perfectly competitive labor market. If the market wage rate is $12, what will be each firm's MWC? What will be their MRPs at their profit-maximizing level of employment? Explain why an efficient allocation of labor will occur in this industry.

7. Complete the following table for a single firm operating in labor market A and product market *AA:*

Units of Labor	Wage Rate (W)	Total Wage Cost	MWC	MRP	VMP
1	$10			$16	$16
2	10			14	15
3	10			12	14
4	10			10	12
5	10			8	10
6	10			6	8

    a. What, if anything, can one conclude about the degree of competition in labor market *A* and product market *AA?*

    b. What is the profit-maximizing level of employment? Explain.

    c. Does this profit-maximizing level of employment yield allocative efficiency? Explain.

8. Use the production data shown here on the left and the labor supply data on the right for a single firm to answer the following questions. Assume that this firm is selling its product for $1 per unit in a perfectly competitive product market.

Units of Labor	Total Product	Units of Labor	Wage Rate
0	0	0	—
1	13	1	$1
2	25	2	2
3	34	3	3
4	42	4	4
5	46	5	5
6	48	6	6

    a. How many workers will this firm choose to employ?

    b. What will be its profit-maximizing wage rate?

    c. What labor market model do these data best describe?

9. Assume a firm *(a)* is a monopsonist in hiring labor, *(b)* is selling its product as a monopolist, and *(c)* faces no union. Portray this market graphically. Correctly label all relevant curves, show the equilibrium wage rate and level of employment, and indicate the efficiency loss (if any).

10. Under what elasticity of labor demand conditions could a union restrict the supply of labor—that is, shift the supply curve leftward—and thereby increase the collective wage income (wage bill) of the workers still employed?

11. Use graphic analysis to explain how a union in a monopsonized labor market might simultaneously enhance *(a)* its wage rate, *(b)* employment, and *(c)* allocative efficiency.

12. Explain why there may be an appearance of chronic shortages in some monopsonized labor markets, while in some bilateral monopoly markets chronic surpluses often exist.

13. Explain how each one of the following contract provisions might affect the elasticity of labor demand during the period of the labor contract:

    a. Layoff and severance pay.

    b. Prevention of subcontracting.

    c. The limiting of plant shutdown or relocation.

14. Use graphical analysis to show how an unexpected decline in labor demand may set off a cobweb adjustment cycle in a labor market for highly trained professionals. In explaining your graph, distinguish between the immediate-period supply curve and the long-run supply curve.

Internet Exercise

Who Is Getting Pay Raises and Who Is Getting Pay Cuts?

Go to the Bureau of Labor Statistics Data Web site **(http://www.bls.gov/data/home.htm)** and select "Series Report." Enter the following ID series numbers: CEU1000000001, CEU4200000001, CEU1000000049, and CEU4200000049. Then click on "All Years." This will retrieve average hourly earnings (in 1982 dollars) and employment for natural resources and mining and retail trade.

What were the average real hourly wage and employment rates in 1979 and 1995 in the retail trade and natural resources and mining industries? What were the percentage changes in the wage rate and employment for both industries? On the basis of the changes in wages and employment, what can you infer about the relative size of the changes in labor demand and labor supply?

What are the average real hourly wages and employment rates for the most recent month shown in the retail trade and natural resources and mining industries? What were the percentage changes between 1995 and the most recent month for the wage rate and employment for both industries? On the basis of the changes in wages and employment, what can you infer about the relative size of the changes in labor demand and labor supply?

Internet Links

The Bureau of Labor Statistics Wages, Earnings, and Benefits Web site contains detailed statistics about wages by state, occupation, and industry **(http://www.bls.gov/bls/wages .htm)**.

The Web site of the World Trade Organization provides extensive information about the organization **(http://www.wto.org)**.

7

Alternative Pay Schemes and Labor Efficiency

Most of you will be seeking full-time employment when you graduate from college. Let's suppose you are offered a job relating to your college major. Before accepting this particular job offer, what information about the compensation package would you want to know? Our surmise is that first you would want to know about the annual salary or the hourly wage. What else? No doubt you would seek information about the fringe benefit package. How good are the medical benefits? Is there disability insurance? Are there paid vacations? Does the firm contribute to a pension plan?

In Chapter 6 we identified and explained several basic models of wage determination. Our assumption in those models was that all compensation was in the form of an hourly wage rate, such as $10 per hour. But as the previous paragraph suggests, in reality fringe benefits constitute an important element of our compensation. Additionally, firms are not indifferent about the composition of the total compensation they pay; for example, they may wish to structure their pay package in special ways to enhance work effort and reduce turnover. The goal of this chapter is to examine pay packages that are more complex in composition and purpose than the standard hourly wage rate.

ECONOMICS OF FRINGE BENEFITS

We begin by analyzing the economics of the fringe benefit portion of total compensation. *Total compensation* comprises wage earnings and the costs of fringe benefits. *Fringe benefits* include public (legally mandated) programs such as Social Security, unemployment compensation, and workers' compensation. They also include many private nonmandatory programs such as private pensions, medical and dental insurance,

FIGURE 7.1

Components of Total Compensation (Wage and Salary Workers, in Percent)

Fringe benefits account for more than one-fourth of the total compensation among wage and salary workers.

(Source: Bureau of Labor Statistics. Data are for March 2006.)

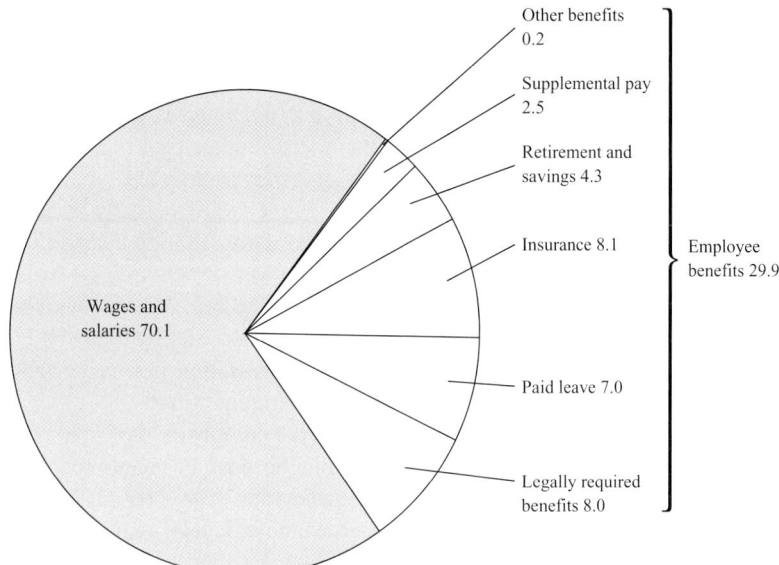

Other benefits 0.2

Supplemental pay 2.5

Retirement and savings 4.3

Insurance 8.1

Employee benefits 29.9

Wages and salaries 70.1

Paid leave 7.0

Legally required benefits 8.0

paid vacations, and sick leave. We will find that fringe benefits can increase the utility workers receive from a given amount of total compensation. Fringe benefits also can benefit the firm by permitting it to retain and attract high-quality workers.

Fringe Benefits: Facts

Fringe benefits constitute a significant portion of total compensation, and they have grown rapidly as a percentage of total compensation during the past several decades.

1 Fringe Benefits as a Proportion of Total Compensation

The Bureau of Labor Statistics (BLS) has broken down employee compensation among wage and salary workers.[1] As shown in Figure 7.1, *wages and salaries* constitute about 70 percent of total compensation among wage and salary workers, while *employee fringe benefits* account for about 30 percent.

It is instructive to examine the various fringe benefit components of the compensation pie. Observe from Figure 7.1 that *legally required benefits* comprise 8 percent of total compensation. These benefits include Social Security, railroad retirement and supplemental retirement, federal and state unemployment insurance, workers' compensation, and state temporary disability insurance benefits. *Paid leaves,* which include paid vacations, paid holidays, paid sick leave, and the like, account for 7.0 percent of total employee compensation. Note that *insurance benefits*—for life, health, and sickness and accident insurance—comprise an 8.1 percent share.

---

[1] U.S. Bureau of Labor Statistics, *Employer Costs for Employee Compensation,* U.S. Department of Labor. News Release 06-1049, June 2006.

The remaining three slices of the employee compensation pie are *retirement and savings benefits* (4.3 percent), which include retirement plans and saving thrift plans; *supplemental pay* (2.5 percent), comprising premium pay for overtime and work on holidays, shift differentials, nonproduction bonuses, and lump-sum payments; and *other benefits* (0.2 percent), which include severance pay, supplemental unemployment benefits, and merchandise discounts in department stores.

The composition of total compensation varies greatly by industry. For example, the fringe benefits proportion of employee compensation is larger (1) in high-paying industries than in low-paying ones; (2) in goods-producing industries compared to service industries; and (3) in transportation and public utilities compared to retail trade. The proportion and specific types of benefits also vary by industry. For example, paid leaves comprise about 8 percent of total compensation in transportation and public utilities, whereas they are only about 4 percent in retail trade.

Finally, the BLS data reveal that the composition of total compensation also differs by occupational group. For example, because of legally mandated fringe benefits, the fringe benefit share of total compensation is greater for blue-collar workers than for white-collar workers. As another example, legally required benefits are a significantly higher percentage of total pay for transportation workers than for executives.

2 Fringe Benefit Growth

Fringe benefits have grown significantly as a component of total employee compensation during the past several decades. This growth is shown in Figure 7.2, where we see

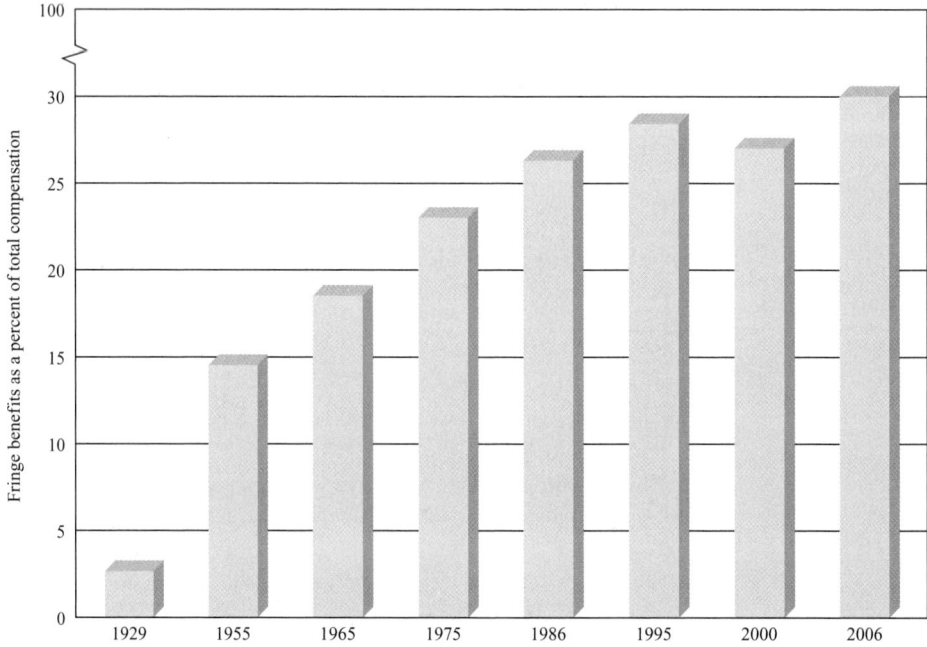

FIGURE 7.2
Relative Growth of Fringe Benefits
Fringe benefits have increased dramatically as a percentage of total compensation since 1929.

Source: Bureau of Labor Statistics, *Employee Benefits in a Changing Economy: A BLS Chartbook,* September 1992, p. 3., updated.

that fringe benefits for all workers have expanded from less than 3 percent of total compensation in 1929 to more than one-quarter of total pay in 2006.

Why are fringe benefits a significant component of total compensation? What explains their rapid growth? A model of optimal fringe benefits will help us answer these questions.

THEORY OF OPTIMAL FRINGE BENEFITS

The theory of optimal fringe benefits is a variation of the income–leisure choice problem encountered in Chapter 2. There we saw that a budget constraint (wage rate line) limited the worker to specific combinations of earnings and leisure (Figure 2.5). The worker chose the single combination of these two "goods" that provided the highest utility. This choice was made on the basis of the worker's subjective evaluation of the trade-off between earnings and leisure in relationship to the objectively determined budget constraint.

In a similar way we might think of a worker facing a choice between wages and fringe benefits. The worker's preferences for these two "goods" are reflected in an *indifference map.* The budget constraint takes the form of the employer's total compensation line, or an *isoprofit curve.*[2]

Worker's Indifference Map

Each indifference curve shown in Figure 7.3 displays combinations of wages and fringe benefits yielding the same level of satisfaction or utility to the worker. Thus a single indifference curve such as I_1 reflects a constant level of total utility. As we move northeast from the origin, each successive indifference curve entails a higher level of total utility.

The downward slope of each indifference curve indicates that workers view wages and fringes as each yielding utility and therefore being somewhat substitutable. At first thought this may seem surprising because most fringes are *in-kind benefits—benefits in the form of a specific kind of good or service.* Would not a worker (consumer) always be better off with—and therefore prefer—an additional dollar's worth of (cash) wages rather than an additional dollar's worth of some specific fringe benefit? One dollar in cash wages represents generalized purchasing power that can be spent on $1 worth of whatever good or service is most preferred by (yields the most marginal utility to) the consumer. An in-kind fringe benefit, on the other hand, ties the individual to the particular good or service. In fact, that good or service may provide little or no marginal utility, or satisfaction, to a particular worker. An on-the-job day care center yields little satisfaction to a worker who does not have children or to an older worker whose children are grown. An older worker with false teeth may derive little or no utility from a program of

[2] The analysis that follows was developed by Ronald G. Ehrenberg and Robert S. Smith. See Smith and Ehrenberg, "Estimating Wage–Fringe Trade-Offs: Some Data Problems," in Jack E. Triplett (ed.), *The Measurement of Labor Cost* (Chicago: University of Chicago Press, 1983), pp. 347–67; and Ehrenberg and Smith, *Modern Labor Economics,* 7th ed. (Reading, MA: Addison-Wesley, 2000), pp. 274–81.

FIGURE 7.3

A Worker's Indifference Map for Wages and Fringe Benefits
Each indifference curve shows the combinations of wages and fringe benefits that yield a specific level of total utility. Indifference curves farther to the northeast in the indifference map represent higher levels of total utility; therefore, they are preferred by the worker.

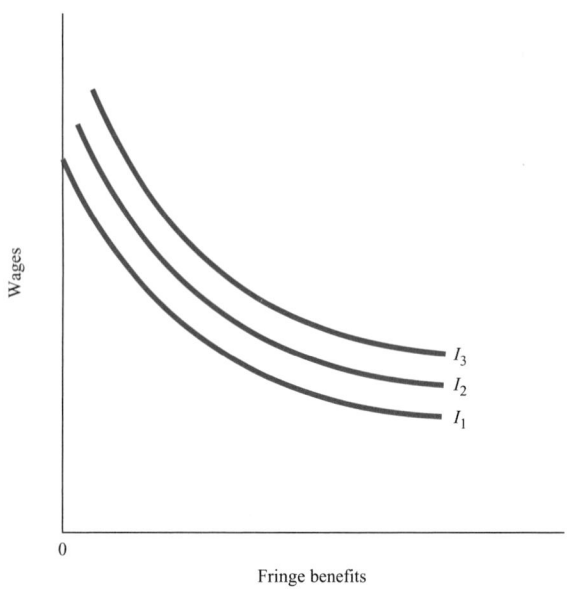

dental insurance. Nevertheless, there are two major reasons that workers are in fact willing to sacrifice some of their wages to obtain a package of fringe benefits.

First, and undoubtedly of greatest consequence, certain fringe benefits entail a large tax advantage to workers. For example, workers do not pay taxes on the deferred income benefits embodied in private pension plans until those benefits are actually received. Pensions allow principal, interest, and dividends to accumulate at a pretax growth rate rather than a posttax pace. Also, because the worker's earned income will likely fall to zero at retirement, the income provided by the pension plan might be taxed at a lower marginal tax rate (say, 15 percent) than the same amount paid as wages during the worker's active work life (for example, 28 or 35 percent). In short, pensions are a means of deferring income to achieve lower tax rates. The after-tax value of $1 of pension contribution is perceived to be greater than the after-tax value of $1 of current wage income. Similarly, premiums paid by employers for health and life insurance are subject to neither the Social Security tax nor the personal income tax.[3]

Second, workers may be willing to substitute fringe benefits for part of their wages to guard against their own tendency to purchase goods that provide more immediate gratification than, say, health insurance or pension annuities. People may realize that their cash earnings tend to get spent on other items such as cars, boats, clothing, and vacations. Thus they are willing to sacrifice some of their earnings to "lock in" health and pension benefits that they know are important for their future. By accepting pay

[3] For studies examining the role of taxes in employee demand for fringe benefits, see Stephen A. Woodbury and Wei-Jang Huang, *The Tax Treatment of Fringe Benefits* (Kalamazoo, MI: W. E. Upjohn Institute, 1991); and David Joulfaian and David Richardson, "Who Takes Advantage of Tax-Deferred Savings Programs? Evidence from Federal Income Tax Data," *National Tax Journal,* September 2001, pp. 669–88.

packages that contain fringe benefits, workers ensure that insurance, pension, and other benefits are available when needed.

Observe that the indifference curves not only slope downward but are convex to the origin (as was the case in our income–leisure diagrams in Chapter 2). Stated technically, the marginal rate of substitution of fringe benefits for wages falls as more benefits are added. When a person has few fringe benefits, he or she is willing to trade off a large amount of wages for an additional unit of fringe benefits. But as the amount of fringe benefits rises, the marginal utility of still more fringe benefits falls, and the person is less willing to sacrifice wage payments to attain still more units of them.

Employer's Isoprofit Curve

For a given level of output, a firm will wish to minimize its total compensation per hour of work to help maximize its profits. In Figure 7.4 we show a firm's *isoprofit curve, WF,* which *indicates the various combinations of wages and fringe benefits providing a given profit.* We assume for simplicity that competition in the product market has resulted in a *normal profit.* We also suppose that competition in the labor market has forced this firm to pay the total compensation indicated by the combinations of wages and fringes demonstrated by curve *WF*. That is, *WF* shows the combinations of wages and fringe benefits that allow the firm to maintain a normal profit, given the "prices" of wages and fringe benefits.

Close inspection of this isoprofit line in Figure 7.4 reveals that its slope is −1. In this example, a $1 reduction in wages accompanied by a $1 increase in fringe benefits leaves the total compensation to the worker—and thus the total profits to the firm—unchanged. The firm's total compensation and profits are the same if it pays 0*W* wages and 0 fringe benefits or 0 wages and 0*F* fringe benefits. Similarly, total compensation is the same for all other combinations of wages and fringe benefits indicated by line *WF*.

FIGURE 7.4   **An Employer's Isoprofit Curve (Normal Profit)**
An isoprofit curve portrays the various combinations of wages and fringe benefits that yield a specific level of profits. We assume that competition will result in a normal profit. Thus *WF* shows the various combinations of wages and fringes the firm can afford to provide, given the "prices" of the alternative forms of compensation.

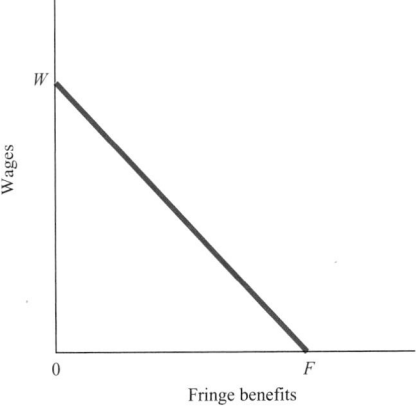

FIGURE 7.5 Wage–Fringe Optimum

The optimal combination of wages and fringe benefits is at *b,* where the isoprofit curve is tangent to the highest attainable indifference curve I_2. Here the firm will provide W_0 wages and F_0 fringe benefits. Points *a* and *c* are also attainable combinations of wages and fringes but yield less total utility, as is evidenced by their locations on the lower indifference curve I_1.

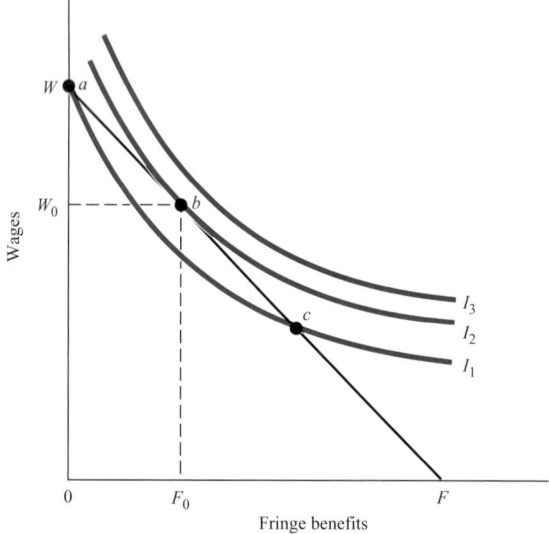

Wage–Fringe Optimum

Noting that the axes of Figure 7.3 and 7.4 are the same, we can now determine the worker's utility-maximizing combination of wages and fringe benefits. Of all the attainable combinations of wages and fringe benefits along line *WF* in Figure 7.5, combination W_0 and F_0 yields the worker the greatest satisfaction, or utility. Specifically, the utility-maximizing combination is the one tangent to the highest attainable indifference curve (I_2 at *b*). To test this proposition, note that points *a* (all wage payments and no fringes) and *c* (relatively low wage payments and high fringes) are inferior to point *b*. That is, at these points the worker is on lower-than-attainable indifference curve I_1. This person can attain the higher indifference curve I_2 if the wages–fringes combination is appropriately adjusted from point *a* or *c* toward *b*.

Although indifference maps vary among individual workers, we will suppose for simplicity that this worker's preferences for wage payments and fringe benefits are representative of the average worker. Differing indifference maps among workers—and therefore differing wage–fringe optimums—are discussed in Chapter 8.

Causes of Fringe Benefit Growth

Let's next consider the implications of a lower "price" for fringe benefits. In Figure 7.6 we have drawn a new normal-profit isoprofit line *WF'* that has a flatter slope than line *WF.* The shift from *WF* to WF' tells us that the relative per-unit cost or "price" of fringe benefits has fallen. Restated, the firm can now supply more fringe benefits at all but the highest wage without increasing its total compensation. Thus it can provide more fringe

FIGURE 7.6   **Fringe Benefit Growth**

A decrease in the price of fringe benefits due to tax advantages, scale economies, and efficiency considerations fans the normal-profit isoprofit line outward. This allows the worker to attain a higher indifference curve (I_3 rather than I_2). In the process, fringe benefits expand from F_0 to F_1.

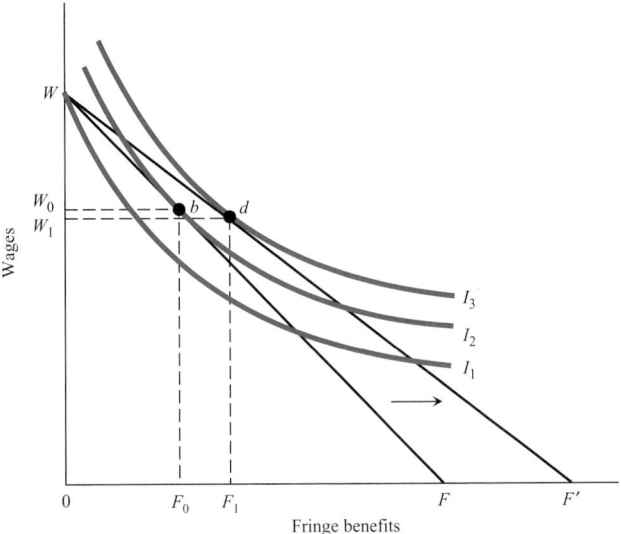

benefits without reducing its profits. The firm can now exchange a dollar's worth of wages for more than a dollar's worth of benefits, even though these benefits cost only a dollar. It will want to offer its workers this better trade-off between wages and fringe benefits to attract and retain the highest-quality employees. In fact, a competitive labor market will dictate that the firm pay compensation to workers as indicated by line WF' because other firms will bid up the level of total compensation to this level.

This new normal-profit isoprofit line results in a new tangency position at point d on a higher indifference curve, I_3. Observe that this representative worker now selects a combination of wages and fringes more heavily weighted in favor of fringe benefits. The decline in the price of fringe benefits has both enabled and enticed the worker to "buy" more fringe benefits. He or she now has more real income (wages plus fringes) and views fringe benefits as being a relatively "better buy" than they were before. Consequently, this worker opts for more fringe benefits and achieves a higher level of utility (I_3 at d rather than I_2 at b).

The obvious question is what might cause the normal-profit isoprofit line to fan outward as indicated in Figure 7.6. What might lower the price of fringe benefits and enable the firm to offer more of them and still retain the same levels of total compensation and normal profits? The answers to these questions provide the basis for a list of reasons fringe benefits have grown historically.

Tax Advantages to the Employer

We have observed that fringe benefits confer tax advantages to the worker. These fringe benefits also reduce taxes owed by the employer. The employer must pay half of the

15.3 percent Social Security payroll tax on worker earnings up to $94,200 (2006) for each employee. For workers earning less than this amount, the firm reduces its payroll tax burden by tilting the pay package away from wage earnings and toward fringe benefits. Suppose a worker earns $30,000 a year. At the 2004 payroll tax rate of 7.65 percent, the employer would have to pay $2,295 of tax. But if the employer instead pays the worker $20,000 in earnings and $10,000 of fringe benefits, the tax burden for the firm falls to $1,530 (= $20,000 × .0765). Multiplied by thousands of workers, the tax savings to a large firm can be considerable. The upshot is that the firm can offer fringe benefits worth more than a dollar for a dollar reduction in direct pay. In Figure 7.6 the normal-profit isoprofit line fans outward as indicated by the shift from *WF* to *WF′*. Because the Social Security tax base and rate have both increased historically, the optimal level of fringe benefits has risen.[4]

Economies of Scale

Significant economies of scale usually exist in the collective purchase of fringe benefits that lower their prices to buyers. In particular, the average administrative costs and agent fees are much less in purchasing medical, life, disability, or dental insurance for a group than for an individual.[5] Additionally, group policies eliminate the *adverse selection problem*—the tendency for individuals who are most likely to draw large benefits to sign up for insurance. As with tax advantages, the "discount prices" on insurance reduce the per-unit cost of fringes and rotate the normal-profit isoprofit line outward, as in Figure 7.6. The result is that a worker is enticed to accept more fringe benefits than previously. To the extent that cost savings have increased historically as the size of firms has grown, the optimal amount of fringe benefits has also grown.

Efficiency Considerations

Employers are interested in protecting their training investments and reducing their recruiting and training costs. They may see fringe benefits as a way to tie workers to jobs and hence to reduce quits. Pension benefits in particular are effective in reducing employee turnover.[6] Lower turnover means that a higher proportion of the firm's workers are experienced workers who are well past the training stage. Consequently, the average productivity of a firm's workforce rises.

7.1

---

[4] For a study examining the impact of taxes on the probability that a worker is eligible for health insurance, see Anne Beeson Royalty, "Tax Preferences for Fringe Benefits and Workers' Eligibility for Employer Health Insurance," *Journal of Public Economics,* February 2000, pp. 209–27. See also Amy Finkelstein, "The Effect of Tax Subsidies to Employer-Provided Supplementary Health Insurance: Evidence from Canada," *Journal of Public Economics,* June 2002, pp. 305–39.

[5] For studies documenting economies of scale in the administration of pension and health plans, see Emily S. Andrews, *Pension Policy and Small Employers: At What Price Coverage?* (Washington, DC: Employee Benefit Research Institute, 1989); See also Teresa Ghilarducci and Kevin Terry, "Scale Economies in Union Pension Plan Administration: 1981–1993," *Industrial Relations,* January 1999, pp. 11–17.

[6] For example, see William E. Even and David A. Macpherson, "Employer Size and Labor Turnover: The Role of Pensions," *Industrial and Labor Relations Review,* July 1996, pp. 707–28; and Alan L. Gustman and Thomas L. Steinmeier, "Pension Portability and Labor Mobility: Evidence from the Survey of Income and Program Participation," *Journal of Public Economics,* March 1993, pp. 299–323.

| 7.1 | **World of Work** | Does Health Insurance Cause "Job Lock"? |

Health insurance coverage may cause some workers to stay on a job they would prefer to leave. Firms that provide health insurance often require waiting periods before covering new workers or completely exclude a new worker's preexisting medical conditions. As a consequence, some workers may be reluctant to change jobs because of concerns about losing health insurance coverage. This reduced job mobility is known as "job lock."

Buchmueller and Valletta examined the empirical importance of this issue by comparing the job mobility of workers with and without health insurance coverage.* Their results provide fairly strong evidence of job lock for both married and single women. Health insurance coverage reduces job mobility for these workers by 35 to 50 percent. The findings were more mixed among men. Married men whose spouses also work appear to suffer from job lock; but among sole-earner married and single men only weak evidence of job lock exists. The authors speculated that the stronger findings of job lock among women reflect their higher health care use compared to that of men.

One public policy solution to the problem of job lock is "continuation of coverage" mandates. Some

states and the federal government require employers to allow ex-employees to purchase health insurance coverage from their former employers for a specified time period after leaving their jobs. To examine the effect of this mandate, Gruber and Madrian compared job mobility for workers across states with different requirements for how long employers must provide coverage (ranging from 2 to 20 months).[†] Also, they compared job mobility before and after the adoption of these laws. They concluded that the mandates do reduce job lock because a 12-month increase in the required continuation of coverage requirement boosts job mobility by approximately 10 percent.

* Thomas C. Buchmueller and Robert G. Valletta, "The Effects of Employer-Provided Health Insurance on Worker Mobility," *Industrial and Labor Relations Review,* April 1996, pp. 439–55. For a survey of earlier studies, see Alan C. Moheit and Philip F. Cooper, "Health Insurance and Job Mobility: Theory and Evidence," *Industrial and Labor Relations Review,* October 1994, pp. 68–85.

[†] Jonathan Gruber and Brigette C. Madrian, "Health Insurance and Job Mobility: The Effects of Public Policy on Job-Lock," *Industrial and Labor Relations Review,* October 1994, pp. 86–102.

Viewed by the firm, pension benefits thus are less costly than their dollar expense. From a dollar outlay the firm must subtract the added revenue resulting from the enhanced productivity arising from the fringe benefit package. A firm can therefore offer more fringe benefits of this kind without suffering a loss of profits.[7] Because the training investments of firms have risen historically, firms increasingly have had an incentive to use fringe benefits to reduce turnover.

[7] Although the overall productivity-enhancing aspects of fringe benefits are thought to dominate, some fringe benefits may reduce productivity. For example, paid sick leave may encourage absenteeism. Also, certain fringe benefits may attract employees who are most likely to draw upon the particular benefits, thus increasing the cost of the fringe benefit program to the employer. For example, a firm that offers parental leave may attract a disproportionate number of employees who have children. For a discussion of the public policy implications of this problem, see Lawrence H. Summers, "Some Simple Economics of Mandated Benefits," *American Economic Review,* May 1989, pp. 177–83.

Other Factors

There are several other reasons fringe benefits have increased historically. Certain fringe benefits are quite *income elastic.* They involve pension coverage and such services as medical and dental care, purchases of which are quite sensitive to increases in income. Thus as worker incomes have grown historically, it is not surprising that the "purchase" of such fringes has also expanded.[8] Also, the federal government has raised mandated fringe benefits such as Social Security and unemployment compensation. Finally, we will find in Chapter 11 that unionization historically has been a factor in the rise in fringe benefits. On average, union workers receive more generous fringe benefits than nonunion workers. Also, nonunion firms often emulate union contracts as a way to deter unionism.

7.1

Quick Review

- Fringe benefits account for more than one-fourth of the total compensation in private industry.
- In the wage–fringe benefit model, the optimal combination of wages and fringe benefits occurs where the isoprofit curve is tangent to the highest attainable indifference curve.
- Favorable tax treatment, economies of scale, and efficiency considerations have reduced the "price" of fringe benefits, expanding their availability and enhancing worker utility.

Your Turn

Suppose the government decides to tax fringe benefits as ordinary income. What would happen to the slopes of the typical worker's indifference curves? How would this affect the optimal amount of fringe benefits? (*Answers:* See page 597.)

THE PRINCIPAL–AGENT PROBLEM

We next turn to a discussion of the relationship between pay and performance. This pay may take the form of either direct cash or fringe benefits. But as a prelude to this topic, we need to explore the nature of the relationship between firms and workers.

We know from our discussion in previous chapters that firms hire employees because workers help produce goods and services that firms can sell for a profit in the marketplace. In this respect workers might be thought of as the firms' *agents—parties who are hired to advance the interests of others.* Alternatively, firms can be conceived of as *principals—parties who hire others to help them achieve their objectives.* In this case the firms' or principals' objective is profits. Employees are willing to help firms earn profits in return for payments of wage income. This income enables workers to buy goods and services that yield utility. Thus the relationship between principals (firms)

---

[8] Stephen Woodbury, "Substitution between Wage and Nonwage Benefits," *American Economic Review,* March 1983, pp. 166–82.

and agents (workers) is based on mutual self-interest; the employment relationship benefits both firms and workers. But to say that principals and agents share common interests is not to say that all their interests are identical. In situations where interests between firms and workers diverge, a so-called principal–agent problem might arise.

The ***principal–agent problem*** *occurs when agents (workers) pursue some of their own objectives in conflict with achieving the goals of the principals (firms).* Firms desire to maximize profits (Chapter 6); workers wish to maximize utility (Chapter 2). Profit maximization requires that employees work all agreed-upon hours at agreed-upon levels of effort. Otherwise output will be reduced, and average and marginal costs of production will be higher. But under many employment circumstances, workers can enhance their own utility by engaging in *opportunistic behavior* that directly conflicts with profit maximization. Specifically, workers can increase their leisure by ***shirking***—that is, by either *taking unauthorized work breaks or giving less than agreed-upon effort during work hours.* If undetected by firms, this shirking permits workers to increase their leisure—through reduced work time and effort—without forfeiting income. In terms of our earlier income–leisure model (Figure 2.5), workers who neglect or evade work can attain greater total utility than that available along their wage rate lines. In effect, undetected shirking allows workers to attain indifference curves like I_3 in Figure 2.5.

An important proposition derives from the principal–agent perspective. *Quite simply, firms (principals) will have a profit incentive to find ways to reduce or eliminate principal–agent problems.* The remainder of this chapter explores various facets of this proposition.

PAY FOR PERFORMANCE

One way that firms might attempt to solve the principal–agent problem is to tie pay directly to output or performance. Some so-called ***incentive pay plans*** have become increasingly popular throughout the economy. These pay schemes include piece rates, commissions and royalties, raises and promotions, bonuses, profit and equity sharing, and tournament pay.[9]

Piece Rates

Piece rates are compensation paid in proportion to the number of units of personal output. This compensation often is found in situations where workers control the pace of work and firms find it expensive to monitor worker effort. For example, apple pickers are paid by the bushel; apparel workers are paid by the piece; and typists are paid by the page. Although piece rates are normally associated with low-paying jobs, this type of pay is more ordinary than commonly thought. Surgeons in private practice set fees on a per-operation basis; tax preparers charge fixed amounts for each simple tax return; and lawyers charge set amounts for the various types of wills they draw up.

---

[9] For an analysis of the determinants of method of pay, see Charles Brown, "Firms' Choice of Method of Pay," *Industrial and Labor Relations Review,* February 1990, pp. S165–S182.

Evidence indicates that workers who are paid piece rates earn 10 to 15 percent more pay than comparable hourly paid workers in the same industry.[10] Nevertheless, piece rates have several drawbacks that have collectively resulted in their declining importance in American industry. First, in industries where technological change is rapid, it can be very difficult for employers to find the profit-maximizing piece rates. Workers can artificially boost the piece rate by agreeing among themselves to make the job seem more difficult and time-consuming than is actually the case.[11] Second, piece rates increase the likelihood of weekly, monthly, and even yearly income variability for workers. Thus to attract workers to piece-rate jobs, firms may have to pay wage premiums (Chapter 8) to compensate workers for this risk of earnings variation. Employers could save the cost of this premium pay by paying a straight hourly wage. Third, where production is complex and team-oriented, it is difficult to ascribe units of output directly to the performance of individuals. Who produces each tube of Colgate toothpaste, can of Campbell's soup, or bottle of Coca-Cola? Fourth, close cooperation among workers is required for successful team performance. Piece rates reward independent work effort and therefore do little to promote this needed cooperation. Finally, piece rates suffer from their own advantage: The rapid production pace they elicit often results in poor product quality. For these reasons piece rates have increasingly given way to *time rates*—*pay based on units of time such as hours, months, or years.*

Commissions and Royalties

Unlike piece rates, which link pay to units of output, commissions and royalties tie pay to the value of sales. *Commissions* are commonly received by realtors, insurance agents, stockbrokers, and sales personnel. A glance at the classified sections of big-city newspapers will reveal several columns of help-wanted advertisements for commissioned workers. *Royalties* also are set as a percentage of sales revenue. They typically are paid to authors, film producers, recording artists, and similar professionals. For instance, about $10 of the price of this textbook—if it is new—accrues to the authors (and we thank you).

Commissions and royalties are efficient where work effort and work hours are difficult to observe. Time rates in these situations would bring forth attendant shirking problems for the firm because observing the worker would be very expensive. By aligning the interests of the firms and the workers, commissions and royalties help overcome the principal–agent problem.

7.2

Raises and Promotions

A sizable proportion of American workers receive time payments as fixed annual salaries. These workers are typically engaged in team production; thus it is not easy to monitor their efforts or measure their outputs. Time payments, rather than piece rates,

[10] Charles Brown, "Wage Levels and Method of Pay," *Rand Journal of Economics,* Autumn 1992, pp. 366–75. For a study reporting a positive effect on productivity and wages for a firm switching from paying hourly wages to paying piece rates, see Edward P. Lazear, "Personnel Economics: Past Lessons and Future Directions," *Journal of Labor Economics,* April 1999, pp. 199–236.

[11] Stephen Jones, *The Economics of Conformism* (New York: Basil Blackwell, 1984).

7.2	World of Work	Why Is There Academic Tenure?*

Tenure is a unique employment system in which college professors can gain almost complete future job security. Near the end of a tenure candidate's probationary period, a committee of peers assesses the credentials of the candidate and recommends for or against tenure. Recommendations go to the university administration, which decides either to grant tenure or to end the person's employment at the university.

The historical purpose of tenure has been to protect faculty members against arbitrary discharge resulting from controversial research or viewpoints. Supporters of tenure claim that it creates a climate of free inquiry essential to the advancement of human knowledge. But tenure also has some potential drawbacks. The job security it provides may reduce the work effort of some professors. Also, tenure may interfere with the optimal assignment of workers to jobs. It is alleged that older, less productive professors may occupy job "slots" that younger, presumably more productive professors are better qualified to fill. Thus, say critics, tenure reduces the total productive effort of the university.

In view of its supposed deficiencies, why has the tenure system prevailed? While most economists would answer, "Because faculties have sufficient political power within institutions to preserve it," Carmichael provides a more novel answer: Tenure endures precisely because it helps solve an unusual principal–agent problem and thereby enhances the overall quality of the faculty. He emphasizes that incumbent members of academic departments largely decide which new faculty to hire. The university entrusts this task to these individuals because they are uniquely qualified to identify the best possible candidates. But without tenure a unique principal–agent problem would arise: Incumbent professors (agents) would have an incentive to recommend to the university (principal) the weakest applicants for job openings! By doing this, senior faculty would reduce the prospect of being replaced by more productive employees, as happens in, say, professional sports. Senior faculty are willing to participate in identifying the top candidates for new academic openings only because of the tenure system. Because of tenure they do not risk losing their own jobs in the future by helping the university identify and employ promising young professors. In short, says Carmichael, the institution of tenure persists because it aligns the interests of universities (principals) and professors (agents) in the hiring process. The result is an improved overall quality of faculty.

This view of tenure is also consistent with other observed practices by universities. Institutions often provide generous early retirement plans to faculty, occasionally buy out the contracts of poorly performing tenured faculty, and sometimes eliminate entire weak departments when faced with budget cutbacks. Each of these practices addresses problems of tenure while preserving the aspects of the tenure system that allegedly solve the aforementioned principal–agent problem.

* H. Lorne Carmichael, "Incentives in Academics: Why Is There Tenure?" *Journal of Political Economy,* June 1988, pp. 453–72.

commissions, or royalties, therefore are optimal. But why fixed annual salaries and not fixed hourly pay? The reason is that managers and professionals are *quasi-fixed resources,* at least for a one-year period.[12] A firm's use of salaried workers is largely independent of its level of production. Salaried workers thus are akin to fixed resources such as capital and land (*quasi-* means "as if"). For example, enterprises need

[12] Walter Oi, "Labor as a Quasi-Fixed Factor," *Journal of Political Economy,* December 1962, pp. 538–55.

accountants, lawyers, managers, and marketing personnel when production and sales are brisk and also when they are slack. In addition, firms incur high search, hiring, and training costs in employing salaried workers. Laying them off would risk quits that would end the firms' opportunities to gain returns on prior expensive investments in specific training [Figure 4.8(b)]. On a more mundane level, high-skilled workers may simply be in a position to demand and receive the greater income security associated with fixed annual salaries.

But for all their benefits, annual salaries present a potential shirking problem. Let's describe this problem and then explore its solution.

Salaries and Work Incentives

In Figure 7.7 we demonstrate the principal–agent problem associated with salaries. Our methodology will be to compare the optimal hours of work under conditions of hourly pay and an annual salary.

1 Hourly Pay First observe wage rate line *WH*, the slope of which indicates a particular level of hourly pay. Given this hourly wage, the worker characterized by the indifference map shown will choose to work h_1 hours and earn an annual income Y_1. This $h_1 Y_1$ combination of work and income permits the worker to attain indifference

FIGURE 7.7   Salaries and Work Incentives

Wage rate line *WH* indicates a specific level of hourly pay that will provide an annual income equal to Y_1 at h_1 hours of work. An equivalent annual salary of Y_1 will allow the worker to obtain higher indifference curve I_2 or I_3 by reducing the actual number of hours worked to h_2 or H. The firm can overcome this incentive problem by offering future raises and promotions to those who work h_1 or more hours.

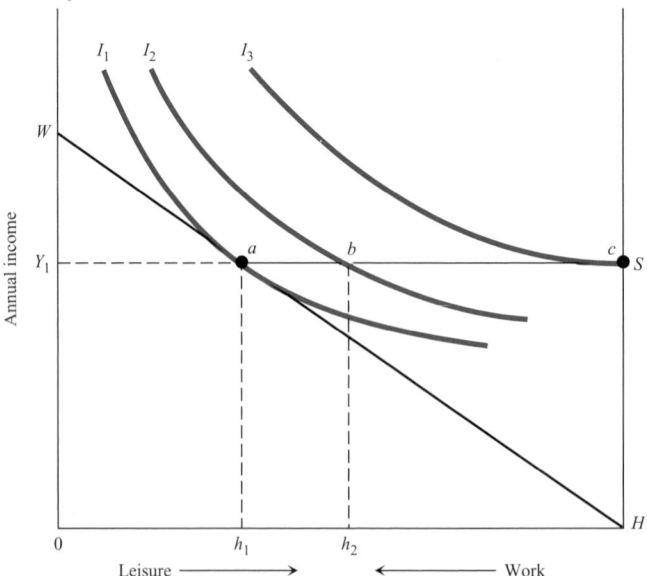

curve I_1 at a, which represents the highest level of total utility possible along the wage rate line. For illustrative purposes let's suppose that h_1 hours of work symbolize annual hours of work resulting from the normal 40-hour week.

2 Annual Salary   Now let's convert the Y_1 income earned by working h_1 hours to an annual salary of the same amount ($=Y_1$). The new budget constraint in Figure 7.7 becomes HSY_1 and indicates this person will receive Y_1 income irrespective of hours of work. Presumably, because of the nature of the job, the number of hours the person actually works while on the job is not easily observed. The worker now can achieve a higher level of utility by shirking. That is, the worker has an incentive to reduce work hours from h_1 to, say, h_2, allowing the worker to reach higher indifference curve I_2 at b. At the extreme, the worker can achieve a still higher level of utility by working zero hours (c on I_3). In both cases the annual salary ensures that the income level remains at Y_1.

Solution: Raises and Promotions

One solution to the salary problem posed in Figure 7.7 is for the firm to establish performance-based raises and promotions. The prospect of future raises and promotions means that the worker's decision about hours of work versus leisure in any given year is *not* based on that year's salary alone. Rather, the salaried worker chooses the optimal hours with a view toward maximizing lifetime utility. Desiring to obtain raises and earn promotions, the worker may decide to work more than h_1 hours this year. In fact, salaried employees work more hours weekly than hourly paid workers. One reason may be the importance of raises and promotions to salaried workers. If the worker gains the reputation of being a low producer, advancement within the firm's job hierarchy is unlikely.[13]

Bonuses

Bonuses are an increasingly popular form of incentive pay. *Bonuses are payments beyond the annual salary based on some factor such as personal or firm performance.* Their advantage to the firm is that they may elicit extra work effort. Another advantage is that they do not permanently raise base salaries or hourly wages, as do raises, promotions, or other forms of merit pay. Therefore, during an economic slump, bonuses can be readily forgone while higher wages or salaries are not readily reduced.

Personal Performance

Some bonuses are geared to personal performance that is formally assessed by superiors. If the superior rates the worker highly, the person receives a bonus. In other instances bonuses are based on some quantifiable output. Professional football players, for example, may receive bonuses for passing for more than a certain number of touchdowns or

---

[13] A competing explanation for the long hours of salaried workers is that these people may gain direct utility from the work they do, independent of compensation. At the extreme, the total utility of some professional workers would decline if they cut back their hours. For a graphical presentation of this phenomenon, see Bevars D. Mabry, *Economics of Manpower and the Labor Market* (New York: Intext Educational Publishers, 1973), pp. 221–29.

getting more than a specified number of quarterback sacks. Such "piece-rate" bonuses are less common in industries where individual performance is less directly measurable.

Bonuses based on individual performance may solve one form of the principal–agent problem, but they may create other kinds. Although this pay system may increase individual effort, it may channel the effort toward behavior that is counter to the employer's overall goals. For example, a basketball player who receives bonuses for assists may tend to pass the ball rather than take wide-open shots. Or a worker whose bonus depends on an evaluation from a superior may spend excessive time pleasing the superior. As a result, the worker may spend less time on, say, developing original product ideas that later might produce higher profits. To repeat: It is relatively easy to structure bonuses to eliminate the shirking problem. But it is difficult to structure bonuses so they do not create other principal–agent problems.

Team Performance

One solution to the problem just discussed is to base individual bonuses on the performance of the team. The team in this case might be an actual team—as in professional sports—or teams such as departments, divisions, or entire enterprises. Once team goals are established, the bonus for each team member depends only on whether the team goals are met. Most formal bonus programs in U.S. enterprises are based on group, rather than personal, contributions to output or profits. Group bonus schemes based on physical output or costs are referred to as *gainsharing schemes.*

Team bonuses have a major drawback in that they create a potential ***free-rider problem.*** As the size of the unit or team increases, the effect of each worker's efforts on achieving the goals of the firm diminishes. Where the number of workers is large, individual workers are tempted to shirk. They realize that their personal shirking will not appreciably reduce the firm's output and profits. Thus if others work hard, the shirker can still obtain a team bonus. It is unclear how workers who work energetically will respond to free riders. One possibility is that they may "punish" the free riders by reducing their own efforts, in which case the bonus plan will surely fail. Alternatively, it is possible that workers may eventually develop a strategy of cooperation—all agreeing to work hard and all monitoring each other to realize the optimal bonuses for all. The point is that depending on the severity of the free-rider problem, team bonuses *may* or *may not* increase team productivity.[14]

Team bonuses are more likely to be successful when they are targeted at a relatively small group of top executives whose decisions directly affect profits. In fact, bonuses based on profitability comprise about half of the total pay for senior executives. Do these large bonuses improve corporate performance? Past research tentatively suggests that the answer is yes. But these studies also indicate that the profit increases attributable to bonuses tend to be relatively small.[15]

[14] For analysis indicating that organizing a large firm into autonomous work groups can induce mutual monitoring among employees and thus overcome the free-riding problems associated with bonuses, see Marc Knez and Duncan Simester, "Firm-Wide Incentives and Mutual Monitoring at Continental Airlines," *Journal of Labor Economics,* October 2001, pp. 743–72.

[15] A representative set of these studies is found in the symposium "Do Compensation Policies Matter?" *Industrial and Labor Relations Review,* special issue, February 1990.

Profit Sharing

Profit sharing is *a pay system that allocates a specified portion of a firm's profits to employees.* This form of pay increased during the 1980s when workers in basic industries such as autos and primary metals accepted profit sharing in lieu of wage increases. Profit sharing also has become increasingly common for senior executives in large corporations. According to the National Center for Employee Ownership, 10.1 million workers participated in profit-sharing plans in 2006.[16] Most participants are in deferred plans, in which profits are credited to employees for distribution at some future date such as retirement.[17]

At first thought the link between profit sharing and productivity seems straight forward. Proponents of profit sharing contend that it transforms workers into minicapitalists who work harder to reap a share of the firm's profits. The extra effort creates extra output and profits, thus making the plan self-financing. Profit sharing therefore aligns the interests of firms and their workforces. That is, profit sharing supposedly overcomes the principal–agent problem.

But in reality the theoretical link between profit sharing and improved efficiency is not so clear-cut.[18] The main reason is that profit sharing is tied to *group* performance. This tie creates the free-rider problem that we identified in our discussion of bonuses. The larger the size of the organization, the greater the possibility that the free-rider problem will short-circuit the profit sharing–productivity link. The success of a profit-sharing plan depends crucially on how well the free-rider problem is resolved.

The effectiveness of profit-sharing plans therefore is an empirical question. Weitzman and Kruse have provided a detailed summary of the considerable amount of research done on this topic. They conclude, "The available evidence on the connection between profit sharing and productivity is not definitive. Yet it is also not neutral—many sources point toward a positive link; the only quarrel seems to be over magnitudes."[19] The Weitzman–Kruse summary suggests that workers under profit-sharing plans are able to overcome the free-rider problem. This conclusion is supported by a major study by Kruse, who reports that the adoption of profit sharing by firms is associated with a 2.5 to 4.2 percent increase in productivity.[20]

---

[16] **http://www.nceo.org.**

[17] Edward M. Coates III, "Profit Sharing Today: Plans and Provisions," *Monthly Labor Review,* April 1991, pp. 19–25. This source lists and discusses the pros and cons of profit-sharing plans.

[18] Martin L. Weitzman and Douglas L. Kruse provide an excellent discussion of the issues surrounding profit sharing. See their "Profit Sharing and Productivity," in Alan S. Blinder (ed.), *Paying for Productivity* (Washington, DC: Brookings Institution, 1990), pp. 95–141. Our previous discussion of the free-rider problem associated with bonuses drew on this source.

[19] Ibid., p. 139. Studies of employee stock ownership plans (ESOPs) tend to find a positive effect on firm performance, but the results are diverse. ESOPs make workers partial owners of the firms for which they work. For a survey of prior studies, see Douglas Kruse and Joseph Blasi, "Employee Ownership, Employee Attitudes, and Firm Performance: A Review of the Evidence," in Daniel J. B. Mitchell, David Lewin, and Mahmood Zaidi (eds.), *Handbook of Human Resource Management* (Greenwich, CT: JAI Press, 1997).

[20] Douglas L. Kruse, "Profit Sharing and Productivity: Microeconomic Evidence from the United States," *Economic Journal,* January 1992 , pp. 24–36. Other studies finding a positive effect on productivity include Edward M. Shepard, III, "Profit Sharing and Productivity: Further Evidence from the Chemicals Industry," *Industrial Relations,* October 1994, pp. 452–66; and Sandeed Bhargava, "Profit Sharing and the Financial Performance of Companies: Evidence from U.K. Panel Data," *Economic Journal,* September 1994, pp. 1044–56.

Global Perspective 7.1

Percentage of Workers in a Profit-Sharing Plan

The percentage of workers participating in a profit-sharing plan varies substantially across countries.

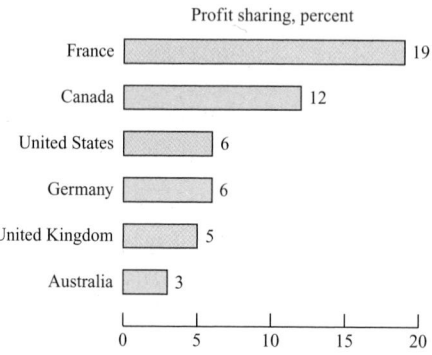

Profit sharing, percent

Country	Percent
France	19
Canada	12
United States	6
Germany	6
United Kingdom	5
Australia	3

Source: OECD, *Employment Outlook*, July 1995, Table 4.1; and Wendy Zellner, Eric Schine, and Geoffrey Smith, "Trickle-Down Is Trickling Down at Work," *BusinessWeek*, March 18, 1996, p. 34.

Equity Compensation

Equity compensation is *a pay scheme where part of the worker's compensation is given or invested in the firm's stock.* An increasingly popular form of equity compensation is **stock options,** which *give an employee the right to purchase a fixed number of shares of stock at a set price for a given time period.*[21] The price at which the option is given is called the *grant price* and is typically set at the market price when the stock option is given to the worker. Workers with stock options can make a profit if the market price rises above the grant price. That is, they can *exercise their option* to purchase the stock from the firm at the grant price and sell it at the market price.

In 2006, 8 percent of all private workers had a stock option.[22] There is substantial variation in the incidence of stock options. The proportion of workers with stock options was 5 percent among workers earning less than $15 per hour and 12 percent among workers earning $15 or more per hour. The percentage of employees with stock options was highest in white-collar occupations (11 percent) and lowest in service occupations (3 percent).

Stock options have a similar incentive effect to profit-sharing plans. That is, stock options mesh the interests of the firm's shareholders with those of the employees.

[21] For information about stock options and less common types of equity compensation, see William J. Wiatrowski, "Putting Stock in Benefits: How Prevalent Is It?" *Compensation and Working Conditions,* Fall 2000, pp. 2–7.

[22] U.S. Bureau of Labor Statistics, "National Compensation Survey: Employee Benefits in Private Industry in the United States, March 2006," Summary 0605, August 2006.

7.3	World of Work	Participant Direction in Pension Plans*

In 1980 about 60 percent of private sector workers with pension coverage had only a defined benefit plan. These pension plans provide a retirement benefit that depends on a worker's earnings and the number of years with the firm. By 2004 about 60 percent of private pension–covered workers had only a defined contribution plan. With defined contribution plans, the contributions by the employer and the employee and the returns on these funds determine the size of retirement benefit.

Over the past 15 years, defined contribution plans have shifted control of investment decisions to workers. Among employees with a defined contribution plan, the percentage who control at least some portion of the assets rose from 29 to 82 between 1990 and 2002.

Why would firms shift control of investment decisions to their workers? Researchers have suggested that new federal regulations making it clearer to firms how to avoid liability for losses resulting from participant

control over assets played an important role. Other factors include technological advances, which reduced the administrative costs of managing accounts for each worker, and the growth of mutual funds, which provide a low-cost way to diversify asset holdings.

Even and Macpherson have examined the impact of participant direction in defined contribution plans and reached several conclusions. First, high-income workers and more educated workers are more likely to have participant-directed plans. Second, the assets in participant-directed plans tend to be less risky. Specifically, participant-directed plans have a smaller share of assets invested in the stock of the employer and a higher share of assets in other types of stock. Third, adjusting for risk, participant-directed plans have a similar rate of return to employer-directed plans.

* Based on William E. Even and David A. Macpherson, "Participant Direction in Defined Contribution Plans," Working Paper, April 2006.

Workers have the incentive to work hard and increase the firm's profits. Greater profits will raise the market price of the firm's stock and thus raise the value of the workers' stock options. However, stock options suffer from the free-rider problem because the value of the stock options is tied to group rather than individual performance.

Tournament Pay

Some incentive pay schemes base compensation on relative performance. Such pay plans are known as *tournament pay.* For example, tennis or golf tournaments structure pay on the basis of where participants finish in the tournament. Typically the first prize is extremely high, with pay dropping a bit but still remaining high for the next few places. Rewards then sink rapidly for rankings well below the top spots. One purpose of this pay scheme is to promote greater performance by *all* participants throughout the rankings. Everyone aspires to the top prize; therefore, everyone works hard to achieve it. Lower pay is tolerated by many because of their opportunity to win one of the few big prizes.[23]

[23] Edward Lazear and Sherwin Rosen, "Rank Order Tournaments as an Optimum Labor Contract," *Journal of Political Economy,* October 1981, pp. 841–64. The interested reader may also wish to refer to Ronald G. Ehrenberg and Michael L. Bognanno, "Do Tournaments Have Incentive Effects?" *Journal of Political Economy,* December 1990, pp. 1307–24; and James G. Lynch, "The Effort Effects of Prizes in the Second Half of Tournaments," *Journal of Economic Behavior and Organization,* May 2005, pp. 115–29.

Global Perspective   7.2 — Chief Executive Officer Compensation

Chief executive officers in the United States are paid substantially more than those in other industrial countries.

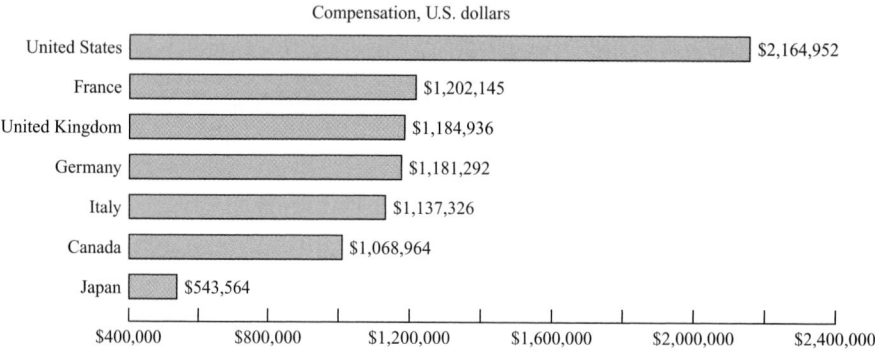

Compensation, U.S. dollars

Country	Compensation
United States	$2,164,952
France	$1,202,145
United Kingdom	$1,184,936
Germany	$1,181,292
Italy	$1,137,326
Canada	$1,068,964
Japan	$543,564

$400,000 $800,000 $1,200,000 $1,600,000 $2,000,000 $2,400,000

Source: Towers Perrin, New York, *Total Worldwide Remuneration,* 2005–2006. The compensation figures are for chief executive officers in firms with approximately $500 million in sales.

Tournament pay may have applications beyond sporting events.[24] Some observers speculate that the multimillion-dollar salaries paid to chief executive officers of large corporations may be equivalent to first-place prizes in a tournament. Indeed, compensation received by CEOs may exceed their personal marginal revenue products. The "excessive" pay (Table 7.1) allegedly may be efficient because it increases the MRPs of younger corporate managers, who aspire to one day become the CEO.

This view of CEO pay is controversial, as we will soon detail; but let's first look at some of its possible implications. First, managers who seek the top spot in the corporation but fall somewhat short will also be paid more than their MRPs. The firm may even tolerate deadwood at the senior level. Firms that gain reputations for arbitrarily firing older, less effective executives may not be able to attract a sufficient number of young workers to the tournament pay scheme. These younger workers may be unwilling to incur the risk of falling short of the top spots after expending years of effort to achieve them. The assurances that other high-paying jobs exist in the hierarchy and that employment is relatively secure may be important to the continuing success of this pay scheme.

[24] For example, see Tor Eriksson, "Executive Compensation and Tournament Theory: Empirical Tests on Danish Data," *Journal of Labor Economics,* April 1999, pp. 262–80; and Michael L. Bognanno, "Corporate Tournaments," *Journal of Labor Economics,* April 2001, pp. 290–315.

TABLE 7.1
**The 10 Highest-
Paid Chief
Executive
Officers, 2005**

Source: *Forbes,*
April 20, 2006.

Name	Company	Total Pay* (in Millions)
1. Richard Fairbank	Capital One Financial	$249.4
2. Terry Semel	Yahoo!	230.6
3. Henry Silverman	Cendant	140.0
4. Bruce Karatz	KB Home	135.5
5. Richard Fuld, Jr.	Lehman Brothers	122.7
6. Ray Irani	Occidental Petroleum	80.7
7. Lawrence Ellison	Oracle	75.3
8. John Thompson	Symantec	71.8
9. Edwin Crawford	Caremark Rx	69.7
10. Angelo Mozilo	Countrywide Financial	69.0

* Includes salaries, bonuses, and long-term payments such as stock options.

Second, tournament pay may help rationalize "golden parachute" provisions in executive compensation contracts. These provisions provide for large lump-sum compensation to executives who lose their jobs as a result of corporate takeovers. Golden parachutes—often worth millions of dollars—allow the executives to float comfortably to the ground.

Several explanations for these provisions have been offered. Perhaps these large sums deter hostile takeovers by making them more expensive. Or perhaps the corporate owners (shareholders) believe these large awards will discourage CEOs from fending off takeovers that bid up stock prices and increase the shareholders' wealth.

Tournament pay provides a complementary explanation. Perhaps golden parachutes are partly insurance against losing the full amount of the CEO prize once it is won. People ascending to CEO positions expect to receive high compensation for several years. But an unforeseen corporate takeover that results in discharge of the present CEO will wipe out part of the compensation prize. This possibility may undermine the desired incentive effects of the compensation scheme. The solution: golden parachutes that ensure against at least part of the lost pay resulting from a takeover.

Finally, tournament pay may help explain why many CEOs have relatively short tenures prior to their retirements. Turnover at the top at relatively frequent intervals is important to open up opportunities for those lower in the corporate hierarchy. Thus CEOs normally are given generous retirement incentives, usually at age 65. In this way the top-to-bottom work incentives created by the pay scheme are maintained.

Critics of the tournament explanation of high CEO pay dismiss the relevance of the theory to executive pay. They assert that such pay schemes are not optimal in corporations, where participants have opportunities to sabotage one another's performance. In this view, a tournament pay scheme within a corporate setting is more likely to promote detrimental strategic behavior by executives. Teamwork allegedly would erode, and overall productivity would decline.

If CEO compensation is not part of a tournament pay scheme, why is this pay so high? Perhaps high CEO pay simply reflects supply-and-demand realities. Because the decisions of CEOs affect entire corporations, their productivity is extremely high. Meanwhile the supply of experienced, top corporate decision makers is low. The labor market result is very high pay, as is true for other superstars, such as those in sports and entertainment.

Critics of high CEO pay dismiss this view, arguing that CEO pay tends to be "excessive" mainly because of the "mutual admiration society" that often develops among CEOs and corporate board members. Many members of corporate boards, themselves CEOs of other corporations, overrate the CEO's importance and worth. In this view some of the profits rightfully belonging to stockholders are instead diverted to extraordinarily high CEO pay. Between 1990 and 1999 chief executive pay increased by 428 percent. During that same period corporate profits rose by only 153 percent and the pay of factory workers increased by 30 percent.[25] In both 2001 and 2002, CEO pay fell substantially. By 2002 CEO pay was back to where it was in 1996 in inflation-adjusted terms. However, CEO pay recovered starting in 2003. In 2005 CEO compensation was 369 times that of the average worker.

This high CEO compensation has drawn considerable complaint from unions, stockholders, and politicians. In response, the Securities and Exchange Commission (SEC) in 1992 established new rules requiring that corporations clearly spell out directly to their stockholders the compensation of their five highest-paid executives. The SEC believes that this informational approach will help stockholders identify and ferret out excessive CEO pay. Also, in 1993 Congress eliminated corporate tax deductions for executive salaries exceeding $1 million annually (with an exception for pay directly tied to the firm's earnings performance).[26]

It is clear that "excessive" CEO pay is highly controversial and will continue to be debated.[27]

EFFICIENCY WAGE PAYMENTS

Pay-for-performance plans are most capable of solving the principal–agent problem in circumstances where individual output can be readily measured. But in many jobs measuring or assessing individual output is at best difficult and at worst impossible. One solution to the principal–agent problem in these circumstances is direct observation of the agents' actions on the job. Firms can reduce shirking by ***monitoring*** the *efforts* of

[25] Based on *BusinessWeek* surveys.
[26] For evidence suggesting that the law made little impact on CEO pay, see Nancy L. Rose and Catherine Wolfram, "Regulating Executive Pay: Using the Tax Code to Influence Chief Executive Compensation," *Journal of Labor Economics,* April 2002, part 2, pp. S138–75.
[27] Recent research on CEO pay includes Rajesh K. Aggarwal and Andrew A. Samwick, "Performance Incentives within Firms: The Effect of Managerial Responsibility," *Journal of Finance,* August 2003, pp. 1613–49; Marianne Bertrand and Sendhil Mullainathan, "Are CEOs Rewarded for Luck? The Ones without Principles Are," *Quarterly Journal of Economics,* August 2001, pp. 901–32; and Kevin J. Murphy and Jan Zabojnik, "CEO Pay and Appointments: A Market-Based Explanation for Recent Trends," *American Economic Review,* May 2004, pp. 192–96.

7.4 World of Work

What Is a Good CEO Worth?*

Some chief executive officers (CEOs) are extremely well-paid. Table 7.1 shows that, in 2005, the 10 highest-paid U.S. CEOs each earned more than $35 million in total compensation. These high figures raise the question of whether CEOs are worth their large compensation packages.

Hayes and Schaefer attempted to answer this question in an innovative way. They argued that the reason for a CEO's departure from his or her firm reveals important information about the manager's ability. CEOs who voluntarily leave because they are bid away by another firm tend to be of high ability. Because accidental death should be a random event among the other CEOs, those who die accidentally should be of average or below-average ability.

To test their hypothesis, Hayes and Schafer analyzed changes in a firm's market value after a manager leaves the firm. If the company loses a manager who is perceived by the stock market as having high ability, then the firm's market value should decline.

The authors' analysis of 158 separations of managers from firms from 1979 to 1994 produced striking results. After the announcement that an executive or the CEO would depart to take a position as a CEO at another company, the market value of the firm fell by an average of 2.8 percent. When the CEO died suddenly, the market value rose by an average of 2.8 percent. Thus Hayes and Schaefer concluded that the difference between a high- and low-ability CEO is worth as much as 5.6 percent of a company's market value. That difference may amount to hundreds of millions of dollars.

* Based on Rachel M. Hayes and Scott Schaefer, "How Much Are Differences in Managerial Ability Worth?" *Journal of Accounting and Economics*, April 1999, pp.125–48.

workers (for example, by hiring supervisors). Fearing the loss of their jobs, most workers will not shirk when they are being observed because presumably those who do will be identified and replaced. Supervision therefore may be an effective way to reduce the principal–agent problem in some circumstances. For this reason many jobs in the economy are supervisory.

Monitoring workers, however, is costly in some employment circumstances. It makes little economic sense, for example, to hire someone to monitor the effort of a security guard, a babysitter, a house painter, or a manager. Also, it may be prohibitively costly to hire a sufficient number of supervisors to monitor the quality of each worker's performance in assembly-line work. As a result, some economists suggest that firms search for approaches other than monitoring or pay for performance to synchronize the interests of the workers with those of the firm.

How might firms deal with the principal–agent problem when supervision is costly and individual output is difficult to measure? One such approach may be to pay workers a wage that is above the market-clearing level.

Wage–Productivity Dependence

In the models discussed in Chapter 6, we explicitly assumed that labor was homogeneous and implicitly assumed that a change in wage rates did not alter the marginal product of labor and hence the location of the labor demand curve. Any change in the wage rate therefore altered the quantity of labor demanded; it did *not* change the location of the demand curve itself. However, under some conditions a wage rise may positively affect labor efficiency, causing a rightward shift of the labor demand curve.

Theories that incorporate the aforementioned possibility—that wage increases may increase productivity—are called *efficiency wage theories*. An **efficiency wage** is *one that minimizes an employer's wage cost per effective unit of labor service employed*. The key phrase is "per *effective* unit of labor service." Under the customary assumptions of competitive labor markets and homogeneous labor inputs, the market-clearing wage (determined where labor supply and demand intersect) *is* the wage that minimizes a firm's wage cost per effective unit of labor service employed. All workers are assumed to be equally and fully effective in the production process. If a firm pays a below-market-clearing wage, the company will not attract the desired number of workers. If it pays an above-market-clearing wage, its wage cost per effective unit of labor will rise because equally efficient units could have been hired at the lower market wage. We will discover, however, that under assumptions of heterogeneous labor and wage–productivity dependence, a firm may find that it can *lower* its wage cost per effective unit of labor service by paying a *higher* wage rate.

A simple numerical example will help demonstrate this general principle. Suppose workers who are fully effective at some task can each produce 10 units of a particular output per hour. Next suppose that the market wage rate is $5 an hour and that for reasons we will discuss shortly, workers each produce only 5 units of output per hour at the $5 wage. In this circumstance we find that each *effective* unit of labor service costs an employer $10 per hour. The firm needs 2 hours of labor services to obtain 10 units of output (= 2 × 5), and each hour costs $5 in wages.

What if the firm discovers that it can obtain fully effective units of labor—those that produce 10 units of hourly output—by paying $8 an hour? This implies that the hourly wage cost per effective unit of labor declines by $2 (= $10 − $8) as the wage rate rises by $3 (= $8 − $5).

The unusual outcome illustrated by our simple example is possible where a higher wage more than proportionately induces greater employee work effort, improves the worker's capabilities, or increases the proportion of highly skilled workers in a particular workforce.

Shirking Model of Efficiency Wages

The shirking model of efficiency wages theorizes that some enterprises pay more than the market-clearing wage to reduce employee shirking. In some situations employers have little information about how diligently workers are performing their duties (for example, night security workers at an office building). Moreover, full supervision and monitoring of such workers may be too costly (hiring other security workers to watch security workers). Under these conditions, the possibility arises that all employees will choose to shirk. To counter this possibility, firms may opt to pay workers more than the market-clearing wage. This higher pay increases the relative value of the job as viewed by each worker. It also raises the cost of being terminated for shirking, should it be detected. In familiar economic wording, the higher opportunity cost (price) of shirking reduces the amount of shirking occurring. Worker productivity improves more than proportionally to the higher wage; the labor demand curve is located farther rightward; and wage costs per effective unit of labor decline.[28]

Other Efficiency Wage Theories

Although less relevant to the principal–agent problem, there are other variations of the efficiency wage idea, two of which are the *nutritional* and the *labor turnover* models.

1 Nutritional Model   In a relatively poor nation, an increase in the real wage might elevate the nutritional and health levels of workers. This will positively affect their physical vigor, mental alertness, and therefore their productivity. Thus real wage increases could shift labor demand curves rightward, benefiting employers as well as employees.[29]

2 Labor Turnover Model   Employers may increase wages to reduce costly **labor turnover,** *the rate at which workers quit their jobs, necessitating their replacement by new workers*. We have seen that employers bear the costs of providing firm-specific training to new workers (Chapter 4). Also, because workers normally "learn by doing," new workers are not initially as proficient as the people they replace.

An above-market-clearing wage raises the workers' costs of quitting their jobs and thus lowers the likelihood that they will quit. Lower labor turnover, in turn, increases worker productivity *on the average,* because it increases the proportion of experienced workers relative to those being trained and still "learning by doing." The result is that the higher wage rate shifts the labor demand curve rightward.

7.5

Implication: Nonclearing Labor Markets

Efficiency wage theories produce several interesting implications, one of which is that permanent unemployment may exist under conditions of equilibrium in labor markets.[30]

---

[28] The reader interested in a more advanced treatment of efficiency wage theories should consult George A. Akerlof and Janet L. Yellen (eds.), *Efficiency Wage Models of the Labor Market* (Cambridge: Cambridge University Press, 1986); Andrew Weiss, *Efficiency Wages: Models of Unemployment, Layoffs, and Wage Dispersions* (Princeton, NJ: Princeton University Press, 1991); and Kevin M. Murphy and Robert H. Topel, "Efficiency Wages Reconsidered: Theory and Evidence," in Yoram Weiss and Gideon Fishelson (eds.), *Advances in Theory and Measurement of Unemployment* (London: MacMillan, 1990).

[29] Harvey Leibenstein, "The Theory of Underemployment in Densely Populated Backward Areas," in Harvey Leibenstein (ed.), *Economic Backwardness and Economic Growth* (New York: John Wiley & Sons, 1963), chap. 6. For a critical review of the empirical evidence on the nutritional model, see John Strauss and Duncan Thomas, "Health, Nutrition, and Economic Development," *Journal of Economic Literature,* June 1998, pp. 766–817.

[30] We explore other implications of the efficiency wage models in later discussions of wage differentials (Chapter 8) and frictional unemployment (Chapter 18).

In 1914 Ford Motor Company made headlines by offering autoworkers the grand sum of $5 per day, up from $2.50 per day. This wage offer was newsworthy because at that time the typical market wage in manufacturing was just $2 to $3 per day.

What was Ford's rationale for offering a higher-than-competitive wage? Statistics indicate that the company was suffering from unusually high quit rates and absenteeism. Ford apparently reasoned that a high wage rate would increase worker productivity by increasing morale and reducing employee turnover. Only workers who had been at Ford for at least 6 months were eligible for the $5 per day wage. Nevertheless, 10,000 workers applied for employment with Ford in the immediate period following the announcement of the wage hike.

According to historians of this era, the Ford strategy succeeded. The $5 wage raised the value of the job to Ford workers, who therefore became loyal to the company and worked hard to retain their high-paying jobs. The quit and absenteeism rates both plummeted, and in 1914 labor productivity at Ford rose by an estimated 51 percent.

How does this increase in productivity relate to economic theory? We know from Chapter 5 that normally a change in the wage rate does not affect labor productivity and therefore does not affect labor demand. Instead the firm responds to a change in the wage rate by altering the quantity of labor it "purchases." This adjustment is shown graphically as a point-to-point movement along the firm's existing labor demand curve. But in the 1914 Ford situation the $2.50 boost in the daily wage increased labor productivity. Stated in economic terms, the $5 wage was an *efficiency wage*. The wage increase to $5 per day raised the marginal product of Ford workers. This translated into an increase in Ford's marginal revenue product schedule, which we know is its demand for labor curve.

In brief, Ford's experience with its $5 daily wage is consistent with the theory that efficiency wages may in some situations be optimal for reducing principal–agent problems.

* This discussion is based in part on Daniel M. G. Raff and Lawrence Summers, "Did Henry Ford Pay Efficiency Wages?" *Journal of Labor Economics*, pt. 2, October 1987, pp. S57–86. For evidence indicating that Henry Ford did *not* intentionally pay efficiency wages, see Jason E. Taylor, "Did Henry Ford Mean to Pay Efficiency Wages?" *Journal of Labor Research*, Fall 2003, pp. 683–94.

We demonstrate this possibility in Figure 7.8, where the initial equilibrium wage rate and level of employment are W_1 and Q_1. Suppose the firm discovers it can reduce its wage cost per effective unit of labor by increasing the wage to W_2 (from *a* to *b*). This decline in the wage cost per effective unit of labor results from the rightward shift of the labor demand curve from D_{L1} to D_{L2}—that is, from an increase in the marginal product of labor. The wage cost per effective unit of labor declines because the extra output of workers presumably rises more than the firm's wage expense. Observe that we have drawn the demand increase such that the firm continues to employ Q_1 workers (at *b*) as before; but the efficiency wage just as reasonably could have shifted the curve to a greater or lesser extent than that shown.[31]

[31] A technical note is required here. Each demand curve in Figure 7.8 is a separate "pseudo-demand curve," which holds worker quality and effort constant and assumes that the firm is hiring labor competitively. In fact, this is a wage-setting firm and as such does not have a labor demand curve (just as a monopolist does not have a supply curve). Demand in this case is actually the single point *b* on D_{L2}.

FIGURE 7.8 Efficiency Wage Model

Under some conditions, an increase in the wage may increase worker efficiency and labor demand. In this situation, we suppose that the firm increases the wage from W_1 to W_2, which shifts labor demand from D_{L1} to D_{L2} and minimizes the firm's wage cost per effective unit of labor. Although W_2 is an equilibrium wage, it is not a market-clearing wage, as shown by the surplus of labor bc.

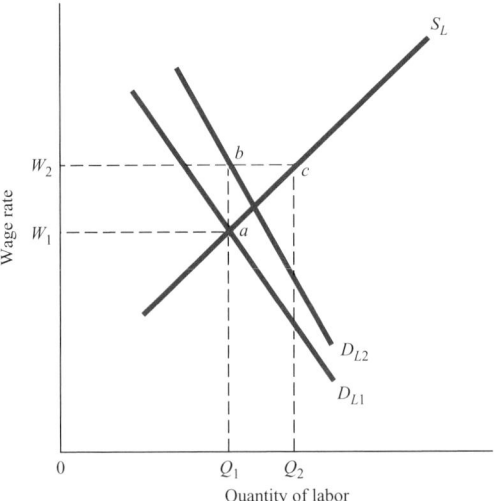

Wage rate W_2 is the new equilibrium wage rate in this market; at b, the firm has no incentive to reduce the wage rate or to increase it further. But observe that this equilibrium wage is *not* the market-clearing wage. At W_2 the firm employs Q_1 workers, whereas we see from point c on the supply curve that Q_2 workers seek employment. Assuming that workers do not find jobs elsewhere, permanent unemployment of bc occurs in this particular labor market. The more elastic the labor demand and supply curves, the greater the unemployment. The closer to c that the efficiency demand curve intersects the labor supply curve, the less equilibrium unemployment.

An additional important point: In the shirking efficiency wage model, the bc unemployment is partly the reason for the wage–productivity dependence in the first place. The threat of losing a relatively high-paying job and of becoming part of the bc unemployed workers serves as a disciplining device to discourage shirking and to encourage full effort. In the absence of the resulting equilibrium unemployment, the labor demand curve might not shift from D_{L1} to D_{L2} in response to the higher wage.

Criticisms

Detractors of efficiency wage theories question whether these models add greatly to our understanding of labor markets in advanced economies. Critics of the shirking model, in particular, point out that several of the pay-for-performance plans discussed earlier in this chapter could serve as alternatives to efficiency wages as ways to guard against poor worker performance. As examples, where monitoring workers is costly, the firm can pay on a piece rate or a commission basis. Where individual performance is difficult to measure, bonus pay based on team performance can be implemented.

Second, critics point out that a firm could require employees to post a bond that they would forfeit if they were found to have been negligent in performing their job duties.

Finally, detractors of the efficiency wage theory note that firms can reduce shirking by establishing pay plans in which part of the workers' pay is deferred until later years or until employees qualify for pensions. Encouraged by the deferred income, workers will work hard to maintain employment within the firm.

Each of these devices, argue the critics, can reduce the principal–agent problem at less expense than paying above-market-clearing wages.[32]

7.2 *Quick Review*	• The principal–agent problem is the conflict of interest that occurs when agents pursue their own objectives to the detriment of meeting the principal's objectives.
	• Pay-for-performance plans such as piece rates, commissions and royalties, raises and promotions, bonuses, profit sharing, and tournament pay are designed to minimize principal–agent problems.
	• Efficiency wages are above-market-clearing wages designed to reduce employee shirking and labor turnover; they are equilibrium wages because, given labor supply and demand, employers have no incentive to change them.
	• Because they are set higher than market-clearing wages, efficiency wages may contribute to permanent unemployment.

Your Turn

What is the major difficulty with profit sharing as a means of overcoming the principal–agent problem? (*Answer:* See page 597)

LABOR MARKET EFFICIENCY REVISITED

The basic supply and demand models in Chapter 6 provide meaningful insights into wages and the efficient allocation of labor. But in this chapter we have seen that the decisions of workers and firms are substantially more complex than our earlier models suggest. A variety of compensation schemes are available, each potentially optimal for a particular type of job and worker. Workers therefore must make choices not only about hours and pay but also about a variety of types of pay. Similarly, firms must not only make hiring and total pay decisions; they must also weigh the costs and benefits of a full range of possible compensation schemes. Some schemes may reduce worker productivity; others may greatly enhance it.

---

[32] For empirical evidence on the efficiency wage idea, see Adriana D. Kugler, "Employee Referrals and Efficiency Wages," *Labour Economics,* October 2003, pp. 531–61; Paul Chen and Per-Anders Edin, "Efficiency Wages and Industrial Wage Differentials: A Comparison Across Methods of Pay," *Review of Economics and Statistics,* November 2002, pp. 617–31; and Scott M. Fuess, Jr., and Meghan Millea, "Do Employers Pay Efficiency Wages? Evidence from Japan," *Journal of Labor Research,* Spring 2002, pp. 279–92.

In this chapter our previous definition of labor market efficiency has been extended. In Chapter 6 we found that efficiency occurred when no worker could be switched from one *job* to another to produce more economic well-being. Now we must append to that definition the following phrase: "Neither can any worker be switched from one *compensation scheme* to another to increase economic well-being." Labor market efficiency requires that workers be allocated to optimal work. It also demands that optimal compensation packages be implemented. Privately optimal compensation choices normally are also socially optimal, the exception being where efficiency wages are paid. Recall that these payments may create unemployment.

Chapter Summary

1. Total compensation consists of wage and fringe benefits. Fringe benefits include *legally required benefits,* such as Social Security contributions, and *voluntary benefits,* such as paid leaves, insurance benefits, and private pensions. More than one-fourth of total pay takes the form of fringe benefits, broadly defined.

2. An employee's preferences for wages and fringe benefits can be set forth in an indifference map. Each indifference curve shows the various combinations of wages and fringe benefits that yield a given level of utility. An employer's normal-profit isoprofit curve displays the various combinations of wages and fringe benefits that yield a normal profit. The worker achieves an optimal or utility-maximizing combination of wages and fringe benefits by selecting the wage–fringe mix that enables the worker to attain the highest possible indifference curve.

3. Several factors explain the historical growth of fringe benefits. These include (1) the tax advantages they confer; (2) the scale economies resulting from their collective purchase; (3) their ability to reduce job turnover and motivate workers; (4) the sensitivity of fringe benefits, such as medical and dental care, to increases in income; (5) legal mandates by the federal government; and (6) the historical growth of union contracts, in which fringe benefits are relatively large.

4. The relationship between firms and workers is one of principals (firms) and agents (workers). Firms will attempt to take actions to reduce the so-called principal–agent problem, which occurs when agents pursue their own goals rather than the objectives of the principals.

5. Piece rates, commissions, and royalties are pay schemes designed to tie pay directly to productivity.

6. Workers receiving annual salaries may have an incentive to reduce work hours below levels that they would work if they were paid by the hour. The prospect of raises and promotions reduces this principal–agent problem.

7. Bonuses can elicit greater work effort and thereby increase productivity. But bonuses attached to personal performance may direct behavior away from team goals. Bonuses based on team or firm performance help solve this problem but create a potential free-rider problem when the team is large. Research indicates that executive bonuses have some positive effect on corporate performance.

8. Assuming minimal free-rider problems, profit-sharing plans and stock options synchronize the interests of firms and their workers. Recent research points toward a positive link between profit sharing and productivity.

9. Tournament pay assigns an extraordinarily high reward to the top performer and is designed to maximize performance by all who are striving to achieve the top spot. Some observers view high CEO pay as an efficient aspect of such pay schemes. Critics dismiss this idea as being a rationalization of excessive CEO pay, arguing instead that high CEO pay has resulted from improper corporate board oversight of stockholders' interests.

10. In situations where supervision of workers is minimal, a dependence between the wage paid and productivity may occur. The firm may find that it can increase its profits by paying an efficiency wage—a wage above the market-clearing wage. An interesting implication of efficiency wage theories is that persistent unemployment may be consistent with equilibrium in the labor market.

Terms and Concepts

fringe benefits, *210*
in-kind benefits, *213*
isoprofit curve, *215*
agents, *220*
principals, *220*
principal–agent
  problem, *221*
shirking, *221*

incentive pay plans, *221*
piece rates, *221*
time rates, *222*
commissions, *222*
royalties, *222*
quasi-fixed resources, *223*
bonuses, *225*
free-rider problem, *226*

profit sharing, *227*
equity compensation, *228*
stock options, *228*
tournament pay, *229*
monitoring, *232*
efficiency wage, *234*
labor turnover, *235*

Questions and Study Suggestions

1. What is an isoprofit curve as it relates to wages and fringe benefits? What is a normal-profit isoprofit curve? In what respect is a normal-profit isoprofit curve a *budget constraint* as viewed by a worker? At which point on the employer's isoprofit curve will a rational worker choose to locate? Explain.

2. In Figure 7.6 the reduction in the cost of fringe benefits resulted in an increase in the amount of fringe benefits and a *reduction* in the wage income received. Redraw the worker's indifference map to demonstrate a circumstance in which fringe benefits would not go up by as much, but wage income would *increase*. Explain the difference between the two situations.

3. The U.S. Office of Management and Budget has estimated that the tax-exempt status of fringe benefits such as pensions and group insurance reduces tax revenue to the Treasury by about $230 billion annually. Some economists have suggested that the federal government recover this tax revenue by taxing fringe benefits as ordinary income. Use Figure 7.5 to explain how this proposal would affect *(a)* the slope of the indifference curves and *(b)* the slope of the isoprofit curve. What would be the likely effect on the optimal level of fringe benefits?

4. Explain what is meant by the term *principal–agent problem.* Have you ever worked in a setting where this problem has arisen? If so, do you think that increased monitoring would have eliminated the problem? Why don't firms simply hire more supervisors to eliminate shirking problems?

5. Identify and explain a separate common problem associated with each of the following pairs of compensation plans:

   a. Piece rates; bonuses tied to individual performance.

   b. Bonuses applied to team performance; profit-sharing plans.

6. Demonstrate graphically why someone guaranteed an annual salary might choose to work fewer hours than someone who could earn that same amount through hourly pay. Reconcile your answer with the fact that salaried workers in general work more hours weekly than people receiving hourly pay.

7. Speculate on what actions workers might take to resolve a free-rider problem arising from a profit-sharing plan.

8. People often sell goods (or raffle tickets) as part of a fund-raising project. These projects typically offer valuable prizes to those who sell over a fixed number of units. Often a grand prize, like a trip to Hawaii, is offered to the person who sells the most units. Why are these prizes offered? Relate this example to the high pay received by chief executive officers of large corporations.

9. Discuss the following statement in relationship to *(a)* the tournament theory of executive pay and *(b)* the "World of Work" 7.2 on faculty tenure: "The new economics of personnel rationalizes whatever exists. If a compensation structure prevails, so goes this view, it *must* be efficient. The policy implication therefore is to 'let it be' *(laissez faire)*. Thus what poses as economic analysis is actually political conservatism."

10. How might payment of an efficiency wage *(a)* reduce shirking by employees and *(b)* reduce employee turnover? What is the implication of the efficiency wage theory for unemployment? In what way are piece rates, commissions, royalties, profit sharing, and stock options substitutes for efficiency wages?

11. What are stock options? How do they relate to the principal–agent problem?

12. As an employer, suppose you find it costly to monitor employee effort 100 percent of the time. What compensation options are available to ensure that you get appropriate levels of employee effort? What factors would you consider in choosing among these options?

Internet Exercise

What Is Happening to Health Insurance?

Go to the Bureau of Labor Statistics National Compensation Survey-Benefits Web site (**http://www.bls.gov/ncs/ebs/home.htm**) and in sequence select "Get Detailed NCS-Benefits Statistics," and "Most Requested Statistics." Then click on "Percent of All Workers Participating in Medical Care Benefits," "Percent of All Workers with Medical Care Required to Contribute Toward Cost of Single Coverage" and "All Years." This will retrieve the percentage of workers with health insurance coverage at private establishments as well as the percentage of covered workers required to help pay for their own coverage.

What was the percentage of workers with health insurance coverage in 1999? What is the figure for the most recent year shown?

What was the percentage of workers with health insurance coverage who were required to help contribute toward the cost of single coverage in 1999? What is the figure for the most recent year shown? What is a possible explanation for the trends in health insurance coverage and the fraction of workers required to help pay for their own coverage?

Provide *one* other specific statistic of your choice from the data on fringe benefits. For example: "In 2006, the percent of all workers at private establishments with access to employer assistance to child care was xx percent."

Internet Links

The Web site of *Forbes* contains an annual special report on the compensation of chief executive officers **(http://www.forbes.com)**.

The National Center for Employee Ownership Web site gives information on employee stock ownership plans and stock options **(http://www.nceo.org)**.

The U.S. Census Bureau Web site provides detailed statistics regarding health insurance coverage **(http://www.census.gov/hhes/www/hlthins.html)**.

The Employee Benefits Research Institute Web site provides summaries of research related to employee benefits **(http://www.ebri.org)**.

Chapter 8

The Wage Structure

As evidence all around us suggests, there are large variations in wages and salaries in the United States. An elite fashion model may earn $2 million annually; her photographer, $90,000; and her makeup artist, $45,000. Meanwhile a teacher's aide glancing at the model in a magazine ad may earn $13,000. A union tile layer may make $48,000 a year, while the secretary at the tile firm earns $22,000. A lawyer charging $200 per hour may pay her babysitter $6.00 per hour. A chemist may earn $80,000 each year; a mixologist (bartender), $20,000. An entertainer from San Diego dressed as a chicken may make $250,000 a year; a deli worker making chicken sandwiches, $20,000.

Many of these wage differences in the economy are *equilibrium wage differentials*—they do not elicit movement of labor from the lower-paying to the higher-paying jobs. Other wage variations are *transitional wage differentials*—they promote worker mobility that eventually reduces the wage disparities. In this chapter we examine the wage structure resulting from the working of labor markets and explain why wage differentials occur and persist. In Chapter 9 we look at labor mobility and migration induced by transitory wage differentials and examine the wage narrowing that eventually results.

PERFECT COMPETITION: HOMOGENEOUS WORKERS AND JOBS

In Chapter 6 we analyzed a perfectly competitive labor market for a *specific type of labor.* Let's now extend the assumption of *homogeneous workers and jobs* to *all* employees and firms in the economy. If information is perfect and job searches and migration are costless, labor resources will flow among various employments and regions of the economy until all workers have the same real wage.

The process whereby wages equalize is demonstrated in Figure 8.1. Initially assume that labor demand and supply are D_a and S_a, respectively, in submarket A and D_b and S_b

FIGURE 8.1 **Wage Equalization in Perfect Competition**

If labor supply and demand are S_a and D_a in labor submarket A and S_b and D_b in submarket B, a $5 wage differential (= $10 in A minus $5 in B) will emerge. Assuming that jobs and workers are homogeneous and information and mobility are costless, workers will leave submarket B for the higher-paying submarket A. The decline of labor supply in B from S_b to S'_b and the increase in submarket A from S_a to S'_a will cause the wage rates in each submarket to equalize at $7.50.

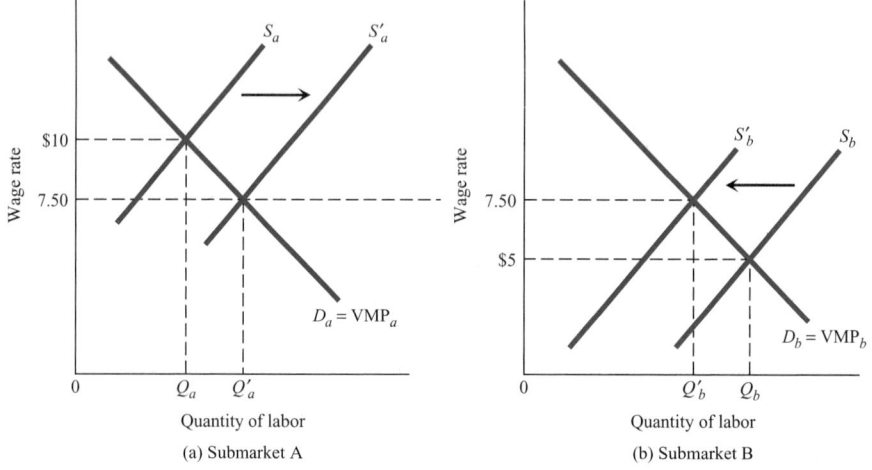

(a) Submarket A

(b) Submarket B

in submarket B. These supply and demand conditions produce a $10 hourly wage in submarket A compared to a $5 wage in B. In each instance the wage rate equals the VMP of labor; but note that the VMP of the Q_b worker in submarket B is less than the wage rate and VMP of the Q_a employee in submarket A. The consequence? Workers will exit submarket B and take jobs in higher-paying A. The decline in labor supply in B from S_b to S'_b and the increase in A from S_a to S'_a will reduce the equilibrium wage in A from $10 to $7.50. The market-clearing wage in submarket B will rise from $5 to $7.50. Following the movement of workers between the two submarkets, the wage rates will be equal ($7.50) and in turn will be equal to the opportunity cost or supply price P_L of the last unit of labor ($7.50) in each market.

We may thus summarize as follows: If all jobs and workers are homogeneous and there is perfect mobility and competition, the **wage structure**—defined as *the array of wage rates paid to workers*—will evidence no variability. The average wage rate will be the *only* wage rate in the economy.

THE WAGE STRUCTURE: OBSERVED DIFFERENTIALS

Casual observation of the economy reveals that in fact wage differentials *do* exist and that many of them persist over time. Table 8.1 shows an overview of occupational wage differentials. Observe that the average hourly earnings of management, business, and financial workers in 2006 were $29.09, while production workers received

TABLE 8.1
Average Hourly Earnings by Occupational Group

Source: Barry T. Hirsch and David A. Macpherson, *Union Membership and Earnings Data Book: Compilations from the Current Population Survey (2007 Edition)* (Washington, DC: Bureau of National Affairs, 2007).

Occupational Group	Average Hourly Earnings
Management, business, and financial workers	$29.09
Professional and related workers	25.33
Installation, maintenance, and repair workers	18.68
Construction and extraction workers	17.18
Sales workers	17.13
Production workers	15.14
Office and administrative support workers	14.83
Transportation and material moving workers	14.28
Service workers	11.84
Farming, fishing, and forestry workers	9.85

$15.14 and service employees $11.84. Hourly earnings also vary within occupational categories such as those shown in Table 8.1. For example, under the category of "service workers," one would discover a difference in hourly earnings between people providing private household services and those providing protective services to corporations. Also, the highest-paid service workers earn more than the lowest-paid workers who are classified as sales workers, even though the average hourly salary is higher for the latter occupational group.

The occupational wage structure is just one of the many wage structures that one can isolate for study. Notice from Tables 8.2 and 8.3 that average hourly gross earnings also differ greatly by industry and geographical location. For example, hourly pay averaged $13.56 in retail trade in 2006 while it was $24.13 in mining. Also observe from Table 18.3 that manufacturing workers in Massachusetts earned an average of $25.04 per hour; in Mississippi, on the other hand, they received $14.65. Finally, as of 2006 female earnings were about 80 percent of male earnings, and the pay for African–Americans was 81 percent of that paid to whites.

What are the sources of these wage differentials, and how can they persist? Why do some wage differences narrow over time while others remain the same or increase? To answer these and related questions we need to abandon several assumptions made

TABLE 8.2
Average Hourly Earnings by Industry Group

Source: Barry T. Hirsch and David A. Macpherson, *Union Membership and Earnings Data Book: Compilations from the Current Population Survey (2007 Edition)* (Washington, DC: Bureau of National Affairs, 2007).

Industry Group	Average Hourly Earnings
Mining	$24.13
Finance, insurance, real estate, rental, and leasing	24.06
Public administration	23.44
Transportation, warehousing, information, and utilities	21.60
Manufacturing	20.67
Wholesale trade	20.58
Construction	18.29
Services	18.10
Retail trade	13.56
Agriculture, forestry, and fisheries	10.94

Global Perspective

8.1

Hourly Pay around the World

Wage differentials are quite pronounced worldwide. The accompanying chart shows the average hourly pay for production workers in U.S. dollars for various nations for 2005. As defined here, hourly pay comprises all payments made directly to the worker, including pay for time worked; pay for vacations, holidays, and other special payments; and in-kind payments. Also included in the figures are employer expenditures for legally required insurance programs and private benefit plans. All wages are before-tax amounts and are converted to U.S. dollars through appropriate exchange rate adjustments.

Several facts stand out from this chart. First, hourly compensation varies greatly around the world. Second, pay for production workers in the United States is not as high as it is in a number of European nations. Finally, hourly wage rates in nations such as Taiwan, Mexico, Brazil, South Korea, and Hong Kong are exceptionally low relative to pay in the more mature industrial nations. *Caution:* Prices of goods and services vary widely among these nations. Because exchange rates do not perfectly reflect this fact, these figures are only rough approximations of actual differences in purchasing power and living standards.

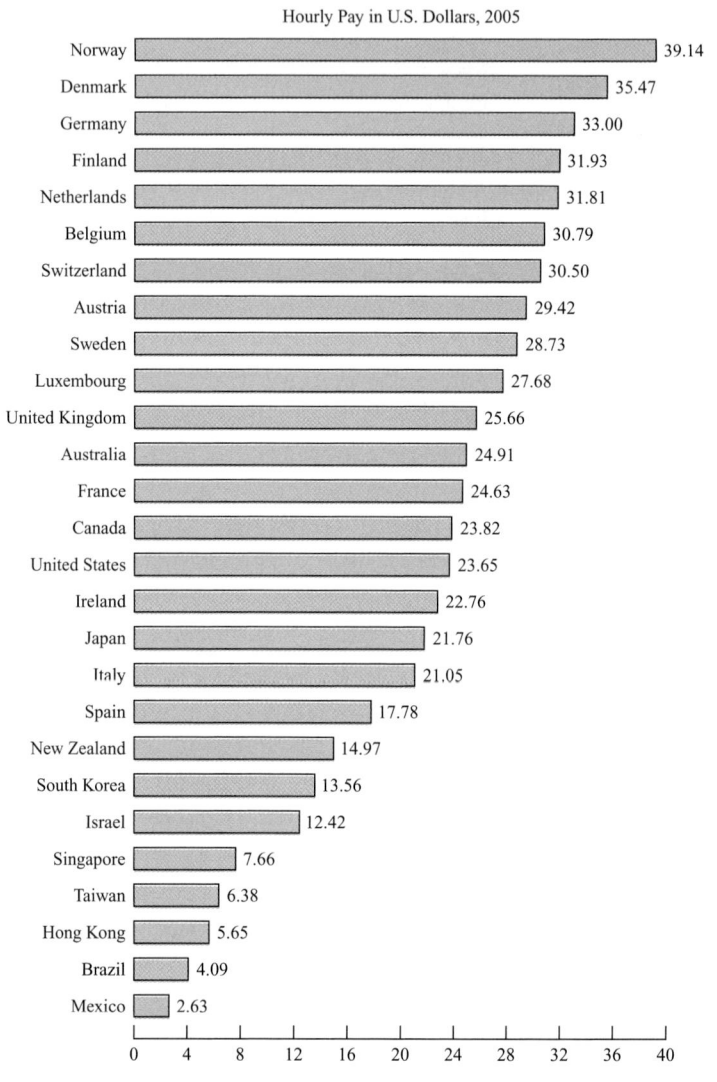

Hourly Pay in U.S. Dollars, 2005

Norway	39.14
Denmark	35.47
Germany	33.00
Finland	31.93
Netherlands	31.81
Belgium	30.79
Switzerland	30.50
Austria	29.42
Sweden	28.73
Luxembourg	27.68
United Kingdom	25.66
Australia	24.91
France	24.63
Canada	23.82
United States	23.65
Ireland	22.76
Japan	21.76
Italy	21.05
Spain	17.78
New Zealand	14.97
South Korea	13.56
Israel	12.42
Singapore	7.66
Taiwan	6.38
Hong Kong	5.65
Brazil	4.09
Mexico	2.63

Source: Data are from *International Comparisons of Hourly Compensation Costs for Production Workers in Manufacturing,* 2005, Bureau of Labor Statistics, News Release 06-2020, November 30, 2006, Table 2.

TABLE 8.3
Average Hourly Earnings of Private Workers in Manufacturing Industries by Selected States

Source: Barry T. Hirsch and David A. Macpherson, *Union Membership and Earnings Data Book: Compilations from the Current Population Survey (2007 Edition)* (Washington, DC: Bureau of National Affairs, 2007).

State	Average Hourly Earnings
Connecticut	$26.54
New Jersey	25.77
Massachusetts	25.04
Michigan	23.94
California	23.51
Texas	20.69
New York	20.65
Pennsylvania	20.62
Ohio	19.20
Florida	18.15
Alabama	17.88
Iowa	16.93
Arkansas	16.42
Mississippi	14.65

in the previous section of this chapter. More specifically, wage differentials occur because (1) jobs are heterogeneous, (2) workers are heterogeneous, and (3) labor markets are imperfect.

WAGE DIFFERENTIALS: HETEROGENEOUS JOBS

In Figure 8.1 we assumed that jobs were identical to one another in all respects. Utility-maximizing employees thus needed to consider only the wage rate itself in deciding where to work. Higher wages in one submarket would attract workers there. But in reality, jobs are heterogeneous rather than homogeneous. In particular, *heterogeneous jobs* have differing nonwage attributes, require different types and degrees of skill, or vary in the efficacy of paying efficiency wages to increase productivity. Employers also vary with respect to such things as union status, firm size, and discriminatory attitudes.

Compensating Differentials

Nonwage aspects of jobs vary greatly and are the source of *compensating wage differentials. These differentials consist of the extra pay that an employer must provide to compensate a worker for some undesirable job characteristic that does not exist in an alternative employment.* Compensating wage differentials are thus equilibrium wage differentials because they do *not* cause workers to shift to the higher-paying jobs and thereby cause wage rates to move toward equality.

Figure 8.1 is useful in showing this concept. In our previous discussion of this figure we assumed that the jobs shown in labor submarkets A and B were homogeneous. Now let's suppose instead that the jobs in submarket A are performed outdoors in freezing weather throughout the year while the work in B occurs indoors in pleasant surroundings. Recall from Table 6.1 that one of the categories of determinants of labor supply consists of the nonwage attributes of employment. Because of the indicated differences in nonwage amenities between submarkets A and B, labor supply will be less in A relative to B. If, for example, S_a is the labor supply curve in submarket A while S_b portrays supply in B, the *equilibrium* wage rate in A will be $10 as contrasted to $5 in submarket B.

The extra $5 paid in A is called a *wage premium, compensating wage differential,* or *equalizing difference.* No movement of workers from B to A will occur, as happened when jobs were assumed to be homogeneous. This $5 wage differential will *persist;* it will change only in response to changes in the other determinants of supply and demand in either of the two labor markets.

Several additional points need to be highlighted here. First, the observed wage disparity—$5—does *not* reflect an actual difference in net advantage or net utility between the two jobs. Taking the nonwage characteristics of the two jobs into account, workers Q_a and Q_b are equally paid; they both *net* $5 of utility from an hour of work: In A, $10 of wage minus $5 of extra disutility equals $5 net; in B, $5 of wage minus $0 of extra disutility equals $5 net.

Second, assuming demand is the same in both markets, employment will be lower where the compensating wage differential must be paid. Notice in Figure 8.1 that only Q_a workers are employed in A as contrasted to Q_b in B.

Finally, it is clear that the compensating wage differential performs the socially useful function of allocating labor resources to a productive task that is not as pleasant as others.

Having established the basic principle of compensating wage differentials, we next examine the types of nonwage aspects of jobs that cause differing labor supply curves and therefore compensating payments. Specifically, let's examine each of the following sources of compensating differentials: (1) risk of job injury and death, (2) fringe benefits, (3) job status, (4) job location, (5) the regularity of earnings, and (6) the prospect for wage advancement.

1 Risk of Job Injury or Death

The greater the risk of being injured or killed on the job, the less the labor supply to a particular occupation. For this reason, jobs that have high risks of accidents relative to others requiring similar skill will command compensating wage differentials. Viscusi has estimated that the average earnings premium for risk of injury and death in the American economy is about 5 percent. Although other studies have produced mixed findings, collectively they confirm the existence of compensating differentials, particularly those associated with higher probabilities of *fatal* injury on the job.[1]

---

[1] W. Kip Viscusi, *Employment Hazards: An Investigation of Market Performance* (Cambridge, MA: Harvard University Press, 1979). In a review he reaches a similar conclusion; see W. Kip Viscusi, "The Value of Risks to Life and Health," *Journal of Economic Literature,* December 1993, pp. 1912–46. See also Robert Sandy and Robert F. Elliott, "Wages: The Impact of the Risk of Occupationally Related Long-Term Illness on Earnings," *Journal of Human Resources,* Summer 2005, pp. 744–68; and John D. Leeth and John Ruser, "Compensating Wage Differentials for Fatal and Nonfatal Injury Risk by Gender and Race," *Journal of Risk and Uncertainty,* December 2003, pp. 257–77.

2 Fringe Benefits

Fringe benefits (Chapter 7) vary greatly among employers who hire similar workers and pay similar wage rates. How might this fact relate to wage differentials? Suppose some firms hiring specific labor pay only $8 an hour while others pay the $8 and provide such fringe benefits as sick leave, paid vacations, and medical and dental insurance. Other things being equal, workers will choose to offer their services to these latter employers. To attract qualified workers, the firms that do not provide fringe benefits will have to pay a compensating wage differential that in effect will equalize the gross hourly compensation between the two groups.[2]

3 Job Status

Some jobs offer high status and prestige and hence attract many willing suppliers; other employment carries with it the social stigma of being mundane, uninspiring, and dirty. As an extreme example, there is more status in being a semiskilled worker in the burgeoning electronics industry than in being a similarly skilled worker in, say, a sewage disposal plant. To the extent that labor supply behavior is affected by status seeking, compensating wage differentials may emerge between low- and high-prestige work.

8.1

Status, of course, is defined culturally, and thus the degree of esteem society places on various jobs is subject to change. For example, in the early 1970s working for the U.S. military commanded limited status, reflecting widespread disapproval of the Vietnam War. On the other hand, the successful U.S military action in the Persian Gulf in 1991 boosted public esteem for those in the military. One result was that supply of labor to the military increased, enabling the military to meet recruitment goals more easily. Similarly, the television show *J.A.G.* is credited with increasing the number of applicants to the military's justice program.

4 Job Location

Similar jobs also differ greatly with respect to their locations, which in turn vary in amenities and living costs. Cities noted for their "livability" may attract a larger supply of workers in a specific occupation than cities mainly noted for their smokestack industries. Consequently, compensating differentials may arise in locations lacking amenities.[3]

---

[2] Although the evidence is far from conclusive, several studies support the idea of a trade-off between wages and fringe benefits. See Craig A. Olson, "Do Workers Accept Lower Wages in Exchange for Health Benefits?" *Journal of Labor Economics,* April 2002, part 2, pp. S91–114. For evidence that a trade-off exists between wages and firm-provided worker's compensation insurance coverage, see Price V. Fishback and Shawn Everett Kantor, "Did Workers Pay for the Passage of Workers' Compensation Laws?" *Quarterly Journal of Economics,* August 1995, pp. 713–42. A similar conclusion is reached for maternity benefits; see Jonathan Gruber, "The Incidence of Mandated Maternity Benefits," *American Economic Review,* June 1994, pp. 622–41.

[3] For evidence on how locational factors such as crime rates and air pollution affect wage differentials, see Jennifer Roback, "Wages, Rents, and the Quality of Life," *Journal of Political Economy,* December 1982, pp. 1257–78. For evidence that wage differentials across cities are much smaller when adjusted for cost of living, see J. Michael DuMond, Barry T. Hirsch, and David A. Macpherson, "Wage Differentials across Labor Markets and Workers: Does Cost of Living Matter?" *Economic Inquiry,* October 1999, pp. 577–98.

8.1 | World of Work

The Economics of the Oldest Profession*

Prostitution is a large business that employs millions of women worldwide. It accounts for between 2 and 14 percent of the gross domestic product in Indonesia, Malaysia, the Philippines, and Thailand. In more developed countries, prostitution is less common. However, 2 percent of women in the United States have indicated that they have sold sex for money at some point in their lives, and a government estimate puts the number of prostitutes at 150,000 in Germany.

Though prostitution is a low-skill occupation, it commands many times the pay of comparably skilled jobs. In 1998 prostitutes in Sweden earned as much as $1,750 per day. Arabic women in the Gulf states could make $2,000 per night.

Why are prostitutes paid so highly? It is not a payment for the risk of engaging in a criminal activity. Petty criminals are notoriously low-paid. Furthermore, the pay premium exists even where prostitution is legal. Nor does the pay premium result from having to forgo earnings increases while engaging in prostitution because the earnings of unskilled workers don't rise much as they become older.

According to Edlund and Korn, the key to the puzzle is that a woman can't be both a wife and a prostitute. If a woman becomes a prostitute, she becomes less desirable in the marriage market. As a result, the pay must be high enough to compensate for forgone income opportunities in the marriage market. Edlund and Korn also analyze two determinants of the degree of prostitution. First, prostitution is less common in developed countries because the higher labor market wages for women in those countries make it less attractive. Second, prostitution is more likely in locations where the male–female ratio is higher because it makes prostitution more profitable relative to marriage. The impact of a higher male–female ratio will be larger if it is the result of men temporarily living in a location. Men in such situations are less likely to be part of the marriage market.

* Based on Lena Edlund and Evelyn Korn, "A Theory of Prostitution," *Journal of Political Economy,* February 2002, pp. 181–214.

Differences in price levels between areas of the country may also result in the need to pay compensating money, or *nominal* wage payments. New York City is a good example. Because the cost of living is so high there, a given nominal wage rate is not equal in purchasing power to the same wage rate in, say, Kansas City. Therefore, relative to labor demand, the number of workers who are willing to supply a particular type of labor at *each nominal wage* is less in New York City than in Kansas City. The labor market result is that the equilibrium nominal wage is higher in New York City. Differentials in nominal wage rates are needed to more closely align *real* wage rates among the two geographical labor markets.

5 Job Security: Regularity of Earnings

Some jobs provide employment security for long periods and explicit or implicit assurances that one will work full weeks throughout the year. Other positions—for example, construction, consulting, and commissioned sales—are characterized by variability of employment, variability of earnings, or both. Because a specific paycheck is not ensured each week of the year, fewer workers may find these occupations attractive and, all else being equal, people who work in these jobs may receive a compensating wage differential. Restated, the hourly wage may be relatively high as compensation for the low probability that it will be earned 40 hours a week for the entire year.

Empirical evidence supports the theoretical conclusion that compensating wage differentials will arise for jobs in which unemployment is more likely. Magnani finds that a one standard deviation increase in the risk of unemployment results in a compensating wage premium between 8.5 and 19 percent.[4] Moretti reports a similar wage differential resulting from unemployment risk.[5] A study by Topel concluded that unemployment insurance greatly reduces compensating wage differentials. In the absence of insurance, an added percentage point of expected unemployment increases a worker's wage rate by about 2.5 percent.[6] Finally, Hamermesh and Wolfe have decomposed the compensating wage differential for unemployment into two parts: that paid for a higher probability of job loss and that resulting from a longer duration of job loss, should it occur. They conclude that nearly all the compensating differential results from the longer duration of job loss, rather than from the higher probability of losing one's job.[7]

6 Prospect of Wage Advancement

Jobs are also heterogeneous with respect to the amount of firm-financed investment in human capital provided over the years. For example, someone entering the banking profession at age 22 might reasonably expect to receive rather continuous on-the-job training leading to promotions to successively higher-paying positions over time. A person that same age who decides to be a carpenter is not likely to experience as large an overall increase in earnings over the years. Assuming that people's time preferences for earnings are the same, at any given wage people will opt for jobs with greater prospects for earnings increases. Thus labor supply will be greater to these jobs and less to employment with flat lifetime earnings streams. This will necessitate a compensating wage differential for *entry-level* pay in the latter type of occupation. In our example we would expect the beginning pay of the bank employee to be less than that of the carpenter. This type of compensating differential is confirmed by research finding that lower starting salaries for inexperienced workers are systematically related to higher rates of wage growth as length of time on the job increases.[8]

Differing Skill Requirements

We have established that one reason for wage differentials in a market economy is differing nonwage aspects of jobs. But jobs are clearly heterogeneous in a second

---

[4] Elisabetta Magnani, "Product Market Volatility and the Adjustment of Earnings to Risk," *Industrial Relations,* April 2002, pp. 304–28.

[5] Enrich Moretti, "Do Wages Compensate for Risk of Unemployment? Parametric and Semiparametric Evidence from Seasonal Jobs," *Journal of Risk and Uncertainty,* January 2000, pp. 45–66.

[6] Robert H. Topel, "Equilibrium Earnings, Turnover, and Unemployment: New Evidence," *Journal of Labor Economics,* October 1984, pp. 500–22.

[7] Daniel S. Hamermesh and John R. Wolfe, "Compensating Wage Differentials and the Duration of Job Loss," *Journal of Labor Economics,* January 1990, pp. S175–97.

[8] David Neumark and Paul Taubman, "Why Do Wage Profiles Slope Upward? Tests of the General Human Capital Model," *Journal of Labor Economics,* October 1995, pp. 736–61.

major way: They have widely different skill requirements. To illustrate, let's compare two hypothetical occupations. Suppose these two jobs have identical nonwage attributes and all workers have similar preferences for current versus future earnings. But suppose job X requires five years of education beyond high school while job Y demands only a high school diploma. If these two occupations paid an identical wage rate, people would have *no* incentive for making occupational choices to select employment X. Why? The unsurprising answer is that occupation X is more costly to enter than Y. Occupation X necessitates much more investment in human capital to meet the skill requirement, and therefore if the hourly pay is the same in both occupations, the return on the investment for the extra five years of education is negative (Chapter 4). That is, the present value of the gained earnings is zero (one receives the same wage after investment as before investment), whereas the present value of the costs is positive and substantial (tuition, books, sacrificed earnings for five years).

The point is that wage equality between occupations X and Y is not sustainable; wage equality would create a disequilibrium. To attract a sufficient flow of people to occupation X, employers must pay these workers more than they pay people in occupation Y. An equilibrium wage differential therefore will persist between the two occupations. The earnings difference created by this wage gap must be just sufficient to produce an internal rate of return r on the investment in five years of education equal to the cost of borrowing i, as discussed in Chapter 4. If the wage differential and therefore r were greater than this i, more people would enter college and pursue the advanced degree. This eventually would expand labor supply, reduce the market wage in occupation X, lower the rate of return, and reduce the wage differential between the two occupations to a sustainable level. On the other hand, if the wage differential were insufficient between occupations X and Y, fewer people would enter occupation X, and eventually the wage differential would rise to the equilibrium one.

To reiterate: Other things being equal, jobs that require large amounts of education and training will pay a higher wage rate than those that do not. The wide variety of skill requirements for various jobs constitutes a major source of wage disparity in the economy. The difference in pay between skilled and unskilled workers is called the *skill differential.*

Wage differentials created by differing skill requirements can either *increase, lessen,* or *reverse* wage variances produced by differences in nonwage aspects of jobs. For example, suppose job A is characterized by a high risk of injury and hence pays a $3 hourly compensating wage premium relative to safe job B. Now let's make two alternative assumptions about the skill differentials between the two jobs. First, suppose the skills necessary to perform dangerous job A are greater than those needed in safe job B. Obviously the actual wage differential will *exceed* the $3 hourly wage premium paid for the risk of injury. Alternatively, suppose the risky job A requires little skill while job B demands costly investment in human capital. In this second case, the actual wage differential between A and B will be *less than* $3 hourly and, depending on the size of the skill differential, may even reverse the pay so that safe job B pays more than dangerous job A. Real-world example: Certified public accountants on average earn more than loggers, even though loggers have a much greater risk of being injured on the job.

Conclusion? The frequent observation that higher-paid workers also seem to have more desirable working conditions does not refute the theory of compensating wage differentials. Rather, this observation simply indicates that in many cases the wage gap created by differences in skills *offsets* the compensating differential working in the opposite direction. Without the compensating differential, the actual wage gap would be even greater. Furthermore, if pleasant working conditions are a normal good ("purchases" of them rise with increases in income), then we would expect to find better working conditions and higher wages positively correlated. Workers who are more highly skilled can afford to "buy" better working conditions as part of their overall compensation package; they can afford to give up some of the relatively high direct wage for more nonwage job amenities. Competition in hiring these highly skilled workers will force employers to offer compensation packages that reflect this greater demand for nonwage amenities.

8.2

Differences Based on Efficiency Wage Payments

We found in Chapter 7 that under some circumstances employers may find it profitable to pay wages above market-clearing levels. Because these circumstances vary *within* and *among* industries, efficiency wages may help explain wage differentials among workers possessing similar qualifications. Pay differentials resulting from efficiency wage payments will be *equilibrium differentials* because the firms will have no incentive to reduce their wages even though qualified people offer to work for lower wages.

Shirking Model and Wage Differentials

The shirking model suggests that firms will pay efficiency wages either where it is costly to monitor the performance of employees or where the employer's cost of poor performance is high. Recall that the above-market wage raises the cost of job loss to workers, which elicits conscientious efforts and reduces the employer's cost per effective unit of labor. On the other hand, where monitoring workers is inexpensive or where the cost of malfeasance by individual workers is low, the cost per effective unit of labor will be minimized at the lower market-clearing wage. These differing circumstances will create wage differentials that are unrelated to skill differentials or to differences in nonwage amenities.

Turnover Model and Wage Differentials

Recall that the turnover version of the efficiency wage model suggested that firms pay above-market-clearing wages where hiring and training costs are large. The above-market-clearing wage increases the value of the job to the worker, thus reducing the turnover rate (quit rate). Consequently, the average level of job experience and the productivity of the firm's labor both rise. The point is that wages may vary across and within industries depending on the efficiency gains, if any, arising from pay strategies that purposely increase the value of the job from the standpoint of the worker.

<table>
<tr><td>8.2</td><td>World
of Work</td><td>Wage Inequality and Skill-Biased Technological Change*</td></tr>
</table>

It is well known that wage inequality among both women and men has increased significantly in the past two decades. Between 1979 and 2005 the hourly earnings of the 90th-percentile worker relative to the 10th-percentile worker increased by about 26 percent for men and 55 percent for women. Wage inequality among males is greater today than at any time since 1940.

This growing wage inequality has several dimensions. We know from Chapter 4, specifically Figure 4.3, that the college wage premium has increased sharply in recent years. For those without college degrees the average wages of older workers have increased relative to those of younger workers. Wage inequality has expanded among individuals of the same age, education, and gender. It also has increased among those working in the same industries and occupations.

We will defer a detailed discussion of the various explanations for the changing wage structure until Chapter 16. Nevertheless, one direct cause of the rising skill differential merits comment here. The past two decades have witnessed an explosion of microcomputers and computer-based technology. This new technology is *skill-biased,* meaning that it does not increase the demand for all skill levels of labor equally. Specifically, the computer revolution has increased the productivity of, and thus the demand for, college-educated and other computer-trained workers.

The fraction of all workers using computers increased from 25 to 56 percent between 1984 and 2003. For college graduates, it rose from 42 to 84 percent. Krueger has estimated that workers who use computers earn 10 to 15 percent more than otherwise similar workers who do not. The wage premium is about 20 percent in the nonunion sector and 8 percent for unionized workers. The lower premium for union workers may have to do with the more standardized wages in the union sector. Autor, Katz, and Krueger find that the increased use of computers

has contributed significantly to earnings inequality. Specifically, they find that computer use explains about one-third of the rise in the demand for higher-skilled workers in manufacturing industries occurring over the 1980s.

Allen confirms the importance of technology improvements in explaining the rise in earnings inequality. Using data from 1979 and 1989, he investigated the impact on wages of measures of technology such as the usage of high-tech capital and the intensity of research and development (R&D). Consistent with Autor, Katz, and Krueger's findings, his analysis reveals that the return to schooling is higher in industries that engage in more R&D and, to a lesser extent, use more high-tech capital. He concludes that technology variables can explain 16 percent of the rise in the earnings gap between college and high school graduates.

The importance of technological change in the rise in wage inequality has been questioned by Card and DiNardo. They note that the rise in wage inequality slowed significantly in the 1990s despite continuing advances in computer technology. They also argue that technological change fails to explain the closing of the gender gap and the stability of the racial wage gap.

* Based on Lawrence F. Katz, "Understanding Recent Changes in the Wage Structure," *NBER Reporter,* Winter 1992–1993, pp. 10–15; Alan B. Krueger, "How Computers Have Changed the Wage Structure: Evidence from Microdata, 1984–1989," *Quarterly Journal of Economics,* February 1993, pp. 33–60; David Autor, Lawrence F. Katz, and Alan B. Krueger, "Computing Inequality: Have Computers Changed the Labor Market?" *Quarterly Journal of Economics,* November 1998, pp. 1169–214; Steven G. Allen, "Technology and the Wage Structure," *Journal of Labor Economics,* April 2001, pp. 440–483; and David Card and John E. DiNardo, "Skill-Biased Technological Change and Rising Wage Inequality: Some Problems and Puzzles," *Journal of Labor Economics,* October 2002, pp. 733–83.

Other Job or Employer Heterogeneities

Although differences in nonwage amenities and disamenities, variations in skill requirements of alternative employment, and efficiency wage payments appear to be the major heterogeneities of jobs that create wage differentials, several other job or employer differences may contribute to this phenomenon. For instance, employers or jobs differ in such things as (1) union status, (2) tendency to discriminate, and (3) absolute and relative firm size.

1 Union Status

We will find in Chapter 11 that empirical evidence suggests that, on the average, unions generate a substantial wage advantage for their members. Part of this differential may be a compensating wage premium for the structured work setting, inflexible hours, and employer-set overtime that are characteristic of unionized firms. Another part may reflect the higher productivity that some economists attribute to unionized labor (Chapter 11). But most economists conclude that the union–nonunion wage differential also includes a separate component of economic rent (Chapter 13) deriving from the ability of unions to exert market power. In this latter respect the existence of both union and nonunion jobs creates a distinct job heterogeneity that helps explain wage disparities.

2 Tendency to Discriminate

We will discover in Chapter 14 that employers may possess varying tendencies to discriminate; that is, some employers are biased toward or against hiring certain classes of workers, say, African–Americans, females, or specific ethnic minorities. Thus direct wage discrimination may occur in some labor markets. The demand for those whom firms prefer will increase; the demand for those whom firms discriminate against will decline; and an observable wage differential will emerge between whites and African–Americans, males and females, and other groups. Much disagreement exists about whether these observed differentials will persist or be eroded by competitive market forces.

8.3

3 Absolute and Relative Firm Size

Several studies indicate that large firms or those with major market shares pay higher wages and salaries in general than smaller firms. There are various possible explanations for this, some involving the previously discussed job heterogeneities. First, large firms are more likely than small firms to be unionized. Second, workers in large firms may be more productive than otherwise comparable workers in small enterprises. This higher productivity may be due to (1) greater amounts and better quality of capital per worker, (2) more on-the-job training necessitated by skill specialization, or (3) the possibility that workers in large firms are "superior" employees who require less supervision than average workers.[9]

---

[9] For more about this topic, see Charles Brown and James Medoff, "The Employer-Size Wage Effect," *Journal of Political Economy,* October 1989, pp. 1027–59; Todd L. Idson and Walter Y. Oi, "Firm Size and Wages," in Orley Ashenfelter and David Card (eds.), *Handbook of Labor Economics,* Volume 3B (Amsterdam: North-Holland, 1999), pp. 2165–2214; Kenneth R. Troske, "Evidence on the Employer Size-Wage Premium from Worker–Establishment Matched Data," *Review of Economics and Statistics,* February 1999, pp. 15–26; and "Firm Size and Wages" Symposium, *American Economic Review,* May 1999, pp. 89–108.

8.3	**World of Work**	Smoking Is Bad for Your Financial Health

Smoking is well known to cause physical health problems such as lung cancer and emphysema. However, it also apparently causes smokers to have worse financial health as well. Levine, Gustafon, and Velenchik examined the impact of cigarette smoking on labor market outcomes by comparing 4,284 nonsmokers and 2,118 smokers aged 27 to 34 in 1991.* Two conclusions emerged from their study. First, smokers earn 4 to 8 percent less than nonsmokers after accounting for differences between the groups. The lower wages of smokers may come from a variety of causes. They could be the result of discrimination. For example, some smokers may be denied raises and promotions because of their smoking habit. Alternatively, smokers' lower wages may be due to a

smoking-related decrease in worker productivity. The productivity decrease could be because of time taken off for smoking breaks or decreased ability to perform manual tasks. Finally, smokers may cost more due to high absenteeism, higher health and fire insurance premiums, higher maintenance costs, and lower worker morale. These higher employee costs for smokers would lead to a compensating decrease in their wages. The second conclusion from this study is that smoking does not affect the probability of employment.

* Philip B. Levine, Tara A. Gustafon, and Ann D. Velenchik, "More Bad News for Smokers? The Effects of Cigarette Smoking on Wages," *Industrial and Labor Relations Review,* April 1997, pp. 493–509.

A third possibility is that the higher pay observed in large firms is a compensating wage premium. Larger firms may be more bureaucratic and less pleasant places to work than smaller companies.[10] Also, larger firms are more likely to be located in major metropolitan areas, where overall living costs, in addition to commuting and parking expenses, are high.

Finally, firms possessing large market shares often make significant economic profits. This may increase workers bargaining power and consequently enable them to secure higher wage rates.[11]

WAGE DIFFERENTIALS: HETEROGENEOUS WORKERS

Having observed that heterogeneities among jobs and employers constitute a major source of wage disparities, we now turn to an equally important factor influencing the wage structure: *heterogeneous workers.* The wage equality initially predicted in

[10] One study reports that one-third of the effect of employer size on wages can be accounted for by differences in the working conditions in large and small firms. See Douglas Kruse, "Supervision, Working Conditions, and the Employer Size-Wage Effect," *Industrial Relations,* Spring 1992, pp. 229–49.
[11] David Blachflower, Andrew Oswald, and Mario Garrett, "Insider Power in Wage Determination," *Economica,* May 1990, pp. 143–70; and S. Nickell, J. Vainiomaki, and Sushil Wadhwani, "Wages and Product Market Power," *Economica,* November 1994, pp. 457–73.

Figure 8.1 relied on our assumption not only that all *jobs* were identical but also that all *workers* in the labor force were equally productive. In reality, people have greatly differing stocks of human capital as well as differing preferences for nonwage aspects of jobs.

Differing Human Capital: Noncompeting Groups

In Chapter 16 we will discuss the personal distribution of earnings as it relates to such characteristics as age, years of education, quality of education, native ability, and family background. That approach points out an important reality: People are not homogeneous. Of particular significance to our discussion of the wage structure is the fact that people possess differing stocks of human capital. At any point in time the labor force consists of numerous **noncompeting groups,** each of which represents one or several occupations for which the members of the group qualify.

Differences in stocks of human capital may result from differing innate abilities to learn and perform. Relatively few people possess the required intellectual or physical endowments to be a nuclear physicist, a professional football quarterback, a petroleum engineer, an opera singer, or a professional model. There is no effective competition in the labor market between these groups and larger groups of skilled and unskilled workers. Nor is there substitutability between nuclear physicists and professional athletes. In fact, even within occupational groups, workers are not always perfectly substitutable. For example, some professional football players command salaries far above the average pay for that occupation. The reason: Other players are only imperfect substitutes because of differences in innate abilities.

More significantly, noncompeting groups result from differences in the type, amount, and quality of education and training that people possess (Chapter 4). For instance, the employment options for recent high school graduates include being a farmworker, a gasoline station attendant, a member of the armed forces, an unskilled construction worker, or a fast-food employee. Each of these categories of workers can be classified into one broad group because each is capable of doing the other jobs. But none of the workers in this group currently offers direct competition to, say, lawyers or accountants, who find themselves in other, more exclusive groups.

Workers can and do move from one noncompeting group to another by investing in human capital. The gasoline attendant may decide to attend college to obtain a degree in accounting. But this presupposes that the person has the financial means and innate intelligence to pursue this degree successfully. To the extent that income, creditworthiness, and native learning skills are unequally distributed, wage differentials between noncompeting groups can persist. Also, bear in mind that the *quality* of education varies. A degree in accounting from a relatively unknown college may not generate the same postinvestment earnings as a degree from a more prestigious university.

To summarize: People have differing stocks of human capital according to native endowments and the type, amount, and quality of education and training they possess. Unsurprisingly, the result is a wide variety of groups, subgroups, or even individuals who are not readily substitutable for one another in the labor market. In the short run, these human capital heterogeneities produce wage differentials due to the varying productivity of workers. People can move toward the higher-paying positions in the long run, but the extent of such movements is limited by differing abilities to finance human capital investments and differing inherent abilities to absorb and apply education and training. Therefore, wage differentials remain.

Differing Individual Preferences

In addition to possessing differing stocks of human capital, people also are heterogeneous with respect to their preferences for such things as (1) present versus future income and (2) various nonwage aspects of work.

Differences in Time Preferences

Some people are highly present-oriented: They discount the future heavily or ignore it entirely. Other people have a great willingness or ability to sacrifice present satisfaction to obtain greater future rewards. In terms of Chapter 4's investment in human capital framework, we are saying that people have differing discount rates—or "i's" in Equation (4.3). People who are highly present-oriented will have high discount rates, or i's. They will not be willing to sacrifice consumption today unless as a result they can obtain substantially more dollars in the future. The higher the i in Equation (4.3), the lower the net present value of the prospective investment and the less the likelihood that people will undertake a given investment in human capital. On the other hand, people who are more future-oriented will be willing to forgo current consumption for the expectation of obtaining relatively small additions to earnings later. In technical terms, such people will have low discount rates (i's) and will perceive a given investment in human capital to have a higher net present value. Consequently, they will obtain more human capital than the more present-oriented individuals.

These differences in time preferences have a significant implication for the theory of noncompeting groups. Specifically, they help explain why people who possess similar innate abilities and access to financing often choose to obtain differing levels of human capital. We have seen that these disparities in amounts of human capital are a major source of wage differentials. Restated, differences in time preferences, which in themselves represent a worker heterogeneity, help explain an even more significant heterogeneity: differing stocks of human capital.[12]

Tastes for Nonwage Aspects of Jobs

We noted earlier that jobs are heterogeneous with respect to such nonwage features as probability of job accidents, fringe benefits, job status, location, regularity of earnings, prospects for wage advance, and control over the work pace. People also differ in their preferences for these nonwage amenities and disamenities: Workers as well as jobs are heterogeneous in this regard. As examples, some workers value job safety highly while

---

[12] For an analysis of differences in time preferences, see John T. Warner and Saul Pleeter, "The Personal Discount Rate: Evidence from Military Downsizing Programs," *American Economic Review,* March 2001, pp. 33–53.

8.4 World of Work

Do Former College Athletes Earn More Than Nonathletes?*

Colleges and universities are making very large investments in their athletic programs. The average National Collegiate Athletic Association (NCAA) Division I-A school loses an average of $600,000 per year. The losses for smaller Division I-AA and I-AAA colleges are even larger. In fact, only 3 percent of the 1,266 NCAA member colleges and universities report a profit from their athletic programs.

Why do colleges support such programs given the large amount of losses? A successful sports program may increase the visibility and image of the school and thus raise the number of applications. Because the number of applications affects a school's academic reputation, this rise will in turn boost the school's academic standing. In addition, donations may rise if a sports program is successful.

Another benefit of college athletic programs is that they may increase the human capital of athletes. Though few college athletes end up with professional sports careers, college athletes may benefit through greater discipline, teamwork skills, a drive to succeed, and a stronger work ethic.

Henderson, Olbrecht, and Polachek have examined how being an athlete during college affects earnings later in life. Their study shows that the average former college athlete earns a 2.8 percent earnings premium relative to nonathletes. However, the distribution of the earnings premium is skewed so that more than half of athletes earn less than nonathletes. The premium varies by occupation. Athletes earn more than nonathletes in business, military, and manual labor. However, athletes earn 8 percent less than nonathletes in teaching, which is a profession that athletes are disproportionately more likely to enter than nonathletes.

* Daniel J. Henderson, Alexandre Olbrecht, Solomon W. Polachek, "Do Former College Athletes Earn More at Work? A Nonparametric Assessment," *Journal of Human Resources*, Summer 2006, pp. 558–77.

others are far less averse to risks; some people desire positions having paid vacations while others find vacations boring and would gladly forgo paid absences for higher hourly pay; and some individuals seek status while others do not care what people think of their occupations.

8.1 Quick Review

- A single wage rate would exist if all workers and jobs were homogeneous, markets were perfectly competitive, and mobility and migration were unimpeded.
- Heterogeneous jobs (differing nonwage attributes, skill requirements, and other features) are a major source of wage differentials.

- Sources of compensating wage differentials include differing risks of injury and death, fringe benefits, job status, job location, regularity of earnings, prospects for wage advancement, and control over the pace of work.
- Wage differentials also arise because workers are heterogeneous; their human capital, time preferences, and tastes for nonwage aspects of jobs differ.

Your Turn

Generally, salaries of state governors are far below those of similarly qualified top executives in the private sector. How can these wage differentials persist? (*Answer:* See page 597.)

THE HEDONIC THEORY OF WAGES

The fact that both jobs *and* workers are heterogeneous is contained in the *hedonic theory of wages.*[13] The term *hedonic* derives from the philosophical concept of hedonism, which hypothesizes that people pursue utility (pleasure), such as wage income, and avoid disutility (pain), such as jobs having unpleasant working conditions. According to the hedonic theory, workers are interested in maximizing *net* utility and therefore are willing to "exchange" that which produces utility to get reductions in something that yields disutility.

The Worker's Indifference Map

The hedonic wage theory often is portrayed in terms of a trade-off between a "good" (the wage) and a work-related "bad" (for example, the probability of injury). However, the *absence* of a "bad" (probability that an injury will not occur) is indeed a "good;" therefore, the theory can also be presented in terms of trading off wages and nonwage amenities. This allows the use of standard indifference curve analysis.

It is reasonable to assume that the typical worker places a positive value on the wage rate being paid and the nonwage amenities that a job offers. In a manner similar to the wage–fringe benefit analysis in Chapter 7, a worker faces a subjective trade-off between two things yielding utility.

Figure 8.2 is illustrative, where the wage rate is measured on the vertical axis and a single nonwage amenity is shown on the horizontal axis. This nonwage amenity may be

FIGURE 8.2   **An Indifference Map for Wages and Nonwage Amenities**
The hedonic indifference map is composed of a number of indifference curves. Each individual curve shows the various combinations of wage rates and a particular nonwage amenity (for example, job safety) that yield a specific level of total utility. Each successive curve to the northeast reflects a higher level of total utility.

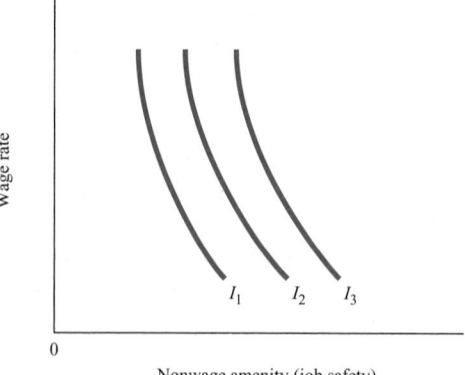

[13] Sherwin Rosen, "Hedonic Prices and Implicit Markets," *Journal of Political Economy,* January–February 1974, pp. 34–55.

any one of several positive job attributes—for example, the probability of *not* being injured on the job, the advantages associated with the job's location, or the expenses saved and leisure gained as commuting time declines.

Let's suppose the particular nonwage amenity measured left to right on the horizontal axis is the degree of job safety (the probability of not being injured on the job). Each indifference curve shows the various combinations of wages and degrees of job safety that will yield some given level of utility or satisfaction to this worker. Recall from Chapter 7 that each point on a specific indifference curve is equally satisfactory, but total utility can be increased by getting to a higher indifference curve—that is, by moving northeasterly from I_1 to I_2 to I_3.

The indifference curves in Figure 8.2 are steep, implying that this individual is highly averse to risks. To understand this conclusion, observe curve I_1 and notice that this person places a high substitution value on extra degrees of job safety. A very large increase in the wage rate is necessary to compensate him or her for a small reduction in safety (small increase in the probability of job injury). But indifference maps vary from person to person; another worker may be far less averse to risk and therefore will have relatively flat indifference curves compared to those in Figure 8.2. Succinctly stated, workers are heterogeneous with respect to their preferences for nonwage amenities.

The Employer's Normal-Profit Isoprofit Curve

It is reasonable to assume that an employer can reduce the probability of job injury or, alternatively stated, increase the safety of the workplace. For example, the employer might provide education programs about job safety, purchase safer machinery, provide protective work gear, or slow the pace of work. But because these steps are costly, the employer faces a trade-off between the wages offered and the degree of job safety provided to workers. To maintain any given level of profits, the firm can either (1) pay lower wages and provide a high degree of job safety or (2) pay higher wages and take fewer actions to reduce the risk of job-related accidents.

Figure 8.3 shows a normal-profit isoprofit curve, which in this case indicates the various combinations of wage rates and degrees of job safety yielding a given normal profit. Observe that this curve is concave; it is not a straight line as was the isoprofit curve for wage rates and fringe benefits in Figure 7.4. Why the difference? In Chapter 7 we assumed that the trade-off between wage rates and fringe benefits was constant. But the concave shape of the isoprofit curve in Figure 8.3 derives from the realistic assumption that each unit of added job safety comes at increasing expense and there-fore results in a successively larger wage reduction. Successive units of expense (wage reduction) yield diminishing returns to job safety. Marginal costs typically rise as more job safety is produced. Therefore, as one moves rightward on *P*, the curve becomes increasingly steep.

But not all employers have identical isoprofit curves; they too are heterogeneous. The isoprofit curve in Figure 8.3 is relatively flat, indicating that this firm can "purchase" job safety at a low marginal cost. Note from *P* that large increments of job safety are

FIGURE 8.3 **Isoprofit Curve**

The employer's isoprofit curve portrays the various combinations of wage rates and job amenities (for example, job safety) that yield a given level of profit. Competition among firms will result in only normal profits (zero economic profit) in the long run; therefore, firms will be forced to make their "wage rate–job amenity" decisions along a curve such as *P*.

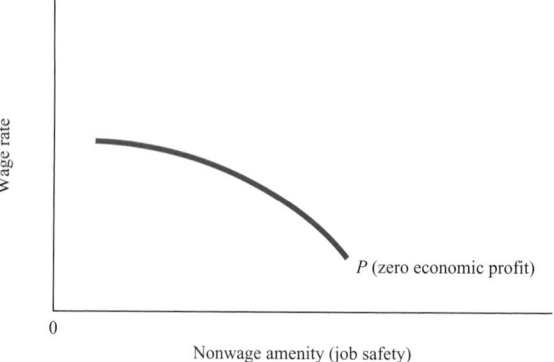

associated with only small reductions in the wage. But other firms may not be so fortunate. Their technological constraints may make it extremely difficult to reduce the risk of accidents and therefore very costly to produce a safe work environment. These firms would face steep normal-profit isoprofit curves.

Matching Workers with Jobs

Figure 8.4 portrays the optimal combination of wage rate and job safety for two distinct sets of employers and workers. Workers A and B possess identical stocks of human capital, but have greatly different tastes for the nonwage amenity job safety. The isoprofit curves P_A in graph (a) and P_B in (b) show the highest profit levels attainable for firms A and B, given the competitive nature of their respective industries. The general slope of isoprofit curve P_A is less steep than that of P_B. This indicates that for technological reasons, the marginal cost of producing job safety is more in firm B than in A. Restated, a specific increase in job safety reduces the wage rate more for firm B than for A.

Now observe the indifference curves I_A and I_B in graphs (a) and (b). These are the highest attainable indifference curves for each worker. Curve I_A is relatively steep, implying that person A is quite averse to the risk of job injury (he values job safety highly). On the other hand, the curve for person B is relatively flat, indicating that B is less concerned about job injury or death than A. Obviously workers A and B have differing tastes for this particular job disamenity.

Each worker maximizes total utility where her or his highest indifference curve is tangent to the employer's zero–economic profit isoprofit curve. Worker A will choose to work for employer A and, as indicated by point *a* in the left graph, will receive wage rate W_A. Along with this low wage, the person will obtain a large quantity of the amenity job safety. Job and worker heterogeneity therefore produce an optimal match between an

FIGURE 8.4   **Matching Heterogeneous Workers and Jobs**

Graph (a) portrays an optimal job match between worker A, who places a high value on job safety at the margin, and firm A, which can produce job safety at relatively low marginal cost. Graph (b) shows the utility-maximizing and profit-maximizing wage rate–nonwage amenity combination (point *b*) for a worker who is less averse to risk and a firm that has high marginal costs of making the workplace safer. Graph (c) plots the optimal wage–job safety combinations shown in (a) and (b). Line *WS* in graph (c) indicates the general relationship between wage rates and job safety in a labor market characterized by many—not just two—heterogeneous workers and jobs. Higher wage rates are associated with lower levels of nonwage amenities, other things being the same.

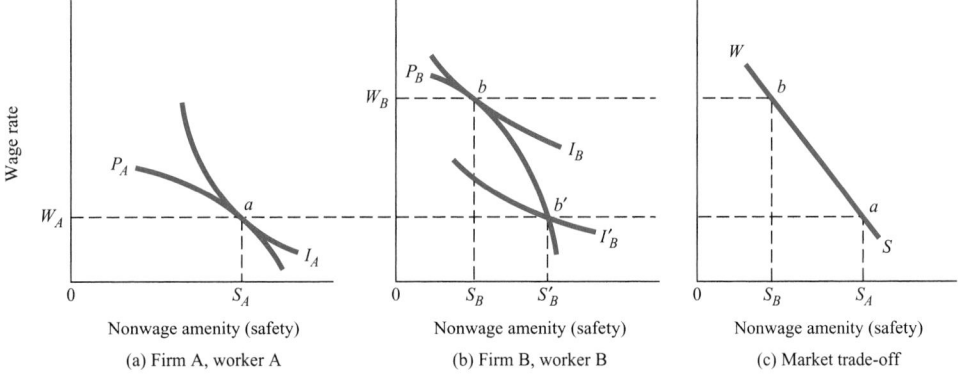

(a) Firm A, worker A   (b) Firm B, worker B   (c) Market trade-off

individual who is highly averse to risk and an employer who has relatively low marginal costs of producing job safety. Similarly, worker B will match up with employer B and receive a higher wage rate W_B but will be employed in a more dangerous work setting. The matching of laborer B and firm B maximizes the interests of both: Employer B has a high marginal cost of producing job safety, and this worker is willing to trade off much of that amenity for a higher wage rate.

Labor Market Implications

The hedonic wage model has some interesting—and in some cases controversial— implications. Let's sample a few.

First, the labor market will generate wage differentials among people who possess identical amounts of human capital. Other things being equal, higher wages will tend to be associated with fewer nonwage amenities. This is shown in graph (c) in Figure 8.4. Line *WS,* which connects points such as *a* and *b* in the two left graphs, indicates the general inverse relationships between wage rates and job safety in a labor market characterized by many—not just two—heterogeneous workers and jobs. The wage differentials possible along this line are persistent, or equilibrium, differentials; they will not create movements of workers among the jobs.

Second, laws that set a minimum standard for nonwage job amenities may actually reduce the utility of some workers. This is shown through reference again to Figure 8.4. If government forces firm B (graph b) to increase its job safety from S_B to, say, S'_B, it

8.5	**World of Work**	Compensating Pay for Shift Work*

In the hedonic theory of wages, compensating wage differentials arise for jobs with onerous working conditions. The market wage in these occupations must increase sufficiently to compensate the last worker employed for the disutility that person associates with the poor working conditions. These compensating wage premiums, however, enable some workers to increase their net utility. Specifically, people who are less averse to the poor working conditions or who are comparatively less productive in normal jobs may enhance their net utility by accepting work under the inferior conditions. For these individuals the utility gain from the extra pay may exceed the utility loss from the poor conditions. In this regard, economists say that some workers "self-select" into occupations having poorer working conditions but paying compensating wage premiums.

Kostiuk has found precisely this outcome for work done at night, commonly called "shift work." Shift work is more prevalent than generally supposed, with about 15 percent of full-time wage and salary workers not working a regular daytime schedule. Using data from supplements to the Census Bureau's *Current Population Survey,* Kostiuk found an 8.2 percent wage premium associated with shift work in manufacturing. Union shift workers received an

18.1 percent wage premium; nonunion shift workers, a 4.3 percent differential.

Kostiuk's findings partly reflect the self-selection mentioned earlier. He discovered that workers with less education had a larger wage premium for shift work than did more educated workers doing similar shift work. This higher relative wage premium for less educated workers enticed more of them to take shift-work jobs. Thought of differently, if the typical night-work employee had instead worked during the day, his or her pay would be less than the pay of typical day-shift workers. On average, night-shift workers are less educated than day-shift workers doing similar work.

The upshot is that the shift-work sector, with its compensating wage differentials, raises the wage of less educated workers and reduces overall wage inequality. Shift work narrows the distribution of earnings on two counts: (1) It provides a compensating wage differential for adverse working conditions, and (2) it attracts workers who have a below-average potential for daytime earnings.

* Based on P. F. Kostiuk, "Compensating Differentials for Shift Work," *Journal of Political Economy,* part 1, October 1990, pp. 1054–75.

will move from point b downward on P_B to b', and worker B will be forced to indifference curve I'_B, which clearly is below I_B.

Third, part of the observed male–female earnings differential (Chapter 14) may reflect differing tastes for positive job amenities such as pleasant working conditions, a short commuting distance, and a low probability of job injury. In terms of Figure 8.4, *if* indifference curves for females as a group tend to be more on the order of I_A rather than I_B, women will match up to a greater extent than men with jobs that have lower pay but also better nonwage amenities. Filer finds evidence to support this possibility. Apparently a portion of the observed male–female earnings differential among similarly trained workers results from compensating differentials.[14]

[14] Randall K. Filer, "Male–Female Wage Differences: The Importance of Compensating Differentials," *Industrial and Labor Relations Review,* April 1985, pp. 426–37.

Finally, the hedonic model extends our earlier discussion of optimal fringe benefits (Figure 7.5) both in terms of worker indifference maps and employer isoprofit curves. Indifference maps of the utility trade-off between wages and fringe benefits vary from worker to worker. Workers who place a high marginal valuation on fringe benefits— that is, have relatively steep indifference curves—will therefore match up with firms offering pay packages containing significant fringe benefits. Conversely, workers whose valuations of cash wages are higher at the margin than valuations of fringe benefits are more likely to opt to work for firms with relatively fewer fringe benefits but higher cash wages.

Additionally, variations in indifference maps among workers help to explain the existence of so-called *cafeteria plans,* which permit workers to choose among a wide range of fringe benefits. These plans allow heterogeneous workers to individually attain higher indifference curves than they could if they had to accept a fixed package of fringe benefits determined by the firm. Examples: A female worker with young children may select child care benefits; an older male worker may opt to have his pension fund enhanced. By increasing the total utility workers receive from any given dollar amount of compensation, cafeteria plans may enable firms to attract and retain higher-quality workers.

The composition of fringe benefits may vary among firms, depending on the marginal cost of providing each fringe benefit. For example, a university may provide free tuition for children of employees, whereas a retail firm may give its workers discounts on merchandise. In each situation, the firm shapes the fringe benefit package in a particular way because of the relatively low marginal cost of providing a specific fringe benefit.

8.2

Quick Review

- In the hedonic wage model, indifference curves show the various combinations of wage rates and levels of a particular nonwage amenity that yield specific levels of total utility.
- The employer's normal-profit isoprofit curve depicts the various combinations of wage rates and specific nonwage amenities that yield a normal profit.
- The optimal job match occurs where the worker's highest attainable indifference curve is tangent to the employer's normal-profit isoprofit curve.
- Workers who have a strong preference for a particular nonwage amenity will tend to match up with employers who can provide the amenity at a relatively low marginal cost. Other things being equal, these workers will receive lower pay than workers who have weak preferences for the nonwage amenity and match up with employers who provide less of it due to its high marginal cost.

Your Turn

8.6   How might a person who actually enjoys working outdoors in extremely cold temperatures benefit from the more general worker preference for employment in climate-controlled buildings or in mild outdoor temperatures? (*Answer:* See page 598.)

| 8.6 | **World of Work** | Placing a Value on Human Life |

Agencies such as the Environmental Protection Agency, Federal Aviation Administration, and Occupational Safety and Health Administration are required by law to determine the expected monetary costs and benefits of any new regulations. Because lives saved are an important benefit of many of the regulations, these federal agencies need to estimate the economic value of human life.

The traditional approach to placing an economic value on human life relies on the concept of human capital (Chapter 4). A so-called wrongful death from, say, an airline crash eliminates earnings over the remaining years of the person's expected work life. Economists use earnings data for similar individuals in the same occupation to estimate the present value of the amount of wages and fringe benefits lost over these years. Although estimates vary by age and occupation, this method places the value of life on average at between $700,000 and $1 million.

A more recent, controversial approach to attaching a value to human life relies on the hedonic wage theory (Figure 8.4). We know that employers must pay compensating wage differentials to induce people to work at dangerous jobs. The size of these differentials reveals information about the amount of money that firms must pay per job-related death. Suppose, for example, that risk-averse behavior of labor suppliers forces firms to pay compensating wages of $1,000 annually for every 0.1 percent ($=.001$) increase in the probability of death on the job. On average, every job-related death therefore costs firms $1 million ($=\$1,000/.001$), a sum that could be thought of as the economic value of each life.

The hedonic method typically yields higher estimates of the value of human life than does the human capital approach. For example, hedonic estimates developed by the federal regulatory agencies range upward to $3.5 million per life saved.

WAGE DIFFERENTIALS: LABOR MARKET IMPERFECTIONS

Wage differences can be explained largely—but not fully—on the basis of heterogeneous jobs, employers, and workers. They also occur because of labor market imperfections that impede labor mobility. Such factors as imperfect information, costly migration, and various other barriers to mobility interact to create and maintain wage differentials.

Imperfect Labor Market Information

We assumed that labor market information was perfect in Figure 8.1, but in reality it is imperfect and costly to obtain. Recognizing that workers are heterogeneous, firms search the labor market to find workers who are best suited for employment. Similarly, workers gather information about prospective job opportunities by scanning help-wanted ads, writing letters, inquiring at business establishments, and so forth. These search efforts by firms and prospective employees involve direct costs and opportunity costs of time. Furthermore, the activity of gaining information eventually will yield diminishing returns. Translated into costs, this implies that the marginal cost of obtaining information will increase as more of it is sought. The fact that information is imperfect and increasingly costly to obtain has important implications for labor market activity and the wage structure.[15] Specifically, it implies that (1) a range of wage rates may exist for any given occupation, independently of compensating differentials, and (2) when changes in demand cause wage differentials, long-run supply adjustments are likely to be slow.

1 Wage Rate Distributions

Once we introduce costly information, job searches, and heterogeneous workers and employers into our analysis, the likelihood there will be a single equilibrium wage (as in Figure 6.1) for each type of labor greatly diminishes. Rather, we can expect to find a *range* of equilibrium wages for each type of labor. This range may be very narrow or quite broad, depending on the individual circumstances within each occupational labor market.

Figure 8.5 portrays one of many possible wage rate distributions. This particular distribution is symmetrical, but other types of distributions are entirely possible. The horizontal axis shows a range of wages, $6.00 through $7.80, and the vertical axis measures the relative frequency of the occurrence of each subrange of wages in the distribution. The area covered by the wage distribution equals 1; there is a 100 percent probability that the wage will fall within the $6.00 to $7.80 range. Likewise, .05 or 5 percent of all wages will be between $6.00 and $6.19, 8 percent will lie between $6.20 and $6.39, and so forth.

How can a wage rate distribution such as that depicted in Figure 8.5 persist? Won't workers move from lower-paying to higher-paying jobs, with a single equilibrium wage rate eventually resulting? The ideas of costly information and costly job searches provide the answers to these questions. Employers will set wages according to their individual circumstances and their estimates of the market wage rate. Some employers may pay slightly more—others, slightly less—than the average wage. But because information is imperfect and costly to obtain, some workers and firms will be unaware that greater or lesser wages are being paid to similar workers. Other employees may recognize that there is a variance in pay but also realize that it is costly to discover which employers of this labor are paying the higher amounts. In technical terms, many workers will judge the marginal cost of obtaining the necessary information to exceed the expected marginal gain from the higher wage. Thus they will remain in their present places of employment, and the wage differentials will persist. *Under conditions of imperfect, costly information, it is entirely possible*

---

[15] It also has important implications for job search (Chapter 15) and unemployment (Chapter 18).

FIGURE 8.5   **A Wage Rate Distribution**

Under conditions of costly information and job searches, competitive labor markets generate an equilibrium distribution of wage rates within a single occupation, rather than an equilibrium hourly wage. In this example, 20 percent of the workers receive a wage rate between $6.80 and $6.99 an hour; but some workers (5 percent) earn as little as $6.00 to $6.19, while another 5 percent make $7.60 to $7.79 an hour. The area under the frequency distribution sums to 1 (100 percent).

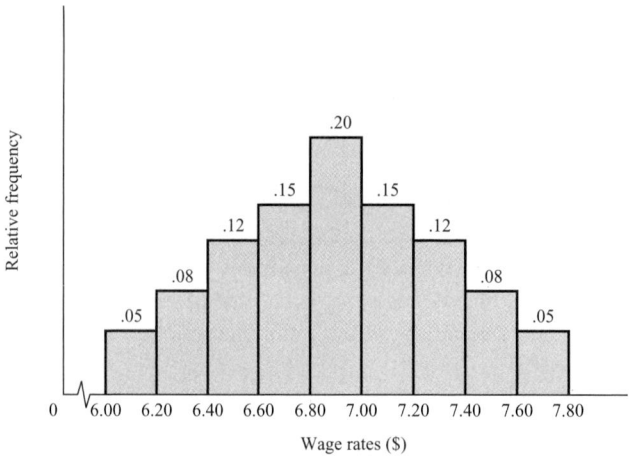

for wage differences within occupations to be equilibrium differentials—that is, differentials that do not evoke job switching.[16]

2 Lengthy Adjustment Periods

A second implication of imperfect, costly information is that long-run supply adjustments to wage differentials created by changes in demand may take months or even years to occur. Suppose, for example, that the demand for labor in occupation X rises sharply. Given an upward-sloping short-run labor supply curve, a wage increase in occupation X will result. But information concerning this new wage is likely to be incompletely disseminated. People choosing the types and amounts of human capital to obtain will learn *gradually* of the higher wage in occupation X. Of course as more time transpires, more information will become known. But even then some potential labor suppliers to X will wonder if this is indeed a permanent wage differential relative to other occupations or one that will quickly evaporate by the time they become qualified.

Once people *do* begin to recognize that the wage rate in occupation X is permanent, some will respond and eventually create a flow of labor into X and away from, say, Y and Z. This will cause the wage narrowing predicted by the pure theory. But

[16] The classic article on this point is George J. Stigler, "Information in the Labor Market," *Journal of Political Economy,* October 1962, pp. S94–105.

FIGURE 8.6   **Wage Rate Adjustment Path**

An increase in labor demand initially may cause a substantial wage increase to, say, W_0 in occupations that require long training periods. But the supply response to the higher wage may create a surplus of labor to the occupation in the subsequent period, driving the wage rate lower, say, to W_1. For a time the wage rate may oscillate above and below the long-run equilibrium wage rate W_e before equilibrium in the market is finally restored. During the transition periods, wage differentials between this occupation and others paying W_e will be observed.

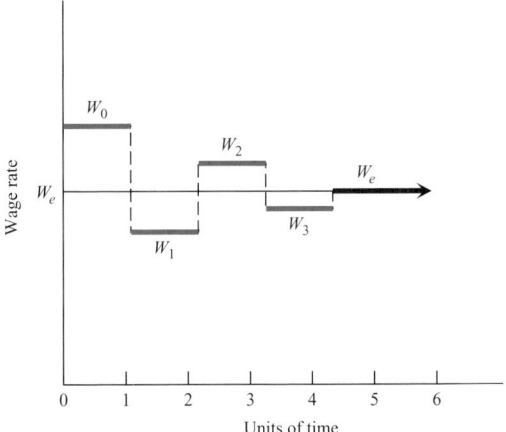

recall from our discussion of the cobweb model in Chapter 6 (Figure 6.12) that in some occupations requiring long training periods—such as law and engineering—the supply response may be so great that the wage differential not only is eliminated but also turns in the opposite direction. Then, in the next period, still another overadjustment may occur, reducing labor supply so dramatically that a positive wage differential again arises. Thus, as shown by the wage rate adjustment path in Figure 8.6, some wage rates may for a time oscillate above and below the long-run equilibrium wage W_e. Note from the diagram that the wage rate shifts from W_0 to W_1 to W_2, and so forth, as units of time transpire. To summarize: Labor markets in which information is imperfect and costly will be characterized by many transitional wage differentials, which exist because of lengthy and occasionally oscillating adjustment paths to final equilibrium.[17]

Immobilities

Labor immobilities, defined simply as *impediments to the movement of labor,* constitute another major reason that wage differentials occur and sometimes persist.

---

[17] For a discussion of alternative wage rate adjustment paths, see Belton M. Fleisher and Thomas J. Kniesner, *Labor Economics: Theory, Evidence, and Policy,* 3rd ed. (Englewood Cliffs, NJ: Prentice-Hall, Inc., 1984), pp. 186–91. Also of interest is Jean Helwege, "Sectoral Shifts and Interindustry Wage Differentials," *Journal of Labor Economics,* January 1992, pp. 55–84.

For convenience, we will classify these barriers to labor mobility as geographic, institutional, and sociological.

1 Geographic Immobilities

We will discover in Chapter 9 that wage differences between geographic areas provide an incentive for workers to migrate. By moving to a high-wage location, a worker can enhance lifetime earnings. But moving also involves costs, such as transportation expenses, forgone earnings during the move, the inconvenience of adjusting to a new job and community, the negative aspects of leaving family and friends, and the possible loss of seniority and pension benefits. If these costs deter migration to the extent that an insufficient number of migrants are attracted to the higher-paying locale, geographic wage differentials will persist.

2 Institutional Immobilities

Restrictions on mobility imposed by such institutions as government and unions may reinforce geographic immobilities. We previously noted in Chapter 6 that government licensing of occupations can restrict the movement of qualified workers among jobs. Also, differing licensing requirements in various states can limit worker mobility geographically. Craft unions also are a factor here; they impede mobility by limiting the access of nonunion workers to union-controlled apprenticeship programs and union-filled jobs. Other institutional immobilities involve pension plans and seniority rights, which reduce people's incentives to move from one job to another.

3 Sociological Immobilities

Finally, there are numerous sociological barriers to labor mobility. In Chapter 14 we examine theories of labor market discrimination by race and gender. For example, females appear to be crowded into certain occupations. This drives down the equilibrium wage in these occupations and raises it elsewhere. To the extent that there are barriers that keep qualified women from moving from these lower-paying positions to higher-paying occupations, wage differentials between the sexes can persist. In the same vein, African–Americans historically were excluded from certain higher-paying occupations either through informal understandings by employers or through formal prohibitions by unions. As an example of the latter, over 20 national unions had constitutional provisions barring African–Americans from membership in 1930. In fact, some unions such as the Locomotive Engineers and the Railway Conductors still excluded African–Americans from membership in 1964, when the Civil Rights Act was passed.[18]

Figure 8.7 provides a schematic overview of the major contributing factors to wage differentials. This diagram merits your careful consideration.

---

[18] F. Ray Marshall, Vernon M. Briggs, Jr., and Allan King, *Labor Economics,* 5th ed. (Homewood, IL: R. D. Irwin, Inc., 1984), p. 567.

FIGURE 8.7
Sources of Wage Differentials: A Review
Wage differentials arise because jobs are heterogeneous, workers are heterogeneous, and markets are imperfect. Heterogeneous jobs *and* heterogeneous workers are the underpinning of the hedonic wage, or job-matching, model.

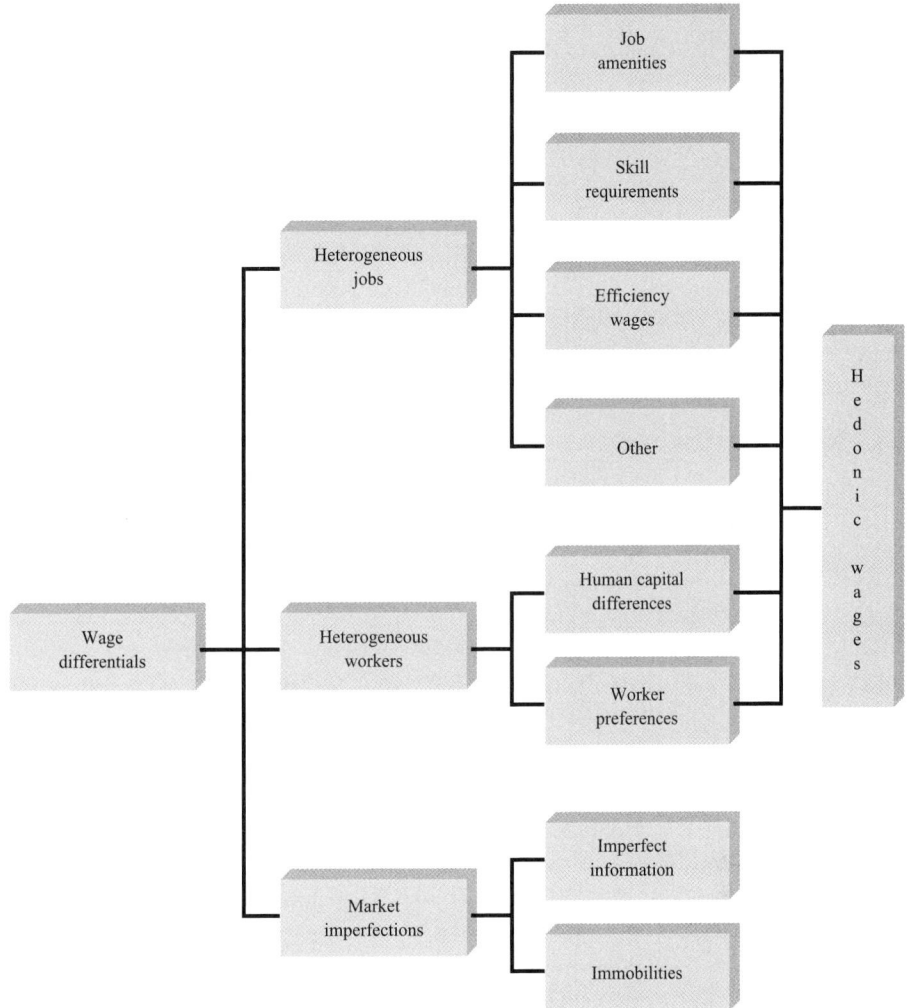

<table>
</table>

Chapter Summary

1. Theoretically, if *all* workers and jobs were homogeneous and all labor markets were perfectly competitive, then workers would move among the various jobs until the wages paid in all markets were identical.

2. Casual and empirical examinations of wage rates and weekly earnings reveal that a variety of wage differentials exist and that many of them persist over time.

3. Several nonwage aspects of jobs influence supply decisions in ways that generate compensating wage differentials. These nonwage factors include *(a)* risk of job injury and death, *(b)* fringe benefits, *(c)* job status, *(d)* job location, *(e)* the regularity of earnings, and *(f)* the prospect for wage advancement.

4. Differences in skill requirements also produce wage differences. Other things being equal, to attract a sufficient flow of laborers to an occupation requiring considerable prior investment in human capital, employers must pay these workers more than they pay less skilled employees.

5. Efficiency wage theories have been advanced to explain pay differences within and among industries. These theories predict that wages will be higher where it is difficult to monitor the performance of workers, where the costs to employers of mistakes by individual workers are large, and where high labor turnover significantly reduces productivity.

6. Another major source of wage disparities is heterogeneous workers. Specifically, workers possess greatly varying stocks of human capital and differing preferences for various nonwage aspects of work. Consequently, the overall labor market is composed of numerous submarkets consisting of groups of workers who offer little competition to other groups.

7. The hedonic theory of wages hypothesizes that workers who possess differing subjective preferences for wages compared to nonwage job amenities seek optimal matches with employers who differ in their costs of providing those nonwage attributes. Among a wide variety of implications that flow from this model is the basic one that labor markets will generate sustained wage differentials, even among people who have similar stocks of human capital.

8. Imperfect and costly market information is another reason that wage differentials exist. Imperfect and costly information creates ranges of wage rates, independent of other factors, and explains why transitional wage differentials often are long-lasting.

9. Labor market immobilities—geographic, institutional, and sociological—also help explain persistent earnings differences among workers.

Terms and Concepts

equilibrium wage
differentials, *243*
transitional wage
differentials, *243*
homogeneous workers
and jobs, *243*

wage structure, *244*
heterogeneous jobs, *247*
compensating wage
differentials, *247*
skill differential, *252*

heterogeneous workers, *256*
noncompeting groups, *257*
hedonic theory of
wages, *260*
labor immobilities, *269*

Questions and Study Suggestions

1. Suppose all workers and jobs in a hypothetical economy are homogeneous. Explain why no wage differentials would exist if this economy were perfectly competitive and information and mobility were costless. Explain why wage differentials would arise if, on the other hand, information and mobility were imperfect and costly.

2. Analyze why college professors generally earn less than their professional PhD counterparts who are employed by corporations.

3. Discuss: "Many of the lowest-paid people in society—for example, short-order cooks—also have relatively poor working conditions. Hence the theory of compensating wage differentials is disproved."

4. Explain why it may be in a worker's *short-term* best interest to have job titles restated to add status: say, becoming a mixologist rather than a bartender or being referred to as a sanitation engineer rather than a garbage worker. Why may such title changes not be in the *long-term* best interest of these workers, however?

5. Explain how the theory of investment in human capital relates to the notion of non-competing groups and how the latter relates to the presence of equilibrium wage differentials.

6. Referring back to Figure 7.8, explain why wage differentials resulting exclusively from efficiency wage payments (shirking model *and* turnover model) will persist rather than erode over time.

7. What is the hedonic theory of wage differentials? Discuss the characteristics of a normal-profit isoprofit curve. Combine isoprofit curves with worker indifference curves to explain how two workers with identical stocks of human capital might be paid different wage rates.

8. Speculate about why the average hourly wage rate paid by manufacturing firms to production workers is so much lower in Mississippi than in Michigan (Table 8.3).

9. Explain how each of the following relates to wage differentials: *(a)* seniority provisions, *(b)* varying state licensing requirements for occupations, *(c)* racial segregation, and *(d)* regional cost-of-living differences.

10. Explain why "pay comparability" legislation requiring that the public sector remunerate government employees at wages equal to private sector counterparts might create excess supplies of labor in public sector labor markets.

11. Suppose that *(a)* employers must pay higher wages to attract workers from wider geographic areas and hence higher wages are associated with longer commuting distances (less of the amenity "closeness of job to home") and *(b)* females have greater tastes for having jobs close to their homes than do males. Use the hedonic wage model to show graphically why a male–female wage differential might emerge, independent of skill differences or gender discrimination.

Internet Exercise

WWW...

Who Earns the Big Bucks? Who Doesn't?

Go to the Bureau of Labor Statistics Occupational Employment Statistics Web site (**http://www.bls.gov/oes/home.htm**) and select "Tables Created by the BLS" and the "Cross-Industry Occupational Employment and Wage Estimates" for the most recent year shown. Provide the mean (average) wage for one relatively high-paying and one relatively low-paying occupation in 10 of the broad occupational categories ("Management Occupation," "Business and Financial Operations Occupations," and so on). What general factors explain the differences you observe within broad occupational categories and among the categories? (Answer in a one-paragraph essay.)

Select the OES Code to view the employment distribution of annual pay for "Brokers, Real Estate" in "Sales and Related Occupations." What is the minimum salary required to be in the top 25 percent of brokers? What is the highest salary a broker can earn and be in the bottom 10 percent of brokers? What might explain these striking differences in pay?

Go to ESPN's Sportszone at **http://sports.espn.go.com/golf/moneyLeaders** to identify the top five leading money winners and their earnings on the men's PGA tour, women's PGA tour (LPGA), Champions tour, Nationwide tour, and European tour. This information can be found by selecting each tour under "Money Leaders" (use either the current earnings or the earnings for the previous year, whichever are listed). What, in general, explains the differences you observe among the top earnings on the five professional tours?

Internet Links

WWW...

The *Forbes* magazine Web site reports the salaries of celebrities, executives, and others (**http://www.forbes.com/lists**).

Chapter

9

Mobility, Migration, and Efficiency

You most likely know someone who has recently changed employers, occupations, or job locations. Indeed, the movement of workers—*labor mobility*—is one of the striking features of labor markets. Alvarez, an auto mechanic, moves from Arizona to Arkansas. Pearson, a public school teacher, quits to become a private detective. Kioski, an executive of a North Carolina firm, gets transferred to New Mexico.

In the real world, changes are common in such things as product demand, labor productivity, levels of human capital, family circumstances, and personal attitudes toward nonwage amenities. These changes induce some workers to switch employers, occupations, geographical locations, or some combination of all three. Also, employers respond to changing economic circumstances by hiring, transferring, or discharging workers; closing or expanding present facilities; or moving operations to new locations.

Combined, these actions of workers and employers produce much movement of labor from employer to employer, occupation to occupation, and place to place. Careful observation often reveals that this mobility arises in response to transitional wage differentials, which tend to erode as markets move toward equilibrium. Mobility is central to the operation of labor markets; it promotes allocative efficiency by shuffling workers to society's highest-valued employments.

TYPES OF LABOR MOBILITY

The boxes in Figure 9.1 categorize several important kinds of labor mobility. The columns of the boxes identify locational characteristics of the employment change, and the rows indicate occupational characteristics. Let's describe the kind of labor mobility associated with each box.

FIGURE 9.1   **Types of Mobility**

Mobility can take several forms, four of which are summarized by boxes I through IV. Specifically, it can involve a job change, but no change in occupation or residence (box I); an occupational change, but no change in residence (box II); a geographic move to a job in the same occupation (box III); or geographic migration accompanied by a change in occupation (box IV).

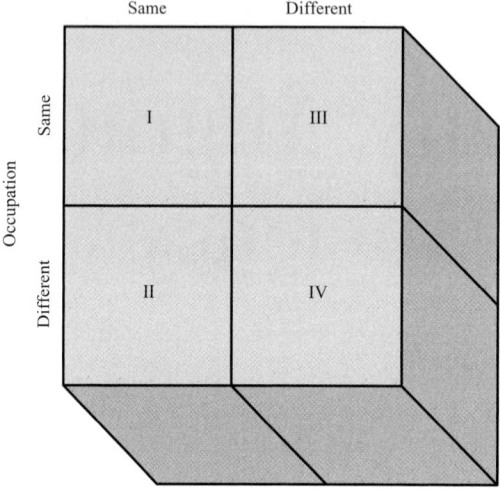

Box I: Job Change/No Change in Occupation or Residence

Box I indicates mobility in which neither the worker's occupation nor residence changes. This form of mobility occurs frequently—for example, when electrical engineers switch employers within California's Silicon Valley or when automobile salespeople quit one dealership to work for another. This category also includes transfers of employees from one of a firm's units to another in the same local area—for example, when a bank employee is reassigned from one branch of a local bank to another.

Box II: Occupational Change/No Change in Residence

This box identifies changes in occupation not accompanied by changes in residence. Much of this *occupational mobility* involves moves to closely related occupations, such as when a carpenter takes a job in a lumberyard or when a production worker is promoted to a supervisory position within a firm. But in other cases, this mobility is characterized by a significant occupational change: For example, a part-time warehouse employee who completes college might accept a job as a securities broker in the same town. Approximately 1 out of 10 workers in the United States is employed in a different occupation than he or she was in the previous year. A vast majority of these changes in occupation are accounted for by people who are less than 35 years old. Many of these changes also involve geographic mobility (box IV).

Box III: Geographic Change/No Change in Occupation

Geographic mobility pertains to movements of workers from a job in one city, state, or nation to another. Between 16 and 18 percent of the total U.S. population changes residences each year. Moves from one county or state to another are involved in 37 percent of these residency changes. Transfers of employees by companies range between 400,000 and 500,000 annually. In recent years net immigration to the United States has been about 1 million people per year.

In many cases geographic moves cause changes in jobs but not changes in occupations. Examples: An executive for an aerospace firm gets transferred from Wichita to Seattle; a farmworker moves from Mexico to the United States; a corporate lawyer leaves a New York City law firm to join one in Boston; a professional football player gets traded from New Orleans to Chicago.

Box IV: Geographic Change/Change in Occupation

Approximately 30 percent of geographic job-related moves are accompanied by changes in occupations. Thus these changes represent both geographic and occupational mobility. For example, a discharged steelworker might leave Pennsylvania to take a job as a construction worker in Arizona. Or perhaps a high school teacher might move from a small town to take a position as an insurance claims adjuster in a distant urban area.

To limit our focus and retain clarity, we will confine our attention to *geographic* mobility (boxes III and IV) in the remainder of the chapter. But much of the analysis that follows can also be directly applied to the other forms of labor mobility.

MIGRATION AS AN INVESTMENT IN HUMAN CAPITAL

Labor migration has been extensively studied by economists, sociologists, demographers, and geographers. One important way economists have contributed to the understanding of geographic mobility is through the development and testing of the human capital model of migration. We know from Chapter 4 that human capital consists of the income-producing skill, knowledge, and experience embodied within individuals. This stock of capital can be increased by specific actions—investments in human capital—that require *present* sacrifices but increase the stream of *future* earnings over one's lifetime. Such actions include obtaining more education, gaining added training, and maintaining one's health. Migration to a higher-paying job is also a human capital investment because it entails present sacrifices to obtain higher future earnings.

Will migration occur in all situations where a potential exists for increased lifetime earnings? The answer is no because there are costs associated with the migration investment that must be weighed against the expected gains. The main costs are transportation expenses, forgone income during the move, psychic costs of leaving family and friends, and the loss of seniority and pension benefits. According to our analysis in Chapter 4, if

9.1	**World of Work**	Determinants of Occupational Tenure*

On average, Americans change occupations several times during their careers. Median occupational tenure—the cumulative length of time a person has worked in her or his current occupation—is about 6.5 years. But occupational mobility varies considerably around this average. Several important factors affect occupational tenure.

Age: Younger workers tend to change occupations more often than do older workers. Median occupational tenure for workers aged 16 to 24 is 2.0 years; for workers aged 55 to 64, it is 17.4 years. Younger workers are still shopping for career paths; older workers have settled into their careers.

Employment trends: Occupational tenure is low in industries with rapidly growing employment and high in industries with slowly growing or declining employment. Growing industries are continually adding new workers, which pulls down the average lengths of occupational tenure. Because slowly growing or stagnant industries hire few new workers, the average tenures of their workforces are high. Example: Median occupational tenure in the fast-growing computer and data processing industry is 5.6 years. This compares to 12.5 years in the stagnating blast furnaces and steel products industry.

Education and training: Occupational mobility declines with educational attainment. Workers with large investments in education for specific occupations stay with their occupations longer than do workers with little human capital. Median occupational tenure for workers with less than 4 years of high school is 5.2 years, compared to 7.9 years for people with 4 or more years of college.

Compensation and benefits: If all else is equal, high pay and long occupational tenures go hand in hand. High pay encourages workers to remain in an occupation.

Gender, race, and ethnicity: Men have longer median occupational tenure (7.7 years) than do women (5.5 years). Whites of both sexes have longer median tenures than African–Americans, and African–Americans have longer tenures than Hispanics.

Self-employed workers: Median occupational tenure is longer for self-employed workers (8.0 years) than for wage and salary workers (5.9 years). Examples of self-employed occupational groups with long tenures include dentists (15.1 years) and barbers (27.2 years).

In short, there are wide variations in occupational mobility among members of the workforce.

* Synopsis of Steven R. Maguire, "Employer and Occupational Tenure: 1991 Update," *Monthly Labor Review,* June 1993, pp. 45–56.

the present value of the expected increased earnings exceeds the present value of these investment costs, the person will choose to move. If the opposite is true, the individual will conclude that it is not worthwhile to migrate, even though the earnings potential in the destination area may be higher than in the present location.[1]

[1] The classic article about this topic is by Larry A. Sjaastad, "The Costs and Returns of Human Migration," *Journal of Political Economy,* suppl., October 1962, pp. 80–93. For a survey of labor mobility models, see Michael J. Greenwood, "Internal Migration in Developed Countries," in Mark. R. Rosenzweig and Oded Stark (eds.), *Handbook of Population and Family Economics* (Amsterdam: Elsevier, 1997), pp. 647–720.

Equation (9.1)—a modification of Equation (4.3) in Chapter 4—gives the net present value of migration:

$$V_p = \sum_{n=1}^{N} \frac{E_2 - E_1}{(1 + i)^n} - \sum_{n=1}^{N} \frac{C}{(1 + i)^n} - Z \qquad \textbf{(9.1)}$$

where V_p = present value of net benefits.

E_2 = earnings from new job in year n.

E_1 = earnings from existing job in year n.

N = length of time expected on new job.

i = interest rate (discount rate).

n = year in which benefits and costs accrue.

C = direct and indirect monetary costs resulting from move in the year n.

Z = net psychic costs of move (psychic costs minus psychic gains).

In Equation (9.1), if $V_p > 0$, implying that the expected earnings gain exceeds the combined monetary and net psychic investment costs, the person will migrate. If, conversely, $V_p < 0$, the person will remain in his or her present job and location. All else being equal, the greater the annual earnings differential ($E_2 - E_1$) between the two jobs, the higher will be the present value of the net benefits (V_p), and the more likely it will be that an individual will migrate.

THE DETERMINANTS OF MIGRATION: A CLOSER LOOK

Various factors besides the annual earnings differential ($E_2 - E_1$) influence the discounted present value of the total earnings and costs streams in Equation (9.1) and thereby affect the present value of the net benefits and the decision to migrate. These factors or ***determinants of migration*** include age, family circumstances, education, distance, and unemployment.

Age

Migration studies consistently find that age is a major factor determining the probability of migration. *All else being equal, the older that a person is, the less likely he or she is to migrate.* There are several reasons for this, each having to do with reducing the gain in net earnings from migrating or increasing the costs of moving.

First, older migrants have fewer years to recoup their investment costs. Given a specific cost of migrating, the shorter the time period one has to gain the annual earnings advantage, the smaller the V_p term in Equation (9.1). A young person may view a relatively small wage differential to be significant over his or her lifetime; a person who is two or three years away from retirement is not likely to incur migration costs to achieve this same short-lived annual differential.

Second, older people tend to have higher levels of human capital that are specific to their present employers. Age, length of time on a job (job tenure), and annual wages are all positively correlated. The longer a person's job tenure, the greater the amount of on-the-job training and employer-financed investment of a specific variety he or she is likely to have. This human capital, by definition, is *not* transferable to other jobs (Chapter 4). Thus the wage one receives after several years of job tenure partially reflects a return on a specific investment in human capital and is likely to be higher than the wage obtainable elsewhere. Regardless of the length of time available to recoup the investment costs, older people may therefore be less likely to migrate.[2]

The cost of moving is a third age-related consideration affecting migration. Older people often have higher migration costs than do younger people. For example, a young person may be able to transport possessions across the country in a 4-by-8-foot U-Haul trailer, whereas an older person may need to hire a professional mover who uses a moving van. Or as another example, a younger person who migrates may lose little seniority or future pension benefits, whereas an older person may incur very large costs of this type.[3] Also, the psychic costs of migration may rise with age. Older people are more likely than younger workers to have roots in their present communities, children in the local school systems, and an extensive network of workplace friends. The higher these net psychic costs—Z in Equation (9.1)—the lower the value of V_p and the less likely one is to migrate.

Finally, the inverse relationship between age and migration exists partially because people are most mobile after completing lengthy investments in human capital. Many people begin "job shopping" at the end of high school—ages 18 to 19—which may result in geographic moves.[4] Migration is even more pronounced for college graduates who enter regional and national labor markets. It therefore is not surprising that the peak age for labor migration in the United States is 23.

Family Factors

The potential costs of migrating multiply as family size increases. Therefore, we would expect married workers to have less tendency to migrate than single people, other factors such as age and education being constant. Furthermore, it seems logical to expect higher migration rates for married workers whose spouses either do not work or work at low pay. If both spouses earn a high wage, the family's cost in forgoing income during the move will be high; and when combined with the possibility that one spouse will not find a job in the destination location, this cost reduces the net present value to the family from migration. Finally, the presence of school-age children can be expected to reduce the likelihood of migration. The parents and children may conclude that the psychic costs associated with the move are too great relative to the expected monetary gain.

[2] Jacob Mincer and Boyan Jovanovic, "Labor Mobility and Wages," in Sherwin Rosen (ed.), *Studies in Labor Markets* (Chicago: University of Chicago Press, 1981), pp. 21–63.
[3] For evidence that the prospect of leaving behind an employer-provided pension constitutes a high cost of changing jobs, see Steven Allen, Robert Clark, and Ann McDermed, "Pensions, Bonding, and Lifetime Jobs," *Journal of Human Resources,* Summer 1993, pp. 463–81.
[4] William Johnson, "A Theory of Job Shopping," *Quarterly Journal of Economics,* May 1978, pp. 261–78.

These particular predictions from the human capital model are supported by empirical evidence. Mincer has found that (1) unmarried people are more likely to move; (2) the wife's employment inhibits family migration; (3) the longer the wife's tenure, the less likely a family will migrate; and (4) the presence of school-age children in the family reduces migration.[5]

Education

Within age groupings, the level of educational attainment beyond high school is a major predictor of how likely one is to migrate within the United States. *The higher one's educational attainment, all else being equal, the more likely it is that one will migrate.*[6] Several reasons have been offered for this relationship. College graduates and those with postgraduate training—MBAs, PhDs, lawyers, CPAs—search for employment in regional and national labor markets in which employers seek qualified employees. These markets often have substantial job information and participants who possess excellent ability to analyze and assess the available information. The potential for economic gain from migration also may be increased by the heterogeneity of many of the workers and positions (Chapter 8).[7] Union wage scales and minimum wage rates reduce wage differentials within occupations not requiring college training. On the other hand, the wide disparities of pay for professional and managerial employees provide more opportunity to move to jobs entailing greater responsibility and pay. Less specialized workers may have a greater opportunity to increase their earnings through *occupational* mobility within their present locale (box II in Figure 9.1). That route may not be open to highly specialized workers, who therefore may use *geographic* migration to achieve gains in earnings.

Other factors are also at work here. College-educated workers are more apt to get transferred to new geographic locations and, if not transferred, are more likely than those with fewer years of schooling to have new jobs already in place upon migrating. Thus the probability of their failing to find a job once they move to the new area is zero, and the expected earnings gain over their lifetimes is increased. Finally, people who have college degrees may attach fewer psychic costs Z to leaving their hometowns. Many college students initially migrate to new areas to attend school in the first place, and this experience may make it easier for them to move again when new economic opportunities are present. Or perhaps the fact that these people moved geographically to attend college indicates that they have lower innate psychic costs of or stronger preferences for migration than those who did not make that same choice

---

[5] Jacob Mincer, "Family Migration Decisions," *Journal of Political Economy,* October 1978, pp. 749–74. Where both the husband and the wife have a college degree, the probability of migration is 4 percent lower when the wife works. See Dora L. Costa and Matthew E. Kahn, "Power Couples: Changes in the Locational Choice of the College Educated, 1940–1990," *Quarterly Journal of Economics,* November 2000, pp. 1287–315.

[6] Larry H. Long, "Migration Differentials by Education and Occupation: Trends and Variations," *Demography,* May 1973, p. 245.

[7] For evidence that regional variations in the returns to schooling are important determinants of migration flows among skilled workers, see George J. Borjas, Stephen G. Bronars, and Stephen J. Trejo, "Self-Selection and Internal Migration in the United States," *Journal of Urban Economics,* September 1992, pp. 159–85.

initially. For whatever reasons, studies show that people who move once are more inclined to migrate again.

Distance

The probability of migrating varies inversely with the distance a person must move. The greater the distance, the less information a potential migrant is likely to possess about the job opportunities available. Also, transportation costs usually increase with distance. Finally, the longer the physical distance of the move, the more probable it is that psychic costs will be substantial. With respect to such costs, it is one matter to move across town, another to move to a nearby state, and still another to migrate across the country or to another nation. Psychic costs may be partially reduced, but not necessarily eliminated, by following "beaten paths" and congregating in specific neighborhoods within the destination area. Migrants often follow the routes previously taken by family, friends, and relatives. These earlier migrants ease the transition for those who follow by providing job information, employment contacts, temporary living quarters, and cultural continuity. But the longer the distance of the move, the less available the information about wage disparities and the greater the psychic cost. Thus the likelihood is less that one will migrate.[8]

Unemployment Rates

On the basis of the human capital model, high unemployment rates in an origin location should increase the net benefits from migrating and *push* workers away. That is, an unemployed person must assess the probability of gaining employment in the *origin* location relative to the probability of gaining employment at the potential *destination.* Although evidence on this matter is surprisingly mixed, studies support the following generalizations: (1) *Families headed by unemployed people are more likely to migrate than others,* and (2) *the rate of unemployment at the origin positively affects out-migration.*[9] Such out-migration may not always be as great as we might expect, however, when the decision makers are mainly older and less educated workers or when unemployment compensation and other income transfers are relatively high.

Does the unemployment rate at the possible destination influence the migration decision by affecting the probability of getting employment and therefore increasing the *expected value* of discounted net benefits? No definitive conclusion can be reached for this question. For one thing, the general unemployment rate does not always reflect the probability that a specific *individual* will find employment. Also, in-migration itself can increase unemployment rates at the destination. Nevertheless, one generalization is possible: Currently unemployed workers tend to migrate to destinations with lower-than-average unemployment rates.

[8] See Henry Herzog, Jr., and Alan M. Schlottmann, "Labor Force Migration and Allocative Efficiency," *Economic Inquiry,* July 1981, pp. 459–75; and Paul S. Davies, Michael J. Greenwood, and Haizheng Li, "A Conditional Logic Approach to U.S. State-to-State Migration," *Journal of Regional Science,* May 2001, pp. 337–60.

[9] See Julie DaVanzo, "Does Unemployment Affect Migration? Evidence from Micro Data," *Review of Economics and Statistics,* November 1978, pp. 32–37; and Davies, Greenwood, and Li, ibid. Also see Joshua Hojvat Gallin, "Net Migration and State Labor Market Dynamics," *Journal of Labor Economics,* January 2004, pp. 1–22.

Other Factors

Many other factors may influence migration, and we list only a few of them here. First, studies show that home ownership deters migration.[10] Second, a higher rate of international immigration into an area tends to reduce in-migration rates and raise out-migration rates among native-born workers.[11] This appears to be result of depressed wages associated with increased international immigration. Third, state and local government policies may influence labor migration. Examples: (1) High personal tax rates that reduce disposable income may impede migration to the high-tax area; (2) high levels of per capita government spending on services may increase in-migration; and (3) government policies that attract new industries are likely to cause greater migration to a particular locale. Fourth, federal defense contracts appear to shift labor regionally in the United States.[12] Fifth, in the case of international migration, the language spoken at the destination is a prime factor affecting mobility. Immigration quotas and emigration prohibitions also greatly influence international migration. Additionally, many international migrants are pushed from their present places of residence by political repression and war. Sixth, union membership may be a determining factor. By providing workers with a voice with which to change undesirable working conditions, unions may reduce voluntary "exits" and reduce mobility and migration (Chapter 11). Or from a different perspective, perhaps the wage gains that unions secure for workers reduce the incentive for members to migrate to new jobs. Seventh, some scholars suggest that people increasingly have placed a high priority on crime and climate in their migration decisions.[13] Although extremely diverse, these factors share a common feature: They all influence V_p in Equation (9.1) by affecting the expected gains from migrating, the expected costs, or some combination of each.[14]

THE CONSEQUENCES OF MIGRATION

The consequences of domestic and international migration have several dimensions. Initially we will examine the individual gains from migration by asking, What is the return on this form of investment in human capital? We then will analyze the increased output accruing to society from migration. There we will also attempt to sort out the distribution of net gains. Who benefits? Who loses?

[10] Richard K. Green and Patric H. Hendershott, "Home Ownership and Unemployment in the U.S." *Urban Studies,* 2001, pp. 1509–20.

[11] George J. Borjas, "Native Internal Migration and the Labor Market Impact of Immigration," *Journal of Human Resources,* Spring 2006, pp. 221–58.

[12] Philip L. Rones, "Moving to the Sun: Regional Job Growth, 1968–1978," *Monthly Labor Review,* March 1980, p. 15. For evidence that government spending on welfare programs does not affect the location decisions of new international immigrants, see Neeraj Kaushal, "New Immigrants' Location Choices: Magnets without Welfare," *Journal of Labor Economics,* January 2005, pp. 59–80.

[13] Richard J. Cebula, "Migration and the Tiebout–Tullock Hypothesis Revisited," *Review of Regional Studies,* Winter–Spring 2002, pp. 87–96.

[14] William J. Kahley provides a very readable summary of the various factors affecting migration in his "Population Migration in the United States: A Survey of Research," *Economic Review* (Federal Reserve Bank of Atlanta), January–February 1991, pp. 12–21.

Personal Gains

People expect to increase their lifetime utility when they *voluntarily* decide to migrate from one area to another. One interesting way to conceptualize this expected gain is to ask, What amount of money would we have to pay to entice the migrant to reject the job opportunity? This dollar amount is an estimate of the migrant's expected gain from moving to the new location.

Empirical Evidence

Empirical studies confirm that migration increases the lifetime earnings of the average mover.[15] The estimated rate of return is similar to that on other forms of investment in human capital, meaning it generally lies in the 10 to 15 percent range.

Caveats

At least five cautions or complications must be mentioned when generalizing about rates of return to migration.

1 Uncertainty and Imperfect Information Migration decisions are based on *expected* net benefits, and most are made under circumstances of uncertainty and imperfect information. High *average* rates of return do not imply positive returns for *all* migrants. In many instances the expected gain from migration simply does not materialize—the anticipated job is not found at the destination, the living costs are higher in the new area than anticipated, the psychic costs of being away from family and friends are greater than expected, the anticipated raises and promotions are not forthcoming. Thus there are major *backflows* in migration patterns.[16] Although this return migration is costly to those involved, it does perform a useful economic function: It increases the availability of information about the destination to other potential migrants, enabling them to assess better the benefits and costs of moving. This makes subsequent migration more efficient.

Also, not all return migration indicates an unprofitable investment in human capital. Some people temporarily migrate to accumulate wealth or enhance their stock of human capital via on-the-job training or after-work education. Most return to their original locations after reaching their financial or human capital goals. For example, most of those who built the Alaskan pipeline returned to the lower 48 states after completion of their task. Also, many illegal aliens who cross the U.S.–Mexican border return to Mexico.[17]

---

[15] For example, see Kristen Keith and Abagail McWilliams, "The Returns to Job Mobility and Job Search by Gender," *Industrial and Labor Relations Review,* April 1999, pp. 460–77.

[16] Among foreign-born immigrants, return migration is more likely among those who do not perform well in the U.S. labor market. See George J. Borjas and Bernt Bratsberg, "Who Leaves? The Outmigration of the Foreign-Born," *Review of Economics and Statistics,* February 1996, pp. 165–76. See also Patricia B. Reagan and Randall J. Olsen, "You Can Go Home Again: Evidence from Longitudinal Data," *Demography,* August 2000, pp. 339–50.

[17] Michael J. Piore, *Birds of Passage: Migrant Labor and Industrial Societies* (Cambridge: Cambridge University Press, 1979), pp. 149–54.

2 Timing of Earnings Gains Lifetime income gains from migration do not necessarily mean that migrants receive gains from earnings during the first few postmigration years. Studies show that some migrants experience reduced earnings in the first few years after moving. These reductions, however, tend to be followed by more than commensurate increases in earnings in later years. Stated differently, some migrants accept a short-term postmigration reduction in earnings as an investment cost for faster-growing future earnings.

3 Earnings Disparities Increases in lifetime earnings do not imply that migrants necessarily will receive annual earnings equal to those received by people already at the destination. The skills that migrants possess are not always perfectly transferable between regions (because of occupational licensure), between employers (because of specific training), or between nations (because of language and other factors). This lack of *skill transferability* may mean that migrants—although perhaps improving their own wage—may be paid less than similarly trained, educated, and employed workers at the destination. For example, McManus has found that differences in English language skills explain a large portion of differences in earnings among U.S. ethnic groups. His research indicates that the cost of English deficiency for most immigrant groups is quite large. The cost of English deficiency, however, appears to be ethnically and occupationally specific. Kossoudji, for example, finds that Hispanics have a higher cost of English language deficiency than Asians at every skill level.[18] Another study finds that immigrants who have less incentive to learn English—for example, those who anticipate returning to their home country or who live in an area where their native language is used extensively—are less likely to learn the new language.[19]

On the other hand, migration tends to be characterized by *self-selection.* Because some migrants choose to move while others with similar skills do not, it is possible that the former have greater motivation for personal economic achievement and greater willingness to sacrifice current consumption for higher levels of later consumption. As Chiswick has pointed out,

> Such self-selected immigrants would tend to have higher earnings than the native born in the destination, if it were not for the disadvantage of being foreign born. Combining the [negative] effects of skill transferability and favorable self-selection suggests that the earnings of the foreign born may eventually equal and then surpass those of the native born.[20]

Do the earnings of immigrants in fact eventually exceed those of native-born Americans? For earlier immigrants, Chiswick found that, given equal amounts of education and premigration labor experience, male immigrants on average achieved earnings parity

---

[18] Walter S. McManus, "Labor Market Assimilation of Immigrants: The Importance of Language Skills," *Contemporary Policy Issues,* Spring 1985, pp. 77–89; and Sherrie A. Kossoudji, "English Language Ability and the Labor Market Opportunities of Hispanic and East Asian Immigrant Men," *Journal of Labor Economics,* April 1988, pp. 205–28. Also see Alberto Davila and Marie T. Mora, "English Language Skills and the Earnings of Self-Employed Immigrants in the United States: A Note," *Industrial Relations,* April 2004, pp. 386–91.

[19] Barry R. Chiswick and Paul W. Miller, "The Endogeneity between Language and Earnings: International Analyses," *Journal of Labor Economics,* April 1995, pp. 246–88.

[20] Barry R. Chiswick, "Immigrant Earning Patterns by Sex, Race, and Ethnic Groupings," *Monthly Labor Review,* October 1980, p. 22.

with their native-born cohorts after 11 to 15 years and after that had higher earnings by as much as 5 percent.[21] However, recent studies have discovered that immigrants arriving in the United States during the second half of the 1970s and the 1980s were on average less skilled than previous immigrants. In addition, the skill disadvantage of new immigrants was larger in the 1980s than in the 1970s. The earnings of these more recent immigrants remain 12 to 20 percent below those of comparable native-born workers. Borjas concludes that these newer immigrants are not likely to achieve wage parity with native workers, even after several decades.[22]

Internal migrants within the United States—as distinct from immigrants from abroad—rather quickly assimilate in their new locales. A recent study indicates that young internal migrants initially earn less than similar natives in the area to which they migrate, but this wage differential disappears within a few years. The initial wage disadvantage is greater the longer the distance moved and the poorer the economic conditions in the destination locale.[23]

4 Earnings of Spouses A gain in family earnings from migration does not necessarily mean a gain in earnings for both working spouses. On the average, migration increases the earnings of husbands but tends to reduce the earnings for wives, at least over the following five-year period.[24] Apparently the higher average earnings and stronger labor force attachment of husbands relative to that of wives entice families to migrate in response to improved earnings for the husband. These moves, on the average, increase the family's income; but they also reduce either the wife's incentive to work (income effect), her market opportunities, or some combination of the two. It is important to note that husbands are more commonly becoming trailing spouses. Recent evidence indicates that the negative labor market effects of being a trailing spouse are similar for both men and women.[25]

5 Wage Reductions from Job Losses A positive rate of return to migration does not necessarily imply higher earnings than would have accrued had past wage rates continued to be earned. Some migrants are pushed into moving by job loss or political repression. For these people job mobility is not totally voluntary. For example, suppose that Smith, a

---

[21] Ibid., p. 23. Also see Chiswick's "The Effect of Americanization of Foreign-Born Men," *Journal of Political Economy,* October 1978, pp. 897–921; and James Long, "The Effect of Americanization on Earnings: Some Evidence for Women," *Journal of Political Economy,* June 1980, pp. 620–29.

[22] George J. Borjas, *Friends or Strangers: The Impact of Immigrants on the U.S. Economy* (New York: Basic Books, 1990), chap. 6; and George J. Borjas, "Assimilation and Changes in Cohort Quality Revisited: What Happened to Immigrant Earnings in the 1980s?" *Journal of Labor Economics,* April 1995, pp. 201–45. However, some evidence exists that the skill of new immigrants increased during the late 1980s. See Edward Funkhouser and Stephen J. Trejo, "The Labor Market Skills of Recent Male Immigrants: Evidence from the Current Population Survey," *Industrial and Labor Relations Review,* July 1995, pp. 792–811.

[23] George J. Borjas, Stephen G. Bonars, and Stephen J. Trejo, "Assimilation and the Earnings of Young Internal Migrants," *Review of Economics and Statistics,* February 1992, pp. 170–75.

[24] For example, see Solomon Polachek and Francis Horvath, "A Life Cycle Approach to Migration," in Ronald G. Ehrenberg (ed.), *Research in Labor Economics* (Greenwich, CT: JAI Press, 1971), pp. 103–49; and Stephen Sandell, "Women and the Economics of Migration," *Review of Economics and Statistics,* November 1977, p. 410.

[25] Thomas J. Cooke and Karen Speirs, "Migration and Employment among the Civilian Spouses of Military Personnel," *Social Science Quarterly,* June 2005, pp. 343–55.

50-year-old Ohio steelworker, earns $18 an hour in wages and fringe benefits, has children in college, and has lived all of his life in the same locale. If Smith is displaced from his job because of a factory shutdown, exhausts his unemployment benefits, and eventually finds a job at $12 an hour in a new occupation in the Southwest, can we conclude that migration enhanced his well-being? Considerable misunderstanding exists about this point. The job loss and its consequences for Smith and his family are indeed severe in that income from work falls to zero. But once this event occurs, Smith faces a new set of prospective earnings streams over the remainder of his work life. For illustrative purposes, let's assume that the highest-paying job he can find in his present locale is at $8 an hour. By migrating to the Southwest where he can earn $12 an hour, Smith does increase his lifetime earnings, other things being equal, even though these earnings are considerably lower than those that would have accrued in the absence of the job loss. Migration increases lifetime earnings for most movers; it does not always increase earnings above levels that existed prior to a job loss.

Wage Narrowing and Efficiency Gains

Economic efficiency exists when a nation achieves the greatest possible real domestic output or income from its available land, labor, capital, and entrepreneurial resources. Labor mobility is crucial in approaching this goal. To illustrate, let's suppose, first, that there are only two labor markets, each perfectly competitive and each situated in a different geographic location. Second, suppose that each labor market contains a fixed number of workers and there is no unemployment in either market. Third, we assume that nonwage job amenities and locational attributes are the same in both areas. A fourth assumption is that capital is immobile. Finally, we assume that workers possess perfect information about wages and working conditions in both markets and that migration between the two markets is costless.

Numerical Illustration

Columns 1_A and 2_A in Table 9.1 display the demand for labor in market A, while columns 1_B and 2_B show it for B. Notice that the wages are given in *annual* terms and that, because of our assumption of perfect competition in the product and labor markets, these wages equal the value of the marginal product (VMP) of labor.[26] Columns 3_A and 3_B cumulate the VMP data to show the value of the total product (VTP) associated with each level of employment. Also, notice that the VMP is greater for each labor input in labor market A than in B. This difference in the strength of labor demand is not crucial to our analysis but presumably arises from a greater capital and technological endowment in A than in B, so that the marginal product of labor is higher in market A.

Now suppose that initially two workers are employed in market A and each earns $23,000 annually (boxed figure), while eight workers, earning $7,000 apiece, are working in B (boxed figure). Next we relax the assumption that these are separate markets and observe that given our other assumptions, workers in B will migrate to labor market A in pursuit of higher earnings.

What will happen to annual earnings in the respective markets as this migration occurs? The number of workers in A will increase, causing the market wage there to

[26] If this is not clear, you may want to review the discussion pertinent to Table 5.2.

TABLE 9.1
Allocative
Efficiency: The
Role of Labor
Mobility

	Labor Market A			Labor Market B	
(1ᴀ) Workers	(2ᴀ) VMPᴀ Annual Wage	(3ᴀ) VTPᴀ	(1ʙ) Workers	(2ʙ) VMPʙ Annual Wage	(3ʙ) VTPʙ
1	$25,000	$ 25,000	1	$21,000	$ 21,000
2	23,000	48,000	2	19,000	40,000
3	21,000	69,000	3	17,000	57,000
4	19,000	88,000	4	15,000	72,000
5	17,000	105,000	5	13,000	85,000
6	15,000	120,000	6	11,000	96,000
7	13,000	133,000	7	9,000	105,000
8	11,000	144,000	8	7,000	112,000
9	9,000	153,000	9	5,000	117,000
10	7,000	160,000	10	3,000	120,000

fall. In region B, the corresponding decline in the quantity of labor will increase the equilibrium wage. Migration will continue until the wage advantage in A is totally eliminated. This occurs in Table 9.1 at $15,000 (circled data). At this annual wage, employers in the highly capital-endowed region A will hire six workers, while those in the less endowed area B will hire four workers. To generalize: *Assuming perfect competition, costless information, and costless migration, market wages will equal the value of the marginal product of labor* ($W = \text{VMP}$), *and labor will relocate until VMPs are equal in all labor markets* ($\text{VMP}_A = \text{VMP}_B$).

Does this migration of labor enhance the total value of output in our hypothetical nation? To determine the answer, again note Table 9.1, columns 3_A and 3_B. Before migration, the value of the total product (VTP) was $48,000 in labor market A and $112,000 in B. Thus the combined premigration VTP was $160,000 (= $48,000 + $112,000). And after migration? A glance at the table shows it to be $192,000. The six workers in A produce a combined output valued at $120,000, while the four workers in B produce $72,000. In this simple model, then, we observe that wage differentials create an incentive for labor to move from one market to another. This mobility, or migration, equalizes wages and results in allocative efficiency [Equation (6.1)]; it generates the highest possible value of total output from the available resources.

Graphic Portrayal

We can easily show graphically both the wage narrowing and the *efficiency gains from migration* that arise. For variety and to extend our focus, let's now employ an international, rather than an interregional, example. Figure 9.2(a) shows the demand for labor in the United States, and graph (b) portrays the labor demand curve for Mexico.

FIGURE 9.2 **The Efficiency Gains from Migration**

The migration of labor from low-wage Mexico (b) to high-wage United States (a) will increase the domestic output and reduce the average wage rate in the United States and produce the opposite effects in Mexico. The output gain of *ebcf* in the United States exceeds the loss of *kijl* in Mexico; therefore, the net value of the combined outputs from the two nations rises.

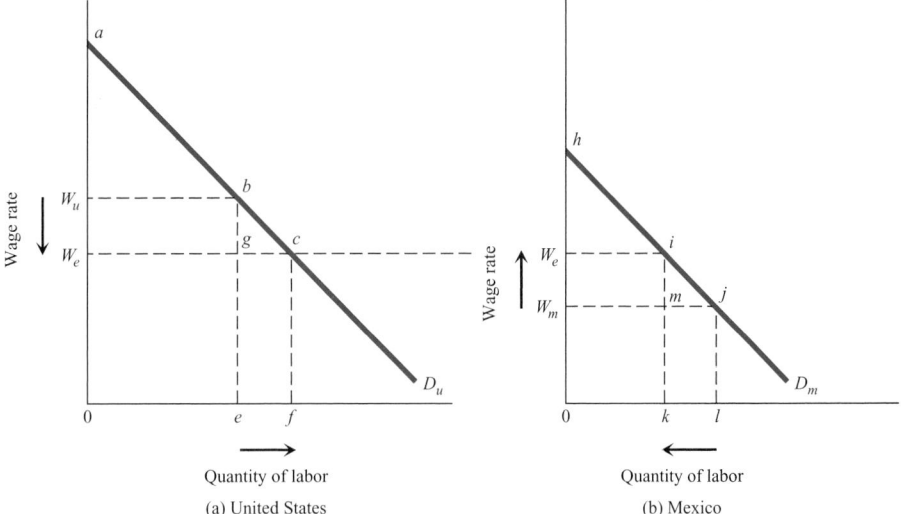

Suppose the employment and wage levels in the United States and Mexico are $0e$, W_u, and $0l$, W_m, respectively. Because information is assumed to be perfect and migration is assumed to be costless, labor will flow from Mexico to the United States until the equilibrium wage of W_e is achieved in each nation. Notice the positive efficiency gains accruing from this migration. The United States *gains* domestic output equal to the area *ebcf* in graph (a), and Mexico *loses* domestic output equivalent to the area *kijl* in graph (b). Because the U.S. gain exceeds the Mexican loss, the total value of the combined output produced by the two nations rises. Stated differently, the sum of the areas $0acf$ in graph (a) and $0hik$ in (b) exceeds the premigration areas $0abe$ plus $0hjl$. Conclusion? Given our assumptions, wage-induced labor migration—whether internal or international—increases the total income and output in the *combined* origin and destination. Quite simply, migration enables a larger total real output to be achieved from a given available amount of resources.

External Effects

The generalization drawn from Table 9.1 and Figure 9.2 raises an important question: If the efficiency gains from migration are so direct and evident, why do so many people in origin and destination locales view migration negatively? Although numerous noneconomic factors are also at work, much of the explanation is economic in character and can be understood by analyzing *migration externalities*, or third-party effects. These externalities can be *real* or *pecuniary* and either positive or negative.

1 Real Negative Externalities

Real negative externalities are effects of private actions spilling over to third parties and creating misallocations of resources (economic inefficiency). An example is water pollution. If a firm produces a product and in the process pollutes a river used by downstream municipalities, recreational enthusiasts, and industries, then the firm fails to cover all the costs of its actions. The price of the firm's product is too low; more resources are devoted to producing this output than is socially optimal; and downstream users incur costs that absorb further resources. In some circumstances mass migration generates similar negative spillovers. As Thurow points out,

> Private incomes may increase enough to more than make up for the costs of moving, but the social costs of accommodating people in a crowded urban area may exceed the net private gain. More public services must be provided, and congestion may increase. Excess capacity, and hence waste, may develop in the production of social services (schools, etc.) in areas from which people are moving, and new investment in social services may be needed in areas to which they are moving.[27]

Put simply, where negative externalities from migration are substantial and diffuse, the private gains to migrants and employers will overstate the net gain to society. Under these circumstances, more migration will occur than is consistent with an optimal allocation of society's resources. For example, this outcome occurs when substantial migration to a rapidly growing area increases congestion, crime, and other external costs.

2 Pecuniary Externalities: Income Redistribution

Most of the expressed opposition to emigration and immigration, however, arises not from these potential real externalities but rather from numerous pecuniary (financial) ones. *Pecuniary externalities may be defined as acts that redistribute income among individuals and groups.* Such redistributive effects typically give rise to active resistance on the part of adversely affected groups and engender heated political debate. Careful analysis of Figure 9.2 reveals several redistributive impacts of migration.

Losses in the Origin Nation   Although immigration from Mexico to the United States *increases* the total product in the United States, it *reduces* it in Mexico. Stated more generally, migration increases the value of the total product produced in the combined economies of the origin and destination; but under most conditions these gains accrue to the destination. There are exceptions, of course. As an extreme example, if the kl workers who migrate to the United States are unemployable (value of marginal product $= 0$), then no increased output is forthcoming, and the destination nation will be the loser by virtue of having to support the migrants. Conversely, the origin nation will gain because its fixed domestic output will be shared among fewer people. Also, many migrants save a large portion of their wages and send these funds home or bring them back as a lump sum at the end of their temporary stay. In these cases the origin nation captures a share of the efficiency gains. But when migration is permanent, is in response to higher

---

[27] Lester C. Thurow, *Investment in Human Capital* (Belmont, CA: Wadsworth Publishing Company, 1970), p. 33.

wages in the destination nation, and involves migrants who leave jobs in the origin nation, the destination nation experiences an increase in national income while the origin nation loses. These distributional impacts partially explain why "brain drains"—the emigration of highly skilled workers—are a source of economic concern for some nations.[28]

Reduced Wage Income to Native Workers   A second consequence of migration on income distribution is also evident from Figure 9.2. Immigration increases the supply of labor in the United States from $0e$ to $0f$, driving down the average wage rate from W_u to W_e and reducing the wage income to native U.S. workers from $0W_u be$ to $0W_e ge$. Notice that immigration may or may not increase the total wage income in the United States: That depends on the elasticity of labor demand (Figure 5.7). It is clear, however, that the influx of the *ef* workers reduces the wage income accruing to the $0e$ native U.S. workers. In Mexico the reduction in labor supply *increases* the wage rate (W_e rather than W_m) for those who remain. Another generalization thus emerges: Immigration is likely to be opposed by laborers in the destination region or nation, whereas workers in the place of origin are likely to support emigration.

This generalization, however, must be accompanied by an important caution relating to our distinction made in Chapter 5 between gross substitutes and gross complements. Immigrants to the United States are *gross substitutes* (substitution effect > output effect) for some labor market groups, reducing the labor demand and wages for these groups. On the other hand, the immigrants are *gross complements* (output effect > substitution effect) for other domestic workers, causing labor demand and wages for these groups to rise. Therefore, not all groups of workers are equally affected by immigration. Overall, a survey of empirical studies concludes that a 10 percent increase in the fraction of immigrants creates at most a 1 percent decrease in the wages of native workers.[29] Immigrants appear to have the largest impact on the wages of high school dropouts and other immigrants.[30]

In this regard, Borjas has shown that immigrants do *not* substantially affect the earnings of *native-born* workers; instead they reduce the earnings of *natives who themselves were immigrants.*[31]

---

[28] Brain drains also are viewed negatively because the origin nation loses the return on investments in human capital that it may have either paid for in full or partially subsidized. For a theoretical discussion of brain drains, see Viem Kevok and Hayne Leland, "An Economic Model of the Brain Drain," *American Economic Review,* March 1982, pp. 91–100. For evidence there is a brain drain from the Caribbean, Central America, and some African and Asian countries, see William J. Carrington and Enrica Detragiache, "How Extensive Is the Brain Drain?" *Finance and Development,* June 1999, pp. 46–49.

[29] Rachel M. Friedberg and Jennifer Hunt, "The Impact of Immigrants on Host Country Wages, Employment and Growth," *Journal of Economic Perspectives,* Spring 1995, pp. 23–44. For another survey reaching a similar conclusion, see T. Paul Schultz, "Immigrant Quality and Assimilation: A Review of the U.S. Literature," *Journal of Population Economics,* May 1998, pp. 239–52.

[30] See George J. Borjas, Richard B. Freeman, and Lawrence Katz, "Searching for the Effect of Immigration on the Labor Market," *American Economic Review,* May 1996, pp. 246–51. See also Maria E. Enchautegui, "Immigration and Wage Changes of High School Dropouts," *Monthly Labor Review,* October 1997, pp. 3–9.

[31] George J. Borjas, "Immigrants, Minorities, and Labor Market Competition," *Industrial and Labor Relations Review,* April 1987, pp. 382–92.

Gains to Owners of Capital   A third potential for opposition to migration by some groups in origin and destination locales arises from the impact of migration on labor income relative to capital income. We again return to Figure 9.2, graph (a). Immigration increases the total nonimmigrant national income in the United States by the triangle *gbc*. To see why, note that the value of the total product rises from 0*abe* to 0*acf* in the United States. Of the total gain (*ebcf*), migrants receive *egcf*. This leaves triangle *gbc* as the increase in total nonimmigrant income. Now recall that in the previous paragraph we concluded that the wage bill to native U.S. workers falls. So who receives the gain that native workers lose? The answer, of course, is U.S. businesses. They gain area $W_e W_u bg$ at the expense of native U.S. workers and also obtain the added product shown by the triangle *gbc*. Thus this simple model suggests that business interests gain added income from immigration—at least in the short run—and conversely actually lose income when substantial out-migration occurs. This helps explain why some U.S. businesses historically have recruited foreign workers to come to the United States. For example, Chinese workers were recruited to help build the railroads, and migrant agricultural workers presently are recruited to help harvest U.S. crops and produce.

The conclusion that businesses gain from migration at the expense of domestic workers must be tempered by the fact that this is a short-run, partial-equilibrium model. The theoretical possibilities become more complicated when a long-run, general-equilibrium approach is used and when various assumptions are relaxed. For example, the new migrants are likely to spend portions of their earnings in the United States. This will increase the demand for many types of labor and may increase wages for workers who are not close substitutes in production for the specific immigrant labor. Additionally, the gain in business income relative to the stock of U.S. capital increases the rate of return on capital. This increase tends to raise domestic investment spending and consequently enlarges the stock of U.S. capital. Under normal production conditions, the marginal product of labor therefore will rise and labor demand will increase. Thus, in the long run, part of the negative impact of immigration on the wage rate may be lessened or eliminated. But the basic point is clear: Differing views of the desirability of open migration policies, illegal aliens, and brain drains can partially be understood in the context of the actual and perceived redistributional effects of migration.

Fiscal Impacts   One final distributional outcome merits discussion. An inflow of immigrants can affect the distribution of disposable income in a destination nation or area through its effect on transfer payments and tax collections. If the immigrants to the United States in Figure 9.2 are highly educated and skilled professionals, for example, we would expect little opposition from the general U.S. public. These workers most probably will be net taxpayers and not major recipients of cash and in-kind transfer payments. However, if the immigrants are illiterate, low-skilled individuals who are not likely to find permanent employment in the United States, then this influx may necessitate increased government spending on transfer payments and social service programs. As a consequence, this specific immigration may produce higher taxes for U.S. citizens, lower average transfer payments to native low-income residents, or some combination of each. Thus taxpayers and low-income residents in the United States may oppose the migration. A real externality might even result from the increased taxes and transfers through a disincentive impact on labor supply (Chapters 2 and 12). This rests on the assumption, of course, that the immigrants are eligible for the transfer programs and extensively use them.

Historically, the immigrant population in the United States was less likely than the native population to receive welfare benefits.[32] But welfare participation by immigrants has greatly increased since the late 1970s and is now greater for immigrants than for natives. Borjas and Trejo attribute this turnabout to the changing mix of immigrants, with fewer skilled immigrants coming from European countries and many unskilled immigrants arriving from Asia and Latin America.[33]

9.1
Quick Review

- Occupational mobility involves workers changing occupations; geographic mobility involves workers moving to jobs in another city, state, or nation.
- The decision to move geographically can be viewed through the investment in human capital framework; a worker will move when the net present value of migration, V_p, is positive.
- Along with the annual earnings differential, important determinants of migration include age, family factors, education, distance, and unemployment rates.
- Migration produces earnings gains for movers, wage narrowing among regions, and real output gains for society. Generally, migration reduces wage income to native workers with skills similar to those of the immigrants and increases the income of owners of capital.

Your Turn

Suppose the E_2 and N values in the net present value equation [Equation (9.1)] fall while the Z value rises. What will happen to V_p and the likelihood of migration? (*Answer:* See page 598.)

CAPITAL AND PRODUCT FLOWS

Table 9.1 and Figure 9.2 overstate the probable extent of labor migration between two regions or nations for reasons other than those associated with the costs of obtaining information and migrating. Through differing rates of investment, capital itself is mobile in the long run. Also, products made in one locale are sold in many others. These facts have considerable significance for labor migration.

---

[32] Francine Blau, "The Use of Transfer Payments for Immigrants," *Industrial and Labor Relations Review,* January 1984, pp. 222–39; and Julian L. Simon, "Immigrants, Taxes, and Welfare in the United States," *Population Development Review,* March 1984, pp. 55–69.

[33] Borjas, *Friends or Strangers,* chap. 9. Also relevant is George J. Borjas and Stephen J. Trejo, "Immigrant Participation in the Welfare System," *Industrial and Labor Relations Review,* January 1991, pp. 195–211; George J. Borjas, "Immigration and Welfare Magnets," *Journal of Labor Economics,* part 1, October 1999, pp. 607–37; and Janet Currie, "Do Children of Immigrants Make Differential Use of Public Health Insurance?" in George Borjas (ed.), *Issues in the Economics of Immigration* (Chicago: University of Chicago Press, 2000).

Capital Flows

The impacts of *capital mobility* and interregional or international trade on wage differentials and therefore on labor migration are illustrated in Figure 9.3. Here we use the United States and South Korea in a simplified example. Notice initially that given the labor demand curves D in each nation, wages in the United States W_u exceed those in South Korea W_k. Our previous analysis implied that this wage differential would induce Korean workers to migrate to the United States. But other forces are also at work. The lower Korean wage rate might cause some U.S. producers to abandon production facilities in the United States and construct new facilities in Korea. We would expect this increase in capital in Korea to increase the marginal product and value of marginal product of labor there. The labor demand curve therefore would shift outward, say to D_1 as shown in graph (b) of Figure 9.3. Conversely, the lower stock of capital in the United States would reduce labor demand from D to D_1 (graph a).

The increase in labor demand from D to D_1 in South Korea raises the market wage from W_k to W_e. In the United States the decline in demand from D to D_1 lowers the wage from W_u to W_e. Capital mobility thus has removed the wage disparity in our model and eliminated the incentive for labor to migrate. But as is true with labor mobility, migration of capital is very costly and is impeded by many real-world economic, political, and legal obstacles. For example, U.S. meat producers would not likely find it profitable to move to South Korea to realize savings in labor costs. Other costs such as transporting livestock to Korean facilities and shipping meat products back to U.S. markets would be too high. Thus although

FIGURE 9.3 **The Impact of Capital and Product Flows on Wage Differentials**
A high wage rate in the United States W_u and a low wage rate in South Korea W_k may cause either (1) flows of capital from the United States toward South Korea or (2) a price advantage for Korean-produced goods. In either case, the demand for labor is likely to increase in South Korea and decline in the United States. Thus the wage rate differential will narrow, and consequently no labor migration will occur.

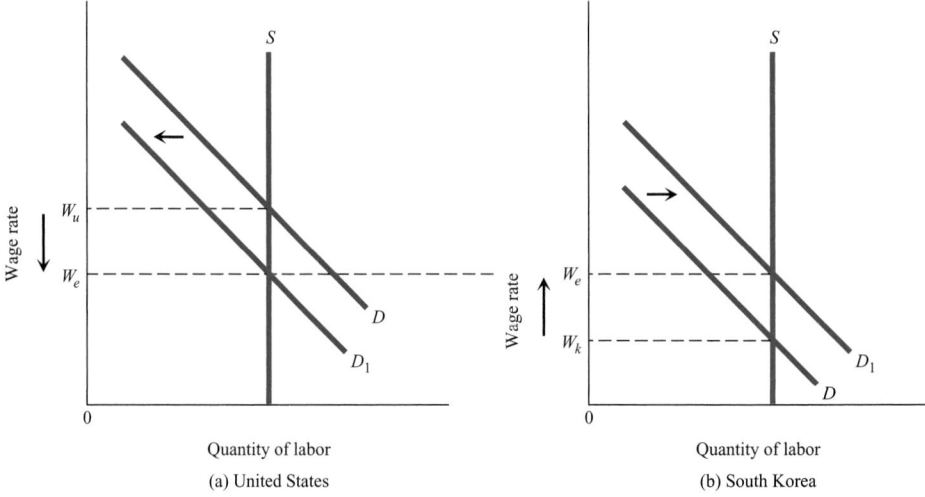

(a) United States

(b) South Korea

significant flows of capital *have* occurred (for example, from the northeast United States to the South and Southwest and from the United States to South Korea, Mexico, and elsewhere), their role in narrowing wage differentials has been somewhat limited. But to the extent that capital is mobile, wage differentials between areas are smaller; and thus less labor migration will occur than if investment is confined to the domestic economy.[34]

Product Flows

Interregional and international trade has a similar potential effect on wage differences and labor mobility. Again return to Figure 9.3. Now suppose that capital and labor are immobile, U.S. and South Korean workers are homogeneous, and the costs of transporting goods between the two nations are zero. What effect will the low Korean wage W_k compared to the high U.S. wage W_u have on the relative competitiveness of Korean versus U.S. goods? Assuming that competition forces product prices down to marginal costs in both nations, U.S. consumers would reallocate their expenditures toward the lower-priced Korean goods. This would increase the total demand for these imports and eventually raise the derived demand for Korean labor. As shown by the outward shift of the labor demand curve from D to D_1 in Figure 9.3(b), this would increase the Korean wage rate. The opposite chain of events would occur in the United States, where reduced product demand would shift the derived demand for U.S. labor leftward from D to D_1 and reduce the wage to W_e. This wage narrowing via product flows diminishes the extent of labor migration if we relax the assumption that labor is immobile. But in reality, transportation costs are so high for many goods and services that shipping them long distances is not economical. Thus trade can be expected to narrow, but not equalize, wages in the long run.

Conclusion: *Labor migration, capital mobility, and trade between regions and nations all complement one another in promoting an efficient allocation of resources.* Labor mobility simply is one aspect of the broader mobility of resources and commodities in the economy. In fact, the U.S. government has at times promoted investment in less developed nations and has reduced trade barriers to slow immigration from those nations into the United States.

U.S. IMMIGRATION POLICY AND ISSUES

Our analysis of the motivations for migration, the efficiency gains produced by this mobility, and the problem of gainers versus losers provides the tools necessary for understanding some of the controversies surrounding U.S. immigration patterns and policies.

History and Scope

Before World War I, immigration to the United States was virtually unimpeded. The great influx of foreign labor occurring in the 19th century contributed to economic growth and to rising levels of per capita income. The flow of immigrants was slowed by World War I and the restrictive Immigration Acts of 1921 and 1924. These acts established immigration quotas for various nationalities based on the number of foreign-born

---

[34] For critical discussion of American capital exports, see Seymour Melman, *Profits without Production* (New York: Alfred A. Knopf, 1983), chap. 1.

people of that nationality in the United States in specific census years. Additionally, the laws allowed several categories of nonquota immigrants to enter the United States. Between 1921 and 1965 only 10 million people entered the United States, and over half were nonquota immigrants, including 900,000 Canadians, 500,000 Mexicans, and thousands of spouses and children of U.S. citizens.

In 1965 amendments to the 1952 Immigration and Nationality Act shifted the preferences of the quota system away from northern and western European immigrants and toward a more evenly balanced set of nationalities. Further amendments established a worldwide annual ceiling of 270,000 immigrants, set an annual limit of 20,000 individuals per nation, and developed a six-point preference system giving priority to people who have specific job skills. Immediate relatives of U.S. citizens, refugees, and people seeking political asylum, however, were exempt from these provisions and ceilings.

Figure 9.4 shows the number of legal immigrants to the United States in selected years. During the 1980s legal immigration ranged from a low of 531,000 in 1980 to a high of 1,091,000 in 1989, but generally was 550,000 to 600,000 each year. The number of legal immigrants jumped considerably in 1989, 1990, and 1991—three years when many former illegal immigrants were granted permanent residence under the amnesty provisions of the Immigration Reform and Control Act of 1986.

To the numbers in Figure 9.4 we must add the illegal aliens who arrived mainly from Mexico, the Caribbean, and Central and South America. The U.S. Census Bureau estimates that the net inflow of illegal aliens averaged about 200,000 annually between 1980 and 1990. Therefore, it was not uncommon for total immigration (legal and illegal) to exceed 750,000 annually during that period.

FIGURE 9.4   Legal Immigration to the United States
Legal immigration increased gradually during the 1970s and 1980s until 1988. The number of legal immigrants rose dramatically from 1989 to 1991 as many former illegal immigrants were permitted to become legal immigrants by the Immigration Reform and Control Act of 1986. In the 1990s and 2000s, legal immigration remained relatively high as the cap on legal immigrants was raised from 500,000 to 700,00 per year.

Source: U.S. Department of Homeland Security, *2005 Yearbook of Immigration Statistics.*

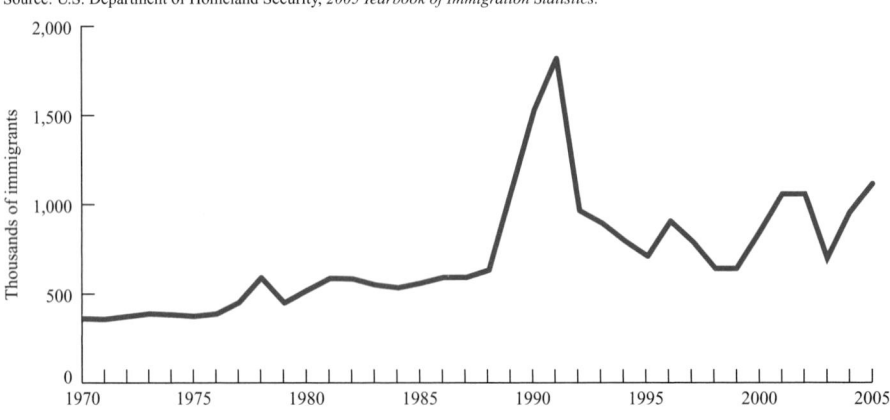

9.2 World of Work

Human Trafficking*

Human trafficking (also known as "modern-day slavery") is a continuing major global problem. Estimates indicate that worldwide there are 600,000 to 800,000 victims per year. In fact, there are 14,500 to 17,500 victims each year in the United States.

Who are the trafficking victims? Half of them are under the age of 18, and about four-fifths are female. Two-thirds of the victims are in the commercial sex industry. The remaining third are in other types of exploitation such as sweatshops.

To combat the problem of human trafficking, Congress enacted the Trafficking Victims Protection Act of 2000. The law authorizes up to 5,000 T-visas to be issued each year to trafficking victims. These visas permit victims to stay in the United States for three years, after which they may apply for permanent resident status. In exchange, the victims must help the government prosecute the traffickers.

The initial results from this law have been mixed. On one hand, fewer than 700 visas had been issued to victims by 2005. The low number of issued visas is likely the result of the requirement that victims must help prosecutors. The victims are apparently deterred by the threat of retaliation by traffickers on family members. On the other hand, the federal government prosecuted 277 cases against traffickers by 2005 and obtained a conviction in each case.

* David Crary, "Human Traffic an Elusive Target," *Journal Star*, October 30, 2005, p. 3A.

Immigration increased further during the 1990s. In late 1990 Congress passed an immigration law raising the legal immigration cap from about 500,000 to 700,000 people annually, not counting refugees. This law reserves 140,000 permanent residency visas each year for high-skilled professional workers. It also grants 10,000 residency slots to immigrants who either invest at least $1 million in the U.S. economy and create 10 or more full-time jobs or who invest $500,000 in targeted depressed areas in the United States.

Meanwhile, despite the passage of the Immigration Reform and Control Act, the flow of illegal immigrants has continued. This law granted amnesty and legal status to undocumented individuals who had lived in the United States since 1982. It also made it illegal for employers to hire undocumented workers.[35] The idea behind the employer sanctions was to diminish or eliminate the demand for the services of undocumented workers, thereby reducing their incentive to enter the country. But illegal immigrants have skirted this law by obtaining counterfeited documents. Thus studies indicate that the law has had no long-term impact on illegal immigration.

9.2

---

[35] For a study examining the wage effects of the Immigration Reform and Control Act, see Julie A. Phillips and Douglas S. Massey, "The New Labor Market: Immigrants and Wages after IRCA," *Demography*, May 1999, pp. 233–46. For evidence regarding the act's impact on illegal immigration, see Pia M. Orrenius and Madeline Zavodny, "Do Amnesty Programs Reduce Undocumented Immigration? Evidence from IRCA," *Demography*, August 2003, pp. 437–50. One study indicates that the act increased discrimination against Latinos. See Cynthia Bansak and Steven Raphael, "Immigration Reform and the Earnings of Latino Workers: Do Employer Sanctions Cause Discrimination?" *Industrial and Labor Relations Review*, January 2001, pp. 275–95.

Global Perspective 9.1

Immigrants as a Percentage of the Labor Force*

Among advanced industrial nations, the percentage of the labor force who are immigrants ranges from 0.3 in Japan to 24.4 in Australia.

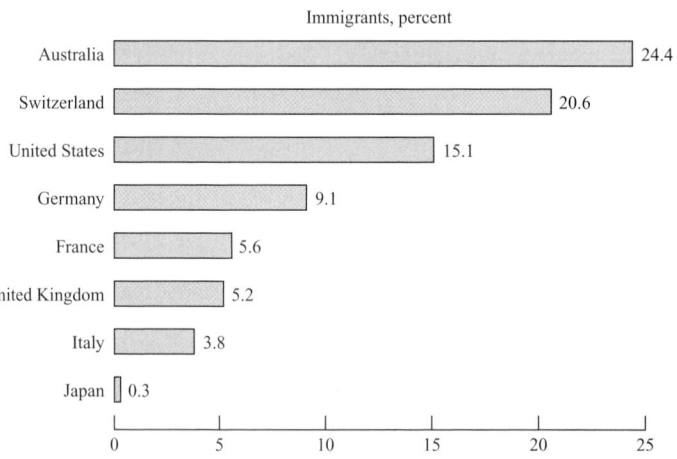

Immigrants, percent

Country	Percent
Australia	24.4
Switzerland	20.6
United States	15.1
Germany	9.1
France	5.6
United Kingdom	5.2
Italy	3.8
Japan	0.3

Source: Organization for Economic Cooperation and Development, *International Migration Outlook, 2006,* Tables A2.2.2 and A2.2.3.

* Data are for 2004 except for Italy, which is for 2002. All data are for the total labor force, except for the United Kingdom and Italy, which are based on employed individuals.

Coupled with the liberalized provisions of the 1990 immigration law, the continued flow of illegal immigrants means that on average about 850,000 immigrants have entered the United States each year since 1992.

Effects of Illegal Immigration

The inflow of *illegal aliens* into the United States over the past two decades has made immigration and immigration policy a major public issue in the United States. The main reason for the general concern is that most undocumented immigrants are unskilled workers. People fear that these individuals and their families reduce employment opportunities for the existing workforce, depress wage rates in already low-wage labor markets, and financially strain U.S. taxpayers via their receipt of transfer payments and use of social service programs. Are these concerns justified? Unfortunately, a simple yes or no answer cannot be provided.

1 Employment Effects

Some observers contend that the employment of illegal aliens decreases the employment of domestic workers on a one-for-one basis. They argue that a given number of jobs exist in the economy and that if one of these positions is taken by an illegal worker, that job is no longer available for a legal resident. At the other extreme is the claim that illegal aliens accept only work that resident workers are unwilling to perform and thus take no jobs from native workers. As we will demonstrate, both views are somewhat simplistic.

Figure 9.5 illustrates a market for unskilled agricultural workers. The curve D is the typical labor demand curve with which we are familiar. Supply curve S_d portrays the labor supply of domestic workers, while curve S_t reflects the total supply of domestic *and* illegal workers. Thus the horizontal distance between S_t and S_d is the number of undocumented workers who will offer their labor services at each wage rate.

Given the presence of the illegal workers, the market wage and level of employment are W_t and Q_t. At this low wage, *no* domestic workers are willing to work. In this case, the reservation wage of domestic workers is simply too high. Perhaps this results from the availability of nonwage income, a high marginal value or opportunity cost associated with leisure, or a perceived lack of possibilities for advancement in the job. Can we therefore conclude that illegal aliens take work that U.S. workers do not want? In Figure 9.5 the answer is yes, *but* only if we add "at the low wage W_t." If all the illegal aliens were

FIGURE 9.5   The Impact of Illegal Aliens on Domestic Jobs and Wages

The presence of illegal aliens in this low-wage labor market shifts the labor supply curve to S_t and reduces the market wage from W_d to W_t. At W_t, all workers hired are illegal aliens. If the illegal aliens were deported, however, Q_d domestic workers would be employed. Thus it is misleading to conclude that illegal aliens accept jobs that domestic workers will not take. It is also misleading to conclude that the deportation of illegal aliens would create employment for native workers on a one-for-one basis.

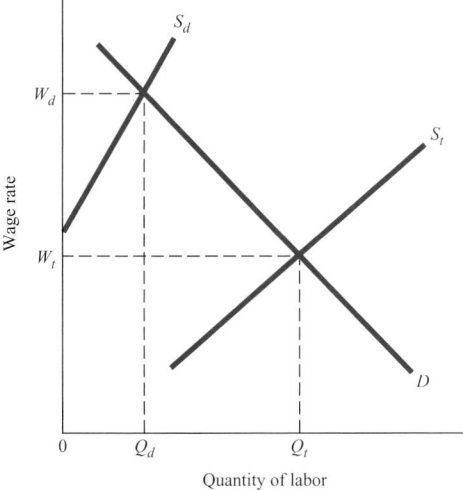

deported, the wage would rise to W_d in this market, and *some* U.S. workers, specifically $0Q_d$, would indeed be willing to do this work. The point is this: So-called undesirable work will attract U.S. workers if the compensating wage premium is sufficiently high (Chapter 8). If the illegal aliens were deported and if employers continued to offer wage rate W_t, there would be a shortage $0Q_t$. But this shortage would occur because the wage rate would not have been allowed to rise to its equilibrium, not because U.S. workers are unwilling to do work that illegal aliens are willing to perform. The willingness to work at any given job depends partly on the wage rate being paid.[36]

The opposite argument, that illegal aliens reduce domestic employment by an amount equal to the employment of illegal aliens, is also misleading. As shown in Figure 9.5, the presence of the undocumented laborers *increases* the total number of jobs in this low-skilled labor market. With the illegal migration, the number of jobs is Q_t; without the inflow, it is only Q_d. It is erroneous to contend that deportation of the Q_t illegal migrants would cause an increase in domestic employment of Q_t. But it is correct to say that native employment would increase by the amount Q_d in this labor market. We conclude that illegal immigration does cause some substitution of illegal aliens for domestic workers but that the amount of displacement most likely is less than the total employment of the illegal aliens.[37]

9.3

2 Wage Effects

There is little doubt that large inflows of migrants—be they legal or illegal—can depress some wage rates. Note in Figure 9.5 that the increase in labor supply reduces the U.S. market wage from W_d to W_t. However, the impact of illegal immigration on wages appears to be minimal at current levels of illegal immigration. The only measurable impact occurs in U.S. border cities.[38]

The overall effect of illegal immigration on the average wage rate in the economy is less clear. Some native workers and illegal immigrants are gross complements. This means that the reduced wage rate associated with the illegal immigration lowers production costs, creating an output effect that increases labor demand for certain native workers. As one example, it is possible that illegal immigration raises the demand for native workers who help transport and merchandise fruit. Also, spending by illegal aliens in

---

[36] Attempted illegal immigration is sensitive to changes in Mexican wages. Higher wages in Mexico reduce illegal immigration; lower wages increase it. See Gordon Hanson and Antonio Spilimbergo, "Illegal Immigration, Border Enforcement, and Relative Wages: Evidence from Apprehensions at U.S.–Mexico Border," *American Economic Review,* December 1999, pp. 1337–57.

[37] For an empirical investigation indicating a low amount of job displacement, see George E. Johnson, "The Labor Market Effects of Immigration," *Industrial and Labor Relations Review,* April 1980, pp. 331–41. A more recent article of interest is Julian L. Simon, Stephen Moore, and Richard Sullivan, "The Effect of Immigration on Aggregate Native Unemployment: An Across-City Estimation," *Journal of Labor Research,* Summer 1993, pp. 299–316. See David Card, "Immigrant Inflows, Native Outflows, and the Local Labor Market Impacts of Higher Immigration," *Journal of Labor Economics,* January 2001, pp. 22–64. Card concludes that immigration flows in the 1980s caused only small drops in employment for low-skilled workers in traditional gateway cities such as Miami and Los Angeles.

[38] Gordon H. Hanson, Raymond Roberston, and Antonio Spilimbergo, "Does Border Enforcement Protect U.S. Workers from Illegal Immigration?" *Review of Economics and Statistics,* February 2002, pp. 73–92.

9.3 World of Work

What Jobs Do Illegal Aliens Hold?*

Illegal alien workers play an important role in the U.S. economy. There are estimated to be 7 million such workers in the United States, making up 5 percent of the total workforce.

Illegal aliens are concentrated in different occupations than are native workers. About three-fifths of native workers are in white-collar occupations, but only one-quarter of illegal alien workers are in such occupations. Illegal alien workers are much more likely to work in occupations that have low education requirements or do not require a license. Illegal aliens are about three times more likely than native workers to be employed in agricultural occupations (4 percent) and construction and extractive occupations (19 percent). The proportion in service occupations (31 percent) is about double that of native workers (16 percent).

An alternative way to view the employment of illegal aliens is to measure how much of an occupation is filled by illegal aliens. In a few occupations, illegal aliens compose a large proportion of all workers employed. For example, illegal aliens make up 24 percent of all workers employed in agricultural occupations. Illegal aliens comprise 17 percent of employment in cleaning occupations, 14 percent in construction industries, and 12 percent in food preparation industries.

* Based on Jeffrey S. Passel, "The Size and Characteristics of the Unauthorized Migrant Population in the U.S.: Estimates Based on the March 2005 Current Population Survey," Pew Hispanic Center Research Report, March 2006.

the United States adds to the demand for products and therefore increases the derived demand for labor. For example, the demand for many workers in the barrios of Los Angeles may be greater because of the presence of illegal workers. On the other hand, this impact is reduced because many illegal aliens remit large portions of their pay to their families living abroad.[39]

So what can we conclude concerning the impact of illegal immigration on wage rates? The safest conclusion—given real-world complexities—is that *large-scale* illegal immigration does reduce the wage rate for substitutable low-skilled domestic workers. But illegal immigration probably has little *net* impact on the average level of wages in the United States.

3 Fiscal Effects

Finally, what are the effects of illegal immigrants on tax revenues, transfer expenditures, and public services? Illegal immigrants legally do not qualify for public assistance from such programs as Medicaid and food stamps. Nevertheless, the easy availability of forged documents has recently increased their participation in these programs. Evidence exists that current illegal immigrants and the families of illegal

[39] For evidence these large remittances are an important source of funds for less-developed countries, see Bilin Neyapti, "Trends in Workers' Remittances: A Worldwide Overview," *Emerging Markets Finance and Trade,* March–April 2004, pp. 83–90.

immigrants granted amnesty in the early 1990s are burdening the social welfare systems of some localities such as Los Angeles. Also, if immigrants displace low-paid native workers, then immigrants may impose an indirect cost on the U.S. welfare and income maintenance programs.[40]

On the other hand, we must remember that most illegal immigrants are young workers without families, whereas eligibility for the major transfer programs depends on such characteristics as old age, illness, disability, or position as female head of a household. And although illegal immigrants do use many local public services such as schools, roads, and parks, most also pay Social Security taxes, user fees, and sales taxes. Most scholars of illegal immigration conclude that these immigrants remain net taxpayers.

Chapter Summary	1. Mobility takes numerous forms, including occupational mobility and geographic mobility.

Chapter Summary

1. Mobility takes numerous forms, including occupational mobility and geographic mobility.

2. The decision to migrate can be viewed from a human capital perspective, by which the present value of expected gains in lifetime earnings is compared to investment costs (transportation expenses, forgone income during the move, and psychic costs).

3. Various factors can influence the decision to migrate. Age is inversely related to the probability of migrating; family status influences the migration decision in several ways; educational attainment and mobility are positively related; the likelihood of migration and the distance of the move are negatively related; unemployed people are more likely to move than those who have jobs; and a high unemployment rate in a destination area reduces the probability that an unemployed worker will migrate there.

4. The average lifetime rate of return on migration is positive and is estimated to be in the 10 to 15 percent range.

5. Labor mobility contributes to allocative efficiency by relocating labor resources away from lower-valued and toward higher-valued employment. Under conditions of perfect competition and costless migration, workers of a given type will relocate until the value of the marginal product of labor (VMP) is the same in all similar employments ($VMP_a = VMP_b = \cdots = VMP_n$), at which point labor is being allocated efficiently.

6. Along with the positive outcomes, migration may generate negative externalities, which if real may reduce the efficiency gains of migration and if pecuniary may alter the distribution of income among various individuals and groups in origin and destination areas.

[40] Evidence suggests, however, that illegal immigration has had very little impact on the unemployment of youth and minority groups. See C. R. Winegarden and Lay B. Khors, "Undocumented Immigration and Unemployment of U.S. Youth and Minority Workers: Econometric Evidence," *Review of Economics and Statistics*, February 1991, pp. 105–12.

7. Wage differentials may generate capital and product flows that tend to equalize wages in the long run and reduce the extent of labor migration.

8. Total annual legal immigration to the United States has averaged about 650,000 during the 1980s and about 850,000 since 1992.

9. Illegal aliens in the United States do not reduce native employment by the full extent of the employment of the illegals, but they do depress wage rates in some labor markets. The overall wage effect of illegal immigration is thought to be slight.

Terms and Concepts

labor mobility, *275*
occupational mobility, *276*
geographic mobility, *277*
determinants of migration, *279*
skill transferability, *285*

self-selection, *285*
efficiency gains from migration, *288*
migration externalities (real versus pecuniary), *289*

capital mobility, *294*
illegal aliens (employment, wage rate, and fiscal impacts), *298*

Questions and Study Suggestions

1. Use Equation (9.1) to explain the likely effect of each of the following on the present value of net benefits from migration: *(a)* age, *(b)* distance, *(c)* education, *(d)* marital status, and *(e)* the discount rate (interest rate).

2. What is meant by the term *beaten paths?* How do such paths increase V_p in Equation (9.1) and thereby increase the likelihood of migration?

3. Why are people who possess *specific* human capital less likely to change jobs, other things being equal, than those who possess *general* human capital? Does this imply that people who possess large amounts of specific human capital will never migrate? Explain.

4. Use Table 9.1 to determine the impact of wage-induced labor migration on
   a. The combined output of the two regions.
   b. Capital versus wage income in the destination region.
   c. The average wage rate in the origin region.
   d. The total wage bill for the native workers in the destination region.

5. Use the variables in Equation (9.1) to cite at least two reasons why it may be rational for a family to migrate from one part of the country to another, even though the hypothetical move produces a decline in family earnings in the first year of work following the move.

6. How might a wage differential between two regions be reduced via movements of capital to the low-wage area?

7. Comment on this statement: "If we deported all illegal aliens who are now in the United States, our total national unemployment would decline by the same number of people."

8. How might labor mobility and migration affect the degree of monopsony power (Chapter 6) in labor markets?

9. Is it consistent to favor the free movement of labor *within* the United States and be opposed to immigration *into* the United States?

10. If one believes in free international trade, then to be consistent, must one also advocate unrestricted international migration of labor?

11. Analyze this statement: "U.S. tariffs on imported products from low-wage foreign nations create an incentive for migration of low-skilled immigrants into the United States." Relate this idea to the North American Free Trade Agreement, discussed in "World of Work" 6.5.

Internet Exercise

Where Are the Immigrants Coming From?

Go to the Department of Homeland Security Publications Web site **(http://www.dhs.gov/ximgtn/statistics/publications)**. Under Annual Flow Reports, select the latest report titled "Legal Permanent Residents" to find information about legal immigrants. Under Annual Population Estimates, select the latest report titled "Estimates of the Unauthorized Immigrant Population Residing in the United States" to find information about illegal immigrants.

For the year shown, from which country did the largest number of legal immigrants come from? From which country is the number of illegal immigrants growing fastest? Offer an explanation for why this country or these countries have such high immigration rates.

Internet Exercise

The U.S. Census Bureau reports internal migration rates for U.S. residents **(http://www.census.gov/population/www/socdemo/migrate.html)**.

Chapter 10

Labor Unions and Collective Bargaining

Experts on etiquette agree that it is unwise to bring up certain topics—politics and religion, for example—in social conversations with new acquaintances. These topics often evoke strong emotions, differing opinions, and the potential for unwanted debate. Unionism is another such topic. A strongly expressed opinion on this subject stated in a social setting may well generate unwanted verbal fireworks.

Opinion, of course, is not fact; nor is opinion always based on sound analysis. In Chapter 6 we examined ways that workers can collectively influence wage rates through unionization. The main objective in this chapter and Chapter 11 is to deepen our understanding of unions, their goals, and their activities. Our approach will be factual and analytical. Thus these two chapters provide useful information that will help you develop an informed opinion about unionism in America.

WHY UNIONS?

Myriad theories have been designed to explain the origins and evolution of labor unions.[1] We will settle for the straightforward historical view that unions are essentially the offspring of industrialization. Most preindustrial workers were self-sufficient, self-employed artisans, craftspeople, or farmers who worked in their own homes and on their own land. These workers were simultaneously employers and employees. Industrialization, however, undermined this system of self-employment and made many workers dependent on factory owners for employment and income. Industrialization also separated the functions of management and labor.

[1] See, for example, Simeon Larson and Bruce Nissen (eds.), *Theories of the Labor Movement* (Detroit Wayne State University Press, 1987). Ray Marshall and Brian Rungeling, *The Role of Unions in the American Economy,* 2nd ed. (New York: Joint Council on Economic Education, 1985), present an excellent elaboration of the theory presented here and a succinct history of the American labor movement.

Although employers may not have purposely mistreated labor, competitive pressures in the product market often forced them to pay meager wages, to work their employees long and hard, to provide minimal on-the-job amenities, and to terminate workers when lagging product demand made them redundant. In short, industrialization forced workers into a position of dependence where their earnings, working conditions, and security were largely beyond their control as individuals. To represent, protect, and enhance their interests, workers formed unions to bargain collectively with employers.

LABOR UNIONISM: FACTS AND FIGURES

Before analyzing the collective bargaining process and its economic implications, it is important that we gain a basic understanding of the scope and character of unionization in the United States. Specifically, let's discuss (1) the distribution of unionized labor by industry, occupation, gender, race, age, and location; (2) the structure of organized labor; and (3) the decline in the relative size of the unionized sector that has occurred over the past several decades.

Who Belongs to Unions?

In 2006 approximately 15.4 million of the 142 million civilian nonagricultural workers belonged to unions. In other words, about 11 percent of American workers were union members. But the likelihood that any given worker will be a union member depends on the occupation and industry with which the worker is associated, personal characteristics (gender, race, and age), and geographic location.

1 Industry and Occupation

Table 10.1 shows the percentage of wage and salary workers who are unionized by industry and occupational classification. Union membership is heavily concentrated in goods-producing industries (mining, construction, and manufacturing) and is relatively low in most service-oriented industries (wholesale and retail trade; finance, insurance, and real estate; and services). The exceptions are the low level of unionization in goods-producing agriculture and the high level in the service-providing transportation, information, and public utilities industries. The high union density in transportation, information, and public utilities partially results because these industries "are typically publicly regulated, highly concentrated within individual labor markets, and capital intensive—all of which lead to low labor demand elasticities, large expected benefits from union representation, and low organizing costs."[2] Also notable is the high level of unionization in public administration, which reflects the facts that almost three-fourths of all postal workers are organized and there has been vigorous growth of public sector unionism at the state and local levels during the past few decades.

[2] Barry T. Hirsch and John T. Addison, *The Economic Analysis of Unions* (Boston: Allen and Unwin, 1986), p. 63.

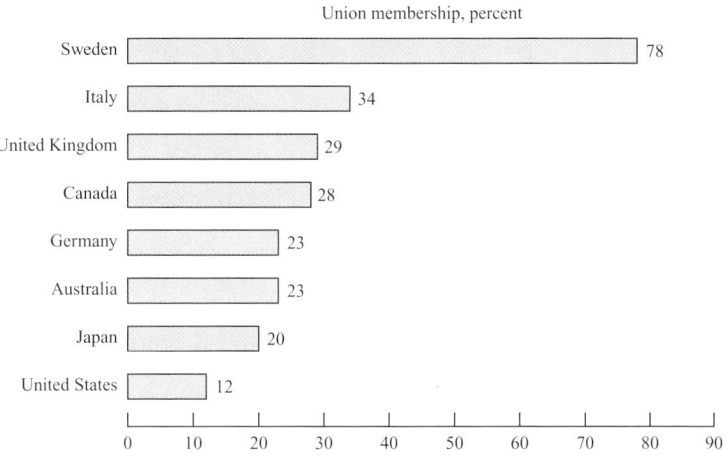

Global Perspective 10.1

Union Membership as a Percentage of Wage and Salary Workers

Union membership varies widely across countries—ranging from 12 percent in the United States to 78 percent in Sweden.

Union membership, percent

Sweden	78
Italy	34
United Kingdom	29
Canada	28
Germany	23
Australia	23
Japan	20
United States	12

Source: Jelle Visser, "Union Membership Statistics in 24 Countries," *Monthly Labor Review,* January 2006, pp. 38–49. Data are for 2003.

Table 10.1 also makes clear that blue-collar workers are much more heavily unionized than white-collar workers. The reasons for this difference include the following: First, some white-collar workers are managers, and under existing labor law, employers are not obligated to bargain with supervisory employees. Second, many white-collar workers identify with management and aspire to move upward from worker to management status. They feel that union membership is "unprofessional" and a potential obstacle to their ambitions. Finally, on the average, white-collar workers enjoy higher wages and better working conditions than blue-collar workers; so the former may feel they have less need for unions.

With some important exceptions, the industrial–occupational pattern of unionization was established by the late 1940s. Industries that were heavily unionized by that time remain so now. Today most workers do *not* become union members by organizing their employers, but rather join a union because they take a job with an already unionized employer.

The previously noted high level of unionization in the public sector merits additional attention. Prior to the 1960s government workers were weakly organized and seemed

TABLE 10.1 **Union Membership by Industry and Occupation**

Source: Barry T. Hirsch and David A. Macpherson, *Union Membership and Earnings Data Book: Compilations from the Current Population Survey (2007 Edition)* (Washington, DC: Bureau of National Affairs, 2007).

Industry	Percentage Union*	Occupation	Percentage Union*
Goods-producing:		**White-collar:**	
Agriculture	3	Professional	18
Mining	8	Managers, business,	
Construction	14	and financial	5
Manufacturing	12	Clerical workers	10
Services-producing:		Sales workers	3
Transportation, information,		**Blue-collar:**	
and public utilities	25	Construction	18
Wholesale and retail trade	5	Installers and	
Finance, insurance, and		repair	16
real estate	3	Production	16
Services	11	Transportation	19
Public administration	31	Service	11

*Percentage of employed wage and salary workers who belong to unions.

destined to remain so because most public sector employment entailed white-collar service jobs *and* a high proportion of government workers were women. Nevertheless, between the mid-1960s and the early 1970s, public sector union membership more than quadrupled, and today we find union density in the public sector to be more than twice as great as for the economy as a whole. This expansion is quite remarkable in view of the fact that private sector unionism has been declining significantly.

What caused this striking spurt of union growth among government workers? Most important, in the 1960s and 1970s a variety of state and local laws were passed that established mechanisms for government employees to vote for or against unionism and required government employers to bargain with unionized workers. Executive orders at the federal level accomplished much the same for federal employees. In short, a new legislative climate gave public sector workers in the 1960s and 1970s the opportunity to join unions—an opportunity private sector workers had enjoyed since the 1930s.

Despite this new legal environment, why did public sector unionism experience such rapid growth while private sector unionism was on the wane? On one hand, a pent-up demand for unionization may have existed that the favorable legal environment simply unleashed. On the other hand, private employers have typically demonstrated considerable resistance to unionization to the extent that they have frequently broken both the spirit and the letter of labor law. In contrast, public sector employers have not fought the unionization of their workers.[3]

[3] This paragraph is based on Richard B. Freeman, "Unionism Comes to the Public Sector," *Journal of Economic Literature,* March 1986, pp. 41–86.

TABLE 10.2
Union Membership by Gender, Race, and Age

Source: Barry T. Hirsch and David A. Macpherson, *Union Membership and Earnings Data Book: Compilations from the Current Population Survey (2007 Edition)* (Washington, DC: Bureau of National Affairs, 2007).

Personal Characteristic	Percentage Union*
Gender:	
Male	13
Female	11
Race:	
White	12
African–American	15
Age:	
Under 25	4
25 and over	13

* Percentage of employed wage and salary workers who belong to

The rapid growth of public sector unionism occurred largely in the 1960–1976 period. Since 1976 there has been little or no growth as membership has leveled off at about 37 percent of all public sector employees. It is probably correct to say that the era of dramatic public sector union growth is now behind us.[4]

2 Personal Characteristics: Gender, Race, and Age

Table 10.2 indicates that personal characteristics are associated with the likelihood of union membership. We observe that men are much more likely than women to be union members. This difference is *not* attributable to any fundamental attitudinal differences based on gender; rather, it occurs because women are disproportionately represented in less unionized industries and occupations. For example, many women are employed in retail sales, food service, and office work, where the levels of unionization are low. Furthermore, women on average have a less permanent attachment than men to the labor force. Thus the present value of the *lifetime* wage gains from unionization will be lower for women than for men, making union membership relatively less attractive to women.[5]

We also see from Table 10.2 that a larger proportion of African–Americans than whites belong to unions. This difference reflects the industrial distribution of workers. Specifically, a disproportionately larger number of African–Americans have blue-collar jobs. Another explanatory factor is that unionization results in larger relative wage gains for African–American workers than for white workers.[6] African–Americans stand to benefit relatively more than whites by belonging to unions.

---

[4] Linda N. Edwards, "The Future of Public Sector Unions: Stagnation or Growth?" *American Economic Review,* May 1989, pp. 161–65.

[5] Two articles addressing the topic of this paragraph are William E. Even and David A. Macpherson, "The Decline of Private-Sector Unionism and the Gender Wage Gap," *Journal of Human Resources,* Spring 1993, pp. 279–96; and Diane S. Sinclair, "The Importance of Sex for the Propensity to Unionize," *British Journal of Industrial Relations,* June 1995, pp. 173–90.

[6] For evidence that African–Americans have a stronger demand for unionization than other groups, see Gregory Defreitas, "Unionization among Racial and Ethnic Minorities," *Industrial and Labor Relations Review,* January 1993, pp. 284–301.

Table 10.2 also reveals that young workers (under 25 years of age) are less likely than older workers to have union cards. Once again, this is largely explainable in terms of the kinds of jobs young workers acquire. Specifically, as we will see momentarily, the traditional blue-collar, goods-producing, unionized sectors of the economy have not been expanding rapidly in recent years and therefore have not been a major source of jobs to youths entering the labor force. Rather, the largely nonunion service sectors have been growing and providing more jobs. Today high school graduates are more likely to take jobs with nonunion fast-food chains; 25 years ago many high school graduates found work in unionized automobile or steel manufacturing plants.

3 Location

To a considerable degree the labor movement in the United States is an urban phenomenon. Six heavily urbanized, heavily industrialized states—New York, California, Pennsylvania, Illinois, Ohio, and Michigan—account for approximately half of all union members.[7] Furthermore, the percentage of workers who are unionized in the South is only about two-thirds that of the rest of the country. This may stem in part from the occupational and industrial makeup of jobs in the South, but it is also claimed that employers and the general populace there simply are more inclined to be antiunion.

Structure of Organized Labor[8]

Figure 10.1 provides a thumbnail sketch of the structure of American labor organizations. There are three major levels of union organizations: the federation, national unions,[9] and local unions.

AFL–CIO

The *American Federation of Labor and Congress of Industrial Organizations,* better known as the *AFL–CIO,* is a loose and voluntary federation of independent and autonomous national unions. We note in Figure 10.1 that 53 national unions with a combined membership of about 8 million workers belonged to the AFL–CIO in 2006, while approximately 64 national unions possessing an aggregate membership of about 3 million were independent of the AFL–CIO. The AFL–CIO does *not* engage in collective bargaining but is the primary political organ of organized labor. The AFL–CIO formulates labor's views on a spectrum of political issues ranging from the minimum wage to foreign

---

[7] Barry T. Hirsch and David A. Macpherson, *Union Membership and Earnings Data Book: Compilations from Current Population Survey (2007 Edition)* (Washington, DC: Bureau of National Affairs, 2007).

[8] The ensuing discussion draws on Marten Estey, *The Unions: Structure, Development and Management,* 3rd ed. (New York: Harcourt Brace Jovanovich, 1981), chap. 3. For a discussion of the labor movement and a detailed consideration of its structure, see John A. Fossum, *Labor Relations: Development, Structure and Process,* 8th ed. (New York: Irwin/McGraw-Hill, 2002), chaps. 2–4.

[9] Some national unions call themselves "international" unions—for example, the International Brotherhood of Electrical Workers (IBEW)—which usually means that there are some affiliated locals in Canada or Puerto Rico.

FIGURE 10.1   The Institutional Organization of American Unionism

Organized labor in the United States consists of the AFL–CIO, Change to Win, and numerous independent unions. The AFL–CIO's basic function is to formulate and promote labor's views on a wide range of economic, social, and political issues. The Change to Win federation is focused on organizing new union members. The national unions generally have responsibility for negotiating collective bargaining agreements, whereas the locals are concerned with administering those agreements.

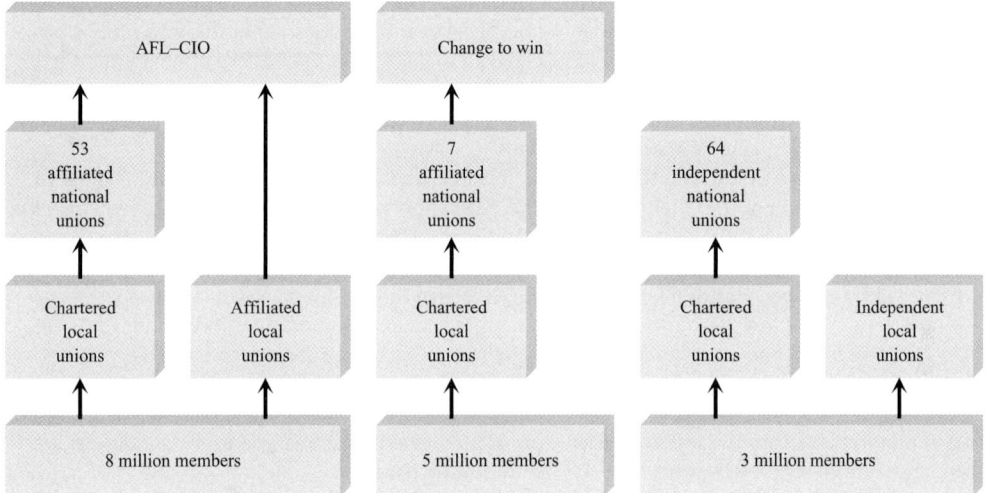

policy, publicizes labor's positions, and engages in political lobbying.[10] The AFL–CIO is also responsible for settling jurisdictional disputes among affiliated national unions; that is, it determines which union has the right to organize a particular group of nonunion workers.

Change to Win

The *Change to Win federation* is a loose federation of seven independent national unions, which was started in 2005. As shown in Figure 10.1, seven national unions, which represent a total of 5 million workers, belong to the Change to Win federation. The federation focuses on organizing new union members.

National Unions

The *national unions* are federations of local unions that are typically in either the same industry ("industrial unions" such as those made up of autoworkers or steelworkers) or the same skilled occupation ("craft unions" such as those representing carpenters and

---

[10] For an analysis of organized labor's effectiveness in the political sphere, see Richard B. Freeman and James L. Medoff, *What Do Unions Do?* (New York: Basic Books, Inc., 1984), chap. 13. See also John T. Delaney, Jack Fiorito, and Paul Jarley, "Evolutionary Politics? Union Differences and Political Activities in the 1990s," *Journal of Labor Research,* Summer 1999, pp. 277–95.

10.1	World of Work	A Divorce in the Union Movement

In 2005 a new labor federation called the Change to Win federation was formed by seven unions that split off from the AFL–CIO. This was a significant blow to the AFL–CIO because these unions represented about 5 million workers—about two-fifths of the total membership in the AFL–CIO. In fact, one of the unions (Service Employees International Union) was the largest union in the AFL–CIO, and another (Teamsters) was the third largest union.

The unions that formed the Change to Win federation felt that the AFL–CIO had not done enough organizing to help reverse the long-term decline in union membership. The federation states that it will devote 75 percent of its resources to organizing new workers. The breakaway unions will focus particularly on organizing immigrants because the unions are in industries with large numbers of immigrants such as restaurants, nursing homes, supermarkets, hotels, and janitorial firms. In addition, they plan to pressure firms to sign neutrality agreements, which state that the firm will recognize a union when a majority of workers sign union authorization cards. This method enables unions to avoid input from firm management, which typically accompanies unionization

elections, about whether to join a union. The federation believes that business opposition to unions has played a major role in the decline of union membership. To increase their leverage, the federation plans to implement this strategy first at partially unionized firms.

It is unclear whether the new informal Change to Win federation will remain a loose confederation or whether it will adopt the formal bureaucracy of the AFL–CIO. The current situation resembles the split of the CIO from the AFL in 1935, which was sparked by disagreement over organizing efforts. After the split, unionization increased rapidly as the CIO mounted extensive and successful organizing campaigns. It remains to be seen whether a similar outcome will occur now when legal and economic conditions are substantially different.

* Based on Steven Greenhouse, "4th Union Quits AFL–CIO in a Dispute over Organizing," *The New York Times*, September 15, 2005; Aaron Bernstein, "Labor's New Face, New Tactics," *BusinessWeek*, September 27, 2005; Steven Greenhouse, "Labor Debates the Future of a Fractured Movement," *The New York Times*, July 27, 2005; and **www.changetowin.org**.

electricians). Table 10.3 lists the largest national unions affiliated with the AFL–CIO. The largest union that is not affiliated with the AFL–CIO is the National Education Association, which has about 3.2 million members.

A national union has two primary functions: (1) organizing the unorganized workers in its craft or industry and (2) negotiating collective bargaining agreements. Responsibility for the latter function, however, may be shared in some cases with local unions, depending on the size of the local and the industry involved. For example, if the relevant product market is local (such as housing construction), the local carpenters, bricklayers, and other craft unions are likely to negotiate their own bargaining contracts. But where the product market is regional or national in scope (for example, textiles or automobiles), contract negotiation is usually performed by the national union rather than its locals. The reasons for this are twofold. Most important, the national union wants to standardize wages—to "take wages out of competition"—so that employers who would pay high union wages would not be penalized by losing sales to other firms paying low

TABLE 10.3
AFL–CIO and Change to Win Affiliated Labor Organizations Reporting 100,000 Members or More (in Thousands)

Source: Barry T. Hirsch and David A. Macpherson, *Union Membership and Earnings Data Book: Compilations from Current Population Survey (2007 Edition)* (Washington, DC: Bureau of National Affairs, 2007); and **www.changetowin.org**.

Labor Organization*	Members
Service Employees (Change to Win)	1,363
State and County Government Workers	1,302
Teamsters (Change to Win)	1,288
Food and Commercial Workers (Change to Win)	1,059
Teachers	1,032
Communication Workers	665
Electrical Workers	630
Aerospace and Autoworkers	624
United Steel Workers	573
Carpenters (Change to Win)	520
Textile, Hotel, and Restaurant Workers (Change to Win)	435
Laborers (Change to Win)	372
Machinists	339
Operating Engineers	280
Postal Workers	233
Firefighters	229
Plumbing and Pipefitting	220
Letter Carriers	210
Government Employees	207
California School Workers	129
Transit Workers	120
Office and Professional Workers	109
Transport Workers	109

*All organizations not identified as Change to Win are affiliated with the AFL–CIO.

union wages. Furthermore, collective bargaining has become very complex and legalistic, requiring skilled negotiators, lawyers, and so forth. Consequently, it is likely that economies of scale are to be gained by relying on national negotiators.

Local Unions

Generally *local unions* are essentially branches or components of the respective national unions. We observe in Figure 10.1, however, that some locals are directly affiliated with the AFL–CIO, and a few are not affiliated with either a national union or the AFL–CIO. The relationship between the locals and the national unions is significantly different from that between the AFL–CIO and the nationals. When they join the federation, the national unions retain their sovereignty and autonomy over their internal affairs. But a local union is usually subservient to its national union. For example, locals are often required to clear a decision to strike with the national before undertaking such action. Furthermore, the national union has the power to suspend or to disband one of its locals.

This is not to downgrade the role of the local union. Locals perform the important functions of administering or policing the bargaining contract and seeking the resolution of worker grievances that may arise in interpreting the contract.

Active, interested, and effective local leadership tends to produce a favorable reaction from the members, and vice versa. In short, the local union *is* the union to the members. Its performance is the basis for many opinions about unions.[11]

Diversity of Bargaining Structures

The term **bargaining structure** refers to *the scope of the employees and employers covered by a collective bargaining agreement;* the bargaining structure tells us who bargains with whom. In the United States a great diversity of bargaining structures exists. The diversity is implicit in Figure 10.1 and in the fact that about 2,000 major collective bargaining contracts (those involving 1,000 or more workers) are currently in force. Thousands of other collective bargaining agreements cover smaller employers.

Many unions negotiate with a single-plant employer. Others bargain on a more centralized basis with multiplant employers. In this case firms with many plants negotiate a "master agreement" with one or more unions, which then applies to workers in all of the firm's plants.[12] Greater centralization is involved in **pattern bargaining,** where the union negotiates a contract with a particular firm in an industry, and this contract—or a slightly modified version—comprises the demands the union seeks to impose on all other employers in that industry. In still other instances, multiemployer bargaining occurs: Employers in a given industry will form an employers' association (for example, the Bituminous Coal Owners Association) and bargain as a group with the union.

Although the determinants of a bargaining structure are manifold and complex,[13] pragmatic considerations and perceived effects on each party's bargaining power are important. For example, where employers are numerous and small and their markets are highly localized, unions are likely to bargain a citywide agreement with an employers' association. Both employers and the union may see advantages in such a bargaining structure. First, there may be some economies of scale in negotiations; it would be costly for the union to have to negotiate separate agreements with a larger number of employers. Second, employers may feel that they can enhance their bargaining power by negotiating as a group rather than individually. Finally—and perhaps most important— by standardizing wage rates through a citywide agreement, each employer avoids the risk of incurring a competitive disadvantage vis-à-vis other firms because of higher wage costs. Similarly, the union "takes wages out of competition" and avoids the problem of job loss in higher-wage union firms.[14] Thus in building construction, hotels and motels, retail trade, and local trucking, citywide agreements are quite common. Regional multiemployer bargaining has also been practiced in trucking, bituminous coal, and the basic steel industry, among others.

---

[11] Estey, op. cit., pp. 50–51.

[12] The master agreement is often supplemented by a local agreement that addresses issues and conditions unique to particular plants.

[13] For a systematic discussion of the determination of bargaining structure, see Harry C. Katz and Thomas A. Kochan, *Introduction to Collective Bargaining and Industrial Relations,* 3rd ed. (New York: Irwin/McGraw-Hill, 2004), chap. 7.

[14] By lessening the ability of consumers to substitute nonunion products for union products, increased union coverage in an industry will lower the elasticity of demand for the products sold by the unionized firms. We know from Chapter 5 that reduced elasticity of product demand reduces the elasticity of labor demand, enabling the union to increase wage rates without experiencing large losses of employment.

Single-company bargaining is common in many basic manufacturing industries where large oligopolistic corporations feel sufficiently strong to "go it alone" in negotiating with the union. But frequently the negotiation of a contract with one firm will establish a pattern for other firms in the same industry. The automobile industry is the most publicized example of pattern bargaining. When contracts terminate every three years, the United Auto Workers selects one of the "Big Three" manufacturers for contract renegotiation. The negotiated contract serves as the standard for dealing with the other automakers. This bargaining structure is advantageous to the union because lost wages during a possible strike will be less if only one firm is struck rather than the entire industry. Furthermore, the firm experiencing the work stoppage will lose sales to its nonstruck competitors, creating pressure on the former to accept the union's demands. The basic point is that there is no such thing as a typical bargaining structure in the United States.

10.1 *Quick* *Review*	• Unions are a by-product of industrialization, through which workers' earnings, working conditions, and security became dependent on decisions of business owners. Unions arose to represent, protect, and enhance the interests of workers. • In 2006 approximately 15.4 million of the 142 million members of the American nonagricultural workforce belonged to unions. • Unionization varies greatly by industry, occupation, gender, race, age, and location. • Organized labor in the United States consists of the AFL–CIO (a federation of 53 affiliated national unions), Change to Win (a federation of seven affiliated national unions), and about 64 independent national unions. **Your Turn** Based on national statistics, who would most likely be a union member: Susan, a white female, age 23, who is a sales worker in Iowa, or Isaiah, an African–American male, age 53, who is a transportation worker in Ohio? (*Answer:* See page 598.)

UNIONISM'S DECLINE

We have just noted that some 15.4 million workers—about 11 percent of civilian nonagricultural workers—belonged to unions in 2006. Figure 10.2 provides a historical overview of trends in union membership. Two points stand out. First, the unionized sector is clearly the minority component of the labor force. Union membership has never exceeded 34 percent of the total labor force. The United States, incidentally, is relatively nonunion compared to most other industrially advanced Western economies. For example, estimates indicate that 78 percent of all wage and salary workers are organized in Sweden. Comparable figures for Australia, Canada, and Japan are 23, 28, and 20 percent, respectively.

The second point is that unionism in the United States is on the decline. In the mid-1940s the percentage of workers belonging to a labor union peaked at 34 percent. The

FIGURE 10.2 **Union Membership in the U.S. among Nonagricultural Workers**
The rate of U.S. union membership has never exceeded 34 percent of the total labor force. It has been declining since the mid-1940s.

Source: Richard B. Freeman, "Spurts in Union Growth: Defining Moments and Social Processes," in Michael Bordo, Claudia Goldin, and Eugene White (eds.), *The Defining Moment: The Great Depression and the American Economy in the Twentieth Century* (Chicago, IL: University of Chicago Press, 1998); and Barry T. Hirsch and David A. Macpherson, *Union Membership and Earnings Data Book: Compilations from the Current Population Survey (2007 Edition)* (Washington, DC: Bureau of National Affairs, 2007).

unionized proportion of the workforce has been steadily falling since then.[15] This decline resulted from union membership's failing to grow as fast as the labor force. Since 1980 the *absolute* number of active union members has also been falling.

Why has this happened? A variety of explanations have been put forth. We will examine the three most widely discussed hypotheses and briefly note several other potential contributors to the wane of unionism.[16]

The Structural Change Hypothesis

The most publicized view, the *structural change hypothesis,* is that a variety of structural changes occurring both in our economy and in the labor force have been unfavorable to the expansion of union membership. This view embraces a number of interrelated observations.

[15] Though the overall rate of union membership has been falling, it was rising in the public sector during this period.
[16] The reader who seeks more detail about this topic should consult Henry S. Farber and Alan B. Krueger, "Union Membership in the United States: The Decline Continues," in Bruce E. Kaufman and Morris M. Kleiner (eds.), *Employee Representation: Alternatives and Future Directions* (Madison, WI: Industrial Relations Research Association, 1993), pp. 105–34; Keith A. Bender, "The Changing Determinants of U.S. Unionism: An Analysis Using Worker-Level Data," *Journal of Labor Research,* Summer 1997, pp. 403–23; and "Symposium on the Future of Private Sector Unions in the United States: Part 1," *Journal of Labor Research,* Spring 2001, pp. 226–354.

First, consumer demand and therefore employment patterns have shifted away from traditional union strongholds. Generally speaking, domestic output has been shifting away from blue-collar manufactured goods (where unions have been strong) to white-collar services (where unions have been weak). This change in the mix of industrial output may be reinforced by increased competition from imports in highly unionized sectors such as automobiles and steel. Growing import competition in these industries has curtailed domestic employment and therefore union membership. As our economy has become increasingly open to low–labor-cost foreign competition, American unionized firms have found themselves at a serious competitive disadvantage.

Second, a disproportionate share of employment growth in recent years has been provided by small firms, which are less likely to be unionized than large firms.

Third, an unusually large proportion of the increase in employment in recent years has been concentrated among women, youths, and part-time workers—groups that have allegedly been difficult to organize because of their less firm attachment to the labor force.

Fourth, spurred by rising energy costs, the long-run trend for industry to shift from the Northeast and the Midwest where unionism is a "way of life" to "hard-to-organize" areas of the South and Southwest may have impeded the expansion of union membership.

A final and ironic possibility is that the relative decline of unionism may in part reflect the greater success unions apparently have had in gaining a wage advantage over nonunion workers. As we will find in the next chapter, there is evidence suggesting that on the average union workers in the 1970s realized an enlarged wage advantage over their nonunion counterparts. Confronted with a growing wage cost disadvantage vis-à-vis nonunion employers, we would expect union employers to accelerate the substitution of capital for labor, subcontract more work to nonunion suppliers, open nonunion plants in less industrialized areas, or have components produced in low-wage nations. These actions reduce the growth of employment opportunities in the union sector as compared to the nonunion sector. Perhaps more important, we would also expect output and employment in lower-cost nonunion firms and industries to increase at the expense of output and employment in higher-cost union firms and industries. In short, union success in raising wages may have changed the composition of industry to the disadvantage of union employment and membership.[17]

Several potential flaws in the structural change hypothesis have been noted.[18] First, other advanced capitalistic countries have experienced structural changes similar to those that have occurred in the United States, and their labor movements continue to grow both absolutely and relatively. Canada is perhaps the most relevant example. Second, historically union growth has been realized in good measure by the unionization of

---

[17] For a discussion and empirical evidence on this point, see Peter D. Linneman, Michael L. Wachter, and William H. Carter, "Evaluating the Evidence on Union Employment and Wages," *Industrial and Labor Relations Review,* October 1990, pp. 34–53; and David G. Blachflower and Richard B. Freeman, "Unionism in the United States and Other Advanced OECD Countries," *Industrial Relations,* Winter 1992, pp. 56–79.

[18] Freeman and Medoff, op. cit., chap. 15.

groups of workers who were once regarded as traditionally nonunion. The unionization of blue-collar workers in the mass-production industries such as automobiles and steel in the 1930s and the organizing of public sector workers more recently are cases in point. Given this history, why can't women workers, young workers, immigrants, and southern workers be brought into the labor movement to spur its continued growth? Finally, surveys indicate that young and female workers—who, we found in Table 10.2, are now less unionized—are in fact as much, or more, prounion as more heavily unionized older and male workers. Yet unions are losing an increasing proportion of National Labor Relations Board (NLRB) elections when workers vote to determine whether they want to be unionized.

Managerial Opposition Hypothesis

Such criticisms have led Freeman and Medoff to question the adequacy of the structural change explanation, arguing that intensified *managerial opposition* to unions has also been a major deterrent to union growth. Freeman and Medoff contend that beginning in the 1970s unions have increased the union wage advantage they enjoy vis-à-vis nonunion workers (Chapter 11), and as a result, union firms have become less profitable than nonunion firms.[19] As a reaction, managerial opposition to unions has crystallized and become more aggressive. This opposition takes a variety of forms, both legal and illegal. Legal antiunion tactics include written and verbal communications with workers indicating that unionism will create an adversarial relationship between labor and management that will be generally detrimental to workers. Similarly, management may suggest that with unionization, strikes will be frequent and costly to workers. Also, as explained in "World of Work" 10.2, firms may hire permanent strikebreakers to replace striking workers. Or management may use various tactics to delay the NLRB union certification election, reasoning correctly that an extension of the election period tends to reduce worker enthusiasm for unionization. It is increasingly common for employers to hire labor–management consultants who specialize in mounting aggressive antiunion drives to dissuade workers from unionizing or, alternatively, to persuade union workers to decertify their union.[20]

Freeman and Medoff contend that the use of illegal antiunion tactics has risen dramatically. In particular, they argue that it has become increasingly common for management to identify and dismiss leading pro-union workers, even though this is prohibited by the Wagner Act. The increasing popularity of this tactic stems from the fact that

---

[19]Although substantial union wage differentials (Chapter 11) induce workers to join unions, the same union wage differentials reduce profits and increase managerial opposition to unionization. Freeman contends that the latter effect outweighs the former and that "as much as one-quarter of the decline in the proportion [of workers] organized through NLRB elections may be attributed to the increased union wage premium of the 1970s and its adverse effects on firm profitability which raised management opposition." See Richard B. Freeman, "The Effect of the Union Wage Differential on Management Opposition and Union Organizing Success," *American Economic Review,* May 1986, pp. 92–96.

[20] An organization called Executive Enterprises Institute claims that 80 percent of the *Fortune* 500 companies send representatives to attend its seminars such as "How to Stay Union Free in the 21st Century."

10.2 World of Work

Should the Right to Hire Permanent Strikebreakers Be Rescinded?

Managerial opposition to unions has increasingly taken the form of threats to hire permanent strikebreakers or the actual employment of such workers. For example, in 1997 the *Detroit News* and *Detroit Free Press* broke a bitter 19-month strike during which the newspapers hired permanent replacements for the striking workers. After the strike ended, the strikers were able to work only as job openings became available.

Earlier, Phelps Dodge, the *Chicago Tribune*, Hormel, Continental Airlines, International Paper, Greyhound, and several other major firms had hired permanent replacements for their striking workers. A few of these firms allegedly "baited" their unions into striking by demanding large, unacceptable wage concessions. The firms then replaced the striking workers with new, permanent employees.

Unions have vigorously sought to change labor relations law to counter these business tactics. In 1992 the U.S. House of Representatives passed legislation banning firms from hiring permanent strikebreakers, but the legislation failed in the Senate. In 1995 President Clinton signed an executive order barring large federal contractors from hiring strikebreaking replacement workers. A year later, his executive order was overturned by a federal appeals court. Despite the efforts of unions, a prohibition on permanent replacement workers remains elusive.

Proponents of the ban on hiring permanent strikebreakers argue that hiring such replacements is akin to firing striking workers. Firing these workers is expressly prohibited under current labor laws;

permanently replacing them is not. Unions and firms must legally bargain with each other in "good faith." But as noted by one commentator, "You can't bargain with a striker whose job is no more." Proponents also note that Japan, Germany, and other key trading competitors bar firms from hiring permanent replacements.

Opponents to the legislation counter by saying that a prohibition on hiring permanent replacement strikebreakers will mean that unions with exorbitant demands could force firms either into bankruptcy or out of the country. They say the possibility of being permanently replaced is simply one of the risks that workers should consider in voting to strike. Also, say opponents, the fact that some corporations can find thousands of qualified permanent replacements reveals the unreasonableness of many union demands.

According to Singh and Jain, the empirical evidence regarding the effects of a ban on hiring permanent replacement workers is somewhat mixed.* On one hand, studies clearly indicate such a ban would shorten strikes, decrease picket line violence, and lower union decertifications. On the other hand, there is inconclusive evidence regarding the effect of a legal prohibition of replacement workers on the number of strikes, wages, and employment.

* Parbudyal Singh and Harish C. Jain, "Striker Replacements in the United States, Canada, and Mexico: A Review of the Law and Empirical Research," *Industrial Relations*, January 2001, pp. 22–53.

when proven guilty, the employers receive only light penalties. Given these antiunion strategies, the labor movement has gone into relative eclipse.

Freeman cites 13 studies of the impact of management antiunion activities on the outcomes of union organizational drives and representation elections. He observes that in 12 of the 13 studies such management activity was found to be effective. He concludes that managerial opposition is critical in determining the success or failure of union organizational campaigns and is a major factor in explaining the deunionization of the American economy.[21]

The Substitution Hypothesis

The *substitution hypothesis* is the notion that other institutions—specifically government and employers—have come to provide the services, benefits, and employment conditions that were historically available to workers only through unionization. This substitution of employer- and government-provided services to workers has allegedly reduced the need for and attractiveness of union membership. Thus Neumann and Rissman note that many of today's public programs that relate to the labor market—such as unemployment insurance, workers' compensation, Social Security, and health and safety laws—were once important goals of labor unions. Their empirical analysis leads them to conclude that historically government has been responsible for providing more and more "unionlike" services, and this has simply lessened the need for workers to join unions.[22]

Similarly, some employers have attempted to install "progressive" labor policies to usurp worker demand for union representation. Such employers establish two-way communication channels with workers, provide for orderly handling of worker grievances, create worker participation schemes, offer seniority protection, pay attractive wages and fringe benefits, and so forth. By averting the major source of pro-union sentiments—job dissatisfaction—employers remain union-free. Here employers are substituting their own benefits for those ordinarily sought through unions and thereby beat unions at their own game.

Examining data on worker attitudes toward unions, Farber observes that workers who are satisfied with their jobs are much less likely to vote for union representation than are dissatisfied workers. His data indicate that the reported levels of satisfaction of nonunion workers with their pay and job security rose dramatically over the 1977–1984 period he examined. Furthermore, nonunion workers' perception of the effectiveness of unions in improving wages and working conditions has diminished. Farber's conclusion is that there has been a significant decline in the demand for union representation among nonunion workers that is independent of structural changes in the labor force and in industry.[23] Farber further supports his view with additional evidence in a controversial paper co-authored with Krueger.[24] The two find that virtually all of the decline in union membership between 1977 and 1991 was caused by a decline in worker demand for union representation, as compared to a decline in the availability of traditionally unionized jobs.

[21] Richard B. Freeman, "Contraction and Expansion: The Divergence of Private Sector and Public Unionism in the United States," *Journal of Economic Perspectives,* Spring 1988, pp. 82–83; and Richard B. Freeman and Morris M. Kleiner, "Employer Behavior in the Face of Union Organizing Drives," *Industrial and Labor Relations Review,* April 1990, pp. 351–65.

[22] George R. Neumann and Ellen R. Rissman, "Where Have All the Union Members Gone?" *Journal of Labor Economics,* April 1984, pp. 175–92. From their empirical work, Neumann and Rissman find that about half of the decrease in union membership that has occurred since 1956 is explainable in terms of changes in the structure of industry.

[23] Henry S. Farber, "Trends in Worker Demand for Union Representation," *American Economic Review,* May 1989, pp. 166–71.

[24] Henry S. Farber and Alan B. Krueger, "Union Membership in the United States: The Decline Continues," in Bruce E. Kaufman and Morris M. Kleiner (eds.), *Employee Representation: Alternatives and Future Directions* (Madison, WI: Industrial Relations Research Association, 1993), pp. 105–34.

Other Factors

Our three hypotheses do not exhaust the factors that might be contributing to the decline of unionism. For example, evidence suggests that union efforts to organize the unorganized have been insufficient.[25] It has also been argued that the basic values of American society, which stress the free market and competitive individualism, do not provide a fertile environment for a strong labor movement.[26] Finally, the public policy environment became increasingly promanagement during the Reagan–Bush era. In particular, NLRB rulings became increasingly antilabor, creating an administrative and legal environment hostile to union growth.

Relative Importance

Interesting attempts have been made to quantify the significance of the various factors that may have contributed to unionism's decline. How important are structural changes—as compared to, say, enhanced managerial opposition or a diminished effort by unions to organize workers—in explaining the labor movement's eclipse? Although quantification is difficult and estimates must be treated with some caution, some reasonable measures are available. For example, Farber has confirmed that structural changes in the economy have been of some significance. He estimates that about 40 percent of the decline in organized labor's relative share of the labor force over the 1956–1978 period resulted from shifts toward more workers in nonmanufacturing jobs, more white-collar workers, more female workers, and the South.[27]

Similarly, Farber and Western conclude that most of the decline in private sector union membership over the 1973–1998 period was due to a greater employment growth rate in the nonunion sector than the union sector.[28] They also find the fall in union organizing activity over the period accounted for only a small part of the decline in unionism. In fact, they report that even if the organizing rate had been *five* times the current rate, the unionization rate would have still fallen between 1973 and 1985 and stabilized since then at about 18 percent.

Freeman[29] has studied the declining success of unions in winning NLRB (Chapter 13) certification elections and estimates that over one-fourth to almost one-half of the decline in union success in organizing workers through NLRB elections is attributable

[25] Paula B. Voos, "Union Organizing: Costs and Benefits," *Industrial and Labor Relations Review,* July 1983, pp. 576–91; and Gary N. Chaison and Dileep G. Dahvale, "A Note on the Severity of the Decline in Union Organizing Activity," *Industrial and Labor Relations Review,* April 1990, pp. 366–73.

[26] See Seymour Martin Lipset, "North American Labor Movements: A Comparative Perspective," in Seymour Martin Lipset (ed.), *Unions in Transition* (San Francisco: ICS Press, 1986), pp. 421–52.

[27] Henry S. Farber, "The Extent of Unionization in the United States," in Thomas A. Kochan (ed.), *Challenges and Choices Facing American Labor* (Cambridge, MA: MIT Press, 1985), pp. 15–43. For a study reaching a similar conclusion, see C. Timothy Koeller, "Union Activity and the Decline in American Trade Union Membership," *Journal of Labor Research,* Winter 1994, pp. 19–32.

[28] Henry S. Farber and Bruce Western, "Accounting for the Decline of Unions in the Private Sector, 1973–1998," *Journal of Labor Research,* Summer 2001, pp. 459–85.

[29] Richard B. Freeman, "Why Are Unions Faring Poorly in NLRB Representation Elections?" in Thomas A. Kochan (ed.), *Challenges and Choices Facing American Labor* (Cambridge, MA: MIT Press, 1985), pp. 45–64.

to managerial opposition. Freeman's overall rough assessment is that about 40 percent of the total decline in unionism is attributable to increased managerial opposition; another 20 percent is the result of reduced efforts by unions to organize nonunion workers; and the remaining 40 percent is due to structural changes in the economy and unknown forces.

Union Responses

How have unions reacted to their declines?

Mergers

A basic response of unions to the relative decline of organized labor has been for unions with similar jurisdictions to merge with one another. Of the more than 136 labor organization mergers that have occurred since the AFL and CIO combined in 1955, about 30 percent took place between 1985 and 1994. While it is true that trade union ideology stresses unity, practical considerations have clearly been paramount in recent mergers. Shrinking membership, declining income from dues, and the desire to achieve a strong and united voice in collective bargaining negotiations have all contributed to the recent impetus for mergers.[30]

Changes in Strategies

Another response by unions to declining membership has been changes in union organizing and negotiation strategies.

Unions have increased their efforts to train union organizers and have attempted to define bargaining demands that appeal to white-collar professionals and to an increasingly female labor force (Chapter 3). For example, some unions are giving a lower priority to wages and working conditions and putting more emphasis on such objectives as parental leave, child care, and flexible work schedules. Many unions have formulated positions on issues such as worker drug testing and AIDS protection that are of concern to potential members. Moreover, unions have begun to offer several nontraditional services, such as low-interest credit cards and job counseling, to both union and nonunion members. The idea is to create union allegiance and associate membership even though a worker may not presently hold a job in a union bargaining unit.

On the negotiation front, unions increasingly have chosen to avoid strikes, which employers frequently countered by hiring permanent strikebreakers who later voted to decertify the union. One alternative to the strike that has gained prominence and some success is the union-sponsored *work slowdown* or "working sitdown." Rather than proceeding with their work as usual, union members "go by the book," which implies working to the very minimum of their job requirements. The decline in production reduces the firm's profitability, much as a strike would; but the employees do not lose their pay or risk replacement by strikebreakers. The goal is to convince management that it is in the firm's interest to negotiate seriously with the union.

10.3

---

[30] Lisa Williamson, "Union Mergers, 1985–1994 Update," *Monthly Labor Review,* February 1995, pp. 18–24.

10.3 World of Work

Will the Internet Help Revive Unions?*

Use of the Internet has exploded over the past decade. More than 70 percent of Americans have used the Internet, and the proportion is still growing. The adoption rate for the Internet is one of the fastest ever for a new technology—similar to that of television in the 1950s.

Wayne Diamond and Richard Freeman argue that increased Internet use will help unions prosper in a variety of ways. The Internet allows unions to provide more personalized service to their members. It can connect the union to its members through online meetings, chat rooms, and e-mail messages. In addition, artificial intelligence programs can provide expert answers to workers' questions about labor laws and work-related issues.

The Internet will create new opportunities for organizing workers. The Web allows workers to read information about the union without fear of retaliation by management and to do so at their convenience. A potentially more dramatic change would be the development of virtual local unions, which are unions that represent a minority of workers and are not formally recognized by the company. An example of such a virtual union is Alliance@IBM (**http://www.allianceibm.org**), which is associated with the Communication Workers of America. Though Alliance@IBM has only a few IBM workers as voting members, it has a larger number of "subscribers" to its e-mail messages and visitors to its Web site. Its Web site provides discussion groups, information about issues at IBM, and relevant links.

Unions may become more democratic and accountable to their members because of the Internet. Web sites can provide information about union policies to all members, not just the few who attend meetings, and the opportunity to debate these policies. In addition, the Internet makes it easier for dissident members, such as Teamsters for a Democratic Union (**http://www.tdu.org**), to readily communicate their views to other union members.

The Internet is altering labor disputes. The Internet allows a union to provide its members and the public its views regarding bargaining issues at low cost. Some unions have used the Web to organize wider protests such as boycotts to help members in a specific location. In addition, aggressive unions have organized "cyber-picketing": overloading a firm's Web site with e-mail protest messages or requests for services.

* Based on Wayne J. Diamond and Richard B. Freeman, "Will Unionism Prosper in Cyberspace? The Promise of the Internet for Employee Organization," *British Journal of Industrial Relations,* September 2002, pp. 569–96.

10.2 Quick Review

- Union membership as a percentage of the labor force has fallen steadily over recent decades; also, the absolute number of union members is lower today than in 1980.

- Three hypotheses—perhaps complementary—have been offered to explain the decline in unionism: *(a)* structural changes in industry composition and location, *(b)* renewed managerial opposition to unions, and *(c)* substitution by government and employers of services formerly provided by unions.

- Unions have responded to their decline by merging and developing creative strategies to serve members' needs.

> **Your Turn**
>
> Which of the following would most likely *increase* union membership as a percentage of the labor force: *(a)* the movement of manufacturing firms from the Northeast to the Southwest, *(b)* a decline in imports, *(c)* expansion of high-technology industries such as computer chips and software, or *(d)* a relative decline in employment in the public sector? (*Answer:* See page 598.)

WHAT DO UNIONS WANT?

With some understanding of the size of the labor movement, the kinds of workers who are most likely to belong to unions, the structure of organized labor, and the possible causes of the relative decline in union membership, let's now turn to the thorny question of union objectives.

Monopoly Union Model

Samuel Gompers, founder of the American Federation of Labor (AFL), is reported to have answered "more, more, more!" when asked what unions wanted. Economists typically believe that the goal of a union is to increase both the wages and employment of its members.[31] As a result, economists usually assume that a union's total utility is positively related to the union wage rate W and the union employment level E. Potential levels of a union's total utility are represented by the union indifference curves I_1, I_2, I_3, and I_4 in Figure 10.3. Each curve shows the combinations of wages and employment at which the union is indifferent. The curves are negatively sloped because if the wage rate increases, the employment level must decrease for total utility to remain constant. The opposite is true for employment increases. The curves are convex to the origin because the union is less willing to trade off additional wages for more employment at low wage levels and is more willing to trade off wages for more employment at high wages. Finally, higher indifference curves (those farther outward from the origin) indicate greater levels of union utility; they represent higher wages *and* greater employment.

Given these indifference curves, what will be the impact of a union on the wage and employment level? Assume that without a union, competitive forces would produce wage rate W_c and employment level Q_c (point c in Figure 10.3). The *monopoly union* model assumes that the union sets the wage rate and the firm determines the level of union employment based on this wage rate. Because the firm is maximizing its profits, it will choose an employment level on its labor demand curve. As a result, the wage and employment combinations available to the union are those on the firm's labor demand curve. In Figure 10.3, the utility-maximizing wage and employment combination for the union is point u, where the union indifference curve I_3 is just tangent to the labor demand curve D_L. The corresponding wage rate is W_u and employment level is Q_u. No other combination of wages and employment provides as much utility to the union as this one. Compared to the nonunion outcome, this combination represents a rise in the wage rate

[31] For a survey of models of union objectives, see Bruce E. Kaufman, "Models of Union Wage Determination: What Have We Learned since Dunlop and Ross?" *Industrial Relations,* January 2002, pp. 110–58.

FIGURE 10.3 **Monopoly Union Model**

In the monopoly union model, the utility-maximizing wage and employment combination for the union is point u, where the union indifference curve I_3 is just tangent to the labor demand curve D_L. The union raises the wage rate from W_c to W_u, the firm decreases employment from Q_c to Q_u, and the union increases its total utility from I_1 to I_3.

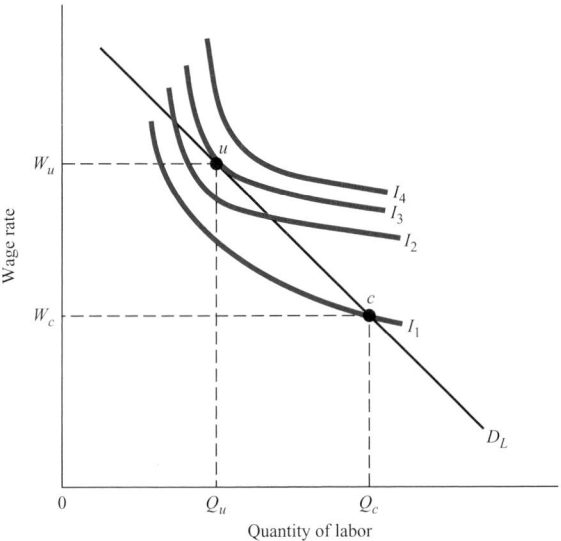

from W_c to W_u, a decrease in employment from Q_c to Q_u, and an increase in the union's total utility from I_1 to I_3.

Efficient Contracts Model

Economists have pointed out that the wage and employment combination under monopoly unionism is not efficient for the two parties. A contract is not efficient if some other wage and employment combination can make at least one party better off without making the other party worse off. If instead of the union setting the wage rate and the firm determining the employment level, the union and firm bargain over the wage rate and employment, then an efficient outcome can occur. The combinations of wage and employment where at least one party can be made better off without the other party being made worse off are called *efficient contracts.* These contracts are efficient in terms of the interests of the two parties. They are not necessarily efficient in terms of the economy's allocation of labor resources.

Figure 10.4 illustrates the efficient contracts model. The figure replicates the union indifference curves I_3 and I_4 and the labor demand curve D_L from Figure 10.3. It also introduces a new family of curves called *isoprofit* curves, π_1, and π_2. The isoprofit curves show combinations of wage rates and employment that yield identical profits from the firm. The maximum profit for a given wage rate is a point on the labor demand curve. Lower isoprofit curves represent *higher* profit levels because wages are lower at each level of employment. Thus a profit-maximizing firm desires to be on the lowest possible isoprofit curve.

Under the monopoly union model, the wage and employment combination would be at point u on the labor demand curve D_L. To see that this outcome is inefficient for the

FIGURE 10.4 Efficient Contracts Model

The outcome of the monopoly union is at point u. This wage (W_u) and employment (Q_u) combination is not efficient for the two parties because at least one of them could be made better off by moving off the labor demand curve. At point x, the union is no worse off than at point u because the union remains on the same indifference curve, but the firm earns higher profits by moving to a lower isoprofit curve. At point y, the union has achieved a higher utility level than at point u by being on a higher indifference curve, and the firm is no worse off because it stays on the same isoprofit curve. The line xy is a contract curve that shows the series of efficient contracts that the union and firm will bargain over.

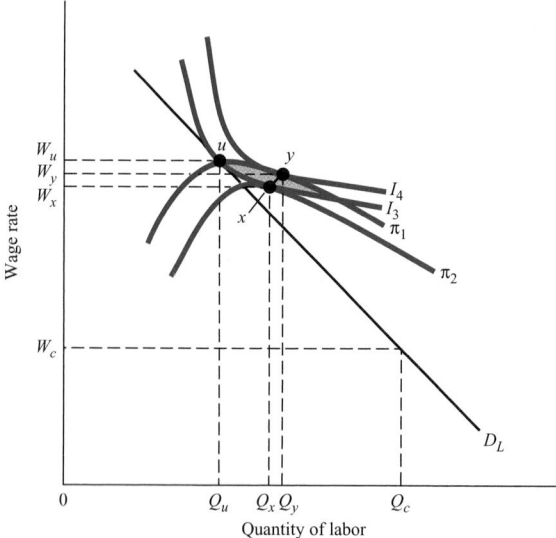

two parties, suppose the firm and the union negotiated a contract that resulted in the wage and employment combination at point x. Compared to the point u result under monopoly unionism, the union is no worse off at point x because it is still on indifference curve I_3; but the firm earns higher profits by being on the lower isoprofit curve π_2 instead of π_1. Alternatively, suppose the negotiated outcome was at point y. Then the union has achieved a higher utility level by being on the higher indifference curve I_4, and the firm is no worse off because it is still on isoprofit curve π_1.

There are a whole set of contracts that the union and firm will find at least as appealing as the monopoly union contract. The shaded area in Figure 10.4 shows these contracts. Among them, the efficient contracts are those where no party can be made better off without making the other party worse off. These efficient wage and employment combinations are those where an isoprofit curve is just tangent to a union indifference curve. The line xy that connects these tangencies between points x and y is called a *contract curve* (or *bargaining curve*).

Although each point on the contract curve xy leaves each party at least as well off as at point u, the parties are not indifferent to where on the curve an agreement is reached. The union would prefer to be closer to point y because it will achieve a higher indifference curve and thus greater total utility. The firm would rather be closer to point x because it gains higher profits (a lower isoprofit curve). The relative bargaining power of the firm and the union will determine where on the contract curve the settlement occurs.

Though the contract curve shown on the line *xy* has a positive slope, the contract curve can be negatively sloped, positively sloped, or vertical. The slope of the contract curve depends on the shapes of the firm's isoprofit curves and the union's indifference curves.

An interesting shape for a potential contract curve is one that is vertical at the competitive employment level. Economists call this type of contract curve a *strongly efficient contract* curve. In this case, the union and firm agree to set the employment at the level that would occur without a union. The total profit level will be maximized at this employment level, and the union and firm bargain over each party's share of the fixed pie of profits. In this context, if the union gets an additional dollar of income though a higher wage, then the firm must get a dollar less of income. The union can raise wages above the competitive level only in industries that earn economic profits. Otherwise the firm would go out of business.

In general, the efficient contract outcome will result in a lower wage and more employment than the monopoly union outcome. Economists have suggested this helps explain the requirements for excess labor in union contracts. These stipulations or "featherbedding" take the form of work rules specifying minimum work crew sizes or narrow job descriptions.

Empirical Evidence

A direct test of the efficient contracts model is whether unions bargain over employment as well as wages. Contrary to the predictions of the efficient contracts model, a survey of the largest U.S. and British labor unions reveals that union contracts almost always allow firms to unilaterally set the employment level.[32] Though unions do not appear to bargain over employment directly, some researchers have suggested they may indirectly affect employment by bargaining over capital–labor ratios.[33] For example, contracts for public school teachers often mandate minimum teacher–student ratios or maximum class sizes. However, this is inconclusive support for the efficient contract model because the firms are allowed to change the level of capital, which would affect the level of employment.

Some studies have attempted indirect tests of the efficient contracts model.[34] These studies rely on the fact that efficient contracts and monopoly union models have different predictions regarding which factors affect the level of union employment. For example, the monopoly union model assumes that the union sets the wage and the firm determines the employment level based on this wage. As a result, the union employment level should be related to the union wage, but it should have no relationship to the competitive wage. The strongly efficient contract model assumes that the level of union employment

[32] Andrew J. Oswald, "Efficient Contracts Are on the Labour Demand Curve: Theory and Facts," *Labour Economics,* June 1993, pp. 85–113.

[33] For example, see George E. Johnson, "Work Rules, Featherbedding, and Pareto–Optimal Union-Management Bargaining," *Journal of Labor Economics,* January 1990, pp. S237–59; and Andrew Clark, "Efficient Bargains and McDonald–Solow Conjecture," *Journal of Labor Economics,* October 1990, pp. 502–28.

[34] For a critical review of these indirect tests, see Alison Booth, *The Economics of Trade Unions* (Cambridge: Cambridge University Press, 1995), pp. 134–41.

is fixed at the level that would occur without a union. Therefore, the union wage should have no effect on the union employment level. Instead the union employment level should be solely determined by the competitive wage.

The findings from these indirect tests yield mixed support for the efficient contracts model. Two studies, using 27 years of data from the printing industry, find that union employment levels are related to the competitive wage rate.[35] This result is consistent with the efficient contracts model. On the other hand, a study using construction data from Sweden finds support for both the monopoly union as well as the efficient contract models.[36] The study's findings vary with the different statistical techniques employed. There is also inconclusive evidence regarding the existence of a vertical contract curve.[37] It is unlikely that a single model can apply to all unions at all points in time.[38]

STRIKES AND THE BARGAINING PROCESS[39]

The threat of a strike is a critical source of bargaining power for a union. A strike imposes costs on both the firm and the union. The firm suffers reduced profits due to the work stoppage, while the union members lose earnings. The party with the greater ability to sustain these costs will have greater bargaining power in contract negotiations. Because the *potential* cost of a strike is large for both the union and firm, nearly all contract negotiations are settled without a strike.

Accident Model

The existence of strikes has been a problem for economists because strikes appear to be an inefficient result of the collective bargaining process. A strike imposes costs, so both the union and the firm could be better off if they agreed to the poststrike settlement before the strike occurred. Thus economists have often viewed strikes as accidents or errors in the negotiating process.

Sir John Hicks developed the most famous *accident model* of strikes.[40] Consider Figure 10.5, which illustrates his model. The Hicks model assumes that the willingness of an employer to make wage concessions rises with the expected length of a strike. The

---

[35] See Thomas E. MaCurdy and John H. Pencavel, "Testing between Competing Models of Wage and Employment Determination in Unionized Markets," *Journal of Political Economy,* June 1986, pp. S3–39; and James N. Brown and Orley Ashenfelter, "Testing the Efficiency of Labor Contracts," *Journal of Political Economy,* June 1986, pp. S40–87. For a study reporting a similar finding, see David Card, "The Efficient Contracts with Costly Adjustment: Short-Run Employment Determination for Airline Mechanics," *American Economic Review,* December 1986, pp. 1045–71.

[36] Thomas Aronsson, Karl-Gustaf Lofgren, and Magnus Wikstrom, "Monopoly Union and Efficient Bargaining: Wage and Employment Determination in the Swedish Construction Sector," *European Journal of Political Economy,* August 1993, pp. 357–70.

[37] For an analysis finding evidence of a strong efficient contract curve, see John M. Abowd, "The Effect of Wage Bargains on the Stock Market Value of the Firm," *American Economic Review,* September 1989, pp. 774–800. For contrary evidence, see MaCurdy and Pencavel, op. cit.

[38] MaCurdy and Pencavel, ibid.

[39] This section draws on Hirsch and Addison, op. cit., chap. 4.

[40] John R. Hicks, *The Theory of Wages,* 2nd ed. (New York: Macmillan, 1963).

FIGURE 10.5   Accident Model

The employer concession curve EC shows the *maximum* wage that the firm would be willing to pay to avoid a strike of a given length. The union resistance curve UR shows the *minimum* wage that a union would be willing to accept to avoid a strike of a given length. If both the union and firm are well informed about the other party's concession curve, the wage settlement will occur at W* where the EC and UR curves intersect, and no strike will occur. If either party misperceives the other party's concession curve, a strike will occur.

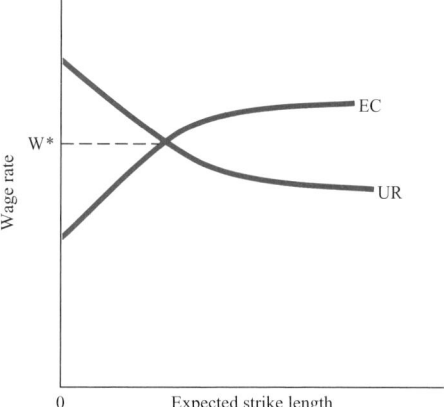

employer concession curve EC shows the *maximum* wage the firm would be willing to pay to avoid a strike of a given length. On the other hand, the model assumes the wage demands of the union fall with the expected length of a strike. The union resistance curve UR shows the *minimum* wage a union would be willing to accept to avoid a strike of a given length. If both the union and firm are well informed about the other party's concession curve, the wage settlement will occur at W* where the EC and UR curves intersect, and no strike will occur.

The shape and position of the firm concession and union resistance curves will determine the wage settlement and the expected strike length. A higher or flatter UR curve, which indicates greater union resistance, will increase both the wage settlement and the expected strike length. Union resistance is likely to be greater when the expected costs of a strike for a union are lower. For example, if a strong labor market enables union members to be temporarily employed elsewhere or striking union members can obtain unemployment benefits, their wage demands are likely to be greater. A lower or flatter EC curve, which indicates greater employer resistance, will lower the wage settlement and increase the expected strike length. Employer resistance will be greater when the demand for union labor is elastic. Elasticity of union labor will be greater when it is easy to substitute away from union labor in the production process, product demand is more elastic, and union labor costs are a large share of total production costs.

Why do strikes occur according to the accident model? They are the result of one or both parties misperceiving the shape or position of the other party's concession curve. Incorrect perceptions of the concession curves will result in disagreement about the expected final wage settlement as well as the expected strike length. For example, if the union perceives that employer resistance will be weaker than it actually is (that is, perceives the EC curve as higher or steeper than the actual one), the union would expect a higher wage than the firm expects to be settled after a strike. This disagreement will cause a strike to occur.

The accident model makes two predictions about when strikes should be more likely. First, they should be more likely when uncertainty is greater about the other party's concession curves.[41] Second, they should be less likely when the *joint* costs of a strike are greater.[42] The distribution of strike costs, which depends on the shape of the concession curves, will determine the wage settlement. However, the distribution of strike costs will not affect the probability of a strike.

Asymmetric Information Models

More recently, two types of strike models based on *asymmetric information* have been developed. The first model type focuses on the information differences between the union leadership and rank-and-file union members.[43] Union leaders are assumed to have a better understanding of the bargaining possibilities than are rank-and-file union members. The union members are assumed to have unrealistic wage demands. Because the union leaders don't want to risk losing their positions by signing a contract with a wage increase less than the rank-and-file members expect, the union leaders may call for a strike. As the strike goes on, the members decrease their wage demands until they match what the firm is willing to offer. The union leadership protects its image of doing all it can to achieve the members' goals. There is some evidence consistent with this conjecture because strikes rose after passage of the Landrum–Griffin Act, which increased union democracy.[44]

The second type of strike model emphasizes the information differences between the union and the firm.[45] This model assumes that the firm has more information about the

---

[41] The empirical evidence indicates that strikes occur because of mistakes. For example, one study indicates that the length and probability of a strike decline as the experience level of bargainers rises. See Edward Montgomery and Mary Ellen Benedict, "The Impact of Bargainer Experience on Teacher Strikes," *Industrial and Labor Relations Review,* April 1989, pp. 380–92. See also Martin J. Mauro, "Strikes as a Result of Imperfect Information," *Industrial and Labor Relations Review,* July 1982, pp. 522–38; and John F. Schnell and Cynthia L. Gramm, "Learning by Striking: Estimates of the Teetotaler Effect," *Journal of Labor Economics,* April 1987, pp. 221–41.

[42] For evidence showing that strikes are less likely when joint costs of a strike are higher, see Melvin W. Reder and George R. Neumann, "Conflict and Contract: The Case of Strikes," *Journal of Political Economy,* October 1980, pp. 867–86; and Barry Sopher, "Bargaining and the Joint Cost Theory of Strikes: An Experimental Study," *Journal of Labor Economics,* January 1990, pp. 48–74.

[43] For a discussion of this model, see Orley Ashenfelter and George Johnson, "Bargaining Theory, Trade Unions, and Industrial Strike Activity," *American Economic Review,* March 1969, pp. 35–49.

[44] Ashenfelter and Johnson, ibid.

[45] For example, see Beth Hayes, "Unions and Strikes with Asymmetric Information," *Journal of Labor Economics,* January 1984, pp. 57–82; and Oliver D. Hart, "Bargaining and Strikes," *Quarterly Journal of Economics,* February 1989, pp. 25–44.

current and future profitability of the firm than the union. The firm has an incentive to understate the profitability of the firm because it can reduce the wage settlement by doing so. In this case, the optimal strategy for a union is to make a wage demand that would be accepted if the profits are high but rejected if they are low. The firm's willingness to accept a costly strike reveals to the union that profits are indeed low. The union lowers its wage demand as the strike progresses.

This asymmetric information model has two implications about strike activity. First, it implies that strikes should be more likely and longer when there is more uncertainty about a firm's profitability. Consistent with this hypothesis, Tracy finds that strikes are more likely and longer when a firm's profitability is more variable over time.[46] Second, the model predicts that the wage settlement will be lower if a contract is signed after a strike than if it is agreed to without a strike. The empirical evidence is consistent with this prediction: Both Canadian and U.S. bargaining data reveal that wage settlements were lower when contracts were signed after strikes.[47]

10.3 *Quick* *Review*	• The monopoly union model assumes that the union sets the wage rate and the firm determines the level of union employment based on this wage rate. Compared to the nonunion outcome, the wage rate will be higher and the employment level will be lower. • The efficient contracts model assumes that the union and firm bargain over the wage rate and employment. In general, the efficient contracts outcome will result in lower wages and more employment than the monopoly union outcome. • In the accident strike model, strikes occur because one or both parties misperceive the willingness of the other party to concede. • Asymmetric information strike models imply that strikes occur because of information differences either between union leaders and the rank-and-file union members or between the union and the firm. **Your Turn** What is likely to happen to the probability of a strike occurring as the number of years that the firm and union are bargaining with each other rises? Explain. (*Answer:* See page 598.)

---

[46] See Joseph S. Tracy, "An Empirical Test of an Asymmetric Information of Strikes," *Journal of Labor Economics,* April 1987, pp. 149–73.

[47] Sheena McConnell, "Strikes, Wages, and Private Information," *American Economic Review,* September 1989, pp. 801–15; and David Card, "Strikes and Wages: A Test of the Asymmetric Information Model," *Quarterly Journal of Economics,* August 1990, pp. 625–59.

Chapter Summary

1. Unions are in part the consequence of industrialization, which changed the economy from one dominated by self-employment to one where labor depends on management for employment and earnings.

2. Approximately 15.4 million workers—about one worker in nine—belong to a labor union. Membership is relatively strong in goods-producing industries and weak in service-providing industries. Unionization is also relatively strong in the public sector.

3. Male, older, and African–American workers are more likely to belong to unions than female, young, and white workers. These differences are largely explained by the industrial and occupational affiliations of these demographic groups.

4. Labor unions are strongest in the heavily urbanized, heavily industrialized states and are relatively weak in the South.

5. The structure of the labor movements reveals three basic levels of union organization. The American Federation of Labor and Congress of Industrial Organizations (AFL–CIO) is concerned with formulating and expressing labor's political views and resolving jurisdictional disputes among national unions. The Change to Win federation focuses on organizing unorganized workers. The national unions negotiate collective bargaining agreements as well as organize workers. The task of administering bargaining agreements falls primarily to the local unions. Bargaining structures are many and diverse.

6. Unionism has been declining relatively in the United States. Some labor economists attribute this to changes in the composition of domestic output and in the demographic structure of the labor force that have been uncongenial to union growth. Others contend that employers, recognizing that unionization lowers profitability, have more aggressively sought by both legal and illegal means to dissuade workers from being union members. Still others feel that government programs and "progressive" labor relations by employers have usurped many of organized labor's traditional functions, lessening workers' perceived need for union membership.

7. The monopoly union model assumes that the union sets the wage rate, and the firm determines the level of union employment based on this wage rate. The model results in a settlement on the firm's labor demand curve. Compared to the nonunion outcome, the wage rate will be higher and the employment level will be lower.

8. The monopoly union model outcome is not efficient for the firm and union because other wage and employment combinations can make at least one party better off without making the other party worse off.

9. The efficient contracts model assumes that the union and firm bargain over the wage rate and employment, rather than just the wage rate. In general, the efficient contract outcome will result in lower wages and more employment than the monopoly union outcome.

10. In the accident strike model, strikes occur because one or both parties misperceive the willingness of the other party to concede.

11. Models of strikes based on asymmetric information imply that strikes result from information differences either between union leaders and the rank-and-file union members or between the union and the firm.

Terms and Concepts

American Federation of Labor and Congress of Industrial Organizations (AFL–CIO), *310*
Change to Win federation, *311*
national unions, *311*
local unions, *313*

bargaining structure, *314*
pattern bargaining, *314*
structural change hypothesis, *316*
managerial opposition hypothesis, *318*
substitution hypothesis, *320*
monopoly union, *324*

efficient contracts, *325*
strongly efficient contract, *327*
accident model, *328*
asymmetric information, *330*

Questions and Study Suggestions

1. Why have unions evolved? To what extent is the civilian labor force unionized? Indicate the *(a)* industrial and *(b)* occupational distribution of union members. Why are relatively fewer white-collar workers organized than blue-collar workers? Briefly explain union membership differences related to gender, race, and age. Evaluate this statement: "Whether an individual worker is a union member depends not so much on the worker's feelings toward membership as on her or his occupational choice."

2. Summarize the organizational structure of the American labor movement, indicating the functions of the AFL–CIO, Change to Win, the national unions, and the local unions.

3. Describe the various bargaining structures that exist in the United States. What might be the advantages of multiemployer bargaining to a union? To employers? What is pattern bargaining?

4. Critically evaluate each of these statements:
   a. "The relative decline of the American labor movement can be explained by the shift from goods-producing to service-providing industries and by the closely related shifts from blue- to white-collar occupations and from male to female employees."
   b. "The success of unions in raising their wages relative to nonunion workers has contributed to the decline of unionism."
   c. "Unionized firms have tended to become less profitable and, therefore, employers are more resistant to unionization."

5. Explain the rapid growth of public sector unionism in the 1960s and early 1970s, despite the general deunionization of the economy during this period.

6. Assume that a union's utility depends on only the wage rate and not the level of employment. In this case, what will be the outcome under the efficient contracts model?

7. How can both the union and the firm be better off by bargaining over the wage rate and employment rather than just the wage rate?

8. Explain the difference between efficient contracts and strongly efficient contracts.

9. Are strikes inefficient for the union and firm? Explain.

10. What role do information differences play in causing strikes?

Internet
Exercise

What Has Happened to Union Membership?

Go to the Bureau of Labor Statistics Current Population Survey Web site **(http://www .bls.gov/cps/)** and select "Union Members" under "Economic News Releases." What percent of wage-earning and salaried workers were union members in the most recent year? What was the unionization rate (percent) for men, women, African–Americans, whites, and Hispanics in the latest year? Provide any other two facts relating to union membership from this source.

Internet
Links

The Unionstats Web site reports unionization rates by industry, occupation, and state **(http://www.unionstats.com/)**.

The AFL–CIO Web site contains information about labor campaigns and strikes as well as policy statements about current political issues **(http://www.aflcio.org/)**.

The Web site of the Institute of Industrial Relations Library provides a directory of links to labor unions, labor union news sources, and many other sites related to the union movement **(http://www.iir.berkeley.edu/library/index.php)**.

Chapter 11

The Economic Impact of Unions

In the previous chapter we focused on (1) the industrial, occupational, and demographic characteristics of organized labor; (2) the institutional structure of the American labor movement; (3) union objectives; and (4) strikes and the bargaining process.

In this chapter we direct our attention to the economic effects of unions and collective bargaining. How large a wage advantage are unions able to gain through collective bargaining? What are the implications of unions and collective bargaining for productivity and allocative efficiency? Do unions affect the profitability of firms? What is the impact of unions on the distribution of earnings?

THE UNION WAGE ADVANTAGE

Most people undoubtedly assume that union workers are paid more than nonunion workers. That is, they assume that unions gain a wage differential or *wage advantage* for their constituents. A union, after all, is able to deprive a firm of its workforce by striking and can thus impose associated costs on the firm. Presumably an employer, within limits, will pay the price of higher wage rates to avoid the costs of a strike. And indeed Bureau of Labor Statistics data reveal that average hourly earnings of union members were $22.38 in 2006 compared to $18.48 for nonunion workers.

Preliminary Complications

Closer examination suggests that this issue is not so clear-cut. In the first place, envision a unionized employer in a perfectly (or at least a highly) competitive industry. If rival firms in the industry are nonunion, other things being equal, this firm will not be able to survive if it pays a higher wage to its employees than competitors are paying to their nonunion workers. Despite its potential to impose strike costs on the employer, the union would face the dilemma of "no wage advantage" or "no firm" in these circumstances. A wage advantage would imply a higher average cost of production than the market-determined product price—that is, an economic loss.

The competitive model implies two additional points. On one hand, the model tells us why unions are anxious to organize not just single firms but entire industries. If *all* firms are unionized and have higher wage costs, then no single firm will be at a competitive disadvantage and therefore faced with the prospect of losing market share to rivals. The United Automobile Workers' intense desire to organize workers of new automobile plants established by foreign manufacturers in the United States is prompted by much more than the goal of adding thousands of workers to UAW ranks. On the other hand, the model implies that unions may fare better in industries where product markets are imperfect, such as government-regulated industries and the oligopolistic industries dominating much of the manufacturing sector of our economy. Such firms realize economic or surplus profits that in part can be expropriated by unions through higher wages without necessarily reducing output and employment.

This leads us to a second complication. Suppose we find a positive association between the degree of unionization and the average level of wage rates in various industries. That is, we discover that strongly unionized industries do in fact pay higher wage rates than weakly unionized industries. How do we know that unions are responsible for the higher wages? Do unions cause higher wages, *or* are unions prone to organizing industries that already pay high wages? The automobile industry, for example, was renowned for paying relatively high wages long before it was unionized in the late 1930s. In fact, one can cite considerations other than the presence of unions that might explain at least a part of the wage advantage that is enjoyed by highly unionized industries.[1] First, female workers generally constitute a larger proportion of the workforce in weakly unionized industries than they do in strongly unionized industries. We will find in Chapter 14 that women—because of discrimination and other considerations—are paid less than men. One can therefore argue that at least some portion of the wage differential found between strongly and weakly unionized industries is due not to the existence of unions but to the differing demographic makeup of the workforces in these industries. Second, strongly unionized industries usually have larger plants *and* are more capital-intensive than weakly unionized industries. The fact that unionized plants tend to be larger raises the possibility that supervision and monitoring may be more costly in such firms, causing employers to seek out and hire "superior" workers who can work effectively with less supervision. Such workers would be paid relatively high wages even if the union were not present. Similarly, capital-intensive production often requires more highly skilled workers who naturally command higher wages.[2] Our basic point is that higher wages in unionized industries might be attributable (at least in part) to factors other than the existence of the union.

---

[1] The following discussion is based on Daniel J. B. Mitchell, *Unions, Wages, and Inflation* (Washington, DC: Brookings Institution, 1980), pp. 83–85.

[2] Of course, one can push the causal relationship back one step further by arguing that highly unionized industries are capital-intensive *because* of union wage pressure that prompts employers to substitute capital for labor.

Measuring the Wage Advantage

Aside from the complications just discussed, there is also a basic conceptual problem in measuring the *pure* union–nonunion differential. This arises because unionization may affect wage rates in nonunion labor markets, pushing them upward or downward and creating a bias in the measurement of the union wage advantage.

To begin, the **pure union wage advantage** is the amount by which the union wage exceeds the nonunion wage that would exist without the union. This difference is expressed as a percentage. In Equation (11.1) the pure union wage advantage is *A:*

$$A = \frac{W_u - W_n}{W_n} \times 100 \qquad\qquad \textbf{(11.1)}$$

where W_u is the union wage and W_n is the nonunion wage. The $(W_u - W_n)/W_n$ term is multiplied by 100 to express the union wage advantage as a percentage. For example, if the union wage were \$12 per hour and the nonunion wage were \$10, the union wage advantage would be 20 percent $[(12 - 10)/10 \times 100]$.

Ideally the union wage advantage should be determined under laboratory conditions in which we compare union and nonunion wages with all other possible influences on wages being constant. Thus in Figure 11.1 we first would want to observe the level of wages before the presence of the union (W_n) and then compare this with the wage rate after the union was added (W_u). We would then use the relevant numbers in our union wage advantage formula as just described. The problem, of course, is that there is no way of conducting such a controlled experiment. In particular, it is impossible to observe what the earnings of unionized workers would be in a given labor market if the union

FIGURE 11.1   **The Union Wage Advantage Measured under Ideal Conditions**
If we could compare wage rates in a given labor market, where all conditions were held constant except for the presence of the union, we could calculate a pure measure of the union's wage advantage. That pure advantage is $(W_u - W_n)/W_n \times 100$.

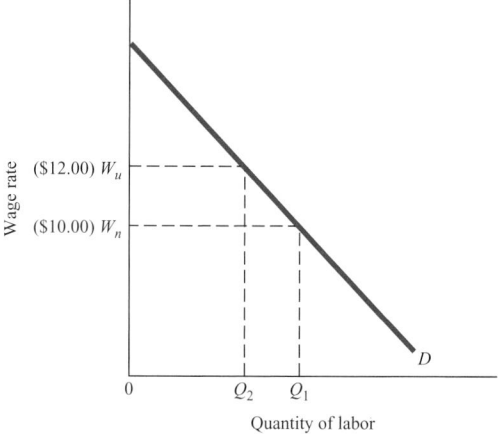

did not exist. We must therefore make real-world comparisons of a more complex and tentative nature.

The best that can be done in this regard is to compare the wages of workers of a specific kind in unionized (or strongly unionized) markets with the wages of workers in nonunion (or weakly unionized) markets. But in making this comparison, our aforementioned conceptual difficulty intrudes. *Unions may influence the wage rates of nonunion workers as well as the wage rates of their own workers.* Furthermore, the potential influence of unions on nonunion wages can take several different forms, so the overall impact is ambiguous. We are theoretically uncertain whether an increase in union wages will cause nonunion wages to rise or fall. Additionally, the union wage may result in more productive workers in union firms. Let's briefly explore several different effects that describe various ways union wage setting may affect nonunion wages and may influence the quality of the unionized workforce.

1 Spillover Effect

The **spillover effect** refers to the decline in nonunion wages that results from displaced union workers supplying their services in nonunion labor markets. The higher wages achieved in the unionized sector of the labor market will be accompanied by a loss of jobs, and displaced workers will "spill over" into the nonunion sector and depress nonunion wages.

The basics of the spillover effect are portrayed in Figure 11.2. Assume that both sectors are initially nonunion and that movement between the two sectors entails a common

FIGURE 11.2   The Spillover Effect, the Threat Effect, and the Measured Wage Advantage
The spillover effect suggests that as a union is able to raise wage rates from W_n to W_u in sector 1, it will reduce employment by Q_1Q_2. Assuming downward wage flexibility, the reemployment of these workers in sector 2 will reduce wages there from W_n to W_s. The measured union wage advantage will be $(W_u - W_s)/W_s \times 100$, which overstates the pure advantage of $(W_u - W_n)/W_n \times 100$. The threat effect indicates that as the union raises wages from W_n to W_u in sector 1, nonunion employers will grant a wage increase from, say, W_n to W_t in sector 2 to counter the threat of unionization. The measured wage advantage will be $(W_u - W_t)/W_t \times 100$, which understates the pure advantage of $(W_u - W_n)/W_n \times 100$.

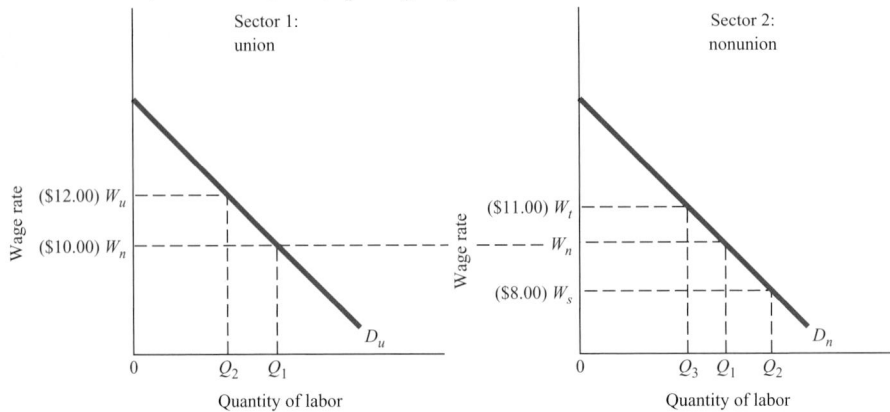

equilibrium wage rate of W_n for this labor. Now assume that sector 1 becomes unionized and that the union is successful in increasing the wage rate to W_u. We observe that the higher wage rate in this sector causes unemployment of Q_1Q_2. The spillover effect assumes that some or all of these unemployed workers will seek and find employment in the nonunion sector. This movement of workers from the union to the nonunion sector will reduce the supply of labor in the union sector and increase the supply in the nonunion sector. If we assume downward flexibility of wages, then wages will fall in the nonunion sector to W_s.

To the extent that the spillover effect occurs, our ***measured union wage advantage***, which is the amount by which the union wage exceeds the *observed* nonunion wage, will *overstate* the pure union wage advantage. We can grasp this by comparing our hypothetical laboratory experiment of Figure 11.1 with the real-world comparison of Figure 11.2 embodying the spillover effect. Specifically, instead of comparing the union wage W_u with the nonunion wage W_n in Figure 11.1 to get the pure union wage advantage of 20 percent, we must compare the union wage W_u ($12) with the nonunion wage W_s ($8). Because W_s is less than W_n due to the spillover effect, the measured wage advantage in this case is 50 percent $[(12 - 8)/8 \times 100]$. The spillover effect depresses observed nonunion wages, so the measured union wage advantage is larger than the pure union wage advantage of 20 percent. To repeat, a spillover effect will cause the union wage advantage to be *overstated*.[3]

2 Threat Effect

In contrast, some labor economists, labeled *institutionalists,* argue that market forces, as described by the spillover effect, are largely subverted or set aside by collective bargaining and that wage rates are determined mainly on the basis of *equitable comparisons*. This implies that wages for any group of workers will be determined on the basis of wages being paid to comparable workers and that union and nonunion wages may be positively linked.

More specifically, the ***threat effect*** refers to an increase in nonunion wages that a nonunion employer offers as a response to the threat of unionization. The reasoning is that nonunion employers will feel increasingly threatened with unionization when workers in union firms obtain wage increases. An enlarged union–nonunion differential will increase the incentive for the workers in the nonunion firms to organize. To meet this threat, the nonunion employer will grant wage increases. Thus if we once again start from the W_n equilibrium wage in both sectors (Figure 11.2), the wage increase from $10 to $12 resulting from the unionization of sector 1 might *increase* nonunion wages in sector 2 from W_n ($10) to, say, W_t ($11). Now the measured union wage advantage will be about 9 percent $[(12 - 11)/11 \times 100]$ rather than the pure advantage of 20 percent (Figure 11.1). To recapitulate: If the threat effect causes union wage increases to pull up

---

[3] For an empirical examination of the spillover effect, see David Neumark and Michael L. Wachter, "Union Effects on Nonunion Wages: Evidence from Panel Data on Industries and Cities," *Industrial and Labor Relations Review,* October 1995, pp. 20–38. They conclude there is mixed evidence regarding the importance of the spillover effect.

nonunion wages, then the measured union wage advantage will *understate* the pure union advantage.[4]

3 Other Effects

Our brief discussions of the spillover and threat effects do not exhaust all the possible ways in which union wages may influence nonunion wages. For example, there may be a *product market effect:* an increase in nonunion wages caused by consumer demand shifting away from relatively high-priced union-produced goods and toward relatively low-priced goods produced by nonunion workers. The product market effect works as follows: A "union pay increase, through its effect on costs and prices, shifts demand to firms in the nonunion sector. The added demand for nonunion output is translated into added demand for nonunion labor, which could have a pay-raising influence."[5]

Other economists question the relevance of the spillover effect by citing the phenomenon of *wait unemployment.* The argument here is that when the union achieves a wage increase in sector 1 of Figure 11.2, the resulting unemployed workers may well remain in sector 1 hoping to be recalled to their high-paying jobs. Encouraged perhaps by the availability of unemployment insurance, they might prefer the probability of being recalled at higher union wages to the alternative of accepting lower-wage jobs in the nonunion sector. If wait unemployment occurs, the downward spillover pressure on nonunion wages does not occur to any great degree in sector 2. This implies that the measured union wage advantage more accurately portrays the pure wage advantage.

There is also the notion of the *superior worker effect.* This idea is that the higher wages paid by union firms will cause workers to queue up for these good union jobs. (Note back in Figure 6.10 that the quantity of labor supplied exceeds the quantity demanded by *be* workers at the union wage rate W_u.) Given the availability of many job seekers, unionized employers will carefully screen these prospective workers for those having the greatest ability, the most motivation, the least need for costly supervision, and other worker traits contributing to high productivity. This means that, in time, high-wage union firms may acquire superior workforces in comparison to nonunion firms.[6] Thus, in seeking to measure the union wage advantage accurately, the researcher is confronted with determining how much of an observed union wage advantage is due to the presence of the union as an institution and how much it reflects the presence of more highly productive workers in the unionized firms. To the extent that superior workers acquire the high-wage union jobs, the measured union wage advantage would be *overstated*. Part of the higher wages paid to such workers is attributable to their higher productivity rather than to the union.

---

[4] For a study finding mixed evidence regarding the magnitude of the threat effect, see Henry S. Farber, "Nonunion Wages and the Threat of Unionization," *Industrial and Labor Relations Review,* April 2005, pp. 335–52.

[5] Mitchell, op. cit., p. 87.

[6] On the other hand, unions may seek higher wages in the future if worker quality improves. See Walter J. Wessels, "Do Unionized Firms Hire Better Workers?" *Economic Inquiry,* October 1994, pp. 616–29. For empirical evidence consistent with Wessels's model, see Barry T. Hirsch and Edward J. Schumacher, "Unions, Wages, and Skills," *Journal of Human Resources,* Winter 1998, pp. 201–19.

TABLE 11.1
Difficulties in Measuring the Pure Union Wage Advantage

Effect	Consequence
Spillover	Lowers nonunion wages, causing measured wage advantage to overstate pure advantage.
Threat	Increases nonunion wages, causing measured wage advantage to understate pure advantage.
Product market	Increases nonunion wages, causing measured wage advantage to understate pure advantage.
Superior worker	Results in more productive workers in union firms, causing measured wage advantage to overstate pure wage advantage.

Finally, part of the union wage advantage may be a *compensating wage differential* that accounts for the fewer amenities in the workplace encountered by union workers. Alternatively stated, some portion of the wage advantage enjoyed by union members may be compensation for the fact that their working conditions are more structured, their working hours are less flexible, and the work pace is faster.[7]

Table 11.1 lists these various effects and summarizes how each biases the measured wage advantage from the pure wage advantage. Although unanimity does not exist on the issue, most studies indicate that the threat and product market effects dominate the spillover effect, meaning that the overall impact of unions on nonunion wages is positive. Furthermore, this positive impact on nonunion wages is more than sufficient to counter any superior worker effect that might be present. As a result, the measured union wage advantage probably understates the pure union wage advantage.[8]

Empirical Evidence

Now that we have some appreciation of the practical and conceptual difficulties in estimating the union wage advantage, let's turn to the available empirical evidence. Hirsch and Macpherson have examined the union wage premium for the 1983–2006 period using a consistent methodology and data source.[9] Their findings are summarized in Figure 11.3. In 2006 the average overall union wage advantage was 17 percent.[10] This estimate is above the 10–15 percent range that Lewis estimated for the 1923–1958 period.[11]

[7] Greg J. Duncan and Frank P. Stafford, "Do Union Members Receive Compensating Wage Differentials?" *American Economic Review,* June 1980, pp. 355–71. See also Stanley W. Siebert and X. Wei, "Compensating Wage Differentials for Workplace Accidents: Evidence for Union and Nonunion Workers in the UK," *Journal of Risk and Uncertainty,* July 1994, pp. 61–76.

[8] Barry T. Hirsch and John T. Addison, *The Economic Analysis of Unions* (Boston: Allen & Unwin, 1986), pp. 120, 176. For some recent evidence that questions the strength of the threat effect, however, see David Neumark and Michael L. Wachter, op. cit.; and Farber, op. cit.

[9] Barry T. Hirsch and David A. Macpherson, *Union Membership and Earnings Data Book: Compilations from the Current Population Survey (2007 Edition)* (Washington, DC: Bureau of National Affairs, 2007).

[10] Errors in the classification of union and nonunion status of workers as well as other data errors may cause the existing estimates of the union wage differential to be too low. See Barry T. Hirsch, "Reconsidering Union Wage Effects: Surveying New Evidence on an Old Topic," *Journal of Labor Research,* Spring 2004, pp. 233–66.

[11] H. Gregg Lewis, *Unionism and Relative Wages in the United States* (Chicago: University of Chicago Press, 1963).

FIGURE 11.3   **Union Wage Advantage**

The union wage advantage averaged 21 percent over the 1983–2006:17.2% period and is currently about 17 percent.

Source: Barry T. Hirsch and David A. Macpherson, *Union Membership and Earnings Data Book: Compilations from the Current Population Survey (2007 Edition)* (Washington, DC: Bureau of National Affairs, 2007).

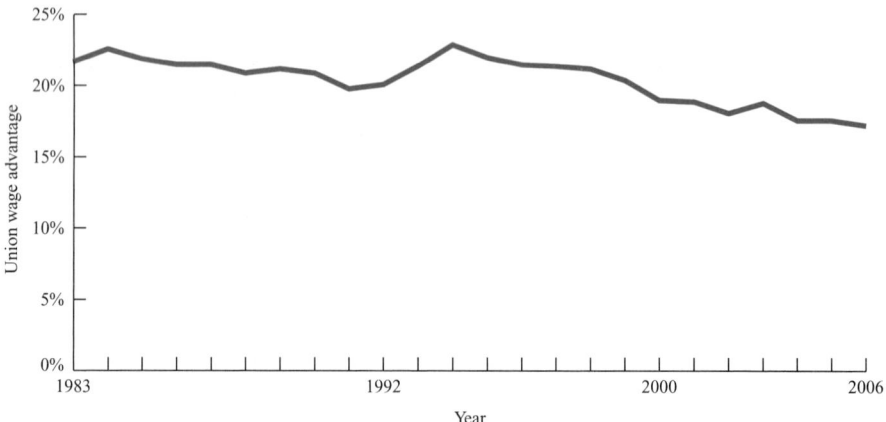

Hirsch and Macpherson also examined the union wage advantage in the public sector, as opposed to the overall wage advantage. They estimate that all else being equal, the pay of unionized government workers is 11 percent higher than that of nonunionized government workers. This union wage advantage is 10 percentage points lower than the advantage commanded by union workers in the private sector.

In the 1970s the union wage advantage was even larger. Lewis found that the union wage advantage pcakcd at 20 percent in 1976.[12] Other researchers have found an even higher union wage premium in the mid-1970s. Mitchell,[13] using three different data sets, surmised that the union wage premium in the mid-1970s was in the range of 20 to 30 percent. Also, Freeman and Medoff, using six data sets for individual workers, found union wage advantages ranging from 21 to 32 percent and concluded that "in the 1970s the archetypical union wage advantage was on the order of 20–30 percent."[14]

The period in question was one of *stagflation*—simultaneous inflation and high unemployment—resulting largely from dramatic oil price increases. Through collective bargaining and cost-of-living adjustments (COLAs) in contracts, union workers were better able than nonunion workers to keep their nominal wages rising with inflation. The loose labor markets (high unemployment) apparently slowed the relative pace of nominal wage increases for nonunion workers. Recall from Chapter 10 that the high union wage advantage of the 1970s is cited as a possible cause of the decline in union employment during the 1980s.

---

[12] H. Gregg Lewis, *Union Relative Wage Effects* (Chicago: University of Chicago Press, 1986).
[13] Mitchell, op. cit., p. 95.
[14] Richard B. Freeman and James L. Medoff, *What Do Unions Do?* (New York: Basic Books, 1984), p. 46.

11.1 | World of Work

A Tale of Two Industries*

Before the late 1970s, both the airline and trucking industries were heavily regulated by the federal government. In both industries, price competition among firms and entry by new firms were severely limited. These regulations reduced product market competition and generated economic rents that were shared with workers in these industries.

This regulatory period ended at about the same time for both the trucking and airline industries. The airline industry was deregulated with the passage of the Airline Deregulation Act of 1978; the trucking industry was officially deregulated with enactment of the Motor Carrier Act of 1980 (it was partially deregulated two years earlier by government regulators).

The impact of deregulation on workers in these industries has been starkly different. In the trucking industry, truck drivers suffered a 15 percent decline in their relative wages after deregulation. A large part of the wage decline resulted from a sharp and rapid fall in the real wages of union drivers (most of the decrease occurred in the first three years after deregulation). In addition, there was a shift in employment away from high-wage union firms toward lower-wage nonunion firms. As a result, the unionization rate among truck drivers fell from 56 percent in 1977–1978 to 33 percent in 1985 and to 17 percent in 2002.

Initially workers in the airline industry fared much better after deregulation. The relative wages of airline industry workers rose about 10 percent between 1979 and 1983. However, since then their relative wages have drifted downward and have fallen by about 15 percent. Most of the decline occurred in the 1990s, many years after the industry was deregulated. The unionization rate in the airline industry fell relatively modestly from 49 percent in 1973–1978 to 38 percent 2002.

There are several reasons for the much slower and less steep decline in wages for airline industry workers. First, the lower airfares resulting from deregulation of prices and entry produced large increases in passenger traffic. Thus the demand for airline workers remained relatively strong. This kept upward pressure on wages: The labor supply of such workers is not very elastic because of their specialized skills. Second, the substantial economies of scale and other entry barriers that exist in the airline industry enabled firms to keep some of their pricing power in the product market. Third, the growth of the number of passengers and persistence of that market power helped unions maintain their organizing ability and bargaining power, slowing the decline in wages for their members.

* Based on Barry T. Hirsch and David A. Macpherson, "Earnings and Employment in Trucking: Deregulating a Naturally Competitive Industry," in James Peoples (ed.), *Regulatory Reform and Labor Markets* (Norwell, MA: Kluwer, 1998); and Barry T. Hirsch and David A. Macpherson, "Earnings, Rents, and Competition in the Airline Labor Market," *Journal of Labor Economics,* January 2000, pp. 125–55.

 The union wage advantage has fallen from its lofty heights in the 1970s. From 1983 to 1994 there was little change in the union wage advantage. Since 1994 the union wage advantage has drifted downward, reflecting a decline in the union wage premium among both private and public sector workers.

Union wage advantages vary greatly by industry, occupation, race, gender, and state of the economy. Although no unassailable generalizations can be drawn from the studies that try to sort out these differences, the following comments seem to be defensible.[15]

[15] For example, see H. Gregg Lewis, 1986, op. cit.; Bernt Bratsberg and James F. Ragan, Jr., "Changes in the Union Wage Premium by Industry," *Industrial and Labor Relations Review,* October 2002, pp. 65–83; and David G. Blanchflower and Alex Bryson, "What Effect Do Unions Have on Wages Now and Would 'What Do Unions Do?' Be Surprised?" *Journal of Labor Research,* Summer 2004, pp. 383–414.

1. The union wage advantage moves countercyclically, increasing during recessions and narrowing during expansions. Union wages are locked in by long-term bargaining contracts that are not readily adjusted. At the same time, nonunion wages are free to rise and fall with changes in the economy and labor market. As a result, nonunion wages rise relative to union wages in economic booms and vice versa during recessions.

2. Craft unions in the construction industry have achieved union wage advantages that are much larger than average. The bargaining power of such unions is great because each craft union represents a small proportion of total building costs (Chapter 5), and construction workers can often find employment in other firms during a strike.

3. African–American males, on average, gain more from being union members than do whites and females.

4. Unions achieve higher wage advantages for blue-collar workers (craftspeople, operatives, laborers) than for white-collar workers (clerical workers, salespeople).

5. Less educated workers have higher union wage premiums than better-educated workers.

Total Compensation: Wages plus Fringe Benefits

We would be remiss not to examine the impact of unions on fringe benefits. Recall from Chapter 7 that *fringe benefits* include public (legally mandated) programs such as Social Security, unemployment compensation, and workers' compensation as well as a wide variety of private nonmandatory programs, including private pensions, medical and dental insurance, and paid vacations and sick leave. *Total compensation* is simply the sum of wage earnings and the value of fringe benefits. If union workers enjoy more generous fringe benefits than nonunion workers, then the overall economic advantage that union workers have over nonunion workers is greater than the wage advantage suggests. On the other hand, if union wage gains are realized at the expense of fringe benefits and nonunion workers receive larger fringe benefits, then the union wage advantage overstates the economic advantage of union workers.

Evidence

How do union fringe benefits compare to those of nonunion workers? The answer is that union workers enjoy a greater variety and higher overall level of fringe benefits than do nonunion workers. Using 2002 data, Budd reports that union members are 31 percentage points and 25 percentage points more likely than their nonunion counterparts to have pension and health insurance coverage, respectively.[16] Wiatrowski finds that the union advantage exists for a wide variety of fringe benefits.[17] Freeman and Medoff have shown that unions gain a larger fringe benefit advantage than wage advantage. Finally, Lewis contends that the inclusion of fringe benefits would raise estimates of the union compensation advantage by 2 or 3 percentage points. In short, substantial agreement exists that union workers generally achieve not only a wage advantage but also a considerable fringe benefit advantage compared to nonunion workers.

Role of Unions

Why do union members receive more generous fringe benefits than nonunion workers? A number of interrelated reasons may be involved. First, union fringes may be higher for the same reason that union wage rates are higher. The union can deprive management of its workforce, and the employer is willing to pay both higher wages *and* larger fringe benefits to avoid the costs of a strike. Second, union workers, by virtue of their higher earnings, may simply choose to "buy" more fringes than lower-income nonunion workers. Third, as a collective-voice institution, a union may formulate fringe benefit proposals, inform its constituents of the details of such proposals, and crystallize worker preferences; the union then communicates these preferences to management. Fourth, older workers are usually more active in the internal politics of a union and are therefore more influential in determining union goals. These older workers are typically more interested in pensions and insurance programs than are younger workers. Fifth, as we will discover momentarily, unionism reduces worker quit rates and thus increases job tenure. Greater tenure in turn increases the probability that workers will actually receive benefits from such fringes as nonvested pensions and life insurance. Finally, there is the simple fact that under collective bargaining law, fringe benefits are a mandatory item on the bargaining agenda, which accords them more serious and systematic attention than in nonunion labor markets.

---

[16] John W. Budd, "Non-Wage Forms of Compensation," *Journal of Labor Research,* Fall 2005, pp. 669–76.
[17] William J. Wiatrowski, "Employee Benefits for Union and Nonunion Workers," *Monthly Labor Review,* February 1994, pp. 34–38.

EFFICIENCY AND PRODUCTIVITY

Are unions a positive or a negative force insofar as economic efficiency and productivity are concerned? How do unions affect the allocation of resources? Although much disagreement exists about the efficiency aspects of unionism, it is useful to consider some of the ways unions might affect efficiency both negatively and positively. We will consider the negative view first.

Negative View

Unions might exert a negative impact on efficiency in three basic ways. First, unions may impose work rules that diminish productivity *within* union firms. Second, strikes may entail a loss of output. Finally, the union wage advantage is a distortion of the wage structure, causing a misallocation of labor *between* union and nonunion firms and industries.

1 Restrictive Work Rules

Perhaps the most apparent way unions might impair productivity and efficiency is by imposing various work rules on management. These "make-work" rules can take a variety of interrelated forms. First, the union may obtain a direct limit on hourly, daily, or weekly output per worker. Example: Allegedly to control output quality, the bricklayers have sought to restrict the number of bricks laid per hour or per day. Second, the union may insist on the use of time-consuming production methods. Illustrations: Painters' unions may prohibit the use of spray guns or limit the width of paint brushes. In past years, the typographers' unions resisted the introduction of computers in setting type. Third, a union may require that unnecessary work be done. Example: Craft unions have sometimes promoted the enactment of building codes requiring that prefabricated housing units be broken down and reassembled on the construction site. Fourth, work crews of excessive size may be required. Examples: Historically the musicians' union insisted on oversized orchestras for musical shows and required that a union standby orchestra be paid by employers using nonunion orchestras. For many years the Brotherhood of Locomotive Firemen and Engineers was able to retain a fireman on train crews, even though the worker's function was eliminated by the shift from steam to diesel engines. Such practices are labeled *featherbedding*.[18] Fifth, unions may impose jurisdictional restrictions on the kinds of jobs workers may perform. Illustration: Sheet metal workers or bricklayers may be prohibited from performing the simple carpentry work often associated with their jobs. Observance of such rules means, in this instance, that unneeded and underutilized carpenters must be available. Finally, unions may restrain management in the assignment of workers to jobs. The most prevalent example is that unions typically insist that workers be promoted in accordance with seniority rather than ability and efficiency.

This recitation of reasons that union work rules might impede intrafirm efficiency merits modification in several respects. To begin, one must not make the mistake of assuming that productivity will necessarily be enhanced by "speeding up the assembly line." A speedup may in fact cause workers to tire and become demoralized and therefore be *less* efficient. Similarly, it is also incorrect to associate featherbedding, unnecessarily large work crews, make-work rules, and the like solely with unionized workers. Although unions may be responsible for codifying and enforcing such practices, the practices themselves are quite common in both union and nonunion sectors of the economy. Peer pressure and the threat of social ostracism can be as effective as a clause in a collective bargaining agreement in controlling the pace of production.[19] Finally, the productivity-reducing practices just outlined often come into being against a backdrop of technological change. Labor and management may agree to a crew size that is reasonable and appropriate at the time the agreement is concluded. But labor-saving technology may then emerge that renders the crew "too large." The union is likely to resist the potential loss of jobs.[20]

2 Strikes

A second way unions may adversely affect efficiency is through strikes. If union and management reach an impasse in their negotiations, a strike will result and the firm's production will generally cease for the strike's duration. The firm will forgo sales and profits, and workers will sacrifice income.

[18] For a discussion of methods of featherbedding, see George E. Johnson, "Work Rules, Featherbedding, and Pareto–Optimal Union–Management Bargaining," *Journal of Labor Economics* Part 2, January 1990, pp. S237–59.
[19] See Paul A. Weinstein (ed.), *Featherbedding and Technological Change* (Boston: D. C. Heath and Company, 1965).
[20] For an analysis of when unions are likely to resist labor-saving technology, see Steve Dowrick and Barbara J. Spencer, "Union Attitudes to Labor-Saving Innovation: When Are Unions Luddites?" *Journal of Labor Economics,* April 1994, pp. 316–44.

FIGURE 11.4

Number of Major Work Stoppages in the United States

There have been only a few major strikes in the United States in recent years.

Source: U.S. Department of Labor, "Major Work Stoppages, 2006," News Release 07-304, February 27, 2007.

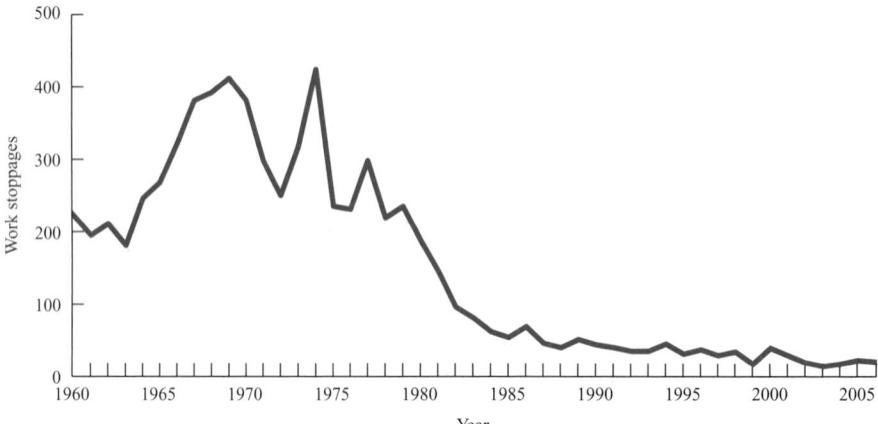

Simple statistics on strike activity suggest that strikes are relatively rare and the associated aggregate economic losses are relatively minimal. Figure 11.4 provides data on the number of major work stoppages, defined as those involving 1,000 or more workers and lasting at least one full day or one work shift. Given that about 700 major collective bargaining agreements are negotiated each year, the number of major work stoppages is surprisingly small. Figure 11.5 presents the percentage of total work time lost due to major strikes in the United States for the 1960–2006 period. Most strikes last only a few days. As a result, the lost work time from major strikes has been consistently far less than one-half of 1 percent of total work time. In fact, over this period the amount of work time lost was typically less than two-tenths of 1 percent of total work time. This loss is the

FIGURE 11.5

Percentage of Total Working Time Lost Due to Major Work Stoppages in the United States

The amount of work time lost due to major strikes in the United States is typically less than two-tenths of 1 percent of total work time.

Source: U.S. Department of Labor, "Major Work Stoppages, 2006," News Release 07-304, February 27, 2007.

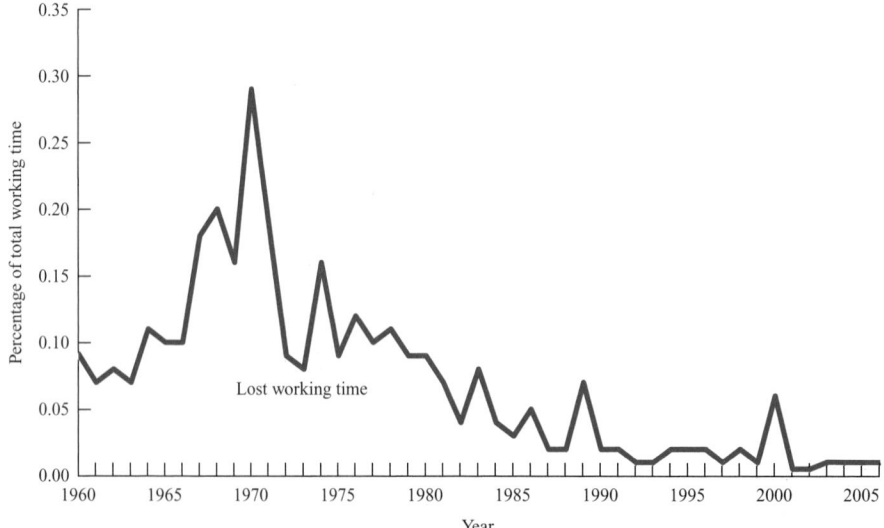

Global Perspective

11.1

Strike Incidence*

The United States has a low proportion of workers involved in strikes compared to other major industrial countries.

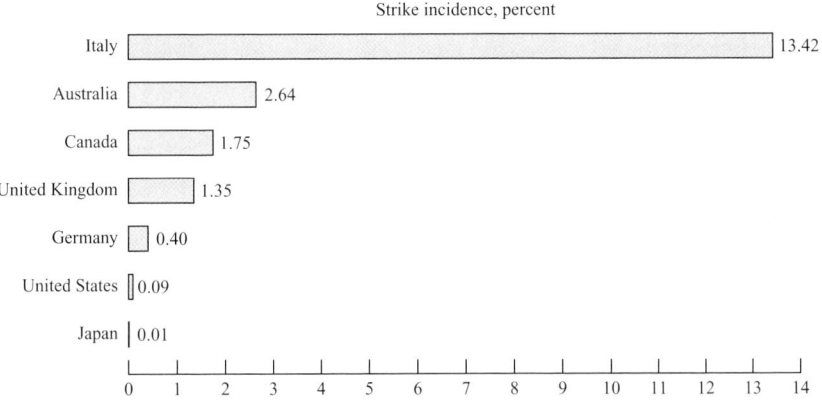

Strike incidence, percent

Italy	13.42
Australia	2.64
Canada	1.75
United Kingdom	1.35
Germany	0.40
United States	0.09
Japan	0.01

Source: International Labour Organization, *Yearbook of Labour Statistics, 2006* (Geneva, Switzerland: International Labour Organization, 2006).

* The strike incidence rate is the annual average of the percentage of wage-earning and salaried workers involved in strikes for the 2001–2005 period. The Japan figure does not include data for 2005.

11.1

equivalent of four hours per worker per year, which is less than five minutes per worker per week.[21]

But these data on time lost from work stoppages can be misleading as a measure of the costliness of a strike. For example, employers in the struck industry may have anticipated the strike and worked their labor force overtime to accumulate inventories to supply customers during the strike period. This means that the overall loss of work time, production, profits, and wages is less than the work time loss figures suggest. Similarly, other nonstruck producers in an industry may have increased their output to offset the loss of production by firms engaged in a strike. In other words, although a strike may impose significant losses on participants, the total output loss to the industry or to society at large may be minuscule or nonexistent. Note, however, that the production adjustments made in anticipation of, or as a consequence of, a strike may entail some efficiency losses. If firms that suffered a strike were able to anticipate perfectly the loss of output and sales and therefore accumulate inventories prior to the strike, this additional

[21] Marten Estey, *The Unions,* 3rd ed. (New York: Harcourt Brace Jovanovich, 1981), p. 140.

production would likely entail the overutilization of productive facilities and thus higher costs (less productivity) per unit of output. Similar efficiency losses may be incurred by firms replacing the output of the firm that is struck. Whereas the data on worker days lost because of strikes may overstate the output loss, a consequent efficiency loss may be concealed.

Furthermore, the amount of production and income lost because of strikes will be greater than suggested by work time loss data when a work stoppage in a specific industry disrupts production in associated industries. These affected industries may either buy inputs from the struck industry or sell output to it. Nonstriking workers in the affected industries may lose work time and the economy may lose their output if a strike depletes these industries of essential inputs or essential buyers. In some instances, a strike could force affected firms to cease or curtail operations.

Alternatively, output in industries linked as purchasers or suppliers to struck industries may decline while paid work time remains steady. If so, labor productivity (output per worker) in the affected industries will fall and the average cost of the output will rise. McHugh[22] finds empirical support for this possible outcome. He suggests that many employers in nonstruck firms affected by strikes retain their workforces during the strike. This "hoarded" labor is redundant; because output falls, these firms experience declines in labor productivity.

As a broad generalization, the adverse effects of a strike on nonstriking firms and customers are likely to be greater when services are involved and less when products are involved. For example, a 10-day strike in 2002 by 10,500 West Coast dockworkers shut down 29 ports from San Diego to Seattle. These ports handle 40 percent of the seaborne cargo in the United States. As a result, the strike cost the U.S. economy an estimated $10 billion. The backlog of cargo created by the strike took weeks to clear up. In contrast, a strike in a durable goods industry is likely to have negligible effects on the public.

Overall it is appropriate to say that, on average, the costs imposed on the immediate parties to a strike and affected firms and consumers are not as great as one might surmise. A study of some 63 manufacturing industries over the 1955–1977 period concluded that strike costs were significant in only 19 of these industries.[23] Furthermore, in these 19 industries the amount of output lost was typically a small fraction of 1 percent of total annual output. The ability of struck firms to draw on inventories and the capacity of nonstruck firms to increase their output apparently make industry output losses minimal.

11.3

Postscript: Strikes are precipitated by the failure of *two* parties—union and management—to reach agreement. In fact, a growing number of work stoppages in recent years have taken the form of lockouts initiated by employers. Popular opinion to the contrary, it is unfair to attribute all of the costs associated with a strike to labor alone.

[22] Richard McHugh, "Productivity Effects of Strikes in Struck and Nonstruck Industries," *Industrial and Labor Relations Review,* July 1991, pp. 722–32.

[23] George R. Neumann and Melvin W. Reder, "Output and Strike Activity in U.S. Manufacturing: How Large Are the Losses?" *Industrial and Labor Relations Review,* January 1984, pp. 197–211. Another study concludes that a strike reduces the stock market value of a struck firm by 3 percent. See John DiNardo and Kevin F. Hallock, "When Unions 'Mattered': Assessing the Impact of Strikes on Financial Markets," *Industrial and Labor Relations Review,* January 2002, pp. 219–33.

11.3	**World of Work**	**Labor Strife and Product Quality***

In 2000, 14.4 million Bridgestone/Firestone tires were recalled. About 6.5 million of the tires were still being used, mostly on Ford Explorers. The National Highway Traffic and Safety Administration issued a statement claiming that the recalled tires were related to 271 deaths and more than 800 injuries. The most frequent reason for failure of the tires was the separation of the rubber tread from the steel belts, which causes a tire to blow out.

Some observers suggested at the time that a long and contentious strike at a Bridgestone/Firestone plant in Decatur, Illinois, may have played a role in causing the tire defects. Tires are still mostly handmade; so human error can lower product quality. Krueger and Mas confirm the speculation that the labor strife lowered product quality. They find that the defect rate was greatest when management requested concessions from workers and when striking workers returned and worked alongside replacement workers hired during the strike. This finding suggests that workers provide more careful work and effort when they feel they are being treated well.

The labor strife imposed costs in various ways. Krueger and Mas estimate that more than 40 deaths were caused by the labor dispute. The number of deaths would have been more than twice as high if the tires had not been recalled. The labor strife also hurt the financial health of Bridgestone/Firestone because tires manufactured at the Decatur plant during the labor dispute were 15 times more likely to have resulted in a financial claim against the company than those manufactured at other Bridgestone/Firestone plants. The market value of the firm dropped from $16.7 billion to $7.5 billion in the four months following the recall. This suggests that good labor relations are beneficial for both management and labor.

* Based on Alan B. Krueger and Alexandre Mas, "Strikes, Scabs, and Tread Separations: Labor Strife and the Production of Defective Bridgestone/Firestone Tires," *Journal of Political Economy,* April 2004, pp. 253–89.

3 Wage Advantage and Labor Misallocation

A third major way unions may adversely affect efficiency is through the wage advantage itself.

A Simple Model   This effect can be seen through reconsideration and extension of the spillover model in Figure 11.2. In Figure 11.6 we have drawn (for simplicity's sake) identical labor demand curves for the unionized and nonunion sectors of the labor market for some particular labor. We assume that the relevant product market is purely competitive so that the labor demand curves reflect not only marginal revenue product (MRP) but also value of marginal product (VMP).[24] If there is no union present, the wage rate that would result from competition in hiring labor is W_n. Now assume that a union establishes itself in sector 1 and increases the wage rate from W_n to W_u. In accordance with our analysis of the spillover effect, the result is that the $Q'_1 Q'_2$ workers who lose their jobs in the union sector move to nonunion sector 2, where we assume they secure employment. These additional workers depress the wage rate from W_n to W_s in nonunion sector 2.

[24] Recall from Chapter 5 that MRP measures the amount that an additional worker adds to a firm's total revenue, while VMP indicates the value of a worker's extra output to society. VMP tells us the dollar amount an extra worker contributes to the domestic output.

FIGURE 11.6 **The Effect of the Union Wage Advantage on the Allocation of Labor**
The higher wage W_u that the union achieves in sector 1 causes the displacement of $Q'_1 Q'_2$ workers. The reemployment of these workers in nonunion sector 2 reduces the wage rate there from W_n to W_s. The associated loss of output in the union sector is the area $Q'_2 abQ'_1$, whereas the gain in the nonunion sector is only area $Q_1 cdQ_2$. Because the shaded areas are of equal size in each diagram, the net loss of output is area $c'abd'$.

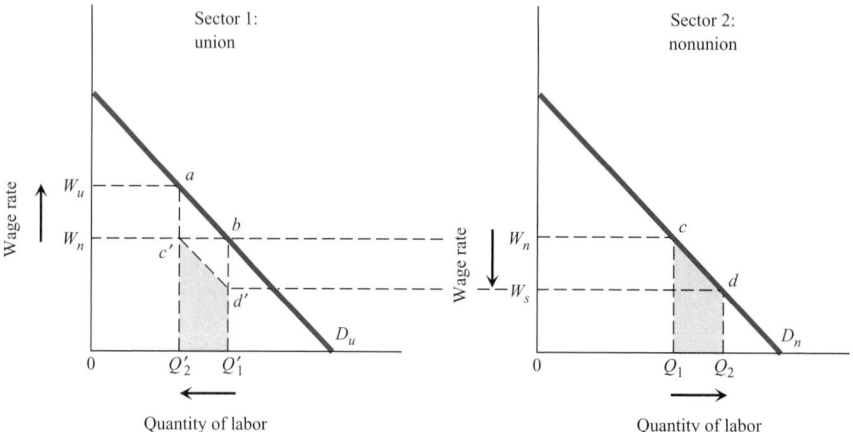

Because we have kept the level of employment unchanged, this simple model allows us to isolate the efficiency or allocative effect of the union wage differential. The area $Q'_2 abQ'_1$ represents the loss of domestic output caused by the $Q'_1 Q'_2$ employment decline in the union sector. This area is the sum of the VMPs—the total contribution to the domestic output—of the workers displaced by the W_n to W_u wage increase achieved by the union. As these workers spill over into nonunion sector 2 and are reemployed, they add to the domestic output the amount indicated by the $Q_1 cdQ_2$ area. Because $Q'_2 abQ'_1$ exceeds $Q_1 cdQ_2$, there is a net loss of domestic output. More precisely, because the shaded areas are equal in each diagram, the net loss of output attributable to the union wage advantage is equal to area $c'abd'$ as shown in the union sector diagram. The same amount of employed labor is now producing a smaller output, so labor is obviously misallocated and inefficiently used. Viewed from a slightly different perspective, *after* the spillover of $Q_1 Q_2$ workers from the union to the nonunion sector has occurred, workers will be paid a wage rate equal to their VMPs in both sectors. But the VMPs of the union workers will be higher than the VMPs of the nonunion workers. The economy will always benefit from a larger domestic output when any given type of labor is reallocated from a relatively low-VMP use to a relatively high-VMP use. But given the union's presence and its ability to maintain the W_u wage rate in its sector, this reallocation from sector 2 to 1 will not occur.

Qualifications Our model of the allocative inefficiency stemming from a union wage advantage is very simplified. Let's briefly call attention to several additional real-world considerations that might cause the efficiency loss to be greater or less than our model suggests.

1. **Unemployment:** Recalling our earlier comments about wait unemployment, what if some workers who lost their jobs because of higher wages in the union sector decided to remain in that sector in the hope of reemployment? The consequence is a net loss of output in excess of $c'abd'$ in Figure 11.6. The reason? While output would decline by area $Q'_2abQ'_1$ in the union sector, it would increase by *less than* Q_1cdQ_2 in the nonunion sector. In the extreme, if all $Q'_1Q'_2$ displaced workers remained unemployed in the union sector, the loss of output to society would be $Q'_2abQ'_1$. The same result might stem from downward wage rigidity in sector 2. If for some reason wages would not decline to W_s, it would not be profitable for sector 2 firms to hire additional workers beyond Q_1. Finally, to the extent that the threat and product market effects increase nonunion wages, workers will be displaced in that sector as well as in the union sector.

2. **Job search costs:** A second and related point is that our model understates the loss of output because it implicitly assumes that workers instantly and costlessly shift from the union to the nonunion sector. Job search by unemployed workers takes time and entails both out-of-pocket costs (paying for advertisements and for the service of employment agencies) and opportunity costs (earnings forgone during the search period). And as we discovered in Chapter 9, the geographic movement that may be involved in shifting from the union to the nonunion sector is also costly.

3. **Bilateral monopoly:** On the other hand, our discussion tends to overstate the detrimental effect that unions may have on allocative efficiency to the extent that unions engage in bargaining with monopsonistic employers. Recall from the discussion of bilateral monopoly in Figure 6.11 that union wage determination may in effect correct the underallocation of labor resources that a monopsonistic employer would find profitable.

4. **Investment behavior and productivity growth:** The model discussed in the preceding section (Figure 11.6) portrays only the *static* or short-run efficiency effects of the union wage advantage. The union wage differential may also have an adverse *dynamic* or long-run effect on efficiency. Specifically, unions may reduce firm and industry profitability, thereby a retarding investment and economic growth. If a powerful union can expropriate a sizable portion of the returns from a firm's investment in either physical capital (machinery and equipment) or in research and development, such investments may diminish. Because the path of labor productivity over time depends heavily on the stock of capital goods per worker and technological progress (Chapters 5 and 17), any significant union encroachment on profits from such investments could be expected to reduce the growth of labor productivity.

Empirical Estimates

Several estimates have been made of the static efficiency loss associated with union wage gains. They are in agreement that the loss is small. In a pioneering study Rees assumed a 15 percent union wage advantage and estimated that approximately

0.14 percent—only about one-seventh of 1 percent—of the domestic output was lost.[25] A more recent estimate by Freeman and Medoff indicates that "union monopoly wage gains cost the economy 0.02 to 0.04 percent of gross national product, which in 1980 amounted to about $5 to $10 billion or $20.00 to $40.00 per person."[26] And in a 1983 study, DeFina estimated that a 15 percent union wage advantage would cause only a 0.08 to 0.09 percentage loss of output.[27]

Positive View

Other economists believe that on balance, unions make a positive contribution to productivity and efficiency.

1 Investment and Technological Progress

One may carry Figure 11.3's discussion of the labor misallocation that stems from the union wage advantage a step further and argue that union wage increases may *accelerate* the substitution of capital for labor and *hasten* the search for cost-reducing (productivity-increasing) technologies. When faced with higher production costs due to the union wage advantage, employers will be prompted to reduce costs by using more machinery and by seeking improved production techniques that use less of both labor and capital per unit of output. In fact, if the product market is reasonably competitive, a unionized firm with labor costs that are, say, 15 to 20 percent higher than those of nonunion competitors will not survive unless productivity can be raised. In short, union wage pressure may inadvertently generate managerial actions that increase domestic productivity. This is essentially the opposite of the argument made a moment ago that higher union wages will reduce profits, inhibit investment in capital goods and innovation, and reduce labor productivity.

2 Unions as a Collective Voice

Freeman and Medoff have stressed the view that on balance, unions contribute to rising productivity in firms by voicing worker grievances and through their effects on labor turnover, worker security, and managerial efficiency.[28]

The Voice Mechanism   The positive impact of unions on productivity occurs in part because unions function as a ***collective voice*** for their members in resolving disputes, improving working conditions, and so forth. If a group of workers is dissatisfied with its conditions of employment, it has two potential means of response. These are the exit mechanism and the voice mechanism. The ***exit mechanism*** refers to the use of

---

[25] Albert Rees, "The Effects of Unions on Resource Allocation," *Journal of Law and Economics,* October 1963, pp. 69–78.

[26] Freeman and Medoff, op. cit., p. 57.

[27] Robert H. DeFina, "Unions, Relative Wages, and Economic Efficiency," *Journal of Labor Economics,* October 1983, pp. 408–29.

[28] Freeman and Medoff, op. cit., chap. 11. For a critical review of the collective voice role of unions, see John T. Addison and Clive R. Belfield, "Union Voice," *Journal of Labor Research,* Fall 2004, pp. 563–96.

the labor market—by leaving or exiting the present job in search of a better one—as a means of reacting to unpleasant employers and working conditions. In contrast, the *voice mechanism* entails communication between workers and the employer to improve working conditions and resolve worker grievances. It may well be risky for *individual* workers to express their dissatisfaction to employers because employers may retaliate by firing such workers as "troublemakers." But unions can give workers a *collective* voice to communicate problems and grievances to management and to press for their satisfactory resolution. This enhances worker job satisfaction and morale and therefore increases productivity. According to Freeman and Medoff, unions can positively affect productivity not only through the voice mechanism but also in a variety of other ways.

Reduced Turnover   Substantial evidence exists that unionization reduces quits and turnovers. On one hand, the collective voice of the union may be effective in correcting job dissatisfaction that otherwise would be resolved by workers through the exit mechanism of changing jobs. On the other hand, other things being the same, the union wage advantage will tend to reduce the quit rates of union workers.

A variety of studies suggest that the decline in quit rates attributable to unionism is very substantial, ranging from 31 to 65 percent.[29] A lower quit rate increases efficiency by producing a more experienced labor force within unionized firms and by reducing the firm's recruitment, screening, and hiring costs. Furthermore, the reduced turnover makes investments in specific training by employers more attractive. Reduced turnover increases the likelihood that the employer will capture a positive return on worker training (Chapter 4).

Seniority and Informal Training

Because of union insistence on the primacy of seniority in such matters as promotion and layoff, worker security is enhanced. Given this security, workers are more willing to pass on their job knowledge and skills to new or subordinate workers through informal on-the-job training (Chapter 15). Obviously this enhances labor quality and productivity.[30]

Managerial Performance

Union wage pressure may precipitate a *shock effect* that is favorable to productivity. Confronted with a strong union and higher wage demands, firms may be forced to

---

[29] Freeman and Medoff, op. cit. pp. 95–96.

[30] The "lifetime" job security that some Japanese firms provide for a portion of their labor force is often cited as an important determinant of their rapid productivity growth. It should be noted, however, that the contention that unionization increases on-the-job training has been challenged. See John M. Barron, Scott M. Fuess, Jr., and Mark A. Loewenstein, "Further Analysis of the Effects of Unions on Training," *Journal of Political Economy*, July 1987, pp. 632–40. However, a British study does find that unionization raises training in Great Britain. See Francis Green, Stephen Machin, and David Wilkinson, "Trade Unions and Training Practices in British Workplaces," *Industrial and Labor Relations Review*, January 1999, pp. 179–95.

adopt better personnel and production methods to meet the union's wage demands and maintain profitability. For example, in his study of the impact of unionization on productivity in the cement industry, Clark observes that after unionization, plant management was improved.[31] He documents a managerial shift to "a more professional, businesslike approach to labor relations." Furthermore, after unionization, greater stress was placed on production goals and the monitoring of worker performance. "Perhaps the most cogent description of the differences in the management process before and after unionization was given by a plant manager who remarked, '. . . before the union this place was run like a family; now we run it like a business.' " Finally, it is worth noting that collective bargaining provides a potential avenue of communication through which the union can point out to management ways of enhancing productivity.

Recapitulation: Unions may improve efficiency by (1) functioning as a collective voice mechanism for resolving worker grievances; (2) reducing worker turnover; (3) enhancing worker security and thereby creating an environment favorable to on-the-job training; and (4) stimulating managerial efficiency through the shock effect.

Empirical Evidence

Many studies have been undertaken to measure the impact of unionization on productivity. These studies attempt to control for labor quality, capital–labor ratios, the newness of capital equipment, and other variables aside from unionization that might contribute to productivity differences. The empirical score on the union–productivity issue is about even. For every study that finds a positive union effect on productivity, another study using different data or techniques concludes that there is a negative effect. In fact, a statistical analysis of existing studies based on U.S. data reveals that the mean effect of unions on productivity is a positive 3 percent.[32] Hirsch in a recent survey concludes that the average union effect on productivity is near zero and at most is slightly positive.[33]

Hirsch argues that two patterns have emerged regarding union productivity effects. First, the impact of unions on productivity tends to be larger in industries where the union wage advantage is largest. This finding is consistent with the shock effect of unions, where firms respond to higher wage costs by operating more efficiently and thus raising productivity. Second, the positive union productivity effects are mostly confined to the private for-profit sector, and the largest productivity effects are in the most competitive industries. For example, there does not appear to be positive productivity effects in public libraries, schools, government agencies, or law enforcement.

---

[31] Kim B. Clark, "The Impact of Unionization on Productivity: A Case Study," *Industrial and Labor Relations Review,* July 1980, pp. 451–69.

[32] Christos Doucouliagos and Patrice Laroche, "What Do Unions Do to Productivity? A Meta-Analysis," *Industrial Relations,* October 2003, pp. 650–91.

[33] Barry T. Hirsch, "What Do Unions Do for Economic Performance?" *Journal of Labor Research,* Summer 2004, pp. 415–55.

11.4 World of Work

Unions and Investment*

Theoretically, the impact of unions on firm investments in physical capital is ambiguous. One possibility is that the union wage advantage may cause firms to substitute toward the relatively cheaper capital and thus increase their investment rate. Alternatively, higher union wages may raise the price of the product and reduce the amount of output sold. This would lower the rate of return on investment and reduce the investment rate. In addition, if unions can extract a large share of the returns to physical capital through higher wages, then firms will reduce their rate of investment.

Fallick and Hassett examine the impact of unions on investment decisions using a sample of over 2,000 firms listed on the New York Stock Exchange. They find that a successful election certifying a new union lowers investment in capital by 30 percent in the year following the election. They note that unionization

has about the same effect as would a doubling of the corporate tax rate of 34 percent. Fallick and Hassett suggest this evidence helps explain why unionized firms tend to merge with other unionized firms, whereas nonunionized firms normally merge with nonunion companies. They argue that these outcomes result from the substantial "tax" that unions place on a firm's investments. If one union firm buys another, this tax will have no effect on the value of the acquired assets. But if a nonunion firm buys a union firm, the assets of the nonunion firm become subject to the tax liability of the union. As a result, nonunion firms are less likely than union firms to merge with a unionized firm.

* Based on Bruce C. Fallick and Kevin A. Hassett, "Investment and Union Certification," *Journal of Labor Economics,* July 1999, pp. 570–82.

Though there is less evidence regarding the long-run effects of unions on productivity, existing empirical evidence suggests that unionized firms have lower productivity growth. Nearly all of the lower productivity growth for unionized firms seems to be due to these firms being in industries that have slow productivity growth.[34] There is apparently no *direct* effect of unions on productivity growth. However, unions *indirectly* lower

productivity growth by reducing the rate of investment in physical capital and research development activity.

FIRM PROFITABILITY

Does unionization raise or lower firm and industry profitability? Do the wage gains of union workers come at the expense of business profits? Or do productivity increases that *may* accompany unionization offset higher wages so that profits are unaffected? Or are unionized firms and industries able to shift their higher wage costs on to consumers through higher product prices and thereby preserve profitability?

Virtually all empirical studies associate unionization with diminished profitability. (Indeed, it would be difficult to reconcile employer resistance to unions if the opposite

[34] Ibid.

were true.) Freeman and Medoff, for example, report significant (17–37 percent) reductions in profits due to unionization.[35] Using data for some 139 manufacturing industries, Voos and Mishell have concluded that unionization reduces profitability by 20 to 23 percent.[36] Two studies using firm-level data report that unionization reduces profitability.[37] Similarly, after examining 16 studies of the union impact on profitability, Addison and Hirsch conclude, "The most striking result of the studies is the common theme of lower profitability in union regimes. . . . Moreover, the magnitude of the reduction in profits is large."[38]

Is this redistribution from profits to wages desirable? There are two polar scenarios. Scenario 1: If the unionized industry is less competitive, the effect of a union may simply be to transfer unwarranted "excess" profits from the pockets of capitalists to those of workers, with no negative effects on economic efficiency. Scenario 2: If the unionized industry is highly competitive and profits are therefore about normal, higher union wage costs may have adverse effects. Specifically, higher wage costs will mean below-normal profits and the impairment of investment in capital equipment and technological progress; and in the long run, firms will leave the industry. The resulting smaller output will mean higher product prices for consumers and less employment for workers. Declining investment in the industry will mean a lower overall rate of economic growth.

Which scenario is more relevant? Empirical findings differ. Some research indicates that unions obtain part of the profits that result from a firm's market power. Specifically, unions appear to capture profits resulting from limited import competition as well as entry restrictions.[39] For example, union workers in the airline and trucking industries received large wage premiums prior to the deregulation of these industries. In other words, these findings seem to support the more socially desirable scenario 1 than the less desirable scenario 2. Other empirical results support the opposite conclusion. These findings suggest that unions achieve wage gains by reducing the return on firm investments in research and development and physical capital.[40] This, of course, lends support to scenario 2.

[35] Freeman and Medoff, op. cit., Table 12.1, p. 183.

[36] Paula B. Voos and Lawrence R. Mishell, "The Union Impact on Profits: Evidence from Industry Price-Cost Margin Data," *Journal of Labor Economics,* January 1986, pp. 105–33.

[37] Barry T. Hirsch, "Union Coverage and Profitability among U.S. Firms," *Review of Economics and Statistics,* February 1991, pp. 69–77; and Stephen G. Bronars, Donald R. Deere, and Joseph S. Tracy, "The Effects of Unions on Firm Behavior: An Empirical Analysis Using Firm-Level Data," *Industrial Relations,* October 1994, pp. 426–51; and Barry T. Hirsch, "Unionization and Economic Performance: Evidence on Productivity, Profits, Investment, and Growth," in Fazil Mihlar (ed.), *Unions and Right-to-Work Laws,* Vancouver, B.C.: The Fraser Institute, 1997, pp. 35–70.

[38] John T. Addison and Barry T. Hirsch, "Union Effects on Productivity, Profits, and Growth: Has the Long Run Arrived?" *Journal of Labor Economics,* January 1989, p. 87. Hirsch, op. cit., chap. 4, pp. 35–68, provides a concise, readable discussion of this topic.

[39] See Hirsch, op. cit., 2004.

[40] See Hirsch, 1991, op. cit; and Brian E. Becker and Craig A. Olson, "Unions and Firm Profits," *Industrial Relations,* Fall 1992, pp. 395–415.

To summarize: There is agreement that, overall, unions reduce firm profitability. But there is no consensus about whether this redistribution reduces economic efficiency.

11.2 *Quick* *Review*	• Unions may impair efficiency and productivity through *(a)* restrictive work rules, *(b)* strikes, and *(c)* labor misallocation resulting from the union wage advantage. • The static efficiency loss from unionism is thought to be relatively small. • Unions may positively contribute to efficiency and productivity through *(a)* inadvertently accelerating the substitution of capital for labor and hastening the search for cost-reducing technologies and *(b)* serving as a collective voice mechanism that reduces labor turnover, enhances worker security, and induces managerial efficiency. • Empirical evidence of the union impact on productivity is mixed and inconclusive. • Studies indicate that unions significantly reduce the profitability of firms. **Your Turn** Explain why the following two statements could be consistent: "Unions enhance productivity"; "Unions reduce firm profitability." (*Answer:* See page 598.)

DISTRIBUTION OF EARNINGS

Some disagreement also arises about the impact of unions on the distribution of earnings. A few economists reason that unions contribute to earnings inequality; most take precisely the opposite view.

Increasing Inequality

Those who argue that unions increase inequality in the distribution of wages contend that unions (1) simultaneously increase the wages of union workers and depress the wages of nonunion workers through the spillover effect; (2) raise the wages of skilled blue-collar workers relative to those of unskilled blue-collar workers; and (3) increase the demand for skilled labor within unionized firms.

Union–Nonunion Wages

Perhaps the simplest argument in support of the position that unions enhance inequality is based on the spillover effect. Recall once again that the higher wage rates realized in the union sector of Figure 11.2 displace workers who then seek reemployment in the nonunion sector. The result of this displacement is that nonunion wage rates are depressed. Thus although we began with equal rates of W_n in both submarkets, the effect of unionism is to generate higher wage rates of W_u for union workers but lower wages of W_s for nonunion workers.

TABLE 11.2
Labor Quality,
Productivity, and
Wage Rates

(1) Type of Labor	(2) Output per Hour	(3) Wage Rate	(4) = (3) ÷ (2) Wage Cost per Unit of Output
A	5	$6.00	$1.20
B	4	4.00	1.00
C	2	2.50	1.25

Blue-Collar Wages

The fact that unionization is more extensive among the more highly skilled, higher-paid blue-collar workers than among less skilled, lower-paid blue-collar workers also suggests that the obtaining of a wage advantage by unions increases the dispersion of earnings.

Skilled Labor Demand

Pettengill[41] has argued that when unions force employers to pay above-equilibrium wage rates, the long-run response is to hire higher-quality workers. This constitutes a shift in the structure of labor demand away from low-quality and toward high-quality workers. The net result is a widening of the dispersion of wages or, in short, greater wage inequality.

Pettengill elaborates his reasoning with the following example shown in Table 11.2. Here we assume that *A, B,* and *C* designate various levels of labor quality—say, high school graduates, high school dropouts, and workers with no high school education, respectively—that are available to a nonunion employer. The productivity or output per hour of each quality level is given in column 2, and wage rates are specified in column 3. By dividing productivity into the wage rate, we obtain wage cost per unit of output as shown in column 4. Given these options, the firm will hire *B* labor at $4 per hour because the associated wage costs per unit of output are minimized.

Now suppose the firm is unionized and the wages of *B* labor increase to $6. What are the consequences? In the short run, the per-unit cost of production rises to $1.50 and the lifetime earnings prospects of *B* workers are enhanced. In the long run, the normal attrition of *B* workers through retirement, voluntary quits, deaths, and so forth will prompt the firm to replace such workers with *A* workers. That is, if the union forces the employer to pay $6 per hour for labor, the firm will seek the best-qualified workers obtainable at that wage rate. Specifically, the firm will now require all of its new employees to have a high school diploma. Note that when all *B* workers are eventually replaced with *A* workers at the $6 wage rate, labor costs per unit of output will have fallen from $1.50 to $1.20 because *A* workers are more productive.

If this scenario is repeated on a wide scale, we find that an increase in the demand for high-quality *A* workers and a decline in the demand for lower-quality *B* workers

---

[41] John S. Pettengill, *Labor Unions and the Inequality of Earned Income* (Amsterdam: North-Holland Publishing Company, 1980).

occur. This causes the ratio of the going wage of high school graduates to increase relative to the going wage of high school dropouts, widening the dispersion of wages and increasing earnings inequality. Less obviously, the higher wages for high school graduates will reduce the incremental income received by college graduates in comparison with high school graduates (see Figure 4.2). This decline in the college premium will reduce the rate of return on an investment in a college education and in time reduce the supply of college graduates. As a result, the wages and salaries received by college graduates will tend to rise, further increasing the dispersion of wages and increasing earnings inequality.

Promoting Equality

Other aspects of union wage policies, however, suggest that unionism promotes greater, not less, equality in the distribution of earnings. What are these other ways in which unions tend to equalize wages?

1 Uniform Wages within Firms

Without unions, employers are apt to pay different wages to individual workers on the same job. These wage differences are based on perceived differences in job performance, length of job tenure, and perhaps favoritism. Unions, on the other hand, have a tradition of seeking uniform wage rates for all workers performing a particular job. In short, while nonunion firms usually assign wage rates to *individual workers,* unions—in the interest of worker allegiance and solidarity—seek to assign wage rates to *jobs.* To the extent that unions are successful, wage and earnings differentials based on supervisory judgments of individual worker performance are eliminated. An important side effect of this standard-wage policy is that wage discrimination against African–Americans, other minorities, and women is likely to be less when a union is present. Recall from Chapter 10 that African–American male workers tend to benefit more from unionization than any other demographic group.

Wage and earnings inequality within a firm may be reduced by unionism for another reason. Industrial unions—those comprising a variety of workers, ranging from unskilled to highly skilled—frequently follow a wage policy of seeking equal *absolute* wage increases for all of their constituents. This means that larger *percentage* increases are realized by less skilled workers, and the earnings gap between unskilled and skilled workers is reduced. Consider this simple illustration. Assume that skilled workers are initially paid $10 and unskilled workers $5 per hour. Suppose the union negotiates equal $2 increases for both groups so that skilled workers now receive $12 and unskilled $7 per hour. Originally unskilled workers earned 50 percent (= $5/$10) of what skilled workers received. But after the wage increase, unskilled workers get about 58 percent (= $7/$12) of skilled wages. Relative wage inequality has diminished.

Why would an industrial union adopt a policy of equal absolute wage increases for workers of different skills? The answer is twofold. On the one hand, it reflects the union's egalitarian ideology. On other hand, it allows union leaders to largely sidestep politically awkward and potentially divisive decisions concerning the relative worth of various groups of constituents.

2 Uniform Wages among Firms

In addition to seeking standard wage rates for given occupational classes *within* firms, unions also seek standard wage rates *among* firms. The rationale for this policy is almost self-evident. The existence of substantial wage differences among competing firms in an industry may undermine the ability of unions to sustain and enhance wage advantages. For example, if one firm in a four-firm oligopoly is allowed to pay significantly lower wages to its union workers, the union is likely to find it difficult to maintain the union wage advantage in the other three firms. In particular, during a recession the high-wage firms are likely to put great pressure on the union to lower wages to the level of the low-wage firm. To avoid this problem, unions seek to "take labor (wages) out of competition" by standardizing wage rates among firms, thereby reducing the degree of wage dispersion. You may recall from Chapter 10 that multi-employer bargaining that culminates in an industrywide contract is an important means of standardizing wage rates.

3 Reducing the White-Collar to Blue-Collar Differential

In examining the empirical evidence on the union wage advantage, we observed that unions achieve larger wage gains for blue-collar workers than for white-collar workers. Because on the average white-collar workers enjoy higher earnings than do blue-collar workers, the larger wage gains that unions achieve for the latter reduce earnings inequalities between blue- and white-collar workers.

Increased Equality?

What is the *net* effect of unionism on the distribution of earnings? There is a rather strong consensus that unions decrease the degree of wage dispersion. Freeman and Medoff have used empirical analysis to conclude that the spillover effect *increases* earnings inequality by about 1 percent, but the standardization of wage rates within and among firms *decreases* inequality by about 4 percent. The net result is a 3 percent decline in earnings inequality due to unionism. Noting that only a relatively small percentage of the labor force is unionized, the authors contend that this 3 percent reduction in inequality should be regarded as "substantial."[42] This conclusion is reinforced by Card,[43] who estimates that unions reduced wage inequality by 7 percent in 1987. He also points to the decline in unionism as a contributor to the recent increase in wage inequality in the United States ("World of Work" 6.4 and Chapter 17). For the 1973–1974 to 1993 period, Card concludes that 15–20 percent of the rise in earnings inequality among male workers and little of the rise in inequality among female workers was due to declining unionism.[44]

---

[42] Freeman and Medoff, op. cit., pp. 90–93, and additional studies cited therein.

[43] David Card, "The Effect of Unions on the Structure of Wages: A Longitudinal Analysis," *Econometrica,* July 1996, pp. 957–79.

[44] David Card, "The Effect of Unions on Wage Inequality in the U.S. Labor Market," *Industrial and Labor Relations Review,* January 2001, pp. 296–315. See also David Card, Thomas Lemieux, and W. Craig Riddell, "Unionization and Wage Inequality: A Comparative Study of the U.S., the U.K., and Canada," National Bureau of Economic Research Working Paper Number 9473, February 2003.

OTHER ISSUES: INFLATION, UNEMPLOYMENT, AND INCOME SHARES

Our discussion of the possible economic impact of unions is not complete. Unions could conceivably affect inflation, employment and unemployment, and the share of national income paid as wages. Let's briefly assess each, necessarily leaving detailed discussion to textbooks about macroeconomics.

Inflation

Economists generally agree that union wage determination is *not* a basic cause of inflation. Most of our serious inflationary episodes have been associated with excess aggregate demand or supply shocks rather than wage push considerations. Specifically, recent inflations can be attributed largely to expansionary fiscal or monetary policies or supply shocks, such as the dramatic Organization of Petroleum Exporting Countries oil price increases of the 1970s. On the other hand, wage determination under collective bargaining may perpetuate an ongoing inflation because unions may seek and receive wage gains in anticipation of future inflation. These actions hinder the effectiveness of anti-inflationary policies.

Unions and Unemployment

The relationship between unionism and unemployment is complex and highly controversial. One view is that unions are a major cause of downward wage inflexibility in our economy.[45] As a result, declines in labor demand affect employment almost exclusively and not wages. Because of the downward inflexibility of wages, wage reduction cannot cushion or ameliorate the impact of recession on unemployment. The counterview is that downward wage rigidity is largely attributable to factors other than unionism. For example, nonunion workers have informal understandings or implicit contracts with employers that obligate employers to maintain wage rates unless economic conditions are so severe as to threaten the firm with bankruptcy. Furthermore, firms may prefer selective layoffs to across-the-board wage reductions during an economic slump. The reason is that the latter might cause higher-skilled, more experienced workers in whom the firm has made large training investments to quit and take other jobs. A fixed-wage-with-layoffs strategy allows employers to hoard these more valuable workers during an economic downturn and to lay off less trained workers who can be more easily and less expensively replaced.

Apart from cyclic changes in labor demand, unions may affect employment in at least two other ways. First, unionism is associated with lower worker turnover, which tends to reduce unemployment rates. Second, by raising wages unions may increase unemployment by attracting additional workers into the labor force (see Figure 6.10 and the accompanying discussion).

Overall, the unionism–unemployment picture is mixed, and no consensus exists about the net effect. It is relevant to note, however, that in one study Montgomery examined data for some 42 metropolitan areas in an attempt to assess the impact of union strength (as measured by both the percentage of workers organized and the size of the union–nonunion

---

[45] See Chapter 18 for a fuller discussion.

wage differential) on employment. He found that greater union strength is associated with a lesser likelihood of employment, but the quantitative effects are very small. For example, a 10 percent increase in the percentage of workers unionized reduces the likelihood of being employed by only 0.2 percent. Similarly, a 10 percent increase in the union wage premium reduces the likelihood of being employed by just 0.06 percent.[46]

Labor's Share

There is no significant evidence to suggest that unions have been able to increase labor's share and decrease the capitalist share of national income. The reasons for this are several. In the first place, as our analysis of the spillover effect implies, higher wages for union workers may come largely at the expense of the wages of nonunion workers (Figure 11.2) and not out of the capitalist share. Second, union wage increases may induce the substitution of capital for labor. Therefore, the potential positive effect that higher union wages have on labor's share in the unionized sector may be offset by the negative effect associated with fewer union jobs. Finally, management may largely escape a redistribution of national income from capital to labor through productivity and price increases. The potential encroachment on profits stemming from wage increases may partially be absorbed or offset by productivity or price increases. The lack of any significant impact on labor's share is undoubtedly related to the fact that only a relatively small percentage of the labor force is unionized.

Chapter Summary	
	1. Considerations other than the presence of unions may explain at least in part why strongly unionized industries pay higher wages than weakly organized industries. These factors include relatively fewer female workers, larger-scale plants, and more capital-intensive production methods in the strongly unionized industries.

Chapter Summary

1. Considerations other than the presence of unions may explain at least in part why strongly unionized industries pay higher wages than weakly organized industries. These factors include relatively fewer female workers, larger-scale plants, and more capital-intensive production methods in the strongly unionized industries.

2. The pure union wage advantage A is equal to $(W_u - W_n)/W_n \times 100$, where W_u is the union wage and W_n the nonunion wage that would exist without unions.

3. The spillover and superior worker effects cause the measured union wage advantage to overstate the pure wage advantage; the threat and product market effects cause the measured union wage advantage to understate the pure wage advantage.

4. Research evidence consistently indicates that unions do achieve a wage advantage for their constituents, although the size of the advantage varies substantially by occupation, industry, race, and gender. Estimates by Lewis for the 1923–1958 period suggest that the average union wage advantage was on the order of 10–15 percent, but the advantage widens during depression and diminishes when unexpected inflation occurs. The union wage advantage widened in the mid-1970s. The advantage has fallen since then to 17 percent.

[46] Edward Montgomery, "Employment and Unemployment Effects of Unions," *Journal of Labor Economics,* April 1989, pp. 170–90.

5. Union workers also generally receive a higher level and greater variety of fringe benefits, causing the union total compensation advantage to exceed the wage advantage.

6. Disagreement exists about whether the net effect of unions on allocative efficiency and productivity is positive or negative. The negative view cites *(a)* the inefficiencies associated with union-imposed work rules, *(b)* the loss of output through strikes, and *(c)* the misallocation of labor created by the union wage advantage.

7. The positive view contends that *(a)* union wage pressure spurs technological advance and the mechanization of the production process and *(b)* as collective voice institutions, unions contribute to rising productivity by resolving worker grievances, reducing labor turnover, enhancing worker security, and inducing greater managerial efficiency.

8. Consensus exists that unions reduce firm profitability, but disagreement arises over whether this reduction has undesirable effects on economic efficiency.

9. Those who contend that unions increase earnings inequality argue that *(a)* unionization increases the wages of union workers but lowers the wages of nonunion workers; *(b)* unions are strongest among highly paid, skilled blue-collar workers but are relatively weak among low-paid, unskilled blue-collar workers; and *(c)* union wage increases generate an increase in the demand for high-quality workers and a decline in the demand for low-quality workers. The opposing view is that unions contribute to greater earnings equality because *(a)* unions seek uniform wages for given jobs within firms, *(b)* unions favor uniform wages among firms, and *(c)* unions have achieved higher wage gains for relatively low-paid blue-collar workers than for relatively high-paid white-collar workers. Recent empirical evidence finds that unionism does reduce wage inequality and that the decline of unionism has contributed to growing wage inequality.

Terms and Concepts

pure union wage advantage, *337*
spillover effect, *338*
measured union wage advantage, *339*

threat effect, *339*
product market effect, *340*
wait unemployment, *340*
superior worker effect, *340*
fringe benefits, *344*

featherbedding, *347*
collective voice, *354*
exit and voice mechanisms, *354–355*
shock effect, *355*

Questions and Study Suggestions

1. What is the commonsense basis for expecting a union wage advantage? Explain how each of the following differences between union and nonunion firms might complicate one's determination of whether unions actually are responsible for an observed wage advantage: *(a)* the demographic makeup of the labor forces, *(b)* plant sizes, and *(c)* the amount of capital equipment used per worker.

2. Evidence suggests that the union wage advantage varies directly with the proportion of a given industry that is organized. Why is this?

3. How is the pure union wage advantage defined? If in a given labor market the wage rate would be $8 without a union and $10 with a union, then what is the pure union wage advantage? Explain how, and in what direction, each of the following might cause the measured union wage advantage to vary from the pure advantage: *(a)* the spillover effect, *(b)* the threat effect, *(c)* the product market effect, and *(d)* the superior worker effect.

4. Indicate the overall size of the measured union wage advantage. Does recent evidence suggest that the advantage has increased or decreased? Comment on and explain cyclic changes in the union wage advantage.

5. Compare the size of the fringe benefits received by union and nonunion workers and indicate why unions might be responsible for any differences.

6. Comment on each of the following statements:
   a. "Unions tie the hands of management and inhibit efficient decision making."
   b. "Unions contribute to economic efficiency in that union wage pressure hastens the weeding out of the high-cost, least efficient producers in each industry."
   c. "Although unions may reduce wage inequality, to the extent that they reduce wage differentials based on individual merit and effort, the outcome may be rightly perceived as both inequitable and inefficient."
   d. "Unions impair the efficiency of our economy indirectly by diminishing profits and thereby reducing investment and economic expansion."

7. Indicate the amount of work time lost each year because of strikes. Cite circumstances under which the amount of work time lost during a specific strike might be a poor indicator of the amount of lost output.

8. "There is an inherent cost to society that accompanies any union wage gain. That cost is the diminished efficiency with which labor resources are allocated." Explain this contention. Do you agree? In your response, distinguish between static and dynamic efficiency.

9. Evidence suggests that firms that sell their products in less competitive product markets are more likely to be unionized than firms selling in highly competitive markets. Recalling from Chapter 5 that the elasticity of product demand is an important determinant of the elasticity of labor demand, how might this affect *(a)* the elasticities of the union and nonunion demand curve in Figure 11.6 and *(b)* the net loss of output due to the union wage advantage?

10. In what specific ways might the presence of a union raise productivity within a firm? Use the exit mechanism and voice mechanism concepts in your response.

11. Describe the various avenues through which unions might alter the distribution of earnings. On balance, do unions enhance or mitigate wage dispersion?

12. Would our economy function better if it were union-free? Explain your answer. Provide a counterargument to your position.

13. What has been the impact of deregulation on the relative wages and employment of unionized workers in the airline and trucking industries? What factors help explain the difference in outcomes between the airline and trucking industries?

**Internet
Exercise**

What Is Up (or Down) with Relative Union Earnings?

Go to the Bureau of Labor Statistics Web site **(http://www.bls.gov)** and select "Economic News Releases." Find and select "Union Members." What are the median weekly earnings of union members compared with the median for nonunion wage-earning and salaried workers for the most recent year? What is the measured union wage advantage?

Provide *one* other statistic of your choice from the data on union and nonunion wages. For example, "In 2006, the measured union wage advantage among government workers was xx.x percent."

**Internet
Link**

The Bureau of Labor Statistics Collective Bargaining Web site reports statistics regarding strikes involving 1,000 or more workers **(http://www.bls.gov/cba/home.htm)**.

Chapter 12

Government and the Labor Market: Employment, Expenditures, and Taxation

In Chapters 6, 10, and 11, we discussed the role of unions in influencing wage rates and employment levels in labor markets. We now turn our attention to another major institution—government—and the various ways it affects wages and employment throughout the economy. Government's participation in the labor market is very substantial. For example, in 2006 the number of Americans working for federal, state, and local governments exceeded the number of workers in manufacturing jobs!

This chapter examines public sector employment and the impacts of government spending and selected taxes on wages and employment in the private sector. In the following chapter we discuss examples of direct government intervention in labor markets via laws and regulations.

PUBLIC SECTOR EMPLOYMENT AND WAGES

Government is a major—or even the sole—employer of specific types of workers in many labor markets. For example, it hires military personnel, antitrust prosecutors, postal workers, air traffic controllers, park rangers, schoolteachers, agency managers, firefighters, and highway maintenance personnel. The demand for these employees is derived from society's demand for the public sector goods and services that these workers help provide. When government employs workers, it "exhausts" or "absorbs" economic resources. More precisely, government employment makes a direct claim on the nation's productive capabilities. For example, when government employs postal workers, those laborers are no longer available to produce other goods and services. Likewise, when the military either drafts personnel or persuades them to enlist voluntarily, society forgoes the private sector output that those resources could have produced. Presumably society values the public sector output or services more highly than the alternative uses for these resources.

Government Employment: Extent and Growth

Figures 12.1 and 12.2 demonstrate the extent and growth of government employment in the United States since 1950. Close examination of the figures reveals several generalizations. First, the absolute number of federal civilian and state and local government employees (Figure 12.1) increased over this period. This is not surprising because total employment in the economy also rose considerably. Second, the growth of federal government employment was much less dramatic than the increase in state and local government employment.

FIGURE 12.1 **Government Employment in the United States**
Government employment rose rapidly between 1950 and 2006, with most of the rise occurring at the state and local levels.

Source: Bureau of Labor Statistics **(http://www.bls.gov)** and U.S. Defense Department, Statistical Information Analysis Division, "Active Duty Military Strength by Service by Fiscal Year."

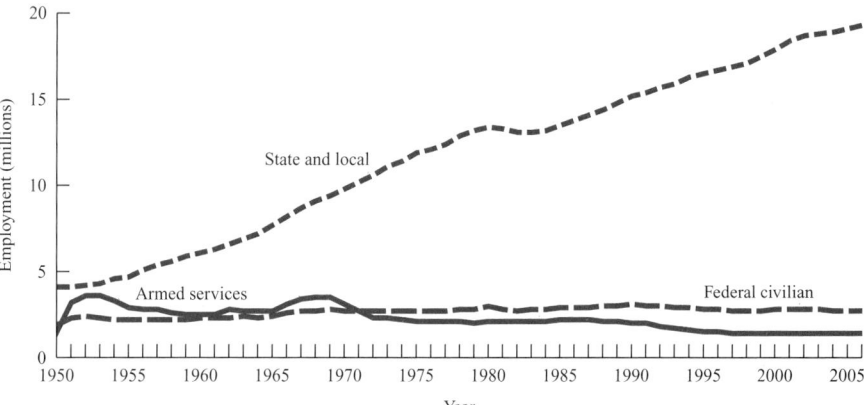

FIGURE 12.2 **Government Employment as a Percentage of Total U.S. Employment**
Relative to total U.S. employment, state and local employment increased sharply over the last half century while federal civilian employment declined slightly.

Source: Bureau of Labor Statistics (**http://www.bls.gov**).

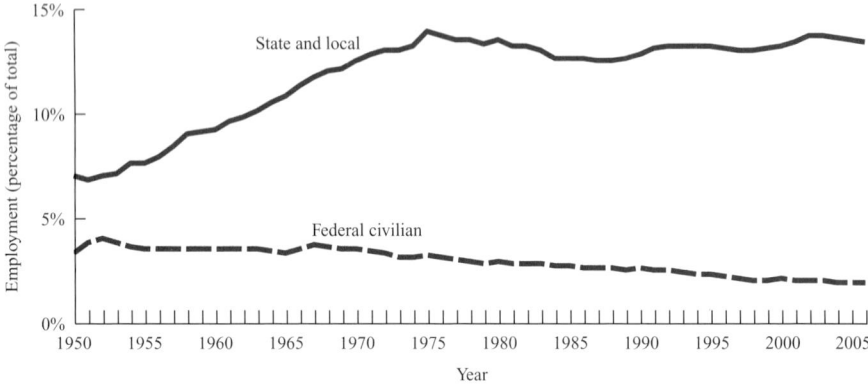

Clearly most of the growth of employment in the public sector since 1950 has occurred at the state and local levels of government. Federal civilian employment as a percentage of total employment fell from 3.2 percent in 1950 to 1.9 percent in 2006 (Figure 12.2). During those same years, state and local employment rose from 7.0 to 13.4 percent of total employment (Figure 12.2). Third, in 1950, one out of seven U.S. workers was employed by government; by 2006 that figure had risen to about one out of six workers. Finally, the number of active-duty personnel in the armed services (Figure 12.1) varied between 1.4 and 3.6 million during these years.

The relative growth of public sector employment over the past several decades can be envisioned in terms of our familiar labor demand and supply model (Figure 6.2). Although labor supply has increased at roughly the same pace in both the public and private sectors, the labor demand curve has shifted to the right more rapidly in the public sector than in the private sector. The result has been a faster rate of equilibrium employment growth in the public sector.

Economists cite several reasons for this relative growth of labor demand in the public sector. In the first place, the attendant needs and problems associated with population growth, urbanization, and urban sprawl increased the demand for many state and local government services. Furthermore, the age composition of the population dramatically changed over this period. The post–World War II baby boom caused a considerable increase in school-age children, which in turn raised demand for public schoolteachers. A third factor at work was the growth of real income in the society, which increased demand for such income-elastic government services as higher education, health services, parks, and a clean environment. Additionally, public sector unions emerged as a more powerful and militant force in the public sector labor market. Some observers contend that public employee unions and professional groups increasingly used their political power—via campaign contributions, organizational support, endorsements, and votes—

12.1	**World of Work**	What Do Government Workers Do?

The type of jobs government workers do depends on the level of government. State and local government employment is focused in education: Over half of such workers are in the education sector. The next

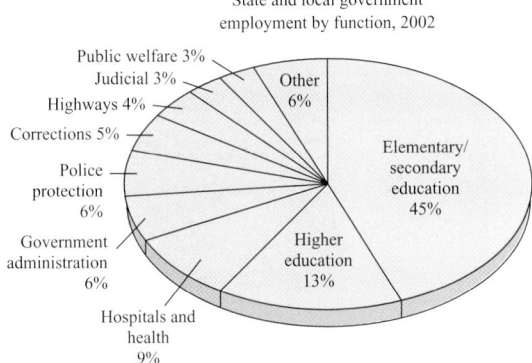

State and local government employment by function, 2002

largest sector is law enforcement, which accounts for about one-seventh of employment. Another large area of employment is hospitals and health, each accounting for about one-tenth of state and local government employment. Smaller sectors such as public welfare and highways together total less than one-tenth of total employment.

Federal government civilian workers are concentrated in different areas than state and local

government workers. Nearly three-fifths of federal government workers are in defense and postal service jobs. One-tenth of workers are in the hospitals and health sector. The natural resources, police, and financial

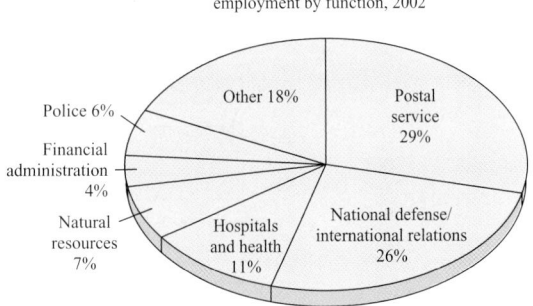

Federal government civilian employment by function, 2002

administration sectors each account for 4 to 7 percent of total employment. The "other" category is composed of workers in areas such as justice and law, corrections, air transportation, and social insurance administration.

Source: U.S. Census Bureau, "State and Local Government Employment and Payroll Data, by State and Function," March 2005; and "Federal Government Employment by Function," December 2005.

to elect government officials who favored greater spending for governmentally provided goods and services. This may have increased the derived demand for public employees.[1] Finally, government's regulatory role in the economy has expanded over the past five decades, and this has also increased the demand for government workers.

---

[1] See Paul Courant, Edward Gramlich, and Daniel Rubinfeld, "Public Employee Market Power and the Level of Government Spending," *American Economic Review,* December 1979, pp. 806–17. Marick F. Masters and John Thomas Delaney provide a good review of the scholarly literature on labor's role in U.S. national politics since 1945 in "Union Political Activities: A Review of the Empirical Literature," *Industrial and Labor Relations Review,* April 1987, pp. 336–53. In particular, see Table 1, pp. 339–42. See also John T. Delaney, Jack Fiorito, and Paul Jarley, "Evolutionary Politics? Union Differences and Political Activities in the 1990s," *Journal of Labor Research,* Summer 1999, pp. 277–95.

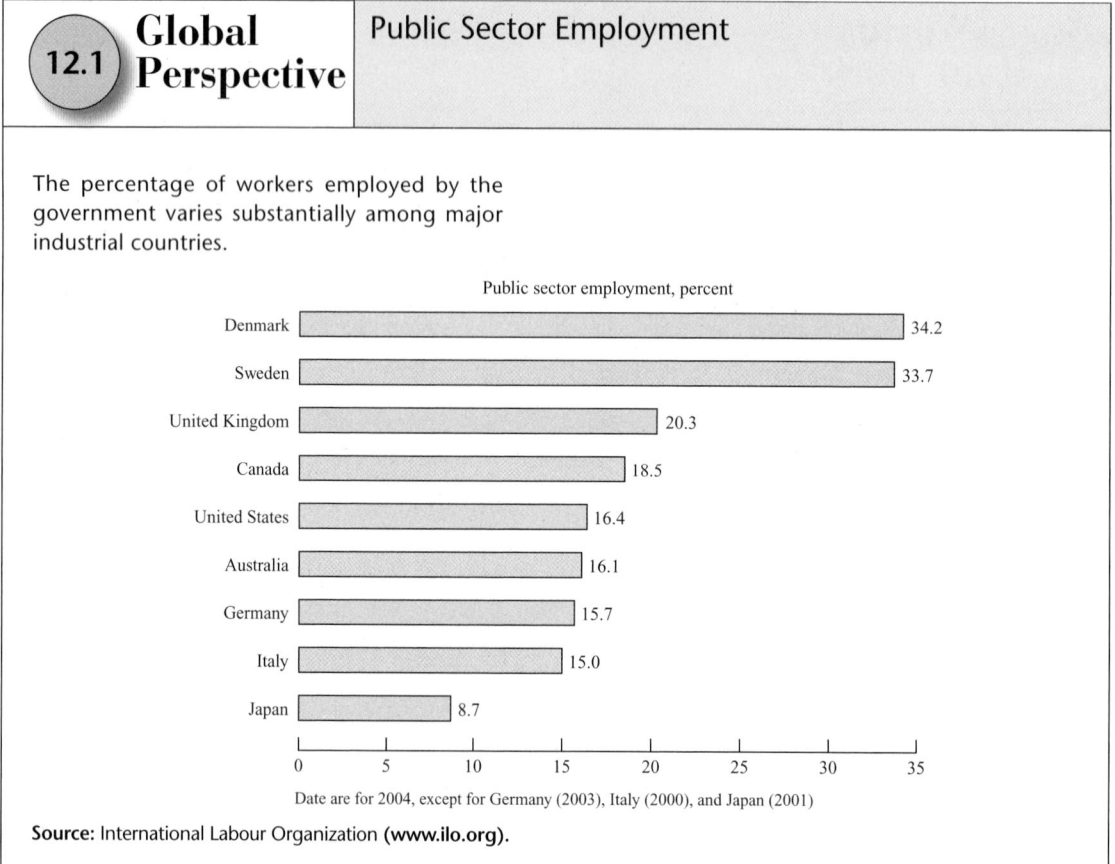

12.1 Global Perspective

Public Sector Employment

The percentage of workers employed by the government varies substantially among major industrial countries.

Public sector employment, percent

Country	Percent
Denmark	34.2
Sweden	33.7
United Kingdom	20.3
Canada	18.5
United States	16.4
Australia	16.1
Germany	15.7
Italy	15.0
Japan	8.7

Date are for 2004, except for Germany (2003), Italy (2000), and Japan (2001)

Source: International Labour Organization (**www.ilo.org**).

Public versus Private Sector Pay

The increase in public sector employment over the 1950–2006 period was accompanied by an increase in public sector pay. In theory, most governmental units adhere to a **prevailing wage rule** (or *comparable wage rule*). That is, they attempt to set public employees' wages equal to those earned by comparably trained and employed private sector workers.[2] In 2006, the average hourly pay of public sector workers was $20.97, while the average for private sector workers was $18.57.[3] But these averages fail to adjust for such factors as differences in union status, education and training, and demographic characteristics (gender, race). Smith undertook a comprehensive study in the mid-1970s to test empirically whether public sector employees did in fact achieve

[2] The prevailing wage principle was codified for federal workers in the Federal Pay Comparability Act of 1970. Many state and local governments have similar formal policies.

[3] Barry T. Hirsch and David A. Macpherson, *Union Membership and Earnings Data Book: Compilations from the Current Population Survey (2006 Edition)* (Washington, DC: Bureau of National Affairs, 2006).

wages comparable to private counterparts, once these other factors were accounted for. She found that in 1975 federal employees received wages that were 13 to 20 percent *higher* than those earned by comparably educated and experienced private sector workers. At the state level, female workers received 6–7 percent more and males 3–11 percent less than similar private sector employees. Local government workers appeared to earn wages nearly equal to their private sector counterparts.[4]

Does the wage differential still exist? The available evidence indicates that the wage premium for public sector workers has declined appreciably since the mid-1970s. Moulton discovered that the federal pay differential had dropped by between 8 and 14 percentage points between 1977–1979 and 1988.[5] Moulton concluded that the federal pay premium is about 3 percent nationally and has disappeared entirely in high-wage urban areas and for administrative and professional occupations.[6] Other studies also indicate that the wage differential has changed by skill levels since the 1970s. Katz and Krueger report that the public sector has not altered relative pay in response to the rising return to education that has occurred in the private sector. As a result, the public sector wage differential has risen for low-skilled workers but fallen for high-skilled workers.[7]

Several additional points are worth noting about public versus private sector pay. First, the percentage of total compensation paid in the form of fringe benefits is higher for public employees than for private workers.[8] Thus wage and salary comparisons alone may be misleading. Second, the rate at which federal government employees quit their jobs is lower than that of comparable workers in the private sector. Some economists conclude that this is an indication that federal workers are overpaid.[9] But others point out that the portion of federal pay taking the form of pensions is very high, which may encourage federal workers to remain in their jobs. If this is the case, quit rates may be poor indexes for judging the adequacy of pay.[10] Third, the occupational wage structure is more egalitarian within government than in the private sector (Chapter 17). Political

[4] Sharon P. Smith, *Equal Pay in the Public Sector: Fact or Fantasy* (Princeton, NJ: Princeton University Press, 1977).

[5] Brent R. Moulton, "A Reexamination of the Federal–Private Wage Differential in the United States," *Journal of Labor Economics,* April 1990, pp. 270–93. For a similar conclusion using data from the 1990s, see Dale Belman and John S. Heywood, "The Structure of Compensation in the Public Sector," in Dale Belman, Morley Gunderson, and Douglas Hyatt (eds.), *Public Sector Employment in a Time of Transition* (Madison, WI: Industrial Relations Research Association, 1996).

[6] For recent evidence indicating that the actual public sector wage differential is reduced substantially if the analysis uses more detailed definitions of occupations, see Dale Belman and John S. Heywood, "Public Wage Differentials and the Treatment of Occupation Differences," *Journal of Policy Analysis and Management,* Winter 2004, pp. 135–52.

[7] Lawrence F. Katz and Alan B. Krueger, "Changes in the Structure of Wages in Public and Private Sectors," *Research in Labor Economics,* 1991, pp. 137–72.

[8] For empirical evidence supporting this point, see John S. Heywood, "Government Employment and the Provision of Fringe Benefits," *Applied Economics,* February 1991, pp. 417–23; and Dale Belman and John S. Heywood, "Changes in the Relative Provision of Public Sector Pension," *Public Finance Review,* July 1997, pp. 426–41.

[9] James Long, "Are Government Workers Overpaid? Alternative Evidence," *Journal of Human Resources,* Winter 1982, pp. 123–31.

[10] Richard A. Ippolito, "Why Federal Workers Don't Quit," *Journal of Human Resources,* Spring 1987, pp. 281–99.

12.2	World of Work	Public Sector Unions: Are They Unique?*

The public sector differs from the private sector in an important way: Governments provide monopoly services in their particular jurisdictions. As a result, the demand for public goods and services in a particular locale is quite inelastic. That is, consumers cannot substitute one provider for another as is true for most private goods and services. The upshot, according to some observers, is that the derived demand for public employees is also highly inelastic. This inelastic demand allegedly gives public sector unions extraordinary bargaining power.

Freeman rejects this claim of extraordinary bargaining power on four grounds:

1. Governments face tax and budget constraints that serve as disciplinary devices similar to market demand in the private sector. Given a fixed budget, any increase in wages will require a reduction in employment.

2. Cities and states are not really monopolies because people who are unhappy with the level of public services in one area can move elsewhere. An exodus of citizens from a particular jurisdiction will reduce the taxable population there and limit the ability of a particular government to pay public sector wages.

3. Workers are almost always forbidden to strike when essential services such as police and fire protection will be disrupted.

4. Strikes by public workers do not block revenue flows to government, whereas strikes by private workers stop these flows to firms. Government may therefore be more willing than private sector firms to resist union demands.

The uniqueness of public sector unions, states Freeman, does not lie in differences in elasticity of labor demand between the private and public sectors. Rather, it derives from the political nature of public sector collective bargaining. Unions use their political power to increase the demand for public services, as well as employing their bargaining power to achieve higher wages. Also, public sector unions place a heavy emphasis on employment because additional employees increase the political power of the unions. Finally, public sector unions operate in a multilateral bargaining environment. Union appeals are made not only to people who sit across the negotiating table but also to elected officials and citizen groups.

In sum, says Freeman, differences between public and private sector unions do indeed exist. Nevertheless, the relative strength of unions in the two sectors cannot be determined by labor demand elasticity alone.

* Based on Richard B. Freeman, "Unionism Comes to the Public Sector," *Journal of Economic Literature,* March 1986, pp. 41–86.

considerations apparently cause government to pay lower-skilled workers relatively more, and elected and appointed officials relatively less, than comparably trained and experienced private sector workers. Finally, studies indicate that female and African–American workers in government receive higher pay than their counterparts in the private sector. Rather than indicating overpayment to workers, however, this higher pay may be the result of a greater relative commitment by government to equal treatment of minorities and women.[11]

[11] This point is discussed in Robert G. Gregory and Jeff Borland, "Recent Developments in Public Sector Labor Markets," in Orley Ashenfelter and David Card (eds.), *Handbook of Labor Economics,* Volume 3C (Amsterdam: North-Holland, 1999).

THE MILITARY SECTOR: THE DRAFT VERSUS THE VOLUNTARY ARMY

Over the past three decades, the number of active-duty military personnel employed by the United States has varied between a high of 3 million in 1970 to a low of 1.4 million in 2006. Before 1973, the United States used the selective service system—commonly called the *draft*—to compel people to serve in the military. These draftees worked alongside *volunteers,* some of whom offered their labor services to the military rather than waiting to be drafted. Under this system of military conscription, wages were below those that many draftees and enlisted personnel could have earned in civilian sector jobs. In 1973 the federal government abandoned the draft in favor of armed services staffed by people recruited voluntarily through wages and benefits that were sufficiently high to attract the required number of employees. In a sense, the military has become a professional, market-based entity, much like the U.S. Postal Service, the Federal Bureau of Investigation, and the National Park Service. In fact, a 2001 study indicated that for most of a male enlistee's military career, his earnings are about the 70th percentile of those for similarly experienced full-time workers who are high school graduates and about the median for full-time workers with some college education.[12] We might add that a part of military earnings may be a compensating wage payment (Chapter 8) for the added risk and poorer working conditions generally associated with jobs in the military.

The voluntary, wage-based army remains somewhat controversial. Calls for a return to the peacetime draft or for establishment of a new system of universal national service are commonplace. Critics of the modern voluntary army argue that it produces an army drawn mainly from the ranks of low-income citizens, creates a racially imbalanced military force, reduces the overall sense of duty to one's country, and increases the cost of the military to taxpayers.

Defenders of the voluntary approach counter that the professional army is better prepared to achieve its goals, minimizes society's overall cost of allocating labor to the services, promotes the use of a more efficient combination of labor and capital in the military, creates employment opportunities for low-skilled workers, provides on-the-job training that is transferable to the private sector, and maximizes individual freedom. These defenders also argue that it is more equitable to have taxpayers, rather than draftees, bear the costs of the armed services; that the voluntary army reduces the military's training costs by lessening the turnover of personnel; and that shortages of skilled personnel or reservists can be eliminated by raising wages in the areas where more personnel are needed.

A comprehensive examination of these pros and cons is well beyond our present discussion. Because our interest is government's role in the labor market, we limit our analysis here to the *labor market* aspects of the two alternatives.

---

[12] Beth J. Asch, James R. Hosek, and John T. Warner, *On Restructuring Enlisted Pay: Analysis in Support of the 9th Quadrennial Review of Military Compensation* (Santa Monica, CA: Rand, 2001).

FIGURE 12.3   The Draft versus the Voluntary Army
If the military drafts the specific group of workers $0G$ and pays each of them $0A$, the wage bill to
taxpayers ($0AfG$) will be less than the total opportunity costs to those drafted ($0BcG$). Under a
voluntary or market-based system, the relevant demand curve becomes D_v, the cost to taxpayers
increases ($0BeH$ as compared to $0AfG$), those who volunteer are fully compensated for their
opportunity costs ($0BeH$), and the military is likely to reduce its total workforce ($0G$ to $0H$). The
true cost of employing any specific group of workers is *independent* of the wage bill.

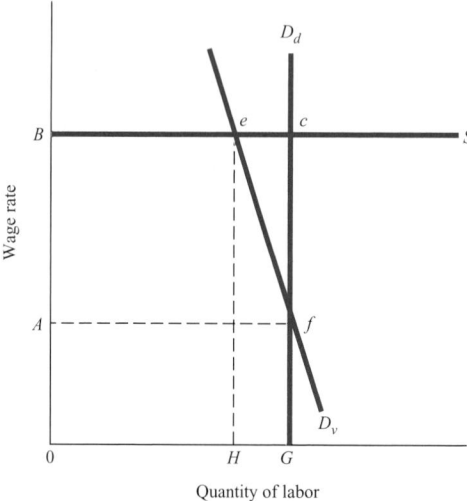

The Economics of Military Conscription

Figure 12.3 shows labor supply and demand as viewed by the military. For simplicity we
assume that the market from which the military drafts personnel is perfectly competitive
and that the nation is not at war. Initially disregard the labor demand curve labeled D_v
and instead concentrate on curves S and D_d. The curve S is a conventional competitive
supply curve as *viewed by an employer.* The perfectly inelastic demand curve D_d is
drawn on the assumption that Congress authorizes the armed services to conscript or
draft $0G$ people and pay each of them wage rate $0A$. Initially suppose that those drafted
are the specific individuals who would have voluntarily enlisted had the wage rate been
at the equilibrium level $0B$ rather than $0A$.

Let's now address two questions. First, what is the total wage bill that the military
(taxpayers) will have to pay under this draft authorization? Second, given our assumptions, what is the overall cost to society of drafting these specific $0G$ workers? The answer to the first question is simple and straightforward. The military's wage bill is the
area $0AfG$, which is found by multiplying the authorized wage $0A$ times the authorized
employment level $0G$.

Is this wage bill also the total cost to society? The answer is no, and we can understand this by examining the labor supply curve. The vertical height of curve S measures
the opportunity cost of using each unit of labor in this employment or, in other words, the

forgone civilian earnings for each of the $0G$ workers drafted. For example, suppose these workers would earn $35,000 a year at wage rate $0B$ and only $20,000 at the military wage rate $0A$. The annual income these individuals sacrifice and the output forgone by society from drafting them is $35,000 times $0G$ draftees. The fact that the military pays these workers $20,000 does *not* reflect the actual costs to either these individuals or to society. By drafting $0G$ workers, the military imposes an opportunity cost on draftees and society equal to the area under the labor supply curve, $0BcG$. It pays the draftees $0AfG$ and imposes the remainder of the cost—$ABcf$—on those drafted. This cost is the difference between what draftees could earn as civilians and the amount earned in the military. To generalize: The true social cost of drafting any specific group of workers into the military is *independent* of the total wage rate that the military pays them. The actual cost consists of the income (output) sacrificed by draftees. *Military conscription* at low pay reduces the military's (taxpayers') personnel costs, but it does *not* lower the costs of the military to society. Rather, it shifts a portion of the true costs—$15,000 per draftee in this case—from taxpayers to those drafted.[13]

Thus far we have assumed that draftees are people who have opportunity costs that are reflected by the perfectly elastic supply curve in Figure 12.3. This assumes that government drafts only those from the low-skilled labor market—people who have low civilian earnings. But what if the military imposes a *lottery* to select the $0G$ draftees? Many of those selected will have higher civilian wage opportunities than $0B$. Stated differently, the collective civilian wage opportunities of the $0G$ draftees selected through a lottery will exceed area $0BcG$. The relevant generalization here is that the true cost to individuals and society of a lottery draft will exceed that of a draft of low-paid civilian workers.

The Voluntary, Market-Based Approach

We can analyze the economic implications of a *voluntary or market-based army* by turning to the demand curve D_v in Figure 12.3. Notice that we have drawn a typical downward-sloping demand curve, as opposed to the perfectly inelastic one used to analyze the draft. This downward-sloping curve reflects a realistic expectation that higher market wages for military personnel will cause the armed services to reduce the number of its employees. As seen by the intersection of D_v and S, the equilibrium military wage and quantity of labor will be $0B$ and $0H$, respectively. The total wage bill to the military will be $0BeH$, which is considerably greater than $0AfG$, the total wage bill under the draft. Assuming that the military's demand for personnel is relatively inelastic, we conclude that a voluntary army will increase the money cost of military personnel to taxpayers. Notice

---

[13] An additional cost to draftees is that military service may lower future civilian earnings. See Joshua D. Angrist, "Lifetime Earnings and the Vietnam Era Draft Lottery: Evidence from Social Security Administrative Records," *American Economic Review,* June 1990, pp. 313–35; and Joshua D. Angrist and Alan B. Krueger, "Why Do World War Two Veterans Earn More Than Nonveterans?" *Journal of Labor Economics,* January 1994, pp. 74–97. On the other hand, voluntary military service (i.e., after the end of the draft) appears to raise the postmilitary earnings of nonwhites and lower the earnings of white veterans. See Joshua D. Angrist, "Estimating the Labor Market Impact of Voluntary Military Service Using Social Security Data on Military Applicants," *Econometrica,* March 1998, pp. 249–88.

that a voluntary army transfers income from taxpayers to military personnel so that the latter are totally compensated for their opportunity costs *0BeH.*

Figure 12.3 shows that *if* the wage rate were at the draft level of *0A,* the voluntary army would hire the same number of employees that it previously drafted (*0G*). But the existence of the voluntary army with a market-determined wage rate reduces military employment from *0G* to *0H.* We assume that this occurs for two reasons. First, as the wage rises from *0A* to *0B,* the military will likely substitute capital for labor. The military can lower its costs by engaging in such activities as purchasing dishwashing machines, procuring more weapons, and computerizing routine paperwork. This will enable the armed services to economize on the use of the higher-priced labor. Second, although the higher wage bill adds nothing to the true cost of the military, it does raise the price of the armed services *as perceived by Congress and taxpayers.* We would expect this price increase to cause Congress to reduce its "output" of military services or reduce the *scale* of the total military establishment, which then would reduce military employment. The alert reader will recognize that we are here referring to both substitution and output effects of a wage rate increase.

A final point is germane to our discussion. The payment to enlistees of an amount equal to the supply price of labor rather than an artificially low wage can be expected to improve military morale and reduce labor turnover. These factors may join those previously discussed in lowering the costs of the military to society.

To summarize: Government's conscription or hiring of personnel for the military is another example of how government influences specific labor markets in the economy. Labor market analysis suggests that (1) the true cost of allocating personnel to the military is independent of the wage paid to those workers; (2) the methods (a lottery versus a draft of low-wage workers) used to obtain labor may affect the total cost of acquiring a given amount of military personnel; (3) the cost of a voluntary army may be less than that of a drafted army because of higher productivity related to reduced turnover and higher morale; (4) a voluntary army is likely to increase the price of the military as viewed by taxpayers; and (5) society can be expected to allocate fewer labor resources to the military under a higher-pay voluntary system than a lower-pay compulsory one.[14] Finally, while labor market analysis *can* help us understand the costs and benefits of various public policy options, it *cannot* determine which option society should select.

> 12.3

NONPAYROLL SPENDING BY GOVERNMENT: IMPACT ON LABOR

We have established that government employment of civilian and military workers is a major factor in the overall labor market. Government's nonpayroll spending also influences wages and employment. This spending is substantial and takes two forms: (1) purchases of

---

[14] For an evaluation of the voluntary army, see John T. Warner and Beth J. Asch, "The Record and Prospects of All-Volunteer Military in the United States," *Journal of Economic Perspectives,* Spring 2001, pp. 169–92.

12.3	World of Work	Private Military Companies*

Recent years have witnessed a rapid growth in the use of private military companies. These firms are hired by other companies or countries to provide military services such as security protection and combat operations. In 2005, 60 private military companies employed an estimated 25,000 workers in Iraq. These workers represented more than 10 percent of the official military forces in Iraq.

Private military companies usually employ elite ex-military personnel who served in units such as Special Forces or Delta Force. These workers are highly compensated: Their typical pay is $400–700 per day. However, they face significant risk of injury or death. By 2005, at least 160 private military company workers had been killed in Iraq.

The use of private military companies is controversial for two reasons. First, private military company workers are often paid several times what U.S. military personnel are paid. There has been concern that this pay differential is causing an exodus of the best military personnel from units such as Special Forces and Delta Force. Special Forces has recently responded by increasing reenlistment bonuses to as much as $150,000. Second, there is little or no regulation regarding the training or conduct of private military personnel. For example, in Iraq, private military personnel are subject to neither court-martial nor Iraqi law. Private military personnel were allegedly involved in prison abuse scandals in Iraq but were not arrested.

* Based on Daniel Bergner, "The Other Army," *The New York Times*, August 14, 2005.

private sector goods and services and (2) transfer payments and subsidies. In 2006 government purchased $2,090 billion of labor, goods, and services. About half of this amount was for goods produced by private industry. Also, government transfers and subsidies were $1,593 billion in 2006. Let's briefly examine selected labor market impacts of each category of expenditure.

Government Purchases of Private Sector Output

Government purchases include procurement of such items as computers, tanks, medical supplies, textbooks, buses, submarines, paper clips, furniture, and weather satellites. This type of spending by government creates a derived demand for specific kinds of private sector workers. In some cases, it creates demands for labor that would not exist—or at least not be nearly as great—without government. We could expect such changes in demand to affect equilibrium wage rates and employment levels. For example, *cuts* in government spending on strategic missiles could be expected to eventually reduce the wages and employment levels of aerospace engineers. Similarly, *increases* in federal construction spending would likely increase the demand for—and the collective bargaining position of—a wide range of construction workers.

Transfer Payments and Subsidies

Government payroll expenditures and nonpayroll spending for private sector goods and services have one common feature. Both are *exhaustive* or resource-absorbing expenditures in that they account for the employment of labor and other economic resources. In contrast, transfer payments and subsidies are *nonexhaustive* because, as such, they do not directly absorb resources or account for production. More precisely, as their name implies, **transfer payments**—such as Social Security benefits to the retired, unemployment compensation, welfare payments, and veterans' benefits—merely transfer income from government to individuals and families. The recipients perform no current productive activities in return; hence transfers are nonexhaustive. Similarly, a **subsidy** is a transfer payment to a firm, institution, or household that consumes or produces some specific product or service. Medicare for the elderly, price supports for farmers, and public education for youth are all examples of governmental subsidies.

Demand Effects

Although transfers and subsidies do not directly exhaust or absorb labor or other resources, they alter the structure of total demand in the economy and therefore affect the derived demands for specific types of labor. For example, cash and in-kind medical transfers provided to older Americans under provisions of the Social Security program increase the demand for products and services that older Americans tend to purchase. More specifically, the transfers increase the demand for such items as prescription and over-the-counter drugs, nursing home services, hospital care, and retirement property. This demand, in turn, increases the derived demand for workers who help produce, deliver, or sell these goods and services. In a similar sense, the cash transfers provided through welfare programs for low-income families increase the demand for a variety of products, including children's clothing, toys, and foodstuffs. Other things being equal, these increases in product demand boost product prices, which then increase the demand for labor in the affected industries (demand determinant 1, Table 6.1).

Subsidies provided to private firms and nonprofit organizations also increase the demand for specific types of workers. For instance, the U.S. government, through the Export–Import Bank, provides loans at below-market interest rates to some foreign buyers of U.S. exports. This reduces the effective price of U.S. exports while leaving the price charged by the exporters intact, thus increasing foreign purchases and ultimately the derived demand for labor in the U.S. export sector. Similarly, the federal government provides subsidies to such nonprofit organizations as private universities, which then demand more workers to deliver their services.

Supply Effects

In addition to their impact on labor demand, transfer payments and subsidies affect short- and long-run labor supply. Recall from our discussion of individual labor supply in Chapter 2 that transfers (for example, a guaranteed income program) generate an *income effect* that tends to reduce the optimal number of work hours offered by the recipient. Put simply, transfer income induces the recipient to buy more normal goods and services, including leisure (Figure 2.12). Also, if the amount of the cash transfer is inversely related to work income—that is, if a benefit reduction rate applies to earned income—then the program creates an accompanying *substitution effect* that further reduces work effort. By reducing the opportunity cost—or price—of leisure, the transfer payment encourages the substitution of the lower-priced leisure for the now relatively higher-priced work.

Transfers and subsidies also influence long-run labor supply decisions (Chapter 4). For example, the existence of cash and in-kind transfers may reduce incentives to invest in human capital. In essence, the present value of the net returns to the investor is reduced because future gains in earned income that result from the training or education are accompanied by the loss of future transfers. Other things being equal, the higher the benefit reduction rate of a transfer plan, the less the actual net rate of return on any given investment in human capital.

Not all transfers and subsidy programs, however, reduce long-run labor supply. Transfers and subsidies that reduce the private cost of investing in human capital produce just the opposite effect. For example, government provides subsidized, below-market interest rates on loans to many college students. Recall that the economic rationale for these loans was outlined in Chapter 4. This subsidy reduces the private cost of investing in a college education, which increases the personal rate of return on this form of human capital. As a direct consequence, the long-run labor supply in various skilled and professional labor markets increases. Additionally, we know that better-educated people stay in the labor force longer than people who have less education. We therefore conclude that government transfers and subsidies may either positively or negatively affect supply in specific labor markets.

LABOR MARKET EFFECTS OF PUBLICLY PROVIDED GOODS AND SERVICES

Thus far we have established that government employment and public sector purchases of private sector output influence wage rates and employment levels in specific labor markets. We next raise an interesting related question: Do publicly provided goods and services affect labor demand and supply *independently* of the public and private employment necessary to provide these items? Publicly provided goods and services range from **pure public goods,** whose benefits are indivisible and therefore impossible to deny to those who have not paid for them, to goods and services provided by government but also sold in the private sector. An example of the former is national defense; an example of the latter is college education. It is clear that some publicly provided goods *do* affect private sector demand for labor. It is also conceivable that these goods and services reduce overall labor supply in the economy. Let's examine each possibility.

Effects on Labor Demand

The provision of public sector goods and services influences labor demand in a variety of ways. For example, suppose government builds a major dam on a river. Assume this project creates multiple benefits such as electricity generation, flood control, irrigation, and recreational opportunities. Government affects the labor market by employing labor and private sector products to construct the dam, power station, irrigation network, and adjacent recreational areas. But the *existence* of the dam also independently affects labor demand. For example, the irrigation system will likely increase the demand for farmworkers; the new recreational opportunities will increase the demand for fishing boats, motors, and water skis, which will increase the derived demand for workers who help produce these products; the availability of cheap electric power may entice manufacturing firms to the area, thereby increasing the demand for specific skilled and unskilled workers; and control of downriver flooding may actually *reduce* the demand for flood insurance agents and claims adjusters. In fact, we may generalize as follows: Other things being equal, the provision of a public good that is a *complement* in either production or consumption to a specific private good will *increase* the derived demand for workers who help produce the private good. Conversely, the provision of a public good that is a *substitute* in production or consumption to a specific private good will *reduce* the derived demand for workers who help produce the private good.

Effects on Labor Supply

A modified version of the basic income–leisure model of short-run individual labor supply suggests that publicly provided goods and services may reduce the quantity of labor supplied. Recall from Chapter 2 that the basic model of income–leisure choice contains a preference map composed of indifference curves, each one showing the various combinations of real income and leisure that yield some specific level of utility. Also recall that the model contains a wage rate, or budget, line indicating the *actual* combination of income and leisure that the individual can obtain given his or her wage.

Figure 12.4 presents a modified version of the basic model. Notice from the vertical axis that we are defining real income as the total amount of private *and* public sector goods and services obtainable from any specific level of work. Suppose that Y_{pu} ($= WW_1$) of public sector goods is available to Green regardless of how much he works. The real income available to him will be Y_{pu} plus the level of private goods that his work income will allow him to obtain. Prior to the provision of Y_{pu} public goods, Green's budget constraint was WW', but the existence of the publicly provided output means that his effective budget constraint is W_1W_1'. This latter line shows the combinations of leisure and goods (private and public sector) available to Green at each level of work, given his wage rate. The vertical distance between the two budget lines measures the value of the public goods available to Green.

If no public goods were available to this individual, he would maximize his utility at *a* by working h_1 hours, from which he would earn Y_1 goods (real income). The existence of the public goods, however, creates an income effect that allows Green to "buy" more

FIGURE 12.4 **Impact of Publicly Provided Goods on Individual Labor Supply**
If real income is defined as the total quantity of public and private goods and services
obtainable from any specific level of work, then the presence of Y_{pu} public sector goods or
services shifts the effective budget constraint upward from WW' to W_1W_1'. Assuming
leisure to be a normal good and disregarding the tax consequences of the increased public
sector provision, this creates an income effect that reduces the optimal number of hours
worked by h_1h_2.

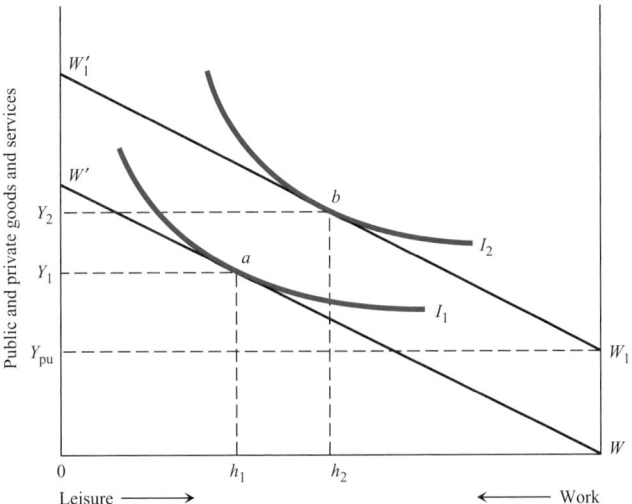

leisure. The provision of the public sector goods Y_{pu} increases his total utility by moving him from a on indifference curve I_1 to b on curve I_2. But in achieving this gain in
utility, Green *reduces* his labor hours from h_1 to h_2.

We thus conclude that the existence of publicly provided goods and services may
reduce individual and overall labor supply in the economy. The more closely the public goods are substitutable for private goods, the greater the reduction in labor supply.
For example, free food provided by the public sector may reduce the incentive to earn
income to buy food. In fact, one study estimated that the federal food stamp program
reduced the labor supply of female heads of households by 9 percent.[15] On the other
hand, the more complementary the public goods are to leisure, the greater the decline
in labor supply. Example: A public golf course conceivably could reduce labor supply
by encouraging more leisure. Finally, the more complementary the public goods are to
work, the less the reduction in labor supply. Example: By reducing the cost of getting
to work, a mass-transit system may augment labor supply.

Our discussion of the labor supply effects of public goods overlooks an important
fact: Government must collect taxes from people to provide the public goods in
question, and these taxes also have potential labor supply impacts. It is to this topic
that we turn next.

---

[15] Thomas Fraker and Robert Moffitt, "The Effect of Food Stamps on Labor Supply: A Bivariate Selection
Model," *Journal of Public Economics,* February 1988, pp. 25–56.

12.1
Quick
Review

- Most of the sizable growth of public sector employment occurring since 1950 has been at the state and local levels of government.

- Although a large federal pay advantage existed a decade or two ago, it is thought to have largely evaporated in recent years.

- A conscripted army at below-market pay does not reduce the cost of the military to society; it simply shifts part of the cost to those drafted. A voluntary, market-based army is likely to be less costly to society because it *(a)* reduces turnover, *(b)* creates higher morale, and *(c)* induces the military to use socially optimal combinations of labor and capital.

- Government transfers (and subsidies) and the existence of publicly provided goods have widespread impacts on labor supply and labor demand.

Your Turn

How might Figure 12.4 relate to the lack of work effort observed under the old Communist regimes of Eastern Europe and Russia? (*Answer:* See page 598.)

INCOME TAXATION AND THE LABOR MARKET

To this point, our emphasis has been on government's influence on labor markets through its spending and hiring decisions. We now examine the effects of selected taxes on the labor market, focusing on the personal *income tax.* Income from wages and salaries constitutes approximately 70 percent of national income in the United States. Because a large portion of this income is subjected to the personal income tax, it is particularly important to ascertain the impact of this tax on labor markets. Specifically, do workers bear the full burden of the tax in the form of lower net, or after-tax, wage rates? Or is it possible that part or all of the tax is borne by employers, who must pay higher market wage rates to attract profit-maximizing quantities of labor? What impact does the income tax have on employment?

The Income Tax: Impact on Wages and Employment

We will discover from the following discussion that given the elasticity of labor demand, the effects of the personal income tax on wages and employment depend principally on the elasticity of labor supply. Figure 12.5(a) and (b) demonstrates this proposition. The labor supply curve in graph (a) is perfectly inelastic, indicating that workers do not collectively change the extent of their labor force participation in response to wage rate changes. In graph (b) the labor supply curve displays some elasticity: people collectively increase their labor hour offerings when the wage rises and reduce them when it falls.

The demand curves in the two graphs are identical and reflect the *before-tax* wage rates and corresponding quantities of labor that firms will desire to employ. The curves labeled D_t lie below the conventional demand curves in each graph and show the

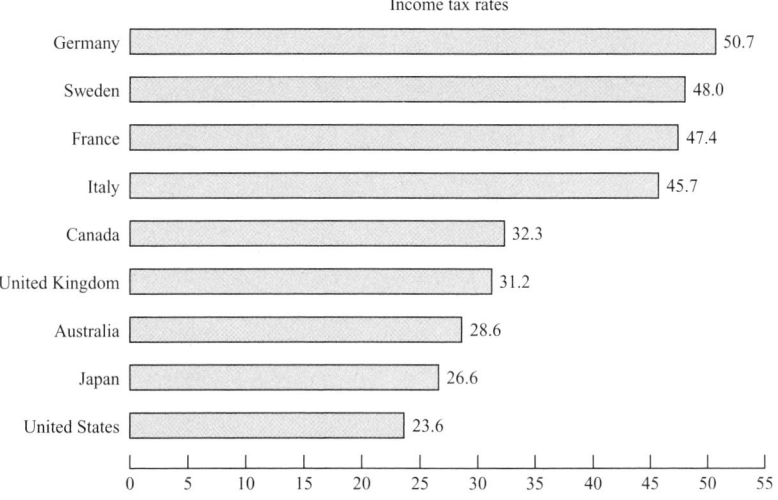

Global Perspective 12.2

Income Tax Rates*

The average income tax for the average production worker who is married and has two children ranges from 23.6 percent in the United States to 50.7 percent in Germany.

Income tax rates

Germany	50.7
Sweden	48.0
France	47.4
Italy	45.7
Canada	32.3
United Kingdom	31.2
Australia	28.6
Japan	26.6
United States	23.6

0 5 10 15 20 25 30 35 40 45 50 55

Source: Organization for Economic Cooperation and Development, *OECD Factbook 2006* (Paris: OECD, 2006).

* The income tax rates include personal income taxes, employer Social Security Contributions, and employees' Social Security contributions.

after-tax wages as viewed by workers. The progressive income tax on labor earnings pivots the after-tax wage rate lines downward from D to D_t by the amount of the tax per hour of work.

Table 12.1 helps us better understand the crucial distinction between the conventional labor demand curve D and the after-tax wage rate line D_t in Figure 12.5(a) and (b). Notice that columns (1) and (2) constitute the before-tax labor demand schedule, which graphically is shown as curve D in each of the figures. Columns (2) and (4) establish the after-tax wage rate lines D_t in the two graphs. Example: If the wage rate is $12 (column 1), firms will employ 3 workers (column 2). Observe from column (3) that the tax per hour is $3.25 at the $12 wage rate. Hence the *net* or *after-tax wage rate* is $8.75 (= $12 − $3.25), as shown in column (4). When plotted graphically against the quantity of labor, the after-tax wage rates shown in column (4) establish the D_t curves in Figure 12.5(a) and (b). The vertical distances between the demand curves and the after-tax wage rate lines measure the tax per hour of work at each particular market wage rate (and at each particular quantity of labor demanded).

FIGURE 12.5 **Impact of the Personal Income Tax on Wages and Employment**
If the aggregate labor supply curve in the economy is perfectly inelastic as in (a), then the personal income tax—measured by the vertical distance between D and D_t—will not affect the market wage ($9) but will reduce the after-tax wage by the amount of the tax per hour. If the labor supply curve displays some elasticity as in (b), the tax reduces the quantity of labor hours supplied and raises the before-tax market wage—in this case from $9 to $10. Given labor demand, the greater the elasticity of labor supply, the greater the increase in the wage rate and the greater the reduction in employment resulting from the tax.

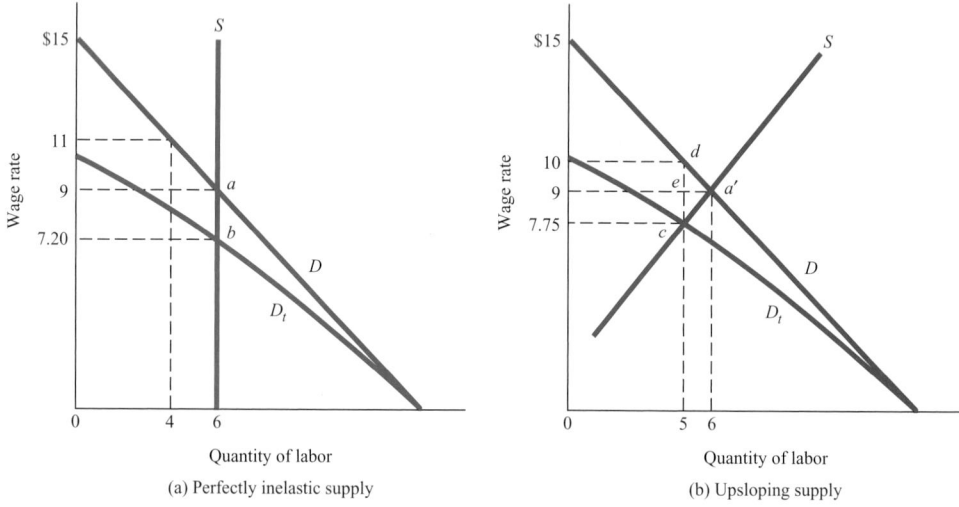

(a) Perfectly inelastic supply

(b) Upsloping supply

Column 5 of Table 12.1 shows the average hourly tax rate ($= T/W$) for each wage rate. Notice that the average tax rate rises as earnings per hour increase, indicating that this tax is progressive. In terms of Figure 12.5(a) and (b), this progressivity is reflected in the fact that the distances between D and D_t increase as a percentage of the wage as the wage rises.

TABLE 12.1
Before-Tax versus After-Tax Earnings per Unit of Labor (Hypothetical Data)

(1) W	(2) Q	(3) T	(4) W − T	(5) T/W (%)
$14	1	$4.25	$9.75	30.4
13	2	3.75	9.25	28.8
12	3	3.25	8.75	27.1
11	4	2.75	8.25	25.0
10	5	2.25	7.75	22.5
9	6	1.80	7.20	20.0
8	7	1.40	6.60	17.5
7	8	1.05	5.95	15.0
6	9	.75	5.25	12.5
5	10	.50	4.50	10.0
4	11	.30	3.70	7.5
3	12	.15	2.85	5.0
2	13	.05	1.95	2.5

Perfectly Inelastic Labor Supply

Let's now focus on graph (a) in Figure 12.5. The before-tax equilibrium market wage and quantity of labor are $9 and 6 units, respectively (point *a*). Once the tax is introduced, however, workers perceive their net wage to be only $7.20 (= $9 − $1.80), as shown by point *b*. But because the supply is perfectly inelastic, the income tax will not affect the collective quantity of labor supplied. Therefore, workers bear the entire burden of the tax; the before-tax wage rate remains at $9, and the after-tax hourly pay falls by the full amount of the tax, $1.80 (= $9 − $7.20).

To confirm this proposition, suppose workers are angered by their *net* wage decline and try to shift the tax to their employers. If they demand, say, $11 (= $9 + $2), employers will seek only 4 units of labor, while workers will continue to offer 6 units. Assuming competition, the excess supply of workers will drive the before-tax wage down to $9, where the labor market will once again clear. It is evident that if the labor supply curve is perfectly inelastic, employees will be unable to pass the tax forward to their employers, and the tax will have no impact on either the market wage rate or equilibrium employment.[16]

Positively Sloped Labor Supply

We next turn our attention to graph (b) in Figure 12.5, where we discover a labor supply curve that displays a positive slope. This implies that workers collectively will respond to wage or income tax changes by adjusting the amount of labor supplied. In the absence of the income tax, the equilibrium wage rate and quantity of labor are $9 and 6 units (point *a'*). How will these workers react to a newly imposed income tax? As we see from the intersection of D_t and S, workers will reduce the amount of labor supplied from 6 to 5 units (point *c*). Employers will encounter a shortage of labor of 1 unit (= 6 − 5) *at the $9 market wage*. This excess demand will drive the wage to $10, and the market will again clear at point *d*—this time at 5 units of labor. Those still working following the tax will receive a before-tax wage rate of $10 rather than $9. The workers' after-tax wage will fall by $1.25 (= $9 − $7.75) to $7.75. Notice that this decline is less than the tax per hour of $2.25 (= $10 − $7.75). The reason is that $1 of the tax is borne indirectly by employers as higher wage rates. That is, of the total tax *dc* in Figure 12.5, *ec* is borne by workers as lower after-tax pay while *ed* is borne by employers as higher wage costs.

To summarize: Other things being equal, if the overall labor supply curve slopes upward, a personal income tax will reduce the quantity of labor supplied, cause the wage rate to rise, and decrease employment. Given the elasticity of demand, the greater the elasticity of supply, the greater the portion of the income tax borne by employers in the form of a higher market wage. You might want to rework the analysis for a *perfectly elastic* labor supply curve to demonstrate that under these conditions the *entire* tax will be borne by employers and that the employment effect will be greater.

---

[16] This is true even in the presence of a strong union, assuming that the union has already bargained for its optimal contract package. If it has squeezed all it can extract from the employers, the sudden enactment of an income tax can do nothing to enhance its ability to gain still more.

The Income Tax and Individual Labor Supply

Which of the two graphs in Figure 12.5 best portrays reality? How elastic is the overall supply of labor? Economists have approached this question both theoretically and empirically.

Theoretical Analysis

The income tax is similar in impact to a wage rate decrease: Both reduce the actual return from an hour of work and lower total net income from any specific number of hours of work. The tax generates income and substitution effects that act in opposing directions. By reducing income at any specific level of work, the tax lowers consumption of all normal goods, including leisure; therefore, the incentive to work increases (the income effect). But the tax also reduces the net return from work or, stated alternatively, decreases the opportunity cost (price) of leisure. This creates an incentive to substitute the relatively lower-priced leisure for the now relatively higher-priced work, so work declines (the substitution effect).

Graphical Depiction   Figure 12.6 illustrates this graphically. The figure shows the indifference maps and budget constraints for Smith (graph a) and Jones (graph b). Notice that each graph portrays two budget lines: *HW,* which is linear, and *HW_t* which lies below *HW* and increases at a diminishing rate as work hours increase from 0 to 24. The *HW* curves shows the *before-tax* income for Smith and Jones at each level of work hours, and the *HW_t* curves depict the *after-tax* income from that specific work effort.

FIGURE 12.6   The Impact of a Personal Income Tax on Individual Labor Supply
A personal income tax shifts the after-tax wage rate line downward to W_t and may cause either an increase or a decrease in a person's optimal supply of labor hours. For Smith (a), the substitution effect generated by the tax overpowers the income effect, resulting in a *decrease* in work from h_1 to h_2. Alternatively, for Jones, the income effect swamps the substitution effect, leading to an *increase* in work hours from h_1 to h_2. The overall effect of the tax on the quantity of labor supplied is indeterminate.

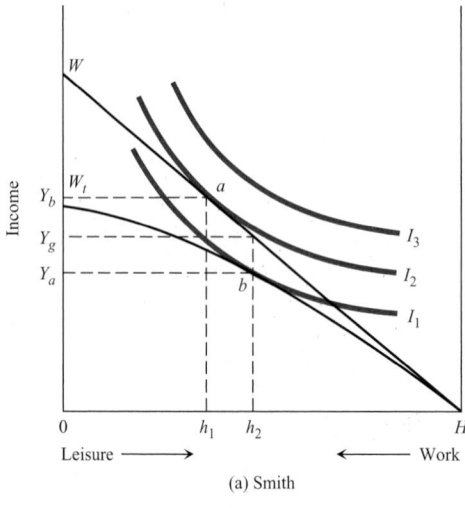

(a) Smith

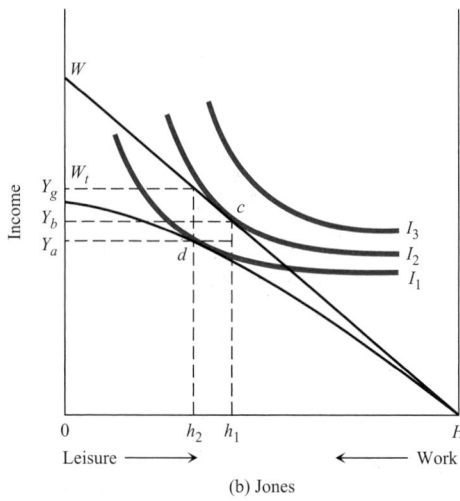

(b) Jones

The vertical distances between HW and HW_t measure the income tax paid at each work–income combination. These distances increase as a percentage of income as income rises, again indicating that the tax is progressive.

Without the tax, Smith (graph a) will choose to work h_1 hours, earn income Y_b, and maximize her utility at point *a* on indifference curve I_2. Once the income tax is imposed, Smith's after-tax wage rate falls as shown by the downward shift of HW to HW_t, and she reacts by *reducing* her work effort to h_2 (point *b*). At this level of work she earns a gross income of Y_g, pays a total tax of Y_gY_a, and receives an after-tax income of Y_a. For Smith, the income tax *reduces* the number of labor hours supplied by h_1h_2.

What is the outcome for Jones (graph b)? By employing the same logic, we find that he reacts to the tax by *increasing* his labor hours. Given his subjective preferences for income versus leisure, he discovers it to be in his interest to increase work from h_1 to h_2 (point *d* rather than *c*), earn a gross income of Y_g, pay a tax equal to the vertical distance of Y_gY_a, and retain an after-tax income of Y_a. Thus Figure 12.6 illustrates a basic point: The progressive income tax (and changes in tax rates) causes some workers to work less, others to work more, and still others to maintain their pretax level of work. For Smith (graph a), the substitution effect outweighs the income effect and she works less; but for Jones (graph b), the income effect swamps the substitution effect, leading him to work more. (Remember from Chapter 2 that the income effect increases hours of work and the substitution effect decreases hours of work when we are considering a reduction in wages.) The basic work–leisure theory of individual labor supply does not permit us to predict whether the aggregate labor supply curve is negatively sloped, perfectly inelastic, or positively sloped. Thus we are uncertain whether the aggregate amount of labor supplied will increase or decrease in response to, say, an income tax reduction.

Caveat

We must note, however, that this matter is not entirely settled. Recall from our previous analysis that government's provision of public goods theoretically can produce income effects that reduce labor hour offerings. These goods are financed partially through the personal income tax and are available to people independent of their work effort. Consequently, workers need not work as much to achieve a given level of real goods or total utility. This income effect may reduce labor hours offered and offset any added work effort generated by the income effect from the imposition of the tax. If so, only a substitution effect remains, and the overall outcome may be less labor supplied.[17]

Empirical Analysis

Many economists have tried to measure the relative strengths of the income and substitution effects and thereby estimate the elasticity of aggregate labor supply in the economy.

---

[17] The view that a tax change produces only a substitution effect on economywide labor supply is found in James Gwartney and Richard Stroup, "Labor Supply and Tax Rates: A Correction of the Record," *American Economic Review,* June 1983, pp. 446–51. The Gwartney–Stroup criticism of the traditional model (Figure 12.6), in turn, has been challenged by several economists. For example, see Firouz Gahvari, "Labor Supply and Tax Rates: Comment," *American Economic Review,* March 1986, pp. 280–83; and David M. Betson and David Greenberg, "Labor Supply and Tax Rates: Comment," *American Economic Review,* June 1986, pp. 551–56.

The task of designing these studies to incorporate and control properly the many inter-correlated influences on labor supply behavior is extremely complex and difficult. The success of existing studies in accomplishing this task is subject to some debate, so their findings must be regarded with caution. Recall from Chapter 2 that most such studies reveal that the income effect slightly exceeds the substitution effect for adult males as a group. This implies that the supply curve for this group is negatively sloped; that is, tax increases (net wage decreases) cause males to increase their work hours slightly. For females, the substitution effect appears to dominate the income effect so that tax increases (wage decreases) create reductions in hours worked. The studies generally find that aggregating various individual labor supply curves yields an overall supply curve that is extremely inelastic. The major portion of U.S. income tax falls squarely on workers. Therefore, the tax has a minimal net impact on work effort, the market wage rate, and equilibrium employment, as shown in Figure 12.5(a).

Specific Individuals and Markets

Although the overall impact of the income tax on labor supply may be negligible, impacts on specific individuals and specific labor markets may be considerable. Examples: Variations in income taxes among states may cause some workers to migrate from high- to low-tax geographic areas;[18] high marginal tax rates may entice some salaried workers to switch to "underground" activity to avoid paying income taxes; and exclusions, deductions, and credits—which are part of the tax code—may influence the composition of labor demand by affecting spending patterns of consumers. With regard to this third example, we point out that the tax deductibility of interest paid on mortgages increases the demand for residential construction workers; the tax deduction for charitable contributions enhances the ability of colleges to provide financial aid, which in turn increases the supply of graduates to such occupations as teaching, medicine, and law; and the complexity of the tax code increases the demand for tax accountants, tax lawyers, and IRS agents.

12.2
Quick Review

- If labor supply is perfectly inelastic, workers will bear the full burden of the personal income tax; if labor supply is positively sloped, some of the tax will be borne by employers through higher wages.
- The impact of the income tax on individual labor supply is indeterminate in terms of theory because the tax creates income and substitution effects having opposite impacts on desired hours of work.
- Empirical studies suggest that labor supply is highly inelastic, meaning that *(a)* workers bear nearly all of the personal income tax and *(b)* the tax has little impact on market wages and employment levels.

Your Turn

In 2001 Congress lowered the maximum marginal tax rate on income from 39.6 to 35 percent. Explain why Stone may work more as a result, whereas Smythe may work less. (*Answer:* See page 598.)

---

[18] See Yu Hsing, "A Note on Interstate Migration and Tax Burdens: New Evidence," *Journal of Applied Business Research,* Winter 1995–1996, pp. 12–14; and Ira S. Saltz, "State Income Tax Policy and Geographic Labour Force Mobility in the United States," *Applied Economics Letters,* October 1998, pp. 599–601.

12.4	**World of Work**	Who Pays the Social Security Payroll Tax?

The federal government levies a flat-rate payroll tax on all earnings below a set minimum to finance the Social Security program (old age, survivors, disability, and health insurance). In 2007 employers and employees each paid a Social Security tax of 7.65 percent of the first $97,500 of wage and salary earnings. Because these taxes are significant and are levied directly on earnings, labor economists are interested in their impact on wages.

The consensus expert opinion is that workers bear more than half of the Social Security tax. How can this be? We have just said that employers and employees are assessed equal Social Security taxes. The answer is that firms "collect" some or all of these tax proceeds from their workers. They "collect" this money by reducing the employees' wages below levels they would have received without the tax.

The part of the Social Security tax levied on employers reduces the after-tax marginal revenue product of labor, as viewed by firms. Suppose, for example, that the pretax wage rate is $10 an hour and the employer is assessed a 7.65 percent Social Security tax (half of 15.3 percent). From the firm's perspective, the workers' MRP thus becomes $9.23 [= $10 − $.77 (= .0765 × $10)]. If labor supply is perfectly inelastic [Figure 12.5(a)] and the wage rate equals MRP, the after-tax hourly pay becomes $9.23, not $10. In this case workers have indirectly paid the employer's $.77 per hour Social Security tax through a $.77 per hour pay cut.

Also, employees must pay the 7.65 percent tax directly levied on their earnings. With the $9.23 market wage, this tax is $.71 per hour (.0765 × $9.23). The after-tax hourly wage therefore falls to $8.52. The Social Security tax reduces the workers' market wage from $10 to $9.23 per hour and lowers their after-tax wage from $10 to $8.52. Thus under these circumstances the workers in effect pay the full Social Security tax.

Empirical studies confirm that employers do not pay their full half of the Social Security tax, although they apparently do pay a small part of it.* These findings imply that the overall labor supply curve may be somewhat elastic rather than perfectly inelastic. As the Social Security tax rises, spouses, teenagers, semi-retired workers, and others who do not have strong attachments to the labor force may reduce their labor offerings. If the overall labor supply curve is somewhat elastic [Figure 12.5(b)], employers cannot reduce workers' wages by the full amount of the employers' portion of the Social Security tax. They will have to bear some of the tax themselves to continue to attract a profit-maximizing number of workers.

* The classic research is John A. Brittain, *The Payroll Tax for Social Security* (Washington, DC: Brookings Institution, 1972). Other research includes Daniel Hamermesh, "New Estimates of the Incidence of the Payroll Tax," *Southern Economic Journal,* February 1979, pp. 1208–19; and Patricia M. Anderson and Bruce D. Meyer, "The Effects of the Unemployment Insurance Payroll Tax on Wages, Employment, Claims and Denials," *Journal of Public Economics,* October 2000, pp. 81–106.

Chapter Summary

1. Government employment has increased both absolutely and as a percentage of total employment since 1950. The growth rate of public sector employment has been greatest at the state and local levels of government.

2. Federal workers had higher wage rates in the 1970s than comparably educated and experienced private sector employees, but that pay differential largely eroded during the 1980s and 1990s.

3. The total economic cost of allocating labor to the military consists of the total value of the alternative output (income) that is forgone. A voluntary army requires that

economic costs be paid by taxpayers; a drafted army at below-market wage rates imposes some of the costs on those who are conscripted.

4. Taken alone, government's provision of goods and services may create an income effect that reduces one's optimal supply of hours of work.

5. Government transfer payments and subsidies affect the composition of labor demand in the economy and also influence labor supply decisions.

6. Other things being equal, the more elastic the overall labor supply in the economy, the greater the extent to which a personal income tax will cause *(a)* a decline in the hours of labor supplied, *(b)* an increase in the market wage, and *(c)* lower overall employment. Most economists, however, judge the aggregate labor supply curve to be highly inelastic.

7. The impact of an income tax on an individual's optimal supply of labor is theoretically indeterminate in that the tax generates income and substitution effects that work in opposite directions with respect to the quantity of labor supplied.

Terms and Concepts

Prevailing wage rule, *372*
military conscription, *377*
voluntary or market-based army, *377*

government purchases, *379*
transfer payments, *380*
subsidy, *380*

pure public goods, *381*
income tax, *384*

Questions and Study Suggestions

1. List and discuss factors that help explain why public sector employment rose faster than private sector employment between 1950 and 2006. At what levels of government has public sector employment increased most dramatically?

2. Comment on this statement: "In general, federal government employees are underpaid compared to similar private sector workers. This is due to the monopsony power of government."

3. Speculate about the reason(s) for each of the following facts about public sector pay:
   a. The pay premium received by federal employees declined in the middle and late 1980s.
   b. Local governments tend to pay less skilled workers more, and more skilled workers less, than comparably trained and experienced private sector workers.
   c. Female and African–American workers in government receive higher pay on average than their equally qualified counterparts in the private sector.

4. Explain why a voluntary army may be less expensive to society than an army composed of draftees. Which will likely be less expensive to taxpayers?

5. Explain why a draft system might cause the U.S. military to overemploy labor and underemploy capital (from society's perspective). Speculate about why the army increasingly contracts out construction and maintenance work to private firms now that it is voluntary.

6. Assuming that income includes both private and public goods and that leisure is a normal good, explain how a major reduction in governmentally provided goods might increase a person's optimal number of hours of work.

7. Explain how the existence of national, state, and city parks might affect
   a. Labor demand in the recreational vehicle industry.
   b. The demand for workers who build and maintain equipment for private recreational theme parks.
   c. The overall supply of labor.

8. Use the following labor market data to determine the answers to *(a)* through *(d)*:

(1) Wage Rate	(2) Quantity Demanded	(3) Quantity Supplied	(4) Tax per Hour
$10	14	22	$3.33
8	18	22	2.67
6	22	22	2.00
4	26	22	1.33
2	30	22	.67

   a. Is this tax progressive? Explain.
   b. What is the before-tax equilibrium wage rate?
   c. What effect does the tax have on the number of hours of work supplied and the market wage rate?
   d. If the labor supply curve were highly elastic, rather than perfectly inelastic, how would your answers to *(c)* change?

Internet Exercise

What Is Up (or Down) with the State and Local Government Compensation Differential?

Go to the Bureau of Labor Statistics Web site **(http://www.bls.gov)** and in sequence select "Get Detailed Statistics" and "Series Report." Then enter the following ID series numbers: CIU3010000000000I and CIU2010000000000I. Last, click on "All Years." This will retrieve indexes of total compensation of state and local government workers and private industry workers (100 = Quarter 4, 2005).

What is the index value for state and local government workers for the most recent quarter shown? What is the index value for private industry workers for the most recent quarter shown?

What is the percentage change in compensation for state and local government workers since Quarter 1, 2001? What is the percentage change in compensation for private industry workers since Quarter 1, 2001? What do these figures indicate has happened to the state and local government compensation differential since Quarter 1, 2001?

Internet Link

The Web site of the Selective Service System provides extensive information about the history of the military draft in the United States as well as a description of what would happen if a draft was reinstituted **(http://www.sss.gov/)**.

Chapter 13

Government and the Labor Market: Legislation and Regulation

Besides directly employing labor, providing public goods, transferring income, and levying taxes (Chapter 12), government engages in the important task of establishing the legal rules for the economy. Many of these laws and regulations directly or indirectly affect wage and employment outcomes. We examine such laws throughout this book; for example, in Chapter 9 we discussed immigration laws. In later chapters we discuss laws outlawing discrimination (Chapter 14) and promoting full employment (Chapter 18).

Laws affecting labor markets are so numerous that we must be highly selective. We limit our analysis here to four main topics: labor relations law, the federal minimum wage, the Occupational Safety and Health Act of 1970, and laws providing workers with increases in economic rent.

LABOR LAW[1]

Laws governing labor relations in general and collective bargaining in particular constitute a significant institutional factor influencing wages, employment, and resource allocation. The major laws in this category are summarized in Table 13.1. A careful reading of this table will complement the discussion that follows. The labor relations

---

[1] Instructors in colleges that offer a separate course in labor relations may wish to skip this section.

TABLE 13.1
A Summary of Basic Labor Relations Laws

The Norris–LaGuardia Act of 1932
1. Increased the difficulty for employers to obtain injunctions against union activity.
2. Declared that yellow-dog contracts were unenforceable. These contracts required employees to agree as a condition of continued employment that they would not join a union.

The Wagner Act of 1935 (National Labor Relations Act—NLRA)
1. Guaranteed the "twin rights" of labor: the right of self-organization and the right to bargain with employers engaged in interstate commerce.
2. Listed a number of "unfair labor practices" on the part of management. Specifically, it *(a)* forbids employers to interfere with the right of workers to form unions; *(b)* outlaws company unions, that is, pseudo-unions, established by firms to discourage the establishment of worker-controlled unions; *(c)* prohibits antiunion discrimination by employers in hiring, firing, and promoting; *(d)* outlaws discrimination against any worker who files charges or gives testimony under the act; and *(e)* obligates employers to bargain in good faith.
3. Established the National Labor Relations Board (NLRB), which was given the authority to investigate unfair labor practices occurring under the act, to issue cease-and-desist orders, and to conduct elections by workers on whether they desire union representation.
4. Made strikes by federal employees illegal and grounds for dismissal.

The Taft–Hartley Act of 1947 (Amendment to the NLRA of 1935)
1. Established "unfair labor practices" on the part of unions. Specifically, it prohibits *(a)* coercion of employees to become union members; *(b)* jurisdictional strikes (disputes between unions over who is authorized to perform a specific job); *(c)* secondary boycotts (refusing to buy or handle products produced by another union or group of workers); *(d)* sympathy strikes (work stoppages by one union designed to assist some other union in gaining employer recognition or some other objective); *(e)* excessive union dues; and *(f)* featherbedding (forcing payment for work not actually performed).
2. Regulated the internal administration of unions—for example, required detailed financial reports to the NLRB.
3. Outlawed the closed shop but made union shops legal in states that do not expressly prohibit them (state "right-to-work" laws).
4. Set up emergency strike procedures allowing the government to stop for up to 80 days a strike that imperils the nation's health and safety.
5. Created the Federal Mediation and Conciliation Service to provide mediators for labor disputes.

The Landrum–Griffin Act of 1959 (Amendment to the NLRA of 1935)
1. Required regularly scheduled elections of union officers and excluded Communists and people convicted of felonies from holding union office.
2. Held union officers strictly accountable for union funds and property.
3. Prevented union leaders from infringing on individual workers' rights to participate in union meetings, vote in union proceedings, and nominate officers.

laws summarized in the table affect the labor market in diverse ways, two of which are (1) by influencing the extent and growth of union membership, which in turn influences the ability of unions to secure wage gains; and (2) by establishing the rules under which collective bargaining transpires.

Labor Law and Union Membership

The effect of labor relations laws and regulations, or the absence thereof, on union membership is not always easy to determine. Such factors as changes in industry structure and altered worker attitudes may create conditions that simultaneously foster both new labor laws *and* changes in union membership. That is, observed changes in union membership may not necessarily result from changes in labor laws. Untangling cause and effect therefore is not an easy task. Nevertheless, there can be no doubt that labor law per se can be an important determinant of union membership. This relationship between labor law and union membership is observable in both the private and public sectors.

1 Labor Law and Private Sector Union Membership

A glance back at Figure 10.2 reveals that union membership was 7 percent of the labor force in 1900 and only 11 percent of the labor force in 1930. Two decades later, union membership stood at over 30 percent of the labor force. Relative to total employment, union membership peaked in the mid-1950s (or in 1970 if members of professional associations are included) and has since declined. Although the reasons for this pattern of union growth and decline are many and varied, the imprint of labor law on these trends is readily discernible.

Pre-1930 Period Prior to the 1930s, union organizers and members were legally unprotected against reprisals by employers or even government itself. Stated bluntly, joining a union might involve job loss, fines, or even bodily harm. Attempts to unionize were met with **discriminatory discharge** in many instances. Those dismissed often were placed on **blacklists** and therefore denied opportunities to gain alternative employment. Workers sometimes were required to sign **yellow-dog contracts** that, as a condition of continued employment, legally prohibited them from joining unions. Violation could result not only in discharge but also in a lawsuit initiated by the employer and a court-imposed fine. Firms also used **lockouts** (plant shutdowns) as a way to stop organizing attempts in their infancies. By closing down the plant for a few weeks, employers could impose high costs on those contemplating joining labor unions. Where workers did successfully organize and attempt to force their employers to bargain, firms often countered strikes by employing **strikebreakers,** who sometimes clashed violently with union workers. The Homestead Strike of 1892 and the Pullman Strike of 1894 are cases in point. Often government intervened with police action on the side of employers during these confrontations.

Court hostility toward unionization was a related factor explaining the low union membership during this period. Without labor laws, courts relied on common law interpretations. This placed unions in the weak position of seeking new legal rights for labor at the expense of long-standing property rights of firms. This court hostility manifested itself in several ways, including the courts' interpretation of antitrust laws and the use of ***injunctions.*** For example, the Supreme Court held that the Sherman Antitrust Act of 1890 applied to unions, even though the intent of the legislation was clearly directed toward prohibiting price fixing and monopolization by firms. Injunctions were readily dispensed as a way of stopping actions such as picketing, striking, and boycotting, which employers claimed would reduce their profits. Lower profits would reduce the capitalized value of the firm's assets and, according to the courts, violate the firm's property rights.

To summarize: Prior to the 1930s, the absence of protective labor legislation allowed firms and the courts to repress union activity and growth. Low union membership translated into an inability of unions, in general, to make a significant impact on the overall labor market.

Post-1930 Period   As evidenced in the summary of labor legislation in Table 13.1, Congress enacted significant labor relations laws during the 1930s. The Norris–LaGuardia Act of 1932 and the Wagner Act of 1935 placed a protective umbrella over the union movement and greatly encouraged growth of union membership. By outlawing yellow-dog contracts, the ***Norris–LaGuardia Act*** significantly reduced the personal costs of becoming a union member and thus made it easier to organize a firm's workforce. Previously the cost of joining a union might be the loss of one's job. Also, the act's provision limiting the use of the court-issued injunction to halt normal union activities such as striking increased the ability of unions to impose costs on firms as a way to obtain higher wage offers. Larger union wage gains, in turn, increased the incentive for workers to become union members.

The ***Wagner Act*** had even greater impact on union membership. In fact, one of the expressed purposes of this law was to promote the growth of unionism. Table 13.1 informs us that this legislation guaranteed unions (1) the right to self-organization, free of interference from employers, and (2) the right to bargain as a unit with employers. Furthermore, the act outlawed several "unfair labor practices" that management had used successfully to thwart unionism. The Wagner Act enabled the American Federation of Labor (AFL) to solidify its power within various crafts and also permitted the rapid growth of industrial unions affiliated with the Congress of Industrial Organizations (CIO). These CIO unions organized millions of less skilled workers employed in mass-production industries such as steel, rubber, and automobiles. By the time of the merger between the AFL and CIO in 1955, union membership had risen to about 17 million.

The dramatic surge in union membership in the two decades following the pro-union legislation of the mid-1930s strengthened the ability of unions to achieve dominance (Chapter 6) of many labor markets and thus secure improvements in wage rates and working conditions. That is, increases in union membership translated into increased union bargaining power and a greater overall impact of unionism on labor market outcomes.

The growing strength of labor unions produced a political backlash against unions, resulting in passage of the ***Taft–Hartley Act*** of 1947 and the ***Landrum–Griffin Act*** of 1959, both of which are annotated in Table 13.1. Union membership continued to grow, however, until the more recent decline in unionism discussed in detail in Chapter 10. Recall that some observers contend that part of the recent decline in unionism can be traced to an increased use of illegal antiunion tactics by management. If this assertion is true, then it might be argued that the *degree of enforcement* of labor laws is also a factor in explaining trends in union membership within the private sector.

2 Labor Law and Public Sector Union Membership

Recall from Chapter 10 that membership in public employee unions spurted during the 1960s and 1970s. The driving force for this growth at the federal level was a set of presidential executive orders that provided for the recognition of unions composed of federal workers. At the state level, the main factors explaining the rapid rise in public employee unionism were (1) laws recognizing the rights of state workers to organize and (2) laws establishing public employee relations boards to conduct elections to determine whether workers desire union representation.[2]

Labor Law and Bargaining Power

The overall body of labor law and specific provisions of the law influence bargaining power independently of effects on the level of union membership. Many provisions of labor law enhance the bargaining power of unions, enabling them to secure higher wage gains; other provisions strengthen the negotiating positions of employers. Let's briefly examine an example of each outcome.

1 Limitation on the Use of the Injunction

The Norris–LaGuardia Act of 1932 limited the use of court-issued injunctions to enjoin picketing, striking, and related union activities. This prohibition clearly strengthened union bargaining power. Because firms could no longer gain legal relief from, say, a work stoppage, threats by unions to strike now became more credible. Previously firms knew they could get the courts to enjoin the strike once it began.

2 Prohibition of Secondary Boycotts

Secondary boycotts are actions by one union to refuse to handle, or to get one's employer to refuse to buy, products made by a firm that is party to a labor dispute. Although the Taft–Hartley Act of 1947 presumably made these secondary pressures illegal, trucking unions continued to demand and obtain "hot-cargo" clauses in their contracts. The courts ruled that such clauses technically did not constitute an illegal secondary boycott. What were these clauses and how did they affect union bargaining power?

Hot-cargo clauses declared that trucking firms would not require unionized truckers to handle or transport products made by an "unfair" employer involved in a labor dispute. For example, suppose a manufacturer of fabricated steel products was being struck by its employees. Unionized transportation firms governed by hot-cargo provisions would refuse to transport these fabricated steel items while the labor dispute

---

[2] Richard Freeman, "Unionism Comes to the Public Sector," *Journal of Economic Literature,* March 1986, pp. 41–86. Table 4 in this article summarizes empirical work supporting the thesis that changes in the legal environment independently encourage membership in public sector unions. For more information on public sector labor laws, see John Lund and Cheryl L. Maranto, "Public Sector Labor Law: An Update," in Dale Belman, Morley Gunderson, and Douglas Hyatt (eds.), *Public Sector Employment in a Time of Transition* (Madison, WI: Industrial Relations Research Association, 1996).

was in progress. The union representing the steel fabricators therefore had more bargaining power than it might otherwise have possessed. The reason is that, as a result of the hot-cargo provisions, the strike would effectively curtail all revenue to the firm, thus causing it to suffer losses; it could not maintain its sales and profits through such actions as hiring strikebreakers, using supervisory personnel, or selling from its inventory. Once struck by a union, the firm could not get its products transported to its customers.

The Landrum–Griffin Act of 1959 declared hot-cargo contracts illegal. Specifically, the act stated that it was an unfair labor practice for a union and employer "to enter into any contract or agreement, express or implied, whereby the employer ceases or refrains or agrees to cease or refrain from handling; using; selling; transporting; or otherwise dealing in any products of any other employer, or to cease doing business with any other persons." Once passed and enforced, this prohibition increased management bargaining power by increasing the union's cost of disagreeing in many labor disputes. Many firms now could continue to maintain their profits during strikes by hiring strikebreakers, using supervisory personnel, or selling previously produced goods.

MINIMUM WAGE LAW

The *Fair Labor Standards Act* of 1938, which established a *minimum wage* of $.25 per hour, is another way government legislation affects the labor market. Before undertaking a detailed analysis of these effects, it will be useful to establish some facts about the minimum wage law and provide a brief synopsis of the alternative positions taken on the wisdom of this government intervention into the labor market.

Facts and Controversy

Congress has amended the Fair Labor Standards Act many times to increase the legal minimum wage in monetary terms. Between 1991 and 1996 the legal minimum wage was $4.25 per hour. Because inflation occurred during this period, the ratio of the minimum wage to the average wage fell from 37.3 percent to 32.4 percent.[3] As a result, in 1996 Congress upped the minimum wage to $5.15 per hour (after September 1997). In mid-2007 Congress raised the minimum wage over two years to $7.25.

Congress has extended the coverage of the minimum wage law over the years. The original legislation placed about 44 percent of all nonsupervisory workers under its coverage; today about 88 percent of all such workers are included. Recent statistics reveal that 37 percent of workers earning the minimum wage are teenagers, 61 percent are women, and 20 percent are African–American. About 91 percent of minimum wage employees work in private sector industries. Approximately 70 percent of those receiving the minimum wage work part-time.[4]

---

[3] Barry T. Hirsch and David A. Macpherson, *Union Membership and Earnings Data Book: Compilations from the Current Population Survey (2004 Edition)* (Washington, DC: Bureau of National Affairs, 2004).
[4] *Statistical Abstract of the United States,* 2007 (Washington, DC: U.S. Government Printing Office, 2006), Table 639.

The minimum wage has been controversial since its inception. Proponents argue that it is needed to ensure that workers receive a "living wage"—one that will provide full-time workers an annual income sufficient to purchase the bare necessities of life. They also contend that this wage floor prevents monopsonistic employers from exploiting low-skilled labor, a disproportionate number of whom are minorities and women.

Opponents of the minimum wage, on the other hand, argue that it increases unemployment, particularly among teenagers, females, and minorities. Second, opponents cite the possibility that the legal wage floor causes a spillover effect (Figure 11.2) that reduces wage rates in sectors of the economy that are not covered by the law. Third, detractors argue that it encourages teenagers to drop out of school. Finally, critics contend that the minimum wage is poorly targeted to reduce poverty; that is, a majority of minimum-wage workers do *not* live in poverty households.

The Competitive Model

The competitive labor supply and demand model is the best starting place for analyzing the possible labor market effects of the minimum wage.[5] Considering Figure 13.1, suppose that all employees in the economy are covered by the minimum wage law and that labor and product markets are perfectly competitive (MRP = VMP = MWC = P_L). The figure depicts the impact of a specific minimum wage W_m on a labor market in which the equilibrium wage and employment levels are W_0 and Q_0. One point needs to be stressed at the outset. *If* the minimum wage W_m is at or below the equilibrium wage W_0, which is true for higher-wage labor markets, then the law is irrelevant and has *no* direct wage and employment consequence. The actual wage and employment outcome will remain at W_0 and Q_0. This is *not* the situation in Figure 13.1, where W_m exceeds the equilibrium wage W_0.

What employment, unemployment, and allocation effects will this government-imposed minimum wage produce? First, observe that at W_m, employers will hire only Q_d workers rather than the original Q_0. Stated differently, the marginal revenue product of the Q_d through Q_0 workers will be less than the minimum wage; therefore, profit-maximizing employers will reduce employment.

Second, the supply curve suggests that the minimum wage will attract Q_s as opposed to Q_0 workers to the market. The minimum wage changes the behavior of employers and labor suppliers so that employment declines by the amount *ba* and unemployment increases by the larger amount *ac*.

Third, the minimum wage W_m creates allocative inefficiency. Notice from segment *ae* of the labor demand curve that the value of the marginal product (VMP) for each

---

[5] The effects of the minimum wage have also been examined in other types of models. For a discussion of its effect in a monopsonistic competition model, see V. Bhaskar and Ted To, "Minimum Wages for Ronald McDonald Monopsonies: A Theory of Monopsonistic Competition," *Economic Journal,* April 1999, pp. 190–203. For an analysis of its impact in an efficiency wage model, see James B. Rebitzer and Lowell J. Taylor, "The Consequences of Minimum Wage Laws: Some New Theoretical Ideas," *Journal of Public Economics,* February 1995, pp. 245–55.

FIGURE 13.1 **Minimum Wage Effects: Competitive Model**

The above-equilibrium minimum wage W_m reduces employment in this low-wage labor market by ab and creates unemployment of ac. The more elastic the labor supply and demand curves, the greater the unemployment consequences of the law.

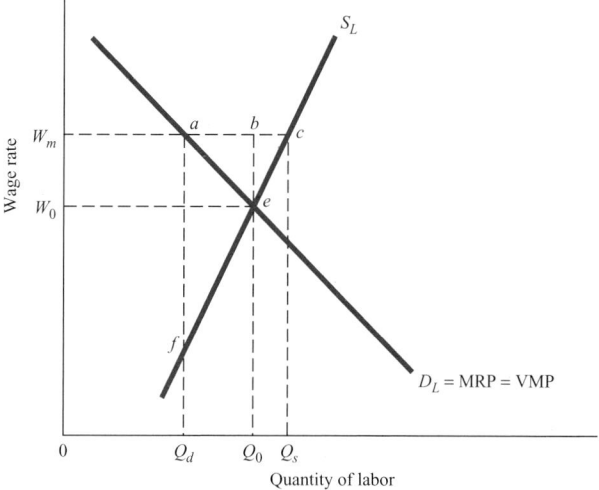

of the Q_d to Q_0 workers exceeds the supply price of these individuals (as shown by segment fe of S_L). This implies that society is giving up output of greater value $(Q_d aeQ_0)$ than the $Q_d Q_0$ displaced workers can contribute in their next most productive employment $(Q_d feQ_0)$. The *net* loss of domestic output is shown then by area $fae (= Q_d aeQ_0 - Q_d feQ_0)$. You should use Figure 13.1 to verify the following generalizations: (1) Other things being equal, the higher the minimum wage relative to the equilibrium wage, the greater the negative employment and allocation effects; and (2) the more elastic the labor supply and demand curves, the greater the unemployment consequences of the law.

Two factors, of course, might dampen the minimum wage effects just mentioned. One such factor is failure on the part of some firms to comply with the minimum wage law.[6] The other factor is the possibility that some firms offset the minimum wage by reducing fringe benefits (say, sick leave or health insurance).[7] In either case, hourly labor cost would not rise in Figure 13.1 by the full amount $W_0 W_m$, and therefore the indicated employment and efficiency effects would be lessened.

---

[6] For evidence of this possibility, see Orley Ashenfelter and Robert S. Smith, "Compliance with the Minimum Wage Law," *Journal of Political Economy,* April 1979, pp. 335–50.

[7] Walter J. Wessels, "The Effect of Minimum Wages in the Presence of Fringe Benefits: An Expanded Model," *Economic Inquiry,* April 1980, pp. 293–313. Also relevant are J. Harold McClure, Jr., "Minimum Wages and the Wessels Effect in a Monopsony Model," *Journal of Labor Research,* Summer 1994, pp. 271–82; and Kosali Ilayperuma Simon and Robert Kaestner, "Do Minimum Wages Affect Nonwage Job Attributes? Evidence on Fringe Benefits," *Industrial and Labor Relations Review,* October 2004, pp. 52–70.

FIGURE 13.2 Minimum Wage Effects: Monopsony

Without the minimum wage, this monopsonist will choose to hire Q_0 workers and pay a wage equal to W_0. Any legal minimum wage above W_0 and below W_2 will transform the firm into a wage taker, and the firm will choose to increase its level of employment. For example, if the minimum wage is W_1, this firm will hire the same number of workers as if competition existed in this labor market. Thus it is possible that a minimum wage might increase employment in some industries.

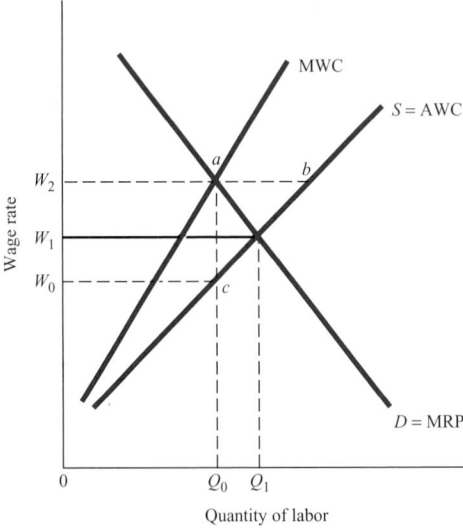

Monopsony

Thus far we have assumed that the low-wage labor market is perfectly competitive. We now dispose of this assumption and analyze the potential employment effects of the minimum wage under conditions of nondiscriminating monopsony. Figure 13.2 portrays a labor market comprising only a single employer of labor services or several employers colluding to set a below-competitive wage. Recall from Figure 6.7 that a monopsonist's marginal wage cost (MWC) exceeds its average wage cost (AWC) at each level of employment. Because it is the only buyer of labor services, the monopsonist faces the typical upward-sloping market supply of labor curve. To hire more workers it must attract them away from other occupations, and it accomplishes this by raising the wage it pays. But because the nondiscriminating monopsonist must pay *all* its workers the same wage, it discovers that its extra cost of hiring one more worker (MWC) exceeds the higher wage payment to that worker alone (AWC).

The monopsonist depicted in Figure 13.2 will use the profit-maximizing hiring rule (MRP = MWC) and employ Q_0 workers. As we see from point c on the labor supply curve, to attract that number of workers it has to pay a wage of W_0. But now suppose that government sets a minimum wage somewhere between W_0 and W_2—say W_1. In effect, the labor supply curve becomes perfectly horizontal at W_1 over the $0Q_1$ range of employment. Because the firm can hire up to Q_1 extra workers at the minimum wage, its marginal wage cost equals its average wage cost over this entire range. Contrast this to the previous situation where it has to raise the wage to attract more workers (MWC > AWC).

With the legal minimum wage of W_1, the monopsonist becomes a wage taker rather than a wage setter and maximizes its profits by hiring Q_1 workers. The additional Q_0 through Q_1 workers are now hired because their MRPs exceed the minimum wage (MWC). In this case, the minimum wage *increases* employment from Q_0 to Q_1 by perfectly countervailing the monopsony power of the employer. Close scrutiny of Figure 13.2 shows that any legal wage above W_0 and below W_2 will increase employment above Q_0. It therefore is possible that a well-chosen and selectively implemented minimum wage might increase employment and improve allocative efficiency. This outcome is the same analytically as Chapter 6's discussion of bilateral monopoly, in which a union-imposed wage rate might increase employment and enhance efficiency (Figure 6.11).

But much caution is needed here. First, if government sets the minimum wage above W_2, employment will decline. Second, even though *employment* may be equal to or greater than Q_0 at minimum wage levels above the monopsony wage W_0, *unemployment* could easily be higher. For example, b laborers seek employment in this market at wage rate W_2, whereas firms hire only a workers. At W_2, although *employment* is the same as at the monopsony wage W_0, the excess supply of workers—*unemployment*—rises from zero to ab. Third, being the only employer of a specific type of low-wage labor, a monopsonist might be able to discriminate—that is, pay each worker a wage just sufficient to attract her or his employment. If so, the MWC curve will coincide with the labor supply curve, and the firm's profit-maximizing level of employment (MRP = MWC) will be the competitive one, Q_1, rather than Q_0. This is true because the firm must pay the higher wage that is necessary to attract each extra worker only to that particular worker. Where discriminating monopsony exists, a minimum wage will either be ineffective or reduce employment; it cannot increase employment. Fourth, empirical studies on this subject find little evidence of monopsony in most labor markets.[8]

Empirical Evidence

Economists have devoted much attention to estimating the effects of the minimum wage on employment. Additionally, they have used statistical studies to try to determine whether the minimum wage influences human capital investment decisions and achieves the goal of creating more equality in the distribution of earnings and household income. The results of several of these studies are summarized as follows.

1 Employment

Many studies have analyzed the employment effects of the minimum wage. Much of this analysis has been devoted to examining teenagers because this is the age group

[8] For a survey of theoretical and empirical studies of monopsony, see William M. Boal and Michael R. Ransom, "Monopsony in the Labor Market," *Journal of Economic Literature,* March 1997, pp. 86–112.

most likely to be affected by the minimum wage. Until recently, a 10 percent increase in the minimum wage typically caused a 1–3 percent decline in the number of jobs held by teenagers, if all other factors were held constant.[9] This long-standing research finding, however, has been challenged by some recent and controversial studies.

Card and Krueger have examined the impact of the 1992 rise in the New Jersey minimum wage on employment in fast-food restaurants in the state.[10] To conduct their research, the authors surveyed managers of 410 fast-food restaurants in New Jersey and eastern Pennsylvania before and after the rise in the minimum wage. They report employment rose faster in New Jersey restaurants than in Pennsylvania restaurants (where the minimum wage did not change). The results also revealed that restaurants in New Jersey that paid high wages before the minimum wage hike did not have faster employment growth than those that paid low wages. Thus the authors concluded that the minimum wage did not decrease employment.

A study by Card of another state minimum wage increase found similar results.[11] He reports that the rise in the minimum wage raised the earnings of California teenagers, but it did not lower their employment rate relative to workers in other states.

Although these and other studies by Card and Krueger have generated strong interest from policy makers, they have also produced warnings that these results should be considered tentative.[12] One criticism of the New Jersey study is that the quality of the data collected by Card and Krueger may be poor. A study by Neumark and Wascher, using actual payroll data collected from fast-food restaurants from New Jersey and Pennsylvania, finds a negative effect of the minimum wage on employment.[13] How-ever, a follow-up study by Card and Krueger, also using a payroll data set, confirms their original conclusion.[14] Another researcher argues that the California study did not appropriately account for the boom that was occurring in California at the time of the minimum wage increase.[15] Critics also point out that the employment declines from new minimum wage legislation could occur before the law takes effect because the

[9] See Charles Brown, "Minimum Wages, Employment, and the Distribution of Income," in Orley Ashenfelter and David Card (eds.), *Handbook of Labor Economics,* Volume 3B (Amsterdam: North-Holland, 1999).

[10] David Card and Alan B. Krueger, "Minimum Wages and Employment: A Case Study of the Fast-Food Industry in New Jersey and Pennsylvania," *American Economic Review,* September 1994, pp. 772–93.

[11] David Card, "Do Minimum Wages Reduce Employment? A Case Study of California, 1987–1989," *Industrial and Labor Relations Review,* October 1992, pp. 38–54.

[12] Much of their research on this topic is summarized in David Card and Alan B. Krueger, *Myth and Measurement: The New Economics of the Minimum Wage* (Princeton, NJ: Princeton University Press, 1995). For a critical review, see "Review Symposium on *Myth and Mismeasurement: The New Economics of the Minimum Wage* by David Card and Alan B. Krueger," *Industrial and Labor Relations Review,* July 1995, pp. 842–48.

[13] David Neumark and William Wascher, "Minimum Wages and Employment: A Case Study of the Fast-Food Industry in New Jersey and Pennsylvania: Comment," *American Economic Review,* December 2000, pp. 1362–96.

[14] David Card and Alan B. Krueger, "Minimum Wages and Employment: A Case Study of the Fast-Food Industry in New Jersey and Pennsylvania: Reply," *American Economic Review,* December 2000, pp. 1397–1420.

[15] See Taeil Kim and Lowell J. Taylor, "The Employment Effect in Retail Trade of California's 1988 Minimum Wage Increase," *Journal of Business and Economic Statistics,* April 1995, pp. 175–82.

13.1 World of Work

Living Wage Laws*

Since 1994 more than 100 cities and counties in the United States have enacted living wage laws. These laws now cover 9 of the 20 largest cities in the United States. Living wage ordinances typically require businesses to pay their employees a wage that would be high enough to a lift a family with one full-time, full-year worker above the poverty line. These laws generally cover employers who are under contract with the local government or are receiving financial assistance from the local government.

Living wage laws differ from minimum wage laws in three critical ways. First, living wages are set much higher than the federal minimum wage. They average about $8.19, which is almost 60 percent higher than the current federal minimum wage. Second, living wage laws usually cover only about 1 percent of residents who are earning a low wage. Third, because these laws are adopted by local governments, officials must worry about employers leaving the city or county or refusing to move in.

Some preliminary conclusions can be drawn from the several studies that Adams and Neumark have conducted regarding the effects of living wage laws. First, living wage laws appear to have sizable positive wage effects for low-paid workers. Second, the ordinances moderately reduce employment among low-skill workers. That evidence is consistent with a trade-off between wages and employment. Finally, the laws modestly reduce the urban poverty rate. Interestingly, the reduction in the poverty rate arises from income gains for individuals with higher wages or skills who are in poor families, rather than those with the lowest wage or skills.

* Based on Timothy Bartik, "Living Wages and Local Governments," W. E. Upjohn Institute for Employment Research *Employment Research,* April 2002, pp. 1–2; David Neumark and Scott Adams, "Detecting Effects of Living Wage Laws," *Industrial Relations,* October 2003, pp. 531–64; David Neumark and Scott Adams, "Do Living Wage Ordinances Reduce Urban Poverty?" *Journal of Human Resources,* Summer 2003, pp. 490–521; and Scott Adams and David Neumark, "Living Wage Effects: New and Improved Evidence," *Economic Development Quarterly,* February 2005, pp. 80–102.

laws are announced well in advance. Alternatively, declines could lag many years behind hikes in the minimum wage.[16] Nevertheless, these findings have renewed empirical interest in the employment effects of minimum wage hikes.[17]

2 Investment in Human Capital

The effect of the minimum wage on investment in human capital is likely negative. The minimum wage probably *reduces* on-the-job training. Recall from Chapter 4 that firms sometimes hire workers and provide them with general on-the-job training. To cover

[16] For evidence consistent with this criticism, see Michael Baker, Dwayne Benjamin, and Shuchita Stanger, "The Highs and Lows of the Minimum Wage Effect: A Time-Series Cross-Section Study of the Canadian Law," *Journal of Labor Economics,* April 1999, pp. 318–50.

[17] Other studies do find a negative effect of the minimum wage on employment. For example, see Richard V. Burkhauser, Kenneth A. Couch, and David C. Wittenberg, "A Reassessment of the New Economics of the Minimum Wage Literature with Monthly Data from the Current Population Survey," *Journal of Labor Economics,* October 2000, pp. 653–80; and Daniel Aaronson and Eric French, "Product Market Evidence on the Employment Effects of the Minimum Wage," *Journal of Labor Economics,* January 2007, pp. 167–200.

the expense, they pay a lower wage during the training period. But the minimum wage places a floor on the wage firms can offer. Therefore, some firms may decide against providing general job training under these circumstances, and thus the minimum wage may reduce the formation of this type of human capital.[18] Also, empirical evidence indicates that a higher minimum wage encourages teenagers to seek employment and drop out of school.[19]

3 Income Inequality and Poverty

The minimum wage does *not* generally alter the overall distribution of family income or appreciably reduce poverty. This somewhat surprising conclusion rests on the empirical evidence that people paid a minimum wage are more likely to be members of middle- or high-income families than low-income families. About 70 percent of minimum-wage workers reside in families that have family income 300 percent above the poverty line. Thus the minimum wage appears to be poorly targeted as an antipoverty weapon.[20] Furthermore, wage growth among the average minimum-wage workers is substantial, rising more than 60 percent above the minimum wage within a year.[21]

Final Remarks

The minimum wage *does* increase the annual earnings of some low-income workers. Perhaps this is the reason for the strong public support for the minimum wage and the fact that the debate over it has largely moved away from the question of whether it should exist and toward the issue of how high it should be set. Economists commonly agree that there is some real minimum wage that would be so high that it would severely reduce employment and economic efficiency. But based on the evidence summarized here, it does not appear that this level has yet been reached. In this regard, one knowledgeable reviewer of the minimum wage literature has concluded that "the minimum wage is overrated: by its critics as well as its supporters."[22]

---

[18] For evidence consistent with this hypothesis, see David Neumark and William Wascher, "Minimum Wages and Training," *Journal of Labor Economics,* July 2001, pp. 563–95. For a study finding no effect on training, see David Fairris and Roberto Pedace, "The Impact of Minimum Wages on Job Training: An Empirical Exploration with Establishment Data," *Southern Economic Journal,* January 2004, pp. 566–83.

[19] See David Neumark and William Wascher, "Minimum Wages and Skill Acquisition: Another Look at Schooling Effects," *Economics of Education Review,* February 2003, pp. 1–10; and Duncan D. Chaplin, "Minimum Wages and School Enrollment of Teenagers: A Look at the 1990s," *Economics of Education Review,* February 2003, pp. 11–21.

[20] See Richard V. Burkhauser, Kenneth A. Couch, and David C. Wittenburg, "Who Gets What from Minimum Wage Hikes: A Reestimation of Card and Krueger's Distributional Analysis in *Myth and Measurement: The New Economics of the Minimum Wage,*" *Industrial and Labor Relations Review,* April 1996, pp. 547–52. See also William E. Even and David A. Macpherson, "Consequences of Minimum Wage Indexing," *Contemporary Economic Policy,* October 1996, pp. 67–77.

[21] See James E. Long, "Updated Estimates of the Wage Mobility of Minimum Wage Workers," *Journal of Labor Research,* Fall 1999, pp. 493–503; and William E. Even and David A. Macpherson, "Wage and Employment Dynamics of Minimum Wage Workers," *Southern Economic Journal,* January 2003, pp. 676–90.

[22] Charles Brown, "Minimum Wage Laws: Are They Overrated?" *Journal of Economic Perspectives,* Summer 1988, pp. 133–45.

13.1 *Quick* *Review*	• The Norris–LaGuardia Act of 1932 and the Wagner Act of 1935 encouraged the growth of U.S. unionism; the Taft–Hartley Act of 1947 and the Landrum–Griffin Act of 1959 sought to restrain union power. • In a competitive labor market, an above-equilibrium minimum wage will reduce employment, increase unemployment, and create an efficiency loss. • Researchers have estimated that a 10 percent increase in the minimum wage causes a 1–3 percent decline in teenage employment. Some question exists, however, of whether the most recent increases in the minimum wage followed this pattern.

Your Turn

Suppose the federal government increases the minimum wage by 25 percent. Based on theory and traditional evidence, predict the impact of this increase on *(a)* the average wage of teenagers, *(b)* teenage employment, and *(c)* teenage unemployment. (*Answers:* See page 598.)

OCCUPATIONAL HEALTH AND SAFETY REGULATION

Another important and controversial area of direct government intervention into the labor market is the regulation of occupational health and safety. This intervention has taken several forms, including state workers' compensation programs and the federal *Occupational Safety and Health Act of 1970.* The former mandated that firms purchase insurance that pays specified benefits to workers injured on the job. The latter, which will be our main focus, requires employers to comply with workplace health and safety standards established under the legislation.

Government regulation of workplace health and safety is worthy of discussion for several reasons. First, statistics show that work is more dangerous than generally perceived. In 2004 5,000 workers died in job-related accidents in the United States, and roughly 3.7 million people incurred injuries that precluded work for a full day or more. As observed in Table 13.2, these accidents varied greatly by industry. Note, for example, that there were 29 deaths per 100,000 workers in agriculture as compared to 2 deaths per 100,000 employees in trade. Second, job safety—or the lack thereof—is an important nonwage aspect of work, which is an important determinant of labor supply (Chapter 6). Therefore, degrees of workplace safety help explain wage differentials among certain occupations (Chapter 8). Finally, just as with such labor market interventions as the minimum wage and affirmative action legislation (Chapter 14), controversy exists over the appropriateness and effectiveness of regulation of workplace health and safety.

This topic will be approached as follows. First we will discuss how a profit-maximizing firm determines how much job safety to provide its workers. Then we will analyze why this level of protection against workplace hazards might be less than society's optimal amount. Finally we will discuss the controversies surrounding the Occupational Safety and Health Act of 1970.

TABLE 13.2
**Occupational
Fatalities and
Disabilities by
Industry**

Source: *Statistical Abstract
of the United States, 2007*
(Washington, DC: U.S.
Government Printing
Office, 2006), Table 638.

Industry Group	Deaths		Number of Disabling Injuries* (in Thousands)
	Number (in Thousands)	Rate per 100,000 Workers	
Agriculture	0.6	29	90
Mining	0.2	28	20
Construction	1.2	12	460
Manufacturing	0.4	3	490
Transportation and utilities	0.8	15	290
Trade	0.4	2	580
Service	0.4	2	550
Government	0.4	2	550
Total	5.0	4	3,700

* Defined as injuries resulting in death, physical impairment, or inability to perform regular duties for a full day beyond the day of injury.

Profit-Maximizing Level of Job Safety[23]

Competition in the product market will force a profit-maximizing firm to minimize its internal costs of producing any specific amount of output. One cost of production is the expenditure necessary to make the workplace safe. The production of job safety normally involves diminishing returns, which, translated into cost terms, means that each dollar of additional expenditure yields successively smaller increases in job safety. More concretely, firms will first use such relatively inexpensive techniques as disseminating safety information and issuing protective gear (say, hard hats) to make the job safer; but to make further gains, they may have to resort to such increasingly costly actions as purchasing safer equipment and slowing the work pace. Therefore, most firms experience a rising *marginal cost of job safety:* Successively higher amounts of direct expense, reduced output, or both will be required to gain additional units of job safety. We depict a marginal cost of safety curve MC_s in Figure 13.3. Each additional unit of job safety, measured on the horizontal axis, costs more than previous units.

Knowing that it is costly to provide job safety, why would a firm choose to offer workers *any* protection from workplace hazards? The answer is provided by the marginal benefit of safety curve MB_s (disregard the curve labeled MB_s' for now). An employer benefits from creating a relatively safe workplace; job safety reduces certain costs that the firm might otherwise incur. Notice, however, that as more units of job safety are produced by this firm, the *marginal benefit from job safety* (MB_s) to the firm falls. Just as individuals experience diminishing marginal utility as successive units of a good are consumed, firms find that the extra benefit (cost savings) of job safety diminishes with every increase in the amount of job safety.

[23] The basic analytical framework for this section and the section that follows was developed by Walter Oi in "An Essay on Workmen's Compensation and Industrial Safety," in *Supplemental Studies for the National Commission on State Workmen's Compensation Laws,* vol. 1, 1974, pp. 41–106.

Global Perspective 13.1

Occupational Injuries*

The United Kingdom has a relatively low proportion of workers affected by occupational injuries, whereas Spain has a substantially higher rate of job injury.

Occupational injuries per 10,000 workers

Country	Injuries per 10,000 workers
Spain	651
France	411
Italy	320
Mexico	303
Canada	224
Hong Kong	183
United States	125
Sweden	84
United Kingdom	61

Source: International Labour Organization (**www.ilo.org**).

* The injury rate is defined as the average annual percentage of workers losing work time due to a job injury.

Canada, Italy, and the United Kingdom statistics include only people losing more than three days of work time. The statistics are based on 2002–2004 data.

Just what are these benefits to the firm? First, lower risks of injury or death enable employers to attract workers at lower wage rates. Because workers value job safety, they are willing to accept a lower wage for work performed in a healthful, relatively safe environment (Chapter 8). Second, a safer workplace reduces the amount of disruption of the production process that job accidents create. Workplace mishaps and the absence of key employees during rehabilitation often halt or slow the production process. Third, a safer workplace reduces the cost of recruiting, screening, and training workers. The fewer workers injured on the job, the fewer resources will be required to hire and train new employees. Fourth, workplace safety helps maintain the firm's return on its specific investment in human capital. Job fatalities and injuries terminate or reduce the firm's returns on its previously financed specific, formal, and on-the-job training. Finally, fewer job-related accidents translate into lower workers' compensation insurance rates. Such rates are determined by the probability and types of accidents experienced in a given firm.

FIGURE 13.3 The Optimal Level of Job Safety

A profit-maximizing firm will provide a level of job safety at which its marginal benefit and marginal cost of safety are equal, say at Q_s, which is determined by the intersection of MB_s and MC_s. If workers have full information about possible work hazards and accurately assess job risks, this level of output will optimize society's well-being. If workers are unaware of workplace danger or underestimate it, they will not be paid a proper wage premium, and the firm will not gain the benefit of lower wages as it provides more safety. Thus the marginal benefit of each unit of job safety will be less (MB_s' rather than MB_s), and the firm will underprovide job safety from society's viewpoint (Q_s' rather than Q_s).

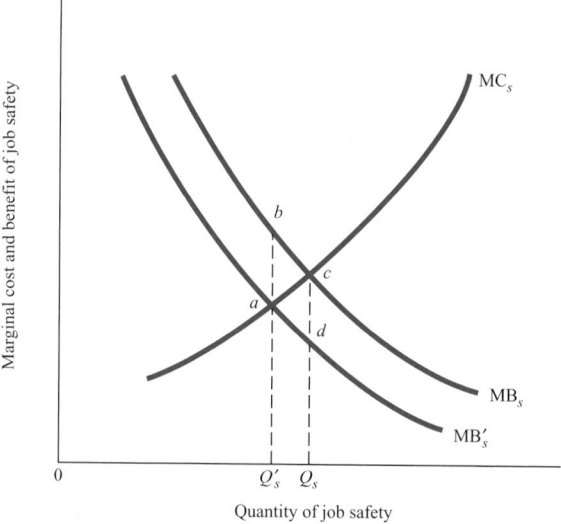

To determine the profit-maximizing level of workplace safety, the cost-minimizing firm will compare the marginal benefit of safety (MB_s) against the marginal cost (MC_s). In so doing, it will use the following decision rule: Provide additional job safety so long as the marginal benefit exceeds the marginal cost. In Figure 13.3 we see that the profit-maximizing level of job safety is Q_s units, at which $MB_s = MC_s$. Conclusion? Even in the absence of government intervention, this firm will find it cost-effective and profitable to provide some degree of job safety. In this case, our firm will provide Q_s units.

Another observation merits comment here. The perception that some jobs, say coal mining and construction, are *inherently* dangerous while others, say accounting and teaching, are innately safe is slightly misleading. A more accurate statement is that given present technology, it is inherently more costly to provide job safety in some occupations than others. Therefore, firms with similar marginal benefit schedules but different marginal costs of safety will offer differing levels of job safety. A firm with the same marginal benefits curve as that in Figure 13.3 but with significantly higher marginal costs of providing job safety than those shown by MC_s would provide much less job safety than Q_s units.

Society's Optimal Level of Job Safety

A firm's profit-maximizing level of job safety *may* or *may not* be society's optimal level of job safety. In addressing this topic, let's first assume that there is perfect information and assessment of job risk, and then examine a situation where this is not the case.

1 Perfect Information and Assessment

If workers have full information about possible work hazards and accurately assess the likelihood of occupational fatality, injury, or disease, then the amount of job safety offered by employers will match the level required to maximize society's well-being. Where workers have full knowledge of job risk, employers providing hazardous work environments will have to pay a wage premium to attract a sufficient number of employees (Chapter 8). The existence of the compensating wage differential will ensure that the employer's extra benefit from providing a safer workplace (including a *reduced* wage premium) will match the extra benefit of job safety from society's perspective.

In Figure 13.3 we are saying that given our assumption of perfect information and assessment, curve MB_s depicts both the private *and* social marginal benefits of job safety. The number of units of job safety shown as Q_s will maximize the firm's profits *and* optimize society's well-being.

2 Imperfect Information and Assessment

Where information about job hazards is limited and/or workers underestimate the personal risk of occupational fatality, injury, or disease, employers will provide less job safety than is socially optimal.

To demonstrate this generalization, suppose workers mistakenly judge the job in question to be risk-free, when in reality one of the substances handled by workers is highly hazardous. Because employees are unaware of the long-term danger, the job hazard will *not* reduce labor supply to this occupation and employer. The market wage therefore will *not* contain a wage premium required to compensate workers for the added job risk. Consequently, the firm's marginal benefit from reducing the health hazard—that is, from providing a safer workplace—will be smaller than it would be if workers had full information about the job danger. Extra units of job safety will fail to reduce the wages paid by this firm because the labor market has not dictated payment of a wage premium to compensate workers for their true risk. From the firm's perspective, the marginal benefit from providing job safety is less than it would be if full information about the long-term health consequences of the job were known.

The marginal benefit schedule of job safety as viewed by the firm in this situation is shown in Figure 13.3 as curve MB'_s. The firm compares MB'_s with its marginal cost of providing safety (MC_s) and settles for Q'_s units of job safety. Result: *Job safety is underprovided from society's viewpoint.* Suppose the true marginal benefits of each added unit of safety are those shown as MB_s rather than MB'_s. Given full information and accurate assessment by workers of the job danger, the firm's relevant marginal benefit curve would be MB_s, and both the profit-maximizing and socially optimal levels of job safety would be Q_s units. As we can observe by extending a vertical line upward from Q'_s to MB_s, and observing the triangle *abc,* the $Q'_s Q_s$ units of job safety generate marginal benefits to society that exceed the marginal costs MC_s. But under conditions of incomplete information or underestimation of risk by workers, and therefore no market wage premium, the firm has no incentive to provide these extra units. From its perspective the marginal benefit is less than the marginal cost. We conclude that a firm's profit-maximizing level of job safety may not always conform to society's optimal level of job safety. In our example, society's welfare loss from this inefficiency is area *abc.*

The Occupational Safety and Health Act

The Occupational Safety and Health Act of 1970 interjected the federal government directly into regulation of workplace hazards. The act's purpose was to reduce the incidence of job injury and illness by identifying and eliminating hazards found in the workplace. The Occupational Safety and Health Administration (OSHA) was given the responsibility of developing safety and health standards and enforcing them through workplace inspections and fines for violations.

The Case for OSHA

OSHA was controversial when passed and remains subject to debate today. Those who support the legislation contend that the costs of providing a healthful and safe workplace are legitimate business costs that should not be transferred to workers. According to this view, imperfect information, underestimation of risk, and barriers to occupational mobility prevent the labor market from making the adjustments that would provide adequate wage premiums for hazardous jobs. Thus, for reasons described earlier, government standards are needed to force firms to provide more job safety than is dictated by their own self-interests. Finally, supporters of OSHA regulation point out that much of the criticism has originated in the corporate community, where resistance is predictable and understandable. To see why, note in Figure 13.3 that under conditions of incomplete information and improper assessment of risk, a minimum safety standard, say of Q_s units, would force this firm to provide $Q'_s Q_s$ units of safety, which, from its perspective, cost more to produce than they generate in private benefits. We see this by comparing the *ac* segment of MC_s to the *ad* segment of MB'_s.

Criticisms of OSHA

Critics of OSHA counter that safety standards and inspections represent an unwarranted, costly government intrusion into the private sector. They point out that even though information about job hazards may be imperfect and workers may inaccurately assess personal risk, no reason exists to expect that workers will systematically underestimate the risk of job hazards. Rather, workers could just as well overestimate the likelihood that they will be the unlucky parties affected by occupational death, injury, or illness, just as many purchasers of state lottery tickets or sweepstake entrants overestimate the probability that they will win. According to this line of reasoning, it is possible that wage premiums for hazardous jobs are greater than they would be if there were perfect information and risk assessment. Restated, the perspective that "it will probably happen to me" may dissuade people from hazardous occupations, driving up the wage rate for those who perform such work. Recall that when such wage premiums exist, the firm's marginal benefit from reducing the job hazard is greater than otherwise, and an under-allocation of resources to job safety is not likely.

Critics of OSHA also assert that workplace standards often bear no relationship to reductions in injury and illness. They point to the numerous trivial standards—wall height rules for fire extinguishers, specified shapes of toilet seats, and so forth—to support this assertion. Additionally, opponents of OSHA cite the complexity of determining just what the standards are. Wiedenbaum has noted OSHA's original definition of an "exit": "That portion of a means of egress which is separated from all other spaces of the building or structure by construction or equipment as required in this subpart to provide a protected way of travel to the exit discharge." Wiedenbaum contrasts this definition with one from a dictionary: An exit is "a passage or way out."[24] In the face of criticism over trivial rules and bureaucratic language, OSHA revoked over 1,100 standards in 1978 and attempted to rewrite remaining standards in simple terms.

Findings and Implications

The controversy over OSHA has been heightened by the mixed findings on whether OSHA standards and inspections have reduced occupational accidents and injuries. Since the passage of OSHA, the rate of fatal injury on the job has declined, but the rate of workdays lost per year from nonfatal injuries has risen.

Studies attempting to sort out OSHA's role in the overall workplace fatality and accident trends are fraught with data and interpretation problems. Nevertheless, several noteworthy attempts have been made. Research looking at early years following passage of OSHA found little indication that OSHA reduced industrial injury rates. Specifically, Viscusi[25] found that OSHA had no significant effect on workplace safety for the years 1972–1975, and Smith and McCaffrey[26] found no effects of OSHA inspections during 1974–1976. These scholars warned, however, that caution needed to be exercised in interpreting their findings. The results may be due to lack of enforcement of the law or inadequate penalties for firms failing to meet the safety standards.

Studies of more recent periods are mixed. In a follow-up study to the earlier Smith and McCaffrey research, Ruser and Smith[27] found that OSHA had little impact on workplace injuries in the early 1980s. On the other hand, a 1986 study by Viscusi[28]

---

[24] Murray L. Wiedenbaum, *Business, Government, and the Public* (Englewood Cliffs, NJ: Prentice-Hall, Inc., 1977), pp. 64–65.

[25] W. Kip Viscusi, "The Impact of Occupational Safety and Health Regulation," *Bell Journal of Economics,* Spring 1978, pp. 117–40.

[26] Robert Smith and David McCaffrey, "An Assessment of OSHA's Recent Effect on Injury Rates," *Journal of Human Resources,* Winter 1983, pp. 131–45.

[27] John W. Ruser and Robert S. Smith, "Reestimating OSHA's Effects: Have the Data Changed?" *Journal of Human Resources,* Spring 1991, pp. 212–35.

[28] W. Kip Viscusi, "Reforming OSHA Regulation of Workplace Risks," in Leonard W. Weiss and Michael W. Klass (eds.), *Regulatory Reform: What Actually Happened?* (Boston: Little, Brown, 1986), p. 262.

covering the 1973–1983 period discovered that OSHA inspections modestly reduced the rate of both occupational injury and lost workdays. Gray and Jones[29] found that OSHA inspections within the manufacturing sector have reduced the number of OSHA citations of safety violations by one-half. However, Gray and Mendeloff,[30] using data from 1979 to 1998, found that the effects of OSHA safety enforcement have declined over time. An OSHA inspection imposing a penalty reduced injuries by about 19 percent in 1979–1985, but this effect fell to 11 percent in 1987–1991 and to 1 percent in 1992–1998.

If OSHA becomes increasingly effective in reducing workplace fatalities, injuries, and diseases in hazardous jobs, existing wage differentials between hazardous and safe jobs should decline over time. Recall from Chapter 6 that one determinant of labor supply to an occupation is the nonwage aspects of employment. By making dangerous jobs safer, effective OSHA standards may increase the supply of labor to the formerly hazardous jobs, eventually reducing the wage premiums paid in those lines of work. Wage premiums for risk of workplace death or injury are one of several sources of wage differentials among workers. Thus, over the long run, highly effective OSHA regulations conceivably could reduce some of the wage disparity among jobs in the economy.

Other subtle labor market effects may possibly result from government regulation of occupational health and safety. For example, the high cost of complying with OSHA standards in some industries may result in the demise of smaller nonunion firms, increased product market share for larger unionized producers, and enhanced bargaining power and wages for union workers.[31] As a second example, the amount of money firms spend to comply with OSHA standards may directly compete with more productive expenditures to improve job safety.[32]

13.2

Questions about the effectiveness of OSHA in relationship to its costs have led some economists to call for alternative or complementary approaches to promoting job safety. As one option, government could accumulate and directly provide information to workers about the injury experience of various employers, much as it publishes the on-time performance of airlines. Alternatively, it could mandate that firms develop and disclose

---

[29] Wayne B. Gray and Carol Adaire Jones, "Longitudinal Patterns of Compliance with OSHA in the Manufacturing Sector," *Journal of Human Resources,* Fall 1991, pp. 623–53. Of related interest is Wayne B. Gray and Carol Adaire Jones, "Are OSHA Health Inspections Effective? A Longitudinal Study in the Manufacturing Sector," *Review of Economics and Statistics,* August 1991, pp. 504–8.

[30] Wayne B. Gray and John M. Mendeloff, "The Declining Effects of OSHA Inspections on Manufacturing Injuries, 1979–1998," *Industrial and Labor Relations Review,* July 2005, pp. 571–87.

[31] For empirical support for this scenario as it relates to the Federal Coal Mine Health and Safety Act of 1969, see Scott Fuess and Mark Lowenstein, "Further Analysis of the Effects of Government Safety Regulation: The Case of the 1969 Coal Mine Health and Safety Act," *Economic Inquiry,* April 1990, pp. 354–89. Also relevant is David Weil, " Are Mandated Health and Safety Committees Substitutes for or Supplements to Labor Unions?" *Industrial and Labor Relations Review,* April 1999, pp. 339–60.

[32] Ann P. Bartel and Lacy Glenn Thomas, "Direct and Indirect Effects of Regulation: A New Look at OSHA's Impact," *Journal of Law and Economics,* April 1985, pp. 1–25.

| 13.2 | World of Work | The Effect of Workers' Compensation on Job Safety |

Each of the 50 states has workers' compensation laws requiring employers to pay legally established benefits to workers injured on the job (or to families of workers who die from work-related accidents). Firms are mandated by law to purchase insurance to finance these benefits.* The insurance premiums the firms must pay vary directly with the risk of accidents at their establishments. For example, logging firms, which typically have higher-than-average accident rates, have larger workers' compensation premiums than, say, fast-food establishments, which have better safety records.

What are the effects of workers' compensation laws on workplace safety? These laws produce two opposing effects. First, the insurance premiums required under the laws create an incentive for firms to make their workplaces safer. By reducing accident rates, firms can lower the workers' compensation premium they must pay. Thus the marginal benefit of providing any given level of safety is greater for the firm in the presence of workers' compensation. Firms therefore discover that it is in their profit interest to increase their levels of job safety. (You should use Figure 13.3 to demonstrate this effect.)

But workers' compensation laws also create an opposing effect—a *moral hazard problem.* Generally defined, this problem is the tendency of one party to a contract to alter his or her behavior in ways that are costly to the other party. As it relates to workers' compensation insurance, the moral hazard problem is that workers may be less careful as they go about their work, knowing they are insured against on-the-job accidents. Taken alone, this change in behavior would lead to higher incidences of job accidents.

In a major study, Moore and Viscusi have found that the workers' compensation laws have had a dramatic effect in reducing job fatalities.[†] This finding implies that the positive incentive effect of the laws swamps the negative moral hazard effect. Specifically, Moore and Viscusi show that fatality risks in American industries would rise by over 40 percent if the workers' compensation program were not in place. They also conclude that the program saves almost 2,000 lives per year. Finally, Moore and Viscusi note that these sizable positive effects stand in contrast to the smaller effects identified in other studies as resulting from direct workplace regulation by the Occupational Safety and Health Administration. This fact suggests that an "injury tax" imposed on employers might be a more efficient way to reduce on-the-job accidents than the present regulatory approach.

* Depending on the state, this insurance may be purchased from a state agency or from private insurance firms. Also, some states allow firms to "self-insure," which means they may establish an insurance plan within their own enterprises.

[†] Michael J. Moore and W. Kip Viscusi, *Compensating Mechanisms for Job Risks: Wages, Workers' Compensation, and Product Liability* (Princeton, NJ: Princeton University Press, 1990).

information about known workplace hazards. In either case, the availability of information would help workers assess risk. This in turn would enable labor markets to establish more appropriate compensating wage differentials.

As a second option, government could impose an "injury tax" on employers based on their incidences of work-related injuries and deaths. By boosting the employers' marginal benefit of job safety, such a tax would provide an incentive for firms to make their workplaces safer.

13.2

Quick Review

- Each year about 5,000 occupational fatalities and about 3.7 million occupational injuries occur in the United States.

- A firm's profit-maximizing level of workplace safety occurs where its marginal cost and marginal benefit of providing safety are equal.

- Profit-maximizing levels of job safety may be lower than socially optimal levels where workers lack information about job risk or underestimate the probability of being hurt or killed.

- The Occupational Safety and Health Act of 1970 remains somewhat controversial; only recently has preliminary evidence emerged finding that OSHA standards and inspections are effective in reducing job injuries.

Your Turn

Suppose a firm's marginal cost of an extra unit of job safety is $250,000; the marginal private benefit, $200,000; and the marginal social benefit, $300,000. Will the firm provide this extra unit of job safety? Should government intervene? If so, what are its policy options? (*Answers:* See page 598.)

GOVERNMENT AS A RENT PROVIDER

Government influences wages and employment in labor markets in more subtle ways than establishing labor laws, imposing a legal minimum wage, and setting occupational safety standards. One such method is through providing economic rent to labor market participants. *Economic rent in the labor market is the difference between the wage paid to a particular worker and the wage just sufficient to keep that person in his or her present employment.* Recall from Chapter 6 that a market labor supply curve such as the one shown in Figure 13.4 is essentially a marginal opportunity cost curve. The curve reflects the value of each worker's next best alternative, whether that be another job, household production, or leisure. Given the market wage of $8 in Figure 13.4, all employed workers with the exception of the marginal one, Q_0, receive economic rent, the total of which is area *abc*. To clarify further, suppose Jones is the worker shown by Q_j and that her marginal opportunity cost is $6 an hour. We can see then that Jones is receiving a $2 per hour "rent" (= $8 − $6).

What would happen to Jones's economic rent if government passed a law that had the effect of increasing the market wage to $10 an hour? She and all other workers who remain employed would receive an *increase* in economic rent of $2 (= $10 − $8). But why might government be interested in providing increases in economic rent to workers? According to some economic and political theorists, the main goal of politicians is to get and stay elected. Consequently, they offer and provide a wide range of publicly provided goods and services that enhance the utility of their constituents. One such service may be the provision or the enhancement of economic rents. According to this controversial theory, groups of workers—for example, professional groups or

FIGURE 13.4   **Economic Rent in Labor Markets**

At the market wage of $8, employers will hire Q_0 workers. The labor supply curve indicates that these Q_0 workers collectively receive economic rent equal to the area *abc*. The Q_j worker receives a $2 per hour rent ($8 minus the person's opportunity cost of $6).

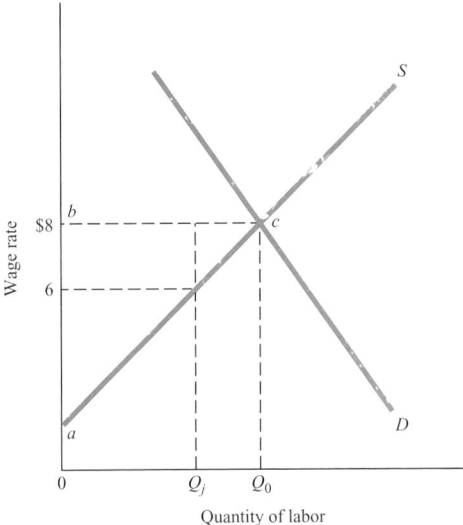

unions—have a demand for economic rent; that is, they are *rent seekers*. Elected officials respond to this demand by supplying the publicly provided service, economic rent; they are *rent providers*.[33]

Admittedly, care must be taken not to oversimplify here. Higher wages provided by law or regulation may produce lower market-determined wages for other workers, higher product prices for consumers, lower corporate dividends for common stockholders, or some combination of all three. These groups are interested in their own rents and may intervene politically to block the provision of rents to a group of workers. But because acquisition of information and political lobbying are costly, people have little incentive to try to block rent provision when they perceive their personal losses to be small. Hence elected officials may find it beneficial to dispense economic rent to highly organized groups of workers.

This concept of rent provision is apparent in some instances of occupational licensure and in legislation that establishes tariffs, quotas, and domestic content laws.

[33] A political scientist once defined *politics* as "who gets what, when, and how." This view of politics has been formalized into a theory of regulation by several economists. See, for example, George J. Stigler, "The Theory of Economic Regulation," *Bell Journal of Economics and Management Science,* Spring 1971, pp. 3–21. See also Sam Peltzman, "Toward a More General Theory of Regulation," *Journal of Law and Economics,* August 1976, pp. 181–210.

TABLE 13.3

Selected Licensed Occupations: State of Washington

Source: Employment Security Department, state of Washington.

Accountants	Dentists	Osteopaths
Agricultural brokers	Dispensing opticians	Oyster farmers
Aircraft pilots	Egg dealers	Pesticide applicators
Ambulance drivers	Embalmers	Pharmacists
Architects	Engineers	Physical therapists
Auditors	Fish dealers	Physician assistants
Barbers	Funeral directors	Physicians and surgeons
Beauticians	Harbor pilots	Proprietary school agents
Blasters	Insurance adjusters	Psychologists
Boathouse operators	Insurance agents	Real estate brokers
Boiler workers	Landscape architects	Real estate sales agents
Boxers	Law clerks	Sanitarians
Boxing managers	Lawyers	Security advisers
Chiropodists	Librarians	Security brokers
Chiropractors	Livestock dealers	Surveyors
Commercial fishers	Marine pilots (inland)	Teachers
Commercial guides	Milk vendors	Veterinarians
Dairy technicians	Naturopaths	Weighers and graders
Debt adjustors	Nurses	Well diggers
Dental hygienists	Optometrists	Wrestlers

Occupational Licensure

In the United States 20 percent of all workers are subject to some form of occupational licensing. In fact, over 800 occupations are licensed in at least one state.[34] Table 13.3 provides a partial list of occupations requiring licenses in one state.

In many instances, licensing of occupational groups (pharmacists, surgeons) is held to be necessary to protect consumers against incompetents who might do irreparable damage. In these circumstances governmental licensing may be the most efficient way to minimize the costs of obtaining information needed by consumers to make optimal buying decisions. But as we first indicated in Chapter 6, in other situations the occupational groups themselves, not consumers, generate the demand for licensing. These groups may wish to restrict access to licenses as a way to obtain economic rent for licensees.

Figure 13.5 demonstrates how occupational licensure can confer economic rent. Suppose the prelicensing equilibrium wage and employment level are $8 and 10,000 workers, respectively. Next assume that licensing has the effect of restricting the total number of licensed workers to 7,000. In effect, the postlicensing labor supply curve is $S_g S_1$, compared to the old curve of SS_0. Notice that licensing increases the market wage to $11 an hour and that total employment falls from 10,000 to 7,000. The $11 wage

---

[34] Morris M. Kleiner, *Licensing Occupations: Ensuring Quality or Restricting Competition?* (Kalamazoo, MI: W.E. Upjohn Institute, 2006).

FIGURE 13.5

Rent Provision through Occupational Licensure
By setting a limit of 7,000 licenses in this labor market, government indirectly increases the wage from $8 to $11, thereby providing licensees collectively with an increase in economic rent of *abce* and creating an efficiency loss of *gcf.*

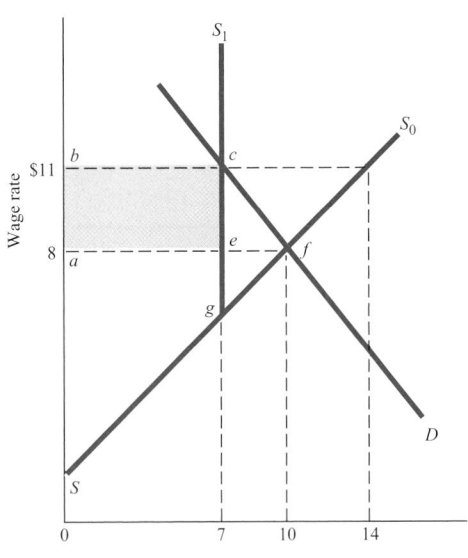

attracts another 4,000 workers (=14,000 − 10,000) who would like to work in this occupation. These 14,000 workers see 7,000 licenses, and those who get licensed receive increases in economic rent of $3 for every hour worked. As a consequence, the government's action *raises* the total rent *to those employed* by $21,000. This can be determined by noting that the total rent was area *Saf* prior to the licensing. Following licensing, the total economic rent increases to *Sbcg.* Thus the *gain* in rent is *abce*—the shaded area in the figure—and the loss of rent to the workers displaced by the licensing is area *gef.*

Close inspection of Figure 13.5 reveals that occupational licensure of a type that restricts labor supply creates an efficiency loss for society—in this case, triangle *gcf.* The 3,000 additional employees who would have been employed in this occupation would contribute more to the value of society's output in this employment (as shown by segment *cf* of the demand curve) than in their most productive alternative uses of time (as shown by segment *gf* of the supply curve). Additionally, the true efficiency loss to society may be greater than area *gcf.* To secure the licensing law and thus the added economic rent, this particular occupational group most likely had to spend large amounts for political lobbying, public relations advertising, and other activities. From society's perspective, these expenditures diverted resources away from potentially higher-valued uses, adding to the overall efficiency cost of the occupational licensing.

To summarize: Occupational licensure of the type restricting labor supply increases the market wage, confers economic rent to licensees, and causes economic inefficiency. We might add that it is possible that the competition for the limited number of licenses will cause the new licensees to expend dollars in an amount equal to the expected rents.

13.3	**World of Work**

Lawyers Attempt to Disbar Competition from Software*

Occupational licensing determines who can and who cannot legally provide certain labor services. It is only natural, therefore, that people who are currently licensed oppose allowing unlicensed individuals to perform licensed tasks.

A licensing battle occurred over a self-help software program called *Quicken Family Lawyer*. The $30 program allows individuals to draft over 100 legal documents such as wills, employment contracts, and rental agreements. In Texas, the Unauthorized Practice of Law Committee sued the program's publisher, arguing that using the program was an unauthorized practice of law.

Federal District Judge Barefoot Sanders agreed with the committee and ruled the program could not be sold in Texas. He stated that because the program guided users on how to create an individualized legal document, it acted as a lawyer. He was also concerned that the program would yield overly simplistic advice. The judge's decision was later overturned by the Texas state legislature, which made an exception to the unauthorized practice of law statute for book and software publishers.

However, this is unlikely to be the last turf war over software and online services. For example, officials have been cracking down on Web sites that offer prescriptions without requiring that a patient see a doctor. Also, securities regulators have been trying to eliminate software and Internet sites that offer bad investment advice.

* Based in part on Barbara Whitaker, "Possible Legal Software Ban Raises Free Speech Issue," *The New York Times,* February 7, 1999.

13.3

Thus those who are automatically granted licenses when the law is passed and those who train potential licensees will be the major beneficiaries of the law.

Existing empirical evidence is consistent with these hypotheses. For example, Kleiner and Krudle, using data on incoming Air Force personnel, report that states with tougher licensing requirements for dentists do not have better dental health.[35] However, prices for dental services are higher in states with stricter licensing requirements due to the reduced competition.

Tariffs, Quotas, and Domestic Content Rules

Collectively, tariffs, quotas, and domestic content rules provide a second example of governmental provision of economic rent to groups of workers. *Tariffs* are excise duties on imported products; *import quotas* are limits on the quantity or total value of imports; and *domestic content rules* are requirements that a specified portion of

[35] See Morris M. Kleiner and Robert T. Krudle, "Does Regulation Affect Economic Outcomes? The Case of Dentistry," *Journal of Law and Economics,* October 2000, pp. 547–82. For a study finding that stricter licensing requirements do not improve audit quality by certified public accountants, see Gary Clobber and Denies Murky, "State Accountancy Regulations, Audit Firm Size, and Auditor Quality: An Empirical Investigation," *Journal of Regulatory Economics,* November 1999, pp. 267–85.

imported products contain domestically produced or domestically assembled components. These laws and regulations tend to increase the prices of foreign goods, raise the sales of the competing protected domestic products, and increase the derived demand for the U.S. workers who help produce the domestic goods. Assuming a competitive labor market in which there is a normal upward-sloping labor supply curve, the increased domestic demand for labor increases the equilibrium wage and employment. If the labor market is imperfectly competitive, the increase in labor demand enhances the bargaining position of the union and increases the probability that the union-negotiated wage will rise. It is therefore perfectly understandable why some U.S. unions—for example, the United Steelworkers and the United Auto Workers—strongly support tariffs, quotas, and domestic content rules. Quite simply, these laws increase economic rent for domestic workers at the expense of foreign producers and domestic consumers.

It is a fairly simple matter to portray this gain in economic rent graphically. Figure 13.6 depicts an initial equilibrium wage of $10 per hour at which firms hire Q_1 workers. The tariff, import quota, or domestic content law increases the derived demand for labor from D to D_1. The increase in labor demand raises the equilibrium wage from $10 to $12 an hour and causes the level of employment to rise to Q_2. Prior to the trade restriction, the total economic rent to workers was *abf*. After the law, it is *ace*. The workers in this market thus collectively gain an increase in economic rent equal to the shaded area *bcef*.

FIGURE 13.6   Rent Provision: Tariffs, Quotas, and Domestic Content Laws
Import restrictions reduce labor demand in foreign nations and increase the demand for specific types of labor in the protected country. These restrictions therefore cause increases in wages in these specific labor markets. In this case the wage rises from $10 to $12, and economic rent increases by the amount *bcef*.

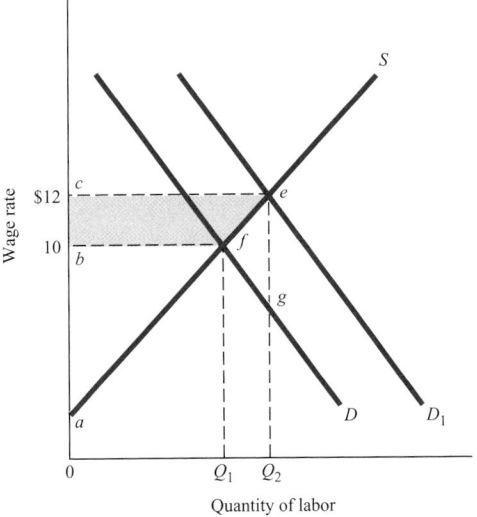

Chapter Summary

1. Labor relations laws and regulations have influenced the growth of both private and public sector unionism in the United States. To the extent that union membership and union bargaining power are positively correlated, labor law influences the determination of wages and employment in labor markets.

2. Labor law in general and specific provisions of labor law in particular influence union bargaining power—and therefore labor market results—independently of impacts on union membership.

3. The basic model of a competitive labor market predicts that an above-equilibrium minimum wage applied to all sections of the economy will reduce employment. The more elastic the supply and demand for labor, the greater the resulting unemployment.

4. The existence of a nondiscriminatory monopsony may cause the negative employment and efficiency consequences predicted by the competitive model to not fully materialize.

5. Empirical evidence indicates that the minimum wage *(a)* reduces employment, particularly for teenagers; *(b)* increases unemployment of teenagers by less than the reduction in employment; *(c)* reduces the amount of on-the-job training offered to low-wage workers; and *(d)* does not greatly alter the degree of family income inequality and extent of poverty.

6. A firm incurs both costs and benefits when it improves the safety of its workplace. A profit-maximizing firm will provide a level of job safety at which its marginal benefit and marginal cost of safety are equal.

7. If workers have full information about possible work hazards and accurately assess job risks, the profit-maximizing level of job safety will tend to be optimal from society's viewpoint. If information is incomplete and job risks are inaccurately assessed, then society's optimal level of job safety may be greater than the level willingly provided by profit-maximizing firms.

8. The Occupational Safety and Health Act imposed a set of workplace safety standards on individual firms. The act is controversial, and the debate over its provisions and methods of enforcement has been heightened by studies that present mixed findings about its effect on the number of work-related accidents.

9. Government affects wages and employment in specific occupations through its rent provision activities. Two examples are *(a)* occupational licensure that restricts labor supply; and *(b)* tariffs, import quotas, and domestic content laws, which increase labor demand for protected domestic workers.

Terms and Concepts

discriminatory
  discharge, *396*
blacklists, *396*
yellow-dog contracts, *396*
lockouts, *396*
strikebreakers, *396*
injunctions, *397*

Norris–LaGuardia Act
  of 1932, *397*
Wagner Act of 1935, *397*
Taft–Hartley Act of
  1947, *397*
Landrum–Griffin Act
  of 1959, *397*

secondary boycotts, *398*
hot-cargo clauses, *398*
Fair Labor Standards Act
  of 1938, *399*
minimum wage, *399*
Occupational Safety and
  Health Act of 1970, *407*

marginal cost of job
  safety, *408*
marginal benefit from job
  safety, *408*

economic rent, *416*
rent seekers and rent
  providers, *417*
tariffs, *420*

import quotas, *420*
domestic content rules, *420*

**Questions
and Study
Suggestions**

1. Explain each of the following statements:
   a. "The Wagner Act of 1935 reduced the costs of providing union services and thereby increased the number of union members."
   b. "The Wagner Act of 1935 increased the demand for union services by increasing the relative bargaining power of unions. This increased union membership."

2. Show graphically how an increase in the minimum wage might affect employment in *(a)* a competitive labor market and *(b)* a labor market characterized by monopsony.

3. Explain how an increase in the minimum wage could
   a. Reduce teenage employment but leave the teenage unemployment rate unaffected.
   b. Reduce investment in human capital.
   c. Leave the poverty rate unchanged.

4. Why are most labor unions—whose constituents receive wages substantially above the minimum wage—strong supporters of the minimum wage? Why might unions composed of skilled workers who are *pure complements in production* (Chapter 5) with raw materials produced by low-skilled workers *oppose* a large increase in the minimum wage?

5. Evaluate this statement: "Profit-maximizing firms lack an incentive to provide job safety, and consequently, the federal government must intervene legislatively to protect workers against the unsafe working conditions that will surely result."

6. Answer these questions on the basis of the information in the accompanying table. The data are for a competitive firm.
   a. What is the profit-maximizing level of job safety as viewed by the firm? Explain.
   b. Assume that information is perfect and that workers accurately assess personal risk. What is the optimal level of job safety from society's perspective? Explain.
   c. Suppose government imposed a minimum safety standard of 5 units. Why would the firm object? Speculate about why some workers might object.
   d. Suppose new technology reduced this firm's marginal cost data to $1, $2, $3, $4, and $5 for the first through fifth units of safety. How would this firm respond?

Marginal Benefit from Safety	Amount of Safety Provided	Marginal Cost of Safety
$60	1	$1
40	2	3
20	3	6
10	4	9
6	5	15

7. How might each of the following be interpreted as an example of rent provision by government?
   a. State laws require that out-of-state big-game hunters be accompanied by one of a limited number of licensed in-state hunting guides.
   b. An increase in the minimum wage increases the likelihood that firms will hire skilled unionized labor rather than unskilled labor.
   c. A state law requires that graduates of dental schools pass a stringent examination, established by a panel of dentists, in order to practice dentistry.

Internet Exercise

Who or What Is the NLRB?

Go to the National Labor Relations Board's home page **(http://www.nlrb.gov)**. Where is the NLRB located? What does it do? How many members are on the board? What is common to all board members' educational backgrounds? What is the main message of the board's most recent press release? List the titles of three recent decisions made by the board.

Internet Links

The Occupational Safety and Health Administration Web site provides detailed information about safety regulations as well as safety inspection statistics **(http://www.osha.gov/)**.

The Department of Labor Web site reports information about the current federal and state minimum wage laws **(http://www.dol.gov/esa/minwage/america.htm)**.

14

Labor Market Discrimination

Few would seriously question the assertion that discrimination based on race, gender, religion, and ethnic background is a fact of American life. Abundant statistical evidence exists to suggest discrimination: Comparison of African–Americans and whites and women and men reveal substantial differences in earnings, unemployment rates, allocations among various occupations, and accumulations of human capital. Also, anecdotal evidence of discrimination can be found in newspaper headlines on an almost daily basis: "Court upholds racial discrimination suit against grocery chain"; "Few jobs for African–American teenagers"; "Minorities excluded from top executive positions"; "Wage gap for women persists"; "Sexual harassment in the workplace." Because of the importance of labor market discrimination as an institutional feature of labor markets, we will devote this chapter to this subject.

Several caveats must be made explicit at the outset. Discrimination is complex, multifaceted, and deeply ingrained in behavior. It is also difficult to measure or quantify. Furthermore, any reasonably complete explanation of discrimination must be interdisciplinary; economic analysis can contribute only insights rather than a full-blown explanation of the phenomenon. In fact, we will find a number of contrasting explanations of discrimination within economics, and these frequently imply different policy prescriptions. Bluntly stated, discrimination constitutes an untidy area of study that is characterized by controversy and a lack of consensus. Finally, to achieve a degree of focus in our discussion, discrimination based on gender (sex) and race is emphasized in this chapter. But keep in mind that age, ethnic origin, religious background, physical disability, and sexual orientation are equally important bases for discrimination and are neglected here only for the sake of brevity.

GENDER AND RACIAL DIFFERENCES

It is not difficult to find statistical discrepancies that lead one to suspect the presence of discrimination based on gender and race.

FIGURE 14.1 **Female to Male Hourly Wage Ratio in the United States**
The ratio of female to male hourly earnings in the United States rose substantially between 1979 and the mid-1990s and has risen slightly since then.

Source: Author calculations from *Current Population Survey.*

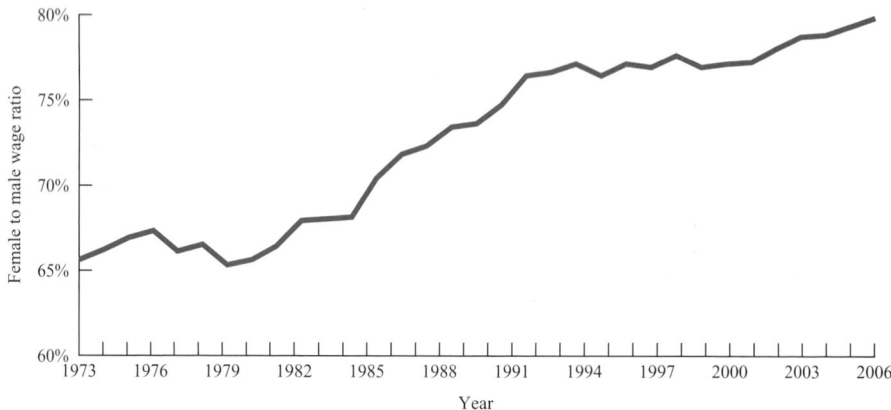

Earnings

Figure 14.1 shows the ratio of female to male hourly wages. We observe that from 1973 to 1978 the hourly earnings of women workers in the United States were about 65 percent of those of men. From 1979 to the mid-1990s the percentage rose significantly, and it has risen slightly since then to about 80 percent.

Several explanations have been given for this narrowing of the gender gap in earnings. First, evidence exists that the skill levels of female workers have increased. Second, labor market discrimination perhaps has declined. Also, the industrial restructuring of the economy away from manufacturing jobs and toward services may have negatively affected the earnings of men more than women. Fourth, the decline in unionism (Chapter 10) may have reduced male pay more than female pay. Finally, the occupational distribution of men and women workers may have changed positively in favor of women.[1]

Figure 14.2 presents the ratio of African–American to white hourly wages. The ratio has shown little change over the past three decades, and a substantial earnings gap remains.[2] In fact, African–American women have lost some ground relative to white women since the mid-1980s.

14.1

[1] This list is drawn from Elaine Sorensen, *Exploring the Reasons behind the Narrowing Gender Gap in Earnings* (Washington, DC: Urban Institute Press, 1991), pp. 129–30. For more on recent earnings trends, see Francine D. Blau and Lawrence M. Kahn, "Gender Differences in Pay," *Journal of Economic Perspectives,* Fall 2000, pp. 75–99; and June O'Neill, "The Gender Gap in Wages, circa 2000," *American Economic Review,* May 2003, pp. 309–14.

[2] Progress was made in the African–American to white earnings ratio prior to the early 1970s. For example, see James P. Smith and Finis Welch, "Black Economic Progress after Myrdal," *Journal of Economic Literature,* June 1989, pp. 519–64. See also James J. Heckman, Thomas M. Lyons, and Petra E. Todd, "Understanding Black–White Wage Differentials, 1960–1990," *American Economic Review,* May 2000, pp. 344–49.

|14.1| **World of Work** | The Gender Pay Gap: An International Comparison* |

The gender pay gap in the United States is greater than in 8 of 16 industrial countries. Specifically, Blau and Kahn find that the female–male weekly earnings ratio among full-time workers is 80–90 percent in Australia, Belgium, France, Italy, New Zealand, and Sweden, compared to 76 percent in the United States. The relatively large U.S. pay gap is particularly surprising because American women compare favorably with women in other countries in terms of education and occupational status. Also, the United States was committed to an equal pay and equal opportunity policy for women before most other countries.

Blau and Kahn help resolve this seeming paradox. They note that pay for lower-skilled workers is lower in the United States than in most other nations. Because women are disproportionately represented in the lower-skilled ranks, the gender pay gap is greater in the United States. In fact, this greater overall wage inequality in the United States more than accounts for the differences in the female–male pay ratios between the United States and countries with higher ratios. That is, the gender earnings gap is lower in the United States than the gap would be in Australia, Britain, and Italy if they had the U.S. overall distribution of earnings.

One of the main reasons Australia, Sweden, and other nations have less overall earnings inequality, and thus smaller gender pay gaps, is because they have more centralized wage setting than in the United

States. For example, in Sweden nearly all workers are unionized, and a single union federation signs wage agreements directly with a single employer's federation. Wage setting is also quite centralized in Australia, where minimum wages are set for various industries by government tribunals. Centralized wage setting by union federations and governmental tribunals tends to compress the market-based wage distribution.

Interestingly, Blau and Kahn find that the pay gap has narrowed much more in the United States than in other countries over the last two decades. They find that the female–male hourly wage ratio narrowed by 14 percent between 1979–1981 and 1994–1998 in the United States, but only by 7 percent in other industrial countries. Blau and Kahn believe that this may have resulted from a faster rise of the relative qualifications and experience of women in the United States than elsewhere. Also, if labor force attachment of women rose faster in the United States than in other countries, then discrimination based on the assumption that women will drop out of the labor force could have fallen relatively more in the United States.

* Based on Francine D. Blau and Lawrence M. Kahn, "Gender Differences in Pay," *Journal of Economic Perspectives,* Fall 2000, pp. 75–99. See also Francine D. Blau and Lawrence M. Kahn, "Understanding International Differences in the Gender Pay Gap," *Journal of Labor Economics,* January 2003, pp. 106–44.

Unemployment

Figure 14.3 shows data on unemployment by race and gender over the past three decades in the United States. During the 1970s, white females were at some disadvantage compared to white males. This gap diminished over time, and there is little difference now.

African–Americans, however, have consistently had unemployment rates roughly twice as great as those of whites. Furthermore, the data understate the disadvantage of African–Americans because a larger percentage of African–Americans than whites have been discouraged workers (Chapters 3 and 18): They have dropped out of the labor force because of poor job prospects and are therefore not counted among the unemployed.

FIGURE 14.2 **African–American to White Hourly Wage Ratio in the United States**
The African–American to white hourly wage ratio in the United States has changed little in the past three decades. Not shown, the ratio increased significantly in the 1960s.

Source: Author calculations from *Current Population Survey.*

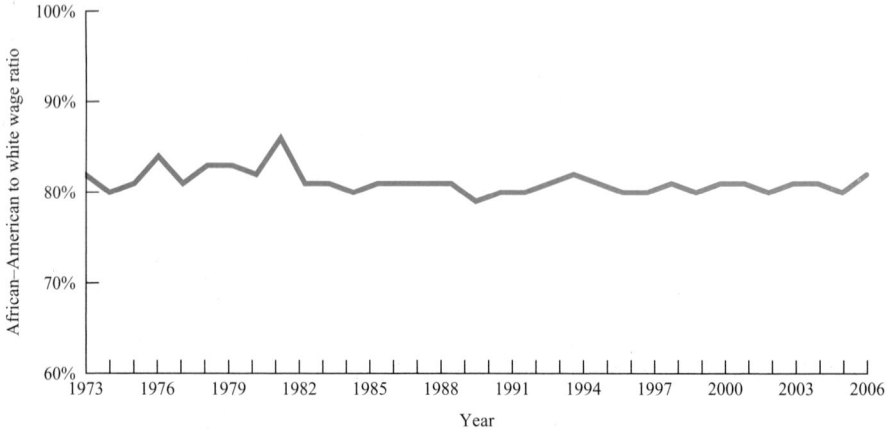

Occupational Distribution

Substantial differences in the occupational distribution of workers by gender and race are revealed in Table 14.1. Women, who constitute about 47 percent of the employed labor force, have been disproportionately concentrated in the following occupations: nursing, public school teaching, clerical work, cashiers, services, secretarial work, and

FIGURE 14.3 **Unemployment Rates by Race and Gender in the United States**
The unemployment rates of African–Americans are about twice those of whites, the unemployment rates of men and women of each race are quite similar.

Source: U.S. Bureau of Labor Statistics (**http://www.bls.gov**).

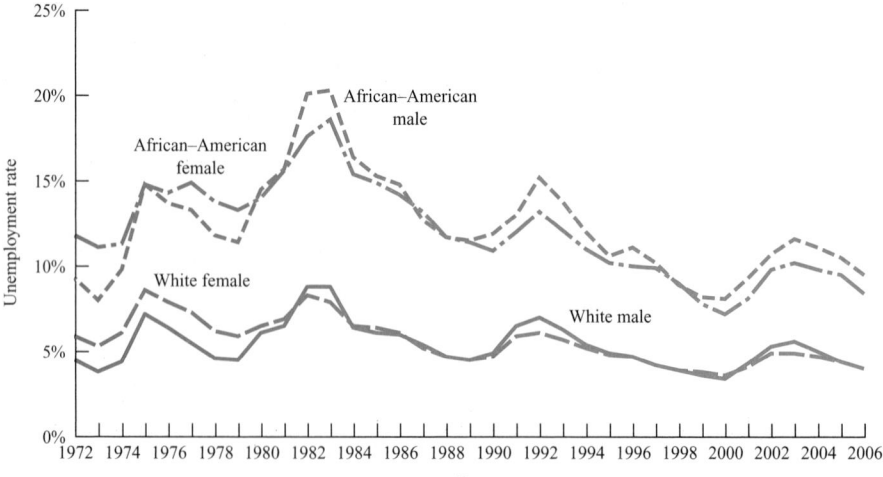

TABLE 14.1
Occupational
Distribution of
Employed
Workers by
Gender and Race

Source: U.S. Department of
Labor, *Employment and
Earnings,* January 2007,
Table 11.

Occupation	Percentage Female	Percentage African–American
Management, business, and financial operations occupations	42	7
Construction managers	8	4
Insurance underwriters	69	16
Professional and related occupations	57	9
Physicians and surgeons	32	5
Dentists	23	3
Registered nurses	91	11
Elementary and middle school teachers	82	10
Service occupations	57	16
Waiters and waitresses	72	7
Nursing, psychiatric, and home health aides	89	34
Janitors and building cleaners	32	19
Child care workers	94	17
Sales occupations	49	9
Cashiers	75	15
Office and administrative support occupations	75	13
Word processors and typists	91	18
Secretaries and administrative assistants	97	10
Receptionists and information clerks	93	11
Construction and extraction occupations	3	7
Brickmasons, blockmasons, and stonemasons	2	7
Construction and building inspectors	9	10
Installation, maintenance, and repair occupations	5	8
Precision instrument and equipment repairers	14	5
Automotive body and related repairers	1	4
Production occupations	30	12
Tool and die makers	1	3
Laundry and dry-cleaning workers	62	18
Transportation and material moving occupations	15	16
Crane and tower operators	2	14
Taxi drivers and chauffeurs	16	24

private household employment. All these occupations rank low in relative earnings. It must be added, however, that women have recently made significant gains in the professions ("World of Work" 14.4).

African–Americans constitute about 11 percent of the total labor force and have also been concentrated in a limited number of low-paying jobs as laundry workers, cleaners, nursing aides, and other manual workers. Conversely, note that women and African–Americans have both been underrepresented among such highly paid professionals as dentists and physicians.

FIGURE 14.4

Selected Measures of the Educational Attainment of the U.S. Population by Race and Gender

In the United States, white males have more education on average than women and African–Americans.

Source: *Statistical Abstract of the United States, 2007,* Table 215.

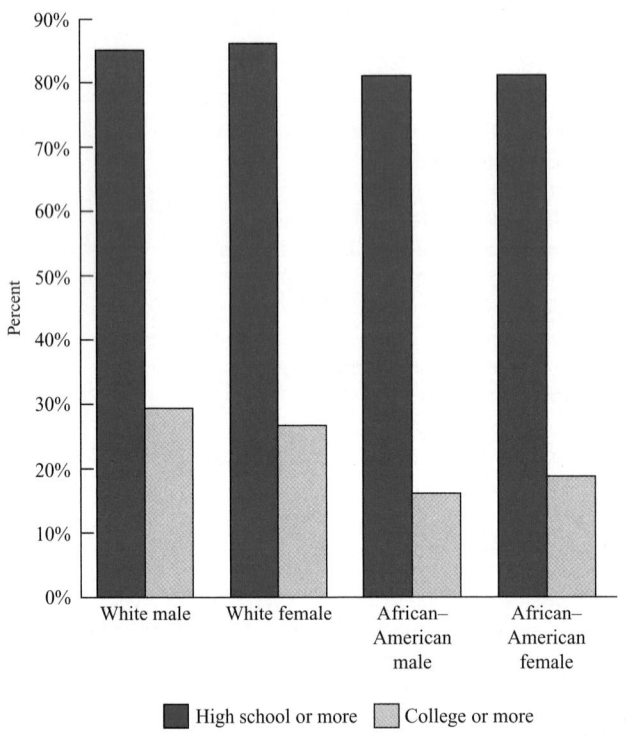

■ High school or more ▢ College or more

Education

Figure 14.4 provides some basic insights into differentials in human capital accumulation, although the data provide no information about apprenticeship programs and on-the-job training. We found in Chapter 4 that individuals who acquire the most formal education also tend to receive the most on-the-job training. The advantages that white males have enjoyed compared to females and African–Americans in obtaining college education have been magnified through the greater access these white males have had to postmarket job training that has increased their productivity and earnings. Furthermore, studies indicate that the quality of education received by African–Americans has been generally inferior to that acquired by whites.

Average Earnings by Educational Attainment

Although Figure 14.4 clearly indicates differences in educational levels by gender and race, it is important to note that these differences do not fully explain the earnings differences observed in Figures 14.1 and 14.2. As shown in Table 14.2, full-time women workers and African–American workers have significantly lower average earnings levels than white male workers at each level of educational attainment. The pattern is clear: On average, white males who work full-time earn more than African–American males at each educational level. African–American males, in turn, earn more than white females and African–American females. These data mean that the age-earnings profiles

TABLE 14.2
Average Earnings of Full-Time Workers (25 Years of Age or Older) by Educational Attainment

Source: U.S. Bureau of the Census, Educational Attainment in the United States, March 2006, Table 9.

	White Male	White Female	African–American Male	African–American Female
No High School Diploma	$29,628	$20,358	$26,501	$20,293
High School Diploma	$43,370	$29,419	$34,147	$25,619
Associate Degree	$54,730	$37,804	$45,801	$35,148
Bachelor's Degree	$78,676	$49,589	$57,586	$48,567
Master's Degree	$99,224	$59,594	$69,001	$56,341
Doctoral Degree	$116,645	$83,800	u	u
Professional Degree	$156,951	$102,907	u	u
Total	$60,452	$39,634	$43,189	$34,611

u = Data unavailable.

for women and African–Americans lie significantly below those displayed earlier in Figure 4.1 (all males).

Related Points

Two additional points must be made concerning this survey of empirical data, each point clarifying potential misinterpretations of the raw numbers.

Nondiscriminatory Factors

Although it is tempting to conclude that the tables and figures shown in this chapter prove the existence of discrimination, the situation is in fact far more complex than this. As will soon become clear from our discussion, a variety of factors other than discrimination may bear on the differences shown in the tables. For example, perhaps women earn less than men not as a result of discrimination, but rather because they freely choose academic programs and jobs that are less valued in the labor market than those chosen by men. Similarly, if African–American professors on average earn less than white professors, is this the result of discrimination or some other factor such as choice of academic discipline or African–Americans having gotten their training and degrees from less prestigious institutions? The point is that simple raw data comparing incomes, unemployment, and occupational distribution by gender or race must be regarded with caution as evidence of discrimination. *Nondiscriminatory factors* may explain part or all of the indicated differentials. Conversely, in some instances raw data indicating workforce integration and comparable *average* salaries can disguise underlying discrimination, once productivity differences are introduced.

Interrelated Data

The second point is that the various gender and racial differences in the earlier tables and figures are interrelated. For example, differences in human capital accumulation shown in Figure 14.4 are undoubtedly an important causal factor in explaining the earnings, unemployment, and occupational differences observed in Figures 14.1 and 14.2 and Table 14.1. Also, the occupational differences shown in Table 14.1 help explain the differences in earnings by education shown in Table 14.2.

14.1

*Quick
Review*

- The ratio of hourly earnings of women to men has risen substantially over the past three decades. However, the African–American to white hourly earnings ratio has changed little during this period.
- Unemployment rates of African–Americans are roughly twice those of whites; unemployment rates of women and men are similar.
- About 29 percent of white males have completed four or more years of college compared to 27 percent of white females, 19 percent of African–American females, and 16 percent of African–American males.
- Compared to white men, women and African–Americans who work full-time have lower average earnings at each level of educational attainment.
- Not all differences in earnings by race and gender result from discrimination. Non-discriminatory factors such as differences in preferences also are at work.

Your Turn

Compare the average earnings of African–American males to those of white males in Table 14.2. Explain how this difference might be responsible for the difference in the percentage of African–American males and white males attending college (Figure 14.4). (*Answers:* See page 598.)

DISCRIMINATION AND ITS DIMENSIONS

Discrimination is easier to define than to discern. *Economic discrimination exists when female or minority workers—who have the same abilities, education, training, and experience as white male workers—are accorded inferior treatment with respect to hiring, occupational access, promotion, wage rate, or working conditions.* Note that discrimination may also take the form of unequal access to formal education, apprenticeships, or on-the-job training programs, each of which enhances one's stock of human capital (Chapter 4).

Types of Discrimination

This definition is sufficiently important to merit elaboration. Implicit in our definition, labor market discrimination can be classified into four general types.[3]

1. *Wage discrimination* means that female (African–American) workers are paid less than male (white) workers for doing the same work. More technically, wage discrimination exists when wage differentials are based on considerations other than productivity differentials.

---

[3] We are concerned here only with those kinds of discrimination that are relevant to the labor market. Although discrimination in access to housing or consumer credit is important, it is less germane to the subject matter of labor economics.

2. *Employment discrimination* occurs when, other things being equal, African–Americans and women bear a disproportionate share of the burden of unemployment. African–Americans in particular have long faced the problem of being the last hired and the first fired.

3. *Occupational* or *job discrimination* means that females (African–Americans) have been arbitrarily restricted or prohibited from entering certain occupations, even though they are as capable as male (white) workers of performing those jobs, and are conversely crowded into other occupations for which they are frequently overqualified.

4. *Human capital discrimination* is in evidence when females (African–Americans) have less access to productivity-increasing opportunities such as formal schooling or on-the-job training. African–Americans in particular often obtain less education and education of inferior quality compared to whites.

The first three categories of discrimination are frequently designated as *postmarket* (also *current* or *direct*) *discrimination* because they are encountered *after* the individual has entered the labor market. Similarly, the fourth category is called *premarket* (also *past* or *indirect*) *discrimination* because it occurs *before* the individual seeks employment.[4]

These distinctions among the various kinds of discrimination are useful for at least two reasons. First, the significance of the various kinds of discrimination varies among African–Americans and women. Generally speaking, African–Americans are subject to a much greater degree of employment discrimination than women. And although African–Americans and women are both subject to occupational segregation, this form of discrimination is especially relevant with respect to women. Second, awareness of the various forms of discrimination helps one understand how discrimination may be self-reinforcing and therefore perpetuate itself. For example, if African–Americans and women anticipate that occupational discrimination will confine them to low-wage, dead-end jobs or that they will be exposed to frequent and prolonged periods of unemployment, they will rationally choose to invest less than otherwise in schooling (Chapter 4). That is, the expectation of postmarket discrimination will reduce the rate of return expected on investments in education and training, which will aggravate the premarket condition of inadequate preparation for many jobs.

Theories of Labor Market Discrimination

As indicated earlier, there is no generally accepted economic theory of discrimination. There are undoubtedly a variety of reasons for this. First, the interest of economists in explaining the phenomenon of discrimination is relatively recent. The pioneering book in

[4] On-the-job training poses a bit of a problem for our pre- and postmarket classification. Although such training is a human capital investment, people do not have access to it until they have entered the labor market. A useful and more detailed taxonomy of discrimination is presented by Brian Chiplin and Peter J. Sloane, "Sexual Discrimination in the Labor Market," in Alice H. Amsden (ed.), *The Economics of Women and Work* (New York: St. Martin's Press, 1980), p. 285.

World of Work

14.2

It Pays to Be Good-Looking

Better-looking men and women earn more than their less beautiful counterparts. Using data from three labor market surveys in which the interviewer rated the respondent on physical looks, Hamermesh and Biddle report that plain people earn 5–10 percent less than average-looking people.* Workers with above-average looks earn a 5 percent premium relative to average-looking people. About half of the men and women were rated as average-looking, while one-third were rated as above average in looks. The effects of appearance are somewhat stronger for men than women.

Why does beauty affect workers' earnings? Hamermesh and Biddle find that attractive people enter occupations in which appearance may be productive (such as a model or flight attendant). However, good looks increase the earnings of individuals even in jobs in which they should not affect productivity (such as a janitor). This result suggests that employers discriminate in favor of better-looking individuals.

Mobius and Rosenblat[†] extend the work of Hamermesh and Biddle by analyzing the causes of the beauty premium in more detail. They set up an experimental labor market where "employers" determined wages of "workers" who performed a maze-solving task, which was not affected by physical attractiveness. Their experiment showed a sizable beauty premium, for which they found three causes. First, physically attractive workers are more confident, and confidence increases wages. This confidence channel explains about 20 percent of the beauty premium. Second, for a given level of confidence, physically attractive workers are incorrectly considered more able by employers. This misperception accounts for about 40 percent of the beauty premium. Third, controlling for worker confidence, physically attractive workers have greater communication and social skills that raise their wages when they interact with employers. These skills explain about 40 percent of the beauty premium.

* Daniel S. Hamermesh and Jeff E. Biddle, "Beauty and the Labor Market," *American Economic Review,* December 1994, pp. 1174–94. For a study on the effects of beauty for lawyers, see Jeff E. Biddle and Daniel S. Hamermesh, "Beauty, Productivity, and Discrimination: Lawyers' Looks and Lucre," *Journal of Labor Economics,* January 1998, pp. 172–201. For a study finding that most spending on beauty represents consumption spending rather than investment spending, see Daniel S. Hamermesh, Xin Meng, and Junsen Zhang, "Dress for Success—Does Primping Pay?" *Labour Economics,* July 2002, pp. 361–73.

[†] Markus M. Mobius and Tanya S. Rosenblat, "Why Beauty Matters," *American Economic Review*, March 2006, pp. 222–35.

the field, Gary Becker's *The Economics of Discrimination,*[5] was published in 1957. Second, discrimination may assume a variety of guises and take different forms for different groups. For example, African–Americans traditionally have been at a substantial disadvantage in obtaining employment, whereas women have had access to jobs but only in a restricted number of occupations. Finally, we noted at the outset that the roots of discrimination are diverse and complex, ranging beyond the boundaries of economics. A discipline such as economics, which predicates its analysis on rational behavior, may be at a severe disadvantage in explaining a phenomenon that many regard as irrational. Nevertheless, economists have contributed important analytical and empirical work on the problem of discrimination, and our immediate goal is to summarize several of the

[5] Chicago: University of Chicago Press, 1957.

more prominent theories: (1) the taste for discrimination model, (2) statistical discrimination, and (3) the crowding model. You should be aware that, for the most part, the models to be discussed apply to all types of discrimination. For example, although we will present the taste for discrimination model in terms of racial discrimination, the model is also useful in explaining discrimination by gender, ethnicity, age, and sexual orientation.

TASTE FOR DISCRIMINATION MODEL

Becker's *taste for discrimination model* envisions discrimination as a preference or "taste" for which the discriminator is willing to pay. Becker uses an analogy based on the theory of international trade. It is well known that a nation can maximize its total output by engaging in free trade based on the principle of comparative advantage. But in fact nations obstruct trade through the use of tariffs, quotas, and a variety of other techniques. Nations are apparently willing to sacrifice economic efficiency to have certain goods produced domestically rather than imported. Society seems to have a preference or taste for domestically produced goods, even though it must pay the price of a diminished national income in exercising that taste. Similarly, Becker argues that unfortunately society also has a taste for discrimination and is willing to forgo productive efficiency—and therefore maximum output and profits—to exercise its prejudices. The price—or opportunity cost—of gender discrimination alone may be on the order of 4 percent of domestic output.[6]

Becker's theory is general because it can be applied to, say, white (male) workers who discriminate against African–American (female) workers, *or* white consumers who discriminate against firms that employ African–American workers or salespeople, *or* white employers who discriminate against African–American workers. The latter aspect of this theory—white employers who exercise their taste for discrimination against African–American workers—is the most relevant to our discussion, so we will concentrate on it. Why do employers discriminate? Employers' tastes for discrimination are based on the idea that they and their employees want to maintain a physical or social distance from certain groups; for example, white employers and their workers may not want to associate with African–American workers. These employers may then choose not to hire African–American workers because they and their employees do not want to work alongside them.

The Discrimination Coefficient

Assuming that African–American and white (male and female) workers are equally productive, a nondiscriminating employer will regard them as perfect substitutes and will hire them at random if their wages are the same. But if a white employer is prejudiced against African–Americans, then the situation is significantly altered. According to Becker, prejudiced white employers have "tastes for discrimination" and behave as if employing African–American workers imposed subjective or psychic costs on the employer. The strength of this psychic cost is reflected in a *discrimination coefficient d,* which can be

---

[6] Carl D. Lantz and Pierre-Daniel G. Sarte, "A Study of U.S. Employment Rates with Emphasis on Gender Considerations," Federal Reserve Bank of Richmond *Economic Quarterly,* Summer 2000, pp. 1–26.

measured in monetary terms. Given that the employer is *not* prejudiced against other whites, the cost of employing a white worker will simply be the wage rate W_w. However, the cost of employing an African–American worker to a prejudiced employer will be regarded as the African–American worker's wage W_{aa} plus the monetary value of the discrimination coefficient—in other words, $W_{aa} + d$. The prejudiced white employer will be indifferent about hiring African–American and white workers when the total cost per worker is the same—that is, when $W_w = W_{aa} + d$. It follows that our prejudiced white employer will hire African–Americans only if their wage rate is *below* that of whites. More precisely, for the prejudiced employer to employ African–Americans, their wage must be less than the wages of whites by the amount of the discrimination coefficient—in other words, $W_{aa} = W_w - d$. For example, if we suppose that the going wage rate for whites is $10 and that the monetary value of the psychic costs the employer attaches to hiring African–Americans is $2 (that is, $d = $2), then that employer will be indifferent about hiring African–Americans or whites only when the African–American wage is $8 ($W_{aa} = W_w - d$ or $8 = $10 − $2).

It is apparent that the larger a white employer's taste for discrimination as reflected in the value of *d,* larger the disparity between white wages and the wages at which African–Americans will be hired. As noted earlier, for a nondiscriminating or "color-blind" employer ($d = 0$), equally productive African–Americans and whites will be hired randomly if their wage rates are the same. At the other extreme, the white employer whose *d* was infinity would refuse to hire African–Americans at any wage rate, no matter how low that wage was in comparison to white wages. But note carefully that we are *not* saying prejudiced employers will refuse to hire African–Americans under all conditions. Thus in our initial example where the monetary value of *d* was $2, the white employer would prefer to hire African–Americans if the actual white to African–American wage gap exceeded $2. For example, if in fact whites could be hired at $10 and equally productive African–Americans at only $7.50 per hour, the employer would choose to hire African–Americans. The prejudiced employer would be willing to pay a wage premium of up to $2 per hour for whites in order to satisfy his or her taste for discrimination, but no more than that. At the $2.50 differential, the employer would choose to hire African–Americans. Conversely, if whites could be hired at $10 and African–Americans at $8.50, whites would be hired. The employer would be willing to pay a wage premium of up to $2 for whites; having to pay only a $1.50 premium means that hiring whites is a "bargain."

Demand and Supply Interpretation

Modified demand and supply analysis is useful in deepening our understanding of Becker's model and, more specifically, in explaining the prevailing wage differential between African–American and white workers. In Figure 14.5 we assume a competitive labor market for some particular occupation. The vertical axis differs from the usual labor market representation in that it measures the ratio of African–American to white wages W_{aa}/W_w, and the horizontal axis shows the quantity of *African–American* workers. The quantity of white workers and their wage rate are assumed to be given. The kinked demand curve for African–American workers D_{aa} is constructed by arraying white employers left to right from lowest to highest discrimination coefficients. Thus we find that the horizontal portion (*ab*) of the demand curve where W_{aa}/W_w equals 1.00 reflects nondiscriminating white employers—those whose *d*'s are zero. These employers do not discriminate between equally

FIGURE 14.5

Wage Discrimination in the Labor Market
The D_{aa} and S_{aa} curves show the demand for and the supply of African–American labor. Their intersection determines the African–American to white wage ratio and the number of African–American workers employed.

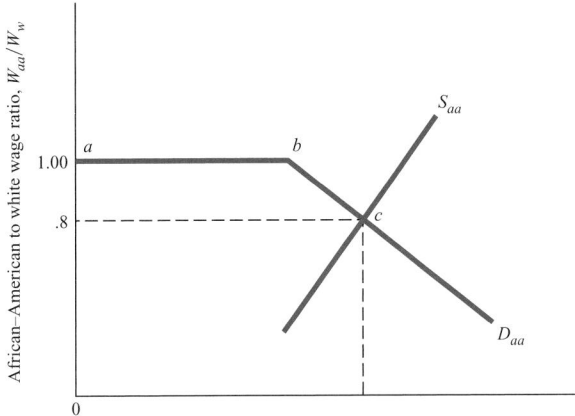

productive African–American and white workers so long as the wage rates of the two groups are equal. The downward-sloping portion of the demand curve (bD_b) reflects discriminating employers, whose d's increase as we move down that segment. On this segment of the curve, W_{aa}/W_w is less than 1.00 and diminishes as we move to the southeast.

To this demand curve we now add the supply of African–American labor. Not surprisingly, this curve is upward-sloping; the quantity of African–American labor supplied increases as W_{aa}/W_w increases. The intersection of the two curves establishes the actual W_{aa}/W_w ratio—that is, the extent of wage discrimination—and the number of African–American workers who will be employed in this occupation. Using the numbers from our initial illustration, let's assume that the actual wage rates being paid to African–Americans and whites are $8 and $10, respectively, so that W_{aa}/W_w is 8/10 or .8. This model suggests that nondiscriminating white employers (segment ab of the demand curve) and those whose d's are less than $2 (segment bc) will hire all African–American workers in this occupation; those shown by the cD_{aa} range of the demand curve have d's greater than $2 and will hire only whites.

Two Generalizations

Two generalizations concerning the size of the African–American to white wage differential emerge from the taste for discrimination model:

1. A change in the shape or location of the demand curve will alter the W_{aa}/W_w ratio. For example, suppose that a change in societal attitudes or antidiscrimination legislation has the effect of reducing the discrimination coefficient of employers. This will extend the horizontal portion of the demand curve farther to the right *and* reduce the slope of the remaining downward-sloping segment. Given the supply of African–American labor, the effect will be to raise the equilibrium W_{aa}/W_w ratio—that is, to reduce the discriminatory wage differential and increase the employment of African–American workers. For example, the equilibrium W_{aa}/W_w ratio in Figure 14.5 may rise from .8 to, say, .85.

2. The size of the discriminatory wage differential varies directly with the supply of minority (African–American) workers. If the supply of African–American labor in

Figure 14.5 were so small as to intersect the horizontal segment of the demand curve, there would be no discriminatory wage differential. If the supply of African–American labor increased to the position shown on the diagram, the differential would be .8 or 8/10. A further increase in supply will lower the W_{aa}/W_w ratio, indicating a widening of the wage differential.

These two generalizations raise an interesting question: Is the greater observed wage differential between African–American and white workers in the South as compared to the North the consequence of a stronger taste for discrimination in the South— that is, a demand curve farther to the left? Or, alternatively, is it the result of a greater relative supply of African–American workers in the South? In either case, of course, the *source* of the discrimination is white prejudice, not the size of the African–American labor force.

Gainers, Losers, and the Persistence of Discrimination

Becker's taste for discrimination model indicates that white workers will gain from discrimination because their wage rates will be higher than otherwise. Just as import restrictions reduce foreign competition to the benefit of domestic producers, discrimination by employers protects white workers from the competition of African–American workers. African–Americans, of course, receive lower wages because of discrimination. Finally, employers who discriminate may injure themselves because they will experience higher costs than necessary. Let's explain why this is so.

Returning to Figure 14.5, let's further assume that all of the employers arrayed on the demand curve are producing the same product. All of the nondiscriminating or less discriminating employers on the demand curve to the left of the intersection point will find themselves with a competitive cost advantage relative to the more discriminating employers on the segment of the demand curve to the right of the intersection. To illustrate: In equilibrium, the W_{aa}/W_w ratio is .8—that is, whites are paid $10 and African–Americans only $8. Remembering the assumption that African–Americans and whites are equally productive workers, a nondiscriminating employer on the horizontal segment would hire an African–American labor force at $8 per hour, whereas a discriminator far down the demand curve would hire all white workers at $10 per hour. The discriminating employer will incur higher wage costs than the nondiscriminating employer. Therefore, nondiscriminating firms will have lower average total costs and product prices than discriminating producers.

An important implication of Becker's model is that competitive market forces will cause discrimination to diminish and disappear over time because the lower-cost nondiscriminating firms can gain a larger share of the market at the expense of less efficient discriminating firms. In fact, in a highly competitive product market, only nondiscriminating firms (least-cost producers) will survive; discriminators will have average total costs that will exceed product price. Thus Becker's theory is consistent with a "conservative" or laissez-faire position toward discrimination; that is, in the long run, the operation of the competitive market will resolve the problem of discrimination, and therefore the only governmental action required is that which promotes

World of Work 14.3

Competition and Discrimination*

The Becker taste for discrimination model has clear predictions about the relationship between competition and discrimination. Employers who discriminate against women will hire relatively fewer of the less highly paid but equally skilled women than nondiscriminating employers. As a result, discriminators will have higher production costs and thus lower profits. This indicates that employer discrimination can exist only in less competitive markets. Therefore, a rise in product market competition in less competitive industries should reduce discrimination as discriminating employers are driven out of business.

Black and Brainerd examine the impact of international trade, which is one source of heightened competitive pressures, on gender discrimination. They find that a 10 percentage point increase in import share lowers the gender wage gap by 6.6 percent in less competitive industries. They conclude that increased international trade accounted for about one-quarter of the decline in gender discrimination in manufacturing during the 1976–93 period.

In another test of the impact of increased competition, Black and Strahan examine the effect of deregulation in the banking industry on discrimination. They report that after deregulation male wages fell by 12 percent, whereas women's wages declined by only 3 percent. The relative rise in the wages of women appears to be partly the result of a movement into

higher-skilled occupations. For example, the proportion of women in managerial positions in the banking industry rose by about 4 percentage points to more than 40 percent female.

Hellerstein, Neumark, and Troske directly test the Becker model's predictions regarding profits and discrimination. Consistent with the model, they find that among plants with high levels of market power, those that hire more women have greater profits. Specifically, a 10 percent increase in the proportion female raises the profit rate by 1.6 percentage points among plants with high market power. Consistent with the prediction that discrimination cannot exist in competitive industries, this relationship does not hold for plants with low levels of market power.

* Based on Sandra E. Black and Elizabeth Brainerd, "Importing Equality? The Impact of Globalization on Gender Discrimination," *Industrial and Labor Relations Review,* July 2004; Sandra E. Black and Philip E. Strahan, "The Division of Spoils: Rent-Sharing and Discrimination in a Regulated Industry," *American Economic Review,* September 2001, pp. 814–31; and Judith K. Hellerstein, David Neumark, and Kenneth R. Troske, "Market Forces and Sex Discrimination," *Journal of Human Resources,* Spring 2002, pp. 353–80. For a study showing reduced racial wage gaps after privatization of public transit systems and deregulation of the trucking industry, see James Peoples, Jr., and Wayne K. Talley, "Black–White Earnings Differentials: Privatization versus Deregulation," *American Economic Review,* May 2001, pp. 164–68.

free occupational choice.[7] Discriminating employers will either have to become nondiscriminators or be driven out of business.

A fundamental criticism of this perspective is that, in fact, progress in eliminating discrimination has been modest. The functioning of the market has *not* eliminated employers' prejudices. Discrimination based on both race and gender has persisted decade after decade. Thus alternative models have been proposed to explain why discrimination has continued.

14.3

[7] That government will be unsuccessful in eliminating discrimination is the major theme of Thomas Sowell, *Markets and Minorities* (New York: Basic Books, Inc., 1981). See also William A. Darity, Jr., and Rhonda M. Williams, "Peddlers Forever? Culture, Competition, and Discrimination," *American Economic Review,* May 1985, pp. 256–61.

<table>
<tr>
<td>

14.2

Quick Review

</td>
<td>

- Labor market discrimination occurs when workers who have the same abilities, education, training, and experience as other workers receive inferior treatment with respect to hiring, occupational access, promotion, or wages.
- Labor market discrimination can be classified as *(a)* wage discrimination, *(b)* employment discrimination, *(c)* occupational or job discrimination, or *(d)* human capital discrimination.
- Becker's taste for discrimination model views discrimination as a preference or "taste" for which the discriminator is willing to pay; the greater this preference, the larger is Becker's discrimination coefficient.
- Employers with high discrimination coefficients will incur higher labor costs than nondiscriminating employers; thus the nondiscriminators will have a cost advantage in competing with discriminators in the marketplace.

Your Turn

Suppose the hourly market wage for specific white workers is $16, while the wage for equally productive African–American workers is $12. What can be inferred about the dollar value of the discrimination coefficient for an employer that hires all white workers under these circumstances? All African–American workers? (*Answers:* See page 599.)

</td>
</tr>
</table>

THEORY OF STATISTICAL DISCRIMINATION

Another theory centers on the concept of *statistical discrimination.*[8] By way of definition, we can say that statistical discrimination

> occurs whenever an individual is judged on the basis of the average characteristics of the group, or groups, to which he or she belongs rather than upon his or her own personal characteristics. The judgments are correct, factual, and objective in the sense that the group actually has the characteristics that are ascribed to it, but the judgments are incorrect with respect to many individuals within the group.[9]

A commonplace non–labor market example of statistical discrimination involves automobile insurance. Insurance rates for teenage males are higher than those for teenage females. This rate differential is based on accumulated factual evidence indicating that, on the average, young males are more likely than females to be involved in accidents. However, many young male drivers are equally or less accident prone than the average of young females, and these males are discriminated against by having to pay higher insurance rates.

---

[8] See Edmund S. Phelps, "The Statistical Theory of Racism and Sexism," *American Economic Review,* September 1972, pp. 659–61; and Dennis J. Aigner and Glen G. Cain, "Statistical Theories of Discrimination in Labor Markets," *Industrial and Labor Relations Review,* January 1977, pp. 175–87. For empirical investigations of statistical discrimination, see Joseph G. Altonji and Charles R. Pierret, "Employer Learning and Statistical Discrimination," *Quarterly Journal of Economics,* February 2001, pp. 313–50; and Joshua C. Pinkston, "A Test of Screening Discrimination with Employer Learning," *Industrial and Labor Relations Review,* January 2006, pp. 267–84.

[9] Lester Thurow, *Generating Inequality* (New York: Basic Books, 1975), p. 172. This entire section draws on chapter 7 of Thurow's work.

It is easy to understand how statistical discrimination would function in labor markets. Employers with job vacancies want to hire the most productive workers available to fill open positions. Thus their personnel departments collect a variety of information concerning each job applicant: for example, an individual's age, education, and prior work experience. Employers supplement this information with scores on preemployment tests that they feel are helpful indicators of potential job performance. But two interrelated considerations pertain to this employee screening process. First, because it is expensive to collect detailed information about each job applicant, only limited data are collected. Second, the limited information available to the employer from job application forms and test scores will *not* permit the employer to predict perfectly which job applicants will be the most productive employees. As a consequence of these two considerations, it is common for employers to use subjective considerations such as race, gender, or age in determining who is hired. In practicing statistical discrimination, the employer is not satisfying a taste for discrimination, but rather is using gender, race, or age as a proxy for production-related attributes of workers that are not easily discernible. Gender, for example, may be used as a proxy for physical strength or job commitment.

To illustrate: An employer may assume that *on the average,* young married women are more likely than males to quit their jobs within, say, two years after hire because they may become pregnant or their husbands may take jobs in different locations. All other things being equal, when choosing between a married female and a male job applicant, the employer may hire the male. Similarly, when considering whether to employ an African–American or a white high school graduate whose age, work experience, and test scores are identical, the employer may hire the white youth because the employer knows that *on the average* African–Americans receive schooling that is qualitatively inferior to that obtained by whites. Note what is happening here: Characteristics that apply to a group are being applied to individuals. *Each* married woman is assumed to behave with respect to employment tenure as the "average" married woman. Similarly, *every* African–American youth is assumed to have the same quality of education as the "average" African–American youth. It is assumed that group or average differences apply in each individual case. As a result, married women who do not plan to have children (or do not plan to quit work if they do) and African–American youths who receive quality education will be discriminated against.

Three further aspects of statistical discrimination merit comment. In the first place, unlike in the taste for discrimination model, the employer is *not* harmed by practicing discrimination. On the contrary, the employer is a beneficiary. An employer will enhance profits by minimizing hiring costs. Given that gathering detailed information about each job applicant is costly, applying perceived group characteristics to job seekers is an inexpensive means of screening employees. Some economists feel that the statistical discrimination theory, which envisions employers as "gainers," is more plausible than the taste for discrimination model, which conceives of them as "losers."

Second, as suggested earlier, the statistical discrimination model does not necessarily indicate that an employer is being malicious in his or her hiring behavior. The decisions made may well be correct, rational, and, as noted, profitable *on the average.* The problem is that many workers who differ from the group average will be discriminated against.

Finally, as noted at the outset, there is no compelling reason statistical discrimination need diminish over time. In contrast to the taste for discrimination model, statistical discrimination may persist because those who practice it are beneficiaries.

Our first and third points merit qualification in one important sense. If the average characteristics of any two groups converge over time—perhaps because of a decline in other aspects of discrimination—statistical discrimination may become increasingly costly to employers. For example, suppose human capital discrimination diminishes and African–American youths now obtain high school education equal in quality to that acquired by white youths. By applying statistical discrimination to employ only whites, the employer will now be making more hiring mistakes. These mistakes will be of two types: hiring more whites who are not qualified and failing to hire African–Americans who are qualified.

Similarly, the increasing availability of child care facilities, higher female pay, and changing female preferences have meant that having children no longer seriously interrupts the work careers of many women. Also, studies reveal that the difference in turnover rates of men and women in similar jobs with similar advancement opportunities is small.[10] Thus employers who base hiring decisions on the average turnover rate of females may make costly hiring mistakes. The cost to the employer of such mistakes is that the most productive workers available are not selected. Employers who make fewer mistakes will have lower production costs and will increase their market share at the expense of rivals.

THE CROWDING MODEL: OCCUPATIONAL SEGREGATION

A glance back at Table 14.1 will reveal that occupational distributions of whites and African–Americans *and* of males and females are substantially different. We have also noted in Chapter 8 that wages differ substantially by occupation, so the occupational structure is an important factor in explaining wages differences across workers. Thus it is no surprise to find that an entire theory of discrimination has been based on the concept of occupational segregation. This *crowding model* uses simple supply and demand concepts to explore the consequences of confining women and African–Americans to a limited number of occupations.[11]

---

[10] Francine D. Blau and Lawrence M. Kahn, "Race and Sex Differences in Quits by Young Workers," *Industrial and Labor Relations Review,* October 1981, pp. 563–77. See also Audrey Light and Manuelita Ureta, "Panel Estimates of Male and Female Job Turnover Behavior: Can Female Nonquitters Be Identified?" *Journal of Labor Economics,* April 1992, pp. 156–81.

[11] For a detailed discussion of the crowding hypothesis by one of its leading exponents, see Barbara R. Bergmann, *The Economic Emergence of Women,* 2nd ed. (New York: Palgrave Macmillan, 2005), chaps. 4–6, and more specifically, pp. 85–90. Elaine Sorensen, "The Crowding Hypothesis and Comparable Worth," *Journal of Human Resources,* Winter 1990, pp. 55–89.

Why does crowding occur? Why do employers practice job segregation based on gender or race? One important reason is that worker productivity is the result of a group or "team" effort. If social interactions on the job are unfavorable, productivity will suffer. Some male (white) workers may become disgruntled when obligated to work along with or to take orders from women (African–Americans). Thus in the interest of productivity and profits, employers decide to segregate men and women (African–Americans and whites) on the job. Furthermore, many employers have preconceived notions concerning the job capabilities of women and minorities. As a result, few women, for example, have jobs driving trucks or selling electronics equipment or automobiles.

Assumptions and Predictions

The following simplifying assumptions will facilitate our discussion of the crowding model:

1. The labor force is equally divided between male and female (or white and African–American) workers. Let's say there are 6 million male and 6 million female workers.

2. The total labor market is composed of three occupations—X, Y, and Z—each having identical labor demand curves as shown in Figure 14.6.

3. Men and women have homogeneous labor force characteristics; males and females are equally productive in each of the three occupations.

4. Product markets are competitive so that the demand curves reflect not only marginal revenue product (MRP) but also value of marginal product (VMP) (Chapter 5).

5. We assume that as a result of occupational segregation, occupations X and Y are "men's jobs" and occupation Z is a "woman's job." Women are confined to occupation Z and systematically excluded from occupations X and Y.

FIGURE 14.6   Occupational Segregation: The Crowding Model
By crowding women into occupation Z, men will receive high wage rates of W_m in occupations X and Y, while women will receive low wage rates of W_f in occupation Z. The abandonment of discrimination will equalize wage rates at W_e and result in a net increase in the domestic output [*(abcd + efgh)* − *ijkl*].

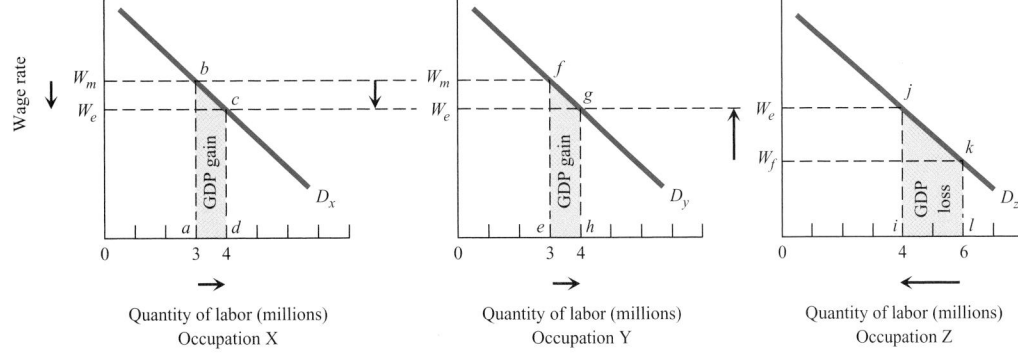

Men will distribute themselves equally among occupations X and Y so that there are 3 million male workers in each and the resulting common wage rate for men is W_m. Assuming no barriers to mobility, any initially different distribution of males between X and Y would result in a wage differential that would prompt labor shifts from low- to high-wage occupations until wage equality was realized. Note that all 6 million women, on the other hand, are crowded into occupation Z and, as a consequence of this occupational segregation, receive a much lower wage rate W_f. Given the reality of discrimination, this is an "equilibrium" situation. Women *cannot,* because of discrimination, reallocate themselves to occupations X and Y in the pursuit of higher wage rates. Although men could presumably enter occupation Z if they so chose, they would not want to do so in the face of Z's lower wage rates.

The net result of occupational segregation is obvious: Men realize higher wage rates and incomes at the expense of women. Note, however, that women are not being disadvantaged as the result of exploitation: They are *not* being paid a wage rate less than their marginal revenue product. In occupation Z women *are* being paid a wage rate equal to their MRP *and* to their contribution to society's output (VMP). Their problem is that by being restricted to only occupation Z, their supply is great relative to demand and their wage rate is therefore low compared to that of males.

Ending Discrimination

Suppose that through legislation or sweeping changes in social attitudes, discrimination disappears. What are the results? Women, attracted by higher wage rates, will shift from Z to X and Y. Specifically, if we assume occupational shifts are costless, 1 million women will shift into X and another 1 million into Y, leaving 4 million workers in Z. At this point, 4 million workers will be in each occupation and wage rates will be equal to W_e in all three occupations; so there is no incentive for further reallocation. This new, nondiscriminatory equilibrium is to the advantage of women, who now receive higher wages, and to the disadvantage of men, who now receive lower wages.

If the elimination of occupational segregation results in both winners (women) and losers (men), it is pertinent to ask whether the gains exceed the losses. That is, does society reap an economic gain by ending occupational segregation? Figure 14.6 reveals that there *is* a net gain to society. Our labor demand curves reflect value of marginal product, the contribution of each successive worker to the domestic output. Hence the movement of 2 million women out of occupation Z yields a *decrease* in domestic output shown by area *ijkl*. But the areas *abcd* and *efgh* for occupations X and Y show the *increases* in domestic output—the market values of the marginal products—realized by adding 1 million women to each of these occupations. We observe that the sum of the additions to domestic output in occupations X and Y exceeds the decline in domestic output that occurs when women leave occupation Z. The conclusion that society gains from the termination of occupational segregation is not unexpected. Women reallocate themselves from occupation Z, where their VMP is relatively low, to occupations X and Y, where their VMPs are relatively high. This reallocation continues until the VMPs of labor in each alternative use are equal—a condition that defines the efficient allocation of labor (Chapter 6). Thus our analysis underscores that discrimination has both equity and efficiency connotations. Discrimination influences not only the distribution but also the size of the domestic income.

14.3
Quick Review

- The theory of statistical discrimination holds that employers often wrongly judge individuals on the basis of the average characteristics of the group to which they belong rather than on their own personal characteristics.
- The crowding model of discrimination suggests that women and minorities are systematically excluded from high-paying occupations and crowded into low-paying ones.

Your Turn

How might statistical discrimination reinforce occupational segregation? (*Answer:* See page 599.)

Index of Segregation

How extensive is crowding or occupational segregation? An *index of segregation* has been devised to quantify occupational segregation. As applied to sex discrimination, *this index is designed to show the percentage of women (or men) who would have to change occupations for women to be distributed among occupations in the same proportions as men.* The hypothetical figures of Table 14.3 are instructive. Suppose the occupational distributions of male and female workers are as shown in columns 2 and 3. To make the distributions identical, *either* 30 percent of the total of *female* workers would have to move *from* occupation C (20 percent going to A and 10 percent to B) *or* 30 percent of the total of *male* workers would have to move *to* occupation C (20 percent coming from A and 10 percent coming from B). Because 30 percent of either female or male workers would have to change occupations for males and females to be distributed in the same proportions among occupations, the index of segregation is 30 percent, or simply 0.30. For more numerous occupational categories, the index can be calculated by determining the absolute value of the percentage differences for each occupation

TABLE 14.3
Determining the Index of Segregation (Hypothetical Data)

(1) Occupation	(2) Male	(3) Female	(4) = (2) − (3) Absolute Differences
A	50%	30%	20%
B	30	20	10
C	20	50	30
	100%	100%	60%

Index of segregation = $\frac{60\%}{2}$ = 30% or 0.30.

FIGURE 14.7 **Index of Occupational Segregation by Gender, United States**
The index of occupational segregation between men and women fell considerably between 1973 and 2006.

Source: Author calculations from *Current Population Survey*.

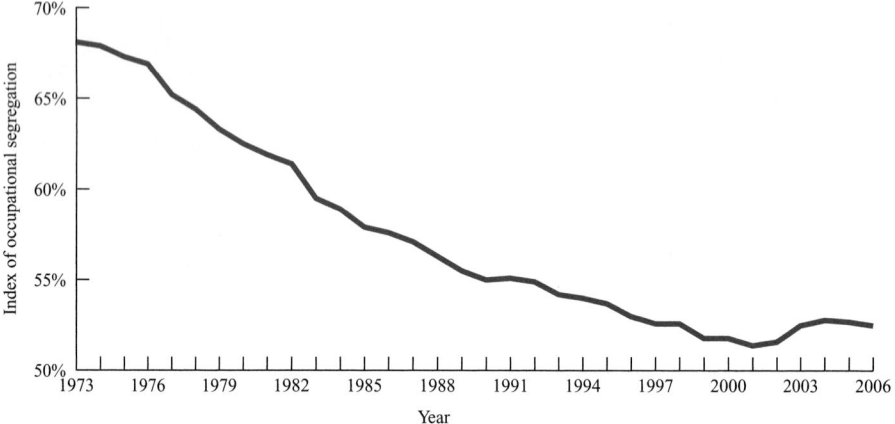

(without regard to sign) and summing these differences as shown in column 4. To obtain the index of segregation, the resulting 60 percent is then divided by 2 because any movement of workers is counted twice: as a movement *out of* one occupation and as a movement *into* another occupation.

The conclusion from our simple hypothetical illustration is that 30 percent of the female (or male) labor force must change occupations for the proportions of men and women in each occupation to be the same. Note that this new distribution would result in an index of segregation of zero. The other extreme where, say, occupations A and B are each populated 50 percent by men and occupation C 100 percent by women yields an index of 100 percent or 1.00. Hence the index of segregation may take on any value ranging from 0 to 1.00, and the higher the value, the greater the extent of occupational segregation.

Evidence

What are the magnitudes of the indexes of occupational segregation based on gender and race for the United States? And what, if anything, has happened to these indexes over time? Figure 14.7 presents the index of occupational segregation between men and women. The index of occupational segregation by gender was 68.1 percent in 1973 and declined to 52.5 percent by 2006.[12] Slightly more than half the women (or men)

[12] For more about gender occupational segregation, see David A. Macpherson and Barry T. Hirsch, "Wages and Gender Composition: Why Do Women's Jobs Pay Less?" *Journal of Labor Economics,* July 1995, pp. 426–71; and Kimberly Bayard, "New Evidence on Sex Segregation and Sex Differences in Wages from Matched Employee–Employer Data," *Journal of Labor Economics,* October 2003, pp. 887–922.

| Global Perspective 14.1 | Occupational Segregation |

The index of occupational segregation for 75 consistent occupations ranges from 44.9 percent in Italy to 63.0 percent in Sweden.

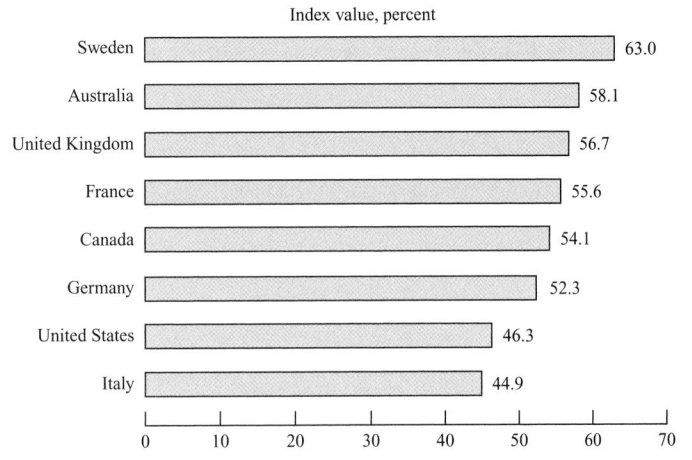

Index value, percent

Sweden	63.0
Australia	58.1
United Kingdom	56.7
France	55.6
Canada	54.1
Germany	52.3
United States	46.3
Italy	44.9

Source: Francine D. Blau, Marianne A. Ferber, and Anne E. Winkler, *The Economics of Women, Men, and Work,* 5th ed. (Englewood Cliffs, NJ: Prentice-Hall, 2006), Table 11.3.

14.4

in the United States would have to change occupations for women to be distributed among occupations in the same proportions as men. This considerable change in the index is consistent with growing evidence that women have made substantial occupational gains in professions such as dentistry, medicine, pharmacy, and law ("World of Work"14.4).[13]

Occupational segregation based on race is less pronounced than that based on gender and has declined noticeably over time. Figure 14.8 presents data for the index of racial occupational segregation by gender. Comparing white women and African–American women, the index of segregation was 37.1 percent in 1973 and fell to 22.2 percent in 2006.[14] This is consistent with a general integration of African–American women into occupations traditionally held by white women. When white men and African–American men are analyzed, the change was slightly more modest: The index fell from 37.0 percent in 1973 to 27.8 percent in 2006.

[13] See Francine D. Blau and Marianne A. Ferber, *The Economics of Women, Men, and Work,* 5th ed. (Englewood Cliffs, NJ: Prentice-Hall, 2006).
[14] For more about racial occupational segregation, see William J. Carrington and Kenneth R. Troske, "Interfirm Segregation and the Black/White Wage Gap," *Journal of Labor Economics,* April 1998, pp. 231–60; and Barry T. Hirsch and David A. Macpherson, "Wages, Sorting on Skill, and Racial Composition of Jobs," *Journal of Labor Economics,* January 2004, pp. 189–210.

<table>
<tr><td>14.4</td><td>World of Work</td><td>Women's Entry into Selected Professions*</td></tr>
</table>

Consistent with the decline in the overall index of occupational segregation during the 1980s and 1990s, women made considerable gains in entering selected professions. This fact is evident from several studies and is implied in the accompanying figure. The light green bars in the figure indicate the overall percentage of women in each particular profession in 2005; the dark green bars show women as a percentage of *new graduates* in each field in 2004.

Note, for example, that while women constituted only 22.5 percent of dentists in 2005; they made up 41.6 percent of the graduates from dental school in the preceding year. In 2004 women were two-thirds of the graduates from pharmacy school, compared to 48.3 percent of pharmacists

in general in 2005. Nearly half of all law school graduates in 2004 were women, which is substantially more than the overall percentage of women lawyers in 2005.

The increase in the number of women entering the professions, of course, is encouraging. Nevertheless, the true test of equality will come as these women progress in their careers. Will some of them drop out of their professions for reasons related to family responsibilities? Will they experience discriminatory barriers—so-called glass ceilings—impeding their advancement to the top positions in their professions? Studies of the hierarchies of professions continue to show that males often dominate the higher-paying professional positions.

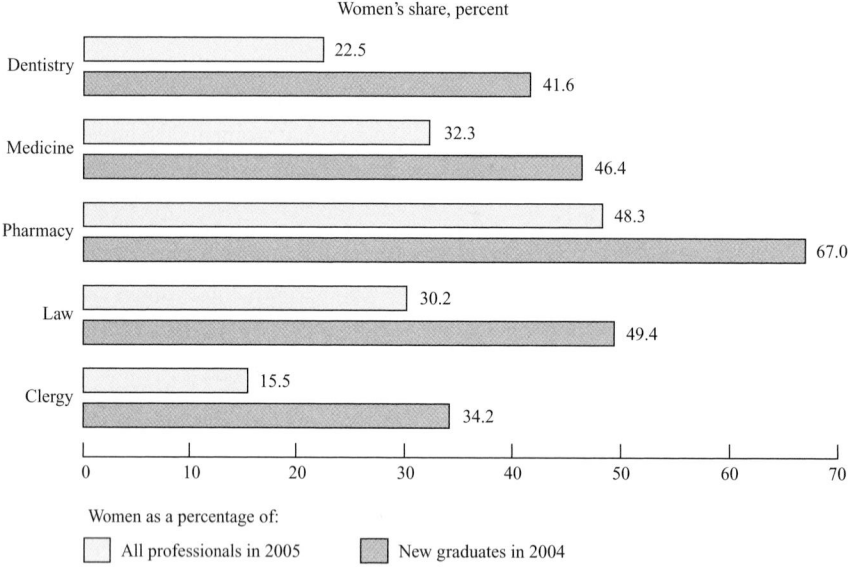

Women's share, percent

Women as a percentage of:
☐ All professionals in 2005   ▨ New graduates in 2004

* Based on Sylvia Nasar, "Women's Progress Stalled? Just Not So?" *The New York Times*, October 18, 1992, Section 3, p. 1. Updated with data from the National Center for Educational Statistics, *Digest of Educational Statistics, 2002* (Washington, DC: NCES, 2002), Table 274, and *Statistical Abstract of the United States, 2007,* Table 602.

FIGURE 14.8 **Index of Racial Occupational Segregation by Gender, United States**
The index of racial occupational segregation fell noticeably for men and women between 1973 and 2005.

Source: Author calculations from *Current Population Survey.*

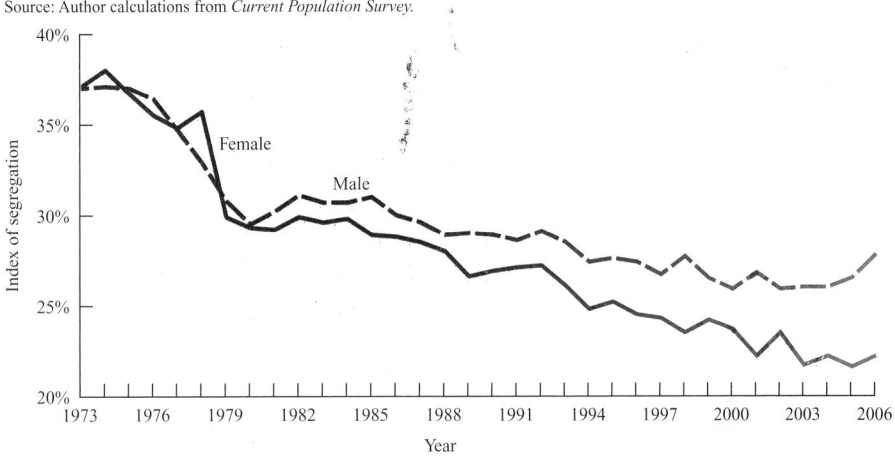

CAUSE AND EFFECT: NONDISCRIMINATORY FACTORS

As we have indicated, economists know that many factors other than discrimination may bear on female to male and African–American to white earnings differentials. Finding that Ms. Anderson earns $20,000 a year while Mr. Alvarez earns $30,000 annually is not necessarily evidence of gender discrimination. This is true even where Ms. Anderson and Mr. Alvarez have equal levels of education or work for the same employer. A variety of considerations that have nothing to do with prejudice may simply cause Alvarez to be more productive than Anderson. More generally, cause-and-effect considerations are difficult to unravel in attempting to isolate the role of discrimination in explaining differences in socioeconomic status. Let's consider this issue in terms of gender discrimination.

Rational Choice versus Discrimination as a Cause

Some economists argue that the inferior economic position of women is basically the result of rational and freely rendered decisions by women. The essence of this view is that most women anticipate marriage and childbearing, and this generates for women a conflict between labor market careers and marriage that explains much of women's economic disadvantage. More specifically, the proponents of this position argue that in attempting to make their traditional homemaking role more compatible with labor market work, women make decisions concerning human capital investments, hours of work, and other job characteristics that result in incomes lower than those earned by men.

The traditional childbearing and family roles of women mean that their participation in the labor market will be discontinuous and truncated. This fact has a variety of implications. First, because women will work fewer lifetime hours, their expected rate of return on human capital investments (education and training) will be lower than that of men. As a result, women as well as their employers may be less willing to invest in education and on-the-job training, causing the productivity and earnings of women to be less than for men. Second, the stock of human capital that women possess may deteriorate when they are out of the labor force, thus lowering their productivity and earnings. Third, it can be argued that occupational segregation is the result of rational choice. Knowing they will not be in the labor force continuously, women may prefer occupations such as nursing or elementary school teaching, which will have the greatest carryover value for productive activity within the home.

Some portion of the male–female earnings differential may be the result of differences in the type of jobs women desire to hold. If women put a high value on, say, shorter hours, job safety, and the location of jobs close to their homes, then the exercise of these preferences may result in lower wages and earnings for women. Stated differently, some portion of the higher earnings of males *may* be a wage differential that compensates them for longer hours and for performing more hazardous and inconveniently located jobs and thus may be unrelated to sex discrimination. In fact, women—particularly married women—are much more likely than men to hold part-time jobs. Additionally, full-time male workers on average work more hours per week than do full-time female workers. Some economists contend that the desire of women to work part-time or shorter hours contributes to occupational segregation—and consequently to lower female earnings—because occupations differ in the opportunities for part-time work and relatively shorter workweeks.

The "rational choice" view suggests that voluntary decisions by women concerning the amounts and types of education and training they receive and the kinds of jobs they choose *cause* them to realize lower earnings than men. Skeptics argue that it is more plausible to reverse the implied cause–effect sequence and thereby assign a primary role to discrimination in explaining female–male earnings differentials. To facilitate our discussion, we will concentrate on the rational choice contention that women freely choose to truncate their labor market careers with the result that it is rational for employers and women themselves to invest less in human capital.

One can argue that women invest in less education and training or invest in types of training that have the greatest carryover value for household production *because* of labor market discrimination and manifest income disparities. For example, the decision of many women to withdraw from the labor force for extended periods may be the consequence of the low opportunity cost of nonparticipation, the latter being the result of low market pay due to discrimination. Poor labor market opportunities for women lower their earnings and increase the relative attractiveness of work in the home. In this interpretation, labor market discrimination *causes* women to choose the amounts and kinds of human capital investment that they do and to withdraw from the labor market for extended periods.

It is also possible that many women who experience sexual harassment and discrimination in the workplace respond by changing careers or having children and working in the home. Thus the truncated careers of women and their resulting lower earnings may be an outcome of discrimination, not the consequence of truly free choice.[15]

---

[15] For evidence of this effect, see David Neumark and Michele McLennon, "Sex Discrimination and Women's Labor Market Interruptions," *Journal of Human Resources,* Fall 1995, pp. 713–40.

Which position is correct? Both views are right. Discrimination entails a complex intermingling of cause and effect. Differences in supply decisions with respect to human capital investment and occupational choice of males and females may *result* from labor market discrimination and existing earnings disparities and simultaneously be a *cause* of these earnings differentials.

Evidence

Despite the difficult cause–effect interrelationships involved, many empirical studies have attempted to disaggregate female to male and African–American to white earnings differentials in the hope of determining what portion of them is due to productivity differences as opposed to discrimination per se. These studies attempt to control for such factors as education, age, training, industry and occupation, union membership, location and continuity of workforce experience, health, and so forth. The reasoning is that these are allegedly nondiscriminatory considerations that cause productivity differences and therefore earnings differences. A comprehensive study by Blau and Kahn found that approximately two-thirds of the female–male earnings differential is attributable to such factors as differences in years of work experience (26 percent), industry (23 percent), occupation (8 percent), and union status (4 percent).[16] That is, males have more work experience, are more likely to be union members, and work in higher-paying industries and occupations. Consequently, their productivity was higher, and this justified two-thirds of the earnings advantage they enjoyed. The remaining third of the earnings gap was unexplained and presumably due, wholly or in part, to discrimination. As Figure 14.1 shows, the female–male hourly earnings ratio rose from 64.6 percent in 1973 to 79.8 percent in 2006. Blau and Kahn found that the earnings differential fell equally between 1972 and 1988 due to an increase in the relative productivity characteristics of women and a decline in the unexplained gap. Borass and Rodgers found that the earnings ratio rose between 1989 and 1999, entirely because of a rise in the relative productivity of women.[17]

Regarding the African–American to white gap, a study by Blau and Kahn found that productivity differences account for 89 percent of the pay differential between African–American and white men.[18] A study by Neal and Johnson found that racial differences in cognitive achievement as measured by the Armed Forces Qualifying Test (AFQT) score alone appear to "explain" about two-thirds of the pay gap between

---

[16] Francine D. Blau and Lawrence M. Kahn, "Swimming Upstream: Trends in the Gender Wage Differential in the 1980s," *Journal of Labor Economics,* January 1997, pp. 1–42. They also report that the productivity differences account for only one-third of the gap when only human capital variables are included in the statistical model (that is, gender differences in industry, occupation, and union status are not accounted for).

[17] Stephanie Borass and William Rodgers III, "How Does Gender Play a Role in the Earnings Gap? An Update," *Monthly Labor Review,* March 2003, pp. 9–15.

[18] Francine D. Blau and Lawrence M. Kahn, "Race and Gender Pay Differentials," in David Lewin, Olivia S. Mitchell, and Peter D. Scherer (eds.), *Research Frontiers in Industrial Relations and Human Resources* (Madison, WI: Industrial Relations Research Association, 1992), pp. 381–416. Evidence exists that the African–American to white difference in productivity characteristics is smaller among working women than among nonworking women. Thus the racial differential in wages among working women is smaller than it would be if all women worked. See Derek Neal, "The Measured Black–White Wage Gap among Women Is Too Small," *Journal of Political Economy,* February 2004, Part 2 Supplement, pp. S1–28.

young African–American and white men.[19] They found that African–American men have lower AFQT scores due to lower-quality schooling and other environmental factors. In contrast to the gender pay gap, the African–American to white pay differential has not narrowed in recent years.[20] The stall in progress for African–American men appears to be partly the result of offsetting factors. On one hand, African–American men have, on average, less education than white men, so the increased payoff to education in the 1990s caused the African–American to white pay gap to expand. On the other hand, the African–American to white gap in education has shrunk, which has tended to diminish the African–American to white earnings differential. The net result has been little change in the African–American to white earnings differential.

Controversy

The interpretation of such studies has been controversial. Some economists feel that the unexplained earnings differential overstates the role of discrimination; others contend that it is an underestimation. Those who feel that the discrimination estimate is too high argue that other productivity-influencing considerations (such as worker motivation, quantitative skills, or course of study in school) have not been taken into account. These factors allegedly increase the productivity of males relative to females and, if included, would reduce the unexplained (discriminatory) portion of the wage differential.[21]

Others, however, take the opposite view and contend that certain omitted variables (for example, men are more likely to smoke and abuse alcohol and drugs, have criminal records, and have bad driving records) suggest that the job performance and productivity of men should be lower than that of females. Taking such variables into account would increase the size of the unexplained female–male earnings gap. A second argument is that in fact many of the control variables—such as formal education, on-the-job training, and occupational placement—reflect discriminatory decisions. Although male productivity may exceed that of females, that higher productivity reflects discriminatory decisions with respect to (1) the quantity and type of education and job training provided men and women and (2) occupational segregation.

Conclusion? "When all is said and done, we cannot make a precise estimate of the proportion of the wage gap that is due to discrimination, but we can say with considerable confidence that the statistical evidence points strongly to discrimination as an important factor in the labor market.[22]

14.5

---

[19] Derek Neal and William Johnson, "The Role of Premarket Factors in Black–White Wage Differences," *Journal of Political Economy,* October 1996, pp. 869–95. Also see Donal O'Neill, Olive Sweetman, and Dirk Van de Gaer, "The Impact of Cognitive Skills on the Distribution of the Black–White Wage Gap," *Labour Economics,* June 2006, pp. 343–56.

[20] See David Card and Thomas Lemieux, "Wage Dispersion, Returns to Skill, and Black–White Wage Differentials," *Journal of Econometrics,* October 1996, pp. 319–61.

[21] For evidence that the lower mathematical content of women's college majors helps explain why female college graduates earn less than their male counterparts, see Catherine J. Weinberger, "Mathematical College Majors and the Gender Gap in Wages," *Industrial Relations,* July 1999, pp. 407–13. See also Charles Brown and Mary Corcoran, "Sex-Based Differences in School Content and the Male–Female Wage Gap," *Journal of Labor Economics,* Part 1, July 1997, pp. 431–65.

[22] Barbara R. Bergmann, *The Economic Emergence of Women,* 2nd ed. (New York: Palgrave Macmillan, 2005), p. 54.

14.5	**World of Work**	The Gender Pay Gap: Slowing Convergence*

After being relatively constant for 30 years, the gender pay gap started to narrow in the 1980s. As shown in Figure 14.1, the female–male ratio in hourly wages rose from 65.6 percent in 1980 to 73.6 percent in 1990, a rise of 8 percentage points. During the next decade, the ratio rose only another 3.5 percentage points to 77.1 percent by 2000. A similar rate of convergence has occurred since 2000 as the ratio rose by another 2.8 percentage points to 79.8 percent by 2006.

Using data from 1979 to 1998, Blau and Kahn investigated the reasons for the slowdown in the convergence in the gender pay gap. They found that a slower rate of increase in women's measured characteristics in the 1990s than the 1980s accounted for roughly one-quarter of the slowdown. In particular, occupational upgrading by women and diminishing of the gender difference in unionization contributed to the shrinking gap in both decades, but to a substantially smaller degree in the 1990s. Interestingly,

the human capital of women increased by a similar amount in both decades and thus did not contribute to the slowdown.

Blau and Kahn assert that the main cause of the slowdown in convergence is that the portion of the gender wage gap that can't be explained by measured worker characteristics declined at a much slower rate in the 1990s. They suggest that three factors are behind this slowdown. First, gender differences in unmeasured worker characteristics diminished at a slower rate in the 1990s than in the 1980s. Second, labor market discrimination against women dropped at a slower pace in the 1990s than in the 1980s. Third, labor demand and labor supply shifts favored women more in the 1980s than during the 1990s.

* Based on Francine D. Blau and Lawrence M. Kahn, "The U.S. Gender Pay Gap: Slowing Convergence," *Industrial and Labor Relations Review*, October 2006, pp. 45–66.

14.4

Quick Review

- Some economists contend that the inferior economic position of women has resulted mainly from educational decisions, occupational choices, interrupted careers, and other voluntary choices made by women.
- Other economists stress discrimination as the root cause of the inferior economic position of women; discriminatory outcomes help explain the economic choices made by women.
- After sorting out nondiscriminatory sources, empirical studies typically find a large, unexplained residual difference in pay by gender and race; many researchers attribute most of this residual to discrimination.
- Controversy remains on the question of how successfully empirical studies have isolated true discriminatory outcomes.

Your Turn

On average, women have less mathematical and quantitative training than do men. Jobs demanding high levels of such training often pay exceptionally high salaries. Relate these factors to each of the arguments made in the first two review points here. (*Answers:* See page 599.)

ANTIDISCRIMINATION POLICIES AND ISSUES

There are several avenues through which government might attack the problem of discrimination.[23] One very general policy is to achieve a tight labor market through the use of appropriate monetary and fiscal policies. On one hand, an expanding economy makes it increasingly expensive for employers to indulge their tastes for discrimination. On the other hand, tight labor markets help to overcome stereotyping. For example, the overfull employment of World War II simultaneously created new labor market opportunities for minorities and women and made it clear that females and African–Americans could effectively perform jobs that heretofore had been closed to them.

A second general policy is to improve the education and training opportunities of those who have been discriminated against. For example, upgrading the quantity and quality of schooling received by African–Americans will enable them to become more competitive with white workers.

The third and most obvious means of dealing with discrimination is through direct governmental intervention. We will focus on this aspect of policy.

Direct governmental intervention has stressed equal employment opportunities for minorities and for women. The purpose has been to deal directly with labor market inequalities by prohibiting certain practices in hiring, promotion, and compensation. Table 14.4 provides a summary of the salient legislation and policies that are the focal point for our discussion.

Equal Pay Act of 1963

This was the first major federal act to deal with sex discrimination. The act makes it illegal for employers to pay men and women different wage rates if they "do equal work on jobs, the performance of which requires equal skill, effort and responsibility, and which are performed under similar working conditions." Although the *Equal Pay Act of 1963* was clearly a landmark piece of legislation, it did not comprehensively deal with all forms of gender discrimination. In particular, we have seen that women workers

TABLE 14.4
A Summary of Antidiscrimination Laws and Policies Relating to Gender and Race

Equal Pay Act of 1963
Mandates equal pay for women and men who perform the same, or highly similar, jobs.

Civil Rights Act of 1964, Title VII
Seeks to eliminate discrimination based on race, gender, color, religion, or national origin in hiring, promoting, firing, and compensating workers.

Executive Orders (1965–1968)
Prohibit federal contractors from discriminating among workers on the basis of race, gender, color, religion, or national origin; require affirmative action programs for firms that underuse women and minorities.

---

[23] For a more detailed discussion of antidiscrimination policies, see Barbara Bergmann, *The Economic Emergence of Women,* 2nd ed., chaps. 7 and 8, op. cit., and her *In Defense of Affirmative Action* (New York: Basic Books, 1996).

are plagued with the problem of occupational segregation as indicated by the crowding model. A discriminating employer could simply dodge the provisions of the act by practicing strict occupational segregation—that is, by *not* employing women and men in the same jobs. In fact, an employer with an all-male labor force would be in compliance with the law.

Civil Rights Act of 1964

Title VII of the *Civil Rights Act of 1964* is the centerpiece of U.S. antidiscrimination policy. This law applies to not only discriminatory wages but also discrimination in hiring and promotions. Specifically, the act made it illegal for any employer "to refuse to hire or to discharge any individual, or otherwise to discriminate against any individual with respect to his compensation, terms, conditions, or privileges or employment, because of such individual's race, color, religion, sex, or national origin." By requiring equal treatment in hiring, firing, promotion, and compensation (including fringe benefits), the law virtually eliminated the ability of employers to practice overt discrimination legally. As amended, the act applies to all employers in interstate commerce with 15 or more workers, to all labor unions with 15 or more members, and to workers employed by educational institutions, state and local governments, and federal agencies. Enforcement rests primarily with the Equal Employment Opportunity Commission (EEOC).

Executive Orders and Federal Contracts

Executive orders issued in 1965 and 1968 attempted to eliminate all discriminatory policies that might be practiced by businesses or other institutions holding government contracts. Thus the executive order of 1968 specifies,

> The contractor will not discriminate against any employee or applicant for employment because of race, color, religion or national origin. The contractor will take *affirmative action* to ensure that applicants are employed, and that employees are treated during employment, without regard to their race, color, religion, sex or national origin. Such action shall include, but not be limited to the following: employment, upgrading, demotion, or transfer; recruitment or recruitment advertising; layoff or termination; rates of pay or other forms of compensation; and selection for training, including apprenticeship.

As revised, the executive orders require firms with contracts totaling $50,000 or more to develop *affirmative action programs.* If on examination it is found that a firm underuses women and minorities compared to their proportions in the available labor force, the firm must establish a program embodying numerical goals and timetables for increasing its employment of women and minorities. In a series of important decisions in 1986 and 1987 involving, among others, sheet metal workers in New York City, firefighters in Cleveland, and the Alabama state police, the Supreme Court upheld the constitutionality of affirmative action programs. More recently, however, the Court's decisions have upheld the constitutionality of affirmative action plans but have limited their scope. For example, in 2003 the Court ruled that the University of Michigan's policy of assigning 20 points to every minority undergraduate applicant out of a possible 150 points necessary to guarantee admission was unconstitutional. However, in another case the Court ruled that the University of Michigan law school, which reviewed applications individually, was permitted to ensure that a "critical mass" of minority students was accepted for admission. On the political scene, in the 1990s voters in the states of California and Washington passed constitutional amendments that ended all state programs giving racial and gender preferences in government hiring and contracting as well as public education. The states of Florida and Michigan instituted similar bans in 2000 and 2006, respectively. It is fair to say that affirmative action is under legal and political attack.

Have Antidiscrimination Policies Worked?

Over the past four decades, there have been increases in the African–American to white and female to male earnings ratios.[24] How much of these increases are explained by antidiscrimination policy? Before an assessment can be made, it is important to isolate the effect of antidiscrimination policies from other factors and policies that might have impacted the relative economic status of women, African–Americans, and whites.

14.6

Three factors other than antidiscrimination policies may have caused the observed rise in the African–American white earnings ratio.[25] First, there was an increase in the quality of education of African–Americans relative to whites during this period. One study estimates that 5–20 percent of the increase in the earnings ratio is due to the improvements in quality of education.[26] Second, the average level of schooling rose relatively more among African–Americans than whites. This rise in schooling has been estimated to account for 20–25 percent of the increase in the earnings ratio.[27] Third, there was a large decline in the labor force participation of low-income African–Americans, which caused the earnings ratio of the remaining workers to rise. This factor has been estimated to account for 10–20 percent of the rise in the earnings ratio.[28]

The unexplained portion of the rise in the African–American to white earnings ratio ranges from 35 to 65 percent. It is difficult to directly attribute the unexplained portion of the increase in the earnings ratio to antidiscrimination policies. However, a couple of factors indicate that antidiscrimination policies played an important role. First, most of the increase in the earnings ratio occurred between 1960 and 1975, when antidiscrimination

---

[24] Note that nearly all of the rise in the African–American to white earnings ratio occurred in the 1960s, and early 1970s, and most of the increase in the female to male earnings ratio took place in the 1980s and early 1990s.

[25] For more about these factors, see John J. Donohue III and James J. Heckman, "Continuous versus Episodic Change: The Impact of Civil Rights Policy on the Economic Status," *Journal of Economic Literature,* December 1991, pp. 1603–43.

[26] David Card and Alan B. Kreuger, "School Quality and Black–White Earnings: A Direct Assessment," *Quarterly Journal of Economics,* February 1992, pp. 151–200.

[27] James P. Smith and Finis Welch, "Black Economic Progress after Myrdal," *Journal of Economic Literature,* June 1989, pp. 519–64.

[28] Donohue and Heckman, op. cit. For a study finding an even larger impact of selective withdrawal from the labor force, see Amitabh Chandra, "Labor-Market Dropouts and the Racial Wage Gap: 1940–1990," *American Economic Review,* May 2000, pp. 333–38.

14.6 World of Work

Orchestrating Impartiality*

Until recently, members of the major symphony orchestras in the United States were mostly hand-picked by the music director. Though the hiring process involved an audition before the conductor and the section leader, most of the applicants were male students of a small group of instructors. As a result, the typical symphony orchestra was less than 10 percent female.

During the 1970s and 1980s, orchestras changed their hiring procedures to make the process more open and systematic. Job openings became widely advertised, and audition committees were expanded to include orchestra members. To increase impartiality, they adopted use of heavy cloth screens descending from the ceiling to hide the identity of the person auditioning. Some orchestras even use a carpet on the stage to muffle footsteps that could reveal the gender of the applicant.

After the change in hiring procedures, there was a substantial increase in the female proportion of major orchestras. At the five highest-ranked orchestras, the female percentage now ranges from 20 to 35 percent. The fraction of new hires that are female is even higher. The empirical evidence indicates that one-quarter to one-third of the rise in the female proportion is due to the use of screens in the audition process.

* Based on Claudia Goldin and Cecilia Rouse, "Orchestrating Impartiality: The Impact of 'Blind' Auditions on Female Musicians," *American Economic Review,* September 2000, pp. 715–41.

policies were instituted. Second, the largest increase in the earnings ratio occurred in the South. This is where antidiscrimination enforcement was initially concentrated and the earnings gap was largest.[29]

The picture painted by the empirical literature on the impact of affirmative action is a bit clearer.[30] Leonard[31] has concluded from a series of studies that affirmative action led to improvements in the employment opportunities of both minorities and females between 1974 and 1980 but that this progress largely ended in the 1980s. Specifically, he statistically compared the changes in the demographic composition of the workforce in more than 68,000 firms, isolating the role of affirmative action by controlling for other factors that might have brought about these changes in demographic composition.

---

[29] Donohue and Heckman, op. cit. For additional evidence that federal antidiscrimination efforts improved the economic situation of African–Americans, see Kenneth Y. Chay, "The Impact of Federal Civil Rights Policy on Black Economic Progress: Evidence from the Equal Employment Opportunity Act of 1972," *Industrial and Labor Relations Review,* July 1998, pp. 608–32.

[30] For a survey of the effects of affirmative action, see Harry Holzer and David Neumark, "Assessing Affirmative Action," *Journal of Economic Literature,* September 2000, pp. 483–568.

[31] Jonathan S. Leonard, "The Impact of Affirmative Action on Employment," *Journal of Labor Economics,* October 1984, pp. 439–63; and Leonard, "Women and Affirmative Action," *Journal of Economic Perspectives,* Winter 1989, pp. 61–75.

Between 1974 and 1980, female and minority shares of employment grew faster in firms obligated to undertake affirmative action than in establishments not subject to this requirement. In this period affirmative action increased the demand for African–American males by 6.5 percent, for other minority males by 11.9 percent, and for white females by 3.5 percent.

But the positive effects of affirmative action apparently ended during the 1980s, when the government's enforcement slackened under the Reagan administration. Leonard reports that, after accounting for other factors, the employment shares of African–Americans actually grew less rapidly over the 1980–1984 period in companies required to practice affirmative action than in firms not covered by the law.

A final comment: We can be quite certain that controversy will continue to surround not only the scope and techniques of antidiscrimination policies but also the question of their actual effectiveness.[32] But these debates should not obfuscate the clear reality that discrimination in America continues to influence labor supply and demand—and therefore wage rates and the allocation of labor. An understanding of discrimination and antidiscrimination policies is essential to a realistic conception of how labor markets work.

Chapter Summary

1. Empirical data suggest that *(a)* the earnings of full-time female and African–American workers are substantially less than those of white male workers; *(b)* African–Americans have higher unemployment rates than whites; *(c)* occupational distributions differ significantly by gender and race; *(d)* there are gender and racial differences in human capital acquisition; and *(e)* women and African–Americans have lower total earnings than white men at each level of educational attainment.

2. Discrimination occurs when female or African–American workers—who have the same abilities, education, training, and experience as male or white workers—are accorded inferior treatment with respect to hiring, occupational access, promotion, or wage rate.

3. Forms of labor market discrimination include wage, employment, occupational, and human capital discrimination.

4. According to Becker, some white employers have a "taste for discrimination" that can be measured by the discrimination coefficient d. Prejudiced white employers will be indifferent to hiring African–Americans only when the wage rate of African–Americans is less than that of whites by the monetary value of d.

[32] For a discussion of seven misperceptions regarding affirmative action, see Roland G. Fryer Jr. and Glenn C. Loury, "Affirmative Action and Its Mythology," *Journal of Economic Perspectives,* Summer 2005, pp. 147–62.

In supply and demand form, the model indicates *(a)* that a decline in the discrimination coefficient will increase the ratio of African–American to white wages and increase African–American employment, and *(b)* that the size of the African–American to white wage differential will vary directly with the supply of African–American workers.

5. The theory of statistical discrimination indicates that because detailed information concerning the potential productivity of job applicants is costly to obtain, profit-seeking employers base employment decisions on the perceived characteristics of groups of workers. The imputation of group characteristics to individuals discriminates against many individuals within those groups.

6. The crowding model focuses on occupational segregation. Using supply and demand analysis, it demonstrates that occupational crowding results in lower wages for women (African–Americans), higher wages for men (whites), and a net loss of domestic output. The index of occupational segregation measures the percentage of women or men who would have to change occupations for the occupational distribution of women to be the same as for men. The index for the United States has declined significantly since 1973.

7. Much disagreement exists about the extent to which earnings differentials based on gender or race are rooted in discrimination per se as opposed to rational decision making by women and African–Americans.

8. Economists have found several nondiscriminatory factors that help explain gender and racial pay differentials. Nevertheless, even after these factors are accounted for, large unexplained pay disadvantages for African–Americans and women remain. Many economists attribute these unexplained pay differences to discrimination.

9. Governmental antidiscrimination legislation, policies, and proposals involving direct labor market intervention include the Equal Pay Act of 1963, the Civil Rights Act of 1964, and executive orders applicable to federal contractors.

10. Statistical evidence suggests that antidiscrimination policy has reduced the racial pay gap. There is also evidence indicating that affirmative action programs have increased African–American employment and earnings in affected industries.

Terms and Concepts

nondiscriminatory factors, *431*

discrimination, *432*

wage discrimination, *432*

employment discrimination, *433*

occupational or job discrimination, *433*

human capital discrimination, *433*

taste for discrimination model, *435*

discrimination coefficient, *435*

statistical discrimination, *440*

crowding model, *442*

index of segregation, *445*

Equal Pay Act of 1963, *454*

Civil Rights Act of 1964, *455*

affirmative action programs, *455*

Questions and Study Suggestions

1. What has been the general secular trend of the weekly earnings of full-time female workers compared to male workers? What factors help explain this trend?

2. Women have increased the amount of education they have achieved relative to men, and average years of schooling completed are now approximately the same for males and females. Human capital theory predicts that this would close the male–female earnings gap. In fact, this has not happened. How can you explain it?

3. In Becker's taste for discrimination model, what is the meaning of the discrimination coefficient d? If the monetary value of d is, say, $3 for a given white employer, will that employer hire African–American or white workers if their actual wage rates are $8 and $10, respectively? Explain. In Becker's model, what effect would a decrease in the supply of African–American labor have on the African–American to white wage ratio and the employment of African–American workers? Use the model to explain the economic effects of an increase in employer prejudice. What are the basic public policy implications of this model?

4. What is statistical discrimination and why does it occur? The theory of statistical discrimination implies that discrimination can persist indefinitely, whereas the taste for discrimination model suggests that discrimination will tend to disappear. Explain the difference.

5. Use simple supply and demand analysis to explain the impact of occupational segregation or "crowding" on the relative wage rates of men and women. Who gains and who loses as a consequence of eliminating occupational segregation? Explain the following statement: "A gender-blind labor market would allocate labor more efficiently throughout the economy, and productivity would be higher on average."

6. Explain the following statement: "In the taste for discrimination model, discrimination is practiced even though it is costly to do so. But in the statistical discrimination model, it is clear that discrimination pays."

7. Assume that the occupational distribution of males and females is as follows:

Occupation	Male	Female
E	60%	5%
F	20	5
G	10	40
H	10	50

Calculate the index of segregation and explain its meaning. Compare the meaning of an index of 0.40 with indexes of 1.00 and 0. As applied to gender, has the index changed significantly over time?

8. Is the following statement true or false? If it's false, explain why. "The unemployment rates for white females and African–American men are considerably higher than the rate for white men."

9. Table 14.2 reveals significant earnings differences by gender and race at each level of education. What nondiscriminatory factors might explain part of the earnings differences between females and males? Between African–Americans and whites? Do you think that nondiscriminatory factors explain all the earnings differences in the table?

10. In what way does discrimination redistribute national income? How does it reduce national income?

11. There has been considerable controversy over the fact that certain pension plans into which males and females make equal contributions pay smaller monthly benefits to women than to men on the grounds that women live longer on average than men. Is this practice discriminatory? Explain. The use of female military personnel in most forms of ground combat is currently prohibited. Do you favor this ban?

12. It has been argued that to correct the inequalities of past discrimination, African–Americans and females should be given preference in employment and promotion. Do you agree? In the famous *Bakke* case, the plaintiff argued that he had been unjustly denied admission to medical school because less qualified African–American applicants were given preference under a quota system. Evaluate the plaintiff's argument: "To discriminate in favor of one individual or group is necessarily to discriminate against some other individual or group." Do you agree?

13. "Wage differences between men and women reflect not discrimination but rather differences in job continuity and rational decisions with respect to education and on-the-job training." Explain why you agree or disagree.

14. Some economists have argued that the unemployment effects associated with the minimum wage have been greater for African–Americans than for whites. Explain why this might be the case.

15. Critically evaluate each of the following statements:

    a. "Affirmative action plans have not worked; there is no evidence that they have increased African–American or female employment and wages."

    b. "The greatest barriers to economic equality between men and women are marriage and children."

16. Although the labor market opportunities for women have improved greatly over the past 30 years, poverty has become increasingly concentrated among women. How can you reconcile these two developments?

Internet Exercise

What Has Happened to the Female–Male Earnings Ratio?

Go to the Census Bureau Historical Income Web site (**http://www.census.gov/hhes/www/income/histinc/histinctb.html**). Under the Current Population Survey heading, click on "People." Then click on "Women's Earnings as a Percentage of Men's Earnings by Race and Hispanic Origin." This will retrieve a historical series of the female/male median earnings ratio.

What are the earnings ratios for 1979, 1995, and the most recent year shown? What was the change in the ratio between 1979 and 1995? What might explain this change? What is the change in the ratio between 1995 and the most recent year?

Internet Links

Harvard University's Project Implicit Web site offers a quiz to test one's conscious and unconscious preferences on over 90 different topics ranging from pets to ethnic groups **(https://implicit.harvard.edu/implicit/research/)**.

The U.S. Equal Employment Opportunity Commission Web site provides detailed information about laws prohibiting discrimination **(http://www.eeoc.gov/)**.

Nonprofit organizations set up to fight discrimination include the Anti-Defamation League **(http://www.adl.org/)**, National Organization for Women **(http://www.now.org/)**, and the National Association for the Advancement of Colored People **(http://www.naacp.org/)**.

Chapter 15

Job Search: External and Internal

A large amount of job switching occurs in the labor market. Nearly two-thirds of young people will work for three or more different employers in their first five years of work experience.[1] Nearly 20 percent of all workers have been with their current employers for less than one year.[2] Individuals also switch jobs without changing employers.

Individuals search for jobs for a variety of reasons. Firms may suffer a decrease in demand and lay off workers who then search for new employment. New high school and college graduates will search for their first permanent employment. Individuals who dropped out of the labor force to raise children may reenter the job market. Workers may search for jobs that are a better match with their abilities.[3] For a given occupation, earnings and other working conditions differ widely within a city or even a firm.[4] As a result, workers search for jobs that offer them better combinations of wages and job characteristics.

Our discussion of the job search process will proceed as follows: We first analyze how workers attempt to find jobs at a new employer (external job search). Then we address the issue of job search within a firm (internal job search) and develop the notion of internal labor markets in some detail.

---

[1] Henry S. Farber, "The Analysis of Interfirm Worker Mobility," *Journal of Labor Economics,* October 1994, pp. 554–93.

[2] Henry S. Farber, "Mobility and Stability: The Dynamics of Job Change in Labor Markets," in Orley Ashenfelter and David Card (eds.), *Handbook of Labor Economics,* Volume 3B (Amsterdam: North-Holland, 1999).

[3] For an analysis of the job matching process, see Boyan Jovanovic, "Job Matching and the Theory of Turnover," *Journal of Political Economy,* October 1979, pp. 972–90; Derek Neal, "The Complexity of Job Mobility among Young Men," *Journal of Human Resources,* April 1999, pp. 237–61; and Margaret Stevens, "Earnings Functions, Specific Human Capital, and Job Matching: Tenure Bias Is Negative," *Journal of Labor Economics,* October 2003, pp. 783–805.

[4] For evidence on the variation in wages, see Stephen G. Bronars and Melissa Famulari, "Wage, Tenure, and Wage Growth Variation within and across Establishments," *Journal of Labor Economics,* April 1997, pp. 285–317.

EXTERNAL JOB SEARCH

Two major characteristics of the labor market contribute to the need for people to search for the best job offer and for firms to search for employees to fill job vacancies. First, as we indicated in our earlier discussion of the wage structure (Chapter 8), workers and jobs are highly heterogeneous. Personalities, levels of motivation, capabilities, and places of residence differ greatly even though individuals may possess similar levels of education, training, and experience. Jobs also are often unique: Employers pay differing wages, offer varying opportunities for advancement, and provide various working conditions, even for similar workers.

Second, market information about such differences in individuals and jobs is imperfect and takes time to obtain. Therefore, job seekers—many of whom are not working elsewhere—and prospective employers find it is in their respective interests to search for information about each other as a way to improve the terms of the transaction. People who are not employed and who are actively seeking work or "job shopping" are officially unemployed. Because there are continuous *flows* to and from the labor force and between jobs, the *stock* of unemployed people is simultaneously being diminished and replenished.[5]

Both expected gains and costs are associated with acquiring job information. Let's examine each in terms of a ***job search model***.[6] Let's assume the job searcher is unemployed and seeking work.[7] Also suppose that the person recognizes that the heterogeneous nature of jobs and employers, together with imperfect market information, generates a wide variance of likely wage offers for his or her occupation. Further assume that this person faces the distribution of wage offers shown in Figure 15.1. This frequency distribution is interpreted as follows: The horizontal axis measures the various wage offers, higher offers being farther to the right; and the vertical axis shows the relative frequency of offers at each wage level. For example, the frequency with which wage offers occur in the lowest *a* to *b* range will be .05. Stated differently, 5 percent of wage offers will be in this range; similarly, 15 percent of the wage offers will fall within the slightly higher *b* to *c* range, 30 percent in the still higher *c* to *d* range, and so on.

Next we assume that this person can roughly estimate the mean and variance of the frequency distribution of wage offers but has no way of knowing which employer has a job opening or which employer is offering which wage. In other words, the worker knows the cards in the deck but recognizes that they have been thoroughly shuffled.[8]

---

[5] See Chapter 18 for a more complete discussion of the definition of unemployment and the stock–flow model of the labor market.

[6] For a nontechnical discussion of a job search model and the empirical estimation of such a model, see Adam M. Zaretsky and Cletus C. Coughlin, "An Introduction to the Theory and Estimation of a Job Search Model," *Federal Reserve Bank of St. Louis Review,* January–February 1995, pp. 53–65.

[7] Only about 20 percent of new hires come directly from another job. For an analysis of job search by employed workers, see Joseph R. Meisenheimer II and Randy E. Ilg, "Looking for a 'Better' Job: Job Search Activity of the Employed," *Monthly Labor Review,* September 2000, pp. 3–14.

[8] Arthur M. Okun, *Prices and Quantities: A Macroeconomic Analysis* (Washington, DC: Brookings Institution, 1981), p. 27.

FIGURE 15.1   Wage Offers, the Acceptance Wage, and Unemployment

Given this frequency distribution of nominal wage offers and the person's acceptance wage W_a, she or he will reject all offers lower than c and accept any offer between c and g. The probability that a specific offer will exceed the acceptance wage is 80 percent (.30 + .30 + .15 + .05). During the period of search for an acceptable wage offer, this person is unemployed.

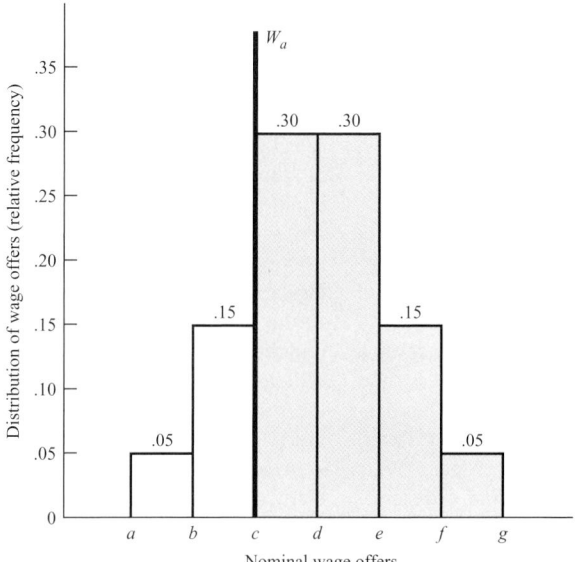

How will job search benefit this worker? Because this person is unemployed, he or she does not have an immediately available wage opportunity. A job search allows people to obtain wage offers and increases the likelihood of discovering wage opportunities in the rightward areas of the distribution shown in Figure 15.1.

And what are the costs of gaining job information? They include costs of such things as "for hire" notices in newspapers and other publications, fees paid to employment agencies, and transportation to and from interviews. But job search also includes significant opportunity costs. For instance, suppose this person searches for one job offer at a time, either getting an offer or not, and if the former, either accepting it or rejecting it before continuing to search for other offers. If this person receives and rejects an offer, that wage opportunity is lost; most wage offers cannot be "stored." Therefore, *a major cost of continued job search is the forgone earnings of the best known opportunity.* As higher wage offers are received, the *marginal* cost of continued search rises.

What decision rule might this person employ in accepting or rejecting a particular wage offer? One approach is to establish a reservation wage (Chapter 2) or, in this context, an *acceptance wage* and reject any wage offer that falls below it. But how would one rationally select such a wage? Theoretically, if a person knows the frequency distribution in Figure 15.1 and can estimate the cost of generating new job offers, she or he can find the wage that equates the expected marginal benefit (MB) and expected marginal cost (MC) from search. If the job seeker is offered an hourly wage above this acceptance wage,

15.1	**World of Work**	Job Search and the Internet*

The explosive growth in the Internet is transforming the job search process. There are now over 3,000 job search sites and 29 million job openings (some are not unique) listed on the Internet. The major job posting site, Monster.com, indicated that 186 million job seekers visited its site and posted 16.4 million new résumés in 2005.

Job posting sites have several advantages over traditional newspaper help-wanted ads. They are easier to search, contain more job openings, and are possibly more current. The cost to employers to advertise open positions is lower. The cost of a 30-day advertisement on Monster.com is less than 5 percent of the cost of a one-time job advertisement in the Sunday edition of *The New York Times*. Job posting sites can also help match employers with job seekers. Software can compare descriptions of open positions with the available résumés. If a suitable match occurs, both parties can be notified.

The Internet is currently used in 15 percent of job searches by unemployed people. Half of those with access to the Internet use it in their job search. The Internet is now used more frequently than traditional approaches such as using private employment agencies and contacting friends or relatives.

The use of the Internet in the job search process is expected to yield significant economic benefits. Job searchers may be able to find jobs more quickly and at less personal expense. The streamlined search could reduce the unemployment rate, although current research does not find that to be true. Productivity should rise because there will be a better match of available jobs with job seekers. The impact on job turnover, however, is unclear. On one hand, better matches between employers and employees should reduce worker turnover. On the other hand, the Internet makes it easier for employed workers to search for a new job, so turnover may rise. In fact, 7 percent of employed workers report that they regularly use the Internet to search for a new job.

* Based on Peter Kuhn and Mikal Skuterud, "Job Search Methods: Internet versus Traditional," *Monthly Labor Review*, October 2000, pp. 3–11; David Autor, "Wiring the Labor Market," *Journal of Economic Perspectives*, Winter 2001, pp. 25–40; and Peter Kuhn and Mikal Skuterud, "Internet Job Search and Unemployment Durations," *American Economic Review*, March 2004, pp. 218–32.

that person will conclude that it is not worthwhile to continue searching (MB < MC); if offered a wage below this amount, the person will reject the offer and continue to look for new offers because the expected marginal benefit of the activity exceeds the expected extra cost (MB > MC).

This optimal acceptance wage is shown as the vertical line W_a in Figure 15.1. The shaded area of the frequency distribution indicates the probability that any single offer will be above the acceptance wage. In this case, the probability is 80 percent (= .30 + .30 + .15 + .05). The probability that this person will accept any wage offer in the c to g range is 100 percent, and the probability that she or he will accept offers in the 0 to c range is zero. During the period of searching for a wage offer that exceeds the acceptance wage, this person is actively seeking work and therefore is officially unemployed. Because of the continuous nature of the labor force flows in the economy, this type of unemployment is always present.

15.1   Several important implications arise from our search model. We will examine two in detail and then briefly list several others.

FIGURE 15.2   **The Impact of Unexpected Inflation on Job Search**

Unexpected inflation results in higher nominal wage offers, and the frequency distribution shifts from that shown in (a) to that seen in (b). Because this person's acceptance wage initially remains at W_a, he or she is more likely to accept the next wage offer—a probability of 95 percent versus 80 percent—and hence the length of job search falls. But once people recognize that the nominal wage offers are no higher in real terms than previously, they adjust their acceptance wages (for example, W_a to W_a'), and the job search length returns to normal.

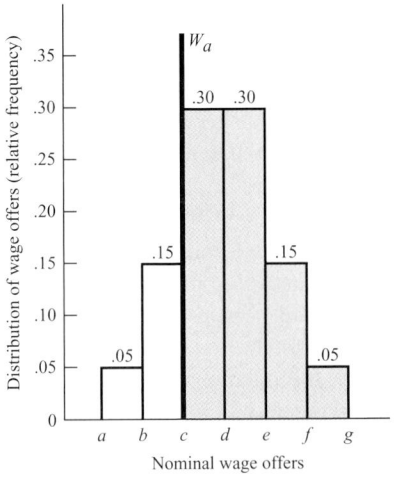

(a) Initial distribution of wage offers

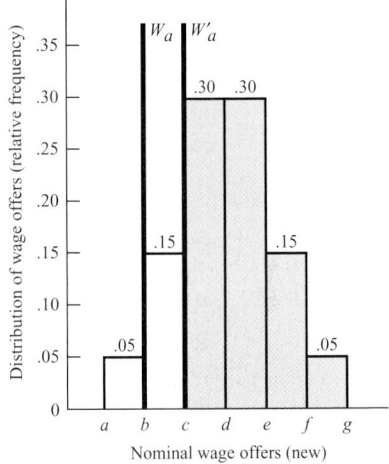

(b) Higher distribution of nominal wage offers

Inflation and Job Search

Will inflation change how long people search for jobs? To answer this question, we assume initially that the rate of inflation is zero and that the economy is operating at its natural levels of output and employment. Now suppose expansionary fiscal and monetary policies increase aggregate demand so that the general price level rises by 5 percent. Also assume that increases in nominal wage offers match this increase in the price level so that real wage offers remain unchanged.

Figure 15.2(a) repeats the frequency distribution of wage offers discussed previously, indicating again that, given the acceptance wage W_a, the probability that the job searcher will accept any specific offer is 80 percent. But now observe from graph (b) that the entire frequency distribution has shifted rightward because nominal wage offers are now 5 percent higher than previously. What impact will this shift have on a person's length of job search? Let's examine two distinct circumstances.

1 Expected Inflation

If the job searcher represented by Figure 15.2(a) and (b) fully anticipates the 5 percent rate of inflation, she or he will simply raise the acceptance wage by 5 percent to keep it constant in real terms. This is shown in graph (b) as the rightward shift of line W_a to W_a'. In this case the worker's expectation that inflation will rise by 5 percent offsets the

5 percent increase in the nominal wage distribution and leaves the probability that any specific wage offer will be accepted at 80 percent (= .30 + .30 + .15 + .05).

To generalize: When the actual rate of inflation matches the expected rate, job searchers will *not* be influenced by the inflation. Their average length of job search will remain constant and, therefore, the unemployment level will stay at the natural rate.

2 Unexpected Inflation

Suppose the present rate of inflation is zero and our job searcher expects this price stability to continue. Also suppose that in the short run, this person does not adjust her expectation to the reality of higher inflation. Under these circumstances, the 5 percent inflation will lead our unemployed job seeker to reduce her search time. As a result, unemployment will decline temporarily below its natural rate.

This is easily demonstrated in Figure 15.2. Expecting inflation to be zero, this individual holds the acceptance wage rate at W_a. But the 5 percent inflation shifts the wage distribution rightward as shown in Figure 15.2(b). We observe that the probability that a new wage offer will be accepted increases from 80 percent to 95 percent (= .15 + .30 + .30 + .15 + .05). This person's duration of job search therefore falls; and if this pattern is widespread, unemployment declines. But according to this **adaptive expectations theory,** the unemployment decline will be short-lived. In the long run, unemployed job searchers will adjust their expectations of future inflation to the actual 5 percent rate. Consequently, they will increase their acceptance wages and lengthen their job searches, causing the unemployment rate to return to its natural level.

Generalization: Actual rates of inflation that exceed expected rates may temporarily reduce unemployment below its natural rate.

Unemployment Compensation and Job Search

A second major implication of our search model is that unemployment benefits provided by government, past employers, or both will increase the extent of unemployment by enabling unemployed people to search for higher wage offers at less *net* cost.[9] Recall that a person's acceptance wage is established at the level where the expected gain from more search just equals the expected cost. Quite understandably, the presence of unemployment compensation increases one's acceptance wage because it *reduces* the expected *net* cost of searching for a higher wage offer. The opportunity cost of continued search is reduced to the existing highest offer minus the unemployment benefits. As portrayed in Figure 15.3, an individual who qualifies for unemployment benefits may have an acceptance wage W'_a rather than W_a, and given the distribution of wage offers, the

---

[9] This is *not* to suggest that such programs are undesirable; in fact, one expressed purpose of these payments is to allow workers to search for positions commensurate with their skills and experience, rather than being forced through economic necessity to take jobs in which they are underemployed. Also, much unemployment occurs in the form of layoffs, and unemployment compensation cushions the decline in earnings while workers wait to be called back.

FIGURE 15.3   **The Impact of Unemployment Benefits on Unemployment**

Unemployment benefits reduce the net opportunity cost of rejecting wage offers and continuing to search for higher-paying employment and thus allow people to increase their acceptance wages. For the person shown, the increase in the acceptance wage from W_a to W_a' means that the probability of receiving an acceptable wage offer in the next attempt falls from 80 to 20 percent $(.15 + .05)$. The length of job search and the amount of unemployment therefore rise.

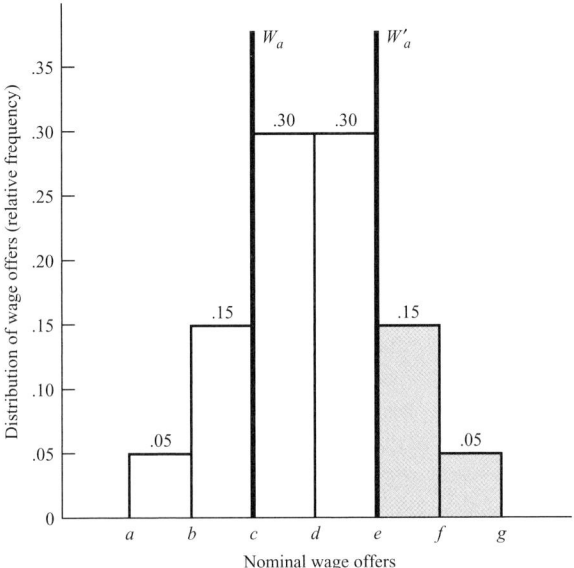

probability that this person will accept the next job offer falls to 20 percent $(= .15 + .05)$ compared to the previous probability of 80 percent $(= .30 + .30 + .15 + .05)$. This person's optimal length of job search therefore increases, and the overall rate of unemployment in the economy rises.

Other Implications of the Search Model

Let's briefly consider several other important implications of the job search theory. First, a prospective worker may not accept the initial job offer or even seek available jobs that pay below the acceptance wage. This fact helps explain the presence of numerous unfilled job vacancies in the presence of considerable overall unemployment. Second, the longer the expected length of tenure on the job, the higher a person's acceptance wage, all else being equal. For instance, suppose a person expects to be employed in a new job for 20 years. The anticipated gain from searching for a high wage offer is greater in this case, and the acceptance wage higher, than if the job searcher expects to work only a month or two for the new employer. Third, random luck will play a part in the wage and earnings distribution in the economy (Chapter 16). One person may receive the highest wage offer in the frequency distribution on the first try; another may get a lower offer, continue to search, and finally accept an offer above the acceptance wage but below the highest wage in the distribution. Fourth, the level of unemployment is partly a function of the overall demand for labor. During recessions, the length of time required to discover each wage offer rises because so few firms are hiring workers. Also, if job searchers perceive a recession to be temporary, they may retain their acceptance wages, thereby prolonging their job search and contributing to a rise in unemployment.

Empirical Evidence

There have been two major strands in studies of the job search process. One line has focused on determinants of the acceptance wage and the other on the length of the job search. Several patterns have emerged regarding the acceptance wage. The acceptance wage falls with time unemployed as individuals become more realistic about the available wage offers.[10] The acceptance wage rates also fall—one estimate is by 15 percent—when people exhaust their unemployment benefits.[11] More highly educated and union workers have a higher acceptance wage.[12] African–American male youth tend to have higher acceptance wages than white male youth.[13] Wealthy people have a somewhat higher acceptance wage.[14]

In a summary of the available evidence, Devine and Kiefer conclude that most studies find that the average acceptance rate of offers is between 80 and 100 percent.[15] Thus most of the variation in the rate of exiting from unemployment results from variations in the rate at which workers receive offers, not from variations in acceptance rates.

Numerous empirical studies indicate that unemployment insurance lengthens the job search process. The consensus estimate is that a 10 percent increase in real monthly unemployment benefits on average lengthens a person's unemployment duration by one-half to one week.[16] Other research is consistent with this finding. Studies using data from other countries show that higher unemployment benefits increase unemployment

[10] Nicholas M. Kiefer and George R. Neumann, "An Empirical Job Search Model with a Test of the Empirical Reservation Wage Hypothesis," *Journal of Political Economy,* February 1979, pp. 89–107.

[11] Raymond Fishe, "Unemployment Insurance and the Reservation Wage of the Unemployed," *Review of Economics and Statistics,* February 1982, pp. 12–17.

[12] Keifer and Neumann, op. cit.

[13] Harry J. Holzer, "Reservation Wages and Their Labor Markets Effects for Black and White Male Youth," *Journal of Human Resources,* Spring 1986, pp. 157–77. Although black male youth have higher acceptance wages, that does not explain their longer duration of unemployment. See Stephen M. Petterson, "Black–White Differences in Reservation Wages and Joblessness: A Replication," *Journal of Human Resources,* Summer 1998, pp. 758–70.

[14] Hans G. Bloemen and Elena G. F. Stancanelli, "Individual Wealth, Reservation Wages, and Transitions into Employment," *Journal of Labor Economics,* April 2001, pp. 400–39.

[15] Theresa J. Devine and Nicholas M. Kiefer, "The Empirical Status of Job Search Theory," *Labour Economics,* June 1993, pp. 3–24.

[16] For a review of some of these studies, see Bruce D. Meyer, "Lessons from U.S. Unemployment Insurance Experiments," *Journal of Economic Literature,* March 1995, pp. 99–131. Also see Peter Fredriksson and Bertil Holmlund, "Improving Incentives in Unemployment Insurance: A Review of Recent Research," *Journal of Economic Surveys,* July 2006, pp. 357–86.

duration.[17] Lengthening the period for which recipients may collect unemployment benefits raises unemployment duration.[18] Finally, the probability of finding work rises sharply after unemployment benefits have ended.[19]

Other factors also influence the duration of job search. African–Americans tend to have a longer job search than whites. Though union workers have a higher acceptance wage, there is only weak evidence that they have a longer job search than nonunion workers.[20] Older workers tend to have longer job searches than younger workers. This likely occurs because they face a wider range in wage offers than younger workers and thus the return to job search is greater.[21]

**15.1
Quick
Review**

- The unemployed worker looking for work determines an acceptance wage based on the expected marginal costs and marginal benefits of longer searches. If a given wage offer exceeds the acceptance wage, the person takes the job; if the wage offer is less than the acceptance wage, the individual rejects the offer.

Your Turn

How do unexpected inflation, anticipated inflation, and unemployment insurance each affect the optimal length of a person's job search? (*Answer:* See page 599.)

INTERNAL LABOR MARKETS

A strict interpretation of neoclassical theory evokes the notion of an auction market in which workers are openly and continuously competing for jobs *and,* conversely, firms persistently bid to attract and retain labor services. Orthodox theory assumes that the firm, as an institution, poses no obstacle or barrier to the competitive pressures of the labor market. It is assumed that the wage rates of every type of labor employed by the firm are determined by market forces. Therefore, the wage structures of all firms employing the same types of workers would be identical. Workers would have access to jobs at all skill levels for which they are qualified, and mobility between firms would be unimpeded and extensive.

---

[17] A positive relationship between unemployment compensation and unemployment duration has been found in Germany. See Jennifer Hunt, "The Effects of Unemployment Compensation on Unemployment Duration in Germany," *Journal of Labor Economics,* January 1995, pp. 88–120. For evidence of the impact of unemployment insurance in Austria, see Rafael Lalive, Jan van Ours, and Josef Zweimuller, "How Changes in Financial Incentives Affect the Duration of Unemployment," *Review of Economic Studies*, October 2006, pp. 1009–38.

[18] Stepan Jurajda and Frederick J. Tannery, "Unemployment Durations and Extended Unemployment Benefits in Local Labor Markets," *Industrial and Labor Relations Review,* January 2003, pp. 324–48. Also see Jan C. van Ours and Milan Vodopivec, "How Shortening the Potential Duration of Unemployment Benefits Affects the Duration of Unemployment: Evidence from a Natural Experiment," *Journal of Labor Economics,* April 2006, pp. 351–78.

[19] Lawrence Katz and Bruce Meyer, "Unemployment Insurance, Recall Expectations, and Unemployment Outcomes," *Quarterly Journal of Economics,* November 1990, pp. 993–1002.

[20] Devine and Kiefer, op. cit.

[21] Solomon W. Polachek and W. Stanley Siebert, *The Economics of Earnings* (Cambridge, England: Cambridge University Press, 1993), pp. 235–36.

15.2	World of Work	Are Long-Term Jobs Vanishing?*

In earlier generations, a worker typically held a long-term job with one firm. But today's workers don't expect to remain with their current employers for the rest of their careers. Between 1983 and 1998, the expected remaining job tenure (how long a worker expects to continue working for his current employer) for the average full-time male worker fell from 18.6 to 14.7 years. The same pattern held for women. Their expected remaining job tenure fell from 15.9 years in 1983 to 12.8 years in 1998.

There has also been a drop in the percentage of workers who are holding long-term jobs. Between 1983 and 2006, the percentage of men 25 and older who had been with their current employers for 10 or more years fell by almost 7 percentage points. The corresponding figure for women rose by nearly 4 percentage points. Men of all age groups experienced a decline in the percentage working 10 years or longer for the same employers. The largest declines were for men aged 40 to 49 and 60 to 64. For women aged 40 to 54, the percentage of women with 10 years or more of tenure rose, but it fell for all other age groups. The rise in the proportion of long-term jobs for women

aged 40 to 54 probably is the result of the increasing labor market attachment of women in recent decades, which more than offsets the trend toward reduced job tenure.

What has caused job tenure to decrease? First, the shift from manufacturing jobs to service sector jobs has tended to reduce job tenure. The median tenure for workers in manufacturing is two years more than for their service sector counterparts. Second, rapid technological progress during the past two decades has decreased job tenure. Between 1983 and 2000, workers in industries that experienced larger increases in productivity growth tended to have lower job tenure. New technologies reduce job tenure by replacing unskilled jobs with machines and making skilled jobs more complex.

* Based on Kristie M. Engemann and Michael T. Owyang, "Your Current Job Probably Won't Be Your Last," *Federal Reserve Bank of St. Louis National Economic Trends,* February 2004; and Leora Friedberg and Michael Owyang, "Explaining the Evolution of Pension Structure and Job Tenure." Working Paper 2002-022b, Federal Reserve Bank of St. Louis, October 2002. Updated.

But critics of orthodox theory contend, and many mainstream economists increasingly agree, that this portrayal is sorely at odds with the real world. The public schoolteacher, the skilled machinist, and the government bureaucrat, to cite but a few, are *not* faced with the daily prospect of being displaced from their jobs by someone who is equally capable and who is willing to work for a slightly lower salary. Workers enjoy "job rights," and employers seek to maintain stable workforces. Although there is considerable occupational and geographic mobility in our economy, the average worker's employment is in fact quite stable. Farber has calculated that among workers aged 35 to 64, 35 percent have been with their current employers 10 or more years.[22] Even for women—who sometimes have problems achieving access to more desirable jobs (Chapter 14)—some 30 percent have been working for the same employers for more than a decade. Indeed, perhaps as much as 50 percent of the workforce participates in "internal labor markets"

[22] Farber, 1999, op. cit.

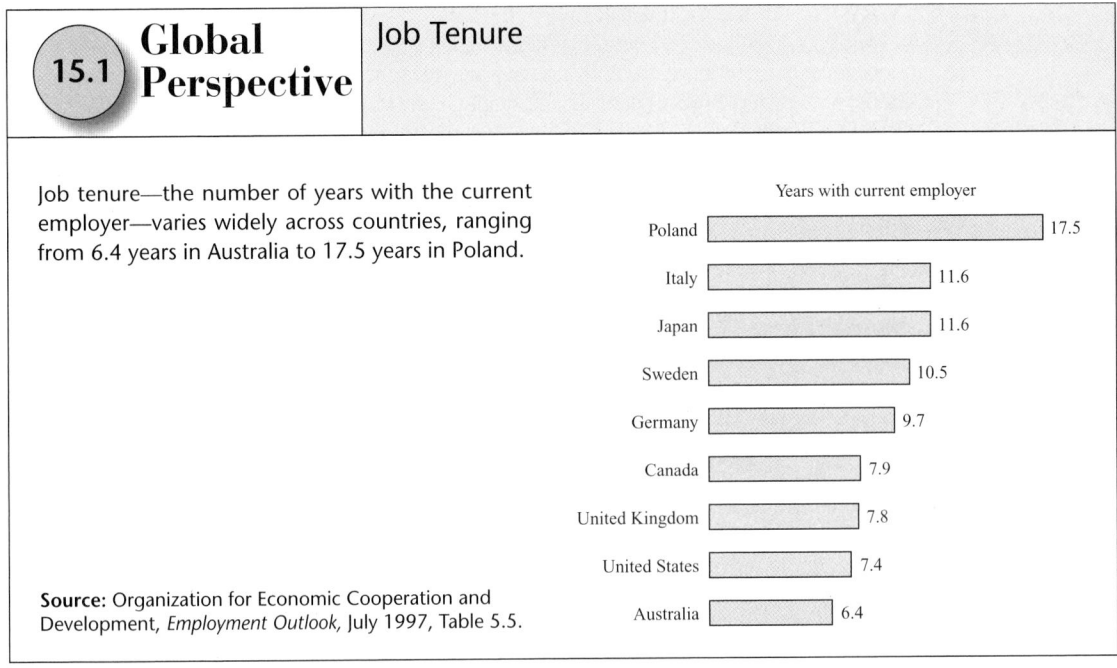

15.1	**Global Perspective**

Job Tenure

Job tenure—the number of years with the current employer—varies widely across countries, ranging from 6.4 years in Australia to 17.5 years in Poland.

Years with current employer

Country	Years
Poland	17.5
Italy	11.6
Japan	11.6
Sweden	10.5
Germany	9.7
Canada	7.9
United Kingdom	7.8
United States	7.4
Australia	6.4

Source: Organization for Economic Cooperation and Development, *Employment Outlook,* July 1997, Table 5.5.

15.1

in which they are substantially shielded from the competitive pressures of the "external labor market."[23]

Characteristics of Internal Labor Markets

What is an internal labor market? How and why do such markets evolve? What are their implications? An ***internal labor market*** is "an administrative unit, such as a manufacturing plant, within which the pricing and allocation of labor is governed by a set of administrative rules and procedures" rather than by economic variables.[24] Within many firms we find more or less elaborate hierarchies of jobs, each of which centers on a certain skill (machinist), a common function (building maintenance), or a single focus of work (the computer). Furthermore, each job hierarchy entails a sequence or progression

---

[23] W. Stanley Siebert and John T. Addison, "Internal Labour Markets: Causes and Consequences," *Oxford Review of Economic Policy,* Spring 1991, pp. 76–92.

[24] Peter B. Doeringer and Michael P. Piore, *Internal Labor markets and Manpower Analysis* (Lexington, MA: D. C. Heath and Company, 1971). The Doeringer and Piore book is a comprehensive discussion of the evolution and character of internal labor markets. For a series of papers analyzing various aspects of internal labor markets, see Isao Ohashi and Toshiaki Tachibanaki (eds.), *Internal Labour Markets, Incentives, and Employment* (New York: St. Martin's Press, 1998). For a critical assessment of internal labor market theory, see George Baker and Bengt Holmstrom, "Internal Labor Markets: Too Many Theories, Too Few Facts," *American Economic Review,* May 1995, pp. 255–59.

FIGURE 15.4 An Internal Labor Market

A worker typically enters an internal labor market at the least skilled port-of-entry job in the job ladder or mobility chain. Whereas the wage rate of the port-of-entry job will be strongly influenced by the forces of demand and supply in the local external labor market, wage rates and the allocation of workers within the internal labor market are governed primarily by administrative rules and procedures.

Source: *Adapted from* Robert M. Fearn, *Labor Economics: The Emerging Synthesis* (Cambridge, MA: Winthrop Publishers, Inc., 1981), p. 142.

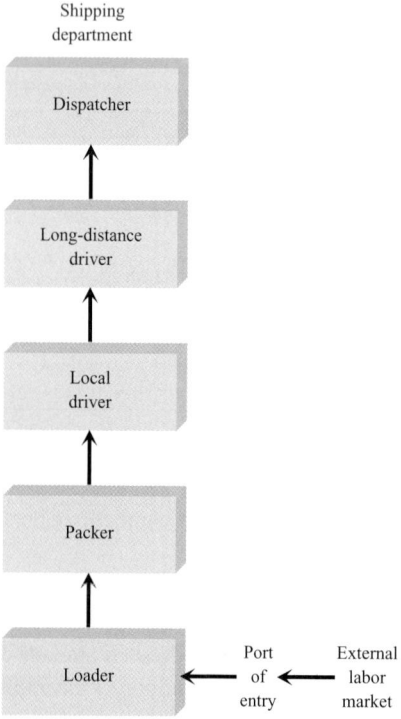

of jobs that forms what is called a mobility chain or *job ladder.* As suggested by Figure 15.4, a new worker will typically enter this job ladder as a trainee in the least skilled job at the bottom of the ladder. The position at which workers gain access to the job ladder is called, for obvious reasons, a *port of entry.* It is through the port of entry that the sequence of jobs that constitutes the job ladder makes contact with the *external labor market.* This external labor market is the "auction market" of orthodox theory. That is, in recruiting workers to fill vacancies for the least skilled position in a job ladder, the firm must compete with other firms that are hiring the same kind of labor. Whereas the market forces of supply and demand may be paramount in determining the wage rate paid for the port-of-entry position, market forces are held to be superseded by administrative rules and procedures in explaining the wages paid for other jobs constituting the job ladder of the internal labor market. The point to be stressed is that within the internal labor market, institutionalized rules and procedures, along with custom and tradition, are foremost in determining how workers are allocated in the job hierarchy and what wage rates they are paid.

Reasons for Internal Labor Markets

Why do internal labor markets exist? The basic answer to this question is that firms typically encounter significant costs in recruiting and training workers, and these costs can be minimized by reducing labor turnover. Let's first consider the matter of training. Internal labor market theorists contend that many job skills are unique and specific to individual enterprises:

> Almost every job involves some specific skills. Even the simplest custodial tasks are facilitated by familiarity with the physical environment specific to the workplace in which they are performed. The apparent routine operation of standard machines can be importantly aided by familiarity with a particular piece of operating equipment. . . . Moreover, performance in some production and most managerial jobs involves a team element, and a critical skill is the ability to operate effectively with the given members of the team. This ability is dependent upon the interaction of the personalities of the members, and the individual's work "skills" are specific in the sense that skills necessary to work on one team are never quite the same as those required on another.[25]

The specificity of job skills and technology to individual firms means that workers require *specific training* that is most efficiently acquired on the job. The cost of such training, you will recall from Chapter 4, is borne by the employer. But to obtain a return on this investment in human capital, the employer must *retain* specifically trained workers *over time*. The job ladder—the core characteristic of internal labor markets—is the mechanism by which the desired workforce stability is achieved.

Advantages to Employers

The mutual advantageousness of the internal labor market to both the firm and the workers merits further comment. As just noted, the reduction of worker turnover increases the return the firm receives on its investments in specific training. Furthermore, the amount of training a firm needs to provide will be reduced by the presence of the internal labor market. If the firm fills a vacancy from the external labor market, it will have to finance *all* of the specific training the worker requires. It can avoid much of this cost by simply promoting an internal applicant who, by virtue of having worked for the firm for some time, has already acquired a portion of the specific training that is prerequisite to the job opening. Similarly, recruitment costs will be larger if a position is filled from the external labor market. The firm—even after interviewing and screening—will have only limited knowledge about the quality of workers in the external labor market. But it will have accumulated a great deal of information about members of its present workforce. Thus promoting from within will greatly reduce recruitment and screening costs and lessen the chances of making an error in filling the job. Another advantage of the

---

[25] Doeringer and Piore, pp. 15–16.

internal labor market to the firm is that the existence of a clearly defined job ladder will provide an incentive for its existing workforce to be disciplined, productive, and continuously motivated to seek new skills. That is, the internal labor market will help solve the principal–agent problem discussed in Chapter 7. Finally, and related, internal labor market configurations may induce greater employee identification with the goals of the organization. Osterman asserts that "this heightened commitment may in turn lead to more effort, more attention to quality, lower turnover rates, and other behaviors which enhance productivity."[26]

Advantages to Workers

Internal labor markets also confer advantages on workers who are accepted into them. Workers who are admitted receive benefits in the form of enhanced job security and built-in opportunities for job training and promotion. Workers need not leave the firm to secure better jobs but rather may ascend a well-defined sequence of jobs that constitute the job ladder. Furthermore, those in the internal labor market are shielded from the competition of workers in the external labor market. In addition, the formalization and codification of the rules and procedures governing both worker allocation and wage rates within the internal labor market protect workers from favoritism and capricious managerial decisions. Workers in internal labor markets are more likely to enjoy due process and equitable treatment with respect to layoffs, promotion, and access to training opportunities.[27]

The Role of Unions

Although the presence of a labor union can accelerate the development of internal labor markets, the cause–effect relationship is rather complicated. Internal labor markets tend to invite unionization; conversely, unions promote or accelerate the evolution of internal labor markets.

On one hand, several reasons make an internal labor market conducive to unionization. First, the enhanced stability of the labor force resulting from an internal labor market promotes unionization. A fluid, unstable workforce is an obstacle to organization, but a stable group of workers develops a community spirit and perhaps a common set of grievances that lead to formalization through a union. Second, workers in internal labor markets possess specific training that endows them with considerable bargaining power. Remember: Employers must retain specifically trained workers to realize a return on their human capital investments. It is only natural that workers might want to express this bargaining power collectively through a union. Finally, the administrative rules and procedures that prevail in the internal labor market define quite clearly the scope and

---

[26] Paul Osterman, "Internal Labor Markets in a Changing Environment: Models and Evidence," in David Lewin, Olivia S. Mitchell, and Peter D. Sherer (eds.), *Research Frontiers in Industrial Relations and Human Resources* (Madison, WI: Industrial Relations Research Association, 1992), pp. 273–337.

[27] For more about the potential benefits of internal labor markets to both employers and employees, see Peter B. Doeringer, "Internal Labor Markets and Noncompeting Groups," *American Economic Review,* May 1986, pp. 48–56. Michael J. Carter and Susan B. Carter detail two interesting case studies of the evolution of internal labor markets in their "Internal Labor Markets in Retailing: The Early Years," *Industrial and Labor Relations Review,* July 1985, pp. 586–98.

character of managerial decisions. Unionization is a logical response to instances where managerial actions are at odds with customary rules and procedures.

On the other hand, the presence of a union can be important in reinforcing the development of an internal labor market. A written collective bargaining agreement codifies, formalizes, and makes more rigid the rules and procedures that prevail in the functioning of an existing internal labor market.

Labor Allocation and the Wage Structure

Let's consider in more detail the promotion process—the allocation of labor—*and* the determination of wages within the internal labor market. The critical point to recall is that in the internal labor market, the pricing and allocation of labor are determined not by the forces of supply and demand but rather by administrative rules and procedures. Thus in the case of promotions, the typical administrative rule is that, other things being roughly equal, the worker who has been on a particular rung of a job ladder for the longest time will be promoted to the next rung when an opening occurs. That is, promotions are generally determined on the basis of *seniority.* Seniority is typically tempered, however, by the presumed ability of the individual to perform the job satisfactorily after a trial period. In short, the rules indicate that the "right" to the promotion resides with the most experienced worker, not necessarily the most able worker available from either the internal or the external labor market. Similarly, layoffs are allocated on the basis of reverse seniority: The newest workers are laid off first (Chapter 18).

The wage structure within an internal labor market is also determined by administrative procedures, through custom and tradition, and by the pattern of mobility that is sought. In terms of Figure 15.4, how should the wage rate of a packer in the shipping department, for example, compare with that of a local driver? Frequently a system of job evaluation is used to establish the wage rate attached to each job in a job ladder. *Job evaluation* is a procedure by which jobs are ranked and wage rates assigned in terms of a set of job characteristics and worker traits. Table 15.1 shows an illustrative job evaluation scheme where points have been assigned, undoubtedly with some degree of arbitrariness, to various job

TABLE 15.1
Model Job Evaluation System

Source: Peter B. Doeringer and Michael J. Piore, *Internal Labor Markets and Manpower Analysis* (Lexington, MA: D. C. Heath and Company), p. 67.

Factor		Maximum Points
Working conditions		15
Noise	5	
Dirt	5	
Smell	5	
Responsibility for equipment		25
Responsibility for other workers		20
Skill		20
Manual dexterity	10	
Experience	10	
Education		35
Physical effort		10
Total		125

characteristics and traits. Thus, using this system, the actual points assigned to a packer's job and a driver's job might be 50 and 75, respectively. This ranking implies that the wage rate of a driver should be 50 percent higher than that of a packer. For example, if packers receive $8 per hour, then drivers should be paid $12. Note in particular that in the internal labor market, wage rates frequently are attached to jobs rather than individuals. Internal labor market theorists are suggesting in effect that productivity often resides in jobs rather than in workers. Also observe that administrative procedure has supplanted the forces of demand and supply.

Once established, custom and tradition intervene to make the internal wage structure rigid: "Any wage rate, set of wage relationships, or wage setting procedure which prevails over a period of time tends to become customary; changes are then viewed as unjust or inequitable, and the work group will exert economic pressure in opposition to them."[28] Recalling the notion of equitable comparisons, we should note that custom and rigidity evolve around wage *relationships* as opposed to specific wage *rates.*

The wage structure is not determined in isolation from the allocative function of the internal labor market. One important constraint is that the wage structure must foster and facilitate the internal allocation of labor that the employer seeks. "The wage on every job must be high enough relative to the job or jobs from which it is supposed to draw its labor and low enough relative to the jobs to which it is supposed to supply labor to induce the desired pattern of internal mobility."[29] In Figure 15.4 the wage of the packer must be sufficiently higher than that of a loader so that the latter will aspire to become the former.

The Efficiency Issue

The question of whether internal labor markets are efficient is intriguing and important. The basic premise of orthodox economics is that competitive pressures result in the efficient use of labor and other inputs. When competition prevails, any given firm must combine labor and other productive resources in the most efficient way, or it will be driven out of business by other firms that are efficient. But the critical feature of the internal labor market is that aside from port-of-entry jobs, workers are shielded from competition. Wages in internal labor markets are determined not by market forces but by rather arbitrary administrative procedures embodied in job evaluation, through custom and tradition, and so forth. Thus, say orthodox economists, it would be only by chance that the various kinds of workers would be paid in accordance with their productivities. Furthermore, workers are promoted (allocated) largely on the basis of seniority, rather than in terms of worker ability (productivity). More senior workers may or may not be more productive than some junior workers. These characteristics imply that the existence of internal labor markets conflicts with society's interest in allocative efficiency.

---

[28] Doeringer and Piore, op. cit., p. 85.

[29] Ibid., p. 78. For a study analyzing the problems pay compression can cause for an internal labor market, see Sherwin Rosen, "The Military as an Internal Labor Market: Some Allocation, Productivity, and Incentive Problems," *Social Science Quarterly,* June 1992, pp. 227–37.

But for several reasons most internal labor market theorists and some mainstream economists rebut this line of reasoning. Internal labor markets and the wage structures embodied in them may exist precisely because they efficiently allocate labor.

In the first place, recall that the internal labor market decreases labor turnover, reducing the costs of training, recruitment, screening, and hiring. Of particular significance, the job ladders of internal labor markets give the employer abundant information about the quality of its workers. Therefore, the firm is less likely to promote a nonproductive worker if it selects that worker from within the internal labor market. In comparison, hiring from the external labor market is based on more limited information, which may increase the risk of obtaining an unproductive worker. It is also noteworthy that the use of seniority in the allocation of labor is *not* necessarily at odds with efficiency. The worker who has been on the job the longest is probably a suitable candidate for promotion. Also, only in a very few instances is internal labor market promotion based *solely* on seniority. The senior worker with the requisite ability and an acceptable performance record typically gets promoted, rather than simply the most senior employee.[30]

A second reason that internal labor markets may be efficient centers on the distinction between static and dynamic efficiency. **Static efficiency** refers to the combining of labor and other resources *of given quality* in the most efficient (least costly) way. **Dynamic efficiency,** on the other hand, has to do with increases in productive efficiency that arise from *improvements in the quality* of labor and other resources. For present purposes, the relevant contention is that internal labor markets promote dynamic efficiency, which is held to be of greater consequence than realizing static efficiency. The gain from using *existing* skills of workers more efficiently is a "one-shot" gain, whereas the gains from *improving* worker knowledge and skills can go on indefinitely.[31] Furthermore, internal labor markets are conducive to dynamic efficiency because providing a greater amount of security to more skilled senior workers makes those workers willing to pass along their knowledge and skills to less skilled colleagues. Highly skilled senior workers will want to conceal their knowledge from less skilled junior workers *if* the latter can become competitors for the formers' jobs. But seniority rules and other security provisions embodied in internal labor markets guarantee that this will not happen. If senior workers are assured that they have priority in promotions, that their wages will not be reduced as more workers acquire knowledge of their jobs, and that they will be the last to be laid off, then senior workers will be amenable to sharing their skills with fellow workers. Internal labor markets may provide these assurances.

Finally, some economists point out that the pay structures within typical internal labor markets may be effective incentive-generating devices, particularly in large firms where it is difficult to monitor the work effort of employees. The wage structure of the internal labor market may be such that not only are senior workers paid more than junior workers, but also senior workers are paid more than their marginal revenue products

[30] Noted, however, that length of service frequently takes priority over ability and performance in promotion. See D. Quinn Mills, "Seniority versus Ability in Promotion Decisions," *Industrial and Labor Relations Review,* April 1985, pp. 421–25.

[31] Lester Thurow, *Investment in Human Capital* (Belmont, CA: Wadsworth Publishing Company, 1970), pp. 194–95.

(MRPs), while junior workers are paid less than their MRPs.[32] The "premium" paid to senior workers is an inducement for younger employees to work hard. By being productive, young workers demonstrate to employers that they deserve to be retained and to progress up the job ladder to higher-paying jobs in which they, too, will enjoy the premium of a wage rate in excess of their MRPs. Young workers presumably accept wages that are initially less than their MRPs for the privilege of participating in a labor market where in time the reverse will be true. This wage structure is also appealing to young workers in that it offers the prospect of higher lifetime earnings. The greater work effort and higher average worker productivity that result from this wage structure increase the firm's profits, in which workers may share through wage bargaining.[33]

15.2 *Quick Review*	• Evidence indicates that many people work for the same employers for numerous years and, in effect, "search" for improved pay and job characteristics through promotions and reassignments within their existing firms. • Internal labor markets are characterized by hierarchies of jobs called job ladders, which workers enter via ports of entry. Only the wages at the ports of entry are truly market-based. • Some economists think that internal labor markets contribute to inefficiency because wages are determined by rigid administrative procedures and rules. • Other economists argue that internal labor markets enhance productivity by (a) reducing recruitment, screening, and training costs; (b) inducing senior workers to share their skills and knowledge with junior workers; and (c) providing younger workers with greater incentives to work productively. **Your Turn** Have you worked in a firm that has a clearly defined job ladder? If so, how much upward mobility did you observe along the ladder? (*Answer:* See page 599.)

Chapter Summary

1. Job search is a natural and often constructive occurrence in a dynamic economy characterized by heterogeneous workers and jobs and by imperfect information.

2. The rational job seeker forms an acceptance wage at a level where the expected marginal costs and benefits of continued search are equal and then compares this wage to actual wage offers.

---

[32] This implies a relationship between wage rate and MRPs that is just the opposite of that shown in Figure 4.8(b).

[33] Edward P. Lazear, "Agency, Earnings Profiles, Productivity, and Hours Restriction," *American Economic Review,* September 1981, pp. 606–20; Lazear, "Why Is There Mandatory Retirement?" *Journal of Political Economy,* December 1979, pp. 1261–84; and Lazear and Sherwin Rosen, "Rank-Order Tournaments as Optimum Labor Contracts," *Journal of Political Economy,* October 1981, pp. 841–64. See also Michael L. Wachter and Randall D. Wright, "The Economics of Internal Labor Markets," *Industrial Relations,* Spring 1990, pp. 240–62.

3. Fully anticipated inflation has no impact on the optimal length of job search because job seekers will adjust their acceptance wages upward at the same rate that nominal wage offers rise. But if job searchers mistakenly view inflation-caused rises in nominal wage offers as real wage increases, they will shorten their job search, and unemployment will temporarily fall.

4. Unemployment benefits extend the optimal length of job search by reducing the net opportunity cost of continuing to seek still higher wage offers.

5. Most firms and plants embody internal labor markets in which wages and the allocation of labor are determined by administrative rules and procedures rather than strictly by supply and demand.

6. Internal labor markets entail hierarchies of jobs called job ladders, which focus on a certain job skill, function, or technology. Having entered the job ladder through a port of entry, internal labor market workers are largely shielded from the competitive pressure of external labor markets.

7. Internal labor markets exist because they generate advantages for both employers and workers. For employers, internal labor markets reduce worker turnover and thereby increase the return on specific training and reduce recruitment and training costs. For workers, internal labor markets provide job security, opportunities for training and promotion, and protection from arbitrary managerial decisions.

8. By providing labor force stability, internal labor markets attract unions; conversely, unions promote and accelerate the development of internal labor markets.

9. It is unclear whether internal labor markets diminish or enhance productive efficiency.

Terms and Concepts

job search model, *464*
acceptance wage, *465*
adaptive expectations theory, *468*

internal labor market, *473*
job ladder, *474*
port of entry, *474*
external labor market, *474*

seniority, *477*
job evaluation, *477*
static and dynamic efficiency, *479*

Questions and Study Suggestions

1. What are the benefits and costs of job search? Why don't job seekers endlessly search for a higher wage offer?

2. What is meant by the term *acceptance wage?* How does a job seeker determine his or her acceptance wage? Why might the acceptance wage for one new college graduate differ from that of another new college graduate?

3. Explain how each of the following would affect the probability that a job searcher will accept the next wage offer and thus affect the expected length of his or her unemployment: *(a)* a decline in the rate of inflation below the expected one and *(b)* a decrease in unemployment benefits.

4. How do you explain the existence of internal labor markets? What are their advantages to employers? To workers?

5. How does a worker search for a better job in an internal labor market? What is the employer's search process within internal labor markets?

6. Explain the following statement: "Unions are both a consequence and a cause of internal labor markets." Why might the presence of internal labor markets in a firm encourage unionization?

7. Do you think internal labor markets enhance or detract from efficiency? How might one argue that the realization of dynamic efficiency is more important than achieving static efficiency? Do you agree?

Internet Exercise

What Is Happening to Long-Term Job Tenure?

Go to the Bureau of Labor Statistics Current Population Survey Web site **(http://www.bls.gov/cps/home.htm)**. Click on "Employee Tenure" under the heading "Economic News Releases."

Go to the table that presents the percentage of workers with 10 years or more of tenure. What are the percentages of all workers with 10 years or more of tenure in 1983 and the most recent year shown? How has job stability changed based on this measure? Replicate the same analysis for men and women. What might explain the gender difference in the change in job stability?

Internet Link

Monster.com is the world's largest job search Web site **(http://www.monster.com/)**.

16

The Distribution of Personal Earnings

Thus far our focus has been mainly on microeconomic aspects of labor markets. Specifically, we have discussed in some detail the labor market decisions of individuals, families, and firms. As illustrated in Figure 1.1, the next three chapters examine the *macroeconomics* of labor markets. Recall that macroeconomics deals with broad aggregates or collections of specific economic units treated as if they were one. The topics in these three chapters include the personal distribution of earnings, aggregate labor productivity, and employment and unemployment.

The micro–macro distinction is clearly evident in the present chapter, where our attention turns away from an analysis of specific wages and toward an examination of the ***distribution of personal earnings.*** This distribution is the national pattern of the shares of individual wage earnings. How unequal is the distribution of wages and salaries? What general factors explain the observed pattern? How much mobility is there within the overall distribution? Why has this distribution become more unequal over the past three decades?

In pursuing these questions we first will discuss alternative ways of describing the earnings distribution and measuring the degree of observed inequality. Second, we will examine theories that help explain the distribution pattern of U.S. earnings. Our focus then shifts to personal earnings mobility, or movements within the aggregate earnings distribution. The chapter concludes with a discussion of the trend toward greater inequality in the earnings distribution over the past 30 years.

DESCRIBING THE DISTRIBUTION OF EARNINGS

The degree of inequality in the distribution of earnings can be described in several ways. Let's examine two graphic portrayals: the frequency distribution and the Lorenz curve.

FIGURE 16.1 **The Distribution of Annual Earnings for Full-Time Wage and Salary Workers**

The personal distribution of annual earnings is highly unequal and is skewed to the right. The histogram (absolute frequency distribution) of earnings is characterized by (1) much bunching around the mode, (2) an extended rightward tail, and (3) a mean (arithmetic average) that exceeds the median (half above, half below).

Source: Author calculations from the March 2006 *Current Population Survey.*

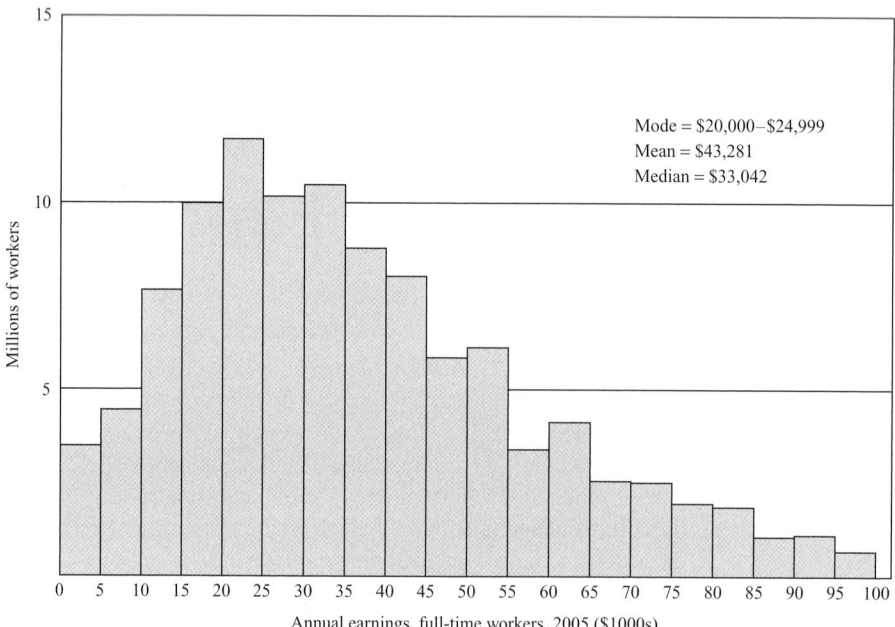

Mode = $20,000–$24,999
Mean = $43,281
Median = $33,042

Millions of workers

Annual earnings, full-time workers, 2005 ($1000s)

Frequency Distribution

The distribution of annual earnings received by full-time U.S. workers in 2005 is shown in Figure 16.1. This *absolute frequency distribution*—or *histogram*—shows the number of full-time wage and salary workers (measured on the vertical axis) whose annual earnings fell within each $5,000 earnings range shown on the horizontal axis. For example, the third bar from the left represents earnings within the $10,000–$14,999 range. We know from the height of this bar that about 7.7 million people had annual earnings in this category in 2005. Or as a second example, the bar representing the $55,000–$59,999 earnings range tells us that 3.4 million people received work income between $55,000 and $59,999 in 2005.

It is equally common to represent the distribution of income in terms of *relative* frequencies, in which case the vertical axis is converted to percentage of total earners rather than being the *absolute* number of such workers, as shown here.

Three measures of location, or central tendency, are commonly used to summarize histograms or absolute frequency distributions such as that in Figure 16.1. The *mode* is the income category occurring with the greatest frequency. The *mean* is the arithmetic average, obtained by dividing the total earnings by the number of workers. Finally, the *median* is the amount of annual work income received by the individual who stands at the midpoint of the array of earnings. Half of those earning wages and salaries receive more than the median, while the other half receive less. With these definitions in mind, note from Figure 16.1 that the distribution of annual earnings for full-time U.S. workers is concentrated around a single leftward mode ($20,000 to $24,999 in 2005); has a median level of earnings ($33,042 in 2005) that is to the right of the mode; and possesses a mean, or average ($43,281 in 2005), that is greater than both the mode and median. The mean exceeds the median because the average is pulled upward by the extremely high earnings of the relatively few workers who have earnings in the long rightward tail of the histogram. This tail is so long that our truncated diagram prevents it from reaching the horizontal axis. These characteristics correctly suggest that most U.S. workers receive earnings in the leftward two-thirds of the overall distribution, while some people receive extraordinarily large annual earnings relative to the median and mean.

Lorenz Curve

The degree of earnings inequality can also be shown by a *Lorenz curve,* such as the one portrayed in Figure 16.2. This curve indicates the *cumulative* percentage of all full-time wage and salary earners from left to right on the horizontal axis and the corresponding

FIGURE 16.2   The Lorenz Curve for Annual Earnings
The Lorenz curve is a useful way of summarizing the distribution of earnings. Line *af* represents perfect equality in the distribution, while the Lorenz curve *abcdef* illustrates the actual earnings distribution for 2005. The greater the area between the line of perfect equality and the Lorenz curve, the more unequal the distribution of earnings.

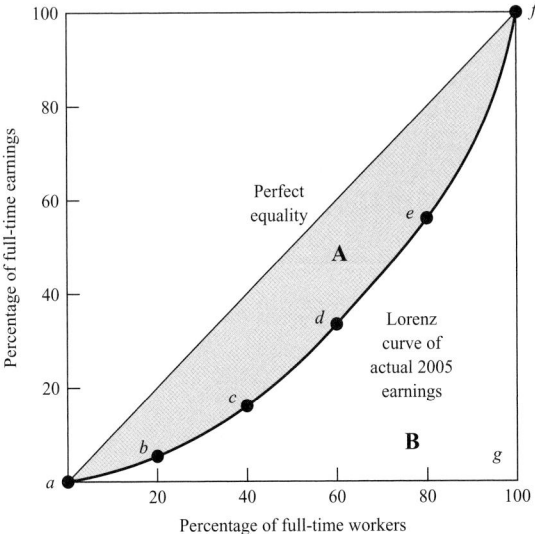

FIGURE 16.3 **The Distribution of Annual Wage and Salary Earnings for Full-Time U.S. Workers**

Over 40 percent of total earnings among full-time workers are received by the top 20 percent of earners.

Source: Author calculations from the March 2006 *Current Population Survey.*

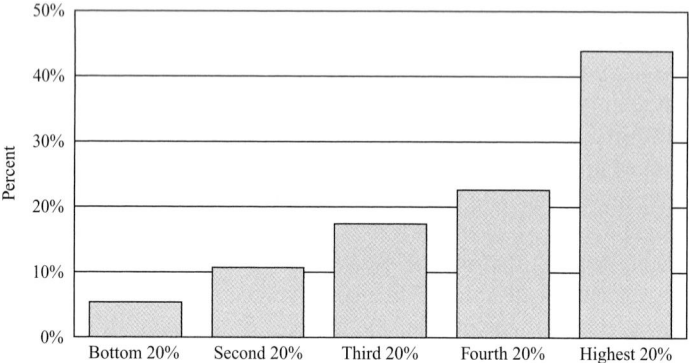

cumulative percentage of the total earnings accruing to that percentage of earners on the vertical axis. If each full-time worker received the average earnings, the Lorenz curve would be the diagonal (45°) line that bisects the graph. Twenty percent of all full-time earners would receive 20 percent of all earnings, 40 percent of the workers would get 40 percent, and so forth. All these points would fall on the diagonal line that we appropriately label *perfect equality.*

The actual Lorenz curve in Figure 16.2 is derived by plotting the data for 2005 from Figure 16.3. This figure shows the percentages of total earnings accruing to five numerically equal groups, or *quintiles.* For 2005 we see that the bottom 20 percent of all full-time workers received 5.4 percent of the total earnings, which plots as point *b* on the Lorenz curve. The bottom 40 percent of the earners received 16.1 percent (= 5.4 + 10.7) of the total earnings, which yields point *c* on the curve, and so forth. The shaded area between the diagonal line of perfect equality of earnings and the Lorenz curve provides a visual measure of the extent of earnings inequality. The larger this area, the greater the degree of disparity in annual earnings. If there were complete inequality—if one person had 100 percent of total earnings—the Lorenz curve would coincide with the horizontal and right vertical axis, forming a 90° angle at point *g.*

Gini Coefficient

The visual measure of earnings inequality just described can be easily transformed into a mathematical measure. The *Gini coefficient,* Equation (16.1), is the ratio of the shaded area of Figure 16.2 to the entire triangle below the diagonal:

$$\text{Gini coefficient} = \frac{\text{area between Lorenz curve and diagonal}}{\text{total area below diagonal}} = \frac{A}{A + B} \quad \textbf{(16.1)}$$

Global Perspective 16.1

Income Inequality*

The United States has the highest degree of income inequality, as measured by the Gini coefficient, among major industrial countries.

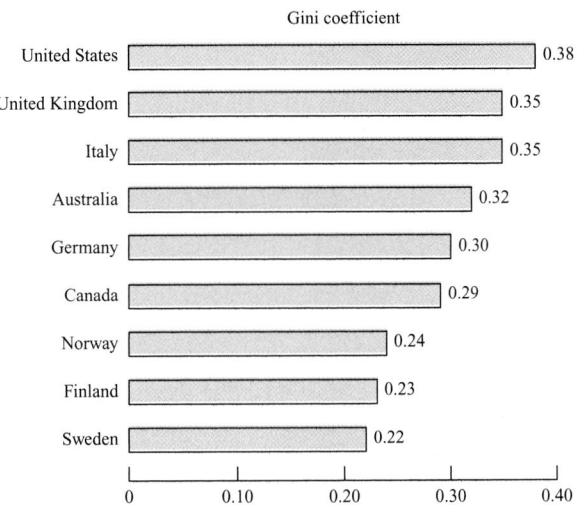

Gini coefficient

United States	0.38
United Kingdom	0.35
Italy	0.35
Australia	0.32
Germany	0.30
Canada	0.29
Norway	0.24
Finland	0.23
Sweden	0.22

Source: Timothy M. Smeeding (with the assistance of Andrej Grodner), "Changing Income Inequality in OECD Countries: Updated Results from the Luxembourg Income Study (LIS)," in R. Hauser and I. Becker (eds.), *The Personal Distribution of Income in an International Perspective* (Berlin, Germany: Springer-Verlag, 2000).

* The data are from the period 1994–1997.

If there were complete equality of earnings, the distance between the diagonal and the Lorenz curve would be zero, and therefore the Gini coefficient also would be zero $(= 0/(A + B))$. On the other hand, if one person had all the income, the area between the Lorenz curve and the diagonal would be equal to $A + B$, and the Gini coefficient would be 1 $(= (A + B)/(A + B))$. The larger the Gini coefficient, the greater the degree of earnings inequality. The Gini coefficient for the 2005 data shown in Figure 16.3 and the Lorenz curve in Figure 16.2 is 0.40.

Cautions

Great care must be exercised in interpreting frequency distributions, Lorenz curves, and Gini coefficients.

1 Full- versus Part-Time Workers

Annual earnings are a product of both wages per hour *and* the number of hours worked in a year. A distribution that includes part-time workers and people who work full-time only portions of the year will display greater variability than distributions that include only full-time workers. The histogram in Figure 16.1 and the Lorenz curve in Figure 16.2 include only *full-time* wage and salary earners.

2 Fringe Benefits

Most earnings data do not include fringe benefits (Chapter 7). The addition of these benefits increases the skewness of the frequency distribution of earnings or, stated differently, increases the sag of the Lorenz curve away from the diagonal and raises the Gini coefficient. Workers who have above-average annual earnings also tend to have higher-than-average fringe benefits as a percentage of their total compensation.[1]

3 Individual versus Family Distributions

Earnings distributions can be shown by either *individual* or *family* wages and salaries. Although the general shape of the family distribution is similar to that for individual workers, the median and average incomes are higher in the family formulation. Also, the family distribution is tighter; that is, the Gini coefficient is lower. The reason is that the income effect (Chapters 2 and 3) produced by the high incomes of some men reduces the likelihood that their wives are labor force participants. This income effect is offset somewhat by the tendency for men with higher earnings to marry women who earn more than the average female salary when they do choose to work.[2]

4 Static Portrayals

Frequency distributions, Lorenz curves, and Gini coefficients are all *static* portrayals or measures of earnings inequality. They do not provide information about the extent of personal movement within the distribution from year to year or over people's lifetimes. We discuss this important topic later in the chapter.

5 Other Income Sources

A final important caution is that annual earnings are only one of several possible sources of individual or family income. People who have high earnings from salaries tend to have disproportionately higher rental, interest, and dividend income than lower-wage workers. Taken alone, the inclusion of these nonwage incomes would make the distribution of individual or family income even more unequal than the distribution of wages and salaries. But government transfer payments such as Social Security benefits, welfare payments, and veterans' benefits offset this added inequality. Individuals and families who have zero or very low wage earnings receive proportionately more transfer income than higher-earnings individuals. The outcome is a slightly less unequal distribution of individual and family income than that based solely on individual or family wage and salary earnings (full-time and part-time workers).

---

[1] For an empirical analysis of the impact of fringe benefits on the distribution of income, see Daniel Slottje, Stephen Woodbury, and Rod Anderson, "Employee Benefits and the Distribution of Income and Wealth," in William T. Alpert and Stephen A. Woodbury (eds.), *Employee Benefits and Labor Markets in Canada and the United States* (Kalamazoo, MI: W. E. Upjohn Institute, 2000).
[2] See Maria Cancian and Deborah Reed, "The Impact of Wives' Earnings on Income Inequality: Issues and Estimates," *Demography,* May 1999, pp. 173–84.

16.1
Quick
Review

- The absolute frequency distribution (histogram) of earnings is a graphical depiction showing the number of employees whose earnings fall within various earnings ranges.
- The Lorenz curve graphically displays the cumulative percentage of all wage and salary earners on the horizontal axis and the corresponding cumulative percentage of total earnings accruing to that group; the farther the curve from the diagonal line of perfect equality, the greater the earnings inequality.
- The Gini coefficient is an arithmetic measure of earnings inequality; it is the area between the Lorenz curve and the diagonal line, divided by the total area beneath the diagonal line. The higher the Gini coefficient, the greater the earnings inequality.
- As measured by the histogram, Lorenz curve, and Gini coefficient, the degree of earnings inequality in the United States is high.

Your Turn

Suppose the Lorenz curve of earnings moves closer to the diagonal line. What has likely happened to the histogram of earnings and the Gini coefficient? (*Answer:* See page 599.)

EXPLAINING THE DISTRIBUTION OF EARNINGS

Human characteristics that we might associate with earnings—intelligence, physical strength, motivation, determination—are thought to be distributed according to the familiar bell-shaped normal curve. So why aren't earnings also distributed in this manner? Numerous theories attempt to explain this paradox.[3] Rather than describing each of these theories, we will approach this topic by first discussing the basic human capital explanation for earnings inequality and then exploring the diversity of alternative explanations by synthesizing several of them into a modified, multifactor model.

Human Capital Theory

The *human capital* model (Chapter 4) provides valuable insights into why the personal distribution of earnings is unequal and has a long rightward tail. Recall that human capital investments take various forms, the two most critical for present purposes being formal education and on-the-job training. Each relates to the earnings distribution.

1 Formal Education: Amount and Quality

Formal education has an investment component in that it requires present sacrifice to enhance future productivity and therefore lifetime earnings. A review of Figure 4.2 reminds us that a given investment will be undertaken only if the present value of the expected stream of enhanced earnings (area 3) equals or exceeds the present value of the sum of the direct and indirect costs (areas 1 + 2). Other things being equal, the

---

[3] For a review of these theories, see Derek Neal and Sherwin Rosen, "Theories of the Distribution of Earnings," in A. B. Atkinson and F. Bourguignon (eds.), *Handbook of Income Distribution* (Amsterdam: North-Holland, 2000).

greater the amount of formal schooling and the better its quality, the higher the investment costs (areas 1 + 2) and thus the greater the enhancement of productivity and the future earnings stream needed to justify the investment. Thus we have a rudimentary theory of earnings inequality. If other things such as ability, nonwage aspects of jobs, uncertainty of earnings, and life expectancies are held constant, earnings will be systematically and positively related to the amount and quality of a person's formal education. An unequal distribution of educational attainment will produce an unequal distribution of personal earnings.

A glance back at Table 14.2 offers casual evidence of the link between the amount of education undertaken and average annual earnings. It reveals that men and women—both African–Americans and whites—who have high school diplomas earn more than people who have obtained less than 12 years of education. Observe that workers with doctorates and professional degrees earn more than those with master's degrees; those with master's degrees earn more than those with bachelor's degrees; and those with bachelor's degrees earn more than those with associate degrees.

Econometric studies that account for other factors confirm the positive relationship between education and earnings shown in Table 14.2. Also, a few studies have found a direct relationship between the quality of formal education and subsequent earnings. For example, Card and Krueger[4] have discovered that, all else being equal, men who were educated in states with higher-quality public schools and who had better-educated teachers experienced a higher average rate of return on their investments in education. Care must be taken, however, not to overstate the importance of the link between education and earnings. Formal schooling explains only about 7 to 12 percent of the observed differences in individual earnings.

2 On-the-Job Training

The explanatory power of the basic human capital model rises appreciably once on-the-job training is added to the analysis. On-the-job training varies from simple "learning by doing" to formal apprenticeships and training programs and, as indicated in Chapter 4, may be either general or specific to the firm. In the case of *general training,* the worker usually bears the investment cost through a reduced wage. The worker's expected gain in future wages, therefore, must be sufficient to produce a rate of return on the investment cost (reduced present wage) equal to what the worker could obtain through alternative investments. With nontransferable *specific training,* the firm will be forced to pay the investment expense. The employer will undertake this investment only if the expected increase in the worker's productivity justifies it. Training is undertaken in both cases in expectation of an increase in productivity and enhanced future earnings. Therefore, we would expect to observe a direct relationship between the amount and quality of on-the-job training and a person's annual earnings.

---

[4] David Card and Alan B. Krueger, "Does School Quality Matter? Returns to Education and the Characteristics of Public Schools in the United States," *Journal of Political Economy,* February 1992, pp. 31–39. Most other studies also find a positive relationship between school quality and earnings. For a survey of such studies, see David Card and Alan B. Krueger, "School Resources and Student Outcomes," *Annals of the American Academy of Political and Social Science,* September 1998, pp. 39–53.

Mincer has shown that about one-half to two-thirds of the variation of personal earnings is explained once postschooling on-the-job training investment is included in the definition of human capital.[5] This inclusion adds so much explanatory power for two reasons. First, taken alone, formal schooling does little to explain why people's earnings typically *rise* with age. That is, education explains why postschooling earnings exceed preschooling pay, but it alone does not explain why earnings rise more rapidly for educated people over their work lives. After all, most people conclude their formal education relatively early in their lives. On-the-job training, on the other hand, provides a basic explanation for the age variations in earnings that are so apparent in the distribution. As a person accumulates more training on the job, productivity and earnings rise. Furthermore, evidence shows that people who possess greater amounts of formal education also receive more on-the-job training from employers. People with the most formal education have demonstrated their ability to absorb training and are the workers firms choose for on-the-job training. Those who have more education therefore have disproportionately greater earnings than less educated workers.

A second reason postschooling investment helps explain the observed inequality in the distribution of earnings is its impact on hours of work. Assuming that in the aggregate the substitution effect dominates the income effect (Chapter 2), people who have more schooling and on-the-job training not only will have higher hourly wage rates but also will choose to work more hours annually than less educated and less trained workers. This will mean that the annual earnings—wage rate × hours worked—will be *disproportionately* greater than the differences in schooling and on-the-job training, implying that the earnings distribution will be skewed to the right.

A Modified Human Capital Model: A Multifactor Approach

The basic human capital explanation of earnings disparities is not without its critics. Of particular interest to our topic is the criticism that schooling and on-the-job training do not sufficiently explain the long, extended rightward tail of the earnings distribution. Many economists believe that we can better understand why the earnings distribution is skewed rightward by modifying the human capital model to include elements beyond the traditional ones of education and on-the-job training. In this ***multifactor approach to the earnings distribution,*** we specifically consider (1) ability, (2) family background, (3) discrimination, and (4) chance and risk taking, as well as education and training.

1 Ability

Ability is broadly defined as "the power to do" and, as used here, consists of something separate and distinct from the skills gained through formal education or on-the-job training. Ability is difficult to isolate and measure but is thought to be normally distributed. In addition, ability is multidimensional; that is, it takes several forms, including intelligence (IQ), physical dexterity, and motivation. It may be either genetic or environmental in origin. Our interest in this discussion is not the source of observed differences

---

[5] Jacob Mincer, *Schooling, Experience, and Earnings* (New York: Columbia University Press, 1974).

in ability but rather the consequences of these differences for the distribution of earnings. Ability can influence earnings directly—in other words, independently of human capital investments—and indirectly, through its impact on the optimal amount and quality of human capital acquired.

Direct Impact   Those who envision a direct effect of ability on earnings argue that in a market economy, people are rewarded in a general way according to their ability to contribute to a firm's output. Other things being equal, the greater one's ability, the greater one's productivity and therefore earnings. Recall from the discussion of the "ability problem" in Chapter 4 that some critics of the human capital theory contend that the observed positive relationship between formal education and earnings largely reflects *self-selection*, which is based on differences in ability. People who possess more intelligence are more likely to choose to attend college than those with less intelligence. Even if these highly intelligent people did not go to college, they could be expected to have higher earnings than less intelligent people who did not attend college. In other words, if we could somehow control for the skills and knowledge gained during college, this high-quality group still would have substantially higher earnings than their less able counterparts. Consequently, much of the inequality of earnings normally attributed to differences in education and training could be the result of differences in ability.

Complementary Elements   A related possibility is that *elements* of differences in ability are complements to one another in the production of earnings. This implies that the addition of one factor will increase the productivity of other elements of ability. In other words, ability differences may act *multiplicatively* to generate the exceptionally high earnings that some people receive. To illustrate, let's suppose that ability consists of several normally distributed complementary elements, two of which are intelligence and the **D-factor,** where D represents drive, dynamism, doggedness, or determination.[6]

With these assumptions, a person who is fortunate enough to be located in the rightward tail of both the normal distribution of intelligence *and* the normal distribution of the D-factor will have earnings that are disproportionately greater than her or his relative position in either of the two distributions. This idea can be illustrated by a simple example. Suppose we could place a cardinal value on intelligence and the D-factor. Next suppose Assad's intelligence is 4 on a scale of 1 to 5 (where 5 is high and 1 is low) while Bates's is 1. Also assume that Assad's D-factor is 4 compared to a rating of 1 for Bates. If intelligence and the D-factor interacted in an *additive* way to determine earnings, we would add $4 + 4$ for Assad ($= 8$) and $1 + 1$ for Bates ($= 2$) and note that Assad could be expected to earn 4 times as much as Bates ($= 8/2$). But we have speculated that the two factors might interact *multiplicatively* to determine earnings; that is, Assad's score will be 16 ($= 4 \times 4$) while Bates's will be 1 ($= 1 \times 1$). In this case, Assad's earnings will be 16 times those of Bates ($= 16/1$). The point is

---

[6] Howard F. Lydall, "Theories of the Distribution of Earnings," in A. B. Atkinson (ed.), *The Personal Distribution of Income* (Boulder, CO: Westview Press, 1976), p. 35.

that if elements of ability are positively correlated and interact in a complementary fashion, a skewed distribution of earnings is entirely consistent with normal distributions of the elements.

Effect on Human Capital Decisions   Perhaps of greater significance is the notion that ability can influence earnings through its effect on the human capital investment decision. You may recall from Figure 4.6 that greater ability enables some people to translate any given investment in human capital, say a year of college or a year of on-the-job training, into a larger increase in labor market productivity and earnings than others. Therefore, the rate of return on each year of schooling or training will be higher for those who possess greater ability.[7] Consequently, these people will have a greater demand for formal education and their employers will possess a stronger desire to train them on the job than will be the case for less able people. The result? People possessing greater ability will tend to have disproportionately greater stocks of human capital and earnings than simple differences in abilities would suggest. Stated simply, people who do well in school because of ability tend to get more schooling; and people who get more education, in turn, tend to receive more on-the-job training than others. These tendencies skew the overall distribution of earnings to the right.

2 Family Background

Differences in family background—indicated by such variables as family income, father's and mother's years of education, father's and mother's occupations, number of children, and so forth—also influence earnings both directly and indirectly.

Direct Effect   The direct effect of family background on earnings often comes through employment of family members in family-owned businesses. A youth born into a family owning a prosperous Mercedes dealership stands a good chance of earning a sizable income later in life. Also, family connections may enable sons and daughters of the wealthy to gain high-paying positions in firms that are owned or managed by their parents' close friends or business associates. Sometimes these networks simply increase a job seeker's access to information about job openings, but in other instances they generate jobs for adult children through intricate reciprocity arrangements among those who interact both socially and commercially with one another.

Effect on Human Capital Decisions   Of perhaps greater significance, however, is the role of family background in influencing the decision of how much formal education to obtain. This influence affects both the demand for human capital and the supply price of investment funds. High-income families tend to provide more preschool education for children, are more likely to live in areas that have better schools, and often stress the importance of higher education as a route toward a professional career. Their children

---

[7] This conclusion must be viewed cautiously. Greater ability also may imply larger forgone earnings during the investment period, in which case the observed greater postinvestment earnings may *not* yield higher rates of return. See John Hause, "Ability and Schooling as Determinants of Lifetime Earnings, or If You're So Smart, Why Ain't You Rich?" in F. Thomas Juster (ed.), *Education, Income and Human Behavior* (New York: McGraw-Hill Book Company, 1975), pp. 123–49.

also may be socialized to think in terms of attending higher-quality educational institutions. Consequently, high-income parents on average have a greater *demand* for human capital for their children, and therefore these offspring obtain more formal education.

Family background may also provide easier financial access to higher education. Wealthier families may be able to finance their children's education from annual earnings or personal savings, incurring only the opportunity cost of forgone goods or interest. Lower-income families most probably will need to borrow funds from imperfect financial markets at high interest rates. Because of these differing supply costs of human capital, the children of wealthier parents will find it optimal to obtain more formal education than children of poorer families (Figure 4.7).[8] These differences in education will combine with *direct* family influences to produce an unequal, rightwardly skewed distribution of earnings.[9]

3 Discrimination

In Chapter 14 we saw that discrimination explains part of the wage inequality between males and females and between whites and minorities in the United States. Discrimination adds to earnings inequality in a number of ways. First, overt pay discrimination and discrimination in promotion directly reduce the pay of those discriminated against. Second, occupational crowding or segregation not only reduces the pay of females and minorities but also increases the pay of males and whites. Both outcomes contribute to greater earnings inequality. Finally, poorer African–American and other minority families are often segregated into city neighborhoods where there is low-cost or public housing. These areas often have lower-quality schools and contain few adult role models with college degrees. Thus children from these areas are much less likely to obtain higher education than are children growing up in higher-income neighborhoods. Adding to this problem is the sheer expense of attending college. This expense deters many African–Americans and Hispanics from obtaining college degrees.

In short, wage and occupational discrimination contribute directly to earnings inequality while human capital discrimination, by reducing the quantity and quality of education and training, further contributes to this inequality.

4 Chance and Risk Taking

Some economists have incorporated the role of random elements such as chance or luck into theories of the distribution of earnings and income. These *stochastic theories* demonstrate how the cumulative impacts of random fortune tend to produce a long rightward tail in the distribution of such nonwage income as profits, rents, and capital gains.

---

[8] Care must be taken not to overstate this effect, however. Financial aid—low-interest loans, scholarships, and so forth—received by students from lower-income families reduces the cost of investment funds for this group. Also, the *implicit* borrowing costs to the rich may not be that much lower than the *actual* borrowing costs to the poor. For a study showing that family income has little impact on the acquisition of human capital, see John Shea, "Does Parents' Money Matter?" *Journal of Public Economics,* August 2000, pp. 155–84.

[9] For a survey of studies examining the relationship between family background and earnings, see Gary Solon, "Intergenerational Mobility in the Labor Market," in Orley Ashenfelter and David Card (eds.), *Handbook of Labor Economics,* Volume 3A (Amsterdam: North-Holland, 1999).

Because this is a text about labor economics, our interest, of course, is strictly in the distribution of earnings, and thus many of the stochastic theories have little relevance.

Nevertheless, according to some economists, stochastic elements offer important insights into why earnings are unequal and why the earnings distribution is skewed to the right. Three examples of ways in which risk and luck might enter into the earnings determination process are as follows. First, suppose that at a specific instant, all people possess a given level of normally distributed earnings plus an opportunity to participate in a lottery. Further suppose that the lottery winnings consist of opportunities to be a premier professional athlete, a rock star, a motion picture celebrity, a major corporate executive, or a best-selling author. These positions are few in number but pay considerably more than the average salaries in society. But there is a catch: You must incur *risk* if you wish to play the lottery; that is, you must buy a lottery ticket. The ticket price may be, say, the cost associated with advocating bold business ventures to your employer only to have one of them fail; the direct and indirect costs of refining your acting, musical, or athletic skills only to discover that the investment does not result in stardom; or the cost of forgoing present job security to become a writer whose uncertain earnings derive from book royalties.

Will all workers of equal ability participate in this lottery? Obviously not. Some people simply are much too averse to risk. Only those who are less averse to risk will decide that the chance of winning the few big prizes is worth the price of the ticket. How then might the distribution of earnings be affected by the lottery? Three distributions, each individually symmetrical, would be observable. First, there would be a distribution of earnings for the many nonparticipants in the lottery. Second, we would observe a distribution, possibly lying to the left of the one for nonparticipants, indicating the earnings of lottery losers. Finally, there would be a distribution lying to the right of that for nonparticipants displaying the very large average earnings of the relatively few lottery winners. Even though each of these three distributions might be normally distributed, the composite distribution of earnings would be skewed to the right.[10]

In Chapter 8 we implied a second way that chance may account for differences in personal earnings. In Figure 8.5 it was observed that differences in pay for the same type of work can exist under circumstances of imperfect wage information and costly job search. Who receives which wage in the frequency distribution shown in the figure is in part determined randomly. For example, suppose that Gomez and Green are equally qualified job seekers who both have the same reservation wage (minimum acceptable wage). Also, assume that each is searching in a random fashion for job openings in the frequency distribution shown in Figure 8.5. Through good luck, Gomez may receive the highest wage offer in the distribution on her first try, while the less fortunate Green may get an offer above her reservation wage but well below the pay received by Gomez.

A final example of the role of chance in theories of personal earnings is provided by Thurow. He contends that "marginal products are inherent in jobs and not individuals.

---

[10] This example is based on a more complex model presented by Milton Friedman, "Choice, Chance, and the Personal Distribution of Income," *Journal of Political Economy,* August 1953, pp. 273–90. For a highly technical criticism of Friedman's article, see S. M. Kanbur, "Of Risk Taking and the Personal Distribution of Income," *Journal of Political Economy,* August 1979, pp. 769–97.

FIGURE 16.4 **Factors Affecting Personal Annual Earnings**

The basic human capital explanation of the personal distribution of annual earnings is shown by the heavy solid arrow that connects education and training to annual earnings. The multifactor approach adds ability, family background, and discrimination as variables that can directly influence earnings (heavy lines) or indirectly affect earnings by having an impact on the amount and quality of education and training that a person receives (thin lines). Luck, or chance, also plays a role in affecting annual earnings (broken line).

Source: Adapted from A. B. Atkinson, *The Economics of Inequality,* 2nd ed. (Oxford: Oxford University Press, 1983), p. 122.

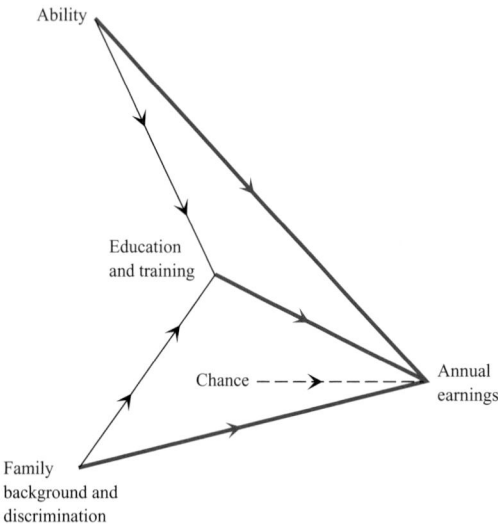

The individual will be trained into the marginal productivity of the job he is slated to hold, but he does not have this marginal productivity independent of the job in question."[11] The implication of this thesis is that workers possessing a particular set of general background characteristics—that is, being equally trainable—will make up a labor pool from which employers will draw randomly. Those who are fortunate will get selected for jobs with high marginal productivity and annual earnings; but because such jobs are few, other equally qualified people will end up in lower-paying occupations. Thus, according to Thurow, "similar individuals will be distributed across a range of job opportunities and earnings. In effect, they will participate in a lottery."[12]

Schematic Summary

Figure 16.4 summarizes the major determinants of earnings just discussed.[13] The basic human capital explanation of earnings is represented by the thick solid line connecting education and training with earnings. The more comprehensive multifactor explanation is

[11] Lester C. Thurow, *Generating Inequality: Mechanisms of Distribution in the U.S. Economy* (New York: Basic Books, Inc., 1975), p. 85.

[12] Ibid., p. 92.

[13] For a fuller discussion of this representation, see A. B. Atkinson, *The Economics of Inequality,* 2nd ed. (Oxford: Clarendon Press, 1983), p. 122.

portrayed by the entire figure. Ability (independent of education) affects earnings directly, as shown by the thick line connecting the two, and indirectly via its impact on the optimal amount and quality of education and training (thin line). Likewise, family background and discrimination have direct and indirect effects on personal earnings. The solid arrow between these factors and earnings represents the roles of family firms, family connections, and wage and occupational discrimination. The thin line from family background and discrimination to education and training illustrates the impact of family education and wealth on the demand for, and the supply price of, human capital. It also captures the effect of racial and gender discrimination on human capital and therefore indirectly on earnings. Finally, the role of chance is portrayed by the broken line leading directly to earnings.

We could easily add more complexity to Figure 16.4. For example, we could connect chance with family background and ability, for in a sense both are partly products of luck. Also, we could add a feedback loop from earnings to education and training, inasmuch as present earnings may help determine how much subsequent education one might find optimal. Then, too, we could recognize the role of compensating wage premiums in causing earnings differences (Chapter 8). Finally, as pointed out by Lydall, Rosen, and others, hierarchical structures of organizations may create large earnings disparities.[14] But these important considerations aside, Figure 16.4 adequately summarizes the major determinants of the personal distribution of earnings.

MOBILITY WITHIN THE EARNINGS DISTRIBUTION

The aggregate personal distribution of earnings is quite rigid from one year to the next and changes only slightly from one decade to the next. But this fact masks the degree of individual movement within that fixed distribution. As Schiller colorfully points out, on one hand, individuals may be highly mobile from year to year and over their lifetimes within the static aggregate distribution, suggesting a game of musical chairs in which the positions of the chairs remain the same but the occupants regularly change. On the other hand, "the rigid shape of the aggregate distribution is equally compatible with a total lack of personal mobility—a game, as it were, that individuals play by remaining in their chairs until the music . . . is over."[15]

Which of these two possibilities best describes reality? The answer appears to be the musical chairs scenario. The evidence suggests that considerable movement or mobility occurs within the rather rigid static distribution. This *earnings mobility* is of two main types: life-cycle mobility and a "churning" that is independent of age.

Life-Cycle Mobility

We know from our previous discussions of age–earnings profiles (Figure 4.1) that people's earnings typically vary systematically with age over the life cycle. Most people

---

[14] Howard Lydall, *The Structure of Earnings* (London: Oxford University Press, 1968); and Sherwin Rosen, "Authority, Control, and the Distribution of Earnings," *Bell Journal of Economics,* Autumn 1982, pp. 311–23.
[15] Bradley R. Schiller, "Relative Earnings Mobility in the United States," *American Economic Review,* December 1977, p. 926.

World of Work 16.1

Cross-Country Differences in Earnings Mobility Across Generations*

Another measure of earnings mobility in a society is the degree to which earnings are transferred from one generation to the next. A large body of literature for the United States indicates that the intergenerational earnings elasticity between a father's earnings and his son's earnings is about 0.4. This elasticity implies that if a father has earnings 10 percent greater than average, his son will earn about 4 percent more than average.

How does U.S. intergenerational earnings elasticity compare to that of other countries? The United States has similar or more intergenerational mobility than the United Kingdom but less than that of several other countries. The estimates for the intergenerational earnings elasticity in the United Kingdom range from .42 to .57. Suggestive evidence indicates that less developed countries also tend to have lower intergenerational mobility. For example, the intergenerational earnings elasticity for South Africa is about .44. In contrast, Canada, Finland, and Sweden are relatively more mobile, by this measure. Their elasticities range from 0.1 to 0.3.

Solon points to several factors that explain these cross-country differences. First, countries with greater earnings inequality at points in time tend to have lower intergenerational earnings mobility. For example, the United States and the United Kingdom have greater income inequality and therefore lower intergenerational earnings mobility than do Sweden and Finland. Second, countries that have greater inheritability of income-producing traits—due to selective mating between individuals with those traits—tend to have less intergenerational earnings mobility. Third, higher returns to investments in education and other forms of human capital increase earnings differentials across generations and thus tend to reduce the intergenerational mobility rate. The United States, in particular, has higher returns to postsecondary education than many other nations. Finally, countries that invest relatively more in the human capital of children from high-earnings households have less intergenerational earnings mobility.

* Based on Gary Solon, "Cross-Country Differences in Intergenerational Earnings Mobility," *Journal of Economic Perspectives,* Summer 2002, pp. 59–66.

have relatively low earnings when they are young; later, during their prime earning years, their earnings rise substantially; and finally, their earnings fall near the time of retirement. Thus even if everyone had an identical stream of earnings over her or his lifetime, we still would observe age-related inequality in the distribution of earnings. In any specific year, the static annual distribution of earnings would include, say, young (low-earnings) workers just beginning their labor force participation, middle-aged (high-earnings) employees in the prime of their careers, and older workers who were phasing into retirement. This inequality of *annual* earnings for a specific year would be present despite complete equality of *lifetime* earnings.

Due to **life-cycle mobility** of earnings, there will be more equality in lifetime earnings than is observed using static cross-sectional annual data.

"Churning" within the Distribution

There is also movement within the earnings distribution that is independent of age itself. Due to **"churning" within the earnings distribution,** people's relative age-adjusted earnings positions change during their lifetimes. For example, a salesperson may have

16.2 World of Work	**Government Employment and the Earnings Distribution**

One out of six U.S. workers is employed by the government. How do the wages paid to these employees affect the distribution of earnings? The answer is that government employment and remuneration reduce overall earnings inequality.

Government agencies and government contractors usually adhere to a prevailing wage rule under which the wages paid to public employees are comparable to the earnings of similar workers in the private sector. But this rule tends to be modified at both the bottom and the top ends of the government pay structure. Blue-collar public employees are paid more than their private sector counterparts, whereas white-collar workers in government—particularly executives—are paid much less. As a consequence, the personal distribution of earnings in the public sector is more egalitarian than in the private sector, causing the overall distribution in society to also be less unequal.

The reasons for the compression of earnings in the public sector are many. For example, elected officials may pay low-wage workers more than their private sector counterparts to avoid the potentially politically embarrassing circumstance of having full-time government workers qualify for government cash and in-kind welfare benefits. Also, it seems probable that low- to middle-wage-earning employees, who are large in number and strong politically, are more likely to secure wage increases than higher-paid managers and professionals, who are few in number. Furthermore, it may be that the large salaries paid to executives in corporations (Table 7.1) simply are not politically feasible when paid to top governmental administrators and elected officials. In this regard, we might note that in a typical year, the total of the combined salaries and bonuses of the 10 highest-paid corporate executives in the United States exceeds the combined salaries of the following government officials: the president of the United States, the vice president, the 100 U.S. senators, the 50 state governors, the 9 Supreme Court justices, and the 50 heads of major regulatory agencies.

relatively small commissions and earnings in the first year of a new job but receive considerably larger annual compensation in subsequent years. Or a manager may get promoted to a new job that pays considerably more than the job previously held. Or as an example of churning in the downward direction, a performer who is highly paid in one year may earn much less during following years.

Evidence

How much movement is there within the earnings distribution? To answer this question, Gottschalk used a sample of men aged 20 to 42 in 1974.[16] He divided the sample into five earnings categories (quintiles), each containing 20 percent of the workers, and then observed the movements of individuals between 1974 and 1991. Gottschalk found that 61 percent of workers changed at least one earnings quintile or one-fifth of the way from one of the ends of the earnings distribution to the other. Some workers had even greater earnings mobility: 24 percent changed two or more quintiles over the 17-year period.

One must not overstate the extent of earnings mobility, however. Gottschalk found that earnings mobility in and out of the *lowest* and *highest* quintiles was lower than to

[16] Peter Gottschalk, "Inequality, Income Growth, and Mobility: The Basic Facts," *Journal of Economic Perspectives,* Spring 1997, pp. 21–40.

and from other categories. In addition, Gittleman and Joyce report that women and African–Americans are more likely to stay in the bottom quintile and less likely to stay in the top quintile.[17] Although there is much movement in the earnings distribution, the extent of this mobility is neither uniform throughout the distribution nor equal for all groups of workers.[18]

Nevertheless, earnings mobility does reduce the amount of inequality in lifetime earnings. Gottschalk found that averaging earnings over the 17-year period reduces inequality by about one-third relative to using data for a single year.[19] Buchinsky and Hunt report that earnings mobility reduces inequality by 12 to 26 percent over a four-year period.[20]

16.2 *Quick* *Review*	• The human capital theory looks to differences in the amount and quality of education and the extent of on-the-job training as the major reasons for earnings inequality. • The multifactor approach to earnings distribution takes into account ability, family background, discrimination, chance, and risk taking, in addition to education and training. • Workers exhibit considerable earnings mobility over their work lives; earnings typically are low in earlier years, rise in prime working years, and then decline. • There is much year-to-year movement of workers across earnings categories, independent of life-cycle aspects of earnings. This mobility is less in the lowest and highest earnings categories.

Your Turn

 Of all the factors explaining earnings inequality, which one do you think is the most significant? (*Answer:* See page 599.)

RISING EARNINGS INEQUALITY

During the past three decades labor economists have devoted much research to tracking and explaining changes in the distribution of earnings in the United States. The initial motivation for this research was the controversial hypothesis expressed in the early 1980s that the middle class in America is shrinking. In its extreme form, this view holds

[17] Maury Gittleman and Mary Joyce, "Earnings Mobility and Long-Run Inequality: An Analysis Using Matched CPS Data," *Industrial Relations,* April 1996, pp. 180–96.
[18] For more evidence on this point, see John Geweke and Michael Keane, "An Empirical Analysis of Earnings Dynamics among Men in the PSID: 1968–1989," *Journal of Econometrics,* June 2000, pp. 293–356.
[19] Gottschalk, op. cit.
[20] Moshe Buchinsky and Jennifer Hunt, "Wage Mobility in the United States," *Review of Economics and Statistics,* August 1999, pp. 351–68. See also Richard V. Burkhauser and John G. Poupore, "A Cross-National Comparison of Permanent Inequality in the United States and Germany," *Review of Economics and Statistics,* February 1997, pp. 10–17; and Richard V. Burkhauser, Douglas Holtz-Eakin, and Stephen E. Rhody, "Labor Earnings Mobility and Inequality in the United States and Germany during the Growth Years of the 1980s," *International Economic Review,* November 1997, pp. 775–94.

FIGURE 16.5 **Wage Inequality, 90–10 Ratio**

Earnings inequality for both men and women has increased in recent decades.

Source: Lawrence Mishel, Jared Bernstein, and Sylvia Allegretto, *State of Working America, 2006/2007* (Washington, DC: Economic Policy Institute, 2006), Tables 3.5 and 3.6.

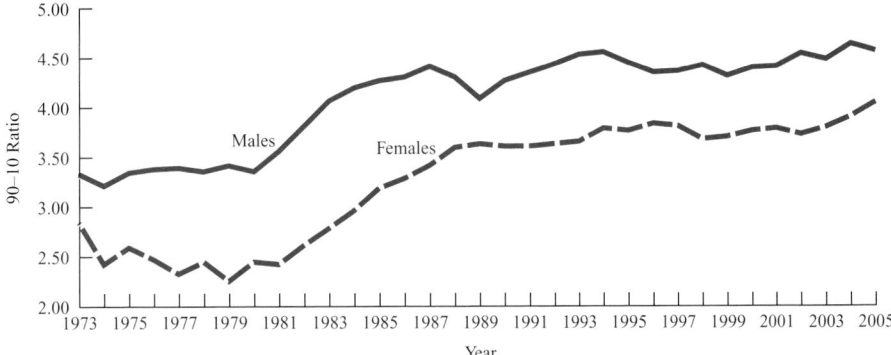

that American employment is being polarized between high-paying positions requiring considerable education and low-paying jobs in the service sector.[21]

Although most labor economists reject the extreme polarization view, a consensus has arisen that the distribution of work and salary earnings has indeed become more unequal.[22] Evidence indicates that earnings inequality has increased over the past 30 years and that this trend has accelerated since 1980.[23]

Trends in Wage Inequality

A useful measure of wage inequality is the ratio of wages at different parts of the wage distribution. For example, a commonly used differential is the 90–10 ratio; that is, the wage at the 90th percentile divided by the wage at the 10th percentile. Figure 16.5 shows the ratio of the hourly wage for wage and salary workers by gender. For men in 1973 the 90–10 ratio was 3.60. This indicates that men at the 90th percentile earned 3.60 times as much as men at the 10th percentile. The ratio rose to 4.63 in 2005, indicating that inequality increased.[24]

[21] Barry Bluestone and Bennett Harrison, *The Deindustrialization of America* (New York: Basic Books, Inc., 1982). Also see Bennett Harrison and Barry Bluestone, *The Great U-Turn: Corporate Restructuring and Polarization of America* (New York: Basic Books, Inc., 1988); and Barry Bluestone, *The Polarization of American Society: Victims, Suspects, and Mysteries to Unravel* (New York: Twentieth Century Fund Press, 1995).

[22] Evidence indicates that inequality among workplace disamenities such as job injuries and shift work is also rising. See Daniel S. Hamermesh, "Changing Inequality in Markets for Workplace Amenities," *Quarterly Journal of Economics,* November 1999, pp. 1085–1123.

[23] Finis Welch (ed.), *The Causes and Consequences of Increasing Inequality* (Chicago: University of Chicago Press, 2001); Daron Acemoglu, "Technical Change, Inequality, and the Labor Market," *Journal of Economic Literature,* March 2002, pp. 7–72; and David H. Autor, Lawrence F. Katz, and Melissa S. Kearney, "The Polarization of the U.S. Labor Market," *American Economic Review,* May 2006, pp. 189–94.

[24] There is evidence that inequality measures are sensitive to the sample of workers examined and the earnings measure. Mark S. Handcock, Martina Morris, and Annette Bernhardt, "Comparing Earnings Inequality Using Two Major Surveys," *Monthly Labor Review,* March 2000, pp. 48–61; and Thomas Lemieux, "Increasing Residual Wage Inequality: Composition Effects, Noisy Data, or Rising Demand for Skill?" *American Economic Review,* June 2006, pp. 461–98.

The rate of increase, however, was not steady over this period. It rose at a modest pace of 0.012 points per year between 1973 and 1979. It increased by a rapid .064 points per year between 1979 and 1994. Between 1994 and 1999, the ratio fell modestly; and it has since risen back to its 1994 value. A further breakdown of the distribution of earnings indicates that the recent relative stability in inequality is due to offsetting factors.[25] On one hand, the wages for males at the low end of the wage distribution have risen relative to those in the middle, which has tended to reduce inequality. On the other hand, the wages of men near the top of the wage distribution have continued to rise relative to those in the middle, which has tended to increase inequality.

Wage inequality has also risen among women. The 90–10 ratio rose from 3.19 in 1973 to 4.20 in 2005. The change in inequality across time was different for women: The 90–10 ratio fell between 1973 and 1979, in contrast to the slight rise for men. On the other hand, the ratio rose one-third faster for women than for men between 1979 and 1994.

Why the Increase in Earnings Inequality?

Economists have advanced several explanations for why earnings inequality has grown over the past three decades. Let's briefly assess four potential explanations.

1 Deindustrialization

Since the mid-1970s employment in the service sector has increased dramatically relative to employment in manufacturing. Because the service sector has a lower average wage and a higher variance of earnings than the manufacturing sector, this tilt toward services has undoubtedly increased earnings inequality.[26]

But economists warn that this is an incomplete explanation. The change in the mix of employment toward services accounts for only a small portion of the overall rise in wage inequality. The vast majority of the rise in earnings inequality is explained by increased wage and salary dispersion *within* industries.[27] This intraindustry increase in earnings inequality is not easily explained by the shift from manufacturing to service employment. Moreover, it is important to remember that several high-growth service industries—for example, law, consulting, accounting, medicine, and education—are high-pay sectors, not low-pay ones.

2 Import Competition and the Decline of Unionism

Strong import competition has severely reduced the demand for workers in several high-wage, unionized industries, including autos and steel. Because union wages have been relatively inflexible downward, these declines in labor demand have produced massive reductions in unionized employment. One result has been a direct decline in the average wage of workers with lower levels of education. Also, the many workers displaced from

---

[25] The source of the statistics in this section is Lawrence Mishel, Jared Bernstein, and Sylvia Allegretto, *State of Working America, 2006/2007* (Washington, DC: Economic Policy Institute, 2006).

[26] Bluestone and Harrison, op. cit.; and Harrison and Bluestone, op. cit. Also relevant is Barry Bluestone, "The Impact of Schooling and Industrial Restructuring on Recent Trends in Wage Inequality in the United States," *American Economic Review,* May 1990, pp. 303–7.

[27] Robert G. Valletta, "The Effects of Industry Employment Shifts on the U.S. Wage Structure, 1979–1995," Federal Reserve Bank of San Francisco *Economic Review,* no. 1 (1997), pp. 16–32.

unionized jobs have increased the labor supply in lower-paying industries. Thus there has been a downward pressure on wages in these industries as well. Another factor is that import competition has induced some high-pay industries to move their operations to nonunion, lower-paying regions of the country. These relocations have further widened earnings inequality and contributed to the decline of unionism.

Research evidence supports this perspective on growing wage inequality. Increases in the trade deficit (more imports than exports) and the related decline of unionism (Chapter 10) have contributed to the rise in earnings inequality.[28]

3 Increased Demand for Skilled Workers

Recall that the college wage premium rose substantially in the 1980s (Chapter 4), implying a growing wage gap between more skilled workers and less skilled workers. One potential explanation for the rising rate of return to higher education and therefore for increased earnings inequality is that the demand for more skilled workers may have sharply increased relative to the demand for less skilled workers. Other things being equal, a relative increase in the demand for more skilled, higher-paid workers will widen the earnings distribution.

Increased demand for more skilled workers may have evidenced itself in two ways. First, the demand for more skilled workers may have occurred *within* industries. Responding to new technologies, industries in general may have changed their production techniques in ways that require comparatively more college-educated workers. For example, manufacturing and service industries alike have expanded their use of computer-aided technologies.[29] Second, a shift in product demand may have occurred *among* industries. Specifically, the derived demand for labor may have shifted in favor of industries that employ a higher proportion of more skilled workers. For instance, the emergence of high-tech industries such as the computer software and biomedicine industries may have increased the overall demand for highly trained workers.

It is also possible that the rise in the college pay premium has resulted from a relative slowdown in the historical increase in the proportion of young people who are attending college. Together with a rising demand for college-educated workers, this would further explain the increase in earnings inequality.[30]

---

[28] For a survey on the link between the trade imbalance and rising inequality, see Gary Burtless, "International Trade and the Rise in Earnings Inequality," *Journal of Economic Literature,* June 1995, pp. 800–16. See also Steven D. Pizer, "Does International Competition Undermine Wage Differentials and Increase Inequality?" *Journal of International Economics,* December 2000, pp. 259–82. For evidence that the decline in unionism has contributed to rising earnings inequality, see David Card, "The Effect of Unions on Wage Inequality in the U.S. Labor Market," *Industrial and Labor Relations Review,* January 2001, pp. 296–315.

[29] See, for instance, "World of Work" 8.2. For evidence regarding the mechanisms by which computer technology increases the demand for skilled workers, see David H. Autor, Frank Levy, and Richard J. Murnane, "The Skill Content of Recent Technological Change: An Empirical Exploration," *Quarterly Journal of Economics,* November 2003, pp. 1279–1333.

[30] For evidence regarding the effects of increased demand for skilled workers, see Chinhui Juhn, "Wage Inequality and Demand for Skill: Evidence from Five Decades," *Industrial and Labor Relations Review,* April 1999, pp. 424–43. For analysis of the impact of computers on inequality, see David H. Autor, Lawrence F. Katz, and Alan B. Krueger, "Computing Inequality: Have Computers Changed the Labor Market?" *Quarterly Journal of Economics,* November 1998, pp. 1169–1213.

4 Demographic Changes

Some economists have looked to the supply side of the aggregate labor market to explain rising earnings inequality. Specifically, they cite changes in the composition of labor supply between more skilled and less skilled workers as an important factor. In particular, the entrance of large numbers of less skilled baby boomers and female workers into the labor market during the 1970s and 1980s may have contributed to increased earnings inequality.

The link between the surge in the number of inexperienced, less skilled workers and earnings inequality has two dimensions. First, this surge may have raised the proportion of low-wage workers to high-wage workers in *all industries,* creating greater wage disparity. Second, the increased supply of young workers and inexperienced female workers in various *lower-wage labor markets* may have depressed the relative earnings of workers in those markets. In either case, the predicted impact would be a rise in the pay differential between less skilled (less experienced) and more skilled workers.

The demographic explanation for rising earnings inequality is logically appealing and often cited. But it is difficult to reconcile this explanation with evidence that increases in aggregate inequality largely result from growing earnings inequality *within* each age group. The research consensus is that the baby boom, the surge of female labor force entrants, and immigration have only modestly contributed to the growing earnings inequality.[31]

Conclusions and Future Prospects

What can we conclude from our discussion of possible sources of growing wage inequality? The main conclusion is that there appears to be no single cause of this phenomenon. The evidence on this matter points to demand-side, supply-side, and institutional factors being at work. The demand for college-trained workers appears to have risen relative to the supply of these workers. The supply of less skilled workers appears to have increased relative to the demand for less skilled workers. Meanwhile, trade deficits and the decline of unionism have reduced traditional mid-paying jobs and channeled workers into lower-paying employment. The result has been a widening distribution of earnings for both women and men.[32]

Will the distribution of earnings continue to widen during the next decade? The tentative answer provided by experts in this area is probably not. Declining labor force growth (Chapter 3) should tighten the aggregate labor market in the future and

---

[31] See Robert H. Topel, "Factor Proportions and Relative Wages: The Supply-Side Determinants of Wage Inequality," *Journal of Economic Perspectives,* Spring 1997, pp. 55–74. See also Robert L. Lerman, "U.S. Wage-Inequality Trends and Recent Immigration," *American Economic Review,* May 1999, pp. 23–28.

[32] A few attempts have been made to evaluate the relative importance of the factors cited. For example, John Bound and George Johnson have concluded from such a study that the major cause of the relative wages changes was a shift in the skill structure of labor demand brought about by technological change that has called for the use of more highly skilled labor. See John Bound and George Johnson, "Changes in the Structure of Wages in the 1980s: An Evaluation of Alternative Explanations," *American Economic Review,* June 1992, pp. 371–92; and Council of Economic Advisers, *Economic Report of the President* (Washington, DC: U.S. Government Printing Office, February 1997), chapter 5.

increase wages for less skilled workers. Also, the rising rate of return to investment in education and training should entice more people to enroll in colleges and encourage firms to invest more in training their employees. Eventually, we would expect the increased supply of more skilled workers to reduce the earnings premium paid to this group.[33] But keep in mind that the factors affecting earnings inequality are manifold and complex. Therefore, predicting the future course of earnings inequality is highly speculative.

Chapter Summary

1. The degree of inequality in personal earnings can be shown by a histogram (absolute frequency distribution), a relative frequency distribution, or a Lorenz curve. A frequency distribution shows either the absolute or the relative number of employed individuals whose annual earnings fall within various ranges of annual earnings. The Lorenz curve portrays the cumulative percentage of all wage and salary earners and their corresponding cumulative percentage of total earnings.

2. The frequency distribution for U.S. earnings evidences considerable bunching around a single mode that is to the left of the median and mean and displays a long rightwardly skewed tail, indicating wide disparities in personal earnings.

3. The Gini coefficient measures the degree of earnings inequality on a scale of zero (complete equality) to 1 (complete inequality). It can be found graphically by comparing the area between the diagonal line and the Lorenz curve to the entire area below the diagonal.

4. Frequency distributions, Lorenz curves, and Gini coefficients of *personal* earnings must be interpreted cautiously because they *(a)* differ depending on whether part-time workers are included or excluded, *(b)* fail to include fringe benefits, *(c)* do not provide information about *family* earnings, and *(d)* display more inequality than when based on income after transfers.

5. According to human capital theorists, approximately one-half to two-thirds of earnings inequality is explained by the interactive differences in people's formal education and on-the-job training.

6. Ability *(a)* is thought by some economists to influence earnings *directly* through enhancement of productivity, *(b)* may take several forms that interact multiplicatively to produce the observed skewed distribution of earnings, and *(c)* may *indirectly* have an impact on earnings by determining the return from—and hence the optimal amount of—investment in human capital.

7. Family background, discrimination, extent of risk taking, and degree of luck also are variables that help explain earnings inequality and the rightwardly skewed tail of the earnings distribution.

[33] For a discussion of this point, see Topel, op. cit.

8. There is considerable movement by individuals within the overall distribution of earnings. This mobility is related to the life cycle, reflecting the generally positive relationship between age and earnings. It can also be of a "churning" nature, in which people with more education, training, ability, or luck rise from lower to higher levels of age-adjusted earnings.

9. The distribution of earnings in the United States has become more unequal over the past 25 years. Potential causes that have been cited include *(a)* deindustrialization, *(b)* import competition and the decline of unionism, *(c)* increased demand for skilled workers, and *(d)* demographic changes. None of these factors alone can explain the increase in wage and salary inequality. It would appear that demand-side, supply-side, and institutional factors all are involved.

Terms and Concepts

distribution of
   personal earnings, *483*
absolute frequency
   distribution, *484*
histogram, *484*
Lorenz curve, *485*

Gini coefficient, *486*
human capital model, *489*
multifactor approach
   to the earnings
   distribution, *491*
self-selection, *492*

D-factor, *492*
stochastic theories, *494*
earnings mobility, *497*
life-cycle mobility, *498*
"churning" within the
   earnings distribution, *498*

Questions and Study Suggestions

1. Suppose a hypothetical economy consists of 20 nonunionized private sector workers who have the following annual earnings: $18,000, $9,000, $82,000, $12,000, $13,000, $76,000, $61,000, $14,000, $22,000, $23,000, $21,000, $46,000, $59,000, $26,000, $27,000, $37,000, $6,000, $41,000, $3,000, and $24,000.

   a. Using annual earnings ranges of $10,000 (that is, 0–$10,000, $10,000–$20,000, and so forth), construct a histogram (absolute frequency distribution) of this economy's distribution of personal earnings. What is the mode of the histogram? What is the average (mean) level of earnings? What is the median level of earnings? Characterize the distribution as being normal, skewed leftward, or skewed rightward. Explain.

   b. Construct a Lorenz curve showing the quintile distribution of earnings for this economy.

   c. What would be the likely impact of unionization of this entire workforce on the Lorenz curve? Explain.

2. Speculate about why a given Gini coefficient is compatible with more than one particular Lorenz curve. Illustrate graphically.

3. Why do people who have more formal education than others also in general tend to receive more on-the-job training during their careers? What is the implication of this fact for the distribution of earnings?

4. Critically evaluate this statement: "Lifetime earnings are less equally distributed than annual earnings."

5. Speculate about how successful attempts by government to tighten the distribution of family *income* through transfers might inadvertently make the distribution of annual *earnings* more unequal.

6. Explain how both ability and family background can *directly* influence earnings, independently of education and training. How do ability and family background *indirectly* determine earnings through the human capital investment decision? How does discrimination contribute to earnings inequality?

7. What has happened to the location of the Lorenz curve of annual earnings over the past 30 years? Make a case that the Lorenz curve will shift leftward over the next 30 years. Make a case that it will shift farther to the right than its present location. Which of your two scenarios do you think is most realistic?

8. Which two of the text's possible explanations for increasing wage and salary inequality seem least consistent with the following fact? The distribution of earnings has become more unequal *within* industries (both goods and service industries) and *within* age groups. Explain.

9. In light of the information presented in this chapter, answer Question 11 at the end of Chapter 4.

Internet Exercise

Is Earnings Inequality Rising or Falling?

Go to the Economic Policy Institute National Data Zone Web site **(http://www.epi.org/content.cfm/datazone_dznational)**. Under Wages and Compensation Trends, click on "Hourly wage decile cutoffs for male workers" and "Hourly wage decile cutoffs for female workers." This will retrieve historical data 90–10 on earnings ratios for male and female workers.

What are the 90–10 earnings ratios for men in 1973, 1979, 1999 and the most recent year shown? What happened to income inequality in the following periods: 1973–1979; 1979–1999; and 1999 to the most recent year? Repeat the same analysis for women.

Internet Link

The United Nations University and United Nations Development Programme has a large database of measures of income inequality for many countries **(http://www.wider.unu.edu/wiid/wiid.htm)**.

Chapter 17

Labor Productivity: Wages, Prices, and Employment

Previous chapters emphasized the determination of wage rates for specific types of workers, explained the complex cluster of individual wages that constitute the wage structure, and examined the distribution of personal earnings. The spotlight now shifts to the long-term trend of the average level of real wages. What propelled the increase in average real wages during the last century? Why did real wage growth in America slow so dramatically between 1979 and 1995? Why has real wage growth rebounded since 1995 ("World of Work" 6.1)?

In answering these questions we will find that the secular expansion of the level of real wages is intimately linked to the growth of labor productivity. Much of the present chapter is thus devoted to productivity growth and its various ramifications.

THE PRODUCTIVITY CONCEPT

In essence, productivity is a simple concept. It is merely a relationship between real output—the quantity of goods and services produced—and the quantity of input used to produce that output. Productivity, in other words, is a measure of resource or input efficiency expressed in terms of a ratio:

$$\text{Productivity} = \frac{\text{output}}{\text{input}} \qquad \textbf{(17.1)}$$

Productivity tells us how many units of output we can obtain from a unit of input. If output per unit of input increases, productivity has risen.

FIGURE 17.1   The Aggregate Production Function and Labor Productivity

The aggregate production functions TP_1 and TP_2 portray the relationship between worker-hour inputs and total product, or real GDP, for two time periods and differing capital stocks. Assuming no change in labor hours, the upward shift of the production function portrays a 50 percent increase in labor productivity.

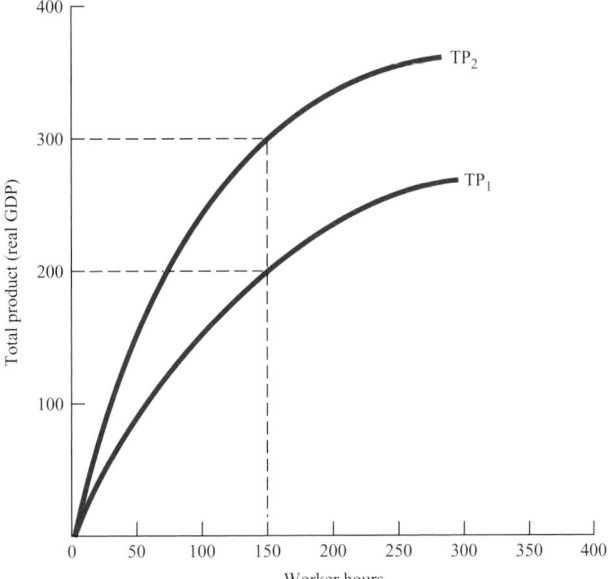

As you might sense from this definition, there is a whole family of productivity measures that vary depending on the specific data chosen for insertion in the numerator and denominator of the productivity equation. The output in the numerator might be the real gross domestic product (GDP), the real output of the private sector, or the real output of a particular industry or plant. Whatever output measure is used in the numerator, it must be stated in *real* rather than nominal terms. The production of more goods and services per unit of input constitutes an increase in productivity; higher prices on a fixed or even declining quantity of output clearly do not. As for the denominator, some productivity analysts combine inputs of both labor and capital to derive a measure of *total factor productivity.* Because labor is the focal point of our discussion, we will be concerned with **labor productivity,** in which worker hours are related to total product, or real GDP.[1]

Measurement

Figure 17.1 provides information enabling us to calculate labor productivity for each of two specific years for a hypothetical economy. The figure shows two aggregate production

[1] For a survey of available productivity measures, see Charles Steindel and Kevin Stiroh, "Productivity: What Is It, and Why Do We Care About It?" *Business Economics,* October 2001, pp. 13–31. See also Bureau of Labor Statistics, *BLS Handbook of Methods* (Washington, DC: Government Printing Office, 1997), chap. 10.

functions, TP_1 and TP_2, each of which represents a specific year and relates quantities of worker hours to total annual real GDP for that period. We will initially focus on the aggregate production function labeled TP_1. This curve reflects two assumptions: first, that the quality of labor, amount of capital, and methods of production are fixed; and second, that production is subject to diminishing marginal returns (Chapter 5). To simplify, we assume diminishing returns over the entire range of output. Thus TP_1 indicates the relationship between worker hours and total product, *other things being equal,* and shows that total product rises at a diminishing rate as added units of labor are used in conjunction with the fixed capital stock.

The input–output information provided by curve TP_1 allows us to measure labor productivity for this hypothetical economy for this particular year. Specifically,

$$\text{Labor productivity} = \frac{\text{total product (real GDP)}}{\text{number of worker hours}} \quad \textbf{(17.2)}$$

Equation (17.2) confirms that labor productivity is simply the average productivity of labor inputs for the economy as a whole. For illustrative purposes, we assume that the number of worker hours—the denominator in Equation (17.2)—is 150. The aggregate production function of Figure 17.1 reveals that the corresponding total product is 200. Dividing 200 by 150, we conclude that labor productivity is 1.33. Equation (17.3) allows us to convert this labor productivity figure to an index number, using this specific year as the base year:

$$\text{Productivity index}_{\text{base year}} = \frac{\text{productivity}_{\text{year 1}}}{\text{productivity}_{\text{base year}}} \times 100 \quad \textbf{(17.3)}$$

Equation (17.3) simply sets labor productivity equal to 100 for the base year. That is, $100 = (1.33/1.33) \times 100$.

We now can turn our attention to the upward shift of the aggregate production function from TP_1 to TP_2 in Figure 17.1. In the long run, other things are *not* equal; that is, labor quality can improve, the capital stock can increase, and more efficient methods for combining resources may be discovered. For example, suppose this economy enlarged its stock of capital goods, which in turn enabled workers to use more machinery and tools in the production process. As illustrated by the upward shift of the aggregate production function from TP_1 to TP_2, this would increase output per unit of labor input. Assuming that the number of worker hours remains constant at 150, total product would rise to 300, and labor productivity would increase to 2 ($= 300/150$). By comparing this new productivity level, 2, to productivity for the base year, 1.33, we can determine the productivity index in year 2:

$$\text{Productivity index}_{\text{year 2}} = \frac{\text{productivity}_{\text{year 2}}}{\text{productivity}_{\text{base year}}} \times 100 \quad \textbf{(17.4)}$$

The new index is 150 [$= (2/1.33) \times 100$], which represents a 50 percent increase relative to the base year index of 100.

FIGURE 17.2 **Index of U.S. Labor Productivity***
Labor productivity has more than doubled over the past 43 years.

Source: Bureau of Labor Statistics (**www.bls.gov**).

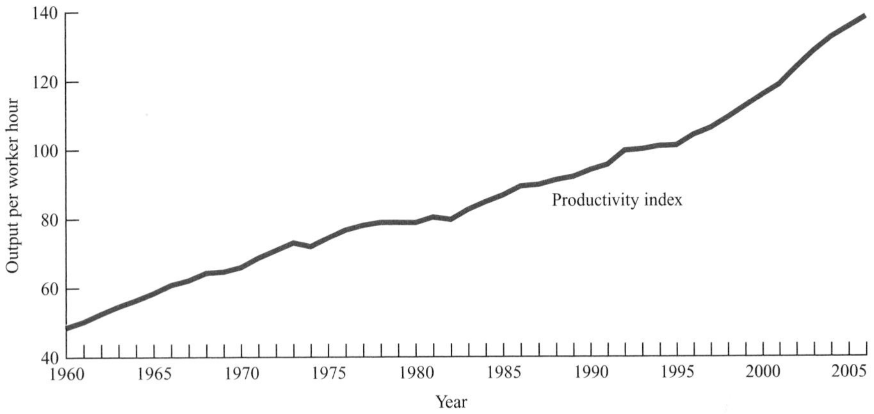

*Business sector.

The BLS Index

The Bureau of Labor Statistics (BLS) publishes an official index of labor productivity for the U.S. economy. Figure 17.2 shows the course of the BLS index of output per worker hour since 1960. Note that 1992 is the base year for the index. Because this *BLS productivity index* is widely used and cited, it is important to be familiar with its characteristics.

First, the index is calculated by dividing constant dollar (real) GDP originating in the private sector by the number of worker hours employed in the private sector. The public sector is excluded from the BLS index for a very practical reason: The public goods and services provided by government—such things as national defense, flood control, police and fire protection—are not sold in a market to individual buyers. Therefore, it is extremely difficult to estimate the economic value of the public sector output. Most productivity experts believe that productivity has grown less rapidly in the public sector than in the private sector. For this reason, the BLS data tend to overstate the entire economy's productivity growth.

Second, the index understates productivity growth because improvements in the *quality* of output are not taken into account. This, of course, is merely a reflection of a shortcoming involved in calculating real output or GDP for the private sector; GDP measures changes in the quantity, but not the quality, of output.

Third, the use of output per worker hour subtly implies that labor alone is responsible for rising productivity. This is not true. As we already indicated in our discussion of Figure 17.1, the factors affecting labor productivity are manifold and diverse. They include improvements in the quality of labor, the use of more capital equipment, improvements in production technologies and managerial organizational techniques, increased specialization as the result of expanding markets, shifts in the structure of the economy, public policies, and societal attitudes. While the BLS index of labor productivity provides information about changes in labor productivity, it does not explain the *causes* of these changes.

Despite its limitations and biases, the BLS index of labor productivity provides a reasonable approximation of how private sector efficiency has changed through time. Indeed, the official BLS measure has certain notable virtues. First, the index is conceptually simple and can quite easily be calculated from available data. Second, because it is calculated on a per worker *hour* basis, the index automatically takes into account changes in the length of the workweek. In contrast, an index of output per worker per year would understate the growth of labor productivity if the length of the average workweek decreased through time. Finally, as a measure of hourly output, the index can be directly compared with hourly wage rates.[2]

IMPORTANCE OF PRODUCTIVITY INCREASES

The growth of labor productivity is important for at least two reasons:

1. Productivity growth is the basic source of improvements in real wages and living standards.

2. Productivity growth is an anti-inflationary force in that it offsets or absorbs increases in nominal wages.

Let's consider these two points in the order stated.

Productivity and Real Wages

Real wage rates have increased in the United States over the past century at an average annual rate of 2 to 3 percent. Figure 17.3 provides an accurate but somewhat superficial explanation for that secular trend. The figure shows that increases in real wages—for example, from $(w/p)_1$ to $(w/p)_2$ to $(w/p)_3$—occur when the demand for labor rises more rapidly than labor supply. As shown in the figure, these rising real wages are fully compatible with increases in the number of worker hours (Q_1 to Q_3).

This simple supply and demand explanation for rising real wages naturally raises a more penetrating question: Why has labor demand increased over the decades? Figure 17.4 identifies the primary source of this increase: rising labor productivity. Notice the extremely close relationship between the increase in output per worker hour and the growth of average real hourly compensation. Increases in labor productivity have increased the demand for labor relative to labor supply and therefore have boosted the average real wage rate. When one recognizes that society's real output *is* its real income, the close relationship between productivity and real compensation is no surprise. Generally, for the economy as a whole, real income per worker per hour can increase at only the same rate as real output per worker per hour; more output per hour

---

[2] For a discussion of the problems involved in measuring productivity, see Edwin R. Dean, "The Accuracy of the BLS Productivity Measures," *Monthly Labor Review,* February 1999, pp. 22–34.

FIGURE 17.3
Real Wage Increases: Labor Supply and Demand Explanation
Increases in real wages occur when the demand for labor rises more rapidly than the labor supply.

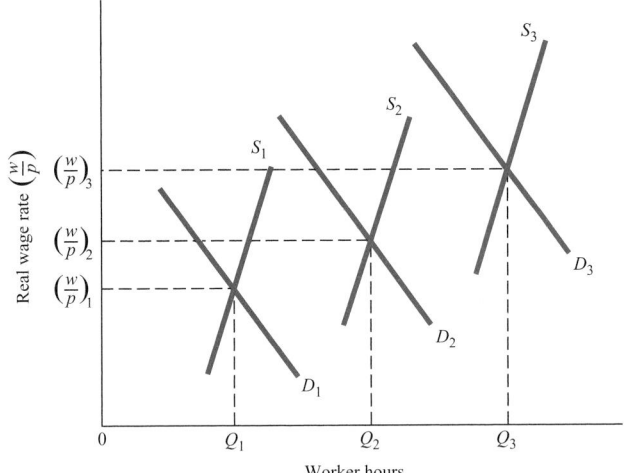

means more real income to distribute for each hour worked. The simplest case is the classic one of Robinson Crusoe on his deserted island. The number of coconuts he can pick or fish he can catch per hour *is* his real income or wage per hour. Crudely stated, what you produce is what you get.

FIGURE 17.4   Labor Productivity and the Average Level of Real Compensation
Because real output *is* real income, the growth of real output per worker hour and the growth of real compensation per hour are very closely related.

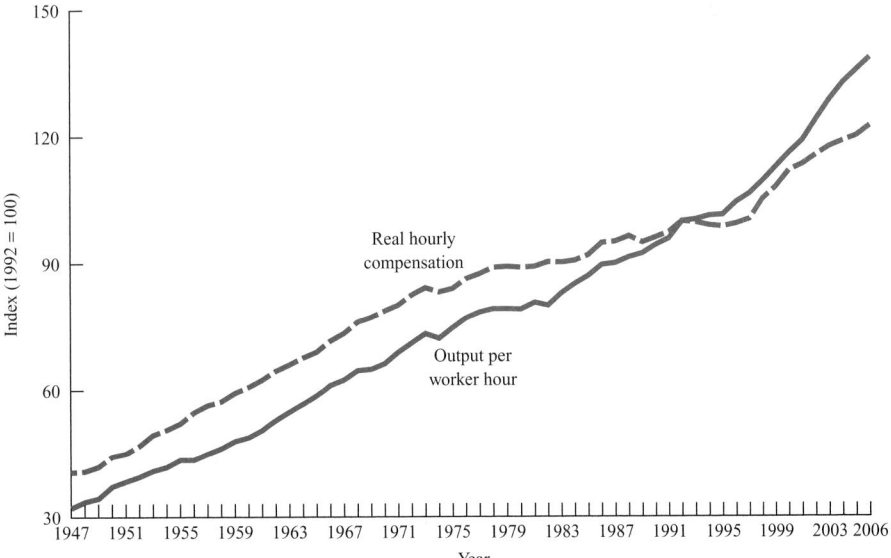

The importance of the contribution that the growth of labor productivity has made to the overall growth of our economy can hardly be overstated. We can rearrange the labor productivity Equation (17.2) as follows:

$$\text{Real GDP} = \text{worker hours} \times \text{labor productivity} \qquad \textbf{(17.5)}$$

Equation (17.5) implies that real output can increase because of an increase in inputs of worker hours *or* because each of those hours of work generates more output. In other words, total product as shown in Figure 17.1 can rise because of a rightward movement along an existing aggregate production function (more inputs of labor hours) or as a result of an upward shift of the function (rising labor productivity). Data indicate that rising productivity has been the more important of the two contributors to the growth of real GDP in the United States. Over the 1960–2006 period, for example, real output increased by 357 percent. During this same period, labor productivity rose by 184 percent, while worker hours of labor increased by 82 percent.

Inflation and Productivity

Although the causes of inflation are complex and controversial, economists acknowledge a link between the rate of productivity growth and the rate of inflation. Other things being equal, rapid productivity growth helps limit the rate of inflation, and slow productivity growth causes the inflation rate to be higher than would otherwise be the case. More specifically, productivity gains offset increases in nominal wages and thereby help restrain increases in unit labor costs and ultimately product prices.

Let's employ several simple numerical examples to grasp the relationship between changes in nominal wages, productivity, and unit labor costs. If, for example, hourly nominal wages are $10.00 and a worker produces 10 units per hour, then unit labor costs—that is, labor cost per unit of output—will be $1.00. If nominal wages increase by 10 percent to $11.00 per hour and productivity also increases by 10 percent to 11 units per hour, then unit labor costs will be unchanged. That is, $10.00/10 = $11.00/11 = $1.00. Generalization: *Equal percentage increases in nominal wages and productivity leave unit labor costs unchanged.*

Similarly, if nominal wages rise by 10 percent and labor productivity does not rise at all, unit labor costs will rise by 10 percent. That is, if the wage is $10.00 initially and output per hour is 10 units, unit labor costs will be $1.00. But with wages now at $11.00 and output still at 10 units per hour, unit labor costs will be $1.10, which is a 10 percent increase. Generalization: *If nominal wage increases exceed the increase in labor productivity, unit labor costs will rise.*

Finally, suppose the nominal wage rate does not rise, but productivity increases by 10 percent. Specifically, if wages remain at $10.00 and productivity increases from 10 to 11 units per hour, then unit labor costs will decline from $1.00 to about $0.91. Generalization: *If productivity increases exceed the increase in nominal wages, unit labor costs will fall.*

Columns 1 through 4 of Table 17.1 show the indicated relationships between changes in the hourly compensation of workers, productivity, and unit labor costs for the 1960–2006 period.

Because labor costs on the average constitute 70 to 75 percent of total production costs and higher production costs eventually cause higher product prices, the link

TABLE 17.1

The Relationship between Changes in Wages, Productivity, Unit Labor Costs, and the Price Level (Annual Percentage Changes)

Source: Bureau of Labor Statistics. Data in columns 2–4 are for the private business sector.

Year	Change in Compensation per Hour	Change in Output per Hour	Change in Unit Labor Costs	Change in Price Level*
1960	4.2	1.7	2.4	1.4
1962	4.4	4.6	−0.1	1.4
1964	3.8	3.4	0.4	1.5
1966	6.7	4	2.6	2.8
1968	8.1	3.4	4.5	4.3
1970	7.7	2	5.6	5.3
1972	6.3	3.2	3	4.3
1974	9.7	−1.6	11.4	9.0
1976	8.6	3.2	5.3	5.8
1978	8.7	1.1	7.5	7.0
1980	10.8	−0.2	11	9.1
1982	7.2	−0.8	8.1	6.1
1984	4.4	2.7	1.7	3.8
1986	5.1	2.9	2.1	2.2
1988	5.1	1.5	3.5	3.4
1990	6.3	2.1	4.1	3.9
1992	5.2	4.3	0.9	2.3
1994	1.4	1	0.4	2.1
1996	3.5	3	0.5	1.9
1998	6.1	2.8	3.2	1.1
2000	7.1	2.9	4.1	2.2
2002	3.6	4.1	−0.5	1.7
2004	3.8	3.1	0.7	2.8
2006	1.6	2.2	2	2.9

* GDP implicit price deflator.

between productivity increases and the rate of inflation is clear. Other things being equal, the 10 percent increase in unit labor costs in our example would translate into a 7.0–7.5 percent increase in total costs. As the data in Table 17.1 suggest, with important exceptions, changes in unit labor costs (column 4) and the rate of inflation (column 5) do track closely. As a rough rule of thumb, in most years changes in unit labor costs are associated with roughly similar changes in the rate of inflation.

We must be careful not to infer from Table 17.1 that the relationship between the growth of nominal wages and the increase in labor productivity is necessarily a primary cause of inflation. Many other factors—the money supply, inappropriate fiscal policy, expectations, supply shocks—are all held by various economists to be of greater significance. Indeed, some economists would argue that the relationship between the growth of real output and increases in the money supply is the primary determinant of changes in the price level. They contend that excessive growth of the money supply causes all prices to rise, including the price of labor: the nominal wage. The great majority of economists believe that both demand and supply (cost) factors can cause inflation, at least in the short term. They believe that the relationship between nominal wages and productivity is an important determinant of the price level. In fact, the U.S. government has at times implemented wage–price policies designed to restrict nominal wage increases to the average labor productivity increase as a means of controlling inflation.

The question of whether increases in unit labor costs cause inflation or are simply a symptom of inflation is subject to debate. Suffice it to say that given the rate of increase in nominal wage rates, the higher the rate of labor productivity, the smaller the rate of inflation.

LONG-RUN TREND OF LABOR PRODUCTIVITY[3]

Data suggest that in the long run—say, over the past century—average annual increases in output per worker hour have been on the order of 2–3 percent. Although these figures may not seem particularly impressive, the "miracle" of compounding translates this annual increase into very large increases in hourly output and income over time. Specifically, a 2.5 percent annual increase in hourly output will double output per worker hour in about 28 years. As we will soon see, the productivity growth since 1995 has been substantially higher than that experienced in the prior two decades.

What causes productivity growth? Generally speaking, the critical determinants of productivity growth can be classified under three headings: (1) the average quality of the labor force; (2) the amount of capital goods employed with each worker hour of labor; and (3) the efficiency with which labor, capital, and other inputs are combined. Figure 17.5 presents Jorgenson, Ho, and Stiroh's estimates of the contributors to the growth of labor productivity for the period 1959–2004. These factors are the focal point of the following discussion.

Improved Labor Quality

The quality of labor depends on its education and training, its health and vitality, and its age–gender composition. Other things being the same, a better-educated, better-trained workforce can produce more output per hour than a less educated, inadequately trained one. Indeed, Chapter 4's discussion of education and training as investments in human capital that increase labor productivity and earnings is highly relevant. Figure 17.6 provides a general overview of the increases in formal educational attainment of the population (25 years of age and older) since 1950. For the 1959–2004 period, Jorgenson, Ho, and Stiroh estimate that approximately 14 percent of the growth of labor productivity was due to enhanced worker education and training (see Figure 17.5).

Investments in human capital that enhance the health and vitality of workers also improve the average quality of labor. Improved nutrition, more and better medical care,

---

[3] For more about productivity growth, see Charles R. Hulten, Edwin R. Dean, and Michael J. Harper (eds.), *New Developments in Productivity Analysis* (Chicago: University of Chicago Press, 2001); and Kevin J. Stiroh, "What Drives Productivity Growth?" Federal Reserve Bank of New York *Economic Policy Review,* March 2001, pp. 37–59.

FIGURE 17.5   Relative Importance of the Causes of U.S. Productivity Growth
Increases in the quantity of capital account for about half of the growth of productivity.
Increased efficiency and improvements in labor quality account for the other half.

Source: Dale W. Jorgenson, Mun S. Ho, and Kevin J. Stiroh, "Potential Growth of the U.S. Economy: Will the Productivity Resurgence
Continue?" *Business Economics,* January 2006, pp. 7–16.

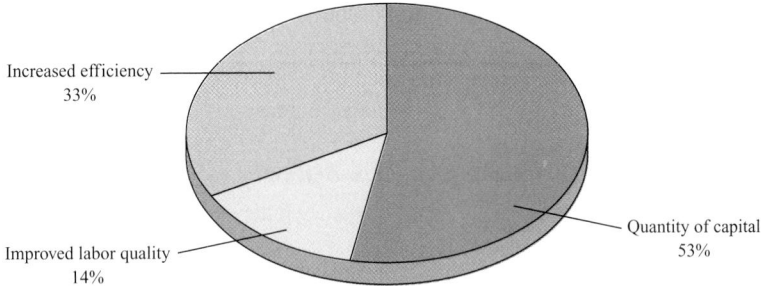

and better general living conditions improve the physical vigor and morale of the labor
force. These same factors enhance worker longevity and contribute to a workforce that
is more productive because it is more experienced.

Finally, changes in the age–gender composition of the labor force may also affect average labor force quality and therefore productivity. For example, historically, increasingly
stringent child labor and school attendance legislation has kept potential young workers—
workers who would be unskilled and relatively unproductive by virtue of their lack of education and work experience—out of the labor force. This exclusion has increased the

**FIGURE 17.6   Educational Attainment Completed by the U.S. Population
(25 years of age or older)**
The percentage of individuals with a high school or college degree has risen over time.

Source: U.S. Census Bureau (**www.census.gov**).

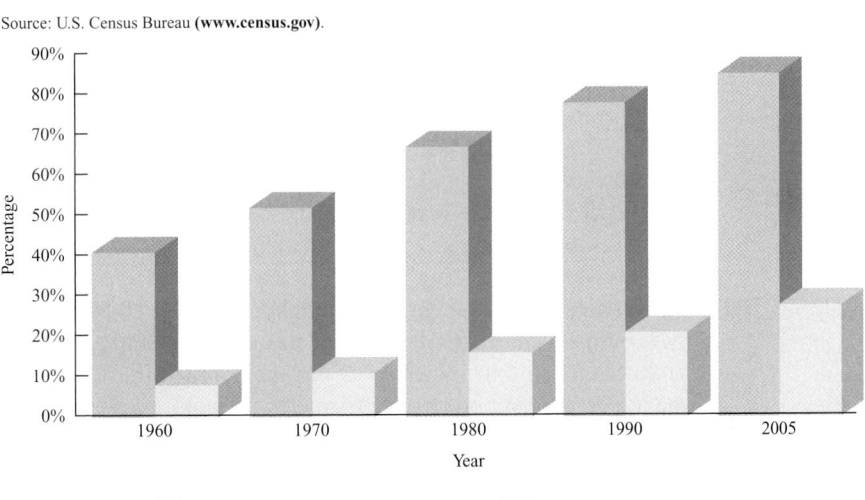

average quality of the labor force. As a second example, changes in the age–gender composition of labor may have lowered productivity growth in the 1970s and 1980s.

A benevolent circle of feedback and self-reinforcement may evolve historically with respect to labor quality. If the productivity of labor rises, real wages also rise. These enhanced earnings permit workers to improve their health and education, which further improves in labor quality and productivity. And so the cycle repeats itself. This circular interaction may be strengthened because the demands for education and health care are both elastic with respect to income. This means that rising national income generates more than proportional percentage increases in expenditures on these items.

Quantity of Physical Capital

The productivity of any given worker will depend on the amount of capital equipment with which he or she is equipped. A construction worker can dig a basement in a much shorter period with a bulldozer than with a hand shovel! A critical relationship with respect to labor productivity is the amount of capital available per unit of labor or, more technically, the capital–labor ratio. This ratio has increased historically. For example, in the 1959–1998 period, the stock of capital goods is estimated to have approximately tripled; and over the same period, labor hours are estimated to have roughly doubled. Thus the quantity of capital goods per labor hour was about 50 percent larger in 1998 than in 1959. Stated differently, the capital–labor ratio increased by half over this 39-year period.[4] Jorgenson, Ho, and Stiroh's estimates for 1959–2004 indicate that approximately 53 percent of the growth of labor productivity was the result of increases in the stock of physical capital (see Figure 17.5).

17.1

Increased Efficiency

The third source of rising productivity is greater efficiency in the use of labor and capital. In the present context, *increased efficiency* is a comprehensive term that includes a variety of both obvious and subtle factors that enhance labor productivity. At a minimum, increased efficiency encompasses (1) technological progress, including that embodied within both improved capital and improved business organization and managerial techniques; (2) greater specialization as the result of scale economies; (3) the reallocation of labor from less to more productive uses; and (4) changes in a society's institutional, cultural, and environmental setting and in its public policies. Note in Figure 17.5 that increased efficiency accounts for about one-third of the productivity gains that occurred over the 1959–2004 period.

Let's comment briefly on each of these factors. First, technological advance involves the development of more efficient techniques of production. The evolution of mass-production assembly-line techniques immediately comes to mind, as do computers, biotechnical developments, xerography, robotics, and containerized shipping. The switch from the old open-hearth process of steelmaking to the oxygen method enhanced productivity in that industry, as did the supplanting of the distillation process by the newer cracking process in petroleum refining. Improved managerial techniques—time-and-motion studies and the creation of new systems of managerial control of

---

[4] Dale W. Jorgenson and Kevin J. Stiroh, "Raising the Speed Limit: U.S. Economic Growth in the Information Age," *Brookings Papers on Economic Activity,* no. 1, 2000, pp. 125–211.

<table>
<tr><td>

17.1

</td><td>

World of Work

</td><td>

Is Public Capital Productive?*

</td></tr>
</table>

The impact of spending on public sector capital such as highways and airports on the productivity growth is controversial. The results from empirical investigations range from public capital having no effect on productivity to it having triple the productivity effect of private capital.

The wide range of productivity estimates arises from several factors. The largest estimates derive from studies based on national data. We should be skeptical of these findings because the studies use broad definitions of public capital goods, and the results vary by estimation technique. Investigations using state–regional data and narrower definitions of public capital yield substantially smaller productivity estimates, but they ignore the positive impact of infrastructure on other states. However, a study by Holtz-Eaken and Schwartz indicates that this bias is small. It is worth noting that all of the empirical estimates are biased downward because they don't account for the complementary effects between public

capital and private capital and labor. In summary, it is likely that public capital does increase productivity but the exact magnitude is unclear.

Should government spending on public capital goods be increased? Not surprisingly, there is wide variance in estimates of the ideal amount of spending on public sector goods. One study suggests that the best amount is 4 percent of GDP, whereas another indicates that it is nearly 20 percent of GDP. The existing figure is 3.3 percent of GDP. Given the uncertainty regarding the preferred amount of public capital goods spending, Lansing argues that we should be wary about increasing investment in public sector capital.

* Based on Kevin J. Lansing, "Is Public Capital Productive?: A Review of the Evidence," Federal Reserve Bank of Cleveland *Economic Commentary*, March 1, 1995; and Douglas Holtz-Eakin and Amy Ellen Schwartz, "Spatial Productivity Spillovers from Public Infrastructure: Evidence from State Highways," *International Tax and Public Finance*, November 1995, pp. 459–68.

production—have similarly enhanced productive efficiency. A variety of worker participation, job enrichment, and profit-sharing plans are being experimented with in the hope that they will enhance worker productivity.

Second, production efficiencies called *economies of scale* are typically derived from growing market and firm size. Market growth allows firms to become mass producers, which in turn permits greater specialization in the use of labor and therefore greater output per worker. Market expansion also enables firms to avail themselves of the most efficient production techniques. For example, a large manufacturer of automobiles can use elaborate assembly lines, featuring computerization and robotics, whereas small producers have to settle for less advanced technologies.

Third, productivity has also been stimulated by the reallocation of labor from less productive to more productive employments. Thus, for example, productivity gains have been realized historically by the reallocation of labor from agriculture, where the average productivity of labor is relatively low, to manufacturing, where the average productivity of labor is relatively high.

Finally, the cultural values of a society, the nature of its institutions, and the character of its public policies affect labor productivity in myriad ways. The fact that American values condone material advance and that the successful inventor, innovator, and business executive are accorded high levels of respect and prestige has been important historically for productivity growth. Similarly, the work ethic is generally held in high esteem. Equally critical is the existence of a complex array of financial institutions that marshal the funds of savers and make them available to investors. On the other hand, recall from Chapter 11 that the impact of unions on productivity is unclear.

Public policies and social attitudes provide a mixed picture with respect to their implications for productivity. For example, while the long-run trend toward freer international trade and the general policy of promoting domestic competition bode well for productivity growth, the many exceptions to both free trade and procompetition policies do not. Tariffs and import quotas shelter American producers from competition and can have the effect of retaining labor and other inputs in relatively inefficient industries. Similarly, we know from Chapter 14 that discrimination based on race, gender, or age is an artificial impediment to allocative efficiency and therefore a barrier to productivity growth.

Two final comments are in order. First, although Jorgenson, Ho, and Stiroh conclude that about half of the increase in labor productivity is due to the use of more capital goods and the other half is the result of increased labor quality and greater efficiency, other experts offer somewhat different estimates. For example, Dean and Harper attribute approximately half of the productivity increase to enhanced efficiency, with labor quality and capital goods accounting for the other half.[5] The second point is that the factors in productivity growth are interrelated. For example, investment in capital equipment is stimulated by technological advance. Similarly, highly educated and well-trained workers cannot be used productively in the absence of sophisticated capital goods.

17.1

Quick Review

- Labor productivity is a measure of output per unit of labor input (worker hours).
- Productivity growth is important for two reasons: It is the basic source of improvements in real wages and living standards, and it helps offset inflationary forces by holding down unit labor costs when nominal wages are rising.
- Productivity growth has averaged between 2 and 3 percent annually since the turn of the century.
- The critical determinants of productivity growth include the average quality of the labor force; the amount of capital goods per worker hour; and the efficiency with which labor, capital, and other inputs are combined. This last category includes technology, economies of scale, improved resource organization, and the legal–human environment.
- Figure 17.5 summarizes the relative weights of the various factors that have contributed to U.S. productivity growth.

Your Turn

Suppose real output in a hypothetical economy is 10 units, 5 units of labor are needed to produce this output, and the price of labor is $2 per unit. What is the economy's labor productivity? What is its unit or average labor cost? (*Answers:* See page 599.)

---

[5] Edwin R. Dean and Michael J. Harper, "The BLS Measurement Program," in Charles R. Hulten, Edwin R. Dean, and Michael J. Harper (eds.), *New Developments in Productivity Analysis* (Chicago: University of Chicago Press, 2001). The Dean and Harper estimates cover the period 1948–1997.

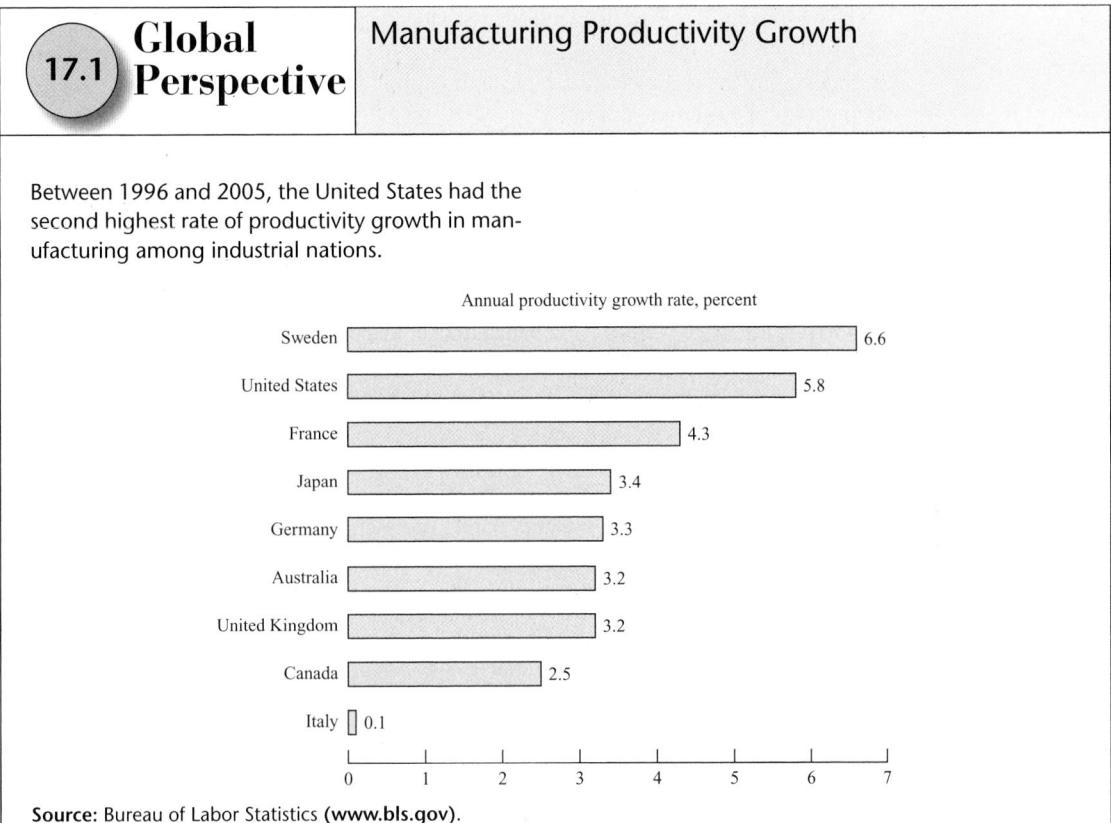

Global Perspective 17.1

Manufacturing Productivity Growth

Between 1996 and 2005, the United States had the second highest rate of productivity growth in manufacturing among industrial nations.

Annual productivity growth rate, percent

Sweden	6.6
United States	5.8
France	4.3
Japan	3.4
Germany	3.3
Australia	3.2
United Kingdom	3.2
Canada	2.5
Italy	0.1

Source: Bureau of Labor Statistics (**www.bls.gov**).

CYCLIC CHANGES IN PRODUCTIVITY

Emphasis thus far has been on the long-term trend of labor productivity. Because of the close relationship between productivity growth and real wages, this attention is entirely appropriate. However, productivity also exhibits a rather systematic short-run or cyclic pattern around the long-term trend.

Labor productivity generally displays a procyclic pattern. That is, productivity growth falls below the long-term trend during a cyclic downturn or recession and rises above the trend during an economic upturn or recovery. For example, over the 1948–2006 period, total real output declined in 8 years and increased in the remaining 51 years. In the 8 years of declining output, the rate of productivity growth was low, averaging 1.2 percent per year; in the 51 years of expanding aggregate output, labor productivity rose by 2.7 percent per year.[6]

---

[6] Author calculations are based on Bureau of Economic Analysis (**www.bea.doc.gov**) output data and Bureau of Labor Statistics (**www.bls.gov**) productivity data.

The reasons for these cyclic changes in productivity are quite detailed. We will simplify the discussion by considering just three factors: (1) changes in the utilization of labor, (2) changes in the utilization of plant and capital equipment, and (3) changes in the composition of aggregate output.[7]

Utilization of Labor

As the economy moves into a downturn or recession, a firm's sales and output will decline more rapidly than its inputs of labor:

> Specifically, during cyclical contractions, employers normally are loath to fire workers—preferring instead to shunt labor into maintenance and other less essential tasks rather than the production of goods—until they are convinced that the downturn is not a temporary aberration. As a consequence, *measured* productivity (the ratio of output to *employed* labor) declines. Analogously, once a recovery starts, employers put these underutilized labor resources back on the production line. So output can expand briskly with little need for new hiring, and measured productivity registers dramatic gains.[8]

Why the reluctance to fire workers during a downswing? Why is labor a quasi-fixed, rather than a completely variable, input? Some employees, of course, are salaried workers or "overhead" labor. Few firms will dispense with top or midlevel executives during a downturn. An internal auditor, a marketing manager, and a personnel director will all be needed, even though output is currently down. Also, the typical firm will have invested in the specific training of its skilled and semiskilled workers. Remember from Chapter 4 that such workers must be retained for the firm to realize a return on its human capital investment. If these workers are furloughed, the firm runs the risk of losing them to other employers. Finally, there are layoff and rehiring costs to contend with, and within limits, it may be less expensive to retain and underutilize workers if layoff and rehiring costs can be avoided by so doing. Thus firms find it to be in their long-run profit-maximizing interest to hoard labor during recession and, from a social perspective, use labor less productively than previously.

DeLong and Waldmann find evidence of **labor hoarding** during cyclic downturns in the United States.[9] Such hoarding diminishes, however, as the unemployment rate rises. Laid-off workers are less likely to find employment at other firms and are more

---

[7] Researchers have also suggested two other explanations for the observed procyclic variations in productivity. First, technological innovations may be procyclic. Second, imperfect competition and increasing returns to scale may lead to rises in productivity when inputs rise. Empirical evidence indicates that the use of inputs rises and falls with the business cycle. However, a recent study indicates that these factors do not play a major role in explaining procyclic productivity. See Susanto Basu and John Fernald, "Why Is Productivity Procyclical? Why Do We Care?" in Charles R. Hulten, Edwin R. Dean, and Michael J. Harper (eds.), *New Developments in Productivity Analysis* (Chicago: University of Chicago Press, 2001).

[8] Alan S. Blinder, *Economic Policy and the Great Stagflation* (New York: Academic Press, 1981), pp. 65–66.

[9] J. Bradford DeLong and Robert J. Waldmann, "Interpreting Procyclical Productivity: Evidence from a Cross-Nation Cross-Industry Panel," Federal Reserve Bank of San Francisco *Economic Review,* no. 1, 1997, pp. 33–52. Other studies finding evidence of labor hoarding include Argia M. Sbordone, "Interpreting the Procyclical Productivity of Manufacturing Sectors: External Effects or Labor Hoarding?" *Journal of Money, Credit, and Banking,* February 1997, pp. 26–45; and Basu and Fernald, op. cit.

likely to be available when the firm wants to rehire them. Thus firms have less incentive to practice labor hoarding when the unemployment rate is high. Consistent with this conjecture, they find that productivity is less procyclic when the unemployment rate is high.

But during the upswing or recovery phase of the cycle, output can be increased substantially by simply correcting this underutilization. Within limits, firms can increase output by taking up the slack in their currently employed labor forces. More output can be obtained from the number of worker hours now being employed so that productivity will rise sharply. It has also been observed that workers are generally more productive when there is more work to be done. For example, checkout personnel at supermarkets work faster when shopper queues are long.[10]

Utilization of Plant and Equipment

A similar point can be made with respect to capital equipment. Competition forces firms to design their plants so that they operate with maximum efficiency during normal times. This means that during a recession, falling output causes the plant and equipment to be used at less than the optimal level, and productivity consequently falls. Conversely, during recovery, plant utilization moves back in the direction of the most efficient level of output, and productivity tends to rise.

Composition of Output

Cyclic fluctuations affect the various sectors of the economy with differing degrees of severity. Specifically, the demand for durable manufactured goods—machinery and equipment and such consumer goods as automobiles, refrigerators, and microwave ovens—is very sensitive to cyclic changes. By way of contrast, the demand for most services is much less responsive to cyclic changes. Thus the *relative* share of manufactured goods in domestic output declines during cyclic downswings and increases during upswings. Because the level of productivity in manufacturing is among the highest of all sectors of the economy, it follows that the relative decline in manufacturing during a recession will reduce overall labor productivity.

Conversely, the relative expansion of manufacturing as a proportion of total output during recovery causes average labor productivity to rise. Note that this effect is independent of other cyclic influences on productivity. Even if no individual firm or industry experienced a productivity change due to a change in the use of labor and capital, the indicated relative shift in the composition of output would cause average labor productivity to vary procyclically.

Implications

Of what consequences are these cyclic changes in productivity? In the first place, they are not merely the result of cyclic fluctuations but rather an integral part of the business

---

[10] George A. Akerlof and Janet L. Yellen, "Introduction," in Akerlof and Yellen (eds.), *Efficiency Wage Models of the Labor Market* (Cambridge, England: Cambridge University Press, 1986), p. 5.

cycle. When the economy lapses into a recession, productivity falls sharply, and this tends to increase unit labor costs. If nominal wage rates continue to rise during the recession, unit labor costs will rise by an even larger amount. Rising costs typically squeeze business profits. This profit decline deters investment spending in two ways: It diminishes the financial resources (undistributed profits) that firms have for investing, *and* it generates pessimistic business expectations. Falling investments, of course, intensify the cyclic downswing. Conversely, rising productivity during recovery stimulates the upturn. Rapidly increasing productivity keeps unit labor costs down and contributes to rising profits. Profit growth is conducive to expanded investment spending, which accelerates the economic expansion.

A second related point is that cyclic changes in productivity have important implications for economic policy. For example, some economists are more or less resigned to the view that to arrest rapid inflation, it is necessary to create a recession through the application of restrictive monetary and fiscal policies. But an understanding of cyclic changes in productivity suggests that any such recession may have to be deep and long to produce its intended effects. Specifically, the decline in productivity that accompanies recession may contribute to rising unit costs, which in turn may contribute to supply, or cost-push, inflation. On the other hand, if the economy is already in a recession and unemployment is high, then the rapid labor productivity increase that occurs in the early stages of recovery may permit policy makers to increase output and employment through expansionary monetary and fiscal measures with less fear of generating added inflation. The reason is that high productivity growth tends to limit cost and price increases.

PRODUCTIVITY AND EMPLOYMENT

Let's now consider the impact of productivity growth on the level of employment. Do employees "work themselves out of their jobs" as they become more productive?

Superficial consideration of the relationship between productivity and employment often leads people to conclude erroneously that productivity growth causes unemployment. The reasoning normally is that an increase in labor productivity means that fewer workers are needed to produce any given level of real output. For example, if a firm employs 50 workers whose average productivity is $10 worth of real output per hour, then $500 worth of output can be produced. If the productivity of the 50 employees were to increase by 25 percent to $12.50 worth of output per hour, the same output could now be produced with only 40 workers ($= 40 \times \$12.50$). Thus 10 of the 50 workers would seem to be redundant.

But this illustration is too simple because it ignores society's desire for additional output and the fact that rising productivity increases aggregate demand. Society's wants tend to exceed its available resources. Productivity increases allow society to achieve higher levels of output—that is, to fulfill more wants—given these limited resources. In terms of the previous example, the 25 percent productivity increase enables society to gain $125 worth of output. The 50 workers now can produce $625 worth of output ($= 50 \times \$12.50$) compared to $500 ($= 50 \times \$10 = \$500$). But will there be sufficient aggregate spending to take this additional output off the market? We know that productivity and real wages are closely correlated. Thus the 25 percent increase in productivity can be expected to increase real incomes, which would increase aggregate spending and generate additional jobs. Although our economy has been characterized by cyclic fluctuations in output and employment (Chapter 18), the long-term historical trend of productivity growth in the United States has *not* given rise to a growing stockpile of unemployed workers. Rather, increases in labor productivity have been associated in the aggregate with both higher real wages *and* higher levels of employment.

Does this positive relationship between productivity and employment also apply on an industry-by-industry basis? In answering this question it will be useful to (1) ascertain the relationship between productivity growth and changes in employment in an industry, given the locations and elasticity of the product demand curves; (2) indicate the complexities that arise once these demand assumptions are relaxed; and (3) present actual data on the relationship between industrial productivity and employment growth in the United States.

Demand Factors Constant

Let's analyze how productivity growth and employment changes in an industry would be related without shifts in, and varying elasticities of, product demand. We must first establish that wage rates in various U.S. industries move more in accord with *national* productivity than with *industry* productivity. As indicated in the right column of Figure 17.7, compensation per hour rises more or less evenly in all industries, even though output per worker hour varies greatly by industry (left column). Why is this the case? If wages began to diverge—rising rapidly in high-productivity-growth industries and increasing slowly in low-productivity-growth industries—the wage structure would be pulled apart. But this doesn't occur because workers respond to the growing wage differentials by leaving the low-growth, low-wage industries to seek the higher wages in the high-growth industries. Similarly, new labor force entrants would choose employment in the high-growth industries and shun the low-growth industries. The increased labor supply would tend to reduce wages in the high-productivity industries, and the diminished labor supply would increase wages in the low-productivity industries. In short, labor supply responses would prevent wages from diverging in the various industries. To repeat: The trend of wages paid by specific industries is dominated by the nationwide trend of productivity primarily because workers respond to wage differentials (Chapter 8).

With this fact in mind, let's now reconsider the productivity–unit labor cost relationship in the context of a simple numerical example designed to illustrate the relationship between productivity growth and employment changes in an industry, *all else being constant.* Assume that (1) the annual rate of productivity growth for the economy as a whole is 3 percent; (2) industry X realizes a 6 percent annual productivity increase, while productivity growth in industry Y is 0 percent; and (3) nominal wage rates and earnings in both industries increase by 3 percent in accordance with the economy's overall rate of productivity growth. We find that unit labor costs would *decrease* in industry X and *increase* in industry Y. Further assuming that changes in unit labor costs result in roughly equivalent price changes, we can expect prices to *fall* by about 3 percent in industry X and to *rise* by approximately 3 percent in industry Y. Specifically, a 3 percent

FIGURE 17.7 **Output per Worker Hour and Compensation per Worker Hour, Selected Industries**
Changes in labor productivity vary considerably by industry on an annual basis, but compensation increases per hour of work tend to be closely matched across industries. Hourly increases in pay per year are more closely related to the average increase in labor productivity for the entire economy than to the change in productivity within specific industries.

Source: Bureau of Labor Statistics (**www.bls.gov**).

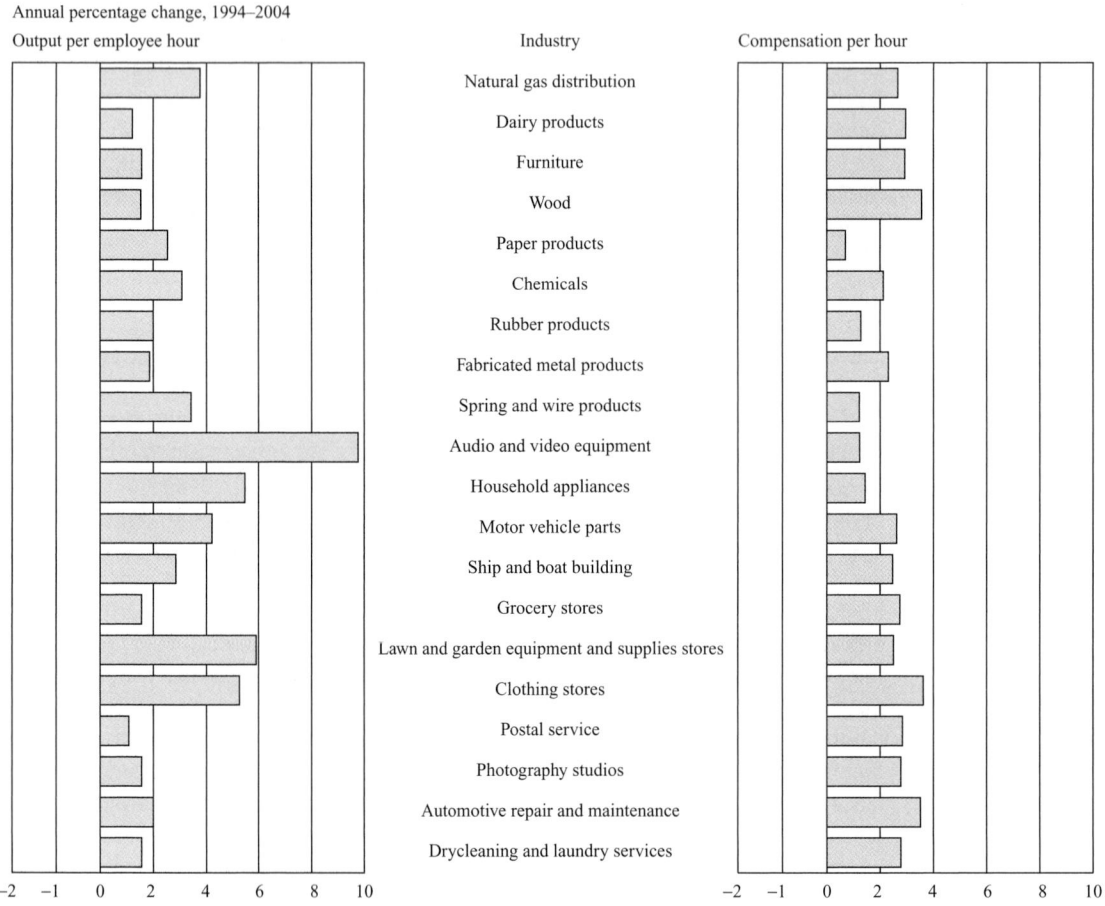

increase in nominal wages in industry X coupled with its 6 percent productivity increase would cause its unit labor costs and product price to fall by about 3 percent. Similarly, the 3 percent increase in nominal wages in industry Y combined with its zero rate of productivity growth would cause unit labor costs and product price to increase by approximately 3 percent. Given the locations and elasticities of the product demand curves for the two industries, output and sales would rise in industry X and decline in Y. Provided that the increase in sales more than compensates for the fact that each unit of output can now be produced with a smaller quantity of labor, an expansion of employment in industry

X would result. Conversely, the price increase for industry Y's product would reduce output and sales, implying the need for fewer workers. Therefore, other things being the same, industries with rapid productivity growth would employ more workers, whereas industries with slow productivity growth would provide less employment.

Demand Factors Variable

It is not realistic to expect that product demand conditions are similar and unchanging for various industries in the economy. In our example, the demands for the products of industries X and Y may have different elasticity characteristics *and* may be changing (shifting) through time in such a way as to undermine the generalization that productivity growth and employment growth are positively related. The price and income elasticities of, and shifts in, product demand curves can and do have profound effects on the cause–effect chain that links productivity and employment.

Industry Growth and Decline

Once again, consider industry X, where productivity is rising by 6 percent and product price is falling by about 3 percent. The consequent increase in output and employment would be especially large *if* the demand for its product is elastic with respect to both price and income. If demand is elastic with respect to price, then the price decline will generate a relatively larger increase in sales. For example, the 3 percent decrease in price may increase sales by 8 or 9 percent. This suggests a relatively large increase in employment. Similarly, if demand is elastic with respect to income,[11] then the growth of income in this economy will cause relatively larger increases in the demand for product X. For example, a 3 percent increase in income—which is the amount by which real income is increasing in our hypothetical two-industry economy—might shift the demand curve to the right so that perhaps 9 or 10 percent more of the product would be purchased at any given price. Of course, industry X's demand curve may shift rightward for reasons other than rising incomes. For example, consumer preferences for the product may become stronger, or the imposition of tariffs or quotas on competing foreign products may have deflected consumer purchases from imports toward domestic production. The point is that increases (rightward shifts) in product demand will enhance output and therefore employment in the industry so as to offset any declines in employment due to the fact that less labor is needed per unit of output.

   In contrast, if the demand for industry X's product is inelastic with respect to both price and income, the increases in output would tend to be small. If sufficiently small, the increase occasioned by the enhancement in sales may fail to offset

[11] Income elasticity is measured as the percentage change in quantity demanded relative to a given percentage change in income. If the percentage increase in the quantity demanded is greater than the percentage increase in the income that triggered the increase in the amount demanded, we say that demand is *income-elastic* or *income-sensitive*. If the percentage increase in quantity demanded is less than the percentage increase in income, then demand is *income-inelastic* or *income-insensitive*. In the special case of an *inferior good,* an *increase* in income *decreases* the demand for the product.

the fact that rising productivity has reduced labor requirements per unit of output. In this case, employment in industry X will decline, despite the high rate of productivity growth.

The worst scenario in terms of adverse employment effects would occur if product X were an *inferior good*—a product of which people buy *less* as their incomes rise—because the resulting decrease (leftward shift) of the product demand curve would reduce employment even though product price is falling. Enhanced foreign competition or declines in the prices of substitute goods are other developments that could also decrease demand and diminish output and employment. To recapitulate: The conditions most conducive to employment growth in an industry experiencing rapid productivity growth are (1) a price- and income-elastic product demand curve and (2) fortuitous circumstances that increase product demand.

Conversely, recall that industry Y, achieving no productivity growth, would find that the price of its product is *rising* by about 3 percent. The adverse effect of this price increase on output and employment will be minimized, or perhaps completely offset, if product demand is inelastic with respect to price and elastic with respect to income. The employment-diminishing effect would be aggravated, however, if demand is price-elastic and income-inelastic. Once again, changes in product demand stemming from a variety of causes other than rising real income may intensify or alleviate the impact on output and employment.

Illustrations

Our analysis can give us insight into the waxing and waning—particularly the waning—of various industries in our economy. For example, productivity in higher education—particularly in teaching—has been relatively constant. The result has been rising educational costs and rising tuition. But the demand for higher education is inelastic with respect to price and elastic with respect to income. As a consequence, higher education has absorbed an expanding proportion of per capita income. As another example, the production of certain highly crafted goods—fine pottery, glassware, and furniture—has also experienced little or no productivity growth. This has resulted in sharply rising prices for such products. But the demand for these products is price-elastic, and the result has been a decline in the total production of high-quality products. A similar analysis applies to the performing arts. (Given the size of the audience, how does one increase the productivity of a string quartet?) The symphonies and community theaters of most cities and towns depend on public and private subsidization. Furthermore, the financial problems of many large cities may be intimately tied to the fact that they provide services—of police, hospital workers, social workers—for which it is difficult to raise productivity. As the wages of public employees rise in accordance with the (higher) productivity growth of the national economy, the cost of government services will necessarily increase. The source of soaring government budgets may lie much more in the low productivity growth associated with public services than with bureaucratic mismanagement or malfeasance.[12]

---

[12] These examples are from William J. Baumol, "Macro-Economics of Unbalanced Growth: The Anatomy of Urban Crisis," *American Economic Review,* June 1967, pp. 415–26.

FIGURE 17.8   Output per Worker Hour and Employment, Selected Industries

Average annual percentage changes in employment within industries are not systematically related to industry average annual productivity changes.

Source: Bureau of Labor Statistics (**www.bls.gov**).

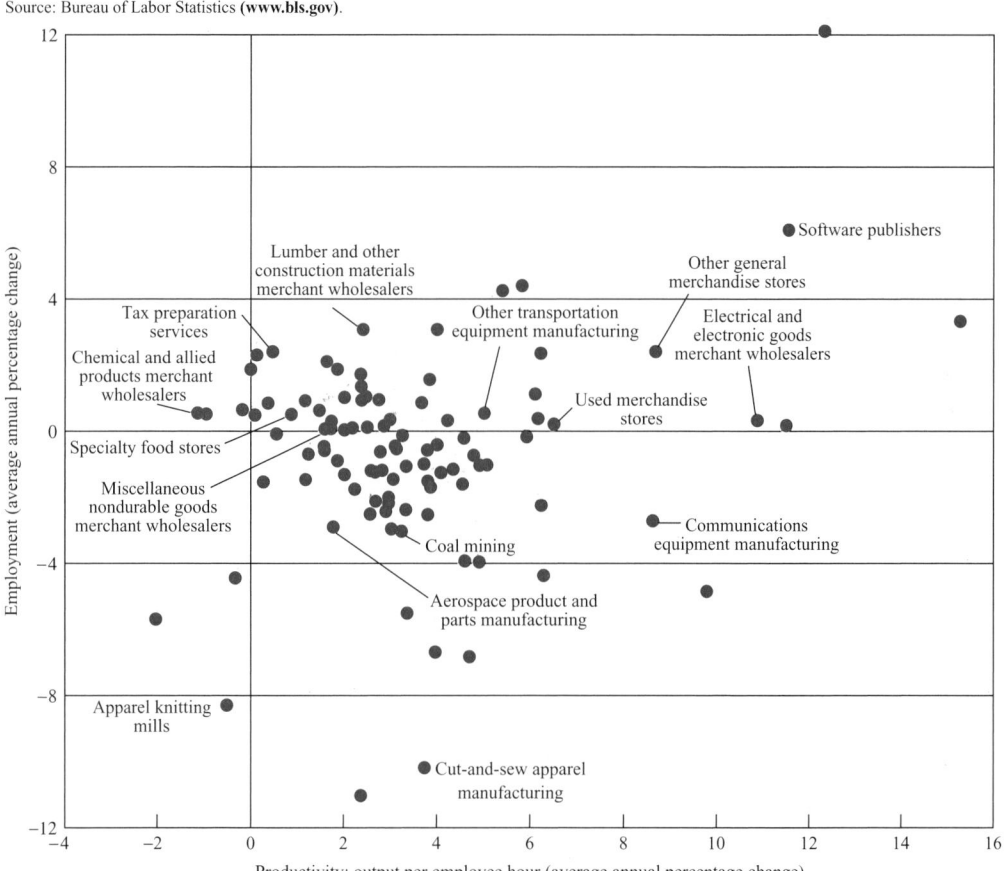

Observed Productivity–Employment Relationship

Figure 17.8 compares for a 10-year period the average annual percentage changes in employment with the average annual percentage changes in productivity for some 100 industries. You will observe that the scattering of industry data points is random; we simply cannot generalize about the relationship between productivity growth and employment growth by industry.

Although productivity increased for 93 of the 100 industries over the 1994–2004 period, employment increased in 44 industries and declined in 56. In some industries rapid productivity growth was associated with declines in employment (footwear, coal mining, and cut-and-sew apparel), whereas other industries experienced both rapid productivity growth and employment growth (software publishers and electronic shopping). Similarly, some industries that have been comparatively stagnant with respect to productivity growth have experienced large employment increases (tax preparation services) while employment has decreased in others (photo finishing).

It is challenging to speculate about the productivity and employment changes shown for specific industries in Figure 17.8. For example, the large fall in employment in the photo finishing services industry, where productivity growth has been slightly negative, might reflect the increased use of digital cameras that occurred in the past two decades. Similarly, we note that in the manufacture of footwear, productivity growth has been quite rapid. The accompanying decline in employment undoubtedly reflects the rise in the import share in the footwear industry that happened in the 1990s. You are urged to use your general knowledge of the economy to ponder the production and employment changes of various other industries shown in Figure 17.8.

17.2
Quick Review

- The rate of productivity growth fluctuates with the business cycle, falling as the economy recedes and rising as the economy expands.
- Although productivity growth means that society can produce its existing output with fewer workers, it also permits society to obtain more total output. Overall, productivity growth has been associated with growing employment, not rising unemployment.
- Compensation per hour rises more or less evenly in all industries, even though output per worker hour varies greatly by industry. Other things being equal, this fact implies rising per-unit costs and reduced output and employment in industries with slow productivity growth, and falling per-unit costs and increased output and employment in industries with high productivity growth.
- Variable demand factors confound the actual relationship between productivity and employment growth within industries; data reveal no systematic relationship between industry productivity growth and industry employment growth.

Your Turn

Productivity growth in both 1990 and 1991 was 0.7 percent; in 1992 it rose to 3.4 percent. Can you think of a possible explanation for this abrupt change? (*Hint:* A recession occurred in 1990–1991.) (*Answer:* See page 599.)

A "NEW ECONOMY"?

Since the mid-1990s the United States has experienced a resurgence of productivity growth. This rekindled productivity growth rate has led some to suggest that the United States is at the beginning of a "new economy." There are three related strands of the new economy perspective. First, some proponents argue that the higher rate of productivity growth permits the U.S. economy to expand at a faster rate without igniting inflation.

Second, other advocates suggest that innovations in information technology are yielding benefits that are spreading throughout the economy. Finally, others claim that recent technological innovations have altered the structure of the economy so that both low unemployment and low inflation can be achieved simultaneously.[13]

Figure 17.9 shows the rate of productivity growth for the 1948–2006 period. Between 1948 and 1973, the United States had a vigorous annual productivity growth rate of 3.2 percent. Productivity grew at less than half that rate during the 1974–1990 and 1991–1995 periods; however, productivity growth rebounded to a rapid 2.9 percent per year between 1996 and 2006.

The effects of this resurgence are those discussed earlier. The standard of living in the United States rose more rapidly in the last half of 1990s and early 2000s than it had in the prior 20 years and more rapidly than in other nations. For example, real compensation per hour rose at an annual rate of 72.0 percent between 1996 and 2006 compared to the sluggish annual rate of only 0.7 percent between 1974 and 1995. Also, according to many economists, the revival in productivity growth contributed to the low inflation experienced in the last half of the 1990s and early 2000s.

Possible Causes

No consensus exists among experts as to whether the increase in the U.S. productivity growth rate is a part of a new long-run trend or simply a temporary aberration. Nevertheless, it is enlightening to survey some possible causes of the productivity resurgence. The following are the primary explanations for the acceleration of productivity.

Increased Use of Information Capital

One possibility is that faster increases in the quantity of capital relating to information technology may have increased productivity growth. In the last half of the 1990s, firms invested heavily in information capital such as computer hardware, software, and communications equipment. In 1999 spending on information capital was responsible for 11 percentage points of the 14 percent real growth in business spending on capital.[14]

Empirical studies indicate that higher spending on information technology played an important role in the increased productivity growth. Jorgenson, Ho, and Stiroh's analysis indicates that 33 percent of the acceleration in productivity growth between 1973–1995 and 1996–2004 was due to increases in the use of information technology.[15] They also found that increased spending on other types of capital contributed 17 percent to the acceleration in productivity.

---

[13] For more about these different new economy perspectives, see Kevin J. Stiroh, "Is There a New Economy?" *Challenge,* July–August 1999, pp. 82–101.

[14] Council of Economic Advisers, *Economic Report of the President, 2001* (Washington, DC: Government Printing Office, 2001), chap. 1.

[15] Dale W. Jorgenson, Mun S. Ho, and Kevin J. Stiroh, "Potential Growth of the U.S. Economy: Will the Productivity Resurgence Continue?" *Business Economics,* January 2006, pp. 7–16.

FIGURE 17.9 **Labor Productivity Growth Rates in the United States**
Productivity growth surged in the 1996-2006 period after being relatively low for two decades.

Source: Bureau of Labor Statistics **(www.bls.gov)**.

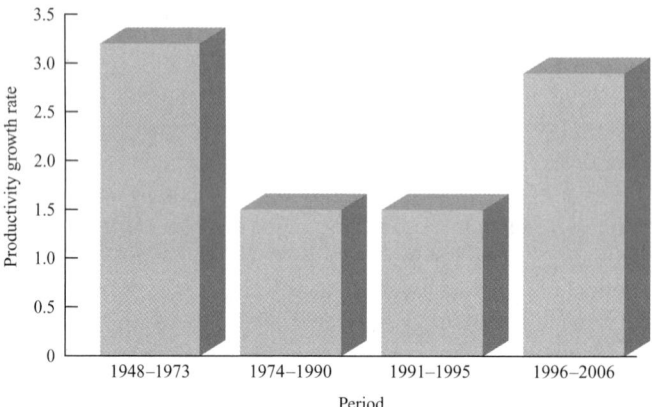

Increased Technological Progress and Efficiency

Another potential explanation is that greater technological progress and efficiency, particularly in information technology (as distinct from simply more capital goods), has increased the productivity growth rate. As measured by prices, the pace of innovations in computer technology has clearly quickened in recent years. Prices for computer equipment fell at a rate of 27 percent per year for 1996–2001 as compared to 18 percent in 1991–1995,[16] reflecting innovation and improved efficiency.

Empirical studies confirm that faster technological progress in high-technology industries played an important role in the speedup of the productivity growth rate. Jorgenson, Ho, and Stiroh find that 18 percent of the productivity acceleration between 1973–1995 and 1996–2004 was caused by increased efficiency in the production of information technology products.[17] They estimate that another 40 percent resulted from technological progress and efficiency gains in the rest of the economy.

The future for productivity growth depends critically on the rate of technological progress. Jorgenson, Ho, and Stiroh estimate that the long-term annual rate of productivity growth will be 2.25 percent if the rate of innovation in the information technology sector falls back to the 1990–2004 average rather than its rapid rate between 1996 and 2004. They forecast a productivity growth rate of 2.97 percent per year if the rate of innovation does not fall from the 1996–2004 average.[18] It remains to be seen what the future rate of innovation will be in the information technology industries.

---

[16] Stephen D. Oliner and Daniel E. Sichel, "Information Technology and Productivity: Where We Are Now and Where We Are Going?" *Journal of Policy Modeling,* July 2003, pp. 477–503.

[17] Jorgenson, Ho, and Stiroh, op. cit.

[18] Jorgenson, Ho, and Stiroh, op. cit.

Chapter Summary

1. Productivity is the relationship between real output and inputs. The "official" Bureau of Labor Statistics (BLS) index of labor productivity is the ratio of real GDP originating in the private sector to the number of worker hours employed in the private sector.

2. The BLS index overstates productivity growth because it excludes the public sector. On the other hand, it understates productivity growth in that quality improvements in output are ignored. The BLS index measures, but does not reveal the causes of, productivity growth.

3. The advantages of the BLS index are that *(a)* it is conceptually simple, *(b)* it automatically takes changes in the length of the workweek into account, and *(c)* it is directly comparable to hourly wage rates.

4. Economists are interested in labor productivity primarily because changes in productivity correlate closely with changes in real wage rates.

5. Other things being equal, productivity growth offsets increases in nominal wages and thereby restrains increases in unit labor costs and product prices.

6. The basic factors that determine productivity growth are *(a)* improvements in the quality of labor, *(b)* increases in the capital–labor ratio, and *(c)* increased efficiency in the use of labor and capital inputs. Increased efficiency is quantitatively the most important factor.

7. Labor productivity falls below the long-term rate of growth during recession and rises above that rate during recovery. Causal factors include cyclic changes in the use of labor and capital and changes in the relative importance of the manufacturing sector.

8. There is no easily discernible relationship between productivity growth and employment changes in various industries. Price and income elasticities of product demand, coupled with demand shifts from changes in such factors as consumer tastes or public policy, make it virtually impossible to predict whether a productivity increase will be associated with increasing or declining employment in any given industry.

9. The rate of productivity growth accelerated dramatically starting in the second half of the 1990s. Possible structural factors in the rise include *(a)* increased use of capital relating to information technology and *(b)* increased technological progress and efficiency.

Terms and Concepts

labor productivity, *509*

BLS productivity index, *511*

labor hoarding, *522*

Questions and Study Suggestions

1. How is *labor productivity* defined? Comment on the shortcomings and advantages of the Bureau of Labor Statistics index of labor productivity.

2. Suppose that in an economy 100 labor hours produce 160 units of output in year 1. In years 2 and 3 labor hours are 120 and 130 and units of output are 216 and 260, respectively. Using year 2 as the base year, calculate *(a)* the productivity index for all three years and *(b)* the rates of productivity growth.

3. How do you account for the close correlation between changes in the rate of productivity growth and changes in real wage rates for the economy as a whole? Does this relationship also hold true on an industry-by-industry basis? Explain.

4. Explain this statement: "High wage rates are both an effect and a cause of high labor productivity."

5. Discuss the relationship between aggregate productivity growth and price inflation. Draw a diagram (similar to Figure 17.8), putting average annual productivity growth on the horizontal axis and average annual price changes on the vertical axis. If you were to plot relevant data for, say, 60 or 70 major industries, what general relationship would you expect? Explain.

6. Suppose in a given year a firm's productivity increases by 2 percent and its nominal wages rise by 5 percent. What would you expect to happen to the firm's unit labor costs and product price?

7. Briefly comment in quantitative terms on the long-term trend of labor productivity in the United States; cite the three primary factors that contributed to that growth, and indicate the relative quantitative importance of each. Discuss the specific factors that have contributed to increased efficiency in the use of labor and capital.

8. Describe and explain the cyclic changes that occur in labor productivity. Of what significance are these changes?

9. Explain the relationship between changes in *(a)* nominal wage rates, *(b)* productivity, *(c)* unit labor costs, and *(d)* product price. What does this relationship suggest about the expected impact of productivity growth on employment in a particular industry? Can you reconcile your generalization with Figure 17.8?

10. Assume that labor productivity is rising by 6 percent in the economy as a whole but by only 1 percent in industry X. Also assume that nominal wages for all industries rise in accordance with the economy's overall rate of productivity increase. Labor costs are 90 percent of total costs in industry X. The demand for industry X's product is highly elastic with respect to price and inelastic with respect to income. Assuming no shifts in demand curves for products in the economy other than those associated with changes in income, forecast the future growth or decline of industry X, specifying all of the steps in your reasoning.

11. Comment on each of the following statements:
    a. "Although most highly productive companies are profitable, not all profitable companies are highly productive."
    b. "Increased public demand for such amenities as clean air and safer workplaces has complicated the comparison of productivity rates over time."
    c. "Rising productivity means that it takes fewer workers to produce a given level of output. Productivity increases are therefore a source of unemployment."

12. U.S. productivity growth accelerated in the second half of the 1990s. How do you account for this speedup? Why is it still impossible to know if this speedup is the start of a long-term trend or simply a transitory change?

Internet Exercise

Has the Resurgence of Productivity Growth Continued?

Go to the Bureau of Labor Statistics Web site **(http://www.bls.gov)** and in sequence select "Get Detailed Statistics" and "Series Report." Then enter the following ID series number: PRS84006091. Last, click on "All Years." This will retrieve the percentage change in output per hour since a year ago (growth in labor productivity).

What was the average rate of increase in labor productivity between 1991 and 1995? Between 1996 and 2006? Between 2006 and the most recent year shown? On the basis of these figures, do proponents of the new economy perspective or their critics have the upper hand in the debate? Explain your answer.

Internet Link

The Bureau of Labor Statistics Labor Productivity Web site has a large amount of information regarding productivity **(http://www.bls.gov/lpc/home.htm)**.

Chapter

18

Employment and Unemployment

Facts: In the 1980s, the U.S. economy created 18 million new jobs; an additional 17 million jobs came into existence in the 1990s; and 8 million more jobs were created between 2000 and 2006. In 2006, 4.6 percent of the U.S. labor force was unemployed, up 0.6 percentage points from six years earlier. Unemployment rates in 2006 fell to 5.5 percent in Canada and 4.2 percent in Japan. Meanwhile, 10.3 percent of the German labor force was unemployed in 2006, up 2.5 percentage points from six years earlier.

Questions! What explains the growth of employment over time? How much unemployment is natural for an economy? What causes higher-than-usual unemployment rates? Who are the unemployed? How long do they remain unemployed? What policies does government use to try to reduce unemployment?

In earlier chapters we analyzed how individuals make short- and long-term labor supply decisions and how firms determine their profit-maximizing levels of employment under varying conditions in labor and product markets. We also examined how unemployment might arise in specific labor markets where a union wage, a legal minimum wage, or an efficiency wage exceeded the market-clearing wage. We now turn our attention to the *aggregate* labor market and to the determinants of the *total* levels of employment and unemployment in the economy.

EMPLOYMENT AND UNEMPLOYMENT STATISTICS

Employment and unemployment statistics are widely used to assess the macroeconomic health of the economy. It is important to know how total employment and unemployment are measured, to be aware of the recent employment and unemployment record, and to understand the limitations of the data as guides to public policy.

Measurement

Each month the Bureau of the Census conducts a current population survey (CPS) commonly referred to as the *Household Survey.* About 60,000 households are selected to represent the U.S. population 16 years of age or older and are interviewed to determine the proportions of the population employed, unemployed, or not in the labor force. The Bureau of Labor Statistics of the U.S. Labor Department then uses the sample data to estimate the number of people in each category in the survey week.

Employed People

Those officially *employed* include people who, during the survey week, were 16 years or older and either (1) were employed by a private firm or government unit; (2) were self-employed; or (3) had jobs but were not working because of illness, bad weather, labor disputes, or vacations.

Once the total employment for the survey week is known, the *employment–population ratio* is easily computed. As shown by Equation (18.1), this ratio is total employment as a percentage of the total noninstitutional population:

$$\text{Employment–population} = \frac{\text{employment}}{\substack{\text{noninstitutional} \\ \text{population}}} \times 100 \quad \textbf{(18.1)}$$

Recall from the discussion of the labor force participation rate in Chapter 3 that the noninstitutional population comprises all people 16 years of age and older who are not in institutions such as prisons, mental hospitals, or homes for the aged.

Unemployed People

People are considered officially *unemployed* if during the survey week they were 16 years of age or older, were not institutionalized, and did not work, *but* were available for work *and* (1) had engaged in some specific job-seeking activity during the past four weeks, (2) were waiting to be called back to a job from which they were temporarily laid off, (3) would have been looking for a job but were temporarily ill, or (4) were waiting to report to a new job within 30 days.

Those who are 16 years or older and not institutionalized but officially neither employed nor unemployed are classified as "not in the labor force." The labor force itself therefore consists of those employed and unemployed:

$$\text{Labor force} = \text{employment} + \text{unemployment} \quad \textbf{(18.2)}$$

The *unemployment rate,* then, is the percentage of the labor force that is unemployed:

$$\substack{\text{Unemployment} \\ \text{rate (\%)}} = \frac{\text{unemployment}}{\text{labor force}} \times 100 \quad \textbf{(18.3)}$$

Recap

Figure 18.1 helps clarify how the BLS breaks down the total population into various components; it also provides a basis for computing values for Equations (18.1) through

FIGURE 18.1 **Total Population, Labor Force, Employment, and Unemployment, in Millions**

Of the total population of 299.4 million people in the United States in 2006, 151.4 million were in the labor force. Of this latter group, 144.4 million workers were employed and 7.0 million people were unemployed. The unemployment rate for 2006 was 4.6 percent, and the employment–population ratio was 63.1 percent.

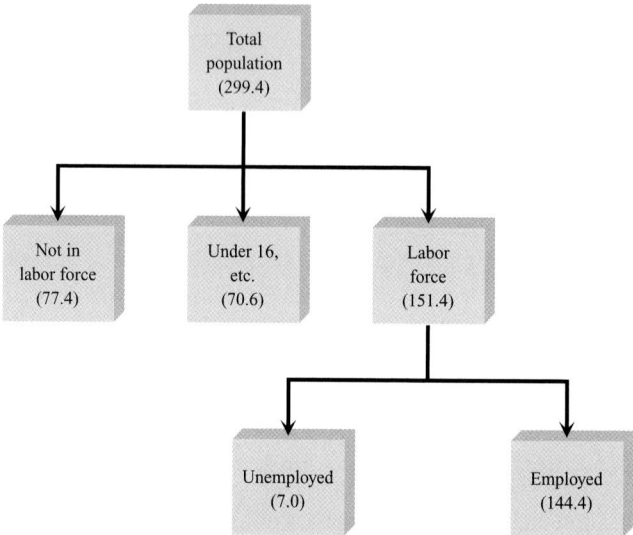

(18.3). The *employment–population ratio* [Equation (18.1)] for 2006 was 63.1 percent. This number is found by dividing the number of people employed (= 144.4 million) by the noninstitutional population of 228.8 million (= 299.4 million − 70.6 million) and multiplying by 100. Consistent with Equation 18.2, we observe that the size of the *labor force* in 2006 was 151.4 million. It is found by adding the number of those employed (= 144.4 million) and the number unemployed (= 7.0 million). The *unemployment rate* [Equation (18.3)] in 2006 was 4.6 percent, calculated by dividing the number of people unemployed (= 7.0 million) by the size of the labor force (= 151.4 million) and multiplying by 100.

Historical Record

Figure 18.2 presents the employment–population ratio since 1960. We see that the ratio is higher in recent years than in 1960, with the 2006 rate being 7.0 percentage points above that of 1960. Figure 18.3 shows the unemployment rate for the last four decades. The unemployment rate has been highly variable during these years: Its low was 3.5 percent in 1968 and its high was 9.7 percent in 1982. Observe that the unemployment rate fell steadily between 1992 and 2000. The 2000 rate of 4.0 percent was the lowest unemployment rate since the early 1970s. After 2000, the unemployment rate rose and reached 6.0 percent by 2003. It fell after 2003 and dropped to 4.6 percent in 2006.

FIGURE 18.2 **Employment–Population Ratio in the United States**
The U.S. employment–population ratio has risen over the past 46 years.

Source: Bureau of Labor Statistics (**www.bls.gov**).

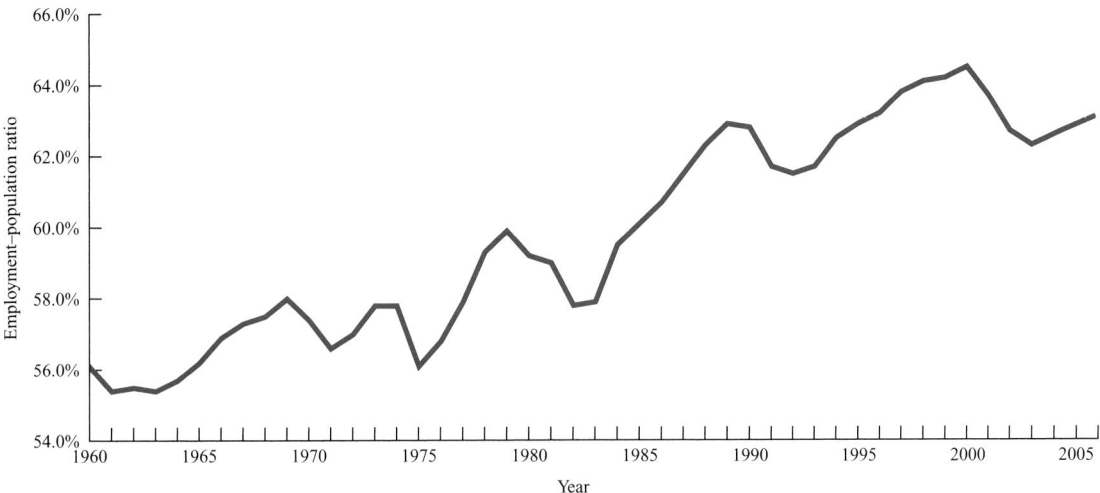

A Critique of the Household Data

The official employment-related statistics based on the CPS household interviews and reported by the BLS possess several notable virtues that make them useful to economists. First, the sampling technique is uniform throughout the nation and, with the

FIGURE 18.3 **U.S. Unemployment Rate**
The U.S. unemployment rate has been highly variable over the past 46 years.

Source: Bureau of Labor Statistics (**www.bls.gov**).

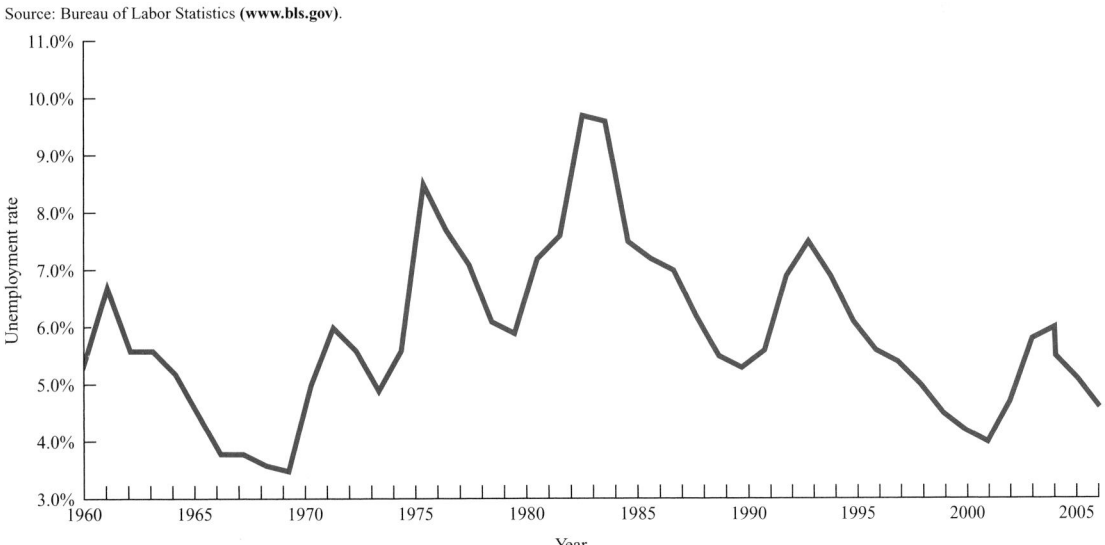

exception of minor changes, has remained consistent over the years. Therefore, economists can compare employment and unemployment rates between periods and track cyclic and secular trends. Second, the time lag between the survey and the reporting of the data is short, and the information is highly accessible through government publications. Third, the data are reported in disaggregated as well as overall forms; for example, unemployment rates are provided by race, age, gender, marital status, occupation, reasons for unemployment, and duration of unemployment. This aids in analyzing the distribution of the burden of unemployment. Finally, the data provide useful clues about the direction of the overall economy during a business cycle.

Unfortunately, however, these official statistics also have limitations. In the first place, the official data include all *part-time workers as fully employed,* when in reality some of these people desire to work full-time. In 2006 about 19.6 million people worked part-time because of personal choice. Another 4.2 million part-time workers either wanted to work full-time but could not find suitable full-time work or were on short hours because of a temporary slack in consumer demand.[1]

A second limitation is that to be counted as unemployed, a person must be actively seeking work. But studies show that after many people unsuccessfully look for work for a time, they become discouraged and then abandon their job search. Specifically, an estimated 381,000 people fell into this category in 2006. These *discouraged workers* (Chapter 3) constitute hidden unemployment.

A third problem is that the data do not measure the *subemployed;* the statistics fail to include people who are forced by economic circumstances to accept employment in occupations that pay lower wages than those they would qualify for in periods of full employment. Each of these three limitations causes the official unemployment statistics to *understate* the extent of underutilization of labor resources and the degree of economic hardship associated with a particular official overall rate of unemployment.

But other problems with the data cause some observers to conclude that the true extent of economic hardship in the nation may be *overstated* by the official unemployment rate. First, it is likely that some respondents to the monthly Household Survey provide false information that increases the official unemployment rate. To present a good image of themselves and family members, interviewees may indicate that household members are actively seeking work when in fact they are not in the labor force.

A second problem is that each unemployed person is counted equally whether he or she is, say, normally a full-time worker who has a strong attachment to the labor force, a semiretired person who wishes to work part-time, or a teenager seeking an after-school job. To the extent that the unemployment statistics include people in the latter two categories, the official unemployment rate may be misleading.[2]

---

[1] For research indicating that the Bureau of Labor Statistics classification of these workers as "involuntarily" part-time is correct, see Leslie S. Stratton, "Are 'Involuntary' Part-Time Workers Indeed Involuntary?" *Industrial and Labor Relations Review,* April 1996, pp. 522–36.

[2] Well over half of all teenagers who are unemployed are enrolled in school and seeking only part-time work.

Moreover, the household data do not contain information about the *minimum acceptable* wages (reservation wages) for those unemployed, some of whom may have recently been discharged from high-paying jobs in declining sectors of the economy. These people may remain unemployed until they accept the reality that they no longer can command their initial reservation wages. Unemployment insurance benefits, supplemental unemployment benefits (SUBs) provided by firms, and severance pay may increase the length of this adjustment period. A closely related criticism of using the official data as an indicator of the social impact of unemployment is that the increase in the number of multiearner families over the past few decades has reduced the amount of poverty corresponding to any specific level of unemployment. The loss of a job by one family member greatly lessens the standard of living of most families, but it does not push as many families into poverty as it once did.[3]

The Stock–Flow Model

One final limitation of the overall unemployment rate requires comment. This rate does not distinguish between people who are experiencing short—perhaps less serious—unemployment spells and those who are going through long periods of unemployment. Suppose, as a simple illustration, that an economy has only 12 members in the labor force. In situation A, each person is unemployed for one separate month during a year; in situation B, one person is unemployed and the rest employed for the entire year. The Household Survey would discover that in each case, 1 out of 12 workers is unemployed *in each month* and therefore the annual employment rate is 8.3 percent (1/12). Yet most observers would judge situation B to be of greater social concern: It leaves one person without any wage income for a full year.

This example demonstrates an important fact: The household data measure *stocks* of people in each of the three important labor force categories—employed, unemployed, and not in the labor force—but do not reveal the continuous movement—or *flows*—of people between the various categories. This movement is captured in the *stock–flow model* of unemployment shown in Figure 18.4. Two things to note from this diagram are that (1) the unemployment rate [$= U/(E + U)$] can remain constant even though the specific people in the unemployment "pool" change, and (2) several distinct flow factors can act independently or interact with one another to change the unemployment rate. As one example of the latter, suppose that the rate of inflow to the unemployment category U by way of layoffs, flow 2, increased, while all other flow rates remained constant. Obviously this would increase the absolute number of people who are unemployed while leaving the size of the labor force ($E + U$) unchanged, thereby causing the unemployment rate to rise.

As a second and more complex example, suppose that the rate of exit from the employed category E via retirements and withdrawals, flow 4, increased while all other flow rates remained unchanged. Once again the unemployment *rate* would rise, but in this case the *absolute* number of unemployed people would remain at its previous level.

[3] S. L. Terry, "Unemployment and Its Effects on Family Income," *Monthly Labor Review,* April 1982, pp. 35–43. See also Adam D. Seitchik, "When Married Men Lose Jobs: Income Replacement within the Family," *Industrial and Labor Relations Review,* July 1991, pp. 692–707.

FIGURE 18.4 **The Stock–Flow Model of Unemployment**

At any point in time, there is a measurable *stock* of people in each of the three boxes that represent categories of labor force status. But these stocks are simultaneously being depleted and replenished by numerous *flows* into and out of each category. Changes in the rates of these flows can significantly affect the unemployment rate.

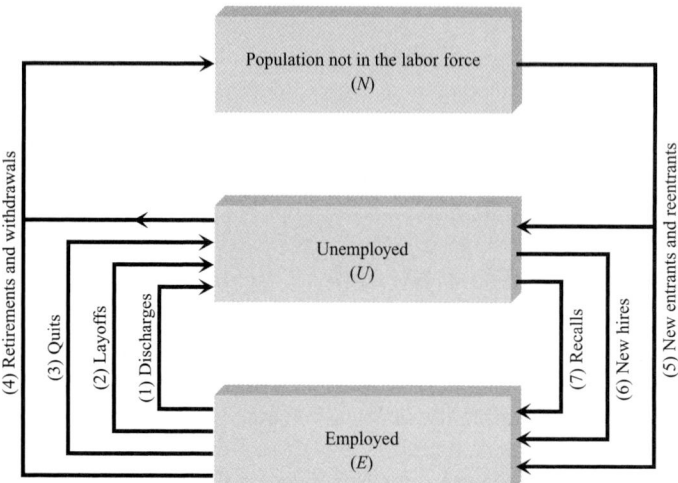

The size of the labor force $(E + U)$ would shrink; and because unemployment (U) would remain constant, the unemployment rate $[= U/(E + U)]$ would rise.

An analysis of the flows between the categories of labor force status helps us understand the length of unemployment spells of individuals and the reasons why unemployment rates rise and fall. The following are examples of insights gleaned from the stock–flow analysis of unemployment rates: (1) Empirical evidence suggests that a considerable amount of unemployment is due to prolonged spells of unemployment for relatively few people.[4] (2) During recessions, the rates of layoffs and discharges rise and the rates of new hires and recalls fall, more than compensating for the decline in voluntary job quits. Consequently, the overall unemployment rate rises. (3) First-time labor force entrants and people reentering the labor force from the "not in the labor force" category typically constitute over one-third of the unemployed. (4) Unemployment rates stay higher than expected during earlier phases of an economic recovery because improved job prospects entice people who are out of the labor force to seek work—that is, to become officially unemployed (Chapter 3).

18.1

Defining Full Employment

Not only is a zero rate of unemployment unachievable in a dynamic economy where information is imperfect and workers and firms heterogeneous, but it may in fact be undesirable. Later in this chapter we will find that some *voluntary* unemployment is a

---

[4] Kim B. Clark and Lawrence H. Summers, "Labor-Market Dynamics and Unemployment: A Reconsideration," *Brookings Papers on Economic Activity,* no. 1, 1979, pp. 13–60.

18.1 World of Work

New Data on Job Gains and Losses*

In 2003 the Bureau of Labor Statistics introduced a new data series called Business Employment Dynamics, which reports on job gains and losses. This data series tracks the number of jobs at establishments that have opened, expanded, contracted, or closed—that is, the flows within the employment stock box in Figure 18.4. The Business Employment Dynamics series is based on data from 6.7 million private sector employers and represents 98 percent of nonfarm private payrolls.

These data show that many jobs are created and eliminated in the comparatively short period of one quarter. For example, in the first quarter of 2006, the number of job gains at opening and expanding establishments was 7.6 million or 6.7 percent of private sector employment. Expanding establishments added 6.2 million jobs, and opening establishments added 1.2 million jobs. The number of job losses at closing and shrinking establishments was 6.8 million or 6.0 percent of private sector employment. Contracting establishments lost 5.5 million jobs, and closing establishments lost 1.2 million jobs.

The net change in employment—the difference between the number of jobs gained and the number of jobs lost—is much smaller than the gross job gains and losses. In the first quarter of 2006, the net change was a gain of only 784,000 jobs or 0.7 percent of private sector employment. However, the net change in employment differed significantly by industry. Job gains exceed job losses in the goods-producing sector of mining, construction, and manufacturing, so the net change in employment in this sector was a gain of 168,000 jobs. The net gain in the service-producing sector was much larger as this sector gained 616,000 jobs.

* Based on "Business Employment Dynamics: First Quarter 2006," U.S. Department of Labor News Release 06-1981, November 17, 2006.

way in which individuals increase their personal earnings and is part of the process through which society enhances its real output and income. We also will observe that some *involuntary* unemployment is an unavoidable by-product of changes in tastes, population shifts, and technological advance. These changes create structural mismatches between labor demand and supply and require adjustments in the allocation of labor resources from some occupations and regions to others.

How much voluntary and unavoidable involuntary unemployment is there in the U.S. economy? What rate of unemployment constitutes **full employment?** In the 1960s economists concluded that a 4 percent unemployment rate was an achievable full-employment policy goal. But in the 1970s and 1980s numerous factors led economists to boost this figure to 5.5 or even 6 percent. Two of the more important factors were (1) a changed composition of the labor force such that groups having high unemployment rates—teenagers, for example—constituted a larger fraction of the overall labor force and (2) evidence that rates of unemployment in the 4 percent range were associated with accelerating rates of inflation.

In the 1990s demographic changes tended to lower the unemployment rate associated with full employment. Of greatest importance, youthful workers declined as a share of the labor force as baby boomers entered middle age. The growth of temporary help agencies and the improved information resulting from the Internet also lowered the

Global Perspective 18.1

Comparative Unemployment Rates

Unemployment rates vary greatly among nations of the world over specific periods. The major reasons for these differences are that nations have different natural rates of unemployment and may be in different phases of their business cycles.

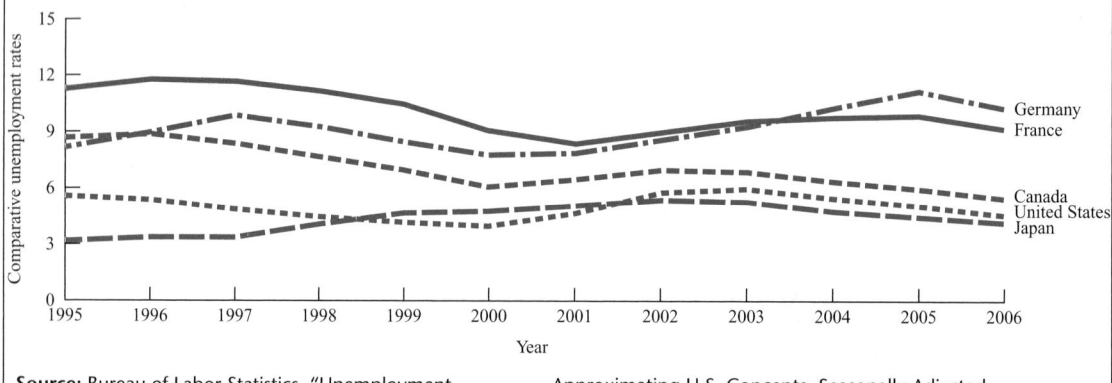

Source: Bureau of Labor Statistics, "Unemployment Rates in Nine Countries, Civilian Labor Force Basis, Approximating U.S. Concepts, Seasonally Adjusted, 1995–2006," February 2007.

unemployment rate. So, too, did the work requirements under the new welfare rules, which moved many people from the ranks of the unemployed to the ranks of the employed. Finally, some economists point out that the doubling of the U.S. prison population since 1985 removed relatively high-unemployment individuals from the labor force and thus lowered the overall unemployment rate.

Today the consensus appears to be that an unemployment rate of about 4.0 to 5.0 percent constitutes "practical" full employment and that attempts to reduce the rate through policies that increase aggregate demand will cause the existing rate of inflation to rise. This "practical" rate is sometimes called the *equilibrium* or *natural rate of unemployment* and is defined as (1) *the unemployment rate at which there is neither excess demand nor excess supply in the overall labor market* or (2) *the unemployment rate that will occur in the long run if expected and actual rates of inflation are equal.*[5] We will defer explanations of the economic rationales for these two definitions to later in this chapter.

[5] For more about changes in the natural rate of unemployment, see "Symposium: The Natural Rate of Unemployment," *Journal of Economic Perspectives,* Winter 1997, pp. 3–108; and Lawrence F. Katz and Alan B. Krueger, "The High-Pressure U.S. Labor Market of the 1990s," *Brookings Papers on Economic Activity,* no. 1, 1999, pp. 1–65.

FIGURE 18.5 **Real Output and Total Employment Determination**

The intersection of the aggregate demand and supply curves D and $S_k\,AS_c$ in graph (a) produces equilibrium price and real output levels P_0 and Q_n. In the aggregate labor market (b), the equilibrium wage rate and level of total employment are determined at the intersection of the aggregate labor demand and supply curves. Employment level E_n is the natural level of employment; it is the amount of labor needed to produce the natural level of real output Q_n.

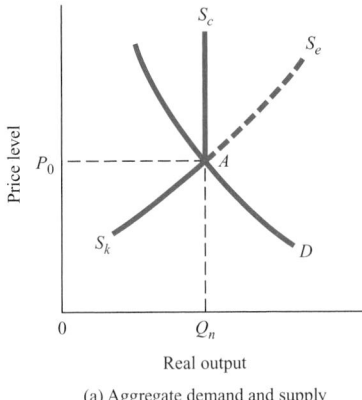

(a) Aggregate demand and supply

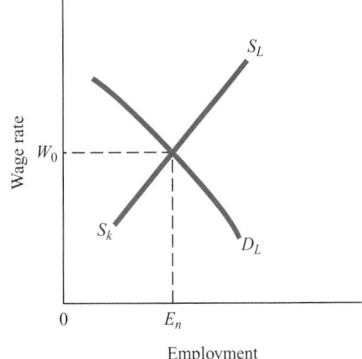

(b) Aggregate labor market

MACROECONOMIC OUTPUT AND EMPLOYMENT DETERMINATION

The macroeconomic models shown as graphs (a) and (b) in Figure 18.5 are central to much of the discussion in this chapter. Therefore, a close look at their components is imperative.

Aggregate Demand and Supply

Graph (a) depicts the familiar aggregate demand and supply curves introduced in principles of macroeconomics textbooks to discuss price level and real output determination. The vertical axis shows the *price level* for a hypothetical economy, and the horizontal axis measures *real output.* Conceptually, real output always equals real income; $1 of output generates $1 of income as wages, rent, interest, and profits. The horizontal axis therefore also measures real income.

Aggregate Demand

Aggregate demand for goods and services is shown as curve D in Figure 18.5(a) and indicates the total quantity of real output that domestic consumers, businesses, government, and foreign buyers will collectively desire to purchase at each price level. As the price level falls (rises), the quantity of goods and services demanded rises (falls).

The negative slope of the aggregate demand curve results from three interacting effects, the first being the *interest rate effect.* As the price level declines, the demand for money drops because fewer dollars are needed to purchase any given quantity of goods and services. If the money supply is fixed, this decrease in money demand will reduce interest rates, which then will increase spending on such interest-sensitive commodities as new autos, homes, and plants and equipment. Thus, other things being equal, the lower the price level, the greater the quantity of output demanded.

The second effect that helps explain the downward slope of the aggregate demand curve is the *wealth* or *real balances effect.* Lower price levels increase the *real value* of such assets as currency, checking deposits, and savings deposits, whose values are fixed in money terms. As the price level falls, the purchasing power of dollar-denominated wealth held by consumers rises, and people increase their spending on normal goods and services.

The final effect at work is the *foreign purchases effect.* As the domestic price level falls relative to prices of products produced abroad, foreign consumers will shift their spending toward U.S. goods. Hence the lower price level will be associated with a greater amount of U.S. real output and income.

Aggregate Supply

Aggregate supply *of goods and services is the relationship between the price level and the total quantity of real output that firms are willing to produce and offer for sale.* The curve in Figure 18.5(a) is a synthesis of varying interpretations of aggregate supply. The solid curve labeled $S_k AS_c$ incorporates traditional Keynesian ($S_k A$) and classical (AS_c) assumptions about the working of the economy. The curve's segment $S_k A$ is explained as follows: As aggregate demand falls (D shifts leftward), firms experience declines in sales and increases in inventories of unsold goods. Because wages are relatively inflexible downward, firms respond by laying off or discharging workers and reducing production. Consequently, output falls.

On the other hand, the AS_c segment of the aggregate supply curve shows that when labor and capital resources are being fully used, as is assumed to be true at the full-employment output level Q_n, increases in aggregate demand boost only the price level. The greater demand and higher prices cannot generate greater output. The *monetary* value of the Q_n output rises because of the higher price level, but *real* output remains constant at Q_n.

Other economists envision a short-run aggregate supply curve as shown by $S_k AS_e$. They assume that in the long run, the economy generates a natural level of output Q_n, but that in the short run, output can be less or greater than that amount depending on the relationship between the actual and expected price levels. We must defer a full discussion of this interpretation to later, but the following constitutes its essence. Suppose the price level is P_0 and workers expect it to remain there. Now suppose unanticipated inflation occurs so that the price level rises above P_0. As a result, the prices firms receive for their products will rise, while nominal wage rates, at least temporarily, will remain fixed at their previously contracted levels. This will mean that real wages will fall and profits will rise, causing firms collectively to increase their employment and output.

Meanwhile, unemployed workers who are searching for jobs will begin to receive inflation-induced higher nominal wage offers and mistakenly think that they are being offered higher real wages. Consequently, they will begin to accept job offers more quickly; the level of employment will rise, unemployment will fall, and real output temporarily will rise above Q_n. Thus the aggregate supply curve will extend upward as shown by the broken line AS_e.

Equilibrium Price Level and Real Output

The equilibrium levels of price and real output occur where the quantities of total output demanded and supplied are equal—that is, where D and $S_k S_c$ in Figure 18.5(a) intersect. Real output and income level Q_n is the full-employment level of real output or, rephrased, the natural level of real output and income.

The Aggregate Labor Market

Graph (b) in Figure 18.5 shows the aggregate labor market. This graph is our familiar labor market diagram "writ large." The labor demand curve D_L in the figure can be thought of as the aggregate marginal revenue product curve for the economy. This curve is found by multiplying the aggregate marginal product of labor by the price level, in this case P_0. This curve tells us the profit-maximizing level of employment associated with each wage rate. The aggregate labor supply curve S_L indicates the amount of labor services people collectively are willing to offer at each nominal wage rate, given the price level. We assume that in the short run, workers expect the existing price level to remain. We observe that the equilibrium wage rate is W_0 and the equilibrium level of employment is E_n. This level of employment is the natural level of employment—or "full employment"—and is just sufficient to produce the Q_n level of real output shown in graph (a). As noted earlier, most economists feel that the natural rate of unemployment associated with E_n and Q_n is 4.0–5.0 percent.

Why is this natural rate of unemployment so high? Why has the actual rate of unemployment in the United States greatly exceeded the natural rate in some years? To answer these questions we must next consider the three major types of unemployment and their causes. Throughout the discussion, bear in mind that the boundaries between unemployment categories are not absolute and that the extent of one type of unemployment may be a function of the amount of one or both of the other types.

FRICTIONAL UNEMPLOYMENT

Even when aggregate demand is sufficient to employ all the labor force and when those who are unemployed possess skills matching those required by firms with job openings, the nation's unemployment rate will remain positive. As implied in our stock–flow model (Figure 18.4), people continuously (1) quit present jobs to shop for new ones, (2) look for new jobs after losing previous ones, (3) enter the labor force to seek work for the first time, (4) reenter the labor force after periods of absence, and (5) move from one job to take another within the next 30 days. Likewise, employers continuously (1) search for replacements for workers who quit or retire, (2) discharge some employees in hopes of finding better ones, and (3) seek new workers to fill jobs created by expansion of their firms. Thus unlike "auction" markets such as stock and wheat exchanges, the overall labor market never fully "clears." At any moment there is considerable *frictional unemployment;* that is, not all active job searchers will have yet found or accepted employment, and not all employers will have yet filled their job vacancies.

Search unemployment is an important source of frictional unemployment. This type of unemployment is created by individuals searching for the best job offer and firms searching for workers to fill job openings. The job search process and its relationship to unemployment compensation and inflation are discussed in Chapter 15.

Not all frictional unemployment is of the search variety. In some instances, unemployed workers willingly wait to be recalled from temporary layoffs or willingly wait in job queues to obtain union jobs (Chapter 11). Additionally, efficiency wages (Chapter 7) may attract workers into the labor force who are forced to wait for such jobs to open. These types of frictional unemployment collectively might best be described as *wait unemployment,* rather than search unemployment. Let's briefly examine each of these potential sources of frictional unemployment.

1 Temporary Layoffs

Although large layoffs are normally associated with recessions, temporary layoffs by firms occur throughout the economy even during periods of robust overall aggregate demand. Such layoffs may account for as much as 1 to 1.5 percentage points of the natural rate of unemployment.[6] Workers on temporary layoff normally do not search for new employment; rather, they wait to be recalled to their former jobs. We know from our discussion of the Household Survey that these workers are counted as unemployed.

Seasonal unemployment might also be thought of as temporary layoff and therefore a type of wait unemployment. Examples: Construction workers often are unemployed during the winter, farmworkers occasionally are unemployed between planting and harvesting seasons, and professional athletes may be unemployed during parts of the year. In each case, these workers are waiting to resume their jobs.

2 Union Job Queues

Unions also contribute to frictional unemployment. Analysis in Chapter 6 demonstrated that union wage scales may contribute to wait unemployment by reducing the number of workers demanded by firms and increasing the number of willing suppliers of labor (Figure 6.10). In brief, some workers may be willing to wait in the employment queue for union jobs rather than take nonunion jobs available at lower pay.

3 Efficiency Wages

Finally, efficiency wages may contribute to the relatively high rate of frictional unemployment. Recall that efficiency wages are those that firms set above the market-clearing levels as a way to elicit hard work, reduce costly labor turnover, or achieve some other desirable end that adds to worker productivity. We observed earlier in Figure 7.8

---

[6] D. M. Lilien, "The Cyclical Pattern of Temporary Layoffs in United States Manufacturing," *Review of Economics and Statistics,* February 1980, pp. 24–31.

that efficiency wage payments and permanent frictional unemployment go hand in hand. As concisely stated by DeFina,

> Unemployed individuals, whether they have quit, have been fired, or have entered the labor force for the first time, might try to get jobs by bidding down the wages of current workers. But in contrast to the simple competitive market situation, firms will not accept those offers. Firms have already weighed the benefits and costs of lower wages and decided that keeping wages high yields them their greatest profit. And because the unemployed cannot bid their way into jobs, they must instead wait until new openings arise from quits, firings, or increases in firms' demands for workers. They must then hope to be chosen over other jobless persons. On the whole, unemployed persons might remain jobless for quite some time.[7]

18.1 *Quick* *Review*	• The employment–population ratio measures total employment as a percentage of the total noninstitutional population; the unemployment rate is the percentage of the labor force that is unemployed.
	• The total level of employment is largely determined by aggregate demand and aggregate supply. Full employment exists when the rate of unemployment is 4.0 to 5.0 percent.
	• Frictional unemployment is the unemployment mainly resulting from voluntary job quits, job switches, and new entrants and reentrants into the labor force.

Your Turn

What factors cause the "official" unemployment rate to overstate the true extent of economic hardship in the United States? What factors cause it to understate economic hardship? (*Answers:* See page 599.)

STRUCTURAL UNEMPLOYMENT

Another type of unemployment that is part of a nation's natural rate of unemployment is *structural unemployment.* This unemployment shares many of the same features as frictional unemployment but is differentiated by being long-lived. It therefore can involve considerable costs to those unemployed and substantial loss of forgone output to society.

Structural unemployment is caused by changes in the *composition* of labor supply and demand; it is a "square pegs, round holes" phenomenon. This unemployment generally has one or both of the following dimensions. First, it may result from a mismatch between the skills needed for available jobs and the skills possessed by those seeking work. Second, structural unemployment may occur because of a geographic mismatch between the locations of job openings and job seekers. Examples of structural unemployment

---

[7] Robert H. DeFina, "Explaining Long-Term Unemployment," *Business Review* (Federal Reserve Bank of Philadelphia), May–June 1987, p. 19. For more about efficiency wages and unemployment, see W. Bentley MacLeod, James M. Malcomson, and Paul Gomme, "Labor Turnover and the Natural Rate of Unemployment: Efficiency Wage versus Frictional Unemployment," *Journal of Labor Economics,* April 1994, pp. 276–315; and Eskander Alvi, "Job Security and Unemployment in an Efficiency-Wage Model," *Journal of Labor Research,* Spring 1998, pp. 387–96.

abound: Robotics technology and the increase in the market share of imports greatly reduced employment in the U.S. textile industry in the 1980s and 1990s. Many of the workers who were displaced did not have the skills required for positions that were open, such as in accounting and computer programming. Similarly, improvements in agricultural technology over the past 100 years caused job losses for many farm operators and laborers who did not possess readily transferable job skills in expanding areas of employment and who were not geographically mobile. Unemployment resulting from job losses associated with the spate of mergers in the United States over the last decade is another example of structural unemployment, as is unemployment resulting from the deregulation of the trucking and airline industries.

Displaced Workers

During the 1980s, 1990s, and early 2000s many of the people who were structurally unemployed were **displaced workers**—individuals who had lost their jobs specifically because of permanent plant closings or job cutbacks. A total of 3.8 million workers 20 years of age and over who had been at their jobs at least three years were displaced between January 2003 and December 2005. By January 2006, 69.9 percent of these workers were reemployed in new jobs. Another 16.7 percent of them had left the labor force. Finally, 13.4 percent of the displaced workers were still unemployed and looking for work. This 13.4 percent figure was more than double the overall unemployment rate in 2006. Of those full-time workers who were back at work, 49.0 percent were earning less than before they were displaced. About one-third were earning 0 to 19 percent more than before, and about one-sixth were earning at least 20 percent more.[8]

Not all plant closures and job cutbacks occur where we would most expect them: in declining industries or industries hurt by import competition. The level of employment within firms is surprisingly volatile from one year to the next, *independent* of the business cycle or major industry trends. Jobs themselves are more unstable than generally thought, implying that much structural unemployment results from workers being in the wrong place at the wrong time. Changes in labor demand within firms alone may account for as much as one-fourth of the natural rate of unemployment.[9]

The extent of structural unemployment depends on the *degree* of the compositional changes in labor demand and supply and the *speed* of the adjustments of the imbalances and mismatches. Training and retraining play a key role in this adjustment process, and efforts to shorten the duration of structural unemployment normally involve retooling of skills to match job vacancies.

[8] "Worker Displacement, 2003–2005," United States Department of Labor, News Release 06-1454, August 17, 2006. These statistics are summarized for the past 20 years in Henry S. Farber, "What Do We Know about Job Loss in the United States? Evidence from the Displaced Workers Survey, 1984–2004," Federal Reserve Bank of Chicago *Economic Perspectives*, 2nd Quarter 2005, pp. 13–28. For a survey of studies examining laid-off workers, see Bruce Fallick, "A Review of Recent Empirical Literature on Displaced Workers," *Industrial and Labor Relations Review*, October 1996, pp. 5–16; and Lori G. Kletzer, "Job Displacement," *Journal of Economic Perspectives*, Winter 1998, pp. 115–36.

[9] Jonathan S. Leonard, "In the Wrong Place at the Wrong Time: The Extent of Frictional and Structural Unemployment," in Kevin Lang and Jonathan S. Leonard (eds.), *Unemployment and the Structure of Labor Markets* (New York: Basil Blackwell, 1987), pp. 141–63.

18.2	World of Work	Downsizing and College Graduates*

In recent years, there have been many well-publicized massive layoffs at large American companies. These layoffs have built up a public perception that firms have been restructuring and reducing their workforces in reaction to increased competition much more now than ever before. It is also typically believed that the laid-off workers are now likely to be college-educated workers and that they suffer severe economic hardship.

Henry Farber assessed the accuracy of these beliefs using data from 1981 to 2003. In all years the job loss rate was actually lower for more educated workers than less educated workers. During the 2001–2003 period, 16 percent of high school dropouts and 10 percent of college graduates suffered a job loss. Consistent with perceptions, there has been an upsurge in the job loss rate among college graduates since the early 1990s. Furthermore, the main cause of the job loss rate rise for college graduates was an increase in the rate of position elimination, rather than layoffs. This is consistent with corporate restructuring.

Farber finds that the economic consequences of job loss are generally less for college graduates. For example, laid-off college graduates were 17 percentage points more likely to be reemployed in the 2001–2003 period than were their counterparts who were high school dropouts. In addition, college educated workers have a greater probability of being reemployed full-time. However, reemployed college graduates have been bearing much larger earnings losses in recent years compared to previous years. Among college-educated full-time workers who were reemployed in full-time jobs, the average worker suffered an earnings decrease of 11 percent in his or her new job during the 1993–1995 period. This decline nearly doubled to 21 percent by the 2001–2003 period.

* Based on Henry S. Farber, "What Do We Know about Job Loss in the United States? Evidence from the Displaced Workers Survey, 1984–2004," Princeton University Industrial Relations Section Working Paper Number 498, January 2005.

Additional Observations

Several additional observations about structural unemployment deserve mention. In the first place, higher levels of general education are associated with lower levels of structural unemployment. For instance, college graduates who are displaced from their employment because of changes in demand or technology have a wider range of job options and usually find retraining to be easier than do people who have little formal education.[10]

A second observation is that structural and cyclic unemployment overlap. When the economy is at full employment and rapidly expanding, firms experiencing shortages of skilled workers often find it profitable to hire people who do not possess the required job skills but who can be trained while on the job. This training reduces the amount of structural unemployment. But when a recession occurs and the overall rate of unemployment rises, firms hiring new or replacement workers can draw skilled workers from the large unemployment pool. Workers who do not possess the required job skills will stay unemployed longer, and structural unemployment will rise.

A final observation is that futurists in nearly every historical period have warned of impending massive increases in technological unemployment. To date, however, the

[10] W. R. Johnson, "The Demand for General and Specific Education with Occupational Mobility," *Review of Economic Studies,* October 1979, pp. 695–705; and Farber, 2005, op. cit.

World of Work 18.3

The Danish Flexicurity Model*

In recent years the Danish economy has outperformed most of the rest of Europe. For example, in 2006 its economy grew by 3 percent. The Danish unemployment rate dropped to 3.8 percent in 2006. In most other European countries the unemployment rate has remained high. The euro-area unemployment rate was 7.8 percent in 2006.

In light of its success, the European Commission has encouraged other countries to adopt Denmark's labor market model, which has been called *flexicurity* due to its ability to provide flexibility in the labor market along with the security of an extensive social safety net. In contrast to most other European countries, Denmark's labor market is quite flexible because employers in the public and private sectors can easily lay off workers. Danish workers have a high degree of social protection with Denmark's generous unemployment benefits. Unemployed Danish workers typically receive about 80 percent of their prior salaries while unemployed. In addition, the government provides a large variety of programs to help unemployed workers get reemployed.

The Danish flexicurity model has mixed effects on unemployment. On one hand, the flexibility of employers to adjust to changing business conditions and the government's labor market programs tend to reduce structural unemployment. On the other

hand, the generous unemployment benefits tend to raise the unemployment rate by reducing the incentive to work. The net effect has been to reduce the unemployment rate since the early 1990s as a result of the flexicurity approach.

Whether other European countries should adopt the Danish labor market model is not clear for three reasons. First, results have not always been good for the Danish model. During the early 1980s unemployment was high until the government reduced unemployment benefits. Second, other approaches to the labor market have also reduced unemployment rates. For example, the United Kingdom, which switched to less generous unemployment benefits and a more flexible labor market, has also reduced its unemployment rate. Third, the tax burden in Denmark associated with its labor market programs and unemployment benefits is quite high (about 5 percent of gross domestic product). Adopting this approach in countries with high unemployment and weak public finances would be difficult because it would be costly to implement, and the reduction in unemployment in the short run would be limited.

* Based on Paul Hilbers and Jianping Zhou, "Danish Flexicurity Model Holds Lessons for the Rest of Europe," *IMF Survey*, October 30, 2006, pp. 316–17; and **ec.europa.eu**.

historical record indicates that on the average, technological change creates more jobs than it destroys and does not greatly alter the overall rate of structural unemployment. More generally, recall the discussion surrounding Figure 17.8, which suggested that no systematic relationship exists between productivity changes and employment changes on an industry-by-industry basis.

But might not the high-technology revolution change this pattern? Most economists doubt that it will. They point out that although specific workers will lose their jobs—and many firms, communities, and perhaps even regions will suffer negative consequences—the new technologies will spur capital investment, spawn secondary industries, and generate output effects that will increase overall labor demand. To fill available positions in the expanding sectors, firms there may need to engage in more concerted on-the-job training. Most economists view the current explosion of new technology as presenting a major challenge to society but not one that is fundamentally different from previous challenges posed by other new technologies.

18.3

DEMAND-DEFICIENT UNEMPLOYMENT

In many years the unemployment rate greatly exceeds the 4.0–5.0 percent natural rate. For example, unemployment was 8.5 percent in 1975, 9.7 percent in 1982, and 7.5 percent in 1992. In the depth of the Great Depression (1933) 24.9 percent of the labor force was unemployed. These high unemployment rates are by-products of recessions and depressions and result from deficiencies in aggregate demand that force firms to lay off and discharge workers. The evidence strongly suggests that decline in aggregate demand—rather than, say, differences between expected and actual inflation rates—are the *primary* cause of cyclic unemployment.[11]

Graphic Analysis

The analytical framework we developed earlier helps clarify *demand-deficient* or *cyclic unemployment.* In Figure 18.6(a) we depict a sharp, unexpected decline in aggregate demand, as shown as the movement from D to D_1. Keynesians view a decline in investment or consumption spending as the usual cause of such a shift, whereas monetarists look to a reduction in the money supply as the underlying culprit. Irrespective of the cause, the fall in aggregate demand decreases real output from the full-employment level Q_n by the amount Q_nQ_1.

As shown in graph (b) of Figure 18.6, the decline in aggregate demand in graph (a) reduces the derived aggregate demand for labor from D_L to D_{L1}. In technical terms, this decline in labor demand occurs because the lower price level P_1 in graph (a) reduces

FIGURE 18.6 Demand-Deficient Unemployment
A decline in the aggregate demand for output [D to D_1 in (a)] reduces the demand for labor [D_L to D_{L1} in (b)]. Assuming a rigid nominal wage W_0, the decline in labor demand results in involuntary demand-deficient unemployment by the amount *ab* in graph (b).

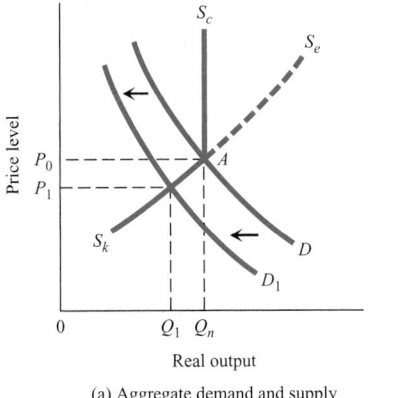
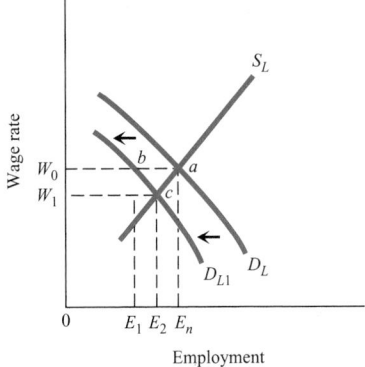

(a) Aggregate demand and supply   (b) Aggregate labor market

[11] Ronald S. Warren, Jr., "Labor Market Contracts, Unanticipated Wages, and Employment Growth," *American Economic Review,* June 1983, pp. 389–97.

revenue to producers; that is, marginal revenue product in the aggregate falls. More generally, firms experience rapid rises in their inventories because they are unable to sell their existing output. They therefore curtail their production and reduce their demand for labor. Put simply, they no longer wish to hire as many workers at each wage rate as previously.

Let's assume, for reasons we will explore shortly, that the wage rate in graph (b) remains at W_0. We note that employment declines from the natural level E_n to the smaller amount E_1. At wage W_0, a individuals desire work—and previously were working—but firms employ only b workers. Thus ab workers are cyclically unemployed.

The full decline in employment and emergence of unemployment rest on the crucial assumption that the wage rate in our model does not fall. If it were to decline to W_1, firms would adjust their employment to E_2 (point c). We note that employment is only E_2 at W_1, compared to E_n at the original W_0 equilibrium. The E_2E_n decline in employment, however, would be voluntary on the part of these workers. As shown by segment ca of the labor supply curve, these workers have reservation wages that exceed the new lower wage W_1. Because the E_2E_n workers voluntarily withdraw from the labor force, they are not officially unemployed.

Just how flexible downward are nominal wages in the U.S. economy? Although nominal wages eventually do fall under pressure of slack aggregate demand, they are relatively rigid downward in the short run. Declines in aggregate demand therefore produce demand-deficient or cyclic unemployment.[12]

Wage Rigidity

Why are nominal wages relatively inflexible downward? Several diverse explanations have been cited.

1 Unions

Unions are one reason why nominal wages are rigid downward. Unions view wage cuts as "givebacks" of previous hard-earned collective bargaining gains and thus vigorously resist wage reductions. Reductions in nominal wages do occur in unionized industries, but normally only *after* severe cutbacks in employment have occurred. Unions appear to prefer layoffs to temporary wage reductions. The latter affect all workers, whereas layoffs usually affect only a small percentage of the firm's workforce and normally involve people with little seniority. Thus a *majority* of workers benefit by a layoff policy as contrasted to wage cuts, and elected union leaders are likely to be responsive to this majority when negotiating wage and layoff provisions.

2 Bias toward Layoffs by Firms

Another reason that nominal wages are inflexible downward is that firms themselves may favor temporary selective layoffs to across-the-board temporary wage reductions. The latter might cause higher-skilled, more experienced workers in whom a firm has

[12] According to Keynes, even if nominal wages did fall, so too would product costs and prices. Therefore, the *real* wage—the nominal wage divided by the price level—would remain constant, and employment would not increase.

invested large amounts of training to quit and take jobs elsewhere. The layoff strategy allows the firm to "inventory" or "hoard" this skilled labor and instead lay off workers who are more easily replaced if they happen to take alternative employment rather than wait for a callback. Furthermore, the existence of unemployment compensation and the way it is financed bias the decision toward layoffs. Those laid off experience a *net* loss of income that is much less than the full decline in wages, and therefore they will be less likely to accept other permanent jobs during this period. Also, because the taxes paid by firms to the unemployment compensation program are not perfectly related to layoff experience, firms that dismiss substantial numbers of workers are subsidized by the tax payments of other firms. Stated technically, the unemployment benefits received by workers who are temporarily unemployed exceed the *incremental* tax cost to the firms that lay them off.[13]

3 Implicit Contracts

A closely related reason that wages appear to be inflexible downward during recessions is that implicit contracts govern many employment relationships. **Implicit contracts** are informal, often unstated, understandings that are "invisible handshakes."[14] One common feature of many implicit contracts is an understanding that the firm will maintain existing nominal wages and pay cost-of-living wage increases except under severe economic conditions, such as impending bankruptcy. In return for this guarantee, employers obtain the right to lay off workers in response to cyclic declines in the demand for their products. By providing "insurance" against wage declines during recessions, employers can attract workers at a lower average wage. Additionally, the "fixed wage–variable employment" contract provides firms with certainty in the reduction of the wage bill (wage $\times$ number of worker hours) compared to the uncertainty associated with a wage reduction, which might cause some highly valued workers to quit. Finally, these contracts may produce positive "reputation effects" that may allow firms to attract better-quality workers who require less supervision.

4 Insider–Outsider Theories

Recently a set of so-called **insider–outsider theories** has emerged that purports to explain downward wage rigidity on the basis of "insiders" and "outsiders."[15] *Insiders* are employed people who have some degree of market power; *outsiders* are unemployed

---

[13] See Martin Feldstein, "The Importance of Temporary Layoffs: An Empirical Analysis," *Brookings Papers on Economic Activity,* no. 3, 1975, pp. 725–44; and Robert H. Topel, "On Layoffs and Unemployment Insurance," *American Economic Review,* September 1983, pp. 541–59. See also Donald R. Deere, "Unemployment Insurance and Employment," *Journal of Labor Economics,* October 1991, pp. 307–24.

[14] A voluminous, but difficult, literature on implicit contracts has developed. The major contributions are surveyed in Costas Azariadis and Joseph E. Stiglitz, "Implicit Contracts and Fixed-Price Equilibria," *Quarterly Journal of Economics,* vol. 98, suppl. 1983, pp. 1–22.

[15] Assar Lindbeck and Dennis Snower, "Wage Setting, Unemployment, and Insider–Outsider Relations," *American Economic Review,* May 1986, pp. 235–39; and Lindbeck and Snower, "Cooperation, Harassment, and Involuntary Unemployment: An Insider–Outsider Approach," *American Economic Review,* March 1988, pp. 167–88. For empirical evidence against the insider–outsider model, see Denise J. Doiron, "A Test of the Insider–Outsider Hypothesis in Union Preferences," *Economica,* August 1995, pp. 281–90.

people who are unable or unwilling to underbid the existing wage rate to gain employment. In terms of Figure 18.6(b), outsiders are represented by distance *ab* at wage W_0.

Why are outsiders unable or unwilling to secure jobs for themselves by bidding down the wage rate to, say, W_1 in Figure 18.6(b)? They may be *unable* to do this because firms may view the cost of hiring them as being prohibitive. Firms may expect that if they hire outsiders at less than the existing wage rate, the remaining incumbent workers will withhold cooperation from those who "stole" jobs. Where workplace cooperation is important in the production process, the firms' output and profits will surely suffer. Moreover, even if firms were willing to hire outsiders, this group may be *unwilling* to offer their services for less than the present wage rate for fear of being harassed by remaining incumbent workers. Outsiders may thus opt to wait for an increase in aggregate demand to obtain or regain employment. Meanwhile, the cyclic unemployment described in Figure 18.6(b) will persist.

THE DISTRIBUTION OF UNEMPLOYMENT

The distribution of unemployment is uneven over the labor force and changes as demand-deficient unemployment rises and falls. In Table 18.1 we present disaggregated civilian unemployment rates by race, age, gender, and duration of unemployment for two different years. These years were selected for contrast: In 1992 a major recession in the previous year had driven the overall unemployment rate to 7.5 percent (civilian

TABLE 18.1
Unemployment Rates for Labor Force Subclassifications, 2006 (Full Employment) versus 1992 (Recession)*

Source: *Employment and Earnings,* January 1993, 2007.

Category	Unemployment Rate, 2006 (%)	Unemployment Rate, 1992 (%)
Occupation		
Managerial and professional	2.1	3.1
Blue-collar	5.9	10.0
Age		
16–19	15.4	20.0
African–American, 16–19	29.1	39.8
White, 16–19	13.2	17.1
Males, 20+	4.0	7.0
Females, 20+	4.1	6.3
Race		
African–American	8.9	14.1
White	4.0	6.5
Gender		
Female	4.6	6.9
Male	4.6	7.8
Duration		
15 weeks +	1.5	2.6
Overall	4.6	7.5

* Civilian labor force data. In 1992 the economy was suffering the lingering unemployment effects of the 1990–1991 recession.

workforce); in 2006 the economy reached full employment, experiencing a 4.6 percent unemployment rate.

Observation of the large variance in the disaggregated rates of unemployment *within each year* and comparison of the rates *between* the two years support several generalizations drawn from more extensive studies of unemployment data. First, the unemployment rates for people in occupations requiring less human capital tend to be higher than those for people in positions requiring more skills. For example, in 2006 the unemployment rate for managers and professionals was 2.1 percent compared to 5.9 percent for blue-collar workers.

As a corollary, the unemployment rate usually is disproportionately higher for lower-skilled workers during a recession. Observe in Table 18.1 that the unemployment rate in 1992 for blue-collar workers was 10.0 percent compared to the 3.1 percent for managerial and professional workers. This 11.0 : 3.1 ratio is greater than the 5.9 : 2.1 ratio occurring in the full-employment year 2006.

The reasons for the differential rates between workers of various skills and the normally rising relative rates for lower-skilled workers during recessions include these: (1) Lower-skilled workers are often subject to more technologically caused unemployment and longer spells of structural unemployment; (2) higher-skilled workers are more likely to be self-employed; and (3) during periods of falling product demand, firms lay off or discharge workers in whom they have invested the least amount of human capital over the years and retain more skilled workers, managers, and professionals.

A second generalization concerning the disaggregated unemployment data shown in Table 18.1 is that the rate of unemployment for 16- to 19-year-olds is considerably higher than that for adults. Additionally, the African–American teenage unemployment rate greatly exceeds that for white teenagers. The overall teenage unemployment rate was 20.0 percent in 1992 and 15.4 percent in 2006, but the African–American teenage rates for the two years were 39.8 and 29.1 percent. Teenagers have low skill levels, high rates of job quits and discharges, little geographic mobility, and frequent transitions to and from the labor force. They therefore have numerous spells of frictional and structural unemployment. Also, some teenage unemployment is attributable to the minimum wage (Chapter 13).[16]

A third broad generalization based on Table 18.1 is that over the years, the unemployment rate for all African–Americans—teenage and adult—has been about two times that for whites. For example, in 2006 the African–American unemployment rate was 8.9 percent compared to the white rate of 4.0 percent. The reasons for the higher rates of African–American unemployment are difficult to sort out, but one factor is that African–Americans are more heavily represented in lower-skilled occupations. Recall from

---

[16] The causes and consequences of unemployment among African–American youths are analyzed in Richard B. Freeman and Harry J. Holzer, *The Black Youth Employment Crisis* (Chicago: University of Chicago Press, 1986). Also of interest are Harry J. Holzer, "Can We Solve Black Youth Unemployment?" *Challenge,* November–December 1988, pp. 43–49; and John Bound and Richard B. Freeman, "What Went Wrong? The Erosion of Relative Earnings and Employment among Young Black Men in the 1980s," *Quarterly Journal of Economics,* February 1992, pp. 201–32.

our prior discussion that such occupations have high rates of frictional and structural unemployment. Also, African–Americans live disproportionately in declining inner cities, where the demand for labor is often insufficient to employ all those seeking work. Finally, discrimination undoubtedly plays an important role in explaining the African–American to white unemployment rate gap. Only 20 to 40 percent of the unemployment rate differential between African–American and white men can be explained by observable characteristics such as education and job experience.[17]

A fourth generalization from the disaggregated unemployment data is that female unemployment rates are very similar to those of males. This has occurred over the past decade as females have moved into positions that are career-oriented and characterized by lower unemployment rates. We see in Table 18.1 that in 2006 the overall unemployment rate was 4.6 for males and females. In 1992 the female unemployment rate actually was lower than that for males. This is explained by the impact of the 1990–1991 recession on unemployment rates in such specific industries as wood products, autos, construction, and steel, which have high male–female employment ratios.

A final generalization concerning the disaggregated data illustrated in Table 18.1 is that the number of people unemployed for long periods—say 15 weeks or more—as a percentage of the labor force is much less than the overall unemployment rate but rises during recessions. The unemployment rate for people without work for 15 weeks or longer was only 1.5 percent in 2006, compared to the overall rate of 4.6 percent. But this rate was 2.6 percent in 1992, indicating that recessions tend to create longer periods of idleness of labor resources and much more social hardship than does the unemployment we associate with the natural rate of unemployment.

18.2 Quick Review

- Structural unemployment results from the mismatch between the skills required for available job openings and the skills possessed by those seeking work; it also results from a geographical mismatch between jobs and job seekers.
- Many displaced workers—those who lose their jobs because of permanent plant closings or job cutbacks—become structurally unemployed.
- Demand-deficient unemployment (also called cyclic unemployment) results from declines in aggregate demand and thus is associated with recessions and depressions.
- Unemployment rates vary by race, age, and occupation; specifically, African–Americans, youth, and lower-skilled workers have disproportionately high unemployment rates.

Your Turn

True or false? The unemployment rate of women typically has been twice that of men in recent years. (*Answer:* See page 599.)

[17] See Leslie S. Stratton, "Racial Differences in Men's Unemployment," *Industrial and Labor Relations Review,* April 1993, pp. 451–63.

REDUCING UNEMPLOYMENT: PUBLIC POLICIES

The U.S. government is officially committed to the goal of full employment. The Employment Act of 1946 proclaimed among other things that "it is the continuing policy of the Federal Government to use all practical means consistent with its needs and obligations and other essential considerations of national policy . . . to promote maximum employment, production, and purchasing power." The Full Employment and Balanced Growth Act of 1978 reaffirmed this goal and required that government (1) establish five-year employment and inflation goals and (2) formulate programs to achieve them.

Table 18.2 deserves careful examination because it summarizes the wide variety of government programs that in full or in part are designed to reduce frictional, structural, and cyclic unemployment. Analysis of each of these approaches is impossible in a single chapter. Therefore, we will confine our attention in the remainder of this chapter to a single topic: stabilization (fiscal and monetary) policy.

Fiscal and Monetary Policy

As defined in Table 18.2, *fiscal policy* is the deliberate manipulation of expenditures and taxes by the federal government for purposes of promoting full employment, price stability, and economic growth. Alternatively, *monetary policy* consists of the deliberate actions taken by the Federal Reserve authorities to adjust the nation's money supply and interest rates to promote these same goals.

The impact of expansionary fiscal and monetary policy on domestic output and unemployment is shown in Figure 18.7. Suppose initially that aggregate demand has fallen from D_1 to D, reducing real output to Q_0 (graph a). This decline in aggregate demand is accompanied by a decline in the demand for labor from D_{L1} to D_L (graph b). For the moment, suppose that labor supply is shown by curve S_L. Because the nominal wage is assumed to be inflexible downward at W_0, the decline in the demand for labor to D_L produces demand-deficient unemployment of ab. If the full-employment level of output in graph (a) is Q_n and the natural rate of employment in graph (b) is E_n, then $E_0 E_n$ represents cyclic unemployment.

Successful fiscal and monetary policy would increase aggregate demand to D_1, which would raise domestic output to its natural level Q_n and, as seen by the intersection of D_{L1} and S_L in graph (b), restore total employment to its natural level E_n.

The increase in aggregate demand to D_1 and the corresponding rise in labor demand to D_{L1} can be accomplished through some combination of (1) tax cuts for individuals to increase personal consumption spending, (2) expansion of the money supply to reduce interest rates and promote investment spending, (3) tax reductions or direct subsidies to firms to increase investment spending, and (4) increases in government expenditures.

Complications

What appears simple in theory—shifting the aggregate demand curve rightward precisely to D_1—is difficult in reality. Timing is crucial, and several time lags make precise management of aggregate demand difficult. Once the administration has recognized that aggregate demand has declined, it must formulate a fiscal policy and submit it to

TABLE 18.2 Government Policies and Programs to Reduce Unemployment*

Frictional Unemployment

Job information and matching: government programs that increase the availability of information concerning job vacancies and skills of those seeking work and help match job applicants and employers. Examples: U.S. Job Service (state employment agencies).

Structural Unemployment

1. *Educational subsidies:* government programs and expenditures that reduce the investment costs of obtaining human capital and thereby enhance people's ability to obtain jobs that are less likely to become obsolete as new technology emerges. Examples: Pell Grants and Guaranteed Student Loans for college students; subsidies under the Vocational Educational Act; funding of primary and secondary schools, community colleges, and state universities.
2. *Equal employment opportunity laws:* laws making it illegal to discriminate in hiring and promotion on the basis of race or gender, thus removing an institutional barrier that creates structural unemployment. Examples: Title VII of Civil Rights Act of 1964; Executive Order 11246.
3. *Job training and retraining:* programs designed to provide skills and work experience for those structurally unemployed. Examples: Manpower Development and Training Act (MDTA), occupational training at skill centers; MDTA on-the-job training programs; Job Corps; Comprehensive Employment and Training Act (CETA) programs aimed at youth, Native Americans, and displaced homemakers; Job Training Partnership Act; Trade Adjustment Assistance.
4. *Public service employment:* direct government hiring and on-the-job training of the long-term structurally unemployed. Examples: CETA, Title II as amended in 1978.
5. *Directed wage subsidies or employment tax credits:* direct payments or tax credits to firms that hire members of specific disadvantaged groups that experience high rates of structural unemployment. Example: Targeted Employment Tax Credit program of 1979; AFDC–WIN program.
6. *Layoff warning:* requirement that firms anticipating plant closures or major layoffs provide advance notice, thus enabling workers to immediately search for new jobs or enroll in retraining programs. Example: Worker Adjustment and Retraining Notification Act of 1988.

Demand-Deficient Unemployment

1. *Fiscal policy:* deliberate manipulations of expenditures and taxes by government for the purposes of increasing aggregate demand and thereby increasing domestic output and employment. Examples: tax cuts in 1964, 1970, 1974, and 2001.
2. *Monetary policy:* deliberate actions taken by the Federal Reserve to increase the nation's supply of money to reduce interest rates and increase aggregate demand for products and services. Examples: monetary expansions in 1982, 1991–1993, and 2001.
3. *Supply-side policies:* deliberate actions taken by the government to increase labor supply, savings, and investment and to reduce the costs of goods and services so that the aggregate supply curve shifts rightward. Examples: Reagan administration 1981 tax cuts; Individual Retirement Accounts; deregulation; Bush 2001 tax cuts.
4. *Public service unemployment:* direct government hiring of people unable to find jobs. Examples: Works Progress Administration in the 1930s; Comprehensive Employment and Training Act; Title VII; Public Service Employment in the 1970s.
5. *Wage subsidies or employment tax credits:* direct payments or tax credits to firms that expand their employment. Example: New Jobs Tax Credit program of 1977.

* Not all of the programs cited as specific examples are currently operating; some examples are historical.

FIGURE 18.7 **Fiscal and Monetary Policy to Reduce Unemployment**

Expansionary fiscal and monetary policy that increases aggregate demand from D to D_1 in graph (a) increases real output from Q_0 to Q_n. In the labor market, the corresponding rise in labor demand from D_L to D_{L1} eliminates cyclic unemployment and raises employment to E_n. But if policy makers mistakenly increase aggregate demand to D_2, labor demand will rise to D_{L2}. Eventually labor suppliers will adjust their behavior to the higher expected price level, their labor supply will decline from S_L to S'_L, and unemployment will then move to its natural level E_n.

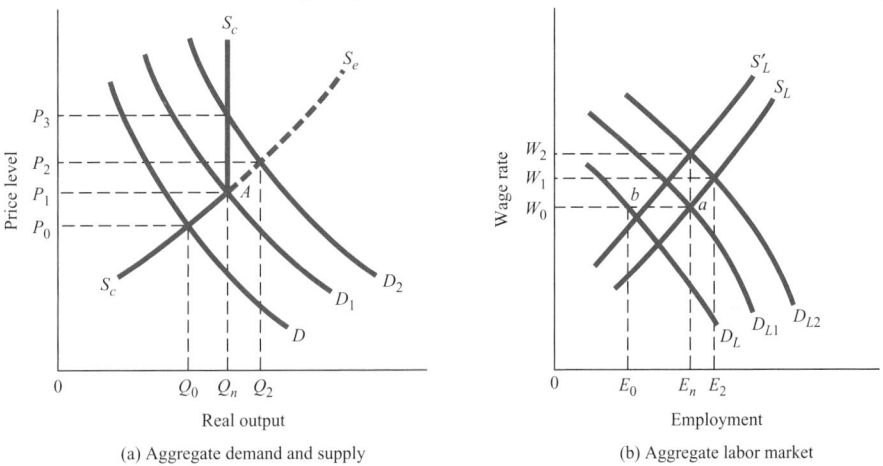

(a) Aggregate demand and supply   (b) Aggregate labor market

Congress. Next Congress must hold hearings on the proposed policy and pass it as law. Once in place, the policy itself takes time to have full impact on the economy. During these lags, factors independent of the fiscal policy can shift the aggregate demand curve further inward or rightward. Thus a specific dose of fiscal policy may turn out to be either inappropriately large or small.

Careful coordination of fiscal and monetary policy is needed to avoid another potential complication of stabilization policy: the ***crowding-out effect.*** This is a problem arising from the federal government's need to borrow funds from the money market to finance the deficits accompanying expansionary fiscal policy. Government borrowing may compete with private borrowing, increasing interest rates and reducing private investment spending. Thus the stimulus of the fiscal policy may be weakened or canceled. To keep this crowding out from occurring, the monetary authorities need to increase the money supply by just enough to offset the deficit-caused rise in the equilibrium interest rate.

Another complication of stabilization policy is that government may overshoot its mark. Because this overshooting has happened in the past, it is worthwhile to examine the implications in aggregate product and labor markets. Let's suppose that expansionary fiscal and monetary policies shift the aggregate demand curve further to the right than expected, say to D_2 rather than D_1, thus causing a higher than expected price level (P_2 rather than P_1). In the short run, this unexpectedly high inflation temporarily may increase real output above its natural level; the economy may move upward along the broken-line segment of AS_e. In the long run, however, real output will return to its natural level Q_n. In the meantime, with aggregate demand at D_2, the price level will continue to rise to its equilibrium level at P_3.

We need to examine closely what is happening in the labor market to understand why real output temporarily rises to Q_2, only to eventually fall back to Q_n. The expansion of aggregate demand to D_2 (graph a) increases the demand for labor to D_{L2} (graph b). Employment temporarily rises above its natural level as firms, which have contracted for existing labor at W_0, expand their hiring. Also, job searchers, who now are being offered nominal wages at W_1, reduce their search time. To repeat: The reason for the rise in employment is that the actual rate of inflation has exceeded the expected rate, reducing frictional unemployment (recall our previous discussion of this topic). But once suppliers of labor recognize that the new price level is higher than previously expected, they readjust their behavior so that labor supply shifts from S_L to S'_L. Why is this so? The answer is that workers will no longer supply as much labor *at each nominal wage* now that the price level is P_2 rather than the expected level of P_1. The *real wage* (nominal wage/price level) associated with *each* nominal wage is now *lower,* and this fact translates into a leftward shift of the labor supply curve.

Observe from the intersection of D_{L2} and S'_L that the nominal wage, which *is* flexible upward, has increased to W_2. At this higher nominal wage, employment returns to its natural level E_n. This employment decline corresponds to the return of real output from Q_2 to Q_n in graph (a). Observe also that both the price level *and* the nominal wage are now higher. The inappropriately expansionary fiscal and monetary policy eliminated cyclic unemployment but also produced price and wage inflation.

Chapter Summary

1. A person is officially unemployed if she or he is 16 years or older, is not institutionalized, and is actively seeking work, waiting to be called back to a job after being laid off, or waiting to report to a new job within 30 days.

2. The official unemployment data have several limitations as measures of economic hardship and as guides to public policy. The stock–flow model sorts out causes of changes in the unemployment rate and provides information about the duration of employment spells for individuals.

3. An unemployment rate of about 4.0–5.0 percent represents a "full" or natural rate of unemployment. At this rate neither an excess demand nor an excess supply of labor occurs, and the actual and expected rates of inflation are equal.

4. Frictional unemployment is a natural and often constructive occurrence in a dynamic economy characterized by heterogeneous workers and jobs, imperfect information, and continuous movements of people among the various categories of labor force status. It can take two basic forms: search unemployment, which is associated with the time required to find a job; and wait unemployment, where workers either wait to be recalled to former jobs or remain in job queues resulting from above-market-clearing wages.

5. Structural unemployment results from a mismatch between the skills needed for available jobs and the skills possessed by those seeking employment. Many of those structurally unemployed are displaced workers who specifically lose their jobs because of permanent plant closings or job cutbacks.

6. Declines in the aggregate demand for goods and services cause a deficiency in the aggregate demand for labor. Wage rates tend to be inflexible downward for a variety of reasons, including the presence of unions, a bias toward layoffs by firms, implicit contracts, and insider–outsider relationships. As a result, involuntary demand-deficient unemployment arises when aggregate demand declines.

7. Unemployment is distributed unevenly in the labor force. For example, the unemployment rate for African–Americans is about twice that for whites.

8. Fiscal policy is a major tool used to combat demand-deficient unemployment, but it is fraught with several complications, including *(a)* time lags, *(b)* the need to coordinate fiscal and monetary policies to avoid the crowding-out effect, and *(c)* tendencies to create inflation.

Terms and Concepts

Household Survey (CPS), *537*
employment–population ratio, *537*
unemployment rate, *537*
discouraged workers, *540*
subemployed, *540*
stock–flow model, *541*
full employment, *543*
equilibrium, *544*

natural rate of unemployment, *544*
aggregate demand, *545*
aggregate supply, *546*
frictional unemployment, *548*
search unemployment, *548*
wait unemployment, *548*
structural unemployment, *549*

displaced workers, *550*
demand-deficient (cyclic) unemployment, *553*
implicit contracts, *555*
insider–outsider theories, *555*
fiscal policy, *559*
monetary policy, *559*
crowding-out effect, *561*

Questions and Study Suggestions

1. Use the following data to calculate *(a)* the size of the labor force, *(b)* the official unemployment rate, and *(c)* the labor force participation rate (Chapter 3) for a hypothetical economy: population = 500; population 16 years or older and noninstitutionalized = 400; people employed full- or part-time = 200; people unemployed and actively seeking work = 20; people who have quit seeking work due to lack of success = 10; part-time workers seeking full-time jobs = 30.

2. What factors tend to *understate* the extent to which the official unemployment rate accurately measures the degree of economic hardship in the nation? What factors lead some observers to conclude that the official unemployment rate *overstates* economic hardship?

3. Use the basic model shown in Figure 18.5 to illustrate graphically each of the following: *(a)* demand-deficient unemployment and *(b)* temporary increases in output and employment beyond their natural, or full-employment, levels.

4. Define the term *structural unemployment* and distinguish it from frictional and demand-deficient unemployment. Why might structural unemployment fall when demand-deficient unemployment declines?

5. Suppose you are an economic adviser to the president, who has asked you to design a program to reduce the amount of unemployment associated with displaced workers. What major elements would your plan include?

6. Why are nominal wages inflexible downward? What is the implication of this characteristic for the ability of involuntary demand-deficient unemployment to persist for a considerable length of time?

7. Assume that the official national unemployment rate rises from 4 percent to 8 percent because of a major recession. What impact do you predict this would have on *(a)* the African–American to white unemployment rate ratio, *(b)* the labor force participation rate, and *(c)* the teenage–adult unemployment rate ratio? Explain.

8. Do you expect the natural rate of unemployment to *(a)* increase, *(b)* decrease, or *(c)* remain at the present level over the next decade? Explain your reasoning.

9. Examine critically this statement: "Unemployment in the United States can be resolved quickly and efficiently. The government should simply provide jobs for everyone who wants to work who cannot find suitable employment in the private sector."

Internet Exercise

The Unemployment Rate

Go to the Bureau of Labor Statistics Web site **(http://www.bls.gov)**. Click on "Unemployment Rate." This will retrieve the latest Bureau of Labor Statistics news release regarding the labor force in the United States.

Use this news release to answer the following questions: What is the unemployment rate for the last two months? How many people were unemployed in each of the last two months? Did the unemployment rate change between the two months because of a change in the size of the labor force or a change in the number of unemployed people? Explain your answers.

Internet Links

The U.S. Department of Labor Unemployment Insurance Web site includes many details about the unemployment benefits program **(http://www.workforcesecurity.doleta.gov/unemploy/)**.

The Bureau of Labor Statistics Local Unemployment Statistics Web site reports employment, unemployment, and labor force data for census regions and divisions, states, counties, metropolitan areas, and many cities **(http://www.bls.gov/lau/home.htm)**.

Appendix

Information Sources in Labor Economics

The purpose of this appendix is to survey significant sources of information about labor economics. This information should prove useful to individuals preparing term papers in this or subsequent courses. In this regard, note the list of potential term paper topics in Appendix Table 1. Also, this appendix provides valuable information about how you might keep your personal and professional knowledge of labor economics current in the years ahead. If you are a business or economics major, we urge you to keep this book (or at least a copy of this appendix) in your personal library.

An overview of the appendix will point our way. First we identify and briefly describe key Internet sites relating to labor economics and labor statistics. Then we annotate print sources of labor statistics. Third, we call your attention to various publications containing articles about labor economics and policy. There we annotate bibliographic indexes, professional journals, compendiums of invited essays, and nontechnical publications. Next several advanced textbooks in labor economics are briefly described. Finally, mention is made of textbooks that cover closely related fields such as labor law, collective bargaining, labor relations, and labor history.

SOURCES OF LABOR STATISTICS

Statistical sources can be classified as being either primary or secondary and as providing either time-series or cross-sectional data. A ***primary statistical source*** is an original source of data such as that generated from the U.S. Bureau of Census' *Current Population Survey* (CPS) and reported by the U.S. Bureau of Labor Statistics (BLS). You may recall from Chapter 18 that this particular survey samples about 60,000 households nationwide each month to obtain information about labor force participation, employment, and unemployment. The CPS data are replicated or summarized in numerous ***secondary statistical sources*** such as handbooks of statistics, business periodicals,

APPENDIX TABLE 1
A Selected List of Term Paper Topics

Worker Absenteeism
Multiple Job Holding (Moonlighting)
The Retirement Decision
Female Labor Force Participation Rates
Discouraged- versus Added-Worker
 Effects
Cyclic and Secular Changes in the
 Average Workweek
Racial Differences in Labor Force
 Participation
Educational Attainment and Earnings,
 Hours of Work, and Unemployment
Trends in Labor Force Participation of
 Older Males
The Economics of Student Loans
Criticisms of Human Capital Theory
The Economic Value of Life
The Firm's Investment in Human Capital:
 On-the-Job Training
Corporate Sponsorship of Education
The Economics of Pensions
CEO Pay
Effectiveness of Public Sector Training
 Programs
Monopsony in Labor Markets
The Market for Nurses
Occupational Licensing
Efficiency Wage Theories
Should Fringe Benefits Be Taxed?
The Decline of Unionism
Determinants of Union Membership
Deregulation and the Labor Market
Theories of Collective Bargaining
Collective Bargaining in Professional
 Sports
The Economics of Seniority
Labor-Owned Enterprises
Incentive Pay Systems
Employee Stock Option Plans (ESOPs)
Compulsory Arbitration
Effects of Right-to-Work Laws
The Economics of Fringe Benefits
Pay, Performance, and Productivity
Unions and Job Turnover
Economic Impacts of Strikes
Trends in Government Employment
Public versus Private Pay
The Impact of Taxes on Labor Supply

National Service Plans
Effects of the Minimum Wage
Labor Market Impacts of OSHA
Sexual Harassment in the Workplace
Earnings Disparities by Race
Trends in the Female–Male Earnings
 Ratio
Occupational Discrimination
Effectiveness of Antidiscrimination Laws
Compensating Wage Differentials
Firm Size and Pay Levels
The Earnings of "Superstars"
Family Background and Human Capital
 Investment in Children
Trends in the Distribution of Earnings
Unions and the Distribution of Earnings
Occupational Mobility
Earnings of Recent Immigrants
Immigration Reform: Labor Market Issues
Plant Closures and Displaced Workers
Are Internal Labor Markets Efficient?
Trends in Real Wage Rates
International Comparisons of Real
 Wages
Productivity Growth and the New
 Economy
International Trends in Productivity
 Growth
Trends in Self-Employment
What Is "Full" Employment?
Theories of Job Search
Technological Unemployment
Implicit Contracts: Theory and
 Implications
Teenage Unemployment
African–American Unemployment
Wage Subsidies: The Earned Income
 Tax Credit
Rational Expectations and Labor
 Markets
Profit Sharing
Labor Market Effects of Unemployment
 Insurance Benefits
International Differences in
 Unemployment Rates
Alternative Work Arrangements:
 Compressed Work, Flextime, and
 Work Sharing

APPENDIX TABLE 1
A Selected List of Term Paper Topics

The North American Free Trade Agreement and American Labor	Occupational Employment Trends in the United States
Lifetime Employment in Japan	Trends in Manufacturing versus Service Employment
Unemployment and Underemployment in the Developing Countries	Trends in the Natural Rate of Unemployment
The Americans with Disabilities Act and the Labor Market	Does Competition Reduce Discrimination?

and textbooks. Secondary sources are normally reliable, but you should be aware that they usually present truncated versions of the data. Therefore, you can often obtain more information by going to the primary source.

Labor statistics are reported as time-series data, cross-sectional data, or some combination of the two. *Time-series data* are ordered chronologically—that is, by some period of time such as month or year. Examples are Figure 3.2, which graphs population and the labor force since 1950; Figure 11.4, which shows the number of work stoppages in the United States since 1960; and Figure 17.2, which chronicles the BLS's annual labor productivity index since 1960.

Cross-sectional data, on the other hand, are measurements of a particular variable at a specific time, but for different economic units or groups. For example, Table 13.2 reports occupational fatalities and injuries in 2004 *by industry.* Similarly, Table 8.3 presents data on the average hourly wages of private workers in manufacturing industries in 2006 *by selected state,* and Table 18.1 summarizes unemployment rates for specific years *by occupation, race, gender, age, and duration.*

What are the major (primary and secondary) sources of time-series and cross-sectional labor statistics? We will approach this topic by annotating each of the following: Internet sites, bibliographies of statistical sources, print sources of general U.S. statistics, print sources of statistics specific to labor economics, and data sets available from research institutes. Where possible, we paraphrase the descriptions supplied by the sources themselves.[1]

Internet Sites

The Internet contains several excellent sources that provide information and statistics relating to labor economics. We list and annotate these sites in Appendix Table 2. We urge you to try out several of the sites listed in the table. (Some of these Internet sites contain full copies of the print sources described here).

Bibliographies of Statistical Sources

Bibliographies of statistical publications index sources of statistical series by topical heading, much as the familiar *Reader's Guide to Periodical Literature* lists magazine articles. Just as the *Reader's Guide* contains no articles itself, bibliographies of statistical sources contain no statistical series themselves. These bibliographies or indexes complement the

---

[1] Our organization in this section roughly follows that used by Charles Helppie, James Gibbons, and Donald Pearson, *Research Guide in Economics* (Morristown, NJ: General Learning Press, 1974), pp. 69–91.

APPENDIX TABLE 2
Internet Sites Relating to Labor Economics

Asset and Health Dynamics among The Oldest-Old (AHEAD)
[http://hrsonline.isr.umich.edu/]
Provides survey data that focus on the relationship between economic and family resources and later life behavior.

Bureau of Economic Analysis
[http://www.bea.gov]
Provides data on GDP and selected tables in the *Survey of Current Business*.

Bureau of Labor Statistics
[http://www.bls.gov]
Includes detailed data on employment, unemployment, prices, productivity, and foreign labor statistics.

Data on the Net
[http://3stages.org/idata]
Permits search by keyword of over 360 Internet sites with downloadable social science statistical data.

EconData
[http://www.econdata.net]
Provides thousands of downloadable data series from the U.S. government.

Economic Journals on the Web
[http://www.oswego.edu/~economic/journals.htm]
Provides an index to Web locations of numerous economics journals.

Economic Report of the President
[http://www.gpoaccess.gov/eop/index.html]
The entire reports for years 1996 and beyond are online. This site also includes statistical tables summarizing important economic data series.

Economic Statistics Briefing Room
[http://www.whitehouse.gov/fsbr/esbr.html]
Contains up-to-date data and historical charts for the major economic data series.

Fedstats
[http://www.fedstats.gov]
Searchable site with links to over 70 federal agencies with statistical data.

Health and Retirement Survey (HRS)
[http://hrsonline.isr.umich.edu/]
Provides survey data on the economic, demographic, and health characteristics of individuals.

Department of Homeland Security
[http://www.dhs.gov/ximgtn]
Provides comprehensive annual immigration statistics for recent years.

Integrated Public Use Micro Data Center
[http://www.ipums.umn.edu]
Contains census data from 1850 to 2000.

National Labor Relations Board
[http://www.nlrb.gov/]
Contains information about the NLRB and its decisions relating to alleged unfair labor practices of firms and unions.

About Guide to Economics
[http://economics.about.com]
Provides Internet links to current economics information. For example, it includes links to economic articles in online versions of magazines such as *BusinessWeek*.

Open Directory Project
[http://dmoz.org/science/social_sciences/economics/labor_economics/]
Supplies many labor economics related links.

Organization for Economic Cooperation and Development
[http://www.oecd.org]
Includes data on selected economic measures for OECD countries.

APPENDIX TABLE 2
Internet Sites Relating to Labor Economics

Panel Study of Income Dynamics [http://psidonline.isr.umich.edu/]
Consists of longitudinal data on the characteristics and labor market behavior of the survey respondents.

Resources for Economists on the Internet [http://rfe.org]
Provides links to more than 700 economics-related Internet sites.

Social Security Administration [http://www.ssa.gov]
Provides statistical information on Social Security programs (e.g., benefit formulas, number of beneficiaries, trust funds, average benefits, etc.).

Statistical Abstract of the United States [http://www.census.gov/compendia/statab]
Tables from the statistical abstract are downloadable.

W. E. Upjohn Institute [http://www.upjohninst.org]
Provides an online catalog of publications as well as working papers.

U.S. Census Bureau [http://www.census.gov]
Comprehensive site with extensive data on topics such as population, earnings, and demographic characteristics. It also provides all Census Bureau Publications data since January 1996. Finally, it includes links to data extraction from data sources such as the Current Population Survey (CPS), American Housing Survey (AHS), and Public Use of Microdata Samples (PUMS) of the census.

Internet as a good place to begin a search for statistical series. For labor economics, you might fruitfully seek listings under such topics as unions, employment, labor, and productivity. Of the several bibliographic guides, the following are particularly useful:

American Statistics Index (Washington, DC: Congressional Information Service). Annual with monthly supplements.

This index provides the most comprehensive print access to U.S. government statistical publications available. It indexes and abstracts all of the statistical publications issued by federal agencies and therefore provides a starting point in searching for specific statistical series.

U.S. Bureau of the Census: *Directory of Federal Statistics for Local Areas: A Guide to Sources* (Washington, DC: U.S. Government Printing Office).

This directory lists sources of federal statistics for metropolitan statistical areas (MSAs). An MSA is a geographic area containing either (1) one city having 50,000 or more inhabitants or (2) an urbanized area of at least 50,000 people *and* a total MSA population of at least 100,000.

U.S. Bureau of the Census: *Statistical Abstract of the United States* (Washington, DC: U.S. Government Printing Office). Appendix, "Guide to Sources of Statistics."

Alphabetically arranged by subject, this appendix contains references to the primary and secondary sources of data summarized in the body of this national data book. Publications listed under each subject are divided into two main groups: "U.S. Government" and "Other."

General Summary Statistics

Several excellent volumes contain summaries of statistical series on a full range of political, economic, social, and demographic variables. These "data books," "statistical abstracts," or "statistical handbooks" contain numerous tables of interest to students of labor economics. A few of the more significant works are the following:

U.S. Bureau of the Census: *Statistical Abstract of the United States* (Washington, DC: U.S. Government Printing Office). Annual.

This previously cited annual edition provides comprehensive summaries of statistics on the social, political, and economic organizations of the United States. It draws on both government and private sources, and many of the more than 1,400 tables present statistics relevant to labor and labor markets. A section of particular significance is titled "Labor Force, Employment, and Earnings." Other useful sections are "Population," "Education," and "Federal Government Finances and Employment."

U.S. Bureau of the Census: *Historical Statistics of the United States, Colonial Times to 1970* (Washington, DC: U.S. Government Printing Office). Issued 1976.

This book contains more than 12,500 statistical time series, largely annual, on American social, economic, political, and geographic developments covering periods from 1610 to 1970. This is an excellent source for backdating series found in the *Statistical Abstract.*

U.S. Office of the President: *Economic Report of the President* (Washington, DC: U.S. Government Printing Office). Annual.

This annual report has an extensive appendix containing statistical data relating to income, the labor force, employment, and production. A section of the appendix that is particularly useful to labor economists is "Population, Employment, Wages, and Productivity." Furthermore, the text of the *Report* usually contains sections or chapters pertaining to recent labor market developments. For example, the 2007 *Report* contains an entire chapter on the recent growth in labor productivity.

Labor-Specific Statistical Sources

Considerable overlap of tables occurs in the various statistical sources. For example, the *Statistical Abstract of the United States* contains many labor-related series also found in the more specialized sources that we are about to annotate. But in general, labor-specific sources contain a wider range of data and statistical series that relate directly to labor economics. Awareness of these specialized sources is therefore critical for finding data that may not be presented elsewhere. Let's examine several excellent publications:

Eva E. Jacobs (ed.): *Handbook of U.S. Labor Statistics* (Lanham, MD: Bernan Press). Periodic.

This publication presents the major series of statistics generated annually by the Bureau of Labor Statistics. The most recent edition (2006) contained tables grouped into the following categories: (1) population, labor force, and employment status; (2) employment and unemployment by industry; (3) hourly and weekly earnings; (4) consumer and producer prices; (5) export and import prices; (6) consumer expenditures by household type; (7) employment costs; (8) productivity; (9) employee benefits; and (10) international comparisons.

Barry T. Hirsch and David A. Macpherson: *Union Membership and Earnings Data Book: Compilations from the Current Population Survey (2007 Edition)* (Washington, DC: Bureau of National Affairs). Annual.

This annual report presents current and historical data on union membership as well as earnings for union and nonunion workers. Breakdowns of these and related measures are provided by state, industry, occupation, and demographic group.

Directory of U.S. Labor Organizations (Washington, DC: Bureau of National Affairs, Inc.). Periodic.

In addition to providing aggregate union membership data for American labor, this publication presents detailed statistics concerning the membership of individual unions and the demographic, occupational, industrial, and geographic characteristics of union members.

U.S. Department of Labor, Bureau of Labor Statistics: *Monthly Labor Review* (Washington, DC: U.S. Government Printing Office). Monthly.

This periodical is a source of current statistics on labor force participation, productivity, employment, unemployment, and consumer prices. An appendix reports the results of the (1) Current Population Survey, (2) Establishment Payroll Survey, and (3) Consumer Price Survey, all of which are conducted monthly.

U.S. Department of Labor, Bureau of Labor Statistics: *Employment and Earnings* (Washington, DC: U.S. Government Printing Office). Monthly.

Employment and Earnings is a monthly publication that provides current information about employment status, characteristics of the employed and unemployed, hours and earnings, productivity, and state and area labor force data. It is worth noting that in 1985 this publication introduced a valuable series—reported in January issues—showing union membership by age, race, gender, occupation, and industry.

U.S. Department of Labor, Bureau of Labor Statistics: *Compensation and Working Conditions* (Washington, DC: U.S. Government Printing Office). Monthly.

This publication, previously titled *Current Wage Developments,* includes data and brief articles on the total compensation package and other aspects of the work environment, such as major collective bargaining settlements, employer costs for employee compensation, union membership, employee benefits, and area wages.

U.S. Department of Commerce, Bureau of the Census: *Money Income of Households, Families, and Persons in the United States.* Current Population Report P–60. Annual.

This publication, found in libraries that are depositories for federal government publications, reports detailed statistics on the functional and personal distribution of income in the United States. The tables summarize data from the Census Bureau's annual *Current Population Survey.*

International Labour Office: *Yearbook of Labour Statistics* (Geneva, Switzerland: ILO Publications). Annual.

This international yearbook contains time series of labor-related data classified by 180 countries or territories.

Research Institute Survey Data

Several sets of primary data from surveys conducted by research institutes are available to scholars wishing to do original research. Three such sources are the following:

Survey Research Center, Institute for Social Research, University of Michigan: *Health and Retirement Survey.*

This survey, conducted biannually, provides information about aspects of work such as working conditions and earnings for people who were age 51 to 62 in 1992.

Survey Research Center, Institute for Social Research, University of Michigan: *Panel Study on Income Dynamics (PSID).*

This survey provides information about employment, earnings, unemployment, fringe benefits, and so forth. Nearly 5,000 families were first surveyed in 1968 and were interviewed annually each year thereafter. When family members leave home and set up new families, the latter also become part of the annual surveys.

U.S. Department of Labor, Employment and Training Administration: *National Longitudinal Survey (NLS).* Conducted by the Center for Human Resource Research, Ohio State University.

The *NLS* collects information from the same group of people periodically over an extended period of time. It provides information about union status, wages, fringe benefits, job separations, and job satisfaction. The availability of extensive personal information allows researchers to control for such factors as education, age, and parents' income.

Updating and Augmenting Tables

Most of the statistical tables found in *Contemporary Labor Economics* are drawn from the general abstracts or labor-specific statistical sources just discussed. These tables can be updated by noting the source cited for each and then finding the most recent edition of that particular publication. Normally, series found in earlier editions are included somewhere within the new ones. Alternatively, you can update many of these tables via the Internet.

For such purposes as writing term papers, tables in the text may not be sufficiently detailed to meet your needs. But keep in mind that the source cited in the table likely contains many more data than those summarized in the table. For example, Table 13.2 provides statistics of occupational fatalities and disabilities by industry for 2004. By referring to the source, *Statistical Abstract of the United States,* you would discover a wealth of information about occupational health and safety, such as (1) production time lost due to workplace accidents and (2) rates of nonfatal job injuries and illnesses by industry. Furthermore, you would discover there that a *primary* source of occupational health and safety information is *Accident Facts* (Itasca, IL: National Safety Council), which contains more information about this subject.

APPLICATIONS, NEW THEORIES, EMERGING EVIDENCE

Our attention now turns to sources in which new developments in labor economics are reported. We will annotate numerous professional journals, compendiums of invited essays, and nontechnical publications in the discussion that follows. But first, let's highlight works that provide indexes or bibliographies of labor-related publications.

Indexes and Bibliographies

Several publications help direct interested people toward specific books and journal articles that treat labor economics. Two useful sources are the following:

American Economic Association: *Index of Economic Articles* (Homewood, IL: Richard D. Irwin). Updated via new volumes.

This series contains bibliographic citations to articles from over 250 economics journals, with each volume covering a particular period. For example, Volume I covers the 1886–1924 period while Volume XIX indexes articles published in 1977. This index is not current, however, and thus those interested in recently published articles should consult the source that follows.

American Economic Association: *Journal of Economic Literature (JEL).* Quarterly.

This publication contains (1) review articles of research on particular topics, (2) reviews of selected books, (3) an annotated listing of new books in economics, and (4) the ***Journal of Economic Literature classification system.*** The "J" listing in the classification system, shown in Appendix Table 3, defines subtopics in labor and demographic economics.

Professional Journals

Scholarly journals contain articles in which economists report new theories, new evidence, new techniques for testing established theories, and the like. The main audiences for these articles are other specialists in economics. Therefore, most undergraduates will find the mathematical models and econometric techniques employed to be formidable. However, the basic conclusions of the articles can be gleaned through careful reading.

Articles about labor economics are found in *general* economics journals and labor-specific journals. Examples of the former include *The American Economic Review, Journal of Political Economy, Review of Economics and Statistics, Quarterly Journal of*

APPENDIX TABLE 3
Journal of Economic Literature Classification System: "J" Listings

J Labor and Demographic Economics

J00 General

J1 Demographic Economics

J10 General

J11 Demographic Trends and Forecasts

J12 Marriage; Marital Dissolution; Family Structure

J13 Fertility; Family Planning; Child Care; Children; Youth

J14 Economics of the Elderly

J15 Economics of Minorities and Races

J16 Economics of Gender

J17 Value of Life; Forgone Income

J18 Public Policy

J19 Other

J2 Time Allocation, Work Behavior, and Employment Determination and Creation

J20 General

J21 Labor Force and Employment, Size, and Structure

J22 Time Allocation and Labor Supply

J23 Employment Determination; Job Creation; Demand for Labor; Self-Employment

J24 Human Capital; Skills; Occupational Choice; Labor Productivity

J26 Retirement; Retirement Policies

J28 Safety; Accidents; Industrial Health; Job Satisfaction; Related Public Policy

J29 Other

J3 Wages, Compensation, and Labor Costs

J30 General

J31 Wage Level and Structure: Wage Differentials by Skill, Training, Occupation, etc.

J32 Nonwage Labor Costs and Benefits; Private Pensions

J33 Compensation Packages; Payment Methods

J38 Public Policy

J39 Other

J4 Particular Labor Markets

J40 General

J41 Contracts: Specific Human Capital, Matching Models, Efficiency Wage Models, and Internal Labor Markets

J42 Monopsony; Segmented Labor Markets

J43 Agricultural Labor Markets

J44 Professional Labor Markets and Occupations

J45 Public Sector Labor Markets

J48 Public Policy

J49 Other

J5 Labor–Management Relations, Trade Unions, and Collective Bargaining

J50 General

J51 Trade Unions: Objectives, Structure, and Effects

J52 Dispute Resolution: Strikes, Arbitration; and Mediation

J53 Labor–Management Relations; Industrial Jurisprudence

J54 Producer Cooperatives; Labor-Managed Firms

J58 Public Policy

J59 Other

J6 Mobility, Unemployment, and Vacancies

J60 General

J61 Geographic Labor Mobility; Immigrant Workers

J62 Occupational and Intergenerational Mobility

J63 Turnover; Vacancies; Layoffs

J64 Unemployment: Models, Duration, Incidence, and Job Search

J65 Unemployment Insurance; Severance Pay; Plant Closings

J68 Public Policy

J69 Other

APPENDIX TABLE 3
Journal of Economic Literature Classification System:"J" Listings

J7 Discrimination	
J70 General	J78 Public Policy
J71 Discrimination	J79 Other
J8 Labor Standards: National and International	
J80 General	J83 Workers' Rights
J81 Working Conditions	J88 Public Policy
J82 Labor Force Composition	J89 Other

Economics, Brookings Papers on Economic Activity, Economic Inquiry, Journal of Economic Issues, Southern Economic Journal, Canadian Journal of Economics, and *Oxford Economic Papers.*[2]

The following are important *labor-specific* journals:

New York State School of Industrial and Labor Relations, Cornell University: *Industrial and Labor Relations Review.* Quarterly.

For example, the April 2004 issue presented research on promotions, wage inequality, job search, affirmative action, retirement, and work hours.

University of Chicago: *Journal of Labor Economics.* Quarterly.

This journal publishes theoretical and applied research on the supply and demand for labor services, compensation, labor markets, the distribution of earnings, labor demographics, unions and collective bargaining, and policy issues in labor economics.

Basil Blackwell: *Industrial Relations.* Triannual.

This cross-disciplinary international journal is a publication of the Institute of Industrial Relations, University of California at Berkeley. It contains papers and original articles, as well as research notes and "current topic" articles, on the employment relationship.

University of Wisconsin: *Journal of Human Resources.* Quarterly.

This excellent journal publishes articles about the role of education and training in enhancing production skills, employment opportunities, and income, as well as human resource development, health, and welfare policies as they relate to the labor market.

International Labour Office, Geneva, Switzerland: *International Labour Review.* Monthly.

This journal contains articles, comparative studies, and research reports about such topics as employment and unemployment, wages and conditions of work, industrial relations, and workers' participation. Authors are international scholars.

George Mason University: *Journal of Labor Research.* Quarterly.

Articles about labor unions, labor economics, labor relations, and related topics appear in this quarterly. Interdisciplinary studies are common, and many papers

[2] For a listing of 130 economics journals, see David N. Laband and Michael J. Piette, "The Relative Impacts of Economics Journals," *Journal of Economic Literature,* June 1994, pp. 640–66.

have a public policy orientation. Occasionally it includes papers from symposia, conferences, and seminars sponsored by the journal.

North-Holland: *Labour Economics: An International Journal.* Quarterly.

This new international journal publishes research in micro and macro labor economics in a balanced mix of theory, empirical testing, and policy applications. Of particular interest are articles that explain the origin of institutional arrangements of national labor markets and the impacts of these institutions on labor market outcomes.

Basil Blackwell: *British Journal of Industrial Relations.* Triannual.

Articles on labor economics, labor relations, and collective bargaining are published in this British journal. For example, a typical issue contained articles titled "Social Partnership or a 'Complete Sellout'? Russian Trade Unions' Responses to Conflict"; "Influences on Trade Union Effectiveness in Britain"; "Works Councils and Plant Closings in Germany"; and "Actual and Preferred Working Hours."

New York University: *Labor History.* Quarterly.

This journal is concerned with research in labor history, the impact of labor problems on ethnic and minority groups, theories of the labor movement, comparative analysis of foreign labor movements, studies of specific unions, and biographical portraits of important labor leaders.

Industrial Relations Research Association: *Proceedings of the Industrial Relations Research Association.* Annual.

These proceedings consist of addresses by distinguished labor experts, contributed papers, and invited papers on topics of interest to industrial and labor relations specialists and practitioners.

Commerce Clearing House: *Labor Law Journal.* Monthly.

This journal contains a survey of important legislative, administrative, and judicial developments in labor law. Articles about subjects pertaining to legal problems in the labor relations field are featured.

Our annotated listing of labor-specific journals is far from exhaustive. Other English-language journals that relate to labor include *Labor Studies Journal, Human Resource Planning, Economic and Industrial Democracy, Women at Work, Journal of Collective Negotiations in the Public Sector, International Journal of Manpower, Journal of Productivity Analysis, Government Union Review, Labour and Society, Japan Labor Bulletin, Journal of Industrial Relations, Work and Occupations,* and *Journal of Population Economics.*

Compendiums of Invited Essays

Several organizations and publishers regularly release edited books that contain invited papers or chapters on current aspects of labor economics. Three examples follows:

Research in Labor Economics: A Research Annual (Amsterdam, Netherlands: Elsevier). Annual. Solomon Polochek, series editor.

Contributions to this series consist of original papers that are longer than normal journal articles but shorter than traditional monographs. The series began in 1977. Contributors include many prominent researchers in labor economics.

Labor and Employment Relations Association Series. Annual.

The Labor and Employment Relations Association (LERA) annually publishes a book made up of papers on a specific topic. Examples include *Theoretical Perspectives on Work and the Employment Relationship,* edited by Bruce Kaufman; *The Ethics of Human Resources and Industrial Relations,* edited by John W. Budd and James G. Scoville; and *Contemporary Issues in Employment Relations,* edited by David Lewin.

Kluwer Law: *Proceedings of New York University Conference on Labor.* Annual. Samuel Estreicher, editor.

This annual publication, which began in 1948, stresses collective bargaining and the labor relations field. Thus recent volumes contain chapters about developments in labor law, arbitration, worker absenteeism and incompetence, age and gender discrimination, public sector bargaining, comparable worth, two-tier wage systems, and so forth.

Nontechnical Publications

Although articles in professional journals are useful, their specialized language and esoteric statistical techniques often diminish their accessibility to undergraduate students. Sometimes of greater usefulness are nontechnical books, journals, magazines, and even newspapers that report and summarize recent theory and research.

1 Nontechnical Books

Many important books in labor economics are directed to wide audiences, not just labor specialists. Some publishing houses specialize in publishing analytical books that are accessible to nonspecialists. The W. E. Upjohn Institute of Employment Research (Kalamazoo, MI), in particular, is noted for books about timely employment topics. Recent examples are Nan L. Maxwell, *The Working Life: The Labor Market for Workers in Low-Skilled Jobs;* Morris M. Kleiner, *Licensing Occupations: Ensuring Quality or Restricting Competition?;* Sandra E. Gleason (editor), *The Shadow Workforce: Perspectives on Contingent Work in the United States, Japan, and Europe;* and Wayne Vroman and Vera Brusentsev, *Unemployment Compensation throughout the World: A Comparative Analysis.* Also, the Brookings Institution occasionally publishes books of interest to students of labor economics. An example is Jack E. Triplett and Barry Bosworth, *Productivity in the U.S. Services Sector: New Sources of Economic Growth.*

2 Hearings Testimony

Testimony before congressional committees is a valuable source of information about important research in labor economics. These volumes, published by the

U.S. Government Printing Office, are located in libraries that are depositories of federal government publications. Although numerous committees hold hearings on legislation relating to labor, two of the more relevant ones are the Senate Human Resources Committee and the House Education and Labor Committee (and subcommittees of each).

3 Nontechnical Journals

A few nontechnical journals are also of interest to students of labor economics. The *Monthly Labor Review* mentioned earlier is of particular importance in this regard. It contains informative and readable articles about such topics as labor markets, wages and earnings, fringe benefits, mobility, unionism, and collective bargaining. Also, the AFL–CIO *Federationist* is a good source of information about organized labor's position on policy issues. Third, the May issue of the *American Economic Review* (previously cited) contains papers delivered at the annual meeting of the American Economics Association. Usually one or two sessions of the conference pertain to labor economics; and because presenters are instructed to keep their papers noneconometric, these discussions usually are accessible to undergraduates. Finally, two journals that contain articles about current economic policy issues are worth checking for discussions of labor topics: *Contemporary Economic Policy* and *Journal of Economic Perspectives.*

4 Magazines and Newspapers

The economics or labor sections of popular magazines such as *BusinessWeek, Newsweek, Time,* and *U.S. News and World Report* occasionally contain stories about current labor economics issues. By mentioning economists who have done research on a particular topic, these articles serve as helpful starting points for identifying academic sources. This is also true of newspaper articles, particularly those found in financial papers such as *The Wall Street Journal.* Listed next are a nontechnical magazine devoted exclusively to economics and two important indexes through which one can identify specific nontechnical magazine and newspaper articles.

Challenge: A Magazine of Economic Affairs. Six issues yearly.

Among other things, *Challenge* contains invited articles about economic policy issues, interviews with leading economists, and a comment section called "The Growlery." It is not uncommon for an issue to contain one or two articles pertinent to labor economics. The articles are written by economics experts but are directed toward all people interested in the topics, not just specialists in the field.

Reader's Guide to Periodical Literature, 1900–present.

This familiar reference source provides a cumulative topic index for articles in over 160 U.S. nontechnical, general, and popular magazines.

The Wall Street Journal Index.

The Wall Street Journal articles are listed by topic and corporation in this index.

TEXTBOOKS AND RESEARCH SURVEYS

There are several advanced textbooks in the "new" labor economics and numerous undergraduate texts in closely related fields. The former strengthen one's *depth* of understanding of labor economics, whereas the latter add *breadth* beyond the topics included in this textbook.

Advanced Texts and Surveys

Advanced textbooks presume more knowledge of mathematics, econometrics, and economic theory than this text. Nevertheless, the diligent reader whose preparation in those areas is modest can gain much from them. The following books are particularly useful in this regard:

Solomon W. Polachek and W. Stanley Seibert: *The Economics of Earnings* (Cambridge, UK: Cambridge University Press, 1993).

   This book covers many of the topics covered in *Contemporary Labor Economics* but treats them with considerably greater analytical rigor. The topics covered include discrimination, training, minimum wage laws, unionism, human capital, and health and safety regulations.

Robert F. Elliott: *Labor Economics: A Comparative Text* (London: McGraw-Hill, 1991).

   Using extensive graphical analysis and some calculus, this British publication treats the economics of labor markets at a slightly higher level than traditional American undergraduate texts. It also contains many tables comparing labor market data among the industrialized nations.

Pierre Cahuc and André Zylberberg: *Labor Economics* (Cambridge, MA: MIT Press, 2004).

   This advanced textbook assumes that readers have substantial training in microeconomics and are familiar with quantitative research techniques. The text discusses topics related to labor supply and demand, wage determination, unemployment, inequality, and labor market policies.

Orley Ashenfelter and Richard Layard (eds.): *Handbook of Labor Economics,* 3 vols. (Amsterdam: North-Holland, 1986, 1999).

   The 53 chapters of this three-volume advanced survey of labor economics are written by prominent labor economists. In volume 1, the supply of labor, the demand for labor, and the wage structure are examined. Volume 2 looks at labor market equilibrium and frictions and discusses institutional structures of labor markets. Volume 3 examines topics related to labor supply, labor demand, emerging labor markets, labor markets and the macroeconomy, and government policy.

Alison L. Booth: *The Economics of the Trade Union* (Cambridge, England: Cambridge University Press, 1995).

   This book surveys, synthesizes, and critically analyzes theoretical and econometric work on the economic effects of unions in the United States and Great Britain.

APPENDIX TABLE 4
Representative Textbooks in Subjects Related to Contemporary Labor Economics

Collective Bargaining
H. C. Katz and T. A. Kochan: *Introduction to Collective Bargaining and Industrial Relations*, 4th ed. (Irwin/McGraw-Hill, 2008).

Labor Economics and Labor Relations
L. G. Reynolds, S. H. Masters, and C. H. Moser: *Labor Economics and Labor Relations*, 11th ed. (Prentice-Hall, 1998).

Human Resource Management
R. L. Mathis and J. H. Jackson: *Human Resource Management: Essential Perspectives*, 4th ed. (South-Western, 2007).

Edward P. Lazear: *Personnel Economics for Managers* (Wiley, 1998).

Labor Law
D. P. Twomey: *Labor Law and Employment Law*, 13th ed. (South-Western, 2007).
J. J. Moran: *Employment Law*, 3rd ed., (Prentice-Hall, 2005).

Social Insurance
G. E. Rejda: *Social Insurance and Economic Security*, 6th ed. (Prentice-Hall, 1999).

Labor History
F. R. Dulles, and M. Dubofsky: *Labor in America*, 6th ed. (Harlan Davidson, 1999).

Texts in Related Fields

High-quality textbooks abound for courses of study related to labor economics. One good way to discover them is to browse in your college bookstore for textbooks required for courses in such fields as collective bargaining, labor law, labor history, labor relations, human resource economics, and social insurance. Appendix Table 4 lists several such books by topic. Numerous other texts are available in each of these subject areas and can be identified by visiting a professor who specializes in the particular field. These textbooks typically are revised on three- to five-year cycles.

Glossary

A

ability problem   The tendency to overestimate rates of return to education if those with more ability tend to obtain more schooling. Earnings differences may reflect differences in ability rather than in education.

absence rate   The ratio of full-time workers with absences from work in a typical week to total full employment. It is usually expressed as a percentage.

absolute frequency distribution   A graphic portrayal (histogram) of the earnings distribution. The horizontal axis shows the various earnings classes, while the heights of the bars indicate the actual numbers of earnings recipients who have earnings in the particular class. *Compare to* relative frequency distribution.

acceptance wage   The lowest wage required to induce an individual to accept an employment offer.

accident model   A model of strikes that assumes they are the result of accidents or errors in the negotiating process.

actual labor force   Those who are either employed or are unemployed but actively seeking work.

actual subsidy payment   The subsidy received by a participant in an income maintenance plan. It is calculated by multiplying the benefit reduction rate times the person's earned income and subtracting the product from the plan's basic benefit.

adaptive expectations theory   Theory that assumes individuals form their expectations about the future based on the recent past.

added-worker effect   The change in the labor force that results from other family members entering the labor force when the primary worker loses his or her job.

administered price   A price or wage rate that is established institutionally rather than through the market forces of supply and demand.

affirmative action programs   Policies that establish targets of employment for women and minorities and a timetable for meeting them.

AFL–CIO   The American Federation of Labor and Congress of Industrial Organizations. It is the largest U.S. federation of autonomous national unions.

age–earnings profile   A graph showing the earnings levels of a specific worker or group of workers at various ages over the life span.

agents   Parties who are hired to help advance the objectives of others. *Compare to* principals.

aggregate demand curve   The curve indicating the total quantity of goods and services that consumers, businesses, government, and foreigners are willing and able to purchase at each price level.

aggregate supply curve   The curve indicating the total real output that producers are willing and able to provide at each price level.

asymmetric information   One party in the bargaining process has more information than the other.

average product (AP)   Output per unit of labor. It is found by dividing total product by the number of labor units or may be measured as the slope of a straight line drawn from the origin to a particular point on the total product curve.

average wage cost   The firm's total wage cost divided by the number of units of labor employed. If all workers are paid the same, it is simply the wage rate.

B

backward-bending labor supply curve   The hours of work supplied as a function of the wage, where the substitution effect dominates at relatively low wages and the income effect dominates at high wages. In the latter region, the supply curve will be negatively sloped.

bargaining power   A measure of the ability of one side to secure, on its own terms, its opponent's agreement to a labor contract.

bargaining structure   The scope of the employees and employers covered by a collective bargaining agreement; the structure determines who bargains with whom.

basic benefit   The amount of subsidy a household receives from an income maintenance plan if it has no earned income.

beaten paths   Migration routes of previous job changers. The information provided by these movers typically reduces the costs of migration and explains why various racial and ethnic groups may cluster in a given area.

Becker's model of the allocation of time   This model assumes households are economic units deciding how best to allocate their time among work, household production, and household consumption to obtain utility-yielding commodities.

benefit reduction rate   The rate at which the household's basic income maintenance benefit is reduced as earned income increases.

bilateral monopoly   A market structure consisting of a monopsonist and a strong industrial union. The wage outcome in such a situation is indeterminate.

blacklist   A directory of individuals known to be union members or sympathizers. Individuals on the list were often denied employment.

bonus   Payment in addition to the annual salary based on some factor such as personal, team, or firm performance.

break-even income   The level of income at which the household's subsidy from an income maintenance plan is reduced to zero. It is calculated by dividing the basic benefit by the benefit reduction rate.

budget constraint   A line plotted on a graph that shows all the combinations of market goods (real income) and leisure that the consumer can obtain at any given wage rate.

Bureau of Labor Statistics productivity index   The measure of productivity reported by the Bureau of Labor Statistics. It is found by dividing real gross domestic product for the private sector by private sector worker hours; it is scaled to have a value of 100 in the base year.

C

cafeteria plan   A fringe benefit package that lets workers choose among a wide range of particular benefits.

capital market imperfections   The bias against lending money for investments in human capital that occurs largely because human beings cannot be used as collateral for loans.

capital mobility   The movement of capital (plant and equipment) from one region or nation to another in response to higher rates of return on investment.

change to win federation   A loose federation of seven independent national unions, which focuses on organizing new union members.

churning   Mobility of individuals within a static earnings distribution independent of life-cycle effects. *Compare to* life-cycle mobility.

Civil Rights Act of 1964   An act of Congress that, among other things, made it illegal to hire, fire, or discriminate on the basis of race, color, religion, gender, or national origin.

coalescing power   The ability of a bilateral monopoly, through tacit collusion between the monopsonist and the union, to suppress competition in the firm's product market.

cobweb model   A labor market characterized by labor supply adjustments that lag behind changes in demand because of the lengthy training periods required. The path of wages and employment in such models traces out a cobweb pattern when plotted on a supply and demand diagram.

collective voice   The role of unions as representatives or agents that speak on behalf of their members in negotiating contracts and resolving disputes.

college wage premium   The average earnings differential enjoyed by college graduates compared to high school graduates.

commissions   Compensation paid to an agent in proportion to the value of sales.

commodity   As defined by Becker, a combination of goods and time that yields utility to the consumer.

comparable worth doctrine   The idea that females in one occupation should receive the same salaries as males in another if the levels of skill, effort, and responsibility and the working conditions in the two occupations are comparable.

compensating wage differential The extra amount an employer must pay to reimburse a worker for an undesirable job characteristic that does not exist in alternative employment. Also called *wage premium* or *equalizing difference*.

Consumer Price Index (CPI) An index number that measures a weighted average of the prices of goods and services consumed by representative consumer families. The percentage change in its level is the most commonly used measure of the rate of inflation.

cost-of-living adjustment (COLA) A labor contract clause that provides automatic increases in nominal wages when the price level rises.

countervailing power The ability of a union to offset the power of a monopsonist in bilateral monopoly in such a way that the resulting wage and employment outcome enhances allocative efficiency.

cross-sectional data A collection of observations of a group of variables at a specific time but for different economic units or groups.

crowding The segregation of women and minorities into low-paying jobs.

crowding model A supply and demand model that suggests that if women (minorities) are crowded into "female" ("minority") occupations, their wages will be driven down by the relatively greater supply of labor to such occupations.

crowding-out effect The reduction in private investment spending due to the upward pressure on interest rates when the government increases its borrowing.

D

***D*-factor** A combination of several personal traits thought to influence an individual's earnings potential. It represents drive, dynamism, doggedness, or determination.

Davis–Bacon Act A law passed in 1931 that requires contractors engaged in federally financed projects to pay prevailing wages, which have primarily been union scale.

deadline The date of termination of a union contract; the probable starting time of a work stoppage if no agreement is reached.

demand-deficient unemployment Unemployment caused by a decline in aggregate demand. Also called *cyclic unemployment.*

demand for human capital curve A curve displaying a negative relationship between the marginal rate of return on investment in human capital and the optimal amount of such investment undertaken.

derived demand The idea that demand curves for labor and other productive inputs are derived from the demand for the product that they are used to produce. For example, the demand for autoworkers is derived from the demand for automobiles.

determinants of labor demand Factors that cause shifts in the labor demand curve, as opposed to a movement along the curve. These include product demand, productivity, number of employers, and the prices of other resources.

determinants of labor supply Factors that cause shifts in the labor supply curve, as opposed to a movement along the curve. These include other wage rates, nonwage income, preferences for work versus leisure, nonwage aspects of jobs, and the number of qualified labor suppliers.

determinants of migration Personal and geographic characteristics, such as age, education, wages, and distance, that affect the decision to migrate.

discount formula The mathematical relationship that defines net present value (V_p) in terms of future values (E_t) and the rate of interest (i):

$$V_p = E_0 + E_1/(1+i) + E_2/(1+i)^2 \\ + \cdots + E_n/(1+i)^n$$

discouraged-worker effect The change in the labor force due to job seekers who drop out of the labor force after becoming pessimistic about their chances of finding suitable employment.

discouraged workers Individuals who have searched unsuccessfully for work, become discouraged, and then abandoned their job search. They are not officially counted as unemployed because they are not in the labor force.

discrimination   According inferior treatment with respect to hiring, occupational access, training, promotion, or wages to the members of one group having the same abilities, education, training, and experience as others.

discrimination coefficient   The amount by which an African–American's (or female's) wage rate is perceived to exceed that of an equally productive white's (or male's). If an employer acts as though the African–American's (female's) wage is equal to W + *d, d* is the discrimination coefficient.

discriminatory discharge   Dismissal of an employee for participation in union activity.

displaced workers   People who lose their jobs specifically because of permanent plant closings or job cutbacks.

domestic content rules   Requirements that imported products contain a specified portion of domestically produced or domestically assembled components.

dynamic efficiency   The combination of resources that produces goods and services at their lowest possible costs over a long time. *Compare to* static efficiency.

E

earnings mobility   Year-to-year movement by individuals from one portion of the earnings distribution to another.

economic perspective   An analytical approach that assumes that resources are scarce relative to wants, individuals make choices by comparing benefits and costs, and people respond to incentives and disincentives.

economic rent   The return to a factor of production in excess of its opportunity cost. Specifically, the difference between a worker's wage and the wage that would be just sufficient to keep that person in his or her present employment. *Compare to* rent.

efficiency gains from migration   The net increase in total output that accrues to society when labor relocates from regions or nations in which its value of marginal product is relatively low to regions or nations in which it is higher.

efficiency wage   A wage rate that minimizes the employer's cost per effective unit of labor employed.

efficient allocation of labor   The state of the economy achieved when the value of goods and services produced is the highest possible given the amount of labor available. This state occurs when the value of marginal product of a given type of labor is the same in all its potential uses and is equal to its opportunity cost (the price of this type of labor).

efficient contracts   The combinations of wage and employment where at least one party can be made better off without the other party being made worse off.

elasticity of labor demand   The responsiveness of the quantity of labor demanded to a change in the wage rate.

employed   An individual who is 16 years of age or older, not institutionalized, and at any time during the survey week *(a)* is employed by a firm or government, *(b)* is self-employed, or *(c)* has a job but is not working due to illness, inclement weather, vacation, or a labor dispute.

employee compensation   The national income account comprising wages and salaries, plus payments into social insurance, and worker pension, health, and welfare funds.

Employment Act of 1946   An act of Congress proclaiming the federal government's goal of promoting "maximum employment, production, and purchasing power."

employment discrimination   Higher-than-average unemployment rates for a particular group after adjusting for differences in education and experience.

employment–population ratio   Total employment as a percentage of the total noninstitutional population.

Equal Pay Act of 1963   A law that made illegal the payment of unequal wages to women and men for equal work.

equilibrium wage differential   A wage differential that does not cause workers to shift their labor supplies to alternative employments.

equity compensation   A pay scheme where part of the worker's compensation is given or invested in the firm's stock.

excess demand   The excess of quantity demanded over quantity supplied at a given wage rate or price.

excess supply   The excess of quantity supplied over quantity demanded at a given wage rate or price.

exclusive unionism   A union structure wherein the members seek to restrict labor supply by excluding potential workers from participating in the trade or profession.

exit mechanism   The process of leaving one's job as a response to dissatisfaction with present working conditions. *Compare to* voice mechanism.

external benefit   A benefit that accrues to a party other than the buyer or seller; also called *social benefit*.

external labor market   The labor market of orthodox economic theory in which wages and employment are determined by the forces of supply and demand.

F

Fair Labor Standards Act of 1938   A law that established the legal minimum wage and maximum hours and mandated time-and-a-half pay for overtime work.

Family and Medical Leave Act of 1993   Legislation that permits workers in firms employing more than 75 workers to take up to 12 weeks a year of unpaid leave to care for a spouse, a child, or their own health. Upon return, those having taken these leaves are guaranteed their original or equivalent positions.

featherbedding   Employment of workers in unnecessary or redundant jobs.

fiscal policy   Deliberate manipulation of federal expenditures and taxes to promote full employment, price stability, and economic growth.

foreign purchases effect   As the domestic price level falls relative to prices abroad, both domestic and foreign consumers will shift their spending toward U.S. goods, thereby increasing the aggregate quantity demanded.

free-rider problem   The incentive for each worker to shirk when individual compensation is based on team performance. As team size grows, each worker's contribution to the team has an increasingly negligible effect on team performance.

frictional unemployment   Unemployment that is due to voluntary quits, job switches, and new entrants or reentrants into the labor force. It is composed of search unemployment and wait unemployment.

fringe benefits   That part of employee compensation other than wages or salary. This includes pensions, insurance benefits, paid vacations, and sick leave.

full employment   The amount of employment consistent with the natural rate of unemployment.

Full Employment and Balanced Growth Act of 1978   A reaffirmation of the Employment Act of 1946, this act also required the federal government to set five-year employment and price level goals and design programs to achieve them.

G

general training   The creation of worker skills that are equally valuable in a number of firms or industries.

geographic mobility   Movement of workers from a job in one city, state, or nation to another. This may or may not also involve a change in occupation.

Gini coefficient   An arithmetic measure of earnings inequality. It is the area between the Lorenz curve and the diagonal line of perfect equality, divided by the total area beneath the diagonal.

golden parachute   A contract provision that provides a large lump-sum payoff to executives who lose their jobs as a result of a corporate takeover.

goods-intensive commodities   Commodities that require a relatively large amount of goods and a small amount of time. *Compare to* time-intensive commodities.

government purchases   Expenditures by federal, state, and local governments on goods, services, and resources.

gross complements   Inputs such that when the price of one changes, the demand for the other changes in the opposite direction because the output effect exceeds the substitution effect.

gross substitutes   Inputs such that when the price of one changes, the demand for the other changes in the same direction because the substitution effect exceeds the output effect.

H

hedonic theory of wages   A model of equilibrium wage differentials that hypothesizes that workers maximize the net utility of their employment by trading changes in wages for changes in nonwage job attributes.

heterogeneous workers and jobs   An assumption that not all workers and not all jobs are identical. As a result, wages will differ to compensate for job and worker differences.

histogram   *See* absolute frequency distribution.

homogeneous workers and jobs   An assumption that all workers and all jobs have identical characteristics. If information were perfect and mobility costless, all workers would receive the same real wage.

hot-cargo clause   A labor contract provision that states that trucking firms will not require unionized truckers to handle or transport products made by an employer involved in a labor dispute. Such clauses were made illegal by the Landrum–Griffin Act of 1959.

Household Survey   A monthly survey conducted by the Bureau of Labor Statistics to determine the number of people who are employed, unemployed, or not in the labor force; also called *Current Population Survey*.

human capital   The accumulation of prior investments in education, on-the-job training, health, and other factors that increase productivity.

human capital discrimination   Unequal access to productivity-increasing opportunities such as formal schooling or on-the-job training.

human capital investment demand curve   The relationship between human capital investment and the marginal rate of return on that investment. It reflects the (individual) optimal amount invested at any given opportunity cost of funds.

human capital investment supply curve   The relationship between human capital investment and the marginal opportunity cost of funds required to finance that investment.

I

illegal aliens   Individuals who unlawfully immigrate into the United States, usually to work; also called *undocumented workers*.

immediate-market-period labor supply curve   A vertical line at the number of workers attracted into a given market by the current wage rate. This number is derived from the long-run supply curve.

Immigration Reform and Control Act of 1986   A sweeping immigration reform bill that granted amnesty to certain illegal aliens, provided sanctions on employers who knowingly hire illegal aliens, and allowed temporary farmworkers into the country to harvest perishable crops.

implicit contracts   Informal, often unstated, understandings about the employment relationship.

in-kind benefits   Benefits that take the form of a specific good or service rather than money—insurance benefits, for example, or a company car.

incentive pay plan   A compensation scheme that ties workers' pay directly to performance. Such plans may include piece rates, commissions and royalties, raises and promotions, bonuses, profit sharing, and tournament pay.

inclusive unionism   A union structure wherein the members seek to include all workers employed in a specific industry.

income effect   The change in the desired hours of work resulting from a change in income, holding the wage rate constant.

income elasticity   The percentage change in quantity demanded divided by the percentage change in income.

income guarantee or basic benefit   The amount of public subsidy an individual or family would be paid if no earned income were received.

income maintenance program   Program whose purpose is to provide some minimum level of income to all families and individuals.

income tax   A broad-based tax on income received from many sources, not just wages and salaries.

indeterminacy problem The idea that if a change in the wage rate changes labor productivity, the position of the labor demand curve becomes indeterminate.

Index of Compensation per Hour (ICH) An index number that measures average hourly compensation of workers, including employer contributions to Social Security and private fringe benefits. The percentage change in its level is a measure of wage inflation.

index of segregation The percentage of women (minorities) who would have to change occupations in order for them to be distributed across occupations in the same proportion as men (whites).

indifference curve A curve that shows the various combinations of two goods (real income and leisure or cash wages and fringe benefits) that will yield some given level of utility or satisfaction to the individual.

indifference map A set of indifference curves that collectively specify an individual's preferences for two goods such as income and leisure or cash wages and fringe benefits.

inferior good A product for which the quantity demanded falls when income rises.

inflation A rising general level of prices in the economy.

injunction A court order to stop a particular activity, such as a strike, boycott, or picketing.

insider–outsider theories Theories that purport to explain downward wage rigidity and thus cyclic unemployment on the basis of the relationships between incumbent workers ("insiders") and unemployed workers ("outsiders") who might be expected to bid down the wage rate to obtain employment.

interest rate effect As the price level falls, the demand for money falls, which in turn reduces interest rates. The subsequent rise in spending on interest-sensitive goods and services increases the aggregate amount of output demanded.

internal labor market A firm or other administrative unit characterized by job ladders. Except for those at the port of entry, jobs are shielded from competitive market pressures in that wages and employment are determined by administrative rules and procedures rather than by the forces of supply and demand.

internal rate of return (r) That rate of discount that equates the present value of future costs and benefits.

An investment is profitable if its internal rate of return exceeds the marginal opportunity cost of the funds as measured by the interest rate (i).

investment in human capital Any action taken to increase the productivity (by improving the skills and abilities) of workers; expenditures made to improve the education, health, or mobility of workers.

isocost curve A curve showing the various combinations of capital and labor that can be purchased with a given outlay, given the prices of capital and labor.

isoprofit curve A curve portraying the various combinations of wages and fringe benefits (or some other nonwage amenity) that yield a specific level of profits.

isoquant A curve showing the various combinations of capital and labor that are capable of producing a specific quantity of total output.

J

job evaluation The procedure by which jobs are ranked and wage rates assigned in terms of a set of job characteristics and worker traits.

job ladder A sequence of jobs within an internal labor market, beginning at a port of entry and progressing through higher levels of skill, responsibility, and wages.

job search model A theory of how workers and firms acquire information concerning employment prospects.

joint monopsony *See* monopsony.

***Journal of Economic Literature* classification system** The system used to classify subfields within economics. The "J" classification identifies labor economics.

L

labor economics The field of economics that examines the organization, functioning, and outcomes of labor markets; the decisions of prospective and present labor market participants; and the public policies relating to the employment and payment of labor resources.

labor force participation rate The percentage of the potential force that is either employed or unemployed.

labor hoarding   The practice by which firms retain more workers during recessions than would be technically necessary, specifically "overhead" workers such as executives, managers, and skilled laborers on whom the firms have spent large sums to recruit and train.

labor immobilities   Geographic, institutional, or sociological barriers to labor mobility. These barriers are a major reason why wage differentials occur and persist.

labor mobility   The movement of workers across employers, occupations, or job locations.

labor productivity   Total product (real GDP) divided by the number of worker hours.

labor turnover   The rate at which workers quit their jobs, necessitating their replacement by new workers.

Landrum–Griffin Act of 1959   An amendment to the Wagner Act that declared hot-cargo clauses illegal, required regularly scheduled elections of union officers, excluded communists and convicted felons from holding union office, held union officers accountable for union funds and property, and prevented union leaders from infringing on individual workers' rights to participate in the governance of the union.

law of diminishing marginal returns   The principle that if technology is unchanged, as more units of a variable resource are combined with one or more fixed resources, the marginal product of the variable resource must eventually decline.

least-cost combination of capital and labor   The point of tangency of an isocost line to a given isoquant. At this point the marginal rate of technical substitution equals the ratio of the price of labor to the price of capital.

life-cycle mobility   The movement of specific individuals within the income distribution over their lifetimes. *Compare to* churning.

line of perfect equality   The Lorenz curve that would result if all individuals in the economy had the same earnings. It is a diagonal line through the origin.

local union   The basic unit of organized labor. Its main functions are administering the labor contract and resolving worker grievances.

lockout   A plant shutdown used as a means of imposing costs on workers who are engaged in union-organizing activity or any other union activity such as a strike.

long run   A period of time sufficient for the firm to vary the levels of all of its factors of production.

long-run demand for labor   The schedule or curve indicating the amount of labor that firms will employ at each possible wage rate when all factors of production are variable.

long-run supply curve   In the cobweb model, this curve indicates the eventual response of labor suppliers to changes in the wage rate.

Lorenz curve   A graphical depiction of the earnings distribution. It indicates the cumulative percentage of all wage and salary earners (ranked from lowest to highest earnings) on the horizontal axis; the vertical axis measures the corresponding cumulative percentage of earnings accruing to that group.

M

macroeconomics   The subfield of economics concerned with the economy as a whole or with the interrelations of basic aggregates of the economy.

managerial opposition hypothesis   The notion that increased managerial opposition to unions has led to the decline in union membership and growth.

marginal cost (benefit) of safety   The cost (benefit) to the firm of increasing job safety by one unit.

marginal internal rate of return   The internal rate of return on additional human capital. Optimal investment occurs where the marginal internal rate of return equals the marginal opportunity cost of the funds.

marginal product (MP)   The change in total product that results from changing labor input by one unit.

marginal rate of substitution of leisure for income (MRS L,Y)   The amount of income one must give up to compensate for the gain of one more unit (hour) of leisure.

marginal rate of technical substitution of labor for capital (MRTS L, K)   The amount by which capital must decline when labor is increased by one unit along an isoquant (equal output curve); the absolute value of the slope of an isoquant.

marginal resource cost (MRC)   The change in the firm's total cost that results from changing its employment of a particular resource by one unit. It is equal to the per-unit cost of the resource in competitive input markets.

marginal revenue product (MRP)   The change in total revenue that results from changing labor input by one unit.

marginal wage cost (MWC)   The change in the firm's total wage cost that results from changing labor input by one unit. It is equal to the wage rate in competitive labor markets.

market demand for labor   The relationship between the quantity of labor demanded by all firms employing a given type of labor and the wage rate for this labor. It is assumed that the amount of labor employed at various wages may have an impact on product price, which is held constant in the derivation of the individual firm's demand for labor.

market sector   That part of the private sector consisting of the millions of small businesses. Firms in this sector are subject to strong competitive forces and have few economies of scale. This sector is associated primarily with the secondary labor market. *Compare to* planning sector.

master agreement   A contract struck between management and one or more local unions that then applies to workers in all of the firm's plants.

mean   The arithmetic average of a distribution. With respect to earnings, it is found by dividing total earnings by the number of earnings recipients.

measured union wage advantage   *See* union wage advantage.

median   The midpoint of a distribution. With respect to earnings, half earn less and half earn more.

microeconomics   The subfield of economics concerned with the decisions of individual economic units and the functioning of specific markets.

midpoints formula   A method employed to calculate the elasticity coefficient:

$$E_d = \frac{(Q_2 - Q_1)/(\text{average } Q)}{(W_2 - W_1)/(\text{average } W)}$$

military conscription   A method of obtaining labor resources for military service that relies on the ability of government to compel people to serve. The alternative is a volunteer or market-based military.

minimum wage   A legally specified minimum rate of pay for labor employed in covered occupations.

mode   The class of a distribution with the greatest frequency.

monetary policy   Deliberate manipulation of the money supply by the Federal Reserve authorities, intended to promote full employment, price stability, and economic growth.

monitoring   Employing supervisors and using other methods to determine which workers, if any, are shirking.

monopoly power   The ability of a firm to set its price, rather than being forced to accept a market-determined price.

monopoly union model   A model that assumes the union sets the wage rate, and the firm determines the level of union employment based on this wage rate.

monopsony   A labor market in which a single firm is the sole employer of a particular type of labor (pure monopsony), or when two or more firms, through collusion, act as the sole employer of a particular type of labor (joint monopsony).

moral-hazard problem   As it relates to workers' compensation insurance, the tendency of workers to be less careful in their jobs, knowing they are insured against workplace accidents.

MRP = MWC rule   A rule specifying the profit-maximizing level of labor employment. With capital fixed, profits are maximized when labor is employed to the point where MRP = MWC.

multiemployer bargaining   A bargaining structure in which employers in a particular industry organize as a group to bargain with the union.

multifactor approach   A method of explaining the earnings distribution that accounts for innate ability, family background, risk taking, chance, and many other factors in addition to schooling and on-the-job training.

N

National Labor Relations Board   A group of individuals empowered by the Wagner Act to ensure that its provisions are carried out.

national union A federation of local unions that typically are in either the same industry or the same skilled occupation.

natural rate of unemployment *(a)* The unemployment rate at which there is neither excess demand nor excess supply in the aggregate labor market; *(b)* the unemployment rate that will occur in the long run if expected and actual rates of inflation are equal. Currently this is estimated to be about 4.0 to 5.0 percent.

net present value The dollar difference between streams of future costs and benefits of an investment that have been discounted to the present at some appropriate rate of interest. *See* discount formula.

noncompeting groups Categories of labor market participants whose members, because of differences in education, training, and skill, are imperfect labor market substitutes for members of other groups.

nondiscriminatory factors Factors other than discrimination that cause differences in earnings by race and gender.

normal-profit isoprofit curve The isoprofit curve consistent with zero economic profits.

Norris–LaGuardia Act of 1932 A law that severely limited the use of injunctions to enjoin labor union activity and outlawed yellow-dog contracts.

O

occupational discrimination Arbitrarily restricting or prohibiting the members of a group from entering certain occupations even though the group members have the requisite skills; also called *job discrimination*.

occupational licensure Laws or regulations by a governmental unit that workers meet certain requirements to practice a specific trade or profession. Tests, standards, and other requirements are established that often have the effect of restricting labor supply to the licensed occupation.

occupational mobility Movement of workers to a different occupation.

Occupational Safety and Health Act of 1970 Legislation that created the Occupational Safety and Health Administration (OSHA), an agency that establishes and enforces workplace health and safety standards.

Old Age, Survivors, Disability, and Health Insurance (OASDHI) A government transfer program. Commonly referred to as the Social Security system, it is financed through a payroll tax on employers and employees.

on-the-job training The accumulation of skills acquired while working at a job.

optimal wage rate–job safety combination The point of tangency between the worker's highest attainable indifference curve and an employer's normal-profit isoprofit curve.

optimal work–leisure position The point on the worker's budget constraint at which the marginal rate of substitution of leisure for income is equal to the wage rate. At this point the budget constraint is tangent to the individual's highest attainable indifference curve.

output effect The change in labor input resulting from the effect of a change in the wage rate on the firm's cost of production and the subsequent change in the desired level of output.

overemployment A situation in which the worker could increase utility by taking more leisure and less income; a level of work where the marginal rate of substitution of leisure for income exceeds the wage rate.

P

pattern bargaining A bargaining structure in which a union negotiates a contract with a particular firm in an industry and then seeks to impose similar terms on all other employers in that industry.

payroll tax A tax on the amount of wages and salaries received.

pecuniary externality Effects of private actions that impose monetary costs or benefits on third parties. Such externalities do not affect economic efficiency but rather redistribute a constant real income.

perfectly competitive labor market A labor market characterized by a large pool of similarly qualified workers independently offering their labor services to a large number of firms, none of which has the power to influence the wage rate. Workers and firms have perfect information, and mobility is costless.

personal distribution of earnings The division of earnings among individuals.

Glossary **591**

piece rates Compensation paid in proportion to the number of units of personal output.

planning sector That part of the private sector consisting of the largest major corporations that carry on the bulk of economic activity. This sector is associated with the primary labor market. *Compare to* market sector.

port of entry The link between the external market and a job ladder within the internal labor market. The market forces of supply and demand determine wages at this lowest level of a job ladder, and those who obtain jobs here are allowed future access to the higher job levels in the internal labor market.

potential labor force All noninstitutionalized persons age 16 and over; also called the *age-eligible population*.

prevailing wage rule The practice by governments of setting public employee wage rates equal to those received by comparably trained and employed private sector workers; also called the *comparable-wage rule*.

price of labor (P_L) The marginal value of alternative work, non–labor market production, or leisure for a given type of labor. P_L measures the opportunity cost of labor.

primary statistical source An original source of data, such as the *Current Population Survey.*

principal–agent problem A conflict of interest that occurs when agents pursue their own objectives to the detriment of meeting the principal's objectives.

principals Parties who hire others to help them advance their objectives. *Compare to* agents.

private perspective Viewing the benefits and costs strictly from the standpoint of an individual who is considering a human capital investment.

product market effect The increase in nonunion wages that is caused by consumer demand shifting away from relatively higher-priced union-produced goods and toward relatively lower-priced goods produced by nonunion workers.

production function The relationship between the various quantities of inputs and the corresponding output, assuming the resources are combined in a technically efficient manner.

productivity Output per unit of input; it is a measure of efficiency of resource use.

profit sharing A compensation scheme that allocates a specified portion of a firm's profits to employees.

progressive tax A tax for which the rate increases with the size of the tax base (particularly if income is the base).

proprietor's income The national income account comprising income received by owners of unincorporated businesses (sole proprietorships and partnerships).

pure complements in production A pair of resources, such as capital and labor, that must be used in direct proportion to one another in producing output. Pure complements in production are always gross complements.

pure monopsony *See* monopsony.

pure public goods Collectively consumed goods or services. For these products use by one person does not diminish the amount available for another's consumption. An example is national defense.

pure union wage advantage *See* union wage advantage.

Q

quality circles Joint labor–management committees on productivity.

quasi-fixed resource A productive resource that has some of the characteristics of both fixed and variable factors. Once made, specific training investments are fixed costs to the firm; thus workers with such training constitute quasi-fixed resources.

quota Limits on the quantity or total value of specific imported goods.

R

real balance effect As the price level falls, the real value of dollar-denominated assets increases. This increase in wealth increases consumption spending and the aggregate amount of output demanded.

real externality Effects of private actions that spill over to third parties, either adding to (external benefits) or detracting from (external costs) economic efficiency.

real wage Worker earnings expressed in terms of purchasing power. It is found by dividing the money or nominal wage by the average price level.

relative frequency distribution A graphic portrayal (histogram) of the earnings distribution. The horizontal axis shows the various earnings classes, while the heights of the bars indicate the percentages of the total number of earnings recipients who have earnings in the particular class. *Compare to* absolute frequency distribution.

relative share The proportion of national income accruing to a particular productive factor.

rent The return to nonreproducible resources (land) that are provided in fixed quantities in nature. *Compare to* economic rent.

rent provision Practices, particularly by government, that yield economic rent to a specific group or individual. Examples include the minimum wage and occupational licensure.

rent-seeking activity Actions by individuals or specific groups that have the effect of increasing their economic rent.

reservation wage The highest wage rate at which an individual chooses not to work; the lowest wage rate at which an individual chooses to enter the labor market.

right-to-work laws State laws (protected by Section 14b of the National Labor Relations Act) that make union shop and agency shop agreements illegal.

royalties An amount, proportional to sales, paid in compensation for allowing an agent to market the principal's product.

S

screening hypothesis The view that education only identifies individuals who are trainable or of high ability rather than increasing productivity per se.

search unemployment Unemployment that is caused by individuals searching for the best job offer and firms searching for workers to fill job openings.

secondary boycott Actions by a union to refuse to handle or to get an employer to refuse to buy products made by a firm that is party to a labor dispute. *See* hot-cargo clause.

secondary statistical source A source that contains data from original sources in abridged or truncated form, such as the *Statistical Abstract of the United States.*

self-selection A type of statistical bias encountered when the effects of individual choices are improperly measured or unaccounted for. For example, if people with more ability are more likely to obtain high earnings, independently of education, and also are more likely to obtain education, failing to account for differences in ability will tend to overstate the effects of education on earnings. With respect to immigration, the idea that those who choose to move tend to have greater motivation for economic gain or greater willingness to sacrifice current for future consumption than those of similar skills who choose not to migrate.

seniority A system of granting economic amenities (higher wage rates, better jobs, protection from layoff) based on length of service (job tenure).

shift work Work done at night, as opposed to during usual daytime work hours.

shirking Attempts by workers to increase utility by taking unauthorized breaks or by giving less than agreed-upon effort during work hours; the act of neglecting or evading work.

shock effect The upward shift in the marginal product schedule that results from managerial responses to an increase in the wage rate.

short run A period of time sufficiently short that the quantity of capital employed by the firm cannot be varied.

short-run labor demand curve The schedule or curve indicating the amount of labor that firms will employ at each possible wage rate assuming a fixed capital stock. It is the part of the marginal revenue product curve that is positive and lies below the average revenue product curve.

skill differential The difference in wages between skilled and unskilled workers.

skill transferability The ability of skills that are appropriate for one job or location to apply in another job or location.

social perspective Viewing the benefits and costs of human capital investment from the standpoint of society.

specific training   The creation of worker skills that are of value only to the particular firm providing the training.

spillover effect   The decline in nonunion wages that results from displaced union workers supplying their services in nonunion labor markets.

static efficiency   The combination of resources of a fixed quality that produces output at the lowest possible cost at a given point in time. ***Compare to*** dynamic efficiency.

statistical discrimination   Judging an individual on the basis of the average characteristics of the group to which he or she belongs rather than on his or her personal characteristics.

stochastic theories   Theories of income distribution that are based on change rather than individual choice or institutional structure.

stock–flow model   A model of labor flows into and out of various categories of labor force status. It is used to analyze changes in the unemployment rate.

stock options   A form of compensation that gives an employee the right to purchase a fixed number of shares of stock at a set price for a given period.

straight-time equivalent wage   The wage that would yield the same income at the same number of hours as the income and hour combination actually chosen by an individual paid an overtime premium.

strikebreaker   A nonunion worker hired by the firm to continue operations during a strike.

strongly efficient contract   A contract where the union and firm agree to set the employment at the level that would occur without a union.

structural change hypothesis   The notion that changes in the composition of the labor force and the industrial mix have led to the decline in union growth and membership.

structural unemployment   Unemployment due to a mismatch between the skills required for available job openings and the skills possessed by those seeking work; a geographical mismatch between jobs and job seekers; displaced workers.

subemployed   Those who are forced by economic circumstances to work in occupations that pay lower wages than those for which they would qualify in periods of full employment.

subminimum training wage   A legally specified minimum rate of pay for teenagers established below the minimum rate for older workers.

subsidy   A transfer payment provided to consumers or producers of a specific good or service.

substitutes in production   A pair of inputs, such as capital and labor, such that a given amount of output can be produced with many different combinations of the two. Substitutes in production will be gross substitutes if the substitution effect outweighs the output effect; the inputs will be gross complements if the output effect outweighs the substitution effect.

substitution effect   As it relates to labor supply, the change in the desired hours of work resulting from a change in the wage rate, keeping income constant. As it relates to production, the change in employment resulting solely from a change in the relative price of labor, output being held constant.

substitution hypothesis   The notion that benefits provided by the government and some employers have substituted for their provision by unions, leading to the decline in union growth and membership.

superior worker effect   The increase in average union wages that arises when union employers carefully screen prospective employees and hire only the most productive workers. This practice is made possible by the queuing of employees for the higher-paying union jobs.

supply of investment funds   A schedule or curve showing the relationship between the marginal opportunity cost of investment funds (the interest rate) and the amount of such funds made available for financing various levels of human capital.

T

Taft–Hartley Act of 1947   An amendment to the Wagner Act, it established unfair labor practices on the part of unions, regulated the internal administration of unions, outlawed the closed shop while upholding state right-to-work laws, and established emergency strike provisions.

tariff   An excise duty on an imported good.

taste for discrimination model   A theory of discrimination developed by Gary Becker that views discrimination as a preference for which employers are willing to pay.

tax incidence   The economic location of the burden of a tax, or the determination of who ultimately pays a tax. The redistributive effects of a tax.

Temporary Assistance for Needy Families (TANF)   Welfare program that requires recipients to return to work after two years of receiving assistance with few exceptions.

threat effect   The increase in nonunion wage rates that a nonunion employer offers as a response to the threat of unionization.

time-intensive commodities   Commodities that require a relatively large amount of time and a small amount of goods. *Compare to* goods-intensive commodities.

time preference   The notion that most people prefer present consumption to future consumption.

time rates   Compensation paid in proportion to time worked such as hours, months, or years.

time-series data   A collection of observations of a group of variables ordered sequentially with respect to time.

total compensation   The sum of wage earnings and the value of fringe benefits.

total factor productivity   Output per standardized unit of combined labor and capital input.

total product (TP)   The total output of the firm, expressed as a function of labor input.

total wage bill   The total wage cost to the firm; the wage rate multiplied by the quantity of labor hours employed.

total wage bill rules   Rules for determining the elasticity of labor demand. Labor demand is elastic (inelastic) if a change in the wage rate causes the total wage bill to move in the opposite (same) direction. If labor demand is unit elastic, then the total wage bill remains constant when the wage rate changes.

tournament pay   A compensation scheme that bases payments on relative performance. Typically first prize is very high, with subsequent prizes sinking rapidly for ranks below the top. If everyone aspires to the top, productivity in the lower ranks is enhanced.

transfer payment   A government expenditure that merely reflects a transfer of income from government to households. Recipients perform no productive activities in exchange.

transitional wage differential   Short-run wage differences that arise from imperfect and costly information as labor markets move toward final equilibrium.

U

underemployment   A situation in which the worker could increase utility by taking less leisure and more income; a level of work wherein the wage rate exceeds the marginal rate of substitution of leisure for income. This term may also refer to a situation in which the worker is employed in a position for which he or she is overqualified.

unemployed   An individual who is 16 years of age or older, is not institutionalized, did not work during the previous week but was available for work, and *(a)* has engaged in some specific job-seeking activity within the previous four weeks, *(b)* is waiting to be called back to a job from which she or he has been laid off, *(c)* would have been looking for a job but was temporarily ill, or *(d)* is waiting to report to a new job within 30 days.

unemployment rate   The percentage of the labor force that is unemployed. It is the ratio of total unemployment to the total labor force, where the latter is the sum of employment and unemployment.

union shop clause   A bargaining agreement that specifies that nonunion workers may be hired but requires that all employees must join the union or pay union dues following a probationary period, usually 60 days.

union wage advantage   The percentage amount by which the union wage exceeds the nonunion wage. The *measured union wage advantage* is $(W_u - W_n)/W_n \times 100$, where W_u is the observed union wage and W_n is the observed nonunion wage. The *pure union wage advantage* is computed in the same manner, but W_n is the nonunion wage that would be observed in the absence of the union.

unit labor cost Total labor cost divided by the quantity of output. It is alternatively computed as the wage rate divided by labor productivity.

utility The ability of goods or leisure to satisfy wants: want-satisfying power.

V

value of marginal product (VMP) The change in the total value of output that results to society from changing labor input by one unit. VMP equals the price of the product times the marginal product ($P \times$ MP).

voice mechanism The process of using communication channels between the employer and employees to express dissatisfaction with present working conditions. Typically these channels are institutionalized through collective bargaining and union grievance procedures. *Compare to* exit mechanism.

voluntary or market-based army An army in which the requisite number of military personnel are attracted through payment of wage rates that are sufficiently high to cover the opportunity costs of those taking the jobs.

W

wage bill The total amount of wages paid by the firm; the wage rate times the number of worker hours.

wage discrimination Basing wage rate differentials on considerations other than productivity differentials.

wage elasticity coefficient (E_d) A measure of the responsiveness of the quantity of labor demanded to a change in the wage rate. E_d equals the percentage change in the quantity of labor demanded divided by the percentage change in the wage rate.

wage elasticity of labor supply (E_s) A measure of the responsiveness of the quantity of labor supplied to a change in the wage rate. E_s equals the percentage change in the quantity of labor supplied divided by the percentage change in the wage rate.

wage–fringe optimum The composition of total compensation that provides maximum attainable utility to the worker.

wage narrowing The overall impact on wages in both the area of origin and area of destination as a result of

migration. Wages tend to rise in the (initially low-wage) origin and fall in the (initially high-wage) destination area.

wage-push inflation An increase in the general level of prices due primarily to decreases in aggregate supply, specifically when total worker compensation rises faster than productivity.

wage structure The observed wage differentials of the economy, broken down by industry, occupation, geographical location, or other job or worker differences.

wage subsidy A direct payment or a reduction in taxes from the government to a firm that expands its employment of low-wage or structurally unemployed workers.

Wagner Act of 1935 (National Labor Relations Act) A law that guaranteed the rights of self-organization and collective bargaining, outlined unfair labor practices on the part of management, established the National Labor Relations Board, and made strikes by federal employees illegal.

wait unemployment The excess supply of workers that results from non–market-clearing wage rates. Workers displaced by union wage gains may prefer unemployment with the likelihood of regaining union employment to employment at the lower nonunion wage rate. Also, the unemployed workers who are forced by efficiency wage payments to wait for jobs to open.

work–leisure optimum The combination of leisure and income that provides the maximum attainable total utility. The point at which the worker is on the highest possible indifference curve given the budget constraint.

Y

yellow-dog contract A labor contract clause that, as a condition of continued employment, prohibited workers from joining a union. Yellow-dog contracts were declared unenforceable by the Norris–LaGuardia Act of 1932.

Z

zone of production Stage II of the production function; quantities of labor input beyond the point of maximum average product but prior to a negative marginal product. In this stage, changes in labor input contribute to increased efficiency by either labor or capital.

Answers to "Your Turn" Questions

Your Turn 1.1: The second statement reflects the economic perspective. Those retiring at age 65 are comparing costs and benefits—that is, responding to incentives and disincentives. Although retirees sacrifice their work earnings, they gain private pension benefits, Social Security benefits, and added leisure, which more than compensate for these forgone earnings.

Your Turn 2.1: If the slope of the budget line is steeper than the slope of the indifference curve that it intersects, the worker should work more hours than those identified by the intersection. Working more hours will allow the person to achieve greater total utility (attain a higher indifference curve). The worker will maximize total utility where the slopes of the budget line and the highest attainable indifference curve are equal.

Your Turn 2.2: When a worker's wage rate declines and the income effect dominates the substitution effect, the person will work more hours. The backward-bending portion of the labor supply curve is the relevant segment here.

Your Turn 2.3: Other things being equal, we would prefer jobs where we can select our work hours. That way we can choose to work the precise number of hours that will maximize our total utility. This optimal number of work hours may differ from that prescribed by an employer. Employer-required hours can lead to either underemployment or overemployment; worker-determined hours cannot.

Your Turn 3.1: The fact that women's real wages and rates of labor force participation have simultaneously increased implies that the Becker substitution effect has exceeded the Becker income effect.

Your Turn 3.2: The labor force size in this hypothetical nation is 60 million (= 53 million employed *plus* 7 million unemployed who are actively seeking work). The potential labor force is 85 million (= 60 million in the labor force *plus* 25 million eligible people who are not in the labor force). The LFPR is 70.6 percent [= (60 million/85 million) × 100].

Your Turn 4.1: If the net present value of an investment is highly positive, then the internal rate of return on the investment typically exceeds the interest cost of borrowing funds to finance the investment.

Your Turn 4.2: The marginal rate of return, r, is indeed the same for each person at the optimal level of education. Both r's equal the cost of borrowing, i. But the person with more ability has a greater r at any particular level of education, leading that person to obtain more education than the individual with less ability.

Your Turn 4.3: MBA education is mainly general training that is applicable to numerous employers. The firm's employees probably indirectly pay for this training through lower dollar salaries than would be paid without this fringe benefit.

Your Turn 5.1: In the competitive situation, MRP is $32 (= 8 units $\times$ the price of $4). Where there is monopoly, MRP will be less than $32. The firm's marginal revenue from each of the extra 8 units sold will be less than $4.

Your Turn 5.2: The high wages paid autoworkers may have accelerated the substitution of industrial robots for workers (substitution effect). Also, these high wages may have contributed to the cost advantage experienced by Japanese auto producers. Partly because of this cost advantage, imports of autos from Japan surged and employment in the American auto industry declined (output effect).

Your Turn 5.3: Capital and labor are gross complements in this scenario. The decline in the price of capital increased the amount of capital purchased, which increased the demand for labor. The output effect of the decline in the price of capital exceeded the substitution effect.

Your Turn 6.1: The increase in labor supply will reduce the market wage rate [the perfectly competitive firms' marginal wage cost (MWC)]. This decline in MWC will entice firms to employ more units of labor. They will stop adding new workers when MRP declines sufficiently to equal the new lower wage rate (= MWC). Equilibrium will be restored where MRP = MWC.

Your Turn 6.2: The monopsonist's MWC curve lies above the market labor supply curve because the monopsonist must pay a higher wage to attract an extra worker and must pay this higher wage to all workers, including those who otherwise could have been paid less. Monopsony is *not* a disadvantage to an employer; it is an advantage because it allows the monopsonist to reduce its wage rate by restricting the number of workers employed.

Your Turn 7.1: The slopes of the typical worker's indifference curves would become flatter. Workers would be less willing to trade off wage earnings for fringe benefits. Thus the optimal amount of fringe benefits would decline.

Your Turn 7.2: The major difficulty of profit sharing as a means of overcoming the principal–agent problem is that it can give rise to free riders who know that they will share in any profits even though they shirk. Seeing free riders, other workers may abandon their efforts to increase productivity, thus undermining the objective of the profit-sharing plan.

Your Turn 8.1: State governors receive compensating wage differentials such as fame, prestige, and power not available to most executives in the private sector. There is a ready supply of qualified, willing candidates for governor, even though the pay is far below that of otherwise similar private sector positions.

Your Turn 8.2: Because most people do not like to work outdoors in freezing temperatures, a compensating wage premium will arise for this type of work. A person who enjoys working in cold temperatures will receive this higher wage without suffering the utility loss experienced by the marginal worker enticed to this occupation by the compensating wage.

Your Turn 9.1: The V_p in the net present value equation will fall, reducing the likelihood that V_p will be positive and that migration will occur.

Your Turn 10.1: Based on personal characteristics, occupation, and location of employment, Isaiah is clearly more likely than Susan to be a union member.

Your Turn 10.2: The correct answer is *(b)*. A decline in imports would probably boost output and sales by domestic, unionized manufacturers. Consequently, domestic employment and union membership would rise.

Your Turn 10.3: The probability of a strike should fall because the likelihood of the firm or the union misperceiving the other party's concession curve will decline.

Your Turn 11.1: The measured union wage advantage is $1 an hour, or 11.1 percent [= ($10 − $9/$9) × 100]; the pure union wage advantage is $2 an hour, or 25 percent [= ($10 − $8/$8) × 100].

Your Turn 11.2: Unions could simultaneously increase the firm's productivity (output per worker) while extracting wage rate increases beyond the productivity gains. If so, the firm's profitability would decline.

Your Turn 12.1: People's incentives to work hard were reduced because the state provided many goods at no charge or at low, highly subsidized prices.

Your Turn 12.2: Stone may work more hours if the substitution effect of the tax decrease (after-tax wage increase) exceeds the income effect. That is, he may work more hours, responding to the fact that leisure is now more expensive. Because of the tax decrease, more after-tax pay is sacrificed in "buying" leisure. In contrast, for Smythe the income effect of the tax decrease may exceed the substitution effect.

Your Turn 13.1: The average wage of teenagers would increase, teenage employment would fall, and teenage unemployment would rise. It is unlikely that adult employment would change.

Your Turn 13.2: The firm will not provide this extra unit of job safety; the marginal benefit of $250,000 is less than the marginal cost of $300,000. But the marginal cost of $250,000 is less than the marginal social benefit of $300,000. Thus a strong case can be made for government intervention. Government could simply require the firm to provide this extra job safety; or alternatively, government could provide workers with information about the safety hazards in their workplaces. Greater awareness by workers of job risks creates compensating wage differences that increase the firm's private benefits of providing job safety.

Your Turn 14.1: Because African–American males earn less than white males at higher levels of education, African–Americans may have a reduced incentive to obtain more education.

Your Turn 14.2: The dollar value of the discrimination coefficient for an employer hiring all white workers must be greater than $4. The coefficient for an employer hiring all African–American workers must be less than $4.

Your Turn 14.3: Statistical differences in group averages might lead employers to reject qualified women and minorities for some jobs, confining those discriminated against to lower-paying, stereotypical jobs. For example, women might be excluded from career tracks in management based on the assumption that family responsibilities will interfere with transfers to new locations and other aspects of job performance. Instead women may be segregated into administrative assistant positions.

Your Turn 14.4: The inferior economic position of women may spring partly from their relative lack of mathematical and quantitative interest and training. Perhaps women have freely chosen to avoid preparing for higher-paying professions requiring these skills. On the other hand, women may possibly have less mathematical training than men because of discrimination. That is, socialization, advising in education, and stereotypical hiring may have pushed them away from this type of training and toward training for "women's jobs."

Your Turn 15.1: Unexpected inflation reduces the length of job search; anticipated inflation has no effect on the length of job search; and unemployment insurance increases the length of job search.

Your Turn 15.2: The job ladder in academia involves only three rungs: assistant professor, associate professor, and full professor. There is considerable upward mobility along the ladder.

Your Turn 16.1: A shift of the Lorenz curve toward the diagonal line represents a decline in earnings inequality. Most likely the histogram of earnings will be compressed, and the Gini coefficient of earnings will decline.

Your Turn 16.2: Although all the factors shown in Figure 16.4 are important, if forced to select one set of factors, we would pick differences in education and training.

Your Turn 17.1: Productivity is 2 (= 10 units of output/5 units of labor). Average labor cost is $1 (= $10 of labor cost/10 units of output).

Your Turn 17.2: As the economy emerged from the recession of 1990–1991, firms collectively increased their output more rapidly than their employment. Therefore, output per worker increased.

Your Turn 18.1: The unemployment rate overstates economic hardship because some survey respondents may falsely claim they are searching for work; it counts people with weak labor market attachment the same as their strongly attached counterparts; and many families have more than one earner. The unemployment rate understates economic hardship because it counts involuntarily part-time workers as fully employed and does not measure either discouraged or subemployed workers.

Your Turn 18.2: False. Recently men and women in the United States have had very similar unemployment rates.

Name Index

Page numbers followed by n indicate material found in notes.

A

Aaronson, Daniel, 61, 405n
Abowd, John M., 328n
Acemoglu, Daron, 501n
Adams, Scott, 405
Adams, Walter, 199
Addison, John T., 79n, 115n, 189n, 306n, 341n, 354n, 358, 473n
Aggarwal, Rajesh K., 232n
Aigner, Dennis J., 440n
Akerlof, George A., 235n, 523n
Allegretto, Sylvia, 501n, 502n
Allen, Steven, 98n, 254, 280n
Alpert, William T., 488n
Altonji, Joseph G., 122, 440n
Alvi, Eskander, 549n
Amsden, Alice H., 433n
Anderson, Patricia M., 391n
Anderson, Rod, 488n
Andrews, Emily S., 218n
Angrist, Joshua D., 377n
Arkes, Jeremy, 119n
Aronsson, Thomas, 328n
Asch, Beth J., 375n, 378n
Ashenfelter, Orley C., 29n, 95n, 97, 121n, 151, 194n, 255n, 328n, 330n, 374n, 401n, 404n, 463n, 494n, 579
Atkinson, A. B., 489n, 492n, 496
Autor, David H., 119n, 157n, 254, 466n, 501n, 503n
Averett, Susan L., 95n
Azariadis, Costas, 555n

B

Bailey, Martha J., 70
Baker, George, 473n
Baker, Michael, 405n
Bansak, Cynthia, 297n

Barrett, Alan, 118n
Barron, John M., 119n, 355n
Bartel, Ann P., 414n
Bartik, Timothy, 405n
Basu, Susanto, 522n
Baum, Charles L., 74n
Baumol, William J., 528n
Bayard, Kimberly, 446n
Becker, Brian E., 358n
Becker, Gary S., 6, 54, 57n, 96n, 434, 435–439
Becker, I., 487n
Belfield, Clive R., 354n
Belman, Dale, 373n, 398n
Benati, Luca, 76n
Bender, Keith A., 316n
Benedict, Mary Ellen, 330n
Benjamin, Dwayne, 405n
Berger, Mark C., 119n
Bergmann, Barbara, 67n, 69n, 442n, 452n, 454n
Bergner, Daniel, 379n
Berkowitz, Ruth, 123
Bernhardt, Annette, 501n
Bernstein, Aaron, 312n
Bernstein, Jared, 38n, 501n, 502n
Bertrand, Marianne, 232n
Betson, David M., 389n
Bhargava, Sandeep, 227n
Bhaskar, V., 400n
Biddle, Jeff E., 30, 434
Blachflower, David G., 189n, 256n, 317n
Black, Dan A., 118n, 119n
Black, Sandra E., 439
Blackburn, McKinley L., 121n
Blanchflower, David G., 343n
Blank, Rebecca M., 44n, 45n
Blasi, Joseph, 227n
Blau, Francine D., 29n, 57n, 67n, 70n, 73n, 74n, 293n, 426n, 427, 442n, 447n, 451, 453
Blinder, Alan S., 227n, 522n
Bloemen, Hans G., 470n
Bluestone, Barry, 501n, 502n

Blundell, Richard E., 29n, 34n
Boal, William M., 186n, 403n
Bognanno, Michael L., 229n
Boissiere, M., 123n
Bonars, Stephen G., 286n
Booth, Alison, 327n, 579
Borass, Stephanie, 451
Bordo, Michael, 316n
Borjas, George J., 281n, 283n, 284n, 286n, 291, 293
Borland, Jeff, 374n
Bosworth, Barry, 577
Boulding, Kenneth E., 39n
Bound, John, 75, 504n, 557n
Bourguignon, F., 489n
Brack, John, 79n
Brainerd, Elizabeth, 439
Bratsberg, Bernt, 284n, 343n
Briggs, Vernon M., Jr., 270n
Brittain, John A., 391n
Brock, James W., 199
Bronars, Stephen G., 281n, 358n, 463n
Brown, Charles, 221n, 222n, 255n, 404n, 406n, 452n
Brown, James N., 328n
Brue, Stanley L., 6n
Brusentsev, Vera, 577
Bryson, Alex, 189n, 343n
Buchinsky, Moshe, 500
Buchmueller, Thomas C., 219
Budd, John W., 345, 577
Burkhauser, Richard V., 405n, 406n, 500n
Burtless, Gary, 44n, 100n, 503n
Burton, Mark L., 95n

C

Cahuc, Pierre, 579
Cain, Glen G., 72n, 440n
Cancian, Maria, 488n
Card, David, 29n, 95n, 100, 107n, 197, 254, 255n, 300n, 328n, 331n, 362, 374n, 404, 452n, 456n, 463n, 490, 494n, 503n

Subject Index

Center for Human Resource Research, Ohio State University, 572

Central tendency measures, 484–485

Centralized wage setting, 427

Challenge: A Magazine of Economic Affairs, 578

Chance, impact on earnings distribution, 494–496, 497

Change to Win federation, 311, 312, 313

Chemical engineering majors, 101

Chemistry majors, 102

Chicago Tribune, 319

Chief executive officer (CEO) compensation, 229–232, 233

Child care, 69

Children
  Becker's view of utility, 6
  impact on labor migration, 280–281
  impact on women's participation rates, 69

Choices underlying labor economics, 4–5

Churning in earnings distribution, 498–499

Citywide agreements, 314

Civil engineering majors, 102

Civil Rights Act of 1964, 454, 455

Clergy, women's gains in, 448

Clerical workers, unionization of, 308

Clinton, Bill, 319

Coalescing power, 199

Cobweb model, 201–204

Codetermination, 190

Collective bargaining; *see also* Unions
  impact of wage elasticity on, 152
  impact on wage rates, 195–197
  national unions' role, 312–313
  strike threat, 328
  structures of, 314–315
  textbooks, 580

Collective voice, unions as, 354–355

College athletes, 259

College degrees; *see also* Education; Human capital theory
  as capital investment decision, 86, 87–88
  impact on job security, 551
  relation to on-the-job training opportunities, 117, 118
  as screening tool, 121–123
  starting salaries for selected fields, 101–102

College faculty, tenure for, 223

College gender gap, 110

College wage premium
  computer skills and, 254

effect of wage increases on, 361

reasons for growth, 503

recent trends, 96–100

Commerce Clearing House, 576

Commissions, 222

Commodities, household, 54–58

Communication Workers of America, 198, 324

Communications majors, 102

Company unions, 395

Comparative advantage, 57, 146

Compensating wage differentials
  common types, 247–251
  in hedonic wage theory, 260–266
  for safety risks, 248, 252–253, 261–263, 266, 411

Compensation; *see also* Distribution of earnings; Fringe benefits; Wage rates
  bonuses, 225–226
  commissions and royalties, 222
  efficiency wage theories, 233–238
  equity, 228–229
  fringe benefit economics, 210–213
  impact on occupational tenure, 278
  importance to work incentive, 10
  labor market efficiency and, 238–239
  optimal fringe benefit model, 213–220
  piece rates, 221–222
  principal-agent problem, 220–221, 223, 224–225
  profit sharing, 227, 228
  raises and promotions, 222–225
  tournament pay, 229–232

Compensation and Working Conditions, 571

Compensation per worker hour, selected industries, 526

Competition, effect on discrimination in Becker's model, 438–439

Competitive model, 400–401

Complements; *see* Gross complements

Composition of output, 523

Computer engineering majors, 101

Computer industry labor demand trends, 157, 158

Computer programming majors, 101

Computer science majors, 101

Computerization; *see also* Technological advances
  effect on income inequalities, 254
  impact on labor productivity, 531–532
  of job searches, 466
  of licensed work, 420

Concession curves, 328–329

Congress of Industrial Organizations, 397

Congressional hearings testimony, 577–578

Connecticut, average hourly earnings, 247

Conscription (military), 375, 376–377

Construction and extraction workers
  average hourly earnings, 245
  distribution by gender and race, 429
  illegal aliens as, 301
  injury risk, 408
  unionization of, 308

Consumption expenditures, college costs as, 119–120

Contemporary Economic Policy, 578

Continental Airlines, 319

Contingent workers, 159

Continuation of coverage mandates, 219

Contraception, 69, 70

Contract curves, 326–327

Convexity of indifference curves, 16–17

Convexity to the origin of isoquant curves, 164–165

Core problem of economics, 1

Cornell University, New York State School of Industrial and Labor Relations, 575

Corporate boards of directors, 232

Cost-benefit analysis, 4–5

Costs of living, 250

Countercyclical nature of union wage advantage, 344

Countervailing power, 199

Countrywide Financial, 231

Courts, hostility to unions, 396–397

Craft unions
  control of labor mobility, 270
  union wage advantage, 344
  work rules promoted by, 346–347

Crime, 6, 75, 103

Cross-country earnings mobility differences, 498

Cross-sectional data, 567

Crowding model, 442–448, 449

Crowding-out effect, 561

Cultural values of productivity, 519–520

Current Population Survey, 537, 565–567, 572

Custom, role in internal labor markets, 478

Cyber-picketing, 323

Cyclical changes in productivity, 521–524

LABOR STATISTICS FOR SELECTED YEARS, 1952–2006

	1985	1986	1987	1988	1989	1990	1991	1992
1. Noninstitutional population, 16 years or older (millions)[a]	178.2	180.6	182.8	184.6	186.4	188.0	189.8	191.6
2. Labor force (millions)[a]	115.7	117.8	119.9	121.7	123.9	124.8	125.3	127.0
3. Labor force participation rate (%)[a]	64.8	65.3	65.6	65.9	66.5	66.4	66.0	66.3
3a. Male (%)[a]	76.3	76.3	76.2	76.2	76.4	76.1	75.5	75.6
3b. Female (%)[a]	54.5	55.3	56.0	56.6	57.4	57.5	57.3	57.8
3c. White (%)[a]	65.0	65.5	65.8	66.2	66.7	66.9	66.6	66.8
3d. African–American and other (%)[a]	63.3	63.7	64.3	64.0	64.7	64.4	63.8	64.6
4. Employment (millions)[a]	107.2	109.6	112.4	115.0	117.3	117.9	116.9	117.6
5. Unemployment (millions)[a]	8.3	8.2	7.4	6.7	6.5	6.9	8.4	9.4
6. Unemployment rate (%)[a]	7.2	7.0	6.2	5.5	5.3	5.5	6.7	7.4
6a. Male (%)[a]	7.0	6.9	6.2	5.5	5.2	5.6	7.0	7.8
6b. Female (%)[a]	7.4	7.1	6.2	5.6	5.4	5.4	6.3	6.9
6c. White (%)[a]	6.2	6.0	5.3	4.7	4.5	4.8	6.1	6.6
6d. African–American and other (%)[a]	13.7	13.1	11.6	10.4	10.0	10.1	11.1	12.7
6e. 16–19-year-olds[a]	18.6	18.3	16.9	15.3	15.0	15.5	18.6	20.0
7. Average hourly earnings (current $)[b]	8.74	8.93	9.14	9.44	9.8	10.2	10.52	10.77
8. Average hours worked per week[b]	34.9	34.7	34.7	34.6	34.5	34.3	34.1	34.2
9. Average earnings per week (1982 $)[b]	277	276	273	271	267	263	259	258
10. Change in earnings per week from year earlier (% in 1982 $)[b]	−1.1	0.0	−1.2	−0.9	−1.2	−1.7	−1.6	−0.2
11. Federal minimum wage rate (current $)	3.35	3.35	3.35	3.35	3.35	3.80	4.25	4.25
12. Change in productivity from year earlier (%)[c]	2.2	2.9	0.5	1.5	1.0	2.1	1.6	4.3
13. Change in hourly compensation from year earlier (%)[c]	1.4	3.2	0.3	1.4	−1.6	1.3	1.3	2.6
14. Change in unit labor cost from year earlier (%)[c]	2.5	2.1	3.2	3.5	1.7	4.1	3.3	0.9
15. Labor union membership (millions)[d]	17.0	17.0	16.9	17.0	17.0	16.7	16.6	16.4
16. Union membership as percentage of nonagricultural workers	17.5	17.1	16.6	16.2	15.7	15.3	15.3	15.1
17. Work stoppages	54	69	46	40	51	44	40	35
18. Strike time as percentage of total work time[e]	.03	.05	.02	.02	.07	.02	.02	.01
19. Employee compensation as percentage of national income	65.1	65.9	65.9	65.2	65.2	65.6	65.9	66.2

[a]Civilian   [b]Total private, nonagricultural industries   [c]Business sector   [d]Includes members of professional associations, 1970–2006

BREAK THROUGH

P9-AFZ-187

To improving results

The Best Preparation for
New State Standards & Assessments

4-2 Prime and Composite Numbers

4-2 Objectives

Students will be able to understand and explain

• Prime and composite numbers.

• The number of divisors of any whole number.

• The Fundamental Theorem of Arithmetic.

• The factorization of whole numbers.

CCSS The grade 4 *Common Core Standards* states that students should be able to:

Find all factor pairs for a whole number in the range 1–100. Recognize that a whole number is a multiple of each of its factors. Determine whether a given whole number in the range 1–100 is a multiple of a given one-digit number. Determine whether a given whole number in the range 1–100 is prime or composite. (p. 29)

One method used in elementary schools to determine the positive factors of a nonzero whole number is to use squares of paper or cubes to represent the number as a rectangle. Such a rectangle resembles a candy bar formed with small squares. The dimensions of the rectangle are divisors or factors of the number. For example, Figure 5 shows rectangles to represent 12.

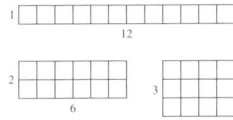

Figure 5

NEW! Relevant excerpts from the **Common Core State Standards** are incorporated throughout the text so that students see how the standards relate to what they are learning.

NEW! Learning objectives are provided for every section to focus student attention on the key ideas.

Extensive problem sets contain many types of exercises that reflect the rigor of the new CCSS assessments.

Each problem set has three parts:

1. **Assessment A** – focused on skills from the section

2. **Assessment B** – parallels Assessment A, with no answers provided in the student text

3. **Mathematical Connections** – rich conceptual exercises of a variety of types that require students to communicate mathematically

Mathematical Connections 4-3

Reasoning

1. Can two nonzero whole numbers have a greatest common multiple? Explain your answer.
2. Is it true that $GCD(a, b, c) \cdot LCM(a, b, c) = abc$? Explain your answer.
3. Suppose that $GCD(a, b, c) = 1$. Is it necessarily true that $GCD(a, b) = GCD(b, c) = 1$? Explain your reasoning.
4. Suppose that $GCD(a, b) = GCD(b, c) = 2$. Does that always imply that $GCD(a, b, c) = 2$? Justify your answer.
5. Is it true that every common divisor of two nonzero whole numbers a and b is a divisor of the $GCD(a, b)$? Explain your answer.
6. How can you tell from the prime factorization of two numbers if their LCM equals the product of the numbers? Explain your reasoning.
7. Can the LCM of two nonzero whole numbers ever be greater than the product of the two numbers? Explain your reasoning.

Open-Ended

8. Find three pairs of numbers for which the LCM of the numbers in a pair is less than the product of the two numbers.
9. Describe infinitely pairs of numbers whose GCD is equal to the following numbers.
   a. 2   b. 6   c. 91
10. A large gear is used to turn a smaller gear. If the larger gear makes 72 revolutions per minute and the smaller gear makes 1500 revolutions per minute, how many teeth does each gear have? Give three different possibilities. What is the least number of teeth possible?

Cooperative Learning

11. a. In your group, discuss whether the Euclidean algorithm for finding the GCD of two numbers should be introduced in middle school (To all students? To some?). Why or why not?
    b. If you decide that it should be introduced in middle school, discuss how it should be introduced. Report your group's decision to the class.

Connecting Mathematics to the Classroom

12. Describe to a sixth-grade student the difference between a divisor and multiple.

13. Eleanor claims that the $GCD(0, a) = 0$. Is she correct? What does she understand about GCD? What does she not understand?
14. Aiko says to find the LCM you can just multiply the two numbers. As a teacher, how do you respond?
15. A student wants to know how many whole numbers between 1 and 10,000 inclusive are either multiples of 3 or multiples of 5. She wonders if it is correct to find the number of those whole numbers that are multiples of 3 and add the number of those that are multiples of 5. How do you respond?

Review Problems

16. Find the greatest digit that makes the following statements true.
    a. $3 | 83\_51$ b. $11 | 8\_691$ c. $23 | 103\_6$
17. Find the prime factorization of the following numbers.
    a. 17,496   b. 32,715   c. $2^4 \cdot 8^2 \cdot 27^3$
18. Is 2223 prime? Justify your answer.
19. Find a number that has exactly five prime factors.
20. Find the least positive number that is divisible by 2, 4, 6, 8, and 10.
21. What is the greatest prime that must be used to determine if 3359 is prime?

National Assessments

National Assessment of Educational Progress (NAEP) Question

The least common multiple of 8, 12, and a third number is 120. Which of the following could be the third number?
A. 15
B. 16
C. 24
D. 32
E. 48

NAEP, Grade 8, 1990

The Best Online Resource — MyMathLab®

VIDEOS

- **NEW!** Common Core in Action – expert faculty shed light on what the standards really mean for classroom teachers

- **UPDATED!** Section Lectures – address the math topics in each section. Students can navigate directly to specific examples within the video.

- Integrating Mathematics and Pedagogy (IMAP) – feature elementary school children working problems

- Classroom Videos - experienced teachers teaching key topics, with commentary by the teacher and college faculty

- Responding to Student Work – analysis and helpful responses to elementary school children's work

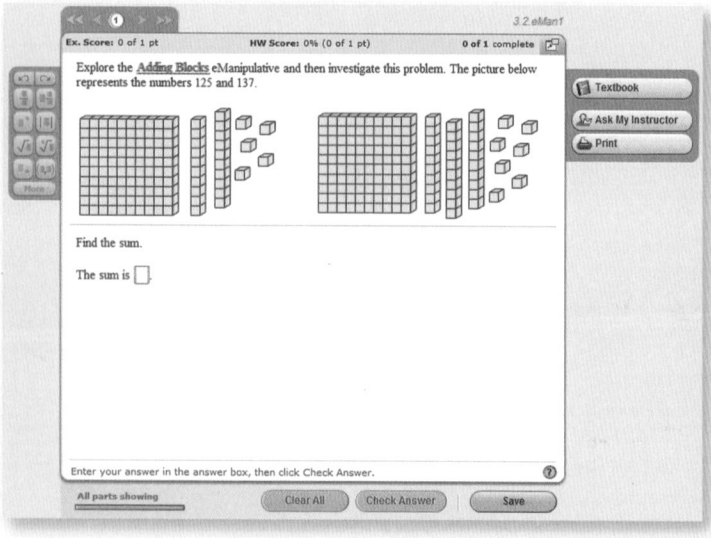

ASSIGNABLE EXERCISES

- **Textbook exercises** - over 2000 algorithmically generated exercises that parallel those in the text

- **E-manipulatives exercises** – require use of electronic manipulatives

- **Integrating Mathematics and Pedagogy (IMAP) video exercises** – require analysis of student work

- **NEW!** Common Core Assessment Analysis exercises – require analysis and interpretation of sample CCSS exercises

- **Assessment exercises** – hundreds of exercises from the test bank

- **Review exercises** – for prerequisite math and geometry skills. Use with MyMathLab's personalized homework functionality to target gaps in prerequisite skills.

VIEW BY STANDARDS

You can toggle between viewing course content organized around the Table of Contents or around other standards, including the Common Core Standards.

12th Edition

A Problem Solving Approach to
Mathematics

for Elementary School Teachers

Rick Billstein
University of Montana

Shlomo Libeskind
University of Oregon

Johnny W. Lott
University of Montana

and

Barbara Boschmans
Northern Arizona University for the chapter on Number Theory

PEARSON

Boston   Columbus   Hoboken   Indianapolis   New York   San Francisco
Amsterdam   Cape Town   Dubai   London   Madrid   Milan   Munich   Paris   Montréal   Toronto
Delhi   Mexico City   São Paulo   Sydney   Hong Kong   Seoul   Singapore   Taipei   Tokyo

Editorial Director: Chris Hoag

Editor in Chief: Anne Kelly

Senior Acquisitions Editor: Marnie Greenhut

Editorial Assistant: Lucia Kim

Program Manager: Patty Bergin

Project Manager: Sherry Berg

Program Management Team Lead:
Karen Wernholm

Project Management Team Lead: Peter Silvia

Media Producer: Nicholas N. Sweeny

TestGen Content Manager: John Flanagan

MathXL Content Developer: Bob Carroll

Executive Marketing Manager: Jeff Weidenaar

Marketing Assistant: Brooke Smith

**Senior Author Support/Technology
Specialist:** Joe Vetere

Rights and Permissions Project Manager:
Julia Tomasella

Senior Procurement Specialist: Carol Melville

Associate Director of Design: Andrea Nix

Program Design Lead: Beth Paquin

Cover and Interior Design: Studio Montage

Production Coordination and Composition:
Lumina Datamatics, Inc.

Illustrations: Lumina Datamatics, Inc.
and Chandler Studios

Library of Congress Cataloging-in-Publication Data
Billstein, Rick.
  A problem solving approach to mathematics for elementary school teachers / Rick Billstein, University of Montana, Shlomo Libeskind, University of Oregon, Johnny W. Lott, University of Montana. —12th edition.
    pages cm
  ISBN 0-321-98729-2 (student edition)—ISBN 0-321-99044-7 (annotated instructor's edition)
  1. Problem solving—Study and teaching (Elementary)   2. Mathematics—Study and teaching (Elementary)
I. Libeskind, Shlomo. II. Lott, Johnny W., 1944-   III. Title.
  QA135.6.B55 2016
  372.7′044--dc23

2014032499

1 2 3 4 5 6 7 8 9 10—CRK—18 17 16 15 14

Annotated Instructor's Edition
ISBN 10:   0-321-99044-7
ISBN 13: 978-0-321-99044-0
ISBN 10:   0-321-98729-2
ISBN 13: 978-0-321-98729-7

PEARSON

Dedication

To my students who for the past 46 years have provided me with enjoyment and challenge.
Each new edition of this book reflects experiences learned in the classroom.
—Rick Billstein

To the American troops in Munich, Germany (1945–1948), who offered hope and
protection to survivors of the Holocaust.
—Shlomo Libeskind

To Carolyn for her support in all endeavors for many years, and to the next generation
of prospective mathematics teachers without whom both students
and mathematics would be in serious trouble.
—Johnny W. Lott

Contents

* MyMathLab or www.pearsonhighered.com/mathstatsresources

* MyMathLab or www.pearsonhighered.com/mathstatsresources

* MyMathLab or www.pearsonhighered.com/mathstatsresources

Preface

The twelfth edition of *A Problem Solving Approach to Mathematics for Elementary School Teachers* is designed to prepare outstanding future elementary and middle school teachers. This edition continues to be heavily concept- and skill-based, with an emphasis on active and collaborative learning. The content has been revised and updated to better prepare students to become teachers in their own classrooms.

National Standards for Mathematics

- **Common Core State Standards for Mathematics** The National Governors Association spearheaded the effort to develop the *Common Core Standards (2010)*; they have been adopted by many states and are used in this text to highlight concepts. The complete text of the *Common Core Standards* is found at www.corestandards.org.
- **Principles and Standards** The National Council of Teachers of Mathematics (NCTM) publication, *Principles and Standards of School Mathematics* (2000) continues to be a guide for the course. The complete text of the NCTM *Principles and Standards* can be found online at www.nctm.org.

Our Goals

- To present appropriate mathematics in an intellectually honest and mathematically correct manner.
- To use problem solving as an integral part of mathematics.
- To approach mathematics in a sequence that instills confidence and challenges students.
- To provide opportunities for alternate forms of teaching and learning.
- To provide communication and technology problems to develop writing skills that allow students to practice reasoning and explanation through mathematical exposition.
- To provide core mathematics for prospective elementary and middle school teachers in a way that challenges them to determine why mathematics is done as it is.
- To provide core mathematics that allows instructors to use methods integrated with content.
- To assist prospective teachers with connecting mathematics, its ideas, and its applications.
- To assist future teachers in becoming familiar with the content and philosophy of the national standards listed above.

The twelfth edition gives instructors a variety of approaches to teaching, encourages discussion and collaboration among future teachers and with their instructors, and aids the integration of projects into the curriculum. Most importantly, it promotes discovery and active learning.

New to This Edition

- At reviewers' suggestions, we **moved topics related to logic** from Chapter 1 to Chapter 2, where sets and the operations of union and intersection are covered.
- **Learning Objectives** are listed at the beginning of every section to focus student attention on the key ideas.
- This text has always reflected the content and processes set forth in today's new state mathematics standards and the Common Core State Standards (CCSS). In the twelfth edition, we have further **tightened the connections to the standards** and made them more explicit in the narrative and exercises:
  - **CCSS are cited within sections** to focus student attention and provide a springboard for discussion of their content.
  - **More exercises that address the CCSS** have been added, particularly in the Mathematical Connections portion of the exercise sets.
  - The **treatment of many topics has been enhanced** to reflect a tighter connection to the CCSS. Examples include:
    - Chapter 1: Expanded the Four-Step Polya Problem solving process with input from Standards for Mathematical Practice. The process is referred to in examples throughout the chapter.
    - Chapter 2: Moved the logic section from Chapter 1 to emphasize the connections to sets and language. Logical reasoning is now an integral part of Chapter 2.
    - Chapter 5: Now includes a definition of addition for integers that uses absolute value—included because it is one of the techniques used in operations on integers in CCSS.

- Chapter 6: The section on ratio and proportion now uses the types of diagrams to set up the proportions that are mentioned in CCSS.
- Chapter 8: Algebraic Thinking is extended to real numbers with greater emphasis on multistep word problems, as described in CCSS.
- Chapter 13: Following CCSS emphasis on transformations and symmetry, these topics are expanded in exposition and in problem sets. New engaging problems were added.
- Chapter 14: All measurement topics are now together in this chapter. Linear measure had been separated out, but because of measurement being highlighted in CCSS, all of the topics are in the same chapter.

- The **text has been streamlined** to help students focus on what's really needed. We made judicious cuts with the student in mind.
- Some of the chapter opener scenarios and exercises have been revised to make them more relevant and engaging.
- The **chapter summary charts have been revised** to make them more comprehensive resources for students as they prepare for tests.

Content Highlights

Chapter 1 An Introduction to Problem Solving

This chapter has been reorganized and shortened to make it friendlier. Much of the detail work on series has been moved to later chapters to allow students to gain a knowledge of problem-solving techniques with less algebraic manipulation at this stage.

Chapter 2 Introduction to Logic and Sets

This chapter has been reorganized to include a section on logic. It works hand in hand with the ideas of set operations and enhances reasoning. Set theory and set operations with properties are introduced as a basis for learning whole number concepts.

Chapter 3 Numeration Systems and Whole Number Operations

This chapter models addition and subtraction of whole numbers. It emphasizes the *missing-addend model*, the definition of subtraction in terms of addition, and discusses various algorithms for addition and subtraction including those in different bases. Models for multiplication and division of whole numbers, properties of these operations with emphasis on the distributive property of multiplication over addition, and various algorithms are covered in depth. Mental mathematics and estimation with whole numbers feature prominently.

Chapter 4 Number Theory

In the twelfth edition, a separate chapter on number theory does not depend on *integers*, which are introduced in Chapter 5. Concepts of divisibility with divisibility tests are discovered. Prime numbers, prime factorization, greatest common divisor and least common multiple as well as the Euclidean Algorithm are explored with many new exercises added. A module on Clock Arithmetic is available online.*

Chapter 5 Integers

This chapter concentrates only on integers, their operations, and properties.

Chapter 6 Rational Numbers and Proportional Reasoning

This chapter has been revised to follow many recommendations in the *Common Core Standards*. Videos showing elementary students learning fraction concepts are included so that future teachers can observe what happens when elementary students absorb what is taught and how they work with those concepts. Proportional reasoning, one of the most important concepts taught in middle school mathematics, is covered in great depth in its natural setting.

Chapter 7 Rational Numbers as Decimals and Percent

This chapter focuses on decimal representation of rational numbers. Discussion of percent includes the computing of simple and compound interest as well as estimation involving percents.

Chapter 8 Real Numbers and Algebraic Thinking

With an introduction to real numbers in the opening sections, the chapter combines knowledge of real numbers with algebraic skills to give a review of algebra needed to teach in grades K through 8. This includes work in the coordinate plane and with spreadsheets. A module on Using Real Numbers in Equations is available online.*

---

*Online modules are availale in MyMathLab or at www.pearsonhighered.com/mathstatsresources

Chapter 9 Probability
This chapter has been reorganized with odds now as an application of probability. *Common Core Standards* have been addressed with content designed to accompany these standards.

Chapter 10 Data Analysis/Statistics: An Introduction
Chapter 10 opens with Designing Experiments/Collecting Data, a section based on *Guidelines for Assessment and Instruction in Statistics Education (GAISE) Report: A preK–12 Curriculum Framework* (2005) by the American Statistical Association. This section, aligned with the *Common Core Standards*, focuses on designing studies and surveys. In the following sections, data, graphs, examples, and assessment exercises have been updated and new material added.

Chapter 11 Introductory Geometry
This chapter has been reorganized to allow students to explore some of the ramifications of different definitions in mathematics used in schools. Linear measure is introduced to emphasize its importance in the curriculum. Also symmetries are now introduced as an early concept that could be used to form geometrical definitions. The Networks module is now offered online.*

Chapter 12 Congruence and Similarity with Constructions
Congruence and constructions sections have been expanded to allow more exploration of circles and quadrilaterals. The concept of similarity is used to reintroduce slope of a line and its properties. Many new exercises have been added. A module on Trigonometric Ratios via Similarity is available online.*

Chapter 13 Congruence and Similarity with Transformations
Because of the prominence of motion geometry in the *Common Core Standards*, this chapter appears earlier among the geometry sections. It focuses on connections among transformations and dilations in congruence and similarity.

Chapter 14 Area, Pythagorean Theorem, and Volume
Chapter 14 continues a reorganization of the geometry chapters. Concepts of linear measure is included with the topics of area, the Pythagorean theorem, and volume. Many topics have been shifted and new material added, for example, the subsection *Comparing Volumes of Similar Figures*. Assessment sets and examples have been updated.

Technology Usage
Virtually all mathematics standards have included the use of technology as a tool for learning mathematics, yet the manner and type of usage in classrooms is as varied as the classrooms and teachers themselves. We strongly support the use of technology as a learning tool and have since the inception of this book. In this edition, online modules discuss the use of technology*. These modules are designed for a brief introduction to the use of spreadsheets and graphing calculators as indicated but it is expected that many instructors using the text will naturally incorporate those tools in their teaching. Additionally, a module on the use of *GeoGebra* is available.

References to the online geometry module problems and lab activities are included in the Mathematical Connections section of the assessments under the heading GeoGebra Activities. It is noted that there are more problems and activities in the online modules than are listed in the text. This is purposefully done to allow instructors to use them in the manner that is most pedagogically and mathematically desirable for their courses.

Features

In creating the 12th edition of this text, we have built upon the strengths of the previous editions, incorporating feedback from users and making extensive improvements to help prepare future teachers for new state standards and the Common Core.

Learning the Mathematics in the New Standards

- **New!** In this edition we have made judicious cuts to even more effectively bring key ideas to the forefront. **A streamlined narrative** keeps students focused on the important ideas.
- **Preliminary Problems** open every chapter with a thought-provoking question that sets the tone and prepares students for the material ahead.
- **New! Learning Objectives** are listed at the beginning of every section to focus student attention on the key ideas.

---

*Online modules are available in MyMathLab or at www.pearsonhighered.com/mathstatsresources

- **Problem-Solving Strategies** are highlighted in italics, and **Problem-Solving Boxes** throughout the text help students put these strategies to work.
- **Chapter Summaries** are organized in a student-friendly chart format, for easy exam preparation. These summaries also provide specific pages references for additional help on individual concepts.
- **Chapter Review** questions allow students to test themselves when preparing for an exam.

Focusing on the Standards for Mathematical Practice

- The **Activity Manual** includes classroom-tested activities and a pouch of perforated, printed color manipulatives.
  - **Activity Manual annotations** in the Annotated Instructor's Edition clarify when specific activities should be used for each lesson, making it easier to teach a more hands-on course.
  - The manual is available as a value-pack option. Ask your Pearson representative for details.
- **Now Try This** exercises, which follow key examples, help students become actively involved in their learning, facilitate the development of critical thinking and problem-solving skills, and stimulate class discussion. Answers are in both the Annotated Instructor's Edition and student text.
- **21 eManipulatives,** available in MyMathLab, allow students to investigate, explore, practice, build conceptual understanding, and solve specific problems, without the mess or cost of physical manipulatives. Annotations in the student edition indicate where these eManipulatives are relevant. Exercises related to the eManipulatives are assignable within MyMathLab.
- **New!** **Integrating Mathematics and Pedagogy (IMAP)** videos, available in MyMathLab, feature elementary school children working problems. Annotations in the student edition indicate where these videos are relevant. Exercises related to the IMAP videos are assignable within MyMathLab.

Teaching the Mathematics in the New Standards

- **New!** **Common Core State Standards (CCSS)** are cited within sections to focus student attention and provide a springboard for discussion of their content.
- **New!** **More exercises** have been added that address the CCSS, particularly in the Mathematical Connections portions of the exercise sets.
- **Connecting Mathematics to the Classroom** exercises require interpretation and analysis of the thinking of typical K-8 students.

- **School book pages** are included to show how various topics are introduced to the K-8 pupil. Icons within the text link the narrative to the appropriate school book page. Students are asked to complete many of the activities on the student pages so they can see what is expected in elementary school.
- **Historical Notes** add context and humanize the mathematics.
- **New!** Enhanced **Common Core State Standards (CCSS)** coverage in MyMathLab encourages students to become familiar with important content and procedures. The **view by standard** functionality in MyMathLab also includes CCSS.

Assessing the New Standards

- **Extensive Problem Sets** are organized into three categories for maximum instructor flexibility when assigning homework that address the standards.
  - **Assessment A** has problems with answers in the text, so that students can check their work.
  - **Assessment B** contains parallel problems to those in Assessment A, but answers are not given in the student text.
  - **Mathematical Connections** problems include the following categories: Reasoning, Open-Ended, Cooperative Learning, Connecting Mathematics to the Classroom, Review Problems, and NAEP sample questions.
- **Hundreds of assignable, algorithmic exercises.** The MyMathLab courses for the Twelfth Edition contains even more assignable exercises to meet students' needs. Assignable exercise types include the following:
  - **Textbook exercises**—over 2,000 algorithmically generated exercises parallel those in the text
  - **New!** **Common Core Assessment Analysis** exercises require analysis and interpretation of sample CCSS exercises.
  - **eManipulative exercises** require use of the eManipulatives within MyMathLab so students can be familiar with this important teaching and learning tool.
  - **Integrating Mathematics and Pedagogy (IMAP)** video exercises require analysis of student work.
  - **Assessment exercises** include hundreds of exercises from the test bank.

Student and Instructor Resources

For the Student

Activities Manual
Mathematics Activities for Elementary School Teachers: A Problem Solving Approach, 12th edition
Dan Dolan, *Project to Increase Mastery of Mathematics and Science, Wesleyan University*; Jim Williamson, *University of Montana*; and Mari Muri, *Project to Increase Mastery of Mathematics and Science, Wesleyan University*
ISBN 0-321-97708-4 | 978-0-321-97708-3

* Provides hands-on, manipulative-based activities keyed to the text that involve future elementary school teachers discovering concepts, solving problems, and exploring mathematical ideas.
* Colorful, perforated paper manipulatives in a convenient storage pouch.
* Activities can also be adapted for use with elementary students at a later time.
* References to these activities are in the margin of the Annotated Instructor's Edition.

Student's Solutions Manual
Barbara Boschmans, *Northern Arizona University* and Brian Beaudrie, *Northern Arizona University*
ISBN 0-321-99056-0 | 978-0321-99056-3

* Provides detailed, worked-out solutions to all of the **odd** problems in Assessments A and B, Review problems from the Mathematical Connections, and **Chapter Review** exercises.

For the Instructor

Annotated Instructor's Edition
ISBN 0-321-99044-7 | 978-0-321-99044-0

* This special edition includes answers to the text exercises on the page where they occur and includes answers to the Preliminary Problems, Now Try This activities, and Mathematical Connections questions.
* Annotations referencing the *Activities Manual* are included in the margins.

Online Supplements
The following instructor material is available for download from Pearson's Instructor Resource Center (www.pearsonhighered.com/irc) or within MyMathLab.

Instructor's Solutions Manual
Barbara Boschmans, *Northern Arizona University* and Brian Beaudrie, *Northern Arizona University*

* Provides detailed, worked-out solutions to all of the **Assessment A & B** exercises, **Review Exercises** from Mathematical Connections, and **Chapter Review** exercises.

Instructor's Testing Manual

* Comprehensive worksheets contain two forms of chapter assessments with answers for each.

Instructor's Guide for
Mathematics Activities for Elementary School Teachers: A Problem Solving Approach, 12th edition
Dan Dolan, *Project to Increase Mastery of Mathematics and Science, Wesleyan University*; Jim Williamson, *University of Montana*; and Mari Muri, *Project to Increase Mastery of Mathematics and Science, Wesleyan University*

* Contains answers for all activities, as well as additional teaching suggestions for some activities.

PowerPoint® Lecture Slides

* Fully editable slides provide section-by-section coverage of key topics and concepts along with examples.
* An Image Resource Library is also available within MyMathLab and contains art files from the text enabling further customization of the PowerPoint lectures.

TestGen®

* TestGen® enables instructors to build, edit, print, and administer tests using a computerized bank of questions developed to cover all the objectives of the text.
* TestGen is algorithmically based, allowing instructors to create multiple but equivalent versions of the same question or test with the click of a button. Instructors can also modify test bank questions or add new questions.

Online Learning

MyMathLab® Online Course (access code required)

MyMathLab from Pearson is the world's leading online resource in mathematics, integrating interactive homework, assessment, and media in a flexible, easy to use format.

MyMathLab delivers **proven results** in helping individual students succeed.

- MyMathLab has a consistently positive impact on student retention, subsequent success, and overall achievement. MyMathLab can be successfully implemented in any environment—lab-based, hybrid, fully online, or traditional.
- MyMathLab has a comprehensive online gradebook that automatically tracks your students' results on tests, quizzes, homework, and in the study plan. You can use the gradebook to quickly intervene if your students have trouble, or to provide positive feedback on a job well done.

MyMathLab provides **engaging experiences** that personalize, stimulate, and measure learning for each student.

- **Personalized Learning:** MyMathLab's personalized homework and adaptive study features allow your students to work more efficiently, spending time where they really need to.
- **Exercises:** The homework and practice exercises in MyMathLab are correlated to the exercises in the textbook, and they regenerate algorithmically to give students unlimited opportunity for practice and mastery. The software offers immediate, helpful feedback when students enter incorrect answers. Assignable exercise types include the following:
  - **Textbook exercises**—over 2,000 algorithmically generated exercises parallel those in the text
  - **New! Common Core Assessment Analysis** exercises in MyMathLab require analysis and interpretation of sample CCSS exercises.
  - **eManipulatives exercises** require use of the eManipulatives within MyMathLab so students can be familiar with this important teaching and learning tool.
  - **Integrating Mathematics and Pedagogy (IMAP)** video exercises require analysis of student work.
  - **Assessment exercises** include hundreds of exercises from the test bank.
- **Multimedia Learning Aids:** Exercises include guided solutions, sample problems, videos, and access to the complete eText access.
- **Complete eText** is available to students for the life of the edition, giving students unlimited access to the eBook within any course that uses that edition of the textbook.
- **eManipulatives** allow students to investigate, explore, practice, build conceptual understanding, and solve specific problems, without the mess or cost of physical manipulatives.
- **New!** Enhanced **Common Core State Standards (CCSS)** coverage in MyMathLab encourages students to become familiar with important content and procedures. The **view by standard** functionality in MyMathLab also includes CCSS.
- **New! Study Skills resources** help students develop good time management skills and deal with stress management.
- **A wide array of videos** meets the unique needs of future teachers.
  - **Integrating Mathematics and Pedagogy (IMAP)** videos feature elementary school children working problems. Exercises related to these videos are assignable within MyMathLab.
  - **New! Section Lecture** videos are revised for this edition—ideal for studying and reviewing.
  - **New! Common Core in Action videos** featuring experienced faculty shedding light on what the CCSS really mean for the classroom and for teachers.
  - **Classroom** videos show experienced teachers teaching key topics, with commentary by the teacher and college faculty.
  - **Responding to Student Work** videos contain analysis and helpful responses to elementary school children's work.
- **Accessibility:** MyMathLab is compatible with the JAWS screen reader and enables multiple-choice and free-response problem types to be read and interacted with via keyboard controls and math notation input. MyMathLab also works with screen enlargers, including ZoomText, MAGic, and SuperNova. And all MyMathLab videos in this course are closed captioned. More information on this functionality is available at http://mymathlab.com/accessibility.

And, MyMathLab comes from an experienced partner with educational expertise and an eye on the future.

- Whether you are just getting started with MyMathLab, or have a question along the way, we're here to help.
- Contact your Pearson representative directly or at www.mymathlab.com.

MyMathLab® Ready to Go Course (access code required)

These new Ready to Go courses provide students with all the same great MyMathLab features that you're used to, but make it easier for instructors to get started. Each course includes pre-assigned homeworks and quizzes to make creating your course even simpler. Ask your Pearson representative about the details for this particular course or to see a copy of this course.

MathXL® Online Course (access code required)

MathXL® is the homework and assessment engine that runs MyMathLab. (MyMathLab is MathXL plus a learning management system.) With MathXL, instructors can:

- Create, edit, and assign online homework and tests using algorithmically generated exercises correlated at the objective level to the textbook.
- Create and assign their own online exercises.
- Maintain records of all student work tracked in MathXL's online gradebook.

With MathXL, students can:

- Take chapter tests in MathXL and receive personalized study plans and/or personalized homework assignments based on their test results.
- Use the study plan and/or the homework to link directly to tutorial exercises for the objectives they need to study.
- Access supplemental animations and video clips directly from selected exercises.

MathXL is available to qualified adopters. For more information, visit the website at www.mathxl.com or contact a Pearson representative.

Acknowledgments

For past editions of this book, many noted and illustrious mathematics educators and mathematicians have served as reviewers. To honor the work of the past as well as to honor the reviewers of this edition, we list all but place asterisks by this edition's reviewers.

Leon J. Ablon
Paul Ache
G.L, Alexanderson
Haldon Anderson
Bernadette Antkoviak
Renee Austin
Richard Avery
Sue H. Baker
Jane Barnard
Joann Becker
Cindy Bernlohr
James Bierden
Jackie Blagg
*Carol Bobbins
Jim Boone
Sue Boren
*James Brandt
Barbara Britton
Beverly R. Broomell
Anne Brown
Jane Buerger
Maurice Burke
David Bush
Laura Cameron
Karen Cannon
Louis J. Chatterley
Phyllis Chinn
*Jose Contreras-Francia
Donald J. Dessart
Ronald Dettmers
Jackie Dewar
Nicole Duvernoy
Amy Edwards
Lauri Edwards
Margaret Ehringer
Rita Eisele
*Rachel Fairhurst
Albert Filano
Marjorie Fitting
Michael Flom
Pari L. Ford
*Marie Franzosa
Martha Gady
Edward A. Gallo
Dwight Galster
*Heather C. Gamel
Melinda Gann

Sandy Geiger
Glenadine Gibb
Don Gilmore
Diane Ginsbach
Elizabeth Gray
*Lorraine Gregory
*Jerrold Grossman
Alice Guckin
Jennifer Hegeman
Joan Henn
Boyd Henry
Linda Hintzman
Alan Hoffer
E. John Hornsby, Jr.
Patricia A. Jaberg
Judith E. Jacobs
*Jay M. Jahangiri
Donald James
Thomas R. Jay
Jeff Johannes
Jerry Johnson
Wilburn C. Jones
Robert Kalin
Sarah Kennedy
Steven D. Kerr
Leland Knauf
Margret F. Kothmann
Kathryn E. Lenz
Hester Lewellen
Ralph A. Liguori
Richard Little
Susan B. Lloyd
Don Loftsgaarden
Sharon Louvier
Carol A. Lucas
Stanley Lukawecki
Lou Ann Martin
Judith Merlau
Barbara Moses
Cynthia Naples
Charles Nelson
Glenn Nelson
Kathy Nickell
*Bethany Noblitt
Dale Oliver
Mark Oursland
Linda Padilla

Dennis Parker
*Priti Patel
Clyde Paul
Keith Peck
Barbara Pence
Glen L. Pfeifer
Debra Pharo
Jack Porter
Edward Rathnell
*Mary Beth Rollick
Sandra Rucker
Jennifer Rutherford
Helen R. Santiz
Sharon Saxton
Sherry Scarborough
Jane Schielack
Barbara Shabell
M. Geralda Shaefer
Nancy Shell
Wade H. Sherard
Gwen Shufelt
Julie Sliva
Ron Smit
Joe K. Smith
William Sparks
Virginia Strawderman
Mary M. Sullivan
Viji Sundar
Sharon Taylor
Jo Temple
C. Ralph Verno
Hubert Voltz
John Wagner
*Catherine Walker
Edward Wallace
Virginia Warfield
Lettie Watford
Mark F. Weiner
Grayson Wheatley
Bill D. Whitmire
Teri Willard
Jim Williamson
Ken Yoder
Jerry L. Young
Deborah Zopf

Chapter 1

An Introduction to Problem Solving

1-1 Mathematics and Problem Solving

1-2 Explorations with Patterns and Algebraic Thinking

Preliminary Problem

Jill received 10 boxes of coins, each box containing 10 identical looking coins. She knows that one box has 10 counterfeit coins, while all the other coins are genuine. She also knows that each fake coin weighs 1 ounce, while a real coin weighs 2 ounces. Jill has a scale and claims it is possible to determine which is the box with fake coins, in one weighing, as follows:

> "Number the boxes 1 through 10, and take 1 coin from the first box, 2 from the second, 3 from the third, and so on until 10 are taken from the last box. Next, I weigh all the coins taken out, and I can determine which box has the fake coins."

Explain why Jill's scheme would work.

If needed, see Hint on page 35.

IMAP Video

Watch Elsie talk about problem-solving with her students.

Problem solving has long been central in the learning of mathematics at all levels. George Pólya (1887–1985), a great mathematician of the twentieth century, is the father of mathematical problem solving. He pointed out that "solving a problem means finding a way out of difficulty, a way around an obstacle, attaining an aim which was not immediately attainable." (Pólya 1981, p. ix)

Polya developed a four-step problem solving process which has been adopted by many. A modified version is given here.

1. Understanding the problem
2. Devising a plan
3. Carrying out the plan
4. Looking back

The *Common Core State Standards for Mathematics* (hereafter referred to as *Common Core Standards* and abbreviated as CCSS) were developed in 2010 through the work of the National Governors Association and the Council of Chief State School Officers. The *Common Core Standards* are built around its *Standards for Mathematical Practice* seen in Table 1.

Table 1

1. Make sense of problems and persevere in solving them.
Mathematically proficient students start by explaining to themselves the meaning of a problem and looking for entry points to its solution. They analyze givens, constraints, relationships, and goals. They make conjectures about the form and meaning of the solution and plan a solution pathway rather than simply jumping in to a solution attempt.

2. Reason abstractly and quantitatively.
Mathematically proficient students make sense of quantities and their relationships in problem situations.

3. Construct viable arguments and critique the reasoning of others.
Mathematically proficient students understand and use stated assumptions, definitions, and previously established results in constructing arguments. They make conjectures and build a logical progression of statements to explore the truth of their conjectures. They are able to analyze situations by breaking them into cases, and can recognize and use counterexamples.

4. Model with mathematics.
Mathematically proficient students can apply the mathematics they know to solve problems arising in everyday life, society, and the workplace. In early grades, this might be as simple as writing an addition equation to describe a situation. In middle grades, a student might apply proportional reasoning to plan a school event or analyze a problem in the community.

5. Use appropriate tools strategically.
Mathematically proficient students consider the available tools when solving a mathematical problem. These tools might include pencil and paper, concrete models, a ruler, a protractor, a calculator, a spreadsheet, a computer algebra system, a statistical package, or dynamic geometry software.

6. Attend to precision.
Mathematically proficient students try to communicate precisely to others. They try to use clear definitions in discussion with others and in their own reasoning. They state the meaning of the symbols they choose, including using the equal sign consistently and appropriately. They are careful about specifying units of measure, and labeling axes to clarify the correspondence with quantities in a problem.

7. Look for and make use of structure.
Mathematically proficient students look closely to discern a pattern or structure. Young students, for example, might notice that three and seven more is the same amount as seven and three more, or they may sort a collection of shapes according to how many sides the shapes have. Later, students will see 7×8 equals the well remembered $7 \times 5 + 7 \times 3$, in preparation for learning about the distributive property. In the expression $x^2 + 9x + 14$, older students can see the 14 as 2×7 and the 9 as $2 + 7$.

8. Look for and express regularity in repeated reasoning.
Mathematically proficient students notice if calculations are repeated, and look both for general methods and for shortcuts. Upper elementary students might notice when dividing 25 by 11 that they are repeating the same calculations over and over again, and conclude they have a repeating decimal.

The *Standards for Mathematical Practice* are used in this book to enhance Polya's four-step process as seen in Table 2.

Table 2

Expanded Four-Step Problem Solving Process with Input from *Standards for Mathematical Practice*

1. **Understanding the problem.**
   - Start by explaining the personal meaning of a problem.
   - Ask if the problem can be stated differently.
   - Analyze goals to identify what is to be found and what is needed.
   - Analyze the givens.
   - Analyze the constraints.
   - Ask what information is missing from the problem.
   - Ask about missing or unneeded information in the problem.
   - Make sense of quantities and their relationships in the problem situation.
   - Look for discernable patterns or structures.

2. **Devising a plan.**
   - Look for a pattern or a structure.
   - Examine related or analogous problems and determine whether the same techniques applied to them can be applied to the current problem.
   - Examine a simpler or special case of the problem to gain insight into the solution of the original problem.
   - Make a table or list.
   - Identify a subgoal.
   - Make a diagram.
   - Use guess and check.
   - Work backward.
   - Write an equation.
   - Abstract a given situation and represent it symbolically.
   - Plan a solution pathway.
   - Make assumptions and approximations to simplify a complicated situation.
   - Use clear definitions.

3. **Carrying out the plan.**
   - State the meaning of any symbols used.
   - Manipulate the representing symbols as if they have a life of their own.
   - Implement the strategy or strategies in step 2 and perform any necessary actions or computations.
   - Attend to the precision in language and mathematics used.
   - Apply the mathematics to solve problems.
   - Check each step of the plan along the way—this may be intuitive checking or formal proof of each step.
   - Keep an accurate record of all work.
   - Map relationships using such tools as diagrams, two-way tables, graphs, flowcharts and formulas.
   - Use appropriate tools strategically.
   - Look for general methods and for shortcuts to calculations.
   - Detect possible errors using estimation and other mathematical knowledge.
   - Specify units of measure.

4. **Looking back.**
   - Check the results in the original problem (in some cases this will require a proof).
   - Interpret the solution in terms of the original problem: Does the answer make sense? Does it answer the question that was asked?
   - Determine whether there is another method of finding the solution.
   - Improve the model if it has not served its purpose.
   - Maintain oversight of the process.
   - Evaluate the reasonableness of intermediate results.
   - Check answers with a different method.
   - Continually ask: "Does this make sense?"
   - Understand different approaches.
   - Identify correspondences among different approaches.
   - Justify conclusions.
   - Communicate conclusions to others.
   - Respond to arguments of others.
   - If possible, determine other related or more general problems for which the technique will work.

Activity Manual

Try *When You Don't Know What to Do* to introduce Polya's four-step problem-solving process.

Students learn mathematics as a result of solving problems. *Exercises* are routine practice for skill building and serve a purpose in learning mathematics, but problem solving must be a focus of school mathematics. A reasonable amount of tension and discomfort improves problem-solving performance. Mathematical problem solving may occur when:

1. Students are presented with a situation that they understand but do not know how to proceed directly to a solution.
2. Students are interested in finding the solution and attempt to do so.
3. Students are required to use mathematical ideas to solve the problem.

We present many opportunities in this text to solve problems. Each chapter opens with a problem that can be solved using concepts developed in the chapter. We give a hint for the solution to the problem at the end of each chapter. Throughout the text, some problems are solved using a four-step process.

Working with others to solve problems enhances problem-solving ability and communication skills. We encourage *cooperative learning* and working in groups whenever possible. To encourage group work and help identify when cooperative learning could be useful, we identify activities and problems where group discussions are especially beneficial for learning mathematics.

1-1 Mathematics and Problem Solving

1-1 Objectives

Students will be able to understand and explain

- The four-step problem-solving process.

- How to solve problems using various problem-solving strategies.

If problems are approached in only one way, a mind-set may be formed. For example, consider the following:

Spell the word spot *three times out loud.* "S-P-O-T! S-P-O-T! S-P-O-T!" *Now answer the question* "What do we do when we come to a green light?" *Write an answer.*

If we answer "Stop," we may be guilty of having formed a mind-set. We do not stop at a *green* light.

Consider the following problem: "A shepherd had 36 sheep. All but 10 died. How many lived?" If we answer "10," we are ready to try some problems. If not, we probably did not understand the question by not reading it carefully. *Understanding the problem* is the first step in the four-step problem-solving process.

▶ **IMAP Video**

Watch Tonya's class model strategies for solving a problem.

Strategies for Problem Solving

We next provide a variety of problems with different contexts to provide experience in problem solving. Strategies are used to discover or construct the means to achieve a solution. For each strategy described, we give an example that can be solved with that strategy. Often, problems can be solved in more than one way. There is no one best strategy to use.

In many of the examples, we use the set of **natural numbers**, 1, 2, 3, ... Note that the first three dots, an *ellipsis*, are used to represent missing terms. The expanded problem-solving steps highlighting some strategies are shown next.

(**Historical Note**)

George Pólya (1887–1985) was born in Hungary, moved to the United States in 1940, and after a brief stay at Brown University, joined the faculty at Stanford University. A preeminent mathematician, he also focused on mathematics education. He published 10 books, including *How To Solve It* (1945), which has been translated into 23 languages.

Strategy: Look for a Pattern

 IMAP Video

Watch a fourth grade class model Gauss's strategy.

Problem Solving **Gauss's Problem**

As a student, Carl Gauss and his fellow classmates were asked to find the sum of the first 100 natural numbers. The teacher expected to keep the class occupied for some time, but Gauss gave the answer almost immediately. How might he have done it?

Understanding the Problem The natural numbers are $1, 2, 3, 4, \ldots$. Thus, the problem is to find the sum $1 + 2 + 3 + 4 + \ldots + 100$.

Devising a Plan The strategy *look for a pattern* is useful here. One story about young Gauss reports that he listed the sum, and wrote the same sum backwards as in Figure 1. If $S = 1 + 2 + 3 + 4 + 5 + \ldots + 98 + 99 + 100$, then Gauss could have seen the following pattern.

$$
\begin{array}{r}
S = \quad 1 + \quad 2 + \quad 3 + \quad 4 + \quad 5 + \ldots + \quad 98 + \quad 99 + 100 \\
+ \ S = 100 + \quad 99 + \quad 98 + \quad 97 + \quad 96 + \ldots + \quad 3 + \quad 2 + \quad 1 \\
\hline
2S = 101 + 101 + 101 + 101 + 101 + \ldots + 101 + 101 + 101
\end{array}
$$

Figure 1

To discover the original sum from the last equation, Gauss could have divided the sum, $2S$, in Figure 1 by 2.

Carrying Out the Plan There are 100 sums of 101. Thus, $2S = 100 \cdot 101$ and $S = \dfrac{100 \cdot 101}{2} = 5050$.

 **Activity Manual**

Try *What's the Pattern?* to introduce the patterns problem-solving strategy.

Looking Back Note that the sum in each pair $(1, 100)$, $(2, 99)$, $(3, 98)$, $\ldots$, $(100, 1)$ is always 101, and there are 100 pairs with this sum. This technique can be used to solve a more general problem of finding the sum of the first n natural numbers $1 + 2 + 3 + 4 + 5 + 6 + \ldots + n$. We use the same plan as before and notice the relationship in Figure 2. Because there are n sums of $n + 1$ we have $2S = n(n + 1)$ and $S = \dfrac{n(n + 1)}{2}$.

$$
\begin{array}{r}
S = \quad 1 + \quad 2 + \quad 3 + \quad 4 + \ldots + \quad n \\
+ \ S = \quad n + (n - 1) + (n - 2) + (n - 3) + \ldots + \quad 1 \\
\hline
2S = (n + 1) + (n + 1) + (n + 1) + (n + 1) + \ldots + (n + 1)
\end{array}
$$

Figure 2

A different strategy for finding a sum of consecutive natural numbers involves the strategy of *making a diagram* and thinking of the sum geometrically as a stack of blocks. This alternative method is explored in exercise 2 of Assessment 1-1A.

▶ **NOW TRY THIS 1**

NTT 1: Answer can be found in Answers at the back of the book.

Explain whether the approach in Gauss's Problem of writing the sum backwards and applying the strategy "Look for a Pattern" will or will not work in finding the following sum: $1^2 + 2^2 + \ldots + 100^2$.

(**Historical Note**)

 Carl Gauss (1777–1855), one of the greatest mathematicians of all time, was born to humble parents in Brunswick, Germany. He was an infant prodigy who later made contributions in many areas of science as well as mathematics. After Gauss's death, the King of Hanover honored him with a commemorative medal with the inscription "Prince of Mathematics." ●

Strategy: Examine a Related Problem

Problem Solving Sums of Even Natural Numbers

Find the sum of the even natural numbers less than or equal to 100. Generalize the result.

Understanding the Problem Even natural numbers are $2, 4, 6, 8, 10, \ldots$. The problem is to find the sum of these numbers: $2 + 4 + 6 + 8 + \ldots + 100$.

Devising a Plan Recognizing that the sum can be *related to Gauss's original problem* helps us devise a plan. Consider the following:

$$2 + 4 + 6 + 8 + \ldots + 100 = 2 \cdot 1 + 2 \cdot 2 + 2 \cdot 3 + 2 \cdot 4 + \ldots + 2 \cdot 50$$
$$= 2(1 + 2 + 3 + 4 + \ldots + 50)$$

Thus, we can use Gauss's method to find the sum of the first 50 natural numbers and then double that result.

Carrying Out the Plan We carry out the plan as follows:

$$2 + 4 + 6 + 8 + \ldots + 100 = 2(1 + 2 + 3 + 4 + \ldots + 50)$$
$$= 2 \left[\frac{50(50 + 1)}{2} \right]$$
$$= 2550$$

Thus, the sum of the even natural numbers less than or equal to 100 is 2550.

Looking Back A different way to approach this problem is to realize that there are 25 sums of 102, as shown in Figure 3. (Why are there 25 sums to consider, and why is the sum in each pair always 102?)

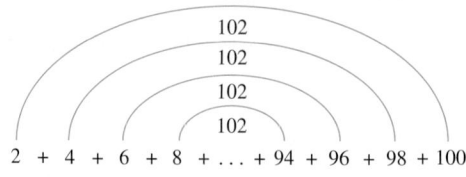

Figure 3

Thus, the sum is $25 \cdot 102 = 2550$.

The numbers $2, 4, 6, 8, \ldots, 100$ are an example of an *arithmetic sequence*—an ordered list of numbers, or *terms*, in which each term starting from the second one differs from the previous term by the same amount—the common difference. The common difference in the above sequence is 2.

▶ NOW TRY THIS 2

Find the sum of consecutive natural numbers shown: $25 + 26 + 27 + \ldots + 120$. Solve this problem in two different ways. 6960

▶ NOW TRY THIS 3

Each of 16 people in a round-robin handball tournament played each other person exactly once. How many games were played? 120 games

Activity Manual

Try *Ten People in a Canoe* to introduce the simplify problem-solving strategy and apply the make a table, make a model, and patterns strategies.

Strategies: Examine a Simpler Case; Make a Table

Often used strategies in problem solving are *examine a simpler case* and *make a table*. A table can be used to look for patterns that emerge in the problem, which in turn can lead to a solution. An example of these strategies is shown on the grade 4 student page below.

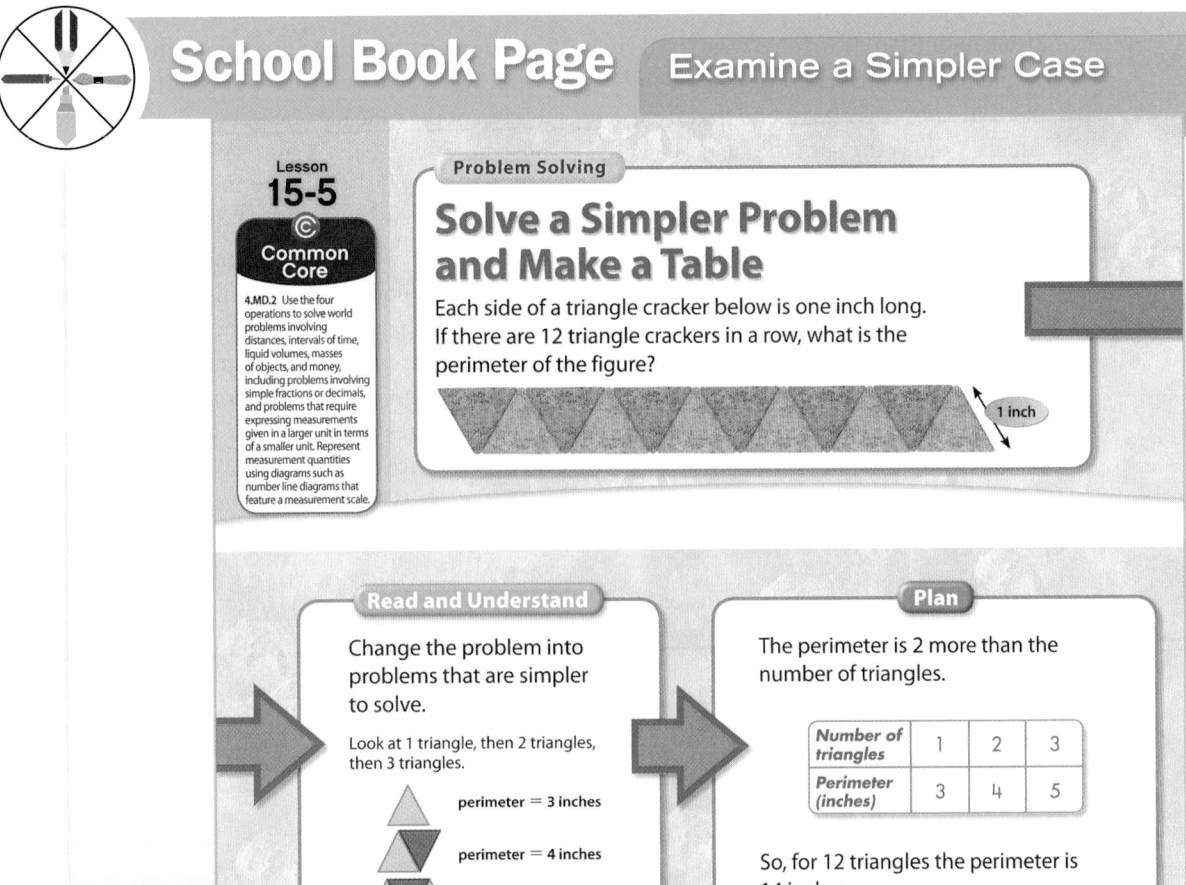

School Book Page   Examine a Simpler Case

Lesson
15-5

Common Core

4.MD.2 Use the four operations to solve world problems involving distances, intervals of time, liquid volumes, masses of objects, and money, including problems involving simple fractions or decimals, and problems that require expressing measurements given in a larger unit in terms of a smaller unit. Represent measurement quantities using diagrams such as number line diagrams that feature a measurement scale.

Problem Solving

Solve a Simpler Problem and Make a Table

Each side of a triangle cracker below is one inch long. If there are 12 triangle crackers in a row, what is the perimeter of the figure?

1 inch

Read and Understand

Change the problem into problems that are simpler to solve.

Look at 1 triangle, then 2 triangles, then 3 triangles.

perimeter = 3 inches

perimeter = 4 inches

perimeter = 5 inches

Plan

The perimeter is 2 more than the number of triangles.

Number of triangles	1	2	3
Perimeter (inches)	3	4	5

So, for 12 triangles the perimeter is 14 inches.

Source: p. 410; From enVisionMATH Common Core (Grade 4). Copyright © 2012 Pearson Education, Inc., or its affiliates. Used by permission. All Rights Reserved.

Activity Manual

Try *What's the Number?* to introduce the make list and elimination problem-solving strategies.

Strategy: Identify a Subgoal

In attempting to devise a plan for solving a problem, a solution to a somewhat easier or more familiar related problem could make it easier. In such a case, finding the solution to the easier problem may become a *subgoal*. The magic square problem on page 8 shows an example of this.

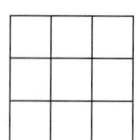

Figure 4

A Magic Square

Arrange the numbers 1 through 9 into a square subdivided into nine smaller squares like the one shown in Figure 4 so that the sum of every row, column, and major diagonal is the same. The result is a *magic square*.

Understanding the Problem Each of the nine numbers $1, 2, 3, \ldots, 9$ must be placed in the small squares, a different number in each square, so that the sums of the numbers in each row, in each column, and in each of the two major diagonals are the same.

Devising a Plan If we knew the fixed sum of the numbers in each row, column, and diagonal, we would have a better idea of which numbers can appear together in a single row, column, or diagonal. Thus *the subgoal* is to find that fixed sum. The sum of the nine numbers, $1 + 2 + 3 + \ldots + 9$, equals 3 times the sum in one row. (Why?) Consequently, the fixed sum can be found using the process developed by Gauss. We have $\dfrac{1 + 2 + 3 + \ldots + 9}{3} = \dfrac{(9 \cdot 10) \div 2}{3} = 15$, so the sum in each row, column, and diagonal must be 15. Next, we need to decide what numbers could occupy the various squares. The number in the center space will appear in four sums, each adding to 15 (two diagonals, the second row, and the second column). Each number in the corners will appear in three sums of 15. (Why?) If we write 15 as a sum of three different numbers 1 through 9 in all possible ways, we could then count how many sums contain each of the numbers 1 through 9. The numbers that appear in at least four sums are candidates for placement in the center square, whereas the numbers that appear in at least three sums are candidates for the corner squares. Thus the new *subgoal* is to write 15 in as many ways as possible as a sum of three different numbers from $1, 2, 3, \ldots, 9$.

Carrying Out the Plan The sums of 15 can be written systematically as follows:

$$9 + 5 + 1$$
$$9 + 4 + 2$$
$$8 + 6 + 1$$
$$8 + 5 + 2$$
$$8 + 4 + 3$$
$$7 + 6 + 2$$
$$7 + 5 + 3$$
$$6 + 5 + 4$$

Note that the order of the numbers in sums like $9 + 5 + 1$ is irrelevant because the order in which additions are done does not matter. In the list, 1 appears in only two sums, 2 in three sums, 3 in two sums, and so on. Table 3 summarizes this information.

Table 3

Number	1	2	3	4	5	6	7	8	9
Number of sums containing the number	2	3	2	3	4	3	2	3	2

The only number that appears in four sums is 5; hence, 5 must be in the center of the square. (Why?) Because 2, 4, 6, and 8 appear 3 times each, they must go in the corners. Suppose we choose 2 for the upper left corner. Then 8 must be in the lower right corner. This is shown in Figure 5(a). Now we could place 6 in the lower left corner or upper right corner. If we choose the upper right corner, we obtain the result in Figure 5(b). The magic square can now be completed, as shown in Figure 5(c).

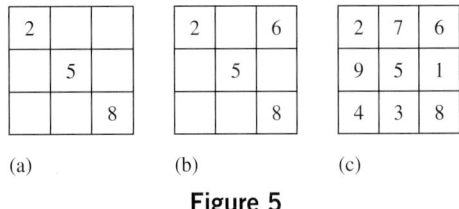

(a)   (b)   (c)

Figure 5

Looking Back We have seen that 5 was the only number among the given numbers that could appear in the center. However, we had various choices for a corner, and so it seems that the magic square we found is not the only one possible. Can you find all the others?

Another way to see that 5 could be in the center square is to consider the sums $1 + 9, 2 + 8, 3 + 7, 4 + 6$, as shown in Figure 6. We could add 5 to each to obtain 15.

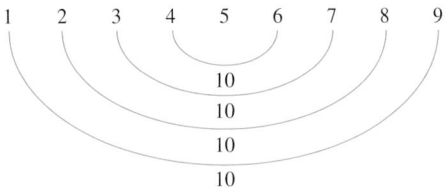

Figure 6

Strategy: Make a Diagram

In the following problem, *making a diagram* helps us to understand the problem and work toward a solution.

Problem Solving	50-m Race Problem

Bill and Jim ran a 50-m race three times. The speed of the runners did not vary. In the first race, Jim was at the 45-m mark when Bill crossed the finish line.

  a. In the second race, Jim started 5 m ahead of Bill, who lined up at the starting line. Who won?

  b. In the third race, Jim started at the starting line and Bill started 5 m behind. Who won?

Understanding the Problem When Bill and Jim ran a 50-m race, Bill won by 5 m; that is, whenever Bill covered 50 m, at the same time Jim covered only 45 m. If Bill started at the starting line and Jim started at the 5-m line or if Jim started at the starting line and Bill started 5 m behind, we are to determine who would win in each case.

Devising a Plan A strategy to determine the winner under each condition is to *make a diagram*. A diagram for the first 50-m race is given in Figure 7(a). In this case, Bill won by 5 m. In the second race, Jim had a 5-m head start and hence when Bill ran 50 m to the finish line, Jim ran only 45 m. Because Jim is 45 m from the finish line, he reached the finish line at the same time as Bill did. This is shown in Figure 7(b). In the third race, because Bill started 5 m behind, we use Figure 7(a) but move Bill back 5 m, as shown in Figure 7(c). From the diagram we determine the results in each case.

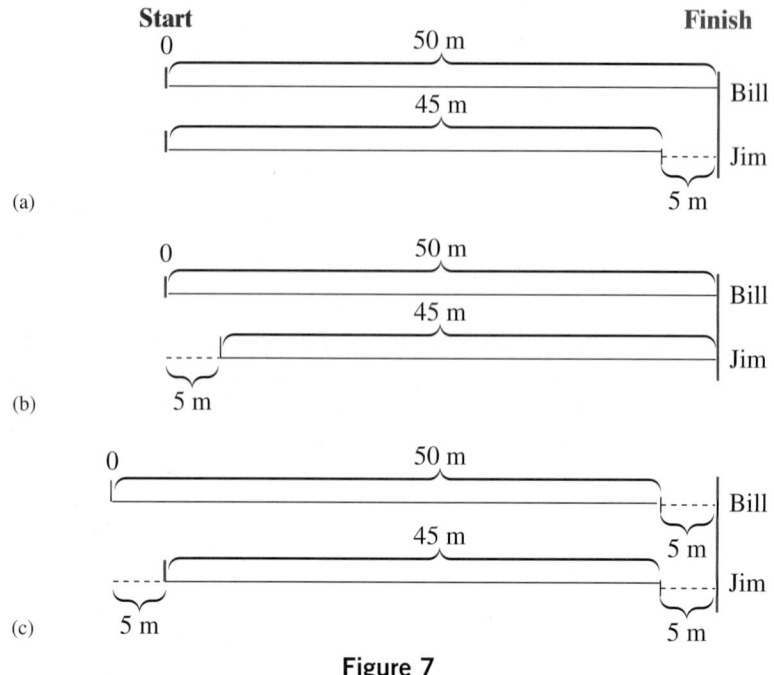

(a)

(b)

(c)

Figure 7

Carrying Out the Plan From Figure 7(b) we see that if Jim had a 5-m head start, then the race ends in a tie. If Bill started 5 m behind Jim, then at 45 m they would be tied. Because Bill is faster than Jim, Bill would cover the last 5 m faster than Jim and win the race.

Looking Back The diagrams show that the solution makes sense and is appropriate. Other problems can be investigated involving racing and handicaps. For example, if Bill and Jim run on a 50-m oval track, how many laps will it take for Bill to lead Jim by one full lap? (Assume the same speeds as earlier.)

▶ **NOW TRY THIS 4**

An elevator stopped at the middle floor of a building. It then moved up 4 floors, stopped, moved down 6 floors, stopped, and then moved up 10 floors and stopped. The elevator was now 3 floors from the top floor. How many floors does the building have? 23 floors

IMAP Video

Watch Arriel use the guess and check strategy.

Strategy: Use Guess and Check

In the strategy of *guess and check*, we first guess at an answer using as reasonable a guess as possible. Then we check to see whether the guess is correct. If not, the next step is to learn as much as possible about the answer based on the guess before making a next guess. This strategy can be regarded as a form of trial and error, in which the information about the error helps us choose what to try next. The guess-and-check strategy is often used when a student does not know how to solve the problem more efficiently or if the student does not yet have the tools to solve the problem in a faster way. Research has suggested that students in grades 1–3 rely primarily on a *guess-and-check* strategy when faced with a mathematical problem. In grades 6–12 this tendency decreases. Older students benefit more from the observed "errors" after a guess when formulating a new "trial."

   The grade 4 student page shown on page 11 gives an example of this strategy, referred to as "try, check, revise."

School Book Page — Try, Check, Revise

| **Try, Check, Revise** | Suzanne spent $27, not including tax, on dog supplies. She bought two of one item and one of another item. What did she buy?

$8 + $8 + $15 = $31
$7 + $7 + $12 = $26
$6 + $6 + $15 = $27 | Use Try, Check, Revise when quantities are being combined to find a total, but you don't know which quantities.

Dog Supplies Sale!
Leash.............................$8
Collar............................$6
Bowls.............................$7
Medium Beds..................$15
Toys...............................$12 |

Source: p. xix; From enVisionMATH Common Core (Grade 4). Copyright © 2012 Pearson Education, Inc., or its affiliates. Used by permission. All Rights Reserved.

Strategy: Work Backward

In some problems, it is easier to start with the result and to *work backward*. This is demonstrated on the grade 6 student page below.

School Book Page — Work Backward

 **Test-Taking Strategies**

Working Backward

The problem-solving strategy *Work Backward* is useful when taking multiple-choice tests. Work backward by testing each choice in the original problem. You will eliminate incorrect answers. Eventually you will find the correct answer.

EXAMPLE

A fruit stand is selling 8 bananas for $1.25. At this rate, how much will 24 bananas cost?

  Ⓐ $1.50   Ⓑ $2.50   Ⓒ $3.75   Ⓓ $5.00

Use mental math to test the choices that are easy to use.

$2.50 is twice $1.25. Twice 8 is only 16, so choice B is not the answer.

$5.00 is four times $1.25. Three times 8 is 24, so choice D is not the correct answer.

Since 24 is between 16 and 32, the cost must be between $2.50 and $5.00. The correct answer is choice C.

Source: p. 199; From enVisionMATH Common Core (Course 1). Copyright © 2013 Pearson Education, Inc., or its affiliates. Used by permission. All Rights Reserved.

Activity Manual

Try *An Ancient Game* to introduce the work backward problem-solving strategy and provide practice using a calculator.

Activity Manual

Try *Magic Number Tricks* to introduce the write an equation problem-solving strategy and reinforce the work backward strategy.

Strategy: Write an Equation

Even though algebraic thinking is involved in the strategy *writing an equation* and may evoke thoughts of traditional algebra, a closer look reveals that algebraic thinking starts very early in students' school lives. For example, finding the missing subtrahend in a problem like

$$\begin{array}{r} 14 \\ -\square \\ \hline 3 \end{array}$$

could be thought of algebraically as $14 - \square = 3$, or as $3 + \square = 14$. In a traditional algebra course, this might be seen as $14 - x = 3$ or $3 + x = 14$ with 11 as a solution. We use such algebraic thinking long before formal algebra is taught. And the strategy of *writing an equation* is used in this text before more formal approaches to algebra are seen in Chapter 8, *Real Numbers and Algebra*.

A student example of *writing an equation* to solve a problem is seen on the grade 6 student page below.

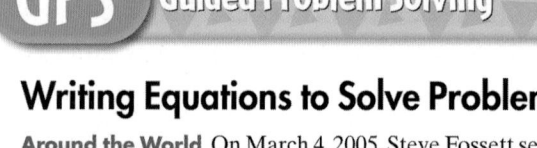
School Book Page   Writing an Equation

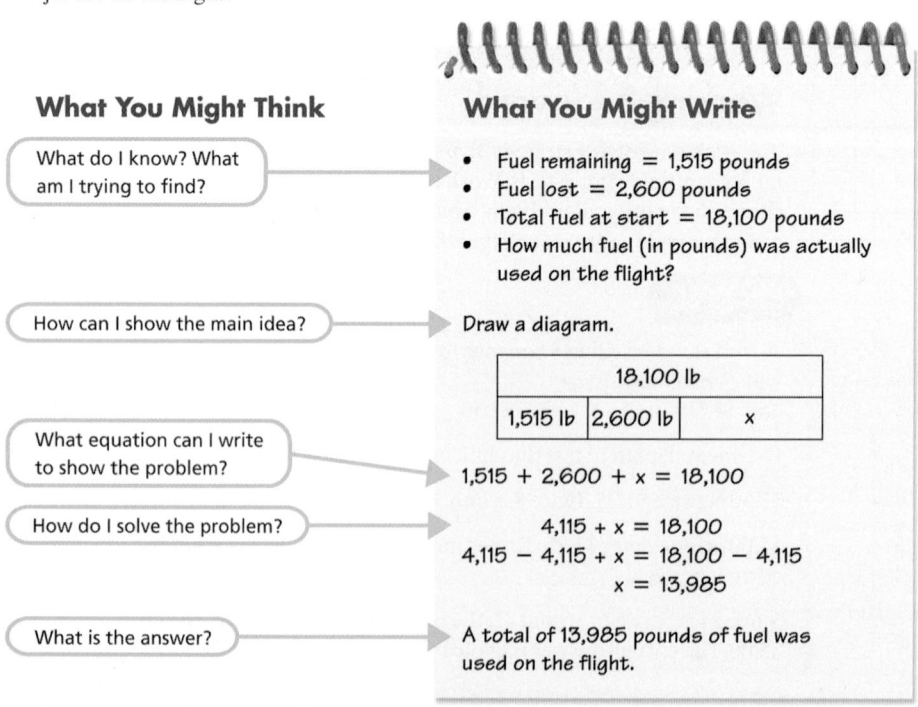

Assessment 1-1A

1. Use the approach in Gauss's Problem to find the following sums of arithmetic sequences (do not use formulas):
   a. $1 + 2 + 3 + 4 + \ldots + 99$ 4950
   b. $1 + 3 + 5 + 7 + \ldots + 1001$ 251,001
   c. $3 + 6 + 9 + 12 + \ldots + 300$ 15,150
   d. $4 + 8 + 12 + 13 + \ldots + 400$ 20,200

2. Use the ideas in drawings (a) and (b) to find the solution to Gauss's Problem for the sum $1 + 2 + 3 + \ldots + n$. Explain your reasoning.   *

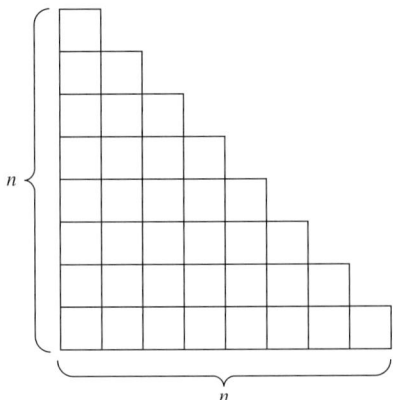

(a)

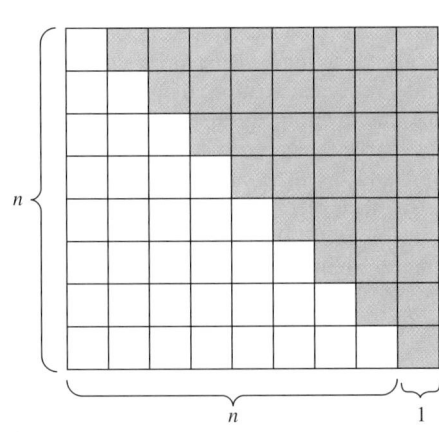

(b)

3. Find the sum $36 + 37 + 38 + 39 + \ldots + 146 + 147$.   10,248

4. Cookies are sold singly or in packages of 2 or 6. With this packaging, how many ways can you buy
   a. 10 cookies?   9
   b. a dozen cookies?   12

5. In a big, red box, there are 7 smaller blue boxes. In each of the blue boxes, there are 7 black boxes. In each of the black boxes, there are 7 yellow boxes. In each of those yellow boxes, there are 7 tiny, gold boxes. How many boxes are there altogether? Explain your answer.   2801

6. How many triangles are in the following figure?   27

7. Without computing each sum of the arithmetic sequence, find which is greater, O or E, and by how much.
$$O = 1 + 3 + 5 + 7 + \ldots + 97$$
$$E = 2 + 4 + 6 + 8 + \ldots + 98 \quad *$$

8. Alababa, Bubba, Cory, and Dandy are in a horse race. Bubba is the slowest; Cory is faster than Alababa but slower than Dandy. Name the finishing order of the horses.   *

9. How many ways can you make change for a $50 bill using $5, $10, and $20 bills?   12

10. The following is a magic square (all rows, columns, and diagonals sum to the same number). Find the value of each letter.   *

17	a	7
12	22	b
c	d	27

11. Debbie and Amy began reading a novel on the same day. Debbie reads 9 pages a day and Amy reads 6 pages a day. If Debbie is on page 72, on what page is Amy?   48

12. The 14 digits of a credit card are written in the boxes shown. If the sum of any three consecutive digits is 20, what is the value of A?   9

A		7									7		4

13. Three closed boxes (A, B, and C) of fruit arrive as a gift from a friend. Each box is mislabeled. How could you choose only one fruit from one box to decide how the boxes should be labeled?   *

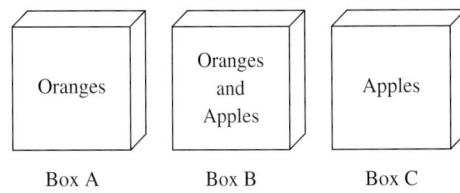

Box A   Box B   Box C

14. An electrician charges $50 per hour and spends $15 a day on gasoline. If she netted $1315 in 4 days, how many hours did she work?   27.5 hours

15. Kathy stood on the middle rung of a ladder. She climbed up three rungs, moved down five rungs, and then climbed up seven rungs. Then she climbed up the remaining six rungs to the top of the ladder. How many rungs are there in the whole ladder?   23

Assessment 1-1B

1. Use the approach in Gauss's Problem to find the following sums of arithmetic sequences (do not use formulas):
   a. $1 + 2 + 3 + 4 + \ldots + 49$ 1225
   b. $1 + 3 + 5 + 7 + \ldots + 2009$ 1,010,025
   c. $6 + 12 + 18 + \ldots + 600$ 30,300
   d. $1000 + 995 + 990 + \ldots + 5$ 100,500

2. Use the diagram below to explain how to find the sum of
   a. the first 100 natural numbers.   *

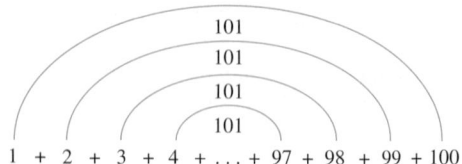

   b. $1 + 2 + 3 + 4 + \ldots + 201$ *

3. Find the sum of $58 + 59 + 60 + 61 + \ldots + 203$.   19,053

4. Eve Merriam* entitled her children's book *12 Ways to Get to 11* (1993). Using only addition and natural numbers, describe 12 ways that one can arrive at the sum of 11.   *

5. Explain why in a drawer containing only two different colors of socks one must draw only three socks to find a matching pair.   *

6. How many squares are in the following figure?   18

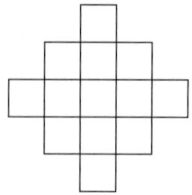

7. If $P = 1 + 3 + 5 + 7 + \ldots + 99$ and $Q = 5 + 7 + 9 + \ldots + 101$ are sums of arithmetic sequences, determine which is greater, P or Q, and by how much.   *

8. The sign says that you are leaving Missoula, Butte is 120 mi away, and Bozeman is 200 mi away. There is a rest stop halfway between Butte and Bozeman. How far is the rest stop from Missoula if both Butte and Bozeman are in the same direction?   160 miles

9. Marc goes to the store with exactly $1.00 in change. He has at least one of each coin less than a half-dollar coin, but he does not have a half-dollar coin.
   a. What is the least number of coins he could have?   11
   b. What is the greatest number of coins he could have?   63

10. Find a 3-by-3 magic square using the numbers 3, 5, 7, 9, 11, 13, 15, 17, and 19.   *

11. Eight marbles look alike, but one is slightly heavier than the others. Using a balance scale, explain how you can determine the heavier one in exactly three weighings.   *

12. Recall the song "The Twelve Days of Christmas":

    On the first day of Christmas my true love gave to me a partridge in a pear tree.
    On the second day of Christmas my true love gave to me two turtle doves and a partridge in a pear tree.
    On the third day of Christmas my true love gave to me three French hens, two turtle doves, and a partridge in a pear tree.

    This pattern continues for 9 more days. After 12 days,
    a. which gifts did my true love give the most? (Yes, you have to remember the song.)   42 geese or 42 swans
    b. how many total gifts did my true love give to me?   364 gifts

13. **a.** Suppose you have quarters, dimes, and pennies with a total value of $1.19. How many of each coin can you have without being able to make change for a dollar?   *
    b. Tell why one of the combinations of coin you have in part (a) is the least number of coins that you can have without being able to make change for a dollar.   *

14. Suppose you buy lunch for the math club. You have enough money to buy 20 salads or 15 sandwiches. The group wants 12 sandwiches. How many salads can you buy?   4

15. One winter night the temperature fell 15 degrees between midnight and 5 A.M. By 9 A.M., the temperature had doubled from what it was at 5 A.M. By noon, it had risen another 10 degrees to 32 degrees. What was the temperature at midnight?   26 degrees

Mathematical Connections 1-1

Answers to Mathematical Connections can be found in the Answers section at the back of the book.

Reasoning

1. Create a 3-by-3 magic square using nine of the ten numbers 20, 21, 22, 23, 24, 25, 26, 27, 28, and 29. Explain your solution and reasoning. List the strategies you have used.

2. In the checkerboard, two squares on opposite corners have been removed. A domino can cover two adjacent squares on the

   board. Can dominoes be arranged in such a way that all the remaining squares on the board can be covered with no dominoes overlapping or hanging off the board? If not, why not? (Hint: Each domino must cover one black and one red square. Compare this with the number of each color of squares on the board.)

3. **a.** If 10 people shake hands with one another exactly once, how many handshakes take place?
   b. Find as many ways as possible to do the problem.
   c. Generalize the solution for n people.

4. Consider a game where you have two distinct piles of objects. Two players alternate moves, each player taking any number (not 0) of objects desired from a single pile. The player who

*Merriam, E. *12 Ways to Get to 11*. New York: Aladdin Paperbacks, 1993.

takes the last object (so nothing is left in either pile) is the winner. If there are *a* objects in one pile and *b* objects in the second, we write (a, b). Given the game $(1, 1)$, the first player loses because if she takes 1 from a pile, the second player takes 1 from the other pile. Answer the following:

a. Show that the first player can win the game $(1, 2)$ as well as $(1, 100)$.

b. Who will win the game $(1, a)$ if $a > 1$? Why?

c. Which player will win the games $(2, 2)$, $(3, 3)$, $(4, 4)$? Why?

d. Which games can the first player always win? Why?

5. Place a half-dollar, a quarter, and a nickel in position *A* as shown in the figure below. Try to move these coins, one at a time, to position *C*. At no time may a larger coin be placed on a smaller coin. Coins may be placed in position *B*.

a. How many moves does it take to get them to position *C*?

b. Now add a penny to the pile and see how many moves are required. This is a simple case of the famous Tower of Hanoi problem, in which ancient Brahman priests were required to move a pile of 64 disks of decreasing size, after which the world would end. How long would it take at a rate of one move per second?

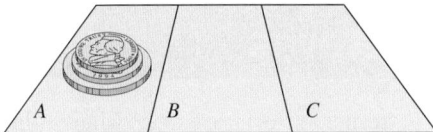

Open-Ended

6. Choose a problem-solving strategy and make up a problem that would use this strategy. Write the solution using Pólya's four-step approach.

7. The distance around the world is approximately 40,000 km. Approximately how many people of average size would it take to stretch around the world if they were holding hands?

Cooperative Learning

8. Work in pairs on the following versions of a game called NIM. A calculator is needed for each pair.

a. Player 1 presses $\boxed{1}$ and $\boxed{+}$ or $\boxed{2}$ and $\boxed{+}$. Player 2 does the same. The players take turns until the target number of 21 is reached. The first player to make the display read 21 is the winner. Determine a strategy for deciding who always wins.

b. Try a game of NIM using the digits 1, 2, 3, and 4, with a target number of 104. The first player to reach 104 wins. What is the winning strategy?

c. Try a game of NIM using the digits 3, 5, and 7, with a target number of 73. The first player to exceed 73 loses. What is the winning strategy?

d. Now play Reverse NIM with the keys $\boxed{1}$ and $\boxed{2}$. Instead of $\boxed{+}$, use $\boxed{-}$. Put 21 on the display. Let the target number be 0. Determine a strategy for winning Reverse NIM.

e. Try Reverse NIM using the digits 1, 2, and 3 and starting with 24 on the display. The target number is 0. What is the winning strategy?

f. Try Reverse NIM using the digits 3, 5, and 7 and starting with 73 on the display. The first player to display a negative number loses. What is the winning strategy?

Connecting Mathematics to the Classroom

9. John asks why the last step of Pólya's four-step problem-solving process, *looking back*, is necessary since he has already given the answer. What could you tell him?

10. A student asks why he just can't make "random guesses" rather than "intelligent guesses" when using the guess-and-check problem-solving strategy. How do you respond?

11. Rob says that it is possible to create a magic square with the numbers 1, 3, 4, 5, 6, 7, 8, 9, and 10. How do you respond?

National Assessments

National Assessment of Educational Progress (NAEP) Questions

1st	2nd	3rd	4th	5th	6th
•	• •	• • •	• • • •	_____	_____
1 dot	3 dots	6 dots	10 dots	__dots	__dots

A pattern of dots is shown above. How many dots would be in the 6th picture?

Answer: _____

Explain how you found your answer.

NAEP, Grade 4, 2009

Susie said, "I have 83¢ but fewer than 10 coins." Show in the chart how many of each coin she could have to total 83¢.

Total number of coins	25¢	10¢	5¢	1¢

NAEP, Grade 4, 2009

Ms. Kim has 45 stickers that she wants to give out to 6 students. The students are sitting in a circle. Ms. Kim gives out one sticker at a time and keeps going around the circle until all the stickers are gone. How many of the students will get more than 7 stickers?

A. 2
B. 3
C. 5
D. 6

NAEP, Grade 4, 2011

Sam folds a piece of paper in half once. There are 2 sections.

Sam folds the paper in half again. There are 4 sections.

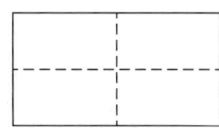

Sam folds the paper in half again. There are 8 sections.

Sam folds the paper in half 2 more times.

Which list shows the number of sections each time Sam folds the paper?
A. 2, 4, 8, 10, 12
B. 2, 4, 8, 12, 24
C. 2, 4, 8, 16, 24
D. 2, 4, 8, 16, 32

NAEP, Grade 4, 2011

1-2 Explorations with Patterns

1-2 Objectives

Students will be able to understand and explain

- Finding patterns and determining if a pattern holds.

- Deductive and inductive reasoning and when to use them.

- Different types of sequences, such as arithmetic, geometric, and Fibonacci.

- Finding the nth term of certain sequences.

- Using differences to find a pattern for neither arithmetic nor geometric sequences.

Mathematics has been described as the study of patterns. Patterns are everywhere—in wallpaper, tiles, traffic, and even television schedules. Police investigators study case files to find the *modus operandi*, or pattern of operation, when a series of crimes are committed. Scientists look for patterns to isolate variables so that they can reach valid conclusions in their research.

Non-numerical patterns abound. For young children, a pattern could appear in non-numerical form as shown in Now Try This 5.

▶ **NOW TRY THIS 5**

a. Find three more terms to continue a pattern:

$$\bigcirc, \triangle, \triangle, \bigcirc, \triangle, \triangle, \bigcirc, \_\_, \_\_, \_\_$$

b. Describe in words the pattern found in part (a).

NTT 5: Answer can be found in Answers at the back of the book.

Patterns can be surprising as seen in the following example.

Example 1

a. Describe any patterns seen in the following:

$$1 + 0 \cdot 9 = 1$$
$$2 + 1 \cdot 9 = 11$$
$$3 + 12 \cdot 9 = 111$$
$$4 + 123 \cdot 9 = 1111$$
$$5 + 1234 \cdot 9 = 11111$$

b. Do the patterns continue? Why or why not?

E-Manipulative Activity

Additional practice with patterns not involving numbers can be found in the *Patterns* activity on the E-Manipulatives disk (or MML). The activity involves completing simple and complex patterns of symbols and colored blocks.

Solution

a. There are several possible patterns. For example, the numbers on the far left are natural numbers. The pattern starts with 1 and continues to the next greater natural number in each successive line. The numbers "in the middle" are products of two numbers, the second of which is 9; the left-most number in the first product is 0; after that the left-most number in each product is formed using successive natural numbers as digits, including an additional digit in each successive line. The five computations given above result in the numbers that are formed using 1s and include an additional 1 in each successive line.

b. The pattern in the complete equation appears to continue for a number of cases, but it does not continue in general; for example,

$$13 + 123456789101112 \cdot 9 = 1{,}111{,}111{,}101{,}910{,}021.$$

This pattern breaks down when the pattern of digits in the number being multiplied by 9 contains previously used digits.

As seen in Example 1, determining a pattern on the basis of a few cases is not reliable. For all patterns found, we should either show the pattern does not hold in general or justify that the pattern always works. Reasoning is used in both cases.

Reasoning

CCSS Some books list various types of reasoning as a problem-solving strategies. However, we think that reasoning underlies problem solving. The *Common Core Standards for Mathematical Practice* lists the following:

- Reason abstractly and quantitatively.
- Construct viable arguments and critique the reasoning of others.
- Look for and express regularity in repeated reasoning. (p. 1)

For students to recognize reasoning and proof as fundamental aspects of mathematics, it is necessary that they use both reasoning and proof in their studies. However, it must be recognized that the level of use depends on the grade level of the students and their understanding of mathematics. For example, from very early ages, students use *inductive reasoning* to look for regularities in patterns based on a very few cases and to develop **conjectures**—statements or conclusions that have not been proven. **Inductive reasoning** is the method of making generalizations based on observations and patterns. Such reasoning may or may not be valid, and conjectures based on inductive reasoning may or may not be true. The validity, or truth, of conjectures in mathematics relies on **deductive reasoning**—the use of definitions, undefined terms, mathematical axioms that are assumed to be true, and previously proved theorems, together with logic to prove these conjectures.

Throughout mathematics, there is a fine interweaving of inductive reasoning and conjecturing to develop conclusions thought to be true. Deductive reasoning is required to prove those statements. In this section we show how inductive reasoning may lead to false conclusions or false conjectures. We show how deductive reasoning is used to prove true conjectures.

Inductive and Deductive Reasoning

Scientists make observations and propose general laws based on patterns. Statisticians use patterns when they draw conclusions based on collected data. This process of *inductive reasoning* may lead to new discoveries; its weakness is that conclusions are drawn only from the collected evidence. If not all cases have been checked, another case may prove the conclusion false. For example, considering only that $0^2 = 0$ and that $1^2 = 1$, we might conjecture that *every number squared is equal to itself.* However, $2^2 \neq 2$. Thus we found an example that contradicts the conjecture. Such an example is a **counterexample**; it shows that the conjecture is false. Sometimes finding a counterexample is difficult, but not finding one immediately does not prove a conjecture is true. A dramatic example of a conjecture that holds true for a very large number of cases but still fails to be true for all cases involves the concept of *perfect squares*. A natural number that is a square of some natural number is a perfect square. For example, 9 is a perfect square because $9 = 3^2$. The conjecture that $1 + 1141n^2$ is never a perfect square is true for every natural number n until $n = 30{,}693{,}385{,}322{,}765{,}657{,}197{,}397{,}208$ when it fails.

Next, consider a pattern that does work and helps solve a problem. How can you find the sum of three consecutive natural numbers without performing the addition? Three examples are given below.

$$14 + 15 + 16; \qquad \text{Sum} = 45$$
$$19 + 20 + 21; \qquad \text{Sum} = 60$$
$$99 + 100 + 101; \qquad \text{Sum} = 300$$

After studying the sums, a pattern of multiplying the middle number by 3 emerges. The pattern suggests other mathematical questions to consider. For example,

1. Does this work for any 3 consecutive natural numbers?
2. How can we find the sum of any odd number of consecutive natural numbers?
3. What happens if there is an even number of consecutive natural numbers?

To answer the first question, we give a proof showing that the sum of three consecutive natural numbers is equal to 3 times the middle number. This proof is an example of *deductive reasoning*.

Proof

Let n be the first of three consecutive natural numbers. Then the three numbers are $n, n + 1$, and $n + 2$. The sum of these three numbers is $n + (n + 1) + (n + 2) = 3n + 3 = 3(n + 1)$. Therefore, the sum of the three consecutive natural numbers is three times the middle number.

A somewhat different way is to let the middle number be m. Then the three consecutive numbers are $m - 1, m$ and $m + 1$. Their sum is $(m - 1) + m + (m + 1) = 3m$, that is, 3 times the middle number. ∎

The Danger of Making Conjectures Based on a Few Cases

The following discussion illustrates the danger of making a conjecture based on a few cases. In Figure 8, we choose points on a circle and connect them to form distinct, nonoverlapping regions. In this figure, 2 points determine 2 regions, 3 points determine 4 regions, and 4 points determine 8 regions. What is the maximum number of regions that would be determined by 10 points?

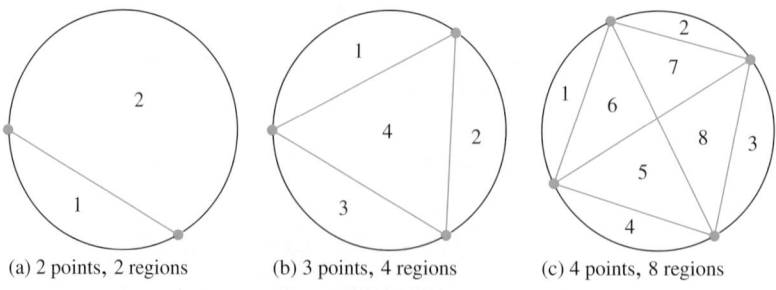

(a) 2 points, 2 regions   (b) 3 points, 4 regions   (c) 4 points, 8 regions

Figure 8

The data from Figure 8 are recorded in Table 4. It appears that each time the number of points increases by 1, the number of regions doubles. If this were true, then for 5 points we would have determined the number of regions by doubling the number of regions with 4 points, or $2 \cdot 8 = 16 = 2^4$, and so on. If we base our conjecture on this pattern, we might believe that for 10 points, we would have 2^9, or 512 regions. (Why?)

Table 4							
Number of points	2	3	4	5	6	. . .	10
Maximum number of regions	2	4	8				?

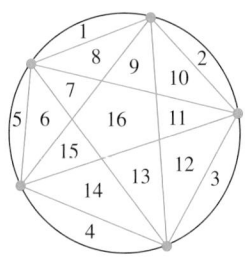

Figure 9

An initial check for this conjecture is to see whether we obtain 16 regions for 5 points. The diagram for 5 points in Figure 9 confirms our guess of 16 regions. For 6 points, the pattern predicts that the number of regions is 32. Choosing the points so that they are neither symmetrically arranged nor equally spaced and counting the regions carefully, we get 31 regions, not 32 as predicted. No matter how the points are located on the circle, the guess of 32 regions is not correct. This counterexample tells us that the doubling pattern is not correct. Note that it does not tell us whether there are 512 regions with 10 points; it tells us only that this conjecture is not true.

▶ **NOW TRY THIS 6**

NTT 6: Answer can be found in Answers at the back of the book.

A *prime number* is a natural number with exactly two distinct positive numbers, 1 and the number itself, that divide it with 0 remainder; for example, 2, 3, 5, 7, 11, and 13 are primes. One day Amy makes a *conjecture* that the formula $y = x^2 + x + 11$ will produce only prime numbers if she substitutes the natural numbers, $1, 2, 3, 4, 5, \ldots$ for x. She shows her work in Table 5 for $x = 1, 2, 3, 4$.

Table 5				
x	1	2	3	4
y	13	17	23	31

   a. What type of reasoning is Amy using?
   b. Try the next several natural numbers and see whether they seem to work.
   c. Show that Amy's conjecture is false for $x = 11$.

Arithmetic Sequences

Activity Manual

Try *What's the Rule?* to investigate arithmetic sequences.

A **sequence** is an ordered arrangement of numbers, figures, or objects. A sequence has items or *terms* identified as *1st, 2nd, 3rd*, and so on. Often, sequences can be classified by their properties. For example, what property do the following first three sequences have that the fourth does not?

   a. $1, 2, 3, 4, 5, 6, \ldots$
   b. $0, 5, 10, 15, 20, 25, \ldots$
   c. $2, 6, 10, 14, 18, 22, \ldots$
   d. $1, 11, 111, 1111, 11111, 111111, \ldots$

In each of the first three sequences, each term—starting from the second term—is obtained from the preceding term by adding a fixed number, the **common difference** or **difference**. In part (a) the difference is 1, in part (b) the difference is 5, and in part (c) the difference is 4. Sequences such as the first three are arithmetic sequences. An **arithmetic sequence** is a sequence in which each successive term from the second term on is obtained from the previous term by the addition or subtraction of a fixed number. The sequence in part (d) is not arithmetic because there is no single fixed number that can be added to or subtracted from the previous term to obtain the next term.

It is convenient to denote the terms of a sequence by a single letter with a subscript. For example in the sequence (b) above $a_1 = 0$, $a_2 = 5$, $a_3 = 10$, and so on. Arithmetic sequences can be generated from objects, as shown in Example 2.

Example 2

Find a numerical pattern in the number of matchsticks required to continue the sequence shown in Figure 10 if each subsequent figure has one more square.

Figure 10

Solution   Assume the matchsticks are arranged, so each figure has one more square on the right than the preceding figure. Note that the addition of a square to an arrangement requires the addition of three matchsticks each time. Thus, with this assumption, the numerical pattern obtained is $4, 7, 10, 13, 16, 19, \ldots$, an arithmetic sequence starting at 4 and having a difference of 3.

An informal description of an arithmetic sequence is one that can be described as an "add d" pattern, where d is the common difference. In Example 2, $d = 3$. In the language of children, the pattern in Example 2 is "add 3." This is an example of a **recursive pattern**. In a recursive pattern, after one or more consecutive terms are given, each successive term of the sequence is obtained from the previous term(s). For example, $11, 14, 17, \ldots$ is another "add 3" sequence starting with 11.

A recursive pattern is typically used in a spreadsheet, as seen in Table 6, where the index column tracks the order of the terms. The headers for the columns are A, B, and so on. The first entry in the A column (in the A1 cell) is 4; to find the term in the A2 cell, we use the number in the A1 cell and add 3. The pattern is continued using the *Fill Down* command. In spreadsheet language, the formula $= A1 + 3$ finds any term after the first by adding 3 to the previous term and using *Fill Down*. A formula based on a recursive pattern is a **recursive formula**. (For more explicit directions on using a spreadsheet, see the Technology Manual, which can be found online at www.pearsonhighered.com/Billstein12einfo.)

Table 6

		A	B
Index Column →	1	4	
	2	7	
	3	10	
	4	13	
	5	16	
	6	19	
	7	22	
	8	25	
	9	28	
	10		
	11		
	12		
	13		

If we want to find the number of matchsticks in the 100th figure in Example 2, we use the spreadsheet or we find an explicit formula or a general rule for finding the number of matchsticks when given the position of the term, the term number. The problem-solving strategy *making a table* is again helpful here.

The spreadsheet in Table 6 provides an easy way to *make a table*. The index column gives the term numbers, and column A gives the terms of the sequence. If we are building such a table without a spreadsheet, it might look like Table 7. Notice that each term is a sum of 4 and a certain number of 3s. We see that the number of 3s is 1 less than the term number. This pattern should continue, since the first term is $4 + 0 \cdot 3$ and each time we increase the number of the term by 1, we add one *more* 3. Thus, it seems that the 100th term is $4 + (100 - 1)3$; and, in general, the ***n*th term** is $4 + (n - 1)3$. Note that $4 + (n - 1)3$ could be written as $3n + 1$.

Table 7

Term Number	Term
1	$4 = 4 + 0 \cdot 3$
2	$7 = 4 + 3 = 4 + 1 \cdot 3$
3	$10 = (4 + 1 \cdot 3) + 3 = 4 + 2 \cdot 3$
4	$13 = (4 + 2 \cdot 3) + 3 = 4 + 3 \cdot 3$
.	.
.	.
.	.
n	$4 + (n - 1)3 = 3n + 1$

Still a different approach to finding the number of matchsticks in the 100th term of Figure 10 might be as follows: If the matchstick figure has 100 squares, we could find the total number of matchsticks by adding the number of horizontal and vertical sticks. There are $2 \cdot 100$ placed horizontally. (Why?) Notice that in the first figure, there are 2 matchsticks placed vertically; in the second, 3; and in the third, 4. In the 100th figure, there should be $100 + 1$ vertical matchsticks. Altogether, there will be $2 \cdot 100 + (100 + 1)$, or 301, matchsticks in the 100th figure. Similarly, in the nth figure, there would be $2n$ horizontal and $n + 1$ vertical matchsticks, for a total of $3n + 1$. This discussion is summarized in Table 8.

Table 8

Term Number	Number of Matchsticks Horizontally	Number of Matchsticks Vertically	Total
1	2	2	4
2	4	3	7
3	6	4	10
4	8	5	13
.	.	.	.
.	.	.	.
.	.	.	.
100	200	101	301
.	.	.	.
.	.	.	.
.	.	.	.
n	$2n$	$n + 1$	$2n + (n + 1) = 3n + 1$

If we are given the value of the term, we can use the formula $3n + 1$ for the nth term in Table 8 to *work backward* and find the term number. For example, given the term 1798, we can write an equation: $3n + 1 = 1798$. Therefore, $3n = 1797$ and $n = 599$. Consequently, 1798 is the 599th term. We could obtain the same answer by solving $4 + (n - 1)3 = 1798$ for n.

In the matchstick problem, we found the nth term of a sequence. If the nth term of a sequence is given, we can find any term of the sequence, as shown in Example 3.

Example 3

Find the first four terms of a sequence, the nth term of which is given by the following, and determine whether the sequence seems to be arithmetic:

a. $4n + 3$ **b.** $n^2 - 1$

Solution

a.

Term Number	Term
1	$4 \cdot 1 + 3 = 7$
2	$4 \cdot 2 + 3 = 11$
3	$4 \cdot 3 + 3 = 15$
4	$4 \cdot 4 + 3 = 19$

Hence, the first four terms of the sequence are 7, 11, 15, 19. This sequence seems arithmetic, with difference 4.

b.

Term Number	Term
1	$1^2 - 1 = 0$
2	$2^2 - 1 = 3$
3	$3^2 - 1 = 8$
4	$4^2 - 1 = 15$

Thus, the first four terms of the sequence are 0, 3, 8, 15. This sequence is not arithmetic, because it has no common difference.

We generalize our work with arithmetic sequences in Chapter 8.

Example 4

The diagrams in Figure 11 show the molecular structure of alkanes, a class of hydrocarbons. C represents a carbon atom and H a hydrogen atom. A connecting segment shows a chemical bond.

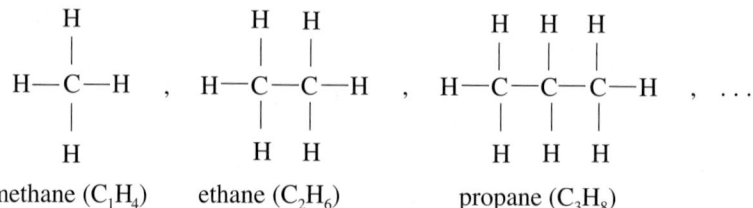

Figure 11

a. Hectane is an alkane with 100 carbon atoms. How many hydrogen atoms does it have?
b. Write a general rule for alkanes C_nH_m showing the relationship between m and n.

Solution

a. To determine the relationship between the number of carbon and hydrogen atoms, we first study the drawing of the alkanes and disregard the extreme left and right hydrogen atoms in each. With this restriction, we see that for every carbon atom, there are two hydrogen atoms. Therefore, there are twice as many hydrogen atoms as carbon atoms plus the two hydrogen atoms at the extremes. For example, when there are 3 carbon atoms, there are $(2 \cdot 3) + 2 = 8$ hydrogen atoms. This notion is summarized in Table 9. If we extend the table for 4 carbon atoms, we get $(2 \cdot 4) + 2$, or 10, hydrogen atoms. For 100 carbon atoms, there are $(2 \cdot 100) + 2$, or 202, hydrogen atoms.

Table 9

No. of Carbon Atoms	No. of Hydrogen Atoms
1	$2 \cdot 1 + 2 = 4$
2	$2 \cdot 2 + 2 = 6$
3	$2 \cdot 3 + 2 = 8$
.	.
.	.
.	.
100	$2 \cdot 100 + 2 = 202$
.	.
.	.
.	.
n	$2n + 2 = m$

b. In general, for n carbon atoms there would be n hydrogen atoms attached above, n attached below, and 2 attached on the sides. Hence, the total number of hydrogen atoms m would be $2n + 2$. It follows that the number of hydrogen atoms is $m = 2n + 2$.

Example 5

A theater is arranged so that there are 20 seats in the first row and 4 additional seats in each consecutive row to the back of the theater, where there are 144 seats. How many rows are there in the theater?

Solution Two strategies lend themselves to this problem. One is to *build a table* and to consider the entries as seen in Table 10.

Table 10

Row Number	Number of Seats
1	20
2	$20 + 4$
3	$20 + 2 \cdot 4$
4	$20 + 3 \cdot 4$
5	$20 + 4 \cdot 4$
.	.
.	.
.	.
n	$20 + (n - 1)4$

Observe that in Table 10 when we write the number of seats as 20 plus the number of additional 4 seats in consecutive rows, the number of 4s added is one less than the number of the row. We know that in the last row there are 144 seats. Thus, we have the following:

$$144 = 20 + (n - 1)4. \quad \text{Subtracting 20 from each side of the equation, we get}$$
$$124 = (n - 1)4 \text{ or } n - 1 = 31.$$

Therefore, $n = 32$, and there are 32 rows in the theater.

A different way to solve the problem is to use a spreadsheet as seen in Table 11, where the number of the row is seen in the index column and the entry in cell A1 indicates 20 seats in that row. Filling down the A column by writing the recursive formula $= A1 + 4$ in cell A2 and using the *Fill Down* command, we find 144 seats in row 32. Thus, there are 32 rows in the theater.

Table 11

Spreadsheet continued.

	A	B			
1	20		19	92	
2	24		20	96	
3	28		21	100	
4	32		22	104	
5	36		23	108	
6	40		24	112	
7	44		25	116	
8	48		26	120	
9	52		27	124	
10	56		28	128	
11	60		29	132	
12	64		30	136	
13	68		31	140	
14	72		32	144	
15	76		33	148	
16	80		34	152	
17	84		35	156	
18	88		36	160	
			37	164	

Activity Manual

Use *Fascinating Fibonacci* to investigate the Fibonacci sequence using a spreadsheet.

Fibonacci Sequence

Dan Brown's popular book *The Da Vinci Code** brought renewed interest to one of the most famous sequences of all time, the **Fibonacci sequence**.

The Fibonacci sequence is

$$1, 1, 2, 3, 5, 8, 13, 21, 34, 55, 89, 144, \ldots.$$

This sequence is not *arithmetic* as there is no fixed difference, d. The first two terms of the Fibonacci sequence are 1, 1 and each subsequent term is the sum of the previous two. If we denote the terms of the Fibonacci sequence by $F_1, F_2, F_3, \ldots$, we have

$$F_1 = F_2 = 1, F_3 = 2, F_4 = 3, F_5 = 5, F_6 = 8, \text{ and so on.}$$

Also $F_3 = F_2 + F_1, F_4 = F_3 + F_2, \ldots$, and in general $F_n = F_{n-1} + F_{n-2}$ for $n = 3, 4, 5, \ldots$. The numbers in the sequence are known as *Fibonacci numbers*.

*Brown, Dan. *The Da Vinci Code*. Doubleday, 2003.

Historical Note

Leonardo de Pisa was born around 1170. His real family name was Bonaccio but he preferred the nickname Fibonacci, derived from *filius Bonacci*, meaning "son of Bonacci." In his book *Liber Abaci* (1202) he described the now-famous rabbit problem, whose solution, the sequence 1, 1, 2, 3, 5, 8, 13, 21, . . . , became known as the *Fibonacci sequence*. ●

Example 6

Consider the two rows of hexagonal cells in Figure 12. The cells in the upper row are numbered by the even natural numbers and the ones in the lower row by the odd natural numbers. You can start at cell 1 or 2 and move to a neighboring cell with a higher number on it. How many different ways are possible to get from start to cell number 7?

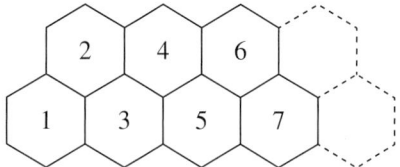

Figure 12

Solution We first use the strategy of *solving a simpler problem*. Since we can start at cell 1 or cell 2, there is only one way to get to cell 1, but two ways to get to cell 2: by starting at cell 2 or via cell 1. There are three ways to get to cell 3: 1–3, 1–2–3, 2–3. There are five ways to cell 4: 2–4, 2–3–4, 1–2–3–4, 1–3–4, 1–2–4.

We can find the number of ways to get to other cells, record the results (see Table 12), and *search for a pattern*.

Table 12	
Cell Number	**Number of Ways to Get to the Cell**
1	1
2	2
3	3
4	5
5	8
6	13

The pattern seems to be similar to the one in the Fibonacci sequence; that is, each term starting from the 3rd is the sum of the preceding two terms. If that is the case, then to reach cell number 7, the number of ways will be 8 + 13 or 21.

But how can we be sure that the pattern exhibited in Table 12 continues as in the Fibonacci sequence? To reach any cell, for example cell 7 in Figure 12, we need to pass through either cell 5 or cell 6 (the two adjacent cells with lower numbers). Thus, the number of ways to reach cell 7 will be the number of ways to reach cell 5, that is, 8 ways, plus the number of ways to reach cell 6, that is, 13 ways. In general, to reach cell number n, we will have to go through cell number $n - 1$ or cell number $n - 2$, that is, we will add the number of ways to reach cell $n - 2$ to the number of ways to reach cell $n - 1$.

▶ **NOW TRY THIS 7**

NTT 7: Answer can be found in Answers at the back of the book.

In Figure 13, we want to know how many different paths there are from point A to point B if one is allowed to walk along the sides or on the indicated diagonals of the squares in the directions indicated by the arrows. Discover a pattern and explain why the pattern continues.

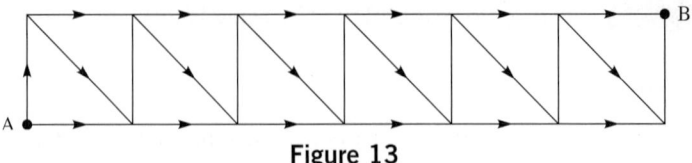

Figure 13

Activity Manual

Try *Paper Powers* and The *King's Problem* to develop understanding of exponents, geometric sequences, and exponential growth.

Geometric Sequences

A child has 2 biological parents, 4 grandparents, 8 great grandparents, 16 great-great grandparents, and so on. The number of generational ancestors form the **geometric sequence** $2, 4, 8, 16, 32, \ldots$. Each successive term of a geometric sequence is obtained from its predecessor by multiplying by a fixed nonzero number, the **ratio**. In this example, both the first term and the ratio are 2. (The ratio is 2 because each person has two parents.) To find the nth term examine the pattern in Table 13.

Table 13

Term Number	Term
1	$2 = 2^1$
2	$4 = 2 \cdot 2 = 2^2$
3	$8 = (2 \cdot 2) \cdot 2 = 2^3$
4	$16 = (2 \cdot 2 \cdot 2) \cdot 2 = 2^4$
5	$32 = (2 \cdot 2 \cdot 2 \cdot 2) \cdot 2 = 2^5$
.	.
.	.
.	.

In Table 13, when the given term is written as a power of 2, the term number is the **exponent**. Following this pattern, the 10th term is 2^{10}, or 1024, the 100th term is 2^{100}, and the nth term is 2^n. Thus, the number of ancestors in the nth previous generation is 2^n. The notation used in Table 13 can be generalized as follows.

Definition of a^n

$$n \text{ factors}$$
If n is a natural number, then $a^n = \overbrace{a \cdot a \cdot a \cdot \ldots \cdot a}$.

If $n = 0$ and $a \neq 0$, then $a^0 = 1$. (This will be motivated in Chapter 2.)

Geometric sequences play an important role in everyday life. For example, suppose we have $1000 in a bank that pays 5% interest annually. (Note that $5\% = 0.05$.) If no money is added or withdrawn, then at the end of the first year we have all of the money we deposited plus 5% more.

Year 1: $\$1000 + 0.05(\$1000) = \$1000(1 + 0.05) = \$1000(1.05) = \$1050$

If no money is added or taken out, then at the end of the second year we would have 5% more money than the previous year.

Year 2: $\$1050 + 0.05(\$1050) = \$1050(1 + 0.05) = \$1050(1.05) = \$1102.50$

The amount of money in the account after any number of years can be found by noting that every dollar invested for one year becomes $1 + 0.05 \cdot 1$, or 1.05 dollars. Therefore, the amount in each year is obtained by multiplying the amount from the previous year by 1.05. The amounts in the bank after each year form a geometric sequence because the amount in each year (starting from year 2) is obtained by multiplying the amount in the previous year by the same number, 1.05. This is summarized in Table 14.

Table 14

Term Number (Year)	Term (Amount at the End of Each Year)
1	$\$1000(1.05)^1$
2	$\$1000(1.05)^2$
3	$\$1000(1.05)^3$
4	$\$1000(1.05)^4$
.	.
.	.
.	.
n	$\$1000(1.05)^n$

NTT 8: a. After 10 hours, there are $2 \cdot 3^{10} = 118,098$ bacteria, and after n hours, there are $2 \cdot 3^n$ bacteria.
b. After 10 hours, there are $2 + 10 \cdot 3 = 32$ bacteria, and after n hours, there are $2 + n \cdot 3$ bacteria. We can see that after only 10 hours geometric growth is much faster than arithmetic growth.

▶ **NOW TRY THIS 8**

a. Two bacteria are in a dish. The number of bacteria triples every hour. Following this pattern, find the number of bacteria in the dish after 10 hours and after n hours.

b. Suppose that instead of increasing geometrically as in part (a), the number of bacteria increases arithmetically by 3 each hour. Compare the growth after 10 hours and after n hours. Comment on the difference in growth of a geometric sequence versus an arithmetic sequence.

Other Sequences

Figurate numbers, based on geometrical patterns, provide examples of sequences that are neither arithmetic nor geometric. Such numbers can be represented by dots arranged in the shape of certain geometric figures. The number 1 is the beginning of most patterns involving figurate numbers. The arrays in Figure 14 represent the first four terms of the sequence of **triangular numbers**.

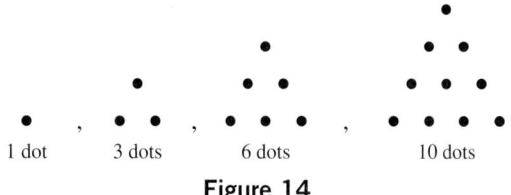

1 dot   3 dots   6 dots   10 dots

Figure 14

The triangular numbers can be written numerically as $1, 3, 6, 10, 15, \ldots$. The sequence $1, 3, 6, 10, 15, \ldots$ is not an arithmetic sequence because there is no common difference, as Figure 15 shows. It is not a geometric sequence because there is no common ratio. It is not the Fibonacci sequence.

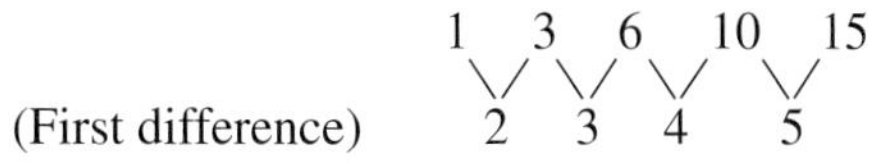

$$\begin{array}{ccccccccc} 1 & & 3 & & 6 & & 10 & & 15 \\ & \diagdown\diagup & & \diagdown\diagup & & \diagdown\diagup & & \diagdown\diagup & \\ \end{array}$$

(First difference)   2   3   4   5

Figure 15

However, the sequence of differences, 2, 3, 4, 5, . . . , appears to form an arithmetic sequence with difference 1, as Figure 16 shows. The next successive terms for the original sequence are shown in color in Figure 16.

$$
\begin{array}{cccccccccccc}
& 1 & & 3 & & 6 & & 10 & & 15 & & 21 & & 28 \\
& & \vee & & \vee & & \vee & & \vee & & \vee & & \vee \\
\text{(First difference)} & & 2 & & 3 & & 4 & & 5 & & 6 & & 7 \\
& & & \vee & & \vee & & \vee & & \vee & & \vee \\
\text{(Second difference)} & & & 1 & & 1 & & 1 & & 1 & & 1
\end{array}
$$

Figure 16

Table 15 suggests a pattern for finding the next terms and the nth term for the triangular numbers. The second term is obtained from the first term by adding 2; the third term is obtained from the second term by adding 3; and so on.

Table 15

Term Number	Term
1	1
2	$3 = 1 + 2$
3	$6 = 1 + 2 + 3$
4	$10 = 1 + 2 + 3 + 4$
5	$15 = 1 + 2 + 3 + 4 + 5$
.	.
.	.
.	.
10	$55 = 1 + 2 + 3 + 4 + 5 + 6 + 7 + 8 + 9 + 10$

We could approach the problem differently without looking for differences. Because the nth triangular number has n dots in the nth row, it is equal to the sum of the dots in the previous triangular number (the $(n - 1)$st one) plus the n dots in the nth row. Following this pattern, the 10th term is $1 + 2 + 3 + 4 + 5 + 6 + 7 + 8 + 9 + 10$, or 55, and the nth term is $1 + 2 + 3 + 4 + 5 + \ldots + (n - 1) + n$. This problem is similar to Gauss's Problem in Section 1-1. Because of the work done in Section 1-1, we know that this sum can be expressed as

$$
\frac{n(n + 1)}{2}.
$$

Next consider the first four *square numbers* in Figure 17. These square numbers, 1, 4, 9, 16 can be written as $1^2, 2^2, 3^2, 4^2$. Continuing, the number of dots in the 10th array would be 10^2, the number of dots in the 100th array would be 100^2, and the number of dots in the nth array would be n^2. The sequence of square numbers is neither arithmetic nor geometric. Investigate whether the sequence of first differences is an arithmetic sequence and tell why.

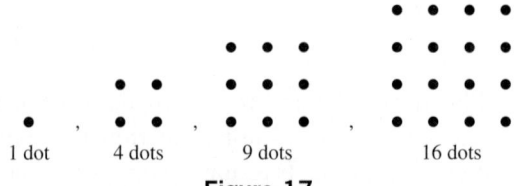

1 dot   4 dots   9 dots   16 dots

Figure 17

When asked to find a pattern for a given sequence, we first look for some easily recognizable pattern and determine whether the sequence is arithmetic or geometric. If a pattern is unclear, taking successive differences may help. *It is possible that none of the methods described reveals a pattern.*

▶ NOW TRY THIS 9

NTT 9: Answer can be found in Answers at the back of the book.

Consider the rectangular numbers in Figure 18 in which the number of columns and the number of rows increase by 1 with each successive "rectangle." What is the 10th rectangular number, and what is the *n*th rectangular number?

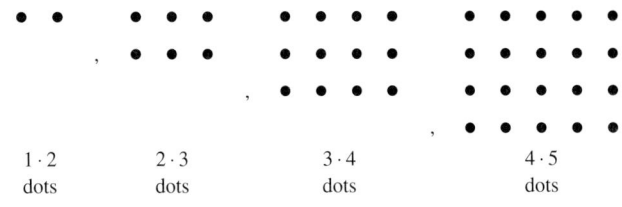

| $1 \cdot 2$ | $2 \cdot 3$ | $3 \cdot 4$ | $4 \cdot 5$ |
| dots | dots | dots | dots |

Figure 18

Example 7

Use differences to find a pattern. Then assuming that the pattern discovered continues, find the seventh term in each of the following sequences:

a. $5, 6, 14, 29, 51, 80, \ldots$ **b.** $2, 3, 9, 23, 48, 87, \ldots$

Solution

a. Figure 19 shows the sequence of first differences.

$$
\begin{array}{ccccccc}
5 & & 6 & & 14 & & 29 & & 51 & & 80 \\
& \vee & & \vee & & \vee & & \vee & & \vee \\
\text{(First difference)} & 1 & & 8 & & 15 & & 22 & & 29
\end{array}
$$

Figure 19

To discover a pattern for the original sequence, we try to find a pattern for the sequence of differences $1, 8, 15, 22, 29, \ldots$. This sequence is an arithmetic sequence with fixed difference 7 as seen in Figure 20.

$$
\begin{array}{ccccccc}
5 & & 6 & & 14 & & 29 & & 51 & & 80 \\
& \vee & & \vee & & \vee & & \vee & & \vee \\
\text{(First difference)} & 1 & & 8 & & 15 & & 22 & & 29 \\
& & \vee & & \vee & & \vee & & \vee \\
\text{(Second difference)} & & 7 & & 7 & & 7 & & 7
\end{array}
$$

Figure 20

Thus, the sixth term in the first difference row is $29 + 7$, or 36, and the seventh term in the original sequence is $80 + 36$, or 116. What number follows 116?

b. Because the second difference is not a fixed number, we go on to the third difference as in Figure 21.

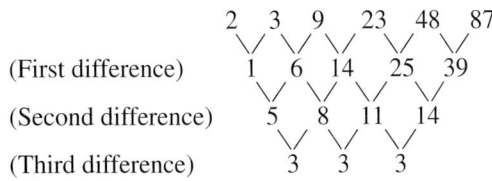

Figure 21

The third difference is a fixed number; therefore, the second difference is an arithmetic sequence. The fifth term in the second-difference sequence is $14 + 3$, or 17; the sixth term in the first-difference sequence is $39 + 17$, or 56; and the seventh term in the original sequence is $87 + 56$, or 143.

Example 8

Figure 22 shows the first three figures of arrays of matchsticks with the number of matchsticks written below the figures. If the next figure consists of a 4-by-4 square arrangement, and each subsequent figure has one more row and one more column of matchsticks squares than the preceding figure, without actually counting, find the number of matchsticks in

   a. the 7th figure
   b. the nth figure.

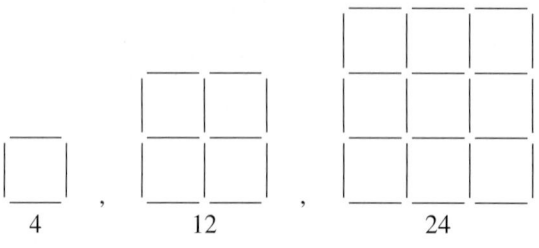

4   12   24

Figure 22

Solution

First Approach

Building the 4th and 5th figures, we find that the number of matchsticks in the figures is 40 and 60 correspondingly.

   To discover a pattern for the original sequence, we use differences. Figure 23 shows first and second differences.

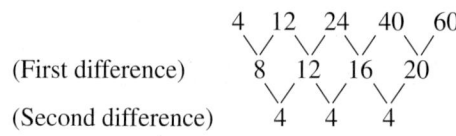

(First difference)

(Second difference)

Figure 23

Thus, the next two terms in the first difference are $20 + 4$ or 24 and $24 + 4 = 28$. Hence the next two terms in the original sequence are $60 + 24$ or 84 and $84 + 28$ or 112. Thus, the answer to part (a) is 112.

   To answer part (b), we use the differences in Figure 21 to write the number of matchsticks in each figure in Table 16.

Table 16

Figure Number	Number of Matchsticks
1	$4 \cdot 1$
2	$12 = 4 + 8 = 4(1 + 2)$
3	$24 = 4 + 8 + 12 = 4(1 + 2 + 3)$
4	$40 = 4 + 8 + 12 + 16 = 4(1 + 2 + 3 + 4)$
5	$60 = 4 + 8 + 12 + 16 + 20 = 4(1 + 2 + 3 + 4 + 5)$
⋮	⋮
n	$4(1 + 2 + 3 + 4 + 5 + \ldots + n)$

Now using Gauss's Problem, we find that the number of matchsticks in the nth figure is

$$4(1 + 2 + 3 + 4 + 5 + \ldots + n) = 4\frac{n(n + 1)}{2} = 2n(n + 1).$$

   Notice that the above solution is based on *inductive reasoning*. Based on a few cases, we decided that the pattern of second differences continues and is always 4. However, we cannot be certain that the second differences continue to be 4. For that reason, we give another approach.

Second Approach

We count the matchsticks in rows and columns. Notice that the number of columns is the same as the number of rows. Thus, we will find the number of matchsticks in the rows and multiply the result by 2. In the first figure, we have 2 rows and 1 matchstick in each. Because we are adding one row and one column to get the subsequent figure, we can write the number of matchsticks in each figure as shown in Table 17.

Table 17

Figure Number	Number of Rows	Number in Each Row	Total in the Rows
1	2	1	$1 \cdot 2$
2	3	2	$2 \cdot 3$
3	4	3	$3 \cdot 4$
4	5	4	$4 \cdot 5$
5	6	5	$5 \cdot 6$
$\vdots$	$\vdots$	$\vdots$	$\vdots$
n	$n + 1$	n	$n(n + 1)$

Because the number of matchsticks in the columns is the same as in the rows, the total number is $2n(n + 1)$. If $n = 7$, then we have the answer for part (a) as $2 \cdot 7(7 + 1)$ or 112.

Assessment 1-2 A

1. For each of the following sequences of figures, determine a possible pattern and draw the next figure according to that pattern:
   a.
   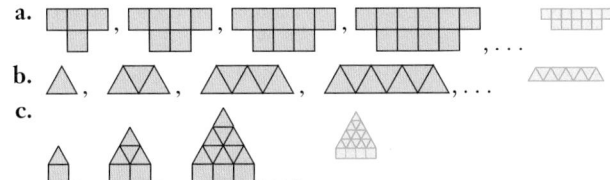
   b. △, △△, △△△, △△△△, ...
   c.

2. Each of the following sequences is either arithmetic or geometric. Identify the sequences and list the next three terms for each.
   a. $1, 5, 9, 13, \ldots$ arithmetic; 17, 21, 25
   b. $70, 120, 170, \ldots$ arithmetic; 220, 270, 320
   c. $1, 3, 9, \ldots$ geometric; 27, 81, 243
   d. $10, 10^3, 10^5, 10^7, \ldots$ geometric; $10^9, 10^{11}, 10^{13}$
   e. $193 + 7 \cdot 2^{30}, 193 + 8 \cdot 2^{30}, 193 + 9 \cdot 2^{30}, \ldots$ *

3. Find the 100th term and the nth term for each of the sequences in exercise 2.   *

4. Use a traditional clock face to determine the next three terms in the following sequence.

   $$1, 6, 11, 4, 9, \ldots \quad 2, 7, 12$$

5. The pattern $1, 8, 27, 64, 125, \ldots$ is a cubic pattern named because $1 = 1 \cdot 1 \cdot 1$ or 1^3, $8 = 2 \cdot 2 \cdot 2$ or 2^3, and so on.
   a. What is the least 4-digit number greater than 1000 in this pattern?   1331

   b. What is the greatest 3-digit number in this pattern?   729
   c. What is the greatest number in this pattern that is less than 10^4?   9261
   d. If this pattern was produced in a normal spreadsheet, what is the number in cell A14?   2744

6. The first windmill has 5 matchstick squares, the second has 9, and the third has 13, as shown. How many matchstick squares are in **(a)** the 10th windmill? **(b)** the nth windmill? **(c)** How many matchsticks will it take to build the nth windmill?   a. 41 b. $4n + 1$ c. $12n + 4$

   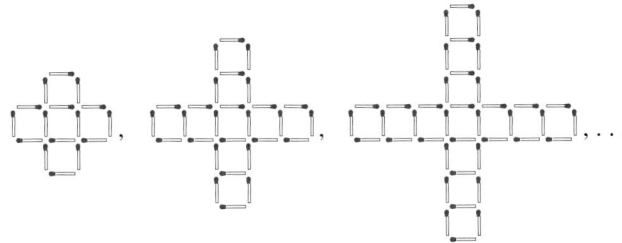

7. In the following sequence, the figures are made of cubes that are glued together. If the exposed surface needs to be painted, how many squares will be painted in **(a)** the 15th figure? **(b)** the nth figure?   a. 62 b. $4n + 2$

8. The school population for a certain school is predicted to increase by 60 students per year for the next 12 years. If the current enrollment is 700 students, what will the enrollment be after 12 years? 1420

9. Joe's annual income has been increasing each year by the same dollar amount. The first year his income was $24,000, and the ninth year his income was $31,680. In which year was his income $45,120? 23rd

10. The first difference of a sequence is the arithmetic sequence $2, 4, 6, 8, 10, \ldots$. Find the first six terms of the original sequence in each of the following cases:
    a. The first term of the original sequence is 3. 3, 5, 9, 15, 23, 33
    b. The sum of the first two terms of the original sequence is 10. 4, 6, 10, 16, 24, 34
    c. The fifth term of the original sequence is 35. *

11. List the next three terms to continue a pattern in each of the following. (Finding differences may be helpful.)
    a. $5, 6, 14, 32, 64, 115, 191$ 299, 447, 644
    b. $0, 2, 6, 12, 20, 30, 42$ 56, 72, 90

12. How many terms are there in each of the following sequences?
    a. $51, 52, 53, 54, \ldots, 251$ 201
    b. $1, 2, 2^2, 2^3, \ldots, 2^{60}$ 61
    c. $10, 20, 30, 40, \ldots, 2000$ 200
    d. $1, 2, 4, 8, 16, 32, \ldots, 1024$ 11

13. Find the first five terms in sequences with the following nth terms.
    a. $n^2 + 2$ 3, 6, 11, 18, 27
    b. $5n + 1$ 6, 11, 16, 21, 26
    c. $10^n - 1$ 9, 99, 999, 9999, 99999
    d. $3n - 2$ 1, 4, 7, 10, 13

14. Find a counterexample for each of the following:
    a. If n is a natural number, then $(n + 5)/5 = n + 1$. *
    b. If n is a natural number, then $(n + 4)^2 = n^2 + 16$. *

15. Assume that the following patterns are built of square tiles and the pattern continues. Answer the questions that follow.

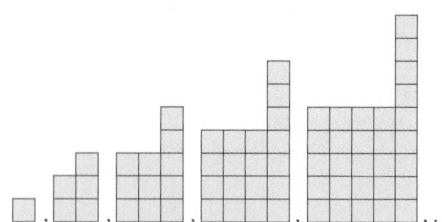

    a. How many square tiles are there in the sixth figure? 41
    b. How many square tiles are in the nth figure? $n^2 + n - 1$
    c. Is there a figure that has exactly 1259 square tiles? If so, which one? (*Hint:* To determine if there is a figure in the

sequence containing exactly 1259 square tiles, first think about the greatest square number less than 1259.) 35th

16. Consider the sequences given in the table below. Find the least number, n, such that the nth term of the geometric sequence is greater than the corresponding term in the arithmetic sequence. 12

Term Number	1	2	3	4	5	6	...	n
Arithmetic	400	600	800	1000	1200	1400	...	
Geometric	2	4	8	16	32	64	...	

17. A sheet of paper is cut into 5 same-size parts. Each of the parts is then cut into 5 same-size parts and so on. Answer the following.
    a. After the 5th cut, how many of the smallest pieces of paper are there? 5^5
    b. After the nth cut, how many of the smallest pieces are there? 5^n

18. Each of the following sequences is labeled either arithmetic or geometric. In each part, find the missing terms.
    a. __, $\underline{39}$, __, __, $\underline{69}$ (arithmetic) 29, 49, 59
    b. __, $\underline{200}$, __, __, $\underline{800}$ (arithmetic) 0, 400, 600
    c. __, $\underline{5^4}$, __, __, $\underline{5^{10}}$ (geometric) $5^2, 5^6, 5^8$

19. A *Fibonacci-type sequence* is a sequence in which the first two terms are arbitrary and in which every term starting from the third is the sum of the two previous terms. Each of the following is a Fibonacci-type sequence. In each part, find the missing terms.
    a. __, __, 1, 1, __, __, __, __ 1, 0, 2, 3, 5, 8
    b. __, __, __, 10, 13, __, 36, 59 $^-$4, 7, 3, 23
    c. $\underline{0}$, $\underline{2}$, __, __, __, __, __, __ 2, 4, 6, 10, 16, 26

20. Starting with 1 and 1 as the first two terms of the Fibonacci sequence, answer the following.
    a. Add the first three terms. The result is one less than which term? *
    b. Add the first four terms. The result is one less than which term? *
    c. Add the first five terms. The result is one less than which term? *
    d. Write a conjecture regarding the sum of the first n terms of the sequence. *
    e. Assuming that your conjecture in part (d) is true, what can you conclude about the sum of the first $n - 2$ terms of the sequence? *

21. A new pair of tennis shoes cost $80. If the price increases each year by 5% of the previous year's price, find the following:
    a. The price after 5 years $102.10
    b. The price after n years $80 \cdot 1.05^n$

Assessment 1-2 B

1. In each of the following, determine a possible pattern and draw the next figure according to that pattern if the sequence continues.
    a.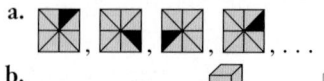
    b.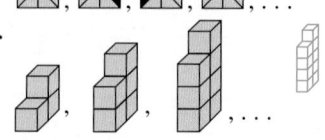

    c.

2. Each of the following sequences is either arithmetic or geometric. Identify the sequences and list the next three terms for each.
    a. $2, 6, 10, 14, \ldots$ *
    b. $0, 13, 26, \ldots$ *
    c. $4, 16, 64, \ldots$ *
    d. $2^2, 2^6, 2^{10}, \ldots$ *
    e. $100 + 4 \cdot 2^{50}, 100 + 6 \cdot 2^{50}, 100 + 8 \cdot 2^{50}, \ldots$ *

3. Find the 100th term and the *n*th term for each of the sequences in exercise 2. *
4. Use a traditional clock face to determine the next three terms in the following sequence:

$$1, 9, 5, 1, \ldots \quad 9, 5, 1$$

5. Observe the following pattern:

$$1 + 3 = 2^2,$$
$$1 + 3 + 5 = 3^2,$$
$$1 + 3 + 5 + 7 = 4^2$$

   a. Conjecture a generalization based on this pattern. *
   b. Based on the generalization in (a), find

$$1 + 3 + 5 + 7 + \ldots + 35. \quad 324$$

6. In the following pattern, one hexagon takes 6 toothpicks to build, two hexagons take 11 toothpicks to build, and so on. How many toothpicks would it take to build
   a. 10 hexagons? 51
   b. *n* hexagons? $5n + 1$

7. Each successive figure below is made of small triangles like the first one in the sequence. Conjecture the number of small triangles needed to make
   a. the 100th figure? 10,000
   b. the *n*th figure? n^2

8. A tank contains 15,360 L of water. At the end of each subsequent day, half of the water is removed and not replaced. How much water is left in the tank after 10 days? 15 liters
9. The Washington Middle School schedule is an arithmetic sequence. Each period is the same length and includes a 4th period lunch. The first three periods begin at 8:10 A.M., 9:00 A.M., and 9:50 A.M., respectively. At what time does the eighth period begin? 2:00 P.M.
10. The first difference of a sequence is 3, 6, 9, 12, 15, . . . Find the first six terms of the original sequence in each of the following cases:
    a. The first term of the original sequence is 3. *
    b. The sum of the first two terms of the original sequence is 7. 2, 5, 11, 20, 32, 47
    c. The fifth term of the original sequence is 34. *
11. List the next three terms to continue a pattern in each of the following. (Finding differences may be helpful.)
    a. 3, 8, 15, 24, 35, 48, . . . 63, 80, 99
    b. 1, 7, 18, 37, 67, 111, . . . 172, 253, 357
12. How many terms are there in each of the following sequences?
    a. $1, 3, 3^2, 3^3, \ldots, 3^{99}$ 100
    b. 9, 13, 17, 21, 25, . . . , 353 87
    c. 38, 39, 40, 41, . . . , 238 201

13. Find the first five terms in sequences with the following *n*th terms.
    a. $5n - 1$ 4, 9, 14, 19, 24
    b. $6n - 2$ 4, 10, 16, 22, 28
    c. $5n + 1$ 6, 11, 16, 21, 26
    d. $n^2 - 1$ 0, 3, 8, 15, 24
14. Find a counterexample for each of the following:
    a. If *n* is a natural number, then $(3 + n)/3 = n$. *
    b. If *n* is a natural number, then $(n - 2)^2 = n^2 - 2^2$. *
15. Assume the following pattern with terms built of square-tiles figures continues and answer the questions that follow.

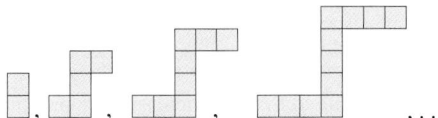

   a. How many square tiles are there in the seventh figure? 20
   b. How many square tiles are in the *n*th figure? $3n - 1$
   c. Is there a figure that has exactly 449 square tiles? If so, which one? Yes, the 150th
16. Consider the sequences given in the table below. Find the least number, *n*, such that the *n*th term of the geometric sequence is greater than the corresponding term in the arithmetic sequence. 9

Term Number	1	2	3	4	5	6	. . .	n
Arithmetic	200	500	800	1100	1400	1700	. . .	
Geometric	1	3	9	27	81	243	. . .	

17. Female bees are born from fertilized eggs, and male bees are born from unfertilized eggs. This means that a male bee has only a mother, whereas a female bee has a mother and a father. If the ancestry of a male bee is traced 10 generations including the generation of the male bee, how many bees are there in all 10 generations? (*Hint:* The Fibonacci sequence might be helpful.) There are 143 bees in all 10 generations.
18. Each of the following sequences is labeled either arithmetic or geometric. In each part, find the missing terms.
    a. __, 49, __, __, 64 (arithmetic) 44, 54, 59
    b. 1, __, __, __, 625 (geometric) 5, 25, 125
    c. __, 3^{10}, __, __, 3^{19} (geometric) $3^7, 3^{13}, 3^{16}$
    d. *a*, __, __, __, 5*a* (arithmetic) 2*a*, 3*a*, 4*a*
19. Each of the following sequences is a Fibonacci-type sequence (see problem 19 Assessment 1-2A). Find the missing terms.
    a. 1, __, __, 7, 11 3, 4
    b. __, 2, __, 4, __ 0, 2, 6
    c. __, __, 3, 4, __ 2, 1, 7
20. Starting with 1 and 1 as the first two terms of the Fibonacci sequence, answer the following.
    a. Check that $F_1 + F_3 = F_4$ *
    b. Compute $F_1 + F_3 + F_5$. The sum is which term? *
    c. Compute $F_1 + F_3 + F_5 + F_7$. The sum is which term? *
    d. Write a conjecture based on the examples in parts (a), (b), and (c). *

Mathematical Connections 1-2

Answers to Mathematical Connections can be found in the Answers section at the back of the book.

Reasoning

1. **a.** If a fixed number is added to each term of an arithmetic sequence, is the resulting sequence an arithmetic sequence? Justify the answer.
   b. If each term of an arithmetic sequence is multiplied by a fixed number, will the resulting sequence always be an arithmetic sequence? Justify the answer.
   c. If the corresponding terms of two arithmetic sequences are added, is the resulting sequence arithmetic?

2. A student says she read that Thomas Robert Malthus (1766–1834), a renowned British economist and demographer, claimed that the increase of population will take place, if unchecked, in a geometric sequence, whereas the supply of food will increase in only an arithmetic sequence. This theory implies that population increases faster than food production. The student is wondering why. How do you respond?

3. Abby and Dan are preparing for a GRE (Graduate Record Exam) to take place in 5 months. Abby starts by studying 10 hours the first week and increases her study by 30 minutes per week. Dan starts at 6 hours per week, but increases his time every week by 45 minutes per week. Answer the following.
   a. How many hours did each student study in week 8?
   b. In which week will Dan first catch up with Abby in the number of hours spent studying per week?

4. The *arithmetic average* of two numbers x and y is $\dfrac{x + y}{2}$. Use *deductive reasoning* to explain why if three numbers a, b, and c form an arithmetic sequence, then b is the arithmetic average of a and c.

5. The numbers $x, y,$ and z are in a Fibonacci-type sequence. If $z = x + y$, use deductive reasoning to find all triples $x, y,$ and z that make an arithmetic sequence as well as consecutive terms in a Fibonacci-type sequence.

6. The figure below shows the first three terms of a sequence of figures containing small square tiles. Some of the tiles are shaded. Notice that the first figure has one shaded tile. The second figure has $2 \cdot 2$, for 2^2, shaded tiles. The third figure has $3 \cdot 3$, or 3^2, shaded tiles. If this pattern of having shaded squares surrounded by white borders continues, answer the following:
   a. How many shaded tiles are there in the nth figure?
   b. How many white tiles are there in the nth figure?

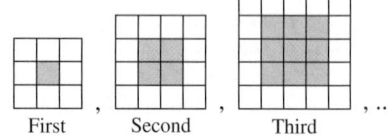

First , Second , Third , ...

Open-Ended

7. Patterns can be used to count the number of dots on the Chinese checkerboard; two patterns are shown here. Determine several other patterns to count the dots.

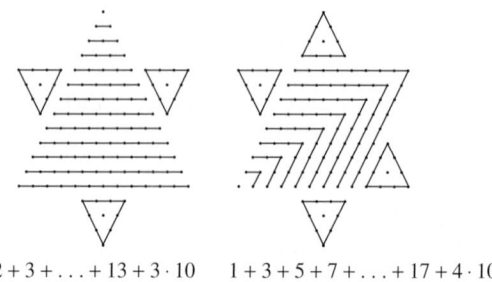

$1 + 2 + 3 + \ldots + 13 + 3 \cdot 10$ $1 + 3 + 5 + 7 + \ldots + 17 + 4 \cdot 10$

8. Make up a pattern involving figurate numbers and find the number of dots in the 100th figure. Describe the pattern and how to find the 100th term.

9. A sequence that follows the same pattern as the Fibonacci sequence but in which the first two terms are any numbers is a Fibonacci type sequence. Choose a few such sequences and compare their behavior to the Fibonacci sequence.

10. Use online sources to find two problems involving the Fibonacci sequence appropriate for the 4th or 5th grades. State the problems and solve them, explaining your solutions in a way appropriate for that level.

Cooperative Learning

11. The following pattern is called *Pascal's triangle*. It was named for the mathematician Blaise Pascal (1623–1662).

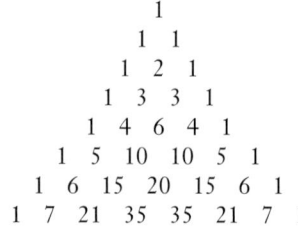

   a. Have each person in the group find four different patterns in the triangle and then share them with the rest of the group.
   b. Add the numbers in each horizontal row. Discuss the pattern that occurs.
   c. Use part (b) to find the sum in the 16th row.
   d. What is the sum of the numbers in the nth row?

12. If the following pattern continued indefinitely, the resulting figure would be called the *Sierpinski triangle*, or *Sierpinski gasket*.

In a group, determine each of the following. Discuss different counting strategies.

a. How many black triangles would be in the fifth figure?
b. How many white triangles would be in the fifth figure?
c. How many black triangles are in the nth figure?

Connecting Mathematics to the Classroom

13. Joey said that 4, 24, 44, and 64 all have remainder 0 when divided by 4, so all numbers that end in 4 must have 0 remainder when divided by 4. How do you respond?
14. Al and Betty were asked to extend the sequence 2, 4, 8, ... Al said his answer of 2, 4, 8, 16, 32, 64, . . . was the correct one. Betty said Al was wrong and it should be 2, 4, 8, 14, 22, 32, 44, ... What do you tell these students?
15. A student claims the sequence 1, 1, 1, 1, . . . is both arithmetic and geometric and would like to know if there are other such sequences. How do you respond?
16. A student claims that she has found an easy way to find the number of terms in an arithmetic sequence: "You take the difference between the last and first terms and divide by the common difference." How do you respond?

Review Problems

17. In a baseball league consisting of 10 teams, each team plays each of the other teams twice. How may games will be played?
18. How many ways can you make change for 40¢ using only nickels, dimes, and quarters?
19. Tents hold 2, 3, 5, 6, or 12 people. What combinations of tents are possible to sleep 26 people if all tents are fully occupied and only one 12-person tent is used?

National Assessments

National Assessment of Educational Progress (NAEP) Questions

The growing number pattern 3, 4, 6, 9, 13, . . . follows a rule. Explain the rule.

Write a new growing pattern beginning with 21 that follows the same rule. 21, _____, _____, _____, _____, _____

NAEP, Grade 4, 2013

Write the next two numbers in the number pattern.

1   6   4   9   7   12   10   ____   ____

Write the rule that you used to find the two numbers you wrote.
NAEP, Grade 4, 2009

A car can seat c adults. A van can seat 4 more than twice as many adults as the car can. In terms of c, how many adults can the van seat?
A. $c + 8$
B. $c + 12$
C. $2c - 4$
D. $2c + 4$
E. $4c + 2$
NAEP, Grade 8, 2013

Which of the following equations has the same solution as the equation $2x + 6 = 32$?
A. $2x = 38$
B. $x - 3 = 16$
C. $x + 6 = 16$
D. $2(x - 3) = 16$
E. $2(x + 3) = 32$
NAEP, Grade 8, 2009

Hint for Solving the Preliminary Problem

Show that if all the coins taken out were genuine, they would weigh 110 ounces. Also notice that if the first box contained all the fake coins, the weight of all the coins would be 109 ounces.

Chapter 1 Summary

KEY CONCEPTS	DEFINITIONS, DESCRIPTIONS, AND THEOREMS
Section 1-1	
Four-step problem-solving process (p. 2)	• Understanding the problem • Carrying out the plan • Devising a plan • Looking Back
Natural numbers (p. 4)	The numbers 1, 2, 3, 4, 5, … The three dots above, called an *ellipsis*, indicate that the pattern of the numbers in the list continues.
Problem-solving strategies (p. 4)	• Look for a pattern • Make a diagram • Examine a related problem • Use guess and check • Examine a simpler case • Work backward • Make a table • Write an equation • Identify a subgoal
Section 1-2	
Conjecture (p. 17)	A statement thought to be true but has not been proven.
Inductive reasoning (p. 17)	Method of making generalizations based on observations and patterns, which may or may not be true.
Deductive reasoning (p. 17)	Method of proving the truth of conjectures through the use of axioms, theorems, undefined terms assumed to be true, and logic.
Counterexample (p. 18)	An example that shows a conjecture is false.
Sequence (p. 19)	An ordered arrangement of numbers, figures, or objects. The individual items of a sequence are the *terms* of the sequence. The *term number* indicates the position of the term in the sequence.
Arithmetic sequence (p. 19)	A sequence in which each successive term from the second term on is obtained from the previous term by adding a fixed number. The fixed number is the *common difference*, or *difference*. An arithmetic sequence involves a *recursive pattern*—each successive term of the sequence is obtained from the previous term(s).
Fibonacci sequence (p. 24)	The sequence in which the first two terms are both 1 and each subsequent term is the sum of the previous two terms: 1, 1, 2, 3, 5, 8, 13, 21, … In general, a sequence in which the first two terms are arbitrary and each subsequent term is the sum of the previous two terms in a *Fibonacci-type sequence*.
Geometric sequence (p. 26)	A sequence in which each successive term from the second term on is obtained from the previous term by multiplying by a fixed nonzero number. The fixed number is the *ratio*.
Exponentiation (p. 26)	If n is a natural number, then $a^n = \underbrace{a \cdot a \cdot a \cdot \ldots \cdot a}_{n \text{ factor}}$. If $n = 0$ and $a \neq 0$, then $a^0 = 1$.
Figurative numbers (p. 27)	Numbers that can be represented by dots arranged in the shape of geometric figures. Figurative numbers provide examples of sequences that are neither arithmetic nor geometric.
Finding common differences (p. 28)	A technique used to discover patterns in sequences.

Chapter 1 Review

1. If today is Sunday, July 4, and next year is not a leap year, what day of the week will July 4 be on next year?   Monday
2. Jackie spent $40 on two items. If she spent $5.90 more on the more expensive item, how much did this item cost? What strategy have you used to solve this problem? $22.95
3. A nursery rhyme states:

   A diller, a dollar, a ten o'clock scholar!
   What makes you come so soon?
   You used to come at ten o'clock,
   But now you come at noon.

   Explain whether the rhyme makes sense mathematically.   *
4. List three more terms that complete a pattern in each of the following; explain your reasoning, and tell whether each sequence is arithmetic or geometric, or neither.
   a. $0, 1, 3, 6, 10,$ ____, ____, ____,   15, 21, 28; neither
   b. $52, 47, 42, 37,$ ____, ____, ____,   32, 27, 22; arithmetic
   c. $6400, 3200, 1600, 800,$ ____, ____, ____,   400, 200, 100; geometric
   d. $1, 2, 3, 5, 8, 13,$ ____, ____, ____,   21, 34, 55; neither
   e. $2, 5, 8, 11, 14,$ ____, ____, ____,   17, 20, 23; arithmetic
   f. $1, 4, 16, 64,$ ____, ____, ____,   256, 1024, 4096; geometric
   g. $0, 4, 8, 12,$ ____, ____, ____,   16, 20, 24; arithmetic
   h. $1, 8, 27, 64,$ ____, ____, ____,   125, 216, 343; neither
5. Find a possible nth term in each of the following.
   a. $5, 8, 11, 14, \ldots$ *
   b. $3, 9, 27, 81, 243, \ldots$ *
   c. $2^2 - 1, 2^3 - 1, 2^4 - 1, 2^5 - 1, \ldots$ *
6. Find the first five terms of the sequences whose nth term is given as follows:
   a. $3n - 2$ 1, 4, 7, 10, 13
   b. $n^2 + n$ 2, 6, 12, 20, 30
   c. $4n - 1$ 3, 7, 11, 15, 19
7. Find the following sums:
   a. $2 + 4 + 6 + 8 + 10 + \ldots + 200$ 10,100
   b. $51 + 52 + 53 + 54 + \ldots + 151$ 10,201
8. Produce a counterexample, if possible, to disprove each of the following. If a statement is true, justify it.
   a. If two odd numbers are added, then the sum is odd. $5 + 3 = 8$; which is not odd.
   b. If a number is odd, then it ends in a 1 or a 3.   *
   c. If two even numbers are added, then the sum is even.   *
9. Complete the following magic square; that is, complete the square so that the sum in each row, column, and diagonal is the same.   *

16	3	2	13
	10		
9		7	12
4		14	

10. How many people can be seated at 12 square tables lined up end to end if each table individually holds four persons?   26
11. Solve the following equations:
    a. $\boxed{} + 2^{60} = 2^{61}$ 2^{60}
    b. $\boxed{}^2 = 625$ 25

12. If fence posts are to be placed in a row 5 m apart, how many posts are needed for 100 m of fence?   21 posts
13. If a complete rotation of a car tire moves a car forward 6 ft, how many rotations of the tire occur before the tire goes off its 50,000 mi warranty?   44,000,000
14. The members of Mrs. Grant's class are standing in a circle; they are evenly spaced and are numbered in order. The student with number 7 is standing directly across from the student with number 17. How many students are in the class?   20
15. A carpenter has three large boxes. Inside each large box are two medium-sized boxes. Inside each medium-sized box are five small boxes. How many boxes are there altogether?   39
16. Use differences to find the next term in the following sequence:

$$5, 15, 37, 77, 141, \_\_\_\_$$ 235

17. An ant farm can hold 100,000 ants. If the farm held 1500 ants on the first day, 3000 ants on the second day, 6000 ants on the third day, and so on forming a geometric sequence, in how many days will the farm be full?   Between the 7th and 8th day.
18. Toma's team entered a mathematics contest where teams of students compete by answering questions that are worth either 3 points or 5 points. No partial credit was given. Toma's team scored 44 points on 12 questions. How many 5-point questions did the team answer correctly?   4
19. Three pieces of wood are needed for a project. They are to be cut from a 90-cm-long piece of wood. The longest piece is to be 3 times as long as the middle-sized piece and the shortest piece is to be 10 cm shorter than the middle-sized piece. How long are the pieces?   10 cm, 20 cm, 60 cm
20. How many four-digit numbers have the same digits as 1993?   12
21. If n and m are natural numbers and $n > m$, how many terms are in the arithmetic sequence $m, m + 1, m + 2, \ldots, n$? (Your answer should be in terms of n and m.) What strategy (or strategies) have you used to answer the question? Why?   *
22. We have two containers, one of which holds 7 cups and the other holds 4 cups. How can we measure exactly 5 cups of water, if we have an unlimited amount of water with which to start?   *
23. The following geometric arrays suggest a sequence of numbers: $2, 6, 12, 20, \ldots$

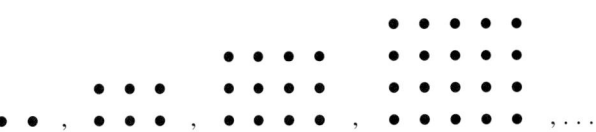

    a. Find the next three terms.   30, 42, 56
    b. Find the 100th term.   10,100
    c. Find the nth term. $n(n + 1)$

24. Each side of each pentagon below is 1 unit long.

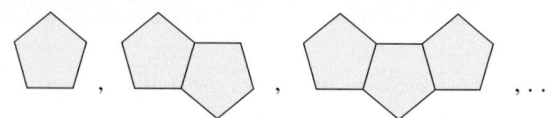

a. Draw a possible next figure in the sequence.   *
b. What is the perimeter (distance around) of each of the first four figures?   5, 8, 11, 14
c. What is the perimeter of the 100th figure?   302
d. What is the perimeter of the nth figure? $3n + 2$

25. a. If every second term in an arithmetic sequence is circled, do the circled terms always constitute an arithmetic sequence? Justify your answer.   *
b. Answer the question in part (a) again, but replace "arithmetic" by "geometric."   *

26. If for every natural number n, the sum of the first n terms of a certain sequence is $n^2 - n$, find the 4th term. Justify your answer.   *

27. Each of the following is a Fibonacci-type sequence. Find the missing terms. In part (c), your answer should be in terms of a. and b.

a. 13 , ___ , ___ , 27   *
b. 137, ___ , ___ , 163   *
c. b , ___ , ___ , a *

Introduction to Logic and Sets

Preliminary Problem

Maria was given the following set of data about 37 college women and invitations to join social organizations: 20 received invitations for Alpha Pi; 21 for Beta Zeta; 12 for Gamma Iota; 10 for Alpha Pi and Beta Zeta; 5 for Beta Zeta and Gamma Iota; 9 for Alpha Pi and Gamma Iota; and 5 received no invitations. She was asked to determine how many women were invited to join all three organizations and how many were invited to Alpha Pi and Beta Zeta but not Gamma Iota. Can you determine the numbers she needs?

If needed, see Hint on page 79.

In this section, tools needed to evaluate arguments are introduced.

2-1 Reasoning and Logic: An Introduction

2-1 Objectives

Students will be able to understand and explain

- Quantifiers and their effects on statements.
- Different forms of statements.
- How to determine if two statements are logically equivalent.
- How to develop logical arguments.
- How to determine whether an argument is valid.

Logic is a tool used in mathematical thinking, reasoning, and sense making. We present some basics of logic in this section and use them in work with set operation in the next section. In logic, a **statement** *is a sentence that is either true or false, but not both*. The following expressions are not statements because their truth values cannot be determined:

1. She has blue eyes.
2. $x + 7 = 18$
3. $2y + 7 > 1$
4. $2 + 3$

5. How are you?
6. Look out!
7. Lincoln was the best president.

Expressions (**1**), (**2**), and (**3**) become statements if, for (**1**), "she" is identified, and for (**2**) and (**3**), values are assigned to x and y, respectively. However, an expression involving he or she or x or y may already be a statement. For example, "If he is over 210 cm tall, then he is over 2 m tall" and "$2(x + y) = 2x + 2y$" are both statements because they are true no matter who *he* is or what the numerical values of x and y are.

Negation and Quantifiers

From a given statement p it is possible to create the **negation** of p, denoted by $\sim p$, which means *not p. If a statement is true, its negation is false; if the statement is false, its negation is true.* Consider the statement "Snow is falling." The negation of this statement may be stated simply as "Snow is not falling."

Example 1

Negate each of the following statements.

  a. $2 + 3 = 5$
  b. A hexagon has six sides.

Solution
  a. $2 + 3 \neq 5$
  b. A hexagon does not have six sides.

At a given time, sentences such as "The shirt I have on is blue" and "The shirt I have on is green" are statements. However, they are not negations of each other. A statement and its negation must have opposite truth values in all possible cases. If the shirt I have on is actually red, then both of the statements are false and, hence, cannot be negations of each other. However, at a given time the statements "The shirt I have on is blue" and "The shirt I have on is not blue" are negations of each other because they have opposite truth values no matter what color the shirt really is.

Some statements involve **quantifiers** and are more complicated to negate. Quantifiers include words such as *all*, *some*, *every*, and *there exists*.

- The quantifiers *all*, *every*, and *no* refer to each and every element and are **universal quantifiers.**
- The quantifiers *some* and *there exists at least one* refer to one or more, or possibly all, of the elements and are **existential quantifiers.**
- *All*, *every*, and *each* have the same mathematical meaning. Similarly, *some* and *there exists at least one* have the same meaning.

Assume the following is true: "Some professors at Paxson University have blue eyes." This means that at least one professor at Paxson University has blue eyes. It does not rule out the possibilities that *all* the Paxson professors have blue eyes or that some of the Paxson professors do not have blue eyes. Because the negation of a true statement is false, neither "Some professors at Paxson University do not have blue eyes" nor "All professors at Paxson have blue eyes" are negations of the original statement. One possible negation of the original statement is "No professors at Paxson University have blue eyes." To discover if one statement is a negation of another, we use arguments to determine whether they have opposite truth values in all possible cases.

Below we give general forms of quantified statements with their corresponding negations.

Statement	**Negation**
Some *a*'s are *b*'s.	No *a* is *b*.
Some *a*'s are not *b*'s.	All *a*'s are *b*'s.
All *a*'s are *b*'s.	Some *a*'s are not *b*'s.
No *a* is *b*.	Some *a*'s are *b*'s.

Example 2

Negate each of the following regardless of its truth value:

a. All students like hamburgers.
b. Some people like mathematics.
c. There exists a natural number n such that $3n = 6$.
d. For all natural numbers n, $3n = 3n$.

Solution
a. Some students do not like hamburgers.
b. No people like mathematics.
c. For all natural numbers n, $3n \neq 6$.
d. There exists a natural number n such that $3n \neq 3n$.

Truth Tables and Compound Statements

To investigate the truth of statements, consider the following puzzle by a foremost writer of logic puzzles, Raymond Smullyan. One of Smullyan's books, *The Lady or the Tiger?*, has a puzzle about a prisoner who must make a choice between two rooms. Each room has a sign on the door and the prisoner knows that exactly *one* of the signs is true. The signs are shown in Figure 1.

IN THIS ROOM THERE IS A LADY AND IN THE OTHER ROOM THERE IS A TIGER.	IN ONE OF THESE ROOMS THERE IS A LADY AND IN ONE OF THESE ROOMS THERE IS A TIGER.
Room 1 Sign	Room 2 Sign

Figure 1

Table 1

Statement	Negation
p	$\sim p$
T	F
F	T

Table 2

		Conjunction
p	q	$p \wedge q$
T	T	T
T	F	F
F	T	F
F	F	F

Table 3

		Disjunction
p	q	$p \vee q$
T	T	T
T	F	T
F	T	T
F	F	F

With the information on the signs in Figure 1, the prisoner can choose the correct room. Consider that if the Room 1 sign is true, then the Room 2 sign must be true. Because this cannot happen, the Room 2 sign must be true, making the Room 1 sign false. Because the Room 1 sign is false, the lady can't be in Room 1 and must be in Room 2.

A symbolic system can help in the study of logic. **Truth tables** are often used to show all possible true-false patterns for statements. Table 1 summarizes the truth table for p and $\sim p$.

From two given statements, it is possible to create a new, *compound statement* by using a connective such as *and*. A **compound statement** may be formed by combining two or more statements. For example, "Snow is falling" and "The ski run is open" together with *and* give "Snow is falling and the ski run is open." Other compound statements can be obtained by using the connective *or*. For example, "Snow is falling or the ski run is open." In logic the symbols $\wedge$ and $\vee$ are used to represent the connectives *and* and *or*, respectively. For example, if p represents "Snow is falling" and q represents "The ski run is open," then "Snow is falling and the ski run is open" is denoted by $p \wedge q$. Similarly, "Snow is falling or the ski run is open" is denoted by $p \vee q$.

The truth value of any compound statement, such as $p \wedge q$, is defined using the truth value of each of the simple statements. Because each of the statements p and q may be either true or false, there are four distinct possibilities in the truth table shown in Table 2. The compound statement $p \wedge q$ is the **conjunction** of p and q and is defined to be true if, and only if, both p and q are true. Otherwise, it is false.

The compound statement $p \vee q$ is the **disjunction** p *or* q. In everyday language, *or* is not always interpreted in the same way. In logic, we use an *inclusive or*. The statement "I will go to a movie or I will read a book" means I will either go to a movie, or read a book, or do both. Hence, in logic, p or q, symbolized $p \vee q$, is defined to be false if both p and q are false and true in all other cases. This is summarized in Table 3.

Example 3

Let p: $2 + 3 = 5$, q: $2 \cdot 3 = 6$, and r: $5 + 3 = 9$.

Classify each of the following statements as true or false.

a. $p \wedge q$ **c.** $\sim p \vee r$ **e.** $\sim (p \wedge q)$
b. $q \vee r$ **d.** $\sim p \wedge \sim q$ **f.** $(p \wedge q) \vee \sim r$

Solution

a. p is true and q is true, so $p \wedge q$ is true.
b. q is true and r is false, so $q \vee r$ is true.
c. $\sim p$ is false and r is false, so $\sim p \vee r$ is false.
d. $\sim p$ is false and $\sim q$ is false, so $\sim p \wedge \sim q$ is false.
e. $p \wedge q$ is true so $\sim (p \wedge q)$ is false.
f. $p \wedge q$ is true and $\sim r$ is true, so $(p \wedge q) \vee \sim r$ is true.

Truth tables are used not only to summarize the truth values of compound statements but also to determine if two statements are *logically equivalent*. *Two statements are* **logically equivalent** *if, and only if, they have the same truth values in every possible situation.* If p and q are logically equivalent, we write $p \equiv q$.

Example 4

Show that $\sim (p \wedge q) \equiv \sim p \vee \sim q$ [First of De Morgan's Laws for logic].

Solution Two compound statements are logically equivalent if they have the same truth values. Truth tables for these statements are given in Table 4.

Table 4

p	q	$p \wedge q$	$\sim(p \wedge q)$	$\sim p$	$\sim q$	$\sim p \vee \sim q$
T	T	T	F	F	F	F
T	F	F	T	F	T	T
F	T	F	T	T	F	T
F	F	F	T	T	T	T

Because the two statements have the same truth values, we know that $\sim (p \wedge q) \equiv \sim p \vee \sim q$.

Example 4 shows that $\sim (p \wedge q) \equiv \sim p \vee \sim q$. In the same way, we can show that $\sim (p \vee q) \equiv \sim p \wedge \sim q$. These equivalencies are **De Morgan's Laws** for logic.

Theorem 2-1: De Morgan's Laws for Logic

a. $\sim (p \wedge q) \equiv \sim p \vee \sim q$
b. $\sim (p \vee q) \equiv \sim p \wedge \sim q$

▶ **NOW TRY THIS 1**

NTT 1: Answer can be found in Answers at the back of the book.

a. Use truth tables to confirm the second De Morgan's Law for logic.
b. Write a sentence showing the use of De Morgan's second law in everyday language.

Conditionals and Biconditionals

Statements expressed in the form "if p, then q" are **conditionals**, or **implications**, and are denoted by $p \rightarrow q$. Such statements also can be read "p implies q." The "if" part of a conditional is the **hypothesis** of the implication and the "then" part is the **conclusion**. Many types of statements can be put in "if-then" form. An example follows:

Statement:	All equilateral triangles have acute angles.
If-then form:	If a triangle is equilateral, then it has acute angles.
	Hypothesis Conclusion

(**Historical Note**)

George Boole (1815–1864), born in Lincoln, England, is called "the father of logic." As a professor at Queens College in Ireland, he used symbols to represent concepts and developed a system of algebraic manipulations to accompany the symbols. His work, a marriage of logic and mathematics, is known as Boolean algebra. ●

An implication may also be thought of as a promise. Suppose Betty makes the promise "If I get a raise, then I will take you to dinner." If Betty keeps her promise, the implication is true; if Betty breaks her promise, the implication is false. Consider the four possibilities in Table 5.

Table 5

Case	p	q	Translation of Symbols	Result
(1)	T	T	Betty gets the raise; she takes you to dinner.	Promise Kept
(2)	T	F	Betty gets the raise; she does not take you to dinner.	Promise Broken
(3)	F	T	Betty does not get the raise; she takes you to dinner.	Promise Kept
(4)	F	F	Betty does not get the raise; she does not take you to dinner.	Promise Kept

Table 6

p	q	Implication $q \to q$
T	T	T
T	F	F
F	T	T
F	F	T

The only case in which Betty breaks her promise is when she gets her raise and fails to take you to dinner, case (2). If she does not get the raise, she can either take you to dinner or not without breaking her promise. The definition of implication is summarized in Table 6. Observe that the only case for which the implication is false is when p is true and q is false.

An implication can be worded in several equivalent ways, as follows:

1. If the sun is shining, then the swimming pool is open. (If p, then q.)
2. If the sun is shining, the swimming pool is open. (If p, q.)
3. The swimming pool is open if the sun is shining. (q if p.)
4. The sun is shining implies the swimming pool is open. (p implies q.)
5. The sun is shining only if the pool is open. (p only if q.)
6. The sun's shining is a sufficient condition for the swimming pool to be open. (p is a sufficient condition for q.)
7. The swimming pool's being open is a necessary condition for the sun to be shining. (q is a necessary condition for p.)

A statement in the form $p \to q$ has three related implication statements, as follows:

Statement:	If p, then q.	$p \to q$
Converse:	If q, then p.	$q \to p$
Inverse:	If not p, then not q.	$\sim p \to \sim q$
Contrapositive:	If not q, then not p.	$\sim q \to \sim p$

Example 5

Write the converse, the inverse, and the contrapositive for the following statement.

If I am in San Francisco, then I am in California.

Solution *Converse:* If I am in California, then I am in San Francisco.
Inverse: If I am not in San Francisco, then I am not in California.
Contrapositive: If I am not in California, then I am not in San Francisco.

Example 5 illustrates that if an implication is true, its converse and inverse are not necessarily true. However, the contrapositive is true. We check these observations on the following true statement: *If a number is a natural number, the number is not 0.* The natural numbers are 1, 2, 3, 4, 5, 6, ... We check the truth of the converse, inverse, and contrapositive.

Converse: *If a number is not 0, then it is a natural number.* This is false; for example, ⁻6 is not 0 and it is not a natural number.

Inverse: *If a number is not a natural number, then it is 0.* This is false; for example, ⁻6 is not a natural number and it also is not 0.

Contrapositive: *If a number is 0, then it is not a natural number.* This is true because the natural numbers are 1, 2, 3, 4, 5, 6 . . . .

The contrapositive of the last statement is the original statement. Hence, the preceding discussion suggests that a statement and its contrapositive are logically equivalent. It follows that a statement and its contrapositive cannot have opposite truth values. We summarize this in the following theorem.

> ### Theorem 2-2: Equivalence of a statement and its contrapositive
>
> The implication $p \rightarrow q$ and its contrapositive $\sim q \rightarrow \sim p$ are logically equivalent; that is, $p \rightarrow q \equiv \sim q \rightarrow \sim p$.

Example 6

Use truth tables to prove that $p \rightarrow q \equiv \sim q \rightarrow \sim p$.

Solution Truth tables for these statements are given in Table 7.

Table 7

p	q	$p \rightarrow q$	$\sim q$	$\sim p$	$\sim q \rightarrow \sim p$
T	T	T	F	F	T
T	F	F	T	F	F
F	T	T	F	T	T
F	F	T	T	T	T

Because the two statements have the same truth values, $p \rightarrow q \equiv \sim q \rightarrow \sim p$.

Connecting a statement and its converse with the connective *and* gives $(p \rightarrow q) \wedge (q \rightarrow p)$. This compound statement can be written as $p \leftrightarrow q$ and usually is read "p if, and only if, q." The statement "p if, and only if, q" is a **biconditional**. *Now Try This 2* considers when a biconditional is true.

▶ **NOW TRY THIS 2**

NTT 2: Answer can be found in Answers at the back of the book.

Build a truth table to determine when a biconditional is true.

Valid Reasoning

In problem solving, the reasoning or argument is said to be **valid** if the conclusion follows unavoidably from the hypotheses. The basis of this determination is a consideration of the possibility of having a true hypothesis and a false conclusion (see Table 6) which yields a false statement or an invalid argument. Consider the following examples:

Hypotheses: All dogs are animals.
                      Goofy is a dog.

Conclusion: Goofy is an animal.

The statement "All dogs are animals" can be pictured with the **Euler diagram** in Figure 2(a).

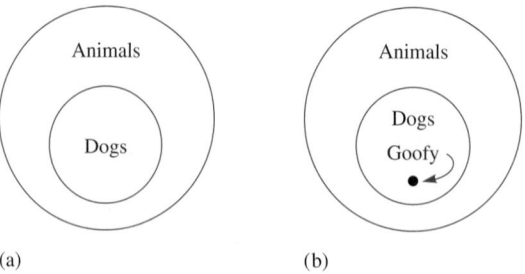

(a)   (b)

Figure 2

The information "Goofy is a dog" implies that Goofy also belongs to the circle containing dogs, as pictured in Figure 2(b). Goofy also belongs to the circle containing animals. Thus, the reasoning is valid because it is impossible to draw a picture that satisfies the hypotheses and contradicts the conclusion.

Consider the following argument.

Hypotheses: All elementary schoolteachers are mathematically literate.
                 Some mathematically literate people are not children.
Conclusion: No elementary schoolteacher is a child.

Let E represent elementary schoolteachers, M represent mathematically literate people, and C represent children. Then the statement "All elementary schoolteachers are mathematically literate" can be pictured as in Figure 3(a). The statement "Some mathematically literate people are not children" can be pictured in several ways. Three of these are illustrated in Figure 3(b) through (d). The conclusion appears to be true with the drawings in Figure 3(b) and (c).

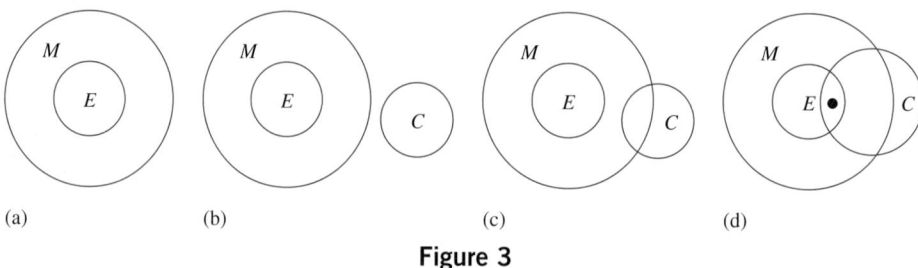

(a)   (b)   (c)   (d)

Figure 3

However, according to Figure 3(d), it is possible that some elementary schoolteachers are children, as noted by the dot placed in the figure and yet the given statements are satisfied. Therefore, the conclusion that "No elementary schoolteacher is a child" does not follow from the given hypotheses. Hence, the reasoning is not valid.

If even one picture can be drawn to satisfy the hypotheses of an argument and contradict the conclusion, the argument is not valid. However, to show that an argument is valid, all possible pictures must show that there are no contradictions. *There must be no way to satisfy the hypotheses and contradict the conclusion if the argument is valid.*

Example 7

Determine whether the following argument is valid:

Hypotheses: In Washington, D.C., all lobbyists have influence.
No one in Washington, D.C., over 6 ft tall has influence.

Conclusion: Persons over 6 ft tall are not lobbyists in Washington, D.C.

Solution   If L represents the lobbyists in Washington, D.C., and I the people who have influence, the first hypothesis is pictured as shown in Figure 4(a). If W represents the people in Washington, D.C., over 6 ft tall, the second hypothesis is pictured in Figure 4(b). Because people over 6 ft tall are outside the circle representing those who have influence and lobbyists are in the circle I, the conclusion is valid and no person over 6 ft tall is a lobbyist in Washington, D.C.

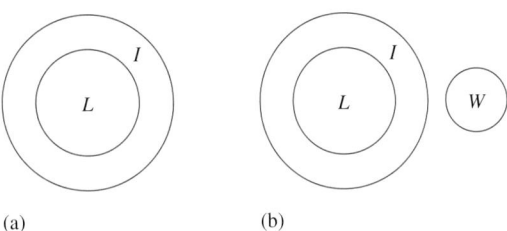

(a)   (b)

Figure 4

A different method for determining whether an argument is valid uses **direct reasoning** and a form of argument called the **law of detachment** (or *modus ponens*). For example, consider the following argument.

Hypotheses: If the sun is shining, then we shall go to the beach.
The sun is shining.

Conclusion: We shall go to the beach.

In general, the law of detachment (or *modus ponens*) is stated as follows.

Theorem 2-3:   Law of Detachment (*Modus Ponens*)

If the statement "if p, then q" is true, and p is true, then q must be true.

Example 8

Show that $[(p \rightarrow q) \wedge p] \rightarrow q$ is always true.

Solution   A truth table for this implication is given in Table 8.

Table 8

p	q	$p \rightarrow q$	$(p \rightarrow q) \wedge p$	$[(p \rightarrow q) \wedge p] \rightarrow q$
T	T	T	T	T
T	F	F	F	T
F	T	T	F	T
F	F	T	F	T

Table 8 is a truth table proof of the law of detachment (*modus ponens*). The statement $[(p \rightarrow q) \wedge p] \rightarrow q$ is a **tautology**, that is, a statement that is true all the time.

Example 9

Determine whether the following argument is valid.

Hypotheses:	If x is a natural number greater than 2, then $x^2 > 4$.
	$x > 2$
Conclusion:	$x^2 > 4$

Solution   Using the law of detachment, *modus ponens*, we see that the conclusion is valid.

A different type of reasoning, **indirect reasoning**, uses a form of argument called the **law of denying the consequent** (or *modus tollens*). For example, consider the following argument.

Hypotheses:	If a figure is a square, then it is a rectangle.
	The figure is not a rectangle.
Conclusion:	The figure cannot be a square.

In general, the law of denying the consequent (or *modus tollens*) is stated as follows:

> **Theorem 2-4:   Law of Denying the Consequent (*Modus Tollens*)**
>
> With a conditional accepted as true but having a false conclusion, the hypothesis must be false. Symbolically if $p \rightarrow q$ is true and q is not true, then p is not true.

The *Law of Denying the Consequent* follows from the fact that an implication and its contrapositive are logically equivalent.

Activity Manual

Try *Eliminate the Impossible* to apply the make a table, make a list, and elimination strategies and introduce the method of indirect reasoning.

Example 10

Determine conclusions for each of the following pairs of true statements:

a. If a person lives in Boston, then the person lives in Massachusetts. Jessica does not live in Massachusetts.

b. If $x = 3$, then $2x \neq 7$. Suppose $2x = 7$.

Solution

a. Jessica does not live in Boston (*modus tollens*).

b. $x \neq 3$ (*modus tollens*)

Finally we consider the **chain rule (*transitivity*)**. Consider the following argument.

Hypotheses:	If I save, I will retire early.
	If I retire early, I will play golf.
Conclusion:	If I save, I will play golf.

In general, the chain rule is stated as follows and proved in the Assessment 2-1A.

Theorem 2-5:   Chain Rule (Transitivity)

If "if p, then q" and "if q, then r" are true, then "if p, then r" is true. Symbolically,
$[(p \rightarrow q) \wedge (q \rightarrow r)] \rightarrow (p \rightarrow r)$.

Example 11

Determine valid conclusions for the following true statements.

   a. If a triangle is equilateral, then it is isosceles. If a triangle is isosceles, it has at least two congruent sides.

   b. If a number is a whole number, then it is an integer. If a number is an integer, then it is a rational number. If a number is a rational number, then it is a real number.

Solution

   a. If a triangle is equilateral, then it has at least two congruent sides.

   b. If a number is a whole number, then it is a real number.

People often draw invalid conclusions based on advertising or other information. Assume, for example, the statement "Healthy people eat Super-Bran cereal" is true. Are the following conclusions valid?

    If a person eats Super-Bran cereal, then the person is healthy.

    If a person is not healthy, the person does not eat Super-Bran cereal.

If the original statement is denoted by $p \rightarrow q$, where p is "a person is healthy" and q is "a person eats Super-Bran cereal," then the first conclusion is the converse of $p \rightarrow q$ (that is, $q \rightarrow p$) and the second conclusion is the inverse of $p \rightarrow q$ (that is, $\sim p \rightarrow \sim q$). Hence, neither is valid.

Assessment 2-1A

1. Determine which of the following are statements and then classify each statement as true or false.
   a. $2 + 4 = 8$ False statement
   b. Los Angeles is a state in the United States.   False statement
   c. What time is it?   Not a statement
   d. $3 \cdot 2 = 6$ True statement

2. Use quantifiers to make each of the following true, where n is a natural number.
   a. $n + 8 = 11$ *   **b.** $n^2 = 4$ *
   c. $n + 3 = 3 + n$ *   **d.** $5n + 4n = 9n$ *

3. Use quantifiers to make each equation in exercise 2 false.   *

4. Write the negation of each of the following statements.
   a. This book has 500 pages.   This book does not have 500 pages.
   b. $3 \cdot 5 = 15$ $3 \cdot 5 \neq 15$
   c. All dogs have four legs.   Some dogs do not have four legs.
   d. Some rectangles are squares.   No rectangles are squares.
   e. Not all rectangles are squares.   All rectangles are squares.
   f. No dogs have fleas.   Some dogs have fleas.

5. Identify the following as true or false.
   a. For some natural numbers n, $n < 6$ and $n > 3$.   True
   b. For all natural numbers n, $n > 0$ or $n < 5$.   True

6. Complete each of the following truth tables.
   a.

p	$\sim p$	$\sim(\sim p)$
T		
F		

   b.

p	$\sim p$	$p \vee \sim p$	$p \wedge \sim p$
T			
F			

   c. Based on part (a), is p logically equivalent to $\sim(\sim p)$?   Yes
   d. Based on part (b), is $p \vee \sim p$ logically equivalent to $p \wedge \sim p$?   No

7. a. Complete the following truth table.   *

p	q	$p \to q$	$\sim p$	$\sim p \vee q$

b. Use columns 3 and 5 to obtain two logically equivalent statement.   *

c. Use your answer to part (b) to write an implication that is logically equivalent to the following: $2 + 3 \neq 5$ or $4 + 6 = 10$.   *

8. If q stands for "This course is easy" and r stands for "Lazy students do not study," write each of the following in symbolic form.

a. This course is easy and lazy students do not study. $q \wedge r$

b. Lazy students do not study or this course is not easy. $r \vee \sim q$

c. It is false that both this course is easy and lazy students do not study. $\sim(q \wedge r)$

d. This course is not easy. $\sim q$

9. Decide on the truth value of each of the following statements.

a. $2 + 3 = 5$ and $4 + 7 = 10$.   False

b. The president of the United States in 2013 was not Barack Obama.   False

c. With every seat filled, the Supreme Court of the United States has 12 justices.   False

d. If a triangle has three sides of the same length, then the triangle has two sides of the same length.   True

e. If a triangle has two sides of the same length, then the triangle has three sides of the same length.   False

10. Write the negation of each statement in exercise 9.   *

11. For each of the following, is the pair of statements logically equivalent?

a. $\sim(p \vee q)$ and $\sim p \vee \sim q$ No

b. $\sim(p \wedge q)$ and $\sim p \wedge \sim q$ No

12. Describe Dr. No as completely as possible.   *

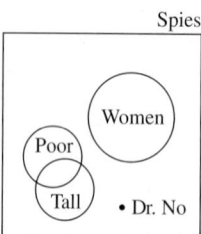

13. Write each of the following in symbolic form if p is the statement "It is raining" and q is the statement "The grass is wet."

a. If it is raining, then the grass is wet. $p \to q$

b. If it is not raining, then the grass is wet. $\sim p \to q$

c. If it is raining, then the grass is not wet. $p \to \sim q$

d. The grass is wet if it is raining. $p \to q$

e. The grass is not wet implies that it is not raining. $\sim q \to \sim p$

f. The grass is wet if, and only if, it is raining. $q \leftrightarrow p$

14. For each of the following implications, write the converse, inverse, and contrapositive.

a. If a triangle is scalene, then it has no two sides of the same length.   *

b. If an angle is not acute, then it is a right angle.   *

c. If Mary is a U.S. citizen, then she is not a citizen of Cuba.   *

d. If a number is a whole number, then it is not a natural number.   *

15. Complete the truth table below to determine whether the negation of $p \wedge \sim q$ is the negation of $p \to q$.   *

p	q	$\sim q$	$p \wedge \sim q$	$\sim(p \wedge \sim q)$	$p \to q$	$\sim(p \to q)$

16. Write a statement logically equivalent to the statement "If a number is a multiple of 8, then it is a multiple of 4."   *

17. Investigate the validity of each of the following arguments.

a. All squares are quadrilaterals.
All quadrilaterals are polygons.
Conclusion: All squares are polygons.   Valid

b. If a student is a freshman, then the student takes mathematics.
Jane is a sophomore.
Conclusion: Jane does not take mathematics.   Invalid

18. Use the truth table below to prove the chain rule (transitivity).   *

p	q	r	$p \to q$	$q \to r$	$(p \to r)$	$(p \to q) \wedge (q \to r)$	$[(p \to q) \wedge (q \to r)] \to (p \to r)$

19. Use the Euler diagram pictured to investigate the validity of the argument that "Some teachers with IQs of 145 are in Mensa."   *

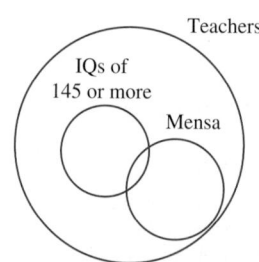

20. For each of the following, form a conclusion that follows logically from the given statements.
   a. Some students in Beta Club are in Integrated Mathematics I. All students who are in Integrated Mathematics I make A's.   *
   b. If I study for the final, then I will pass the final. If I pass the final, then I will pass the course. If I pass the course, then I will look for a teaching job.   *
   c. Every equilateral triangle is isosceles. There exist triangles that are equilateral.   *

21. Write the following in if-then form.
   a. Every figure that is a square is a rectangle.   *
   b. All integers are rational numbers.   *
   c. Polygons with exactly three sides are triangles.   *

22. Use De Morgan's Laws to write a negation of each of the following.
   a. $3 \cdot 2 = 6$ and $1 + 1 \neq 3$. $3 \cdot 2 \neq 6$ or $1 + 1 = 3$.
   b. You can pay me now or you can pay me later.   You cannot pay me now and you cannot pay me later.

Assessment 2-1B

1. Determine which of the following are statements and then classify each statement as true or false:
   a. Shut the window.   Not a statement
   b. He is in town.   Not a statement
   c. $2 \cdot 2 = 2 + 2$ True statement
   d. $2 + 3 = 8$ False statement
   e. Stay put!   Not a statement

2. Use quantifiers to make each of the following true, where n is a natural number:
   a. $n + 0 = n$ *
   b. $n + 1 = n + 2$ *
   c. $3(n + 2) = 12$ *
   d. $n^3 = 8$ *

3. Use quantifiers to make each equation in exercise 2 false.   *

4. Write the negation of each of the following statements.
   a. $6 < 8$ 6 is not less than 8.
   b. Some cats do not have nine lives.   *
   c. All squares are rectangles.   *
   d. Not all numbers are positive.   All numbers are positive.
   e. Some people have blond hair.   All people have blond hair.

5. Identify the following as true or false.
   a. For some natural numbers n, $n > 5$ and $n > 2$.   True
   b. For all natural numbers n, $n > 5$ or $n < 5$.   False

6. **a.** If you know that p is true, what can you conclude about the truth value of $p \vee q$, even if you don't know the truth value of q? $p \vee q$ is true.
   b. If you know that p is false, what can you conclude about the truth value of $p \rightarrow q$? $p \rightarrow q$ is true.

7. If q stands for "You said goodbye" and r stands for "I said hello," write each of the following in symbolic form.
   a. You said goodbye and I said hello. $q \wedge r$
   b. You said goodbye and I did not say hello. $q \wedge \sim r$
   c. I did not say hello or you did not say goodbye. $\sim r \vee \sim q$
   d. It is false that both you said goodbye and I said hello. $\sim(q \wedge r)$

8. Decide on the truth value of each of the following statements.
   a. $4 + 6 = 10$ or $2 + 3 = 5$.   True
   b. A National Football League team can have more than 11 players on the field while a game is in progress.   False
   c. The first president of the United States was George Washington.   True

d. If a quadrilateral has three sides of the same length, the quadrilateral has four sides of the same length.   False
   e. If a rectangle has four sides of the same length, then it has three sides of the same length.   True

9. Write the negation of each statement in exercise 8.   *

10. For each of the following, is the pair of statements logically equivalent?
   a. $\sim(p \vee q)$ and $\sim p \wedge \sim q$ Yes
   b. $\sim(p \wedge q)$ and $\sim p \vee \sim q$ Yes

11. Use the Euler diagram to describe Ms. Makeover as completely as possible.   *

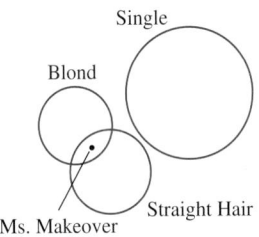

12. Write each of the following in symbolic form if p is the statement "You build it" and q is the statement "They will come."
   a. If you build it, they will come. $p \rightarrow q$
   b. If you do not build it, then they will come. $\sim p \rightarrow q$
   c. If you build it, they will not come. $p \rightarrow \sim q$
   d. They will come if you build it. $p \rightarrow q$
   e. If you do not build it, then they will not come. $\sim p \rightarrow \sim q$
   f. If they will not come, then you do not build it. $\sim q \rightarrow \sim p$

13. For each of the following implications, state the converse, inverse, and contrapositive.
   a. If $x = 3$, then $x^2 = 9$.   *
   b. If it snows, then classes are canceled.   *

14. Iris makes the true statement "If it rains, then I am going to the movies." Does it follow logically that "if it does not rain, then Iris does not go to the movies?"   No, this is the inverse.

15. Investigate the validity of each of the following arguments.
   a. All women are mortal. Hypatia was a woman. Conclusion: Hypatia was mortal.   Valid

b. All of the original Harry Potter books were written by J. K. Rowling.
Dirty Harry was not written by J. K. Rowling.
Conclusion: *Dirty Harry* is not an original Harry Potter book.   Valid

c. Some whole numbers are natural numbers.
Seven is a whole number.
Conclusion: Seven is a natural number.   *

16. For each of the following, form a conclusion that follows logically from the given statements.   Answers vary.

a. All students in Integrated Mathematics I are in Kappa Mu Epsilon.
Helen is in Integrated Mathematics I.   *

b. All engineers need mathematics.
Ron does not need mathematics.   Ron is not an engineer.

c. All bicycles have tires.
All tires use rubber.   All bicycles use rubber.

17. Write each of the following in if-then form.
a. All natural numbers are real numbers.   *
b. Every circle is a closed figure.   *

18. Use De Morgan's Laws to write a negation of each of the following.
a. $3 + 5 \neq 9$ and $3 \cdot 5 = 15$. $3 + 5 = 9$ or $3 \cdot 5 \neq 15$
b. I am going or she is going.   *

19. Use the chain rule to form a logical conclusion based on the following statements.
A square is a rectangle. A rectangle is a parallelogram.
A square is a parallelogram.

Mathematical Connections 2-1

Answers to Mathematical Connections can be found in the Answers section at the back of the book.

Reasoning

1. Explain why commands and questions are not statements.

2. Explain how to write the negation of a quantified statement in the form "Some A's are B's."

3. a. Describe under what conditions a disjunction is true.
b. Describe under what conditions an implication is true.

4. Consider the nursery rhyme.

For want of a nail, the shoe was lost.
For want of a shoe, the horse was lost.
For want of a horse, the rider was lost.
For want of a rider, the battle was lost.
For want of a battle, the war was lost.
Therefore, for want of a nail, the war was lost.

a. Write each line as an *if-then* statement.
b. Does the conclusion (the *therefore* statement) follow logically. Why?

5. In an e-mail address line, a comma or a semicolon is used to separate addresses. From an e-mail sender's standpoint, explain the logical meaning of the punctuation mark.

6. If a statement and its converse are both true, which of the other forms, inverse and contrapositive, are also true, if any?

Open-Ended

7. Table 5 shows a situation used to motivate the definition of the truth values for the implication $p \rightarrow q$. Describe a similar situation that could be used to motivate this same implication.

8. A student in a logic class suggested that one could take the negation of "both sides" of a tautology and construct another tautology. Is this correct? Justify your answer.

Cooperative Learning

9. Discuss the paradox arising from the following set of statements.
(a) This textbook is 2000 pages long.
(b) The author of this textbook is Dante.
(c) The statements (a), (b), and (c) are all false.

10. With classmates divided into small groups, each group should write a series of statements and give them to another group to have the second group write any possible conclusions. The material with conclusions should then be returned to the original writing group for evaluation of the conclusions. The original statements, possible conclusions, and evaluations should all be shared with the class.

Connecting Mathematics to the Classroom

11. Write an explanation for a seventh grader showing how you could explain that even with a false hypothesis, an argument can still be valid.

12. Analyze the following argument that was presented by a sixth-grade student.
Joe said, "Mr. Johnson said that some of us could go to recess at 10:00 A.M., and all got to go but me. He lied."
Describe circumstances in the situation where Mr. Johnson would have lied.

2-2 Describing Sets

Students will be able to understand and explain

- Set language and structure as applied to elementary mathematics.

- Connections between finite sets and whole numbers.

- Uses of one-to-one correspondence.

 In the *Common Core Standards for Mathematical Practice*, we find the following:

Mathematically proficient students make sense of quantities and their relationships in problem situations. They bring two complementary abilities to bear on problems involving quantitative relationships: the ability to decontextualize—to abstract a given situation and represent it symbolically and manipulate the representing symbols as if they have a life of their own, without necessarily attending to their referents—and the ability to contextualize, to pause as needed during the manipulation process in order to probe into the referents for symbols involved. (p. 6)

In this chapter, the groundwork is laid for an understanding of the structure of sets and the logic needed to reason abstractly. This entails both making sense of quantities and their relationships in problem situations and understanding how one begins to "use stated assumptions, definitions, and previously established results in constructing arguments." (p. 6)

In the years from 1871 through 1884, Georg Cantor created *set theory*, which had a profound effect on research and mathematics teaching. Sets, and relations between sets, form a basis for teaching children the *concept* of the set of whole numbers, $\{0, 1, 2, 3, \ldots\}$, and the concept of "less than" as well as addition, subtraction, and multiplication of whole numbers. Understanding whole numbers and operations on whole numbers can be enhanced by the notion of sets. In this section we introduce set notation and relations between sets.

Activity Manual

Try *What's in the Loop* to introduce the concept of a set and to explore the concepts of universal set, complement, equivalent sets, equal sets, and the cardinal number of a set.

The Language of Sets

A **set** is understood to be any collection of objects. Individual objects in a set are **elements**, or **members**, of the set. For example, each letter is an element of the set of letters in the English language. Capital letters are generally used to name sets. The elements of the set are listed inside a pair of braces, $\{\ \}$. The set A of lowercase letters of the English alphabet can be written in set notation as follows:

$$A = \{a, b, c, d, e, f, g, h, i, j, k, l, m, n, o, p, q, r, s, t, u, v, w, x, y, z\}$$

The order in which the elements are written makes no difference, and *each element is listed only once*. Thus, $\{b, o, k\}$ and $\{k, o, b\}$ are considered to be the same set.

We show that an element belongs to a set by using the symbol $\in$. Thus, if $A = \{a, b, c\}$, then $b \in A$. If an element does not belong to a set, we use the symbol $\notin$. For example, $3 \notin A$. In mathematics, the same letter, one lowercase and the other uppercase, cannot be freely interchanged. For example, we have $b \in A$ but $B \notin A$.

A set must be **well defined**; that is, if we are given a set and some particular object, then we must be able to tell whether the object does or does not belong to the set. For example, the set of all citizens of Pasadena, California, who ate rice on January 1, 2014, is well defined. We

---

(**Historical Note**)

Georg Cantor (1845–1918) obtained his doctorate in mathematics in Berlin at age 22. Most of his academic career was spent at the University of Halle. His hope of becoming a professor at the University of Berlin did not materialize because his work gained little recognition during his lifetime. After his death Cantor's work in set theory was praised as an astonishing product of mathematical thought, one of the most beautiful realizations of human activity. ●

personally may not know if a particular resident of Pasadena ate rice or not, but that resident either belongs or does not belong to the set. On the other hand, the set of all tall people is not well defined because there is no clear meaning of "tall."

We may use sets to define mathematical terms. For example from Chapter 1, we have the set of natural numbers in $N = \{0, 1, 2, 3, \ldots\}$. Two common methods of describing sets are the **listing**, or **roster method**, and **set-builder notation**, as seen in the examples:

Listing, or roster method: $C = \{1, 2, 3, 4\}$
Set-builder notation: $C = \{x \mid x \in N, x < 5\}$
The latter notation is read as follows:

C	$=$	$\{$	x	$\mid$	$x \in N,$	$x < 5\}$
Set C	is	the	all	such	x is an element	x is less
	equal	set	elements	that	of the natural	than 5
	to	of	x		numbers, and	

In the set-builder notation $C = \{x \mid x \in N \text{ and } x < 5\}$; the comma is often a place holder for "and." With this notation both conditions, $x \in N$ and $x < 5$, must be true.

In set-builder notation any lowercase letter can be used to represent a general element. Set-builder notation is useful when the individual elements of a set are not known or they are too numerous to list. For example, the set of decimals between 0 and 1 can be written as

$$D = \{x \mid x \text{ is a decimal between 0 and 1}\}.$$

It would be impossible to list all the elements of D. Hence the set-builder notation is indispensable here.

Example 12

Use set-builder notation to write the following sets whose elements are terms of arithmetic sequences.

a. $\{2, 4, 6, 8, 10, \ldots\}$ **b.** $\{1, 3, 5, 7, \ldots\}$

Solution
a. $\{x \mid x \text{ is an even natural number}\}$. Because every even natural number can be written as 2 times some natural number, this set can also be written as $\{x \mid x = 2n, n \in N\}$, or $\{2n \mid n \in N\}$.
b. $\{x \mid x \text{ is an odd natural number}\}$. Because every odd natural number can be written as some even number minus 1, this set can also be written as $\{x \mid x = 2n - 1, n \in N\}$, or $\{2n - 1 \mid n \in N\}$.

In Example 12, we note that the elements in the sets of parts (a) and (b) constitute sequences where elements are ordered.

Example 13

Each of the following sets is described in set-builder notation. Write each of the sets by listing its elements.

a. $C = \{2k + 1 \mid k = 3, 4, 5\}$
b. $D = \{x \mid x \text{ is an even natural number less than 8}\}$

Solution

a. We substitute 3, 4, and 5 for k in $2k + 1$ and obtain the corresponding values shown in Table 9. Thus, $C = \{7, 9, 11\}$.

Table 9

k	$2k + 1$
3	$2 \cdot 3 + 1 = 7$
4	$2 \cdot 4 + 1 = 9$
5	$2 \cdot 5 + 1 = 11$

b. $D = \{2, 4, 6\}$

As noted earlier, the order in which the elements are listed does not matter. If sets A and B are **equal**, written $A = B$, then every element of A is an element of B, and every element of B is an element of A. If A does not equal B, we write $A \neq B$.

Definition of Equal Sets

Two sets are **equal** if, and only if, they contain exactly the same elements.

One-to-One Correspondence

One of the most useful concepts in set theory is a **one-to-one correspondence** between two sets. For example, consider the set of people $P = \{$ Tomas, Dick, Mari $\}$ and the set of swimming lanes $S = \{1, 2, 3\}$. Suppose each person in P is to swim in a lane numbered 1, 2, or 3 so that no two people swim in the same lane. Such a person-lane pairing is a one-to-one correspondence. One way to exhibit a one-to-one correspondence is shown in Figure 5 with arrows connecting corresponding elements.

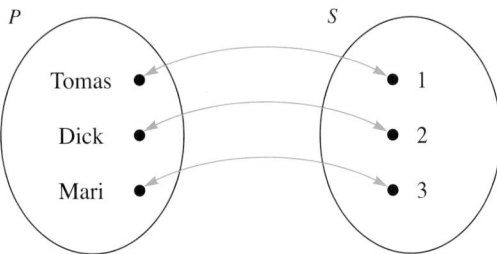

Figure 5

Other possible one-to-one correspondences exist between the sets P and S. All six possible one-to-one correspondences between sets P and S can be listed as follows:

1. Tomas $\leftrightarrow$ 1	**2.** Tomas $\leftrightarrow$ 1	**3.** Tomas $\leftrightarrow$ 2
Dick $\leftrightarrow$ 2	Dick $\leftrightarrow$ 3	Dick $\leftrightarrow$ 1
Mari $\leftrightarrow$ 3	Mari $\leftrightarrow$ 2	Mari $\leftrightarrow$ 3
4. Tomas $\leftrightarrow$ 2	**5.** Tomas $\leftrightarrow$ 3	**6.** Tomas $\leftrightarrow$ 3
Dick $\leftrightarrow$ 3	Dick $\leftrightarrow$ 1	Dick $\leftrightarrow$ 2
Mari $\leftrightarrow$ 1	Mari $\leftrightarrow$ 2	Mari $\leftrightarrow$ 1

Notice that each listing 1–6 represents a single one-to-one correspondence between the sets P and S. A complete set of one-to-one correspondences between sets P and S can also be listed using a table as in Table 10.

Table 10			
		Lanes	
Pairings	**1**	**2**	**3**
1.	Tomas	Dick	Mari
2.	Tomas	Mari	Dick
3.	Dick	Tomas	Mari
4.	Dick	Mari	Tomas
5.	Mari	Tomas	Dick
6.	Mari	Dick	Tomas

The general definition of one-to-one correspondence between two sets follows.

Definition of One-to-One Correspondence

If the elements of sets P and S can be paired so that for each element of P there is exactly one element of S and for each element of S there is exactly one element of P, then the two sets P and S are in **one-to-one correspondence**.

▶ **NOW TRY THIS 3**

NTT 3: Answer can be found in Answers at the back of the book.

Consider a set of four people $\{A, B, C, D\}$ and a set of four swimming lanes $\{1, 2, 3, 4\}$.

  a. Exhibit all the one-to-one correspondences between the two sets.
  b. How many such one-to-one correspondences are there?
  c. Find the number of one-to-one correspondences between two sets with five elements each and explain your reasoning.

Figure 6 shows all possible one-to-one correspondences from Table 10. To read the tree diagram and see the one-to-one correspondence, we follow each branch. The person occupying a specific lane in a correspondence is listed below the lane number. For example, the top branch gives the pairing (Tomas, 1), (Dick, 2), and (Mari, 3).

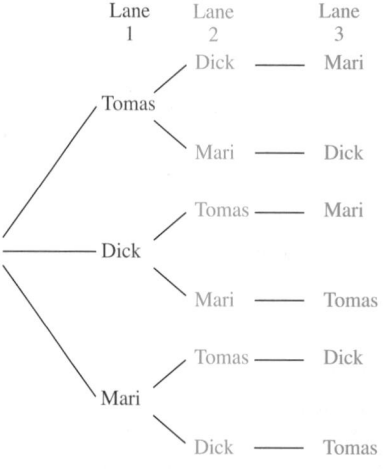

Figure 6

Observe in Figure 6 when assigning a swimmer to lane 1, we have a choice of three people: Tomas, Dick, or Mari. If we put Tomas in lane 1, then he cannot be in lane 2, and hence the second lane must be occupied by either Dick or Mari. In the same way, we see that if Dick is in lane 1, then there are two choices for lane 2: Tomas or Mari. Similarly, if Mari is in lane 1, then again there are two choices for the second lane: Tomas or Dick. Thus, for each of the three ways we can fill the first lane, there are two subsequent ways to fill the second lane, and hence there are $2 + 2 + 2$, or $3 \cdot 2$, or 6 ways to arrange the swimmers in the first two lanes. For each arrangement of the swimmers in the first two lanes, there remains only one possible swimmer to fill the third lane. For example, if Mari fills the first lane and Dick fills the second, then Tomas must be in the third. Thus, the total number of arrangements for the three swimmers is equal to $3 \cdot 2 \cdot 1$, or 6.

Similar reasoning can be used to find how many ice-cream arrangements are possible on a two-scoop cone if 10 flavors are offered. If we count chocolate and vanilla (chocolate on bottom and vanilla on top) different from vanilla and chocolate (vanilla on bottom and chocolate on top) and allow two scoops to be of the same flavor, we proceed as follows. There are 10 choices for the first scoop, and for each of these 10 choices there are 10 subsequent choices for the second scoop. Thus, the total number of arrangements is $10 \cdot 10$, or 100.

The counting argument used to find the number of possible one-to-one correspondences between the set of swimmers and the set of lanes and the previous problem about ice-cream-scoop arrangements are examples of the Fundamental Counting Principle.

Theorem 2-6:   Fundamental Counting Principle

If event M can occur in m ways and, after it has occurred, event N can occur in n ways, then event M followed by event N can occur in $m \cdot n$ ways.

▶ **NOW TRY THIS 4**

Write a mathematical expression showing how many one-to-one correspondences there are between two sets with 17 elements each. $17 \cdot 16 \cdot 15 \cdot \ldots \cdot 3 \cdot 2 \cdot 1$

Equivalent Sets

Closely associated with one-to-one correspondences is the concept of **equivalent sets**. For example, suppose a room contains 20 chairs with one student is sitting in each chair and no one standing. There is a one-to-one correspondence between the set of chairs and the set of students in the room. In this case, the set of chairs and the set of students are not equal sets because the elements are different, but they are considered equivalent sets.

Definition of Equivalent Sets

Two sets A and B are **equivalent**, written $A \sim B$, if, and only if, there exists a one-to-one correspondence between the sets.

The term *equivalent* should not be confused with *equal*. The difference is seen in Example 14.

Example 14

Let

$$A = \{p, q, r, s\}, \qquad B = \{a, b, c\}, \qquad C = \{x, y, z\}, \qquad \text{and} \qquad D = \{b, a, c\}.$$

Compare the sets, using the terms *equal* and *equivalent*.

Solution

Each set is both equivalent to and equal to itself.

Sets A and B are not equivalent ($A \nsim B$) and not equal ($A \neq B$).

Sets A and C are not equivalent ($A \nsim C$) and not equal ($A \neq C$).

Sets A and D are not equivalent ($A \nsim D$) and not equal ($A \neq D$).

Sets B and C are equivalent ($B \sim C$) but not equal ($B \neq C$).

Sets B and D are equivalent ($B \sim D$) and equal ($B = D$).

Sets C and D are equivalent ($C \sim D$) but not equal ($C \neq D$).

Cardinal Numbers

Without knowing how to count, a child might tell that there are as many fingers on the left hand as on the right hand by matching the fingers on one hand with the fingers on the other hand, as in Figure 7. Naturally placing the fingers so that the left thumb touches the right thumb, the left index finger touches the right index finger, and so on, exhibits a one-to-one correspondence between the fingers of the two hands. Similarly, without counting, children realize that if every student in a class sits in a chair and no chairs are empty, there are as many chairs as students, and vice versa.

A one-to-one correspondence between sets helps explain the concept of a number. Consider the five sets $\{a, b\}$, $\{p, q\}$, $\{x, y\}$, $\{b, a\}$, and $\{*, \#\}$; the sets are equivalent to one another and share the property of "twoness"; that is, these sets have the same *cardinal number*, namely, 2. The **cardinal number** of a set S, denoted $n(S)$, indicates the number of elements in the set S. If $S = \{a, b\}$, the cardinal number of S is 2, and we write $n(S) = 2$. *If two sets, A and B, are equivalent, then A and B have the same cardinal number; that is, $n(A) = n(B)$.*

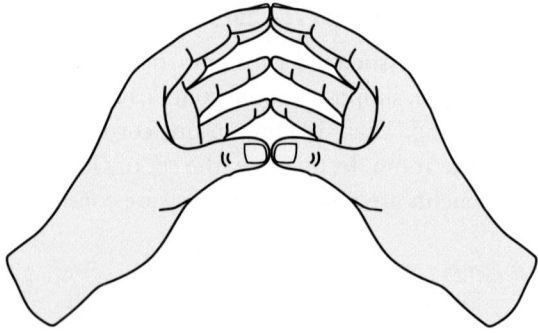

Figure 7

The Empty Set

A set that contains no elements has cardinal number 0 and is an **empty**, or **null, set**. The empty set is designated by the symbol $\varnothing$ or $\{\ \}$. Two examples of empty sets follow.

$$C = \{x \,|\, x \text{ was a state of the United States before 1200 CE}\}$$
$$D = \{x \,|\, x \text{ is a natural number such that } x^2 = 17\}$$

The empty set is often incorrectly written as $\{\varnothing\}$. This set is not empty because it contains one element, namely $\varnothing$. Likewise, $\{0\}$ does not represent the empty set. Why?

A set is a **finite set** if the cardinal number of the set is zero or a natural number. The set N of natural numbers is an **infinite set**; it is not finite. The set W, containing all the natural numbers and 0, is the set of **whole numbers**: $W = \{0, 1, 2, 3, \ldots\}$. W is an infinite set.

▶ **NOW TRY THIS 5**

NTT 5: Answer can be found in Answers at the back of the book.

Explain why there can be no greatest natural number; that is, explain why the set of natural numbers is not a finite set.

More About Sets

The **universal set**, or the **universe**, denoted U, is the set that contains all elements being considered in a given discussion. Suppose $U = \{x \,|\, x \text{ is a person living in California}\}$ and $F = \{x \,|\, x \text{ is a female living in California}\}$. The universal set, U, and set F can be represented by a diagram, as in Figure 8(a). The universal set is represented by a large rectangle, and F is indicated by the circle inside the rectangle, as shown in Figure 8(a). This figure is an example of a **Venn diagram**, named after the British logician and philosopher John Venn (1834–1923). The set of elements in the universe that are not in F, denoted by $\overline{F}$, is the set of males living in California and is the **complement** of F. It is represented by the shaded region in Figure 8(b).

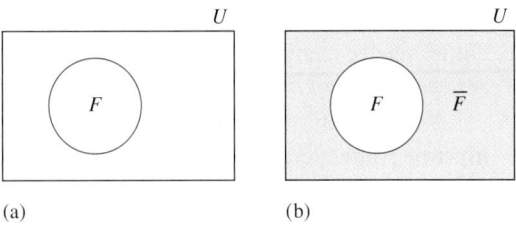

(a)   (b)

Figure 8

Definition of Set Complement

The **complement** of a set A, written $\overline{A}$, is the set of all elements in a given universal set U that are not in A; that is, $\overline{A} = \{x \,|\, x \in U \text{ and } x \notin A\}$.

Example 15

a. If $U = \{a, b, c, d\}$ and $B = \{c, d\}$, find $\overline{B}, \overline{U}$, and $\overline{\varnothing}$.
b. If $U = \{x \,|\, x \text{ is an animal in the zoo}\}$ and $S = \{x \,|\, x \text{ is a snake in the zoo}\}$, describe $\overline{S}$.
c. If $U = N$, $E = \{2, 4, 6, 8, \ldots\}$, and $O = \{1, 3, 5, 7, \ldots\}$, find $\overline{E}$, and $\overline{O}$.

Solution
a. $\overline{B} = \{a, b\}$, $\overline{U} = \varnothing$, and $\overline{\varnothing} = U$
b. $\overline{S} = \{x \,|\, x \text{ is an animal in the zoo and } x \text{ is not a snake}\}$
c. $\overline{E} = O$ and $\overline{O} = E$

Subsets

Consider the sets $A = \{1, 2, 3, 4, 5, 6\}$ and $B = \{2, 4, 6\}$. All the elements of B are contained in A and we say that B is a **subset** of A. We write $B \subseteq A$. In general, we have the following:

> **Definition of Subset**
>
> B is a **subset** of A, written $B \subseteq A$, if, and only if, every element of B is an element of A.

This definition allows B to be equal to A. The definition is written with the phrase "if, and only if," which means "if B is a subset of A, then every element of B is an element of A, and if every element of B is an element of A, then B is a subset of A." An alternate definition follows.

> **Alternate Definition of Set Equality**
>
> Two sets A and B are equal if, and only if, $A \subseteq B$ and $B \subseteq A$.

When a set A is not a subset of another set B, we write $A \not\subseteq B$. To show that $A \not\subseteq B$, we must find at least one element of A that is not in B. If $A = \{1, 3, 5\}$ and $B = \{1, 2, 3\}$, then A is not a subset of B because 5 is an element of A but not of B. Likewise, $B \not\subseteq A$ because 2 belongs to B but not to A.

The Empty Set as a Subset of Every Set

It is not obvious how the empty set fits the definition of a subset because no elements in the empty set are elements of another set. To investigate this problem, we use the strategies of *indirect reasoning* and *looking at a special case*.

For the set $\{1, 2\}$, either $\varnothing \subseteq \{1, 2\}$ or $\varnothing \not\subseteq \{1, 2\}$. Suppose $\varnothing \not\subseteq \{1, 2\}$. Then there must be some element in $\varnothing$ that is not in $\{1, 2\}$. Because the empty set has no elements, there cannot be an element in the empty set that is not in $\{1, 2\}$. Consequently, $\varnothing \not\subseteq \{1, 2\}$ is false. Therefore, the only other possibility, $\varnothing \subseteq \{1, 2\}$, is true. The same reasoning can be applied in the case of the empty set and any other set. Therefore, *the empty set is a subset of every set.*

Proper Subsets

For sets $A = \{a, b, c\}$ and $B = \{c, b, a\}$, we have $B \subseteq A$, $A \subseteq B$, and $B = A$. If C is a subset of A and C is not equal to A, then C is a **proper subset** of A, written $C \subset A$. This means that every element of C is contained in A and there is at least one element of A that is not in C. For example, if $X = \{1, 2\}$ and $Y = \{1, 2, 3\}$ then $X \subset Y$.

> **Definition of Proper Subset**
>
> For all sets A and B, B is a **proper subset** of A, written $B \subset A$, if, and only if, $B \subseteq A$ and $B \neq A$; that is, every element of B is an element of A, and there is at least one element of A that is not an element of B.

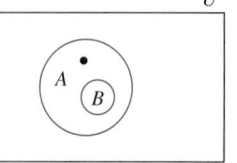

Figure 9

To indicate a proper subset, sometimes a Venn diagram like the one shown in Figure 9 is used, showing a dot (an element) in A that is not in B. The empty set is a proper subset of every non-empty set. (Why?)

Example 16

Let $A = \{1, 2, 3, 4, 5\}$, $B = \{1, 3\}$, and $P = (x \mid x = 2^n - 1, n \in N)$.

a. Identify all the subset relationships that occur among these sets.
b. Identify all the proper subset relationships that occur among these sets.
c. If $C = \{2k \mid k \in N\}$ and $D = \{4k \mid k \in N\}$, show that one of the sets is a subset of the other.

Solution

a. Because $2^1 - 1 = 1$, $2^2 - 1 = 3$, $2^3 - 1 = 7$, $2^4 - 1 = 15$, $2^5 - 1 = 31$, and so on, $P = \{1, 3, 7, 15, 31, \ldots\}$. Thus, $B \subseteq P$. Also $B \subseteq A$, $A \subseteq A$, $B \subseteq B$ and $P \subseteq P$.
b. $B \subset A$ and $B \subset P$.
c. $C = \{2 \cdot 1, 2 \cdot 2, 2 \cdot 3, 2 \cdot 4, \ldots\} = \{2, 4, 6, 8, \ldots\}$ and $D = \{4 \cdot 1, 4 \cdot 2, 4 \cdot 3, 4 \cdot 4, \ldots\} = \{4, 8, 12, 16, \ldots\}$. Each element in D appears in C. This is true because $4k = 2(2k)$. Therefore, every element of D is an element of C and $D \subseteq C$.

Subsets and elements of sets are often confused. We say that $2 \in \{1, 2, 3\}$. But because 2 is not a set, we cannot substitute the symbol $\subseteq$ for $\in$. However, $\{2\} \subseteq \{1, 2, 3\}$ and $\{2\} \subset \{1, 2, 3\}$. Notice that $\{2\} \notin \{1, 2, 3\}$ and $2 \not\subseteq \{1, 2, 3\}$.

Inequalities: An Application of Set Concepts

The notion of proper subset and the concept of one-to-one correspondence can be used to define the concept of "less than" among natural numbers. The set $\{a, b, c\}$ has fewer elements than the set $\{w, x, y, z\}$ because when we try to pair the elements of the two sets, as in

$$\{a, b, c\}$$
$$\uparrow\downarrow \ \uparrow\downarrow \ \uparrow\downarrow$$
$$\{x, y, z, w\}$$

we see that there is at least one element of the second set that is not paired with an element of the first set. The set $\{a, b, c\}$ is equivalent to $\{x, y, z\}$, a proper subset of the set $\{x, y, z, w\}$. The generalization leads to a definition of **less than**.

Definition of Less Than and Greater Than
If A and B are finite sets, A has fewer elements than B if A is equivalent to a proper subset of B.

We say that $n(A)$ is **less than** $n(B)$ and write $n(A) < n(B)$. We say that b is **greater than** a, written $b > a$, if, and only if, $a < b$.

If A and B are finite sets and $A \subset B$, then A has fewer elements than B and it is not possible to find a one-to-one correspondence between the sets. Consequently, A and B are not equivalent. However, when both sets are infinite and $A \subset B$, the sets could be equivalent. For example, consider the set N of natural numbers and the set E of even natural numbers. $E \subset N$, but it is still possible to find a one-to-one correspondence between the sets. To do so, we correspond each number in set N to a number in set E that is twice as great; that is, $n \in N$ corresponds to $2n \in E$, as shown next.

$$N = \{1, 2, 3, 4, 5, \ldots, n, \ldots\}$$

$$E = \{2, 4, 6, 8, 10, \ldots, 2n, \ldots\}$$

Notice that in the correspondence, every element of N corresponds to a unique element in E and, conversely, every element of E corresponds to a unique element in N. For example, 11 in N corresponds to $2 \cdot 11$, or 22, in E. And 100 in E corresponds to $100 \div 2$, or 50, in N. Thus, $N \sim E$; that is, N and E are equivalent.

Students sometimes have difficulty with infinite sets and especially with their cardinal numbers, called **transfinite numbers**. As shown, E is a proper subset of N, but because they can be placed in a one-to-one correspondence, they are equivalent and have the same cardinal number. Georg Cantor was the first to introduce the concept of a transfinite number. He used the first letter of the Hebrew alphabet $\aleph_0$ (aleph-null) for the cardinal number of the set N.

Problem Solving Passing a Senate Measure

A committee of senators consists of Abel, Baro, Carni, and Davis. Suppose each member of the committee has one vote and a simple majority is needed to either pass or reject any measure. A measure that is neither passed nor rejected is considered to be blocked and will be voted on again. Determine the number of ways a measure could be passed or rejected and the number of ways a measure could be blocked.

Understanding the Problem We are asked to determine how many ways the committee of four could pass or reject a measure and how many ways the committee of four could block a measure. To pass or reject a measure requires a winning coalition, that is, a group of senators who can pass or reject the measure, regardless of what the others do. To block a proposal, there must be a blocking coalition, that is, a group who can prevent any measure from passing but who cannot reject the measure.

Devising a Plan To solve the problem, we can *make a list* of subsets of the set of senators. Any subset of the set of senators with three or four members will form a winning coalition. Any subset of the set of senators with exactly two members will form a blocking coalition.

Carrying Out the Plan We list all subsets of the set $S = \{$Abel, Baro, Carni, Davis$\}$. For ease, we identify the members as follows: A—Abel, B—Baro, C—Carni, D—Davis.

$$\varnothing \quad \{A\} \quad \{A, B\} \quad \{A, B, C\} \quad \{A, B, C, D\}$$
$$\{B\} \quad \{A, C\} \quad \{A, B, D\}$$
$$\{C\} \quad \{A, D\} \quad \{A, C, D\}$$
$$\{D\} \quad \{B, C\} \quad \{B, C, D\}$$
$$\{B, D\}$$
$$\{C, D\}$$

There are five subsets with at least three members that can form a winning coalition to pass or reject a measure and six subsets with exactly two members that can block a measure.

Looking Back Other questions that might be considered include:

1. How many minimal winning coalitions are there? In other words, how many subsets are there of which no proper subset could pass a measure?
2. Devise a method to solve this problem without listing all subsets.
3. In "Carrying Out the Plan," 16 subsets of $\{A, B, C, D\}$ are listed. Use that result to systematically list all the subsets of a committee of five senators. Can you find the number of subsets of the 5-member committee without actually counting the subsets?

Number of Subsets of a Finite Set

How many subsets can be made from a set containing n elements? To obtain a general formula, we use the strategy of *examine a simpler case* first.

1. If $P = \{a\}$, then P has two subsets, $\varnothing$ and $\{a\}$.
2. If $Q = \{a, b\}$, then Q has four subsets, $\varnothing$, $\{a\}$, $\{b\}$, and $\{a, b\}$.
3. If $R = \{a, b, c\}$, then R has eight subsets, $\varnothing$, $\{a\}$, $\{b\}$, $\{c\}$, $\{a, b\}$, $\{a, c\}$, $\{b, c\}$, and $\{a, b, c\}$.

We could list all the subsets of a given set by using a tree diagram. For example, tree diagrams for the subsets of $Q = \{a, b\}$ and $R = \{a, b, c\}$ are given in Figure 10(a) and (b) respectively.

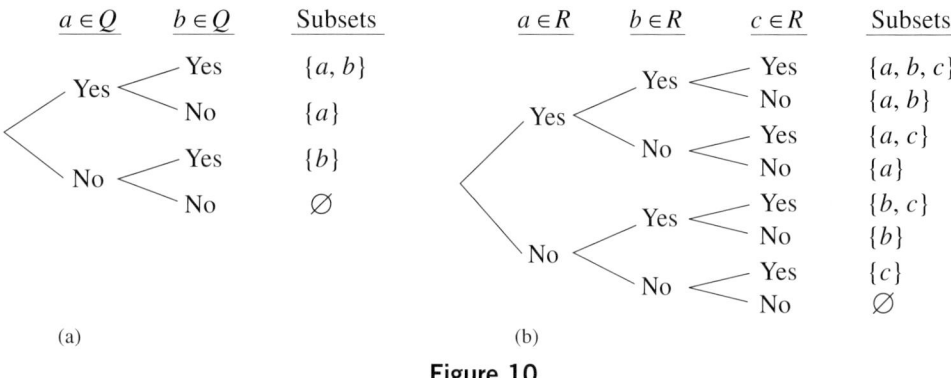

(a)   (b)

Figure 10

Using the information from these cases, we *make a table* and *search for a pattern*, as in Table 11.

Table 11	
Number of Elements	**Number of Subsets**
1	2, or 2^1
2	4, or 2^2
3	8, or 2^3
.	.
.	.
.	.

Table 11 suggests that for four elements, there might be 2^4, or 16, subsets. Is this correct? If $S = \{a, b, c, d\}$, then all the subsets of $R = \{a, b, c\}$ are also subsets of S. Eight new subsets are also formed by including the element d in each of the eight subsets of R. The eight new subsets are $\{d\}$, $\{a, d\}$, $\{b, d\}$, $\{c, d\}$, $\{a, b, d\}$, $\{a, c, d\}$, $\{b, c, d\}$, and $\{a, b, c, d\}$. Thus, there are twice as many subsets of set S (with four elements) as there are of set R (with three elements). Consequently, there are $2 \cdot 8$, or 2^4, subsets of a set with four elements. Because including one more element in a finite set doubles the number of possible subsets of the new set, a set with five elements will have $2 \cdot 2^4$, or 2^5, subsets, and so on. In each case, the number of elements and the power of 2 used to obtain the number of subsets are equal. *Therefore, if there are n elements in a set, 2^n subsets can be formed.* If we apply this formula to the empty set; that is, when $n = 0$, we have $2^0 = 1$. The pattern is meaningful because the empty set has only one subset—itself.

▶ **NOW TRY THIS 6**

NTT 6: Answer can be found in Answers at the back of the book.

a. How many proper subsets does a set with five elements have?

b. Write a formula to show how many proper subsets a set with n elements has. Explain your reasoning.

Assessment 2-2A

1. Write the following sets using the listing (roster) method or using set-builder notation.
   a. The set of letters in the word *assessment*   *
   b. The set of natural numbers greater than 20   *
2. Rewrite the following using mathematical symbols.
   a. P is equal to the set containing p, q, r, and s.   *
   b. The set consisting of the elements 1 and 2 is a proper subset of $\{1, 2, 3\}$. $\{1,2\} \subset \{1,2,3\}$
   c. The set consisting of the elements 0 and 1 is not a subset of $\{1, 2, 3\}$. $\{0,1\} \not\subseteq \{1,2,3\}$
3. Which of the following pairs of sets can be placed in one-to-one correspondence?
   a. $\{1, 2, 3, 4, 5\}$ and $\{m, n, o, p, q\}$ Yes
   b. $\{a, b, c, d, e, f, \ldots, m\}$ and $\{1, 2, 3, 4, 5, 6, \ldots, 13\}$ Yes
   c. $\{x \mid x$ is a letter in the word *mathematics*$\}$ and $\{1, 2, 3, 4, \ldots, 11\}$ No
4. How many one-to-one correspondences are there between two sets with
   a. 6 elements each?   720
   b. n elements each? Explain your reasoning.   *
5. How many one-to-one correspondences are there between the sets $\{x, y, z, u, v\}$ and $\{1, 2, 3, 4, 5\}$ if in each correspondence
   a. x must correspond to 5?   24
   b. x must correspond to 5 and y to 1?   6
   c. x, y, and z must correspond to odd numbers?   12
6. Which of the following represent equal sets?
   $A = \{a, b, c, d\}$ $B = \{x, y, z, w\}$
   $C = \{c, d, a, b\}$ $D = \{x \mid 1 \leq x \leq 4 \text{ and } x \in N\}$
   $E = \varnothing$ $F = \{\varnothing\}$
   $G = \{0\}$ $H = \{\ \}$
   $I = \{x \mid x = 2n + 1 \text{ and } n \in W\}$
   $L = \{x \mid x = 2n - 1 \text{ and } n \in N\}$ $A = C; E = H; I = L$
7. Find the cardinal number of each of the following sets. Assume the pattern of elements continues in each part in the order given.
   a. $\{201, 202, 203, \ldots, 1100\}$ 900
   b. $\{1, 3, 5, \ldots, 101\}$ 51
   c. $\{1, 2, 4, 8, 16, \ldots, 1024\}$ 10
   d. $\{x \mid x = k^3, k = 1, 2, 3, \ldots, 100\}$ 100
8. If U is the set of all college students and A is the set of all college students with a straight-A average, describe $\overline{A}$.   *
9. Suppose B is a proper subset of C.
   a. If $n(C) = 8$, what is the maximum number of elements in B?   7
   b. If $n(B) = 8$, what is the maximum number of elements in C?   *

10. Suppose C is a subset of D and D is a subset of C.
    a. If $n(C) = 5$, find $n(D)$.   5
    b. What other relationship exists between sets C and D?   *
11. If $A = \{a, b, c, d, e\}$,
    a. how many subsets does A have?   32
    b. how many proper subsets does A have?   31
    c. how many subsets does A have that include the elements a and e?   8
12. If a set has 127 proper subsets, how many elements are in the set?   7
13. Identify all the possible proper subset relationships that occur among the following sets.
    $A = \{3n \mid n \in N\}$, $B = \{6n \mid n \in N\}$, $C = \{12n \mid n \in N\}$. $B \subset A, C \subset A, C \subset B$
14. Indicate which symbol, $\in$ or $\notin$, makes each of the following statements true.
    a. 0 _____ $\varnothing$ $\notin$
    b. 1024 _____ $\{x \mid x = 2^n \text{ and } n \in N\}$ $\in$
    c. 3002 _____ $\{x \mid x = 3n - 1 \text{ and } n \in N\}$ $\in$
    d. x _____ $\{x \mid x = 2^n \text{ and } n \in N\}$ $\notin$
15. Indicate which symbol, $\subseteq$ or $\not\subseteq$, makes each part of problem 14 true.   a. $\not\subseteq$ b. $\not\subseteq$ c. $\not\subseteq$ d. $\not\subseteq$
16. Answer each of the following. If your answer is *no*, tell why.
    a. If $A = B$, can we always conclude that $A \subseteq B$?   Yes
    b. If $A \subseteq B$, can we always conclude that $A \subset B$?   *
    c. If $A \subset B$, can we always conclude that $A \subseteq B$?   Yes
    d. If $A \subseteq B$, can we always conclude that $A = B$?   *
17. Use the definition of *less than* to show each of the following.
    a. $3 < 100$ *
    b. $0 < 3$ *
18. On a certain senate committee there are seven senators: Abel, Brooke, Cox, Dean, Eggers, Funk, and Gage. Three of these members are to be appointed to a subcommittee. How many possible subcommittees are there?   35
19. Name two infinite sets that are equivalent but not equal.   *
20. Write an argument to show that the set of even natural numbers and the set of odd natural numbers should have the same cardinal number.   *
21. Draw a Venn diagram showing the relationship between the set of natural numbers and the set of whole numbers.   *
22. Draw a Venn diagram depicting the Adamsville Beta Club, the officers of the Beta Club, and a member Sanna who is not an officer of the Beta Club.   *
23. If the set of officers of the Adamsville Beta Club is equivalent to the set of members of the Adamsville Beta Club, what can you infer?   *

Assessment 2-2B

1. Write the following sets using the listing (roster) method or set-builder notation.
   a. The set of letters in the word *algebra*   *
   b. The set of natural numbers less than 10   *
2. Rewrite the following using mathematical symbols.
   a. Q is equal to the set whose elements are q, r, and s.   *
   b. The set containing 1 and 3 is equal to the set containing 3 and 1. $\{1, 3\} = \{3, 1\}$
   c. The set containing 1 and 3 only is not a proper subset of $\{1, 4, 6\}$ $\{1, 3\} \not\subset \{1, 4, 6\}$
3. Which of the following pairs of sets can be placed in a one-to-one correspondence?
   a. $\{1, 2, 3, 4\}$ and $\{w, c, y, z\}$ Yes
   b. $\{1, 2, 3, \ldots, 25\}$ and $\{a, b, c, d, \ldots, x, y\}$ Yes
   c. $\{x \mid x$ is a letter in the word *geometry*$\}$ and $\{1, 2, 3, 4, 5, 6, 7, 8\}$ No
4. How many one-to-one correspondences exist between two sets with
   a. 8 elements each?   40,320
   b. $n - 1$ elements each? Explain your reasoning.   *
5. How many one-to-one correspondences are there between the sets $\{a, b, c, d\}$ and $\{1, 2, 3, 4\}$ if in each correspondence
   a. b must correspond to 3?   6
   b. b must correspond to 3 and d to 4?   2
   c. a and c must correspond to even numbers?   4
6. Which of the following represent equal sets? $A = C$
   $A = \{a, b, c\}$ $B = \{x, y\}$
   $C = \{c, a, b\}$ $D = \{x \mid 1 \le x \le 3 \text{ and } x \in N\}$
   $I = \{x \mid x = 2n \text{ and } n \in W\}$,
   $K = \{2, 4, 6, 8, 10, 12, \ldots\}$
   $L = \{x \mid x = 2n - 1 \text{ and } n \in N\}$
7. Find the cardinal number of each of the following sets. Assume the pattern continues in each part.
   a. $\{19, 20, 21, \ldots, 99\}$ 81
   b. $\{2, 4, 6, 8, \ldots, 1002\}$ 501
   c. $\{x^2 \mid x = 1, 3, 5, 7, \ldots, 99\}$ 99
   d. $\{x \mid x = x + 1 \text{ and } x \in N\}$ 0
8. If U is the set of all women and G is the set of alumnae of Georgia State University, describe $\overline{G}$.   *
9. Suppose $A \subseteq B$.
   a. Explain why $n(A)$ could equal 0.   *
   b. Is it possible for set B to be the empty set? If so, give an example of sets A and B satisfying this. If not, explain why not.   *
10. If two sets are subsets of each other, what other relationships must they have?   They are equal and equivalent.
11. If $A = \{1, 2, 3, 4, 5, 6, 7, 8, 9\}$,
    a. how many subsets does A have?   512
    b. how many proper subsets does A have?   511

12. If a set has 16 subsets, how many elements are in the set?   4
13. Identify all possible proper subset relationships that occur among the following sets.
    $A = \{3n + 1 \mid n \in N\}$, $B = \{6n + 1 \mid n \in N\}$,
    $C = \{12n + 1 \mid n \in N\}$ $B \subset A, C \subset A, C \subset B$
14. Indicate which symbol, $\in$ or $\notin$, makes each of the following statements true.
    a. $\varnothing$_____$\{\varnothing\}$ $\in$
    b. 1022_____$\{s \mid s = 2^n - 2 \text{ and } n \in N\}$ $\in$
    c. 3004_____$\{x \mid x = 3n + 1 \text{ and } n \in N\}$ $\in$
    d. 17_____N $\in$
15. Answer each of the following. If your answer is *no*, tell why.
    a. If $A \subseteq B$, can we always conclude that $A = B$?   *
    b. If $A \subset B$, can we conclude that $A = B$?   *
    c. If A and B can be placed in a one-to-one correspondence, must $A = B$?   *
    d. If A and B can be placed in a one-to-one correspondence, must $A \subseteq B$?   No; for example, $A = \{1\}$ and $B = \{2\}$.
16. Use the definition of *less than* to show each of the following.
    a. $0 < 2$ *
    b. $99 < 100$ *
17. How many ways are there to stack an ice-cream cone with 4 scoops if the choices are
    a. vanilla, chocolate, rhubarb, and strawberry and each scoop must be different?   24
    b. vanilla, chocolate, rhubarb, and strawberry and there are no restrictions on different scoops?   256
18. If two sets have 720 one-to-one correspondences pairing them, how many elements are in each set?   6
19. Write an argument showing that the set of whole numbers can be placed in a one-to-one correspondence with the set of natural numbers.   *
20. Draw a Venn diagram showing the members of Congress of the United States, the members of the House of Representatives, and the members of the Senate.   *
21. In a state swim meet, if the set of swimmers in the 100-m butterfly race is equal to the set of swimmers from the Maryville Swim Team, what can you infer?   *
22. In some states of the United States, to vote in a primary election, one has to declare a party affiliation of Republican or Democrat. Draw a Venn diagram depicting this information for such a state.   *
23. If set A and set B are such that set B has one more element than set A, describe a possible relationship between the two sets using some of the following words: *subset, proper subset, equivalent*, and *equal*.   *
24. Find an infinite set A such that
    a. $\overline{A}$ is finite.   *
    b. $\overline{A}$ is infinite.   *

Mathematical Connections 2-2

Answers to Mathematical Connections can be found in the Answers section at the back of the book.

Reasoning

1. Explain the difference between a well-defined set and one that is not. Give examples.
2. Which of the following sets are not well defined? Explain.
   a. The set of wealthy schoolteachers
   b. The set of great books
   c. The set of natural numbers greater than 100
   d. The set of subsets of $\{1, 2, 3, 4, 5, 6\}$
   e. The set $\{x \mid x \neq x \text{ and } x \in N\}$
3. Explain why the empty set cannot be put in a one-to-one correspondence with any non-empty set.
4. Explain why $\{\varnothing\}$ has $\varnothing$ as an element and also as a subset.
5. For sets A and B, tell how you would show that $A \not\subseteq B$.
6. Explain why the word "finite" was used in the definition of *less than*.
7. Define *less than or equal to* in a way similar to the definition of *less than*.

Open-Ended

8. a. Give three examples of sets A and B and a universal set U such that $A \subset B$; find $\overline{A}$ and $\overline{B}$.
   b. Based on your observations, conjecture a relationship between $\overline{B}$ and $\overline{A}$.
   c. Demonstrate your conjecture in (b) using a Venn diagram.
9. Draw a Venn diagram depicting $\overline{A}$. Shade $\overline{\overline{A}}$. What is the simplest symbol to use for the area you shaded? Why?
10. A set has elements in an arithmetic sequence $\{3, 5, 7, 9, \ldots, 1009\}$. Show how a one-to-one correspondence might be used to find the number of elements in this set. Show the correspondence and any patterns used to find the cardinal number of the sequence.
11. A set of 100 people on a tour includes only men and women. If there is at least one person of each sex on the tour, draw a Venn diagram showing all the information you can deduce and write all number sentences and set relationships you can find.

Cooperative Learning

12. Choose 4 people from your class and have them stand in a row in front of the class. Give each of the people one of the numbers on a sheet of paper: 1, 2, 3, or 4. As a class, gather and re-distribute the sheets of paper as many times as you can to exhibit all the possible arrangements of the symbols 1, 2, 3, and 4. How many arrangements are possible?

Connecting Mathematics to the Classroom

13. A student asks if A is a subset of B and B is a subset of C, do we know that A is a subset of C? How do you respond?

14. A student states that given any two sets A and B, either A is a subset of B or B is a subset of A. What assumptions might the student be making?
15. A third grader asked his teacher whether infinite sets could be compared. How might you respond?

Review Problems

16. If p is false and q is true, find the truth values for each of the following.
    a. $p \wedge q$
    b. $\sim q$
    c. $\sim p \wedge q$
    d. $\sim (p \wedge q)$
    e. $\sim q \wedge \sim p$
17. Find the truth value for each statement in exercise 16 if p is true and q is false.
18. Complete the following truth table.

p	q	$\sim q$	$p \vee \sim q$
T	T		
T	F		
F	T		
F	F		

National Assessments

National Assessment of Educational Progress (NAEP) Question

Four people—A, X, Y, and Z—go to a movie and sit in adjacent seats. If A sits in the aisle seat, list all possible arrangements of the other three people. One of the arrangements is shown below.

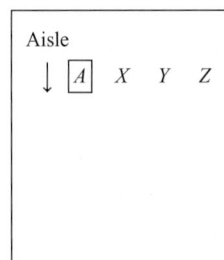

NAEP, Grade 12, 1996

2-3 Other Set Operations and Their Properties

2-3 Objectives

Students will be able to understand and explain

- Relations between set operations and logic connectives.
- Properties of set and logic operations.
- Venn diagrams to sort and reason with data.

In the grade 1 *Common Core Standards*, we find that students should "organize, represent, and interpret data with up to three categories; ask and answer questions about the total number of data points, how many in each category, and how many more or less are in one category than in another." (p. 16)

In this section we examine different operations and tools to aid in this type of work. What is presented here should give tools to future teachers to use with organizing, representing, and interpreting small amounts of data. One operation, finding the complement of a set, used in this regard was seen in Section 2-2.

Finding the complement of a set is an operation that acts on only one set at a time. In this section, we consider binary operations that act on two sets at a time and use such logic terms as *and* and *or*.

Set Intersection

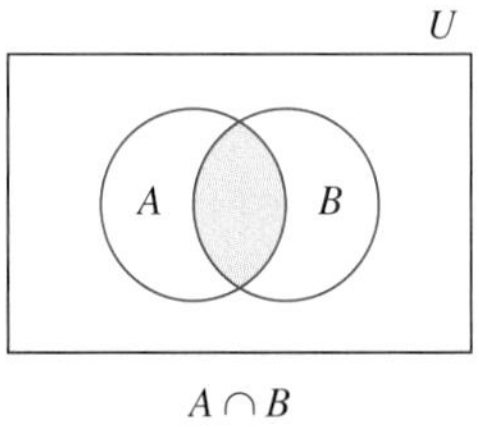

U

$A \cap B$

Figure 11

Suppose that during the fall quarter, a college wants to mail a survey to all its students who are enrolled in both art and biology classes. To do this, the school officials must identify those students who are taking both classes. If A and B are the set of students taking art courses and the set of students taking biology courses, respectively, during the fall quarter, then the desired set of students includes those common to A *and* B, or the **intersection** of A and B. The intersection of sets A and B is the shaded region in Figure 11, which depicts the possibility of A and B containing common elements. The intersection might contain no elements.

Activity Manual

Try *Loop de Loops* to explore the concepts of union, intersection, empty set, and subset.

> **Definition of Set Intersection**
>
> The **intersection** of two sets A and B, written $A \cap B$, is the set of all elements common to both A and B; $A \cap B = \{x \mid x \in A \text{ and } x \in B\}$.

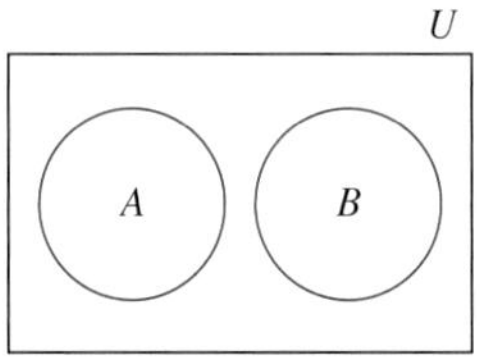

U

A B

Figure 12

For all sets A and B, $A \cap B \subseteq A$ and $A \cap B \subseteq B$. The key word in the definition of *intersection* is *and* (see Section 2-1). In everyday language, as in mathematics, *and* implies that both conditions must be met. In the example, the desired set is the set of those students enrolled in both art and biology.

If sets such as A and B have no elements in common, they are *disjoint sets*. In other words, two sets A and B are **disjoint** if, and only if, $A \cap B = \varnothing$. For example, if there are no students that are taking both art (A) and biology (B), then the sets are disjoint. The Venn diagram for this situation could be drawn as in Figure 12.

Example 17

Find $A \cap B$ in each of the following.

  a. $A = \{1, 2, 3, 4\}$, $B = \{3, 4, 5, 6\}$
  b. $A = \{0, 2, 4, 6, \ldots\}$, $B = \{1, 3, 5, 7, \ldots\}$
  c. $A = \{2, 4, 6, 8, \ldots\}$, $B = \{1, 2, 3, 4, \ldots\}$

Solution
  a. $A \cap B = \{3, 4\}$
  b. $A \cap B = \varnothing$; therefore A and B are disjoint.
  c. $A \cap B = A$ because all the elements of A are also in B.

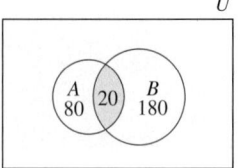

Figure 13

Suppose A represents all students enrolled in art classes and B all students enrolled in biology classes. We may use a Venn diagram to illustrate the previous statement taking into account that some students may be enrolled in both subjects. If we know that 100 students are enrolled in art and 200 in biology and that 20 of these students are enrolled in both art and biology, then $100 - 20$, or 80, students are enrolled in art but not in biology and $200 - 20$, or 180, are enrolled in biology but not art. We record this information as in Figure 13. The total number of students in set A is 100, and the total in set B is 200.

Set Union

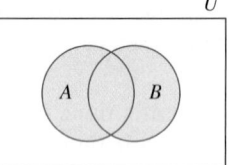

$A \cup B$

Figure 14

If A is the set of students taking art courses during the fall quarter and B is the set of students taking biology courses during the fall quarter, then the set of students taking art *or* biology or both during the fall quarter is the *union* of sets A and B. The **union** of sets A and B is pictured in Figure 14.

> **Definition of Set Union**
> The **union** of two sets A and B, written $A \cup B$, is the set of all elements in A or in B;
> $A \cup B = \{x \mid x \in A \text{ or } x \in B\}$.

For all sets A and B, $A \subseteq A \cup B$, $B \subseteq A \cup B$, and $A \cap B \subseteq A \cup B$. The key word in the definition of *union* is *or* (see Section 2-1). In mathematics, *or* usually means "one or the other or both." This is known as the *inclusive or*.

Example 18

Find $A \cup B$ for each of the following.

 a. $A = \{1, 2, 3, 4\}$, $B = \{3, 4, 5, 6\}$
 b. $A = \{0, 2, 4, 6, \ldots\}$, $B = \{1, 3, 5, 7, \ldots\}$
 c. $A = \{2, 4, 6, 8, \ldots\}$, $B = \{1, 2, 3, 4, \ldots\}$

Solution
 a. $A \cup B = \{1, 2, 3, 4, 5, 6\}$ b. $A \cup B = \{0, 1, 2, 3, 4, \ldots\}$
 c. Because every element of A is already in B, we have $A \cup B = B$.

Example 19

Find each of the following if $A = \{a, b, c\}$.

 a. $A \cap \varnothing$ b. $A \cup \varnothing$ c. $\varnothing \cap \varnothing$ d. $\varnothing \cup \varnothing$

Solution
 a. $\varnothing$ b. A c. $\varnothing$ d. $\varnothing$

Set Difference

During the fall quarter if A is the set of students taking art classes and B is the set of students taking biology classes, then the set of all students taking biology but not art is the **complement of A relative to B**, or the **set difference** of B and A.

Definition of Relative Complement

The **complement of A relative to B**, written $B - A$, is the set of all elements in B that are not in A;
$B - A = \{x \mid x \in B \text{ and } x \notin A\}$.

Note that $B - A$ is not read as "B minus A." The symbol used here is the same for both subtraction and set difference, but it should not be read as "minus." *Set difference* is an operation on sets. A Venn diagram representing $B - A$ is shown in Figure 15(a). The shaded region represents all the elements that are in B but not in A. A Venn diagram for $B \cap \overline{A}$ is given in Figure 15(b). The shaded region represents all the elements that are in B *and* in $\overline{A}$. Notice that $B - A = B \cap \overline{A}$ because $B \cap \overline{A}$ is, by definitions of intersection and complement, the set of all elements in B and not in A.

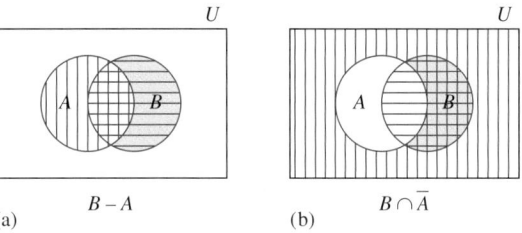

(a) $B - A$ (b) $B \cap \overline{A}$

Figure 15

Example 20

Let $A = \{d, e, f\}$, $B = \{a, b, c, d, e, f\}$, and $C = \{a, b, c\}$. Find or answer each of the following.

a. $A - B$
b. $B - A$
c. $B - C$
d. $C - B$
e. To answer parts (a)–(d), does it matter what the universal set is?
f. Let $D = \{c, d, e, f\}$. Find $C - D$.

Solution

a. $A - B = \varnothing$
b. $B - A = \{a, b, c\}$
c. $B - C = \{d, e, f\}$
d. $C - B = \varnothing$
e. Parts (a)–(d) can be answered independently of the universal set. The definition of set difference relates one set to another, independent of the universal set.
f. $C - D = \{a, b\}$

Properties of Set Operations

Because the order of elements in a set is not important, $A \cap B$ is equal to $B \cap A$. It does not matter in which order we write the sets when the intersection of two sets is involved. Similarly, $A \cup B = B \cup A$. These properties are stated formally next.

Theorem 2-7:   Commutative Property of Set Intersection and Commutative Property of Set Union

For all sets A and B, $A \cap B = B \cap A$. For all sets A and B, $A \cup B = B \cup A$.

▶ **NOW TRY THIS 7**

Use Venn diagrams or other means to find whether grouping is important when the same operation is involved. For example, is it always true that $A \cap (B \cap C) = (A \cap B) \cap C$? Investigate similar questions involving union and set difference.

In answering Now Try This 7, the following properties become evident:

> **Theorem 2-8:   Associative Property of Set Intersection and Associative Property of Set Union**
>
> For all sets A, B, and C, $A \cap (B \cap C) = (A \cap B) \cap C$. For all sets A and B, $A \cup (B \cup C) = (A \cup B) \cup C$.

Example 21

Is grouping important when two different set operations are involved? For example, is it true that $A \cap (B \cup C) = (A \cap B) \cup C$?

Solution
To investigate this, let $A = \{a, b, c\}$, $B = \{c, d\}$, and $C = \{d, e, f\}$.

$$A \cap (B \cup C) = \{a, b, c\} \cap (\{c, d\} \cup \{d, e, f\})$$
$$= \{a, b, c\} \cap \{c, d, e, f\}$$
$$= \{c\}$$

$$(A \cap B) \cup C = (\{a, b, c\} \cap \{c, d\}) \cup \{d, e, f\}$$
$$= \{c\} \cup \{d, e, f\}$$
$$= \{c, d, e, f\}$$

In this case, $A \cap (B \cup C) \neq (A \cap B) \cup C$. We have found a counterexample, that is, an example illustrating that the general statement is not always true.

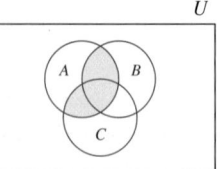

Figure 16

To discover an expression that is equal to $A \cap (B \cup C)$, consider the Venn diagram for $A \cap (B \cup C)$ shown by the shaded region in Figure 16. In the figure, $A \cap B$ and $A \cap C$ are subsets of the shaded region. The union of $A \cap B$ and $A \cap C$ is the entire shaded region. Thus, $A \cap (B \cup C) = (A \cap B) \cup (A \cap C)$.

> **Theorem 2-9:   Distributive Property of Set Intersection over Set Union**
>
> For all sets A, B, and C, $A \cap (B \cup C) = (A \cap B) \cup (A \cap C)$.

Theorems 2-7, 2-8, and 2-9 can be proved using the definition of set intersection and set union and the rules of logic.

▶ **NOW TRY THIS 8**

In the distributive property of set intersection over set union, if the symbol $\cap$ is replaced by $\cup$ and the symbol $\cup$ is replaced by $\cap$, is the new property true? Explain why. What should this property be called?

Example 22

Use set notation to describe the shaded portions of the Venn diagrams in Figure 17.

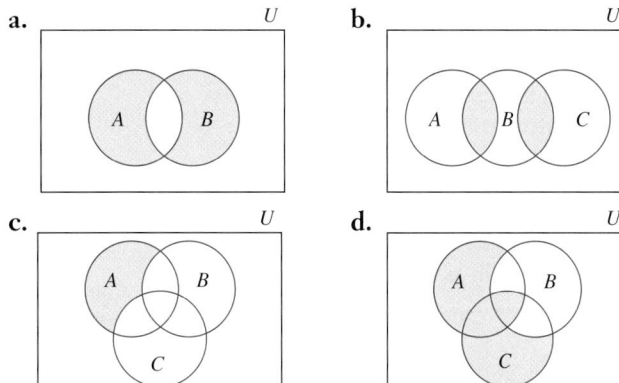

Figure 17

Solution

The solutions can be described in many different, but equivalent, forms. Some possible answers follow.

a. $(A \cup B) - (A \cap B)$ or $(A \cup B) \cap \overline{A \cap B}$ or $(A - B) \cup (B - A)$
b. $(A \cap B) \cup (B \cap C)$ or $B \cap (A \cup C)$
c. $(A - B) - C$ or $A - (B \cup C)$ or $(A - (A \cap B)) - (A \cap C)$
d. $((A \cup C) - B) \cup (A \cap B \cap C)$ or $(A - (B \cup C)) \cup (C - (A \cup B)) \cup (A \cap C)$

Using Venn Diagrams as a Problem-Solving Tool

Venn diagrams can be used as a problem-solving tool for modeling information, as shown in the following examples and on the student page shown on page 72.

Example 23

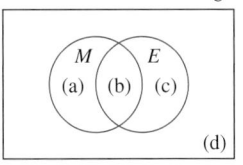

Figure 18

Suppose M is the set of all students taking mathematics and E is the set of all students taking English. Identify in words and using set notation the students described by each region in Figure 18.

Solution
Answers vary.

Region (a) contains all students taking mathematics but not English or $M - E$.

Region (b) contains all students taking both mathematics and English or $M \cap E$.

Region (c) contains all students taking English but not mathematics or $E - M$.

Region (d) contains all students taking neither mathematics nor English or $\overline{M \cup E}$ or $\overline{M} \cap \overline{E}$.

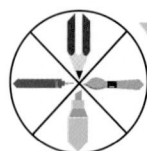

School Book Page   Venn Diagrams

Venn Diagrams

A Venn diagram uses circles, loops, or other shapes to show relationships between sets. Sets are described by the data or objects they contain. Circles overlap, or intersect, when some data belong to more than one set. The Venn diagram below relates parallelograms. Notice that squares are a subset of both rectangles and rhombuses.

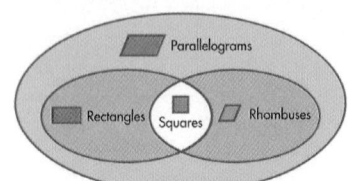

Example: Describe the sets shown in the Venn diagram below.

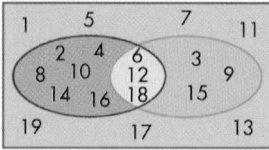

Counting numbers less than 20 are shown in the rectangle. The numbers in the red loop are divisible by 2. The numbers in the green loop are divisible by 3. The numbers divisible by both 2 and 3 are a subset of both loops.

Source: p. 123; From enVisionMATH Common Core (Grade 6). Copyright © 2012 Pearson Education, Inc., or its affiliates. Used by permission. All Rights Reserved.

Example 24

In a survey that investigated the high school backgrounds of 110 college freshmen, the following information was gathered.

  25 took physics
  45 took biology
  48 took mathematics
  10 took physics and mathematics
  8 took biology and mathematics
  6 took physics and biology
  5 took all three subjects

a. How many students took biology but neither physics nor mathematics?
b. How many took physics, biology, or mathematics?
c. How many did not take any of the three subjects?

Solution

To solve this problem, we *build a model* using sets. Because there are three distinct subjects, we should use three circles. In Figure 19, P is the set of students taking physics, B is the set of students taking biology, and M is the set of students taking mathematics. The shaded region represents the 5 students who took all three subjects. The lined region represents the students who took physics and mathematics, but who did not take biology.

Part (a) asks for the number of students in the subset of B that has no element in common with either P or M, that is, $B - (P \cup M)$. Part (b) asks for the number of elements in $P \cup B \cup M$. Finally, part (c) asks for the number of students in $\overline{P \cup B \cup M}$, or $U - (P \cup B \cup M)$. Our strategy is to find the number of students in each of the eight nonoverlapping regions.

One mind set to be aware of in this problem is thinking that the 25 students who took physics took only physics. That is not necessarily the case.

a. Because a total of 10 students took physics and mathematics and 5 of those also took biology, $10 - 5 = 5$ students took physics and mathematics but not biology. Similarly, because 8 students took biology and mathematics and 5 took all three subjects, $8 - 5 = 3$ took biology

Figure 19

and mathematics but not physics. Also $6 - 5 = 1$ student took physics and biology but not mathematics. To find the number of students who took biology but neither physics nor mathematics, we subtract from 45 (the total number who took biology) the number of those that are in the distinct regions that include biology and other subjects; that is, $1 + 5 + 3 = 9$. Because $45 - 9 = 36$, we know that 36 students took biology but neither physics nor mathematics.

b. To find the number of students in all the remaining distinct regions in P, M, or B, we proceed as follows. The number of students who took physics but neither mathematics nor biology is $25 - (1 + 5 + 5) = 14$. The number of students who took mathematics but neither physics nor biology is $48 - (5 + 5 + 3) = 35$. Hence the number of students who took mathematics, physics, or biology is $35 + 14 + 36 + 3 + 5 + 5 + 1 = 99$.

c. Because the total number of students is 110, the number of students who did not take any of the three subjects is $110 - 99 = 11$.

E-Manipulative Activity
Additional work with Venn Diagrams can be found in the *Venn Diagrams* activity on the E-Manipulatives disk (or MML).

Cartesian Products

Another way to produce a set from two given sets is by forming the **Cartesian product**. This formation pairs the elements of one set with the elements of another set in a specific way to create elements in a new set. Suppose a person has three pairs of pants, $P = \{$blue, white, green$\}$, and two shirts, $S = \{$blue, white$\}$. According to the Fundamental Counting Principle, there are $3 \cdot 2 = 6$ possible different pants-and-shirt pairs, as shown in Figure 20.

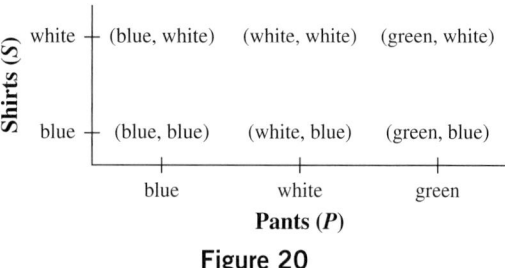

Figure 20

The pants-shirt combinations are elements of the set of all possible pairs in which the first member of the pair is an element of set P and the second member is an element of set S. The set of all possible pairs is given in Figure 20. Because the first component in each pair represents pants and the second component in each pair represents shirts, the order in which the components are written is important. Thus (white, blue) represents white pants and a blue shirt, whereas (blue, white) represents blue pants and a white shirt. Therefore, the two pairs represent different outfits. Because the order in each pair is important, the pairs are **ordered pairs**. The positions that the ordered pairs occupy within the set of outfits is immaterial. Only the order of the **components** within each pair is significant. The pants-and-shirt pairs suggest the following definition of **equality for ordered pairs**: $(x, y) = (m, n)$ *if, and only if, the first components are equal and the second components are equal.* In symbols, $(x, y) = (m, n)$ if, and only if, $x = m$ and $y = n$. The set of six ordered pairs shown in Figure 20, denoted $P \times S$, is an example of a Cartesian product. A formal definition follows.

Definition of Cartesian Product

For any sets A and B, the **Cartesian product** of A and B, written $A \times B$, is the set of all ordered pairs such that the first component of each pair is an element of A and the second component of each pair is an element of B.

$$A \times B = \{(x, y) \mid x \in A \text{ and } y \in B\}$$

$A \times B$ is commonly read as "A cross B" and should never be read "A times B."

Example 25

If $A = \{a, b, c\}$ and $B = \{1, 2, 3\}$, find each of the following:

a. $A \times B$
b. $B \times A$
c. $A \times A$

Solution

a. $A \times B = \{(a, 1), (a, 2), (a, 3), (b, 1), (b, 2), (b, 3), (c, 1), (c, 2), (c, 3)\}$
b. $B \times A = \{(1, a), (1, b), (1, c), (2, a), (2, b), (2, c), (3, a), (3, b), (3, c)\}$
c. $A \times A = \{(a, a), (a, b), (a, c), (b, a), (b, b), (b, c), (c, a), (c, b), (c, c)\}$

It is possible to form a Cartesian product involving the empty set. Suppose $A = \{1, 2\}$. Because there are no elements in $\varnothing$, no ordered pairs (x, y) with $x \in A$ and $y \in \varnothing$ are possible, so $A \times \varnothing = \varnothing$. This is true for all sets A. Similarly, $\varnothing \times A = \varnothing$ for all sets A. There is an analogy between the last equation and the multiplication fact that $0 \cdot a = 0$, where a is a whole number. In Chapter 3 we use the concept of Cartesian product to define multiplication of whole numbers.

Assessment 2-3A

1. If $N = \{1, 2, 3, 4, \ldots\}$, $A = \{x \mid x = 2n - 1, n \in N\}$, $B = \{x \mid x = 2n, n \in N\}$, and $C = \{x \mid x = 2n + 1, n = 0$ or $n \in N\}$, find the simplest possible expression for each of the following.
   a. $A \cup C$ *A or C*
   b. $A \cup B$ *N*
   c. $A \cap B$ $\varnothing$

2. Decide whether the following pairs of sets are always equal.
   a. $A - A$ and $\varnothing$ *Yes*
   b. $B - A$ and $B \cap \overline{A}$ *Yes*
   c. $B - A$ and $B \cap A$ if $A \subseteq B$ *No*
   d. $A \cup A$ and $A \cup \varnothing$ *Yes*

3. Tell whether each of the following is true for all sets A and B. If false, give a counterexample.
   a. $A \cup \varnothing = A$ *True*
   b. $A - B = B - A$ *
   c. $\overline{A \cap B} = \overline{A} \cap \overline{B}$ *
   d. $(A \cup B) - A = B$ *
   e. $(A - B) \cup A = (A - B) \cup (B - A)$ *

4. If $B \subseteq A$, find a simpler expression for each of the following.
   a. $A \cap B$ *B*
   b. $A \cup B$ *A*

5. For each of the following, shade the portion of the Venn diagram that illustrates the set.
   a. $(A \cap B) \cup (A \cap C)$ *
   b. $(A \cup B) \cap \overline{C}$ *
   c. $(A \cap B) \cup C$ *

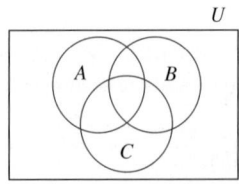

6. If S is a subset of universe U, find each of the following.
   a. $S \cup \overline{S}$ *U*
   b. $\overline{U}$ $\varnothing$
   c. $S \cap \overline{S}$ $\varnothing$
   d. $\varnothing \cap S$ $\varnothing$

7. For each of the following conditions, find $A - B$.
   a. $A \cap B = \varnothing$ *A*
   b. $B = \varnothing$ *A*
   c. $B = U$ $\varnothing$

8. If for sets A and B we know that $A - B = \varnothing$, is it necessarily true that $A \subseteq B$? Justify your answer.   *

9. Use set notation to identify each of the following shaded regions: *Answers vary.*

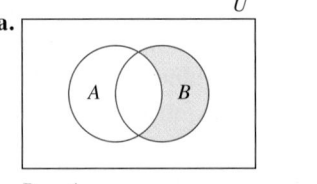

$B - A$

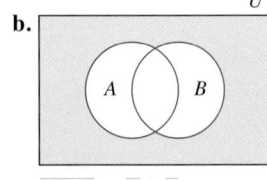

$\overline{A \cup B}$ or $\overline{A} \cap \overline{B}$

c.

$(A \cap B) - C$ or $(A \cap B) \cap \overline{C}$

10. a. In the following, shade the portion of the Venn diagram that represents the given set. *

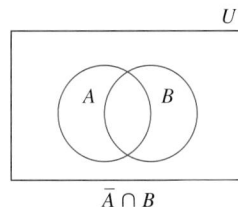

$\overline{A} \cap B$

b. Find another expression for $\overline{A} \cap B$. *

11. Use Venn diagrams to determine if each of the following is true.
a. $A \cup (B \cap C) = (A \cup B) \cap C$ *
b. $A - (B - C) = (A - B) - C$ *

12. a. If an element is in $A \cap B$, must it be in $A \cup B$? Explain your answer with an example. *
b. If an element is in $\overline{A - B}$, can it be in A? Explain your answer with an example. *

13. a. If A has three elements and B has two elements, what is the greatest number of elements possible in (i) $A \cup B$? (ii) $A \cap B$? (iii) $B - A$? (iv) $A - B$? *
b. If A has n elements and B has m elements, what is the greatest number of elements possible in (i) $A \cup B$? (ii) $A \cap B$? (iii) $B - A$? (iv) $A - B$? *

14. If $n(A) = 4, n(B) = 5$, and $n(C) = 6$, what is the greatest and least number of elements possible in
a. $A \cup B \cup C$? Greatest is 15; least is 6.
b. $A \cap B \cap C$? Greatest is 4; least is 0.

15. In 2012, the population of the United States was about 321.8 million; of that population about 2.6 million were Muslim. A total of the number of people who were identified as being of some faith was about 150.6 million. Find the number of each of the following in 2012.
a. The non-Muslims in the United States *
b. The people of some faith who were non-Muslims *

16. Given that the universe is the set of all humans, $B = \{x \mid x \text{ is a college basketball player}\}$, and $S = \{x \mid x \text{ is a college student more than 200 cm tall}\}$, describe each of the following in words:
a. $B \cap S$ *
b. $\overline{S}$ *
c. $B \cup S$ *
d. $\overline{B \cup S}$ *
e. $\overline{B} \cap S$ *
f. $B \cap \overline{S}$ *

17. Of the eighth graders at the Paxson School, 7 played basketball, 9 played volleyball, 10 played soccer, 1 played basketball and volleyball only, 1 played basketball and soccer only, 2 played volleyball and soccer only, and 2 played volleyball, basketball, and soccer. How many played one or more of the three sports? 18

18. In a sorority with 40 members, 18 take mathematics, 5 take both mathematics and biology, and 8 take neither mathematics nor biology. How many take biology but not mathematics? 14

19. In Paul's bicycle shop, 50 bicycles were inspected. If 20 needed new tires and 30 needed gear repairs, answer the following.
a. What is the greatest number of bikes that could have needed both? 20

b. What is the least number of bikes that could have needed both? 0
c. What is the greatest number of bikes that could have needed neither? 20

20. The Red Cross looks for three types of antigens in blood tests: A, B, and Rh. When the antigen A or B is present, it is listed, but if both of these antigens are absent, the blood is type O. If the Rh antigen is present, the blood is positive; otherwise, it is negative. If a laboratory technician reports the following results after testing the blood samples of 200 people, how many were classified as O negative? 92

Number of Samples	Antigen in Blood
50	A
18	B
82	Rh
5	A and B
31	A and Rh
10	B and Rh
4	A, B, and Rh

21. John has applied for the registrar's job at a small college. He submitted the following report to the hiring committee on a survey he did of 100 students: 45 take mathematics; 40 take chemistry; 47 take physics; 20 take mathematics and chemistry; 15 take chemistry and physics; 10 take mathematics and physics; 8 take all three of these subjects; and 10 students take none of these three subjects. Do you think John should be hired on the basis of his report? Explain why. *

22. Three announcers each try to predict the winners of next Sunday's professional football games. The only team not picked that is playing Sunday is the Giants. The choices for each person were as follows:

Phyllis: Cowboys, Steelers, Vikings, Bills
Paula: Steelers, Packers, Cowboys, Redskins
Rashid: Redskins, Vikings, Jets, Cowboys
If the only teams playing Sunday are those just mentioned, which teams will play which other teams? *

23. The table below contains the 10 most popular candy bars in the United States in 2013 with the primary ingredients listed.

Favorite Candies	Chocolate (C)	Nuts/Peanut Butter (N)	Caramel (R)
Snickers	Yes	Yes	Yes
Toblerone	Yes	No	No
Cadbury Chocolate Bars	Yes	No	No
Hershey	Yes	No	No
Butterfinger	Yes	Yes	No
Baby Ruth	Yes	Yes	Yes
Mars Bar	Yes	No	Yes
Milky Way	Yes	No	Yes
3 Musketeers	Yes	No	No
KitKat	Yes	No	No

a. Draw a Venn diagram sorting the brands according to the three listed ingredients with the universal set (U) being the set of candy bars. *

b. How many candy bars are in each of the following sets? What bars are in each set?

   i. $\overline{C} \cap R$ 0

   ii. $\overline{C} - N$ 0

   iii. Of the bars listed, what is the most popular of the listed ingredients? The most unpopular? *

   iv. If you were a manufacturer of candy bars and using only this list, write an argument for which ingredients your new candy bar would contain. *

24. When the *Titanic* sank, the following data about the 324 first-class passengers were reported in newspapers.

- 146 women and children were first-class passengers who survived with only 4 lost.
- 117 men were lost.   57

How many men who were first-class passengers survived?

25. Two families, each having three children, are at a birthday party. Each of the six children has either blue or brown eyes and brown or blond hair. In a family, children differ by at most one characteristic. The following are descriptions of the six children. *

- Tom: blue eyes, brown hair
- Dick: brown eyes, blond hair
- Mary: brown eyes, brown hair
- Harry: blue eyes, blond hair
- Jane: blue eyes, brown hair
- Abby: blue eyes, blond hair

Separate the children into families.

26. Let $A = \{x, y\}$ and $B = \{a, b, c\}$. Find each of the following.

a. $A \times B$ $\{(x,a),(x,b),(x,c),(y,a),(y,b),(y,c)\}$

b. $B \times A$ $\{(a,x),(a,y),(b,x),(b,y),(c,x),(c,y)\}$

c. Does $A \times B = B \times A$?   No

27. For each of the following, the Cartesian product $C \times D$ is given by the sets listed. Find C and D.

a. $\{(a,b),(a,c),(a,d),(a,e)\}$ $C = \{a\}, D = \{b,c,d,e\}$

b. $\{(1,1),(1,2),(1,3),(2,1),(2,2),(2,3)\}$ *

c. $\{(0,1),(0,0),(1,1),(1,0)\}$ $C = D = \{0,1\}$

Assessment 2-3B

1. If $W = \{0, 1, 2, 3, \ldots\}$, $A = \{x \mid x = 2n + 1 \text{ and } n \in W\}$, $B = \{x \mid x = 2n \text{ and } n \in W\}$, and $N = \{1, 2, 3, \ldots\}$, find the simplest possible expression for each of the following.

a. $W - A$ B

b. $A \cap B$ $\varnothing$

c. $W \cap N$ N

2. Decide whether the following pairs of sets are always equal. If not equal, give a counterexample.

a. $A - B$ and $B - A$ *

b. $A - B$ and $A \cap \overline{B}$ Yes

c. $B - A$ and $B \cup A$ if $B \subseteq A$ *

d. $B \cup \varnothing$ and $B \cap B$ Yes

3. Tell whether each of the following is true for all sets A, B, and C. If false, give a counterexample.

a. $A - B = A - \varnothing$ *

b. $\overline{A \cup B} = \overline{A} \cup \overline{B}$ *

c. $A \cap (B \cup C) = (A \cap B) \cup C$ *

d. $(A - B) \cap A = A$ *

e. $A - (B \cap C) = (A - B) \cap (A - C)$ *

4. If $X \subseteq Y$, find a simpler expression for each of the following.

a. $X - Y$ $\varnothing$

b. $X \cap \overline{Y}$ $\varnothing$

5. For each of the following, shade the portion of the Venn diagram that illustrates the set.

a. $A \cap \overline{C}$ *

b. $(A \cap B) \cup (B \cap C)$ *

c. $A \cup (B \cap C)$ *

d. $A \cup \overline{B} \cap \overline{C}$ *

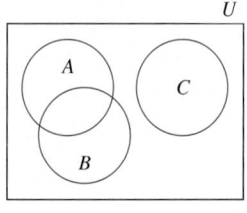

6. If A is a subset of universe U, find each of the following.

a. $A \cup U$ U

b. $U - A$ $\overline{A}$

c. $A - \varnothing$ A

d. $\overline{\varnothing} \cap A$ A

7. For each of the following conditions, find $B - A$.

a. $A = B$ $\varnothing$

b. $B \subseteq A$ $\varnothing$

8. Use set notation to identify each of the following shaded regions: Answers vary.

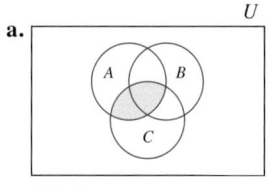

$A \cap C$ $(A \cap C) \cup (B \cap C)$

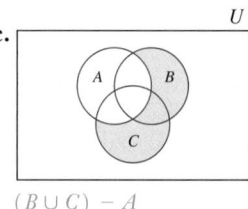

$(B \cup C) - A$

9. a. In the following, shade the portion of the Venn diagram that represents the given set: *

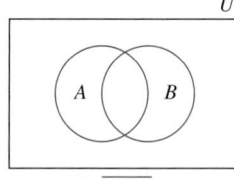

$\overline{A \cup B}$

b. Find another expression for $\overline{A \cup B}$. *

10. Use Venn diagrams to determine whether each of the following is true.
  a. $A - (B \cap C) = (A - B) \cap (A - C)$ *
  b. $A - (B \cup C) = (A - B) \cup (A - C)$ *

11. In a police bulletin, it was reported that a suspect had blond hair, green eyes, and a beard. A second report said that the suspect had blond hair and green eyes. Use your knowledge of set operations to explain which report should have the fewest number of people fitting the descriptions. *

12. **a.** If $n(A \cup B) = 23$, $n(A \cap B) = 9$, and $n(B) = 12$, find $n(A)$. 20
  b. If $n(A) = 9$, $n(B) = 13$, and $n(A \cap B) = 5$, find $n(A \cup B)$. 17

13. The equation $\overline{A \cup B} = \overline{A} \cap \overline{B}$ and a similar equation for $\overline{A \cap B}$ are referred to as *De Morgan's Laws* for sets (see Section 2-1).
  a. Discover an equation involving $\overline{A \cap B}$, $\overline{A}$, and $\overline{B}$. Use Venn diagrams to show that the equation holds. *
  b. Verify the equation in (a) for specific sets. *

14. Suppose P is the set of all eighth-grade students at the Paxson School, with B the set of all students in the band and C the set of all students in the choir. Identify in words the students described by each region of the following figure. *

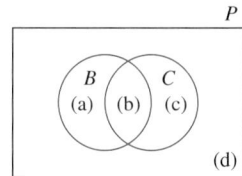

15. Fill in the Venn diagram with the appropriate numbers based on the following information. *
  $n(A) = 26$ $n(B \cap C) = 12$
  $n(B) = 32$ $n(A \cap C) = 8$
  $n(C) = 23$ $n(A \cap B \cap C) = 3$
  $n(A \cap B) = 10$ $n(U) = 65$

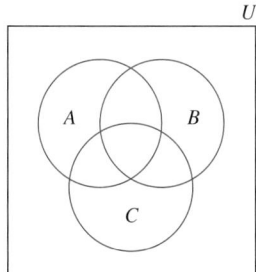

16. Write the letters in the appropriate sections of the following Venn diagram using the following information (ignore the case of the letters).

Set A contains the letters in the word *Iowa*.
Set B contains the letters in the word *Hawaii*.
Set C contains the letters in the word *Ohio*.

The universal set U contains the letters in the word *Washington*. *

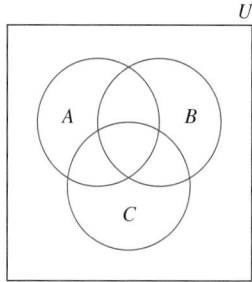

17. Students at Hellgate High School were asked if they were taking courses in algebra (A), biology (B), or chemistry (C). Use the diagram to answer the following questions.
  a. Which region (or regions) represents the students who do not take algebra? (List the letters.) c, f, g, h
  b. Which region (or regions) represents the students who take biology or chemistry? (List the letters.) b, c, e, f, d, g
  c. A student who took both algebra and biology could be in which region (or regions)? (List the letters.) b, e
  d. How would you describe region (a) in sentence form? *
  e. How would you describe region (f) in sentence form? *
  f. Describe region (f) using set notation. *
  g. If we were to combine regions (d) and (g) to form one large region, describe it using set notation. *
  h. Describe region (g) using set notation. *

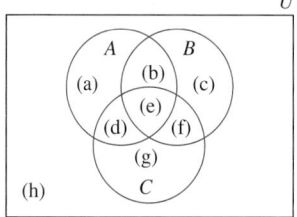

18. A pollster interviewed 600 university seniors who owned credit cards. She reported that 290 owned Goldcard, 300 had Supercard, and 270 had Thriftcard. Of those seniors, the report said that 80 owned only a Goldcard and a Supercard, 70 owned only a Goldcard and a Thriftcard, 60 owned only a Supercard and a Thriftcard, and 50 owned all three cards. When the report was submitted for publication in the local campus newspaper, the editor refused to publish it, claiming the poll was not accurate. Was the editor right? Why or why not? *

19. In a survey of 1000 investors, it was determined that 600 invested in stocks, 575 in bonds, and 300 in both stocks and bonds.
  a. How many invested only in stocks? 300
  b. How many invested in stocks or bonds? 875
  c. How many did not invest in either stocks or bonds? 125

20. In a survey of 150 students, 90 were taking algebra and 30 were taking biology.
  a. What is the least number of students who could have been taking both courses? 0
  b. What is the greatest number of students who could be taking both courses? 30
  c. What is the greatest number of students who could have been taking neither course? 60

21. In 2012, the population of the United States was about 321.8 million (denoted U); of that population about 4.2 million identified themselves as religious Jews. A total of the number of people who were identified as being of some

faith was about 150.6 million. Find the number of each of the following in 2012.
a. The people of some faith who were not religious Jews *
b. The non-faith people in the United States   *

22. At the end of a tour, several guides discussed the people on the latest Canadian-American tour. The guides could not remember the total number in the group; however, they compiled the following data about the group.
- 26 Canadian females
- 17 American women
- 17 American males
- 29 girls
- 44 Canadian citizens
- 29 women
- 24 Canadian adults

Find the total number of people in the group.   93

23. Tell whether each of the following is true or false and explain why:
a. $(2,5) = (5,2)$ *
b. $(2,5) = \{2,5\}$ *

24. Answer each of the following.
a. If A has five elements and B has four elements, how many elements are in $A \times B$?   20
b. If A has m elements and B has n elements, how many elements are in $A \times B$?   mn
c. If A has m elements, B has n elements, and C has p elements, how many elements are in $(A \times B) \times C$?   mnp

Mathematical Connections 2-3

Answers to Mathematical Connections can be found in the Answers section at the back of the book.

Reasoning

1. Answer each of the following and justify your answer.
a. If $a \in A \cup B$, is it true that $a \in A \cap B$?
b. If $A \cup B = A \cup C$, then is $B = C$?
c. If $A \cap B = A \cap C$, then is $B = C$?
2. Given two sets identify conditions under which the complements of the two sets could be equal.
3. Is the operation of forming Cartesian products commutative? Explain why or why not.
4. If A and B are sets, is it always true that $n(A - B) = n(A) - n(B)$? Explain.
5. Explain whether the following could be true: In a survey of 220 students, 110 were taking algebra, 90 were taking biology, and 20 were taking neither of the two subjects.
6. If you were looking for a book in the library on mathematical biology, name the first two items you might type in the search line of a browser. Explain how a search engine might use operations on sets to locate a book.

Open-Ended

7. Describe a real-life situation that can be represented by each of the following:
a. $A \cap \overline{B}$
b. $A \cap B \cap C$
c. $A - (B \cup C)$

Cooperative Learning

8. A set of attribute blocks consists of 32 blocks. Each block is identified by its own shape, size, and color. The four shapes in a set are square, triangle, rhombus, and circle; the four colors are red, yellow, blue, and green; the two sizes are large and small. In addition to the blocks, each set contains a group of 20 cards. Ten cards specify one of the attributes of the blocks (for example, red, large, square). The other 10 cards are negation cards and specify the lack of an attribute (for example, not green, not circle). Many set-type problems can be studied with these blocks. For example, let A be the set of all green blocks and B be the set of all large blocks. As a

group using the set of all blocks as the universal set, describe elements in each set listed here to determine which are equal.
a. $A \cup B$ and $B \cup A$
b. $\overline{A \cap B}$ and $\overline{A} \cap \overline{B}$
c. $\overline{A \cap B}$ and $\overline{A} \cup \overline{B}$
d. $A - B$ and $A \cap \overline{B}$

9. In small groups, identify three characteristics that at least one person in the group has. Write these on paper. Distribute the papers to the other groups. Have the group that wrote the characteristics stand and see if the rest of the class can identify each person based on the written characteristics. Explain how this activity uses set operations.

Connecting Mathematics to the Classroom

10. A student asks, "If $A = \{a,b,c\}$ and $B = \{b,c,d\}$, why isn't it true that $A \cup B = \{a,b,c,b,c,d\}$?" What is your response?
11. A student is asked to find all one-to-one correspondences between two given sets. He finds the Cartesian product of the sets and claims that his answer is correct because it includes all possible pairings between the elements of the sets. How do you respond?
12. A student argues that adding two sets $A + B$, and taking the union of two sets $A \cup B$ is the same thing. How do you respond?
13. The symbol "$\leq$" is read as "less than or equal to." How could this be explained to students using set concepts and terms?

Review Problems

14. Describe the contrapositive of the contrapositive of a statement.
15. Write a conclusion for each of the following.
a. If Mary is elected class president, she will change the lunch menu. Mary is elected class president.
b. Samuel is a student in the class play. All the students in the class play stay after school.
c. If the lake is frozen, we can go ice skating. We cannot go ice skating.

16. In the diagram, suppose statements p and q are represented by the circles with each region of circle p being where p is true, and similarly the regions of circle q showing where q is true. Write a paragraph showing that the diagram could be used to show all possible truth values of combinations of p and q.

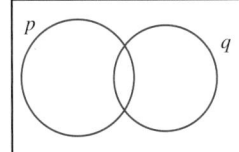

17. **a.** Write $\{4, 5, 6, 7, 8, 9\}$ using set-builder notation.
    b. Write $\{x \mid x = 5n, n = 3, 6, \text{ or } 9\}$ using the listing method.
18. Find the number of elements in the following sets:
    a. $\{x \mid x \text{ is a letter in the phrase } common\ core\}$
    b. The set of letters appearing in the word *committee*
19. If $A = \{1, 2, 3, 4\}$ and $B = \{1, 2, 3, 4, 5\}$, answer the following questions.
    a. How many subsets of A do not contain the element 1?
    b. How many subsets of A contain the element 1?
    c. How many subsets of A contain either the element 1 or 2?
    d. How many subsets of A contain neither the element 1 nor 2?
    e. How many subsets of B contain the element 5 and how many do not?
20. Give examples from real life for each of the following:
    a. A one-to-one correspondence between two sets
    b. A correspondence between two sets that is not one-to-one
21. José has three pairs of slacks, four shirts, and five sweaters. From how many combinations can he choose if he chooses a pair of slacks, a shirt, and a sweater each day?

National Assessments

National Assessment of Educational Progress (NAEP) Question

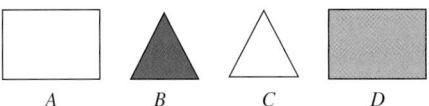

Melissa chose one of the figures above.

- The figure she chose was shaded.
- The figure she chose was *not* a triangle.

Which figure did she choose?
A. *A*
B. *B*
C. *C*
D. *D*

NAEP, Grade 4, 2007

Hint for Solving the Preliminary Problem

As a first step to answering the questions, organize the data using a Venn diagram with circles representing Alpha Pi, Beta Zeta, and Gamma Iota. Sorting the information into the various sections representing each bit of information will help determine the information Maria needs.

Chapter 2 Summary

KEY CONCEPTS	DEFINITIONS, DESCRIPTIONS, AND THEOREMS
Section 2-1	
Statement (p. 40)	A sentence that is either true or false but not both.
Negation of a statement (p. 40)	A statement that has the opposite truth value of a given statement. The negation of statement p is $\sim p$, which means not p.
Quantifiers (p. 41)	*Universal quantifiers*—words that refer to each and every element in a set, such as *all*, *every*, and *no*. *Existential quantifiers*—words or phrases that refer to one or more, or possibly all, of the elements in a set, such as *some* and *there exists at least one*.
Compound statement (p. 42)	A statement formed by combining two or more statements.
Truth table (p. 42)	A chart that shows all possible true-false patterns for statements.
Conjunction (p. 42)	A compound statement in the form "*p and q*," which uses the connective *and* (denoted by $\wedge$). The *conjunction* $p \wedge q$ is defined to be true if, and only if, both p and q are true.
Disjunction (p. 42)	A compound statement in the form "*p or q*," which uses the connective *or* (denoted by $\vee$). The *disjunction* $p \vee q$ is defined to be true if, and only if, either p or q, or both, are true.
Logically equivalent statements (p. 42)	Statements with the same truth value in every possible situation (denoted by $\equiv$).
De Morgan's laws for logic (p. 43)	• $\sim(p \wedge q) \equiv \sim p \vee \sim q$ • $\sim(p \vee q) \equiv \sim p \wedge \sim q$
Conditional statement (p. 43)	A compound statement in the form "*if p, then q*" (denoted by $p \rightarrow q$). The *conditional*, or *implication*, $p \rightarrow q$ is defined to be true unless p is true and q is false. The conditional $p \rightarrow q$ has three related implication statements. • *Converse*: If q, then p (denoted by $q \rightarrow p$). • *Inverse*: If not p, then not q (denoted by $\sim p \rightarrow \sim q$). • *Contrapositive*: If not q, then not p (denoted by $\sim q \rightarrow \sim p$). A conditional and its contrapositive are logically equivalent.
Biconditional (p. 45)	The conjunction of a conditional statement and its converse: $(p \rightarrow q) \wedge (q \rightarrow p)$. This compound statement can be written as $p \leftrightarrow q$, which is read "p, if, and only if, q," or equivalently "q if, and only if, p."
Law of detachment (*modus ponens*) (p. 47)	If the statement "*if p, then q*" is true and p is true, then q must be true.
Law of denying the consequent (*modus tollens*) (p. 48)	If the statement "*if p, then q*" is true and q is not true, then p is not true.
Tautology (p. 48)	A statement that is always true.
Chain rule (transitivity) (p. 48)	If the statements "*if p, then q*" and "*if q, then r*" are both true, then the statement "*if p, then r*" is true. If $(p \rightarrow q) \wedge (q \rightarrow r)$, then $p \rightarrow r$ is a tautology.

Section 2-2

Set (p. 53)	Any collection of objects.
Element (member) (p. 53)	Any individual object in a set (denoted by $\in$).
Well-defined set (p. 53)	Given a set and some particular object, it must be possible to say whether the object does or does not belong to the set.
Describing a set (p. 54)	*Listing*, or *roster method*: $A = \{1, 2, 3\}$ *Set-builder notation*: $A = \{x \mid x \in N \text{ and } x < 4\}$
Equal sets (p. 55)	Sets that have exactly the same elements, or equivalently $A = B$, if, and only if, $A \subseteq B$ and $B \subseteq A$.
One-to-one correspondence between two sets (p. 55)	Pair the elements of sets A and B so that for each element of A there is exactly one element of B and for each element of B there is exactly one element of A.
Fundamental Counting Principle (p. 57)	If event M can occur in m ways and, after it has occurred, event N can occur in n ways, then event M followed by event N can occur in $m \cdot n$ ways.
Equivalent sets (p. 57)	Sets that can be placed in a one-to-one correspondence.
Cardinal number of a set (p. 58)	The number of elements in a set S, denoted by $n(S)$.
Special sets (p. 58)	• *Empty* (or *null*) *set*—a set with no elements. • *Universal set* (or the *universe*)—the set that contains all of the elements under discussion.
Complement of a set (p. 59)	The set of elements in the universe that are not in set A, denoted by $\overline{A}$.
Subset of a set (p. 60)	Set B is a subset of set A, written $B \subseteq A$, if, and only if, every element of set B is an element of set A. For all sets A, $\varnothing \subseteq A$.
Proper subset (p. 60)	Set B is a proper subset of A, written $B \subset A$, if, and only if, $B \subseteq A$ and there exists at least one element of A not in B; that is, $B \neq A$. The empty set is a proper subset of every set except itself.
Number of subsets of a finite set (p. 63)	If a set has n elements, then it has 2^n subsets.
Inequalities (defined by sets) (p. 61)	• *Less than*—If A and B are finite sets such that $A \subset B$, then A has fewer elements than B; that is, $n(A) < n(B)$. • *Greater than*—B has more elements than A, that is, $n(B) > n(A)$ if, and only if, $n(A) < n(B)$.

Section 2-3

Intersection of sets *A* and *B* (p. 67)	For any two sets A and B, the set of all elements common to both A and B. The intersection of A and B is denoted by $A \cap B$. $A \cap B = \{x \mid x \in A \text{ and } x \in B\}$.
Union of sets *A* and *B* (p. 68)	For any two sets A and B, the set of all elements in either A or B, or both. The union of A and B is denoted by $A \cup B$. $A \cup B = \{x \mid x \in A \text{ or } x \in B\}$.
Complement of *A* relative to *B* (p. 69)	The set of all elements in B that are not in A. The complement of A relative to B is the *set difference* of B and A, denoted by $B - A$. $B - A = \{x \mid x \in B \text{ and } x \notin A\}$.

Section 2-3

Properties of set operations (p. 69)	• *Commutative property*—for all sets A and B, set intersection: $A \cap B = B \cap A$ set union: $A \cup B = B \cup A$ • *Associative property*—for all sets A, B, and C, set intersection: $A \cap (B \cap C) = (A \cap B) \cap C$ set union: $A \cup (B \cup C) = (A \cup B) \cup C$ • *Distributive property*—for all sets A, B, and C, set intersection over set union: $A \cap (B \cup C) = (A \cap B) \cup (A \cap C)$ set union over set intersection: $A \cup (B \cap C) = (A \cup B) \cap (A \cup C)$
Venn diagram (p. 71)	A problem-solving tool using sets to model information.
Cartesian product of two sets (p. 73)	For any sets A and B, the *Cartesian product* of A and B (written as $A \times B$ and read as "A cross B") is the set of all ordered pairs such that the first component of each pair is an element of A and the second component of each pair is an element of B: $A \times B = \{(x, y) \mid x \in A$ and $x \in B\}$.

Chapter 2 Review

1. Write an example of a statement and an example of a sentence that is not a statement.   *
2. Explain the difference between the following two statements: (i) All students made at least C's on the final exam. (ii) Some students made at least C's on the final exam.   *
3. Which of the following are statements?
   a. $3 + 5 = 9$ Yes
   b. $n + 5 = 15$ No
   c. Some men have Ph.D.'s in mathematics.   Yes
4. Negate each of the following:
   a. No women smoke.   Some women smoke.
   b. $3 + 5 \neq 8$ $3 + 5 = 8$
   c. Bach wrote only classical music.   *
5. Write the converse, inverse, and contrapositive of the following. If the whole world is tweeting, someone will read a tweet.   *
6. Use a truth table to show that $(\sim p \rightarrow q) \equiv (q \rightarrow p)$.   *
7. Construct truth tables for each of the following.
   a. $(p \vee \sim q) \wedge (p \vee q)$ *
   b. $[(p \vee \sim q) \wedge \sim q)] \rightarrow p$ *
8. Find valid conclusions for the following hypotheses.
   a. All Eurasians love Mom and apple pie.
      Alfinia is a Eurasian.   *
   b. Marble and granite eventually crack.
      The Washington Monument is made of marble and granite.   *
   c. Josef passed the math for elementary teachers course or Josef dropped out of school.
      Josef did not drop out of school.   *
9. Write the following argument symbolically and then determine its validity.
   If you pass your classes, your parents will allow you to go to the dance.   *
   If your parents allow you to go to the dance, you will not sit in a corner.   *
   You do sit in a corner.   *
   Conclusion: You do not pass your classes.   *

10. State whether the conclusion is valid and explain your answer: If Bob passes the course, he scored at least 75 on the final exam.
    Bob scored less than 75 on the final exam.
    Conclusion: Bob did not pass the course.   *
11. How many proper subsets does $A = \{a, b, c, d\}$ have?   15
12. List all the subsets of $\{m, a, t, h\}$.   *
13. Let
    $U = \{u, n, i, v, e, r, s, a, l\}$
    $A = \{r, a, v, e\}$ $C = \{l, i, n, e\}$
    $B = \{a, r, e\}$ $D = \{s, a, l, e\}$
    Find each of the following.
    a. $A \cup B$ A
    b. $C \cap D$ $\{l, e\}$
    c. $\overline{D}$ $\{u, n, i, v, r\}$
    d. $A \cap \overline{D}$ $\{r, v\}$
    e. $\overline{B \cup C}$ $\{s, v, u\}$
    f. $(B \cup C) \cap D$ $\{l, e, a\}$
    g. $(\overline{A} \cup B) \cap (C \cap \overline{D})$ $\{i, n\}$
    h. $(C \cap D) \cap A$ $\{e\}$
    i. $n(B - A)$ 0
    j. $n(\overline{C})$ 5
    k. $n(C \times D)$ 16
14. Indicate the following sets by shading part of the figure.
    a. $A \cap (B \cup C)$ *   b. $\overline{A \cup B} \cap C$ *

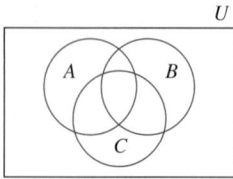

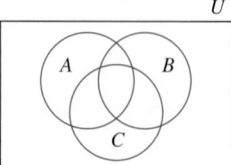

15. Suppose you are playing a word game with five distinct letters. How many different arrangements of the five letters can there be?   120

16. **a.** If $D = \{t, b, e\}$ and $E = \{e, n, d\}$, show one possible one-to-one correspondence between sets D and E.   *
    b. How many one-to-one correspondences between sets D and E are possible?   6

17. Use a Venn diagram to determine whether $A \cup (B - C) = (A \cup B) - C$ for all sets A, B, and C.   *

18. If $A \subseteq B$, which of the following are always true? Give a counterexample if false.
    a. $\overline{A} \subseteq \overline{B}$ *
    b. $\overline{B} \subseteq \overline{A}$ True
    c. $A \cup B = B$ True
    d. $A \cap B = A$ True
    e. $\overline{A} \cap \overline{B} = \overline{B}$ True
    f. $\overline{A} \cup \overline{B} = \overline{A}$ True

19. Tell whether each of the following is true or false. If false, give a counterexample.
    a. If $A - B = A - C$, then $B = C$.   *
    b. If $A \times B = A \times C$, then $B = C$.   *

20. Simplify each of the following: Answers vary.
    a. $(A \cap B) \cup (A \cap \overline{B})$ A
    b. $(A \cap B) \cup \overline{B}$ $A \cup \overline{B}$

21. Classify each of the following as true or false. If false, tell why.
    a. For all sets A and B, either $A \subseteq B$ or $B \subseteq A$.   *
    b. The empty set is a proper subset of every set.   *
    c. For all sets A and B, if $A \sim B$, then $A = B$.   *
    d. The set $\{5, 10, 15, 20, \ldots\}$ is a finite set.   *
    e. No set is equivalent to a proper subset of itself.   *
    f. If A is an infinite set and $B \subseteq A$, then B also is an infinite set.   *
    g. For all finite sets A and B, if $A \cap B \neq \emptyset$, then $n(A \cup B) \neq n(A) + n(B)$.   True
    h. If A and B are sets such that $A \cap B = \emptyset$, then $A = \emptyset$ or $B = \emptyset$.   *

22. Decide whether each of the following is always true for finite sets A and B.
    a. $n(A \cup B) = n(A - B) + n(B - A) + n(A \cap B)$ *
    b. $n(A \cup B) = n(A - B) + n(B) = n(B - A) + n(A)$ *

23. Suppose P and Q are equivalent sets and $n(P) = 17$.
    a. What is the minimum number of elements in $P \cup Q$?   17
    b. What is the maximum number of elements in $P \cup Q$?   34

    c. What is the minimum number of elements in $P \cap Q$?   0
    d. What is the maximum number of elements in $P \cap Q$?   17

24. If $n(A) = 3$, $n(B) = 4$, and $n(c) = 2$, find $n(A \times B \times C)$.   24

25. Case Eastern Junior College awarded 26 varsity letters in crew, 15 in swimming, and 16 in soccer. If awards went to 46 students and only 2 lettered in all sports, how many students lettered in just two of the three sports?   7

26. According to a student survey, 16 students liked history, 19 liked English, 18 liked mathematics, 8 liked mathematics and English, 5 liked history and English, 7 liked history and mathematics, 3 liked all three subjects, and every student liked at least one of the subjects. Draw a Venn diagram describing this information and answer the following questions.   *
    a. How many students were in the survey?   36
    b. How many students liked only mathematics?   6
    c. How many students liked English and mathematics but not history?   5

27. Describe, using symbols, the shaded portion in each of the following figures: *

    a.   **b.**
    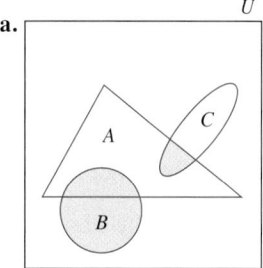   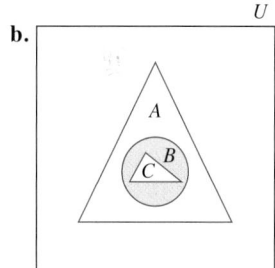

28. Heidi has a brown pair and a gray pair of slacks; a brown blouse, a yellow blouse, and a white blouse; and a blue sweater and a white sweater. How many different outfits does she have if each outfit she wears consists of slacks, a blouse, and a sweater?   12 outfits

29. Using the definitions of less than or greater than, show that each of the following inequalities is true.
    a. $3 < 13$ *
    b. $12 > 9$ *

Numeration Systems and Whole Number Operations

Preliminary Problem

If the sums of the values of each symbol are shown in the respective rows and columns, find the value of each symbol.

□	△	□	35
○	□	□	32
△	□	○	37
△	△	□	40
52	50	42	

If needed, see Hint on page 168.

In the introduction to the *Common Core Standards*, we find the following comment assessing coherence of the standards.

... to be coherent, a set of content standards must evolve from particulars (e.g., the meaning and operations of whole numbers, including simple math facts and routine computational procedures associated with whole numbers and fractions) to deeper structures inherent in the discipline. ...

These Standards endeavor to follow such a design, not only by stressing conceptual understanding of key ideas, but also by continually returning to organizing principles such as place value or the properties of operations to structure those ideas. (p. 4)

In Chapter 3, the conceptual understanding of whole numbers and operations on whole numbers are developed along with estimation and mental mathematics techniques. This foundation lays the groundwork for later work involving the real number system and its properties. We begin the chapter by introducing several counting systems that allow students to compare numeration systems throughout the ages.

3-1 Numeration Systems

3-1 Objectives

Students will be able to understand and explain

- Numbers, their origin, and their representation in numerals and models.

- Different numeration systems including the Hindu-Arabic system.

- Place value and counting in base ten and other bases.

- Issues in learning with different numeration systems.

We introduce various numeration systems to allow comparison to the system used in the United States. Comparing ancient systems helps to develop a clearer appreciation of the U.S. system. The commonly used base-ten system relies on 10 digits—0, 1, 2, 3, 4, 5, 6, 7, 8, and 9. Grouping into sets of 10 probably occurred because we have 10 "digits" on our two hands. The word *digit* means "finger" or "toe" in ancient Latin. The written symbols for the digits, such as 2 or 5, are **numerals**. Different cultures developed different numerals for representing numbers. Table 1 shows other representations for the digits 0 through 9.

Table 1

Babylonian		▼	▼▼	▼▼▼	▼▼▼▼	▼▼▼ ▼▼	▼▼▼ ▼▼▼	▼▼▼▼ ▼▼▼	▼▼▼▼ ▼▼▼▼	▼▼▼▼▼ ▼▼▼▼	<
Egyptian		I	II	III	IIII	II/II	III/II	IIII/II	III/III	III/III	∩
Mayan	👁	•	••	•••	••••	—	•̲	••̲	•••̲	••••̲	═
Greek		α	β	γ	δ	∈	φ	ζ	η	υ	ι
Roman		I	II	III	IV	V	VI	VII	VIII	IX	X
Hindu		0	1	2	3	4	5	6	7	8	9
Arabic		.	١	٢	٣	٤	٥	٦	٧	٨	٩
Hindu-Arabic		0	1	2	3	4	5	6	7	8	9	10

Table 1 shows rudiments of different sets of numbers. A **numeration system** is a collection of properties and symbols agreed upon to represent numbers systematically. Through the study of various numeration systems, we explore the evolution of the Hindu-Arabic system in U.S. usage.

Hindu-Arabic Numeration System

The **Hindu-Arabic numeration system** was developed by the Hindus and transported to Europe by the Arabs—hence, the name *Hindu-Arabic*. The Hindu-Arabic system relies on the following properties:

1. All numerals are constructed from the 10 digits—0, 1, 2, 3, 4, 5, 6, 7, 8, and 9.
2. Place value is based on powers of 10, the *number base* of the system.

IMAP Video

Watch Zenaida discuss the place value of 32, 120 and 316 and watch Maryann's students discuss place value.

Because the Hindu-Arabic system is based on powers of 10, the system is a base ten or *decimal system*. **Place value** assigns a value to a digit depending on its placement in a numeral. To find the value of a digit, placed in a numeral, we multiply the place value of the digit by its **face value**. For example, in the numeral 65,984, the 6 has place value "ten thousand," the 5 has place value "thousand," the 9 has place value "hundred," the 8 has place value "ten," and the 4 has place value "one" as seen in Figure 1. The values of the respective digits are $6 \cdot 10{,}000 = 60{,}000$, $5 \cdot 1000 = 5000$, $9 \cdot 100 = 900$, $8 \cdot 10 = 80$, and $4 \cdot 1 = 4$.

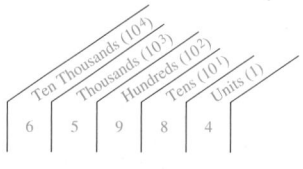

Figure 1

The number 65,984 is read "sixty-five thousand, nine hundred eighty-four." The word *and* does not appear in the name of the number as it is reserved for decimals to separate the decimal portion from the rest of a number. A comma is used to separate groups of three digits. Internationally, commas are omitted and single spaces are used to separate groups of three digits. In some countries commas are used as the United States uses decimal points. We could write 65,984 in **expanded form** as $6 \cdot 10^4 + 5 \cdot 10^3 + 9 \cdot 10^2 + 8 \cdot 10 + 4 \cdot 1$. The expanded form of 65,984 uses exponents. For example, 10,000, or $10 \cdot 10 \cdot 10 \cdot 10$ is written as 10^4. In this case, 10 is a **factor** of the product 10^4. In general, we have the following:

Definition of a^n

If a is any number and n is any natural number, then

$$a^n = \underbrace{a \cdot a \cdot a \cdot \ldots \cdot a}_{n \text{ factors}}.$$

If $a \neq 0$, then $a^0 = 1$.

A set of base-ten blocks (or Dienes blocks), shown in Figure 2, can be used in representing place value. The blocks consist of *units*, *longs*, *flats*, and *blocks*, representing 1's, 10's, 100's, and 1000's, respectively.

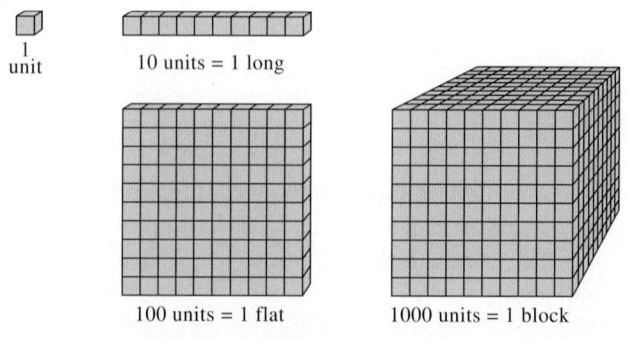

Figure 2

Activity Manual

Use *Regrouping Numbers* and *Find the Missing Numbers* to reinforce place value concepts.

$$1 \text{ unit} \rightarrow 10^0 = 1 \text{ unit}$$
$$1 \text{ long} \rightarrow 10^1 = 10 \text{ units}$$
$$1 \text{ flat} \rightarrow 10^2 = 10 \text{ longs, or } 100 \text{ units}$$
$$1 \text{ block} \rightarrow 10^3 = 10 \text{ flats, or } 100 \text{ longs, or } 1000 \text{ units}$$

Students trade blocks by regrouping. That is, they take a set of base-ten blocks representing a number and trade them until they have the fewest possible pieces representing the same number. For example, suppose we have 58 units and want to trade them for other base-ten blocks. We start trading the units for as many longs as possible. Five sets of 10 units each can be traded for 5 longs. Thus, 58 units can be traded for 5 longs and 8 units. This is analogous to rewriting 58 as $5 \cdot 10 + 8 \cdot 1$.

Example 1

Fair exchange 11 flats, 17 longs, and 16 units to obtain the fewest blocks possible.

Solution

	11 flats	17 longs	16 units	(16 units = 1 long and 6 units)
		1 long	6 units	(Trade)
	11 flats	18 longs	6 units	(After the first trade)
	11 flats	18 longs	6 units	(18 longs = 1 flat and 8 longs)
	1 flat	8 longs		(Trade)
	12 flats	8 longs	6 units	(After the second trade)
	12 flats	8 longs	6 units	(12 flats = 1 block and 2 flats)
1 block	2 flats			(Trade)
1 block	2 flats	8 longs	6 units	(After the third trade)

As a result of the trading we obtain 1 block, 2 flats, 8 longs, and 6 units. This exchange yields the fewest number of pieces, $1 + 2 + 8 + 6 = 17$.

▶ **NOW TRY THIS 1**

NTT 1: Answer can be found in Answers at the back of the book.

a. Trade base-ten blocks (as shown in Figure 2) to write 3 blocks, 12 flats, 11 longs, and 17 units with the fewest number of blocks. What Hindu-Arabic numeral is represented by these blocks?
b. Write 3282 in expanded form.

Other numeration systems provide a historical perspective and help us better understand the United States system.

Tally Numeration System

The **tally numeration system** uses single strokes, or tally marks, to represent each object counted; for example, the first 10 counting numbers are:

$$|, ||, |||, ||||, |||||, ||||||, |||||||, ||||||||, |||||||||, ||||||||||$$

Historical Note

The invention of the Hindu-Arabic numeration system is one of the most important developments in mathematics. The system was introduced in India and then transmitted by the Arabs to North Africa and Spain and then to the rest of Europe. Historians trace the use of zero as a placeholder to the fourth century BCE (Before the Common Era). Arab mathematicians extended the decimal system to include fractions.

A tally system has a one-to-one correspondence between the marks and the items being counted. The system is simple, but it requires many symbols when the numbers are large. As numbers become greater, the tally marks for them are harder to read. The tally system can be improved by *grouping*. Tallies are grouped into fives by placing a diagonal across four tallies to make a group of five. Grouping makes it easier to read the numeral.

$$||||| \rightarrow \text{\cancel{||||}}, \quad ||||||| \rightarrow \text{\cancel{||||}}\,||$$

Egyptian Numeration System

The Egyptian numeration system, dating to about 3400 BCE, used tally marks for the first nine numerals. Egyptians improved on the system based only on tally marks by developing a *grouping system*. For example, the Egyptians used a heel bone symbol, ∩, to stand for a grouping of 10 tally marks.

$$||||||||| \rightarrow \cap$$

Table 2 shows other numerals that the Egyptians used. Some of the symbols from the Karnak temple in Luxor are depicted in Figure 3.

Table 2		
Egyptian Numeral	**Description**	**Hindu-Arabic Equivalent**
		Vertical staff	1
∩	Heel bone	10
9	Scroll	100
⸚	Lotus flower	1000
⌀	Pointing finger	10,000
⌒	Polliwog or burbot	100,000
⚇	Astonished man	1,000,000

Figure 3

In its simplest form, the Egyptian system involved an **additive property** where the value of a number was the sum of the face values of the numerals. The Egyptians customarily wrote the numerals in decreasing order from left to right, as in ⌐999∩∩||. This number can be converted to base ten as shown below:

⌐	represents	100,000	
999	represents	300	(100 + 100 + 100)
∩∩	represents	20	(10 + 10)
||	represents	2	(1 + 1)
⌐999∩∩||	represents	100,322	

▶ **NOW TRY THIS 2**

NTT 2: Answers can be found in Answers at the back of the book.

a. Use the Egyptian system to represent 1,312,322.
b. Use the Hindu-Arabic system to represent ⌐⌐⌐ ƒƒƒ∩∩∩||||.
c. What disadvantages do you see in the Egyptian system compared to the Hindu-Arabic system?

Babylonian Numeration System

The Babylonian numeration system was developed about the same time as the Egyptian system. The symbols in Table 3 were made using a stylus either vertically or horizontally on clay tablets.

Table 3	
Babylonian Numeral	**Hindu-Arabic Equivalent**
▼	1
<	10

The clay tablets were heated and dried to preserve a permanent record. Babylonian symbols on a clay tablet are pictured in Figure 4.

Figure 4

Babylonian numerals 1 through 59 were similar to Egyptian numerals, but the vertical staff and the heel bone were replaced by symbols shown in Table 3. For example, **<< ▼▼▼** represented 23.

The Babylonian numeration system used a *place-value system*. Numbers greater than 59 were represented by repeated groupings of 60, much as we use groupings of 10 today. For example, **▼▼ <<** represents $2 \cdot 60 + 20 \cdot 1 = 140$. The space indicates that **▼▼** represents $2 \cdot 60$ rather than 2. Numerals immediately to the left of a second space have a value $60 \cdot 60 = 60^2$ times their face value, and so on.

<< ▼	represents	$20 \cdot 60 + 1 \cdot 1 = 1201$
<▼ <▼ ▼	represents	$11 \cdot 60 \cdot 60 + 11 \cdot 60 + 1 \cdot 1 = 11 \cdot 60^2 + 11 \cdot 60 + 1 \cdot 1 = 40{,}261$
▼ <▼ <▼ ▼	represents	$1 \cdot 60 \cdot 60 \cdot 60 + 11 \cdot 60 \cdot 60 + 11 \cdot 60 + 1 \cdot 1 = 1 \cdot 60^3 + 11 \cdot 60^2 + 11 \cdot 60 + 1 \cdot 1 = 256{,}261$

The initial Babylonian system was inadequate by today's standards. For example, the symbol **▼▼** could have represented 2 or $2 \cdot 60$. Later, the Babylonians introduced the symbol **⚡** as a placeholder for missing position values. Using this symbol, **< <<▼** represented $10 \cdot 60 + 21 \cdot 1$ and **< ⚡ <<▼** represented $10 \cdot 60^2 + 0 \cdot 60 + 21 \cdot 1$. In this sense, **⚡** represented 0.

▶ **NOW TRY THIS 3**

NTT 3: Answers can be found in Answers at the back of the book.

a. Use the Babylonian system to represent 12,321.
b. Use the Hindu-Arabic system to represent **▼▼ <▼ ▼**.
c. What advantages does the Hindu-Arabic system have over the Babylonian system?

Mayan Numeration System

In the early development of numeration systems, people frequently used parts of their bodies to count. Fingers could be matched to objects to stand for one, two, three, four, or five objects. Two hands could then stand for a set of ten objects. In warmer climates where people went barefoot, people may have used their toes as well as their fingers for counting. The Mayans introduced an attribute that was not present in the Egyptian or early Babylonian systems, namely, a symbol for zero. The Mayan system used only three symbols shown in Table 4, and based their system primarily on 20 with vertical groupings.

Table 4	
Mayan Numeral	**Hindu-Arabic Equivalent**
 ⬯	0
•	1
—	5

The symbols for 11 numbers (beginning with zero) in the Mayan system are shown in Table 1. Notice the groupings of five, where each horizontal bar represents a group of five. Thus, the symbol for 19 was ≣••••, or three 5s and four 1s. The symbol for 20 was ⬯̇, which represents one group of 20 plus zero 1s. Remember that vertical groupings are used. In Figure 5(a), we have $2 \cdot 5 + 3 \cdot 1 = 13$ groups of 20 plus $2 \cdot 5 + 1 \cdot 1 = 11$, for a total of $260 + 11 = 271$. In Figure 5(b), we have $3 \cdot 5 + 1 \cdot 1 = 16$ groups of 20 and zero 1s, for a total of 320.

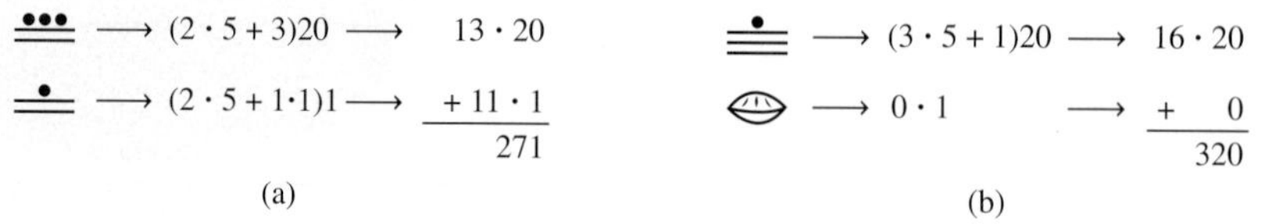

≣••• ⟶ $(2 \cdot 5 + 3)20$ ⟶ $13 \cdot 20$			≣• ⟶ $(3 \cdot 5 + 1)20$ ⟶ $16 \cdot 20$		
≣• ⟶ $(2 \cdot 5 + 1 \cdot 1)1$ ⟶ $\dfrac{+ 11 \cdot 1}{271}$			⬯ ⟶ $0 \cdot 1$ ⟶ $\dfrac{+ \quad 0}{320}$		
(a)			(b)		

Figure 5

For a number written using three rows in a true base-twenty system, the place value of the symbols in the top row should represent one group of 20^2, or 400. However, the Mayans used $20 \cdot 18 = 360$ instead of 400. (The number 360 is an approximation of the length of a calendar year, which consisted of 18 months of 20 days each, plus 5 "unlucky" days.) Thus, instead of place values of 1, 20, 20^2, 20^3, 20^4, and so on, the Mayans used 1, 20, $20 \cdot 18$, $20^2 \cdot 18$, $20^3 \cdot 18$, and so on. For example, in Figure 6(a), we have $5 + 1 = 6$ groups of 360, plus $2 \cdot 5 + 2 = 12$ groups of 20, and $5 + 4 = 9$ groups of 1, for a total of $2400 + 9 = 2409$. In Figure 6(b), we have $2 \cdot 5$ (or 10) groups of 360, plus 0 groups of 20, plus two 1s, for a total of 3602. Spacing is important in the Mayan system. For example, if two horizontal bars are placed close together, as in $=$, the symbols represent $5 + 5 = 10$. If the bars are spaced apart, as in $=$, then the value is $5 \cdot 20 + 5 \cdot 1 = 105$.

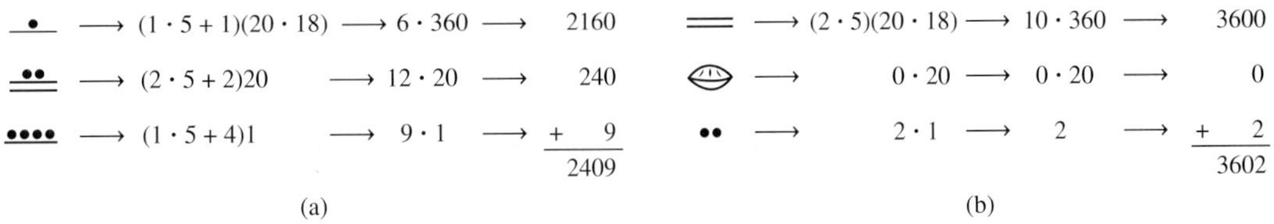

•̄	$\longrightarrow$ $(1 \cdot 5 + 1)(20 \cdot 18)$ $\longrightarrow$ $6 \cdot 360$ $\longrightarrow$ 2160			$=$	$\longrightarrow$ $(2 \cdot 5)(20 \cdot 18)$ $\longrightarrow$ $10 \cdot 360$ $\longrightarrow$ 3600		

$$\overset{\bullet\bullet}{\overline{}} \longrightarrow (2 \cdot 5 + 2)20 \longrightarrow 12 \cdot 20 \longrightarrow 240$$

$$\overset{\bullet\bullet\bullet\bullet}{} \longrightarrow (1 \cdot 5 + 4)1 \longrightarrow 9 \cdot 1 \longrightarrow \underline{+\quad 9}$$
$$2409$$

$$\text{(a)}$$

$$\langle\!\!\langle\rangle\!\!\rangle \longrightarrow 0 \cdot 20 \longrightarrow 0 \cdot 20 \longrightarrow 0$$

$$\bullet\bullet \longrightarrow 2 \cdot 1 \longrightarrow 2 \longrightarrow \underline{+\quad 2}$$
$$3602$$

$$\text{(b)}$$

Figure 6

Roman Numeration System

The Roman numeration system was used in Europe in its early form from the third century BCE. It is still seen today on cornerstones, on the opening pages of books, and on the faces of some clocks. The Roman system uses only the symbols shown in Table 5.

Table 5

Roman Numeral	Hindu-Arabic Equivalent
I	1
V	5
X	10
L	50
C	100
D	500
M	1000

Roman numerals can be written using an additive property. For example, MDCLXVI represents $1000 + 500 + 100 + 50 + 10 + 5 + 1 = 1666$, CCCXXVIII represents 328, and VI represents 6.

To avoid repeating a symbol more than three times, as in IIII, a **subtractive property** was introduced in the Middle Ages. For example, I is less than V, so if it is to the immediate left of V, it is subtracted. Thus, IV has a value of $5 - 1 = 4$, and XC represents $100 - 10 = 90$. Some extensions of the subtractive property could lead to ambiguous results. For example, IXC could be 91 or 89. By custom, 91 is written XCI and 89 is written LXXXIX. In general, only one lesser number symbol can be to the left of a greater number symbol, and the pair must be one of those listed in Table 6.

Table 6

Roman Numeral	Hindu-Arabic Equivalent
IV	$5 - 1 = 4$
IX	$10 - 1 = 9$
XL	$50 - 10 = 40$
XC	$100 - 10 = 90$
CD	$500 - 100 = 400$
CM	$1000 - 100 = 900$

In the Middle Ages, a bar was placed over a Roman numeral to multiply it by 1000. The use of bars is based on a **multiplicative property**. For example, $\overline{V}$ represents $5 \cdot 1000 = 5000$, and $\overline{CDX}$ represents $410 \cdot 1000 = 410,000$. To indicate even greater numbers, more bars appear. For example, $\overline{\overline{V}}$ represents $(5 \cdot 1000)1000 = 5,000,000$; $\overline{\overline{CXI}}$ represents $111 \cdot 1000^3 = 111,000,000,000$; and $\overline{CXI}$ represents $110 \cdot 1000 + 1 = 110,001$.

Several properties might be combined to represent some numbers, for example:

$$\overline{DCLIX} = \underbrace{\underbrace{(500 \cdot 1000)}_{\text{Multiplicative}} + \underbrace{(100 + 50)}_{\text{Additive}} + \underbrace{(10 - 1)}_{\text{Subtractive}}}_{\text{Additive}} = 500,159$$

> ### NOW TRY THIS 4
>
> **a.** Write CCXLIX as a Hindu-Arabic numeral.   249
> **b.** Use Roman numerals to represent each of the following
>   **(i)** 1634   MDCXXXIV   **(ii)** 5280 $\overline{V}$CCLXXX   **(iii)** 88   LXXXVIII
> **c.** Use Mayan numerals to represent each of the following
>   **(i)** 684   **(ii)** 164

NTT 4: c. (i)

(ii)

Other Number-base Systems

To investigate some problems students encounter learning the Hindu-Arabic system, we investigate systems that have different number bases.

Base Five

Activity Manual

Try *A Visit to Fouria* to investigate place value, addition, and subtraction in base four.

The Luo peoples of Kenya used a *quinary*, or base-five, system. A system of this type can be modeled by counting with only one hand. The digits available for counting are 0, 1, 2, 3, and 4. In the "one-hand system," or base-five system, we count 0, 1, 2, 3, 4, 10, where 10 *represents one hand and no additional fingers*. Counting in base five proceeds as shown in Figure 7. We write the subscript "five" as a reminder that the numeral is written in base five. **If no base is written, a numeral is assumed to be in base ten.** Also note that 0, 1, 2, 3, 4 are the same, and have the same meaning, in both base five and base ten.

One-Hand System	Base-Five Symbol	Base-Five Blocks
0 fingers	0_{five}	
1 finger	1_{five}	▱
2 fingers	2_{five}	▱ ▱
3 fingers	3_{five}	▱ ▱ ▱
4 fingers	4_{five}	▱ ▱ ▱ ▱
1 hand and 0 fingers	10_{five}	▭
1 hand and 1 finger	11_{five}	▭ ▱
1 hand and 2 fingers	12_{five}	▭ ▱ ▱
1 hand and 3 fingers	13_{five}	▭ ▱ ▱ ▱
1 hand and 4 fingers	14_{five}	▭ ▱ ▱ ▱ ▱
2 hands and 0 fingers	20_{five}	▭ ▭
2 hands and 1 finger	21_{five}	▭ ▭ ▱

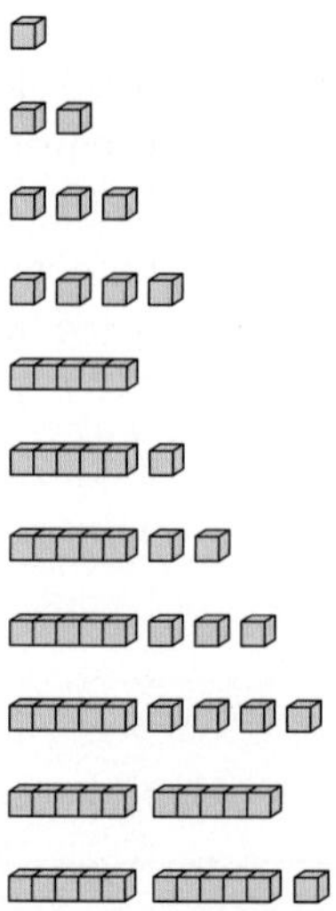

Figure 7

Counting in base five is similar to counting in base ten. Because we have only five digits, 4_{five} plays a role similar to 9 in base ten. Figure 8 shows how to find the number that comes after 34_{five} using base-five blocks. If we add one more unit block to 34_{five} and perform a trade as shown in Figure 8, we obtain 40_{five}. This numeral is read "four zero base five" and not "forty base five" because forty is a base-ten word.

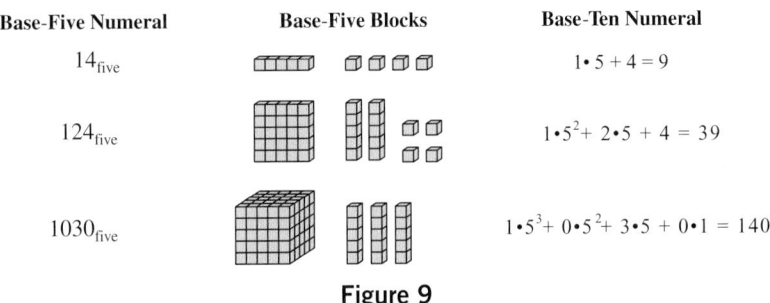

Figure 8

What number follows 44_{five}? There are no more two-digit numerals in the system after 44_{five}. In base ten, the same situation occurs at 99, where we use 100 to represent ten 10s, or one hundred. In the base-five system, we need a numeral to represent five 5s. To continue the analogy with base ten, we use 100_{five} to represent one group of five 5s or 5^2, zero groups of five, and zero units. The name for 100_{five} is read "one zero zero base five." The numeral 100 means $1 \cdot 10^2 + 0 \cdot 10^1 + 0 \cdot 1$, whereas the numeral 100_{five} means $(1 \cdot 10^2 + 0 \cdot 10^1 + 0)_{five}$, or $1 \cdot 5^2 + 0 \cdot 5^1 + 0 = 25$.

Examples of base-five numerals along with their base-five block representations and conversions to base ten are given in Figure 9.

Base-Five Numeral	Base-Five Blocks	Base-Ten Numeral
14_{five}		$1 \cdot 5 + 4 = 9$
124_{five}		$1 \cdot 5^2 + 2 \cdot 5 + 4 = 39$
1030_{five}		$1 \cdot 5^3 + 0 \cdot 5^2 + 3 \cdot 5 + 0 \cdot 1 = 140$

Figure 9

Example 2

Convert 11244_{five} to base ten.

Solution

$$11244_{five} = 1 \cdot 5^4 + 1 \cdot 5^3 + 2 \cdot 5^2 + 4 \cdot 5^1 + 4 \cdot 1$$
$$= 1 \cdot 625 + 1 \cdot 125 + 2 \cdot 25 + 4 \cdot 5 + 4 \cdot 1$$
$$= 625 + 125 + 50 + 20 + 4$$
$$= 824$$

Example 2 suggests a method for changing a base-five numeral to a base-ten numeral using powers of 5. To convert 824 to base five, we consider how to write 824 using powers of 5. We first determine the greatest power of 5 less than or equal to 824. Because $5^4 = 625$ and $5^5 = 3125$, the greatest power is 5^4. How many 5^4s are contained in 824? There is only one, so we have $824 = 1 \cdot 5^4 + 199$. Next we find the greatest power of 5 in 199. How many 5^3s are in 199? There is only one giving us $824 = 1 \cdot 5^4 + 1 \cdot 5^3 + 74$. Similarly, there are two 5^2s in 74 with 24 remaining, giving $824 = 1 \cdot 5^4 + 1 \cdot 5^3 + 2 \cdot 5^2 + 24$. Because there are four 5s in 24 with

4 remaining, we have $824 = 1 \cdot 5^4 + 1 \cdot 5^3 + 2 \cdot 5^2 + 4 \cdot 5^1 + 4 \cdot 1$. Therefore, $824 = 11244_{\text{five}}$. A shorthand method for recording this conversion follows.

$$5^4 = 625 \rightarrow 625 \overline{) 824 } \, 1 \qquad \text{How many groups of 625 in 824?}$$
$$ -625$$

$$5^3 = 125 \rightarrow 125 \overline{) 199 } \, 1 \qquad \text{How many groups of 125 in 199?}$$
$$ -125$$

$$5^2 = 25 \rightarrow 25 \overline{) 74 } \, 2 \qquad \text{How many groups of 25 in 74?}$$
$$ -50$$

$$5^1 = 5 \rightarrow 5 \overline{) 24 } \, 4 \qquad \text{How many groups of 5 in 24?}$$
$$ -20$$

$$5^0 = 1 \rightarrow 1 \overline{) 4 } \, 4 \qquad \text{How many 1s in 4?}$$
$$ -4$$
$$ 0$$

Thus, $824 = 11244_{\text{five}}$.

▶ **NOW TRY THIS 5**

A different method of converting 824 to base five is shown using successive divisions by 5. The quotient in each case is placed below the dividend and the remainder is placed on the right, on the same line with the quotient. The answer is read from bottom to top, that is, as 11244_{five}. Use this method to convert 728 to base five.

$$
\begin{array}{ll}
5 \, \underline{|824} & \\
5 \, \underline{|164} & 4 \\
5 \, \underline{|32} & 4 \\
5 \, \underline{|6} & 2 \\
1 & 1
\end{array}
\qquad
\begin{array}{ll}
5 \, \underline{|728} & \quad \text{Thus, the answer} \\
5 \, \underline{|145} & 3 \quad \text{is } 10403_{\text{five}}. \\
5 \, \underline{|29} & 0 \\
5 \, \underline{|5} & 4 \\
1 & 0
\end{array}
$$

Base Two

Historians tell of early tribes that used base two. Some aboriginal tribes still count "one, two, two and one, two twos, two twos and one, ..." Because base two has only two digits, it is called the **binary system**. In a technological setting, such as a computer or when sending data over the internet, one of the two digits can be represented by the presence of an electrical signal and the other by the absence of an electrical signal. Although base two works well for some purposes, it is inefficient for everyday use because multidigit numbers are reached very rapidly in counting in this system.

Conversions from base two to base ten, and vice versa, can be accomplished in a manner similar to that used for base five conversions.

Example 3

a. Convert 10111_{two} to base ten.
b. Convert 27 to base two.

Solution

a. $10111_{\text{two}} = 1 \cdot 2^4 + 0 \cdot 2^3 + 1 \cdot 2^2 + 1 \cdot 2^1 + 1$
$\phantom{10111_{\text{two}}} = 16 + 0 + 4 + 2 + 1$
$\phantom{10111_{\text{two}}} = 23$

b. $16\overline{)\,27\,}\underline{1}$ How many groups of $2^4 = 16$ in 27?
$\qquad -16$
$\qquad 8\overline{)\,11\,}\underline{1}$ How many groups of $2^3 = 8$ in 11?
$\qquad\quad -8$
$\qquad\quad 4\overline{)\,3\,}\underline{0}$ How many groups of $2^2 = 4$ in 3?
$\qquad\qquad -0$
$\qquad\qquad 2\overline{)\,3\,}\underline{1}$ How many groups of 2 in 3?
$\qquad\qquad\quad -2$
$\qquad\qquad\quad 1\overline{)\,1\,}\underline{1}$ How many 1s in 1?
$\qquad\qquad\qquad -1$
$\qquad\qquad\qquad\quad 0$

Alternative Solution:

$2\underline{|27}$
$2\underline{|13}\quad 1$
$2\underline{|6}\quad 1$
$2\underline{|3}\quad 0$
$\quad 1\quad 1$

Thus, 27 is equivalent to 11011_{two}.

Base Twelve

Another commonly used number-base system is the base twelve, or the duodecimal ("dozens"), system. Eggs are bought by the dozen, and pencils are bought by the *gross* (a dozen dozen). In base twelve, there are 12 digits, just as there are 10 digits in base ten, 5 digits in base five, and 2 digits in base two. In base twelve, new symbols are needed to represent the following groups of *x*'s:

$$\overbrace{xxxxxxxxxx}^{10\ x's} \quad \text{and} \quad \overbrace{xxxxxxxxxxx}^{11\ x's}$$

The new symbols chosen are T and E, respectively, so that the base twelve digits are $(0, 1, 2, 3, 4, 5, 6, 7, 8, 9, T, E)_{\text{twelve}}$. Thus, in base twelve we count $(1, 2, 3, 4, 5, 6, 7, 8, 9, T, E, 10, 11, 12, \ldots, 17, 18, 19, 1T, 1E, 20, 21, 22, \ldots, 28, 29, 2T, 2E, 30, \ldots)_{\text{twelve}}$.

Example 4

a. Convert $E2T_{\text{twelve}}$ to base ten.
b. Convert 1277 to base twelve.

Solution

a. $\begin{aligned} E2T_{\text{twelve}} &= 11 \cdot 12^2 + 2 \cdot 12^1 + 10 \cdot 1 \\ &= 11 \cdot 144 + 24 + 10 \\ &= 1584 + 24 + 10 \\ &= 1618 \end{aligned}$

b. $144\overline{)\,1277\,}\underline{8}$ How many groups of $12^2 = 144$ in 1277?
$\qquad -1152$
$\qquad\quad 12\overline{)\,125\,}\underline{T}$ How many groups of 12 in 125?
$\qquad\qquad -120$
$\qquad\qquad\quad 1\overline{)\,5\,}\underline{5}$ How many 1s in 5?
$\qquad\qquad\qquad -5$
$\qquad\qquad\qquad\quad 0$

Thus, $1277 = 8T5_{\text{twelve}}$.

Example 5

Rob used base twelve to write the following:

$$g36_{twelve} = 1050_{ten}$$

What is the value of g? Check your answer.

Solution   We could write the following equations:

$$g \cdot 12^2 + 3 \cdot 12 + 6 \cdot 1 = 1050$$
$$144g + 36 + 6 = 1050$$
$$144g + 42 = 1050$$
$$144g = 1008$$
$$g = 7$$

Check $736_{twelve} = 7 \cdot 12^2 + 3 \cdot 12 + 6 \cdot 1 = 1050$

Assessment 3-1A

1. Write the following numerals in words.
   a. 56,283,914 *
   b. 5,365,295,234 *
2. Indicate which digit in 234,518 has place value
   a. hundreds 5
   b. ten thousands. 3
3. For each of the following base-ten numerals, give the place value of the underlined digit.
   a. 827,367 Hundreds
   b. 8,421,000 Tens
4. Rewrite each of the following as a base-ten numeral.
   a. $3 \cdot 10^6 + 4 \cdot 10^3 + 5$ 3,004,005
   b. $2 \cdot 10^4 + 1$ 20,001
5. If □, △, and ○ each represent different non-zero base-ten digits, order the numerals from least to greatest.
   a. □; △□○; □△ *
   b. △□○; □□; □□△△ *
6. How many digits are there in the standard form of the numeral representing $625 \cdot 10^{12}$? 15
7. A certain three-digit natural number has the following properties: The hundreds digit is greater than 7; the tens digit is an odd number; and the sum of the three digits is 10. What could the number be? 811 or 910
8. For each of the following pairs of numerals tell which numeral represents the greater number.
   a. $\overline{\text{MCDXXIV}}$ and $\overline{\text{MCDXXIV}}$ $\overline{\text{MCDXXIV}}$
   b. 4632 and 46,032 46,032
   c. ⟨▼▼ and ⟨ ▼▼ ⟨ ▼▼
   d. 999∩∩ⅠⅠ and 𝓁∩Ⅰ 𝓁∩Ⅰ
   e. ⚏ and ◡ ◡
9. For each of the following numerals write both the succeeding and the preceding numerals (one more and one less).
   a. MCMXLIX *
   b. ⟨⟨ ⟨▼ *
   c. 𝓁99 *
   d. ⚏ *

10. A cornerstone representing when a building was built reads MCMXXII. When was this building built? 1922
11. Write each of the following numerals in Roman symbols.
    a. 121 CXXI   b. 42 XLII
    c. 91 XCI   d. 2014 MMXIV
12. Complete the following table, which compares symbols for numbers in different numeration systems: *

	Hindu-Arabic	Babylonian	Egyptian	Roman	Mayan
a.	72	▼ ⟨▼▼	∩∩∩∩∩∩ⅠⅠ	LXXII	••• ⚏
b.	602	⟨ ▼▼	999 999 ⅠⅠ	DCII	• ⚏ ••
c.	1223	⟨⟨ ⟨⟨▼▼▼	𝓁99∩∩Ⅰ‖‖	MCCXXIII	•• ⚏ •••

13. In the counting frame, the value of each dot is represented by the number in the box below the dot. For example, the following figure represents the number 154.

••	•••	••
64	8	1

What numbers are represented in the following frames?

a.

•••	••	•	86
25	5	1	

b.

•		•	•	11
8	4	2	1	

14. Write the base-four numeral for the representation shown. 2112₍four₎

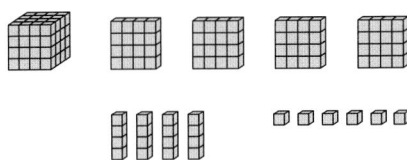

15. Write the first 15 counting numerals for each of the following bases.
    a. Two *
    b. Four *
16. How many different digits are needed for the base-twenty system? 20 digits
17. Write 2032₍four₎ in expanded notation and then convert it to base ten. *
18. Determine the greatest three-digit number in each of the following bases.
    a. Base two 111₍two₎
    b. Base twelve EEE₍twelve₎
19. Find the numeral preceding and succeeding each of the following numerals.
    a. EE0₍twelve₎ ETE₍twelve₎; EE1₍twelve₎
    b. 100000₍two₎ 11111₍two₎; 100001₍two₎
    c. 555₍six₎ 554₍six₎; 1000₍six₎
20. What, if anything, is wrong with the following numerals?
    a. 204₍four₎ There is no numeral 4 in base four.
    b. 607₍five₎ There are no numerals 6 or 7 in base five.
21. What is the least number of base-four blocks needed to represent 214? 7; three blocks, one flat, one long, and two units
22. Draw base-five blocks to represent 231₍five₎. *
23. Use only quarters, nickels, and pennies to answer the following questions.
    a. What is the fewest number of quarters, nickels, and pennies you can receive in a fair exchange for two quarters, nine nickels, and eight pennies? *
    b. How could you use the approach in (a) to write 73 in base five? *
24. Without converting to base ten, tell which is the lesser in each of the following pairs.
    a. 3030₍four₎ or 3100₍four₎ 3030₍four₎
    b. E0TE₍twelve₎ or E0ET₍twelve₎ E0ET₍twelve₎
25. Recall that with base-ten blocks: 1 long = 10 units, 1 flat = 10 longs, and 1 block = 10 flats. Make all possible exchanges to obtain the fewest number of pieces, and write the corresponding number in the given base in the following.
    a. Ten flats in base ten 1000
    b. Twenty flats in base twelve 1800₍twelve₎
26. Convert each of the following base-ten numerals to a numeral in the indicated bases.
    a. 456 in base five 3311₍five₎
    b. 1782 in base twelve 1046₍twelve₎
    c. 32 in base two 100000₍two₎
27. Write each of the following numerals in base ten.
    a. 432₍five₎ 117
    b. 101101₍two₎ 45
    c. 92E₍twelve₎ 1331
28. Represent abcd₍six₎, a base-six numeral, in expanded form. *
29. In what base does 12₍b₎ + 26₍b₎ = 41₍b₎? Seven
30. The hexadecimal numeration system in computer programming is a base-sixteen system using the symbols 0, 1, 2, 3, 4, 5, 6, 7, 8, 9, A, B, C, D, E, F. Convert the following to base ten.
    a. 256₍sixteen₎ 598
    b. 3ACD₍sixteen₎ 15,053
31. Write 584 in base sixteen. (See exercises 30.) 248₍sixteen₎
32. You are asked to distribute $900 in prize money. The dollar amounts for the prizes are $625, $125, $25, $5, and $1. How should this $900 be distributed in order to give the fewest number of prizes? *
33. Convert each of the following quantities.
    a. 58 days to weeks and days 8 weeks and 2 days
    b. 29 hours to days and hours 1 day and 5 hours
34. For each of the following, find b if possible. If not possible, tell why.
    a. b2₍seven₎ = 44 6
    b. 5b2₍twelve₎ = 734 1
35. Write the following numerals in the indicated base without multiplying out the powers.
    a. $3 \cdot 5^4 + 3 \cdot 5^2$ in base five 30300₍five₎
    b. $2 \cdot 12^5 + 8 \cdot 12^3 + 12$ in base twelve 208010₍twelve₎
36. In a game called WIPEOUT, we are to "wipe out" digits from a calculator's display without changing any of the other digits. "Wipe out" in this case means to replace the chosen digit(s) with a 0. For example, if the initial number is 54,321 and we are to wipe out the 4, we could subtract 4000 to obtain 50,321. Complete the following two parts and then try other numbers or challenge another person to wipe out a number from the number you have placed on the screen.
    a. Wipe out the 2s from 32,420. *
    b. Wipe out the 5 from 67,357. *

Assessment 3-1B

1. Write the following in words.
    a. 253,243,810 *
    b. 62,355,288,432 *
2. Indicate which digit in 2,345,925 has place value
    a. thousands 5
    b. hundred thousands 3
3. For each of the following base-ten numerals, give the place value of the underlined digit.
    a. 9̲7,998 Thousands
    b. 8̲10,485 Hundred thousands
4. Rewrite each of the following as a base-ten numeral.
    a. $3 \cdot 10^3 + 5 \cdot 10^2 + 6 \cdot 10$ 3560
    b. $9 \cdot 10^6 + 9 \cdot 10 + 9$ 9,000,099
5. If □, △, and ○ represent different non-zero base-ten digits, order the numerals from least to greatest.
    a. ○○; □△○; ○ ○, ○○, □△○
    b. □□□□; △△; □△○ △△, □△○, □□□□
6. How many digits are there in the standard form of $5250 \cdot 10^{15}$? 19

7. A two-digit number has the property that the units digit is 4 less than the tens digit, and the tens digit is twice the units digit. What is the number?   84

8. For each of the following pairs, tell which represents the greater number and why.
   a. $\overline{\text{MDCXXIV}}$ and $\overline{\text{MCDXXIV}}$ *
   b. 3456 and 30,456   *
   c. ❮▼ and ❮ ▼▼   *
   d. 99∩| and 999   *
   e. ⬌ and ☺   *

9. For each of the following name both the preceding and the succeeding numbers (one more and one less).
   a. $\overline{\text{MI}}$ $\overline{\text{M}}$; $\overline{\text{MII}}$
   b. CMXCIX   CMXCVIII; M
   c. ❮ ❮▼   ❮ ❮; ❮ ❮▼▼
   d. 𝕀9   𝕀∩∩∩∩∩∩∩∩∩∩|||||||||| ; 𝕀9|
   e. •••   ⬌

10. On the United States one-dollar bill, the number MDCCLXXVI is written on the base of the pyramid. What year does this represent?   1776

11. Write each of the following in Roman numerals.
    a. 89   LXXXIX   b. 5202 $\overline{\text{V}}$CCII
    c. 32   XXXII   d. 102   CII

12. Complete the following table, which compares symbols for numbers in different numeration systems.

	Hindu-Arabic	Babylonian	Egyptian	Roman	Mayan
a.	78	▼ ❮ ▼▼▼▼ / ▼▼▼▼	*	*	••• / ⬌
b.	601	❮ ▼	*	DCI	*
c.	1111	*	𝕀9∩|	MCXI	*

13. A number is represented on the following counting frame. What might the number be? Explain your reasoning.   *

•	••	••
27	9	1

14. Write the base-three numeral for the base-three representation shown. 1222_{three}

15. Write the first 10 counting numerals for each of the following bases.
    a. Base three $(1, 2, 10, 11, 12, 20, 21, 22, 100, 101)_{\text{three}}$
    b. Base eight $(1, 2, 3, 4, 5, 6, 7, 10, 11, 12)_{\text{eight}}$

16. How many different digits are used in base eighteen?   18

17. Write 2022_{three} in expanded form and then convert it to base ten.   *

18. Determine the greatest three-digit number in each of the following bases.
    a. Base three 222_{three} b. Base seven 666_{seven}

19. Find the numeral preceding and succeeding each of the following numerals.
    a. 100_{seven} 66_{seven}; 101_{seven}
    b. 1000_{two} 111_{two}; 1001_{two}
    c. 101_{two} 100_{two}; 110_{two}

20. What, if anything, is wrong with the following.
    a. 306_{four} There is no numeral 6 in base four.
    b. 1023_{two} There are no numerals 2 and 3 in base two.

21. What is the fewest number of base-three blocks needed to represent 79?   7; two blocks, two flats, two longs, and one unit

22. Draw base-two blocks to represent 1001_{two}.   ▣ ▫

23. Using a number system based on dozen and gross, how would you describe the representation for 277?   *

24. Without converting to base ten, tell which is the greater for each of the following pairs and explain why.
    a. $EET9E_{\text{twelve}}$ or $EOT9E_{\text{twelve}}$ *
    b. 1011011_{two} or 101011_{two} *
    c. 50555_{six} or 51000_{six} *

25. What is the fewest number of multibase blocks that can be used to represent the corresponding numeral in the given base?
    a. 10 longs in base four   4: 2 flats and 2 longs
    b. 10 longs in base three   2: 1 block and 1 long

26. Convert each of the following base-ten numerals to a numeral in the indicated base.
    a. 234 in base four 3222_{four}
    b. 1876 in base twelve 1104_{twelve}
    c. 303 in base three 102020_{three}
    d. 22 in base two 10110_{two}

27. Write each of the following numerals in base ten.
    a. 432_{six} 164
    b. 11011_{two} 27
    c. $E29_{\text{twelve}}$ 1617

28. Represent $abcd_{\text{eight}}$ as a base-ten numeral in expanded form. $a \cdot 8^3 + b \cdot 8^2 + c \cdot 8^1 + d \cdot 1$

29. In what base does $54_b + 45_b = 132_b$?   Seven

30. The hexadecimal numeration system is used in computer programming. It is a base-sixteen system and uses the symbols 0, 1, 2, 3, 4, 5, 6, 7, 8, 9, A, B, C, D, E, F. Convert the following to base ten.
    a. 864_{sixteen} 2,148
    b. $2CDE_{\text{sixteen}}$ 11,486

31. Write 256 in base sixteen. (See exercises 30.) 100_{sixteen}

32. *Who Wants the Money*, a game show, distributes prizes that are powers of 2. What is the minimum number of prizes that could be distributed from $900?   4

33. A coffee shop sold 1 cup, 1 pint, and 1 quart of coffee. Express the number of cups sold in base two. 111_{two}

34. For each of the following numerals find b, if possible. If not possible, tell why.
    a. $b3_{\text{four}} = 31_{\text{ten}}$ Not possible. There is no digit 7 in base four.
    b. $1b2_{\text{twelve}} = 1534_{\text{six}}$ Not possible

35. Using only the number keys on a calculator, fill the display to show the greatest four-digit number if each key can be used only once.   9876

36. The English word MIX has value $1000 + 9 = 1009$ in Roman numerals. Find other English words that can be converted to base ten if the letters are Roman numerals.   *

Mathematical Connections 3-1

Answers to Mathematical Connections can be found in the Answers section at the back of the book.

Reasoning

1. Explain why a number and a numeral are considered different.
2. If a numeration system has place value, what does this mean?
3. Explain the difference between zero and nothing.
4. What are the major drawbacks to each of the following systems?
   a. Egyptian
   b. Babylonian
   c. Roman
5. a. Why are large numbers in the United States written with commas separating groups of three digits?
   b. Find examples from other countries that do not use commas to separate groups of three digits.
6. In the Roman numeral system explain (a) when you add values, (b) when you subtract values, and (c) when you multiply values. Give an example to illustrate each case.

Open-Ended

7. Research an abacus and discuss how it uses place value.
8. An inspector of weights and measures uses a special set of weights to check the accuracy of scales. Various weights are placed on a scale to check accuracy of any amount from 1 oz through 15 oz. What is the fewest number of weights the inspector needs? What weights are needed to check the accuracy of scales from 1 oz through 15 oz? From 1 oz through 31 oz? Discuss the pattern forming here and find possible extensions.

Cooperative Learning

9. a. Create a numeration system with unique symbols, and write a paragraph explaining the properties of the system.
   b. Complete the following table using the system in part (a).

Hindu-Arabic Numeral	Your System Numeral
1	
5	
10	
50	
100	
5000	
10,000	
115,280	

Connecting Mathematics to the Classroom

10. Joanne asks if the year is 2015, why isn't it in the 20th century? How do you respond?

11. Allie added the Babylonian numbers below as shown.

How would you help her?

12. Betty asks how the two 3s in the numeral 32,356 are different. How do you respond?
13. A student claims that the Roman system is a base-ten system since it has symbols for 10, 100, and 1000. How do you respond?
14. When using Roman numerals, a student asks whether it is correct to write I̅I̅, as well as MI for 1001. How do you reply?

National Assessments

National Assessment of Educational Progress (NAEP) Questions

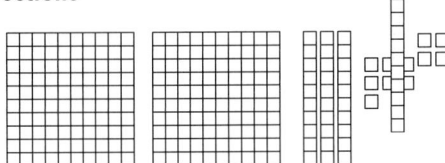

The figure above represents 237. Which number is more than 237?
A. 244
B. 249
C. 251
D. 377
NAEP, Grade 4, 2007

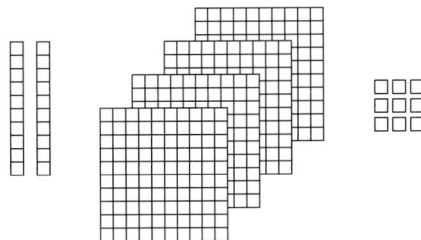

Each small square (□) above is equal to 1. There are 10 small squares in each strip. There are 100 small squares in each large square. What number is shown?
A. 4,029
B. 492
C. 429
D. 249
NAEP, Grade 4, 2003

3-2 Addition and Subtraction of Whole Numbers

Students will be able to understand and explain

- Number relationships including comparing and ordering.

- The meaning of addition and subtraction by studying various models and in turn learn addition and subtraction facts.

- Properties of addition and subtraction and how to use them to develop computational strategies.

- The inverse relationship between addition and subtraction.

> **CCSS** In the grade 1 *Common Core Standards*, we find the following:
>
> Add and subtract within 20, demonstrating fluency for addition and subtraction within 10. Use strategies such as counting on; making ten (e.g., $8 + 6 = 8 + 2 + 4 = 10 + 4 = 14$); decomposing a number leading to a ten (e.g., $13 - 4 = 13 - 3 - 1 = 10 - 1 = 9$); using the relationship between addition and subtraction (e.g., knowing that $8 + 4 = 12$, one knows $12 - 8 = 4$); and creating equivalent but easier or known sums (e.g., adding $6 + 7$ by creating the known equivalent $6 + 6 + 1 = 12 + 1 = 13$). (p. 15)

When 0 is included with the set of natural numbers $N = \{1, 2, 3, 4, 5, \ldots\}$, we have the set of whole numbers, denoted $W = \{0, 1, 2, 3, 4, 5, \ldots\}$. In the first part of this section, we develop the strategies mentioned above for adding and subtracting whole numbers. Later in the section, we show how to use properties of addition and subtraction to create and use additional strategies for these operations. Addition and subtraction are **binary operations** because *two* numbers are combined to form another number.

Addition of Whole Numbers

Counting On

Children encounter addition in their preschool years by combining sets of objects and wanting to know how many objects are in the combined set. They may count the objects to find the cardinal number of the combined set, or they may "count on." *Counting on* is an addition strategy where addition is performed by counting on from one of the numbers, for example, $5 + 3$ can be computed by starting at 5 and counting 6, 7, 8. The addition $7 + 4$ can be performed by starting at 7 and counting 8, 9, 10, 11.

Set Model

A set model is one way to represent addition of whole numbers. Suppose Jane has 4 blocks in one pile and 3 in another. If she combines the two groups, how many objects are there in the combined group? Figure 10 shows the solution. The combined set of blocks is the union of the disjoint sets of 4 blocks and 3 blocks. *Note the importance of the sets being disjoint or having no elements in common.* If the sets have common elements, then an incorrect conclusion can be drawn when using the set model.

Historical Note

Historians think that the word *zero* originated from the Hindu word *sūnya*, which means "void." Then *sūnya* was translated into the Arabic *sifr*, which when translated to Latin became *zephirum*, from which the word *zero* was derived. ●

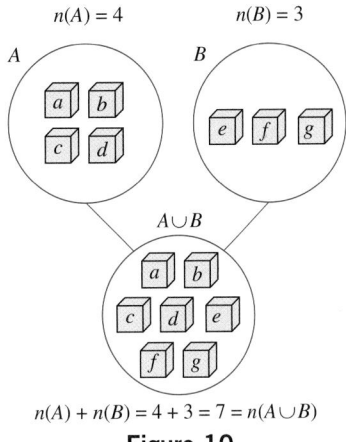

$$n(A) + n(B) = 4 + 3 = 7 = n(A \cup B)$$

Figure 10

We define addition formally using set terminology.

> ### Definition of Addition of Whole Numbers
> Let A and B be two disjoint finite sets. If $n(A) = a$ and $n(B) = b$, then $a + b = n(A \cup B)$.

The numbers a and b are the **addends** and $a + b$ is the **sum**.

▶ **NOW TRY THIS 6**

NTT 6: Answers can be found in Answers at the back of the book.

If the sets in the preceding definition of addition of whole numbers are not disjoint, explain why the definition is incorrect.

Number Line (Measurement) Model

The set model for addition is not always the best model for addition. For example, consider the following addition problems.

1. Josh has 4 feet of red ribbon and 3 feet of white ribbon. How many feet of ribbon does he have altogether?
2. One day, Gail drank 4 ounces of orange juice in the morning and 3 ounces at lunchtime. If she drank no other orange juice that day, how many ounces of orange juice did she drink for the entire day?

A *number line* can be used to model the preceding and other whole-number additions. Any line marked with two fundamental points, one representing 0 and the other representing 1, can be represented by a number line. The points representing 0 and 1 mark the ends of a *unit segment*. Other points can be marked and labeled, as shown in Figure 11. Any two consecutive whole numbers on the number line in Figure 11 mark the ends of a segment that has the same length as the unit segment.

(Historical Note)

The symbol "+" first appeared in a 1417 manuscript and was a short way of writing the Latin word *et*, which means "and." The word *minus* means "less" in Latin. First written as an *m*, it was later shortened to a horizontal bar. In a printed book in 1489, the symbols + and − referred only to surpluses and deficits in business problems.   ●

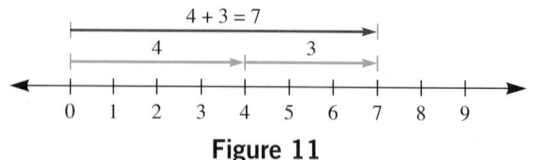

Figure 11

Addition problems may be modeled using directed arrows (*vectors*) on the number line. For example, the sum of 4 + 3 is shown in Figure 11. Arrows representing the addends, 4 and 3, are combined into one arrow representing the sum 4 + 3.

Students need to understand that the sum represented by any two directed arrows can be found by placing the endpoint of the first directed arrow at 0 and then joining to it the directed arrow for the second number with no gaps or overlaps. The sum of the numbers can then be read. We have depicted the addends as arrows (or vectors) above the number line, but students typically concatenate (connect) the arrows directly on the line. Figure 11 poses an inherent problem for students. If an arrow starting at 0 and ending at 3 represents 3, why should an arrow starting at 4 and ending at 7 also represent 3?

▶ **NOW TRY THIS 7**

NTT 7: Answers can be found in Answers at the back of the book.

A common error is that students represent 3 as an arrow on the number line sometimes starting at 1, as shown in Figure 12. Explain why this is not appropriate.

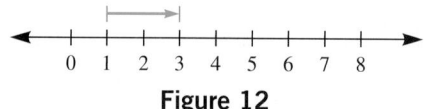

Figure 12

Ordering Whole Numbers

CCSS In the kindergarten *Common Core Standards*, we find that students should be able to:

Identify whether the number of objects in one group is greater than, less than, or equal to the number of objects in another group, e.g., by using matching and counting strategies.

Compare two numbers between 1 and 10 presented as written numerals. (p. 11)

In Chapter 2, we used the concept of a set and one-to-one correspondence to define *less than* and *greater than* relations. A horizontal number line can also be used to describe **greater than** and **less than** relations on the set of whole numbers. For example, in Figure 11, notice that 4 is to the left of 7 on the number line. We say, "four is less than seven," and we write 4 < 7. Equivalently we also say "seven is greater than four" and write 7 > 4. Because 4 is less than 7, there is a natural number that can be added to 4 to get 7, namely 3. Thus, 4 < 7 because 4 + 3 = 7. This discussion can be generalized to form the following definition of *less than*.

Definition of Less Than

For any whole numbers a and b, a is **less than** b, written $a < b$, if, and only if, there exists a natural number k such that $a + k = b$.

Sometimes equality is combined with the inequalities, greater than and less than, to give the relations **greater than or equal to** and **less than or equal to**, denoted $\geq$ and $\leq$, respectively. Thus, $a \leq b$ means $a < b$ or $a = b$. The emphasis with respect to these symbols is on the meaning of *or* in logic. Thus $3 \leq 5$, $5 \geq 3$, and $3 \geq 3$ are all true statements.

Whole-Number Addition Properties

 In the grade 1 *Common Core Standards*, we find that students should:

use properties of addition to add whole numbers and to create and use increasingly sophisticated strategies based on these properties (e.g., "making tens") to solve addition and subtraction problems within 20. By comparing a variety of solution strategies, children build their understanding of the relationship between addition and subtraction. (p. 13)

We next develop properties of whole number addition.

Whenever two whole numbers are added, a unique whole number is obtained. We say that "the set of whole numbers is *closed under addition*."

Theorem 3-1:   Closure Property of Addition of Whole Numbers

If a and b are whole numbers, then $a + b$ is a whole number.

The closure property implies that the sum of two whole numbers *exists*, and that the sum is a *unique whole number*; for example, $5 + 2$ is a unique whole number, and that number is 7.

▶ **NOW TRY THIS 8**

Determine whether each of the following sets is closed under addition: If not, tell why not.

a. $E = \{2n \mid n \in W\}$ Closed; an even number plus an even number is always even.
b. $F = \{2n + 1 \mid n \in W\}$ Not closed; for example, $1 + 3 = 4$, and 4 is not an element of *F*.
c. $G = \{0, 2\}$ Not closed; $2 + 2 = 4$ and 4 is not in *G*.

Figure 13(a) shows two additions. Pictured above the number line is $3 + 5$ and below the number line is $5 + 3$. The sums are the same. Figure 13(b) shows the same sums obtained with colored rods. Both illustrations in Figure 13 demonstrate the idea that when two whole numbers are added in either order, we obtain the same answer. This property is true in general and is the *commutative property of addition of whole numbers.*

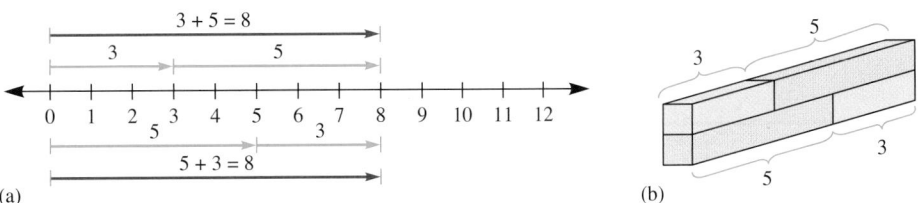

Figure 13

Theorem 3-2:   Commutative Property of Addition of Whole Numbers

If a and b are any whole numbers, then $a + b = b + a$.

We say that "addition of whole numbers is commutative." The word *commutative* is derived from *commute*, which means "to interchange."

The commutative property of addition of whole numbers is not obvious to many young children. They may be able to find the sum $9 + 2$ and not be able to find the sum $2 + 9$. Using *counting on*, $9 + 2$ can be computed by starting at 9 and then counting on two more as "ten" and "eleven." To compute $2 + 9$ without the commutative property, the *counting on* is more involved. Students need to understand that $2 + 9$ is another name for $9 + 2$.

▶ **NOW TRY THIS 9**

NTT 9: Answers can be found in Answers at the back of the book.

a. Use a set model to show the commutative property for $3 + 5 = 5 + 3$.
b. Use a number line model to show that $4 + 2 = 2 + 4$.
c. Which model do you prefer? Why?

⊙ IMAP Video

Watch Connor use the associative and commutative properties of addition to find the sum of whole numbers.

Another property of addition is demonstrated when selecting the order in which to add three or more numbers. For example, we could compute $24 + 8 + 2$ by grouping the 24 and the 8 together: $(24 + 8) + 2 = 32 + 2 = 34$. (The parentheses indicate that the first two numbers are grouped together.) We might also recognize that it is easy to add any number to 10 and compute it as $24 + (8 + 2) = 24 + 10 = 34$. This example illustrates the *associative property of addition of whole numbers*. The word *associative* is derived from the word *associate*, which means "to unite."

Theorem 3-3: Associative Property of Addition of Whole Numbers

If a, b, and c are whole numbers, then $(a + b) + c = a + (b + c)$.

When several numbers are being added, the parentheses are usually omitted because the grouping does not alter the result.

Another property of addition of whole numbers is seen when one addend is 0. In Figure 14, set A has 5 blocks and set B has 0 blocks. The union of sets A and B has only 5 blocks.

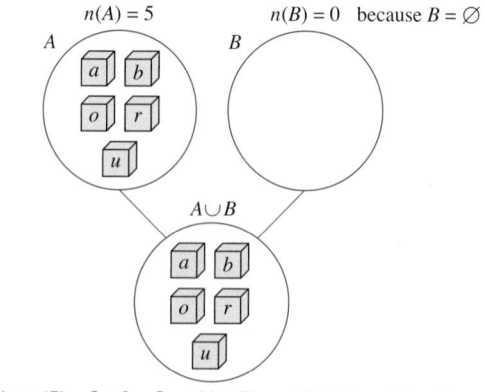

$$n(A) + n(B) = 5 + 0 = 5 = n(A \cup B) = n(A \cup \varnothing) = n(A) = 5$$

Figure 14

The set model illustrates the following property of whole numbers:

Theorem 3-4: Identity Property of Addition of Whole Numbers

There is a unique whole number 0, called the **additive identity**, such that for any whole number a, $a + 0 = a = 0 + a$.

The commutative, associative, and identity properties are introduced on the following partial grade 3 student page.

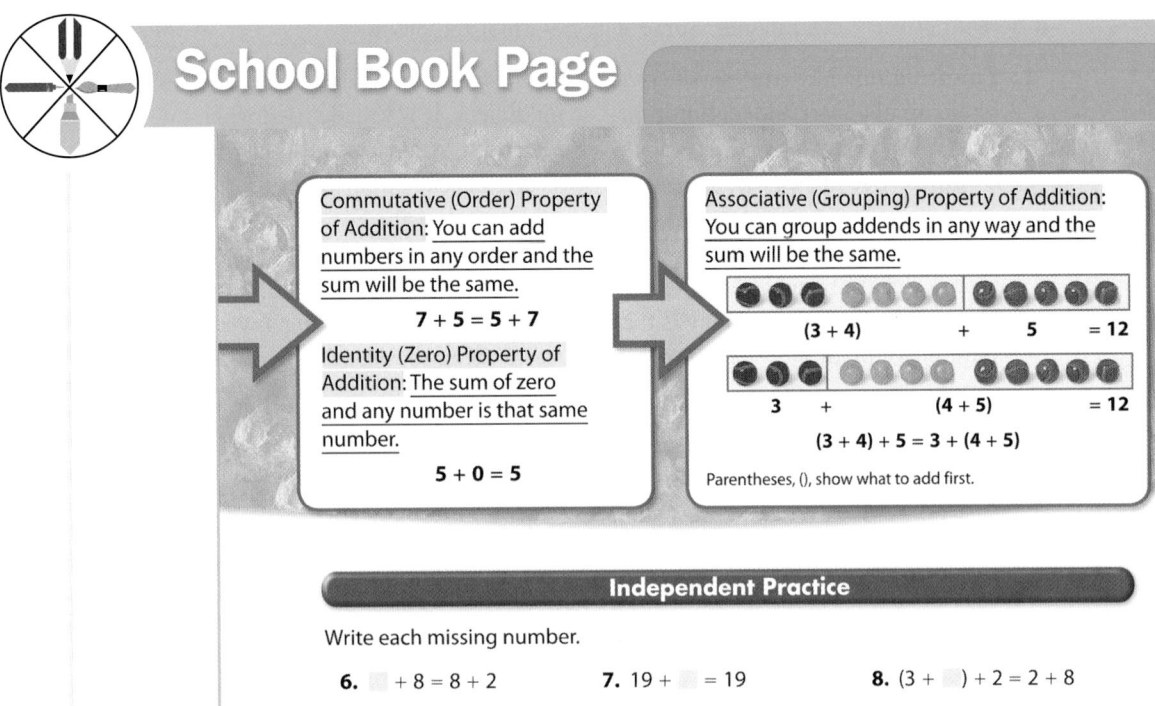

School Book Page

Commutative (Order) Property of Addition: You can add numbers in any order and the sum will be the same.

$$7 + 5 = 5 + 7$$

Identity (Zero) Property of Addition: The sum of zero and any number is that same number.

$$5 + 0 = 5$$

Associative (Grouping) Property of Addition: You can group addends in any way and the sum will be the same.

(3 + 4)   +   5   = 12

3   +   (4 + 5)   = 12

$$(3 + 4) + 5 = 3 + (4 + 5)$$

Parentheses, (), show what to add first.

Independent Practice

Write each missing number.

6. ▢ + 8 = 8 + 2   **7.** 19 + ▢ = 19   **8.** (3 + ▢) + 2 = 2 + 8

9. 4 + (2 + 3) = 4 + ▢   **10.** 7 + 3 = ▢ + 7   **11.** ▢ + 25 = 25

12. (3 + ▢) + 6 = 3 + (4 + 6)   **13.** (6 + 2) + ▢ = 8 + 7

Source: p. 33; From enVisionMATH Common Core (Grade 3). Copyright © 2012 Pearson Education, Inc., or its affiliates. Used by permission. All Rights Reserved.

Example 6

Which properties of whole numbers are illustrated in each of the following statements?

a. 5 + 7 = 7 + 5
b. 1001 + 733 is a unique whole number.
c. (3 + 5) + 7 = (5 + 3) + 7
d. (8 + 5) + 2 = 2 + (8 + 5) = (2 + 8) + 5

Solution
a. Commutative property of addition
b. Closure property of addition
c. Commutative property of addition
d. Commutative and then associative properties of addition

Mastering Basic Addition Facts

Certain mathematical facts are *basic addition facts*. Basic addition facts are those involving a single digit plus a single digit. One method of learning the basic facts is to organize them according to different derived fact strategies. Some stategies are listed below.

1. **Counting on.** The strategy of counting on from one of the addends can be used any time whole numbers are added, but it may be inefficient. It is usually used when one addend is 1, 2, or 3. For example, $9 + 2$ can be computed by starting at 9 and then counting on 10, 11.

2. **Doubles.** Use of *doubles*, such as $3 + 3$, receive special attention. After students master doubles, *doubles* + 1 and *doubles* + 2 can be learned easily. For example, if a student knows $6 + 6 = 12$, then using the associative property $6 + 7 = 6 + (6 + 1) = (6 + 6) + 1$, or 1 more than the double of 6, or 13.

3. **Making 10.** Another strategy is that of *making* 10 and then adding any remaining. For example, think of $8 + 5$ as shown in Figure 15 using the associative property of addition.

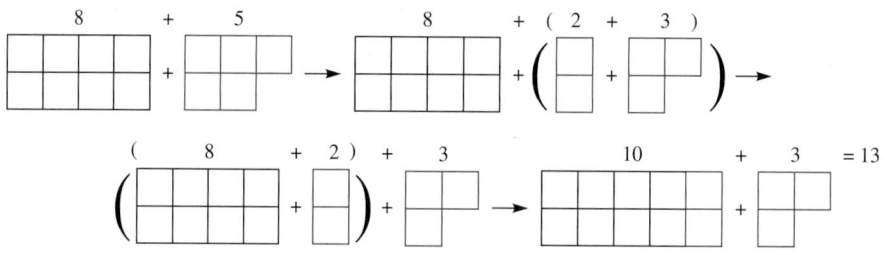

Figure 15

4. **Counting back.** The strategy of *counting back* is usually used when one number is 1 or 2 less than 10. For example, because 9 is 1 less than 10, then $9 + 7$ is 1 less than $10 + 7$. In symbols, this is $9 + 7 = (10 + 7) - 1 = 17 - 1 = 16$.

Many basic facts might be classified under more than one strategy. For $9 + 8$, we use *making* 10 as $9 + (1 + 7) = (9 + 1) + 7 = 10 + 7 = 17$ or use a *double* + 1 as $(8 + 8) + 1$.

Subtraction of Whole Numbers

In elementary school, operations that "undo" each other are **inverse operations**. Subtraction is the inverse operation of addition. It is sometimes hard for children to understand this inverse relationship. Subtraction of whole numbers models include the *take-away* model, the *missing addend* model, the *comparison* model, and the *number line (measurement)* model.

Take-Away Model

To model addition, we imagine a second set of objects as being joined to a first set, but in subtraction, we imagine a subset being *taken away* from a first set. For example, suppose from a set of 8 blocks 3 are taken away. This is illustrated in Figure 16 and the process is recorded as $8 - 3 = 5$.

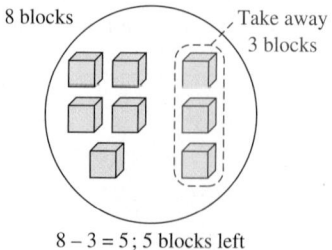

$8 - 3 = 5$; 5 blocks left

Figure 16

▶ NOW TRY THIS 10

NTT 10: Answers can be found in Answers at the back of the book.

Recall how addition of whole numbers was defined using the concept of union of two disjoint sets. Similarly, write a definition of subtraction of whole numbers using the concepts of subsets and set difference.

Missing Addend Model

The *missing addend* model for subtraction relates subtraction and addition. In Figure 17(a) suppose set A has 8 blocks but only 3 are visible. How many blocks must be in the set to have a total of 8? The answer is $8 - 3$, but this can also be thought of as the number of blocks that could be added to 3 blocks in order to get 8 blocks; that is,

$$3 + \boxed{8 - 3} = 8.$$

The number $\boxed{8 - 3} = 5$ is the **missing addend** in the equation

$$3 + \square = 8.$$

We demonstrate the *missing addend* approach using a number line. The subtraction $8 - 3$ is illustrated in Figure 17(a) using sets and in Figure 17(b) using the number line.

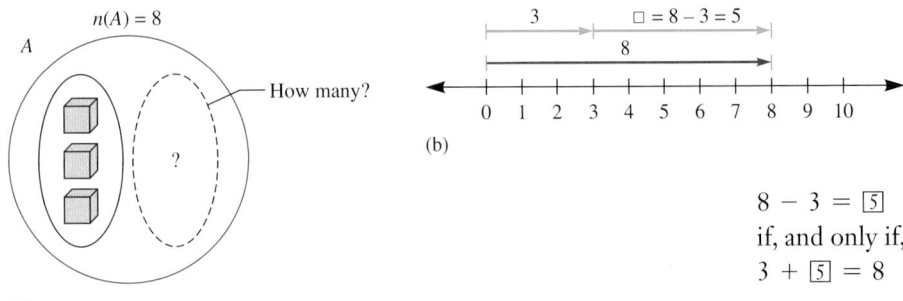

$$8 - 3 = \boxed{5}$$
if, and only if,
$$3 + \boxed{5} = 8$$

Figure 17

 IMAP Video

Watch Arriel solve a problem using the missing-addend model.

The missing addend model gives elementary school students an opportunity to use algebraic thinking because the concept of the unknown plays a key role in this model.

Cashiers often use the missing-addend model. For example, if the bill for a movie is $8 and you give the cashier $10, the cashier might calculate the change by saying "8 and 2 is 10." This idea can be generalized: *For any whole numbers a and b such that $a \geq b$, $a - b$ is the unique whole number such that $b + (a - b) = a$.* That is, $a - b$ is the unique solution of the equation $b + \square = a$. The definition can be written as follows:

> **Definition of Subtraction of Whole Numbers**
> For any whole numbers a and b such that $a \geq b$, $a - b$ is the unique whole number c such that $b + c = a$.

An alternative but equivalent definition for subtraction can be given without stipulating that $a \geq b$: "For any whole numbers a and b, $a - b$ is the unique whole number c, if it exists, such that $b + c = a$." Notice that "$a \geq b$" has been deleted and "if it exists" added.

 Refer to the partial student page shown on page 108 to see how grade 3 students are shown how addition and subtraction are related using a **fact family**.

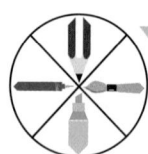

School Book Page

Another Example Subtract to find a missing addend.

Rick plans on making 13 flags. How many more flags does he need?

The parts and the whole show how addition and subtraction are related.

13 flags in all

| 8 | ? |

A fact family is a group of related facts using the same numbers.

The missing part is 5. This means Rick needs to make 5 more flags.

$8 + \blacksquare = 13$

You can write a fact family when you know the parts and the whole.

$5 + 8 = 13$ $8 + 5 = 13$
$13 - 8 = 5$ $13 - 5 = 8$

The difference is the answer when subtracting two numbers.

Source: p. 34; From enVisionMATH Common Core (Grade 3). Copyright © 2012 Pearson Education, Inc., or its affiliates. Used by permission. All Rights Reserved.

▶ **NOW TRY THIS 11**

NTT 11: Answers can be found in Answers at the back of the book.

The following is an *Addition/Subtraction Fact Triangle*. It emphasizes fact families. It has two addends and a sum.

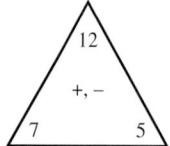

Fact Family	
$7 + 5 = 12$	$5 + 7 = 12$
$12 - 5 = 7$	$12 - 7 = 5$

Develop an *Addition/Subtraction Fact Triangle* for each of the following and write the fact family for each case

a. 7, 8, 15

b. 4, 7, 11

Comparison Model

Another way to consider subtraction is by using a *comparison* model. Suppose Juan has 8 blocks, Susan has 3 blocks, and we want to know how many more blocks Juan has than Susan. We can pair Susan's blocks with some of Juan's blocks, as shown in Figure 18, and determine that Juan has 5 more blocks than Susan. We also write this as $8 - 3 = 5$.

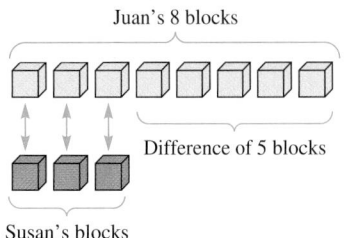

Figure 18

Number Line (Measurement) Model

Subtraction of whole numbers can also be modeled on a number line using directed arrows, as suggested in Figure 19, which shows that $5 - 3 = 2$.

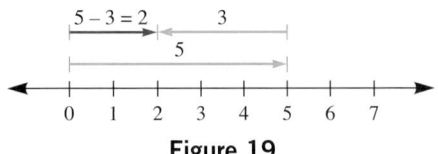

Figure 19

Properties of Subtraction

In an attempt to find $3 - 5$, we use the definition of subtraction: $3 - 5 = c$ if, and only if, $c + 5 = 3$. Since there is no whole number c that satisfies the equation, $3 - 5$ is not meaningful in the set of whole numbers. In general, if $a < b$, then $a - b$ is not meaningful in the set of whole numbers. Therefore, the set of whole numbers is not closed under subtraction.

▶ NOW TRY THIS 12

NTT 12: Answers can be found in Answers at the back of the book.

Which of the following properties hold for subtraction of whole numbers? Explain.

a. Closure property   **b.** Associative property
c. Commutative property   **d.** Identity property

Using Whole-Number Addition and Subtraction in Equations

Sentences such as $9 + 5 = \square$ and $12 - \Delta = 4$ can be true or false depending on the values of $\square$ and Δ. For example, if $\square = 10$, then $9 + 5 = \square$ is false. If $\Delta = 8$, then $12 - \Delta = 4$ is true. A value that makes an equation true is a **solution** to the equation. Thus, $8 - 5 = 3$ is the solution to $\square + 5 = 8$.

▶ NOW TRY THIS 13

Find the solution for each of the following where x is a whole number.

a. $x + 8 = 13$ 5   **b.** $15 - x = 8$ 7   **c.** $x > 9$ and $x < 11$ 10
d. $x + b = a$ if $a \geq b$, a and b are whole numbers $a - b$

Assessment 3-2A

1. A student uses the *counting on* strategy for adding two numbers. She says "thirteen, fourteen, fifteen, sixteen, seventeen." What two numbers is she adding?   *

2. For which of the following sets is it true that $n(A) + n(B) = n(A \cup B)$?
   a. $A = \{a,b,c\}, B = \{d,e\}$ True
   b. $A = \{a,b,c\}, B = \{b,c\}$ False
   c. $A = \{a,b,c\}, B = \varnothing$ True

3. If $n(A) = 3$, $n(B) = 5$, and $n(A \cup B) = 6$, what do you know about $n(A \cap B)$? $n(A \cap B) = 2$

4. Give an example to show why, in the definition of addition, sets A and B must be disjoint.   *

5. If $n(A) = 3$ and $n(A \cup B) = 6$, answer the following questions.
   a. What are the possible values for $n(B)$?   3, 4, 5, 6
   b. If in addition $A \cap B = \varnothing$, what are the possible values of $n(B)$?   3

6. Which of the following sets are closed under addition? If a set is not closed under addition explain why not.
   a. $B = \{0\}$ Closed
   b. $T = \{3n \mid n \in W\}$ Closed
   c. $N = \{1, 2, 3, 4, 5, \dots \}$ Closed
   d. $V = \{3, 5, 7\}$ Not Closed. $3 + 5 \notin V$
   e. $A = \{x \mid x \in W \text{ and } x > 10\}$ Closed
   f. $C = \{0, 1\}$ Not Closed. $1 + 1 \notin C$

7. Set A is closed under addition and contains the numbers 2 and 3. List six additional numbers, three even and three odd, that must be in A.   *

8. Set A contains the elements 2 and 3 and is closed under addition. What whole numbers might be missing from A?   *

9. Each of the following equations illustrates an example of one of the properties of whole-number addition. Fill in the blank to make a true statement and identify the property or properties.
   a. $9 + 1 = \underline{\quad} + 9$ *
   b. $7 + (3 + 5) = (3 + 5) + \underline{\quad}$ *
   c. $a + \underline{\quad} = a = \underline{\quad} + a$ *
   d. $7 + (3 + 5) = (3 + \underline{\quad}) + 5$ *

10. Each of the following illustrates a property of addition of whole numbers. Identify the property illustrated.
    a. $6 + 3 = 3 + 6$ Commutative property of addition
    b. $(6 + 3) + 5 = 6 + (3 + 5)$ *
    c. $(6 + 3) + 5 = (3 + 6) + 5$ *
    d. $5 + 0 = 5 = 0 + 5$ Identity property of addition
    e. $5 + 0 = 0 + 5$ Commutative property of addition
    f. $(a + c) + d = a + (c + d)$ *
    g. $5 + 0$ is a unique whole number   *

11. In the definition of *less than*, can the natural number k be replaced by the whole number k? Why or why not?   *

12. Give a definition of *less than* and *greater than* using the concept of subtraction.   *

13. Find the next three terms in each of the following arithmetic sequences.
    a. 8, 13, 18, 23, 28, _33, 38, 43_
    b. 98, 91, 84, 77, 70, 63, _56, 49, 42_

14. Complete the following magic square using the whole numbers 1–9. (Each row, column, and diagonal must have the same sum.)   *

8		
	5	
		2

15. If A, B, and C each stand for a different single digit from 1 to 9, answer the following if

$$A + B = C.$$

   a. What is the greatest digit that C could be?   9
   b. What is the greatest digit that A could be?   8
   c. What is the least digit that C could be?   3
   d. If A, B, and C are even, what number(s) could C be?   6 or 8
   e. If C is 5 more than A, what number(s) could B be?   5
   f. If A is 3 times B, what number(s) could C be?   4 or 8
   g. If A is odd and A is 5 more than B, what number(s) could C be?   9

16. A special domino set contains all number pairs from double-0 to double-8, with each number pair occurring only once. For example, the following domino counts as 1-4 and 4-1. How many dominos are in the set?   45

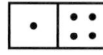

17. **a.** At a volleyball game, the players stood in a row ordered by height. If Kent is shorter than Mischa, Sally is taller than Mischa, and Vera is taller than Sally, who is the tallest and who is the shortest?   *
    b. Write possible heights for the players in part (a).   *

18. Rewrite each of the following subtraction problems as an equivalent addition problem:
    a. $9 - 7 = x$ $9 = 7 + x$ or $9 = x + 7$
    b. $x - 6 = 3$ $x = 6 + 3$ or $x = 3 + 6$
    c. $9 - x = 2$ $9 = x + 2$ or $9 = 2 + x$

19. Illustrate $8 - 5 = 3$ using each of the following models:
    a. Take-away   *   **b.** Missing addend   *
    c. Comparison   *   **d.** Number line   *

20. Write a word problem that corresponds well to each of the following models for subtraction.   Answers vary.
    a. Take-away   **b.** Number line
    c. Comparison   **d.** Missing addend

21. **a.** Solve for x in each of the following equations.
    i. $15 - 9 = 15 - 10 + x$ 1
    ii. $27 - 9 = 27 - 10 + x$ 1
    iii. $32 - 9 = 32 - 10 + x$ 1
    b. What strategy does this suggest for subtracting 9 from a whole number?   Subtract 10 and add 1.

22. **a.** One fact in a fact family is $6 + 5 = 11$. What are the other three members of this fact family?   *
    b. Draw four number line models to illustrate each of the number facts in part (a).   *

23. What conditions, if any, must be placed on a, b, and c in each of the following to make sure that the operations can be performed within the set of whole numbers?
  a. $a - b$ $a \geq b$
  b. $a - (b - c)$ $b \geq c$ and $a \geq b - c$
24. Show that each of the following is true. Give a property of addition to justify each step in your argument.
  a. $x + (y + z) = z + (x + y)$ *
  b. $x + (y + z) = y + (x + z)$ *
25. Find the solution in the set W for each of the following equations
  a. $3 + (4 + 7) = (3 + x) + 7$ 4
  b. $8 + 0 = x$ 8

  c. $5 + 8 = 8 + x$ 5
  d. $x + 8 = 12 + 5$ 9
  e. $x + 8 = 5 + (x + 3)$ All whole numbers
  f. $x - 2 = 9$ 11
  g. $x - 3 = x + 1$ No solution
  h. $0 + x = x + 0$ All whole numbers
26. Kelsey has a marbles, Gena has b marbles, and Noah has c marbles. If Kelsey has more marbles than Gena and Noah combined, write an expression (using a, b, and c) that shows how many more marbles Kelsey has than Gena and Noah combined.   *
27. Is set $B = \{5, 10, 15, 20, 25, \ldots\}$ or $B = \{5n \mid n \in W\}$ closed with respect to addition? Why?   *

Assessment 3-2B

1. A student uses the *counting on* strategy for adding two numbers. He says "fifteen, sixteen, seventeen, eighteen." What two numbers is he adding? $15 + 3$
2. For which of the following sets is it true that $n(A) + n(B) = n(A \cup B)$?
  a. $A = \{a, b\}, B = \{d, e\}$ True
  b. $A = \{a, b, c\}, B = \{b, c, d\}$ False
  c. $A = \{a\}, B = \emptyset$ True
3. If $n(A) = 3, n(B) = 5$, and $n(A \cap B) = 1$, what do you know about $n(A \cup B)$? $n(A \cup B) = 7$
4. If $n(A) - n(B)$ is defined as $n(A - B)$, what must $A \cap B$ equal? B
5. If $n(B) = 4$ and $n(A \cup B) = 6$, answer the following.
  a. What are the possible values of $n(A)$?   2, 3, 4, 5, or 6
  b. If in addition $n(A \cap B) = 0$, what are the possible values of $n(A)$?   2
6. Explain whether the following sets are closed under addition.
  a. $B = \{0, 1\}$ Not closed
  b. $T = \{0, 4, 8, 12, 16, \ldots\}$ Closed
  c. $F = \{5, 6, 7, 8, 9, 10, \ldots\}$ Closed
  d. $H = \{x \mid x \in W \text{ and } x > 100\}$ Closed
7. **a.** Set A is closed under addition and contains the numbers 2, 5, and 8. List six other elements that must be in A.   *
  b. Set A contains the element 1. What other whole numbers must be in set A for it to be closed under addition?   *
8. The set A contains the elements 2 and 4 and is closed under addition. What whole numbers must necessarily be elements of A?   *
9. Each of the following equations is an example of one of the properties of whole-number addition. Fill in the blank to make a true statement, and identify the property.
  a. $3 + 4 = \underline{\quad} + 3$ *
  b. $5 + (4 + 3) = (4 + 3) + \underline{\quad}$ *
  c. $8 + \underline{\quad} = 8$ *
  d. $3 + (4 + 5) = (3 + \underline{\quad}) + 5$ *
10. Each of the following illustrates a property of addition of whole numbers. Identify the property illustrated.
  a. $6 + 8 = 8 + 6$ Commutative property of addition
  b. $(6 + 3) + 0 = 6 + 3$ Identity property of addition
  c. $(6 + 8) + 2 = (8 + 6) + 2$ *
  d. $(5 + 3) + 2 = 5 + (3 + 2)$ *

11. Complete the following statement: $a \leq b$ if, and only if, $b = a + k$ for some $\underline{\qquad}$ number k.   Whole
12. Use the concept of subtraction to define $a \geq b$.   *
13. Find the next three terms in each of the following arithmetic sequences.
  a. 5, 12, 19, 26, 33,   40, 47, 54
  b. 63, 59, 55, 51, 47,   43, 39, 35
14. Complete the following magic square using the whole numbers 1–9. (Each row, column, and diagonal must have the same sum.)   *

6		
1		
8		

15. If A, B, C, and D each represent a different single digit from 1 to 9, answer each of the following if

$$\begin{array}{r} A \\ + B \\ \hline CD \end{array}$$

  a. What is the value of C?   1
  b. Can D be 1? Why?   No, because $C = 1$.
  c. If D is 7, what values can A be?   8 or 9
  d. If A is 6 greater than B, what is the value of D?   2
16. **a.** A domino set contains all number pairs from double-0 to double-6, with each number pair occurring only once; for example, the following domino counts as 2-4 and 4-2. How many dominos are in the set?   28

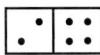

  b. When considering the sum of all dots on a single domino in an ordinary set of dominos, explain how the commutative property might be important.   *
17. If $a < b, c > b, d > c$, and $c < e < d$, order the letters from the least to the greatest.   *
18. Rewrite each of the following subtraction problems as an equivalent addition problem.
  a. $9 - 3 = x$ $9 = 3 + x$ or $9 = x + 3$
  b. $x - 5 = 8$ $x = 5 + 8$ or $x = 8 + 5$
  c. $11 - x = 2$ $11 = x + 2$ or $11 = 2 + x$

19. Illustrate $7 - 3 = 4$ using each of the following models.
  a. Take-away *
  b. Missing addend *
  c. Comparison *
  d. Number line *

20. Write a word problem that corresponds to each of the following models for subtraction. Answers vary.
  a. Take-away
  b. Number line
  c. Comparison
  d. Missing addend

21. Use the *doubles plus* strategy for adding the following.
  a. $11 + 7$ *
  b. $24 + 28$ *
  c. $35 + 37$ *

22. a. One fact in a fact family is $11 + 5 = 16$. What are the other three members of this fact family? *
  b. Draw four number line models to illustrate each of the number facts in part (a). *

23. What conditions, if any, must be placed on a, b, and c in each of the following expressions to make sure the operations can be performed within the set of whole numbers?
  a. $b - a$ *
  b. $b - (a - 3)$ *

24. Show that each of the following is true. Give a property of addition to justify each step.
  a. $a + (b + c) = c + (a + b)$ *
  b. $a + (b + c) = (c + b) + a$ *

25. Find the solution in the set W for each of the following equations.
  a. $12 - x = x + 6$ 3
  b. $(9 - x) - 6 = 1$ 2
  c. $3 + x = x + 3$ All whole numbers
  d. $11 - x = 0$ 11
  e. $14 - x = 7 - x$ No solution.
  f. $x - 3 = 17$ 20
  g. $x + 3 = x - 1$ No solution
  h. $0 + x = x - 0$ All whole numbers

26. Rob has 11 pencils. Kelly has 5 pencils. Which number sentence shows how many more pencils Rob has than Kelly?   (iii) $11 - 5 = 6$
  (i) $11 + 5 = 16$
  (ii) $16 - 5 = 11$
  (iii) $11 - 5 = 6$
  (iv) $11 - 6 = 5$

27. Is the set $B = \{7, 14, 21, 28, 35, \ldots\}$ or $B = \{7n \mid n \in W\}$ closed with respect to addition? Why? *

Mathematical Connections 3-2

Answers to Mathematical Connections can be found in the Answers section at the back of the book.

Reasoning

1. In a survey of 52 students, 22 said they were taking algebra and 30 said they were taking biology. Are there necessarily 52 students taking algebra or biology? Why?

2. To find $9 + 7$, a student says she thinks of $9 + 7$ as $9 + (1 + 6) = (9 + 1) + 6 = 10 + 6 = 16$. What property or properties is she using?

3. Explain in two different ways why if $a > b$ and c is a whole number, then $a + c > b + c$.

4. When subtraction and addition appear in an expression without parentheses, it is agreed that the operations are performed in order of their appearance from left to right. Taking this into account, and assuming that all expressions are meaningful, use an appropriate real-world model for subtraction to explain why each of the following statements is true.
  a. $a - b - c = a - c - b$
  b. $a - b - c = a - (b + c)$
  c. $(a + b) - c = a + (b - c)$
  d. $a + b - c = a - c + b$

5. Explain whether it is important for elementary students to learn more than one model for the operations of addition and subtraction.

6. Do elementary students still have to learn their basic facts when the calculator is part of the curriculum? Explain.

7. Explain how the model shown can be used to illustrate each of the following family of facts.
  a. $9 + 4 = 13$
  b. $4 + 9 = 13$
  c. $4 = 13 - 9$
  d. $9 = 13 - 4$

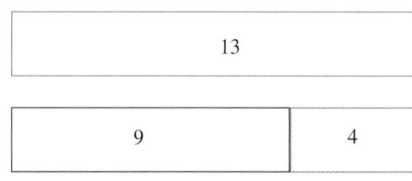

8. How are addition and subtraction related? Explain.

9. Is there a non-empty subset of the whole numbers that is closed under subtraction? If no, tell why not. If yes, give an example.

10. Use the figure below to design an *unmagic square*. That is, use each of the digits 1, 2, 3, 4, 5, 6, 7, 8, and 9 exactly once so that every column, row, and diagonal adds to a different sum. Explain how you constructed your square.

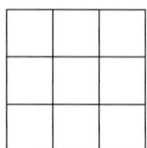

Open-Ended

11. Describe any model not in this text that you might use to teach addition to students.

12. Suppose $A \subseteq B$. If $n(A) = a$ and $n(B) = b$, then $b - a$ is defined as $n(B - A)$. Choose two sets A and B and illustrate this definition.

13. a. Create a word problem in which the set model would be appropriate to show $25 + 8 = 33$.

b. Create a word problem in which the number-line (measurement) model would be appropriate to show $25 + 8 = 33$.

c. Create a word problem or a diagram that explains why $a - (b - c) = a - b + c$ (where all operations result in whole numbers).

Cooperative Learning

14. Use the basic addition fact table for whole numbers shown and discuss with your group each of the following questions.

+	0	1	2	3	4	5	6	7	8	9
0	0	1	2	3	4	5	6	7	8	9
1	1	2	3	4	5	6	7	8	9	10
2	2	3	4	5	6	7	8	9	10	11
3	3	4	5	6	7	8	9	10	11	12
4	4	5	6	7	8	9	10	11	12	13
5	5	6	7	8	9	10	11	12	13	14
6	6	7	8	9	10	11	12	13	14	15
7	7	8	9	10	11	12	13	14	15	16
8	8	9	10	11	12	13	14	15	16	17
9	9	10	11	12	13	14	15	16	17	18

a. How does the table illustrate the closure property?
b. How does the table illustrate the commutative property?
c. How does the table illustrate the identity property?
d. How do the addition properties help students learn their basic facts?

15. Suppose that a mathematical system uses only four symbols, $a, b, c,$ and d, and the operation Δ as shown in the table. Discuss with your group each of the following questions.

Δ	a	b	c	d
a	a	b	c	d
b	b	c	d	a
c	c	d	a	b
d	d	a	b	c

a. Is the system closed? Why?
b. Is the operation commutative? Why?
c. Does the operation have an identity? If so, what is it?
d. Use several examples to investigate whether the operation is associative.

16. Have each person in your group choose a different grade textbook that does whole number operations and report on when and how subtraction of whole numbers is introduced. Compare with the different ways subtraction is introduced in this section.

Connecting Mathematics to the Classroom

17. A student says that 0 is the identity for subtraction because if $a \in W$, then $a - 0 = a$. How do you respond?

18. A student asks why we use subtraction to determine how many more pencils Sam has than Karly if nothing is being taken away. How do you respond?

19. A student claims that the set of whole numbers is closed with respect to subtraction. To show this is true, she shows that $8 - 5 = 3, 5 - 2 = 3, 6 - 1 = 5,$ and $12 - 7 = 5$ and says she can show examples like this all day that yield whole numbers when the subtraction is performed. How do you respond?

20. John claims that he can get the same answer to the problem below by adding up (begin with $4 + 7$) or by adding down (begin with $8 + 7$). He wants to know why and if this works all the time. How do you respond?

$$\begin{array}{r} 8 \\ 7 \\ + \ 4 \\ \hline \end{array}$$

21. A first grader claims that $2 - 4 = 0$ because you can't have less than nothing. How do you respond?

22. A first grader claims that $2 - 4 = 2$ because you just turn the numbers around. How do you respond?

23. Al claims that if he has 8 cookies and eats 3 of them and later eats 2 more, this is the same as having 8 cookies and eating 2 of them and later eating 3 of them. He says that this is just the commutative property of subtraction. How do you respond?

24. Jane and Mark started with the same number of pencils. Jane gave Mark two pencils and claims that Mark now has two more pencils than she has. How do you respond?

Review Problems

25. Write 5280 in expanded form.
26. What is the value of MCDX in Hindu-Arabic numerals?
27. Convert each of the following to base ten:
   a. $E0T_{\text{twelve}}$
   b. 1011_{two}
   c. 43_{five}
28. Write $12^4 + 12^2 + 13$ in base twelve.

National Assessments

National Assessment of Educational Progress (NAEP) Questions

$\square - 8 = 21$

What number should be put in the box to make the number sentence above true?

Answer: _____
NAEP, Grade 4, 2009

Fill in the four missing numbers on the number line above.
NAEP, Grade 4, 2005

3-3 Multiplication and Division of Whole Numbers

 CCSS In the grade 3 *Common Core Standards*, we find:

> Students develop an understanding of the meanings of multiplication and division of whole numbers through activities and problems involving equal-sized groups, arrays, and area models; multiplication is finding an unknown product, and division is finding an unknown factor in these situations. For equal-sized group situations, division can require finding the unknown number of groups or the unknown group size. Students use properties of operations to calculate products of whole numbers, using increasingly sophisticated strategies based on these properties to solve multiplication and division problems involving single-digit factors. By comparing a variety of solution strategies, students learn the relationship between multiplication and division. (p. 21)

This quote sets the tone and agenda for this section. If multiplication and division facts are only memorized, they may be forgotten. If students have a conceptual understanding of the basic facts, then the basic facts can be determined even if not automatically recalled. We discuss models used to help students understand the meanings of multiplication and division. We then develop the distributive property of multiplication over addition and the relationship of multiplication and division as inverse operations.

Repeated-Addition and Number-Line (Measurement) Models

CCSS In the grade 3 *Common Core Standards*, we find that students should be able to:

> Interpret products of whole numbers, e.g., interpret 5 × 7 as the total number of objects in 5 groups of 7 objects each. *For example, describe a context in which a total number of objects can be expressed as 5 × 7.* (p. 23)

One way to interpret products of whole numbers uses a *repeated-addition* model.

The student page shown on page 115 shows that if there are 3 groups of 8 goldfish, addition can put the groups together. When equal-sized groups are put together, we can use multiplication. Think of this as combining 3 sets of 8 objects into a single set. The 3 sets of 8 suggest the following addition:

$$\underbrace{8 + 8 + 8}_{\text{three } 8s} = 24$$

 Activity Manual

Use *Multiplication Arrays* to investigate multiplication as repeated addition.

(**Historical Note**)

 William Oughtred (1574–1660), an English mathematician, was the first to introduce the "St. Andrew's cross" (×) as the symbol for multiplication. This symbol was not readily adopted because, as Gottfried Wilhelm von Leibniz (1646–1716) objected, it was too easily confused with the letter *x*. Leibniz used the dot (·) for multiplication, which has become common.   ●

School Book Page — Multiplication as Repeated Addition

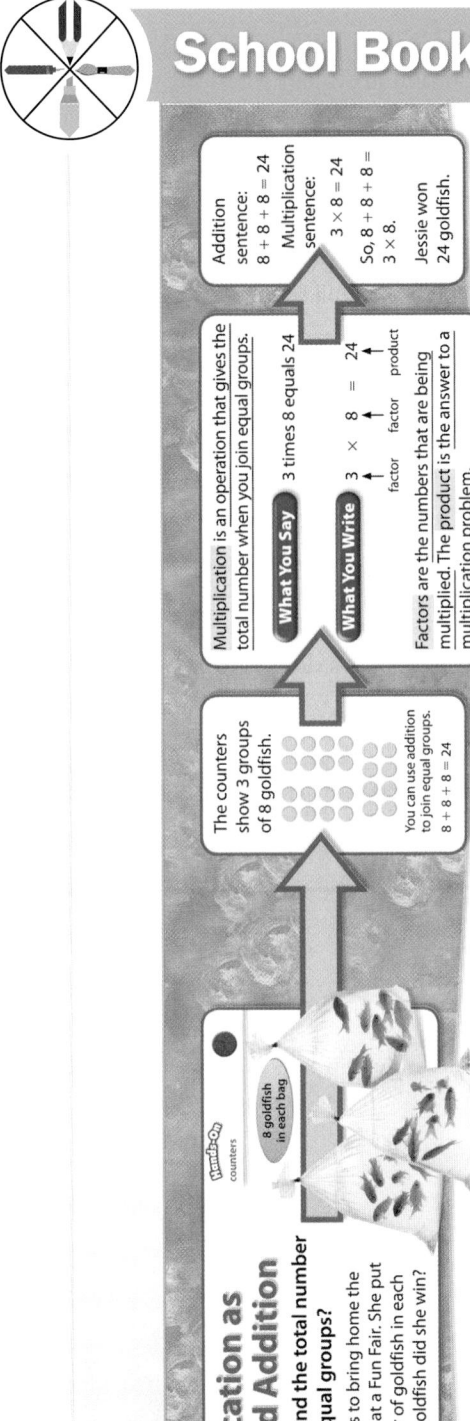

Lesson
4-1

Common Core

3.OA.1 Interpret products of whole numbers, e.g., interpret 5 × 7 as the total number of objects in 5 groups of 7 objects each. Also 3.OA.3, 3.OA.5

Multiplication as Repeated Addition

How can you find the total number of objects in equal groups?

Jessie used 3 bags to bring home the goldfish she won at a Fun Fair. She put the same number of goldfish in each bag. How many goldfish did she win?

8 goldfish in each bag

The counters show 3 groups of 8 goldfish.

You can use addition to join equal groups.
8 + 8 + 8 = 24

Multiplication is an operation that gives the total number when you join equal groups.

What You Say   3 times 8 equals 24

What You Write
$$3 \times 8 = 24$$
factor   factor   product

Factors are the numbers that are being multiplied. The product is the answer to a multiplication problem.

Addition sentence:
8 + 8 + 8 = 24
Multiplication sentence:
3 × 8 = 24
So, 8 + 8 + 8 = 3 × 8.
Jessie won 24 goldfish.

Guided Practice*

Do you know HOW?

Copy and complete. Use counters.

1. 2 groups of
    4 + 4 = ⬚
    2 × ⬚ = ⬚

2. ⬚ groups of 5
    5 + ⬚ + ⬚ = ⬚
    3 × ⬚ = ⬚

Do you UNDERSTAND?

3. Can you write 3 + 3 + 3 + 3 as a multiplication sentence? Explain.

4. **Reason** Can 3 + 5 + 6 = 14 be written as a multiplication sentence? Explain.

5. **Model** Write an addition sentence and a multiplication sentence to solve this problem:

Jessie bought 4 packages of colorful stones to put in the fish bowl. There were 6 stones in each package. How many stones did Jessie buy?

Independent Practice

Use Tools Copy and complete. Use counters or draw a picture to help.

6. 2 groups of
    6 + ⬚ = ⬚
    2 × ⬚ = ⬚

7. 3 groups of
    7 + ⬚ + ⬚ = ⬚
    3 × ⬚ = ⬚

Animated Glossary, eTools
www.pearsonsuccessnet.com

*For another example, see Set A on page 110.

100

Copy and complete each number sentence. Use counters or draw a picture to help.

8. 2 + 2 + 2 + 2 = 4 × ⬚
9. ⬚ + ⬚ + ⬚ = 3 × 7
10. 9 + ⬚ = ⬚ × 9
11. 6 + 6 + 6 + 6 + 6 = ⬚ × ⬚

Persevere Write +, −, or × for each ⬚.

12. 4 ⬚ 3 = 12
13. 3 ⬚ 6 = 9
14. 4 ⬚ 4 = 0
15. 6 ⬚ 4 = 10
16. 5 ⬚ 3 = 2
17. 2 ⬚ 4 = 8

Problem Solving

18. What number sentence shows how to find the total number of erasers?

A 5 + 5 = ⬚
B 15 − 5 = ⬚
C 15 ÷ 5 = ⬚
D 3 × 5 = ⬚

19. **Model** Write an addition sentence and a multiplication sentence to solve the problem below.

Maria has 6 new flashlights. Each flashlight takes 3 batteries. How many batteries will Maria need for the flashlights?

20. **Communicate** Luke says that you can add or multiply to join groups. Is he correct? Explain.

21. Which picture shows 3 groups of 2?

A   B   C   D

Lesson 4-1

101

We write $8 + 8 + 8$ as $3 \cdot 8$ and say "three times eight" or "eight multiplied by three." The advantage of the multiplication notation over repeated addition is evident when the number of addends is great; for example, with 25 groups of 8 goldfish, we could find the total number of goldfish by adding twenty-five 8s or writing this as $25 \cdot 8$. As seen on the student page the numbers 3 and 8 are **factors** and 24 is the **product**. Work through the exercises on the student page.

The *repeated-addition* model can be illustrated in several ways. For example, using colored rods of length 4, the combined length of five rods can be found by joining the rods end-to-end, as in Figure 20(a). Figure 20(b) shows the process using arrows on a number line.

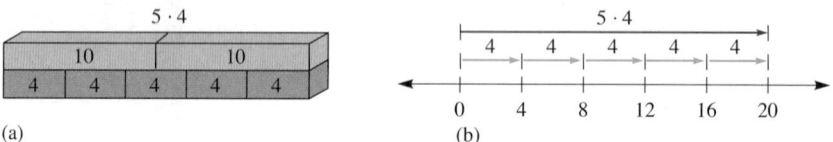

Figure 20

 The constant feature on a calculator can help relate multiplication to addition. Students can find products on the calculator without using the $\boxed{\times}$ key. For example, if a calculator has the *constant feature*, then 5×3 can be found by starting with 0 and pressing $\boxed{+}\ \boxed{3}\ \boxed{=}\ \boxed{=}\ \boxed{=}\ \boxed{=}\ \boxed{=}$. Each press of the equal sign adds 3 to the display. (Some calculators work differently.)

The repeated-addition model motivates the following definition.

Definition of Multiplication of Whole Numbers: Repeated-Addition Model

For any whole numbers a and natural number n,

$$n \cdot a = \underbrace{a + a + a + \ldots + a}_{n \text{ terms}}.$$

Rectangular-Array and Area Models

Another representation useful in exploring multiplication of whole numbers is an *array*. An array is suggested when objects are arranged with the same numbers of objects in each row and column as in Figure 21.

Figure 21

In Figure 22(a), sticks are crossed to create intersection points, thus forming an array of points. The number of intersection points on a single vertical stick is 4 and there are 5 sticks, forming a total of $5 \cdot 4$ points in the array. In Figure 22(b), the *area* model is shown as a 4-by-5 grid. The number of unit squares required to fill in the grid is 20.

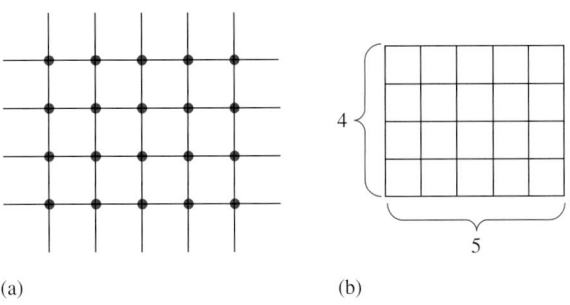

(a)   (b)

Figure 22

Cartesian-Product Model

The *Cartesian-product* model offers another way to discuss multiplication. Suppose you can order a soyburger on light or dark bread with one condiment: mustard, catsup, or horseradish. To show the number of different soyburger orders that a waiter could write for the cook, we use a *tree diagram*. The ways of writing the order are listed in Figure 23, where the bread is chosen from the set $B = \{\text{light}, \text{dark}\}$ and the condiment is chosen from the set $C = \{\text{mustard}, \text{catsup}, \text{horseradish}\}$.

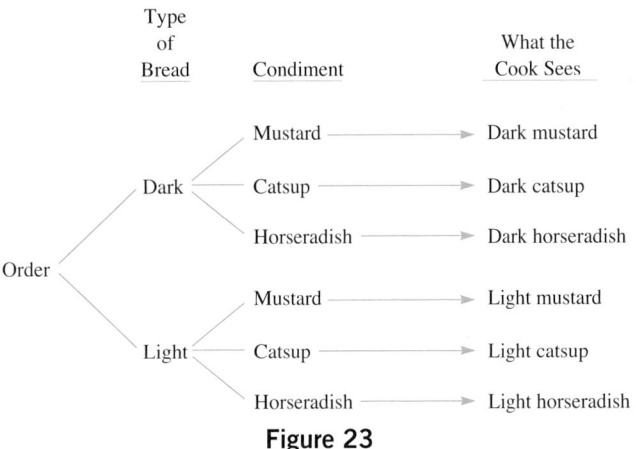

Figure 23

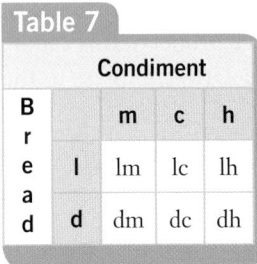

Table 7

Each order can be written as an ordered pair, for example, (dark, mustard). The set of ordered pairs forms the Cartesian product $B \times C$. The Fundamental Counting Principle tells us that the number of ordered pairs in $B \times C$ is $2 \cdot 3$ or 6.

A table is another way to model this example. Let $B = \{l, d\}$ and $C = \{m, c, h\}$ where the elements of B represent the types of bread (light, dark) and the elements of C represent the set of condiments (mustard, catsup, horseradish). Table 7 shows the six possible combinations.

The preceding discussion demonstrates how multiplication of whole numbers can be defined in terms of Cartesian products. Thus, an equivalent definition of multiplication of whole numbers follows:

Definition of Multiplication of Whole Numbers: Cartesian Product Model

For finite sets A and B, if $n(A) = a$ and $n(B) = b$, then $a \cdot b = n(A \times B)$.

In this definition, sets A and B do not have to be disjoint. The expression $a \cdot b$, or simply ab, is the **product** of a and b, and a and b are **factors**. Note that $A \times B$ indicates the Cartesian product, not multiplication. Numbers are multiplied, sets are not.

Properties of Whole-Number Multiplication

CCSS The grade 3 *Common Core Standards* recognize the importance of applying the properties of whole numbers to multiply and divide.

Apply properties of operations as strategies to multiply and divide. Examples: If 6 × 4 = 24 is known, then 4 × 6 = 24 is also known. (Commutative property of multiplication.) 3 × 5 × 2 can be found by 3 × 5 = 15, then 15 × 2 = 30, or by 5 × 2 = 10, then 3 × 10 = 30. (Associative property of multiplication.) Knowing that 8 × 5 = 40 and 8 × 2 = 16, one can find 8 × 7 as 8 × (5 + 2) = (8 × 5) + (8 × 2) = 40 + 16 = 56. (Distributive property.) (p. 23)

Next we discuss properties of whole-number multiplication.

The set of whole numbers is *closed* under multiplication. That is, if we multiply any two whole numbers, the result is a unique whole number. This property is referred to as the *closure property of multiplication of whole numbers*. Multiplication on the set of whole numbers, like addition, has the closure, commutative, associative, and identity properties.

Theorem 3-5:   Properties of Multiplication of Whole Numbers

Closure property of multiplication of whole numbers   For whole numbers a and b, $a \cdot b$ is a unique whole number.

Commutative property of multiplication of whole numbers   For whole numbers a and b, $a \cdot b = b \cdot a$.

Associative property of multiplication of whole numbers   For whole numbers a, b, and c, $(a \cdot b) \cdot c = a \cdot (b \cdot c)$.

Identity property of multiplication of whole numbers   There is a unique whole number 1, the *multiplicative identity*, such that for every whole number a, $a \cdot 1 = a = 1 \cdot a$.

3 · 5 = 15

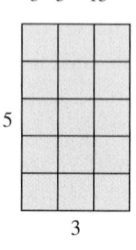

5 · 3 = 15

Figure 24

E-Manipulative Activity

Practice using the area model to perform multiplication can be found in the *Multiplication* activity.

The *commutative property of multiplication of whole numbers* is illustrated easily by building a 3-by-5 grid and then turning it sideways, as shown in Figure 24. We see that the number of 1×1 squares present in either case is 15; that is, $3 \cdot 5 = 15 = 5 \cdot 3$. The commutative property can be verified by showing that for sets with $n(A) = a$ and $n(B) = b$, $n(A \times B) = n(B \times A)$.

The *associative property of multiplication of whole numbers* can be illustrated as follows. Suppose $a = 3$, $b = 5$, and $c = 4$. In Figure 25(a), we see a picture of $3(5 \cdot 4)$ blocks. In Figure 25(b), we see the same blocks, this time arranged as $4(3 \cdot 5)$. By the commutative property, this can be written as $(3 \cdot 5)4$. Because both sets of blocks in Figure 25(a) and Figure 25(b) compress to the set shown in Figure 25(c), we see that $3(5 \cdot 4) = (3 \cdot 5)4$.

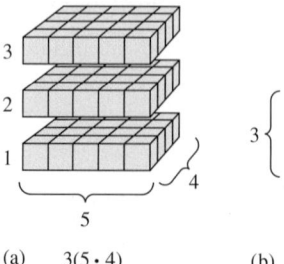

(a)   3(5 · 4)

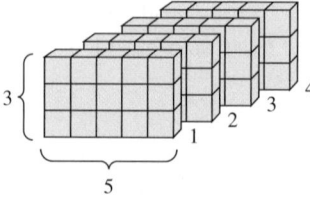

(b)   (3 · 5)4

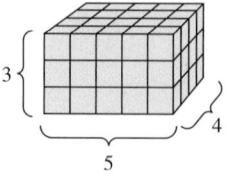

(c) 3(5 · 4) = (3 · 5)4

Figure 25

The associative property is useful in computations such as the following:

$$4 \cdot 60 = 4(6 \cdot 10) = (4 \cdot 6)10 = 24 \cdot 10 = 240$$

The *multiplicative identity for whole numbers* is 1. For example, $3 \cdot 1 = 1 + 1 + 1 = 3$. In general, for any whole number a,

$$a \cdot 1 = \underbrace{1 + 1 + 1 + \ldots + 1}_{a \text{ terms}} = a.$$

Thus, $a \cdot 1 = a$, and using the commutative property for multiplication, we have $a \cdot 1 = a = 1 \cdot a$. Cartesian products can also be used to show that $a \cdot 1 = a = 1 \cdot a$.

Next, consider multiplication involving 0. For example, $0 \cdot 6$ by definition means we have zero 6s or 0. Also $6 \cdot 0 = 0 + 0 + 0 + 0 + 0 + 0 = 0$. Thus, we see that multiplying 0 by 6 or 6 by 0 yields a product of 0. This is an example of the *multiplication property of 0*. This property can also be verified by using the definition of multiplication in terms of Cartesian products. In algebra, $3x$ means 3 x's or $x + x + x$. Similarly, $0 \cdot x$ means 0 x's or 0. Thus the following is true.

> **Theorem 3-6: Multiplication Property of 0 for Whole Numbers**
>
> **Multiplication property of 0 for whole numbers**   For every whole number a, $a \cdot 0 = 0 = 0 \cdot a$.

IMAP Video

Watch Ally use the distributive property of multiplication over addition to find the product of two whole numbers.

The Distributive Property of Multiplication over Addition and Subtraction

Operations of multiplication and addition combine to form the basis for understanding multiplication algorithms for whole numbers. The area of the large rectangle in Figure 26 equals the sum of the areas of the two smaller rectangles and therefore $5(3 + 4) = 5 \cdot 3 + 5 \cdot 4$.

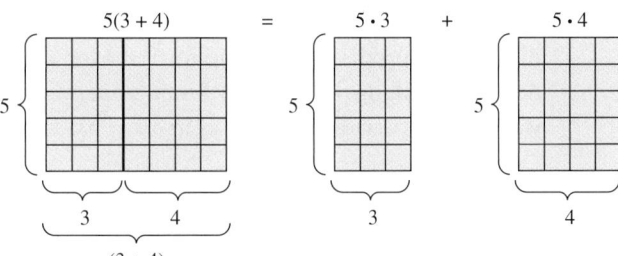

Figure 26

Properties of addition and the definition of multiplication of whole numbers also can be used to justify the above result:

$$5(3 + 4) = \underbrace{(3 + 4) + (3 + 4) + (3 + 4) + (3 + 4) + (3 + 4)}_{\text{Five terms}}$$

$$= (3 + 3 + 3 + 3 + 3) + (4 + 4 + 4 + 4 + 4)$$

Commutative and associative properties of addition

$$= 5 \cdot 3 + 5 \cdot 4 \qquad \text{Definition of multiplication}$$

This example illustrates the *distributive property of multiplication over addition* for whole numbers. A similar property of multiplication over subtraction is also true. The distributive property of multiplication over addition and the distributive property of multiplication over subtraction are stated as follows.

> **Theorem 3-7:   Distributive Property of Multiplication over Addition for Whole Numbers**
>
> For all whole numbers a, b, and c,
>
> $$a(b + c) = ab + ac.$$

> **Theorem 3-8:   Distributive Property of Multiplication over Subtraction for Whole Numbers**
>
> For all whole numbers a, b, and c with $b \geq c$,
>
> $$a(b - c) = ab - ac.$$

Theorem 3-7 can be proved using the definition of multiplication, and Theorem 3-8 can be proved using Theorem 3-7. Note that in Theorem 3-8 the condition $b \geq c$ is included to ensure that the subtraction is defined in whole numbers. Because the commutative property of multiplication of whole numbers holds, the distributive property of multiplication over addition can be rewritten as $(b + c)a = ba + ca$. The distributive property can also be generalized to any finite number of terms. For example, $a(b + c + d) = ab + ac + ad$.

The distributive property can be written as

$$ab + ac = a(b + c).$$

This is commonly referred to as *factoring*. Thus, the factors of $ab + ac$ are a and $(b + c)$.

Students find the distributive property of multiplication over addition useful when doing mental computation. For example, $13 \cdot 7 = (10 + 3)7 = 10 \cdot 7 + 3 \cdot 7 = 70 + 21 = 91$. The distributive property of multiplication over addition is important in the study of algebra and in developing algorithms for arithmetic operations. For example, it is used to combine like terms when we work with variables, as in $3x + 5x = (3 + 5)x = 8x$.

Example 7

a. Use an area model to show that $(x + y)(z + w) = xz + xw + yz + yw$.
b. Use the distributive property of multiplication over addition to justify the result in part (a).

Solution

a. Consider the rectangle in Figure 27, whose height is $x + y$ and whose length is $z + w$. The area of the entire rectangle is $(x + y)(z + w)$. If we divide the rectangle into smaller rectangles as shown, we notice that the sum of the areas of the four smaller rectangles is $xz + xw + yz + yw$. Because the area of the original rectangle equals the sum of the areas of the smaller rectangles, the statement is true.

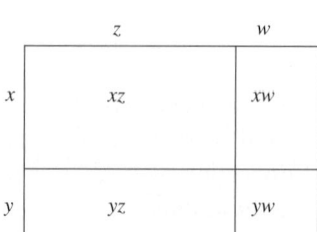

Figure 27

b. To apply the distributive property of multiplication over addition, think of $x + y$ as one number (closure property) and proceed as follows:

$$(x + y)(z + w) = (x + y)z + (x + y)w \qquad \text{The distributive property of}$$
$$\text{multiplication over addition}$$

$$= (xz + yz) + (xw + yw) \qquad \text{The distributive property of}$$
$$\text{multiplication over addition}$$

$$= xz + xw + yz + yw \qquad \text{The commutative and associative}$$
$$\text{properties of addition}$$

Example 8

Prove that $A = \{6n \mid n \in W\}$ is closed under addition.

Proof Suppose $a, b \in A$. Then $a = 6j$ and $b = 6k$, for some $j, k \in W$. By using the distributive property of multiplication over addition, $a + b = 6j + 6k = 6(j + k)$. Because $a + b \in A$, A is closed under addition.

The properties of whole-number multiplication reduce the 100 basic multiplication facts involving numbers 0–9. For example, 19 facts involve multiplication by 0, and 17 more have a factor of 1. Therefore, knowing the multiplication property of 0 and the identity property of multiplication allows students to know 36 facts. The commutative property cuts this number in half, because if students know $7 \cdot 9$, then they know $9 \cdot 7$. Knowing some multiplication facts, students can use the associative and distributive properties to figure out other products. For example, $6 \cdot 5$ can be thought of as $(5 + 1)5 = 5 \cdot 5 + 1 \cdot 5 = 25 + 5 = 30$.

Division of Whole Numbers

We use three models for division: the *set (partition)* model, the *missing-factor* model, and the *repeated-subtraction* model.

Activity Manual
Use *Find the Missing Factor* to investigate division as equal sharing.

CCSS In the grade 3 *Common Core Standards*, we find that students should be able to:

Interpret whole-number quotients of whole numbers, e.g., interpret 56 ÷ 8 as the number of objects in each share when 56 objects are partitioned equally into 8 shares, or as a number of shares when 56 objects are partitioned into equal shares of 8 objects each. *For example, describe a context in which a number of shares or a number of groups can be expressed as 56 ÷ 8.* (p. 23)

▶ **IMAP Video**

Watch Cheyenne use the set (partition) model to answer a story problem.

We introduce division using the set (partition) model.

E-Manipulative Activity
Practice using the set (partition) model to perform divisions can be found in the *Divisions* activity.

Set (Partition) Model

Suppose we have 18 cookies and want to give an equal number of cookies to each of 3 friends: Bob, Dean, and Charlie. How many should each person receive? If we draw a picture, we can see that we can divide (or partition) the 18 cookies into 3 sets, with an equal number of cookies in each set. Figure 28 shows that each friend receives 6 cookies.

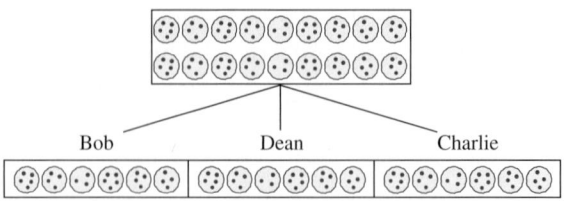

Figure 28

The answer may be symbolized as $18 \div 3 = 6$. Thus, $18 \div 3$ is the number of cookies in each of three disjoint sets whose union has 18 cookies. In this approach to division, we partition a set into a number of equivalent subsets.

Missing-Factor Model

Another strategy for dividing 18 cookies among 3 friends is to use the *missing-factor* model. If each friend receives c cookies, then the 3 friends receive $3c$, or 18, cookies. Hence, $3c = 18$. Because $3 \cdot 6 = 18$, $c = 6$. We have modeled a division problem by using multiplication. This leads to the following definition of division of whole numbers:

> **Definition of Division of Whole Numbers: Missing-Factor Model**
>
> For any whole numbers a and b, with $b \neq 0$, $a \div b = c$ if, and only if, c is the unique whole number such that $b \cdot c = a$.

The number a is the **dividend**, b is the **divisor**, and c is the **quotient**. Note that $a \div b$ can also be written as $\dfrac{a}{b}$, $b\overline{)a}$ or a/b.

Activity Manual

Use *Find the Missing Factor* and *How Many Cookies?* to investigate division as equal sharing and as repeated subtraction.

Repeated-Subtraction Model

Suppose we have 18 cookies and want to package them in cookie boxes that hold 6 cookies each. How many boxes are needed? We could reason that if one box is filled, then we have $18 - 6$ (or 12) cookies left. If one more box is filled, then there are $12 - 6$ (or 6) cookies left. Finally, we place the last 6 cookies in a third box. This discussion is summarized by writing $18 - 6 - 6 - 6 = 0$. We found by repeated subtraction that $18 \div 6 = 3$. Treating division as repeated subtraction works well if there are no cookies remaining. If there are cookies remaining, a non-zero remainder arises.

Calculators illustrate the repeated subtraction operation. For example, consider $135 \div 15$. If the calculator has a constant key, $\boxed{K}$, press $\boxed{1}\,\boxed{5}\,\boxed{-}\,\boxed{K}\,\boxed{1}\,\boxed{3}\,\boxed{5}\,\boxed{=}$ . . . and then count how many times the $\boxed{=}$ key must be pressed to make the display read 0. Calculators with a different constant feature may require a different sequence of entries. For example, on some calculators, we press $\boxed{1}\,\boxed{3}\,\boxed{5}\,\boxed{-}\,\boxed{1}\,\boxed{5}\,\boxed{=}$ and count the number of times the $\boxed{=}$ key is pressed to make the display read $\boxed{0}$.

The Division Algorithm

The set of whole numbers is not closed under division. For example, to find $27 \div 5$, look for a whole number c such that $5c = 27$. Table 8 shows several products of whole numbers times 5. Since 27 is between 25 and 30, there is no whole number c such that $5c = 27$. Because no whole number c satisfies this equation, $27 \div 5$ has no meaning in the set of whole numbers, and the set of whole numbers is not closed under division.

Table 8					
$5 \cdot 1$	$5 \cdot 2$	$5 \cdot 3$	$5 \cdot 4$	$5 \cdot 5$	$5 \cdot 6$
5	10	15	20	25	30

Even though the set of whole numbers is not closed under division, practical applications with whole number divisions are common. For example, if 32 apples were to be divided among 6 students, each student would receive 5 apples and 2 apples would remain. The number 2 is the **remainder**. Thus, 32 contains six 5s with a remainder of 2. Observe that the remainder is a whole number less than 6. This operation is illustrated in Figure 29. The concept illustrated is the **division algorithm**.

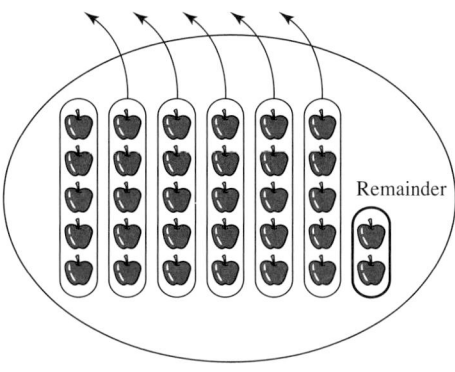

$$32 = 6 \cdot 5 + 2 \text{ with } 0 \leq 2 < 6$$

Figure 29

The above is frequently written as $32 \div 6 = 5 \text{ R}2$, which means $32 = 5 \cdot 6 + 2$. In general as shown below when we divide a by b, $b \neq 0$, we get a quotient q and a remainder r.

Division Algorithm

Given any whole numbers a and b with $b \neq 0$, there exist unique whole numbers q (quotient) and r (remainder) such that

$$a = bq + r \qquad \text{with } 0 \leq r < b.$$

When a is divided by b and the remainder is 0, we say a is *divisible* by b, or b is a *divisor* of a, or b *divides* a. By the division algorithm, a is divisible by b if $a = bq$ for a unique whole number q. Thus, 63 is divisible by 9 because $63 = 9 \cdot 7$ and the remainder is 0. Notice that 63 is also divisible by 7 and the remainder is 0.

Example 9

If 123 is divided by a number and the remainder is 13, what are the possible divisors?

Solution   If 123 is divided by b and the quotient is q, then by the division algorithm

$$123 = bq + 13 \quad \text{and} \quad b > 13.$$

Therefore, $bq = 123 - 13$, and hence $110 = bq$. Now we look for two numbers whose product is 110, where one number is greater than 13. Table 9 shows the pairs of whole numbers whose product is 110.

Table 9

1	110
2	55
5	22
10	11

The only possible values for b are 110, 55, and 22 because each is greater than 13.

Relating Multiplication and Division as Inverse Operations

In Section 3-2, subtraction and addition were related as inverse operations. In a similar way, division with remainder 0 and multiplication are related. Division is the inverse of multiplication. This relationship can be seen by looking at fact families as shown on the grade 4 student page shown on page 125. Answer the questions on the student page.

Next consider how the four operations of addition, subtraction, multiplication, and division are related on the set of whole numbers. This is shown in Figure 30. Note that addition and subtraction are inverses of each other, as are multiplication and division with remainder 0. Also multiplication can be viewed as repeated addition, and division can be accomplished using repeated subtraction when the remainder is 0.

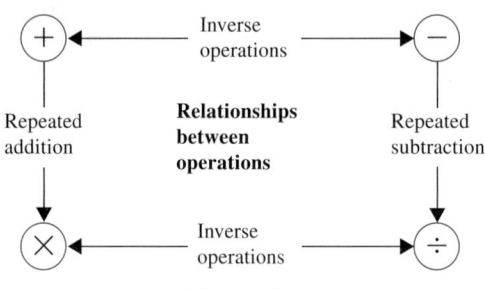

Figure 30

In Section 3-2, it was shown that the set of whole numbers is closed under addition that addition is commutative and associative, and there is an identity. On the other hand, subtraction did not have these properties. In this section, we have seen that multiplication has some of the same properties that hold for addition. Does it follow that division behaves like subtraction? Investigate this question in Now Try This 14.

▶ **NOW TRY THIS 14**

NTT 14: Answers can be found in Answers at the back of the book.

a. Provide counterexamples to show that the set of whole numbers is not closed under division and that division is neither commutative nor associative.
b. Why is 1 not the identity for division?

Division by 0 and 1

Division by 0 and by 1 are frequently misunderstood by students. Try to find the values of the following three expressions.

1. $3 \div 0$ **2.** $0 \div 3$ **3.** $0 \div 0$

Consider the following explanations:

1. By definition, $3 \div 0 = c$ if, and only if, c is the unique whole number such that $0 \cdot c = 3$. Since the multiplication property of 0 states that $0 \cdot c = 0$ for any whole number c, there is no whole number c such that $0 \cdot c = 3$. Because there is no answer to the equivalent multiplication problem, $3 \div 0$ is undefined.

2. By definition, $0 \div 3 = c$ if, and only if, c is the unique whole number such that $3 \cdot c = 0$. Because $3 \cdot 0 = 0$, $c = 0$ and $0 \div 3 = 0$. Note that $c = 0$ is the only number that satisfies $3 \cdot c = 0$.

3. By definition, $0 \div 0 = c$ if, and only if, c is the unique whole number such that $0 \cdot c = 0$. Notice that for *any* c, $0 \cdot c = 0$. According to the definition of division, c must be unique. Since there is no *unique* number c such that $0 \cdot c = 0$, it follows that $0 \div 0$ is undefined.

School Book Page — Relating Multiplication and Division

Lesson 1-7

Common Core

4.OA.1 Interpret a multiplication equation as a comparison, e.g., interpret 35 = 5 × 7 as a statement that 35 is 5 times as many as 7 and 7 times as many as 5. Represent verbal statements of multiplicative comparisons as multiplication equations.

Relating Multiplication and Division

Operations that undo each other are inverse operations. Multiplying by 3 and dividing by 3 are inverse operations.

Each trading card sheet has 3 rows with 2 pockets in each row. How many pockets are on each sheet?

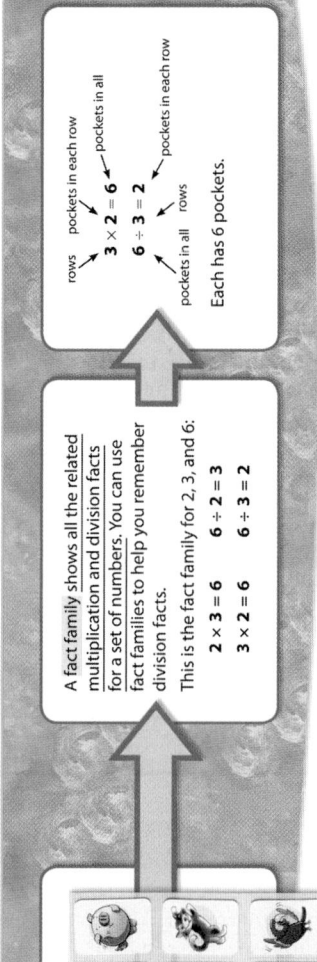

3 rows of 2

A fact family shows all the related multiplication and division facts for a set of numbers. You can use fact families to help you remember division facts.

This is the fact family for 2, 3, and 6:

$2 \times 3 = 6 \qquad 6 \div 2 = 3$
$3 \times 2 = 6 \qquad 6 \div 3 = 2$

rows pockets in each row
$3 \times 2 = 6$ ← pockets in all

pockets in all
$6 \div 3 = 2$ rows pockets in each row

Each has 6 pockets.

Guided Practice*

MATHEMATICAL PRACTICES

Do you know HOW?

In **1** and **2**, copy and complete each fact family.

1. $8 \times \square = 32$ **2.** $6 \times 9 = \square$
$32 \div \square = 4$ $54 \div \square = 9$
$32 \div \square = \square$ $54 \div 9 = \square$
$\square \times \square = 32$ $9 \times \square = \square$

In **3** and **4**, write the fact family for each set of numbers.

3. 3, 6, 18 **4.** 5, 7, 35

Do you UNDERSTAND?

5. Why are there four number sentences in the example above?

6. Is $2 \times 6 = 12$ part of the fact family from the example above?

7. Why is $3 + 3 = 6$ **NOT** in the fact family of 2, 3, and 6?

8. Reason If you know $7 \times 9 = 63$, what division facts do you know?

Independent Practice

Leveled Practice In **9** through **12**, copy and complete each fact family.

9. $5 \times \square = 35$ **10.** $9 \times \square = 72$ **11.** $3 \times \square = 18$ **12.** $2 \times \square = 24$
$35 \div 7 = \square$ $72 \div 8 = \square$ $18 \div 6 = \square$ $24 \div 12 = \square$
$\square \times \square = 35$ $\square \times \square = 72$ $\square \times \square = 18$ $\square \times \square = 24$
$35 \div \square = \square$ $72 \div \square = \square$ $18 \div \square = \square$ $24 \div \square = \square$

Animated Glossary
www.pearsonsuccessnet.com

DIGITAL

*For another example, see Set E on page 33.

In **13** through **20**, write a fact family for each set of numbers.

13. 7, 8, 56 **14.** 2, 8, 16 **15.** 6, 7, 42 **16.** 6, 6, 36

17. 3, 8, 24 **18.** 7, 10, 70 **19.** 6, 5, 30 **20.** 5, 8, 40

Problem Solving

MATHEMATICAL PRACTICES

21. Persevere How many years did it take to release all 50 quarters? Write a division fact you can use to find this quotient.

State Quarters

First quarters released	1999
Number of new quarters each year	5

22. In the fact family for the numbers 5, 6, 30, which term does **NOT** describe 5 or 6?

A factor **C** product
B divisor **D** quotient

23. Josh practiced his drums two hours before dinner and three hours after dinner. How many hours did he practice in all?

A 3 hours **C** 5 hours
B 4 hours **D** 6 hours

24. Model Write the fact family that has 9 as a factor and 45 as a product.

25. Reason Why does the fact family for 64 and 8 have only two number sentences?

Division involving 0 may be summarized as follows. Let n be any non-zero whole number. Then,

1. $n \div 0$ is undefined.   **2.** $0 \div n = 0$.   **3.** $0 \div 0$ is undefined.

In general, division by 0 is undefined.

Recall that $n \cdot 1 = n$ for any whole number n. Thus, by the definition of division, $n \div 1 = n$. For example, $3 \div 1 = 3, 1 \div 1 = 1$, and $0 \div 1 = 0$.

Order of Operations

Difficulties involving the order of arithmetic operations sometimes arise. For example, many students treat $2 + 3 \cdot 6$ as $(2 + 3)6$, whereas others treat it as $2 + (3 \cdot 6)$. In the first case, the value is 30; in the second case, the value is 20. To avoid confusion, mathematicians agree that when no parentheses are present, multiplications and divisions are performed *before* additions and subtractions. The multiplications and divisions are performed in the order they occur from left to right, and then the additions and subtractions are performed in the order they occur from left to right. Thus, $2 + 3 \cdot 6 = 2 + 18 = 20$. If parentheses are present, the computations in parentheses are done first. This order of operations is not built into calculators that display an incorrect answer of 30.

The computation $8 - 9 \div 3 \cdot 2 + 3$ is performed as follows.

$$8 - 9 \div 3 \cdot 2 + 3 = 8 - 3 \cdot 2 + 3$$
$$= 8 - 6 + 3$$
$$= 2 + 3$$
$$= 5$$

Assessment 3-3A

1. Show that $3 \cdot 4 = 12$ using each of the following models.
   a. Repeated-addition number line   *
   b. Rectangular array   *
   c. Area   *
   d. Cartesian product   *
2. If $A = \{a, b\}$ and $B = \{x, y, z\}$, find each of the following.
   a. $A \times B$ *
   b. $n(A \times B)$ 6
   c. Write a multiplication equation using numerals related to the answers in parts (a) and (b). $2 \cdot 3 = 6$
3. What multiplication is suggested by the following models?
   a.
   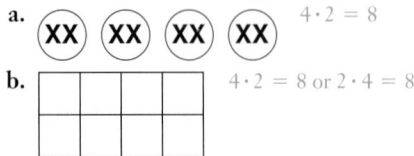
   $4 \cdot 2 = 8$
   b.
   $4 \cdot 2 = 8$ or $2 \cdot 4 = 8$
4. For each of the following find, if possible, a whole number that makes the equation true.
   a. $3 \cdot \square = 15$ 5   **b.** $18 = 6 + 3 \cdot \square$ 4
   c. $\square \cdot (5 + 6) = \square \cdot 5 + \square \cdot 6$ Any whole number
5. Determine whether the following sets are closed under multiplication.
   a. $\{0, 1\}$ Closed   **b.** $\{2, 4, 6, 8, 10, \ldots\}$ Closed
   c. $\{1, 4, 7, 10, 13, \ldots\}$ Closed

6. **a.** If 5 is removed from the set of whole numbers, is the set closed with respect to addition? Explain.   *
   b. If 5 is removed from the set of whole numbers, is the set closed with respect to multiplication? Explain.   *
7. Rename each of the following using the distributive property of multiplication over addition so there are no parentheses in the final answer:
   a. $(a + b)(c + d)$ $ac + ad + bc + bd$
   b. $\square(\triangle + \bigcirc)$ $\square \cdot \triangle + \square \cdot \bigcirc$
   c. $a(b + c) - ac$ $ab + ac - ac$ or ab
8. Place parentheses, if needed, to make each of the following equations true.
   a. $5 + 6 \cdot 3 = 33$ $(5 + 6) \cdot 3 = 33$
   b. $8 + 7 - 3 = 12$ No parentheses are needed.
   c. $6 + 8 - 2 \div 2 = 13$ No parentheses are needed.
   d. $9 + 6 \div 3 = 5$ $(9 + 6) \div 3 = 5$
9. Using the distributive property of multiplication over addition, we can factor as in $x^2 + xy = x(x + y)$. Use the distributive property and other multiplication properties to factor each of the following expressions.
   a. $xy + y^2$ $y(x + y)$ or $(x + y)y$ **b.** $xy + x$ $x(y + 1)$ or $(y + 1)x$
   c. $a^2b + ab^2$ $ab(a + b)$ or $(a + b)ab$
10. For each of the following equations, find whole numbers to make the statement true, if possible.
   a. $18 \div 3 = \square$ 6   **b.** $\square \div 76 = 0$ 0
   c. $28 \div \square = 7$ 4

11. A sporting goods store has designs for 6 shirts, 4 pairs of pants, and 3 vests. How many different shirt-pants-vest outfits are possible?   72

12. Which property is illustrated in each of the following equations.
    a. $6(5 \cdot 4) = (6 \cdot 5)4$ Associative property of multiplication
    b. $6(5 \cdot 4) = 6(4 \cdot 5)$ Commutative property of multiplication
    c. $6(5 \cdot 4) = (5 \cdot 4)6$ Commutative property of multiplication
    d. $1 \cdot (5 \cdot 4) = 5 \cdot 4$ Identity property of multiplication
    e. $(3 + 4) \cdot 0 = 0$ Multiplication property of 0
    f. $(3 + 4)(5 + 6) = (3 + 4)5 + (3 + 4)6$ *

13. Students are overheard making the following statements. What properties justify their statements?
    a. I know that $9 \cdot 7$ is either 63 or 69, and I know they can't both be right.   Closure property of multiplication
    b. I know that $9 \cdot 0$ is 0 because I know that any number times 0 is 0.   Multiplication property of 0
    c. Any number times 1 is the same as the number we started with, so $9 \cdot 1$ is 9.   Identity property of multiplication

14. The product $6 \cdot 14$ can be found by thinking of the problem as $6(10 + 4) = 6 \cdot 10 + 6 \cdot 4 = 60 + 24 = 84$.
    a. What properties are being used?   *
    b. Use this technique to mentally compute $32 \cdot 12$.   *

15. Use the distributive property of multiplication over subtraction to compute each of the following expressions.
    a. $9(10 - 2)$ $9(10 - 2) = 9 \cdot 10 - 9 \cdot 2 = 90 - 18 = 72$
    b. $20(8 - 3)$ $20(8 - 3) = 20 \cdot 8 - 20 \cdot 3 = 160 - 60 = 100$

16. Show that $(a + b)^2 = a^2 + 2ab + b^2$ using
    a. the distributive property of multiplication over addition and other properties.   *
    b. an area model.   *

17. If a and b are whole numbers with $a > b$, use the rectangles in the figure to explain why $(a + b)^2 - (a - b)^2 = 4ab$.   *

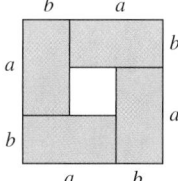

18. Use the property $(a + b)^2 = a^2 + 2ab + b^2$ to compute the following expressions.
    a. 51^2 *
    b. 102^2 *

19. In each of the following equations, show that the left side of the equation is equal to the right side and give a reason for every step.
    a. $(ab)c = (ca)b$ *
    b. $(a + b)c = c(b + a)$ *

20. Factor each of the following expressions.
    a. $xy - y^2$ $xy - y^2 = y(x - y)$
    b. $47 \cdot 101 - 47$ $47 \cdot 101 - 47 = 47(101 - 1) = 47 \cdot 100 = 4700$
    c. $ab^2 - ba^2$ $ab^2 - ba^2 = ab(b - a)$

21. Rewrite each of the following division problems as a multiplication problem.
    a. $40 \div 8 = 5$ $40 = 8 \cdot 5$
    b. $326 \div 2 = x$ $326 = 2x$

22. If $108/a = b$, then find $108/b$. a

23. Write the complete fact family for $72/8 = 9$.   *

24. Think of a number. Multiply it by 5. Add 5. Divide by 5 and then subtract 1. How does the result compare with your original number? Will this work all the time? Justify your answer.   *

25. Show that, in general, each of the following is false if a, b, and c are whole numbers.
    a. $(a \div b) \div c = a \div (b \div c)$ *
    b. $a \div (b + c) = (a \div b) + (a \div c)$ *

26. Suppose all of the operations result in whole numbers. Explain why $(a + b) \div c = (a \div c) + (b \div c)$.   *

27. Find the solution for each of the following equations.
    a. $5x + 2 = 22$ 4
    b. $3x + 7 = x + 13$ 3
    c. $3(x + 4) = 18$ 2
    d. $(x - 5) \div 10 = 9$ 95

28. A new model of car is available in 4 exterior colors and 3 interior colors. Use a tree diagram and specific colors to show how many color schemes are possible for the car.   *

29. Is it possible to find a whole number less than 100 that when divided by 10 has remainder 4 and when divided by 47 has remainder 17?   Yes, 64

30. Students were divided into 10 teams with 12 on each team. Later, the same students were divided into teams with 8 on each team. How many teams were there then?   15

31. In each of the following, tell what computation must be done last:
    a. $5(16 - 7) - 18$ $45 - 18$
    b. $54/(10 - 5 + 4)$ $54 \div 9$
    c. $(14 - 3) + (24 \cdot 2)$ $11 + 48$
    d. $21,045/345 + 8$ $8 + 61$

32. Find infinitely many whole numbers that leave remainder 1 upon division by 4. $\{4n + 1 \mid n \in W\} = \{1,5,9,13, \ldots\}$

33. The operation $\odot$ is defined on the set $S = \{a, b, c\}$, as shown in the following table. For example, $a \odot b = b$ and $b \odot a = b$.

$\odot$	a	b	c
a	a	b	c
b	b	c	a
c	c	a	b

    a. Is S closed with respect to $\odot$?   Yes
    b. Is $\odot$ commutative on S?   Yes
    c. Is there an identity for $\odot$ on S? If yes, what is it?   Yes, a
    d. Try several examples to investigate the associative property for $\odot$ on S.   All examples should work.

34. If $a, b \in W$, is the operation # commutative if $a \# b = a + b + 4$? Explain why.   *

35. At a certain concert, the audience was allowed to enter in a certain way. The first time a bell rang only 1 person was allowed to enter and choose his or her seat. The second time the bell rang 3 people were allowed to enter. On each successive ring the group that enters has two more people than the previous group.
    a. How many people have entered after the 25th ring of the bell?
    b. How many have entered after the nth ring?
    c. After how many rings will there be at least 1000 people?   *

Assessment 3-3B

1. Show that $5 \cdot 3 = 15$ using each of the following models.
   a. Repeated-addition number line *
   b. Rectangular array *
   c. Area *
   d. Cartesian product model *

2. If $A = \{a, b, c, d\}$ and $B = \{x, y, z\}$, find each of the following.
   a. $A \times B$ *   b. $n(A \times B)$ *
   c. Write a multiplication equation involving numerals related to the answers in parts (a) and (b). *

3. What multiplication is suggested by the following models?
   a. 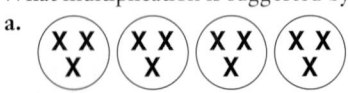 $4 \cdot 3 = 12$
   b. ▦▦▦ $3 \cdot 7 = 21$ or $7 \cdot 3 = 21$

4. For each of the following, find, if possible, a whole number that makes the equation true.
   a. $8 \cdot \square = 24$ 3   b. $28 = 4 + 6 \cdot \square$ 4
   c. $\square \cdot (8 + 6) = \square \cdot 8 + \square \cdot 6$ Any whole number

5. Determine if the following sets are closed under multiplication.
   a. $\{1, 2\}$ Not closed
   b. $\{2k + 1 \mid k \in W\}$ Closed
   c. $\{2^{k+1} \mid k \in W\}$ Closed

6. a. If 2 is removed from the set of whole numbers, is the set closed with respect to addition? Explain. *
   b. If 1 is removed from the set of whole numbers, is the set closed with respect to multiplication? Explain. *

7. Rename each of the following using the distributive property of multiplication over addition so there are no parentheses in the final answer. Use other properties to simplify when possible.
   a. $3(x + y + 5)$ $3x + 3y + 15$
   b. $(x + y)(x + y + z)$ $x^2 + 2xy + xz + y^2 + yz$
   c. $x(y + 1) - x$ xy

8. Place parentheses, if needed, to make each of the following equations true:
   a. $4 + 3 \cdot 2 = 14$ $(4 + 3)2 = 14$
   b. $9 \div 3 + 1 = 4$ Parentheses are unnecessary.
   c. $5 + 4 + 9 \div 3 = 6$ $(5 + 4 + 9) \div 3 = 6$
   d. $3 + 6 - 2 \div 1 = 7$ Parentheses are unnecessary.

9. Using the distributive property of multiplication over addition, we can factor as in $x^2 + xy = x(x + y)$. Use the distributive property and other multiplication properties to factor each of the following.   Answers vary.
   a. $47 \cdot 99 + 47$ $47(99 + 1)$
   b. $(x + 1)y + (x + 1)$ $(x + 1)(y + 1)$
   c. $x^2y + zx^3$ $x^2(y + zx)$

10. For each of the following equations, find whole numbers to make the statement true, if possible.
    a. $27 \div 9 = \square$ 3   b. $\square \div 52 = 1$ 52
    c. $13 \div \square = 13$ 1

11. A new car comes in 5 exterior colors and 3 interior colors. How many different looking cars are possible?   15

12. Which property of whole numbers is illustrated in each of the following equations?
    a. $(5 \cdot 4)0 = 0$ Multiplication property of 0
    b. $7(3 \cdot 4) = 7(4 \cdot 3)$ Commutative property of multiplication

c. $7(3 \cdot 4) = (3 \cdot 4)7$ Commutative property of multiplication
d. $(3 + 4)1 = 3 + 4$ Identity property of multiplication
e. $(3 + 4)5 = 3 \cdot 5 + 4 \cdot 5$ *
f. $(1 + 2)(3 + 4) = (1 + 2)3 + (1 + 2)4$ *

13. Students are overheard making the following statements. What properties justify their statements?
    a. I know if I remember what $7 \cdot 9$ is, then I also know what $9 \cdot 7$ is.   Commutative property of multiplication
    b. To find $9 \cdot 6$, I just remember that $9 \cdot 5$ is 45, so $9 \cdot 6$ is just 9 more than 45, or 54. *

14. The product $5 \cdot 24$ can be found by thinking of the computation as $5(20 + 4) = 5 \cdot 20 + 5 \cdot 4 = 100 + 20 = 120$.
    a. What property is being used? *
    b. Use this technique to mentally compute $8 \cdot 34$. *

15. Use the distributive property of multiplication over subtraction to compute each of the following.
    a. $15(10 - 2)$ *   b. $30(9 - 2)$ *

16. Show that if $b > c$, then $a(b - c) = ab - ac$ using an area model suggested by the given figure (express the shaded area in two different ways). *

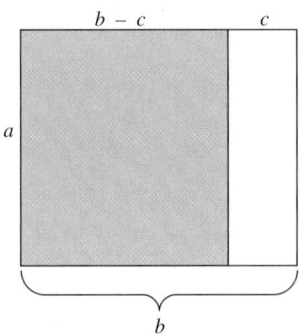

17. Use an area model suggested by the following figure to explain why $(a + b)(a - b) = a^2 - b^2$. *

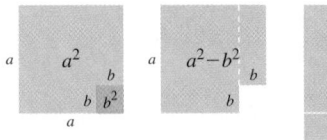

18. Use the formula $(a + b)(a - b) = a^2 - b^2$ to compute the following.
    a. $19 \cdot 21$ *   b. $25 \cdot 15$ *
    c. $99 \cdot 101$ *   d. $101^2 - 99^2$ *

19. Show that the left-hand side of the equation is equal to the right-hand side and give a reason for every step.
    a. $(ab)c = b(ac)$ *   b. $a(b + c) = ac + ab$ *

20. Factor each of the following:
    a. $xy - y$ *
    b. $(x + 1)y - (x + 1)$ *
    c. $a^2b^3 - ab^2$ *

21. Rewrite each of the following division problems as a multiplication problem.
    a. $48 \div x = 16$ $48 = x \cdot 16$
    b. $x \div 5 = 17$ $x = 5 \cdot 17$

22. If $\dfrac{64}{a} = b$, then find $\dfrac{64}{b}$. a

23. Write the complete fact family for $30/6 = 5$. *

24. Think of a number. Multiply it by 2. Add 2. Divide by 2. Subtract 1. **(a)** How does the result compare with your original number? **(b)** Will this work all the time? Explain your answer. *

25. Show that, in general, each of the following is false if a and b are whole numbers.
    a. $a \div b = b \div a$ *
    b. $a - b = b - a$ *

26. Suppose all operations result in whole numbers. Explain why $(a - b) \div c = (a \div c) - (b \div c)$. *

27. Find the solution for each of the following equations.
    a. $5x + 8 = 28$ 4
    b. $5x + 6 = x + 14$ 2
    c. $5(x + 3) = 35$ 4
    d. $(x - 6) \div 3 = 1$ 9

28. String art is formed by connecting evenly spaced nails on the vertical and horizontal axes by segments of string. Connect the nail farthest from the origin on the vertical axis with the nail closest to the origin on the horizontal axis. Continue until all nails are connected, as shown in the figure that follows. How many intersection points (red dots) are created with 10 nails on each axis? 45

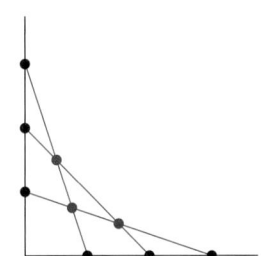

3 nails per axis
3 intersections

29. Jonah has a large collection of marbles. He notices that if he borrows 5 marbles from a friend, he can arrange the marbles in rows of 13 each. What is the remainder when he divides his original number of marbles by 13? 8

30. Students were divided into eight teams with nine on each team. Later, the same students were divided into teams with six on each team. How many teams were there then? 12

31. In each of the following, tell what computation must be done last.
    a. $5 \cdot 6 - 3 \cdot 4 + 2$ $18 + 2$
    b. $19 - 3 \cdot 4 + 9 \div 3$ $7 + 3$
    c. $15 - 6 \div 2 \cdot 4$ $15 - 12$
    d. $5 + (8 - 2)3$ $5 + 18$

32. Find infinitely many whole numbers that leave remainder 3 upon division by 5. $3, 8, 13, 18, \ldots$

33. The operation $\odot$ is defined on the set $S = \{a, b, c\}$, as shown in the following table. For example, $a \odot b = b$ and $b \odot a = b$.

$\odot$	a	b	c
a	a	b	c
b	b	a	c
c	c	c	c

   a. Is S closed with respect to $\odot$? Yes
   b. Is $\odot$ commutative on S? Yes
   c. Is there an identity for $\odot$ on S? If yes, what is it? Yes, a
   d. Try several examples to investigate the associative property for $\odot$ on S. All examples should work.

34. If $a, b \in W$, is the operation # commutative if $a \# b = 0$, if either a or b or both are odd and $a \# b = 1$, if a and b are both even? *

35. When a marching band was placed in rows of 5, one member remained. When the members were placed in rows of 6, there was still one member remaining. However, when they were placed in rows of 7, nobody remained. What is the least number of members that could have been in the band? 91

Mathematical Connections 3-3

Answers to Mathematical Connections can be found in the Answers section at the back of the book.

Reasoning

1. Why is an odd number times an odd number always odd?
2. Can 0 be the identity for multiplication? Explain why or why not.
3. Suppose you forgot the product of $9 \cdot 7$. Give several ways that you could find the product using different multiplication facts and properties.
4. Is $x \div x$ always equal to 1? Explain your answer.
5. Is $x \cdot x$ ever equal to x? Explain your answer.
6. Describe all pairs of whole numbers whose sum and product are the same.
7. In the *Common Core Standards* quote at the beginning of this section it states that students should learn the relationship between multiplication and division. Explain this relationship.
8. Explain how the distributive property of multiplication over addition would be helpful to mentally perform the following computation.

$$37 \cdot 52 + 37 \cdot 48$$

Open-Ended

9. Create word problems using each model for multiplication and division.

10. Describe a real-life situation that could be represented by the expression $3 + 2 \cdot 6$.

Cooperative Learning

11. Multiplication facts that most children have memorized can be stated in the following table that is partially filled.

$\times$	1	2	3	4	5	6	7	8	9
1									
2									
3									
4				16					
5							35		
6									
7									
8									72
9									81

a. Complete the table of multiplication facts. Find as many patterns as you can. List all the patterns that your group discovered and explain why some of those patterns occur in the table.

b. How can the multiplication table be used to solve division problems?

c. Consider the odd number 35 shown in the multiplication table. Consider all the numbers that surround it. Note that they are all even. Does this happen for all odd numbers in the table? Explain why or why not.

12. Enter a natural number less than 20 on a calculator. If the number is even, divide it by 2; if it is odd, multiply it by 3 and add 1. Next, follow the same directions for the number on the display. Keep repeating the process.

a. Will the display eventually reach 1?

b. Which number less than 20 takes the most steps before reaching 1?

c. Do even or odd numbers reach 1 more quickly?

d. Investigate what happens with numbers greater than 20.

Connecting Mathematics to the Classroom

13. Suppose a student argued that $0 \div 0 = 1$ because every number divided by itself is 1. How would you help that student?

14. Sue claims the following is true by the distributive law, where a and b are whole numbers.

$$3(ab) = (3a)(3b)$$

How might you help her?

15. A student claims that for all whole numbers $(ab) \div b = a$. How do you respond?

16. A student says that 1 is the identity for division because $a \div 1 = a$ for all whole numbers a. How do you respond?

17. Amy claims that no finite set of whole numbers is closed under multiplication. How do you respond?

18. Linda performed the following calculations.

$$2 + 3 \cdot 4 = 2 + 12 = 14 \quad \text{and} \quad 2(3 + 4) = 2 \cdot 7 = 14.$$

From this she concluded that if $a, b, c \in W$, then $a + bc = a(b + c)$. How do you respond?

Review Problems

19. Give an infinite set of even numbers that is not closed under addition.

20. Is the operation of subtraction for whole numbers commutative? If not, give a counterexample.

21. In base two, does the number "two" exist? Explain.

22. Write 81 in base three.

National Assessments

National Assessment of Educational Progress (NAEP) Question

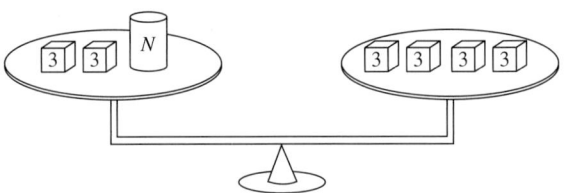

The weights on the scale above are balanced. Each cube weighs 3 pounds. The cylinder weighs N pounds. Which number sentence best describes this situation?

A. $6 + N = 12$

B. $6 + N = 4$

C. $2 + N = 12$

D. $2 + N = 4$

NAEP, Grade 4, 2007

3-4 Addition and Subtraction Algorithms, Mental Computation, and Estimation

3-4 Objectives

Students will be able to understand and explain

- Models to develop algorithms for addition and subtraction.

- Addition and subtraction algorithms including the standard algorithms and how to use them to solve problems.

(continued on next page)

CCSS The grade 2 *Common Core Standards* state that students at this level should be able to:

Use place value understanding and properties of operations to add and subtract.

Fluently add and subtract within 100 using strategies based on place value, properties of operations, and/or the relationship between addition and subtraction.

Add up to four two-digit numbers using strategies based on place value and properties of operations.

Add and subtract within 1000, using concrete models or drawings and strategies based on place value, properties of operations, and/or the relationship between addition and subtraction; relate the strategy to a written method. Understand that in adding or subtracting three-digit numbers, one adds or subtracts hundreds and hundreds, tens and tens, ones and ones; and sometimes it is necessary to compose or decompose tens or hundreds.

Mentally add 10 or 100 to a given number 100–900, and mentally subtract 10 or 100 from a given number 100–900. (p. 19)

- Number bases other than ten to provide insight into base-ten algorithms.
- Mental addition and subtraction computational skills and estimation techniques to check reasonableness of answers.

Activity Manual

Use *It All Adds Up* to develop an understanding of addition of multi-digit numbers.

CCSS

IMAP Video

Watch Andrew discuss and algorithm for adding whole numbers he invented himself.

E-Manipulative Activity

Practice using base-ten blocks to perform additions can be found in the *Adding Blocks* activity.

Section 3-2 introduced the operations of addition and subtraction of whole numbers, and now it is time to focus on *computational fluency*—having and using efficient and accurate methods for computing. Standard algorithms are one means to achieve this fluency. An **algorithm** is a step-by-step procedure for solving a problem or performing a computation. The word is derived from the name of the Persian mathematician, astronomer, and geographer al-Khwarizmi (780–850 CE).

This section focuses on developing and understanding algorithms involving addition and subtraction along with mental mathematics and estimation associated with those operations.

Addition Algorithms

To help children understand algorithms, they should explore addition using manipulatives. If children can touch and move around items such as chips, bean sticks, and an abacus or use base-ten blocks, they often proceed naturally on their own to the creation of algorithms for addition. In the following, we use base-ten blocks to illustrate the development of the standard algorithm for whole-number addition. The grade 4 *Common Core Standards* state that students should "fluently add and subtract multi-digit whole numbers using the standard algorithm." (p. 29)

To add $14 + 23$, we start with a concrete model as in Figure 31(a), move to the expanded algorithm in Figure 31(b), and then to the standard algorithm in Figure 31(c).

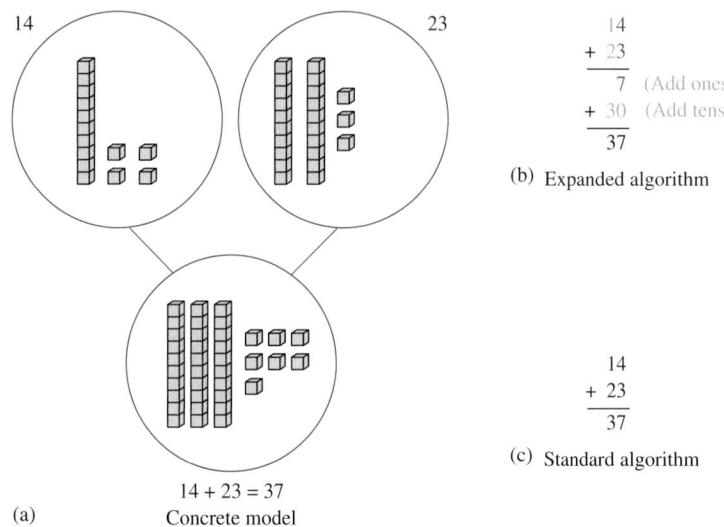

(b) Expanded algorithm

(c) Standard algorithm

(a)   Concrete model
$14 + 23 = 37$

Figure 31

A more formal justification for this addition, not usually presented at the elementary school level, is the following:

$$14 + 23 = (1 \cdot 10 + 4) + (2 \cdot 10 + 3) \quad \text{Expanded form}$$
$$= (1 \cdot 10 + 2 \cdot 10) + (4 + 3) \quad \text{Commutative and associative properties of addition}$$
$$= (1 + 2)10 + (4 + 3) \quad \text{Distributive property of multiplication over addition}$$
$$= 3 \cdot 10 + 7 \quad \text{Single-digit addition facts}$$
$$= 37 \quad \text{Place value}$$

The student page shown on page 132 shows an example of adding two-digit numbers with regrouping using base-ten blocks. Kim's way leads to the expanded algorithm, and Henry's way leads to the standard algorithm. On the student page, students are asked to estimate their answers before performing an algorithm. This is good practice and leads to the development of number sense and also makes students consider whether their answers are reasonable.

School Book Page | Adding Two-Digit Numbers

Lesson 3-1

Key Idea
You can break apart numbers, using place value, to add.

Vocabulary
• regroup

Think It Through
• I should **estimate** so I will know if my answer is reasonable.
• I can **use place-value blocks** to show addition.

Adding Two-Digit Numbers

✓ **WARM UP**
Use mental math.
1. 48 + 20   2. 63 + 11
3. 71 + 8   4. 53 + 5

LEARN

How do you add two-digit numbers?

Example

Cal counted 46 ladybugs on a log and 78 more on some bushes. How many ladybugs did he count all together?

Find 46 + 78.

Estimate: 46 rounds to 50. 78 rounds to 80.

50 + 80 = 130, so the answer should be about 130.

What You **Think**	What You **Write**

Kim's Way
• Add the ones.
  6 + 8 = 14 ones
• Add the tens.
  4 tens + 7 tens =
  11 tens = 110
• Find the sum.

11 tens   14 ones

$$\begin{array}{r} 46 \\ +\ 78 \\ \hline 14 \\ 110 \\ \hline 124 \end{array}$$

Henry's Way
• Add the ones.
  6 + 8 = 14 ones
• **Regroup** 14 ones into 1 ten 4 ones.
• Add the tens.
  1 ten + 4 tens +
  7 tens = 12 tens
• Find the sum.

14 ones = 1 ten 4 ones

$$\begin{array}{r} 1 \\ 46 \\ +\ 78 \\ \hline 124 \end{array}$$

Cal counted 124 ladybugs all together.

✓ **Talk About It**

1. Why did Henry write a small 1 above the 4 in the tens place?

2. Why should you estimate when adding two-digit numbers?

Once children have mastered concrete models, they should be ready to use the expanded and standard algorithms. Figure 32 shows the computation $37 + 28$ using both algorithms. In Figure 32(b), notice that when there were more than 10 ones, we regrouped 10 ones as a ten and then added the tens. The words *regroup* or *trade* are now commonly used in the elementary classroom to describe what was called *carrying* in the past. The reason for this is that *regroup* and *trade* match more closely the physical actions done with manipulatives.

$$
\begin{array}{r}
37 \\
+\ 28 \\
\hline
15 \quad \text{(Add ones)} \\
+\ 50 \quad \text{(Add tens)} \\
\hline
65
\end{array}
$$

(a)   Expanded algorithm

$$
\begin{array}{r}
\overset{1}{3}7 \\
+\ 28 \\
\hline
65 \quad \text{(Add the ones, regroup, and add the tens.)}
\end{array}
$$

(b)   Standard algorithm

Figure 32

Next we add two three-digit numbers involving two regroupings. Figure 33 shows how to add $186 + 127$ using base-ten blocks and how this concrete model relates to the standard algorithm.

	Concrete Mode	**Standard Algorithm**

1. Add the ones and regroup.
  6 ones + 7 ones = 13 ones
  13 ones = 1 ten + 3 ones

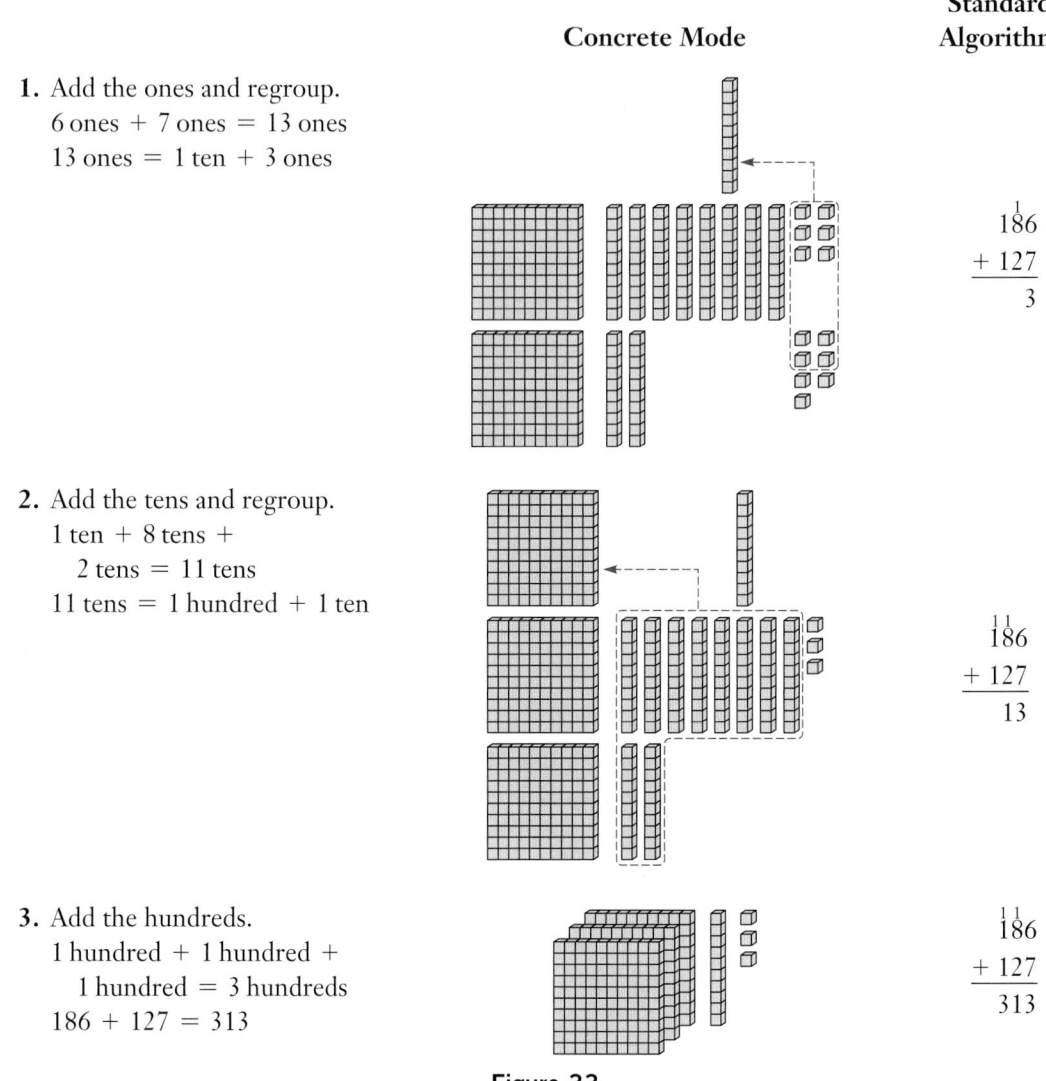

$$
\begin{array}{r}
\overset{1}{1}86 \\
+\ 127 \\
\hline
3
\end{array}
$$

2. Add the tens and regroup.
  1 ten + 8 tens +
    2 tens = 11 tens
  11 tens = 1 hundred + 1 ten

$$
\begin{array}{r}
\overset{1\ 1}{1}86 \\
+\ 127 \\
\hline
13
\end{array}
$$

3. Add the hundreds.
  1 hundred + 1 hundred +
    1 hundred = 3 hundreds
  $186 + 127 = 313$

$$
\begin{array}{r}
\overset{1\ 1}{1}86 \\
+\ 127 \\
\hline
313
\end{array}
$$

Figure 33

Addition of whole numbers using blocks has a natural carryover to the expanded form and trading used earlier. Consider the following addition:

$$
\begin{array}{r}
376 \\
459 \\
+\ 8716 \\
\end{array}
\quad\text{or}\quad
\begin{array}{r}
3\cdot 10^2 +\ \ 7\cdot 10 +\ \ 6 \\
4\cdot 10^2 +\ \ 5\cdot 10 +\ \ 9 \\
+\ 8\cdot 10^3 +\ \ 7\cdot 10^2 +\ \ 1\cdot 10 +\ \ 6 \\
\hline
8\cdot 10^3 +\ 14\cdot 10^2 +\ 13\cdot 10 +\ 21 \\
\end{array}
$$

To complete the addition, trading is used.

Consider an analogous algebra problem of adding polynomials:

$$
(3x^2 + 7x + 6) + (4x^2 + 5x + 9) + (8x^3 + 7x^2 + x + 6) \quad\text{or}\quad
\begin{array}{r}
3x^2 +\ \ 7x +\ \ 6 \\
4x^2 +\ \ 5x +\ \ 9 \\
+\ 8x^3 +\ \ 7x^2 +\ \ x +\ \ 6 \\
\hline
8x^3 + 14x^2 + 13x + 21 \\
\end{array}
$$

Note that if $x = 10$, the addition is the same as given earlier. Knowledge of place value in addition problems aids in algebraic thinking. Next we explore several algorithms that have been used throughout history.

IMAP Video

Watch Gilberto use the left-to-right Algorithm to answer a story problem.

Left-to-Right Algorithm for Addition (Partial Sums Algorithm)

Because children learn to read from left to right, it might seem natural that they add from left to right. When working with base-ten blocks, many children in fact do combine the larger pieces first and then move to combining the smaller pieces. This method has the advantage of emphasizing place value. An example of the use of left-to-right algorithm follows:

$$
\begin{array}{r}
568 \\
+\ 757 \\
\hline
\end{array}
\qquad
\begin{array}{r}
568 \\
+\ 757 \\
\hline
\end{array}
$$

$$
\begin{array}{rcr}
(500 + 700) & \rightarrow & 1200 \\
(60 + 50) & \rightarrow & 110 \\
(8 + 7) & \rightarrow & 15 \\
\hline
& & 1325 \\
\end{array}
\quad\longrightarrow\quad 1\overset{3}{2}\overset{2}{7}5 \quad\rightarrow\quad 1325
$$

Lattice Algorithm for Addition

We demonstrate the lattice algorithm using an addition involving two four-digit numbers. For example,

$$
\begin{array}{r}
3\ \ 5\ \ 6\ \ 7 \\
+\ 5\ \ 6\ \ 7\ \ 8 \\
\end{array}
$$

$$
9\ \ 2\ \ 4\ \ 5
$$

To use the algorithm, add the single-digit numbers by place value on top to the single-digit numbers on the bottom and record the results in a lattice. Then add the sums along the diagonals, as shown. This is very similar to the expanded algorithm introduced earlier. This method is useful with some students because it does not matter if you start left, right, or in between; the regrouping is handled by placement and diagonals. For example in the lattice, the cell separates 15 units into 1 ten and 5 units, and the cell separates 130 units into 1 hundred and 3 tens, allowing addition along diagonals.

Scratch Algorithm for Addition

The *scratch algorithm* for addition is often referred to as a *low-stress algorithm* because it allows students to perform complicated additions by doing a series of additions that involve only two single digits. An example follows:

1.
$$\begin{array}{r} 87 \\ 65\!\!\!/_2 \\ +\,49 \\ \hline \end{array}$$
Add the numbers in the units place starting at the top. When the sum is 10 or more, record this sum by scratching a line through the last digit added and writing the number of units next to the scratched digit. For example, since $7 + 5 = 12$, the "scratch" represents 10 and the 2 represents the units.

2.
$$\begin{array}{r} 87 \\ 65\!\!\!/_2 \\ +\,49\!\!\!/_1 \\ \hline \end{array}$$
Continue adding the units, including any new digits written. When the addition again results in a sum of 10 or more, as with $2 + 9 = 11$, repeat the process described in step (1).

3.
$$\begin{array}{r} {}^2 87 \\ 65\!\!\!/_2 \\ +\,49\!\!\!/_1 \\ \hline 1 \end{array}$$
When the first column of additions is completed, write the number of units, 1, below the addition line in the proper place value position. Count the number of scratches, 2, and add this number to the second column.

4.
$$\begin{array}{r} {}^2 8\!\!\!/_0\, 7 \\ 6\ \ 5\!\!\!/_2 \\ 4\!\!\!/_0\, 9\!\!\!/_1 \\ \hline 2\ \ 0\ \ 1 \end{array}$$
Repeat the procedure for each successive column until the last column with non-zero values. At this stage, sum the scratches in that column and place the number to the left of the current value.

Subtraction Algorithms

As with addition, we use base-ten blocks to provide a concrete model for subtraction. Consider how the base-ten blocks are used to perform the subtraction $243 - 61$. First we represent 243 with 2 flats, 4 longs, and 3 units, as shown in Figure 34.

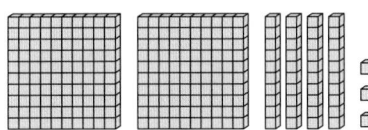

Figure 34

To subtract 61 from 243, we try to remove 6 longs and 1 unit from the blocks in Figure 34. We can remove 1 unit, as in Figure 35.

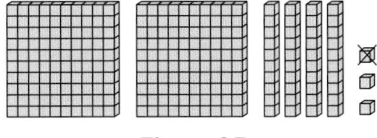

Figure 35

E-Manipulative Activity
 Practice using base-ten blocks to perform subtractions can be found in the *Subtracting Blocks* activity.

To remove 6 longs from Figure 35, we have to trade 1 flat for 10 longs, as shown in Figure 36.

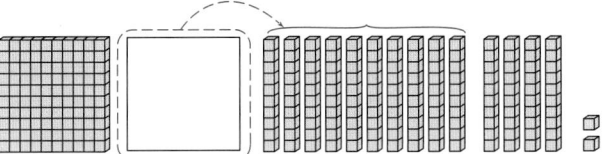

Figure 36

Now we can remove, or "take away," 6 longs, leaving 1 flat, 8 longs, and 2 units, or 182, as shown in Figure 37.

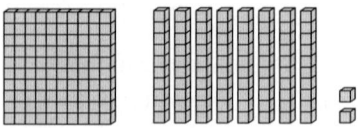

Figure 37

Student work with base-ten blocks along with discussions and recorded work lead to the development of the standard algorithm as seen on the student page shown on page 137.

Subtraction of whole numbers using blocks carries over to the expanded form and trading. For example, consider the following subtraction problem done earlier with blocks:

$$
\begin{array}{c}
243 \\
-61
\end{array}
\longrightarrow
\begin{array}{c}
2 \cdot 10^2 + 4 \cdot 10 + 3 \\
-(6 \cdot 10 + 1)
\end{array}
\longrightarrow
\begin{array}{c}
1 \cdot 10^2 + \quad 14 \cdot 10 + 3 \\
- \quad (6 \cdot 10 + 1) \\
\hline
1 \cdot 10^2 + (14 - 6)10 + (3 - 1)
\end{array}
$$

$$= 1 \cdot 10^2 + 8 \cdot 10 + 2$$

$$= 182$$

Note that to complete the subtraction, trading was used.

Equal-Additions Algorithm

The equal-additions algorithm for subtraction is based on the fact that the difference between two numbers does not change if we add the same amount to both numbers. For example, $93 - 27 = (93 + 3) - (27 + 3)$. Thus, the difference can be computed as $96 - 30 = 66$. Using this approach, subtraction could be performed as follows:

$$
\begin{array}{c}
255 \\
-163
\end{array}
\rightarrow
\begin{array}{c}
255 + 7 \\
-(163 + 7)
\end{array}
\rightarrow
\begin{array}{c}
262 \\
-170
\end{array}
\rightarrow
\begin{array}{c}
262 + 30 \\
-(170 + 30)
\end{array}
\rightarrow
\begin{array}{c}
292 \\
-200 \\
\hline
92
\end{array}
$$

▶ **NOW TRY THIS 15**

NTT 15: Answers can be found in Answers at the back of the book.

Jessica claims that a method similar to *equal additions* for subtraction also works for addition. She says that in an addition problem, "you may add the same amount to one number as you subtract from the other. For example, $68 + 29 = (68 - 1) + (29 + 1)$. Thus, the sum can be computed as $67 + 30 = 97$ or as $(68 + 2) + (29 - 2) = 70 + 27 = 97$." **(i)** Explain why this method is valid and **(ii)** use it to compute $97 + 69$.

Understanding Addition and Subtraction in Bases Other Than Ten

A look at computation in other bases provides insight into computation in base ten. Use of multi-base blocks helps in building an addition table for different bases. Table 10 is a base-five addition table.

School Book Page — Subtracting 3-Digit Numbers

Subtracting 3-Digit Numbers

How can you use subtraction to solve problems?

Mike and Linda are playing a game. How many more points does Mike have than Linda?

Find 528 – 341.

Estimate: 530 – 340 = 190

place-value blocks

MIKE 528   341 LINDA

Subtract the ones.

8 ones > 1 one
You do not regroup.

$$\begin{array}{r} 5\ 2\ 8 \\ -\ 3\ 4\ 1 \\ \hline 7 \end{array}$$

8 ones – 1 one = 7 ones

Subtract the tens.

Since 2 tens < 4 tens, regroup 1 hundred into 10 tens.

$$\begin{array}{r} {\scriptstyle 4\ 12} \\ \cancel{5}\ \cancel{2}\ 8 \\ -\ 3\ 4\ 1 \\ \hline 8\ 7 \end{array}$$

12 tens – 4 tens = 8 tens

Subtract the hundreds.

4 hundreds – 3 hundreds = 1 hundred

$$\begin{array}{r} {\scriptstyle 4\ 12} \\ \cancel{5}\ \cancel{2}\ 8 \\ -\ 3\ 4\ 1 \\ \hline 1\ 8\ 7 \end{array}$$

Mike has 187 more points. 187 is close to the estimate of 190. The answer is reasonable.

Another Example How do you subtract with two regroupings?

Find 356 – 189.
Estimate: 400 – 200 = 200

Step 1
Subtract the ones.
Regroup if needed.

6 ones < 9 ones. So, regroup 1 ten into 10 ones.

$$\begin{array}{r} {\scriptstyle 4\ 16} \\ 3\ \cancel{5}\ \cancel{6} \\ -\ 1\ 8\ 9 \\ \hline 7 \end{array}$$

Step 2
Subtract the tens.
Regroup if needed.

4 tens < 8 tens. So, regroup 1 hundred into 10 tens.

$$\begin{array}{r} {\scriptstyle 2\ 14\ 16} \\ \cancel{3}\ \cancel{5}\ \cancel{6} \\ -\ 1\ 8\ 9 \\ \hline 6\ 7 \end{array}$$

Step 3
Subtract the hundreds.

$$\begin{array}{r} {\scriptstyle 2\ 14\ 16} \\ \cancel{3}\ \cancel{5}\ \cancel{6} \\ -\ 1\ 8\ 9 \\ \hline 1\ 6\ 7 \end{array}$$

The answer 167 is reasonable because it is close to the estimate.

Explain It

1. Why do you need to regroup both a ten and a hundred?

2. **Reason** How is 3 hundreds 5 tens 6 ones the same as 3 hundreds 4 tens 16 ones? How is 3 hundreds 4 tens 16 ones the same as 2 hundreds 14 tens 16 ones?

82

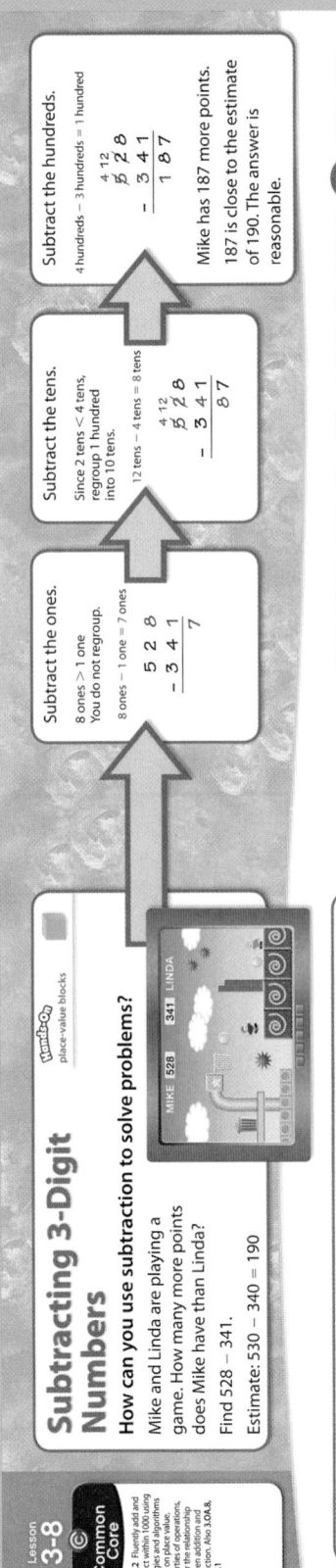

Guided Practice*

MATHEMATICAL PRACTICES

Do you know HOW?

In 1–6, subtract. Use place-value blocks, if you wish.

1.   374
   – 176

2.   431
   – 145

3.   568
   – 269

4.   327
   – 238

5. 574 – 86

6. 410 – 257

Do you UNDERSTAND?

7. **Communicate** In the example above, explain how to decide if regrouping is needed.

8. At the end of their game, Lora had 426 points, and Lou had 158 points. How many more points did Lora have than Lou?

a Write a number sentence.

b Estimate the answer.

c Solve the problem.

d Explain why your answer is reasonable.

Independent Practice

Estimate. Then find each difference. Check answers for reasonableness.

9.   385
   – 296

10.   276
    – 97

11.   516
    – 238

12.   629
    – 453

13.   948
    – 569

eTools   www.pearsonsuccessnet.com

Lesson 3-8   83

*For another example, see Set D on page 93.

Source: pp. 82–83; From enVisionMATH Common Core (Grade 3). Copyright © 2012 Pearson Education, Inc., or its affiliates. Used by permission. All Rights Reserved.

Table 10		Base-Five Addition Table			
+	**0**	**1**	**2**	**3**	**4**
0	0	1	2	3	4
1	1	2	3	4	10
2	2	3	4	10	11
3	3	4	10	11	12
4	4	10	11	12	13

Using the addition facts in Table 10, we apply the algorithms that we developed for base-ten addition to base-five addition. We show the computation using a concrete model in Figure 38(a); in Figure 38(b), we use an expanded algorithm; in Figure 38(c), we use the standard algorithm.

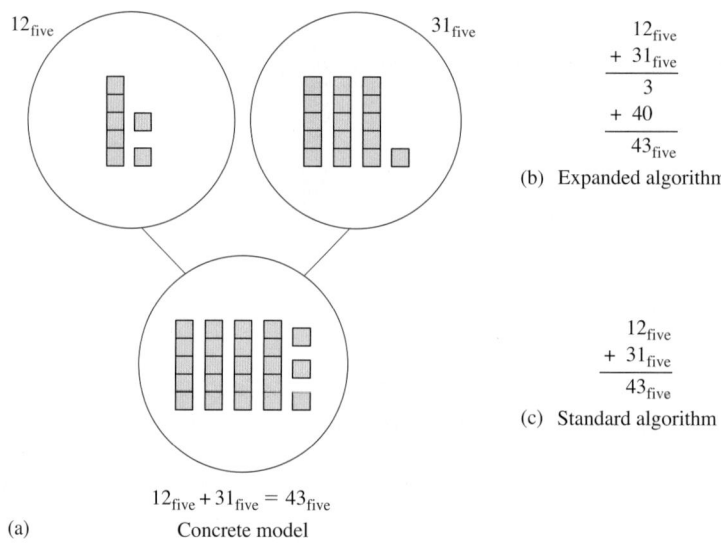

(b) Expanded algorithm

(c) Standard algorithm

(a)   Concrete model

Figure 38

The subtraction facts for base five can also be derived from the addition facts table by using the definition of subtraction. For example, to find $12_{five} - 4_{five}$, recall that $12_{five} - 4_{five} = c$ if, and only if, $c + 4_{five} = 12_{five}$. From Table 10, we see that $c = 3_{five}$. An example of subtraction involving regrouping, $32_{five} - 14_{five}$, is developed in Figure 39.

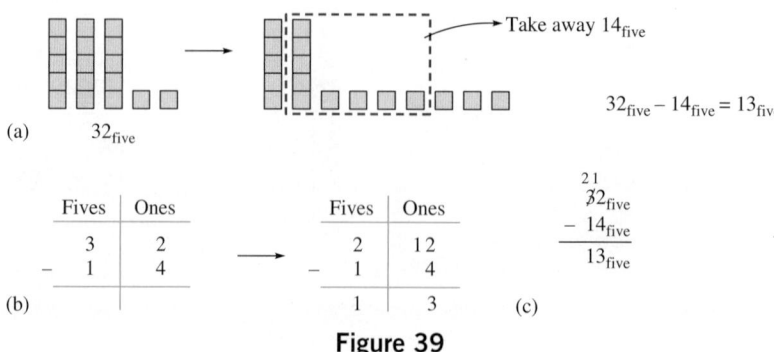

Figure 39

The equal additions algorithm for subtraction and other algorithms be used in base-ten computations can also be efficiently used in other bases. For example, consider $432_{\text{five}} - 43_{\text{five}}$:

$$
\begin{array}{r}
432_{\text{five}} \\
- \quad 43_{\text{five}}
\end{array}
\rightarrow
\begin{array}{r}
432_{\text{five}} + 2 \\
-(43_{\text{five}} + 2)
\end{array}
\rightarrow
\begin{array}{r}
434_{\text{five}} \\
-100_{\text{five}} \\
\hline
334_{\text{five}}
\end{array}
$$

 NOW TRY THIS 16

NTT 16: Answers can be found in Answers at the back of the book.

a. Build an addition table for base two.
b. Use the addition table from part (a) to perform: **(i)** $1111_{\text{two}} + 111_{\text{two}}$ **(ii)** $1101_{\text{two}} - 111_{\text{two}}$.

Mental Computation and Estimation for Whole-Number Addition and Subtraction

CCSS According to the grade 4 *Core Curriculum Standards*, students should be able to:

Assess the reasonableness of answers using mental computation and estimation strategies including rounding. (p. 29)

 **IMAP Video**

Watch Estephania demonstrate the differences between computational strategies and mental mathematics.

Earlier, we focused mainly on paper-and-pencil computational strategies. Now we focus on mental computation and computational estimation. **Mental computation** is the process of producing an answer to a computation without using physical computational aids. **Computational estimation** is the process of forming an *approximate* answer to a numerical problem. Facility with estimation strategies helps to determine whether an answer is reasonable. Proficiency in mental computation can help in everyday estimation skills. It is essential to have these skills even in a time when calculators are readily available. We must be able to judge the reasonableness of calculator answers. Mental computation uses a variety of strategies and properties. We consider several of the most common algorithms for performing operations mentally on whole numbers.

Mental Computation: Addition

1. *Adding from the left*

    a.   67   60 + 30 = 90   (Add the tens.)
         + 36   7 + 6 = 13   (Add the units.)
              90 + 13 = 103   (Add the two sums.)

    b.   36   30 + 30 = 60   (Double 30.)
         + 36   6 + 6 = 12   (Double 6.)
              60 + 12 = 72   (Add the doubles.)

2. *Breaking up and bridging*

       67   67 + 30 = 97   (Add the first number to the tens in the second number.)
     + 36   97 + 6 = 103   (Add this sum to the units in the second number.)

3. *Trading off*

    a.   67   67 + 3 = 70   (Add 3 to make a multiple of 10.)
         + 36   36 − 3 = 33   (Subtract 3 to compensate for the 3 that was added.)
              70 + 33 = 103   (Add the two sums.)

b.   67 $67 + 30 = 97$ (Add 30 [next multiple of 10 greater than 29].)
      $+\ 29$ $97 - 1 = 96$ (Subtract 1 to compensate for the 1 that was added.)

The *trading off* algorithm is just the *equal additions* algorithm discussed earlier.

4. *Using compatible numbers*
Compatible numbers are numbers whose sums are easy to calculate mentally.

$130 + 70 = 200$
$50 + 50 = 100$
$100 + 200 = 300$ (add the two sums)
$300 + 20 = 320$ (add the remaining number)

▶ **IMAP Video**

Watch Johanna make compatible numbers as she finds the sum of three whole numbers.

5. *Making compatible numbers*

   25     $25 + 75 = 100$ (Add $25 + 75$.)
   $+\ 79$ $100 + \ 4 = 104$ (Add 4 more units.)

Mental Computation: Subtraction

1. *Breaking up and bridging*

   67     $67 - 30 = 37$ (Subtract the tens in the second number from the first number.)
   $-\ 36$ $37 - \ 6 = 31$ (Subtract the units in the second number from the difference.)

2. *Trading off*

   71     $71 + \ 1 = 72; 39 + 1 = 40$ (Add 1 to both numbers.)
   -39 $72 - 40 = 32$ (Perform the subtraction, which is easier than the original problem.)

Notice that adding 1 to both numbers does not change the answer. (Why?)

3. *Drop the zeros*

   8700 $87 - 5 = 82$ (Drop these zeros and perform the computation.)
   $-\ 500$ $82 \rightarrow 8200$ (Replace the two zeros to obtain proper place value.)

Another mental computation technique for subtraction is called *adding up*. This method is based on the *missing addend* approach and is sometimes referred to as the *cashier's algorithm*. An example follows.

Example 10

Noah owed $11 for his groceries. He used a $50 bill to pay. While handing Noah the change, the cashier said, "11, 12, 13, 14, 15, 20, 30, 50." How much change did Noah receive?

Solution   Table 11 shows what the cashier said and how much money Noah received each time. Since $11 plus $1 is $12, Noah must have received $1 when the cashier said $12. The same reasoning follows for $13, $14, and so on. Thus, the total amount of change that Noah received is given by $1 + $1 + $1 + $1 + $5 + $10 + $20 = $39. In other words, $50 - $11 = $39 because $39 + $11 = $50.

Table 11

What the Cashier Said	$11	$12	$13	$14	$15	$20	$30	$50
Amount of Money Noah Received Each Time	0	$1	$1	$1	$1	$5	$10	$20

▶ NOW TRY THIS 17

Perform each of the following computations mentally and explain what technique you used to find the answer:

Answers vary. For example,

a. 40 + 160 + 29 + 31   40 + 160 = 200 and 29 + 31 = 60, so the sum is 260.
b. 3679 − 474   3679 − 400 = 3279 and 3279 − 74 = 3205.
c. 75 + 28   75 + 25 = 100 and 100 + 3 = 103.
d. 2500 − 700   2500 − 500 = 2000, and 2000 − 200 = 1800.

Computational Estimation

Computational estimation may help determine whether or not an answer is reasonable. This is especially useful when the computation is done on a calculator. Some common estimation strategies for addition are given next.

1. *Front-end with adjustment*
   Front-end with adjustment estimation begins by focusing on the lead, or front, digits of the addition. These front, or lead, digits are added and assigned an appropriate place value. At this point we may have an underestimate that needs to be adjusted. The adjustment is made by focusing on the next group of digits. The following example shows how front-end estimation works:

   4 + 3 + 5
   12 hundred

   423 —— 20
   338 ——> 120
   + 561 ——> 100

   Steps: (1) **Add front-end digits**
   4 + 3 + 5 = 12.
   (2) **Place value** = 100.
   (3) **Adjust** 61 + 38 ≈ 100 and 20 + 100 is 120.
   (4) **Adjusted estimate** is 1200 + 120 = 1320.

2. *Grouping to nice numbers*
   The strategy used to obtain the adjustment in the preceding example is the *grouping to nice numbers* strategy, which means that numbers that "nicely" fit together are grouped. Another example is given here.

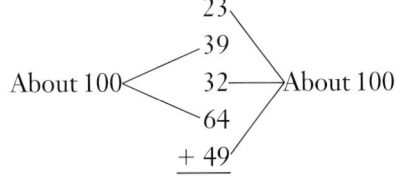

   About 100
   23
   39
   32 ——> About 100
   64
   + 49

   Therefore, the sum is about 100 + 100 = 200.

3. *Clustering*
   Clustering is used when a group of numbers cluster around a common value. This strategy is limited to certain kinds of computations. In this example, the numbers seem to cluster around 6000.

   6200
   5842
   6512
   5521
   +6319

   Estimate the "average"—about 6000.

   Multiply the average by the number of values to obtain $5 \cdot 6000 = 30{,}000$.

4. *Rounding*

Rounding is a way of changing numbers so they are easier to handle. Rounding enables us to find approximate answers to calculations, as follows:

4724	5000	(Round 4724 to 5000.)
+3192	+3000	(Round 3192 to 3000.)
	8000	(Add the rounded numbers.)
1267	1300	(Round 1267 to 1300.)
− 510	− 500	(Round 510 to 500.)
	800	(Subtract the rounded numbers.)

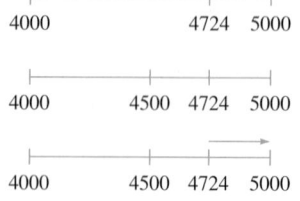

Figure 40

Performing estimations requires a knowledge of place value and rounding techniques. We illustrate a rounding procedure that can be generalized to all rounding situations. For example, suppose we wish to round 4724 to the nearest thousand. We may proceed in four steps (see also Figure 40).

a. Determine between which two consecutive thousands the number lies.
b. Determine the midpoint between the thousands.
c. Determine which thousand the number is closer to by observing whether it is greater than or less than the midpoint. (*Not all texts use the same rule for rounding when a number falls at a midpoint.*)
d. If the number to be rounded is greater than or equal to the midpoint, round the given number to the greater thousand; otherwise, round to the lesser thousand. In this case, 4724 rounds to 5000.

5. *Using the range*

It is often useful to know into what *range* an answer falls. The range is determined by finding a low estimate and a high estimate and reporting that the answer falls in this interval. An example follows:

Problem	Low Estimate	High Estimate
378	300	400
+ 524	+ 500	+ 600
	800	1000

Thus, a range for this problem is from 800 to 1000.

 The student page shown on page 143 shows both the *rounding* and *front-end* estimation strategies applied to a problem.

Assessment 3-4A

1. Find the missing digits in each of the following addition problems.

a.
```
  _ _ 1      981
+ 4  2   =  +421
─ 4  0  2    1402
```

b.
```
  _ 0  2  5     2025
  1 1  _  6     1196
+ 3 1  4  8    +3148
  6 _  6  _     6369
```

2. Make a drawing similar to the one in Figure 33 to show the use of base-ten blocks to compute 29 + 37. *

3. Place the digits 7, 6, 8, 3, 5, and 2 in the boxes to obtain
a. the greatest sum. *
b. the least sum. *

```
   □ □ □
+  □ □ □
```

4. In the following problem, the sum is correct but the order of the digits in each addend has been scrambled. Correct the addends to obtain the correct sum. *

```
  2 8 3 4        □ □ □ □
+ 6 3 1 5      + □ □ □ □
  9 0 5 9        9 0 5 9
```

School Book Page   Estimating Sums and Differences

Lesson 1-9

Key Idea
There is more than one way to estimate sums and differences.

Vocabulary
• front-end estimation
• rounding (p. 26)

Think It Through
I only need an **estimate** because it asks about how many pounds.

Estimating Sums and Differences

LEARN

How can you estimate sums?

Students at Skyline Elementary collected aluminum cans for recycling. About how many pounds of cans did they collect in all?

Recycling Cans				
Grade	3rd	4th	5th	6th
Pounds Collected	398	257	285	318

You can estimate 398 + 257 + 285 + 318 two ways.

Jon used **rounding**.

I'll round each number to the nearest hundred.

398 → 400
257 → 300
285 → 300
+ 318 → + 300
           1,300

About 1,300 pounds

Kylie used **front-end estimation** and adjusted the estimate.

I'll first add the front-end digits.
398 → 300
257 → 200
285 → 200
+ 318 → + 300
            1,000
Then I'll adjust to include the remaining numbers.
98 → 100.
85 → 100.
57 + 18 → 100.
Less than 1,300 pounds

28

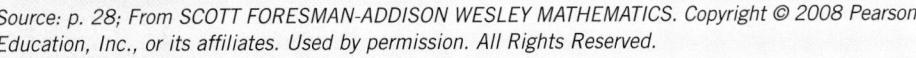

5. Use the equal-additions approach to compute each of the following subtraction problems.

a.

$$\begin{array}{r} 93 \\ -37 \end{array} \quad \begin{array}{r} 93 \\ -37 \end{array} \rightarrow \begin{array}{r} 93+3 \\ -(37+3) \end{array} \rightarrow \begin{array}{r} 96 \\ -40 \\ \hline 56 \end{array}$$

b. $\begin{array}{r} 321 \quad {}^* \\ -\ 38 \\ \hline \end{array}$

6. Janet worked her addition problems by placing the partial sums as shown here:

$$\begin{array}{r} 569 \\ +\ 645 \\ \hline 14 \\ 10 \\ 11 \\ \hline 1214 \end{array}$$

a. Use this method to work the following addition problems.

  i. $\begin{array}{r} 687 \quad {}^* \\ +\ 549 \\ \hline \end{array}$ **ii.** $\begin{array}{r} 359 \quad {}^* \\ +\ 673 \\ \hline \end{array}$

b. Explain why this algorithm works.   *

7. Analyze the following computations. Explain what is wrong in each case.

a. $\begin{array}{r} 28 \quad {}^* \\ +75 \\ \hline 913 \end{array}$ **b.** $\begin{array}{r} \overset{3}{28} \quad {}^* \\ +75 \\ \hline 121 \end{array}$

c. $\begin{array}{r} 305 \quad {}^* \\ -259 \\ \hline 154 \end{array}$ **d.** $\begin{array}{r} \overset{2}{\cancel{3}}\overset{10}{0}5 \quad {}^* \\ -259 \\ \hline 56 \end{array}$

8. Tom's diet allows only 1500 calories per day. For breakfast, Tom had skim milk (90 calories), a waffle with no syrup (120 calories), and a banana (119 calories). For lunch, he had $\frac{1}{2}$ cup of salad (185 calories) with mayonnaise (110 calories) and tea (0 calories). He had pecan pie (570 calories). Can he have dinner consisting of fish (250 calories), $\frac{1}{2}$ cup of salad with no mayonnaise, and tea?   *

9. Give reasons for each of the following steps.   *

$$\begin{aligned} 16 + 31 &= (1 \cdot 10 + 6) + (3 \cdot 10 + 1) \\ &= (1 \cdot 10 + 3 \cdot 10) + (6 + 1) \\ &= (1 + 3)10 + (6 + 1) \\ &= 4 \cdot 10 + 7 \\ &= 47 \end{aligned}$$

10. In each of the following addition problems, justify the standard addition algorithm using place value of the numbers, the commutative and associative properties of addition, and the distributive property of multiplication over addition.

a. $66 + 23$ *   **b.** $124 + 235$ *

11. Use the lattice algorithm to perform each of the following addition problems.

a. $4358 + 3864$ *   **b.** $4923 + 9897$ *

12. Perform each of the following operations using the bases shown and check your answers using a different algorithm.

a. $43_{five} + 23_{five}$ 121_{five} **b.** $43_{five} - 23_{five}$ 20_{five}
c. $432_{five} + 23_{five}$ 1010_{five} **d.** $42_{five} - 23_{five}$ 14_{five}
e. $110_{two} + 11_{two}$ 1001_{two}
f. $10001_{two} - 111_{two}$ 1010_{two}

13. Construct an addition table for base eight and then perform each of the following computations.

a. $573_{eight} - 77_{eight}$ *   **b.** $765_{eight} - 76_{eight}$ *

14. Perform each of the following operations:

a. $\begin{array}{r} 3 \text{ hr } 36 \text{ min } 58 \text{ sec} \\ +\ 5 \text{ hr } 56 \text{ min } 27 \text{ sec} \\ \hline \end{array}$ 9 hr 33 min 25 sec

b. $\begin{array}{r} 5 \text{ hr } 36 \text{ min } 38 \text{ sec} \\ -\ 3 \text{ hr } 56 \text{ min } 58 \text{ sec} \\ \hline \end{array}$ 1 hr 39 min 40 sec

15. The following is a supermagic square.

1	15	14	4
12	6	7	9
8	10	11	5
13	3	2	16

a. Find the sum of each row, the sum of each column, and the sum of each diagonal.   34; 34; 34
b. Find the sum of the four numbers in the center.   34
c. Find the sum of the four numbers in the corners.   34
d. Add 5 to each number in the square. Is the square still a magic square?   Yes
e. Subtract 1 from each number in the square. Is the square still a magic square?   Yes

16. Use scratch addition to perform the following addition problems.

a. $\begin{array}{r} 432 \\ 976 \\ +\ 1418 \\ \hline \end{array}$ $\begin{array}{r} {}^1 4 \ {}^1 3 \ 2 \\ 9_4 \ 7_1 \ 6 \\ +\ {}^1 \ 1 \ 4 \ 1 \ 8 \\ \hline 2 \ 8 \ 2 \ 6 \end{array}$

b. $\begin{array}{r} 32_{five} \\ 13_{five} \\ 22_{five} \\ 43_{five} \\ 23_{five} \\ +\ 12_{five} \\ \hline \end{array}$ $\begin{array}{r} {}^3 \overset{}{\cancel{3}}_1 2 \ {}_{five} \\ 1 \ \overset{}{\cancel{3}}_0 \ {}_{five} \\ 2 \ 2 \ {}_{five} \\ 4_3 \overset{}{\cancel{3}}_0 \ {}_{five} \\ 2_0 3 \ {}_{five} \\ +\ 1 \ 2_0 \ {}_{five} \\ \hline 3 \ 1 \ 0 \ {}_{five} \end{array}$

17. Determine what is wrong with the following addition problem.

$$\begin{array}{r} 22_{five} \quad {}^* \\ +\ 33_{five} \\ \hline 55_{five} \end{array}$$

18. Find the number to put in the blank to make each equation true. Do not convert to base ten.

a. $3423_{five} - \underline{\hspace{1cm}} = 2132_{five}$ 1241_{five}
b. $11011_{two} + \underline{\hspace{1cm}} = 100000_{two}$ 101_{two}
c. $TEE_{twelve} - \underline{\hspace{1cm}} = 1$ TET_{twelve}
d. $1000_{five} + \underline{\hspace{1cm}} = 10000_{five}$ 4000_{five}

19. The Hawks played the Elks in a basketball game. Based on the following information, complete the scoreboard showing the number of points scored by each team during each quarter and the final score of the game.

Teams	Quarters				Final Score
	1	2	3	4	
Hawks	14	22	36	48	120
Elks	18	23	36	54	131

a. The Hawks scored 14 points in the first quarter.
b. The Hawks were behind by 4 points at the end of the first quarter.
c. The Elks scored 5 more points in the second quarter than they did in the first quarter.
d. The Hawks scored 1 fewer point than the Elks in the second quarter.
e. The Elks outscored the Hawks by 6 points in the fourth quarter.
f. The Hawks scored a total of 120 points in the game.
g. The Hawks scored twice as many points in the third quarter as the Elks did in the first quarter.
h. The Elks scored as many points in the third quarter as the Hawks did in the first two quarters combined.

20. a. Place the numbers 1 through 9 in the following circles so that the sums are the same along each segment.   *

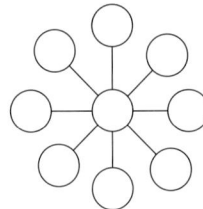

b. How many different numbers can be placed in the middle to obtain a solution?   Three, (5, 1, 9).

21. A palindrome is any number that reads the same backward as forward, for example, 121 and 2332. Try the following: Begin with any multi-digit number. Is it a palindrome? If not, reverse the digits and add this reversed number to the original number. Is the result a palindrome? If not, repeat the procedure until a palindrome is obtained. For example, start with 78. Because 78 is not a palindrome, we add: $78 + 87 = 165$. Because 165 is not a palindrome, we add: $165 + 561 = 726$. Again, 726 is not a palindrome, so we add $726 + 627$ to obtain 1353. Finally, $1353 + 3531$ yields 4884, which is a palindrome.
    Try this method with the following numbers:
    a. 93   *   b. 588   *   c. 2003   *

22. Compute each of the following mentally.
    a. $180 + 97 - 23 + 20 - 140 + 26$ 160
    b. $87 - 42 + 70 - 38 + 43$ 120

23. Compute each of the following mentally and describe your approach.
    a. $475 + 49 + 525$ *   b. $375 - 76$ *
    c. $230 + 60 + 70 + 44 + 6$ *

24. Use breaking up and bridging to compute each of the following mentally.
    a. $567 + 38$ *   b. $418 + 215$ *

25. Use trading off to compute each of the following mentally.
    a. $85 - 49$ *   b. $87 + 33$ *
    c. $143 - 97$ *   d. $58 + 39$ *

26. Compute each of the following using the *adding up* (cashier's) algorithm.
    a. $53 - 28$ *   b. $63 - 47$ *

27. Round each number to the place value indicated by the digit in bold.
    a. **5**280   5300   b. 1**1**5,234   100,000
    c. 115,**2**34   120,000   d. 2,3**2**5   2330

28. Estimate each answer by rounding.   Answers vary. For example:
    a. $878 + 2340$ $900 + 2300 = 3200$
    b. $25,201 - 19,987$ $25,000 - 20,000 = 5000$
    c. $2215 + 3023 + 5967 + 975$ *

29. Use front-end estimation with adjustment to estimate each of the following.
    a. $2215 + 3023 + 5987 + 975$ *
    b. $234 + 478 + 987 + 319 + 469$ *

30. a. Would the clustering strategy of estimation be a good one to use in each of the following cases? Why or why not?   *

	(i)		(ii)
	474		483
	1467		475
	64		530
	+ 2445		503
			+ 528

    b. Estimate each part of (a) using the following strategies: *
       (i) Front-end
       (ii) Grouping to nice numbers
       (iii) Rounding

31. Use the range strategy to estimate each of the following. Explain how you arrived at your estimates.
    a. $145 + 678$ *   b. $278 + 36$ *

32. Suppose you had a balance of $3287 in your checking account and you wrote checks for $85, $297, $403, and $523. Estimate your balance and tell what you did.   *

33. The following is a list of the areas in square miles of Europe's largest countries. Mentally use this information to decide if each of the given statements is true.

France	211,207
Spain	194,896
Sweden	173,731
Finland	130,119
Norway	125,181

    a. Sweden is less than $40,000 \text{ mi}^2$ larger than Finland.   *
    b. France is more than twice the size of Norway.   *
    c. France is more than $100,000 \text{ mi}^2$ larger than Norway.   *
    d. Spain is about $21,000 \text{ mi}^2$ larger than Sweden   *

34. The attendance at a World's Fair for one week follows.

Monday	72,250
Tuesday	63,891
Wednesday	67,490
Thursday	73,180
Friday	74,918
Saturday	68,480

    Estimate the week's attendance and tell what strategy you used.   *

Assessment 3-4B

1. Find the missing digits in each of the following subtraction problems.

   a.
   $$\begin{array}{r} 3\ \_\ \_ \\ -\ 1\ 5\ 9 \quad * \\ \hline \_\ 2\ 4 \end{array}$$

   b.
   $$\begin{array}{r} 1\ \_\ \_\ \_\ 6 \\ -\ \ \ 8\ 3\ 0\ 9 \quad * \\ \hline 4\ 9\ 8\ 7 \end{array}$$

2. Make an appropriate drawing like the one in Figure 33 to show the use of base-ten blocks to compute 46 + 38. *

3. Place the digits 7, 6, 8, 3, 5, and 2 in the boxes to obtain
   a. the greatest difference. *
   b. the least positive difference. *

   $$\begin{array}{r} \square\square\square \\ -\ \square\square\square \end{array}$$

4. In the following problem, the sum is correct but the order of the digits in each addend has been scrambled. Correct the addends to obtain the correct sum.

   $$\begin{array}{r} 8\,3\,5\,4 \\ +\,3\,4\,5\,6 \\ \hline 1\,1\,7\,2\,9 \end{array} \qquad \begin{array}{r} \square\square\square\square \\ +\square\square\square\square \quad * \\ \hline 1\ 1\ 7\ 2\ 9 \end{array}$$

5. Use the equal-additions approach to compute each of the following subtraction problems.

   a.
   $$\begin{array}{r} 86 \quad * \\ -\ 38 \\ \hline \end{array}$$

   b.
   $$\begin{array}{r} 5\,8\,2 \quad * \\ -\,4\,4 \\ \hline \end{array}$$

6. Janet computed her addition problems by placing the partial sums as shown here:

   $$\begin{array}{r} 768 \\ +\ 647 \\ \hline 15 \\ 10 \\ 13 \\ \hline 1415 \end{array}$$

   Use this method to work the following addition problems.

   a.
   $$\begin{array}{r} 987 \quad * \\ +\ 356 \\ \hline \end{array}$$

   b.
   $$\begin{array}{r} 415 \quad * \\ +\ 79 \\ \hline \end{array}$$

7. Analyze the following computations. Explain what is wrong in each case.

   a.
   $$\begin{array}{r} 135 \quad * \\ +\ 47 \\ \hline 172 \end{array}$$

   b.
   $$\begin{array}{r} 87 \quad * \\ +\ 25 \\ \hline 1012 \end{array}$$

   c.
   $$\begin{array}{r} 57 \quad * \\ -\ 38 \\ \hline 21 \end{array}$$

   d.
   $$\begin{array}{r} 56 \quad * \\ -\ 18 \\ \hline 48 \end{array}$$

8. George is cooking a meal for Thanksgiving. He can cook only one thing at a time in his microwave oven. His turkey takes 75 min; the pumpkin pie takes 18 min; rolls take 45 sec; and a cup of coffee takes 30 sec to heat. How much time does he need to cook the meal? When does he need to start in order to complete the cooking at 4 P.M.? *

9. Give reasons for each of the following steps:

   $$\begin{aligned} 123 + 45 &= (1\cdot 10^2 + 2\cdot 10 + 3) + (4\cdot 10 + 5) \\ &= 1\cdot 10^2 + (2\cdot 10 + 4\cdot 10) + (3 + 5) \\ &= 1\cdot 10^2 + (2 + 4)10 + (3 + 5) \\ &= 1\cdot 10^2 + 6\cdot 10 + 8 \\ &= 168 \quad * \end{aligned}$$

10. In each of the following addition problems justify the standard addition algorithm using place value of the numbers, the commutative and associative properties of addition, and the distributive property of multiplication over addition:
    a. 46 + 32 *
    b. 3214 + 783 *

11. Use the lattice algorithm to perform each of the following addition problems.
    a. 2345 + 8888 *
    b. 8713 + 4214 *

12. Perform each of the following operations using the bases shown:
    a. $43_{five} - 24_{five}$ 14_{five}
    b. $143_{five} + 23_{five}$ 221_{five}
    c. $32_{five} - 23_{five}$ 4_{five}
    d. $232_{five} + 43_{five}$ 330_{five}
    e. $110_{two} + 111_{two}$ 1101_{two}
    f. $10001_{two} - 101_{two}$ 1100_{two}

13. Construct an addition table for base six, and then perform each of the following subtractions, and check your answers by computing an equivalent addition problem.
    a. $231_{six} - 144_{six}$ *
    b. $342_{six} - 144_{six}$ *

14. Perform each of the following operations (2 c = 1 pt, 2 pt = 1 qt, 4 qt = 1 gal).

    a.
    $$\begin{array}{r} 1\ qt\ 1\ pt\ 1\ c \\ +\quad 1\ pt\ 1\ c \\ \hline \end{array}$$
    2 qt 1 pt

    b.
    $$\begin{array}{r} 1\ qt\qquad 1c \\ -\quad 1\ pt\ \ 1c \\ \hline \end{array}$$
    1 pt

    c.
    $$\begin{array}{r} 1\ gal\ 3\ qt\ 1\ c \\ -\quad\quad 4\ qt\ 2\ c \\ \hline \end{array}$$
    2 qt 1 pt 1 c

15. The following is a supermagic square taken from an engraving called *Melancholia* by Dürer. Notice 1514 in the bottom row, the year the engraving was made.

16	3	2	13
5	10	11	8
9	6	7	12
4	15	14	1

    a. Find the sum of each row, the sum of each column, and the sum of each diagonal.   34; 34; 34
    b. Find the sum of the four numbers in the center.   34
    c. Find the sum of the four numbers in the corners.   34
    d. Add 11 to each number in the square. Is the square still a magic square?   Yes
    e. Subtract 11 from each number in the square. Is the square still a magic square?   Yes

16. Use scratch addition to perform the following addition problems.

    a.   537   *
           318
       + 2345

    b. 41_{six} *
         32_{six}
         22_{six}
         43_{six}
         22_{six}
       $+54_{\text{six}}$

17. Determine what is wrong with the following addition problem.

$$23_{\text{six}} \quad *$$
$$+ \ 43_{\text{six}}$$
$$66_{\text{six}}$$

18. Find the number to put in the blank to make each equation true. Do not convert to base ten.
    a. $342_{\text{five}} -$ _____ $= 213_{\text{five}}$ 124_{five}
    b. $1101_{\text{two}} -$ _____ $= 1011_{\text{two}}$ 10_{two}
    c. $E08_{\text{twelve}} -$ _____ $= 9_{\text{twelve}}$ TEE_{twelve}
    d. $100_{\text{two}} +$ _____ $= 10000_{\text{two}}$ 1100_{two}

19. The Hawks played the Elks in a basketball game. Based on the following information, complete the scoreboard showing the number of points scored by each team during each quarter and the final score of the game.

Teams	Quarters				Final Score
	1	2	3	4	
Hawks	15	32	40	33	120
Elks	20	25	47	39	131

    a. The Hawks scored 15 points in the first quarter.
    b. The Hawks were behind by 5 points at the end of the first quarter.
    c. The Elks scored 5 more points in the second quarter than they did in the first quarter.
    d. The Hawks scored 7 more points than the Elks in the second quarter.
    e. The Elks outscored the Hawks by 6 points in the fourth quarter.
    f. The Hawks scored a total of 120 points in the game.
    g. The Hawks scored twice as many points in the third quarter as the Elks did in the first quarter.
    h. The Elks scored as many points in the third quarter as the Hawks did in the first two quarters combined.

20. **a.** Place the numbers 24 through 32 in the following circles so that the sums are the same along each segment. *

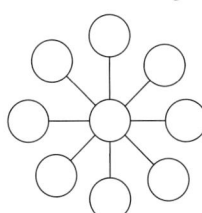

    b. How many different numbers can be placed in the middle to obtain a solution? Three, (24, 28, 32).

21. What is the greatest possible addend that can be placed in the boxes to make this a correct computation?

$$8\ 7 \quad 99$$
$$7\ 8$$
$$+ \square\square$$
$$2\ \square\square$$

22. Compute each of the following mentally.
    a. $160 + 92 - 32 + 40 - 18$ 242
    b. $36 + 97 - 80 + 44$ 97

23. Supply reasons for each of the first four steps given here. *

$$(525 + 37) + 75 = 525 + (37 + 75)$$
$$= 525 + (75 + 37)$$
$$= (525 + 75) + 37$$
$$= 600 + 37$$
$$= 637$$

24. Use breaking and bridging to compute each of the following mentally.
    a. $997 - 32$ *
    b. $560 + 136$ *

25. Use trading off to compute each of the following mentally.
    a. $75 - 38$ *
    b. $57 + 35$ *
    c. $137 - 29$ *
    d. $78 + 49$ *

26. Compute each of the following using the *adding up* (cashier's) algorithm.
    a. $74 - 63$ *
    b. $73 - 57$ *

27. Round each number to the place value indicated by the digit in bold.
    a. **3**587 3600
    b. **1**48,213 100,000
    c. 23,**7**85 24,000
    d. 2,3**5**7 2360

28. Estimate each answer by rounding. Answers vary. For example:
    a. $937 + 28$ $940 + 30 = 970$
    b. $32,285 - 18,988$ $32,000 - 19,000 = 13,000$
    c. $3215 + 3789 + 5987$ $3000 + 4000 + 6000 = 13,000$

29. Use front-end estimation with adjustment to estimate each of the following.
    a. $2345 + 5250 + 4210 + 910$ *
    b. $345 + 518 + 655 + 270$ *

30. **a.** Would the clustering strategy of estimation be a good one to use in each of the following cases? Why or why not? *

    (i)   318
          2314
            57
       + 3489

    (ii)   2350
          1987
          2036
          2103
       + 1890

    b. Estimate each part of (a) using the following strategies: *
      (i) Front-end with adjustment
      (ii) Grouping to nice numbers
      (iii) Rounding

31. Use the range strategy to estimate each of the following. Explain how you arrived at your estimates.
    a. $123 + 780$ *
    b. $482 + 246$ *

32. Suppose you had a balance of $1237 in your checking account and you wrote checks for $65, $190, $45, $212, and $420. Estimate your balance and tell what you did.

33. In each of the following, answer the question using estimation methods if possible. If estimation is not appropriate, explain why not.
    a. Josh has $380 in his checking account. He wants to write checks for $39, $28, $59, and $250. Will he have enough money in his account to cover these checks? *
    b. Gila deposited two checks into her account, one for $981 and the other for $1140. Does she have enough money in

her account to cover a check for $2000 if we know she has a positive starting balance to start with? *

c. Alberto and Juan are running for city council. They receive votes from two districts. Alberto receives 3473 votes from one district and 5615 votes from the other district. Juan receives 3463 votes from the first district and 5616 from the second. Who gets elected? *

34. The attendance at a County Fair for six days follows:

Monday	71,150
Tuesday	64,993
Wednesday	68,490
Thursday	72,980
Friday	84,968
Saturday	69,495

Estimate the total attendance for the six days. *

Mathematical Connections 3-4

Answers to Mathematical Connections can be found in the Answers section at the back of the book.

Reasoning

1. Discuss the merit of the following expanded algorithm for addition where we first add the ones, then the tens, then the hundreds, and then the total.

$$
\begin{array}{r}
479 \\
+\ 385 \\
\hline
14 \\
150 \\
+\ 700 \\
\hline
864
\end{array}
$$

2. The following example uses a regrouping approach to subtraction. Discuss the merit of this approach in teaching subtraction.

$$
\begin{array}{r}
843 \\
-\ 568 \\
\hline
\end{array}
\rightarrow
\begin{array}{r}
800 + 40 + 3 \\
-\ (500 + 60 + 8) \\
\hline
\end{array}
\rightarrow
$$

$$
\begin{array}{r}
800 + 30 + 13 \\
-\ (500 + 60 + \ 8) \\
\hline
\end{array}
\rightarrow
\begin{array}{r}
700 + 130 + 13 \\
-\ (500 + \ 60 + \ 8) \\
\hline
200 + \ 70 + \ 5 \ = 275
\end{array}
$$

3. Explain why the scratch addition algorithm works.
4. Consider the following subtraction algorithm.

$$
\begin{aligned}
585 - 277 &= 585 - 200 - \ 77 \\
&= 385 - \ 77 \\
&= 385 - 100 + \ 23 \\
&= 285 + \ 23 = 308
\end{aligned}
$$

 a. Explain why it works.
 b. Use this algorithm to find $787 - 398$.

5. Explain why in paper-and-pencil addition and subtraction the terms *trading* and *regrouping* are used instead of the terms *carrying* and *borrowing*.
6. Is the front-end estimate for addition before adjustment always less than the exact sum? Explain why or why not.
7. In the new textbooks, there is an emphasis on mental mathematics and estimation. Explain why these topics are important for today's students.
8. Suppose x and y are positive (greater than 0) whole numbers. If x is greater than y and you estimate $x - y$ by rounding x up and y down, will your estimate always be too high or too low or could it be either? Explain.

Open-Ended

9. Search for or develop an algorithm for whole-number addition or subtraction, and write a description of your algorithm so that others can understand and use it.
10. Give several examples from real-world situations where an estimate, rather than an exact answer, is sufficient.
11. a. Give a numerical example of when front-end estimation and rounding can produce the same estimate.
 b. Give an example of when they can produce a different estimate.

Cooperative Learning

12. In this section you have been exposed to many different algorithms. Discuss in your group whether children should be encouraged to develop and use their own algorithms for whole-number addition and subtraction or whether they should be taught only one algorithm per operation and all students should use only one algorithm.
13. Prepare a grocery list of 10 items with prices, and find the total price using a calculator. Give the list to each member of your group without revealing the total price. Ask them to estimate the total price in one minute. Find who came closest to the total price. Take turns preparing a list.
14. Play the following game with a partner or teams of two. Make a deck of 32 cards to include four each of the numbers 1 through 9. (You could use a playing deck of cards and use the ace for a 1.) Two players draw alternately from the deck and after each draw place the card in either the *tens* column or the *ones* column. The player or team closest to a sum of 100 after 5 draws is the winner. For example, if you drew 6, 1, 5, 3, 5 and placed them as shown, your total would be 101.

tens	ones
6	1
3	5
	5

Connecting Mathematics to the Classroom

15. Tira, a fourth grader, performs addition by adding and subtracting the same number. She added as follows:

$$
\begin{array}{r}
39 \\
+\ 84 \\
\hline
\end{array}
\rightarrow
\begin{array}{r}
39 + 1 \\
+\ 84 - 1 \\
\hline
\end{array}
\rightarrow
\begin{array}{r}
40 \\
+\ 83 \\
\hline
123
\end{array}
$$

How would you respond if you were her teacher?

16. Cathy found her own algorithm for subtraction. She subtracted as follows:

$$\begin{array}{r} 97 \\ -28 \\ \hline -1 \\ +70 \\ \hline 69 \end{array}$$

short 1

How would you respond if you were her teacher?

17. To find $68 - 19$, Joe began by finding $6 - 1$ and then $9 - 8$ and wrote 51 as the answer. How would you respond?

18. Jill subtracted $415 - 212$ by writing $4 - 2 = 2$ and $15 - 12 = 3$ and wrote 23 as the answer. How would you help her?

19. Betsy found $518 - 49 = 469$. She was not sure she was correct, so she tried to check her answer by adding $518 + 49$. How could you help her?

20. A child is asked to compute $7 + 2 + 3 + 8 + 11$ and writes $7 + 2 = 9 + 3 = 12 + 8 = 20 + 11 = 31$. Noticing that the answer is correct, if you were the teacher how would you react?

21. When Richie was asked to round 2568 to the nearest ten, he wrote 2578. How would you respond?

22. When Ashley was asked to round 345 to the nearest 100, she rounded 345 to 350 and then rounded 350 to 400. Billie claimed the answer was 300. How would you respond to these students?

23. Pauli subtracted 549 from 5004 as follows. How would you respond?

$$\begin{array}{r} \overset{499}{5\overset{\cancel{0}\cancel{0}}{0}4} \\ -549 \\ \hline 4455 \end{array}$$

24. Molly computed $261 - 48$ by first subtracting 50 from 261 to obtain 211; then, to make up for adding 2 to 48, she subtracted 2 from 211 to obtain an answer of 209. Is her thinking correct? If not, how could you help her?

25. A student asks why he has to learn about any estimation strategy other than rounding. What is your response?

26. In order to finish her homework quickly, an elementary student does her estimation problems by using a calculator to find the exact answers and then rounds them to get her estimate. What do you tell her?

Review Problems

27. What is the value of MCDX in Hindu-Arabic numerals?

28. Convert each of the following to base ten.
   a. $E0T_{twelve}$ **b.** 1011_{two} **c.** 43_{five}

29. Is the set $\{1, 2, 3\}$ closed under addition? Why?

30. Give an example of the associative property of addition of whole numbers.

31. Find all whole numbers for which the following statements are true.
   a. $20 - x = x$
   b. $20 - x - 6 = 0$
   c. $x + 4 = 3 + x + 1$

National Assessments

National Assessment of Educational Progress (NAEP) Questions

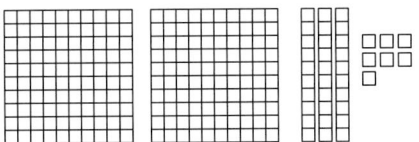

The figure above represents 237. Which number is

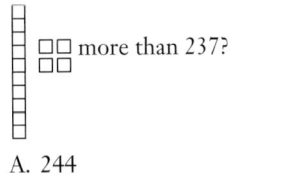

more than 237?

A. 244   B. 249
C. 251   D. 377

NAEP, Grade 4, 2007

There are 30 people in the music room. There are 74 people in the cafeteria. How many more people are in the cafeteria than in the music room?

A. 40   B. 44
C. 54   D. 104

NAEP, Grade 4, 2009

Audrey used only the number tiles with the digits 2, 3, 4, 6, and 9. She placed one tile in each box below so the difference was 921.

Write the numbers in the boxes below to show where Audrey placed the tiles.

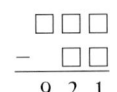

NAEP Grade 4, 2005

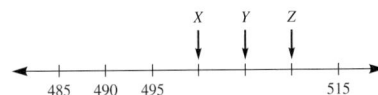

On the number line above, what is the sum of the numbers to which the arrows X, Y, and Z point?

A. 1,491   B. 1,515
C. 1,530   D. 1,545

Did you use the calculator on this question?

NAEP Grade 4, 2011

3-5 Multiplication and Division Algorithms, Mental Computation, and Estimation

3-5 Objectives

Students will be able to understand and explain

- Properties of exponents and how these can be used to develop multiplication and division algorithms.

- Models to develop algorithms for multiplication and division.

- Multiplication and division algorithms and how to use them to solve problems.

- Bases other than ten to provide insight into base-ten multiplication and division.

- Mental multiplication and division skills and estimation techniques.

CCSS In the grade 4 *Common Core Standards*, we find the following:

Students generalize their understanding of place value to 1,000,000, understanding the relative sizes of numbers in each place. They apply their understanding of models for multiplication (equal-sized groups, arrays, area models), place value, and properties of operations, in particular the distributive property, as they develop, discuss, and use efficient, accurate, and generalizable methods to compute products of multi-digit whole numbers. Depending on the numbers and the context, they select and accurately apply appropriate methods to estimate or mentally calculate products. They develop fluency with efficient procedures for multiplying whole numbers; understand and explain why the procedures work based on place value and properties of operations; and use them to solve problems. (p. 27)

In this section we discuss the use of efficient, accurate, and generalizable methods to compute products and quotients. We also discuss appropriate methods to estimate and mentally calculate products and quotients. We begin with a discussion of the properties of exponents.

Properties of Exponents

Some properties of exponents are used in this section and in the following chapters.

Definition of a^n

If a, the base, and n, the exponent, are whole numbers and $n \neq 0$, then

$$a^n = \underbrace{a \cdot a \cdot \ldots \cdot a}_{n \text{ factors}}.$$

When multiplying powers of 10, the definition of exponents is used; for example, $10^2 \cdot 10^1 = (10 \cdot 10) \cdot 10 = 10^3 = 10^{2+1}$. In general, where a is a whole number and m and n are natural numbers, $a^m \cdot a^n$ is given by the following:

$$a^m \cdot a^n = \underbrace{(a \cdot a \cdot a \cdot \ldots \cdot a)}_{m \text{ factors}} \cdot \underbrace{(a \cdot a \cdot a \cdot \ldots \cdot a)}_{n \text{ factors}}$$

$$= \underbrace{a \cdot a \cdot a \cdot \ldots \cdot a}_{m + n \text{ factors}} = a^{m+n}$$

Consequently, $a^m \cdot a^n = a^{m+n}$.

Therefore we have the following theorem.

Theorem 3-9

For every whole number a and natural numbers m and n:

$$a^m \cdot a^n = a^{m+n}$$

The definition of exponents and Theorem 3-9 can be used to rewrite an expression such as $(5^2)^3$ using a single exponent:

$$(5^2)^3 = 5^2 \cdot 5^2 \cdot 5^2 = 5^{2+2+2} = 5^{3 \cdot 2} = 5^6$$

This suggests the following theorem:

Theorem 3-10

For every whole number a, and natural numbers m and n:

$$(a^m)^n = a^{mn}$$

Proof

$$(a^m)^n = \underbrace{a^m \cdot a^m \cdot \ldots \cdot a^m}_{n \text{ factors}} = a^{\overbrace{m+m+\ldots+m}^{n \text{ terms}}} = a^{mn}$$

The preceding theorems involve exponents and multiplication. However, corresponding properties for exponents and addition do not exist; for example $2^5 + 2^3 \neq 2^{5+3}$.

Sometimes it is convenient to write a product such as $2^3 \cdot 5^3$ with a single exponent:

$$2^3 \cdot 5^3 = 2 \cdot 2 \cdot 2 \cdot 5 \cdot 5 \cdot 5 = (2 \cdot 5)(2 \cdot 5)(2 \cdot 5) = (2 \cdot 5)^3 = 10^3$$

In general we have Theorem 3-11.

Theorem 3-11

For whole numbers a and b, and natural numbers n:

$$a^n \cdot b^n = (ab)^n$$

The proof of this theorem is similar to the one in the previous example and is left as an exercise. It is often useful to divide exponential expressions with the same base. Consider writing $2^6 \div 2^2$ with a single exponent. Using the definition of division, $2^6 \div 2^2 = \square$ if, and only if, $\square \cdot 2^2 = 2^6$. Since $\boxed{2^4} \cdot 2^2 = 2^6$, it follows that $2^6 \div 2^2 = 2^4$. This example suggests the following theorem:

Theorem 3-12

If a, m, and n are natural numbers with $m > n$, then

$$a^m \div a^n = a^{m-n}.$$

Proof

By definition of division, $a^m \div a^n = a^x$ if, and only if, $a^x \cdot a^n = a^m$. We want to find x in terms of m and n. By Theorem 3-9, $a^{x+n} = a^m$. Hence $x + n = m$, so $x = m - n$. Thus $a^m \div a^n = a^{m-n}$. ∎

If the laws of exponents for natural numbers are to hold for the exponent 0, then $a^0 \cdot a^n = a^{0+n} = a^n$. Because $a^0 \cdot a^n = a^n$ we have $a^0 = 1$. However, 0^0 is considered to be undefined.

Definition of a^0 for natural number a

If a is a natural number, then

$$a^0 = 1.$$

Example 11

Write each of the following with only one exponent.

    a. $2^6 \cdot 8^5 \cdot 16^3$ **b.** $(9^4 \cdot 36^5) \div 3^{18}$

Solution

a. $2^6 \cdot 8^5 \cdot 16^3 = 2^6 \cdot (2^3)^5 \cdot (2^4)^3 = 2^6 \cdot 2^{15} \cdot 2^{12}$
$$= 2^{6+15+12} = 2^{33}$$

b. $9^4 \cdot 36^5 = (3^2)^4 \cdot (2^2 \cdot 3^2)^5 = 3^{2 \cdot 4} \cdot (2^2)^5 \cdot (3^2)^5$
$$= 3^8 \cdot 2^{10} \cdot 3^{10}$$
$$= 3^8 \cdot 3^{10} \cdot 2^{10}$$
$$= 3^{18} \cdot 2^{10}$$

    Thus $(9^4 \cdot 36^5) \div 3^{18} = (3^{18} \cdot 2^{10}) \div 3^{18}$
$$= 2^{10}.$$

▶ **IMAP Video**

Watch Brooke discuss an algorithm for multiplying whole numbers she invented herself.

Multiplication Algorithms

To develop algorithms for multiplying multi-digit whole numbers, we look at a simple example. Consider $4 \cdot 12$. This computation could be pictured as in Figure 41(a) with 4 rows of 12 blocks, or 48 blocks. These blocks in Figure 41(a) can also be partitioned to show that $4 \cdot 12 = 4(10 + 2) = 4 \cdot 10 + 4 \cdot 2$. The numbers $4 \cdot 10$ and $4 \cdot 2$ are *partial products*. This technique is often referred to as the **partial products algorithm**.

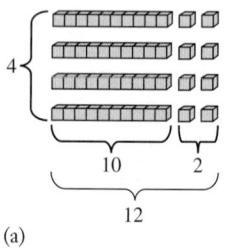

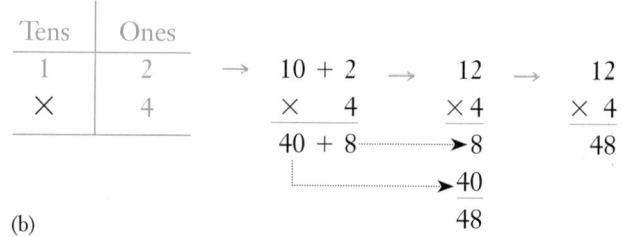

Figure 41

    Figure 41(a) illustrates the distributive property of multiplication over addition on the set of whole numbers. The process leading to an algorithm for multiplying $4 \cdot 12$ is seen in Figure 41(b). There is similarity between the multiplication in Figure 41 and the following algebra multiplication:

$$4(x + 2) = 4x + 4 \cdot 2$$
$$= 4x + 8$$

Similarly there is an analogy between the products

$$23 \cdot 14 = (2 \cdot 10 + 3)(1 \cdot 10 + 4) \quad \text{and} \quad (2x + 3)(x + 4).$$

The analogy is continued as shown:

$$
\begin{array}{r}
2 \cdot 10 + 3 \\
\times \, (1 \cdot 10 + 4) \\
\hline
12 \\
8 \cdot 10 \\
3 \cdot 10 \\
2 \cdot 10^2 \\
\hline
2 \cdot 10^2 + 11 \cdot 10 + 12
\end{array}
\qquad
\begin{array}{r}
2x + 3 \\
\times \, (x + 4) \\
\hline
12 \\
8x \\
3x \\
2x^2 \\
\hline
2x^2 + 11x + 12
\end{array}
$$

Multiplication of a three-digit number by a one-digit factor will be explored after discussing multiplication by a power of 10.

Multiplication by 10^n

Consider multiplication by powers of 10. What happens when a given number is multiplied by 10, such as $10 \cdot 23$? If we begin with the base-ten block representation of 23, we have 2 longs and 3 units. To multiply by 10, we must replace each piece with a base-ten piece that represents the next higher power of 10. This is shown in Figure 42. Notice that the 3 units in 23 when multiplied by 10 become 3 longs or 3 tens. Therefore, after multiplication by 10 there are no units and hence we have 0 in the units place. In general, if we multiply any natural number by 10, we append a 0 to the right of the original number.

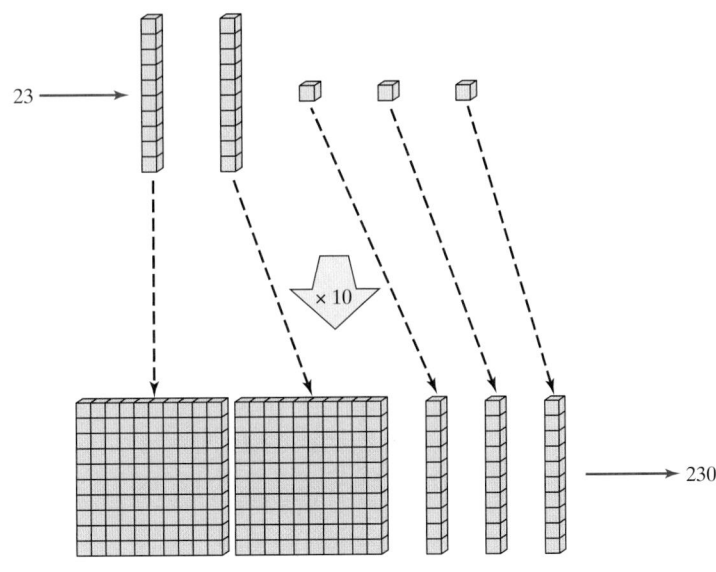

Figure 42

The computation $23 \cdot 10$ from Figure 42 can be shown as follows:

$$
\begin{aligned}
23 \cdot 10 &= (2 \cdot 10 + 3)\,10 \\
&= (2 \cdot 10)\,10 + 3 \cdot 10 \\
&= 2\,(10 \cdot 10) + 3 \cdot 10 \\
&= 2 \cdot 10^2 + 3 \cdot 10 \\
&= 2 \cdot 10^2 + 3 \cdot 10 + 0 \cdot 1 \\
&= 230
\end{aligned}
$$

To compute products such as $3 \cdot 200$, proceed as follows:

$$\begin{aligned} 3 \cdot 200 &= 3(2 \cdot 10^2) \\ &= (3 \cdot 2)10^2 \\ &= 6 \cdot 10^2 \\ &= 6 \cdot 10^2 + 0 \cdot 10 + 0 \cdot 1 \\ &= 600 \end{aligned}$$

Multiplying 6 by 10^2 results in appending two zeros to the right of 6. This idea can be generalized to the statement that *multiplication of any natural number by 10^n where n is a whole number, results in appending n zeros to the right of the number*.

The appending of n zeros to a natural number when multiplying by 10^n can also be explained as follows. First multiply by 10, resulting in appending one zero (as in $23 \cdot 10 = 230$). Then multiply by another 10, resulting in appending another zero (as in $230 \cdot 10 = 2300$). Since we multiply n times by 10, n zeros are appended to the right of the original natural number. Note that if $n = 0$, then $10^0 = 1$ appending no zeros.

Multiplication by a power of 10 is helpful in calculating the product of a one-digit number and a three-digit number. In the following example, we assume the previously developed algorithm for multiplying a one-digit number times a two-digit number:

$$\begin{aligned} 4 \cdot 367 &= 4(3 \cdot 10^2 + 6 \cdot 10 + 7) \\ &= 4(3 \cdot 10^2) + 4(6 \cdot 10) + 4 \cdot 7 \\ &= (4 \cdot 3)10^2 + (4 \cdot 6)10 + 4 \cdot 7 \\ &= 12 \cdot 10^2 + 24 \cdot 10 + 28 \\ &= 1200 + 240 + 28 \\ &= 1468 \end{aligned}$$

$$\begin{array}{r} 367 \\ \times\ 4 \\ \hline 28 \\ 240 \\ 1200 \\ \hline 1468 \end{array}$$

Multiplication with Two-Digit Factors

 **Activity Manual**

Use *Multi-digit Multiplication* to develop an algorithm for multiplying multi-digit numbers.

Consider $14 \cdot 23$. Model this computation by first using base-ten blocks, as shown in Figure 43(a), and then showing all the *partial products* and adding, as shown in Figure 43(b).

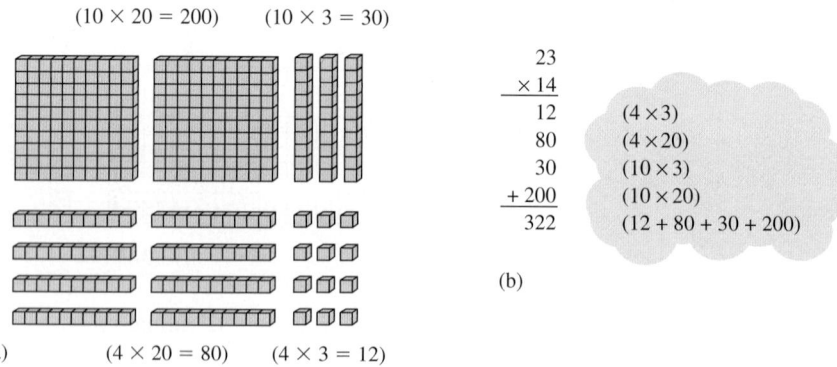

Figure 43

Figure 43(b) leads to an algorithm for multiplication:

$$\begin{array}{r} 23 \\ \times\ 14 \\ \hline 92 \\ 230 \\ \hline 322 \end{array} \quad \begin{array}{l} (4 \cdot 23) \\ (10 \cdot 23) \end{array} \quad \text{or} \quad \begin{array}{r} 23 \\ \times\ 14 \\ \hline 92 \\ 23 \\ \hline 322 \end{array}$$

It is not uncommon to see the partial product 230 written without the zero, as 23. The placement of 23 with 3 in the tens column obviates having to write the 0 in the units column. We encourage the inclusion of the zero. This promotes better understanding and helps to avoid errors.

The distributive property of multiplication over addition can be used to explain why the algorithm for multiplication works. Again, consider $14 \cdot 23$.

$$14 \cdot 23 = (10 + 4)23$$
$$= 10 \cdot 23 + 4 \cdot 23$$
$$= 230 + 92$$
$$= 322$$

Because algorithms are powerful, there is sometimes a tendency to overapply them or to use paper and pencil for a task that should be done mentally. For example, consider the following example.

$$
\begin{array}{r}
213 \\
\times\ 1000 \\
\hline
000 \\
000 \\
000 \\
213 \\
\hline
213000
\end{array}
$$

This application is not wrong but is inefficient.

Mental computation and estimation are important skills in learning mathematics and should be practiced in addition to paper-and-pencil computations. Children should be encouraged to *estimate* whether their answers are reasonable. For example, in the computation $14 \cdot 23$, we know that the answer must be between $10 \cdot 20 = 200$ and $20 \cdot 30 = 600$ because $10 < 14 < 20$ and $20 < 23 < 30$. Also, since 14 is close to 10 and 23 is close to 20, the product should be close to 200.

Lattice Multiplication

Lattice multiplication has the advantage of delaying all additions until the single-digit multiplications are complete. Because of this, it is sometimes referred to as a *low-stress algorithm*. Students like this algorithm, perhaps because of the structure provided by the lattice. The lattice multiplication algorithm for multiplying 14 and 23 is shown in Figure 44. (Determining the reasons why lattice multiplication works is left as an exercise.)

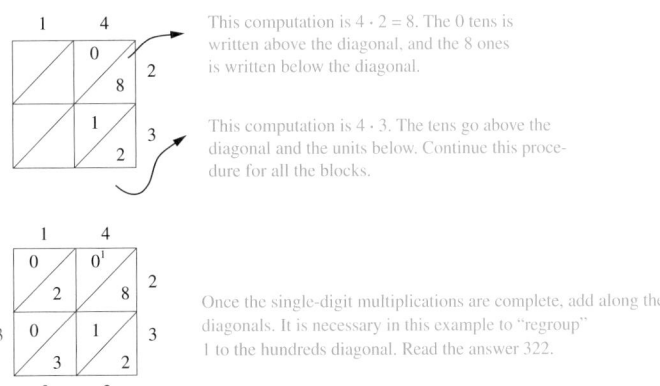

This computation is $4 \cdot 2 = 8$. The 0 tens is written above the diagonal, and the 8 ones is written below the diagonal.

This computation is $4 \cdot 3$. The tens go above the diagonal and the units below. Continue this procedure for all the blocks.

Once the single-digit multiplications are complete, add along the diagonals. It is necessary in this example to "regroup" 1 to the hundreds diagonal. Read the answer 322.

Figure 44

Activity Manual

Use *Multi-digit Division* to help develop an algorithm for division.

Division Algorithms

Using Repeated Subtraction to Develop the Standard Division Algorithm

As we have seen in Section 3-3, division of whole numbers can be modeled by repeated subtraction. We use this approach in the following question.

A shopkeeper is packaging juice in cartons that hold 6 bottles each. She has 726 bottles. How many cartons does she need?

We reason that if 1 carton holds 6 bottles, then 10 cartons hold 60 bottles and 100 cartons hold 600 bottles. If 100 cartons are filled, there are $726 - 100 \cdot 6$, or 126, bottles remaining. If 10 more cartons are filled, then $126 - 10 \cdot 6$, or 66, bottles remain. Similarly, if 10 more cartons are filled, $66 - 10 \cdot 6$, or 6, bottles remain. Finally, 1 carton will hold the remaining 6 bottles. The total number of cartons necessary is $100 + 10 + 10 + 1$, or 121. This procedure is summarized in Figure 45(a). This method is sometimes called the **partial quotients algorithm**. A more efficient method is shown in Figure 45(b).

$$
\begin{array}{rl}
6\overline{)726} & \\
-600 & \quad 100 \text{ sixes} \\
\hline
126 & \\
-60 & \quad 10 \text{ sixes} \\
\hline
66 & \\
-60 & \quad 10 \text{ sixes} \\
\hline
6 & \\
-6 & \quad \underline{1 \text{ six}} \\
\hline
0 & \quad 121 \text{ sixes}
\end{array}
$$

(a)

$$
\begin{array}{rl}
6\overline{)726} & \\
-600 & \quad 100 \text{ sixes} \\
\hline
126 & \\
-120 & \quad 20 \text{ sixes} \\
\hline
6 & \\
-6 & \quad \underline{1 \text{ six}} \\
\hline
0 & \quad 121 \text{ sixes}
\end{array}
$$

(b)

Figure 45

▶ **NOW TRY THIS 18**

Study the following division, and explain what was done in each step.

$$
\begin{array}{r}
97 \ \text{R}14 \\
45\overline{)4379} \\
-2250 \\
\hline
2129 \\
-1800 \\
\hline
329 \\
-270 \\
\hline
59 \\
-45 \\
\hline
14
\end{array}
\qquad
\begin{array}{r}
\\
\\
50 \\
\\
40 \\
\\
6 \\
\\
\underline{1} \\
97
\end{array}
$$

Answers vary. In the first step 50 45s = 2250 were subtracted from 4379 leaving 2129. Then 40 45s were subtracted leaving 329. Then 6 45s were subtracted leaving 59, and finally 1 45 was subtracted leaving 14. Altogether 50 + 40 + 6 + 1 = 97 45s were subtracted leaving 14. Therefore, 4379 ÷ 45 = 97R14.

Historical Note

Lattice multiplication dates back to tenth-century India. This algorithm was imported to Europe and was popular in the fourteenth and fifteenth centuries. Napier's rods (or bones), developed by John Napier in the early 1600s, were modeled on lattice multiplication. ●

Divisions such as the one in Figure 45 are usually shown in elementary school texts in the most efficient form, as in Figure 46(b), in which the numbers in color in Figure 46(a) are omitted. The technique used in Figure 46(a) is often called the **scaffold algorithm** and may be used as a preliminary step to achieving the standard algorithm, as in Figure 46(b). Scaffolding takes the numbers on the right in Figure 45(b), and places them on the top as in Figure 46(a). The scaffolding shows place value. Place value is important to understanding the standard algorithm.

$$
\begin{array}{r}
121 \\
\hline
1 \\
20 \\
100 \\
6\overline{)726} \\
-600 \\
\hline
126 \\
-120 \\
\hline
6 \\
-6 \\
\hline
0
\end{array}
\qquad
\begin{array}{r}
121 \\
6\overline{)726} \\
-6 \\
\hline
12 \\
-12 \\
\hline
6 \\
-6 \\
\hline
0
\end{array}
$$

(a)   (b)

Figure 46

Using Base-ten Blocks to Develop the Standard Division Algorithm

Students need to see why each move in an algorithm is appropriate rather than just knowing which sequence of moves to make. Below we use base-ten blocks to justify why each move in the standard algorithm is appropriate. In Table 12 we perform the division $726 \div 6$. The base-ten block model is on the left with the corresponding steps in the standard algorithm on the right.

Table 12

Base-ten Blocks	Algorithm
1. First represent 726 with base-ten blocks. 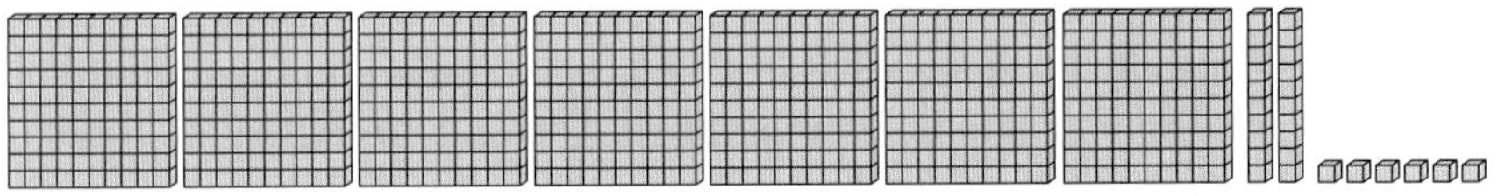	$6\overline{)726}$
2. Next determine how many sets of 6 flats (hundreds) there are in the representation. There is 1 set of 6 flats with 1 flat, 2 longs (tens), and 6 units (ones) remaining. 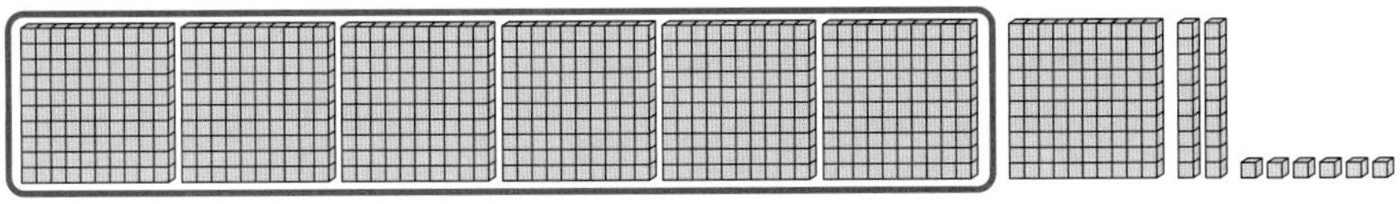	1 set of 6 flats $\begin{array}{r} 1 \\ 6\overline{)726} \\ -6 \\ \hline 1 \end{array}$ 1 flat 2 longs 6 units remaining
3. Next, convert the one remaining flat to 10 longs (tens), giving 12 longs (tens) and 6 units (ones). 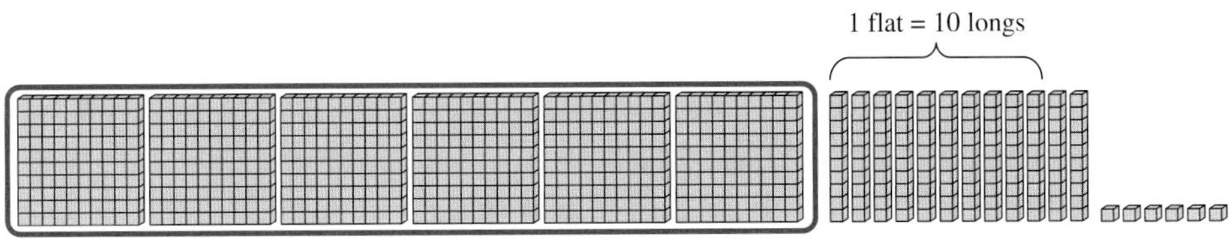 1 flat = 10 longs	1 set of 6 flats $\begin{array}{r} 1 \\ 6\overline{)726} \\ -6 \\ \hline 12 \end{array}$ 12 longs 6 units remaining

(continued)

Table 12 (continued)

Base-ten Blocks	Algorithm
4. Then determine how many sets of 6 longs (tens) there are in 12 longs and 6 units, giving 2 sets of 6 longs and 6 units left over.	1 set of 6 flats 2 sets of 6 longs $\dfrac{12}{6\overline{)726}}$ $\underline{-6}$ 12 $\underline{-12}$ 6 6 units left over
5. Finally determine how many sets of 6 units (ones) there are in the 6 remaining units. There is 1 set of 6 units with no units left over (the remainder is 0).	1 set of 6 flats 2 sets of 6 longs 1 set of 6 units 121 $6\overline{)726}$ $\underline{-6}$ 12 $\underline{-12}$ 6 $\underline{-6}$ 0 0 remainder

Therefore, in the base-ten block representation of 726, there is 1 group of 6 flats (hundreds), 2 groups of 6 longs (tens), and 1 group of 6 units (ones) with none left over. Hence, the quotient is 121 with a remainder of 0. The steps in the algorithm are shown alongside the work with the base-ten blocks.

Using an Area Model to Develop the Standard Division Algorithm

The division $726 \div 6$ can be viewed using an area model. We can think of this as finding the unknown side length of a rectangular region with area 726 square units and side length 6 units as shown in Figure 47. The amount of hundreds is found, then tens, then ones. This yields three regions of dimensions 6 by 100, 6 by 20, and 6 by 1 as seen in Figure 47(b). It can be connected with the decomposition of 726 as $6 \cdot 100, 6 \cdot 20$, and $6 \cdot 1$. By the distributive property, this is $6(100 + 20 + 1) = 6 \cdot 121 = 726$, so the unknown side length is 121. This can be recorded as in Figure 46(a).

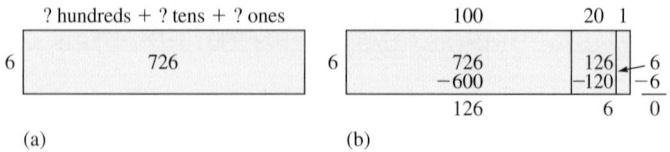

Figure 47

▶ **NOW TRY THIS 19**

NTT 19: Answer can be found in Answers at the back of the book.

Using base-ten blocks, perform the division $726 \div 6$ by dividing the blocks into 6 equal piles. Compare your answer to that in Table 12. Which technique do you prefer? Why?

Short Division

The process used in Table 12 is usually referred to as "long" division. Another technique, called the **short division algorithm**, can be used when the divisor is a one-digit number and most of the work is done mentally. An example of the short division algorithm is given in Figure 48.

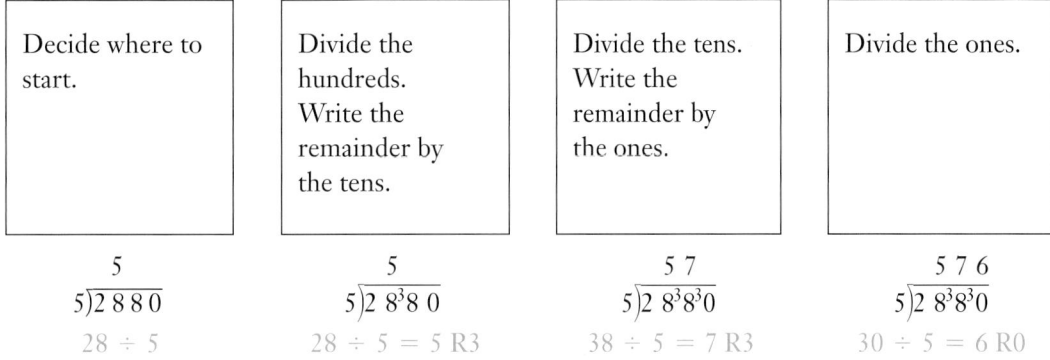

Figure 48

Division by a Two-digit Divisor

An example of division by a divisor of more than one digit is given next. Consider $32\overline{)2618}$.

1. Estimate the quotient in $32\overline{)2618}$. Because $1 \cdot 32 = 32$, $10 \cdot 32 = 320$, and $100 \cdot 32 = 3200$, the quotient is between 10 and 100.
2. Find the number of tens in the quotient. Because $26 \div 3$ is approximately 8, 26 hundreds divided by 3 tens is approximately 8 tens. Then write the 8 in the tens place, as shown:

$$
\begin{array}{r}
80 \\
32\overline{)2618} \\
-2560 \quad (32 \cdot 80) \\
\hline
58
\end{array}
$$

3. Find the number of units in the quotient. Because $5 \div 3$ is approximately 1, 5 tens divided by 3 tens is approximately 1. This is shown on the left, with the standard algorithm shown on the right.

$$
\begin{array}{r}
81 \\
\hline
1 \\
80 \\
32\overline{)2618} \\
-2560 \\
\hline
58 \\
-32 \quad (32 \cdot 1) \\
\hline
26
\end{array}
\qquad \rightarrow \qquad
\begin{array}{r}
81 \text{ R}26 \\
32\overline{)2618} \\
-256 \\
\hline
58 \\
-32 \\
\hline
26
\end{array}
$$

Normally grade-school books show the format on the right, which places the remainder beside the quotient.

4. Check: $32 \cdot 81 + 26 = 2618$.

Multiplication and Division in Different Bases

In multiplication, as with addition and subtraction, we identify the basic facts of single-digit multiplication before developing any algorithms. The multiplication facts for base five are given in Table 13. These facts can be derived by using repeated addition.

Table 13 Base Five Multiplication Table

×	0	1	2	3	4
0	0	0	0	0	0
1	0	1	2	3	4
2	0	2	4	11	13
3	0	3	11	14	22
4	0	4	13	22	31

There are various ways to compute the product $21_{five} \cdot 3_{five}$.

Fives	Ones
2	1
×	3

$$\rightarrow \begin{array}{r} (20 + 1)_{five} \\ \times \quad 3_{five} \\ \hline (110 + 3)_{five} \end{array} \rightarrow \begin{array}{r} 21_{five} \\ \times 3_{five} \\ \hline 3 \\ 110 \\ \hline 113_{five} \end{array} \rightarrow \begin{array}{r} 21_{five} \\ \times\ 3_{five} \\ \hline 113_{five} \end{array}$$

The multiplication of a two-digit number by a two-digit number is developed next:

$$\begin{array}{rl} 23_{five} & \\ \times 14_{five} & \\ \hline 22 & (4 \cdot 3)_{five} \\ 130 & (4 \cdot 20)_{five} \\ 30 & (10 \cdot 3)_{five} \\ 200 & (10 \cdot 20)_{five} \\ \hline 432_{five} & \end{array} \qquad \begin{array}{r} 23_{five} \\ \times 14_{five} \\ \hline 202 \\ 230 \\ \hline 432_{five} \end{array}$$

Lattice multiplication can also be used to multiply numbers in various number bases. This is explored in Assessments 3-5A and B.

Division in different bases can be performed using the multiplication facts and the definition of division. For example, $22_{five} \div 3_{five} = c$ if, and only if, $c \cdot 3_{five} = 22_{five}$. From Table 13, we see that $c = 4_{five}$. As in base ten, computing multi-digit divisions efficiently in different bases requires practice. The ideas behind the algorithms for division can be developed by using subtraction. For example, $3241_{five} \div 43_{five}$ is computed by means of the subtraction technique in Figure 49(a) and by means of the standard algorithm in Figure 49(b). Thus, $3241_{five} \div 43_{five}$ results in quotient 34_{five} and remainder 14_{five}. Using the **division algorithm**, this can be written as $3241_{five} = 34_{five} \cdot 43_{five} + 14_{five}$.

$$\begin{array}{rl} 43_{five}\overline{)3241_{five}} & \\ -430 & (10 \cdot 43)_{five} \\ \hline 2311 & \\ -430 & (10 \cdot 43)_{five} \\ \hline 1331 & \\ -430 & (10 \cdot 43)_{five} \\ \hline 401 & \\ -141 & (2 \cdot 43)_{five} \\ \hline -210 & \\ -141 & (2 \cdot 43)_{five} \\ \hline 14 & (34 \cdot 43)_{five} \end{array}$$

(a)

$$\begin{array}{r} 34_{five}\text{R}14_{five} \\ 43_{five}\overline{)3241_{five}} \\ -234 \\ \hline 401 \\ -332 \\ \hline 14_{five} \end{array}$$

(b)

Figure 49

Computations involving base two are demonstrated in Example 12.

Example 12

a. Multiply:

$$101_{two}$$
$$\times\ 11_{two}$$

b. Divide:

$$101_{two}\overline{)110110_{two}}$$

Solution

a.

$$101_{two}$$
$$\underline{\times 11_{two}}$$
$$101$$
$$\underline{101}$$
$$1111_{two}$$

b.

$$101_{two}\overline{)110110_{two}}^{\ \ \ 1010_{two}R100_{two}}$$
$$\underline{-101}$$
$$\ \ \ \ 111$$
$$\ \ \underline{-101}$$
$$\ \ \ \ 100_{two}$$

IMAP Video

Watch Gilberto find the product of whole numbers using the Front-end multiplying strategy.

Mental Computation: Multiplication

As with addition and subtraction, mental computation is useful for multiplication. For example, consider $8 \cdot 26$. Students may think of this computation in a variety of ways, as shown here.

$26 = 20 + 6$	$26 = 25 + 1$	$26 = 30 - 4$
$8 \cdot 20$ is 160;	$8 \cdot 25$ is 200;	$8 \cdot 30$ is 240;
$8 \cdot 6$ is 48, so	$8 \cdot 1$ is 8, so	subtract $8 \cdot 4 = 32$.
$8 \cdot 26$ is $160 + 48 = 208$	$8 \cdot 26$ is $200 + 8 = 208$	$8 \cdot 26 = 240 - 32 = 208$

Next we consider several of the most common strategies for performing mental computation using multiplication.

1. *Front-end multiplying*

$$\begin{array}{r} 64 \\ \underline{\times 5} \end{array}$$

$60 \cdot 5 = 300$ (Multiply the number of tens in the first number by 5.)
$\ 4 \cdot 5 = \ \ 20$ (Multiply the number of units in the first number by 5.)
$300 + 20 = 320$ (Add the two products.)

2. *Using compatible numbers*

$$2 \cdot 9 \cdot 5 \cdot 20 \cdot 5$$

Rearrange as $9 \cdot (2 \cdot 5) \cdot (20 \cdot 5) = 9 \cdot 10 \cdot 100 = 9000$.

3. *Thinking money*

a.
$$\begin{array}{r} 64 \\ \underline{\times 5} \end{array}$$
(Think of the product as 64 nickels, which can be thought of as 32 dimes, which is $32 \times 10 = 320$ cents.)

b.
$$\begin{array}{r} 64 \\ \underline{\times 50} \end{array}$$
(Think of the product as 64 half-dollars, which is 32 dollars, or 3200 cents.)

c.
$$\begin{array}{r} 64 \\ \underline{\times 25} \end{array}$$
(Think of the product as 64 quarters, which is 32 half-dollars, or 16 dollars. Thus, we have 1600 cents.)

Mental Computation: Division

1. *Breaking up the dividend*

$$7\overline{)4256} \quad 7\overline{)42\,|\,56}$$ (Break up the dividend into parts.)

$$\begin{array}{c} 600 + 8 \\ \hline 7\overline{)4200 + 56} \end{array}$$ (Divide both parts by 7.)

$$600 + 8 = 608$$ (Add the answers together.)

2. *Using compatible numbers*

  a. $3\overline{)105}$ $105 = 90 + 15$ (Look for numbers that you recognize as divisible by 3 and having a sum of 105.)

$$\begin{array}{c} 30 + 5 \\ \hline 3\overline{)90 + 15} \end{array} \quad \text{Thus } 105 \div 3 = 35.$$ (Divide both parts and add the answers.)

  b. $8\overline{)232}$ $232 = 240 - 8$ (Look for numbers that are easily divisible by 8 and whose difference is 232.)

$$\begin{array}{c} 30 - 1 \\ \hline 8\overline{)240 - 8} \end{array} \quad \text{Thus } 232 \div 8 = 29.$$ (Divide both parts and take the difference.)

Computational Estimation

Activity Manual

Use *Target Number* to reinforce the inverse relationship between multiplication and division and to develop estimation skills.

Computational estimation may help determine whether an answer is reasonable or not. This is especially useful when the computation is done on a calculator. Some common estimation strategies for multiplication and division are given next.

1. *Front-end*

$$\begin{array}{r} 524 \\ \times 8 \\ \hline \end{array}$$ $500 \cdot 8 = 4000$ (Start multiplying at the front to obtain a first estimate.)

$$20 \cdot 8 = 160$$ (Multiply the next important digit by 8.)

$$4000 + 160 = 4160$$ (Adjust the first estimate by adding the two numbers.)

2. *Compatible numbers*

$$5\overline{)4163} \quad 5\overline{)4000}$$ (Change 4163 to a number close to it that you know is divisible by 5.)

$$\begin{array}{c} 800 \\ 5\overline{)4000} \end{array}$$ (Carry out the division and obtain the first estimate of 800. Various techniques can be used to adjust the first estimate.)

▶ **NOW TRY THIS 20**

NTT 20: Answers can be found in Answers at the back of the book.

Estimate each of the following mentally, and explain what technique you used to find the answer.

  a. A sold-out concert was held in a theater with a capacity of 4525 people. Tickets were sold for $9 each. Approximately how much money was collected?

  b. Fliers are to be delivered to 3625 houses, and there are 42 people who will be doing the distribution. If distributed equally, approximately how many houses will each person visit?

Assessment 3-5A

1. Simplify each of the following multiplications using properties of exponents. Leave answers as powers.
   a. $5^7 \cdot 5^{12}$ 5^{19}
   b. $6^{10} \cdot 6^2 \cdot 6^3$ 6^{15}
   c. $10^{296} \cdot 10^{17}$ 10^{313}
   d. $2^7 \cdot 10^5 \cdot 5^7$ 10^{12}
2. a. Which is greater, $2^{80} + 2^{80}$ or 2^{100}? Why?   *
   b. Which is greatest, $4 \cdot 2^{99}$, $3 \cdot 2^{100}$, or 2^{102}? Why?   *
3. Illustrate how to use base-ten blocks to compute $3 \cdot 42$.   *
4. The following model illustrates $22 \cdot 13$.

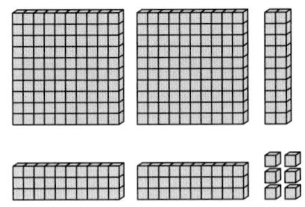

   a. Explain how the partial products are shown in the figure.   *
   b. Draw a similar model for $15 \cdot 21$.   *
   c. Draw a similar base-five model for the product $43_{\text{five}} \cdot 23_{\text{five}}$. Explain how the model can be used to find the answer in base five.   *
5. Fill in the missing numbers in each of the following computations.

   a.
   ```
       4_6
     × 783
     ─────
     1_78
     3408
      982
     ─────
    3335_8
   ```
   $\quad$
   ```
     4 2 6
   ×  7 8 3
   ───────
   1 2 7 8
   3 4 0 8
   2 9 8 2
   ───────
   3 3 3 5 5 8
   ```

   b.
   ```
      327
    × 9_1
    ─────
      327
    1_08
     _9_3
    ─────
   30_ _07
   ```
   $\quad$
   ```
     3 2 7
   ×  9 4 1
   ───────
     3 2 7
   1 3 0 8
   2 9 4 3
   ───────
   3 0 7 7 0 7
   ```

6. Perform the following multiplications using the lattice multiplication algorithm:
   a.
   ```
    728   *
   × 94
   ```
   b.
   ```
    306   *
   × 24
   ```
7. The following chart displays the average daily water use per person for various countries; an approximate population for the countries is also given. Compute the daily total water use in each country.   *

Country/population	Daily Water Use per Person in Liters
India/1,200,000,000	140
Brazil/200,000,000	200
Nigeria/160,000,000	40
Japan/130,000,000	375
Australia/23,000,000	500
Kuwait/3,000,000	500
Bahrain/800,000	450

8. a. Use the distributive property of multiplication over addition to explain why multiplication of a natural number in base two by 10_{two} results in appending 0 to the number.   *
   b. Use part (b) to explain why multiplication in base two by 100_{two} results in appending 00 to the number.   *
   c. Use the distributive property of multiplication over addition and parts (a) and (b) to compute $110_{\text{two}} \cdot 11_{\text{two}}$.   *
9. The Russian peasant algorithm for multiplying $27 \cdot 68$ follows. (Disregard remainders when halving.)

Halves			Doubles	
	→	27 ×	⟨68⟩	
Halve 27	→	13	⟨136⟩	Double 68
Halve 13	→	6	272	Double 136
Halve 6	→	3	⟨544⟩	Double 272
Halve 3	→	1	⟨1088⟩	Double 544

   In the "Halves" column, choose the odd numbers marked by an arrow. In the "Doubles" column, circle the numbers paired with the odds from the "Halves" column. Add the circled numbers.

   $\quad$ 68
   $\quad$ 136
   $\quad$ 544
   $\quad$ 1088
   $\quad$ ─────
   $\quad$ 1836   This is the product of $27 \cdot 68$.

   Try the Russian peasant algorithm for $17 \cdot 63$.   *

10. Answer the following questions based on the activity chart provided:

Activity	Calories Burned per Hour
Playing tennis	462
Snowshoeing	708
Cross-country skiing	444
Playing volleyball	198

   a. How many calories are burned during 3 hours of cross-country skiing?   1332
   b. Jane played tennis for 2 hours while Carolyn played volleyball for 3 hours. Who burned more calories, and how many more?   Jane, 330 more
   c. Lyle went snowshoeing for 3 hours and Maurice went cross-country skiing for 5 hours. Who burned more calories, and how many more?   Maurice, 96 more
11. On a 14-day vacation, Glenn increased his caloric intake by 1500 calories per day. He also worked out more than usual by swimming 2 hours a day. Swimming burns 666 calories per hour, and a net gain of 3500 calories adds 1 lb of weight. Did Glenn gain at least 1 lb during his vacation?   No

12. Dave purchased a $50,000 life insurance policy at the price of $30 for each $1000 of coverage. If he pays the annual premium quarterly, how much is each installment? $375

13. Perform each of the following divisions using both the repeated-subtraction and standard algorithms.
    a. $8\overline{)623}$ *
    b. $36\overline{)298}$ *
    c. $391\overline{)4001}$ *

14. Place the digits 4, 5, 7, and 3 in the boxes $\square\overline{)\square\square\square}$ to obtain
    a. the greatest quotient. $3\overline{)754}$
    b. the least quotient. $7\overline{)345}$

15. Using a calculator, Ralph multiplied by 10 when he should have divided by 10. The display read 300. What should the correct answer be? 3

16. Consider the following multiplications. Notice that when the digits in the factors are reversed, the products are the same.

$$\begin{array}{cc} 36 & 63 \\ \times\, 42 & \times\, 24 \\ \hline 1512 & 1512 \end{array}$$

    a. Find other multiplications where this procedure works. *
    b. Find a pattern for the numbers that work in this way. *

17. Dan has 4520 pennies in three boxes. He says that there are 3 times as many pennies in the first box as in the third and twice as many in the second box as in the first. How much does he have in each box? 1356; 2712; and 452

18. Gina buys apples from an orchard and then sells them at a country fair in bags 3 for $1. She bought 50 boxes of apples, 36 apples in a box, and paid $452. If she sold all but 18 apples, what was her total profit? $142

19. Discuss possible error patterns in each of the following computations.
    a. $\begin{array}{r} 35 \\ \times\, 26 \\ \hline 90 \end{array}$ *
    b. $\begin{array}{r} 53 \\ 5\overline{)2515} \\ -25 \\ \hline 15 \\ -15 \\ \hline 0 \end{array}$ *

20. Give reasons for each of the following steps. *
$$\begin{aligned} 56\cdot 10 &= (5\cdot 10 + 6)\cdot 10 \\ &= (5\cdot 10)\cdot 10 + 6\cdot 10 \\ &= 5\cdot(10\cdot 10) + 6\cdot 10 \\ &= 5\cdot 10^2 + 6\cdot 10 \\ &= 5\cdot 10^2 + 6\cdot 10 + 0\cdot 1 \\ &= 560 \end{aligned}$$

21. **a.** Find all whole numbers that leave remainder 3 upon division by 4. Write your answer using set-builder notation. $\{4n + 3 \mid n \in W\}$

    b. Write the numbers from part (a) in a sequence in increasing order. $3, 7, 11, 15, 19, \ldots$
    c. What kind of sequence is this? Why? *

22. For what possible bases are each of the following computations correct?
    a. $\begin{array}{r} 213 \quad \text{Nine} \\ +\, 308 \\ \hline 522 \end{array}$
    b. $\begin{array}{r} 213 \quad \text{Six} \\ \times\, 32 \\ \hline 430 \\ 1043 \\ \hline 11300 \end{array}$

23. Use lattice multiplication to compute $323_{\text{five}} \cdot 42_{\text{five}}$. *

24. Find the least values of a and b such that $32_a = 23_b$. Explain your reasoning. *

25. Place the digits 7, 6, 8, and 3 in the boxes to obtain

$$\begin{array}{c} \square\square\square \\ \times\ \square \end{array}$$

    a. the greatest product. *
    b. the least product. *

26. Perform each of these operations using the bases shown.
    a. $32_{\text{five}} \cdot 4_{\text{five}}$ 233_{five}
    b. $32_{\text{five}} \div 4_{\text{five}}$ $4_{\text{five}}\, \text{R} 1_{\text{five}}$
    c. $43_{\text{six}} \cdot 23_{\text{six}}$ 1513_{six}
    d. $143_{\text{five}} \div 3_{\text{five}}$ 31_{five}
    e. $10010_{\text{two}} \div 11_{\text{two}}$ 110_{two}
    f. $10110_{\text{two}} \cdot 101_{\text{two}}$ 1101110_{two}

27. A car trip took 8 hr of driving at an average of 62 mph. Mentally compute the total number of miles traveled. 496 mi

28. A theater has 38 rows with 23 seats in each row. Estimate the number of seats in the theater and tell how you arrived at your estimate. *

29. Without computing, tell which of the following have the same answer. Describe your reasoning.
    a. $44\cdot 22$ and $22\cdot 11$ *
    b. $22\cdot 32$ and $11\cdot 64$ *
    c. $13\cdot 33$ and $39\cdot 11$ *

30. In each of the following, determine whether the estimate given in parentheses is high (higher than the actual answer) or low (lower than the actual answer). Justify your answers without computing the exact values.
    a. $299\cdot 300$ $(90,000)$ *
    b. $6001 \div 299$ (20) *
    c. $6000 \div 299$ (20) *
    d. $999 \div 99$ (10) *

31. Use your calculator to calculate $25^2, 35^2, 45^2$, and 55^2, and then see if you can find a pattern that will let you find 65^2 and 75^2 mentally. *

32. A student uses front-end estimation to estimate the product of two numbers as 42,000. List a pair of possible factors. *

Assessment 3-5B

1. Simplify each of the following multiplications using properties of exponents. Leave answers as powers.
   a. $3^8 \cdot 3^4$ 3^{12} **b.** $5^2 \cdot 5^4 \cdot 5^2$ 5^8
   c. $6^2 \cdot 2^2 \cdot 3^2$ 6^4 **d.** $4^8 \cdot 8^4 \cdot 32^5$ 2^{53}
2. **a.** Which is greater, $2^{20} + 2^{20}$ or 2^{21}? Why? *
   b. Which is greatest, 3^{31}, $9 \cdot 3^{30}$, or $3 \cdot 3^{32}$? Why? *
3. Illustrate how to use base-ten blocks to compute $4 \cdot 13$. *
4. The following model illustrates $13 \cdot 12$.

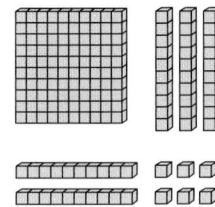

   a. Explain how the partial products are shown in the figure. *
   b. Draw a similar model for $12 \cdot 22$. *
   c. Draw a similar base-five model for the product $14_{\text{five}} \cdot 23_{\text{five}}$. Explain how the model can be used to find the answer in base five. *
5. Fill in the missing numbers in the following.

$$
\begin{array}{r}
4\_4 \\
\times\,327 \\
\hline
3\_88 \\
968 \\
\underline{\_452} \\
1582\_8
\end{array}
\qquad
\begin{array}{r}
484 \\
\times\,327 \\
\hline
3388 \\
968 \\
\underline{1452} \\
158268
\end{array}
$$

6. Perform the following multiplications using the lattice multiplication algorithm.
   a. $\begin{array}{r} 327 \\ \times\,43 \\ \hline \end{array}$ *   **b.** $\begin{array}{r} 2618 \\ \times\,137 \\ \hline \end{array}$ *
7. The following chart gives average water usage for various activities for one person for one day. *

Use	Average Amount
Taking bath	110 L (liters)
Taking shower	75 L
Flushing toilet	22 L
Washing hands, face	7 L
Getting a drink	1 L
Brushing teeth	1 L
Doing dishes (one meal)	30 L
Cooking (one meal)	18 L

   a. Use the chart to calculate how much water you use each day. Answers vary.

8. **b.** An average American uses approximately 200 L of water per day and there are approximately 310,000,000 people in the United States. On average approximately how much water is used in the United States per day? 62,000,000,000 L/day
8. **a.** Use the distributive property of multiplication over addition to explain why multiplication of a natural number in base five by 10_{five} results in appending 0 to the number. *
   b. Use part (b) to explain why multiplication of a natural number in base five by 100_{five} results in appending two 0s to the number. *
   c. Use the distributive property of multiplication over addition and part (b) to compute $14_{\text{five}} \cdot 23_{\text{five}}$. *
9. Use the Russian peasant algorithm from exercise 9 in Assessment 3-5A to find $31 \cdot 69$. *
10. Answer the following questions based on the activity chart.

Activity	Calories Burned per Hour
Playing tennis	462
Snowshoeing	708
Cross-country skiing	444
Playing volleyball	198

   a. How many calories are burned during 4 hours of cross-country skiing? 1776
   b. Jane played tennis for 3 hours while Carolyn played volleyball for 4 hours. Who burned more calories, and how many more? Jane, 594 more
   c. Lyle went snowshoeing for 4 hours and Maurice went cross-country skiing for 5 hours. Who burned more calories, and how many more? Lyle, 612 more

11. On a 14-day vacation, Glenn increased his calorie intake by 1800 calories per day. He also worked out more than usual by swimming 3 hours a day. Swimming burns 666 calories per hour, and a net gain of 3500 calories adds 1 lb of weight. Did Glenn gain at least 1 lb during his vacation? No
12. Sue purchased a $30,000 life-insurance policy at the price of $24 for each $1000 of coverage. If she pays the premium in 12 monthly installments, how much is each installment? $60
13. Perform each of the following divisions using both the repeated-subtraction and the standard algorithms.
   a. $7\overline{)392}$ *   **b.** $37\overline{)925}$ *
   c. $423\overline{)5002}$ *
14. Place the digits 7, 6, 8, and 3 in the boxes $\square)\overline{\square\square\square}$ to obtain
   a. the greatest quotient. $3\overline{)876}$
   b. the least quotient. $8\overline{)367}$

15. Using a calculator, Jody multiplied by 5 when she should have divided by 5. The display read 250. What should the correct answer be?   10

16. A student wrote the following addition problem to his parents.

$$
\begin{array}{r}
\text{SEND} \\
+ \text{ MORE} \\
\hline
\text{MONEY}
\end{array}
$$

If each letter represents a different digit how much money did the student request? $10,652

17. Debbie has 340 dimes in three boxes. She says that there are 4 times as many dimes in the first box as in the second and 3 times as many in the third box as in the first. How much money in dollars does she have in each box?   *

18. Xuan saved $5340 in 3 years. If he saved $95 per month in the first year and a fixed amount per month for the next 2 years, how much did he save per month during the last 2 years? $175

19. Discuss possible error patterns in each of the following multiplications

a.
$$
\begin{array}{r}
34 \\
\times 8 \quad * \\
\hline
2432
\end{array}
$$

b.
$$
\begin{array}{r}
34 \\
\times 6 \quad * \\
\hline
114
\end{array}
$$

20. Give reasons for each of the following steps.   *

$$
\begin{aligned}
35 \cdot 100 &= (3 \cdot 10 + 5)\,100 \\
&= (3 \cdot 10 + 5)\,10^2 \\
&= (3 \cdot 10)\,10^2 + 5 \cdot 10^2 \\
&= 3\,(10 \cdot 10^2) + 5 \cdot 10^2 \\
&= 3 \cdot 10^3 + 5 \cdot 10^2 \\
&= 3 \cdot 10^3 + 5 \cdot 10^2 + 0 \cdot 10 + 0 \cdot 1 \\
&= 3500
\end{aligned}
$$

21. a. Find all the whole numbers that leave remainder 1 upon division by 4. Write your answer using set-builder notation. $\{x \mid x = 4n + 1, n \in W\}$

b. Write the numbers from part (a) in a sequence in increasing order. $1, 5, 9, 13, 17, 21, \ldots$

c. What kind of sequence is this?   *

22. For what possible bases are each of the following computations correct?

a.
$$
\begin{array}{r}
322 \quad \text{Four} \\
- 233 \\
\hline
23
\end{array}
$$

b.
$$
\begin{array}{r}
101 \quad \text{Any base greater} \\
11)\overline{1111} \quad \text{than or equal to two} \\
- 11 \\
\hline
11 \\
- 11 \\
\hline
0
\end{array}
$$

23. Use lattice multiplication to compute $423_{\text{five}} \cdot 23_{\text{five}}$.   *

24. Find the least values of a and b such that $41_a = 14_b$. $a = 5, b = 17$

25. Place the digits 7, 6, 8, 3, and 2 in the boxes to obtain

$$
\begin{array}{r}
\square\square\square \\
\times \quad \square\square
\end{array}
$$

a. the greatest product.   *   **b.** the least product.   *

26. Perform each of these operations using the bases shown.

a. $42_{\text{five}} \cdot 3_{\text{five}}$ 231_{five} **b.** $22_{\text{five}} \div 4_{\text{five}}$ 3_{five}
c. $32_{\text{five}} \cdot 42_{\text{five}}$ 2444_{five} **d.** $1313_{\text{five}} \div 23_{\text{five}}$ 31_{five}
e. $101_{\text{two}} \cdot 101_{\text{two}}$ 11001_{two} **f.** $1001_{\text{two}} \div 11_{\text{two}}$ 11_{two}

27. A car trip took 6 hours at an average of 65 mph. Mentally compute the total number of miles traveled.   *

28. About 3540 calories must be burned to lose 1 lb of body weight. Estimate how many calories must be burned to lose 6 lb.   *

29. Without computing, tell which of the following have the same answer. Describe your reasoning.

a. $88 \cdot 44$ and $44 \cdot 22$ *   **b.** $93 \cdot 15$ and $31 \cdot 45$ *
c. $12 \cdot 18$ and $20 \cdot 17$ *

30. In each of the following, determine if the estimate given in parentheses is high (higher than the actual answer) or low (lower than the actual answer). Justify your answers without computing the exact values.

a. $398 \cdot 500$ (200,000)   *   **b.** $8001 \div 398$ (20)   *
c. $10,000 \div 999$ (10)   *   **d.** $1999 \div 201$ (10)   *

31. Use your calculator to multiply several two-digit numbers by 99. Then see if you can find a pattern that will let you find the product of any two-digit number and 99 mentally.   *

32. A student uses front-end estimation to estimate the product of two numbers as 2400. List a pair of possible factors.   *

Mathematical Connections 3-5

Answers to Mathematical Connections can be found in the Answers section at the back of the book.

Reasoning

1. How would you explain to students how to multiply $345 \cdot 678$, assuming that they know and understand multiplication by a single digit and multiplication by a power of 10?

2. What happens when you multiply any two-digit number by 101? Explain why this happens.

3. Pick a number. Double it. Multiply the result by 3. Add 24. Divide by 6. Subtract your original number. Is the result always the same? Write a convincing argument for what happens.

4. Do you think it is valuable for students to see more than one method of doing computation problems? Why or why not?

5. Tom claims that long division should receive reduced attention in elementary classrooms. Do you agree or disagree? Defend your answer. (Check the web for related research.)

6. For the given computation, answer the following questions.

$$
\begin{array}{r}
122\,R37 \\
43)\overline{5283} \\
-43 \\
\hline
98 \\
-86 \\
\hline
123 \\
-86 \\
\hline
37
\end{array}
$$

a. Why is the 1 in the quotient above the 2 in the dividend?
b. Why can we just bring down the 8 to obtain 98?
c. Why can we just bring down the 3 to obtain 123?
d. What does R37 mean?

7. For the base-five computation below, answer the following questions.

$$31_{\text{five}} \overline{)\,4\,0\,2\,1_{\text{five}}}$$
$$\underline{-3\,1}$$
$$4$$

a. What does the 4 in the subtraction represent?
b. Complete the division.

Open-Ended

8. If a student presented a new "algorithm" for computing with whole numbers, describe the process you would recommend to the student to determine whether the algorithm would always work.

9. Dina calculated each of the following mentally:

$$49 \cdot 51 + 49 \cdot 49 = 4900$$
$$98 \cdot 37 + 2 \cdot 37 = 3700$$
$$99 \cdot 37 + 37 = 3700$$

Explain how she performed the calculations and why her method works. Then give three similar calculations based on the same approach and find the answers mentally.

Cooperative Learning

10. The traditional sequence for teaching operations in the elementary school is first addition, then subtraction, followed by multiplication, and finally division. Some educators advocate teaching addition followed by multiplication, then subtraction followed by division. Within your group, prepare arguments for teaching the operations in either order listed.

11. a. Without actually finding the answers determine which is greater: 19,876 · 43 or 19,875 · 44. Explain your approach. Compare the explanations with other members in your group.
    b. Come up with three similar pairs of products and determine which is greater. Justify your answers. Compare your answers with the other students in your group.

12. Messages can be coded on paper tape in base two. A hole in the tape represents 1, whereas the absence of a hole represents 0. The value of each hole depends on its position; from left to right, the values are 16, 8, 4, 2, 1 (all powers of 2). Letters of the alphabet may be coded in base two according to their position in the alphabet. For example, G is the seventh letter. Since $7 = 1 \cdot 4 + 1 \cdot 2 + 1$, the holes appear as they do below.

○	○	○
16 8	4	2	1

a. Decode the message below.

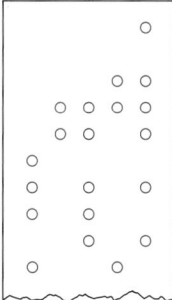

b. Write your name on a tape using base two.
c. Consider the cards, which are modeled on base-two representations.

Card E		**Card D**		**Card C**	
16	24	8	24	4	20
17	25	9	25	5	21
18	26	10	26	6	22
19	27	11	27	7	23
20	28	12	28	12	28
21	29	13	29	13	29
22	30	14	30	14	30
23	31	15	31	15	31

Card B		**Card A**	
2	18	1	17
3	19	3	19
6	22	5	21
7	23	7	23
10	26	9	25
11	27	11	27
14	30	13	29
15	31	15	31

(i) Suppose a person in your group under 32 tells you that his age appears on cards E, C, and B. How can you use that information to find the person's age? Explain how the system works in general.
(ii) Design card F and redesign cards A to E so that the numbers 1 through 63 appear on the cards.

Connecting Mathematics to the Classroom

13. A student asks why she should learn the standard long division algorithm if she can get a correct answer using repeated subtraction. How do you respond?

14. A student divides as follows. How do you help?

$$6\overline{)36}$$
$$15$$
$$\underline{-6}$$
$$30$$
$$\underline{30}$$

15. A student asks how you can find the quotient and the remainder in a division problem like 593 ÷ 36 using a calculator that can perform only the four basic operations. How do you respond?

16. A student claims that to divide a number with the units digit 0 by 10, she just crosses out the 0 to get the answer. She wants to know if this is always true and if the 0 has to be the units digit. How do you respond?

17. a. A student notices that $39 + 41 = 40 + 40$ and wonders if it is also true that $39 \cdot 41 = 40 \cdot 40$. How do you reply?
    b. Another student says that he knows that $39 \cdot 41 \neq 40 \cdot 40$ but he found that $39 \cdot 41 = 40 \cdot 40 - 1$. He also found that $49 \cdot 51 = 50 \cdot 50 - 1$. He wants to know if this pattern continues. How would you respond?

18. Howard is having trouble finding a number to fill in the box below. What might be his problem, and how do you help him?

$$\Box \div 5 = 6$$

19. What errors do you think the student is making in each of the following? How would you help these students?

a.
$$4\overline{)682} \quad 120$$

b.
$$5\overline{)906} \quad 19R1$$
$$\underline{-5}$$
$$4\ 6$$
$$\underline{-4\ 5}$$
$$1$$

20. A student performs the following computation.

$$\begin{array}{r} \overset{3}{}\overset{4}{6}8 \\ \times\ 5 \\ \hline 340 \end{array}$$

a. Explain the meaning of the 4 above the 6.
b. Explain the meaning of the 3 in the hundreds place.

21. A student performs the following computation in base five.

$$\begin{array}{r} \overset{3}{}34_{\text{five}} \\ \times\ 4_{\text{five}} \\ \hline 301_{\text{five}} \end{array}$$

Explain the meaning of the 3 above the 3.

Review Problems

22. Illustrate the identity property of addition for whole numbers.

23. Rename each of the following using the distributive property of multiplication over addition.
a. $ax + bx + 2x$
b. $3(a + b) + x(a + b)$

24. At the beginning of a trip, the mileage odometer registered 52,281. At the end of the trip, the odometer registered 59,260. How many miles were traveled on this trip?

25. Write each of the following division problems as a multiplication problem.
a. $36 \div 4 = 9$
b. $112 \div 2 = x$
c. $48 \div x = 6$
d. $x \div 7 = 17$

National Assessments

National Assessment of Educational Progress (NAEP) Questions

There will be 58 people at a breakfast and each person will eat 2 eggs. There are 12 eggs in each carton. How many cartons of eggs will be needed for the breakfast?
A. 9
B. 10
C. 72
D. 116

NAEP, Grade 4, 2007

Which of these would be easiest to solve by using mental math?
A. $\$65.12 - \$28.19$
B. 358×2
C. $1,625 \div 3$
D. $\$100.00 + \$10.00$

NAEP, Grade 4, 2007

A student had to multiply 328×41. The student's answer was 4,598. Use estimation to explain why this answer is not reasonable.

NAEP, Grade 4, 2007

Hint for Solving the Preliminary Problem

Look at the columns and rows that have only two symbols. Compare these columns and rows. Look for a pattern.

Chapter 3 Summary

KEY CONCEPTS	DEFINITIONS, DESCRIPTIONS, AND THEOREMS
Section 3-1	
Numeration system (p. 85)	A collection of properties and symbols agreed upon to represent numbers.
Hindu-Arabic numeration system (p. 86)	A base-ten system constructed from the ten digits 0, 1, 2, 3, 4, 5, 6, 7, 8, and 9. *Numerals*—symbols representing numbers.
Place value (p. 86)	The value assigned to a digit depending on its placement in a numeral.
Face value (p. 86)	The value of the digit.
Exponent (p. 86)	If a is any number and n is any natural number, then $a^n = \underbrace{a \cdot a \cdot a \cdot \ldots \cdot a}_{n \text{ factors}},$ where a is the *base* and n is the *exponent*. If $a \neq 0$, then $a^0 = 1$.
Different numeration systems (p. 87)	*Tally numeration system*—single strokes or tally marks used to represent numbers.
	Egyptian numeration system—a grouping system, consisting of seven basic symbols used to represent certain sets of numbers.
	Babylonian numeration system—a place-value system based on 60 using two basic symbols to represent numbers.
	Mayan numeration system—a place-value system based primarily on 20 using three basic symbols and vertical groupings.
	Roman numeration system—a system, consisting of seven symbols, that used *additive*, *subtractive*, and *multiplicative* properties.
	Other number-base system—a place-value system based on a number other than ten, which is studied to understand the base-ten system. Examples of such systems are *base two*, *base five*, and *base twelve*.
Section 3-2	
Addition of whole numbers (p. 101)	Let A and B be two disjoint finite sets. If $n(A) = a$ and $n(B) = b$, then $a + b = n(A \cup B)$.
Models for addition (p. 101)	• *Set* • *Number line*
Ordering whole numbers (p. 102)	*Less than*—for any whole numbers a and b, a is less than b, written $a < b$, if, and only if, there exists a natural number k such that $a + k = b$.
	Greater than—for any whole numbers a and b, a is greater than b, written $a > b$, if, and only if, $b < a$.
Addition properties for whole numbers (p. 103)	• *Closure*—if a and b are any whole numbers, then $a + b$ is a unique whole number.
	• *Commutative*—if a and b are any whole numbers, then $a + b = b + a$.
	• *Associative*—if $a, b,$ and c are any whole numbers, then $(a + b) + c = a + (b + c)$.
	• *Identity*—there is a unique whole number 0, the *additive identity*, such that for any whole number a, $a + 0 = a = 0 + a$.
Subtraction of whole numbers (p. 106)	For any whole numbers a and b, such that $a \geq b$, $a - b$ is the unique whole number c such that $b + c = a$.
Models for subtraction (p. 106)	• *Take-away* • *Comparison* • *Missing addend* • *Number line*

Section 3-3

Multiplication of whole numbers (p. 116)	*Repeated addition approach*—for any whole number a and $n \neq 0$, $n \cdot a = \underbrace{a + a + a + \ldots + a}_{n \text{ terms}} = na$. If $n = 0$, then $0 \cdot a = 0$. $a \cdot b$, or ab, is the *product*, and a and b are *factors*. *Cartesian product approach*—for finite sets A and B, if $n(A) = a$ and $n(B) = b$, then $a \cdot b = n(A \times B)$.
Models for multiplication	• *Repeated addition* • *Rectangular array* • *Number line* • *Area* • *Cartesian product*
Multiplication properties for whole numbers (p. 118)	• *Closure*—if a and b are any whole numbers, then $a \cdot b$ is a unique whole number. • *Commutative*—if a and b are any whole numbers, then $a \cdot b = b \cdot a$. • *Associative*—if a, b, and c are any whole numbers, then $(a \cdot b) \cdot c = a \cdot (b \cdot c)$. • *Identity*—there is a unique whole number 1, the *multiplicative identity*, such that for any whole number a, $a \cdot 1 = a = 1 \cdot a$. • *Property of 0*—if a is any whole number, then $a \cdot 0 = 0 = 0 \cdot a$.
Distributive property of multiplication over addition or subtraction (p. 119)	If a, b, and c are any whole numbers, then $a(b + c) = ab + ac$. If a, b, and c are any whole numbers with $b \geq c$, then $a(b - c) = ab - ac$.
Division of whole numbers (p. 122)	*Missing-factor approach*—for any whole numbers a and b, with $b \neq 0$, $a \div b = c$ if, and only if, c is the unique whole number such that $b \cdot c = a$. The number a is the *dividend*, b is the *divisor*, and c is the *quotient*.
Models for division (p. 121)	• *Set (partition)* • *Repeated subtraction* • *Missing-factor*
Division Algorithm (p. 122)	For any whole numbers a and b with $b \neq 0$, there exist unique whole numbers q (quotient) and r (remainder) such that $a = bq + r$, with $0 \leq r < b$.
Relating multiplication and division (p. 124)	Whole number multiplication and division with remainder 0 are inverses of each other.
Division by 0 and 1 (p. 124)	• For any nonzero whole number n, $n \div 0$ is undefined and $0 \div n = 0$. • $0 \div 0$ is undefined. • For any whole number n, $n \div 1 = n$.
Order of operations (p. 126)	Multiplications and divisions are performed in the order they occur from left to right, and then the additions and subtractions are performed in the order they occur from left to right. Computations in parentheses are done first.

Section 3-4

Addition algorithms (p. 131)	• *Concrete model* • *Lattice* • *Left-to-right* • *Scratch*
Subtraction algorithms (p. 135)	• *Concrete model* • *Equal additions*
Addition and subtraction in bases other than ten	Computations involving a number-base system other than base ten are studied to better understand base-ten system algorithms.
Mental computation algorithms for addition (p. 139)	• *Adding from the left* • *Breaking and bridging* • *Trading off* • *Using compatible numbers* • *Making compatible numbers*

Section 3-4

Mental computation algorithms for subtraction (p. 140)	• *Breaking and bridging* • *Trading off*	• *Drop the zeros* • *Making compatible numbers*
Estimation algorithms for addition and subtraction (p. 141)	• *Front-end with adjustment* • *Grouping to nice numbers* • *Clustering*	• *Rounding* • *Using the range*

Section 3-5

Definition of a^n

If a and n are whole numbers and $n \neq 0$, then $a^n = \underbrace{a \cdot a \cdot a \cdot \ldots \cdot a}_{n \text{ factors}}$.

Properties of whole number exponents (p. 150)

$a^1 = a$
If $a \neq 0$, then $a^0 = 1$.
For whole numbers a, and natural numbers m, and n, $a^m \cdot a^n = a^{m+n}$.
For whole numbers a, and natural numbers m, and n, $(a^m)^n = a^{mn}$.
For whole numbers a and b, natural numbers n, $a^n \cdot b^n = (ab)^n$.
For natural numbers a, m, and n with $m \geq n$, $a^m \div a^n = a^{m-n}$.

Multiplication algorithms (p. 152)

• *Multiplication by 10^n*—results in appending n zeros
• *Multiplication with two-digit factors*
• *Lattice multiplication*

Division algorithms (p. 156)

• *Using repeated subtraction*
• *Using base-ten blocks, developing the standard division algorithm*
• *Short division*
• *Division by a two-digit divisor*

Multiplication and division in bases other than ten

Computations involving a number-base system other than base ten are studied to understand better base-ten system algorithms.

Mental computation algorithms for multiplication (p. 161)

• *Front-end multiplying*   • *Thinking money*
• *Using compatible numbers*

Mental computation algorithms for division (p. 161)

• *Breaking up the dividend*   • *Using compatible numbers*

Estimation algorithms for multiplication and division (p. 162)

• *Front-end multiplication*   • *Compatible number division*

Chapter 3 Review

1. For each of the following base-ten numerals, tell the place value for the underlined digits.
   a. 4<u>3</u>2   Tens
   b. <u>3</u>432   Thousands
   c. 1<u>9</u>324   Hundreds
2. Convert each of the following to a base-ten number.
   a. $\overline{\text{CD}}$XLIV   400,044
   b. 432_{five} 117
   c. $ET0_{\text{twelve}}$ 1704
   d. 1011_{two} 11
   e. 4136_{seven} 1448

3. Convert each of the following to a number in the indicated system.
   a. 999 to Roman   CMXCIX
   b. 86 to Egyptian   ∩∩∩∩∩∩∩∩|||||
   c. 123 to Mayan
   d. 346_{ten} to base five 2341_{five}
   e. 27 to base two 11011_{two}
4. Simplify each of the following products, if possible. Write your answers in exponential form, a^b.
   a. $3^4 \cdot 3^7 \cdot 3^6$ 3^{17}
   b. $2^{10} \cdot 2^{11}$ 2^{21}

5. Write the base-three numeral for the base-three blocks shown.

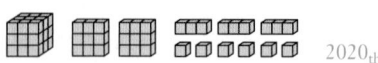

2020_{three}

6. What is the fewest number of base-three blocks needed to represent 51? 1 block, 2 flats, 2 longs, 0 units, so 5 blocks

7. Draw multibase blocks to represent each of the following.
   a. 123_{four} *
   b. 24_{five} *

8. a. The first digit from the left (the lead digit) of a base-ten numeral is 4 followed by 10 zeros. What is the place value of 4? 10^{10}
   b. A number in base five has 10 digits. What is the place value of the second digit from the left? 5^8
   c. A number in base two has lead digit 1 followed by 30 zeros and units digit 1. What is the place value of the lead digit? 2^{31}

9. Write the following base-ten numerals in the indicated base without performing any multiplications.
   a. $10^{10} + 23$ in base ten 10,000,000,023
   b. $2^{10} + 1$ in base two $10,000,000,001_{two}$
   c. $5^{10} + 1$ in base five $10,000,000,001_{five}$
   d. $10^{10} - 1$ in base ten 9,999,999,999
   e. $2^{10} - 1$ in base two $1,111,111,111_{two}$
   f. $12^5 - 1$ in base twelve $EEEEE_{twelve}$
   g. $7 \cdot 5^6 + 3 \cdot 5^4 + 11$ in base five. 12030021_{five}

10. Give an example of a base other than ten used in a real-life situation. How is it used? *

11. Describe the important characteristics of each of the following systems.
   a. Egyptian *
   b. Babylonian *
   c. Roman *
   d. Hindu-Arabic *

12. Write 128 in each of the following bases.
   a. Five 1003_{five}
   b. Two 10000000_{two}
   c. Twelve $T8_{twelve}$

13. Write each of the following numerals in the indicated bases without multiplying the various powers.
   a. $2^{10} + 2^3$ in base two 10000001000_{two}
   b. $11 \cdot 12^5 + 10 \cdot 12^3 + 20$ in base twelve *

14. If $123_b = 83$, solve for b. eight

15. For each of the following equations where $a, b \in W$, identify the properties of the operation(s) for whole numbers illustrated.
   a. $3(a + b) = 3a + 3b$ *
   b. $2 + a = a + 2$ *
   c. $16 \cdot 1 = 1 \cdot 16 = 16$ *
   d. $6(12 + 3) = 6 \cdot 12 + 6 \cdot 3$ *
   e. $3(a \cdot 2) = 3(2a)$ *
   f. $3(2a) = (3 \cdot 2)a$ *

16. Using the definitions of less than or greater than given in this chapter, prove that each of the following inequalities is true.
   a. $3 < 13$ *
   b. $12 > 9$ *

17. For each of the following equations, find all possible replacements to make the statement true for whole numbers.
   a. $4 \cdot \square - 37 < 27$ $0, 1, 2, \ldots, 15$
   b. $398 = \square \cdot 37 + 28$ 10
   c. $\square \cdot (3 + 4) = \square \cdot 3 + \square \cdot 4$ Any whole number
   d. $42 - \square \geq 16$ $0, 1, 2, \ldots, 26$

18. Use the distributive property of multiplication over addition, other multiplication properties, and addition facts, if possible, to rename each of the following where $a, b, x, y \in W$.
   a. $3a + 7a + 5a$ $15a$ Answers vary
   b. $3x^2 + 7x^2 - 5x^2$ $5x^2$
   c. $x(a + b + y)$ $xa + xb + xy$
   d. $(x + 5)3 + (x + 5)y$ $(x + 5)(3 + y)$
   e. $3x^2 + x$ $x(3x + 1)$
   f. $2x^5 + x^3$ $x^3(2x^2 + 1)$

19. How many 12-oz cans of juice would it take to give 60 people one 8-oz serving each? 40 cans

20. Heidi has a brown pair and a gray pair of slacks; a brown blouse, a yellow blouse, and a white blouse; and a blue sweater and a white sweater. How many different outfits does she have if each outfit she wears consists of slacks, a blouse, and a sweater? 12 outfits

21. I am thinking of a whole number. If I divide it by 13, then multiply the answer by 12, then subtract 20, and then add 89, the result is 93. What was my original number? 26

22. A ski resort offers a weekend ski package for $80 per person or $6000 for a group of 80 people. Which would be the less expensive option for a group of 80? $6000 for 80 people is cheaper.

23. Josi has a job in which she works 30 hr/wk and gets paid $5/hr. If she works more than 30 hr in a week, she receives $8/hr for each hour over 30 hr. If she worked 38 hr this week, how much did she earn? $214

24. In a television game show, there are five questions to answer. Each question is worth twice as much as the previous question. If the last question was worth $6400, what was the first question worth? $400

25. a. Think of a number.
   Add 17.
   Double the result.
   Subtract 4.
   Double the result.
   Add 20.
   Divide by 4.
   Subtract 20.
   Your answer will be your original number. Explain how this trick works. *
   b. Fill in two more steps that will take you back to your original number.
   Think of a number.
   Add 18.
   Multiply by 4.
   Subtract 7.
   ·
   ·
   · *
   c. Make up a series of instructions such that you will always get back to your original number. *

26. Use both the scratch and the traditional algorithms to compute the following sum.

$$\begin{array}{r} 316 \\ 712 \\ + \ 91 \\ \hline \end{array}$$ *

27. Use both the traditional and the lattice multiplication algorithms to compute the following multiplication.

$$\begin{array}{r} 613 \\ \times \ 98 \\ \hline \end{array}$$ *

28. Use both the repeated-subtraction and the conventional algorithms to perform the following divisions.
    a. $912\overline{)4803}$ *
    b. $11\overline{)1011}$ *
    c. $23_{\text{five}}\overline{)3312}_{\text{five}}$ *
    d. $11_{\text{two}}\overline{)1011}_{\text{two}}$ *
29. Use the Division Algorithm to check your answers in exercise 28.   *
30. In some calculations a combination of mental math and a calculator is most appropriate. For example, because
    $$200 \cdot 97 \cdot 146 \cdot 5 = 97 \cdot 146 (200 \cdot 5)$$
    $$= 97 \cdot 146 \cdot 1000,$$
    we can calculate $97 \cdot 146$ on a calculator and then mentally multiply by 1000. Show how to calculate each of the following products using a combination of mental math and a calculator.
    a. $19 \cdot 5 \cdot 194 \cdot 2$ $(19 \cdot 194) \cdot 10 = 36,860$
    b. $379 \cdot 4 \cdot 193 \cdot 25$ $(379 \cdot 193) \cdot 100 = 7,314,700$
    c. $8 \cdot 481 \cdot 73 \cdot 125$ *
    d. $374 \cdot 200 \cdot 893 \cdot 50$ *
31. Jim was paid $320 a month for 6 months and $410 a month for 6 month. What were his total earnings for the year? $4380
32. A soft-drink manufacturer produces 15,600 cans of product each hour. Cans are packed 24 to a case. How many cases could be filled with the cans produced in 4 hours?   2600 cases
33. Apples normally sell for 32¢ each. They go on sale for 3 for 69¢. How much money is saved if you purchase 2 dozen apples while they are on sale? $2.16
34. The owner of a bicycle shop reported his inventory of bicycles and tricycles in an unusual way. He said he counted 126 wheels and 108 pedals. How many bikes and how many trikes did he have?   18 tricycles, 36 bicycles
35. Perform each of the following computations.
    a. 123_{five} 212_{five}
        $+ 34_{\text{five}}$
    b. 1010_{two} 101_{two}
        -101_{two}
    c. 23_{five} 1442_{five}
        $\times 34_{\text{five}}$
    d. 1001_{two} 101101_{two}
        $\times 101_{\text{two}}$
36. Use the distributive property of multiplication over addition to compute $44_{\text{five}} \cdot 34_{\text{five}}$.   *
37. Use repeated subtraction to find $434_{\text{five}} \div 4_{\text{five}}$ without first converting to base ten. Write the answer using the Division Algorithm.   *
38. Tell how to use compatible numbers mentally to perform each of the following operations.
    a. $26 + 37 + 24 - 7$ *
    b. $4 \cdot 7 \cdot 9 \cdot 25$ *
39. Compute each of the following operations mentally. Name the strategy you used to perform your mental math.
    a. $63 \cdot 7$ *
    b. $85 - 49$ *
    c. $(18 \cdot 5)2$ *
    d. $2436 \div 6$ *

40. Estimate the following addition using **(a)** front-end estimation with adjustment and **(b)** rounding.
    $$543$$
    $$398$$
    $$255$$ *
    $$408$$
    $$+\ 998$$
41. Using clustering, estimate the sum $2345 + 2854 + 2234 + 2203$.   *
42. In some cases, the distributive property of multiplication over addition or distributive property of multiplication over subtraction can be used to obtain an answer quickly. Compute each of the following.
    a. $999 \cdot 47 + 47$ *
    b. $43 \cdot 59 + 41 \cdot 43$ *
    c. $1003 \cdot 79 - 3 \cdot 79$ *
    d. $1001 \cdot 113 - 113$ *
    e. $101 \cdot 35$ *
    f. $98 \cdot 35$ *
43. Recall that addition problems like $3478 + 521$ can be written and computed using expanded notation as shown here, and answer the questions that follow.
    $$3 \cdot 10^3 + 4 \cdot 10^2 + 7 \cdot 10 + 8$$
    $$+ \qquad\quad 5 \cdot 10^2 + 2 \cdot 10 + 1$$
    $$\overline{3 \cdot 10^3 + 9 \cdot 10^2 + 9 \cdot 10 + 9}$$
    a. Write a corresponding addition algebra problem (use x for 10) and find the answer.   *
    b. Write a subtraction problem and the corresponding algebra problem and find the answer.   *
    c. Write a multiplication problem and the corresponding algebra problem and compute the answer.   *
44. Prove that $B = \{5n \mid n \in W\}$ is closed under addition.   *
45. The Washington School PTA set up a phone tree in order to reach all of its members. Each person's responsibility, after receiving a call, is to call two other assigned members until all members have been called. Assume that everyone is home and answers the phone and that each phone call takes 30 seconds. If one of the 85 members, the PTA president, makes the first phone call and starts the clock, what is the least amount of time necessary to reach all 85 members of the group?   5 min
46. Abby baked 124 cookies. While they were cooling, she stepped outside. She saw a group of children run into the kitchen and run back out with cookies in their hands. When she returned to the kitchen, she found only 7 cookies left on the cooking racks. If each child took the same number of cookies, and the number of children who took cookies was more than 10 and fewer than 30, how many were in the group?   13 children
47. The number on a license plate consists of five digits. When the license plate is looked at upside down, you can still read it, but the value of the upside-down number is 78,633 greater than the real license number. What is the license number?   10968

Number Theory

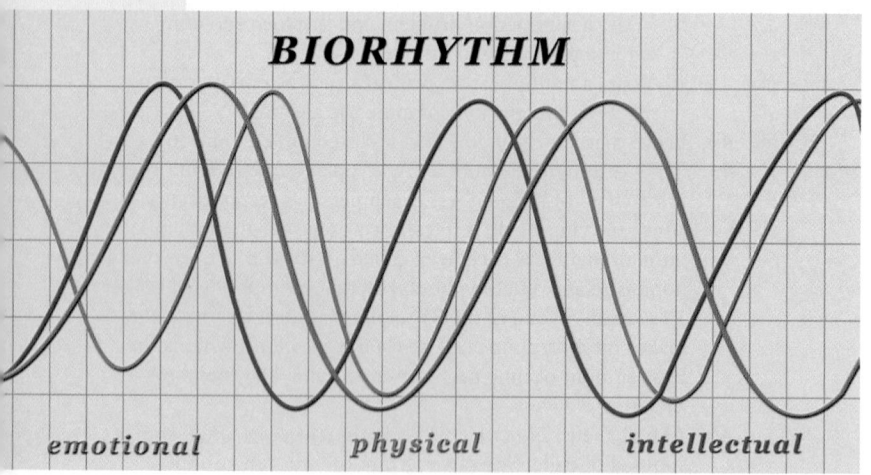

Preliminary Problem

The theory of biorhythms states that there are three "cycles" to life, and each peaks at different times: the physical cycle peaks every 23 days, the emotional cycle peaks every 28 days, and the intellectual cycle peaks every 33 days.

Suppose that today the three cycles are all at their peak. In how many days will they all be at their peak again?

If needed, see Hint on page 215.

Number theory started to flourish in the seventeenth century with the work of Pierre de Fermat (1601–1665). Topics in number theory that occur in the elementary school curriculum include factors, multiples, divisibility tests, prime numbers, prime factorizations, greatest common divisors, and least common multiples. The topic of congruences, introduced by Carl Gauss (1777–1855), is also incorporated into the elementary curriculum through clock arithmetic and modular arithmetic. Clock and modular arithmetic (available online) give students a look at mathematical systems.

4-1 Divisibility

4-1 Objectives

Students will be able to understand and explain

- Divisibility, factors, and multiples.
- Divisibility tests for 2, 3, 4, 5, 6, 8, 9, 10, and 11.
- That the set of factors is finite, and the set of multiples is infinite for any given natural number.

Activity Manual

Use *Odd and Even Patterns* to explore the sums of odd and even numbers and discover the relationship the addends and the sum.

CCSS The grade 2 *Common Core Standards* state that students should be able to:

Determine whether a group of objects (up to 20) has an odd or even number of members, for example, by pairing objects or counting them by 2s; write an equation to express an even number as a sum of two equal addends. (p. 19)

The concepts *even* and *odd* for whole numbers are commonly used. For example, during summer water shortages in some parts of the country, houses with even-number addresses water on even-numbered days of the month, and houses with odd-number addresses water on odd-numbered days. An **even** whole number is a whole number that has remainder 0 when divided by 2. An **odd** whole number is a whole number that has remainder 1 when divided by 2. From the Division Algorithm if n is even then $n = 2q$ for some whole number q (the remainder is 0). If n is odd, then $n = 2q + 1$ (why?). In the Division Algorithm if the remainder is 0 when m is divided by n, m is **divisible by** n.

The fact that 2 divides 12 can be stated in the following equivalent statements in the left column.

Example	**General Statement**
12 is divisible by 2.	a is divisible by b.
2 is a divisor of 12.	b is a divisor of a.
12 is a multiple of 2.	a is a multiple of b.
2 is a factor of 12.	b is a factor of a.
2 divides 12.	b divides a.

The statement that "2 divides 12" is written with a vertical segment, as in $2\,|\,12$, where the vertical segment means **divides**. Likewise for $a, b \in W$, "b divides a" is written $b\,|\,a$. Each statement in the right column above can be written $b\,|\,a$. We write $5 \nmid 12$ to symbolize that 5 does not divide 12 or that 12 is not divisible by 5. The notation $5 \nmid 12$ also implies that 12 is not a multiple of 5 and 5 is not a factor of 12.

In general, if a is a whole number and b is a nonzero whole number, then a is divisible by b or equivalently b divides a if, and only if, the remainder when a is divided by b is 0. Using the Division Algorithm, this means that there is a unique whole number q (quotient) such that $a = bq$. Thus we have the following definition.

Definition of Divides

For any whole numbers a and b, where $b \neq 0$, b divides a, if, and only if, there is a unique whole number q such that $a = bq$.

If $b\,|\,a$, then b is a **factor**, or a **divisor**, of a, and a is a **multiple** of b.

Do not confuse $b\,|\,a$ with b/a, which means b divided by a (also written as $b \div a$). The former expresses a relation and is either true or false. The latter, b/a, expresses an operation on whole numbers and has a numerical value if $a \neq 0$. Note that if a/b is a whole number, then $b\,|\,a$. Also note that for whole numbers $b \nmid a$ is equivalent to saying that the remainder when a is divided by b is not 0.

Example 1

Classify each of the following as true or false. Explain your answers.

a. $3\,|\,12$

b. $0\,|\,2$

c. 0 is even.

d. $8 \nmid 2$

e. For all whole numbers a, $1\,|\,a$.

f. For all nonzero whole numbers a, $a^2\,|\,a^5$.

g. $3\,|\,6n$ for all whole numbers n.

h. $3 \nmid (5 \cdot 7 \cdot 9 \cdot 11 + 1)$

i. $0\,|\,0$

Solution

a. $3\,|\,12$ is true because $12 = 4 \cdot 3$.

b. $0\,|\,2$ is false because there is no whole number c such that $2 = c \cdot 0$.

c. 0 is even is true because $0 = 0 \cdot 2$.

d. $8 \nmid 2$ is true because there is no whole number c such that $2 = c \cdot 8$.

e. $1\,|\,a$ is true for all whole numbers a because $a = a \cdot 1$.

f. True, because $a^5 = a^2 \cdot a^3$.

g. $3\,|\,6n$ is true. Because $6n = 3(2n)$, $6n$ is a multiple of 3 and hence $3\,|\,6n$.

h. True, because $5 \cdot 7 \cdot 9 \cdot 11 + 1 = 3(5 \cdot 7 \cdot 3 \cdot 11) + 1$, so $5 \cdot 7 \cdot 9 \cdot 11 + 1$ leaves remainder 1 when divided by 3.

i. $0\,|\,0$ is false because $0 = 0 \cdot q$ for all whole numbers q, so q is not unique.

Suppose we have one pack of gum and we know that the number of pieces, a, is divisible by 5. Then if we had two packs, the total number of pieces of gum is still divisible by 5. The same is true if we had 10 packs, or 100 packs, or in general n packs where n is any whole number. We could record this observation as follows:

If $5\,|\,a$, then $5\,|\,na$, where a and n are whole numbers.

The above statement is generalized in the following theorem.

Theorem 4-1

For any whole numbers a and d, if $d\,|\,a$ and n is any whole number, then $d\,|\,na$.

Historical Note

Pierre de Fermat (1601–1665) was a French lawyer who devoted his leisure time to mathematics—a subject in which he had no formal training. After his death, his son published an edition of Diophantus's *Arithmetica* with Fermat's notes. One of the margin notes asserted that the equation $x^n + y^n = z^n$ has no natural number solutions if n is greater than 2 and commented, "I have found an admirable proof of this, but the margin is too narrow to contain it." Only in 1995 did Andrew Wiles, a Princeton University mathematician, prove the theorem.

The theorem can be stated in an equivalent form:

If d is a factor of a, then d is a factor of any multiple of a.

Figure 1

Next consider two different brands of chewing gum each having five pieces, as in Figure 1. We can divide each pack of gum equally among five students. In addition, if we opened both packs and put all of the pieces in a bag, we could still divide the number of pieces of gum equally among the five students. To generalize this notion, if we buy gum in larger packages with a pieces in one package and b pieces in a second package with both a and b divisible by 5, we record the preceding discussion as follows:

$$\text{If } 5 \,|\, a \text{ and } 5 \,|\, b, \text{ then } 5 \,|\, (a + b).$$

If the number a of pieces of gum in one package is divisible by 5, but the number b of pieces in the other package is not, then the total $a + b$ cannot be divided equally among the five students. This is recorded as

$$\text{If } 5 \,|\, a \text{ and } 5 \nmid b, \text{ then } 5 \nmid (a + b).$$

▶ **NOW TRY THIS 1**

NTT 1: Answers can be found in Answers at the back of the book.

For any whole numbers a and b, determine the truth of the statement: if $5 \nmid a$ and $5 \nmid b$, then $5 \nmid (a + b)$.

Since subtraction can be defined in terms of addition, results similar to those for addition hold for subtraction. These ideas are generalized in Theorem 4-2.

Theorem 4-2

For any whole numbers a, b, and $d \neq 0$:

a. If $d \,|\, a$ and $d \,|\, b$, then $d \,|\, (a + b)$.
b. If $d \,|\, a$ and $d \nmid b$, then $d \nmid (a + b)$.
c. If $d \,|\, a$, $d \,|\, b$, and $a > b$, then $d \,|\, (a - b)$.
d. If $d \,|\, a$, $d \nmid b$, and $a > b$, then $d \nmid (a - b)$.
e. If $d \nmid a$, $d \,|\, b$, and $a > b$, then $d \nmid (a - b)$.

Theorem 4-2 can be extended. For example, if a, b, c, and d are whole numbers, with $d \neq 0$, then,

$$\text{If } d \,|\, a, d \,|\, b, \text{ and } d \,|\, c, \text{ then } d \,|\, (a + b + c).$$

The proofs of several theorems in this section are left as exercises, but the proofs of Theorem 4-2(a) and (b) are given as illustrations.

Proof

Theorem 4-2(a) is equivalent to the following.

If a is a multiple of d and b is a multiple of d, then a + b is a multiple of d.

Notice that "a is a multiple of d" means $a = md$, for some whole number m. Similarly "b is a multiple of d" means $b = nd$, for some whole number n. To show that $a + b$ is a multiple of d, we add as follows:

$$a + b = md + nd$$

Is $md + nd$ a multiple of d? Because $md + nd = (m + n)d$, then $a + b = (m + n)d$. By the closure property of whole number addition, $m + n$ is a whole number. Consequently, $a + b$ is a multiple of d, and therefore $d \,|\, (a + b)$. ∎

To prove Theorem 4-2(b), we proceed as follows:

Because $d\,|\,a$, $a = md$ for some $m \in W$. Because $d \nmid b$, when b is divided by d the remainder is not 0; that is, $b = qd + r$, where $q, r \in W$ and $0 < r < d$. Thus,

$$a + b = md + qd + r$$
$$= (m + q)d + r.$$

Consequently when $a + b$ is divided by d, the quotient is $m + q$ and the remainder is r. Because $r \neq 0$, $d \nmid (a + b)$.   ■

Example 2

Classify each of the following as true or false, where x, y, and z are whole numbers. If a statement is true, prove it. If a statement is false, provide a counterexample.

a. If $3\,|\,x$ and $3\,|\,y$, then $3\,|\,xy$.   **b.** If $3\,|\,(x + y)$, then $3\,|\,x$ and $3\,|\,y$.
c. If $9 \nmid a$, then $3 \nmid a$.

Solution
a. True; by Theorem 4-1, if $3\,|\,x$, then, for any whole number y, $3\,|\,yx$ or $3\,|\,xy$.
b. False; for example, $3\,|\,(7 + 2)$, but $3 \nmid 7$ and $3 \nmid 2$.
c. False; for example, $9 \nmid 21$, but $3\,|\,21$.

▶ **NOW TRY THIS 2**

NTT 2: Yes, it is true. If $3\,|\,x$, then 3 divides x times any whole number.

If $x, y \in W$, and $3\,|\,x$, is it true that $3\,|\,xy$ regardless of whether $3\,|\,y$ or $3 \nmid y$? Why?

Example 3

Figure 2

Coach Edgerton bought nine pairs of basketball shoes for team players. She gave the bag of shoes to the student manager with the instructions, "Make sure each player pays for the shoes. Each pair costs the same, and the receipt is in the bag, so you'll be able to figure out how much to charge each player."

However, when the student manager pulled out the receipt from the bag, she realized it had gotten wet, and the last digit had been erased. The cost said $53__. Despite this, the manager figured out what to charge each player for the shoes. How did she do it? What is the missing digit?

Solution
We know there are 9 pairs of basketball shoes for $53__. We can divide 9 into 530 and see that it would be 58 with 8 left over. We reason that we need to add 1 to 8 is to have a whole 9 which is divisible by 9. So $(9 \cdot 58) + 9 = 531$. The missing digit is 1.

Divisibility Rules

As shown in Example 3, sometimes it is convenient to know whether one number is divisible by another. We used division and remainders to find the answer, but it would be convenient to have a rule that would allow us to know if one number is divisible by another just by looking at the number or by performing a simple test. Following are some of these divisibility rules.

It is possible to determine whether 1734 is divisible by 17, either by using pencil and paper or a calculator. To avoid decimals, we can use a calculator with an $\boxed{\text{INT}\div}$ button. On such a calculator, division can be performed using the following sequence of buttons:

$$\boxed{1}\ \boxed{7}\ \boxed{3}\ \boxed{4}\ \boxed{\text{INT}\div}\ \boxed{1}\ \boxed{7}\ \boxed{=}$$

to obtain the display $\underset{\underset{Q}{\longmapsto}}{102} \quad \underset{\underset{R}{\longmapsto}}{0.}$

This implies $1734/17 = 102$ with a remainder of 0, which, in turn, implies $17 \mid 1734$.

We could reach the conclusion mentally by considering the following:

$$1734 = 1700 + 34$$

Because $17 \mid 1700$ and $17 \mid 34$, by Theorem 4-2(a), we have $17 \mid (1700 + 34)$, or $17 \mid 1734$. Similarly, we could determine mentally that $17 \nmid 1735$.

Divisibility Tests for 2, 5, and 10

To determine whether a given whole number n is divisible by a whole number d without the use of a calculator, we express n as a sum or difference of two whole numbers, of which at least one is divisible by d. We use a concrete example to get an idea of how this works. Consider the number 1362. This number can be represented as in Figure 3. Because 10 and every power of 10 has a factor of two, 2 divides each part of the figure (see dashed segments). Since 2 divides each part of the figure, by the extension of Theorem 4-2, 2 divides the sum of all of the parts and hence $2 \mid 1362$.

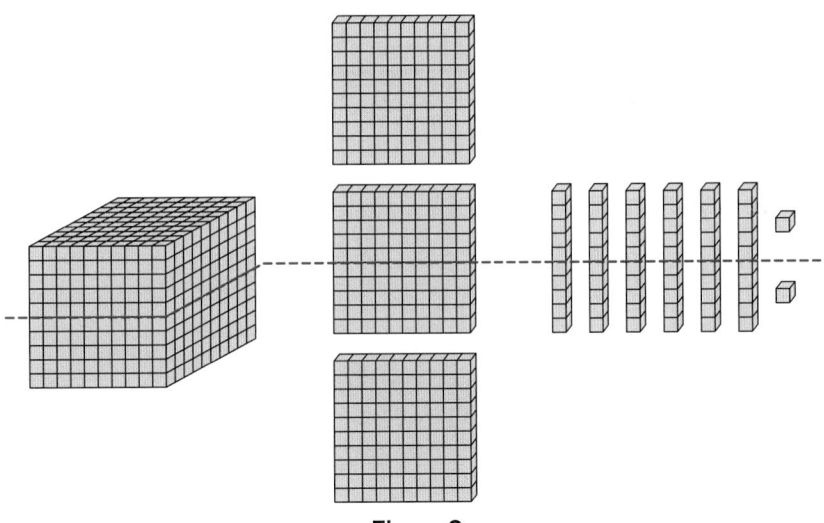

Figure 3

If the original number were 1363, then $2 \mid 1362$ and $2 \nmid 1$, so $2 \nmid 1363$. All we have to do is to determine whether the units digit is divisible by 2 in order to determine whether the number is divisible by 2. Similar tests for divisibility by 5 and 10 hold.

Theorem 4-3:   Divisibility Test for 2

A whole number is divisible by 2 if, and only if, its units digit is divisible by 2; that is, if and only if, the units digit is even.

Theorem 4-4: Divisibility Test for 5

A whole number is divisible by 5 if, and only if, its units digit is divisible by 5; that is, if, and only if, the units digit is 0 or 5.

Theorem 4-5: Divisibility Test for 10

A whole number is divisible by 10 if, and only if, its units digit is divisible by 10; that is, if, and only if, the units digit is 0.

Divisibility Tests for 4 and 8

When we consider divisibility tests for 4 and 8, we see that $4 \nmid 10$ and $8 \nmid 10$, so it is not a matter of checking the units digit for divisibility by 4 or 8. However, 4 (which is 2^2) divides 10^2, and 8 (which is 2^3) divides 10^3.

We first develop a divisibility rule for 4. Consider any four-digit whole number n such that $n = a \cdot 10^3 + b \cdot 10^2 + c \cdot 10 + d$. The *subgoal* is to *write the given number as a sum of two numbers*, one of which is as great as possible and divisible by 4. We know that $4 \mid 10^2$ because $10^2 = 4 \cdot 25$ and, consequently, $4 \mid 10^3$. Because $4 \mid 10^2$, then $4 \mid b \cdot 10^2$; and because $4 \mid 10^3$, then $4 \mid a \cdot 10^3$. Finally, $4 \mid a \cdot 10^3$ and $4 \mid b \cdot 10^2$ imply $4 \mid (a \cdot 10^3 + b \cdot 10^2)$. Now the divisibility of $a \cdot 10^3 + b \cdot 10^2 + c \cdot 10 + d$ by 4 depends on the divisibility of $(c \cdot 10 + d)$ by 4. The number represented by the last two digits in the given number n is $c \cdot 10 + d$.

The preceding derivation of the divisibility test for 4 can be somewhat shortened by observing that if *abcd* is a base ten numeral (*a, b, c, d* are the digits), then $abcd = ab00 + cd = ab \cdot 100 + cd$. Since $4 \mid 100$, by Theorem 4-1 this implies that $4 \mid ab \cdot 100$. Thus, if $4 \mid cd$, then by Theorem 4-2(a), $4 \mid ab \cdot 100 + cd$; that is, $4 \mid abcd$. If, however, $4 \nmid cd$, then Theorem 4-2(b) implies that $4 \nmid ab \cdot 100 + cd$; that is, $4 \nmid abcd$. We summarize this in the following theorem.

Theorem 4-6: Divisibility Test for 4

A whole number is divisible by 4 if, and only if, the last two digits of the number represent a number divisible by 4.

To investigate divisibility by 8, we note that the least positive power of 10 divisible by 8 is 10^3 since $10^3 = 8 \cdot 125$. Consequently by Theorem 4-1, all whole number powers of 10 greater than 10^3 also are divisible by 8. Hence, the following is a divisibility test for 8.

Theorem 4-7: Divisibility Test for 8

A whole number is divisible by 8 if, and only if, the last three digits of the whole number represent a number divisible by 8.

Example 4

a. Determine whether 97,128 is divisible by 2, 4, and 8.
b. Determine whether 83,026 is divisible by 2, 4, and 8.

Solution

a. $2 \mid 97{,}128$ because $2 \mid 8$
   $4 \mid 97{,}128$ because $4 \mid 28$
   $8 \mid 97{,}128$ because $8 \mid 128$

b. $2 \mid 83{,}026$ because $2 \mid 6$
   $4 \nmid 83{,}026$ because $4 \nmid 26$
   $8 \nmid 83{,}026$ because $8 \nmid 026$

Example 5

Use Theorems 4-1 and 4-2 to show why the divisibility test for 8 works in Example 4(a).

Solution   We write 97,128 as 97,000 + 128. Because $8\,|\,1000$, then $8\,|\,97\cdot1000$ or $8\,|\,97{,}000$ (Theorem 4-1). Next check if $8\,|\,128$. It does, so $8\,|\,(97{,}000 + 128)$ or $8\,|\,97{,}128$ (Theorem 4-2).

In Example 4(a), it would have been sufficient to check that the given whole number a is divisible by 8 because if $8\,|\,a$, then $a = 8k$ for some whole number k. Hence $a = 2(4k)$ and $a = 4(2k)$, which implies that $2\,|\,a$ and $4\,|\,a$. This relationship is shown in Figure 4.

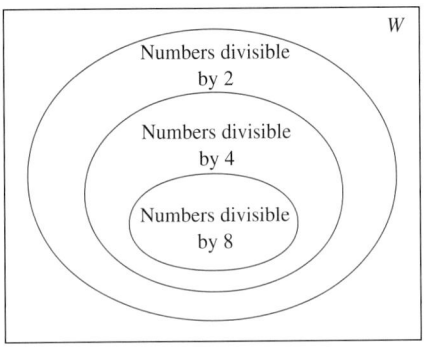

Figure 4

Notice that if $8 \nmid a$, we cannot conclude that $4 \nmid a$ or $2 \nmid a$. (Why?)

Divisibility Tests for 3 and 9

Consider a divisibility test for 3. No power of 10 is divisible by 3, but the numbers 9, and 99, and 999, and other similar numbers are divisible by 3. For example, to determine whether 5721 is divisible by 3, we rewrite the number using 999, 99, and 9, as follows:

$$
\begin{aligned}
5721 &= 5\cdot10^3 + 7\cdot10^2 + 2\cdot10 + 1 \\
&= 5(999 + 1) + 7(99 + 1) + 2(9 + 1) + 1 \\
&= 5\cdot999 + 5\cdot1 + 7\cdot99 + 7\cdot1 + 2\cdot9 + 2\cdot1 + 1 \\
&= (5\cdot999 + 7\cdot99 + 2\cdot9) + (5 + 7 + 2 + 1)
\end{aligned}
$$

The sum in the first set of parentheses in the last line is divisible by 3, so the divisibility of 5721 by 3 depends on the sum in the second set of parentheses. In this case, $5 + 7 + 2 + 1 = 15$ and $3\,|\,15$, so by Theorem 4-2(a), $3\,|\,5721$. Hence, to test 5721 for divisibility by 3, we test $5 + 7 + 2 + 1$ for divisibility by 3. Notice that $5 + 7 + 2 + 1$ is the sum of the digits of 5721. This suggests the following test for divisibility by 3.

> **Theorem 4-8:   Divisibility Test for 3**
>
> A whole number is divisible by 3 if, and only if, the sum of its digits is divisible by 3.

Proof

A proof similar to the above argument for 5721 works for any whole number. We illustrate the proof for any four-digit whole number $n = a\cdot10^3 + b\cdot10^2 + c\cdot10 + d$. Even though

$a \cdot 10^3 + b \cdot 10^2 + c \cdot 10 + d$ is not necessarily divisible by 3, the number $a \cdot 999 + b \cdot 99 + c \cdot 9$ is divisible by 3. We have:

$$a \cdot 10^3 + b \cdot 10^2 + c \cdot 10 + d = a \cdot 1000 + b \cdot 100 + c \cdot 10 + d$$
$$= a \cdot (999 + 1) + b \cdot (99 + 1) + c \cdot (9 + 1) + d$$
$$= (a \cdot 999 + b \cdot 99 + c \cdot 9) + (a \cdot 1 + b \cdot 1 + c \cdot 1 + d)$$
$$= (a \cdot 999 + b \cdot 99 + c \cdot 9) + (a + b + c + d)$$

Because $3|9, 3|99$, and $3|999$, it follows that $3|(a \cdot 999 + b \cdot 99 + c \cdot 9)$. If $3|(a + b + c + d)$, then $3|[(a \cdot 999 + b \cdot 99 + c \cdot 9) + (a + b + c + d)]$; that is, $3|n$. If, on the other hand, $3 \nmid (a + b + c + d)$, it follows from Theorem 4-2(b) that $3 \nmid n$. ∎

Since $9|9, 9|99, 9|999$, and so on, a test similar to that for divisibility by 3 applies to divisibility by 9. (Why?)

Activity Manual

Use the *Great Divide Game* for more practice with divisibility rules.

> **Theorem 4-9:   Divisibility Test for 9**
>
> A whole number is divisible by 9 if, and only if, the sum of the digits of the whole number is divisible by 9.

Example 6

Use divisibility tests to determine whether each of the following numbers is divisible by 3 and divisible by 9.

   a. 1002 **b.** 14,238

Solution

   a. Because $1 + 0 + 0 + 2 = 3$ and $3|3$, it follows that $3|1002$. Because $9 \nmid 3$, it follows that $9 \nmid 1002$.

   b. Because $1 + 4 + 2 + 3 + 8 = 18$ and $3|18$, it follows that $3|14{,}238$. Because $9|18$, it follows that $9|14{,}238$.

Example 7

The store manager has an invoice for 72 calculators. The first and last digits on the invoice are illegible. The manager can read

$$\$ \blacksquare 67.9 \blacksquare .$$

What are the missing digits, and what is the cost of each calculator?

Solution

Let the missing digits be x and y so that the base ten notation for the number is $x67.9y$ dollars, or $x679y$ cents. Because there were 72 calculators sold, the number on the invoice must be divisible by 72. Because the number is divisible by 72 and $72 = 8 \cdot 9$, it must be divisible by 8 and 9, which are factors of 72. For the number on the invoice to be divisible by 8, the three-digit number $79y$ must be divisible by 8. Because $79y$ must be divisible by 8, it is an even number. Therefore, $79y$ must be either 790, 792, 794, 796, or 798. Only the number 792 is divisible by 8, so the last digit, y, on the invoice must be 2.

Because the number on the invoice must be divisible by 9, we know that 9 must divide $x + 6 + 7 + 9 + 2$, or $(x + 24)$. Since 3 is the only single digit that will make $(x + 24)$ divisible by 9, then x must be 3. Therefore, the number on the invoice must be \$367.92. The calculators must cost $\$367.92/72 = \$5.11$ each.

Divisibility Tests for 11 and 6

The divisibility test for 7 is usually harder to use than actually performing the division, so we omit the test.

To develop a test for divisibility by 11, we search for numbers close to powers of 10 that are divisible by 11. Notice that $11 \mid 11, 11 \mid 99, 11 \mid 1001, 11 \mid 9999, \ldots$. As for divisibility by 3 and 9, we illustrate our argument on a four-digit number n and split it into two parts, one divisible by 11 and the other to be tested.

$$n = a \cdot 10^3 + b \cdot 10^2 + c \cdot 10 + d$$
$$= a(1001 - 1) + b(99 + 1) + c(11 - 1) + d$$
$$= (a \cdot 1001 + b \cdot 99 + c \cdot 11) + (b + d - a - c)$$

Because 11 divides the number in the first parentheses, the test depends on whether $b + d - a - c = b + d - (a + c)$ is divisible by 11 or not. Thus we have the following theorem.

Theorem 4-10: Divisibility Test for 11

A whole number is divisible by 11 if, and only if, the sum of the digits in the places that are even powers of 10 minus the sum of the digits in the places that are odd powers of 10 is divisible by 11. (If the sums are different, then subtract the lesser from the greater.)

For example, to test whether 8,471,986 is divisible by 11, we check whether 11 divides the difference $(6 + 9 + 7 + 8) - (8 + 1 + 4) = 17$. Because $11 \nmid 17$, it follows from the divisibility test for 11 that $11 \nmid 8,471,986$. A number like 2772 is divisible by 11 because $(2 + 7) - (7 + 2) = 9 - 9 = 0$ and 0 is divisible by 11.

The divisibility test for 6 is related to the divisibility tests for 2 and 3. In Section 4-2, we show that if $2 \mid n$ and $3 \mid n$, then $(2 \cdot 3) \mid n$, and in general: if a and b have no factors in common and if $a \mid n$ and $b \mid n$, then we can conclude that $ab \mid n$. Consequently, the following divisibility test is true.

Theorem 4-11: Divisibility Test for 6

A whole number is divisible by 6 if, and only if, the whole number is divisible by both 2 and 3.

Example 8

The number 57,729,364,583 has too many digits for most calculator displays. Determine whether it is divisible by each of the following:

a. 2   **b.** 3   **c.** 5   **d.** 6   **e.** 8   **f.** 9   **g.** 10   **h.** 11

Solution
  a. No; the units digit 3 is not divisible by 2.
  b. No; the sum of the digits is 59, which is not divisible by 3.
  c. No; the units digit is neither 0 nor 5.
  d. No; the number is not divisible by 2 (see Theorem 4-11).
  e. No; the number formed by the last three digits is 583, which is not divisible by 8.
  f. No; the sum of the digits is 59, which is not divisible by 9.
  g. No; the units digit is not 0.
  h. Yes; $(3 + 5 + 6 + 9 + 7 + 5) - (8 + 4 + 3 + 2 + 7) = 35 - 24 = 11$ and 11 is divisible by 11.

Divisibility tests for other numbers are explored in Assessments 4-1A and 4-1B. The student page shown on page 184 illustrates divisibility rules.

School Book Page · Factors, Multiples, and Divisibility

Factors, Multiples, and Divisibility

How are factors and divisibility related?

How many different ways can Raul build a dog pen that has an area of 36 square feet and has sides measured in whole feet?

Choose an Operation Divide to find the possible measurements.

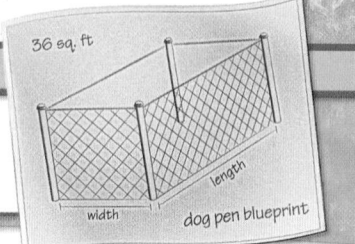

36 sq. ft

length

width   dog pen blueprint

Another Example How can you use divisibility rules?

Is 126 divisible by 2, 3, 4, 6, 9, or 10? You can use divisibility rules to find out.

Divisibility Rules

A whole number is divisible by	Examples:	Is 126 divisible by the number?
2 if the ones digit is an even number.	10; 6; 108	Yes, the ones digit is even.
3 if the sum of the digits is divisible by 3.	3; 627; 891	Yes, 1 + 2 + 6 = 9. 9 is divisible by 3.
4 if the last two digits of the number are divisible by 4.	64; 5,888	No, 26 is not divisible by 4.
5 if the ones digit is 0 or 5.	380; 9,005	No, the ones digit is 6.
6 if the number is divisible by both 2 and 3.	240; 8,982	Yes, 126 is divisible by both 2 and 3.
9 if the sum of the digits is divisible by 9.	189; 1,035	Yes, 1 + 2 + 6 = 9. 9 is divisible by 9.
10 if the ones digit is 0.	170; 1,380	No, the ones digit is not 0.

What is a multiple of a number?

Is 126 a multiple of 7? A multiple of a given number is <u>a product of that number and a whole number greater than 0.</u>

Since 126 ÷ 7 = 18, 126 is the product of 7 and 18. So, 126 is a multiple of 7. Other multiples of 7 are 7, 14, 21, 28, 35, 42, 49, and so on.

Explain It

1. Is 53,802 a multiple of 9? Explain your answer.

120

Historical Note

A twentieth century mathematician who did research in number theory was American Julia Robinson (1919–1985). Robinson was the first woman mathematician to be elected to the National Academy of Sciences and the first woman president of the American Mathematical Society.

Problem Solving Maple Syrup

In a maple syrup bottling warehouse in New Hampshire, bottles are packed with 12 bottles in a case or 6 bottles in a case. The manager checks the inventory and notices that there are 12,338 bottles in the warehouse. He immediately knows that this is wrong. How does he know?

Understanding the Problem The problem is to determine how the manager knows 12,338 cannot be the correct inventory. To solve the problem, we assume that each case contains exactly 12 or 6 bottles.

Devising a Plan Because the cases are for 6 or 12, the total number of bottles has to be divisible by 6 or 12. Since 6 divides 12, we only need to check for divisibility by 6.

Carrying Out the Plan We can see that 6 divides 12,000 and only need to determine if 6 divides 338. Furthermore, knowing that 6 divides 300 would leave us to check if 6 divides 38, and since it does not, we conclude that the manager is correct and 12,338 is the incorrect inventory.

Looking Back Another way to look at the problem is to create an equation to model the total number of bottles. If we let n be the number of cases with 6 bottles and m be the number of cases with 12 bottles, then we have a total of $6n + 12m$ bottles. The manager claimed the total was incorrect, so $6n + 12m \neq 12,338$. We need to show that these are not equal. We can factor $6n + 12m = 6(n + 2m)$. If the total 12,338 is correct, it would have to be divisible by the factor 6. The divisibility test for 6 states that a number is divisible by 6 if, and only if, the number is divisible by both 2 and 3. Because 12,338 ends in 8, it is divisible by 2. However, 3 does not divide the sum of the digits $1 + 2 + 3 + 3 + 8 = 17$. So $6 \nmid 12338$, and therefore, the manager's claim was correct.

Assessment 4-1A

1. If you multiply an even number by 2 and add 1, is your answer even or odd? Odd
2. Classify each of the following statements as true or false. If false, tell why. False; there is no value $c \in W$ such
   a. 5 is a multiple of 24. that $24c = 5$.
   b. 10 is a divisor of 30. True
   c. $8 \mid 324$ False; there is no value $c \in W$ such that $8c = 324$.
   d. 24 is divisible by 0. False; there is no value $c \in W$ such that $0c = 24$.
3. Without using a calculator, test each of the following numbers for divisibility by 2, 3, 4, 5, 6, 8, 9, 10, and 11.
   a. 4,201,012 2, 4
   b. 1573 11
   c. 15,810 2, 3, 5, 6, 10
4. Using divisibility tests, solve each of the following problems.
   a. There are 1379 children signed up in a baseball league. If exactly 9 players are to be placed on each team, will any team be short of players? Yes

   b. An orchard has 1354 apple trees to be planted. Can the apple trees be planted in rows of 11? No; $11 \nmid 1354$.
   c. If there are 1216 pencils in a box and 8 classrooms, can each classroom receive the same number of pencils? *
5. Find all possible single digits that can be placed in the square so that the number $1,427,4\square2$ is divisible by the given number.
   a. 2 0, 1, 2, 3, 4, 5, 6, 7, 8, 9   b. 3 1, 4, 7
   c. 4 1, 3, 5, 7, 9   d. 9 7
6. Fill each of the following blanks with the greatest digit that makes the statement true.
   a. $3 \mid 74\_\_$ 7   b. $9 \mid 83\_45$ 7
   c. $11 \mid 6\_55$ 6   d. $5 \mid 136\_\_$ 5
   e. $6 \mid 2\_44$ 8   f. $8 \mid 38\_4$ 6
7. Justify each of the following statements.
   a. $7 \mid 280$ $280 = 7 \cdot 40$ b. $19 \mid (3800 + 19)$ *
   c. $15 \mid 2^4 \cdot 3^5 \cdot 5$ $15 \mid (3 \cdot 5) \cdot 2^4 \cdot 3^4$ d. $19 \nmid (3800 + 37)$ $19 \mid 3800$ but $19 \nmid 37$

8. Without using a calculator, classify each of the following statements as true or false. Justify your answers.
   a. $13 \mid 390{,}026$ *
   b. $13 \nmid 260{,}033$ *
   c. $17 \mid 34{,}015$ *
   d. $17 \mid 34{,}051$ *
   e. $19 \mid 19{,}031$ *
   f. $31 \mid 93^{11}$. *

9. Classify each of the following statements as true or false, for all whole numbers a, b, and c, with $b \neq 0$.
   a. $7 \mid 21$ implies $7 \mid 21^2$.   True
   b. If $b \mid a$, then $(b + c) \mid (a + c)$.   False
   c. If $b \mid a$, then $b^2 \mid a^3$.   True
   d. If $b \mid a$, then $b \mid (a + b)$.   True

10. Find a whole number solution that makes each of the following true.
    a. Divisible by 2 and 3 but not by 5.   Answers vary. For example, 6.
    b. Divisible by 2 and 4 but not by 8.   Answers vary. For example, 12.
    c. Divisible by 5 and 10 but not by 2.   Does not exist.

11. A group of people ordered pencils. The bill was $2.09. If the original price of each pencil was 12¢ and the price has risen, how much does each cost?   Each pencil costs 19¢.

12. Classify each of the following statements as true or false.
    a. The product of three consecutive whole numbers is divisible by 3.   True
    b. The product of two consecutive whole numbers is divisible by 4.   False

13. An archery target consists of five concentric circles as shown below. The value of the arrow landing in each region starting from the inner circle is 9, 7, 5, 3, 1 points. In how many ways could five scoring arrows earn 29 points?   11 ways

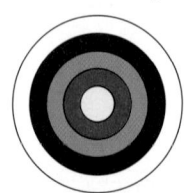

14. Classify each of the following statements as true or false.
    a. If every digit of a number is divisible by 3, then the number is divisible by 3.   True
    b. If a number is divisible by 3, then every digit of the number is divisible by 3.   False
    c. A number is divisible by 3 if, and only if, every digit of the number is a multiple of 3.   False

15. To find the remainder when a number is divided by 3 you could use long division. Alternatively, you could find the sum of the digits and then find the remainder when that sum is divided by 3.
    a. Find the remainder when 7,242,815 is divided by 3 using long division and then using the sum of the digits.   *
    b. Explain why the sum of the digits approach is valid.   *
    c. Will the sum of the digits approach work to find the remainder when a number is divided by 9? Justify your answer.   *

16. If $45 \mid n$, what other whole numbers divide n? Why? *

17. Devise a test for divisibility by 16. *

18. A test for checking arithmetic calculations is called *casting out nines*. Consider the sum $193 + 24 + 786 = 1003$. The remainders when 193, 24, and 786 are divided by 9 are 4, 6, and 3, respectively. The sum of the remainders, 13, has a remainder of 4 when divided by 9, as does 1003. Checking the remainders in this manner provides a quasi-check for the computation. Find the following sums and use *casting out nines* to check the sums:
    a. $12{,}343 + 4546 + 56$ *
    b. $987 + 456 + 8765$ *
    c. Try the check on the subtraction $1003 - 46$. *
    d. Try the check on the multiplication $345 \cdot 56$. *
    e. Would it make sense to try the check on division? Why or why not? *

19. A palindrome is a number that reads the same forward as backward.
    a. Are all five digit palindromes divisible by 11? Why or why not?   No. For example $11 \nmid 10{,}001$
    b. Are all six-digit palindromes divisible by 11? Why or why not? *

20. Prove the test for divisibility by 9 for any-five-digit whole number. *

Assessment 4-1B

1. If you multiply an odd number by 2 and add, 1 is your answer even or odd?   Odd

2. Classify each of the following statements as true or false. If false, tell why.
   a. 5 is a divisor of 20.   True
   b. 10 is a multiple of 20.   False; there is no value $c \in W$ such that $20c = 10$.
   c. $5 \mid 20$ True
   d. 30 is divisor of 6.   False; there is no value $c \in W$ such that $30c = 6$.

3. Without using a calculator, test each of the following numbers for divisibility by 2, 3, 4, 5, 6, 8, 9, 10, and 11.
   a. 7163   None
   b. 34,200   2, 3, 4, 5, 6, 8, 9, 10
   c. 199,990   2, 5, 10

4. Using divisibility tests, solve each of the following problems.
   a. Nine friends win the lottery. The payoff is $1,111,500. Can the money be divided equally?   Yes; $9 \mid 1{,}111{,}500$.
   b. There are 548 students at a baseball game. Can they be divided equally into four sections?   Yes; $4 \mid 548$.
   c. The average amount of student loan debt is $26,600. Can this amount be paid back equally over 12 years?   No; $12 \nmid 26{,}600$.

5. Find all possible single digits that can be placed in the square so that the number $1{,}182{,}1\square6$ is divisible by the given number.
   a. 2   0, 1, 2, 3, 4, 5, 6, 7, 8, 9
   b. 3   2, 5, 8
   c. 4   1, 3, 5, 7, 9
   d. 9   8

6. Without using a calculator, classify each of the following statements as true or false. Justify your answers.
   a. $5 \mid (2 \cdot 3 \cdot 5 \cdot 7)$ *
   b. $5 \mid (2 \cdot 3 \cdot 5 \cdot 7) + 1$ *
   c. $6 \mid (2^3 \cdot 3^2 \cdot 17^4)$ *
   d. $7 \nmid 4222$ *

7. Justify each of the following statements.
   a. $26 \mid (13^4 \cdot 100)$ $13^4 \cdot 100 = (13 \cdot 2) \cdot 13^3 \cdot 50 = 26 \cdot (13^3 \cdot 50)$
   b. $13 \nmid (2^4 \cdot 5^3 \cdot 26 + 1)$ $13 \mid (2^4 \cdot 5^3 \cdot 26)$ but $13 \nmid 1$
   c. $2^4 \nmid (2 \cdot 4 \cdot 6 \cdot 8 \cdot 17^{10} + 1)$ *
   d. $2^4 \mid (10^4 + 6^4)$ *

8. Without using a calculator, classify each of the following statements as true or false. Justify your answers.
   a. $12 \mid 24{,}013$ *
   b. $12 \mid 24{,}036$ *
   c. $19 \mid 38{,}037$ *
   d. $19 \nmid 3{,}800{,}018$ *
   e. $23 \nmid 23{,}023$ *
   f. $23 \mid 46^{10}$ *

9. Classify each of the following statements as true or false, assuming that a, b, and c are whole numbers.
   a. $3 \nmid 50$ and $3 \mid 30$ imply $3 \nmid (50 + 30)$.   True
   b. $3 \nmid 50$ and $3 \mid 30$ imply $3 \nmid (50 \cdot 30)$.   False
   c. $3 \mid (a + b)$ and $3 \nmid c$ imply $3 \nmid (a + b + c)$.   True
   d. $3 \mid b$ implies $3 \mid b^2$.   True

10. Answer each of the following questions without actually performing the division. Explain how you did it in each case.
    a. Is 24,013 divisible by 12? *
    b. Is 24,036 divisible by 12? *
    c. Is 17,034 divisible by 17? *
    d. Is $2 \cdot 3 \cdot 5 \cdot 7$ divisible by 3? *
    e. Is $(2 \cdot 3 \cdot 5 \cdot 7) + 1$ divisible by 6? *

11. The bookstore marked some notepads down from $2.00 but still kept the price over $1.00. It sold all of them. The total amount of money from the sale of the pads was $31.45. How many notepads were sold? What was the price of each notepad?   17 notepads; $1.85 each.

12. Classify each of the following statements as true or false.
    a. The sum of every three consecutive numbers is divisible by 3. *
    b. The sum of every four consecutive numbers is divisible by 4. *

13. In a football game, a touchdown with an extra point is worth 7 points and a field goal is worth 3 points. Suppose that in a game the only scoring done by teams are touchdowns with extra points and field goals.
    a. Which of the scores 1 to 25 are impossible for a team to score?   1; 2; 4; 5; 8; 11

b. List all possible ways for a team to score 40 points. *
c. A team scored 57 points with 6 touchdowns and 6 extra points. How many field goals did the team score? *

14. Classify each of the following statements as true or false.
    a. If a number is divisible by 6, then it is divisible by 2 and 3. *
    b. If a number is divisible by 2 and 3, then it is divisible by 6. *
    c. If a number is divisible by 2 and 4, then it is divisible by 8. *
    d. If a number is divisible by 8, then it is divisible by 2 and 4. *
    e. A number is divisible by 8 if, and only if, it is divisible by 2 and by 4.   False

15. Complete the following table where n is the given whole number.

n	Remainder when n is divided by 9	Sum of the digits of n	Remainder when the sum of the digits of n is divided by 9
a. 31	4	4	4
b. 143	8	8	8
c. 345	3	12	3
d. 2987	8	26	8
e. 7652	2	20	2

   f. Make a conjecture about the remainders when a whole number and the sum of its digits are divided by 9. *

16. If $28 \mid n$, what other whole numbers divide n? Why? *

17. Devise a test for divisibility by 25. *

18. Use the casting out nines approach outlined in exercise 18 of Assessment 4-1 A to show that the following computations are wrong.
    a. $99 + 28 = 227$ *
    b. $11{,}199 - 21 = 11{,}168$ *
    c. $99 \cdot 26 = 2575$ *

19. A palindrome is a number that reads the same forward as backward.
    a. Check the following four-digit palindromes for divisibility by 11.
       i. 4554 *
       ii. 9339 *
       iii. 2002 *
       iv. 2222 *
    b. Are all four-digit palindromes divisible by 11?   Yes

20. Prove the test for divisibility by 9 for any four-digit number. *

Mathematical Connections 4-1

Answers to Mathematical Connections can be found in the Answers section at the back of the book.

Reasoning

1. Prove the following statements, assuming n is a natural number.
   a. If n^2 is odd, then n is odd.
   b. If n^2 is even, then n is even.

2. A customer wants to mail a package. The postal clerk determines the cost of the package to be $18.95, but only 5¢ and 10¢ stamps are available. Can the available stamps be used for the exact amount of postage for the package? Why or why not?

3. a. Jim uses his calculator to see if a number n having eight or fewer digits is divisible by a number d. He finds that $n \div d$ has a display of 32 digits. Does $d \mid n$? Why or why not?
   b. If $n \div d$ gives a display of 16.8, does $d \mid n$? Why or why not?

4. Is the area (in cm²) of each of the following rectangles divisible by 4? The area is the length times the width. Explain why or why not.
   a.
   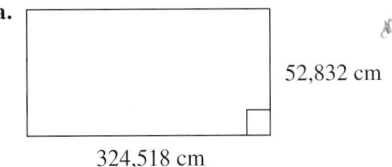
   52,832 cm
   324,518 cm
   b.
   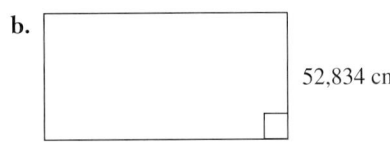
   52,834 cm
   324,514 cm

5. Answer each of the following and justify your answers.
   a. If a number is not divisible by 5, can it be divisible by 10?
   b. If a number is not divisible by 10, can it be divisible by 5?

6. A number in which each digit except 0 appears exactly 3 times is divisible by 3. For example, 777,555,222 and 414,143,313 are divisible by 3. Explain why this statement is true.

7. Enter any three-digit number on the calculator; for example, enter 243. Repeat it: 243,243. Divide by 7. Divide by 11. Divide by 13. What is the answer? Try it again with any other three-digit number. Will this always work? Why?

8. Arrange the digits 0 through 9 so that the number formed by the first (left) digit is divisible by 1, the number formed by the first 2 digits is divisible by 2, the number formed by the first 3 digits is divisible by 3, and so forth. What is the 10-digit number? If you were only allowed to use the digits 1 through, what would the 9-digit number be?

9. Three tiles marked X, Y, and Z need three different nonzero digits painted on them. The whole numbers XYZ, as well as ZXY and YZX, are all divisible by 6 and 9. What are the values of X, Y, and Z?

Open-Ended

10. A breakfast-food company had a contest in which the numbers were placed in breakfast-food boxes. A prize of $1000 was awarded to anyone who could collect numbers whose sum was 100. The company had thousands of cards made with the following numbers on them:

3	12	15	18	27	33
45	51	66	75	84	90

    a. If the company did not make any more cards, is there a winning combination?
    b. If the company is going to add one more number to the list and it wants to make sure the contest has at most 1000 winners, suggest a strategy for it to use.

11. How would you use concrete materials to explain the following to young children?
    a. The concept of even and odd numbers.
    b. A number being divisible by 3 or not being divisible by 3.
    c. If $9\,|\,a$, then $3\,|\,a$.

Cooperative Learning

12. In your group, discuss if the sum of two consecutive numbers is divisible by 2, the sum of three consecutive numbers is divisible by 3, the sum of four consecutive numbers is divisible by 4, etc. Make a general statement about the sum of n consecutive numbers and its divisibility by n.

13. In your groups use base-ten blocks to illustrate the divisibility rules for 3, 4, 5, 8, 9, and 10. Use a three-digit number as your example.

Connecting Mathematics to the Classroom

14. Amy claims 10 is both even and odd because it is divisible by the even number 2 and the odd number 5. How would you respond?

15. Jane claimed that a number is divisible by 4 if each of the last two digits is divisible by 4. Is this claim correct? If not, how would you suggest that Jane change it?

16. Your seventh-grade class has just completed a unit on divisibility rules. One student asks why divisibility by 6 cannot be tested by dividing the sum of the digits by 6. How do you respond?

17. A student claims that a number is divisible by 24 if, and only if, it is divisible by 6 and by 4, and, in general, a number is divisible by $a \cdot b$ if, and only if, it is divisible by a and by b. What is your response?

18. Brian claims zero is neither even nor odd because in order to be even, zero would have to be divided into two equal piles and in order to be odd, zero would not be able to be divided into two equal piles. What is your response to Brian to convince him that zero is even?

National Assessments

National Assessment of Educational Progress (NAEP) Questions

Andy has three cards, A, B, and C. Each card has one number on it.

One card has the number 4 on it.
One card has the number 6 on it.
One card has the number 10 on it.

The number on card B is a factor of 8, and the number on card C is a factor of 12.

Write the correct number on each of the cards below so that they are the same as Andy's cards.

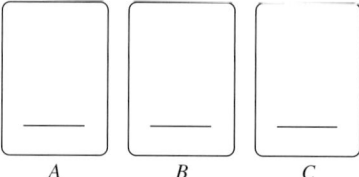

$$A \qquad B \qquad C$$

NAEP, Grade 4, 2013

Sam did the following problems.

$$2 + 1 = 3$$
$$6 + 1 = 7$$

Sam concluded that when he adds 1 to any whole number, his answer will always be odd.

   Is Sam correct? _____
   Explain your answer.

NAEP, Grade 4, 2009

4-2 Prime and Composite Numbers

4-2 Objectives

Students will be able to understand and explain

- Prime and composite numbers.
- The number of divisors of any whole number.
- The Fundamental Theorem of Arithmetic.
- The factorization of whole numbers.

Activity Manual

Use *A Square Experiment* to develop the concepts of prime, composite, and square numbers.

CCSS The grade 4 *Common Core Standards* states that students should be able to:

Find all factor pairs for a whole number in the range 1–100. Recognize that a whole number is a multiple of each of its factors. Determine whether a given whole number in the range 1–100 is a multiple of a given one-digit number. Determine whether a given whole number in the range 1–100 is prime or composite. (p. 29)

One method used in elementary schools to determine the positive factors of a nonzero whole number is to use squares of paper or cubes to represent the number as a rectangle. Such a rectangle resembles a candy bar formed with small squares. The dimensions of the rectangle are divisors or factors of the number. For example, Figure 5 shows rectangles to represent 12.

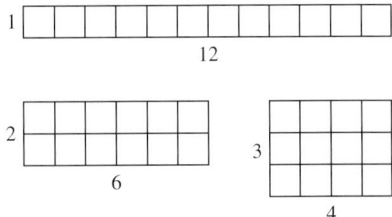

Figure 5

As seen in Figure 5, the number 12 has six positive divisors: 1, 2, 3, 4, 6, and 12. If we use rectangles to find the divisors of 7, then we would find only a 1 × 7 rectangle, as shown in Figure 6. Thus, 7 has exactly two divisors: 1 and 7.

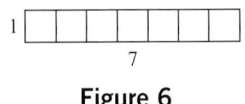

Figure 6

Table 1 illustrates the number of positive divisors of a nonzero whole number. Below each number listed across the top, we identify the numbers less than or equal to 37 that have that number of whole number divisors. For example, 12 is in the 6 column because it has six divisors, and 7 is in the 2 column because it has only two divisors.

▶ **NOW TRY THIS 3**

NTT 3: Answers can be found in Answers at the back of the book.

a. Will there be other entries in the 1 column? Why?
b. What are the next three numbers in the 3 column?
c. What is the next number in the 5 column?
d. Find an entry for the 7 column.
e. What kinds of numbers have an odd number of factors? Why?
f. What other patterns do you see in Table 1?

The numbers in the 2 column in Table 1 are of particular importance: they have exactly two positive divisors, namely, 1 and themselves. Any positive integer with exactly two distinct, positive divisors is a *prime number*, or a **prime**. Any whole number greater than 1 that has a positive factor

Table 1

Number of Positive Divisors								
1	**2**	**3**	**4**	**5**	**6**	**7**	**8**	**9**
1	2	4	6	16	12		24	36
	3	9	8		18		30	
	5	25	10		20			
	7		14		28			
	11		15		32			
	13		21					
	17		22					
	19		26					
	23		27					
	29		33					
	31		34					
	37		35					

other than 1 and itself is a *composite number*, or a **composite**. For example, 4, 6, and 16 are composites because they have positive factors other than 1 and themselves. The number 1 has only one positive factor, so it is neither prime nor composite. From the 2 column in Table 1, we see that the first 12 primes are 2, 3, 5, 7, 11, 13, 17, 19, 23, 29, 31, and 37. The number 2 is sometimes called the "oddest" prime because it is the only even prime.

Example 9

Show that the following numbers are composite.

a. 1564

b. 2781

c. 1001

d. $3 \cdot 5 \cdot 7 \cdot 11 \cdot 13 + 1$

Solution

a. Since $2 \mid 4$, 1564 is divisible by 2 and is composite.

b. Since $3 \mid (2 + 7 + 8 + 1)$, 2781 is divisible by 3 and is composite.

c. Since $11 \mid [(1 + 0) - (0 + 1)]$, 1001 is divisible by 11 and is composite.

d. Because a product of odd numbers is odd (why?), $3 \cdot 5 \cdot 7 \cdot 11 \cdot 13$ is odd. If we add 1 to an odd number, the sum is even. Any even natural number has a factor of 2 besides 1 and itself, and is therefore composite.

Prime Factorization

Activity Manual

Use *The Factor Game* to introduce the prime factorization of a number.

Composite numbers can be expressed as products of two or more whole numbers greater than 1. For example, $18 = 2 \cdot 9$, $18 = 3 \cdot 6$, or $18 = 2 \cdot 3 \cdot 3$. Each expression of 18 as a product of factors is a **factorization**.

A factorization containing only prime numbers is a **prime factorization**. To find a prime factorization of a given composite number, we first rewrite the number as a product of two whole numbers greater than 1. We continue the process, factoring these numbers until all factors are primes. For example, consider 260:

$$260 = 26 \cdot 10 = (2 \cdot 13)(2 \cdot 5) = 2 \cdot 2 \cdot 5 \cdot 13 = 2^2 \cdot 5 \cdot 13$$

The procedure for finding a prime factorization of a number can be organized using a **factor tree**, as Figure 7(a) demonstrates. The last branches of the tree display the prime factors of 260.

A second way to factor 260 is shown in Figure 7(b). The two trees produce the same prime factorization.

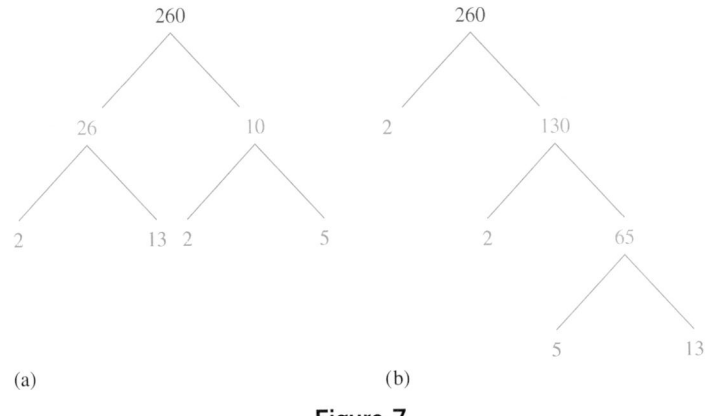

(a)   (b)

Figure 7

The *Fundamental Theorem of Arithmetic*, or the *Unique Factorization Theorem*, states that in general, if order is disregarded, the prime factorization of a number is unique.

Theorem 4-12:   Fundamental Theorem of Arithmetic

Each composite number can be written as a product of primes in one, and only one, way except for the order of the prime factors in the product.

The Fundamental Theorem of Arithmetic assures that once we find a prime factorization of a number, a different prime factorization of the same number cannot be found. For example, consider 260. We start with the least prime, 2, and see whether it divides 260. If not, we try the next greater prime and check for divisibility by this prime. Once we find a prime that divides the number in question, we must find the quotient when the number is divided by the prime. This step in the prime factorization of 260 is shown in Figure 8(a). Next, if the quotient is a composite number, we check whether the prime divides the quotient. If so, we repeat the process; if not, we try the next greater prime, 3, and check to see if it divides the quotient. We see that 130 divided by 2 yields 65, as shown in Figure 8(b). We continue the procedure, using greater primes, until a quotient of 1 is reached. The original number is the product of all the prime divisors used. The complete procedure for 260 is shown in Figure 8(c). An alternative form of this procedure is shown in Figure 8(d).

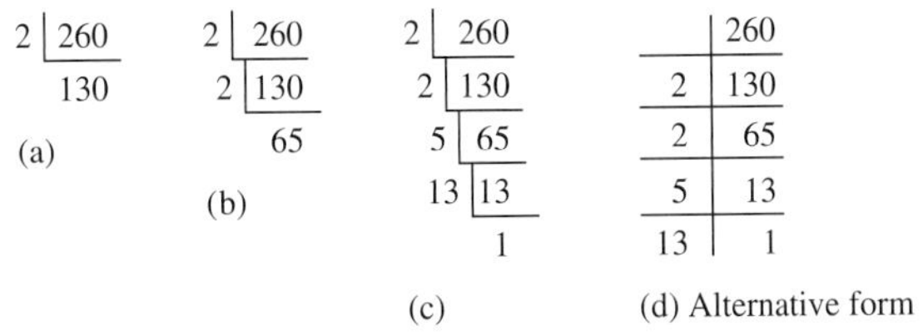

$$
\begin{array}{cccc}
2\,\lfloor\underline{260} & 2\,\lfloor\underline{260} & 2\,\lfloor\underline{260} & \lfloor\underline{260} \\
\quad 130 & 2\,\lfloor\underline{130} & 2\,\lfloor\underline{130} & 2\,\lfloor\,130 \\
\text{(a)} & \quad 65 & 5\,\lfloor\underline{65} & 2\,\lfloor\,65 \\
& \text{(b)} & 13\,\lfloor\underline{13} & 5\,\lfloor\,13 \\
& & \qquad 1 & 13\,\lfloor\,1 \\
& & \text{(c)} & \text{(d) Alternative form}
\end{array}
$$

Figure 8

The primes in the prime factorization of a number are typically listed in increasing order from left to right, and if a prime appears in a product more than once, exponential notation is used. Thus, the factorization of 260 is written as $2^2 \cdot 5 \cdot 13$. Prime factorization is demonstrated in the student page shown on page 192. Notice that the factor tree is developed in two different ways leading to the same result.

School Book Page   Prime Factorization

Lesson
5-2

© Common Core

This lesson reinforces concepts and skills required for Topic 9.

Prime Factorization

How can you write the prime factorization of a number?

Whole numbers greater than 1 are either prime or composite numbers.

A prime number has exactly two factors, 1 and itself. The numbers 2, 3, and 5 are prime numbers.

Model	Dimension	Factors
	1×2	1, 2
	1×3	1, 3
	1×4	1, 4
	2×2	2
	1×5	1, 5

A composite number has more than two factors and can be written as the product of its prime factors. This is called its prime factorization.

4 is a composite number. The factors of 4 are 1, 2, and 4. 2 is its only prime factor. The prime factorization of 4 is 2×2, or 2^2.

To find the prime factorization of 60, write its factors, beginning with the smallest prime factor.

$60 = 2 \times 30$ ← 2 is a factor of 60.

$= 2 \times 2 \times 15$ ← 2 is a factor again.

$= 2 \times 2 \times 3 \times 5$ ← 3 and 5 are factors.

$= 2^2 \times 3 \times 5$ ← Use exponents.

Another Example   How can you use a factor tree to find the prime factorization of a number?

One Way

To find the prime factorization of 72, begin with the smallest prime factor. Write factors until all the factors are prime numbers.

```
        72
       /  \
      2 × 36
         /  \
      2 × 2 × 18
            /  \
      2 × 2 × 2 × 9
                /  \
      2 × 2 × 2 × 3 × 3
```

$72 = 2 \times 2 \times 2 \times 3 \times 3$
$72 = 2^3 \times 3^2$

Another Way

To find the prime factorization of 72, begin with any two factors of 72. Write factors until all the factors are prime numbers.

Arrange prime factors in order.

```
        72
       /  \
      6  × 12
     / \   / \
   2 × 3 3 × 4
              / \
   2 × 3 × 3 × 2 × 2
```

$72 = 2 \times 2 \times 2 \times 3 \times 3$
$72 = 2^3 \times 3^2$

There is only one prime factorization for any number.

NTT 4: c. Only one white rod can be used for prime numbers.

NOW TRY THIS 4

Colored rods are used in the elementary-school classroom to teach many concepts. The rods vary in length from 1 cm to 10 cm. Various lengths have different colors; for example, the 5 rod is yellow. The rods and their colors are shown in Figure 9(a). A row with all the same color rods is called a *one-color train*.

a. What rods can be used to form a one-color train for 18? 1, 2, 3, 6, 9

b. What one-color trains are possible for 24? 1, 2, 3, 4, 6, 8

c. How many one-color trains of two or more rods are possible for each prime number?

d. In Figure 9(b), a number represented by an all-red train, an all-green train, and an all-purple train is shown. How many factors does this number have? What are the factors?
The number must have 6 factors: 1, 2, 3, 4, 6, 12.

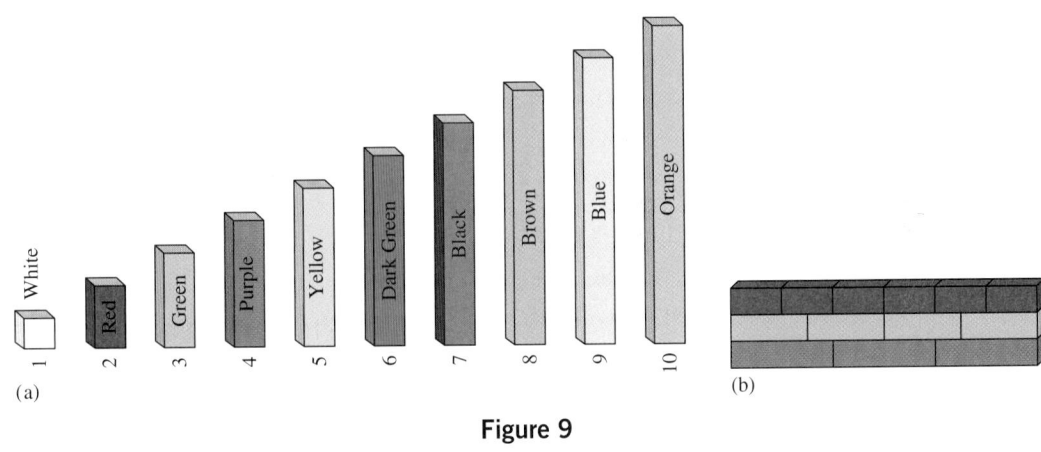

Figure 9

Number of Whole Number Divisors

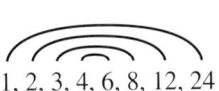

1, 2, 3, 4, 6, 8, 12, 24

Figure 10

How many whole number divisors does 24 have? To aid in answering the question, we group divisors as in Figure 10. The whole number divisors of 24 occur in pairs, where the product of the divisors in each pair is 24. If 3 is a divisor of 24, then $24/3 = 8$, is also a divisor of 24. In general, if a whole number k is a divisor of 24, then $24/k$ is also a divisor of 24.

Another way to think of the number of whole number divisors of 24 is to consider the prime factorization $24 = 2^3 \cdot 3$. The whole number divisors of 2^3 are $2^0, 2^1, 2^2$, and 2^3. The whole number divisors of 3 are 3^0 and 3^1. We know that 2^3 has $(3 + 1) = 4$ divisors and 3^1 has $(1 + 1) = 2$ divisors. Because each divisor of 24 is the product of a divisor of 2^3 and a divisor of 3^1, we use the Fundamental Counting Principle to conclude that 24 has $4 \cdot 2 = 8$ positive divisors. This is summarized in Table 2.

Table 2

Divisors of 2^3	$2^0 = 1$	$2^1 = 2$	$2^2 = 4$	$2^3 = 8$
Divisors of 3^1	$3^0 = 1$	$3^1 = 3$		
Divisors of $3^1 \cdot 2^3$ (Divisors of 24)	$3^0 \cdot 2^0 = 1$ $3^1 \cdot 2^0 = 3$	$3^0 \cdot 2^1 = 2$ $3^1 \cdot 2^1 = 6$	$3^0 \cdot 2^2 = 4$ $3^1 \cdot 2^2 = 12$	$3^0 \cdot 2^3 = 8$ $3^1 \cdot 2^3 = 24$

This discussion can be generalized as follows: If p is any prime and n is any whole number, then the whole number divisors of p^n are $p^0, p^1, p^2, p^3, \ldots, p^n$. Therefore, there are $(n + 1)$ whole number divisors of p^n. Using the Fundamental Counting Principle, we can find the number of divisors of any number whose prime factorization is known.

Theorem 4-13

If p and q are different primes, and n, m are whole numbers, then $p^n q^m$ has $(n + 1)(m + 1)$ whole number divisors. In general, if $p_1, p_2, \ldots, p_k$ are primes and $n_1, n_2, \ldots, n_k$ are whole numbers, then $p_1^{n_1} \cdot p_2^{n_2} \cdot \ldots \cdot p_k^{n_k}$ has $(n_1 + 1)(n_2 + 1) \cdot \ldots \cdot (n_k + 1)$ whole number divisors.

Example 10

Find the number of whole number divisors of each given value.

a. 1,000,000   **b.** 210^{10}

Solution

a. We first find the prime factorization of 1,000,000.

$$1{,}000{,}000 = 10^6 = (2 \cdot 5)^6 = (2 \cdot 5)(2 \cdot 5)(2 \cdot 5)(2 \cdot 5)(2 \cdot 5)(2 \cdot 5)$$
$$= (2 \cdot 2 \cdot 2 \cdot 2 \cdot 2 \cdot 2)(5 \cdot 5 \cdot 5 \cdot 5 \cdot 5 \cdot 5)$$
$$= 2^6 \cdot 5^6$$

Because 2^6 has $6 + 1$ divisors and 5^6 has $6 + 1$ divisors, then by Theorem 4-13, $2^6 \cdot 5^6$ has $(6 + 1)(6 + 1) = 49$ divisors.

b. We first find the prime factorization of 210^{10}:

$$210 = 21 \cdot 10 = 3 \cdot 7 \cdot 2 \cdot 5 = 2 \cdot 3 \cdot 5 \cdot 7,$$
$$210^{10} = (2 \cdot 3 \cdot 5 \cdot 7)^{10} = 2^{10} \cdot 3^{10} \cdot 5^{10} \cdot 7^{10}$$

By Theorem 4-13, the number of divisors of 210^{10} is $(10 + 1)(10 + 1)(10 + 1)(10 + 1) = 11^4 = 14{,}641$.

Determining Whether a Number Is Prime

Suppose we want to check whether 97 is prime and we find that 2, 3, 5, and 7 do not divide 97. Could a greater prime divide 97? If p is a prime greater than 7, then $p \geq 11$. If $p \mid 97$, then $97/p$ also divides 97. However, because $p \geq 11$ then $97/p$ must be less than 9 and hence cannot divide 97. (Why?) We see that there is no need to check for divisibility by numbers other than 2, 3, 5, and 7. These ideas are generalized in the following theorems.

Theorem 4-14

If d is a divisor of n, where $n \neq 0$, then $\dfrac{n}{d}$ is also a divisor of n.

Suppose that p is the *least* divisor of a composite number n and $p \neq 1$. Such a divisor must be prime. (Why?) Then $n = pk$, for some whole number k, $k \neq 1$. Since $k \mid n$ and p was the least divisor of n, $k \geq p$. Therefore, $n = pk \geq pp = p^2$. Since $n \geq p^2$, we have $p^2 \leq n$. This idea is summarized in the following theorem.

Theorem 4-15

If n is composite, then n has a prime factor p such that $p^2 \leq n$.

Theorem 4-15 can be used to help determine whether a given number is prime or composite. For example, consider the number 109. If 109 is composite, it must have a prime divisor p such that $p^2 \leq 109$. The primes whose squares do not exceed 109 are 2, 3, 5, and 7. Mentally, we can see that $2 \nmid 109$, $3 \nmid 109$, $5 \nmid 109$, and $7 \nmid 109$. Hence, 109 is prime. The argument used leads to the following theorem.

Theorem 4-16

If n is a whole number greater than 1 and not divisible by any prime p such that $p^2 \leq n$, then n is prime.

Example 11

a. Is 397 composite or prime?

b. Is 91 composite or prime?

Solution

a. The possible primes p such that $p^2 \leq 397$ are 2, 3, 5, 7, 11, 13, 17, and 19. Because $2 \nmid 397, 3 \nmid 397, 5 \nmid 397, 7 \nmid 397, 11 \nmid 397, 13 \nmid 397, 17 \nmid 397$, and $19 \nmid 397$, the number 397 is prime.

b. The possible primes p such that $p^2 \leq 91$ are 2, 3, 5, and 7. Because 91 is divisible by 7, it is composite.

▶ NOW TRY THIS 5

The cartoon below concerns divisibility and prime numbers. Answer the following questions based on the cartoon.

a. Find all the factors of the numbers shown. What can you conclude?   The numbers are prime.

b. How many numbers in all did she say?   100 in all.

Activity Manual

Use *A Sieve of Another Sort* to investigate primes, composites, multiples, and prime factorizations.

One way to find all the primes less than a given number is to use the *Sieve of Eratosthenes*, named after the Greek mathematician Eratosthenes (ca. 276–194 BCE). If all the whole numbers greater than 1 are considered (or placed in the sieve), the numbers that are not prime are methodically crossed out (or drop through the holes of the sieve). The remaining numbers are prime. The partial student page shown on page 196 illustrates this process.

Historical Note

Eratosthenes (276–194 BCE) spent most of his life in Alexandria as a chief librarian. In mathematics Eratosthenes is best known for his "sieve"—a systematic procedure for isolating the prime numbers—and for a simple method for calculating the circumference of the Earth. ●

School Book Page   Problem Solving

Problem Solving   MATHEMATICAL PRACTICES

36. Use the following steps devised by the Greek mathematician Eratosthenes to create a list of prime numbers from 1 to 100. How many prime numbers are there between 1 and 100?

- Write all the numbers from 1 to 100.
- Draw a triangle around number 1; it is not prime nor composite.
- Circle 2 and cross out all other multiples of 2.
- Circle 3 and cross out all other multiples of 3.
- Circle 5, the next number that is not crossed out. Cross out other multiples of 5.
- Continue in the same way. When you have finished, the circled numbers are prime.

Lesson 11-2   **261**

Source: p. 261; From enVisionMATH Common Core (Grade 4). Copyright © 2012 Pearson Education, Inc., or its affiliates. Used by permission. All Rights Reserved.

The Sieve of Eratosthenes is another way to demonstrate Theorem 4-16. Notice the observations from the sieve in Table 3 as we crossed out numbers.

Table 3

Prime	Observation
2	Once 2 is circled, the first number not crossed out that 2 divides is $4 = 2^2$.
3	Once 3 is circled, the first number not crossed out that 3 divides is $9 = 3^2$.
5	Once 5 is circled, the first number not crossed out that 5 divides is $25 = 5^2$.
7	Once 7 is circled, the first number not crossed out that 7 divides is $49 = 7^2$.

Problem Solving   Perfect Squares

A perfect square is a whole number that is a square of a whole number. For example, 81 is a perfect square because $81 = 9^2$. Show that a nonzero whole number is a perfect square if, and only if, it has an odd number of divisors.

Understanding the Problem We need to show that all perfect squares—such as 36—have an odd number of divisors, and if a number is not a perfect square—such as 24—then it has an even number of divisors. Indeed, $36 = 6^2 = 2^2 \cdot 3^2$ and it has $(2 + 1)(2 + 1) = 9$ divisors, which is odd. In contrast, $24 = 4 \cdot 6 = 2^3 \cdot 3^1$ has $(3 + 1)(1 + 1) = 8$ divisors, an even number. We need to prove the statement in the problem for all nonzero whole numbers.

Devising a Plan We write the prime factorization of a perfect square and use Theorem 4-13 to find an expression for the number of divisors. Similarly, if a number is not a perfect square, we characterize its prime factorization and again use Theorem 4-13.

Carrying Out the Plan Every perfect square can be written as m^2, where m is a whole number. If the prime factorization of m is $p_1^{n_1} p_2^{n_2} \cdot \ldots \cdot p_k^{n_k}$, then $m^2 = p_1^{2n_1} p_2^{2n_2} \cdot \ldots \cdot p_k^{2n_k}$. Theorem 4-13 tells us that the number of divisors of m^2 is $(2n_1 + 1)(2n_2 + 1) \cdot \ldots \cdot (2n_k + 1)$. Each of these factors is odd. Since a product of odd numbers is odd, the above product is odd.

If a number is not a perfect square, then the exponents to which the primes in its prime factorization are raised cannot be all even. If they were all even, the number would be a perfect square. Thus, at least one of the exponents is odd. Suppose that exponent is n_j; then by Theorem 4-13, the number of divisors would be a product in which one of the factors in that product is $n_j + 1$. Since n_j is odd, $n_j + 1$ is even. When an even whole number is multiplied by any whole number, the result is even and hence the product is even.

Looking Back We could approach the problem differently. Theorem 4-14 states that if $d\,|\,n$, where $n \neq 0$, then n/d is also a divisor of n. Consequently, if for all divisors d of n, $d \neq n/d$, then each divisor can be paired with a different divisor of n. Therefore n must have an even number of divisors. If for some divisor d, $d = n/d$, then $n = d^2$, and all the divisors of n except d are paired with a different divisor. Hence the number of divisors is odd. It follows that n has an even number of divisors if, and only if, n is a perfect square.

More About Primes

There are infinitely many whole numbers, infinitely many odd whole numbers, and infinitely many even whole numbers. Are there infinitely many primes? The answer to this question is not obvious. Euclid was the first to prove that there are infinitely many primes.

Mathematicians have long looked for a formula that produces only primes, but no one has found one. One result was the expression $n^2 - n + 41$, where n is a whole number. Substituting $0, 1, 2, 3, \ldots, 40$ for n in the expression always results in a prime number. However, substituting 41 for n gives $41^2 - 41 + 41 = 41^2$, which is a composite number. In 1998, Roland Clarkson, a 19-year-old student at California State University, showed that $2^{3,021,377} - 1$ is prime. The number has 909,526 digits. The full decimal expansion of the number would fill several hundred pages. Since then, more large primes have been discovered, including $2^{57,885,161} - 1$ (17,425,170 digits) in 2013. The latest primes are examples of *Mersenne primes*. A Mersenne prime, named after the French monk Marin Mersenne (1588–1648), is a prime of the form $2^n - 1$, where n is prime.

Another type of interesting prime is a *Sophie Germain prime*, which is an odd prime p for which $2p + 1$ is also a prime. Notice that $p = 3$ is a Sophie Germain prime, since $2 \cdot 3 + 1$, or 7, is also a prime. Check that 5, 11, and 23 are also such primes. The primes were named after the French mathematician Sophie Germain. The greatest Sophie Germain prime discovered as of 2012 is $18{,}543{,}637{,}900{,}515 \cdot 2^{666{,}667} - 1$ with 200,701 digits.

Problem Solving   How Many Bears?

A large toy store carries one kind of stuffed bear. On Monday the store sold a certain number of the stuffed bears for $1843, and on Tuesday, without changing the price, the store sold a certain number of the stuffed bears for $1957. How many toy bears were sold each day if the price of each bear is a whole number and greater than $1?

Understanding the Problem One day a store sold a number of stuffed bears for $1843 and on the next day a number of them for a total of $1957. We don't know the number of stuffed bears sold on each day nor do we know the cost.

However, we know the following:

Day 1: number of bears sold times the cost per bear is $1843.

Day 2: number of bears sold times the cost per bear is $1957.

The total for two days is (number of bears sold on day 1 plus number of bears sold on day 2) times the cost per bear is $1843 + $1957.

We need to find the number of bears sold each day.

Devising a Plan If x bears were sold the first day and y bears the second day, and if the price of each bear was c dollars, we would have $cx = 1843$ and $cy = 1957$. Thus, 1843 and 1957 should have a common factor—the price c. We could factor each number and find the possible factors. If the problem is to have a unique solution, the two numbers should have only one common factor other than 1. Any common factor of 1957 and 1843 will also be a factor of $1957 - 1843 = 114$ and the factors of 114 are easier to find.

Carrying Out the Plan We have $114 = 2 \cdot 57 = 2 \cdot 3 \cdot 19$. Thus, if 1957 and 1843 have a common prime factor, it must be 2, 3, or 19. Neither 2 nor 3 divides 1957 or 1843. Hence the only possible common factor is 19. We divide each number by 19 and find

$$1843 = 19 \cdot 97$$
$$1957 = 19 \cdot 103.$$

Consequently, the price of each bear is $19. The first day 97 bears were sold, and the next day 103 bears were sold.

Looking Back The problem has a unique solution because the only common factor (greater than 1) of the two numbers is 19. We could create similar problems by having the price of the item be a prime number and the number of items sold each day also be prime numbers. For example, the total sale on the first day could have been $23 \cdot 101$, or $2323, and on the second day $23 \cdot 107$, or $2461 (23, 101, and 107 are prime numbers).

To find a common factor of 1957 and 1843, we found all the common factors of $1957 - 1843 = 114 = 2 \cdot 3 \cdot 19$ and checked which of the factors of the difference was a common factor of the original numbers. We used Theorem 4-2(c): If $d \mid a$ and $d \mid b$, then $d \mid (a - b)$. This theorem assures that every common factor of a and b is also a factor of $a - b$ if $a \geq b$. Thus the set of all common factors of a and b is a subset of all the factors of $a - b$.

Assessment 4-2A

1. **a.** Fill in the missing numbers in the following factor tree. *

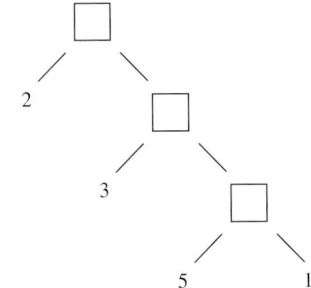

   b. How could you find the top number without finding the other two numbers? $2 \cdot 3 \cdot 5 \cdot 11 = 330$

2. Use a factor tree to find the prime factorization for each of the following numbers.
   a. 504 *   **b.** 2475 *   **c.** 11,250 *

3. Find the prime factorization of the following numbers.
   a. $1 \cdot 2 \cdot 3 \cdot 4 \cdot 5 \cdot 6 \cdot 7 \cdot 8 \cdot 9$ $2^7 \cdot 3^4 \cdot 5 \cdot 7$
   b. $10^2 \cdot 13 \cdot 49^{10}$ $2^2 \cdot 5^2 \cdot 7^{20} \cdot 13$
   c. 251   251
   d. 100^{10} $2^{20} \cdot 5^{20}$

4. What is the greatest prime that must be considered to test whether 769 is prime?   23

5. Determine which of the following numbers are primes.
   a. 103   Prime   **b.** 119   Not prime
   c. 31   Prime   **d.** 303   Not prime
   e. 463   Prime   **f.** 97   Prime
   g. $2 \cdot 3 \cdot 5 \cdot 7 + 1$ Prime
   h. $2 \cdot 3 \cdot 5 \cdot 7 + 11$ Not prime

6. Find the least natural number that is divisible by three different primes.   30

7. Find the least three-digit whole number that has exactly five positive factors.   625

8. **a.** Use the Fundamental Theorem of Arithmetic to justify that if $2 \mid n$ and $3 \mid n$, then $6 \mid n$. *
   b. Is it always true that if $a \mid n$ and $b \mid n$, then $ab \mid n^2$? Either prove the statement or give a counterexample. *

9. Find the prime factorization of each of the following numbers.
   a. $36^{10} \cdot 49^{20} \cdot 6^{15}$ $2^{35} \cdot 3^{35} \cdot 7^{40}$
   b. $100^{60} \cdot 300^{40}$ $2^{200} \cdot 3^{40} \cdot 5^{200}$
   c. $2 \cdot 3^4 \cdot 5^{110} \cdot 7 + 4 \cdot 3^4 \cdot 5^{110}$ $2 \cdot 3^6 \cdot 5^{110}$
   d. $2 \cdot 3 \cdot 5 \cdot 7 \cdot 11 + 1$ 2311

10. Explain why $2^3 \cdot 3^2 \cdot 25^3$ is not a prime factorization and find the prime factorization of the number. *

11. Is it possible to find nonzero whole numbers x, y, and z such that $3^x \cdot 5^y = 8^z$? Justify your answer. *

12. If $32n = 2^6 \cdot 3^5 \cdot 5^4 \cdot 7^3 \cdot 11^7$, explain why $2 \cdot 3 \cdot 5 \cdot 7 \cdot 11^6$ is a factor of n. *

13. Is $7^4 \cdot 11^3$ a factor of $7^5 \cdot 11^3$? Explain why or why not. *

14. **a.** When the U.S. flag had 48 stars, the stars formed a 6 by 8 rectangular array. In what other rectangular arrays could they have been arranged? *
    b. How many rectangular arrays of stars could there be if there were only 47 states? *

15. Miss Cotton wants to put her classroom in a rectangular array. For each of the following number of desks, find all possible numbers of rows if each row has the same number of desks.
    a. 30 *   **b.** 28 *   **c.** 23 *   **d.** 120 *

16. Briah and Emma are on the same swim team for the summer. The coach placed each team member on a different training schedule. As a result, Briah swims laps every other day and Emma swims laps every three days. The schedule begins on the first day of summer, with both girls swimming laps. How many times will Briah and Emma swim laps on the same day during the first ten weeks of summer?   12 times

17. A woman with a basket of eggs finds that if she removes the eggs from the basket 3 or 5 at a time, there is always 1 egg left. However, if she removes the eggs 7 at a time, there are no eggs left. If the basket holds up to 100 eggs, how many eggs does she have?   91 eggs

18. A band of 17 pirates stole a sack of golden coins. When they tried to divide them into equal portions there were 3 leftover. In the brawl over who would get the extra 3 coins a pirate was killed. They tried to divide the coins into equal portions again, but this time 10 coins were left over. Again there was a brawl and another pirate was killed. Now when the coins were divided none were left over. What is the least number of coins the pirates stole?   224 coins

19. A license plate is in two parts, a two-digit number and a three-digit number. The two-digit number is prime and the sum of the two digits is a two-digit prime. The tens digit is greater than the units digit. In the three digit part, the digits are all odd and different. The sum of the three digits is palindromic. The sum of the first and third digit is one-half the sum of the first and second. Determine the license plate number.   83-173

20. The prime numbers 11 and 13 are called *twin primes* because they differ by 2. (The existence of infinitely many twin primes has not been proved.) Find all the twin primes less than 200. *

21. A whole number is a *perfect* number if the sum of its factors (other than the number itself) is equal to the number. For example, 6 is a perfect number because its factors sum to 6; that is, $1 + 2 + 3 = 6$.
    a. Determine which of the following numbers are perfect.   ii. 28 is perfect
    i. 12   **ii.** 28   **iii.** 35
    b. Find at least one more number that is perfect.   Answers vary. For example, 496.

Assessment 4-2B

1. a. Fill in the missing numbers in the following factor tree. *

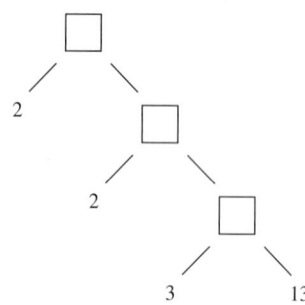

   b. How could you find the top number without finding the other two numbers? $2 \cdot 2 \cdot 3 \cdot 13 = 156$

2. Use a factor tree to find the prime factorization for each of the following numbers.

   a. 544 $2^5 \cdot 17$ **b.** 3010   *   **c.** 9550   *

3. Find the prime factorization of the following numbers.

   a. 1001 $7 \cdot 11 \cdot 13$

   b. 1001^2 $7^2 \cdot 11^2 \cdot 13^2$

   c. 999^{10} $3^{30} \cdot 37^{10}$

   d. $111^{10} - 111^9$ $2 \cdot 3^9 \cdot 5 \cdot 11 \cdot 37^9$

4. What is the greatest prime that must be considered to test whether 671 is prime?   23

5. Determine which of the following numbers are primes.

   a. 101   Prime   **b.** 113   Prime

   c. 153   Not prime   **d.** 189   Not prime

   e. 541   Prime   **f.** 601   Prime

   g. $2 \cdot 3 \cdot 5 \cdot 7 + 5$ *   **h.** $2 \cdot 3 \cdot 5 \cdot 7 - 5$ *

6. Find the least natural number that is divisible by four different primes.   210

7. Find the greatest four-digit whole number that has exactly three positive factors.   9409

8. Use the Fundamental Theorem of Arithmetic to prove that if $4 \mid n$ and $9 \mid n$, then $36 \mid n$.   *

9. Find the prime factorization of each of the following numbers.

   a. $16^4 \cdot 81^4 \cdot 6^6$ $2^{22} \cdot 3^{22}$

   b. $8^4 \cdot 32^5$ 2^{37}

   c. $2^2 \cdot 3^5 \cdot 7^{55} + 2^4 \cdot 3^4 \cdot 7^{55}$ $2^2 \cdot 3^4 \cdot 7^{56}$

   d. $2 \cdot 3 \cdot 5 \cdot 7 \cdot 13 + 1$ 2731

10. Explain why $2^2 \cdot 5^3 \cdot 9^2$ is not a prime factorization and find the prime factorization of the number.   *

11. Is it possible to find nonzero whole numbers x, y, and z such that $2^x \cdot 3^y = 5^z$? Justify your answer.   *

12. If $2n = 2^6 \cdot 3^5 \cdot 5^4 \cdot 7^3 \cdot 11^7$, explain why $2 \cdot 3 \cdot 5 \cdot 7 \cdot 11$ is a factor of n.   *

13. Is $3^2 \cdot 2^4$ a factor of $3^3 \cdot 2^2$? Explain why or why not.   *

14. a. A rectangular solar panel is made up of small squares. A particular solar panel is 4 squares by 6 squares. In what other rectangular arrays could the squares have been arranged?   *

   b. If there were 43 squares, how many rectangular arrays can there be?   *

15. Mr. Todd wants to build a new rectangular patio. For each of the following numbers of square tiles, find all possible lengths and widths.

   a. 15   *   **b.** 24   *   **c.** 17   *   **d.** 200   *

16. Barbara is getting in shape, and every other day she goes for a run and every fifth day she goes to dance class. How many times in a 30-day month does she run and dance in the same day?   3 times

17. Jose has fewer than 100 baseball cards. If he puts them in piles of 2, 3, 4, 5, or 6 he has one card left over each time. How many baseball cards does Jose have?   61 cards

18. Isabelle, Noelle, and Juliette acquired a pile of chocolate coins. They go to bed, leaving their dad to guard the coins. An hour later Juliette gets up, gives two chocolate coins from the pile to her dad as hush money, divides the remaining pile of coins evenly into three parts, takes one part, and goes back to bed. A little later, Noelle gets up, gives two chocolate coins to her dad as hush money, divides the remaining pile evenly into three parts, takes one part, and goes back to bed. A little later, Isabelle gets up and does the very same thing as her siblings. In the morning, when they count the remaining chocolate coins, there are 100 of them left. How many were in the pile originally?   347 coins

19. Anya had a collection of red, green, and blue beads. She noticed that the number of beads in each color was a prime number and that the numbers were all different. She also observed that if she multiplied the number of red beads by the total number of red and green beads she obtained a number exactly 120 greater than the number of blue beads. How many beads of each color did she have?   *

20. A prime such as 7331 is a *superprime* because any integers obtained by deleting digits from the right of 7331 are prime, namely, 733, 73, and 7.

   a. For a prime to be a superprime, what digit(s) cannot appear in the number?   0, 4, 6, 8

   b. Of the digits that can appear in a superprime, what digit(s) cannot be the leftmost digit of a superprime?   1, 9

   c. Find all two-digit superprimes.   *

   d. Find a three-digit superprime other than 733.   *

21. A whole number is an *abundant* number if the sum of its factors (other than the number itself) is greater than the number itself. A *deficient* number is a number with factors (other than the number itself) whose sum is less than the number itself.

   a. Determine which of the following numbers are abundant or deficient.   *

     i. 12   **ii.** 28   **iii.** 35

   b. Find at least one more number that is deficient and one that is abundant.   Answers vary. For example, 14 is deficient and 18 is abundant.

Mathematical Connections 4-2

Reasoning

1. Explain why the product of any three consecutive whole numbers is divisible by 6.

2. Explain why the product of any four consecutive whole numbers is divisible by 24.

3. In the Sieve of Eratosthenes for numbers less than 100, explain why, after crossing out all the multiples of 2, 3, 5, and 7, the remaining numbers are prime.

4. Let $M = 2 \cdot 3 \cdot 5 \cdot 7 + 11 \cdot 13 \cdot 17 \cdot 19$. Without multiplying, show that none of the primes less than or equal to 19 divides M.

5. The numbers 2, 3, 5, 7, 11, 13, and 17 are not factors of 353. Explain why it is possible to conclude that 353 is prime without checking for more prime factors.

6. Explain why, when a number is composite, its least whole number divisor, other than 1, must be prime.

7. Euclid proved that given any finite list of primes, there exists a prime not in the list. Read the following argument and answer the questions that follow.

    Let $2, 3, 5, 7, \ldots, p$ be a list of all primes less than or equal to a certain prime p. We will show that there exists a prime not on the list. Consider the product

    $$2 \cdot 3 \cdot 5 \cdot 7 \cdot \ldots \cdot p$$

    Every prime in the list divides that product. However, if we add 1 to the product, that is, form the number $n = (2 \cdot 3 \cdot 5 \cdot 7 \cdot \ldots \cdot p) + 1$, then none of the primes in the list will divide n. Whether n is prime or composite, some prime q must divide n. Because no prime in the list divides n, q is not one of the primes in the list. Consequently $q > p$. We have shown that there exists a prime greater than p.

    a. Explain why no prime in the list will divide n.

    b. Explain why some prime must divide n.

    c. Does the argument show that there are infinitely many primes? Why or why not?

8. A class of 23 students was using square tiles to build rectangular shapes. Each student had more than 1 tile and each had a different number of tiles. Each student was able to build only one shape of rectangle. All tiles had to be used to build a rectangle and the rectangle could not have holes. For example, a 2 by 6 rectangle uses 12 tiles and is considered the same as a 6 by 2 rectangle but is different from a 3 by 4 rectangle. The class did the activity using the least number of tiles. How many tiles did the class use? Explore the various rectangles that could be made.

9. Explain why each of the following numbers is composite.

    a. $3 \cdot 5 \cdot 7 \cdot 11 \cdot 13$

    b. $(3 \cdot 4 \cdot 5 \cdot 6 \cdot 7 \cdot 8) + 2$

    c. $(3 \cdot 5 \cdot 7 \cdot 11 \cdot 13) + 5$

    d. $10! + 7$ (*Note:* $10! = 10 \cdot 9 \cdot 8 \cdot 7 \cdot 6 \cdot 5 \cdot 4 \cdot 3 \cdot 2 \cdot 1$.)

10. After a game of marbles with his three friends, Jacob said, "If only I had 1 more marble, I would have 4 times as many as Felipe, 5 times as many as Bella, and 7 times as many as Jessie." What is the least number of marbles Jacob could have had?

11. When students asked their teacher how old her children were, she said, "I have three children. The product of their ages is 72 and the sum of their ages is the number of this room." The children then asked for the door to be opened to verify the room number. Then Carly told the teacher she needed more information to solve the problem. The teacher said, "My oldest child is good at math." Then Carly announced the correct ages of her teacher's children. What are the ages of the teacher's children?

Open-Ended

12. **a.** In which of the following intervals are there more primes? Why?

    i. 0–99   **ii.** 100–199

    b. What is the longest string of consecutive composite numbers in the intervals?

    c. How many twin primes are there in each interval?

    d. What patterns, if any, do you see for any of the preceding questions? Predict what might happen in other intervals.

Cooperative Learning

13. There are 100 people waiting in line for a baseball spring training game. The manager gives each person a free hat and then asks them to participate in a contest where the people with their hats on at the end of the game win free admission. The manager asks the first person in line and then every person after that to put on their hat and then asks the second person in line and then every other person after that to take their hat off, every third person to change their status (if they had their hat on, they take it off and if they had their hat off they put it on), every fourth person to change their status, and so on. All 100 people played the game. Which people won free admission? Work in your group to come up with a strategy to solve this problem and write out the solution.

14. In the game *Catch the Divisors*, player A circles a number on the grid in blue and player B circles all the divisors of the number in red. Player A's score is the number they circled and player B's score is the sum of the divisors they circled. Once a number is circled it cannot be used again. The game is done when all numbers are circled and the winner is the player with the highest total score. Play the game in pairs and discuss winning strategies.

1	2	2	2	2	2	3
3	3	3	3	4	4	4
4	5	5	5	5	6	6
6	7	7	8	8	9	9
10	10	11	12	13	14	15
16	17	18	19	20	21	22
23	24	25	26	27	28	30
32	33	34	35	36	38	39
40	42	44	45	46	48	49
50	51	52	54	55	56	60

Connecting Mathematics to the Classroom

15. In order to test for divisibility by 12, one student checked to determine divisibility by 3 and 4; another checked for divisibility by 2 and 6. Are both students using a correct approach to divisibility by 12? Why or why not?

16. In the book *A Remainder of One* by Elinor J. Pinczes (1995), ant soldier Joe is part of the 25th squadron. If the squadron divides into 2, 3, 4, and 5 queues, how many soldiers are in each queue? Make all possible arrays with 25 ants and find the one without a remainder. Discuss how modeling this story can help students find a solution.

17. Mary says that her factor tree for 72 begins with 3 and 24 so her prime factors will be different from Larry's because he is going to start with 8 and 9. What do you tell Mary?

18. Bob says that to check whether a number is prime he just uses the divisibility rules he knows for 2, 3, 4, 5, 6, 8, and 10. He says if the number is not divisible by these numbers, then it is prime. How do you respond?

19. Joe says that every odd number greater than 3 can be written as the sum of two primes. To convince the class, he wrote $7 = 2 + 5, 5 = 2 + 3$, and $9 = 7 + 2$. How do you respond?

20. A sixth-grade student argues that there are infinitely many primes because "there is no end to numbers." How do you respond?

21. A student claims 1 is prime because it only has 1 and itself as factors. How do you respond?

Review Problems

22. Classify the following statements as true or false.
    a. 13 is a factor of 130.
    b. 1001 is a multiple of 11.
    c. $7 \mid 1001$ and $7 \nmid 12$ imply $7 \nmid (1001 - 12)$.

23. Check each of the following numbers for divisibility by 2, 3, 4, 5, 6, 7, 8, 9, 10, and 11.
    a. 438,162
    b. 2,345,678,910

24. Prove that if a number is divisible by 15, then it is divisible by 3.

National Assessments

National Assessment of Educational Progress (NAEP) Questions

A. If c and d are different prime numbers less than 10 and the sum $c + d$ is a composite number greater than 10, what is one possible pair of values for c and d?

$c =$ _____ $d =$ _____

B. If j and k are different prime numbers less than 10 and the sum $j + k$ is a prime number less than 10, what is one possible pair of values for j and k?

$j =$ _____ $k =$ _____

C. If s and t are different prime numbers greater than 10, explain why the sum $s + t$ cannot be a prime number.

$s =$ _____ $t =$ _____

NAEP, Grade 8, 2013

Which of the following true statements proves that 119 is not a prime number?
A. $17 \cdot 7 = 119$
B. $119 \cdot 1 = 119$
C. 119 is greater than 100.
D. 119 is an odd number.
E. 119 is not divisible by 3.

NAEP, Grade 8, 2011

4-3 Greatest Common Divisor and Least Common Multiple

4-3 Objectives

Students will be able to understand and explain

- The greatest common divisor and least common multiple of two or more whole numbers by using a variety of methods.

- Applications of GCD and LCM to word problems and their solutions.

- The Euclidean Algorithm in relation to the greatest common divisor.

CCSS In the grade 6 *Common Core Standards*, students

find the greatest common factor of two whole numbers less than or equal to 100 and the least common multiple of two whole numbers less than or equal to 12." Furthermore they are asked to "use the distributive property to express a sum of two whole numbers 1–100 with a common factor as a multiple of a sum of two whole numbers with no common factor. For example, express $36 + 8$ as $4(9 + 2)$. (p. 42)

Consider the following problem:

There are two fourth-grade classrooms at Haven Elementary School. Class 4-A has 24 students and class 4-B has 30 students. During recess, the two classes will play many games with each other, but they have to pick teams based on the following rules:

1. Teams must consist of students from the same class.
2. All teams must be of equal size.
3. Every student must be on exactly one team.
4. Teams should have as many students as possible.

How many teams can be made? How many students will be on each team?

The students could be in teams of 2, but this does not satisfy the condition of having the largest team possible. The number of students must divide both 24 and 30. (Why?). Numbers that divide both 24 and 30 are 1, 2, 3, and 6. The greatest of these numbers is 6, so there should be 6 students on each team. Class 4-A would have 4 teams and class 4-B would have 5 teams. In this problem, we have found the greatest number that divides both 24 and 30, that is, the *greatest common divisor* (GCD) of 24 and 30. We denote this as $GCD(24, 30) = 6$. Another name for the greatest common divisor is the *greatest common factor* (GCF).

> **Definition**
>
> The **greatest common divisor (GCD)** or the **greatest common factor (GCF)** of two whole numbers a and b, not both 0, is the greatest whole number that divides both a and b.

We provide several methods for finding GCDs.

Colored Rods Method

We can build a model of two or more nonzero whole numbers with colored rods to determine their GCD. For example, find the GCD of 6 and 8 using the 6 rod and the 8 rod, as in Figure 11.

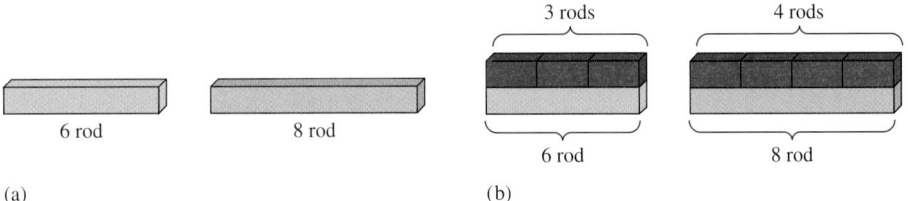

(a)   (b)

Figure 11

To find the GCD of 6 and 8, we must find the longest rod such that we can use multiples of that rod to build both the 6 rod and the 8 rod. The 2 rods can be used to build both the 6 and 8 rods, as shown in Figure 11(b); the 3 rods can be used to build the 6 rod but not the 8 rod; the 4 rods can be used to build the 8 rod but not the 6 rod; the 5 rods can be used to build neither; and the 6 rods cannot be used to build the 8 rod. Therefore, the GCD of 6 and 8 is 2. We denote this as $GCD(6, 8) = 2$.

The Intersection of Sets Method

In the *intersection of sets* method, we list all members of the set of whole number divisors of the two numbers, then find the set of all *common divisors*, and, finally, pick the *greatest* element in that set. For example, to find the GCD of 20 and 32, we write the sets of divisors of 20 and 32, denoted by D_{20} and D_{32}, respectively.

$$D_{20} = \{1, 2, 4, 5, 10, 20\}$$

$$D_{32} = \{1, 2, 4, 8, 16, 32\}$$

The set of all common whole number divisors of 20 and 32 is

$$D_{20} \cap D_{32} = \{1, 2, 4\}.$$

Because the greatest number in the set of common whole number divisors is 4, $GCD(20, 32) = 4$.

▶ **NOW TRY THIS 6**

The Venn diagram in Figure 12 shows the factors of 24 and 40.

a. What is the meaning of each of the shaded regions shown?

b. Which factor is the GCD of 24 and 40?

c. Draw a similar Venn diagram to find the GCD of 36 and 44.

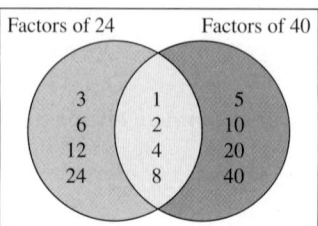

Figure 12

The Prime Factorization Method

The intersection of sets method is rather time consuming and tedious if the numbers have many divisors. Another, more efficient, method is the *prime factorization method*. To find GCD(180, 168), we first consider the prime factorization of the numbers:

$$180 = 2 \cdot 2 \cdot 3 \cdot 3 \cdot 5 = (2^2 \cdot 3)3 \cdot 5$$

and

$$168 = 2 \cdot 2 \cdot 2 \cdot 3 \cdot 7 = (2^2 \cdot 3)2 \cdot 7$$

We see that 180 and 168 have two factors of 2 and one of 3 in common. These common primes divide both 180 and 168. In fact, the only numbers other than 1 that divide both 180 and 168 must have no more than two 2s and one 3 and no other prime factors in their prime factorizations. The possible common divisors are $1, 2, 2^2, 3, 2 \cdot 3$, and $2^2 \cdot 3$. Hence, the greatest common divisor of 180 and 168 is $2^2 \cdot 3$ or 12. The procedure for finding the GCD of two or more numbers by using the prime factorization method is summarized as follows:

> *To find the GCD of two or more nonzero whole numbers, first find the prime factorizations of the given numbers and then identify each common prime factor of the given numbers. The GCD is the product of the common prime factors, each raised to the lowest power of that prime that occurs in any of the prime factorizations.*

If we apply the prime factorization technique to finding GCD(4, 9), we see that 4 and 9 have no common prime factors. But that does not mean there is no GCD. We still have 1 as a common divisor, so GCD(4, 9) = 1. Numbers, such as 4 and 9, whose GCD is 1 are said to be **relatively prime**. Both the intersection of sets method and the prime factorization method are found on the student page shown on page 205.

School Book Page   Greatest Common Factor

4-4   Greatest Common Factor

Check Skills You'll Need

1. **Vocabulary Review** Write a sentence about math using the words *factor* and *product*.

Find the prime factorization.

2. 45
3. 21
4. 99

GO for Help
Lesson 4-3

What You'll Learn

To find the GCF of two or more numbers

◀)) **New Vocabulary** common factor, greatest common factor (GCF)

Why Learn This?

A stamp club president distributes equally one set of 18 stamps and another set of 30 stamps to members present at a meeting. No stamps are left over. You can use factors to find the greatest possible number of club members at the meeting.

To find the greatest possible number of club members, you can find the factors that 18 and 30 share. A factor that two or more numbers share is a **common factor**.

The **greatest common factor (GCF)** of two or more numbers is the greatest factor shared by all the numbers. You can find the GCF of two numbers by listing their factors.

EXAMPLE   Using Lists of Factors

① Find the greatest common factor of 18 and 30.

List the factors of 18 and the factors of 30. Then circle the common factors.

Factors of 18: ①, ②, ③, ⑥, 9, 18   ← The common factors
Factors of 30: ①, ②, ③, 5, ⑥, 10, 15, 30   are 1, 2, 3, and 6.

The greatest common factor (GCF) is 6.

EXAMPLE   Using Factor Trees

③ A volunteer divides 18 adults, 27 girls, and 36 boys into groups to clean up the park. He divides the adults, girls, and boys equally among the groups. What is the largest possible number of groups he can make?

Make a factor tree for each number.

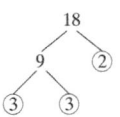 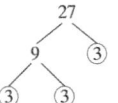 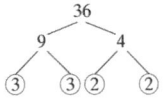

18 = ③ × ③ × 2   ← Write the prime factorization
27 = 3 × 3 × 3   for each number.
36 = ③ × ③ × 2 × 2
                              ← Identify common factors.

The GCF of 18, 27, and 36 is 9. The largest number of groups is 9.

EXAMPLE 12

Find each of the following:

    a. $\text{GCD}(108, 72)$ **b.** $\text{GCD}(0, 13)$

    c. $\text{GCD}(x, y)$ if $x = 2^3 \cdot 7^2 \cdot 11 \cdot 13$ and $y = 2 \cdot 7^3 \cdot 13 \cdot 17$

    d. $\text{GCD}(x, y, z)$ if $z = 2^2 \cdot 7$, using x and y from part (c)

    e. $\text{GCD}(x, y)$, where $x = 5^4 \cdot 13^{10}$ and $y = 3^{10} \cdot 11^{20}$

Solution

    a. Since $108 = 2^2 \cdot 3^3$ and $72 = 2^3 \cdot 3^2$, it follows that $\text{GCD}(108, 72) = 2^2 \cdot 3^2 = 36$.

    b. Because $13 \mid 0$ and $13 \mid 13$, it follows that $\text{GCD}(0, 13) = 13$.

    c. $\text{GCD}(x, y) = 2 \cdot 7^2 \cdot 13 = 1274$.

    d. Because $x = 2^3 \cdot 7^2 \cdot 11 \cdot 13$, $y = 2 \cdot 7^3 \cdot 13 \cdot 17$, and $z = 2^2 \cdot 7$, the $\text{GCD}(x, y, z) = 2 \cdot 7 = 14$. Notice that $\text{GCD}(x, y, z)$ can also be obtained by finding the GCD of z and 1274, the answer from part (c).

    e. Because x and y have no common prime factors, $\text{GCD}(x, y) = 1$.

Calculator Method

Calculators with a $\boxed{\text{Simp}}$ key can be used to find the GCD of two numbers. For example, to find $\text{GCD}(120, 180)$, use the following sequence of buttons to start: First, press $\boxed{1}\boxed{2}\boxed{0}\boxed{/}\boxed{1}\boxed{8}\boxed{0}$ $\boxed{\text{Simp}}\boxed{=}$ to obtain the display $\boxed{\text{N/D} \rightarrow \text{n/d } 60/90}$. By pressing the $\boxed{x \circ y}$ button, we see $\boxed{2}$ on the display as a common divisor of 120 and 180. By pressing the $\boxed{x \circ y}$ button again and pressing $\boxed{\text{Simp}}\boxed{=}\boxed{x \circ y}$, we see 2 again as a factor. The process is repeated to reveal 3 and 5 as other common factors. The GCD of 120 and 180 is the product of the common prime factors $2 \cdot 2 \cdot 3 \cdot 5$, or 60.

    Some calculators have a built-in GCD feature, probably found in the *MATH* menu. With this feature, select GCD and enter the numbers separated by a comma and enclosed within parentheses; for example, $\text{GCD}(120, 180)$. When the $\boxed{=}$ is pressed, the GCD of 60 will be displayed.

Euclidean Algorithm Method

For large numbers, a more efficient method than factorization for finding the GCD is available. For example, suppose we want to find $\text{GCD}(676, 221)$. If we could find two smaller numbers whose GCD is the same as $\text{GCD}(676, 221)$, the task would be easier. From Theorem 4-2(c), every divisor of 676 and 221 is also a divisor of $676 - 221$ and 221. Conversely, every divisor of $676 - 221$ and 221 is also a divisor of 676 and 221. Thus, the set of all the common divisors of 676 and 221 is the same as the set of all common divisors of $676 - 221$ and 221. Consequently, $\text{GCD}(676, 221) = \text{GCD}(676 - 221, 221)$. This process can be continued to subtract three 221s from 676 so that $\text{GCD}(676, 221) = \text{GCD}(676 - 3 \cdot 221, 221) = \text{GCD}(13, 221)$. Because 13 is a prime, we can conclude now that the GCD is either 1 or 13. Since $13 \mid 221$, $\text{GCD}(13, 221) = 13$. However, it is often advantageous to continue the process until the remainder 0 is obtained: $\text{GCD}(13, 221) = \text{GCD}(221, 13) = \text{GCD}(221 - 17 \cdot 13, 13) = \text{GCD}(0, 13) = 13$. Consequently $\text{GCD}(676, 221) = 13$. To determine how many 221s can be subtracted from 676, and how many 13s from 221, we could have divided as follows:

$$\begin{array}{cc} 3 \text{ R } 13 & 17 \text{ R } 0 \\ 221\overline{)676} & 13\overline{)221} \end{array}$$

When 0 is reached as a remainder, the divisions are complete. Based on this illustration, the following generalization is given in Theorem 4-17.

> **Theorem 4-17**
>
> If a and b are any whole numbers with $b \neq 0$ and $a \geq b$, then $\text{GCD}(a, b) = \text{GCD}(r, b)$, where r is the remainder when a is divided by b.

Because $GCD(x, y) = GCD(y, x)$ for all whole numbers x and y, not both 0, Theorem 4-17 can be written

$$GCD(a, b) = GCD(b, r).$$

We have seen that $GCD(676, 221) = GCD(676 - 221, 221)$

$$= GCD(676 - 3 \cdot 221, 221).$$

This is true in general, as stated in Theorem 4-18:

Theorem 4-18

If a and b are any nonzero whole numbers and $a \geq b$, then:

a. $GCD(a, b) = GCD(a - b, b)$
b. $GCD(a, b) = GCD(a - kb, b)$ for any whole number k for which $a - kb$ is a whole number.

Finding the GCD of two numbers by repeatedly using Theorem 4-17 until the remainder 0 is reached is referred to as the **Euclidean algorithm**. This method is found in Book VII of Euclid's *Elements* (300 BCE). Figure 13 is a flowchart for using the Euclidean algorithm.

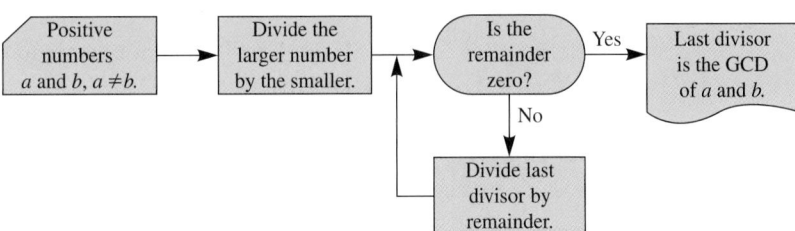

Figure 13

EXAMPLE 13

Use the Euclidean algorithm to find $GCD(10764, 2300)$.

Solution

$$
\begin{array}{r}
4 \\
2300)\overline{10764} \\
-9200 \\
\hline
1564
\end{array}
$$
Thus, $GCD(10764, 2300) = GCD(2300, 1564)$.

$$
\begin{array}{r}
1 \\
1564)\overline{2300} \\
-1564 \\
\hline
736
\end{array}
$$
Thus, $GCD(2300, 1564) = GCD(1564, 736)$.

$$
\begin{array}{r}
2 \\
736)\overline{1564} \\
-1472 \\
\hline
92
\end{array}
$$
Thus, $GCD(1564, 736) = GCD(736, 92)$.

$$
\begin{array}{r}
8 \\
92)\overline{736} \\
-736 \\
\hline
0
\end{array}
$$
Thus, $GCD(736, 92) = GCD(92, 0)$.

Because $GCD(92, 0) = 92$, it follows that $GCD(10764, 2300) = 92$.

The procedure for finding the GCD by using the Euclidean algorithm can be stopped at any step at which the GCD is obvious. Sometimes shortcuts can be used to find the GCD of two or more numbers, as seen in the following example.

EXAMPLE 14

Find each of the following:

a. GCD(134791, 6341, 6339)
b. The GCD of any two consecutive whole numbers

Solution

a. Any common divisor of three numbers is also a common divisor of any two of them (why?). Consequently, the GCD of three numbers cannot be greater than the GCD of any two of the numbers. The numbers 6341 and 6339 are close to each other, and therefore it is easy to find their GCD:

$$GCD(6341, 6339) = GCD(6341 - 6339, 6339)$$
$$= GCD(2, 6339)$$
$$= 1$$

Because GCD(134791, 6341, 6339) cannot be greater than 1, it follows that it must equal 1.

b. GCD(4, 5) = 1, GCD(5, 6) = 1, GCD(6, 7) = 1, and GCD(99, 100) = 1. It seems that the GCD of any two consecutive whole numbers is 1. To justify this conjecture, we show that for all whole numbers n, GCD($n, n + 1$) = 1. Using Theorem 4-18 we have:

$$GCD(n, n + 1) = GCD(n + 1, n) = GCD(n + 1 - n, n)$$
$$= GCD(1, n)$$
$$= 1$$

Activity Manual

Use *Pool Factors* to apply GCD, LCM, and relatively prime numbers in a geometric problem situation.

Least Common Multiple

Consider the following problem:

It is Morgan's birthday and we need to buy cups and plates for the party. Plastic cups are sold in packages of 8 and paper plates are sold in packages of 12. What is the least number of each we need to buy to have an equal number of plates and cups? The number of cups that we need to buy are the multiples of 8, that is, 8, 16, 24, 32, 40, ... Likewise the number of plates we need to buy are multiples of 12, that is, 12, 24, 36, 48, ... In this problem we are interested in the least number we need to buy, which is 24. So, we need to buy 3 packages of cups and 2 packages of plates. We found the **least common multiple (LCM)** of 8 and 12, that is LCM(8, 12) = 24.

> **Definition**
> The **least common multiple (LCM)** of two nonzero whole numbers a and b is the least nonzero whole number that is simultaneously a multiple of a and a multiple of b.

As with GCDs, there are several methods for finding least common multiples.

Number Line Method

A number line can be used to find the LCM of two numbers. For example, to find $LCM(3, 4)$, we show the multiples of 3 and 4 on the number line using intervals of 3 and 4, as shown in Figure 14.

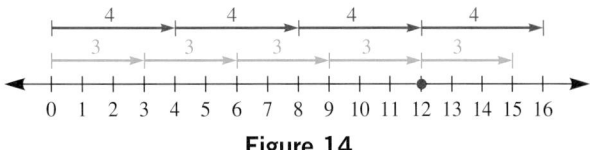

Figure 14

Beginning at 0, the arrows do not coincide until the point 12 on the number line. If the line were continued, the arrows would coincide again at 24, 36, 48, and so on. There are an infinite number of common multiples of 3 and 4, but the least common multiple is 12. This number line approach is instructive and promotes understanding but is not practical for large numbers.

Colored Rods Method

Colored rods are used to determine the LCM of two numbers. For example, consider the 3 rod and the 4 rod in Figure 15(a). Build trains of 3 rods and 4 rods until they are the same length, as shown in Figure 15(b). The LCM is the common length of the train.

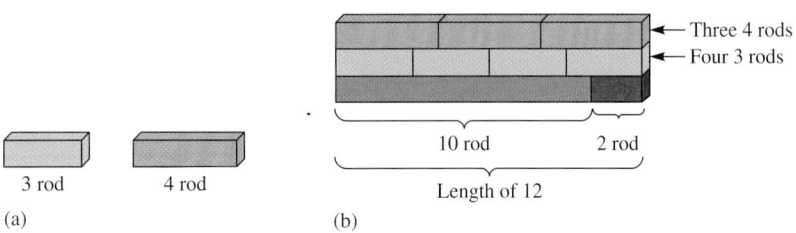

Figure 15

The Intersection of Sets Method

In the *intersection of sets* method, we first find the set of all positive *multiples* of both the first and second numbers, then find the set of all *common multiples* of both numbers, and finally pick the *least* element in that set. For example, to find the LCM of 8 and 12, we denote the sets of nonzero whole number multiples of 8 and 12 by M_8 and M_{12}, respectively.

$$M_8 = \{8, 16, 24, 32, 40, 48, 56, 64, 72, \dots\}$$

$$M_{12} = \{12, 24, 36, 48, 60, 72, 84, 96, 108, \dots\}$$

The set of common multiples is

$$M_8 \cap M_{12} = \{24, 48, 72, \dots\}.$$

Because the least number in $M_8 \cap M_{12}$ is 24, the LCM of 8 and 12 is 24, or $LCM(8, 12) = 24$.

▶ **NOW TRY THIS 7**

NTT 7: Answers can be found in Answers at the back of the book.

Draw a Venn diagram showing M_8 and M_{12} and show how to find $LCM(8, 12)$ using the diagram.

The Prime Factorization Method

The intersection of sets method for finding the LCM is often lengthy, especially when it is used to find the LCM of three or more nonzero whole numbers. Another, more efficient, method for finding the LCM of several numbers is the *prime factorization method*. For example, to find LCM$(40, 12)$, we first find the prime factorizations of 40 and 12: $40 = 2^3 \cdot 5$ and $12 = 2^2 \cdot 3$.

If $m =$ LCM$(40, 12)$, then m is a multiple of 40 and must contain both 2^3 and 5 as factors. Also, m is a multiple of 12 and must contain 2^2 and 3 as factors. Since 2^3 is a multiple of 2^2, then $m = 2^3 \cdot 5 \cdot 3 = 120$. In general, we have the following:

> *To find the LCM of two nonzero whole numbers, we first find the prime factorization of each number. Then we take each of the primes that are factors of either of the given numbers. The LCM is the product of these primes, each raised to the greatest power of the prime that occurs in either of the prime factorizations.*

EXAMPLE 15

Find the LCM of 2520 and 10,530.

Solution

$$2520 = 2^3 \cdot 3^2 \cdot 5 \cdot 7$$
$$10{,}530 = 2 \cdot 3^4 \cdot 5 \cdot 13$$
$$\text{LCM}(2520, 10{,}530) = 2^3 \cdot 3^4 \cdot 5 \cdot 7 \cdot 13 = 294{,}840$$

The prime factorization method can also be used to find the LCM of more than two numbers. For example, to find LCM$(12, 108, 120)$, we proceed as follows:

$$12 = 2^2 \cdot 3$$
$$108 = 2^2 \cdot 3^3$$
$$120 = 2^3 \cdot 3 \cdot 5$$

Then, LCM$(12, 108, 120) = 2^3 \cdot 3^3 \cdot 5 = 1080$.

The GCD-LCM Product Method

To see the connection between the GCD and LCM, we consider the GCD and LCM of 24 and 30. The prime factorizations of these numbers are

$$24 = 2^3 \cdot 3$$
$$30 = 2 \cdot 3 \cdot 5.$$

Figure 16 shows a diagram with the prime factors.

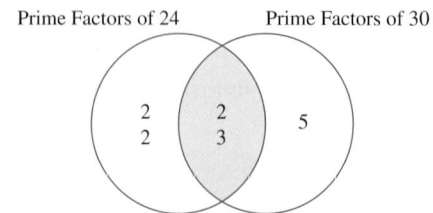

Prime Factors of 24   Prime Factors of 30

Figure 16

GCD$(24, 30) = 2 \cdot 3$ and is the product of the factors in the shaded region, and LCM$(24, 30) = 2^3 \cdot 3 \cdot 5$ is the product of the prime factors in the combined regions. Also:

$$\text{GCD}(24, 30) \cdot \text{LCM}(24, 30) = (2 \cdot 3)(2^3 \cdot 3 \cdot 5) = (2^3 \cdot 3)(2 \cdot 3 \cdot 5) = 24 \cdot 30$$

This shows that the product of the GCD and LCM of 24 and 30 is equal to $24 \cdot 30$. In general, the connection between the GCD and LCM of any pair of nonzero whole numbers is given by Theorem 4-19.

Theorem 4-19

For any two nonzero whole numbers a and b,

$$\text{GCD}(a, b) \cdot \text{LCM}(a, b) = ab.$$

Theorem 4-19 can be justified in several ways. A specific example suggesting how the theorem might be proved is given below:

$$\text{Let} \quad a = 5^{13} \cdot 7^{20} \cdot 11^4 \quad \text{and} \quad b = 5^{10} \cdot 7^{25} \cdot 11^6 \cdot 13.$$

$$\text{Then, } \text{LCM}(a, b) = 5^{13} \cdot 7^{25} \cdot 11^6 \cdot 13 \quad \text{and} \quad \text{GCD}(a, b) = 5^{10} \cdot 7^{20} \cdot 11^4.$$

We have $\text{LCM}(a, b) \cdot \text{GCD}(a, b) = 5^{13+10} \cdot 7^{25+20} \cdot 11^{6+4} \cdot 13$ and $ab = 5^{13+10} \cdot 7^{20+25} \cdot 11^{6+4} \cdot 13$.

For the preceding values of a and b, Theorem 4-19 is true. However, in general we reason as follows: in the product $\text{LCM}(a, b) \cdot \text{GCD}(a, b)$, we have all the powers of the primes appearing in a or in b, because for the LCM we take the greater of the powers of the common primes and for the GCD the lesser. Also, ab contains all the powers of the primes appearing in a or b. Hence, Theorem 4-19 is true in general.

The Euclidean Algorithm Method

Theorem 4-19 is useful for finding the LCM of two numbers a and b when their prime factorizations are not easy to find. $\text{GCD}(a, b)$ can be found by the Euclidean algorithm, the product ab can be found by multiplication, and $\text{LCM}(a, b)$ can be found by division.

EXAMPLE 16

a. Find $\text{LCM}(731, 952)$.
b. If $b \mid a$, find $\text{LCM}(a, b)$ in terms of a or b.

Solution

a. By the Euclidean algorithm, $\text{GCD}(731, 952) = 17$. By Theorem 4-19,

$$17 \cdot \text{LCM}(731, 952) = 731 \cdot 952.$$

Consequently,

$$\text{LCM}(731, 952) = \frac{731 \cdot 952}{17} = 40{,}936.$$

b. Because $b \mid a$, a is a multiple of b; thus $\text{LCM}(a, b) = a$.

The Division-by-Primes Method

Another procedure for finding the LCM of several nonzero whole numbers involves *division by primes*. For example, to find $\text{LCM}(12, 75, 120)$, start with the least prime that divides at least one of the given numbers and divide as follows:

$$2 \lfloor \underline{12, 75, 120} $$
$$6, 75, \ \ 60$$

Because 2 does not divide 75, we simply bring down the 75. To obtain the LCM using this procedure, we continue the division process until the row of answers consists of relatively prime numbers.

$$
\begin{array}{r|rrr}
2 & 12, & 75, & 120 \\
\hline
2 & 6, & 75, & 60 \\
\hline
2 & 3, & 75, & 30 \\
\hline
3 & 3, & 75, & 15 \\
\hline
5 & 1, & 25, & 5 \\
\hline
& 1, & 5, & 1
\end{array}
$$

Thus, $\text{LCM}(12, 75, 120) = 2 \cdot 2 \cdot 2 \cdot 3 \cdot 5 \cdot 1 \cdot 5 \cdot 1 = 2^3 \cdot 3 \cdot 5^2 = 600$.

Assessment 4-3A

1. Use colored rods to find the GCD and the LCM of 6 and 8. *
2. Find the GCD and the LCM for each of the following groups of numbers using the intersection-of-sets method.
   a. 18 and 12 *   b. 20 and 36 *
   c. 8, 24, and 64 *   d. 7 and 9 *
3. Find the GCD and the LCM for each of the following groups of numbers using the prime factorization method.
   a. 132 and 504 *   b. 65 and 1690 *
   c. 96, 900, and 630 *   d. 108 and 360 *
4. Find the GCD for each of the following groups of numbers using the Euclidean algorithm.
   a. 220 and 2924 *   b. 14,595 and 10,856 *
5. Find the LCM for each of the following groups of numbers using any method.
   a. 24 and 36 *
   b. 72, 90, and 96 *
   c. 90, 105, and 315 *
   d. 16^{100} and 25^{100} *
6. The product of two numbers is 1734 and their GCD is 17. Find their LCM.   102
7. The GCD of two numbers is 19 and their LCM is 228. One of the numbers is 57. Find the other number.   76
8. Assume a and b are natural numbers and answer the following questions.
   a. If $\text{GCD}(a, b) = 1$, find $\text{LCM}(a, b)$. $\text{LCM}(a, b) = ab$
   b. Find $\text{GCD}(a, a)$ and $\text{LCM}(a, a)$. *
   c. Find $\text{GCD}(a^2, a)$ and $\text{LCM}(a^2, a)$. *
   d. If $a \mid b$, find $\text{GCD}(a, b)$ and $\text{LCM}(a, b)$. *
9. Classify each of the following statements as true or false where a and b are whole numbers.
   a. If $\text{GCD}(a, b) = 1$, then a and b cannot both be even.   True
   b. If $\text{GCD}(a, b) = 2$, then both a and b are even.   True
   c. If a and b are even, then $\text{GCD}(a, b) = 2$.   False
10. To find $\text{GCD}(24, 20, 12)$, it is possible to find $\text{GCD}(24, 20)$, which is 4, and then find $\text{GCD}(4, 12)$, which is 4. Use this approach and the Euclidean algorithm to compute the following.
    a. $\text{GCD}(120, 75, 105)$ 15   b. $\text{GCD}(34578, 4618, 4619)$ 1

11. Show that 97,219,988,751 and 4 are relatively prime. *
12. Draw Venn diagrams to show the prime factors for each of the following sets of three numbers.
    a. 10, 15, 60 *   b. 8, 16, 24 *
13. Find three pairs (a, b) such that $\text{LCM}(a, b) = 48$. *
14. Find all whole numbers x such that $\text{GCD}(49, x) = 1$ and $1 \le x \le 49$.   All, except 7, 14, 21, 28, 35, 42, 49
15. In Quinn's dormitory room, there are three snooze-alarm clocks, each of which is set at a different time. Clock A goes off every 15 min, clock B goes off every 40 min, and clock C goes off every 60 min. If all three clocks go off at 6:00 A.M., answer the following questions.
    a. How long will it be before the clocks go off simultaneously again after 6:00 A.M.?   120 minutes
    b. Would the answer to (a) be different if clock B went off every 15 min and clock A went off every 40 min?   No
16. A company is running a promotion on Facebook. Every twelfth and thirteenth "like" earns a badge and every twentieth "like" wins free movie tickets. Which "like" will be first to get two badges and a free movie ticket?   780th "like"
17. If there were to be 9 boys and 6 girls at a party and the host wanted each to be given exactly the same number of candies that could be bought in packages containing 12 candies, what is the fewest number of packages that could be bought? *
18. Three motorcyclists ride around a circular course starting at the same place and the same time. The first passes the starting point every 12 min, the second every 18 min, and the third every 16 min. After how many minutes will all three pass the starting point again at the same time? Explain your reasoning. *
19. Anna has made 42 chocolate chip cookies and 54 sugar cookies. She wants to put them in bags for her friends with the same number of cookies in each bag, the same kind of cookies in each bag, and no cookies left over. What is the greatest number of cookies she can put in each bag? *
20. The front wheel of a tricycle has a circumference of 100 in. and the back wheels have a circumference of 18 in. If points P and Q are both touching the sidewalk when Jose starts to ride, how many ft will the tricycle

travel before P and Q first touch the sidewalk at the same time again?   900 in. = 75 ft

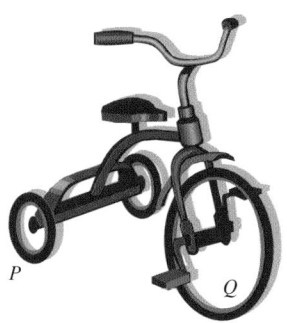

P   Q

21. Jazz has 72 yd of red ribbon and 42 yd of blue ribbon. What are the largest possible pieces of ribbon Jazz can cut so that each piece is the same length and all the ribbon is used?   6 yd

Assessment 4-3B

1. Use colored rods to find the GCD and the LCM of 4 and 10.   *
2. Find the GCD and the LCM for each of the following groups of numbers using the intersection-of-sets method.
   a. 12 and 30   *   **b.** 18 and 58   *
   c. 6, 18, and 24   *   **d.** 36 and 13   *
3. Find the GCD and the LCM for each of the following groups of numbers using the prime factorization method.
   a. 11 and 19   *   **b.** 140 and 320   *
   c. 800, 75, and 450   *   **d.** 103 and 320   *
4. Find the GCD for each of the following groups of numbers using the Euclidean algorithm.
   a. 14,560 and 8250   10
   b. 8424 and 2520   72
5. Find the LCM for each of the following groups of numbers using any method.
   a. 25 and 36   900
   b. 82, 90, and 50   18,450
   c. 80, 105, and 315   5040
   d. 8^{100} and 50^{100} $2^{300} \cdot 5^{200}$
6. The product of two numbers is 5880 and their GCD is 14. Find their LCM.   420
7. The GCD of two numbers is 11 and their LCM is 330. One of the numbers is 66. Find the other number.   55
8. Assume a and b are natural numbers and answer the following questions.
   a. If a and b are two different primes, find $GCD(a, b)$ and $LCM(a, b)$. $GCD(a, b) = 1$; $LCM(a, b) = ab$
   b. What is the relationship between a and b if $GCD(a, b) = a$? $a \mid b$
   c. What is the relationship between a and b if $LCM(a, b) = a$? $b \mid a$
9. Classify each of the following statements as true or false where a and b are distinct natural numbers.
   a. $LCM(a, b) \mid GCD(a, b)$ False
   b. $LCM(a, b) \mid ab$ True
   c. $GCD(a, b) \leq a$ True
   d. $LCM(a, b) \geq a$ True
10. To find $GCD(24, 20, 12)$, it is possible to find $GCD(24, 20)$, which is 4, and then find $GCD(4,12)$, which is 4. Use this approach and the Euclidean algorithm to find the following.
    a. $GCD(180, 240, 306)$ 6
    b. $GCD(5284, 1250, 1280)$ 2
11. Show that 181,345,913 and 11 are relatively prime.   *
12. Draw Venn diagrams to show the prime factors for each of the following sets of three numbers.
    a. 12, 14, 70   *   **b.** 6, 8, 18   *
13. Find three pairs (a, b) such that $LCM(a, b) = 60$.   *
14. Find all whole numbers x such that $GCD(25, x) = 1$ and $1 \leq x \leq 25$.   All except: 5, 10, 15, 20, 25
15. A light display has three colored lights, each of which flashes on for an instant at regular intervals. The yellow one flashes 15 times per minute, the blue one flashes 6 times per minute, and the red one flashes on 12 times per minute. You see all three lights flash on simultaneously. How much longer must you wait before the three lights flash on simultaneously again?   20 seconds
16. A movie rental store gives a free popcorn to every 15th customer and a free movie rental to every 40th customer. Which customer was the first to win both prizes?   *
17. Brian purchases 245 white bouncy balls, 238 yellow bouncy balls, and 84 orange bouncy balls. He asked his son to divide them up into bags, so that each bag of balls had at least one of each color in them, and that each bag had the same number of total balls, and that there were no balls left over. What is the greatest number of balls he can put into each bag?   81 balls
18. A college runs two different bus routes starting at 7:00 A.M. Route A takes 75 min, while route B takes 90 min. If they take off from the same location, when will both busses be there at that same location again?   *
19. By selling cookies at 24¢ each, Jose made enough money to buy several cans of pop costing 45¢ per can. If he had no money left over after buying the pop, what is the least number of cookies he could have sold?   15 cookies

20. Determine how many complete revolutions each gear in the following diagram must make before the red arrows are lined up again.   Gear 1: 3; Gear 2: 5; Gear 3: 2

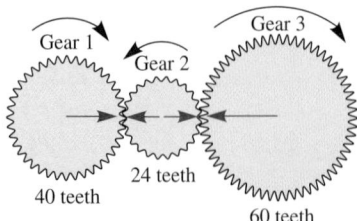

Gear 1
Gear 2
Gear 3
40 teeth
24 teeth
60 teeth

21. Kobe has collected 300 football cards and 264 baseball cards. He wants to divide them into piles so that each pile has only one type of card, there is the same number of cards in each pile, and each pile has the greatest possible number of cards. How many cards will be in each pile?   12 cards

Mathematical Connections 4-3

Answers to Mathematical Connections can be found in the Answers section at the back of the book.

Reasoning

1. Can two nonzero whole numbers have a greatest common multiple? Explain your answer.

2. Is it true that $GCD(a, b, c) \cdot LCM(a, b, c) = abc$? Explain your answer.

3. Suppose that $GCD(a, b, c) = 1$. Is it necessarily true that $GCD(a, b) = GCD(b, c) = 1$? Explain your reasoning.

4. Suppose that $GCD(a, b) = GCD(b, c) = 2$. Does that always imply that $GCD(a, b, c) = 2$? Justify your answer.

5. Is it true that every common divisor of two nonzero whole numbers a and b is a divisor of the $GCD(a, b)$? Explain your answer.

6. How can you tell from the prime factorization of two numbers if their LCM equals the product of the numbers? Explain your reasoning.

7. Can the LCM of two nonzero whole numbers ever be greater than the product of the two numbers? Explain your reasoning.

Open-Ended

8. Find three pairs of numbers for which the LCM of the numbers in a pair is less than the product of the two numbers.

9. Describe infinitely pairs of numbers whose GCD is equal to the following numbers.
   a. 2   **b.** 6   **c.** 91

10. A large gear is used to turn a smaller gear. If the larger gear makes 72 revolutions per minute and the smaller gear makes 1500 revolutions per minute, how many teeth does each gear have? Give three different possibilities. What is the least number of teeth possible?

Cooperative Learning

11. a. In your group, discuss whether the Euclidean algorithm for finding the GCD of two numbers should be introduced in middle school (To all students? To some?). Why or why not?
   b. If you decide that it should be introduced in middle school, discuss how it should be introduced. Report your group's decision to the class.

Connecting Mathematics to the Classroom

12. Describe to a sixth-grade student the difference between a divisor and multiple.

13. Eleanor claims that the $GCD(0, a) = 0$. Is she correct? What does she understand about GCD? What does she not understand?

14. Aiko says to find the LCM you can just multiply the two numbers. As a teacher, how do you respond?

15. A student wants to know how many whole numbers between 1 and 10,000 inclusive are either multiples of 3 or multiples of 5. She wonders if it is correct to find the number of those whole numbers that are multiples of 3 and add the number of those that are multiples of 5. How do you respond?

Review Problems

16. Find the greatest digit that makes the following statements true.
   a. $3 \,|\, 83\_51$ **b.** $11 \,|\, 8\_691$ **c.** $23 \,|\, 103\_6$

17. Find the prime factorization of the following numbers.
   a. 17,496   **b.** 32,715   **c.** $2^4 \cdot 8^2 \cdot 27^3$

18. Is 2223 prime? Justify your answer.

19. Find a number that has exactly five prime factors.

20. Find the least positive number that is divisible by 2, 4, 6, 8, and 10.

21. What is the greatest prime that must be used to determine if 3359 is prime?

National Assessments

National Assessment of Educational Progress (NAEP) Question

The least common multiple of 8, 12, and a third number is 120. Which of the following could be the third number?

A. 15
B. 16
C. 24
D. 32
E. 48

NAEP, Grade 8, 1990

Hint for Solving the Preliminary Problem

Try to find in how many days two cycles peak before finding when all three cycles peak again.

Chapter 4 Summary

KEY CONCEPTS	DEFINITIONS, DESCRIPTIONS, AND THEOREMS
Section 4-1	
Even whole number (p. 175)	A whole number that has remainder 0 when divided by 2.
Odd whole number (p. 175)	A whole number that has remainder 1 when divided by 2.
Divides (p. 175)	For any whole numbers a and b, where $b \neq 0$, b divides a (written $b \mid a$), if, and only if, there is a unique whole number q such that $a = bq$. If a and b are any whole numbers and $b \neq 0$, then b does *not* divide a, written $b \nmid a$ if, and only if, the remainder when a is divided by b is not 0.
Terms for divisibility (p. 177)	If $b \mid a$, then • b *divides* a. • b is a *factor* of a. • b is a *divisor* of a. • a is *divisible by* b. • a is a *multiple* of b.
Divisibility theorems (p. 177)	*Theorem:* For any whole numbers a and d, if $d \mid a$ and n is any whole number, then $d \mid na$. *Theorem:* For any whole numbers a, b, and d, • If $d \mid a$ and $d \mid b$, then $d \mid (a + b)$. • If $d \mid a$ and $d \nmid b$, then $d \nmid (a + b)$. • If $d \mid a$, $d \mid b$, and $a > b$, then $d \mid (a - b)$. • If $d \mid a$, $d \nmid b$, and $a > b$, then $d \nmid (a - b)$. • If $d \nmid a$, $d \mid b$, and $a > b$, then $d \nmid (a - b)$.
Divisibility rules (p. 179)	*Divisibility Tests* *for 2:* A whole number is divisible by 2 if, and only if, its units digits is divisible by 2; that is if, and only if, the units digit is even. *for 5:* A whole number is divisible by 5 if, and only if, its units digits is divisible by 5; that is if, and only if, the units digit is 0 or 5. *for 10:* A whole number is divisible by 10 if, and only if, its units digits is divisible by 10; that is if, and only if, the units digit is 0. *for 4:* A whole number is divisible by 4 if, and only if, the last two digits of the number represent a number divisible by 4. *for 8* A whole number is divisible by 8 if, and only if, the last three digits of the number represent a number divisible by 8. *for 3:* A whole number is divisible by 3 if, and only if, the sum of its digits is divisible by 3. *for 9* A whole number is divisible by 9 if, and only if, the sum of its digits is divisible by 9. *for 11:* A whole number is divisible by 11 if, and only if, the sum of the digits in the places that are even powers of 10 minus the sum of the digits in the places that are odd powers of 10 is divisible by 11. (If the sums are different, then subtract the smaller from the greater.) *for 6:* A whole number is divisible by 6 if, and only if, the number is divisible by 2 and 3.

Section 4-2

Prime number (p. 190)	Any whole number with exactly two divisors.
Composite number (p. 190)	Any whole number greater than 1 that is not prime.
Prime factorization (p. 190)	A *factorization* (a product of factors) containing only prime numbers. A prime factorization of any composite number can be found by using a *factor tree*.
Fundamental Theorem of Arithmetic (p. 191)	Each composite number can be written as a product of primes in one, and only one way, except for the order of the prime factors in the product.
Finding prime numbers (p. 191)	*Theorem*: If d is a divisor of n, where $n \neq 0$, then $\frac{n}{d}$ is also a divisor of n. *Theorem*: If n is composite, then n has a prime factor p such that $p^2 \leq n$. *Theorem*: If n is a whole number greater than 1 and not divisible by any prime p such that $p^2 \leq n$, then n is prime. *Sieve of Eratosthenes*: A method of finding all the primes less than a given number.

Section 4-3

The greatest common divisor (GCD) (p. 203)	For two whole numbers a and b, not both 0, the greatest whole number that divides both a and b.

Methods for finding the GCD (p. 203)	• *Colored rods*
	• *Intersection of sets*
	• *Prime factorization*
	• *Calculator*
	• *Euclidean Algorithm*
	
	  Theorem: If a and b are any whole numbers with $b \neq 0$, and $a \geq b$, then $\mathrm{GCD}(a,b) = \mathrm{GCD}(r,b)$, where r is the remainder when a is divided by b.
	  Theorem: If a and b are any nonzero whole numbers and $a \geq b$, then
	    • $\mathrm{GCD}(a,b) = \mathrm{GCD}(a-b,b)$.
	    • $\mathrm{GCD}(a,b) = \mathrm{GCD}(a-kb,b)$ for any whole number k for which $a-kb$ is a whole number.

Relatively prime (p. 204)	Two whole numbers are relatively prime if they share no common positive divisors except 1.
The least common multiple (LCM) (p. 208)	For two nonzero whole numbers a and b, the least natural number that is simultaneously a multiple of both a and b.
Methods for finding the LCM (p. 210)	• *Number line* • *Colored rods* • *Intersection of sets* • *Prime factorization* • *The GCD-LCM product* *Theorem*: For any two nonzero whole numbers a and b, $\mathrm{GCD}(a,b) \cdot \mathrm{LCM}(a,b) = ab$. • *Division-by-primes*

Chapter 4 Review

1. Classify each of the following statements as true or false.
   a. $12 \mid 4$ False
   b. $0 \mid 8$ False
   c. $8 \mid 0$ True
   d. If a number is divisible by 4 and by 6, then it is divisible by 24.   False
   e. If a number is not divisible by 12, then it is not divisible by 3.   False

2. Test each of the following numbers for divisibility by 2, 3, 4, 5, 6, 8, 9, 10, and 11.
   a. 125,160 $2, 3, 4, 5, 6, 8, 10$
   b. 12,193   none

3. Find the greatest digit to make each of the following statements true.
   a. $6 \mid 87\_4$ 8
   b. $24 \mid 4\_856$ 7
   c. $29 \mid 87\_\_4$ 75

4. A student claims that the sum of five consecutive whole numbers is always divisible by 5.
   a. Check the student's claim for a few cases.   True
   b. Prove or disprove the student's claim.   *

5. How can you tell if a number is divisible by 24? Check 4152 for divisibility by 24.   *

6. Construct a number that has exactly five positive divisors. Explain your construction.   *

7. Find all the positive divisors of 144.   *

8. Prove the test for divisibility by 9 using a three-digit number n such that $n = a \cdot 10^2 + b \cdot 10 + c$.   *

9. If 1009 is prime, prove that 1026 is not divisible by 17.   *

10. Determine whether each of the following numbers is prime or composite.
    a. 147   Composite
    b. 373   Prime

11. Explain why each of the following numbers is composite.
    a. $7 \cdot 11 \cdot 13 \cdot 17 + 17$ *
    b. $10! + k$ where $k = 2, 3, 4, 5, 6, 7, 8, 9,$ or 10
        (*Note*: $10! = 10 \cdot 9 \cdot 8 \cdot 7 \cdot 6 \cdot 5 \cdot 4 \cdot 3 \cdot 2 \cdot 1$.)   *

12. The triplets 3, 5, 7 consist of consecutive odd whole numbers that are all prime. Give a convincing argument that this is the only triplet of consecutive odd integers that are all prime. (*Hint*: use the division algorithm.)   *

13. Find the prime factorization of each of the following numbers.
    a. 111 $3 \cdot 37$
    b. 144 $2^4 \cdot 3^2$
    c. 188 $2^2 \cdot 47$
    d. 520 $2^3 \cdot 5 \cdot 13$

14. Find the prime factorization of each of the following numbers.
    a. 10^{10} $2^{10} \cdot 5^{10}$
    b. 89^4 89^4
    c. $8^3 \cdot 6^4 \cdot 13^2$ $2^{13} \cdot 3^4 \cdot 13^2$
    d. $2^3 \cdot 3^2 + 2^4 \cdot 3^3 \cdot 7$ $2^3 \cdot 3^2 \cdot 43$
    e. $2^4 \cdot 3 \cdot 5^7 + 2^4 \cdot 5^6$ $2^8 \cdot 5^6$

15. Find the least nonzero whole number that is divisible by every nonzero whole number less than or equal to 10.   2520

16. Find the GCD for each of the following pairs of numbers.
    a. 24 and 52   4
    b. 5767 and 4453   73

17. Find the LCM for each of the following groups of numbers.
    a. $2^3 \cdot 5^2 \cdot 7^3, 2 \cdot 5^3 \cdot 7^2 \cdot 13$ and $2^4 \cdot 5 \cdot 7^4 \cdot 29$ $2^4 \cdot 5^3 \cdot 7^4 \cdot 13 \cdot 29$
    b. 277 and 278   77006

18. Is the LCM of two numbers always greater than the GCD of the numbers? Justify your answer.   *

19. Explain how to find the LCM of three numbers with the help of the Euclidean algorithm.   *

20. If the GCD of two positive whole numbers is 1, what can you say about the LCM of the two numbers? Explain your reasoning.   *

21. Candy bars priced at 50¢ each were not selling, so the price was reduced. Then they all sold in one day for a total of $31.93. What was the reduced price of each candy bar?   31¢ or 1¢

22. June, an owner of a coffee stand, marked down the price of a latte between 7:00 A.M. and 8:00 A.M. from $2.00 a cup. If she grossed $98.69 from the latte sale and we know that she never sells a latte for less than a dollar, how many lattes did she sell between 7:00 A.M. and 8:00 A.M.? Explain your reasoning. (*Note*: $71 \mid 9869$.)   *

23. Two bells ring at 8:00 A.M. For the remainder of the day, one bell rings every half hour and the other bell rings every 45 min. What time will it be when the bells ring together again?   9:30 A.M.

24. Midas has 120 gold coins and 144 silver coins. He wants to place his gold coins and his silver coins in stacks so that there are the same number of coins in each stack. What is the greatest number of coins that he can place in each stack?   24 coins

25. Jane and Ramon are running laps on a track. If they start at the same time and place and go in the same direction, with Jane running a lap in 5 min and Ramon running a lap in 3 min, how long will it take for them to be at the starting place at the same time if they continue to run at these speeds?   15 min

26. There are 60 oranges and 24 apples in Ivan's house. These fruits have to be kept in separate plastic bags containing the same kind and number in each. Find the greatest number of possible fruits in each plastic bag.   12 fruits

27. Determine how many complete revolutions Gear 2 in the following diagram must make before the arrows are lined up again.   12 revolutions

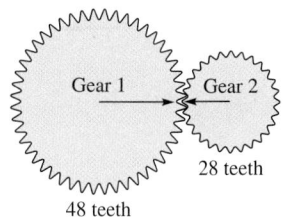

Chapter **5**

Integers

Preliminary Problem

In a research study, seventh-grade students were paired according to ability, based on previously taken tests. An experimental teaching method was used, and tests were given at the end of the experiment to determine how the paired students had fared. Pairs of numbers were used to represent the scores of paired students with the first number in each pair being the score of the student having the experimental treatment and the second number being the control student without the experimental treatment. Use sums of the differences of the pairs to explain whether you would call the experiment a success and why. The scores are (20, 17), (15, 18), (21, 19), (17, 22), (18, 18), (19, 15), (16, 14), (20, 18), (21, 20), and (18, 25).

If needed, see Hint on page 252.

Mount Everest is 29,028 ft above sea level, and the Dead Sea is 1293 ft below sea level. We may symbolize these elevations as 29,028 and $^-$1293.

In mathematics, the need for negative integers arises because subtractions cannot always be performed in the set of whole numbers. To compute $4 - 6$ using the definition of subtraction for whole numbers, we must find a whole number n such that $6 + n = 4$. There is no such whole number n. To perform the computation, we must invent a new number, a *negative integer*. If we attempt to calculate $4 - 6$ on a number line, we must draw intervals to the left of 0. In Figure 1, $4 - 6$ is pictured as an arrow that starts at 0 and ends 2 units to the left of 0. The new number that corresponds to the point 2 units to the left of 0 is *negative two*, symbolized by $^-2$.

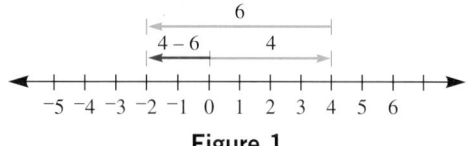

Figure 1

Other numbers to the left of 0 are created similarly. The new set of numbers $\{^-1, ^-2, ^-3, ^-4, \ldots\}$ is the set of **negative integers**. The set $\{1, 2, 3, 4, \ldots\}$ is the set of **positive integers**. The integer 0 is neither positive nor negative.

Definition

The union of the set of negative integers, the set of positive integers, and $\{0\}$ is the set of **integers**, denoted by I.

$$I = \{\ldots, ^-4, ^-3, ^-2, ^-1, 0, 1, 2, 3, 4, \ldots\}$$

Historical Note

The Hindu mathematician Brahmagupta (ca. 598–665 CE) provided the first systematic treatment of negative numbers and of zero. Only about 1000 years later did the Italian mathematician Gerolamo Cardano (1501–1576) consider negative solutions of equations. Still uncomfortable with the concept of negative numbers, he called them "fictitious" numbers.   ●

5-1 Addition and Subtraction of Integers

Representations of Integers

It is unfortunate that the symbol "−" is used to indicate both a subtraction and a negative sign. To reduce confusion between the uses of this symbol in this text, a raised "−" sign is used for negative numbers, as in $^-2$, and for the opposite of a number (described later), in contrast to the lower sign for subtraction. To emphasize that an integer is positive, sometimes a raised plus sign is used, as in $^+3$. In this text, we use the plus sign for addition only and write $^+3$ simply as 3.

The negative integers are **opposites** of the positive integers. For example, the opposite of 5 is $^-5$. Similarly, the positive integers are the opposites of the negative integers. As depicted in Figure 1, opposites are on "opposite" sides of 0 and the same number of units from 0. Because the opposite of 4 is denoted $^-4$, the opposite of $^-4$ can be denoted $^-(^-4)$, which equals 4. The opposite of 0 is 0. In the set of integers I, every element has an opposite that is also in I. In grade 6 *Common Core Standards* as in Example 1(b), students should "recognize that the opposite of the opposite of a number is the number itself." (p. 43) Using addition of integers, we shall soon see that when the opposite of an integer is added to the integer the sum is 0. In fact, ^-a can be defined as the solution of $x + a = 0$.

Example 1

For each of the following equations, find the opposite of x.

   a. $x = 3$ **b.** $x = ^-5$ **c.** $x = 0$

Solution
   a. $^-x = ^-3$
   b. $^-x = ^-(^-5) = 5$
   c. $^-x = ^-0 = 0$

The value of ^-x in Example 1(b) is 5. Note that ^-x is the opposite of x and might *not represent a negative number*. In other words, x is a variable that can be replaced by some number either positive, zero, or negative. *Note: ^-x is read "the opposite of x" not "minus x" or "negative x."*

We next investigate informal ways to introduce operations on integers, beginning with the addition of integers.

Historical Note

The dash has not always been used for both the subtraction operation and the negative sign. Other notations were developed but never adopted universally. One such notation was used by Abu al-Khwarizmi (ca. 825), who indicated a negative number by placing a small circle over it. For example, $^-4$ was recorded as 4̊. The Hindus denoted a negative number by enclosing it in a circle; for example, $^-4$ was recorded as ④. The symbols + and − first appeared in print in European mathematics in the late fifteenth century, at which time the symbols referred not to addition or subtraction nor positive or negative numbers, but to surpluses and deficits in business problems.

Integer Addition

Hands-on materials can be an aid when working with integers. Several models are presented to illustrate integer addition.

Chip Model for Addition

In the chip model, positive integers are represented by black chips and negative integers by red chips. One red chip neutralizes one black chip. Hence, the integer ⁻1 can be represented by 1 red chip, or 2 red and 1 black, or 3 red and 2 black, and so on. Similarly, every integer can be represented in many ways using chips, as shown in Figure 2.

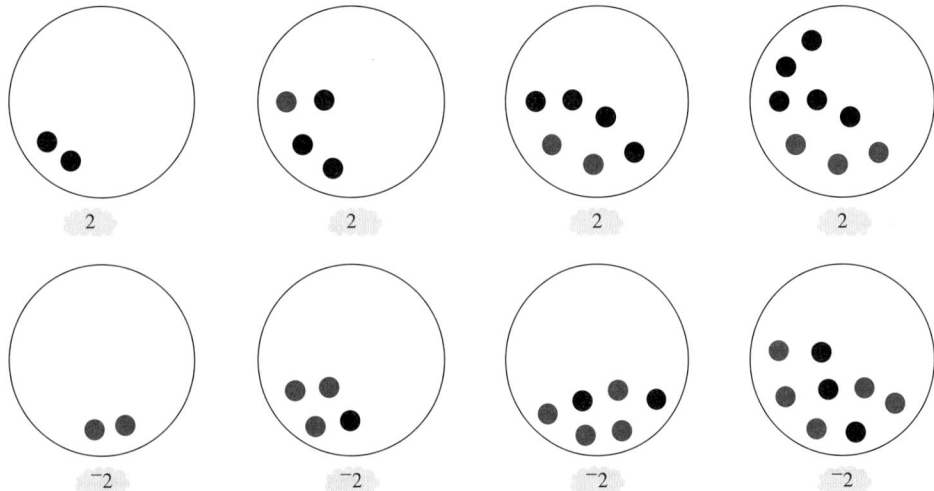

Figure 2

An example of the use of colored chips for modeling integer addition is seen on the student page shown on page 222.

On the student page, note the sentence, *"To add integers with different signs, use zero pairs."* Observe that one chip of each of two different colors pair to equal 0. Also, note the sentence, *"Removing a zero pair does not change the sum."* Additionally, as seen later in the chapter, adding zero pairs to aid in computation with integers does not change the computation.

Figure 3 shows a chip model for the addition ⁻4 + 3. Place 4 red chips together with 3 black chips. Because 3 red chips neutralize 3 black ones, Figure 3 represents the equivalent of 1 red chip or ⁻1.

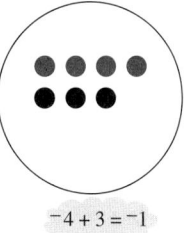

$$^-4 + 3 = {}^-1$$

Figure 3

Charged-Field Model for Addition

A model similar to the chip model uses positive and negative charges. A field has 0 charge if it has the same number of positive (+) and negative (−) charges. As in the chip model, a given integer

School Book Page   Modeling Integer Addition and Subtraction

1-2a   Activity Lab

Modeling Integer Addition and Subtraction

You can use models to add and subtract integers. Use chips of two different colors. Let one color represent positive integers and the other color represent negative integers.

ACTIVITY

1. Find 5 + 2.

Show 5 "+" chips. Then add 2 "+" chips.

There are 7 "+" chips. So 5 + 2 = 7.

2. Find −5 + (−2).

Show 5 "−" chips. Then add 2 "−" chips.

There are 7 "−" chips. So −5 + (−2) = −7.

To add integers with different signs, use zero pairs. These chips 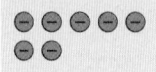 are a *zero pair* because 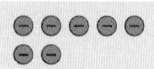 = 0. Removing a zero pair does not change the sum.

3. Find 5 + (−2).

Show 5 "+" chips. Then add 2 "−" chips.

Pair the "+" and "−" chips. Remove the pairs.

There are 3 "+" chips left. So 5 + (−2) = 3.

4. Find −5 + 2.

Show 5 "−" chips. Then add 2 "+" chips.

Pair the "+" and "−" chips. Remove the pairs.

There are 3 "−" chips left. So −5 + 2 = −3.

8   Activity Lab   Modeling Integer Addition and Subtraction

Activity Manual

Use *A Clown on a Tightrope* to develop algorithms for integer addition and subtraction using a number line model.

E-Manipulative Activity

Use the *Number Line* activity to illustrate the number-line model.

can be represented in many ways using the charged-field model. Figure 4 uses the model for 3 + ⁻5. Because 3 positive charges "neutralize" 3 negative charges, the net result is 2 negative ones. Hence, 3 + ⁻5 = ⁻2.

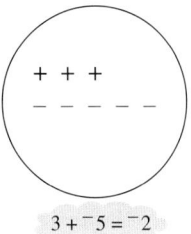

3 + ⁻5 = ⁻2

Figure 4

Number-Line Model for Addition

Another model for addition of integers involves a number line, and it can be introduced with the idea of a hiker walking the number line, as seen in Figure 5(a) illustrating 3 + 2 = 5 and in Figure 5(b) illustrating ⁻3 + ⁻2 = ⁻5. Without the hiker, ⁻3 + ⁻5 = ⁻8 is pictured in Figure 6(a) and 3 + ⁻5 = ⁻2 is in Figure 6(b).

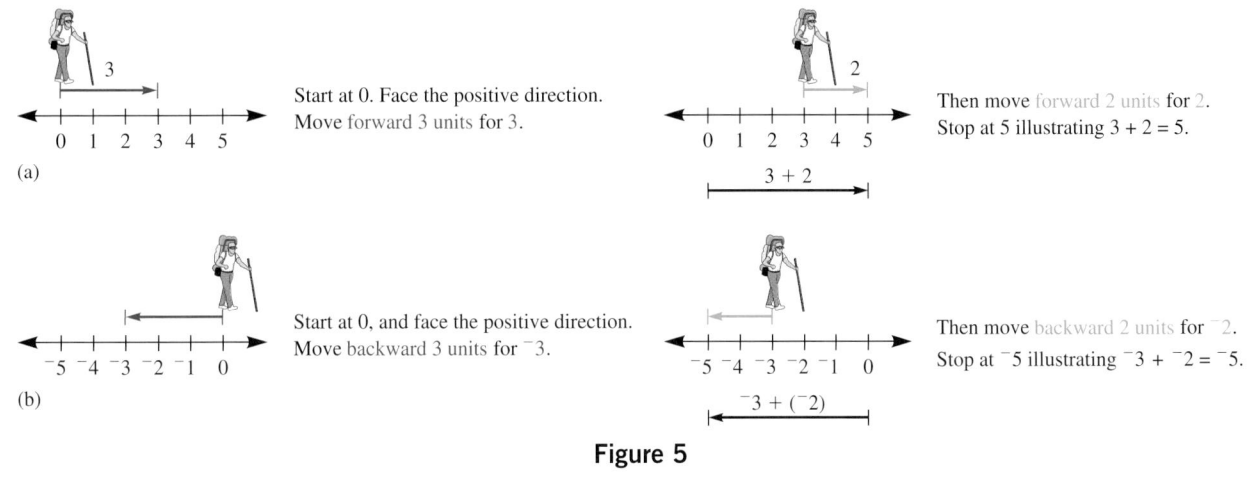

Figure 5

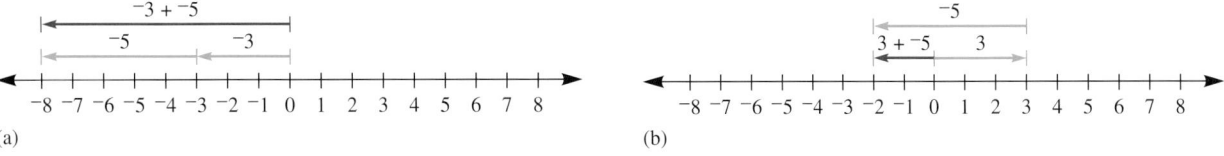

Figure 6

▶ NOW TRY THIS 1

NTT 1: Answers can be found in Answers at the back of the book.

Explain whether the sum of two negative integers is always negative.

Example 2 involves a thermometer with a scale in the form of a vertical number line.

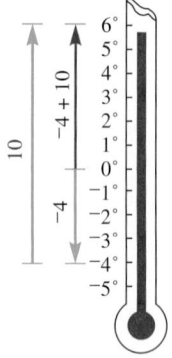

Figure 7

Example 2

The temperature was ⁻4°C. In an hour, it rose 10°C. What is the new temperature?

Solution   Figure 7 shows that the new temperature is 6°C and that ⁻4 + 10 = 6.

Pattern Model for Addition

Addition of whole numbers was discussed in Chapter 3. Addition of integers can also be motivated using patterns of addition of whole numbers. Notice in the left column of Table 1, the first four facts are known from whole number addition. Also notice that as the 4 stays fixed and the numbers added to 4 decrease by 1, the sum decreases by 1. Following this pattern, we get 4 + ⁻1 = 3, and we can continue the pattern as shown. Similar inductive reasoning can be used to complete the computations in the right column of Table 1, where ⁻2 stays fixed and the other numbers decrease by 1 each time.

Table 1	
4 + 3 = 7	⁻2 + 4 = 2
4 + 2 = 6	⁻2 + 3 = 1
4 + 1 = 5	⁻2 + 2 = 0
4 + 0 = 4	⁻2 + 1 = ⁻1
4 + ⁻1 = 3	⁻2 + 0 = ⁻2
4 + ⁻2 = 2	⁻2 + ⁻1 = ⁻3
4 + ⁻3 = 1	⁻2 + ⁻2 = ⁻4
4 + ⁻4 = 0	⁻2 + ⁻3 = ⁻5
4 + ⁻5 = ⁻1	⁻2 + ⁻4 = ⁻6
4 + ⁻6 = ⁻2	⁻2 + ⁻5 = ⁻7

However, we know that the inductive reasoning shown in Table 1 does not constitute a proof that the sums are correct.

Absolute Value

Because 4 and ⁻4 are opposites, they are on opposite sides of 0 on the number line and are the same distance (4 units) from 0, as shown in Figure 8.

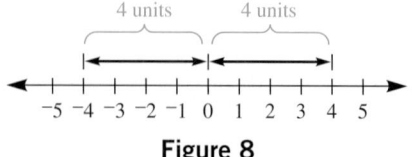

Figure 8

Distance is always a positive number or zero. The distance between the point corresponding to an integer and 0 is the **absolute value** of the integer. Thus, the absolute value of both 4 and ⁻4 is 4, written $|4| = 4$ and $|⁻4| = 4$, respectively. Notice that if $x \geq 0$, then $|x| = x$, and if $x < 0$, then ⁻x is positive. Therefore, we have the following definition.

Definition of Absolute Value

For any integer x,

$$|x| = x, \text{ if } x \geq 0.$$
$$|x| = {}^-x, \text{ if } x < 0.$$

Example 3

Evaluate each of the following expressions.

a. $|20|$ b. $|{}^-5|$ c. $|0|$
d. ${}^-|{}^-3|$ e. $|2 + {}^-5|$

Solution

a. $|20| = 20$ b. $|{}^-5| = 5$ c. $|0| = 0$
d. ${}^-|{}^-3| = {}^-3$ e. $|2 + {}^-5| = |{}^-3| = 3$

CCSS In grade 6 *Common Core Standards*, we find that students should

understand the absolute value of a rational number [integer] as its distance from 0 on the number line; interpret absolute value as magnitude for a positive or negative quantity in a real-world situation. (p. 43)

Example 4

If Omar's bank balance is ${}^-\$75$, what could be said about his indebtedness to the bank?

Solution

Because the bank balance is ${}^-\$75$, we could interpret his indebtedness as $|{}^-75| = 75$. We might say that he is in debt $75.

In Example 4, indebtedness is reported as a positive number $75 while Omar's balance is ${}^-\$75$. This different use of positives and negatives at the same time in discussions of real-world applications has to be carefully considered as it may cause confusion.

▶ **NOW TRY THIS 2**

Write each of the following in simplest form without the absolute value notation in the final answer. Show your work.

a. $|x| + x$ if $x \leq 0$ Since $x \leq 0$, $|x| = {}^-x$ and $|x| + x = {}^-x + x = 0$.
b. ${}^-|x| + x$ if $x \leq 0$ Since $x \leq 0$, ${}^-|x| + x = {}^-({}^-x) + x = 2x$.
c. ${}^-|x| + x$ if $x \geq 0$ Since $x \geq 0$, ${}^-|x| + x = {}^-x + x = 0$.

Integer Addition

Addition of two integers can be defined in cases using what we have learned with the hands-on models in this section. Because the set of integers includes the set of whole numbers, any definition of addition of integers should be valid for the addition of whole numbers.

Examples taken from the models are seen in Table 2. With a knowledge of addition of whole numbers, the definition of opposites for integers, and the model examples, generalizations for addition of integers are also given in Table 2.

Table 2

Examples from Models	Generalizations
$^-2 + 0 = ^-2 = 0 + ^-2$	$m + 0 = m = 0 + m$ for all integers m
$4 + 3 = 7$	If m and n are nonnegative integers, they are added as whole numbers.
$^-3 + ^-5 = ^-(3 + 5)$	If $m \geq 0$ and $n \geq 0$, then $^-m + ^-n = ^-(m + n)$.
$4 + ^-3 = 4 - 3$	If $n > 0$ and $m \geq n$, then $m + ^-n = m - n$.
$3 + ^-5 = ^-(5 - 3)$	If $n > m$ and $m \geq 0$, then $m + ^-n = ^-(n - m)$.

The generalizations for addition of integers in Table 2 do not conflict with the addition of whole numbers and are used in the following definition.

Definition of Addition of Integers

Let m and n be any integers as described.

a. If m is any integer, then $0 + m = m = m + 0$.
b. If $m \geq 0$ and $n \geq 0$, then $m + n$ is defined using addition of whole numbers.
c. If $m \geq 0$ and $n \geq 0$, then $^-m + ^-n = ^-(m + n)$.
d. If $n > 0$ and $m \geq n$, then $m + ^-n = ^-n + m = m - n$.
e. If $n > m$ and $m \geq 0$, then $m + ^-n = ^-n + m = ^-(n - m)$.

CCSS The *Common Core Standards* for grade 7 indicate that students should

understand $p + q$ as the number located a distance $|q|$ from p, in the positive or negative direction depending on whether q is positive or negative. (p. 48)

While not a definition, the statement provides an understanding of how integers may be added. The ideas here lead to a definition of integer addition using absolute values as follows:

To add two integers with the same sign, add the absolute values of the integers. The sum has the same sign as the integers being added.

To add two integers with different signs, subtract the lesser absolute value from the greater one. The sum has the same sign as the integer with the greater absolute value.

Thus, an alternative definition of integer addition using absolute values is given below.

Definition of Integer Addition Using Absolute Values

Let m and n be any integers as described.

If m is any integer, then $m + 0 = m = 0 + m$.
If m and n are non-negative integers, then $m + n$ is the sum of whole numbers m and n.
If m and n are negative integers, then $m + n = ^-(|m| + |n|)$.
If m is a positive integer and n is a negative integer, then $m + n$ is defined as follows:

If $|m| \geq |n|$, then $m + n = n + m = |m| - |n|$.
If $|m| < |n|$, then $m + n = n + m = ^-(|n| - |m|)$.

The use of absolute values to compute integer addition is seen on the partial student page.

School Book Page   Adding Integers

KEY CONCEPTS **Adding Integers**

Start at zero. Move to the first integer. Find the absolute value of
the second integer and move that distance. If the second integer is
positive, move in the positive direction (right). If negative, move in
the negative direction (left).

Examples $3 + 5 = 8$ $-3 + (-5) = -8$

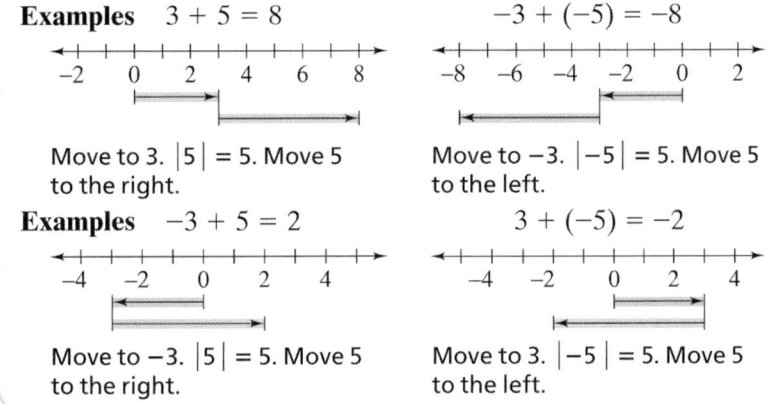

Move to 3. $|5| = 5$. Move 5   Move to −3. $|-5| = 5$. Move 5
to the right.   to the left.

Examples $-3 + 5 = 2$ $3 + (-5) = -2$

Move to −3. $|5| = 5$. Move 5   Move to 3. $|-5| = 5$. Move 5
to the right.   to the left.

Properties of Integer Addition

Integer addition has all the properties of whole number addition. These properties can all be
proved using the definition of addition of integers.

Theorem 5-1:   Properties of Integer Addition

For all integers a, b, and c,

   a. **Closure property of addition of integers** $a + b$ is a unique integer.
   b. **Commutative property of addition of integers** $a + b = b + a$.
   c. **Associative property of addition of integers** $(a + b) + c = a + (b + c)$.
   d. **Identity property of addition of integers**   0 is the unique integer, the **additive identity**,
      such that, for all integers a, $0 + a = a = a + 0$.

   We have seen that every integer has an opposite. This opposite is the **additive inverse** of the
integer. The fact that each integer has a unique (one and only one) additive inverse is stated in
Theorem 5-2.

Theorem 5-2:   Additive Inverse Property of Integers

For every integer a, there exists a unique integer ^-a, the **additive inverse** of a, such that
$a + {}^-a = 0 = {}^-a + a$.

By definition, the additive inverse, ^-a, is the solution of the equation $x + a = 0$. The fact that the additive inverse is unique is equivalent to saying that the preceding equation has only one solution. In fact, for any integers a and b, the equation $x + a = b$ has a unique solution, $b + ^-a$.

The uniqueness of additive inverses can be used to justify other theorems; for example: The opposite, or the additive inverse, of ^-a can be written $^-(^-a)$. However, because $a + ^-a = 0$, the additive inverse of ^-a is also a. Because the additive inverse of ^-a must be unique, we have $^-(^-a) = a$. ∎

Other theorems of addition of integers can be investigated by considering previously discussed notions. For example, if we have two representations of the same integer, we may use the number line or other models to show that if we add the same integer to each representation, we have equal results. For example, we know that if $3 + ^-4 = ^-2 + 1$, then $(3 + ^-4) + 3 = (^-2 + 1) + 3$. This is generalized in Theorem 5-3(b) as the Addition Property of Equality for Integers. Also, we saw that $^-2 + ^-4 = ^-(2 + 4)$. This relationship is true in general and is stated in Theorem 5-3(c).

Theorem 5-3

Let $a, b,$ and c be any integers.

   a. $^-(^-a) = a$

   b. **Addition Property of Equality for Integers:** If $a = b$, then $a + c = b + c$.

   c. $^-a + ^-b = ^-(a + b)$

We prove Theorem 5-3(c) as follows:

By definition $^-(a + b)$ is the additive inverse of $(a + b)$; that is, $(a + b) + ^-(a + b) = 0$. If we could show that $^-a + ^-b$ is also the additive inverse of $a + b$, the uniqueness of the additive inverse implies that $^-(a + b)$ and $^-a + ^-b$ are equal. To show that $^-a + ^-b$ is the additive inverse of $a + b$, we need only to show that their sum is 0. Using the associative and commutative properties of integer addition and the definition of the additive inverse, we have the following:

$$(a + b) + (^-a + ^-b) = (a + b) + (^-b + ^-a)$$
$$= [(a + b) + ^-b] + ^-a$$
$$= [a + (b + ^-b)] + ^-a$$
$$= (a + 0) + ^-a$$
$$= a + ^-a$$
$$= 0$$

Since $(a + b) + (^-a + ^-b) = 0$ and $(a + b) + ^-(a + b) = 0$, by the uniqueness of the additive inverse we have $^-(a + b) = ^-a + ^-b$. ∎

Example 5

Find the additive inverse of each of the following expressions.

   a. $^-(3 + x)$ b. $a + ^-4$ c. $^-3 + ^-x$

Solution

   a. $3 + x$

   b. $^-(a + ^-4)$, which can be written as $^-a + ^-(^-4)$, or $^-a + 4$

   c. $^-(^-3 + ^-x)$, which can be written $^-(^-3) + ^-(^-x)$, or $3 + x$

Integer Subtraction

As with integer addition, we explore several models for integer subtraction.

Chip Model for Subtraction

To find $3 - {}^-2$, we want to subtract $^-2$ (take away 2 red chips) from 3 black chips. As seen in Figure 9(a), if we just have 3 black chips, we cannot take away 2 red ones. Therefore, we need to represent 3 so that at least 2 red chips are present using zero pairs. To insure the problem does not change because we need 2 red chips, we can add 2 black chips and 2 red chips forming two zero pairs. In Figure 9(b), we now see 3 represented using 5 black chips and 2 red chips. Now when the 2 red chips are "taken away," in Figure 9(c), 5 black chips are left and hence, $3 - {}^-2 = 5$.

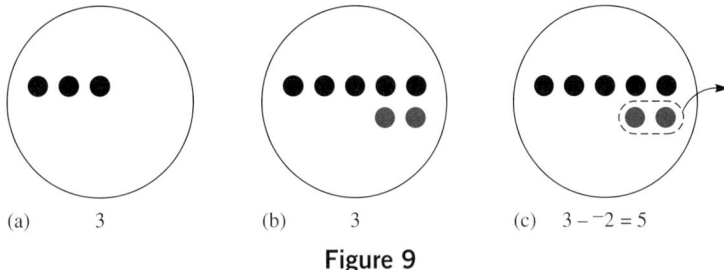

(a)   3   (b)   3   (c) $3 - {}^-2 = 5$

Figure 9

Charged-Field Model for Subtraction

Integer subtraction can be modeled with a charged field. For example, consider $^-3 - {}^-5$. To subtract $^-5$ from $^-3$, we represent $^-3$ in Figure 10(a) so at least 5 negative charges are present as in Figure 10(b). To subtract $^-5$, remove the 5 negative charges as in Figure 10(c), leaving 2 positive charges, as in Figure 10(d). Hence, $^-3 - {}^-5 = 2$.

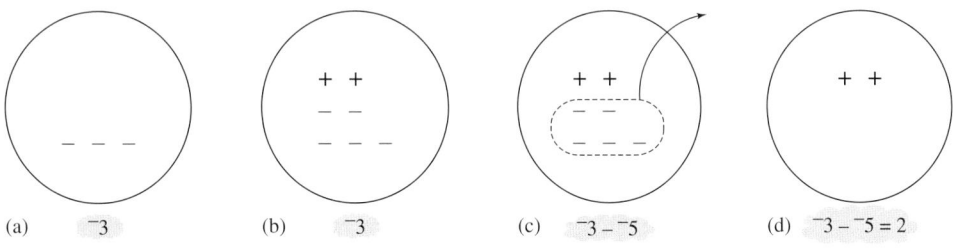

(a) $^-3$ (b) $^-3$ (c) $^-3 - {}^-5$ (d) $^-3 - {}^-5 = 2$

Figure 10

Number-Line Model for Subtraction

The number-line model used for integer addition can also be used to model integer subtraction. While integer addition is modeled by maintaining the same direction and moving forward or backward depending on whether a positive or negative integer is added, subtraction is modeled by turning around. This is seen in Figure 11 with $3 - {}^-2$.

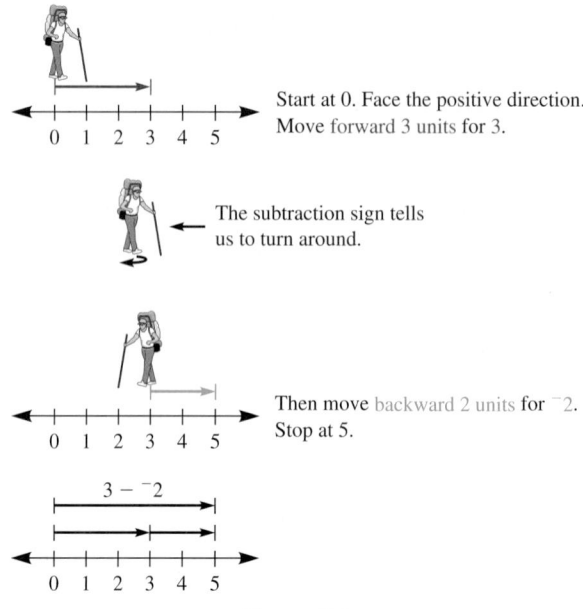

Start at 0. Face the positive direction.
Move forward 3 units for 3.

The subtraction sign tells
us to turn around.

Then move backward 2 units for ⁻2.
Stop at 5.

$3 - {}^-2$

Figure 11

▶ **NOW TRY THIS 3**

NTT 3: Answers can be
found in Answers at the
back of the book.

Model the subtraction $4 - {}^-3$ on a number line.

Example 6

   a. Suppose a mail carrier brings us three letters, one with a check for $25, and the other two
      with bills for $15 and $20, respectively. What is the result to our balance?
   b. Suppose the very next day, we find that the bill for $20 was mis-delivered, and we give it
      back to the mail carrier. What is our new balance?

Solution
   a. We record the transaction as $25 + {}^-15 + {}^-20 = {}^-10$. Thus, we have $10 less than we had
      initially.
   b. From part (a), we have the ⁻10 less than the original balance to start but a bill for $20 was
      taken away so the transaction results in ${}^-10 - {}^-20 = 10$. Thus, we have $10 more than the
      original balance.

Pattern Model for Subtraction

Activity Manual

Use *Subtraction Patterns*
to develop an algorithm
for integer subtraction by
exploring patterns.

By using inductive reasoning, we find the difference of two integers by considering the patterns
that result from subtractions we know. Both the following pattern on the left and the pattern on
the right of Table 3 start with $3 - 2 = 1$.

Table 3

$3 - 2 = 1$	$3 - 2 = 1$
$3 - 3 = 0$	$3 - 1 = 2$
$3 - 4 = ?$	$3 - 0 = 3$
$3 - 5 = ?$	$3 - {}^-1 = ?$
$3 - 6 = ?$	$3 - {}^-2 = ?$

In the pattern on the left, the difference decreases by 1. If we continue the pattern, we have
$3 - 4 = {}^-1, 3 - 5 = {}^-2$, and $3 - 6 = {}^-3$. In the pattern on the right, the difference increases
by 1. If we continue the pattern, we have $3 - {}^-1 = 4$ and $3 - {}^-2 = 5$.

Defining Integer Subtraction

Subtraction of integers, like subtraction of whole numbers, can be defined in terms of addition. Using the missing-addend approach, $5 - 3$ can be computed by finding a whole number n as follows:

$$5 - 3 = n \quad \text{if, and only if,} \quad 5 = 3 + n$$

Because $3 + 2 = 5$, $n = 2$.

Similarly, we compute $3 - 5$ as follows:

$$3 - 5 = n \quad \text{if, and only if,} \quad 3 = 5 + n$$

Because $5 + {}^-2 = 3$, $n = {}^-2$. In general, for integers a and b, we have the following definition of subtraction.

> ### Definition of Integer Subtraction
> For all integers a and b, $a - b$ is the unique integer n such that $a = b + n$.

Addition is the inverse of subtraction; it "undoes" subtraction; that is, $(a - b) + b = a$. Also, subtraction "undoes" addition; that is, $(a + b) - b = a$.

Example 7

Use the definition of subtraction to compute the following subtractions:

  a. $3 - 10$ **b.** ${}^-2 - 10$

Solution

  a. Let $3 - 10 = n$. Then $n + 10 = 3$, so $n = {}^-7$. Therefore, $3 - 10 = {}^-7$.
  b. Let ${}^-2 - 10 = n$. Then $n + 10 = {}^-2$, so $n = {}^-12$. Therefore, ${}^-2 - 10 = {}^-12$.

Subtraction Using Adding the Opposite Approach

In grade 7 *Common Core Standards*, we find that students should "understand subtraction of rational numbers [integers] as adding the additive inverse, $p - q = p + {}^-q$." (p. 48)

This approach is shown with a number line on the partial student page shown on page 232.

From previous work, we know that $3 - 5 = {}^-2$ and $3 + {}^-5 = {}^-2$. Hence, $3 - 5 = 3 + {}^-5$. In general, the following is true.

> ### Theorem 5-4
> For all integers a and b, $a - b = a + {}^-b$.

The preceding theorem can be justified using the fact that the equation $b + x = a$ has a unique solution for x. From the definition of subtraction, the solution of the equation is $a - b$. To show that $a - b = a + {}^-b$, we show that $a + {}^-b$ is also a solution to $b + x = a$ by checking whether $b + (a + {}^-b) = a$:

$$b + (a + {}^-b) = b + ({}^-b + a)$$
$$= (b + {}^-b) + a$$
$$= 0 + a$$
$$= a$$

Consequently, $a - b = a + {}^-b$.

Theorem 5-4 is frequently used as an alternative definition of subtraction.

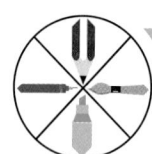

EXAMPLES Subtracting Integers

3 Find $4 - 6$.

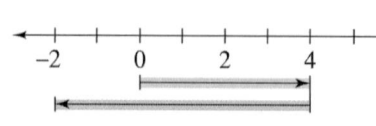

Start at 0. Move to 4.
Then add the opposite of 6,
which is -6.

$$4 - 6 = 4 + (-6) = -2$$

4 Find $-2 - (-5)$.

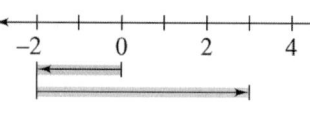

Start at 0. Move to -2.
Then add the opposite of -5,
which is 5.

$$-2 - (-5) = -2 + 5 = 3$$

Source: p. 7; From MATHEMATICS Common Core (Course 2). Copyright © 2013 Pearson Education, Inc., or its affiliates. Used by permission. All Rights Reserved.

▶ **NOW TRY THIS 4**

NTT 4: Answers can be found in Answers at the back of the book.

a. Is the set of integers closed under subtraction? Why?

b. Do the commutative, associative, or identity properties hold for subtraction of integers? Why?

Example 8

Using the fact that $a - b = a + {}^-b$, compute each of the following.

a. $2 - 8$ **b.** $2 - {}^-8$ **c.** ${}^-12 - {}^-5$ **d.** ${}^-12 - 5$

Solution

a. $2 - 8 = 2 + {}^-8 = {}^-6$

b. $2 - {}^-8 = 2 + {}^-({}^-8) = 2 + 8 = 10$

c. ${}^-12 - {}^-5 = {}^-12 + {}^-({}^-5) = {}^-12 + 5 = {}^-7$

d. ${}^-12 - 5 = {}^-12 + {}^-5 = {}^-17$

Example 9

Rewrite each expression without parentheses.

a. ${}^-(b - c)$

b. $a - (b + c)$

Solution

a. ${}^-(b - c) = {}^-(b + {}^-c) = {}^-b + {}^-({}^-c) = {}^-b + c$

b. $a - (b + c) = a + {}^-(b + c) = a + ({}^-b + {}^-c) = (a + {}^-b) + {}^-c = a + {}^-b + {}^-c$

$\qquad\qquad = a - b - c$

Example 10

Simplify each of the following expressions.

   a. $2 - (5 - x)$ **b.** $5 - (x - 3)$ **c.** $^-(x - y) - y$

Solution

a.
$$
\begin{aligned}
2 - (5 - x) &= 2 + {}^-(5 + {}^-x) \\
&= 2 + {}^-5 + {}^-({}^-x) \\
&= 2 + {}^-5 + x \\
&= {}^-3 + x \text{ or } x + {}^-3 \text{ or } x - 3
\end{aligned}
$$

b.
$$
\begin{aligned}
5 - (x - 3) &= 5 + {}^-(x + {}^-3) \\
&= 5 + {}^-x + {}^-({}^-3) \\
&= 5 + {}^-x + 3 \\
&= 8 + {}^-x \\
&= 8 - x
\end{aligned}
$$

c.
$$
\begin{aligned}
{}^-(x - y) - y &= {}^-(x + {}^-y) + {}^-y \\
&= [{}^-x + {}^-({}^-y)] + {}^-y \\
&= ({}^-x + y) + {}^-y \\
&= {}^-x + (y + {}^-y) \\
&= {}^-x + 0 \\
&= {}^-x
\end{aligned}
$$

Subtraction of Integers on a Calculator

Many calculators have a change of sign key, either $\boxed{\text{CHS}}$, $\boxed{+/-}$, or use $\boxed{(-)}$, a key that allows computation with integers. For example, to compute $8 - ({}^-3)$, we press $\boxed{8}\boxed{-}\boxed{3}\boxed{+/-}\boxed{=}$. Investigate what happens if you press $\boxed{8}\boxed{-}\boxed{-}\boxed{3}\boxed{=}$.

Order of Operations

Subtraction in the set of integers is neither commutative nor associative, as illustrated in these counterexamples:

$$5 - 3 \neq 3 - 5 \quad \text{because} \quad 2 \neq {}^-2$$
$$(3 - 15) - 8 \neq 3 - (15 - 8) \quad \text{because} \quad {}^-20 \neq {}^-4$$

An expression such as $3 - 15 - 8$ is ambiguous unless we know in which order to perform the subtractions. Mathematicians agree that $3 - 15 - 8$ means $(3 - 15) - 8$; that is, the subtractions in $3 - 15 - 8$ are performed in order from left to right. Similarly, $3 - 4 + 5$ means $(3 - 4) + 5$ and not $3 - (4 + 5)$. Thus, $(a - b) - c$ may be written without parentheses as $a - b - c$. Order of operations for integers will be revisited after multiplication and division are discussed.

Example 11

Compute each of the following.

   a. $2 - 5 - 5$ **b.** $3 - 7 + 3$ **c.** $3 - (7 - 3)$

Solution

   a. $2 - 5 - 5 = {}^-3 - 5 = {}^-8$
   b. $3 - 7 + 3 = {}^-4 + 3 = {}^-1$
   c. $3 - (7 - 3) = 3 - 4 = {}^-1$

Assessment 5-1A

1. Find the additive inverse of each of the following integers. Write the answer in the simplest possible form.
   a. 2 ⁻2
   b. ⁻6 6
   c. m ⁻m
   d. 0 0
   e. ⁻m m
   f. $a + b$ *
2. Simplify each of the following expressions.
   a. ⁻(⁻2) 2
   b. ⁻(⁻m) m
   c. ⁻0 0
3. Evaluate each of the following expressions.
   a. |⁻5| 5
   b. |10| 10
   c. ⁻|⁻5| ⁻5
   d. ⁻|5| ⁻5
4. Demonstrate each of the following additions using the charged-field or chip model.
   a. 5 + ⁻3 *
   b. ⁻2 + 3 *
   c. ⁻3 + 2 *
   d. ⁻3 + ⁻2 *
5. Demonstrate each of the additions in exercise 4 using a number-line model. *
6. Use the absolute value definition of addition to find the following sums.
   a. 7 + ⁻13 *
   b. ⁻7 + ⁻13 *
7. Compute each of the following subtractions using $a - b = a + ⁻b$.
   a. 3 − ⁻2 5
   b. ⁻3 − 2 ⁻5
   c. ⁻3 − ⁻2 ⁻1
8. Answer each part of exercise 7 using subtraction with the missing-addend approach. *
9. Write an addition equation that corresponds to each of the following sentences and then answer the question.
   a. A certain stock dropped 17 points and the following day gained 20 points. What was the net change in the stock's worth? ⁻17 + 20 = 3 giving a net change of 3 points
   b. The temperature was ⁻10°C and then it rose by 8°C. What is the new temperature? ⁻10 + 8 = ⁻2 giving a rise of 2°C
   c. The plane was at 35,000 ft and dropped 1000 ft. What is the new altitude of the plane? *
10. On January 1, Jane's bank balance was $300. During the month, she wrote checks for $45, $55, $165, $35, and $100 and made deposits of $75, $25, and $400.
    a. If a check is represented by a negative integer and a deposit by a positive integer, express Jane's transactions as a sum of positive and negative integers. *
    b. What was the balance in Jane's account at the end of the month? $400
11. Use a number-line model to compute the following subtractions.
    a. ⁻4 − ⁻1 *
    b. ⁻4 − ⁻3 *
12. Use patterns to show the following statements.
    a. ⁻4 − ⁻1 = ⁻3 *
    b. ⁻2 − 1 = ⁻3 *
13. Do exercise 12 using the charged-field model. *
14. Compute each of the following expressions.
    a. ⁻2 + (3 − 10) ⁻9
    b. (8 − ⁻5) − 10 3
    c. ⁻2 − 7 + 10 1
15. In each of the following problems, write both a subtraction and an addition expression that correspond to the question and then answer the question.
    a. The temperature is 55°F and is supposed to drop 60°F by midnight. What is the expected midnight temperature? 55 − 60; 55 + ⁻60; ⁻5°F

b. Moses has overdraft privileges at his bank. If he had $200 in his checking account and he wrote a $220 check, what would be his balance if the bank allowed the overdraft? *
16. Simplify each of the following expressions as much as possible. Show all work.
    a. 3 − (2 − 4x) *
    b. $x − (⁻x − y)$ *
17. For which integers a, b, and c, does $a − b + c = a − (b − c)$? Justify your answer. *
18. Let W stand for the set of whole numbers, I the set of integers, I^+ the set of positive integers, and I^- the set of negative integers. Find each of the following sets.
    a. $W \cup I$ I
    b. $W \cap I$ W
    c. $I^+ \cap I^-$ ∅
    d. $W − I$ ∅
19. Place the integers ⁻4, ⁻3, ⁻2, ⁻1, 0, 1, 2, 3, 4 in the grid to make a magic square. Answers vary.

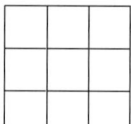

20. Let $y = ⁻x − 1$. Find the value of y (in parts (a)–(d)) when x has the following values.
    a. ⁻1 0
    b. 100 ⁻101
    c. ⁻2 1
    d. ⁻a $a − 1$
    e. For which values of x will y be 3? ⁻4
21. Determine the number of terms in the arithmetic and geometric sequences below.
    a. ⁻40, ⁻39, ⁻38, . . . , 37, 38, 39, 40 81
    b. $2^5, 2^6, 2^7, . . . , 4096$ 8
22. Explain how you could use the Gauss method from Chapter 1 to find the sum of the first 100 negative integers. *
23. Find the sum of the terms in the following arithmetic sequence: ⁻40, ⁻39, ⁻38, . . . , 37, 38, 39, 40. 0
24. How could you explain the time change from the eastern coast of the United States to the western coast of the United States in terms of integers? *
25. On an automobile trip, the speed limit on one stretch of the road was 55 mph. A driver was driving at the speed limit and then drove 10 mph over the limit, 7 mph under the limit, and finally, 13 mph under the limit. Interpret the speed using integers and determine his speed when last reported. *
26. Par in golf acts like zero in the set of integers. An eagle is 2 under par, a birdie is 1 under par, a bogey is one over par, and a double bogey is 2 over par. If Leonine Trees shot a bogey on hole 1, par on hole 2, an eagle on hole 3, a double bogey on hole 4, a birdie on hole 5 and a hole-in-one on par 4 hole 6, describe his total score in terms of integers and report his final score in relation to par. *
27. Find all integers x, if there are any, such that the following are true.
    a. ⁻x is positive. All negative integers
    b. ⁻x is negative. All positive integers
    c. ⁻x − 1 is positive. All integers less than ⁻1
    d. |x| = 2 2 or ⁻2

* Answers can be found in the Answers section at the back of the book.

28. In each of the following equations, find all integers x satisfying the given equation.
   a. $|x - 6| = 6$ 0 or 12
   b. $|x| + 2 = 10$ ⁻8 or 8
   c. $|⁻x| = |x|$ All integers

29. An arithmetic sequence may have a positive or negative difference. In each of the following arithmetic sequences, find the difference and write the next two terms.
   a. $0, ⁻3, ⁻6, ⁻9$ $d = ⁻3$; next terms: ⁻12, ⁻15
   b. $x + y, x, x - y$ $d = ⁻y$; next terms: $x - 2y, x - 3y$

30. Classify each of the following as true or false. If false, show a counterexample that makes it false.
   a. $|⁻x| = |x|$ True

b. $|x - y| = |y - x|$ True
c. $|⁻x + ⁻y| = |x + y|$ True

31. Solve the following equations.
   a. $x + 7 = 3$ ⁻4
   b. $⁻10 + x = ⁻7$ 3
   c. $⁻x = 5$ ⁻5

32. Estimate each of the following and then compute the actual answer.   Estimates vary.
   a. $327 + ⁻52 - 398$ ⁻125; ⁻123
   b. $⁻1772 + 2005 - 503$ ⁻270; ⁻270
   c. $996 - ⁻10,007 - 102$ 10,900; 10,901
   d. $⁻303 - ⁻1203 + 4997$ 5900; 5897

Assessment 5-1B

1. Find the additive inverse of each of the following integers. Write the answer in the simplest possible form.
   a. 3   ⁻3
   b. ⁻8   8
   c. q $⁻q$
   d. 6   ⁻6
   e. ⁻n n
   f. $3 + x$ $⁻3 - x$

2. Simplify each of the following expressions.
   a. $⁻(⁻5)$ 5
   b. $⁻(⁻x)$ x

3. Evaluate each of the following expressions.
   a. $|⁻3|$ 3
   b. $|15|$ 15
   c. $⁻|⁻3|$ ⁻3
   d. $⁻|6|$ ⁻6

4. Demonstrate each of the following additions using the charged-field or chip model.
   a. $⁻2 + 5$ *
   b. $⁻5 + 2$ *
   c. $⁻3 + ⁻3$ *
   d. $6 + ⁻4$ *

5. Demonstrate each of the additions in exercise 4 using a number-line model.   *

6. Use the absolute value definition of addition to find the following sums.
   a. $5 + ⁻31$ *
   b. $⁻5 + ⁻31$ *

7. Compute each of the following using $a - b = a + ⁻b$.
   a. $⁻3 - 5$ *
   b. $5 - (⁻3)$ *
   c. $⁻2 - ⁻3$ $⁻2 - ⁻3 = ⁻2 + 3 = 1$

8. Answer each part of exercise 7 using the missing-addend approach.   *

9. Write an addition equation that corresponds to each of the following sentences and then answer the question.
   a. A visitor in a Las Vegas casino lost $200, won $100, and then lost $50. What is the change in the gambler's net worth? $⁻200 + 100 + ⁻50 = ⁻150$. Thus, he lost $150.
   b. In four downs, the football team lost 2 yd, gained 7 yd, gained 0 yd, and lost 8 yd. What is the total gain or loss? $⁻2 + 7 + 0 + ⁻8 = ⁻3$. Thus, the team lost 3 yd.
   c. In a game of Triominoes, Jack's scores in five successive turns are 17, ⁻8, ⁻9, 14, and 45. What is his total at the end of five turns? $17 + ⁻8 + ⁻9 + 14 + 45 = 59$. The total is 59.

10. a. The largest bubble chamber in the world is 15 ft in diameter and contains 7259 gal of liquid hydrogen at a temperature of ⁻247°C. If the temperature is dropped by 11°C per hour for 2 consecutive hours, what is the new temperature?   ⁻269°C
   b. The greatest recorded temperature ranges in the world are around the "cold pole" in Siberia. Temperatures in Verkhoyansk have varied from ⁻94°F to 98°F. What is the difference between the high and low temperatures in Verkhoyansk?   192°F

11. Use a number-line model to find the following differences.
   a. $⁻3 - ⁻2$ *
   b. $⁻4 - 3$ *

12. Use patterns to show the following results.
   a. $⁻2 - ⁻3 = 1$ *
   b. $⁻3 - 2 = ⁻5$ *

13. Do exercise 12 using the charged-field model.   *

14. Compute each of the following.
   a. $⁻2 - (7 + 10)$ ⁻19
   b. $8 - 11 - 10$ ⁻13
   c. $⁻2 - 7 + 3$ ⁻6

15. Motor oils protect car engines over a range of temperatures. These oils have names like 10W–40 or 5W–30. The following graph shows the temperatures, in degrees Fahrenheit, at which the engine is protected by a particular oil. Using the graph, find which oils can be used for the following temperatures.
   a. Between ⁻5° and 90°   10W–40 or 10W–30
   b. Below ⁻20°   5W–30
   c. Between ⁻10° and 50°   10W–40, 5W–30, or 10W–30
   d. From ⁻20° to over 100°   None
   e. From ⁻8° to 90°   10W–30 or 10W–40

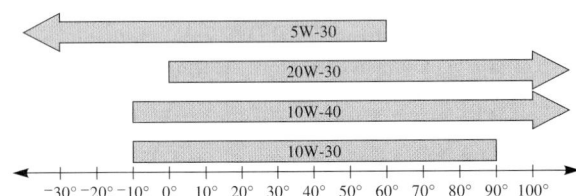

16. Simplify each of the following expressions as much as possible. Show all work.
   a. $4x - 2 - 3x$ *
   b. $4x - (2 - 3x)$ *

17. a. Prove that for all integers x and y, $⁻x - y = ⁻y - x$.   *
   b. Does part (a) imply that subtraction is commutative? Explain.   *

18. Let W stand for the set of whole numbers, I the set of integers, I^+ the set of positive integers, and I^- the set of negative integers. Find each of the following.
   a. $W - I^+$ {0}
   b. $W - I^-$ W
   c. $I \cap I$ I
   d. $I - W$ I^-

19. Complete the magic square using the following integers: ⁻13, ⁻10, ⁻7, ⁻4, 2, 5, 8, 11.   Answers vary.

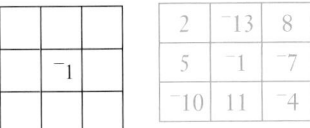

20. Let $y = {}^-3x - 2$. Find the value of y (in parts (a)–(d)) for each of the following values of x.

    a. ${}^-1$ 1   **b.** 100 ${}^-302$

    c. ${}^-2$ 4   **d.** ${}^-a$ in terms of a $3a - 2$

    e. For which values of x will y be ${}^-11$?   3

21. Determine the number of terms in the arithmetic and geometric sequences below.

    a. ${}^-27, {}^-26, {}^-25, \ldots, 50, 51, 52$ 80

    b. $3^3, 3^4, 3^5, 3^6, \ldots, 3^{10}$ 8

22. Find the sum of the following arithmetic sequence.

    ${}^-27, {}^-26, {}^-25, \ldots, 50, 51, 52.$ 1000

23. On *The Biggest Loser*, a person weighed 372 lbs, lost 9 lbs, gained 4 lbs, lost 13 lbs, and lost 24 lbs. Describe this weight fluctuation with a sum of integers and find the final weight of the contestant.   Answers vary. $372 + {}^-9 + 4 + {}^-13 + {}^-24 = 330$ lbs

24. In swimming, a competitor at any level trains to better his best time. If Hamilton swam the 100-m backstroke in 65 sec in his last race and in the next training session bettered the time by 4 sec, express this discussion using a sum of integers and show what the time in the training sessions was. $65 + {}^-4 = 61$ seconds

25. When one downloads a file to a computer, memory space is taken up on the computer. When one deletes a file, one gains a certain amount of memory space on the computer. If Sarai downloaded a program of 3.6 MB to her computer and deleted a picture file of 7.2 MB, explain this in terms of integers and the resulting effect on her computer memory.   *

26. Find all integers x, if there are any, such that the following are true.

    a. ${}^-|x| = 2$ None   **b.** ${}^-|x|$ is negative.   *

    c. ${}^-|x|$ is positive.   None   **d.** ${}^-x + 1$ is positive.   *

    e. ${}^-x - 1$ is negative. $x > {}^-1$

27. Let $y = |x - 5|$. Find the value of y (in parts (a)–(b)) for each of the following values of x.

    a. 10   5   **b.** ${}^-1$ 6

    c. Find all the values of x for which y is 7.   12 or ${}^-2$

28. By the definition of absolute value, the equation $y = |x|$ can be written as follows:

$$y = \begin{cases} x, & \text{if } x \geq 0 \\ {}^-x, & \text{if } x < 0 \end{cases}$$

Write $y = |x - 6|$ in a similar way without absolute value.   *

29. An arithmetic sequence may have a positive or negative difference. In each of the following arithmetic sequences, find the difference and write the next two terms:

    a. $7, 3, {}^-1, {}^-5$ ${}^-4; {}^-9, {}^-13$

    b. $1 - 3x, 1 - x, 1 + x$ $2x; 1 + 3x; 1 + 5x$

30. Classify each of the following as true or false. If false, show a counterexample that makes it false.

    a. $|x^2| = x^2$ True   **b.** $|x^3| = x^3$ *

    c. $|x^3| = x^2|x|$ True

31. Solve the following equations:

    a. ${}^-x + 5 = 7$ ${}^-2$ **b.** $1 - x = {}^-13$ 14

    c. ${}^-x - 8 = {}^-9$ 1

32. Estimate each of the following.   Estimates vary.

    a. $343 + {}^-42 - 402$ ${}^-101$

    b. ${}^-1992 + 3005 - 497$ 516

    c. $992 - {}^-10,003 - 101$ 10,894

    d. ${}^-301 - {}^-1303 + 4993$ 5995

Mathematical Connections 5-1

Answers to Mathematical Connections can be found in the Answers section at the back of the book.

Reasoning

1. A turnpike driver had car trouble. He knew that he had driven 12 mi from milepost 68 before the trouble started. Assuming he is confused and disoriented when he calls on his cellular phone for help, explain how he can determine his possible location.

2. Dolores claims that a way to understand that $a - b = a + {}^-b$, for all integers a and b, is to show that when you add b to each expression you get equal answers. Explain why Dolores's claim is true.

3. Explain why $b - a$ and $a - b$ are additive inverses of each other.

4. The absolute value of an integer is never negative. Does this contradict the fact that the absolute value of x could be equal to ${}^-x$? Explain why or why not.

5. If an integer a is pictured on the number line, then the distance from the point on the number line that represents the integer to the origin is $|a|$. Using this idea, explain why $|a - b|$ is the distance between the points that represent the integers a and b.

6. Recall the definition of less than for whole numbers using addition and define $a < b$ for any integers a and b. Use your definition to show that ${}^-8 < {}^-7$.

Open-Ended

7. Describe a realistic word problem that models ${}^-50 + {}^-85 - {}^-30$.

8. In a library some floors are below ground level and others are above ground level. If the ground-level floor is designated the zero floor, design a system to number the floors.

9. a. I choose an integer. I then subtract 10 from the integer, take the opposite of the result, add ${}^-3$, and find the opposite of the new result. My result is ${}^-3$. What is the original number?

    b. Judy wants to do the activity in part (a) with her classmates. Each classmate probably chooses a different number, and Judy wants to tell each classmate quickly what number was chosen. Judy figures out that the only thing she needs to do is to add 7 to each answer she gets. Does this always work? Explain why or why not.

    c. Come up with your own "trick" similar to the one in part (b) that works for each answer you get from your classmates.

10. Investigate how tides are measured and design an appropriate system to talk about negative, positive, and 0 tides.

Cooperative Learning

11. Look at several history of mathematics books and the Internet and report in your group on when and how negative integers were first introduced.

12. On 21 3×5 cards, write the integers ${}^-10$ to 10 using one integer per card. Lay the cards on the floor to form a number line. Choose someone from your group to act like the hiker in integer addition and subtraction. Give directions to walk the number line to solve exercises 4 and 11 in Assessment 5-lA. Try other addition and subtraction problems to make sure that the number-line model is understood by everyone in your group and could be used in an elementary classroom.

Connecting Mathematics to the Classroom

13. A fourth-grade student devised the following algorithm for subtracting $84 - 27$:

4 minus 7 equals negative 3.

$$
\begin{array}{r}
84 \\
-\ 27 \\
\hline
^-3
\end{array}
$$

80 minus 20 equals 60.

$$
\begin{array}{r}
84 \\
-\ 27 \\
\hline
^-3 \\
60
\end{array}
$$

60 plus negative 3 equals 57.

$$
\begin{array}{r}
84 \\
-\ 27 \\
\hline
^-3 \\
+\ 60 \\
\hline
57
\end{array}
$$

Thus, the answer is 57. How should you respond as a teacher? Will this technique always work?

14. An eighth-grade student claims she can prove that subtraction of integers is commutative. She points out that if a and b are integers, then $a - b = a + {}^-b$. Since addition is commutative, so is subtraction. What is your response?

15. A student had the following picture of an integer and its opposite. Other students in the class objected, saying that ^-a should be to the left of 0. How do you respond?

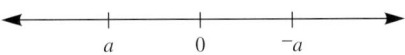

16. If the digits 1 through 9 are written in order, it is possible to place plus and minus signs between the numbers or to use no operation symbol at all to obtain a total of 100. For example, $1 + 2 + 3 - 4 + 5 + 6 + 78 + 9 = 100$. Can you obtain a total of 100 using fewer plus or minus signs than in the given example? Note that digits, such as 7 and 8 in the example, may be combined.

17. Mary wants to know more about absolute value. "Why can it be used to discuss distance? Is distance always positive?" she asks. How would you respond?

National Assessments

National Assessment of Educational Progress (NAEP) Questions

Paco had 32 trading cards. He gave N trading cards to his friend. Which expression tells how many trading cards Paco has now?
A. $32 + N$
B. $32 - N$
C. $N - 32$
D. $32 \div N$

NAEP, Grade 4, 2007

The lowest point of the St. Lawrence River is 294 feet below sea level. The top of Mt. Jacques Cartier is 1,277 feet above sea level. How many feet higher is the top of Mt. Jacques Cartier than the lowest point of the St. Lawrence River? Show your work.

NAEP, Grade 8, 1996

5-2 Multiplication and Division of Integers

5-2 Objectives

Students will be able to understand and explain

- Models for multiplication of integers.
- Properties of multiplication of integers.
- Integer division.
- Order of operations on integers.
- Inequalities with integers.

Multiplication of integers is approached through a variety of models: *patterns*, *charged-field*, *chip*, and *number-line*. Reasoning with these models is inductive and is used to motivate the operations.

Patterns Model for Multiplication of Integers

We may approach multiplication of integers using repeated addition. For example, if a running back lost 2 yd on each of three carries in a football game, then there was a net loss of $^-2 + {}^-2 + {}^-2$, or $^-6$, yards. Since $^-2 + {}^-2 + {}^-2$ can be written as $3(^-2)$, we have $3(^-2) = {}^-6$ by using repeated addition.

Activity Manual

Use *Multiplication and Division Patterns* to develop algorithms for multiplying and dividing integers by exploring patterns and inverse operations.

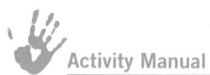

Consider $(^-2)3$. It is meaningless to say that there are $^-2$ threes in a sum. But if the commutative property of multiplication is to hold for all integers, then $(^-2)3 = 3(^-2) = {}^-6$.

To find $(^-3)(^-2)$, we develop the following pattern:

$$\begin{aligned} 3(^-2) &= {}^-6 \\ 2(^-2) &= {}^-4 \\ 1(^-2) &= {}^-2 \\ 0(^-2) &= 0 \\ {}^-1(^-2) &= ? \\ {}^-2(^-2) &= ? \\ {}^-3(^-2) &= ? \end{aligned}$$

The first four products, $^-6$, $^-4$, $^-2$, and 0, are terms in an arithmetic sequence with a fixed difference of 2. If the pattern continues, the next three terms in the sequence are 2, 4, and 6. Thus, it appears that $(^-3)(^-2) = 6$. Likewise, $(^-2)(^-3) = 6$. We used inductive reasoning to reach the results but will use deductive reasoning later to justify the generalized product.

Example 12

On a spreadsheet, in column A enter 5 as the first entry and then write a formula to add $^-1$ to 5 for the second entry. Then add $^-1$ to the second entry and fill down until there are 20 terms continuing the pattern. In column B, repeat the process. In column C, find the product of the respective entries in columns A and B. What patterns do you observe?

Solution

The described spreadsheet is seen in Figure 12.

	A	B	C
1	5	5	25
2	4	4	16
3	3	3	9
4	2	2	4
5	1	1	1
6	0	0	0
7	-1	-1	1
8	-2	-2	4
9	-3	-3	9
10	-4	-4	16
11	-5	-5	25
12	-6	-6	36
13	-7	-7	49
14	-8	-8	64
15	-9	-9	81
16	-10	-10	100
17	-11	-11	121
18	-12	-12	144
19	-13	-13	189
20	-14	-14	196

Figure 12

Patterns found may vary, but we see that any number squared is either positive or zero. Additionally, we have positive numbers times positive numbers having a positive product, and negative numbers times negative numbers having a positive product. The spreadsheet only depicts examples of the generalizations made and does not constitute a proof.

Multiplication of integers is approached using the chip model, the charged-field model, and the number-line model. In all of these models we start with 0, represented in various ways.

Chip Model and Charged-Field Model for Multiplication

The chip model and the charged-field model can both be used to illustrate multiplication of integers. Consider Figure 13(a), where $3(^-2)$ is pictured using a chip model. The product $3(^-2)$ is interpreted as putting in 3 groups of 2 red chips each. In Figure 13(b), $3(^-2)$ is pictured as 3 groups of 2 negative charges.

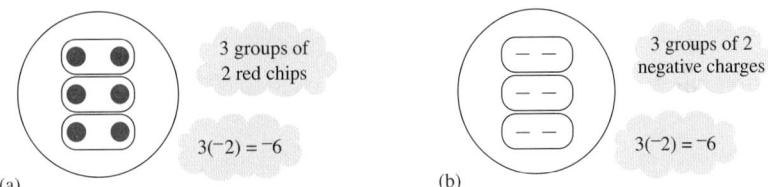

Figure 13

To find $(^-3)(^-2)$ using the chip model, we interpret the signs as follows: $^-3$ is taken to mean *"remove 3 groups of"*; and $^-2$ is taken to mean *"2 red chips."* To do this, we start with a value of 0 that includes at least 6 red chips, as shown in Figure 14(a). When we remove 6 red chips, we are left with 6 black chips. The result is a positive 6, so $(^-3)(^-2) = 6$. Similar reasoning can be used in Figure 14(b) with the charged-field model.

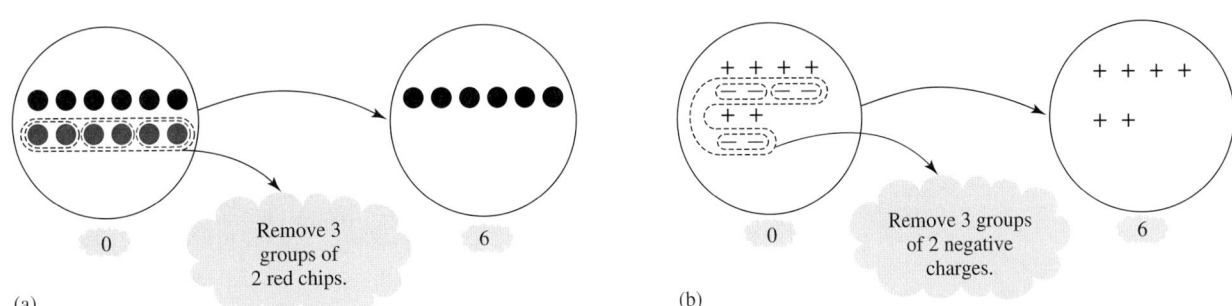

Figure 14

Number-Line Model

As with addition and subtraction, we demonstrate multiplication by using a hiker moving along a number line, according to the following rules:

1. Traveling to the left (west) means moving in the negative direction, and traveling to the right (east) means moving in the positive direction.
2. Time in the future is denoted by a positive value, and time in the past is denoted by a negative value.

Consider the number line shown in Figure 15. Various cases using this number line are given next.

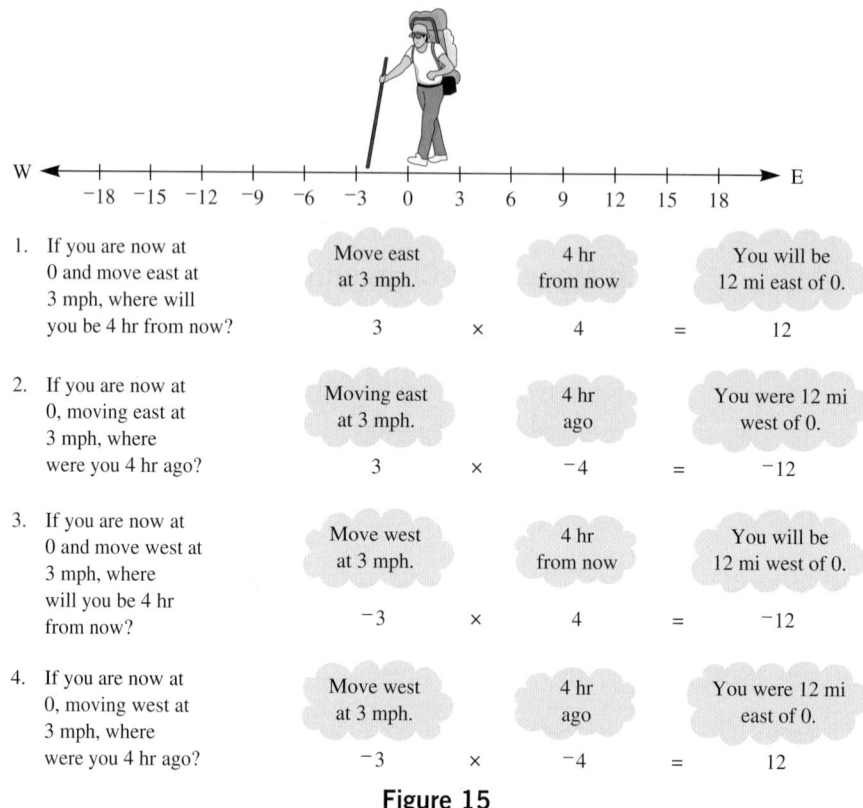

1. If you are now at 0 and move east at 3 mph, where will you be 4 hr from now?

   Move east at 3 mph.

   4 hr from now

   You will be 12 mi east of 0.

   3 × 4 = 12

2. If you are now at 0, moving east at 3 mph, where were you 4 hr ago?

   Moving east at 3 mph.

   4 hr ago

   You were 12 mi west of 0.

   3 × $^-4$ = $^-12$

3. If you are now at 0 and move west at 3 mph, where will you be 4 hr from now?

   Move west at 3 mph.

   4 hr from now

   You will be 12 mi west of 0.

   $^-3$ × 4 = $^-12$

4. If you are now at 0, moving west at 3 mph, where were you 4 hr ago?

   Move west at 3 mph.

   4 hr ago

   You were 12 mi east of 0.

   $^-3$ × $^-4$ = 12

Figure 15

 An alternative use of the number line to show multiplication of integers is seen on the following student shown on page 241. Observe how $^-3(^-2)$ is performed.

The models presented earlier in this section suggest ways to define the multiplication of integers. We give a formal definition using absolute values in the following:

Definition of Integer Multiplication

Let a and b be any integers.

a. If either $a \geq 0$ and $b \geq 0$, then a and b are whole numbers with product ab.
b. If $a \leq 0$ and $b \leq 0$, then $ab = |a||b|$.
c. If one of a or b is less than 0 while the other is greater than 0, then $ab = {}^-|a||b|$.

Properties of Integer Multiplication

CCSS In grade 7 *Common Core Standards*, students should

understand that multiplication is extended . . . by requiring that operations continue to satisfy the properties of operations [of addition and multiplication on whole numbers], particularly the distributive property leading to products such as $(^-1)(^-1) = 1$ and the rules for multiplying signed numbers. (p. 48)

School Book Page Multiply and Divide Integers

What You'll Learn
To multiply and divide integers and to solve problems involving integers

Why Learn This?
Balloonists watch their altitude when they fly. You can multiply integers to find change in altitude.

A balloon descends at a rate of 4 ft/min for 3 min. To multiply integers, think of multiplication as repeated addition.

$$3(-4) = (-4) + (-4) + (-4) = -12 \quad \leftarrow \text{The balloon descends 12 ft.}$$

You can use number lines to multiply integers.

3(2) means three groups of 2.

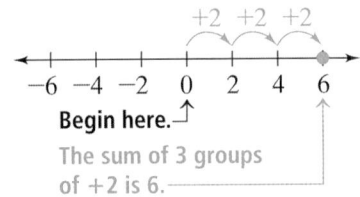

Begin here.
The sum of 3 groups of +2 is 6.

3(−2) means three groups of −2.

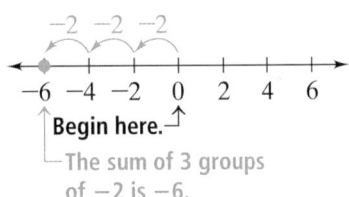

Begin here.
The sum of 3 groups of −2 is −6.

−3(2) is the opposite of three groups of 2.

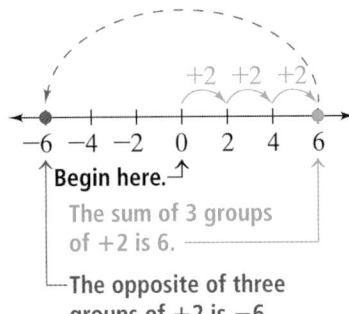

Begin here.
The sum of 3 groups of +2 is 6.
The opposite of three groups of +2 is −6.

−3(−2) is the opposite of three groups of −2.

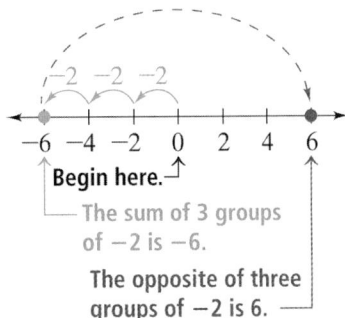

Begin here.
The sum of 3 groups of −2 is −6.
The opposite of three groups of −2 is 6.

This pattern suggests the rules for multiplying integers.

The set of integers has properties under multiplication analogous to those of the set of whole numbers under multiplication, these properties are summarized in Theorem 5-5.

Theorem 5-5:   Properties of Integer Multiplication

The set of integers I satisfies the following properties of multiplication for all integers $a, b, c \in I$:

Closure property of multiplication of integers ab is a unique integer.

Commutative property of multiplication of integers $ab = ba$.

Associative property of multiplication of integers $(ab)c = a(bc)$.

Identity property of multiplication of integers   1 is the unique integer such that for all integers a, $1 \cdot a = a = a \cdot 1$.

Distributive properties of multiplication over addition for integers $a(b + c) = ab + ac$ and $(b + c)a = ba + ca$.

Zero property of multiplication of integers   0 is the unique integer such that for all integers a, $a \cdot 0 = 0 = 0 \cdot a$.

Theorem 5-6 is another convenient theorem that follows from the definition of multiplication of integers and the properties in Theorem 5-5.

Theorem 5-6

For every integer a, $(^-1)a = {}^-a$.

It is important to keep in mind that $(^-1)a = {}^-a$ is true for all integers a. Thus, if we substitute $^-1$ for a, we get $(^-1)(^-1) = {}^-(^-1)$. Because $^-(^-1) = 1$, we have justification for the fact that $(^-1)(^-1) = 1$. Using this result, the preceding theorem, and the properties of integers listed earlier, we show that for all integers a and b, $(^-a)b = {}^-(ab)$ and $(^-a)(^-b) = ab$ as follows:

$$
\begin{aligned}
(^-a)b &= [(^-1)a]b \\
&= (^-1)(ab) \\
&= {}^-(ab)
\end{aligned}
$$

Also:

$$
\begin{aligned}
(^-a)(^-b) &= [(^-1)a][(^-1)b] \\
&= [(^-1)(^-1)](ab) \\
&= 1(ab) \\
&= ab
\end{aligned}
$$

We have established the following theorem:

Theorem 5-7

For all integers a and b,
    a. $(^-a)b = {}^-(ab)$
    b. $(^-a)(^-b) = ab$

The distributive property of multiplication over subtraction follows from the distributive property of multiplication over addition:

$$
\begin{aligned}
a(b - c) &= a(b + {}^-c) \\
&= ab + a(^-c) \\
&= ab + {}^-(ac) \\
&= ab - ac
\end{aligned}
$$

Consequently, $a(b - c) = ab - ac$. From this and the commutative property of multiplication, it follows that $(b - c)a = ba - ca$.

Theorem 5-8: Distributive Property of Multiplication over Subtraction for Integers

For all integers a, b, and c,

    a. $a(b - c) = ab - ac$

    b. $(b - c)a = ba - ca$

Example 13

Simplify each of the following expressions so there are no parentheses in the final answer.

    a. $(^-3)(x - 2)$ **b.** $(a + b)(a - b)$

Solution

    a. $(^-3)(x - 2) = (^-3)x - (^-3)(2) = {}^-3x - (^-6) = {}^-3x + {}^-(^-6) = {}^-3x + 6$

    b. $\begin{aligned}(a + b)(a - b) &= (a + b)a - (a + b)b \\ &= (a^2 + ba) - (ab + b^2) \\ &= a^2 + ba + {}^-(ab + b^2) \\ &= a^2 + ab + {}^-(ab) + {}^-b^2 \quad (\text{Note: } {}^-b^2 \text{ means } {}^-(b^2).) \\ &= a^2 + 0 + {}^-b^2 \\ &= a^2 - b^2\end{aligned}$

    Thus, $(a + b)(a - b) = a^2 - b^2$.

The result $(a + b)(a - b) = a^2 - b^2$ in Example 13(b) is used so often that we call it the **difference-of-squares** formula and list it as Theorem 5-9.

Theorem 5-9: Difference of Squares Formula

For all expressions a and b, $(a + b)(a - b) = a^2 - b^2$.

Example 14

Use the difference-of-squares formula to simplify the following expressions.

    a. $(4 + b)(4 - b)$ **b.** $(^-4 + b)(^-4 - b)$ **c.** $(x + 3)^2 - (x - 3)^2$

Solution

    a. $(4 + b)(4 - b) = 4^2 - b^2 = 16 - b^2$

    b. $(^-4 + b)(^-4 - b) = (^-4)^2 - b^2 = 16 - b^2$

    c. $\begin{aligned}(x + 3)^2 - (x - 3)^2 &= [(x + 3) + (x - 3)][(x + 3) - (x - 3)] \\ &= 2x(x + 3 - x + 3) \\ &= 2x(x + 3 + {}^-x + 3) \\ &= 2x(6) \\ &= 12x\end{aligned}$

When the distributive property of multiplication over subtraction is written in reverse order as

$$ab - ac = a(b - c) \quad \text{and} \quad ba - ca = (b - c)a$$

and similarly for addition, the expressions on the right of each equation are in *factored* form. We say that the common factor a has been *factored out*. Both the difference-of-squares formula and the distributive properties of multiplication over addition and subtraction can be used for factoring.

Example 15

Factor each of the following expressions completely.

a. $x^2 - 9$ **b.** $(x + y)^2 - z^2$ **c.** $^-3x + 5xy$ **d.** $3x - 6$ **e.** $5x^2 - 2x^2$

Solution

a. $x^2 - 9 = x^2 - 3^2 = (x + 3)(x - 3)$
b. $(x + y)^2 - z^2 = (x + y + z)(x + y - z)$
c. $^-3x + 5xy = ^-3x + 5yx = (^-3 + 5y)x$
d. $3x - 6 = 3x - 3 \cdot 2 = 3(x - 2)$
e. $5x^2 - 2x^2 = (5 - 2)x^2 = 3x^2$

Problem Solving **Barrel Problem**

In the 1400s, European merchants used integers to label barrels of flour. For example, a barrel labeled $^+3$ meant the barrel was 3 lb overweight, while a barrel labeled $^-5$ meant the barrel was 5 lb underweight. A worker who had labeled 100-lb barrels turned in a weight sheet knowing that the total of the weight was off 53 lbs. He had used only 5s and 6s to label the barrels, but he forgot how many of the labels were positive and how many were negative. He was certain that there were fewer than 20 barrels. How might the barrels have been labeled?

 Understanding the Problem In understanding the problem, one may start by explaining to oneself "the meaning of a problem and looking for entry points to its solution" as suggested in the *Common Core Standards* for mathematical practice. (p. 6) In this problem, we recognize that all barrels were labeled using 5s and 6s, but we do not know whether these were positive or negative. Thus, both will have to be considered. Additionally the total weight of all the barrels is off 53 lb, and there were fewer than 20 barrels total. All of these facts must be taken into account as a solution is sought.

 Devising a Plan If we reason quantitatively about this problem, we see that we are looking for combinations of multiples of 5, 6, $^-5$, and $^-6$. As mentioned in the *Common Core Standards* for mathematical practice (p. 6), we must "attend to the meaning of the quantities," or in this case the "positiveness" and "negativeness" of the quantities as we look for combinations to find the desired weight of 53 with 20 or fewer combinations of multiples for each possible solution. One way to manage this search is to create a table of values showing the multiples of the possible used quantities.

Carrying Out the Plan The construction of a table may be aided by a spreadsheet, but construction can be achieved without it as seen in Table 4.

Table 4

Multiples of 6	Multiples of 5	Total Barrels	Total Weight
$8 \cdot 6 = 48$	$1 \cdot 5 = 5$	9	53
$3 \cdot 6 = 18$	$7 \cdot 5 = 35$	10	53
Multiples of $^-6$	**Multiples of 5**	**Total Barrels**	**Total Weight**
$2 \cdot ^-6 = ^-12$	$13 \cdot 5 = 65$	15	53
$13 \cdot ^-6 = ^-78$	$5 \cdot 5 = 25$	18	$^-53$
Multiples of 6	**Multiples of $^-5$**	**Total Barrels**	**Total Weight**
$2 \cdot 6 = 12$	$13 \cdot ^-5 = ^-65$	15	$^-53$
$13 \cdot 6 = 78$	$5 \cdot ^-5 = ^-25$	18	53
Multiples of $^-6$	**Multiples of $^-5$**	**Total Barrels**	**Total Weight**
$8 \cdot ^-6 = ^-48$	$1 \cdot ^-5 = ^-5$	9	$^-53$
$3 \cdot ^-6 = ^-18$	$7 \cdot ^-5 = ^-35$	10	$^-53$

Activity Manual

Use *Integer × and ÷ Contig* to reinforce integer multiplication and division.

Thus, there are eight possible ways that the barrels could have been labeled as seen above.

Looking Back There are many possible ways to change this problem. One is to use different sets of values of weights that the barrels could be off. A different way is to change the number of barrels used. The problem provides many different avenues for exploration.

Integer Division

In the set of whole numbers, where $b \neq 0$, $a \div b$ is the unique whole number c such that $a = bc$. If such a whole number c does not exist, then $a \div b$ is undefined. Division on the set of integers is defined analogously with division by 0 undefined.

> **Definition of Integer Division**
>
> For all integers a and b, $a \div b$ is the unique integer c, if it exists, such that $a = bc$.

Notice that $a \div b$, if it exists, is the solution of $a = bx$. If $a \div b$ is an integer, then we can extend the concept of divisibility introduced in Chapter 4 as follows:

> **Definition of Divisibility for Integers**
>
> For any integers a and b, if $a \div b$ is a unique integer, then a is **divisible** by b, or equivalently b **divides** a, written as $b \mid a$.

Example 16

Use the definition of integer division, if possible, to evaluate each of the following.

a. $12 \div (^-4)$ **b.** $^-12 \div 4$ **c.** $^-12 \div (^-4)$
d. $^-12 \div 5$ **e.** $(ab) \div b, b \neq 0$ **f.** $(ab) \div a, a \neq 0$

Solution
a. Let $12 \div (^-4) = c$. Then $12 = ^-4c$ and consequently $c = ^-3$. Thus, $12 \div (^-4) = ^-3$.
b. Let $^-12 \div 4 = c$. Then $^-12 = 4c$ and therefore $c = ^-3$. Thus, $^-12 \div 4 = ^-3$.
c. Let $^-12 \div (^-4) = c$. Then $^-12 = ^-4c$ and consequently $c = 3$. Thus, $^-12 \div (^-4) = 3$.
d. Let $^-12 \div 5 = c$. Then $^-12 = 5c$. Because no integer c exists to satisfy this equation (why?), we say that $^-12 \div 5$ is undefined over the set of integers.
e. Let $(ab) \div b = x$. Then $ab = bx$ and consequently $x = a$.
f. Let $(ab) \div a = x$. Then $ab = ax$ and hence $x = b$.

Example 16 suggests that *the quotient of two negative integers, if it exists, is a positive integer, and the quotient of a positive and a negative integer, if it exists, or of a negative and a positive integer, if it exists, is negative.*

Example 17

Division by 0 in the set of whole numbers is undefined. Use the definition of division for integers to show that dividing by 0 is not possible.

Solution
We know that $a \div 0 = x$ if, and only if, $0x = a$ and x is unique. Because $0x = 0$ for all integers, the equation has no solution if $a \neq 0$. If $a = 0$ then for all integers x, $0x = a$. Because the solution is not unique, $0 \div 0$ is not defined.

Algorithm for Division Extended

The division process for whole numbers can be extended to work with integers as seen in the following division: $12{,}985 \div 17$.

$$
\begin{array}{r}
763 \\
\hline
3 \\
60 \\
{}^-200 \\
900 \\
17\overline{)12985} \\
-15300 \\
\hline
{}^-2315 \\
-({}^-3400) \\
\hline
1085 \\
-(1020) \\
\hline
65 \\
-51 \\
\hline
14
\end{array}
$$

Though not efficient as a standard division, the end result that $12{,}985 = 17 \cdot 763 + 14$ still holds with 763 as the quotient and 14 as the remainder.

Order of Operations on Integers

When addition, subtraction, multiplication, division, and exponentiation appear without parentheses, exponentiation is done first in order from right to left, then multiplications and divisions in the order of their appearance from left to right, and then additions and subtractions in the order of their appearance from left to right. Arithmetic operations that appear inside parentheses must be done first.

Example 18

Evaluate each of the following.

a. $2 - 5 \cdot 4 + 1$ **b.** $(2 - 5)4 + 1$ **c.** $2 - 3 \cdot 4 + 5 \cdot 2 - 1 + 5$
d. $2 + 16 \div 4 \cdot 2 + 8$ **e.** $({}^-3)^4$ **f.** ${}^-3^4$

Solution

a. $2 - 5 \cdot 4 + 1 = 2 - 20 + 1 = {}^-18 + 1 = {}^-17$
b. $(2 - 5)4 + 1 = ({}^-3)4 + 1 = {}^-12 + 1 = {}^-11$
c. $2 - 3 \cdot 4 + 5 \cdot 2 - 1 + 5 = 2 - 12 + 10 - 1 + 5 = 4$
d. $2 + 16 \div 4 \cdot 2 + 8 = 2 + 4 \cdot 2 + 8 = 2 + 8 + 8 = 10 + 8 = 18$
e. $({}^-3)^4 = ({}^-3)({}^-3)({}^-3)({}^-3) = 81$
f. ${}^-3^4 = {}^-(3^4) = {}^-(81) = {}^-81$

From Example 18(e) and (f), we have $({}^-3)^4 \neq {}^-3^4$. By convention, $({}^-x)^4$ means $({}^-x)({}^-x)({}^-x)({}^-x)$ and ${}^-x^4$ means ${}^-(x^4)$ and equals ${}^-(x \cdot x \cdot x \cdot x)$.

With the meaning of exponentiation given, the properties of exponents given in Chapter 3 hold for all integers when their exponents are whole numbers. Negative integer exponents will be explored in Chapter 6.

Ordering Integers

As with whole numbers, a number line as shown in Figure 16 can be used to describe greater than and less than relations for the set of integers. Because $^-5$ is to the left of $^-3$ on the number line, we say that "$^-5$ is less than $^-3$," and write $^-5 < \, ^-3$. We also say that "$^-3$ is greater than $^-5$," and we write $^-3 > \, ^-5$.

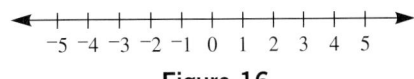

Figure 16

Notice that since $^-5$ is to the left of $^-3$, there is a positive integer that can be added to $^-5$ to get $^-3$, namely, 2. Thus, $^-5 < \, ^-3$ because $^-5 + 2 = \, ^-3$. The definition of *less than* for integers is similar to that for whole numbers.

> ### Definition of Less Than for Integers
> For all integers a and b, a is less than b, written $a < b$, if, and only if, there exists a positive integer k such that $a + k = b$.

The last equation implies that $k = b - a$. Thus, we have proved the following theorem:

> ### Theorem 5-10
> For integers a and b, $a < b$ (or equivalently, $b > a$) if, and only if, $b - a$ is equal to a positive integer; that is, $b - a > 0$, or equivalently $a - b < 0$.

Using Theorem 5-10, $^-5 < \, ^-3$ because $^-3 - (^-5) = \, ^-3 + \, ^-(^-5) = \, ^-3 + 5 = 2 > 0$. Theorem 5-10 can also be used to justify each of the following.

> ### Theorem 5-11
> Let x, y, n be any integers.
>   **a.** If $x < y$, then $x + n < y + n$.
>   **b.** If $x < y$, then $^-x > \, ^-y$.
>   **c.** If $x < y$ and $n > 0$, then $nx < ny$.
>   **d.** If $x < y$ and $n < 0$, then $nx > ny$.

The justifications are given next.

a. To show that $x + n < y + n$, we need to show that $(y + n) - (x + n) > 0$. We have
$y + n - (x + n) = y + n - x - n = y - x$. Because $x < y$, $y - x > 0$ and we have
$y + n - (x + n) > 0$; hence $x + n < y + n$.

b. To show that $^-x > \, ^-y$, we need to show that $^-x - (^-y) > 0$. We have $^-x - (^-y) =$
$^-x + \, ^-(^-y) = \, ^-x + y = y + \, ^-x = y - x$. Because $x < y$, $y - x > 0$ and we have
$^-x - (^-y) > 0$; hence $^-x > \, ^-y$.

c. To show that $nx < ny$, we need to show that $ny - nx > 0$. We have $ny - nx = n(y - x)$.
Because n is a positive integer, $x < y$, and $y - x > 0$, $n(y - x)$ must also be positive.
Because $ny - nx > 0$, we have $nx < ny$.

d. To show that $nx > ny$, we show that $nx - ny > 0$. We have $nx - ny = n(x - y)$. Since
$y - x > 0$, $x - y < 0$ (why?). Because $n < 0$ and $x - y < 0$, $n(x - y)$ is positive. Thus,
$nx - ny > 0$ and hence, $nx > ny$.

Example 19

Use the theorems developed above to find all integers x that satisfy the inequalities parts (a) and (b).

   a. $x + 3 < {}^-2$
   b. ${}^-x - 3 < 5$
   c. If $x \leq {}^-2$, find the values of $5 - 3x$ when x is an integer.

Solution

   a. If $x + 3 < {}^-2$, then by Theorem 5–11(a),

   $$x + 3 + {}^-3 < {}^-2 + {}^-3$$
   $$x < {}^-5, \quad x \text{ is an integer.}$$

   We can also write the solution set (the set of all solutions) as $\{{}^-6, {}^-7, {}^-8, {}^-9, \ldots\}$.

   Strictly speaking, we have only shown that every x that satisfies the first inequality also satisfies $x < {}^-5$. To be sure that $x < {}^-5$ represents all the solutions, we need to show the converse; that is, if $x < {}^-5$ then $x + 3 < {}^-2$. This can be easily done by adding 3 to both sides of $x < {}^-5$.

   b. If ${}^-x - 3 < 5$, then

   $${}^-x - 3 + 3 < 5 + 3$$
   $${}^-x < 8$$
   $${}^-({}^-x) > {}^-8 \quad \text{by Theorem 5–11(b)}$$
   $$x > {}^-8, \quad x \text{ is an integer; that is, all the integers in the set } \{{}^-7, {}^-6, {}^-5, \ldots\}.$$

   c. If $x \leq {}^-2$, then to find an inequality for $5 - 3x$, we proceed as follows.

   $${}^-3x \geq {}^-3({}^-2)$$
   $${}^-3x \geq 6$$
   $$5 + {}^-3x \geq 5 + 6$$
   $$5 - 3x \geq 5 + 6$$
   $$5 - 3x \geq 11; \text{ that is, all integers in the set } \{11, 12, 13, 14, \ldots\}.$$

Assessment 5-2A

1. Use patterns to show that $({}^-1)({}^-1) = 1$. *
2. Use the charged-field model to show that $({}^-4)({}^-2) = 8$. *
3. Use the number-line model to show that $2({}^-4) = {}^-8$. *
4. In each of the following charged-field models, the encircled charges are removed. Write the corresponding integer multiplication problem with its solution based on the model.

   a.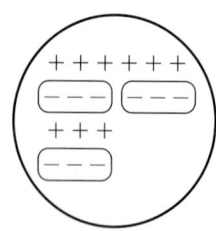

   $({}^-3)({}^-3) = 9$

   b.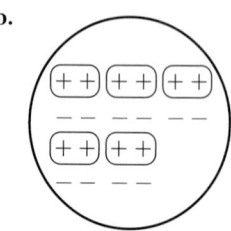

   $({}^-5)2 = {}^-10$

5. The number of students eating in the school cafeteria has been decreasing at the rate of 30 per year for many years. Assuming this trend continues, write a multiplication problem that describes the change in the number of students eating in the school cafeteria for each of the following situations.

   a. The change over the next 4 years $4({}^-30) = {}^-120$
   b. The situation 4 years ago $({}^-4)({}^-30) = 120$ more
   c. The change over the next n years $(n)({}^-30) = {}^-30n$
   d. The situation n years ago $({}^-n)({}^-30) = 30n$ more
6. Use the definition of division to find each quotient, if possible. If a quotient is not defined, explain why.
   a. ${}^-40 \div {}^-5$ ${}^-5x = {}^-40$, so $x = 8$
   b. ${}^-143 \div 13$ $13x = {}^-143$, so $x = {}^-11$
   c. ${}^-5 \div 0$ Undefined because division by 0 is undefined.
7. Evaluate each of the following expressions, if possible.
   a. $({}^-10 \div {}^-2)({}^-2)$ ${}^-10$
   b. $({}^-10 \cdot 5) \div 5$ ${}^-10$
   c. ${}^-8 \div ({}^-8 + 8)$ Not defined
   d. $({}^-6 + 6) \div ({}^-2 + 2)$ Undefined
   e. $|{}^-24| \div [4(9 - 15)]$ 1
8. Evaluate each of the following products and then, if possible, write two division statements that are equivalent to the given multiplication statement. If two division statements are not possible, explain why.
   a. $({}^-6)5$ ${}^-30$; ${}^-30 \div {}^-6 = 5$; ${}^-30 \div 5 = {}^-6$
   b. $({}^-5)({}^-4)$ 20; $20 \div {}^-5 = {}^-4$; $20 \div {}^-4 = {}^-5$
   c. $({}^-3)0$ 0; $0 \div {}^-3 = 0$; division by 0 is undefined.

* Answers can be found in the Answers section at the back of the book.

9. In each of the following, x and y are integers; $y \neq 0$. Use the definition of division in terms of multiplication to perform the indicated operations. Write your answers in simplest form.
   a. $(4x) \div 4$ *   **b.** $(^-xy) \div y$ *

10. In a lab, the temperature of various chemical reactions is changing by a fixed number of degrees per minute. Write a numeric expression that describes each of the following if all times are on the same day.
    a. The temperature at 8:00 P.M. is 32°C. If it drops 1°C per minute, what will the temperature be at 8:30 P.M.? $32 + (^-1)30 = 2°C$
    b. The temperature at 8:20 P.M. is 0°C. If it has dropped 2°C per minute, what was the temperature at 7:55 P.M.? $0 + (^-2)(^-25) = 50°C$
    c. The temperature at 8:00 P.M. is $^-20°C$. If it has dropped 2°C per minute, what was the temperature at 7:30 P.M.? $^-20 + (^-2)(^-30) = 40°C$
    d. The temperature at 8:00 P.M. is 25°C. If it has been increasing every minute by 2°C, what was the temperature at 7:40 P.M.? $25 + 2(^-20) = ^-15°C$

11. The farmland acreage lost to family dwellings over the next 8 years will be 12,000 acres per year. How much acreage would be lost to homes during this time period?   96,000 acres

12. Illustrate the distributive property of multiplication over subtraction, $a(b - c) = ab - ac$, using $a = ^-1, b = ^-4$, and $c = ^-2$. $^-1(^-4 - ^-2) = ^-1(^-4) - (^-1)(^-2) = 4 - 2 = 2$

13. Compute each of the following.
    a. $(^-2)^3$ $^-8$ **b.** $(^-2)^4$ 16
    c. $(^-10)^5 \div (^-10)^2$ $^-1000$ **d.** $(^-3)^5 \div (^-3)$ 81
    e. $(^-1)^{50}$ 1 **f.** $(^-1)^{151}$ $^-1$
    g. $^-2 + 3 \cdot 5 - 1$ 12 **h.** $10 - 3 \cdot 7 - 4(^-2) + 3$ 0
    i. $(^-2)^{64} - 2^{64}$ 0 **j.** $^-2^8 + 2^8$ 0

14. If x is an integer and $x \neq 0$, which of the following expressions are always positive and which are always negative?
    a. $^-x^2$ Negative   **b.** x^2 Positive
    c. $(^-x)^2$ Positive   **d.** $^-x^3$ Neither
    e. $(^-x)^3$ Neither

15. Find all integer values of x for which the following are true.
    a. $^-x^2 = x^2$ 0 **b.** $^-x^3 = (^-x)^3$ All integers

16. If $48 \div x$ is an integer, what are the possible values of x? $^-48, ^-24, ^-16, ^-12, ^-8, ^-6, ^-4, ^-3, ^-2, ^-1, 1, 2, 3, 4, 6, 8, 12, 16, 24, 48$

17. Identify the property of integers being illustrated in each of the following.
    a. $(^-3)(4 + 5) = (4 + 5)(^-3)$ *
    b. $(^-4)(^-7) \in I$ Closure property of multiplication
    c. $5[4(^-3)] = (5 \cdot 4)(^-3)$ *
    d. $(^-9)[5 + (^-8)] = (^-9)5 + (^-9)(^-8)$ *

18. Simplify each of the following expressions.
    a. $(^-x)(^-y)$ xy **b.** $^-2x(^-y)$ $2xy$
    c. $^-2(^-x + y) + x + y$ $3x - y$ **d.** ^-1x ^-x

19. Multiply each of the following and combine terms where possible.
    a. $^-2(x - y)$ $^-2x + 2y$ **b.** $x(x - y)$ $x^2 - xy$
    c. $^-x(x - y)$ $^-x^2 + xy$ **d.** $^-2(x + y - z)$ $^-2x - 2y + 2z$

20. Find all integers x (if any) that make each of the following true.
    a. $^-3x = 6$ $^-2$
    b. $^-2x = 0$ 0
    c. $x \div 3 = ^-12$ $^-36$
    d. $x \div (^-3) = ^-2$ 6
    e. $x \div (^-x) = ^-1$ $x \in I, x \neq 0$
    f. $^-3x - 8 = 7$ $^-5$
    g. $^-2(5x - 3) = 26$ $^-2$
    h. $3x - x - 2x = 3$ None
    i. $^-2(5x - 6) - 30 = ^-x$ $^-2$
    j. $x^2 = 4$ 2 or $^-2$
    k. $(x - 1)^2 = 9$ 4 or $^-2$
    l. $(x - 1)^2 = (x + 3)^2$ $^-1$
    m. $(x - 1)(x + 3) = 0$ 1 or $^-3$

21. Use the difference-of-squares formula to simplify each of the following, if possible.
    a. $52 \cdot 48$ $(50 + 2)(50 - 2) = 50^2 - 2^2 = 2500 - 4 = 2496$
    b. $(5 - 100)(5 + 100)$ $5^2 - 100^2 = 25 - 10,000 = ^-9975$
    c. $(^-x - y)(^-x + y)$ $x^2 - y^2$

22. Factor each of the following expressions completely.
    a. $3x + 5x$ $(3 + 5)x = 8x$
    b. $xy + x$ $x(y + 1)$
    c. $x^2 + xy$ $x(x + y)$
    d. $3xy + 2x - xz$ $x(3y + 2 - z)$
    e. $abc + ab - a$ $a(bc + b - 1)$
    f. $16 - a^2$ $(4 + a)(4 - a)$
    g. $4x^2 - 25y^2$ $(2x + 5y)(2x - 5y)$

23. Use the distributive property of multiplication over addition or over subtraction and other properties to show that
    $$(a - b)^2 = a^2 - 2ab + b^2$$ *

24. In each of the following, find the next two terms. Assume each sequence is arithmetic or geometric, and find its common difference or ratio and the nth term.
    a. $^-10, ^-7, ^-4, ^-1, 2, 5, \ldots$ $8, 11, d = 3, n$th term is $3n - 13$
    b. $^-2, ^-4, ^-8, ^-16, ^-32, ^-64, \ldots$ $^-128, ^-256, r = 2, n$th term is $^-2^n$
    c. $2, ^-2^2, 2^3, ^-2^4, 2^5, ^-2^6, \ldots$ *

25. Find the missing terms in the following arithmetic or geometric sequences.
    a. $^-3, ^-9, \_\_, \_\_, ^-243$ $^-27, ^-81$
    b. $\_\_, 32, ^-16, 8, \_\_$ $^-64, ^-4$

26. A hot air balloon descends at the rate of 5 ft per minute for 6 minutes and then rises at the rate of 3 ft per minute for 8 minutes. Write this information using integers and give the net result on balloon height.   *

27. A paper cup is 7 in. tall with 1 in. of that height being the rim. The cups nest together with the non-rim part (6″) fitting in a cup below. Write an expression for the total height of n nested cups using $^-6$ to represent each of the unseen nested portions of the cups.   Answers vary. $7n + (^-6)(n - 1) = n + 6$

Assessment 5-2B

1. Use patterns to show that $(^-2)(^-2) = 4$.   *
2. Use the charged-field model to show that $(^-2)(^-3) = 6$.   *
3. Use the number-line model to show that $2(^-3) = ^-6$.   *
4. In each of the following charged-field models, the encircled charges are removed. Write the corresponding integer multiplication problem with its solution based on the model.

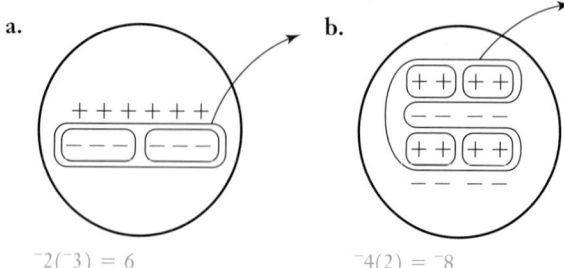

a.   b.

$^-2(^-3) = 6$ $^-4(2) = ^-8$

5. The number of students taking sophomore mathematics at Union College has been decreasing at the rate of 20 per year for many years. Assuming this trend continues, write a multiplication problem that describes the change in the number of sophomores taking mathematics at Union for each of the following situations.
    a. The change over the next 4 years   *
    b. The situation 5 years ago   *
    c. The change over the next n years   *
    d. The situation n years ago   *
6. Use the definition of division to find each quotient, if possible. If a quotient is not defined, explain why.
    a. $143 \div (^-10)$ *
    b. $0 \div (^-6)$ 0
7. Evaluate each of the following, if possible.
    a. $(a \div b)b$ a if $b \neq 0$ b. $(ab) \div b$ a if $b \neq 0$
    c. $(^-8 + 8) \div 8$ 0   d. $(^-23 - ^-7) \div 4$ $^-4$
    e. $|^-28| \div (2|^-7|)$ 2
8. Evaluate each of the following products and then, if possible, write two division statements that are equivalent to the given multiplication statement. If two division statements are not possible, explain why.
    a. $(^-5)4$ $^-20$; $^-20 \div 4 = ^-5$ and $^-20 \div ^-5 = 4$
    b. $(^-4)(^-3)$ 12; $12 \div ^-4 = ^-3$ and $12 \div ^-3 = ^-4$
    c. $0 \cdot 0$ *
9. In each of the following, x and y are integers. Use the definition of division in terms of multiplication to perform the indicated operations. Write your answers in simplest form.
    a. $(^-4x) \div x$ $xn = ^-4x; n = ^-4$ as long as $x \neq 0$
    b. $(^-10x + 5) \div 5$ $5n = ^-10x + 5; n = ^-2x + 1$
10. In a lab, the temperature of various chemical reactions is changing by a fixed number of degrees per minute. Write a numeric expression that describes each of the following situations.
    a. The temperature at 8:00 A.M. is $^-5°C$. If it increases by d degrees per minute, what will the temperature be m minutes later? $^-5 + dm$
    b. The temperature at 8:00 P.M. is $0°C$. If it has been dropping by d degrees per minute, what was the temperature m minutes before? $0 + (^-d)(^-m) = dm$
    c. The temperature at 8:00 P.M. is $20°C$. If it has been increasing every minute by d degrees, what was the temperature m minutes before? $20 + d(^-m) = 20 - dm$

11. a. On each of four consecutive plays in a football game, a team lost 11 yd. If lost yardage is interpreted as a negative integer, write the information as a product of integers and determine the total number of yards lost.   *
    b. If Jack Jones lost a total of 66 yd in 11 plays, how many yards, on the average, did he lose on each play? $^-66 \div 11 = ^-6$; he lost 6 yd per play
12. Illustrate the distributive property of multiplication over subtraction, $a(b - c) = ab - ac$, using $a = ^-1, b = 4$, and $c = ^-2$. $^-1(4 - ^-2) = ^-1(4) - (^-1)(^-2) = ^-4 - 2 = ^-6$
13. Compute each of the following.
    a. $10 - 3 - 12$ $^-5$ b. $10 - (3 - 12)$ 19
    c. $(^-3)^2$ 9 d. $^-3^2$ $^-9$
    e. $^-5^2 + 3(^-2)^2$ $^-13$ f. $^-2^3$ $^-8$
    g. $(^-2)^5$ $^-32$ h. $^-2^4$ $^-16$
    i. $^-2^{63} + 2^{64}$ 2^{63} j. $7^5 + ^-7^5$ 0
14. If x is an integer and $x \neq 0$, which of the following expressions are always positive and which are always negative?
    a. $^-x^4$ Negative   b. $(^-x)^4$ Positive
    c. x^4 Positive   d. x Neither
    e. ^-x Neither
15. Identify the property of integers being illustrated in each of the following.
    a. $(^-2)(3) \in I$ Closure property of multiplication
    b. $(^-4)0 = 0$ Zero property of multiplication
    c. $^-2(3 + 4) = ^-2(3) + (^-2)4$ *
    d. $(^-2)3 = 3(^-2)$ Commutative property of multiplication
16. Simplify each of the following.
    a. $x - 2(^-y)$ $x + 2y$
    b. $a - (a - b)(^-1)$ $2a - b$
    c. $y - (y - x)(^-2)$ $3y - 2x$
    d. $^-1(x - y) + x$ y
17. Multiply each of the following and combine terms where possible.
    a. $^-x(x - y - 3)$ $^-x^2 + xy + 3x$
    b. $(^-5 - x)(5 + x)$ $^-25 - 10x - x^2$
    c. $(x - y - 1)(x + y + 1)$ $x^2 - y^2 - 2y - 1$
18. Find all integers x (if any) that make the statements in parts (a)–(k) true.
    a. $x^2 = 9$ $3, ^-3$
    b. $x^2 = ^-9$ No solution
    c. $^-x \div ^-x = 1$ All integers except 0
    d. $^-x^2$ is negative.   All integers except 0
    e. $^-(1 - x) = x - 1$ All integers
    f. $x - 3x = ^-2x$ All integers
    g. $^-3(x + 2) = ^-3x + 6$ No solutions
    h. $(2x - 1)^2 = (1 - 2x)^2$ All integers
    i. $x^3 = ^-2^9$ $^-2^3$ or $^-8$
    j. $^-6x > ^-x + 20$ $x < ^-4$
    k. $^-5(x - 3) > ^-5$ $x < 4$
    l. If $x > ^-2$, find the values of $3 - 5x$. $\{12, 11, 10, \dots\}$
    m. If $x < 0$, find the values of $2 - 7x$. $\{3, 4, 5, 6, \dots\}$
19. Use the difference-of-squares formula to simplify or compute each of the following, if possible.
    a. $(2 + 3x)(2 - 3x)$ $4 - 9x^2$
    b. $(x - 1)(1 + x)$ $x^2 - 1$
    c. $213^2 - 13^2$ $(213 + 13)(213 - 13) = 226(200) = 45,200$

20. Factor each of the following expressions completely and then simplify, if possible.
    a. $ax + 2x$ $(a + 2)x$
    b. $ax - 2x$ $(a - 2)x$
    c. $3x - 4x + 7x$ $(3 - 4 + 7)x = 6x$
    d. $3x^2 + xy - x$ $x(3x + y - 1)$
    e. $(a + b)(c + 1) - (a + b)$ $(a + b)(c + 1 - 1) = (a + b)c$
    f. $x^2 - 9y^2$ $(x + 3y)(x - 3y)$
    g. $(x^2 - y^2) + x + y$ $(x + y)(x - y) + (x + y) = (x + y)(x - y + 1)$
21. Show that $(a - 1)^2 = a^2 - 2a + 1$.   *
22. In each of the following, find the next two terms. Assume the sequence is arithmetic or geometric, and find its common difference or ratio and the nth term.
    a. $10, 7, 4, 1, ^-2, ^-5, \ldots$ $^-8, ^-11; d = ^-3$; nth term is $^-3n + 13$
    b. $^-2, 4, ^-8, 16, ^-32, 64, \ldots$ $^-128, 256; r = ^-2$; nth term is $(^-2)^n$
23. Find all integer values of x for which the following are true.
    a. $^-x = x^2$ $0, ^-1$ b. $^-x^2 = (^-x)^3$ $0, 1$

24. If $54 \div x$ is an integer, what are the possible values of x?   *
25. Find the missing terms in the following arithmetic or geometric sequences.
    a. $^-4, ^-16, \_, \_, ^-1024$ $^-64, ^-256$
    b. $\_, 27, ^-9, 3, \_$ $^-81, ^-1$
26. A hot air balloon descends at the rate of 4 ft per minute for 6 minutes and then rises at the rate of 2 ft per minute for 8 minutes. Write this information using integers and give the net result on balloon height.   *
27. A paper cup is 8 in. tall with 2 in. of that height being the rim. The cups nest together with the non-rim part ($6''$) fitting in a cup below. Write an expression for the total height of n nested cups using $^-6$ to represent each of the unseen nested portion of the cups.   *

Mathematical Connections 5-2

Answers to Mathematical Connections can be found in the Answers section at the back of the book.

Reasoning

1. Explain whether $(^-x - y)(x + y)$ can be multiplied by using the difference-of-squares formula.
2. We use the equation $(a + b)^2 = a^2 + 2ab + b^2$ to find a similar equation for $(a - b)^2$. Supply any missing steps or justifications.
$$(a - b)^2 = [a + (^-b)]^2$$
$$= a^2 + 2a(^-b) + (^-b)^2$$
$$= a^2 - 2ab + b^2$$
3. Consider the argument to show that $(^-a)b = ^-(ab)$ for all integers a and b: I know that $(^-1)a = ^-a$ and a could be a variable to be replaced by ab so that $(^-1)(ab) = ^-(ab)$ and $(^-1)(ab) = (^-1 \cdot a)b$ by the associative property. Also $(^-1 \cdot a)b = (^-a)b$. Therefore, $(^-a)b = ^-(ab)$. If the argument is valid, give reasons for each step; if it is not valid, explain why not.
4. Evaluate the "proof" that $a - b = a + ^-b$.
$$a - b = a + ^-b$$
$$(a - b) + b = (a + ^-b) + b$$
$$a = a + (^-b + b)$$
$$a = a + 0$$
$$a = a$$
Since we obtain a true statement we have $a - b = a + ^-b$.
5. Explain how to find the number of integers between x and y if $x < y$.
6. Explain why $^-500$ is less than 7.
7. The Swiss mathematician Leonhard Euler (1707–1783) argued that $(^-1)(^-1) = 1$ as follows: "The result must be either $^-1$ or 1. If it is $^-1$, then $(^-1)(^-1) = ^-1$. Because $^-1 = (^-1)1$, we have $(^-1)(^-1) = (^-1)1$. Now dividing both sides of the last equation by $^-1$ we get $^-1 = 1$, which of course cannot be true. Hence $(^-1)(^-1)$ must be equal to 1."
    a. What is your reaction to this argument? Is it logical? Why or why not?
    b. Can Euler's approach be used to justify other properties of integers? Explain.

Open-Ended

8. On a national mathematics competition, scoring is accomplished using the formula 4 times the number answered correctly minus the number answered incorrectly. In this scheme, problems left blank are considered neither correct nor incorrect. Devise a scenario that would allow a student to have a negative score.
9. Choose two integers and illustrate the algorithm for division on page 246. Be careful with positive and negative signs in the computation.
10. Express each of the numbers from 1 through 10 using four 4s and any operations. For example,
$$1 = 44 \div 44, \text{ or}$$
$$1 = (4 \div 4)^{44}, \text{ or}$$
$$1 = ^-4 + 4 + (4 \div 4).$$
11. In modeling the division algorithm, explain how any integer estimate may be used to find the first quotient and the resulting effect on the remainder of the division.

Cooperative Learning

12. a. How would you introduce multiplication of integers in a middle-school class and how would you explain that a product of two negative numbers is positive? Write a rationale for your approach.
    b. Present your answers and compare them to those of another class group and together decide the most appropriate way to introduce the concepts.
13. In your group, discuss each person's favorite approach to justify $(^-1)(^-1) = 1$.

Connecting Mathematics to the Classroom

14. A seventh-grade student does not believe that $^-5 < ^-2$. The student argues that a debt of $5 is greater than a debt of $2. How do you respond?
15. A student computes $^-8 - 2(^-3)$ by writing $^-10(^-3) = 30$. How would you help this student?

16. A student says that his father showed him a very simple method for dealing with expressions like $^-(a - b + 1)$ and $x - (2x - 3)$. The rule is, if there is a negative sign before the parentheses, change the signs of the expressions inside the parentheses. Thus, $^-(a - b + 1) = {^-a} + b - 1$ and $x - (2x - 3) = x - 2x + 3$. What is your response?

17. Mariana felt that using absolute values with multiplications were too hard to be taught to middle school students. How would you respond based on the *Common Core Standards?*

Review Problems

18. Illustrate $^-8 + {^-5}$ on a number line.

19. Find the additive inverse of each of the following.
  a. $^-5$
  b. 7
  c. 0

20. Compute each of the following.
  a. $|^-14|$
  b. $|^-14| + 7$
  c. $8 - |^-12|$
  d. $|11| + |^-11|$

21. Solve for integers x in each of the following equations or inequalities.
  a. $|x - 7| = 0$
  b. $|x - 7| < 0$
  c. $|x - 7| > 0$

22. Is the set of integers closed under subtraction?

National Assessments

National Assessment of Educational Progress (NAEP) Questions

What are all values of n for which $^-2n \geq n + 6$?
A. $n \leq {^-2}$
B. $n \geq {^-2}$

NAEP, Grade 8, 2013

If $a > 0$ and $b < 0$, which of the following *must* be true?
A. $ab > 0$
B. $a - b > 0$
C. $b - a > 0$

NAEP, Grade 8, 2011

Hint for Preliminary Problem

One method of considering the issue is to find the differences in the first component of the ordered pair minus the second component of the ordered pair and look at those differences.

Chapter 5 Summary

KEY CONCEPTS	DEFINITIONS, DESCRIPTIONS, AND THEOREMS
Section 5-1	
Set of integers (p. 219)	$\{\ldots, {}^-3, {}^-2, {}^-1, 0, 1, 2, 3, \ldots\}$ Set of *positive integers*: $\{1, 2, 3, \ldots\}$ Set of *negative integers*: $\{\ldots, {}^-3, {}^-2, {}^-1\}$
Opposites (p. 220)	Pairs of numbers that are the same distance from 0 on the number line. The negative integers are the *opposites* of the positive integers, and vice versa.
Models for integer addition (p. 221)	• *Chip* • *Charged-field* • *Number-line* • *Pattern* • *Absolute value*
Absolute value (p. 224)	Absolute value of a number is its distance from 0 on a number line. For any integer x, $\lvert x \rvert = x$, if $x \geq 0$ and $\lvert x \rvert = {}^-x$, if $x < 0$.
Integer addition (p. 225)	Let m and n be any integers, as described. $\quad 0 + m = m = m + 0$ If $m \geq 0$ and $n \geq 0$, then $m + n$ is defined using addition of whole numbers. If $m \geq 0$ and $n \geq 0$, then ${}^-m + {}^-n = {}^-(m + n)$. If $n > 0$ and $m \geq n$, then $m + {}^-n = m - n$. If $n > m$ and $m \geq 0$, then $m + {}^-n = {}^-(n - m)$.

Integer addition using absolute values (p. 226)	Let m and n be any integers, as described.
	  If m and n are non-negative integers, then $m + n$ is the sum of whole numbers m and n.
	  If m and n are negative integers, then $m + n = {}^-(\lvert m \rvert + \lvert n \rvert)$.
	  If m is a positive integer and n is a negative integer, then $m + n$ is defined as:
	    If $\lvert m \rvert > \lvert n \rvert$, then $m + n = \lvert m \rvert - \lvert n \rvert$.
	    If $\lvert m \rvert < \lvert n \rvert$, then $m + n = {}^-(\lvert n \rvert - \lvert m \rvert)$.

Addition properties for integers (p. 227)	• *Closure*—for all integers a and b, $a + b$ is a unique integer. • *Commutative*—for all integers a and b, $a + b = b + a$. • *Associative*—for all integers a, b, and c, $(a + b) + c = a + (b + c)$. • *Identity*—there is a unique integer 0, the *additive identity*, such that for all integers a, $0 + a = a = a + 0$. • *Additive inverse*—for every integer a, there is a unique integer ${}^-a$, the *additive inverse* of a, such that $a + {}^-a = 0 = {}^-a + a$. • *Theorem: Opposite of the opposite of an integer*—for every integer a, ${}^-({}^-a) = a$. • *Theorem: Addition property of equality*—for any integers a, b, and c, if $a = b$, then $a + c = b + c$. • *Theorem: Addition of opposites*—for any integers a and b, ${}^-a + {}^-b = {}^-(a + b)$.
Integer subtraction (p. 229)	For integers a and b, $a - b$ is the unique integer n such that $a = b + n$ or $b + n = a$. For all integers a and b, $a - b = a + {}^-b$.
Models for integer subtraction (p. 229)	• *Chip* • *Charged-field* • *Number-line* • *Pattern* • *Missing-addend* • *Adding the opposite*

Section 5-2

Models for integer multiplication (p. 237)	• *Pattern* • *Chip* • *Charged-field* • *Number-line*
Integer multiplication (p. 240)	Let a and b be any integers. If either $a \geq 0$ and $b \geq 0$, then a and b are whole numbers with the product ab. If $a \leq 0$ and $b \leq 0$, then $ab = \lvert a \rvert \lvert b \rvert$. If one of a or b is less than 0 while the other is greater than 0, then $ab = {}^{-}\lvert a \rvert \lvert b \rvert$.
Multiplication properties for integers (p. 242)	• *Closure*—for all integers a and b, ab is a unique integer. • *Commutative*—for all integers a and b, $ab = ba$. • *Associative*—for all integers a, b, and c, $(ab)c = a(bc)$. • *Identity*—there is a unique integer 1, the *multiplicative identity*, such that for all integers a, $1 \cdot a = a = a \cdot 1$. • *Zero multiplication*—there is a unique integer 0 such that for every integer a, $0 \cdot a = 0 = a \cdot 0$.
Distributive property of multiplication over addition or subtraction (p. 242)	For any integers a, b, and c, $a(b + c) = ab + ac$ and $(b + c)a = ba + ca$. For any integers a, b, and c, $a(b - c) = ab - ac$.
Multiplication for integers theorems (p. 242)	*Theorem:* For every integer a, $({}^{-}1)(a) = {}^{-}a$. *Theorem:* For all integers a and b, $({}^{-}a)b = {}^{-}(ab)$. *Theorem:* For all integers a and b, $({}^{-}a)({}^{-}b) = ab$.
Difference of squares (p. 243)	For all integers a and b, $(a + b)(a - b) = a^2 - b^2$.
Integer division (p. 245)	For all integers a and b with $b \neq 0$, $a \div b$ is the unique integer c, if it exists, such that $a = bc$. For any integers a and b with $b \neq 0$, if $a \div b$ is a unique integer, then a *is divisible by* b, or equivalently b *divides* a, written as $b \mid a$.
Order of operations for integers (p. 246)	With no parentheses present, exponentiations are performed first in order from right to left, then multiplications and divisions are performed in the order they occur from left to right, and then the additions and subtractions are performed in the order they occur from left to right. Arithmetic operations inside parentheses must be performed before other operations.
Less than for integers (p. 247)	For any integers a and b, a is less than b, written $a < b$, if, and only if, there exists a positive integer k such that $a + k = b$.
Inequality for integers theorems (p. 247)	*Theorem:* For all integers a and b, $a < b$ (or equivalently $b > a$) if, and only if, $b - a$ is equal to a positive integer; that is, $b - a > 0$. *Theorem:* Let x, y, and n be any integers. If $x < y$, then $x + n < y + n$. If $x < y$, then ${}^{-}x > {}^{-}y$. If $x < y$ and $n > 0$, then $nx < ny$. If $x < y$ and $n < 0$, then $nx > ny$.

Chapter 5 Review

1. Find the additive inverse of each of the following.
  a. 3   ⁻3
  b. ⁻a   a
  c. ⁻2 + 3   ⁻1
  d. x + y   ⁻x − y
  e. ⁻x + y   x − y
  f. ⁻x − y   x + y
  g. (⁻2)⁵   ⁻32
  h. ⁻2⁵   32

2. Perform each of the following operations.
  a. (⁻2 + ⁻8) + 3   ⁻7
  b. ⁻2 − (⁻5) + 5   8
  c. ⁻3(⁻2) + 2   8
  d. ⁻3(⁻5 + 5)   0
  e. ⁻40 ÷ (⁻5)   8
  f. (⁻25 ÷ 5)(⁻3)   15

3. For each of the following, find all possible integer values of x that make the given equation true.
  a. ⁻x + 3 = 0   3
  b. ⁻2x = 10   ⁻5
  c. 0 ÷ (⁻x) = 0   *
  d. ⁻x ÷ 0 = ⁻1   No values
  e. 3x − 1 = ⁻124   ⁻41
  f. ⁻2x + 3x = x   *

4. Use a pattern approach to explain why (⁻2)(⁻3) = 6.   *

5. In each of the following chip models, the encircled chips are removed. Write the corresponding integer problem with its solution.

  a.
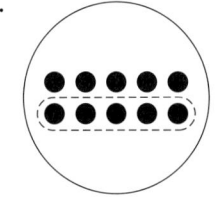
       b.
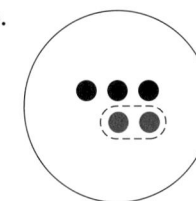

  10 − 5 = 5   1 − (⁻2) = 3

6. Simplify each of the following expressions.
  a. ⁻1x   ⁻x
  b. (⁻1)(x − y)   y − x or ⁻x + y
  c. 2x − (1 − x)   3x − 1
  d. (⁻x)² + x²   2x²
  e. (⁻x)³ + x³   0
  f. (⁻3 − x)(3 + x)   ⁻x² − 6x − 9
  g. (⁻2 − x)(⁻2 + x)   4 − x²

7. Factor each of the following expressions and then simplify, if possible.
  a. x − 3x   ⁻2x
  b. x² + x   x(x + 1)
  c. x² − 36   (x + 6)(x − 6)
  d. 81y⁴ − 16x⁴   (9y² + 4x²) = (3y + 2x)(3y − 2x)
  e. 5 + 5x   5(1 + x)
  f. (x − y)(x + 1) − (x − y)   (x − y)x

8. Classify each of the following statements as true or false (all letters represent integers). If false, tell why.
  a. |x| always is positive.   False; it is not positive for x = 0.
  b. For all x and y, |x + y| = |x| + |y|.   *
  c. If a < ⁻b, then a < 0.   False; let a = 2 and b = ⁻5.
  d. For all x and y, (x − y)² = (y − x)².   True

9. Find a counterexample to disprove each of the following properties on the set of integers.   Answers vary.
  a. Commutative property for division   1 ÷ 2 ≠ 2 ÷ 1
  b. Associative property for subtraction   *
  c. Closure for division   1 ÷ 2 is not an integer
  d. Distributive property of division over subtraction   *

10. Solve each of the following for x, where x is an integer.
  a. x + 3 = ⁻x − 17   ⁻10
  b. 2x = ⁻2¹⁰⁰   ⁻2⁹⁹
  c. 2¹⁰x = 2⁹⁹   2⁸⁹
  d. ⁻x = x   0
  e. |⁻x| = 3   3 or ⁻3
  f. |x| = ⁻x   x ≤ 0; that is, {0, ⁻1, ⁻2, ⁻3, . . .}
  g. |x| > 3   *
  h. (x − 1)² = 100   11 or ⁻9

11. Write the first six terms of each of the sequences whose nth term is given.
  a. (⁻1)ⁿ   ⁻1, 1, ⁻1, 1 ⁻1, 1
  b. (⁻2)ⁿ   ⁻2, 4, ⁻8, 16, ⁻32, 64
  c. ⁻2 − 3n   ⁻5, ⁻8, ⁻11, ⁻14, ⁻17, ⁻20

12. In each part of exercise 11, if a sequence is arithmetic, find its difference, and if it is geometric, find its ratio.   *

13. Find the missing terms in the arithmetic, geometric, or Fibonacci-type sequences below.
  a. ⁻1, 1, 0, _, _, _, 3   1, 1, 2
  b. ⁻49, 98, ⁻196, _, _, _   392, ⁻784, 1568
  c. ⁻49, 98, 245, _, _, _   392, 539, 686

14. Find the sum of each of the finite sequences in exercise 13.   *

15. How many terms are missing by the indicated ellipsis in each of the following arithmetic or geometric sequences?
  a. 101, 99, 97, . . . , ⁻101, ⁻103   98
  b. 5, ⁻25, 125, . . . , ⁻15625   2

16. Find the difference or ratio of each of the sequences in exercise 15.   **a.** Difference is ⁻2.   **b.** Ratio is ⁻5.

17. On a college test, students receive 4 points for every question answered correctly and a penalty of 7 points when a question is answered incorrectly. On this particular test, Terry answered 87 questions correctly and 46 questions incorrectly. What is Terry's score for this test?   26

18. The following states' lowest temperatures on record are given below. Order the given states according to their lowest temperatures from lowest to highest.   *

State	Temperature in degree Celsius
Alabama	⁻33
Arizona	⁻40
California	⁻43
Iowa	⁻44
Nevada	⁻46
Ohio	⁻39
Oregon	⁻48
West Virginia	⁻38

19. In 1971, the lowest recorded temperature in the United States, ⁻62°C, was in Prospect Creek Camp, Alaska. That same year, Arizona recorded a low temperature of ⁻40°C at Hawley Lake. Alaska's temperature was recorded at an elevation of 1100 ft above sea level while Arizona's was recorded at 8180 ft above sea level.

a. What is the low temperature difference between Alaska and Arizona?   22

b. What is the high elevation difference between Arizona and Alaska where the low temperatures were measured?   7080

c. Hawaii's lowest temperature on record is ⁻11°C. What would you expect to be true about the elevation of the site where this temperature was measured?   *

20. Two states record their lowest points below sea level, one at ⁻282 ft and one at ⁻8 ft.

a. What is the difference in elevation between the lowest points of the two states?   *

b. Which two states do you think these are and why?   *

21. The average depth of the Pacific Ocean is 3963 m. Interpret this number in relation to sea level.   *

22. In the metric system there are two official temperature scales: degree Celsius and kelvin. The kelvin temperature scale is obtained by shifting the Celsius scale so that 0 kelvin corresponds to absolute zero, the absence of any heat whatsoever. An equation approximating the relationship between the two scales follows:

$$\text{kelvin} \approx \text{degree Celsius} + 273°$$

a. Write an equation to find degree Celsius in terms of kelvin.   degree Celsius = kelvin − 273

b. If the boiling point of water in Celsius is 100°, what is the comparable temperature in kelvin?   373 kelvin

c. ⁻40° is the point on a thermometer at which both degree Celsius and degree Fahrenheit are the same. What is this temperature in kelvin?   233 kelvin

23. In the Battle of Gettysburg, it was estimated that there were 75,000 Confederate forces engaged and 82,289 Union forces engaged. The number of casualties were estimated at 23,049 for the Union and 28,063 for the Confederates.

a. How might positive and negative integers be used to describe these numbers?   *

b. Using positive and negative numbers, describe the total casualties.   ⁻51,112 or 51,112 casualties

24. The drawing below depicts an elevator. Explain what ⁻2 might mean as a floor number.   *

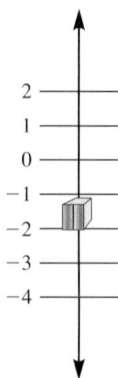

25. Find any common solutions to the following pairs of inequalities.

a. ⁻2x < 14 and 3x > ⁻15   x > ⁻5

b. $x^2 < 9$ and $x^2 \le 1$ ⁻1, 0, 1

c. |x| > ⁻4 and |x| < ⁻1   No solution

26. Joaquin said to his sister, "I'm thinking of your IQ and subtract 30 from it, take the opposite of the result, add ⁻14, and find the opposite of the new result. My final answer is 6." What is Joaquin suggesting is his sister's IQ?   22

27. Describe how you could use the difference of squares formula to compute 96 · 104.   *

28. Find the first five terms of the sequence whose nth term is given.

a. $n^2 - 4$ ⁻3, 0, 5, 12, 21

b. ⁻5n − (⁻3)   ⁻2, ⁻7, ⁻12 ⁻17, ⁻22

c. ⁻n^2 − 4   ⁻5, ⁻8, ⁻13, ⁻20, ⁻29

29. Evaluate each expression.

a. $(⁻1)^{2n}$ 1, for all integer values of n

b. $(⁻1)^{2n+1}$ ⁻1, for all integer values of n

30. Consider the sequence 1, ⁻2, 3, ⁻4, 5, ⁻6, ...

a. Find the nth term of the sequence. $(⁻1)^{n+1}(n)$

b. Find the sum of the first 100 terms of the sequence.   ⁻50

Rational Numbers and Proportional Reasoning

Preliminary Problem

A special rubber washer is made with two holes cut out as pictured. The area of the smaller of the two holes is $\frac{1}{7}$ of the whole piece of rubber while the area of the larger hole is $\frac{1}{4}$ of the whole. If the area of the original piece of rubber was $1\frac{3}{8}$ in^2, what is the area of the finished washer?

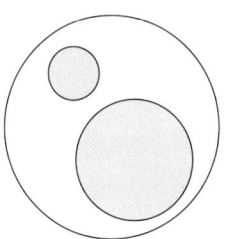

If needed, see Hint on page 323.

Integers such as $^-5$ were invented to solve equations like $x + 5 = 0$. Similarly, a different type of number is needed to solve the equation $2x = 1$. We need notation for this new number. If multiplication is to work with this new type of number as with whole numbers, then $2x = x + x = 1$. In other words, the number $\frac{1}{2}$ (*one-half*) created to solve the equation must have the property that when added to itself, the result is 1. It is an element of the set of numbers of the form $\frac{a}{b}$, where $b \neq 0$ and a and b are integers. More generally, numbers of the form $\frac{a}{b}$ are solutions to equations of the form $bx = a$. This set Q of **rational numbers** is defined as follows:

$$Q = \left\{ \frac{a}{b} \mid a \text{ and } b \text{ are integers and } b \neq 0 \right\}$$

Each member of Q is a *fraction*. In general, fractions are of the form $\frac{a}{b}$, where $b \neq 0$ but a and b are not necessarily integers. Each element $\frac{a}{b}$ of set Q has a as the **numerator** and b as the **denominator**.

The English words used for denominators of rational numbers are similar to words to tell "order," for example, the *fourth* person in a line, and the glass is three-fourths full. In contrast, $\frac{3}{4}$ is read "out of four parts, (take) three" in Chinese. The Chinese model enforces the idea of partitioning quantities into equal parts and choosing some number of these parts. The concept of sharing quantities and comparing sizes of shares provides entry points to introduce students to rational numbers.

 As early as grade 3 in the *Common Core Standards*, we find that students should "develop an understanding of fractions, beginning with unit fractions . . . view fractions as being built out of unit fractions . . . use fractions along with visual fraction models to represent parts of a whole." (p. 21) Additionally by grade 4, students should "understand a fraction as a number on the number line." (p. 24)

REMARK A unit fraction has a numerator of 1.

6-1 The Set of Rational Numbers

6-1 Objectives

Students will be able to understand and explain

- Different representations for rational numbers.

- Equal fractions, equivalent fractions, and the simplest form of fractions.

- Ordering of rational numbers.

- Denseness property of rational numbers.

The rational number $\frac{a}{b}$ may also be represented as a/b or $a \div b$. The word *fraction* is derived from the Latin word *fractus*, meaning "broken." The word *numerator* comes from a Latin word meaning "numberer," and *denominator* comes from a Latin word meaning "namer." Frequently it is only in the upper grades of middle school that students begin to use integers for the parts of rational numbers, but prospective teachers should know and recognize that rational numbers are negative as well as positive and zero. Some uses of rational numbers that will be considered in this chapter are seen in Table 1.

Table 1

Use	Example
Division problem or solution to a multiplication problem	The solution to $2x = 3$ is $\frac{3}{2}$.
Portion, or part, of a whole	Joe received $\frac{1}{2}$ of Mary's salary each month for alimony.
Ratio	The ratio of Republicans to Democrats on a Senate committee is three to five.
Probability	When you toss a fair coin, the probability of getting heads is $\frac{1}{2}$.

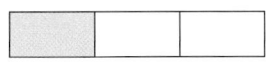

(a) Bar model or area model

0 1

(b) Number-line model

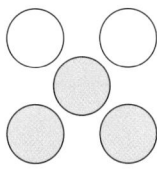

(c) Set model

Figure 1

Activity Manual

Use *What is a Fraction?* and *Square Fractions* to reinforce the concept of a fraction using concrete models.

 **IMAP Video**

Watch three students explore part-to-whole relationships.

Figure 1 illustrates the use of rational numbers as equal-sized parts of a whole in part (a), a distance on a number line in part (b), and a part of a given set in part (c). The simplest representation is from part (a) where 1 part of 3 equal-sized parts is shaded. The fractional representation for this part is $\frac{1}{3}$ where *the entire bar represents 1 unit and the shaded part is $\frac{1}{3}$ of the unit whole.* [Later the bar model of part (a) will be extended to an area model where the shape may be different than the rectangular bar. Additionally, the bar model is helpful when we consider proportional reasoning later in the chapter.]

An extension of the thinking in the bar model is seen in the remaining parts of Figure 1. For example, part (b) could represent two one-thirds of the unit length, or two-thirds of the unit segment. Part (c) could represent three one-fifths of the whole set, or three-fifths of the whole set.

Early student exposure to rational numbers as fractions usually takes the form of description rather than mathematical notation. They hear phrases such as "one-half of a pizza," "one-third of a cake," or "three-fourths of a pie." They encounter such questions as "If three identical fruit bars are distributed equally among four friends, how much does each receive?" The answer is that each receives $\frac{3}{4}$ of a bar.

When rational numbers are introduced as fractions that represent a part of a whole, we must pay attention to the whole from which a rational number is derived. For example, if we talk about $\frac{3}{4}$ of a pizza, then the amount of pizza depends on the size of the pizza, for example, 10″ or 12″, and the fractional part, $\frac{3}{4}$.

To understand the meaning of any fraction, $\frac{a}{b}$, where $a, b \in W$ and $b \neq 0$, using the parts-to-whole model, we must consider each of the following:

1. The *whole* being considered.
2. The number b of equal-size parts into which the whole has been divided.
3. The number a of parts of the whole that are selected.

A fraction $\frac{a}{b}$, where $0 \leq a < b$, is a **proper fraction**. A proper fraction is less than 1. For example, $\frac{4}{7}$ is a proper fraction, but $\frac{7}{4}, \frac{4}{4}$, and $\frac{9}{7}$ are not; $\frac{7}{4}$ is an **improper fraction**. In general $\frac{a}{b}$ is an improper fraction if $a \geq b > 0$. An improper fraction is greater than or equal to 1.

(**Historical Note**)

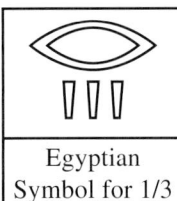

Egyptian Symbol for 1/3

The early Egyptian numeration system had symbols for fractions with numerators of 1 (unit fractions). Most fractions with other numerators were expressed as a sum of unit fractions, for example, $\frac{7}{12} = \frac{1}{3} + \frac{1}{4}$.

Fractions with denominator 60 or powers of 60 were seen in Babylon about 2000 BCE, where 12,35 meant $12 + \frac{35}{60}$. This usage was adopted by the Greek astronomer Ptolemy (approximately 125 CE), was used in Islamic and European countries, and is presently used in the measurements of angles.

The modern notation for fractions—a bar between numerator and denominator—is of Hindu origin. It came into general use in Europe in sixteenth-century books. ●

Other meanings of fractions can be considered using *whole-to-part* and *part-to-part* references. For example whole-to-part might give us an improper fraction and part-to-part allows us to write, for example, the ratio of the number of band students in the school to the number of non-band students in the school.

The *Common Core Standards* state that grade 3 students should "express whole numbers as fractions, and recognize fractions that are equivalent to whole numbers." (p. 24)

Later students learn that every integer n can be represented as a rational number because $n = \dfrac{nk}{k}$, where k is any nonzero integer. In particular, $0 = \dfrac{0 \cdot k}{k} = \dfrac{0}{k}$.

Rational Numbers on a Number Line

In the grade 3 *Common Core Standards*, we find the following standard:

Represent a fraction $\dfrac{a}{b}$ on a number line by marking off a lengths of $\dfrac{1}{b}$ from 0. Recognize that the resulting interval has size $\dfrac{a}{b}$ and that its endpoint locates the number $\dfrac{a}{b}$ on the number line. (p. 24)

Once the integers 0 and 1 are assigned to points on a line, the unit segment is defined and every other rational number is assigned to a specific point. For example, to represent $\dfrac{3}{4}$ on the number line, we divide the segment from 0 to 1 into 4 segments of equal length and mark the line accordingly. Then, starting from 0, we count 3 of these segments and stop at the mark corresponding to the right endpoint of the third segment to obtain the point assigned to the rational number $\dfrac{3}{4}$.

The *Common Core Standards* for grade 3 talk about a lengths of $\dfrac{1}{b}$, where a and b are both positive (or a could be 0), but we also use integers as numerators or denominators of rational numbers, though negative integers are not used to talk about lengths. We think of the positive fractions described in the *Common Core Standards* as marked on a number line on the right side, and as with integers, we can consider the opposites of those fractions reflected over 0 to the left side of the number line as seen in Figure 2. We adopt two conventions for negative fractions, either $\dfrac{^-a}{b}$ or $-\dfrac{a}{b}$.

Figure 2 shows the points that correspond to $^-2, -\dfrac{5}{4} = \dfrac{^-5}{4}, ^-1, -\dfrac{3}{4} = \dfrac{^-3}{4}, 0, \dfrac{3}{4}, 1, \dfrac{5}{4}$, and 2.

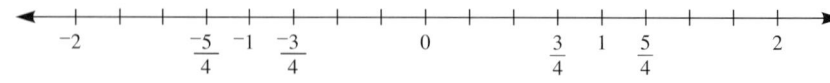

Figure 2

Example 1

Describe how to locate the following numbers on the number line of Figure 3: $\dfrac{1}{2}, -\dfrac{1}{2}, \dfrac{7}{4}$, and $-\dfrac{7}{4}$.

Figure 3

Solution   To decide how to find the point on the number line representing $\frac{1}{2}$, we consider the unit length 1. We find the point that would be the rightmost endpoint of the segment starting at 0 and ending at the point marking the middle of the unit segment. This is seen in Figure 4.

To find the point on the number line representing $-\frac{1}{2}$, we find the mirror image of $\frac{1}{2}$ on the left side of the number line as seen in Figure 4 when it is reflected in 0.

To find the location of $-\frac{7}{4}$, we first find the image or $\frac{7}{4}$ on the right side of 0 by marking the unit length in four parts, duplicating the four parts to mark points between 1 and 2, and then counting 7 of those parts starting at 0. Once $\frac{7}{4}$ is found on the right side of 0, then its reflection image in 0 gives the point where $-\frac{7}{4} = \frac{^-7}{4}$ should be marked. This is seen in Figure 4.

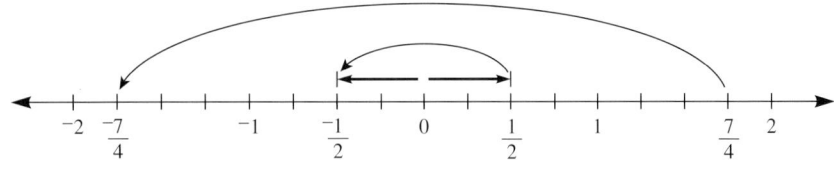

Figure 4

Equivalent or Equal Fractions

Activity Manual

Use *Equivalent Fractions* to reinforce the concept of equivalent fractions.

CCSS The grade 4 *Common Core Standards* state that students should be able to:

Explain why a fraction $\frac{a}{b}$ is equivalent to a fraction $\frac{na}{nb}$ by using visual fraction models with attention to how the number and the size of the parts differ even though the two fractions themselves are the same size. Use the principle to recognize and generate equivalent fractions. (p. 30)

Fractions may be introduced in the classroom through a concrete activity such as paperfolding. In Figure 5(a), 1 of 3 congruent parts, or $\frac{1}{3}$, is shaded. In this case, the whole is the rectangle. In Figure 5(b), each of the thirds has been folded in half so that now we have 6 sections, and 2 of 6 congruent parts, or $\frac{2}{6}$, are shaded. Thus, both $\frac{1}{3}$ and $\frac{2}{6}$ represent exactly the same shaded portion. Although the symbols $\frac{1}{3}$ and $\frac{2}{6}$ do not look alike, they represent the same rational number and are **equivalent fractions**, or **equal fractions**. *Equivalent fractions are numbers that represent the same point on a number line.* Because they represent equal amounts, we write $\frac{1}{3} = \frac{2}{6}$ and say that "$\frac{1}{3}$ equals $\frac{2}{6}$."

E-Manipulative Activity

For practice with the concept of fractions, see the *Naming Fractions* and *Visualizing Fractions* modules on the E-manipulatives disc.

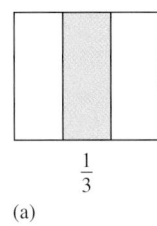
$\frac{1}{3}$
(a)

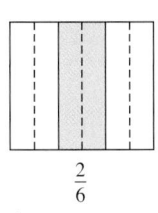
$\frac{2}{6}$
(b)

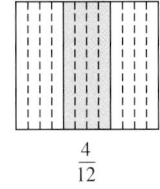
$\frac{4}{12}$
(c)

Figure 5

Figure 5(c) shows the rectangle with each of the original thirds folded into 4 equal parts with 4 of the 12 parts now shaded. Thus, $\frac{1}{3}$ is equal to $\frac{4}{12}$ because the same portion of the model is shaded. Similarly, we could illustrate that $\frac{1}{3}, \frac{2}{6}, \frac{3}{9}, \frac{4}{12}, \frac{5}{15}, \ldots$ are all equal.

Fraction strips can be used for generating equivalent fractions, as seen on the student page below. This technique makes use of the Fundamental Law of Fractions, which can be stated as follows: *The value of a fraction does not change if its numerator and denominator are multiplied by the same nonzero integer.* Under certain assumptions this Law of Fractions can be proved and is stated as a theorem.

Theorem 6-1:   Fundamental Law of Fractions

If $\frac{a}{b}$ is a fraction and n a nonzero number, then $\frac{a}{b} = \frac{an}{bn}$.

School Book Page   Equivalent Fractions

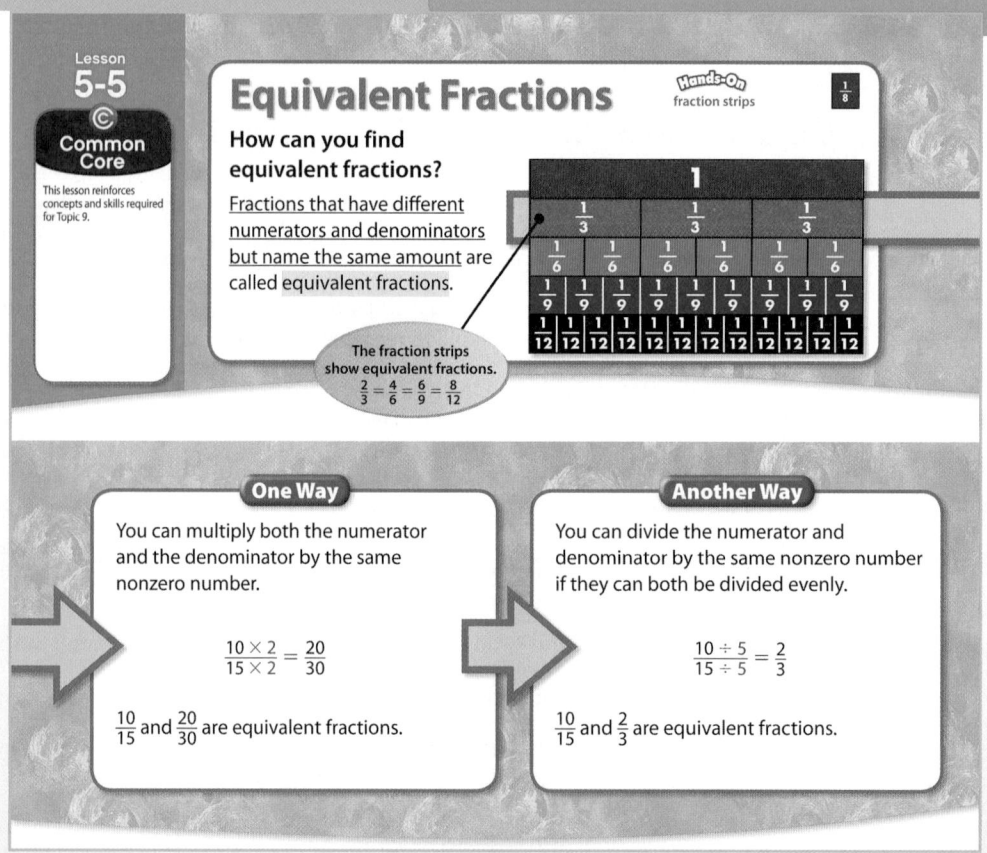

From the Fundamental Law of Fractions, $\frac{7}{^{-}15} = \frac{^{-}7}{15}$ because $\frac{7}{^{-}15} = \frac{7(^{-}1)}{^{-}15(^{-}1)} = \frac{^{-}7}{15}$. Similarly, $\frac{a}{^{-}b} = \frac{^{-}a}{b}$. *The form* $\frac{^{-}a}{b}$*, where b is a positive number, is usually preferred.*

Simplifying Fractions

Theorem 6-1 implies that if d is a common factor of a and b, then $\frac{a}{b} = \frac{a \div d}{b \div d}$. Because d is a divisor of both a and b, we know that $a \div d = m$ is a nonzero integer. Also $b \div d = n$ is a nonzero integer. Thus, we have the following:

$$\frac{a}{b} = \frac{a \div d}{b \div d} = \frac{m}{n}$$

Hence, we have two equivalent forms of the same rational number. A numerical example is given next.

$$\frac{60}{210} = \frac{60 \div 10}{210 \div 10} = \frac{6}{21}$$

This process is referred to as **simplifying a fraction**. A slightly different look is seen below.

$$\frac{60}{210} = \frac{6 \cdot 10}{21 \cdot 10} = \frac{6}{21}$$

Also,

$$\frac{6}{21} = \frac{2 \cdot 3}{7 \cdot 3} = \frac{2}{7}.$$

We can simplify $\frac{60}{210}$ because the numerator and denominator have a common factor of 10. We can simplify $\frac{6}{21}$ because 6 and 21 have a common factor of 3. However, we cannot simplify $\frac{2}{7}$ because 2 and 7 have no positive common factor other than 1. We could also simplify $\frac{60}{210}$ in one step: $\frac{60}{210} = \frac{2 \cdot 30}{7 \cdot 30} = \frac{2}{7}$. Notice that $\frac{2}{7}$ is the **simplest form** of $\frac{60}{210}$ because both 60 and 210 have been divided by their greatest common divisor, 30.

Suppose we wanted to simplify the rational number $-\frac{60}{210}$ or its equivalent $\frac{^{-}60}{210}$. The problem could be addressed by simplifying $\frac{60}{210}$ as above and then taking the opposite of the result. This could be thought of as considering $-\frac{60}{210} = -\left|\frac{60}{210}\right| = -\frac{2}{7}$. Note that the same result could have been found using $-\frac{60}{210} = -\frac{|60|}{|210|} = -\frac{2}{7}$.

Definition of Simplest Form

A rational number $\frac{a}{b}$ is in **simplest form** or **lowest terms** if, and only if, $GCD(a, b) = 1$, that is, if a and b have no common factor greater than 1.

Scientific/fraction calculators can simplify fractions. For example, to simplify $\dfrac{6}{12}$, we enter

$\boxed{6}\ \boxed{/}\ \boxed{1}\ \boxed{2}$ and press $\boxed{\text{SIMP}}\ \boxed{=}$, and $\dfrac{3}{6}$ appears on the screen. At this point, an indicator tells us

that this is not in simplest form, so we press $\boxed{\text{SIMP}}\ \boxed{=}$ again to obtain $\dfrac{1}{2}$. At any time, we can view

the factor that was removed by pressing the $\boxed{x \bigcirc y}$ key.

Example 2

Find a value for x such that $\dfrac{12}{42} = \dfrac{x}{210}$.

Solution We use the mathematical practice of reasoning to see that because $210 \div 42 = 5$, we

can use the Fundamental Law of Fractions to obtain $\dfrac{12}{42} = \dfrac{12 \cdot 5}{42 \cdot 5} = \dfrac{60}{210}$. Hence, $\dfrac{x}{210} = \dfrac{60}{210}$, and

$x = 60$.

Alternative approach: $\dfrac{12}{42} = \dfrac{2 \cdot 6}{7 \cdot 6} = \dfrac{2}{7} = \dfrac{2 \cdot 30}{7 \cdot 30} = \dfrac{60}{210}$. Therefore $x = 60$.

Example 3

Write each of the following fractions in simplest form if they are not already.

a. $\dfrac{28ab^2}{42a^2b^2}$ b. $\dfrac{(a+b)^2}{3a+3b}$ c. $\dfrac{x^2+x}{x+1}$ d. $\dfrac{3+x^2}{3x^2}$

e. $\dfrac{3+3x^2}{3x^2}$ f. $\dfrac{a^2-b^2}{a-b}$ g. $\dfrac{a^2+b^2}{a+b}$

Solution

a. $\dfrac{28ab^2}{42a^2b^2} = \dfrac{2(14ab^2)}{3a(14ab^2)} = \dfrac{2}{3a}$

b. $\dfrac{(a+b)^2}{3a+3b} = \dfrac{(a+b)(a+b)}{3(a+b)} = \dfrac{a+b}{3}$

c. $\dfrac{x^2+x}{x+1} = \dfrac{x(x+1)}{x+1} = \dfrac{x(x+1)}{1(x+1)} = \dfrac{x}{1} = x$

d. $\dfrac{3+x^2}{3x^2}$ cannot be simplified because $3+x^2$ and $3x^2$ have no factors in common except 1.

e. $\dfrac{3+3x^2}{3x^2} = \dfrac{3(1+x^2)}{3x^2} = \dfrac{1+x^2}{x^2}$

f. Recall the difference of squares formula from Chapter 5: $a^2 - b^2 = (a-b)(a+b)$. Thus,
$$\dfrac{a^2-b^2}{a-b} = \dfrac{(a-b)(a+b)}{(a-b)1} = \dfrac{a+b}{1} = a+b.$$

g. The fraction is already in simplest form because $a^2 + b^2$ does not have $(a+b)$ as a factor. Notice that $a^2 + b^2 \neq (a+b)^2$.

When an algebraic expression is written as a fraction, the denominator may not be 0. Thus, when the fraction is simplified, this restriction has to be maintained. For example, in part (c) of Example 3, $\dfrac{x^2 + x}{x + 1} = x$ if $x \neq {}^-1$, and in part (f) the result holds if $a - b \neq 0$, that is, if $a \neq b$.

Some students think of the Fundamental Law of Fractions as a *cancellation property* and "simplify" an expression like $\dfrac{6 + a^2}{3a}$ by thinking of it as $\dfrac{2 \cdot 3 + a \cdot a}{3a}$ and "canceling" equal numbers in the products to obtain $2 + a$ as the answer. Emphasizing the factor approach that neither 3 nor a is a factor of $6 + a^2$ may help to avoid such mistakes.

Equality of Fractions

We use three equivalent methods to show that two fractions, such as $\dfrac{12}{42}$ and $\dfrac{10}{35}$, are equal.

1. Simplify both fractions to simplest form.

$$\frac{12}{42} = \frac{2^2 \cdot 3}{2 \cdot 3 \cdot 7} = \frac{2}{7} \quad \text{and} \quad \frac{10}{35} = \frac{5 \cdot 2}{5 \cdot 7} = \frac{2}{7}$$

Thus,

$$\frac{12}{42} = \frac{10}{35}.$$

2. Rewrite both fractions with the same least common denominator. Since $\text{LCM}(42, 35) = 210$, then

$$\frac{12}{42} = \frac{60}{210} \quad \text{and} \quad \frac{10}{35} = \frac{60}{210}.$$

Thus,

$$\frac{12}{42} = \frac{10}{35}.$$

3. Rewrite both fractions with a common denominator (not necessarily the least). A common multiple of 42 and 35 may be found by finding the product $42 \cdot 35 = 1470$.

$$\frac{12}{42} = \frac{420}{1470} \quad \text{and} \quad \frac{10}{35} = \frac{420}{1470}.$$

Hence,

$$\frac{12}{42} = \frac{10}{35}.$$

E-Manipulative Activity

Additional practice with ordering fractions is available in the *Ranking Fractions* module on the E-Manipulative disc.

The third method suggests a general algorithm for determining whether two fractions $\dfrac{a}{b}$ and $\dfrac{c}{d}$ are equal. Rewrite both fractions with common denominator bd; that is,

$$\frac{a}{b} = \frac{ad}{bd} \quad \text{and} \quad \frac{c}{d} = \frac{bc}{bd}.$$

Because the denominators are the same, $\dfrac{ad}{bd} = \dfrac{bc}{bd}$ if, and only if, $ad = bc$. For example, $\dfrac{24}{36} = \dfrac{6}{9}$ because $24 \cdot 9 = 216 = 36 \cdot 6$. In general, the following theorem holds.

> ### Theorem 6-2:   Equality of Fractions
>
> Two fractions $\dfrac{a}{b}$ and $\dfrac{c}{d}$, with $b \neq 0$ and $d \neq 0$, are equal if, and only if, $ad = bc$.

Using a calculator, we determine whether two fractions are equal by using Theorem 6-2. Since both $\boxed{2}\,\boxed{\times}\,\boxed{2}\,\boxed{1}\,\boxed{9}\,\boxed{6}\,\boxed{=}$ and $\boxed{4}\,\boxed{\times}\,\boxed{1}\,\boxed{0}\,\boxed{9}\,\boxed{8}\,\boxed{=}$ yield a display of 4392, we see that $\dfrac{2}{4} = \dfrac{1098}{2196}$.

Ordering Rational Numbers

> **CCSS** The grade 4 *Common Core Standards* state that a student should compare two fractions with different numerators and different denominators, e.g., by creating common denominators or numerators, or by comparing to a benchmark fraction such as $\dfrac{1}{2}$. Recognize that comparisons are valid only when two fractions refer to the same whole. (p. 30)

Example 4

Activity Manual

Use *How Big Is It?* for practice estimating the magnitude of fractions.

Jim claims that $\dfrac{1}{3} > \dfrac{1}{2}$ because in Figure 6 the shaded portion for $\dfrac{1}{3}$ is larger than the shaded portion for $\dfrac{1}{2}$. How would you help him?

Solution   Jim needs to understand as noted in the *Common Core Standards* that comparisons of two fractions are valid only when they refer to the same whole. In Figure 6, the circle is clearly larger than the square so the two wholes are not the same.

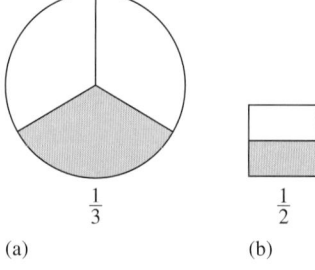

$\dfrac{1}{3}$

$\dfrac{1}{2}$

(a)   (b)

Figure 6

In order to compare two fractions referring to the same whole, it is easiest to compare fractions with like denominators. Children know that $\dfrac{7}{8} > \dfrac{5}{8}$ because if a pizza is divided into 8 parts of equal size, then 7 parts of the pizza is more than 5 parts. Similarly, $\dfrac{3}{7} < \dfrac{4}{7}$. Thus, given two fractions with common positive denominators, the one with the greater numerator is the greater fraction. To make ordering of rational numbers consistent with the ordering of whole numbers and integers we have the following definition.

> ### Definition of Greater Than for Rational Numbers with Like Denominators
>
> If a, b, and c are integers and $b > 0$, then $\dfrac{a}{b} > \dfrac{c}{b}$ if, and only if, $a > c$.

IMAP Video

Watch Jace compare $\frac{1}{5}$ and $\frac{1}{8}$.

To compare fractions with unlike denominators, some students may incorrectly reason that $\frac{1}{8} > \frac{1}{7}$ because 8 is greater than 7. In another case, they might falsely believe that $\frac{6}{7}$ is equal to $\frac{7}{8}$ because in both fractions the difference between the numerator and the denominator is 1. Comparing positive fractions with unlike denominators may be aided by using fraction strips to compare the fractions visually. For example, consider the fractions $\frac{4}{5}$ and $\frac{11}{12}$ shown in Figure 7.

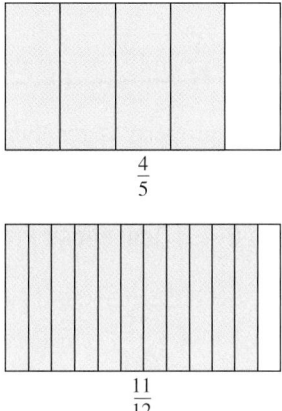

$$\frac{4}{5}$$

$$\frac{11}{12}$$

Figure 7

 Activity Manual

Use *What Comes First?* To introduce comparing and ordering fractions.

 IMAP Video

Watch Jacky use fraction strips to compare fractions and a practicing teacher explain Jacky's misconceptions.

From Figure 7, students see that each fraction is one piece less than the same-size whole unit. However, they see that the missing piece for $\frac{11}{12}$ is smaller than the missing piece for $\frac{4}{5}$, so $\frac{11}{12}$ must be greater than $\frac{4}{5}$.

Comparing any fractions with unlike denominators can be accomplished by rewriting the fractions with the same positive common denominator. Using the common denominator bd, we can write the fractions $\frac{a}{b}$ and $\frac{c}{d}$ as $\frac{ad}{bd}$ and $\frac{bc}{bd}$. Because $b > 0$ and $d > 0$, then $bd > 0$; and we have the following:

$$\frac{a}{b} > \frac{c}{d} \text{ if, and only if, } \frac{ad}{bd} > \frac{bc}{bd}; \quad \text{and} \quad \frac{ad}{bd} > \frac{bc}{bd} \text{ if, and only if, } ad > bc.$$

Therefore, we have the following theorem.

Theorem 6-3

If $a, b, c,$ and d are integers with $b > 0$ and $d > 0$, then $\frac{a}{b} > \frac{c}{d}$ if, and only if, $ad > bc$.

 Activity Manual

Use *Fraction War* to reinforce comparison of fractions.

Next consider two fractions with both numerators and denominators positive and with numerators that are the same. For example, consider $\frac{3}{4}$ and $\frac{3}{10}$. If the whole is the same for both fractions, this means that we have three $\frac{1}{4}$ s and three $\frac{1}{10}$ s. Because $\frac{1}{4}$ is greater than $\frac{1}{10}$, three of the larger parts is greater than three of the smaller parts. Thus, $\frac{3}{4} > \frac{3}{10}$.

Denseness of Rational Numbers

The set of rational numbers has a property unlike the set of whole numbers and the set of integers. Consider $\frac{1}{2}$ and $\frac{2}{3}$. To find a rational number between $\frac{1}{2}$ and $\frac{2}{3}$, we first rewrite the fractions with a common denominator, as $\frac{3}{6}$ and $\frac{4}{6}$. Because there is no whole number between the numerators 3 and 4, we next find two fractions equal, respectively, to $\frac{1}{2}$ and $\frac{2}{3}$ with greater denominators. For example, $\frac{1}{2} = \frac{6}{12}$ and $\frac{2}{3} = \frac{8}{12}$, and $\frac{7}{12}$ is between the two fractions $\frac{6}{12}$ and $\frac{8}{12}$. So $\frac{7}{12}$ is between $\frac{1}{2}$ and $\frac{2}{3}$. This property is generalized as follows and stated as a theorem.

Theorem 6-4:   Denseness Property for Rational Numbers

Given any two different rational numbers $\frac{a}{b}$ and $\frac{c}{d}$, there is another rational number between these two numbers.

▶ **NOW TRY THIS 1**

NTT 1: Answers can be found in Answers at the back of the book.

Explain why there are infinitely many rational numbers between any two rational numbers.

Example 5

a. Find two fractions between $\frac{7}{18}$ and $\frac{1}{2}$.

b. Show that the sequence $\frac{1}{2}, \frac{2}{3}, \frac{3}{4}, \frac{4}{5}, \ldots, \frac{n}{n+1} \ldots$, where $n \in N$, is an *increasing sequence*; that is, that each term starting from the second term is greater than the preceding term.

Solution

a. Because $\frac{1}{2} = \frac{1 \cdot 9}{2 \cdot 9} = \frac{9}{18}$, we see that $\frac{8}{18}$, or $\frac{4}{9}$, is between $\frac{7}{18}$ and $\frac{9}{18}$. To find another fraction between the given fractions, we find two fractions equal to $\frac{7}{18}$ and $\frac{9}{18}$, respectively, but with greater denominators; for example, $\frac{7}{18} = \frac{14}{36}$ and $\frac{9}{18} = \frac{18}{36}$.

We now see that $\frac{15}{36}, \frac{16}{36}$, and $\frac{17}{36}$ are all between $\frac{14}{36}$ and $\frac{18}{36}$ and thus between $\frac{7}{18}$ and $\frac{1}{2}$.

b. Because the nth term of the sequence is $\frac{n}{n+1}$, the next term is $\frac{n+1}{(n+1)+1}$, or $\frac{n+1}{n+2}$. We need to show that for all positive integers n, $\frac{n+1}{n+2} > \frac{n}{n+1}$.

The terms of the sequence are positive. The inequality will be true if, and only if, $(n+1)(n+1) > n(n+2)$. This inequality is equivalent to

$$n^2 + 2n + 1 > n^2 + 2n$$
$$2n + 1 > 2n$$
$$1 > 0, \text{ which is true.}$$

Therefore we have an increasing sequence.

Another way to find a number between any two rational numbers involves adding numerators and adding denominators. In Example 5(a), to find a number between $\frac{7}{18}$ and $\frac{1}{2}$ we could add the numerators and add the denominators to produce $\frac{7+1}{18+2} = \frac{8}{20}$. We see that $\frac{7}{18} < \frac{8}{20}$ because $140 < 144$. Also, $\frac{8}{20} < \frac{1}{2}$ because $16 < 20$. The general property is stated in the following theorem and explored in Now Try This 2.

Theorem 6-5

Let $\frac{a}{b}$ and $\frac{c}{d}$ be any rational numbers with positive denominators such that $\frac{a}{b} < \frac{c}{d}$. Then,

$$\frac{a}{b} < \frac{a+c}{b+d} < \frac{c}{d}.$$

▶ NOW TRY THIS 2

NTT 2: Answers can be found in Answers at the back of the book.

Prove Theorem 6-5. $\left(\textit{Hint:} \text{ Prove that } \frac{a}{b} < \frac{a+c}{b+d} \text{ and } \frac{a+c}{b+d} < \frac{c}{d}. \right)$

The proof of Theorem 6-5 suggested in Now Try This 2 also proves Theorem 6-4.

Assessment 6-1A

1. Write a sentence that illustrates the use of $\frac{7}{8}$ in each of the following ways.   Answers vary.
   a. As a division problem   The solution to $8x = 7$ is $\frac{7}{8}$.
   b. As part of a whole   Jane ate $\frac{7}{8}$ of the pizza.
   c. As a ratio   The ratio of boys to girls is 7 to 8.

2. For each of the following, write a fraction to approximate the shaded portion as part of the whole.

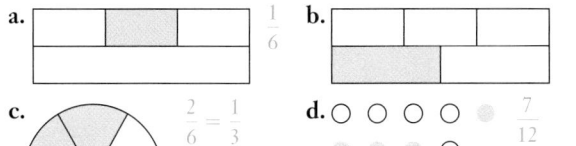
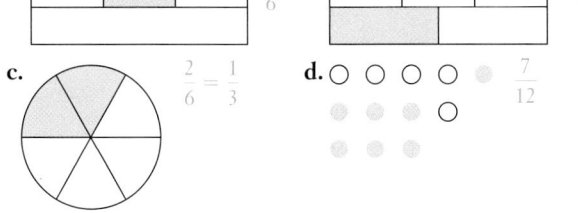

3. If the entire rectangle is a whole, what fraction represents the shaded portion of the figure?

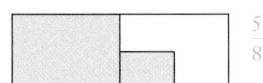

$\frac{5}{8}$

4. For each of the following four squares, write a fraction to describe the shaded portion. What property of fractions does the diagram illustrate?   *

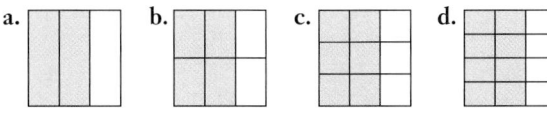

5. Based on your observations, could the shaded portions in the following figures represent the indicated fractions? If not, tell why.

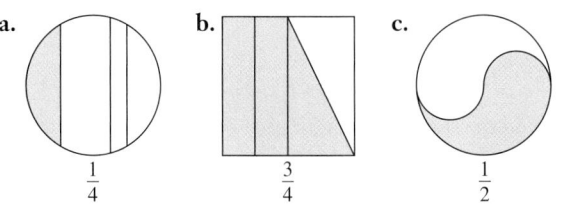

   a. No, the parts do not have equal areas. The shaded part could be $\frac{1}{4}$ of the circle, but we can't tell from the figure.   **b.** Yes   **c.** Yes

6. In each case, subdivide the *whole* shown on the right to show the equivalent fraction.   Answers vary.

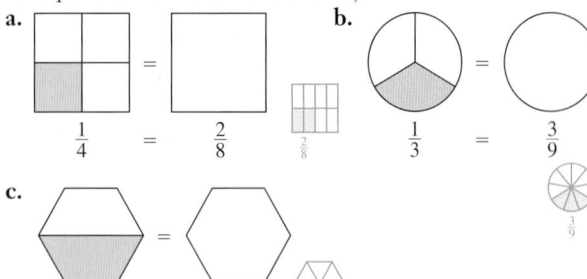

a. $\frac{1}{4} = \frac{2}{8}$

b. $\frac{1}{3} = \frac{3}{9}$

c.   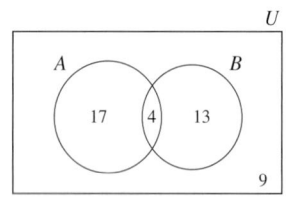 $\frac{1}{2} = \frac{3}{6}$

7. Referring to the figure, represent each of the following quantities as a fraction.

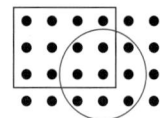

a. The dots in the interior of the circle as a part of all the dots $\frac{9}{24} = \frac{3}{8}$
b. The dots in the interior of the rectangle as a part of all the dots $\frac{12}{24} = \frac{1}{2}$
c. The dots in the intersection of the interiors of the rectangle and the circle as a part of all the dots $\frac{4}{24} = \frac{1}{6}$
d. The dots outside the circular region but inside the rectangular region as part of all the dots $\frac{8}{24} = \frac{1}{3}$

8. Use the Venn diagram pictured with A representing the people in an arts class and B representing the people in a botany class to express the fraction of elements in the indicated sets as a part of the universal set.

U, A 17 4 13 B, 9

a. $A \cap B$ *
b. $A - B$ *
c. U 1
d. $\overline{A \cap B}$ *

9. For each of the following fractions, write three equal fractions.   Answers vary.

a. $\frac{2}{9}$ $\frac{4}{18}, \frac{6}{27}, \frac{8}{36}$
b. $\frac{^-2}{5}$ $\frac{^-4}{10}, \frac{2}{^-5}, \frac{^-10}{25}$
c. $\frac{0}{3}$ $\frac{0}{1}, \frac{0}{2}, \frac{0}{4}$
d. $\frac{a}{2}$ $\frac{2a}{4}, \frac{3a}{6}, \frac{4a}{8}$

10. Find the simplest form for each of the following fractions.

a. $\frac{156}{93}$ $\frac{52}{31}$
b. $\frac{27}{45}$ $\frac{3}{5}$
c. $\frac{^-65}{91}$ $\frac{^-5}{7}$

11. For each of the following fractions, choose the expression in parentheses that equals or describes best the given fraction.

a. $\frac{0}{0}$ (1, undefined, 0)   Undefined

b. $\frac{5}{0}$ (undefined, 5, 0)   Undefined

c. $\frac{0}{5}$ (undefined, 5, 0)   0

d. $\frac{2 + a}{a}$ (2, 3, cannot be simplified)   Cannot be simplified

e. $\frac{15 + x}{3x}$ $\left(\frac{5 + x}{x}, 5, \text{cannot be simplified}\right)$ Cannot be simplified

12. Find the simplest form for each of the following fractions.

a. $\frac{a^2 - b^2}{3a + 3b}$ $\frac{a - b}{3}$
b. $\frac{14x^2y}{63xy^2}$ $\frac{2x}{9y}$

13. Determine whether the following pairs are equal.

a. $\frac{3}{8}$ and $\frac{375}{1000}$ Equal
b. $\frac{18}{54}$ and $\frac{23}{69}$ Equal

14. Determine whether the following pairs are equal by changing both to have the same denominator.

a. $\frac{10}{16}$ and $\frac{12}{18}$ Not equal
b. $\frac{^-21}{86}$ and $\frac{^-51}{215}$ Not equal

15. Draw an area model to show that $\frac{3}{4} = \frac{6}{8}$.   *

16. If a fraction is equal to $\frac{3}{4}$ and the sum of the numerator and denominator is 84, what is the fraction? $\frac{36}{48}$

17. Mr. Gomez filled his car's 16 gal gas tank. He took a trip and used $\frac{7}{8}$ of the gas.

a. Draw an arrow in the following figure to show what his gas gauge looked like after the trip: *

b. How many gallons of gas were used?   14 gallons

18. Solve for x in each of the following.

a. $\frac{2}{3} = \frac{x}{16}$ $\frac{32}{3}$
b. $\frac{3}{4} = \frac{^-27}{x}$ $^-36$

19. For each of the following pairs of fractions, replace the comma with the correct symbol ($<$, $=$, $>$) to make a true statement:

a. $\frac{7}{8}, \frac{5}{6}$ $>$
b. $\frac{^-7}{8}, \frac{^-4}{5}$ $<$

20. Arrange each of the following in decreasing order.

a. $\frac{11}{22}, \frac{11}{16}, \frac{11}{13}$ $\frac{11}{13}, \frac{11}{16}, \frac{11}{22}$
b. $\frac{^-1}{5}, \frac{^-19}{36}, \frac{^-17}{30}$ $\frac{^-1}{5}, \frac{^-19}{36}, \frac{^-17}{30}$

21. For each of the following, find two rational numbers between the given fractions.   Answers vary.

a. $\frac{3}{7}$ and $\frac{4}{7}$ $\frac{10}{21}, \frac{11}{21}$
b. $\frac{^-7}{9}$ and $\frac{^-8}{9}$ $\frac{^-22}{27}, \frac{^-23}{27}$

22. a. 6 oz is what part of a pound? A ton?   *
   b. A dime is what fraction of a dollar?   *
   c. 15 min is what fraction of an hour?   *
   d. 8 hr is what fraction of a day?   *

23. Determine whether the following is true: If a, b, c are integers and $b < 0$, then $\frac{a}{b} > \frac{c}{b}$ if, and only if, $a > c$.   False

24. Based on your visual observation write a fraction to represent the shaded portion. $\frac{1}{6}$

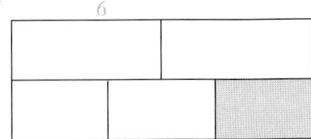

25. Fill in missing numbers for $x, y, z,$ and w to create a sequence with each term being greater than the preceding term.   Answers vary.

   a. $\frac{1}{3}, \frac{x}{4}, \frac{y}{5}, \frac{z}{6}$ 2, 3, 4
   b. $\frac{^-3}{x}, \frac{^-4}{y}, \frac{^-5}{z}, \frac{^-6}{w}$ 3, 5, 7, 9

26. Explain why in the Fundamental Law of Fractions (Theorem 6-1), n must be nonzero.   *

27. Prove that any integer n can be written as a fraction.   *

28. A typical English ruler is marked in sixteenths of an inch. Sketch a ruler marking $\frac{3}{8}$ in.   *

29. Ten light bulbs were in a chandelier. One-fifth of the bulbs were not shining. How many light bulbs were not shining?   2

30. At a party, there were 35 guests. Two-fifths of the guests were men. What fraction of the guests were women? $\frac{3}{5}$

Assessment 6-1B

1. Write a sentence that illustrates the use of $\frac{7}{10}$ in each of the following ways: Answers vary.
   a. As a division problem   The solution to $10x = 7$ is $\frac{7}{10}$.
   b. As part of a whole   Jane ate $\frac{7}{10}$ of her pizza.
   c. As a ratio   The ratio of boys to girls is 7 to 10.

2. For each of the following, write a fraction to approximate the shaded portion of the whole.

   a. 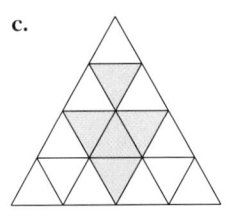 $\frac{1}{3}$

   b. 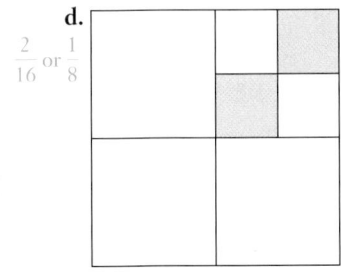 $\frac{9}{12}$ or $\frac{3}{4}$

   c. 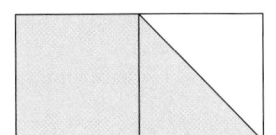 $\frac{5}{16}$

   d.  $\frac{2}{16}$ or $\frac{1}{8}$

3. If the entire rectangle is a whole, what fraction represents the shaded portion of the figure?

   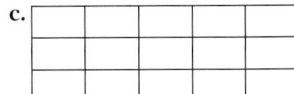 $\frac{3}{4}$

4. Complete each of the following figures so that it illustrates $\frac{3}{5}$.

   a.    *
   b. 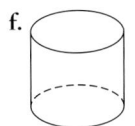   *

   c. *   d. *

   e. *   f. *

5. Based on your observations, could the shaded portions in the following figures represent the indicated fractions? Tell why.

   a. 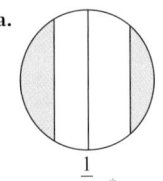 $\frac{1}{2}$ *
   b. 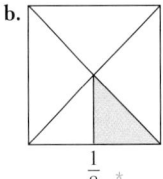 $\frac{1}{8}$ *
   c. 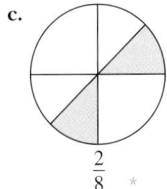 $\frac{2}{8}$ *

6. If each of the following models represents the given fraction, draw a model that represents the *whole*. Shade your answer.

   a. 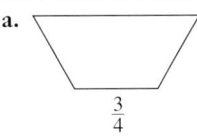   * $\frac{3}{4}$
   b. 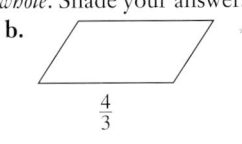   * $\frac{4}{3}$

   c. 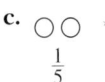   * $\frac{1}{5}$
   d. 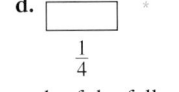   * $\frac{1}{4}$

7. Referring to the figure, represent each of the following quantities as a fraction.

   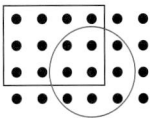

   a. The dots outside the circular region as a part of all the dots $\frac{15}{24} = \frac{5}{8}$

   b. The dots outside the rectangular region as a part of all the dots $\frac{12}{24} = \frac{1}{2}$

   c. The dots in the union of the rectangular and the circular regions as a part of all the dots $\frac{17}{24}$

   d. The dots inside the circular region but outside the rectangular region as a part of all the dots. $\frac{5}{24}$

8. Use the Venn diagram pictured with A representing the people in an algebra class and B representing the people in a biology class to express the fraction of elements in the indicated sets as a part of the universal set.

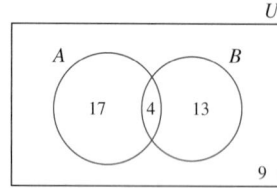

   a. $A \cup B$ *
   b. $A - \overline{B}$ *
   c. $\varnothing$ 0
   d. $\overline{A \cup B}$ *

9. For each of the following, write three fractions equal to the given fractions.   Answers vary.

   a. $\dfrac{1}{3}$ $\dfrac{2}{6}, \dfrac{3}{9}, \dfrac{4}{12}$
   b. $\dfrac{4}{5}$ $\dfrac{8}{10}, \dfrac{12}{15}, \dfrac{16}{20}$
   c. $\dfrac{^-3}{7}$ $\dfrac{^-6}{14}, \dfrac{^-9}{21}, \dfrac{^-12}{28}$
   d. $\dfrac{a}{3}$ $\dfrac{2a}{6}, \dfrac{3a}{9}, \dfrac{4a}{12}$

10. Find the simplest form for each of the following fractions.

   a. $\dfrac{0}{68}$ $\dfrac{0}{1} = 0$
   b. $\dfrac{84^2}{91^2}$ $\dfrac{144}{169}$
   c. $\dfrac{662}{703}$ Simplified

11. For each of the following, choose the expression in parentheses that equals or describes best the given fraction.

   a. $\dfrac{6 + x}{3x}$ $\left(\dfrac{2 + x}{x}, 3, \text{cannot be simplified} \right)$ Cannot be simplified
   b. $\dfrac{2^6 + 2^5}{2^4 + 2^7}$ $\left(1, \dfrac{2}{3}, \text{cannot be simplified} \right)$ $\dfrac{2}{3}$
   c. $\dfrac{2^{100} + 2^{98}}{2^{100} - 2^{98}}$ $\left(2^{196}, \dfrac{5}{3}, \text{too large to simplify} \right)$ $\dfrac{5}{3}$

12. Find the simplest form for each of the following fractions.

   a. $\dfrac{a^2 + ab}{a + b}$ a
   b. $\dfrac{a}{3a + ab}$ $\dfrac{1}{3 + b}$

13. Determine whether the following pairs are equal.

   a. $\dfrac{6}{16}$ and $\dfrac{3,750}{10,000}$ Equal
   b. $\dfrac{17}{27}$ and $\dfrac{25}{45}$ Not equal

14. Determine whether the following pairs are equal by changing both to the same denominator.

   a. $\dfrac{3}{^-12}$ and $\dfrac{^-36}{144}$ Equal
   b. $\dfrac{^-21}{430}$ and $\dfrac{^-51}{215}$ Not equal

15. Draw an area model to show that $\dfrac{2}{3} = \dfrac{6}{9}$.   *

16. A board is needed that is exactly $\dfrac{11}{32}$ in. wide to fit a hole. Can a board that is $\dfrac{3}{8}$ in. be shaved down to fit the hole? If so, how much must be shaved from the board?   Yes, $\dfrac{1}{32}$ in.

17. The following two parking meters are next to each other with the times left as shown. Which meter has more time left on it? How much more?   Meter A, 3 min

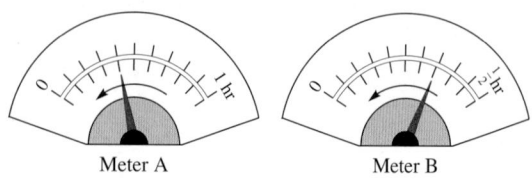

18. Solve for x in each of the following.

   a. $\dfrac{2}{3} = \dfrac{x}{18}$ 12
   b. $\dfrac{3}{x} = \dfrac{3x}{x^2}$ x is any number except 0

19. For each of the following pairs of fractions, replace the comma with the correct symbol ($<, =, >$) to make a true statement.

   a. $\dfrac{1}{^-7}, \dfrac{1}{^-8}$ $<$
   b. $\dfrac{2}{5}, \dfrac{4}{10}$ $=$
   c. $\dfrac{0}{7}, \dfrac{0}{17}$ $=$

20. For each of the following, find two rational numbers between the given fractions.   Answers vary.

   a. $\dfrac{5}{6}$ and $\dfrac{83}{100}$ $\dfrac{997}{1200}, \dfrac{998}{1200}$
   b. $\dfrac{^-1}{3}$ and $\dfrac{3}{4}$ $0, \dfrac{1}{2}$

21. a. 12 oz is what part of a pound?   *
    b. A nickel is what fraction of a dollar?   *
    c. 25 min is what fraction of an hour?   *
    d. 16 hr is what fraction of a 24-hr day?   *

22. Read each measurement as shown on the following ruler.

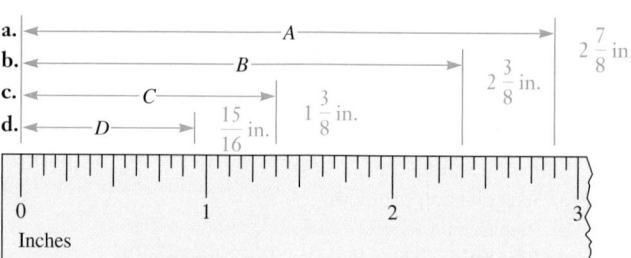

23. Fill in missing numbers for $x, y, z,$ and w to create a sequence with each term being less than the preceding term.   Answers vary.

   a. $\dfrac{1}{3}, \dfrac{x}{4}, \dfrac{y}{5}, \dfrac{z}{6}$ $0, ^-1, ^-2$
   b. $\dfrac{^-3}{x}, \dfrac{^-4}{y}, \dfrac{^-5}{z}, \dfrac{^-6}{w}$ $6, 5, 4, 3$

24. Use the Fundamental Law of Fractions (Theorem 6-1) to show that 0 could be written in infinitely many ways.   *

25. Prove that a negative integer n can be written as a fraction with a positive denominator. $n = \dfrac{n}{1}$

26. A typical metric ruler is marked in millimeters (mm) where $1 \text{ mm} = \dfrac{1}{1000}$ m (where m is the designation of meter). How many millimeters would 5 meters be?   5000 m

27. Ten light bulbs were in a chandelier. Three-fifth of the bulbs were shining. What fraction of the light bulbs were not shining? $\dfrac{2}{5}$

28. At a party, there were 40 guests. One-fifth of the guests were men. What fraction of the guests were women? $\dfrac{4}{5}$

29. Answer each of the following.

   a. If the area of the entire square is 1 square unit, find the area of each tangram piece.   *
   b. If the area of piece a is 1 square unit, find the area of each tangram piece.   *

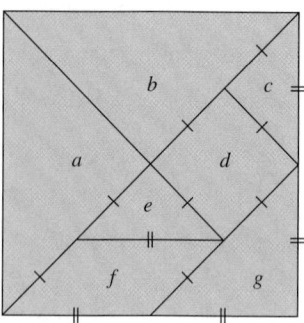

Mathematical Connections 6-1

Answers to Mathematical Connections can be found in the Answers section at the back of the book.

Reasoning

1. Explain why 25 cents is one-fourth of a dollar, yet 15 minutes is one-fourth of an hour. Why should these one-fourths not be equal?

2. In each of two different fourth-grade classes, $\frac{1}{3}$ of the members are girls. Does each class have the same number of girls? Explain your answer.

3. Consider the set of all fractions equal to $\frac{1}{2}$. If you take any 10 of those fractions, add their numerators to obtain the numerator of a new fraction and add their denominators to obtain the denominator of a new fraction, how does the new fraction relate to $\frac{1}{2}$? Generalize what you found and explain.

4. Draw a Venn diagram showing the relationship among natural numbers, whole numbers, integers, and rational numbers. Use subset relations to explain your Venn diagram.

Open-Ended

5. Make three statements about yourself or your environment and use fractions in each. Explain why your statements are true. For example, your parents have three children, two of whom live at home; hence $\frac{2}{3}$ of their children live at home.

6. Consider the demographics of your class including gender and ethnicity. Write fractions to describe the demographics of the class.

7. Sketch four different windows having different numbers of window panes in each. Shade $\frac{3}{4}$ of the panes in each window.

Cooperative Learning

8. Assume that the shortest person in your group is 1 unit tall and do the following:
   a. Find rational numbers to approximately represent the heights of other members of the group.
   b. Make a number line and plot the rational number for each person ordered according to height.

9. Assume the tallest person in your group is 1 unit tall and do the following.
   a. Find rational numbers to approximately represent the heights of other members of the group.
   b. Make a number line and plot the rational number for each person ordered according to height.

Connecting Mathematics to the Classroom

10. A student asks if $\frac{0}{6}$ is in its simplest form. How do you respond?

11. A student writes $\frac{15}{53} < \frac{1}{3}$ because $3 \cdot 15 < 53 \cdot 1$. Another student writes $\frac{1\cancel{5}}{\cancel{5}3} = \frac{1}{3}$. Where is the fallacy?

12. A student claims that there are no numbers between $\frac{999}{1000}$ and 1 because they are so close together. What is your response?

13. A student argued that a pizza cut into 12 pieces was more than a pizza cut into 6 pieces. How would you respond?

14. Ann claims that she cannot show $\frac{3}{4}$ of the following faces because some are big and some are small. What do you tell her?

15. How would you respond to each of the following students?
   a. Iris claims that if we have two positive rational numbers, the one with the greater numerator is the greater.
   b. Shirley claims that if we have two positive rational numbers, the one with the greater denominator is the lesser.

16. Steve claims that the shaded circles below cannot represent $\frac{2}{3}$ since there are 10 circles shaded and $\frac{2}{3}$ is less than 1. How do you respond?

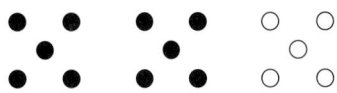

17. Carl says that $\frac{3}{8} > \frac{2}{3}$ because $3 > 2$ and $8 > 3$. How would you help Carl?

18. Mr. Jimenez and Ms. Cortez gave the same test. In Mr. Jimenez's class, 20 out of 25 students passed, and in Ms. Cortez's class, 24 of 30 passed. One of Ms. Cortez's students claimed that the classes did equally well. How could you explain the student's reasoning?

National Assessments

National Assessment of Educational Progress (NAEP) Questions

What fraction of the figure is shaded?

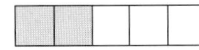

NAEP, Grade 4, 2007

In which of the following are the three fractions arranged from least to greatest?

A. $\frac{2}{7}, \frac{1}{2}, \frac{5}{9}$ B. $\frac{1}{2}, \frac{2}{7}, \frac{5}{9}$ C. $\frac{1}{2}, \frac{5}{9}, \frac{2}{7}$

D. $\frac{5}{9}, \frac{1}{2}, \frac{2}{7}$ E. $\frac{5}{9}, \frac{2}{7}, \frac{1}{2}$

NAEP, Grade 8, 2007

Kim, Les, Mario, and Nina each had a string 10 feet long.

    Kim cut hers into fifths.
    Les cut his into fourths.
    Mario cut his into sixths.
    Nina cut hers into thirds.

After the cuts were made, who had the longest pieces of string?

A. Kim
B. **Les**
C. Mario
D. **Nina**

NAEP, Grade 4, 2013

Which fraction has a value closest to $\frac{1}{2}$?

A. $\frac{5}{8}$

B. $\frac{1}{6}$

C. $\frac{2}{2}$

D. $\frac{1}{5}$

NAEP, Grade 4, 2011

6-2 Addition, Subtraction, and Estimation with Rational Numbers

6-2 Objectives

Students will be able to understand and explain

- Addition of rational numbers with like and unlike denominators.

- Rational numbers as mixed numbers.

- Subtraction of rational numbers with like and unlike denominators.

- Properties of addition and subtraction of rational numbers.

- Addition properties of equality.

- Estimation with rational numbers.

Addition and subtraction of rational numbers is very much like addition and subtraction of whole numbers and integers. We first demonstrate the addition of two rational numbers with like denominators, $\frac{2}{5} + \frac{1}{5}$, using an area model in Figure 8(a) and a number line model in Figure 8(b).

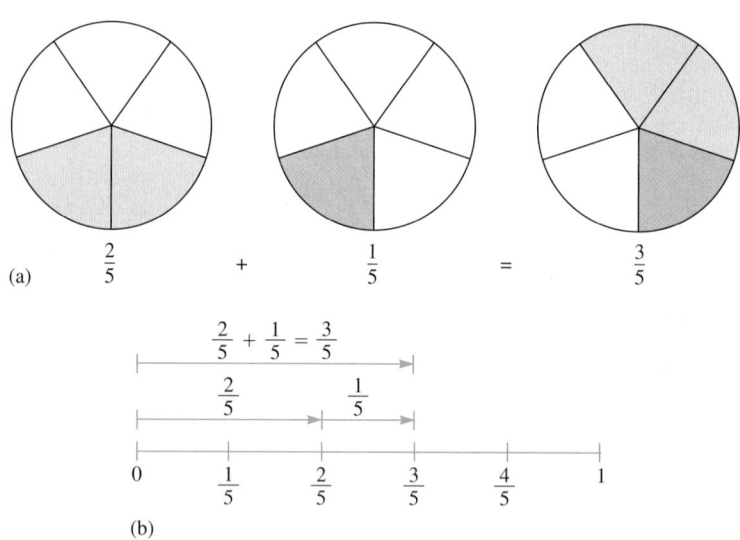

Figure 8

▶ **IMAP Video**

Watch Felisha use an area model to add rational numbers.

Why does the area model in Figure 8(a) make sense? Suppose that someone gives us $\frac{2}{5}$ of a pie initially and then gives us another $\frac{1}{5}$ of the pie. In Figure 8(a), $\frac{2}{5}$ is represented by 2 pieces when the pie is cut into 5 equal-size pieces, and $\frac{1}{5}$ is represented by 1 piece of the 5 equal-size pieces. So

you have $2 + 1 = 3$ pieces of the 5 equal-size pieces, or $\frac{3}{5}$ of the total (whole) pie. The number line model in Figure 8(b) works the same as the number line model for whole numbers.

Using a bar model, the addition $\frac{3}{5} + \frac{4}{5}$ is depicted in Figure 9.

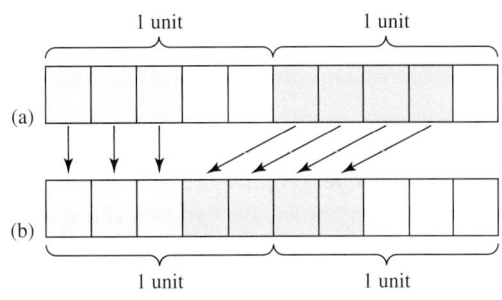

Figure 9

In Figure 9(a), we have $\frac{3}{5}$ and $\frac{4}{5}$ pictured as parts of two equal-sized wholes where each whole consists of five parts. In Figure 9(b), we have $\frac{3}{5} + \frac{4}{5}$ again pictured as parts of two equal-sized wholes, where each whole consists of five parts. We see that there is one whole and two parts of another whole shaded. Additionally, we see that there are seven of the one-fifth parts shaded. Thus, we could say that $\frac{3}{5} + \frac{4}{5} = \frac{7}{5}$. Also $\frac{3}{5} + \frac{4}{5} = 1 + \frac{2}{5}$, which could be written as $1\frac{2}{5}$. The latter representation is a *mixed number*, which is discussed later in the section.

The ideas illustrated in Figures 8 and 9 are summarized in the following definition.

Definition of Addition of Rational Numbers with Like Denominators

If $\frac{a}{b}$ and $\frac{c}{b}$ are rational numbers, then $\frac{a}{b} + \frac{c}{b} = \frac{a + c}{b}$.

CCSS In the grade 5 *Common Core Standards*, we find that students should be able to:

Add and subtract fractions with unlike denominators (including mixed numbers) by replacing given fractions with equivalent fractions in such a way as to produce an equivalent sum or difference of fractions with like denominators. (p. 36)

CCSS We use the four-step process and *Common Core Standards* practices to develop this concept.

Problem Solving   **Adding Rational Numbers Problem**

Determine how to add the rational numbers $\frac{2}{3}$ and $\frac{1}{4}$.

Understanding the Problem We model $\frac{2}{3}$ and $\frac{1}{4}$ as parts of the same-sized whole, as seen in Figure 10, but we need a way to combine the two drawings to find the sum.

IMAP Video

Watch Felisha use an area model to solve a story problem.

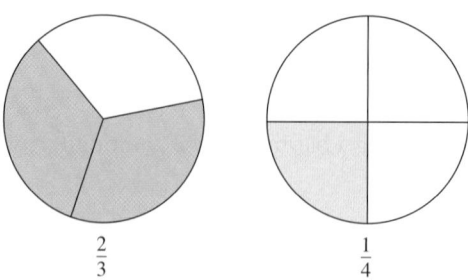

$$\frac{2}{3} \qquad \frac{1}{4}$$

Figure 10

Devising a Plan We use the strategy of *solving a related problem*: adding rational numbers with the same denominators. We can find the sum using reasoning to write each fraction with a common denominator and then complete the computation.

Carrying Out the Plan We know that $\frac{2}{3}$ has infinitely many representations, including $\frac{4}{6}, \frac{6}{9}, \frac{8}{12}$, and so on. Also $\frac{1}{4}$ has infinitely many representations, including $\frac{2}{8}, \frac{3}{12}, \frac{4}{16}$, and so on. We see that $\frac{8}{12}$ and $\frac{3}{12}$ have the same denominator. One is 8 parts of 12 equal parts, while the other is 3 parts of 12 equal parts. Consequently, the sum is $\frac{2}{3} + \frac{1}{4} = \frac{8}{12} + \frac{3}{12} = \frac{11}{12}$. Figure 11 illustrates the addition.

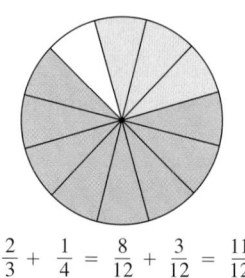

$$\frac{2}{3} + \frac{1}{4} = \frac{8}{12} + \frac{3}{12} = \frac{11}{12}$$

Figure 11

Looking Back To add two rational numbers with unlike denominators, we considered equal rational numbers with like denominators. A common denominator for $\frac{2}{3}$ and $\frac{1}{4}$ is 12. This is also the least common denominator, or the LCM, of 3 and 4. To add two fractions with unequal denominators such as $\frac{5}{12}$ and $\frac{7}{18}$, we could find equal fractions with LCM(12, 18) = 36 as the denominator. However, any common denominator will work as well, for example, 72 or even 12 · 18.

By considering the sum $\frac{2}{3} + \frac{1}{4} = \frac{2 \cdot 4}{3 \cdot 4} + \frac{1 \cdot 3}{4 \cdot 3} = \frac{8}{12} + \frac{3}{12} = \frac{8 + 3}{12} = \frac{11}{12}$, we can generalize to find the sum of two rational numbers with unlike denominators, as in the following.

Alternate Definition of Addition of Rational Numbers with Unlike Denominators

If $\frac{a}{b}$ and $\frac{c}{d}$ are rational numbers, then $\frac{a}{b} + \frac{c}{d} = \frac{ad + bc}{bd}$.

The definition of addition of rational numbers with unlike denominators can be applied to like denominators as seen below.

$$\frac{a}{b} + \frac{c}{b} = \frac{ab + cb}{b \cdot b} = \frac{(a + c)b}{b \cdot b} = \frac{a + c}{b}$$

Example 6

Find each of the following sums.

a. $\dfrac{2}{15} + \dfrac{4}{21}$ **b.** $\dfrac{2}{-3} + \dfrac{1}{5}$ **c.** $\left(\dfrac{3}{4} + \dfrac{1}{5}\right) + \dfrac{1}{6}$ **d.** $\dfrac{3}{x} + \dfrac{4}{y}$ **e.** $\dfrac{2}{a^2b} + \dfrac{3}{ab^2}$

Solution

a. $\text{LCM}(15, 21) = 3 \cdot 5 \cdot 7;\ \dfrac{2}{15} + \dfrac{4}{21} = \dfrac{2 \cdot 7}{15 \cdot 7} + \dfrac{4 \cdot 5}{21 \cdot 5} = \dfrac{14}{105} + \dfrac{20}{105} = \dfrac{34}{105}$

b. $\dfrac{2}{-3} + \dfrac{1}{5} = \dfrac{(2)(5) + (-3)(1)}{(-3)(5)} = \dfrac{10 + {}^-3}{{}^-15} = \dfrac{7}{{}^-15} = \dfrac{7({}^-1)}{{}^-15({}^-1)} = \dfrac{{}^-7}{15}$

c. $\dfrac{3}{4} + \dfrac{1}{5} = \dfrac{3 \cdot 5 + 4 \cdot 1}{4 \cdot 5} = \dfrac{19}{20};$

$\left(\dfrac{3}{4} + \dfrac{1}{5}\right) + \dfrac{1}{6} = \dfrac{19}{20} + \dfrac{1}{6} = \dfrac{19 \cdot 6 + 20 \cdot 1}{20 \cdot 6} = \dfrac{134}{120} = \dfrac{67}{60}$

d. $\dfrac{3}{x} + \dfrac{4}{y} = \dfrac{3y}{xy} + \dfrac{4x}{xy} = \dfrac{3y + 4x}{xy}$

e. $\text{LCM}(a^2b, ab^2) = a^2b^2;\ \dfrac{2}{a^2b} + \dfrac{3}{ab^2} = \dfrac{2b}{(a^2b)b} + \dfrac{3a}{a(ab^2)} = \dfrac{2b + 3a}{a^2b^2}$

Mixed Numbers

In everyday life, we often use **mixed numbers**, that is, numbers that are made up of an integer and a proper fraction. Figure 12 shows a nail that is $2\frac{3}{4}$ in. long. The mixed number $2\frac{3}{4}$ means $2 + \frac{3}{4}$. Students may infer that $2\frac{3}{4}$ means 2 times $\frac{3}{4}$, since xy means $x \cdot y$, but this is not correct. Also, the number ${}^-4\frac{3}{4}$ means ${}^-\left(4\frac{3}{4}\right) = {}^-4 - \frac{3}{4}$, not ${}^-4 + \frac{3}{4}$.

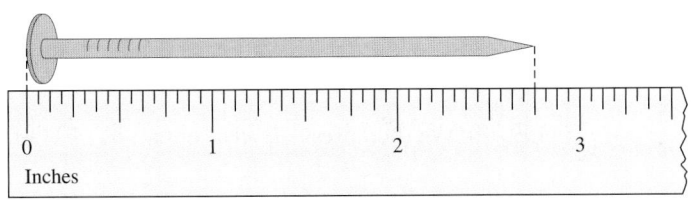

Figure 12

IMAP Video

Watch Rachel correct her own misconception about converting mixed numbers to improper fractions using an area model.

A mixed number is a rational number because it can always be written in the form $\frac{a}{b}$. For example,

$$2\frac{3}{4} = 2 + \frac{3}{4} = \frac{2}{1} + \frac{3}{4} = \frac{2 \cdot 4 + 1 \cdot 3}{1 \cdot 4} = \frac{8 + 3}{4} = \frac{11}{4}.$$

Example 7

Change each of the following mixed numbers to the form $\dfrac{a}{b}$, where a and b are integers:

a. $4\dfrac{1}{3}$ b. $^-3\dfrac{2}{5}$

Solution

a. $4\dfrac{1}{3} = 4 + \dfrac{1}{3} = \dfrac{4}{1} + \dfrac{1}{3} = \dfrac{4 \cdot 3 + 1 \cdot 1}{1 \cdot 3} = \dfrac{12 + 1}{3} = \dfrac{13}{3}$

b. $^-3\dfrac{2}{5} = {}^-\left(3 + \dfrac{2}{5}\right) = {}^-\left(\dfrac{3}{1} + \dfrac{2}{5}\right) = {}^-\left(\dfrac{3 \cdot 5 + 1 \cdot 2}{1 \cdot 5}\right) = {}^-\left(\dfrac{17}{5}\right) = \dfrac{^-17}{5}$

Example 8

Change $\dfrac{39}{5}$ to a mixed number.

Solution   We divide 39 by 5 and use the division algorithm as follows:

$$\dfrac{39}{5} = \dfrac{7 \cdot 5 + 4}{5} = \dfrac{7 \cdot 5}{5} + \dfrac{4}{5} = 7 + \dfrac{4}{5} = 7\dfrac{4}{5}$$

In elementary schools, problems like Example 8 are usually computed using division, as follows:

$$\begin{array}{r} 5 \\ 5\overline{)29} \\ \underline{25} \\ 4 \end{array}$$

Hence, $\dfrac{29}{5} = 5 + \dfrac{4}{5} = 5\dfrac{4}{5}$. The remainder of 4 in the division actually represents $\dfrac{4}{5}$ of a unit when put in context.

Scientific/fraction calculators can change improper fractions to mixed numbers. For example, if we enter $\boxed{2}\boxed{9}\boxed{/}\boxed{5}$ and press $\boxed{Ab/c}$, then $5 \sqcup 4/5$ appears, which means $5\dfrac{4}{5}$.

We can also use scientific/fraction calculators to add mixed numbers. For example, to add $2\dfrac{4}{5} + 3\dfrac{5}{6}$, we enter $\boxed{2}\boxed{\text{Unit}}\boxed{4}\boxed{/}\boxed{5}\boxed{+}\boxed{3}\boxed{\text{Unit}}\boxed{5}\boxed{/}\boxed{6}\boxed{=}$, and the display reads $5 \sqcup 49/30$. We then press $\boxed{Ab/c}$ to obtain $6 \sqcup 19/30$, which means $6\dfrac{19}{30}$.

Adding Mixed Numbers

Because mixed numbers are rational numbers, the method of adding rationals can be used to include mixed numbers. The student page shown on page 279 shows a method for computing sums of mixed numbers that uses the commutative and associative properties discussed later in the next section.

School Book Page Equivalent Fractions

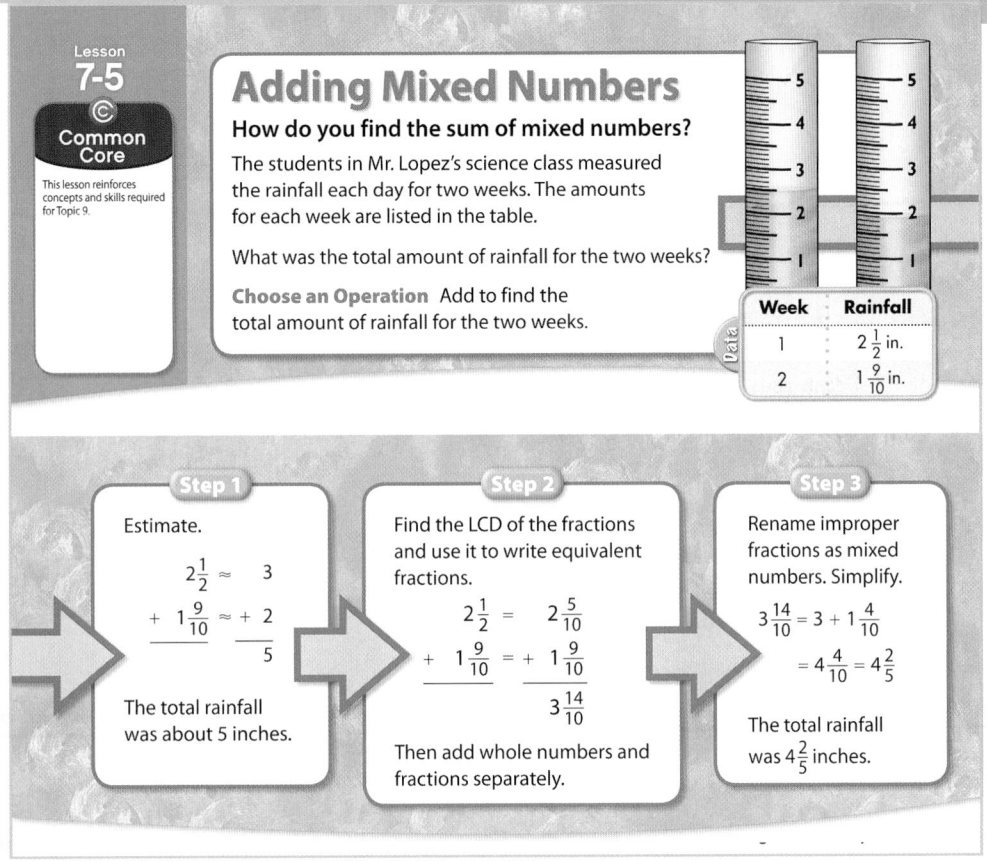

Lesson
7-5

Common Core

This lesson reinforces concepts and skills required for Topic 9.

Adding Mixed Numbers

How do you find the sum of mixed numbers?

The students in Mr. Lopez's science class measured the rainfall each day for two weeks. The amounts for each week are listed in the table.

What was the total amount of rainfall for the two weeks?

Choose an Operation Add to find the total amount of rainfall for the two weeks.

Week	Rainfall
1	$2\frac{1}{2}$ in.
2	$1\frac{9}{10}$ in.

Step 1

Estimate.

$2\frac{1}{2} \approx 3$

$+ 1\frac{9}{10} \approx + 2$

$\overline{5}$

The total rainfall was about 5 inches.

Step 2

Find the LCD of the fractions and use it to write equivalent fractions.

$2\frac{1}{2} = 2\frac{5}{10}$

$+ 1\frac{9}{10} = + 1\frac{9}{10}$

$\overline{3\frac{14}{10}}$

Then add whole numbers and fractions separately.

Step 3

Rename improper fractions as mixed numbers. Simplify.

$3\frac{14}{10} = 3 + 1\frac{4}{10}$

$= 4\frac{4}{10} = 4\frac{2}{5}$

The total rainfall was $4\frac{2}{5}$ inches.

Source: pp. 172–173; From enVisionMATH Common Core (Grade 6). Copyright © 2013 Pearson Education, Inc., or its affiliates. Used by permission. All Rights Reserved.

Properties of Addition for Rational Numbers

Rational numbers have the following properties for addition: *closure, commutative, associative, additive identity*, and *additive inverse*. To emphasize the additive inverse property of rational numbers, we state it explicitly, as follows.

Theorem 6-6: Additive Inverse Property of Rational Numbers

For any rational number $\frac{a}{b}$, there exists a unique rational number $-\frac{a}{b}$, the additive inverse of $\frac{a}{b}$, such that

$$\frac{a}{b} + \left(-\frac{a}{b}\right) = 0 = \left(-\frac{a}{b}\right) + \frac{a}{b}.$$

As mentioned earlier, another form of $-\dfrac{a}{b}$ can be found by considering the sum $\dfrac{a}{b} + \dfrac{^-a}{b}$. Because

$$\dfrac{a}{b} + \dfrac{^-a}{b} = \dfrac{a + ^-a}{b} = \dfrac{0}{b} = 0,$$

it follows that $-\dfrac{a}{b}$ and $\dfrac{^-a}{b}$ are both additive inverses of $\dfrac{a}{b}$, so $-\dfrac{a}{b} = \dfrac{^-a}{b}$.

Example 9

Find the additive inverses for each of the following:

a. $\dfrac{3}{5}$ **b.** $\dfrac{^-5}{11}$ **c.** $4\dfrac{1}{2}$

Solution

a. $-\dfrac{3}{5}$ or $\dfrac{^-3}{5}$ **b.** $-\left(\dfrac{^-5}{11}\right) = \dfrac{^-(^-5)}{11} = \dfrac{5}{11}$ **c.** $^-4\dfrac{1}{2}$, or $\dfrac{^-9}{2}$

Properties of the additive inverse for rational numbers are analogous to those of the additive inverse for integers, as shown in Table 2.

Table 2

Integers	Rational Numbers
1. $^-(^-a) = a$	**1.** $-\left(\dfrac{^-a}{b}\right) = \dfrac{a}{b}$
2. $^-(a + b) = ^-a + ^-b$	**2.** $-\left(\dfrac{a}{b} + \dfrac{c}{d}\right) = \dfrac{^-a}{b} + \dfrac{^-c}{d}$

The set of rational numbers has the addition property of equality, which says that the same number can be added to both sides of an equation.

Theorem 6-7:   Addition Property of Equality of Rational Numbers

If $\dfrac{a}{b}$ and $\dfrac{c}{d}$ are any rational numbers such that $\dfrac{a}{b} = \dfrac{c}{d}$ and $\dfrac{e}{f}$ is any rational number, then

$$\dfrac{a}{b} + \dfrac{e}{f} = \dfrac{c}{d} + \dfrac{e}{f}.$$

IMAP Video

Watch Francisco use the take-away model with rational numbers.

Subtraction of Rational Numbers

In elementary school, subtraction of rational numbers is usually introduced by using a take-away model. If we have $\dfrac{6}{7}$ of a pizza and $\dfrac{2}{7}$ of the original pizza is taken away, $\dfrac{4}{7}$ of the pizza remains; that is, $\dfrac{6}{7} - \dfrac{2}{7} = \dfrac{6 - 2}{7} = \dfrac{4}{7}$. In general, subtraction of rational numbers with like denominators is determined as follows:

$$\dfrac{a}{b} - \dfrac{c}{b} = \dfrac{a - c}{b}.$$

As with integers, a number line can be used to model subtraction of nonnegative rational numbers. If a line is marked off in units of length $\frac{1}{b}$ and $a \geq c$, then $\frac{a}{b} - \frac{c}{b}$ is equal to $(a - c)$ units of length $\frac{1}{b}$, which implies that $\frac{a}{b} - \frac{c}{b} = \frac{a-c}{b}$.

When the denominators are not the same, we can perform the subtraction by finding a common denominator. For example,

$$\frac{3}{4} - \frac{2}{3} = \frac{3 \cdot 3}{4 \cdot 3} - \frac{2 \cdot 4}{3 \cdot 4} = \frac{9}{12} - \frac{8}{12} = \frac{9-8}{12} = \frac{1}{12}.$$

Subtraction of rational numbers, like subtraction of integers, can be defined in terms of addition as follows.

Definition of Subtraction of Rational Numbers in Terms of Addition

If $\frac{a}{b}$ and $\frac{c}{d}$ are any rational numbers, then $\frac{a}{b} - \frac{c}{d}$ is the unique rational number $\frac{e}{f}$ such that $\frac{a}{b} = \frac{c}{d} + \frac{e}{f}$.

As with integers, we can see that subtraction of rational numbers can be performed by adding the additive inverses as stated in the following theorem.

Theorem 6-8

If $\frac{a}{b}$ and $\frac{c}{d}$ are any rational numbers, then $\frac{a}{b} - \frac{c}{d} = \frac{a}{b} + \frac{^-c}{d}$.

Now, using Theorem 6-8, we obtain the following.

$$\frac{a}{b} - \frac{c}{d} = \frac{a}{b} + \frac{^-c}{d}$$

$$= \frac{ad + b(^-c)}{bd}$$

$$= \frac{ad + {}^-(bc)}{bd}$$

$$= \frac{ad - bc}{bd}$$

We proved the following theorem, which is sometimes given as a definition of subtraction.

Theorem 6-9

If $\frac{a}{b}$ and $\frac{c}{d}$ are any rational numbers, then $\frac{a}{b} - \frac{c}{d} = \frac{ad - bc}{bd}$.

Example 10

Find each difference.

a. $\dfrac{5}{8} - \dfrac{1}{4}$ b. $5\dfrac{1}{3} - 2\dfrac{3}{4}$

Solution

a. One approach is to find the LCM for the denominators. LCM$(8, 4) = 8$.

$$\frac{5}{8} - \frac{1}{4} = \frac{5}{8} - \frac{2}{8} = \frac{3}{8}$$

An alternative approach follows.

$$\frac{5}{8} - \frac{1}{4} = \frac{5 \cdot 4 - 8 \cdot 1}{8 \cdot 4} = \frac{20 - 8}{32} = \frac{12}{32} = \frac{3}{8}$$

b. Two methods of solution are given.

$$\begin{array}{l} 5\dfrac{1}{3} = \;\; 5\dfrac{4}{12} = 4 + 1\dfrac{4}{12} = \;\; 4\dfrac{16}{12} \\[2mm] \underline{-2\dfrac{3}{4} = -2\dfrac{9}{12} = \quad\; -2\dfrac{9}{12} \quad = -2\dfrac{9}{12}} \\[2mm] \hspace{7cm} 2\dfrac{7}{12} \end{array} \qquad \begin{aligned} 5\dfrac{1}{3} - 2\dfrac{3}{4} &= \dfrac{16}{3} - \dfrac{11}{4} \\[2mm] &= \dfrac{16 \cdot 4 - 3 \cdot 11}{3 \cdot 4} \\[2mm] &= \dfrac{64 - 33}{12} \\[2mm] &= \dfrac{31}{12} = 2\dfrac{7}{12} \end{aligned}$$

The following examples show the use of fractions in algebra.

Example 11

Add or subtract, writing your answer in simplest form.

a. $\dfrac{x}{2} + \dfrac{x}{3}$ b. $\dfrac{2 - x}{6 - 3x} + \dfrac{4 - 2x}{3x - 6}$

c. $\dfrac{2}{a + b} - \dfrac{2}{a - b}$ d. $\dfrac{1}{x} - \dfrac{1}{2x^2}$

Solution

a. $\dfrac{x}{2} + \dfrac{x}{3} = \dfrac{3x}{3 \cdot 2} + \dfrac{2x}{2 \cdot 3}$

$= \dfrac{3x + 2x}{6} = \dfrac{5x}{6}$

b. We first write each fraction in simplest form.

$$\frac{2 - x}{6 - 3x} = \frac{2 - x}{3(2 - x)} = \frac{1(2 - x)}{3(2 - x)} = \frac{1}{3}$$

$$\frac{4 - 2x}{3x - 6} = \frac{^-2(x - 2)}{3(x - 2)} = \frac{^-2}{3}$$

Thus, the sum is $\dfrac{1}{3} + \dfrac{^-2}{3} = \dfrac{^-1}{3}$.

c. We use Theorem 6-9.

$$\frac{2}{a+b} - \frac{2}{a-b} = \frac{2(a-b) - 2(a+b)}{(a+b)(a-b)}$$

$$= \frac{2a - 2b - 2a - 2b}{(a+b)(a-b)}$$

$$= \frac{^-4b}{(a+b)(a-b)} = \frac{^-4b}{a^2 - b^2}$$

d.
$$\frac{1}{x} - \frac{1}{2x^2} = \frac{2x \cdot 1}{2x \cdot x} - \frac{1}{2x^2}$$

$$= \frac{2x}{2x^2} - \frac{1}{2x^2}$$

$$= \frac{2x - 1}{2x^2}$$

Estimation with Rational Numbers

Estimation helps us make practical decisions in our everyday lives. For example, suppose we need to double a recipe that calls for $\frac{3}{4}$ of a cup of flour. Will we need more or less than a cup of flour?

Many of the estimation and mental math techniques that we learned to use with whole numbers also work with rational numbers.

The grade 5 *Common Core Standards* calls for students to "use benchmark fraction and number sense of fractions to estimate mentally and assess the reasonableness of answers." (p. 36) Estimation plays an important role in judging the reasonableness of computations.

▶ **NOW TRY THIS 3**

NTT 3: Answers can be found in Answers at the back of the book.

A student added $\frac{3}{4} + \frac{1}{2}$ and obtained $\frac{4}{6}$. How would you use estimation to show that this answer could not be correct?

Sometimes to obtain an estimate it is desirable to round fractions to a ***convenient*** or ***benchmark*** fraction, such as $\frac{1}{2}, \frac{1}{3}, \frac{1}{4}, \frac{1}{5}, \frac{2}{3}, \frac{3}{4}$, or 1. For example, if a student had 59 correct answers out of 80 questions, the student answered $\frac{59}{80}$ of the questions correctly, which is approximately $\frac{60}{80}$, or $\frac{3}{4}$. We know $\frac{60}{80}$ is greater than $\frac{59}{80}$. The estimate $\frac{3}{4}$ for $\frac{59}{80}$ is a high estimate. In a similar way, we can estimate $\frac{31}{90}$ by $\frac{30}{90}$, or $\frac{1}{3}$. In this case, the estimate of $\frac{1}{3}$ is a low estimate of $\frac{31}{90}$.

An example of benchmark estimation is seen on the student page shown on page 284.

School Book Page

Another Example   **How can you use benchmark fractions such as $\frac{1}{4}, \frac{1}{3}, \frac{1}{2}, \frac{2}{3},$ and $\frac{3}{4}$ to estimate?**

Estimate $\frac{5}{8} - \frac{3}{16}$.

$\frac{5}{8}$ is close to $\frac{6}{8}$, and $\frac{6}{8} = \frac{3}{4}$.

$\frac{3}{16}$ is close to $\frac{4}{16}$, and $\frac{4}{16} = \frac{1}{4}$.

So, $\frac{5}{8} - \frac{3}{16}$ is close to $\frac{3}{4} - \frac{1}{4}$.

$\frac{3}{4} - \frac{1}{4} = \frac{2}{4}$ or $\frac{1}{2}$

So, $\frac{5}{8} - \frac{3}{16} \approx \frac{1}{2}$.

Source: p. 170; From enVisionMATH Common Core (Grade 6). Copyright © 2013 Pearson Education, Inc., or its affiliates. Used by permission. All Rights Reserved.

Example 12

A sixth-grade class is collecting cans to take to the recycling center. Becky's group brought the following amounts (in pounds). About how many pounds does her group have all together?

$$1\frac{1}{8}, 3\frac{4}{10}, 5\frac{7}{8}, \frac{6}{10}$$

Solution   We can estimate the amount by using front-end estimation with the adjustment made by using 0 which is close to $\frac{1}{8}$, $\frac{1}{2}$ which is close to $\frac{4}{10}$ and $\frac{6}{10}$, and 1 which is close to $\frac{7}{8}$ as benchmark fractions. The front-end estimate is $1 + 3 + 5 = 9$. The adjustment is $0 + \frac{1}{2} + 1 + \frac{1}{2}$, or 2. An adjusted estimate would be $9 + 2 = 11$ lb.

Example 13

Estimate each of the following additions.

a. $\frac{27}{13} + \frac{10}{9}$ **b.** $3\frac{9}{10} + 2\frac{7}{8} + \frac{11}{12}$ **c.** $3\frac{7}{8} + 11\frac{1}{2} + 2\frac{2}{5} + 5\frac{1}{16}$

Solution

a. Because $\frac{27}{13}$ is slightly more than 2 and $\frac{10}{9}$ is slightly more than 1, an estimate might be 3. We know the estimate is low.

b. We first add the whole-number parts to obtain $3 + 2 = 5$. Because each of the fractions, $\frac{9}{10}, \frac{7}{8},$ and $\frac{11}{12}$, is close to but less than 1, their sum is close to but less than 3. The approximate answer is $5 + 3 = 8$. The estimate is high.

c. Using *grouping to nice numbers*, we group $\left(3\frac{7}{8} + 5\frac{1}{16}\right)$ and $\left(11\frac{1}{2} + 2\frac{2}{5}\right)$ to obtain approximately $9 + 14 = 23$. The estimate is high. (Why?)

Assessment 6-2A

1. Perform the following additions or subtractions.

   a. $\dfrac{1}{2} + \dfrac{2}{3}$ $\dfrac{7}{6} = 1\dfrac{1}{6}$

   b. $\dfrac{4}{12} - \dfrac{2}{3}$ $\dfrac{^-4}{12} = \dfrac{^-1}{3}$

   c. $\dfrac{5}{x} + \dfrac{^-3}{y}$ $\dfrac{5y - 3x}{xy}$

   d. $\dfrac{^-3}{2x^2y} + \dfrac{5}{2xy^2} + \dfrac{7}{x^2}$ $\dfrac{^-3y + 5x + 14y^2}{2x^2y^2}$

   e. $\dfrac{5}{6} + 2\dfrac{1}{8}$ $\dfrac{71}{24} = 2\dfrac{23}{24}$

   f. $^-4\dfrac{1}{2} - 3\dfrac{1}{6}$ $\dfrac{^-23}{3} = ^-7\dfrac{2}{3}$

   g. $7\dfrac{1}{4} + 3\dfrac{5}{12} - 2\dfrac{1}{3}$ $8\dfrac{4}{12} = 8\dfrac{1}{3}$

2. Change each of the following fractions to a mixed number.

   a. $\dfrac{56}{3}$ $18\dfrac{2}{3}$

   b. $-\dfrac{293}{100}$ $^-2\dfrac{93}{100}$

3. Change each of the following mixed numbers to a fraction in the form $\dfrac{a}{b}$, where a and b are integers and $b \neq 0$.   Answers vary.

   a. $6\dfrac{3}{4}$ $\dfrac{27}{4}$

   b. $^-3\dfrac{5}{8}$ $\dfrac{^-29}{8}$

4. Approximate each of the following situations with a benchmark fraction. Tell whether your estimate is high or low.   Answers vary.

   a. Giorgio had 15 base hits out of 46 times at bat. $\dfrac{1}{3}$, high

   b. Ruth made 7 goals out of 41 shots.   *

   c. Laura answered 62 problems correctly out of 80. $\dfrac{3}{4}$, low

   d. Jonathan made 9 baskets out of 19.   *

5. Use the information in the table to answer each of the following questions.

Team	Games Played	Games Won
Ducks	22	10
Beavers	19	10
Tigers	28	9
Bears	23	8
Lions	27	7
Wildcats	25	6
Badgers	21	5

   a. Which team won more than $\dfrac{1}{2}$ of its games and was closest to winning $\dfrac{1}{2}$ of its games?   Beavers

   b. Which team won less than $\dfrac{1}{2}$ of its games and was closest to winning $\dfrac{1}{2}$ of its games?   Ducks

   c. Which team won more than $\dfrac{1}{3}$ of its games and was closest to winning $\dfrac{1}{3}$ of its games?   Bears

6. Sort the following fraction cards into the ovals by estimating in which oval the fraction belongs.   *

   Sort these fraction cards.   About 0   About $\dfrac{1}{2}$ About 1

    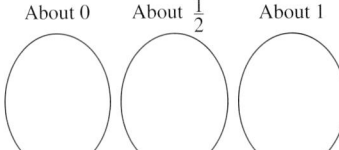

7. Approximate each of the following fractions by $0, \dfrac{1}{4}, \dfrac{1}{2}, \dfrac{3}{4}$, or 1. Tell whether your estimate is high or low.

   a. $\dfrac{19}{39}$ $\dfrac{1}{2}$, high

   b. $\dfrac{3}{197}$ 0, low

   c. $\dfrac{150}{201}$ $\dfrac{3}{4}$, high

   d. $\dfrac{8}{9}$ 1, high

8. Without actually finding the exact answer, state which of the numbers given in parentheses is the best approximation for the given sum.

   a. $\dfrac{6}{13} + \dfrac{7}{15} + \dfrac{11}{23} + \dfrac{17}{35}$ $\left(1, 2, 3, 3\dfrac{1}{2}\right)$ 2

   b. $\dfrac{30}{41} + \dfrac{1}{1000} + \dfrac{3}{2000}$ $\left(\dfrac{3}{8}, \dfrac{3}{4}, 1, 2\right)$ $\dfrac{3}{4}$

9. Compute each of the following mentally.

   a. $1 - \dfrac{3}{4}$ $\dfrac{1}{4}$

   b. $3\dfrac{3}{8} + 2\dfrac{1}{4} - 5\dfrac{5}{8}$ 0

10. The following ruler has regions marked M, A, T, H.

    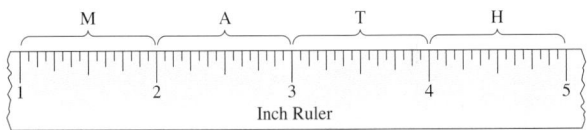

    Use estimation to determine into which region on the ruler each of the following measurements falls. For example, $\dfrac{12}{5}$ in. falls into region A.

    a. $\dfrac{20}{8}$ in.   A

    b. $\dfrac{36}{8}$ in.   H

    c. $\dfrac{60}{16}$ in.   T

    d. $\dfrac{18}{4}$ in.   H

11. Use *clustering* to estimate the following sum.   Answers vary.

    $3\dfrac{1}{3} + 3\dfrac{1}{5} + 2\dfrac{7}{8} + 2\dfrac{7}{9}$ Approximately $4 \cdot 3 = 12$

12. A class consists of $\dfrac{2}{5}$ freshmen, $\dfrac{1}{4}$ sophomores, and $\dfrac{1}{10}$ juniors; the rest are seniors. What fraction of the class is seniors? $\dfrac{1}{4}$

13. A clerk sold three pieces of one type of ribbon to different customers. One piece was $\dfrac{1}{3}$ yd long, another was $2\dfrac{3}{4}$ yd long, and the third was $3\dfrac{1}{2}$ yd long. What was the total length of that type of ribbon sold? $6\dfrac{7}{12}$ yd

14. Martine bought $8\frac{3}{4}$ yd of fabric. She wants to make a skirt using $1\frac{7}{8}$ yd, pants using $2\frac{3}{8}$ yd, and a vest using $1\frac{2}{3}$ yd. How much fabric will be left over? $2\frac{5}{6}$ yd

15. Give an example illustrating each of the following properties of rational number addition.
  a. Closure *   **b.** Commutative * **c.** Associative *

16. Insert five fractions between the numbers 1 and 2 so that the seven numbers (including 1 and 2) constitute part of an arithmetic sequence. *

17. a. Check that each of the following statements is true.

   i. $\frac{1}{3} = \frac{1}{4} + \frac{1}{3 \cdot 4}$ $\frac{1}{4} + \frac{1}{3 \cdot 4} = \frac{1}{4} + \frac{1}{12} = \frac{16}{48} = \frac{1}{3}$

   ii. $\frac{1}{4} = \frac{1}{5} + \frac{1}{4 \cdot 5}$ $\frac{1}{5} + \frac{1}{4 \cdot 5} = \frac{1}{5} + \frac{1}{20} = \frac{25}{100} = \frac{1}{4}$

   iii. $\frac{1}{5} = \frac{1}{6} + \frac{1}{5 \cdot 6}$ $\frac{1}{6} + \frac{1}{5 \cdot 6} = \frac{1}{6} + \frac{1}{30} = \frac{36}{180} = \frac{1}{5}$

  b. Based on the examples in (a), write $\frac{1}{n}$ as a sum of two unit fractions; that is, as a sum of fractions with numerator 1. *

18. Solve for x.

  a. $x + 2\frac{1}{2} = 3\frac{1}{3}$ $\frac{5}{6}$

  b. $x - 2\frac{2}{3} = \frac{5}{6}$ $\frac{21}{6} = 3\frac{1}{2} = \frac{7}{2}$

19. Al runs $\frac{5}{8}$ mi in 10 min. Bill runs $\frac{7}{8}$ mi in 10 min. If both runners continue to run at the same rate, how much farther can Bill run than Al in 20 min? $\frac{1}{2}$ mi

20. One recipe calls for $1\frac{3}{4}$ cups of milk and a second recipe calls for $1\frac{1}{2}$ cups of milk. If you only have 3 cups of milk, can you make both recipes? Why?   No, you need $\frac{1}{4}$ cup more milk.

21. The table below shows census data from the state of Pennsylvania for 2011.

Population	2011
Total 8-yr. old	150,155
Boys	76,432
Girls	73,723
Total 9-yr. old	149,904
Boys	76,503
Girls	73,401
Total 10-yr. old	154,144
Boys	78,672
Girls	75,472

Data from 2011 Census taken from http://www.census.gov/schools/facts/pennsylvania.html

Answers vary.

  a. About what part of the total population is 8- to 10-year-old boys?   About $\frac{23}{45}$

  b. About what part of the total population is 8- to 10-year-old girls?   About $\frac{22}{45}$

  c. If the population of the entire state of Pennsylvania in 2011 was 12,742,886, about what part of the population was boys of ages 8- to 10-year-olds?   About $\frac{2}{127}$

22. According to the US Census Bureau, in October 2012, there were about 633,000 3- and 4-year-olds enrolled in schools. Additionally there were about 1,186,000 16- and 17-year-olds enrolled in schools. In the respective ages there were about 1,193,000 and 1,259,000 total. Which age group had the greater fraction in school?   The 16- and 17-year-olds

23. There are 360° in a circle graph. If 40° of the graph represents rent and 5° of the graph represents savings, what fractional portion of the whole graph is represented by rent and savings? $\frac{1}{8}$

24. The energy sources for the US in 2012 included $\frac{37}{100}$ coal, $\frac{3}{10}$ natural gas, $\frac{19}{100}$ nuclear, and $\frac{7}{100}$ hydropower. How much is unaccounted for in this list? $\frac{7}{100}$

Assessment 6-2B

1. Perform the following additions or subtractions.

  a. $\frac{-1}{2} + \frac{2}{3}$ $\frac{1}{6}$

  b. $\frac{5}{12} - \frac{2}{3}$ $\frac{-1}{4}$

  c. $\frac{5}{4x} + \frac{-3}{2y}$ $\frac{5y - 6x}{4xy}$

  d. $\frac{-3}{2x^2y^2} + \frac{5}{2xy^2} + \frac{7}{x^2y}$ $\frac{-3 + 5x + 14y}{2x^2y^2}$

  e. $\frac{5}{6} - 2\frac{1}{8}$ $\frac{-31}{24} = -1\frac{7}{24}$

  f. $-4\frac{1}{2} + 3\frac{1}{6}$ $\frac{-4}{3} = -1\frac{1}{3}$

  g. $5\frac{1}{3} + 5\frac{5}{6} - 3\frac{1}{9}$ $8\frac{1}{18} = \frac{145}{18}$

2. Change each of the following fractions to a mixed number.

  a. $\frac{14}{5}$ $2\frac{4}{5}$ **b.** $-\frac{47}{8}$ $-5\frac{7}{8}$

3. Change each of the following mixed numbers to a fraction in the form $\frac{a}{b}$, where a and b are integers and $b \neq 0$.   Answers vary.

  a. $7\frac{1}{2}$ $\frac{15}{2}$ **b.** $-4\frac{2}{3}$ $\frac{-14}{3}$

4. Place the numbers 2, 5, 6, and 8 in the following boxes to make the equation true.

$$\frac{\square}{\square} + \frac{\square}{\square} = \frac{23}{24} \qquad \frac{2}{6} + \frac{5}{8} = \frac{23}{24}$$

5. Use the information in the table to answer each of the following questions.

Team	Games Played	Games Won
Ducks	22	10
Beavers	19	10
Tigers	28	9
Bears	23	8
Lions	27	7
Wildcats	25	6
Badgers	21	5

   a. Which team won less than $\frac{1}{3}$ of its games and was closest to winning $\frac{1}{3}$ of its games?   Tigers

   b. Which team won more than $\frac{1}{4}$ of its games and was closest to winning of $\frac{1}{4}$ of its games?   Lions

   c. Which teams won less than $\frac{1}{4}$ of their games?
   Wildcats, Badgers

6. Sort the following fraction cards into the ovals by estimating in which oval the fraction belongs.   *

Sort these fraction cards.

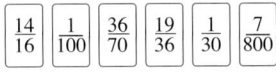

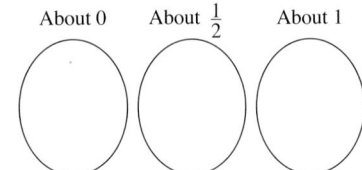

7. Approximate each of the following fractions by $0, \frac{1}{4}, \frac{1}{2}, \frac{3}{4}$, or 1. Tell whether your estimate is high or low.

   a. $\frac{113}{100}$ 1, low

   b. $\frac{3}{1978}$ 0, low

   c. $\frac{150}{198}$ $\frac{3}{4}$, low

   d. $\frac{8}{9}$ 1, high

8. Without actually finding the exact answer, state which of the numbers given in parentheses is the best approximation for the given sum.

   a. $\frac{2}{13} + \frac{7}{15} + \frac{12}{23} + \frac{33}{35}$ $\left(1, 2, 3, 3\frac{1}{2}\right)$ 2

   b. $\frac{30}{41} + \frac{220}{1000} + \frac{5}{2000}$ $\left(\frac{3}{8}, \frac{3}{4}, 1, 2\right)$ 1

9. Compute each of the following mentally.

   a. $6 - \frac{7}{8}$ $5\frac{1}{8}$

   b. $2\frac{3}{5} + 4\frac{1}{10} + 3\frac{3}{10}$ 10

10. The following ruler has regions marked M, A, T, H.

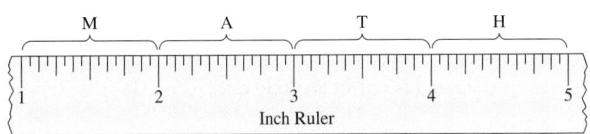

Use mental mathematics and estimation to determine into which region on the ruler each of the following measurements falls. For example, $\frac{12}{5}$ in. falls into region A.

   a. $\frac{9}{8}$ in.   M

   b. $\frac{18}{8}$ in.   A

   c. $\frac{50}{16}$ in.   T

   d. $\frac{17}{4}$ in.   H

11. A class consists of $\frac{1}{4}$ freshmen, $\frac{1}{5}$ sophomores, and $\frac{1}{10}$ juniors; the rest are seniors. What fraction of the class is seniors? $\frac{9}{20}$

12. The Naturals Company sells its products in many countries. The following two circle graphs show the fractions of the company's earnings for 2012 and 2014. Based on this information, answer the following questions.

   a. In 2012, how much greater was the fraction of sales for Japan than for Canada? $\frac{1}{30}$

   b. In 2014, how much less was the fraction of sales for England than for the United States? $\frac{2}{20}$ or $\frac{1}{10}$

   c. How much greater was the fraction of total sales for the United States in 2014 than in 2012? $\frac{1}{60}$

   d. Is it true that the amount of sales in dollars in Australia was less in 2012 than in 2014? Why?   *

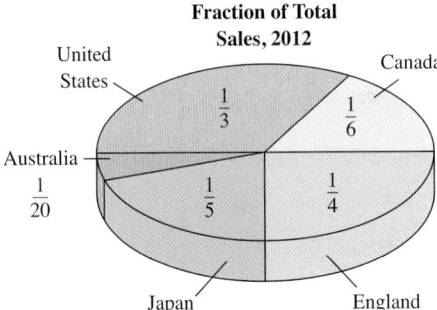

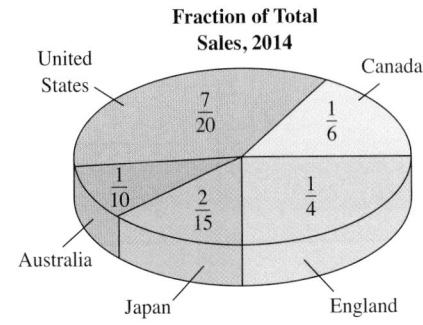

13. A recipe requires $3\frac{1}{2}$ cups of milk. Ran put in $1\frac{3}{4}$ cups in a bowl. How much more milk does he need? $1\frac{3}{4}$ cups

14. A $15\frac{3}{4}$ in. board is cut in a single cut from a $38\frac{1}{4}$ in. board. The saw cut takes $\frac{3}{8}$ in. How much of the $38\frac{1}{4}$ in. board is left after cutting? $22\frac{1}{8}$ in.

15. Students from Rattlesnake School formed four teams to collect cans for recycling during the months of April and May. A record of their efforts follows.

Number of Pounds Collected

	Team 1	Team 2	Team 3	Team 4
April	$28\frac{3}{4}$	$32\frac{7}{8}$	$28\frac{1}{2}$	$35\frac{3}{16}$
May	$33\frac{1}{3}$	$28\frac{5}{12}$	$25\frac{3}{4}$	$41\frac{1}{2}$

a. Which team collected the most for the 2-month period? How much did they collect?   Team 4; $76\frac{11}{16}$ lb

b. What was the difference between the total pounds collected in April and the total pounds collected in May? $3\frac{11}{16}$ lb

16. Insert four fractions between the numbers 1 and 3 so that the six numbers (including 1 and 3) constitute part of an arithmetic sequence.   *

17. Solve for x in each of the following.

a. $x - \frac{5}{6} = \frac{2}{3}$ $\frac{9}{6} = \frac{3}{2} = 1\frac{1}{2}$

b. $x - \frac{7}{2^3 \cdot 3^2} = \frac{5}{2^2 \cdot 3^2}$ $\frac{17}{2^3 \cdot 3^2} = \frac{17}{72}$

18. Joe has $\frac{3}{4}$ cup of paint in a container. He uses $\frac{1}{3}$ cup on a project and then adds another $\frac{1}{2}$ cup. How much paint does he have now? $\frac{11}{12}$ cup

19. a. Find $\frac{1}{2} + \frac{1}{4}$. $\frac{3}{4}$

b. Find $\frac{1}{2} + \frac{1}{4} + \frac{1}{8}$. $\frac{7}{8}$

c. Find $\frac{1}{2} + \frac{1}{4} + \frac{1}{8} + \frac{1}{16}$. $\frac{15}{16}$

d. If you continue in this pattern with powers of 2 in the denominator, will the sum ever become greater than 1? Why?   *

20. The table below shows census data from the state of Pennsylvania for 2011.

Population	2011
Total 8-yr. old	150,155
Boys	76,432
Girls	73,723
Total 9-yr. old	149,904
Boys	76,503
Girls	73,401
Total 10-yr. old	154,144
Boys	78,672
Girls	75,472

Data from 2011 Census taken from http://www.census.gov/schools/facts/pennsylvania.html

Answers vary.

a. About what fraction more of girls is there in the 8-year-olds are there than in the 10-year-olds?   *

b. About what part of the total population of 8- to 9-year-olds are girls?   *

c. If the population of the entire state of Pennsylvania in 2011 was 12,742,886, about what part of the population was girls of ages 8–10?   *

21. According to the US Census Bureau in October 2012, there were about 633,000 3- and 4-year olds enrolled in schools. Additionally there were about 1,186,000 16- and 17-year-olds enrolled in schools. In the respective ages there were about 1,193,000 and 1,259,000 total. Which of these age groups had the lesser fraction in school?   The 3- and 4-year-olds

22. There are 360° in a circle graph. If 50° of the graph represents rent and 7° of the graph represents savings, what fractional portion of the whole graph is not represented by rent and savings?   *

23. The energy sources for the United States in 2012 included $\frac{37}{100}$ coal, $\frac{3}{10}$ natural gas, $\frac{19}{100}$ nuclear, and $\frac{7}{100}$ hydropower. What fraction more coal than natural gas is used? $\frac{7}{100}$

Mathematical Connections 6-2

Answers to Mathematical Connections can be found in the Answers section at the back of the book.

Reasoning

1. Suppose a large pizza is divided into 3 equal-size pieces and a small pizza is divided into 4 equal-size pieces and you get 1 piece from each pizza. Does $\frac{1}{3} + \frac{1}{4}$ represent the amount that you received? Explain why or why not.

2. a. When we add two fractions with unlike denominators and convert them to fractions with the same denominator, must we use the least common denominator? What are the advantages of using the least common denominator?

   b. When the least common denominator is used in adding or subtracting fractions, is the result always a fraction in simplest form?

3. Explain why we can do the following to convert $5\frac{3}{4}$ to a mixed number.

$$\frac{5 \cdot 4 + 3}{4} = \frac{23}{4}$$

4. Kara spent $\frac{1}{2}$ of her allowance on Saturday and $\frac{1}{3}$ of what she had left on Sunday. Can this situation be modeled as $\frac{1}{2} - \frac{1}{3}$? Explain why or why not.

5. Compute $3\frac{3}{4} + 5\frac{1}{3}$ in two different ways and leave your answer as a mixed number. Tell which way you prefer and why.

6. Explain whether each of the following properties holds for subtraction of rational numbers.
   a. Closure   b. Commutative
   c. Associative   d. Identity
   e. Inverse

Open-Ended

7. Write a story problem for $\frac{2}{3} - \frac{1}{4}$.

8. a. Write two fractions whose sum is 1. If one of the fractions is $\frac{a}{b}$, what is the other?
   b. Write three fractions whose sum is 1.
   c. Write two fractions whose difference is very close to 1 but not exactly 1.

9. a. With the exception of $\frac{2}{3}$, the Egyptians used only unit fractions (fractions that have numerators of 1). Every unit fraction can be expressed as the sum of two unit fractions in more than one way, for example, $\frac{1}{2} = \frac{1}{4} + \frac{1}{4}$ and $\frac{1}{2} = \frac{1}{3} + \frac{1}{6}$. Find at least two different unit fraction representations for each of the following.
   i. $\frac{1}{3}$ ii. $\frac{1}{7}$
   b. Show that $\frac{1}{n} - \frac{1}{n+1} = \frac{1}{n(n+1)}$.
   c. Rewrite the equation in part (b) as a sum and then use the sum to answer part (a).
   d. Write $\frac{1}{17}$ as a sum of two different unit fractions.

Cooperative Learning

10. Interview 10 people and ask them if and when they add and subtract fractions in their lives. Combine their responses with those of the rest of the class to get a view of how "ordinary" people use computation of rational numbers in their daily lives.

Connecting Mathematics to the Classroom

11. Kendra showed that $\frac{1}{3} + \frac{3}{4} = \frac{4}{7}$ by using the following figure. How would you help her?

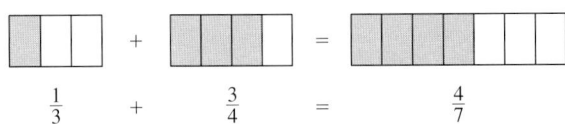

$$\frac{1}{3} \qquad + \qquad \frac{3}{4} \qquad = \qquad \frac{4}{7}$$

12. To show $2\frac{3}{4} = \frac{11}{4}$, the teacher drew the following picture. Ken said this shows a picture of $\frac{11}{12}$, not $\frac{11}{4}$. What is Ken thinking and how should the teacher respond?

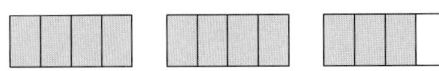

13. Jill claims that for positive fractions, $\frac{a}{b} + \frac{a}{c} = \frac{a}{b+c}$ because the fractions have a common numerator. How do you respond?

14. Explain the error pattern on Jon's test.
   a. $\frac{13}{35} = \frac{1}{5}, \quad \frac{27}{73} = \frac{2}{3}, \quad \frac{16}{64} = \frac{1}{4}$
   b. $\frac{4}{5} + \frac{2}{3} = \frac{6}{8}, \quad \frac{2}{5} + \frac{3}{4} = \frac{5}{9}, \quad \frac{7}{8} + \frac{1}{3} = \frac{8}{11}$
   c. $8\frac{3}{8} - 6\frac{1}{4} = 2\frac{2}{4}, \quad 5\frac{3}{8} - 2\frac{2}{3} = 3\frac{1}{5}, \quad 2\frac{2}{7} - 1\frac{1}{3} = 1\frac{1}{4}$

Review Problems

15. Simplify each rational number if possible.
   a. $\frac{14}{21}$ b. $\frac{117}{153}$
   c. $\frac{5^2}{7^2}$ d. $\frac{a^2 + a}{1 + a}$
   e. $\frac{a^2 + 1}{a + 1}$ f. $\frac{a^2 - b^2}{a - b}$

16. Determine whether the fractions in each of the following pairs are equal.
   a. $\frac{a^2}{b}$ and $\frac{a^2 b}{b^2}$
   b. $\frac{377}{400}$ and $\frac{378}{401}$
   c. $\frac{0}{10}$ and $\frac{0}{-10}$
   d. $\frac{a}{b}$ and $\frac{a+1}{b+1}$, where $a \ne b$

17. There are 206 bones in the body. Can the fraction $\frac{27}{103}$ represent the number of bones in both hands as a part of the total number of bones in the body? Explain your answer.

18. Explain why there are infinitely many fractions equivalent to $\frac{3}{5}$.

19. Mary ate $\frac{3}{5}$ of the cookies and left the rest for Suzanne. What fraction of the cookies are left for Suzanne?

20. On a number line, explain why $\frac{^{-}1}{100}$ is greater than $\frac{^{-}1}{10}$.

National Assessments

National Assessment of Educational Progress (NAEP) Questions

$$\frac{1}{20}, \frac{4}{20}, \frac{7}{20}, \frac{10}{20}, \frac{13}{20}, \cdots$$

If the pattern shown continues, what is the first fraction in the pattern that will be greater than 1?

A. $\frac{20}{20}$ 　　　　　　　B. $\frac{21}{20}$

C. $\frac{22}{20}$ 　　　　　　　D. $\frac{25}{20}$

NAEP, Grade 4, 2013

$\frac{1}{4}$ Cup 　　 $\frac{1}{3}$ Cup 　　 $\frac{1}{2}$ Cup

A recipe requires $1\frac{1}{3}$ cups of sugar. Which of the following ways describes how the measuring cups shown can be used to measure $1\frac{1}{3}$ cups of sugar accurately?

A. Use the $\frac{1}{2}$ cup three times.

B. Use the $\frac{1}{4}$ cup three times.

C. Use the $\frac{1}{2}$ cup twice and the $\frac{1}{3}$ cup once.

D. Use the $\frac{1}{3}$ cup twice and the $\frac{1}{2}$ cup once.

E. Use the $\frac{1}{4}$ cup once, the $\frac{1}{3}$ cup once, and the $\frac{1}{2}$ cup once.

NAEP, Grade 8, 2011

6-3 Multiplication, Division, and Estimation with Rational Numbers

6-3 Objectives

Students will be able to understand and explain

• Multiplication and division of rational numbers.

• Properties of multiplication and division of rational numbers.

• Estimation of multiplication and division with rational numbers.

• Extension of exponents to include negative integers.

Multiplication of Rational Numbers

To motivate the definition of multiplication of rational numbers, we use the interpretation of multiplication as repeated addition. Using repeated addition, we interpret $3\left(\frac{3}{4}\right)$ as follows:

$$3\left(\frac{3}{4}\right) = \frac{3}{4} + \frac{3}{4} + \frac{3}{4} = \frac{9}{4} = 2\frac{1}{4}$$

The area model in Figure 13 is another way to calculate this product.

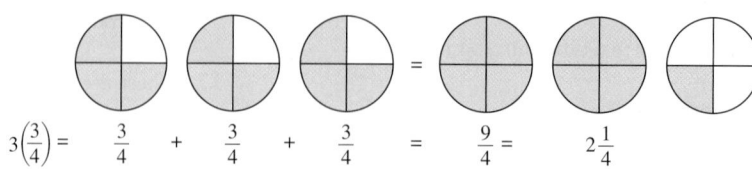

$$3\left(\frac{3}{4}\right) = \quad \frac{3}{4} \quad + \quad \frac{3}{4} \quad + \quad \frac{3}{4} \quad = \quad \frac{9}{4} = \quad 2\frac{1}{4}$$

Figure 13

We next consider $\left(\frac{3}{4}\right)3$. How should this product be interpreted? If the commutative property of multiplication of rational numbers is to hold, then $\left(\frac{3}{4}\right)3 = 3\left(\frac{3}{4}\right) = \frac{9}{4}$.

Next, we consider another interpretation of multiplication. What is $\frac{3}{4}$ of 3? In Figure 14(a) consider the 1-unit bar broken into fourths. Thus, there are four equal parts of the 1 unit, each of length $\frac{1}{4}$ unit. In Figure 14(b) suppose the length of the bar was 3 units. We want the same type of action to occur so it is divided into three-fourths using the same strategy. But analogously, each part would be 3 times the length of the bars in Figure 13(a). If this strategy is used then $\frac{3}{4}$ of 3 is seen as the shaded portion and $\frac{3}{4} \cdot 3 = \frac{9}{4}$ of 1 or simply $\frac{9}{4}$ is $\frac{3}{4}$ of 3.

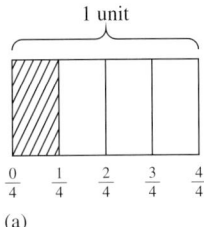

(a)

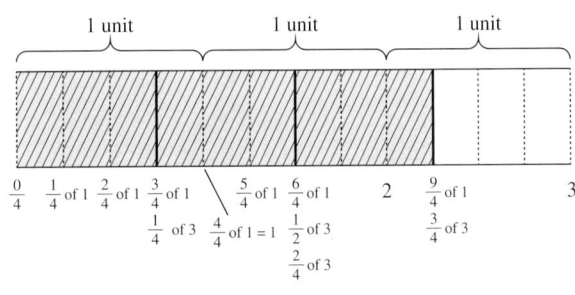

(b)

Figure 14

If forests once covered about $\frac{3}{5}$ of Earth's land and only about $\frac{1}{2}$ of these forests remain, what fraction of Earth is covered with forests today? We need to find $\frac{1}{2}$ of $\frac{3}{5}$, and can use an area model to find the answer.

Figure 15(a) shows a rectangle representing the *whole* separated into fifths, with $\frac{3}{5}$ shaded.

To find $\frac{1}{2}$ of $\frac{3}{5}$, we divide the shaded portion of the rectangle in Figure 15(a) into two congruent parts and take one of those parts. The result would be the green portion of Figure 15(b). However, the green portion represents 3 parts out of 10, or $\frac{3}{10}$, of the whole. Thus,

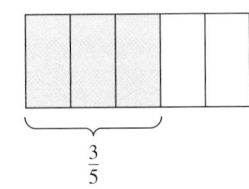

$\frac{3}{5}$

(a)

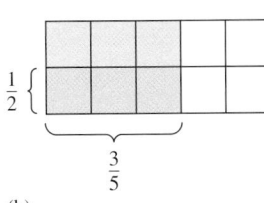

$\frac{3}{5}$

(b)

Figure 15

$$\frac{1}{2} \text{ of } \frac{3}{5} = \frac{1}{2} \cdot \frac{3}{5} = \frac{3}{10} = \frac{1 \cdot 3}{2 \cdot 5}.$$

An area model like the one in Figure 14 is used on the student page shown on page 292.

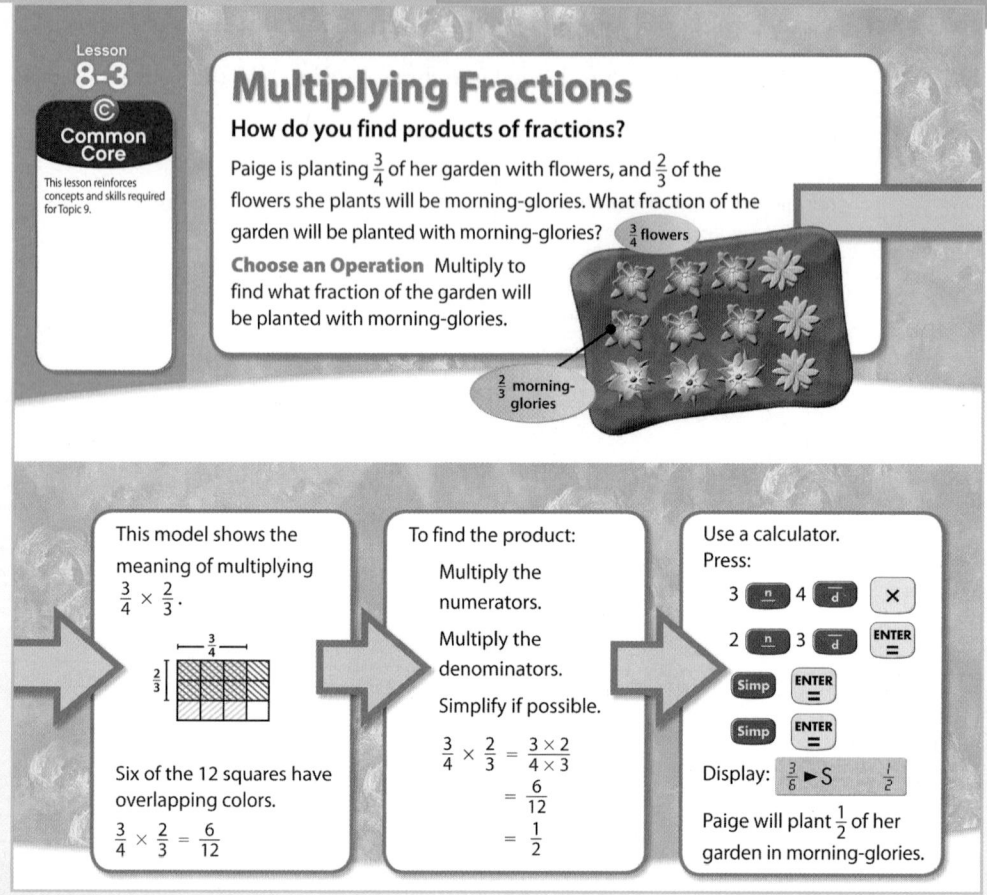

Source: pp. 190–191; From enVisionMATH Common Core (Grade 6). Copyright © 2013 Pearson Education, Inc., or its affiliates. Used by permission. All Rights Reserved.

This discussion leads to the following definition of multiplication for rational numbers.

Definition of Multiplication of Rational Numbers

If $\dfrac{a}{b}$ and $\dfrac{c}{d}$ are any rational numbers, then $\dfrac{a}{b} \cdot \dfrac{c}{d} = \dfrac{ac}{bd}$.

Example 14

If $\dfrac{5}{6}$ of the population of a certain city are college graduates and $\dfrac{7}{11}$ of the city's college graduates are female, what fraction of the population of that city is female college graduates?

Solution   The fraction should be $\dfrac{7}{11}$ of $\dfrac{5}{6}$, or $\dfrac{7}{11} \cdot \dfrac{5}{6} = \dfrac{7 \cdot 5}{11 \cdot 6} = \dfrac{35}{66}$.

The fraction of the population who are female college graduates is $\dfrac{35}{66}$.

Properties of Multiplication of Rational Numbers

Multiplication of rational numbers has properties analogous to the properties of multiplication of integers. These include the following properties for multiplication: closure, commutative, associative, and multiplicative identity. When we expand from the set of integers to the set of rationals, we pick up an additional property; that is, the multiplicative inverse property. For emphasis, we list the last two properties.

Theorem 6-10: Identity and Inverse Properties of Multiplication of Rational Numbers

Multiplicative Identity Property of Rational Numbers

The rational number 1 is the unique number such that for every rational number $\dfrac{a}{b}$,

$$1 \cdot \frac{a}{b} = \frac{a}{b} = \frac{a}{b} \cdot 1.$$

Multiplicative Inverse Property of Rational Numbers

For any nonzero rational number $\dfrac{a}{b}$, the multiplicative inverse (**reciprocal**) is the unique rational number $\dfrac{b}{a}$ such that

$$\frac{a}{b} \cdot \frac{b}{a} = 1 = \frac{b}{a} \cdot \frac{a}{b}.$$

Example 15

Find the multiplicative inverse, if possible, for each of the following rational numbers.

   a. $\dfrac{2}{3}$ **b.** $\dfrac{^-2}{5}$ **c.** 4   **d.** 0   **e.** $6\dfrac{1}{2}$

Solution

   a. $\dfrac{3}{2}$

   b. $\dfrac{5}{^-2}$, or $\dfrac{^-5}{2}$

   c. Because $4 = \dfrac{4}{1}$, the multiplicative inverse of 4 is $\dfrac{1}{4}$.

   d. Even though $0 = \dfrac{0}{1}, \dfrac{1}{0}$ is undefined; there is no multiplicative inverse of 0.

   e. Because $6\dfrac{1}{2} = \dfrac{13}{2}$, the multiplicative inverse of $6\dfrac{1}{2}$ is $\dfrac{2}{13}$.

Multiplication and addition are connected through the distributive property of multiplication over addition. Also, there are multiplication properties of equality and inequality for rational numbers and a multiplication property of zero similar to those for whole numbers and integers. These properties can be proved using the definition of operations on rational numbers and properties of integers. They are stated in the following theorem.

Theorem 6-11:   Properties of Rational Number Operations

Distributive Properties of Multiplication Over Addition and Subtraction for Rational Numbers

Let $\dfrac{a}{b}, \dfrac{c}{d}$, and $\dfrac{e}{f}$ be any rational numbers. Then

$$\frac{a}{b}\left(\frac{c}{d} + \frac{e}{f}\right) = \frac{a}{b} \cdot \frac{c}{d} + \frac{a}{b} \cdot \frac{e}{f}; \text{ and } \frac{a}{b}\left(\frac{c}{d} - \frac{e}{f}\right) = \frac{a}{b} \cdot \frac{c}{d} - \frac{a}{b} \cdot \frac{e}{f}.$$

Multiplication Property of Equality for Rational Numbers

Let $\dfrac{a}{b}, \dfrac{c}{d}$, and $\dfrac{e}{f}$ be any rational numbers such that $\dfrac{a}{b} = \dfrac{c}{d}$; then $\dfrac{a}{b} \cdot \dfrac{e}{f} = \dfrac{c}{d} \cdot \dfrac{e}{f}$.

Multiplication Properties of Inequality for Rational Numbers

Let $\dfrac{a}{b}, \dfrac{c}{d}$, and $\dfrac{e}{f}$ be any rational numbers. Then

a. $\dfrac{a}{b} > \dfrac{c}{d}$ and $\dfrac{e}{f} > 0$, then $\dfrac{a}{b} \cdot \dfrac{e}{f} > \dfrac{c}{d} \cdot \dfrac{e}{f}$.

b. $\dfrac{a}{b} > \dfrac{c}{d}$ and $\dfrac{e}{f} < 0$, then $\dfrac{a}{b} \cdot \dfrac{e}{f} < \dfrac{c}{d} \cdot \dfrac{e}{f}$.

Multiplication Property of Zero for Rational Numbers

Let $\dfrac{a}{b}$ be any rational number; then $\dfrac{a}{b} \cdot 0 = 0 = 0 \cdot \dfrac{a}{b}$.

Example 16

A bicycle is on sale at $\dfrac{3}{4}$ of its original price. If the sale price is \$330, what was the original price?

Solution   Let x be the original price. Then $\dfrac{3}{4}$ of the original price is $\dfrac{3}{4}x$. Because the sale price is \$330, we have $\dfrac{3}{4}x = 330$. Solving for x gives

$$\frac{4}{3} \cdot \frac{3}{4}x = \frac{4}{3} \cdot 330$$
$$1 \cdot x = 440$$
$$x = 440.$$

Thus, the original price was \$440.

An alternative approach follows. Suppose the bar in Figure 16 represents the original price. We know that $\dfrac{3}{4}$ of the original price is the sale price \$330 as shown. We have 3 of the $\dfrac{1}{4}$ parts of the original price is \$330, and one part, $\dfrac{1}{4}$ of the original price, must be \$110. Thus, the original price is \$330 + \$110 = \$440.

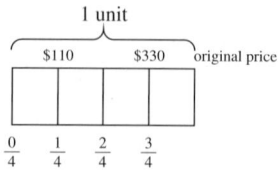

Figure 16

Multiplication with Mixed Numbers

In Figure 17, Johnny just figured out how to multiply mixed numbers while his colleagues seem to be struggling. How might we help them?

I JUST FIGURED OUT HOW TO MULTIPLY 2 1/2 X 2 1/2!

Figure 17

In Figure 17, Johnny may have decided one way to multiply $2\frac{1}{2} \cdot 2\frac{1}{2}$ is to change the mixed numbers to improper fractions and use the definition of multiplication as shown.

$$2\frac{1}{2} \cdot 2\frac{1}{2} = \frac{5}{2} \cdot \frac{5}{2} = \frac{25}{4}$$

We could then change $\frac{25}{4}$ to the mixed number $6\frac{1}{4}$.

Another way to multiply mixed numbers uses the distributive property of multiplication over addition, as seen below.

$$2\frac{1}{2} \cdot 2\frac{1}{2} = \left(2 + \frac{1}{2}\right)\left(2 + \frac{1}{2}\right)$$

$$= \left(2 + \frac{1}{2}\right)2 + \left(2 + \frac{1}{2}\right)\frac{1}{2}$$

$$= 2 \cdot 2 + \frac{1}{2} \cdot 2 + 2 \cdot \frac{1}{2} + \frac{1}{2} \cdot \frac{1}{2}$$

$$= 4 + 1 + 1 + \frac{1}{4}$$

$$= 6 + \frac{1}{4}$$

$$= 6\frac{1}{4}$$

Multiplication of fractions enables us to obtain equivalent fractions, to perform addition and subtraction of fractions, as well as to solve equations in a different way, as shown in the following example.

Example 17

Use the definition of multiplication of fractions and its properties to justify the following.

a. The Fundamental Law of Fractions: $\dfrac{a}{b} = \dfrac{an}{bn}$ if $b \neq 0, n \neq 0$.

b. Addition of fractions using a common denominator.

Solution

a. $\dfrac{a}{b} = \dfrac{a}{b} \cdot 1 = \dfrac{a}{b} \cdot \dfrac{n}{n} = \dfrac{an}{bn}$

b. $\dfrac{a}{b} + \dfrac{c}{d} = \dfrac{a}{b} \cdot \dfrac{d}{d} + \dfrac{c}{d} \cdot \dfrac{b}{b}$

$= \dfrac{ad}{bd} + \dfrac{bc}{bd}$

$= \dfrac{ad + bc}{bd}$

Division of Rational Numbers

CCSS In the grade 6 *Common Core Standards*, we find the following concerning division of rational numbers:

Apply and extend previous understandings of multiplication and division to divide fractions by fractions.

1. Interpret and compute quotients of fractions and solve word problems involving division of fractions by fractions, e.g., by using visual fraction models and equations to represent the problem. (p. 42)

IMAP Video

Watch Trina to see why it is important to build a conceptual understanding as well as a procedural understanding of mathematical concepts.

IMAP Video

Watch Shelby explain how she determined 12 divided by $\dfrac{1}{2}$.

Activity Manual

Use *Dividing Fractions* to reinforce the meaning of division with fractions.

We apply and extend division of whole numbers by recalling that $6 \div 3$ means "How many 3s are there in 6?" We found that $6 \div 3 = 2$ because $3 \cdot 2 = 6$ and, in general, when $a, b, c \in W$, $a \div b = c$ if, and only if, c is the unique whole number such that $bc = a$. Consider $3 \div \left(\dfrac{1}{2}\right)$, which is equivalent to finding how many halves there are in 3. We see from the area model in Figure 18 that there are 6 half pieces in the 3 whole pieces. We record this as $3 \div \left(\dfrac{1}{2}\right) = 6$. This is true because $\left(\dfrac{1}{2}\right)6 = 3$.

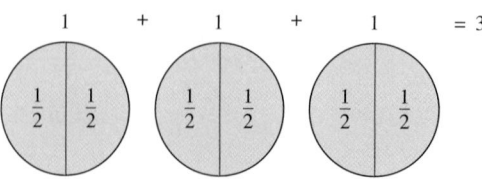

Figure 18

Another way to show that $3 \div \left(\dfrac{1}{2}\right) = 6$ is on a ruler. In Figure 19 we see that there are six $\dfrac{1}{2}$s in 3.

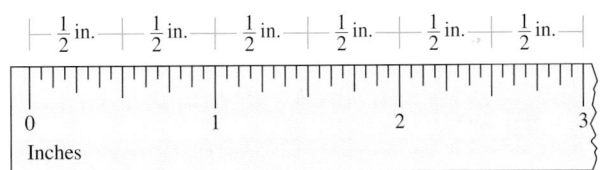

Figure 19

With whole numbers, one way to think about division is in terms of *repeated subtraction*. We found that $6 \div 2 = 3$ because 2 could be subtracted from 6 three times; that is, $6 - 3 \cdot 2 = 0$. Similarly, with $3 \div \dfrac{1}{2}$, we want to know how many halves can be subtracted from 3. Because $3 - 6\left(\dfrac{1}{2}\right) = 0$, we know that $3 \div \dfrac{1}{2} = 6$.

Next, consider $\dfrac{3}{4} \div \dfrac{1}{8}$. This means "How many $\dfrac{1}{8}$s are in $\dfrac{3}{4}$?" Figure 20 shows that there are six $\dfrac{1}{8}$s in the shaded portion, which represents $\dfrac{3}{4}$ of the whole. Therefore, $\dfrac{3}{4} \div \dfrac{1}{8} = 6$. This is true because $\left(\dfrac{1}{8}\right)6 = \dfrac{3}{4}$.

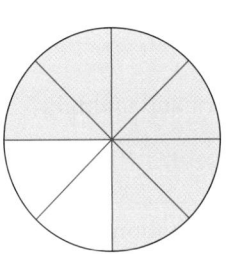

Figure 20

The measurement, or number-line, model may be used to understand division of fractions. For example, consider $\dfrac{7}{8} \div \dfrac{3}{4}$. First we draw a number line divided into eighths, as shown in Figure 21. Next we want to know how many $\dfrac{3}{4}$s there are in $\dfrac{7}{8}$. The bar of length $\dfrac{3}{4}$ is made up of 6 equal-size pieces of length $\dfrac{1}{8}$. We see that there is at least one length of $\dfrac{3}{4}$ in $\dfrac{7}{8}$. If we put another bar of length $\dfrac{3}{4}$ on the number line, we see there is 1 more of the 6 equal-length segments needed to make $\dfrac{7}{8}$. Therefore, the answer is $1\dfrac{1}{6}$, or $\dfrac{7}{6}$.

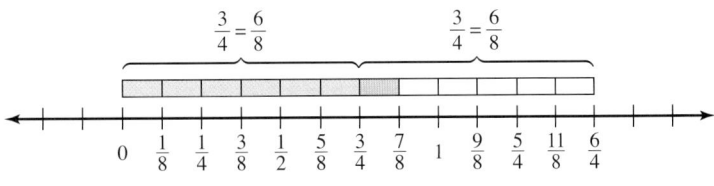

Figure 21

Additionally we know that $\dfrac{3}{4} \cdot \dfrac{7}{6} = \dfrac{21}{24} = \dfrac{7}{8}$, so the answer is correct.

In the previous examples, we saw a relationship between division and multiplication of rational numbers. We can define division for rational numbers formally in terms of multiplication in the same way that we defined division for whole numbers.

Definition of Division of Rational Numbers

Let $\dfrac{a}{b}, \dfrac{c}{d}$, and $\dfrac{e}{f}$ be rational numbers such that $\dfrac{c}{d} \neq 0$. Then $\dfrac{a}{b} \div \dfrac{c}{d} = \dfrac{e}{f}$ if, and only if, $\dfrac{e}{f}$ is the unique rational number such that $\dfrac{c}{d} \cdot \dfrac{e}{f} = \dfrac{a}{b}$.

In the above definition of division, $\frac{c}{d} \neq 0$ because division by 0 is not defined.

▶ **NOW TRY THIS 4**

NTT 4: Answers can be found in Answers at the back of the book.

Students often confuse finding half of a number with dividing by one-half. Notice that

$a \div 2 = \frac{a}{2} = \frac{1}{2}a$, but $a \div \frac{1}{2} = x$ if, and only if, $\frac{1}{2}x = a$ which implies $2\left(\frac{1}{2}x\right) = 2a$ and $x = 2a$.

Write a real-life story that will help students see the difference between finding half of a number and division by $\frac{1}{2}$.

The partial student page below illustrates a method for dividing called "invert and multiply."

Algorithm for Division of Rational Numbers

Does the *invert-and-multiply* method make sense based on what we know about rational numbers? Consider what such a division might mean. For example, using the definition of division of rational numbers,

$$\frac{2}{3} \div \frac{5}{7} = x \quad \text{if, and only if,} \quad \frac{2}{3} = \frac{5}{7}x.$$

To solve for x, we multiply both sides of the equation by $\frac{7}{5}$, the reciprocal of $\frac{5}{7}$. Thus,

$$\frac{7}{5} \cdot \frac{2}{3} = \frac{7}{5}\left(\frac{5}{7}x\right) = \left(\frac{7}{5} \cdot \frac{5}{7}\right)x = 1 \cdot x = x.$$

Therefore, $\frac{2}{3} \div \frac{5}{7} = \frac{2}{3} \cdot \frac{7}{5}$. This illustrates the "invert-and-multiply" method, or the "use the reciprocal and multiply" method.

School Book Page

To divide by a fraction, multiply by the reciprocal of the fraction. You can remember this by thinking "invert and multiply."

KEY CONCEPTS   **Dividing Fractions**

Arithmetic	**Algebra**
$\frac{3}{5} \div \frac{1}{3} = \frac{3}{5} \cdot \frac{3}{1}$	$\frac{a}{b} \div \frac{c}{d} = \frac{a}{b} \cdot \frac{d}{c}$, where b, c, and d are not 0.

A traditional justification of this rule follows. The algorithm for division of fractions is usually justified in the middle grades by using the Fundamental Law of Fractions, $\frac{a}{b} = \frac{ac}{bc}$, where a, b, and c are fractions, or equivalently, the identity property of multiplication. For example,

$$\frac{2}{3} \div \frac{5}{7} = \frac{\frac{2}{3}}{\frac{5}{7}} = \frac{\frac{2}{3}}{\frac{5}{7}} \cdot 1 = \frac{\frac{2}{3}}{\frac{5}{7}} \cdot \frac{\frac{7}{5}}{\frac{7}{5}} = \frac{\frac{2}{3} \cdot \frac{7}{5}}{1} = \frac{2}{3} \cdot \frac{7}{5}.$$

Theorem 6-12:   Algorithm for Division of Fractions

If $\frac{a}{b}$ and $\frac{c}{d}$ are any rational numbers with $\frac{c}{d} \neq 0$, then

$$\frac{a}{b} \div \frac{c}{d} = \frac{a}{b} \cdot \frac{d}{c}.$$

Alternative Algorithm for Division of Rational Numbers

An alternative algorithm for division of fractions can be found by first dividing fractions that have equal denominators. For example, $\frac{9}{10} \div \frac{3}{10} = \frac{9}{10} \cdot \frac{10}{3} = \frac{9}{3}$ and $\frac{15}{23} \div \frac{5}{23} = \frac{15}{23} \cdot \frac{23}{5} = \frac{15}{5}$. These examples suggest that when two fractions with the same denominator are divided, the result can be obtained by dividing the numerator of the first fraction by the numerator of the second; that is, $\frac{a}{b} \div \frac{c}{b} = \frac{a}{c}$. To divide fractions with different denominators, we rename the fractions so that the denominators are equal. Thus,

$$\frac{a}{b} \div \frac{c}{d} = \frac{ad}{bd} \div \frac{bc}{bd} = \frac{ad}{bd} \cdot \frac{bd}{bc} = \frac{ad}{bc}.$$

▶ **NOW TRY THIS 5**

NTT 5: Answers can be found in Answers at the back of the book.

Show that $\frac{a}{b} \div \frac{c}{d}$ and $\frac{a \div c}{b \div d}$ are equal.

The next three examples illustrate the use of division of rational numbers.

Example 18

A radio station provides 36 min for public service announcements for every 24 hr of broadcasting.

a. What part of the 24-hr broadcasting day is allotted to public service announcements?

b. How many $\frac{3}{4}$-min public service announcements can be broadcast in the 36 min?

Solution

a. There are 60 min in an hour and $60 \cdot 24$ min in the broadcasting day. Thus, $36 \div (60 \cdot 24)$, or $\frac{1}{40}$, of the day is allotted for the announcements.

b. $36 \div \left(\frac{3}{4}\right) = 36\left(\frac{4}{3}\right) = 48$ announcements are broadcast.

Example 19

We have $35\frac{1}{2}$ yd of material available to make towels. Each towel requires $\frac{3}{8}$ yd of material.

   a. How many towels can be made?
   b. How much material will remain?

Solution

   a. We need to find the integer part of the answer to $35\frac{1}{2} \div \frac{3}{8}$.

$$35\frac{1}{2} \div \frac{3}{8} = \frac{71}{2} \cdot \frac{8}{3} = \frac{284}{3} = 94\frac{2}{3}$$

   Thus, we can make 94 towels.

   b. Because the division in part (a) was by $\frac{3}{8}$, the amount of material remaining is $\frac{2}{3}$ of $\frac{3}{8}$, or

$$\frac{2}{3} \cdot \frac{3}{8} = \frac{1}{4} \text{ yd.}$$

Example 20

A bookstore has a shelf that is $37\frac{1}{2}$ in. long. Each book that is to be placed on the shelf is $1\frac{1}{4}$ in. thick. How many books can be placed on the shelf?

Solution   We need to find how many $1\frac{1}{4}$s there are in $37\frac{1}{2}$.

$$\frac{37\frac{1}{2}}{1\frac{1}{4}} = \frac{75}{2} \div \frac{5}{4}$$

$$= \frac{75}{2} \cdot \frac{4}{5}$$

$$= \frac{300}{10}$$

$$= 30$$

Note that we could compute $\frac{75}{2} \cdot \frac{4}{5}$ by first eliminating common factors; that is, $\frac{75}{2} \cdot \frac{4}{5} = \frac{15 \cdot 2}{1 \cdot 1} = \frac{30}{1} = 30$.

   Therefore, 30 books can be placed on the shelf.

Mental Math and Estimation with Rational Numbers

Mental math strategies developed with whole numbers can also be used with rational numbers.

Example 21

Use rational number properties to mentally compute the following products.

  a. $(12 \cdot 25)\dfrac{1}{4}$ **b.** $\left(5\dfrac{1}{6}\right)12$ **c.** $\dfrac{4}{5}(20)$

Solution   Each computation shown is a possible approach.

  a. $(12 \cdot 25)\dfrac{1}{4} = 25\left(12 \cdot \dfrac{1}{4}\right) = 25 \cdot 3 = 75$

  b. $\left(5\dfrac{1}{6}\right)12 = \left(5 + \dfrac{1}{6}\right)12 = 5 \cdot 12 + \dfrac{1}{6} \cdot 12 = 60 + 2 = 62$

  c. $\dfrac{4}{5}(20) = 4\left(\dfrac{1}{5} \cdot 20\right) = 4 \cdot 4 = 16$

Similarly, estimation strategies developed with whole number can be used with rational numbers.

Example 22

Estimate each of the following.

  a. $3\dfrac{1}{4} \cdot 7\dfrac{8}{9}$ **b.** $24\dfrac{5}{7} \div 4\dfrac{1}{8}$

Solution
  a. Using rounding, the product will be close to $3 \cdot 8 = 24$. If we use the range strategy, we can say the product must be between $3 \cdot 7 = 21$ and $4 \cdot 8 = 32$.
  b. We can use compatible numbers and think of the estimate as $24 \div 4 = 6$ or $25 \div 5 = 5$.

Extending the Notion of Exponents

Recall that a^m was defined for any whole number a and any natural number m as the product of m a's. We define a^m for any rational number a in a similar way as follows.

Definition of a to the mth Power

$a^m = \underbrace{a \cdot a \cdot a \cdot \ldots \cdot a}_{m \text{ factors}}$, where a is any rational number and m is any natural number.

From the definition, $a^3 \cdot a^2 = (a \cdot a \cdot a)(a \cdot a) = a^{3+2} = a^5$. In a similar way, it follows that

Statement 1: If a is a rational number and m and n are any natural numbers, $a^m \cdot a^n = a^{m+n}$.
  If Statement 1 is to be true for all whole numbers m and n, then because $a^1 \cdot a^0 = a^{1+0} = a^1$, we must have $a^0 = 1$. Hence, it is useful to give meaning to a^0 when $a \neq 0$ as follows.

Statement 2: For any nonzero rational number a, $a^0 = 1$.
  If $a^m \cdot a^n = a^{m+n}$ is extended to all integer powers of a, then how should a^{-3} be defined? If Statement 1 is to be true for all integers m and n, then $a^{-3} \cdot a^3 = a^{-3+3} = a^0 = 1$. Therefore,

  $a^{-3} = \dfrac{1}{a^3}$. This is true in general and we have the following.

Statement 3: Definition: For any nonzero rational number a and any natural number n, $a^{-n} = \dfrac{1}{a^n}$.

In elementary grades the definition of a^{-n} is typically motivated by looking at patterns. Notice that as the following exponents decrease by 1, the numbers on the right are divided by 10. Thus, the pattern might be continued, as shown.

$$10^3 = 10 \cdot 10 \cdot 10$$
$$10^2 = 10 \cdot 10$$
$$10^1 = 10$$
$$10^0 = 1$$
$$10^{-1} = \frac{1}{10} = \frac{1}{10^1}$$
$$10^{-2} = \frac{1}{10} \cdot \frac{1}{10} = \frac{1}{10^2}$$
$$10^{-3} = \frac{1}{10^2} \cdot \frac{1}{10} = \frac{1}{10^3}$$

If the pattern is extended in this way, then we would predict that $10^{-n} = \frac{1}{10^n}$. Notice that this is inductive reasoning and hence is not a mathematical justification.

Consider whether the property $a^m \cdot a^n = a^{m+n}$ can be extended to include all powers of a, where the exponents are integers. For example, is it true that $2^4 \cdot 2^{-3} = 2^{4+^-3} = 2^1$? The definitions of 2^{-3} and the properties of nonnegative exponents ensure this is true, as shown next.

$$2^4 \cdot 2^{-3} = 2^4 \cdot \frac{1}{2^3} = \frac{2^4}{2^3} = \frac{2^1 \cdot 2^3}{2^3} = 2^1$$

Similarly, $2^{-4} \cdot 2^{-3} = 2^{-4+^-3} = 2^{-7}$ is true because

$$2^{-4} \cdot 2^{-3} = \frac{1}{2^4} \cdot \frac{1}{2^3} = \frac{1 \cdot 1}{2^4 \cdot 2^3} = \frac{1}{2^{4+3}} = \frac{1}{2^7} = 2^{-7}.$$

In general, with integer exponents, the following theorem holds.

Theorem 6-13

For any nonzero rational number a and any integers m and n, $a^m \cdot a^n = a^{m+n}$.

If $a = 0$ and either m or n is negative, then $a^m \cdot a^n$ is undefined.

Other properties of exponents can be developed by using the properties of rational numbers. For example,

$$\frac{2^5}{2^3} = \frac{2^3 \cdot 2^2}{2^3} = 2^2 = 2^{5-3} \quad \text{and} \quad \frac{2^5}{2^8} = \frac{2^5}{2^5 \cdot 2^3} = \frac{1}{2^3} = 2^{-3} = 2^{5-8}.$$

With integer exponents, the following theorem holds.

Theorem 6-14

For any nonzero rational number a and any integers m and n, $\frac{a^m}{a^n} = a^{m-n}$.

At times, we may encounter an expression like $(2^4)^3$. This expression can be written as a single power of 2 as follows:

$$(2^4)^3 = 2^4 \cdot 2^4 \cdot 2^4 = 2^{4+4+4} = 2^{3 \cdot 4} = 2^{12}$$

In general, if a is any rational number and m and n are positive integers, then

$$(a^m)^n = \underbrace{a^m \cdot a^m \cdot \ldots \cdot a^m}_{n \text{ factors}} = \overbrace{a^{m+m+\ldots+m}}^{n \text{ terms}} = a^{nm} = a^{mn}.$$

Does this theorem hold for negative-integer exponents? For example, does $(2^3)^{-4} = 2^{(3)(-4)} = 2^{-12}$? The answer is yes because $(2^3)^{-4} = \dfrac{1}{(2^3)^4} = \dfrac{1}{2^{12}} = 2^{-12}$. Also, $(2^{-3})^4 = \left(\dfrac{1}{2^3}\right)^4 = \dfrac{1}{2^3} \cdot \dfrac{1}{2^3} \cdot \dfrac{1}{2^3} \cdot \dfrac{1}{2^3} = \dfrac{1^4}{(2^3)^4} = \dfrac{1}{2^{12}} = 2^{-12}$.

Theorem 6-15

For any nonzero rational number a and any integers m and n,

$$(a^m)^n = a^{mn}.$$

Using the definitions and theorems developed, we derive additional properties. For example:

$$\left(\frac{2}{3}\right)^4 = \frac{2}{3} \cdot \frac{2}{3} \cdot \frac{2}{3} \cdot \frac{2}{3} = \frac{2 \cdot 2 \cdot 2 \cdot 2}{3 \cdot 3 \cdot 3 \cdot 3} = \frac{2^4}{3^4}$$

This property is generalized as follows.

Theorem 6-16

For any nonzero rational number $\dfrac{a}{b}$ and any integer m,

$$\left(\frac{a}{b}\right)^m = \frac{a^m}{b^m}.$$

From the definition of negative exponents, the preceding theorem, and division of fractions, we have

$$\left(\frac{a}{b}\right)^{-m} = \frac{1}{\left(\dfrac{a}{b}\right)^m} = \frac{1}{\dfrac{a^m}{b^m}} = \frac{b^m}{a^m} = \left(\frac{b}{a}\right)^m.$$

Theorem 6-17

For any nonzero rational number $\dfrac{a}{b}$ and any integer m, $\left(\dfrac{a}{b}\right)^{-m} = \left(\dfrac{b}{a}\right)^m.$

A property similar to the one in Theorem 6-16 holds for multiplication. For example,

$$(2 \cdot 3)^{-3} = \frac{1}{(2 \cdot 3)^3} = \frac{1}{2^3 \cdot 3^3} = \left(\frac{1}{2^3}\right) \cdot \left(\frac{1}{3^3}\right) = 2^{-3} \cdot 3^{-3}.$$

Theorem 6-18 considers the distributive property of exponentiation over multiplication.

Theorem 6-18

For any nonzero rational numbers a and b and any integer m,

$$(a \cdot b)^m = a^m \cdot b^m.$$

Theorem 6-18 is also true when a or $b = 0$ and $m > 0$.

The properties of exponents are summarized below.

Theorem 6-19: Properties of Exponents

For any nonzero rational numbers a and b and integers m and n, the following are true.

a. $a^0 = 1$

b. $a^{-m} = \dfrac{1}{a^m}$

c. $a^m \cdot a^n = a^{m+n}$

d. $\dfrac{a^m}{a^n} = a^{m-n}$

e. $(a^m)^n = a^{mn}$

f. $\left(\dfrac{a}{b}\right)^m = \dfrac{a^m}{b^m}$

g. $\left(\dfrac{a}{b}\right)^{-m} = \left(\dfrac{b}{a}\right)^m$

h. $(ab)^m = a^m b^m$

Notice that property (h) is for multiplication. Analogous properties do not hold for addition and subtraction. For example, in general, $(a + b)^{-1} \neq a^{-1} + b^{-1}$. To see why, a numerical example is sufficient, but it is instructive to write each side with positive exponents:

$$(a + b)^{-1} = \frac{1}{a + b}$$

$$a^{-1} + b^{-1} = \frac{1}{a} + \frac{1}{b}$$

We know from addition of fractions, $\dfrac{1}{a + b} \neq \dfrac{1}{a} + \dfrac{1}{b}$. Therefore, $(a + b)^{-1} \neq a^{-1} + b^{-1}$.

Example 23

In each of the following statements, show each equality or inequality is true in general for non-zero rational numbers x, a, and b.

a. $(^-x)^{-2} \neq {}^-x^{-2}$

b. $(^-x)^{-3} = {}^-x^{-3}$

c. $ab^{-1} \neq (ab)^{-1}$ unless $a = 1$ or $a = {}^-1$

d. $(a^{-2}b^{-2})^{-1} = a^2 b^2$

e. $(a^{-2} + b^{-2})^{-1} \neq a^2 + b^2$

Solution

a. $(^-x)^{-2} = \dfrac{1}{(^-x)^2} = \dfrac{1}{x^2}$

$^-x^{-2} = -(x^{-2}) = {}^-\left(\dfrac{1}{x^2}\right) = \dfrac{^-1}{x^2}$

Hence, $(^-x)^{-2} \neq {}^-x^{-2}$.

b. $(^-x)^{-3} = \dfrac{1}{(^-x)^3} = \dfrac{1}{^-x^3} = {}^-\left(\dfrac{1}{x^3}\right)$

$^-x^{-3} = {}^-(x^{-3}) = {}^-\left(\dfrac{1}{x^3}\right)$

Hence, $(^-x)^{-3} = {}^-x^{-3}$.

c. $ab^{-1} = a(b^{-1}) = a \cdot \dfrac{1}{b} = \dfrac{a}{b}$, but $(ab)^{-1} = \dfrac{1}{ab}$. Hence, $ab^{-1} \neq (ab)^{-1}$.

d. $(a^{-2}b^{-2})^{-1} = (a^{-2})^{-1}(b^{-2})^{-1}$

$= a^{(^-2)(^-1)}b^{(^-2)(^-1)}$

$= a^2b^2$

e. $(a^{-2} + b^{-2})^{-1} = \left(\dfrac{1}{a^2} + \dfrac{1}{b^2}\right)^{-1} = \left(\dfrac{a^2 + b^2}{a^2 b^2}\right)^{-1} = \dfrac{a^2 b^2}{a^2 + b^2} \neq a^2 + b^2$

Observe that all the properties of exponents refer to powers with either the same base or the same exponent. To evaluate expressions using exponents where different bases and powers are used, perform all the computations or rewrite the expressions in either the same base or the same exponent, if possible. For example, $\dfrac{27^4}{81^3}$ can be rewritten $\dfrac{27^4}{81^3} = \dfrac{(3^3)^4}{(3^4)^3} = \dfrac{3^{12}}{3^{12}} = 1$.

Example 24

Perform the following computations and express your answers without negative exponents.

a. $16^2 \cdot 8^{-3}$

b. $20^2 \div 2^4$

c. $(10^{-1} + 5 \cdot 10^{-2} + 3 \cdot 10^{-3})10^3$

d. $(x^3y^{-2})^{-4}$

Solution

a. $16^2 \cdot 8^{-3} = (2^4)^2 \cdot (2^3)^{-3} = 2^8 \cdot 2^{-9} = 2^{8+^-9} = 2^{-1} = \dfrac{1}{2}$

b. $\dfrac{20^2}{2^4} = \dfrac{(2^2 \cdot 5)^2}{2^4} = \dfrac{2^4 \cdot 5^2}{2^4} = 5^2$ or 25

c. $(10^{-1} + 5 \cdot 10^{-2} + 3 \cdot 10^{-3})10^3 = 10^{-1} \cdot 10^3 + 5 \cdot 10^{-2} \cdot 10^3 + 3 \cdot 10^{-3} \cdot 10^3$

$= 10^{-1+3} + 5 \cdot 10^{-2+3} + 3 \cdot 10^{-3+3}$

$= 10^2 + 5 \cdot 10^1 + 3 \cdot 10^0$

$= 153$

d. $(x^3y^{-2})^{-4} = (x^3)^{-4} \cdot (y^{-2})^{-4} = x^{3(^-4)} \cdot y^{(^-2)(^-4)} = x^{-12}y^8 = \left(\dfrac{1}{x^{12}}\right)y^8 = \dfrac{y^8}{x^{12}}$, if $x, y \neq 0$

Assessment 6-3A

1. In the following figures, a unit rectangle is used to illustrate the product of two fractions. Name the fractions and their products.

   a. 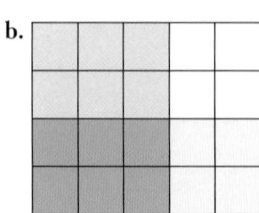 *   b. *

2. Use a rectangular region to illustrate each of the following products.

   a. $\dfrac{1}{3} \cdot \dfrac{3}{4}$ *

   b. $\dfrac{2}{3} \cdot \dfrac{1}{5}$ *

3. Find each of the following products. Write your answers in simplest form.

   a. $\dfrac{49}{65} \cdot \dfrac{26}{98}$ $\frac{1}{5}$ b. $\dfrac{a}{b} \cdot \dfrac{b^2}{a^2}$ $\frac{b}{a}$ c. $\dfrac{xy}{z} \cdot \dfrac{z^2 a}{x^3 y^2}$ $\frac{za}{x^2 y}$

4. Use the distributive property of multiplication over addition to find each product.

   a. $4\dfrac{1}{2} \cdot 2\dfrac{1}{3}$ $10\frac{1}{2}$

   b. $3\dfrac{1}{3} \cdot 2\dfrac{1}{2}$ $8\frac{1}{3}$

5. Find the multiplicative inverse of each of the following.

   a. $\dfrac{^-1}{3}$ $^-3$ b. $3\dfrac{1}{3}$ $\frac{3}{10}$

   c. $\dfrac{x}{y}$, if $x \neq 0$ $\frac{y}{x}$ d. $^-7$ $\frac{^-1}{7}$

6. Solve for x.

   a. $\dfrac{2}{3}x = \dfrac{7}{6}$ $\frac{21}{12} = \frac{7}{4}$

   b. $\dfrac{3}{4} \div x = \dfrac{1}{2}$ $\frac{6}{4} = \frac{3}{2}$

   c. $\dfrac{5}{6} + \dfrac{2}{3}x = \dfrac{3}{4}$ $\frac{^-1}{8}$

   d. $\dfrac{2x}{3} - \dfrac{1}{4} = \dfrac{x}{6} + \dfrac{1}{2}$ $\frac{3}{2}$

7. Show that the following properties do not hold for the division of rational numbers.   Answers vary. For example,
   a. Commutative $6 \div 2 \neq 2 \div 6$
   b. Associative $(8 \div 4) \div 2 \neq 8 \div (4 \div 2)$

8. Compute the following mentally. Find the exact answers.

   a. $3\dfrac{1}{4} \cdot 8$ 26

   b. $7\dfrac{1}{4} \cdot 4$ 29

   c. $9\dfrac{1}{5} \cdot 10$ 92

   d. $8 \cdot 2\dfrac{1}{4}$ 18

9. Choose from among the numbers in parentheses the number that best approximates each of the following.

   a. $3\dfrac{11}{12} \cdot 5\dfrac{3}{100}$ $(8, 20, 15, 16)$ 20

   b. $2\dfrac{1}{10} \cdot 7\dfrac{7}{8}$ $(16, 14, 4, 3)$ 16

   c. $\dfrac{1}{101} \div \dfrac{1}{103}$ $\left(0, 1, \dfrac{1}{2}, \dfrac{1}{4}\right)$ 1

10. Without actually doing the computations, choose the phrase in parentheses that correctly describes each.

   a. $\dfrac{13}{14} \cdot \dfrac{17}{19}$ (greater than 1, less than 1) Less than 1

   b. $3\dfrac{2}{7} \div 5\dfrac{1}{9}$ (greater than 1, less than 1) Less than 1

   c. $4\dfrac{1}{3} \div 2\dfrac{3}{100}$ (greater than 2, less than 2) Greater than 2

11. A sewing project requires $6\dfrac{1}{8}$ yd of material that sells for $4 per yard and $3\dfrac{1}{4}$ yd of material that sells for $3 per yard.

    Choose the best estimate for the cost of the project: d
    a. Between $30 and $40
    b. Between $20 and $34
    c. Between $36 and $40
    d. Between $33 and $40

12. Five-eighths of the students at Salem State College live in dormitories. If 6000 students at the college live in dormitories, how many students are there in the college?   9600 students

13. Alberto owns $\dfrac{5}{9}$ of the stock in the N.W. Tofu Company. His sister Renatta owns half as much stock as Alberto. What part of the stock is owned by neither Alberto nor Renatta? $\frac{1}{6}$

14. A suit is on sale for $180.00. What was the original price of the suit if the discount was $\dfrac{1}{4}$ of the original price? $240

15. John took all his money out of his savings account. He spent $50.00 on a radio and $\dfrac{3}{5}$ of what remained on presents. Half of what was left he put in his checking account, and the remaining $35.00 he donated to charity. How much money did John originally have in his savings account? $225

16. Al gives $\frac{1}{2}$ of his marbles to Bev. Bev gives $\frac{1}{2}$ of these to Carl. Carl gives $\frac{1}{2}$ of these to Dani. If Dani was given four marbles, how many did Al have originally?   *32 marbles*

17. Write each of the following in simplest form using positive exponents in the final answer.
  a. $3^{-7} \cdot 3^{-6}$ $\frac{1}{3^{13}}$
  b. $3^7 \cdot 3^6$ 3^{13}
  c. $5^{15} \div 5^4$ 5^{11} 3^{13}
  d. $5^{15} \div 5^{-4}$ 5^{19}
  e. $(^-5)^{-2}$ $\frac{1}{5^2}$
  f. $\frac{a^2}{a^{-3}}$ a^5

18. Write each of the following in simplest form using positive exponents in the final answer.
  a. $\left(\frac{1}{2}\right)^3 \cdot \left(\frac{1}{2}\right)^7$ $\left(\frac{1}{2}\right)^{10} = \frac{1}{2^{10}}$
  b. $\left(\frac{1}{2}\right)^9 \div \left(\frac{1}{2}\right)^6$ $\left(\frac{1}{2}\right)^3$
  c. $\left(\frac{2}{3}\right)^5 \cdot \left(\frac{4}{9}\right)^2$ $\left(\frac{2}{3}\right)^9$
  d. $\left(\frac{3}{5}\right)^7 \div \left(\frac{3}{5}\right)^7$ 1

19. If a and b are rational numbers, with $a \neq 0$ and $b \neq 0$, and if m and n are integers, which of the following statements are always true? Justify your answers.
  a. $a^m \cdot b^n = (ab)^{m+n}$ *
  b. $a^m \cdot b^n = (ab)^{mn}$ *
  c. $a^m \cdot b^m = (ab)^{2m}$ *
  d. $(ab)^0 = 1$ *
  e. $(a+b)^m = a^m + b^m$ *
  f. $(a+b)^{-m} = \frac{1}{a^m} + \frac{1}{b^m}$ *

20. Solve for the integer n in each of the following.
  a. $2^n = 32$ 5
  b. $n^2 = 36$ 6 or $^-6$
  c. $2^n \cdot 2^7 = 2^5$ $^-2$
  d. $2^n \cdot 2^7 = 8$ $^-4$

21. Solve each of the following inequalities for x, where x is an integer.
  a. $3^x \leq 9$ $x \leq 2$
  b. $25^x < 125$ $x < 2$
  c. $3^{2x} > 27$ $x \geq 2$
  d. $4^x > 1$ $x \geq 1$

22. Determine which fraction in each of the following pairs is greater.
  a. $\left(\frac{1}{2}\right)^3$ or $\left(\frac{1}{2}\right)^4$ $\left(\frac{1}{2}\right)^3$
  b. $\left(\frac{3}{4}\right)^{10}$ or $\left(\frac{3}{4}\right)^8$ $\left(\frac{3}{4}\right)^8$
  c. $\left(\frac{4}{3}\right)^{10}$ or $\left(\frac{4}{3}\right)^8$ $\left(\frac{4}{3}\right)^{10}$
  d. $\left(\frac{3}{4}\right)^{10}$ or $\left(\frac{4}{5}\right)^{10}$ *
  e. 32^{50} or 4^{100} 32^{50}
  f. $(^-27)^{-15}$ or $(^-3)^{-75}$ $(^-3)^{-75}$

23. Show that the arithmetic mean of two rational numbers is between the two numbers; that is, prove if $\frac{a}{b} < \frac{c}{d}$, then
$$\frac{a}{b} < \frac{1}{2}\left(\frac{a}{b} + \frac{c}{d}\right) < \frac{c}{d}.$$ *

24. In the Corcoran School of Design in 2014, $\frac{17}{25}$ of the students were male.
  a. What fraction were female? $\frac{8}{25}$
  b. Does this imply 17 students are male?   *

25. The reported tax revenue in dollars for Washington DC in 2011 is shown below.

Corporate Income	$36,802,396
Personal Income	32,020,924
Social Security & Other Taxes	620,501
Hotel Tax	212,565,755
Property Taxes	183,005,144
Excise & Fees	21,723,515
Sales Tax	187,656,061
Restaurant	119,487,765
Retail	58,122,531
Airport	7,155,614
Car Rental	2,890,151
Total	**674,394,296**

  a. Approximately what is the fractional part of the total tax is the difference in restaurant sales tax and retail sales tax?   *
  b. If the sales tax were abolished, approximately what fraction of the total tax package would be lost?   *

26. According to the Washington DC City Government, the following lists the number of homicides in the city since 2004.

2013	2012	2011	2010	2009	2008	2007	2006	2005	2004
104	88	108	132	144	186	181	169	196	198

  a. What year showed the greatest fractional increase from the previous year?   *2012 to 2013*
  b. What year showed the greatest fractional decrease from the previous year?   *2008 to 2009*

27. If $\frac{1}{33}$ of all deer in the United States are in Mississippi and $\frac{2}{7}$ of the deer are in Montana, what total fractional part of the deer population is in those two states? $\frac{73}{231}$

28. If $\frac{1}{4}$ of an estate is to be distributed equally to 8 cousins, what fractional part of the entire estate does each cousin receive? $\frac{1}{32}$

Assessment 6-3B

1. In the following figure a unit rectangle is used to illustrate the product of two fractions. Name the fractions and their products.

a. 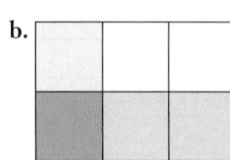 *   b.   *

2. Use a rectangular region to illustrate each of the following products.

a. $\dfrac{2}{5} \cdot \dfrac{1}{3}$ *   b. $\dfrac{2}{3} \cdot \dfrac{2}{3}$ *

3. Find each of the following products of rational numbers. Write your answers in simplest form.

a. $2\dfrac{1}{3} \cdot 3\dfrac{3}{4}$ $\dfrac{35}{4} = 8\dfrac{3}{4}$ b. $\dfrac{22}{7} \cdot 4\dfrac{2}{3}$ $\dfrac{44}{3} = 14\dfrac{2}{3}$

c. $\dfrac{^{-}5}{2} \cdot 2\dfrac{1}{2}$ $\dfrac{^{-}25}{4} = {}^{-}6\dfrac{1}{4}$ d. $2\dfrac{3}{4} \cdot 2\dfrac{1}{3}$ $\dfrac{77}{12} = 6\dfrac{5}{12}$

e. $\dfrac{a^2}{b^3} \cdot \dfrac{b^2}{a^3}$ $\dfrac{1}{ab}$ f. $\dfrac{x^3 y^2}{z} \cdot \dfrac{z}{x^2 y}$ xy

4. Use the distributive property to find each product of rational numbers.

a. $2\dfrac{1}{3} \cdot 4\dfrac{3}{5}$ $10\dfrac{11}{15}$ b. $\left(\dfrac{x}{y} + 1\right)\left(\dfrac{y}{x} - 1\right)$ *

c. $248\dfrac{2}{5} \cdot 100\dfrac{1}{8}$ $24871\dfrac{1}{20}$

5. Find the multiplicative inverse of each of the following.

a. $\dfrac{6}{7}$ $\dfrac{7}{6}$ b. 8 $\dfrac{1}{8}$ c. $4\dfrac{1}{5}$ $\dfrac{5}{21}$ d. $^{-}1\dfrac{1}{2}$ $\dfrac{^{-}2}{3}$

6. Solve for x.

a. $\dfrac{2}{3}x = \dfrac{11}{6}$ $\dfrac{11}{4}$ or $2\dfrac{3}{4}$ b. $\dfrac{3}{4} \div x = \dfrac{1}{3}$ $\dfrac{9}{4}$ or $2\dfrac{1}{4}$

c. $\dfrac{5}{6} - \dfrac{2}{3}x = \dfrac{3}{4}$ $\dfrac{1}{8}$ d. $\dfrac{2x}{3} + \dfrac{1}{4} = \dfrac{x}{6} - \dfrac{1}{2}$ *

7. Find a fraction such that if you add the denominator to the numerator and place the sum over the original denominator, the new fraction has triple the value of the original fraction.   Answers vary; for example, $\dfrac{1}{2}$

8. Compute the following mentally; find the exact answers.

a. $3\dfrac{1}{2} \cdot 8$ 28 b. $7\dfrac{3}{4} \cdot 4$ 31

c. $9\dfrac{1}{5} \cdot 6$ $55\dfrac{1}{5}$ d. $8 \cdot 2\dfrac{1}{3}$ $18\dfrac{2}{3}$

e. $3 \div \dfrac{1}{2}$ 6 f. $3\dfrac{1}{2} \div \dfrac{1}{2}$ 7

g. $3 \div \dfrac{1}{3}$ 9 h. $4\dfrac{1}{2} \div 2$ $2\dfrac{1}{4}$

9. Choose from among the numbers in parentheses the number that best approximates each of the following.

a. $20\dfrac{2}{3} \div 9\dfrac{7}{8} \left(2, 180, \dfrac{1}{2}, 10\right)$ 2

b. $3\dfrac{1}{20} \cdot 7\dfrac{77}{100} \left(21, 24, \dfrac{1}{20}, 32\right)$ 24

c. $\dfrac{1}{10^3} \div \dfrac{1}{1001} \left(\dfrac{1}{10^3}, 1, 1001, 0\right)$ 1

10. Without actually doing the computations, choose the phrase in parentheses that correctly describes each.

a. $4\dfrac{1}{3} \div 2\dfrac{13}{100}$ (greater than 2, less than 2)   Greater than 2

b. $16 \div 4\dfrac{3}{18}$ (greater than 4, less than 4)   Less than 4

c. $16 \div 3\dfrac{8}{9}$ (greater than 4, less than 4)   Greater than 4

11. When you multiply a certain number by 3 and then subtract $\dfrac{7}{18}$, you get the same result as when you multiply the number by 2 and add $\dfrac{5}{12}$. What is the number? $\dfrac{29}{36}$

12. Di Paloma University had a faculty reduction and lost $\dfrac{1}{5}$ of its faculty. If 320 faculty members were left after the reduction, how many members were there originally?   400 members

13. A person has $29\dfrac{1}{2}$ yd of material available to make doll outfits. Each outfit requires $\dfrac{3}{4}$ yd of material.

a. How many outfits can be made?   39 outfits
b. How much material will be left over? $\dfrac{1}{4}$ yd

14. Every employee's salary at the Sunrise Software Company increases each year by $\dfrac{1}{10}$ of that person's salary the previous year.

a. If Martha's present annual salary is $100,000, what will her salary be in 2 yr? $121,000
b. If Aaron's present salary is $99,000, what was his salary 1 yr ago? $90,000
c. If Juanita's present salary is $363,000, what was her salary 2 yr ago? $300,000

15. Jasmine is reading a book. She has finished $\dfrac{3}{4}$ of the book and has 82 pages left to read. How many pages has she read?   246 pages

16. Peter, Paul, and Mary start at the same time walking around a circular track in the same direction. Peter takes $\dfrac{1}{2}$ hr to walk around the track. Paul takes $\dfrac{5}{12}$ hr, and Mary takes $\dfrac{1}{3}$ hr.

a. How many minutes does it take each person to walk around the track?   Peter, 30 min; Paul, 25 min; Mary, 20 min
b. How many times will each person go around the track before all three meet again at the starting line?   Peter, 10; Paul, 12; Mary, 15

17. Write each of the following rational numbers in simplest form using positive exponents in the final answer.

 a. $\left(\dfrac{1}{3}\right)^{-1}$ 3   b. $\dfrac{a^{-3}}{a}$ $\dfrac{1}{a^4}$ c. $\dfrac{(a^{-4})^3}{a^{-4}}$ $\dfrac{1}{a^8}$

 d. $\dfrac{a}{a^{-1}}$ a^2 e. $\dfrac{a^{-3}}{a^{-2}}$ $\dfrac{1}{a}$

18. Write each of the following in simplest form using positive exponents in the final answer.

 a. $\left(\dfrac{1}{2}\right)^{10} \div \left(\dfrac{1}{2}\right)^{2}$ $\left(\dfrac{1}{2}\right)^{8} = \dfrac{1}{2^8}$

 b. $\left(\dfrac{2}{3}\right)^{5}\left(\dfrac{4}{9}\right)^{-2}$ $\dfrac{2}{3}$

 c. $\left(\dfrac{3}{5}\right)^{7} \div \left(\dfrac{5}{3}\right)^{4}$ $\left(\dfrac{3}{5}\right)^{11}$

 d. $\left[\left(\dfrac{5}{6}\right)^{7}\right]^{3}$ $\left(\dfrac{5}{6}\right)^{21}$

19. If a and b are rational numbers, with $a \neq 0$ and $b \neq 0$, and if m and n are integers, which of the following statements are always true? Justify your answers.

 a. $\dfrac{a^m}{b^n} = \left(\dfrac{a}{b}\right)^{m-n}$ *

 b. $(ab)^{-m} = \dfrac{1}{a^m} \cdot \dfrac{1}{b^m}$ *

 c. $\left(\dfrac{2}{a^{-1}+b^{-1}}\right)^{-1} = \dfrac{1}{2} \cdot \dfrac{1}{a+b}$ *

 d. $2(a^{-1}+b^{-1})^{-1} = \dfrac{2ab}{a+b}$ *

 e. $a^{mn} = a^m \cdot a^n$ *

 f. $\left(\dfrac{a}{b}\right)^{-1} = \dfrac{b}{a}$ *

20. Solve, if possible, for n where n is an integer in each of the following.

 a. $2^n = {}^-32$ *   b. $n^3 = \dfrac{{}^-1}{27}$ no integer solution

 c. $2^n \cdot 2^7 = 1024$ 3   d. $2^n \cdot 2^7 = 64$ $^-1$

 e. $(2+n)^2 = 2^2 + n^2$ 0   f. $3^n = 27^5$ 15

21. Solve each of the following inequalities for x, where x is an integer.

 a. $3^x \geq 81$ $x \geq 4$ b. $4^x \geq 8$ $x \geq 2$

 c. $3^{2x} \leq 27$ $x \leq 1$ d. $2^x < 1$ $x < 0$

22. Determine which fraction in each of the following pairs is greater.

 a. $\left(\dfrac{4}{3}\right)^{10}$ or $\left(\dfrac{4}{3}\right)^{8}$ $\left(\dfrac{4}{3}\right)^{10}$

 b. $\left(\dfrac{3}{4}\right)^{10}$ or $\left(\dfrac{4}{5}\right)^{10}$ $\left(\dfrac{4}{5}\right)^{10}$

 c. $\left(\dfrac{4}{3}\right)^{10}$ or $\left(\dfrac{5}{4}\right)^{10}$ $\left(\dfrac{4}{3}\right)^{10}$

 d. $\left(\dfrac{3}{4}\right)^{100}$ or $\left(\dfrac{3}{4}\cdot\dfrac{9}{10}\right)^{100}$ $\left(\dfrac{3}{4}\right)^{100}$

23. In the following, determine which number is greater.

 a. 32^{100} or 4^{200} 32^{100}

 b. $(^-27)^{15}$ or $(^-3)^{50}$ $(^-3)^{-50}$

24. Brandy bought a horse for $270 and immediately started paying for his keep. She sold the horse for $540. Considering the cost of his keep she found that she had lost an amount equal to half of what she paid for the horse plus one-fourth of the cost of his keep. How much did Brandy lose on the horse? $270

25. In 2014 in the Corcoran School of Design, $\dfrac{8}{25}$ of the students were female. What fraction was male? $\dfrac{17}{25}$

26. The reported tax revenue in dollars for Washington DC in 2011 is shown below.

Corporate Income	$36,802,396
Personal Income	32,020,924
Social Security & Other Taxes	620,501
Hotel Tax	212,565,755
Property Taxes	183,005,144
Excise & Fees	21,723,515
Sales Tax	187,656,061
Restaurant	119,487,765
Retail	58,122,531
Airport	7,155,614
Car Rental	2,890,151
Total	**674,394,296**

 a. Approximately what is the fractional part of the total tax is the difference in hotel tax and property tax? *

 b. If the sales tax was increased $\dfrac{1}{11}$, approximately what fraction of the total tax package would be gained? *

27. According to the Washington DC City Government, the following lists the number of homicides in the city since 2004.

2013	2012	2011	2010	2009	2008	2007	2006	2005	2004
104	88	108	132	144	186	181	169	196	198

 a. What is the fractional decrease in homicides from 2005 to 2012? $\dfrac{27}{49}$

 b. What is the fractional increase in homicides from 2012 to 2013? $\dfrac{2}{11}$

28. If $\dfrac{1}{33}$ of all deer in the United States are in Mississippi, and $\dfrac{2}{7}$ of the deer are in Montana, what fractional part of the deer population is not in those two states? $\dfrac{158}{231}$

29. If $\dfrac{1}{4}$ of an estate consists of $\dfrac{2}{5}$ stocks and $\dfrac{3}{5}$ bonds, what part of the estate is each of the stocks and bonds? *

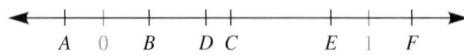

Answers to Mathematical Connections can be found in the Answers section at the back of the book.

Reasoning

1. Suppose you divide a natural number n by a positive rational number less than 1. Will the answer always be less than n, sometimes less than n, or never less than n? Why?

2. If the fractions represented by points C and D on the following number line are multiplied, what point best represents the product? Explain why.

```
◄──┼──┼──┼──┼┼──┼──┼──┼──►
   A  0  B  D C     E  1  F
```

3. If the product of two numbers is 1 and one of the numbers is greater than 1, what do you know about the other number? Explain your answer.

Open-Ended

4. Write a story or model for $1\frac{3}{4} \div \frac{1}{2}$.

5. Complete a survey of your class asking questions such as their favorite color, favorite type of shoe, and favorite math concept. Use fractions to summarize your information and find any differences in male and female preference.

6. Consider the demographics of students in each undergraduate class (freshman, sophomore, junior, and senior) at your university. Describe the fractional differences in males and females in each class.

Cooperative Learning

7. Choose a brick building on your campus. Measure the height of one brick and the thickness of mortar between bricks. Estimate the height of the building and then calculate the height of the building. Were rational numbers used in your computations?

8. Have each student in your group choose a state or city and find the demographics on taxes as in Exercise 26 in Assessment 6-3B. Compare fractions representing sales taxes for each chosen location. Which has the highest? Lowest?

9. In each group of a class, describe your group using fractions in the explanation. Use at least three sets of fractions in your description. Pass the descriptions to the teacher who will then distribute the descriptions to a different group. The goal is to describe your group well enough that others can identify the groups.

Connecting Mathematics to the Classroom

10. Bente says to do the problem $12\frac{1}{4} \div 3\frac{3}{4}$ you just find $12 \div 3 = 4$ and $\frac{1}{4} \div \frac{3}{4} = \frac{1}{3}$ to get $4\frac{1}{3}$. How do you respond?

11. Amy says that dividing a number by $\frac{1}{2}$ is the same as taking half of a number. How do you respond?

12. Dani says that if we have $\frac{3}{4} \cdot \frac{2}{5}$, we could just multiply $\frac{3}{5} \cdot \frac{2}{4} = \frac{3}{5} \cdot \frac{1}{2} = \frac{3}{10}$. Is she correct? Explain why.

13. Noah says that dividing a number by 2 is the same as multiplying it by $\frac{1}{2}$. He wants to know if he is right, and if so, why. How do you respond?

14. Jim is not sure when to use multiplication by a fraction and when to use division. He has the following list of problems. How would you help him solve these problems in a way that would enable him to solve similar problems on his own?

   a. $\frac{3}{4}$ of a package of sugar fills $\frac{1}{2}$ c. How many cups of sugar are in a full package of sugar?

   b. How many packages of sugar are needed to fill 2 c?

   c. If $\frac{1}{3}$ c sugar is required to make two loaves of challah, how many cups of sugar are needed for three loaves?

   d. If $\frac{3}{4}$ c sugar is required for 1 gal of punch, how many gallons can be made with 2 c of sugar?

   e. If you have $22\frac{3}{8}$ in. of ribbon, and need $1\frac{1}{4}$ in. to decorate one doll, how many dolls can be decorated, and how much ribbon will be left over?

15. A student claims that division always makes things smaller so $5 \div \left(\frac{1}{2}\right)$ cannot be 10 because 10 is greater than the number 5 she started with. How do you respond?

16. A student simplified the fraction $\frac{m+n}{p+n}$ to $\frac{m}{p}$. How would you help this student?

17. Jillian says she learned that 17 divided by 5 can be written as $17 \div 5 = 3$ R2, but she thinks that writing $17 \div 5 = \frac{17}{5} = 3\frac{2}{5}$ is much better. How do you respond?

Review Problems

18. Perform each of the following computations. Leave your answers in simplest form or as mixed numbers.

   a. $\frac{^-3}{16} + \frac{7}{4}$

   b. $\frac{1}{6} + \frac{^-4}{9} + \frac{5}{3}$

   c. $\frac{^-5}{2^3 \cdot 3^2} - \frac{^-5}{2 \cdot 3^3}$

   d. $3\frac{4}{5} + 4\frac{5}{6}$

   e. $5\frac{1}{6} - 3\frac{5}{8}$

   f. $^-4\frac{1}{3} - 5\frac{5}{12}$

19. Each student at Sussex Elementary School takes one foreign language. Two-thirds of the students take Spanish, $\frac{1}{9}$ take French, $\frac{1}{18}$ take German, and the rest take some other foreign language. If there are 720 students in the school, how many do not take Spanish, French, or German?

20. Find each sum or difference; simplify if possible.

   a. $\frac{3x}{xy^2} + \frac{y}{x^2}$

   b. $\frac{a}{xy^2} - \frac{b}{xyz}$

   c. $\frac{a^2}{a^2 - b^2} - \frac{a-b}{a+b}$

21. Determine which of the following is always correct.

 a. $\dfrac{ab + c}{b} = a + c$

 b. $\dfrac{a + b}{a + c} = \dfrac{b}{c}$

 c. $\dfrac{ab + ac}{ac} = \dfrac{b + c}{c}$

National Assessments

National Assessment of Educational Progress (NAEP) Questions

Both figures below show the same scale. The marks on the scale have no labels except the zero point.

The weight of the cheese is $\dfrac{1}{2}$ pound. What is the total weight of the two apples?

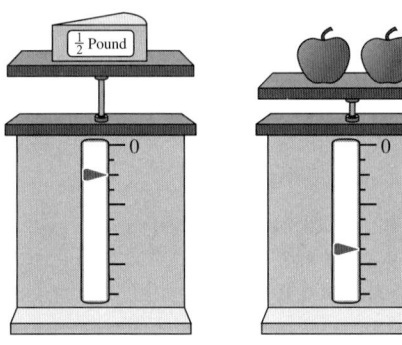

NAEP, Grade 8, 2007

Jim has $\dfrac{3}{4}$ of a yard of string which he wishes to divide into pieces each $\dfrac{1}{8}$ of a yard long. How many pieces will he have?

A. 3
B. 4
C. 6
D. 8

NAEP, Grade 8, 2003

Nick has a whole pizza.

Nick says he will eat $\dfrac{1}{2}$ of the pizza.

He says he will give $\dfrac{3}{8}$ of the pizza to Sam and $\dfrac{3}{8}$ of the pizza to Joe.

Can Nick do what he says?

◯ Yes   ◯ No

NAEP, Grade 4, 2013

6-4 Proportional Reasoning

6-4 Objectives

Students will be able to understand and explain

- Ratios and their relation to rational numbers.
- Proportions and their properties.
- Constant of proportionality.
- Scaling.

Proportional reasoning is an extremely important concept taught in grades K–8. Proportionality has connections to most, if not all, of the other foundational middle-school topics and can provide a context to study these topics.

For grade 7, the *Common Core Standards* state that students should "analyze proportional relationships and use them to solve real-world and mathematical problems." Additionally we find that students should "decide whether two quantities are in a proportional relationship," "identify the constant of proportionality (unit rate) in tables, graphs, equations, diagrams and verbal descriptions," represent proportional relationships in equations," and "use proportional relationships to solve multistep ratio and percent problems." (p. 48)

Ratios are encountered in everyday life. For example, there may be a 2-to-3 ratio of Democrats to Republicans on a certain legislative committee, a friend may be given a speeding ticket for driving 69 miles per hour, or eggs may cost $2.40 a dozen. Each of these illustrates a **ratio**.

Definition of Ratio

A **ratio**, denoted as $\dfrac{a}{b}$, a/b, or $a{:}b$, where a and b are rational numbers, is a comparison of two quantities.

Activity Manual

Use *Professors Short* and *Tall* to introduce the concepts of ratio and equivalent ratios.

A ratio of 1:3 for boys to girls in a class means that the number of boys is $\frac{1}{3}$ that of girls; that is, there is 1 boy for every 3 girls. We could also say that the ratio of girls to boys is 3:1, or that there are 3 times as many girls as boys. Ratios can represent **part-to-whole** or **whole-to-part** comparisons. For example, if the ratio of boys to girls in a class is 1:3, then the ratio of boys (part) to children (whole) is 1:4. If there are b boys and g girls, then $\frac{b}{g} = \frac{1}{3}$ and $g = 3b$. Also, the ratio of boys to the entire class is $\frac{b}{b+g} = \frac{b}{b+3b} = \frac{b}{4b} = \frac{1}{4}$. We could also say that the ratio of all children (whole) to boys (part) is 4:1. Some ratios give **part-to-part** comparisons, such as the ratio of the number of boys to girls or the number of students to one teacher. For example, a school might say that the average ratio of students to teachers cannot exceed 24:1.

The ratio of 1:3 for boys to girls in a class does not tell us how many boys and how many girls there are in the class. It only tells us the relative size of the groups. There could be 2 boys and 6 girls, or 3 boys and 9 girls, or 4 boys and 12 girls, or some other numbers that give a ratio equal to $\frac{1}{3}$.

Example 25

There were 7 males and 12 females in the Dew Drop Inn on Monday evening. In the game room next door were 14 males and 24 females.

  a. Express the number of males to females at the inn as a ratio (part-to-part).
  b. Express the number of males to females at the game room as a ratio (part-to-part).
  c. Express the number of males in the game room to the number of people in the game room as a ratio (part-to-whole).

Solution

  a. The ratio is $\frac{7}{12}$.

  b. The ratio is $\frac{14}{24} = \frac{7}{12}$.

  c. The ratio is $\frac{14}{38} = \frac{7}{19}$.

Proportions

In a study, children were shown a picture of a carton of orange juice and were told that the orange juice was made from orange concentrate and water. Then they were shown two glasses—a large glass and a small glass—and they were told that both glasses were filled with orange juice from the carton. They were then asked if the orange juice from each of the two glasses would taste equally "orangey" or if one would taste more "orangey." About half of the students said they were not equally orangey. Of those about half the students said the larger glass would be more "orangey" and about half said the smaller glass would be more "orangey." These students may have been thinking of only one quantity—the water alone or the orange concentrate alone.

Suppose Recipe A for an orange drink calls for 2 cans of orange concentrate for every 3 cans of water. We could say that the ratio of cans of orange concentrate to cans of water is 2:3.

We represent this pictorially in Figure 22(a), where O represents a can of orange concentrate and W represents a can of water. In Figure 22(b) and (c), we continue the process of adding 2 cans of orange concentrate for every 3 cans of water.

Recipe A

(a)	(b)		(c)		
O O	O O	O O	O O	O O	O O
W W W	W W W	W W W	W W W	W W W	W W W

Figure 22

From Figure 22 we could develop and continue the **ratio table**, as shown in Table 3.

Table 3

Cans of Orange Concentrate	2	4	6	8	10	12
Cans of Water	3	6	9	?	?	?

In Table 3, the ratios $\frac{2}{3}$ and $\frac{4}{6}$ are equal. The equation $\frac{2}{3} = \frac{4}{6}$ is a proportion. In general, we have the following definition.

Definition of a Proportion

A **proportion** is a statement that two given ratios are equal.

If Recipe B calls for 4 cans of orange concentrate for every 8 cans of water, then the ratio of cans of orange concentrate to cans of water for this recipe is 4:8. We picture this in Figure 23(a).

Recipe B

(a)	(b)	
O O O O	O O	O O
W W W W	W W	W W
W W W W	W W	W W

Figure 23

Which of the two recipes produces a drink that tastes more "orangey"? In Figure 22(a), we see that in Recipe A there are 2 cans of orange concentrate for every 3 cans of water. In Figure 23(a), we see that in Recipe B there are 4 cans of orange concentrate for every 8 cans of water.

To compare the two recipes, we need either the same number of cans of orange concentrate or the same number of cans of water. Either is possible. Figure 22(b) shows that for Recipe A there are 4 cans of orange concentrate for every 6 cans of water. In Recipe B, for 4 cans of orange concentrate there are 8 cans of water. Recipe B calls for more water per 4 cans of orange concentrate, so it is less "orangey." An alternative is to observe that in Figure 23(b), Recipe B shows that there are 2 cans of orange concentrate for every 4 cans of water. We compare this with Figure 22(a), showing 2 cans of orange concentrate for every 3 cans of water, and reach the same conclusion.

From our work in Section 6-1, we know that $\frac{2}{3} = \frac{4}{6}$ because $2 \cdot 6 = 3 \cdot 4$. Hence $\frac{2}{3} = \frac{4}{6}$ is a proportion. Also $\frac{2}{3} \neq \frac{4}{8}$ because $2 \cdot 8 \neq 3 \cdot 4$; this is not a proportion. In general, we have the following theorem that follows from Theorem 6-2 developed in Section 6-1.

> ### Theorem 6-20
> If a, b, c, and d are rational numbers and $b \neq 0$ and $d \neq 0$, then
>
> $$\frac{a}{b} = \frac{c}{d} \text{ is a proportion if, and only if, } ad = bc.$$

The proportion $\frac{a}{b} = \frac{c}{d}$ may be read as "a is to b as c is to d."

Students in the lower grades typically experience problems that are *additive*. Consider the problem below.

Allie and Bente type at the same speed. Allie started typing first. When Allie had typed 8 pages, Bente had typed 4 pages. When Bente has typed 10 pages, how many has Allie typed?

This is an example of an *additive* relationship. Students should reason that since the two people type at the same speed, when Bente has typed an additional 6 pages, Allie should have also typed an additional 6 pages, so she should have typed 8 + 6, or 14, pages.

Next consider the following problem:

Carl can type 8 pages for every 4 pages that Dan can type. If Dan has typed 12 pages, how many pages has Carl typed?

If students try an *additive* approach, they will conclude that since Dan has typed 8 more pages than in the original relationship, then Carl should have typed an additional 8 pages for a total of 16 pages. However, the correct reasoning is that since Carl types twice as fast as Dan he will type twice as many pages as Dan. Therefore, when Dan has typed 12 pages, Carl has typed 24 pages. The relationship between the ratios is *multiplicative*. Another way to solve this problem is to set up the proportion $\frac{8}{4} = \frac{x}{12}$, where x is the number of pages that Carl will type, and solve for x. Because $\frac{8}{4} = \frac{8 \cdot 3}{4 \cdot 3} = \frac{24}{12}$, then $x = 24$ pages.

In the problem above, one term in the proportion is missing:

$$\frac{8}{4} = \frac{x}{12}$$

One way to solve the equation is to multiply both sides by 12, as follows:

$$\frac{8}{4} \cdot 12 = \frac{x}{12} \cdot 12$$
$$8 \cdot 3 = x$$
$$24 = x$$

Another method of solution uses Theorem 6-20. This is often called the *cross-multiplication method*. The equation $\frac{8}{4} = \frac{x}{12}$ is a proportion if, and only if,

$$8 \cdot 12 = 4x$$
$$96 = 4x$$
$$24 = x.$$

Example 26

If there are 3 cars for every 8 students at a high school, how many cars are there for 1200 students?

Solution   We use the strategy of *setting up a table*, as shown in Table 4.

Table 4

Number of cars	3	x
Number of students	8	1200

The ratio of cars to students is always the same:

$$\text{Cars} \to \frac{3}{8} = \frac{x}{1200} \leftarrow \text{Students}$$
$$3 \cdot 1200 = 8x$$
$$3600 = 8x$$
$$450 = x$$

Thus, there are 450 cars.

Next consider two car rental companies where the rates for 1–4 days are given in Table 5.

Table 5

(a) Ace Car Rental		(b) Better Car Rental	
Days	Cost	Days	Cost
1	$20	1	$20
2	$40	2	$35
3	$60	3	$48
4	$80	4	$52

The first two days for Ace Car Rental rates can be used to write a proportion because $\frac{1\ day}{\$20} = \frac{2\ days}{\$40}$. In a proportion, the units of measure must be in the same relative positions. In this case, the numbers of days are in the numerators and the costs are in the denominators.

For the Better Car Rental we see that $\frac{1\ day}{\$20} \neq \frac{2\ days}{\$35}$, so a proportion is not formed.

Consider Table 6, which is a ratio table built from the values for Ace Car Rental.

Table 6				
Days (d)	1	2	3	4
Cost (c)	20	40	60	80

The ratios $\dfrac{d}{c}$ are all equal, that is, $\dfrac{1}{20} = \dfrac{2}{40} = \dfrac{3}{60} = \dfrac{4}{80}$. Thus, each pair of ratios forms a proportion. In this case, $\dfrac{d}{c} = \dfrac{1}{20}$ for all values of c and d. This is expressed by saying that d *is proportional to* c or *d varies proportionally to c* or *d varies directly with c*. In this case, $d = \dfrac{1}{20}c$ for every c and d. The number $\dfrac{1}{20}$ is the **constant of proportionality**. We can say that *gas used by a car is proportional to the miles traveled* or *lottery profits vary directly with the number of tickets sold*.

> ### Definition of Constant of Proportionality
>
> If the variables x and y are related by the equality $y = kx$ $\left(\text{or } k = \dfrac{y}{x} \right)$, then **$y$ is proportional to x** and k is the **constant of proportionality** between y and x.

A central idea in proportional reasoning is that a relationship between two quantities is such that the ratio of one quantity to the other remains unchanged as the numerical values of both quantities change.

It is important to remember that in the ratio $a{:}b$ or $\dfrac{a}{b}$, a and b do not have to be whole numbers. For example, if in Eugene, Oregon, $\dfrac{7}{10}$ of the population exercise regularly, then $\dfrac{3}{10}$ of the population do not exercise regularly, and the ratio of those who do to those who do not is $\dfrac{7}{10}{:}\dfrac{3}{10}$. This ratio can be written $7{:}3$.

It is important to pay special attention to units of measure when working with proportions. For example, if a turtle travels 5 in. every 10 sec, how many feet does it travel in 50 sec? If units of measure are ignored, we might set up the following proportion:

$$\frac{5}{10} = \frac{x}{50}$$

In this proportion the units of measure are not listed. A more informative proportion that often prevents errors is the following:

$$\frac{5 \text{ in.}}{10 \text{ sec}} = \frac{x \text{ in.}}{50 \text{ sec}}$$

This implies that $x = 25$. Consequently, since 12 in. = 1 ft, the turtle travels $\dfrac{25}{12}$ ft, or $2\dfrac{1}{12}$ ft, or 2 ft 1 in. in 50 sec.

Another approach for solving proportions uses the **scaling strategy**. Suppose we are asked whether it is better to buy 12 tickets for $15.00 or 20 tickets for $23.00. One way to approach the problem is to find the cost of a common number of tickets from each scenario.

Because LCM(12, 20) = 60, we could choose to find the cost of 60 tickets under each plan.

In the first plan, since 12 tickets cost $15.00, then 60 tickets cost $75.00.

In the second plan, since 20 tickets cost $23.00, then 60 tickets cost $69.00.

Therefore, the second plan is a better buy.

The **unit-rate strategy** for solving this problem involves finding the cost of one ticket under each plan and then comparing unit costs.

In the first plan, since 12 tickets cost $15.00, then 1 ticket costs $1.25.

In the second plan, since 20 tickets cost $23.00, then 1 ticket costs $1.15.

CCSS The grade 6 *Common Core Standards* state the following:

Solve unit rate problems including those involving unit pricing and constant speed. For example, if it took 7 hours to mow 4 lawns, then at that rate how many lawns could be mowed in 35 hours? (p. 42)

▶ NOW TRY THIS 6

Work the problem posed in the grade 6 *Common Core Standards*.   20 lawns

---

Example 27

Kai, Paulus, and Judy made $2520 for painting a house. Kai worked 30 hr, Paulus worked 50 hr, and Judy worked 60 hr. They divided the money in proportion to the number of hours worked. If they all earn the same rate of pay, how much did each earn?

Solution   Let x be the unit rate or the rate of pay per hour. Then $30x$ denotes the amount of money that Kai received; Paulus received $50x$ and Judy received $60x$. Because the total amount of money received is $30x + 50x + 60x$, we have

$$30x + 50x + 60x = 2520$$
$$140x = 2520$$
$$x = 18 \text{ (dollars per hour)}.$$

Hence,

$$\text{Kai received } 30x = 30 \cdot 18, \text{ or } \$540.$$
$$\text{Paulus received } 50x = 50 \cdot 18, \text{ or } \$900.$$
$$\text{Judy received } 60x = 60 \cdot 18, \text{ or } \$1080.$$

Dividing each of the amounts by 18 shows that the proportion is as required.

Consider the proportion $\frac{15}{30} = \frac{3}{6}$. Because the ratios in the proportion are equal and because equal nonzero fractions have equal reciprocals, it follows that $\frac{30}{15} = \frac{6}{3}$. Also notice that the proportions are true because each results in $15 \cdot 6 = 30 \cdot 3$. In general, we have the following theorem.

Theorem 6-21

For any rational numbers $\frac{a}{b}$ and $\frac{c}{d}$, with $a \neq 0$ and $c \neq 0$, $\frac{a}{b} = \frac{c}{d}$ if, and only if, $\frac{b}{a} = \frac{d}{c}$.

Consider $\frac{15}{30} = \frac{3}{6}$ again. Notice that $\frac{15}{3} = \frac{30}{6}$; that is, the ratio of the numerators is equal to the ratio of the corresponding denominators. In general, we have the following theorem.

Theorem 6-22

For any rational numbers $\frac{a}{b}$ and $\frac{c}{d}$, with $c \neq 0$, $\frac{a}{b} = \frac{c}{d}$ if, and only if, $\frac{a}{c} = \frac{b}{d}$.

Scale Drawings

Ratios and proportions are used in scale drawings. For example, if the scale is $1:300$, then the length of 1 cm in such a drawing represents 300 cm, or 3 m in true size. The **scale** is the ratio of the size of the drawing to the size of the object. The following example shows the use of scale drawings.

Example 28

The floor plan of the main floor of a house in Figure 24 is drawn in the scale of $1:300$. Find the dimensions in meters of the living room.

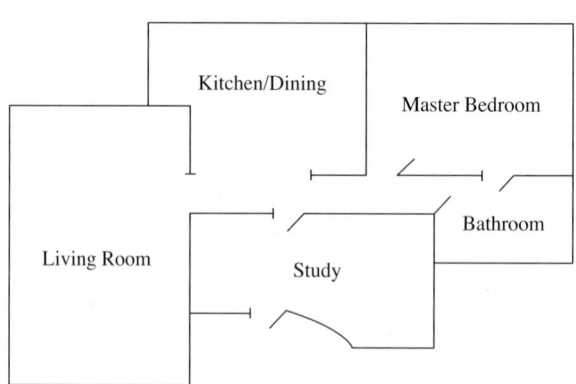

Figure 24

Solution If the dimensions of the living room are approximately 3 cm by 2 cm. Because the scale is $1:300$, 1 cm in the drawing represents 300 cm, or 3 m in true size. Hence, 3 cm represents $3 \cdot 3 = 9$ m, and 2 cm represents $2 \cdot 3 = 6$ m. Hence, the dimensions of the living room are approximately 9 m by 6 m.

Example 29

The ratio of men to women at a party was 5:2 before 14 more women appeared. At that point, the ratio was 4:3. How many men and how many women were at the party?

Solution We find the solution using a *bar method*. In Figure 25 each unit of men and women contain the same number of people giving the ratio 5:2.

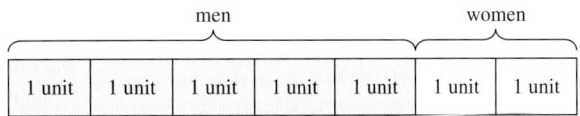

Figure 25

When 14 women joined the group, we have the situation in Figure 26(a). Additionally the ratio is now 4:3, and the number of people in each original unit has changed. The number of men has not changed so 5 of the original units equal 4 of the new ones.

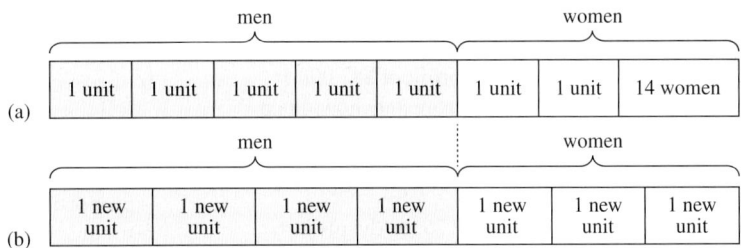

Figure 26

Thus, we have the following equations.

    For the men: 5 original units = 4 new units.

    For the women: 2 original units + 14 = 3 new units.

    Adding the two together we get

    7 original units + 14 = 7 new units, or

    1 original unit + 2 = 1 new unit.

    Equivalently, 4 original units + 8 = 4 new units.

    Substituting we have, 4 old units + 8 = 5 old units, or 8 = 1 original unit.

In the Figure 25, there are 5 units of men at 8 men per unit = 40 men, and 2 units of women at 8 women per unit for 16 women. Thus, there were 56 people at the party originally. When 14 more women joined, there were 70 total.

Assessment 6-4A

1. Answer the following regarding the English alphabet.
   a. Determine the ratio of vowels to consonants.   5:21
   b. What is the ratio of consonants to vowels?   21:5
   c. What is the ratio of consonants to letters?   21:26
   d. Write a word that has a ratio of 2:3 of vowels to consonants.   Answers vary. For example, minor.

2. Solve for x in each of the following proportions.
   a. $\dfrac{12}{x} = \dfrac{18}{45}$ 30
   b. $\dfrac{x}{7} = \dfrac{^-10}{21}$ $^-3\frac{1}{3}$
   c. $\dfrac{5}{7} = \dfrac{3x}{98}$ $23\frac{1}{3}$
   d. $3\frac{1}{2}$ is to 5 as x is to 15. $10\frac{1}{2}$

3. a. If the ratio of boys to girls in a class is 2:3, what is the ratio of boys to all the students in the class? Why? *
   b. If the ratio of boys to girls in a class is *m:n*, what is the ratio of boys to all the students in the class?   *m:(m + n)*
   c. If $\frac{3}{5}$ of the class are girls, what is the ratio of girls to boys?   *3:2*

4. There are approximately 2 lb of muscle for every 5 lb of body weight. For a 90-lb person, approximately how much of the weight is muscle?   *36 lb*

5. Which is a better buy—4 grapefruits for 80¢ or 12 grapefruits for $2?   *12 grapefruits for $2*

6. On a map, $\frac{1}{3}$ in. represents 5 mi. If New York and Aluossim are 18 in. apart on the map, what is the actual distance between them?   *270 mi*

7. David reads 40 pages of a book in 50 min. How many pages should he be able to read in 80 min if he reads at a constant rate?   *64 pages*

8. Two numbers are in the ratio 3:4. Find the numbers if
   a. their sum is 98.   *42, 56*
   b. their product is 768.   *24 and 32, or ⁻24 and ⁻32*

9. Gary, Bill, and Carmella invested in a corporation in the ratio of 2:3:5, respectively. If they divide the profit of $82,000 proportionally to their investment, approximately how much will each receive?   *$16,400; $24,000; $41,000*

10. Sheila and Dora worked $3\frac{1}{2}$ hr and $4\frac{1}{2}$ hr, respectively, on a programming project. They were paid $176 for the project. How much did each earn if they are both paid at the same rate?   *$77 and $99*

11. Vonna scored 75 goals in her soccer kicking practice. If her success-to-failure rate is 5:4, how many times did she attempt a goal?   *135*

12. Express each of the following ratios in the form $\frac{a}{b}$, where *a* and *b* are natural numbers.
   a. $\frac{1}{6}:1$ $\frac{1}{6}$
   b. $\frac{1}{3}:\frac{1}{3}$ $\frac{1}{1}$
   c. $\frac{1}{6}:\frac{2}{7}$ $\frac{7}{12}$

13. Use Theorems 6-21 and 6-22 to write three other proportions that follow from the following proportion.
$$\frac{12¢}{36 \text{ oz}} = \frac{16¢}{48 \text{ oz}} \quad *$$

14. The *rise* and *span* for a house roof are identified as shown on the drawing. The *pitch* of a roof is the ratio of the rise to the half-span.
   a. If the rise is 10 ft and the span is 28 ft, what is the pitch? $\frac{5}{7}$

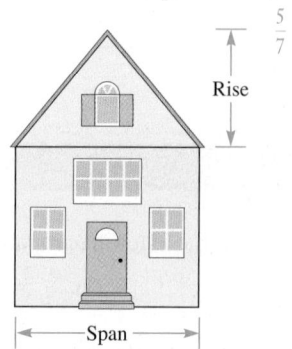

Rise

Span

   b. If the span is 16 ft and the pitch is $\frac{3}{4}$, what is the rise?   *6 ft*

15. Gear ratios are used in industry. A gear ratio is the comparison of the number of teeth on two gears. When two gears are meshed, the revolutions per minute (rpm) are inversely proportional to the number of teeth; that is,
$$\frac{\text{rpm of large gear}}{\text{rpm of small gear}} = \frac{\text{Number of teeth on small gear}}{\text{Number of teeth on large gear}}.$$
   a. The rpm ratio of the large gear to the small gear is 4:6. If the small gear has 18 teeth, how many teeth does the large gear have?   *27*
   b. The large gear revolves at 200 rpm and has 60 teeth. How many teeth are there on the small gear, which has an rpm of 600?   *20*

16. A Boeing 747 jet is approximately 230 ft long and has a wingspan of 195 ft. If a scale model of the plane is about 40 cm long, approximately what is the model's wingspan?   *Approximately 34 cm*

17. A recipe calls for 1 tsp of mustard seeds, 3 c of tomato sauce, $1\frac{1}{2}$ c of chopped scallions, and $3\frac{1}{4}$ c of beans. If one ingredient is altered as specified, how must the other ingredients be changed to keep the proportions the same?
   a. 2 c of tomato sauce $\frac{2}{3}$ tsp mustard seeds, 1 c scallions, $2\frac{1}{6}$ c beans
   b. 1 c of chopped scallions $\frac{2}{3}$ tsp mustard seeds, 2 c tomato sauce, $2\frac{1}{6}$ c beans
   c. $1\frac{3}{4}$ c of beans $\frac{7}{13}$ tsp mustard seeds, $1\frac{8}{13}$ c tomato sauce, $\frac{21}{26}$ c scallions

18. The electrical resistance of a wire, measured in ohms (Ω), is proportional to the length of the wire. If the electrical resistance of a 5-ft wire is 4 Ω, what is the resistance of 20 ft of the same wire?   *16 ohms*

19. In a photograph of a father and his daughter, the daughter's height is 2 cm and the father's height is 6 cm. If the father is actually 183 cm tall, how tall is the daughter?   *61 cm*

20. The amount of gold in jewelry and other products is measured in karats (K), where 24K represents pure gold. The mark 14K on a chain indicates that the ratio between the mass of the gold in the chain and the mass of the chain is 14:24. If a gold ring is marked 18K and it weighs 4 oz, what is the value of the gold in the ring if pure gold is valued at $1800 per oz?   *

21. If Amber is paid $8 per hour for typing, the table shows how much she earns.

Hours (*h*)	1	2	3	4	5
Wages (*w*)	$8	$16	$24	$32	$40

   a. How much would Amber make for a 40-hr work week?   *$320*
   b. What is the constant of proportionality?   *8*

22. a. In Room A there are 1 man and 2 women; in Room B there are 2 men and 4 women; and in Room C there are 5 men and 10 women. If all the people in Rooms B and C go to Room A, what will be the ratio of men to women in Room A?   *1:2*
   b. Prove the following generalization of the proportions used in part (a).
   If $\frac{a}{b} = \frac{c}{d} = \frac{e}{f}$, then $\frac{a}{b} = \frac{c}{d} = \frac{e}{f} = \frac{a + c + e}{b + d + f}$.   *

23. Use the bar method of Example 29 to solve the following exercise. One-half of the length of stick A is $\frac{2}{3}$ of the length of stick B. Stick B is 18 cm shorter than stick A. What is the length of both sticks?   *

24. A car travels about 26 miles on 1 gallon of gas while a truck travels about 250 miles on 14 gallons of gas. Which gets the better gas mileage?   The car
25. Susan bikes 20 miles in 2 hours while Nick bikes 32 miles in 3 hours. Who travels faster?   Nick
26. There are 40 students in a classroom, and the desired ratio of students to computers is 3:1. How many computers are needed for the classroom to achieve the desired ratio?   14 computers

27. The ratio of oblong tables to round tables at a conference is 5:1. The total number of tables at the conference is 102. How many of each type are there?   17 round ones and 85 oblong ones
28. A recipe uses $1\frac{1}{2}$ c flour to make 2 dozen cookies. Is 4 c flour enough to make 6 dozen cookies with this recipe? Explain your answer.   No. 6 dozen cookies would take $4\frac{1}{2}$ c flour.

Assessment 6-4B

1. Answer the following regarding the letters in the word *Mississippi*.
   a. Determine the ratio of vowels to consonants.   4:7
   b. What is the ratio of consonants to vowels?   7:4
   c. What is the ratio of consonants to letters?   7:11
2. Solve for x in each of the following proportions.

   a. $\dfrac{5}{x} = \dfrac{30}{42}$ 7

   b. $\dfrac{x}{8} = \dfrac{^-12}{32}$ $^-3$

   c. $\dfrac{7}{8} = \dfrac{3x}{48}$ 14

   d. $3\frac{1}{2}$ is to 8 as x is to 24 $10\frac{1}{2}$

3. There are 5 adult drivers to each teenage driver in Aluossim. If there are 12,345 adult drivers in Aluossim, how many teenage drivers are there?   2469
4. A candle is 30 in. long. After burning for 12 min, the candle is 25 in. long. If it continues to burn at the same rate, how long will it take for the whole candle to burn?   72 min
5. A rectangular yard has a width-to-length ratio of 5:9. If the distance around the yard is 2800 ft, what are the dimensions of the yard?   500 ft × 900 ft
6. A grasshopper can jump 20 times its length. If jumping ability in humans (height) were proportional to a grasshopper's (length), how far could a 6-ft-tall person jump?   120 ft
7. Jim found out that after working for 9 months he had earned 6 days of vacation time. How many days per year does he earn at this rate?   8 days
8. At Rattlesnake School the teacher–student ratio is 1:30. If the school has 1200 students, how many additional teachers must be hired to change the ratio to 1:20?   20
9. At a particular time, the ratio of the height of an object that is perpendicular to the ground to the length of its shadow is the same for all objects. If a 30-ft tree casts a shadow of 12 ft, how tall is a tree that casts a shadow of 14 ft?   35 ft
10. The following table shows several possible widths W and corresponding lengths L of a rectangle whose area is 10 ft².

Width (W) (Feet)	Length (L) (Feet)	Area (Square Feet)
$\frac{1}{2}$	20	$\frac{1}{2} \cdot 20 = 10$
1	10	$1 \cdot 10 = 10$
2	5	$2 \cdot 5 = 10$
$2\frac{1}{2}$	4	$2\frac{1}{2} \cdot 4 = 10$
4	$2\frac{1}{2}$	$4 \cdot 2\frac{1}{2} = 10$
5	2	$5 \cdot 2 = 10$
10	1	$10 \cdot 1 = 10$
20	$\frac{1}{2}$	$20 \cdot \frac{1}{2} = 10$

L

Area $= 10$ ft² W

   a. Use the values in the table and some additional values to graph the length L on the vertical axis versus the width W on the horizontal axis.   *
   b. What is the algebraic relationship between L and W? $WL = 10$
11. Find three sets of x- and y-values for the following proportions.

$$\frac{4 \text{ tickets}}{\$20} = \frac{x \text{ tickets}}{\$y}$$ *

12. If rent is \$850 for each 2 weeks, how much is the rent for 7 weeks?   \$2975
13. Leonardo da Vinci in his drawing *Vitruvian Man* showed that the man's armspan was equal to the man's height. Some other ratios are listed below.

$$\frac{\text{Length of hand}}{\text{Length of foot}} = \frac{7}{9}$$

$$\frac{\text{Distance from elbow to end of hand}}{\text{Distance from shoulder to elbow}} = \frac{8}{5}$$

$$\frac{\text{Length of hand}}{\text{Length of big toe}} = \frac{14}{3}$$

   Using the ratios above, answer the following questions.
   a. If the length of a big toe is 6 cm, how long should the hand be?   28 cm
   b. If a hand is 21 cm, how long is the foot?   27 cm
14. On a city map, a rectangular park has a length of 4 in. If the actual length and width of the park are 300 ft and 200 ft, respectively, how wide is the park on the map? $\frac{8}{3}$ in.
15. Jim's car will travel 240 mi on 15 gal of gas. How far can he expect to go on 3 gal of gas?   48 mi
16. Some model railroads use an O scale in replicas of actual trains. The O scale uses the ratio 1 in./48 in. How many feet long is the actual locomotive if an O scale replica is 18 in. long?   72 ft
17. a. On an American flag, what is the ratio of stars to stripes?
    b. What is the ratio of stripes to stars?   13:50
18. On an American flag, the ratio of the length of the flag to its width must be 19:10.
    a. If a flag is to be $9\frac{1}{2}$ ft long, how wide should it be?   5 ft   *
    b. The flag that was placed on the Moon measured 5 ft by 3 ft. Does this ratio form a proportion with the official length-to-width ratio? Why?   No; $\frac{19}{10} \neq \frac{5}{3}$ because $19 \cdot 3 \neq 10 \cdot 5$
19. If $\dfrac{x}{y} = \dfrac{a}{b}$, $a \neq 0$, $x \neq 0$, is true, what other proportions do you know are true?   Answers vary. $\dfrac{y}{x} = \dfrac{b}{a}$, $\dfrac{x}{a} = \dfrac{y}{b}$ and $\dfrac{a}{x} = \dfrac{b}{y}$

20. If a certain recipe takes $1\frac{1}{2}$ c flour and 4 c milk, how much milk should be used if the cook only has 1 c flour? $2\frac{2}{3}$ c

21. To estimate the number of fish in a lake, scientists use a tagging and recapturing technique. A number of fish are captured, tagged, and then released back into the lake. After a while, some fish are captured and the number of tagged fish is counted.

    Let T be the total number of fish captured, tagged, and released into the lake, n the number of fish in a recaptured sample, and t the number of fish found tagged in that sample. Finally, let x be the number of fish in the lake. The assumption is that the ratio between tagged fish and the total number of fish in any sample is approximately the same, and hence scientists assume $\frac{t}{n} = \frac{T}{x}$. Suppose 173 fish were captured, tagged, and released. Then 68 fish were recaptured and among them 21 were found to be tagged. Estimate the number of fish in the lake.   560 fish

22. A car travels about 36 miles on 1 gallon of gas while a truck travels about 200 miles on 14 gallons of gas. Which gets the better gas mileage?   The car

23. Susan bikes 18 miles in 2 hours while Nick bikes 30 miles in 3 hours. Who travels faster?   Nick

24. There are 32 students in a classroom, and the desired ratio of students to computers is 3:1. How many computers are needed for the classroom to achieve the desired ratio?   11 computers

25. The ratio of oblong tables to round tables at a conference is 6:1. The total number of tables at the conference is 112. How many of each type are there?   96 oblong tables and 16 round tables

26. A recipe uses $1\frac{1}{2}$ c flour to make 3 dozen cookies. Is 4 c flour enough to make 6 dozen cookies with this recipe? Explain your answer.   Yes. 6 dozen cookies require 3c flour.

27. Jennifer weighs 160 lb on Earth and 416 lb on Jupiter. Find Amy's weight on Jupiter if she weights 120 lb on Earth.   312 lb

Mathematical Connections 6-4

Answers to Mathematical Connections can be found in the Answers section at the back of the book.

Reasoning

1. Iris has found some dinosaur bones and a fossil footprint. The length of the footprint is 40 cm, the length of the thigh bone is 100 cm, and the length of the body is 700 cm.
   a. Iris found a new track that she believes was made by the same species of dinosaur. If the footprint was 30 cm long and if the same ratio of foot length to body length holds, how long is the dinosaur?
   b. In the same area, Iris also found a 50-cm thigh bone. Do you think this thigh bone belonged to the same dinosaur that made the 30-cm footprint that Iris found? Why or why not?

2. Suppose a 10-in. circular pizza costs $4.00. To find the price, x, of a 14-in. circular pizza, is it correct to set up the proportion $\frac{x}{4} = \frac{14}{10}$? Why or why not?

3. Prove that if $\frac{a}{b} = \frac{c}{d}$ and $a \neq {}^{-}b$, then the following are true.
   a. $\frac{a + b}{b} = \frac{c + d}{d}$ $\left(\text{Hint:}\frac{a}{b} + 1 = \frac{c}{d} + 1\right)$
   b. $\frac{a}{a + b} = \frac{c}{c + d}$ c. $\frac{a - b}{a + b} = \frac{c - d}{c + d}$
   d. $\frac{d}{c - d} = \frac{b}{a - b}.$

4. Nell said she can tell just by looking at the ratios 15:7 and 15:8 that these do not form a proportion. Is she correct? Why?

5. Sol had photographs that were 4 in. by 6 in., 5 in. by 7 in., and 8 in. by 10 in. Do the dimensions vary proportionately? Explain why.

6. Can $\frac{a}{b}$ and $\frac{a + b}{b}$ ever form a proportion? Why?

7. In a condo complex, $\frac{2}{3}$ of the men were married to $\frac{3}{4}$ of the women. What is the ratio of married people to the total adult population of the condo complex? Explain how you can obtain this ratio without knowing the actual number of men or women.

Open-Ended

8. List three real-world situations that involve ratio and proportion.

9. Find the ratio of Democrats to Republicans in the U.S. House of Representatives and the U.S. Senate. Determine how many each party would need to hold a majority and how many would be needed to stop a filibuster under the existing rules.

10. Most fertilizers used for gardening and crops are listed with a ratio of 1:2:1. Research the meaning of this ratio and find an acceptable mixture for flowers and foliage. If a fertilizer package showed a ratio of 10:20:10, what would be the meaning of this?

11. Research the golden ratio that the Greeks may have used in the design of the Parthenon. Write a report on this ratio and include a drawing of a golden rectangle.

Cooperative Learning

12. In *Gulliver's Travels* by Jonathan Swift we find the following:

    The seamstresses took my measure as I lay on the ground, one standing at my neck and another at mid-leg, with a strong cord extended, that each held by the end, while the third measured the length of the cord with a rule of an inch long. Then they measured my right thumb and desired no more; for by a mathematical computation, that twice around the thumb is once around the wrist, and so on to the neck and the waist; and with the help of my old shirt, which I displayed on the ground before them for a pattern, they fitted me exactly.

    a. Explore the measurements of those in your group to see if you believe the ratios mentioned for Gulliver.
    b. Suppose the distance around a person's thumb is 9 cm. What is the distance around the person's neck?

c. What ratio could be used to compare a person's height to armspan?

d. Do you think there is a ratio between foot length and height? If so, what might it be?

e. Estimate other body ratios and then see how close you are to actual measurements.

Connecting Mathematics to the Classroom

13. Mary is working with measurements and writes the following proportion.

$$\frac{12 \text{ in.}}{1 \text{ ft}} = \frac{5 \text{ ft}}{60 \text{ in.}}$$

How would you help her?

14. Nora said she can use division to decide whether two ratios form a proportion; for example, 32:8 and 40:10 form a proportion because $32 \div 8 = 4$ and $40 \div 10 = 4$. Is she correct? Why?

15. Al is 5 ft tall and has a shadow that is 18 in. long. At the same time, a tree has a shadow that is 15 ft long. Al sets up and solves the proportion as follows:

$$\frac{5 \text{ ft}}{15 \text{ ft}} = \frac{18 \text{ in.}}{x}, \quad \text{so } x = 54 \text{ in.}$$

How would you help him?

16. Mandy read that the arm of the Statue of Liberty is 42 ft long. She would like to know how long the Statue of Liberty's nose is. How would you advise her to proceed?

17. One student in the class says that her sister is in a school using the Singapore math materials and much of the work with fractions is done with bars. The student continues, saying, "I don't understand how bars can help me understand it with an exercise like that found in exercise 13 above." Can you help her?

Review Problems

18. If the numerator of a rational number is 6 times the denominator and the numerator is also 5 more than the denominator, what are the numerator and denominator?

19. Explain whether $\frac{3}{4}$ is a proper fraction or an improper fraction and why.

20. Explain why any integer is a rational number.

21. A student says that $\frac{20}{30}$ can be simplified by crossing out the 0s and that in general, this procedure works for simplifying fractions. Explain whether or not the statement is true using the rational number $\frac{25}{35}$.

22. In an old Sam Loyd puzzle, a watch is described as having stopped when the minute and hour hands formed a straight line and the second hand was not on 12. At what time can this happen?

23. If $\frac{2}{3}$ of a class was absent due to illness and $\frac{4}{5}$ of the school was absent due to illness, is the fractional portion of the absent class equivalent to the fractional portion of the school absenteeism?

24. Prove that $\frac{99}{98}$ is less than $\frac{97}{96}$.

25. a. Amal can finish a job in $\frac{1}{2}$ of a day working by herself. Her son Sharif can finish the same job in $\frac{1}{4}$ of a day working alone. How long will it take to finish the job if they work together?

    b. If Amal can finish a job in a hours and Sharif in b hours, then how long will it take to finish the job if they work together?

National Assessments

National Assessment of Educational Progress (NAEP) Questions

Sarah has a part-time job at Better Burgers restaurant and is paid $5.50 for each hour she works. She has made the chart below to reflect her earnings but needs your help to complete it.

A. Fill in the missing entries in the chart.

Hours Worked	Money Earned (in dollars)
1	$5.50
4	
	$38.50
$7\frac{3}{4}$	$42.63

B. If Sarah works h hours, then in terms of h, how much will she earn?

NAEP, Grade 8, 2007

The length of a photograph is 5 inches and its width is 3 inches. The photograph is enlarged proportionally. The length of the enlarged photograph is 10 inches. What is the width of the enlarged photograph?

A. 6 inches

B. 7 inches

C. 9 inches

D. 15 inches

E. $16\frac{2}{3}$ inches

NAEP, Grade 8, 2013

Hint for Solving the Preliminary Problem

Find the fraction of the whole washer that the two holes represent and then find the portion not represented by the holes. This should aid in finding the area of the washer.

Chapter 6 Summary

KEY CONCEPTS	DEFINITIONS, DESCRIPTIONS, AND THEOREMS
Section 6-1	
Rational number (p. 258)	A number in the form $\frac{a}{b}$, or a/b, where a and b are integers and $b \neq 0$. In the rational number $\frac{a}{b}$, a is the *numerator* and b is the *denominator*.
Uses of rational numbers (p. 258)	• Division problem • Portion, or part, of a whole • Ratio • Probability
Types of fractions (p. 259)	*Proper fraction*—any fraction $\frac{a}{b}$, where $0 \leq a < b$; a proper fraction is always less than 1. *Improper fraction*—any fraction $\frac{a}{b}$, where $a \geq b > 0$; an improper fraction is always greater than or equal to 1. *Equivalent, or equal, fractions*—numbers that represent the same point on a number line.
Fundamental Law of Fractions (p. 263)	*Theorem:* If $\frac{a}{b}$ is a fraction and n is a nonzero rational number, then $\frac{a}{b} = \frac{an}{bn}$.
Simplest form (p. 263)	A rational number $\frac{a}{b}$ is in *simplest form*, or *lowest terms* if, and only if, $\text{GCD}(a, b) = 1$; that is, if a and b have no common factor greater than 1.
Equality of fractions (p. 266)	Two fractions $\frac{a}{b}$ and $\frac{c}{d}$, where $b \neq 0$ and $d \neq 0$, are *equal* (or *equivalent*) if, and only if, $ad = bc$.
Ordering of rational numbers (p. 267)	*Like denominators*—If a, b, and c are any integers and $b > 0$, then $\frac{a}{b} > \frac{c}{b}$ if, and only if, $a > c$. *Unlike denominators*—If a, b, c, and d are any integers such that $b > 0$ and $d > 0$, then $\frac{a}{b} > \frac{c}{d}$ if, and only if $ad > bc$.
Denseness property for rational numbers (p. 268)	Given any two different rational numbers $\frac{a}{b}$ and $\frac{c}{d}$, there is another rational numbers between these two numbers. *Theorem:* Let $\frac{a}{b}$ and $\frac{c}{d}$ be any rational numbers with positive denominators, where $\frac{a}{b} < \frac{c}{d}$. Then $\frac{a}{b} < \frac{a+c}{b+d} < \frac{c}{d}$.
Section 6-2	
Addition of rational numbers (p. 275)	*Like denominators*—If $\frac{a}{b}$ and $\frac{c}{b}$ are rational numbers, then $\frac{a}{b} + \frac{c}{b} = \frac{a+c}{b}$. *Unlike denominators*—If $\frac{a}{b}$ and $\frac{c}{d}$ are rational numbers, then $\frac{a}{b} + \frac{c}{d} = \frac{ad+bc}{bd}$.

Section 6-2

Addition properties for rational numbers (p. 279)

- *Additive inverse*—for any rational number $\frac{a}{b}$, there exists a unique rational number $-\frac{a}{b}$ such that $\frac{a}{b} + \left(-\frac{a}{b}\right) = 0 = \left(-\frac{a}{b}\right) + \frac{a}{b}$.

- *Property of equality*—if $\frac{a}{b}$ and $\frac{c}{d}$ are any rational numbers such that $\frac{a}{b} = \frac{c}{d}$ and $\frac{e}{f}$ is any rational number, then $\frac{a}{b} + \frac{e}{f} = \frac{c}{d} + \frac{e}{f}$.

Subtraction of rational numbers (p. 281)

If $\frac{a}{b}$ and $\frac{c}{d}$ are any rational numbers, then $\frac{a}{b} - \frac{c}{d}$ is the unique rational number $\frac{e}{f}$ such that $\frac{a}{b} = \frac{c}{d} + \frac{e}{f}$.

If $\frac{a}{b}$ and $\frac{c}{d}$ are any rational numbers, then $\frac{a}{b} - \frac{c}{d} = \frac{a}{b} + \frac{^-c}{d}$.

If $\frac{a}{b}$ and $\frac{c}{d}$ are any rational numbers, then $\frac{a}{b} - \frac{c}{d} = \frac{ad - bc}{bd}$.

Estimation with rational numbers (p. 283)

Round fractions to *convenient*, or *benchmark* numbers, such as $\frac{1}{2}, \frac{1}{3}, \frac{1}{4}, \frac{1}{5}, \frac{2}{3}, \frac{3}{4}$, or 1.

Section 6-3

Multiplication of rational numbers (p. 292)

If $\frac{a}{b}$ and $\frac{c}{d}$ are any rational numbers, then $\frac{a}{b} \cdot \frac{c}{d} = \frac{ac}{bd}$.

Multiplication properties for rational numbers (p. 293)

- *Multiplicative identity*—the rational number 1 is the unique number such that for every rational number $\frac{a}{b}$, $1 \cdot \frac{a}{b} = \frac{a}{b} = \frac{a}{b} \cdot 1$.

- *Multiplicative inverse*—for any nonzero rational number $\frac{a}{b}$, the multiplicative inverse (reciprocal) is the unique rational number $\frac{b}{a}$ such that $\frac{a}{b} \cdot \frac{b}{a} = 1 = \frac{b}{a} \cdot \frac{a}{b}$.

- *Property of 0*—let $\frac{a}{b}$ be any rational number. Then $\frac{a}{b} \cdot 0 = 0 = 0 \cdot \frac{a}{b}$.

- *Property of equality*—let $\frac{a}{b}, \frac{c}{d}$, and $\frac{e}{f}$ be any rational numbers such that $\frac{a}{b} = \frac{c}{d}$. Then $\frac{a}{b} \cdot \frac{e}{f} = \frac{c}{d} \cdot \frac{e}{f}$.

- *Properties of inequality*—let $\frac{a}{b}, \frac{c}{d}$, and $\frac{e}{f}$ be any rational numbers:

  If $\frac{a}{b} > \frac{c}{d}$ and $\frac{e}{f} > 0$, then $\frac{a}{b} \cdot \frac{e}{f} > \frac{c}{d} \cdot \frac{e}{f}$.

  If $\frac{a}{b} > \frac{c}{d}$ and $\frac{e}{f} < 0$, then $\frac{a}{b} \cdot \frac{e}{f} < \frac{c}{d} \cdot \frac{e}{f}$.

Distributive property of multiplication over addition or subtraction (p. 294)

Let $\frac{a}{b}, \frac{c}{d}$, and $\frac{e}{f}$ be any rational numbers. Then

$$\frac{a}{b}\left(\frac{c}{d} + \frac{e}{f}\right) = \frac{a}{b} \cdot \frac{c}{d} + \frac{a}{b} \cdot \frac{e}{f} \quad \text{and} \quad \frac{a}{b}\left(\frac{c}{d} - \frac{e}{f}\right) = \frac{a}{b} \cdot \frac{c}{d} - \frac{a}{b} \cdot \frac{e}{f}.$$

Division of rational numbers (p. 297)

If $\frac{a}{b}$ and $\frac{c}{d}$ are any rational numbers, with $\frac{c}{d} \neq 0$, then $\frac{a}{b} \div \frac{c}{d} = \frac{e}{f}$ if, and only if, $\frac{e}{f}$ is the unique rational number such that $\frac{c}{d} \cdot \frac{e}{f} = \frac{a}{b}$.

Algorithm for Division of Fractions (p. 299)

If $\frac{a}{b}$ and $\frac{c}{d}$ are any rational numbers, with $\frac{c}{d} \neq 0$, then $\frac{a}{b} \div \frac{c}{d} = \frac{a}{b} \cdot \frac{d}{c}$.

Section 6-3

a^m (p. 301)	If a is any rational number and m is any natural number, then $a^m = \underbrace{a \cdot a \cdot a \cdot \ldots \cdot a}_{m \text{ factors}}.$
a^{-n} (p. 302)	For any nonzero rational number a and any natural number n, $a^{-n} = \dfrac{1}{a^n}.$
Exponents of rational numbers theorems (p. 302)	*Theorem:* For any nonzero rational number a and any integers m and n, $a^m \cdot a^n = a^{m+n}.$ *Theorem:* For any nonzero rational number a and any integers m and n, $\dfrac{a^m}{a^n} = a^{m-n}.$ *Theorem:* For any nonzero rational number a and any integers m and n, $(a^m)^n = a^{mn}.$ *Theorem:* For any nonzero rational number $\dfrac{a}{b}$ and any integer m, $\left(\dfrac{a}{b}\right)^m = \dfrac{a^m}{b^m}.$ *Theorem:* For any nonzero rational number $\dfrac{a}{b}$ and any integer m, $\left(\dfrac{a}{b}\right)^{-m} = \left(\dfrac{b}{a}\right)^m.$ *Theorem:* For any nonzero rational numbers a and b and any integer m, $(a \cdot b)^m = a^m \cdot b^m.$

Section 6-4

Ratio (p. 311)	A comparison of two quantities a and b, where a and b are rational numbers, denoted as $\dfrac{a}{b}$, a/b, or $a{:}b$ and read as "a to b".
Proportion (p. 313)	A statement that two given ratios are equal. *Theorem:* If a, b, c, and d are rational numbers and $b \neq 0$ and $d \neq 0$, then $\dfrac{a}{b} = \dfrac{c}{d}$ if, and only if, $ad = bc$.
Constant of Proportionality (p. 316)	If the variables x and y are related by the equality $y = kx$, or $k = \dfrac{y}{x}$, then y *is proportional to* x and k is the *constant of proportionality* between y and x.
Proportionality theorems (p. 318)	*Theorem:* For any rational numbers $\dfrac{a}{b}$ and $\dfrac{c}{d}$, with $a \neq 0$ and $c \neq 0$, $\dfrac{a}{b} = \dfrac{c}{d}$ if, and only if, $\dfrac{b}{a} = \dfrac{d}{c}$. *Theorem:* For any rational numbers $\dfrac{a}{b}$ and $\dfrac{c}{d}$, with $c \neq 0$, $\dfrac{a}{b} = \dfrac{c}{d}$ if, and only if, $\dfrac{a}{c} = \dfrac{b}{d}$.

Chapter 6 Review

1. For each of the following, draw a diagram illustrating the fraction. Answers vary.
   a. $\dfrac{3}{4}$
   b. $\dfrac{2}{3}$
   c. $\dfrac{3}{4} \cdot \dfrac{2}{3}$ *

2. Write three rational numbers equal to $\dfrac{5}{6}$. *

3. Write each of the following rational numbers in simplest form.
   a. $\dfrac{24}{28}$ $\dfrac{6}{7}$
   b. $\dfrac{ax^2}{bx}$ $\dfrac{ax}{b}$
   c. $\dfrac{0}{17}$ $\dfrac{0}{1} = 0$
   d. $\dfrac{45}{81}$ $\dfrac{5}{9}$
   e. $\dfrac{b^2 + bx}{b + x}$ b
   f. $\dfrac{16}{216}$ $\dfrac{2}{27}$
   g. $\dfrac{x + a}{x - a}$ Cannot be simplified
   h. $\dfrac{xa}{x + a}$ Cannot be simplified

4. In each of the following pairs, replace the comma with $>$, $<$, or $=$ to make a true statement.

   a. $\dfrac{6}{10}, \dfrac{120}{200}$ $=$

   b. $\dfrac{^-3}{4}, \dfrac{^-5}{6}$ $>$

   c. $\left(\dfrac{4}{5}\right)^{10}, \left(\dfrac{4}{5}\right)^{20}$ $>$

   d. $\left(1 + \dfrac{1}{3}\right)^2, \left(1 + \dfrac{1}{3}\right)^3$ $<$

5. Find the additive and multiplicative inverses for each of the following.

   a. 3 $^-3, \dfrac{1}{3}$

   b. $3\dfrac{1}{7}$ $^-3\dfrac{1}{7}, \dfrac{7}{22}$

   c. $\dfrac{5}{6}$ $\dfrac{^-5}{6}, \dfrac{6}{5}$

   d. $-\dfrac{3}{4}$ $\dfrac{3}{4}, \dfrac{^-4}{3}$

6. Order the following numbers from least to greatest.   *

   $$^-1\dfrac{7}{8}, 0, ^-2\dfrac{1}{3}, \dfrac{69}{140}, \dfrac{71}{140}, \left(\dfrac{71}{140}\right)^{300}, \dfrac{1}{2}, \left(\dfrac{74}{73}\right)^{300}$$

7. Can $\dfrac{4}{5} \cdot \dfrac{7}{8} \cdot \dfrac{5}{14}$ be written as $\dfrac{4}{8} \cdot \dfrac{7}{14} \cdot \dfrac{5}{5}$ to obtain the same answer? Why or why not?   *

8. Use mental math to compute the following. Explain your method.

   a. $\dfrac{1}{3} \cdot (8 \cdot 9)$ *

   b. $36 \cdot 1\dfrac{5}{6}$ *

9. John has $54\dfrac{1}{4}$ yd of material.

   a. If he needs to cut the cloth into pieces that are $3\dfrac{1}{12}$ yd long, how many pieces can he cut?   17 pieces

   b. How much material will be left over? $1\dfrac{5}{6}$ yd

10. Without actually performing the given operations, choose the most appropriate estimate (among the numbers in parentheses) for the following expressions.

    a. $\dfrac{30\dfrac{3}{8}}{4\dfrac{1}{9}} \cdot \dfrac{8\dfrac{1}{3}}{3\dfrac{8}{9}}$ $(15, 20, 8)$ 15

    b. $\left(\dfrac{3}{800} + \dfrac{4}{5000} + \dfrac{15}{6}\right)6$ $(15, 0, 132)$ 15

    c. $\dfrac{1}{407} \div \dfrac{1}{1609}$ $\left(\dfrac{1}{4}, 4, 0\right)$ 4

11. Write a story problem that models $4\dfrac{5}{8} \div \dfrac{1}{2}$. Solve the problem by drawing appropriate diagrams.   Answers vary.

12. Find two rational numbers between $\dfrac{3}{4}$ and $\dfrac{4}{5}$.   *

13. Suppose the $\div$ button on your calculator is broken, but the $\boxed{1/x}$ button works. Explain how you could compute $504792/23$. $\boxed{5}\boxed{0}\boxed{4}\boxed{7}\boxed{9}\boxed{2}\boxed{\times}\boxed{2}\boxed{3}\boxed{1/x}\boxed{=}$

14. Jim is starting a diet. When he arrived home, he ate $\dfrac{1}{3}$ of the half of a pizza that was left from the previous night. The whole pizza contains approximately 2000 calories. How many calories did Jim consume?   Approximately 333 calories

15. If a person got heads on a flip of a fair coin one-half the time and obtained 376 heads, how many times was the coin flipped?   752 times

16. If a person obtained 240 heads when flipping a coin 1000 times, what fraction of the time did the person obtain heads? Put the answer in simplest form. $\dfrac{240}{1000} = \dfrac{6}{25}$

17. If the University of New Mexico won $\dfrac{3}{4}$ of its women's basketball games and $\dfrac{5}{8}$ of its men's basketball games, explain whether it is reasonable to say that the university won $\dfrac{3}{4} + \dfrac{5}{8}$ of its basketball games.   *

18. The carvings of the faces at Mount Rushmore in South Dakota measure 60 ft from chin to forehead. If the distance from chin to forehead is typically 9 in., and the distance between the pupils of the eyes is typically $2\dfrac{1}{2}$ in., what is the approximate distance between the pupils on the carving of George Washington's head? $16\dfrac{2}{3}$ ft

19. A student argues that the following fraction is not a rational number because it is not the quotient of two integers:

    $$\dfrac{\dfrac{2}{3}}{\dfrac{3}{4}}$$

    You should show him that the given fraction could be written as an integer over an integer. In this case, the result is $\dfrac{8}{9}$.

    How would you respond?

20. Molly wants to fertilize 12 acres of park land. If it takes $9\dfrac{1}{3}$ bags for each acre, how many bags does she need?   112 bags

21. If $\dfrac{2}{3}$ of all students in the academy are female and $\dfrac{2}{5}$ of those are blondes, what fraction describes the number of blond females in the academy? $\dfrac{4}{15}$

22. Explain which is greater: $\dfrac{^-11}{9}$ or $\dfrac{^-12}{10}$.   *

23. Solve for x in each of the following.

    a. $7^x = 343$ 3

    b. $2^{-3x} = \dfrac{1}{512}$ 3

    c. $2x - \dfrac{5}{3} = \dfrac{5}{6}$ $\dfrac{5}{4}$ or $1\dfrac{1}{4}$

    d. $x + 2\dfrac{1}{2} = 5\dfrac{2}{3}$ $\dfrac{19}{6}$ or $3\dfrac{1}{6}$

    e. $\dfrac{20 + x}{x} = \dfrac{4}{5}$ $^-100$

    f. $2x + 4 = 3x - \dfrac{1}{3}$ $\dfrac{13}{3}$ or $4\dfrac{1}{3}$

24. Write each of the following in simplest form. Leave all answers with positive exponents.

    a. $\dfrac{(x^3 a^{-1})^{-2}}{xa^{-1}}$ $\dfrac{a^3}{x^7}$

    b. $\left(\dfrac{x^2 y^{-2}}{x^{-3} y^2}\right)^{-2}$ $\dfrac{y^8}{x^{10}}$

25. Find each sum or difference.

    a. $\dfrac{3a}{xy^2} + \dfrac{b}{x^2 y^2}$ $\dfrac{3ax + b}{x^2 y^2}$

    b. $\dfrac{5}{xy^2} - \dfrac{2}{3x}$ $\dfrac{15 - 2y^2}{3xy^2}$

    c. $\dfrac{a}{x^3 y^2 z} - \dfrac{b}{xyz}$ $\dfrac{a - bx^2 y}{x^3 y^2 z}$

    d. $\dfrac{7}{2^3 3^2} + \dfrac{5}{2^2 3^3}$ $\dfrac{31}{216}$

26. Mike drew the following picture to find out how many pieces of ribbon $\frac{1}{2}$ yd long could be cut from a strip of ribbon $1\frac{3}{4}$ yd long.

From the picture he concluded that $1\frac{3}{4} \div \frac{1}{2}$ is 3 pieces with $\frac{1}{4}$ yd left over, so the answer is $3\frac{1}{4}$ pieces. He checked this using the algorithm $\frac{7}{4} \cdot \frac{2}{1} = \frac{14}{4} = 3\frac{1}{2}$ and is confused why he has two different answers. How would you help him? *

27. Tom tossed a coin 30 times and got 17 heads.
    a. What is the ratio of heads to coin tosses?   17:30
    b. What is the ratio of heads to tails?   17:13
    c. What is the ratio of tails to heads?   13:17

28. Which bottle of juice is a better buy (cost per fluid ounce): 48 fl oz for $3 or 64 fl oz for $4?   Neither; same price

29. Eighteen-karat gold contains 18 parts (grams) gold and 6 parts (grams) other metals. Amy's new ring contains 12 parts gold and 3 parts other metals. Is the ring 18-karat gold? Why?   No, $\frac{18}{6} \neq \frac{12}{3}$

30. A recipe for fruit salad serves 4 people. It calls for 3 oranges and 16 grapes. How many oranges and grapes do you need to serve 11 people? $8\frac{1}{4}$ oranges and 44 grapes

31. If the scale on a drawing of a house is 1 cm to $2\frac{1}{2}$ m, what is the length of the house if it measures 3 cm on the scale drawing? $7\frac{1}{2}$ m

32. In water (H_2O), the ratio of the weight of oxygen to the weight of hydrogen is approximately 8:1. How many ounces of hydrogen are in 1 lb of water?   *

33. A manufacturer produces the same kind of computer chip in two plants. In the first plant, the ratio of defective chips to good chips is 15:100 and in the second plant, that ratio is 12:100. A buyer of a large number of chips is aware that some come from the first plant and some from the second. However, she is not aware of how many come from each. The buyer would like to know the ratio of defective chips to good chips in any given order. Can she determine that ratio? If so, explain how. If not, explain why not.   *

34. Suppose the ratio of the lengths of the sides in two squares is $1:r$. What is the ratio of their areas? ($A = s^2$) $1:r^2$

35. The Grizzlies won 18 games and lost 7.
    a. What is the ratio of games won to games lost?   18:7
    b. What is the ratio of games won to games played?   18:25

36. Express each of the following as a ratio $\frac{a}{b}$ where a and b are whole numbers.
    a. $\frac{1}{5}:1$ 1:5
    b. $\frac{2}{5}:\frac{3}{4}$ 8:15

37. The ratio of boys to girls in Mr. Good's class is 3 to 5, the ratio of boys to girls in Ms. Garcia's is the same, and you know that there are 15 girls in Ms. Garcia's class. How many boys are in Ms. Garcia's class?   9

38. If the ratio of the number of states of the United States using the *Common Core Standards* to those not using it is 9:10, how many states are not using these *Standards*?   5 states

39. From about 1978 to 1985, there was a trend towards conservatism among university professors with about $\frac{1}{20}$ of professors identifying themselves as strongly left-wing, about a third identifying themselves as liberals, about $\frac{1}{4}$ identifying themselves as moderates, $\frac{1}{4}$ as conservative, and $\frac{1}{20}$ as strongly conservative. What fraction identified themselves with none of the labels? $\frac{1}{15}$

40. Since 1985, the fraction of liberal professors has grown steadily, with research finding somewhere between 7 to 9 liberals for each professor of another political persuasion. What statement with ratios could you make about professors of other political persuasions?   *

41. In an equilateral triangle, all sides have the same length and the perimeter is the sum of those lengths. What is the ratio of the perimeters of two equilateral (all sides of equal length) triangles whose sides each have lengths 6 cm and 10 cm respectively?   The ratio of perimeters is 3:5.

42. If a cup of coffee with 1 oz of cream is compared to another cup with $\frac{9}{10}$ oz cream, which has more cream?   *

43. In a package of tulip bulbs, the seller guarantees that at least $\frac{45}{99}$ of the bulbs will bloom. If you planted a package of 121 bulbs, at least how many would be expected not to bloom?   66

44. A woman's will decreed that her cats be shared among her three daughters as follows: $\frac{1}{2}$ of the cats to the eldest daughter, $\frac{1}{3}$ of the cats to the middle daughter, and $\frac{1}{9}$ of the cats to the youngest daughter. Since the woman had 17 cats, the daughters decided that they could not carry out their mother's wishes. The judge who held the will agreed to lend the daughters a cat so that they could share the cats as their mother wished. Now, $\frac{1}{2}$ of 18 is 9; $\frac{1}{3}$ of 18 is 6; and $\frac{1}{9}$ of 18 is 2. Since $9 + 6 + 2 = 17$, the daughters were able to divide the 17 cats and return the borrowed cat. They obviously did not need the extra cat to carry out their mother's bequest, but they could not divide 17 into halves, thirds, and ninths. Has the woman's will really been followed?   *

45. Prince Juan was allowed to take a number of bags of gold as he went into exile. However, a guard at the first bridge he crossed demanded half the bags of gold plus one more bag. Juan met this demand and proceeded to the next bridge. Guards at the second, third, and fourth bridges made identical demands, all of which the prince met. When Juan finally crossed all the bridges, a single bag of gold was left. With how many bags did Juan start?   46 bags.

Chapter 7

Rational Numbers as Decimals and Percent

Preliminary Problem

On a photocopy machine, you can alter an original by entering a percentage for the copy. If you enter 200%, the machine will double all the dimensions of the original. Debbie set the machine to 150% and copied a 3 cm by 6 cm photo. She decided the copy was not large enough, so she placed the copy into the machine and left the setting on 150%. (a) What are the dimensions of the new copy? (b) If she wanted to reproduce another photo to the same size of the new copy and do it using only one step, what setting should she use? (c) If she had a copy that had been enlarged using a setting of 150%, what setting should she use to reduce the copy to its original size?

If needed, see Hint on page 383.

Although the Hindu-Arabic numeration system discussed in Chapter 3 was used in many regions around the sixth century, the extension of the system to decimals by Dutchman Simon Stevin did not take place until approximately a thousand years later. The only significant improvement in the system since Stevin's time has been in notation. Even today, there is no universally accepted form of writing a decimal. For example, in the United States, we write 6.75; in England, this number is written $6 \cdot 75$; and in Germany and France, it is written 6,75.

 In the grade 4 *Common Core Standards*, we find that students should:

Use decimal notation for fractions with denominators 10 or 100. For example, rewrite 0.62 as $\frac{62}{100}$; describe a length as 0.62 meters; locate 0.62 on a number line diagram. (p. 31)

In Section 7-1, we explore relationships between fractions and decimals and show how decimals are an extension of the base-ten system. Later in the chapter, we consider operations on decimals, properties of decimals, and percents.

7-1 Introduction to Finite Decimals

7-1 Objectives

Students will be able to understand and explain

- Decimal notation.
- Connections between fractions and decimals using various models and strategies.
- Why terminating decimals occur and how to tell if a decimal will terminate.
- Ordering of terminating decimals.

The word *decimal* comes from the Latin *decem*, meaning "ten." Thus, integers written in base ten are technically decimals, although most people do not think of them as such.

 In the grade 5 *Common Core Standards*, we find that students should:

Read and write decimals to thousandths using base-ten numerals, number names, and expanded form, e.g., $347.392 = 3 \times 100 + 4 \times 10 + 7 \times 1 + 3 \times \left(\frac{1}{10}\right) + 9 \times \left(\frac{1}{100}\right) + 2 \times \left(\frac{1}{1000}\right)$. (p. 35)

We encounter decimals when dealing with money. For example, if a bike costs \$128.95, the dot in \$128.95 is the **decimal point**. Because \$0.95 is $\frac{95}{100}$ of a dollar, $128.95 = 128 + \frac{95}{100}$.

Historical Note

In 1584, Simon Stevin (1548–1620), a Dutch quartermaster general, wrote *La Thiende (The Tenth)*, giving rules for computing with decimals. He not only stated these rules but also suggested practical applications for decimals and recommended that his government adopt them. To show place value, Stevin used circled numerals between digits. For example, he wrote 0.4789 as 4 ① 7 ② 8 ③ 9 ④.

dollars. Also because \$0.95 is 9 dimes and 5 cents, 1 dime is $\frac{1}{10}$ of a dollar, and 1 cent is $\frac{1}{100}$ of a dollar, we see that \$0.95 is $9 \cdot \frac{1}{10} + 5 \cdot \frac{1}{100}$ dollars. Consequently,

$$128.95 = 1 \cdot 10^2 + 2 \cdot 10 + 8 \cdot 1 + 9 \cdot \frac{1}{10} + 5 \cdot \frac{1}{10^2}.$$

The digits in 128.95 correspond, respectively, to the following place values: 10^2, 10, 1, $\frac{1}{10^1}$, and $\frac{1}{10^2}$.
Similarly, 12.61843 represents

$$1 \cdot 10 + 2 \cdot 1 + \frac{6}{10^1} + \frac{1}{10^2} + \frac{8}{10^3} + \frac{4}{10^4} + \frac{3}{10^5}.$$

Since $1 \cdot 10 + 2 \cdot 1 = 12$ and

$$\frac{6}{10^1} + \frac{1}{10^2} + \frac{8}{10^3} + \frac{4}{10^4} + \frac{3}{10^5} = \frac{6 \cdot 10^4}{10^1 \cdot 10^4} + \frac{1 \cdot 10^3}{10^2 \cdot 10^3} + \frac{8 \cdot 10^2}{10^3 \cdot 10^2} + \frac{4 \cdot 10^1}{10^4 \cdot 10^1} + \frac{3}{10^5}$$

$$= \frac{6 \cdot 10^4 + 1 \cdot 10^3 + 8 \cdot 10^2 + 4 \cdot 10^1 + 3}{10^5}$$

$$= \frac{61,843}{100,000},$$

we can write $12.61843 = 1 \cdot 10 + 2 \cdot 1 + \frac{6}{10^1} + \frac{1}{10^2} + \frac{8}{10^3} + \frac{4}{10^4} + \frac{3}{10^5}$ as $12\frac{61,843}{100,000}$.

Technically the decimal 12.61843 is read "twelve and sixty-one thousand eight hundred forty-three hundred-thousandths" although most people will say "twelve point six, one, eight, four, three." The word "and" is used only to represent the decimal point. Each place of a decimal may be named by its power of 10. For example, the places of 12.61843 can be named as shown in Table 1.

Table 1

1	2	.	6	1	8	4	3
Tens	Units	and	Tenths	Hundredths	Thousandths	Ten-thousandths	Hundred-thousandths

In most U.S. school mathematics programs, fractions are introduced before decimals. Children see $2\frac{1}{4}$ before they see 2.25, although they both represent the same number. With the introduction of the metric system, decimals become even more important.

The three main ideas in this section are:

1. Decimal numerals are another way of writing selected fractions. Connections between fractions and decimals and how they are represented are important concepts in elementary school.
2. The decimal point indicates a separating point between the *units* digit and parts of a unit.
3. The base-ten place-value system extends two directions from the decimal point. In one direction, the values become greater; in the other direction, the values become lesser.

Decimals can be introduced with concrete materials. For example, suppose that a long in the base-ten block set represents 1 unit instead of letting the cube represent 1 unit. Then the cube represents $\frac{1}{10}$ and 5.4 could be represented as in Figure 1(a).

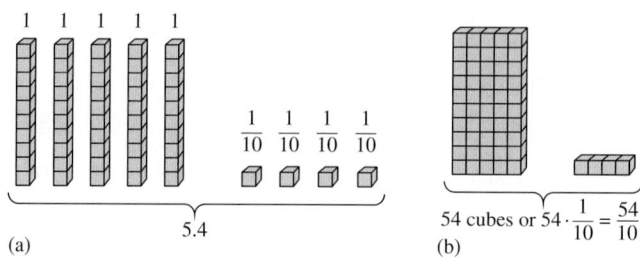

Figure 1

We could use Figure 1(b) to obtain a different interpretation of 5.4 and see that 5.4 is also equivalent to 54 tenths, or $\frac{54}{10}$. This equivalence can be stated symbolically as

$$5.4 = 5 + 0.4 = 5 + \frac{4}{10} = \frac{50}{10} + \frac{4}{10} = \frac{54}{10}.$$

This approach gives students a concrete connection between fractions and decimals.

▶ **NOW TRY THIS 1**

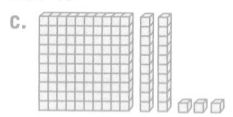
NTT 1:
c.

In a set of base-ten blocks, let 1 flat represent 1 unit.

  a. What does 1 long represent? $\frac{1}{10}$ or 0.1
  b. What does 1 cube represent? $\frac{1}{100}$ or 0.01
  c. Represent 1.23 using the blocks with these representations.

To represent a decimal such as 2.235, think of a block shown in Figure 2(a) as a unit. Then a flat represents $\frac{1}{10}$, a long represents $\frac{1}{100}$, and a cube represents $\frac{1}{1000}$. Using these objects, we show a representation of 2.235 in Figure 2(b).

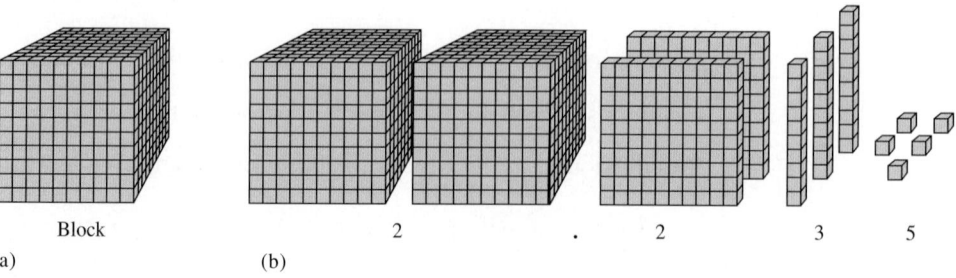

Block

(a)   (b)   2   .   2   3   5

Figure 2

Table 2 shows other examples of decimals, their fractional meanings, and their common fraction notations.

Table 2		
Decimal	**Expanded Fractional Meaning**	**Common Fraction Notation**
5.3	$5 + \dfrac{3}{10}$	$5\dfrac{3}{10} = \dfrac{53}{10}$
0.02	$0 + \dfrac{0}{10} + \dfrac{2}{100}$	$\dfrac{2}{100}$
2.0103	$2 + \dfrac{0}{10} + \dfrac{1}{100} + \dfrac{0}{1000} + \dfrac{3}{10,000}$	$2\dfrac{103}{10,000} = \dfrac{20,103}{10,000}$
$^-3.6$	$^-\left(3 + \dfrac{6}{10}\right)$	$^-3\dfrac{6}{10} = -\dfrac{36}{10}$

Decimals in standard form can be written in expanded form using place value and negative exponents. For example,

$$12.61843 = 1 \cdot 10^1 + 2 \cdot 10^0 + 6 \cdot 10^{-1} + 1 \cdot 10^{-2} + 8 \cdot 10^{-3} + 4 \cdot 10^{-4} + 3 \cdot 10^{-5}.$$

From the student page "Decimal Place Value" shown on page 334, we see that in grade 5, students learn equivalent forms of decimals.

Example 1 shows how to convert rational numbers whose denominators are powers of 10 to decimals.

Example 1

Convert each of the following to decimals.

a. $\dfrac{25}{10}$ b. $\dfrac{56}{100}$ c. $\dfrac{205}{10,000}$

Solution

a. $\dfrac{25}{10} = \dfrac{2 \cdot 10 + 5}{10} = \dfrac{2 \cdot 10}{10} + \dfrac{5}{10} = 2 + \dfrac{5}{10} = 2.5$

b. $\dfrac{56}{100} = \dfrac{5 \cdot 10 + 6}{10^2} = \dfrac{5 \cdot 10}{10^2} + \dfrac{6}{10^2} = 0 + \dfrac{5}{10^1} + \dfrac{6}{10^2} = 0.56$

c. $\dfrac{205}{10,000} = \dfrac{2 \cdot 10^2 + 0 \cdot 10^1 + 5}{10^4} = \dfrac{2 \cdot 10^2}{10^4} + \dfrac{0 \cdot 10^1}{10^4} + \dfrac{5}{10^4}$

$\quad = \dfrac{2}{10^2} + \dfrac{0}{10^3} + \dfrac{5}{10^4} = 0 + \dfrac{0}{10^1} + \dfrac{2}{10^2} + \dfrac{0}{10^3} + \dfrac{5}{10^4} = 0.0205$

The conversions in Example 1 can also be performed using negative exponents. For example,

$$\dfrac{25}{10} = (2 \cdot 10 + 5) \cdot 10^{-1} = (2 \cdot 10) \cdot 10^{-1} + 5 \cdot 10^{-1} = 2 \cdot (10 \cdot 10^{-1}) + 5 \cdot 10^{-1}$$

$$= 2 \cdot 10^0 + 5 \cdot 10^{-1} = 2 \cdot 1 + 5 \cdot 10^{-1} = 2.5.$$

School Book Page   Decimal Place Value

Lesson 1-4

Common Core
5.NBT.3.a Read and write decimals to thousandths using base-ten numerals, number names, and expanded form.

Decimal Place Value

How can you represent decimals?

Jo picked a seed from her flower. The seed measured 0.245 gram. What are some different ways you can represent 0.245?

A single seed of certain orchids can measure 0.245 gram.

ones	.	tenths	hundredths	thousandths
0	.	2	4	5

The 5 is in the thousandths place. Its value is 0.005.

Standard Form: 0.245

Expanded Form: 0.2 + 0.04 + 0.005

Word Form: two hundred forty-five thousandths

Another Example What are equivalent decimals?

Equivalent decimals name the same amount.

Name two other decimals equivalent to 1.4.

One and four tenths is the same as one and forty hundredths.
So, 1.4 = 1.40.

One and four tenths is the same as one and four hundred thousandths.
So, 1.4 = 1.400.

So, 1.4 = 1.40 = 1.400.

1 whole

4 columns = 4 tenths
40 small squares = 40 hundredths
                 = 400 thousandths

Guided Practice*

MATHEMATICAL PRACTICES

Do you know HOW?

Write the word form for each number and give the value of the underlined digit.

1. 4.7**3**7
2. 9.80**6**

Write each number in standard form.

3. 6 + 0.6 + 0.03 + 0.007
4. four and sixty-eight hundredths

Write two decimals that are equivalent to the given decimal.

5. 3.700
6. 5.60

Do you UNDERSTAND?

7. **Reason** The number 3.453 has two 3s. Why does each 3 have a different value?

8. How do you read the decimal point in word form?

9. **Generalize** José finished a race in 2.6 hours and Pavel finished the same race in 2.60 hours. Which runner finished the race first?

*For another example, see Set D on page 23.

14

Independent Practice

Write the word form for each number and give the value of the underlined digit.

10. 2.**3**00
11. 9.**2**07
12. 1.982
13. 6.178

Write each number in standard form.

14. two and six thousandths
15. five and one hundred four thousandths
16. 3 + 0.3 + 0.009
17. 7 + 0.6 + 0.05 + 0.007

Write two decimals that are equivalent to the given decimal.

18. 2.200
19. 8.1
20. 9.50
21. 4.200

Problem Solving

MATHEMATICAL PRACTICES

22. **Be Precise** Kay is buying juice at the market. She has $9 and each bottle of juice costs $2. Does she have enough money to buy 5 bottles of juice? Explain.

23. **Model** Which point on the number line below best represents 0.368?

0.350   W X   Y   Z   0.370

A W   B X   C Y   D Z

24. The Borneo stick insect has a total length, including legs, of 21.5 inches. Write 21.5 in word form.

25. Worker leafcutter ants can measure 0.5 inches. Name two decimals that are equivalent to 0.5.

26. **Generalize** Why are 7.630 and 7.63 equivalent?

Animated Glossary, eTools
www.pearsonsuccessnet.com

Lesson 1-4   15

Source: pp. 14–15; From enVisionMATH Common Core (Grade 5). Copyright © 2012 Pearson Education, Inc., or its affiliates. Used by permission. All Rights Reserved.

The ideas in Example 1 are reinforced with a calculator. In Example 1(b), press [5] [6] [÷] [1] [0] [0] [=] and watch the display. Next divide by 10 again and look at the new placement of the decimal point. Once more, divide by 10 (which amounts to dividing the original number, 56, by 10,000) and note the placement of the decimal point. This leads to the general rule for dividing or multiplying a decimal by a positive integer power of 10:

> To divide a decimal by 10^n where n is a positive integer, start at the decimal point, count n place values to the left, adjoining zeros if necessary, and insert the decimal point to the left of the nth place value counted.

> To multiply a decimal by 10^n where n is a positive integer, move the decimal point n places to the right adjoining zeros, if needed.

The fractions in Example 1 are easy to convert to decimals because the denominators are powers of 10. If the denominator of a fraction is not a power of 10, as in $\frac{3}{5}$, we use the problem-solving strategy of *converting the problem to one that we already know how to do.* First, we rewrite $\frac{3}{5}$ as a fraction in which the denominator is a power of 10, and then we convert the fraction to a decimal.

$$\frac{3}{5} = \frac{3 \cdot 2}{5 \cdot 2} = \frac{6}{10} = 0.6$$

The reason for multiplying the numerator and the denominator by 2 is apparent when we observe that $10 = 5 \cdot 2$ or $2 \cdot 5$.

When the denominator of a fraction is a power of 10, converting the fraction to a decimal is a simple use of division of a whole number by a power of 10. Any power of 10 is of the form 10^n, and in general, because $10^n = (2 \cdot 5)^n = 2^n \cdot 5^n$, the prime factorization of the denominator that is a power of 10^n must be $2^n \cdot 5^n$. We use this idea in Example 2.

Example 2

Express each of the following as decimals.

a. $\dfrac{7}{2^6}$ **b.** $\dfrac{1}{2^3 \cdot 5^4}$ **c.** $\dfrac{1}{125}$ **d.** $\dfrac{7}{250}$

Solution

a. $\dfrac{7}{2^6} = \dfrac{7 \cdot 5^6}{2^6 \cdot 5^6} = \dfrac{7 \cdot 15{,}625}{(2 \cdot 5)^6} = \dfrac{109{,}375}{10^6} = 0.109375$

b. $\dfrac{1}{2^3 \cdot 5^4} = \dfrac{1 \cdot 2^1}{2^3 \cdot 5^4 \cdot 2^1} = \dfrac{2}{2^4 \cdot 5^4} = \dfrac{2}{(2 \cdot 5)^4} = \dfrac{2}{10^4} = 0.0002$

c. $\dfrac{1}{125} = \dfrac{1}{5^3} = \dfrac{1 \cdot 2^3}{5^3 \cdot 2^3} = \dfrac{8}{(5 \cdot 2)^3} = \dfrac{8}{10^3} = 0.008$

d. $\dfrac{7}{250} = \dfrac{7}{2 \cdot 5^3} = \dfrac{7 \cdot 2^2}{2 \cdot 5^3 \cdot 2^2} = \dfrac{28}{(2 \cdot 5)^3} = \dfrac{28}{10^3} = 0.028$

A calculator quickly converts fractions to decimals. For example, to find $\dfrac{7}{2^6}$, press [7] [÷] [2] [y^x] [6] [=]. To convert $\dfrac{1}{125}$ to a decimal, press [1] [÷] [1] [2] [5] [=] or press [1] [2] [5] [1/x] [=].

The given calculator answers, as well as the answers in Example 2, are illustrations of **terminating decimals**—*decimals that can be written with a finite number of places to the right of the decimal point.* Not every rational number can be written as a terminating decimal. For example, if we attempt to rewrite $\frac{2}{11}$ as a terminating decimal using the method just developed, we try to find a natural number b such that the following holds:

$$\frac{2}{11} = \frac{2b}{11b}, \quad \text{where } 11b \text{ is a power of 10}$$

The only prime factors of a power of 10 are 2 and 5. Because $11b$ has 11 as a factor, by the Fundamental Theorem of Arithmetic, we cannot write $11b$ as a power of 10. Therefore, it seems that $\frac{2}{11}$ cannot be written as a terminating decimal. A similar argument using the Fundamental Theorem of Arithmetic holds in general, so we have the following theorem.

Theorem 7-1

A rational number $\frac{a}{b}$ in simplest form can be written as a terminating decimal if, and only if, the prime factorization of the denominator contains no primes other than 2 or 5.

Example 3

Which of the following fractions can be written as terminating decimals?

a. $\frac{7}{8}$ b. $\frac{11}{250}$ c. $\frac{21}{28}$ d. $\frac{37}{768}$

Solution

a. Because the denominator, 8, is 2^3, and the fraction is in simplest form, $\frac{7}{8}$ can be written as a terminating decimal.

b. Because the denominator, 250, is $2 \cdot 5^3$, and the fraction is in simplest form, $\frac{11}{250}$ can be written as a terminating decimal.

c. $\frac{21}{28}$ can be written in simplest form as $\frac{21}{28} = \frac{3 \cdot 7}{2^2 \cdot 7} = \frac{3}{2^2}$. The denominator is now 2^2, so $\frac{21}{28}$ can be written as a terminating decimal.

d. In simplest form, the fraction $\frac{37}{768} = \frac{37}{2^8 \cdot 3}$ has a denominator with a factor of 3, so $\frac{37}{768}$ cannot be written as a terminating decimal.

REMARK As Example 3(c) shows, to determine whether a rational number $\frac{a}{b}$ can be represented as a terminating decimal, we consider the prime factorization of the denominator *only* if the fraction is in simplest form.

Ordering Terminating Decimals

 In the grade 4 *Common Core Standards*, **we find that students should be able to:**

compare two decimals to hundredths by reasoning about their size. Recognize that comparisons are valid only when the two decimals refer to the same whole. Record the results of comparisons with the symbols >, =, or <, and justify the conclusions, e.g., by using a visual model. (p. 31)

Given two numbers, the one located farther to the right on a standard horizontal number line is the greater. A terminating decimal is easily located on a number line because it can be represented as a rational number $\frac{a}{b}$ and b is a power of 10. For example, consider 0.56, or $\frac{56}{100}$. One way to think about $\frac{56}{100}$ is as the rightmost endpoint of the 56th part of a unit segment divided into 100 equal parts, as in Figure 3.

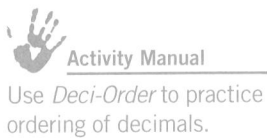 Use *Deci-Order* to practice ordering of decimals.

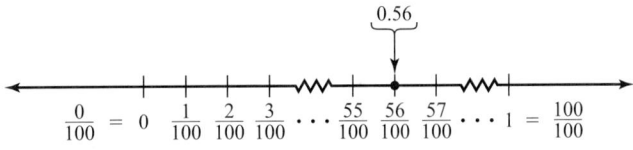

Figure 3

Two terminating decimals can be ordered by converting each to rational numbers in the form $\frac{a}{b}$ and determining which is greater. For example, because $0.36 = \frac{36}{100}$, $0.9 = 0.90 = \frac{90}{100}$, and $\frac{90}{100} > \frac{36}{100}$, it follows that $0.9 > 0.36$. One could also tell that $0.9 > 0.36$ because $0.90 is 90¢ and $0.36 is 36¢ and 90¢ > 36¢.

 IMAP Video

Watch Madison compare decimals and see a common misconception about ordering decimals.

Comparing 0.36 and 0.9 as above suggests a method for comparing any two decimals. For example, consider the decimals 0.345 and 0.1474. Note that 0.345 is a decimal with thousandths as the least place value, and 0.1474 has ten-thousandths as its least place value. To compare the decimals, we could write both with ten-thousandths as the least place value. Note that 0.345 could be written as 0.3450. Now, we have 0.3450 and 0.1474 both with ten-thousandths as the least place value. These decimals could be written as follows:

$$\frac{3450}{10,000} \quad \text{and} \quad \frac{1474}{10,000}$$

These two fractions can be compared by looking only at the numerators. Because 3450 is greater than 1474, $\frac{3450}{10,000} > \frac{1474}{10,000}$, and hence $0.345 > 0.1474$.

This process is frequently shortened by looking only at the decimals lined up as follows:

$$0.3450 = 0.345$$
$$0.1474 = 0.1474$$

With the decimals lined up in this fashion, 3 tenths is greater than 1 tenth. Thus, $0.345 > 0.1474$. This suggests a way to order terminating decimals without conversion to fractions. The steps used to compare terminating decimals are similar to those for comparing whole numbers.

1. *Line up the numbers by place value and append zeros, if necessary.*
2. *Start at the left and find the first place where the face values are different.*
3. *Compare these digits. The digit with the greater face value in this place represents the greater of the two numbers.*

Assessment 7-1A

1. Write each of the following as a sum in expanded place value form.
   a. 0.023 *
   b. 206.06 *
   c. 312.0103 *
   d. 0.000132 *

2. Rewrite each of the following as a decimal.
   a. $4 \cdot 10^3 + 3 \cdot 10^2 + 5 \cdot 10 + 6 + 7 \cdot 10^{-1} + 8 \cdot 10^{-2}$ 4356.78
   b. $4 \cdot 10^3 + 6 \cdot 10^{-1} + 8 \cdot 10^{-3}$ 4000.608
   c. $4 \cdot 10^4 + 3 \cdot 10^{-2}$ 40,000.03
   d. $2 \cdot 10^{-1} + 4 \cdot 10^{-4} + 7 \cdot 10^{-7}$ 0.2004007

3. Write each of the following as a decimal.
   a. Five hundred thirty-six and seventy-six ten-thousandths   536.0076
   b. Three and eight thousandths   3.008
   c. Four hundred thirty-six millionths   0.000436
   d. Five million and two tenths   5,000,000.2

4. Write each of the following numerals in words.
   a. 0.34   thirty-four hundredths
   b. 20.34   twenty and thirty-four hundredths
   c. 2.034   two and thirty-four thousandths
   d. 0.000034   thirty-four millionths

5. Write each of the following terminating decimals as $\frac{a}{b}$ in simplest form where $a, b \in I$ and $b \neq 0$.
   a. 0.436 *
   b. 25.16 *
   c. ‾316.027 *
   d. 28.1902 *
   e. ‾4.3 *
   f. ‾62.01 *

6. Mentally determine which of the following can be represented as a terminating decimal. *
   a. $\frac{4}{5}$
   b. $\frac{61}{2^2 \cdot 5}$
   c. $\frac{3}{6}$
   d. $\frac{1}{2^5}$
   e. $\frac{4}{34}$
   f. $\frac{133}{625}$

7. Where possible, write each of the numbers in exercise 6 as a terminating decimal. *

8. Seven minutes is part of an hour. If 7 min were to be expressed as a decimal part of an hour, explain whether it would be a terminating decimal. *

9. Given the U.S. monetary system, what reason can you think of for having coins only for a penny, nickel, dime, quarter, and half-dollar as coins less than $1.00? *

10. In each of the following, order the decimals from greatest to least:
    a. 13.4919, 13.492, 13.49183, 13.49199 *
    b. ‾1.453, ‾1.45, ‾1.4053, ‾1.493 *

11. Write the numbers in each of the following sentences as decimals.
    a. A mite has body length of about fourteen thousandths of an inch.   0.014
    b. The Earth orbits the Sun once every three hundred sixty-five and twenty-four hundredths days.   365.24

12. Use a grid with 100 squares and represent 0.32. Explain your representation. *

13. If the decimals 0.804, 0.84, and 0.8399 are arranged on a typical horizontal number line, which is furthest to the right?   0.84

14. Write a decimal that has a ten-thousandths place and is between 8.34 and 8.341. *

15. a. Show that between any two terminating decimals, there is another terminating decimal. *
    b. Argue that part (a) can be used to show that there are infinitely many terminating decimals between any two terminating decimals. *

16. If "decimals" in other number bases work the same as in base ten, explain the meaning of 3.145_{six}. *

17. The five top swimmers in an event had the following times:

Emily	64.54 sec	Kathy	64.02 sec
Molly	64.46 sec	Rhonda	63.54 sec
Martha	63.59 sec		

    List them in the order they placed with the "best" time first (least time is best here).   Rhonda, Martha, Kathy, Molly, Emily

18. Suppose a carpenter's ruler was marked in thirty-seconds. What would be the fraction and its decimal equivalent for the mark on the ruler between $\frac{1}{16}$ and $\frac{2}{16}$? $\frac{3}{32} = 0.09375$

Assessment 7-1B

1. Write each of the following as a sum in expanded place value form.
   a. 0.045 *
   b. 103.03 *
   c. 245.6701 *
   d. 0.00034 *

2. Rewrite each of the following as a decimal.
   a. $5 \cdot 10^3 + 2 \cdot 10^2 + 4 \cdot 10^{-1}$ 5200.4
   b. $4 \cdot 10^{-3} + 2 \cdot 10^4$ 20,000.004
   c. $2 \cdot 10^2 + 3 \cdot 10^4$ 30,200
   d. $10^{-3} + 10^{-5}$ 0.00101

3. Write each of the following as a decimal.
   a. Two thousand twenty-seven thousandths   2.027
   b. Two thousand and twenty-seven thousandths   2000.027
   c. Two thousand twenty and seven thousandths   2020.007
   d. Four hundred-thousandths   0.00004

4. Write each of the following numerals in words.
   a. 0.45   forty-five hundredths
   b. 2.035   two and thirty-five thousandths
   c. 45.0006   forty-five and six ten-thousandths
   d. 0.0000445   four hundred forty-five ten-millionths

5. Write each of the following terminating decimals as $\frac{a}{b}$ in simplest form where $a, b \in I$ and $b \neq 0$.
   a. 28.32 *   b. 34.1736 *   c. ⁻27.32 *
6. Mentally determine which of the following represent terminating decimals.
   a. $\frac{4}{8}$ Terminating   b. $\frac{1}{2^6}$ Terminating
   c. $\frac{137}{625}$ Terminating   d. $\frac{1}{17}$ Not terminating
   e. $\frac{3}{25}$ Terminating   f. $\frac{14}{35}$ Terminating
7. Where possible, write each of the numbers in exercise 6 as a terminating decimal. *
8. What whole numbers of minutes (less than 60) could be expressed as terminating decimal parts of an hour? *
9. If in a set of base-ten-blocks, one block represented $\frac{1}{10}$, what is the value of each of the following?
   a. 1 cube   one ten-thousandth
   b. 1 flat   one hundredth
   c. 1 long   one thousandth
   d. 3 blocks, 1 long, and 4 cubes *
10. In each of the following, order the decimals from least to greatest:
   a. 24.9419, 24.942, 24.94189, 24.94199 *
   b. ⁻34.25, ⁻34.251, ⁻34.205, ⁻34.2519 *

11. Write the numbers in each of the following sentences as decimals.
   a. A flea has a body length about one sixteenth of an inch.   0.0625
   b. Venus orbits the sun about once every 224 and $\frac{7006}{10,000}$ days.   224.7006
12. Use a grid with 100 squares and represent 0.23. *
13. If the decimals 0.8114, 0.8119, 0.82 are arranged on a typical number line, which is furthest to the right?   0.82
14. Write a decimal that is between 8.345 and 8.3456. *
15. Argue that there are infinitely many terminating decimals between any two specific terminating decimals such as 0.0625 and 0.125. *
16. If "decimals" in other number bases work the same as in base ten, explain the meaning of 0.00334_{seven}. *
17. The five top swimmers in an event had the following times:

Eddie	63.51 sec	Karl	62.99 sec
Marius	63.43 sec	Ricky	62.51 sec
Michael	62.56 sec		

   List them in the order they placed with the "best" time first (least time is best here).   Ricky, Michael, Karl, Marius, Eddie
18. A normal carpenter's ruler marked off in sixteenths. What would be the values at each of the marks in decimal form? *

Mathematical Connections 7-1

Answers to Mathematical Connections can be found in the Answers section at the back of the book.

Reasoning

1. Using Simon Stevin's notation (see Historical Note), how would you write the following decimals?
   a. 0.3256
   b. 0.0032
2. If 1 mL is 0.001 L, how should 18 mL be expressed as a terminating decimal number of liters (L stands for liter)?
3. Explain whether 1 day can be expressed as a terminating decimal part of a 365-day year.
4. Using the number line model to depict terminating decimals, explain whether or not you think there is a greatest terminating decimal less than 1. Explain.
5. Explain why you think a sign on a copy machine reading ".05¢ a copy" is put up by mistake.
6. Explain how you could use base-ten blocks to represent two and three hundred forty-five thousandths.
7. Explain why in Theorem 7-1 the rational number must be in simplest form before examining the denominator.
8. Explain why appending any number of zeros to the right of a finite decimal does not change its value. For example, 0.34 = 0.340 = 0.3400.
9. How can you tell each of the following is incorrect just by looking at them?
   a. $\frac{1}{5} = 2.0$
   b. $\frac{2}{3} = 0.6$

Open-Ended

10. Determine how decimal notation is symbolized in different countries.
11. Examine three elementary school textbooks and report how the introductions of the topics of exponents and decimals differ, if they do. Report the grade level that decimals are introduced.

Cooperative Learning

12. Using base-five blocks similar to base-ten blocks, in your group discuss how you might introduce a "decimal" notation in base five.
13. In small groups, research the history of decimals to find contributions of the Arabs, the Chinese, and the people of Renaissance Europe. Explain whether you believe Stevin "invented" the decimal system.
14. With your group, play the *Where's the Best Place* game below. The object of the game is to build the greatest number possible.
   • Each player builds a number chart like the one shown.
     0 . ☐ ☐ ☐ ☐
   • Number ten cards 0 through 9, shuffle and place them face down in a pile.
   • One player draws a card and each player must decide where to place the card in his or her number chart. After a

digit is written, it cannot be erased, and the digit cannot be used again in that game.

- The game is over when each place in the number chart is filled. The player with the greatest number wins the game.
  a. Suppose a 9 is drawn first. Where should it be placed? Why?
  b. Suppose a 0 is drawn first. Where should it be placed? Why?
  c. The number charts for four players are shown below.
     (i) Can Ann win the game? (ii) Can Ben win the game?
  d. Suppose 2 is drawn next. Who will win the game?

Ann 0 . 6 7 ☐ 5   Ben 0 . 6 5 ☐ 7
Carl 0 . 6 7 5 ☐   Dani 0 . 6 5 7 ☐

Connecting Mathematics to the Classroom

15. A student claims that 0.86 is greater than 0.9 because 86 is greater than 9. How do you respond?
16. A student argues that fractions should no longer be taught once students learn how to work with decimal numbers. How do you respond?
17. A student claims that 0.304 = 0.34 because 0 is nothing. How do you respond?
18. A student claims that because 0.1, 0.01, 0.001, . . . is a geometric sequence so is 1.1, 1.01, 1.001, ... How do you respond?

National Assessments

National Assessment of Educational Progress (NAEP) Questions

Joe rode his bicycle from his house to his friend's house. He rode 1.7 miles along the path below. The path is marked every 0.5 mile. Put an X on the path to show how far Joe rode to his friend's house.

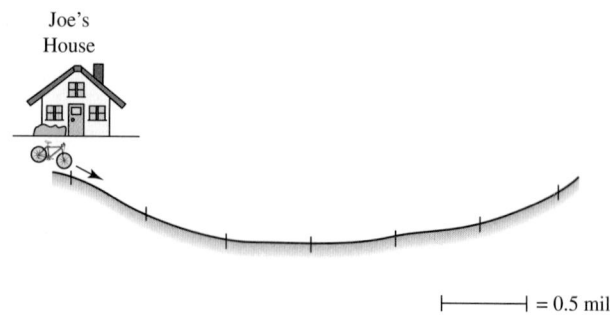

Joe's House

⊢————⊣ = 0.5 mile

NAEP, Grade 4, 2011

50-YARD RACE

Girl	Time (seconds)
Christa	8.28
Kelly	7.82
Lorinda	7.9
Sonja	8.31
Tanya	8.2

The table shows the times for five girls who ran a 50-yard race. The goal was for each girl to run the race in less than 8.25 seconds. Which girls met this goal?

A. Christa and Sonja
B. Christa and Tanya
C. Kelly, Lorinda, and Sonja
D. Kelly, Lorinda, and Tanya

NAEP, Grade 4, 2013

The diameter of a red blood cell, in inches, is 3×10^{-4}. This expression is the same as which of the following numbers?

A. 0.00003
B. 0.0003
C. 0.003
D. 3,000
E. 30,000

Did you use the calculator on this question?
NAEP, Grade 8, 2003

7-2 Operations on Decimals

7-2 Objectives

Students will be able to understand and explain

- How concrete models, drawings, and strategies can be used to develop efficient algorithms for decimal operations.

- Exponential and scientific notation for decimals.

- Strategies for decimal mental computations and estimations.

CCSS Grade 5 *Common Core Standards* expects students to:

add, subtract, multiply, and divide decimals to hundredths, using concrete models or drawings and strategies based on place value, properties of operations, and/or the relationship between addition and subtraction; relate the strategy to a written method and explain the reasoning used. (p. 35)

Adding Decimals

To develop an algorithm for addition of terminating decimals, consider the sum 2.16 + 1.73. In elementary school, base-ten blocks are recommended to demonstrate such an addition problem. Figure 4 shows how the addition can be performed.

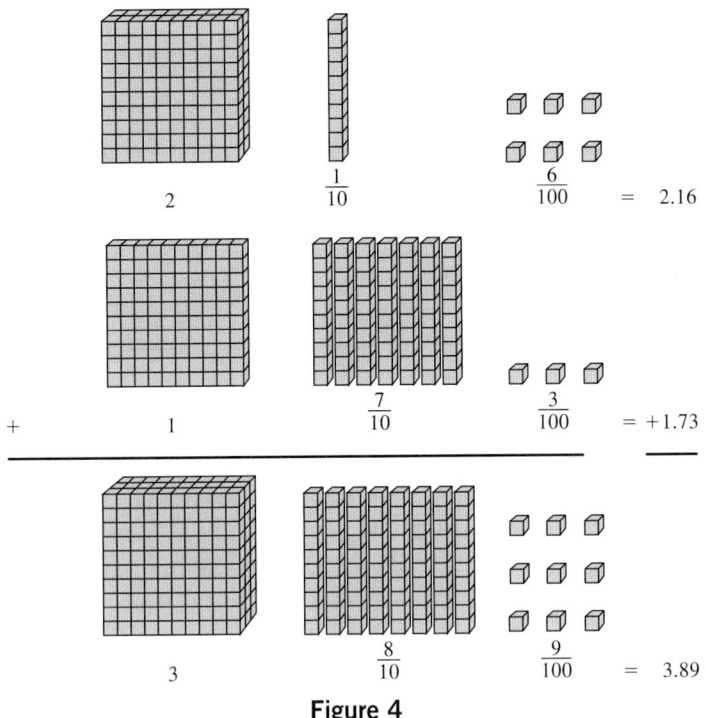

Figure 4

The computation in Figure 4 can be explained by *changing it to a problem we already know how to solve*; that is, to a sum involving fractions. We then use the commutative and associative properties of addition to aid in the computation as follows:

$$2.16 + 1.73 = \left(2 + \frac{1}{10} + \frac{6}{100}\right) + \left(1 + \frac{7}{10} + \frac{3}{100}\right)$$

$$= (2 + 1) + \left(\frac{1}{10} + \frac{7}{10}\right) + \left(\frac{6}{100} + \frac{3}{100}\right)$$

$$= 3 + \frac{8}{10} + \frac{9}{100}$$

$$= 3.89$$

A different way of looking at the addition $2.16 + 1.73$ uses a different representation of the decimals as fractions with denominators that are powers of 10 as shown in the following:

$$2.16 = \frac{216}{100} \quad \text{and} \quad 1.73 = \frac{173}{100} \quad \text{so } 2.16 + 1.73 = \frac{216}{100} + \frac{173}{100}$$

$$= \frac{216 + 173}{100} = \frac{389}{100} = 3.89$$

Similarly, $2.1 + 1.73 = \frac{21}{10} + \frac{173}{100} = \frac{210}{100} + \frac{173}{100} = \frac{383}{100} = 3.83.$

In each case, the decimals are converted to fractions with the same denominator that is a power of 10. Once this is done, the numerators can be added as whole numbers to form the numerator of the answer fraction, which can then be converted back to a decimal. If these decimals are written as shown below, we "line up the decimal points" and add as we do with whole numbers, placing the decimal point in the appropriate place in the answer.

$$\begin{array}{r} 2.16 \\ +1.73 \\ \hline 3.89 \end{array} \quad \text{and} \quad \begin{array}{r} 2.1 \\ +1.73 \\ \hline 3.83 \end{array} \quad \text{or} \quad \begin{array}{r} 2.10 \\ +1.73 \\ \hline 3.83 \end{array}$$

In the preceding computations, we add units to units, tenths to tenths, and hundredths to hundredths. The lining-up-the-decimal-points technique works for both addition and subtraction.

Activity Manual

Use *Decimal Arrays* and *Decimal Multiplication* to model multiplication of decimals using Base Ten Blocks.

Multiplying Decimals

Just as in the presented algorithms for adding terminating decimals by representing them as fractions, we develop and explain an algorithm for multiplication of decimals. Consider the product $4.62 \cdot 2.4$ shown below:

$$(4.62)(2.4) = \frac{462}{100} \cdot \frac{24}{10} = \frac{462}{10^2} \cdot \frac{24}{10^1} = \frac{462 \cdot 24}{10^2 \cdot 10^1} = \frac{11{,}088}{10^3} = 11.088$$

The answer to this computation was obtained by multiplying the whole numbers 462 and 24 and then dividing the result by 10^3.

On the student page shown on page 343, observe how multiplication of a whole number times a decimal can be accomplished by first shading 0.36 four times. The product is the sum of all the shaded portions: 1.44. In this manner, multiplication of a whole number times a decimal is interpreted almost exactly as the multiplication of a whole number by a whole number. Consider the shading method in the *Another Example* of the student page to show why $0.5 \times 0.3 = 0.15$.

An algorithm for multiplying decimals can be stated as follows:

If there are n digits to the right of the decimal point in one number and m digits to the right of the decimal point in a second number, multiply the two numbers, ignoring the decimals, and then place the decimal point so that there are n + m digits to the right of the decimal point in the product.

Example 4

Compute each of the following:

  a. $(6.2)(1.43)$ **b.** $(0.02)(0.013)$ **c.** $(1000)(3.6)$

Solution

a.   1.4 3   (2 digits after the decimal point)
    $\times$ 6.2   (1 digit after the decimal point)
    2 8 6
    8 5 8
    8.8 6 6   (2 + 1, or 3 digits after the decimal point)

b.   0.0 1 3   **c.**   3.6
   $\times$ 0.0 2 $\times$ 1 0 0 0
   0.0 0 0 2 6   3 6 0 0.0

Some people feel that teaching pencil-and-paper computation with decimal multiplication and division cannot be justified in light of readily available calculators and computers. Instead they suggest that more emphasis be placed on estimation skills. Estimation would then be used to place the decimal point in the multiplication or division. With this in mind the following algorithm is suggested.

Ignore the decimal points and do the multiplication or division as if all numbers were whole numbers. When finished, place the decimal point in the result by estimation.

For example, we would multiply $8.2 \cdot 2.63$ by multiplying $82 \cdot 263 = 21566$. Since $8 \cdot 2 = 16$ and $8 \cdot 3 = 24$, the decimal point is placed as 21.566.

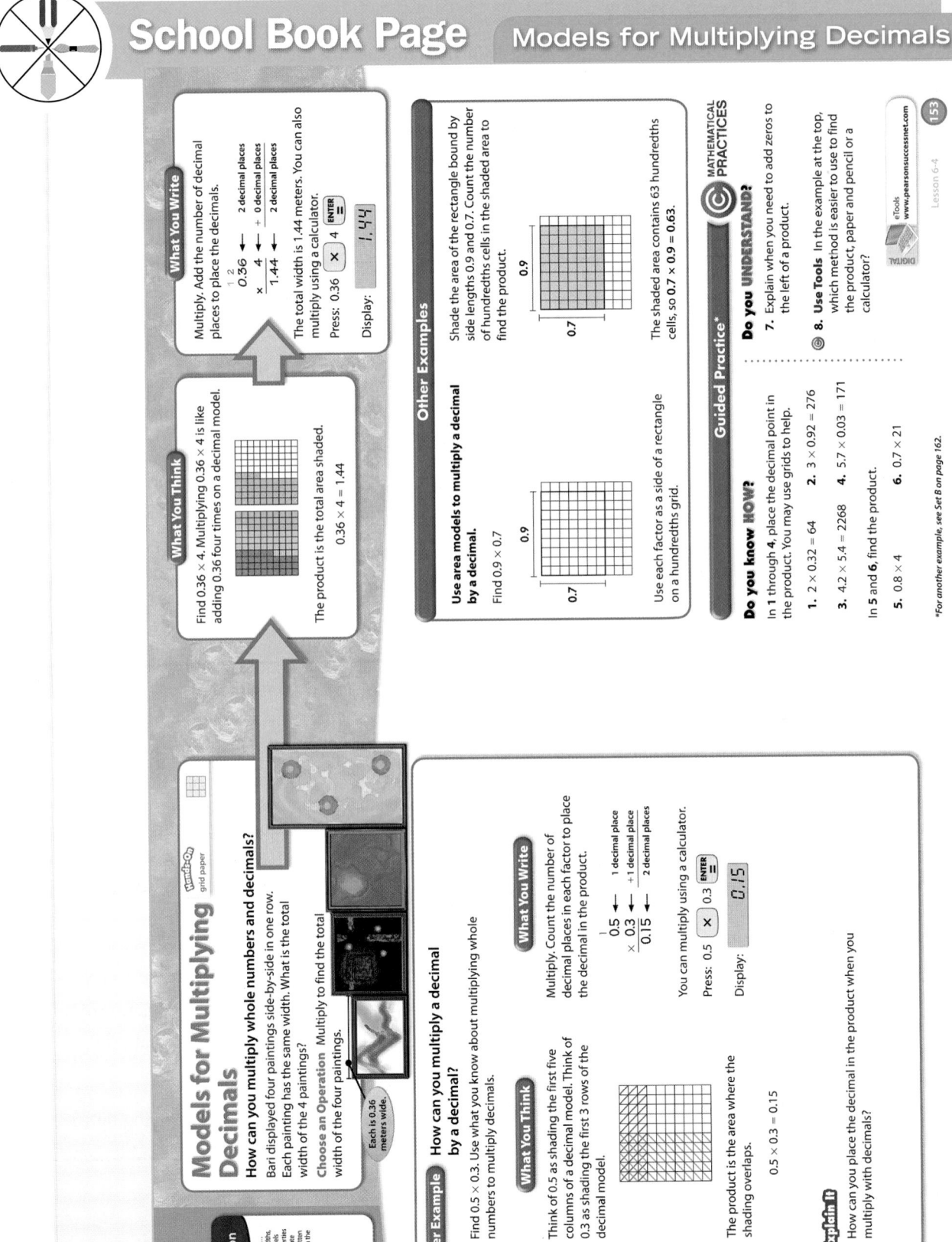

School Book Page — Models for Multiplying Decimals

Lesson 6-4

Common Core

5.NBT.7 ...Multiply... decimals to hundredths, using concrete models or drawings... relate the strategy to a written method and explain the reasoning used.

Models for Multiplying Decimals

How can you multiply whole numbers and decimals?

Bari displayed four paintings side-by-side in one row. Each painting has the same width. What is the total width of the 4 paintings?

Choose an Operation Multiply to find the total width of the four paintings.

Each is 0.36 meters wide.

What You Think

Find 0.36 × 4. Multiplying 0.36 × 4 is like adding 0.36 four times on a decimal model.

The product is the total area shaded.

$$0.36 \times 4 = 1.44$$

What You Write

Multiply. Add the number of decimal places to place the decimals.

$$
\begin{array}{r}
\overset{1\ 2}{0.36} \quad \leftarrow \text{2 decimal places} \\
\times \quad 4 \quad \leftarrow \text{0 decimal places} \\
\hline
1.44 \quad \leftarrow \text{2 decimal places}
\end{array}
$$

The total width is 1.44 meters. You can also multiply using a calculator.

Press: 0.36 [×] 4 [ENTER =]

Display: 1.44

Another Example **How can you multiply a decimal by a decimal?**

Find 0.5 × 0.3. Use what you know about multiplying whole numbers to multiply decimals.

What You Think

Think of 0.5 as shading the first five columns of a decimal model. Think of 0.3 as shading the first 3 rows of the decimal model.

The product is the area where the shading overlaps.

$$0.5 \times 0.3 = 0.15$$

What You Write

Multiply. Count the number of decimal places in each factor to place the decimal in the product.

$$
\begin{array}{r}
\overset{1}{0.5} \quad \leftarrow \text{1 decimal place} \\
\times \ 0.3 \quad \leftarrow \text{+1 decimal place} \\
\hline
0.15 \quad \leftarrow \text{2 decimal places}
\end{array}
$$

You can multiply using a calculator.

Press: 0.5 [×] 0.3 [ENTER =]

Display: 0.15

Explain It

1. How can you place the decimal in the product when you multiply with decimals?

152

Other Examples

Use area models to multiply a decimal by a decimal.

Find 0.9 × 0.7.

Shade the area of the rectangle bound by side lengths 0.9 and 0.7. Count the number of hundredths cells in the shaded area to find the product.

The shaded area contains 63 hundredths cells, so **0.7 × 0.9 = 0.63.**

Use each factor as a side of a rectangle on a hundredths grid.

Guided Practice*

Do you know HOW?

In **1** through **4**, place the decimal point in the product. You may use grids to help.

1. 2 × 0.32 = 64   **2.** 3 × 0.92 = 276

3. 4.2 × 5.4 = 2268   **4.** 5.7 × 0.03 = 171

In **5** and **6**, find the product.

5. 0.8 × 4   **6.** 0.7 × 21

Do you UNDERSTAND?

7. Explain when you need to add zeros to the left of a product.

8. Use Tools In the example at the top, which method is easier to use to find the product, paper and pencil or a calculator?

*For another example, see Set B on page 162.

MATHEMATICAL PRACTICES

DIGITAL — eTools   www.pearsonsuccessnet.com

Lesson 6-4   153

▶ NOW TRY THIS 2

NTT 2: Answers can be found in Answers at the back of the book.

a. Try the above technique using estimation to place the decimal point with the parts of Example 4.

b. Example 4(c) suggests that multiplication by 1000, or 10^3, results in moving the decimal point in the product three places to the right. **(i)** Explain why this is true using expanded notation and the distributive property of multiplication over addition for rational numbers. **(ii)** In general, how does multiplication by 10^n, where n is a positive integer, affect the product? Why?

Scientific Notation

Many calculators display the decimals for the fractions $\frac{3}{45,689}$ and $\frac{5}{76,146}$ as $\boxed{6.5661319 \quad -05}$ and $\boxed{6.566333 \quad -05}$, respectively. The displays are in **scientific notation**. The first display is a notation for $6.5661319 \cdot 10^{-5}$ and the second for $6.566333 \cdot 10^{-5}$.

Scientists use scientific notation to express either very small or very large numbers. For example, "the Sun is 93,000,000 mi from Earth" is expressed as "the Sun is $9.3 \cdot 10^7$ mi from Earth." A micron, a metric unit of measure that is 0.000001 m, is written $1 \cdot 10^{-6}$ m.

> **Definition of Scientific Notation**
>
> In **scientific notation**, a positive number is written as the product of a number greater than or equal to 1 and less than 10 and an integer power of 10. To write a negative number in scientific notation, treat the number as a positive number and adjoin the negative sign in front of the result.

The following numerals are in scientific notation:

$$8.3 \cdot 10^8, \quad 1.2 \cdot 10^{10}, \quad {}^{-}7.32 \cdot 10^8, \quad \text{and} \quad 7.84 \cdot 10^{-6}$$

The numbers $0.43 \cdot 10^9$ and $12.3 \cdot 10^{-6}$ are not in scientific notation because 0.43 and 12.3 are not greater than or equal to 1 and less than 10. To write a number like 934.5 in scientific notation, we divide by 10^2 to get 9.345 and then multiply by 10^2 to retain the value of the original number:

$$934.5 = \left(\frac{934.5}{10^2}\right)10^2 = 9.345 \cdot 10^2$$

This results in moving the decimal point two places to the left (dividing by 10^2) and then multiplying by 10^2. Similarly, to write 0.000078 in scientific notation, we first multiply by 10^5 to obtain 7.8 and then divide by 10^5 (or, equivalently, multiply by 10^{-5}) to keep the original value:

$$0.000078 = (0.000078 \cdot 10^5)10^{-5} = 7.8 \cdot 10^{-5}$$

This amounts to moving the decimal point five places to the right and multiplying by 10^{-5}.

Example 5

Write each of the following in scientific notation.

a. 413,682,000   **b.** 0.0000231   **c.** 83.7

d. $^{-}$10,000,000   **e.** $0.34 \cdot 10^{-6}$

Solution

a. $413{,}682{,}000 = \left(\dfrac{413{,}682{,}000}{10^8}\right)10^8 = 4.13682 \cdot 10^8$

b. $0.0000231 = (0.0000231 \cdot 10^5)10^{-5} = 2.31 \cdot 10^{-5}$

c. $83.7 = 8.37 \cdot 10^1$ (Move the decimal point one place to the left and multiply by 10.)

d. $^-10{,}000{,}000 = \dfrac{^-10{,}000{,}000}{10^7} \cdot 10^7 = {}^-1 \cdot 10^7$

e. $0.34 \cdot 10^{-6} = (3.4 \cdot 10^{-1}) \cdot 10^{-6} = 3.4 \cdot (10^{-1} \cdot 10^{-6}) = 3.4 \cdot 10^{-7}$

Example 6

Convert the following to standard numerals.

a. $6.84 \cdot 10^{-5}$ b. $3.12 \cdot 10^7$ c. $^-4.08 \cdot 10^4$

Solution

a. $6.84 \cdot 10^{-5} = 6.84\left(\dfrac{1}{10^5}\right) = 0.0000684$

b. $3.12 \cdot 10^7 = 31{,}200{,}000$

c. $^-4.08 \cdot 10^4 = {}^-40{,}800$

Computations involving scientific notation make use of the laws of exponents. For example, $(5.6 \cdot 10^5)(6 \cdot 10^4)$ can be rewritten $(5.6 \cdot 6)(10^5 \cdot 10^4) = 33.6 \cdot 10^9$, which is $3.36 \cdot 10^{10}$ in scientific notation. Also,

$$(2.35 \cdot 10^{-15})(2 \cdot 10^8) = (2.35 \cdot 2)(10^{-15} \cdot 10^8) = 4.7 \cdot 10^{-7}.$$

 Calculators with an $\boxed{\text{EE}}$ key can be used to represent numbers in scientific notation. For example, to find $(5.2 \cdot 10^{16})(9.37 \cdot 10^4)$, press

$$\boxed{5}\,\boxed{\cdot}\,\boxed{2}\,\boxed{\text{EE}}\,\boxed{1}\,\boxed{6}\,\boxed{\times}\,\boxed{9}\,\boxed{\cdot}\,\boxed{3}\,\boxed{7}\,\boxed{\text{EE}}\,\boxed{4}\,\boxed{=}.$$

Dividing Decimals

The set of nonzero whole numbers and the set of nonzero integers are not closed under division. However, the set of nonzero rational numbers is closed under division (why?).

The following examples deal with terminating decimals. Consider $75.45 \div 3$.

$$75.45 \div 3 = \frac{7545}{100} \div \frac{3}{1} = \frac{7545}{100} \cdot \frac{1}{3} = \frac{7545}{3} \cdot \frac{1}{100} = 2515 \cdot \frac{1}{100} = 25.15$$

By writing the dividend as a fraction whose denominator is a power of 10 and using the commutative property of multiplication, the division is changed into a division of whole numbers $(7545 \div 3)$ times a power of 10, namely, $\dfrac{1}{100}$, or 10^{-2}. A different method of accomplishing the change of the division into whole number division is to multiply the dividend and the divisor by the same power of 10, as follows:

$$75.45 \div 3 = \frac{75.45}{3} = \frac{75.45 \cdot 10^2}{3 \cdot 10^2} = \frac{7545}{300} = 25\frac{45}{300} = 25\frac{15}{100} = 25.15$$

When the divisor is a whole number as shown above, the division can be handled as with whole number division and the decimal point placed directly over the decimal point in the dividend. When the divisor is not a whole number, as in $1.2032 \div 0.32$, we can obtain a whole-number divisor by expressing the quotient as a fraction and then multiplying the numerator and denominator of the fraction by a power of 10 as seen on the student page shown on page 347. This corresponds to rewriting the division problem in form (a) as an equivalent problem in form (b), as follows:

(a) $0.32\overline{)1.2032}$ (b) $32\overline{)120.32}$

In elementary school texts, this process is usually described as "moving" the decimal point two places to the right in both the dividend and the divisor. It is usually indicated with arrows, as shown in the following.

$$
\begin{array}{r}
3.7\,6 \\
0.3\,2\overline{)1.2\,0\,3\,2} \\
\underline{9\,6} \\
2\,4\,3 \\
\underline{2\,2\,4} \\
1\,9\,2 \\
\underline{1\,9\,2} \\
0
\end{array}
$$ Multiply divisor and dividend by 100.

As seen above, in some cases of division of decimals, just as in division of whole numbers, the remainder for the division is 0.

Activity Manual

Use *Dice and Decimals* to reinforce operations with decimals.

Example 7

Compute each of the following.

  a. $13.169 \div 0.13$ **b.** $9 \div 0.75$

Solution

a.
$$
\begin{array}{r}
1\,0\,1.3 \\
0.1\,3\overline{)1\,3.1\,6\,9} \\
\underline{1\,3} \\
1\,6 \\
\underline{1\,3} \\
3\,9 \\
\underline{3\,9} \\
0
\end{array}
$$

b.
$$
\begin{array}{r}
1\,2 \\
0.7\,5\overline{)9.0\,0} \\
\underline{7\,5} \\
1\,5\,0 \\
\underline{1\,5\,0} \\
0
\end{array}
$$

In Example 7(b), we appended two zeros in the dividend because $\dfrac{9}{0.75} = \dfrac{9 \cdot 100}{0.75 \cdot 100} = \dfrac{900}{75}$.

School Book Page — Dividing a Decimal by a Decimal

Lesson 7-6
Common Core
5.NBT.7 ... divide decimals to hundredths, using concrete models or drawings and strategies based on place value... relate the strategy to a written method and explain the reasoning used.

Dividing a Decimal by a Decimal

How can you divide a decimal using a decimal divisor?

Michelle purchases several bottles of water. Before tax is added, the total cost is $3.60 and the cost of each bottle is $1.20. How many bottles did she buy?

Choose an Operation
Divide 3.60 by 1.20.

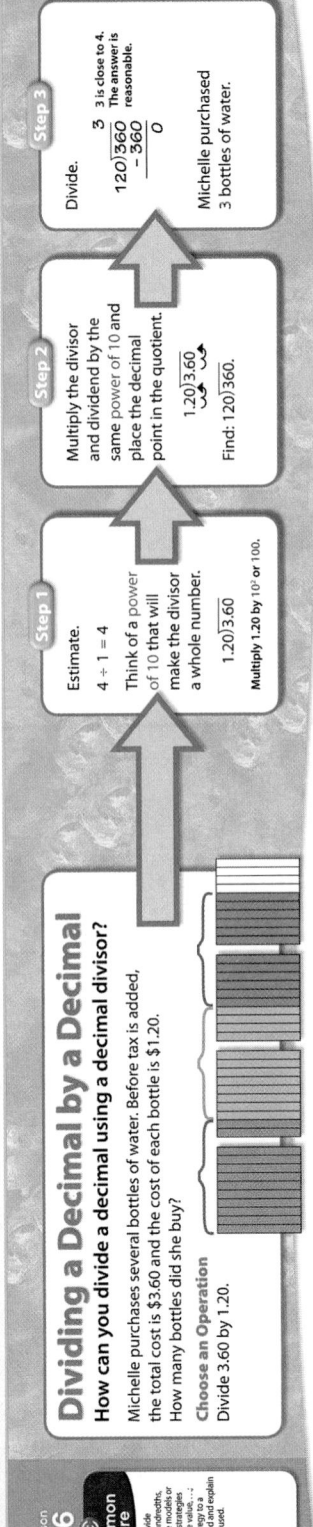

Step 1
Estimate.
$4 \div 1 = 4$
Think of a power of 10 that will make the divisor a whole number.
$1.20\overline{)3.60}$
Multiply 1.20 by 10^2 or 100.

Step 2
Multiply the divisor and dividend by the same power of 10 and place the decimal point in the quotient.
$1.20\overline{)3.60}$
Find: $120\overline{)360.}$

Step 3
3 is close to 4. The answer is reasonable.
$$\begin{array}{r} 3 \\ 120\overline{)360} \\ -360 \\ \hline 0 \end{array}$$
Michelle purchased 3 bottles of water.

Another Example
How can you divide a decimal by a decimal?

Find $0.021 \div 0.35$.

Step 1
Use multiplication to estimate.
$\square \times 0.35 = 0.021.$
You know:
$1 \times 0.35 = 0.35$ and
$0.1 \times 0.35 = 0.035.$
So, the quotient is < 0.1.

Step 2
Multiply the divisor and dividend by the same power of 10 to make the divisor a whole number, and place the decimal point in the quotient.
$0.35\overline{)0.021} = 35\overline{)2.1}$

Step 3
Divide. Annex zeros as needed.
$$\begin{array}{r} 0.06 \\ 35\overline{)2.10} \\ -2\ 10 \\ \hline 0 \end{array}$$
Since $0.06 < 0.1$, the answer is reasonable.

MATHEMATICAL PRACTICES

Guided Practice*

Do you know HOW?
Find each quotient.
1. $2 \div 0.5$
2. $1.25 \div 0.25$
3. $2.1 \div 0.7$
4. $6.6 \div 0.3$

TIP: Use estimation to check answers for reasonableness.

Do you UNDERSTAND?
5. **Look for Patterns** When dividing by a decimal, why can you multiply the divisor and dividend by the same power of 10?
6. **Communicate** Why is a zero added to the dividend in Step 3 of the example above?

*For another example, see Set D on page 187.

180

Independent Practice

Leveled Practice In **7** through **10**, estimate each quotient.
7. $3.6 \div 0.7$
8. $9.8 \div 0.2$
9. $17.8 \div 3.1$
10. $89.05 \div 4.8$

In **11** through **22**, find each quotient.
11. $62 \div 0.25$
12. $48.4 \div 0.02$
13. $0.02 \div 0.05$
14. $182.88 \div 0.08$
15. $107.25 \div 0.03$
16. $5.68 \div 8$
17. $624 \div 0.6$
18. $23.1 \div 0.7$
19. $24.2 \div 55$
20. $0.3567 \div 8.7$
21. $3.6 \div 9$
22. $4.788 \div 0.42$

Problem Solving

23. **Critique Reasoning/Arguments** Susan solves $1.4 \div 0.2$ using the diagram at the right. Is her reasoning correct? Explain her thinking.

24. **Communicate** Tim estimates that $60 \div 5.7$ is about 10. Will the actual quotient be greater than or less than 10? Explain.

25. **Reason** Dex estimates that $49{,}892 \div 0.89$ is about 5,000. Is his estimate reasonable? Why or why not?

26. **Think About the Structure** What value should you multiply the divisor and dividend by to begin dividing 89 by 0.04?
A 1
B 10
C 100
D 1,000

MATHEMATICAL PRACTICES

Lesson 7-6

Example 8

An owner of a gasoline station must collect a gasoline tax of $0.11 on each gallon of gasoline sold. One week, the owner paid $1595.00 in gasoline taxes. The pump price of a gallon of gas that week was $3.35.

a. How many gallons of gas were sold during the week?
b. What was the revenue after taxes for the week?

Solution

a. To find the number of gallons of gas sold during the week, we must divide the total gas tax bill by the amount of the tax per gallon.

$$\frac{1595}{0.11} = \frac{159500}{11} = 14,500$$

Thus, 14,500 gallons were sold.

b. To obtain the revenue after taxes, first determine the revenue before taxes. To do so, multiply the number of gallons sold by the cost per gallon:

$$(14,500)(\$3.35) = \$48,575$$

Next, subtract the gasoline taxes from the total revenue.

$$\$48,575 - \$1,595 = \$46,980$$

Thus, the revenue after gasoline taxes is $46,980.

Next consider a division resulting in a nonzero remainder as shown below.

```
             3.6 4    Quotient
    0.3 3)1.2 0 3 2
              9 9
            2 1 3
            1 9 8
            1 5 2
            1 3 2
              2 0    Remainder
```

Activity Manual

Use *Target Number Revisited* to develop number and operation sense, estimation skills, and increased understanding of multiplication and division of decimals.

Note that all digits in the dividend are used, and the remainder 20 is shown at the bottom of the division. The quotient is 3.64 and the remainder shown as 20 actually represents 0.0020, as can be seen by the original decimal alignment. This could be verified by checking: $3.64 \cdot 0.33 + 0.0020 = 1.2032$. In the next section, we will show how to write $\frac{12032}{33}$ as an infinite repeating decimal.

Mental Computation

CCSS In the grade 5 *Common Core Standards*, we find that students "apply their understanding of models for decimals, decimal notation, and properties of operations to add and subtract decimals to hundredths. They develop fluency in these computations and make reasonable estimates of their results." (p. 33)

Some of the tools used for mental computations with whole numbers can be used to perform mental computations with decimals, as seen in the following:

1. *Breaking and bridging*

$$1.5 + 3.7 + 4.48 \qquad \boxed{1.5 + 3 = 4.5}$$

$$= 4.5 + 0.7 + 4.48 \qquad \boxed{4.5 + 0.7 = 5.2}$$

$$= 5.2 + 4.48 \qquad \boxed{5.2 + 4 = 9.2}$$

$$= 9.2 + 0.48 = 9.68 \qquad \boxed{9.2 + 0.48 = 9.68}$$

2. *Using compatible numbers*

Decimal numbers are compatible when they add to a whole number.

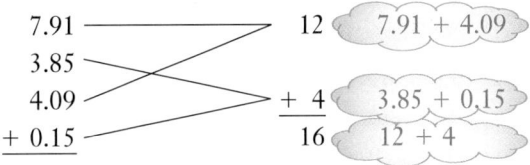

$$
\begin{array}{l}
7.91 \\
3.85 \\
4.09 \\
+\,0.15
\end{array}
\qquad
\begin{array}{r}
12 \\
\\
+\,4 \\
\hline
16
\end{array}
\qquad
\begin{array}{l}
\boxed{7.91 + 4.09} \\
\\
\boxed{3.85 + 0.15} \\
\boxed{12 + 4}
\end{array}
$$

3. *Making compatible numbers*

$$
\begin{array}{rl}
9.27 = & 9.25 + 0.02 \\
+3.79 = & 3.75 + 0.04 \\
\hline
& 13.00 + 0.06 = 13.06
\end{array}
$$

4. *Balancing with decimals in subtraction*

$$
\begin{array}{c}
4.63 \\
-\,1.97 \\
\end{array}
\ \text{or}\
\begin{array}{rl}
4.63 + 0.03 = & 4.66 \\
-(1.97 + 0.03) = & -2.00 \\
\hline
& 2.66
\end{array}
$$

5. *Balancing with decimals in division*

$$0.25\overline{)8}$$
$$\times 4 \qquad \times 4$$
$$\left(\begin{array}{c} 32 \\ 1\overline{)32} \end{array} \right)$$

REMARK Balancing with decimals in division uses the property $\dfrac{a}{b} = \dfrac{ac}{bc}$, if $c \neq 0$.

Rounding Decimals

Frequently, it is not necessary to know the exact numerical answer to a question. For example, if we want to know the distance to the Moon or the population of New York City, the approximate answers of 239,000 mi and 8,300,000 people, respectively, may be adequate.

Often a situation determines how you should round. For example, suppose a purchase came to $38.65, and the cashier used a calculator to determine the 6% sales tax by multiplying $0.06 \cdot 38.65$. The display showed 2.319. Because the display is between 2.31 and 2.32, and it is closer to 2.32, the cashier rounds up the sales tax to $2.32.

Suppose a display of 8.7345649 needs to be reported to the nearest hundredth. The display is between 8.73 and 8.74 but is closer to 8.73, so we round it down to 8.73. Next suppose the number 6.8675 needs to be rounded to the nearest thousandth. Notice that 6.8675 is exactly halfway between 6.867 and 6.868. *In such cases, it is common practice to round up*; therefore the answer to the nearest thousandth is 6.868. We write this as $6.8675 \approx 6.868$ and say 6.8675 is approximately equal to 6.868. You may encounter different rounding rules when the number is exactly half way between two values.

Example 9

Round each of the following numbers.

   a. 7.456 to the nearest hundredth
   b. 7.456 to the nearest tenth
   c. 7.456 to the nearest unit
   d. 7456 to the nearest thousand
   e. 745 to the nearest ten
   f. 74.56 to the nearest ten

Solution
   a. $7.456 \approx 7.46$
   b. $7.456 \approx 7.5$
   c. $7.456 \approx 7$
   d. $7456 \approx 7000$
   e. $745 \approx 750$
   f. $74.56 \approx 70$

 Rounding can also be done on some calculators using the $\boxed{\text{FIX}}$ key. If we want the number 2.3669 to be rounded to thousandths, we enter $\boxed{\text{FIX}}\ \boxed{3}$. The display will show 0.000. If we then enter 2.3669 and press the $\boxed{=}$ key, the display will show 2.367.

Estimating Decimal Computations Using Rounding

Rounded numbers can be useful for estimating answers to computations. For example, consider each of the following:

   1. Karly goes to the grocery store to buy items that cost the following amounts. She estimates the total cost by rounding each amount to the nearest dollar and adding the rounded numbers.

$$
\begin{array}{rcl}
\$2.39 & \rightarrow & \$2 \\
0.89 & \rightarrow & 1 \\
6.13 & \rightarrow & 6 \\
4.75 & \rightarrow & 5 \\
+\ 5.05 & \rightarrow & \underline{5} \\
& & \$19
\end{array}
$$

Thus, Karly's estimate for her grocery bill is $19.

   2. Karly's bill for car repairs was $72.80, and she has a coupon for $17.50 off. She can estimate her total cost by rounding each amount to the nearest 10 dollars and subtracting.

$$
\begin{array}{rcl}
\$72.80 & \rightarrow & \$70 \\
-\ 17.50 & \rightarrow & \underline{-\ 20} \\
& & \$50
\end{array}
$$

Thus, an estimate for the repair bill is $50. Notice that this is not a very good estimate. A better estimate is obtained by finding $73 - 18$, which is $55.

3. Karly sees a flash of lightning and hears the thunder 3.2 sec later. She knows that sound travels at 0.33 km/sec. She may estimate the distance she is from the lightning by rounding the time to the nearest unit and the speed to the nearest tenth and multiplying.

$$
\begin{array}{ccc}
0.33 & \to & 0.3 \\
\underline{\times\,3.2} & \to & \underline{\times\,3} \\
 & & 0.9
\end{array}
$$

Thus, Karly estimates that she is approximately 0.9 km from the lightning.

An alternative approach is to recognize that $0.33 \approx \dfrac{1}{3}$ and 3.2 is close to 3.3, so an

approximation using compatible numbers is $\left(\dfrac{1}{3}\right)3.3$, or 1.1 km.

4. Karly wants to estimate the number of miles she gets per gallon of gas. She started with a full tank. If she had driven 298 mi and it took 12.4 gal to refill the gas tank, she rounds and divides as follows:

$$
12.4\overline{)298} \quad \to \quad 12\overline{)300}^{\,25}
$$

Thus, she estimates about 25 mi/gal.

5. Karly wanted to place the decimal point in a product resulting from the multiplication estimation when she bought 21.45 lb of sesame seeds to grind for tahini at \$3.40 per pound. The multiplication (without a decimal) resulted in 7293. She knew that very rough estimates could be obtained by rounding 21.45 to 20 and \$3.40 to \$3. The product had to be in the neighborhood of 20 × 3, or 60. So her placement of the decimal point was \$72.93.

▶ **NOW TRY THIS 3**

NTT 3: Answers can be found in Answers at the back of the book.

Other estimation strategies, such as front-end, clustering, and grouping to convenient numbers, that we investigated with whole numbers also work with decimals. Take Karly's grocery store bill in exercise 1 on the preceding page and use a front-end-with-adjustment strategy to estimate the bill.

Do you prefer rounding or front-end estimation? Why?

Round-off Errors

Round-off errors are typically compounded when computations are involved. For example, if two distances 42.6 mi and 22.4 mi are rounded to the nearest tenth, then the sum of the distances appears to be 42.6 + 22.4, or 65.0 mi. To the nearest hundredth, the distances might have been more accurately reported as 42.55 and 22.35 mi, respectively. The sum of these distances is 64.9 mi. Alternatively, the original distances may have been rounded from 42.64 and 22.44 mi. The sum now is 65.08, or 65.1 rounded to the nearest tenth. The original sum of 65.0 mi is between 64.9 and 65.1 mi, but the exact answer need not be 65.0 mi to the nearest tenth.

The *greatest possible error* in measuring is defined as one half of the measuring unit. For example, if we measure a length to be 4.7 cm, then because the measurement was made to the nearest tenth, the greatest possible error is $\dfrac{1}{2}$ of 0.1 cm or 0.05 cm.

Similar errors arise in other arithmetic operations.

When computations are done with approximate numbers, the final result should not be reported using more significant digits than the number used with the fewest significant digits.

Nonzero digits are always significant. Zeros before other digits are non significant. Zeros between other nonzero digits are significant. Zeros to the right of a decimal point are significant.

Assessment 7-2A

1. Use base-ten blocks to model 3.2 + 2.32. *
2. Write the decimals as fractions and then add. Write your answer in decimal form.
   a. 8.6 + 23.1 + 0.92 *   **b.** 2.32 + 21.008 *
3. Write the decimals as fractions and then multiply. Write your answer in decimal form. Show all work.
   a. 0.5 · 0.6 *   **b.** 203 · 0.03 *   **c.** 0.003 · 0.006 *
4. Assume the multiplication shown below is correct except for the placement of the decimal point in the product.

   $$934.23 \cdot 3.2 = 2989536$$

   a. Insert the decimal point in the correct position without actually performing the multiplication. Describe the process you used to place the decimal point. *
   b. Describe a second way to determine where to place the decimal point. *
5. John's calculator calculates correctly but does not display decimal points. Use estimation to place the decimal point in the correct position for each of the following.
   a. 6 · 854.14 = 512484   5124.84
   b. 81.6 · 212.34 = 17326944   17326.944
   c. 137.025/1.75 = 783   78.3
6. Multiply each number below by 0.01 using mental computation.
   a. 2586   25.86   **b.** 34.79   0.3479
   c. 0.24   0.0024   **d.** 0.0037   0.000037
7. When you multiply a natural number by a decimal,
   a. when do you get a result less that the natural number?   When the decimal is less than 1
   b. when do you get a result greater than the natural number?   When the decimal is greater than 1
8. If Maura went to the store and bought a chair for $17.95, a lawn rake for $13.59, a spade for $14.86, a lawn mower for $179.98, and two six-packs of mineral water for $2.43 each, what was the bill? $231.24
9. **a.** Complete the following magic square; that is, make the sum of every row, column, and diagonal the same.

8.2		
3.7	5.5	
	9.1	2.8

8.2	1.9	6.4
3.7	5.5	7.3
4.6	9.1	2.8

   b. If each cell of the magic square has 0.85 added to it, is the square still magic?   Yes
   c. If the answer to part (b) is "yes," what is the sum of each row?   19.05
10. Karin bought 25 lb of peaches at $4.00/lb and 15 lb of apples at $2.00/lb. If she wanted to buy 10 more pounds of another kind of fruit to make the average price per pound equal to $3.50, what price should she pay for the additional 10 lb? $4.50/lb or $45

11. Automobile engines were once measured in cubic inches (in.^{3}) but are now usually measured in cubic centimeters (cm^3). Susan's 1963 Thunderbird has a 390 in.^{3} engine. If 2.54 cm is equivalent to 1 in., approximately how many cubic centimeters is this?   6,391 cm^3
12. A stock rose $0.24 in the market on Thursday. If the resulting price was $73.245, what was the price of the stock before the rise? $73.005
13. A U.S. $1 bill was valued at 1.046 Canadian dollars in November, 2013. What was the value of 27.32 American dollars in Canadian dollars that day? *
14. A kilowatt hour means 1000 watts of electricity are being used continuously for 1 hr. The electric utility company in Laura's town charges $0.06715 for each kilowatt hour used. Laura heats her house with three electric wall heaters that use 1200 watts each.
   a. How much does it cost to heat her house for 1 day? $5.80
   b. How many hours would a 75-watt lightbulb have to stay on to result in $1 for electricity charges?   Approximately 199 hours
15. If one liter is 4.224 cups, how many liters is 36.5 cups? *
16. If each of the following sequences is arithmetic, continue the decimal patterns for 3 more terms.
   a. 0.9, 1.8, 2.7, 3.6, 4.5,   5.4, 6.3, 7.2
   b. 0.3, 0.5, 0.7, 0.9, 1.1,   1.3, 1.5, 1.7
17. If the first term of a geometric sequence is 0.9 and its ratio is 0.2, what is the sum of the first five terms?   1.12464
18. Interpret 0.2222 as a sum of a finite geometric sequence whose first term is 0.2. (*Hint:* Write 0.2222 as the sum of fractions whose denominators are powers of 10.) *
19. Estimate the placement of each of the following values on the given number line by placing the letter for each computation in the appropriate box.
   a. 0.3 ÷ 0.31 *
   b. 0.3 · 0.31 *

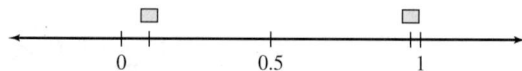

20. A bank statement from a local bank shows that a checking account has a balance of $83.62. The balance recorded in the checkbook shows only $21.69. After checking the canceled checks against the record of these checks, the customer finds that the bank has not yet recorded six checks in the amounts of $3.21, $14.56, $12.44, $6.98, $9.51, and $7.49. Is the bank record correct? (Assume the person's checkbook records *are* correct.)   No, the bank is over by $7.74.
21. Mike's class is building a model of the new World Trade Center (WTC) in New York City. They used a scale of 0.005 for their model; that is, each measure of the actual building is multiplied by 0.005 to find the measure of the corresponding part on the model. If the height of the WTC is 1776 ft, what is the height of the model?   8.88 ft

22. Suppose that to predict how tall a four-year-old will be at age 12, you multiply his or her height by 1.5. If Allie is 102.3 cm when she turns 4, predict how tall she will be when she turns 12. *

23. The value of a yen in Japan in November 2013 was given by the equation $1 = 99.925$ yen.
    a. What was the value of $150? 14988.75 yen
    b. Pauli saw a shirt marked at 3500 yen in November 2013. What was the price in U.S. dollars? Approximately $35.03

24. There are 2.54 cm in 1 in.
    a. Estimate the number of inches in 35 cm. *
    b. Compute the number of inches in 35 cm to the nearest hundredth. 13.78
    c. Jamie is 154.5 cm tall. What is her height in inches? Approximately 60.83

25. A kilometer is approximately 0.62 miles. Answers vary.
    a. Molly ran a 30-km race. How many miles is this? *
    b. In Canada, the speed limit for a certain stretch of road was marked 90 km/hr. What is the corresponding speed limit in mi/hr? Approximately 55.8
    c. If the speed limit is 75 mi/hr, what is it in km/hr? *

26. Convert each of the following to standard form.
    a. $3.2 \cdot 10^{-9}$ 0.0000000032
    b. $3.2 \cdot 10^{9}$ 3,200,000,000
    c. $4.2 \cdot 10^{-1}$ 0.42
    d. $6.2 \cdot 10^{5}$ 620,000

27. Write the numerals in each of the following sentences in scientific notation.
    a. The diameter of Earth is about 12,700,000 m. $1.27 \cdot 10^{7}$
    b. The distance from Pluto to the Sun is about 4,486,000,000 km. $4.486 \cdot 10^{9}$
    c. Each year, about 50,000,000 cans are discarded in the United States. $5 \cdot 10^{7}$

28. Solve the following for x where x is a decimal.
    a. $8.56 = 3 - 2x$ $^-$2.78
    b. $2.3x - 2 = x + 2.55$ 3.5

29. Write the numerals in each of the following sentences in standard form.
    a. The mass of a dust particle is $7.53 \cdot 10^{-10}$ g. 0.000000000753 g
    b. The speed of light is approximately $2.98 \cdot 10^{5}$ km/sec. 298,000 km per sec
    c. Jupiter is approximately $7.7857 \cdot 10^{8}$ km from the Sun. 778,570,000 km

30. Write the results of each of the following in scientific notation.
    a. $(8 \cdot 10^{12})(6 \cdot 10^{15})$ $4.8 \cdot 10^{28}$
    b. $(16 \cdot 10^{12}) \div (4 \cdot 10^{5})$ $4 \cdot 10^{7}$
    c. $(5 \cdot 10^{8})(6 \cdot 10^{9}) \div (15 \cdot 10^{15})$ $2 \cdot 10^{2}$

31. Round each of the following numbers as specified.
    a. 203.651 to the nearest hundred 200
    b. 203.651 to the nearest ten 200
    c. 203.651 to the nearest unit 204
    d. 203.651 to the nearest tenth 203.7
    e. 203.651 to the nearest hundredth 203.65

32. Jane's car travels 243 mi on 12 gal of gas. How many miles to the gallon does her car get? 20.25 mpg

33. Audrey wants to buy some camera equipment to take pictures on her daughter's birthday. To estimate the total cost, she rounds each price to the nearest dollar and adds the rounded prices. What is her estimate for the items listed?

Camera	$54.56
Film	$4.50
Case	$17.85

    $78

34. Estimate the sum or difference in each of the following by using (i) rounding and (ii) front-end estimation. Then perform the computations to see how close your estimates are to the actual answers. Answers vary. Exact answers follow.
    a.   65.84 122.06
         24.29
         12.18
       + 19.75

    b.   89.47 57.31
       − 32.16

    c.   5.85 25.40
         6.13
         9.10
       + 4.32

    d.   223.75 136.15
       − 87.60

35. Find the least and the greatest possible products for the expression using the digits 1 through 9. Each digit may be used only once in each case. $2.3 \cdot 1 = 2.3; 8.7 \cdot 9 = 78.3$

36. Some digits in the following number are covered by squares.
    $4\Box\Box3\Box.\Box\Box8\Box$

    If each of the digits 1 through 9 is used exactly once in the number, determine the greatest possible number. 49,736.5281

37. Iris worked a 40-hour week at $8.25/hr. Mentally compute her salary for the week and explain how you did it. *

38. Mentally compute the number to fill in the blank in each of the following equations.
    a. $8.4 \cdot 6 = 4.2 \cdot$ __12__
    b. $10.2 \div 0.3 = 20.4 \div$ __0.6__
    c. $ab = (a/2) \cdot$ __2b__
    d. $a \div b = (2a) \div$ __2b__

39. Which of the following result in equal quotients?
    i. $7 \div 0.25$
    ii. $70 \div 2.5$
    iii. $0.7 \div 0.25$
    iv. $700 \div 25$ (i), (ii), and (iv) have equal quotients.

40. a. Fill in the parentheses in each of the following to write a true equation.
    $$2 \cdot 1 + 0.25 = (\ \ )^2$$
    $$3 \cdot 2 + 0.25 = (\ \ )^2$$
    Conjecture what the next two equations in this pattern will be. *
    b. Generalize your answer in part (a) by filling in an appropriate expression in the equation
    $$n(n-1) + 0.25 = (\ \ )^2,$$
    where $n = 2, 3, 4, \ldots$ and prove it is true. *

Assessment 7-2B

1. Use base-ten blocks to model 3.7 + 1.22. *
2. Write the decimals as fractions and then add. Write your answer in decimal form.
   a. 5.3 + 13.2 + 0.86 *   **b.** 5.42 + 32.005 *
3. Write the decimals as fractions and then multiply. Write your answer in decimal form. Show all work.
   a. 0.3 · 0.8 *   **b.** 502 · 0.04 *   **c.** 0.004 · 0.06 *
4. Assume the multiplication shown below is correct except for the placement of the decimal point in the product.

   $$564.23 \cdot 6.7 = 3780341$$

   a. Insert the decimal point in the correct position without actually performing the multiplication. Describe the process you used to place the decimal point. *
   b. Describe a second way to determine where to place the decimal point? *
5. John's calculator calculates correctly but does not display decimal points. Use estimation to place the decimal point in the correct position for each of the following.
   a. 5 · 254.15 = 127075   1270.75
   b. 31.6 · 122.34 = 3865944   3865.944
   c. 813.45 ÷ 4.25 = 1914   191.4
6. Multiply each number below by 0.001 using mental computation.
   a. 5280   5.280   **b.** 54.56   0.05456
   c. 0.275   0.000275   **d.** 0.78   0.00078
7. When you multiply a positive decimal less than 1 by a decimal greater than 1, will the result always be greater than 1? Explain.   No, for example 0.5 · 1.5 = 0.75 and 0.75 < 1.
8. At a store, Samuel bought a bouquet for $14.99, a candy bar for 79¢, a memory stick for $49.99, and a bottle of water for $1.49. What was this total? $67.26
9. **a.** Complete the following magic square; that is, make the sum of every row, column, and diagonal the same.

7.5		
3.0	4.8	
	8.4	2.1

7.5	1.2	5.7
3.0	4.8	6.6
3.9	8.4	2.1

   b. If each cell of the original magic square is multiplied by 0.5, is the square still magic? If "yes," what is the sum of each row?   Yes, 7.2
10. Keith bought 30 lb of nuts at $3.00/lb and 20 lb of nuts at $5.00/lb. If he wanted to buy 10 more pounds of a different kind of nut to make the average price per pound equal to $4.50, what price should he pay for the additional 10 lb? $8/lb or $80
11. Automobile engines were once measured in cubic inches (in.³) but are now usually measured in cubic centimeters (cm³). Dan's 1991 Taurus has a 3000 cm³ engine. If 2.54 cm is equivalent to 1 in., approximately how many cubic inches is this?   Approximately 183 in.³
12. A stock's price dropped from $63.28 per share to $27.45. What was the loss on a single share of the stock? $35.83

13. A U.S. $1 bill was valued at 1.046 Canadian dollars on November 10, 2013. What was the value of 28.43 American dollars in Canadian dollars that day?   Approximately $29.74 Canadian
14. If one quart is 4 cups, how many quarts is 18.5 cups?   4.625
15. If each of the following sequences is either arithmetic or geometric, continue the decimal patterns for 3 more terms.
    a. 1, 0.5, 0.25, 0.125,   0.0625, 0.03125, 0.015625
    b. 0.2, 1.5, 2.8, 4.1, 5.4,   6.7, 8, 9.3
16. If the first term of a finite geometric sequence is 0.4 and its ratio is 0.3, what is the sum of the first five terms?   0.57004
17. Interpret the decimal 0.3333333 as a sum of a finite geometric sequence whose first term is 0.3. (*Hint:* Write 0.3333333 as the sum of fractions whose denominators are powers of 10.) *
18. Estimate the placement of each of the following values on the given number line by placing the letter for each computation in the appropriate box.
    a. 0.3 + 0.31 *
    b. 0.3 − 0.31 *

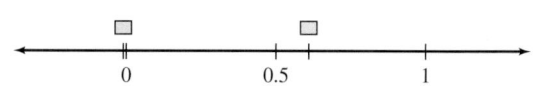

19. Mary Kim invested $964 in 18 shares of stock. A month later, she sold the 18 shares at $61.48 per share. She also invested in 350 shares of another stock for $27,422.50. She sold this stock for $85.35 a share and paid $495 in commissions. What was Mary Kim's profit or loss on the transactions to the nearest dollar?   A profit of $2098
20. Mike's class is building a model of the Willis Tower (formerly Sears Tower). They used a scale of 0.005 for their model; that is, each measure of the actual building is multiplied by 0.005 to find the measure of the corresponding part on the model. If the height of the Willis Tower is 1451 ft, what is the height of the model?   7.255 ft
21. Suppose that to predict how tall a four-year-old will be at age 12, you multiply his or her height by 1.5. If Allie is 105.2 cm when she turns 4, predict how tall she will be when she turns 12.   157.8 cm
22. The value of a yen in Japan in November 2013 was given by the equation $1 = 99.925 yen.
    a. What is the value of $200?   19,985 yen
    b. Pauli saw a shirt marked at 7000 yen in November 2013. What was the price in U.S. dollars?   Approximately $70.05
23. There are 2.54 cm in 1 in.
    a. Estimate the number of inches in 160 cm. *
    b. Compute the number of inches in 160 cm to the nearest hundredth.   Approximately 62.99
    c. Jamie is 182 cm tall. What is her height in inches?
24. One kilometer is approximately 0.62 miles.   Approximately 71.65
    a. Molly ran a 50-km race. How many miles is this?   31
    b. In Canada, the speed limit for a certain stretch of road was marked 120 km/hr. What is the corresponding speed limit in mi/hr?   74.4
    c. If the speed limit is 50 mi/hr, what is it in km/hr?   Approximately 81

25. Convert each of the following to standard numerals:
   a. $3.5 \cdot 10^7$ 35,000,000
   b. $3.5 \cdot 10^{-7}$ 0.00000035
   c. $^-2.4 \cdot 10^{-3}$ $^-0.0024$
26. Write the numerals in each of the following sentences in scientific notation.
   a. The population of Montana is 998,199 people. $9.98199 \cdot 10^5$
   b. The area of North America is 24,490,000 mi^2. $2.449 \cdot 10^7$
27. Solve the following for x where x is a decimal.
   a. $2x + 1.3 = 4.1$ 1.4
   b. $4.2 - 3x = 10.2$ $^-2$
28. Write the numerals in each of the following sentences in standard form.
   a. A computer requires $4.4 \cdot 10^{-6}$ sec to do an addition problem.   0.0000044
   b. There are about $1.99 \cdot 10^4$ km of coastline in the United States.   19,900
   c. Earth has existed for approximately $3 \cdot 10^9$ yr.   *
29. Write the results of each of the following in scientific notation.
   a. $(5 \cdot 10^7)(7 \cdot 10^{12})$ $3.5 \cdot 10^{20}$
   b. $(^-13 \cdot 10^4) \div 65$ $^-2 \cdot 10^3$
   c. $(3 \cdot 10^7)(4 \cdot 10^5) \div (6 \cdot 10^{-7})$ $2 \cdot 10^{19}$
30. Round each of the following numbers as specified.
   a. 715.04 to the nearest hundred   700
   b. 715.04 to the nearest tenth   715.0
   c. 715.04 to the nearest unit   715
   d. 715.04 to the nearest ten   720
   e. 715.04 to the nearest thousand   1000
31. Jane drives at a constant speed of 55.5 mph. How far should she expect to drive in $\frac{3}{4}$ hr?   41.625 miles
32. Use estimation to choose a decimal to multiply by 9 in order to get within 1 of 93. Explain how you made your choice and check your estimate.   *
33. Estimate the sum or difference in each of the following by using (i) rounding and (ii) front-end estimation. Then perform the computation to see how close your estimates are to the actual answers.   Answers vary. Exact answers follow.
   a.   47.62   96.36
        27.99
        13.14
      + 7.61
   b.   79.86   52.49
      − 27.37

c.   5.85   25.35
     6.17
     9.1
   + 4.23

d.   232.65   153.73
   − 78.92

34. Find the least and the greatest possible products for the expression using the digits 1 through 9. Each digit may be used only once in each case.

$$\square . \square \times \square . \square$$

Least: $1.3 \cdot 2.4 = 3.12$ Greatest: $8.7 \cdot 9.6 = 83.52$

35. Some digits in the following number are covered by squares:

$$4\,\square\,\square\,3\,\square\,.\,\square\,\square\,8\,\square$$

If each of the digits 1 through 9 is used exactly once in the number, determine the least possible number.   41,235.6789

36. Iris worked a 40-hour week at \$6.25/hr. Mentally compute her salary for the week and explain how you did it.   *
37. Mentally compute the number to fill in the blank in each of the following equations.
   a. $12.4 \cdot 7 = 6.2 \cdot$ __14__
   b. $12.4 \div 0.2 =$ __6.2__ $\div 0.1$
   c. $ab = (a \cdot 10^{-1}) \cdot$ __10b__
   d. $12.3 = 10^{-2} \cdot$ __1230__
38. Which of the following result in equal quotients?
   (i) $9 \div 0.35$
   (ii) $90 \div 3.5$
   (iii) $900 \div 35$
   (iv) $0.9 \div 0.035$ (i), (ii), (iii), and (iv) have the same quotient.
39. a. Fill in the parentheses in each of the following to write a true equation.

$$1 \cdot 2 + 0.25 = (\ \ )^2$$
$$2 \cdot 3 + 0.25 = (\ \ )^2$$

   Conjecture what the next two equations in this pattern will be. $1.5^2; 2.5^2; 3 \cdot 4 + 0.25 = 3.5^2; 4 \cdot 5 + 0.25 = 4.5^2$
   b. Do the computations to determine if your next two equations are correct.   The above equations are correct.
   c. Generalize your answer in part (a) by filling in an appropriate expression in the equation

$$n(n + 1) + 0.25 = (\ \ )^2$$

   where $n = 1, 2, 3, \ldots$. $n(n + 1) + 0.25 = (n + 0.5)^2$

Mathematical Connections 7-2

Answers to Mathematical Connections can be found in the Answers section at the back of the book.

Reasoning

1. How much greater is $0.76 \cdot 3$ than $0.75 \cdot 3$? How can you tell without actually multiplying each product?
2. How is multiplication of decimals like multiplication of whole numbers? How is it different?
3. Why are estimation skills important in dividing decimals?
4. In the text, multiplication and division were done using both fractional and decimal forms. Discuss the advantages and disadvantages of each.
5. Explain why subtraction of terminating decimals can be accomplished by lining up the decimal points, subtracting as if the numbers were whole numbers, and then placing the decimal point in the difference.
6. Is a product of two positive decimals each less than 1 always less than each of the decimals? Justify your answer.

7. What is the significance of the 1 above the 6 in the addition shown below?

$$\begin{array}{r} \overset{1}{2}1.67 \\ + \ 6.28 \\ \hline 27.95 \end{array}$$

Open-Ended

8. Find several examples of the use of decimals in the newspaper. Tell whether you think the numbers are exact or estimates. Also tell why you think decimals were used instead of fractions.
9. How could a calculator be used to develop or reinforce the understanding of multiplication of decimals?
10. Do you think that decimals should always be converted to fractions to explain computational procedures?

Cooperative Learning

11. In your group, decide on all the prerequisite skills that students need before learning to perform arithmetic operations on decimals.

12. In your group, each person will write a test of 5 questions that examines students' ability to estimate products of decimals. Next, compare the tests to choose the best questions, and then cooperate to devise a single test.

Connecting Mathematics to the Classroom

13. In multiplying $0.125 \cdot 0.08$, Roger knew the rule that says he should multiply $125 \cdot 8$ and then move the decimal point $3 + 2 = 5$ places. When he did the calculation on the calculator he saw the answer was 0.01. He was confused on whether the rule really works. How do you help him?

14. Jamal wants to know why 0.3 and 0.30 are equal. How do you respond?

15. Fred says that to multiply $32.7 \cdot 2.6$, he just multiplies $327 \cdot 26 = 8502$, and then because $33 \cdot 3 = 99$, he records the answer as 85.02. What is your response?

16. A student multiplies $(6.5)(8.5)$ to obtain the following:

$$
\begin{array}{r}
8.5 \\
\times\, 6.5 \\
\hline
4\,2\,5 \\
5\,1\,0 \\
\hline
5\,5.2\,5
\end{array}
$$

However, when the student multiplies $8\frac{1}{2} \cdot 6\frac{1}{2}$, she obtains the following:

$$
\begin{array}{r}
8\frac{1}{2} \\
\times\, 6\frac{1}{2} \\
\hline
4\frac{1}{4} \quad \left(\frac{1}{2} \cdot 8\frac{1}{2}\right) \\
48 \quad (6 \cdot 8) \\
\hline
52\frac{1}{4}
\end{array}
$$

How is this possible?

17. A student tries to calculate $0.999^{10,000}$ on a calculator and finds the answer to be $4.5173346 \cdot 10^{-5}$. The student wonders how it could be that when a number so close to 1 is raised to the 10,000 power the result is a number close to 0. How do you respond?

18. How would you respond to the following situations?

    a. A student claims that $\dfrac{9443}{9444}$ and $\dfrac{9444}{9445}$ are equal because each fraction equals approximately 0.9998941.

    b. Another student claims that the fractions are not equal and wants to know if there is any way the same calculator can determine which is greater.

Review Problems

19. Write 14.0479 in expanded form.

20. Without dividing, determine which of the following represent terminating decimal.

    a. $\dfrac{24}{36}$

    b. $\dfrac{49}{56}$

21. If the denominator of a fraction is 26, is it possible that the fraction could be written as a terminating decimal? Why or why not?

22. $\dfrac{35}{56}$ can be written as a terminating decimal. Explain why.

National Assessments

National Assessment of Educational Progress (NAEP) Questions

It costs $0.25 to operate a clothes dryer for 10 minutes at a laundromat. What is the total cost to operate one clothes dryer for 30 minutes, a second for 40 minutes, and a third for 50 minutes?

A. $3.25   B. $3.00   C. $2.75   D. $2.00   E. $1.20

Add the numbers $\dfrac{7}{10}$, $\dfrac{7}{100}$, and $\dfrac{7}{1,000}$. Write this sum as a decimal.

NAEP, Grade 8, 2007

Sales Tax Table	
Amount of Sales	Amount of Tax
$6.00	$0.36
6.20	0.37
6.40	0.38
6.60	0.40
6.80	0.41
7.00	0.42
7.20	0.43
7.40	0.44
7.60	0.46
7.80	0.47
8.00	0.48

Carlos bought the cereal and milk shown. Use the table to find out the total amount Carlos spent, including tax.
Total amount spent: _____

Show how you found your answer.

NAEP, Grade 4, 2007

Which of these would be easiest to solve by using mental math?

A. $65.12 − $28.19
B. 358×2
C. $1,625 \div 3$
D. $100.00 + $10.00

NAEP, Grade 4, 2007

7-3 Repeating Decimals

Students will be able to understand and explain

- Why repeating decimals occur and how to tell if a decimal will repeat.

- How a fraction can be converted to a repeating decimal and vice versa.

- Ordering repeating decimals efficiently.

- That $0.\overline{9} = 1$ and investigate various ways to show this is true.

CCSS In the grade 7 *Common Core Standards*, we find that students should be able to "convert a rational number to a decimal using long division; know that the decimal form of a rational number terminates in 0s or eventually repeats." (p. 49)

Earlier in the chapter, we developed procedures for converting some rational numbers to decimals. For example, $\frac{7}{8}$ can be written as a terminating decimal as follows:

$$\frac{7}{8} = \frac{7}{2^3} = \frac{7 \cdot 5^3}{2^3 \cdot 5^3} = \frac{875}{1000} = 0.875$$

The decimal for $\frac{7}{8}$ can also be found by division:

$$
\begin{array}{r}
0.875 \\
8\overline{)7.000} \\
\underline{6\,4} \\
60 \\
\underline{56} \\
40 \\
\underline{40} \\
0
\end{array}
$$

However, we showed that $\frac{2}{11}$ was not a terminating decimal. In the following discussion, we investigate nonterminating repeating decimals.

Repeating Decimals

If we use a calculator to find a decimal representation for $\frac{2}{11}$, the calculator may display 0.1818181. It seems that the block of numbers 18 repeats. To examine what digits, if any, the calculator did not display, consider the following division:

$$
\begin{array}{r}
0.18 \\
11\overline{)2.00} \\
\underline{1\,1} \\
90 \\
\underline{88} \\
2
\end{array}
$$

Activity Manual

Use *Repeating Decimals* to discover the decimal equivalent for proper fractions whose denominators contain only 9s or a combination of 9s followed by 0s and to investigate nonterminating decimals.

At this point, if the division is continued, the division pattern repeats, since the remainder 2 divided by 11 repeats the division. Thus, the quotient is 0.181818 . . . . A decimal of this type is a **repeating decimal**, and the repeating block of digits is the **repetend**. The repeating decimal is written $0.\overline{18}$, where the bar indicates that the block of digits underneath is repeated continuously. The **period** of the repetend is the number of digits that repeat. In $0.\overline{18}$ the period is 2. We use the least number of digits possible in the repetend to represent the decimal. For example, the numeral 3.21515151515 . . . is written $3.2\overline{15}$ rather than $3.2\overline{1515}$ or $3.215\overline{1}$. A repeating decimal such as $0.\overline{18}$ is the infinite sum $0.18 + 0.0018 + 0.000018 + \ldots$. Because we can't add infinitely many numbers, we need to define the meaning of such a sum. We interpret it by looking at partial finite sums: $0.18, 0.18 + 0.0018, 0.18 + 0.0018 + 0.000018, \ldots$. The more terms we add, the closer the partial sums get to a specific number; the partial sums given above get closer and closer to $\frac{2}{11}$. The value of the infinite sum is defined as that number.

Example 10

Use a calculator to convert the following to decimals.

a. $\frac{1}{7}$ b. $\frac{2}{13}$ c. $\frac{5}{18}$

Solution   When we use a calculator to divide, it seems that the division pattern repeats.

a. $\frac{1}{7} = 0.\overline{142857}$ b. $\frac{2}{13} = 0.\overline{153846}$ c. $\frac{5}{18} = 0.2\overline{7}$

To see why in Example 10 the division pattern repeats as predicted, consider the following divisions:

a.
$$
\begin{array}{r}
0.142857 \\
7\overline{)1.000000} \\
\underline{7} \\
30 \\
\underline{28} \\
20 \\
\underline{14} \\
60 \\
\underline{56} \\
40 \\
\underline{35} \\
50 \\
\underline{49} \\
1
\end{array}
$$

b.
$$
\begin{array}{r}
0.153846 \\
13\overline{)2.000000} \\
\underline{1\,3} \\
70 \\
\underline{65} \\
50 \\
\underline{39} \\
110 \\
\underline{104} \\
60 \\
\underline{52} \\
80 \\
\underline{78} \\
2
\end{array}
$$

c.
$$
\begin{array}{r}
0.27 \\
18\overline{)5.0000} \\
\underline{36} \\
140 \\
\underline{126} \\
14
\end{array}
$$

In $\frac{1}{7}$, the remainders obtained in the division are 3, 2, 6, 4, 5, and 1. These are all the possible nonzero remainders that can be obtained when dividing by 7. If we had obtained a remainder of 0, the decimal would terminate. Consequently, the seventh division cannot produce a new remainder. Whenever a remainder recurs, the process repeats itself. Using similar reasoning, we could predict that the repetend for $\frac{2}{13}$ could not have more than 12 digits, because there are only 12 possible nonzero remainders. However, one of the remainders could repeat sooner than that, which was actually the case in part (b). In part (c), we could not have more than 17 nonzero re-mainders. The remainder 14 begins repeating after one step, and the repeating part is not directly after the decimal point. In general, if $\frac{a}{b}$ is any rational number in simplest form with $b \neq 0$ and $b > a$, and it does not represent a terminating decimal, the repetend has at most $b - 1$ digits. Therefore, a *rational number may always be represented either as a terminating decimal or as a repeating decimal.*

Students frequently forget to simplify a given rational number before determining the possible length of the repetend. For example, consider $\frac{6}{21}$. Even though the denominator is 21, the maximum possible length of the repetend is not 20. Because $\frac{6}{21} = \frac{2}{7}$, the maximum possible length of the repetend is 6.

▶ NOW TRY THIS 4

a. Write $\frac{1}{9}$ as a decimal. $\frac{1}{9} = 0.\overline{1}$

b. Based on your answer in part (a), mentally compute the decimal representation for each of the following.

i. $\frac{2}{9}$ **ii.** $\frac{3}{9}$ **iii.** $\frac{5}{9}$ **iv.** $\frac{8}{9}$

i. $\frac{2}{9} = 2(0.\overline{1}) = 0.\overline{2}$ ii. $\frac{3}{9} = 3(0.\overline{1}) = 0.\overline{3}$

iii. $\frac{5}{9} = 5(0.\overline{1}) = 0.\overline{5}$ iv. $\frac{8}{9} = 8(0.\overline{1}) = 0.\overline{8}$

Example 11

Use a calculator to convert $\frac{1}{17}$ to a repeating decimal.

Solution   In using a calculator, if we press $\boxed{1}\ \boxed{\div}\ \boxed{1}\ \boxed{7}\ \boxed{=}$, we obtain the following, shown as part of a division problem:

$$\begin{array}{r} 0.0588235 \\ 17\overline{)1.} \end{array}$$

Without knowing whether the calculator has an internal round-off feature and with the calculator's having an eight-digit display, we find the greatest number of digits to be trusted in the quotient is six following the decimal point. (Why?) If we use those six places and multiply 0.058823 times 17, we may continue the operation as follows:

$$\boxed{\cdot}\ \boxed{0}\ \boxed{5}\ \boxed{8}\ \boxed{8}\ \boxed{2}\ \boxed{3}\ \boxed{\times}\ \boxed{1}\ \boxed{7}\ \boxed{=}$$

We then obtain 0.999991, which we may place in the preceding division:

$$\begin{array}{r} 0.0\,5\,8\,8\,2\,3 \\ 1\,7\overline{)1.0\,0\,0\,0\,0\,0} \\ \underline{9\,9\,9\,9\,9\,1} \\ 9 \end{array}$$

What is left to divide is $1 - 0.999991$. Next, we divide 9 by 17 to obtain 0.5294118. Again ignoring the rightmost digit, we continue as before, completing the division as follows, where the repeating pattern is apparent:

$$\begin{array}{r} 0.0588235294117647058823 \\ 17\overline{)1.0000000000000000000000} \\ \underline{999991} \\ 9000000 \\ \underline{8999987} \\ 13000000 \\ \underline{12999985} \\ 15 \end{array}$$

Thus, $\frac{1}{17} = 0.\overline{0588235294117647}$, and the repetend is 16 digits long.

Example 11 illustrates how a calculator with only a finite display of digits can be used to do division beyond what the calculator was designed to do. A common suggestion for elementary students is that they only use the division algorithm selectively to learn the process. The calculator example given and similar ones are used to see if we truly understand the division process and the place values involved along the way.

Writing a Repeating Decimal in the Form $\frac{a}{b}$, where $a, b \in I, b \neq 0$

We have already considered how to write terminating decimals in the form $\frac{a}{b}$, where a, b are integers and $b \neq 0$. For example,

$$0.55 = \frac{55}{10^2} = \frac{55}{100}.$$

To write $0.\overline{5}$ in a similar way, we see that because the repeating decimal has infinitely many digits, the denominator cannot be written as a single power of 10. To overcome this difficulty, we must somehow eliminate the infinitely repeating part of the decimal. If we let $n = 0.\overline{5}$, then the *subgoal* is to write an equation for n without a repeating decimal. It can be shown that $10(0.555\ldots) = 5.555\ldots = 5.\overline{5}$. Hence, $10n = 5.\overline{5}$. Using this information, we subtract the corresponding sides of the equations to obtain an equation whose solution can be written without a repeating decimal.

$$\begin{array}{r} 10n = 5.\overline{5} \\ -\quad n = 0.\overline{5} \\ \hline 9n = 5 \\ n = \dfrac{5}{9} \end{array}$$

Performing the subtraction gives an equation that contains only integers. The repeating blocks "cancel" each other. Thus, $0.\overline{5} = \dfrac{5}{9}$. This result can be checked by performing the division $5 \div 9$.

Suppose a decimal has a repetend of more than one digit such as $0.\overline{235}$. One approach is to multiply the decimal $0.\overline{235}$ by 10^3, since there is a three-digit repetend. Let $n = 0.\overline{235}$. Our *subgoal* is to write an equation for n without the repeating decimal:

$$\begin{array}{r} 1000n = 235.\overline{235} \\ -\quad n = 0.\overline{235} \\ \hline 999n = 235 \\ n = \dfrac{235}{999} \end{array}$$

Thus, $0.\overline{235} = \dfrac{235}{999}$.

We generalize the above method by first noticing that because $0.\overline{5}$ repeats in one-digit blocks to write it in the form $\frac{a}{b}$, we first multiply by 10^1. Because $0.\overline{235}$ repeats in three-digit blocks, we first multiply by 10^3. In general, *if the repetend is immediately to the right of the decimal point, first multiply by 10^m, where m is the number of digits in the repetend, and then continue as in the preceding cases.*

The above approach to finding the fraction equivalent of a repeating decimal is seen on the partial student page shown on page 361.

1-1b Activity Lab

Repeating Decimals

In Lesson 1-1, you learned how to write a terminating decimal as a fraction. You use algebra to write a repeating decimal as a fraction.

EXAMPLE **Writing a Repeating Decimal as a Fraction**

In a recent survey, $0.\overline{45}$ of those asked chose blue as their favorite color. Write $0.\overline{45}$ as a fraction in simplest form.

Step 1 Represent the given decimal with a variable.

$$n = 0.\overline{45}$$

Step 2 Multiply by 10^d, where $d =$ the number of digits that repeat. In this case, multiply by 10^2 or 100. Since 2 digits repeat in $0.\overline{45}$.

$$100n = 45.\overline{45}$$

Step 3 Subtract to eliminate the repeating part.

$$
\begin{aligned}
100n &= 45.454545\ldots \\
- \quad n &= - \ 0.454545\ldots \qquad \leftarrow \text{Use the Subtraction Property of Equality.}\\
99n &= 45.000000\ldots \qquad \leftarrow \text{Simplify.}\\
99n &= 45
\end{aligned}
$$

Step 4 Solve the new equation.

$$\frac{99n}{99} = \frac{45}{99} \qquad \leftarrow \text{Divide each side by 99.}$$

$$n = \frac{45}{99} = \frac{5}{11} \qquad \leftarrow \text{Simplify using the GCF, 9.}$$

● The repeating decimal $0.\overline{45}$ equals $\frac{5}{11}$.

Now, suppose the repeating block does *not* occur immediately after the decimal point. For example, let $n = 2.3\overline{45}$. A strategy for solving this problem is to *change it to a related problem* we know how to solve; that is, change it to a problem where the repeating block immediately follows the decimal point. This becomes a *subgoal*. To accomplish this, we multiply both sides by 10:

$$n = 2.3\overline{45}$$
$$10n = 23.\overline{45}$$

We now proceed as with previous problems. Because $10n = 23.\overline{45}$ and the number of digits in the repetend is 2, we multiply by 10^2 as follows:

$$100(10n) = 2345.\overline{45}$$

Thus,

$$
\begin{aligned}
1000n &= 2345.\overline{45} \\
- \quad 10n &= \quad\ 23.\overline{45} \\
990n &= 2322
\end{aligned}
$$

$$n = \frac{2322}{990}, \text{or } \frac{129}{55}.$$

Hence, $2.3\overline{45} = \dfrac{2322}{990} = \dfrac{129}{55} = 2\dfrac{19}{55}$. We can check that the answer is correct by using a calculator to convert $\dfrac{129}{59}$ back to decimal form.

A Surprising Result

To find the $\frac{a}{b}$ form of $0.\overline{9}$, we proceed as follows. Let $n = 0.\overline{9}$; then $10n = 9.\overline{9}$. Next we subtract and continue to solve for n:

$$10n = 9.\overline{9}$$
$$-\quad n = 0.\overline{9}$$
$$9n = 9$$
$$n = 1$$

Hence, $0.\overline{9} = 1$. This approach to the problem may not be convincing. Another approach to show that $0.\overline{9}$ is really another name for 1 is shown next:

$$\frac{1}{3} = 0.3333\ldots$$
$$+\ \frac{2}{3} = 0.6666\ldots$$
$$1 = 0.9999\ldots \text{ or } 0.\overline{9} = 1$$

This last decimal represents the infinite sum $\dfrac{9}{10} + \dfrac{9}{10^2} + \dfrac{9}{10^3} + \ldots$.

Still another approach is as follows:

$$\frac{1}{9} = 0.11111111\ldots$$
$$1 = 9 \cdot \frac{1}{9} = 9 \cdot 0.11111111\ldots$$
$$= 0.999999\ldots$$

Some may prefer a visual approach to show that $0.\overline{9} = 1$. Consider the number line in Figure 5(a). Most would agree that $0.\overline{9}$ would be between 0.9 and 1.0, so we start there. Then $0.\overline{9}$ is between 0.99 and 1.0, as in Figure 5(b).

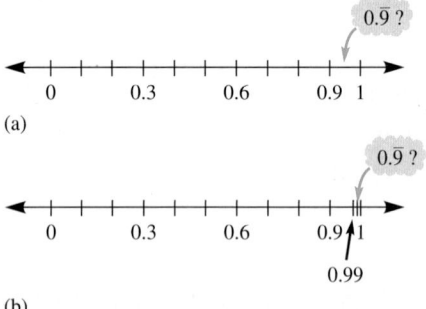

(a)

(b)

Figure 5

Then we can proceed similarly to argue that $0.\overline{9}$ would be between 0.999 and 1, and so forth. Next, it is reasonable to ask if there is any tiny amount a such that $0.\overline{9} + a = 1$? The answer has to be no. (Why?) If there is no such number a, then $0.\overline{9}$ cannot be less than 1. Because $0.\overline{9}$ cannot be greater than 1, we know that $0.\overline{9} = 1$. In more advanced mathematics courses, sums like $0.\overline{9}$, or $0.9 + 0.09 + 0.009 + \ldots$, are defined as the *limits of finite sums*.

Ordering Repeating Decimals

We now know that any repeating decimal can be written as a rational number in the form $\frac{a}{b}$, where $b \neq 0$. Thus, any repeating decimal can be represented on a number line in a manner similar to the way that terminating decimals can be placed on the number line. Also, because we have seen that between any two rational numbers in $\frac{a}{b}$ form there are infinitely many more rational numbers of that form (denseness property), it is reasonable that there should be infinitely many repeating decimals between any two other decimals.

To order repeating decimals, we consider where a repeating decimal might lie on a number line, or we compare them using place value in a manner similar to how we ordered terminating decimals. For example, to order repeating decimals such as $1.\overline{3478}$ and $1.34\overline{7821}$ we write the decimals one under the other, in their equivalent forms without the bars, and line up the decimal points (or place values) as follows:

$$1.34783478\ldots$$
$$1.34782178\ldots$$

The digit to the left of the decimal points and the first four digits after the decimal points are the same in each of the numbers. However, since the digit in the hundred-thousandths place of the top number, which is 3, is greater than the digit 2 in the hundred-thousandths place of the bottom number, $1.\overline{3478}$ is greater than $1.34\overline{7821}$.

It is easy to compare two fractions, such as $\frac{21}{43}$ and $\frac{37}{75}$, using a calculator. We convert each to a decimal and then compare the decimals.

$$\boxed{2}\,\boxed{1}\,\boxed{\div}\,\boxed{4}\,\boxed{3}\,\boxed{=} \rightarrow 0.4883721$$

$$\boxed{3}\,\boxed{7}\,\boxed{\div}\,\boxed{7}\,\boxed{5}\,\boxed{=} \rightarrow 0.4933333$$

Examining the digits in the hundredths place, we see that

$$\frac{37}{75} > \frac{21}{43}.$$

Example 12

Find a rational number in decimal form between $0.\overline{35}$ and $0.\overline{351}$.

Solution First, line up the decimals.

$$0.353535\ldots$$
$$0.351351\ldots$$

Then, to find a decimal between these two, observe that starting from the left, the first place at which the two numbers differ is the thousandths place. Clearly, one decimal between these two is 0.352. Others include 0.3514, 0.35$\overline{15}$, and 0.35136. In fact, there are infinitely many others.

Assessment 7-3A

1. Will $\dfrac{1}{123456789}$ be a terminating decimal? Explain how you know. *

2. **a.** Do $0.45\overline{7}77, 0.45\overline{77}$, and $0.45\overline{7}$ represent different numbers? Explain. *
   b. Which is the preferred form in part (a)? $0.45\overline{7}$
   c. What is the period of the decimal in part (b)?   1

3. Write the first 10 decimal places for each of the following.
   a. $0.\overline{123}$ 0.1231231231
   b. $0.1\overline{23}$ 0.1232323232
   c. $0.12\overline{3}$ 0.1233333333
   d. $0.123\overline{43}$ 0.1234343434

4. Which of the following is greater: $0.3\overline{625}$ or $0.36\overline{25}$? $0.3\overline{625}$

5. Write the following using a bar to indicate the repetend and give the period of each repetend.
   a. $0.4444\ldots$ $0.\overline{4}, 1$
   b. $0.36454545\ldots$ $0.36\overline{45}, 2$
   c. $0.18273273273\ldots$ $0.18\overline{273}, 3$

6. Find the decimal representation for each of the following.
   a. $\dfrac{4}{9}$ $0.\overline{4}$
   b. $\dfrac{2}{7}$ $0.\overline{285714}$
   c. $\dfrac{3}{11}$ $0.\overline{27}$
   d. $\dfrac{1}{15}$ $0.0\overline{6}$
   e. $\dfrac{2}{75}$ $0.02\overline{6}$
   f. $\dfrac{1}{99}$ $0.\overline{01}$
   g. $\dfrac{5}{6}$ $0.8\overline{3}$
   h. $\dfrac{1}{13}$ $0.\overline{076923}$
   i. $\dfrac{1}{21}$ $0.\overline{047619}$
   j. $\dfrac{3}{19}$ $0.\overline{157894736842105263}$

7. Convert each of the following repeating decimals to $\frac{a}{b}$ form, where a, b are integers and $b \neq 0$.
   a. $0.\overline{4}$ $\frac{4}{9}$
   b. $0.\overline{61}$ *
   c. $1.3\overline{96}$ $\frac{461}{330}$
   d. $0.5\overline{5}$ $\frac{5}{9}$
   e. $^-2.3\overline{4}$ $\frac{^-211}{90}$
   f. $^-0.0\overline{2}$ *

8. Express 1 min as a repeating decimal part of an hour. $0.01\overline{6}$ hr

9. Order the following decimals from greatest to least.   *

   $$^-1.45\overline{4}, ^-1.\overline{454}, ^-1.4\overline{5}, ^-1.4\overline{54}, ^-1.454$$

10. Find three more terms for the following sequence.   *

    $$0, 0.5, 0.\overline{6}, 0.75, 0.8, 0.8\overline{3}, \underline{\qquad}, \underline{\qquad}, \underline{\qquad}$$

11. Write $(0.\overline{5})^2$ as a repeating decimal. $0.\overline{308641975}$

12. Give an argument why $3\frac{1}{7}$ must be a repeating decimal.   *

13. Suppose $a = 0.\overline{32}$ and $b = 0.\overline{123}$. Find $a + b$ by adding from left to right. How many digits are in the repetend of the sum? $0.\overline{446355}, 6$

14. Explain whether a terminating decimal could ever be written as a repeating decimal.   *

15. Find three decimals between each of the following pairs of decimals.   Answers vary. For example, 3.221, 3.2211, 3.22111.
    a. $3.\overline{2}$ and 3.22
    b. $462.\overline{24}$ and 462.243 Answers vary. For example, 462.2425, 462.2426, 462.2427

16. Find the decimal halfway between the decimals $0.\overline{4}$ and 0.5. $0.47\overline{2}$

17. a. Find three rational numbers between $\frac{3}{4}$ and $0.7\overline{5}$.   *

    b. Find three rational numbers between $\frac{1}{3}$ and $0.3\overline{4}$.   *

18. a. What is the 21st digit in the decimal expansion of $\frac{3}{7}$?   8

    b. What is the 5280th digit in the decimal expansion of $\frac{1}{17}$?   7

19. a. Write each of the following as a fraction in the form $\frac{a}{b}$, where a and b are integers and $b \neq 0$.
    i. $0.\overline{1}$ $\frac{1}{9}$
    ii. $0.\overline{01}$ $\frac{1}{99}$
    iii. $0.\overline{001}$ $\frac{1}{999}$

    b. What fraction would you expect represents $0.\overline{0001}$?   *

    c. Mentally compute the decimal equivalent for $\frac{1}{90}$. $0.0\overline{1}$

20. Use the fact that $0.\overline{9} = 1$ to find the terminating decimal equal to the following.
    a. $0.0\overline{9}$ 0.1
    b. $0.3\overline{9}$ 0.4
    c. $9.\overline{99}$ 10

21. Use the fact that $0.\overline{1} = \frac{1}{9}$ to convert each of the following into rational numbers.
    a. $0.\overline{2}$ $\frac{2}{9}$
    b. $0.\overline{3}$ $\frac{3}{9}$ or $\frac{1}{3}$
    c. $9.\overline{9}$ 10

22. Use the fact that $0.\overline{01} = \frac{1}{99}$ and $0.\overline{001} = \frac{1}{999}$ to mentally convert each of the following to rational numbers. $\frac{3}{}$
    a. $0.\overline{05}$ $\frac{5}{99}$
    b. $0.\overline{003}$ $\frac{3}{999}$ or $\frac{1}{333}$

23. Find the sum of the finite geometric sequence whose first term is 0.4, whose ratio is 0.5, and which has five terms. 0.775

24. Find a rational number in the form $\frac{a}{b}$, where a and b are integers and $b \neq 0$, for the following repeating decimals.
    a. $0.2\overline{9}$ $\frac{3}{10}$
    b. $2.0\overline{29}$ $\frac{2009}{990}$

25. Consider the repeating decimals $0.\overline{235}$ and $0.2\overline{356}$. How many places do you expect in the repetend of the sum of the two decimals? Why?   12, to make the repeating parts match

26. Find values of x such that each of the following is true. Write answers both in $\frac{a}{b}$ form, where a and b are integers and $b \neq 0$, and as decimals.
    a. $1 - 3x = 8$ $\frac{^-7}{3}$ or $^-2.\overline{3}$
    b. $1 = 3x + 8$ Same as a.
    c. $1 = 8 - 3x$ $\frac{7}{3}$ or $2.\overline{3}$

27. If a, b, and c are digits, write $0.\overline{abc}$ as a fraction. $\frac{abc}{999}$

28. What is the repetend of $\frac{1}{333,333}$? $0.\overline{000003}$

29. If $\frac{9}{23} = 0.\overline{3913043478260869565217}$, what is the 100th digit in the decimal expansion?   6

Assessment 7-3B

1. Will $\frac{3}{1234567}$ be a terminating decimal? Explain how you know.   *

2. a. Do $0.34\overline{666}, 0.34\overline{66}$, and $0.34\overline{6}$ represent different numbers? Explain.   *
   b. Which is the preferred form in part (a)? $0.34\overline{6}$
   c. What is the period of the decimal in part (a)?   1

3. Write the first 10 decimal places for each of the following.
   a. $0.\overline{246}$ 0.2462462462
   b. $0.2\overline{46}$ 0.2464646464
   c. $0.24\overline{6}$ 0.2466666666
   d. $0.24\overline{68}$ 0.2468686868

4. Which of the following is greater: $0.5\overline{789}$ or $0.57\overline{89}$? $0.5\overline{789}$

5. Write the following using a bar to indicate the repetend and give the period of each repetend.
   a. $0.9999\ldots$ $0.\overline{9}, 1$
   b. $0.567323232\ldots$ $0.567\overline{32}, 2$
   c. $0.1827482748274\ldots$ $0.18\overline{2748}, 4$

6. Find the decimal representation for each of the following.
   a. $\frac{2}{3}$ $0.\overline{6}$
   b. $\frac{7}{9}$ $0.\overline{7}$
   c. $\frac{1}{24}$ $0.041\overline{6}$
   d. $\frac{3}{60}$ 0.05
   e. $\frac{2}{99}$ $0.\overline{02}$
   f. $\frac{7}{6}$ $1.1\overline{6}$
   g. $\frac{2}{21}$ $0.\overline{095238}$
   h. $\frac{4}{19}$ *

7. Convert each of the following repeating decimals to $\frac{a}{b}$ form, where a and b are integers and $b \neq 0$.
   a. $0.\overline{7}$ $\frac{7}{9}$
   b. $0.\overline{46}$ $\frac{46}{99}$
   c. $2.\overline{37}$ $\frac{235}{99}$
   d. $2.3\overline{4}$ $\frac{211}{90}$
   e. $^-4.\overline{34}$ $\frac{^-391}{90}$
   f. $^-0.0\overline{3}$ $\frac{^-1}{30}$

8. Express 1 sec as a repeating decimal part of an hour. $0.0002\overline{7}$ hr

9. Order the following decimals from least to greatest.   *

   $$^-4.3\overline{4}, ^-4.\overline{34}, ^-4.3\overline{4}, ^-4.3\overline{43}, ^-4.4\overline{34}$$
   $$^-4.4\overline{34}, ^-4.3\overline{4}, ^-4.\overline{34} = ^-4.3\overline{4}, ^-4.3\overline{43}, ^-4.34$$

10. List the next three terms in the following arithmetic sequence.

    $$0, 0.\overline{3}, 0.\overline{6}, 1, 1.\overline{3}, \quad 1.\overline{6}, 2, 2.\overline{3}$$

11. Write $0.4\overline{9} \cdot 0.\overline{62}$ as a repeating decimal. $0.\overline{31}$

12. Give an argument why $\frac{2}{26}$ must be a repeating decimal. What can you say about length of the repetend without performing the division.?   *

13. Find $a + b$ if $a = 1.2\overline{34}$ and $b = 0.\overline{1234}$. Is the answer a rational number? How many digits are in the repetend?   *

14. Explain whether a repeating decimal could ever be written as a terminating decimal.
Answers vary. Yes if, and only if, the repeating part is 0 or 9. For example, $0.5000\ldots = 0.49999\ldots = 0.5$.

15. Find three decimals between each of the following pairs of decimals.
   a. $4.\overline{3}$ and 4.3 *Answers vary; for example, 4.31, 4.32, and 4.33.*
   b. $203.\overline{76}$ and $203.\overline{7}$ *

16. Find the decimal halfway between $0.\overline{9}$ and 1.1.   *1.05*

17. Find three rational numbers between the following.
   a. $\frac{2}{3}$ and 0.67 *Answers vary.*
   For example, 0.6671,
   b. $\frac{2}{3}$ and $0.6\overline{7}$ *Same as a.*
   0.6672, and 0.6673

18. What is the 23rd decimal in the expansion of $\frac{1}{17}$?   *5*

19. a. Write each of the following as a fraction in the form $\frac{a}{b}$, where a and b are integers and $b \neq 0$.   *
   i. $0.\overline{2}$ ii. $0.0\overline{2}$ iii. $0.00\overline{2}$
   b. What fraction would you expect represents $0.000\overline{2}$?   *
   c. Mentally compute the decimal equivalent for $\frac{4}{90}$.   *$0.0\overline{4}$*

20. Use the fact that $0.\overline{9} = 1$, to find the terminating decimal equal to the following.
   a. $1.\overline{9}$ *2*   b. $0.00\overline{9}$ *0.01*   c. $0.3\overline{9}$ *0.4*

21. Use the fact that $0.\overline{1} = \frac{1}{9}$, $0.\overline{01} = \frac{1}{99}$, and $0.\overline{001} = \frac{1}{999}$ to convert each of the following mentally to the form $\frac{a}{b}$, where a and b are integers and $b \neq 0$.
   a. $0.\overline{4}$ *$\frac{4}{9}$*   b. $0.\overline{12}$ *$\frac{12}{99}$, or $\frac{4}{33}$*   c. $0.\overline{111}$ *$\frac{111}{999}$, or $\frac{1}{9}$*

22. Use the fact that $0.\overline{01} = \frac{1}{99}$ and $0.\overline{001} = \frac{1}{999}$ to convert each of the following to a rational number $\frac{a}{b}$, where a and b are integers and $b \neq 0$.
   a. $3.\overline{25}$ *$\frac{322}{99}$*   b. $3.\overline{125}$ *$\frac{3122}{999}$*

23. Find the sum of the finite geometric sequence whose first term is 0.1, whose ratio is 0.3, and which has four terms.   *0.1417*

24. Find the $\frac{a}{b}$ form, where a and b are integers and $b \neq 0$, for each of the following.
   a. $0.\overline{29}$ *$\frac{29}{99}$*   b. $0.0002\overline{9}$ *$\frac{29}{99,000}$*

25. Consider the repeating decimals $0.\overline{23}$ and $0.\overline{235}$. How many places do you expect in the repetend of the sum of the two decimals? Why?   *6; to make the repeating parts match*

26. Find values of x such that each of the following is true. Write answers both in $\frac{a}{b}$ form, where a and b are integers and $b \neq 0$, and as decimals.
   a. $3x = 8$ *$\frac{8}{3}$, or $2.\overline{6}$*   b. $3x + 1 = 8$ *$\frac{7}{3}$, or $2.\overline{3}$*   c. $3x - 1 = 8$ *$\frac{3}{1}$, or 3*

27. If a and b are digits, write $0.\overline{ab}$ as a fraction.   *$\frac{ab}{99}$*

28. What is the repetend of $\frac{1}{333,333,333}$?   *0.000000003*

29. If $\frac{9}{23} = 0.\overline{3913043478260869565217}$, what is the 900th digit in the decimal expansion?   *2*

Mathematical Connections 7-3

Answers to Mathematical Connections can be found in the Answers section at the back of the book.

Reasoning

1. a. If a grocery store advertised three lemons for $2.00, what is the cost of one lemon?
   b. If you choose to buy exactly one lemon at the cost given in part (a), what will the grocery store charge?
   c. How is the store treating the repeating decimal cost of one lemon?
   d. Explain whether or not a grocery store would ever use a repeating decimal as a cost for an item.
   e. Explain whether you think cash registers ever work with repeating decimals.

2. A friend claims that every finite decimal is equal to some infinite decimal. Is the claim true? Explain why or why not.

3. Some addition problems are easier to compute with fractions and some are easier to do with decimals. For example,
   $\frac{1}{7} + \frac{5}{7}$ is easier to compute than $0.\overline{142857} + 0.\overline{714285}$
   and $0.4 + 0.25$ is easier to compute than $\frac{2}{5} + \frac{1}{4}$. Describe situations in which you think it would be easier to compute the additions with fractions than with decimals, and vice versa.

4. Find decimal expansions of $\frac{1}{11}$, $\frac{1}{111}$, and $\frac{1}{1111}$, and then guess the decimal expansion of $\frac{1}{11111}$. Explain your reasoning and check your answer with a calculator.

Open-Ended

5. Notice that $\frac{1}{7} = 0.\overline{142857}$, $\frac{2}{7} = 0.\overline{285714}$, $\frac{3}{7} = 0.\overline{428571}$, $\frac{4}{7} = 0.\overline{571428}$, $\frac{5}{7} = 0.\overline{714285}$, and $\frac{6}{7} = 0.\overline{857142}$.
   a. Describe a common property that all of these repeating decimals share.
   b. Suppose you memorized the decimal form for $\frac{1}{7}$. How could you quickly find the answers for the decimal expansions of the five fractions above? Describe as many ways as you can.
   c. Find some other fractions that behave like $\frac{1}{7}$. In what way is the behavior similar?

6. a. Multiply each of the following, giving your answer as a decimal in simplest form.
      i. $2 \cdot 0.\overline{3}$ ii. $3 \cdot 0.\overline{3}$ iii. $3 \cdot 0.\overline{35}$
   b. Explain whether the traditional algorithm for multiplying decimals can be used for multiplying repeating decimals.
   c. Explain whether repeating decimals can be multiplied.

7. a. Does your calculator allow you to enter repeating decimals? If so, in what form?
   b. Explain whether repeating decimal arithmetic can be performed on your calculator.

8. Explain whether we would rather have the solution to $3x = 7$ expressed as a fraction or as a repeating decimal.

Cooperative Learning

9. Choose a partner and play the following game. Write a repeating decimal of the form $0.\overline{abcdef}$. Tell your partner that the decimal is of that form but do not reveal the specific values for the digits. Your partner's objective is to find your repeating decimal. Your partner is allowed to ask you for the values of six digits that are at the 100th or greater places after the decimal point but not the digits in consecutive places. For example, your opponent may ask for the 100th, 200th, 300th, ... digits but may not ask for the 100th and 101st digit. Switch roles at least once. After playing the game, discuss in your group a strategy for asking your partner the least number of questions that will allow you to find your partner's repetend.

Connecting Mathematics to the Classroom

10. A student argues that repeating decimals are of little value because no calculator will handle computations with repeating decimals, and in real life decimals do not have an infinite number of digits. How do you respond?
11. A student asks if a sum of two repeating decimals is always a repeating decimal. How do you respond?
12. A student needs to find $0.3333 \cdot 48$ without using a calculator. She finds $\frac{1}{3}$ of 48 and gets 16 as the answer. How do you respond?
13. Joe says terminating decimals are those with repetend 0 and nonterminating decimals are those with nonzero repetends. Is this correct? Explain.

14. Bob uses a calculator to compute $\frac{1}{7}$ as 0.142857142. He then multiplies this decimal by 2 to get the decimal approximation for $\frac{2}{7}$. Is this correct? How would you help him?

15. A student says that $0.\overline{4} = \frac{4}{9}$ and $0.\overline{44} = \frac{44}{99}$, so $0.\overline{4} \neq 0.\overline{44}$. How do you respond?

Review Problems

16. Jill received a bonus totaled $27,849.50 and deposited it in a new checking account. She wrote checks for $1520.63, $723.30, and $2843.62. What was the balance in her new checking account?
17. The speed of light is approximately 186,000 mi/sec. It takes light from the nearest star, Alpha Centauri, approximately 4 years to reach Earth. How many miles away is Alpha Centauri from Earth? Express the answer in scientific notation.
18. Find the product of 0.22 and 0.35 on a calculator. How does the placement of the decimal point in the answer on the calculator compare with the placement of the decimal point using the rule in this chapter? Explain.
19. a. Find a number to add to $^{-}0.023$ to obtain a sum greater than 3 but less than 4.
    b. Find a number to subtract from $^{-}0.023$ to obtain a difference greater than 3 but less than 4.
    c. Find a number to multiply times 0.023 to obtain a product greater than 3 but less than 4.
    d. Find a number to divide into 0.023 to obtain a quotient greater than 3 but less than 4.

7-4 Percents and Interest

7-4 Objectives

Students will be able to understand and explain

- Fractions, decimals, and percents as representations of rational numbers with conversions from one form to another.

- Proportional relationships to solve percent problems.

- Techniques to solve problems including discounts, interest, compound interest, and percent increase and percent decrease.

- Strategies for percent mental computation and estimation.

CCSS In the grade 7 *Common Core Standards*, we find the following:

> Students develop a unified understanding of number, recognizing fractions, decimals (that have a finite or a repeating decimal representation), and percents as different representations of rational numbers. (p. 46)

Percents are very useful in conveying information. People hear that there is a 60% chance of rain or that their savings account is drawing 2% annual interest. Percents are special kinds of fractions—namely, fractions with a denominator of 100. The word **percent** comes from the Latin phrase *per centum*, which means *per hundred*. A bank that pays 2% annual simple interest on a savings account pays $2 for each $100 in the account for one year; that is, it pays 2/100 of whatever amount is in the account for one year. The symbol % indicates percent; 2% means 2 for each 100. Hence, to find 2% of $400, we determine how many hundreds are in 400. There are 4 hundreds in 400, so 2% of 400 is $2 \cdot 4 = 8$. Therefore, 2% of $400 = $8.

Definition of Percent

$$n\% = \frac{n}{100}, \text{ where } n \text{ is any nonnegative number.}$$

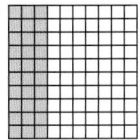

Figure 6

Thus, $n\%$ of a quantity is $\dfrac{n}{100}$ of the quantity, or $\dfrac{n}{100}$ times the quantity. Therefore, 1% is one hundredth of a whole, and 100% represents the entire quantity. Similarly, 200% represents $\dfrac{200}{100}$, or 2, times, the given quantity. Percents can be illustrated by using a hundreds grid. For example, in Figure 6, because 30 out of the 100, or $\dfrac{30}{100}$, of the squares are shaded, we say that 30% of the grid is shaded. Likewise we say that 70% of the grid is not shaded.

▶ **NOW TRY THIS 5**

NTT 5: (a) $\dfrac{11}{20}$, 55%

(b) $\dfrac{3}{5}$, 60%

(c) $\dfrac{13}{25}$, 52%

(d) $\dfrac{1}{5}$, 20%

In each part of Figure 7 write the fraction that represents the shaded portion of the large square in lowest terms and its equivalent percent.

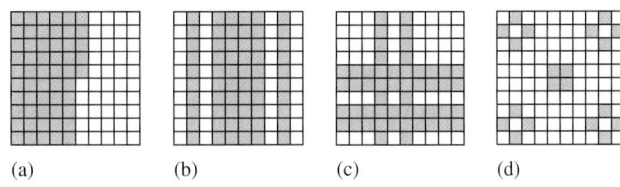

(a)   (b)   (c)   (d)

Figure 7

E-Manipulative Activity

For more help with the percents using a hundreds grid, see the *Percents* module.

Because $n\% = \dfrac{n}{100}$, one way to convert a number to a percent is to write it as a fraction with denominator 100; the numerator gives the amount of the percent. For example,

$\dfrac{3}{4} = \dfrac{3 \cdot 25}{4 \cdot 25} = \dfrac{75}{100}$. Hence, $\dfrac{3}{4} = 75\%$, but $\dfrac{3}{4}\% = \dfrac{\frac{3}{4}}{100} = \dfrac{0.75}{100} = 0.0075$.

Example 13

Write each of the following as a percent.

  a. 0.03   **b.** $0.\overline{3}$ **c.** 1.2   **d.** 0.00042

  e. 1   **f.** $\dfrac{3}{5}$ **g.** $\dfrac{2}{3}$ **h.** $2\dfrac{1}{7}$

Activity Manual

Use *What is Percent?* to develop the concept of percent and the relationships among fractions, decimals, and percents.

Solution

a. $0.03 = \dfrac{3}{100} = 3\%$

b. $0.\overline{3} = \dfrac{33.\overline{3}}{100} = 33.\overline{3}\%$

c. $1.2 = \dfrac{120}{100} = 120\%$

d. $0.00042 = \dfrac{0.042}{100} = 0.042\%$

e. $1 = \dfrac{100}{100} = 100\%$

f. $\dfrac{3}{5} = \dfrac{3 \cdot 20}{5 \cdot 20} = \dfrac{60}{100} = 60\%$

g. $\dfrac{2}{3} = 100\left[\dfrac{\left(\frac{2}{3}\right)}{100}\right] = \dfrac{\left(\frac{200}{3}\right)}{100} = \dfrac{66.\overline{6}}{100} = 66.\overline{6}\%$

h. $2\dfrac{1}{7} = 100\left[\dfrac{\left(2\frac{1}{7}\right)}{100}\right] = \dfrac{\left(\frac{1500}{7}\right)}{100} = \dfrac{1500}{7}\%$ or $214\dfrac{2}{7}\%$.

Still another way to convert a number to a percent is to recall that $1 = 100\%$. Thus, for example, $\dfrac{3}{4} = \dfrac{3}{4} \cdot 1 = \dfrac{3}{4} \cdot 100\% = 75\%$.

The % symbol is crucial in identifying the meaning of a number. For example, $\dfrac{1}{2}$ and $\dfrac{1}{2}\%$ are different numbers: $\dfrac{1}{2} = 50\%$, which is not equal to $\dfrac{1}{2}\% = 0.5\%$. Similarly, 0.01 is different from 0.01%, which is 0.0001.

Converting percents to decimals can be done by writing the percent as a fraction in the form $\dfrac{n}{100}$ and then converting the fraction to a decimal. Percents less than 1% and percents greater than 100% are examined in Example 14.

Example 14

Write each of the following percents as a decimal.

a. 5%   **b.** 6.3%   **c.** 100%   **d.** 250%   **e.** $\dfrac{2}{3}\%$ **f.** $33\dfrac{1}{3}\%$

Solution

a. $5\% = \dfrac{5}{100} = 0.05$ **b.** $6.3\% = \dfrac{6.3}{100} = 0.063$

c. $100\% = \dfrac{100}{100} = 1$ **d.** $250\% = \dfrac{250}{100} = 2.5$

e. $\dfrac{2}{3}\% = \dfrac{\frac{2}{3}}{100} = \dfrac{0.\overline{6}}{100} = 0.00\overline{6}$ **f.** $33\dfrac{1}{3}\% = \dfrac{33\frac{1}{3}}{100} = \dfrac{33.\overline{3}}{100} = 0.3\overline{3}$

Another approach to converting a percent to a decimal is to first convert 1% to a decimal. Because $1\% = \dfrac{1}{100} = 0.01$, we conclude that $5\% = 5 \cdot 1\% = 5 \cdot 0.01 = 0.05$ and that $6.3\% = 6.3 \cdot 0.01 = 0.063$.

NTT 6: **a.** Answers vary. For example, most calculators will convert the decimal form of a number to a percent by moving the decimal point two places to the left. Other calculators actually place a $\boxed{\%}$ symbol in the display when the % key is pushed.

▶ **NOW TRY THIS 6**

a. Investigate how your calculator handles percents and explain what the calculator does when the $\boxed{\%}$ key is pushed.

b. Use your calculator to change $\dfrac{1}{3}$ to a percent. $33.\overline{3}\%$

Applications Involving Percents

 In grade 6 *Common Core Standard*, we find that students are expected to be able to accomplish the following:

Find a percent of a quantity as a rate per 100 (e.g., 30% of a quantity means 30/100 times the quantity); solve problems involving finding the whole, given a part and the percent. (p. 42)

Application problems that involve percents usually take one of the following forms:

1. Finding a percent of a number
2. Finding what percent one number is of another
3. Finding a number when a percent of that number is known

Before we consider examples illustrating these forms, recall what it means to find a fraction "of" a number. For example, $\frac{2}{3}$ of 70 equals $\frac{2}{3} \cdot 70$. Similarly, to find 40% of 70, we have $\frac{40}{100}$ of 70, which equals $\frac{40}{100} \cdot 70$, or $0.40 \cdot 70 = 28$.

A *percent bar* can be used as a model for understanding what 100% of a number means as well as understanding other percents. In Figure 8, consider the percent bar that represents 100% of the whole with 40% of the whole shaded. Note that 100% of the bar represents 70.

| | Bar |
Percentage	Length
0%	0
10%	
20%	
30%	
40%	?
50%	35
60%	
70%	
80%	
90%	
100%	70

Table 3

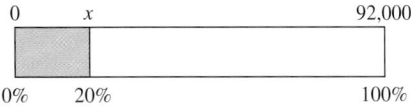

Figure 8

Also, half of the percent bar (50% denoted by the dotted segment) represents half of 70, or 35. Thus, we know that 40% of the bar (or 40% of 70) is less than 35. In fact, if the bottom of the bar is thought of as being marked off in 1% intervals, there are 100 intervals marking whole numbers of percentages. If at the same time the top of the bar is considered to be marked in intervals of 1, there would be only 70 intervals marked at the bottom.

Suppose in Table 3 we know that 0% of 70 is 0, 50% of 70 is 35, and 100% of 70 is 70. What percentages of 70 are 10%, 20%, 30%, and so on? If there are 100 intervals marking percentages compared to only 70 intervals marking the corresponding length, there must be a ratio of $\frac{70}{100}$, or $\frac{7}{10}$. Thus, 10% of 70 is 7, 20% of 70 is $2 \cdot 7$, or 14, and so on. Hence, 40% of 70 is $4 \cdot 7$, or 28.

Percent bars for the three types of percent problems are shown on the partial student page on page 370.

Example 15

A house that sells for $92,000 requires a 20% down payment. What is the amount of the down payment?

Solution   The amount of the down payment is 20% of $92,000 $= 0.20 \cdot \$92{,}000 = \$18{,}400$.
A percent bar for this example is given in Figure 9.

$$0 \qquad x \qquad\qquad\qquad\qquad 92{,}000$$

$$0\% \qquad 20\% \qquad\qquad\qquad 100\%$$

Figure 9

The percent bar leads to the following proportion.

$$\frac{x}{20} = \frac{92{,}000}{100}$$

$$100x = 92{,}000(20)$$

$$x = \$18{,}400$$

School Book Page   Key Concepts

KEY CONCEPTS   Percents and Proportions

Finding a Percent	**Finding a Part**	**Finding a Whole**
What percent of 25 is 5?	What is 20% of 25?	20% of what is 5?

$$\frac{5}{25} = \frac{n}{100}$$

$$n = 20$$

5 is 20% of 25.

$$\frac{n}{25} = \frac{20}{100}$$

$$n = 5$$

5 is 20% of 25.

$$\frac{5}{n} = \frac{20}{100}$$

$$n = 25$$

20% of 25 is 5.

Example 16

If Alberto has 45 correct answers on an 80-question test, what percent of his answers are correct?

Solution   Alberto has $\frac{45}{80}$ of the answers correct. To find the percent of correct answers, we need to convert $\frac{45}{80}$ to a percent. We can do this by multiplying the fraction by 100 and attaching the % symbol as follows:

$$\frac{45}{80} = 100 \cdot \frac{45}{80}\%$$

$$= 56.25\%$$

Thus, 56.25% of the answers are correct.

A percent bar for this example is given in Figure 10.

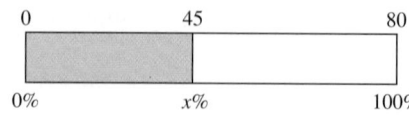

Figure 10

The percent bar leads to the following proportion.

$$\frac{45}{x} = \frac{80}{100}$$

$$80x = 45(100)$$

$$x = 56.25$$

Example 17

Forty-two percent of the parents of the schoolchildren in the Paxson School District are employed at Di Paloma University. If the number of parents employed by the university is 168, how many parents are in the school district?

Solution   Let n be the number of parents in the school district. Then 42% of n is 168. We translate this information into an equation and solve for n.

$$42\% \text{ of } n = 168$$

$$\frac{42}{100}n = 168$$

$$0.42n = 168$$

$$n = \frac{168}{0.42} = 400$$

There are 400 parents in the school district.

A percent bar for this example is given in Figure 11.

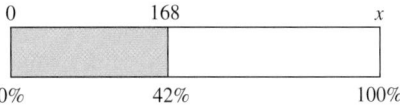

Figure 11

The percent bar leads to the following proportion.

$$\frac{168}{42} = \frac{x}{100}$$

$$42x = 168(100)$$

$$x = 400$$

We can also solve Example 17 as follows:

$$42\% \text{ of } n \text{ is } 168$$

$$1\% \text{ of } n \text{ is } \frac{168}{42}$$

$$100\% \text{ of } n \text{ is } 100\left(\frac{168}{42}\right)$$

Therefore,

$$n = 100\left(\frac{168}{42}\right), \text{ or } 400.$$

Example 18

Kelly bought a bicycle and a year later sold it for 20% less than what she paid for it. If she sold the bike for \$144, what did she pay for it?

Solution   We are looking for the original price P that Kelly paid for the bike. We know that she sold the bike for \$144 and that this included a 20% loss. Thus, we can write the following equation:

$$144 = P - \text{Kelly's loss}$$

Because Kelly's loss is 20% of P, we proceed as follows:

$$144 = P - 20\% \cdot P$$
$$144 = P - 0.20P$$
$$144 = (1 - 0.20)P$$
$$144 = 0.80P$$
$$\frac{144}{0.80} = P$$
$$180 = P$$

Thus, she paid $180 for the bike.

A percent bar for this example is given in Figure 12.

Figure 12

The percent bar leads to the following proportion.

$$\frac{144}{80} = \frac{x}{100}$$
$$80x = 144(100)$$
$$x = 180$$

Alternatively, we can argue that since Kelly lost 20% of the original price, she sold the bike for $100\% - 20\%$ or 80% of the original price. Thus,

$$144 = 80\% \text{ of } P$$
$$144 = 0.8P$$
$$P = 180.$$

We can also approach the problem as follows:

$$80\% \text{ of } P \text{ is } 144.$$
$$1\% \text{ of } P \text{ is } \frac{144}{80}.$$
$$100\% \text{ of } P \text{ is } 100 \cdot \frac{144}{80} \text{ or } 180.$$

Example 19

Westerner's Clothing Store advertised a suit for 10% off, for a savings of $15. Later, the manager marked the suit at 30% off the original price. What is the amount of the current discount?

Solution A 10% discount amounts to a $15 savings. We could find the amount of the current discount if we knew the original price P. Thus, finding the original price becomes our *subgoal*. Because 10% of P is $15, we have the following:

$$10\% \cdot P = 15$$
$$0.10P = 15$$
$$P = 150$$

To find the current discount, we calculate 30% of $150. Because $0.30 \cdot \$150 = \$45$, the amount of the 30% discount is $45.

In the *Looking Back* stage of problem solving, we check the answer and look for other ways to solve the problem. A different approach leads to a more efficient solution and confirms the answer. If 10% of the price is $15, then 30% of the price is 3 times $15, or $45.

Mental Math with Percents

Mental math may be helpful when working with percents. Below we give two techniques.

1. *Using fraction equivalents*
   Knowing fraction equivalents for some percents can make some computations easier. Table 4 gives several fraction equivalents.

Table 4

Percent	25%	50%	75%	$33\frac{1}{3}$%	$66\frac{2}{3}$%	10%	1%
Fraction Equivalent	$\frac{1}{4}$	$\frac{1}{2}$	$\frac{3}{4}$	$\frac{1}{3}$	$\frac{2}{3}$	$\frac{1}{10}$	$\frac{1}{100}$

These equivalents can be used in such computations as the following.

$$50\% \text{ of } 80 = \left(\frac{1}{2}\right)80 = 40$$

$$66\frac{2}{3}\% \text{ of } 90 = \left(\frac{2}{3}\right)90 = 60$$

2. *Using a known percent*
   Frequently, we may not know a percent of something, but we know a close percent of it. For example, to find 55% of 62, we might do the following.

$$50\% \text{ of } 62 = \left(\frac{1}{2}\right)(62) = 31$$

$$5\% \text{ of } 62 = \left(\frac{1}{2}\right)(10\%)(62) = \left(\frac{1}{2}\right)(6.2) = 3.1$$

Adding, we see that 55% of 62 is $31 + 3.1 = 34.1$.

Estimations with Percents

Estimations with percents can be used to determine whether answers are reasonable. Here are two examples.

1. To estimate 27% of 598, note that 27% of 598 is a little more than 25% of 598, but 25% of 598 is approximately the same as 25% of 600, or $\frac{1}{4}$ of 600, or 150. Here, we adjusted 27% downward and 598 upward, so 150 should be a reasonable estimate. A better estimate might be obtained by estimating 30% of 600 and then subtracting 3% of 600 to obtain 27% of 600, giving $180 - 18$, or 162.
2. To estimate 148% of 500, note that 148% of 500 should be slightly less than 150% of 500. 150% of 500 is $1.5(500) = 750$. Thus, 148% of 500 should be a little less than 750.

Example 20

Laura wants to buy a blouse originally priced at $26.50 but now on sale at 40% off. She has $17 in her wallet, and wonders if she has enough cash. How can she mentally determine this? (Ignore the sales tax.)

Solution   It is easier to find 40% of $25 (versus $26.50) mentally. One way is to find 10% of $25, which is $2.50. Now, 40% is 4 times that much, that is, $4 \cdot \$2.50$, or $10. Thus, Laura estimates that the blouse will cost $26.50 − $10, or $16.50. Since the actual discount is greater than $10 (40% of 26.50 is greater than 40% of 25), Laura will have to pay less than $16.50 for the blouse. She has enough cash.

Sometimes it may not be clear which operations to perform with percent. The following example investigates this.

Example 21

Which of the following statements could be true and which are false? Explain your answers.

a. Leonardo got a 10% raise at the end of his first year on the job and a 10% raise after another year. His total raise was 20% of his original salary.
b. Jung and Dina paid 45% of their first department store bill of $620 and 48% of the second department store bill of $380. They paid 45% + 48% = 93% of the total bill of $1000.
c. Bill spent 25% of his salary on food and 40% on housing. Bill spent 25% + 40% = 65% of his salary on food and housing.
d. In Bordertown, 65% of the adult population work in town, 25% work across the border, 15% are unemployed, and everyone in town is in exactly one of these categories.
e. In Clean City, the fine for various polluting activities is a certain percentage of one's monthly income. The fine for smoking in public places is 40%, for driving a polluting car is 50%, and for littering is 30%. Mr. Schmutz committed all three polluting crimes in one day and paid a fine of 120% of his monthly income.

Solution
a. In applications, percent has meaning only when it represents part of a quantity. For example, 10% of a quantity plus another 10% of the same quantity is 20% of that quantity. In Leonardo's case, the first 10% raise was calculated based on his original salary, and the second 10% raise was calculated on his new salary. Consequently, the percentages cannot be added, and the statement is false. He received a 21% raise.
b. The last statement does not make sense; 45% of one bill plus 48% of the other bill is not 93% of the total bill because the bills are different.
c. Because the percentages are of the same quantity, the statement is true.
d. Because the percentages are of the same quantity (the number of adults), we can add them: 65% + 25% + 15% = 105%. But 105% of the population accounts for more than the town's population (actually 5% more), which is impossible. Hence, the statement is false.
e. Again, the percentages are of the same quantity; that is, the individual's monthly income. Hence, we can add them: 120% of one's monthly income is a stiff fine, but possible.

Computing Interest

In the grade 7 *Common Core Standards*, we find that "students use their understanding of ratios and proportionality to solve a wide variety of percent problems, including those involving discounts, interest, taxes, tips, and percent increase or decrease." (p. 46) We next investigate the topic of interest.

When a bank advertises a $5\frac{1}{2}$% interest rate on a loan, the **interest** is the amount of money you will pay for using the bank's money. The original amount borrowed is the **principal**. The percent used to determine the interest is the **interest rate**. Interest rates are given for specific periods of time, such as years, months, or days. Interest computed on the original principal is **simple interest**. For example, suppose we borrow $5000 from a bank at an annual simple interest rate of 9% for 1 year. The interest we owe on the loan for 1 year is 9% of $5000, or $0.09 \cdot \$5000 = \$450$. In general, *if a principal, P, is invested at an annual interest rate of r, then the simple interest after 1 year is $Pr \cdot 1$; after t years, it is Prt.* Thus, if *I* represents simple interest, we have

$$I = Prt.$$

The amount needed to pay off a $5000 loan at 9% annual simple interest for 1 year is the $5000 borrowed plus the interest on the $5000; that is, $5000 + 5000 \cdot 0.09 = \$5450$. In general, *an* **amount** (*or* **balance**) *A is equal to the principal P plus the interest I:*

$$A = P + I = P + Prt = P(1 + rt)$$

| Example 22 |

Vera opened a savings account that pays simple interest at the rate of $5\frac{1}{4}$% per year. If she deposits $2000 and makes no other deposits, find the interest and the final amount for the following time periods:

  a. 1 yr
  b. 90 days

Solution
  a. To find the interest for 1 yr, we proceed as follows.

$$I = \$2000 \cdot 5\frac{1}{4}\% \cdot 1 = \$2000 \cdot 0.0525 \cdot 1 = \$105$$

Her final amount at the end of 1 yr is

$$\$2000 + \$105 = \$2105.$$

  b. When the interest rate is annual and the interest period is given in days, we represent the time as a fractional part of a year by dividing the number of days by 365. Thus,

$$I = \$2000 \cdot 5\frac{1}{4}\% \cdot \frac{90}{365}$$

$$= \$2000 \cdot 0.0525 \cdot \frac{90}{365} \approx \$25.89.$$

Hence,

$$A \approx \$2000 + \$25.89$$
$$A \approx \$2025.89.$$

Thus, Vera's amount after 90 days is approximately $2026.

Example 23

Find the annual interest rate if a principal of $10,000 increased to $10,900 at the end of 1 yr.

Solution   Let the annual interest rate be x%. We know that x% of $10,000 is the increase. Because the increase is $10,900 - $10,000 = $900, we use the strategy of *writing an equation* for x as follows:

$$x\% \text{ of } 10{,}000 = 900$$

$$\frac{x}{100} \cdot 10{,}000 = 900$$

$$x = 9$$

Thus, the annual interest rate is 9%. We can also solve this problem mentally by asking, "What percent of 10,000 is 900?" Because 1% of 10,000 is 100, to obtain 900, we take 9% of 10,000.

Compound Interest

In business transactions, interest is sometimes calculated daily (365 times a year). In the case of savings, the earned interest is added daily to the principal, and each day the interest is earned on a different amount; that is, it is earned on the previous interest as well as the principal. Interest earned in this way is **compound interest**. Compounding is usually done annually (once a year), semiannually (twice a year), quarterly (4 times a year), or monthly (12 times a year). Though common in the past for banks to compound interest quarterly, today banks compound interest monthly, daily, or even continuously. However, even when the interest is compounded, it is given as an annual rate. For example, if the annual rate is 6% compounded monthly, the interest per month is $\frac{6}{12}$%, or 0.5%. If it is compounded daily, the interest rate per day is $\frac{6}{365}$%. In general, *the interest rate per period is the annual interest rate divided by the number of periods in a year.*

If we invest $100 at 8% annual interest compounded quarterly, how much will we have in the account after 1 yr? The quarterly interest rate is $\frac{1}{4} \cdot 8\%$, or 2%. It seems that we would have to calculate the interest 4 times. But we can also reason as follows. If at the beginning of any of the four periods there are x dollars in the account, at the end of that period there will be

$$x + 2\% \text{ of } x = x + 0.02x$$
$$= x(1 + 0.02)$$
$$= x(1.02) \text{ dollars.}$$

 Hence, to find the amount at the end of any period, we need only multiply the amount at the beginning of the period by 1.02. From Table 5, we see that the amount at the end of the fourth period is $100 \cdot 1.02^4$. On a scientific calculator, we can find the amount using $\boxed{1}\,\boxed{0}\,\boxed{0}\,\boxed{\times}$ $\boxed{1}\,\boxed{.}\,\boxed{0}\,\boxed{2}\,\boxed{y^x}\,\boxed{4}\,\boxed{=}$. The calculator displays 108.24322. Thus, the amount at the end of 1 yr is approximately $108.24.

Table 5

Period	Initial Amount	Final Amount
1	100	$100 \cdot 1.02$
2	$100 \cdot 1.02$	$(100 \cdot 1.02)1.02$, or $100 \cdot 1.02^2$
3	$100 \cdot 1.02^2$	$(100 \cdot 1.02^2)1.02$, or $100 \cdot 1.02^3$
4	$100 \cdot 1.02^3$	$(100 \cdot 1.02^3)1.02$, or $100 \cdot 1.02^4$

Finding the final amount at the end of the nth period becomes finding the nth term of a geometric sequence whose first term is $100 \cdot 1.02$ (amount at the end of the first period) and whose ratio is 1.02. Thus, the amount at the end of the nth period is given by $(100 \cdot 1.02)(1.02)^{n-1} = 100 \cdot 1.02^n$. We can generalize this discussion. If the principal is P and the interest rate per period is r, then the amount A after n periods is $P(1 + r)(1 + r)^{n-1} = P(1 + r)^n$. Therefore, the *formula for computing the amount at the end of the nth period is*

$$A = P(1 + r)^n.$$

For convenient comparison, banks are required to report the **effective annual** yield, also called **annual** percentage yield or APY. The effective annual yield on an investment is the simple interest rate that after 1 yr would pay the same amount as the given compound rate compounded at given intervals.

Example 24

Suppose you deposit $1000 in a savings account that pays 6% annual interest compounded quarterly.

   a. What is the balance at the end of 1 yr?
   b. What is the *effective annual yield* on this investment?

Solution

   a. An annual interest rate of 6% earns $\frac{1}{4}$ of 6%, or an interest rate of $\frac{0.06}{4}$, in 1 quarter. Because there are 4 periods, we have the following:

$$A = 1000\left(1 + \frac{0.06}{4}\right)^4 \approx \$1061.36$$

   The balance at the end of 1 yr is approximately $1061.36.
   b. Because the interest earned is $1061.36 - \$1000.00 = \$61.36$, the effective annual yield can be computed by using the simple interest formula, $I = Prt$.

$$61.36 = 1000 \cdot r \cdot 1$$

$$\frac{61.36}{1000} = r$$

$$0.06136 = r$$

$$6.136\% = r$$

The effective annual yield is 6.136%.

Example 25

To save for their child's college education, a couple deposits $3000 into an account that pays 7% annual interest compounded daily. Find the amount in this account after 8 yr.

Solution   The principal in the problem is $3000, the daily rate i is $0.07/365$, and the number of compounding periods is $8 \cdot 365$, or 2920. Thus, we have

$$A = \$3000\left(1 + \frac{0.07}{365}\right)^{2920} \approx \$5251.74.$$

Thus, the amount in the account is approximately $5251.74.

Assessment 7-4A

1. Estimate the percent of the square that is shaded.

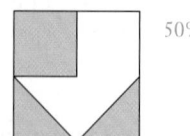

50%

2. Copy the number line and fill in the blanks so that each tick mark is labeled with a percent, a fraction, and a decimal. Write fractions in lowest terms.   *

   0% 50%   250% 300%

   0   1   2   3

   0   0.5   1   1.5   2   2.5   3   3.5

3. Express each of the following as a percent.
   a. 7.89   789%
   b. 193.1   19,310%
   c. $\frac{5}{6}$ $83\frac{1}{3}\%$
   d. $\frac{1}{8}$ 12.5%
   e. $\frac{5}{8}$ 62.5%
   f. $\frac{4}{5}$ 80%

4. Convert each of the following percents to a decimal.
   a. 16%   0.16
   b. $\frac{1}{5}\%$ 0.002
   c. $13\frac{2}{3}\%$ $0.13\overline{6}$
   d. $\frac{1}{3}\%$ $0.00\overline{3}$

5. Fill in the following blanks to find other expressions for 4%.
   a. ____4____ for every 100
   b. ____2____ for every 50
   c. 1 for every ____25____
   d. 8 for every ____200____
   e. 0.5 for every ____12.5____

6. Draw a percent bar to represent 125% of 60. Set up a proportion from the percent bar and solve it.   *

7. Answer each of the following questions.
   a. What is 6% of 34?   2.04
   b. 17 is what percent of 34?   50%
   c. 18 is 30% of what number?   60
   d. What is 7% of 49?   3.43

8. a. Write a fraction representing 5% of x. $\frac{5x}{100} = \frac{x}{20}$
   b. If 10% of an amount is a, what is the amount in terms of a?   10a

9. Marc had 84 boxes of candy to sell. He sold 75% of the boxes. How many did he sell?   63 boxes

10. Gail received a 7% raise last year. If her salary is now $27,285, what was her salary last year? $25,500

11. Joe sold 180 newspapers out of 200. Bill sold 85% of his 260 newspapers. Ron sold 212 newspapers, 80% of those he had.
    a. Who sold the most newspapers? How many?   Bill, 221
    b. Who sold the greatest percentage of his newspapers? What percent?   Joe, 90%
    c. Who started with the greatest number of newspapers? How many?   Ron, 265.

12. If a dress that normally sells for $35 is on sale for $28, what is the "percent off"? (This could be called a *percent of decrease*, or a *discount*.)   20%

13. Mort bought his house in 2006 for $359,000. It was recently appraised at $195,000. What is the approximate *percent of decrease* in value to the nearest percent?   About 46%

14. Sally bought a dress marked 20% off. If the regular price was $28.00, what was the sale price? $22.40

15. An airline ticket costs $320 without the tax. If the tax rate is 5%, what is the total bill for the airline ticket? $336

16. Bill got 52 correct answers on an 80-question test. What percent of the questions did he answer incorrectly?   35%

17. If $66\frac{2}{3}\%$ of 1800 employees favored a new insurance program, how many employees favored the new program?   1200

18. Which represents the greater percent: $\frac{325}{500}$ or $\frac{600}{1000}$? How can you tell?   *

19. An advertisement reads that if you buy 10 items, you get 20% off your total purchase price. You need 8 items that cost $9.50 each.
    a. How much would 8 items cost? 10 items? $76; $76
    b. Is it more economical to buy 8 items or 10 items?   *

20. John paid $330 for a new mountain bicycle to sell in his shop. He wants to price it so that he can offer a 10% discount and still make 20% of the price he paid for it. At what price should the bike be marked? $440

21. Solve each of the following using mental mathematics.   Techniques may vary:
    a. 15% of $22 $3.30
    b. 20% of $120 $24
    c. 5% of $38 $1.90
    d. 25% of $98 $24.50

22. A crew consists of one apprentice, one journeyman, and one master carpenter. The crew receives a check for $4200 for a job they just finished. A journeyman makes 200% of what an apprentice makes, and a master makes 150% of what a journeyman makes. How much does each person in the crew earn?   *

23. a. In an incoming freshman class of 500 students, only 20 claimed to be math majors. What percent of the freshman class is this?   4%
    b. When the survey was repeated the next year, 5% of nonmath majors had decided to switch and become math majors.
       i. How many math majors are there now?   44
       ii. What percent of the former freshman class do they represent?   8.8%

24. Ms. Price has received a 10% raise in salary in each of the last 2 yr. If her annual salary this year is $100,000, what was her salary 2 yr ago, rounded to the nearest penny? $82,644.63

25. When the U.S. Congress was sent a $2.57 trillion budget, it was reported that one would have to purchase a $100 item every second for 815 yr to spend that much money.
  a. Decide whether or not you believe this report. *
  b. Assuming that exactly 815 yr are required to spend the entire $2.57 trillion, what percentage of the money is spent each year? Approximately 0.12%

26. If you wanted to spend 25% of your monthly salary on entertainment and 56% of the salary on rent, could those amounts be $500 and $950? Why or why not? *

27. An organization has 100,000 members. A bylaw change can be made at the annual business meeting held once each year, and a bylaw change must be approved by a majority of those attending the meeting. The chair of the meeting cannot vote unless there is a tie vote but does count as an attendee at the meeting.
  a. With these rules, what is the minimum number required at the meeting to make a bylaw change? 3
  b. Based on your answer to part (a), what percentage of the membership can change the bylaws of the organization? 0.002%

28. A tip in a restaurant has been typically figured at 15% of the total bill.
  a. If the bill is $30, what would be the typical tip? $4.50
  b. If the patron receiving the bill gave a tip that was half the bill, what is the percentage of the tip? 50%
  c. If the patron receiving the bill gave a tip that was equal to the bill, what is the percentage of the tip? 100%

29. Suppose the percent bar below shows the number of students in a school who do not favor dress codes. How many students are in the school? 550

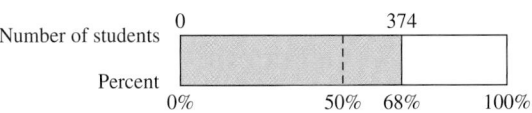

30. Consider the natural numbers 1 through 50.
  a. What percent of these numbers have two digits? 82%
  b. What percent are multiples of 9? 10%
  c. What percent are even? 50%
  d. What percent are prime? 30%
  e. What percent are even and prime? 2%

31. Sunscreens block ultraviolet (UV) rays produced by the sun. These rays are harmful and each sunscreen has a Sun Protection Factor (SPF) that tells you how long you can be exposed before you receive 1 minute of UV rays. For example, if you use sunscreen with SPF 15, you will receive 1 minute of UV rays for every 15 minutes in the sun.
  a. A sunscreen with SPF 15 blocks $\frac{14}{15}$ of the sun's UV rays. What percent is this? $93\frac{1}{3}\%$
  b. Suppose a sunscreen blocks 80% of the sun's UV rays. What fraction of the sun's UV rays does it block? $\frac{4}{5}$
  c. What is the SPF for the sunscreen in part (b)? 5
  d. Carol bought sunscreen with a SPF 30 label. The label claims it block about 97% of the sun's UV rays. If the SPF 30 label is accurate, is the claim true? Explain. Yes, it blocks $96\frac{2}{3}\%$.

32. Complete the following compound interest chart.

Compounding Period	Principal	Annual Rate	Length of Time (Years)	Interest Rate per Period	Number of Periods	Amount of Interest Paid	Total Amount in Account
a. Semiannual	$1000	6%	2	3%	4	$125.51	$1125.51
b. Quarterly	$1000	8%	3	2%	12	$268.24	$1268.24
c. Monthly	$1000	10%	5	*	60	$645.31	$1645.31
d. Daily	$1000	12%	4	*	1460	$615.95	$1615.95

33. Ms. Jackson borrowed $42,000 at 8.75% annual simple interest. If exactly 1 yr later she was able to repay the loan without penalty, how much interest would she owe? $3675

34. Falafel King will need $50,000 in 5 yr for a new addition. To meet this goal, the company deposits money in an account today that pays 3% annual interest compounded quarterly. Find the amount that should be invested to total $50,000 in 5 yr. Approximately $43,059.49

35. To save for their retirement, a couple deposits $4000 in an account that pays 5.9% annual interest compounded quarterly. What will be the value of their investment after 20 yr? $12,905.80

36. Adrien and Jarrell deposit $300 on January 1 in a holiday savings account that pays 1.1% per month interest. What is the effective annual yield? Approximately 14.03%

37. An amount of $3000 was deposited in a bank at a rate of 2% annual interest compounded quarterly for 3 yr. The rate then increased to 3% annual interest and was compounded quarterly for the next 3 yr. If no money was withdrawn, what was the balance at the end of this time? $3483.81

38. The New Age Savings Bank advertises 4% annual interest rates compounded daily, while the Pay More Bank pays 5.2% annual interest compounded annually. Which bank offers a better rate for a customer who plans to leave her money in for exactly 1 yr? Pay More bank offers the better rate.

39. Amy is charged 12% annual interest compounded monthly on the unpaid balance of a $2000 loan. She did not make any payments for 2 yr. Her friend said the amount she owed had more than doubled. Is this correct? How much does she now owe? No, now she owes $2539.47.

Assessment 7-4B

1. Estimate the percent of the square that is shaded.

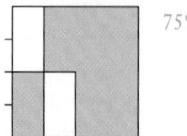   75%

2. Copy the number line and fill in the blanks so that each tick mark is labeled with a percent, a fraction, and a decimal. Write fractions in lowest terms.   *

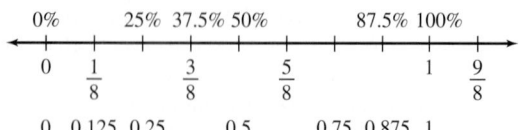

3. Express each of the following as a percent.
   a. 0.032   3.2%
   b. 0.2   20%
   c. $\frac{3}{20}$ 15%
   d. $\frac{13}{8}$ 162.5%
   e. $\frac{1}{6}$ $16\frac{2}{3}\%$
   f. $\frac{1}{40}$ 2.5%

4. Convert each of the following percents to a decimal.
   a. $4\frac{1}{2}\%$ 0.045
   b. $\frac{2}{7}\%$ $0.00\overline{285714}$
   c. 125%   1.25
   d. $\frac{1}{4}\%$ 0.0025

5. Fill in the following blanks to find other expressions for 5%.
   a. ___5___ for every 100
   b. ___2.5___ for every 50
   c. 1 for every ___20___
   d. 8 for every ___160___
   e. 0.5 for every ___10___

6. Draw a percent bar to represent 150% of 60. Set up a proportion from the percent bar and solve it.   *

7. Answer each of the following questions.
   a. 63 is 30% of what number?   210
   b. What is 7% of 150?   10.5
   c. 61.5 is what percent of 20.5?   300%
   d. 16 is 40% of what number?   40

8. a. Write a fraction representing 0.5% of x. $\frac{5x}{1000}$ or $\frac{x}{200}$
   b. If 0.1% of an amount is a, what is the amount in terms of a?   1000a

9. What is the sale price of a softball, if the regular price is $6.80, and there is a 25% discount? $5.10

10. Brandy received a 10% raise last year. If her salary is now $60,000, what was her salary last year? $54,545.45

11. A line segment X is 3 in. long. This segment represents 50% of another segment Y. Find the length of each of the following.
    a. A segment that represents 100% of segment Y.   6 in.
    b. A segment that represents 25% of the segment in part (a).   *
    c. A segment that represents 150% of segment in part (a).   9 in.

12. A used car originally cost $1700. One year later, it was worth $1400. What is the percentage of depreciation?   *

13. On a certain day in Glacier Park, 728 eagles were counted. Five years later, 594 were counted. What was the percentage of decrease in the number of eagles counted?   *

14. A salesperson earns a weekly salary of $900 plus a commission rate of 4% on all sales. What did the person make for a week with total sales of $1800? $972

15. If you buy a new bicycle for $380 and the sales tax is 9%, what is your total bill? $414.20

16. The number of known living species is about 1.7 million. About 4500 species are mammals. What percent of known living species are mammals?   *

17. Jim bought two shirts that were originally marked at $40 each. One shirt was discounted 20% and the other was discounted 25%. The sales tax was 4.5%. How much did he spend in all? $64.79

18. Without multiplying out find which number represents the greater percent: 0.625 or $(0.625)^2$?   0.625

19. a. It is recommended that no more than 30% of your calorie intake should be from fat. If you consumed about 2400 calories daily, what is the maximum amount of fat calories you should consume?   720 calories
    b. If one cookie contains 140 calories, and 70 calories in the cookie are fat calories, could you eat 3 cookies and not exceed the recommended amount of fat calories for the day?   Yes, you would have $720 - 210 = 510$ fat calories remaining.

20. The price of a suit that sells for $200 is reduced by 25%. By what percent must the price of the suit be increased to bring the price back to $200? $33\frac{1}{3}\%$

21. Solve each of the following using mental mathematics.   Techniques may vary.
    a. 15% of $42 $6.30
    b. 20% of $280 $56
    c. 5% of $28 $1.40
    d. 25% of $84 $21

22. If a $\frac{1}{4}$-cup serving of Crunchies breakfast food has 0.5% of the minimum daily requirement of vitamin C, how many cups would you have to eat to obtain the minimum daily requirement of vitamin C?   50 cups

23. The car Elsie bought 1 yr ago has depreciated by $1116.88, which is 12.13% of the price she paid for it. How much did she pay for the car, to the nearest dollar?   Approximately $9208

24. If you add 20% of a number to the number itself, what percent of the result would you have to subtract to get the original number back? $16\frac{2}{3}\%$

25. If we build a 10 × 10 model with blocks, as shown in the following figure, and paint the entire model, what percent of the cubes will have each of the following?

a. Four faces painted 4%   **b.** Three faces painted 32%
c. Two faces painted 64%

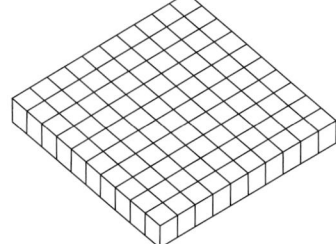

26. Cartons of milk in a store are labeled "2% milk" or "98% fat free." The data for 1 cup of whole milk shows it has 8 g of fat while 1 cup of 2% milk as 5 g of fat. What is percent of reduction in fat for 1 cup of 2% milk over whole milk? 37.5%
27. There are 80 coins in a piggy bank of which 20% are quarters. What is the least possible amount of money that could be in the piggy bank? $4.64
28. According to a *TV Guide* survey, 46% of people in the United States said they would not stop watching television for anything less than a million dollars. Use the percent bar for

the U.S. population to estimate the number of people who would not stop watching television for anything less than a million dollars. About 139 million people

People (millions)	0	151	302

Percent 0% 46% 50% 100%

29. Consider the natural numbers 1 through 50.
   a. What percent are greater than 9? 82%
   b. What percent are factors of 12? 12%
   c. What percent have only even digits? 28%
   d. What percent have only odd digits? 30%
30. Jake bought an antique clock for $30. The following year the clock had increased in value by 20%.
   a. How many dollars did the clock increase in value? $6
   b. What is the clock worth now? $36
   c. You could calculate the worth of the clock by calculating the amount of increase in value and then add it to the original price. How would you calculate the answer in part (b) in only one step? Show the answers are the same and explain why the one-step method works. *

31. Complete the following compound interest chart.

Compounding Period	Principal	Annual Rate	Length of Time (Years)	Interest Rate per Period	Number of Periods	Amount of Interest Paid	Total Amount in Account
a. Semiannual	$1000	4%	2	2%	4	$82.43	$1082.43
b. Quarterly	$1000	6%	3	1.5%	12	$195.62	$1195.62
c. Monthly	$1000	18%	5	1.5%	60	$1443.22	$2443.22
d. Daily	$1000	18%	4	*	1460	$1054.07	$2054.07

32. A man collected $28,500 on a loan of $25,000 he made 4 yr ago. If he charged simple interest, what was the rate he charged? 3.5%
33. Green Energy store will need $100,000 in 5 yr for a new addition. To meet this goal, the company deposits money in an account that pays 3% annual interest compounded quarterly. Find the amount that should be invested to total $100,000 in 5 yr. $86,118.99
34. Sara invested money at a bank that paid 3.5% annual interest compounded quarterly. If she had $4650 at the end of 4 yr, what was her initial investment? Approximately $4044.98
35. A bank pays 2% annual interest compounded daily. What is the value of $10,000 after 15 yr? $13,498.48
36. If a saving account pays 0.5% per month interest, what is the effective annual yield? Approximately 6.17%

37. If a publishing company signed an agreement to allow a textbook (1st edition with 500 pages) to expand over several editions to 1000 pages, and the book was growing at approximately 10% in the number of pages over each edition, how many editions could be published before it reached the contractual limit? 8 editions
38. Al invests $1000 at 6% annual interest compounded daily and Betty invests $1000 at 7% simple interest. After how many whole years will Al's investments be worth more than Betty's investment? *
39. The number of trees in a rain forest decreases each month by 0.5%. If the forest has approximately $2.34 \cdot 10^9$ trees, how many trees will be left after 20 yr? Approximately $7.03 \cdot 10^8$

Mathematical Connections 7-4

Answers to Mathematical Connections can be found in the Answers section at the back of the book.

Reasoning
1. Use mental math to find 11% of 850. Explain your method.
2. Does 0.4 = 0.4%? Explain.
3. What does it mean to reach 125% of your savings goal?
4. Is 4% of 98 the same as 98% of 4? Explain.

5. **a.** If 25% of a number is 55, is the number greater than or less than 55? Explain.
   b. If 150% of a number is 55, is the number greater than or less than 55? Explain.
6. Can 35% of one number be greater than 55% of another number? Explain.

7. Why does one picture have so much more shaded area when they both show 50%?

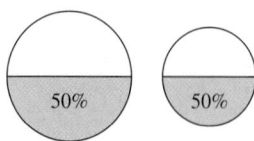

8. Why is it possible to have an increase of 150% in price but not a 150% decrease in price?

9. Two equal amounts of money were invested in two different stocks. The value of the first stock increased by 15% the first year and then decreased by 15% the second year. The second stock decreased by 15% the first year and increased by 15% the second year. Was one investment better than the other? Explain your reasoning.

10. Because of a recession, the value of a new house depreciated 10% each year for 3 yr in a row. Then, for the next 3 yr, the value of the house increased 10% each year. Had the value of the house increased or decreased after 6 yr? Explain.

11. Approximate the number of years it would take for any amount of money to double if it were deposited at a 2% annual interest rate compounded annually. Explain your reasoning.

12. Each year a car's value depreciated 20% from the previous year. Mike claims that after 5 yr the car would depreciate 100% and would not be worth anything. Is Mike correct? Explain why or why not. If not, find the actual percent the car would depreciate after 5 yr.

13. If 70% of the girls in a class wanted to have a prom and 60% of the boys wanted a prom, is it possible that only 50% of the students in the class wanted a prom? Explain your answer.

14. If 70% of the girls in a class wanted to have a prom and 40% of the boys wanted a prom, is it possible that only 50% of the students in the class wanted a prom? Explain your answer.

15. Abe and Barb were shopping at a department store. Abe looked at his receipt and noted that the total before the discount was $75 but he paid only $56.25. Barb's total before the discount was $52 but she paid only $31.20. Who saved the greater percentage off the original price? Explain.

16. Dan claims that the sales tax going from 5% to 6% is only increasing the sales tax by 1 percentage point. Stan says that the sales tax is going up by 20%. Who is correct? Why?

Open-Ended

17. Write and solve a word problem whose solution involves the following. If any of these tasks is impossible, explain why.
    a. Addition of percent
    b. Subtraction of percent
    c. Multiplication of percent
    d. Division of percent
    e. A percent whose decimal representation is raised to the second power
    f. A percent greater than 100

18. Look at newspapers and magazines for information given in percents.
    a. Based on your findings, write a problem that involves social science as well as mathematics.
    b. Write a clear solution to your problem in part (a).

19. Write a percentage problem whose answer is the solution of each of the following equations.
    a. $\dfrac{37}{100} = \dfrac{115}{x}$
    b. $\dfrac{p}{100} = \dfrac{a}{x}$

20. The effect of depreciation can be computed using a formula similar to the formula for compound interest.
    a. Assume depreciation is the same each month. Write a problem involving depreciation and solve it.
    b. Develop a general formula for depreciation defining what each variable in the formula represents.

21. Find four large cities around the world and an approximate percentage rate of population growth for the cities. Estimate the population in each of the four cities in 25 yr.

Cooperative Learning

22. Al read that 80% of supermarket prices end in 9 or 5. Investigate this in your group and report percentages to back up your findings.

23. Find the percentage of students in your class who engage in each of the following activities:

a. **Studying and Doing Homework**

Number of Hours per Week (h)	Percent
$h < 1$	
$1 \le h < 3$	
$3 \le h < 5$	
$5 \le h < 10$	
$h \ge 10$	
Total	

b. **Watching TV**

Number of Hours per Week (h)	Percent
$h < 1$	
$1 \le h < 5$	
$5 \le h < 10$	
$h \ge 10$	
Total	

c. Did your totals add up to 100% in each table? Why or why not?

24. The federal Truth in Lending Act, passed in 1969, requires lending institutions to quote an annual percentage rate (APR) that helps consumers compare the true cost of loans regardless of how each lending institution computes the interest and adds on costs.
    a. Call different banks and ask for their APR on some loans and the meaning of APR.
    b. Based on your findings in part (a), write a definition of APR.
    c. Use the information given by your credit card (you may need to call the bank) and compute the APR on cash advances. Is your answer the same as that given by the bank? Compare the APR for different credit cards.

Connecting Mathematics to the Classroom

25. Jamal says that since there are 48% girls at Washington School and 52% girls at Jefferson School there must be more girls at Jefferson School. Is he correct? How would you help him?

26. A student claims that if prices at a store can increase 120%, then a candidate should be able to get 120% of the votes in an election. How do you respond?

27. A student says that $3\frac{1}{4}\% = 0.03 + 0.25 = 0.28$. Is this correct? Why?

28. A student argues that a $p\%$ increase in salary followed by a $q\%$ decrease is equivalent to a $q\%$ decrease followed by a $p\%$ increase because of the commutative property of multiplication. How do you respond?

29. Noel read that women used to make 75¢ for every dollar that men made. She says that this means that men were paid 25% more than women. Is she correct? Why?

30. A student claims that if the value of an item increases by 100% each year from its value the previous year, and the original price is d dollars, then the value after n years will be $d \cdot 2^n$ dollars. Is the student correct? Why or why not?

Review Problems

31. a. Human bones make up 0.18 of a person's body weight. How much do the bones of a 120 lb person weigh?
   b. Muscles make up about 0.4 of a person's body weight. How much do the muscles of a 120 lb person weigh?

32. Write each of the following decimals in the form $\frac{a}{b}$, where $a, b \in I, b \neq 0$ and $\frac{a}{b}$ is in simplest terms.
   a. 16.72
   b. 0.003
   c. ⁻5.07
   d. 0.123

33. Write a repeating decimal equal to each of the following without using more than one zero.
   a. 5
   b. 5.1
   c. $\frac{1}{2}$

34. Write 0.00024 as a fraction in simplest form.

35. Write $0.\overline{24}$ as a fraction in simplest form.

36. Write each of the following as a standard numeral.
   a. $2.08 \cdot 10^5$
   b. $3.8 \cdot 10^{-4}$

National Assessments

National Assessment of Educational Progress (NAEP) Questions

There were 90 employees in a company last year. This year the number of employees increased by 10 percent. How many employees are in the company this year?

A. 9
B. 81
C. 91
D. 99
E. 100

NAEP, Grade 8, 2005

One store, Price Pleasers, reduces the price *each week* of a $100 stereo by 10 percent of *the original* price.

Another store, Bargains Plus, reduces the price *each week* of the same $100 stereo by 10 percent of *the previous week's* price.

After 2 weeks, how will the prices at the two stores compare?

A. The price will be cheaper at Price Pleasers.
B. The price will be the same at both stores.
C. The price will be cheaper at Bargains Plus.

Explain your reasoning.
NAEP, Grade 8, 2003

Helga's process of calculating the tip to leave in a restaurant starts with the bill for food and drink.

• First, she rounds the bill to the nearest ten cents.
• Then she moves the decimal point in the rounded total one place to the left.
• Finally, she doubles that amount.

Helga's process calculates approximately what percent of the original bill?

A. 2%
B. 5%
C. 10%
D. 15%
E. 20%

NAEP, Grade 8, 2013

Hint for Solving the Preliminary Problem

The first two questions can be answered by direct computations involving percents. The third question can be investigated in several ways. One way is to try the calculations with a specific number such as 100. Another strategy is to write an equation and solve it. The answer can be checked to make sure it is correct.

Chapter 7 Summary

KEY CONCEPTS	DEFINITIONS, DESCRIPTIONS, AND THEOREMS
Section 7-1	
Decimal point (p. 330)	A dot used to separate the whole number part from the fractional part of a decimal number. The dot in the decimal 12.618 is the *decimal point*.
Standard (or expanded) form of a decimal (p. 333)	Decimals in standard form can be expanded using place value and powers of 10. The decimal 12.618 in standard form is written as $$12.618 = 1 \cdot 10^1 + 2 \cdot 10^0 + 6 \cdot 10^{-1} + 1 \cdot 10^{-2} + 8 \cdot 10^{-3}.$$
Multiplying or dividing by 10^n (p. 335)	For any decimal and any natural number n: *Multiplying by 10^n*—Move the decimal point n places *to the right*, adjoining zeros as needed. *Dividing by 10^n*—Move the decimal point n places *to the left*, adjoining zeros as needed.
Terminating decimal (p. 336)	Any decimal that can be written with only a finite number of places to the right of the decimal point. *Theorem:* A rational number $\frac{a}{b}$ in simplest form can be written as a terminating decimal if, and only if, the prime factorization of the denominator contains no primes other than 2 or 5.
Comparing terminating decimals (p. 337)	• Write the decimals as rational numbers with a common denominator that is a power of 10, and then compare the numerators. • Line up the decimals by place value (appending zeros as necessary). Starting at the left, find the first place where the digits are different. In comparing these digits, the digit with the greater face value represents the greater of the two decimals.
Section 7-2	
Adding terminating decimals (p. 340)	• Write the decimals as fractions with denominators that are a power of 10, and then add or subtract. • Line up the decimals points in the decimals, and then add or subtract as we do with whole numbers, placing the decimal point of the answers in line with the other decimal points.
Multiplying terminating decimals (p. 342)	Multiply the two numbers, ignoring the decimal points. If there are n digits after the decimal point in the first number and m digits after the decimal point in the second number, then place the decimal point in the resulting product so there are $m + n$ digits after the decimal point.
Scientific notation (p. 344)	Any positive number written as the product of a number greater than or equal to 1 and less than 10 and an integer power of 10. To write a negative number in scientific notation, treat the number as a positive number and adjoin the negative sign in front of the result.
Writing a number in scientific notation (p. 344)	Move the decimal point so that there is only one nonzero digit to the left of the decimal point. If the decimal point is moved *to the left* n places, then multiply the resulting number by 10^n. If the decimal point is moved *to the right* n places, then multiply the resulting number by 10^{-n}.

Section 7-2

Dividing terminating decimals (p. 345)

Multiply the divisor and dividend by the power of 10 that gives a whole number divisor. Then divide, lining up the decimal point in the quotient with the decimal point in the dividend.

Mental computation algorithms for decimals (p. 348)

- *Breaking and bridging*
- *Using compatible numbers*
- *Making compatible numbers*
- *Balancing with decimals (in subtraction)*
- *Balancing with decimals (in division)*

Estimating decimal computations using rounding (p. 349)

Round numbers appropriately to estimate answers for quick computation.

Round-off error (p. 351)

An error that arises when computing with approximate numbers. The final result should not be reported using more significant digits than the number with the fewest significant digits used in the computation.

Section 7-3

Repeating decimal (p. 357)

Any decimal that has a repeating block of digits, called a *repetend*. The number of digits that repeat is the *period* of the repetend.

Writing a repeating decimal as a fraction (p. 360)

A repeating decimal can be written in the form $\frac{a}{b}$, where a and b are integers and $b \neq 0$.

There are several ways to show that $0.\overline{9} = 1$.

Ordering repeating decimals (p. 362)

- Consider where the repeating decimals might lie on a number line.
- Compare the decimals using place value similarly to how terminating decimals are compared.

Section 7-4

Percent (p. 366)

$n\% = \frac{n}{100}$, where n is a nonnegative number.

Percent application problems (p. 368)

Application problems involving percents take one of the following forms:

- *Finding a percent of a number*
- *Finding what percent one number is of another number*
- *Finding a number when a percent of that number is known*

Percent bar (p. 369)

A graphical model that can be used for understanding what a given percent of a number means.

Mental computation algorithms for percents (p. 373)

- *Using fraction equivalents*
- *Using known percents*

Computing interest (p. 374)

Principal—the original amount deposited or loaned.

Interest—the amount of money the bank will pay or charge.

Interest rate—the percent used to determine the interest.

Simple interest—the interest computed using the formula $I = Prt$, where P is the principal, r is the annual interest rate, and t is the time in years.

Compound interest—the interest based on using both the principal and the accrued interest; it is computed using the formula $A = P(1 + r)^n$, where A is the balance, P is the principal, r is the interest rate per period, and n is the number of periods.

Chapter 7 Review

1. a. On the number line, find the decimals that correspond to points A, B, and C. $A(0.02), B(0.05), C(0.11)$
   b. Indicate by D the point that corresponds to 0.09 and by E the point that corresponds to 0.15.   *

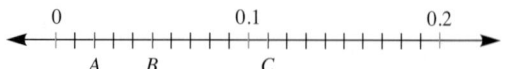

2. Write each of the following as a rational number in the form $\frac{a}{b}$, where a and b are integers and $b \neq 0$ and $\frac{a}{b}$ is in simplest form.
   a. 32.012 $\frac{8003}{250}$ **b.** 0.00103 $\frac{103}{100,000}$

3. Describe a test to determine whether a fraction can be written as a terminating decimal without actually performing the division.   *

4. A board is 442.4 cm long. How many shelves can be cut from it if each shelf is 55.3 cm long? (Disregard the width of the cuts.)   8 shelves.

5. Write each of the following as a decimal.
   a. $\frac{4}{7}$ *   **b.** $\frac{1}{8}$ *   **c.** $\frac{2}{3}$ *   **d.** $\frac{5}{8}$ *

6. Write each of the following as a fraction in simplest form.   *
   a. 0.28   **b.** ‾6.07   **c.** $0.\overline{3}$ **d.** $2.0\overline{8}$

7. Round each of the following numbers as specified.
   a. 307.625 to the nearest hundredth   307.63
   b. 307.625 to the nearest tenth   307.6
   c. 307.625 to the nearest unit   308
   d. 307.625 to the nearest hundred   300

8. Rewrite each of the following in scientific notation.
   a. 426,000 $4.26 \cdot 10^5$ **b.** $324 \cdot 10^{-6}$ $3.24 \cdot 10^{-4}$
   c. 0.00000237 $2.37 \cdot 10^{-6}$ **d.** ‾0.325 $-3.25 \cdot 10^{-1}$

9. Order the following decimals from greatest to least.   *
   $1.4\overline{519}$, $1.451\overline{9}$, 1.4519, $1.45\overline{19}$,   ‾0.134,
   ‾$0.13\overline{401}$, $0.13\overline{401}$

10. Write each of the following in scientific notation without using a calculator.
   a. 1783411.56 $1.78341156 \cdot 10^6$
   b. $\frac{347}{10^8}$ $3.47 \cdot 10^{-6}$
   c. $49.3 \cdot 10^8$ $4.93 \cdot 10^9$
   d. $29.4 \cdot \frac{10^{12}}{10^{-4}}$ $2.94 \cdot 10^{17}$
   e. $0.47 \cdot 1000^{12}$ $4.7 \cdot 10^{35}$
   f. $\frac{3}{5^9}$ $1.536 \cdot 10^{-6}$

11. a. Find five decimals between 0.1 and 0.11 and order them from greatest to least.   *
   b. Find four decimals between 0 and 0.1 listed from least to greatest, so each decimal starting from the second is twice as large as the preceding one.   *
   c. Find four decimals between 0.1 and 0.2 and list them in increasing order, so the first one is halfway between 0.1 and 0.2, the second halfway between the first and 0.2, the third halfway between the second and 0.2, and similarly for the fourth one.   0.15, 0.175, 0.1875, 0.19375

12. Answer each of the following questions.
   a. 6 is what percent of 24?   25%
   b. What is 320% of 60?   192
   c. 17 is 30% of what number? $56.\overline{6}$
   d. 0.2 is what percent of 1?   20%

13. Change each of the following to a percent.
   a. $\frac{1}{8}$ 12.5%   **b.** $\frac{3}{40}$ 7.5%
   c. 6.27   627%   **d.** 0.0123   1.23%
   e. $\frac{3}{2}$ 150%

14. Change each of the following percents to a decimal.
   a. 60%   0.60 or 0.6   **b.** $\frac{2}{3}$% $0.00\overline{6}$ **c.** 100%   1

15. Sandy received a dividend that equals 11% of the value of her investment. If her dividend was $1020.80, how much was her investment? $9280

16. Five computers in a shipment of 150 were found to be defective. What percent of the computers were defective? $3.\overline{3}$%

17. On a mathematics examination, a student missed 8 of 70 questions. What percent of the questions, rounded to the nearest tenth of a percent, did the student answer correctly?   88.6%

18. A used car costs $3450 at present. This is 60% of the cost 4 yr ago. What was the cost of the car 4 yr ago? $5750

19. If, on a purchase of one new suit, you are offered successive discounts of 5%, 10%, or 20% in any order you wish, what order should you choose?   *

20. Jane bought a bicycle and sold it for 30% more than she paid for it. She sold it for $104. How much did she pay for it? $80

21. The student bookstore had a textbook for sale at $89.95. A student found the book on eBay for $62.00. If the student bought the book on eBay, what percentage of the cost of the bookstore book did she save?   Approximately 31%

22. When a store had a 60% off sale, Dori had a coupon for an additional 40% off any item and thought she should be able to obtain the dress that she wanted for free. If you were the store manager, how would you explain the mathematics of the situation to her?   *

23. A store marks up an item by adding 30% to the wholesale price. Later the store has a sale and marks the item down 30% from the retail price. Is the store breaking even on the item, making a profit, or losing money on the item?   *

24. A company was offered a $30,000 loan at a 12.5% annual simple interest rate for 4 yr. Find the simple interest due on the loan at the end of 4 yr. $15,000

25. A fund pays 14% annual interest compounded quarterly. What is the value of a $10,000 investment after 3 yr? $15,110.69

26. The crust of a certain pumpkin pie is 25% of the pie. By what percent should the amount of crust be reduced in order to make it constitute 20% of the pie?   25%

Real Numbers and Algebraic Thinking

Preliminary Problem

A sheet of paper of the international standard size (used in most countries other than the United States and Canada) has the ratio of length (the longer side) to width (the shorter side) such that when cut or folded widthwise, the halves have the same length to width ratio.

a. What is that ratio?

b. what will the ratio of length to width of a larger sheet of paper be if two such standard sheets are joined along their length?

If needed, see Hint on page 461.

The development of numbers was inspired by such commercial uses as negative numbers to indicate debts and to think about fractions as parts of a whole. The development of real numbers was comparable. The Pythagoreans knew a right triangle with two sides of length 1 had to have a new type of number to describe the length of the third side. Ancient Greeks struggled with finding a number to describe the ratio of the circumference of a circle to its diameter. These examples involve irrational numbers, but the formal definition of a real number came long after such numbers began to be used.

The grade 8 *Common Core Standards* recognize that students need to know that "there are numbers that are not rational, and [how to] approximate them by rational numbers." (p. 54)

In this chapter, we explore real numbers and examine aspects of algebra including the analysis and solution of linear equations, pairs of simultaneous linear equations, and other algebraic notions including functions, and the coordinate system.

These topics are reflected in the grade 8 *Common Core Standards* in the following:

- Work with radicals and integer exponents
- Analyze and solve linear equations and pairs of simultaneous linear equations. (p. 53)

8-1 Real Numbers

8-1 Objectives

Students will be able to understand and explain

- Real numbers
- Operations on real numbers
- *n*th roots and in particular square root.
- How $a^{1/n}$ and $a^{n/m}$ are defined and why they are defined in this way.
- Expressions involving radicals and radical exponents.

In Chapter 7, we saw that every rational number can be represented either as a terminating decimal or as a repeating decimal. But the ancient Greeks discovered numbers that are not rational, that is, numbers with a decimal representation that neither terminates nor repeats. To find such decimals, consider their characteristics.

1. There must be an infinite number of nonzero digits to the right of the decimal point.
2. There cannot be a repeating block of digits (a *repetend*).

One way to construct a nonterminating, nonrepeating decimal is to devise a pattern of infinite digits so that there is no repetend. For example, consider the number 0.1010010001 . . . . If the pattern continues, the next groups of digits are four 0's followed by 1, five 0's followed by 1, and so on. Because this decimal is nonterminating and nonrepeating, it cannot represent a rational number. Numbers that are not rational numbers are **irrational numbers**, and there are infinitely many of them. In the mid-eighteenth century, it was proved that the ratio of the circumference of a circle to its diameter, symbolized by **π (pi)**, is an irrational number. The numbers $\frac{22}{7}$, 3.14, or 3.14159 are rational number approximations of π. The value of π has been computed to over 5 trillion decimal places and the digits appear to be random.

(Historical Note)

Although the Pythagoreans seem to have known about some irrational numbers, it was not until 1872 that German mathematician Richard Dedekind introduced a method of constructing irrational numbers from sets of rational numbers by showing that an irrational number could be thought of as a cut in a number line that separates the set of rational numbers into two disjoint non-empty subsets, one of which has no least element and the other of which has no greatest element, with all elements of one set less than the elements of the other set.   ●

The set of **real numbers** is the union of the set of rational and irrational numbers. Every real number can be represented as a decimal and corresponds to a point on a number line.

> ### Definition of Real Numbers
> A **real number** is any number that can be represented by a decimal.

Square Roots

Irrational numbers occur in the study of area. For example, to find the area of a square as in Figure 1(a), we could use the formula $A = s^2$, where A is the area and s is the length of a side of the square. If a side of a square is 3 cm long as in Figure 1(b), then the area of the square is 9 cm^2 (square centimeters).

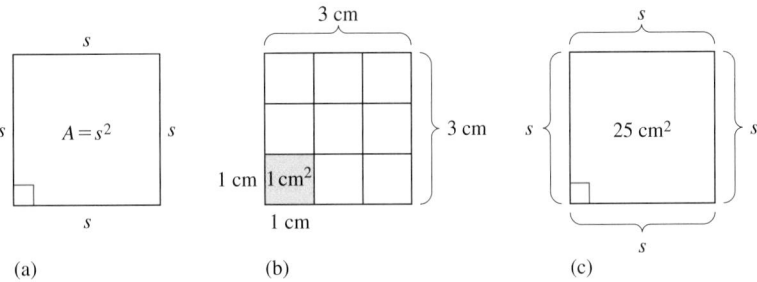

Figure 1

Conversely, given the area, we can use the formula to find the length s of a side of a square. If the area of a square is 25 cm^2 as in Figure 1(c), then $s^2 = 25$ and hence $s = 5$ or $s = {}^-5$.

Each of these solutions is a **square root** of 25. However, because lengths are always non-negative, 5 is the only possible solution to the equation. The non-negative solution of $s^2 = 25$ (namely, 5) is the **principal square root** of 25 and is denoted $\sqrt{25}$. Similarly, the principal square root of 2 is denoted $\sqrt{2}$. Also $\sqrt{16} \neq {}^-4$ because $^-4$ is not the principal square root of 16.

> ### Definition of the Square Root and Principal Square Root
> 1. A **square root** of non-negative number a is a number x, such that $x^2 = a$.
> 2. If a is any non-negative number, the **principal square root** of a (denoted $\sqrt{a}$) is the non-negative number x such that $x^2 = a$.

> **REMARK** The phrase "the square root of a" is commonly used to mean the principal square root of a.

Example 1

Find the following:

a. The square roots of 144

b. $\sqrt{144}$

c. $\sqrt{\dfrac{4}{9}}$

d. The solutions of $x^2 = 5$.

Solution

a. The square roots of 144 are 12 and $^-12$.

b. $\sqrt{144} = 12$

c. $\sqrt{\dfrac{4}{9}} = \dfrac{2}{3}$

d. $\sqrt{5}$ or $^-\sqrt{5}$

Other Roots

We have seen that the non-negative solution to $s^2 = 25$ is denoted $\sqrt{25}$. Similarly, the non-negative solution to $s^4 = 25$ is denoted $\sqrt[4]{25}$. In general, if n is even, the positive solution to $x^n = 25$ is $\sqrt[n]{25}$ and is the principal **nth root** of 25. The number n is the **index**. In the expression $\sqrt{25}$, the index 2 is understood and not written. In general, *the non-negative solution to $x^n = b$, where b is non-negative, is $\sqrt[n]{b}$.* Thus if b is non-negative, $\sqrt[n]{b}$ is a non-negative number, which raised to the nth power results in b. Hence:

$$\left(\sqrt[n]{b}\right)^n = b$$

If b is negative and n is even, $\sqrt[n]{b}$ is not a real number. For example, $\sqrt[4]{^-16}$. If $\sqrt[4]{^-16} = x$, then $x^4 = ^-16$. Because any nonzero real number raised to the fourth power is positive, there is no real-number solution to $x^4 = ^-16$ and therefore $\sqrt[4]{^-16}$ is not a real number. Similarly, if we are restricted to real numbers, it is not possible to find *any* even root of a negative number. However, the value $^-2$ is the only real number solution to the equation $x^3 = ^-8$. We write, $\sqrt[3]{^-8} = ^-2$. Because there is only one real number solution to $x^3 = ^-8$, $\sqrt[3]{^-8}$ is the cube root of $^-8$, and there is no meaning to "principle cube root of $^-8$." *In general, the odd root of a negative number is a negative number.*

Because $\sqrt{a}$, if it exists, is non-negative by definition, $\sqrt{(^-3)^2} = \sqrt{9} = 3$. In general,

$$\sqrt{a^2} = |a|.$$

Similarly, $\sqrt[4]{a^4} = |a|$ and $\sqrt[6]{a^6} = |a|$, but $\sqrt[3]{a^3} = a$ for all a. (Why?) Notice that when n is even and $b > 0$, the equation $x^n = b$ has two real-number solutions, $\sqrt[n]{b}$ and $^-\sqrt[n]{b}$. If n is odd, the equation has only one real-number solution, $\sqrt[n]{b}$, for any real number b.

(**Historical Note**)

Evaluating square roots may have been known by Vedic Hindu scholars before 600 BCE. Sanskrit texts contain incredibly accurate approximations for some square roots. The discovery of irrational numbers by members of the Pythagorean Society was kept secret. Legend has it that a society member was drowned because the secret was relayed to persons outside the society. In 1525, Christoff Rudolff, a German mathematician, became the first to use the symbol $\sqrt{}$ for a radical or a root.

Irrationality of Square Roots and Other Roots

Some square roots are rational numbers. Others, like $\sqrt{2}$, are irrational numbers. To see this, we note that $1^2 = 1$ and $2^2 = 4$ and that there is no whole number s such that $s^2 = 2$. Is there a rational number $\frac{a}{b}$ such that $\left(\frac{a}{b}\right)^2 = 2$? To decide, we use the strategy of *indirect reasoning*. If we assume there is such a rational number $\frac{a}{b}$, then the following must be true:

$$\left(\frac{a}{b}\right)^2 = 2$$

$$\frac{a^2}{b^2} = 2$$

$$a^2 = 2b^2$$

If $a^2 = 2b^2$, then by the Fundamental Theorem of Arithmetic, the prime factorizations of a^2 and $2b^2$ must be the same. In particular, the prime 2 appears the same number of times in the prime factorization of a^2 as it does in the factorization of $2b^2$. Because $b^2 = bb$, no matter how many times 2 appears in the prime factorization of b, it appears twice as many times in bb.

Also, a^2 has an even number of 2s for the same reason b^2 does. In $2b^2$, another factor of 2 is introduced, resulting in an odd number of 2s in the prime factorization of $2b^2$. Because $a^2 = 2b^2$, we have 2 appearing both an odd number of times and an even number of times on different sides of the equality, and thus there is a contradiction.

This contradiction could have been caused only by the assumption that $\sqrt{2}$ is a rational number. Consequently, $\sqrt{2}$ cannot be rational and therefore, $\sqrt{2}$ must be an irrational number. We can use a similar argument to show that $\sqrt{3}$ is irrational or $\sqrt{n}$ is irrational, where n is a whole number greater than 1 but not the square of a whole number.

Example 2

Show that if $\frac{a}{b}$ and $\frac{c}{d}$ are rational numbers (a, b, c, and d integers), then $\frac{a}{b} + \frac{c}{d}\sqrt{2}$ is an irrational number.

Solution We use *indirect reasoning*. Suppose the expression is a rational number; then $\frac{a}{b} + \frac{c}{d}\sqrt{2} = \frac{e}{f}$, where e and f are integers. We can obtain a contradiction by expressing $\sqrt{2}$ in terms of the integers a, b, c, d, e, and f, which will show that $\sqrt{2}$ is rational. This would be a contradiction to the fact that $\sqrt{2}$ is an irrational number. It would follow then that the assumption that $\frac{a}{b} + \frac{c}{d}\sqrt{2}$ is a rational number is wrong and consequently that it is an irrational number. We proceed according to this plan.

$$\frac{a}{b} + \frac{c}{d}\sqrt{2} = \frac{e}{f} \quad \text{implies}$$

$$\frac{c}{d}\sqrt{2} = \frac{e}{f} - \frac{a}{b} = \frac{eb - af}{bf}$$

We multiply both sides of the above equation by $\dfrac{d}{c}$ to isolate $\sqrt{2}$.

$$\frac{d}{c} \cdot \frac{c}{d}\sqrt{2} = \frac{d}{c} \cdot \frac{eb - af}{bf}$$

$$\sqrt{2} = \frac{deb - daf}{cbf}$$

Because all the letters are integers, it follows that $\sqrt{2}$ is a rational number, a contradiction. Consequently, $\dfrac{a}{b} + \dfrac{c}{d}\sqrt{2}$ is an irrational number.

Many irrational numbers can be interpreted geometrically. For example, we find a point on a number line to represent $\sqrt{2}$ by using the **Pythagorean Theorem**. That is, *if a and b are the lengths of the shorter sides (legs) of a right triangle and c is the length of the longer side (hypotenuse), then* $a^2 + b^2 = c^2$, as shown in Figure 2.

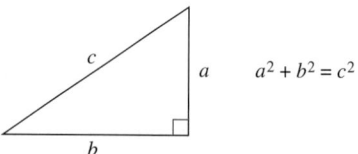

Figure 2

Figure 3 shows a segment 1 unit long constructed perpendicular to a number line at point P. Thus two sides of the triangle shown are each 1 unit long. If $a = b = 1$, then $c^2 = 2$ and $c = \sqrt{2}$. To find a point on the number line that corresponds to $\sqrt{2}$, we need to find a point Q on the number line such that the distance from 0 to Q is $\sqrt{2}$. Because $\sqrt{2}$ is the length of the hypotenuse, the point Q can be found by marking an arc with center 0 and radius c. The intersection of the positive number line with the arc is point Q.

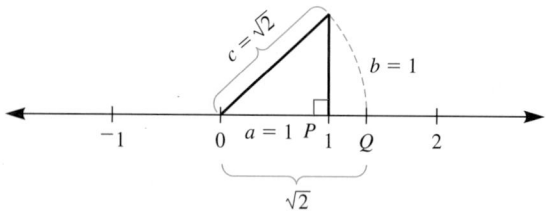

Figure 3

Similarly, other principal square roots can be constructed, as shown in Figure 4 and placed on a number line using the method of Figure 3. Also, their opposites can then be constructed, as shown in Figure 4.

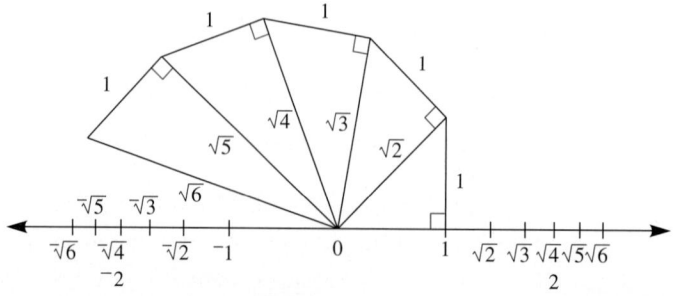

Figure 4

Estimating a Square Root

From Figure 4, we see that $\sqrt{2}$ must have a value between 1 and 2; that is, $1 < \sqrt{2} < 2$. To obtain a closer approximation of $\sqrt{2}$, we attempt to "squeeze" $\sqrt{2}$ between two numbers that are between 1 and 2. Because $(1.4)^2 = 1.96$ and $(1.5)^2 = 2.25$, it follows that $1.4 < \sqrt{2} < 1.5$. Because a^2 can be interpreted as the area of a square with side of length a, this discussion can be pictured geometrically, as in Figure 5.

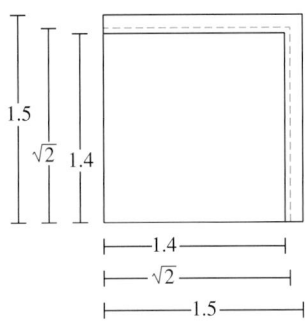

Figure 5

For a more accurate approximation for $\sqrt{2}$, we continue this squeezing process. We see that $(1.4)^2 = 1.96$, is closer to 2 than is $(1.5)^2 = 2.25$, so we choose numbers closer to 1.4 to find the next approximation. We find the following:

$$(1.42)^2 = 2.0164$$
$$(1.41)^2 = 1.9981$$

Thus, $1.41 < \sqrt{2} < 1.42$. We continue this process until we obtain the desired approximation. If a calculator has a square-root key, we can obtain an approximation directly. In fact, $\sqrt{2}$ is approximately 1.41421356.

▶ **NOW TRY THIS 1**

NTT 1: Answers can be found in Answers at the back of the book.

One algorithm for calculating square roots is sometimes attributed to Archimedes though the Babylonians had a similar method. The method is also referred to as Newton's method. The algorithm finds closer and closer estimates to the square root. To find the square root of a positive number, n, we first make a positive number guess, *Guess*1. Now compute as follows:

Step 1. Divide n by *Guess*1.
Step 2. Now add *Guess*1 to the quotient obtained in step 1.
Step 3. Divide the sum in step 2 by 2. The quotient becomes *Guess*2.
Step 4. Repeat steps 1–3 using *Guess*2 to obtain a successive guess.
Step 5. The process may be repeated until the desired accuracy is achieved.

  a. Use the method described to find the square root of 13 to three decimal places.
  b. Write the steps for the algorithm in a recursive formula.

The System of Real Numbers, Operations, and Their Properties

Real numbers can be represented as, terminating, repeating, or nonterminating and nonrepeating decimals.

Every integer is a rational number as well as a real number. Every rational number is a real number, but not every real number is rational, as has been shown with $\sqrt{2}$. The relationships among sets of numbers are summarized in the diagram in Figure 6.

Real Numbers: $R = \{x \mid x \text{ can be written as a decimal}\}$

Irrational Numbers:

$S = \{x \mid x \text{ is a non-repeating and non terminating decimal}\}$

Rationals: $Q = \left\{x \mid x = \dfrac{a}{b}, \text{ where } a, b \in I \text{ and } b \neq 0\right\}$

Integers: $I = \{\ldots, {}^-3, {}^-2, {}^-1, 0, 1, 2, 3, \ldots\}$

Whole Numbers: $W = \{0, 1, 2, 3, 4, \ldots\}$

Natural Numbers: $N = \{1, 2, 3, 4, 5, \ldots\}$

Figure 6

The set of fractions can be extended to be of the form $\dfrac{a}{b}$, where a and b are real numbers with $b \neq 0$, such as $\dfrac{\sqrt{3}}{5}$.

Addition, subtraction, multiplication, and division are defined on the set of real numbers in such a way that all the properties of these operations on rationals still hold. The properties are summarized next.

Theorem 8-1:   Properties of Operations on Real Numbers

Closure properties	For real numbers a and b, $a + b$ and ab are unique real numbers.
Commutative properties	For real numbers a and b, $a + b = b + a$ and $ab = ba$.
Associative properties	For real numbers a, b, and c, $a + (b + c) = (a + b) + c$ and $a(bc) = (ab)c$.
Identity properties	The number 0 is the unique additive identity because for any real number a, $a + 0 = a = 0 + a$.
	The number 1 is the unique multiplicative identity because for any real number a, $a \cdot 1 = a = 1 \cdot a$.
Inverse properties	For every real number a, ${}^-a$ is its unique additive inverse; that is, $a + {}^-a = 0 = {}^-a + a$.
	For every nonzero real number a, $\dfrac{1}{a}$ (or a^{-1}) is its unique multiplicative inverse; that is, $a\left(\dfrac{1}{a}\right) = 1 = \left(\dfrac{1}{a}\right)a$.
Distributive property of multiplication over addition and subtraction	For real numbers a, b, and c, $a(b + c) = ab + ac$; $a(b - c) = ab - ac$.
Multiplication property of zero	For all real numbers a, $a \cdot 0 = 0 = 0 \cdot a$.
Density property for real numbers	For real numbers a and b with $a < b$, there exists a real number c such that $a < c < b$.
Inverse properties	For every real number a, ${}^-a$ is it unique additive inverse; that is $a + {}^-a = 0 = {}^-a + a$.
	For every nonzero real number a, $\dfrac{1}{a}$ (or a^{-1}) is its unique multiplicative inverse, that is, $a\left(\dfrac{1}{a}\right) = 1 = \left(\dfrac{1}{a}\right)a$.

By the denseness property, we can always find a real number between any two other real numbers. This leads to infinitely many real numbers.

Order of Operations

The set of real numbers follows the same order of operations given earlier; that is, when addition, subtraction, multiplication, division, and exponentiation appear without parentheses, exponentiation is done first in order from right to left, then multiplications and divisions in the order of their appearance from left to right, and then additions and subtractions in the order of their appearance from left to right. Arithmetic operations that appear inside parentheses must be done first.

Radicals and Rational Exponents

Scientific calculators have a $\boxed{y^x}$ key with which we find the values of expressions like $4^{1/2}$ and $3.41^{2/3}$. What does $4^{1/2}$ mean? By extending the properties of exponents previously developed for integer exponents,

$$4^{1/2} \cdot 4^{1/2} = 4^{(1/2+1/2)} = 4^1$$

$$(4^{1/2})^2 = 4^1 = 4$$

and consequently, $4^{1/2}$ must be a square root of 4. To obtain a unique value, it is defined to be the principal square root, that is:

$$4^{1/2} = \sqrt{4}$$

In general, if x is a nonnegative real number, then $x^{1/2} = \sqrt{x}$. Similarly, $(x^{1/3})^3 = x^{(1/3)3} = x^1$ and $x^{1/3} = \sqrt[3]{x}$. This discussion leads to the following definitions.

Definition of Real Number Raised to Rational Exponent

If x is a real number, n is a positive integer and m is an integer then:

1. $x^{1/n} = \sqrt[n]{x}$, when $\sqrt[n]{x}$ is meaningful.

2. $x^{m/n} = \sqrt[n]{x^m}$, if $\text{GCD}(m, n) = 1$ and $\sqrt[n]{x^m}$ is meaningful.

From part (1) it follows that $(x^m)^{1/n} = \sqrt[n]{x^m}$ if $\sqrt[n]{x^m}$ is meaningful. If n is odd then $\sqrt[n]{x^n} = x$ for all real x, but if n is even then $\sqrt[n]{x^n} = |x|$. For example $\sqrt[4]{(^-2)^4} = \sqrt[4]{16} = 2$.

More about Properties of Exponents

It can be shown that the properties of integer exponents also hold for rational exponents. These properties are equivalent to the corresponding properties of radicals *if the expressions involving radicals are meaningful.*

Let r and s be any rational numbers, x and y be any real numbers, and n a positive integer. If all the expressions are meaningful then,

a. $x^{-r} = \dfrac{1}{x^r}$.

b. $(xy)^r = x^r y^r$ which implies $(xy)^{1/n} = x^{1/n} y^{1/n}$ and $\sqrt[n]{xy} = \sqrt[n]{x}\sqrt[n]{y}$.

c. $\left(\dfrac{x}{y}\right)^r = \dfrac{x^r}{y^r}$ which implies $\left(\dfrac{x}{y}\right)^{1/n} = \dfrac{x^{1/n}}{y^{1/n}}$ and $\sqrt[n]{\dfrac{x}{y}} = \dfrac{\sqrt[n]{x}}{\sqrt[n]{y}}$.

d. $(x^r)^s = x^{rs}$ which implies $(x^{1/n})^p = x^{p/n}$ and hence $(\sqrt[n]{x})^p = \sqrt[n]{x^p}$, where p is an integer.

The preceding properties can be used to write equivalent and simplified expressions for many roots. For example, $\sqrt{96} = \sqrt{16 \cdot 6} = \sqrt{16}\sqrt{6} = 4\sqrt{6}$. Similarly, $\sqrt[3]{54} = \sqrt[3]{27 \cdot 2} = \sqrt[3]{27}\sqrt[3]{2} = 3\sqrt[3]{2}$.

Example 3

Simplify each of the following if possible.

a. $16^{1/4}$　　　**b.** $16^{5/4}$　　　**c.** $(^-8)^{1/3}$

d. $125^{-4/3}$　　**e.** $(^-16)^{1/4}$

Solution

a. $16^{1/4} = (2^4)^{1/4} = 2^1 = 2$. Also $16^{1/4} = \sqrt[4]{16} = 2$

b. $16^{5/4} = 16^{(1/4)5} = (16^{1/4})^5 = 2^5 = 32$

c. $(^-8)^{1/3} = ((^-2)^3)^{1/3} = (^-2)^1 = ^-2$ or $(^-8)^{1/3} = \sqrt[3]{^-8} = ^-2$

d. $125^{-4/3} = (5^3)^{-4/3} = 5^{-4} = \dfrac{1}{5^4} = \dfrac{1}{625}$

e. Because every real number raised to the fourth power is positive, $\sqrt[4]{^-16}$ is not a real number. Consequently, $(^-16)^{1/4}$ is not a real number. A simplification is not possible.

▶ **NOW TRY THIS 2**

NTT 2: Answers can be found in Answers at the back of the book.

Compute $\sqrt[8]{10}$ on a calculator using the following sequence of keys:

$$\boxed{10}\ \boxed{\sqrt{\ }}\ \boxed{\sqrt{\ }}\ \boxed{\sqrt{\ }}$$

a. Explain why this approach works.

b. For what values of n can $\sqrt[n]{10}$ be computed using only the $\boxed{\sqrt{\ }}$ key? Why?

▶ **NOW TRY THIS 3**

NTT 3: Answers can be found in Answers at the back of the book.

The properties of integer exponents were extended to rational exponents and can be extended to real number exponents. Consider a base with a decimal exponent such as $8^{0.\overline{3}}$ and $8^{0.101001\ldots}$. Write an explanation for a possible meaning of these decimal exponents.

Assessment 8-1A

1. Write an irrational number whose digits are 2s and 3s. *
2. Use the Pythagorean Theorem to find the value for x.

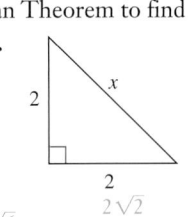
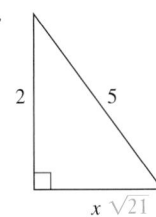

a.   b.   c.

3. Arrange the following real numbers in order from greatest to least. $0.9, 0.998, \sqrt{0.98}, 0.\overline{98}, 0.\overline{9}, 0.\overline{898}$

$$0.9, \quad 0.\overline{9}, \quad 0.\overline{98}, \quad 0.9\overline{88}, \quad 0.9\overline{98}, \quad 0.\overline{898}, \quad \sqrt{0.98}$$

4. Determine which of the following represent irrational numbers.
   a. $\sqrt{51}$ Yes
   b. $\sqrt{64}$ No
   c. $\sqrt{324}$ No
   d. $\sqrt{325}$ Yes
   e. $2 + 3\sqrt{2}$ Yes
   f. $\sqrt{2} \div 5$ Yes
5. If possible, find each of the following without using a calculator.
   a. The principal square root of 225   15
   b. $\sqrt{169}$ 13
   c. $^-\sqrt{81}$ $^-9$
   d. $\sqrt{625}$ 25
   e. $\sqrt{\dfrac{1}{4}}$ $\dfrac{1}{2}$
   f. $\sqrt{0.0001}$ 0.01
6. Find the approximate square root of each of the following, rounded to hundredths, using the squeezing method.
   a. 7   2.65
   b. 0.0120   0.11
7. Classify each of the following statements as true or false. If false, give a counterexample.
   a. The sum of any rational number and any irrational number is a rational number.   False: $\sqrt{2} + 0 = \sqrt{2}$
   b. The sum of any two irrational numbers is an irrational number.   False: $^-\sqrt{2} + \sqrt{2} = 0$
   c. The product of any two irrational numbers is an irrational number.   False: $\sqrt{2} \cdot \sqrt{2} = 2$
   d. The difference of two irrational numbers could be a rational number.   True
8. Find three irrational numbers between each of the following pairs of rational numbers.
   a. 1 and 3   Answers vary. For example: $\sqrt{2}, \sqrt{3},$ and $\sqrt{5}$.
   b. $0.\overline{54}$ and $0.\overline{55}$ *
   c. $\dfrac{1}{2}$ and $\dfrac{1}{3}$ *
9. Based on your answers in exercise 8, argue that there are infinitely many irrational numbers.   *
10. If R is the set of real numbers, Q is the set of rational numbers, I is the set of integers, W is the set of whole numbers, and S is the set of irrational numbers, find each of the following:
    a. $Q \cup S$ R
    b. $Q \cap S$ $\varnothing$
    c. $Q \cap R$ Q
    d. $S \cap W$ $\varnothing$
    e. $W \cup R$ R
    f. $Q \cup R$ R

11. The letters in the following table correspond to the sets listed in exercise 10. Complete the table by placing checkmarks in the appropriate columns. (N is the set of natural numbers.)

	N	*I*	*Q*	*S*	*R*
a. 6.7			✓		✓
b. 5	✓	✓	✓		✓
c. $\sqrt{2}$				✓	✓
d. $^-5$		✓	✓		✓
e. $3\dfrac{1}{7}$			✓		✓

12. The letters in following table correspond to the sets listed in exercise 10. Put a checkmark under each set of numbers for which a solution to the problem exists. (N is the set of natural numbers.)

	N	*I*	*Q*	*S*	*R*
a. $x^2 + 1 = 5$	✓	✓	✓	✓	✓
b. $2x - 1 = 32$			✓		✓
c. $x^2 = 3$				✓	✓
d. $\sqrt{x} = ^-1$					
e. $\dfrac{3}{4}x = 0.\overline{4}$			✓		✓

13. Determine for what real number values of x, if any, each of the following statements is true.
    a. $\sqrt{x} = 8$ 64
    b. $\sqrt{x} = ^-8$ None
    c. $\sqrt{x} = 8$ $^-64$
    d. $\sqrt{x} = ^-8$ None
    e. $\sqrt{x} > 0$ *
    f. $\sqrt{x} < 0$ None
14. Write each of the following roots in the form $a\sqrt{b}$, where a and b are integers and b has the least value possible.
    a. $\sqrt{180}$ $6\sqrt{5}$
    b. $\sqrt{363}$ $11\sqrt{3}$
    c. $\sqrt{252}$ $6\sqrt{7}$
15. Write each of the following in the simplest form or as $a\sqrt[n]{b}$, where a and b are integers, $b > 0$, and b has the least value possible.
    a. $\sqrt[3]{54}$ $^-3\sqrt[3]{2}$
    b. $\sqrt[5]{96}$ $2\sqrt[5]{3}$
    c. $\sqrt[3]{250}$ $5\sqrt[3]{2}$
    d. $\sqrt[5]{243}$ $^-3$
16. If each of the following is a part of a geometric sequence, find the missing terms.
    a. 5, ____, ____, 10   *
    b. 2, ____, ____, ____, 1   *
    c. ____, 5, ____, 3   *
    d. ____, $^-2$, ____, $^-3$ *

17. The expression $2^{10} \cdot 16^t$ approximates the number of bacteria after t hr.
    a. What is the initial number of bacteria, that is, the number when $t = 0$? 2^{10}
    b. After $\dfrac{1}{4}$ hr, how many bacteria are there? 2^{11}
    c. After $\dfrac{1}{2}$ hr, how many bacteria are there? 2^{12}

18. Evaluate each of the following without using a calculator.
    a. $(0.008)^{\frac{2}{3}}$ $\dfrac{1}{25}$
    b. $(6.25)^{\frac{3}{2}}$ $\dfrac{125}{8}$
    c. $\left(\dfrac{25}{81}\right)^{-\frac{3}{2}}$ $\dfrac{729}{125}$
    d. $(0.0000128)^{\frac{3}{7}}$ $\dfrac{1}{125}$
    e. $(^-27)^{-\frac{4}{3}}$ $\dfrac{1}{81}$
    f. $^-(27)^{-\frac{4}{3}}$ $-\dfrac{1}{81}$

19. In each of the following, find all real numbers x that satisfy the given equation. If none satisfy the equation, then state the answer as "None."
    a. $3^x = 243$ 5
    b. $9^{-x} = 27$ $-\dfrac{3}{2}$

    c. $\left(\dfrac{9}{4}\right)^{3x} = \dfrac{32}{243}$ $-\dfrac{5}{6}$
    d. $\sqrt{^-x} = 3\sqrt{2}$ $^-18$
    e. $x^{-\frac{3}{4}} = 2$ $2^{-\frac{4}{3}}$
    f. $(x - 1)^2 = 2$ $1 \pm \sqrt{2}$

20. Write an equation in x not involving radical signs or fractional exponents with the following as a solution.   Answers vary
    a. $\sqrt[5]{20}$ $x^5 - 20 = 0$
    b. $\sqrt[3]{-2}$ $x^3 + 2 = 0$
    c. $\sqrt[3]{10} - 1$ $(x + 1)^3 - 10 = 0$
    d. $\dfrac{\sqrt{2}}{\sqrt{3}}$ $3x^2 - 2 = 0$

21. Use the "guess and check" strategy to approximate $\sqrt[3]{103}$ to the nearest whole number.   *

22. Determine which of the following are irrational.
    a. $\dfrac{\sqrt{500}}{\sqrt{20}}$ Rational
    b. $8^{\frac{1}{3}} + 8^{-\frac{1}{3}}$ Rational
    c. $\dfrac{2}{\sqrt{2}} - \sqrt{2}$ Rational
    d. $\sqrt{1000}$ Irrational

Assessment 8-1B

1. Write an irrational number whose digits are 4s and 5s.   *
2. Use the Pythagorean Theorem to find x.

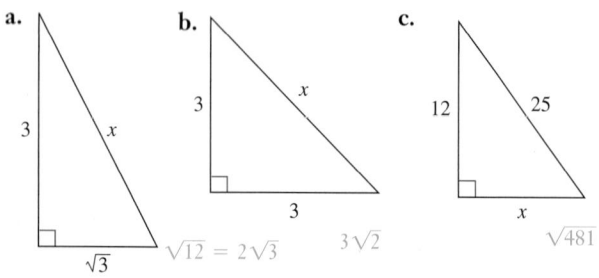

    a. $\sqrt{3}$
    b. $\sqrt{12} = 2\sqrt{3}$ $3\sqrt{2}$
    c. $\sqrt{481}$

3. Arrange the following real numbers in order from greatest to least. $0.\overline{89}, 0.8\overline{89}, 0.\overline{8}, \sqrt{0.7744}, 0.8$

$$0.8, 0.\overline{8}, 0.\overline{89}, 0.8\overline{89}, \sqrt{0.7744}$$

4. Determine which of the following represent irrational numbers.
    a. $\sqrt{78}$ Yes
    b. $\sqrt{81}$ No
    c. $\sqrt[3]{343}$ No
    d. $3 + \sqrt{81}$ No
    e. $2 \div \sqrt{2}$ Yes

5. If possible, find each of the following without using a calculator.
    a. The principle square root of 256   16
    b. $\sqrt{324}$ 18
    c. $\sqrt[4]{-1}$ Not possible
    d. All x such that $x^2 = 1024$ 32

6. Find the approximate principal square root for each of the following, rounded to hundredths, using the squeezing method.
    a. 20.3   4.51
    b. 1.64   1.28

7. Classify each of the following statements as true or false. If false, give a counterexample.

    a. The sum of any two rational numbers is a rational number.   True
    b. The difference of any two irrational numbers is an irrational number.   False; $0 \cdot \sqrt{2} = 0$
    c. The product of any rational number and any irrational number is an irrational number.   False; $0 \cdot \sqrt{2} = 0$

8. Find three irrational numbers between each of the following pairs of numbers.
    a. 3 and 4   *
    b. $0.\overline{55}$ and $0.\overline{56}$ *
    c. 0.01 and 0.011   *

9. Describe infinitely many irrational numbers between 1 and 2 in terms of $\sqrt{2}$.   *

10. If R is the set of real numbers, Q is the set of rational numbers, I is the set of integers, W is the set of whole numbers, N is the set of natural numbers, and S is the set of irrational numbers, simplify or answer the following.
    a. $Q \cap I$ I
    b. $S - Q$ S
    c. $R \cup S$ R
    d. Which of the sets could be a universal set for the rest of the sets? R
    e. If the universal set is R, how would you describe $\overline{S}$?   *

11. The letters in the table correspond to the sets listed in exercise 10. Complete the following table by placing checkmarks in the appropriate columns.

	N	I	Q	S	R
a. $\sqrt{3}$				✓	✓
b. $4\dfrac{1}{2}$			✓		✓
c. $^-3\dfrac{1}{7}$			✓		✓

12. The letters in the following table correspond to the sets listed in exercise 10. Put a checkmark under each set of numbers for which a solution to the problem exists.

	N	I	Q	S	R
a. $x^2 + 2 = 4$				✓	✓
b. $1 - 2x = 32$			✓		✓
c. $x^3 = 4$				✓	✓
d. $\sqrt{x} = {}^-2$					
e. $0.\overline{7}x = 5$			✓		✓

13. Determine for what real values of x, if any, each of the following statements is true.
  a. $\sqrt{x} = 5$ $x = 25$
  b. $\sqrt{x} = {}^-7$ No solution
  c. $\sqrt{{}^-x} = 5$ $x = {}^-25$
  d. ${}^-\sqrt{x} = 7$ No solution
  e. ${}^-\sqrt{x} = {}^-5$ $x = 25$

14. Write each of the following square roots in the form $a\sqrt{b}$, where a and b are integers and b has the least value possible.
  a. $\sqrt{360}$ $6\sqrt{10}$
  b. $\sqrt{40}$ $2\sqrt{10}$
  c. $\sqrt{240}$ $4\sqrt{15}$

15. Write each of the following in the simplest form or as $a\sqrt[n]{b}$, where a and b are integers and $b > 0$ and b is as small as possible.
  a. $\sqrt[3]{{}^-102}$ ${}^-\sqrt[3]{102}$
  b. $\sqrt[6]{64}$ 2
  c. $\sqrt[3]{64}$ 4

16. If each of the following is a part of a geometric sequence, find the missing terms.
  a. $4, \underline{\quad}, \underline{\quad}, 8$ *
  b. $1, \underline{\quad}, \underline{\quad}, 2$ *
  c. $\underline{\quad}, \underline{\quad}, 2, \sqrt{2}$ *
  d. $\underline{\quad}, 1, \underline{\quad}, 2$ *

17. In the expression 8^t, let t represents time in hours.
  a. What is the value of the expression when $t = 0$?   1
  b. After $\dfrac{1}{3}$ hour what is the value of the expression?   2

18. Evaluate each of the following without using a calculator.
  a. $(0.008)^{-\frac{2}{3}}$ 25
  b. $(0.04)^{\frac{3}{2}}$ $\dfrac{1}{125}$
  c. $\left(\dfrac{{}^-8}{27}\right)^{-\frac{2}{3}}$ $\dfrac{9}{4}$
  d. $(0.00000256)^{\frac{3}{8}}$ $\dfrac{1}{125}$
  e. $({}^-32)^{-\frac{4}{5}}$ $\dfrac{1}{16}$
  f. ${}^-(32)^{-\frac{4}{5}}$ $\dfrac{1}{16}$

19. In each of the following, find all real numbers x that satisfy the given equation. If none satisfy the equation, then state the answer as "None."
  a. $3^x = {}^-243$ None
  b. $81^{-x} = 27$ $-\dfrac{3}{4}$
  c. $\left(\dfrac{4}{9}\right)^{-3x} = \dfrac{32}{243}$ $-\dfrac{5}{6}$
  d. $\sqrt[3]{x} = 2\sqrt{3}$ -24
  e. $x^{-\frac{2}{5}} = 2$ $2^{\frac{5}{2}}$ or $-2^{\frac{5}{2}}$
  f. $(x + 1)^2 = 2$ ${}^-1 \pm \sqrt{2}$

20. Write an equation in x not involving radical signs or fractional exponents with the following as a solution.   Answers vary.
  a. $\sqrt[3]{5}$ $x^3 - 5 = 0$
  b. $\sqrt[5]{{}^-2}$ $x^5 + 2 = 0$
  c. $\sqrt{2} - 1$ $(x + 1)^2 - 2 = 0$
  d. $\dfrac{\sqrt{2}}{\sqrt[3]{2}}$ $x^6 - 2 = 0$

21. Use the "guess and check" strategy to approximate $\sqrt[3]{2001}$ to the nearest whole number.   *

22. Determine which of the following irrational.
  a. $\dfrac{\sqrt{320}}{\sqrt{20}}$ Rational
  b. $2\sqrt{50} - 8\sqrt{5}$ Irrational
  c. $\dfrac{\sqrt{2}}{2} - \sqrt{2}$ Irrational
  d. $\sqrt{10^9}$ Irrational

Mathematical Connections 8-1

Answers to Mathematical Connections can be found in the Answers section at the back of the book.

Reasoning

1. Use the fact that each prime in the prime factorization of a^3 (a is a whole number) appears a number of times that is a multiple of 3 to prove that $\sqrt[3]{2}$ is irrational.

2. Find the value of $\sqrt{3}$ on a calculator. Explain why this cannot be the exact value of $\sqrt{3}$.

3. Is it true that $\sqrt{a + b} = \sqrt{a} + \sqrt{b}$ for all a and b? If not, find all the values of a and b for which it is true. Explain.

4. The number $\dfrac{22}{7}$ can be written as an infinite repeating decimal. Could $\pi = \dfrac{22}{7}$? Why or why not?

5. a. Use the fact that if a prime p appears in the prime factorization of a perfect square then it must appear an even number of times, to prove that for all primes p, $\sqrt{p}$ is irrational.
  b. Prove that $\sqrt{\dfrac{7}{2}}$ is irrational.

6. Without using a calculator, order the following. Explain your reasoning.

$$(4/25)^{-1/3}, (25/4)^{1/3}, (4/25)^{-1/4}$$

7. a. To prove that $\dfrac{2}{\sqrt{3}} < \dfrac{3}{\sqrt{5}}$ a student wrote the following:

$$\dfrac{3}{\sqrt{5}} - \dfrac{2}{\sqrt{3}} = \dfrac{3\sqrt{3} - 2\sqrt{5}}{\sqrt{15}} = \dfrac{\sqrt{9} \cdot \sqrt{3} - \sqrt{4} \cdot \sqrt{5}}{\sqrt{15}}$$

$$= \dfrac{\sqrt{27} - \sqrt{20}}{\sqrt{15}} > 0$$

  Explain why this proves that $\dfrac{2}{\sqrt{3}} < \dfrac{3}{\sqrt{5}}$.

  b. Prove that $\dfrac{5}{\sqrt{6}} < \dfrac{6}{\sqrt{7}}$, using the approach in part(a).

Open-Ended

8. The sequence 1, 1.01, 1.001, 1.0001, . . . is an infinite sequence of rational numbers (each term has one more zero between the ones than the preceding term).
  a. Describe several other infinite sequences of rational numbers.
  b. Describe an infinite sequence of irrational numbers.

9. **a.** Define three irrational numbers between $\frac{1}{2}$ and $\frac{3}{4}$, each of which has the form $\frac{a}{b}\sqrt{2}$ where a and b are integers.

   b. Describe an infinite sequence of irrational numbers between $\frac{1}{2}$ and $\frac{3}{4}$.

Cooperative Learning

10. Let each member of a group choose a number between 0 and 1 on a calculator and check what happens when the $\boxed{x^2}$ key is pressed in succession until it is clear that there is no reason to go on.

    a. Compare your answers and write a conjecture based on what you observe.

    b. Use other keys on the calculator in a similar way. Describe the process and state a corresponding conjecture.

    c. Why do you get the result you do in parts (a) and (b)?

11. A calculator displays the following: $(3.7)^{2.4} = 23.103838$. In your group, discuss the meaning of the expression $(3.7)^{2.4}$ in view of what you know about exponents. Compare your findings with those of other groups.

Connecting Mathematics to the Classroom

12. Jim asked, if $\sqrt{2}$ can be written as $\frac{\sqrt{2}}{1}$, why is it not rational? How would you answer him?

13. A student claims that $(\sqrt{a} + \sqrt{b})^2 = a + b$ because $(\sqrt{a})^2 = a$ and $(\sqrt{b})^2 = b$. How would you help the student?

14. A student wants to know how to write $\sqrt{\sqrt{\sqrt{2}}}$ with a single radical sign. How would you help the student?

15. A student says that she saw online that the solution of $x^2 = 2$ was written as $x = \pm\sqrt{2}$. She claims that if this is true then $\sqrt{2}$ has two values: one positive and one negative. How would you respond?

16. A student noticed that $\sqrt[3]{5} < \sqrt{5}$ and wants to know if whenever $a > 0$, $\sqrt[3]{a} < \sqrt{a}$. How do you respond?

17. Jose says that the equation $\sqrt{-x} = 3$ has no solution, since the square root of a negative number does not exist. How would you help him?

18. A student wants to know what is wrong with the following "proof" that $^-1 = 1$. How do you respond?

$$\sqrt{a}\sqrt{b} = \sqrt{ab}$$
$$\text{Let } a = b = \,^-1.$$
$$\sqrt{^-1}\sqrt{^-1} = \sqrt{(^-1)(^-1)} = \sqrt{1} = 1$$
$$\text{But also } \sqrt{^-1}\sqrt{^-1} = \,^-1.$$
$$\text{Thus, } ^-1 = 1.$$

8-2 Variables

8-2 Objectives

Students will be able to understand and explain

- Variables to translate word phrases into algebraic expressions.

- Solving equations and word problems.

- The formulas for the nth term of arithmetic and geometric sequences.

Algebraic thinking is important in mathematics at all levels—from the early grades on. In this section, we focus not only on patterns (introduced in Chapter 1) but on other features of algebraic thinking as well, including solving equations, word problems.

Today, the importance of integrating algebraic thinking and problem solving at all levels begins with kindergarten.

CCSS In grade 4, *Common Core Standards* emphasizes using algebraic equations and says that students should:

Multiply or divide to solve word problems involving multiplicative comparison, for instance by using drawings and equations with a symbol for the unknown number to represent the problem, distinguishing multiplicative comparison from additive comparison. Solve multistep word problems posed with whole numbers and having whole-number answers using the four operations, including problems in which remainders must be interpreted. Represent these problems using equations with a letter standing for the unknown quantity. Assess the reasonableness of answers using mental computation and estimation strategies including rounding. (p. 29)

Grade 6 *Common Core Standards* suggests that students:

use variables to represent numbers and write expressions when solving a real-world or mathematical problem. . . . (p. 44)

Historical Note

al-Khowarizmi

Fibonacci

The word *algebra* comes from the book *Hidab al-jabr wa'l muqabalah*, written by Mohammed ibn Musa al-Khowarizmi (ca. 825 CE). In his book he synthesized Hindu work on the notions of algebra and used the words *jabr* and *muqubalah* to designate two basic operations in solving equations: *jabr* meant to transpose subtracted terms to the other side of the equation; *muqubalah* meant to cancel like terms on opposite sides of the equation.

Another contributor to the development of algebra was Diophantus (ca. 200–284 CE) whose *Arithmetica* is the most prominent work on algebra in Greek mathematics. About 900 years later, Leonardo di Pisa (Fibonacci) (ca. 1170–1250) introduced algebra to Europe.

A fourth contributor to algebra was François Viète (1540–1603), known as "the father of modern algebra," who introduced the first systematic algebraic notation in his book *In Artem Analyticam Isagoge*.   ●

Algebra is a branch of mathematics in which symbols, usually letters, represent numbers or members of a given set. Elementary algebra is used to generalize arithmetic. For example, the fact that $7 + (3 + 5) = (7 + 3) + 5$, or that $9 + (3 + 8) = (9 + 3) + 8$, are special cases of $a + (b + c) = (a + b) + c$, where a, b, and c are numbers from a given set; whole numbers, integers, rational numbers, or real numbers. Similarly, $2 + 3 = 3 + 2$ and $2 \cdot 3 = 3 \cdot 2$ are special cases of $a + b = b + a$ and $a \cdot b = b \cdot a$ for all whole numbers a and b.

A major concept of algebraic thinking is that of **variable**. In basic arithmetic we have fixed numbers, or **constants**, as in $4 + 3 = 7$, but in algebra we have values that vary—hence the term *variable*.

- A variable may stand for a missing element or unknown, as in $x + 2 = 5$.
- A variable can represent more than one thing. For example, in a group of children, we could say that their heights vary with their ages. If h represents height and a represents age, then both h and a can have different values for different children in the group. Here a variable represents a changing quantity.
- A variable can be used in generalizations of patterns.
- A variable can be an element of a set, or a set itself. For example, in the definition of the intersection of two sets $A \cap B = \{x \mid x \in A \text{ and } x \in B\}$, x is any element that belongs to both sets.

To apply algebra in solving problems, we frequently need to translate given information into a mathematical expression involving variables designated by letters or words. In all such examples, we may name the variables as we choose.

In the student page shown on page 402, simple word statements are translated into **algebraic expressions**.

Historical Note

Mary Everest Boole

Mary Everest Boole (1832–1916), born in England and raised in France, was a self-taught mathematician and is most well-known for her works on mathematics and science education. In *Philosophy and Fun of Algebra* (London: C. W. Daniel, LTD, 1909), a book for children, she writes:

But when we come to the end of our arithmetic we do not content ourselves with guesses; we proceed to algebra—that is to say, to dealing logically with the fact of our own ignorance. . . .

Instead of guessing whether we are to call it nine, or seven, or a hundred and twenty, or a thousand and fifty, let us agree to call it x, and let us always remember that x stands for the Unknown. . . . This method of solving problems by honest confession of one's ignorance is called Algebra.   ●

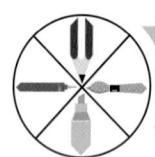

School Book Page — Using Variables to Write Expressions

Step-UP
Lesson
2

Common
Core

5.OA.2 Write simple
expressions that record
calculations with numbers,
and interpret numerical
expressions without
evaluating them.

Using Variables to Write Expressions

How can you write an algebraic expression?

Donnie bought CDs for $10 each. How can you represent the total cost of the CDs?

A **variable** is <u>a quantity that can change or vary and is often represented with a letter</u>. Variables help you translate word phrases into algebraic expressions.

$10 each

CDs cost $10 each. The operation is multiplication.

Number of CDs	Total Cost
1	$10 × 1
2	$10 × 2
3	$10 × 3
4	$10 × 4

Use the variable n to represent the number of CDs and write an algebraic expression.

$$\$10 \times n$$

An **algebraic expression** is <u>a mathematical phrase that has at least one variable and one operation</u>. The total cost of the CDs is represented by

$$10 \times n$$
or $10n$.

The operation is multiplication. The variable is n.

Other Examples

The table shows algebraic expressions for given situations.

Word Phrase	Operation	Algebraic Expression
5 dollars more than cost c	addition	$c + 5$
eleven pencils decreased by a number n	subtraction	$11 - n$
six times a distance d	multiplication	$6 \times d$ or $6d$
b bananas divided by seven	division	$b \div 7$ or $\frac{b}{7}$
four less than two times an amount x	multiplication and subtraction	$2x - 4$

Example 4

In each of the following descriptions, translate the given information into a symbolic expression involving variables.

  a. The cost of renting a car for any number of days if the charge per day is $40
  b. The distance a car traveled at a constant speed of 65 mph for any number of hours
  c. One weekend, a store sold twice as many CDs as full-size DVDs and 25 fewer mini DVDs than CDs. If the store sold d full-size DVDs, how many mini DVDs and CDs did it sell?
  d. French fries have about 12 calories apiece. A hamburger has about 600 calories. Akiva is on a diet of 2000 calories per day. If he ate f french fries and one hamburger, how many more calories can he consume that day?

Solution

  a. If d is the number of days, the cost of renting the car for d days at $40 per day is $40d$ dollars.
  b. If h is the number of hours traveled at 65 mph, the total distance traveled in h hours is $65h$ miles.
  c. Because d full-size DVDs were sold, twice as many CDs as full-size DVDs implies $2d$ CDs. Thus, 25 fewer mini DVDs than CDs implies $2d - 25$ mini DVDs.
  d. First, find how many calories Akiva consumed eating f french fries and one hamburger. Then, to find how many more calories he can consume, subtract this expression from 2000.

  1 french fry $\rightarrow$ 12 calories

  f french fries $\rightarrow$ $12f$ calories

  Therefore, the number of calories in f french fries and one hamburger is $600 + 12f$.

  The number of calories left for the day is $2000 - (600 + 12f)$, or $2000 - 600 - 12f$, or $1400 - 12f$.

Example 5

Activity Manual

Use *Patterns and Expressions* to practice writing algebraic expressions that describe patterns.

A teacher asked her class to do the following:

  Take any real number and add 15 to it. Now multiply that sum by 4. Next subtract 8 and divide the difference by 4. Now subtract 12 from the quotient and tell me the answer. I will tell you the original number.

Analyze the instructions to see whether the teacher can determine the original number.

Solution   Translate the information into an algebraic expression as seen in Table 1.

Table 1

Instructions	Discussion	Symbols/Algebraic Expressions
Take any real number.	Since any number is used, we need a variable to represent the number. Let n be that variable.	n
Add 15 to it.	We are told to add 15 to "it." "It" refers to the variable n.	$n + 15$
Multiply that sum by 4.	We are told to multiply "that sum" by 4. "That sum" is $n + 15$.	$4(n + 15)$
Subtract 8.	We are told to subtract 8 from the product.	$4(n + 15) - 8$
Divide the difference by 4.	The difference is $4(n + 15) - 8$. Divide it by 4.	$\dfrac{4(n + 15) - 8}{4}$
Subtract 12 from the quotient and tell me the answer.	We are told to subtract 12 from the quotient.	$\dfrac{4(n + 15) - 8}{4} - 12$

Translating what the teacher asked the class to do results in the algebraic expression $\dfrac{4(n+15)-8}{4} - 12$. We are to determine whether the teacher can take a given student answer and produce the original number. We use the strategy of *working backward* to help with this determination. Suppose a student gives the teacher an answer of r. Think about how r was obtained and reverse the steps in Table 1. Just before obtaining "r," the student had subtracted 12. To reverse that operation, add 12 to obtain $r + 12$. Prior to that, the student had divided by 4. To reverse that, multiply by 4 to obtain $4r + 48$. To get that result, the student had subtracted 8, so now add 8 to obtain $4r + 56$. Just prior to that, the student had multiplied by 4, so now divide $4r + 56$ by 4 to obtain $r + 14$. The first operation had been to add 15, so now subtract 15 from $r + 14$ to get $r - 1$. Thus, the teacher knows when the student tells the final result of r, it is 1 more than the number with which the student started, or the number with which the student started n is the result minus 1.

This analysis can also be shown in a different way as follows:

$$\frac{4(n+15)-8}{4} - 12 = \frac{4(n+15-2)}{4} - 12$$
$$= (n+13) - 12$$
$$= n + 1$$

Therefore $n + 1 = r$ and $n = r - 1$.

▶ NOW TRY THIS 4

Noah has some white square tiles and some blue square tiles. They are all the same size. He first makes a row of white tiles and then surrounds the white tiles with a single layer of blue tiles, as shown in Figure 7.

How many blue tiles docs he need:

Figure 7

a. to surround a row of 100 white tiles?   206
b. to surround a row of n white tiles? $2n + 6$

Generalizations for Arithmetic Sequences

In Chapter 1 we saw examples of arithmetic sequences, and we were able to determine their nth terms. We now generalize this work and find the nth term of any arithmetic sequence.

An arithmetic sequence is determined by its first term and the difference. Suppose the first term of an arithmetic sequence is a_1, and the difference is d. The strategy of *making a table* can be used to find the general term for the sequence $a_1, a_1 + d, a_1 + 2d, a_1 + 3d, \ldots$, as shown in Table 2.

Table 2	
Number of Term	**Term**
1	a_1
2	$a_2 = a_1 + d = a_1 + (2-1)d$
3	$a_3 = a_1 + 2d = a_1 + (3-1)d$
4	$a_4 = a_1 + 3d = a_1 + (4-1)d$
5	$a_5 = a_1 + 4d = a_1 + (5-1)d$
$\vdots$	$\vdots$
n	$a_n = a_1 + (n-1)d$

Observe that the number of ds in the given terms is 1 less than the number of the term. This pattern continues since we add d to get the next term. Thus, the *nth term of any arithmetic sequence with first term a_1 and difference d is given by $a_n = a_1 + (n - 1)d$, where n is a natural number.*

For example, in the arithmetic sequence $5, 9, 13, 17, 21, 25, \ldots$, the first term a_1 is 5, and the difference d is 4. Thus, the nth term is given by $a_n = 5 + (n - 1)4$. Simplifying, we obtain $a_n = 5 + (n - 1)4 = 5 + 4n - 4 = 4n + 1$.

> **Example 6**
>
> In an arithmetic sequence with the second term 11 and the fifth term 23, find the 100th term.
>
> **Solution**   We know that in the arithmetic sequence $a_2 = 11, a_5 = 23$, and we need to find a_{100}. To find the 100th term, we use the formula developed in Table 2: $a_{100} = a_1 + (100 - 1)d = a_1 + 99d$. Thus to find a_{100}, we need to know a_1 and d. This becomes our *subgoal*. We have $a_2 = 11$ and $a_5 = 23$. Hence, $11 = a_2 = a_1 + d$ and $23 = a_5 = a_1 + (5 - 1)d = a_1 + 4d$. Thus,
>
> $$a_1 + d = 11 \quad \text{and}$$
> $$a_1 + 4d = 23.$$
>
> Because we know that $11 = a_1 + d$, we write
>
> $$a_1 + 4d = (a_1 + d) + 3d = 23$$
> $$11 + 3d = 23$$
> $$3d = 12$$
> $$d = 4.$$
>
> To find the first term, we have $11 = a_1 + d$, so
>
> $$11 = a_1 + 4, \text{or } a_1 = 7.$$
>
> To find the 100th term, we know that $a_{100} = a_1 + (100 - 1)d$, or that $a_{100} = 7 + (100 - 1)4 = 403$.

Generalizations for Geometric Sequences

It is possible to find the nth term, a_n, of any geometric sequence when given the first term and the ratio as mentioned in Chapter 1. For example, in the geometric sequence $3, 12, 48, 192, \ldots$, the first term is 3, and the ratio is 4. To generalize geometric sequences, let the first term be a_1 and the ratio be r, so that the third term is $a_1 r^2$, and the fourth term is $a_1 r^3$ as seen in Table 3.

Table 3

Number of Term	Term
1	a_1
2	$a_1 r$
3	$a_1 rr = a_1 r^2$
4	$a_1 r^2 r = a_1 r^3$
5	$a_1 r^3 r = a_1 r^4$
$\vdots$	$\vdots$
n	$a_1 r^{n-1}$

The power of r in each term is 1 less than the number of the term. This pattern continues since we multiply by r to get the next term. Thus, *the nth term a_n, of a geometric sequence, is $a_n = a_1 r^{n-1}$.* In the geometric sequence $3, 12, 48, 192, \ldots$, the first term is 3, and the ratio is 4, so the nth term is $a_n = 3 \cdot 4^{n-1}$.

Example 7

a. Find the nth term of the geometric sequence $2, 3, \dfrac{9}{2}, \dfrac{27}{4}, \ldots$.

b. If a geometric sequence has first term 3 and ratio $\sqrt{2}$, find its 10th term.

Solution

a. By dividing any term from the 2nd on by its previous term, we can find the ratio r of the geometric sequence. For this sequence, $r = \dfrac{3}{2}$. Thus, the nth term is

$$a_n = a_1 r^{n-1} = 2\left(\frac{3}{2}\right)^{n-1}.$$

b. The 10th term is computed as follows:

$$a_{10} = 3(\sqrt{2})^{10-1} = 3(\sqrt{2})^9 = 3(2^{9/2}) = 3(2^{8/2})(2^{1/2}) = 3 \cdot 2^4 \cdot 2^{1/2} = 48\sqrt{2}$$

▶ **NOW TRY THIS 5**

NTT 5: Answers can be found in Answers at the back of the book.

a. Two bacteria are in a dish. The number of bacteria triples every hour. Following this pattern, find the number of bacteria in the dish after 10 hours and after n hours.

b. Suppose that instead of increasing geometrically as in part (a), the number of bacteria increases arithmetically by 3 bacteria each hour. Compare the geometric and arithmetic sequences after 10 hours and after n hours. Comment on the growth of a geometric sequence versus an arithmetic sequence.

The Fibonacci Sequence

Both arithmetic and geometric sequences may be defined *recursively*. A sequence is defined recursively when one or more initial terms are given, and each subsequent term is defined in terms of the preceeding term or terms (see also p. 20.) In a geometric sequence a_1 is given and $a_n = a_{n-1} r$, for $n = 2, 3, \ldots$. In an arithmetic sequence, a_1 is given and $a_n = a_{n-1} + d$, for $n = 2, 3, \ldots$. Similarly the Fibonacci sequence (see Section 1-2) is defined recursively. Fibonacci sequence has F_1 as the first term, F_2 as the second term, and in general, F_n as the nth term. The two terms before the nth, F_n, are F_{n-1} and F_{n-2}. With this notation, the rule for generating the Fibonacci sequence can be written as follows:

$$F_n = F_{n-1} + F_{n-2}, \text{ for } n = 3, 4, \ldots$$

This rule cannot be applied to the first two Fibonacci terms. Because $F_1 = 1$ and $F_2 = 1$, then $F_3 = 1 + 1$, or 2. The beginning terms, or seeds, $F_1 = 1$ and $F_2 = 1$ and the equation $F_n = F_{n-1} + F_{n-2}$ for $n \geq 3$ is a recursive definition because the rule for the sequence defines each term after the first two using previous terms in the same sequence.

More Algebraic Thinking

Algebraic thinking can occur in different ways. One example that uses pictures is seen in Example 8.

Example 8

At a local farmer's market, three purchases were made for the prices shown in Figure 8. What is the cost of each object?

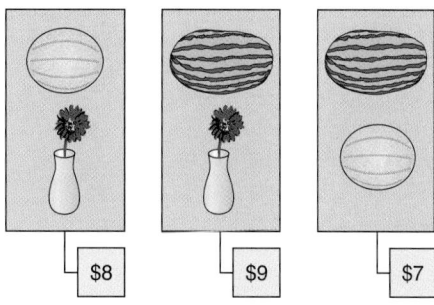

Figure 8

Solution Approaches to this problem may vary. For example, if the objects in the first two purchases are put together, the total cost would be $8 + $9, or $17. That cost would be for two vases with flowers and one each of the cantaloupe and watermelon, as in Figure 9.

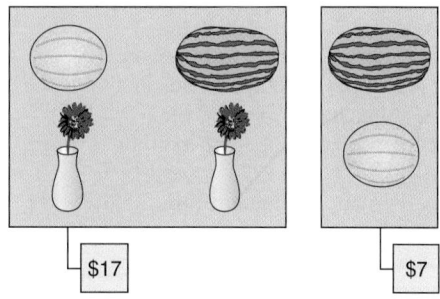

Figure 9

Now if the cantaloupe and watermelon are taken away from that total, then according to the cost of those two objects from the tag on the right, the cost should be reduced to $10 for two vases with flowers. That means each of the two vases costs $5. This in turn tells us that the cantaloupe costs $8 − $5, or $3, and the watermelon costs $9 − $5, or $4.

Assessment 8-2A

1. Translate the following phrases into algebraic expressions:
   a. The 4th term of an arithmetic sequence whose first term is 10 and whose difference is d $10 + 3d$
   b. 15 less than twice a number $2n − 15$
   c. 15 times the square of a number $15n^2$
   d. The difference between the square of a number and twice the number $n^2 − 2n$
2. a. Translate the following instructions into an algebraic expression: Take any number, add $\sqrt{3}$ to it, multiply the sum by 7, subtract 14, and divide the difference by 7. Finally, subtract the original number. $\dfrac{7(n + \sqrt{3}) − 14}{7} − n$
   b. Simplify your answer in part (a). $\sqrt{3} − 2$

3. In the tile pattern sequence of figures shown, each figure starting from the second has two more blue squares than the preceding one. The pattern represents an arithmetic sequence.

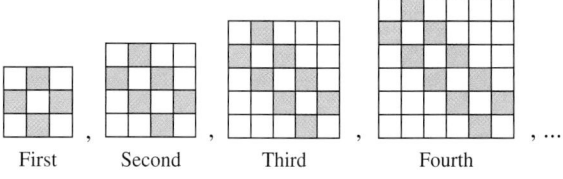

First, Second, Third, Fourth, ...

Answer the following questions.

a. How many blue tiles are there in the nth figure if this arithmetic sequence continues? $2(n + 1)$

b. If the pattern of large square tiles with shaded blue ones continues, how many white tiles are there in the nth figure? $(n + 2)^2 - 2(n + 1)$ or $n^2 + 2n + 2$

4. In the following descriptions, write an expression in terms of the given variable that represents the indicated quantity.

a. The cost of having a plumber spend h hours at your house if the plumber charges $50 for coming to the house and $60 per hour for labor $50 + 60h$ dollars

b. The amount of money in cents in a jar containing d dimes and some nickels and quarters if there are 3 times as many nickels as dimes and 3 times as many quarters as nickels $250d$ cents

c. The sum of three consecutive integers if the least integer is x $3x + 3$

d. The amount of bacteria after n min if the initial amount of bacteria is q and the amount of bacteria doubles every minute (*Hint:* The answer should contain q as well as n.)   *

e. The temperature after t hr if the initial temperature is 40°F and each hour it drops by 3°F $(40 - 3t)$ degrees F

f. Pawel's total earnings after 3 yr if the first year his salary was s dollars, the second year it was $5000.00 higher, and the third year it was twice as much as the second year   *

g. The sum of three consecutive odd natural numbers if the least is x $3x + 6$

h. The sum of three consecutive natural numbers if the middle is m $3m$

5. In a college, there are P professors and S students. There are 45 times as many students as professors. Write an algebraic equation that shows this relationship. $S = 45P$

6. Suppose a class has g girls and b boys, and there are 5 more girls than boys. Write an algebraic equation that shows this relationship. $g = b + 5$

7. Ryan is building matchstick sequences as shown. How many matchsticks will he use for the nth figure if the pattern of adding one new square horizontally and one vertically continues? $6n + 7$

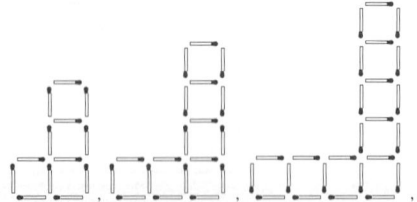

8. Write an algebraic equation relating the variables described in each of the following situations:

a. The pay, P, for t hr if you are paid $8 an hour $P = 12t$

b. The pay, P, for t hr if you are paid $15 for the first hour and $10 for each additional hour $P = 12(t - 1) + 15$

9. For a particular event, a student pays $5 per ticket and a nonstudent pays $13 per ticket. If x students and 100 nonstudents buy tickets, find the total revenue from the sale of the tickets in terms of x. $5x + 1300$ dollars

10. Suppose a will decreed that three siblings will each receive a cash inheritance according to the following: The eldest receives 3 times as much as the youngest, and twice as much as the middle sibling. Answer the following.

a. If the youngest sibling receives $$x$, how much do the other two receive in terms of x?   Eldest $3x$; middle $\frac{3x}{2}$;

b. If the middle sibling receives $$y$, how much do the other two receive in terms of y?   Eldest $2y$; youngest $\frac{2y}{3}$

c. If the oldest sibling receives $$z$, how much do the other two receive in terms of z?   Middle $\frac{1}{2}z$; youngest $\frac{1}{3}z$

11. In each of the following arithmetic sequences, find (i) the 100th term; (ii) the nth term.

a. $0, ^-3, ^-6, \ldots$ $^-297; ^-3(n - 1)$

b. $1 - \sqrt{2}, 1 + \sqrt{2}, \ldots$ $1 + 197\sqrt{2}; (1 - \sqrt{2}) + 2\sqrt{2}(n - 1)$

c. $\sqrt{3} + 0.5, \sqrt{3} + 2.5, \sqrt{3} + 4.5, \ldots$ *

12. In each of the following geometric sequences, find an expression for (i) the 17th term; (ii) for the nth term.   Answers vary

a. $2, 2\sqrt{3}, 6, \ldots$ $13,122; 2(\sqrt{3})^{n-1}$

b. $2, ^-2\sqrt{2}, \ldots$ $512; 2(^-\sqrt{2})^{n-1}$

c. $^-\sqrt{5}, 5, \ldots$ $^-\sqrt{5} \cdot 5^8; (^-\sqrt{5})^n$

13. Find the first term and the difference in an arithmetic sequence, if the 100th term is $\sqrt{2}$ and the 200th term is $\sqrt{3}$.   *

14. Find the first term in a geometric sequence, if the 11th term is $^-128$ and the ratio is $^-\sqrt{2}$. $^-4$

15. A ball is dropped from a height of 10 ft and bounces 80% of its previous height on each bounce. How high off the ground is the ball at the top of the 5th bounce?   3.3 ft

16. Jake bought contact lenses and was told to wear them only 2 hours the first day and to increase the length of time by 20 minutes each day. On what day will Jake be able to wear the contacts for 12 hours?   Day 31

17. In a Fibonacci-like sequence, the first term is $\sqrt{2}$, the second is $\sqrt{3}$, and each subsequent term is the sum of two previous terms. Find the following.

a. The first 10 terms in simplest form without computing $\sqrt{2}$ or $\sqrt{3}$.   *

b. If the terms in the Fibonacci sequence are $F_1, F_2, F_3, \ldots$, and the terms in the Fibonacci-like sequence in this question are $L_1, L_2, L_3, \ldots$, answer the following.

   i. Verify that $L_7 = F_5\sqrt{2} + F_6\sqrt{3}$.   *

   ii. Write L_8, L_9, and L_{10} using the terms of the Fibonacci sequence, $\sqrt{2}$, and $\sqrt{3}$.   *

   iii. Use your answers in the previous part to conjecture an expression for L_n in terms of $\sqrt{2}, \sqrt{3}$, and Fibonacci terms. $L_n = F_{n-2}\sqrt{2} + F_{n-1}\sqrt{3}$

Assessment 8-2B

1. Translate the following phrases into algebraic expressions.

a. 10 more than a number $n + 10$

b. 10 less than a number $n - 10$

c. half a number $\frac{1}{2}n$

d. The sum of a number and 10 $n + 10$

e. The difference between the cube of a number and the square of the number $n^3 - n^2$

2. **a.** Translate the following instructions into an algebraic expression: Take any number, add 25 to it, multiply the sum by 4, subtract 60, and divide the difference by 4. Finally, add 5.   *

b. Simplify your answer in part (a). $n + 15$

3. Discover a possible tile pattern in the following sequence and answer the following.

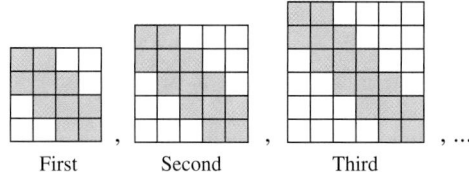

First   Second   Third

  a. How many shaded tiles are there in the nth figure of your pattern if the arithmetic sequence of shaded tiles continues? $3n + 7$
  b. How many white tiles are there in the nth figure of your pattern? $(n + 3)^2 - (3n + 7)$ or $n^2 + 3n + 2$
4. In the following descriptions, write an expression in terms of the given variables that represents the indicated quantity:
  a. The cost of having a plumber spend h hours at your house if the plumber charges \$30 for coming to the house and \$$x$ per hour for labor $30 + hx$ dollars
  b. The amount of money in cents in a jar containing some nickels and d dimes and some quarters if there are 4 times as many nickels as dimes and 3 times as many quarters as nickels $330d$ cents
  c. The sum of three consecutive integers if the greatest integer is x $3x - 3$
  d. The amount of bacteria after n min if the initial amount of bacteria is q and the amount of bacteria triples every 20 sec. (The answer should contain q as well as n.) $A = q \cdot 3^{3n}$
  e. The temperature t hr ago if the present temperature is 40°F and each hour it drops by 3°F $(40 + 3t)$ degrees F
  f. Pawel's total earnings after 3 yr if the first year his salary was s dollars, the second year it was \$5000 higher, and the third year it was twice as much as the first year $4s + 5000$ dollars
  g. The sum of three consecutive even whole numbers if the greatest is x $3x - 6$
5. If a school has w women and m men and you know that there are 100 more men than women, write an algebraic equation relating w and m. $m = w + 100$, answers vary
6. Suppose there are c chairs and t tables in a classroom and there are 15 more chairs than tables. Write an algebraic equation relating c and t. $c = t + 15$
7. Ryan is building triangle sequences so that one triangle is added to the right each time, as shown. How many matchsticks will he use for the nth figure and for the figure one before the nth? $2n + 1$ and $2n - 1$

△, ◁▷, ◁▷▷, ...

8. Write an algebraic equation relating the variables described in each of the following situations:
  a. The pay, P, for t hours if you are paid \$$d$ an hour   *
  b. The pay, P, for t hours if you are paid \$25 for the first hour and \$$k$ for each additional hour $P = 25 + k(t - 1)$
  c. The total pay, P, for a visit and t hours of gardening if you are paid \$30 for the visit and \$10 for each hour of gardening $P = 30 + 10t$

  d. The total cost, C, of membership in a health club that charges a \$300 initiation fee and \$4 for each of n days attended   *
  e. The cost, C, of renting a midsized car for 1 day of driving m mi if the rent is \$30 per day plus 35¢ per mile $C = 30 + 0.35m$
9. For a particular event, students pay \$$d$ per ticket and non-students pay twice as much. If x students and 100 nonstudents buy tickets, find the total revenue from the sale of the tickets in terms of x and d. $dx + 2d \cdot 100 = dx + 200d$ dollars
10. Matt has twice as many stickers as David. If David has d stickers, and Matt gives David 10 stickers, how many stickers does each have in terms of d?   *
11. In each of the following arithmetic sequences, find (i) the 100th term; (ii) the nth term.
  a. $0, ^-5, ^-10, \ldots$ $^-495$; $^-5n + 5$
  b. $1 + \sqrt{2}, 1 - \sqrt{2}, \ldots$ *
  c. $x + \sqrt{3}, 2x + 3\sqrt{3}, \ldots$ *
12. In each of the following geometric sequences, find an expression for (i) the 20th term; (ii) for the nth term.   Answers vary
  a. $\sqrt{\dfrac{3}{2}}, \sqrt{3}, \ldots$ $512\sqrt{3}$; $\sqrt{\dfrac{3}{2}}(\sqrt{2})^{n-1}$
  b. $\sqrt{2}, 2, 2\sqrt{2} \ldots$ 2^{10}; $(\sqrt{2})^n$
  c. $^-\sqrt{3}, 3, \ldots$ 3^{10}; $(^-\sqrt{3})^n$
  d. $3, ^-3\sqrt{3}, \ldots$ $^-\sqrt{3} \cdot 3^{10}$; $(^-\sqrt{3})^{n+1}$
13. In a geometric sequence, find the first term and the ratio if the 10th term is 25 and the 20th term is 100.   *
14. a. Find the difference in the arithmetic sequence whose nth term is $3n + 5$. 3
  b. Find the ratio of a geometric sequence whose nth term is $3^{\frac{3}{2}n}$. $3^{3/2}$
15. A ball is dropped from a height of 20 meters and bounces 90% of its previous height on each bounce. How high off the ground is the ball at the top of the 4th bounce?   13.122 meters
16. Consider the following arithmetic sequences. Determine the first time when a term of the first sequence is greater than the corresponding term of the second.

$0.01, 0.11, 0.21, \ldots$

$100, 100.01, 100.02, \ldots$ The 1113th term of the first sequence is greater than the 1113th term of the second.

17. Find the following.
  a. The first seven terms of the Fibonacci-type sequence with seeds 1, 2   1, 2, 3, 5, 8, 13, 21
  b. The sum of the first three terms of the sequence in part (a)   6
  c. The sum of the first four terms of the sequence in part (a)   11
  d. The sum of the first five terms of the sequence in part (a)   19
  e. The sum of the first six terms of the sequence in part (a)   32
  f. The sum of the first seven terms of the sequence in part (a)   53
  g. A pattern for the sums in parts (b)–(f).   *
  h. A rule for the pattern found in part (g) using the notation for Fibonacci terms.   *

Mathematical Connections 8-2

Answers to Mathematical Connections can be found in the Answers section at the back of the book.

Reasoning

1. Students were asked to write an algebraic expression for the sum of five consecutive natural numbers. One student wrote $x + (x + 1) + (x + 2) + (x + 3) + (x + 4) = 5x + 10$. Another wrote $(x - 2) + (x - 1) + x + (x + 1) + (x + 2) = 5x$.
   a. Explain who is correct and why.
   b. Does either approach prove that the sum of five consecutive integers equals 5 times the middle integer?
   c. Does the statement in part (b) generalize to the sum of five consecutive terms in every arithmetic sequence? Justify your answer.

2. a. Choose seven consecutive terms in any arithmetic sequence and check that the arithmetic average (the sum of the seven terms divided by 7) equals the middle term.
   b. Prove that the result in part (a) is true for every arithmetic sequence.

3. A teacher instructed her class as follows:

   Take any number, multiply it by 4, add 16, and divide the result by 2. Subtract 7 from the quotient and tell me your answer. I will tell you the original number.

   Explain how the teacher was able to tell each student's original number.

Open-Ended

4. A teacher instructed her class to take any number and perform a series of computations using that number. The teacher was able to tell each student's original number by subtracting 1 from the student's answer. Create similar instructions for students so that the teacher needs to do only the following to obtain the student's original number.
   a. Add 1 to the answer.
   b. Multiply the answer by 2.
   c. Multiply the answer by 1.

5. Give an example of a geometric sequence whose first 3 terms are very close to 1 but whose terms are eventually very close to 0. Use a calculator to check that your sequence has the desired property.

Cooperative Learning

6. Examine several elementary school textbooks for grades 1 through 5 and report on which algebraic concepts involving variables are introduced at each grade level.

Connecting Mathematics to the Classroom

7. A student writes $a(bc) = (ab)(ac)$. How do you respond?
8. A student wonders if sets can ever be considered as variables. What do you tell her?
9. A student thinks that if A and B are sets, then the statements $A \cup B = B \cup A$ and $A \cap B = B \cap A$ are set properties in a way similar to the statements $a + b = b + a$ and $ab = ba$ are arithmetic properties of numbers. How do you respond?
10. A student wants to know how can she prove that a sequence whose nth term is $5n + 4$ is arithmetic and a sequence whose nth term is $5 \cdot 3^{\frac{n}{2}}$ is geometric. How do you respond?

Review Problems

11. Find two rational numbers and two irrational numbers between 1.41 and $\sqrt{2}$.
12. Determine which of the following are rational and which are irrational numbers.
    a. $\sqrt[3]{728}$
    b. $\dfrac{2}{\sqrt{2}}$
    c. $\sqrt[3]{2^9 \cdot 3^{12}}$
    d. $\sqrt[3]{2} \cdot \sqrt[3]{4}$
    e. $(\sqrt{3} - \sqrt{2})(\sqrt{3} + \sqrt{2})$
    f. $(\sqrt{3} - \sqrt{2})^2$
13. Compute the following, if possible. If a number is not a real number, write "not real."
    a. $\left(\dfrac{^-8}{27}\right)^{-\frac{2}{3}}$
    b. $\left(\dfrac{^-9}{4}\right)^{\frac{3}{2}}$
    c. $^-\left(\dfrac{9}{4}\right)^{\frac{3}{2}}$
14. Find all real number values for x, if possible. If there is no real solution, write "None."
    a. $\sqrt{^-x} = 5$
    b. $\sqrt{x^2} = {}^-x$
    c. $(^-x)^{\frac{3}{2}} = 125$
15. Find all integers n such that $n < \sqrt[3]{50} < n + 1$.

National Assessments

National Assessment of Educational Progress (NAEP) Questions

A yellow box holds 72 pencils.

    $\boxed{\text{Y}}$ is the same as $\boxed{72}$.

Two red boxes hold as many pencils as 1 yellow box.

    $\boxed{\text{R}}\,\boxed{\text{R}}$ is the same as $\boxed{\text{Y}}$.

Three blue boxes hold as many pencils as 1 red box.

    $\boxed{\text{B}}\,\boxed{\text{B}}\,\boxed{\text{B}}$ is the same as $\boxed{\text{R}}$.

How many pencils does 1 blue box hold?

Answer: _____

Show or explain how you got your answer.

NAEP, Grade 4, 2013

$2 + n$	5
$3 + n$	6
$4 + n$	7
$5 + n$	8

What number does n represent in the table?
A. 2
B. 3
C. 4
D. 5

NAEP, Grade 4, 2009

A. If c and d are different prime numbers less than 10 and the sum $c + d$ is a *composite* number greater than 10, what is one possible pair of values for c and d?

$c =$ _____ $d =$ _____

B. If j and k are different prime numbers less than 10 and the sum $j + k$ is a *prime* number less than 10, what is one possible pair of values for j and k?

$j =$ _____ $k =$ _____

C. If s and t are different prime numbers greater than 10, explain why the sum $s + t$ cannot be a prime number.

NAEP, Grade 8, 2013

8-3 Equations

With variables w and c, we consider equations such as $w + c = \sqrt{7}$. The equal sign indicates that the values on both sides of the equation are the same even though they do not look the same.

To solve equations, we need several properties of equality. Many of these can be discovered by using a balance scale. For example, consider two objects a and b of the same weight on the balances, as in Figure 10(a). If the balance is level, then $a = b$. When we add an equal amount of weight, c, to both sides, the balance is still level, as in Figure 10(b).

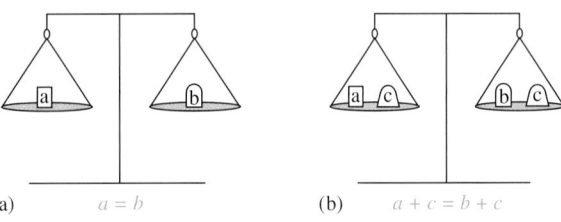

(a) $a = b$ (b) $a + c = b + c$

Figure 10

This demonstrates that *if $a = b$, then $a + c = b + c$*, which is *the addition property of equality*.

Similarly, if the scale is balanced with amounts a and b, as in Figure 11(a), and we put additional a's on one side and an equal number of b's on the other side, the scale remains level, as in Figure 11(b).

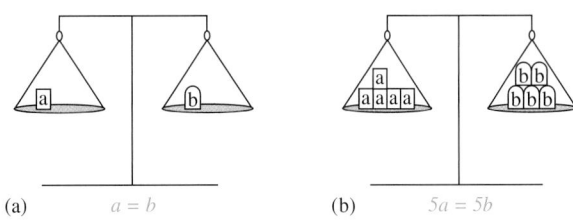

(a) $a = b$ (b) $5a = 5b$

Figure 11

Figure 11 suggests that *if c is any natural number and $a = b$, then $ac = bc$*. This property can be extended to all real numbers c. The extension is the *multiplication property of equality*. These properties are summarized in the next theorem.

Theorem 8-2: The Addition and Multiplication Properties of Equality

a. For any real numbers a, b, and c, if $a = b$, then $a + c = b + c$.

b. For any real numbers a, b, and c, if $a = b$, then $ac = bc$.

Because $a - c = a + (^-c)$ and if $c \neq 0$ then $\dfrac{a}{c} = a \cdot \dfrac{1}{c}$, Theorem 8-2 implies the subtraction and division properties of equality.

Equality is not affected if we substitute a number for its equal. This property is referred to as the **substitution property**. Examples of substitution follow:

   a. If $a + b = c + d$ and $d = 5$, then $a + b = c + 5$.
   b. If $a + b = c + d$, $b = e$, and $d = f$, then $a + e = c + f$.

Using the substitution property, we can see that equations can be added or subtracted as stated in the following theorem.

> **Theorem 8-3: Addition and Subtraction Property of Equations**
>
> If a, b, c, d are real numbers, $a = b$ and $c = d$, then $a + c = b + d$ and $a - c = b - d$.

Theorem 8-2 implies that we may add the same real number to both sides of an equation or multiply both sides of the equation by the same real number without affecting the equality. If $a + c = b + c$ and $ac = bc$, the cancellation properties of equality can be developed by adding ^-c to both sides of the first equation and multiplying both sides by $\dfrac{1}{c}$, where $c \neq 0$, in the second equation.

> **Theorem 8-4: Cancellation Properties of Equality**
>
> **a.** For any real numbers a, b, and c, if $a + c = b + c$, then $a = b$.
> **b.** For any real numbers a, b, and c, with $c \neq 0$, if $ac = bc$, then $a = b$.

If $ab = 0$, then at least one factor, a or b, must be 0. Thus, we have the following: *For any real numbers a and b, if ab = 0, then a = 0 or b = 0.*

An algebraic use of the italized statement is seen when we find a solution to an equation like $(x - 3)(x - 5) = 0$. We know that $x - 3 = 0$ or $x - 5 = 0$. Hence $x = 3$ or $x = 5$. The above theorems and properties for real numbers also hold for algebraic expressions.

As mentioned in an earlier chapter, when using the commutative property of multiplication, each of the distributive properties can be written in the equivalent forms:

$$ab + ac = a(b + c)$$
$$ab - ac = a(b - c)$$

When the distributive properties are written in the above equivalent forms, we refer to them as *factoring* and say that a has been "factored out."

Solving Equations with One Variable

Finding solutions to equations is a major part of algebra. Use of tangible objects can increase students' engagement and comprehension when they work with equations. A balance-scale model fosters understanding of the basic concepts used in solving equations and inequalities.

For example, consider Figure 12. If we release the pan on the left, what happens? Upon release, the scale tilts down on the right side and we have an *inequality*, $2 \cdot 3 < 3 + (2 \cdot 2)$.

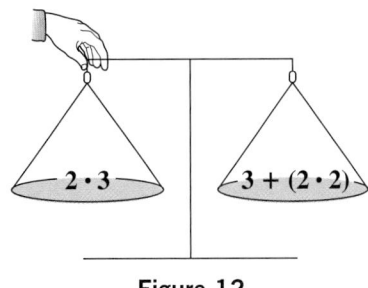

Figure 12

Next consider Figure 13. If we release the pan, then the sides will balance and we have the *equality* $2 \cdot 3 = (1 + 1) + 4$.

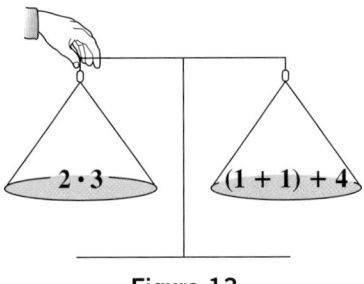

Figure 13

A balance scale can also be used to reinforce the idea of a replacement set for a variable. Name some solutions in Figure 14 that keep the scale balanced. For example, $3(5/2)$ balances $2(15/4)$, $3\sqrt{16}$ balances $2 \cdot 6 = 12$, and so on.

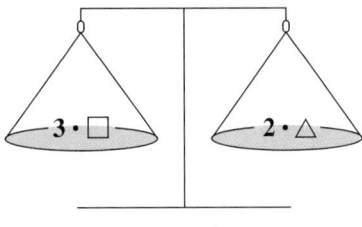

Figure 14

Other types of balance scale problems may help students with algebra. Work through Now Try This 6 before proceeding.

▶ **NOW TRY THIS 6**

What are the values of □ and △ in parts (a) and (b) below?

a.

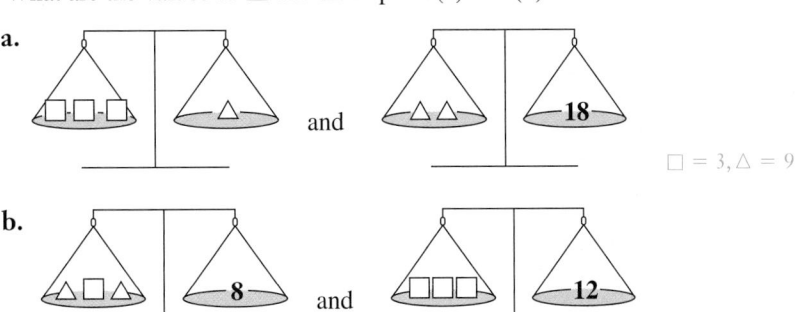

$□ = 3, △ = 9$

b.

$□ = 4, △ = 2$

To solve equations, we may think of the properties of equality used on a balance pan. Consider $3x - 14 = 1$. Put the equal expressions on the opposite pans of the balance scale. Because the expressions are equal, the pans should be level, as in Figure 15.

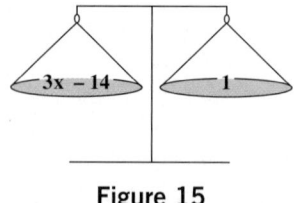

Figure 15

To solve for x, we use the properties of equality to manipulate the expressions on the scale so that after each step, the scale remains level and, at the final step, only an x remains on one side of the scale. The number on the other side of the scale represents the solution to the original equation. To find x in the equation of Figure 15, consider the scales pictured in successive steps in Figure 16, where each successive scale represents an equation that is equivalent to the original equation; that is, each has the same solution as the original. The last scale shows $x = 5$. To check that 5 is the correct solution, we substitute 5 for x in the original equation. Because $3 \cdot 5 - 14 = 1$ is a true statement, 5 is the solution to the original equation.

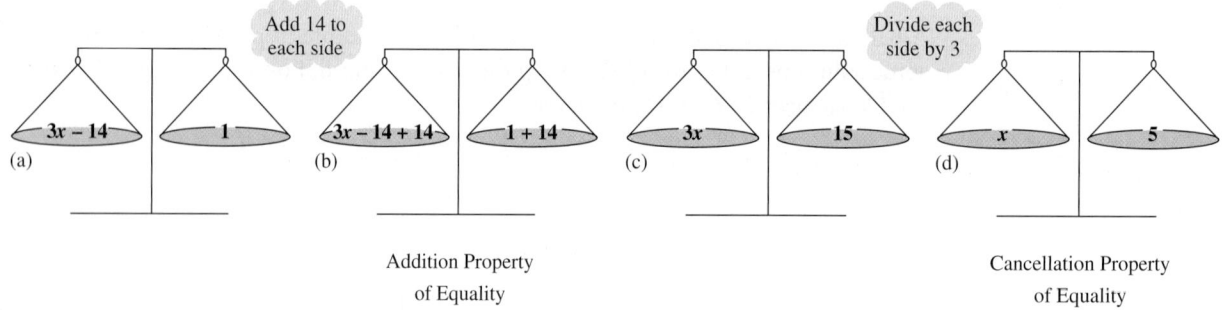

Figure 16

 Concrete objects are used in solving equations on the student page shown on page 415.

3-5a **Activity Lab** **Hands On**

Modeling Equations

To solve an equation using models, get the variable by itself on one side.

EXAMPLE **Addition Equations**

Solve $x + 7 = 15$.

$$x + 7 = 15$$ ← Model the equation.

$$x + 7 - 7 = 15 - 7$$ ← Remove 7 tiles from each side. This will keep the equation balanced.

$$x = 8$$ ← Find the solution.

Exercises

Solve each equation by drawing models or using tiles.

1. $x + 2 = 7$ **2.** $5 + c = 35$ **3.** $7 + m = 21$ **4.** $8 = n + 5$

Example 9

Solve each of the following equations for x.

a. $x + \sqrt[3]{4} = 20$

b. $3x = x + \sqrt{10}$

c. $\dfrac{4}{3}x = 33x - \dfrac{1}{3}$

d. $4(x + 3) + 5(x + 3) = 99$

Solution

a.
$$x + \sqrt[3]{4} = 20$$
$$\left(x + \sqrt[3]{4}\right) - \sqrt[3]{4} = 20 - \sqrt[3]{4}$$
$$x = 20 - \sqrt[3]{4}$$

b.
$$3x = x + \sqrt{10}$$
$$3x - x = (x + \sqrt{10}) - x$$
$$(3 - 1)x = (\sqrt{10} + x) - x$$
$$2x = \sqrt{10}$$
$$x = \frac{\sqrt{10}}{2}$$

c.

$$\frac{4}{3}x = 33x - \frac{1}{3}$$

$$3 \cdot \frac{4}{3}x = 3\left(33x - \frac{1}{3}\right)$$

$$4x = 99x - 1$$

$$4x + 1 = 99x - 1 + 1$$

$$4x + 1 = 99x$$

$$^-4x + (4x + 1) = {}^-4x + 99x$$

$$1 = (^-4 + 99)x$$

$$1 = 95x$$

$$\frac{1}{95} = x$$

d.
$$4(x + 3) + 5(x + 3) = 99$$
$$(4 + 5)(x + 3) = 99 \,(\text{Why?})$$
$$9(x + 3) = 99$$
$$x + 3 = 11$$
$$x = 8$$

Application Problems

Figure 17 demonstrates a method for solving application problems with a third-grade example: formulate the problem with a mathematical model, solve that mathematical model, and interpret the solution in terms of the original problem.

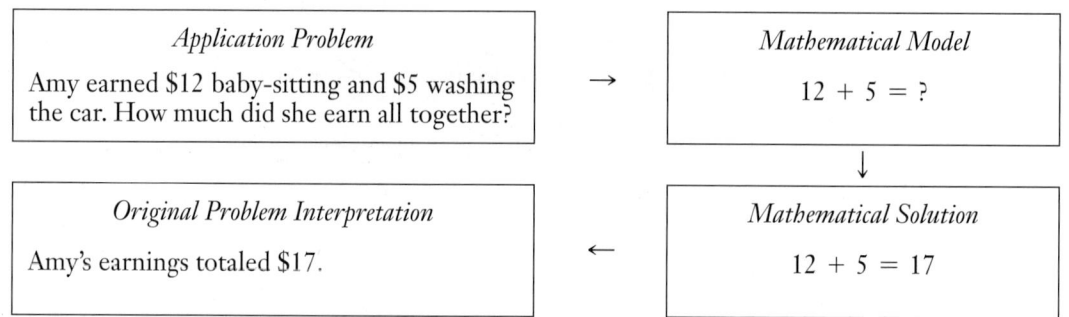

Figure 17

We apply the four-step problem-solving process to solving word problems with algebraic thinking. In Understanding the Problem, we identify what is given and what is to be found. In Devising a Plan, we assign letters to the unknown quantities and try to translate the information in the problem into a model involving equations. In Carrying Out the Plan, we solve the equations or inequalities. In Looking Back, we interpret and check the solution in terms of the original problem.

Problem Solving   Overdue Books

Bruno has five books overdue at the library. The fine for overdue books is 10¢ a day per book. He remembers that he checked out an astronomy book a week before he checked out four novels. If his total fine was $8.70, how long was each book overdue?

Understanding the Problem Bruno has five books overdue. The astronomy book was checked out seven days before the four novels. The fine per day for each book is 10¢, and the total fine was $8.70. We need to find out how many days each book is overdue.

Devising a Plan Let d be the number of days that each of the four novels is overdue. The astronomy book was due seven days before the novels so it is $(d + 7)$ days overdue. To *write an equation* using d, we express the total fine in two ways. The total fine is \$8.70. This fine in cents equals the fine for the four novels, plus the fine for the astronomy book.

$$\text{Fine for each of the novels} = \underbrace{\text{Fine per day}}_{10} \underbrace{\text{times}}_{\cdot} \underbrace{\text{number of overdue days}}_{d}$$

$$\text{Fine for the four novels} = \underbrace{\text{1 day's fine for novels}}_{4 \cdot 10} \underbrace{\text{times}}_{\cdot} \underbrace{\text{number of overdue days}}_{d}$$

$$= (4 \cdot 10)d$$

$$= 40d$$

$$\text{Fine for the astronomy book} = \underbrace{\text{Fine per day}}_{10} \underbrace{\text{times}}_{\cdot} \underbrace{\text{number of overdue days}}_{(d + 7)}$$

$$= 10(d + 7)$$

Because each of the expressions is in cents, we write the total fine of \$8.70 as 870¢ to produce the following:

$$\text{Fine for the four novels} + \text{Fine for the astronomy book} = \text{Total fine}$$

$$40d \qquad + \qquad 10(d + 7) \qquad = 870$$

Carrying Out the Plan Solve the equation for d.

$$40d + 10(d + 7) = 870$$
$$40d + 10d + 70 = 870$$
$$50d + 70 = 870$$
$$50d = 800$$
$$d = 16$$

Thus, each of the four novels was 16 days overdue, and the astronomy book was overdue $d + 7 = 23$ days.

Looking Back To check the answer, follow the original information. Each of the four novels was 16 days overdue, and the astronomy book was 23 days overdue. Because the fine was 10¢ per day per book, the fine for each of the novels was $16 \cdot 10$¢, or 160¢. Hence, the fine for all four novels was $4 \cdot 160$¢, or 640¢. The fine for the astronomy book was $23 \cdot 10$¢, or 230¢. Consequently, the total fine was 640¢ + 230¢, or 870¢, which agrees with the given information of \$8.70 as the total fine.

Problem Solving Newspaper Delivery

In a small town, 3 children deliver all the newspapers. Abby delivers 3 times as many papers as Bob, and Connie delivers 13 more than Abby. If the 3 children deliver a total of 496 papers, how many papers does each deliver?

Understanding the Problem The problem asks for the number of papers each child delivers. We are given information comparing the number of papers that each child delivers as well as the total number of papers delivered in the town.

Devising a Plan Let a, b, and c be the number of papers delivered by Abby, Bob, and Connie, respectively. We translate the given information into *algebraic equations* as follows:

Abby delivers 3 times as many papers as Bob: $a = 3b$

Connie delivers 13 more papers than Abby: $c = a + 13$

Total delivery is 496: $a + b + c = 496$

To reduce the number of variables, substitute $3b$ for a in the second and third equations:

$c = a + 13$ becomes $c = 3b + 13$

$a + b + c = 496$ becomes $3b + b + c = 496$

Next, make an equation in one variable, b, by substituting $3b + 13$ for c in the equation $3b + b + c = 496$; solve for b; and then find a and c.

Carrying Out the Plan

$$3b + b + 3b + 13 = 496$$
$$7b + 13 = 496$$
$$7b = 483$$
$$b = 69$$

Thus, $a = 3b = 3 \cdot 69 = 207$. Also, $c = a + 13 = 207 + 13 = 220$. So, Abby delivers 207 papers, Bob delivers 69 papers, and Connie delivers 220 papers.

Looking Back To check the answers, follow the original information, using $a = 207, b = 69$, and $c = 220$. The information in the first sentence, "Abby delivers 3 times as many papers as Bob," checks, since $207 = 3 \cdot 69$. The second sentence, "Connie delivers 13 more papers than Abby," is true because $220 = 207 + 13$. The information on the total delivery checks, since $207 + 69 + 220 = 496$.

▶ **NOW TRY THIS 7**

NTT 7: Answers can be found in Answers at the back of the book.

Solve the *Newspaper Delivery* problem above by introducing only one unknown for the number of newspapers Bob delivered.

Assessment 8-3A

1. Consider the balances: $\bigcirc = 3, \triangle = 8, \square = 4$

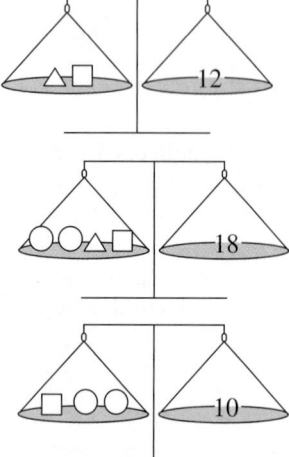

What is the value of each shape?

2. Solve each of the following if x is a real number. If a real number solution does not exist, write "No solution."
   a. $x + \sqrt{3} = 2\sqrt{3} - x$ $\dfrac{\sqrt{3}}{2}$
   b. $\dfrac{3}{2}x - 3 = x + \sqrt{2}$ $2(3 + \sqrt{2}) = 6 + 2\sqrt{2}$
   c. $5(2x + \sqrt{2}) + 7(2x + \sqrt{2}) = 12$ $\dfrac{1 - \sqrt{2}}{2}$
   d. $3(\sqrt{x} - 3) = 5(\sqrt{x} - 3)$ 9
   e. $(\sqrt{x} - 5)^2 = 9$ $4; 64$

3. Ryan is building matchstick square sequences so that one square is added to the right each time a new figure is formed, as shown. He used 67 matchsticks to form the last figure in his sequence. How many squares are in this last figure? 22

4. For a particular event, 812 tickets were sold for a total of $1912. If students paid $2 per ticket and non-students paid $3 per ticket, how many student tickets were sold? 524

5. An estate of $486,000 is left to three siblings. The eldest receives 3 times as much as the youngest. The middle sibling receives $14,000 more than the youngest. How much did each receive?   *

6. A 10 ft board is to be cut into three pieces, two equal-length ones and the third 3 in. shorter than each of the other two. If the cutting does not result in any length being lost, how long are the pieces?   3ft 5 in, 3ft 5 in, 3 ft 2 in

7. A box contains 67 coins, only dimes and nickels. The amount of money in the box is $4.20. How many dimes and how many nickels are in the box?   *

8. Miriam is 10 years older than Ricardo. Two years ago, Miriam was 3 times as old as Ricardo is now. How old are they now?   Ricardo, 4; Miriam, 14

9. In a college, 20 times as many undergraduate students as graduate students are enrolled. If the total student enrollment at the college is 21,000, how many graduate students are there?   1000

10. A farmer has 1200 yd of fencing to enclose a rectangular pasture for her goats. Since one side of the pasture borders a river, that side does not need to be fenced. Side b must be twice as long as side a. Find the dimensions of the rectangular pasture. $a = 300$ yd., $b = 600$ yd.

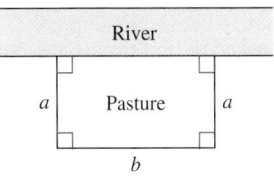

11. The sum of three consecutive terms in the arithmetic sequence 1, 4, 7, 10, . . . is 903; find these three terms.   298, 301, 304

12. The perimeter of a rectangle (the sum of the lengths of the 4 sides) is 100 feet and the shorter side is $\frac{1}{3}$ of the length of the longer side. Find the length of the diagonal. (Use the Pythagorean Theorem on p. 392.) $12.5\sqrt{10}$ ft

Assessment 8-3B

1. Consider the following balances:

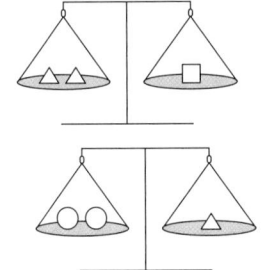

   a. Which shape weighs the most? Tell why.   *
   b. Which shape weighs the least? Tell why.   *

2. Solve each of the following if x is a real number and if a real number solution does not exist, write "no real solution."
   a. $x - \sqrt{2} = 3\sqrt{2} - x$ $2\sqrt{2}$
   b. $-\frac{3}{2}x - 2 = x - \sqrt{2}$ $\frac{2}{5}(\sqrt{2} - 2)$
   c. $5(2x - \sqrt{3}) - 7(2x - \sqrt{3}) = 2$ $\frac{\sqrt{3} - 1}{2}$
   d. $2(x^2 - 3) = x^2 - 3$ $\sqrt{3}$ or $^-\sqrt{3}$
   e. $(\sqrt{x} - 5)^2 = 9$ 4; 64

3. Ryan is building matchstick square sequences, as shown. He used 599 matchsticks to form the last two figures in his sequence. How many matchsticks did he use in each of the last two figures?   298 and 301 respectively

4. At the Out-Rage Benefit Concert, 723 tickets were sold for $3/student and $5/non-student. The benefit raised $2815. How many non-student tickets were sold?   323

5. An estate of $2,000,000 is left to four siblings. The eldest is to receive 3 times as much as the youngest. The other two siblings are each to receive $16,000 more than the youngest. How much will each receive?   *

6. Ten years from now Alex's age will be 3 times her present age. Find Alex's age now.   5

7. Matt has twice as many stickers as David. How many stickers must Matt give David so that they will each have 120 stickers? Check that your answer is correct.   *

8. Miriam is four years older than Ricardo. Ten years ago Miriam was 3 times as old as Ricardo was then.
   a. How old are they now?   Miriam is 16; Ricardo is 12
   b. Determine whether your answer is correct by checking that it satisfies the conditions of the problem. $16 = 12 + 4$; $16 - 10 = 6$; $12 - 10 = 2$; $6 = 3 \cdot 2$

9. In a college there are 13 times as many students as professors. If together the students and professors number 28,000, how many students are there in the college?   2000 professors; 26,000 students.

10. A farmer has 800 yd of fencing to enclose a rectangular pasture. One side of the pasture borders a river and does not need to be fenced. If side a must be twice as long as side b parallel to the river, what are the dimensions of the rectangular pasture? (see drawing in exercise 10 Assessment 8-3A)   160 yd by 320 yd

11. The sum of the first two terms of a geometric sequence is 100 times the first term. What is the common ratio?   99

12. In a rectangle, one side is $\frac{1}{3}$ of the length of the other side and the length of a diagonal is 9 feet, how long are the sides of the rectangle? $\frac{9}{\sqrt{10}}$ ft; $\frac{27}{\sqrt{10}}$ ft

Mathematical Connections 8-3

Answers to Mathematical Connections can be found in the Answers section at the back of the book.

Reasoning

1. Students were asked to find three consecutive whole numbers whose sum is 393. One student wrote the equation $x + (x + 1) + (x + 2) = 393$. Another wrote $(x - 1) + x + (x + 1) = 393$. Explain whether either approach works to find the answer to the question.

2. Explain how to solve the equation $3x + 5 = 5x - 3$ using a balance scale.

3. Rails lengthen in hot weather. Clips anchor the welded rails to concrete or steel sleepers. Without these clips a one mile length of track might expand 2 ft. and buckle in an arc as shown. Use AC as an approximation of half of the bow to estimate the height h of the buckle.

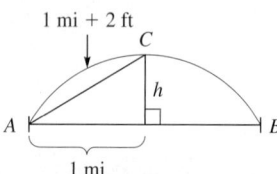

4. **a.** A pipe can fill a pool in 12 hours. Another pipe can fill the pool in 18 hours. How long will it take for the two pipes to fill the pool if they operate simultaneously?
   b. Answer the question in part (a) if the first pipe can fill the pool in a hours and the second in b hours. Write your answer in as simple a form as possible in terms of a and b.

Open-Ended

5. Create an equation with x on both sides of the equation for each of the following.
   a. Every real number is a solution.
   b. No real number is a solution.
   c. 0 is a solution.

6. Create an equation not involving radicals or fractional exponents for each of the following.
   a. $\sqrt{3}$ and $^-\sqrt{3}$ are the solutions
   b. $\sqrt[3]{2}$ is the only solution

Cooperative Learning

7. Examine several elementary school textbooks for grades 1 through 5 and report how algebraic concepts involving equations are introduced in each grade level.

8. Each person in your group is to search the Internet for two word problems that seem interesting and somewhat challenging, and bring them back to the group. Next, the group is to discuss the problems and choose which one is most interesting. Each person then is to create a clear, well-written solution. The group should discuss the different solutions and choose the best one. Discuss what makes the chosen solution good.

Connecting Mathematics to the Classroom

9. A student claims that the equation $3x = 5x$ has no solution because $3 \neq 5$. How do you respond?

10. A student claims that because in the following problem we need to find three unknown quantities, he must set up equations with three unknowns. How do you respond?
    Abby delivers twice as many papers as Jillian, and Brandy delivers 50 more papers than Abby. How many papers does each deliver if the total number of papers delivered is 550?

11. A student was told that in order to check a solution to a word problem like the one in exercise 10, it is not enough to check that the solution found satisfies the equation set up, but rather that it is necessary to check the answer against the original problem. She would like to know why. How do you respond?

12. On a test, a student was asked to solve the equation $4x + 5 = 3(x + 15)$. He proceeded as follows:

    $$4x + 5 = 3x + 45 = x + 5 = 45 = x = 40$$

    Hence, $x = 40$. He checked that $x = 40$ satisfies the original equation; however, he did not get full credit for the problem and wants to know why. How do you respond?

Review Problems

13. If the number of sophomores, juniors, and seniors combined is denoted by x and it is 3 times the number of freshmen, denoted by y, write an algebraic equation that shows the relationship.

14. Write the sum of five consecutive even numbers if the middle one is $2n$. Simplify your answer.

15. If Julie has twice as many CDs as Jack and Tyto has 3 times as many as Julie, write an algebraic expression for the number of CDs each has in terms of one variable.

16. Write an algebraic equation relating the variables described in each of the following.
    a. The total pay P for 3 hours if you are paid $30 for the first hour and $$d$ more than the preceding hour for each hour thereafter.
    b. Jimmy's total pay P after 4 years if the first year his salary was d dollars and then each year thereafter his salary is twice as much as in the preceding year

17. **a.** Show that the sum of every three consecutive terms in every arithmetic sequence equals 3 times the middle term.
    b. State and justify a statement similar to the one in part(a) for a product of every three consecutive terms in every geometric sequence.

18. If the first term of a geometric sequence is $\sqrt{5}$ and the ratio is 0.5, find the 6th term of the sequence.

19. In a geometric sequence, the first term is 12 and the 4th term is $\sqrt{5}$. Find the ratio.

National Assessments

National Assessment of Educational Progress (NAEP) Questions

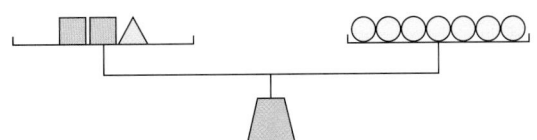

The objects on the scale above make it balance exactly. According to this scale, if △ balances ◯◯◯, then ▢ balances which of the following?

A. ◯
B. ◯◯
C. ◯◯◯
D. ◯◯◯◯

NAEP, Grade 8, 2013

While she was on vacation, Tara sent 14 friends either a letter or a postcard. She spent $3.84 on postage. If it costs $0.20 to mail a postcard and $0.33 to mail a letter, how many letters did Tara send? Show what you did to get your answer.

NAEP, Grade 8, 2013

8-4 Functions

8-4 Objectives

Students will be able to understand and explain

- The concept of a function including domain and range.

- Different representations of functions.

- Derivation of the formulas for the sum of n terms of arithmetic and geometric sequences.

- The concept of a relation.

CCSS The concept of a function is central to all of mathematics and particularly to algebra, as elaborated in the following excerpt from grade 8 *Common Core Standards*. We find that students should:

- **Define, evaluate, and compare functions.**
- **Use functions to model relationships between quantities. (p. 53)**

Functions can model many real-world phenomena. In this section, we explore different ways to represent functions—as *rules, machines, equations, arrow diagrams, tables, ordered pairs, and graphs.* It is important that students see a variety of ways of representing functions.

Functions as Rules Between Two Sets

The following problem is an example of a game called "guess my rule," and often used to introduce the concept of a function.

> When Tom said 2, Noah said 5. When Dick said 4, Noah said 7. When Mary said 10, Noah said 13. When Liz said 6, what did Noah say? What is Noah's rule?

The answer to the first question may be 9, and the rule could be "Take the original number and add 3"; that is, for any number n, Noah's answer is $n + 3$.

IMAP Video

Watch students in a 4th grade classroom develop a rule for summing consecutive natural numbers.

Example 10

Activity Manual

Use *What's My Function?* to practice determining functions and representing them in multiple ways.

Guess the teacher's rule for the following responses:

a.

Student	Teacher
1	3
0	0
4	12
10	30

b.

Student	Teacher
2	5
3	7
5	11
10	21

c.

Student	Teacher
2	0
4	0
7	1
21	1

Solution

a. The teacher's rule could be "Multiply the given number n by 3"; that is, for any number n the teacher's answer is $3n$.

b. The teacher's rule could be "Double the original number n and add 1;" that is, for any number n the teacher's answer is $2n + 1$.

c. The teacher's rule could be "If the number n is even, answer 0; if the number is odd, answer 1." Another possible rule is "If the number is less than 5, answer 0; if greater than or equal to 5, answer 1."

■

Note that in Example 10, the rule connects the set describing what the student says to the set describing the teacher's responses.

Functions as Machines

Another way to prepare students for the concept of a function is by using a "function machine." Functions are commonly given letter names, in particular f or g. The following partial student page shows an example of a function machine. What goes into the machine is referred to as *input* and what comes out as *output*. On the student page below, if the input to the function, f, is 3, the output is 12. For any input element x, the output could be denoted as $f(x)$, read "f of x." For the function in the example on the student page, one possibility is to write it as $f(x) = 4x$, where x is a real number.

School Book Page   Why Learn This?

Why Learn This?

Pretend you have a machine. You can put any number, or input, into the machine. The machine performs an operation on the number and provides a result, or output. A **function** is a rule that assigns exactly one output value to each input value.

Input

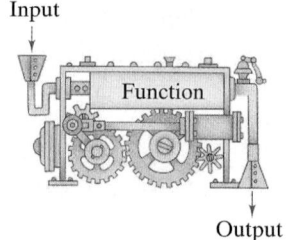

Function

Output

Suppose you tell the machine to multiply by 4. A function table, such as the one at the right, shows the input and output values.

Input	Output
3	12
−7	−28

Historical Note

Leonhard Euler

The Babylonians of Mesopotamia (ca. 2000 BCE) developed a precursor to a function. To them, a function was a table or a correspondence.

In his book *Geometry* (1637), René Descartes (1596–1650) used functions to describe many mathematical relationships. Almost 50 years after the publication of Descartes's book, Gottfried Wilhelm Leibniz (1646–1716) introduced the term *function*. Function was further formalized by Leonhard Euler (pronounced "oiler," 1707–1783), who introduced the notation $y = f(x)$. In the early twenty-first century, on most graphing calculators, Y1, Y2, Y3, . . . serve as function notations where Y1 acts like $f(x)$ if the function rule is written in terms of x.   ●

Example 11

Consider the function machine in Figure 18. For the function named f, what happens when the numbers 0, 1, 3, 4, and 6 are input?

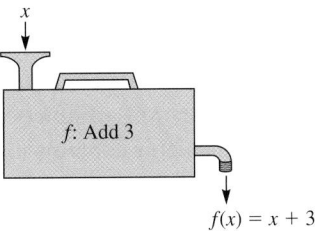

$$f(x) = x + 3$$

Figure 18

Solution For the given values of x, the corresponding values $f(x)$ are described in Table 4.

Table 4	
x	$f(x)$
0	3
1	4
3	6
4	7
6	9

Functions as Equations

The equation $f(x) = x + 3$ describes the function in Example 11. The output values can be obtained by substituting the values 0, 1, 3, 4, and 6 for x in $f(x) = x + 3$, as shown:

$$f(0) = 0 + 3 = 3$$
$$f(1) = 1 + 3 = 4$$
$$f(3) = 3 + 3 = 6$$
$$f(4) = 4 + 3 = 7$$
$$f(6) = 6 + 3 = 9$$

In many applications, both the inputs and the outputs of a function machine are numbers. However, inputs and outputs can be any objects. For example, consider a particular candy machine that accepts only 25¢, 50¢, and 75¢ and outputs one of three types of candy with costs of 25¢, 50¢, and 75¢, respectively. A function machine associates *exactly one output with each input*. If we enter some element x as input and obtain $f(x)$ as output, then every time we enter the same x as input, we obtain the same $f(x)$ as output. The idea of a function machine associating exactly one output with each input according to some rule leads to a definition of a function as a relation between two sets as seen below.

E-Manipulative Activity

Additional practice with function machines can be found in *Function Machine* on the E-Manipulative Disk.

Definition of Function

A **function** from set A to set B is a correspondence from A to B in which each element of A is paired with one, and only one, element of B.

From the definition it follows that f is a function from set A to set B if for every $x \in A$, x is paired with a single element in B, denoted by $f(x)$ the image of x. Later in this section we will see that functions are sets of ordered pairs.

The set, A, of all allowable inputs in the definition of a function is the **domain** of the function. Normally, *if no domain is given to describe a function, then the domain is assumed to contain all elements for which the rule is meaningful.* Set B, the **codomain**, is any set that includes all the possible outputs. The set of all actual outputs is the **range** of the function. Set B includes the range and could be the range itself. The distinction is made for convenience sake, since sometimes the range is not easy to find. Students frequently have trouble with the language of functions (for example, *image, domain, range,* and *one-to-one*), which subsequently impacts their ability to work with graphical representations of functions.

A typical calculator contains many functions. For example, the $\boxed{\pi}$ button always displays an approximation for π, such as 3.1415927; the $\boxed{+/-}$ button either displays a negative sign in front of a number or removes an existing negative sign; and the $\boxed{x^2}$ and $\boxed{\sqrt{}}$ buttons square numbers and take the principal square root of numbers, respectively.

Not all input-output machines are function machines. Consider the machine in Figure 19. For any *natural-number* input x, the machine outputs a number that is less than x. If, for example, the number 10 is input, the machine may output 9, since 9 is less than 10. If 10 is input again, the machine may output 3, since 3 is less than 10. Such a machine is not a function machine because the same input may have different outputs; it is an example of a *relation*.

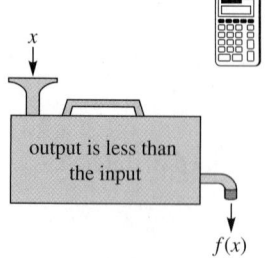

x

output is less than the input

$f(x)$

Figure 19

Example 12

A bicycle manufacturer incurs a daily fixed cost of $1400 for overhead expenses and a cost of $500 per bike manufactured.

a. Find the total cost $C(x)$ of manufacturing x bikes in a day.
b. If the manufacturer sells each bike for $700 and the profit (or loss) in producing and selling x bikes in a day is $P(x)$, find $P(x)$ in terms of x.
c. Find the break-even point, that is, the number of bikes x produced and sold that will result in neither a profit nor a loss.

Solution

a. Since the cost of producing each bike is $500, the cost of producing x bikes is $500x$ dollars. Because of the fixed cost of $1400 per day, the total cost, $C(x)$ in dollars, of producing x bikes in a given day is $C(x) = 500x + 1400$.

b. $P(x) = $ Income from selling x bikes $-$ total cost of manufacturing x bikes

$P(x) = 700x - (500x + 1400)$

$ = 200x - 1400$

c. We need the number of bikes x to be produced so that $P(x) = 0$; that is, we need to solve $200x - 1400 = 0$.

$$200x - 1400 = 0$$
$$200x = 1400$$
$$x = \frac{1400}{200} = 7$$

Thus, the manufacturer needs to produce and sell 7 bikes to break even.

Functions as Arrow Diagrams

Arrow diagrams can be used to examine whether a correspondence represents a function. This representation is normally used when sets A and B are finite sets with few elements. Example 13 shows how arrow diagrams can be used to examine both functions and nonfunctions.

Example 13

Which, if any, of the parts of Figure 20 exhibit a function from A to B? If a correspondence is a function from A to B, find the range of the function.

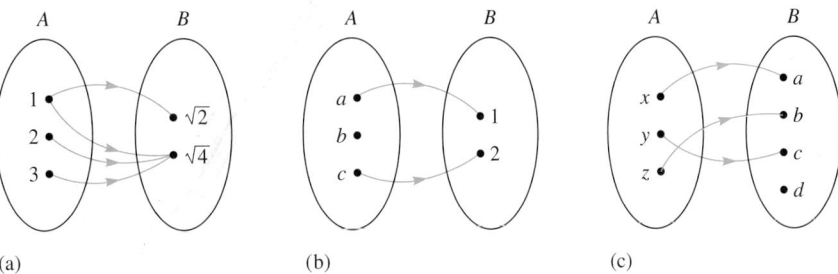

(a)   (b)   (c)

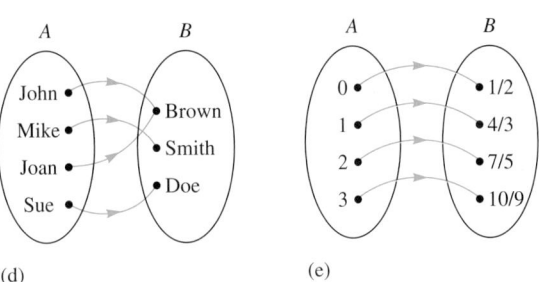

(d)   (e)

Figure 20

Solution

a. Figure 20(a) does not define a function from A to B, because the element 1 is paired with both $\sqrt{2}$ and $\sqrt{4}$.

b. Figure 20(b) does not define a function from A to B, since the element b is not paired with any element of B. (It is a function from a subset of A to B.)

c. Figure 20(c) does define a function from A to B, since there is one, and only one, arrow leaving each element of A. The fact that d, an element of B, is not paired with any element in the domain does not violate the definition. The range is $\{a, b, c\}$ and does not include d because d is not an output of this function, as no element of A is paired with d.

d. Figure 20(d) illustrates a function from A to B, since there is one, and only one, arrow leaving each element in A. It does not matter that an element of set B, Brown, has two arrows pointing to it. The range is {Brown, Smith, Doe}.

e. Figure 20(e) illustrates a function from A to B whose range is $\left\{ \dfrac{1}{2}, \dfrac{4}{3}, \dfrac{7}{5}, \dfrac{10}{9} \right\}$.

Figure 20(e) also illustrates a **one-to-one correspondence between A and B**. In fact, *any one-to-one correspondence between A and B defines a function from A to B as well as a function from B to A.*

▶ **NOW TRY THIS 8**

NTT 8: Answers can be found in Answers at the back of the book.

Determine which of the following are functions from the set of natural numbers to $\{0, 1\}$.

a. For every natural-number input, the output is 0.

b. For every natural-number input, the output is 0 if the input is an even number, and the output is 1 if the input is an odd number.

Functions as Tables and Ordered Pairs

One way to describe a function is with a table. Consider the information in Table 5 relating the amounts spent on advertising and the resulting sales in a given month for a small business. The information is given in thousands of dollars. We could define a function between the set of amounts of dollars, A, spent in Advertising and the set of amounts of dollars in Sales, S, or we could simply define the function as follows. If $A = \{0, 1, 2, 3, 4\}$ and $S = \{1, 3, 5, 7, 9\}$, the table describes a function from A to S, where A represents thousands of dollars in advertising and S represents thousands of dollars in sales. For example, $(2, 5)$ means $2000 was spent on advertising resulting in $5000 in sales.

Table 5	
Amount of Advertising (in $1000s)	Amount of Sales (in $1000s)
0	1
1	3
2	5
3	7
4	9

The function could be given using *ordered pairs* (discussed in Chapter 2) as $\{(0, 1), (1, 3), (2, 5), (3, 7), \text{ and } (4, 9)\}$. The first component in each ordered pair is the *input* and the second is the *output*.

Example 14

Which of the following sets of ordered pairs represent functions? If a set represents a function, give its domain and range. If it does not, explain why.

a. $\{(1, 2), (1, 3), (2, 3), (3, 4)\}$

b. $\left\{\left(1, \frac{1}{2}\right), \left(2, \frac{1}{3}\right), \left(3, \frac{1}{4}\right), \left(4, \frac{1}{5}\right)\right\}$

c. $\{(1, 0), (2, 0), (3, 0), (4, 4)\}$

d. $\{(a, b) \mid a \in N \text{ and } b = 2a\}$

Solution

a. This is not a function because the input 1 has two different outputs.

b. This is a function with domain $\{1, 2, 3, 4\}$. Because the range is the set of outputs corresponding to these inputs set of outputs, the range is $\left\{\frac{1}{2}, \frac{1}{3}, \frac{1}{4}, \frac{1}{5}\right\}$.

c. This is a function with domain $\{1, 2, 3, 4\}$ and range $\{0, 4\}$. The output 0 appears more than once, but this does not contradict the definition of a function in that each input corresponds to only one output.

d. This is a function with domain N and range, the set of all even natural numbers.

Activity Manual

Use *Graphing Rectangles* to explore the use of graphs for representing functions.

Functions as Graphs

A sequence can be viewed as a function whose domain, is the set of natural numbers. For example in Figure 21(a), we see a partial *graph* of the arithmetic sequence: $3, 5, 7, 9, 11, \ldots, 2n + 1, \ldots$. The graph of this sequence is depicted on the grid with points given as $(1, 3), (2, 5), (3, 7), (4, 9),$ and $(5, 11)$. Each ordered pair (a, b) is paired with a point on the grid. The horizontal axis in this case is used for the inputs (the numbers of the terms) and the vertical scale depicts the outputs (the terms of the sequence).

In general, to plot an ordered pair (a, b), we move to the point a (the **abscissa**) on the horizontal scale, and then move (up or down) to the point b (the **ordinate**) along the vertical line that goes through a.

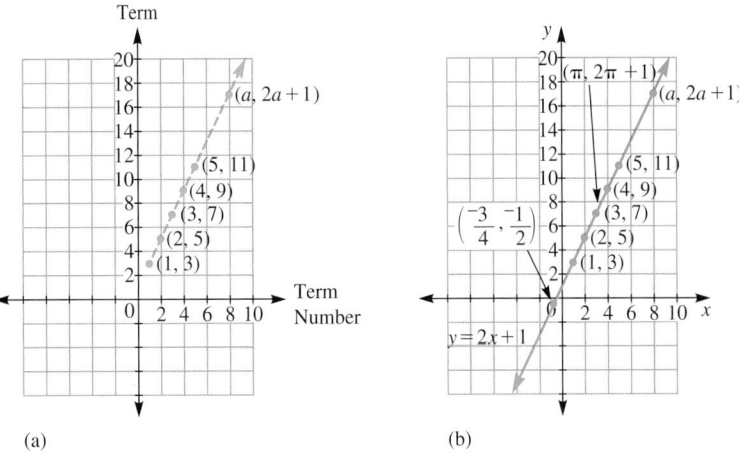

Figure 21

For example, to mark the point corresponding to $(1, 3)$, we start at 1 on the horizontal scale and move up 3 units on the vertical grid line through 1. Marking the point that corresponds to an ordered pair is referred to as **graphing** the ordered pair. The set of all points corresponding to all ordered pairs is the **graph** of the function or relation. In the graph of 21(a) the points are connected by a dashed ray to emphasize that they lie on a straight line, but not every point on the ray belongs to the graph.

Using all real numbers in the domain of the function, $y = 2x + 1$ is depicted in Figure 21(b) and the graph is drawn as a solid line because for every real number a, there is a corresponding real number $2a + 1$ resulting in the ordered pair $(a, 2a + 1)$, which lies on that line. For example, $(\pi, 2\pi + 1)$ and $(^-3/4, ^-1/2)$ are points on the line. The domain and range in this case are each the set of real numbers. Additionally, the horizontal scale in this case is the **x-axis**; the vertical scale is the **y-axis**.

Example 15

Explain why a telephone company would not set rates for telephone calls as depicted on the graph in Figure 22.

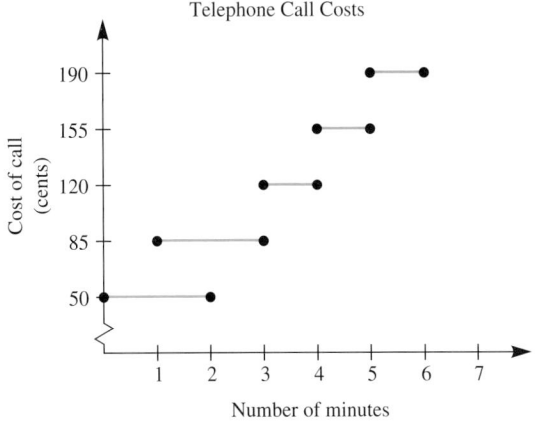

Figure 22

Solution   The graph does not depict a function. For example, a customer could be charged either $0.50 or $0.85 for a 2-min call; hence, not every input has a unique output.

Sequences as Functions

As mentioned earlier, arithmetic, geometric, and other sequences can be thought of as functions whose inputs are natural numbers and whose outputs are the terms of the particular sequences. For example, an arithmetic sequence $2, 4, 6, 8, \ldots$, whose nth term a_n is $2n$ can be described as a function from the set N (natural numbers) to the set E (even natural numbers) using the rule $f(n) = 2n$, where n is a natural number representing the number of the term and $f(n)$ stands for the value of the nth term, a_n. Thus, $f(n) = a_n$.

Example 16

If $f(n)$ denotes the nth term of a sequence, find $f(n)$ in terms of n for each of the following:

a. An arithmetic sequence whose first term is 3 and whose difference is 3.
b. A geometric sequence whose first term is 3 and whose ratio is 3.

Solution

a. $a_n = a_1 + (n - 1)d = 3 + (n - 1)3 = 3 + n \cdot 3 - 3 = 3n$. Thus, $f(n) = 3n$, where n is a natural number.
b. $a_n = a_1 r^{n-1} = 3 \cdot 3^{n-1} = 3^n$. Hence, $f(n) = 3^n$, where n is a natural number.

Sums of Sequences as Functions

Gauss's Problem in Chapter 1 to find the sum of $1 + 2 + 3 + \ldots + 100$ is an example of finding the sum of an arithmetic sequence with 100 terms. Recall that one way to find this sum was to write it twice as follows:

$$S = \quad 1 + \quad 2 + \quad 3 + \ldots + 100$$
$$S = 100 + 99 + 98 + \ldots + \quad 1$$

Adding equals to equals:

$$S + S = (1 + 100) + (2 + 99) + (3 + 98) + \ldots + (100 + 1)$$
$$2S = 100 \cdot 101$$
$$S = \frac{100 \cdot 101}{2} = 5050$$

The same process can be used to find the sum of the first n terms of any arithmetic sequence. $a_1 + (a_1 + d) + (a_1 + 2d) + (a_1 + 3d) + \ldots + (a_1 + (n - 1)d)$. We observe that the sum could also be written backwards as $a_n + (a_n - d) + (a_n - 2d) + (a_n - 3d) + \ldots + (a_n - (n - 1)d)$. (Why?) Using $S(n)$ as a function notation to represent the sum of n terms, we have.

$$S(n) = a_1 + (a_1 + d) + (a_1 + 2d) + \ldots + (a_1 + (n - 1)d)$$
$$S(n) = a_n + (a_n - d) + (a_n - 2d) + \ldots + (a_n - (n - 1)d)$$

Adding as before:

$$S(n) + S(n) = (a_1 + a_n) + (a_1 + a_n) + (a_1 + a_n) + \ldots + (a_1 + a_n)$$

Thus, $2S(n) = n(a_1 + a_n)$ and therefore

$$S(n) = \left(\frac{n}{2}\right)(a_1 + a_n) = \left(\frac{a_1 + a_n}{2}\right)n.$$

This proves Theorem 8-5.

Theorem 8-5

The sum S_n of the first n terms of an arithmetic sequence with first term a_1 and nth term a_n is given by

$$S(n) = \left(\frac{a_1 + a_n}{2}\right)n = \frac{(a_1 + a_n)n}{2}.$$

Because $a_n = a_1 + (n-1)d$, we may substitute for a_n to obtain an equivalent expression for the sum:

$$S(n) = \left(\frac{a_1 + a_1 + (n-1)d}{2}\right)n = \left(\frac{2a_1 + (n-1)d}{2}\right)n = a_1 n + \frac{n(n-1)}{2}d$$

The sum can be thought of as a function of n where n is the number of terms of the sequence. In this case the domain is the set of natural numbers and the output for input n is the sum of the first n terms of the sequence. There is no need to memorize the above two formulas for $S(n)$. Knowing Theorem 8-5 and the expression $a_n = a_1 + (n-1)d$ is sufficient.

Example 17

Find the sum of the first 100 terms of the following arithmetic sequence: $3, 7, 11, 15, 19, \ldots$.

Solution   In this arithmetic sequence $a_1 = 3$ and $d = 7 - 3 = 4$.

From Theorem 8-5, we have $S(100) = \left(\dfrac{a_1 + a_{100}}{2}\right)100 = \left(\dfrac{3 + a_{100}}{2}\right)100$. Thus, our *subgoal*

is to compute a_{100}. We have $a_{100} = 3 + (100 - 1)4 = 399$. Thus, $S(100) = \left(\dfrac{3 + 399}{2}\right)100$

$= 20,100$.

Similarly, we can find the sum of the first n terms of a geometric sequence. Consider the geometric sequence $a_1, a_1 r, a_1 r^2, a_1 r^3, \ldots, a_1 r^{(n-1)}$. Let

$$S(n) = a_1 + a_1 r + a_1 r^2 + \ldots + a_1 r^{n-1}.$$

Because the terms are very similar, suppose we multiply both sides of the equation by r obtaining $rS_n = a_1 r + a_1 rr + a_1 r^2 r + \ldots + a_1 r^{n-1}r = a_1 r + a_1 r^2 + a_1 r^3 + \ldots + a_1 r^n$. Then:

$$S(n) = a_1 + a_1 r + a_1 r^2 + \ldots + a_1 r^{n-1}$$
$$rS(n) = \qquad a_1 r + a_1 r^2 + a_1 r^3 + \ldots + a_1 r^n$$

Subtracting, we obtain:

$$S(n) - rS(n) = a_1 - a_1 r^n$$
$$S(n)(1 - r) = a_1(1 - r^n)$$
$$S(n) = a_1 \frac{1 - r^n}{1 - r}$$

Note that in the above formula, $r \neq 1$ because division by 0 is not defined.

This proves Theorem 8-6.

Theorem 8-6

The sum of the first n terms of a geometric sequence whose first term is a_1, and whose ratio is $r \neq 1$ is

$$S(n) = a_1 \frac{1 - r^n}{1 - r}.$$

If the sum of n terms of a geometric sequence is multiplied by $(^-1)/(^-1)$, it can be written as $S(n) = a_1\left(\dfrac{r^n - 1}{r - 1}\right)$. As with the arithmetic sequence sum, the sum of the first n terms of a geometric sequence is a function of n, the number of terms. It is common to write the sum of n terms of a sequence as S_n, we used $S(n)$ to emphasize that the sum is a function of n.

Example 18

Find the sum of the first 10 terms of the geometric sequence: $3, -\dfrac{3}{2}, \dfrac{3}{4}, -\dfrac{3}{8}, \ldots$.

Solution The geometric sequence has first term 3 and ratio $\dfrac{-\dfrac{3}{2}}{3} = -\dfrac{1}{2}$. Thus, the sum of the first

10 terms is $S(10) = 3\left(\dfrac{1 - \left(-\dfrac{1}{2}\right)^{10}}{1 - \left(-\dfrac{1}{2}\right)}\right) = 3\left(\dfrac{1 - \left(\dfrac{1}{2}\right)^{10}}{\dfrac{3}{2}}\right) = 2\left(1 - \left(\dfrac{1}{2}\right)^{10}\right) = \dfrac{1023}{512} \doteq 1.998.$

Problem Solving **Computer Chips Problem**

Employees working at the same rate produce an order for computer chips. If all were to start at the same time they would complete the job in 3 hours. However, the employees did not start at the same time; each (starting from the second) came to work a fixed number of hours after the first employee so that the one who arrived first worked 11 times longer than the one who arrived last. If they all stayed working until the job was done, how many hours did the first employee work?

Understanding the Problem We know that the first employee worked the most, 11 times more than the last. We designate the number of hours that the last employee worked by b. Then the first worked $11b$ hours. Each employee thereafter worked a certain number of hours, d less than the proceeding one. Thus, the number of hours that each employee worked is an arithmetic sequence. We subtract a fixed number to see how much the next employee worked; that is add ^-d. We also know that if all employees were to start the job at the same time, they would have completed it in 24 hours.

Devising a Plan Suppose there were n employees. We write expressions for the total number of working hours in terms of the unknowns introduced. On the one hand, the total number of working hours is $3n$. (Each of the n employees would work 3 hours until the job was finished.) On the other hand, the total working hours is the sum of the hours that each employee worked. Because the hours that each employee worked form an arithmetic sequence, we know that the sum is $\dfrac{(b + 11b)n}{2}$. We now write an equation and solve it for b.

Carrying Out the Plan Equating the total number of working hours to complete the job we get:

$$3n = \frac{(b + 11b)n}{2}$$

$$3n = \frac{12bn}{2}$$

$$3n = 6bn$$

We divide both sides of the equation by n:

$$3 = 6b$$

$$\frac{1}{2} = b$$

Thus, $11b = 11 \cdot \frac{1}{2} = 5\frac{1}{2}$ and therefore the first employee worked $5\frac{1}{2}$ hours.

Looking Back We notice that the answer to the problem is the same regardless of the number of employees. We also did not have to know d, the number of hours that an employee, starting from the second one, worked less than the preceding one. However, d can be found if n is known. Show that $d = \dfrac{5}{n-1}$.

Composition of Functions

Consider the function machines in Figure 23. If 2 is entered in the top machine, then $f(2) = 2 + 4 = 6$. The number 6 is then entered in the second machine and $g(6) = 2 \cdot 6 = 12$. The functions in Figure 23 illustrate the **composition of two functions**. In the composition of two functions, the range of the first function must be a subset of the domain of the second function.

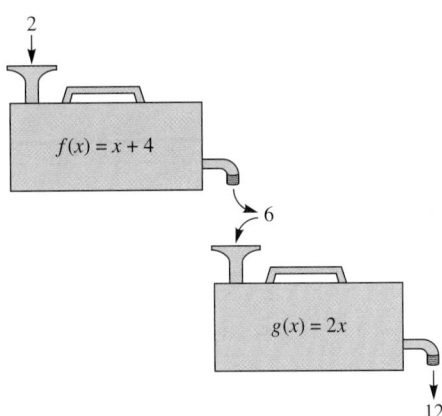

Figure 23

If the first function f is followed by a second function g, as in Figure 23, we symbolize the composition of the functions as $g \circ f$. If we input 3 in the function machines of Figure 23, then the output is symbolized by $(g \circ f)(3)$. Because f acts first on 3, to compute $(g \circ f)(3)$ we find $f(3) = 3 + 4 = 7$ and then $g(7) = 2 \cdot 7 = 14$. Hence, $(g \circ f)(3) = 14$. Observe that $(g \circ f)(3) = g(f(3))$, which is read as "g of f of 3." Also $(g \circ f)(x) = g(f(x)) = 2f(x) = 2(x + 4)$ and hence $g(f(3)) = 2(3 + 4) = 14$.

Example 19

If $f(x) = 2x + 3$ and $g(x) = x - 3$, find the following outputs:

a. $(f \circ g)(3)$ b. $(g \circ f)(3)$ c. $(f \circ g)(x)$ d. $(g \circ f)(x)$

Solution

a. $(f \circ g)(3) = f(g(3)) = f(3 - 3) = f(0) = 2 \cdot 0 + 3 = 3$
b. $(g \circ f)(3) = g(f(3)) = g(2 \cdot 3 + 3) = g(9) = 9 - 3 = 6$
c. $(f \circ g)(x) = f(g(x)) = 2g(x) + 3 = 2(x - 3) + 3 = 2x - 6 + 3 = 2x - 3$
d. $(g \circ f)(x) = g(f(x)) = f(x) - 3 = (2x + 3) - 3 = 2x$

Example 19 shows that composition of functions is not commutative, since $(f \circ g)(3) \neq (g \circ f)(3)$.

Calculator or Computer Representation of a Function

A function can be represented in a variety of ways: pictures of sets with arrows, function machines, tables, equations, or graphs. Depending on the situation, one representation may be more useful than another. For example, if the domain of a function has many elements, a table is not a convenient representation. Graphing calculators or computer graphing applications can be used to display a graph of most functions given by equations with specified domains.

A sketch of the function $f(x) = 2x + 1$ is shown in Figure 24 using a graphing calculator downloaded on a computer. Note that on this graphing calculator $f(x)$ is depicted as y_1, and the domain was automatically chosen.

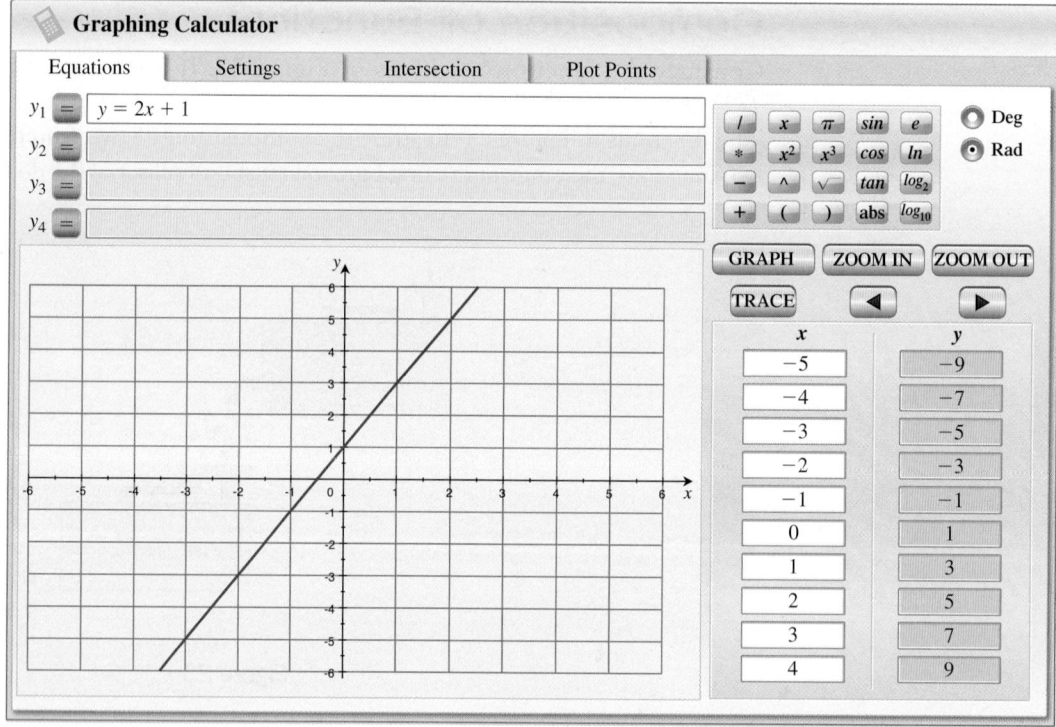

Figure 24

Because $f(x) = 2x + 1$ in Figure 24 and x is the only variable; we say that f is a function of *single variable*. However, we can also have functions of two or more variables. For example, the function that assigns to each ordered pair (x, y) the number $x + y$ is written $f(x, y) = x + y$, and is a function of two variables. If a particle moves at a speed V miles per hour for t hours, the distance S that it travels is Vt. If we let V as well as t vary, then $S(V, t) = Vt$ is a function of two variables. The function $f(x, y, z) = (x + y)z$ is an example of a function of three variables.

Relations

A function from set A to set B is a form of a *relation from set A to set B*. In a relation from A to B, there is a correspondence between elements of A and elements of B, but we do not require that each element of A be paired with one, and only one, element of B. Consequently, any set of ordered pairs is a relation. With appropriate set definitions, examples of relations include the following:

"is a daughter of"   "is the same color as"
"is less than"   "is greater than or equal to"

Consider the relation "is a sister of". Figure 25 illustrates this relation among children on a playground, with letters A through J representing the children. An arrow from I to J indicates that I "is a sister of " J. The arrows from F to G and from G to F indicate that F is a sister of G and G is a sister of F. This implies that F and G are girls. On the other hand, the absence of an arrow from J to I implies that J is not a sister of I. Thus, I is a girl and J is a boy.

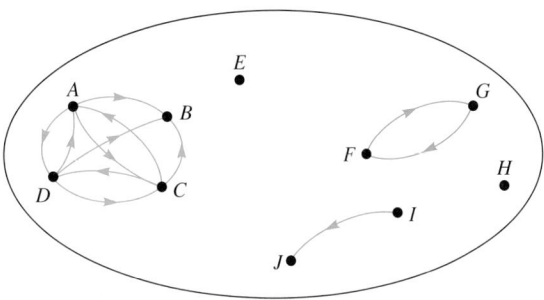

Figure 25

▶ NOW TRY THIS 9

NTT 9: Answers can be found in Answers at the back of the book.

All sister relationships are indicated in Figure 25.

  a. Which children are boys and which are girls?
  b. For which children is there not enough information to determine gender?

Another way to depict the arrow relation "A is a sister of B" is as an ordered pair (A, B). Using this notation, the relation "is a sister of " can be described for the children on the playground in Figure 26 as the set

$$\{(A,B), (A,C), (A,D), (C,A), (C,B), (C,D), (D,A), (D,B), (D,C), (F,G), (G,F), (I,J)\}.$$

This set is a subset of the Cartesian product $\{A, B, C, D, E, F, G, H, I, J\} \times \{A, B, C, D, E, F, G, H, I, J\}$.

This observation motivates the following definition of a relation.

Definition of a Relation from Set _A_ to Set _B_

Given any two sets A and B, a **relation** from A to B is a subset of $A \times B$; that is, R is a relation from set A to set B if, and only if, $R \subseteq A \times B$.

In the definition, if $A = B$, we say that the **relation is on** A. Using the concept of a relation a function from set A to set B can be defined as a relation from set A to set B such that:

- for each $a \in A$, there exist some element $b \in B$ such that (a, b) is in the relation and,
- two different ordered pairs in the relation cannot have the same first component.

Properties of Relations

Figure 26 represents a set of children in a small group. The children have drawn all possible arrows representing the relation "has the same first letter in his or her name as." Three properties of relations are illustrated in Figure 26.

Definition of the Reflexive Property

A relation R on a set X is **reflexive** if, and only if, for every element $a \in X$, a is related to a; that is, for every $a \in X$, $(a, a) \in R$.

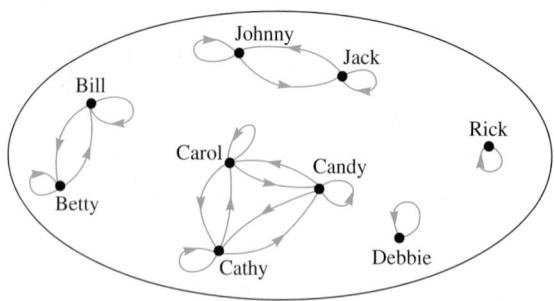

Figure 26

In the diagram, there is a loop at every point. For example, Rick has the same first initial as himself, namely R. A relation such as "is taller than" is not reflexive because people cannot be taller than themselves.

Definition of the Symmetric Property

A relation R on a set X is **symmetric** if, and only if, for all elements a and b in X, whenever a is related to b, then b also is related to a; that is, if $(a, b) \in R$, then $(b, a) \in R$.

In terms of the diagram, every pair of points that has an arrow headed in one direction also has a return arrow. For example, if Bill has the same first initial as Betty, then Betty has the same first initial as Bill. A relation such as "is a brother of" is not symmetric since Dick can be a brother of Jane, but Jane cannot be a brother of Dick.

Definition of the Transitive Property

A relation R on a set X is **transitive** if, and only if, for all elements a, b, and c of X, whenever a is related to b and b is related to c, then a is related to c. That is, if $(a, b) \in R$ and $(b, c) \in R$, then $(a, c) \in R$.

In the definitions for the symmetric and transitive properties, a, b, and c are variables and do not have to be different.

The relation in Figure 26 is transitive. For example, if Carol has the same first initial as Candy, and Candy has the same first initial as Cathy, then Carol has the same first initial as Cathy. A relation such as "is the father of" is not transitive since, if Tom Jones is the father of Tom Jones, Jr. and Tom Jones, Jr. is the father of Joe Jones, then Tom Jones is not the father of Joe Jones. He is, instead, the grandfather of Joe Jones.

The relation "is the same color as" is reflexive, symmetric, and transitive. In general, relations that satisfy all three properties are **equivalence relations**.

Definition of the Equivalence Relation

An **equivalence relation** is any relation R that satisfies the reflexive, symmetric, and transitive properties.

The most natural equivalence relation encountered in elementary school is "is equal to" on the set of all numbers. The relation on W (the set of whole numbers) defined by "have the same remainder upon division by m ($m \geq 2$)" is an equivalence relation. (Why?) For example if $m = 3$, W is partitioned into three disjoint subsets by this relation, all the elements of W that have remainder 0 when divided by 3, remainder 1 when divided by 3, and those that have remainder 2 when divided by 3.

Equivalence relations are useful in mathematics because of the property that an equivalence relation on a set S partitions the set into disjoint subsets whose union is S. In subsequent chapters, we will see other examples of equivalence relations, such as congruence and similarity in geometry.

Assessment 8-4A

1. The following sets of ordered pairs are functions. Give a rule that could describe each function.
   a. $\{(^-1,2),(0,0),(1,^-2),(2^{\frac{1}{2}},^-2^{\frac{1}{2}})\}$ Multiply the input by -2.
   b. $\{(^-6,0),(0,6),(5,11),(\sqrt{3},\sqrt{3}+6)\}$ Add 6 to the input.
   c. $\{(^-1,1),(1,1),(2,4),(\sqrt{3},3)\}$ Square the input.
2. Which of the following are functions from the set $\{1,2,3\}$ to the set $\{a,b,c,d\}$? If the set of ordered pairs is not a function, explain why not.   This is not a function, since the input
   a. $\{(1,a),(2,b),(3,c),(1,d)\}$ 1 is paired with two outputs (a and d).
   b. $\{(1,a),(2,b),(3,a)\}$ Function
   c. $\{(1,a),(2,a),(3,a)\}$ Function
   d. $\{(1,a),(2,b),(3,b)\}$ Function
3. a. Draw an arrow diagram of a function with domain $\{1,2,3,4,5\}$ and range $\{a,b\}$.   *
   b. How many possible functions are there for part (a)?   30
4. Suppose $f(x)=2x+1$ and the domain is $\{0,1,\sqrt{2},\sqrt{3},4\}$. Describe the function in the following ways.
   a. Draw an arrow diagram involving two sets.   *
   b. Use ordered pairs.   *
   c. Make a table.   *
   d. Draw a graph to depict the function.   *
5. Determine which of the following are functions from the set of real numbers, R, or a subset of R, to R. If your answer is that it is not a function, explain why not.
   a. $f(x)=2$ for all $x \in R$ Function
   b. $f(x)=\sqrt{x}$ Function
   c. $\{(x,y)\,|\,x=y^2, x \geq 0\}$ *
   d. $\{(x,y)\,|\,x=y^3\}$ Function
6. a. Make an arrow diagram for each of the following.
      i. Rule: "when doubled is"   *

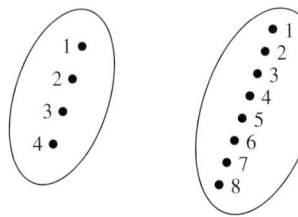

      ii. Rule: "is greater than"   *

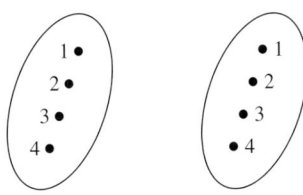

   b. Which, if any, of the parts in (a) exhibits a function from A to B? If it is a function, tell why and find the range of the function.   *

7. The dosage of a certain drug is related to the weight of a child as follows: 50 mg of the drug and an additional 15 mg for each 2 lb or fraction of 2 lb of body weight above 30 lb. Sketch the graph of the dosage as a function of the weight of a child for children who weigh between 20 and 40 lb.   *
8. For each of the following, guess what might be Latifah's rule. In each case, if n is your input and $L(n)$ is Latifah's answer, express $L(n)$ in terms of n.

   a.

   | You | Latifah | *
   |-----|---------|
   | 3 | 8 |
   | 4 | 11 |
   | 5 | 14 |
   | 10 | 29 |

   b.

   | You | Latifah | *
   |-----|---------|
   | 0 | 1 |
   | 3 | 10 |
   | 5 | 26 |
   | 8 | 65 |

9. Quick-Talk advertises monthly cellular phone service for $0.50 a minute for the first 60 minutes but only $0.10 a minute for each minute thereafter. Quick-Talk charges for the exact amount of time used. Answer the following.
   a. Make one graph showing the cost per minute as a function of number of minutes and the other showing the total cost for calls as a function of the number of minutes up to 100 min.   *
   b. If you connect the points in the second graph in part (a), what kind of assumption needs to be made about the way the telephone company charges phone calls?   *
   c. Why does the total cost for calls consist of two line segments? Why is one part steeper than the other?   *
   d. The function representing the total cost for calls as a function of number of minutes talked can be represented by two equations. Write these equations.   *
10. For each of the following sequences (either arithmetic or geometric), find a possible function $f(n)$ whose domain is the set of natural numbers and whose outputs are the terms of the sequence.
    a. $3,8,13,18,23,\ldots$ $f(n)=5n-2$
    b. $3,9,27,81,243,\ldots$ $f(n)=3^n$
    c. $3,3,3,3,\ldots$ $f(n)=3$
    d. $3,3^{\frac{4}{3}},3^{\frac{5}{3}},3^2,\ldots$ $f(n)=3^{\frac{n+2}{3}}$
11. Consider the following two function machines. Find the final output for each of the following inputs.
    a. 6   37
    b. 10   65
    c. $\sqrt{10}$ $7\sqrt{10}-5$
    d. 0 $^-5$
    e. $\dfrac{5}{8}$ $\dfrac{^-5}{8}$
    f. n $7n-5$

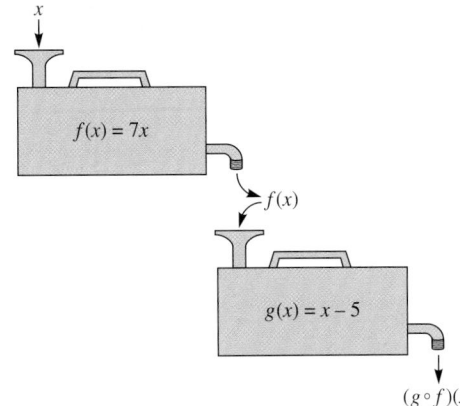

12. In problem 11, find all inputs for which the final output equals twice the input.   1

13. a. Repeat problem 11 when the bottom machine $g(x) = x - 5$ is on top and the top machine $f(x) = 7x$ is at the bottom. (In this case, the final output is $(f \circ g)(x)$.)   *
   b. Find all x for which $(f \circ g)(x) = x$. $\frac{35}{6}$

14. Consider the function $f(x) = {}^-x + b$, where b is a constant, and find the following.
   a. $f(f(0))$ 0   **b.** $f(f(2))$ 2
   c. All inputs x for which the final output is x, that is, $f(f(x)) = x$.   All real numbers

15. Let $t(n)$ represent the nth term of a sequence for $n \in N$. Answer the following.
   a. If $t(n) = 4n - 3$, determine which of the following are output values of the function: (i), (ii), and (iii)
      i. 1   **ii.** 385   **iii.** 389   **iv.** 392
   b. If $t(n) = n^2$, determine which of the following are output values of the function.   (ii) and (iii)
      i. 0   **ii.** 25   **iii.** 625   **iv.** 1000   **v.** 90
   c. If $t(n) = n(n - 1)$, determine which of the following are in the range of the function.
      i. 0   **ii.** 2   **iii.** 20   **iv.** 999   (i), (ii), and (iii)

16. a. If $f(x) = x^2$ and the output is 2 find all possible inputs.   *
   b. Repeat (a) if $f(x) = x^3$ $\sqrt[3]{2}$

17. Consider a function machine that accepts inputs as ordered pairs. Suppose the components of the ordered pairs are natural numbers and the first component is the length of a rectangle and the second is its width. The following machine computes the perimeter (the distance around a figure) of the rectangle. Thus, for a rectangle whose length, l, is 3 and whose width, w, is 2, the input is (3, 2) and the output is $2 \cdot 3 + 2 \cdot 2$, or 10.

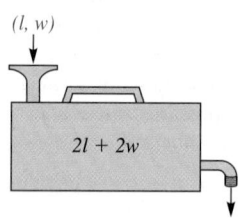

(l, w)

$2l + 2w$

   a. For each of the following inputs, find the corresponding output: $(1, 7), (2, 6), (6, 2), (\sqrt{5}, \sqrt{5})$.   16; 16; 16; $4\sqrt{5}$
   b. Find the set of all the inputs for which the output is 20.   *
   c. What is the domain and the range of the function?   *

18. The following graph shows the relationship between the number of cars on a certain road and the time of day for times between 5:00 A.M. and 9:00 A.M.:

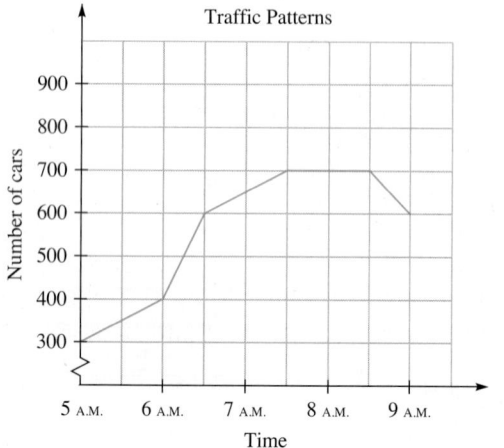

Traffic Patterns

Number of cars

5 A.M.   6 A.M.   7 A.M.   8 A.M.   9 A.M.

Time

a. What was the increase in the number of cars on the road between 6:30 A.M. and 7:00 A.M.?   50 cars
b. During which half hour was the increase in the number of cars the greatest?   Between 6 and 6:30 A.M.
c. What was the increase in the number of cars between 8:00 A.M. and 8:30 A.M.?   0
d. During which half hour(s) did the number of cars decrease? By how much?   Between 8:30 A.M. and 9 A.M., 100 cars
e. The graph for this problem is composed of segments rather than just points. Why do you think segments are used here instead of just points?   *

19. A ball is shot out of a cannon at ground level. Its height H in feet after t sec is given by the function $H(t) = 128t - 16t^2$.
   a. Find $H(2), H(6), H(3)$, and $H(5)$. Why are some of the outputs equal?   *
   b. Graph the function and from the graph find at what instant the ball is at its highest point. What is its height at that instant?   *
   c. How long does it take for the ball to hit the ground?   8 sec
   d. What is the domain of H? $0 \leq t \leq 8$
   e. What is the range of H? $0 \leq H(t) \leq 256$

20. In the following sequence of matchstick figures assume a possible pattern and, let $S(n)$ be the function giving the total number of matchsticks in the nth figure. Find $S(n)$ in terms of n.   *

21. Assume the pattern continues for the following sequence of square tile figures; that is each square is divided into four squares in the subsequent figure. Let $S(n)$ be the function giving the total number of tiles in the nth figure. Find a formula for $S(n)$ in terms of n. 4^{n-1}

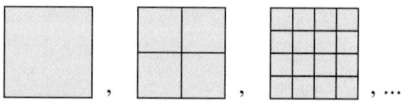

22. Which of the following equations or inequalities represent functions and which do not? In each case x and y are real numbers; x is in the domain and y in the range. If your answer is "not a function" explain why not.   *
   a. $x + y = 2$ **b.** $x - y < 2$
   c. $y = x^3 + x$ **d.** $xy = 2, x \neq 0$
   e. $y = |x|$ **f.** $|y| = x$
   g. $x^2 + y^2 = 1$ **h.** $y = \sqrt{{}^-x}$

23. Which of the following are graphs of functions and which are not? If a graph is not a graph of function explain why not.
   a.

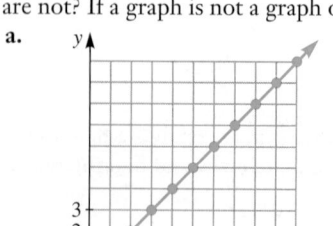

Only (b) is not. For $x = 1$ there are many values of y.

b. 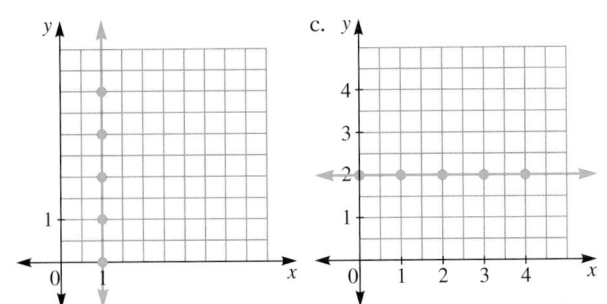   **c.**

24. Suppose each point and letter in the figure represents a child on a playground, and an arrow going from I to J means that I is the sister of J.

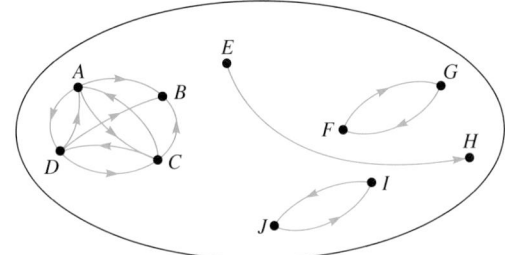

a. Based on the information in the figure, who are definitely girls and who are definitely boys?   *

b. Suppose we write "A is the sister of B" as an ordered pair (A, B). Based on the information in the diagram, write the set of all such ordered pairs.   *

c. Is the set of all ordered pairs in (b) a function with the domain equal to the set of all first components of the ordered pairs and with the range equal to the set of all second components?   No

25. **a.** Consider the relation consisting of ordered pairs (x, y) such that y is the biological mother of x. Is this a function whose domain is the set of all people born on January 1, 2015?   Yes

b. Use the same information as in part (a) but now y is a brother of x. Is the relation a function from the set of all boys to the set of all boys?   No

26. Tell whether each of the following is reflexive, symmetric, or transitive on the set of all people. Which are equivalence relations?

a. "Is a parent of"   None; No

b. "Is the same age as"   *

c. "Has the same last name as"   *

d. "Is the same height as"   *

e. "Is married to"   Symmetric; No

f. "Lives within 10 mi of"   Reflexive and symmetric; No

g. "Is older than"   Transitive; No

Assessment 8-4B

1. The following sets of ordered pairs are functions. Give a rule that could describe each function.

a. $\{(^{-}1, 3), (0, 0), (1, ^{-}3), (3^{-\frac{1}{2}}, ^{-}3^{\frac{1}{2}})\}$ *

b. $\{(^{-}5, 0), (0, 5), (5, 10), (\sqrt{5}, \sqrt{5} + 5)\}$ Add 5 to the input

c. $\left\{(0, 0), (\sqrt{3}, 3), (^{-}\sqrt{5}, 5), \left(\dfrac{1}{\sqrt{6}}, \dfrac{1}{6}\right)\right\}$ Square the input

2. Which of the following are functions from the set $\{1, 2, 3\}$ to the set $\{a, b, c, d\}$? If the set of ordered pairs is not a function, explain why not.

a. $\{(1, c), (3, d)\}$ *   **b.** $\{(1, a), (1, b), (1, c)\}$ *

c. $\{(1, b), (2, b), (3, b)\}$ *   **d.** $\{(1, a), (2, b), (2, c), (3, d)\}$ *

3. **a.** Draw an arrow diagram of a function with domain $\{1, 2, 3\}$ and range $\{a, b\}$.   *

b. How many possible functions are there for part (a)?   6

4. Suppose $f(x) = 2(x - 1)$ and the domain is $\{0, 1, \sqrt{2}, \sqrt{3}, 4\}$. Describe the function in the following ways.

a. Draw an arrow diagram involving two sets.   *

b. Use ordered pairs.   *

c. Make a table.   *

d. Draw a graph to depict the function.   *

5. Determine which of the following are functions from the set of real numbers, R, or a subset of R, to R. If your answer is that it is not a function, explain why not.

a. $f(x) = 0$ if $x \in \{0, 1, 2, 3\}$, and $f(x) = 3$ if $x \notin \{0, 1, 2, 3\}$ Function

b. $f(x) = 0$ for all $x \in R$ and $f(x) = 1$ if $x \in \{3, 4, 5, 6, \ldots\}$ *

c. $\{(x, y) \mid y = |x|\}$ Function

d. $\{(x, y) \mid x = \sqrt{y^2}\}$ *

6. Given the following arrow diagrams for functions from A to B, give a possible rule for the function.

a. 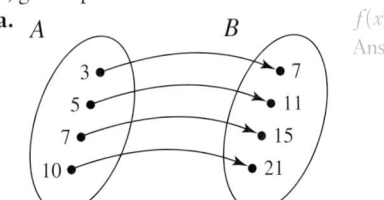 $f(x) = 2x + 1$ Answers vary

b. 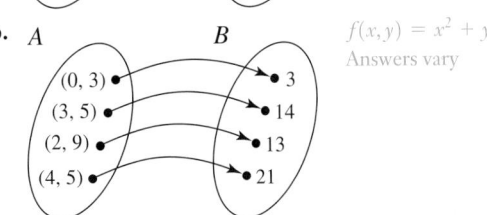 $f(x, y) = x^2 + y$ Answers vary

7. According to wildlife experts, the rate at which crickets chirp is a function of the temperature; specifically, $C = T - 40$, where C is the number of chirps every 15 sec and T is the temperature in degrees Fahrenheit.

a. How many chirps does the cricket make per second if the temperature is 70°F?   2 chirps per second

b. What is the temperature if the cricket chirps 40 times in 1 min?   50°F

8. For each of the following, guess what might be Latifah's rule. In each case, if *n* is your input and *L*(*n*) is Latifah's answer, express *L*(*n*) in terms of *n*.   *

   a.

You	Latifah
6	42
0	0
8	72
2	6

   b.

You	Latifah
0	1
1	2
5	32
6	64
10	1024

9. ChitChat charges $0.45 a minute for cellular phone calls. The cost per minute does not change, but the total cost changes as the telephone is used.

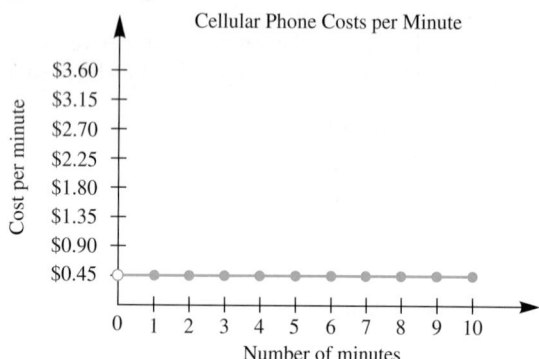

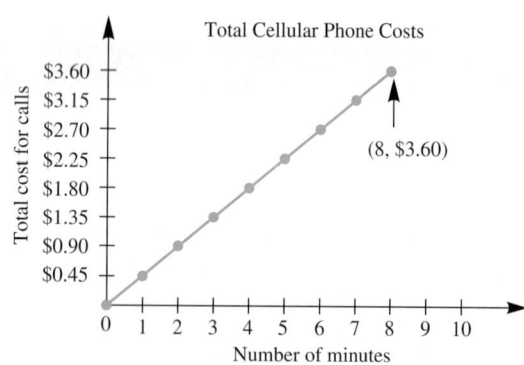

   a. When the number of minutes is 6, what do the values of the corresponding point on each graph represent?   *
   b. What kind of assumption about the charges needs to be made to allow the connection of the points on each graph? Explain.   *
   c. If the time in minutes is *t* and the cost in dollars for calls is *c*, write *c* as a function of *t* for each graph.   *

10. For each of the following (arithmetic or geometric) sequences, discover the pattern and find a function whose domain is the set of natural numbers and whose outputs are the terms of the sequence:

    a. $2, 4, 6, 8, 10, \ldots$ $f(n) = 2n$ b. $1, 3, 9, 27, 81, \ldots$ $f(n) = 3^{n-1}$
    c. $\sqrt{3}, \sqrt{3}, \sqrt{3}, \sqrt{3}, \ldots$ d. $3^{-1}, 3^{-\frac{1}{2}}, 1, 3^{\frac{1}{2}}, 3, \ldots$
    $f(n) = \sqrt{3}$ $f(n) = 3^{\frac{n-3}{2}}$

11. Consider two function machines that are placed as shown. Find the final output for each of the following inputs.

    a. 5 28   b. $\sqrt{3}$ $7\sqrt{3} - 7$
    c. 10 63   d. *a* $7(a - 1)$
    e. $\dfrac{7}{6}$ $\dfrac{7}{6}$

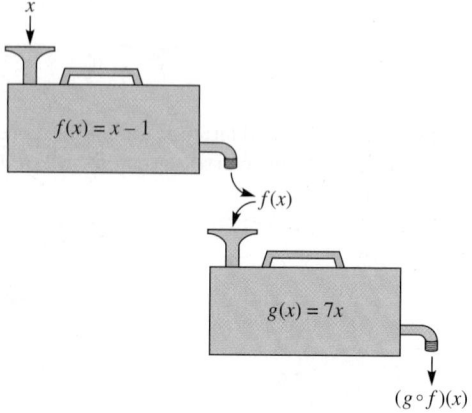

12. In problem 11, find all inputs for which the final output equals twice the input. $\dfrac{7}{5}$
13. a. Repeat problem 11 when the bottom machine $g(x) = 7x$ is on top and the top machine $f(x) = x - 1$ is at the bottom. (In this case, the final output is $(f \circ g)(x)$.)   *
    b. Find all *x* for which $(f \circ g)(x) = x$. $\dfrac{1}{6}$
14. Consider the function $f(x) = {}^-(x + b)$, where *b* is a constant, and find the following (simplify your answers).
    a. $f(f(0))$ 0
    b. $f(f(\sqrt{2}))$ $\sqrt{2}$
    c. All inputs *x* for which the final output is *x*, that is, $f(f(x)) = x$ *
15. Consider the function $f(x) = \dfrac{2x - 1}{2x + 1}$ and find, all possible, inputs for the following outputs.
    a. 2 $\dfrac{3}{2}$ b. 0 $\dfrac{1}{2}$
    c. $-\dfrac{1}{2}$ $\dfrac{1}{6}$ d. 1 Not possible.
16. Let $t(n)$ represent the *n*th term of a sequence for $n \in N$.
    a. If $t(n) = n^2$, determine which of the following are output values of the function: (i), (ii), (iii), and (v)
       i. 1   ii. 4   iii. 9   iv. 10   v. 900
    b. If $t(n) = n(n + 1)$, determine which of the following are in the range of the function: (i), (ii), and (iii)
       i. 2   ii. 12   iii. 2550   iv. 2600
17. Consider a function machine that accepts inputs as ordered pairs. Suppose the components of the ordered pairs are natural numbers and the first component is the length of a rectangle and the second is its width. The following machine computes the perimeter (the distance around a figure) of the rectangle. Thus, for a rectangle whose length, *l*, is 3 and whose width, *w*, is 1, the input is (3, 1) and the output is $2 \cdot 3 + 2 \cdot 1$, or 8.

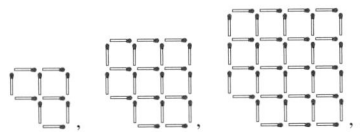

a. For each of the following inputs, find the corresponding output: $(1, 4), (2, 1), (1, 2), (\sqrt{3}, \sqrt{3}), (x, y)$. *
b. Find the set of all the inputs for which the output is 20. *
c. Is $(2, 2)$ a possible output? Explain your answer. *

18. A health club charges a one-time initiation fee of $100.00 plus a membership fee of $40.00 per month.
   a. Write an expression for the cost function $C(x)$ that gives the total cost for membership at the health club for x months. $C(x) = 100 + 40x$
   b. Draw the graph of the function in (a). *
   c. The health club decided to give its members an option of a higher initiation fee but a lower monthly membership charge. If the initiation fee is $300 and the monthly membership fee is $30, use a different color and draw on the same set of axes the cost graph under this plan. *
   d. Determine after how many months the second plan is less expensive for the member. After 20 months

19. A ball is shot straight up at ground level. Its height H in feet after t sec is given by the function $H(t) = 128t - 16t^2$.
   a. Graph the function and from the graph find at what instant the ball is at its highest point. What is its height at that instant? *
   b. Find from the graph all t such that $H(t) = H(1)$. *
   c. Use your graph to find how long it takes the ball to hit the ground. 8 sec
   d. What is the domain of H? $0 \le t \le 8$
   e. What is the range of H? $0 \le H(t) \le 256$

20. In the following sequence of matchstick figures, assume that your discovered pattern continues and let $S(n)$ be the function giving the total number of matchsticks in the nth figure.
   a. Find the total number of matchsticks in the fourth figure. 58
   b. Find a formula for $S(n)$ in terms of n. $2(n + 1)(n + 2) - 2$

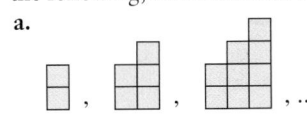

21. Assume the pattern continues for each of the following sequences of square tile figures. Let $S(n)$ be the function giving the total number of tiles in the nth figure. For each of the following, find a formula for $S(n)$ in terms of n. *
   a.

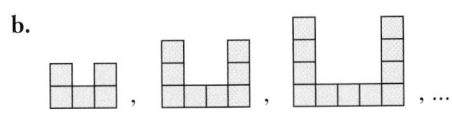

   b.

22. Which of the following equations or inequalities represent functions and which do not? In each case x and y are real numbers; x is in the domain and y in the range. If your answer is "not a function" explain why not. *
   a. $x - y = 2$ b. $x + y < 20$
   c. $y = 2x^2$ d. $y = x^3 - 1$
   e. $y = {}^-|x|$ f. $|y| = |x|$
   g. $x^2 - y^2 = 1$ h. $y = {}^-\sqrt{x}$

23. Which of the following are graphs of functions and which are not? Justify your answers. *
   a.

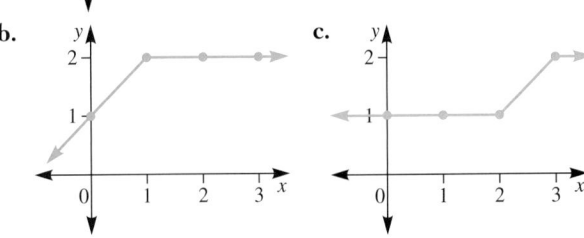

   b.   c.

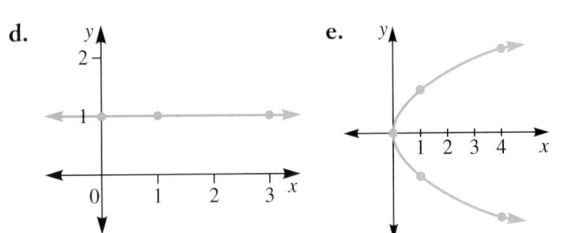

   d.   e.

24. a. Which of the following relations from the set W of whole numbers to W have the symmetric property? Justify your answers. *
       i. $x + y = 10$
       ii. $x - y = 100$
       iii. $xy = 100$
       iv. $y = x$
       v. $y = x^2$
   b. Which of the relations in part (a) are functions? Justify your answer. *

25. Suppose each point and letter in the figure represents a child on a playground, and an arrow going from I to J means that I "is the sister of" J.

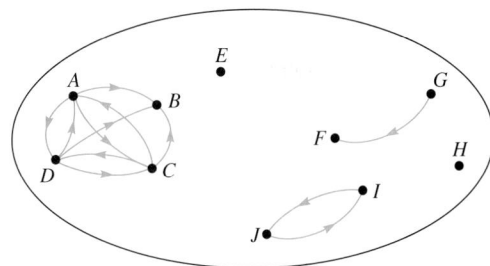

   a. Based on the information in the figure, who are definitely girls and who are definitely boys? *

b. Suppose we write "A is the sister of B" as an ordered pair (A, B). Based on the information in the diagram, write the set of all such ordered pairs. *

c. Is the set of all ordered pairs in (b) a function with the domain equal to the set of all first components of the ordered pairs and with the range equal to the set of all second components? *

26. Which of the following are functions and which are relations but not functions from the set of first components of the ordered pairs to the set of second components?

a. {(Montana, Helena), (Oregon, Salem), (Illinois, Springfield), (Arkansas, Little Rock)}   Function and relation

b. {(Pennsylvania, Philadelphia), (New York, Albany), (New York, Niagara Falls), (Florida, Ft. Lauderdale)} *

c. $\{(x, y) \mid x$ resides in Birmingham, Alabama, and x is the mother of y, where y is a U.S. resident} *

d. $\{(1, 1), (2, 4), (3, 9), (4, 16)\}$ Relation and a function

e. $\{(x, y) \mid x$ and y are natural numbers and $x + y$ is an even number}   Relation but not a function

27. Tell whether each of the following is reflexive, symmetric, or transitive on the set of subsets of a nonempty set. Which are equivalence relations?

a. "Is equal to" *

b. "Is a proper subset of "   Transitive; No

c. "Is not equal to"   Symmetric; No

d. "Has the same cardinal number as" *

Mathematical Connections 8-4

Answers to Mathematical Connections can be found in the Answers section at the back of the book.

Reasoning

1. Does the diagram define a function from A to B? Why or why not?

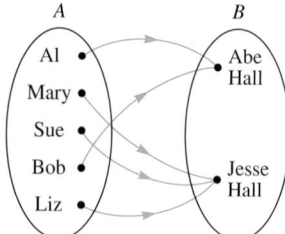

2. Is a one-to-one correspondence a function? Explain your answer and give an example.

3. Which of the following are functions from A to B? If your answer is "not a function," explain why not.

a. A is the set of mathematics faculty at the university. B is the set of all mathematics classes. To each mathematics faculty member, we associate a class that person is teaching during a given term.

b. A is the set of mathematics classes at the university. B is the set of mathematics faculty. To each mathematics class, we associate the teacher who is teaching the class.

c. A is the set of all U.S. senators and B is the set of all senate committees. We associate each senator to a committee of which the senator is chairperson.

4. If S is the set of students in Ms. Carmel's class, and A is any subset of S, we define: $f(A) = \overline{A}$ (where $\overline{A}$ is the complement of A). Notice that the input in this function is a subset of S and the output is a subset of S. Answer the following.

a. Explain why f is a function and describe the domain and the range of f.

b. If there are 20 children in the class, what are the number of elements in the domain and the number in the range? Explain.

c. Is the function in this question a one-to-one correspondence? Justify your answer.

5. Answer the following about $f(x) = 2^x$, an exponential function.

a. What do you think $f(x) = 2^{3.14}$ means?

b. What could $2^{\sqrt{3}}$ mean?

c. What is the domain of $f(x)$? Why?

d. What is the range of $f(x)$? Why?

6. A sum of money is invested for a certain length of time in an account earning interest at a certain rate. Explain how the balance in the account at the end of that time can be considered a function of three variables. Clearly identify the variables and derive a formula for the balance in terms of these three variables.

7. Is every set of ordered pairs a function whose domain is the set of first components and whose range is the set of second components? Justify your answer.

Open-Ended

8. Examine several newspapers and magazines and describe at least three examples of functions that you find. What is the domain and range of each function?

9. Give at least three examples of functions from A to B, where neither A nor B is a set of numbers.

10. Draw a sequence of matchstick figures and describe the pattern in words. Find as simple an expression as possible for $S(n)$, the total number of matchsticks in the nth figure.

11. A function whose output is always the same regardless of the input is a *constant function*. Give several examples of constant functions from real life.

12. A function whose output is the same as its input is an *identity function*. Give several concrete examples of identity functions.

13. Define three functions $f(x), g(x)$, and $h(x)$ that are placed in a way similar to the two machines in exercise 11 of Assessment 8-4B. Draw a figure depicting the machines and find $(h \circ g \circ f)(x)$ for the following inputs.

a. 1

b. $\sqrt{3}$

c. n

Cooperative Learning

14. Each person in a group picks a natural number and uses it as an input in the following function machine:

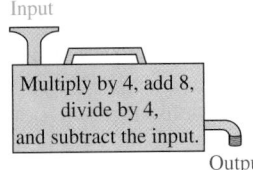

Input

Multiply by 4, add 8, divide by 4, and subtract the input.

Output

   a. Compare your answers. Based on the answers, make a conjecture about the range of the function.
   b. Based on your answer in (a), graph the function.
   c. Write the function in the simplest possible way using $f(x)$ notation.
   d. Justify your conjecture in (a).
   e. Make up similar function machines and try different inputs in your group.
   f. Devise a function machine in which the machine performs several operations but the output is always the same as the input. Exchange your answer with someone in the group and check that the other person's function machine performs as required.

15. In a group of four, work through the following. You will need a metric tape or meterstick.
   a. Place your mathematics book on the edge of a desk and measure the distance (to the nearest centimeter) from the floor to the top of the book. Record the distance.
   b. Place a second mathematics book on top of the first and measure the distance (to the nearest centimeter) from the floor to the top of the second book. Record the distance.
   c. Continue this procedure for all four of your mathematics books and complete the following table and graph:

Number of books	Distance from floor
1	
2	
3	
4	

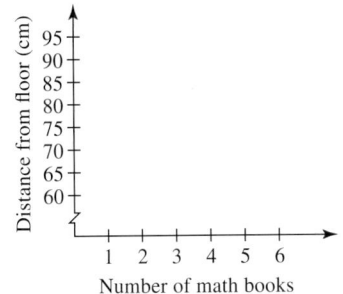

   d. Without measuring, what is the distance from the floor with 0 books? 5 books?
   e. Write a rule or function for $d(x)$, where $d(x)$ is the distance above the floor to the top of the stack of books and x is the number of books.
   f. Suppose the distance from the floor to the ceiling is 2.5 m. If you stack the books as described above, how many books would be needed to reach the ceiling?
   g. The function $h(x) = 34x + 70$ represents the height of another stack of x mathematics books (in centimeters) of

the same thickness in a cabinet. What does the function tell you about the height of the cabinet?
   h. Suppose that a table with a stack of similar mathematics books (more than 10) is 200 cm high. If the top mathematics book is removed, the height is 197 cm. If a second book is removed, the height is 194 cm. What is the height if 5 books are removed?
   i. Write a function $h(x)$ for the height of the stack in part (h) after x books are removed.

16. As a teacher you noticed that several students in your class assumed that if f is a function, then $f(a + b) = f(a) + f(b)$ whenever $a, b,$ and $a + b$ are in the domain of the function. How do you respond?

Connecting Mathematics to the Classroom

17. A student claims that the following machine does not represent a function machine because it accepts two inputs at once rather than a single input. How do you respond?

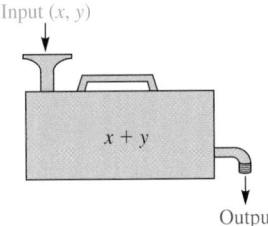

Input (x, y)

$x + y$

Output

18. A student claims that the following does not represent a function, since all the values of x correspond to the same number.

x	0	1	2	3	4	5
y	1	1	1	1	1	1

How do you respond?
19. A student asks if the function $f(x) = 3x + 5$ with domain the set of real numbers is a one-to-one correspondence between the sets of real numbers. How do you respond?
20. A student wants to know why sometimes it is incorrect to connect points on the graph of a function. How do you respond?
21. A student does not understand why $\{(x, y) \mid y = x^2, x \in R\}$ is a function but $\{(x, y) \mid x = y^2, x \in R, x \geq 0\}$ is not. How do you respond?

Review Problems

22. Solve the following equations for x.
   a. $2\sqrt{2} - \sqrt{2}x = x$ **b.** $\dfrac{3}{4}x = \dfrac{\sqrt{2}}{2}x + 3$

   c. $(x - 1)^2 = 2$ **d.** $\sqrt{2}(2x - 3) = \sqrt{3}(2x - 3)$
   e. $\sqrt{(x - 1)^2} = x - 1$ **f.** $\sqrt{(x - 1)^2} = 1 - x$
23. Solve the following problem by setting up an appropriate equation:
     Two cars, each traveling at a constant speed—one 60 mph and the other 70 mph—start at the same time from the same point traveling in the same direction. After how many hours will the distance between them be 40 mi?
24. a. Find two rational numbers between $\sqrt{3}$ and 2.
    b. Find two irrational numbers between $\dfrac{11}{13}$ and $\dfrac{12}{13}$.
25. Show that the set of irrational numbers is not closed under addition.

National Assessments

National Assessment of Educational Progress (NAEP) Questions

In	Out
2	5
3	7
4	9
5	11
15	31
38	

The table shows how the "In" numbers are related to the "Out" numbers. When 38 goes in, what number comes out?
A. 41
B. 51
C. 54
D. 77

NAEP, Grade 4, 2007

Each figure in the pattern below is made of hexagons that measure 1 centimeter on each side.

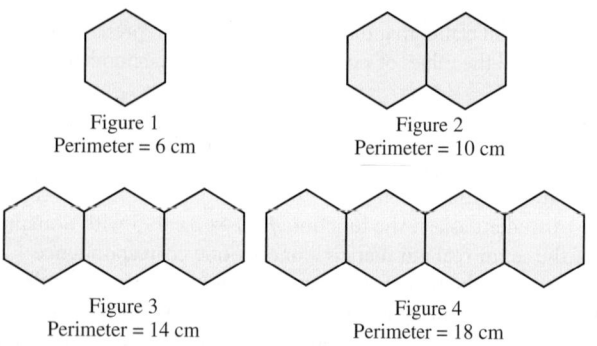

Figure 1
Perimeter = 6 cm

Figure 2
Perimeter = 10 cm

Figure 3
Perimeter = 14 cm

Figure 4
Perimeter = 18 cm

If the pattern of adding one hexagon to each figure is continued, what will be the perimeter of the 25th figure in the pattern? Show how you got your answer.
NAEP, Grade 8, 2007

Old Faithful is one of hundreds of geysers in Yellowstone National Park. Predicting when Old Faithful will erupt next can be done by timing the previous eruption.

If an eruption lasts t minutes, then the next eruption will occur approximately $12.5t + 33$ minutes after the eruption ends. If the previous eruption lasted 6 minutes and ended at 1:23 P.M., when is the next eruption expected to occur?

Answer: _____

Show how you found your answer.
NAEP, Grade 8, 2012

8-5 Objectives

8-5 Equations in a Cartesian Coordinate System

Students will be able to understand and explain

- Equations of lines.

- The slope of a line and the slope formula.

- Graphic and algebraic solutions for systems of linear equations.

- Ways to determine if a system of linear equations has a unique solution, infinitely many solutions, or no solution.

The Cartesian coordinate system (named for René Descartes) enables us to combine geometry and algebra. The **Cartesian coordinate system**, is constructed by placing two number lines perpendicular to each other, as shown in Figure 27. The intersection point of the two lines is the **origin**, the horizontal line is the x-axis, and the vertical line is the y-axis. The location of any point P can be described by an ordered pair of numbers (a, b), where a perpendicular from P to the x-axis intersects at a point with coordinate a and a perpendicular from P to the y-axis intersects at a point with coordinate b; the point is identified as $P(a, b)$. A line is **perpendicular** to another line if they form a 90° angle (right angle). There is a one-to-one correspondence between all the points in the plane and all the ordered pairs of real numbers. For example, in Figure 27, Q has coordinates $(^-4, ^-3)$, written $Q(^-4, ^-3)$.

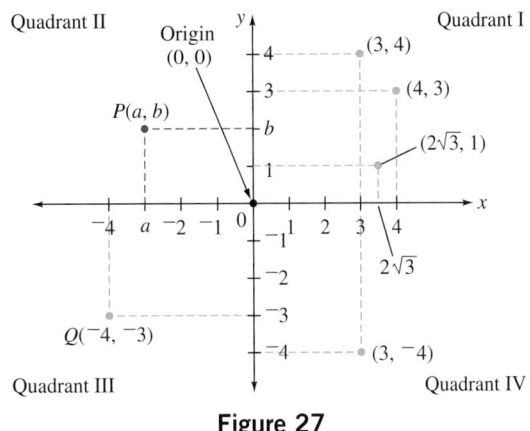

Figure 27

In Figure 27, the axes separate the plane into four **quadrants** numbered counterclockwise.

Equations of Vertical and Horizontal Lines

Every point on the x-axis has a y-coordinate of zero. Thus, the x-axis can be described as the set of all points (x, y) such that $y = 0$. *The x-axis has the equation $y = 0$.* Similarly, *the y-axis can be described as the set of all points (x, y) such that $x = 0$ and y is an arbitrary real number. Thus, $x = 0$ is the equation of the y-axis.* Using set notation, the x-axis is the set of points $\{(x, 0) \mid x \text{ is a real number}\}$ and the y-axis is the set of points $\{(0, y) \mid y \text{ is a real number}\}$.

Example 20

Sketch the graph for each of the following on a Cartesian coordinate system.

  a. $x = 2$
  b. $y = 3$
  c. $\{(x, y) \mid x < 2 \text{ and } y = 3\}$

Solution
  a. The equation $x = 2$ represents the set of all points (x, y) for which $x = 2$ and y is any real number, as in Figure 28(a).

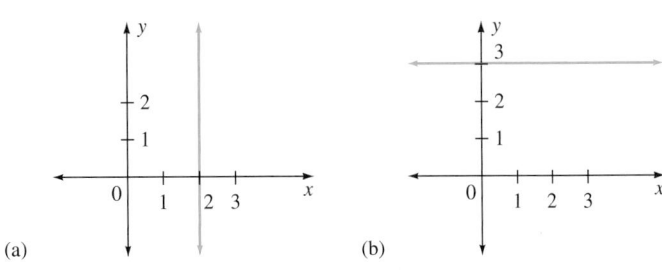

Figure 28

  b. The equation $y = 3$ represents the set of all points (x, y) for which $y = 3$ and x is any real number, as in Figure 28(b).

c. The statements in part (c) represent the set of all points (x, y) for which $x < 2$, but $y = 3$. The set is part of a line, as shown in Figure 29. Note that the hollow dot at $(2, 3)$ indicates that this point is not included in the solution set.

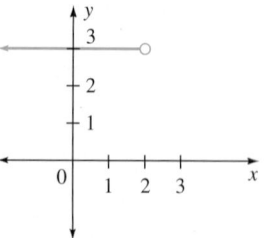

Figure 29

As seen in Example 20(a) and (b) *the graph of the equation* $x = a$, *where a is some real number, is the line perpendicular to the x-axis through the point with coordinates* $(a, 0)$. Similarly, *the graph of the equation* $y = b$ *is the line perpendicular to the y-axis through the point with coordinates* $(0, b)$.

Equations of Lines

Activity Manual

Use *Exploring Linear Functions* to develop the concept of slope and explore the graphs and equations of lines.

The arithmetic sequence $4, 7, 10, 13, \ldots$ in Table 6 has xth term $3x + 1$. If the number of the term is the x-coordinate and the corresponding term the y-coordinate, the set of points appear to lie on a line that is parallel to neither the x-axis nor the y-axis, as in Figure 30.

Table 6	
Number of Term	**Term**
1	4
2	7
3	10
4	13
⋮	⋮
x	$3x + 1$

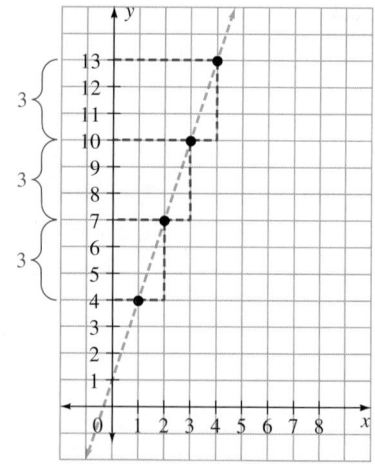

Figure 30

In Table 6, we see that there is a difference of 3 in the y-coordinates of the marked points. Correspondingly, there is a difference of 1 in the number of the term on the x-axis. Hence, we might say that the rate of change of the term with respect to the number of the term is 3, or the ratio is 3 to 1. Does something comparable happen with other arithmetic sequences?

To help answer this question, we consider the following sequences in Table 7.

Table 7					
Number of Term x	$1x = x$	$2x$	$\frac{1}{2}x$	$(^-1)x = {}^-x$	$(^-2)x = {}^-2x$
1	1	2	$\frac{1}{2}$	$^-1$	$^-2$
2	2	4	1	$^-2$	$^-4$
3	3	6	$\frac{3}{2}$	$^-3$	$^-6$
4	4	8	2	$^-4$	$^-8$
5	5	10	$\frac{5}{2}$	$^-5$	$^-10$
6	6	12	3	$^-6$	$^-12$
⋮	⋮	⋮	⋮	⋮	⋮
x	x	$2x$	$\frac{1}{2}x$	^-x	^-2x

Figure 31 shows the sets of ordered pairs (x, y) in Table 7 plotted on a graph so that the number of the term is the x-coordinate and the corresponding term is the y-coordinate. Again the separate sets of points appear to lie on straight lines.

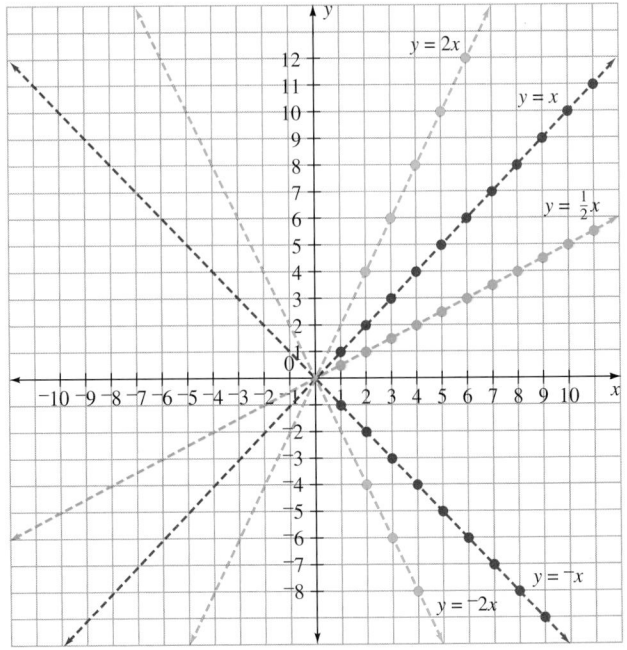

Figure 31

All dashed lines in Figure 31 have equations of the form $y = mx$, where m takes the values 1, 2, $\frac{1}{2}$, $^-1$, and $^-2$. If we consider the equations but allow x to be any real number, then all the points (x, y) that satisfy the equation lie along a given dashed line and all the points on that line satisfy the equation. The number m is a measure of steepness and is the **slope** of the line whose equation is $y = mx$. The graph goes up from left to right (y increases as x increases) if m is positive, and it goes down from left to right (y decreases as x increases) if m is negative.

a. In the equation $y = mx$, if m is 0, what happens to the line?
b. What happens to the line as m increases from 0?
c. What happens to the line when m decreases from 0?

All dashed lines in Figure 31 pass through the origin. This is true for any line whose equation is $y = mx$. If $x = 0$, then $y = m \cdot 0 = 0$, and $(0,0)$ is a point on the graph of $y = mx$. Conversely, it is possible to show that any nonvertical line passing through the origin has an equation of the form $y = mx$ for some value of m.

Example 21

Find the equation of the line that contains $(0,0)$ and $(2,3)$.

Solution   The line goes through the origin so its equation has the form $y = mx$. To find the equation of the line, we find the value of m. The line contains $(2,3)$, so we substitute 2 for x and 3 for y in the equation $y = mx$ to obtain $3 = m \cdot 2$, and thus $m = \dfrac{3}{2}$. The required equation is $y = \dfrac{3}{2}x$.

Next, we consider equations of the form $y = mx + b$, where b is a real number. We do this by first examining the graphs of $y = x$, $y = x + 2$ and $y = x - 2$. Given the graph of $y = x$, we obtain the graph of $y = x + 2$ by "raising" each point on the graph of $y = x$ by 2 units. This is shown in Figure 32(a). Similarly, to sketch the graph of $y = x - 2$, we first draw the graph of $y = x$ and then lower each point vertically by 2 units, as shown in Figure 32(a).

The graphs of $y = x$, $y = x + 2$, and $y = x - 2$ are parallel lines. In general, *for a given value of m, the graph of $y = mx + b$ is a straight line through $(0, b)$ and parallel to the line whose equation is $y = mx$.*

Thus, the graph of the line $y = mx + b$ can be obtained from the graph of $y = mx$ by sliding $y = mx$ up b units if $b > 0$ and down $|b|$ units if $b < 0$, as shown in Figure 32(b). In general, *any two parallel lines have the same slope it will be shown later in this section that* vertical lines have no slope.

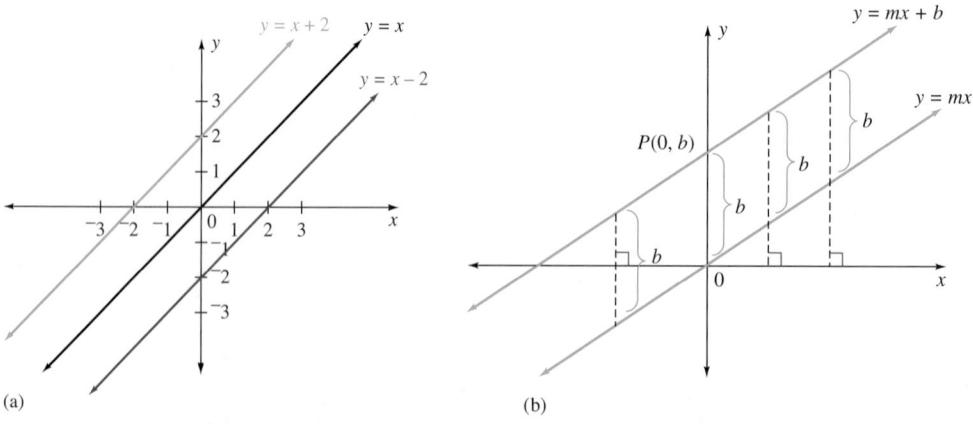

Figure 32

The graph of $y = mx + b$ in Figure 32(b) crosses the y-axis at point $P(0, b)$. The value of y at the point of intersection of any line with the y-axis is the **y-intercept**. Thus, b is the y-intercept of $y = mx + b$; this form of an equation of a straight line is the **slope-intercept form**. Similarly, the value of x at the point of intersection of a line with the x-axis is the **x-intercept**.

Example 22

Given the equation $y - 3x = {}^-6$, answer the following.

   a. Find the slope of the line.
   b. Find the y-intercept.
   c. Find the x-intercept.
   d. Sketch the graph of the equation.

Solution

   a. We write the equation in the form $y = mx + b$ by adding $3x$ to both sides of the given equa-tion: $y = 3x + ({}^-6)$. Hence, the slope is 3.
   b. The form $y = 3x + ({}^-6)$ shows that $b = {}^-6$, which is the y-intercept. The y-intercept can also be found directly by substituting $x = 0$ in the equation and finding the corresponding value of y.
   c. The x-intercept is the x-coordinate of the point where the graph intersects the x-axis. At that point, $y = 0$. Substituting 0 for y in $y = 3x - 6$ gives 2 as the x-intercept.
   d. Knowing the y-intercept and the x-intercept gives us two points, $(0, {}^-6)$ and $(2, 0)$, on the line. We may plot these points and draw the line through them to obtain the desired graph in Figure 33.

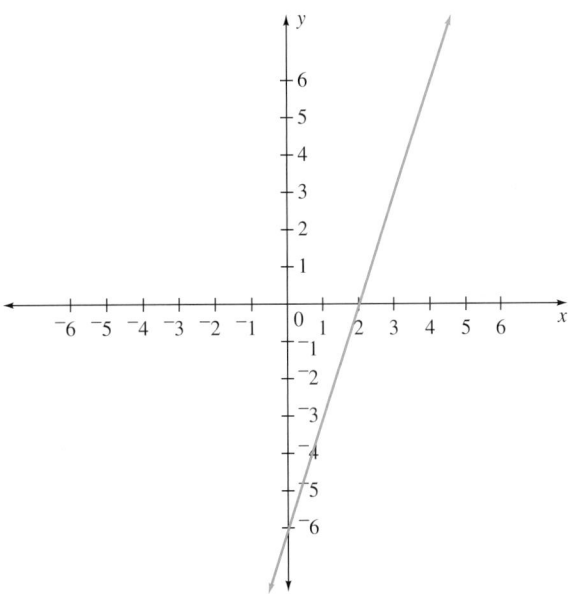

Figure 33

Any vertical line has equation $x = a$ for some real number a, and cannot be written in slope-intercept form. A horizontal line has slope of 0, and can be written in a slope intercept form as $y = 0 \cdot x + b = b$. In general, *every line has an equation of the form either $y = mx + b$ or $x = a$.* Any equation that can be put in one of these forms is a **linear equation**. Equations of the form $ax + by + c = 0$, where a, b, c are real numbers, are linear equations and may be written in slope intercept form if $b \neq 0$. (Why?) If $b = 0$ and $a \neq 0$, we get the equation $x = \dfrac{{}^-c}{a}$, which is an equation of a vertical line.

Theorem 8-7:   Equation of a Line

Every line has an equation of the form either $y = mx + b$ or $x = a$, where m is the slope and b is the y-intercept. In the equation $x = a$, a is the x-intercept.

▶ **NOW TRY THIS 11**

NTT 11: Answers can be found in Answers at the back of the book.

The nth term of an arithmetic sequence is given as $a_n = a_1 + (n - 1)d$. Explain why this is considered a *linear relationship*.

Determining Slope

We defined the slope of a line with equation $y = mx + b$ to be m. The slope is a measure of steepness of a line. A different way to discuss the steepness of a line is to consider the rate of change in y-values in relation to their corresponding x-values. In Figure 34, line k has a greater rate of change than line ℓ. In other words, line k rises faster than line ℓ for the same horizontal run.

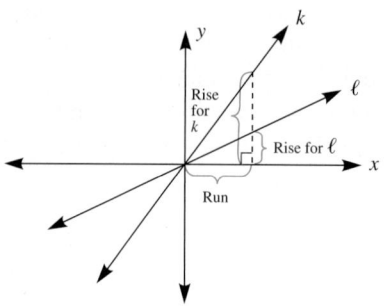

Figure 34

Thus, we could express the rate of change, or steepness, as the ratio $\dfrac{\text{change in } y\text{-values}}{\text{corresponding change in } x\text{-values}}$. The rate is frequently expressed as $\dfrac{rise}{run}$.

Given two points $A(x_1, y_1)$ and $B(x_2, y_2)$ the difference $x_2 - x_1$ is the *run*, and the difference $y_2 - y_1$ is the *rise*. The values of *rise* and *run* depend on the points chosen on the line and hence vary. However, the ratio $\dfrac{y_2 - y_1}{x_2 - x_1}$ is always the same, regardless of which two points on a given nonvertical line are chosen, and equals the slope of the line. This can be shown as follows:

$$\frac{y_2 - y_1}{x_2 - x_1} = \frac{(mx_2 + b) - (mx_1 + b)}{x_2 - x_1}$$

$$= \frac{mx_2 - mx_1 + b - b}{x_2 - x_1}$$

$$= \frac{m(x_2 - x_1)}{x_2 - x_1}$$

$$= m$$

Thus, as seen in Figure 35, we can define the slope of a nonvertical line as $\dfrac{rise}{run}$.

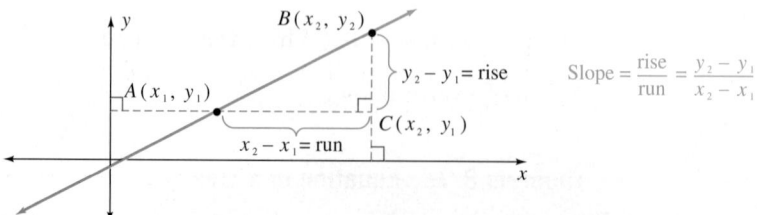

Figure 35

The discussion of slope is summarized in the following definition for the slope of a line.

> ### Definition of Slope (Slope Formula)
>
> Given two points $A(x_1, y_1)$ and $B(x_2, y_2)$ with $x_1 \neq x_2$, the slope m of the line through A and B is
>
> $$m = \frac{y_2 - y_1}{x_2 - x_1}.$$

In the above definition, if we multiply both the numerator and the denominator on the right side of the slope formula by $^{-}1$, we obtain

$$m = \frac{y_2 - y_1}{x_2 - x_1} = \frac{(y_2 - y_1)(^{-}1)}{(x_2 - x_1)(^{-}1)} = \frac{y_1 - y_2}{x_1 - x_2}.$$

Thus, it does not matter which point is named (x_1, y_1) and which is named (x_2, y_2); *the order of the coordinates in the subtraction must be the same.*

▶ NOW TRY THIS 12

NTT 12: Answers can be found in Answers at the back of the book.

   a. Use the slope formula to find the slope of any horizontal line.
   b. What happens when we attempt to use the slope formula for a vertical line? What is your conclusion about the slope of a vertical line?

When a line is inclined downward from the left to the right, the slope is negative. This is illustrated in Figure 36, where the graph of the line $y = {}^{-}2x$ is shown.

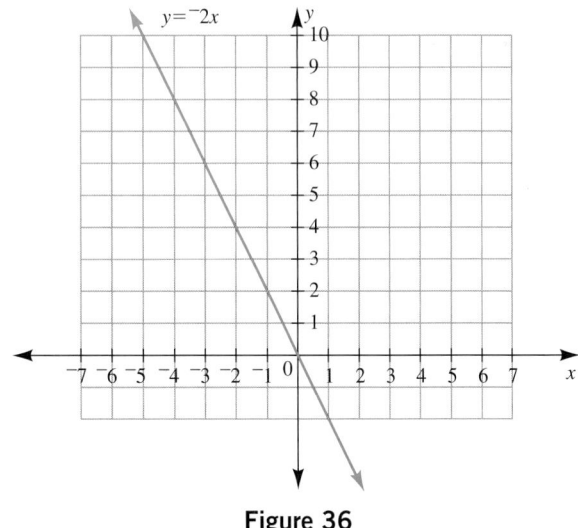

Figure 36

Example 23

   a. Given $A(3, 1)$ and $B(5, 4)$, find the slope of $\overleftrightarrow{AB}$ (the line through A and B).
   b. Find the slope of the line passing through the points $A({}^{-}3, 4)$ and $B({}^{-}1, 0)$.
   c. In Figure 37, find the slope of $\overleftrightarrow{OA}$ (the line through O and A).

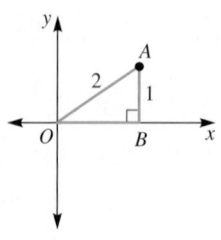

Figure 37

Solution

a. $m = \dfrac{4 - 1}{5 - 3} = \dfrac{3}{2}$

b. $m = \dfrac{4 - 0}{^-3 - (^-1)} = \dfrac{4}{^-2} = {}^-2$

c. OB (the distance from O to B) is the run while AB, or 1, is the rise.
$(OB)^2 + 1^2 = 2^2$ in right triangle OAB, using the Pythagorean theorem.
$(OB)^2 + 1 = 4$
$(OB)^2 = 4 - 1 = 3$
$OB = \sqrt{3}$

The slope of $\overleftrightarrow{OA}$ (the line through O and A) is $\dfrac{1}{\sqrt{3}}$, which is sometimes written as

$\dfrac{1}{\sqrt{3}} \cdot \dfrac{\sqrt{3}}{\sqrt{3}} = \dfrac{\sqrt{3}}{3}$.

Given two points on a nonvertical line, we use the slope formula to find the slope of the line and its equation as demonstrated in the following example.

Example 24

In Figure 38, the points $(^-4, 0)$ and $(1, 4)$ are on the line ℓ. Find:

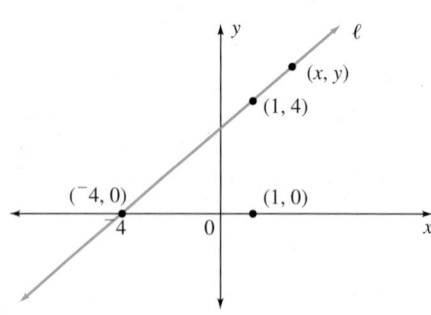

Figure 38

a. The slope of the line
b. The equation of the line

Solution

a. $m = \dfrac{4 - 0}{1 - (^-4)} = \dfrac{4}{5}$

b. Any point (x, y) on ℓ different from $(^-4, 0)$ can be found using the slope $\frac{4}{5}$ determined by points $(^-4, 0)$ and (x, y). Thus,

$$\frac{y - 0}{x - (^-4)} = \frac{4}{5}$$

$$\frac{y}{x + 4} = \frac{4}{5}$$

$$y = \frac{4}{5}(x + 4).$$

The equation of the line is $y = \frac{4}{5}x + \frac{16}{5}$.

Systems of Linear Equations

The mathematical descriptions of many problems involve more than one equation, each having more than one unknown. To solve such problems, we must find a common solution to the equations, if it exists. An example is given below and on the student page shown on page 452.

Example 25

May Chin paid $18 for three soyburgers and twelve orders of fries. Another time she had paid $12 for four soyburgers and four orders of fries. Assume the prices have not changed. Set up a system of equations with two unknowns representing the prices of a soyburger and an order of fries, respectively.

Solution Let x be the price in dollars of a soyburger and y be the price in dollars of an order of fries. Three soyburgers cost $3x$ dollars, and twelve orders of fries cost $12y$ dollars. Because May paid $18 for her entire order, we have $3x + 12y = 18$, or, after dividing each side by 3, $x + 4y = 6$. Similarly, $4x + 4y = 12$ is equivalent to $x + y = 3$. The system of equations is $x + 4y = 6$ and $x + y = 3$.

An ordered pair satisfying the two linear equations in Example 25 is a point that belongs to each of the lines. Figure 39 shows the graphs of $x + 4y = 6$ and $x + y = 3$. The price x of the soyburger and the price y of an order of fries satisfy both equations; that is, (x, y) is a point on both lines. The two lines appear to intersect at $(2, 1)$. Thus, $(2, 1)$ seems to be the solution of the given system of equations. This solution can be checked by substituting 2 for x and 1 for y in each equation. Because two distinct lines intersect in only one point, $(2, 1)$ is the only solution to the system. Therefore, in Example 25 a soyburger costs $2 and fries cost $1.

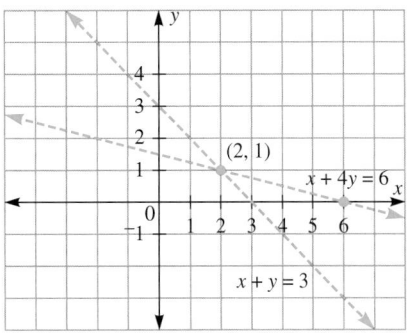

Figure 39

Because costs of the soyburger and an order of fries cannot be negative, parts of the lines are dashed.

School Book Page — Linear Functions

 **Guided Problem Solving**

Linear Functions

For each rental plan, represent the relationship between the number of miles (from 20 to 45) and the cost. Use a linear function, a table of ordered pairs, and a graph (using the same coordinate grid). What conclusions can you draw about these plans?

Car Rental Plan **1**
$15 per day
plus
$.25 per mile

Car Rental Plan **2**
$8 per day
plus
$.45 per mile

What You Might Think

What do I know? What do I want to find out?

How can I write a function rule for each plan?

How can I make a table and graph?

What conclusions can be stated?

What You Might Write

Plan 1 costs $15 plus $.25 per mile. Plan 2 costs $8 plus $.45 per mile. I want to compare the two plans using function rules, tables, and graphs.

Let m = the number of miles driven. Let C = the cost of the rental in dollars.

Plan 1: $C_1 = \$.25m + 15$

Plan 2: $C_2 = \$.45m + 8$

I can use the function rule to get data points for the table. Then I can graph those points.

m	C_1	C_2
20	20	17
30	22.5	21.5
35	23.75	23.75
45	26.25	28.25

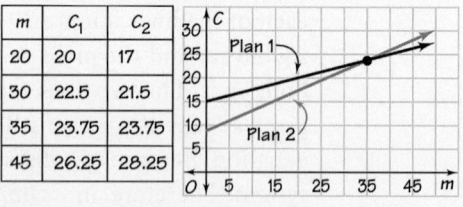

The lines intersect at (35, 23.75). Plan 2 is better if you drive less than 35 miles.

Plan 1 is better if you drive more than 35 miles. The costs of Plans 1 and 2 are equal if you drive exactly 35 miles.

Substitution Method

The graphing method for solving systems of equations is not practical when the point of intersection of the lines cannot be accurately identified. There are algebraic methods for solving systems of equations. One such method is the **substitution method**. The equations

$$x + 4y = 6 \quad \text{and} \quad x + y = 3$$

can be solved by finding x in terms of y (or vice versa) from one of the equations and substituting in the other. From the second equation, we have $x = 3 - y$. Substituting for x in the first equation we get the equivalent equations: $3 - y + 4y = 6, 3 + 3y = 6, 3y = 3, y = 1$. Substituting $y = 1$ in $x + y = 3$, we get $x + 1 = 3$ and hence $x = 2$. Thus, $x = 2$ and $y = 1$ is the solution to the system. Example 26 demonstrates the substitution method in another system of equations.

Example 26

Solve the following system using the substitution method.

$$3x - 4y = 5$$
$$2x + 5y = 1$$

Solution   First, rewrite one equation, expressing y in terms of x.

$$y = \frac{3x - 5}{4}$$

Because we are looking for x and y that satisfy each equation, we substitute $\dfrac{3x - 5}{4}$ for y in the other original equation and solve the resulting equation for x.

$$2x + 5\left(\frac{3x - 5}{4}\right) = 1$$
$$4\left[2x + 5\left(\frac{3x - 5}{4}\right)\right] = 4 \cdot 1$$
$$8x + 5(3x - 5) = 4$$
$$8x + 15x - 25 = 4$$
$$23x = 4 + 25$$
$$x = \frac{29}{23}$$

Substituting $\dfrac{29}{23}$ for x in $y = \dfrac{3x - 5}{4}$ gives $y = \dfrac{^-7}{23}$. Hence, $x = \dfrac{29}{23}$ and $y = \dfrac{^-7}{23}$. This can be checked by substituting the values for x and y in the original equations.

Elimination Method

The **elimination method** for solving two equations with two unknowns is based on eliminating one of the variables by adding or subtracting the original or equivalent equations. For example, consider the following system:

$$x - y = {}^-3$$
$$x + y = 7$$

By adding the two equations, we can eliminate the variable y. The resulting equation can then be solved for x.

$$\begin{array}{r} x - y = {}^-3 \\ \underline{x + y = 7} \\ 2x = 4 \\ x = 2 \end{array}$$

Substituting 2 for x in the first equation (either equation may be used) gives $y = 5$. Checking this result shows that $x = 2$ and $y = 5$, or $(2, 5)$, is the solution to the system.

Often, another operation is required before equations are added so that an unknown can be eliminated. For example, consider the following system:

$$3x + 2y = 5$$
$$5x - 4y = 3$$

Neither adding nor subtracting the equations eliminates an unknown. However, if the first equation contained $4y$ rather than $2y$, the variable y could be eliminated by adding. To obtain $4y$ in the first equation, we multiply both sides of the equation by 2 to obtain the equivalent equation $6x + 4y = 10$. Adding the equations in the equivalent system gives the following:

$$\begin{array}{r} 6x + 4y = 10 \\ \underline{5x - 4y = 3} \\ 11x = 13 \\ x = \dfrac{13}{11} \end{array}$$

To find the corresponding value of y, we substitute $\dfrac{13}{11}$ for x in either of the original equations and solve for y. We get $y = \dfrac{8}{11}$.

Consequently, $x = \dfrac{13}{11}$ and $y = \dfrac{8}{11}$, or equivalently $\left(\dfrac{13}{11}, \dfrac{8}{11} \right)$ is the solution of the original system. This solution, as always, should be checked by substitution in the original equations.

Solutions to Various Systems of Linear Equations

All examples thus far have had unique solutions. However, other situations may arise. Geometrically, a system of two linear equations can be characterized as follows:

1. *The system has a unique solution if, and only if, the graphs of the equations intersect in a single point.*
2. *The system has no solution if, and only if, the equations represent distinct parallel lines.* Two distinct lines in a plane are parallel if they do not intersect.
3. *The system has infinitely many solutions if, and only if, the equations represent the same line.* A line is considered parallel to itself.

Consider the following system and assume it has a solution.

$$2x - 3y = 1$$
$${}^-4x + 6y = 5$$

In an attempt to solve for x, we multiply the first equation by 2 and then add as follows:

$$\begin{array}{r} 4x - 6y = 2 \\ \underline{{}^-4x + 6y = 5} \\ 0 = 7 \end{array}$$

A false statement results from the assumption that the system had a solution. That assumption caused a false statement; therefore, the assumption itself must be false. Hence, the system has no solution. In other words, the solution set is $\varnothing$. This situation arises if, and only if, the corresponding lines are parallel and different. The lines are parallel because their equations can be written as $y = \frac{2}{3}x - \frac{1}{3}$ and $y = \frac{2}{3}x + \frac{5}{6}$, which shows that the slope of each line is $\frac{2}{3}$.

Next, consider the following system:

$$2x - 3y = 1$$
$$^{-}4x + 6y = {}^{-}2$$

To solve this system, we multiply the first equation by 2 and add as follows:

$$4x - 6y = 2$$
$$\underline{{}^{-}4x + 6y = {}^{-}2}$$
$$0 = 0$$

The resulting statement, $0 = 0$, is always true. In the original system, if we multiply by $^{-}2$ both sides of the first equation, the result would be the second equation. Thus, the graphs are exactly the same or the graph is a single line. All pairs of x and y that correspond to points on the line $2x - 3y = 1$ also satisfy the equivalent equation $^{-}4x + 6y = {}^{-}2$.

Thus, one way to determine that a system of two equations in two unknowns has infinitely many solutions is by checking whether each of the original equations represents the same line. It can be shown that a system has infinitely many solutions if, and only if, we get $0 = 0$ by trying to eliminate one of the variables and adding or subtracting the equations side by side. The statement $0 = 0$ originated from $0 \cdot x + 0 \cdot y = 0$, which is satisfied by all x and y.

Example 27

Identify each of the following systems as having a unique solution, no solution, or infinitely many solutions:

a. $2x - 3y = 5$
$\frac{1}{2}x - y = 1$

b. $\frac{x}{3} - \frac{y}{4} = 1$
$3y - 4x + 12 = 0$

c. $6x - 9y = 5$
$^{-}8x + 12y = 7$

Different methods are illustrated in the solutions.

Solution   One method is to attempt to solve each system. Another method is to write each equation in the slope-intercept form and interpret the system geometrically.

a. *First method.*   To eliminate x, multiply the second equation by $^{-}4$ and add the equations.

$$2x - 3y = 5$$
$$\underline{{}^{-}2x + 4y = {}^{-}4}$$
$$y = 1$$

Substituting 1 for y in either equation gives $x = 4$. Thus $x = 4$ and $y = 1$, or $(4, 1)$ is the unique solution of the system.

Second method.   In slope-intercept form, the first equation is $y = \frac{2}{3}x - \frac{5}{3}$. The second equation is $y = \frac{1}{2}x - 1$. The slopes of the corresponding lines are $\frac{2}{3}$ and $\frac{1}{2}$, respectively. Consequently, the lines are distinct and are not parallel and, therefore, intersect in a single point whose coordinates are the unique solution to the original system.

b. *First method.* Multiply the first equation by 12 and rewrite the second equation as $^-4x + 3y = ^-12$. Then, adding the resulting equations gives the following:

$$4x - 3y = 12$$
$$\underline{^-4x + 3y = ^-12}$$
$$0 = 0$$

Hence, the two equations represent the same line, and the original system has infinitely many solutions (all the points on the line).

Second method.   In slope-intercept form, both equations are

$$y = \frac{4}{3}x - 4.$$

Thus, the two lines are identical, so the system has infinitely many solutions.

c. *First method.*   To eliminate y, multiply the first equation by 4 and the second by 3; then, add the resulting equations.

$$24x - 36y = 20$$
$$\underline{^-24x + 36y = 21}$$
$$0 = 41$$

This is a contradiction (no pair of numbers x and y satisfy $0 \cdot x + 0 \cdot y = 41$), so this equation has no solutions, and, consequently, the original system has no solutions.

Second method.   In slope-intercept form, the first equation is $y = \frac{2}{3}x - \frac{5}{9}$. The second equation is $y = \frac{2}{3}x + \frac{7}{12}$. The corresponding lines have the same slope, $\frac{2}{3}$, but different y-intercepts.

Consequently, the lines are distinct and parallel, and the original system has no solution.

▶ **NOW TRY THIS 13**

NTT 13: Answers can be found in Answers at the back of the book.

Find all solutions (if any) of each of the following systems.

a. $x - y = 1$ **b.** $2x - y = 1$ **c.** $2x - y = 1$
$\ 2x - y = 5$ $\ 2y - 4x = 3$ $\ 2y - 4x = ^-2$

Substitution and elimination methods may be used to solve systems with 3 or more variables. Consider the problem in Example 28. We use the strategy of writing an equation.

Example 28

At a local farmer's market, three purchases were made for the following prices:

- cantaloupe and a vase for $8
- watermelon and an identical vase for $9
- same-priced watermelon and a same-priced cantaloupe for $7

What is the cost of each object?

Solution   If the cost of the cantaloupe is c dollars, the cost of the vase is v dollars, and the cost of the watermelon is w dollars, we have the following system of 3 equations with 3 unknowns.

$$c + v = 8$$
$$w + v = 9$$
$$w + c = 7$$

We can eliminate the unknown w by subtracting the third equation from the second:
$(v + w) - (c + w) = 9 - 7$ or equivalently $v - c = 2$.

Now we have a system of two equations with two unknowns: $c + v = 8$ and $v - c = 2$. Adding the equations we get $2v = 10$ or $v = 5$. Substituting $v = 5$ into the first equation, we get $c + 5 = 8$ or $c = 3$. Substituting $v = 5$ into the second equation, we get $w + 5 = 9$ or $w = 4$. Thus, the vase costs \$5, a cantaloupe \$3, and a watermelon \$4.

Assessment 8-5A

1. The graph of $y = mx$ is given in the following figure. Sketch the graphs for each of the following on the same figure. Explain your answers.
   a. $y = mx + 3$ *
   b. $y = mx - 3$ *
   c. $y = 3mx$ *
   d. $y = {}^-3mx$ *

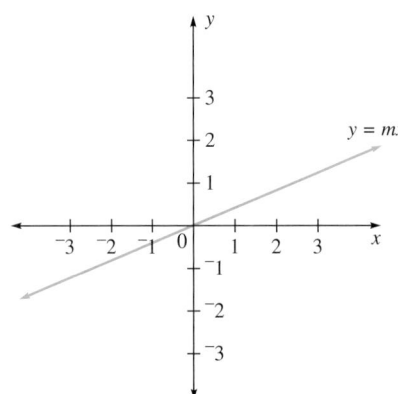

2. Sketch the graphs for each of the following equations:
   a. $y = \dfrac{{}^-3}{4}x + 3$ *
   b. $y = {}^-3$ *
   c. $y = 15x - 30$ *
3. Find the x-intercept and y-intercept for the equations in exercise 2, if they exist.   *
4. In the following figure, part (i) shows a dual-scale thermometer and part (ii) shows the corresponding points plotted on a graph.

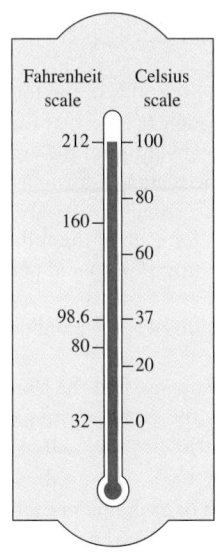

(i)

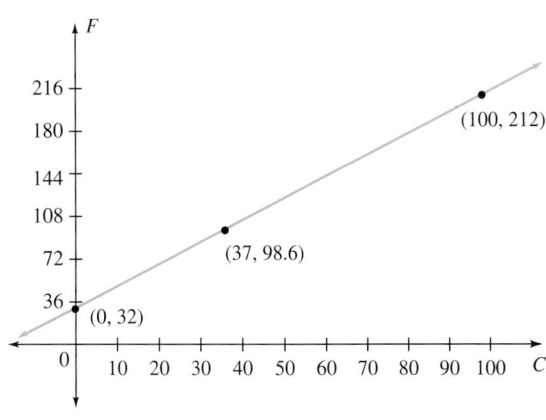

(ii)

a. Use the points $(0, 32)$ and $(100, 212)$ to develop a formula for conversion from degrees Celsius (C) to degrees Fahrenheit (F). *

b. Use your answer in (a) to find a formula for converting from degrees F to degrees C. *

c. Is there a point where degree Celsius and degree Fahrenheit are the same? If so, find it. $(^{-}40°, ^{-}40°)$

5. Write each of the following equations in slope-intercept form and identify the slope and y-intercept.

a. $3y - x = 0$ *   **b.** $x + y = 3$ *   **c.** $x = 3y$ *

6. For each of the following, write the equation of the line determined by the given pair of points in slope-intercept form or in the form $x = a$ or $y = b$.

a. $(^{-}4, 3)$ and $(1, ^{-}2)$ $y = ^{-}x - 1$

b. $(0, 0)$ and $(2, 1)$ *

c. $\left(0, \dfrac{^{-}1}{2}\right)$ and $\left(\dfrac{1}{2}, 0\right)$ $y = x - \dfrac{1}{2}$

d. $(0, ^{-}3)$ and $(^{-}1, ^{-}3)$ $y = ^{-}3$

7. Find the coordinates of two other **collinear** points (on the same line) with each of the following pairs of given points.   Answers vary.

a. $P(2, 2)$, $Q(4, 2)$ **b.** $P(0, 0)$, $Q(0, 1)$

8. For each of the following, give as much information as possible about x and y.

a. The ordered pairs $(^{-}2, 0)$, $(^{-}2, 1)$, and (x, y) represent collinear points. $x = ^{-}2$; y is any real number.

b. The ordered pair (x, y) is in the fourth quadrant. *

9. Consider lines through $P(2, 4)$ that form $90°$ angles with the x- and y-axes, respectively. Find the area and the perimeter of the rectangle formed by these lines and the axes.   Perimeter: 12 units   Area: 8 sq. units

10. Find the equations for each of the following lines.

a. The line containing $P(3, 0)$ and perpendicular to the x-axis $x = 3$

b. The line containing $P(^{-}4, 5)$ and parallel to the x-axis $y = 5$

11. For each of the following, find the slope, if it exists, of the line determined by the given pair of points.

a. $(4, 3)$ and $(^{-}5, 0)$ $\dfrac{1}{3}$ **b.** $(\sqrt{5}, 2)$ and $(1, 2)$ 0

c. (a, a) and (b, b) 1 **d.** $(\sqrt{5}, 2)$ and $(\sqrt{5}, ^{-}2)$ *

12. Write the equation of each line in exercise 11. *

13. Wildlife experts found that the number of chirps a cricket makes in a 15-sec interval is related to the temperature T in degrees Fahrenheit, as shown in the following graph:

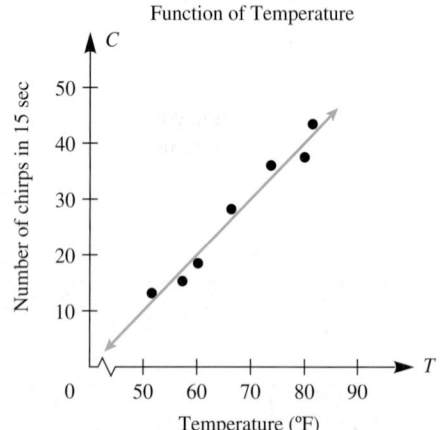

Number of Chirps as a Function of Temperature

a. If C is the number of chirps in 15 sec, write a formula for C in terms of T (temperature in degrees Fahrenheit) that seems to fit the data best. *

b. Use the equation in (a) to predict the number of chirps in 15 sec when the temperature is 90°.   Answers vary 48 chirps in 15 sec

c. If N is the number of chirps per minute, write a formula for N in terms of T.   Answers vary $N = 4T - 168$

14. The lines $\overleftrightarrow{AB}$ and $\overleftrightarrow{BC}$ shown in the figure are graphs of $y = 2x - 20$ and $y = 4 - 2x$. Through the point C, a vertical line (parallel to the y-axis) was drawn intersecting $\overleftrightarrow{AB}$ at D.

a. Which graph corresponds to which line? Justify your answer. $y = 2x - 20$ is line $\overleftrightarrow{BC}$ and $y = 4 - 2x$ is $\overleftrightarrow{AB}$.

b. Find the coordinates of point D. $(10, ^{-}16)$

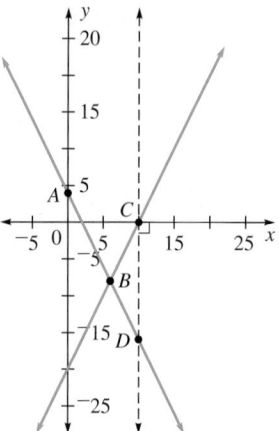

15. What do the graphs of the following equations have in common?

a. $y = m(x + 3)$ for different real number values of m? *

b. $y = m(1 - x)$ for different real number values of m? *

c. $\dfrac{x}{a} + \dfrac{y}{2a} = 1$ for different non-zero values of a? *

d. $x + y = a$ for different values of a? *

16. Suppose a car is traveling at a constant speed of 60 mph.

a. Draw a graph showing the relation between the distance traveled and the amount of time that it takes to travel the distance. *

b. What is the slope of the line that you drew in part (a)?   60

17. Solve each of the following systems, if possible. Indicate whether the system has a unique solution, infinitely many solutions, or no solution.

a. $y = 3x - 1$
$y = x + 3$ Unique solution, $(2, 5)$

b. $3x + 4y = ^{-}17$
$2x + 3y = ^{-}13$ Unique solution, $(1, ^{-}5)$

c. $2x - 3y = ^{-}1$
$\dfrac{^{-}2}{3}x + y = \dfrac{1}{3}$ *

d. $y = 1 - x$
$y = x - 1$ Unique solution, $(1, 0)$

18. The owner of a 5000-gal oil truck loads the truck with gasoline and kerosene. The profit on each gallon of gasoline is 13¢ and on each gallon of kerosene it is 12¢. How many gallons of each fuel did the owner load if the profit was $640.00?   4000 gal of gasoline; 1000 gal of kerosene

19. Josephine's bank contains 27 coins. If all the coins are either dimes or quarters and the value of the coins is $5.25, how many of each kind of coin are there?   17 quarters, 10 dimes

Assessment 8-5B

1. The graph of $y = mx + 5$ is given in the following figure. Sketch the graphs for each of the following equations on the same figure. Explain your answers.
   a. $y = mx$ *
   b. $y = mx - 5$ *
   c. $y = {}^-mx$ *
   d. $y = 2mx$ *

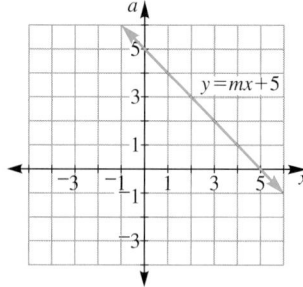

2. Sketch the graphs for each of the following equations:
   a. $x = {}^-2$ *
   b. $y = 3x - 1$ *
   c. $y = \dfrac{1}{20}x$ *

3. Find the x-intercept and y-intercept for the equations in exercise 2, if they exist.   *

4. On a ruler that measures both metric and English units, we see that 1 m = 39.37 in. Use this information to write an equation to convert x m to y in. meters. $y = 39.37x$

5. Write each of the following equations in slope-intercept form and identify the slope and y-intercept.
   a. $\dfrac{x}{3} + \dfrac{y}{4} = 1$ $y = \dfrac{{}^-4}{3}x + 4;$ slope $\dfrac{{}^-4}{3};$ y intercept 4
   b. $3x - 4y + 7 = 0$ *
   c. $x - y = 4(x - y)$ $y = x;$ slope 1; y-intercept 0

6. For each of the following, write the equation of the line determined by the given pair of points in slope-intercept form or in the form $x = a$ or $y = b$.
   a. $(0, 1)$ and $(2, 1)$ $y = 1$
   b. $(2, 1)$ and $(2, {}^-1)$ $x = 2$
   c. $({}^-a, 0)$ and $(a, 0), a \neq 0$ $y = 0$
   d. $(0, {}^-\sqrt{3})$ and $({}^-1, {}^-\sqrt{3})$ $y = {}^-\sqrt{3}$

7. Find the coordinates of two other collinear points (on the same line) with each of the following pairs of given points: Answers vary.
   a. $P({}^-1, 0), Q({}^-1, 2)$ **b.** $P(0, 0), Q(1, 1)$

8. Give as much information as possible about x and y in the following.
   a. The ordered pairs $({}^-2, 1)$, $(0, 1)$, and (x, y) represent collinear points. x is any real number; $y = 1$
   b. (x, y), $(0, 0)$ and $({}^-1, {}^-1)$ are collinear   *

9. A rectangle has two vertices on the x-axis, two vertices on the y-axis, and one vertex at the point with coordinates $(4, 6)$.
   a. Make a sketch showing that there is a rectangle with these characteristics.   *
   b. Write the coordinates of each of the other three vertices. $(0, 0), (0, 6), (4, 0)$
   c. Write the equations of the diagonals of the rectangle.   *
   d. Find the coordinates of the point of intersection of the diagonals. $(2, 3)$

10. Find the equation for each of the following lines.
    a. The line containing $P(0, {}^-2)$ and parallel to the x-axis   *
    b. The line containing $P({}^-4, 5)$ and parallel to the y-axis   *

11. For each of the following, find the slope, if it exists, of the line determined by the given pair of points:
    a. $({}^-4, 1)$ and $(5, 2)$ $\dfrac{1}{9}$
    b. $({}^-3, 81)$ and $({}^-3, 198)$ Undefined
    c. $(1.0001, 12)$ and $(1, 10)$ 20,000
    d. $(2, \sqrt{5})$ and $({}^-2, \sqrt{5})$ 0

12. Write the equation of each line in exercise 11.   *

13. At the end of 10 months, the balance of an account earning annual simple interest is $2100.
    a. If, at the end of 18 mo, the balance is $2180, how much money was originally in the account? $2000
    b. What is the annual rate of interest?   6% annually

14. The lines $\overleftrightarrow{AB}$ and $\overleftrightarrow{BC}$ shown in the figure are graphs of $y = 2 - 2x$ and $y = x - 4$, respectively. The line $\overleftrightarrow{CD}$ goes through $D(0, 5)$ and is parallel to the x-axis. Find the coordinates of $A, B,$ and C.   *

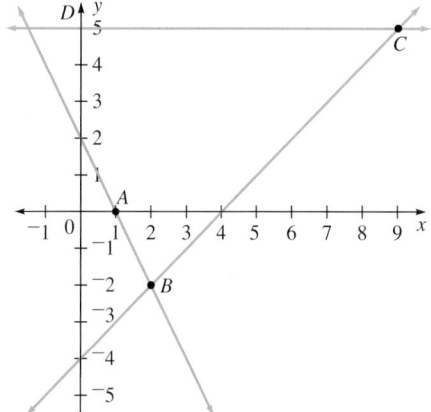

15. What do the graphs of the following equations under the given conditions in each part of the problem have in common?
    a. $y = m(x - 3)$, for different real number values of m?   *
    b. $y = m(3 - x)$, for different real number values of m?   *
    c. $x - y = a$, for different real number values of a?   *
    d. $y = m(x - 1) + 1$, for different real number values of m?   *

16. Suppose a car is traveling at a constant speed of 45 mph.
    a. Draw a graph showing the relation between the distance traveled and the amount of time that it takes to travel the distance.   *
    b. What is the slope of the line you drew in part (a)?   45

17. Solve each of the following systems, if possible. Indicate whether the system has a unique solution, infinitely many solutions, or no solution.
    a. $2x - 6y = 7$
       $3x - 9y = 10$ *
    b. $4x - 6y = 1$
       $6x - 9y = 1.5$ *
    c. $y = 2 - x$
       $y = x - 2$ *
    d. $3x - 2y = {}^-1$
       $\dfrac{{}^-3}{2}x + y = \dfrac{1}{2}$ *

18. The vertices of a triangle are given by $(0, 0)$, $(10, 0)$, and $(6, 8)$. Show that the segments connecting $(5, 0)$ and $(6, 8)$, $(10, 0)$ and $(3, 4)$, and $(0, 0)$ and $(8, 4)$ intersect at a common point.   *

Mathematical Connections 8-5

Answers to Mathematical Connections can be found in the Answers section at the back of the book.

Reasoning

1. In this chapter, an arithmetic sequence was associated with a linear graph. Explain whether a geometric sequence should be associated with a linear graph.
2. Explain why two lines with the same slope and different y intercepts, are parallel.
3. Given the equations $y = mx + b$ and $y = nx + a$ answer the following.
   a. Assuming that the lines intersect in a single point, find the coordinates of this point in terms of m, n, and a and b.
   b. Under what condition (in terms of m, n, a and b) do the lines intersect in a single point? Find the answer using part (a) and interpret it using the graphs of the lines.
4. Given the lines in problem 3, once x is found, y can be found by substituting the value of x into either equation. Explain why it does not matter which one.
5. Draw graphs for the following. Justify your solution.
   a. $(x + y)^2 = 4$
   b. $|x + y| = 1$
   c. $|x| = 1$ and y is any real number
   d. $|y| = 1$ and x is any real number
6. Explain why there exist lines with irrational numbers as slopes.

Open-Ended

7. Look for situations in books or the internet that can be modeled by equations whose graphs are straight lines.
8. a. Write equations of two lines that intersect but when graphed look parallel.
   b. At what point do those two lines intersect?

Cooperative Learning

9. Play the following game between your group and another group. Each group makes up four linear equations that have a common property and presents the equations to the other group. For example, one group could present the equations $2x - y = 0$, $4x - 2y = 3$, $y - 2x = 3$, and $3y - 6x = 5$. If the second group discovers a common property that the equations share, such as the graphs of the equations are four parallel lines, they get 1 point. Each group takes a specified number of turns.
10. Consider equations of the form $ax + by = c$, where not both a and b equal 0. Each group should choose three such equations so that a, b, and c are consecutive terms in arithmetic sequence and answer the following.
   a. In your group, choose all pairs of your equations (there are 3 pairs) and solve each pair simultaneously. What do the solutions have in common?
   b. Compare the answers from different groups.
   c. Explain why what you discovered in parts (a) and (b) is always true. Compare the arguments from different groups and choose the best argument. What makes it best?

Connecting Mathematics to the Classroom

11. A student would like to know why it is impossible to find the slope of a vertical line. How do you respond?

12. Jonah tried to solve the equation $^-5x + y = 20$ by adding 5 to both sides. He wrote $5 - 5x + y = 5 + 20$ or $0 \cdot x + y = 25$ and finally $y = 25$. How would you help Jonah?
13. Jill would like to know why two lines with an undefined slope are parallel. How would you respond?
14. Janis noticed that in the simultaneous equations

$$2x - 3y - 5 = 0$$
$$^-4x + 6y + 10 = 0,$$

$\dfrac{2}{^-4} = \dfrac{^-3}{6} = \dfrac{^-5}{10}$ and the system has infinitely-many solutions.

She would like to know whether, if a similar situation occurs in other systems of two equations in two unknowns, the corresponding system will have infinitely many solutions. How do you respond?

Review Problems

15. Write the following with algebraic expressions or equations.
   a. The cube root of a number is 3 less than its square.
   b. The sum of the squares of two numbers is 36.
   c. $\sqrt{0.\overline{9}}$ has 1 as its principal square root.
16. Give an approximation of $\sqrt{6}$ correct to hundredths.
17. Solve the following for x.
   a. $x\sqrt{2} = ^-3\sqrt{2}x + 2$
   b. $x^2 - 81 = 0$
   c. $3x < ^-\sqrt{7}$
18. Find $f(x)$ for each given value of x when $f(x) = x\sqrt{7} - \sqrt{7}$.
   a. 3
   b. $\sqrt{7}$
   c. $^-4$
19. If $f(x) = 12$ when $f(x) = 3x - \sqrt{2}$, find x.
20. What are the domains for each of the following functions?
   a. $f(x) = \sqrt{x + 1}$
   b. $f(x) = \sqrt{^-x}$

National Assessments

National Assessment of Educational Progress (NAEP) Questions

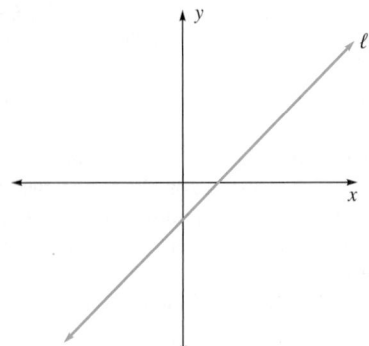

Which of the following statements is true about line ℓ shown above?

A. Line ℓ has a positive slope and a positive y-intercept.
B. Line ℓ has a positive slope and a negative y-intercept.
C. Line ℓ has zero slope and a negative y-intercept.
D. Line ℓ has a negative slope and a positive y-intercept.
E. Line ℓ has a negative slope and a negative y-intercept.

NAEP, Grade 8, 2013

Two large storage tanks, T and W, contain water. T starts losing water at the same time additional water starts flowing into W. The graph below shows the amount of water in each tank over a period of hours.

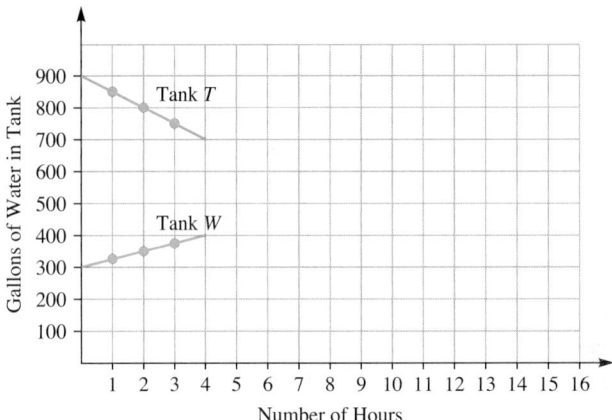

Assume that the rates of water loss and water gain continue as shown. At what number of hours will the amount of water in T be equal to the amount of water in W?

Show or explain how you found your answer.

NAEP, Grade 8, 2013

Hint for Solving the Preliminary Problem

Use Figure 40 to write a proportion and slove for $\dfrac{l}{w}$

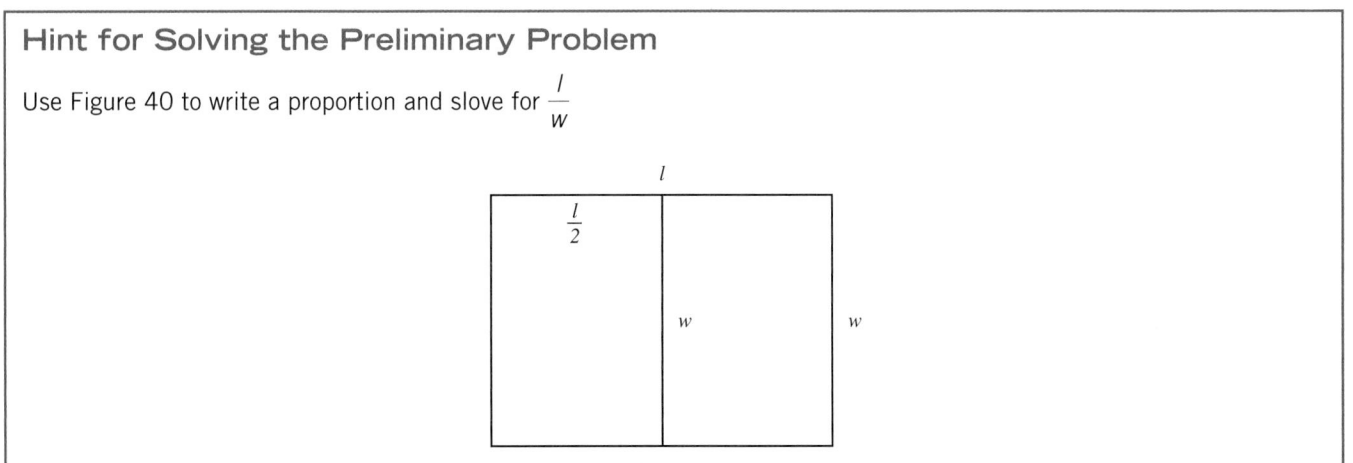

Figure 40

Chapter 8 Summary

KEY CONCEPTS	DEFINITIONS, DESCRIPTIONS, AND THEOREMS
Section 8-1	
Irrational number (p. 388)	Any number that is not rational.
Real number (p. 389)	Any rational or irrational number. Every real number can be represented as a decimal.
Square root (p. 389)	If a is any nonnegative number, a *square root of a* is a number x such that $x^2 = a$. For example, 9 has square roots 3 and $^-3$. If a is any nonnegative number, the *principal square root of a* (denoted $\sqrt{a}$) is the nonnegative number x such that $x^2 = a$. For example, $\sqrt{9} = 3$.
Principal *n*th root (p. 390)	If n is even and b is any nonnegative real number, then the *principal nth root* of b (denoted as $\sqrt[n]{b}$) is the positive solution of $x^n = b$. If n is odd and b is any real number, the *nth root* of b (or $\sqrt[n]{b}$) is the unique solution of $x^n = b$.
Pythagorean Theorem (p. 392)	If a and b are the lengths of the shorter sides (legs) of a right triangle and c is the length of the hypotenuse (the side opposite the right angle), then $a^2 + b^2 = c^2$.
Fraction (p. 394)	Any real number of the form $\dfrac{a}{b}$, where a and b are real numbers with $b \neq 0$.
Addition and multiplication properties for real numbers (p. 394)	• *Closure*—for all real numbers a and b, $a + b$ and ab are unique real numbers. • *Commutative*—for all real numbers a and b, $a + b = b + a$ and $ab = ba$. • *Associative*—for all real numbers a, b, and c, $(a + b) + c = a + (b + c)$ and $(ab)c = a(bc)$. • *Identity*—for all real numbers a; 0 is the (unique) *additive identity* such that $a + 0 = 0 + a$, 1 is the (unique) *multiplicative identity* such that $a \cdot 1 = 1 \cdot a = a$. • *Inverse*—for every real number a, there is an unique real number $-a$, the *additive inverse of a*, such that $a + \,^-a = 0 = \,^-a + a$. For every nonzero real number a, there is an unique real number $\dfrac{1}{a}$, the *multiplicative inverse of a*, such that $a \cdot \dfrac{1}{a} = 1 = \dfrac{1}{a} \cdot a$. • *Multiplicative Property of* 0—for all real number a, $a \cdot 0 = 0 \cdot a = 0$. • *Distributive property of multiplication over addition*—for all real numbers a, b, and c, $a(b + c) = ab + ac$.
Density property for real numbers (p. 394)	For all real numbers a and b with $a < b$, there exists a real number c such that $a < c < b$.
Rational exponents (p. 395)	For any positive integer n and any integer m, $x^{1/n} = \sqrt[n]{x}$, if $\sqrt[n]{x}$ is a real number, and $x^{m/n} = \sqrt[n]{x^m}$, if $\text{GCD}(m, n) = 1$ and $\sqrt[n]{x^m}$ is a real number.

Section 8-1

Properties of exponents (p. 395)

Let r and s be any rational numbers, x and y be any real numbers, and n be any nonzero integer. (Assume the following expressions are meaningful.)

- $x^{-r} = \dfrac{1}{x^r}, x^{-1/n} = \dfrac{1}{x^{1/n}} = \dfrac{1}{\sqrt[n]{x}}$

- $(xy)^r = x^r y^r$, $(xy)^{1/n} = x^{1/n} y^{1/n}$ and $\sqrt[n]{xy} = \sqrt[n]{x}\,\sqrt[n]{y}$

- $\left(\dfrac{x}{y}\right)^r = \dfrac{x^r}{y^r}, \left(\dfrac{x}{y}\right)^{1/n} = \dfrac{x^{1/n}}{y^{1/n}}$ and $\sqrt[n]{\dfrac{x}{y}} = \dfrac{\sqrt[n]{x}}{\sqrt[n]{y}}$

- $(x^r)^s = x^{rs}$, $\left(x^{1/n}\right)^p = x^{p/n}$ and $\left(\sqrt[n]{x}\right)^p = \sqrt[n]{x^p}$ where p is an integer.

Section 8-2

Constant (p. 401)

A fixed number or other fixed mathematical object

Variable (p. 401)

A quantity that varies.

A variable may

(1) represent a missing element or an unknown,

(2) stand for more than one thing,

(3) be used in generalizations of patterns, and

(4) be an element of a set, or a set itself.

nth term of an arithmetic sequence (p. 404)

$a_n = a_1 + (n - 1)d$, where a_1 is the first term and d is the difference.

nth term of an geometric sequence (p. 405)

$a_n = a_1 r^{n-1}$, where a_1 is the first term and r is the ratio.

Fibonacci sequence (p. 406)

A sequence in which $F_1 = F_2 = 1$ and $F_n = F_{n-1} + F_{n-2}$ for $n \geq 3$.

Section 8-3

Properties of equality and equations (p. 412)

- *Addition*—for all real numbers a, b, and c, if $a = b$, then $a + c = b + c$.
- *Multiplication*—for all real numbers a, b, and c, if $a = b$, then $ac = bc$.
- *Cancellation*—For any real numbers a, b, and c,

    if $a + c = b + c$, then $a = b$.

    if $c \neq 0$ and $ac = bc$, then $a = b$.

- *Substitution*—equality is not affected if we substitute a number for its equal.

Section 8-4

Function (p. 423)

A correspondence from set A to set B in which each element of A is paired with one, and only one, element of B.

Let f be a function from A to B. If $x \in A$, then $f(x)$, the value of the function f at x (or the *image of x*) is the element in B that corresponds to x.

Set A is the *domain* of the function, and set B is the *codomain* (or the set of all possible outputs) of the function. The *range* of the function is the set of all outputs of the function.

Section 8-4

Function models (p. 424)	Functions may be modeled in various ways: • as a rule between two sets • as a machine relating inputs and outputs • as an equation relating two variables • as a table relating two variables • as an arrow diagram showing the correspondence between elements of two sets • as a set of ordered pairs • as a graph in two dimensions
Sum of the first n terms, $S(n)$, of an arithmetic sequence (p. 428)	$S(n) = \left(\dfrac{a_1 + a_n}{2}\right)n$ or $S(n) = a_1 n + \dfrac{n(n-1)d}{2}$, where a_1 is the first term, a_n is the last term, d is the difference, and n is the number of terms.
Sum of the first n terms, $S(n)$, of a geometric sequence (p. 429)	$S(n) = \dfrac{a_1(1 - r^n)}{1 - r}$, where a_1 is the first term, r is the ratio ($r \neq 1$), and n is the number of terms.
Composition of functions (p. 431)	Given the functions f and g, the composition of f with g is the function $g \circ f$ such that $(g \circ f)(x) = g(f(x))$.
Relation (p. 433)	A *relation from set A to set B* is any set of ordered pairs; that is, a subset of $A \times B$. A *relation* is a *function* from set A to set B if for every $a \in A$, there is a unique $b \in B$ such that (a, b) is in the relation.
Properties of relations (p. 433)	*Reflexive*—a relation R on a set X is *reflexive* if, and only if, for every element $a \in X$, a is related to a; that is, for every $a \in X$, $(a, a) \in R$. *Symmetric*—a relation R on a set X is *symmetric* if, and only if, for all elements a and b in X, whenever a is related to b, then b also is related to a; that is, if $(a, b) \in R$, then $(b, a) \in R$. *Transitive*— a relation R on a set X is *transitive* if, and only if, for all elements a, b, and c in X, whenever a is related to b and b is related to c, then a is related to c; that is, if $(a, b) \in R$ and $(b, c) \in R$, then $(a, c) \in R$.
Equivalence relation (p. 434)	Any relation that has the reflexive, symmetric, and transitive properties.

Section 8-5

Cartesian coordinate system (p. 442)	A system constructed by placing two number lines perpendicular to each other. The intersection point of the two lines is the *origin*. The two perpendicular lines are commonly called the *x-axis*, and the *y-axis*.
Slope (p. 445, 449)	The measure of steepness (denoted by m) of a line. Give two points $A(x_1, y_1)$ and $B(x_2, y_2)$ with $x_1 \neq x_2$, the *slope m* of the line through A and B is $$m = \dfrac{\text{rise}}{\text{run}} = \dfrac{y_2 - y_1}{x_2 - x_1} = \dfrac{y_1 - y_2}{x_1 - x_2}.$$
x-intercept and y-intercept (p.446)	The value of x at the point of intersection of a line with the x-axis is the *x-intercept*. The value of y at the point of intersection of a line with the y-axis is the *y-intercept*.
Equation of a line (p. 447)	Every nonvertical line has an equation of the form $y = mx + b$ (*slope-intercept form*), where m is the *slope* and b is the *y-intercept*. A vertical line has undefined slope and the equation $x = a$. A horizontal line has 0 slope and the equation $y = b$.

Section 8-5

Solving a system of equations (p. 451)	A system of two equations in two unknowns may be solved using any of the following methods:
	• *Graphing*
	• *Substitution*
	• *Elimination*
Number of solutions of a system of two equations in two variables (p. 454)	The system has *a unique solution* if, and only if, the graphs of the equations intersect in a single point.
	The system has *no solution* if, and only if, the equations represent distinct parallel lines.
	The system has *infinitely many solutions* if, and only if, the equations represent the same line.

Chapter 8 Review

1. Classify each of the following as rational or irrational (assume the patterns shown continue):
   a. 2.19119911999119999119 . . .   Irrational
   b. $\dfrac{1}{\sqrt{2}}$ Irrational
   c. $\dfrac{4}{9}$ Rational
   d. 0.0011001100110011 . . .   Rational
   e. 0.001100011000011 . . .   Irrational

2. Write each of the following in the form $a\sqrt{b}$ or $a\sqrt[n]{b}$, where a and b are positive integers and b has the least value possible:
   a. $\sqrt{484}$ 22
   b. $\sqrt{288}$ $12\sqrt{2}$
   c. $\sqrt{180}$ $6\sqrt{5}$
   d. $\sqrt[3]{162}$ $3\sqrt[3]{6}$

3. Answer each of the following and explain your answers.
   a. Is the set of irrational numbers closed under addition?   No; $\sqrt{2} + (^-\sqrt{2})$ is rational
   b. Is the set of irrational numbers closed under subtraction?   No; $\sqrt{2} - \sqrt{2} = 0$
   c. Is the set of irrational numbers closed under multiplication?   No; $\sqrt{2} \cdot \sqrt{2}$ is rational
   d. Is the set of irrational numbers closed under division?   No; $\sqrt{2}/\sqrt{2}$ is rational.

4. Find an approximation for $\sqrt{23}$ correct to three decimal places without using the $\boxed{y^x}$ or the $\boxed{\sqrt{}}$ keys on a calculator.   4.796

5. Approximate $\sqrt[3]{2}$ to two decimal places by using the squeezing method.   1.26

6. Each of the following is a geometric sequence. Find the missing terms.
   a. 5, _____, 10 $5\sqrt{2}$ or $^-5\sqrt{2}$
   b. 1, _____, _____, _____, 1/4   *

7. In a geometric sequence, if the nth term is $\sqrt{7}(^-1)^n$, what is the 10th term and what is the ratio? $\sqrt{7}; r = ^-1$

8. If the first two terms of an arithmetic sequence are 1 and $\sqrt{2}$, what is an algebraic expression for the nth term? $1 + (n - 1)(\sqrt{2} - 1)$

9. There are 13 times as many students as professors at a college. Use S for the number of students and P for the number of professors to represent the given information. $S = 13P$

10. Write a sentence that gives the same information as the following equation: $A = 103B$, where A is the number of girls in a neighborhood and B is the number of boys.   There are 103 times as many girls as boys.

11. Write an equation to find the number of feet given the number of yards (let f be the number of feet and y be the number of yards). $f = 3y$

12. The sum of n whole numbers is S. If each number is multiplied by 10 and then decreased by 10, what is the sum of the new numbers in terms of n and S? $10S - 10n$

13. I am thinking of a whole number. If I divide it by 13, then multiply the answer by 12, then subtract 20, and then add 89, I end up with 93. What was my original number?   26

14. a. Think of a number.
       Add 17.
       Double the result.
       Subtract 4.
       Double the result.
       Add 20.
       Divide by 4.
       Subtract 20.
       Your answer will be your original number. Explain how this "trick" works.   *
   b. Fill in two more steps that will take you back to your original number.
       Think of a number.
       Add 18.
       Multiply by 4.
       Subtract 7.
       .
       .
       .
       .   *

15. Find all the values of x that satisfy the following equations write your answers in simplified form:
   a. $4(7x - 21) = 14(7x - 21)$ 3
   b. $3(\sqrt{x} - 1) = \sqrt{9x} + 5$ No solution
   c. $2(3x + 5) = 6x + 11$ No solution
   d. $2(x + \sqrt{3}) = 3(x - \sqrt{3})$ $5\sqrt{3}$

16. Mike has 3 times as many baseball cards as Jordan, who has twice as many cards as Paige. Together, the three children have 999 cards. Find how many cards each child has.   Paige 111, Jordan 222, and Mike 666

17. Jeannie has 10 books overdue at the library. She remembers she checked out 2 science books two weeks before she checked out 8 children's books. The daily fine per book is $0.20. If her total fine was $11.60, how long was each book overdue?   Science books 17 days, other books 3 days

18. Three children deliver all the newspapers in a small town. Jacobo delivers twice as many papers as Dahlia, who delivers 100 more papers than Rashid. If altogether 500 papers are delivered, how many papers does each child deliver?   Rashid 50, Dahlia 150, Jacobo 300

19. Which of the following sets of ordered pairs are functions from the set of first components to the set of second components?
    a. $\{(a,b),(c,d),(e,a),(f,g)\}$ Function
    b. $\{(a,b),(a,c),(b,b),(b,c)\}$ Not a function
    c. $\{(a,b),(b,a)\}$ Function
    d. $\{(x,y)\mid x \text{ is any real number}, y = 2\}$ Function

20. Given the following function rules and the domains, find the associated ranges:
    a. $f(x) = x + 3$; domain $= \{0,1,2,3\}$ Range $= \{3,4,5,6\}$
    b. $f(x) = 3x - 1$; domain is R (all real numbers)   All real numbers
    c. $f(x) = x^2$; domain is R (all real numbers)   *
    d. $f(x) = x^2 + 3x + 5$; domain $= \{0,1,2\}$ Range $= \{5,9,15\}$

21. Which of the following correspondences from A to B describe a function? If a correspondence is a function, find its range. Justify your answers.
    a. A is the set of college students, and B is the set of majors. To each college student corresponds his or her major.   *
    b. A is the set of books in the library, and B is the set N of natural numbers. To each book corresponds the number of pages in the book.   *
    c. $A = \{(a,b)\mid a \in N \text{ and } b \in N\}$, and $B = N$. To each element (a,b) of A corresponds the number $4a + 2b$.   *
    d. $A = N$ and $B = N$. If x is even, then $f(x) = 0$, and if x is odd, then $f(x) = 1$.   *
    e. $A = N$ and $B = N$. To each natural number corresponds the sum of its digits.   *

22. A health club charges an initiation fee of $200, which gives 1 month of free membership, and then charges $55 per month.
    a. If $C(x)$ is the total cost of membership in the club for x months, express $C(x)$ in terms of x.   *
    b. Graph $C(x)$ for the first 12 months.   *
    c. Use the graph in (b) to find when the total cost of membership in the club will exceed $600.   *
    d. When will the total cost of membership exceed $6000?   *

23. For each of the following functions, find possible inputs x, if $f(x)$ is as given.
    a. $f(x) = 4x - 5; f(x) = 15$ 5
    b. $f(x) = x^2 - 1; f(x) = 2$ $\sqrt{3}$ or $^-\sqrt{3}$
    c. $f(x) = \sqrt{x}; f(x) = 3$ ⁻9
    d. $f(x) = \sqrt{x}; f(x) = ^-3$ No
    e. $f(x) = \dfrac{x+1}{x+2}; f(x) = ^-1$ $-\dfrac{3}{2}$
    f. $f(x) = \dfrac{x+1}{x+2}; f(x) = 1$ No input

24. Which of the following graphs represent functions? Tell why.
    a. 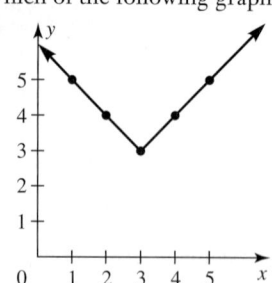   Yes, each input has exactly one output
    b. 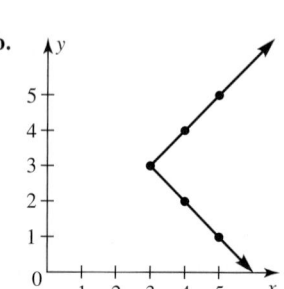   No, for $x = 4$, there are two value of y.
    c. 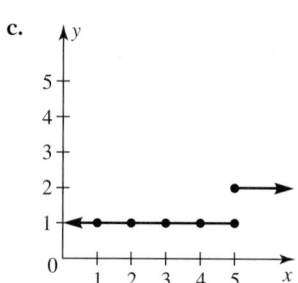   No, for $x = 5$, there are two value of y.

25. a. Jilly is building towers with cubes, placing one cube on top of another and painting the tower (including the top and the bottom, but not the faces touching each other). Find the number of square faces that Jilly needs to paint for towers made of 1, 2, 3, 4, 5, and 6 cubes by filling in the following table: 14, 18, 22, 26

# of Cubes	# of Squares to Paint
1	6
2	10
3	
4	
5	
6	

   b. Graph the information you found in part (a) where the number of cubes in a tower is on the horizontal x-axis and the number of squares to be painted is on the vertical axis.   *
   c. If x is the number of cubes in a tower and y is the corresponding number of squares to be painted, write an equation that gives y as a function of x.   *
   d. Is the graph describing the number of squares as a function of the number of cubes used a straight line?   *

26. Graph each of the following equations:

    a. $y = {}^-2x + 5$ *

    b. $-\dfrac{x}{3} + \dfrac{y}{5} = 1$ *

    c. $y = {}^-x\sqrt{2}$ *

27. The following are graphs of $x - y - 1 = 0$ and of $4x + 3y - 12 = 0$. Answer the following.

    a. Which equation is the graph of $\overleftrightarrow{CD}$?   *

    b. If line $\overleftrightarrow{ED}$ is parallel to the x-axis, find the coordinates of E.   *

    c. If line $\overleftrightarrow{BF}$ is parallel to the x-axis, find the length of segment $\overline{BF}$. $\dfrac{15}{4}$

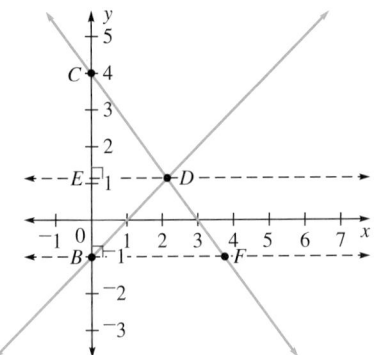

28. Solve the following equations if possible(s).

    a. ${}^-3x + 12 = 23$ $\dfrac{{}^-11}{3}$

    b. $\sqrt{2}x - 5 = \sqrt{8}x + {}^31$ $\dfrac{6}{\sqrt{2}} = {}^-3\sqrt{2}$

    c. $x^3 = {}^-2$ $\sqrt[3]{2} = {}^-\sqrt[3]{2}$

    d. $4x^2 - 33 = 3$ 3 or ${}^-3$

    e. $(x - 1)^3 = 2$ $1 + \sqrt[3]{2}$

    f. $(2x + 1)^4 = 5$ $\dfrac{\sqrt[4]{5} - 1}{2}$, or $\dfrac{{}^-\sqrt[4]{5} - 1}{2}$

    g. $(2x - 1)(x - 1) = {}^-0$ $\dfrac{1}{2}$ or 1

29. If we take the third root of every term of a geometric sequence is the resulting sequence also geometric? If so, what is its ratio? Justify your answer.   Yes. The new ratio is the cube root of the original ratio. if x and y are successive terms in the original sequence with ratio r, so that $\dfrac{y}{x} = r$, then $\dfrac{\sqrt[3]{y}}{\sqrt[3]{x}} = \sqrt[3]{\dfrac{y}{x}} = \sqrt[3]{r}$, which constant.

Chapter 9

Probability

Preliminary Problem

Fifty people are boarding a 50-passenger bus. All have assigned seats listed on their boarding passes. The first person boarding lost the boarding pass and took a random seat. After that, each person takes the assigned seat if it is unoccupied, and a random unoccupied seat otherwise. What is the probability that the 50th person to board gets to sit in his/her assigned seat?

If needed, see Hint on page 530.

Probability is used in predicting sales, planning political campaigns, determining insurance premiums, making investment decisions, and testing experimental drugs. Some uses of probability in conversations include the following:

> What is the probability that the Chicago Cubs will win the World Series?
>
> There is no chance you will get a raise.
>
> There is a 50% chance of rain today.

 In the *Common Core Standards*, only grade 7 has specific standards dealing with probability. The overall probability standard says that students should "investigate chance processes and develop, use, and evaluate probability models." (p. 50)

In this chapter, we introduce probability topics and use tree diagrams and geometric probabilities (area models) to solve problems and to analyze games that involve spinners, cards, and dice. Additionally we introduce counting techniques and discuss the role of simulations in probability.

9-1 Determining Probabilities

9-1 Objectives

Students will be able to understand and explain

- How probabilities are determined.

- Experimental or empirical probabilities versus theoretical probabilities.

- Properties of probabilities.

- Mutually exclusive and non-mutually exclusive events.

- Geometric probabilities.

Probabilities are ratios, expressed as fractions, decimals, or percents, determined by considering results or outcomes of experiments. An **experiment** is an activity whose results are **outcomes** of the experiment. For example, if we toss a typical coin that cannot land on its edge, there are two distinct possible outcomes: heads (H) and tails (T).

The set of all possible outcomes for an experiment is a **sample space**. The outcomes in the sample space cannot overlap. In a single coin toss of a typical coin, the sample space S is given by $S = \{H, T\}$ where H is for heads and T is for tails. The sample space can be modeled by a **tree diagram**, as shown in Figure 1. Each outcome of the experiment is designated by a separate branch in the tree diagram. The sample space S for rolling a standard die as in Figure 2(a), is typically written as $S = \{1, 2, 3, 4, 5, 6\}$ instead of showing the dots (pips). Figure 2(b) gives a tree diagram for that sample space.

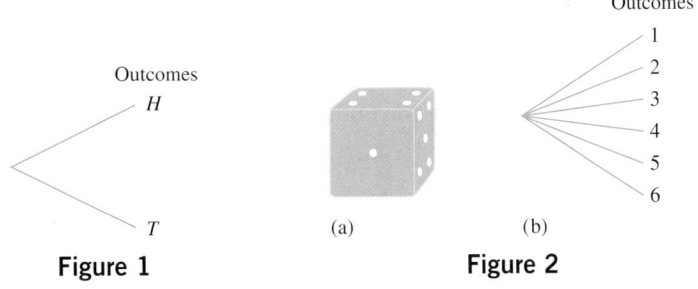

Figure 1   **Figure 2**

Historical Note

 Most mathematics historians think that probability originated from an unfinished dice game. The French mathematician Blaise Pascal (1623–1669) was asked by his friend Chevalier de Méré, a professional gambler, how to divide the stakes if two players start, but fail to complete, a game consisting of five matches in which the winner is the one who wins three out of five matches and players were to divide the stakes according to their chances of winning the game. Pascal shared the problem with Pierre de Fermat (1601–1665), and together they solved the problem, which led to the development of probability. Since the work of the French mathematician Pierre Simon de Laplace (1749–1827), probability theory has become a major branch of mathematics. ●

Any subset of a sample space is an **event**. For example, the set of all even-numbered rolls of a die $\{2, 4, 6\}$ is an event and is a subset of all possible rolls $\{1, 2, 3, 4, 5, 6\}$. Because events are subsets of a sample space and a sample space is a set, we commonly use letters such as A, B, C to represent events. We see this in Example 1.

Example 1

Suppose an experiment consists of drawing 1 slip of paper from a jar containing 12 slips of paper, each with a different month of the year written on it. Find each of the following:

a. Sample space S for the experiment
b. Event A consisting of outcomes having a month name beginning with J
c. Event B consisting of outcomes having a month name that has exactly four letters
d. Event C consisting of outcomes having a month name that begins with M or N

Solution

a. $S = \{$January, February, March, April, May, June, July, August, September, October, November, December$\}$
b. $A = \{$January, June, July$\}$
c. $B = \{$June, July$\}$
d. $C = \{$March, May, November$\}$

Determining Probabilities

CCSS According to the grade 7 *Common Core Standards*, students should be able to:

Approximate the probability of a chance event by collecting data on the chance process that produces it and observing its long-run relative frequency, and predict the approximate relative frequency given the probability. *For example, when rolling a number cube 600 times, predict that a 3 or 6 would be rolled roughly 200 times, but probably not exactly 200 times.* (p. 51)

Around 1900, the English statistician Karl Pearson collected data on the chance process of obtaining a head or a tail on a coin toss. He tossed a coin 24,000 times and recorded 12,012 heads. During World War II, John Kerrich, a Dane and a prisoner of war, tossed a coin 10,000 times. A subset of his results is shown in Table 1. The *relative frequency* column on the right is obtained by dividing the number of heads by the number of tosses of the coin.

Activity Manual

Use *The Spinner Game* to introduce experimental probability, fair games, and mutually exclusive, complementary, certain, and impossible events.

Table 1

Number of Tosses	Number of Heads	Relative Frequency (rounded)
10	4	0.400
50	25	0.500
100	44	0.440
500	255	0.510
1,000	502	0.502
5,000	2,533	0.507
8,000	4,034	0.504
10,000	5,067	0.507

As the number of Kerrich's tosses increased, he obtained heads close to half the time. The relative frequency for Pearson's 24,000 tosses gave a similar result of $\frac{12,012}{24,000}$, or approximately $\frac{1}{2}$. Kerrich used the relative frequency interpretation of probability. In this interpretation, *the experimental probability of an event is the long-run relative frequency that an event will occur given many repetitions under identical circumstances.*

   The **experimental (or empirical) probability** of an event is an estimate of the likelihood that the event will happen based on the observed outcomes of several trials of the experiment. The experimental probability of an event is an estimate of the probability that the event happens, based on the observed outcomes of repeated trials. If the experiment is performed few times, the experimental probability might not be accurate in predicting the probability of the event. For example, if a fair coin was tossed 4 times and 4 heads were observed, the experimental probability of obtaining a head on the coin toss is $\frac{4}{4}$ or 1, which is far from the theoretical probability. A *fair coin* is a coin that is just as likely to land "heads" as it is to land "tails." So the experimental probability based on 4 tosses is considered an anomaly. If, as Pearson and Kerrich did, the coin is tossed many times, the experimental probability of obtaining "heads" is close to $\frac{1}{2}$. This discussion leads to the fact that a probability only suggests what will happen in the "long run" if the experiment is repeated many times. This concept is called *the Law of Large Numbers*, or sometimes *Bernoulli's Theorem*, and is given as Theorem 9-1.

Activity Manual

Use *Theoretical Probability* to introduce theoretical probability and equally likely events.

> **Theorem 9-1:   Law of Large Numbers (Bernoulli's Theorem)**
>
> As the number of trials of an experiment increases, the *experimental* or *empirical* probability of a particular event approaches a fixed number, the *theoretical probability* of that event.

   In this text, we use "*probability*" and "*theoretical probability*" interchangeably unless it is explicitly stated to be an experimental or empirical probability.

   We could argue that since a fair coin marked heads (H) and tails (T) is symmetric and has two sides, each side should appear about the same number of times if the coin is tossed many times. If $H = \{H\}$ and $T = \{T\}$ in the sample space $S = \{H, T\}$, then we write the probability of event H as $P(H)$, the probability of event T as $P(T)$ and assign the theoretical probability of $\frac{1}{2}$ to each.

$$P(H) = P(T) = \frac{1}{2}$$

When one outcome is just as likely as another, as in fair coin tossing, the outcomes are **equally likely**. If an experiment is repeated many times, the experimental probability of the event's occurring should be approximately equal to the theoretical probability of the event's occurring.

   A *fair* die, as seen flattened in Figure 3, is a die that is just as likely to land showing any of the numbers of dots 1 through 6 on any toss.

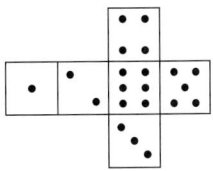

Figure 3

───(**Historical Note**)──────────────────────────────────────

Jakob Bernoulli (1654–1705) was a member of the Bernoulli family of mathematicians. After completing a theology degree, Jakob traveled for 7 years studying mathematics, then returned to Basel, Switzerland, in 1683. In 1687 he became the chair of mathematics at the University of Basel. His greatest and most original work, *Ars Conjectandi* (*The Art of Conjecturing*), laid the foundation for the modern theory of probability. He is responsible for Bernoulli's Theorem, stated here as Theorem 9-1.   ●

Its sample space S is listed by $S = \{1, 2, 3, 4, 5, 6\}$. We use a shorthand notation to denote, for example, $P(\{1\})$ as $P(1)$ so that $P(1) = P(2) = P(3) = P(4) = P(5) = P(6) = \frac{1}{6}$. The probability of rolling an even number, that is, the probability of the event $E = \{2, 4, 6\}$, is $\frac{3}{6} = \frac{1}{2}$.

Note that probabilities are typically as simplified fractions or decimals. For a sample space with equally likely outcomes, the probability of an event A can be defined as shown.

Definition of Probability of an Event in a Sample Space with Equally Likely Outcomes

For an experiment with non-empty finite sample space S with equally likely outcomes, the **probability of an event A** is given by

$$P(A) = \frac{\text{Number of elements of } A}{\text{Number of elements of } S} = \frac{n(A)}{n(S)}.$$

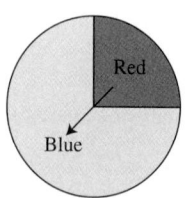

Figure 4

The above definition of the probability of an event applies only to a sample space that has equally likely outcomes. If each possible outcome of the sample space is equally likely, the sample space is a **uniform sample space**. Thus, in a uniform sample space with n outcomes, the probability of each outcome is $\frac{1}{n}$. Applying the definition of probability given above to a sample space with outcomes that are not equally likely (non-uniform) leads to incorrect conclusions. For example, the sample space for spinning the spinner in Figure 4 is given by $S = \{\text{Red, Blue}\}$, but Blue is more likely to occur than Red. If the spinner were spun 100 times, we could reasonably expect that about $\frac{1}{4}$ of $100 = 25$, of the outcomes would be Red, whereas about $\frac{3}{4}$ of $100 = 75$, of the outcomes would be Blue.

▶ NOW TRY THIS 1

NTT 1: Answer can be found in Answers at the back of the book.

a. In an experiment of tossing a fair die once, what is the sum of the probabilities of all the distinct outcomes in the sample space?
b. Does the sum of the probabilities of all the distinct outcomes of any sample space always result in the same number?
c. What is the probability of the spinner in Figure 5 landing on Red? Why?

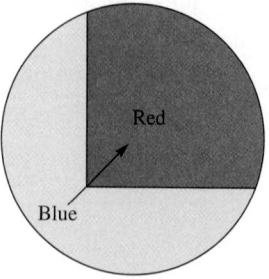

Figure 5

Use *It's in the Bag* to investigate theoretical and experimental probabilities, random sampling, and making predictions.

Activity Manual

CCSS In the grade 7 *Common Core Standards*, we find that students should be able to:

understand that the probability of a chance event is a number between 0 and 1 that expresses the likelihood of the event occurring. Larger numbers indicate greater likelihood. A probability near 0 indicates an unlikely event, a probability around $\frac{1}{2}$ indicates an event that is neither unlikely nor likely, and a probability near 1 indicates a likely event. (p. 50)

Example 2

Let $S = \{1, 2, 3, 4, 5, \ldots, 25\}$. If a number is chosen at **random**, with the same chance of being drawn as all other numbers in the set, calculate each of the following probabilities:

 a. The event A that an even number is drawn.
 b. The event B that a number less than 10 and greater than 20 is drawn.
 c. The event C that a number less than 26 is drawn.
 d. The event D that a prime number is drawn.
 e. The event E that a number both even and prime is drawn.

Solution   Each of the 25 numbers in set S has an equal chance of being drawn.

 a. $A = \{2, 4, 6, 8, 10, 12, 14, 16, 18, 20, 22, 24\}$, so $n(A) = 12$. Thus, $P(A) = \dfrac{n(A)}{n(S)} = \dfrac{12}{25}$.

 b. $B = \varnothing$, so $n(B) = 0$. Thus, $P(B) = \dfrac{0}{25} = 0$.

 c. $C = S$ and $n(C) = 25$. Thus, $P(C) = \dfrac{25}{25} = 1$.

 d. $D = \{2, 3, 5, 7, 11, 13, 17, 19, 23\}$, so $n(D) = 9$. Thus, $P(D) = \dfrac{n(D)}{n(S)} = \dfrac{9}{25}$.

 e. $E = \{2\}$, so $n(E) = 1$. Thus, $P(E) = \dfrac{1}{25}$.

In Example 2(b), event B is the empty set. *Any event with no outcomes, such as B, is an* ***impossible event*** *and has probability 0.* If the word *and* were replaced by *or* in Example 2(b), then event B would no longer be the empty set. If event B is the empty set, $\varnothing$, then it has no elements and its probability is the ratio $P(B) = \dfrac{n(\varnothing)}{n(S)} = \dfrac{0}{n(S)} = 0$. [An assumption is made that the sample space does not have 0 elements.] In Example 2(c), event C consists of drawing a number less than 26 on a single draw. Because every number in S is less than 26, $P(C) = \dfrac{25}{25} = 1$.
An event that has probability 1 is a ***certain event***.

If A is a subset of the finite sample space S with equally likely outcomes, the greatest number of elements that A can have is the number of elements in the sample space S. So the probability of A in this case would be $P(A) = \dfrac{n(A)}{n(S)} = \dfrac{n(S)}{n(S)} = 1$. For any set A that is a proper subset of S, $n(A)$ is greater than or equal to 0 but less than $n(S)$. Hence $P(A) = \dfrac{n(A)}{n(S)} < 1$. We summarize this discussion in the following theorem.

Theorem 9-2

If A is any event and S is the sample space, then $0 \leq P(A) \leq 1$.

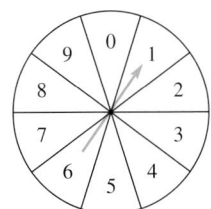

Figure 6

Consider one spin of the number wheel shown in Figure 6, where each sector of the circle is determined by angles with the same measure. For this experiment, $S = \{0, 1, 2, 3, 4, 5, 6, 7, 8, 9\}$. If A is the event of spinning a number in the set $\{0, 1, 2, 3, 4\}$ and B is the event of spinning a number in the set $\{5, 7\}$, then using the definition of probability of an event when the sample space has equally likely outcomes, $P(A) = \dfrac{n(A)}{n(S)} = \dfrac{5}{10} = \dfrac{1}{2}$ and $P(B) = \dfrac{n(B)}{n(S)} = \dfrac{2}{10} = \dfrac{1}{5}$. The probability of an event can be found by adding the probabilities of disjoint events representing the various outcomes in the set. For example, event $B = \{5, 7\}$ can be represented as the union of two disjoint events, that is, spinning a 5 or spinning a 7. Then $P(B)$ can be found by adding the probabilities of each event.

$$P(B) = \frac{1}{10} + \frac{1}{10} = \frac{2}{10} = \frac{1}{5}$$

Likewise,

$$P(A) = \frac{1}{10} + \frac{1}{10} + \frac{1}{10} + \frac{1}{10} + \frac{1}{10} = \frac{5}{10} = \frac{1}{2}.$$

These are special cases of the following theorem.

> **Theorem 9-3**
> The probability of an event is equal to the sum of the probabilities of disjoint events whose union is the event.

Example 3

An ordinary deck of playing cards consists of four suits: spades, hearts, diamonds, and clubs. There are 13 cards in each suit; spades and clubs are black; hearts and diamonds are red. The 13 cards in each suit include the ace, 2, 3, 4, 5, 6, 7, 8, 9, 10, and the three face cards (king, queen, and jack). If we draw a card at random from an ordinary deck of playing cards, find the probability that the

a. card is an ace.
b. card is an ace or a queen.

Solution

a. There are 52 cards in a deck, 4 of which are aces. If event A is drawing an ace, then $A = \{♠, ♣, ♦, ♥\}$. We use the definition of probability of an event in a sample space with equally likely outcomes to compute the probability of drawing an ace.

$$P(A) = \frac{n(A)}{n(S)} = \frac{4}{52} = \frac{1}{13}$$

An alternative approach is to find the sum of the probabilities of the disjoint events containing each of the outcomes in the event, where the probability of the event of drawing any single ace from the deck is $\frac{1}{52}$.

$$P(A) = \frac{1}{52} + \frac{1}{52} + \frac{1}{52} + \frac{1}{52} = \frac{4}{52} = \frac{1}{13}$$

b. From part (a), $P(A) = \frac{4}{52} = \frac{1}{13}$. By similar reasoning if event B is drawing a queen then $P(B) = \frac{4}{52} = \frac{1}{13}$. Therefore the probability of the union of these disjoint sets is $\frac{4}{52} + \frac{4}{52} = \frac{8}{52} = \frac{2}{13}$.

Mutually Exclusive Events

Consider one spin of the wheel in Figure 7(a). For this experiment, $S = \{0, 1, 2, 3, 4, 5, 6, 7, 8, 9\}$. If $A = \{0, 1, 2, 3, 4\}$ and $B = \{5, 7\}$, then $A \cap B = \emptyset$. (See Figure 7(b).) Events A and B are **mutually exclusive** events. If event A occurs, then event B cannot occur, and we have the following definition.

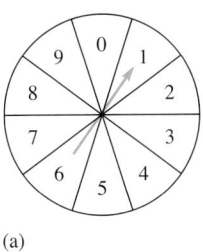

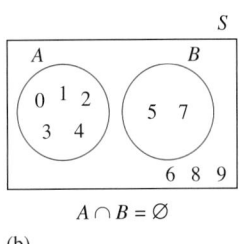

$A \cap B = \emptyset$

(a)   (b)

Figure 7

Definition of Mutually Exclusive Events

Events A and B are **mutually exclusive** if and only if, they have no elements in common; that is, $A \cap B = \emptyset$.

Each outcome in the above sample space $S = \{0, 1, 2, 3, 4, 5, 6, 7, 8, 9\}$ is equally likely. The probability of an event with a single outcome in S is $\frac{1}{10}$. With mutually exclusive events A and B, we write the probability of A or B as $P(A \cup B)$, and have the following:

$$P(A \cup B) = \frac{n(A \cup B)}{n(S)} = \frac{7}{10} = \frac{5+2}{10} = \frac{5}{10} + \frac{2}{10}$$

$$= \frac{n(A)}{n(S)} + \frac{n(B)}{n(S)} = P(A) + P(B)$$

The result developed in this example is true for all mutually exclusive events. In general, we have the following theorem.

Theorem 9-4

If events A and B are mutually exclusive, then $P(A \text{ or } B) = P(A \cup B) = P(A) + P(B)$.

For a sample space with equally likely outcomes, this theorem follows immediately from the fact that if $A \cap B = \emptyset$, then $n(A \cup B) = n(A) + n(B)$.

Complementary Events

If the weather forecaster tells us that the probability of rain is 25%, what is the probability that it will not rain? The two events—rain and not rain—are **complements** of each other. Therefore, if the probability of rain is 25%, or $\frac{1}{4}$, the probability it will not rain is $100\% - 25\% = 75\%$, or $1 - \frac{1}{4} = \frac{3}{4}$. Also $P(\text{no rain}) = 1 - P(\text{rain})$. The two events "rain" and "no rain" are mutually exclusive because if one happens, the other cannot. *Two mutually exclusive events whose union is the sample space are* **complementary events**. If A is an event, the complement of A, written $\overline{A}$, is also an event. For example, consider the event $A = \{2, 4\}$ of tossing a 2 or a 4 using a standard die. The complement of A is the set $\overline{A} = \{1, 3, 5, 6\}$. Because the sample space is $S = \{1, 2, 3, 4, 5, 6\}$, we have $P(A) = \frac{2}{6}$ and $P(\overline{A}) = \frac{4}{6}$. Notice that $P(A) + P(\overline{A}) = \frac{2}{6} + \frac{4}{6} = 1$. This is true in general for any set A and its complement, $\overline{A}$.

Theorem 9-5

If A is an event and $\overline{A}$ is its complement, then

$$P(\overline{A}) = 1 - P(A).$$

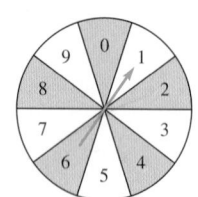

Figure 8

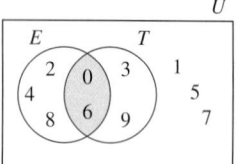

Figure 9

Non-Mutually Exclusive Events

Consider the spinner in Figure 8. Let E be the event of spinning an even number and T the event of spinning a number divisible by 3; that is,

$$E = \{0, 2, 4, 6, 8\}$$
$$T = \{0, 3, 6, 9\}.$$

The event of spinning an even number and a number divisible by 3 is $E \cap T$. Because $E \cap T = \{0, 6\}$, as seen in Figure 9, E and T are not mutually exclusive and $P(E \cup T) \neq P(E) + P(T)$. However, because each outcome is equally likely, we compute the probability of E or T as follows:

$$P(E \cup T) = \frac{n(E \cup T)}{n(S)}$$

Because $E \cup T = \{0, 2, 4, 6, 8, 3, 9\}, n(E \cup T) = 7$. With, $n(S) = 10$, we have $P(E \cup T) = \frac{7}{10}$.

In general, we compute the probability of E or T by using a result from Chapter 2.

$$n(E \cup T) = n(E) + n(T) - n(E \cap T)$$

Therefore, for a sample space with equally likely outcomes,

$$P(E \cup T) = \frac{n(E \cup T)}{n(S)}$$
$$= \frac{n(E) + n(T) - n(E \cap T)}{n(S)}$$
$$= \frac{n(E)}{n(S)} + \frac{n(T)}{n(S)} - \frac{n(E \cap T)}{n(S)}$$
$$= P(E) + P(T) - P(E \cap T).$$

This result, although given for events in a sample space with equally likely outcomes, is true in general. This and other results of probability are summarized next.

Summary of Probability Properties

1. $P(\varnothing) = 0$ (impossible event).
2. $P(S) = 1$, where S is the sample space (certain event).
3. For any event $A, 0 \leq P(A) \leq 1$.
4. If A and B are mutually exclusive events, then $P(A \cup B) = P(A) + P(B)$.
5. If A and B are any events, then $P(A \cup B) = P(A) + P(B) - P(A \cap B)$.
6. If A is an event, then $P(\overline{A}) = 1 - P(A)$.

Example 4

A golf bag contains 2 red tees, 4 blue tees, and 5 white tees.

a. What is the probability of the event R that a tee drawn at random is red?
b. What is the probability of the event "not R," that is, a tee drawn at random is not red?
c. What is the probability of the event that a tee drawn at random is either red (R) or blue (B), that is, $P(R \cup B)$?

Solution

a. Because the bag contains a total of $2 + 4 + 5 = 11$ tees and 2 tees are red, $P(R) = \dfrac{2}{11}$.

b. The bag contains 11 tees and 9 are not red, so the probability of "not R" is $\dfrac{9}{11}$. Observe that

$$P(\overline{R}) = 1 - P(R) = 1 - \dfrac{2}{11} = \dfrac{9}{11}.$$

c. The bag contains 2 red tees and 4 blue tees and $R \cap B = \varnothing$, so $P(R \cup B) = \dfrac{2}{11} + \dfrac{4}{11} = \dfrac{6}{11}$.

Other Views of Probability

On the student page below, events are categorized as "less likely" if the probability of the event is near 0 and "more likely" if the event has probability close to 1.

School Book Page

All probabilities range from 0 to 1. The probability of rolling a 7 on a number cube is 0, so that is an *impossible* event. The probability of rolling a positive integer less than 7 is 1, so that is a *certain* event.

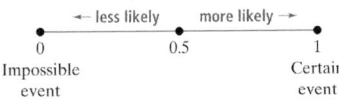

The **complement** of an event is the collection of outcomes not contained in the event. The sum of the probabilities of an event and its complement is 1. So $P(\text{event}) + P(\text{not event}) = 1$.

EXAMPLES   **Finding Probabilities From 0 to 1**

2 **Clothes** The picture shows the jeans in Juanita's closet. She selects a pair of jeans with her eyes shut. Find $P(\text{dark color})$.

There are 8 possible outcomes. Since there are 3 black pairs and 2 blue pairs, the event *dark color* has 5 favorable outcomes.

$$P(\text{dark color}) = \dfrac{5}{8} \quad \begin{array}{l} \leftarrow \text{number of favorable outcomes} \\ \leftarrow \text{total number of possible outcomes} \end{array}$$

3 Refer to Juanita's closet. Find $P(\text{red})$.

The event *red* has no favorable outcome.

$$P(\text{red}) = \dfrac{0}{8}, \text{ or } 0 \quad \begin{array}{l} \leftarrow \text{number of favorable outcomes} \\ \leftarrow \text{total number of possible outcomes} \end{array}$$

4 Refer to Juanita's closet. Find $P(\text{not dark color})$.

$$P(\text{dark color}) + P(\text{not dark color}) = 1 \quad \leftarrow \begin{array}{l} \text{The sum of probabilities of an} \\ \text{event and its complement is 1.} \end{array}$$

$$\dfrac{5}{8} + P(\text{not dark color}) = 1 \quad \leftarrow \text{Substitute } \tfrac{5}{8} \text{ for } P(\text{dark color}).$$

$$\dfrac{5}{8} - \dfrac{5}{8} + P(\text{not dark color}) = 1 - \dfrac{5}{8} \quad \leftarrow \begin{array}{l} \text{Subtract } \tfrac{5}{8} \text{ from} \\ \text{each side.} \end{array}$$

$$P(\text{not dark color}) = \dfrac{3}{8} \quad \leftarrow \text{Simplify.}$$

Also on the student page, the probability of an event is the ratio of the "number of favorable outcomes" compared to the "total number of possible outcomes."

Alternative Definition of Probability of an Event from Sample Space with Equally Likely Outcomes

$$P(\text{event}) = \frac{\text{number of favorable outcomes}}{\text{total number of possible outcomes}}$$

Geometric Probability (Area Models)

A probability model that uses geometric shapes is an **area model**. When area models are used to determine probabilities geometrically, outcomes are associated with points chosen at random in a geometric region that represents a sample space. This process is referred to as finding **geometric probabilities**.

Suppose we throw darts at a square target 2 units long on a side and divided into 4 congruent triangles, as shown in Figure 10. If the dart must hit the target somewhere and no part of the square is favored, what is the probability of the event that the dart will land in the shaded region? The entire target, which has an area of $2 \cdot 2 = 4$ square units, represents the sample space. The shaded area is the event of a successful toss. The area of the shaded part is $\frac{1}{4}$ of the sample space. The probability of the dart's landing in the shaded region is the ratio of the area of the event to the area of the sample space, or $\frac{1}{4}$. In general when computing the probability of an event geometrically, we find the ratio of the area of the region representing an event to the area of the region representing the sample space.

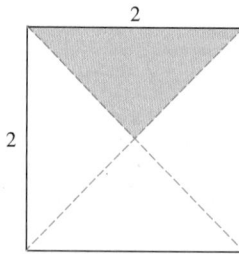

Figure 10

Example 5

Design a geometric model for the following experiments.

 a. Tossing a fair coin
 b. Rolling a fair die

Solution   Answers may vary on the geometric models chosen.

 a. Because we expect a fair coin to have $P(H) = \frac{1}{2} = P(T)$, one model might be to create a square spinner divided into parts of equal area by a diagonal as in Figure 11. The spin models the coin toss.

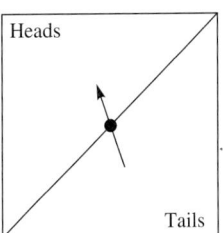

Figure 11

b. Because we expect the sides of a fair die to be equilikely when it is tossed, we might model it with a regular hexagonal spinner constructed of six equilateral triangles as shown in Figure 12. The spin models a roll of the die.

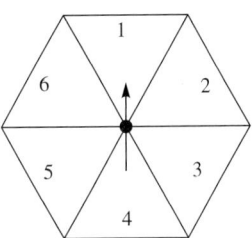

Figure 12

Assessment 9-1A

1. Consider the experiment of drawing a single card from a standard deck of 52 cards and determine which are uniform sample spaces, that is, sample spaces with equally likely outcomes.
   a. {face card, not face card} No
   b. {club, diamond, heart, spade} Yes
   c. {black, red} Yes
   d. {king, queen, jack, ace, even-numbered card, odd-numbered card} No

2. Is it likely that a number drawn from the first 1000 whole numbers is not a natural number? Explain your answer. *

3. Each letter of the alphabet is written on a separate piece of paper and placed in a box and then one piece is drawn at random.
   a. What is the probability that the selected piece of paper has a vowel written on it? (Assume *y* is not a vowel.)
   b. What is the probability that it has a consonant written on it?
   c. What is the probability that the paper has a vowel on it or a letter from the word *probability*? $\frac{11}{26}$

4. The spinner shown is spun.

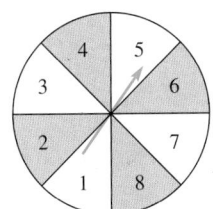

Find the probability of each of the following events.
   a. *A*: the number is a factor of 35
   b. *B*: the number is a multiple of 3
   c. *C*: the number is even
   d. *D*: the number is 6 or 2
   e. *E*: the number is 11
   f. *F*: the number is composite
   g. *G*: the number is neither a prime nor a composite $\frac{1}{8}$

5. A card is selected from an ordinary deck of 52 cards. Find the probabilities of the following events.
   a. Red card $\frac{1}{2}$
   b. Face card $\frac{3}{13}$
   c. Red card or a 10 $\frac{7}{13}$
   d. Queen $\frac{1}{13}$
   e. Not a queen $\frac{12}{13}$
   f. Face card or a club $\frac{11}{26}$
   g. Face card and a club $\frac{3}{52}$
   h. Not a face card and not a club $\frac{15}{26}$

6. Suppose a drawer contains six black socks, four brown socks, and two green socks. We draw one sock from the drawer and it is equally likely that any one of the socks is drawn. Find the probabilities of the events in parts (a–d).
   a. Sock is brown $\frac{1}{3}$
   b. Sock is either black or green $\frac{2}{3}$
   c. Sock is red 0
   d. Sock is not black $\frac{1}{2}$
   e. We reach into the drawer without looking to pull out four socks. What is the probability that we get at least two socks of the same color?

7. Riena has six unmarked files on her computer, one file dedicated to each of English, mathematics, French, American history, chemistry, and computer science.
  a. If she chooses a file at random, what is the probability of the event that she chooses the English file? $\frac{1}{6}$
  b. What is the probability of the event that she chooses a file that is neither mathematics nor chemistry? $\frac{2}{3}$

8. According to a weather report, there is a 30% chance it will rain tomorrow.
  a. Design a geometric model for this probability.   *
  b. What is the probability of the event that it will not rain tomorrow? Explain your answer.   *

9. A set of dolls is in a packing crate: 17 with blond hair, 13 with black hair, and 12 with red hair. If one doll is drawn at random from the crate, what is the probability that the doll's hair is not red? $\frac{5}{7}$

10. The plays generally considered the tragedies by William Shakespeare are *Antony and Cleopatra, Coriolanus, Hamlet, Julius Caesar, King Lear, Macbeth, Othello, Romeo and Juliet, Timon of Athens,* and *Titus Andronicus.* Find the probabilities of the events shown.
  a. The title of the play contains the word "King" $\frac{1}{10}$
  b. The title of the play begins with the letter "T" $\frac{1}{5}$
  c. The title of the play contains the letter "Q"   0
  d. The title of the play contains the names of two people $\frac{1}{5}$

11. In the children's song "Old MacDonald Had a Farm," what is the probability of choosing an "*o*" from all the letters in the five vowel refrain "*e-i-e-i-o*"? $\frac{1}{5}$

12. In Sentinel High School, there are 350 freshmen, 320 sophomores, 310 juniors, and 400 seniors. If a student is chosen at random from the student body to represent the school, what is the probability of the event that the chosen student is a freshman? $\frac{35}{138}$

13. If *A* and *B* are mutually exclusive, $P(A) = 0.3$, and $P(B) = 0.4$, what is $P(A \cup B)$?   0.7

14. A calculus class is composed of 35 men and 45 women. There are 20 business majors, 30 biology majors, 10 computer science majors, and 20 mathematics majors. No person has a double major. If a single student is chosen from the class, what is the probability of the event that the student is
  a. female? $\frac{9}{16}$
  b. a computer science major? $\frac{1}{8}$
  c. not a mathematics major? $\frac{3}{4}$
  d. a computer science major or a mathematics major? $\frac{3}{8}$

15. A box contains five white balls, three black balls, and two red balls.
  a. If only red balls are added to the box, how many must be added so that the probability of the event of drawing a red ball is $\frac{3}{4}$?   22
  b. If only black balls are added to the original box, how many balls must be added so that the probability of the event of drawing a white ball is $\frac{1}{4}$?   10

16. Zoe is playing a game in which she draws one ball from one of the boxes shown. She wins if she draws a white ball from either box #1 or box #2. She says that in order to maximize her chances of winning she will always pick box #2 because it has more white balls. Is she correct? Why?   *

#1   #2

17. If you flipped a fair coin 15 times and got 15 heads, what is the probability of the event of getting a head on the 16th toss? Explain your answer.   *

18. Consider the letters in the word *numbers.* If one letter is drawn at random, find the probabilities of the events listed below.
  a. Letter is a vowel. $\frac{2}{7}$
  b. Letter is a consonant. $\frac{5}{7}$

19. A witness identified all the digits on a license plate except the rightmost one. If the witness guesses at random what that digit is, what is the probability that the witness is correct? $\frac{1}{10}$

20. The line with the smallest type on an eye chart typically has nine letters. On many of these lines, there is exactly one vowel. If the letter were randomly assigned, what is the probability of the event that the first letter in the line with the smallest type is a vowel? $\frac{1}{9}$

21. The experimental probability of rolling a 4 on a single die was obtained by rolling the die 100 times and obtaining 24 4s. What is the numerical difference between this experimental probability and the theoretical probability of rolling a 4 when the die is tossed once? $\frac{11}{150}$

22. How many times would you expect to obtain a 4 on a roll of a die if you rolled it 1000 times?   About 167

Assessment 9-1B

1. When a thumbtack is dropped, it will land point up (⊥) or point down (⋏). This experiment was repeated 80 times with the following results: point up: 56 times; point down: 24 times.
  a. What is the experimental probability that the thumbtack will land point up? $\frac{7}{10}$
  b. What is the experimental probability that the thumbtack will land point down? $\frac{3}{10}$
  c. If you were to try this experiment another 80 times, would you get the same results? Why?   *

  d. Would you expect to get nearly the same results on a second trial? Why?   *

2. An experiment consists of selecting the rightmost digit of a telephone number from a telephone book. Assume that each of the 10 digits is equally likely to appear as this digit. List each of the following sets in parts a–d.
  a. The sample space   {0, 1, 2, 3, 4, 5, 6, 7, 8, 9}
  b. The event consisting of outcomes for which the digit is less than 5   {0, 1, 2, 3, 4}

c. The event consisting of outcomes for which the digit is odd   {1, 3, 5, 7, 9}

d. The event consisting of outcomes for which the digit is not 2   {0, 1, 3, 4, 5, 6, 7, 8, 9}

e. Find the probability of each of the events in (b) through (d). $\frac{1}{2}, \frac{1}{2}, \frac{9}{10}$

3. The name of a member of the U.S. Congress is drawn at random. Which is more likely: drawing a member of the House of Representatives or a member of the Senate? Why?   *

4. In the United States, if a person is chosen at random, the probability is about $\frac{3}{4}$ that the person has corrected vision. If the United States has about 300 million people, about how many have corrected vision?   225 million

5. In a refrigerator there are 16 bottles of diet soda, 8 bottles of regular soda, and 4 bottles of water. Find the probabilities for the events listed below.

a. Choosing a bottle of diet soda when a bottle is chosen at random $\frac{4}{7}$

b. Choosing a bottle of regular soda when a bottle is chosen at random $\frac{2}{7}$

c. Choosing a bottle of water when a bottle is chosen at random $\frac{1}{7}$

6. A bag contains n cards, each having a natural number less than or equal to n written on it, with each number being used once. The probability of drawing a card with a number less than or equal to 10 is $\frac{4}{10}$. How many cards are in the bag?   25

7. Determine whether each player has an equal chance of winning each of the following games.

a. Toss a fair coin. If a head appears, I win; if a tail appears, you lose.   No

b. Toss a fair coin. If a head appears, I win; otherwise, you win.   Yes

c. Toss a fair die numbered 1 through 6. If 1 appears, I win; if 6 appears, you win.   Yes

d. Toss a fair die numbered 1 through 6. If an even number appears, I win; if an odd number appears, you win.   Yes

e. Toss a fair die numbered 1 through 6. If a number greater than or equal to 3 appears, I win; otherwise, you win.   No

f. Toss two fair dice numbered 1 through 6. If a 1 appears on each die, I win; if a 6 appears on each die, you win.   Yes

g. Toss two fair dice numbered 1 through 6. If the sum is 3, I win; if the sum is 2, you win.   No

8. In each of the following scenarios, sketch a single spinner with the given characteristics.

a. The outcomes M, A, T, and H are each equally likely.   *

b. The outcomes are R, A, and T with $P(R) = \frac{3}{4}$, $P(A) = \frac{1}{8}$, and $P(T) = \frac{1}{8}$.   *

9. In the game of "Between," two cards are dealt and not replaced in the deck. You then pick a third card from the deck. To win, you must pick a card that has a value between the other two cards. The order of values is 2, 3, 4, 5, 6, 7, 8, 9, 10, J, Q, K, A, where the letters represent a jack, queen, king, and ace, respectively. Determine the probability of your winning if the first two cards dealt are the following.

a. 5 and jack. $\frac{2}{5}$

b. 2 and king. $\frac{4}{5}$

c. 5 and 6.   0

10. Let the universal set, U, be the set of students at Central High, A be the set of students taking algebra, and C be the set of students taking chemistry. If a student is selected at random, describe in words what is meant by each of the following probabilities.

a. $P(A \cup C)$ The probability of a student taking algebra or chemistry

b. $P(A \cap C)$ The probability of a student taking algebra and chemistry

c. $1 - P(C)$ The probability of a student not taking chemistry

11. A box contains 25% black balls and 75% white balls. The same number of black balls as were in the box are added (so the new number of black balls is twice the original number). A ball is now drawn from the box at random. What is the probability of the event that the ball chosen is black? $\frac{2}{5}$

12. A teacher gave students three questions and wrote that she would randomly choose one of the three questions for an exam. If Harry prepared for only one of the questions, what is the probability that he did not study for the question that the teacher put on the exam? $\frac{2}{3}$

13. Nanci has 15 files in a filing cabinet labeled A, B, C, . . . O, one file per label. If she chooses one file at random, find the probabilities for the following events.

a. A file with the label B $\frac{1}{15}$

b. A file not labeled B $\frac{14}{15}$

14. Suppose we have a box containing five white balls, three black balls, and two red balls. Is it possible to add the same number of balls of each color to the box so that when a ball is drawn at random, the probability of the event that it is a black ball is the following? Explain.

a. $\frac{1}{3}$ *

b. 0.32   *

15. Sylvia decided to model the probability of the birth of a boy or a girl by spinning a spinner with the numbers 1–7 on the seven equally divided sectors of the spinner. Suppose the birth of a boy is represented by spinning an odd number and a girl is represented by spinning an even number. If the chance of the birth of a boy is approximately equal to the chance for the birth of a girl, explain whether the spinner described is a good tool to simulate the birth.   *

16. Describe each of the following events as likely or unlikely in 2014.

a. The probability that a current U.S. Supreme Court Justice chosen at random is a man.   Likely

b. The probability that a current member of the U.S. Senate chosen at random is African-American.   Unlikely

17. You have the choice of flipping a fair coin and winning a game when heads appear, or you can roll a single standard die and you win if an even number appears. Explain why the choice of coin or die does not matter in regard to your winning.   Both winning events have probability $\frac{1}{2}$

18. If you are choosing one state at random, are you more likely to choose a state whose name begins with a consonant or a vowel? What is the probability of each?   *

19. What is the probability of choosing a continent at random whose name does not start with a vowel? $\frac{2}{7}$

20. If you are doing a traffic survey looking at the types and ages of cars on the road today, how would you describe the probability of seeing a car built before 1940: likely or unlikely?   Unlikely

21. The experimental probability of rolling a 6 on a single die was obtained by rolling the die 100 times and obtaining 16 6s.

What is the numerical difference between this probability and the theoretical probability of rolling a 6 when the die is tossed once?   *

22. How many times would you expect to obtain a 6 on a roll of a die if you rolled it 1000 times?   About 167

Mathematical Connections 9-1

Answers to Mathematical Connections can be found in the Answers section at the back of the book.

Reasoning

1. Explain whether you think that when dialing a seven-digit phone number without its area code, each digit 0–9 has an equal chance of being chosen as the lead number.

2. Events A and B are from the same sample space, and $P(A) = 0.8$ and $P(B) = 0.9$. Explain whether events A and B can be mutually exclusive.

3. Bobbie says that when she shoots a free throw in basketball, she will either make it or miss it. Because there are only two outcomes and one of them is making a basket, Bobbie claims the probability of her making a free throw is $\frac{1}{2}$. Explain whether Bobbie's reasoning is correct.

4. Consider a page of a newspaper as a sample of letters in the English language, and choose one letter at random. Which letter do you expect to have the highest probability of being chosen? Why?

5. If a die is thrown 1000 times and a 6 appears on each toss, explain whether you believe the die is fair.

Open-Ended

6. Prepare a card with the numbers printed on it as shown.

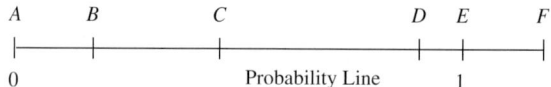

Show the card to 10 people and ask each of them to pick a single digit listed on the card and tell you what number they picked. Record the results. Pool the results with 4 other people and answer the following questions.

a. What is the probability of selecting a 3 from the card if the choice was made at random?

b. Based on the data you gathered, what is the experimental probability of selecting a 3 based on the sample of 10? Based on the sample of 50?

c. Why might the theoretical probability based on the assumption that the choice was made at random not agree with the experimental probability?

d. Conjecture what will happen if the numbers 1, 2, 3, 4, 5 are printed on the card and a similar experiment is repeated. Test the conjecture.

7. Select any book, go to the first complete paragraph in it, and count the number of words the paragraph has. Now count the number of words that start with a vowel. If the paragraph has fewer than 100 words, continue to count words until there are more than 100 words from the start. What is the experimental probability that a word chosen at random from the book starts with a vowel? Open the book to any page and

choose a paragraph with more than 100 words. Count the words. Predict how many words in the paragraph start with a vowel, and then count to see how close the prediction is.

8. List three real-world situations that do not involve weather or gambling where probability might be used.

9. If possible, for each of the following letters, describe an event, that has the approximate probability marked by the letter on the probability line.

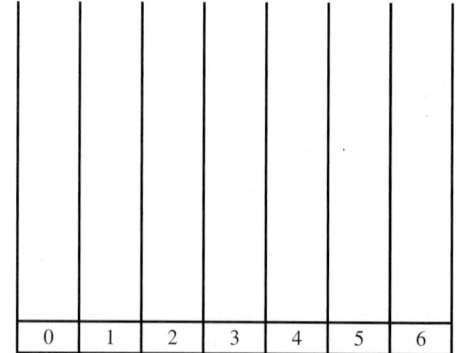

Cooperative Learning

10. Form groups of three or four students. Each group has a pair of dice. Each player needs 18 markers and a sheet of paper with a gameboard drawn on it similar to the following gameboard.

At the beginning of each game, each player places his or her markers on the boards in any arrangement above the numbers. Two players then take turns rolling the dice. The result of each roll is the positive difference between the greater and the smaller of the two numbers. All players who have a marker on the number that represents the difference can remove one marker. Only one marker can be removed each roll. The first player to remove all of the markers is the winner. The game may be stopped if it is clear that there can be no winner.

a. Play the game twice. What differences seem to occur most often? Least often?

b. Roll the dice 20 times and record how often the various differences occur. Using this information, explain how to distribute the 18 markers to win.

c. Compute the theoretical probabilities for each possible difference.

d. Use the answers to (c) to explain how to arrange the markers to obtain the best chance of winning.

11. The following game is played with two players and a single fair die numbered 1 through 6. The die is rolled and one person receives a score that is the square of the number appearing on the die. The other person will receive a score of 4 times the value showing on the die. The person with the greater score wins.

  a. Play the game several times to see if it appears to be a *fair game*, that is, a game in which each player has an equal chance of winning.

  b. Determine if this is a fair game. If it is not fair, who has the advantage? Explain the answer.

12. Complete the following activities.

  a. Suppose a paper cup is tossed in the air. The different ways it can land are shown below. Toss a cup 100 times and record each result. From this information, calculate the experimental probability of each outcome. Do the outcomes appear to be equally likely? Using experimental probabilities, predict how many times the cup will land on its side if tossed 100 times.

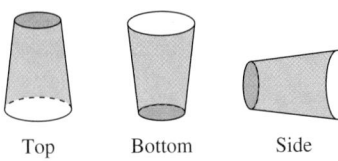

Top   Bottom   Side

  b. Toss a fair coin 200 times and record the results. From this information, calculate the experimental probability of getting heads on a particular toss. Does the experimental result agree with the expected theoretical probability of $\frac{1}{2}$?

  c. Hold a coin upright on its edge under your forefinger on a hard surface and then spin it with your other finger so that it spins before landing. Repeat this experiment 100 times and calculate the experimental probability of the coin's landing on heads on a particular spin. Compare your experimental probabilities with those in part (b).

Connecting Mathematics to the Classroom

13. A student claims that if a fair coin is tossed and comes up heads 5 times in a row, then, according to the law of averages, the probability of tails on the next toss is greater than the probability of heads. What is your reply?

14. A student observes the following spinner and claims that the color red has the highest probability of appearing, since there are two red areas on the spinner. What is your reply?

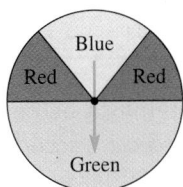

15. A student tosses a coin 3 times, and a head appears each time. The student concludes that the coin is not fair. What is your response?

16. A student wonders why probabilities cannot be negative. What is your response?

17. A student claims that "if the probability of an event is $\frac{3}{5}$, then there are three ways the event can occur and only five elements in the sample space." How do you respond?

18. Joe claims that if the following spinner is spun 100 times, the number 4 will occur most often because the greatest area of the spinner is covered by the number 4. What would you tell Joe about his conjecture? What is the probability that a 4 will occur on any spin?

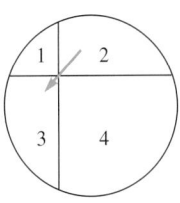

19. Suppose the figure in exercise 14 is a dartboard with no spinner. Would you expect each color space to have the same probability of being hit with a dart on a random throw? Explain your answer.

20. Mari argues that if one chooses a page at random from a typical English language dictionary, the probability of choosing a page with words that begin with the letter Q is $\frac{1}{26}$ because there are 26 letters in the alphabet. How might you respond?

National Assessments

National Assessment of Educational Progress (NAEP) Questions

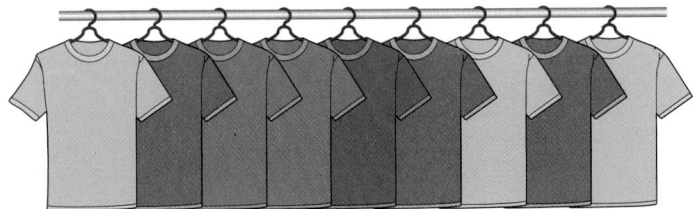

Mark has nine shirts in his closet as shown.

If Mark picks a shirt out of the closet without looking, which two colors have the greatest chance of being picked?

A. Blue and purple   B. Green and blue
C. Red and blue   D. Red and green

NAEP, Grade 4, 2013

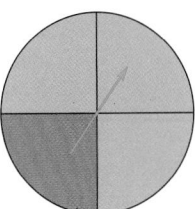

Ms. Livingston's class spins the arrow on the spinner 92 times. Of the following, which is the most likely result?

A. 66 green, 26 blue   B. 46 green, 46 blue
C. 23 green, 69 blue   D. 2 green, 90 blue

NAEP, Grade 4, 2013

Each of the 6 faces of a certain cube is labeled either R or S. When the cube is tossed, the probability of the cube landing with an R face up is $\frac{1}{3}$.

How many faces are labeled R?
A. Five
B. Four
C. Three
D. Two
E. One

NAEP, Grade 8, 2005

A bag contains two red candies and one yellow candy. Kim takes out one candy and eats it, and then Jeff takes out one candy. For

each sentence below, fill in the circle to indicate whether it is possible or not possible.

Possible	Not Possible	
○	○	Kim's candy is red and Jeff's candy is red.
○	○	Kim's candy is red and Jeff's candy is yellow.
○	○	Kim's candy is yellow and Jeff's candy is red.
○	○	Kim's candy is yellow and Jeff's candy is yellow.

NAEP, Grade 8, 1996

9-2 Multistage Experiments and Modeling Games

In Section 9-1, we considered **one-stage experiments** completed in one step. For example, drawing one ball at random from the box containing a red, white, and green ball in Figure 13(a) is a one-stage experiment. A tree diagram for this experiment is shown in Figure 13(b).

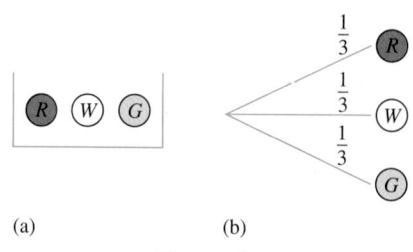

(a)   (b)

Figure 13

CCSS According to the grade 7 *Common Core Standards*, students should be able to:

Find probabilities of compound events using organized lists, tables, tree diagrams, and simulation.

a. Understand that, just as with simple events, the probability of a compound event is the fraction of outcomes in the sample space for which the compound event occurs.
b. Represent sample spaces for compound events using methods such as organized lists, tables, and tree diagrams. For an event described in everyday language (e.g., "rolling double sixes"), identify the outcomes in the sample space which compose the event. (p. 51)

Next we consider **multistage experiments**. For example, a ball is drawn from the box in Figure 13(a) and its color is recorded. Then the ball is *replaced*, a second ball is drawn, and its color is recorded. A tree diagram for this two-stage experiment is given in Figure 14. The tree diagram can be used to generate the sample space { *RR, RW, RG, WR, WW, WG, GR, GW, GG* }.

Each of the outcomes in the sample space is equally likely and there are nine total outcomes, so the probability of the event containing each separate outcome is $\frac{1}{9}$.

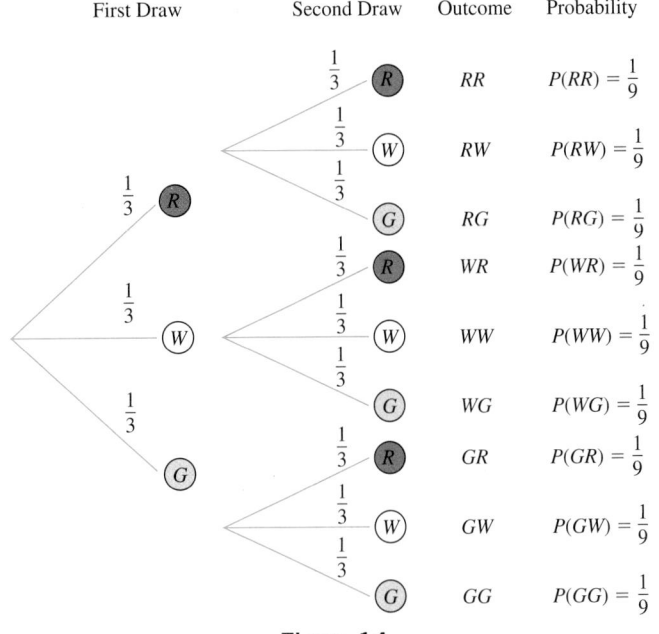

Figure 14

Tree diagrams are useful in determining probabilities. Using the tree diagram of Figure 14 to determine the probability of choosing a white ball (W) on the first draw and a red ball (R) on the second draw, we expect to obtain $W\frac{1}{3}$ of the time on the first draw. Then of that $\frac{1}{3}$ of the time that we obtain W, we expect to obtain $R\frac{1}{3}$ of the time. That is, we expect $\left(\frac{1}{3}\right)\left(\frac{1}{3}\right) = \frac{1}{9}$ of the time to obtain WR as an outcome of the two draws. The other probabilities at the far right side of the tree are obtained similarly.

Example 6

Use the tree diagram in Figure 14 to obtain the probabilities of

  a. obtaining GR.
  b. obtaining either GR or RG.
  c. obtaining R on the second draw.

Solution

  a. $P(GR) = \dfrac{1}{3} \cdot \dfrac{1}{3} = \dfrac{1}{9}$

  b. $P(GR \text{ or } RG) = \dfrac{1}{9} + \dfrac{1}{9} = \dfrac{2}{9}$

  c. $P(R \text{ on the second draw}) = \dfrac{1}{9} + \dfrac{1}{9} + \dfrac{1}{9} = \dfrac{3}{9} = \dfrac{1}{3}$

Observe that in Example 6(c), the probability of obtaining a R on the second draw does not depend on the first draw. The same probability could have been obtained only by looking at the second draw where $P(R) = \dfrac{1}{3}$.

An alternative way to generate the sample space is to use a table, as shown in Table 2.

Table 2			
		Second Draw	
	R	**W**	**G**
R	RR	RW	RG
W	WR	WW	WG
G	GR	GW	GG

First Draw appears to the left of the R, W, G row labels.

▶ **NOW TRY THIS 2**

1. Use the tree diagram in Figure 14 to determine the probability of each of the following events when two balls are drawn with replacement from the box.

   a. Both balls are red. $\frac{1}{9}$
   b. No ball is red. $\frac{4}{9}$
   c. At least one ball is red. $\frac{5}{9}$
   d. At most one ball is red. $\frac{8}{9}$
   e. Both balls are the same color. $\frac{1}{3}$

2. Answer each part of question 1 using Table 2.   The answers are the same as in part 1.

Example 7

Suppose we toss a fair coin 3 times and record the results in order. Find the

   a. sample space for this experiment.
   b. event A of tossing 2 heads and 1 tail.
   c. event B of tossing no tails.
   d. event C of tossing a head on the last toss.

Solution
   a. $S = \{HHH, HHT, HTH, HTT, THH, TTT, TTH, THT\}$
   b. $A = \{HHT, HTH, THH\}$
   c. $B = \{HHH\}$
   d. $C = \{HHH, HTH, THH, TTH\}$

  The previous quote from *Common Core Standards* mentions the event of "rolling double sixes" when rolling a pair of fair dice. We can think of this as a two-stage experiment. We explore various probabilities in Example 8.

Example 8

A pair of *fair* dice is rolled. Find the probability of each of the following events.

   a. Event A—rolling double sixes.
   b. Event B—rolling a sum of 7 or 11.

Solution   To solve this problem, we use the strategy of *making a table*. Figure 15(a) shows all possible outcomes of tossing the dice. We know that there are 6 possible results from tossing the first die and 6 possible results from tossing the second die, so by the Fundamental Counting Principle (Chapter 2), there are $6 \cdot 6 = 36$ entries.

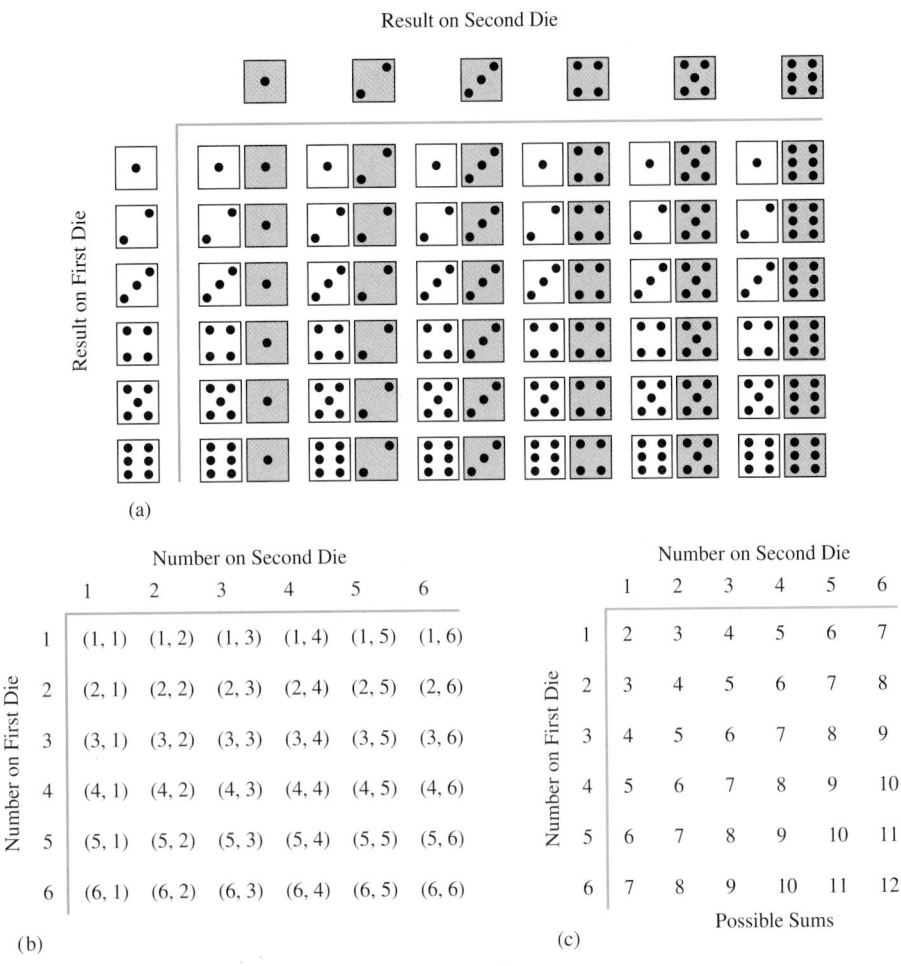

Figure 15

a. In Figure 15(a) we see that event A, "double sixes," appears only one time out of 36 possible outcomes. Therefore $P(A) = \dfrac{1}{36}$.

b. It may be easier to read the results when they are recorded as ordered pairs, as in Figure 15(b), where the first component represents the number on the first die and the second component represents the number on the second die. We show the possible sums from rolling the pair of dice in Figure 15(c). In Figure 15(c), we see that a sum of 7 appears 6 times. Hence, the event "a sum of 7" arises from the following subset of the set of ordered pairs in Figure 15(b):

$$\{(6, 1), (5, 2), (4, 3), (3, 4), (2, 5), (1, 6)\}$$

Each outcome in this set is equally likely and hence, $P(\text{a sum of } 7) = \dfrac{6}{36}$. Similarly, P(a sum of 11) $= \dfrac{2}{36}$. The probabilities of each of the possible sums can be calculated in the same way. From Figure 15(c), the sample space for the experiment "roll the pair of dice and record the sum" is $\{2, 3, 4, 5, 6, 7, 8, 9, 10, 11, 12\}$, but the sample space is not uniform (the probabilities of the given sums are not equal). A **probability distribution** as in Table 3 summarizes these probabilities.

Table 3

Outcome	2	3	4	5	6	7	8	9	10	11	12
Probability	$\dfrac{1}{36}$	$\dfrac{2}{36}$	$\dfrac{3}{36}$	$\dfrac{4}{36}$	$\dfrac{5}{36}$	$\dfrac{6}{36}$	$\dfrac{5}{36}$	$\dfrac{4}{36}$	$\dfrac{3}{36}$	$\dfrac{2}{36}$	$\dfrac{1}{36}$

The probability of event B "rolling a sum of 7 or 11" is given by $P(B) = P(\text{sum of 7 or sum of 11}) = P(\text{sum of 7}) + P(\text{sum of 11}) = \dfrac{6}{36} + \dfrac{2}{36} = \dfrac{8}{36} = \dfrac{2}{9}.$

A fair pair of dice is rolled and the sum recorded. Let E be the event of rolling a sum that is an even number and F the event of rolling a sum that is a prime number. Find the probability of rolling a sum that is even *or* prime, that is, $P(E \cup F)$.

Solution   To solve this problem, we use Table 3. Note that $E \cup F = \{2, 4, 6, 8, 10, 12, 3, 5, 7, 11\}$. Therefore, we have

$$P(E \cup F) = P(2) + P(4) + P(6) + P(8) + P(10) + P(12) + P(3)$$
$$+ P(5) + P(7) + P(11)$$
$$= \frac{1}{36} + \frac{3}{36} + \frac{5}{36} + \frac{5}{36} + \frac{3}{36} + \frac{1}{36} + \frac{2}{36} + \frac{4}{36} + \frac{6}{36} + \frac{2}{36}$$
$$= \frac{32}{36} = \frac{8}{9}.$$

Another approach is to use a property of probabilities. We know that events E and F are not mutually exclusive because $E = \{2, 4, 6, 8, 10, 12\}$, $F = \{2, 3, 5, 7, 11\}$, and $E \cap F = \{2\}$. Therefore,

$$P(E \cup F) = P(E) + P(F) - P(E \cap F)$$
$$= \frac{18}{36} + \frac{15}{36} - \frac{1}{36}$$
$$= \frac{32}{36} = \frac{8}{9}.$$

A third approach to finding $P(E \cup F)$ is to find $P(\overline{E \cup F})$ and subtract this probability from 1. Because $E \cup F = \{2, 3, 4, 5, 6, 7, 8, 10, 11, 12\}$, then $\overline{E \cup F} = \{9\}$ and $P(\overline{E \cup F}) = \dfrac{4}{36}$. Hence,

$$P(E \cup F) = 1 - P(\overline{E \cup F}) = 1 - \frac{4}{36} = \frac{32}{36} = \frac{8}{9}.$$

More Multistage Experiments

The box in Figure 16(a) contains one black ball and two white balls. If a ball is drawn at random from the box and the color recorded, a tree diagram for the experiment is shown in Figure 16(b). Because each ball has the same chance of being drawn, we combine the branches and obtain the tree diagram shown in Figure 16(c). Combining branches in this way is a common practice because it simplifies tree diagrams.

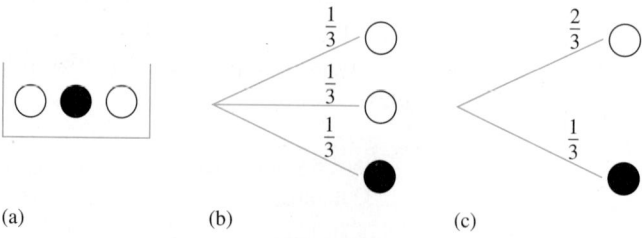

(a)   (b)   (c)

Figure 16

Suppose a ball is drawn at random from the box in Figure 16(a) and its color recorded. The ball is then *replaced*, and a second ball is drawn and its color recorded. The sample space for this two-stage experiment may be recorded using ordered pairs as $\{(\bullet, \bullet), (\bullet, \bigcirc), (\bigcirc, \bullet), (\bigcirc, \bigcirc)\}$ or, more commonly, as $\{\bullet\bullet, \bullet\bigcirc, \bigcirc\bullet, \bigcirc\bigcirc\}$, as shown in the tree diagram in Figure 17.

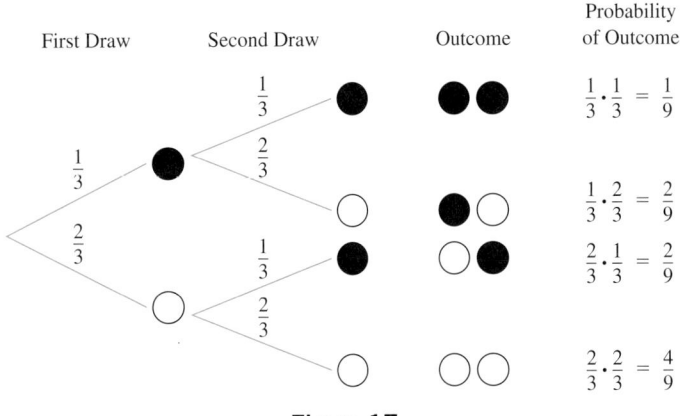

Figure 17

To assign the probability of the outcomes in this experiment, consider the path for the outcome $\bullet\bigcirc$. In the first draw, the probability of the event of obtaining a black ball is $\frac{1}{3}$. Then, the probability of obtaining a white ball in the second draw is $\frac{2}{3}$. Thus, we expect to obtain a black ball on the first draw $\frac{1}{3}$ of the time, and then on the second draw to obtain a white ball $\frac{2}{3}$ of those times that we obtained a black ball on the first draw; that is, $\frac{2}{3}$ of $\frac{1}{3}$, or $\frac{2}{3} \cdot \frac{1}{3}$. This product can be obtained by multiplying the probabilities along the branches used for the path leading to $\bullet\bigcirc$; that is, $\frac{1}{3} \cdot \frac{2}{3} = \frac{2}{9}$. The probabilities shown in Figure 17 are obtained by following the paths leading to each of the four outcomes and multiplying the probabilities along the paths. The sum of the probabilities on all the branches from any point always equals 1, and the sum of the probabilities for all the possible outcomes must also be 1. This procedure is an instance of the following general theorem.

Theorem 9-6: Multiplication Rule for Probabilities for Tree Diagrams
For all multistage experiments, the probability of the outcome along any path of a tree diagram is equal to the product of all the probabilities along the path.

Look again at the box pictured in Figure 16(a). This time, suppose two balls are drawn one-by-one *without replacement*. A tree diagram for this experiment, along with the set of possible outcomes, is shown in Figure 18. The branch showing the second draw, with probability $\frac{0}{2}$, is added here for completeness. As seen later, the branch could be deleted, as could any unneeded branches of a tree diagram. Compare this figure to the one in Figure 18. How are they different?

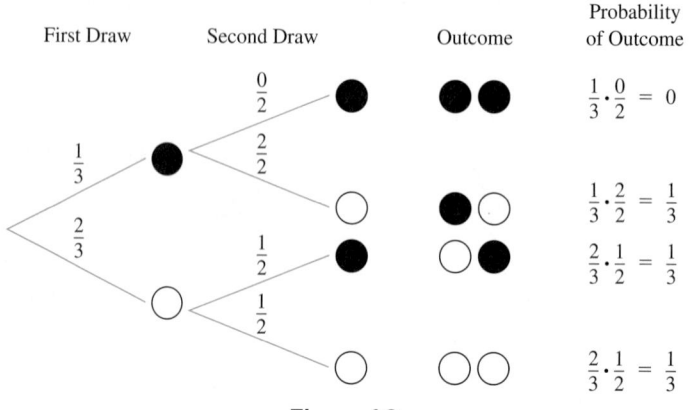

Figure 18

The denominators of the fractions in the second draw are all 2. Because the draws are made without replacement, only two balls remain for the second draw.

Consider event A, consisting of the outcomes for drawing exactly one black ball in the two draws without replacement. This event is given by $A = \{\bullet\bigcirc, \bigcirc\bullet\}$. Since the outcome $\bullet\bigcirc$ appears $\frac{1}{3}$ of the time, and the outcome $\bigcirc\bullet$ appears $\frac{1}{3}$ of the time, then either $\bullet\bigcirc$ or $\bigcirc\bullet$ will appear $\frac{2}{3}$ of the time. Thus, $P(A) = \frac{1}{3} + \frac{1}{3} = \frac{2}{3}$.

Event B, consisting of outcomes for drawing *at least* one black ball, could be recorded as $B = \{\bullet\bigcirc, \bigcirc\bullet, \bullet\bullet\}$. Because $P(\bullet\bigcirc) = \frac{1}{3}, P(\bigcirc\bullet) = \frac{1}{3}$, and $P(\bullet\bullet) = 0$, we have $P(B) = \frac{1}{3} + \frac{1}{3} + 0 = \frac{2}{3}$. Because $\overline{B} = \{\bigcirc\bigcirc\}$ and $P(\overline{B}) = \frac{1}{3}$, the probability of B could have been computed as follows: $P(B) = 1 - P(\overline{B}) = 1 - \frac{1}{3} = \frac{2}{3}$.

Independent Events

![hand] Activity Manual

Use *Pascal's Probabilities* to find theoretical probabilities for independent events using tree diagrams and Pascal's triangle.

In Figure 18, the fact that the first ball was not replaced affects the probability of the color of the second ball drawn. When the occurrence or nonoccurrence of event A has no influence on the outcome of event B, the events A and B are **independent**. For example, if two coins are flipped and if event E_1 is obtaining a head on the first coin and E_2 is obtaining a tail on the second coin, then E_1 and E_2 are independent events because one event has no influence on the second. Figure 19(a) depicts a tree diagram for flipping the coins. In Figure 19(b), the tree diagram is abbreviated to show the branch of interest. Notice that $P(E_1) = \frac{1}{2}, P(E_2) = \frac{1}{2}$, and $P(E_1 \cap E_2) = \frac{1}{4}$. So in this case, $P(E_1 \cap E_2) = P(E_1) \cdot P(E_2)$.

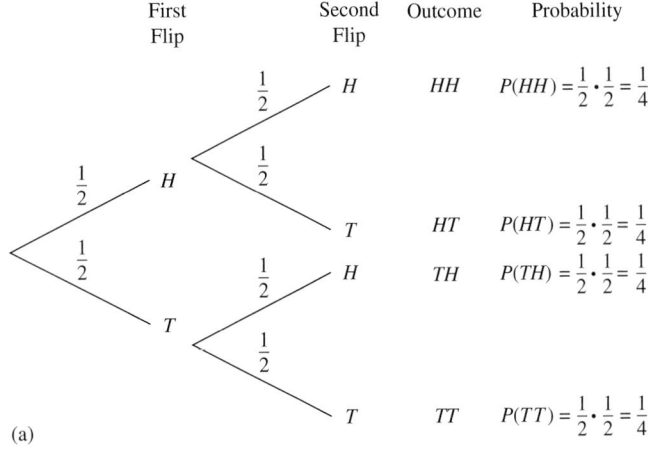

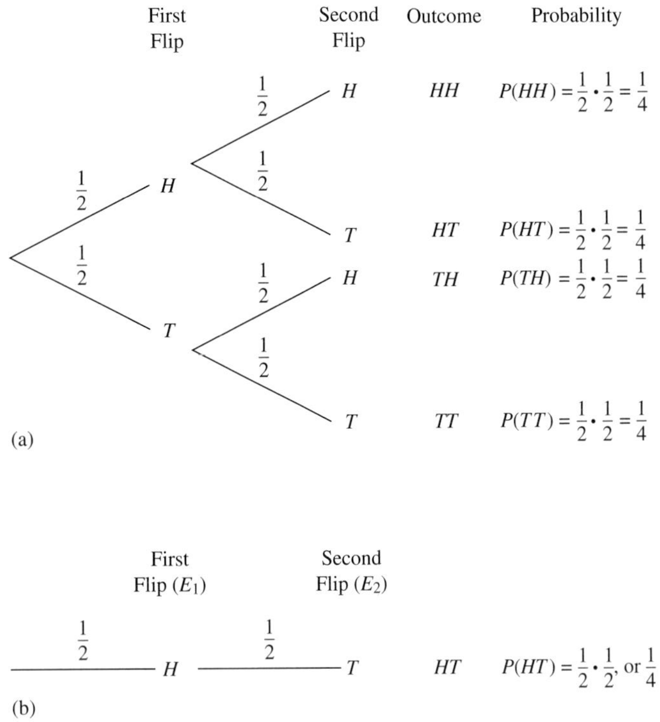

First Flip   Second Flip   Outcome   Probability

$\frac{1}{2}$ H   HH $P(HH) = \frac{1}{2} \cdot \frac{1}{2} = \frac{1}{4}$

$\frac{1}{2}$ T   HT $P(HT) = \frac{1}{2} \cdot \frac{1}{2} = \frac{1}{4}$

$\frac{1}{2}$ H   TH $P(TH) = \frac{1}{2} \cdot \frac{1}{2} = \frac{1}{4}$

$\frac{1}{2}$ T   TT $P(TT) = \frac{1}{2} \cdot \frac{1}{2} = \frac{1}{4}$

(a)

First Flip (E_1)   Second Flip (E_2)

$\frac{1}{2}$ H $\frac{1}{2}$ T   HT $P(HT) = \frac{1}{2} \cdot \frac{1}{2}$, or $\frac{1}{4}$

(b)

Figure 19

Next, consider two boxes in Figure 20. Box 1 contains two white and two black balls, and box 2 contains two white balls and three black balls. We draw one ball from each box and record their respective colors. Let B_1 be the event of drawing a black ball from box 1 and B_2 the event of drawing a black ball from box 2. B_1 and B_2 are independent. Suppose a ball is drawn from each box and we are interested in the probability of the event that each ball is black, that is, $P(B_1 \cap B_2)$. We know that $P(B_1) = \frac{2}{4} = \frac{1}{2}$, and $P(B_2) = \frac{3}{5}$.

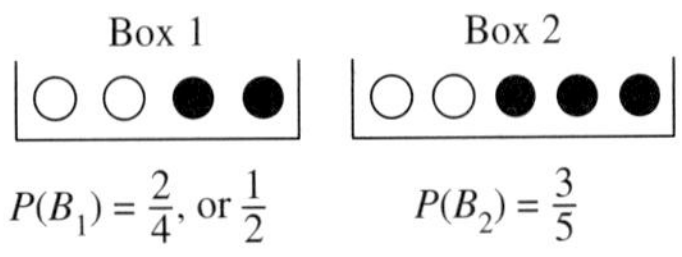

Box 1   Box 2

○ ○ ● ●   ○ ○ ● ● ●

$P(B_1) = \frac{2}{4}$, or $\frac{1}{2}$ $P(B_2) = \frac{3}{5}$

Figure 20

Is $P(B_1 \cap B_2) = P(B_1) \cdot P(B_2)$ in this case as well? We answer this question by computing $P(B_1 \cap B_2)$ using a familiar approach. If we consider all the black balls to be different and all the white balls to be different, there are $4 \cdot 5$ different pairs of balls. (Why?) Among these pairs, we are interested in pairs consisting only of black balls. There are $2 \cdot 3$ such pairs. (Why?) Hence,

$$P(B_1 \cap B_2) = \frac{2 \cdot 3}{4 \cdot 5} = \frac{2}{4} \cdot \frac{3}{5} = \frac{1}{2} \cdot \frac{3}{5}.$$

Thus, we see that for the independent events B_1 and B_2, we have $P(B_1 \cap B_2) = P(B_1) \cdot P(B_2)$. This discussion can be generalized as follows.

Theorem 9-7

For any independent events E_1 and E_2,

$$P(E_1 \cap E_2) = P(E_1) \cdot P(E_2).$$

NOW TRY THIS 3

NTT 3: Answers may vary depending on the interpretation of the last sentence in the caption. If it is ignored, the answers may be as seen. **a.** $\frac{1}{8}$ **b.** $\frac{3}{8}$ **c.** $\frac{1}{2}$ **d.** $\frac{5}{8}$ **e.** They are likely not independent events as the snow may be a part of the same weather front moving through an area.

In the following cartoon, assume that the events are independent.

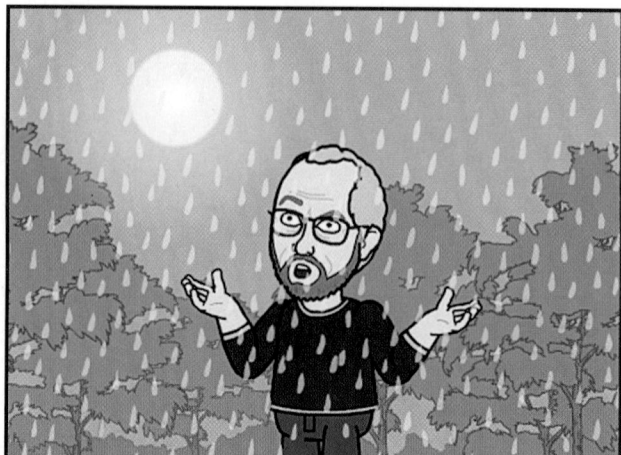

There is a 25% chance of snow tonight and 50% chance of snow tomorrow. I think that there is a 75% chance of error.

a. What is the probability of snow both times?
b. What is the probability that it will not snow either of the times?
c. What is the probability that it will snow exactly one of the times?
d. What is the probability that it will snow at least one of the times?
e. In real life, do you think that the events of snow tonight and snow tomorrow are independent events? Why or why not?

Example 10

Figure 21 shows a box with 11 letters. Some letters are repeated. Suppose 4 letters are drawn at random from the box one-by-one *without replacement*. What is the probability of the event consisting of the outcome *BABY*, with the letters chosen in exactly the order given?

PROBABILITY

Figure 21

Solution The portion of the tree branch leading to the outcome *BABY* is shown in Figure 22.

$$\xrightarrow{\frac{2}{11}} B \xrightarrow{\frac{1}{10}} A \xrightarrow{\frac{1}{9}} B \xrightarrow{\frac{1}{8}} Y \qquad \text{Probability of Outcome: } \frac{2}{11}\cdot\frac{1}{10}\cdot\frac{1}{9}\cdot\frac{1}{8} = \frac{2}{7920} = \frac{1}{3960}$$

Figure 22

The probability of the event that the first letter is B is $\frac{2}{11}$ because there are 2 B's out of 11 letters. The probability of the event of the second B is $\frac{1}{9}$ because there are 9 letters left after 1 B and 1 A have been chosen. Thus, $P(BABY)$ is $\frac{2}{7920} = \frac{1}{3960}$.

In Example 10, suppose 4 letters are drawn one-by-one from the box and the letters are chosen with replacement after each drawing. In this case, the branch needed to find $P(BABY)$ in the order drawn is pictured in Figure 23. Thus, $P(BABY) = \dfrac{2}{11} \cdot \dfrac{1}{11} \cdot \dfrac{2}{11} \cdot \dfrac{1}{11} = \dfrac{4}{14{,}641}$.

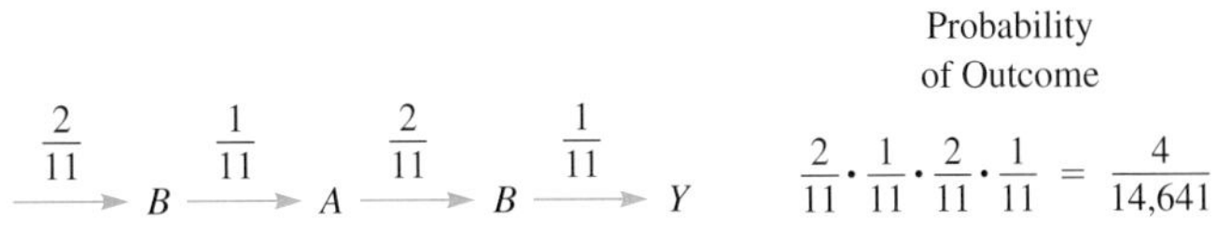

Probability
of Outcome

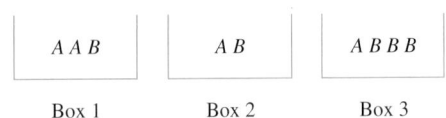

$\dfrac{2}{11} \cdot \dfrac{1}{11} \cdot \dfrac{2}{11} \cdot \dfrac{1}{11} = \dfrac{4}{14{,}641}$

Figure 23

Example 11

Consider the three boxes in Figure 24. A letter is drawn from box 1 and placed in box 2. Then, a letter is drawn from box 2 and placed in box 3. Finally, a letter is drawn from box 3. What is the probability of the event that the letter drawn from box 3 is B?

$A\ A\ B$	$A\ B$	$A\ B\ B\ B$
Box 1	Box 2	Box 3

Figure 24

Solution A tree diagram for this experiment is given in Figure 25. The denominators in the second stage are 3 rather than 2 because in this stage, there are now three letters in box 2. The denominators in the third stage are 5 because in this stage, there are five letters in box 3. To find the probability that a B is drawn from box 3, add the probabilities for the outcomes AAB, ABB, BAB, and BBB that make up this event.

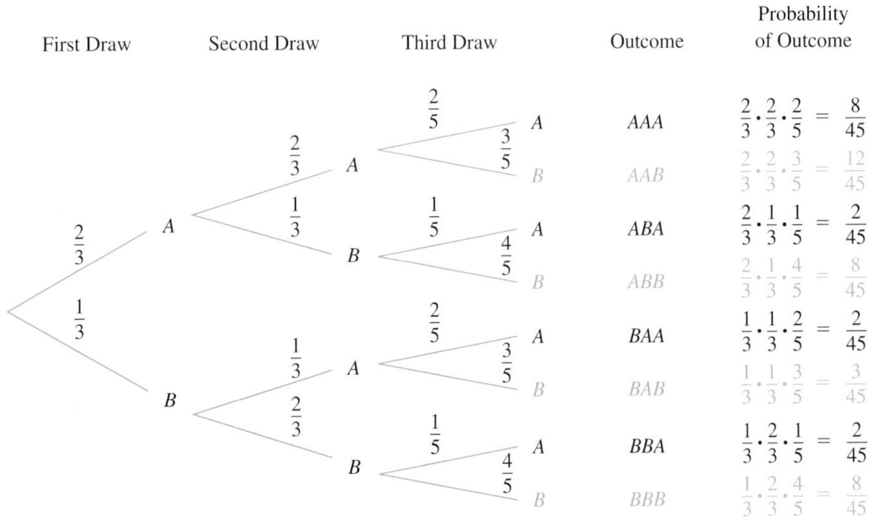

First Draw	Second Draw	Third Draw	Outcome	Probability of Outcome
		$\dfrac{2}{5}$ A	AAA	$\dfrac{2}{3} \cdot \dfrac{2}{3} \cdot \dfrac{2}{5} = \dfrac{8}{45}$
	$\dfrac{2}{3}$ A $\dfrac{3}{5}$	B	AAB	$\dfrac{2}{3} \cdot \dfrac{2}{3} \cdot \dfrac{3}{5} = \dfrac{12}{45}$
$\dfrac{2}{3}$ A	$\dfrac{1}{3}$	$\dfrac{1}{5}$ A	ABA	$\dfrac{2}{3} \cdot \dfrac{1}{3} \cdot \dfrac{1}{5} = \dfrac{2}{45}$
	B	$\dfrac{4}{5}$ B	ABB	$\dfrac{2}{3} \cdot \dfrac{1}{3} \cdot \dfrac{4}{5} = \dfrac{8}{45}$
$\dfrac{1}{3}$		$\dfrac{2}{5}$ A	BAA	$\dfrac{1}{3} \cdot \dfrac{1}{3} \cdot \dfrac{2}{5} = \dfrac{2}{45}$
	$\dfrac{1}{3}$ A $\dfrac{3}{5}$	B	BAB	$\dfrac{1}{3} \cdot \dfrac{1}{3} \cdot \dfrac{3}{5} = \dfrac{3}{45}$
B	$\dfrac{2}{3}$	$\dfrac{1}{5}$ A	BBA	$\dfrac{1}{3} \cdot \dfrac{2}{3} \cdot \dfrac{1}{5} = \dfrac{2}{45}$
	B	$\dfrac{4}{5}$ B	BBB	$\dfrac{1}{3} \cdot \dfrac{2}{3} \cdot \dfrac{4}{5} = \dfrac{8}{45}$

Figure 25

Thus, the probability of the event of obtaining a B on the draw from box 3 in this experiment is

$$\dfrac{12}{45} + \dfrac{8}{45} + \dfrac{3}{45} + \dfrac{8}{45} = \dfrac{31}{45}.$$

Conditional Probabilities

When the sample space of an experiment is affected by additional information, the new sample space often is reduced in size. For example, suppose we toss a fair coin 3 times and consider the following events:

A: getting a tail on the first toss

B: getting a tail on all 3 tosses

Let S be the sample space in Figure 26. We see that $P(A) = \dfrac{4}{8} = \dfrac{1}{2}$ and $P(B) = \dfrac{1}{8}$.

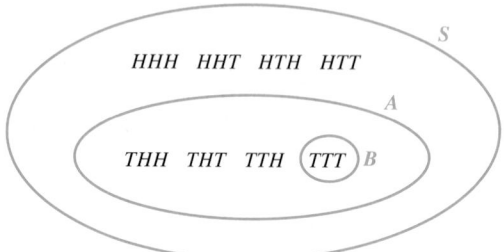

Figure 26

If event A has occurred (that is, a tail occurred on the first toss), how does that change $P(B)$? The sample space is reduced to $\{THH, THT, TTH, TTT\}$. The probability of the event that all three tosses are tails given that the first toss is a tail is $\dfrac{1}{4}$. (Note that $A \cap B = \{TTT\}$.) The notation used for this situation is $P(B|A)$, read "the probability of the event B given event A," and we write $P(B|A) = \dfrac{1}{4}$. Note that

$$P(B|A) = \frac{1}{4} = \frac{\frac{1}{8}}{\frac{4}{8}} = \frac{P(A \cap B)}{P(A)}.$$

This is true in general and we have the following definition.

> **Definition of Conditional Probability**
>
> If A and B are events in sample space S and $P(A) \neq 0$, then the **conditional probability** that event B occurs, given that event A has occurred, is given by
>
> $$P(B|A) = \frac{P(A \cap B)}{P(A)}.$$

Example 12

What is the probability of the event of rolling a 6 on a fair die if we know that the roll is an even number?

Solution   If event B is rolling a 6 and event A is rolling an even number, then

$$P(B|A) = \frac{P(A \cap B)}{P(A)} = \frac{\frac{1}{6}}{\frac{1}{2}} = \frac{1}{3}.$$

It is not really necessary to use the formula for conditional probability to answer the question because the new sample space is $\{2, 4, 6\}$, and so $P(6) = \dfrac{1}{3}$.

Modeling Games

We use models to analyze games that involve probability. Consider the game that Arthur and Gwen play: There are two black marbles and one white marble in a box, as in Figure 27(a). Gwen mixes the marbles, and Arthur draws two marbles at random without replacement. If the two marbles match, Arthur wins; otherwise, Gwen wins. Does each player have an equal chance of winning?

We *develop a model* to analyze the game. One model is a tree diagram, as shown in Figure 27(b). Because the outcome ○ ○ cannot happen, the tree diagram could be shortened as in Figure 27(c).

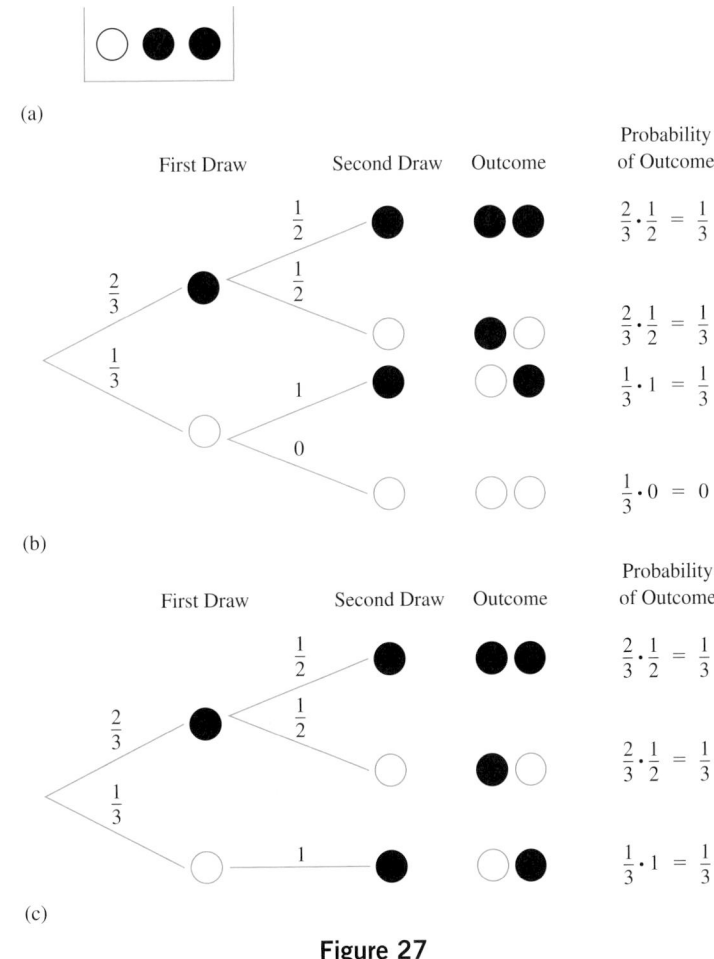

Figure 27

The probability that the marbles are the same color is $\dfrac{1}{3} + 0 = \dfrac{1}{3}$, and the probability that they are not the same color is $\dfrac{1}{3} + \dfrac{1}{3} = \dfrac{2}{3}$. Because $\dfrac{1}{3} \neq \dfrac{2}{3}$, the players do not have the same chance of winning.

An alternative model for analyzing this game is given in Figure 28(a), where the black and white marbles are shown along with the possible ways of drawing two marbles. Each line segment in the diagram represents one pair of marbles that could be drawn. S indicates that the marbles in the pair are the same color, and D indicates that the marbles are different colors. Because there are two D's in Figure 28(a), the probability of drawing two different-colored marbles is $\frac{2}{3}$. Likewise, the probability of drawing two marbles of the same color is $\frac{1}{3}$. Because $\frac{2}{3} \neq \frac{1}{3}$, the players do not have an equal chance of winning.

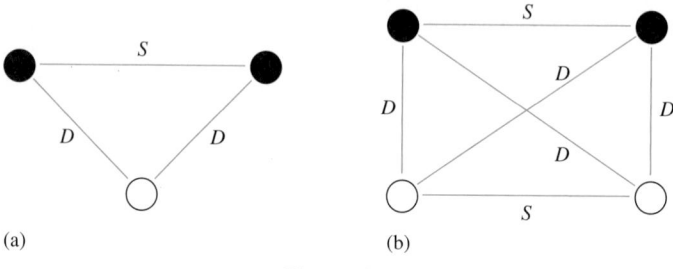

(a)   (b)

Figure 28

Will adding another white marble give each player an equal chance of winning? With two white and two black marbles, we have the model in Figure 28(b). Therefore, $P(D) = \frac{4}{6} = \frac{2}{3}$, and $P(S) = \frac{2}{6} = \frac{1}{3}$. We see that adding a white marble does not change the probabilities.

Next, consider a game with the same rules but using three black marbles and one white marble. Figure 29 shows a model for this situation. The probability of drawing two marbles of the same color is $\frac{3}{6}$, and the probability of drawing two marbles of different colors is $\frac{3}{6}$. Finally, we have a game in which each player has an equal chance of winning.

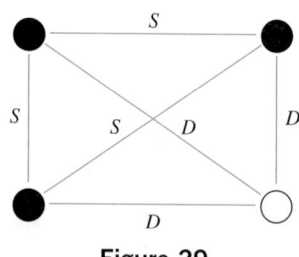

Figure 29

▶ **NOW TRY THIS 4**

NTT 4: Answer can be found in Answers at the back of the book.

Referring to the game described above, answer the following.

a. Does each player have an equal chance of winning if only one white marble and one black marble are used and the marble is replaced after the first draw?

b. Find games that involve different numbers of marbles in which each player has an equal chance of winning.

c. Find a pattern for the numbers of black and white marbles that allow each player to have an equal chance of winning.

Problem Solving **A String-Tying Game**

In a party game, a child has six strings, as shown in Figure 30(a). Another child ties the top ends two at a time, forming three separate knots, and the bottom ends, forming three separate knots, as in Figure 30(b). If the strings form one closed ring, as in Figure 30(c), the child tying the knots wins a prize. What is the probability of the event that the child wins a prize on the first try? Guess the probability before reading the solution.

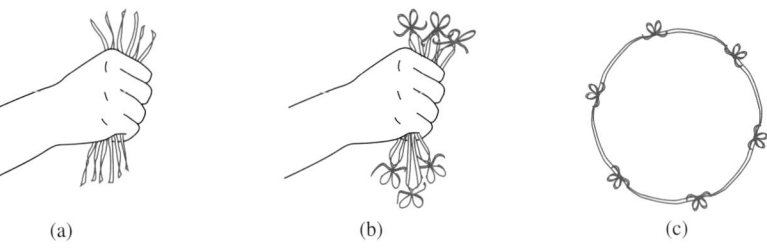

(a)   (b)   (c)

Figure 30

Understanding the Problem   The problem is to determine the probability of the event that one closed ring will be formed. One closed ring means that all six pieces are joined end-to-end to form one, and only one, ring, as shown in Figure 30(c).

Devising a Plan   Figure 31(a) shows what happens when the ends of the strings of one set are tied in pairs at the top. Notice that no matter in what order those ends are tied, the result appears as in Figure 31(a).

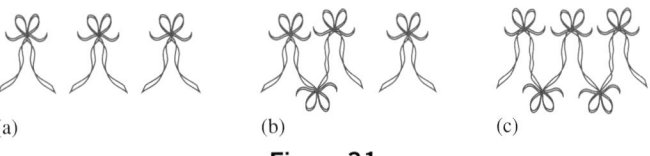

(a)   (b)   (c)

Figure 31

Then, the other ends are tied in a three-stage experiment. If we pick any string in the first stage, then there are five choices for its mate. Four of these choices are favorable choices for forming a ring. (Why?) Thus, the probability of the event of forming a favorable first tie is $\frac{4}{5}$. Figure 31(b) shows a favorable tie at the first stage.

For any one of the remaining four strings, there are three choices for its mate. Two of these choices are favorable ones. (Why?) Thus, the probability of the event of forming a favorable second tie after forming a favorable first tie is $\frac{2}{3}$. Figure 31(c) shows a favorable tie at the second stage.

Now, two ends remain. Since nothing can go wrong at the third stage, the probability of the event of making a favorable tie after making favorable ties at the first two stages is 1. If we use the probabilities completed at each stage and a single branch of a tree diagram, we calculate the probability of performing three successful ties in a row and hence the probability of the event of forming one closed ring.

Carrying Out the Plan   If we let S represent a successful tie at each stage, then the branch of the tree with which we are concerned is the one shown in Figure 32.

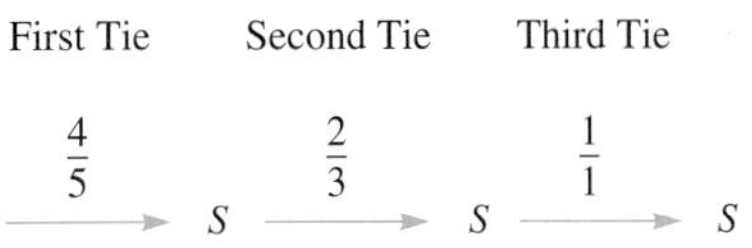

First Tie   Second Tie   Third Tie

$\frac{4}{5}$ $\frac{2}{3}$ $\frac{1}{1}$

$\xrightarrow{\hspace{1.5cm}} S \xrightarrow{\hspace{1.5cm}} S \xrightarrow{\hspace{1.5cm}} S$

Figure 32

Thus, the probability of the event of forming one ring is $P(\text{ring}) = \frac{4}{5} \cdot \frac{2}{3} \cdot \frac{1}{1} = \frac{8}{15}$.

Looking Back The probability of the event that a child will form a ring on the first try is $\frac{8}{15}$. A class might simulate this problem several times with strings to see how the fraction of successes compares with the theoretical probability of $\frac{8}{15}$.

Related problems that could be posed for solution include the following:

1. If a child fails to get a ring 10 times in a row, the child may not play again. What is the probability of such a streak of bad luck?
2. If the number of strings is reduced to three and the rule is that an upper end must be tied to a lower end, what is the probability of the event of forming a single ring?
3. If the number of strings is three, but an upper end can be tied to either an upper or a lower end, what is the probability of the event of forming a single ring?
4. What is the probability of the event of forming three rings in the original problem?
5. What is the probability of the event of forming two rings in the original problem?

Problem Solving   A Quiz-Show Game

On a quiz show, a contestant stands at the entrance to a maze that opens into two rooms, labeled *A* and *B* in Figure 33. The master of ceremonies' assistant is to place a new car in one room and a donkey in the other. The contestant must walk through the maze into one of the rooms and will win whatever is in that room. If the contestant makes each decision in the maze at random, in which room should the assistant place the car to give the contestant the best chance to win?

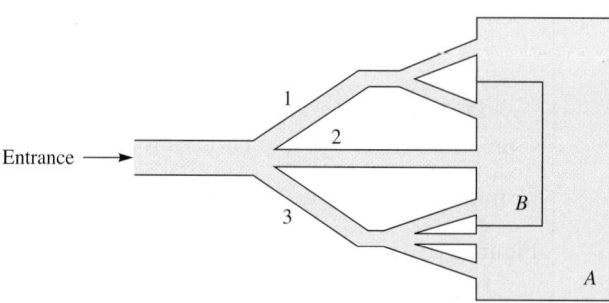

Figure 33

Understanding the Problem The contestant must first choose one of the paths marked 1, 2, or 3 and then choose another path as she proceeds through the maze. To determine the room the contestant is most likely to choose, the assistant must be able to determine the probability of the contestant's reaching each room.

Devising a Plan One way to determine where the car should be placed is to *model the choices with a tree diagram* and to compute the probabilities along the branches of the tree.

Carrying Out the Plan A tree diagram for the maze is shown in Figure 34, along with the possible outcomes and the probabilities of each branch.

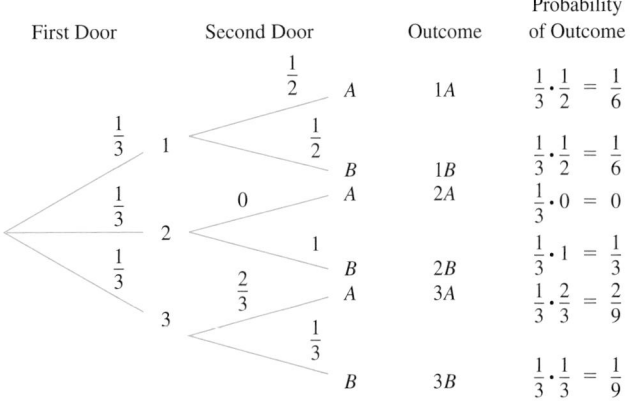

Figure 34

The probability of the event that room A is chosen is $\dfrac{1}{6} + 0 + \dfrac{2}{9} = \dfrac{7}{18}$. Hence the probability of the event that room B is chosen is $1 - \dfrac{7}{18} = \dfrac{11}{18}$. Thus, room B has the greater probability of being chosen. This is where the car should be placed for the contestant to have the best chance of winning it.

Looking Back An alternative model for this problem and for many probability problems is an area model. The rectangle in Figure 35(a) represents the first three choices that the contestant can make. Because each choice is equally likely, each is represented by an equal area. If the contestant chooses the upper path, then rooms A and B have an equal chance of being chosen. If she chooses the middle path, then only room B can be entered. If she chooses the lower path, then room A is entered $\dfrac{2}{3}$ of the time. This can be expressed in terms of the area model shown in Figure 35(b). Dividing the rectangle into pieces of equal area, we obtain the model in Figure 35(c), in which the area representing room B is shaded. Because the area representing room B is greater than the area representing room A, room B has the greater probability of being chosen. Figure 35(c) can enable us to find the probability of choosing room B. Because the shaded area consists of 11 rectangles out of a total of 18 rectangles, the probability of the event of choosing room B is $\dfrac{11}{18}$. We can vary the problem by changing the maze or by changing the locations of the rooms.

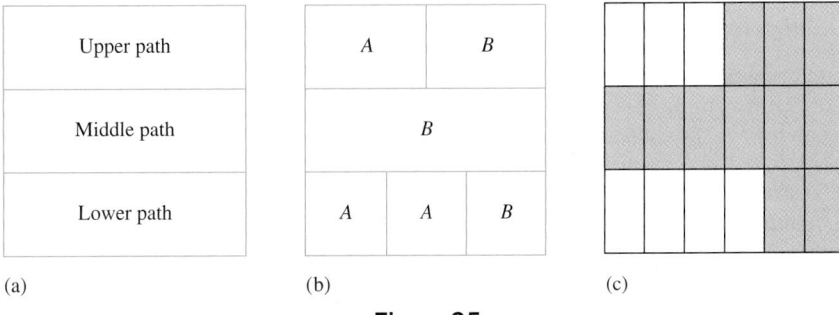

(a)   (b)   (c)

Figure 35

Assessment 9-2A

1. **a.** A box contains three white balls and two black balls. A ball is drawn at random from the box and not replaced. Then a second ball is drawn from the box. Draw a tree diagram for this experiment and find the probability of the event that the two balls are of different colors.   *

b. Suppose that a ball is drawn at random from the box in part (a), its color is recorded, and then the ball is put back in the box. Draw a tree diagram for this experiment and find the probability of the event that the two balls are of different colors.   *

2. A box contains the six letters shown.

$$\boxed{R\ A\ N\ D\ O\ M}$$

What is the probability of the event *DAN* is obtained in that order if three letters are drawn one-by-one:
a. With replacement? $\frac{1}{216}$
b. Without replacement? $\frac{1}{120}$

3. An executive committee consisted of 10 members: 4 women and 6 men. Three members were selected at random to be sent to a meeting in Hawaii. A blindfolded woman drew 3 of the 10 names from a hat to determine who would go. All 3 names drawn were women's. What was the probability of such luck? $\frac{1}{30}$

4. Following are three boxes containing balls. Draw a ball from box 1 and place it in box 2. Then draw a ball from box 2 and place it in box 3. Finally, draw a ball from box 3.

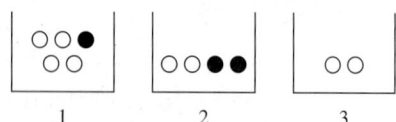

a. What is the probability of the event that the last ball, drawn from box 3, is white? $\frac{64}{75}$
b. What is the probability of the event that the last ball drawn is black? $\frac{11}{75}$

5. Assume the probability is $\frac{1}{2}$ that a child born at any time is a boy and births are independent. What is the probability of the event that if a family has four children, they are all boys? $\frac{1}{16}$

6. A box contains five slips of paper. Each slip has one of the numbers 4, 6, 7, 8, or 9 written on it and all numbers are used. Al reaches into the box and draws two slips and adds the two numbers. If the sum is even, Al wins a prize.
a. What is the probability of the event that Al wins a prize?
b. Does the probability change if the two numbers are multiplied? Explain.   Yes, now P(Even) =

7. In a game, there are one black marble and one white marble in a bag. A marble is drawn from the bag and the color recorded. The marble is replaced and another is drawn and the color recorded. If the two marbles match, Arthur wins,

but if the marbles do not match, Gwen wins. Explain whether this is a fair game.   Yes, the game is fair; the probabilities are equal.

8. You play a game in which you first choose one of the two spinners shown. You then spin your spinner and a second person spins the other spinner. The one with the greater number wins.

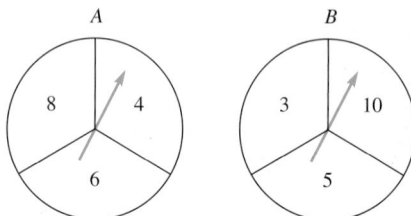

a. Which spinner should you choose? Why?   *
b. The sum of the numbers on each spinner is 18. Design two spinners with unequal sums so that choosing the spinner with the lesser sum will give the player a greater probability of winning.   *

9. If a person takes a five-question true-false test, what is the probability of the event that the score is 100% correct if the person guesses on every question? $\frac{1}{32}$

10. Rattlesnake and Paxson Colleges play four games against each other in a chess tournament. The probabilities that Rattlesnake and Paxson will win each game are $\frac{2}{3}$ and $\frac{1}{3}$, respectively. Determine the probabilities of the following events.
a. Paxson loses all four games. $\frac{16}{81}$
b. The match is a draw with each school winning two games. $\frac{8}{27}$

11. Consider the following dartboard where all quadrilaterals are squares and the *x*'s represent equal lengths.

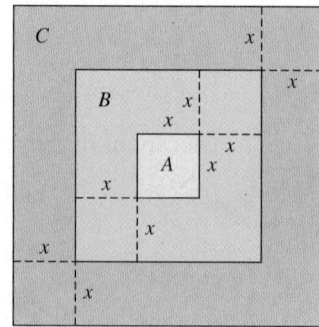

If a dart may land in any region on the board with probability determined by the ratio of the area of the chosen region to the whole, what is the probability that it will land in
a. section *A*? $\frac{1}{25}$
b. section *B*? $\frac{8}{25}$
c. section *C*? $\frac{16}{25}$

12. An electric clock is stopped by a power failure. What is the probability of the event that the second hand is stopped between the 3 and the 4? $\frac{1}{12}$

13. There are 40 employees in a certain firm. We know that 28 of these employees are males, 2 of these males are secretaries, and 10 secretaries are employed by the firm. What is the probability of the event that an employee chosen at random is a secretary, given that the person is a male? $\frac{1}{14}$

14. Four blue socks, four white socks, and four gray socks are mixed in a drawer. You pull out two socks, one at a time, without looking.
   a. Draw a tree diagram along with the possible outcomes and the probabilities of each outcome. *
   b. What is the probability of the event of getting a pair of socks of the same color? *
   c. What is the probability of the event of getting two gray socks? *
   d. Suppose that, instead of pulling out two socks, you pull out four socks. What is the probability of the event of getting at least two socks of the same color? 1

15. When you toss a quarter 4 times, what is the probability of the event that you get
   a. at least as many heads as tails? $\frac{11}{16}$
   b. at least as many tails as heads? $\frac{11}{16}$

16. A manufacturer found that among 500 randomly selected smoke detectors only 450 worked properly. Based on this information, how many smoke detectors would you have to install to be sure that the probability that at least one of them will work will be at least 99.99%? 4

17. Bob leaves the top of Snow Mountain for his last ski run of the day. There are 6 trails to the base of the mountain. He would like to end up at the lodge but it is snowing and he cannot tell one trail from another. If he chooses a path at random at each fork, what is the probability of the event that he will end up at the lodge? $\frac{7}{12}$

Snow mountain

Ski lift   Lodge   Parking lot

18. Carolyn wins a large prize if she wins two tennis games in a row out of three games. She is to play alternately against Billie and Bobby. She may choose to play Billie-Bobby-Billie or Bobby-Billie-Bobby. Assume she wins against Billie 50% of the time and against Bobby 80% of the time. Which alternative should she choose? *

19. A bag contains 3 blue marbles, 4 red marbles, and 3 yellow marbles. The probability of drawing a blue marble out of the bag is 3/10 or 30%. How many of what color of marbles must be added to the bag so that the probability of a blue marble being drawn at random from the bag is 75%? *

20. A pair of dice is rolled. One die lands on the tabletop and shows a 1. The other rolls under the table. What is the probability that the sum showing on the pair of dice is 2? $\frac{1}{6}$

21. A pair of dice is rolled. What is the probability that the sum showing on a pair of dice will be greater than 9 given that the first die shows a 6? $\frac{1}{2}$

22. The table shows the numbers of students in grades 6, 7, and 8 identifying their favorite winter sports. Use the table to find the given probabilities.

Grade	Snowboarding	Skiing
Sixth	27	18
Seventh	22	16
Eighth	20	23
Total	69	57

$\frac{69}{126} = \frac{23}{42}$

   a. What is the probability a student chooses snowboarding?
   b. Given that a student is in the sixth grade, what is the probability that the student chooses skiing? *
   c. If a brother–sister combination of students is in grade seven and grade eight, respectively, what is the probability that both choose snowboarding? $\frac{440}{1634} = \frac{220}{817}$
   d. In the scenario of part (c), if you know that the brother in grade seven chooses snowboarding, what is the probability of both choosing snowboarding? $\frac{20}{43}$

Assessment 9-2B

1. Suppose an experiment consists of spinning X and then spinning Y, as follows:

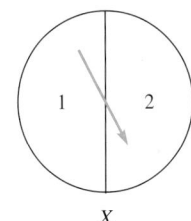

X

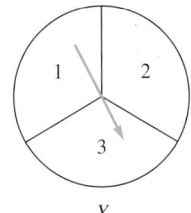

Y

Find
   a. the sample space S for the experiment. *
   b. the event A consisting of outcomes from spinning an even number followed by an even number. {(2,2)}

   c. the event B consisting of outcomes from spinning at least one 2 on either spinner. {(1,2),(2,1),(2,2),(2,3)}
   d. the event C consisting of outcomes from spinning exactly one 2 on either spinner. {(1,2),(2,1),(2,3)}

2. Following are three boxes containing specific letters.

   |MATH| |AND| |HISTORY|
      1   2   3

   a. From box 1, three letters are drawn one-by-one without replacement and recorded in order. What is the probability that the outcome is *HAT*? $\frac{1}{24}$
   b. From box 1, three letters are drawn one-by-one with replacement and recorded in order. What is the probability that the outcome is *HAT*? $\frac{1}{64}$

c. One letter is drawn at random from box 1, then another from box 2, and then another from box 3, with the results recorded in order. What is the probability that the outcome is *HAT*? $\frac{1}{84}$

d. If a box is chosen at random and then a letter is drawn at random from the box, what is the probability of the event that the outcome is *A*? $\frac{7}{36}$

3. A penny, a nickel, a dime, and a quarter are tossed.

a. What is the probability of the event of obtaining at least three heads on the tosses? $\frac{5}{16}$

b. What is the probability of obtaining three heads if the first toss is a head? $\frac{3}{8}$

4. Two boxes with given letters are shown. Choose a box and draw three letters at random, one-by-one, without replacement. If the outcome is SOS, you win a prize.

S O S	S O S S O S
1	2

a. Which box should you choose? *

b. Which box would you choose if the letters are to be drawn with replacement? Either, with probability $\frac{4}{27}$

5. An assembly line has two inspectors. The probability that the first inspector will miss a defective item is 0.05. If the defective item passes the first inspector, the probability that the second inspector will miss it is 0.01. If the events are independent, what is the probability of the event that a defective item will pass by both inspectors? 0.0005

6. Following are two boxes containing black and white balls. A ball is drawn at random from box 1. Then a ball is drawn at random from box 2, and the colors of the balls from both boxes are recorded in order.

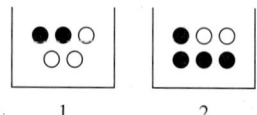

1	2

Find the probability of each of the following events.

a. Two white balls $\frac{1}{5}$

b. At least one black ball $\frac{4}{5}$ $\frac{11}{15}$

c. At most one black ball $\frac{8}{15}$

d. ● ○ or ○ ● $\frac{8}{15}$

7. The following questions refer to a very popular dice game, craps, in which a player rolls two dice.

a. Rolling a sum of 7 or 11 on the first roll of the dice is a win. What is the probability of the event of winning on the first roll? $\frac{2}{9}$

b. Rolling a sum of 2, 3, or 12 on the first roll of the dice is a loss. What is the probability of the event of losing on the first roll? $\frac{1}{9}$

c. Rolling a sum of 4, 5, 6, 8, 9, or 10 on the first roll is neither a win nor a loss. What is the probability of the event of neither winning nor losing on the first roll? $\frac{2}{3}$

d. After rolling a sum of 4, 5, 6, 8, 9, or 10, to win a player must roll the same sum again before rolling a sum of 7. Which sum—4, 5, 6, 8, 9, or 10—has the highest probability of occurring again? 6 and 8 both have probability $\frac{5}{36}$.

e. What is the probability of the event of rolling a sum of 1 on any roll of the dice? 0

f. What is the probability of the event of rolling a sum less than 13 on any roll of the dice? 1

g. If the two dice are rolled 60 times, predict about how many times a sum of 7 will be rolled. 10 times

8. Suppose we spin the following spinner with the first spin giving the numerator and the second spin giving the denominator of a fraction. What is the probability of the event that the fraction will be greater than $1\frac{1}{2}$? $\frac{1}{8}$

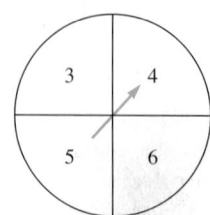

9. Brittany is going to ascend a four-step staircase. At any time, she is just as likely to stride up one step or two steps. Find the probability of the event that she will ascend the four steps in

a. two strides. $\frac{1}{4}$

b. three strides. $\frac{5}{8}$

c. four strides. $\frac{1}{8}$

10. An experiment consists of spinning the spinner shown and then flipping a coin with sides numbered 1 and 2.

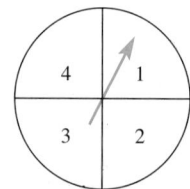

What is the probability of the events that

a. the number on the spinner will be greater than the number on the coin? $\frac{5}{8}$

b. the outcome will consist of two consecutive integers in any order? $\frac{3}{8}$

11. In the following square dartboard, suppose a dart is equally likely to land in any small square of the board.

Points are given as shown in the table.

Region	Points
A	10
B	8
C	6
D	4
E	2

a. What is the total area of the board?   100 square units
b. What is the probability of the event of a dart's landing in each lettered region of the board?   *
c. If two darts are tossed, what is the probability of the event of scoring 20 points? $\frac{1}{625}$
d. What is the probability of the event that a dart will land in neither *D* nor *E*? $\frac{9}{25}$

12. The combinations on the lockers at the high school consist of three numbers, each ranging from 0 to 39. If a combination is chosen at random, what is the probability of the event that the first two numbers are each multiples of 9 and the third number is a multiple of 4? $\frac{1}{256}$

13. The following box contains the 11 letters shown. The letters are drawn one-by-one without replacement, and the results are recorded in order. Find the probability of the event MISSISSIPPI. $\frac{1}{34,650}$

$$\boxed{\text{M I I I I P P S S S S}}$$

14. The land area of Earth is approximately 57,500,000 mi². The water area of Earth is approximately 139,600,000 mi². If a meteor lands at random on the planet, what is the probability, to the nearest tenth, that it will hit water?

15. A husband and wife discover that there is a 10% probability of their passing on a hereditary disease to any child they have. If they plan to have three children and passing on the disease to the children are independent events, what is the probability at least one child will inherit the disease?   27.1%

16. At a certain hospital, 40 patients have lung cancer, 30 patients smoke, and 25 have lung cancer and smoke. Suppose the hospital contains 200 patients. If a patient chosen at random is known to smoke, what is the probability that the patient has lung cancer? $\frac{5}{6}$

17. Solve the Quiz-Show Game in this section by replacing Figure 33 with the following maze.   *

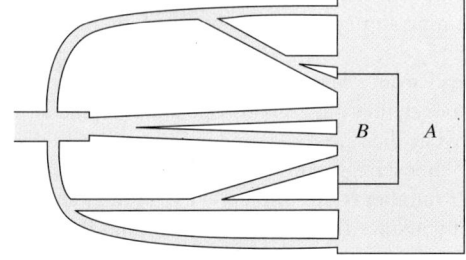

18. Jane has two tennis serves, a hard serve and a soft serve. Her hard serve is in (a good serve) 50% of the time, and her soft serve is in (good) 75% of the time. If her hard serve is in, she wins 75% of her points. If her soft serve is in, she wins 50% of her points. Since she is allowed to re-serve one time if her first serve is out, what should her serving strategy be? That is, should she serve hard followed by soft; both hard; soft followed by hard; or both soft? Note that two bad serves is a lost point.   *

19. In a certain population of caribou, the probability of an animal's being sickly is $\frac{1}{20}$. If a caribou is sickly, the probability of its being eaten by wolves is $\frac{1}{3}$. If a caribou is not sickly, the probability of its being eaten by wolves is $\frac{1}{150}$. If a caribou is chosen at random from the herd, what is the probability of the event that it will be eaten by wolves? $\frac{23}{1000}$

20. A pair of dice is rolled. The sum of the faces shown is 11. If one die is showing a 6, what is the probability that the other die shows a 4?   0

21. A pair of dice is rolled. What is the probability that the sum showing on a pair of dice will be less than 7 given that the first die shows a 3? $\frac{1}{2}$

22. The table shows the numbers of students in grades 6, 7, and 8 identifying their favorite winter sports. Use the table to find the given probabilities.

Grade	Snowboarding	Skiing
Sixth	27	18
Seventh	22	16
Eighth	20	23
Total	69	57

a. What is the probability a student chooses skiing? $\frac{19}{42}$
b. Given that a student is in the seventh grade, what is the probability that the student chooses snowboarding? $\frac{22}{38} = \frac{11}{19}$
c. If a brother–sister combination of students is in grade 6 and grade 8, respectively, what is the probability that both choose skiing? $\frac{46}{215}$
d. In the scenario of part (c), if you know that the brother in grade 6 chooses skiing, what is the probability of both choosing skiing? $\frac{23}{43}$

Mathematical Connections 9-2

Answers to Mathematical Connections can be found in the Answers section at the back of the book.

Reasoning

1. Jim rolled a fair die 5 times and obtained a 3 every time. He concluded that on the next roll, a 3 is more likely to occur than the other numbers. Explain why this is not true.

2. A witness to a crime observed that the criminal had blond hair and blue eyes and drove a red car. When the police looks for a suspect, is the probability greater that they will find someone with blond hair and blue eyes or that they will find someone with blond hair and blue eyes who drives a red car? Explain your answer.

3. You are given three white balls, one red ball, and two identical boxes. You are asked to distribute the balls in the boxes in any way you like. You then are asked to select a box (after the boxes have been shuffled) and without looking pick a ball at random from that box. If the ball is red, you win a prize. How should you distribute the balls in the boxes to maximize your chances of winning? Justify your reasoning.

4. A fair coin is tossed and a fair die is thrown. Which has the greater probability when the event is obtaining a head and a 6 if (1) you know that a head has already been obtained, or (2) you know a 6 has already been obtained?

5. Could the probability of two independent events occurring, and a conditional probability involving the two events occurring be equal?

Open-Ended

6. Make up a game in which the players have an equal chance of winning and the game involves rolling two regular dice.

7. How can the faces of two cubes be numbered so that when they are rolled, the resulting sum is one of the numbers 1 to 12 and each sum has the same probability?

8. Use graph paper to design a dartboard such that the probability of hitting a certain part of the board is $\frac{3}{5}$. Explain your reasoning.

9. Design a pair of six-sided number cubes so that each possible sum is equiprobable.

Cooperative Learning

10. Use two spinners divided into four equal areas numbered 1–4. A player spins both spinners and computes the product of the two numbers. If the product is 1, 2, 3, or 4, player A wins. In the same way, player B wins if the product is 6, 8, 9, 12, or 16. The game ends when 20 plays have been made. Each player receives 1 point for each win, and the game winner is the person with the most points when the game ends.

   a. Do you think the game looks fair; that is, both players have the same chance of winning? Why or why not? If not, who do you think has the best chance of winning?

   b. Play the game to see if it seems fair. Do you think it is fair based on playing it? Why?

   c. Complete the following table to determine possible products.

		2nd spin		
×	1	2	3	4
1				
2				
3				12
4				

   1st spin

   d. Based on the table in part (c), is this a fair game? Explain why.

11. Replace the spinners in the game of exercise 10 with ones divided into six equal areas with the numbers 1, 2, 3, 4, 5, and 6 in the regions. Design a similar game and decide what products each player should use so that this is a fair game. Explain how your game is fair.

12. Play the following game in pairs. One player chooses one of four equally likely outcomes from the set $\{HH, HT, TH, TT\}$, which is the sample space for the experiment of tossing a fair coin twice. The other player then chooses one of the other outcomes. A coin is flipped until either player's choice appears. For example, the first player chooses TT and the second player chooses HT. If the first two flips yield TH, then no one wins and the game continues. If, after five flips, the string $THHHT$ appears, the second player is the winner because the sequence HT finally appeared. Play the game 10 times. Does each player appear to have the same chance of winning? Analyze the game for the case in which the first player chooses TT and the second HT, and explain whether the game is fair for all choices made by the two players. (*Hint*: Find the probability that the first player wins the game by showing that the first player will win if, and only if, tails appears on the first and on the second flip.)

13. Consider the three spinners A, B, and C shown in the following figure:

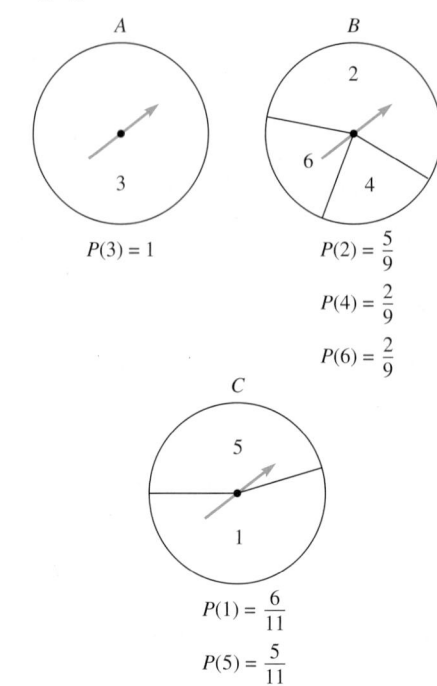

$P(3) = 1$

$P(2) = \frac{5}{9}$

$P(4) = \frac{2}{9}$

$P(6) = \frac{2}{9}$

$P(1) = \frac{6}{11}$

$P(5) = \frac{5}{11}$

   a. Suppose there are only two players and that the first player chooses a spinner, then the second player chooses a different spinner, and each person spins his or her spinner, with the greater number winning. Play the game several times to get a feeling for it. Determine if each player appears to have the same chances of winning the game. If not, which spinner should you choose in order to win?

   b. This time play the same game with three players. If each player must choose a different spinner and spin it, is the winning strategy the same as it was in (a)? Why or why not?

14. Bradley Efron, a Stanford University statistician, designed a set of nonstandard dice whose faces are numbered as shown below. The dice are to be used in a game in which each player chooses a die and then rolls it. Whoever rolls the greater number is the winner. What strategy should you use so that you have the best chance of winning this game?

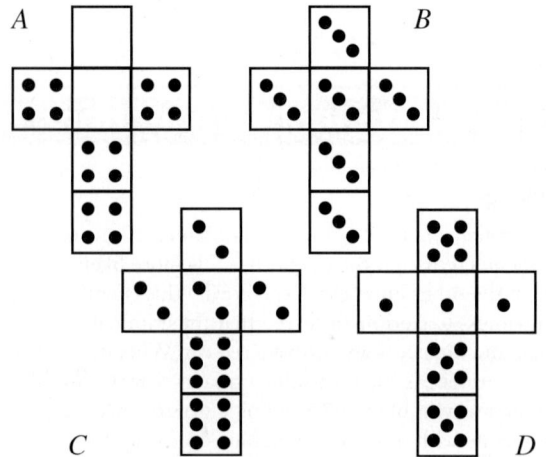

Connecting Mathematics to the Classroom

15. An experiment consists of tossing a fair coin twice. The student reasons that there are three possible outcomes: two heads, one head and one tail, or two tails. Thus, $P(HH) = \frac{1}{3}$. What is your reply?

16. A student would like to know the difference between two events being independent and two events being mutually exclusive. How would you answer her?

17. In response to the question "If a fair die is rolled twice, what is the probability of the event of rolling a pair of 5s?" a student replies, "One-third, because $\frac{1}{6} + \frac{1}{6} = \frac{1}{3}$." How do you respond?

18. A student is not sure when to add and when to multiply probabilities. How do you respond?

19. Alberto is to spin the spinners shown and compute the probability of getting two blacks. He looks at the spinners and says the answer is $\frac{1}{2}$ because $\frac{1}{2}$ of the areas of the circles are black. How do you respond?

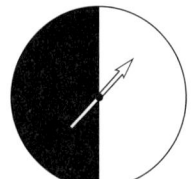 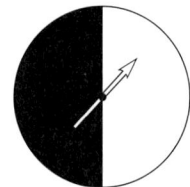

20. There are two bags each containing red balls and yellow balls. Bag A contains 1 red and 4 yellow balls. Bag B contains 3 red and 13 yellow balls. Alva says that if we choose one bag and draw one ball from that bag, we should always choose bag B if trying to draw a red ball because these are more red balls than in bag B in bag A. How do you respond?

Review Problems

21. Match the following phrase to the probability that describes it:

    a. A certain event   **i.** $\frac{1}{1000}$

    b. An impossible event   **ii.** $\frac{999}{1000}$

    c. A very likely event   **iii.** 0

    d. An unlikely event   **iv.** $\frac{1}{2}$

    e. A 50% chance   **v.** 1

22. A date in the month of April is chosen at random. Find the probability of the event of the date's being each of the following:
    a. April 7
    b. April 31
    c. Before April 20

23. Three men were walking down a street talking when they met a fourth man. If the fourth man knew that two of the men always lied and the third always told the truth and he asked the three a question, what is the probability that he got a truthful answer when only one man answered?

24. A roulette wheel has 38 slots around the rim; 36 slots are numbered from 1 to 36. Half of these 36 slots are red, and the other half are black. The remaining 2 slots are numbered 0 and 00 and are green. As the roulette wheel is spun in one direction, a small ivory ball is rolled along the rim in the opposite direction. The ball has an equally likely chance of falling into any one of the 38 slots. Find the probabilities of the events listed below.
    a. Ball lands in a black slot.
    b. Ball lands on 0 or 00.
    c. Ball does not land on a number from 1 through 12.
    d. Ball lands on an odd number or on a green slot.

25. If the roulette wheel in exercise 24 is spun 190 times, predict about how many times the ball can be expected to land on 0 or 00.

National Assessments

National Assessment of Educational Progress (NAEP) Questions

A package of candies contained only 10 red candies, 10 blue candies, and 10 green candies. Bill shook up the package, opened it, and started taking out one candy at a time and eating it. The first 2 candies he took out and ate were blue. Bill thinks the probability of getting a blue candy on his third try is $\frac{10}{30}$ or $\frac{1}{3}$.

Is Bill correct or incorrect?

Explain your answer.

NAEP, Grade 8, 2005

Leroy has one quarter, one dime, one nickel, and one penny. Two of the coins are in his left pocket and the other two coins are in his right pocket. The coins have been randomly placed in the two pockets.

What is the probability that Leroy will be able to purchase a 30-cent candy bar with two coins in his left pocket?

Using the coins, explain your reasoning.

NAEP, Grade 8, 2007

9-3 Simulations and Applications in Probability

9-3 Objectives

Students will be able to understand and explain

- Simulations in probability.
- Odds.
- Expected value.

Activity Manual

Use *Simulate It* to analyze probability situations using simulations.

Students may often encounter complex probabilistic situations. To analyze those, simulations may be used.

Simulations

A **simulation** is a technique used to act out a situation by conducting an experiment whose outcomes are analogous to the original situation. Using simulations, students typically estimate a probability using many trials rather than determine probabilities theoretically. Simulations can take various forms.

> **CCSS** According to the grade 7 *Common Core Standards*, students should be able to:
>
> Design and use a simulation to generate frequencies for compound events. *For example, use random digits as a simulation tool to approximate the answer to the question: If 40% of donors have type A blood, what is the probability that it will take at least 4 donors to find one with type A blood?* (p. 51)

In Section 9-1, Table 1, we saw partial results of John Kerrich's coin tosses. It would take considerable time to toss a coin 10,000 times as he did. But suppose we could simulate those tosses without having to flip a coin that many times. If that could be done, then we could make predictions based on the simulation, which, if the simulation was correct, would be very much like the experimental results Kerrich found. So how can we simulate a coin toss?

Because the probabilities of tossing a fair coin and obtaining a head or a tail are each $\frac{1}{2}$, it is sensible to devise a system that has two outcomes, each of which is expected to have a probability of $\frac{1}{2}$. Consider the following possibilities (and there are many more):

Scenario 1: Take an ordinary deck of playing cards. There are 52 cards (without jokers) in the deck; half are red and half are black. One simulation for the coin toss is simply to draw a card at random from the deck. Assign red to mean "a head appears," and assign black to mean "a tail appears." The probability of the event of drawing a red (or obtaining a head) is $\frac{1}{2}$, and the probability of obtaining a black (or a tail) is $\frac{1}{2}$. No coin has to be used, but the flipping of a coin could be simulated by drawing a card.

Scenario 2: Take an ordinary die with six faces, half are even and half are odd. We assign an even number as a "head," and an odd number as a "tail." Rolling the die then becomes a simulation for flipping a coin.

Scenario 3: We could use a **random-number table** as in Table 4. The digits in the table have been chosen at random, often by a computer or a calculator. To simulate the coin toss, we pick a number at random to start, and then read across the table, letting an even digit represent "heads", and an odd digit represent "tails." By keeping a record of what we obtain as we read, we simulate the probability of the event of tossing heads as the ratio of the number of even digits found to the total number read.

Table 4	Random Digits								
36422	93239	76046	81114	77412	86557	19549	98473	15221	87856
78496	47197	37961	67568	14861	61077	85210	51264	49975	71785
95384	59596	05081	39968	80495	00192	94679	18307	16265	48888
37957	89199	10816	24260	52302	69592	55019	94127	71721	70673
31422	27529	95051	83157	96377	33723	52902	51302	86370	50452
07443	15346	40653	84238	24430	88834	77318	07486	33950	61598
41348	86255	92715	96656	49693	99286	83447	20215	16040	41085
12398	95111	45663	55020	57159	58010	43162	98878	73337	35571
77229	92095	44305	09285	73256	02968	31129	66588	48126	52700
61175	53014	60304	13976	96312	42442	96713	43940	92516	81421
16825	27482	97858	05642	88047	68960	52991	67703	29805	42701
84656	03089	05166	67571	25545	26603	40243	55482	38341	97782
03872	31767	23729	89523	73654	24626	78393	77172	41328	95633
40488	70426	04034	46618	55102	93408	10965	69744	80766	14889
98322	25528	43808	05935	78338	77881	90139	72375	50624	91385
13366	52764	02407	14202	74172	58770	65348	24115	44277	96735
86711	27764	86789	43800	87582	09298	17880	75507	35217	08352
53886	50358	62738	91783	71944	90221	79403	75139	09102	77826
99348	21186	42266	01531	44325	61042	13453	61917	90426	12437
49985	08787	59448	82680	52929	19077	98518	06251	58451	91140
49807	32863	69984	20102	09523	47827	08374	79849	19352	62726
46569	00365	23591	44317	55054	99835	20633	66215	46668	53587
09988	44203	43532	54538	16619	45444	11957	69184	98398	96508
32916	00567	82881	59753	54761	39404	90756	91760	18698	42852
93285	32297	27254	27198	99093	97821	46277	10439	30389	45372
03222	39951	12738	50303	25017	84207	52123	88637	19369	58289
87002	61789	96250	99337	14144	00027	43542	87030	14773	73087
68840	94259	01961	42552	91843	33855	00824	48733	81297	80411
88323	28828	64765	08244	53077	50897	91937	08871	91517	19668
55170	71062	64159	79364	53088	21536	39451	95649	65256	23950

The scenarios above are for expected single outcomes of an experiment. Suppose we simulate the probability of a couple having two girls (*GG*) in an expected family. If we assume the birth of a boy and the birth of a girl are equally likely and assume successive births are independent, we could use the random-digit table with an even digit representing a girl and an odd digit representing a boy. Because there are two children, we need to consider pairs of digits. If we examine 100 pairs, then the simulated probability of *GG* will be the number of pairs of even digits divided by 100, the total number of pairs considered.

Example 13

A baseball player, Reggie, has a batting average of 0.400. This gives his experimental probability of getting a hit on any particular time at bat. Estimate the probability of the event that he will get at least one hit in his next three times at bat if the at bats are independent events.

Solution We use a random-digit table to simulate this situation. We choose a starting point and place the random digits in groups of three. Because Reggie's probability of getting a hit on any particular time at bat is 0.400, we use the occurrence of four specific numbers from 0 through 9 to represent a hit. Suppose a hit is represented by 0, 1, 2, and 3. At least one hit is obtained in three times at bat if, in any sequence of three digits, a 0, 1, 2, or 3 appears. Data for 50 trials are given next:

780	862	760	580	783	720	590	506	021	366
848	118	073	077	042	254	063	667	374	153
377	883	573	683	780	115	662	591	685	274
279	652	754	909	754	892	310	673	964	351
803	034	799	915	059	006	774	640	298	961

We see that a 0, 1, 2, or 3 appears in 42 out of the 50 trials. Thus, an estimate for the probability of the event of at least one hit on Reggie's next three times at bat is $\frac{42}{50} = 0.84$.

▶ **NOW TRY THIS 5**

NTT 5: Answer can be found in Answers at the back of the book.

a. Use the random-digit table to estimate the probability of the event that a couple that plans to have three children will have two girls and one boy.
b. Determine the theoretical probability of the event described in part (a).
c. Should the answers in parts (a) and (b) always be exactly the same? Why?

The partial student page shown on page 509 explores designing a simulation with random digits. The exercise on the student page asks how random numbers can be used to simulate blood type problems as referred to in the *Common Core Standards* quote on p. 506.

The following simulation problem concerns how many chips there are in chocolate chip cookies.

Example 14

Suppose Corey makes enough batter for exactly 100 chocolate chip cookies and mixes 100 chocolate chips into the batter. If the chips are distributed at random and Johnny chooses a cookie at random from the 100 cookies, estimate the probability that it will contain exactly one chocolate chip.

School Book Page

EXAMPLE **Using Random Digits as a Simulation Tool**

3 **Journalism** In an election, 52% of voters chose Mayor Garner. Use random digits as a simulation tool to estimate the probability that a reporter will ask more than 2 voters before finding one who voted for Garner.

52% of voters, or $\frac{52}{100}$, chose Garner.

Use a simulation tool with 100 equally likely outcomes. You can use 2-digit random numbers from 00 to 99.

52 of the possible outcomes should represent voters for Garner. Use the numbers 00 to 51.

Each row of random numbers at the right represents one trial.

If either or both numbers are between 00 and 51, the reporter will need to ask 1 or 2 voters.

If neither number is between 00 and 51, the reporter will need to ask more than 2 voters.

Out of 10 trials, 3 resulted in more than 2 voters being asked.

So, the probability that a reporter will have to ask more than 2 voters before finding one who voted for Garner is approximately $\frac{3}{10}$.

Random Numbers	Outcome
06 82	← 1 voter
80 17	← 2 voters
87 65	← > 2 voters
96 96	← > 2 voters
60 68	← > 2 voters
47 39	← 1 voter
40 31	← 1 voter
66 17	← 2 voters
30 33	← 1 voter
20 68	← 1 voter

Medicine
91 04 81 49
72 45 45 96
54 93 14 81
70 28 66 00
67 37 29 45
33 77 57 22
58 84 14 80
49 45 20 59
78 05 88 88
21 83 16 98

✓ **Quick Check**

3. Medicine In the U.S., 42% of blood donors have type A blood. Use the random numbers at the left as a tool to estimate the probability that it will take at least 4 donors to find one with type A blood.

Solution We use a simulation to estimate the probability of choosing a cookie with exactly one chocolate chip. We construct a 10×10 grid, as in Figure 36(a), to represent the 100 cookies Corey made. Each square (cookie) can be associated with some ordered pair, where the first component is for the horizontal scale and the second is for the vertical scale. For example, the squares $(0, 2)$ and $(5, 3)$ are pictured in Figure 36(a). Using the random-digit Table 4, we close our eyes and then take a pencil and point to one number to start. Look at the number and the number immediately following it. Consider these numbers an ordered pair and continue until we obtain 100 ordered pairs to represent the locations of the 100 chips. For example, suppose we start at a 3 and the numbers following 3 are as follows:

$$39968 \qquad 80495 \qquad 00192 \ldots$$

Then the ordered pairs would be given as $(3, 9), (9, 6), (8, 8), (0, 4)$, and so on. We use each pair of numbers as the coordinates for the square (cookie) and place a tally on the grid to represent each chip, as shown in Figure 36(b). We estimate the probability of the event that a cookie has exactly one chip by counting the number of squares with exactly one tally and dividing by 100.

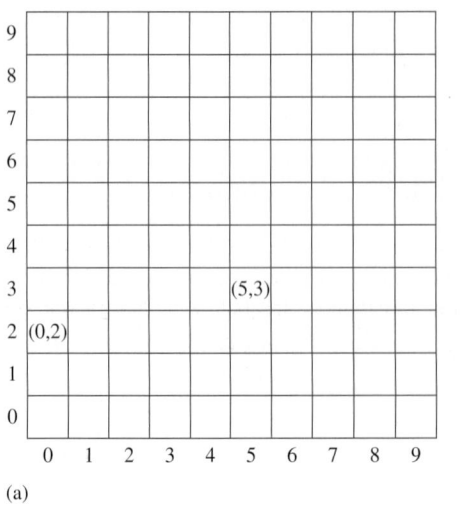 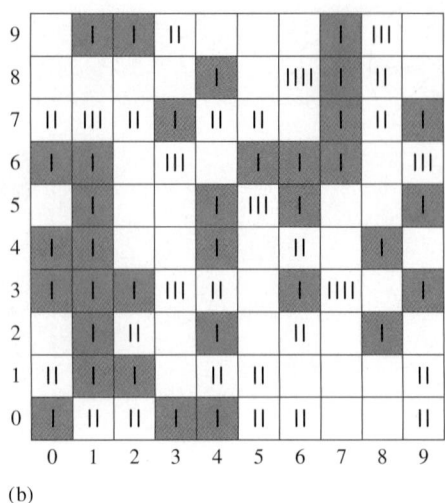

(a) (b)

Figure 36

Table 5 shows the results of one simulation. Thus, an estimate for the probability of Johnny receiving a cookie with exactly one chip is $\frac{34}{100}$.

Table 5

Number of Chips	Number of Cookies
0	38
1	34
2	20
3	6
≥4	2

The results given in Table 6 were obtained using theoretical methods beyond the scope of this text.

Table 6

Number of Chips	Number of Cookies
0	36.8
1	36.8
2	18.4
3	6.1
≥4	1.9

Odds: An Application of Probabilities

People talk about the *odds in favor of* and the *odds against* a particular event's happening. For example, if the odds in favor of an event are 4:1, this means that if circumstances surrounding the event are to occur many times, for every 5 times the circumstances occur, we expect the event to happen 4 of those times and not to happen 1 time. This interpretation gives the following intuitive results:

$$P(\text{event happens}) = \frac{4}{5}$$

$$P(\text{event does not happen}) = \frac{1}{5}$$

We could start with probabilities and work to get odds as follows:

$$\frac{P(\text{event happens})}{P(\text{event does not happen})} = \frac{\dfrac{4}{5}}{\dfrac{1}{5}} = \frac{4}{5} \div \frac{1}{5} = \frac{4}{5} \cdot \frac{5}{1} = \frac{4}{1}$$

When the **odds in favor** of the president being reelected are 4 to 1, this refers to the ratio showing how likely the president is to win the election relative to how likely the president is to lose. The probability of the event of the president's winning is 4 times the probability of the event of the president's losing. If W represents the event the president wins the election and L represents the event the president loses, then

$$P(W) = 4P(L)$$
$$\frac{P(W)}{P(L)} = \frac{4}{1}, \text{ or } 4{:}1.$$

Because W and L are complements of each other, $L = \overline{W}$ and $P(\overline{W}) = 1 - P(W)$, so

$$\frac{P(W)}{P(\overline{W})} = \frac{P(W)}{1 - P(W)} = \frac{4}{1}, \text{ or } 4{:}1.$$

The **odds against** the president's winning are how likely the president is to lose relative to how likely the president is to win. Using the preceding information, we have

$$\frac{P(L)}{P(W)} = \frac{P(\overline{W})}{P(W)} = \frac{1 - P(W)}{P(W)} = \frac{1}{4}, \text{ or } 1{:}4.$$

Formally, odds are defined as follows.

> ### Definition of Odds
> Let $P(A)$ be the probability that event A occurs and $P(\overline{A})$ be the probability that event A does not occur. Then the **odds in favor** of event A occurring are
> $$\frac{P(A)}{P(\overline{A})} = \frac{P(A)}{1 - P(A)}$$
> and the **odds against** event A occurring are
> $$\frac{P(\overline{A})}{P(A)} = \frac{1 - P(A)}{P(A)}.$$

When odds are calculated for equally likely outcomes, we have the following:

$$\text{Odds in favor of an event } A{:} \quad \frac{P(A)}{P(\overline{A})} = \frac{n(A)}{n(S)} \div \frac{n(\overline{A})}{n(S)} = \frac{n(A)}{n(S)} \cdot \frac{n(S)}{n(\overline{A})} = \frac{n(A)}{n(\overline{A})}$$

$$\text{Odds against an event } A{:} \quad \frac{n(\overline{A})}{n(A)}$$

Thus, in the case of equally likely outcomes, we have

$$\text{Odds in favor} = \frac{\text{Number of favorable outcomes}}{\text{Number of unfavorable outcomes}}$$

$$\text{Odds against} = \frac{\text{Number of unfavorable outcomes}}{\text{Number of favorable outcomes}}.$$

Example 15

For each of the following, find the odds in favor of the given event.

  a. Rolling a number less than 5 on a die.
  b. Tossing heads on a fair coin.
  c. Drawing an ace from an ordinary 52-card deck.
  d. Drawing a heart from an ordinary 52-card deck.

Solution

  a. The probability of the event of rolling a number less than 5 is $\frac{4}{6}$; the probability of the event of rolling a number not less than 5 is $\frac{2}{6}$. The odds in favor of rolling a number less than 5 are $\frac{4}{6} \div \frac{2}{6}$, or 4:2, or 2:1.

  b. $P(H) = \frac{1}{2}$ and $P(\overline{H}) = \frac{1}{2}$. The odds in favor of getting heads are $\frac{1}{2} \div \frac{1}{2}$, or 1:1.

  c. The probability of the event of drawing an ace is $\frac{4}{52}$, and the probability of the event of not drawing an ace is $\frac{48}{52}$. The odds in favor of drawing an ace are $\frac{4}{52} \div \frac{48}{52}$, or 4:48, or 1:12.

  d. The probability of the event of drawing a heart is $\frac{13}{52} = \frac{1}{4}$, and the probability of the event of not drawing a heart is $\frac{39}{52} = \frac{3}{4}$. The odds in favor of drawing a heart are $\frac{1}{4} \div \frac{3}{4}$, or 1:3.

▶ **NOW TRY THIS 6**

NTT 6: Answer can be found in Answers at the back of the book.

In Example 15(a), there are 4 ways to roll a number less than 5 on a die (favorable outcomes) and 2 ways of not rolling a number less than 5 (unfavorable outcomes), so the odds in favor of rolling a number less than 5 are 4:2, or 2:1. Work the other three parts of Example 15 using this approach.

In Example 15(d), the odds in favor of drawing a heart are 1:3. Therefore, the ratio of favorable outcomes to unfavorable outcomes is $\frac{1}{3}$. Thus, in a sample space modeling this situation with four elements, there would be 1 favorable outcome and 3 unfavorable outcomes and $P(\text{drawing a heart}) = \frac{1}{1+3} = \frac{1}{4}$. In general, we have the following.

Theorem 9-8

If the *odds in favor* of event E are $m:n$, then $P(E) = \frac{m}{m+n}$.

If the *odds against* event E are $m:n$, then $P(E) = \frac{n}{m+n}$.

Expected Value Using Probabilities

Racetracks use odds for betting purposes. If the odds against Fast Jack are 3:1, this means the track will pay $3 for every $1 you bet. If Fast Jack wins, then for a $5 bet, the track will return your $5 plus $3 · $5, or $15, for a total of $20. The 3:1 odds means Fast Jack is expected to lose 3 out of 4 times in this situation. If the stated odds of 3:1 against Fast Jack are accurate, then the probability of Fast Jack's losing the race is $\frac{3}{4}$ and of Fast Jack's winning, $\frac{1}{4}$. If we compute the expected average winnings (expected value) over the long run, the gain is $3 for every $1 bet for a win, and a loss of $1 otherwise. The expected value, E, is computed as follows:

$$E = 3\left(\frac{1}{4}\right) + {}^{-}1\left(\frac{3}{4}\right) = 0$$

Therefore, the expected value is $0. (If a racetrack gave accurate odds, it could not cover its expenses and make a profit. Thus, usually the track overestimates a horse's chance of winning by about 20% and uses "house odds.")

As another example of using expected value, consider the spinner in Figure 37; the payoff is in each sector of the circle. Using area models, we assign the following probabilities to each region:

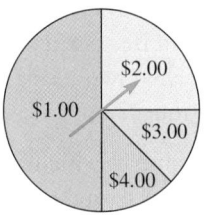

$$P(\$1.00) = \frac{1}{2} \qquad P(\$2.00) = \frac{1}{4} \qquad P(\$3.00) = \frac{1}{8} \qquad P(\$4.00) = \frac{1}{8}$$

Should the owner of this spinner expect to make money over an extended period of time if the charge is $2.00 per spin?

To determine the average payoff over the long run, we find the product of the probability of the event of landing on the payoff and the payoff itself and then find the sum of the products. This computation is given by

$$E = \left(\frac{1}{2}\right)1 + \left(\frac{1}{4}\right)2 + \left(\frac{1}{8}\right)3 + \left(\frac{1}{8}\right)4 = 1.875.$$

Figure 37

The owner expects to pay out about $1.88 per spin. This is less than the $2.00 charge, so the owner should make a profit if the spinner is used many times. The sum of the products in this example, $1.875, is the **expected value**, or **mathematical expectation**, of the experiment of spinning the wheel in Figure 37. The owner's expected average earnings are $2.00 − $1.875 = $0.125 per spin, and the player's expected average earnings (loss) are ${}^{-}$0.125. The expected value does not need to be one of the individual possible outcomes so it might never be the actual amount won on any trial.

The expected value is an average of winnings over the long run. Expected value was also used to predict the average winnings in the horse-race example above. *An expected value, however, cannot be used to determine the outcome of any single experiment.*

Definition of Expected Value

If, in an experiment, the possible outcomes are numbers $a_1, a_2, \ldots, a_n$, occurring with probabilities $p_1, p_2, \ldots, p_n$, respectively, then the **expected value (mathematical expectation)** E is given by the equation

$$E = a_1 \cdot p_1 + a_2 \cdot p_2 + a_3 \cdot p_3 + \ldots + a_n \cdot p_n.$$

When payoffs in a game are involved and the expected value minus cost to play a game of chance is $0, the game is a **fair game**. Previously, a *fair game* was defined as a game in which each player has an equal chance of winning. If there are two players and each has the same probability of winning a given number of dollars from the other, it follows that the expected value minus the cost to play (net winnings) for each player is $0.

Example 16

It costs $5.00 to play a game when two coins are tossed. We receive $10 if two heads occur, $5 if exactly one head occurs, and nothing if no heads appear. Is this a fair game? That is, are the net winnings $0?

Solution   Before we determine the net winning, recall that $P(HH) = \dfrac{1}{4}$, $P(HT \text{ or } TH) = \dfrac{1}{2}$, and $P(TT) = \dfrac{1}{4}$. To find the expected value, we compute

$$E = \left(\frac{1}{4}\right)(\$10) + \left(\frac{1}{2}\right)(\$5) + \left(\frac{1}{4}\right)(\$0) = \$5.$$

Since the cost of the game is $5, then the net winnings are $0. This is a fair game.

Problem Solving   **A Coin-Tossing Game**

Al and Betsy play a coin-tossing game in which a fair coin is tossed until a total of either three heads or three tails occurred. Al wins when a total of three heads are tossed, and Betsy wins when a total of three tails are tossed. Each bet $50 on the game. If the coin is lost when two heads and one tail occurred, how should the stakes be fairly split if the game is not continued?

Understanding the Problem   Al and Betsy each bet $50 on a coin-tossing game in which a fair coin is tossed. Al wins when a total of three heads is obtained; Betsy wins when a total of three tails is obtained. When two heads and one tail had occurred, the coin was lost. The problem is how to split the stakes fairly.

There are different interpretations of what "splitting fairly" means. Possibly, the best interpretation is to split the pot in proportion to the probabilities of each player's winning the game when play is halted. We calculate the expected value for each player and split the pot accordingly.

Devising a Plan   A third head makes Al the winner, whereas Betsy needs two more tails to win. We use a tree diagram to analyze the completion of the game and find the probabilities. Once we find the probabilities, we multiply the probabilities by the amount of the pot, $100, to determine each player's fair share.

Carrying Out the Plan   The tree diagram in Figure 38 shows the possibilities for game winners if the game is completed. We find the probabilities of the events of each player winning.

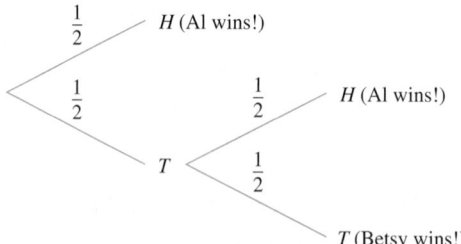

Figure 38

$$P(\text{Betsy wins}) = \frac{1}{2} \cdot \frac{1}{2} = \frac{1}{4}$$

$$P(\text{Al wins}) = 1 - \frac{1}{4} = \frac{3}{4}$$

Hence, the fair way to split the stakes is for Al to receive $\dfrac{3}{4}$ of $100, or $75, and for Betsy to receive $\dfrac{1}{4}$ of $100, or $25.

Looking Back The problem could be made even more interesting by assuming that the coin is not fair so that the probability is not $\frac{1}{2}$ for each branch in the tree diagram. Other possibilities arise if the players have unequal amounts of money in the pot or if more tosses are required in order to win.

This game is reminiscent of the original game that marked the beginning of the development of probability as part of mathematical science. (See p. 469.)

Assessment 9-3A

1. Could we use a thumb tack to simulate the birth of boys and girls? Why or why not? *
2. How could we use a random-number table to estimate the probability that two cards drawn from a standard deck of cards with replacement will be of the same suit? *
3. How might we use a random-digit table to simulate each of the following events?
   a. Tossing a single die *
   b. Choosing three people at random from a group of 20 people *
   c. Spinning the spinner, where the probability of each color is as shown in the following figure *

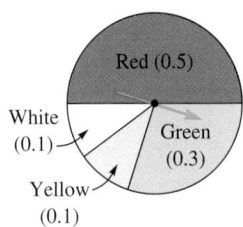

4. A school has 500 students. The principal is to pick 30 students at random from the school to go to the Rose Bowl. How can this be done using a random-digit table? *
5. In a certain city, the probability of the event that it will rain on a certain day is 0.8 if it rained the day before. The probability of the event that it will be dry on a certain day is 0.3 if it was dry the day before. It is now Sunday, and it is raining. Use the random-digit table to simulate the weather for the rest of the week. *
6. It is reported that 15% of people who come into contact with a person infected with strep throat contract the disease. How might we use the random-digit table to estimate the probability that at least one child in a three-child family will catch the disease, given that each child has come into contact with an infected person? *
7. Pick a block of two digits from the random-digit table. What is the probability of the event that the block picked is less than 30? $\frac{3}{10}$
8. An estimate of the fish population of a certain pond was found by catching 200 fish and marking and returning them to the pond. The next day, 300 fish were caught, of which 50 had been marked the previous day. Estimate the fish population of the pond. 1200 fish

9. Suppose that in the World Series, the two teams are evenly matched and the outcomes of successive games are independent events. The two teams play until one team wins four games, and no ties are possible.
   a. What is the maximum number of games that could be played? 7
   b. Use simulation to approximate the probabilities of the event that the series will end in (i) four games and in (ii) seven games. *
10. Assume Carmen Smith, a basketball player, makes free throws with 80% probability of success and is placed in a one-and-one situation where she is given a second foul shot if, and only if, the first shot goes through the basket. If you assume successive shots are independent, simulate the 25 attempts from the foul line in one-and-one situations to determine how many times we would expect Carmen to score 0 points, 1 point, and 2 points. *
11. **a.** What are the odds in favor of drawing a face card from an ordinary deck of playing cards? 3 to 10
    b. What are the odds against drawing a face card? 10 to 3
12. On a single roll of a pair of dice, what are the odds against rolling a sum of 7? 30 to 6 or 5 to 1
13. If the probability of a boy's being born is $\frac{1}{2}$, and a family plans to have four children, what are the odds against having all boys? 15 to 1
14. If the odds against Deborah's winning first prize in a chess tournament are 3 to 5, what is the probability of the event that she will win first prize? $\frac{5}{8}$
15. If the probability of the event that a randomly chosen household has a cat is 0.27, what are the odds against a chosen household having a cat? 73:27
16. From a set of eight marbles, five red and three white, we choose one at random. What are the odds in favor of choosing a red marble? 5:3
17. In exercise 16, what are the odds against choosing a red marble? 3:5
18. If the odds in favor of achieving a Grand Slam golf sweep are 2:9, what is the probability of the event of achieving the sweep? $\frac{2}{11}$
19. A regular die has 1–6 dots, respectively, on its faces. When a die is tossed, what are the odds in favor of obtaining a prime number? 1:1
20. If the probability of an event happening is $\frac{88}{93}$, what are the odds against its happening? 5:88

21. If the probability of the event of rain for the day is 90%, what are the odds in favor of rain?   9:1

22. What are the odds in favor of rolling double sixes on a single roll of a fair pair of dice?   1:35

23. Suppose five quarters, five dimes, five nickels, and ten pennies are in a box. One coin is selected at random. What is the   8.4 cents   expected value of the amount of money drawn from the bag?

24. If the odds in favor of Fast Leg winning a horse race are 5 to 2 and the first prize is $14,000, what is the expected value of Fast Leg's monetary winnings in this race? $10,000

25. Suppose it costs $8 to roll a pair of dice. We get paid the sum of the numbers in dollars that appear on the dice. Is it a fair game?   No, the expected value is ⁻$1

26. A container has three white balls and two red balls. A first ball is drawn at random and not replaced. Then a second

ball is drawn. Given the following conditions, what is the probability of the event that the second ball was red?
  a. The first ball was white. $\frac{1}{2}$
  b. The first ball was red. $\frac{1}{4}$

27. If the ratio of men to women in a room is 5:4, what are the odds of a man being chosen if a person in the room is chosen at random?   5:4

28. If the probability of spilling soup on your tie is $\frac{1}{3}$, then what are the odds of not spilling soup on your tie?   2:1

29. A bag of grass seed is advertised as having 98% of the seeds germinate. What are the odds of having a seed chosen at random in the bag germinate?   98:2 or 49:1

30. There are 58 consonants in a traditional Scrabble game containing 100 tiles. How could you use a random digit table to simulate choosing a consonant at random from the game?   *

Assessment 9-3B

1. How could we use a spinner as shown below to simulate the birth of boys and girls?   *

2. How could we use a random-digit generator or random-number table to simulate the event of rain if you knew that 60% of the time with conditions as you have today, it will rain?   *

3. How could you use a random-digit generator or a random-number table to simulate choosing 4 people at random from a group of 25 people?   *

4. In a school with 200 students, the band director chooses four people at random to carry a banner. If she uses a random-digit table or a random-number generator, how could this be done?   *

5. Simulate tossing two fair coins 25 times and obtaining the outcome TT, where T represents tails. What is your simulated probability?   *

6. An estimate of the frog population in a certain pond was found by catching 30 frogs, marking them, and returning them to the pond. The next day, 50 frogs were caught, of which 14 had been marked the previous day. Estimate the frog population of the pond.   About 107 frogs

7. Suppose a dot is placed at random in a 10 × 10 graph grid in which squares have been numbered from 1 to 100 with no number repeated. Now simulate choosing 100 numbers at random between 1 and 100 inclusive. How many numbers might you expect to match the square with the dot?   1

8. In a class of seven students, a teacher spins a seven-sectored spinner (with equal-sized sectors) to determine which students to ask questions. Determine about how many times a student can expect to be called on when 100 questions are asked.   *

9. Use a random digit table to estimate the probability of the event that at least 2 people in a group of 5 people have the same zodiac sign. There are 12 zodiac signs. Assume each sign is equally likely for each person.   *

10. In the United States, about 45% of the people have blood type O. Assuming that donors arrive independently and randomly at a local blood bank, use a simulation to answer each of the following questions.
  a. If 10 donors come to the blood bank one day, what is the probability of the event that at least four have blood type O?   *
  b. How many donors on average should the bank expect to see in order to obtain exactly four people with blood type O?   *

11. **a.** Susan said that the odds in favor of drawing a black card from a normal deck of 52 cards was 2:1. Do you agree?   No; the odds are 1:1.
  b. Explain what is meant by "the odds in favor of drawing a black card from the normal deck of 52 cards."   *

12. Diane tossed a coin 9 times and got 9 tails. Assume that Diane's coin is fair and answer each of the questions.
  a. What is the probability of the event of tossing a tail on the 10th toss? $\frac{1}{2}$
  b. What is the probability of the event of tossing 10 more tails in a row? $\frac{1}{1024}$
  c. What are the odds against tossing 10 more tails in a row?   *

13. If a family has one girl and plans to have another child, answer the following if the probability of the event of a girl being born is $\frac{1}{2}$, and births are independent events.
  a. What is the probability of the event of the second child's being a boy? $\frac{1}{2}$
  b. What are the odds in favor of having one girl and one boy given their current family?   1:1

14. Suppose the odds against winning the lottery are exactly 55 million to 1. What is the probability of the event of winning the lottery? $\frac{1}{55,000,001}$

15. What are the odds in favor of tossing at least 2 heads if a fair coin is tossed 3 times?   1:1

16. What are the odds in favor of randomly drawing the letter S from the letters in the word MISSISSIPPI?   4:7   7:4

17. In exercise 16, what are the odds against choosing the letter S?

18. If a whole number less than 10 is chosen at random, what are the odds in favor of the number being greater than 5?   4:6 or 2:3

19. If the probability of an event is $0.\overline{3}$, what are the odds against the event?   2:1

20. The following spinner is spun. What is the probability of the event that the spinner

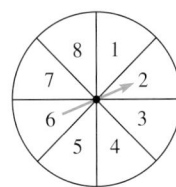

a. lands on an odd number? $\frac{1}{2}$
b. lands on a number divisible by 3? $\frac{1}{4}$
c. does not land on 5, 6, or 7? $\frac{5}{8}$
d. lands on a number less than 4? $\frac{3}{8}$

21. If the probability of the event of rain for the day is 60%, what are the odds against rain?   4:6 or 2:3

22. On a roulette wheel, half of the slots numbered 1 through 36 are red and half are black. Two slots, numbered 0 and 00, are green. What are the odds against a ball landing in a red slot on any spin of the wheel?   20:18 or 10:9

23. On a roulette wheel are 36 slots numbered 1 through 36 and 2 slots numbered 0 and 00. You can bet on a single number. If the ball lands on your number, you receive 35 chips plus the chip you played.
a. What is the probability of the event that the ball will land on 17? $\frac{1}{38}$

b. What are the odds against the ball landing on 17?   37 to 1
c. If each chip is worth $1, what is the expected result for a player who plays the number 17 for a long time?   *

24. We play a game in which two dice are rolled. If a sum of 7 appears, we win $10; otherwise, we lose $2.00. If we intend to play this game for a long time, should we expect to make money, lose money, or come out about even? Explain.   *

25. Suppose a standard six-sided die is rolled and you receive $1 for every dot showing on the top of the die. What should the cost of playing the game be in order to make it a fair game? $3.50

26. A family with 3 children can have 0, 1, 2, or 3 girls. What is the expected value for the number of girls in this family assuming the probability of a girl being born is $\frac{1}{2}$?   1.5 girls

27. If the ratio of men to women in a room is 5:4, what are the odds of a woman being chosen if a person in the room is chosen at random?   4:5

28. If the probability of spilling soup on your tie is $\frac{1}{3}$, then what are the odds of spilling soup on your tie?   1:2

29. A bag of grass seed is advertised as having 98% of the seeds germinate. What are the odds of having a seed in the bag chosen at random not germinate?   1 to 49

30. There are 42 vowels in a traditional Scrabble game containing 100 tiles. How could you use a random-digit table to simulate choosing a vowel at random from the game?   *

Mathematical Connections 9-3

Reasoning

1. In an attempt to reduce the growth of its population, China instituted a policy limiting a family to one child. Rural Chinese suggested revising the policy to limit families to one son. Assuming the suggested policy is adopted and that any birth is as likely to produce a boy as a girl, and that successive births are independent, explain how to use simulation to answer the following questions.
a. What would be the average family size?
b. What would be the ratio of newborn boys to newborn girls?

2. Consider a "walk" on the following grid starting at the origin O and "walking" 1 unit (block) north, and at each intersection turning left with probability $\frac{1}{2}$, turning right with probability $\frac{1}{6}$, and moving straight with probability $\frac{1}{3}$. Explain how to simulate the "walk" using a regular six-sided die.

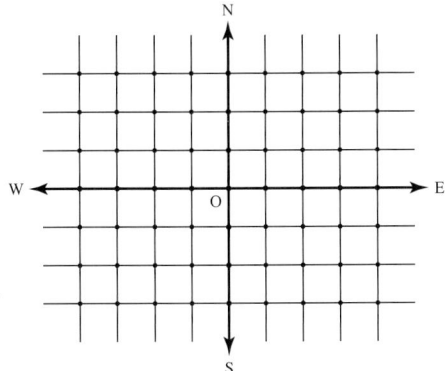

3. A game involves tossing two coins. A player wins $1.00 if both tosses result in heads. What should you pay to play this game in order to make it a fair game? Explain your reasoning.

Open-Ended

4. What is the probability of the event that in a group of five people chosen at random, at least two will have birthdays in the same month? Assume all months are equally likely for birth days. Design a simulation for this situation and try it 10 times.

5. The probability of the event of the home team's winning a basketball game is 80%. Describe a simulation of the event that the home team will win three home games in a row.

6. Montana duck hunters are all perfect shots. Ten Montana hunters are in a duck blind when 10 ducks fly over. All 10 hunters pick a random duck at which to shoot, and all 10 hunters fire at the same time. How many ducks could be expected to escape, on the average, if this experiment were repeated a large number of times? How could this situation be simulated?

7. Suppose we toss two fair coins. Design a fair game with a payoff based on the results of the toss.

8. An insurance company sells a policy that pays $50,000.00 in case of accidental death. According to company figures, the rate of accidental death is 47 per 100,000 population each year. What annual premium should the company charge for this coverage?

9. Write a game-type problem about odds and payoffs so that the odds in favor of an event are 2:3 and the game is a fair game.

Cooperative Learning

10. The sixth-grade class decided that an ideal family of four children has two boys and two girls.
    a. As a group, design a simulation to determine the probability of the event of two boys and two girls in a family with four kids.
    b. Have each person in the group try the simulation 25 times and compare the probabilities.
    c. Combine the results of all the group members and use this information to find a simulated probability.
    d. Compute the theoretical probability of the event of having two boys and two girls in a family of four and compare your answer to the simulated probability.

11. Have you ever wondered how you would score on a 10-item true-false test if you guessed at every answer?
    a. Simulate a score by tossing a coin 10 times, with heads representing true and tails representing false. Check the answers by using the following key to score the test.

1	2	3	4	5	6	7	8	9	10
F	T	F	F	T	F	T	T	T	F

    b. Combine all results in the group to find the average (mean) number of correct answers for the group.
    c. How many items would you expect to get correct if the number of items were 30 instead of 10?
    d. What is the theoretical probability of getting all the answers correct on a 10-item true-false test if all answers were chosen by flipping a coin?

12. a. Guess how many cards you would expect to have to draw on the average in an ordinary playing deck before an ace appears.
    b. Have each person in the group repeat the experiment 10 times or simulate it for 10 trials. Then find the average number of cards turned before an ace appears.
    c. Combine the results of all the group members and find the average number of cards that are turned before an ace appears. How does this average compare to each individual estimate?

13. A cereal company places a coupon bearing a number from 1 to 9 in each box of cereal. If the numbers are distributed at random in the boxes, estimate the number of boxes you would have to purchase in order to obtain all nine numbers. Explain how the random-digit table could be used to estimate the number of boxes. Each person in the group should simulate 10 trials, and the results in the group should be combined to find the estimate.

14. As a group, explore the random-number features on graphing calculators.
    a. On some graphing calculators, if we choose the MATH menu and then select PRB, which stands for PROBABILITY, we find **RANDINT**, the random integer feature. RANDINT(generates a random integer within a specified range. It requires two inputs, which are the upper and lower boundaries for the integers. For example, RANDINT(1, 10) generates a random integer from 1 through 10.
        i. How could we use RANDINT(to simulate tossing a single die?
        ii. How could we use RANDINT(to simulate the sum of the numbers when tossing two dice?

    b. Some graphing calculators have a **RAND** function. RAND generates a random number greater than 0 and less than 1. For example, RAND might produce the numbers .5956605, .049599836, or .876572691. To have RAND produce random numbers from 1 to 10 as in part (a), we enter int (10 *RAND) + 1. The **INT** (greatest integer) feature is found in the MATH menu under NUM. The feature int returns the greatest integer less than or equal to a number.
        i. How could we use RAND to simulate tossing a single die?
        ii. How could we use RAND to simulate tossing two dice and taking the sum of the numbers?
    c. Use one of these random features to simulate tossing two dice 30 times. Based on our simulation, what is the probability of the event that a sum of 7 will occur?

15. As a group, design a game that involves cards, dice, or spinners.
    a. Write the rules so that any person who wants to play can understand the game.
    b. Write a description explaining whether the game is fair.
    c. Calculate the odds in favor of each player's winning.
    d. If betting is involved, discuss expected values.
    e. Exchange games and analyze them in groups.

Connecting Mathematics to the Classroom

16. Maximilian said that he could make up an experimental probability answer to a homework question about simulations and no one would ever know. How do you react?

17. A student claims that if the odds in favor of winning a game are $a:b$, then out of every $a + b$ games she would win a games. Hence, the probability of the event of winning the game is $\frac{a}{a + b}$. Is the student's reasoning correct? Why or why not?

18. A student wants to know why if the odds in favor of an event are $3:4$, the probability of the event occurring is not $\frac{3}{4}$. How do you respond?

19. Maria wants at least 51% of her class to vote for her. To achieve this, she decides that there is a probability of $\frac{1}{3}$ that an individual student will not vote. Also, she promises 24 of the 48 students that she will do what they individually want if she is elected; so that she is reasonably sure they will vote for her. Would you advise her that she is on safe ground for winning with this strategy?

Review Problems

20. In a two-person game, four coins are tossed. If exactly two heads come up, one player wins. If anything else comes up, the other player wins. Does each player have an equal chance of winning the game? Explain why or why not.

21. A single card is drawn from an ordinary deck. What is the probability of each of the following events?
    a. Club
    b. Queen and a spade
    c. Not a queen
    d. Not a heart
    e. Spade or a heart
    f. 6 of diamonds
    g. Queen or a spade
    h. Either red or black

22. From a sack containing seven red marbles, eight blue marbles, and four white marbles, marbles are drawn at random for several experiments. Determine the probability of each of the following events.
  a. One marble drawn at random is either red or blue.
  b. The first draw is red and the second is blue, where one marble is drawn at random, its color is recorded, the marble is replaced, and another marble is drawn.
  c. The event in (b) where the first marble is not replaced.
23. A basketball player shoots free throws and makes them with probability $\frac{1}{3}$. If you assume successive shots are independent, what is the probability the player will miss three in a row?
24. Refer to the following spinners and write a sample space for each of the following experiments:

Spinner 1

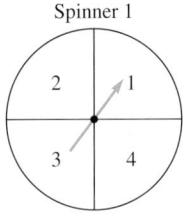

Spinner 2

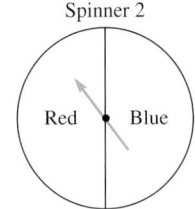

  a. Spin spinner 1 once.
  b. Spin spinner 2 once.
  c. Spin spinner 1 once and then spin spinner 2 once.
  d. Spin spinner 2 once and then roll a normal die.
  e. Spin spinner 1 twice.
  f. Spin spinner 2 twice.
25. Draw a spinner with two sections, red and blue, such that the probability of the event of getting (Blue, Blue) on two spins is $\frac{25}{36}$.
26. Find the probability of the event of getting two vowels when someone draws two letters from the English alphabet with replacement.

9-4 Permutations and Combinations in Probability

9-4 Objectives

Students will be able to understand and explain

- Permutations.
- Permutations of like objects.
- Combinations.
- Use of permutations and combinations in probability problems.

 Activity Manual

Use *How Many Arrangements?* to investigate permutations and combinations.

Permutations of Unlike Objects

An arrangement of things in a definite order with no repetitions is a **permutation**. For example, different arrangements of the three letters R, A, and T are seen in Figure 39.

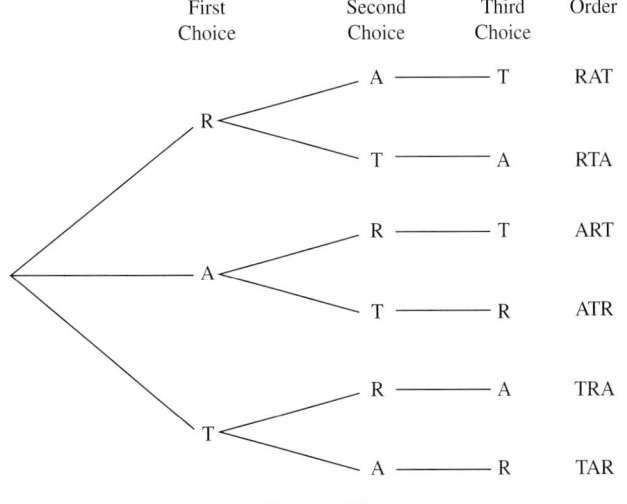

Figure 39

Order is important in a permutation and there are no repetitions in the arrangements. Determining the number of possible arrangements of the three letters without making a list is done using the Fundamental Counting Principle. Recall that the Fundamental Counting Principle states that *if an event M can occur in m ways and, after M has occurred, event N can occur in n ways, then event M followed by event N can occur in mn ways.* There are three ways to choose the first letter in Figure 39, and for each of these choices, there are two ways to choose the second letter. Thus far, there are $3 \cdot 2$ ways to choose the first two letters. Next, for each of the $3 \cdot 2$ choices, there is one way to choose the third letter, so there are $3 \cdot 2 \cdot 1$, or 6, ways to arrange the letters. It is common to record and say the number of permutations of three objects taken three at a time is $_3P_3$. Therefore, $_3P_3 = 6$.

Consider how many ways the owner of an ice cream parlor can display 10 flavors in a row along the front of the display case. The first position can be filled in 10 ways, the second position in 9 ways, the third position in 8 ways, and so on. By the Fundamental Counting Principle, there are $10 \cdot 9 \cdot 8 \cdot 7 \cdot 6 \cdot 5 \cdot 4 \cdot 3 \cdot 2 \cdot 1$, or 3,628,800, ways to display the flavors. If there were 16 flavors, there would be $16 \cdot 15 \cdot 14 \cdot 13 \cdot \ldots \cdot 3 \cdot 2 \cdot 1$ ways to arrange them.

In general, *if there are n objects, then the number of possible ways to arrange the objects in a row is the product of all the natural numbers from n to 1, inclusive.* This expression, *n* **factorial**, is denoted *n*! as shown.

$$n! = n(n - 1)(n - 2) \cdot \ldots \cdot 3 \cdot 2 \cdot 1$$

For example, $5! = 5 \cdot 4 \cdot 3 \cdot 2 \cdot 1$; $3! = 3 \cdot 2 \cdot 1$; and $1! = 1$.

 Many calculators have a factorial key such as $\boxed{x!}$. To use this key, enter a whole number and then press the factorial key. For example, to compute 5! press $\boxed{5}$ $\boxed{x!}$ and 120 appears on the display.

Consider the set of people in a small club, {Al, Betty, Carl, Dan}. How many ways are there to elect a president and a secretary for the club? One way to answer the question is to agree that the choice "Al, Betty" denotes Al as president and Betty as secretary, while the choice "Betty, Al" indicates that Betty is president and Al is secretary. Order is important and no repetitions are possible. Consequently, counting the number of possibilities is a permutation problem. Since there are four ways of choosing a president, and then for each of these choices, there are three ways of choosing a secretary, by the Fundamental Counting Principle, there are $4 \cdot 3$, or 12, ways of choosing a president and a secretary. Choosing two officers from a club of four is a permutation of four people chosen two at a time. The number of possible permutations of four objects taken two at a time, denoted $_4P_2$, may be counted using the Fundamental Counting Principle. Therefore, we have $_4P_2 = 4 \cdot 3$, or 12.

▶ **NOW TRY THIS 7**

  a. Write $_nP_2$, $_nP_3$, and $_nP_4$ in terms of *n*. $n(n - 1), n(n - 1)(n - 2), n(n - 1)(n - 2)(n - 3)$
  b. Based on your answers in part (a), write $_nP_r$ in terms of *n* and *r*. $n(n - 1)(n - 2) \cdot \ldots \cdot (n - r + 1)$
  c. In the club mentioned above, how many ways are there to elect a president, vice president, and secretary? $4 \cdot 3 \cdot 2 = 24$

Any number of permutations can be written in terms of factorials. Consider the number of permutations of 20 objects chosen 3 at a time.

$$_{20}P_3 = 20 \cdot 19 \cdot 18$$
$$= \frac{20 \cdot 19 \cdot 18 \cdot (17 \cdot \ldots \cdot 3 \cdot 2 \cdot 1)}{17 \cdot \ldots \cdot 3 \cdot 2 \cdot 1}$$
$$= \frac{20!}{17!}$$
$$= \frac{20!}{(20 - 3)!}$$

This is generalized as follows.

Permutations of Objects in a Set

The number of permutations of r objects chosen from a set of n objects, where $0 \le r \le n$, is denoted by $_nP_r$ and is given by

$$_nP_r = n(n-1)(n-2) \cdot \ldots \cdot (n-(r-1)) = \frac{n!}{(n-r)!}.$$

Recall that $_nP_n$ is the number of permutations of n objects chosen n at a time, that is, the number of ways of rearranging all n objects in a row. We have seen that this number is $n!$. If we use the formula for $_nP_r$ to compute $_nP_n$, we obtain

$$_nP_n = \frac{n!}{(n-n)!} = \frac{n!}{0!}.$$

Consequently, $n! = \frac{n!}{0!}$. Thus, *we define* $0! = 1$ for the formula to be true.

Many calculators, especially graphing calculators, can calculate the number of permutations of n objects taken r at a time. This feature is usually denoted $\boxed{_nP_r}$. To use this key, enter the value of n, then press $\boxed{_nP_r}$, followed by the value of r. If you then press $\boxed{=}$ or $\boxed{\text{ENTER}}$, the number of permutations is displayed.

▶ **NOW TRY THIS 8**

NTT 8: Answer can be found in Answers at the back of the book.

a. Use a factorial key $\boxed{x!}$ on a calculator to compute $\frac{100!}{98!}$. What happens? Why?

b. Without using a calculator, use the definition of factorials to compute the expression in part (a).

Example 17

a. A baseball team has nine players. Find the number of ways the manager can arrange the batting order.

b. Find the number of ways of choosing three initials from the English alphabet if none of the letters can be repeated.

Solution

a. Because there are nine ways to choose the first batter, eight ways to choose the second batter, and so on, there are $9 \cdot 8 \cdot 7 \cdot \ldots \cdot 2 \cdot 1 = 9! = 362{,}880$ ways of arranging the batting order.

Using the formula for permutations, we have $_9P_9 = \frac{9!}{0!} = 362{,}880$.

b. There are 26 ways of choosing the first letter, 25 ways of choosing the second letter, and 24 ways of choosing the third letter. Hence, there are $26 \cdot 25 \cdot 24 = 15{,}600$, ways of choosing the three letters. Alternatively, if we use the formula for permutations, we have

$$_{26}P_3 = \frac{26!}{23!} = \frac{26 \cdot 25 \cdot 24 \cdot (23 \cdot 22 \cdot 21 \cdot \ldots \cdot 1)}{23 \cdot 22 \cdot 21 \cdot \ldots \cdot 1}$$

$$= 26 \cdot 25 \cdot 24$$

$$= 15{,}600.$$

Permutations Involving Like Objects

In the previous counting examples, each object to be counted was distinct. Suppose we wanted to arrange the letters in the word *ZOO*. How many choices would we have? If the *O*'s were distinguishable, a tree diagram, as in Figure 40, suggests that there might be $3 \cdot 2 \cdot 1 = 3! = 6$, possibilities. However, looking at the list of possibilities shows that *ZOO*, *OZO*, and *OOZ* each appear twice because the *O*'s are not different. To determine how to remove the duplication in arrangements where some objects are the same, we eliminate the duplication by dividing by the number of ways the two *O*'s can be rearranged, which is 2!. Consequently, there are $\dfrac{3!}{2!} = 3$, ways of arranging the letters in *ZOO*. The arrangements are *ZOO*, *OZO*, and *OOZ*.

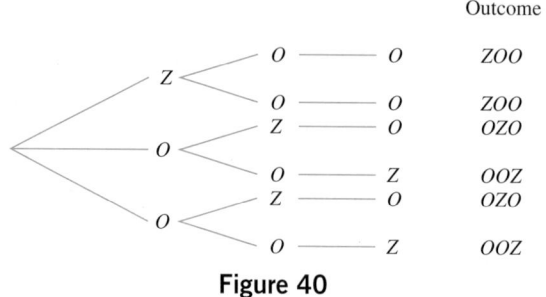

Figure 40

This discussion is generalized in the following.

Permutations of Like Objects

If there are n objects, of which r_1 are alike, r_2 are alike, and so on through r_k, then the number of different arrangements of all n objects, where alike objects are indistinguishable, is equal to

$$\frac{n!}{r_1! \cdot r_2! \cdot r_3! \cdot \ldots \cdot r_k!}$$

Example 18

Find the number of arrangements of the letters in each of the following words.

   a. *bubble*   **b.** *statistics*

Solution

  a. There are 6 letters with *b* repeated 3 times. Hence, the number of arrangements is

$$\frac{6!}{3!} = 6 \cdot 5 \cdot 4 = 120.$$

  b. There are 10 letters in the word *statistics*, with three *s*'s, three *t*'s, and two *i*'s in the word. Hence, the number of arrangements is

$$\frac{10!}{3! \cdot 3! \cdot 2!} = \frac{10 \cdot 9 \cdot 8 \cdot 7 \cdot 6 \cdot 5 \cdot 4 \cdot 3 \cdot 2 \cdot 1}{3 \cdot 2 \cdot 1 \cdot 3 \cdot 2 \cdot 1 \cdot 2 \cdot 1} = 50,400.$$

Combinations

Reconsider the club {Al, Betty, Carl, Dan}. Suppose a two-person committee is selected with no chair. In this case, order is not important, and an Al-Betty choice is the same as a Betty-Al choice. An arrangement of objects in which the order makes no difference is a **combination**.

A comparison of the results of electing a president and a secretary for the club and the results of simply selecting a two-person committee are shown in Figure 41. Because each two permutations "shrink" into one combination, we see that the number of combinations is the number of permutations divided by 2, or $\dfrac{4 \cdot 3}{2} = 6$.

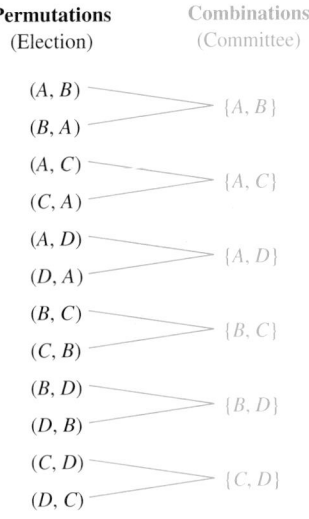

Permutations
(Election)

Combinations
(Committee)

Figure 41

In how many ways can a committee of three people be selected from the club {Al, Betty, Carl, Dan}? To solve this problem, we proceed as we did earlier and find the number of ways to select three people from a group of four for three offices, say president, vice president, and secretary (a permutation problem) and then use this result to see how many combinations of people are possible for the committee. Figure 42 shows two examples from the whole list.

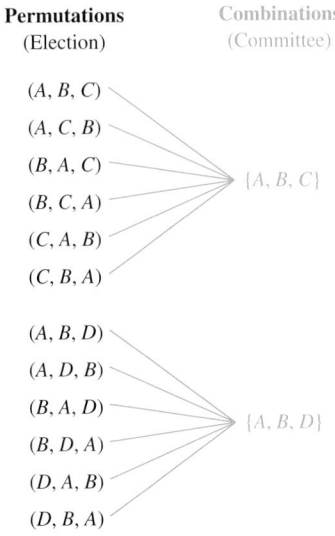

Permutations
(Election)

Combinations
(Committee)

Figure 42

By the Fundamental Counting Principle, if order is important, the number of ways to choose three people from the list of four is $4 \cdot 3 \cdot 2 = 24$. However, with each triple chosen, there are 3!, or 6, ways to arrange the triple, as in Figure 42. Therefore, there are 3! times as many permutations as combinations, or equivalently each $3! = 6$, permutations "shrink" into one combination. Therefore, to find the number of combinations, we divide the number of permutations, 24, by $3! = 6$, to obtain 4. The four committees are $\{A, B, C\}$, $\{A, B, D\}$, $\{A, C, D\}$, and $\{B, C, D\}$.

To find the number of combinations possible in a counting problem, first use the Fundamental Counting Principle to find the number of permutations and then divide by the number of ways in which each choice can be arranged. A general formula follows.

> ## Combinations of Objects in a Set
>
> The number of combinations of r objects chosen from a set of n objects, where $0 \le r \le n$, is denoted by $_nC_r$ and is given by:
>
> $$_nC_r = \frac{_nP_r}{_rP_r} = \frac{\frac{n!}{(n-r)!}}{r!} = \frac{n!}{r!(n-r)!} = \frac{n(n-1)(n-2)\cdot\ldots\cdot(n-r+1)}{r!}$$

It is not necessary to memorize the formula above; we can always find the number of combinations by using the Fundamental Counting Principle and the reasoning developed in the committee example.

Example 19

The Library of Science Book Club offers 3 free books from a list of 42 books. How many possible combinations are there?

Solution   Order is not important, so this is a combination problem. By the Fundamental Counting Principle, there are $42 \cdot 41 \cdot 40$ ways to choose the 3 free books regardless of order. Because each set of 3 books could be arranged in $3 \cdot 2 \cdot 1$ ways, there is an extra factor of 3! in the original $42 \cdot 41 \cdot 40$ ways. Therefore, the number of combinations possible for 3 books is

$$\frac{42 \cdot 41 \cdot 40}{3!} = 11{,}480.$$

If we use the formula for $_nC_r$, we have $_{42}C_3 = \frac{42!}{3! \cdot 39!} = \frac{42 \cdot 41 \cdot 40 \cdot 39!}{3 \cdot 2 \cdot 1 \cdot 39!} = \frac{42 \cdot 41 \cdot 40}{6} = 11{,}480.$

Example 20

At the beginning of the first semester of a mathematics class for elementary school teachers, each of the class's 25 students shook hands with each other student exactly once. How many handshakes took place?

Solution   Since the handshake between persons A and B is the same as that between persons B and A, this is a problem of choosing combinations of 25 people 2 at a time. There are

$$_{25}C_2 = \frac{25 \cdot 24}{2!} = 300$$

different handshakes.

Example 21

Given a class of 12 girls and 10 boys, answer each of the following questions.

a. In how many ways can a committee of 5 consisting of 3 girls and 2 boys be chosen?
b. What is the probability of the event that a committee of 5, chosen at random from the class, consists of 3 girls and 2 boys?
c. How many of the possible committees of 5 have no boys?
d. What is the probability of the event that a committee of 5, chosen at random from the class, consists only of girls?

Solution

a. Based on the information given, the order of the children on the committee does not matter. From 12 girls we can choose 3 girls in $_{12}C_3$ ways. Each of these choices can be paired with $_{10}C_2$ combinations of boys. By the Fundamental Counting Principle, the total number of committees is

$$_{12}C_3 \cdot {}_{10}C_2 = \frac{12 \cdot 11 \cdot 10}{3!} \cdot \frac{10 \cdot 9}{2} = 9900.$$

b. The total number of committees of 5 is $_{22}C_5$, or 26,334. Using part (a), the probability of the event that a committee of 5 will consist of 3 girls and 2 boys is

$$\frac{_{12}C_3 \cdot {}_{10}C_2}{_{22}C_5} = \frac{9900}{26,334} \approx 0.376.$$

c. The number of ways to choose 0 boys from the 10 boys and 5 girls from the 12 girls in the class is

$$_{10}C_0 \cdot {}_{12}C_5 = 1 \cdot {}_{12}C_5 = \frac{12 \cdot 11 \cdot 10 \cdot 9 \cdot 8}{5 \cdot 4 \cdot 3 \cdot 2 \cdot 1} = 792.$$

d. $\dfrac{_{12}C_5}{_{22}C_5} = \dfrac{792}{26,334} \approx 0.030$

Problem Solving   **A True-False Test Problem**

In the cartoon, suppose Johnny took a six-question true-false test. If he answered each question true or false at random, what is the probability of the event that he answered exactly 50% of the questions correctly?

I HAD A 50-50 CHANCE
ON EVERY TRUE/FALSE QUESTION!
BUT MY GRADE IS 50!

Understanding the Problem A score of 50% indicates that Johnny answered $\frac{1}{2}$ of the six questions, or three questions, correctly. He answered the questions true or false at random, so the probability that he answered a given question correctly is $\frac{1}{2}$. We are asked to determine the probability of the event that Johnny answered exactly three of the questions correctly.

Devising a Plan We do not know which three questions Johnny missed. He could have missed any three out of six on the test. Suppose he answered questions 2, 4, and 5 incorrectly. In this case, he would have answered questions 1, 3, and 6 correctly. We compute the probability of answering questions 1, 3, and 6 correctly by using a branch of a tree diagram, as in Figure 43, where C represents a correct answer and I represents an incorrect answer.

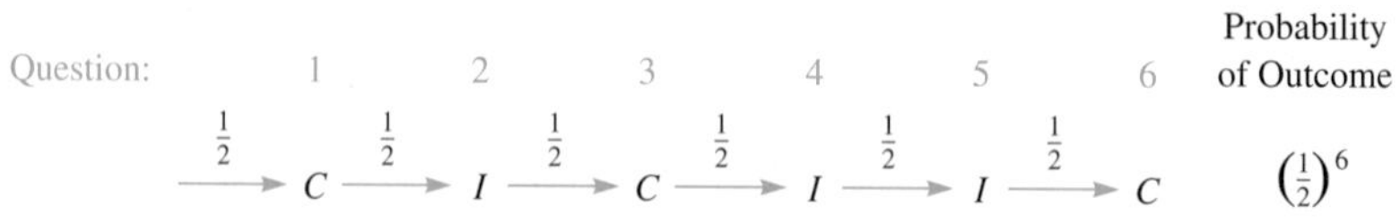

Question: 1   2   3   4   5   6   Probability of Outcome

$\xrightarrow{\frac{1}{2}}$ C $\xrightarrow{\frac{1}{2}}$ I $\xrightarrow{\frac{1}{2}}$ C $\xrightarrow{\frac{1}{2}}$ I $\xrightarrow{\frac{1}{2}}$ I $\xrightarrow{\frac{1}{2}}$ C $\left(\frac{1}{2}\right)^6$

Figure 43

Multiplying the probabilities along the branches, we obtain $\left(\frac{1}{2}\right)^6$ as the probability of answering questions 1 through 6 in the following way: $C\,I\,C\,I\,I\,C$. There are other ways to answer exactly three questions correctly: for example, $C\,C\,C\,I\,I\,I$. The probability of answering questions 1 through 6 in this way is also $\left(\frac{1}{2}\right)^6$. The number of ways to answer exactly three of the questions correctly is simply the number of ways of arranging three C's and three I's in a row, which is also the number of ways of choosing three correct questions out of six, that is, $_6C_3$. Because all these arrangements give Johnny a score of 50%, the desired probability is the sum of the probabilities for each arrangement.

Carrying Out the Plan There are $_6C_3$, or 20, sets of answers similar to the one in Figure 43, with three correct and three incorrect answers. The product of the probabilities for each of these sets of answers is $\left(\frac{1}{2}\right)^6$, so the sum of the probabilities for all 20 sets is $20\left(\frac{1}{2}\right)^6$, or 0.3125. Thus, Johnny has a probability of 0.3125 of obtaining a score of exactly 50% on the test.

Looking Back It may seem strange to learn that the probability of the event of obtaining a score of 50% on a six-question true-false test is not close to $\frac{1}{2}$. As an extension of the problem, suppose a passing score is a score of at least 70%. Now what is the probability of the event that Johnny will pass? What is the probability of the event of him obtaining a score of at least 50% on the test? If the test is a six-question multiple-choice test with five alternative answers for each question, what is the probability of the event of obtaining a score of at least 50% by random guessing?

Problem Solving **Matching Letters to Envelopes**

Stephen placed three letters in envelopes while he was having a telephone conversation. He addressed the envelopes and sealed them without checking whether each letter was in the correct envelope. What is the probability of the event that each of the letters was inserted correctly?

Understanding the Problem Stephen sealed three letters in addressed envelopes without checking to see if each was in the correct envelope. We are to determine the probability of the event that each of the three letters was placed correctly. This probability could be found if we knew the sample space, or at least how many elements are in the sample space.

Devising a Plan To aid in solving the problem, we represent the respective letters as a, b, and c and the respective addressed envelopes as A, B, and C. For example, a correctly placed letter a

would be in envelope *A*. To construct the sample space, we use the strategy of *making a table*. The table should show all the possible permutations of letters in envelopes. Once the table is completed, we can determine the probability of the event that each letter is placed correctly.

Carrying Out the Plan   Table 7 is constructed by using the envelope labels *A*, *B*, and *C* as headings and listing all ways that letters *a*, *b*, and *c* could be placed in the envelopes. The first arrangement in the list is the only one out of six in which each of the envelopes is labeled correctly, so the probability of the event that each envelope is labeled correctly is $\frac{1}{6}$.

Table 7

A	B	C
a	*b*	*c*
a	*c*	*b*
b	*a*	*c*
b	*c*	*a*
c	*a*	*b*
c	*b*	*a*

} Envelopes

} Envelope contents

Looking Back   We also could have used a counting argument to solve the problem. Given an envelope, there is only one correct letter to place in the envelope. Thus, there is $1 \cdot 1 \cdot 1$ or one correct way to place the letters in the envelopes. By the Fundamental Counting Principle, there are $3 \cdot 2 \cdot 1$ ways of choosing the letters to place in the envelopes, so the probability of the event of having the letters correctly placed is $\frac{1}{6}$. Is the probability of having each letter placed incorrectly the same as the probability of having each letter placed correctly? A first guess might be that the probabilities are the same, but that is not true. Why?

Assessment 9-4A

1. The eighth-grade class at a grade school has 16 girls and 14 boys. How many different boy-girl partners can be arranged?   224
2. The telephone prefix for a university is 243. The prefix is followed by four digits. How many different telephone numbers are possible before a new prefix is needed?   10,000
3. Carlin's Pizza House offers 3 kinds of salad, 15 kinds of pizza, and 4 kinds of dessert. How many different three-course meals consisting of a salad, pizza, and dessert can be ordered?   ▬
4. Decide whether each of the following statements is true. If false, demonstrate why.
   a. $6! = 6 \cdot 5!$ True
   b. $3! + 3! = 6!$ False; $3! + 3! = 2(3!) = 12 \neq 6!$
   c. $\frac{6!}{3!} = 2!$ False; $120 \neq 2! = 2$
5. Find the number of ways to arrange the letters in the following words:
   a. *SCRAMBLE*   40,320
   b. *PERMUTATION*   19,958,400

6. How many two-person committees can be formed from a group of six people?   15
7. Assume a class has 30 members.
   a. In how many ways can a president, a vice president, and a secretary be selected?   24,360
   b. How many committees of three people can be chosen?   4060
8. A five-volume numbered set of books is placed randomly on a shelf. What is the probability of the event that the books will be numbered in the correct order from left to right? $\frac{1}{120}$
9. There are 10 points in a plane, no 3 of them on a line. How many straight lines can be drawn if each line is drawn through a pair of points?   45
10. Sally has four red flags, three green flags, and two white flags. Each arrangement of flags is a different signal. How many nine-flag signals can she run up a flagpole?   1260
11. At a party, 28 handshakes took place. Each person shook hands exactly once with each of the others present. How many people were at the party?   8
12. How many different 5-card hands can be dealt from a standard deck of 52 playing cards?   2,598,960

13. In a certain lottery game, 54 numbers are randomly mixed and 6 are selected. A person must pick all 6 numbers to win. Order is not important. What is the probability of winning? $\frac{1}{25,827,165}$

14. From a group of 10 boys and 12 girls, a committee of 4 students is chosen at random. What is the probability that
  a. all 4 members on the committee will be girls? *
  b. all 4 members of the committee will be boys? $\frac{6}{209}$
  c. there will be at least 1 girl on the committee? $\frac{203}{209}$

15. From a group of 20 Britons, 21 Italians, and 4 Danes, a committee of 8 people is chosen at random. Expressing your answers using the notation for combinations, find the probability that
  a. the committee will consist of 2 Britons, 4 Italians, and 2 Danes. ▓▓▓▓▓.
  b. the committee will have no Britons. ▓▓▓▓▓▓
  c. there will be at least one Briton on the committee. *
  d. all members of the committee will be Britons. *

16. Stephen placed five letters in envelopes while he was watching television and addressed the envelopes without checking whether each letter was in the correct envelope. What is the probability of the event that all five letters were in the correct envelopes? $\frac{1}{120}$

17. A company is setting up four-digit ID numbers for employees.
  a. How many four-digit numbers are there if numbers can start with 0 and digits can be repeated? 10,000
  b. How many four-digit numbers are there if numbers can start with 0 and all the digits must be different? 5040
  c. If you randomly assign a four-digit ID number that can start with 0 and digits can be repeated, what is the probability that all the digits are even? $\frac{1}{16}$

18. A company president presents identical awards to four out of six finalists. In how many ways can she present the awards? 15

19. Your English teacher asks that you read any three of the eight books on his reading list. How many choices do you have for the set of three books you read? 56

20. How many arrangements of the letters in the word "equation" can be made if the vowels all must stay in the same positions? 6

21. How many arrangements can be made from the letters of the word "quick" if
  a. all the letters are used? 120
  b. three of the letters are used? 60
  c. four of the letters are used? 120

22. In how many ways can a group of seven people stand in a line at a ticket booth? 5040

Assessment 9-4B

1. If a coin is tossed 5 times, in how many different ways can the sequence of heads and tails appear? 32

2. Radio stations in the United States have call letters that begin with either *K* or *W*. Some have three letters; others have four letters.
  a. How many three-letter call letters are possible? 1352
  b. How many four-letter call letters are possible? 35,152

3. Three men and four women stand in line at a checkout counter at a store. In how many ways can they stand in the line if we consider only their gender? 35

4. Classify each of the following statements as true or false. If false, demonstrate why.
  a. $\frac{6!}{3} = 2!$ False; $240 \neq 2$
  b. $\frac{6!}{5!} = 6!$ False; $6 \neq 720$
  c. $\frac{6!}{4!2!} = 15$ True
  d. $n!(n + 1) = (n + 1)!$ True

5. Find the number of ways to arrange the letters in the following words.
  a. *OHIO*   12
  b. *ALABAMA*   210
  c. *ILLINOIS*   3360
  d. *MISSISSIPPI*   34,650
  e. *TENNESSEE*   3780

6. In a car race, there are 6 Chevrolets, 4 Fords, and 2 Hondas. In how many ways can the 12 cars finish if we consider only the makes of the cars? 13,860

7. A basketball coach was criticized in the newspaper for not trying every combination of players. If the team roster has 12 players, how many 5-player combinations are possible? 792

8. Seven performers, *A, B, C, D, E, F,* and *G*, are to appear in a talent contest. The order of appearance is by random selection. Find the probability that
  a. *C* will perform first $\frac{1}{7}$
  b. *F* or *G* will perform first $\frac{2}{7}$
  c. They will appear in the order *C, D, E, A, B, F, G*. $\frac{1}{5040}$

9. Find the number of shortest paths from point *A* to point *B* along the edges of the cubes in each of the following diagrams. (For example, in (a) one shortest path is *A-C-D-B*.)

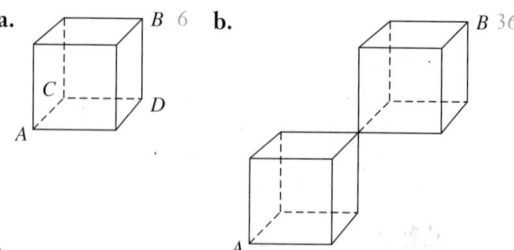

  a. *B* 6   **b.** *B* 36

10. License plates in a certain state have three letters followed by three digits. How many different plates are possible if no repetitions of letters or digits are allowed? 11,232,000

11. How many different 12-person juries can be selected from a pool of 24 people? 2,704,156

12. Social Security numbers are in the form ###-##-####, where each symbol represents a number 0 through 9. How many Social Security numbers are possible using this format? 1,000,000,000

13. A fair die is rolled 8 times. What is the probability of getting
  a. 1 on each of the 8 rolls? $\frac{1}{1,679,616}$
  b. 6 exactly twice in the 8 rolls? About 0.260
  c. 6 at least once in the 8 rolls? About 0.767

14. A committee of three people is selected at random from a set consisting of seven Americans, five French people, and three English people.
  a. What is the probability of the event that the committee consists of all Americans? $\frac{1}{13}$
  b. What is the probability of the event that the committee has no Americans? $\frac{8}{65}$

15. A club selects an executive committee of 5 and from the 5, one of the group becomes the president. If the club has a membership of 32, how many ways are there to choose an executive committee and a president? 1,006,880

16. Assume the probability of the event of a basketball player's making a free throw successfully each time she tries is $\frac{2}{3}$ and the outcomes are independent. If the player attempts 10 free throws in a game, what is the probability that exactly 6 are made? About 0.228

17. What are the odds against a royal flush in poker, that is, a 10, jack, queen, king, and ace all of the same suit? *

18. At the American Kennel Club, there are 36 dogs entered in a show where there will be a first-, second-, and third-place award. How many possibilities are there for these awards? 42,840

19. Two fair dice are rolled five times and the sum of the numbers that come up on each roll is recorded. Find the probability of getting
  a. a sum of 7 on each of the five rolls. About 0.00013
  b. a sum of 7 exactly twice in the five rolls. About 0.161

20. How many arrangements of the letters in the word "equation" can be made if the consonants all must stay in their original positions? 120

21. How many arrangements can be made from the letters of the word "french" if
  a. all the letters are used? 720
  b. three of the letters are used? 120
  c. four of the letters are used? 360

22. In how many ways can a group of 9 people stand in a line at a ticket booth? 362,880

Mathematical Connections 9-4

Answers to Mathematical Connections can be found in the Answers section at the back of the book.

Reasoning

1. The terms *Fundamental Counting Principle*, *permutations*, and *combinations* are all used to work with counting problems. In your own words, explain how all these terms are related and how they are used.

2. A bicycle lock has three reels, each of which contains the numbers 0 through 9. To open the lock, you must enter the numbers in the correct order, such as 369 or 455, where one number is chosen from each reel. Explain how many different possibilities there are for the numbers to open the lock.

3. a. Ten people are to be seated on 10 chairs in a line. Among them is a family of 3 that does not want to be separated. How many different seating arrangements are possible? Explain how you arrived at your answer.
  b. How many possible seating arrangements are there in part (a) in which the family members do not all sit together? Explain how you arrived at your answer.

4. In how many ways can five couples be seated in a row of 10 chairs if no couple is separated? Explain how you arrived at your answer.

5. Which number do you expect to be greater, a combination or a permutation of n objects taken r at a time? Why?

Open-Ended

6. Suppose the Department of Motor Vehicles uses six digits and the numbers 0 through 9 to create its license plates with digits allowed to repeat.
  a. How many license plates are possible?
  b. If you were in charge of making license plates for the state of California, describe the method you would use to ensure you would have enough license plates.

7. Write an essay to defend a position as to whether combinations and permutations should be included in a grade 7 or 8 curriculum as recommended in the *Common Core Standards*.

Cooperative Learning

8. The following triangular array of numbers is a part of **Pascal's triangle:**

													Row
						1							(0)
					1		1						(1)
				1		2		1					(2)
			1		3		3		1				(3)
		1		4		6		4		1			(4)
	1		5		10		10		5		1		(5)
1		6		15		20		15		6		1	(6)

  a. In your group, decide how the triangle was constructed and complete the next two rows.
  b. Describe at least three number patterns in Pascal's triangle.
  c. Find the sum of the numbers in each row. Predict the sum of the numbers in row 10.
  d. The entries in row 2 are just $_2C_0$, $_2C_1$, and $_2C_2$. Have different members of your group investigate whether a similar pattern holds for other rows in Pascal's triangle.
  e. Describe how you could use combinations to find any entry in Pascal's triangle.

9. In your group, demonstrate which number is greater; the arrangements of 4 students in a line, or the number of arrangement of 4 students at a round table.

Connecting Mathematics to the Classroom

10. A student does not understand the meaning of $_4P_0$. He wants to know how we can consider permutations of four objects chosen zero at a time. How do you respond?

11. A student wants to know why, if we can define 0! as 1, we cannot define $\frac{1}{0}$ as 1. How do you respond?

12. A student claims that he does not need to define permutations because he knows the Fundamental Counting Principle. What do you say?

Review Problems

13. Two cards are drawn at random without replacement from a deck of 52 cards. What is the probability of the event that
    a. at least 1 card is an ace?
    b. exactly 1 card is red?

14. If two regular dice are tossed, what is the probability of the event of tossing a sum greater than 10?

15. Two coins are tossed. You win $5.00 if both coins are heads, $3.00 if both coins are tails, and lose $4.00 if the coins do not match. What is the expected value of this game? Is this a fair game?

16. On a roulette wheel, the probability of the event of winning when you pick a particular number is $\frac{1}{38}$. Suppose you bet $1.00 to play the game, and if your number is picked, you get back $35.00 plus the $1.00 that you bet.
    a. Is this a fair game?
    b. What would happen if you played this game a large number of times?

17. It is your first day of class; your class has 40 students. A friend who does not know any students in your class bets you that at least 2 of them share a birthday (month and day). What are your friend's chances of winning the bet?

National Assessments

National Assessment of Educational Progress (NAEP) Questions

How many different three-digit whole numbers can be written using each of the digits 4, 5, and 6 exactly once?
A. 3
B. 6
C. 9
D. 24
E. 27

NAEP, Grade 4, 2011

Li's English book weighs 3 pounds, her math book weighs 5 pounds, her history book weighs 4 pounds, and her science book weighs 6 pounds. How many different combinations of one or more books can Li pack in her backpack so that the total weight of the books is 12 pounds or less?
A. 9
B. 10
C. 11
D. 12
E. 18

NAEP, Grade 8, 2011

Hint for Solving the Preliminary Problem

Consider what happens, for example, when any person after the first enters the bus. If the seat assigned is not taken, then the person sits in the correct seat. If not, the person might choose the seat assigned to the first person or the 50th person with probability $\frac{1}{2}$. See if you can generalize.

Chapter 9 Summary

KEY CONCEPTS	DEFINITIONS, DESCRIPTIONS, AND THEOREMS
Section 9-1	
Experiment (p. 469)	An activity whose results are its *outcomes*.
Sample space (p. 469)	The set of all possible outcomes for an experiment.
Tree diagram (p. 469)	A model for a sample space in which each outcome of an experiment is shown on a separate branch.
Event (p. 470)	Any subset of a sample space.
Probability (or theoretical probability) of an event (p. 472)	The likelihood that an event will happen. The number of ways that a given event can occur divided by the total number of outcomes from a sample space of equally likely outcomes.
Experimental (or empirical) probability (p. 471)	An estimate of the probability that the event happens, based on observed outcomes of repeated trials. The number of times an event occurs divided by the total number of trials.
Law of Large Numbers (Bernoulli's Theorem) (p. 471)	*Theorem:* As the number of trials of an experiment increases, the *experimental probability* of a particular event approaches a fixed number, which is the *theoretical probability* of that event.
Probability of an event in a sample space with equally likely outcomes (p. 472)	For an experiment with nonempty sample space S with equally likely outcomes, the probability of an event A is given by $$P(A) = \frac{\text{Number of elements of } A}{\text{Number of elements of } S} = \frac{n(A)}{n(S)}$$ $$P(\text{event}) = \frac{\text{Number of favorable outcomes}}{\text{Total number of possible outcomes}}.$$
Uniform sample space (p. 472)	A sample space in which each outcome is equally likely.
Probability properties (p. 473)	<ul><li>$P(\varnothing) = 0$ (*impossible event*)</li><li>$P(S) = 1$, where S is the sample space (*certain event*)</li><li>*Theorem:* For any event A, $0 \leq P(A) \leq 1$.</li><li>If A and B are mutually exclusive events, then $$P(A \cup B) = P(A) + P(B).$$</li><li>If A and B are any events, then $$P(A \cup B) = P(A) + P(B) - P(A \cap B).$$</li><li>*Theorem:* If A is any event and $\overline{A}$ is its complement, then $P(\overline{A}) = 1 - P(A)$.</li></ul> *Theorem:* The probability of an event is equal to the sum of the probabilities of disjoint events whose union is the event.
Mutually exclusive events (p. 475)	Events that have no elements in common; that is, for events A and B, $A \cap B = \varnothing$. *Theorem:* If events A and B are mutually exclusive, then $$P(A \text{ or } B) = P(A \cup B) = P(A) + P(B).$$
Complementary events (p. 475)	Two mutually exclusive events whose union is the sample space.
Models for probability (p. 478)	<ul><li>*Tree diagrams*</li><li>*Geometric* or *area models*</li></ul>

Section 9-2

Types of experiments (p. 484)	• One-stage—completed after one step. • Multistage—completed after two or more steps.
Multiplication rule for tree diagrams (p. 489)	*Theorem:* For all multistage experiments, the probability of the outcome along any path of a tree diagram is equal to the product of all the probabilities along the path.
Independent events (p. 491)	*Theorem:* Two events such that the occurrence or nonoccurrence of the first event has no influence on the outcome of the second event. *Theorem:* For any independent events E_1 and E_2, $$P(E_1 \cap E_2) = P(E_1) \cdot P(E_2).$$
Conditional probability (p. 494)	If A and B are events in sample space S and $P(A) \neq 0$, then the *conditional probability* that event B occurs, given that event A has occurred, is given by $$P(B|A) = \frac{P(A \cap B)}{P(A)}.$$
Analyzing games (p. 495–496)	We can use models that involve probability to analyze games.

Section 9-3

Simulation (p. 506)	A technique used to act out a situation by conducting experiments whose outcomes are analogous to the original situation.
Random-number (or random-digit) table (p. 506)	A table whose digits have been generated randomly.
Odds (p. 511)	Let $P(A)$ be the probability that event A occurs and $P(\overline{A})$ be the probability that event A does not occur. Then the *odds in favor* of event A occurring are $\dfrac{P(A)}{P(\overline{A})} = \dfrac{P(A)}{1 - P(A)}$, and the *odds against* event A occurring are $\dfrac{P(\overline{A})}{P(A)} = \dfrac{1 - P(A)}{P(A)}.$ *Theorem:* If the *odds in favor* of event E are $m{:}n$, then $P(E) = \dfrac{m}{m + n}.$ *Theorem:* If the *odds against* of event E are $m{:}n$, then $P(E) = \dfrac{n}{m + n}.$
Expected value (p. 513)	If the possible outcomes in an experiment are numbers $a_1, a_2, \ldots, a_n$ occurring with probabilities $p_1, p_2, \ldots, p_n$, then the *expected value*, or *mathematical expectation*, E is given by the equation $E = a_1 \cdot p_1 + a_2 \cdot p_2 + \cdots + a_n \cdot p_n.$
Fair game (p. 513)	A game in which the mathematical expectation is 0. With more than one player, each player has the same chance of winning.

Section 9-4

Permutation (p. 519)	An arrangement of things in a definite order with no repetitions.
***n* factorial** (p. 520)	$n! = n(n - 1)(n - 2) \cdot \ldots \cdot 3 \cdot 2 \cdot 1$ $0! = 1$
Permutations of objects in a set (p. 521)	The number of permutations of r objects chosen from a set of n objects, where $0 \leq r \leq n$, denoted by $_nP_r$, is given by $$_nP_r = \frac{n!}{(n - r)!}.$$

Section 9-4

Permutations of like objects (p. 522)	If there are n objects, of which r_1 are alike, r_2 are alike, and so on through r_k, then the number of different arrangements of all n objects, where alike objects are indistinguishable, is equal to $$\frac{n!}{r_1! \cdot r_2! \cdot \ldots \cdot r_k!}.$$
Combination (p. 522)	An arrangement of objects in which the order makes no difference.
Combinations of objects in a set (p. 524)	The number of combinations of r objects chosen from a set of n objects, where $0 \le r \le n$, denoted by $_nC_r$, is given by $$_nC_r = \frac{_nP_r}{_rP_r} = \frac{\frac{n!}{(n-r)!}}{r!} = \frac{n!}{r!(n-r)!}.$$

Chapter 9 Review

1. A coin is flipped 3 times and heads (H) or tails (T) are recorded.
   a. List all the elements in the sample space.   *
   b. List the elements in the event "at least two heads appear." {HHH, HHT, HTH, THH}
   c. Find the probability that the event in part (b) occurs. $\frac{1}{2}$
2. Suppose the names of the days of the week are placed in a box and one name is drawn at random.
   a. List the sample space for this experiment.   *
   b. List the event consisting of outcomes that the day drawn starts with the letter T.   {Tuesday, Thursday}
   c. What is the probability of the event of drawing a day that starts with T? $\frac{2}{7}$
3. If you have a jar of 1000 red and blue jelly beans and you know that $P(\text{Blue}) = \frac{4}{5}$ and $P(\text{Red}) = \frac{1}{8}$, list several mathematical observations you can make about the number of beans in the jar. *
4. In the 2012 election, Barack Obama received 65,899,660 votes and Mitt Romney received 60,932,152 votes. In this election, if a voter for either Obama or Romney is chosen at random, answer the following:
   a. What is the probability of the event that the voter opted for Romney? Approximately 0.480
   b. What is the probability that the voter opted for Obama? Approximately 0.520
   c. What are the odds in favor of this voter not voting for Obama? About 12 to 13
5. A box contains three red balls, five black balls, and four white balls. Suppose one ball is drawn at random. Find the probability of each event.
   a. Black ball is drawn. $\frac{5}{12}$
   b. Black or a white ball is drawn. $\frac{3}{4}$
   c. Neither a red nor a white ball is drawn. $\frac{5}{12}$
   d. Red ball is not drawn. $\frac{3}{4}$

   e. Black ball and a white ball are drawn. 0
   f. Black or white or red ball is drawn. 1
6. One card is selected at random from an ordinary set of 52 cards. Find the probability of each event.
   a. Club is drawn. *
   b. Spade and a 5 are drawn. $\frac{1}{52}$
   c. Heart or a face card is drawn. $\frac{11}{26}$
   d. Jack is not drawn. *
7. A box contains five colored balls and four white balls. If three balls are drawn one by one, find the probability of the event that they are all white if the draws are made
   a. with replacement. *
   b. without replacement. $\frac{1}{21}$
8. Consider the following two boxes. If a letter is drawn from box 1 and placed into box 2 and then a letter is drawn from box 2, what is the probability of the event that the letter is an L? $\frac{6}{25}$

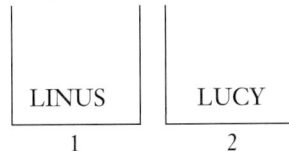

9. Use the following boxes for a two-stage experiment. First select a box at random and then select a letter at random from the box. What is the probability of the event of drawing an A? $\frac{7}{40}$

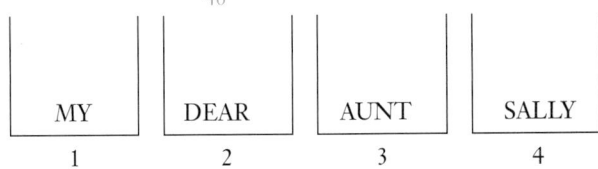

10. Consider the following boxes. Draw a ball from box 1 and put it into box 2. Then draw a ball from box 2 and put it into

box 3. Finally, draw a ball from box 3. Calculate the
probability of the event that the last ball chosen is black. $\frac{7}{45}$

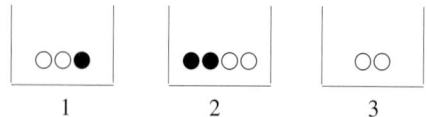

11. What are the odds in favor of drawing a jack when one card
is drawn from an ordinary deck of playing cards?   *
12. A fair normal die is rolled once. What are the odds against
rolling a prime number?   3 to 3 or 1 to 1
13. If the odds in favor of a particular event are 3 to 5, what is
the probability that the event will occur? $\frac{3}{8}$
14. A game consists of rolling two dice. Rolling double ones pays
$7.20. Rolling double sixes pays $3.60. Any other roll pays
nothing. What is the expected value for this game? $0.30
15. A total of 3000 tickets have been sold for a drawing. If one
ticket is drawn for a single prize of $1000, what is a fair price
for a ticket?   *
16. In a special raffle, a ticket costs $2. You mark any four digits
on a card (repetition and 0 are allowed). A random four-digit
number is selected. If yours matches, you win $15,000. What
is the expected value of winning the money?   *
17. How many four-digit numbers can be formed if the first digit
cannot be 0 and the last digit must be 2?   900
18. A club consists of 10 members. In how many different ways can
a group of 3 people be selected to go on a European trip?   120
19. Find the number of ways that 4 flags can be displayed on
a flagpole, one above the other, if 10 different flags are
available.   5040
20. Five women live together in an apartment. Two have blue
eyes. If two of the women are chosen at random, what is the
probability of the event that they both have blue eyes? $\frac{1}{10}$
21. Five evenly matched horses (Applefarm, Bandy, Cash, Dead-
beat, and Egglegs) run in a race.
    a. In how many ways can the first-, second-, and third-place
    horses be determined?   60
    b. Find the probability of the event that Deadbeat finishes
    first and Bandy finishes second in the race. $\frac{1}{20}$
    c. Find the probability of the event that the first-, second-,
    and third-place horses are Deadbeat, Egglegs, and Cash,
    in that order. $\frac{1}{60}$
22. Al and Ruby each roll an ordinary die once. What is the
probability of the event that the number of Ruby's roll is
greater than the number of Al's roll? $\frac{5}{12}$
23. Amy has a quiz on which she is to answer any three of the
five questions. If she is equally well versed on all questions and chooses three questions at random, what is the
probability of the event that question 1 is not chosen? $\frac{2}{5}$
24. How many batting lineups are there for the nine players of
a baseball team if the center fielder must bat fourth and the
pitcher last?   5040
25. On a certain street are three traffic lights. Assume that the
probability of the event at any given time, that any given
light at any given time is green is 0.3 independent of the
status of the other lights. What is the probability of the
event that a person will hit all three lights when they are
green?   0.027
26. A three-stage rocket has the following probabilities for failure: The probability for failure at stage one is $\frac{1}{6}$; at stage two,

$\frac{1}{8}$; and at stage three, $\frac{1}{10}$. What is the probability of the event
of a successful flight, given that the first stage was successful,
and all stages are independent? $\frac{63}{80}$
27. How could each of the following events be simulated by
using a random-digit table?
    a. Tossing a fair die   *
    b. Picking 3 different months at random from the
    12 months of the year   *
    c. Spinning the spinner shown   *

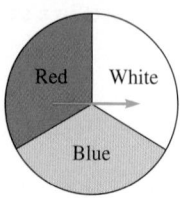

28. Otto says that if you toss three coins you get 3H, 2H, 1H, or
0H, so the probability of the event of getting three heads is $\frac{1}{4}$.
How do you respond?   *
29. If a dart is thrown at the following tangram dartboard and
we assume the dart lands at random on the board, what is the
probability of the event of its landing in each of the following areas?
    a. Area A   *
    b. Area B $\frac{1}{4}$
    c. Area C $\frac{1}{16}$

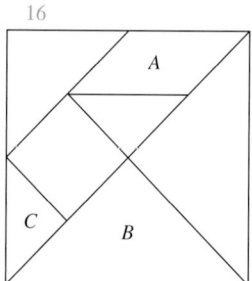

30. The points M, N, O, P, and Q in the following figure represent
exits on a highway (the numbers represent miles). An accident
occurs at random between points M and Q. What is the probability of the event that it has occurred between N and O? $\frac{2}{5}$

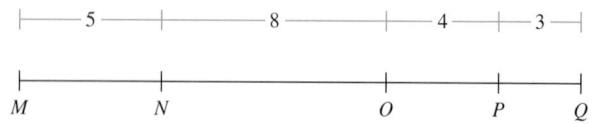

31. If three cards are drawn at random from a standard deck of
52 playing cards without replacement, what is the probability
that at least one of the cards is a face card: that is, one of the
cards is a king, queen, or jack?   About 0.553
32. In a box of 64 Crayola crayons in 2012, the following
shades of yellow were found: Yellow, Green Yellow, Lemon
Yellow, Orange Yellow, Yellow Green, Yellow Orange, and
Goldenrod. If a crayon is chosen at random from this box
of 64, what is the probability that it is not a shade
of yellow? $\frac{57}{64}$
33. Blue, red, violet, and green had consistently been chosen the
most used colors in a Crayola box in 2012. In a box of

64 Crayola crayons, if two are drawn at random without replacement, what is the probability that the choice includes at least one of the most used colors?   About 0.122

34. In a survey of countries with the most zoos in the world, the United States had 350 and Germany had 414. If you choose one of the two countries at random and one of the zoos is chosen at random from the country, what is the probability that you chose some well-known zoo in the United States? $\frac{1}{700}$

35. The following table shows the numbers of symbols on each of the three dials of a standard slot machine.

Symbol	Dial 1	Dial 2	Dial 3
Bar	1	3	1
Bell	1	3	3
Plum	5	1	5
Orange	3	6	7
Cherry	7	7	0
Lemon	3	0	4
Total	**20**	**20**	**20**

Find the probability for each of the following events.
- **a.** Three plums $\frac{1}{320}$
- **b.** Three oranges $\frac{63}{4000}$
- **c.** Three lemons   0
- **d.** No plums $\frac{171}{320}$

36. An airplane can complete its flight if at least $\frac{1}{2}$ of its engines are working. If the probability that an engine fails is 0.01 and the failures of different engines are independent, what is the probability of the event of a successful flight if the plane has
- **a.** two engines?   *
- **b.** four engines?   *

37. Al tosses one quarter and at the same time Betty tosses two quarters. What is the probability that Betty gets the same number of heads as Al?   *

Data Analysis/Statistics: An Introduction

Preliminary Problem

At his birthday party, Calvin presented his guests with a riddle: how to discover his age without being told what it was. As guests arrived, he had them reveal their ages to the group. When the last guest arrived, he computed the arithmetic average of the ages of everyone present (including himself) and announced the result. Explain how his guests would be able to determine Calvin's age from this information.

If needed, see Hint on page 613.

Data analysis typically refers to an informal approach to statistics. Today, much of statistics involves making sense of data.

In *Guidelines for Assessment and Instruction in Statistics Education (GAISE) Report: A PreK–12 Curriculum Framework* (March 2005) (hereafter referred to as the *Statistics Framework*), presented to the American Statistical Association, recommendations are made for statistics education. In the *Statistics Framework*, specific data analysis recommendations are divided into three parts—A, B, and C—with the more intuitive parts for early grades being in part A and the more advanced ideas being in part C. According to the *Statistics Framework*, "Sound statistical reasoning skills take a long time to develop. . . . The surest way to reach the necessary skill level is to begin the educational process in the elementary grades and keep strengthening and expanding these skills throughout the middle and high school years." (p. 3)

In the *Common Core Standards*, we see that students in the early grades should explore the basic ideas of statistics by collecting data, organizing the data pictorially, and then interpreting information. The ideas of gathering, representing, and analyzing data are expanded in the later grades.

In this chapter, we deal with categorical and numerical data, representations of data, and key statistical concepts, including measures of central tendency and of variation. Additionally, some uses and misuses of statistics are discussed.

10-1 Designing Experiments/Collecting Data

10-1 Objectives

Students will be able to understand and explain

- Designing experiments to collect data.
- Variability in data and how it relates to the study of statistics.
- The difference between a survey population and a sample population.
- Biased questions.
- Simple data analysis methods and interpretation across grade levels.

Variability

CCSS The grade 6 *Common Core Standards* point out that students should be able to:

Recognize a statistical question as one that anticipates variability in the data related to the question and accounts for it in the answers. *For example, "How old am I?" is not a statistical question, but "How old are the students in my school?" is a statistical question because one anticipates variability in students' ages.* (p. 45)

Much of the study of statistics deals with **variability** of data, that is, the amount by which the pieces of data in a data set differ. It is important to understand different types of variability when designing experiments and examining data. Below we give several types of variability:

Measurement variability: For example, suppose 20 students measure the length of a board. In a perfect world, all the measurements would be the same. However, simple human fallibility will produce different results. Questions for the statistician might be "How much difference could be expected in such a measurement? Are the different measures drastically different or close enough to be considered acceptable?"

Natural variability: It has been said that nature abhors a vacuum, but it might also be said that nature loves differences. For example, any two individuals are different; even genetically identical twins differ in personality, aptitude, and so on.

(Historical Note)

The seventeenth-century work on birth and death records of John Graunt (1620–1674) and the nineteenth-century work on crime and mortality of Adolph Quetelet (1796–1874) involved making predictions from data. Florence Nightingale (1820–1910) worked with mortality tables during the Crimean War to improve hospital care. Other notables in data collection and analysis include Sir Francis Galton (1822–1911), Gregor Mendel (1822–1884), Ronald Fisher (1890–1962), and Andrei Nikolaevich Kolmogorov (1903–1987). ●

Induced variability: Induced variability is frequently studied to see, for example, how individuals react to certain stimuli or how bean plants grow based on the amount of food, water, and sunlight they receive.

Sampling variability: If we want to choose, for example, a set of college students to see how they react to a question, we could do so in many ways. Some selections might elicit a reaction that could be judged as representative of the entire student population; other selection methods might produce a very biased result. Suppose only one class is interviewed; would you expect the same reaction from a graduate class in mathematics as a freshman class in English composition?

In each type of variability, the role of context is important when considering how much variability is acceptable. To make generalizations from a sample, one might want to choose a group that could be deemed highly representative of the population from which it was taken. The student page shown below describes how pollsters use surveys to understand group preferences.

School Book Page   Random Samples and Surveys

11-4 Random Samples and Surveys

Check Skills You'll Need

1. **Vocabulary Review**
   A _?_ is a ratio that compares a number to 100.

   Write each ratio as a percent.

2. 4 out of 5

3. 10 out of 40

4. 14 out of 200

GO for Help
Lesson 6-1

What You'll Learn

To identify a random sample and to write a survey question

🔊 **New Vocabulary** population, sample, random sample, biased question

Why Learn This?

You can use a survey to gather information from a group of people. Pollsters use surveys to understand group preferences.

A **population** is a group of objects or people. The population of an election is all the people who vote in that election. It is not practical to ask all the voters how they expect to vote. Pollsters select a **sample**, or a part of the population. A sample is called a **random sample** when each member of a population has the same chance of being selected.

EXAMPLE   Identifying a Random Sample

1. You survey customers at a mall. You want to know which stores they shop at the most. Which sample is more likely to be random? Explain.

   a. You survey shoppers in a computer store.

      Customers that shop in a particular store may not represent all the shoppers in the entire mall. This sample is not random.

   b. You walk around the mall and survey shoppers.

      By walking around, you give everyone in the mall the same chance to be surveyed. This sample is more likely to be random.

A **population** is the total group of objects or people involved, and a **sample** is a subset of the population.

> **CCSS** The grade 7 *Common Core Standards* point out that students should be able to:
>
> 1. Understand that statistics can be used to gain information about a population by examining a sample of the population; generalizations about a population from a sample are valid only if the sample is representative of that population. Understand that random sampling tends to produce representative samples and support valid inferences.
>
> 2. Use data from a random sample to draw inferences about a population with an unknown characteristic of interest. Generate multiple samples (or simulated samples) of the same size to gauge the variation in estimates or predictions. *For example, estimate the mean word length in a book by randomly sampling words from the book; predict the winner of a school election based on randomly sampled survey data. Gauge how far off the estimate or prediction might be.* (p. 50)

A **simple random sample** is a sample such that any subset of the population has the same chance of being the sample as any other subset of the same size. A *random sample* is sometimes defined as on the student page (p. 540).

In this section we consider issues of formulating questions and designing studies to collect and analyze data that can be used to find possible resolutions to various issues.

Underlying Issues in Designing Studies

Suppose 8-year-old Tyto wants to check the advertising claim on a can of nuts that less than half of the nuts are peanuts. Tyto can count the number of nuts and the types of nuts in a specific can to check the claim. However, the company might still be allowed to make that claim without violating regulations of the Federal Trade Commission (FTC). For students in the lower grades, Tyto's approach is very reasonable. In the middle and higher grades, it would not be sufficient. How, then, do we approach advertising and other issues that may be considered statistically at different grade levels or as adults?

From the FTC standpoint, the claim on the can label can legitimately be made if the company has evidence that, in general, the claim is true, the claim does not "injure" the consumer, and the consumer would likely buy the product even if the claim were not true in every instance, such as in Tyto's can. Evaluating a claim such as this from a company's standpoint might rely on the selection of a random sample of cans from the production line and having a very high percentage of the cans from the sample meet the advertised standard. Few can visit assembly lines to check advertising claims. However, students can become very aware of the process necessary to evaluate statistical claims. The following framework for statistical problem solving was suggested for the classroom.

a. Formulate questions	**b.** Collect data
c. Analyze the data	**d.** Interpret the results

We consider each in turn.

Formulating Questions

For any given problem where data are needed to determine either an answer or an approach to an answer, it is important that the problem is clarified to the extent that meaningful data can be collected. For example, if we wanted to collect data on the appearance of an average fifth grader, we must clarify what "the appearance of an average fifth grader means". By appearance, do we mean clothing; do we mean size; or do we mean something entirely different? If we mean size, then what exactly is meant by size? Is it height? Is it weight? Is it a combination of height and weight? Or is it something else? The point is that we must have a clear understanding of exactly what we want to know when we mention "the appearance of an average fifth grader." And we may need several questions to get at what we want. All of that has to be decided before data are collected to try to determine an answer.

In the early grades, teachers, not students, may pose questions to be examined and restrict data collection to the classroom or possibly to families. In middle grades, students pose their own questions and collect data beyond the classroom, and in the higher grades, students may pose questions from which generalizations can be made. As pointed out on the student page shown below, we must be careful when formulating questions so that they are not **biased**. Read through the *EXAMPLE* on the student page to see *biased* and *fair* questions.

▶ **NOW TRY THIS 1**

NTT 1: Quick Check:
2a-biased, 2b-fair.

On the student page shown below, work through the *Quick Check* questions.

A formulation of unbiased questions on questionnaires for surveys requires careful consideration. Example 1 poses a question about survey methods.

School Book Page

Vocabulary Tip

Bias means "slant."
A biased question slants the answers in one direction.

When you conduct a survey, ask questions that do not influence the answer. A **biased question** is a question that makes an unjustified assumption or makes some answers appear better than others.

EXAMPLE   **Identifying Biased Questions**

2 **Music** Is each question *biased* or *fair*? Explain.

a. "Do you think that soothing classical music is more pleasing than the loud, obnoxious pop music that teenagers listen to?"

This question is biased against pop music. It implies that all pop music is loud and that only teenagers listen to it. The adjectives "soothing" and "obnoxious" may also influence responses.

b. "Which do you think is the most common age group of people who like pop music?"

This question is fair. It does not assume that listeners of pop music fall into only one age group.

c. "Do you prefer classical music or pop music?"

This question is fair. It does not make any assumptions about classical music, pop music, or people.

✓ **Quick Check**

2. Is each question *biased* or *fair*? Explain.
   a. Do you prefer greasy meat or healthy vegetables on your pizza?
   b. Which pizza topping do you like best?

Example 1

The IM Reliable Polling Company plans to conduct a survey of college students to determine their favorite movies in 2014–2015. What are some survey methods that could be used to obtain information from the students?

Solution   Answers vary. One possibility is to have randomly selected students list their favorite movies in 2014–2015. A second possibility is to provide a list of movies from the time period and ask randomly selected students to rate them from most favored to least favored using a numerical scale.

In Example 1, the type of questions asked will have some influence on the responses. For example, if a list of movies is provided, then someone who knows nothing about the movies may rate them anyway and return the survey. All such possibilities have to be considered when adopting a survey method. Examples for different levels follow.

Early Grades: How many pets does each student in the class have?

Middle Grades: Does the number of each student's pets change from Mr. Smith's grade 1 class to Mrs. Oneida's grade 2 class?

Higher Grades: Do students have more pets per student as they progress from grade 1 to grade 2?

Collect Data

Once questions are formulated, the next step is to develop a plan for collecting the data needed to answer the questions. In the process, we identify types of variability to determine a minimal expectation from eventual results. When we think about collecting data, an immediate question is from whom or where the data have to be collected. Are we talking about data from humans, from animals, even from data based on other data? The list could go on. The context is most important. To continue the example about the appearance of an average fifth grader, do we want to examine medical records to make this determination? Do we want to choose a sample group of students and make generalizations from the sample? If we want a sample, what geographical factors, if any, might need to be considered? Do all fifth graders "have the same appearance" in Montana? in the United States? in the world? In any event, a plan has to be devised and then implemented to collect the desired data.

In the early grades, there will likely be few plans to address variability in data collected because questions are fairly simple. In the middle grades, students may begin to use random selection for samples and choose students from the entire school as subjects. In later grades, experimental designs for study will include randomization to a wider audience. Using the same pet data questions as before, we illustrate collection methods for the different levels.

Early Grades: How many pets does each student in the class have?

The number of pets for each student is collected and recorded.

Middle Grades: Does the number of each student's pets change from Mr. Smith's grade 1 class to Mrs. Oneida's grade 2 class?

A simple random sample of the two classes might be used to compare the two classes. An important consideration is how to choose the samples.

Higher Grades: Do students have more pets per student as they progress from grade 1 to grade 2?

A random sample from first- and second-grade classes across a school system or a state might be used to help answer this question. Just how this is to be done is one of the major issues.

Analyze the Data

In analyzing collected data, we must make a decision about how to display the data or whether to report numbers to summarize them. Sections 10-2 and 10-3 deal with graphics for displaying data, and Section 10-4 discusses summaries of data. Often, decisions about how to analyze data are made with the data in hand. However, a good plan for collecting data should include some consideration of how the data will be analyzed once it is collected.

In the early grades, individual data may be compared to other individual data or to all the collected data for the entire group. In the middle grades, students may consider distributions and their associated properties. For example, groups may be compared to other groups using box plots (discussed in the next section). It is possible that students at this level may recognize sampling errors when analyzing data or begin to associate one variable with another. For example, students may consider the relationship between age and weight of children. In higher grades, students will analyze variability by considering numerical summaries of data.

Using the pet data questions, types of data analysis and display are considered at different levels.

Early Grades: How many pets does each student in the class have?

Simple bar graphs or graphical displays may be used to illustrate the data.

Middle Grades: Does the number of each student's pets change from Mr. Smith's grade 1 class to Mrs. Oneida's grade 2 class?

Double bar graphs might be used on the same scale so that differences can be seen. Also double stem and leaf plots might be used at this stage.

Higher Grades: Do students have more pets per student as they progress from grade 1 to grade 2?

Here, the bar graphs of the middle grades might be used or the stem and leaf plots (discussed in the next section) might be used, but students would also consider margins of error as a result of sampling techniques.

Interpret the Results

The results of data analysis must be interpreted. Some interpretations are clear-cut; others sometimes misuse data, a topic discussed in the final section of the chapter. In any event, the interpretation must be related to the original questions.

Early Grades: How many pets does each student in the class have?

An interpretation at this level might be as simple as reading and understanding a graph of the data.

Middle Grades: Does the number of each student's pets change from Mr. Smith's grade 1 class to Mrs. Oneida's grade 2 class?

From double bar graphs or the stem and leaf plots, or possibly even box plots, students can compare the numbers and might acknowledge that this is only for the given classes and not generalizable.

Higher Grades: Do students have more pets per student as they progress from grade 1 to grade 2?

The interpretation at this level might include all the interpretation at the middle-grades level but would consider generalizing across schools or the state.

Assessments 10-1A and 10-1B are basically communication exercises designed to interact about designing experiments and collecting data.

Assessment 10-1A

1. A second-grade class has a project to determine how many houses are on the blocks where they live. Formulate questions that might be asked, how the data might be collected, how it might be analyzed, and how it might be interpreted. *
2. Students in a middle-school class decide to determine if they are more physically active than their parents. What are possible questions for investigation? *
3. An eighth-grade class wants to determine if the temperature in their school varies by classroom. What are some considerations? *
4. To determine the most popular book among students at an elementary school, which sample is more likely to be random? Why? *
   (i) Ask students from different grades at the school.
   (ii) Ask a group of friends sitting in the library.
5. Decide whether each of the following questions is *biased* or *fair* and why.
   a. What is your favorite subject in school? Fair
   b. Do you enjoy the refreshing taste of ice-cold soda on a hot day? *
   c. How much sleep do you get on average on a week night? *
6. A group of adults remarked that they could "tell the difference between Coke and Pepsi." How might students design a study to test this claim if the students were
   a. elementary-grade students? *
   b. middle-grade students? *
7. If a class were to investigate how many countries students have visited, what are potential issues to be resolved before the investigation begins? *
8. In 1936, *The Literary Digest* predicted from questionnaires sent to owners of telephones and automobiles that Alfred Landon would win the U.S. presidency over Franklin Roosevelt. Clearly that prediction was incorrect. What are some likely errors made by the *Literary Digest*? *
9. In a set of student evaluations of their professors, one university lists the "three most positive comments and the three most negative comments" on its website. Discuss this listing and its usefulness in evaluating a professor's class. *

10. Suppose you want to choose a sample of 50 students from a school of 400. Explain why the following samples fail at drawing a representative sample.
    a. The first 50 students who arrive at school in the morning. *
    b. The first 50 students of all students lined up in a row. *
    c. Any 50 students at Friday's home soccer game. *
    d. 50 of all student responses to a questionnaire placed in a drop box at school. *
11. If a bar graph like the one shown here were used to depict data for second graders, what observations might be realistic for students to make in analyzing the graph? *

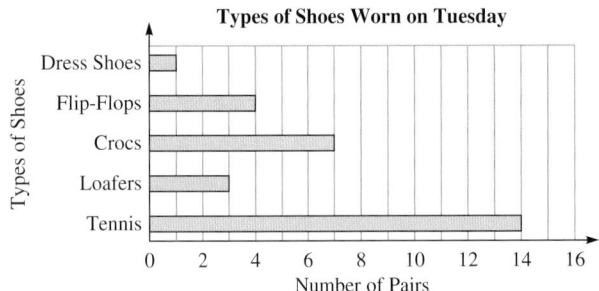

12. Determine the population in each of the following surveys and whether the sample is representative of that population.
    a. You ask 50 soccer fans sitting in seat numbers randomly chosen by a computer to rate the new stadium lights. *
    b. To find the average distance students have to travel to get to school, you survey the first 75 students coming through the main gate in the morning. *
    c. To find the average number of bicycles owned by a typical household in your town, you poll every student at your school. *
    d. You randomly select 5 students from each grade and measure their heights to get a better idea of the average height of students at your school. *

Assessment 10-1B

1. A second-grade class has a project to determine how many pets are owned by the students in each grade at their school. Formulate questions that might be asked, how the data might be collected, how it might be analyzed, and how it might be interpreted. *
2. An elementary school class decides to determine whether adult family members were lazier than students. What are possible questions for investigation? *

3. A seventh-grade class wants to determine if the students on one floor of the school are more affluent than those on another floor. What are some types of questions to consider? *
4. To determine student computer use, which sample is more likely to be representative? *
   (i) The students who are eating lunch.
   (ii) The students entering the library on Friday night.

5. Tell whether each of the following questions is *biased* or *fair* and why.
   a. Given the great tradition of space exploration in the United States, do you favor continued funding for space flights? Biased
   b. Do you think middle school students should be required to wear uniforms? Fair
   c. With just under 2% of the school budget going to the sciences, what do you think about the decision to build a new sports complex? *
   d. How many hours do you spend per week on average at the city public library? *

6. Some adults said different types of chocolate had distinctive flavors. How might students design a study to test whether the adults could tell the difference between types of chocolate if the students were
   a. elementary-grade students? *
   b. middle-grade students? *

7. A class wants to investigate how many different sporting events students have attended. What are some of the potential issues to be resolved before the investigation begins? *

8. Many predictions for the winner of the 2008 Super Bowl were incorrect. According to *The Arizona Republic* of February 3, 2008, "Giants pull off Super upset: With bruising defense and one brilliant drive, Giants stun Patriots." The predictions were based on the fact that the New England Patriots had won 18 games in a row. What data might be studied to help predict the winner before the game? *

9. A university professor used a rating scale to evaluate her classes: 1. Excellent class; 2. Good class; 3. Above-average class. Discuss the rating scale and its usefulness in evaluating a class. *

10. Suppose a poll is to be conducted in an elementary school by interviewing 50 students. Explain whether or not the following samples are representative of the students at the school.
    a. The first 50 students leaving the cafeteria. *
    b. Fifty randomly chosen names from a computer-generated list of names of all students at the school. *
    c. Ten students randomly chosen from each of the 5 areas of campus. *
    d. Five students from 10 teachers' classes. *

11. A teacher used a large grid printed on plastic, labeled the axes as kinds of shoes and number of wearers, respectively, had his students put one of their shoes on the grid, and proceeded to analyze the data with the class. What types of observation might it be reasonable for first graders to make? *

12. Determine the population and the sample in the following surveys. Is the sample representative?
    a. You ask 50 students who have segregated their recyclables at lunch time whether or not they recycle at home. *
    b. To determine the favorite drink (coffee or tea) among the staff at your school, you ask each teacher, principal, and administrative assistant to write their choice on a card provided and then tally the responses. *
    c. To determine how many children have seen the new action hero movie over the weekend, you interview 50 children in the school library on the following Monday afternoon. *
    d. To determine the most popular color of cars in your city, you sit at the only thoroughfare connecting the largest residential district with downtown and tally the colors of passing cars during peak hours on several weekdays. *

Mathematical Connections 10-1

Answers to Mathematical Connections can be found in the Answers section at the back of the book.

Reasoning

1. Which is more likely to produce a representative sample of math texts written in the United States, a college library or the U.S. Library of Congress? Why?

2. Read about basic ideas of statistics in *Common Core Standards* for grades 3–5, and discuss why students at these grade levels should be studying data analysis.

Open-Ended

3. Choose a grade and design a grade-appropriate question that students could investigate using statistics.

4. Suggest how students at different grades might investigate the length of words in a textbook.

Cooperative Learning

5. Examine grade-school books to see what types of data analysis are introduced and when they are introduced.

6. What are the Nielsen ratings? How does the survey determine how many people viewed a television show airing last night?

7. How might a sample not be representative of the population in a study? Look through a textbook on statistics or search online for several types of sampling biases. Create a list and compare with your classmates.

Connecting Mathematics to the Classroom

8. A student asks if the precision with which manufacturers must calibrate their tools is at all related to statistics. How do you respond?

9. Steve asks what an exit poll is and whether they are effective at predicting results in an election. What do you tell him?

10. Garth asks about the taste-testers a popular pizza restaurant chain employs. He wants to know how their opinion affects styles of pizza on the menu and whether this is at all related to statistics. How do you respond?

11. Sandra wonders how potato chip companies ensure the right levels of salt and spices and crunchiness in the thousands of bags of chips produced each day. How do you respond?

National Assessments

National Assessment of Educational Progress (NAEP) Questions

Zoo Attendance		
Day	Adults	Children
Thursday	757	649
Friday	774	742
Saturday	792	788
Sunday	801	726

The table shows the number of adults and children who went to the zoo.

On what day was the number of adults who went to the zoo about the same as the number of children who went to the zoo?
A. Thursday
B. Friday
C. Saturday
D. Sunday

NAEP, Grade 4, 2011

The fourth graders voted for a name for their pet. The graph shows the result of the vote.

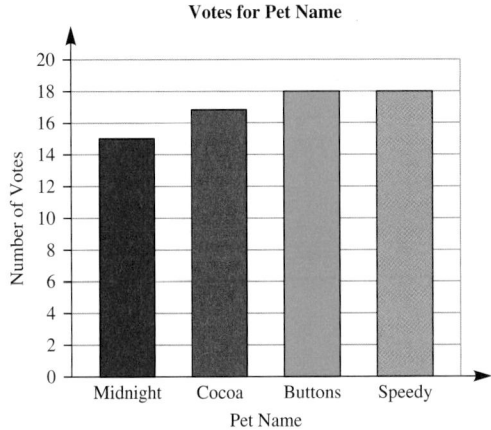

Votes for Pet Name

The students voted a second time. For the second vote, 4 students changed their vote from Buttons to Midnight. All other students voted for the same name they voted for the first time. Which name had the most votes the second time?
A. Midnight
B. Cocoa
C. Buttons
D. Speedy

◯ Yes   ◯ No

NAEP, Grade 4, 2013

10-2 Displaying Data: Part I

10-2 Objectives

Students will be able to understand and explain

- Categorical and numerical data.
- Simple plots and graphs.
- Stem and leaf plots.
- Histograms and bar graphs.
- Circle graphs.

Once data have been collected, their organization and visual illustrations are important. Such visual illustrations or graphs take many forms: *pictographs, circle graphs* (pie charts), *dot plots* (line plots), *scatterplots, stem and leaf plots, box plots, frequency tables, histograms, bar graphs,* and *frequency polygons* (line graphs). A *graph* is a picture that displays data. Graphs are used to tell a story.

What message is the *Bureau of Labor Statistics* trying to get across in the following graph?

Earnings and Unemployment Rates by Educational Attainment

Unemployment rate in 2013 (%)

2.2	Doctoral degree
2.3	Professional degree
3.4	Master's degree
4.0	Bachelor's degree
5.4	Associate's degree
7.0	Some college, no degree
7.5	High school diploma
11.0	Less than a high school diploma

All workers: 6.1%

Median weekly earnings in 2013 ($)

Doctoral degree	1,623
Professional degree	1,714
Master's degree	1,329
Bachelor's degree	1,108
Associate's degree	777
Some college, no degree	727
High school diploma	651
Less than a high school diploma	472

All workers: $827

Source: Bureau of Labor Statistics, 2014.

As the above graph shows, those with the highest unemployment rate and the lowest median weekly earnings are those with the least education.

Data: Categorical and Numerical

Statistical thinking begins in early grades with a need to know such things as "the most popular" pet, the favorite type of shoe, the most used color to paint, and so on. Data may be collected to find answers to such questions. Data collected may be either ***categorical*** or ***numerical*** depending on the questions being answered. For example, according to the *Statistics Framework*, in the elementary grades, students may

> *be interested in the favorite type of music among students at a certain grade level. . . . The class might investigate the question:* What type of music is most popular among students? *. . . The characteristic, favorite music type is a categorical variable—each child in that grade would be placed in a particular nonnumerical category based on his or her favorite music type. The resulting data are often called Categorical Data. (p. 22)*

Categorical data are data that represent characteristics of objects or individuals in groups (or categories), such as black or white, inside or outside, male or female. **Numerical data** are data collected on numerical variables. For example, in grade school, students may ask whether there is a difference in the distance that girls and boys can jump. The distance jumped is a numerical variables, and the collected data are *numerical*.

Some representations are used for both categorical and numerical data. We see different representations for both types of data in the following subsections.

Pictographs

An elementary student might use a picture graph, or **pictograph**, to represent tallies of categories such as their favorite pets. Pictographs are often seen in newspapers and magazines.

In Figure 1, categorical data might be seen in the determination of the month in which the most newspapers were recycled. The month is the *category*. In a pictograph, a symbol or an icon is used to represent a quantity of items. A *legend* tells what the symbol represents. Pictographs are used frequently to show comparisons of quantities among different categories (Figure 1). A major disadvantage of pictographs is evident in Figure 1. The month of September contains a partial bundle of newspapers. It is impossible to tell from the graph the weight of that partial bundle with any accuracy.

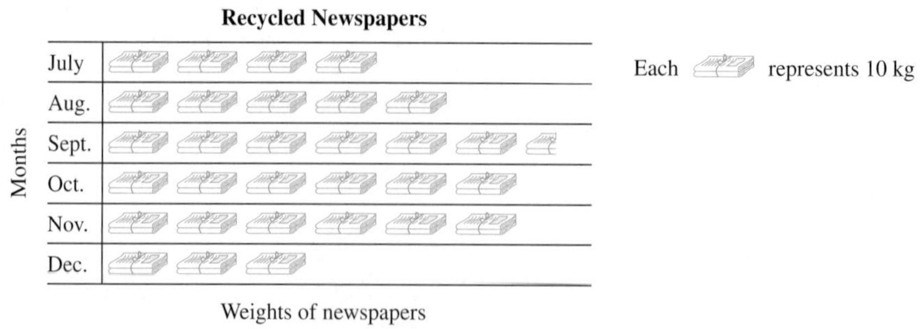

Figure 1

The number of students in each teacher's fifth-grade class at Hillview School is depicted in the tabular representation in Table 1. Each teacher is a category and the frequency/count table provides a method to summarize the categorical data. Figure 2 depicts the information in a pictograph. All graphs need titles; and if applicable, legends should be shown.

Table 1	Number of Students in Each Teacher's Fifth-Grade Hillview School	
Teacher	**Frequency or Count**	
Ames	20	
Ball	20	
Cox	15	
Day	25	
Eves	15	
Fagin	10	

**Hillview Fifth-Grade
Student Distribution**

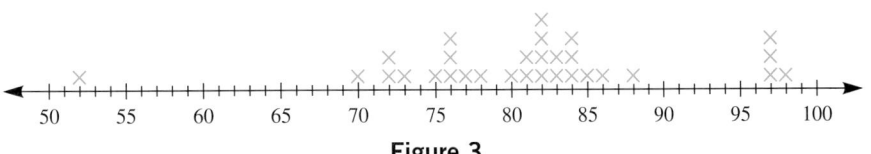

Figure 2

 Activity Manual

Use *Graphing m&m's®* to explore relationships among data using pictographs, dot plots, and bar graphs.

Dot Plots (Line Plots)

Next we examine a **dot plot**, sometimes called a **line plot**. Dot plots provide a quick, simple way of organizing data. Typically, we use them when there is only one group of data with fewer than 50 values.

Suppose the 30 students in Abel's class received the following test scores:

82 97 70 72 83 75 76 84 76 88 80 81 81 52 82

82 73 98 83 72 84 84 76 85 86 78 97 97 82 77

A dot plot for the class scores consists of a horizontal number line on which each score is denoted by a dot, or an ✕, above the corresponding number-line value, as shown in Figure 3. The number of ✕'s above each score indicates how many times each score occurred.

Figure 3 yields information about Abel's class exam scores. For example, three students scored 76 and four scored greater than 90. We also see that the low score was 52 and the high score was 98. Several features of the data become more obvious when dot plots are used. For example, outliers, clusters, and gaps are apparent. An **outlier** is a data point whose value is significantly greater or less than other values, such as the score of 52 in Figure 3. (Outliers are discussed in more detail in a later section.) A **cluster** is an isolated group of points, such as the one located at the scores 97 and 98. A **gap** is a large space between points, such as the one between 88 and 97.

Scores on Abel's Class Test

Figure 3

Another feature of the data is the score that appears most often in the data set. In Figure 3, 82 is the score that appears the most number of times. A data value that appears most often is the **mode**. Modes are discussed in more detail later.

If a dot plot is constructed on grid paper, then shading in the squares with ×'s and adding a vertical axis depicting the scale allows the formation of a *histogram*, as in Figure 4. The break in the horizontal axis between 0 and 50 is denoted by a squiggle and indicates that a part of the number line is missing.

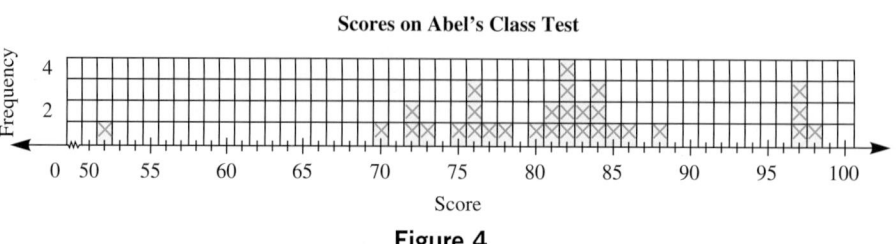

Scores on Abel's Class Test

Figure 4

Activity Manual

Use *Grouped Data* to explore the use of frequency tables, histograms, stem and leaf plots, and circle graphs to display data.

Stem-and-Leaf Plots

A **stem and leaf plot** is akin to a dot plot, but the scale is usually vertical, and digits are used rather than ×'s. A stem and leaf plot of test scores for Abel's class is shown in Figure 5. The numbers on the left side of the vertical segment are the **stems**, and the numbers on the right side are the **leaves**. In Figure 5, the stems are the tens digits of the scores on the test and the leaves are the units digits. In this case, the legend, "9|7 represents 97," shows how to read the plot.

In an **ordered stem-and-leaf plot**, the data values are given in order from least to greatest in each row as in Figure 5. Stem-and-leaf plots are sometimes first constructed with leaf values written in the order they are encounted in the raw data. To make the plot more useful and easier to read the leaf values are often ordered in each row.

Scores for Abel's Class

```
5 | 2

6 |

7 | 0223566678

8 | 011222233444568        9 | 7 represents 97

9 | 7778
```

Figure 5

Historical Note

John Tukey

Stem and leaf plots evolved from Arthur Bowley's work in the early 1900s and are a useful tool in exploratory data analysis. John Tukey (1915–2000), an American statistician, published *Exploratory Data Analysis* in 1977. This publication led to the common usage of stem and leaf plots in data analysis.

Smaller numbers are usually placed at the top so that when the plot is turned counterclockwise 90°, it resembles a bar graph or a histogram. Important advantages of stem and leaf plots are that they can be created by hand rather easily and they do not become unmanageable when the number of values becomes large. Moreover, no original values are lost in a stem and leaf plot. For example, in the stem and leaf plot of Figure 5, we know that one score was 75 and that exactly three students scored 97.

A summary of how to construct a stem and leaf plot is given below.

1. Find the high and low values of the data.
2. Decide on the stems.
3. List the stems in a column from least to greatest.
4. Use each piece of data to create leaves to the right of the stems on the appropriate rows.
5. If the plot is to be ordered, list the leaves in order from least to greatest.
6. Add a legend identifying the values represented by the stems and leaves.
7. Add a title explaining what the graph is about.

> ▶ NOW TRY THIS 2

NTT 2: Answers can be found in Answers at the back of the book.

Construct a stem and leaf plot using the data in Table 2, which lists the presidents of the United States and their ages at death.

Table 2

President	Age at Death	President	Age at Death	President	Age at Death
George Washington	67	Franklin Pierce	64	Woodrow Wilson	67
John Adams	90	James Buchanan	77	Warren Harding	57
Thomas Jefferson	83	Abraham Lincoln	56	Calvin Coolidge	60
James Madison	85	Andrew Johnson	66	Herbert Hoover	90
James Monroe	73	Ulysses Grant	63	Franklin Roosevelt	63
John Q. Adams	80	Rutherford Hayes	70	Harry Truman	88
Andrew Jackson	78	James Garfield	49	Dwight Eisenhower	78
Martin Van Buren	79	Chester Arthur	57	John Kennedy	46
William H. Harrison	68	Grover Cleveland	71	Lyndon Johnson	64
John Tyler	71	Benjamin Harrison	67	Richard Nixon	81
James K. Polk	53	William McKinley	58	Gerald Ford	93
Zachary Taylor	65	Theodore Roosevelt	60	Ronald Reagan	93
Millard Fillmore	74	William Taft	72		

Back-to-Back Stem and Leaf Plots

If two sets of related data with a similar number of data values are to be compared, a *back-to-back stem and leaf plot* can be used. In this case, two plots are made: one with leaves to the right, and one with leaves to the left. For example, if Abel gave the same test to two classes, he might prepare a back-to-back stem and leaf plot, as shown in Figure 6, where the data for the first class are on the left and for the second class are on the right.

Abel's Class Test Scores

Second-period Class			Fifth-period Class
20	5	2	
531	6	24	
99987542	7	1257	
875420	8	4456999	
0|5| represents a score of 50 1	9	2457	|5|2 represents a score of 52
	10	0	

Figure 6

NTT 3: Answers can be found in Answers at the back of the book.

▶ **NOW TRY THIS 3**

In the stem and leaf plots in Figure 6, which class do you think did better on the test? Why?

Example 2

Group the presidents in Table 2 into two groups, the first consisting of George Washington to Rutherford Hayes and the second consisting of James Garfield to Ronald Reagan.

a. Create a back-to-back stem and leaf plot of the two groups and see if there appears to be a difference in ages at death between the two groups.
b. Which group of presidents seems to have lived longer?

Solution

a. Because the ages at death vary from 46 to 93, the stems vary from 4 to 9. In Figure 7, the first 19 presidents are listed on the left and the remaining 19 on the right.

Ages of Presidents at Death

Early Presidents			Later Presidents
	4	96	
63	5	787	
364587	6	707034	|6|7 represents 67 years old
0741983	7	128	
3|8| represents 83 years old 053	8	81	
0	9	033	

Figure 7

b. The early presidents seem, on average, to have lived longer because the ages at the high end, especially in the 70s through 90s, come more often from the early presidents. The ages at the lower end come more often from the later presidents. For the stems in the 50s and 60s, the numbers of leaves are about equal.

A stem and leaf plot shows how wide a range of values the data cover, where the values are concentrated, whether the data have any symmetry, where gaps in the data are, and whether any data points are decidedly different from the rest of the data.

Grouped Frequency Tables

The stem and leaf plot in Figure 5 naturally groups scores into intervals or **classes**. For the data in Figure 5, the following classes are used: 50–59, 60–69, 70–79, 80–89, and 90–99. Thus each class has interval size 10. To compute an interval size we subtract the lower limit of one interval from the lower limit of the next higher interval; we get $60 - 50 = 10, 70 - 60 = 10$, and so on. Students often incorrectly report the interval size as 9 because $59 - 50 = 9$.

A **grouped frequency table** shows how many times data occur in a range. For example, consider the data in Table 2 for the ages of the presidents at death. These results are summarized in Table 3.

Table 3	Ages of Presidents at Death	
Ages at Death	**Tally**	**Frequency**
40–49	||	2
50–59	⊬⊤⊤	5
60–69	⊬⊤⊤ ⊬⊤⊤ ||	12
70–79	⊬⊤⊤ ⊬⊤⊤	10
80–89	⊬⊤⊤	5
90–99	||||	4
	Total	38

Table 3 shows that 12 presidents had ages at death in the interval 60–69, but it does not show the particular ages at which the presidents died. As the interval size increases, information is lost. Choices of interval size may vary. Classes should be chosen to accommodate all the data and each item should fit into only one class; that is, the classes should not overlap. Data from frequency tables can be graphed, as will be shown next.

Histograms and Bar Graphs

The data in Table 3 could be pictured graphically using a **histogram**. Figure 8(a) shows a histogram of the frequencies in Table 3. A histogram is made up of adjoining rectangles, or bars. In this case, the death ages are shown on the horizontal axis and the numbers along the vertical axis give the scale for the frequency. The frequencies of the death ages are shown by the bars, which are all the same width. The scale on the vertical axis must be uniform. In some reports the midpoints of the bars in a histogram are marked instead of the intervals.

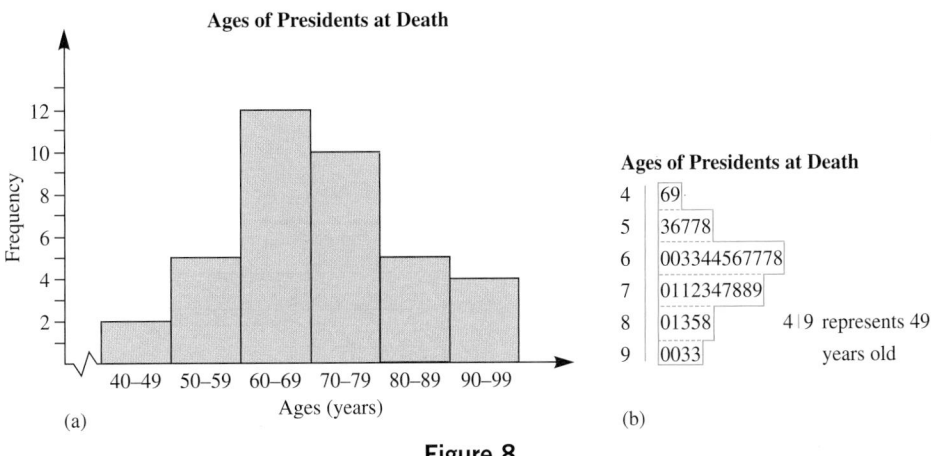

Figure 8

Histograms can be made easily from single-sided stem and leaf plots. For example, if we take the stem-and-leaf plot in Figure 8(b) and enclose each row (set of leaves) in a bar, we have what looks like a histogram. Histograms show gaps and clusters just as stem and leaf plots do. However, with a histogram we cannot retrieve data as we can in a stem and leaf plot. Another disadvantage of a histogram is that it is often necessary to estimate the heights of the bars. The student page shown on page 553 shows a dot plot (line plot), a frequency table, and a histogram.

▶ **NOW TRY THIS 4**

a. Work *Quick Checks* 2 and 3 on the student page shown on p. 553.
b. In the histogram for Atlantic Ocean hurricanes on the student page do, you think there should be space on the horizontal axis to represent the interval 0–1? Why?

E-Manipulative Activity
Use the activity *Bar Graphs* to create and analyze date in a bar graph.

A **bar graph** is somewhat like a histogram. It typically has spaces between the bars and is used to depict categorical data. A bar graph showing the heights in centimeters of five students appears in Figure 9. The height of each bar represents the height in centimeters of each student named on the horizontal axis. Each space between bars is usually one-half the width of a bar.

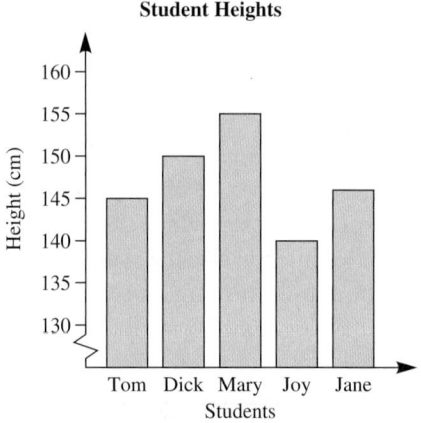

Student Heights

Figure 9

Note that in Figure 9 the bars representing Tom, Dick, Mary, Joy, and Jane could be placed in any order, whereas in Figure 8(a), the order cannot be changed without losing the continuity of the numbering along the horizontal axis. A distinguishing feature between histograms and bar graphs is that there is no ordering that has to be done among the bars of the bar graph, whereas there is an order for a histogram.

Double-bar graphs can be used to make comparisons in data. For example, the data in the back-to-back stem and leaf plot of Figure 7 can be pictured as shown in Figure 10. The green bars represent the later presidents, and the blue bars represent the earlier presidents.

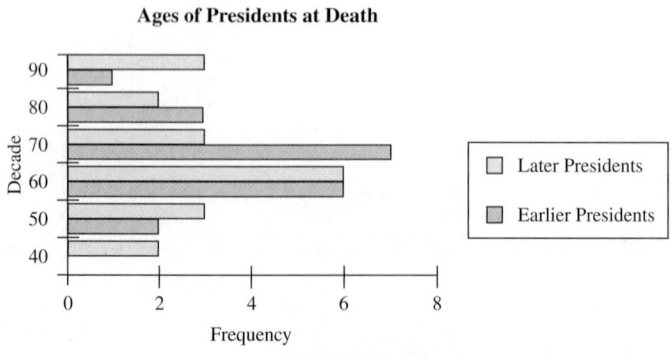

Ages of Presidents at Death

Figure 10

School Book Page
Making Line Plots and Histograms

A **line plot** is a graph that shows the shape of a data set by stacking **✗**'s above each data value on a number line.

EXAMPLE **Making a Line Plot**

② Make a line plot of the data in Example 1.

Step 1 Draw a number line from the least to the greatest value (from 2 to 11).

Step 2 Write an **✗** above each value for each time the value occurs in the data.

Atlantic Ocean Hurricanes

```
            ✗
            ✗   ✗
            ✗   ✗           ✗
        ✗   ✗   ✗       ✗   ✗   ✗
    ✗   ✗   ✗   ✗   ✗   ✗   ✗   ✗
    ✗   ✗   ✗   ✗   ✗   ✗   ✗   ✗   ✗   ✗
    2   3   4   5   6   7   8   9   10  11
```

✓ Quick Check

2. Make a line plot of the number of students in math classes: 24 27 21 25 25 28 22 23 25 25 28 22 23 25 22 24 25 28 27 22.

A **histogram** is a bar graph with no spaces between the bars. The height of each bar shows the frequency of data within that interval. The intervals of a histogram are of equal size and do not overlap.

EXAMPLE **Making a Histogram**

③ Make a histogram of the data in Example 1.

Make a frequency table. Use the equal-sized intervals 2–3, 4–5, 6–7, 8–9, and 10–11. Then make a histogram.

Atlantic Ocean Hurricanes

Number	Frequency
2–3	ⅢⅡ
4–5	ⅢⅡ ⅢⅡ Ⅰ
6–7	ⅢⅡ Ⅰ
8–9	ⅢⅡ Ⅰ
10–11	ⅡⅠ

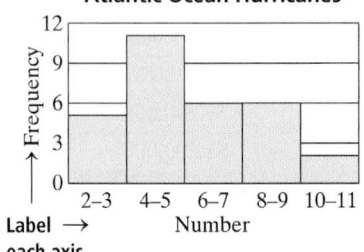

Label → each axis.

✓ Quick Check

3. Make a histogram of the ages of employees at a retail store: 28 20 44 72 65 40 59 29 22 36 28 61 30 27 33 55 48 24 28 32.

Other Bar Graphs

Table 4 shows various types of shoes worn by students in one class and the approximate percentages of students who wore them. Figure 11 depicts a **percentage bar graph** with that same data.

Table 4	Number of Students and Percentage Wearing the Type of Shoes	
Shoe Type	**Frequency**	***Percentage**
Dress	1	4%
Flip-Flops	4	14%
Crocs	7	24%
Loafers	3	10%
Tennis	14	48%

Note: percentages are approximate to sum to 100%.

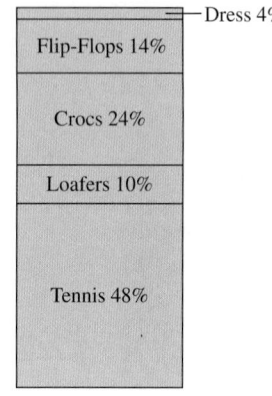

Figure 11

Table 5 shows information about the expenditures of a business over a period of years. These data are depicted in a **stacked bar graph** in Figure 12.

Table 5	Expenditures of a Business Over a Period of Years	
Years	**Materials**	**Labor**
1970–1979	$ 795,000	$1,500,000
1980–1989	$ 950,000	$1,900,000
1990–1999	$1,230,000	$2,400,000
2000–2009	$1,500,000	$2,400,000

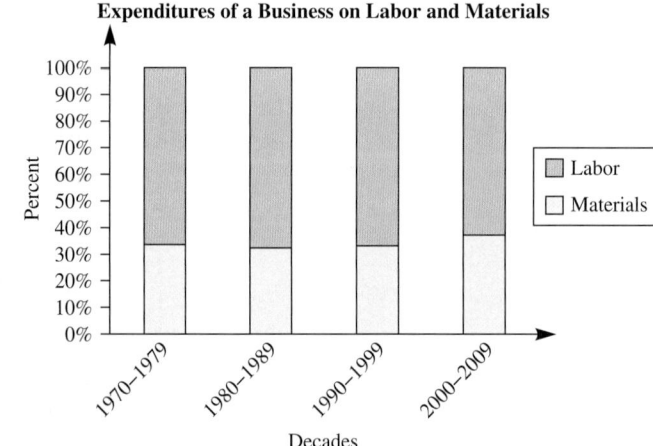

Figure 12

Circle Graphs (Pie Charts)

A **circle graph**, or **pie chart**, consists of a circular region partitioned into sectors, with each sector representing a part or percentage of the whole. A circle graph shows how parts are related to the whole. An example of a circle graph is given in Figure 13.

E-Manipulative Activity

Use the activity *Pie Graphs* to create and analyze data in a pie chart.

U.S. Population by Age, 2008

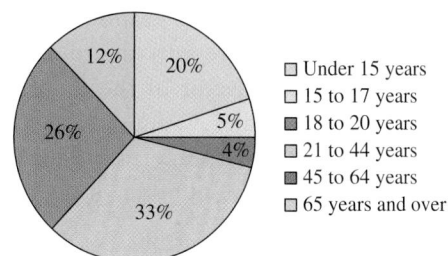

☐ Under 15 years
☐ 15 to 17 years
■ 18 to 20 years
☐ 21 to 44 years
■ 45 to 64 years
☐ 65 years and over

Source: U.S. Census Bureau. Current Population Survey, Annual Social and Economic Supplement, 2009.

Figure 13

In Figure 13 the measure of the central angle (an angle whose vertex is at the center of the circle) of each sector of the graph is proportional to the fraction or percentage of the population the section represents. For example, the measure of the angle for the sector for the under-15 group is approximately 20% of the circle. Because the entire circle is 360°, then 20% of 360°, which is 72°, should be devoted to the Under-15 group. Similarly, we can compute the number of degrees for each age group, as shown in Table 6.

The Number of Degrees in the Pie Chart for Each Age Group

Table 6		
Age	**Approximate Percent**	**Approximate Degrees**
Under 15	20	72
15–17	5	18
18–20	4	14
21–44	33	119
45–64	26	94
65 and Over	12	43
Total	100	360

Example 3

The information in Table 7 is based on the survival and death rates of the crew and passengers in the various ticket classes on the *Titanic* when it sank. The numbers in the table reflect the numbers of people who survived or died in each class.

a. Construct circle graphs (pie charts) for the survival group and the death group to make comparisons.
b. Construct stacked bar graphs for the survival group and the death group to make comparisons.
c. Which class fared best in terms of survival? Why?

Survival and Death on the Titanic by Class

Table 7		Class			
	1st	**2nd**	**3rd**	**Crew**	**Total**
Survival	202	118	178	212	710
Death	123	167	528	673	1491

Source: HistoryontheNet.com

Solution

a. We construct a circle graph for the survival passengers based on the data in Table 7. The entire circle represents the total 710 people who survived. The measure of the central angle of each sector of the graph is proportional to the fraction or percentage of the passengers and crew the section represents. The measure of the angle for the sector for the first-class passengers is 202/710 or approximately 28.5% of the circle. Similarly, we can compute the number of degrees for each group listed in Table 7. This is given in Table 8.

Table 8	Survival Percentage by Class		
	Survival Group		
Class	**Ratio**	**Approximate Percent**	**Approximate Degrees**
1st	$\frac{202}{710}$	28.5%	103°
2nd	$\frac{118}{710}$	16.6%	60°
3rd	$\frac{178}{710}$	25.1%	90°
Crew	$\frac{212}{710}$	29.9%	108°

The percents and degrees in Table 8 are only approximate. Appropriate software or a compass and protractor can be used to draw the sectors in the circle graph. Similar reasoning can be used to construct a circle graph for the death groups of the *Titanic*. The two circle graphs are given in Figure 14. The circle graphs show that for ticketed passengers the chance of survival depended upon the class of ticket.

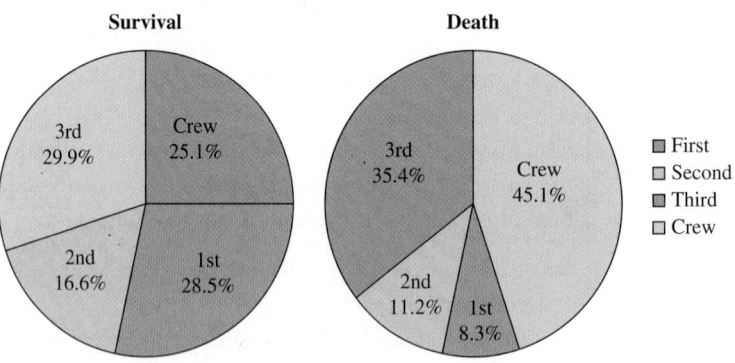

Figure 14

b. For the stacked bar graphs in Figure 15, each bar represents the whole (100%) and is divided proportionally based on the percentages given in Figure 14. Again, we see from the graph that the rate of survival seemed to depend on the ticket class of a passenger.

Survival and Death Depicted in Stacked Bar Graphs

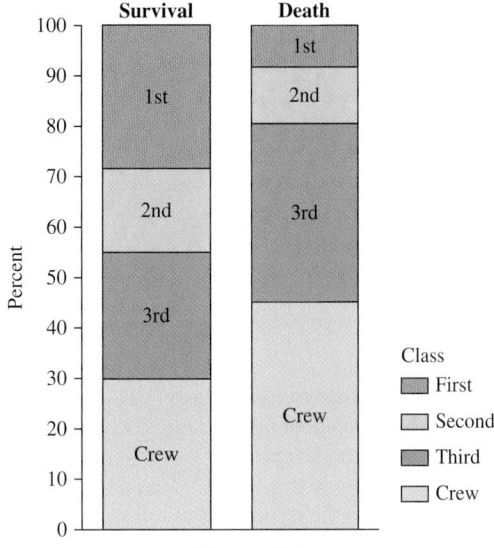

Figure 15

c. Notice that the above data, although true, may be misleading. The survival and death percentages given are computed using the ratios of the numbers of passengers that survived or died in given classes of passengers, to the total number of Titanic passengers that survived or died. For example, the 28.5% of first class passengers that survived is the percentage of first class that survived out of the total 710 passengers that survived. If we want to know the percentage of first-class that survived out of the total 325 first class passengers, we get $\frac{202}{325} \approx 62.2\%$. Similarly, the percentage of second-class passengers that survived is $\frac{118}{285} \approx 41.4\%$. For third class we get $\frac{178}{706} \approx 25.2\%$, and for the crew $\frac{212}{885} \approx 24.0\%$. This data clearly shows that first class fared the best.

Assessment 10-2A

1. The following pictograph shows the approximate number of pieces of mail processed at the Townville post office over a five-day week.
   a. On what day were the most pieces processed? Tuesday
   b. About how many more pieces of mail were processed on Tuesday than on Monday? Approximately 1500
   c. How many symbols would be used to represent 3000 pieces of mail? 3

**Number of Pieces of Mail Processed
by the Townville Post Office**

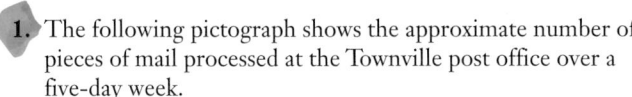

Each ▱ represents 1000 pieces of mail

2. Make a pictograph to represent the categorical data in the following table. Use 🥤 to represent 10 glasses of lemonade sold. *

Glasses of Lemonade Sold		
Day	**Tally**	**Frequency**
Monday	╫╫ ╫╫ ╫╫	15
Tuesday	╫╫ ╫╫ ╫╫ ╫╫	20
Wednesday	╫╫ ╫╫ ╫╫ ╫╫ ╫╫ ╫╫	30
Thursday	╫╫	5
Friday	╫╫ ╫╫	10

3. Sixth-grade students reported the number of apps that they downloaded to their smartphones. Construct a dot plot from the results given below. *

12, 5, 7, 3, 0, 2, 0, 10, 12, 9, 0, 0, 15, 17, 25, 7, 8, 10, 12, 13, 0, 0, 10, 14, 0

4. The following stem and leaf plot gives the weights in pounds of all 15 students in the Algebra 1 class at East Junior High:

Weights of Students in East Junior High Algebra 1 Class

```
 7 | 24
 8 | 112578
 9 | 2478
10 | 3          10|3 represents
11 |            103 lb
12 | 35
```

a. Write the weights of the 15 students. *
b. What is the weight of the lightest student in the class? 72 lbs.
c. What is the weight of the heaviest student in the class? 125 lbs.

5. Draw a histogram based on the stem and leaf plot in exercise 4. *

6. Roll a six-sided die 30 times and record the result of each roll.
a. Construct a dot plot for the data. *
b. Draw a bar graph for the data. *

7. The following figure shows a bar graph of the rainfall in centimeters in the city of Centerville during the last school year:

Rainfall Last School Year in Centerville

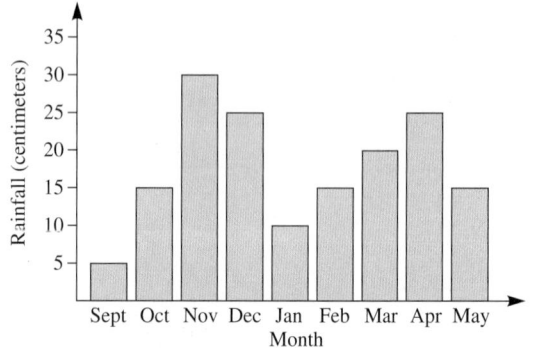

a. Which month had the most rainfall, and how much did it have? November, 30 cm
b. How much total rain fell in October, December, and January? 50 cm

8. HKM Company employs 40 people of the following ages:

```
34  58  21  63  48  52  24  52  37  23
23  34  45  46  23  26  21  18  41  27
23  45  32  63  20  19  21  23  54  62
41  32  26  41  25  18  23  34  29  26
```

a. Draw a stem and leaf plot for the data. *
b. Are more employees in their 40s or in their 50s? *
c. How many employees are less than 30 years old? 20
d. What percentage of the people are 50 years or older? 17.5%

9. Five coins are tossed 64 times. A distribution for the number of heads obtained is shown in the following table. Draw a bar graph for the data. *

Number of Heads	0	1	2	3	4	5
Frequency	2	10	20	20	10	2

10. Use a 3-inch-long rectangle to create a percentage bar graph for the monthly family budget below. Their total monthly income is $5400. *

Rent	$2050
Food	$1700
Utilities	$800
Transportation	$400
Recreation	$200
Savings	(the remainder)

11. Seniors at Sierra High were asked about their preferred online social networking service. The following are the percentages of students in the top five responses and those with none of the five responses.

Facebook	64%
Twitter	22%
Myspace	2%
Google+	1%
LinkedIn	1%
none	10%

Construct a circle graph for the data. *

12. a. In a circle graph, a sector containing 65° represents what percentage of the data? Approximately 18%
b. In a circle graph, 32% of data can be represented by a sector of how many degrees? 115.2°

13. a. A 2-inch-long rectangle serves as a percentage bar chart. What percentage of the data does one $\frac{1}{4}$-in. subrectangle represent? 12.5%
b. In the percentage bar chart in part (a), 16% of data can be represented by how long a subrectangle? 0.32 inches

14. A class of eighth graders undertook an ambitious project to compile the most dominant color of uniforms for all 241 middle school sports teams in their state this year. The circle graph below shows the results. Approximately how many teams are represented in each sector?

Dominant Color of Middle School Sport Team Uniforms

5% 12% 17% 24% 22% 20%

Approximately:

black 58
navy blue 53
white 48
gray 41
maroon 29
other 12

15. a. If the number of people reading mysteries in different age groups in a survey are depicted as in the given bar graph, explain whether or not you think that the graph is accurate and why. *
b. Based on the data in the graph, in what age decade do people read the most? *

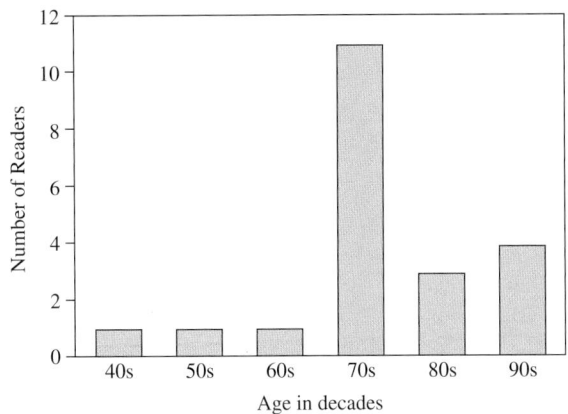

Number of Mystery Readers by Age in Decades

16. The following are the amounts (to the nearest $10) paid by 25 college students for textbooks during the fall term:

240	440	240	260	250
340	350	320	360	540
130	340	420	350	450
250	540	350	460	540
450	440	160	530	220

a. Draw an ordered stem and leaf plot to illustrate the data. *
b. Construct a grouped frequency table for the data, starting the first class at $100 with intervals of $50. *
c. Draw a bar graph of the data. *

17. The following bar graph shows the life expectancies for men and women:

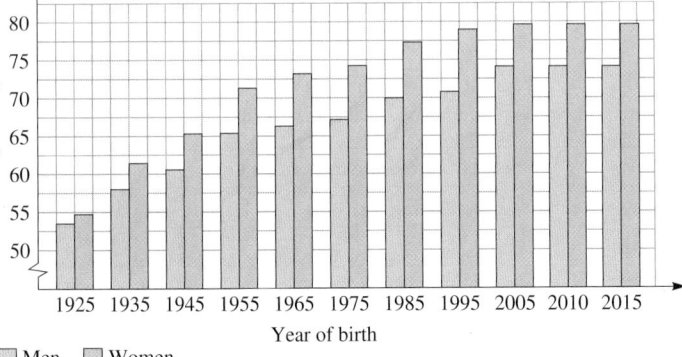

Life Expectancy at Birth

☐ Men ☐ Women

a. What kind of bar graph is this? Double-bar graph
b. Whose life expectancy has changed the most since 1925? Women
c. In 1925, about how much longer was a woman expected to live than a man? Approximately 2 yrs.
d. In 2010, about how much longer was a woman expected to live than a man? Approximately 5 yrs.

18. A percentage bar graph is drawn to depict the information in the table. If the bar is 8 cm, what is the length of each section? *

Savings	Rent	Food	Auto Payment	Tuition
10%	30%	12%	27%	$x\%$

19. The following bar graph shows the 2012–13 average starting teacher salaries reported by the National Education Association in 2014.

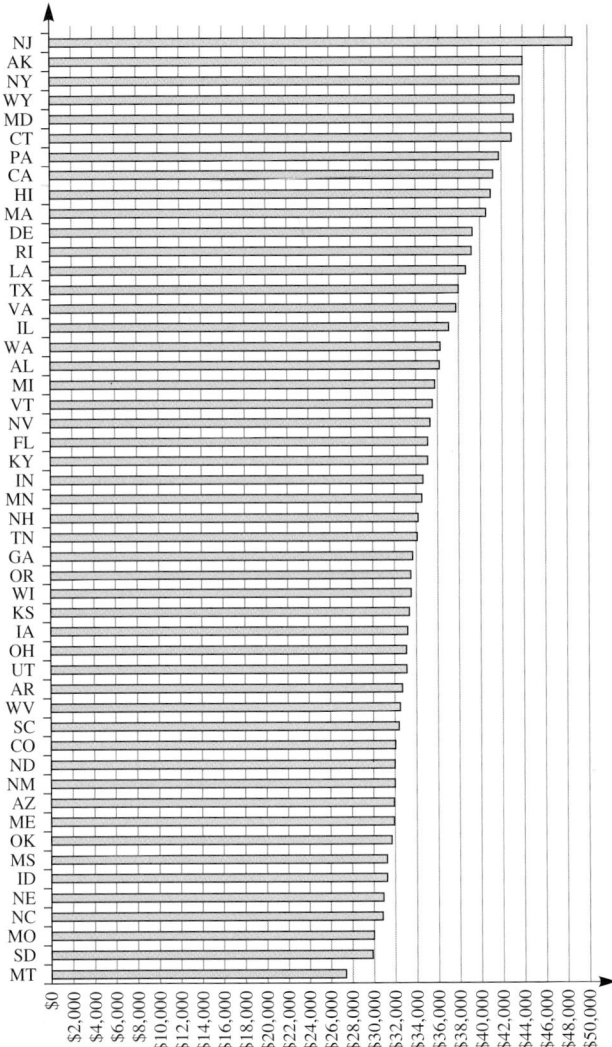

2012–2013 Average Starting Teacher Salaries by State Reported by the NEA in 2014

Source: http://www.nea.org/home/2012-2013-average-starting-teacher-salary.html

a. Which state pays the highest average teacher salaries? New Jersey
b. Which state pays the lowest average teacher salaries? Montana
c. Estimate the median average salary; that is, the salary where half the states pay more and half the states pay less. Approximately $34,500
d. About what percent more in average salary does New Jersey pay than Montana? Approximately 72%

Assessment 10-2B

1. The following pictograph shows the approximate attendance at four Big Sky High School winter sporting events. Estimate how many attended each event.   Boy's soccer, 4500; Girl's soccer, 2250; Boy's basketball, 4750; Girl's basketball, 4000.

Attendance at Big Sky High School Sporting Events

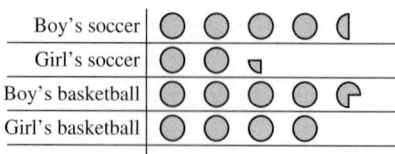

Each ⬤ represents 1000 people

2. Display the following information about the status of selected hardware sold in the United States in 2010 in a pictograph where an icon represents $5 million in sales.   *

Hardware	Sales (in millions of dollars)
Computers	26,060
Smartphones	20,607
Digital video recorders	4668
Digital cameras	2442
Camcorders	6345
Portable media/MP3 players	5400

Source: Consumer Electronics Association, 2010.

3. Following are the GPA's of the 30 students from Washington University who participated in the NCAA track meet. Draw a dot plot to better display the data.   *

3.2	2.8	2.0	1.9	3.0
3.3	2.9	2.2	2.0	4.0
3.5	3.0	3.1	2.1	3.4
4.0	3.1	3.3	2.8	3.9
3.9	3.7	2.5	2.9	3.7
2.7	3.0	2.7	2.9	3.9

4. The heights reached by 15 model rockets launched by the students in Mr. Ford's science class are shown in the stem and leaf plot below.

Height reached by rockets (in feet)

1	90
2	24 38
2	75 89 98 99 (2|75 represents 275 ft.)
3	10 12 19 20 25
3	52 55
4	02

  a. What is the least height reached by one of the rockets?   190 ft
  b. What is the greatest height reached?   402 ft
  c. What percentage of the rockets flew above 300 feet?
     Approximately 53%

5. Draw a histogram based on the stem and leaf plot in exercise 4.   *
6. Toss four pennies 30 times and record the number of heads in each toss.
  a. Construct a dot plot for the data.   *
  b. Draw a bar graph for the data.   *
7. Given the following bar graph, estimate the length of the following rivers.
  a. **Mississippi**   Approximately 3800 km
  b. **Columbia**   Approximately 1900 km

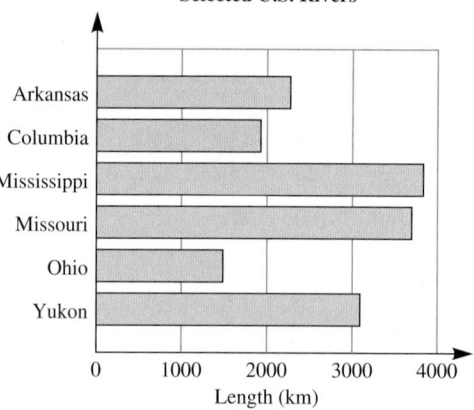

8. The data below show the number of car thefts in a city for a period of 20 days.

    50, 62, 69, 56, 52, 66, 53, 49, 72, 35
    65, 53, 78, 66, 55, 48, 82, 78, 72, 75

  a. Draw an ordered stem and leaf plot for the data.   *
  b. What percent of the 20 days had more than 70 cars stolen?   30%
9. Two dice are tossed 65 times and the sums of the numbers are recorded in the table. Draw a bar graph for the data.   *

Frequency of Sums on Dice											
Sums on Dice	2	3	4	5	6	7	8	9	10	11	12
Frequency	2	3	5	8	10	12	9	6	7	2	1

10. The following table shows the grade distribution for the final examination in the mathematics course for elementary teachers. Draw a percentage bar graph for the data.   *

Grade	Frequency
A	6
B	10
C	36
D	6
F	2

11. Draw a circle graph for the data in exercise 10.   *

12. Use the circle graph to answer the following questions:

Earth's Land

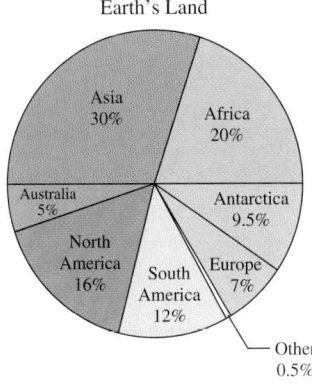

a. Which is the largest continent? Asia

b. Which continent is about twice the size of Antarctica? Africa

c. How does Africa compare in size to Asia? *

d. Which two continents make up about half of Earth's land area? Asia and Africa

e. What is the ratio of the size of Australia to North America? 5:16

f. If Europe has approximately 4.1 million mi² of land, what is the total area of the land on Earth? *

13. a. In a circle graph, a sector containing 82° represents what percentage of the data? Approximately 23%

b. In a circle graph, 0.05% of data can be represented by a sector of how many degrees? 0.18°

14. a. A 5 cm long rectangle serves as a percentage bar chart. What percentage of the data does one 1.5 cm section represent? 30%

b. In the percentage bar chart in part (a), 20% of data can be represented by how long a section? 1 cm

15. A list of presidents, with the number of children for each, follows:

1. Washington, 0	23. B. Harrison, 3
2. J. Adams, 5	24. McKinley, 2
3. Jefferson, 6	25. T. Roosevelt, 6
4. Madison, 0	26. Taft, 3
5. Monroe, 2	27. Wilson, 3
6. J. Q. Adams, 4	28. Harding, 0
7. Jackson, 0	29. Coolidge, 2
8. Van Buren, 4	30. Hoover, 2
9. W. H. Harrison, 10	31. F. D. Roosevelt, 6
10. Tyler, 15	32. Truman, 1
11. Polk, 0	33. Eisenhower, 2
12. Taylor, 6	34. Kennedy, 4
13. Fillmore, 2	35. L. B. Johnson, 2
14. Pierce, 3	36. Nixon, 2
15. Buchanan, 0	37. Ford, 4
16. Lincoln, 4	38. Carter, 4
17. A. Johnson, 5	39. Reagan, 4
18. Grant, 4	40. G. Bush, 5
19. Hayes, 8	41. Clinton, 1
20. Garfield, 7	42. G. W. Bush, 2
21. Arthur, 3	43. Obama, 2
22. Cleveland, 5	

a. Construct a dot plot for these data. *

b. Make a frequency table for these data. *

c. What is the most frequent number of children? 2

16. The double bar graph below shows the *2015 Quarterly Report of Income and Expenses for Acme Toy Company.*

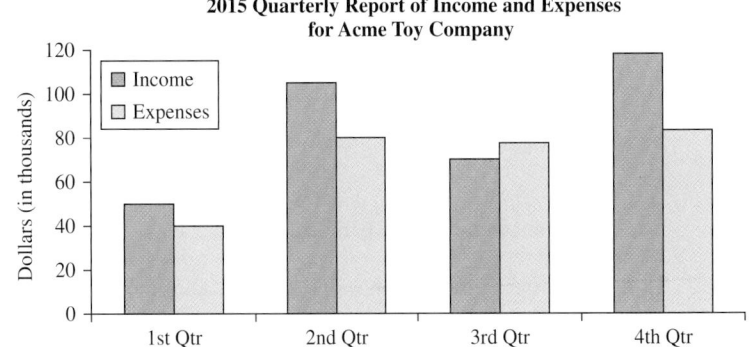

a. In what quarters did the company experience its greatest profit and the greatest loss? *

b. Overall, did Acme Toy Company experience a profit or a loss for the year? Why? *

c. Is it true that if Acme's quarter income is over $60,000, then it's expenses are over $60,000 that quarter? *

17. The table below depicts the number of deaths in the United States from Acquired Immunodeficiency Syndrome (AIDS) by age in 2007, 2008, 2009 and 2010.

a. Choose and construct a graph to display the data. *

b. Are any patterns of difference evident in the comparison of the two groups of data? *

Death from AIDS by Age and Year				
Age (yr)	**2007**	**2008**	**2009**	**2010**
< 13	8	6	6	4
13–19	53	48	34	36
20–29	720	700	668	533
30–39	3016	2517	2208	1730
40–49	7019	6268	5622	4623
50–59	5102	5612	5507	4963
≥ 60	2170	2804	3023	2867

Source: Centers for Disease Control and Prevention 2011 http://www.cdc.gov/hiv/pdf/statistics_2011_HIV_Surveillance_Report_vol_23.pdf#Page=40

18. The histogram below shows the number of books read by 20 people in a book club over a 3-month period.

Number of Books Read in 3 Months

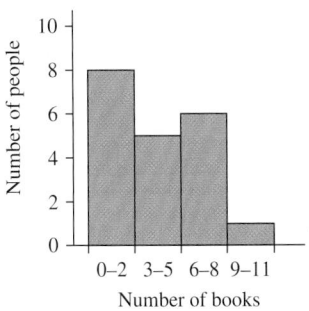

a. How many people read 3–5 books during this period? 5

b. How many people read more than 5 books? 7

c. What would you estimate for the number of books read by a person in this club? About 4

Mathematical Connections 10-2

Answers to Mathematical Connections can be found in the Answers section at the back of the book.

Reasoning

1. **a.** Discuss when a pictograph might be more appropriate than a circle graph.
   b. Discuss when a circle graph might be more appropriate than a bar graph.
   c. Give an example of a set of data for which a stem and leaf plot would be more informative than a histogram.

2. Explain whether a circle graph would change if the amount of data in each category were doubled.

3. Explain why the sum of the percents in a circle graph should always be 100%. How could it happen that the sum is only close to 100%?

4. The federal budget for one year is typically depicted with one type of visual representation. Which one is used and why?

5. Tell whether it is appropriate to use a bar graph for each of the following. If so, draw the appropriate graph.
   a. U.S. population

Year	U.S. Population
1920	105,710,620
1930	122,775,046
1940	131,669,275
1950	150,697,361
1960	179,323,175
1970	203,302,031
1980	226,542,203
1990	248,765,170
2000	281,421,906
2010	308,745,538
2013	316,128,839

   b. Continents of the world

Continent	Area in Square Miles (mi²)
Africa	11,694,000
Antarctica	5,100,000
Asia	16,968,000
Australia	2,966,000
Europe	4,066,000
North America	9,363,000
South America	6,886,000

6. Car sales from 1990 to 2015 for a large city are given below. Discuss the trend in car sales based on the information in the given circle graphs.

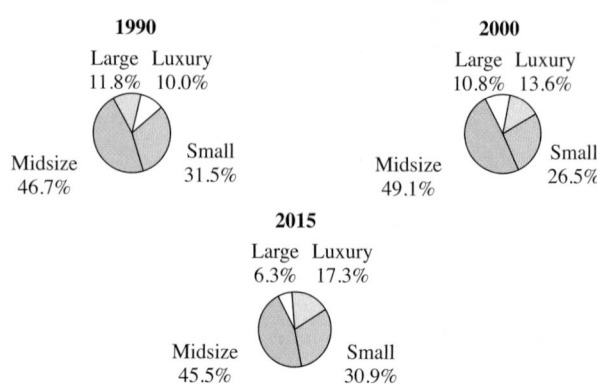

Car Sales by Vehicle Size and Type

7. The following data are the average weights of backpacks collected from students as they left school in the afternoon once per week, over a period of 3 years. Organize the data into an appropriate display and draw some meaningful conclusions.

Average Weights of Students Backpacks			
	Year 1	Year 2	Year 3
Freshmen	2.4	2.0	0.8
Sophomores	3.2	2.8	1.1
Juniors	3.4	2.9	1.3
Seniors	2.7	2.1	0.9

Open-Ended

8. Find five examples of visual representations of data from current events in the media. Discuss the merits of each.

9. Choose a topic that interests you or a question you would like to attempt to answer. Describe how you would go about collecting data on the topic, and then explain how you would display your data in a graph. Tell why you chose the particular graph.

10. A graph similar to the following one was depicted on a package of cigarettes in Canada.

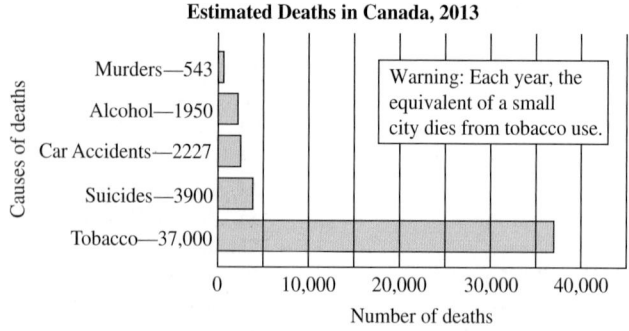

Estimated Deaths in Canada, 2013

   a. Make a circle graph of the data.
   b. Explain which graph, bar graph or circle graph, you think is more effective.

Cooperative Learning

11. Decide on and give a rationale for the type of graph that you would use to show the percentage of working time that professors spend on teaching, service, and research.

12. Choose one page of this text. Find the word length of every word on the page. Draw a graph depicting these data. If you chose another page of the book at random, what would you expect the most common word length to be? Why?

Connecting Mathematics to the Classroom

13. Jackson asks whether a stem and leaf plot should be constructed with the greatest numbers at the bottom and the least ones at the top and why this should or should not be done. How do you respond?

14. Aliene says that she constructed the following graph on a spreadsheet and wants to know if it is an acceptable type of graph to be used to depict data regarding the types of cars owned by a certain subset of the population. How do you react?

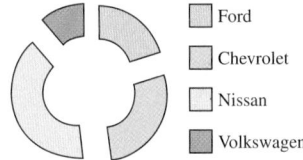

☐ Ford
☐ Chevrolet
☐ Nissan
☐ Volkswagen

15. Paul asks how to create a stem and leaf plot when the data consists of numbers with two places after the decimal point. How do you respond?

Review Problems

16. Classify the following questions as biased or fair.
    a. Do you agree or disagree with the statement "There is a need for stricter gun laws"?
    b. Many people have said there is a need for stricter laws on dangerous weapons. Do you agree?
    c. Do you like this pair of pants?
    d. You don't like this pair of pants, do you?
    e. Do you agree that this new law is a problem?
    f. Do you agree or disagree that this new law is a problem?

17. The owners of a restaurant want to address their concerns of declining customer satisfaction. Examine the following sampling methods for bias. Which would provide good feedback? Why?
    (i) A postcard questionnaire is placed with every bill in hopes that patrons fill it out at home and mail it back.
    (ii) Servers are instructed to encourage patrons to visit the web site, the address of which is printed on the bottom of the receipt, hosting a short survey.
    (iii) Patrons can fill out a questionnaire at the bar and drop it in a locked box, thereby entering a drawing for a free dinner for two.
    (iv) A pollster is hired to stand outside the restaurant and ask every other exiting patron some questions.

National Assessments

National Assessment of Educational Progress (NAEP) Questions

The graph below shows students' favorite fruits.

Use these clues to label the bars with the correct fruit.

- Twice as many students chose apples as grapes.
- Five more students chose peaches than apples.
- Ten more students chose bananas than peaches.

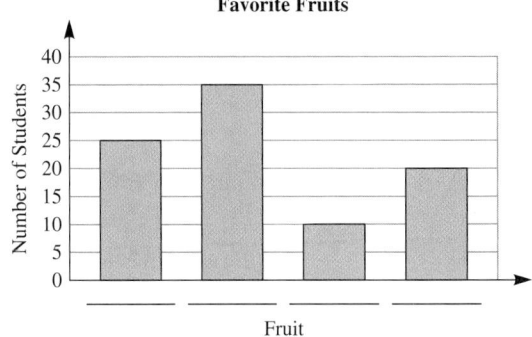

Favorite Fruits

Write the correct fruit on the lines above.

NAEP, Grade 4, 2011

Favorite Ice-Cream Flavors of Fourth Graders		
Class	Number Who Chose Vanilla	Number Who Chose Chocolate
Mr. Kennedy	6	12
Ms. Ying	8	10
Mrs. Delgado	7	13
Mrs. Findley	9	15

The table lists the favorite ice-cream flavors of four classes of fourth graders. On the graph below, use one ☺ to represent 10 children. Draw the correct number of faces on the graph to show the favorite flavors of the fourth graders.

Favorite Ice-Cream Flavors	
Number Who Chose Vanilla	
Number Who Chose Chocolate	

☺ = 10 children

NAEP, Grade 4, 2011

The stem-and-leaf plot below shows the number of seconds it took each student in a class of 18 to complete a word search.

Seconds to Complete Word Search

1	2 4 5 8 9 9
2	0 1 1 1 2 5 7 7 7 7
3	2 3

Key: 1|2 represents a time of 12 seconds.

How many students took more than 25 seconds to complete the word search?

A. 4
B. 5
C. 6
D. 7
E. 10

NAEP, Grade 8, 2013

10-3 Objectives

Students will be able to understand and explain

- Line graphs.

- Scatterplots for two variables.

- Relationship between a pair of variables using a scatterplot.

- Trend lines.

- Positive association, negative association, and no association.

- How to choose a data display.

10-3 Displaying Data: Part II

In the previous section, we examined some graphical depictions of data. In this section, we explore other graphical displays: line graphs, scatterplots, and trend lines.

Line Graphs

A graphical form used to present numerical data is a line graph (or a broken-line graph). A **line graph** typically shows the trend of a variable over time. Time is usually marked on the horizontal axis, with the variable being considered marked on the vertical axis. An example is seen in Figure 16, where Sanna's weight over 9 years is depicted. Observe that consecutive data points are connected by line segments.

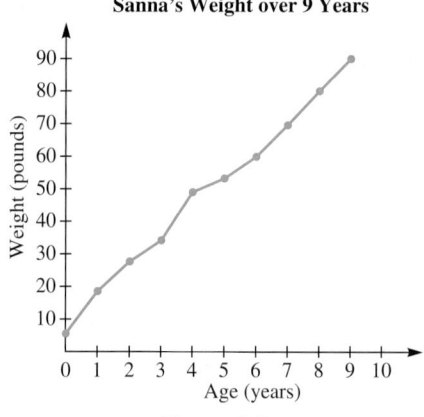

Sanna's Weight over 9 Years

Figure 16

Figure 16 is an example of a depiction of **continuous data**. Though the dots mark only Sanna's weight at given years, we know that she had a weight at every age along the horizontal axis. It is for this reason that it makes sense to connect the given data points with a set of line segments. Much data examined thus far have been **discrete data**. For example, in Figure 9 of the previous section, it would make no sense to connect the points at the tops of the bars representing the heights of five students. These are discrete data that essentially stand as individual pieces of information. They are graphed together to examine the set of information, but connecting them would have no mathematical or statistical meaning. It is sometimes done to "prettify" a graph.

 On the grade 6 partial student page shown on page 565, line graphs are drawn that depict the distances covered by a house boat and a ski boat. Observe that in these graphs, the line is continuous because the boats move over a period of time.

School Book Page

Algebra Connections

Comparing Line Graphs

Remember that a line graph often represents data collected over time. The double-line graph, below on the right, compares the rates of two boats. Use what you know about rates to describe the trends and compare their speeds.

Use the graph to answer **1** through **4**.

1. What is the unit rate of speed of the ski boat? At this rate, how far will it travel in 6 hours?

2. How much farther does the ski boat travel than the houseboat travels in 2 hours?

3. Let x = the number of times faster the ski boat travels than the houseboat travels. Solve 30 = 10x.

4. Based on the trends shown, is it reasonable to predict that the ski boat will always travel farther than the houseboat in the same amount of time?

Example: What is the speed, as a unit rate, of the houseboat in the double-line graph below? If the houseboat continues at this speed, how far will it travel in 6 hours?

The speed is the distance that the houseboat travels in 1 hour. It travels 10 miles per hour (mph).

$$\frac{10\ mi}{1\ hr} = \frac{x}{6\ hrs}$$
$$\frac{10}{1} = \frac{x}{6}$$
$$x = 60\ mi$$

The houseboat can travel 60 miles in 6 hours.

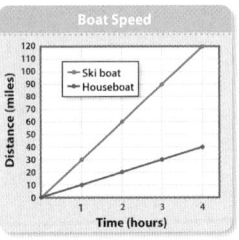

Use Are Women Catching Up? to analyze data using line graphs, scatterplots, and median fit lines.

Scatterplots

Sometimes a relationship between variables cannot be easily depicted by any type of line. Frequently, a **scatterplot** is used. Figure 17 shows a scatterplot depicting the relationship between the number of hours studied and quiz scores. The highest score is a 10 and the lowest is 1.

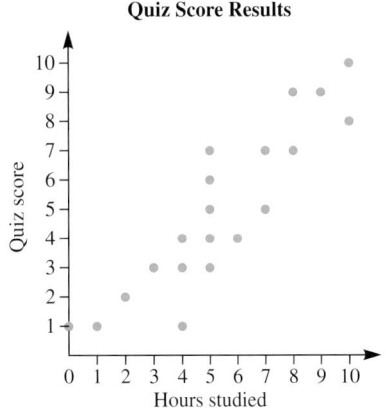

Figure 17

In a scatterplot like that in Figure 17, we frequently try to discern patterns. In this case it appears that the more hours studied, the higher the quiz score.

Before examining such a relationship (as in Figure 17), we consider a simpler discrete set of data that second or third graders may recognize. Imagine an arithmetic sequence determined by skip counting by 2 to obtain 2, 4, 6, 8, 10, ... We know that 2 is the first term in the sequence, 4 is the second term, 6 is the third term, and we could continue. We summarize the data in Table 9.

Table 9	Arithmetic Sequence of Even Counting Numbers		
Number of the Term	Term	Number of the Term	Term
1	2	6	12
2	4	7	14
3	6	8	16
4	8	9	18
5	10	10	20

In earlier chapters, we described the value of the term using two different methods: a recursive method, and a closed-form method. In the recursive method, we recognized the following:

First term is 2.

Each next term is 2 more than the previous term.

In the closed-form method, we observed the constant difference of 2 in the terms and learned that this was an arithmetic sequence such that the value of the term was twice the number of the term. We wrote this as $f(n) = 2n$, where n was the number of the term and $f(n)$ is the value of the term.

Now consider what might happen if we plotted the same data with a scatterplot, as in Figure 18.

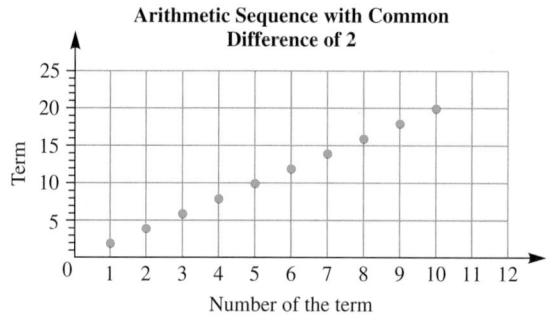

Figure 18

The graph of Figure 18 is depicted as a set of discrete data in a scatterplot. But this scatterplot is unlike the one of Figure 17. All of the points in Figure 18 appear to lie along a line. If we draw the line, as in Figure 19, then that line is the line of best fit for the data.

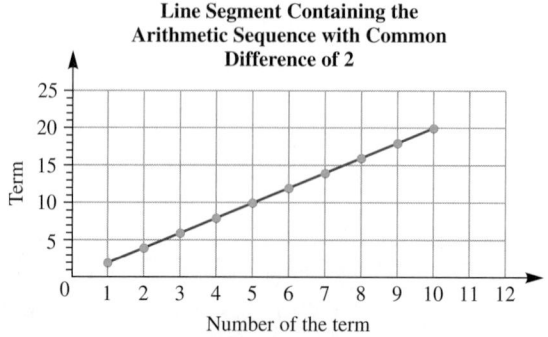

Figure 19

A point in Figure 19 depicting the arithmetic sequence lies along this line if the term is twice the term number. The second, or "y-coordinate," is twice the first, or "x-coordinate." (Note that this description makes sense only if the vertical axis is the "y-axis" and the horizontal axis is the "x-axis.") Generalizing to continuous data, we have $y = 2x$ for all real numbers x. With this representation, we moved from the discrete case, and lost the sequence notation, but for any value of x given, we could predict the corresponding value of y. The line itself is a **trend line**, *a line that closely fits the data and can be used to describe it*. In this case, all the given data fall on this line.

> **NOW TRY THIS 5**

NTT 5: Answer can be found in Answers at the back of the book.

Consider a sequence of data points formed using the following recursive formula:

The first term is $^-10$ and thereafter each term is 4 more than the previous term.

a. Construct a table of values for this recursive relation.
b. Draw a scatterplot for the relation with the trend line.
c. Identify by formula the "best" trend line for the data.

In cases where not all the data are given we try to find a trend line that can be used to approximate the data.

 In the grade 8 *Common Core Standards*, we find that students should:

Know that straight lines are widely used to model relationships between two quantitative variables. For scatter plots that suggest a linear association, informally fit a straight line, and informally assess the model fit by judging the closeness of the data points to the line. (p. 56)

In the scatterplot of Figure 20(a) for the quiz scores, is it possible to identify a "good" trend line for this data? And if so, how might it be done? Clearly, there is no single line that contains all of the data points in the graph of Figure 20(a). However, we could consider moving a line across the data to define a line that follows the general pattern of the data. If we used this technique with Figure 20(a), we might produce the trend line as seen in Figure 20(b). Could we find the equation of this line?

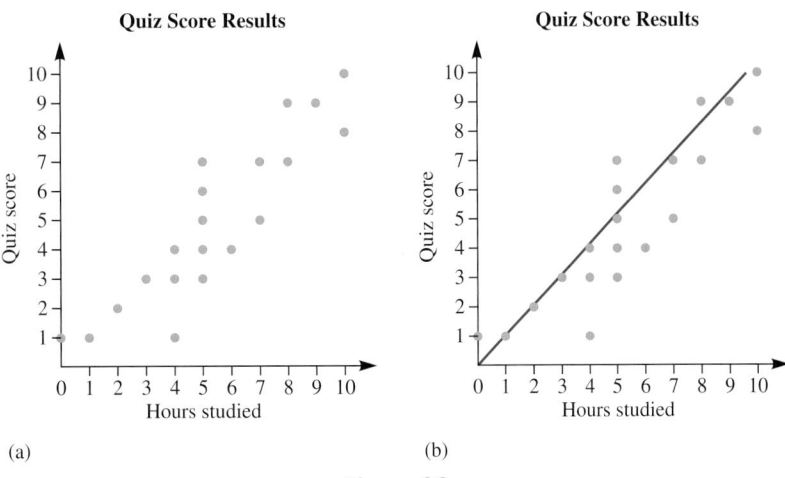

Figure 20

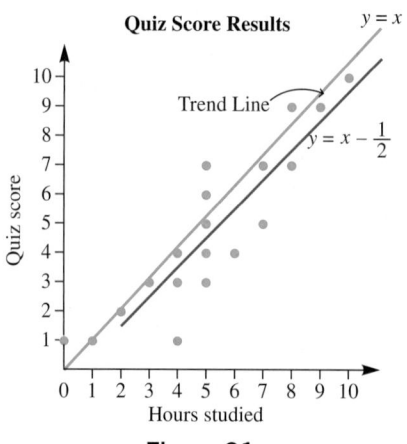

Figure 21

Attempting to find an equation of the line in Figure 20(b), we realize that the line approximately goes through points with coordinates $(2, 2)$ and $(7, 7)$. The slope of the line through the points is $\frac{7 - 2}{7 - 2}$ or 1. The line also goes through $(0, 0)$ so the y-intercept is 0 and the line has equation $y = 1 \cdot x + 0$ or $y = x$.

If we plot the equation $y = x$ on the graph, we see that it is a bit higher than the trend line, shown in Figure 21. We could "lower" the line in Figure 20(b) by "moving" it down $\frac{1}{2}$ unit, yielding the equation $y = x - \frac{1}{2}$, as seen in Figure 21.

A trend line can be used to make predictions. If a trend line slopes up from left to right, as in Figure 21, then there is a **positive association** between the number of hours studied and the quiz score. From the trend line in Figure 21, we would predict that students who studied 7 hours might score about $6\frac{1}{2}$. The student page shown below describes a method for drawing a trend line when two sets of data seem to have a linear association.

School Book Page   Modeling Data with Lines

EXAMPLE   Drawing Trend Lines

Tree Height and Circumference

Height (ft)	Circumference (in.)
19	10
32	63
57	72
43	111
75	150
97	185
110	214

1 The table at the left shows the circumference and height of a variety of trees. Use a scatter plot to predict the height of a tree that has a circumference of 175 in.

Step 1 Plot each data pair.

Step 2 The plotted points go up from left to right. This scatter plot shows a positive, linear association.

Step 3 Draw a line with positive slope. Make sure there are about as many points above the line as there are below it.

Step 4 Find 175 on the horizontal axis. Move up to the trend line. Then move left to the vertical axis.

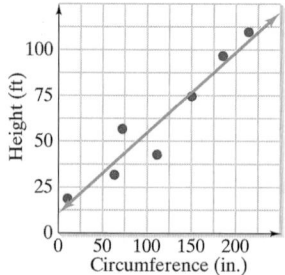

In Figure 21, note that the student who studied 4 hours and received a score of 1 did no better than the student who did not study. Although there is a possible association between studying and scoring well on a quiz, we cannot deduce cause and effect based on scatterplots and trend lines.

If the trend line slopes downward to the right, we can also make predictions; there is *a negative association*. If the points do not approximately fall about any line, there is *no association*. Scatterplots also show clusters of points and outliers. Examples of various associations are given in Figure 22.

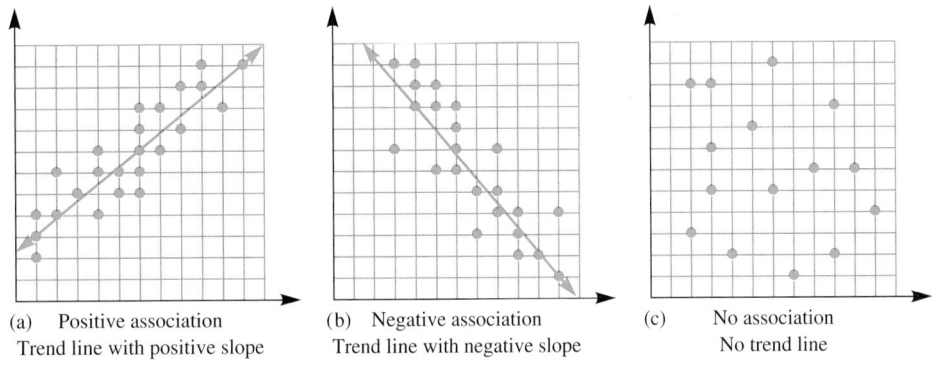

| (a) Positive association | (b) Negative association | (c) No association |
| Trend line with positive slope | Trend line with negative slope | No trend line |

Figure 22

Multiple-Line Graphs

Frequently, **multiple-line graphs** are used to demonstrate different sets of data where comparisons may be made. For example, Figure 23 shows the population growth in Florida, Georgia, Alabama, N. Carolina, and S. Carolina between 1900 and 2010. Notice the difference in population growth for Florida over this time period in comparison to the other states.

			State		
Year	**Florida**	**Alabama**	**Georgia**	**N. Carolina**	**S. Carolina**
1900	529	1829	2216	1894	1340
1910	753	2138	2609	2206	1515
1920	968	2348	2896	2559	1684
1930	1468	2646	2909	3170	1739
1940	1897	2833	3124	3572	1900
1950	2771	3062	3445	4062	2117
1960	4952	3267	3943	4556	2383
1970	6789	3444	4590	5082	2591
1980	9746	3894	5463	5882	3122
1990	12938	4040	6478	6632	3486
2000	15982	4447	8186	8049	4012
2010	18801	4780	9688	9535	4625

Population (thousands)

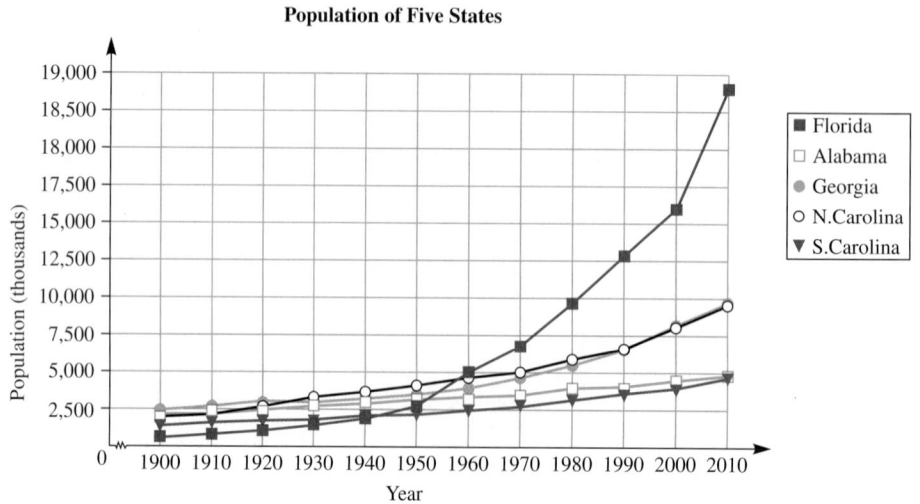

Figure 23

▶ **NOW TRY THIS 6**

NTT 6: Answers can be
found in Answers at the
back of the book.

Consider the line graphs in Figure 24.

a. Write an equation for the "bicycling" line.
b. Estimate how many calories a 150-pound person bicycling for 2 hours burns.
c. Write an equation for the "sitting" line.
d. Estimate how many calories a 150-pound person sitting for 4 hours burns.
e. Estimate how many calories a 150-pound person bicycling for 4 hours and then sitting for 3 hours burns.
f. Describe a line graph for burning calories if a 150-pound person sits for an hour and then bikes for 3 hours.

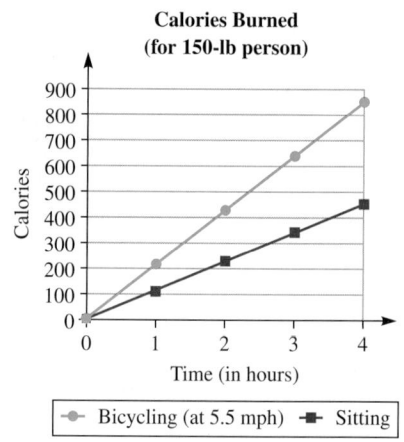

Figure 24

Choosing a Data Display

Each type of graph is suitable for presenting certain kinds of data. In this chapter, we explored pictographs, dot plots (line plots), stem and leaf plots, histograms, bar graphs, line graphs, scatterplots, and circle graphs (pie charts). Some types of display and uses follow:

Bar graph—Used to compare numbers of data items in grouped categories.

Histogram—Used to compare numbers of data items typically grouped in numerical intervals; order matters in the data depicted.

Stem and leaf plot—Used to show each value in a data set and to group values into intervals.

Scatterplot—Used to show the relationship between two variables.

Line graph—Used to show how data values change over time; normally used for continuous data.

Circle graph—Used to show the division of a whole into parts.

▶ NOW TRY THIS 7

a. Which graph, Figure 25(a) or (b), displays the data more effectively? Why?

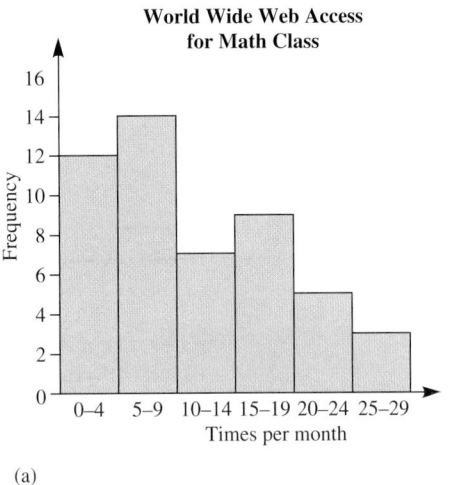

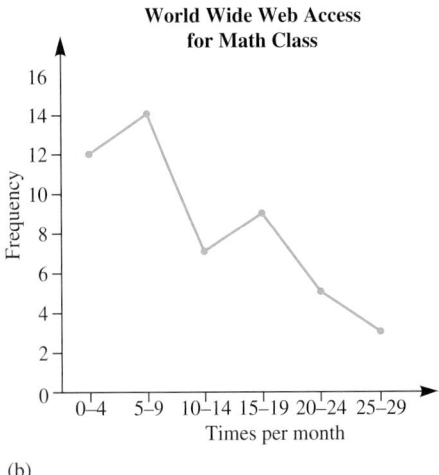

(a)   (b)

Figure 25

Note: Figure 25(b) was formed by connecting the midpoints of the tops of the bars in Figure 25(a).

b. Explain whether connecting the dots with line segments as in Figure 25(b) is meaningful.

c. To show each of the following, which graph is the best choice: line graph, bar graph, or circle graph? Why?

    i. The percentage of a college student's budget devoted to housing, clothing, food, tuition and books, taxes

    ii. Showing the change in the cost of living over the past 12 months

Assessment 10-3A

1. The following graph shows how the value of a car depreciates each year. This graph allows us to find the trade-in value of a car for each of 5 years. The percents given in the graph are based on the selling price of the new car.

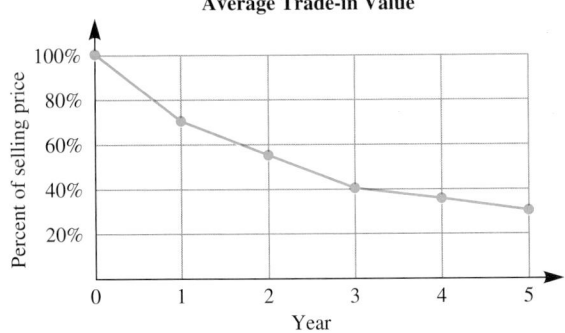

a. What is the approximate trade-in value of a $12,000 car after 1 yr? *Approximately $8400*

b. How much has a $20,000 car depreciated after 5 yr? *

c. What is the approximate trade-in value of a $20,000 car after 4 yr? *Approximately $7000*

d. Dani wants to trade in her car before it loses half its value. When should she do this? *After two years*

2. The graph below shows the population of the United States in the years 1790–1830.

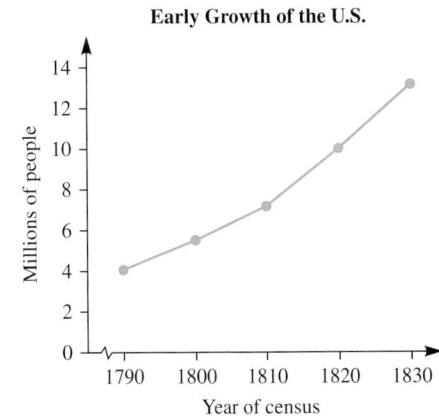

a. Estimate what year the population was about 6,000,000. *

b. Estimate the population in 1830. *About 13,000,000*

c. Did the U.S. population increase more between 1790 and 1800 or between 1810 and 1820? How can you tell? *

3. The graph below shows the number of snow shovels sold in winter months at a store in 2010 and 2015.
   a. During which month did the store sell the most snow shovels in 2015?   January
   b. During which month did the store sell the fewest snow shovels in 2010?   March
   c. Based on snow shovel sales, which year, 2010 or 2015, seems to have had the most snow in the store's locale?   2015

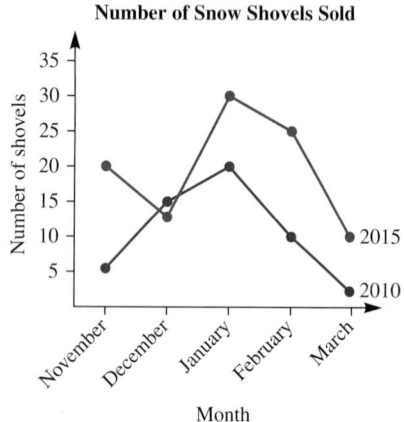

Number of Snow Shovels Sold

4. Which of the following statements are true for the time periods listed?

Average Retail Price (in dollars) of Regular Unleaded Gasoline in Last Half of 2013.		
Month	**CA**	**NY**
June	4.003	3.704
July	4.008	3.799
August	3.871	3.842
Sept	3.942	3.785
Oct	3.781	3.594
Nov	3.594	3.530
Dec	3.594	3.637

www.eia.gov (US Energy Information Administration)

   a. During which month was the price of gasoline in California the highest?   July
   b. Which statement was true for the period of time shown above?   (ii)
      (i) The price of gasoline is always higher in California.
      (ii) The price of gasoline in both states decreases during the Fall.
      (iii) In September, the price of gasoline is higher in New York.
      (iv) The price of gasoline in the summer months in New York doesn't get above $3.50 per gallon.

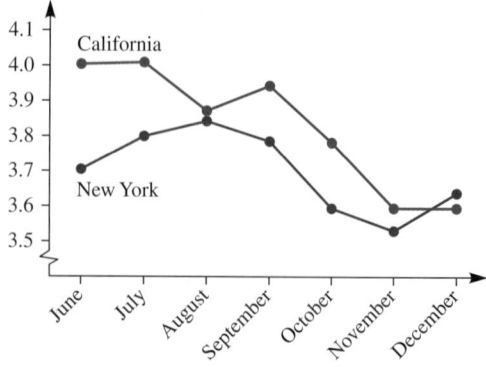

Average Retail Price (in dollars) of Gasoline in Last Half of 2013

5. Coach Lewis kept track of the basketball team's jumping records for a 10-year period, as shown below. Draw a line graph for the data.   *

Year	2003	2004	2005	2006	2007	2008
Record (nearest in.)	65	67	67	68	70	74

Year	2009	2010	2011	2012
Record (nearest in.)	77	78	80	81

6. Refer to the following scatterplot regarding movie attendance in a certain city. Each dot represents one person and this person's movie habits.

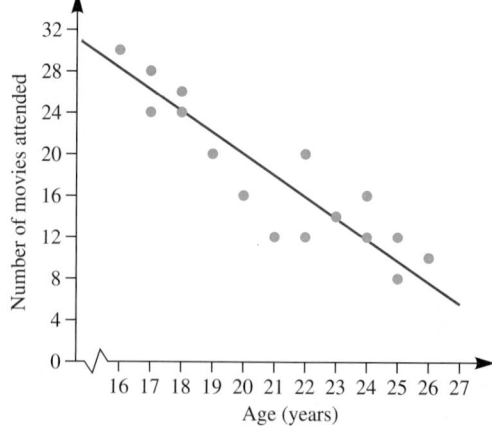

Yearly Movie Attendance

   a. What type of association exists for these data?   Negative
   b. About how many movies does an average 25-year-old attend?   Approximately 10
   c. From the data in the scatterplot, conjecture how old you think a person is who attends 16 movies a year.   *

7. Consider an arithmetic sequence with first term of 3 and difference 5.
   a. Plot the sequence as a scatterplot.   *
   b. Sketch a trend line.   *
   c. Find an equation for the trend line you sketched in part (b).   Answers vary. $y = 5(x - 1) + 3 = 5x - 2$

8. For each of the scatterplots below, answer the following.
   i. What type of association, if any, can you identify? *
   ii. Is there an identifiable trend line? If so, sketch it. *
   a.

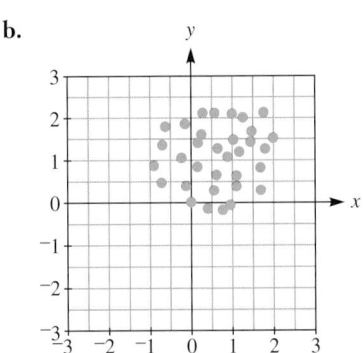

   b.   No association

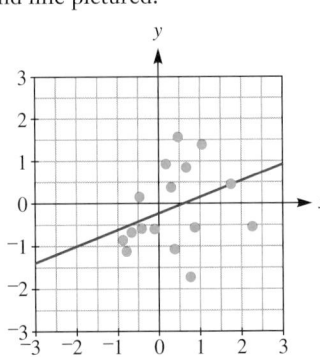

9. In the following scatterplots, estimate an equation of the trend line pictured.
   a. $y = \frac{3}{8}x - \frac{3}{10}$

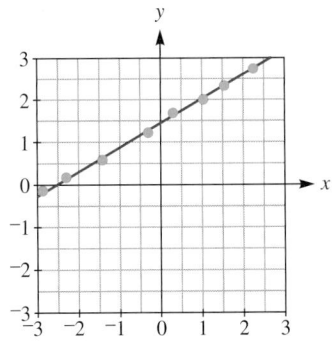

   b. $y = \frac{1}{2}x + \frac{3}{2}$

c.

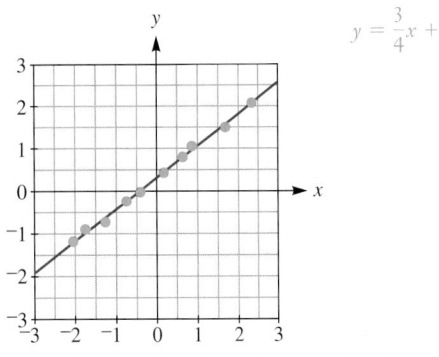

$y = \frac{3}{4}x + \frac{1}{2}$

10. The following data show the cost of various diamonds of weights (measured in carats). *

The Cost of Diamonds Compared to Their Weight			
Carats	Cost($)	Carats	Cost($)
0.17	355	0.32	919
0.16	328	0.15	298
0.17	350	0.16	339
0.18	325	0.16	338
0.25	642	0.23	595
0.16	342	0.2	498
0.15	322	0.23	595
0.19	485	0.29	860
0.21	483	0.12	223
0.15	323	0.26	663
0.18	462	0.25	750
0.28	823	0.27	720
0.16	336	0.18	468
0.17	353	0.23	553
0.18	438	0.17	345
0.17	318	0.33	945
0.18	419	0.25	655
0.17	346	0.35	1086
0.15	315	0.18	443
0.17	350	0.25	678
0.32	918	0.25	675

Source: Singfat Chu. "Diamond Ring Pricing Using Linear Regression." Journal of Statistics Education *4 (1996).*

Draw a scatterplot of the data and determine if there is a trend line that could be used to predict the cost of 0.5 carat of a diamond. *

11. If a trend line has equation $y = 3.2x - 0.11$, what y-value would you expect to obtain when x has the following values?
    a. 1   3.09   b. 0   ⁻0.11
    c. 10 31.89   d. 20.3 64.85

12. If a trend line has equation $y = 15 - 0.8x$, what could you say about the data?   There seems to be a negative linear association.

Assessment 10-3B

1. The graph below shows the average age at which women in the United States married for the first time from 1890 to 2010.

Women's Average Age of First Marriage

Source: U.S. Census Bureau, 2010.

a. What was the approximate average age for a woman's first marriage in
   i. 1890. 22
   ii. 1950. 20.4
   iii. 2010. 25.4
b. During what 10-year period was there the greatest decrease in the average age of first marriage? 1940–1950
c. During what 10-year period was there the greatest increase in the average age of first marriage? 1980–1990

2. Answer the following questions based on the line graph below.

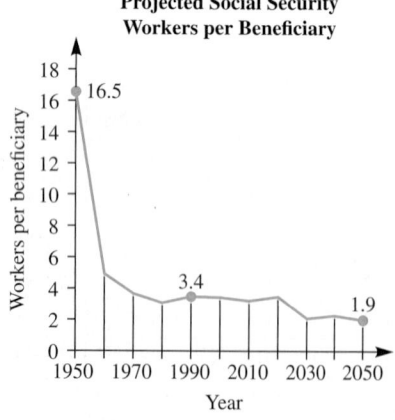

Projected Social Security Workers per Beneficiary

Source: Social Security Administration

a. What does the line graph tell us about Social Security after 2050? *
b. About how many workers were there per beneficiary in 1960? About 5
c. About how many workers will there be per beneficiary in 2030? About 2

3. The graph below shows line graphs for participation in National Collegiate Athletic Association (NCAA) sports for both men and women.

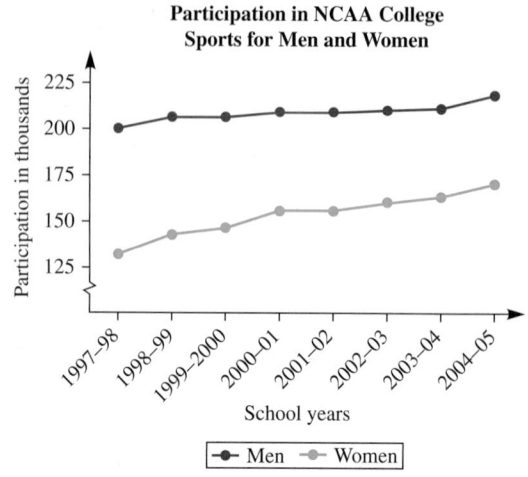

Participation in NCAA College Sports for Men and Women

a. About how many more men than women participated in NCAA sports in 2004–05? About 50,000
b. Between what years did the number of participants not change for both men's and women's sports? *
c. What seems to be the trend for both men and women's participation in NCAA sports? *

4. The graph depicts the spelling results from Mr. DiMaso's class.

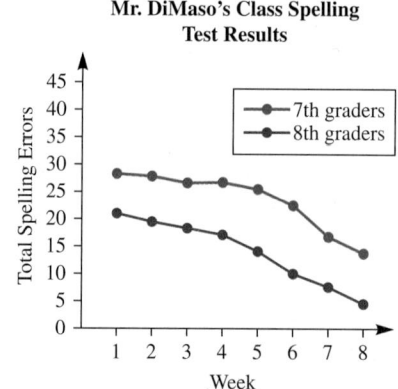

Mr. DiMaso's Class Spelling Test Results

a. Describe any trends you observe. *
b. What conclusions might you draw about Mr. DiMaso's teaching program? It appears to be working.
c. Make a prediction as to the total number of spelling errors the 7th and 8th grade classes might make in week 9. *

5. Use the following data to draw a line graph. Then use your graph to tell the story of a heated container of ice. *

Time (minutes)	Temperature in (°F)
0	14
1	32
2	32
3	86
4	212
5	212

(continued)

Time (minutes)	Temperature in (°F)
6	212
7	212
8	212
9	284
10	302

6. Refer to the following scatterplot regarding fuel efficiency.

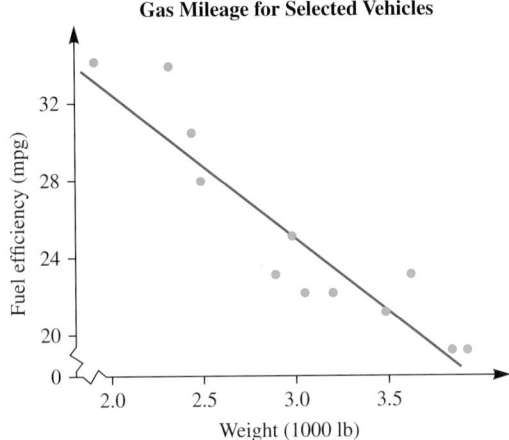

Gas Mileage for Selected Vehicles

a. What type of association exists for these data? *
b. About how many miles per gallon would you expect for a 2000-pound vehicle? About 32 mpg

7. Consider an arithmetic sequence with first term 20 and difference ⁻3
  a. Plot this sequence as a scatterplot. *
  b. Sketch a trend line. *
  c. Find an equation for the trend line you sketched in part (b). *

8. Use the scatterplots shown to answer the following.
  i. What type of association, if any, can you identify? *
  ii. Sketch a trend line for the data if one exists. *

a.

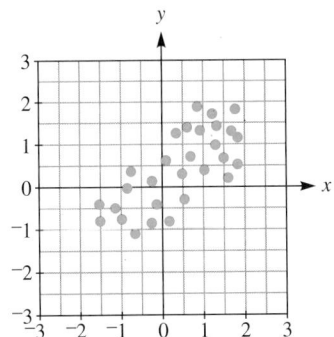

b.

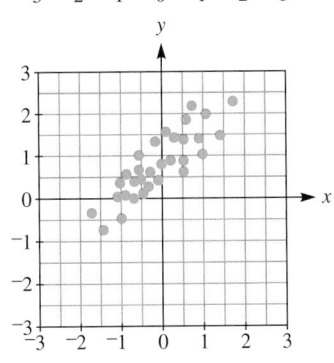

9. In the following scatterplots, find an equation to estimate the trend line pictured:

a.

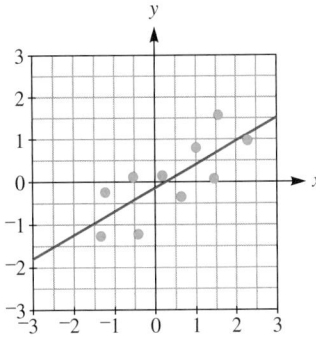

Answers vary.
$y = \frac{1}{2}x$

b.

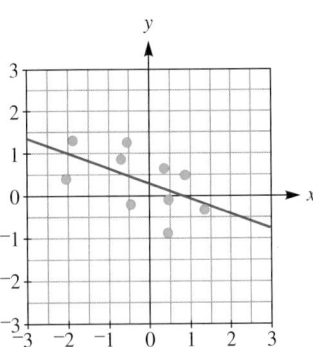

Answers vary.
$y = \frac{-2}{5}x + \frac{3}{5}$

10. The data show the number of flea eggs produced over a period of days.

Day	No. of Eggs	Day	No. of Eggs
1	436	15	550
2	495	16	487
3	575	17	585
4	444	18	549
5	754	19	475
6	915	20	435
7	945	21	523
8	655	22	390
9	782	23	425
10	704	24	415
11	590	25	450
12	411	26	395
13	547	27	405
14	584		

Source: Moore D., and McCabe G. (2005). Introduction to the Practice of Statistics, p. 27.

a. Draw a line graph of the given data. *
b. Predict how many eggs there might be on day 28. *

11. If a trend line has equation $y = ⁻3.2x + 0.11$, what y-value would you expect to obtain when x has the following values?
  a. 10 ⁻31.89
  b. 0 0.11
  c. 4.3 ⁻13.65
  d. 7.2 ⁻22.93

12. If a trend line has equation $y = 15 + 0.8x$, what type of association would you expect the data to have? *

13. If a trend line has equation $y = 0.0001x + 12$, what could you say about the data?   *

14. For each of the following pairs of variables, determine the association, if any, between them. (Assume that you have obtained information on 50 subjects in your study).

  a. The span of person's right hand and her/his left hand span.   Positive association

  b. Temperature in the summer and amount of ice cream sold   Positive association

  c. Incident of vaccination in a city and incidence of illness in that city.   Negative association

---

Mathematical Connections 10-3

Answers to Mathematical Connections can be found in the Answers section at the back of the book.

Reasoning

1. Explain the concept of *association* as it is understood in statistics so that a middle school student could understand.

Cooperative Learning

2. With your group, examine several sixth-, seventh-, and eighth-grade mathematics textbooks to learn more about the ways that association between a pair of variables and resulting scatterplots are presented. Summarize your findings.

3. The International Association of Athletics Federations (IAAF) has been the official record keeper for the mile run since 1913. Why is a line graph, as you have learned about it in this section, with *years* on the horizontal axis not an appropriate way to display this data? Find the 32 records and determine an appropriate way to present the data graphically. Present your graph to the class.

Open-Ended

4. With your group, examine several sixth-, seventh-, and eighth-grade mathematics textbooks to learn more about the ways how linear equations and trend lines are presented there. Summarize your findings.

5. Report on several variants of line graphs, for example, polygon plots, ogives, and time series. Provide an example for each type that you find. Compare and contrast them. For what kind of data is each line graph not an appropriate display?

Connecting Mathematics to the Classroom

6. Jacquie argued that scatterplots had little value because rarely does a single trend line fit the data. How do you respond?

7. Merle says that there is no reason to practice drawing graphs because spreadsheets can be used to draw any images desired. How do you respond?

Review Problems

8. The Smith family drew a circle graph of their budget that contained the following:

Taxes, 20%
Rent, 32%
Food, 20%
Utilities, 5%
Gas, 13%
Miscellaneous, 12%

What would you tell the family concerning the data?

9. Adjust the miscellaneous percentage in exercise 8 to 10% and draw a stacked bar graph of the entire data set.

10. The following are the number of home runs hit by Mark McGwire during the 1986–2001 seasons.

$3, 49, 32, 33, 39, 22, 42, 9, 9, 39, 52, 58, 70, 65, 32, 29$

  a. Draw an ordered stem and leaf plot for the data.

  b. Describe the distribution.

National Assessments

National Assessment of Educational Progress (NAEP) Question

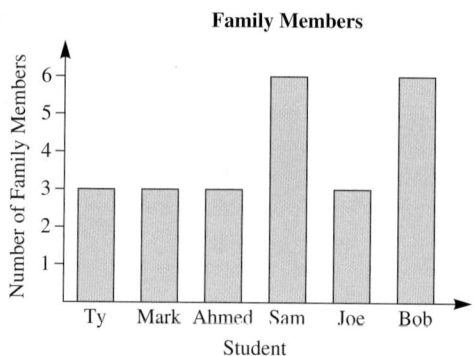

The graph above shows the number of family members for six students. Which graph below is the best summary of the data?

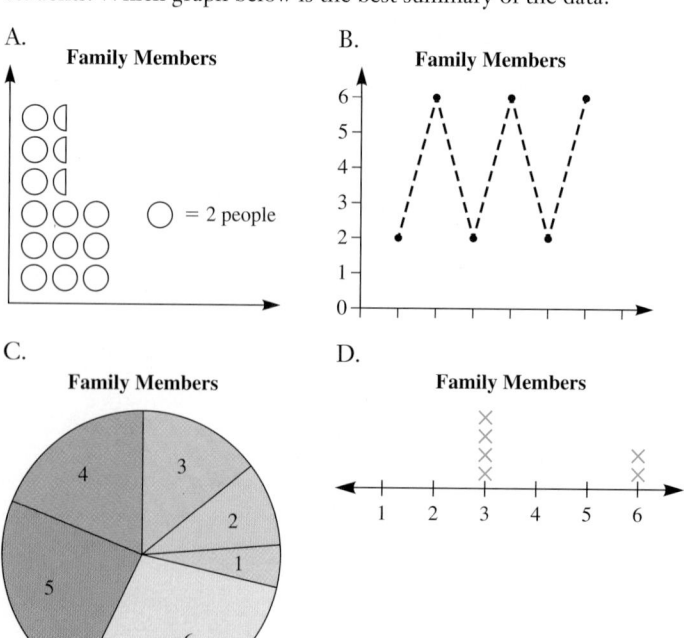

NAEP, Grade 4, 2013

10-4 Measures of Central Tendency and Variation

10-4 Objectives

Students will be able to understand and explain

- Central tendency and variation (spread).
- Computing the mean.
- Median and mode of a data set.
- Appropriate measures of central tendency.
- Measures of spread.
- Boxplots and comparing sets of data.
- Variance and standard deviation.
- Normal distribution.
- Percentiles, quantiles, and deciles.

 CCSS The grade 6 *Common Core Standards* suggest that all students should be able to:

Summarize numerical data sets in relation to their context, such as by: . . . Giving quantitative measures of center (median and/or mean) and variability (interquartile range and/or mean absolute deviation), as well as describing any overall pattern and any striking deviations from the overall pattern with reference to the context in which the data were gathered. (p. 45)

Two important aspects of data are *center* and *spread*. The *mean* and *median* are **measures of central tendency** that describe where data are centered. Each of these measures is a single number that describes the data. The *range, interquartile range, variance, mean absolute deviation,* and *standard deviation* introduced later in this section describe the spread of data and should be used with measures of central tendency.

A word that is often used in statistics is *average*. To explore averages, examine the following set of data for three teachers, each of whom claims that his or her class scored better *on the average* than the other two classes did:

Mr. Smith:	62, 94, 95, 98, 98
Mr. Jones:	62, 62, 98, 99, 100
Ms. Rivera:	40, 62, 85, 99, 99

All of these teacher's assertions are reasonable based on a different numbers to characterize the scores in the class. In the following, we examine how each teacher's claim can be justified.

 **Activity Manual**

Use *What's the Average?* to investigate means, medians, and modes.

Means

A commonly used number characterizing a set of data is the **arithmetic mean**, frequently called the **average**, or the **mean**. To find the mean of scores for each of the teachers given previously, we find the sum of the scores in each case and divide by 5, the number of scores.

$$\text{Mean (Smith):} \quad \frac{62 + 94 + 95 + 98 + 98}{5} = \frac{447}{5} = 89.4$$

$$\text{Mean (Jones):} \quad \frac{62 + 62 + 98 + 99 + 100}{5} = \frac{421}{5} = 84.2$$

$$\text{Mean (Rivera):} \quad \frac{40 + 62 + 85 + 99 + 99}{5} = \frac{385}{5} = 77$$

In terms of the mean, Mr. Smith's class scored better than the others. In general, we define the *arithmetic mean* as follows.

Definition of Arithmetic Mean

The **arithmetic mean** of the numbers $x_1, x_2, \ldots, x_n$, denoted $\bar{x}$ and read "x bar," is given by

$$\bar{x} = \frac{x_1 + x_2 + x_3 + \ldots + x_n}{n}.$$

Understanding the Mean as a Balance Point

A model for thinking about a mean is seen next. A student reports that the mean number of pets for six students in a group is 5. The distribution of these pets is unknown. All six students could have exactly five pets, as shown in the dot plot in Figure 26(a).

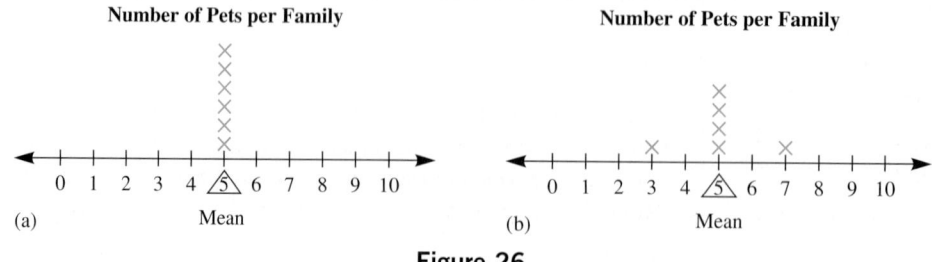

Figure 26

If we change the dot plot as shown in Figure 26(b), the mean is still 5. The new dot plot could be obtained by moving one value from Figure 26(a) 2 units to the right and then balancing this by moving one value 2 units to the left. The mean is a *balance point*.

Figure 27 shows the number of children for each family in a group. The mean of 5 is the balance point where the sum of the distances from the mean to the data points *above* the mean equals the sum of the distances from the mean to the data points *below* the mean. The sum of the distances above the mean is $3 + 5$, or 8. The sum of the distances below the mean is $1 + 2 + 2 + 3$, or 8. In this case, we see that the data are centered about the mean, but the mean is not in the data set.

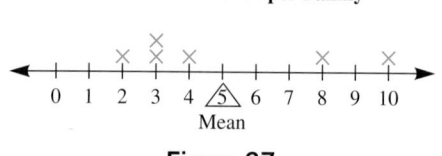

Figure 27

Knowing that the mean is a balance point as depicted in Figure 27 also shows the importance of not reporting the mean as a single number to summarize data. Using the data in Figure 27, it is possible to find a second data set consisting of six points and having the same mean but be spread very differently. See for example, the data, independent of context, given as Case 1 in Table 10. Case 2 of Table 10 has 5 subtracted from each of the data points to the left of the mean while 10 is added to each of the data points to the right of the mean. The means of each of the sets of data in the two cases are exactly the same but the data are differently spread. Later, we use a measure of spread the range along with the mean to describe the data.

Table 10		
	Case 1	Case 2
	2	⁻3
	3	⁻2
	3	⁻2
	4	⁻1
	8	18
	10	20
Mean	$(2 + 3 + 3 + 4 + 8 + 10)/6 = 5$	$(^-3 + {}^-2 + {}^-2 + {}^-1 + 18 + 20)/6 = 5$

Problem Solving The Missing Grades

Students of Dr. Van Horn were asked to keep track of their own grades. One day, Dr. Van Horn asked the students to report their grades. One student had lost the papers but claims to remember the grades on four of six assignments: 100, 82, 74, and 60. In addition, the student remembered that the mean of all six papers was 69, and the other two papers had identical grades. What were the grades on the other two homework papers?

Understanding the Problem The student had scores of 100, 82, 74, and 60 on four of six papers. The mean of all six papers was 69, and two identical scores were missing.

Devising a Plan To find the missing grades, we use the strategy of *writing an equation*. The mean is obtained by finding the sum of the scores and then dividing by the number of scores, which is 6. So if we let x stand for each of the two missing grades, we have

$$69 = \frac{100 + 82 + 74 + 60 + x + x}{6}.$$

To find the missing grades we solve for x.

Carrying Out the Plan We now solve the equation as follows.

$$69 = \frac{100 + 82 + 74 + 60 + x + x}{6}$$

$$69 = \frac{316 + 2x}{6}$$

$$49 = x$$

Since the solution to the equation is $x = 49$, each of the two missing scores was 49.

Looking Back The answer of 49 seems reasonable. We can check this by computing the mean of the scores 100, 82, 74, 60, 49, 49 and showing that it is 69.

▶ NOW TRY THIS 8

NTT 8: Answer can be found in Answers at the back of the book.

a. A litter of six puppies was born with a mean weight of 7 lb. List two possible data sets for the weights of the puppies.
b. Could the mean of a set of scores ever be equal to the greatest score? The least score? Explain your answers.
c. Using the data in Figure 27, move the data points until a single "balance point" (the mean) can be found or estimated. For example, move the value 10 two units left to 8 and counterbalance that by moving the value 2 two units right to 4. Continue until a single balance point is determined. What is the mean?

Medians

The value in the middle of an ordered set of numbers is the **median**. To find the median for the teachers' scores on page 577, we arrange each of their scores in increasing or decreasing order and pick the middle score.

Median (Smith): 62, 94, 95, 98, 98   median = 95
Median (Jones): 62, 62, 98, 99, 100   median = 98
Median (Rivera): 40, 62, 85, 99, 99   median = 85

In terms of the median, Mr. Jones's class scored better than the others.

With an odd number of scores, as in the present example, the median is the middle score. With an even number of scores, however, the median is defined as the mean of the middle two scores. Thus, to find the median, we add the middle two scores and divide by 2. For example, the median of the scores

$$64, 68, \boxed{70, 74,} 82, 90$$

is given by

$$\frac{70 + 74}{2}, \text{ or } 72.$$

In general, to find the median for a set of *n* numbers, we proceed as follows:

1. Arrange the numbers in order from least to greatest.
2. a. If *n* is odd, the median is the middle number.
   b. If *n* is even, the median is the mean of the two middle numbers.

Just as the mean needs a measure of spread to help describe a set of data, the median needs such a measure as well. For example, if we consider Jones's students' scores 62, 62, 98, 99, and 100, the median is 98. If the scores were 32, 32, 98, 99, and 100, the median is still 98 but the two sets of scores are very different. A median is often reported with the *interquartile range*, a measure of spread is discussed later in this section. The two together form a much better pair to describe the data than the median alone.

Modes

The **mode** of a set of data is sometimes reported as a measure of central tendency, but it is frequently misused. *The mode of a set of data is the value if there is one, that appears most frequently.* Examples of this follow. A mode is frequently reported with categorical data. In some distributions, no data item appears more than once. In other distributions, there may be more than one mode. Saying that there is no mode does not imply there are no measures of central tendency.

The set of scores 64, 79, 80, 82, 90 has no mode. Some would say that this set of data has five modes, but because no one score appears more than another, we prefer to say there is no mode. The set of scores 64, 75, 75, 82, 90, 90, 98 is **bimodal** (two modes) because both 75 and 90 are modes. It is possible for a set of data to have too many modes for this type of number to be useful in describing the data. For the three classes listed previously, if the mode were used as the criterion for an average, Ms. Rivera's class scored better than the others. This example is technically correct but the modes do not describe the data well.

Mode (Smith): 62, 94, 95, 98, 98   mode = 98

Mode (Jones): 62, 62, 98, 99, 100   mode = 62

Mode (Rivera): 40, 62, 85, 99, 99   mode = 99

Example 4

Find (a) the mean, (b) the median, and (c) the mode for the data shown:

$$60, \quad 60, \quad 70, \quad 95, \quad 95, \quad 100.$$

Solution

a. $\bar{x} = \dfrac{60 + 60 + 70 + 95 + 95 + 100}{6} = \dfrac{480}{6} = 80$

b. The median is $\dfrac{70 + 95}{2} = 82.5$.

c. The set of data is bimodal and has both 60 and 95 as modes.

▶ **NOW TRY THIS 9**

Describe a situation in which not all the data points are the same, but the mean, median, and mode are still the same.

▶ **NOW TRY THIS 10**

a. Suppose the average number of children per family for the employees of the university in a certain city is 2.58. Could this be a mean? Median? Mode? Explain why.
b. Answer the questions in (a) if the average number of children was reported to be 2.5.

Choosing the Most Appropriate Measure of Central Tendency

Although the *mean* is commonly used to describe a set of data, it may not always be the most appropriate choice.

Example 5

Suppose a company employs 20 people. The president of the company earns $200,000, the vice president earns $75,000, and 18 part-time employees earn $10,000 each. Is the mean the best number to choose to represent the "average" salary for the company?

Solution   The mean salary for this company is

$$\frac{\$200{,}000 + \$75{,}000 + 18(\$10{,}000)}{20} = \frac{\$455{,}000}{20} = \$22{,}750.$$

In this case, the mean salary of $22,750 is not representative. Either the median or mode, both of which are $10,000, would describe the typical salary better.

In Example 5, notice that *the mean is affected by extreme values*. In most cases, the *median* is not affected by extreme values. The median, however, can also be misleading, as shown in the following example.

Example 6

Suppose nine students make the following scores on a test:

$$30, 35, 40, 40, 92, 92, 93, 98, 99$$

Is the median the appropriate "average" to represent the set of scores?

Solution   The median score is 92, yet 92 is certainly not a typical score. The mean of approximately 69 might be more appropriate than the median. However, with the spread of the scores, neither is very appropriate for this distribution. A more appropriate description is that the data is bimodal, having 40 and 92 as modes.

As mentioned earlier, the *mode*, too, can be misleading in describing a set of data with very few items that occur frequently, as shown in the following example.

Example 7

Is the mode an appropriate "average" for the following test scores?

$$40, 42, 50, 62, 63, 65, 98, 98$$

Solution   The mode of the set of scores is 98 because this score occurs most frequently. The score of 98 is not representative of the set of data because of the large spread of scores and the much lower mean (and median).

The choice of which number to use to represent a particular set of data is not always easy. In the example involving the three teachers, each teacher chose the number that best suited his or her claim. The measure of central tendency should always be specified along with a measure of spread.

▶ NOW TRY THIS 11

NTT 11: Answers can be found in Answers at the back of the book.

Mr. Ramirez and Ms. Jonsey gave tests to their classes with the results seen in Table 11.

Table 11

	Overall Mean	Mean for Females	Mean for Males	Percent Females
Ramirez	218	230	205	
Jonsey	221	224		88

What are the missing entries? For an overall mean, Ms. Jonsey's class is higher, but for females, the mean is higher in Mr. Ramirez's class. Is it possible that the mean for males is higher in Mr. Ramirez's class as well?

Measures of Spread

CCSS The grade 6 *Common Core Standards* suggests that all students:

Recognize that a measure of center for a numerical data set summarizes all of its values with a single number, while a measure of variation describes how its values vary with a single number. (p. 45)

The mean and median are measures of center or central tendency that provide limited information about a data set. For example, if you sit in a sauna for 30 minutes and then in a refrigerated room for 30 minutes, an average temperature of your surroundings for that hour might sound comfortable. To tell how much the data are scattered, we develop measures of *spread* or *dispersion*. The easiest measure of spread is the **range**, the difference between the greatest and the least values in a data set. For example, the range in the set of data 1, 3, 7, 8, 10 is $10 - 1 = 9$. However, just because the ranges of two sets of data are the same, the data do not have to have the same dispersion. For example, the data set 1, 10, 10, 10, 10 also has a range of 9 and is spread quite differently from the first collection of data. For this reason we need other measures of spread besides the range.

Another measure of spread is the **interquartile range (IQR)**. Consider the following set of test scores:

$$20 \quad 25 \quad 40 \quad 50 \quad 50 \quad 60 \quad 70 \quad 75 \quad 80 \quad 80 \quad 90 \quad 100 \quad 100$$

The range for this set of scores is $100 - 20 = 80$. The median score for this set of data is 70. We mark this location with a vertical bar between the 7 and the 0 and circle the data point for emphasis, as shown.

$$20 \quad 25 \quad 40 \quad 50 \quad 50 \quad 60 \quad \boxed{7 \mid 0} \quad 75 \quad 80 \quad 80 \quad 90 \quad 100 \quad 100$$

Next, we consider only the data values to the left of the **vertical bar** and draw another vertical bar where the median of those values is located:

$$20 \quad 25 \quad 40 \mid 50 \quad 50 \quad 60$$

The score of $(40 + 50)/2 = 45$ is the median of the lower half of the scores and is the **lower quartile**. The lower quartile, or the **first quartile**, is denoted Q_1. Approximately one quarter, or 25%, of the scores lie at or below Q_1. Similarly, we can find the upper, or third, quartile (Q_3), which is $(80 + 90)/2$, or 85. The **upper quartile** (Q_3) is the median of the upper half of all scores. Approximately three-quarters, or 75%, of the scores lie at or below Q_3. The median is the **second quartile** or Q_2. Thus we have divided the scores into five groups, four of three scores each and fifth with the single median score.

$$
\begin{array}{ccc}
& 45 & & & 85 \\
20 \quad 25 \quad 40 \mid 50 & 50 \quad 60 & \boxed{7 \mid 0} & 75 \quad 80 \quad 80 \mid 90 & 100 \quad 100
\end{array}
$$

Lower extreme — Lower quartile, Q_1 — Median, Q_2 — Upper quartile, Q_3 — Upper extreme

The interquartile range (IQR) is the difference between the upper quartile and the lower quartile. In this case, IQR $= 85 - 45 = 40$. The IQR is a useful measure of spread because it is less influenced by extreme values.

The interquartile range is the measure of spread most often reported with the median. This is done because the median marks the center of the data. However, as we saw earlier, the same median could be reported with two sets of data that have very different spreads. With the interquartile range reported along with the median, not only do we know the middle, we know how spread out the middle 50% of the data are. If they have a wide spread, then we are aware of it and can assess and use the data accordingly. For example, in the data set just presented, the median of 70 should be reported with the interquartile range of 40.

▶ **NOW TRY THIS 12**

Create a set of data that ranges from 0 to 100 has median 70 and an interquartile range 50. One possible set is 0, 0, 40, 40, 40, 70, 70, 80, 90, 90, 100.

Activity Manual

Use *Finger-Snapping Time* to investigate box-and-whisker plots.

Box Plots

A **box plot** (or a **box-and-whisker plot**) is a way to display data visually and draw informal conclusions. Box plots show only certain data; they are visual representations of the *five-number summary* of the data. The five numbers are the median, the upper and lower quartiles (the interquartile range information), and the least and greatest values in the distribution. The center, the spread, and the overall range are immediately evident by looking at the plot.

To construct a box plot, we use the five-number summary. To construct the box, we draw bars at the upper and lower quartiles. We draw segments from each end of the box to the extreme values to form the whiskers. The box plot can be either vertical or horizontal. A vertical version of the box plot for the given data is shown in Figure 28.

The box plot gives a fairly clear picture of the spread of the data examined on p. 583. We have found that the median is 70, the maximum value is 100, the minimum value is 20, and the upper and lower quartiles are 45 and 85. This information is recorded in a box plot in Figure 28.

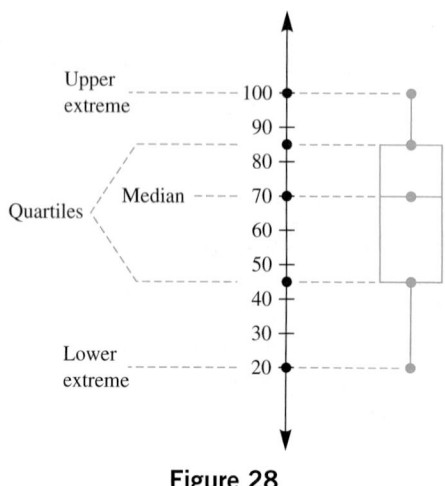

Figure 28

The partial student page shown below outlines the steps for constructing a box-and-whisker plot.

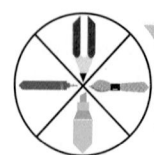

School Book Page   Box-and-Whisker Plots

EXAMPLE   Constructing a Box-and-Whisker Plot

1 A girls' basketball team had the following scores: 7, 10, 16, 18, 20, 22, 22, 25, 30, 37, 43. Construct a box-and-whisker plot to represent the data.

There are 11 observations in the data set. List the data in order to identify the five key values. The unit of measurement for this data set is points per game.

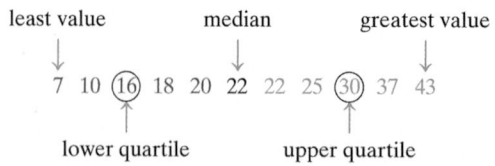

Graph the five key values above a number line. Label the number line with the unit of measurement. Draw a box from the lower to the upper quartile. Draw a vertical line inside at the median. Connect the least and greatest values to the box for the "whiskers."

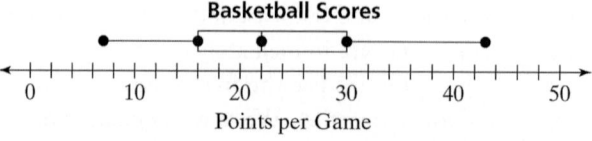

Example 8

What are the minimum and maximum values, the median, and the lower and upper quartiles of the data set whose box plot is shown in Figure 29?

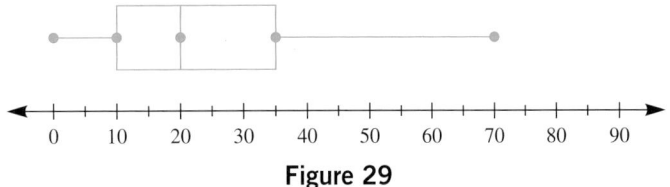

Figure 29

Solution   The minimum value is 0, the maximum value is 70, the median is 20, the lower quartile is 10, and the upper quartile is 35.

Outliers

An *outlier* is a value widely separated from the rest of a group of data. For example, in a set of scores such as

91   92   92   93   93   93   94

all data are grouped close together and no values are widely separated. However, in a set of scores such as

21   92   92   93   93   93   95   150

both 21 and 150 are widely separated from the rest of the data. These values are potential outliers. The upper and lower extreme values are not necessarily outliers. For data such as

75   90   91   92   92   93   93

it is not easy to decide, so we develop a convention for determining outliers. *An* **outlier** *is any value that is more than* 1.5 *times the interquartile range above the upper quartile or below the lower quartile.* Statisticians sometimes use values different from 1.5 to determine outliers.

It is common practice to indicate outliers in box plots with asterisks. Whiskers are then drawn to the extreme points that are not *outliers.* To investigate how this works, consider Example 9.

Example 9

Draw a box plot of the data in Table 12 and identify possible outliers.

Table 12		
Final Medal Standings for Top 20 Countries—2012 Summer Olympics		
United States	104	
China	88	
Russia	82	
Great Britain	65	
Germany	44	$Q_3 = 42.5$
Japan	38	
Australia	35	
France	34	
South Korea	28	
Italy	28	Median $(Q_2) = 24$
Netherlands	20	

(continued)

Final Medal Standings for Top 20 Countries—2012 Summer Olympics		
Ukraine	20	
Canada	18	
Hungary	18	
Spain	17	$Q_1 = 17$
Brazil	17	
Cuba	15	
Kazakhstan	13	
New Zealand	13	
Jamaica	12	

Solution   The extreme scores are 12 and 104, the median is 24, $Q_1 = 17$, and $Q_3 = 42.5$. The IQR is $42.5 - 17 = 25.5$. Outliers are scores that are greater than $42.5 + 1.5 \cdot 25.5 = 80.75$, or less than $17 - 1.5 \cdot 25.5 = {}^-21.25$. Therefore in this data 82, 88, and 104 are the only outliers. A box plot is given in Figure 30. The whisker stops at the extreme point on the lower end and at 65 on the upper end. Outliers are indicated with asterisks.

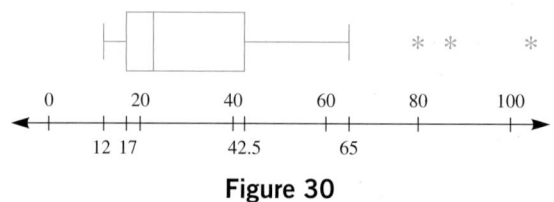

Figure 30

Comparing Sets of Data

Box plots are used primarily for large data sets or for comparing several distributions. The stem and leaf plot is usually a much clearer display for a single distribution if the data set is not to large. Parallel box plots drawn using the same number line provide the easiest comparison of medians, extreme scores, and the quartiles for the sets of data. As an example, we construct parallel box plots comparing the data in Table 13.

Table 13   **Gas Mileage by Car Size for 2014**

Fuel Economy of 2014 Compact Cars	Fuel Economy of 2014 Midsize Cars	Fuel Economy of 2014 Standard SUV 2WD
25	19	16
19	29	16
30	24	12
23	29	16
32	30	15
32	32	19
24	20	12
30	25	17
26	22	12
23	19	15
25	23	16

(continued)

Fuel Economy of 2014 Compact Cars	Fuel Economy of 2014 Midsize Cars	Fuel Economy of 2014 Standard SUV 2WD
26	24	23
26	31	15
27	40	11
23	14	17
33	31	25
26	13	12
22	20	16
33	11	19

Source: http://www.fueleconomy.gov/feg/byclass/2014ClassList.shtml

Before constructing parallel box plots, we find the five important values for each group of data. These values are given in Table 14.

Table 14

Value	Compact	Midsize	SUV
Maximum	33	40	25
Q_3	30	30	17
Median	26	24	16
Q_1	23	19	12
Minimum	19	11	11

In this example, the IQR for compact is 7, for midsize is 11, and for SUV is 5.

Next we draw the horizontal scale and construct the box plots for the compact, midsize, and SUV data in Table 14, as shown in Figure 31. Grid lines are used to emphasize the value for the important dots.

2014 Gas Mileage by Car Size

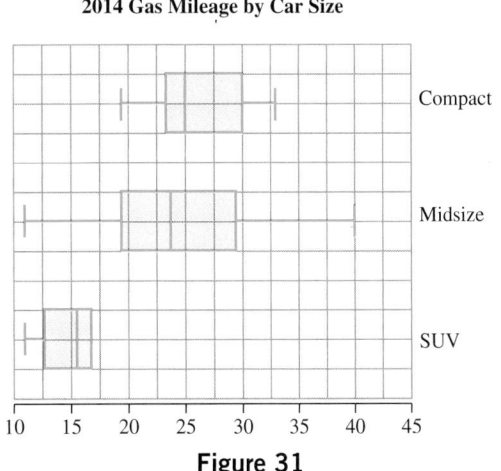

Figure 31

From the box plots we see that the median gas mileage for compacts is higher than that for midsize or SUV cars. The data for SUV cars is less spread out than for the other two groups and the midsize cars have the most spread.

Although we cannot spot clusters or gaps in box plots as we can with stem and leaf or line plots, we can more easily compare data from different sets. With box plots, we do not need to have sets of data that are approximately the same size, as we did for back-to-back stem and leaf plots. To compare data from two or more sets using their box plots, we first study the boxes to see whether they are located in approximately the same places. Next, we consider the lengths of the boxes to see whether the variability of the data is about the same. We also check whether the median, the quartiles, and the extreme values in one set are greater than those in another set. If they are, the data are greater than those of the other set, no matter how we compare them. If they are not, we can continue to study the data for other similarities and differences.

Variation: Mean Absolute Deviation, Variance, and Standard Deviation

Earlier in the section, we noted that a measure of spread is needed when data are summarized with a single number, such as the mean or median. There are many measures of spread that are generally discussed and each has a different use. To examine these measures of spread, we start again with a simple test-score example.

Suppose Professors Abel and Babel each taught a section of a graduate statistics course and each had six students. Both professors gave the same final exam. The results, along with the means for each group of scores, are given in Table 15, with stem and leaf plots in Figure 32(a) and (b), respectively. As the stem and leaf plots show, the sets of data are very different. The first is more

Table 15	
Abel's Class Scores	**Babel's Class Scores**
100	70
80	70
70	60
50	60
50	60
10	40
$\bar{x} = \dfrac{360}{6} = 60$	$\bar{x} = \dfrac{360}{6} = 60$

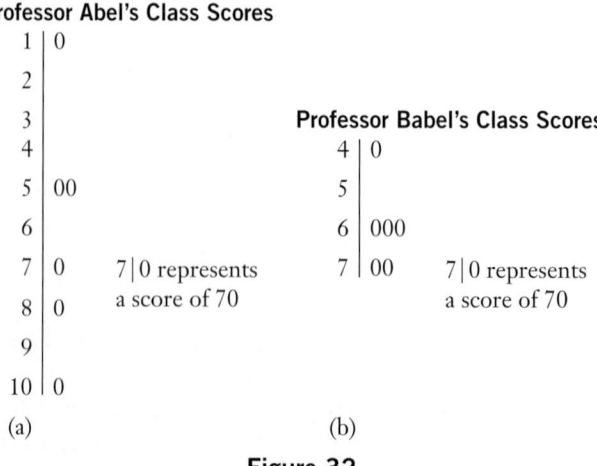

Professor Abel's Class Scores

```
 1 | 0
 2 |
 3 |
 4 |
 5 | 00
 6 |
 7 | 0      7|0 represents
 8 | 0      a score of 70
 9 |
10 | 0
```

Professor Babel's Class Scores

```
 4 | 0
 5 |
 6 | 000
 7 | 00     7|0 represents
          a score of 70
```

(a)   (b)

Figure 32

spread out, or varies more, than the second. However, each set has 60 as the mean. Each median also equals 60. Although the mean and the median for these two groups are the same, the two distributions of scores are very different.

As we have seen, there are many ways to measure the spread of data. The simplest way is to find the range. The range for Professor Abel's class is $100 - 10$, or 90. The range for Professor Babel's class is $70 - 40$, or 30. If we use the range as the measure of dispersion, we see that Abel's class is much more spread out than Babel's class. If we use the interquartile range, the IQR for Abel's class is 30, and for Babel's class, 10. Again, these measures of spread show more of a spread for Abel's class than for Babel's. A disadvantage of the range is that it uses only extreme values.

Mean Absolute Deviation

A basic way to measure the spread of data is to measure the distance that each data point is away from the mean. The **mean absolute deviation (MAD)** makes use of the absolute value to find the distance each data point is away from the mean; then the mean of those distances is found to give an "average distance from the mean" for each of the points. We find the mean absolute deviation of the scores by using the following steps:

- Measure the distance from the mean by calculating the score minus the mean.
- Find the absolute value of each difference.
- Sum those absolute values (the absolute deviation).
- Find the mean absolute deviation (MAD) by dividing the sum by the number of scores.

Table 16 contains a sample set of data.

Table 16

Test Scores	|Test Score − Mean|
99	$\|99 - 83.2\|$, or 15.8
67	$\|67 - 83.2\|$, or 16.2
84	$\|84 - 83.2\|$, or 0.8
99	$\|99 - 83.2\|$, or 15.8
67	$\|67 - 83.2\|$, or 16.2
$\bar{x} = \dfrac{(99 + 67 + 84 + 99 + 67)}{5} = 83.2$	Sum of absolute deviations = 64.8 $\text{MAD} = \dfrac{64.8}{5}$, or 12.96

Definition of Mean Absolute Deviation (MAD)

The **mean absolute deviation (MAD)** for the numbers $x_1, x_2, x_3, \ldots, x_n$, where $\bar{x}$ is the mean of the numbers, is

$$\text{MAD} = \frac{|x_1 - \bar{x}| + |x_2 - \bar{x}| + \ldots + |x_n - \bar{x}|}{n}.$$

Visual pictures of the MAD for the given set of test scores are given in Figure 33(a) and (b).

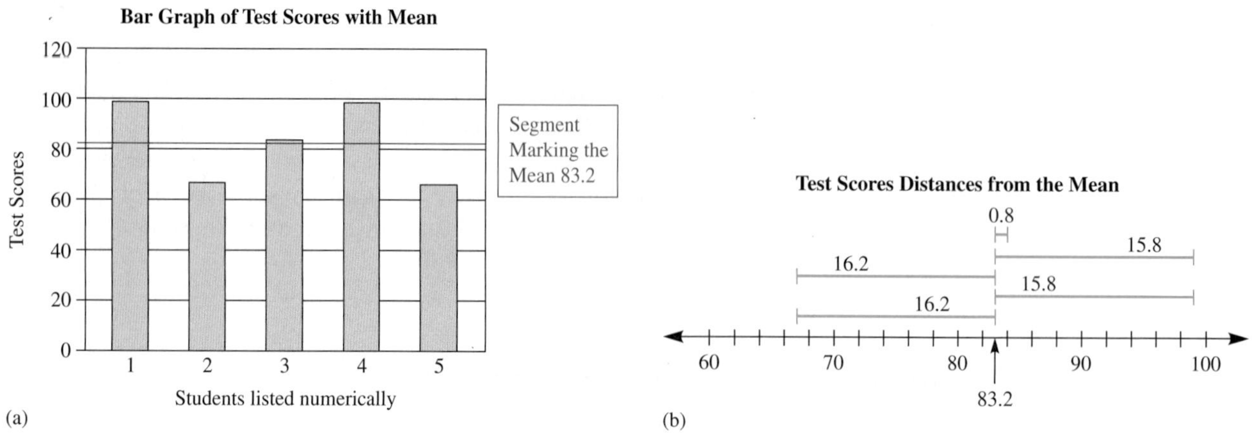

Figure 33

The MAD is a measure of the average distance that a score is from the mean and hence gives an idea of how far away from the mean the test scores are. The MAD is recommended for use in *Statistics Framework* (p. 43), and serves as a precursor to the standard deviation. The MAD does give a measure of spread that works well for some data sets. It handles fairly large deviations. Consider the data for Abel from Table 16 and displayed in Table 17.

Table 17

Abel's Class Scores	|Abel's Scores − 60|	Babel's Class Scores	|Babel's Scores − 60|
100	40	70	10
80	20	70	10
70	10	60	0
50	10	60	0
50	10	60	0
10	50	40	20
Mean = 60	$\text{MAD} = \dfrac{140}{6} \approx 23.3$	Mean = 60	$\text{MAD} = \dfrac{40}{6} \approx 6.7$

Using the MAD on the two sets of scores, it is easy to see that even though the means are 60, the spreads are very different. For Abel's class, the scores are an average of 23.3 points from the mean, whereas in Babel's class, the scores are an average of 6.7 points from the mean. Babel's test scores are "less spread out."

Variance and Standard Deviation

Statisticians commonly use two other measures of spread: the *variance* and the *standard deviation*. These measures are also based on how far the scores are from the mean. To find out how far each value differs from the mean, we subtract each value in the data from the mean to obtain the deviation. Some deviations may be positive, and others may be negative. Because the mean is the balance point, the total of the deviations above the mean equals the total of the deviations below the mean. (The mean of the deviations is 0 because the sum of the deviations is 0.) Squaring the deviations makes them all positive. *The mean of the squared deviations is the **variance**. Because the* variance involves squaring the deviations, it does not have the same units of measurement as the original observations. For example, lengths measured in feet have a variance measured in square feet. To obtain the same units as the original observations, we take the square root of the variance and obtain the **standard deviation**.

The steps involved in calculating the variance v and standard deviation s of n numbers are as follows.

1. Find the mean of the numbers.
2. Subtract the mean from each number.
3. Square each difference found in Step 2.
4. Find the sum of the squares in Step 3.
5. Divide by n to obtain the variance v.
6. Find the square root of v to obtain the standard deviation s.

Definition of Standard Deviation and Variance

The **standard deviation** for the numbers $x_1, x_2, x_3, \ldots, x_n$, where $\bar{x}$ is the mean of these numbers and v is the **variance**, is

$$s = \sqrt{v} = \sqrt{\frac{(x_1 - \bar{x})^2 + (x_2 - \bar{x})^2 + (x_3 - \bar{x})^2 + \ldots + (x_n - \bar{x})^2}{n}}$$

In some textbooks, the formula for standard deviation and variance involves division by $n - 1$ instead of by n. Division by $n - 1$ is more useful for advanced work in statistics. Notice that $v = s^2$, which is a common notation for variance.

The variances and standard deviations for the final exam data from the classes of Professors Abel and Babel are calculated using Table 18(a) and (b), respectively.

Table 18 (a) Abel's Class Scores

x	$x - \bar{x}$	$(x - \bar{x})^2$
100	40	1600
80	20	400
70	10	100
50	⁻10	100
50	⁻10	100
10	⁻50	2500
Totals: 360	0	4800

(b) Babel's Class Scores

x	$x - \bar{x}$	$(x - \bar{x})^2$
70	10	100
70	10	100
60	0	0
60	0	0
60	0	0
40	⁻20	400
Totals: 360	0	600

$\bar{x} = \dfrac{360}{6} = 60$

$v = \dfrac{4800}{6} = 800$

$s = \sqrt{800} \approx 28.3$

$\bar{x} = \dfrac{360}{6} = 60$

$v = \dfrac{600}{6} = 100$

$s = \sqrt{100} = 10$

Values far from the mean on either side have greater positive squared deviations, whereas values close to the mean have lesser positive squared deviations. Therefore, the standard deviation is a greater number when the values from a set of data are widely spread and a lesser number (close to 0) when the data values are close together.

Example 10

Professor Abel gave two group exams. Exam A had grades of 0, 0, 0, 100, 100, 100, and Exam B had grades of 50, 50, 50, 50, 50, 50. Find the following values for each exam.

a. Mean   b. Range   c. Mean absolute deviation
d. Standard deviation   e. Median   f. Interquartile range

Solution

a. The means for exams A and B are each 50.
b. The range for exams A and B are 100 and 0, respectively.
c. The mean absolute deviations for the two exams are as follows:

$$\text{MAD}_A = \frac{|0-50| + |0-50| + |0-50| + |100-50| + |100-50| + |100-50|}{6} = 50$$

$$\text{MAD}_B = \frac{|50-50| + |50-50| + |50-50| + |50-50| + |50-50| + |50-50|}{6} = 0$$

d. The standard deviations for exams A and B are as follows:

$$s_A = \sqrt{\frac{3(0-50)^2 + 3(100-50)^2}{6}} = 50$$

$$s_B = \sqrt{\frac{6(50-50)^2}{6}} = 0$$

e. The medians for the exams are each 50.
f. The interquartile range for Exams A and B, respectively, are 100 and 0.

In Example 10, exam A has mean 50, mean absolute deviation of 50, and standard deviation of 50. Exam A also had median 50 and interquartile range 100. Reporting the three measures of spread together in each case demonstrates that the scores are widely spread away from the mean and median. Exam B has mean 50, mean absolute deviation 0, and standard deviation of 0. Its median is 50 with interquartile range 0. All of the descriptors for Exam B show that there is very little spread of data from the mean and median. (In this case there is none.) Example 10 was chosen with extreme scores to illustrate what can happen with measures of central tendency and measures of spread. Normally, one can tell more about the distribution of data points when the mean, mean absolute deviation, or standard deviation are reported together, as well as when the median and interquartile range are reported together.

Normal Distributions

To better understand how standard deviations are used as measures of spread, we next consider normal distributions. The graphs of normal distributions are bell-shaped curves or *normal curves*. Normal distribution arises naturally in many real-world situations. Human heights, gestation, test scores, IQ scores, experimental measurements all have approximate normal distributions when a large population is considered.

A **normal curve** is a smooth, bell-shaped curve that depicts frequency values distributed symmetrically about the mean. The normal curve is a theoretical distribution that extends infinitely in both directions. It gets closer and closer to the x-axis but never reaches it. On a normal curve, about 68% of the values lie within 1 standard deviation of the mean, about 95% lie within 2 standard deviations, and about 99.7% are within 3 standard deviations. The percentages represent approximations of the total percent of area under the curve. The curve and the percentages are illustrated in Figure 34.

Normal Curve Distribution

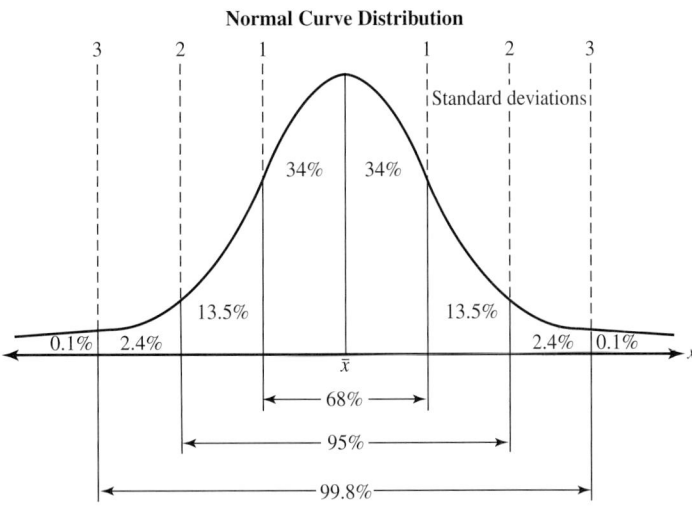

Figure 34

Suppose the area under the curve represents the population of the United States. Psychologists claim that the mean IQ is 100 and the standard deviation is 15. They also claim that an IQ score of over 130 represents a superior score. Because 130 is equal to the mean plus 2 standard deviations, we see from Figure 34 that only 2.5% of the population have IQ's 130 or greater.

Example 11

When a standardized test was scored, there was a mean of 500 and a standard deviation of 100. Suppose that 10,000 students took the test and their scores had a bell-shaped distribution, making it possible to use a normal curve to approximate the distribution.

  a. How many scored between 400 and 600?
  b. How many scored between 300 and 700?
  c. How many scored between 200 and 800?
  d. How many scored above 800?

Solution
  a. Since 1 standard deviation on either side of the mean is from 400 to 600, about 68% of the scores fall in this interval. Thus, 0.68(10,000), or 6800, students scored between 400 and 600.
  b. About 95% of 10,000, or 9500, students scored between 300 and 700.
  c. About 99.8% of 10,000, or 9980, students scored between 200 and 800.
  d. About 0.1% of 10,000, or 10, students scored above 800.

About 0.2%, or 20, of the students' scores in Example 11 fall outside 3 standard deviations. About 10 of these students did very well on the test, and about 10 students did very poorly.

Application of the Normal Curve

Suppose that a group of students asked their teacher to grade "on a curve." If the teacher gave a test to 200 students and the mean on the test was 71, with a standard deviation of 7, the graph in Figure 35 shows how the grades could be assigned. In Figure 35, the teacher has used the normal curve in grading. The use of the normal curve presupposes that the teacher had a bell-shaped distribution of scores and also that the teacher arbitrarily decided to use the lines marking standard deviations to determine the boundaries of the A's, B's, C's, D's, and F's. Thus, based on the normal curve in Figure 35, Table 19 shows the range of grades that the teacher might assign if the grades are rounded. Some students who ask their teachers to grade on the curve may wish to reconsider if the normal curve is to be used.

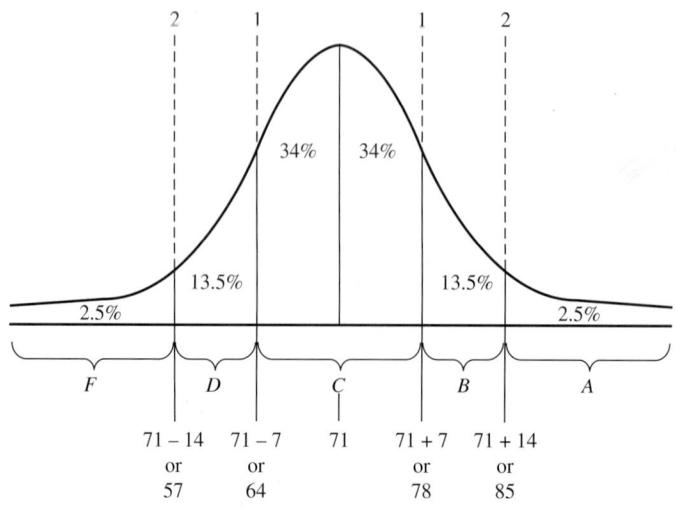

Figure 35

Table 19			
Test Score	Grade	Number of People per Grade	Percentage Receiving Grade
85 and above	A	5	2.5%
78–84	B	27	13.5%
64–77	C	136	68%
57–63	D	27	13.5%
Below 57	F	5	2.5%

Percentiles

Standardized test scores on the ACT or SAT are often reported in **percentiles**. A percentile shows a person's score relative to other scores. For example, if a student's score is at the 82nd percentile, this means that approximately 82% of those taking the test scored lower than the student and approximately 18% had higher scores.

One application of percentiles is to make comparisons. For example, consider Kristy and Kim as they applied for a job. On the application, Kristy wrote that she finished 15th in her class. Kim reported that she finished 40th in her class. Does Kristy's class rank imply that she is a better student than Kim? Suppose that there were 50 students in Kristy's class and 400 students in Kim's

class. In such a case, we need a common method of comparing their rankings. In order to make a balanced comparison, we can find Kristy's and Kim's percentile ranks, or percentiles, in their respective classes. In Kristy's class, there were $50 - 15$, or 35, students ranked below her, so Kristy ranked at the 70th percentile $\left(\dfrac{35}{50} = 70\%\right)$. Similarly, $\dfrac{(400 - 40)}{400}$, or 90%, of the students ranked below Kim. Kim ranked at the 90th percentile for her school. Thus, comparatively, Kim ranked higher in her class than Kristy did in hers.

As the name implies, percentiles divide the set of data into 100 equal parts. For example, if Tomas reports that he scored at the 50th percentile (the median, or Q_2) on the SAT, he is saying that he scored better than 50% of the people taking the test. In general, *the rth percentile is denoted by P_r*. In a case where the distribution is normal, we could use the percentages in Figure 34 to determine percentiles. For example, someone scoring 2 standard deviations above the median is at the $(0.1 + 2.4 + 13.5 + 34 + 34 + 13.5)$ percentile, or better than 97.5% of the population. Because percentiles are typically reported using whole percentages, that places the person at the 98th percentile. In some sets of test scores, a particular percentile may not be represented. With small data sets, percentiles are not useful.

Percentiles can be found from distributions that are not normal. This can be done by constructing a frequency table, determining the number of scores less than the score for which we are trying to determine a percentile, and then dividing that number by the total number of scores in the set of data. This is investigated further in the assessment set.

Deciles are points that divide a distribution into 10 equally spaced sections. There are nine deciles, denoted $D_1, D_2, \ldots, D_9$, and $D_1 = P_{10}, D_2 = P_{20}, \ldots, D_9 = P_{90}$. Quartiles were defined similarly earlier.

Example 12

A standardized test that was distributed along a normal curve had a median (and mean) of 500 and a standard deviation of 100. The 16th percentile, P_{16}, is 400 because 400 is 1 standard deviation below the median. Find each of the following percentiles.

a. P_{50}
b. P_{84}

Solution
a. Since 500 is the median, 50% of the distribution is less than 500. Thus, $P_{50} = 500$.
b. Since 600 is 1 standard deviation above the median, 84% of the distribution is less than 600. Thus, $P_{84} = 600$.

Example 13

a. Ossie was ranked 25th in a class of 250. What was his percentile rank?
b. In a class of 50, Cathy has a percentile rank of 60. What is her class standing?

Solution
a. There were $250 - 25$, or 225, students ranked below Ossie. Hence, $225/250$, or 90%, of the class ranked below him. Therefore, Ossie ranked at the 90th percentile.
b. Cathy's percentile rank is 60. Thus 60% of the class ranks below her. Because 60% of 50 is 30, 30 students ranked below Cathy. Therefore, Cathy is 20th in her class.

Assessment 10-4A

1. Calculate the mean, the median, and the mode for each of the following data sets.
   a. $3, 7, 7, 8, 6, 7, 11, 4$ Mean = 6.625; median = 7; mode = 7
   b. $10.5, 12.5, 12.5, 14.5, 20.5, 16.5, 12.5, 14.5, 11.5$ *
   c. $3, \overline{6}.2, \overline{7}.4, 4.2, \overline{2}, 1.2, 8.3, \overline{1}.1$ *
   d. $80, 85, 93, 85, 79, 82, 0$ Mean = 72; median = 82; mode = 85

2. a. Find an example of a data set with seven observations for which the mode is not a good descriptor for the typical data values.   *
   b. Find an example of a data set with seven observations for which the median is not a good descriptor of the center of the data.   *

3. a. If three students scored 75 on a test and three other students scored 88 on the same test, find each of the following related to the test scores:
   i. mean   81.5   ii. median   81.5   iii. mode   *
   b. The mean score on a set of 20 tests is 75. What is the sum of the 20 test scores?   1500

4. The mean for a set of 28 scores is 80. Suppose two more students take the test and score 60 and 50. What is the new mean?   Approximately 78.3

5. Suppose in Selina's class there were four students who scored 98 and eleven who scored 60. What is the mean of the scores in the class?   70.13

6. Suppose there were m students in a class who scored 100 and n students who scored 50. Write an algebraic expression for the mean in terms of m and n.   *

7. A table showing Jon's fall-quarter grades follows. Find his grade point average for the term (A = 4, B = 3, C = 2, D = 1, F = 0).   Approximately 2.59

Course	Credits	Grade
Math	5	B
English	3	A
Physics	5	C
German	3	D
Handball	1	A

8. If the mean weight of seven linemen on a team is 230 lb and the mean weight of the four backfield members is 190 lb, what is the mean weight of the 11-person team?   Approximately 215 lbs

9. The following table gives the annual salaries of the 50 faculty and staff at Mountain Unified School District.

Salary ($)	Faculty/Staff
18,000	2
22,000	6
32,000	24
48,000	15
80,000	2
150,000	1

   a. Find the mean annual salary for the employees. $39,320
   b. Find the median annual salary. $32,000
   c. Find the mode. $32,000

10. Use the data in exercise 9 to find the following.
    a. Range $132,000
    b. Mean absolute deviation $12,889.60
    c. Standard deviation   Approximately $20,339.56
    d. Interquartile range $16,000

11. Use the data in exercise 9 and the values in exercise 10 to answer the following.
    a. Which values from exercise 10 should be reported to best describe the data in exercise 9?   *
    b. Explain why you made the choice you did in part (a).   *

12. Maria filled her car's gas tank. The mileage odometer read 42,800 mi. When the odometer read 43,030, Maria filled the tank with 12 gal. At the end of the trip, she filled the tank with 18 gal and the odometer read 43,390 mi. How many miles per gallon did she get for the entire trip? $19\frac{2}{3}$ mpg

13. The youngest person in a company is 24 years old. The range of ages is 34 years. How old is the oldest person in the company?   58 years old

14. To receive an A in a class, Willie needs at least a mean of 90 on five exams. Willie's grades on the first four exams were 84, 95, 86, and 94. What minimum score does he need on the fifth exam to receive an A in the class?   91

15. Following are box plots comparing the ticket prices of two performing arts theaters:

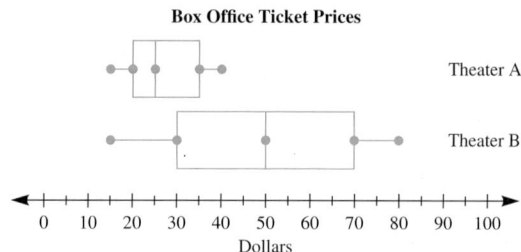

Box Office Ticket Prices

    a. What is the median ticket price for each theater?   *
    b. Which theater has the greatest range of prices?   B
    c. What is the highest ticket price at either theater? $80 at B
    d. Make some statements comparing the ticket prices at the two theaters.   *

16. Construct a box plot for the following set of quiz scores. Indicate outliers, if any, with asterisks.   *

    $20, 92, 88, 70, 75, 80, 69, 72, 83, 90$

17. The following table shows the heights in feet of the 8 tallest buildings in St. Louis, Missouri, and in Los Angeles, California.

Los Angeles	St. Louis
858	593
750	588
735	540
699	434
625	420
620	398
578	392
571	375

a. Draw horizontal box plots to compare the data.   *
b. Based on your box plots from (a), make some comparisons of the heights of the buildings in the two cities.   *

18. What is the standard deviation of the heights of seven trapeze artists if their heights are 175 cm, 182 cm, 190 cm, 180 cm, 192 cm, 172 cm, and 190 cm?   7.3 cm

19. In a Math 131 class at DiPaloma University, the grades on the first exam were as follows:

   96 71 43 77 75 76 61
   83 71 58 97 76 74 91
   74 71 77 83 87 93 79

   a. Find the mean.   Approximately 76.8
   b. Find the median.   76
   c. Find the mode.   71
   d. Find the IQR.   14
   e. Find the variance of the scores.   Approximately 156.8
   f. Find the standard deviation of the scores.   Approximately 12.5
   g. Find the mean absolute deviation of the scores.   *

20. Assume that the heights of American women are approximately normally distributed with a mean of 65.5 in. and a standard deviation of 2.5 in. Within what range are the heights of 95% of American women?   Between 60.5 in. and 70.5 in.

21. Assume a normal distribution and that the average phone call in a certain town lasted 3 min, with a standard deviation of 1 min. What percentage of the calls lasted less than 1 min?   16%

22. If a standardized test with scores distributed normally has a mean of 65 and a standard deviation of 12, find the following:
   a. Q_2 65
   b. P_{16} 53
   c. P_{84} 77
   d. D_5 65

23. For certain workers, the mean wage is $7.50/hr with a standard deviation of $0.75. If a worker is chosen at random, what is the probability that the worker's wage is between $6.75 and $8.25? Assume a normal distribution of wages.   *

24. On a certain exam, the mean is 79 and the standard deviation is 5.5. If a grade of A is given to any student who scores at least 2 standard deviations above the mean, what is the lowest score that a person could receive and still get an A?   *

25. A standardized test given to 10,000 students had scores normally distributed. Al scored 648. The mean was 518 and the standard deviation was 130. About how many students scored below him?   8400 students.

26. In a class of 45 students, Al has a rank of 14. At what percentile is he?   69th percentile

27. Jack was 70th in a class of 200; whereas Jill who is in the same class has a percentile rank of 70. Which student has the higher standing in the class? Why?   *

Assessment 10-4B

1. Calculate the mean, the median, and the mode for each of the following data sets:
   a. 85, 83, 66, 78, 95, 83, 95, 93, 83, 83   *
   b. 2, 2, 2, 2, 2, 12   Mean = 3.67; median = 2; mode = 2
   c. 5, ⁻4.2, ⁻5.4, 6.2, ⁻4, ⁻1.2, 6.3, ⁻3.1   *
   d. 5.99, 12.99, 19.99, 7.99, 10.99, 18.99   *

2. Find an example of a data set with seven observations for which the mean is not a good descriptor of the center of the data.   Answers vary.

3. a. If each of seven students scored 80 on a test, find each of the following for the scores:
      i. mean   80
      ii. median   80
      iii. mode   80
   b. Make up another set of six scores that are not all the same but in which the mean, median, and mode are all 80.   *

4. The tram at a ski area has a capacity of 50 people with a load limit of 7500 lb. What is the mean weight of the passengers if the tram is loaded to its weight limit and capacity?   150 lbs.

5. The names and ages for each person in a family of five follow:

Name	Dick	Jane	Kirk	Jean	Scott
Age	42	36	10	8	4

   a. What is the mean age?   20
   b. Find the mean of the ages 10 yrs from now.   30
   c. Find the mean 20 yrs from now.   40
   d. Describe the relationships among the means found in (a), (b), and (c).   *

6. Suppose there were n students in a class; h of them scored 100 and the rest scored 50. Write an algebraic expression for the mean for the class in terms of n and h.   *

7. a. Mr. Alberto wanted to count the score on a term paper as 60% of a final grade, homework as 25% of the grade, and the final exam as the remainder of the grade. A student in the class made 85 on the term paper, had a 78 average on homework, and scored 90 on the final exam. What number could Mr. Alberto use to determine the student's grade if he used his grading scheme?   84
   b. Write an algebraic expression to generalize the scoring procedure for Mr. Alberto's class to allow him to use any percentages he likes for the scoring scheme. Clearly describe what the variables represent.   *

8. If 99 people had a mean income of $13,500, how much is the mean income increased by the addition of a single income of $210,000? $1965

9. Refer to the following chart. In a gymnastics competition, each competitor receives six scores. The highest and lowest scores are eliminated, and the official score is the mean of the four remaining scores.

Gymnast	Scores					
Balance Beam						
Meta	9.2	9.2	9.1	9.3	9.8	9.6
Lisa	9.3	9.1	9.4	9.6	9.9	9.4
Olga	9.4	9.5	9.6	9.6	9.9	9.6
Uneven Bars						
Meta	9.2	9.1	9.3	9.2	9.4	9.5
Lisa	10.0	9.8	9.9	9.7	9.9	9.8
Olga	9.4	9.6	9.5	9.4	9.4	9.4
Floor Exercises						
Meta	9.7	9.8	9.4	9.8	9.8	9.7
Lisa	10.0	9.9	9.8	10.0	9.7	10.0
Olga	9.4	9.3	9.6	9.4	9.5	9.4

a. If the only events in the competition are the balance beam, the uneven bars, and the floor exercise, find the winner of each event.   *

b. Find the overall winner of the competition if the overall winner is the person with the highest combined official scores.   Lisa (29.20)

10. Choose the data set(s) that fit the descriptions given in each of the following:

a. The mean is 6.
The range is 6.
Set *A*: 3, 5, 7, 9
Set *B*: 2, 4, 6, 8
Set *C*: 2, 3, 4, 15   A

b. The mean is 11.
The median is 11.
The mode is 11.
Set *A*: 9, 10, 10, 11, 12, 12, 13
Set *B*: 11, 11, 11, 11, 11, 11, 11
Set *C*: 9, 11, 11, 11, 11, 12, 12   B and C

c. The mean is 3.
The median is 3.
It has no mode.
Set *A*: $0, 2\frac{1}{2}, 6\frac{1}{2}$
Set *B*: 3, 3, 3, 3
Set *C*: 1, 2, 4, 5   C

d. Match the data set with the box plot shown below.

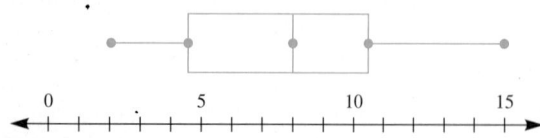

Set *A*: 2, 3, 4, 4, 6, 6, 7, 15
Set *B*: 2, 3, 6, 6, 8, 9, 12, 14, 15
Set *C*: 2, 4.5, 8, 13, 15
Set *D*: 2, 3, 6, 6, 8, 9, 10, 11, 15   D

11. The mean of five numbers is 6. If one of the five numbers is removed, the mean becomes 7. What is the value of the number that was removed?   2

12. a. Find the mean and the median of the following arithmetic sequences:

i. 2, 4, 6, 8, . . . , 200   Mean = 101; median = 101
ii. 1, 3, 5, 7, 9, . . . , 199   Mean = 100; median = 100
iii. 5, 13, 21, 29, . . . , 157   Mean = 81; median = 81

b. Based on your answers in (a), make a conjecture about the mean and the median of any arithmetic sequence.   *

13. The youngest person in a company is 21. The oldest is 66.
a. What is the range?   45
b. Is the range a good measure of spread for the ages in the company? Why?   *

14. Ginny's median score on three tests was 90. Her mean score was 92 and her range was 6. What were her three test scores?   96, 90, 90

15. Following are box plots comparing ages at first marriage for a sample of U.S. citizens.

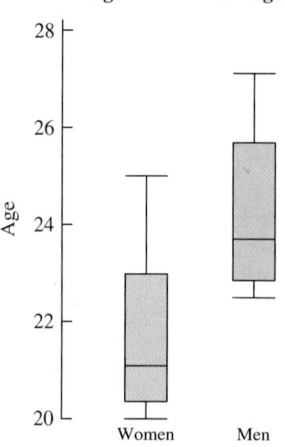

Age at First Marriage

a. What is the median age of first marriage for men?   About 23.7
b. What is the median age of first marriage for women?   *
c. Which group has the greater range?   *
d. Compare the first marriage age for men and women.   *

16. Construct a box plot for the following gas mileages per gallon of various company cars: *

25, 21, 17, 31, 33, 15, 41, 25, 33, 42, 23, 21, 17, 19, 13

17. The following table shows the heights in feet of the tallest 10 buildings in Los Angeles and in Minneapolis:

Los Angeles	Minneapolis
858	950
750	775
735	668
699	579
625	561
620	447
578	440
571	416
534	403
516	366

a. Draw horizontal box plots to compare the data.   *
b. Are there any outliers in this data? If so, which values are they?   There are no outliers.
c. Based on your box plots from (a), make some comparisons of the heights of the buildings in the two cities.   *

18. a. If all the numbers in a set are equal, what is the standard deviation? $s = 0$
    b. If the standard deviation of a set of numbers is zero, must all the numbers in the set be equal?   Yes

19. In a school system, teachers start at a salary of $25,200 and have a top salary of $51,800. The teachers' union is bargaining with the school district for next year's salary increment.
    a. If every teacher is given a $1000 raise, what happens to each of the following?
       i. Mean   Increase by $1000
       ii. Median   Increase by $1000
       iii. Extremes   Increase by $1000
       iv. Quartiles   Increase by $1000
       v. Standard deviation   Stays the same
       vi. IQR   Stays the same
    b. If every teacher received a 5% raise, what does this do to the following?
       i. Mean   Increase by 5%
       ii. Standard deviation   Increase by 5%

20. The mean IQ score for 1500 students is 100, with a standard deviation of 15. Assuming the scores have a normal distribution, answer the following.
    a. How many have an IQ between 85 and 115?   1020
    b. How many have an IQ between 70 and 130?   1425
    c. How many have an IQ over 145?   1.5, so 1 or 2 people

21. Sugar Plops boxes say they hold 16 oz. To make sure they do, the manufacturer fills the box to a mean weight of 16.1 oz, with a standard deviation of 0.05 oz. If the weights have a normal distribution, what percentage of the boxes actually contain 16 oz or more?   97.5%

22. According to psychologists, IQs are normally distributed, with a mean of 100 and a standard deviation of 15.
    a. What percentage of the population has IQs between 100 and 130?   47.5%
    b. What percentage of the population has IQs lower than 85?   16%

23. The weights of newborn babies in a certain country are distributed normally, with a mean of approximately 90 oz and a standard deviation of 18 oz. If a newborn is selected at random, what is the probability that the baby weighs more than 108 oz?   0.16

24. A tire company tests a particular model of tire and finds the tires to be normally distributed with respect to wear. The mean is 56,000 mi and the standard deviation is 3500 mi. If 1,500 tires are tested, about how many are likely to wear out before 49,000 mi?   Approximately 37 tires.

25. A standardized mathematics test given to 14,000 students had the scores normally distributed. The mean was 850 and the standard deviation was 75. A student scoring below 775 points was deficient in mathematics. About how many students were rated deficient?   2240 students

26. In a class of 35 students, Steve has a rank of 35th. At what percentile is he?   *

27. Jill was 80th in a class of 200, whereas Nathan, who is in the same class, has a percentile rank of 80. Which student has the higher standing in the class?   Nathan; Jill has a percentile rank of 60.

Mathematical Connections 10-4

Answers to Mathematical Connections can be found in the Answers section at the back of the book.

Reasoning

1. Suppose you own a hat shop and decide to order hats in only *one* size for the coming season. To decide which size to order, you look at last year's sales figures, which are itemized according to size. Should you find the mean, median, or mode for the data? Why?

2. A movie chain conducts a popcorn poll in which each person entering a theater and buying a box of popcorn is asked a yes-no question. Which "average" do you think is used to report the result and why?

3. When a government agency reports the average rainfall for a state for a year, which "average" do you think it uses and why?

4. Carl had scores of 90, 95, 85, and 90 on his first four tests.
   a. Find the median, mean, and mode.
   b. Carl scored a 20 on his fifth exam. Which of the three averages would Carl want the instructor to use to compute his grade? Why?
   c. Which measure is affected most by an extreme score?

5. The mean of the five numbers given is 50:

$$20 \quad 35 \quad 50 \quad 60 \quad 85$$

   a. Add four numbers to the list so that the mean of the nine numbers is still 50.
   b. Explain how you could choose the four numbers to add to the list so that the mean does not change.
   c. How does the mean of the four numbers you added to the list compare to the original mean of 50?

6. Selina claimed that in her class all of the scores on a test were either 100 or 50, so the mean must be 75.
   a. Explain with an example how Selina may have reasoned.
   b. Explain whether this reasoning is valid.

7. Sue drives 5 mi at 30 mph and then 5 mi at 50 mph. Is the mean speed for the trip 40 mph? Why or why not?

8. Explain why the mode could be a less-than-adequate measure of center for a data set.

9. If you were to make an argument that there were not enough women's bathrooms in a theater, what type of data would you use and why? Explain the types of measures of center and spread that you would report for your data.

10. The mean of 5, 7, 9 is 7. The mean of 67, 72, 77 is 72.
    a. Find two more examples where the mean of an ordered set of data is the "middle" data point.
    b. Suppose that a data set consists of $a_1, a_2, a_3, \ldots, a_n$, an arithmetic sequence. Explain why the mean of this data set is $\dfrac{a_1 + a_n}{2}$.

11. If each number in a set of data is multiplied by a constant answer the following.
    a. How is the new mean related to the original mean?
    b. How is the new standard deviation related to the original standard deviation?

12. What does a large standard deviation imply about a data set?

13. In each pair of variables below, select the one that can be assumed to be normally distributed.
    a. Salaries of employees at a high school; shoe sizes of students at a high school
    b. The exam scores on a statistics midterm; the heights of 25-years-old adults
    c. SAT scores; the frequency of numbers appearing in weekly lotteries for the past 5 years

Open-Ended

14. Use the data in the following table to compare the number of people living in the United States from 1820 through 1900 and the number living in the United States from 1920 through 2010. Use any form of graphical representation to make the comparison and explain why you chose the representation that you did.

Year	Number (thousands)	Year	Number (thousands)
1820	9,638	1930	123,202
1830	12,866	1940	132,164
1840	17,068	1950	151,325
1850	23,191	1960	179,323
1860	31,443	1970	203,302
1870	38,558	1980	226,542
1880	50,189	1990	248,765
1890	62,979	2000	281,422
1900	76,212	2012	313,914
1920	106,021		

Data taken from The World Almanac and Book of Facts 2002, *World Almanac Books, 2014.*

Cooperative Learning

15. In small groups, scrutinize a daily newspaper or weekly magazine for averages. Based on your findings, write a report defending or criticizing the types of averages used in the contexts.

16. In small groups, create one numerical data set by surveying the other students in the class about a topic that interests you. Then create three more data sets by (a) adding 5 to each data point in the original set, (b) subtracting 5, and (c) multiplying by 5. What can you say about the means of each of these three data sets? What about the median?

Connecting Mathematics to the Classroom

17. A student asks, "If the mean income of 10 people is $10,000 and one person gets a raise of $10,000, is the median, the mean, or the mode changed and, if so, by how much?"

18. Jose asks, "Why can a median number of children not be 3.8?" How do you respond?

19. Suppose the class takes a test and the following averages are obtained: mean, 80; median, 90; and mode, 70. Tom, who scored 80, would like to know if he did better than half the class. What is your response?

20. A student asks if it is possible to find the mode for data in a grouped frequency table. What is your response?

21. A student asks if she can draw any conclusions about a set of data if she knows that the mean for the data is less than the median. How do you answer?

22. A student asks if it is possible to have a standard deviation of ⁻5. How do you respond?

23. Mel's mean on 10 tests for the quarter was 89. She complained to the teacher that she should be given an A because she missed the cutoff of 90 by only a single point. Explain whether it is clear that she really missed an A by only a single point if each test was based on 100 points.

Review Problems

24. Consider the following circle graph. What is the number of degrees in each sector of the graph?

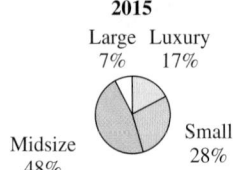

U.S. Car Sales by Vehicle Size and Type for Ali Auto Sales

25. Given the bar graph shown, answer the following.
    a. Which mountain is the highest? Approximately how high is it?
    b. Which mountains are higher than 6000 m?

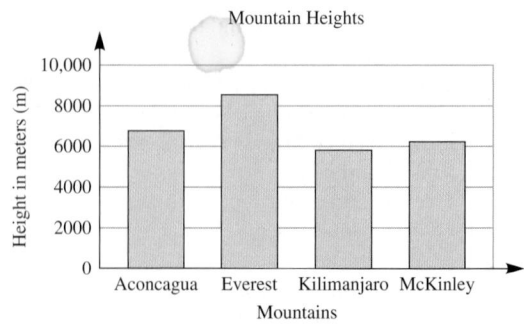

26. Following are raw test scores from a history test:

$$86 \quad 85 \quad 87 \quad 96 \quad 55$$
$$90 \quad 94 \quad 82 \quad 68 \quad 77$$
$$88 \quad 89 \quad 85 \quad 74 \quad 90$$
$$72 \quad 80 \quad 76 \quad 88 \quad 73$$
$$64 \quad 79 \quad 73 \quad 85 \quad 93$$

  a. Construct an ordered stem and leaf plot for the given data.
  b. Construct a grouped frequency table for these scores with intervals of 5, starting the first class at 55.
  c. Draw a histogram of the data.
  d. If a circle graph of the grouped data in (b) were drawn, how many degrees would be in the section representing the 85 through 89 interval?

National Assessments

National Assessment of Educational Progress (NAEP) Questions

Rick has earned a total of 581 points on all of his science tests. His overall test average (mean) is 83. How many tests has Rick taken?
A. 6
B. 7
C. 8
D. 9
E. 10
NAEP, Grade 8, 2013

Last month Bonnie recorded the weights of 11 dogs. Statistics for these weights are given below.

Weights of Dogs Last Month	
Minimum	31 pounds
Maximum	93 pounds
Mean	81 pounds
Mode	88 pounds
First Quartile	78 pounds
Median	88 pounds
Third Quartile	90 pounds

This month, Bonnie weighed the 11 dogs again. The weight of one dog changed from 31 pounds to 27 pounds. The weights of all the other dogs stayed the same.

Which of the following statistics changed from last month to this month?
A. Maximum
B. Mean
C. Mode
D. First Quartile
E. Median
NAEP, Grade 8, 2013

Tetsu rides his bicycle x miles the first day, y miles the second day, and z miles the third day. Which of the following expressions represents the average number of miles per day that Tetsu travels?
A. $x + y + z$ B. xyz C. $3(x + y + z)$
D. $3(xyz)$ E. $(x + y + z)/3$
NAEP, Grade 8, 2003

10-5 Abuses of Statistics

10-5 Objectives

Students will be able to understand and explain

• Misuses and abuses of statistics based on samples and populations.

• Valid and invalid inferences.

• Misuses of graphs.

• Misuses of numerical data.

Statistics are frequently abused. Benjamin Disraeli (1804–1881), an English prime minister, once remarked, "There are three kinds of lies: lies, damned lies, and statistics." People sometimes deliberately use statistics to mislead others. This can be seen in advertising. More often, however, the misuse of statistics is the result of misinterpreting what the data and statistics mean.

Misuses Based on Samples/Population

Consider an advertisement reporting that of the people responding to a recent survey, 98% said that Buffepain is the most effective pain reliever of headaches and arthritis. To certify that the statistics are not being misused, the following information should have been reported:

  1. The questions being asked
  2. The number of people surveyed
  3. The number of people who responded
  4. How the people who participated in the survey were chosen
  5. The number and type of pain relievers tested
  6. How the answers were interpreted

Without the information listed, the following situations are possible, all of which could cause the advertisement to be misleading.

1. Suppose 1,000,000 people nationwide were sent the survey, and only 50 responded. This would mean that there was only a 0.005% response, which would certainly cause mistrust in the ad.

2. Of the 50 responding in (1), suppose 49 responses were affirmative. The 98% claim is true, but 999,950 people did not respond.

3. Suppose a survey sentence read, "Buffepain is the best pain reliever I've tried for headaches and arthritis," and there were no questions about the kind and type of other pain relievers tried.

4. Suppose all the people who received the survey were chosen from a town in which the major industry was the manufacture of Buffepain. It is very doubtful that the survey would represent an unbiased sample.

5. Suppose only two "pain relievers" were tested: Buffepain, whose active ingredient is 100% aspirin, and a placebo containing only powdered sugar.

This is not to say that advertisements of this type are all misleading or dishonest, but simply that data interpretations may mislead.

In the Buffepain report, a primary issue deals with the survey conducted, the number of people involved in the survey, how they were chosen, and how results of the survey were interpreted. Surveys are common for gaining information from a population. However, there are classic examples in history of how surveys and survey information have been either misused or misinterpreted. A well-known example was seen in the predictions of the winner of the Harry S. Truman/Thomas E. Dewey 1948 U.S. presidential election. A leading pollster, Elmo Roper, was so confident of a loss by Truman that on September 9, 1948, approximately 2 months before the election, he announced that there would be no more polls on the election. Additionally, while Truman was still on the campaign trail, *Newsweek*, after polling 50 key political experts, stated on October 11, 1948, approximately 1 month before the election, that Dewey would win. In the *Newsweek* survey, a very select group was surveyed. Questions that should have been asked include (1) How was the group chosen? (2) Was the group representative of the voters in the United States? and (3) Could the result of this survey appropriately have been generalized to all voters? All of these types of questions are important to surveyors. What is the population to which the results are being generalized? Is the entire population to be surveyed, or is the survey given only to a sample of the population? If only a sample will be used, how is the sample chosen? Is the sample of the population randomly chosen so that each person being surveyed has an equally likely chance of being chosen? How large is the population and how large a sample must be used so that the sample is representative of the population?

▶ **NOW TRY THIS 13**

NTT 13: Answers can be found in Answers at the back of the book.

Based on the graph in Figure 36, write arguments to determine whether or not the following inferences are correct:

a. 82% of the parents surveyed say that there is not too much focus on preparing for tests.

b. Only 9% of the parents say that learning is thwarted.

c. 12% of the parents say test questions are too difficult and that expectations are unreasonable.

d. At least 89% of the parents believe that schools require too many tests.

e. The vast majority of parents say that teachers are not putting too much academic pressure on their children.

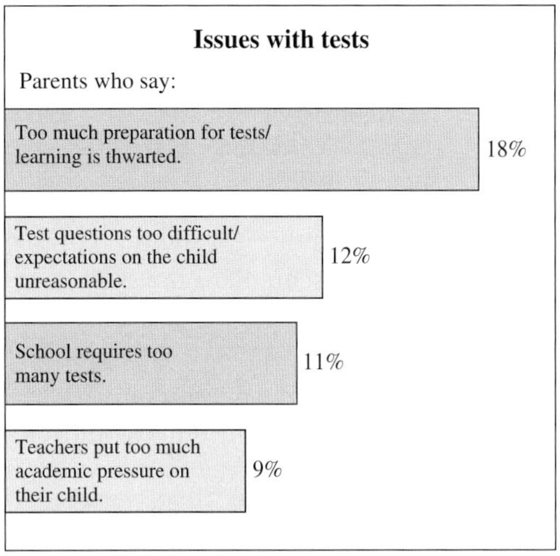

Issues with tests
Parents who say:
Too much preparation for tests/ learning is thwarted.
18%
Test questions too difficult/ expectations on the child unreasonable.
12%
School requires too many tests.
11%
Teachers put too much academic pressure on their child.
9%

Figure 36

Misuses Based on Graphs

A different type of misuse of data and statistics involves graphs. Among the things to look for in a graph are the following items. If they are not there, then the graph may be misleading.

1. Title
2. Labels on both axes of a line or bar chart and on all sections of a pie chart
3. Source of the data
4. Key to a pictograph
5. Uniform size of symbols in a pictograph
6. Scale: Does it start with zero? If not, is there a break shown?
7. Scale: Are the numbers equally spaced?

To see an example of a misleading use of graphs, consider how graphs can be used to distort data or exaggerate certain pieces of information. Graphs using a break in the vertical axis can be used to create different visual impressions, which are sometimes misleading. For example, consider the two graphs in Figure 37, which represent the number of girls trying out for basketball at each of three middle schools. As we can see, the graph in Figure 37(a) portrays a different picture from the one in Figure 37(b) because the scalings are different.

Number of Girls Trying Out for Basketball
Number of Girls
70
60
50
40
30
20
10
Wilson
Taft
Lincoln
Schools
(a)
Number of Girls Trying Out for Basketball
Number of Girls
62
60
58
56
54
52
50
Wilson
Taft
Lincoln
Schools
(b)

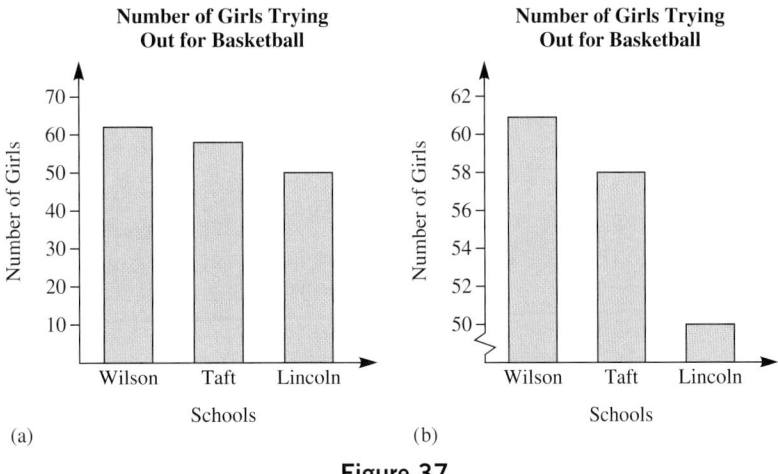

Figure 37

A line graph, histogram, or bar graph can be altered by changing the scale of the graph. For example, consider the data in Table 20 for the number of graduates from a community college for the years 2011 through 2015.

Table 20					
Year	2011	2012	2013	2014	2015
Number of Graduates	140	180	200	210	160

The graphs in Figure 38(a) and (b) represent the same data, but different scales are used in each. The statistics presented are the same, but these graphs do not convey the same psychological message. In Figure 38(b), the spacing of the years on the horizontal axis of the graph is more spread out and the spacing of the numbers on the vertical axis is more condensed than in Figure 38(a). Both of these changes minimize the variability of the data. A college administrator might use a graph like the one in Figure 38(b) to convince people that the college was not in serious enrollment trouble.

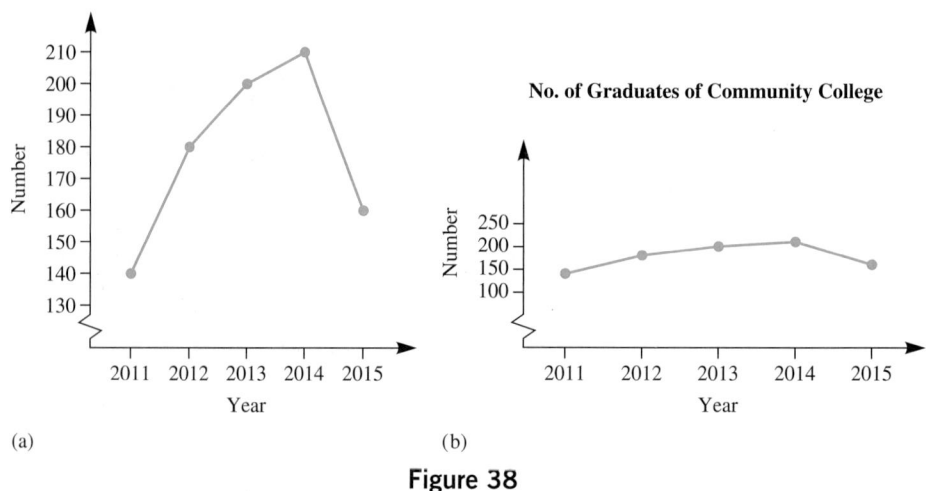

Figure 38

Another error that frequently occurs is the use of continuous graphs, as in Figure 39, to depict data that are discrete (a finite number of data values). In Figure 39, we see the enrollment in Math 206 for five semesters. The bar graph accurately depicts the enrollment data, but if this graph is replaced with the continuous line in Figure 39 but without the bars, then many points along the line are meaningless.

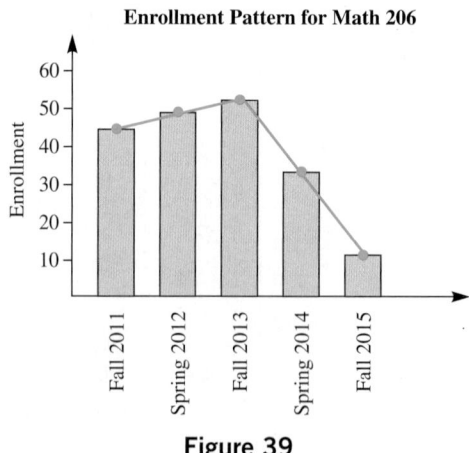

Figure 39

Other ways to distort graphs include omitting a scale, as in Figure 40(a). The scale is given in Figure 40(b).

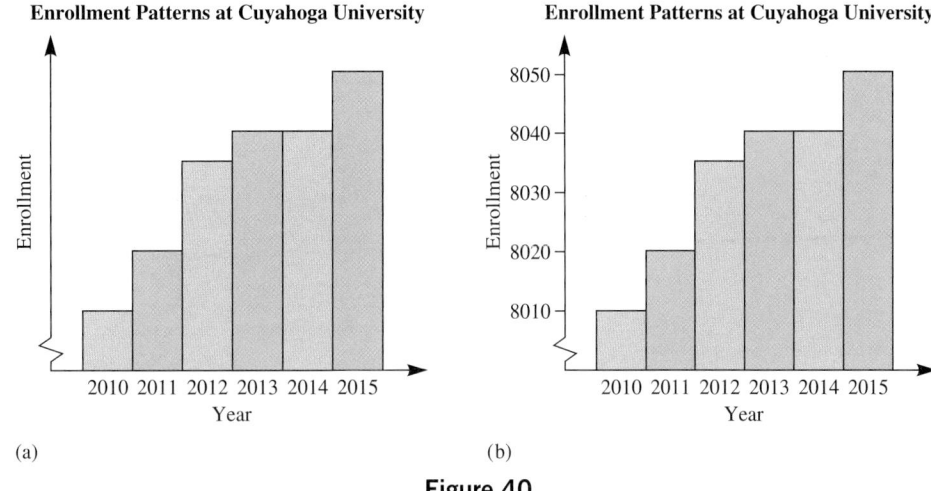

(a)   (b)

Figure 40

Other graphs can also be misleading. Suppose, for example, that the number of boxes of cereal sold by Sugar Plops last year was 2 million and the number of boxes of cereal sold by Korn Krisps was 8 million. The Korn Krisps executives prepared the graph in Figure 41 to demonstrate the data. The Sugar Plops people objected. Do you see why?

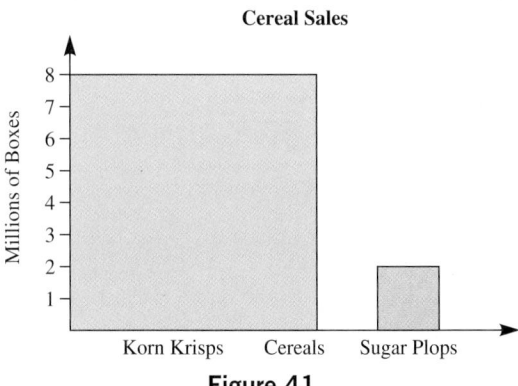

Figure 41

The graph in Figure 41 clearly distorts the data, since the figure for Korn Krisps is both 4 times as high and 4 times as wide as the bar for Sugar Plops. Thus, the area of the bar representing Korn Krisps is 16 times the comparable area representing Sugar Plops, rather than 4 times the area, as would be justified by the original data. To depict the data accurately, the length of a side of the Sugar Plops bar should be 4 units. Then four of these bars would "fit" in the Korn Krisps bar. Figure 42 shows how the comparison of Sugar Plops and Korn Krisps cereals might look if the figures were made three-dimensional. The figure for Korn Krisps has a volume 64 times the volume of the Sugar Plops figure.

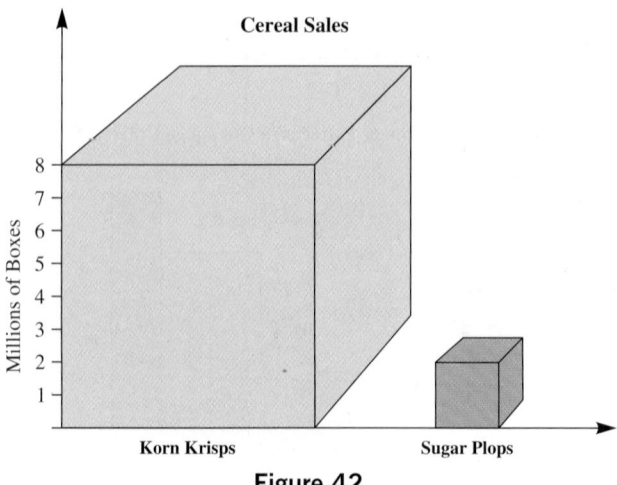

Figure 42

Graphs easily become misleading when attempts are made to depict them as three-dimensional. Many graphs of this type do not acknowledge either the variable thickness of the depiction or the distortion due to perspective. Observe that the 27% sector pictured in Figure 43(a) looks much greater than the 23% sector, although they should be very nearly the same size. In Figure 43(b) the three-dimensional bar graph is more attractive but it is harder to read the true values of the data. These three-dimensional graphs are typically created with computer software.

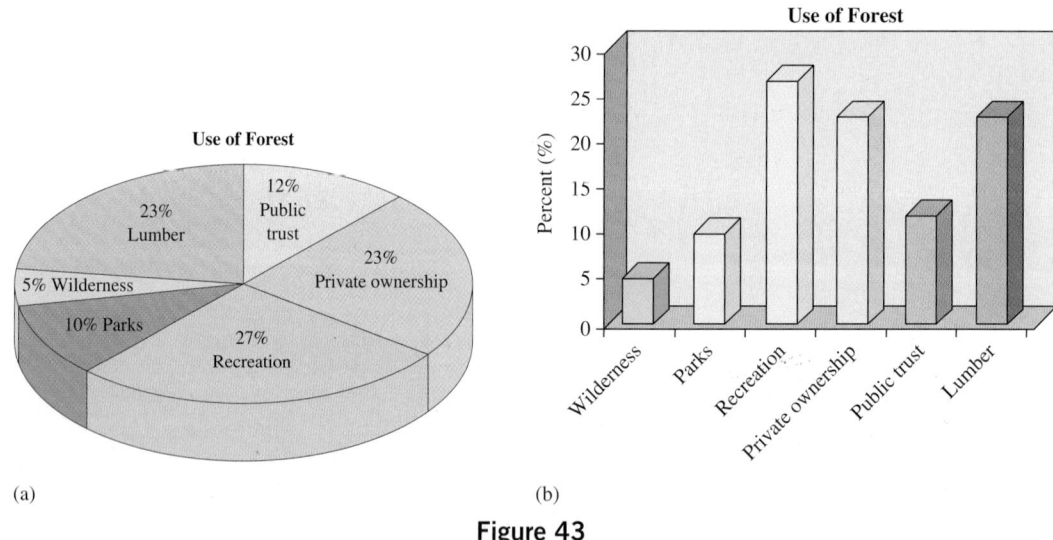

Figure 43

Misuses with Numbers Representing Data

The final examples of the misuses of statistics involve misleading uses of mean, median, and mode. All these are "averages" and can be used to suit a person's purposes. As discussed in Section 10-4 in the example involving the teachers Smith, Jones, and Rivera, each teacher had reported that his or her class had done better than the other two. Each of the teachers used a different number to represent the test scores.

As another example, company administrators wishing to portray to prospective employees a rosy salary picture may find a mean salary of $58,000 for line workers as well as upper management in the schedule of salaries. At the same time, a union that is bargaining for salaries may include part-time employees as well as line workers and will exclude management personnel in order to present a mean salary of $29,000 at the bargaining table. The important thing to watch for when a mean is reported is disparate cases in the reference group. If the sample is small, then a few extremely high or low scores can have a great influence on the mean. Figure 44 shows the salaries of both management and line workers of the company. If the median is being used as the average, then the median might be $43,500, which is representative of neither major group of employees. The bimodal distribution means the median is nonrepresentative of the distribution.

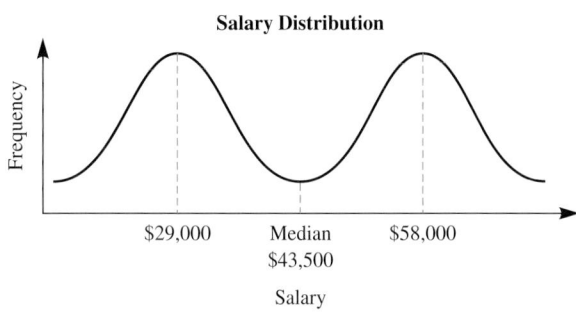

Figure 44

To conclude our comments on the misuse of statistics, consider a quote from Darrell Huff's book *How to Lie with Statistics* (p. 8):

So it is with much that you read and hear. Averages and relationships and trends and graphs are not always what they seem. There may be more in them than meets the eye, and there may be a good deal less.

The secret language of statistics, so appealing in a fact-minded culture, is employed to sensationalize, inflate, confuse, and oversimplify. Statistical methods and statistical terms are necessary in reporting the mass data of social and economic trends, business conditions, "opinion" polls, the census. But without writers who use the words with honesty and understanding and readers who know what they mean, the result can be semantic "nonsense."

Assessment 10-5A

This entire set of assessment items is appropriate for reasoning and cooperative learning. Many items are open-ended and several lend themselves to further investigation. *

1. Find the potential misuse (or abuse) of statistics in the following.
   a. An ad reads, "Work from home. Earn an average of $500 weekly." *
   b. The same five questions appear in the same order on all the questionnaires printed for Acme Foods. *
   c. A company spokesperson made the claim that 3 out of 4 dentists prefer their dental products. *
   d. A news host brought the discussion on an education topic to viewers at home by asking them to send a text message containing a yes/no response to the toll free number displayed on their screen. *
   e. A survey question reads, "Do you support the district's decision to fund the school's much-needed science facility?" *

2. The city of Podunk advertised itself as having the most ideal temperature in the state because its mean temperature was 82°. What possible misconception could people draw from this claim? *

3. A student read that 9 out of 10 pickup trucks sold in the last 10 years are still on the road. She concluded that the average life of a pickup is around 10 yr. Is she correct? *

4. What is wrong with the following line graph? *

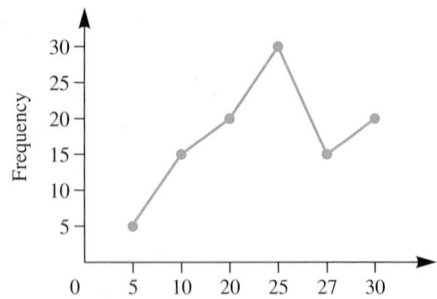

5. Doug's Dog Food Company wanted to impress the public with the magnitude of the company's growth. Sales of Doug's Dog Food had doubled from 2014 to 2015, so the company displayed the following graph, in which the radius of the base and the height of the 2015 can are double those of the 2014 can. What does the graph really show with respect to the growth of the company? (*Hint:* The volume of a cylinder is given by $V = \pi r^2 h$, where r is the radius of the base and h is the height.) *

Doug's Dog Food Sales

2015

2014

6. Refer to the following circle graph.

Drivers in Fatal Accidents

Men   Women

Ms. McNulty claims that on the basis of this information, we can conclude that men are worse drivers than women. Discuss whether you can reach that conclusion from the circle graph or you need more information. If more information is needed, what would you like to know? *

7. Can you draw any conclusion about average secretary salary knowing that the mean annual salary at the company is $100,000? *

8. The following two graphs were prepared by a department store's advertising agency to display a competitor's price of a particular brand of LCD television over the course of six months. Which graph will most likely draw potential customers away from the competition? *

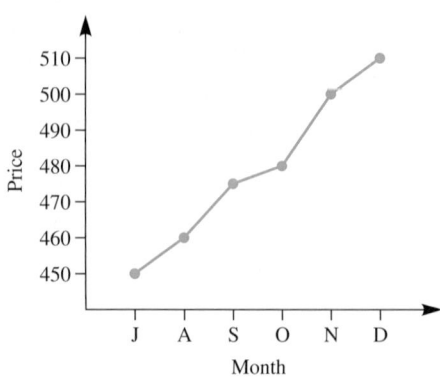

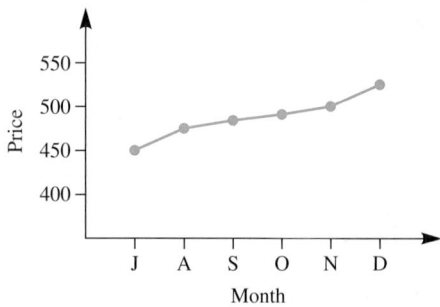

9. The following table gives the number of accidents per year on a certain highway for a 5-yr period.

Year	2011	2012	2013	2014	2015
Number of Accidents	24	26	30	32	38

a. Draw a bar graph to convince people that the number of accidents is on the rise and that something should be done about it. *

b. Draw a bar graph to show that the rate of accidents is almost constant, and that nothing needs to be done. *

10. Write a list of scores for which the mean and median are not representative of the list. *

11. Consider a state such as Montana that has both mountains and prairies. What numbers might you report to depict the height above sea level of such a state? Why? *

12. A student read in the newspaper that the pill form of a drug taken once per day is up to 92% effective in warding off the flu. She concludes that if she takes the pill 8% more times per day, she will be 100% safe from contracting the flu. Explain whether you agree with her and why. *

13. a. Suppose you are a student doing a survey of eating habits in a high school. If you sit in the hall and ask each student who passes you in 1 hr questions about their eating habits, explain whether or not you think you have a representative sample of the school population. *

b. If you are conducting the survey mentioned in part (a) and interview students in the cafeteria at noon, explain whether or not you think that you have a representative sample of the school population. *

c. For this survey, explain how you could choose a sample to be reasonably sure that you got a representative sample of the population. *

14. The following chart lists the number of complaints received about airlines as reported in *The New York Times*, 2010.

Most complaints, 2010	
American	517
Delta	403
United	176
Fewest	
U.S. Airways	131
Southwest Airlines	118
Alaska	62

Discuss whether you think that American, Delta, and United are the worst airlines and U. S. Airways, Southwest, and Alaska are the best based on the above information. *

15. In the graphic shown, two states are compared using their students' SAT scores and the spending ranking per pupil by those states. What are some erroneous conclusions that could be reached? *

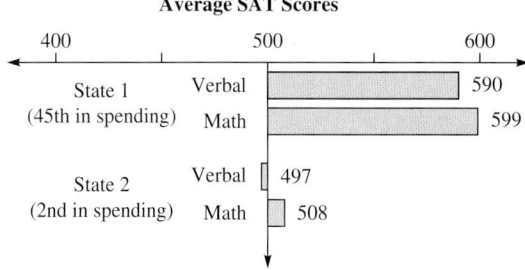

Average SAT Scores

16. Which of the following pieces of information would not be helpful in deciding the type of automobile that is the most economical to drive?   Only part (b) might not be helpful.
   a. Range of insurance costs
   b. Modes of drivers' ages for specific vehicle types
   c. Mean miles per gallon
   d. Typical cost of repairs per year
   e. Cost of routine maintenance

Assessment 10-5B

1. Find the potential misuse (or abuse) of statistics in the following.
   a. A motorcycle manufacturer claims that more than 95% of its cycles sold in the state of Texas in the last 15 years are still on the road. *
   b. The floor manager of a car dealership tells you that a car will get up to 30 mpg. *
   c. A study claims that taking a dietary supplement will reduce cholesterol in some people. *
   d. A sticker on a certain brand of bread reads "40% fresher."   Fresher than what? 40% of what?
   e. More than 95% of the people who fly to a certain city do so on Airline A. Therefore, most people prefer Airline A to other airlines.   Is there another airline flying to the city?
   f. Most accidents occur in the home. Therefore, to be safer, you should stay out of your house as much as possible. *

2. General Cooster once asked a person by the side of a river if the river was too deep to ride his horse across. The person responded that the average depth was 2 ft. If General Cooster rode out across the river, what assumptions did he make on the basis of the person's information? *

3. Jenny read that 80% of those responding to a survey in her school favored 2 hours of homework per night. What, if anything, might be wrong with this claim? *

4. What is wrong with the following line graph? *

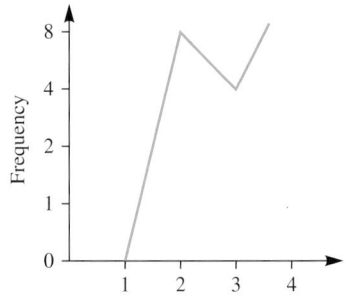

5. A histogram of the data for the number of cars sold by Acme Car Lot is given in Figure (a) below. A three-dimensional version of the histogram as shown in Figure (b) was given out by the company. What is wrong or misleading about the graph in Figure (b)? *

a. **Number of Cars Sold by Acme Car Lot**

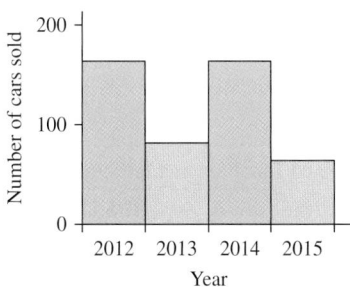

b. **Number of Cars Sold by Acme Car Lot**

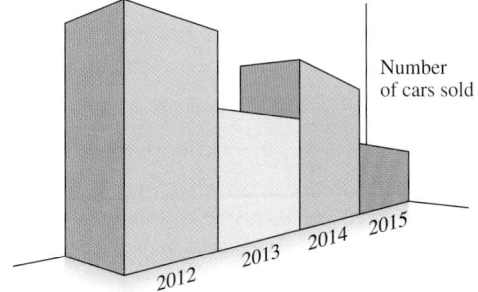

6. Suppose the following circle graphs are used to illustrate the fact that the number of elementary teaching majors at teachers' colleges has doubled between 2005 and 2015, while the percentage of male elementary teaching majors

has stayed the same. What is misleading about the way the graphs are constructed?   *

400 Elementary Teaching Majors   **800 Elementary Teaching Majors**

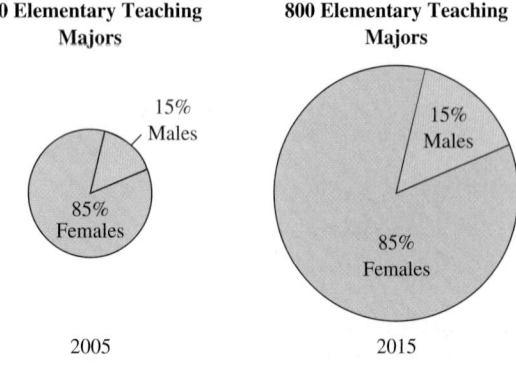

2005   2015

7. Jenny averaged 70 on her quizzes during the first part of the quarter and 80 on her quizzes during the second part of the quarter. When she found out that her final average for the quarter was not 75, she went to argue with her teacher. Give a possible explanation for Jenny's misunderstanding.   *

8. Explain what is wrong with the following graph.   *

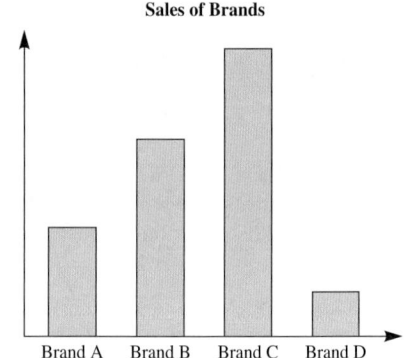

Sales of Brands

9. In a recent survey, teachers rated their mathematics textbooks as shown in the following table.

National Survey of Teachers of Mathematics		
	Grades K–4 (percentage)	Grades 5–8 (percentage)
Very poor	1	2
Poor	3	5
Fair	18	16
Good	35	33
Very good	36	33
Excellent	8	10

At about the same time that the survey was being done, newspapers printed articles saying that national experts in mathematics have been very critical of mathematics textbooks at all levels.

a. What is your reaction to the survey and the reports?   *

b. Does the national survey agree with the newspaper articles? Explain your thinking as you react.   *

10. A student got 99 on a quiz and was ecstatic over the grade. What other information might you need in order to decide if the student was justified in being happy?   *

11. a. Use the following data to justify the amount of time that you expect to assign for weekly homework to classes in grades K–4 and grades 5–8.   *

National Survey of Teachers Concerning the Amount of Homework Assigned per Week		
	K–4 (percentages)	5–8 (percentages)
0–30 min	48	8
31–60 min	27	21
61–90 min	13	26
91–120 min	8	24
2–3 hr	3	17
More than 3 hr	1	5

b. How might the survey data be misused to justify assigning at least 2 hr of homework per week?   *

12. If the mean and the median in a data set are equal can you conclude that the data is symmetric? Justify your answer.   *

13. Write a list of scores for which the mean is representative of the list, but the median is not.   *

14. Is it possible for a state or country to have a mean sea level that is negative? If so, what might such a region look like?   *

15. What are the characteristics that you think a sample might have to have to be representative of an entire population of students at a university?   *

16. The two headlines shown here were written based on exactly the same data set.
"Obesity has increased over 30%."
"On the average, Americans' weight has increased by less than 10 pounds."   *

a. As a reporter, which headline would you use?   *

b. As a reader, which headline would have the greatest impact?   The first headline does grab one's attention.

c. As an educated reader, which headline might you consider the most accurate knowing that both were written based on the same data set? Explain your answer.   *

17. In a British study around 1950, a group of 649 men with lung cancer were surveyed. A control group of the same size was established from a set of men who did not have lung cancer. The groups were matched according to ethnicity, age, and socioeconomic status. The statistics from the survey follow.

	Lung Cancer Cases	Controls	Totals
Smokers	647	622	1269
Nonsmokers	2	27	29

a. What fraction of the men with lung cancer were smokers?   *

b. What fraction of the men in the control group were smokers?   *

c. If one person is chosen at random from each of the two groups (smokers and nonsmokers), what is the probability that a randomly chosen smoker has cancer? What is the probability that a randomly chosen nonsmoker has cancer?   *

d. Do you think that this evidence is conclusive that smoking causes lung cancer?
   (Problem taken from *Statistics Framework*)   *

18. The following graph shows the mean center of population of the United States as it has shifted from 1790 to 2010. Based solely on this graph, could you conclude that the population of the West Coast has increased since 1790?   *

Source: U.S. Bureau of the Census, 2000 Census of Population and Housing, Population and Housing Unit Counts, United States (2010 CPH-2-1).   *

19. In the figure shown, monthly sales of three departments (dairy, fish, produce) are compared. What are some erroneous conclusions that could be reached?   *

Monthly Sales by Department

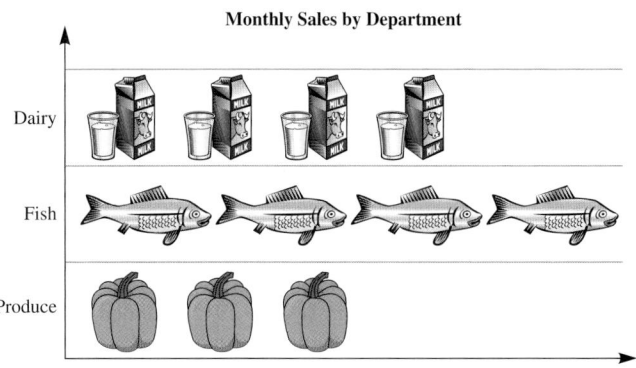

20. Compare the two figures below for impact. What impression does each leave on you? How did the artist go about creating the effect?   *

Monthly Sales in Dollars

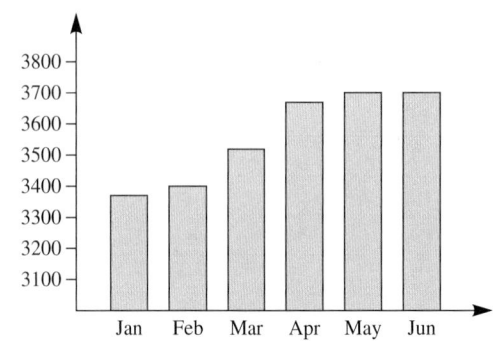

Monthly Sales in Dollars

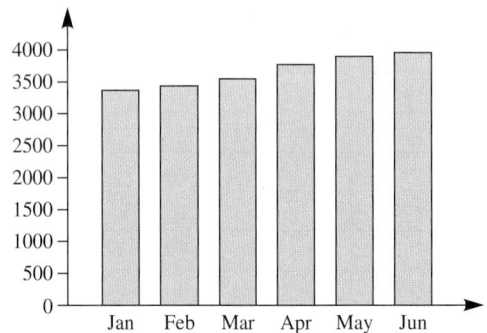

Mathematical Connections 10-5

Answers to Mathematical Connections can be found in the Answers section at the back of the book.

Open-Ended

1. Discuss the effect on the appearance of a graph when its dimensions are changed.

2. Words such as "may" (as in "may help with reading comprehension"), "some" ("lowers heart disease risk in some people"), and "suggest" ("studies suggest. . . .") imply a conclusion that may not be valid in general. Come up with a list of additional such dubious words and give an example of how each can be misused.

Review Problems

3. On the English 100 exam, the scores were as follows:

43	91	73	65
56	77	84	91
82	65	98	65

a. Find the mean.
b. Find the median.
c. Find the mode.

d. Find the variance.
e. Find the standard deviation.
f. Find the mean absolute deviation.
4. If the mean of a set of 36 scores is 27 and two more scores of 40 and 42 are added, what is the new mean?
5. On a certain exam, Tony corrected 10 papers and found the mean for his group to be 70. Alice corrected the remaining 20 papers and found that the mean for her group was 80. What is the mean of the combined group of 30 students?
6. Following are the men's gold-medal times for the 100-m run in the Olympic games from 1896 to 2012, rounded to the nearest tenth of a second. Construct an ordered stem-and-leaf plot for the data.

Year	Time (sec), rounded
1896	12.0
1900	11.0
1904	11.0
1908	10.8
1912	10.8
1920	10.8
1924	10.6
1928	10.8
1932	10.3
1936	10.3
1948	10.3
1952	10.4
1956	10.5
1960	10.2
1964	10.0
1968	10.0
1972	10.1
1976	10.1
1980	10.3
1984	10.0
1988	9.9
1992	9.7
1996	9.8
2000	9.9
2004	9.8
2008	9.7
2012	9.6

7. Following are the record swimming times of the women's 100-m freestyle and 100-m butterfly in the Olympics from 1960 to 2012. Draw parallel box plots of the two sets of data to compare them.

Year	Time—100-m Freestyle (sec)	Time—100-m Butterfly (sec)
1960	61.20	69.50
1964	59.50	64.70
1968	60.00	65.50
1972	58.59	63.34
1976	55.65	60.13
1980	54.79	60.42
1984	55.92	59.26
1988	54.93	59.00
1992	54.64	58.62
1996	54.50	59.13
2000	53.83	56.61
2004	53.84	57.72
2008	53.12	56.73
2012	53.00	55.98

National Assessments

National Assessment of Educational Progress (NAEP) Questions

Elements That Make Up the Earth's Crust

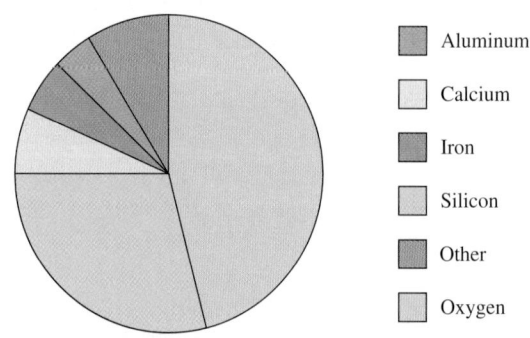

Aluminum
Calcium
Iron
Silicon
Other
Oxygen

According to the graph, which element forms the second greatest portion of the earth's crust?
A. Oxygen
B. Silicon
C. Aluminum
D. Iron
E. Calcium

NAEP, Grade 8, 2007

Richard wants to estimate the average (mean) monthly temperature of the United States last year. He will choose one of the following two methods to do this.

Method I: Richard selects his state and 9 other states that are near his state. Then he finds the average (mean) monthly temperature of each of those 10 states and uses those numbers to compute the average monthly temperature of the United States.

Method II: Richard selects 10 different states by writing the names of all 50 states on cards, with one state's name on each card. Then he places all of the cards in a hat and takes out 10 cards without looking. Finally, he finds the average (mean) monthly temperature of each of those 10 states and uses those numbers to compute the average monthly temperature of the United States.

Which method is better, I or II?

Explain why.

NAEP, Grade 8, 2013

Liz is conducting an experiment to see whether students learn vocabulary words by a new method faster than they learn them by the old method. Fifty students will participate in the experiment. She pairs off the 50 students so that the two students in each pair have similar levels of vocabulary. One student in each pair then learns words by the old method. The other student in the pair learns words by the new method. Why did Liz pair off her 50 students instead of just having all 50 of them use the new method?

NAEP, Grade 8, 2013

Hint for Solving the Preliminary Problem

One way to approach this problem is to start with an example. Suppose the party consisted of 10 people, Calvin being one of them. Make up ages for each of the guests as well as an age for Calvin and compute the mean. Now, pretend you don't know Calvin's age. How can you use what you have to find his age?

Chapter 10 Summary

KEY CONCEPTS	DEFINITIONS, DESCRIPTIONS, AND THEOREMS
Section 10-1	
Variability (p. 537)	The amount by which data differ. Types of variability—*measurement, natural, induced, sampling.*
Population (p. 538)	A group of objects or people in total.
Sample (p. 538)	Any subset of a population.
Simple random sample (p. 539)	A sample such that any subset of the population has the same chance of being the sample as any other subset of the same size.
Section 10-2	
Types of data (p. 546)	*Categorical*—data that represent characteristics of objects or individuals in groups (categories). *Numerical*—data collected on numerical variables.
Representations for data (p. 546)	• *Pictographs* • *Frequency tables* • *Dot plots (line plots)* • *Stem-and-leaf plots* • *Grouped frequency tables* • *Histograms* • *Bar graphs* • *Circle graphs (pie charts)*
Section 10-3	
Line graph (p. 564)	A graph of numerical data that typically shows a variable over time.
Scatterplot (p. 564)	A graph of numerical data that shows a relationship between two variables.
Trend line (p. 567)	A line that closely fits the data in a scatterplot and can be used to describe it.
Types of association between two variables (p. 568)	*Positive association*—when the values of one variable have the tendency to increase as the values of the other variable increase; the trend line slopes upward from left to right. *Negative association*—when the values of one variable have the tendency to decrease as the values of the other variable increase; the trend line slopes downward from left to right. *No association*—when the data points do not approximately fall about any non-horizontal line.
Section 10-4	
Central tendency (p. 577)	Describes where the data are centered in a data set.
Measures of central tendency (p. 578)	*Mean*—the sum of the numbers in a data set divided by the numbers of elements in the set. *Median*—the middle number of a data set if the numbers are arranged in numerical order; if there is no middle number, the median is the mean of the two middle numbers. *Mode*—the data value or values that occur most frequently in a data set; there may be no mode for a data set.

Section 10-4

Spread (or variation) (p. 582)

Describes how much the data are scattered.

Measures of spread (p. 582)

Range—the difference between the greatest and the least values in a data set.

Interquartile range (IQR)—is the difference between the upper quartile and the lower quartile.

Lower quartile—the median of the lower half of all the data values.

Upper quartile—the median of the upper half of all the data values.

Box plot (or box-and-whisker plot) (p. 583)

A graphical summary of the median, the lower and upper quartiles, and the lower and upper extreme values.

Outlier (p. 585)

A value widely separated from the rest of the values in a set of data.

Any value that is more than 1.5 times the IQR above the upper quartile or more than 1.5 times the IQR below the lower quartile.

Measures of variation (or spread) (p. 590)

Mean absolute deviation (MAD)—the mean of the absolute values of the differences between each data value and the mean; that is, the average distance that a data value is from the mean.

Variance—the number found by subtracting the mean from each data value, squaring each of these differences, finding the sum of these squares, and then dividing by the total number of data values in the set.

Standard deviation—the square root of the variance.

Normal curve (p. 592)

A smooth, bell-shaped curve that depicts frequency values distributed symmetrically about the mean, as shown:

Percentiles (p. 595)

Values that shows a specific score relative to other scores in a large distribution.

Percentiles divide a set of data into 100 equal parts.

Deciles (p. 596)

Deciles divide a set of data into 10 equally spaced sections.

Section 10-5

Abuses of statistics (p. 601)

Misleading or dishonest interpretations of data caused by poor sample selections or incorrect population choices, misleading graphs, and misleading uses of mean, median, or mode.

Chapter 10 Review

1. Suppose you read that "the average family in Rattlesnake Gulch has 2.41 children." What average is being used to describe the data? Explain your answer. Suppose the sentence had said 2.5. Then what are the possibilities? *

2. At Bug's Bar-B-Q restaurant, the average (mean) weekly wage for full-time workers is $250. There are 10 part-time employees whose average weekly salary is $100, and the total weekly payroll is $4000. How many full-time employees are there?   12

3. Find the mean, the median, and the mode for each of the following groups of data.
   a. 10, 50, 30, 40, 10, 60, 10 *
   b. 5, 8, 6, 3, 5, 4, 3, 6, 1, 9 *
   c. 100, 100, 100, 100, 200, 200, 200, 200 *
   d. 12.2, 13.7, 11.9, 10.0, 13.2, 11.1, 28.5, 12.1, 12.3, 13.5, 10.1, 10.7, 13.6, 12.9, 11.5, 10.9 *

4. Find the range, mean absolute deviation, interquartile range, variance, and standard deviation for each set of scores in exercise 3. *

5. The mass, in kilograms, of each child in Ms. Rider's class follows.

   40 49 43 48 46 42 49 39 47 49
   42 41 42 39 41 40 45 43 44 42

   a. Make a dot plot for the data. *
   b. Make an ordered stem and leaf plot for the data. *
   c. Make a frequency table for the data. *
   d. Make a bar graph of the data. *

6. The grades on a test for 30 students follow:

   96 73 61   76 77 84
   78 98 98   80 67 82
   61 75 79   90 73 80
   85 63 86   100 94 77
   86 84 91   62 77 64

   a. Make a grouped frequency table for these scores, using four classes and starting the first class at 61. *
   b. Draw a histogram of the grouped data. *

7. The budget for the Wegetem Crime Co. is $2,000,000. Draw a circle graph to indicate how the company spends its money, where $600,000 is spent on bribes, $400,000 for legal fees, $300,000 for bail money, $300,000 for contracts, and $400,000 for public relations. Indicate percentages on your graph. *

8. What, if anything, is wrong with the following bar graph? *

Monthly Health Club Costs

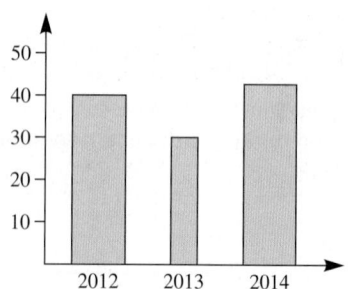

9. The mean salary of 24 people is $9000. How much will one additional salary of $80,000 increase the mean salary? $2840

10. The following data are the gold medal counts from the 2014 Winter Olympics in Sochi. Construct a pie chart for the top 10 countries. *

Rank	Country	Gold
1	Russian Fed	13
2	Norway	11
3	Canada	10
4	United States	9
5	Netherlands	8
6	Germany	8
7	Switzerland	6
8	Belarus	5
9	Austria	4
10	France	4

11. The life expectancies at birth for males and females in the United States are approximated in the following table:

Year	Male	Female	Year	Male	Female
1970	67.1	74.7	1991	72.0	78.9
1971	67.4	75.0	1992	72.1	78.9
1972	67.4	75.1	1993	72.1	78.9
1973	67.6	75.3	1994	72.4	79.0
1974	68.2	75.9	1995	72.5	78.9
1975	68.8	76.6	1996	73.1	79.1
1976	69.1	76.8	1997	73.6	79.2
1977	69.5	77.2	1998	73.8	79.5
1978	69.6	77.3	1999	73.9	79.4
1979	70.0	77.8	2000	74.1	79.3
1980	70.0	77.5	2001	74.2	79.4
1981	70.4	77.8	2002	74.3	79.5
1982	70.9	78.1	2003	74.5	79.6
1983	71.0	78.1	2004	74.9	79.9
1984	71.2	78.2	2005	74.9	79.9
1985	71.2	78.2	2006	75.1	80.2
1986	71.3	78.3	2007	75.4	80.4
1987	71.5	78.4	2008	75.6	80.6
1988	71.5	78.3	2009	76.0	80.9
1989	71.7	78.5	2010	76.2	81.0
1990	71.8	78.8	2011	76.3	81.1

Source: The World Almanac, 2014. National Center for Health Statistics.

a. Draw back-to-back ordered stem and leaf plots to compare the data. *
b. Draw box plots to compare the data. *

12. Larry and Marc took the same courses last quarter. Each bet that he would receive the better grades. Their courses and grades are as follows:

Course	Larry's Grades	Marc's Grades
Math (4 credits)	A	C
Chemistry (4 credits)	A	C
English (3 credits)	B	B
Psychology (3 credits)	C	A
Tennis (1 credit)	C	A

Marc claimed that the results constituted a tie, since both received 2 A's, 1 B, and 2 C's. Larry said that he won the bet because he had the higher grade-point average for the quarter. Who is correct? (Allow 4 points for an A, 3 points for a B, 2 points for a C, 1 point for a D, and 0 points for an F.) *

13. Following are the lengths in yards of the nine holes of the University Golf Course:

$$160 \quad 360 \quad 330$$
$$350 \quad 180 \quad 460$$
$$480 \quad 450 \quad 380$$

Find each of the following measures with respect to the lengths of the holes:
a. Median 360
b. Mode None
c. Mean 350
d. Standard deviation About 108.2
e. Range 320
f. Interquartile range 200
g. Variance About 11,711.1
h. Mean absolute deviation 84.4

14. The speeds in miles per hour of 30 cars were checked by radar. The data are as follows:

$$62 \quad 67 \quad 69 \quad 72 \quad 75 \quad 60 \quad 58 \quad 86 \quad 74 \quad 68$$
$$56 \quad 67 \quad 82 \quad 88 \quad 90 \quad 54 \quad 67 \quad 65 \quad 64 \quad 68$$
$$74 \quad 65 \quad 58 \quad 75 \quad 67 \quad 65 \quad 66 \quad 64 \quad 45 \quad 64$$

a. Find the median. 67 mph
b. Find the upper and lower quartiles. $Q_1 = 64, Q_3 = 74$
c. Draw a box plot for the data and indicate outliers (if any) with asterisks. *
d. If every person driving faster than 70 mph received a ticket, what percentage of the drivers received speeding tickets? 30%
e. Describe the spread of the data. *
f. Find P_{25}, P_{75}, and D_5. 64; 74; 67

15. The following scattergram was developed with information obtained from the girls trying out for the high school basketball team:

Heights and Weights of Girls' Basketball Team Tryout Players

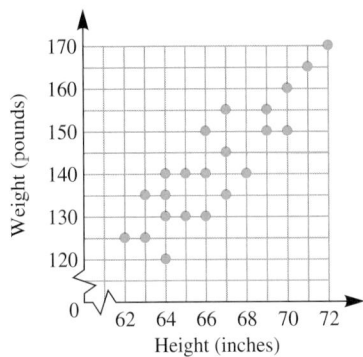

a. What kind of association exists between the heights and weights that are listed? Positive
b. What is the weight of the girl who is 72 in. tall? 170 lbs
c. How tall is the girl who weighs 145 lb? 67 in.
d. What is the mode of the heights? 64 in.
e. What is the range of the weights? 50 lbs

16. The following table shows statistics for two grade-school basketball players. Collette is the leading scorer for the girls, while Rudy is the leading scorer for the boys.

	Collette	Rudy
Mean points per game	24	24
Mean absolute deviation (in points per game)	6	14
Points scored in the final game	36	36

a. Explain whether Collette or Rudy is the more consistent scorer. *
b. For each player, identify the range of values within 1 MAD of the mean. Collette: 18–30; Rudy: 10–38
c. Explain which player's performance was more impressive in the last game. *

17. If the test scores were distributed normally, what is the probability that a student scores more than 2 standard deviations above the mean? 2.5%

18. If every person on an academic team had exactly the same score, describe the following.
a. The mean of the scores The score for each
b. The median of the scores Same as (a)
c. The mode of the scores Same as (a)
d. The standard deviation of the scores 0
e. The mean absolute deviation of the scores 0

19. If one tossed a fair die 500 times and drew a bar graph showing the frequencies of the resulting tosses, describe what you think the graph would look like. *

20. A cereal company has an advertisement on one of its boxes that says, "Lose up to 6 lb in 2 weeks."

   a. How much might a person who weighs 175 lb when he starts the plan expect to weigh in 1 yr if this rate could be continued?   19 lbs.

   b. Explain whether or not you believe your mathematical answer to part (a) is possible for weight loss.   *

   c. A disclaimer on the box says that the "average weight loss is 5.0 lb." On what basis do you think that the cereal company could make the two claims?   *

21. Tell which graph is more appropriate for this data and explain why.   *

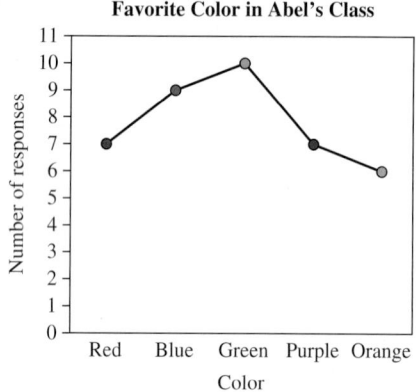

Favorite Color in Abel's Class

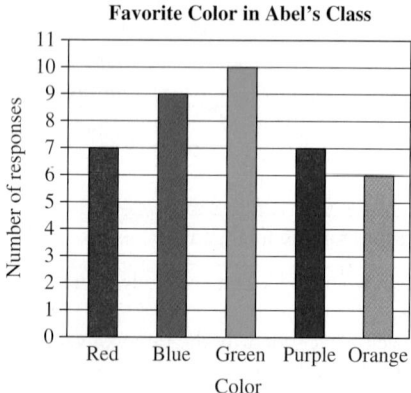

Favorite Color in Abel's Class

22. Explain whether or not it is reasonable to use a single number to describe the "average" depth of a swimming pool that includes a diving pool as a part of the swimming pool.   *

23. A box of cereal is labeled as weighing 138 g. How might the company have determined the weight to make that claim on all comparable boxes to ensure reasonable accuracy of weight?   *

24. a. In box plots showing the ages of students at two different universities, the interquartile range for one was 3 (from 17 to 20) and the other was 5 (from 24 to 29). If you were a typical high school graduating senior and were trying to decide between the two universities using these data, which would you choose and why?   *

   b. If you were a student at one of the two universities and were 23 years old, at which university might you expect to appear belonging to a whisker part in the box plot?   The first

25. From an unlabeled USDA food pyramid such as the one below, how could you come to the erroneous conclusion to eat as many sweets (the top triangle) as diary products?   *

26. The Nielsen Television Index rating of 30 means that an estimated 30% of American televisions are tuned to the show with that rating. The ratings are based on the preferences of a scientifically selected sample of 1200 homes.

   a. Discuss possible ways in which viewers could bias this sample.   *

   b. How could networks attempt to bias the results?   *

27. Give examples of several ways to misuse statistics graphically.   *

28. Given the graph below, answer the following questions.

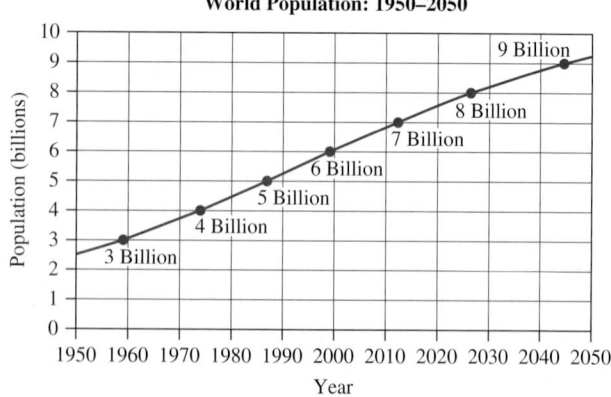

World Population: 1950–2050

Source: U.S. Census Bureau, International Data Base, December 2010 Update.

a. What was the world population in 1959? About 3 billion

b. What was the world population in 1999? About 6 billion

c. What was the growth factor for the 40-year period from 1959 to 1999? The population doubled

d. Estimate the world population in 2049. About 9.3 billion

e. What is the estimated percent growth for the 50-year period from 1999 to 2049? About 55%

29. The heights of 1000 girls at East High School were measured, and the mean was found to be 64 in., with a standard deviation of 2 in. If the heights are approximately normally distributed, about how many of the girls are

a. over 68 in. tall? 25

b. between 60 and 64 in. tall? 475

c. If a girl is selected at random at East High School, what is the probability that she will be over 66 in. tall? 0.16

30. A standardized test has a mean of 600 and a standard deviation of 75. If 1000 students took the test and their scores approximated a normal curve, how many scored between 600 and 750? 475

31. Use the information in problem 30 to find:

a. P_{16} 525

b. D_5 600

c. P_{84} 675

32. The graph below was shown on national television. What is wrong with this graph? *

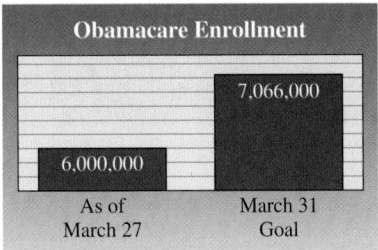

Source: HHS

33. At a class reunion five friends were talking and wanted to know their mean salary. However, not one was willing to tell any of the others any specific salary information. They had a calculator and needed to find a way to compute the mean salary without anyone revealing any person's salary to the other four. How could it be done? *

Introductory Geometry

Preliminary Problem

A graphic designer needs to know the measurement of each of the shaded angles at the vertices of the 5-pointed star shown below. All the sides and all the shaded angles are congruent. How can he find the exact measurement of the angles without using a protractor?

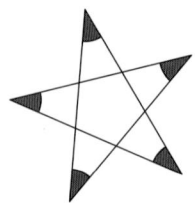

If needed, see Hint on page 695.

The origins of geometry date back to ancient Egypt, when yearly flooding of the Nile River required resurveys of surrounding land for taxation purposes. Later, the Babylonians added to geometrical knowledge with an approximation of π. Centuries later, two Greek words—*geo* ("earth") and *metron* ("measure")—were combined to give this science of land measurement a name. With the work of the Greek geometer Euclid (ca. 300 BCE), geometry began to move from the practical to the theoretical, as revealed in his *Elements* (see historical note on page 622). Euclid began with a list of statements called *axioms* or *postulates* that he assumed to be true and then showed that geometric statements followed directly from his assumptions. Euclid defined a *point* as that which has no part and a line as "breadthless length," but neither "part" nor "breadth" were defined. Over the years, geometry progressed from providing the knowledge of surveying, to measurements between planets, to Mandelbrot's work with fractals.

In the early grades, *Common Core Standards* recommends that students begin to analyze, create, compare, and compose shapes (kindergarten, p. 10), reason with shapes (grades 1–3, pp. 14, 19, 22), identify lines and angles (grade 4, p. 28), and classify two-dimensional figures (grade 5, p. 32). All of these topics and more are addressed in this chapter.

Much of the geometry instruction in U.S. schools in the past several decades is based, at least in part, on the 1950s research of two Dutch educators, Dina van Hiele-Geldof (?–1959) and her husband, Pierre van Hiele (1909–2010). The pair identified five levels through which students may progress in developing geometric reasoning. The levels are hierarchical and sequential so that to obtain one level, students are presumed to have passed through all preceding levels. However, other research suggests that with different experiences and instruction, individual students may be at different levels with different geometrical topics. The following van Hiele levels have been adapted based on additional work by Clements and Battista[1] (1992) and Battista[2] (2007):

Level 1: Visual-Holistic Reasoning

At this level, students identify, describe, and reason about geometrical objects based on appearance as whole objects. For example, a rectangle may be described as such because it looks like a carpet runner. Some students in this level are able to identify common shapes, while others are not.

Level 2: Descriptive-Analytic Reasoning

At this level, students may describe structures by analyzing shape parts; their definitions are typically not minimal; they begin to use more formal geometric concepts to consider relationships among parts of geometric structures or figures. Still at this level, language and descriptions vary widely in sophistication.

Level 3: Relational-Inferential Reasoning

At this level, students begin to infer relationships among shapes or figures. Much of this inference is based upon empirical evidence and looking at some cases. Simple logical inferences begin to be made and increasingly students begin to develop minimal definitions, but the sophistication levels of students still vary widely.

Level 4: Formal Deductive Proof

At this level, students can produce proofs in an axiomatic system. It is at this level that most secondary high school geometry courses are taught.

Level 5: Rigor

At this level, students understand and can use alternative axiomatic systems, typically found at the university level.

[1]Clements, D., and M. Battista. "Geometry and Spacial Reasoning." In *Handbook of Research on Mathematics Teaching and Learning*, edited by D. Grouws. New York: MacMillan, 1992.

[2]Battista, M. "The Development of Geometry and Spatial Thinking." In *Second Handbook of Research on Mathematics Teaching and Learning*, edited by F. Lester, Jr. Charlotte, NC: Information Age Publishing, 2007.

Legend says that Euclid of Alexandria (ca. 300 BCE) studied geometry for its beauty and logic. He is best known for the *Elements*, a work so systematic and encompassing that many earlier mathematical works were discarded. The *Elements*, comprising 13 books, includes not only geometry but also arithmetic and topics in algebra. In the *Elements*, Euclid developed a deductive system by starting with a set of statements, assumed to be true, and then showed that geometric discoveries followed logically from these assumptions. ●

Though the van Hieles influenced geometric study in the United States, their theory is only one of many. Prospective teachers in grades K–8 should understand that other research, beyond the van Hieles', has been done to examine geometrical learning.

11-1 Basic Notions

11-1 Objectives

Students will be able to understand and explain

- Basic undefined and defined terms of geometry.

- Basic geometrical shapes and learn the notation associated with each shape.

- Attributes and properties of basic geometrical shapes and the relationships among them.

- Names, classifications, and measurement of angles.

The fundamental building blocks of geometry are *points*, *lines*, and *planes*. Ironically, the building blocks are *undefined terms* in order to avoid circular definitions. Instead of defining *point*, *line*, and *plane*, we describe the relationships among them. An intuitive notion and notation of these undefined terms appears in the illustrations of Table 1.

Table 1

Term/Symbolism	Illustration
points A, B, and C	
line ℓ	
line m, line AB, $\overleftrightarrow{AB}$, or $\overleftrightarrow{BA}$	
plane α	
plane ABC or plane γ	

A mathematical point has no size. It only has location. Drawings of points are simply models representing points. A line extends forever in two directions, but has no thickness, and *it is uniquely determined by two points; that is, given two distinct points, there is one, and only one, line that connects these points.* A basic concept in geometry is that of a *distance.* If P and Q are any two distinct points, we create a number line $\overleftrightarrow{PQ}$ such that there is one-to-one correspondence between the points on the line and real numbers. Moreover, if P corresponds to the real number 0 and Q corresponds to a positive real number, the **distance** between P and Q, written PQ, is the real number that corresponds to Q. Table 2 illustrates and defines many commonly used terms in geometry.

Statements that cannot be proven are **axioms**. Some axioms of Euclidean geometry follow:

1. Axiom: There is exactly one line that contains any two distinct points.
2. Axiom: If two points lie in a plane, then the line containing the points lies in the plane.
3. Axiom: There is exactly one plane that contains any three distinct noncollinear points.

Theorems are statements that can be deduced using logic, undefined terms, axioms, definitions, and previously proved theorems. In mathematics, a *definition* is stated as simply as possible

Table 2	
Term	**Illustration and Symbolism**
Collinear points are points on the same line.	 Line ℓ contains points A, B, and C. Points A, B, and C belong to line ℓ. Points A, B, and C are collinear. Points A, B, and D are not collinear (or are noncollinear).
If A, B, and C are three distinct collinear points, then B is **between** A and C if, and only if, $AB + BC = AC$.	 Point D is not between A and C. AB is the distance between points A and B.
A **line segment**, or **segment**, is a subset of a line that contains two points of the line and all points between those two points.	 $\overline{AB}$ or $\overline{BA}$ (closed segment)
Subsets of segments that are sometimes identified include a **closed segment** (a segment with endpoints), a **half-open** or **half-closed segment** (a segment without one endpoint) and an **open segment** (a segment without its endpoints).	 $\overline{AB}$ (half-open or half-closed segment) $\overline{AB}$ (open segment)
A ray, $\overrightarrow{AB}$, is a subset of the line, $\overleftrightarrow{AB}$, that contains the endpoint A, the point B, all the points between A and B, and all points C on the line such that B is between A and C.	 $\overleftrightarrow{AB}$ contains $\overrightarrow{AB}$ $\overrightarrow{BA}$ and $\overrightarrow{BC}$ are **opposite rays.**
A **half-line** is a ray without the endpoint. A point separates a line into three parts: two half-lines and the point itself.	 Parts of $\overleftrightarrow{AC}$ are: half-line BA, denoted $\overset{\circ}{\overrightarrow{BA}}$; half-line BC, denoted $\overset{\circ}{\overrightarrow{BC}}$; and point B.

with properties that can be proven omitted. Sometimes a geometric object can be defined in different ways, but they must be consistent in usage.

▶ **NOW TRY THIS 1**

NTT 1: Answers can be found in Answers at the back of the book.

a. Explain whether every three points must be collinear.
b. In Table 2, it is stated that B is between points A and C if A, B, and C are collinear and $AB + BC = AC$. If A, B, and C are three different points, is it possible to have $AB + BC = AC$ and to have the points noncollinear?
c. If we think of lines, segments, and rays as sets of points, find:

    i. $\overline{AB} \cup \overline{BA}$ **iii.** $\overleftrightarrow{AB} \cup \overleftrightarrow{BA}$ **v.** $\overleftrightarrow{AB} \cap \overrightarrow{AB}$
    ii. $\overline{AB} \cap \overline{BA}$ **iv.** $\overleftrightarrow{AB} \cup \overrightarrow{AB}$ **vi.** $\overleftrightarrow{AB} \cap \overleftrightarrow{BA}$

Problem Solving   **Lines Through Points**

Given 15 points, no three of which are collinear, how many lines are determined by pairs of those points?

Understanding the Problem Because two points determine exactly one line, we consider ways to find out how many lines are determined by 15 points, no 3 of which are collinear.

Devising a Plan We use the strategy of *examining related simpler cases* of the problem in order to think through the original problem. Figure 1 shows that 3 noncollinear points determine 3 lines, 4 determine 6 lines, 5 determine 10 lines, and 6 determine 15 lines.

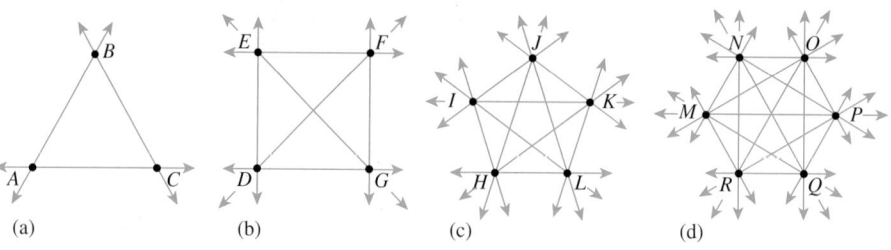

(a)   (b)   (c)   (d)

Figure 1

Examining Figure 1(d), we see that through any one of the 6 points, we draw only 5 lines to connect to the other 5 points. If 5 lines are drawn through each point, there seem to be $6 \cdot 5$, or 30, lines. But in this approach, each line is counted twice; for example, $\overleftrightarrow{NO}$ is counted as 1 of the 5 lines through N and also as 1 of the 5 lines through O. Thus, there are $\dfrac{6 \cdot 5}{2}$, or 15, lines in the figure. We use this information to determine the solution for 15 points.

Carrying Out the Plan Each of the 15 points can be paired with all points other than itself to determine a line; that is, each point can be paired with the other 14 points to determine 14 lines. If we do this and account for counting each line twice, we see that there are $\dfrac{15 \cdot 14}{2} = 105$ lines.

Looking Back Using the above reasoning, the number of lines determined by n points, no 3 of which are collinear, is $\dfrac{n(n-1)}{2}$.

An alternative solution to this problem uses the notion of combinations found in Chapter 9. The number of ways that n points, no 3 of which are collinear, can be chosen 2 at a time to form lines is $_nC_2$, or $\dfrac{n(n-1)}{2}$.

Another approach also uses the strategy of *solving a simpler problem*. Two points determine exactly 1 line. When we add a third point so that the 3 points are not collinear as in Figure 1(a), we connect that point to the 2 existing points and create 2 new lines for a total of $1 + 2$ lines. When a fourth point is added (so that no 3 of the 4 points are collinear), it can be connected to the 3 existing points to obtain 3 additional lines, for a total of $1 + 2 + 3$ lines. Continuing in this way so that no 3 points are collinear, when the 15th point is added to the existing 14 points, 14 new lines are created for a total of $1 + 2 + 3 + \ldots + 14$ lines. Using what we know about the sum of an arithmetic sequence we get

$$1 + 2 + 3 + \ldots + 14 = \frac{14(14 + 1)}{2} = \frac{14 \cdot 15}{2} = 105 \text{ lines.}$$

In general, when the nth point is added, we connect it to the $n - 1$ existing points to obtain $n - 1$ new lines. Using the formula for the sum of an arithmetic sequence developed in Chapter 8, the number of lines determined by n points, no 3 of which are collinear, is

$$1 + 2 + 3 + \ldots + (n - 1) = \frac{(n - 1)(n - 1 + 1)}{2} = \frac{(n - 1)n}{2}.$$

Planar Notions

A plane has no thickness, extends indefinitely, and *is uniquely determined by three noncollinear points*. In other words, *given three distinct noncollinear points, there is one, and only one, plane that contains these points*. Table 3 illustrates and defines intuitive planar notions.

Table 3	
Term	**Illustration and Symbolism**
Coplanar points are points in the same plane.	Points D, E, and G are coplanar.
Noncoplanar points cannot be placed in a single plane.	Points D, E, G, and F are noncoplanar.
Coplanar lines are lines in the same plane.	$\overleftrightarrow{DE}$, $\overleftrightarrow{DF}$, and $\overleftrightarrow{FE}$ are coplanar. $\overleftrightarrow{DE}$, $\overleftrightarrow{DG}$, and $\overleftrightarrow{EG}$ are coplanar.
Intersecting lines are lines with exactly one point in common.	$\overleftrightarrow{DE}$ and $\overleftrightarrow{GE}$ are intersecting lines; they intersect at point E.
Skew lines are lines that cannot be contained in a single plane; they are noncoplanar.	$\overleftrightarrow{GF}$ and $\overleftrightarrow{DE}$ are skew lines.
Concurrent lines are lines that intersect in a single point.	$\overleftrightarrow{DE}$, $\overleftrightarrow{EG}$, and $\overleftrightarrow{EF}$ are concurrent.
Two distinct coplanar lines are **parallel** if they have no point in common. A line is parallel to itself. Two segments or rays are parallel if they lie on parallel lines.	m is parallel to n, written $m \parallel n$; also, $m \parallel m$ and $n \parallel n$.

Table 4 depicts relationships among planes and lines.

Table 4

Term	Illustration and Symbolism
Two distinct **planes that intersect** have a single line in common.	 $\alpha \cap \beta = \overleftrightarrow{AB}$
Two distinct planes are **parallel** if they are not intersecting planes. A plane is parallel to itself. A line is either wholly contained in a plane, intersects it in one point, or has no points in common with the plane.	 $\alpha \parallel \beta$ $\overleftrightarrow{FG} \cap \alpha = \{F\}$ $\overleftrightarrow{FG} \cap \beta = \{G\}$ $\overleftrightarrow{HG} \subseteq \beta$ $\overleftrightarrow{HG} \cap \alpha = \varnothing$
A line and a plane are **parallel** if their intersection is the empty set (they do not intersect) or if the line is in the plane.	 $\ell \parallel \alpha; \; m \parallel \alpha$
A line contained in a plane separates the plane into three mutually disjoint sets: two half-planes and the line itself. A **half-plane** is a subset of a plane that consists of all points in the plane on one side of a line.	 ℓ separates plane α into half-planes, $A\text{-}\overleftrightarrow{BC}$ and $D\text{-}\overleftrightarrow{BC}$, and $\overleftrightarrow{BC}$.

▶ NOW TRY THIS 2

Just as a point separates a line into three parts, a line separates a plane into three parts: the line and two half-planes as shown in Table 4. Two lines can separate a plane into a maximum of 4 parts, and so on. Figure 2 shows the first few cases. Conjecture an expression for the maximum number of regions into which n lines in a plane separate the plane, if the lines themselves are not included. $\frac{n^2}{2} + \frac{n}{2} + 1$ is a correct conjecture.

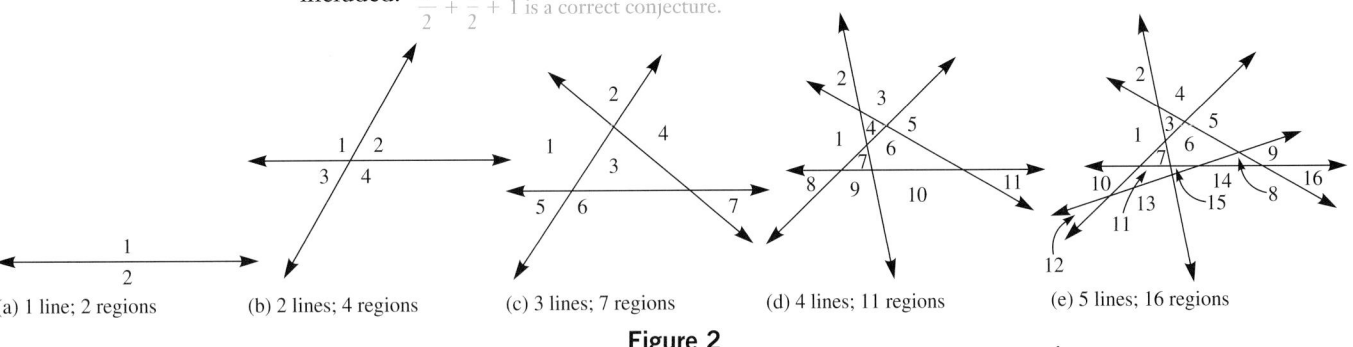

(a) 1 line; 2 regions   (b) 2 lines; 4 regions   (c) 3 lines; 7 regions   (d) 4 lines; 11 regions   (e) 5 lines; 16 regions

Figure 2

▶ NOW TRY THIS 3

NTT 3: Answers can be found in Answers at the back of the book.

a. Can skew lines have a point in common? Why?
b. Can skew lines be parallel? Why?
c. Identify skew and parallel lines among the lines marked in Figure 3.

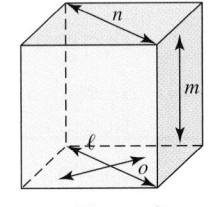

o contains a diagonal of the base

Figure 3

Angles

The concept of an **angle** in geometry has many interpretations, including the idea of rotation and a subset of a plane formed by rays. More definition are given in Table 5.

Table 5	
An **angle** is the union of two distinct rays that share only an endpoint. The rays of the angle are the **sides** of the angle, and the common endpoint is the **vertex** of the angle.	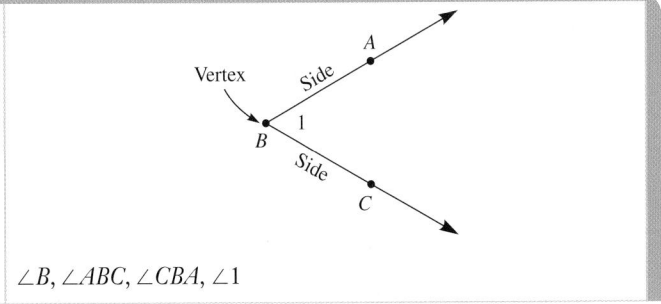
	$\angle B, \angle ABC, \angle CBA, \angle 1$

(continued)

Table 5 (*continued*)	
The **interior of an angle** whose sides do not lie in a straight line is the region in the plane encompassed by the two sides of the angle. The interior of $\angle ABC$ is the set of all points in the intersection of the half-plane determined by $\overleftrightarrow{BC}$ and point A, and the half-plane determined by $\overleftrightarrow{AB}$ and point C.	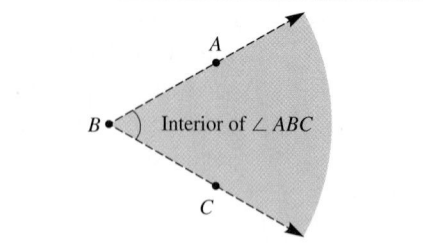 Points A, B, and C are not in the interior of $\angle ABC$.
Adjacent angles are angles that share a common vertex and a common side, but whose interiors do not overlap.	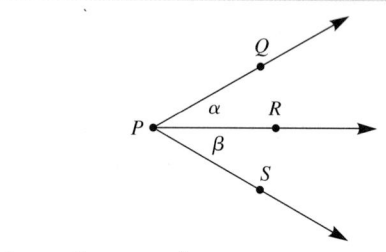 α and β are adjacent angles.

Angle Measurement

An angle is measured by the amount of "opening" between its sides. The **degree** is commonly used to measure angles. A complete rotation about a point has a measure of 360 degrees, written 360°. One degree is $\frac{1}{360}$ of a complete rotation. Figure 4 shows that $\angle BAC$ has a measure of 30 degrees, written $m(\angle BAC) = 30°$. The measuring device pictured in the figure is a **protractor**. A degree is subdivided into 60 equal parts—**minutes**—and each minute is further divided into 60 equal parts—**seconds**. The measurement 29 degrees, 47 minutes, 13 seconds is written 29°47′13″.

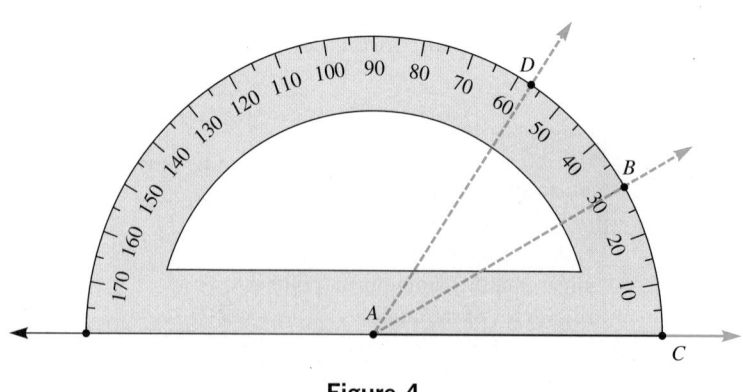

Figure 4

▶ NOW TRY THIS 4

NTT 4: Answers can be found in Answers at the back of the book.

Convert 8.42° to degrees, minutes, and seconds.

Historical Note

The French mathematician and astronomer Pierre Herigone (1580–1643) used a symbol for angle in 1634 and the Mathematical Association of America recommended this symbol to become the standard for angle in the United States in 1923. The use of 360° to measure angles seems to date to the Babylonians (4000–3000 BCE).

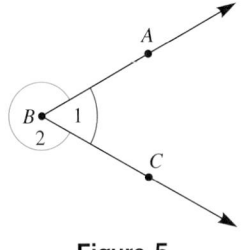

Figure 5

The protractor in Figure 4 shows measures from 0° to 180°, but by the definition of an angle from Table 4, there is no reason to limit the measure of an angle as the protractor shows. When we refer to an angle, as ∠*ABC* in Figure 5, we typically mean the "smaller" of the two openings (pictured as ∠1), but we could also refer to ∠2. The "larger" opening, one whose measure is greater than 180° but less than 360°, is a **reflex angle**.

To measure a reflex angle, a circular protractor as in Figure 6 is sometimes used. Instead of being marked from 0 to 360 degrees, this model is marked from 0 to 90 on quarters.

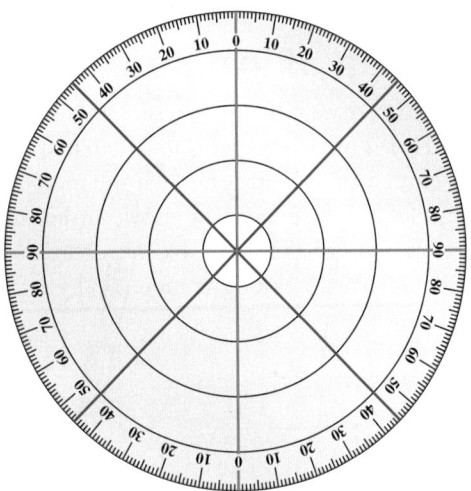

Figure 6

Example 1

a. In Figure 7, find the measure of ∠*BAC* if $m(\angle 1) = 47°45'$ and $m(\angle 2) = 29°58'$.

b. Express $47°45'36''$ as a number of degrees.

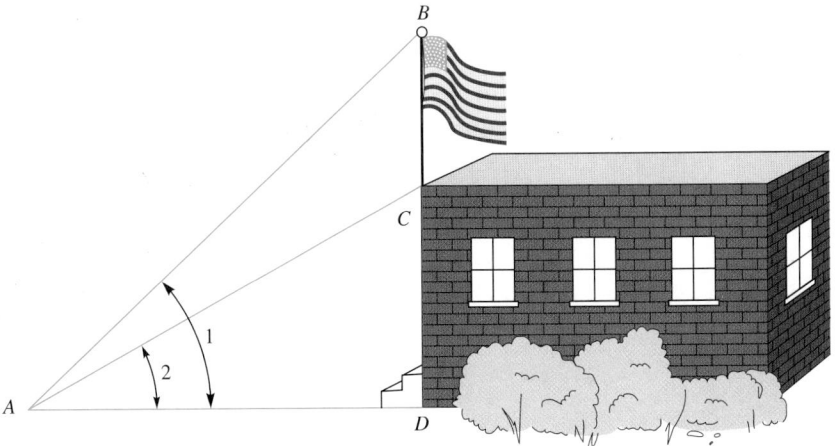

Figure 7

Solution

a. $m(\angle BAC) = 47°45' - 29°58'$
$= 46°(60 + 45)' - 29°58'$
$= 46°105' - 29°58'$
$= (46 - 29)° + (105 - 58)'$
$= 17°47'$

b. $45' = \left(\dfrac{45}{60}\right)° = 0.75°$

$36'' = \left(\dfrac{36}{60}\right)' = \left(\dfrac{1}{60} \cdot \dfrac{36}{60}\right)°$
$= 0.01°$

Thus, $47°45'36'' = 47° + 0.75° + 0.01° = 47.76°$.

$1° = 60'$

Types of Angles

We can create different types of angles by paperfolding. Consider the folds shown in Figure 8(a) and (b). A piece of paper is folded in half and then reopened. If any point on the fold line, labeled ℓ, is chosen as the vertex O, then the measure of the angle pictured is 180°. If the paper is refolded and folded once more, as shown in Figure 8(c), and then is reopened, as shown in Figure 8(d), four angles of the same size are created. Each angle has measure 90° and is a right angle. The symbol ⌐ denotes a right angle. (Why is the measure of each of these angles 90°?)

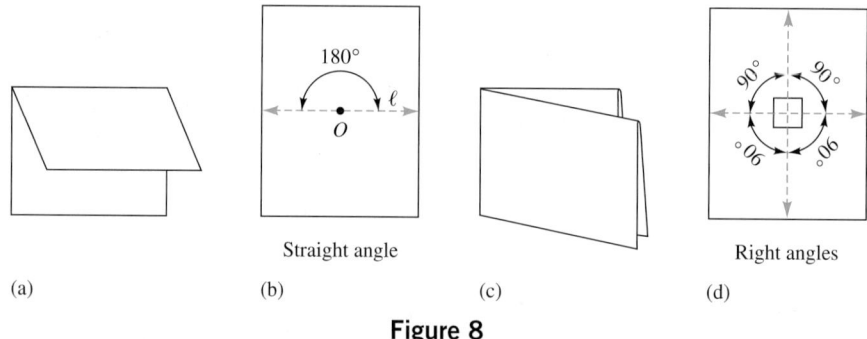

(a)   (b) Straight angle   (c)   (d) Right angles

Figure 8

If the paper is folded as shown in Figure 9 and reopened, then angles α and β are formed with measures that are less than 90° and greater than 90°, respectively. (Note that angle β has measure less than 180°.) Angle α is an **acute** angle, and angle β is an **obtuse** angle. In Figure 9(b), the measures of angles α and β sum to 180°. Any two angles the sum of whose measures is 180° are **supplementary** angles. We say that each angle is a **supplement** of the other.

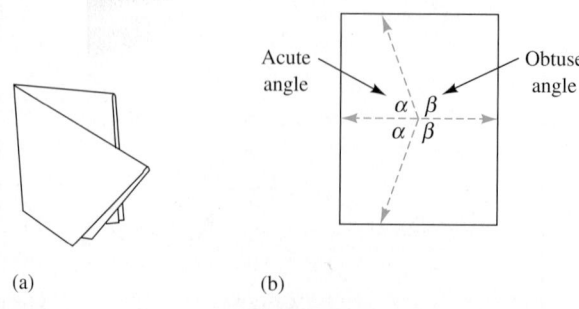

(a)   (b)

Figure 9

The types of planar angles and their definitions are shown in Figure 10.

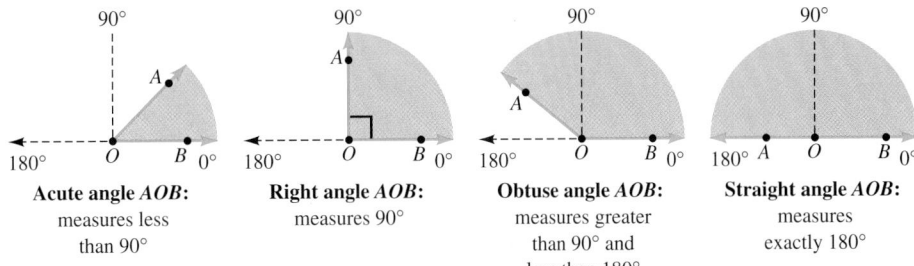

Acute angle *AOB*:
measures less
than 90°

Right angle *AOB*:
measures 90°

Obtuse angle *AOB*:
measures greater
than 90° and
less than 180°

Straight angle *AOB*:
measures
exactly 180°

Figure 10

A straight angle can be described without referring to degree measure: *A straight angle is an angle whose sides are opposite rays forming a straight line.* A model of a straight angle can be obtained by folding a page in half, as previously shown in Figure 8.

Circles and Angle Measurement

In higher mathematics and in scientific applications, an angle may be viewed as being created by a ray rotating about its endpoint. If the ray makes one full rotation, it sweeps an angle of 360°. Angles with positive measure are created by a counterclockwise rotation, and angles with negative measure by a clockwise rotation. Angles whose measures are greater than 360° are created when the ray makes more than one full rotation about its endpoint.

Circles and Arcs

If an angle were to be viewed as being created by a ray rotating around its endpoint, we might also consider a point (not the endpoint) and the path that it follows as the ray rotates. The path produced by the point is one of the most pleasing shapes in geometry, the **circle**. Not only did circles intrigue ancient mathematicians, they continue to fascinate people around the world as seen in the crop circle from Sweden in Figure 11.

Figure 11

A **circle** *is the set of all points in a plane that are the same distance (the **radius**) from a given point (the **center**). An* **arc** *of a circle is any part of the circle that can be drawn without lifting a pencil.* A circle and associated arcs are shown in Figure 12(b).

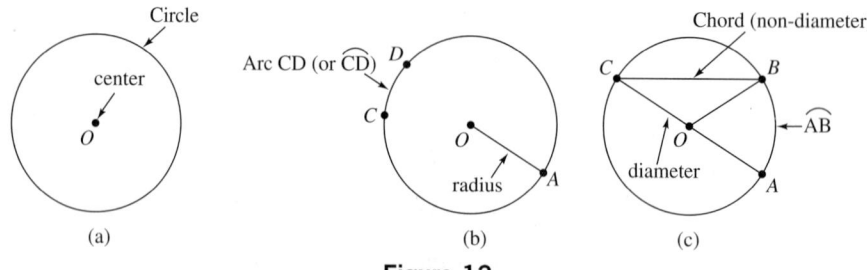

Figure 12

In Figure 12(a), we refer to circle O to indicate all points on the circle. *Radius* is a term frequently used to name any segment with one endpoint at the center of the circle and the other endpoint on the circle, as well as the length of that segment. For example, in Figure 12(b), $\overline{OA}$ is a radius of circle O and refers to the segment with endpoints O and A, while OA refers to the length of that segment. In a similar way, any segment with endpoints on the circle is a **chord** of the circle. If a chord contains the center of the circle, it is a **diameter** of the circle. "Diameter" can also refer to the length of the segment depending on the context in which the term is used. In Figure 12(c) $\overline{AC}$ is a diameter of circle O while $\overline{BC}$ is a chord but not a diameter.

Additionally, in Figure 12(c), arc AB (denoted $\overarc{AB}$) is considered to have center O because it is a part of circle O. $\overarc{AB}$ is associated with $\angle AOB$, a **central angle** of circle O. A central angle of a circle has its vertex at the center of the circle. Figure 13 shows some arcs and associated central angles. Arcs are frequently measured in degrees. The degree measure of an arc is the measure of the associated central angle. This is not the same as the *length* of an arc which depends on the size of the circle.

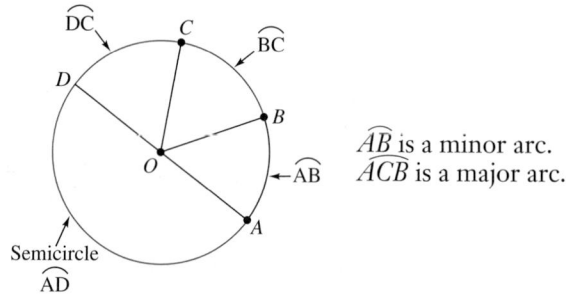

$\overarc{AB}$ is a minor arc.
$\overarc{ACB}$ is a major arc.

Figure 13

In Figure 13, central angle $\angle AOB$ determines two arcs, $\overarc{AB}$ and $\overarc{ACB}$, a minor and major arc, respectively. A **minor arc** is one determined by a central angle whose measure is less than 180°, while a **major arc** is determined by a reflex angle whose measure is greater than 180°. Depending on the context, *a central angle and its associated arc have the same degree measure.*

An arc determined by a diameter is a **semicircle**. A semicircle of circle O in Figure 13 also is considered to have center O.

Example 2

Find the following in Figure 14.

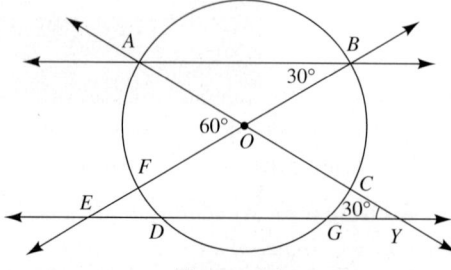

Figure 14

a. $m(\widehat{AB})$ associated with central angle AOB
b. $m(\widehat{AF})$ associated with central angle AOF
c. $m(\widehat{BC})$ associated with central angle BOC
d. $m(\widehat{FDC})$ associated with central angle FOC

Solution
a. $m(\widehat{AB}) = 180° - 60° = 120°$ **b.** $m(\widehat{AF}) = m(\angle AOF) = 60°$
c. $m(\widehat{BC}) = m(\angle BOC) = 60°$ **d.** $m(\widehat{FDC}) = 180° - 60° = 120°$

Perpendicular Lines

When two lines intersect so that the angles formed are right angles, as in Figure 15, the lines are **perpendicular lines**. In Figure 15 where lines m and n are perpendicular, we write $m \perp n$. Note the use of the "⌐" symbol to indicate a right angle. Two intersecting segments, two intersecting rays, one segment and one ray, a segment and a line, or a ray and a line that intersect are perpendicular if they lie on perpendicular lines. For example, in Figure 15, $\overline{AB} \perp \overline{BC}$, $\overrightarrow{BA} \perp \overrightarrow{BC}$, and $\overleftrightarrow{AB} \perp \overrightarrow{BC}$.

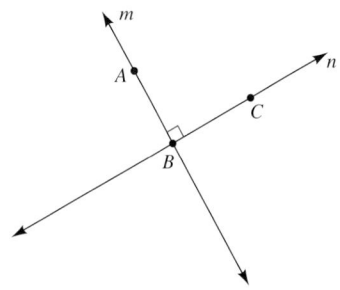

Figure 15

▶ **NOW TRY THIS 5**

Consider the construction of perpendicular lines with paper folding in Figure 16 and answer the questions that follow.

 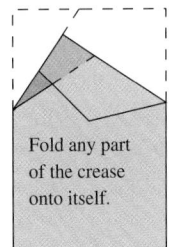 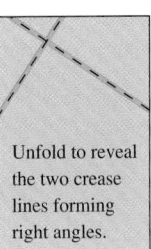

Figure 16

a. Explain why the two crease lines are perpendicular.
b. Use a sheet of paper and follow the instructions in Figure 16 to create two pairs of perpendicular lines.
c. Use paper folding to create angles with the following measures:
   i. 45°   **ii.** 135°   **iii.** 22°30′
d. Cut out a large circle; fold it in half by creasing along a line through the center of the circle. Fold the resulting half circle in half again. Unfold and tell what is the measure of the smallest angle created by the creases.
e. Suppose you continue folding in half as in part (d); what is the measure of the smallest angle created after three folds?
f. What is the measure of the smallest angle created after n folds?

A Line Perpendicular to a Plane

If a line and a plane intersect, they can be perpendicular. For example, in Figure 17, planes β and γ represent two walls. The intersection of planes γ and β is part of $\overleftrightarrow{AB}$. The edge $\overleftrightarrow{AB}$ is perpendicular to the floor. Also, every line in the plane of the floor (plane α) passing through point A is perpendicular to $\overleftrightarrow{AB}$. A **line perpendicular to a plane** is a line that is perpendicular to every line in the plane through its intersection with the plane.

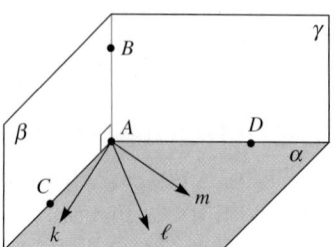

Figure 17

▶ **NOW TRY THIS 6**

NTT 6: Answers can be found in Answers at the back of the book.

   a. Is it possible for a line intersecting a plane to be perpendicular to exactly one line in the plane through its intersection with the plane? Explain by making an appropriate drawing.

   b. Is it possible for a line intersecting a plane to be perpendicular to two distinct lines in a plane going through its point of intersection with the plane, and yet not be perpendicular to the plane?

   c. Can a line be perpendicular to infinitely many lines?

   d. If a line ℓ intersecting a plane α at point A is perpendicular to two distinct lines in the plane through A, what seems to be true about ℓ and α?

Perpendicular Planes and Dihedral Angles

If we view Figure 18(a) as the union of two half-planes with common line AD, we have a **dihedral angle** that measures 90°; one way to denote the angle is Q-AD-S. Figure 18(a) shows two perpendicular planes α and β, which can be modeled by two pages of a book opened at 90°. If $\overline{AB}$ and $\overline{AC}$ represent edges of the book, then each is perpendicular to the binding $\overline{AD}$, and $\angle BAC$ is a right angle. If P is any point on $\overleftrightarrow{AD}$, Q is in plane α, and S is in plane β so that $\overrightarrow{PQ} \perp \overleftrightarrow{AD}$ and $\overrightarrow{PS} \perp \overleftrightarrow{AD}$, then $\angle QPS$ is also a right angle. Since $\angle QPS$ measures 90°, we say that the **planes are perpendicular.**

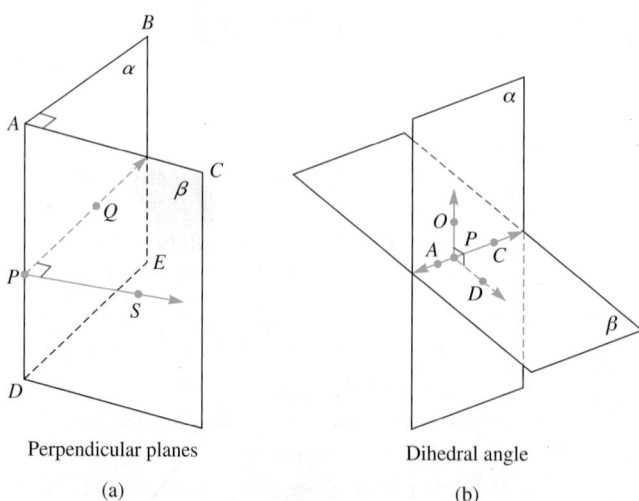

Perpendicular planes

(a)

Dihedral angle

(b)

Figure 18

In general, a *dihedral angle is formed by the union of two half-planes and the common line defining the half-planes.* (Remember that the common line belongs to neither half-plane.) In Figure 18(b), the dihedral angle *O-AC-D* is formed by the intersecting planes α and β. Note that the point O is in the plane α, $\overleftrightarrow{AC}$ is the edge of the dihedral angle, and point D is in plane β. A dihedral angle is measured by any of the associated planar angles such as $\angle OPD$, where $\overrightarrow{PO} \perp \overleftrightarrow{AC}$ and $\overrightarrow{PD} \perp \overleftrightarrow{AC}$. If any of the four dihedral angles created by the intersecting planes measures 90°, then all four dihedral angles measure 90° and the planes α and β are perpendicular. We compare the definition of a planar angle and a dihedral angle: a planar angle is a union of two rays with a common endpoint, whereas a dihedral angle is the union of two half-planes and a common line.

Assessment 11-1A

1. Name two rays that contain

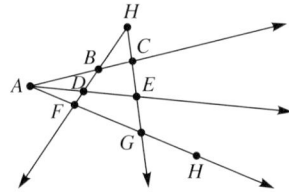

 a. $\overleftrightarrow{BC}$.   Answers vary, $\overrightarrow{BC}, \overrightarrow{AC}, \overrightarrow{CB}, \overrightarrow{CA}$.
 b. $\overleftrightarrow{EG}$.   Answers vary, $\overrightarrow{EG}, \overrightarrow{CG}, \overrightarrow{GE}, \overrightarrow{GC}$.

2. Let S be the set of lines, skew to a given line, and P be the set of lines parallel to that line. Draw a Venn diagram for sets S and P.   *

3. Label each of the following as true or false. If false, explain why.
 a. Two intersecting lines are coplanar.   True
 b. Three noncollinear points are always coplanar.   True
 c. Two planes can intersect in exactly one point.   *
 d. A line segment contains an infinite number of points.   True
 e. The union of two rays is always a line.   *

4. a. Points A, B, C, and D are collinear. In how many ways can the line be named using only these points? (Assume that different order means different name.)
 b. Points A, B, C, D, and E are coplanar and no three are collinear. In how many ways can the plane be named using only these points?

5. The following figure is a rectangular box in which *EFGH* and *ABCD* are rectangles with $\overline{BF}$ and $\overline{DH}$ perpendicular to planes *FGH* and *BCD*. Answer the following.

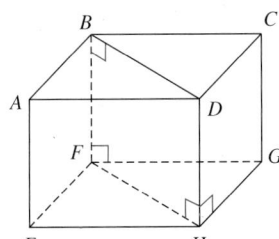

 a. Name two pairs of skew lines.   *
 b. Are $\overleftrightarrow{BD}$ and $\overleftrightarrow{FH}$ parallel, skew, or intersecting lines?
   Parallel

 c. Are $\overleftrightarrow{BD}$ and $\overleftrightarrow{GH}$ parallel?   No
 d. Find the intersection of $\overleftrightarrow{BD}$ and plane *EFG*. $\varnothing$
 e. Explain why planes *BDH* and *FHG* are perpendicular.   *

6. Use the following drawing of one of the Great Pyramids of Egypt (with square base) to find the following.

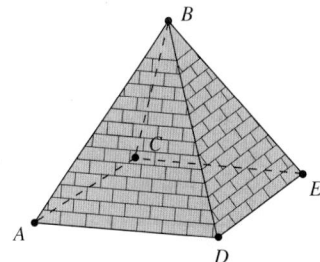

 a. The intersection of $\overline{AD}$ and $\overline{CE}$ $\varnothing$
 b. The intersection of planes *ABC*, *ACE*, and *BCE*   Point *C*
 c. The intersection of $\overrightarrow{AD}$ and $\overleftrightarrow{CA}$ Point *A*
 d. A pair of skew lines   *
 e. A pair of distinct parallel lines $\overleftrightarrow{AC}$ and $\overleftrightarrow{DE}$ or $\overleftrightarrow{AD}$ and $\overleftrightarrow{CE}$
 f. A plane not determined by one of the triangular faces or by the base   Planes *BCD* or *BEA*

7. Determine how many acute angles are determined in the following figure.

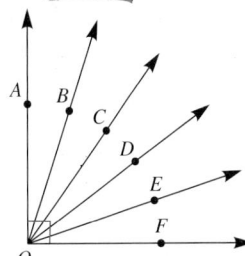

8. Identify a physical model for each of the following.
 a. Perpendicular lines   *
 b. An acute angle   *
 c. An obtuse angle   *

9. Find the measure of each of the following
angles.   As measured on the protractor:
a. ∠*EAB*   110°   **b.** ∠*EAD*   40°
c. ∠*GAF*   20°   **d.** ∠*CAF*   130°

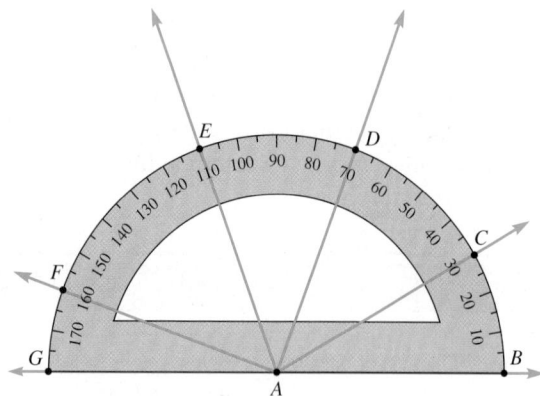

10. a. Perform each of the following operations. Leave your
answers in simplest form.
  i. 18°35′29″ + 22°55′41″   41°31′10″
  ii. 15°29′ − 3°45′   11°44′
b. Express the following measurement using degrees,
minutes, and seconds, without decimals.
  i. 0.9°   0°54′00″
  ii. 15.13°   15°7′48″

11. Consider a correctly set clock that starts ticking at noon.
a. Find the measure of the angle swept by the hour hand by
the time it reaches
  i. 3 P.M.   90°
  ii. 12:25 P.M.   12.5° = 12°30′
  iii. 6:50 P.M.   205°
b. Find the exact angle measure between the minute and the
hour hands at 1:15 P.M.   52.5° = 52°30′

12. In parts (a) and (b) of the following figures, relationships
among marked angles are given below the figure. Find the
measure of the marked angles. In part (c), find only the
measure of ∠*BOC* and tell why the exact values of *x* and *y*
cannot be determined.   *

a.   **b.**

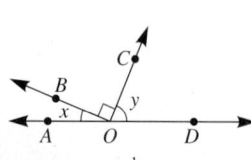   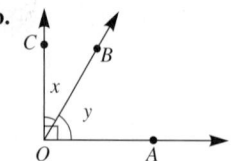

$m(\angle AOB) = \frac{1}{3}m(\angle COD)$ $m(\angle AOB)$ is 35° less than $3m(\angle BOC)$

c.

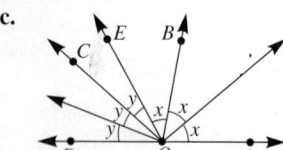

13. Given three collinear points *A*, *B*, *C*, with *B* between *A* and
C, four different rays can be named using these points: $\overrightarrow{AB}$,
$\overrightarrow{BA}$, $\overrightarrow{BC}$, and $\overrightarrow{CB}$. Determine how many different rays can be
named given each of the following.
a. Four collinear points
b. Five collinear points
c. *n* collinear points

14. Refer to the following table.

Number of Intersection Points of Coplanar Lines

	0	1	2	3	4	5
2		✕	Not possible	Not possible	Not possible	Not possible
3					Not possible	Not possible
4						
5						
6						

(Number of Lines)

a. Sketch the possible intersections of the given number of
lines. Three sketches are given.   *
b. Given *n* lines, find a formula for determining the $\frac{n(n-1)}{2}$
greatest possible number of intersection points.

15. Trace each of the following drawings. In your tracings, use
dashed lines for segments that would not be seen and solid
lines for segments that would be seen.   *

a.   **b.**

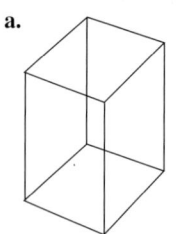   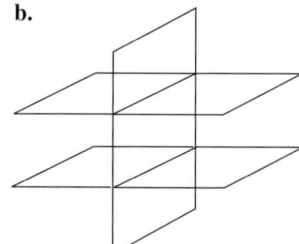

c.

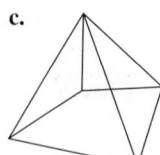

16. Draw pictures illustrating a real-world example of the
following.   *
a. Three planes intersecting in a common line
b. Three planes intersecting in a common point
c. A central angle of a circle

17. In the figure below, *O* is the center of the circle. Find the
measures of the following arcs.

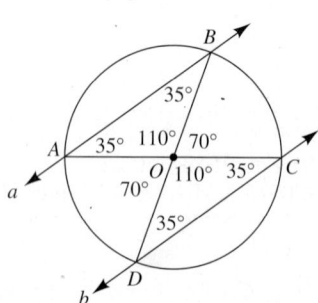

a. $\overparen{BC}$ 70°   b. $\overparen{CD}$ 110°.   c. $\overparen{AD}$ 70°.
d. $\overparen{AB}$ 110°   e. $\overparen{ADC}$ 180°.

d. $\overline{CE} \cap \angle BEC$ $\overline{CE}$
f. $\overrightarrow{EB} \cap \overleftrightarrow{EC}$ {E}

e. $\overleftrightarrow{AE} \cap \overleftrightarrow{DE}$ $\overrightarrow{DE}$
g. interior $\angle BEC \cap \overrightarrow{BE}$ ∅

18. The measure of $\angle A$ is 30° more than 4 times the measure of $\angle B$ and the sum of the measures of the two angles is 170°. What is the measure of each angle? $m(\angle A) = 142°; m(\angle B) = 28°$

19. Describe each of the following sets of points with reference to the given figure.
   a. (plane AFD) ∩ (plane XYE) $\overrightarrow{AE}, \overrightarrow{AD},$ or $\overrightarrow{DE}$
   b. (Plane XYE) ∩ $\overleftrightarrow{AE}$ $\overrightarrow{AE}$
   c. $\overleftrightarrow{BE} \cap \overleftrightarrow{CE}$ {E}

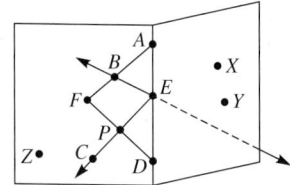

Assessment 11-1B

1. Name 3 points that are not collinear.
   Answers vary; for example, A, B, E; B, C, E; C, E, D

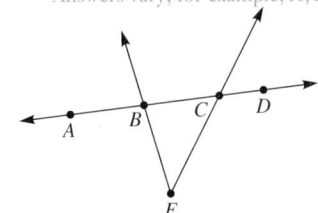

2. Let C be the set of coplanar lines with a given line, S be the set of lines, skew to that line, and P be the set of lines parallel to that line. Draw a Venn diagram for sets C, S, and P. *

3. Label each of the following as true or false. If false, explain why.
   a. Any two distinct lines that do not intersect are parallel. *
   b. If a plane contains one point of a line, then it must contain the entire line. *
   c. For any two distinct points $\overleftrightarrow{AB} = \overrightarrow{AB}$ *
   d. A ray contains no endpoints.   False; a ray has 1 endpoint.
   e. Two skew lines can be coplanar. *

4. Coplanar points A, B, C, and D are such that no three are collinear. How many distinct angles less than 180° do they determine? Explain. *

5. The following figure is a box in which the top and bottom are rectangles with $\overline{BF}$ and $\overline{DH}$ perpendicular to planes FGH and BCD.

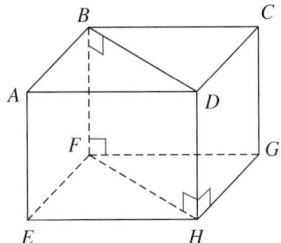

   a. Find the intersection of $\overleftrightarrow{BH}$ and plane DCG.   Point H
   b. Name two pairs of perpendicular planes. *
   c. Name two lines that are perpendicular to plane EFH. *
   d. What is the measure of dihedral angle D-HG-F? 90°

6. Use the following drawing of a triangular pyramid (Each triangle creating the pyramid determines a face.) to find the following.

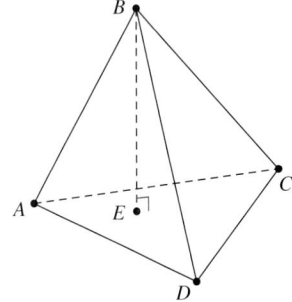

   a. The intersection of $\overline{AD}$ and $\overline{BE}$ ∅
   b. The intersection of planes ABD and ACD $\overleftrightarrow{AD}$
   c. The intersection of $\overleftrightarrow{BC}$ and $\overleftrightarrow{AC}$ Point C
   d. A pair of skew lines   Answers vary, for example, $\overleftrightarrow{BE}$ and $\overleftrightarrow{CD}$
   e. A pair of distinct parallel lines if possible   *
   f. A plane not determined by one of the four triangular faces *

7. Determine the number of obtuse angles in the following.   6

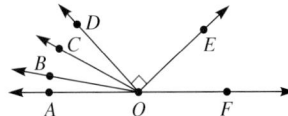

8. Identify a physical model for each of the following. Answers vary.
   a. Parallel lines   Railroad tracks
   b. A right angle   The corners of a room in your home
   c. Parallel planes   Two opposite facing walls in your home

9. Find the measures of each of the following angles:

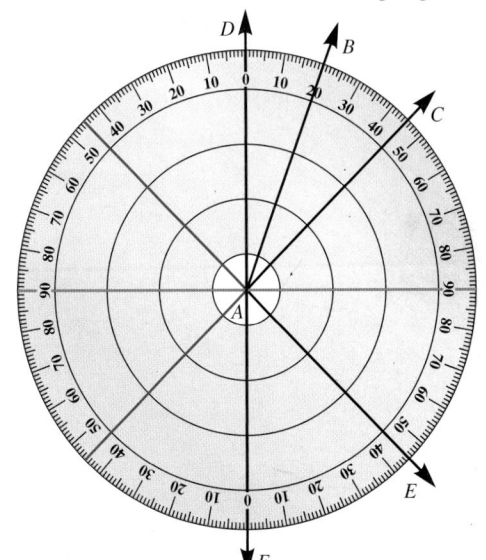

   a. ∠*BAC*   25°
   b. ∠*DAE*   135°
   c. ∠*CAF*   135°
   d. Reflex angle, ∠*BAE*   245°
10. a. Perform the following operations. Leave your answers as simple as possible.
   i. 21°35′31″ + 49°51′32″   71°27′3″
   ii. 93°38′14″ − 13°49′27″   79°48′47″
   b. Express the following measurements in degrees, minutes, and seconds without decimals.
   i. 10.3°   10°18′
   ii. 15.14°   15°8′24″
11. Consider a correctly functioning clock that starts ticking at noon and find the time between 12 noon and 1 P.M. when the angle measure between the hands is 180°.   About 12:32:44
12. In each of the following figures, relationships among marked angles are given. Find the measures of the marked angles.

a.

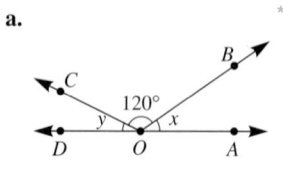

$m(\angle DOC) = \frac{3}{4}m(\angle BOA)$

b.

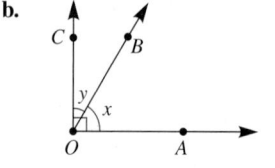

m(∠*AOB*) is 30° less than 2*m*(∠*BOC*)
   m(∠*BOC*) = 40°
   m(∠*AOB*) = 50°

c.

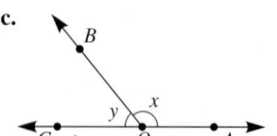

m(∠*AOB*) − *m*(∠*BOC*) = 50°
   m(∠*AOB*) = 115°
   m(∠*BOC*) = 65°

13. a. How many planes are determined by three noncollinear points?   1
   b. How many planes are determined by four points that are not coplanar?   4
   c. How many planes are determined by *n* points, no four of which are coplanar?   *
14. In each of the following pairs, determine whether the symbols name the same geometric figure.
   a. $\overrightarrow{AB}$ and $\overrightarrow{BA}$ No
   b. $\overline{AB}$ and $\overline{BA}$ Yes
   c. $\overleftrightarrow{AB}$ and $\overleftrightarrow{BA}$ Yes
15. Trace each of the following drawings of three-dimensional figures. In your tracings, use dashes for segments that would not be seen and solid drawings for segments that would be seen. (Different people may have different perspectives.)

a.

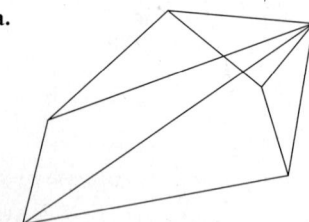

b.

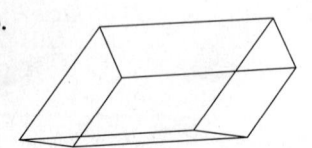

16. On the dot paper below, draw all possible segments parallel to $\overline{PQ}$ that have dots as endpoints.   Six parallel segments can be drawn including $\overline{PQ}$.

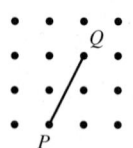

17. In the figure below, *O* is the center of the circle and *m*(∠*ACB*) = 90°. Find the following measures.

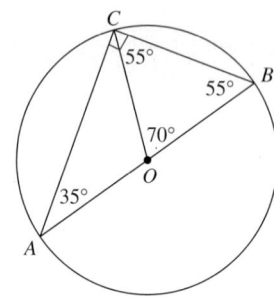

   a. *m*(∠*ACO*)   35°
   b. *m*($\overset{\frown}{AC}$)   110°
   c. *m*($\overset{\frown}{CB}$)   70°
   d. *m*($\overset{\frown}{AB}$)   180°
   e. *m*($\overset{\frown}{CBA}$)   250°
18. If the measure of ∠*A* is 30° more than twice the measure of ∠*B*, and the sum of the measures of the two angles is 180°, what is the measure of each angle?   *m*(∠*A*) = 130°, *m*(∠*B*) = 50°
19. Describe each of the following sets of points with reference to the given figure.

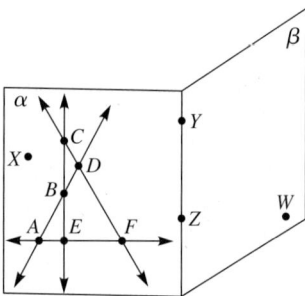

   a. α ∩ β $\overleftrightarrow{YZ}$
   b. ∠*ADF* ∩ $\overleftrightarrow{BE}$ {*B*}
   c. $\overleftrightarrow{AF}$ ∩ $\overleftrightarrow{BE}$ {*E*}
   d. ∠*CEF* ∩ $\overrightarrow{CF}$ {*C, F*}
   e. $\overline{AE}$ ∪ $\overline{FE}$ $\overline{FE}$ or $\overline{EF}$
   f. $\overrightarrow{BD}$ ∪ $\overrightarrow{BA}$ $\overleftrightarrow{AD}$
   g. $\overrightarrow{AE}$ ∩ $\overrightarrow{AF}$ $\overrightarrow{AE}$
   h. $\overline{AE}$ ∪ $\overline{EF}$ $\overline{AF}$ or $\overline{FA}$

Mathematical Connections 11-1

Answers to Mathematical Connections can be found in the Answers section at the back of the book.

Reasoning

1. Answer each of the following and explain your answer.
   a. How many lines can contain a particular segment?
   b. How many rays can contain a particular segment?
   c. How many planes can contain a given line?
   d. Is it possible for 3 points to be noncoplanar?
2. Given a line and a point not on the line, explain why there is only one plane containing the point and the line.
3. How are pairs of parallel lines and skew lines
   a. similar?
   b. different?
4. Is it possible for ∠ABC to have vertex C? Why?
5. If planes α and β are distinct planes having points A, B, and C in common, what conclusion can you make about points A, B, and C?
6. Forest rangers use degree measures to identify directions and locate fires. In the drawing, a ranger at tower A observes smoke at a bearing of 149° (clockwise from the north), while another ranger at tower B observes the same source of smoke at a bearing of 250° (clockwise from the north).

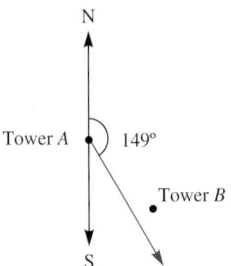

   a. On a blank sheet of paper, choose two locations for A and B and use the bearings and a protractor and a straightedge to locate the source of the smoke.
   b. Explain how the rangers find the location of the fire.
   c. Describe other situations in which location can be determined by similar methods.
7. Is it possible to locate four points in a plane such that the number of lines determined by the points is not exactly 1, 4, or 6? Explain.
8. A line n is perpendicular to plane α, and plane β contains n (n is in plane β). Must planes α and β be perpendicular? Explain why or why not.

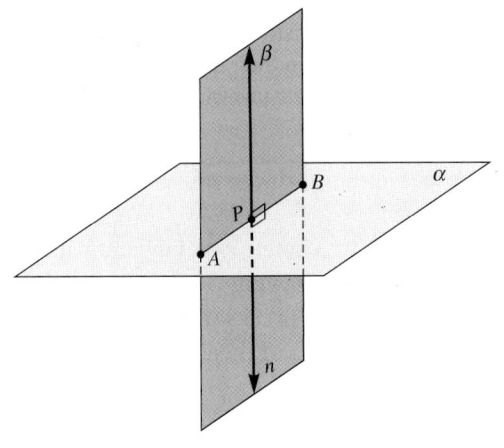

9. Mario was studying right angles and wondered if during his math class the minute and hour hands of the clock formed a right angle. If his class meets from 2:00 P.M. to 2:50 P.M., is a right angle formed? If it is, figure out to the nearest second when the hands form the right angle.

Open-Ended

10. a. Sketch three rays that share a common vertex. Label the vertex A and label another point on each ray. Explain why you can't name any of the angles, ∠A.
    b. Sketch and name two angles that have a common vertex and a common side but are not adjacent angles.
11. Identify a physical object within the classroom to represent each of the following.
    a. Parallel lines
    b. Parallel planes
    c. Skew lines
    d. A right angle
12. On a sheet of dot paper or on a geoboard like the one shown, create the following.
    a. Right angle
    b. Acute angle
    c. Obtuse angle
    d. Adjacent angles
    e. Parallel segments
    f. Intersecting segments

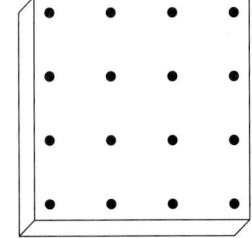

Cooperative Learning

13. Let each member of your group use a protractor to make a triangle out of cardboard that has one angle measuring 30° and another 50°. Answer the following and compare your solutions with other members of your group.
    a. Show how to use the triangle (without a protractor) to draw an angle with measure 40°.
    b. Is there more than one way to draw an angle of 40° using the triangle? Explain.
    c. What other angles can be drawn with the triangle? Why?

Connecting Mathematics to the Classroom

14. Allie says that $\overline{AB}$ and $\overline{CD}$ are parallel because they do not intersect. How do you respond?

15. Bonnie named the line below as $\overleftrightarrow{ABC}$. How do you respond?

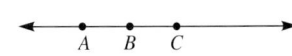

16. A student says that $\overline{AB} \neq \overline{BA}$ because $\overline{AB}$ starts at A and ends at B and $\overline{BA}$ starts at B and ends at A. How do you respond?

17. Henry claims that a line segment has a finite number of points because it has two endpoints. How do you respond?

18. A student claims that if any two planes that do not intersect are parallel, then any two lines that do not intersect should also be parallel. How do you respond?

19. A student says that it is actually impossible to measure an angle, since each angle is the union of two rays that extend infinitely and therefore continue forever. What is your response?

20. Maggie claims that to make the measure of an angle greater, you just extend the rays. How do you respond?

21. A student says there can be only 360 different rays emanating from a point since there are only 360° in a circle. How do you respond?

22. A student asks why an angle is not defined as the union of two half-lines and a common point. How do you respond?

National Assessments

National Assessment of Educational Progress (NAEP) Questions

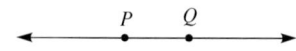

What is the intersection of rays PQ and QP in the figure above?
A. Segment PQ B. Line PQ
C. Point P D. Point Q
E. The empty set

NAEP, Grade 8, 2007

Lines a and b are parallel to each other. Line c is perpendicular to these lines. Jan correctly draws lines a, b, and c. Which of these could be Jan's drawing?

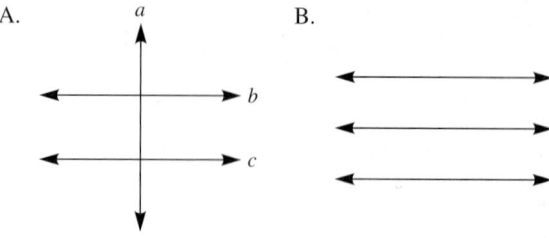

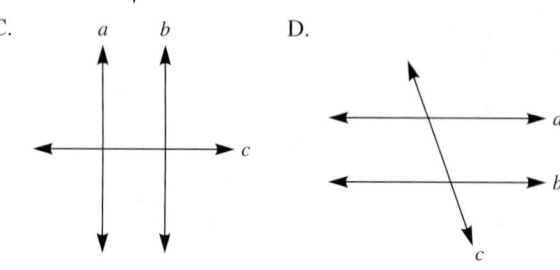

NAEP, Grade 4, 2011

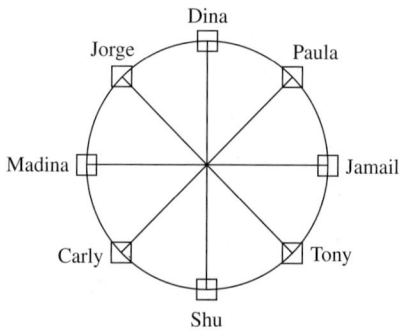

The figure above shows a Ferris wheel stopped with Dina at the top. Who will be at the top after a 135° clockwise rotation?
A. Tony   B. Carly   C. Madina
D. Jorge   E. Paula

NAEP, Grade 8, 2013

11-2 Curves, Polygons, and Symmetry

11-2 Objectives

Students will be able to understand and explain

- Simple, closed, and convex curves including polygons.

- Naming and classifying triangles and quadrilatrals.

- Hierarchy among selected polygons.

- Symmetries and their relation to planar figures.

CCSS In the grade 4 *Common Core Standards*, we find:

Students describe, analyze, compare, and classify two-dimensional shapes. Through building, drawing, and analyzing two-dimensional shapes, students deepen their understanding of properties of two-dimensional objects and the use of them to solve problems involving symmetry. (p. 27)

In this section we work with two-dimensional shapes and introduce symmetry and its relation to planar figures.

With a pencil, draw a path on a piece of paper without lifting the pencil and without retracing any part of the path except single points. The resulting drawing is restricted to the plane of the paper, and not lifting the pencil implies that there are no breaks in the drawing. The drawing is **connected** and is a **curve**. Table 6 shows sample curves and their classifications. A check is placed in a box if the curve has the attribute listed at the top.

Table 6

Curve	Simple	Closed	Polygon	Convex	Concave
(curve)	✔				
(curve)	✔				
(curve)	✔	✔			✔
(circle)	✔	✔		✔	
(hourglass)		✔			
(quadrilateral)	✔	✔	✔	✔	
(arrow polygon)	✔	✔	✔		✔

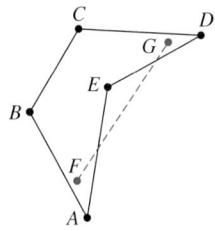

Figure 19

A **simple** curve does not intersect itself, except the starting and stopping points may be the same when the curve is traced. A **closed** curve can be drawn starting and stopping at the same point. A curve can be classified as simple, nonsimple, closed, nonclosed, and so on. A **polygon** is a simple closed curve with only segments as *sides*. A point where two sides of a polygon meet is a *vertex*. A **convex** curve is simple and closed and has the property that *the segment connecting any two points in the interior of the curve is wholly contained in the interior of the curve*. A **concave** curve is simple, closed, and not convex; that is, it is possible for a line segment connecting two interior points to contain a point or points outside the interior of the curve as shown in Figure 19.

▶ NOW TRY THIS 7

An alternative definition of a concave polygon is a polygon is convex if every diagonal (a segment connecting nonadjacent vertices) is entirely in the interior. Which definition do you prefer? Why?   Answers vary.

Figure 20(a), shows a polygon with a side and vertex marked. As in Figure 20(b), every simple closed curve separates the plane into three disjoint subsets: the interior of the curve, the exterior of the curve, and the curve itself. Of specific interest are polygons and their interiors, together called **polygonal regions**. Figure 20(c), shows a polygonal region.

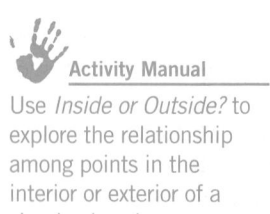

Activity Manual

Use *Inside or Outside?* to explore the relationship among points in the interior or exterior of a simple closed curve.

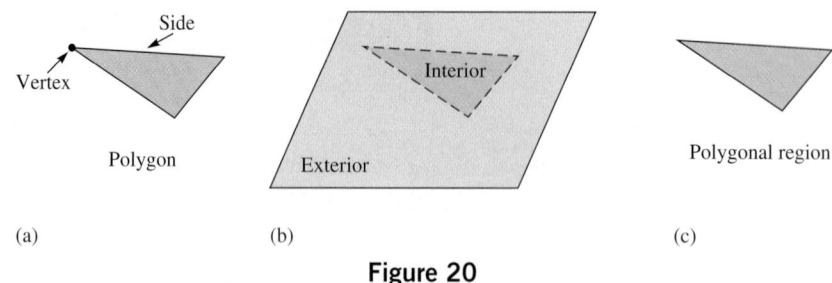

(a)   (b)   (c)

Figure 20

Whether a point is inside or outside a curve is not always obvious. This is explored in Now Try This 8.

▶ **NOW TRY THIS 8**

NTT 8: Answers can be found in Answers at the back of the book.

Determine whether point X is inside or outside the simple closed curve of Figure 21. Explain your reasoning so that it can be generalized to other simple closed curves.

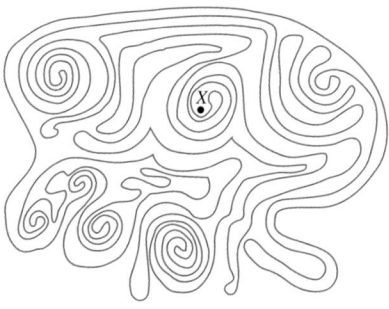

Figure 21

More About Polygons

Polygons are classified according to the number of sides or vertices they have. Consider the polygons listed in Table 7.

Table 7	
Polygon	**Number of Sides or Vertices**
Triangle	3
Quadrilateral	4
Pentagon	5
Hexagon	6
Heptagon	7
Octagon	8
Nonagon	9
Decagon	10
*Hendecagon	11
Dodecagon	12
⋮	⋮
n-gon	n

*not often used

Two vertices of a polygon such as *A* and *B* in Figure 22 connected by a side are *consecutive vertices*. Two angles that share a side, such as ∠*A* and ∠*B* in Figure 22, are *consecutive angles*, and two sides that share a vertex are *consecutive sides*. A polygon is referred to by the capital letters that represent its consecutive vertices, such as *ABCD* or *CDAB* shown in Figure 22(a). Any two sides of a convex polygon having a common vertex determine an **interior angle**, or **angle of the polygon**, such as ∠1 of polygon *ABCD* in Figure 22(a). An **exterior angle of a convex polygon** is determined by a side of the polygon and the extension of a contiguous side of the polygon. An example is ∠2 in Figure 22(b). Any line segment connecting nonconsecutive vertices of a polygon, such as $\overline{AC}$ in Figure 22(a), is a **diagonal** of the polygon.

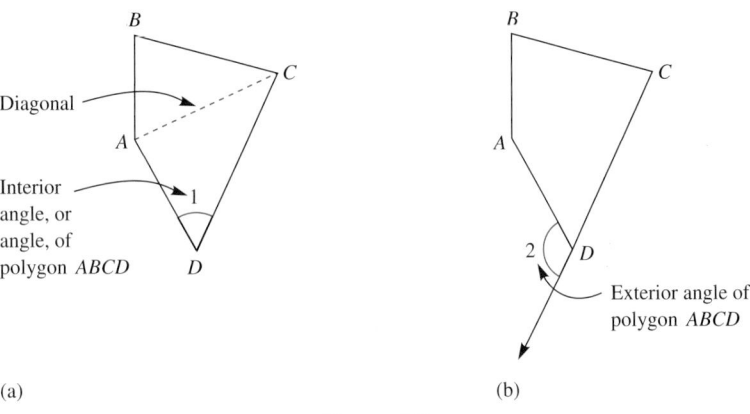

(a)   (b)

Figure 22

Congruent Segments and Angles

Most modern industries operate on the notion of creating **congruent parts**—parts that are of the same size and shape. For example, the specifications for the bodies of particular cars are the same, and all parts produced for those cars are basically the same. Usually congruent figures refer to figures in a plane. For example, two line **segments** are **congruent** ($\cong$) if a tracing of one can be fitted exactly on top of the other. If $\overline{AB}$ is congruent to $\overline{CD}$, we write $\overline{AB} \cong \overline{CD}$. Congruent segments have the same measure and we write $m(\overline{AB}) = m(\overline{CD})$. Two **angles** are **congruent** if they have the same measure. Congruent segments and congruent angles are shown in Figure 23(a) and (b), respectively.

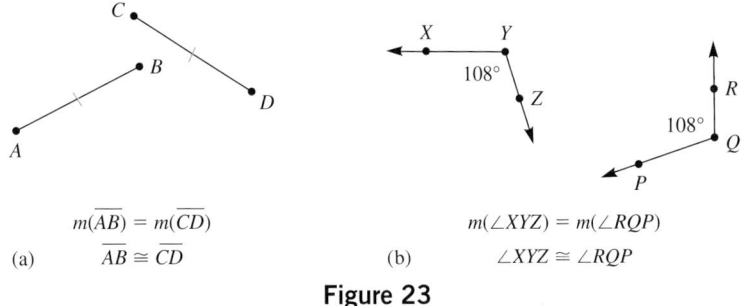

$m(\overline{AB}) = m(\overline{CD})$		$m(\angle XYZ) = m(\angle RQP)$
(a) $\overline{AB} \cong \overline{CD}$	(b)	$\angle XYZ \cong \angle RQP$

Figure 23

In Figure 23(a), $\overline{AB} = \overline{BA}$, but $\overline{AB} \neq \overline{CD}$ because the segments contain different sets of points. However, $\overline{AB} \cong \overline{CD}$. In geometry, *we use the equal sign "=" to mean the same set of points.*

Regular Polygons

Convex polygons in which all the interior angles are congruent (**equiangular**) and all the sides are congruent (**equilateral**) are **regular polygons**. Thus, a *regular polygon is both equiangular and equilateral.* A regular triangle is an equilateral triangle. A regular quadrilateral is a square.

A regular pentagon and a regular hexagon are illustrated in Figure 24. The congruent sides and congruent angles are marked.

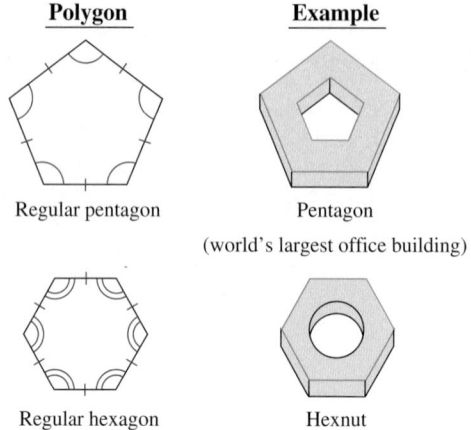

Polygon	Example
Regular pentagon	Pentagon (world's largest office building)
Regular hexagon	Hexnut

Figure 24

▶ **NOW TRY THIS 9**

NTT 9: Answers can be found in Answers at the back of the book.

Sketch the following polygons.

a. A polygon that is equiangular but not equilateral.
b. A polygon that is equilateral but not equiangular.

Activity Manual

Use *Name That Polygon* to reinforce geometric vocabulary and the properties of polygons.

Triangles and Quadrilaterals

Triangles and quadrilaterals are polygons and may be classified according to their angle measures or according to their side length, as shown in Table 8. The definitions in this table were chosen carefully; others are possible. Later in the chapter we see that many of the polygons here could also be defined by their symmetries.

Table 8

Definition	Illustration	Example
A triangle containing one right angle is a **right triangle**.		
A triangle in which all the angles are acute is an **acute triangle**.		YIELD
A triangle containing one obtuse angle is an **obtuse triangle**.		
A triangle with no congruent sides is a **scalene triangle.**		
A triangle with at least two congruent sides is an **isosceles triangle**.		

(continued)

Table 8 *(continued)*		
Definition	**Illustration**	**Example**
A triangle with three congruent sides is an **equilateral triangle**.		
A **trapezoid** is a quadrilateral with at least one pair of parallel sides.		
A **kite** is a quadrilateral with two adjacent sides congruent and the other two sides also congruent.		
An **isosceles trapezoid** is a trapezoid with congruent base angles.		
A **parallelogram** is a quadrilateral in which each pair of opposite sides is parallel.		
A **rectangle** is a parallelogram with a right angle.		
A **rhombus** is a parallelogram with two adjacent sides congruent.		
A **square** is a rectangle with two adjacent sides congruent.		

Hierarchy Among Selected Polygons

From the definitions in this text, we get a hierarchy as seen in Figure 25. Using set concepts, we note that the set of triangles is a proper subset of the set of polygons. Also, the set of equilateral triangles is a proper subset of the set of isosceles triangles. In Figure 25, more general terms appear above more specific ones.

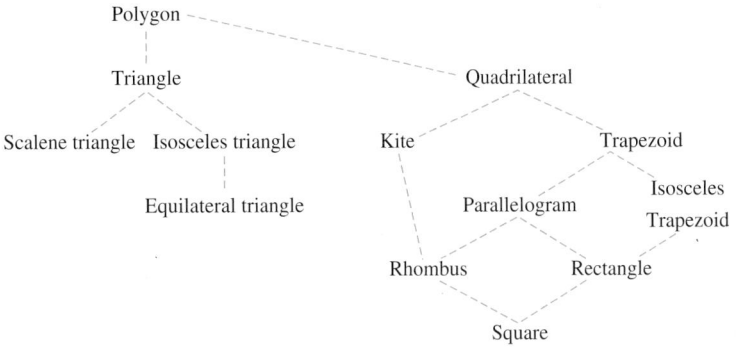

Figure 25

There are different definitions for trapezoids and other figures. For example, many elementary texts define a trapezoid as a quadrilateral with *exactly* one pair of parallel sides and an isosceles triangle with exactly one pair of congruent sides. Note the definition of a trapezoid on the following partial student page. If these different definitions are used, the hierarchy in Figure 25 would change to that shown on the student page below. How are the "trees" different? Why?

School Book Page — Classifying Quadrilaterals

Many special **quadrilaterals** have special **properties**.

A **trapezoid** has exactly one pair of parallel sides.

A **parallelogram** has two pairs of equal parallel sides.

A **rectangle** is a parallelogram with 4 right angles.

A **rhombus** is a parallelogram with 4 equal sides.

A **square** is a parallelogram with 4 right angles and 4 equal sides.

Trapezoid   Parallelogram   Rectangle   Rhombus   Square

Identify each quadrilateral. Describe each quadrilateral by as many names as possible.

1.
2.
3.
4.

Set E, pages 380–381

How are special quadrilaterals related to each other?

This "family tree" shows how special quadrilaterals are related to each other.

Quadrilaterals
Parallelogram   Trapezoid
Rectangle   Rhombus
Square

Tell whether each statement is true or false.

1. All squares are rectangles.

2. Every parallelogram is a rectangle.

3. Rhombuses are special parallelograms.

4. All trapezoids are quadrilaterals.

Source: p. 385; From enVisionMATH Common Core (Grade 5). Copyright © 2012 Pearson Education, Inc., or its affiliates. Used by permission. All Rights Reserved.

▶ **NOW TRY THIS 10**

Use the definitions in Table 8 and several drawings to conjecture which of the following are true.

1. An equilateral triangle is isosceles.   True
2. A square is a regular quadrilateral.   True
3. If one angle of a rhombus is a right angle, then all the angles of the rhombus are right angles.   True
4. A square is a rhombus with a right angle.   True
5. All the angles of a rectangle are right angles.   True
6. A rectangle is an isosceles trapezoid.   True
7. Some isosceles trapezoids are kites.   True
8. If a kite has a right angle, then it must be a square.   False

Symmetry and Its Relation to Planar Figures

CCSS In the grade 4 *Common Core Standards*, we find that students should:

Recognize a line of symmetry for a two-dimensional figure as a line across the figure such that the figure can be folded along the line into matching parts. Identify line-symmetric figures and draw lines of symmetry. (p. 32)

Paperfolding can be used to introduce the concept of symmetry. Consider Figure 26 where folds on the dashed lines allow the figures to match with themselves.

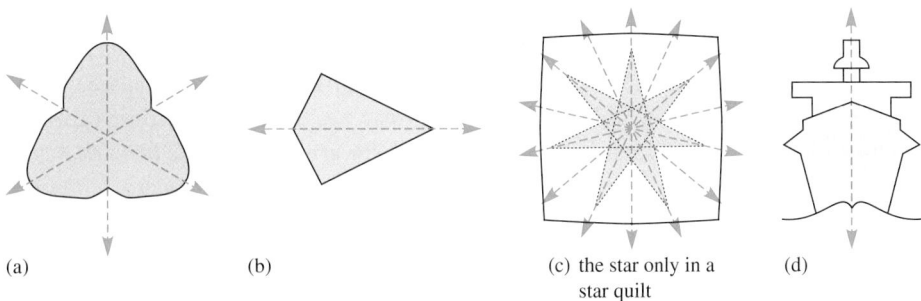

(a)   (b)   (c) the star only in a   (d)
                                         star quilt

Figure 26

A geometric figure has a line of symmetry if it is its own image when folded along the line. (This concept using paperfolding can be done much more precisely using reflections introduced in Chapter 13.)

Example 3

How many lines of symmetry does each drawing in Figure 27 have?

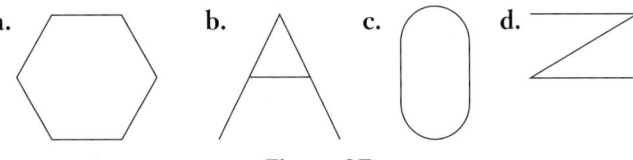

a.   b.   c.   d.

Figure 27

Solution
  a. 6   **b.** 1   **c.** 2   **d.** 0

As mentioned, symmetry may be used to define different polygons. For example, as seen in Figure 28(a), a *rectangle could be defined as a quadrilateral with two lines of symmetry through the midpoints of the opposite sides*. Figure 28(b) shows a rhombus could be defined as a quadrilateral with two lines of symmetry containing its diagonals.

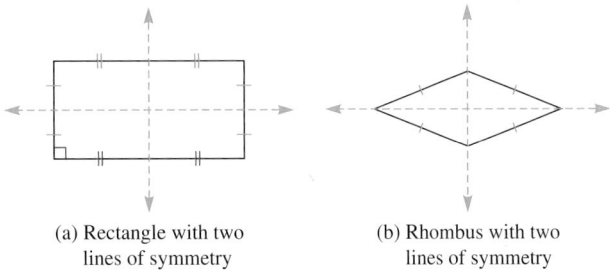

(a) Rectangle with two   (b) Rhombus with two
    lines of symmetry   lines of symmetry

Figure 28

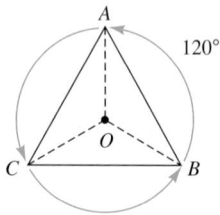

Figure 29

▶ **NOW TRY THIS 11**

Use the information from Figure 28 and the hierarchy of Figure 25 to define a square in terms of line symmetry.

Turn (Rotational) Symmetries

A figure has **turn symmetry** (or **rotational symmetry**) when a tracing of the figure can be rotated more than 0° and less than 360° about some point (the **center of the turn**) so that it matches the original figure. (The condition "more than 0° and less than 360°" is necessary because any figure will coincide with itself if it is rotated 360° about any point.) In Figure 29, the equilateral triangle coincides with itself after a turn of 120° about point O. Hence, we say that the triangle has 120° turn symmetry. Also in Figure 29, if we were to rotate the triangle another 120°, we would find again that it matches the original. So we can say that the triangle also has 240° turn symmetry. (*Turns counterclockwise are positive while turns clockwise are negative.*)

In general, *if a figure has α degrees turn symmetry, it also will coincide with itself when rotated by nα degrees for any integer n.* For this reason in turn symmetry, it is sufficient to report the least possible positive angle measure that turns the figure onto itself. A circle has a turn symmetry by any turn around its center. Thus, *a circle has infinitely many turn symmetries.* This is often called *circular symmetry.*

Other examples of figures that have turn symmetry are shown in Figure 30. Figures 30(a), (b), (c), and (d) have 72°, 90°, 180°, and 180° turn symmetries, respectively [(a) and (b) also have other turn symmetries].

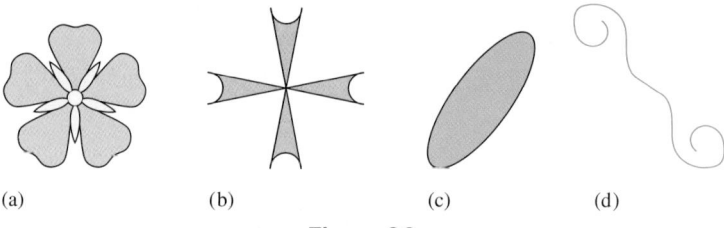

Figure 30

We can often determine whether a figure has turn symmetry by tracing it and turning the tracing about a point (the center of the figure) to see if it aligns on the figure before the tracing has turned in a complete circle, or 360°. The amount of turning is determined by measuring the *turn angle ∠POP′* through which a point P is rotated around a point O to match another point $P′$ when the figures align. Such an angle, ∠POP′, is labeled with points P, O, and $P′$ in Figure 31 and has measure 120°. Point O, the point held fixed when the tracing is turned, is the *turn center.*

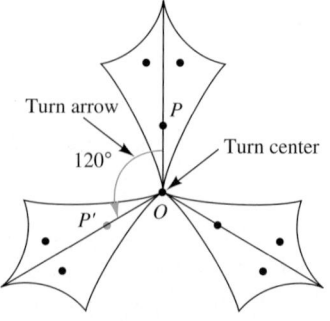

Figure 31

Example 4

Determine the turn angle measures for the rotational symmetries of each part of Figure 32. Assume the turns are about the "center" of each drawing.

a. 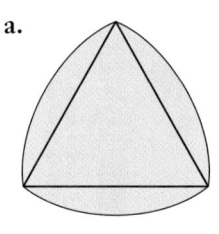   b.    c.

Figure 32

Solution

a. The turn angle measures are $\dfrac{360°}{3} = 120°$ and $240°$.

b. The turn angle measure is $180°$.

c. The turn angle measures are $60°$, $120°$, $180°$, $240°$, and $300°$.

 On the student page shown on page 650, students verify experimentally the properties of turn and line symmetries.

Point Symmetry

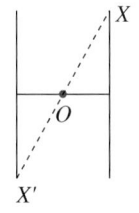

Figure 33

The turns in Figure 32(b) and (c) exemplify yet another type of symmetry, namely, point symmetry. Any figure that has $180°$ turn symmetry is said to have **point symmetry** about the turn center. The turn center of a figure with point symmetry may be found as in Figure 33 where X is connected to its symmetrical point X' with O being the turn center and midpoint of $\overline{XX'}$. Some figures with point symmetry are shown in Figure 34.

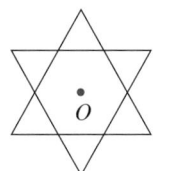 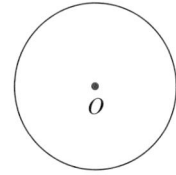 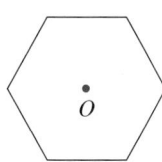 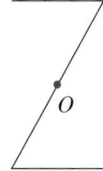

Figure 34

Classification of Polygons by Their Symmetries

Geometric figures in a plane can be classified according to the number of symmetries they have. Consider a triangle described as having exactly one line of symmetry and no turn symmetries. What could the triangle look like? The only possibility is a triangle in which exactly two sides are congruent, that is, an isosceles triangle that is not equilateral. The line of symmetry passes

School Book Page — Symmetry

Step-Up Lesson **11-8**

Common Core

6.G.1 Verify experimentally the properties of rotations, reflections, and translations.

Symmetry

What are symmetric figures?

Aria is creating a square mosaic tile design in art class. The art teacher said to create a design that has at least two lines of symmetry.

Does Aria's tile design have at least two lines of symmetry?

A figure has reflection symmetry if it can be reflected onto itself. The line of reflection is a line of symmetry. Some figures have more than one line of symmetry.

Aria's design has four lines of symmetry. Her design meets her art teacher's directions.

Another Example — What is rotational symmetry?

When a figure rotates onto itself in less than a full turn, the figure has rotational symmetry. The shapes below have rotational symmetry.

180° ($\frac{1}{2}$ turn)
rotational symmetry

120° ($\frac{1}{3}$ turn)
rotational symmetry

90° ($\frac{1}{4}$ turn)
rotational symmetry

45° ($\frac{1}{8}$ turn)
rotational symmetry

Guided Practice*

Do you know HOW?

For **1** and **2**, identify the type(s) of symmetry; tell the number of lines of symmetry or smallest turn needed for rotational symmetry.

1.

2.

3. How many lines of symmetry, if any, do each of the figures in Another Example have?

Do you UNDERSTAND?

4. Persevere How could you check to see if a paper shape has reflection symmetry?

5. Describe the symmetry of a regular hexagon.

6. Does Aria's mosaic tile design have rotational symmetry? Explain.

Animated Glossary www.pearsonsuccessnet.com **DIGITAL**

Independent Practice

In **7** through **10**, tell if each figure has reflection symmetry, rotational symmetry, or both. If it has reflection symmetry, how many lines of symmetry are there? If it has rotational symmetry, what is the smallest turn that will rotate the figure onto itself?

7.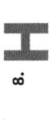

8.

9.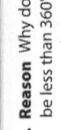

10.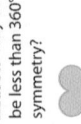

MATHEMATICAL PRACTICES

Problem Solving

11. Draw a picture of a scalene triangle and its reflection over a vertical line.

12. Reason Why does a rotation have to be less than 360° to show rotational symmetry?

13. How many times does Caleb have to turn this figure 90° to get it back to its original position?

14. Writing to Explain How many lines of symmetry does a circle have? Explain.

15. Perservere Elli wants to draw a figure that has reflection symmetry but not rotation symmetry. What shape might Elli draw?

16. This sea star has 5 arms. How many lines of symmetry does it have?

17. Which shape has exactly 2 lines of symmetry?

A T
B E
C N
D I

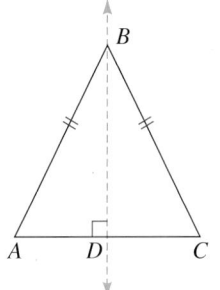

Figure 35

through a vertex, as shown in Figure 35. We can describe equilateral and scalene triangles in terms of the number of lines of symmetry they have.

A square, as in Figure 36, can be described as a four-sided polygon with four lines of symmetry—d_1, d_2, h, and v—and three turn symmetries about point O. In fact, we can use lines of symmetry and turn symmetries to define various types of quadrilaterals normally used in geometry.

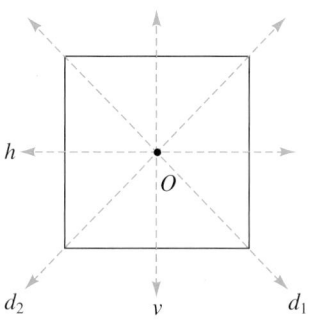

Figure 36

Assessment 11-2A

1. Determine which of the following figures labeled (1) through (10) can be classified under the given description.
  a. Simple closed curve   1, 4, 6, 7, 8
  b. Polygon   1, 6, 7, 8
  c. Convex polygon   6, 7
  d. Concave polygon   1, 8

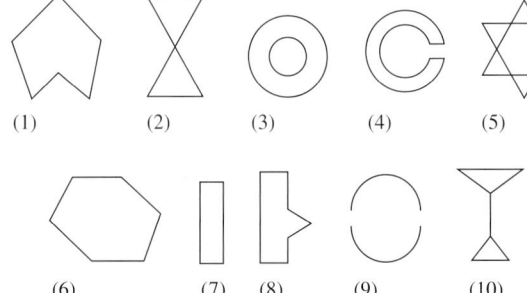

(1)   (2)   (3)   (4)   (5)

(6)   (7) (8)   (9)   (10)

2. What is the maximum number of intersection points between a quadrilateral and a triangle (where no sides of the polygons are on the same line)?   8

3. What type of polygon must have a diagonal such that at least part of the diagonal falls in the exterior of the polygon?   Concave polygon

4. Which of the following figures are convex and which are concave?   a. Convex b. Concave c. Convex d. Concave
  a.
  b.

  c.
  d.

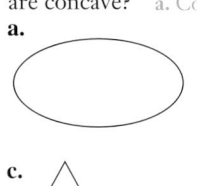
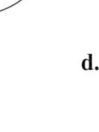
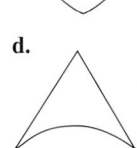

5. Describe the shaded region as simply as possible.   Squares

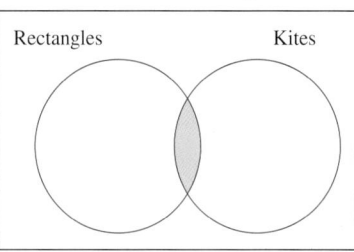

6. If possible, draw the following triangles. If it is not possible, state why.
  a. An obtuse scalene triangle   *
  b. A right scalene triangle   *
  c. An obtuse equilateral triangle   *
  d. A right equilateral triangle   *
  e. An obtuse isosceles triangle   *

7. Determine how many diagonals each of the following polygons has.
  a. Pentagon
  b. Decagon
  c. 20-gon
  d. n-gon

8. Draw all lines of symmetry (if any exist) for each of the following figures.
  a.   *   **b.**   *

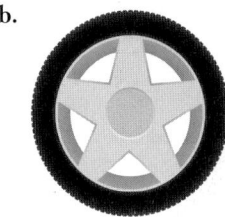

* Answers can be found in the Answers section at the back of the book.

9. Identify each of the following triangles as scalene, isosceles, or equilateral. There may be more than one term that applies to these triangles.

a.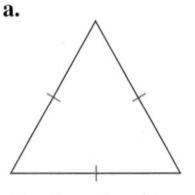
Equilateral and isosceles

b.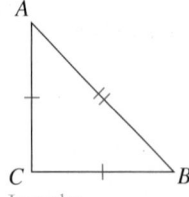
Isosceles

c.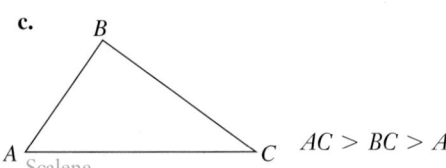
Scalene $AC > BC > AB$

10. Various international signs have symmetries. Determine which of the following figures, if any, have (i) line symmetry, (ii) turn symmetry, and/or (iii) point symmetry. *

a.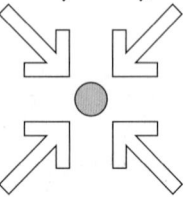
Rendezvous point

b.
Light switch

11. Find all lines of symmetries for the figures in exercise 10. *

12. Design symbols that have each of the following symmetries, if possible. *
   a. Line symmetry but not turn symmetry *
   b. Turn symmetry but not point symmetry *
   c. Rotational symmetry but not line symmetry *

13. In each of the following figures, complete the sketches so that they have line symmetry about ℓ.

a.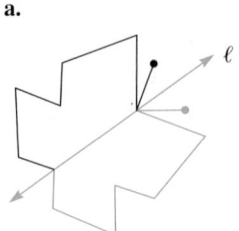

b.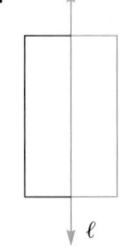

14. Given the digits **0, 1, 2, 3, 4,** which of these have the following symmetries? *
   a. Line symmetry (if so, how many?)
   b. Point symmetry

15. Determine the measures of the angles of turn symmetry for each of the following figures. *

a.

b.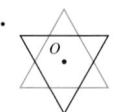

16. Complete the following figures so that they have point symmetry about point O.

a.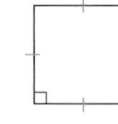

b.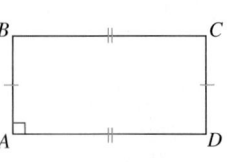

17. Give the most general name for the quadrilaterals having the given symmetries.
   a. Exactly 4 lines of symmetry   Square
   b. A line of symmetry through a pair of opposite vertices   kite
   c. 180 degree rotational symmetry   Parallelogram

Assessment 11-2B

1. Determine which of the following figures (if any) labeled (1) through (10) can be classified under the given description.
   a. Isosceles triangle   1, 2
   b. Isosceles but not equilateral triangle   1
   c. Equilateral but not isosceles triangle   None
   d. Parallelogram but not a trapezoid   None
   e. A trapezoid but not a parallelogram   5
   f. A rectangle but not a square   7
   g. A square but not a rectangle   None
   h. A square but not a trapezoid   None
   i. A rhombus but not a kite   None
   j. A rhombus   4, 6
   k. A kite   4, 6, 8, 9

(1)

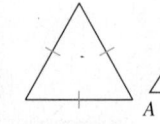
(2)

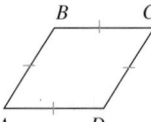
(3) $\overline{AB} \parallel \overline{CD}$,
$\overline{AD} \parallel \overline{BC}$

(4) Opposite sides parallel; all sides congruent.

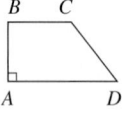 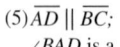
(5) $\overline{AD} \parallel \overline{BC}$; $\angle BAD$ is a right angle.

(6) Square

(7) Rectangle, $AB \neq BC$

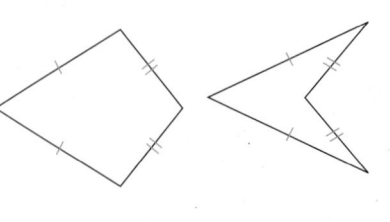
(8)   (9)

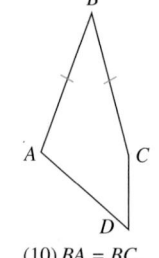
(10) $BA = BC$, $AD \neq CD$, not a trapezoid

2. What is the maximum number of intersection points between two triangles, where no sides of the triangles are on the same line? ⬛

3. A pentagon has only two diagonals that intersect at a given vertex. Determine how many diagonals intersect at a given vertex in each of the following polygons.
  a. Hexagon   3
  b. Decagon   7
  c. 20-gon   17
  d. n-gon $n - 3$

4. Which of the following figures are convex and which are concave? Why? *
  a. 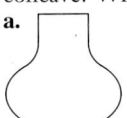   **b.** 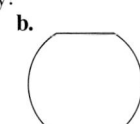   **c.** 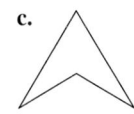   **d.**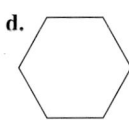

5. Describe the shaded region as simply as possible.   Squares

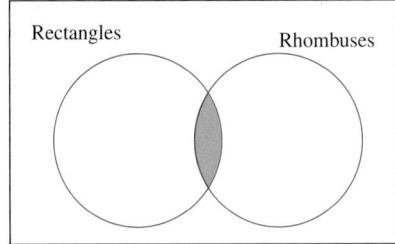

6. If possible, draw the following triangles. If it is not possible, state why.   Answers vary.
  a. An acute scalene triangle   *
  b. A right isosceles triangle   *
  c. A scalene equiangular triangle   *
  d. An equilateral equiangular triangle   *
  e. An acute isosceles triangle   *

7. Determine how many diagonals each of the following polygons has.
  a. Hexagon   9   **b.** 11-gon   44   **c.** 18-gon   135

8. Find the lines of symmetry, if any, for each of the following figures.
  a. BOOHOOED   *
  b. 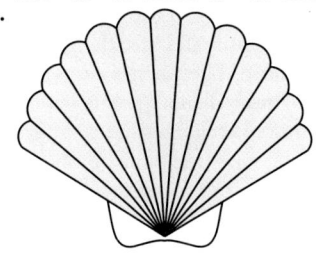   *

9. Identify each of the following triangles as acute, obtuse, right, or equiangular. There may be more than one term that applies to these triangles.
  a. 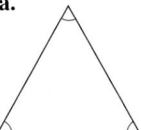   **b.** 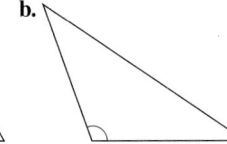   **c.**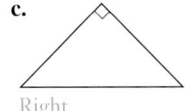
  Equiangular   Obtuse   Right
  and acute

10. Various international signs have symmetries. Determine which of the following figures, if any, have (i) line symmetry, (ii) turn symmetry, and/or (iii) point symmetry:
  a. 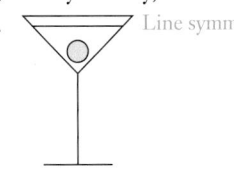 Line symmetry   **b.** 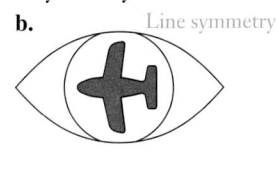 Line symmetry
      Bar   Observation deck

11. Determine the types of symmetry that each separate quilt pattern below has (line, turn, point), if any.   *
  a. 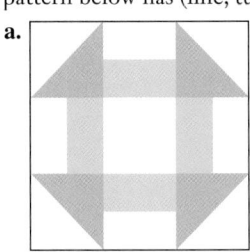   **b.**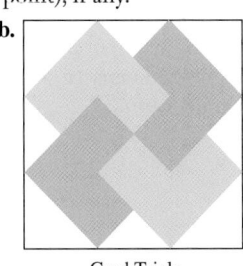
     Churn Dash   Card Trick

  c. 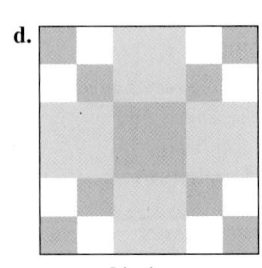   **d.**
     Friendship Star   Linoleum

12. How many lines of symmetry exist for each of the following.
  a.    **b.** 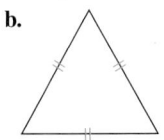   **c.**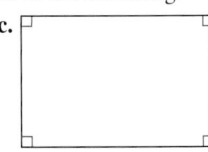
  An isosceles, but not   Equilateral triangle   Rectangle, but not
  equilateral triangle   a square

  d. 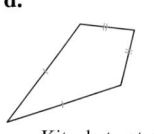   **e.** 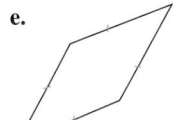   **f.**
  Kite, but not a   Rhombus, but not   Isosceles trapezoid, but
  rhombus   a square   not a rectangle

  g. 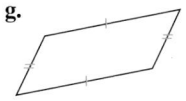   **h.**    **i.**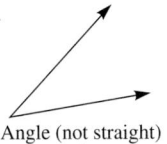
  Parallelogram, but neither   Trapezoid, but not   Angle (not straight)
  a rectangle nor a rhombus   a rectangle
  a. 1   **b.** 3   **c.** 2   **d.** 1   **e.** 2   **f.** 1   **g.** None   **h.** None   **i.** 1

13. In each of the following figures, complete the sketches so that they have line symmetry about ℓ.
   a.   b.

   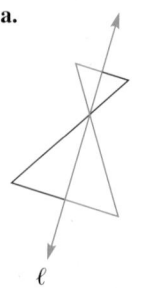   

   ℓ   ℓ

14. Given the digits **5, 6, 7, 8, 9**, which of these have the following symmetries?
   a. Line symmetry (if so, how many?)   *
   b. Point symmetry   *

15. Determine the measures of the angles of turn symmetry for each of the following figures.
   a.   b.

   72°, 144°, 216°, 280°   90°, 180°, 270°

16. Complete the following figures so that they have point symmetry about point *O*.
   a. [*o•*]   b. (☻) *o•* (☺)

17. Give the most general name for the quadrilaterals having the given symmetries.
   a. Two lines of symmetry each through a pair of opposite vertices   Rhombus
   b. Two lines of symmetry each through a pair of midpoints of opposite sides   Rectangle
   c. A line of symmetry through a pair of midpoints of opposite sides   Isosceles trapezoid

Mathematical Connections 11-2

Answers to Mathematical Connections can be found in the Answers section at the back of the book.

Reasoning

1. a. Fold a rectangular piece of paper to create a square. Describe your procedure in writing. Explain why your approach creates a square.
   b. Crease the square in (a) so that the two diagonals are shown. Use paperfolding to show that the diagonals of a square are congruent and perpendicular and divide each other into congruent parts. Describe your procedure and explain why it works.
2. Can a regular polygon be concave? Explain.
3. Are all equilateral triangles isosceles? Explain.
4. Classify each of the following as true or false. If false, explain why.
   a. Every regular polygon is equilateral.
   b. Every equilateral polygon is regular.
   c. A diagonal of a convex polygon can lie outside the polygon.
   d. Every equilateral polygon is convex.

Open-Ended

5. Copy and complete sketches if possible for each of the polygons described in the table below.

Polygon	Triangle	Quadrilateral	Pentagon
Concave			
Convex			
Regular			
Equilateral only			
Equiangular only			

6. On a geoboard or dot paper, construct each of the following polygons.
   a. A scalene triangle
   b. An obtuse triangle

   c. An isosceles trapezoid
   d. A trapezoid that is not isosceles
   e. A convex hexagon
   f. A concave quadrilateral
   g. A parallelogram
   h. A rhombus that is not a square.

   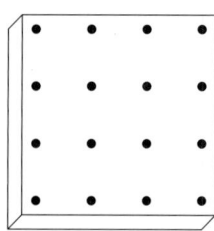

Cooperative Learning

7. Work with a partner. One constructs a figure on a geoboard or draws it on a piece of paper and identifies it. Do not show the figure to the partner but tell the partner sufficient properties of the figure to identify it. Have the partner identify the constructed figure. The partner earns 1 point if the figure is correctly identified and 2 points if a figure is found that has all the required attributes but is different from the one drawn. Each person takes the same number of turns. Try this with each of the following figures.
   a. Scalene triangle
   b. Isosceles triangle
   c. Square
   d. Parallelogram
   e. Trapezoid
   f. Rectangle
   g. Regular polygon
   h. Rhombus
   i. Isosceles trapezoid
   j. A kite that is not a rhombus

8. Work with partners to create a Venn diagram with the universal set being all triangles and the subsets being isosceles, equilateral, and right triangles.

9. Work with partners to create a Venn diagram representing the relationship among polygons, quadrilaterals, trapezoids, parallelograms, rhombuses, rectangles, and squares.

10. Fold a sheet of paper into fourths as shown and cut off the folded corner. Predict what shape you think you will have when you unfold the paper. Check to see if you were correct.

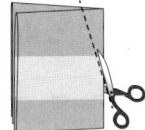

Is it possible to cut the folded sheet so that you obtain each of the following figures. If not, discuss why not.
  a. A parallelogram that is not a rhombus
  b. A rectangle that is not a square
  c. A square

11. The six pattern blocks shown below are manipulatives that can be used to explore polygons and their angles. Given these blocks work in a group to answer the following questions.

  a. Which shapes are (i) quadrilaterals (ii) parallelograms (iii) rhombuses (iv) regular polygons?
  b. The interior angles of pattern blocks can be determined by creating designs such as those shown below. Explain how to use these designs to determine the measures of the interior angles of each pattern block.

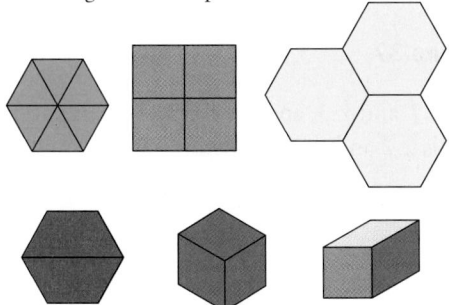

  c. Create pattern-block designs that have various line symmetries and turn symmetries and discuss the symmetries in your group.

Connecting Mathematics to the Classroom

12. A student asks whether a polygon whose sides are congruent is necessarily a regular polygon and whether a polygon with all angles congruent is necessarily a regular polygon. How do you answer?

13. One student says, "My sister's high school geometry book talked about equal angles. Why don't we use the term 'equal angles' instead of 'congruent angles'?" How do you reply?

14. Millie claims that a rhombus is regular because all of its sides are congruent. How do you respond?

15. Jane heard a student say that all squares are rectangles but not all rectangles are squares. She said this did not sound correct. How do you respond?

16. A student asks if $ABCD$ is a valid name for the rectangle below, then is $ACBD$ also valid?

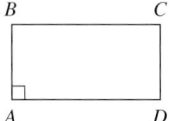

17. A student claims that all figures with four congruent sides are squares. How do you respond?

18. Two students are thinking about squares. One student says that a square is just an equiangular rhombus. Another student says that a square is just an equilateral rectangle. Explain who is correct.

GeoGebra Activities

19. Use GeoGebra Lab-2 to construct quadrilaterals.

Review Problems

20. If three distinct rays with the same vertex are drawn as shown in the following figure, then the angles $\angle AOB$, $\angle AOC$, and $\angle BOC$ are formed.

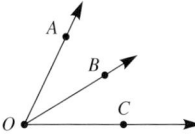

What is the maximum number of angles, measuring less than 180°, formed by using
  a. 10 distinct noncollinear rays with the same vertex?
  b. n distinct noncollinear rays with the same vertex?

21. Determine the possible intersection sets of a line and an angle.

22. Classify the following statements as true or false. If false, tell why.
  a. A ray has two endpoints.
  b. For any points M and N, $\overrightarrow{MN} = \overrightarrow{NM}$.
  c. Skew lines are coplanar.
  d. $\overleftrightarrow{MN} = \overleftrightarrow{NM}$
  e. A line segment contains an infinite number of points.
  f. If two distinct planes intersect, their intersection is a line segment.

National Assessments

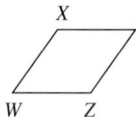

In the figure above, *WXYZ* is a parallelogram. Which of the following is NOT necessarily true?

A. Side *WX* is parallel to side *ZY*.
B. Side *XY* is parallel to side *WZ*.
C. The measures of angles *W* and *Y* are equal.
D. The lengths of sides *WX* and *ZY* are equal.
E. The lengths of sides *WX* and *XY* are equal.

NAEP, Grade 8, 2003

Which statement is true about all four shapes shown?
A. Each shape is a rectangle.
B. Each shape is a quadrilateral.
C. Each shape has two pairs of parallel sides.
D. Each shape has one or more right angles.

NAEP, Grade 4, 2013

Draw two lines of symmetry for the rhombus below.

NAEP, Grade 8, 2013

11-3 More About Angles

11-3 Objectives

Students will be able to understand and explain

- Vertical, supplementary, and complementary angles.

- Parallel lines and angles associated with them.

- Measures of interior and exterior angles of polygons.

CCSS In the grade 7 *Common Core Standards*, we find the following.

Use facts about supplementary, complementary, vertical, and adjacent angles in a multi-step problem to write and solve simple equations for an unknown angle in a figure. (p. 50)

In Figure 37 two lines intersect and form the angles marked 1, 2, 3, and 4.

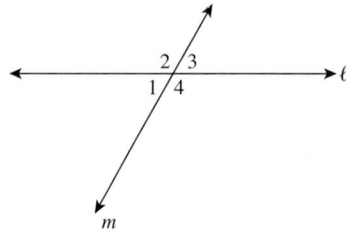

Figure 37

Vertical angles are pairs of angles such as $\angle 1$ and $\angle 3$, and are formed when two lines intersect. Another pair of vertical angles in Figure 37 is $\angle 2$ and $\angle 4$. We define vertical angles as follows.

> **Definition of Vertical Angles**
>
> **Vertical angles**, created by intersecting lines, are a pair of angles whose sides are two pairs of opposite rays.

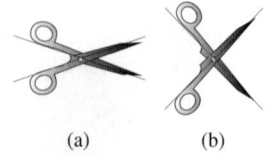

(a)   (b)

Figure 38

Consider a pair of scissors as shown in Figure 38. The scissors form vertical angles. The angle between the blades stays congruent to the angle between the handles when you open or close the scissors as seen in Figure 38(a) and (b). The vertical angles appear congruent. This leads to the following theorem and its proof.

Theorem 11-1

Vertical angles are congruent.

Proof

In Figure 37, we must show that $\angle 1 \cong \angle 3$ and $\angle 2 \cong \angle 4$. We see that $m(\angle 1) + m(\angle 2) = 180°$ and $m(\angle 3) + m(\angle 2) = 180°$. Thus,

$$m(\angle 1) = 180° - m(\angle 2)$$
$$m(\angle 3) = 180° - m(\angle 2).$$

Consequently, $m\angle 1 = m\angle 3$. In a similar way we can show that $m(\angle 2) = m(\angle 4)$. ∎

Specific names are given to other pairs of angles that occur frequently, as seen in Table 9.

Table 9

Supplementary angles are two angles such that the sum of their measures is 180°. Each angle is a *supplement* of the other. (Supplementary angles do not need to be adjacent.)	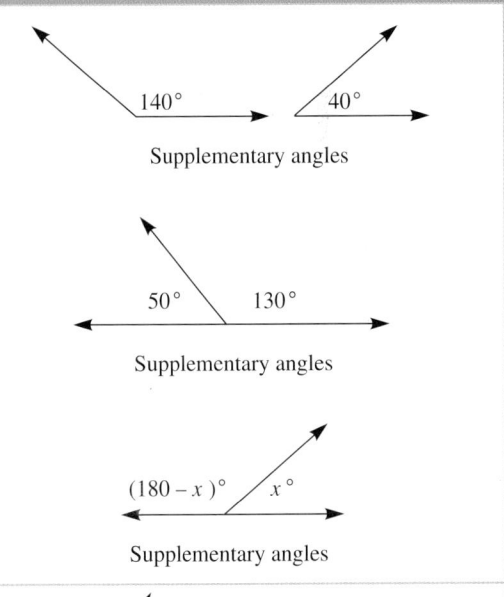
Complementary angles are two angles such that the sum of their measures is 90°. Each angle is a *complement* of the other. (Complementary angles do not need to be adjacent.)	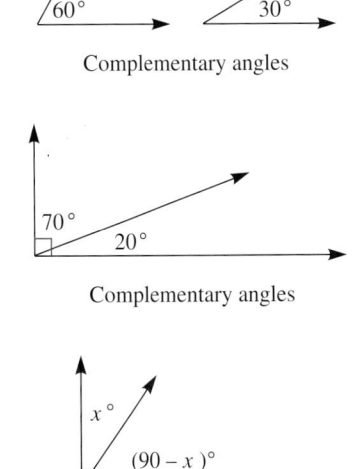

Angles formed when a line (a **transversal**) intersects two distinct lines are named according to their placement in relation to the transversal and the two given lines. Table 10 shows these angles.

Table 10	
	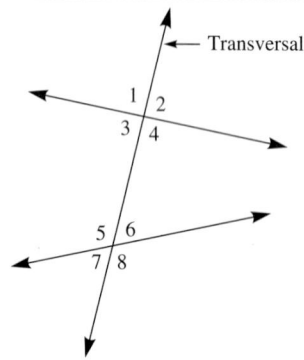
Interior angles are "between" two lines cut by a transversal.	Interior angles are $\angle 3$, $\angle 4$, $\angle 5$, and $\angle 6$.
Exterior angles are not "between" two lines cut by a transversal.	Exterior angles are $\angle 1$, $\angle 2$, $\angle 7$, and $\angle 8$.
Alternate interior angles are between two lines cut by a transversal and are on opposite sides of the transversal.	Alternate interior angles are pairs: $\angle 3$ and $\angle 6$, $\angle 4$ and $\angle 5$.
Alternate exterior angles are not "between" two lines cut by a transversal and are on opposite sides of the transversal.	Alternate exterior angles are pairs: $\angle 1$ and $\angle 8$, $\angle 2$ and $\angle 7$.
Corresponding angles are in the same relative position when two lines are cut by a transversal.	Corresponding angles are pairs: $\angle 1$ and $\angle 5$, $\angle 2$ and $\angle 6$, $\angle 3$ and $\angle 7$, and $\angle 4$ and $\angle 8$.

Suppose corresponding angles such as $\angle 1$ and $\angle 5$ are congruent as in Figure 39. With this assumption, and because $\angle 1$ and $\angle 4$ are congruent vertical angles, we know that the pair of alternate interior angles, $\angle 4$ and $\angle 5$, are also congruent. Similarly, each pair of corresponding angles, alternate interior angles, and alternate exterior angles are congruent.

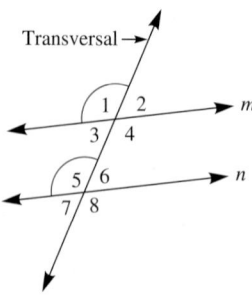

Figure 39

If we examine Figure 39 further, we might conjecture that lines m and n would be parallel when $\angle 1$ is congruent to $\angle 5$. Conversely, if the lines are parallel, the pairs of angles mentioned in Table 10 are congruent. These conjectures are true and are summarized in the following theorem.

Theorem 11-2: Angles and Parallel Lines

If any two distinct coplanar lines are cut by a transversal, then a pair of corresponding angles, alternate interior angles, or alternate exterior angles are congruent if, and only if, the lines are parallel.

Constructing Parallel Lines

Grade 4 *Common Core Standards* state that students should "draw and identify lines and angles, and classify shapes by properties of their lines and angles" (p. 32). Early school drawings lead to later constructions. For example, a method which was commonly used by architects to construct a line ℓ through a given point P parallel to a given line m is shown in Figure 40. Place the side $\overline{AB}$ of triangle ABC on line m, as shown in Figure 40(a). Next, place a ruler on side $\overline{AC}$. Keeping the ruler stationary, slide triangle ABC along the ruler's edge until its side $\overline{AB}$ (marked $\overline{A'B'}$) contains point P, as in Figure 40(b). Use the side $\overline{A'B'}$ to draw the line ℓ through P parallel to m.

To show that the construction produces parallel lines, notice that when triangle ABC slides, the measures of its angles are unchanged. The angles of triangle ABC and triangle A'B'C' in Figure 40(b) are corresponding congruent angles. ∠A and ∠A' are corresponding angles formed by m and ℓ and the transversal $\overline{EF}$. By Theorem 11–2, because corresponding angles are congruent, ℓ ∥ m. In Chapter 12, we will show how to construct parallel lines using only a compass and straightedge.

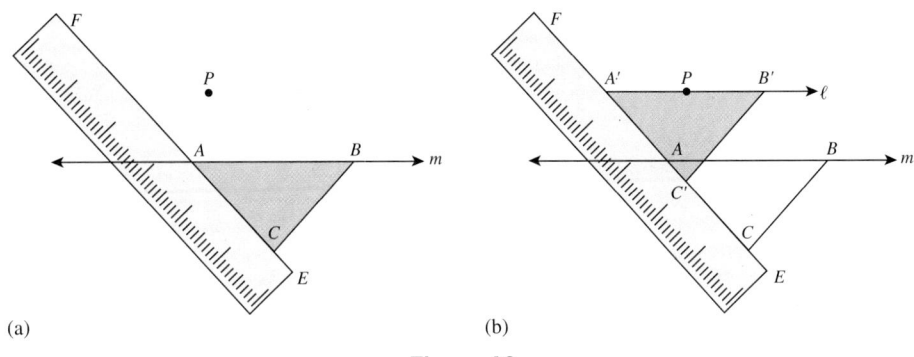

(a)   (b)

Figure 40

Use *Triangle Properties-Angles* to reinforce the angle sum of a triangle theorem and the construction of triangles using a protractor and ruler.

The Sum of the Measures of the Angles of a Triangle

The sum of the measures of the angles in a triangle is observed to be 180°. We see this by using a torn triangle, as shown in Figure 41. Angles 1, 2, and 3 of triangle ABC in Figure 41(a) are torn as pictured and then replaced as shown in Figure 41(b). The three angles seem to lie along a single line ℓ.

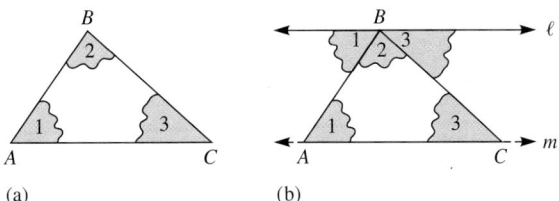

(a)   (b)

Figure 41

If we repeat the procedure for several different triangles, the angle measures always seem to sum to 180° or a straight angle. This conclusion is only a conjecture. We use *deductive reasoning* to prove that a statement is true using given information, previously defined and undefined terms, theorems or statements assumed to be true, and logic. A conclusion based on *deductive reasoning* must be true if the hypothesis is true. We state the triangle sum as a theorem and provide a proof.

Theorem 11-3

The sum of the measures of the interior angles of any triangle is 180°.

Proof

In Figure 42(a), $\triangle ABC$ has interior angles 1, 2, and 3; we want to prove $m(\angle 1) + m(\angle 2) + m(\angle 3) = 180°$. Motivated by the experiment in Figure 41, we place $\angle 4$ in Figure 42(b) so that $\angle 4 \cong \angle 1$. We next extend $\overrightarrow{BD}$ to form line ℓ. In this way, $\angle 5$ is formed. If we could show that $\angle 5 \cong \angle 3$, the proof would be completed. Because we constructed $\angle 4$ so that $\angle 4 \cong \angle 1$, we have a pair of congruent alternate interior angles created by lines ℓ and m and transversal $\overleftrightarrow{AB}$. Thus, $\ell \parallel m$ and therefore $\angle 5 \cong \angle 3$, as these are alternate interior angles created by the parallel lines ℓ and m and the transversal $\overleftrightarrow{BC}$. Consequently,

$$m(\angle 1) + m(\angle 2) + m(\angle 3) = m(\angle 4) + m(\angle 2) + m(\angle 5) = 180°, \text{or}$$

$$m(\angle 1) + m(\angle 2) + m(\angle 3) = 180°.$$

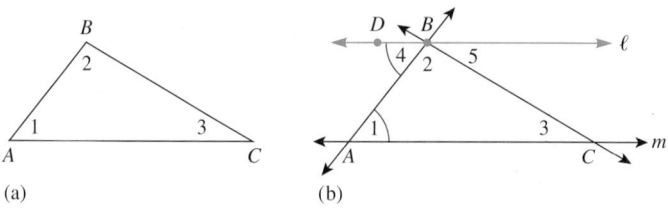

(a)   (b)

Figure 42   ∎

Example 5

From the framework for a tire jack shown in Figure 43(a), parallelogram $ABCD$ is drawn in Figure 43(b). If $\angle ADC$ of the parallelogram measures 50°, what are the measures of the other angles of the parallelogram?

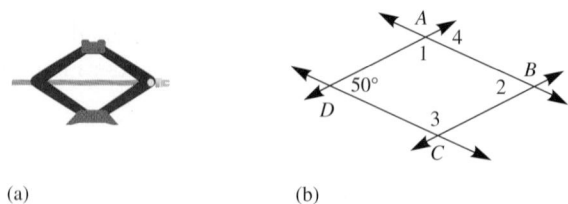

(a)   (b)

Figure 43

Solution In Figure 43(b), we draw lines containing the sides of parallelogram $ABCD$. $\angle ADC$ has a measure of 50°, and $\angle 4$ and $\angle ADC$ are corresponding angles formed by parallel lines $\overleftrightarrow{AB}$ and $\overleftrightarrow{DC}$ cut by transversal $\overleftrightarrow{AD}$. So it follows that $m(\angle 4) = 50°$. Because $\angle 1$ and $\angle 4$ are supplementary, $m(\angle 1) = 180° - 50° = 130°$. Using similar reasoning, we find that $m(\angle 2) = 50°$ and $m(\angle 3) = 130°$.

In Figure 44, $m \| n$ and k is a transversal. Explain why interior angles, $\angle 1$ and $\angle 2$ are supplementary.

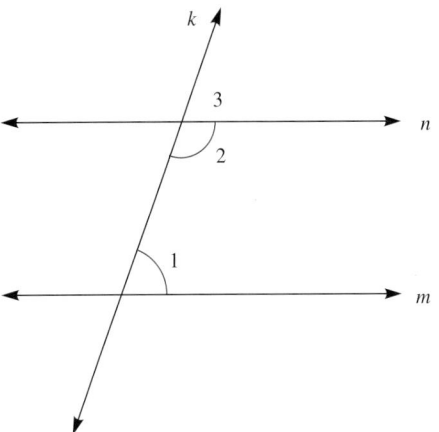

Figure 44

Solution Because $\angle 1$ and $\angle 3$ are corresponding angles when parallel lines m and n are cut by transversal k, $m(\angle 1) = m(\angle 3)$. Also because $\angle 2$ and $\angle 3$ are supplementary angles, $m(\angle 2) + m(\angle 3) = 180°$. Substituting $m(\angle 1)$ for $m(\angle 3)$, we have $m(\angle 2) + m(\angle 1) = 180°$ and therefore $\angle 1$ and $\angle 2$ are supplementary.

Example 6 leads to the following theorem.

Theorem 11-4

The sum of the measures of the interior angles on the same side of a transversal and formed when two parallel lines are cut by the transversal is 180°; the angles are supplementary.

The Sum of the Measures of the Interior Angles of a Convex Polygon with *n* Sides

We study the sum of the measures of all the interior angles in any convex *n*-gon by considering several special cases. From any vertex of a polygon, diagonals can be drawn from the vertex to form adjacent, nonoverlapping triangular regions. In the quadrilateral in Figure 45(a), the diagonal from *B* partitions the quadrilateral into two triangles.

Use Angles on Pattern Blocks and Sum of Interior/Exterior Angles to develop the relationships between the number of sides of a convex polygon and the sum of the measures of its interior angles and the sum of the measures of its exterior angles.

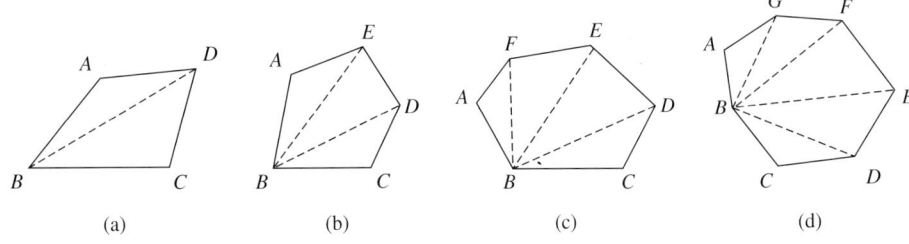

Figure 45

In the pentagon in Figure 45(b), the diagonals from *B* partition the pentagon into three triangles. In the hexagon in Figure 45(c), the diagonals from *B* partition the hexagon into four triangles. In each of the polygons in Figure 45, the number of triangles is two less than the number of sides because when we increase the number of sides by 1, we add one triangle leaving the number of triangles still 2 less than the number of sides. This is illustrated in the heptagon of Figure 45(d), which has one more side than the hexagon in Figure 45(c).

The number of triangles in a convex n-gon created by all the diagonals from a single vertex is $n - 2$. To find the sum of the measures of all the interior angles in any convex polygon, we add the measures of all the interior angles in the triangles. Since the sum of the measures of the angles in any triangle is 180°, the sum of the measures of the interior angles in any convex n-gon is $(n - 2)180°$, proving the following theorem.

> **Theorem 11-5**
>
> The sum of the measures of the interior angles of any convex n-gon is $(n - 2)180°$.

The Sum of the Measures of the Exterior Angles of a Convex n-gon

Figure 46 shows interior and exterior angles (in blue) of a pentagon. The measures of the interior angles are $\alpha_1, \alpha_2, \alpha_3, \alpha_4, \alpha_5$ and of the exterior angles are $\beta_1, \beta_2, \beta_3, \beta_4, \beta_5$. Since the exterior and interior angle at a vertex are supplementary, and the sum of the measure of the interior angles in a pentagon is $(5 - 2)180°$, we have:

$$(\alpha_1 + \beta_1) + (\alpha_2 + \beta_2) + (\alpha_3 + \beta_3) + (\alpha_4 + \beta_4) + (\alpha_5 + \beta_5) = 5 \cdot 180°$$
$$(\alpha_1 + \alpha_2 + \alpha_3 + \alpha_4 + \alpha_5) + (\beta_1 + \beta_2 + \beta_3 + \beta_4 + \beta_5) = 5 \cdot 180°$$
$$(5 - 2)180° + (\beta_1 + \beta_2 + \beta_3 + \beta_4 + \beta_5) = 5 \cdot 180°$$
$$\beta_1 + \beta_2 + \beta_3 + \beta_4 + \beta_5 = 5 \cdot 180° - 3 \cdot 180°$$
$$= 2 \cdot 180°$$
$$= 360°$$

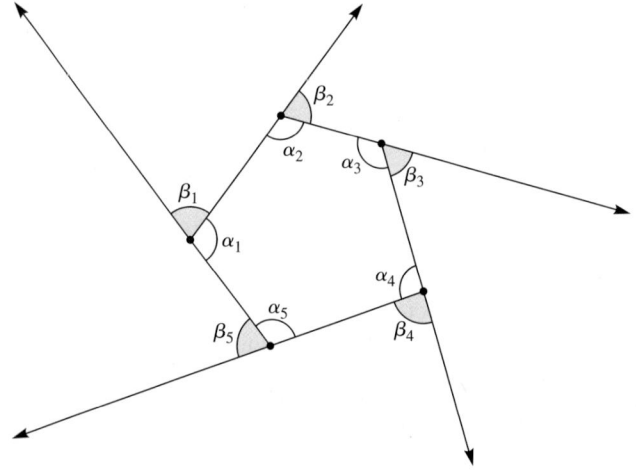

Figure 46

Thus, the sum of the measures of the exterior angles in a pentagon is 360°.

An analogous approach works for any convex n-gon. Let S be the sum of the measures of the interior angles and E the sum of the measures of the exterior angles. We know that $S + E = n \cdot 180°$. Because $S = (n - 2)180°$, we get

$$(n - 2)180° + E = n \cdot 180°$$
$$E = n \cdot 180° - (n - 2)180°$$
$$= [n - (n - 2)]180°$$
$$= 2 \cdot 180°$$
$$= 360°.$$

Thus, we have proved Theorem 11–6.

Theorem 11-6
The sum of the measures of the exterior angles of any convex *n*-gon is 360°.

An intuitive justification of Theorem 11-6 is shown in Figure 47. Imagine walking clockwise around the convex pentagon starting at vertex *A*. At each vertex we need to turn by an exterior angle as in Figure 47(a). At the end of the walk we are at *A*, heading in the direction of the red arrow as in Figure 47(b). To return to the original starting direction we turn through one more exterior angle as in Figure 47(c). Thus, it seems that our total turn is through 360°, whether we walk around a convex pentagon or any other convex polygon. This may be clearer if we extend the sides of the exterior angles and look at the figure from afar. Because the sides are infinite and the polygon is small, the figure will look like the one in Figure 47(d).

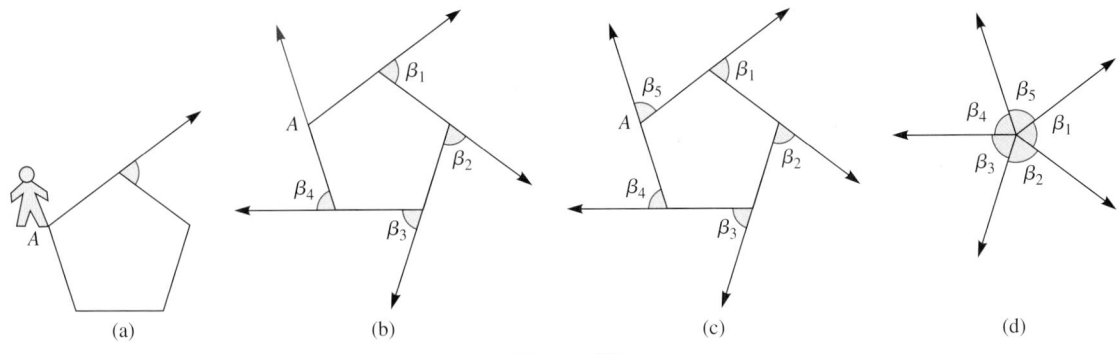

(a)   (b)   (c)   (d)

Figure 47

▶ **NOW TRY THIS 12**

NTT 12: Answers can be found in Answers at the back of the book.

a. Using the fact that the sum of the measures of the exterior angles in a convex *n*-gon is 360°, derive the formula for the sum of the interior angles.
b. Express the measure of a single interior angle of a regular *n*-gon in terms of *n*.

Example 7

a. Find the measure of each interior angle of a regular decagon.
b. Find the number of sides of a regular polygon each of whose interior angles has a measure of 175°.

Solution

a. Because a decagon has 10 sides, the sum of the measures of the interior angles of a decagon is $(10 - 2)180° = 8 \cdot 180° = 1440°$. A regular decagon has 10 angles, all of which are congruent, so each one has a measure of $\dfrac{1440°}{10}$, or 144°. As an alternative solution using the approach in Now Try This 12, each exterior angle is $\dfrac{360°}{10}$, or 36°. Hence, each interior angle is $180° - 36°$, or 144°.

b. Each interior angle of the regular polygon is 175°. Thus, the measure of each exterior angle of the polygon is $180° - 175°$, or 5°. Because the sum of the measures of all exterior angles of a convex polygon is 360°, the number of exterior angles is $\dfrac{360}{5}$, or 72. Hence, the number of sides is 72.

Example 8

In Figure 48, lines k and l are parallel. Measures of some of the angles are shown. Find x, the measure of $\angle BCA$.

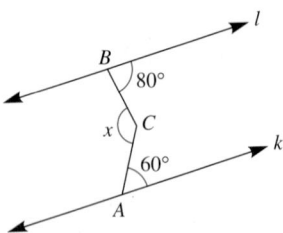

Figure 48

Solution   Using the strategy of *examining a related problem*, if we had a transversal intersecting the parallel lines, we could consider congruent corresponding or alternate interior angles. To obtain a transversal we extend either $\overline{BC}$ or $\overline{AC}$. In Figure 49(a), transversal $\overleftrightarrow{BC}$ intersects line k at D. The marked angles with vertices at B and D are congruent alternate interior angles created by the parallel lines and the transversal, and hence $\angle BDA$ measures 80°. The measure of the third angle in $\triangle ACD$ is $180° - (60° + 80°) = 40°$. Thus, $x = 180° - 40° = 140°$.

An alternative approach is suggested in Figure 49(b), where line m is constructed parallel to ℓ.

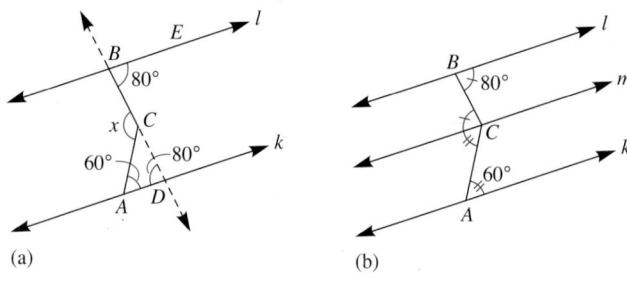

(a)   (b)

Figure 49

Assessment 11-3A

1. If three lines all meet in a single point, how many pairs of vertical angles are formed?   6
2. Find the measure of the third angle in each of the following triangles.

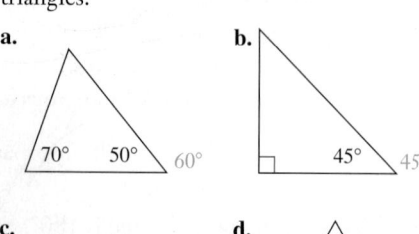

a.

b.

70°   50°   60°

45°   45°

c.

d.

30°   60°

60°   60°   60°

3. Find the measure of a complementary angle, a supplementary angle, and a vertical angle for the following measures.
   a. $m(\angle A) = 30°$ Complementary, 60°; supplementary, 150°; vertical, 30°
   b. $m(\angle B) = x°$ Complementary, $90° - x°$; supplementary, $180° - x°$; vertical, $x°$

$m(\angle A) = 18°, m(\angle B) = 54°, m(\angle C) = 108°$

4. In $\triangle ABC$, the measure of $\angle B$ is three times the measure of $\angle A$ and the measure of $\angle C$ is twice the measure of $\angle B$. Find the measure of each angle.
5. What is the measure of the complement of the supplement of a 150° angle?   60°
6. If the measure of an angle is 23°17'18", what is the measure of its supplement?   156° 42' 42"
7. If $9x°$ and $(5x + 62)°$ are the measure of complementary angles, what is the measure of each angle?   18° and 72°
8. For each of the following figures, determine whether m and n are parallel lines. Justify your answers.

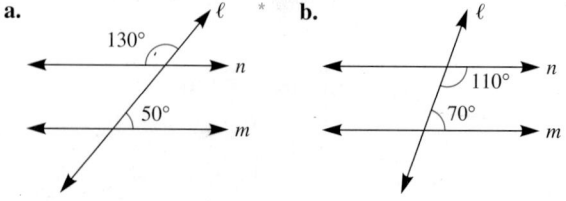

a.

130°

50°

b.

110°

70°

c.

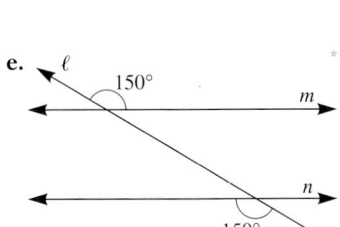

d.

e.

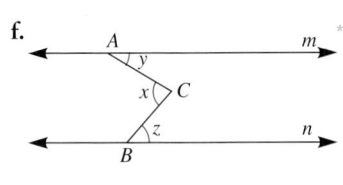

f.

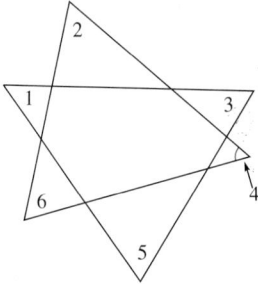

$x = y + z$

9. Two angles are complementary and the ratio of their measures is 7:2. What are the angle measures? 70° and 20°

10. In a regular polygon, the measure of each interior angle is 162°. How many sides does the polygon have? 20

11. Find the sum of the measures of the marked angles in the following figure. 360°

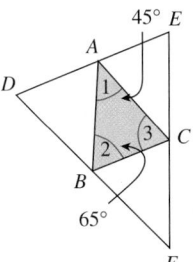

12. If the interior angles of a hexagon form an arithmetic sequence with the greatest measure being 130°, find the measure of each angle.

13. In the following figure, $\overleftrightarrow{DE} \parallel \overleftrightarrow{BC}$, $\overleftrightarrow{EF} \parallel \overleftrightarrow{AB}$, and $\overleftrightarrow{DF} \parallel \overleftrightarrow{AC}$. Also, $m(\angle 1) = 45°$ and $m(\angle 2) = 65°$. Find each of the following angle measures.
  a. $m(\angle 3)$ 70°
  b. $m(\angle D)$ 70°
  c. $m(\angle E)$ 65°
  d. $m(\angle F)$ 45°

14. In the following figures, solve for x.
  a.

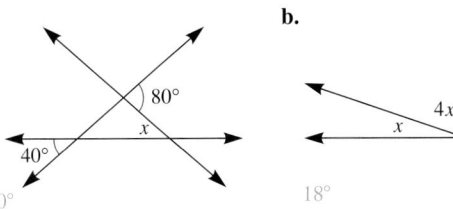

  40°

  b.

  18°

  c.

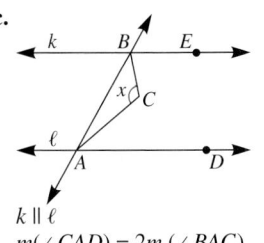

  $k \parallel \ell$
  $m(\angle CAD) = 2m(\angle BAC)$
  $m(\angle CBE) = 2m(\angle ABC)$ 120°

15. a. Determine the measure of an angle whose measure is twice that of its complement. 60°
  b. If two angles of a triangle are complementary, what is the measure of the third angle? 90°

16. Find the sum of the measures of the marked angles in the following figure. 360°

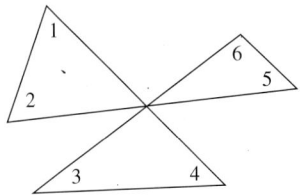

17. Find x in the following figure. 111°

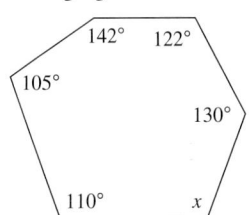

18. Find the measures of angles 1, 2, and 3 given that $TRAP$ is a trapezoid with $\overline{TR} \parallel \overline{PA}$.

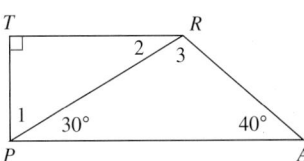

$m(\angle 1) = 60°; m(\angle 2) = 30°; m(\angle 3) = 110°$

19. Use the following figure to answer the following.

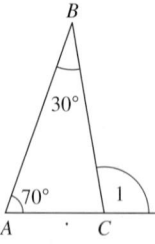

a. Find $m(\angle 1)$.   100°

b. $\angle 1$ is an exterior angle of $\triangle ABC$. Use your answer in (a) to make a conjecture concerning the measure of an exterior angle of a triangle. Justify your conjecture.   *

20. In the figure, x, y, z, and w are measures of the angles as shown. If $y = 2x = \frac{1}{2}z = \frac{1}{3}w$, find x, y, z, and w.   *

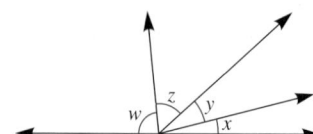

21. If m is parallel to n, find the measures of each numbered angle.   *

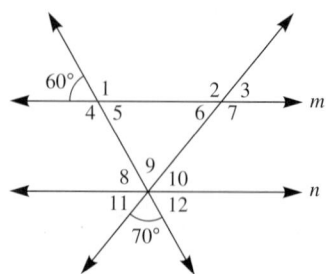

22. If $m(\angle 2) = m(\angle 3)$, prove $m(\angle 1) = m(\angle 4)$.

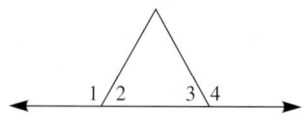

$m(\angle 1) + m(\angle 2) = 180°$ (straight angle)
$m(\angle 3) + m(\angle 4) = 180°$ (straight angle)
Then $m(\angle 1) + m(\angle 2) = m(\angle 3) + m(\angle 4)$ and since
$m(\angle 2) = m(\angle 3)$, we have $m(\angle 1) + m(\angle 3) = m(\angle 3) + m(\angle 4)$.
Subtracting $m(\angle 3)$ from both sides, we have $m(\angle 1) = m(\angle 4)$.

Assessment 11-3B

1. If two planes intersect in a single line forming dihedral angles, how would you define vertical dihedral angles?   *

2. Find the measure of the angle marked x in each of the following triangles.

a.

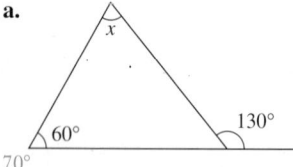

b.

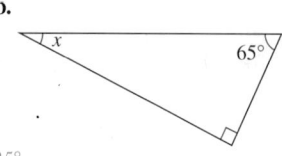

c.

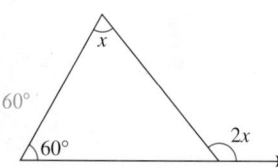

d.

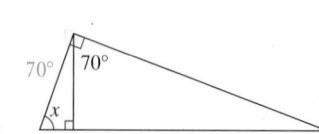

3. Find the measure of a complementary angle, a supplementary angle, and a vertical angle for the following measures.
  a. $m(\angle A) = 20°$ *   **b.** $m(\angle B) = 10° + x°$ *

4. An angle measures 15° more than 4 times the measure of its complementary angle. What is the measure of the angle?   75°

5. What is the measure of the supplement of the complement of a 20° angle?   110°

6. If the measure of an angle is 128°19′28″, what is the measure of its supplement?   51°40′32″

7. If $3x°$ and $(6x + 18)°$ are the measures of supplementary angles, what is the measure of each angle?   54° and 126°

8. In part (a) prove that $k \parallel \ell$. In parts (b) and (c), solve for x given that $k \parallel \ell$.
  a.   *

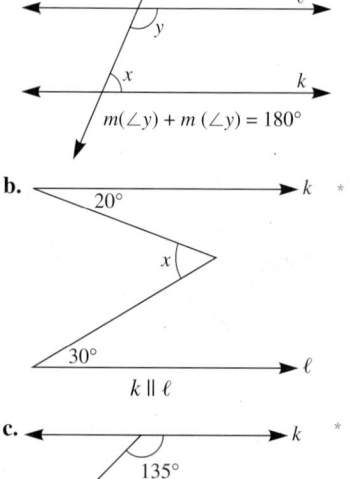

$m(\angle y) + m(\angle y) = 180°$

  b.

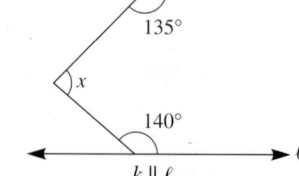

$k \parallel \ell$

  c.   *

$k \parallel \ell$

9. Determine the measure of an angle whose measure is $\frac{2}{3}$ of its complement.   36°

10. Find the measure of each of the interior angles of a regular dodecagon (12-sided polygon).   150°

11. Find the sum of the measures of the numbered angles in the following figure.   360°

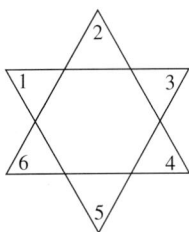

12. Calculate the measure of each angle of a pentagon, where the measures of the angles form an arithmetic sequence and the least measure is 60°.   60°, 84°, 108°, 132°, 156°

13. The sides of △DEF are parallel to the sides of △BCA. If the measures of two angles of △ABC are 60° and 70° as shown, find the measures of angles of △DEF.
$m(\angle D) = 50°; m(\angle E) = 70°; m(\angle F) = 60°$

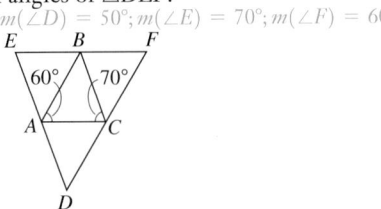

14. In each of the following figures, find the measures of the marked angles.

a.

b.

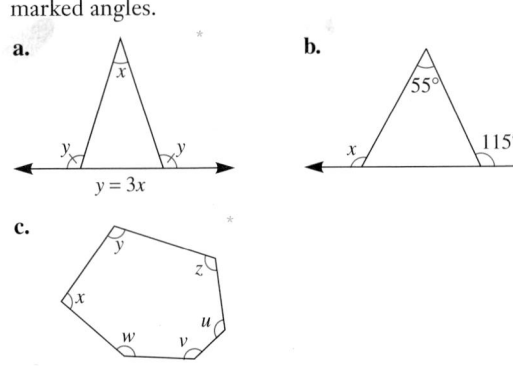

c.

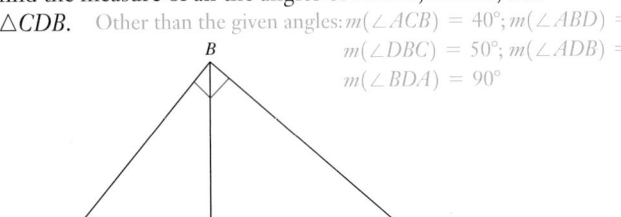

The sequence x, y, z, u, v, w is an arithmetic sequence and v = 136°.

15. **a.** If $m(\angle ABC) = 90°$ and $\overline{BD} \perp \overline{AC}$ and $m(\angle A) = 50°$, find the measure of all the angles of △ABC, △ADB, and △CDB.   Other than the given angles: $m(\angle ACB) = 40°; m(\angle ABD) = 40°;$
$m(\angle DBC) = 50°; m(\angle ADB) = 90°;$
$m(\angle BDA) = 90°$

b. If $m(\angle A) = \alpha$ in (a), find the measures of all the angles of △ABC, △ADB, and △CDB in terms of α.
Other than the given angles:
$m(\angle ACB) = 90° - \alpha; m(\angle ABD) = 90° - \alpha;$
$m(\angle ABD) = 90° - \alpha; m(\angle DBC) = \alpha;$
$m(\angle BDA) = 90°$

16. Two sides of a regular octagon are extended as shown in the following figure. Find the measure of ∠1.

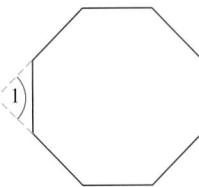

17. Home plate on a baseball field has three right angles and two other congruent angles. Refer to the following figure and find the measures of each of these two other congruent angles.

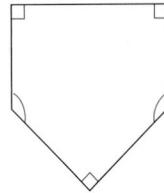

18. Find the measure of ∠x in the figure below.   135°

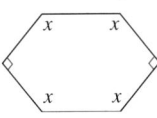

19. ABCD is a quadrilateral in which opposite angles have the same measure, as indicated in the following figure. What kind of quadrilateral is ABCD? Justify your answer.   *

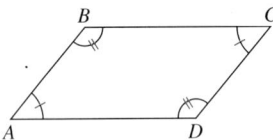

20. Find the measure of the unknown marked angles.

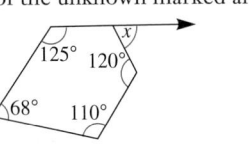

21. Given the figure shown with $\overleftrightarrow{AX} \parallel \overleftrightarrow{DY}$, find the measures of each numbered angle.   *

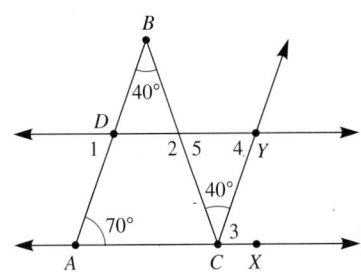

22. If $m(\angle 2) = m(\angle 3)$, prove $m(\angle 1) = m(\angle 4)$.   *

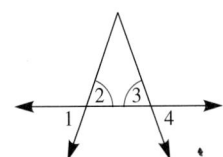

Mathematical Connections 11-3

Answers to Mathematical Connections can be found in the Answers section at the back of the book.

Reasoning

1. **a.** If one angle of a triangle is obtuse, can another also be obtuse? Why or why not?
   b. If one angle in a triangle is acute, can the other two angles also be acute? Why or why not?
   c. If a triangle has one acute angle, is the triangle necessarily acute? Why or why not?
   d. Can two angles of a triangle be supplementary? Why or why not.

2. In the following figure, A is a point not on line ℓ. Is it possible to have two distinct perpendicular segments from A to ℓ in a plane? Why or why not?

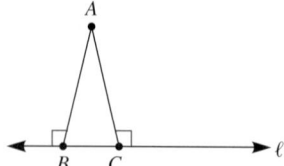

3. Can the measures of the interior angles in a convex polygon be $60°, 80°, 90°,$ and $135°$? Explain your answer.

4. Can each of the following be the sum of the measures of the interior angles of a polygon? If not, tell why not.
   a. $2700°$ **b.** $1400°$ **c.** $1260°$

5. In the figure below, how is the measure of $\angle 4$ related to the sum of the measures of $\angle 1$ and $\angle 2$? Prove your answer.

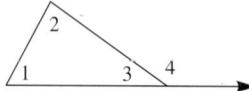

6. **a.** Explain how to find the sum of the measures of the interior angles of any convex pentagon by choosing any point P in the interior and constructing triangles, as shown in the following figure.

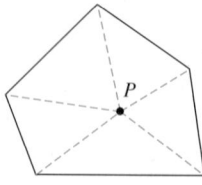

   b. Using the method suggested by the diagram in (a), explain how to find the sum of the measures of the angles of any convex n-gon. Is your answer the same as the one already obtained in this section, $(n - 2)180°$?

7. Explain how, through paperfolding, you would show each of the following statements.
   a. In an isosceles triangle, the angles opposite congruent sides are congruent.
   b. If two angles of a triangle are congruent, the triangle is isosceles.
   c. In an equilateral triangle, all the interior angles are congruent.
   d. An isosceles trapezoid has two pairs of congruent angles.

8. **a.** Explain how to find the sum of the measures of the marked interior angles of a concave quadrilateral like the following.

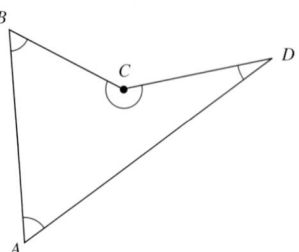

   b. Conjecture whether the theorem for the sum of the measures of the interior angles of a convex polygon is true for concave polygons.
   c. Justify your conjecture in (b) for pentagons and hexagons and explain why your conjecture is true in general.

9. Regular hexagons have been used to tile floors. Can a floor be tiled using only regular pentagons? Why or why not?

10. Lines a and b are cut by transversals c and d. If $m(\angle 1) = m(\angle 3)$ and $m(\angle 2) = m(\angle 4)$, can you conclude that a and b are parallel? Justify your answer.

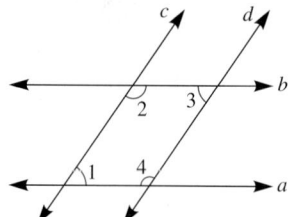

11. A beam of light from A hits the surface of a mirror at point B, is reflected, and then hits a perpendicular mirror and is reflected again. If $\angle 1 \cong \angle 2$ and $\angle 3 \cong \angle 4$, prove that the reflected beam is parallel to the incoming beam, that is, that the rays $\overrightarrow{AB}$ and $\overrightarrow{CD}$ are parallel.

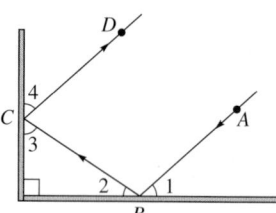

Open-Ended

12. Find a possible set of measures of the interior angles of a non-regular octagon.

13. Draw three different concave polygons. When you walk around a polygon, at each vertex you need to turn either right (clockwise) or left (counterclockwise). A turn to the left is measured by a positive number of degrees and a turn to the right by a negative number of degrees. Find the sum of the measures of the turn angles of the polygons you drew. Assume you start at a vertex facing in the direction of a side, walk around the polygon, and end up at the same vertex facing in the same direction as when you started.

14. Draw three concave polygons. Measure all the interior angles, including any reflex angles. Conjecture a statement about the sum of the interior angles of any concave polygon.

Cooperative Learning

15. In $\triangle ABC$, $\overrightarrow{AD}$ and $\overrightarrow{BD}$ are *angle bisectors*; that is, they divide the angles at A and B respectively into congruent angles.
    a. If the measures of $\angle A$ and $\angle B$ are known, then $m(\angle D)$ can be found. Explain how.

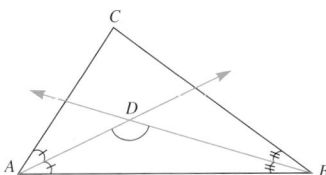

    b. Suppose $m(\angle A)$ and $m(\angle B)$ are not known but that of $m(\angle C)$ is. Can $m(\angle D)$ be found? If so, find $m(\angle D)$ in terms of $m(\angle C)$. To answer this question, assign each member of your group a triangle with different angles but with the same measure for $\angle C$. Each person should compute $m(\angle D)$. Use the results to make a conjecture related to the previous question.
    c. Discuss a strategy for answering the question in part (b) and write a solution to be distributed to the entire class.

16. Each person should draw a large triangle like $\triangle ABC$ in the following figure and cut it out. Fold the crease $\overline{BB'}$ so that A falls on some point A' on $\overline{AC}$. Next, unfold and fold the top B along $\overline{BB'}$ so that B falls on B'. Then fold vertices A and C along $\overline{AC}$ to match point B', as shown in the following figures.

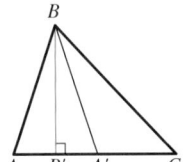 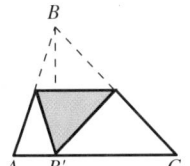 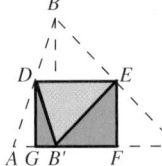

    a. Why is $\overline{BB'}$ perpendicular to $\overline{AC}$?
    b. What theorem does the folded figure illustrate? Why?
    c. The folded figure seems to be a rectangle. Explain why.
    d. What is the length of $\overline{GF}$ in terms of the length of the base $\overline{AC}$ of $\triangle ABC$? Why?

Connecting Mathematics to the Classroom

17. Jan, wants to make tiles in the shape of a convex polygon with all interior angles acute. She is wondering if there are any such polygons besides triangles. How do you respond?

18. A student wonders if there exists a convex decagon with exactly four right angles. How do you respond?

19. A student wants to know if a triangle can have two right angles. How do you respond?

Review Problems

20. In each of the following, name the required properties. If this is not possible, explain why.
    a. Two properties that hold true for all rectangles but not for all rhombuses
    b. Two properties that hold true for all squares but not for all isosceles trapezoids

c. Two properties that hold true for all parallelograms but not for all squares

21. Sort the following shapes according to the given attributes they must have.
    a. Number of parallel sides
    b. Number of right angles
    c. Number of congruent sides

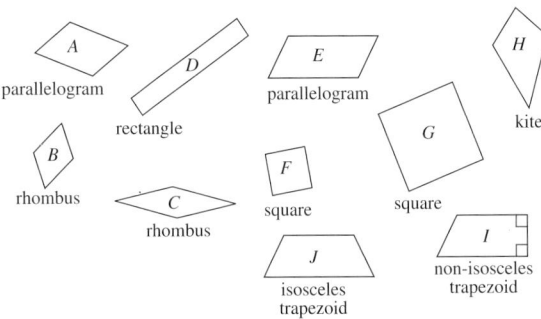

22. What geometric properties make SOS a good choice for the international distress symbol?

23. Design symbols that have each of the following symmetries, if possible:
    a. Turn symmetry but not line symmetry
    b. Line, turn, and point symmetry

24. a. Determine the number of lines of symmetry, if any, in each of the following flags.
    b. Sketch the lines of symmetry for each, if they exist.

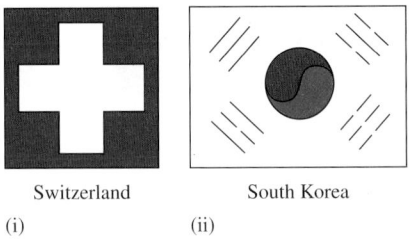

Switzerland   South Korea
   (i)   (ii)

25. Explain whether the following quilt patterns have turn symmetry, and, if so, identify the turn center.

a. 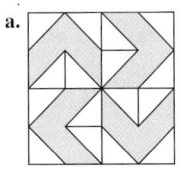   b.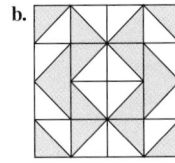

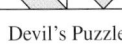

Devil's Puzzle   Empire Star

26. Find the lines of symmetry, if any, for each of the following:

a. 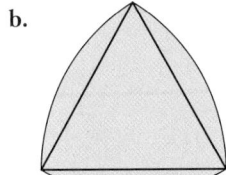   b.

National Assessments

National Assessment of Educational Progress (NAEP) Questions

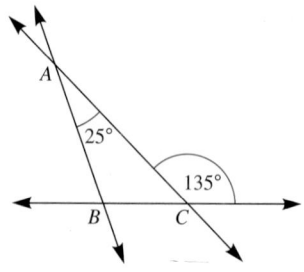

In the triangle, what is the degree measure of ∠*ABC*?

A. 45   B. 100   C. 110

D. 135   E. 160

NAEP, Grade 8, 2003

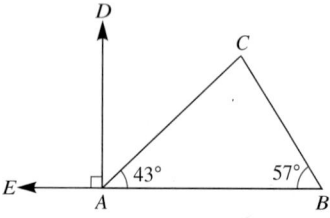

In the figure, what is the measure of angle *DAC*?

A. 47°   B. 57°   C. 80°

D. 90°   E. 137°

NAEP, Grade 8, 2007

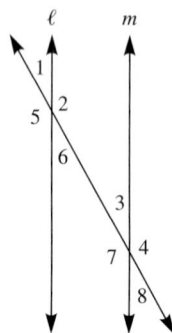

In the figure above, line ℓ is parallel to line *m*. Which of the following pairs of angles must have the same measure?

A. Angles 1 and 2

B. Angles 1 and 5

C. Angles 2 and 3

D. Angles 4 and 5

E. Angles 4 and 8

NAEP, Grade 8, 2011

11-4 Geometry in Three Dimensions

Simple Closed Surfaces

11-4 Objectives

Students will be able to understand and explain

- Simple closed surfaces and polyhedra.
- How to draw three-dimensional shapes.
- Why there are only five regular polyhedra.
- Simple closed surfaces that are not polyhedra.

CCSS In the kindergarten *Common Core Standards*, we find the following.

Students describe their physical world using geometric ideas (e.g., shape, orientation, spatial relations) and vocabulary. They identify, name, and describe basic two-dimensional shapes, such as squares, triangles, circles, rectangles, and hexagons, presented in a variety of ways (e.g., with different sizes and orientations), as well as three-dimensional shapes such as cubes, cones, cylinders, and spheres. They use basic shapes and spatial reasoning to model objects in their environment and to construct more complex shapes. (p. 9)

In previous sections we identified, named, and described two-dimensional shapes. In this section, we expand to three-dimensional shapes.

A visit to the grocery store exposes us to many three-dimensional objects that have simple closed surfaces. Figure 50 shows some examples.

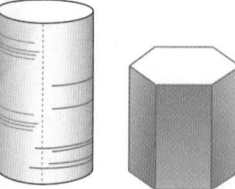 

Figure 50

A **simple closed surface** has a connected interior, has no holes, and is hollow. A simple closed surface partitions space into three disjoint sets: the points on the surface, its interior, and its exterior. The set of all points on a simple closed surface together with all interior points is a **solid**. Figure 51(a), (b), (c), and (d) are examples of simple closed surfaces; (e) and (f) are not. (Why?)

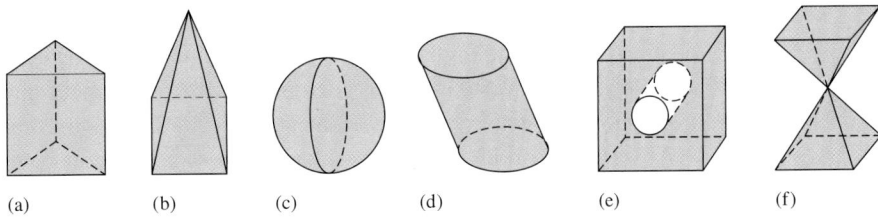

Figure 51

A **polyhedron** (*polyhedra* is the plural) is a simple closed surface made up of polygonal regions, or **faces**. The vertices of the polygonal regions are the **vertices** (*vertex* is the singular) of the polyhedron, and the sides of each polygonal region are the **edges** of the polyhedron. A **sphere** is the set of all points at a given distance from a given point, the **center**. Figure 51(a) and (b) are examples of polyhedra but (c), (d), (e), and (f) are not.

A **prism** is a polyhedron in which two congruent polygonal faces (bases) lie in parallel planes and the remaining faces are formed by the union of the line segments joining corresponding points in the two bases. The shaded parallel faces of a prism are the **bases** of the prism. Any cross section of the prism that is parallel to the bases will be congruent to the bases. Figure 52 shows four different prisms. A prism is usually named after its bases, as noted.

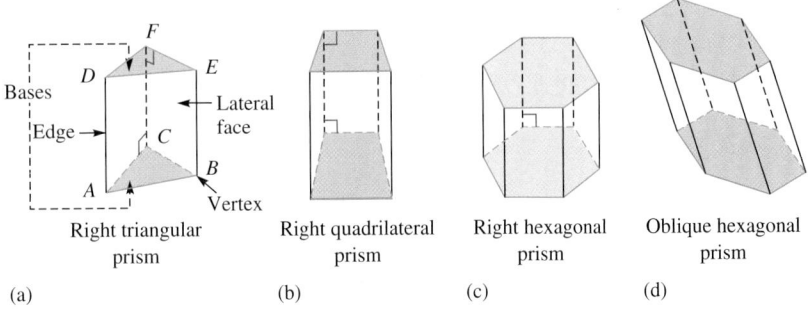

Figure 52

The faces other than the bases are the **lateral faces** of a prism and are parallelograms. If the lateral faces of a prism are all bounded by rectangles, the prism is a **right prism**, as in Figure 52(a)–(c). In a right prism the line segments joining corresponding points in the bases are perpendicular to the planes of the bases. Figure 52(d) is an **oblique prism** because some of its lateral faces are *not* bounded by rectangles.

Students often have difficulty drawing three-dimensional figures. Figure 53 gives an example of how to draw a pentagonal right prism.

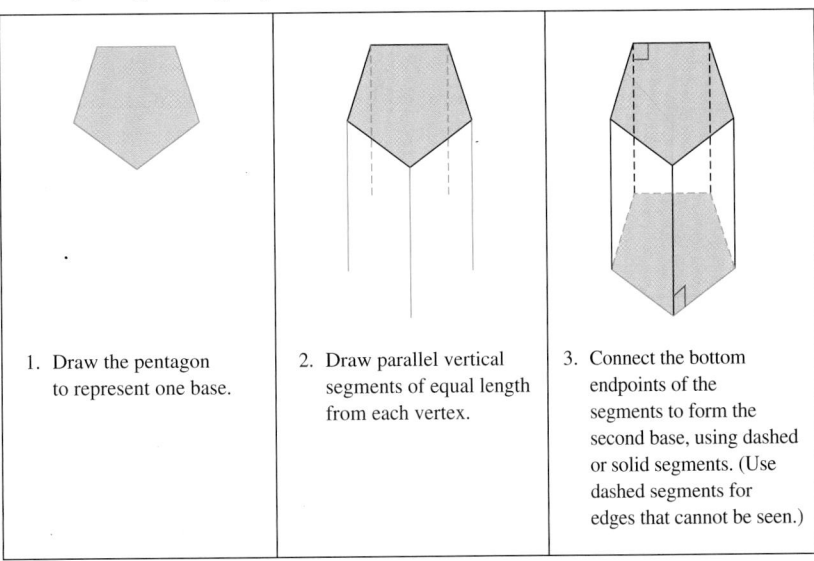

1. Draw the pentagon to represent one base.

2. Draw parallel vertical segments of equal length from each vertex.

3. Connect the bottom endpoints of the segments to form the second base, using dashed or solid segments. (Use dashed segments for edges that cannot be seen.)

Figure 53

A **pyramid** is a polyhedron determined by a polygon and a point not in the plane of the polygon. The pyramid consists of the triangular regions determined by the point and each pair of consecutive vertices of the polygon and the polygonal region determined by the polygon. The polygonal region is the **base** of the pyramid, and the point not in the plane of the base is the **apex**. As with a prism, the faces other than the base are **lateral faces**. Pyramids are classified according to their bases, which are shaded in Figure 54. The **altitude** of the pyramid is the line segment from the apex to the plane of the base, perpendicular to the plane of the base. A **right regular pyramid** has an altitude intersecting the regular polygonal base at the center of the circle passing through all vertices of the base. In a right regular pyramid the base is a regular polygon, and the lateral faces are formed by congruent isosceles triangles.

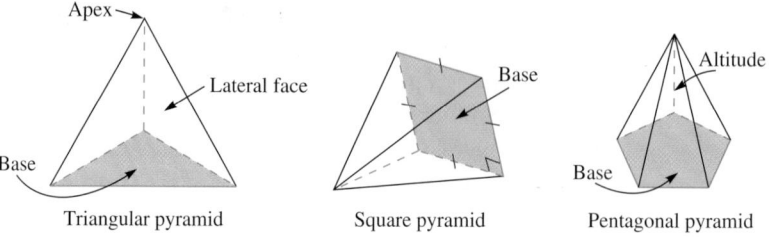

Triangular pyramid   Square pyramid   Pentagonal pyramid

Figure 54

To draw a pyramid, follow the steps in Figure 55.

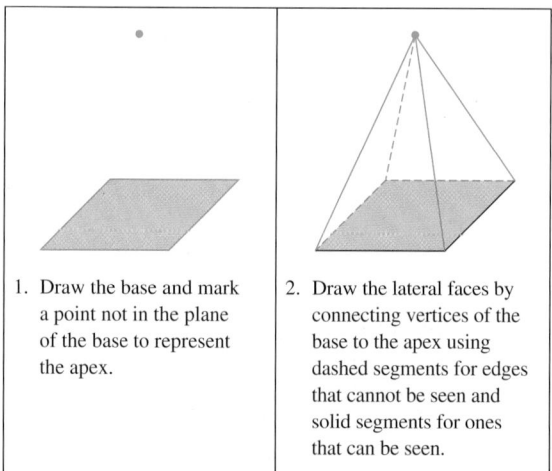

1. Draw the base and mark a point not in the plane of the base to represent the apex.

2. Draw the lateral faces by connecting vertices of the base to the apex using dashed segments for edges that cannot be seen and solid segments for ones that can be seen.

Figure 55

If one (or more) corners of a polyhedron are removed by an intersecting plane or planes and the removed portion replaced by a polygonal region, the polyhedron is a **truncated polyhedron**. Figure 56 shows several truncated polyhedra.

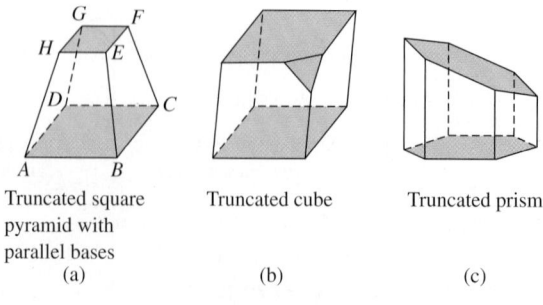

Truncated square pyramid with parallel bases
(a)

Truncated cube
(b)

Truncated prism
(c)

Figure 56

(Historical Note)

The regular polyhedra with their interiors are known as **Platonic solids**, after the Greek philosopher Plato (ca. 350 BCE). Plato suggested that the smallest particles of earth have the form of a cube, those of air an octahedron, those of fire a tetrahedron, those of water an icosahedron, and those of the universe a dodecahedron (see Figure 58). ●

Regular Polyhedra

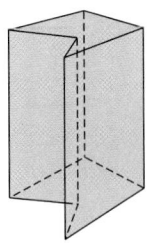

Concave polyhedron

Figure 57

A polyhedron is a **convex polyhedron** if, and only if, the segment connecting any two points in the interior of the polyhedron is itself in the interior. A polyhedron that is not convex is concave. Figure 57 shows a concave polyhedron. A **regular polyhedron** is a convex polyhedron whose faces are congruent regular polygonal regions such that the number of edges that meet at each vertex is the same for all the vertices of the polyhedron.

Regular polyhedra, shown in Figure 58, have fascinated mathematicians for centuries. At least three of the polyhedra were identified by the Pythagoreans (ca. 500 BCE). Two other polyhedra were known to the followers of Plato (ca. 350 BCE). Three of the five polyhedra occur in nature in the form of crystals of sodium sulphantimoniate, sodium chloride (common salt), and chrome alum. The other two do not occur in crystalline form but have been observed as skeletons of microscopic sea animals called *radiolaria*.

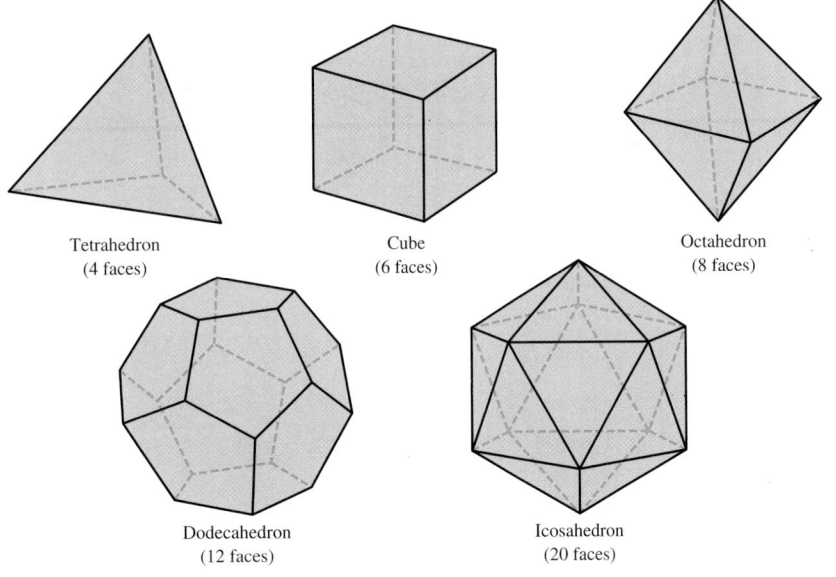

Tetrahedron
(4 faces)

Cube
(6 faces)

Octahedron
(8 faces)

Dodecahedron
(12 faces)

Icosahedron
(20 faces)

Figure 58

Problem Solving   **How Many Regular Polyhedra?**

How many regular polyhedra are there?

Understanding the Problem   Each face of a regular polyhedron is congruent to each of the other faces of that polyhedron, and each face is bounded by a regular polygon. We are to find the number of different regular polyhedra.

Devising a Plan   The sum of the measures of all the angles of the faces at a vertex of a regular polyhedron must be less than 360°. (Why?) We examine the measures of the interior angles of regular polygons to determine which of the polygons could be faces of a regular polyhedron. We then try to determine how many types of polyhedra there are.

Carrying Out the Plan We determine the size of an angle of some regular polygons, as shown in Table 11. Could a regular heptagon be a face of a regular polyhedron? At least three figures must fit together at a vertex to make a polyhedron. (Why?) If three angles of a regular heptagon were together at one vertex, then the sum of the measures of these angles would be $\dfrac{3 \cdot 900°}{7}$, or $\dfrac{2700°}{7}$, which is greater than 360°. Similarly, more than three angles cannot be used at a vertex. Thus, a heptagon cannot be used to make a regular polyhedron.

Table 11

Regular Polygon	Measure of an Interior Angle
Triangle	60°
Square	90°
Pentagon	108°
Hexagon	120°
Heptagon	$\left(\dfrac{900}{7}\right)^\circ$

As shown in Table 11, the measure of an interior angle of a regular polygon increases as the number of sides of the polygon increases. (Why?) Thus, any polygon with more than six sides has an interior angle greater than 120°. If three angles were to fit together at a vertex, the sum of the measures of the angles would be greater than 360°. This means that the only polygons that might be used to make regular polyhedra are equilateral triangles, squares, regular pentagons, and regular hexagons. Consider the possibilities given in Table 12.

Table 12

Regular Polygon	Measure of an Interior Angle	Number of Polygons at a Vertex	Sum of the Angles at the Vertex	Name of Polyhedron Formed	Model
Triangle	60°	3	180°	**Tetrahedron**	
Triangle	60°	4	240°	**Octahedron**	
Triangle	60°	5	300°	**Icosahedron**	
Square	90°	3	270°	**Cube**	
Pentagon	108°	3	324°	**Dodecahedron**	

We are not able to use six equilateral triangles to make a polyhedron because $6 \cdot 60° = 360°$, so the triangles would lie in a plane. Similarly, we cannot use four squares or three hexagons. We cannot use more than three pentagons because if we did, the sum of the measures of the angles would be more than 360°.

Looking Back   Interested readers may want to investigate **semiregular polyhedra**. These are also formed by using regular polygonal regions as faces, but the regular polygons used need not have the same number of sides. In addition at each vertex semiregular polyhedra have the same number of faces of each kind. Two semiregular polyhedra are shown in Figure 59(a) and (b).

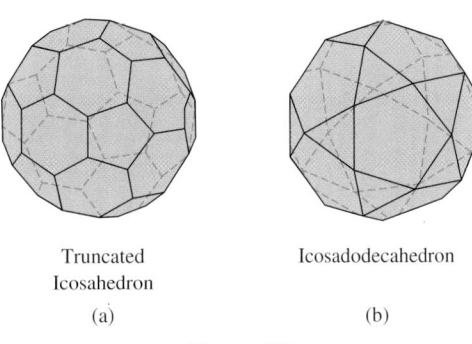

Truncated
Icosahedron

(a)

Icosadodecahedron

(b)

Figure 59

A **net** is a pattern used to construct a polyhedron. The patterns (nets) in Figure 60 can be used to construct the five regular polyhedra. It is left as an exercise to determine other nets for constructing the regular polyhedra.

Activity Manual

Use *Spatial Visualization* to develop spatial perception by exploring polyhedrons and their corresponding polyhedral nets.

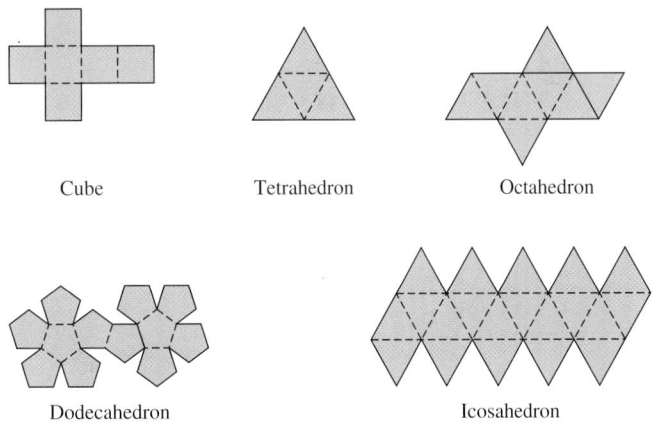

Cube   Tetrahedron   Octahedron

Dodecahedron   Icosahedron

Figure 60

(**Historical Note**)

Leonhard Euler went blind in 1766 and for the remaining 17 years of his life continued to do mathematics by dictating to a secretary and by writing formulas in chalk on a slate for his secretary to copy down. He published 530 papers in his lifetime and left enough work to supply the *Proceedings of the St. Petersburg Academy* for the next 47 years.

▶ NOW TRY THIS 13

A simple relationship among the number of faces, the number of edges, and the number of vertices of any polyhedron was discovered by the French mathematician and philosopher René Descartes (1596–1650) and rediscovered by the Swiss mathematician Leonhard Euler (1707–1783). Table 13 suggests a relationship among the numbers of vertices (V), edges (E), and faces (F) of any polyhedra. This relationship is known as Euler's formula. Determine Euler's formula and verify that the relationship holds for the three truncated polyhedra in Figure 56.

Table 13

Name	V	F	E
Tetrahedron	4	4	6
Cube	8	6	12
Octahedron	6	8	12
Dodecahedron	20	12	30
Icosahedron	12	20	30

Cylinders and Cones

A *cylinder* is an example of a simple closed surface that is *not* a polyhedron. Cylinders are similar to prisms in that as the number of sides of a prism increases, the prism approaches the shape of a cylinder. Like prisms, cylinders have two congruent parallel bases. Consider two congruent simple closed curves that are contained in parallel planes. A **cylinder** is the union of the line segments joining the corresponding points on the two parallel simple closed curves and the interiors of the simple closed curves. The simple closed curves, along with their interiors, are the **bases** of the cylinder, and the remaining points constitute the **lateral surface**.

If a base of a cylinder is a circular region, as in Figure 61(a) and (b), the cylinder is a **circular cylinder**. If a line segment connecting a point on one base to its corresponding point on the other base is perpendicular to the planes of the bases then the cylinder is a **right cylinder**. Cylinders that are not right cylinders are **oblique cylinders**. The cylinder in Figure 61(a) is a right cylinder; those in Figure 61(b) and (c) show oblique cylinders.

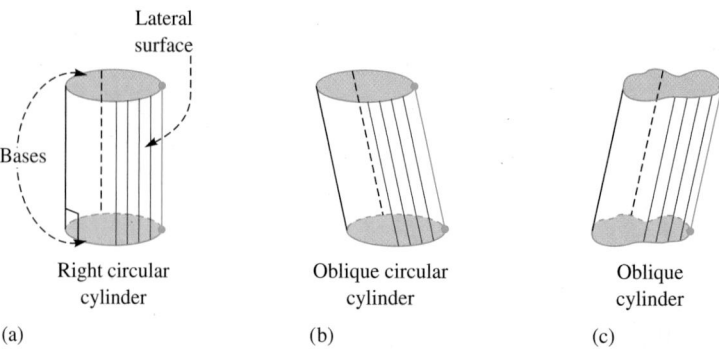

Right circular cylinder
(a)

Oblique circular cylinder
(b)

Oblique cylinder
(c)

Figure 61

Suppose we have a simple closed curve, other than a polygon, in a plane and a point P not in the plane of the curve. The union of line segments connecting point P to each point of the curve, the curve itself, and the interior of the curve is a **cone**. Cones are pictured in Figure 62. Point P is the **apex** of the cone. The points of the cone not in the base constitute the *lateral surface of the cone* as seen in Figure 62(a). The line segment from vertex P to the plane of the base perpendicular to the plane of the base, is the **altitude**. A **right circular cone**, such as the one in Figure 62(b), is a cone whose altitude intersects the base (a circular region) at the center of the circle. Figure 62(c) illustrates an **oblique circular cone**.

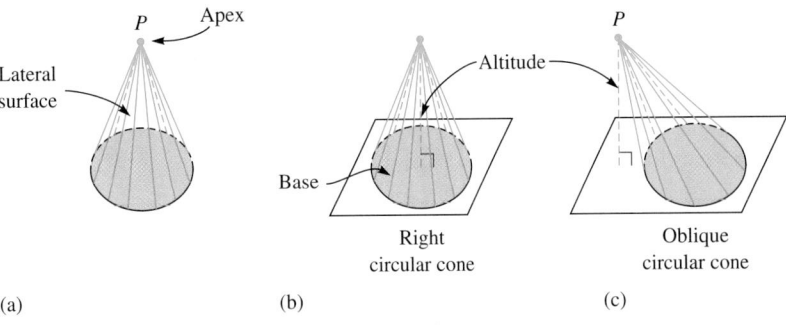

(a)   (b)   (c)

Figure 62

Assessment 11-4A

1. Identify each of the following polyhedra. If a polyhedron can be described in more than one way, give as many names as possible. *

   a. 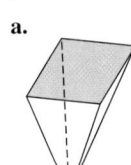   **b.** 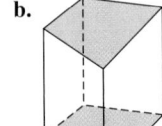   **c.**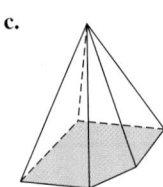

2. The following are pictures of stacks of solid cubes. In each case, determine the number of cubes in the stack and the number of faces that are glued together. *

   a.    **b.**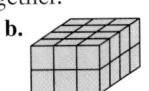

3. Given the tetrahedron shown, name the following.
   a. Vertices A, D, R, W
   b. Edges $\overline{AR}, \overline{RD}, \overline{AD}, \overline{AW}, \overline{WR}, \overline{WD}$
   c. Faces   Triangular regions: $\triangle ARD, \triangle DAW, \triangle AWR, \triangle DRW$
   d. Intersection of face DRW and edge $\overline{RA}$ R
   e. Intersection of face DRW and face DAW $\overline{DW}$

   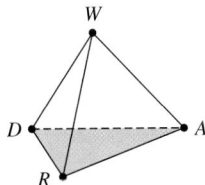

4. How many possible pairs of bases are there in a triangular prism? Explain.   1, the two bases that lie in parallel planes

5. The base of a prism has n sides.
   a. How many lateral faces does it have? n
   b. How many faces does it have? $n + 2$

6. Determine the minimum number of faces possible for each of the following polyhedra.
   a. Prism   5   **b.** Pyramid   4   **c.** Polyhedron   4

7. Classify each of the following statements as true or false. If false, tell why.
   a. If the lateral faces of a prism are bounded by rectangles, it is a right prism.   True
   b. Every pyramid is a prism.   *
   c. Some pyramids are polyhedra.   True
   d. The bases of a prism lie in perpendicular planes.   *
   e. A prism can have a single base.   *
   f. A cylinder has 2 congruent bases.   True

8. If possible, sketch the given polyhedron.
   a. An oblique square prism   *
   b. An oblique square pyramid   *

9. Sketch the top, side, and front views of each of the following shapes. *

   a.    **b.**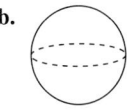

10. Sketch a pyramid that is a hexahedron (six faces).   *

11. Name each polyhedron that can be constructed using the described nets.   *

   a.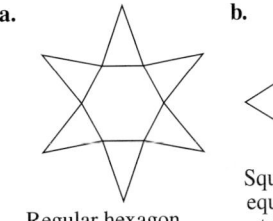
   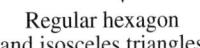
   Regular hexagon and isosceles triangles

   b.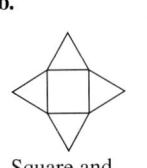
   Square and equilateral triangle

   c.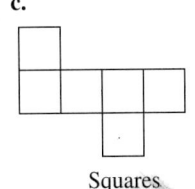
   Squares

d. **e.**

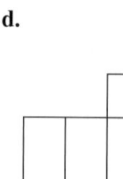 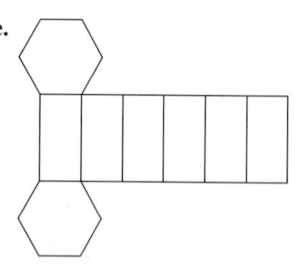

Rectangles and squares   Rectangles and regular hexagons

12. Is each of the following a net for a polyhedron? If not, tell why not. *

a. **b.**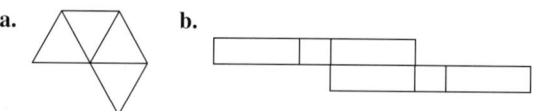

13. Sketch a prism whose base is an obtuse triangle. *

14. A die (singular of dice) as shown below is a cube with faces labeled with dots 1 through 6. The faces are labeled so that the sum of the number of dots on any two opposite faces is 7.

a. How many dots are on the (i) bottom of die (ii) left side of the die? (i) 4 (ii) 5

b. Sketch a net for the die shown above indicating the number of dots on each side. *

15. The figure on the left in each of the following represents a card attached to a wire, as shown. Match each figure on the left with what it would look like if you were to revolve it by spinning the wire between your fingers.

a. (iv)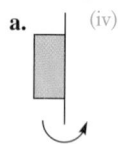

(i)   (ii)   (iii)   (iv)

b. (ii)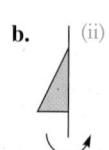

(i)   (ii)   (iii)   (iv)

16. Which of the following three-dimensional figures could be used to make a shadow like the polygonal region given on the left.

a.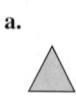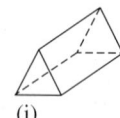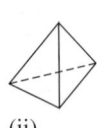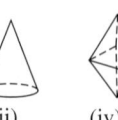

(i)   (ii)   (iii)   (iv)

(i) end view, (ii) top view, (iii) side view

b.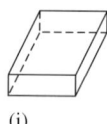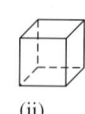

(i)   (ii)   (iii)   (iv)

(i), (ii), (iii), (iv) top view

17. Name the intersection of each of the following three-dimensional figure with the plane shown: *

a.

Cube

b.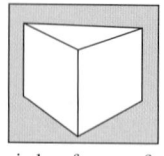

Remainder of unseen figure completes the cube

c.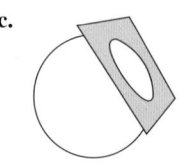

Sphere

18. The right hexagonal prism shown has regular hexagons as bases.

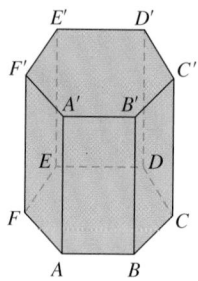

a. Name all the pairs of parallel lateral faces. (Faces are parallel if the planes containing the faces are parallel.) *

b. What is the measure of the dihedral angle between two adjacent lateral faces? Why? 120°

19. For each of the following figures, find $V + F - E$, where V, E, and F stand, respectively, for the number of vertices, edges, and faces:

a. 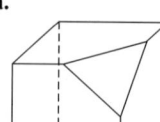 **b.**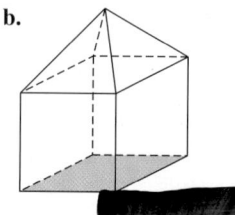

20. The polyhedron below has 14 faces made up of 8 triangles and 6 octagons. How many vertices does it have?

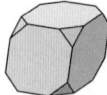

Assessment 11-4B

1. Identify each of the following three-dimensional figures: *

   a. 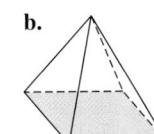   **b.** 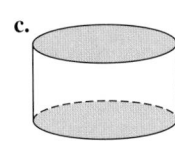   **c.**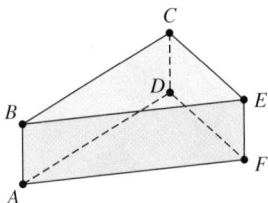

2. The following are pictures of solid cubes lying on a flat surface. In each case, determine the number of cubes in the stack and the number of faces that are glued together. *

   a. 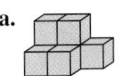   **b.**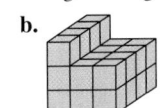

3. Given the prism shown, name the following.

   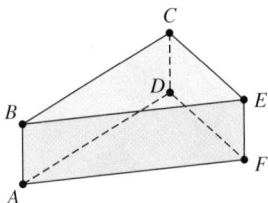

   a. Vertices   *A, B, C, D, E, F*
   b. Edges $\overline{AB}, \overline{BC}, \overline{CE}, \overline{BE}, \overline{EF}, \overline{CD}, \overline{AD}, \overline{DF}, \overline{AF}$
   c. Faces   *
   d. Intersection of face *BCE* and edge $\overline{EF}$.   *E*
   e. Intersection of face *BCE* and face *ADF*. $\varnothing$

4. How many lateral faces does an octagonal prism have? Explain.   8, one lateral face for each side of the octagonal base

5. The base of a pyramid has *n* sides.
   a. How many lateral faces does it have?   *n*
   b. How many faces does it have?   *n* + 1

6. Determine the minimum number of edges possible for each of the following polyhedra.
   a. Prism   9   **b.** Pyramid   6   **c.** Polyhedron   6

7. Classify each of the following statements as true or false. If false, tell why.
   a. The bases of all cones are circles.   *
   b. A cylinder has only one base.   False. It has two bases.
   c. All lateral faces of an oblique prism are rectangular regions.   *
   d. All regular polyhedra are convex.   True
   e. A cube has congruent edges.   True
   f. Any pair of opposite faces of a rectangular prism can be bases.   True

8. For each of the following polygons, draw a prism and a pyramid with the polygonal region as a base.   *
   a. Triangle   *
   b. Pentagon   *
   c. Regular hexagon   *

9. Sketch the top, side, and front views of each of the following shapes.   *
   a.   **b.**

10. Sketch a prism that is an octahedron (eight faces).   *

11. Name the polyhedron that can be constructed using the given net. Assume squares and equilateral triangles were used to form each net.

    a. 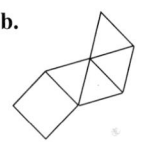   **b.**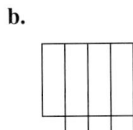

    Right equilateral triangular prism   Right square pyramid

12. Is each of the following a net for a polyhedron? If not, tell why not.   *

    a. 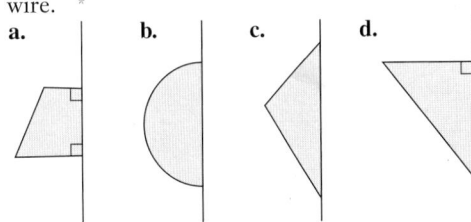   **b.**

13. Sketch a triangular prism. Label one of its bases and one of its lateral faces.   *

14. **a.** In a prism, what is the relationship between the number of edges (*E*) and the number of sides in the polygonal base (*n*)?   *E* = 3*n*
    b. Could a prism have 17 edges? Why?   *
    c. What is the relationship between the number of vertices (*V*) and *n*?   *V* = 2*n*
    d. Could a prism have 23 vertices? Why?   *

15. The following figures represent cards attached to a wire, as shown. For each card, sketch and name the three-dimensional figure resulting from revolving it about the wire.   *

    a.   **b.**   **c.**   **d.**

16. On the left of each of the following figures is a net for a three-dimensional object. On the right are several objects. Which object will the net fold to make?

    a.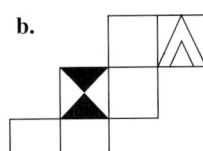

    (i)   (ii)   (iii)   (iv)

    Object (ii)

    b.

    (i)   (ii)   (iii)   (iv)

    Object (iv)

17. Sketch the intersection of each of the following three-dimensional figures with the plane shown: *

a.

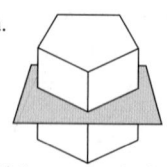

Right pentagonal prism

b.

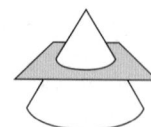

Right circular cone
(plane parallel to base)

c.

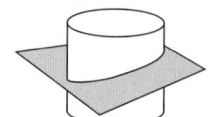

Right circular cylinder
(plane not parallel to base)

18. Draw a right pentagonal prism with bases $ABCDE$ and $A'B'C'D'E'$.
   a. Name all the pairs of parallel lateral faces. (Faces are parallel if the planes containing the faces are parallel.)   None
   b. What is the measure of the dihedral angle between two adjacent lateral faces? Why?   108°

19. Answer each of the following questions about a pyramid and a prism, each having an n-gon as a base.
   a. How many faces does each have?   *
   b. How many vertices does each have?   *
   c. How many edges does each have?   *
   d. Use your answers to (a), (b), and (c) to verify Euler's formula $V + F - E = 2$ for all pyramids and all prisms.   *

20. A diagonal of a prism is any segment determined by two vertices that do not lie in the same face, as shown in the following figure.

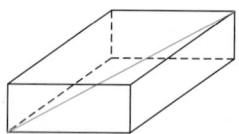

Complete the following table showing the total number of diagonals for various prisms:

Prism	Vertices per Base	Diagonals per Vertex	Total Number of Diagonals
Quadrilateral	4	1	4
Pentagonal	5	2	10
Hexagonal	6	3	18
Heptagonal	7	4	28
Octagonal	8	5	40
⋮	⋮	⋮	⋮
n-gonal	n	$(n-3)$	$n(n-3)$

21. A soccer ball resembles a polyhedron with 32 faces made up of 20 regular hexagons and 12 regular pentagons. How many vertices are there?   60

Mathematical Connections 11-4

Answers to Mathematical Connections can be found in the Answers section at the back of the book.

Reasoning

1. How many possible pairs of bases does a rectangular prism have? Explain.

2. A circle can be approximated by a "many-sided" regular polygon. Use this notion to describe the relationship between each of the following:
   a. A pyramid and a cone
   b. A prism and a cylinder

3. Can either or both of the following be drawings of a quadrilateral pyramid? If yes, where would you be standing in each case? Explain why.

a.

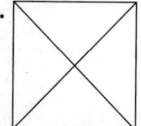

b.

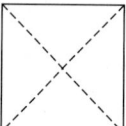

4. What is the name of a pyramid that has 9 vertices? Explain.

5. Write a note to another student explaining the difference between a right prism and an oblique prism.

6. What is the minimum number of faces that intersect to form the vertices of a polyhedron? Explain.

7. When a plane intersects a three-dimensional object, a cross section is created. Sketch a cube and show how each of the following cross sections can be obtained. Explain your reasoning:
   a. An equilateral triangle
   b. A scalene triangle
   c. A rectangle
   d. A square
   e. A pentagon
   f. A hexagon
   g. A parallelogram that is not a rectangle
   h. A rhombus that is not a square

8. The following is a picture of a right rectangular prism. *M* and *N* are points on two edges such that $\overline{MN} \parallel \overline{AD}$. Answer the following questions and explain your reasoning.

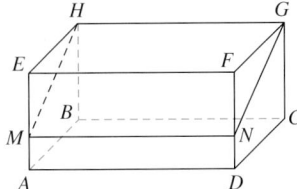

   a. Is *HGNM* a rectangle or a parallelogram that is not a rectangle?
   b. If the vertex *H* is connected to each of the vertices *A*, *B*, *C*, and *D*, a rectangular pyramid is formed. Is it a right regular pyramid?

Open-Ended

9. Sketch at least 2 nets for the prism shown below.

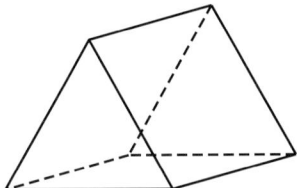

10. When a box in the shape of a right rectangular prism, like the one in the following figure, is cut by a plane halfway between the opposite sides and parallel to these sides, that plane is a *plane of symmetry*. If a mirror is placed at the plane of symmetry, the reflection of the front part of the box will look just like the back part. Draw several space figures and find the number of planes of symmetry for each. Summarize your results in a table. Can you identify any figures with infinitely many planes of symmetry?

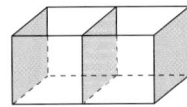

Cooperative Learning

11. Work with a partner. Sketch a polyhedron without showing it to the other person. Describe the figure and have your partner sketch your figure based on your description. Compare sketches making sure to compare dashed segments. If the figures are different, discuss how the description might have been changed to more accurately portray the original figure. Reverse roles with your partner.
12. In a two-person game, draw a three-dimensional figure without showing it to your partner. Tell your partner the shape of all possible cross sections of your figure sufficient to identify the figure. If your partner can identify your figure, one point is earned by your partner. If a figure is identified that has all the cross sections listed but that figure is not your figure, two points are earned by your partner. Each of you should take an equal number of turns.
13. Some of the following nets can be folded into cubes. Have each person in your group draw all the nets that can be

folded into cubes. Share your findings with the group and decide how many different such nets there are. Discuss what "different" means in this case. Finally, compare your group's answers with those of other groups.

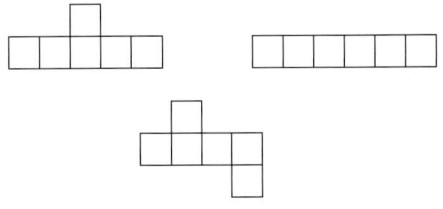

14. Choose different triples of points on the edges of each of the following figures. Then find the cross section of where a plane through each triple of points intersects the figure. (The following figures show only a few examples.) List possible figures that can be obtained in this manner.

   a.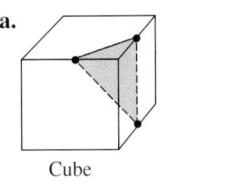
   Cube

   b.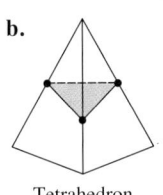
   Tetrahedron

Connecting Mathematics to the Classroom

15. Joni asks why a sphere is not a polyhedron. How do you respond?
16. Trevor said a cube has 3 faces, 7 vertices, and 9 edges. He drew a picture to show he was correct. How would you respond?

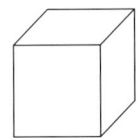

17. Bonnie said the figure below is a rectangular prism because it has a rectangle as a base. How do you respond?

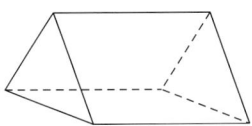

18. Joey asks if his soccer ball is a regular polyhedron. How do you respond?
19. Jodi has a model of a tetrahedron (shown below) and would like to know how many different nets exist for the tetrahedron. How do you respond?

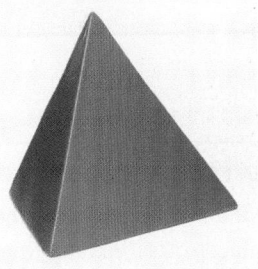

Review Problems

20. Find the supplement of $18°13'42''$.

21. Determine the following given the figure below.

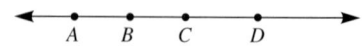

    a. $\overrightarrow{AB} \cap \overrightarrow{BA}$ **b.** $\overleftrightarrow{AC} \cup \overrightarrow{BC}$

    c. $\overrightarrow{BC} \cup \overrightarrow{DC}$ **d.** $\overrightarrow{BC} \cap \overline{CD}$

22. Can two adjacent angles be vertical angles? Explain.

23. Draw a figure that has line symmetry but not turn symmetry.

24. How many diagonals are there in a decagon?

25. In a regular 20-gon, what is the measure of each interior angle?

26. If $m \parallel n$, find $m(\angle 1)$.

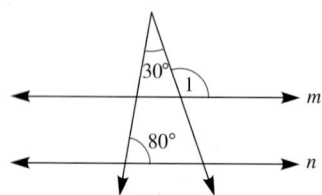

National Assessments

National Assessment of Educational Progress (NAEP) Questions

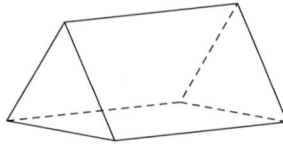

Which of the following can be folded to form the prism above?

A.
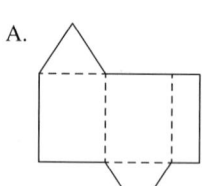
B.
C.
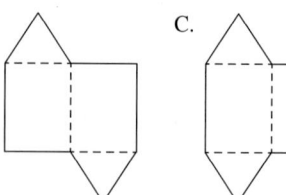

D.
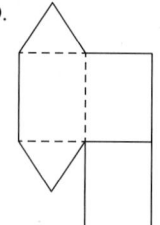
E.
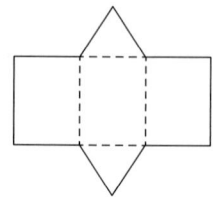

NAEP, Grade 8, 2005

Kyle makes a 3-dimensional shape using 3 rectangles and 2 triangles as the faces. Which of these could be his shape?

A.
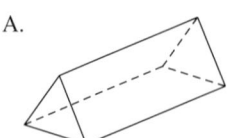
B.
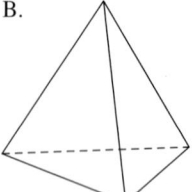

C.
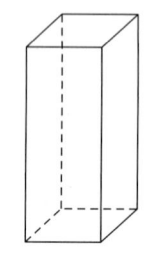
D.
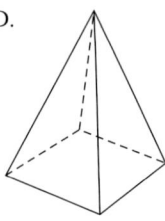

NAEP, Grade 4, 2013

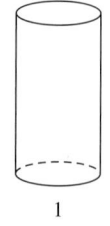
   1   2   3   4

Which of these shapes are cylinders?

A. 1 and 2   B. 1 and 3

C. 2 and 4   D. 3 and 4

NAEP, Grade 8, 2005

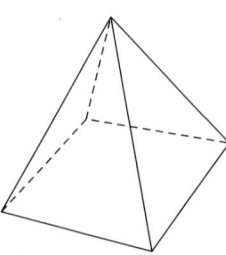

The figure above shows a pyramid with a square base. How many edges does the pyramid have?

A. Three   B. Four   C. Five

D. Seven   E. Eight

NAEP, Grade 8, 2011

Hint for the Preliminary Problem

Find the sum of the interior angles of the pentagon inside the star. Use this information to find the measure of each interior angle of the pentagon. Use this information and the isosceles triangle adjacent to each side of the pentagon to determine the measure of each shaded angle.

Chapter 11 Summary

KEY CONCEPTS	DEFINITIONS, DESCRIPTIONS, AND THEOREMS
Section 11-1	
Undefined terms (p. 622)	*Points*, *lines*, and *planes* are the fundamental building blocks of geometry and are left undefined.

Basic defined terms (p. 623)	*Collinear points*—points on the same line.
	A point *between* two points—Point B is *between* points A and C if, and only if, $$AB + BC = AC.$$
	Line segment—subset of a line that contains two points of the line and all the points between those two points.
	    Closed line segment—a segment with its endpoints. $(\overline{AB})$
	    Half-open (or half-closed) line segment—a segment without one endpoint. $(\overset{\circ}{AB}\ \text{or}\ A\overset{\circ}{B})$
	    Open line segment—a segment without its endpoints. $(\overset{\circ}{A}\overset{\circ}{B})$
	Ray—A ray $\overrightarrow{AB}$, is a subset of $\overleftrightarrow{AB}$ that contains the endpoint A, the point B, all the points between A and B, and all points C, on $\overleftrightarrow{AB}$ such that B is between A and C.
	Half-line—a ray that doesn't include the endpoint.

Planar defined terms (p. 625)	*Coplanar points*—points that are in the same plane.
	Noncoplanar points—points that cannot be placed in a single plane.
	Coplanar lines—lines that are in the same plane.
	    Intersecting lines—lines with exactly one point in common.
	    Skew lines—lines that cannot be contained in a single plane.
	    Concurrent lines—distinct lines that have a single point in common.
	Parallel lines—two coplanar lines that have no points in common or all points in common.
	    A line is *parallel* to itself.
	    Two segments or rays are *parallel* if they lie on parallel lines.

Relationships among planes and lines (p. 626)	*Intersecting planes*—Two distinct planes that have a single line in common.
	Parallel planes—two distinct planes that do not intersect.
	    A plane is *parallel* to itself.
	    A line and a plane are *parallel* if their intersection is the empty set or if the line is in the plane.
	Half-plane—a subset of a plane that consists of all points on one side of a line.
	    A line contained in a plane separates the plane into three mutually disjoint sets: two half-planes and the line itself.

Angle (p. 627)	The union of two rays that share an endpoint.
	    Sides of an angle—the rays of the angle.
	    Vertex—the common endpoint of the rays.
	    Interior of an angle—the region in the plane between the two sides of the angle.
	An angle can be measured in *degrees*, *minutes*, and *seconds*.

Types of angles (p. 629)	*Reflex angle*—an angle whose measure is greater than 180° and less than 360°. *Acute* angle—an angle whose measure is greater than 0° and less than 90°. *Right angle*—an angle whose measure is 90°. *Obtuse angle*—an angle whose measure is greater than 90° but less than 180°. *Straight angle*—an angle whose measure is 180°. *Adjacent angles*—angles that share a common vertex and a common side, but their interiors do not overlap.

Section 11-1

Circle (p. 631)	The set of all points in a plane that are the same distance from a fixed point.
	  Center—the given fixed point.
	  Radius—the segment connecting any point on the circle with the center. Also, the distance from the center to a point on the circle.
	  Chord—a segment whose endpoints are on the circle.
	  Diameter—a chord containing the center of the circle. Also, the length of such a chord.
	  Central angle—an angle whose vertex is at the center of the circle and whose sides contain radii.
	  Arc—a connected part of the circle. Each arc of a circle is associated with a central angle.

Perpendicular lines (p. 633)	Intersecting lines that form a right angle. A *line is perpendicular to a plane* if it is perpendicular to every line in the plane through its intersection with the plane.
Dihedral angle (p. 634)	The union of two half-planes with a common line.
Perpendicular planes (p. 634)	Two planes that form a dihedral angle whose measure is 90°.

Section 11-2

Curve (p. 640)	A part that can be drawn on a piece of paper without lifting the pencil and without retracing any part of the path except single points. *Simple curve*—a curve that does not intersect itself; except the starting and stopping points may be the same when the curve is traced. *Closed curve*—a curve that can be drawn starting and stopping at the same point. *Convex curve*—a simple and closed curve such that the segment connecting any two points in the interior of the curve is wholly contained in the interior of the curve. *Concave curve*—a simple, closed curve that is not convex.
Polygon (p. 641)	A simple closed curve with only segments as sides. *Polygonal region*—the union of a polygon and its interior.
Angle of a polygon (p. 643)	*Interior angle*—the angle formed by the rays containing any two sides of a convex polygon having a common vertex. *Exterior angle*—the angle formed by a ray containing a side of a convex polygon and the extension of a contiguous side of the polygon.
Diagonal (p. 643)	Any line segment connecting nonconsecutive vertices of a polygon.
Congruent figures (p. 643)	*Congruent segments*—two segments such that a tracing of one can be fitted exactly on top of the other; they have the same measure. *Congruent angles*—two angles that have the same measure.
Regular polygon (p. 643)	A polygon that is both equilateral and equiangular.
Types of triangles (p. 644)	*Right triangle*—a triangle containing one right angle. *Acute triangle*—a triangle whose angles are all acute. *Obtuse triangle*—a triangle containing an obtuse angle. *Scalene triangle*—a triangle with no congruent sides. *Isosceles triangle*—a triangle with at least two congruent sides. *Equilateral triangle*—a triangle with three congruent sides.

Section 11-2

Types of quadrilaterals (p. 645)	*Trapezoid*—a quadrilateral with at least one pair of parallel sides.
	Isosceles trapezoid—a trapezoid with congruent base angles.
	Kite—a quadrilateral with two adjacent sides congruent and the other two sides also congruent.
	Parallelogram—a quadrilateral in which each pair of opposite sides is parallel.
	Rhombus—a parallelogram with two adjacent sides congruent.
	Rectangle—a parallelogram with a right angle.
	Square—a rectangle with two adjacent sides congruent.
Types of symmetries (p. 647)	*Line of symmetry*—a geometric figure is its own image when folded along this line.
	Turn (rotational) symmetry—a geometric figure is its own image when rotated less than 360° about some point (the *turn center*). The amount of turning is measured by the *turn angle*.
	Point symmetry—a 180° turn symmetry.

Section 11-3

Vertical angles (p. 656)	A pair of angles, created by intersecting lines, whose sides are two pairs of opposite rays.
	Theorem: Vertical angles are congruent.
More types of angles (p. 657)	*Supplementary angles*—two angles the sum of whose measures is 180°.
	Complementary angles—two angles the sum of whose measure is 90°.
	Angles that are formed when two lines are cut by a *transversal* are *interior*, *exterior*, *alternate interior*, *alternate exterior*, and *corresponding* angles.
Angles and parallel lines (p. 659)	If any two distinct coplanar lines are cut by a transversal, then a pair of corresponding angles, alternate interior angles, or alternate exterior angles are congruent if, and only if, the lines are parallel.
Angles of a polygon (p. 660)	*Theorem:* The sum of the measures of the interior angles of any triangle is 180°.
	Theorem: The sum of the measures of the interior angles of any convex n-gon is $(n - 2)180°$.
	Theorem: The sum of the measures of the exterior angles of any convex n-gon is 360°.

Section 11-4

Simple closed surface (p. 670)	Has a corrected interior, has no holes, and is hollow.
	Solid—the union of a simple closed surface and its interior.
Sphere (p. 671)	The set of all points at a given distance from a given point, the *center*.
Polyhedron (p. 671)	A simple closed surface consisting of polygonal regions.
	Faces—the polygonal regions of the polyhedron.
	Vertices—the vertices of the polygonal regions.
	Edges—the sides of the polygonal regions.
Prism (p. 671)	A polyhedron in which two congruent polygonal faces lie in parallel planes and the remaining faces are formed by the union of the line segments joining the corresponding points in the two bases. Any cross section of the prism that is parallel to the base will be congruent to the bases.
	Bases—the parallel congruent polygonal faces of the prism.
	Lateral faces—the faces that are not bases.
	Right prism—a prism whose lateral faces are bounded by rectangles.
	Oblique prism—a prism that is not a right prism.

Section 11-4

Pyramid (p. 672)

A polyhedron determined by a polygon and a point not in the plane of the polygon. The pyramid consists of the triangular regions determined by the point and each pair of consecutive vertices of the polygon, and the polygon region determined by the polygon.

Base—the polygonal region of the pyramid.

Apex—the point not in the plane of the base.

Lateral faces—the triangular regions determined by the apex and each pair of consecutive vertices of the base.

Altitude—the line segment from the apex to the plane of the base, perpendicular to the plane of the base.

Right regular pyramid—a pyramid that has a regular polygonal region as the base and lateral faces that are polygonal regions formed by congruent isosceles triangles. It has an altitude intersecting the regular polygonal base at the center of the circle passing through all vertices of the base.

Truncated polyhedron (p. 672)

A polyhedron with one or more corners removed by an intersecting plane or planes and the removed portion replaced by a polygonal region.

Convex polyhedron (p. 673)

A polyhedron such that the segment connecting any two points in the interior of the polyhedron is itself in the interior.

Concave polyhedron—a polyhedron that is not convex.

Regular polyhedron (p. 673)

A convex polyhedron whose faces are congruent regular polygonal regions such that the number of edges that meet at each vertex is the same for all vertices of the polyhedron.

There are only five *regular polyhedra*: cube, tetrahedron, octahedron, dodecahedron, and icosahedron.

Net (p. 675)

A planar pattern used to construct a polyhedron.

Euler's formula for polyhedra (p. 676)

Theorem: $V + F - E = 2$, where V stands for the number of vertices, F stands for the number of faces, and E stands for the number of edges.

Cylinder (p. 676)

A simple closed surface that is the union of line segments joining corresponding points of two congruent, parallel simple closed curves, and the interiors of the simple closed curves.

Bases—the simple closed curves along with their interiors.

Lateral surface—the remaining points not in the bases.

Circular cylinder—a cylinder whose base is a circular region.

Right cylinder—a cylinder such that any line segment connecting a point of one base to its corresponding point on the other base is perpendicular to the bases.

Oblique cylinder—a cylinder that is not a right cylinder.

Cone (p. 676)

A simple closed surface that is the union of line segments connecting a fixed point not in the plane of a simple closed curve that is not a polygon to each point of the simple closed curve, and the interior of the curve.

Base—the simple closed curve and its interior.

Apex—the fixed point that is not in the plane of the base.

Altitude—the line segment from the apex of the cone to the plane of the base, perpendicular to the plane of the base.

Lateral surface—the points of the cone not in the base.

Right circular cone—a cone whose altitude intersects the base (circular region) at its center.

Oblique circular cone—a circular cone that is not a right circular cone.

Chapter 11 Review

1. Refer to the following line *m*.

   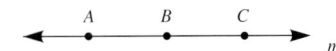

   a. Other than *m* list three more names for the line. $\overleftrightarrow{AB}, \overleftrightarrow{BC}, \overleftrightarrow{AC}$
   b. Name two rays on *m* that have endpoint *B*. $\overrightarrow{BA}$ and $\overrightarrow{BC}$
   c. Find $\overrightarrow{AB} \cap \overrightarrow{BA}$. $\overline{AB}$
   d. Find $\overrightarrow{BA} \cap \overrightarrow{AC}$. $\overrightarrow{AB}$
2. In the given figure, $\overleftrightarrow{PQ}$ is perpendicular to the plane α.
   Answer the following.   Answers vary, for example, $\overleftrightarrow{PQ}$
   a. Name a pair of skew lines.   and $\overleftrightarrow{AB}$.
   b. Using only the letters in the figure, name as many planes as
      possible that are perpendicular to α.   Planes *APQ* and *BPQ*
   c. What is the intersection of planes *APQ* and β? $\overrightarrow{AQ}$
   d. Is there a single plane containing *A*, *B*, *P*, and *Q*? Explain
      your answer.   No, $\overleftrightarrow{AB}$ and $\overleftrightarrow{PQ}$ are skew lines, so no single plane
         contains them.

   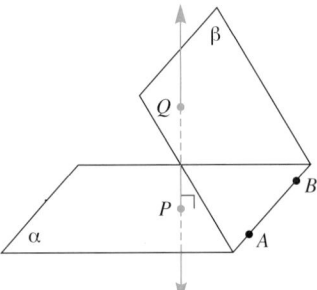

3. Perform each of the following computations.
   a. $113°57' + 18°14'$ $132°11'$
   b. $84°13' - 27°45'$ $56°28'$
   c. $113°57' + 18.4°$ $132°21'$
   d. $0.75°$ in minutes and seconds $0°45'0''$
   e. $6°48'59'' + 28°19'36''$ $35°8'35''$
4. In the accompanying figure, planes α and β intersect in line
   AB. The dihedral angle *S-AB-Q* measures 90°. The lines *PS*
   and *PQ* determine a new plane γ.
   a. Why is plane γ perpendicular to α as well as to β?   *
   b. Why is line *AB* perpendicular to γ?   *

   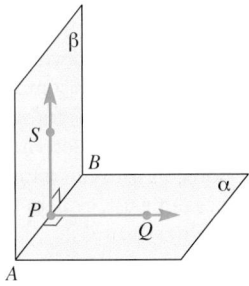

5. Draw each of the following curves.
   a. A simple closed curve   *
   b. A closed curve that is not simple   *
   c. A concave hexagon   *
   d. A convex decagon   *
   e. An equilateral pentagon that is not regular   *
   f. An equiangular quadrilateral that is not a square   *

6. a. Can a triangle have two obtuse angles? Justify your answer.
   b. Can a parallelogram have four acute angles? Justify your
      answer.   *
7. In a certain triangle, the measure of one angle is twice the   18°, 36°, 126°
   measure of the smallest angle. The measure of the third
   angle is 7 times as great as the measure of the smallest angle.
   Find the measures of each of the angles in the triangle.
8. If *ABC* is a right triangle and $m(\angle A) = 42°$, what is the
   measure of the other acute angle?   48°
9. In a certain regular polygon, the measure of each interior
   angle is 176°. How many sides does the polygon have?   90
10. In a periscope, a pair of mirrors are parallel. If the dotted
    line in the following figure represents a path of light and
    $m(\angle 1) = m(\angle 2) = 45°$, find $m(\angle 3)$ and $m(\angle 4)$. $m(\angle 3) = m(\angle 4) = 45°$

    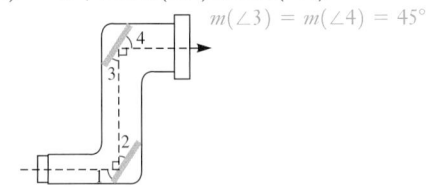

11. In the figure, ℓ is parallel to *m*, and $m(\angle 1) = 60°$. Find each
    of the following angle measures.
    a. $m(\angle 3)$ b. $m(\angle 6)$ c. $m(\angle 8)$
       60°   120°   120°

    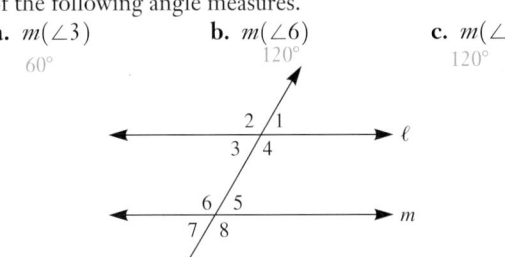

12. If $\angle ACB$ is a right angle as shown, and the other angles are
    as indicated in the figure, find *x*, the measure of $\angle DCB$.   55°

    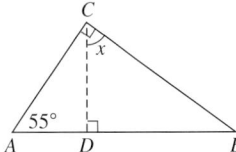

13. For each of the following figures, determine *x* if the lines *a*
    and *b* are parallel.
    a.   40°

    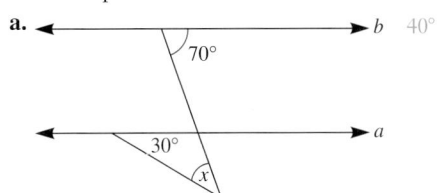

    b.   55°

    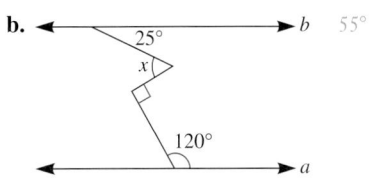

14. In the following figures, find the measures of the angles marked x and y:

a.

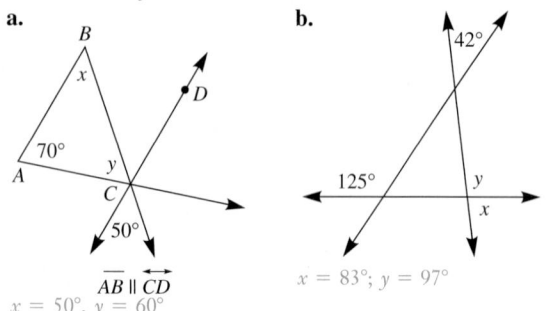

$\overline{AB} \parallel \overleftrightarrow{CD}$
$x = 50°, \ y = 60°$

b.

$x = 83°; \ y = 97°$

15. In $\triangle ABC$, line DE is parallel to line AB, and line DF is parallel to line AC. If $m(\angle C) = 70°$ and $m(\angle B) = 45°$, find the measures of the angles labeled 1, 2, 3, 4, and 5.

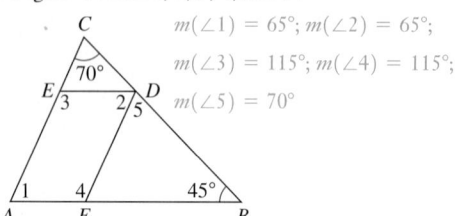

$m(\angle 1) = 65°; \ m(\angle 2) = 65°;$
$m(\angle 3) = 115°; \ m(\angle 4) = 115°;$
$m(\angle 5) = 70°$

16. The polygon $ABCDE$ contains a point P in its interior that can be joined to all the vertices by segments entirely in the interior of the polygon. In this way, the polygon has been "divided" into five triangles. Use such a division into triangles to do the following.

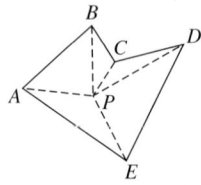

a. Find the sum of the measures of the interior angles of the polygon $ABCDE$. 540°

b. If an n-gon can be subdivided into triangles in a similar way, explain how to derive the formula for the sum of the measures of the interior angles of the n-gon in terms of n. *

c. Explain how to find the sum of the measures of the interior angles of the following polygon. *

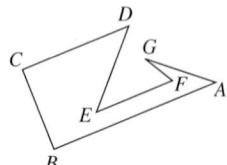

17. Draw a large triangle ABC and tear off $\angle B$. Fit the torn-off angle as $\angle BAD$, as shown in the following figure.

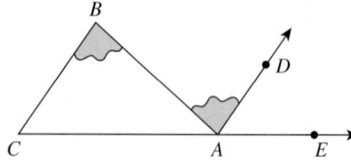

a. Why is $\overleftrightarrow{AD} \parallel \overleftrightarrow{CB}$? *

b. Why is $\angle DAE \cong \angle C$? *

c. Use parts (a) and (b) to show that the sum of the measures of the interior angles of a triangle is 180°. *

18. Prove the transitive property for parallelism, that is, if $a \parallel b$ and $b \parallel c$, then $a \parallel c$. *

19. Wally claims that he can easily prove that the sum of measures of the interior angles in any triangle is 180°. He says that any right triangle is half of a rectangle. Because a rectangle has four right angles, its angles add up to 360°, so the angles of a right triangle add up to half of 360°, or 180°. Next he claims that he can divide any triangle into two right triangles and use what he proved for right triangles to prove the theorem for any triangle. Is Wally's approach correct? Explain why or why not. *

20. Prove that if $x = y + z$, then $a \parallel b$. *

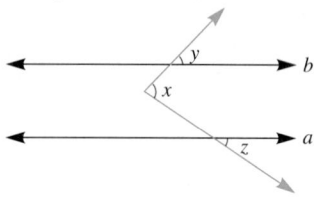

21. In the following figure, $\angle 1 \cong \angle 2$.

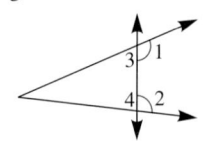

a. Prove that $\angle 3 \cong \angle 4$. *

b. Suppose $m(\angle 1) < m(\angle 2)$. What can you conclude about $m(\angle 3)$ and $m(\angle 4)$? Justify your answer. *

22. In the figure below, find the following measures.

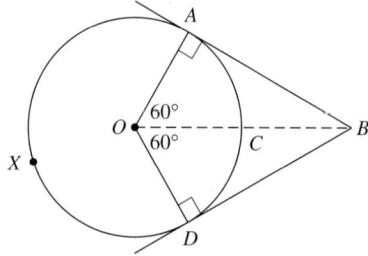

a. $m(\angle ABO)$ 30°

b. $m(\angle ABD)$ 60°

c. $m(\overarc{AXD})$ 240°

23. Sketch three planes that intersect in a point. *

24. a. Given 10 points in the plane, no 3 of which are collinear, how many triangles can be drawn whose vertices are the given points? Explain your reasoning. *

b. Generalize and answer part (a) for n points. *

25. In each of the following figures, determine the number of sides of a regular polygon with the stated property. If such a regular polygon does not exist, explain why.

a. Each exterior angle measures 20°. *

b. Each exterior angle measures 25°. *

c. The sum of all the exterior angles is 3600°. *

d. The total number of diagonals is 4860. *

26. Determine how many lines of symmetry, if any, each of the following figures has.

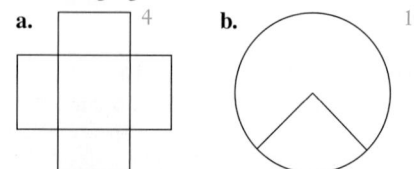

a. 4   **b.** 1

c. 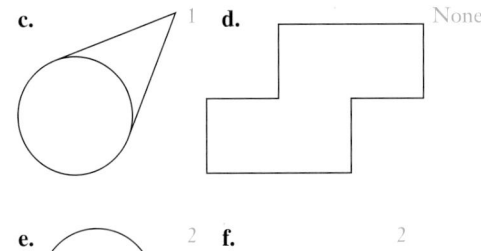   1   **d.**   None

e. 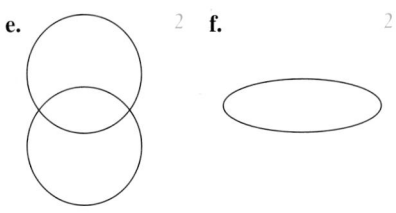   2   **f.**   2

27. For each of the following figures, identify the types of symmetry (line, turn, or point) it possesses.   *

a. 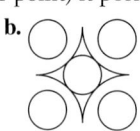   **b.**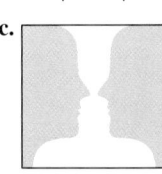

c.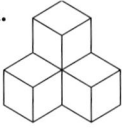

28. In the following figures, draw in dotted lines for the unseen segments.

a. 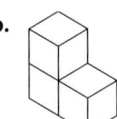   *   **b.** 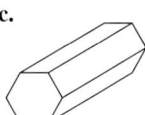   *   **c.** 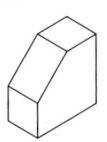   *

d. 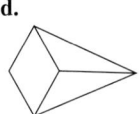   *   **e.** 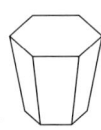   *   **f.**   *

29. In the figure below, $a \parallel b$. Find the following measures.

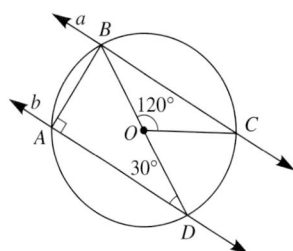

    a. $m(\angle ABD)$ 60°
    b. $m(\angle DBC)$ 30°
    c. $m(\angle BCO)$ 30°
    d. $m(\angle COD)$ 60°
    e. $m(\overset{\frown}{CD})$ 60°
    f. $m(\overset{\frown}{BC})$ 120°

30. If a pyramid has an octagon for a base, how many lateral faces does it have?   8

31. Carefully draw nets that can be folded into each of the following. Cut the nets out and fold them.
    a. Tetrahedron   *
    b. Square pyramid   *
    c. Right rectangular prism   *
    d. Right circular cylinder   *

32. a. Draw as many different nets as possible that can be folded into an open cube (a cube without a top).   *
    b. How many different nets are possible in part (a)? Explain what "different" means to you.   *

33. Verify Euler's formula ($V - E + F = 2$, see NTT 13) for figures d, e, and f in exercise 28.   *

12

Congruence and Similarity with Constructions

Preliminary Problem

In real estate, lots that have more "ocean frontage" (property that touches the ocean) usually have more value. Find the ocean frontage for each of the three lots shown if the total ocean front-age of the three lots is 130 m. Assume the non-water property lines that do not lie on Ocean Drive are perpendicular to Ocean Drive. Which lot has the highest selling price?

130 m

Lot A

Lot B

Lot C

40 m

34 m

30 m

Ocean Drive

If needed, see Hint on page 749.

The grade 7 *Common Core Standards* states that students should:

- Draw, construct, and describe geometrical figures and describe the relationship between them. (p. 49)
- Solve problems involving scale drawings of geometric figures, including computing actual lengths and areas from a scale drawing and reproducing a scale drawing at a different scale. (p. 49)
- Draw (freehand, with ruler and protractor, and with technology) geometric shapes with given conditions. Focus on constructing triangles from three measures of angles or sides, noticing when the conditions determine a unique triangle, more than one triangle, or no triangle. (p. 50)

In this chapter, we introduce the concepts of congruence and similarity through constructions and visualization.

12-1 Congruence Through Constructions

12-1 Objectives

The student will be able to understand and explain

- Geometric constructions leading to the SSS, SAS, and HL congruence properties.
- Isosceles triangle properties.
- Altitudes and perpendicular bisectors.
- Circles circumscribing triangles and quadrilaterals.

In mathematics, **similar** ($\sim$) objects have the same shape but not necessarily the same size; **congruent** ($\cong$) objects have the same size as well as the same shape. Whenever two figures are congruent, they are also similar. However, the converse is not true. A 100% photocopy of a two-dimensional object is congruent to the original. When we photocopy and either reduce or enlarge the image, we get a similar object. Examples of similar and congruent objects are seen in Figure 1.

(a)

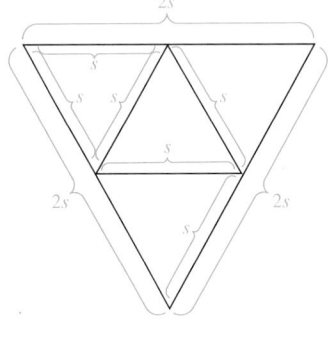

(b)

Figure 1

The Escher print in Figure 1(a) shows congruent fish and congruent birds. Figure 1(b) contains both congruent and similar equilateral triangles. The smaller triangles are both similar to and congruent to each other. They also are similar to the large triangle that contains them. Figure 1(b) contains an example of a **rep-tile**, a figure that is used to construct a larger, similar figure by using repetition. In Figure 1(b), one of the smaller equilateral triangles is a rep-tile.

Figure 2(a) shows two circles with the same shape but different sizes. Circles with equal radii as in Figure 2(b) are congruent. All circles are similar to each other.

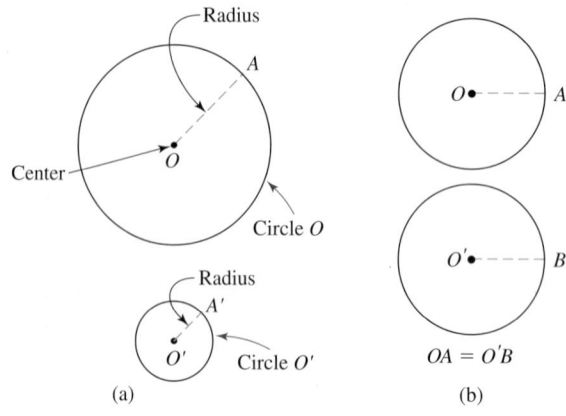

Figure 2

Before studying congruent and similar figures, we first consider some notation and review definitions from Chapter 11. For example, *any two line segments are congruent if, and only if, a tracing of one can be fitted exactly on top of the other.* Congruent segments have the same measure. *Two angles are congruent if, and only if, they have the same measure.* The length of line segment $\overline{AB}$ is denoted AB.

Definition of Congruent Segments and Angles

$\overline{AB} \cong \overline{CD}$ if, and only if, $AB = CD$.

$\angle ABC \cong \angle DEF$ if, and only if, $m(\angle ABC) = m(\angle DEF)$.

Geometric Constructions

Geometric constructions are useful in drafting and design. Designers most frequently use computers and computer software in their work; manual tools such as the compass, ruler, triangle, and protractor are used infrequently. In Euclid's time, mathematicians required that constructions be done using only a compass and a straightedge—an unmarked ruler. Euclidean constructions follow these rules:

1. Given two points, a unique straight line can be drawn containing the points as well as a unique segment connecting the points.
2. A circle can be drawn given its center and radius.
3. Any number of points can be chosen on a given line, segment, or circle.
4. Points of intersection of two lines, two circles, or a line and a circle can be used to construct segments, lines, or circles.
5. No other instruments (such as a marked ruler, triangle, or protractor) can be used to perform Euclidean constructions.

In reality, compass and straightedge constructions are subject to error. For example, a geometric line is an ideal line with zero width. However, a drawing of a line, no matter how sharp the pencil or how good the straightedge, has a nonzero width.

Figure 3 shows a modern compass that can be used to mark off and duplicate lengths and to construct circles or arcs with a radius of a given measure. To draw a circle when given the radius PQ of a circle, we follow the steps illustrated in Figure 3.

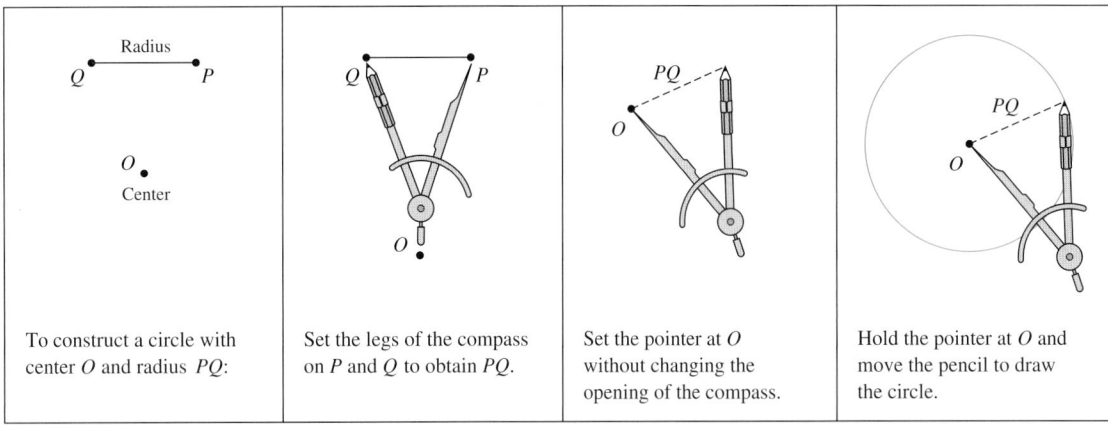

Figure 3 Constructing a circle given its center and radius

Constructing Segments

There are many ways to draw a segment congruent to a given segment $\overline{AB}$. A natural approach is to use a ruler, measure $\overline{AB}$, and then draw a congruent segment. A different way is to trace $\overline{AB}$ onto a piece of paper. A third method is to use a straightedge and a compass, and construct it as in Figure 4.

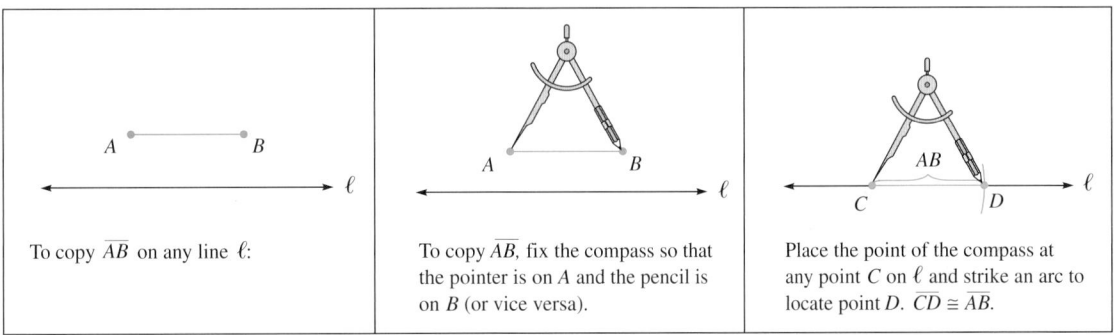

Figure 4 Constructing a line segment congruent to a given segment

Triangle Congruence

Informally, two figures are congruent if it is possible to slide, flip, turn, or a combination of these, one figure onto the other so all matching parts coincide. In Figure 5, $\triangle ABC$ and $\triangle A'B'C'$ have corresponding congruent parts. Tick marks are used to show congruent segments and angles in the triangles. If we were to trace $\triangle ABC$ in Figure 5 and put the tracing over $\triangle A'B'C'$ so that the tracing of A is over A', the tracing of B is over B', and the tracing of C is over C', then $\triangle ABC$ would coincide with $\triangle A'B'C'$. Comparable tick marks indicate congruent parts. This suggests the following definition of congruent triangles.

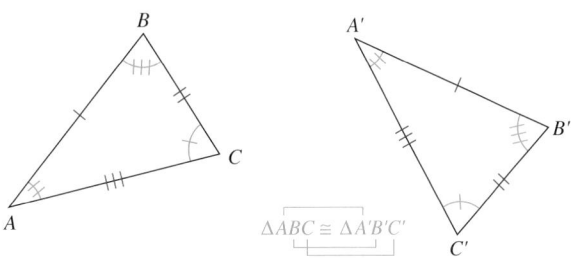

Figure 5

Definition of Congruent Triangles

$\triangle ABC$ is congruent to $\triangle A'B'C'$, written $\triangle ABC \cong \triangle A'B'C'$, if, and only if, $\angle A \cong \angle A'$, $\angle B \cong \angle B'$, $\angle C \cong \angle C'$, $\overline{AB} \cong \overline{A'B'}$, $\overline{BC} \cong \overline{B'C'}$, and $\overline{AC} \cong \overline{A'C'}$.

In the definition of congruent triangles $\triangle ABC$ and $\triangle A'B'C'$, the order of the vertices is such that the listed congruent angles and congruent sides correspond, leading to the statement: *"Corresponding parts of congruent triangles are congruent,"* abbreviated as *CPCTC*. When writing congruence statements for polygons, order is also important as seen on the following student page.

School Book Page — Congruent Figures

7-3 Congruent Figures

What You'll Learn

To identify congruent figures and use them to solve problems

🔊 **New Vocabulary** congruent polygons

Why Learn This?

Land surveyors measure angles and distances on land. To do so, they may use congruent polygons.

Congruent polygons are polygons that have the same size and shape. The symbol $\cong$ means "is congruent to." When two polygons are congruent, you can slide, flip, or turn one so that it fits exactly on top of the other one.

Corresponding angles and corresponding sides of congruent polygons are congruent. The two polygons below are congruent.

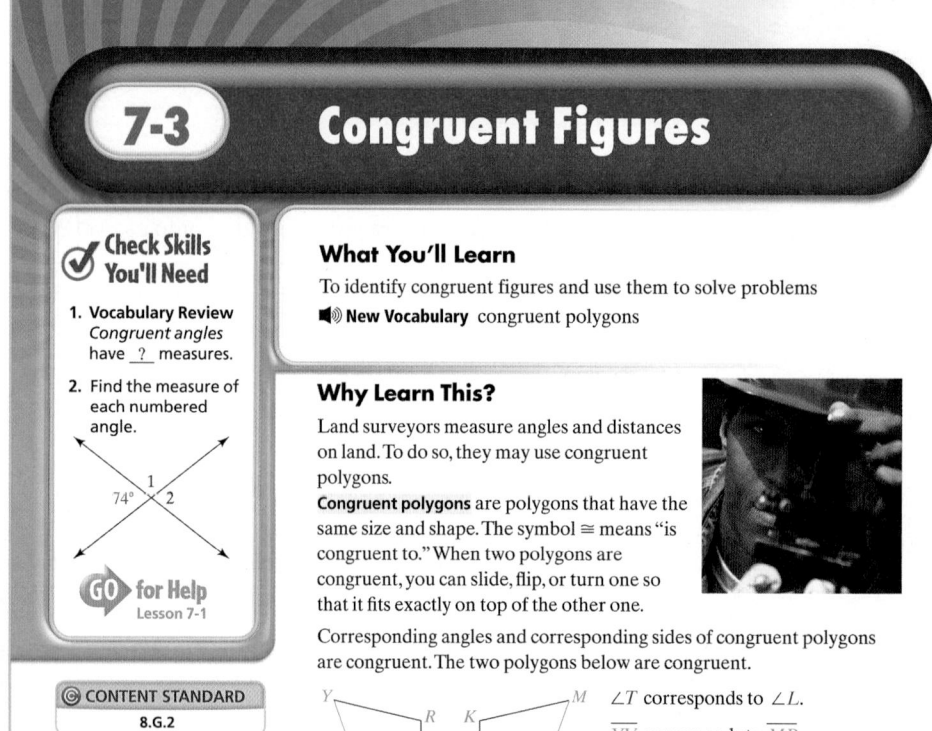

$\angle T$ corresponds to $\angle L$.

$\overline{YV}$ corresponds to $\overline{MP}$.

R corresponds to K.

You can write $VTRY \cong PLKM$.

The tick marks in the diagram tell you which sides are congruent. The arcs tell you which angles are congruent. When you name congruent polygons, you must list the corresponding vertices in the same order.

EXAMPLE Writing Congruence Statements

1. Write a congruence statement for the congruent figures at the right.

$\angle R \cong \angle L$, $\angle S \cong \angle K$, $\angle T \cong \angle J$, and $\angle W \cong \angle N$. So $RSTW \cong LKJN$.

✓ **Quick Check**

1. Write a congruence statement for the congruent figures at the right.

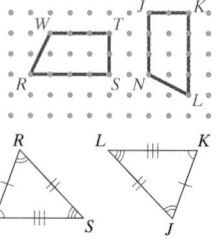

The straight line and circle were considered the basic geometric figures by the Greeks, and the straightedge and compass are their physical analogs. It is believed that the Greek philosopher Plato (427–347 BCE) rejected the use of mechanical devices other than the straightedge and compass for geometric constructions because use of other tools emphasized practicality rather than "ideas." ●

▶ **NOW TRY THIS 1**

NTT 1: Answers can be found in Answers at the back of the book.

Assume △*ABC* ≅ △*DEF*.

a. List the congruent angles and congruent sides.
b. List all possible ways that the congruence can be symbolized.

Example 1

Write an appropriate symbolic congruence for each of the pairs of congruent triangles in Figure 6.

a.
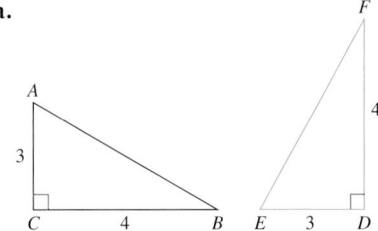

b.
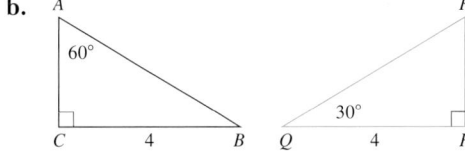

Figure 6

Solution

a. Because it is given that the triangles are congruent, vertex *C* corresponds to *D* because ∠*C* and ∠*D* are right angles. Because *CB* = *DF* = 4, we have $\overline{CB} \cong \overline{DF}$ and because *C* corresponds to *D*, *B* must correspond to *F*. Also, $\overline{AC} \cong \overline{ED}$. Consequently, *A* corresponds to *E*. Thus, △*ABC* ≅ △*EFD*.

b. Because *BC* = *QP* = 4, we have $\overline{BC} \cong \overline{QP}$. Vertex *C* corresponds to *P* because ∠*C* and ∠*P* are right angles. To establish the other correspondences, we first find the missing angle measures in the triangles. We see that *m*(∠*B*) = 90° − 60° = 30° and *m*(∠*R*) = 90° − 30° = 60°. Because *m*(∠*A*) = *m*(∠*R*) = 60°, *A* corresponds to *R*. Because *m*(∠*B*) = *m*(∠*Q*) = 30°, *B* corresponds to *Q*. Thus, △*ABC* ≅ △*RQP*.

Activity Manual

Use *Triangle Properties— Sides* to develop the SSS congruence theorem and the triangle inequality.

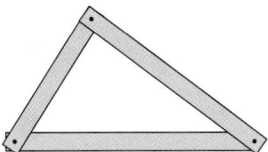

Triangle determined by its three sides

Figure 7

Side, Side, Side Congruence (SSS)

In considering congruence of figures in geometry, we look for minimal conditions that assure congruence. If three sides and three angles of one triangle are congruent to the corresponding three sides and three angles of another triangle, then by definition the triangles are congruent. However, do we need to know that all six parts of one triangle are congruent to the corresponding parts of the second triangle in order to conclude that the triangles are congruent? What if we know only five parts, or four parts, or just three parts to be congruent? In this section and in the next section, we will show when three parts are sufficient to determine triangle congruency and when they are not.

Consider the triangle formed by attaching three segments, as in Figure 7. Such a triangle is *rigid;* that is, its size and shape cannot be changed. Because of this property, a manufacturer can make duplicates if the lengths of the sides are known. Once the sides are known, all the angles are automatically determined.

Many bridges and other structures that have exposed triangular frameworks demonstrate the practical use of the rigidity of triangles, as seen in Figure 8.

Figure 8

A triangle is completely determined by its three sides. Under certain assumptions the following theorem can be proved.

> **Theorem 12-1: Side, Side, Side (SSS) Congruence**
> If the three sides of one triangle are congruent, respectively, to the three sides of a second triangle, then the triangles are congruent.

Example 2

For each part in Figure 9, use SSS to explain why the given triangles are congruent.

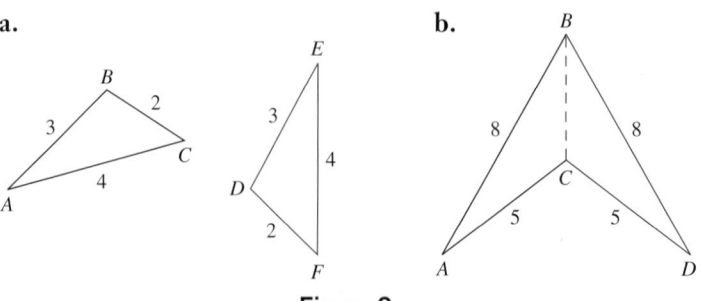

Figure 9

Solution

a. $\triangle ABC \cong \triangle EDF$ by SSS because $\overline{AB} \cong \overline{ED}$, $\overline{BC} \cong \overline{DF}$, and $\overline{AC} \cong \overline{EF}$.

b. $\triangle ABC \cong \triangle DBC$ by SSS because $\overline{AB} \cong \overline{DB}$, $\overline{AC} \cong \overline{DC}$, and $\overline{BC} \cong \overline{BC}$.

Constructing a Triangle Congruent to a Given Triangle

We can construct a triangle $A'B'C'$ congruent to a given triangle ABC if we know the lengths of the three sides. We illustrate this in Figure 10.

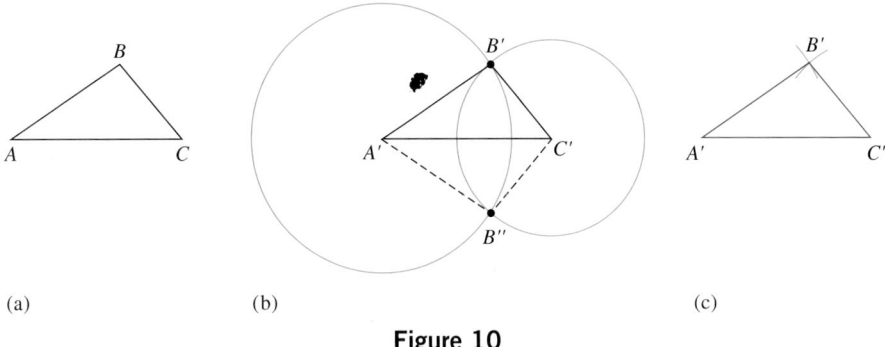

(a) (b) (c)

Figure 10

First, in Figure 10(b) we construct a segment congruent to one of the three segments of Figure 10(a): for example, $\overline{A'C'}$ congruent to $\overline{AC}$. To complete the triangle construction, we must locate the other vertex, B'. The distance from A' to B' is AB. All points at a distance AB from A' are on a circle with center at A' and radius of length AB. Similarly, B' must be on a circle with center C' and radius of length BC. The only possible locations for B' are at the points where the two circles intersect. Either point B' or B'' is acceptable. Usually, a picture of the construction shows only one possibility and the construction uses only arcs, as seen in Figure 10(c). By SSS, $\triangle ABC \cong \triangle A'B'C'$.

The above construction of a triangle may lead us to believe that a triangle can always be constructed given any three lengths for sides. However, it is not always possible to construct a triangle whose sides will be congruent to the given segments. For example, if the sides are 8, 14, and 5 units long, then $8 + 14 > 5$ and $14 + 5 > 8$, but since $8 + 5 < 14$, a triangle with such side lengths does not exist. (Why?) In general, given three segments of lengths a, b, and c, respectively, it is possible to construct a triangle whose sides are congruent to the given segments if, and only if, $a + b > c$, $a + c > b$, and $b + c > a$.

Constructing Congruent Angles

We use the SSS notion of congruent triangles to construct an angle congruent to a given angle, $\angle B$, by making $\angle B$ a part of an isosceles triangle and then reproducing this triangle, as in Figure 11.

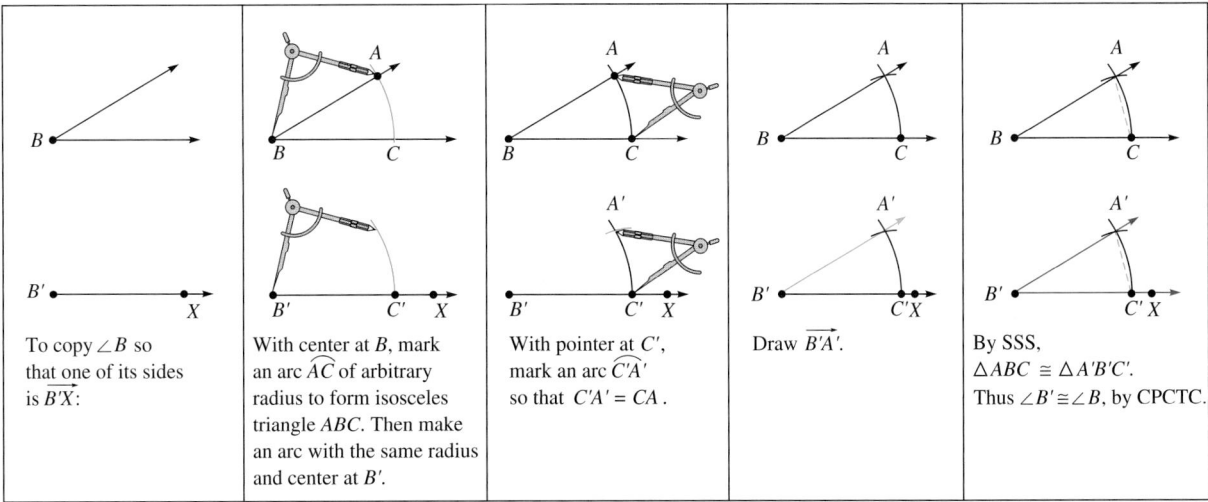

| To copy $\angle B$ so that one of its sides is $\overrightarrow{B'X}$: | With center at B, mark an arc $\overset{\frown}{AC}$ of arbitrary radius to form isosceles triangle ABC. Then make an arc with the same radius and center at B'. | With pointer at C', mark an arc $\overset{\frown}{C'A'}$ so that $C'A' = CA$. | Draw $\overrightarrow{B'A'}$. | By SSS, $\triangle ABC \cong \triangle A'B'C'$. Thus $\angle B' \cong \angle B$, by CPCTC. |

Figure 11 Copying an angle

With the compass and straightedge alone, it is impossible in general to construct an angle if given only its measure. For example, an angle of measure 20° cannot be constructed with a compass and a straightedge only. Instead, a protractor or a geometry drawing utility or some other measuring tool must be used. Some angles such as 90°, 60°, 45°, 30°, and 15° can be constructed with compass and straightedge only.

Activity Manual

Use *To Be or Not to Be Congruent?* to develop the triangle congruence theorems using constructions.

Side, Angle, Side Congruence (SAS)

We have seen that, given three segments, only one triangle can be constructed in the sense that all other triangles will be congruent to the one constructed. When given only two segments, more than one triangle can be constructed with sides congruent to these segments. Consider Figure 12(b), which shows three different triangles with sides congruent to the segments given in Figure 12(a). The length of the third side depends on the measure of the **included angle**, the angle between the two given sides.

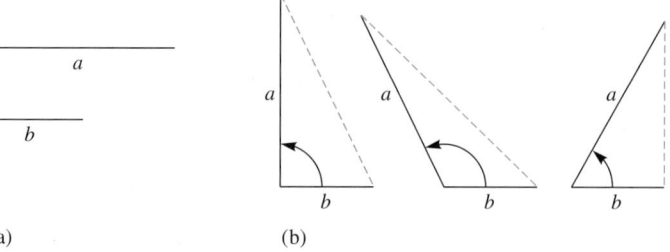

Figure 12

Constructions Involving Two Sides and an Included Angle of a Triangle

Figure 13 shows how to construct a triangle congruent to $\triangle ABC$ using two sides $\overline{AB}$ and $\overline{AC}$ and the included angle, $\angle A$, formed by these sides. First, a ray with an arbitrary endpoint A' is drawn, and $\overline{A'C'}$ is constructed congruent to $\overline{AC}$. Then, $\angle A'$ is constructed so that $\angle A' \cong \angle A$, and B' is marked on the side of $\angle A'$ not containing C' so that $\overline{A'B'} \cong \overline{AB}$. Connecting B' and C' completes $\triangle A'B'C'$ so that $\triangle A'B'C'$ is congruent to $\triangle ABC$.

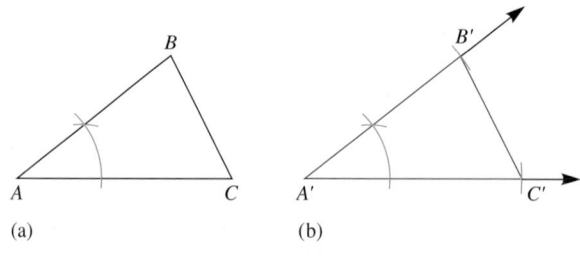

Figure 13

Therefore, if we have lengths of two sides and the measure of the angle included between them, we can construct a unique triangle. We express this as the **Side, Angle, Side (SAS)** congruence theorem. This theorem can be proved using SSS congruence and is stated in Theorem 12-2.

Theorem 12-2:   Side, Angle, Side Congruence (SAS)

If two sides and the included angle of one triangle are congruent to two sides and the included angle of another triangle, respectively, then the two triangles are congruent.

Example 3

For each part of Figure 14, use SAS to show that the given pair of triangles are congruent.

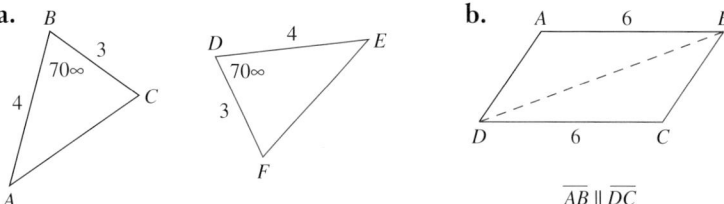

Figure 14

$\overline{AB} \parallel \overline{DC}$

Solution
a. $\triangle ABC \cong \triangle EDF$ by SAS because $\overline{AB} \cong \overline{ED}$, $\angle B \cong \angle D$ (the included angles), and $\overline{BC} \cong \overline{DF}$.
b. Because $\overline{AB} \cong \overline{CD}$ and $\overline{DB} \cong \overline{BD}$, we need either another side or a specific angle to show that the triangles are congruent. It is given that $\overline{AB} \parallel \overline{DC}$. Since parallel segments $\overline{AB}$ and $\overline{DC}$ are cut by transversal $\overline{BD}$, we have congruent alternate interior angles $\angle ABD$ and $\angle CDB$. Therefore $\triangle ABD \cong \triangle CDB$ by SAS.

We have seen that two pairs of congruent sides and a pair of included angles (SAS) determine congruent triangles. What if the angle is not an included angle? In Figure 15, $\triangle ABC$ and $\triangle ABD$ have two pairs of congruent sides and a common angle. They share $\overline{AB}$, $\overline{BC} \cong \overline{BD}$ (radii), and $\angle A$ appears in both triangles. However, $\triangle ABC$ is not congruent to $\triangle ABD$. Thus, Side-Side-Angle (SSA), which specifies two sides and a non-included angle, does not assure congruence.

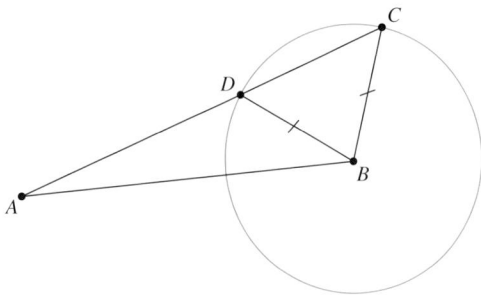

Figure 15

Nevertheless, if the angle in SSA is a right angle, then we have two right triangles with two pairs of congruent sides, one of which is opposite the right angle, as shown in Figure 16. The side opposite the right angle in a right triangle is the **hypotenuse**, and the other two sides are **legs**. In this case the triangles are congruent.

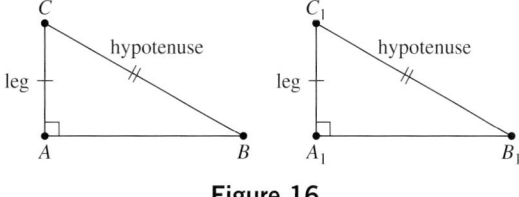

Figure 16

This congruence condition is referred to as the **Hypotenuse-Leg (HL)** congruence condition and because it can be proved we state it as a theorem.

> ### Theorem 12-3:   Hypotenuse-Leg (HL) Congruence
> If the hypotenuse and a leg of one right triangle are congruent to the hypotenuse and a leg of another right triangle, then the triangles are congruent.

It can be shown that the SSA theorem is also valid when the non-included angle is obtuse. Other congruence and noncongruence conditions for triangles are explored in Section 12-2.

Isosceles Triangle Theorems

Conditions for congruence allow us to investigate a number of properties of triangles. For example in Figure 17, consider isosceles triangle ABC with $\overline{AB} \cong \overline{AC}$. The symmetry of an isosceles triangle allows us to paperfold $\angle A$ into two congruent angles. We crease the triangle through vertex A so that vertex B "falls" on vertex C (this can be done because $\overline{AB} \cong \overline{AC}$). If point D is the intersection of the crease and $\overline{BC}$, then our folding assures that $\angle BAD \cong \angle CAD$. Notice that the fold line $\overleftrightarrow{AD}$ is a line of symmetry of the isosceles triangle. If we flip $\triangle ABC$ about $\overleftrightarrow{AD}$, we obtain congruent triangles. A ray such as $\overrightarrow{AD}$, that separates an angle into two congruent angles is the **angle bisector** of the original angle. (Instead of paperfolding, we could start here by considering the angle bisector $\overrightarrow{AD}$ of $\angle A$). Thus, by SAS, $\triangle ABD \cong \triangle ACD$. Because corresponding parts must be congruent, $\angle B \cong \angle C$, $\overline{BD} \cong \overline{CD}$, and $\angle BDA \cong \angle CDA$. Because the last pair of angles are supplementary, it follows that each is a right angle. Consequently, $\overline{AD}$ is perpendicular to $\overline{BC}$ and bisects $\overline{BC}$. A line that is perpendicular to a segment and bisects it is the **perpendicular bisector** of the segment.

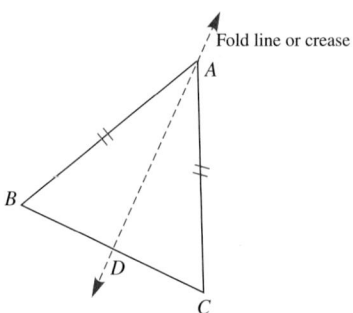

Figure 17

In Figure 17, notice that if point A is equidistant from the endpoints B and C, then A is on the perpendicular bisector of $\overline{BC}$. The converse of this statement is also true. The statement and its converse are given in Theorem 12-4.

The findings related to Figure 17 are summarized in Theorems 12-4 and 12-5.

> ### Theorem 12-4
> **a.** Any point equidistant from the endpoints of a segment is on the perpendicular bisector of the segment.
> **b.** Any point on the perpendicular bisector of a segment is equidistant from the endpoints of the segment.

> ### Theorem 12-5
> For every isosceles triangle,
> **a.** the angles opposite the congruent sides are congruent (base angles of an isosceles triangle are congruent);
> **b.** the angle bisector of an angle formed by two congruent sides lies on the perpendicular bisector of the third side of the triangle.

The converse of Theorem 12-5(a) is also true; that is: *If two angles of a triangle are congruent, the sides opposite these angles are congruent, and the triangle is isosceles.* This proof will be explored in the problem set.

Altitudes of a Triangle

An **altitude** of a triangle is the perpendicular segment from a vertex of the triangle to the line containing the opposite side of the triangle. In Figure 17 we see that in an isosceles triangle not only does the altitude to $\overline{BC}$ lie on the perpendicular bisector of $\overline{BC}$, but it also lies on the angle bisector of the opposite angle. Figure 18(a) and (b) shows the three altitudes $\overline{AE}$, $\overline{BF}$, and $\overline{CD}$ of an acute triangle and an obtuse triangle. Notice that in Figure 18(b), by definition the altitude $\overline{AE}$ is the perpendicular segment from the vertex A to the line containing the opposite side of the triangle. Similarly, the altitude $\overline{CD}$ is the perpendicular segment from vertex C to the line containing the opposite side, $\overline{AB}$. In Figure 18(a), we see that the three altitudes intersect in a single point P in the interior of the triangle. In Figure 18(b), the three lines containing the altitudes intersect in a single point P in the exterior of the triangle.

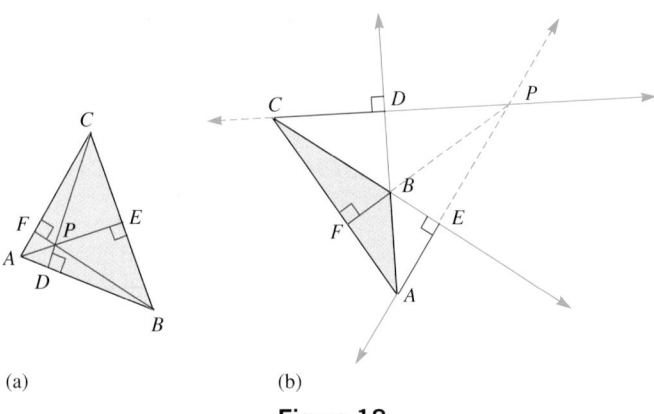

(a)   (b)

Figure 18

The concepts of altitude and height are directly related to the concept of the **distance between a point and a line**, which is the length of the perpendicular segment from the point to the line. Thus, in Figure 18(a), the heights AE, BF, and CD are respectively the distances from the vertices A, B, and C to the opposite sides. In Figure 18(b), the height AE of $\triangle ABC$ is the distance from A to $\overleftrightarrow{BC}$, the height CD is the distance from C to $\overleftrightarrow{AB}$, and BF is the distance from B to $\overleftrightarrow{AC}$. It can be shown that the distance from a point to a line is the length of the shortest segment among all the segments connecting the given point to points on the line.

Activity Manual

Use *Paper Folding Constructions* to develop various constructions.

Construction of the Perpendicular Bisector of a Segment

Theorem 12-4 can be used to construct the perpendicular bisector of a segment by constructing any two points equidistant from the endpoints of the segment. Each point not on the segment is a vertex of an isosceles triangle, and the two points determine the perpendicular bisector of the segment. In Figure 19(a) we have constructed point P equidistant from A and B by drawing intersecting arcs with the same radius—one with center at A, and the other with center at B. Point Q is constructed similarly with two intersecting arcs. By Theorem 12-4(a), each point is on the perpendicular bisector of $\overline{AB}$. Because two points determine a unique line, $\overleftrightarrow{PQ}$ must be the perpendicular bisector of $\overline{AB}$. The construction can be achieved with fewer arcs as shown in Figure 19(b). We construct two intersecting arcs with the same radius—one with center at A and the other with center at B. The arcs intersect in points P and Q, each equidistant from A and B.

Hence $\overleftrightarrow{PQ}$ is the perpendicular bisector of $\overline{AB}$. $\overleftrightarrow{PQ}$ is the perpendicular bisector of $\overline{AB}$ because $AP = PB = BQ = AQ$, $APBQ$ is a rhombus, and the diagonals of a rhombus are perpendicular bisectors of each other.

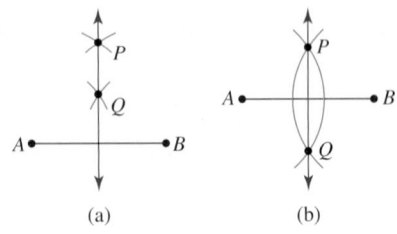

Figure 19

> ▶ **NOW TRY THIS 2**

NTT 2: Answers can be found in Answers at the back of the book.

Theorem 12-4 and the above construction can be used to construct the perpendicular to a given line through a point on the line. Draw a line ℓ and mark a point P on the line and construct the perpendicular to the line through the point.

Construction of a Circle Circumscribed About a Triangle

In Figure 20(a), a circle is **circumscribed** about a given $\triangle ABC$; that is, every vertex of the triangle is on the circle ($\triangle ABC$ is **inscribed** in the circle). How can such a **circumcircle** be constructed?

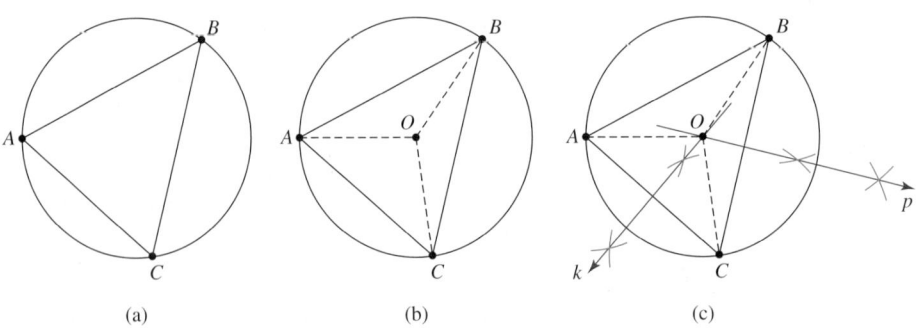

Figure 20

Suppose we know the location of center O of the circle, as in Figure 20(b). Because O is the center of the circle circumscribed about $\triangle ABC$, $OA = OC = OB$. The fact that $OA = OC$ implies that O is equidistant from the endpoints of segment $\overline{AC}$. Hence, by Theorem 12-4(a), O is on the perpendicular bisector, k, of $\overline{AC}$, as shown in Figure 20(c). Similarly, because $OC = OB$, O is on the perpendicular bisector, p, of $\overline{BC}$. Because O is on k and on p, it is the point of intersection of the two perpendicular bisectors. Thus, given $\triangle ABC$, we can construct the center of the circumscribed circle by constructing perpendicular bisectors of any two sides of the triangle. The point where the perpendicular bisectors intersect is the **circumcenter**. Thus, the required circle is the circle with the center at O and radius OA (the **circumradius**). The construction is shown in Figure 20(c).

Notice that because $OA = OB$, O is also on the perpendicular bisector of $\overline{AB}$; therefore the three perpendicular bisectors of a triangle are **concurrent,** that is, intersect in a single point.

▶ **NOW TRY THIS 3**

Construct an obtuse triangle, and then use the above reasoning to find the center of the circumcircle and construct the circle.   Construction

Problem Solving **Archaeological Find**

At the site of an ancient settlement, archaeologists found a fragment of a saucer, as shown in Figure 21. To restore the saucer, the archaeologists needed to determine the radius of the original saucer. How can they do this?

Figure 21

Understanding the Problem A portion of the border of the shard shown in Figure 21 is part of a circle. To reconstruct the saucer, we want to determine the center and the radius of the circle which the shard determines.

Devising a Plan We use a *model* to determine the radius. We begin tracing an outline of the circular edge of the three-dimensional shard on a piece of paper. The result is an arc of a circle, as shown in Figure 22. To determine the radius, we must find the center O. We know that by connecting O to points of the circle, we obtain congruent radii. Also, each pair of radii determines an isosceles triangle. Consider points A, B, and O. Triangle ABO is isosceles, and O is on the perpendicular bisector of $\overline{AB}$.

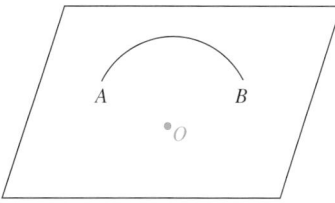

Figure 22

Carrying Out the Plan To find a line containing point O, construct a perpendicular bisector of $\overline{AB}$, as in Figure 23(a). Similarly, any other segment (for example, $\overline{AC}$) with endpoints on $\overparen{AB}$ has a perpendicular bisector containing O, as in Figure 23(b). The point of intersection of the two perpendicular bisectors is point O. To complete the problem, measure the length of either $\overline{OB}$ or $\overline{OA}$.

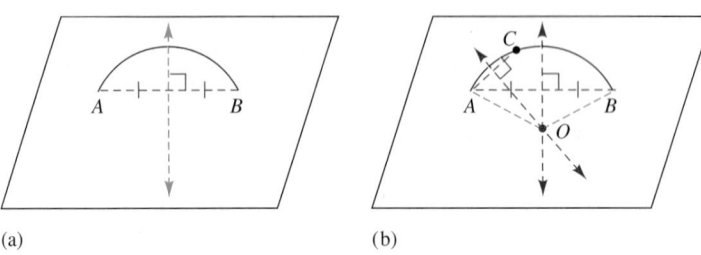

(a) (b)

Figure 23

Looking Back Alternatively we can use the fact that a circle has infinitely many lines of symmetry, each containing the center of the circle. Thus, we can find two lines of symmetry (by folding the arc onto itself and folding again a part of the arc onto itself) and the center of the circle is the point of intersection of the two lines. A related problem is, What would happen if the piece of pottery had been part of a sphere? Would the same ideas still work?

Circle Circumscribed About Some Quadrilaterals

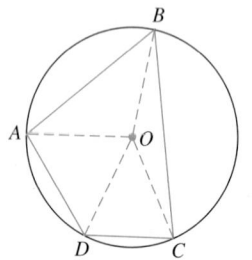

Figure 24

If a circle with center O is circumscribed about a quadrilateral $ABCD$ as in Figure 24, then the center O is equidistant from the endpoints of each of the sides and hence is on each of the four perpendicular bisectors of the sides. However, unlike in a triangle, the perpendicular bisectors of the sides of an arbitrary quadrilateral are not always concurrent (intersect in a single point) and hence it is not always possible to construct a circle circumscribed around every quadrilateral. For example, the four perpendicular bisectors of the sides of a parallelogram that is not a rectangle are not concurrent (Why?). If, on the other hand, the perpendicular bisectors of the sides of a quadrilateral are concurrent at some point, then that point is the center of the circle that circumscribes the quadrilateral. The radius of the circle is the distance from the point to any of the vertices.

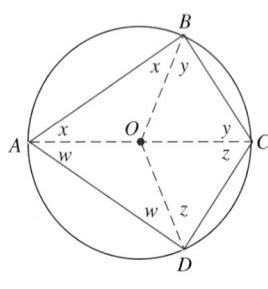

Figure 25

We next investigate a different criterion involving the angles of a convex quadrilateral for the quadrilateral to have a circumcircle. Suppose quadrilateral $ABCD$ has a circumcircle with center O as in Figure 25. To find a relationship among the angles of the quadrilateral, the measures of congruent base angles of the isosceles triangles AOB, BOC, COD, and DOA have been marked by x, y, z, and w, respectively. Notice that the sum of the measures of the opposite angles of the quadrilateral at B and D is

$$m(\angle B) + m(D) = x + y + w + z.$$

However, the sum of the measures of all the interior angles of any quadrilateral is $360°$. Thus,

$$(x + y) + (y + z) + (z + w) + (w + x) = 360°$$
$$2x + 2y + 2z + 2w = 360°$$
$$x + y + z + w = 180°.$$

Thus, we have proved part (a) of Theorem 12-6 for the case when the center O is in the interior of the quadrilateral (if the center O of the circle is in the exterior of the quadrilateral or on a side, the result still holds and the proofs are similar). In part (b), we state the converse of Theorem 12-6(a). The proof is beyond the scope of this text.

Theorem 12-6

    a. If a circle can be circumscribed about a convex quadrilateral, then the sum of the measures of a pair of opposite angles of the quadrilateral is 180°; that is, the angles are supplementary.

Conversely,

    b. If the sum of the measures of a pair of opposite angles of a convex quadrilateral is 180° (that is, the angles are supplementary), then a circle can be circumscribed about the quadrilateral.

Notice that one pair of opposite angles of a quadrilateral are supplementary if, and only if, the other pair are supplementary (Why?).

▶ **NOW TRY THIS 4**

NTT 4: Answers can be found in Answers at the back of the book.

Construct the following quadrilaterals and the perpendicular bisectors of their sides. Based on your constructions why is there no circle that circumscribes the quadrilaterals?

    a. A parallelogram that is not a rectangle
    b. A non-isosceles trapezoid

Example 4

Use Theorem 12-6 to find convex kites for which it is possible to construct a circumcircle.

Solution   Let $ABCD$ be a convex kite as in Figure 26. By constructing the diagonal $\overline{AC}$ we obtain two isosceles triangles. Because the angles opposite congruent sides in each of the isosceles triangles are congruent, we have $\angle BAC \cong \angle BCA$ and $\angle DAC \cong \angle DCA$. Using these we can show $\angle BAD \cong \angle BCD$. By Theorem 12-6, a circumscribed circle exists if, and only if, $m(\angle BAD) + m(\angle BCD) = 180°$. Because $m(\angle BAD) = m(\angle BCD)$, we have $m(\angle BAD) + m(\angle BAD) = 180°$ and hence $m(\angle BAD) = 90°$.

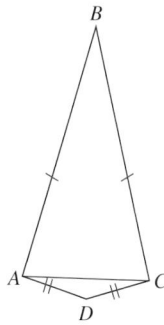

Figure 26

Thus, a circle can be circumscribed about a kite if, and only if, the congruent angles of the kite are right angles.

Assessment 12-1A

1. If $\triangle CAT \cong \triangle DOG$, which of the following, if any, is necessarily true. Explain why.
   a. $\overline{CT} = \overline{DG}$ *   b. $\angle A \cong \angle D$ *   c. $\overline{AT} \cong \overline{DO}$ *

2. In $\triangle TRI$ and $\triangle ABC$, $\overline{TR} \cong \overline{AB}$, $\overline{RI} \cong \overline{BC}$, and $\overline{IT} \cong \overline{CA}$. Which angle is congruent to $\angle R$? $\angle B$

3. Find two congruent triangles in the following figure and write a symbolic congruence for the corresponding congruent angles and sides.   *

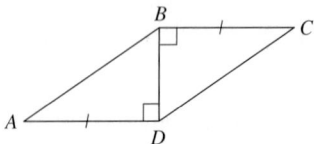

4. A truss used in house construction to strengthen roofs is shown below. Name two congruent triangles and tell why they are congruent. $\triangle ABD \cong \triangle CBD$ by SAS

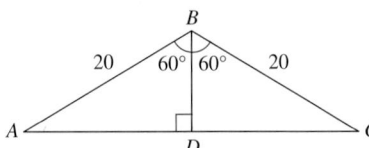

5. Given the two triangles below, are they necessarily congruent? Explain why or why not.
   No, AAA is not sufficient for congruence. One triangle might be larger than the other.

6. Prove $\overline{AB} \| \overline{DE}$.   *

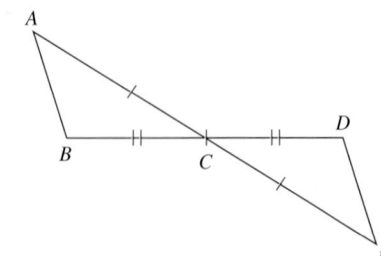

7. If ℓ is the perpendicular bisector of $\overline{AC}$ solve for x in each of the following figures.   a. $x = 4$ b. $x = 6$
   a.

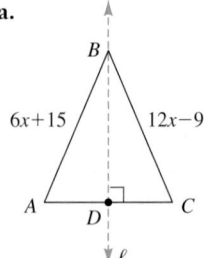

   b.

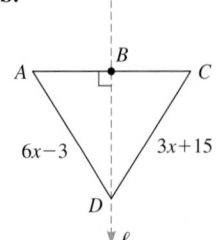

8. In the figure below, assume $\overline{AB} \cong \overline{BC}$ and $\overline{AD} \cong \overline{CD}$. Prove $\angle ABD \cong \angle CBD$.   *

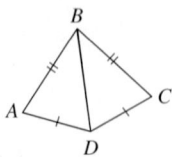

9. Given three points in the plane, is it always possible to find a point equidistant from the three points? Explain why.   *

10. For what kind of triangles will the perpendicular bisectors of the sides intersect in the exterior of the triangle?   Obtuse triangles

11. a. Use any tool to draw triangle ABC in which BC is greater than AC. Measure the angles opposite $\overline{BC}$ and $\overline{AC}$. Compare the angle measures. Repeat for different triangle. What did you find? $m(\angle A) > m(B)$
    b. Based on your finding in (a), make a conjecture concerning the lengths of sides and the measures of angles of a triangle.   *

12. Prove that $ABCD$ is a parallelogram.   *

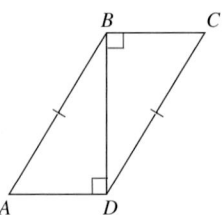

13. Use any tools to construct each of the following, if possible:
    a. A segment congruent to $\overline{AB}$ and an angle congruent to $\angle CAB$ *

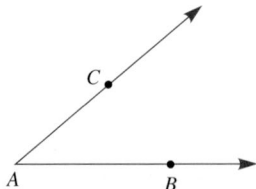

    b. A triangle with sides of lengths 2 cm, 3 cm, and 4 cm   *
    c. A triangle with sides of lengths 4 cm, 3 cm, and 5 cm (What kind of triangle is it?)   Scalene right triangle
    d. A triangle with sides 4 cm, 5 cm, and 10 cm   Not possible
    e. An equilateral triangle with sides 5 cm   Proceed as in part (b).
    f. A triangle with sides 6 cm and 7 cm and an included angle of measure 75°   *
    g. A triangle with sides 6 cm and 7 cm and a nonincluded angle of measure 40°   *
    h. A triangle with sides 6 cm and 6 cm and a nonincluded angle of measure 40°   *

i. A right triangle with legs 4 cm and 8 cm (the legs include the right angle)   *
j. For each of the conditions in exercise 13(b) through (i), does the given information determine a unique triangle? Explain why or why not.   *

14. Use the fact that the perpendicular bisector of the base of an isosceles triangle is also the angle bisector of the opposite angle to construct a 45° angle.   *

15. Refer to the figure shown and, using only a compass and a straightedge, perform each of the following constructions.

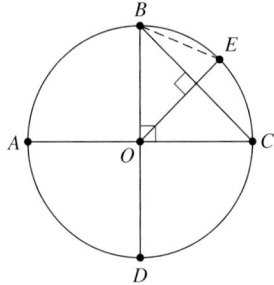

a. Construct ∠C so that $m(\angle C) = m(\angle A) + m(\angle B)$.   *
b. Construct ∠C so that $m(\angle C) = m(\angle B) - m(\angle A)$.   *

16. Is it possible to construct a right triangle with all sides congruent? Justify your answer.   *

17. Use the figure below to answer the following questions.

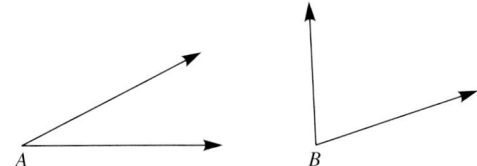

a. Construct a circle with center O and two perpendicular diameters $\overline{AC}$ and $\overline{BD}$ of the circle. Why are the endpoints of the diameter vertices of a square inscribed in the circle?   *

b. Construct the perpendicular bisector of $\overline{BC}$. Why is $\overline{BE}$ a side of a regular octagon inscribed in the circle.   *
c. Use part (b) to construct the octagon.   *

18. If you have a paper cutout of a square, how could you use only paperfolding to find the center of the circumscribing circle? What would be the radius of the circle?   *

19. Draw a line m and mark two points A and B on the line. Then use only a compass and straightedge to construct point C on m so that $AC = BC$. Describe how C can be found.   *

20. Draw a segment. Then use any instruments to construct a square whose side is congruent to the given segment. Then, using only a compass and a straightedge, construct the circle that circumscribes the square.   *

21. For which of the following figures is it possible to find a circle that circumscribes the figure? If it is possible to find such a circle, draw the figure and construct the circumscribing circle.
a. A right triangle   Yes
b. A regular hexagon   Yes
c. A parallelogram that is not a rectangle   No

22. Use a compass and straightedge to perform each of the following constructions.
a. Equilateral triangle with the following side $\overline{AB}$:   *

b. 60° angle   *
c. 120° angle   *

23. Use the fact that an isosceles triangle is congruent to itself to answer the following.
a. Write a congruence correspondence between an isosceles △ABC and itself when $AC = BC$. Answers vary. $\triangle CAB \cong \triangle CBA$
b. Use your answer in part (a) to show that the base angles in an isosceles triangle are congruent.   *

24. Given three points in the plane, is it always possible to find a fourth point that is the same distance from each of the three points? Justify your answer.   No. This is possible if, and only if, the three points are not collinear.

Assessment 12-1B

1. If △CAT ≅ △DOG, which of the following, if any, is necessarily true. Explain why.
a. ∠A ≅ ∠O   *   **b.** $\overline{CT} \cong \overline{DG}$ *   **c.** $\overline{CA} \cong \overline{DG}$ *

2. In △TRI and △ABC, $\overline{TR} \cong \overline{AB}$, ∠A ≅ ∠T, and $\overline{IT} \cong \overline{CA}$. Which side is congruent to $\overline{RI}$?   BC

3. Find two congruent triangles in the following figure and write the symbolic congruence for the corresponding congruent angles and sides.   *

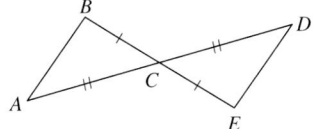

4. Name two congruent triangles in the figure below and tell why they are congruent.   △ABD ≅ △CBD by SSS

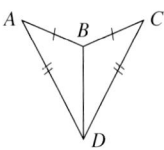

5. Prove that if the convex quadrilateral ABCD has opposite sides congruent, then the opposite sides are parallel. (*Hint*: Draw $\overline{BD}$.)   *

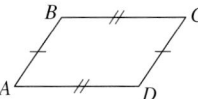

6. Find the measure of $\angle C$ in the following figure. $m(\angle C) = 100°$

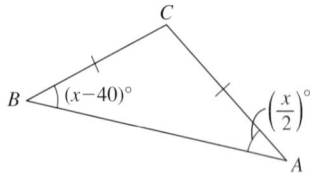

7. Given that polygon $ABCD \cong EFGH$, complete the following.
  a. polygon $GHEF \cong$ _____ $CDAB$
  b. $x =$ _____, $y =$ _____, $z =$ _____ $x = 20, y = 4, z = 22$

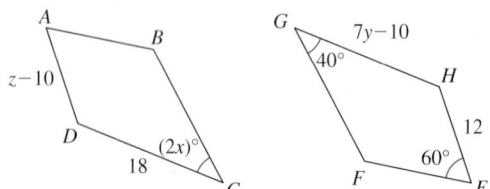

8. Congruent sides are marked on the figure below. Find the values of x and y. $x = 60, y = 30$

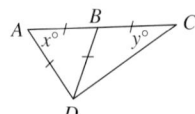

9. For each of the following, determine whether the given conditions are sufficient to prove that $\triangle PQR \cong \triangle MNO$. Justify your answers.
  a. $\overline{PQ} \cong \overline{MN}, \overline{PR} \cong \overline{MO}, \angle P \cong \angle M$ Yes, SAS
  b. $\overline{PQ} \cong \overline{MN}, \overline{PR} \cong \overline{MO}, \overline{QR} \cong \overline{NO}$ Yes, SSS
  c. $\overline{PQ} \cong \overline{MN}, \overline{PR} \cong \overline{MO}, \angle Q \cong \angle N$ No, not an included angle

10. Given four points in the plane, no three of which are collinear, is it always possible to find a point in the same plane equidistant from the four points? Explain why or why not.   *

11. In the plane is it possible to find four points equidistant from each other? Explain why or why not.   *

12. **a.** Construct a triangle with one of the angles greater than another. Measure the sides opposite these angles. Repeat for different triangles.   Construction
  b. Based on your finding in part (a), make a conjecture concerning the measure of angles in a triangle and the lengths of sides.   *
  c. Based on your conjecture in part (b), explain why the hypotenuse is the longest side in a right triangle.   *

13. An antenna is held in place by three guy wires, as shown in the following figure.

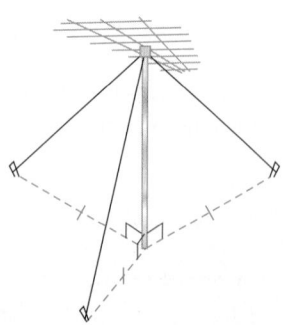

a. If the stakes are on level ground and the distances from the stakes to the base of the antenna are the same, what is true about the lengths of the wires? Why?   *
b. If the stakes are not on level ground yet are the same distance from the base of the antenna, explain whether you can make the same conclusion regarding the lengths of the wires.   *

14. Use the fact that the perpendicular bisector of the base of an isosceles triangle is also the angle bisector of the opposite angle, to construct a 30° angle using only a compass and straightedge.   *

15. Refer to the figure shown and, using only a compass and a straightedge, perform each of the following constructions.
Construction

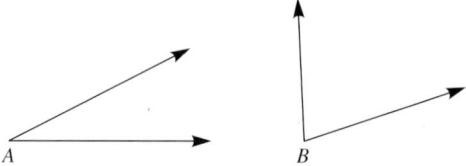

a. Construct $\angle C$ so that $m(\angle C) = 2m(\angle A) + m(\angle B)$.
b. Construct $\angle C$ so that $m(\angle C) = 2m(\angle B) - m(\angle A)$.

16. Construct an equilateral triangle and one of its altitudes to obtain two congruent triangles, and answer the following questions.
  a. Why are the two triangles congruent?   *
  b. What can you conclude about the length of the leg opposite the 30° angle in a right triangle in relation to its hypotenuse? Explain.   *

17. **a.** $ABCDEF$ is a regular hexagon inscribed in a circle of radius r. The perpendicular bisector of $\overline{BC}$ intersects the arc $\overset{\frown}{BC}$ at G. Explain why $\overline{BG}$ is a side of a regular dodecagon (12-gon) inscribed in the circle.   *
  b. Prove that $\triangle BOC$ is equilateral.   *
  c. Construct a regular dodecagon.
  Hint: Use part (b) to construct the hexagon and then part (a) to construct the 12-gon.

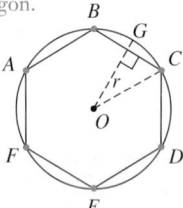

18. Let $ABCD$ be a square with diagonals $\overline{AC}$ and $\overline{BD}$ intersecting in point F, as shown in the figure.

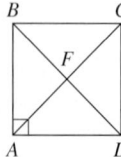

a. What is the relationship between point F and the diagonals $\overline{BD}$ and $\overline{AC}$? Why?   *
b. What are the measures of angles BFA and AFD? Why?   90°. They are congruent and supplementary.

19. Describe how to construct the center of a given circle if the center is not marked.   *

20. Construct a rectangle that is not a square. Then, using only a compass and a straightedge, construct the circle that circumscribes the rectangle. *

21. For which of the following figures is it possible to find a circle that circumscribes the figure? If it is possible to find such a circle, draw the figure using any tools and construct the circumscribing circle.
    a. A rhombus *   **b.** A regular decagon *

22. Use only a compass and straightedge to construct the following figures.
    a. An isosceles triangle in which one of the angles measures 120°.   Construct an equilateral triangle and use an exterior angle.
    b. A 150° angle. *

23. **a.** Write all possible true congruence correspondences between an equilateral triangle and itself. *
    b. Write all possible true congruence correspondences between a rectangle and itself. *

24. **a.** Construct any right triangle *ABC*.   Construction
    b. Construct the circle that circumscribes the triangle in part (a) and conjecture the location of the center. *
    c. Based on your conjecture in part (b) find the radius of the circle in terms of the hypotenuse. *

Mathematical Connections 12-1

Answers to Mathematical Connections can be found in the Answers section at the back of the book.

Reasoning

1. If quadrilateral *ABCD* ≅ *EFGH*, then complete the following; quadrilateral *CDAB* ≅ _____.

2. Can you construct a triangle using the lengths 5 cm, 4 cm, and 12 cm? Why or why not?

3. A triangle has two sides of length 10 cm and 14 cm. What can you say about the length of the third side?

4. For the figure below, answer the following.

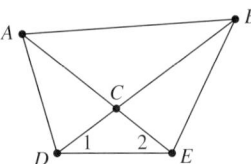

   a. If ∠1 ≅ ∠2, name two congruent sides.
   b. If $\overline{AC} \cong \overline{BC}$, name two congruent angles besides ∠1 and ∠2.
   c. If △*ACB* and △*DCE* are both isosceles, are △*ACB* and △*DCE* necessarily congruent? Why?
   d. If △*ACB* and △*DCE* are both isosceles, are △*ACD* and △*BCE* congruent? Why?

5. In a circle with center *A* and radius *AB*, let *P* be a point on $\overline{AB}$ that is not an endpoint. Explain whether or not *P* is on the circle.

6. Write an argument to convince the class that Theorem 12-5 is true.

7. In the following kite, congruent segments are shown with tick marks.

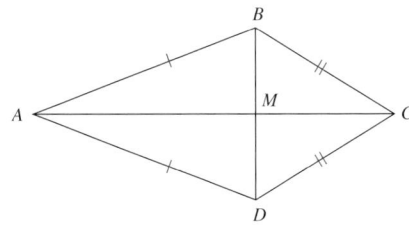

   a. Argue that the diagonal $\overline{AC}$ bisects ∠*A* and ∠*C*.
   b. Let *M* be the point on which the diagonals of kite *ABCD* intersect. Measure ∠*AMD* and make a conjecture concerning an angle formed by the diagonals of a kite. Justify your conjecture.
   c. Show that $\overline{BM} \cong \overline{MD}$.

8. If the kite in Exercise 7 were concave, do the same answers to parts (a) through (c) hold? Justify your answer.

9. Are all rectangles whose diagonals are 19 in. long congruent? Justify your answer.

10. Explain why the quadrilateral *ABCD* is a kite.

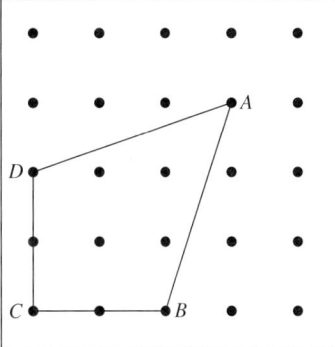

11. To construct the perpendicular to a line ℓ through a point *P* on the line, use a drafting triangle to align one of the legs of the triangle with the line, as shown in the figure. Next move the triangle along the leg until the other leg passes through the given point, *P*. The line *m* is perpendicular to line ℓ. Will the construction described above work if the point *P* is not on line ℓ? Why or why not?

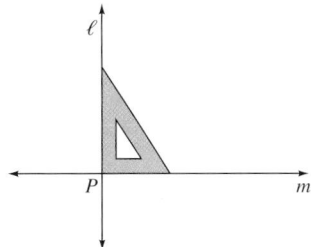

12. In the following drawing, a compass is used to draw circle *O*. A point *P* is marked on the circle. Using the compass with the same setting that was used to draw the circle and using point *P* as the center, draw an arc that intersects the original

circle in two points *A* and *B*. Repeat the process using points *A* and *B* on the circle. Continue this process.

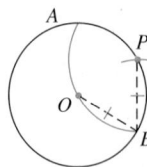

a. What do you observe?
b. If you connected the points on the circle in order with line segments, starting at *P* and going in a clockwise fashion around the circle, what figure would you draw? Why?

Open-Ended

13. Using only a compass and straightedge, construct a triangle congruent to triangle △*TRI*.

14. Below are two sides and the included angle between the sides. Using only a compass and straightedge, construct △*ABC*.

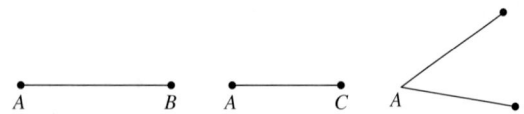

15. Thales' theorem (named after Thales of Miletus) states that if *A*, *B*, and *C* are points on a circle where $\overline{AC}$ is a diameter of the circle, then the angle ∠*ABC* is a right angle. Thales' theorem is a special case of the inscribed angle theorem, and is mentioned and proved as the 33rd proposition in the third book of Euclid's Elements. Prove the special case of Thales theorem. (*Hint*: Draw a radius from *O*, the center of the circle, to a point *B*, on the circle and use isosceles triangles to prove the theorem.)

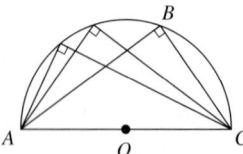

16. a. Find at least five examples of congruent objects.
   b. Find at least five examples of similar objects that are not congruent.
17. Design a quilt pattern that involves rep-tiles or find a pattern and describe the rep-tiles involved.
18. Use △*AFB* and △*CED* shown on the following dot paper to verify that $\overline{AB}$ and $\overline{CD}$ are

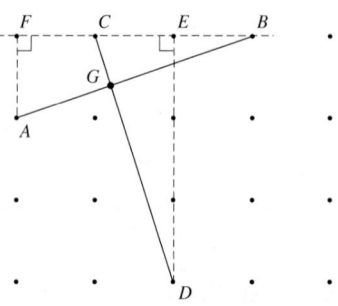

a. congruent.
b. perpendicular to each other (consider the angles in △*BGC*).
19. Use the theorem (not in the text) that in a triangle the side opposite the greatest angle is longer than the side opposite the least angle to answer the following.
   a. Explain why the hypotenuse of a right triangle is longer than a leg of the triangle.
   b. Define the distance between a point not on a line and the line. Use part (a) to show that it is the length of the shortest segment among all the segments connecting the given point to points on the line.

Cooperative Learning

20. Have each member of your group draw quadrilateral *ABCD* with *AB* = 5 cm, *BC* = 7 cm, *CD* = 9 cm, and *DA* = 11 cm. Compare your quadrilaterals in your group. Are all the quadrilaterals congruent? Decide whether you think there is an SSSS congruence theorem for quadrilateral congruence.

Connecting Mathematics to the Classroom

21. A student claims that all squares are congruent to each other. How do you respond?
22. Joel claims the following triangles are congruent by SAS. How do you respond?

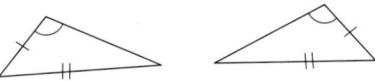

23. On a test, a student wrote *AB* ≅ *CD* instead of $\overline{AB}$ ≅ $\overline{CD}$. Is this answer correct? Why?
24. A student asks for a mathematical definition of congruence that holds for all figures. How do you respond?
25. Zara claims that in spite of the fact that every triangle is congruent to itself, the statement △*ABC* ≅ △*BAC* is generally false. However, if *AC* = *BC*, the statement is true. Is she correct? If so, why?

GeoGebra Activities

26. Use GeoGebra Lab 4 activities 1–7 to investigate congruence and noncongruence of triangles.
27. a. Use GeoGebra Lab 1 activities 10 and 11 as well as Lab 2 activity 1 or GeoGebra Lab 3 activities 1–4 to investigate measuring segments and angles.
   b. Use GeoGebra to display a grid (choose View > Grid in GeoGebra). Then construct the triangles in problem 18 above and measure some of their sides and angles as well as ∠*CGB* to verify the claims in parts (a) and (b) of the problem.
28. Use GeoGebra Lab 5 activities 1–4 to investigate the construction of a circle circumscribed about a triangle.
29. Use GeoGebra activities 1–3 to investigate circles circumscribing rectangles and quadrilaterals.

National Assessments

National Assessment of Educational Progress (NAEP) Questions

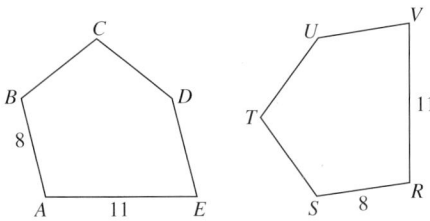

In the figure above, polygons *ABCDE* and *RSTUV* are congruent. Which side must have the same length as side $\overline{BC}$?

A. $\overline{CD}$
B. $\overline{DE}$
C. $\overline{ST}$
D. $\overline{TU}$
E. $\overline{UV}$

NAEP, Grade 8, 2009

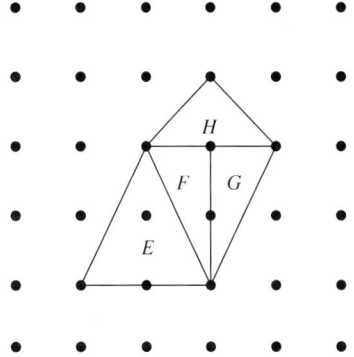

Which two figures are congruent?
A. *E* and *H*
B. *F* and *G*
C. *F* and *H*
D. *G* and *H*

NAEP, Grade 4, 2013

12-2 Additional Congruence Theorems

12-2 Objectives

The student will be able to understand and explain

- Geometric constructions leading to the ASA and AAS congruence properties.

- Properties of quadrilaterals.

Angle, Side, Angle Congruence (ASA)

Triangles can be determined to be congruent by SSS and SAS. Can a triangle be constructed congruent to a given triangle by using two angles and the side included between these angles? Figure 27 shows the construction of a triangle $A'B'C'$ such that $\overline{A'C'} \cong \overline{AC}$, $\angle A' \cong \angle A$, and $\angle C' \cong \angle C$. It seems that $\triangle A'B'C' \cong \triangle ABC$. This construction illustrates the **Angle, Side, Angle (ASA)** congruence theorem.

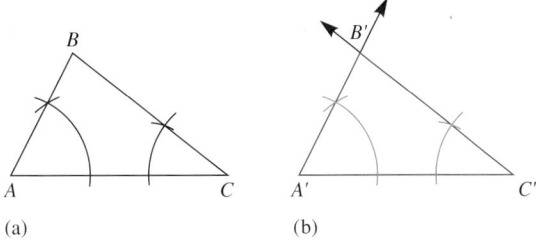

(a)   (b)

Figure 27

Theorem 12-7:   Angle, Side, Angle Congruence (ASA)

If two angles and the included side of one triangle are congruent to two angles and the included side of another triangle, then the triangles are congruent.

Example 5

In Figure 28, $\triangle ABC$ and $\triangle DEF$ have two pairs of angles congruent and a pair of sides congruent. Show that the triangles are congruent.

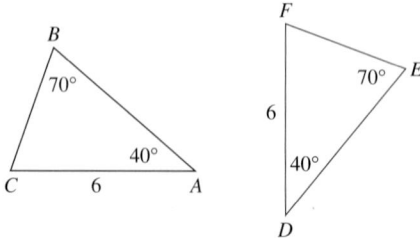

Figure 28

Solution Notice that $\angle A \cong \angle D$ and $\angle B \cong \angle E$, which implies that $\angle C \cong \angle F$ because the measure of each is $180° - (70 + 40)°$. Then, since $\overline{AC} \cong \overline{DF}$, we have $\triangle ABC \cong \triangle DEF$ by ASA.

Example 5 is a special case of the following theorem which can be justified in a similar way.

Theorem 12-8:   Angle, Angle, Side Congruence (AAS)

If two angles and a side opposite one of these two angles of a triangle are congruent to the two corresponding angles and the corresponding side in another triangle, then the two triangles are congruent.

Notice in Theorem 12-8 the emphasis that the side in one triangle must correspond to the side in the other triangle. If that is not the case, two angles and a side do not ensure congruence, as shown in Figure 29, where a side and two angles in $\triangle ABC$ are congruent to a side and two angles in $\triangle DEF$. In that figure, $\overline{AB} \cong \overline{EF}$, $\angle A \cong \angle D$, and $\angle B \cong \angle E$, but the triangles are not congruent. Side $\overline{AB}$ is not corresponding to one of the angles mentioned. Consequently, the condition AAS does not ensure congruence unless the side is corresponding to one of the two angles.

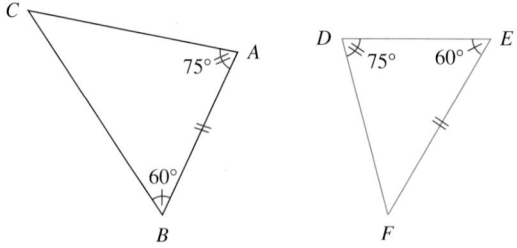

Figure 29

Example 6

Show that the triangles in each part of Figure 30 are congruent.

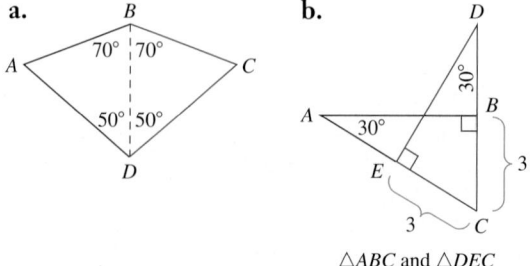

$\triangle ABC$ and $\triangle DEC$

Figure 30

Solution
  a. $\angle ABD \cong \angle CBD, \overline{BD} \cong \overline{BD},$ and $\angle ADB \cong \angle CDB.$ Consequently, by ASA, $\triangle ABD \cong$
     $\triangle CBD.$
  b. Since $\angle C \cong \angle C, \angle ABC \cong \angle DEC,$ and $\overline{EC} \cong \overline{BC},$ by AAS, $\triangle ABC \cong \triangle DEC.$

The ASA congruency theorem can be used to prove that in a parallelogram (a quadrilateral with each pair of opposite sides parallel) opposite sides and opposite angles are congruent. In Figure 31 $ABCD$ is a parallelogram. Because a diagonal divides the parallelogram into two triangles, we construct the diagonal $\overline{AC}$. Now $\triangle ABC \cong \triangle CDA$ by ASA because $\overline{AC} \cong \overline{CA}$ and the pairs of equally marked angles are congruent as they are alternate interior angles created by pairs of parallel sides and the transversal $\overleftrightarrow{AC}$. Therefore $\overline{AB} \cong \overline{CD}$ and $\overline{BC} \cong \overline{DA}$, by CPCTC. From the same congruent triangles $\angle B \cong \angle D$. By constructing the diagonal $\overline{BD}$ instead of $\overline{AC}$ we can show that $\angle BAD \cong \angle DCB$.

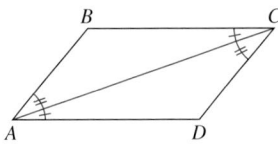

Figure 31

Thus, we have proved the following theorem.

Theorem 12-9
The opposite sides and the opposite angles of a parallelogram are congruent.

Example 7

  a. Use the definition of a parallelogram and Theorem 12-9 to prove that the diagonals of a parallelogram bisect each other; that is, in Figure 32(a), show that $AO = OC$ and $BO = OD$.

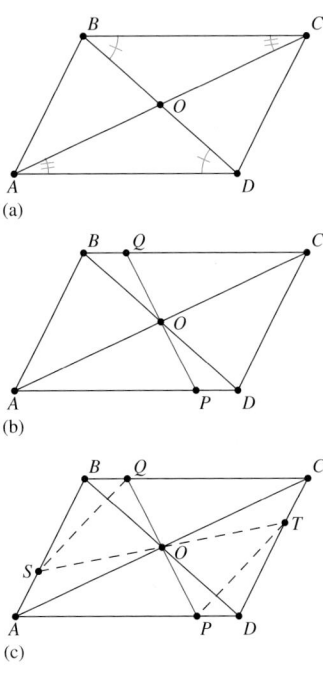

Figure 32

b. Draw a line through the point O where the diagonals of a parallelogram intersect, as in Figure 32(b). The line intersects the opposite sides of the parallelogram at points P and Q. Prove that $\overline{OP} \cong \overline{OQ}$.

c. In Figure 32(c) prove that $\overline{SQ} \cong \overline{TP}$.

Solution

a. In Figure 32(a), we want to show that $\overline{AO} \cong \overline{OC}$ and $\overline{BO} \cong \overline{OD}$. These segments appear in two pairs of triangles that seem to be congruent. One pair is $\triangle AOD$ and $\triangle COB$. To prove these triangles congruent, we use Theorem 12-9 to conclude that $\overline{AD} \cong \overline{CB}$. We have no information about the other corresponding sides; however, we know that $\overline{BC} \parallel \overline{AD}$. Consequently, $\angle ADO \cong \angle CBO$, as these are alternate interior angles formed by the parallel lines and the transversal $\overleftrightarrow{BD}$. Similarly, using the transversal $\overleftrightarrow{AC}$, we have $\angle OAD \cong \angle OCB$ (congruent angles have been similarly marked in Figure 32(a)). Now $\triangle AOD \cong \triangle COB$ by ASA. Corresponding parts in these triangles are congruent so $\overline{AO} \cong \overline{OC}$ and $\overline{BO} \cong \overline{OD}$, and therefore $AO = OC$ and $BO = OD$.

b. As in part (a), there are two pairs of triangles that have segments $\overline{OQ}$ and $\overline{OP}$ as sides; one such pair is $\triangle AOP$ and $\triangle COQ$. In these triangles, $\overline{AO} \cong \overline{CO}$ (as was proved in part (a)). As in part (a), $\angle OAP \cong \angle OCQ$. Also, $\angle AOP \cong \angle COQ$ because these are vertical angles. Thus, $\triangle AOP \cong \triangle COQ$ by ASA and $\overline{OP} \cong \overline{OQ}$ because these are corresponding parts in these congruent triangles.

c. $\overline{OS} \cong \overline{OT}$ and $\overline{OQ} \cong \overline{OP}$ (using the same reasoning as part (b)). $\angle SOQ \cong \angle TOP$ because these are vertical angles. These imply $\triangle SQO \cong \triangle TPO$ by SAS. Consequently $\overline{SQ} \cong \overline{TP}$ by CPCTC.

▶ **NOW TRY THIS 5**

NTT 5: Answers can be found in Answers at the back of the book.

If the diagonals of a quadrilateral bisect each other, must the quadrilateral be a parallelogram? Explain why or why not.

Using properties of congruent triangles, we can deduce various properties of quadrilaterals. Table 1 summarizes the definitions and lists some properties of six quadrilaterals, not all of which have been proved. These and other properties of quadrilaterals are further investigated in Assessment 12-2.

Table 1

Quadrilateral and Its Definition	Theorems about the Quadrilateral
Trapezoid: A quadrilateral with at least one pair of parallel sides	Consecutive angles between parallel sides are supplementary.
Isosceles trapezoid: A trapezoid with a pair of congruent base angles	**a.** Each pair of base angles are congruent. **b.** A pair of opposite sides are congruent. **c.** If a trapezoid has congruent diagonals, it is isosceles.

(continued)

Table 1 (continued)	
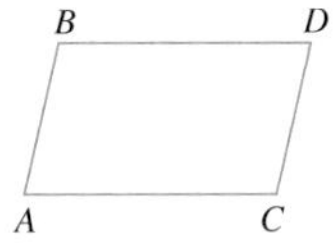 *Parallelogram:* A quadrilateral in which each pair of opposite sides is parallel	**a.** A parallelogram is a trapezoid in which each pair of opposite sides are parallel. **b.** Opposite sides are congruent. **c.** Opposite angles are congruent. **d.** Diagonals bisect each other. **e.** A quadrilateral in which the diagonals bisect each other is a parallelogram.
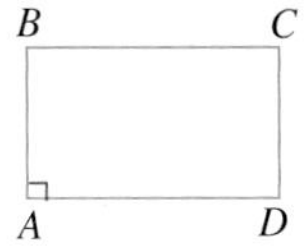 *Rectangle:* A parallelogram with a right angle	**a.** A rectangle has all the properties of a parallelogram. **b.** All the angles of a rectangle are right angles. **c.** A quadrilateral in which all the angles are right angles is a rectangle. **d.** The diagonals of a rectangle are congruent and bisect each other. **e.** A quadrilateral in which the diagonals are congruent and bisect each other is a rectangle.
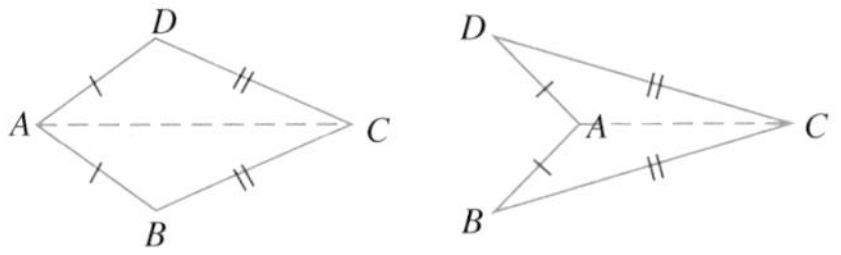 convex kite concave kite *Kite:* A quadrilateral with two adjacent sides congruent and the other two sides also congruent	**a.** Lines containing the diagonals are perpendicular to each other. **b.** A line containing one diagonal ($\overline{AC}$ in the figure) is a bisector of the other diagonal. **c.** One diagonal ($\overline{AC}$ in the figure) bisects nonconsecutive angles. **d.** A quadrilateral in which the line containing one diagonal is the perpendicular bisector of the other diagonal is a kite.
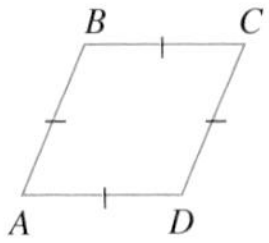 *Rhombus:* A parallelogram with two adjacent sides congruent	**a.** A rhombus has all the properties of a parallelogram and a kite. **b.** A quadrilateral is a rhombus if, and only if, all four sides are congruent. **c.** The diagonals of a rhombus are perpendicular to and bisect each other. Each diagonal bisects opposite angles. **d.** A quadrilateral in which the diagonals are perpendicular to and bisect each other is a rhombus.
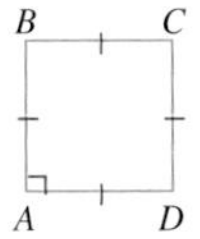 *Square:* A rectangle with two adjacent sides congruent	**a.** A square has all the properties of a parallelogram, a rectangle, and a rhombus. **b.** A rhombus with a right angle is a square.

The proofs of some of the theorems listed in Table 1 will be explored in the Assessments; meanwhile, in the following examples we assume some theorems from the table and prove other theorems.

Example 8

Prove that a parallelogram whose diagonals are congruent is a rectangle.

Solution We need to prove that one of the angles of the parallelogram in Figure 33 is a right angle (see definition of a rectangle). We show that ∠*BAD* in Figure 33 is a right angle. What do we know about the angles of *ABCD*? Because it is a parallelogram, ∠*BAD* and ∠*CDA* are supplementary (see Table 1). Thus, to show that each is a right angle, it will suffice to prove that the angles are congruent. These angles are in $\triangle ABD$ and $\triangle DCA$, which are congruent by SSS since $\overline{AB} \cong \overline{DC}$ (in a parallelogram opposite sides are congruent), $\overline{AD} \cong \overline{DA}$, and $\overline{BD} \cong \overline{CA}$ (given). Therefore, $\angle BAD \cong \angle CDA$ by CPCTC. Since these angles are supplementary and congruent, each must be a right angle. Therefore, $ABCD$ is a rectangle.

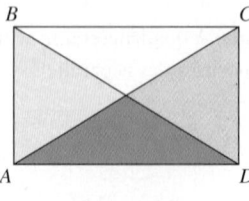

Figure 33

Example 9

In Figure 34(a), $\triangle ABC$ is a right triangle, and $\overline{CD}$ is a **median** (segment connecting a vertex to the midpoint of the opposite side). Prove that the median containing the vertex of the right triangle is half the length of the hypotenuse.

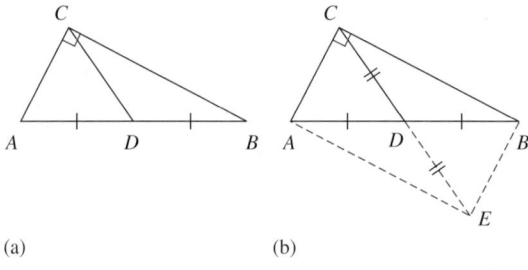

(a)   (b)

Figure 34

Solution   We are given that $\angle C$ is a right angle and D is the midpoint of $\overline{AB}$. We need to prove that $2CD = AB$. In Figure 34(b), we extend $\overline{CD}$ by its length to obtain $CE = 2CD$. Because D is the midpoint of $\overline{AB}$ and also the midpoint of $\overline{CE}$ (by our construction), the diagonals $\overline{AB}$ and $\overline{CE}$ of quadrilateral $ACBE$ bisect each other. Thus, $ACBE$ is a parallelogram (theorem (e) for a parallelogram in Table 1). We also know that $\angle C$ is a right angle (given). Thus, $ACBE$ is a rectangle. Because the diagonals of a rectangle are congruent (theorem (d) for rectangles in Table 1), $CE = AB$ and therefore $2CD = AB$, or $CD = \frac{1}{2}AB$.

Congruence of Quadrilaterals

What minimum conditions determine congruence of quadrilaterals? For example, does the SSS condition for triangles extend to the SSSS condition for quadrilaterals? Figure 35 shows a parallelogram $ABCD$ with hinges at all the vertices and vertices A and D fixed so that their position cannot change. Dragging side $\overline{BC}$ to the right gives a new parallelogram AB_1C_1D with the same sides lengths but different angles, and therefore infinitely many noncongruent parallelograms. Thus, knowing four sides does not determine a unique quadrilateral. Therefore there is no SSSS congruency condition for quadrilaterals.

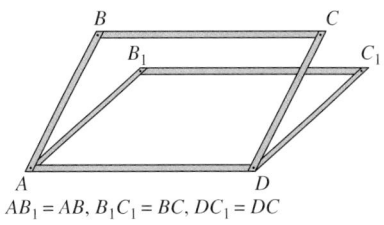

$AB_1 = AB, B_1C_1 = BC, DC_1 = DC$

Figure 35

One way to determine a quadrilateral is to give directions for drawing it. Start with a side and tell by what angle to turn at the end of each side to draw the next side (the turn is by an exterior angle). Thus, SASAS seems to be a valid congruence condition for quadrilaterals (this condition can be proved by dividing a quadrilateral into triangles and using what we know about congruence of triangles).

Assessment 12-2A

Construction

1. Construct each of the following figures, if possible.
   a. A triangle with angles measuring 60° and 70° and an included side of 8 in.
   b. A triangle with angles measuring 60° and 70° and a nonincluded side of 8 cm on a side of the 60° angle
   c. A triangle with angles measuring 30°, 70°, and 80°
2. For each of the conditions in exercises 1(a) through (c), is it possible to construct two noncongruent triangles? Explain why or why not. *
3. For each of the following, determine whether the given conditions are sufficient to prove that $\triangle PQR \cong \triangle MNO$. Justify your answers.
   a. $\angle Q \cong \angle N, \angle P \cong \angle M, \overline{PQ} \cong \overline{MN}$ Yes, ASA
   b. $\angle R \cong \angle O, \angle P \cong \angle M, \overline{QR} \cong \overline{NO}$ Yes, AAS
4. A parallel ruler, shown as follows, can be used to draw parallel lines. The distance between the parallel segments $\overline{AB}$ and $\overline{DC}$ can vary. The ruler is constructed so that the distance between A and B equals the distance between D and C. The distance between A and C is the same as the distance between B and D. Explain why $\overline{AB}$ and $\overline{DC}$ are always parallel. *

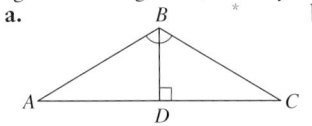
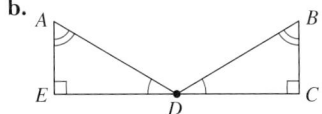

5. List congruent triangles, if any, for each of the following figures. If congruent, tell why.
   a.   *   b.

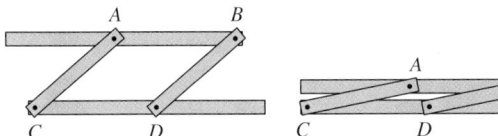

6. In $\triangle ABC$ and $\triangle DEF$, a student knows $\angle B \cong \angle E$ and $\overline{BC} \cong \overline{EF}$. What else does he need to know to establish congruence?

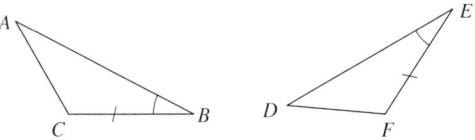

7. Suppose $\triangle ABC \cong \triangle DEF$, find the following measures.

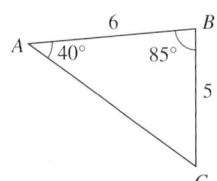

   a. $m(\angle E)$ 85°   b. $m(\angle F)$ 55°
   c. $m(\overline{DE})$ 6   d. $m(\overline{EF})$ 5
8. In the figure below, $\angle ABC \cong \angle DEF$ and are right angles. Also $\overline{AB} \cong \overline{DE}, \overline{BC} \cong \overline{EF}$. Prove $\angle BAC \cong \angle EDF$. *

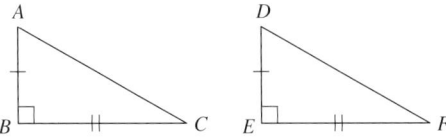

9. Given $\overline{AD} \| \overline{EC}$, and $\overline{BD} \cong \overline{BC}$, prove $\triangle ABD \cong \triangle EBC$. *

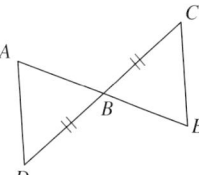

10. In the figure below, $ABCD \cong EFGH$. Solve for x and y.

$x = 7$ and $y = 9$

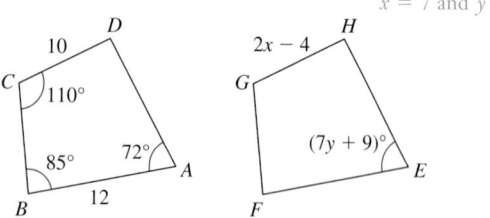

11. In each of the following statements, identify the word in the set {*parallelogram, rectangle, rhombus, trapezoid, kite,* or *square*} needed to make the resulting sentence true. If none of the words makes the sentence true, answer "none".
  a. A quadrilateral is a _____ if, and only if, its diagonals bisect each other.   Parallelogram
  b. A quadrilateral is a _____ if, and only if, its diagonals are congruent.   None
  c. A quadrilateral is a _____ if, and only if, its diagonals are perpendicular.   None

12. Create several trapezoids that have a pair of opposite nonparallel sides congruent. Measure all angles and make a conjecture about the relationships among pairs of angles.   *

13. Classify each of the following statements as true or false. If the statement is false, provide a counterexample.
  a. The diagonals of a square are perpendicular bisectors of each other.   True
  b. If all sides of a quadrilateral are congruent, the quadrilateral is a rhombus.   True
  c. If a rhombus is a square, it must also be a rectangle.   True
  d. Every trapezoid is a parallelogram.   *

14. a. Construct quadrilaterals having exactly one, two, or four right angles.   Construction
  b. Can a quadrilateral have exactly three right angles? Why?   *
  c. Can a parallelogram have exactly two right angles? Why?   *

15. Quadrilateral $ABCD$ pictured is a kite. Prove that $\overleftrightarrow{BD} \perp \overleftrightarrow{AC}$.   *

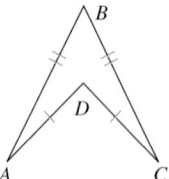

16. Classify each of the following figures formed from regular hexagon $ABCDEF$.

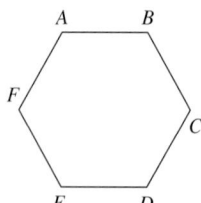

  a. Quadrilateral $ABDE$ Rectangle
  b. Quadrilateral $ABEF$ Isosceles trapezoid

17. The game of Triominoes has equilateral-triangular playing pieces with numbers at each vertex as shown.

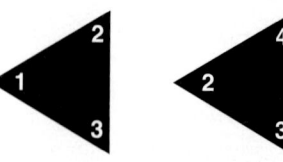

If two pieces are placed together as shown in the following figure, explain what type of quadrilateral is formed:

The figure is a rhombus, because all the sides are congruent.

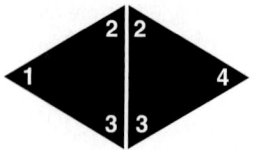

18. A **sector** of a circle is a section shaped like a piece of pie, bounded by two radii and an arc. What is a minimal set of conditions for determining that two sectors of the same circle are congruent?   *

19. In the rectangle $ABCD$ shown, X and Y are midpoints of the given sides and $DP = AQ$.

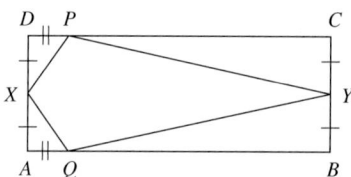

  a. What type of quadrilateral is $PYQX$? Prove your answer.   *
  b. If points P and Q are moved at a constant rate and in the same direction along $\overline{DC}$ and $\overline{AB}$, respectively, does this change your answer in part (a)? Why or why not?   *

20. Draw two quadrilaterals such that two angles and an included side in one quadrilateral are congruent, respectively, to two angles and an included side in the other quadrilateral but, the quadrilaterals are not congruent.   *

21. Construct any convex kite. Then construct a second convex kite that is not congruent to the first but whose sides are congruent to the corresponding sides of the first kite.   *

22. What type of figure is formed by joining the midpoints of a rectangle (see the following figure)? Justify your answer.

Rhombus; use SAS to prove that $\triangle ECF \cong \triangle GBF \cong \triangle EDH \cong \triangle GAH$.

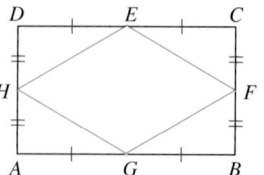

23. What minimum information is sufficient to determine congruency for each of the following?
  a. Two squares   The lengths of one side of each square must be equal.
  b. Two rectangles   *
  c. Two parallelograms   *

24. Prove each of the following statements.
    a. A quadrilateral with a pair of opposite sides parallel and congruent is a parallelogram.   *
    b. A quadrilateral whose diagonals bisect each other is a parallelogram.   *

25. Describe a set of minimal conditions to determine whether two regular polygons are congruent.   *

Assessment 12-2B

1. Construct each of the following figures, if possible.
   a. A right triangle with one acute angle measuring 75° and a leg of 5 cm on a side of the 75° angle   Construction
   b. A triangle with angles measuring 30°, 60°, and 90°   *
2. For each of the conditions in exercises 1(a) and (b), is it possible to construct two noncongruent triangles? Explain why or why not.   *
3. For each of the following, determine whether the given conditions are sufficient to prove that $\triangle PQR \cong \triangle MNO$. Justify your answers.   No; SSA does not ensure congruence.
   a. $\overline{PQ} \cong \overline{MN}, \overline{PR} \cong \overline{MO}, \angle N \cong \angle Q$
   b. $\angle P \cong \angle M, \angle Q \cong \angle N, \angle R \cong \angle O$ *
4. k and ℓ are two lines with A and C on k and B and D on ℓ. If $\overline{AB} \cong \overline{CD}$ and $\overline{AB}$ and $\overline{CD}$ are perpendicular to line k, why must lines k and ℓ be parallel?   *

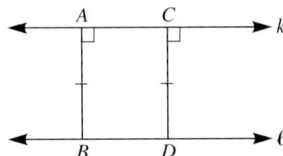

5. List congruent triangles, if any, for each of the following figures. If congruent, tell why.
   a.   *   b.   *

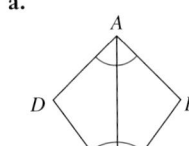   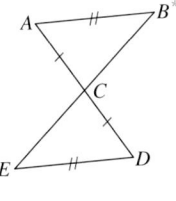

6. Given $\triangle ABC$ and $\triangle DEC$ with congruent parts as marked, what else do you need to know to show congruence?   *

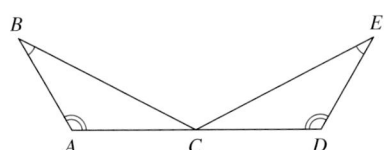

7. Given circle O in the figure below, find each angle measure.   *

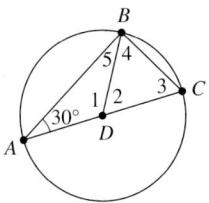

8. In the figure below, $\overline{PQ} \parallel \overline{RS}$ and $\angle P \cong \angle R$. Prove $\overline{PQ} \cong \overline{RS}$.   *

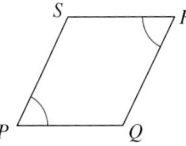

9. $\triangle ISO$ and $\triangle ANG$ are isosceles triangles. Prove $\triangle ISO \cong \triangle ANG$.   *

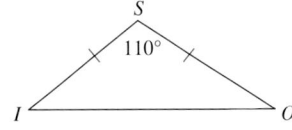   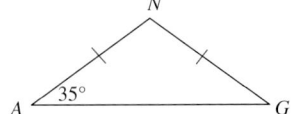

10. In the figure below, $\triangle ABC \cong \triangle DEF$. Find the values of x and y. $x = 13, y = 13$

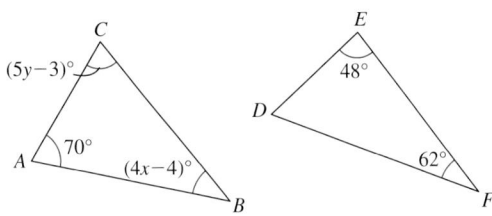

11. In each of the following statements, choose one word, *parallelogram, rectangle, rhombus, trapezoid, kite,* or *square,* so that the resulting sentence is true. If none of the words makes the sentence true, answer "none."
    a. A quadrilateral is a _____ if, and only if, its diagonals are congruent and bisect each other.   Rectangle
    b. A quadrilateral is a _____ if, and only if, its diagonals are perpendicular and bisect each other.   Rhombus
    c. A quadrilateral is a _____ if, and only if, its diagonals are congruent and perpendicular and they bisect each other.   Square
    d. A quadrilateral is a _____ if, and only if, a pair of opposite sides are parallel and congruent.   Parallelogram
12. $ABCD$ in the following figure is a trapezoid in which $\overline{AD} \parallel \overline{BC}$ and $AD > BC$. Prove that if $AB = CD$, then $\angle A \cong \angle D$. (*Hint:* Through C draw a line parallel to $\overline{AB}$.)   *

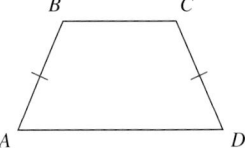

13. Classify each of the following statements as true or false. If the statement is false, provide a counterexample.
    a. No rectangle is a rhombus.   *
    b. No trapezoid is a square.   False, a square is a trapezoid.
    c. Some squares are trapezoids.   *
    d. A rhombus is a parallelogram.   True
    e. A square is a rhombus.   True

14. a. Construct a pentagon with all sides congruent and exactly two right angles.   *
    b. Can a quadrilateral have four acute angles? Why?   *
    c. Can a kite have exactly two right angles? Why?   *

15. Are ∠*BAD* and ∠*BCD* congruent? Explain why or why not.
    Yes, because △*ABD* ≅ △*CBD* by SSS and ∠*BAD* ≅ ∠*BCD* by CPCTC.

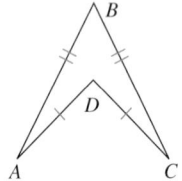

16. Classify each of the figures obtained from regular hexagon *ABCDEF*.

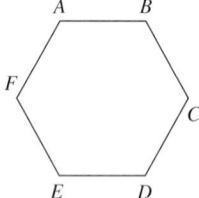

    a. Quadrilateral *ABCD*   Isosceles trapezoid
    b. Quadrilateral *ABCE*   Kite

17. a. Construct a convex kite.   Construction
    b. Construct a rectangle so that the vertices of the kite from part (a) are on the sides of the rectangle.   Construction

18. Draw two noncongruent quadrilaterals such that two 45° angles and an included side in one quadrilateral are congruent, respectively, to two angles and an included side in the other quadrilateral.   *

19. a. Prove that a quadrilateral whose diagonals are congruent and bisect each other is a rectangle.   *
    b. Use part (a) and only a compass and straightedge to construct any rectangle.   *
    c. Construct another rectangle not congruent to the rectangle in part (b) but whose diagonals are congruent to the diagonals of the rectangle in part (b). Why are the rectangles not congruent?   *

20. a. What type of figure is formed by joining the midpoints of the sides of a parallelogram?   Parallelogram
    b. Justify your answer to part (a).   *

21. What minimum information is sufficient to determine congruency for each of the following figures?
    a. Two rectangles   *
    b. Two kites   *
    c. Two isosceles triangles   *

22. Suppose polygon *ABCD* shown in the following figure is any parallelogram:

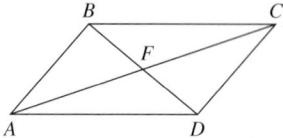

    Use congruent triangles to justify each of the following.
    a. ∠*A* ≅ ∠*C* and ∠*B* ≅ ∠*D* (opposite angles are congruent).   *
    b. $\overline{BC}$ ≅ $\overline{AD}$ and $\overline{AB}$ ≅ $\overline{CD}$ (opposite sides are congruent).   *
    c. $\overline{BF}$ ≅ $\overline{DF}$ and $\overline{AF}$ ≅ $\overline{CF}$ (the diagonals bisect each other).   *
    d. ∠*DAB* and ∠*ABC* are supplementary.   *

23. Describe a set of minimal conditions to determine whether two rhombuses are congruent.   *

Mathematical Connections 12-2

Answers to Mathematical Connections can be found in the Answers section at the back of the book.

Reasoning

1. a. If you know 4 parts (angles and sides) of one triangle are congruent to the corresponding 4 parts of another triangle, are the triangles congruent? Why?
   b. If you know 3 parts (angles and sides) of one triangle are congruent to the corresponding 3 parts of another triangle, are the triangles congruent? Why?

2. List all the methods you know to prove that two triangles are congruent.

3. A surveyor wanted to know the length of a bridge ($\overline{AB}$) over water. He designed the figure below. Explain how he can use his diagram to find the length of the bridge.

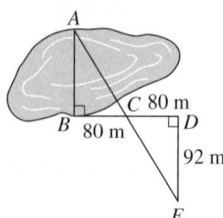

4. In making a quilt block out of congruent right triangles, you mark a right angle and the length of each leg as shown. How do you know the fabric triangles are congruent?

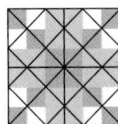
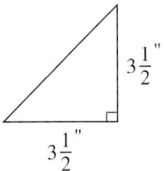

5. Quadrilateral *ABCD* is congruent to quadrilateral *EFGH*. Answer each of the following.
   a. ∠*CDA* ≅ _____
   b. $\overline{CD}$ ≅ _____
   c. Why is △*BCD* ≅ △*FGH*?

6. Stan is standing on the bank of a river wearing a baseball cap. Standing erect and looking directly at the other bank, he pulls the bill of his cap down until it just obscures his vision of the opposite bank. He then turns around, being careful not to disturb the cap, and picks out a spot that is just obscured by the bill of his cap. He then paces off the distance to this spot and claims that the distance across the river is approximately equal to the distance he paced. Is Stan's claim true? Why?

7. Most ironing boards are collapsible for storage and can be adjusted to fit the height of the person using them. The surface of the board, though, remains parallel to the floor regardless of the height. Explain how to construct the legs of an ironing board to ensure that the surface is always parallel to the floor.

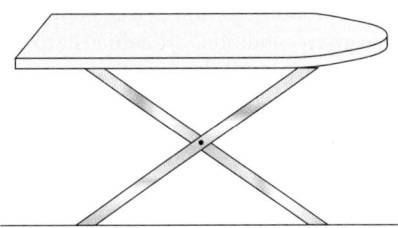

8. Using the fact that the perpendicular bisector of the base of an isosceles triangle is also the angle bisector to explain how to construct the angle bisector of a given angle using only a straightedge and a compass.

9. The marked angles and a side in the two triangles are congruent. Can you conclude that the triangles are congruent? Why or why not?

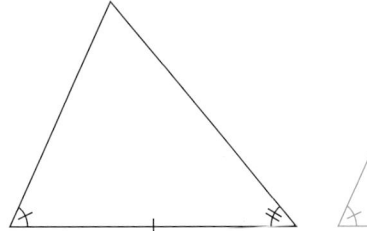
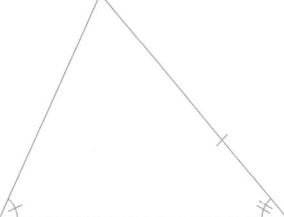

10. In the following figure, point *P* is on the angle bisector of ∠*A*. The distance from *P* to one of the sides of the angle is *PB* and to the other side it is *PC*. It seems that *PB* = *PC*.
    a. Pick another point on the angle bisector and construct the distances from that point to the sides of the angle. What seems to be true about the distances?

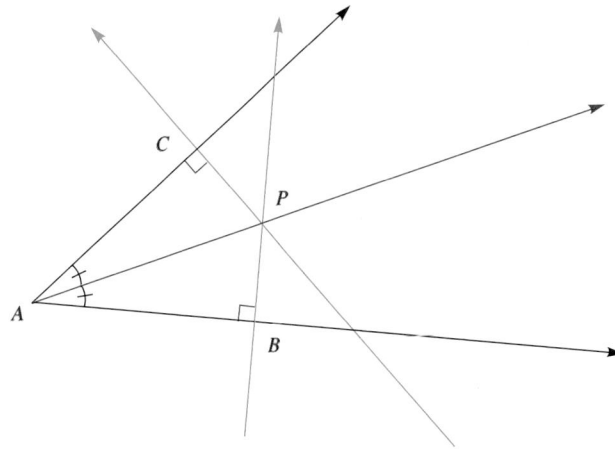

   b. State a conjecture about the points on the angle bisector of an angle by completing the following sentence:

   The distances from every point on the angle bisector of an angle. . .

   c. Prove your conjecture in part (b).
   d. State and prove the converse of your statement in part (b).

11. By definition, two quadrilaterals are congruent if there is a one-to-one correspondence between the vertices such that corresponding angles are congruent and corresponding sides are congruent. Thus, there are eight relations—four between sides and four between angles. If the following number of these conditions hold, explain whether the quadrilaterals are congruent.
    a. 7
    b. 4

Open-Ended

12. On a square geoboard or dot paper (with 16 nails or dots), create and answer questions about the following.
    a. Congruent triangles
    b. Isosceles trapezoids
    c. Noncongruent squares

Cooperative Learning

13. a. Record the definitions of *trapezoid* and *kite* given in different grade 6–8 and secondary-school geometry textbooks.
    b. Compare the definitions found with those in this text and with those other groups found.
    c. Describe the advantages and disadvantages of one definition over another.

Connecting Mathematics to the Classroom

14. A student claims that polygon *ABCD* in the following drawing is a parallelogram if ∠1 ≅ ∠2. Is he correct? Why?

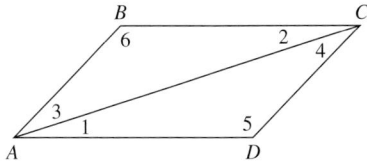

15. A student asks why "congruent" rather than "equal" is used to discuss triangles that have the same size and shape. What do you say?

16. A student asks why triangles often appear in structures such as bridges, building frames, and trusses. How do you respond?

17. A student says that she knows that a parallelogram has two altitudes but when it is long and narrow like the one shown, she does not know how to construct the altitude to the shorter sides. How do you respond?

18. A student claims that if a line ℓ is drawn through vertex A of $\triangle ABC$ parallel to $\overline{BC}$ and a new point A' is chosen anywhere on ℓ, then the height of $\triangle A'BC$ to side $\overline{BC}$ is the same as the height of $\triangle ABC$ to side $\overline{BC}$. He would like to know whether this is true and if so, why. How do you respond?

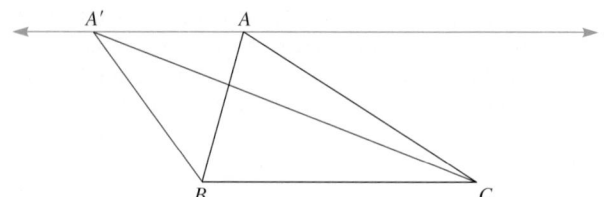

19. Ellen had the following figure drawn on her paper. The teacher walked by and told her that her picture could not possibly be correct. How did the teacher know? Explain.

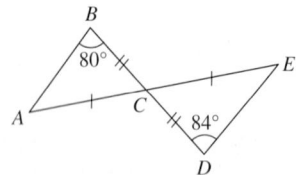

GeoGebra Activities

20. Use Geogebra Lab 1 activities 6–10 and Lab 2 activity 1 or Geogebra Lab 2 activity 2 and Lab 3 activities 1–4 to show the following using inductive reasoning.
    a. The opposite sides and opposite angles of a parallelogram are congruent.
    b. The diagonals of a parallelogram bisect each other.
    c. The diagonals of a rhombus are perpendicular bisectors of each other.
    d. If one pair of sides of a quadrilateral are congruent and parallel, then the quadrilateral is a parallelogram. Prove this statement.

Review Problems

21. In the following regular pentagon, use the existing vertices to find all the triangles congruent to $\triangle ABC$. Show that the triangles actually are congruent.

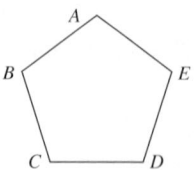

22. If possible, construct a triangle that has the three segments a, b, and c shown here as its sides; if not possible, explain why not.

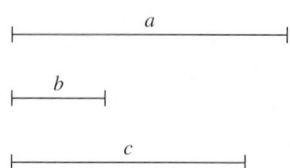

23. Construct an equilateral triangle whose sides are congruent to the following segment:

24. For each of the following pairs of triangles, determine whether the given conditions are sufficient to show that the triangles are congruent. If the triangles are congruent, tell which property can be used to verify this fact.

a.   b.

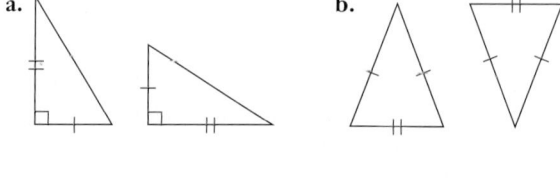

c.

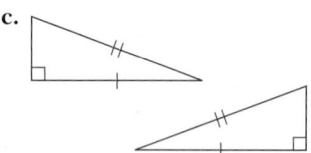

12-3 Additional Constructions

We use the definition of a rhombus and the following theorems (also listed in Table 1) to accomplish basic compass-and-straightedge constructions:

1. A rhombus is a parallelogram in which all the sides are congruent.
2. A quadrilateral is a rhombus if, and only if, all four sides are congruent.
3. Each diagonal of a rhombus bisects the opposite angles.
4. The diagonals of a rhombus are perpendicular.
5. The diagonals of a rhombus bisect each other.

Constructing Parallel Lines

To construct a line parallel to a given line ℓ through a point P not on ℓ, as in the leftmost panel of Figure 36, our strategy is to construct a rhombus (using Theorem 12-2 listed above) with one of its vertices at P and one of its sides on line ℓ. Because the opposite sides of a rhombus are parallel, one of the sides through P will be parallel to ℓ. The complete construction is shown in Figure 36.

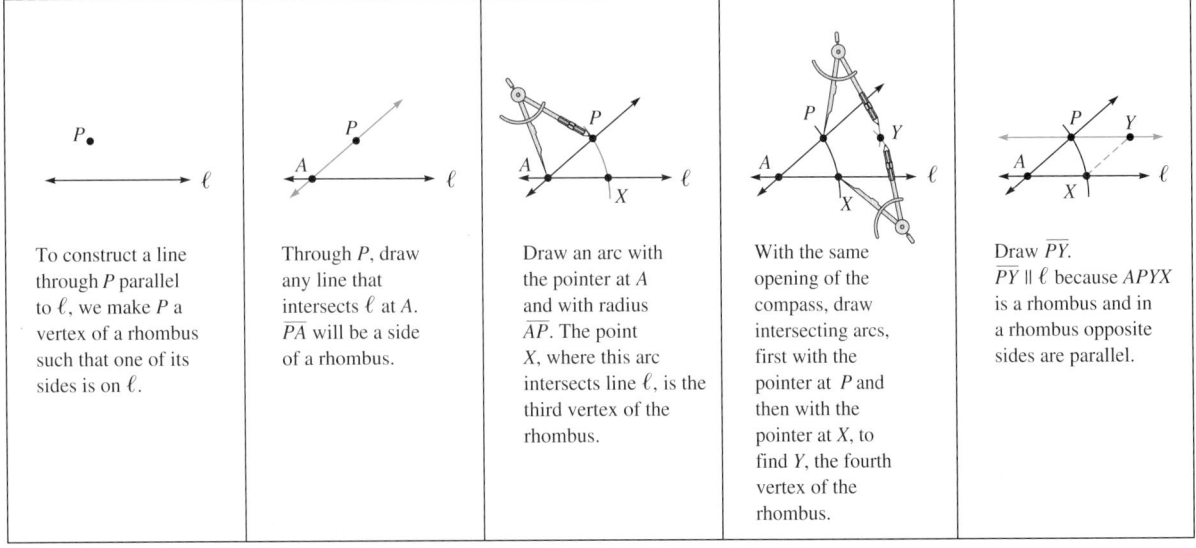

To construct a line through P parallel to ℓ, we make P a vertex of a rhombus such that one of its sides is on ℓ.

Through P, draw any line that intersects ℓ at A. $\overline{PA}$ will be a side of a rhombus.

Draw an arc with the pointer at A and with radius $\overline{AP}$. The point X, where this arc intersects line ℓ, is the third vertex of the rhombus.

With the same opening of the compass, draw intersecting arcs, first with the pointer at P and then with the pointer at X, to find Y, the fourth vertex of the rhombus.

Draw $\overline{PY}$. $\overline{PY} \parallel \ell$ because $APYX$ is a rhombus and in a rhombus opposite sides are parallel.

Figure 36 Constructing parallel lines (rhombus method)

Figure 37 shows another way to construct parallel lines. If congruent corresponding angles are formed by a transversal cutting two lines, then the lines are parallel. Thus, the first step is to draw a transversal through P that intersects ℓ. The angle marked α is formed by the transversal and line ℓ. By constructing an angle with a vertex at P congruent to α, we create congruent corresponding angles; therefore, $\overrightarrow{PQ} \parallel \ell$.

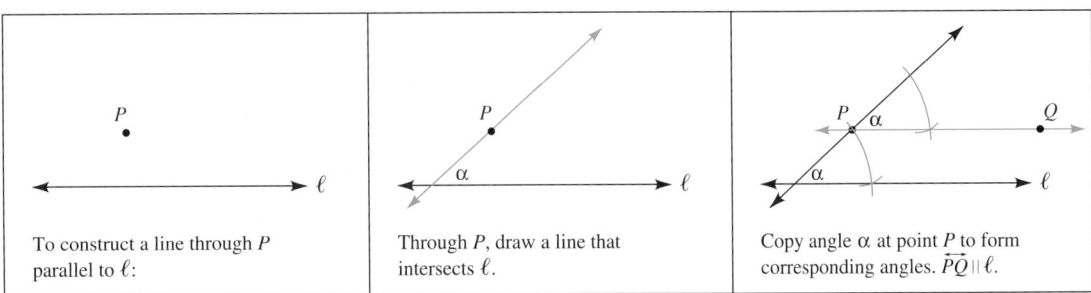

To construct a line through P parallel to ℓ:

Through P, draw a line that intersects ℓ.

Copy angle α at point P to form corresponding angles. $\overrightarrow{PQ} \parallel \ell$.

Figure 37 Constructing parallel lines (corresponding angle method)

Parallel lines are frequently constructed using either a ruler and one triangle or two triangles. If a ruler and a triangle are used, the ruler is left fixed and the triangle is slid so that one side of the triangle touches the ruler at all times. In Figure 38, the hypotenuses of the right triangles are all parallel (also the legs not on the ruler are all parallel).

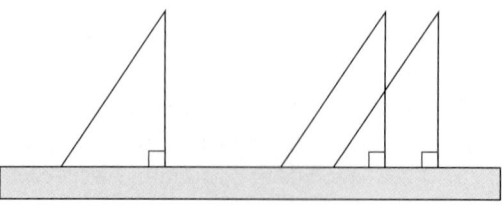

Figure 38

a. How can this method be used to construct a line parallel to a given line through a given point?
b. Why are the hypotenuses parallel?

Paperfolding can be used to construct parallel lines. For example in Figure 39(a) to construct a line m parallel to line p through point Q, we can fold a perpendicular to line p so that the fold line does not contain point Q, as shown in Figure 39(b). Then by marking the image of point Q and connecting point Q and its image, Q', we have $\overleftrightarrow{QQ'}$ parallel to line p (why?), as in Figure 39(c).

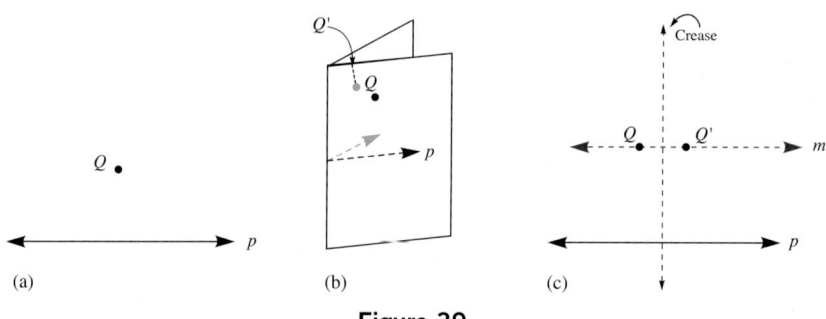

Figure 39

Constructing an Angle Bisector

Another construction based on a property of a rhombus is the construction of an angle bisector, (a ray that separates an angle into two congruent angles). The construction is shown in Figure 40. The diagonal of a rhombus with vertex A bisects $\angle A$.

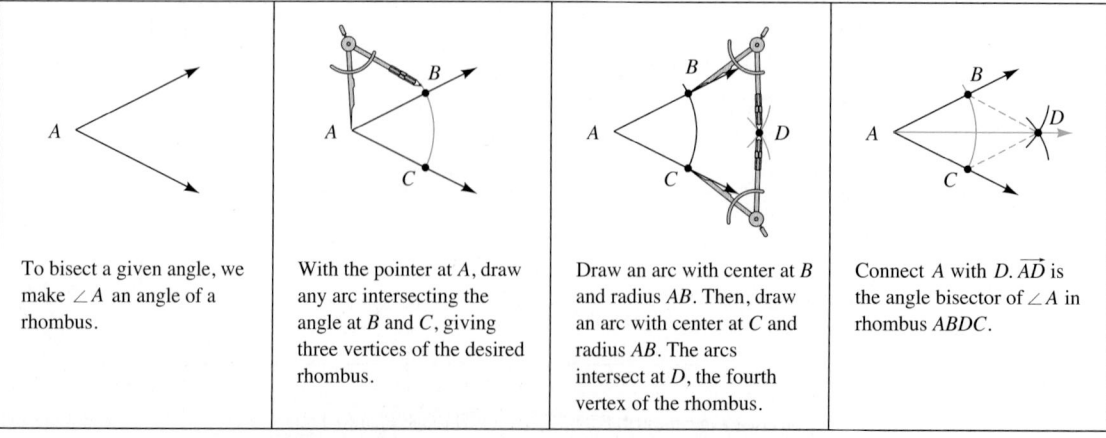

To bisect a given angle, we make $\angle A$ an angle of a rhombus.	With the pointer at A, draw any arc intersecting the angle at B and C, giving three vertices of the desired rhombus.	Draw an arc with center at B and radius AB. Then, draw an arc with center at C and radius AB. The arcs intersect at D, the fourth vertex of the rhombus.	Connect A with D. $\overrightarrow{AD}$ is the angle bisector of $\angle A$ in rhombus $ABDC$.

Figure 40   Bisecting an angle (rhombus method)

Another way to bisect an angle can be devised by using the fact that a perpendicular bisector of the base of an isosceles triangle contains the vertex and is the angle bisector of the opposite angle. Actually, the steps of the construction can be the same as in Figure 40, where $\triangle BAC$ is an isosceles triangle and $\overleftrightarrow{AD}$ is the perpendicular bisector of $\overline{BC}$, because both A and D are equidistant from the endpoints of $\overline{BC}$.

Paperfolding can be used to bisect an angle. Fold a line through the vertex so that one side of the angle folds onto the other side. For example, in Figure 41 we bisect $\angle ABC$ by folding and creasing the paper through the vertex B so that $\overrightarrow{BC}$ coincides with $\overrightarrow{BA}$.

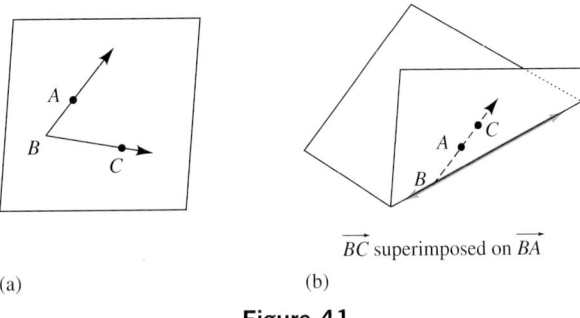

(a) $\overrightarrow{BC}$ superimposed on $\overrightarrow{BA}$ (b)

Figure 41

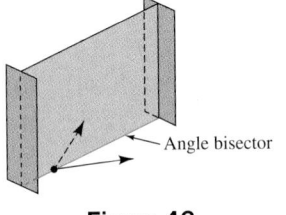

Figure 42

A Mira is a plastic device that acts as a reflector so that the image of an object can be seen behind the Mira. The drawing edge of the Mira acts as a folding line on paper. Any construction demonstrated in this text using paperfolding can also be done with a Mira. To construct the bisector of an angle with a Mira, we place the drawing edge of the Mira on the vertex of the angle and reflect one side of the angle onto the other, as shown in Figure 42. Notice that the Mira shows symmetry of an angle about the angle bisector—the reflection line.

Constructing Perpendicular Lines

To construct a line through P perpendicular to line ℓ, where P is not a point on ℓ, as in Figure 43, we use the fact that the diagonals of a rhombus are perpendicular to each other. If we construct a rhombus with a vertex at P and a diagonal on ℓ, as in Figure 43, the segment connecting the fourth vertex Q to P is perpendicular to ℓ.

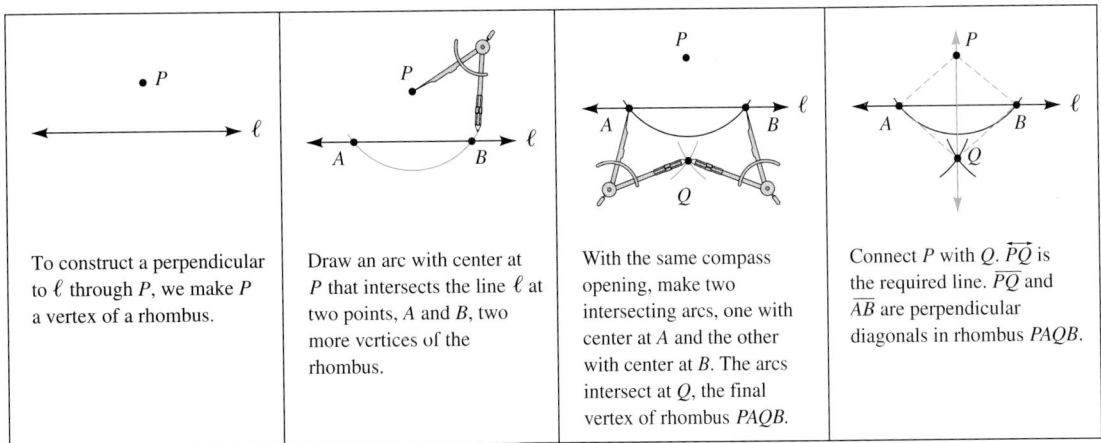

To construct a perpendicular to ℓ through P, we make P a vertex of a rhombus.	Draw an arc with center at P that intersects the line ℓ at two points, A and B, two more vertices of the rhombus.	With the same compass opening, make two intersecting arcs, one with center at A and the other with center at B. The arcs intersect at Q, the final vertex of rhombus $PAQB$.	Connect P with Q. $\overrightarrow{PQ}$ is the required line. $\overrightarrow{PQ}$ and $\overline{AB}$ are perpendicular diagonals in rhombus $PAQB$.

Figure 43   Constructing a perpendicular to a line from a point not on the line (rhombus method)

In Section 12-1 we saw how to construct the perpendicular bisector of a segment using a property of a perpendicular bisector stated in Theorem 12-3. Here we show how a property of a rhombus can also be used for constructing the perpendicular bisector of a segment.

To construct the perpendicular bisector of a line segment, as in Figure 44, we use the fact that the diagonals of a rhombus are perpendicular bisectors of each other.

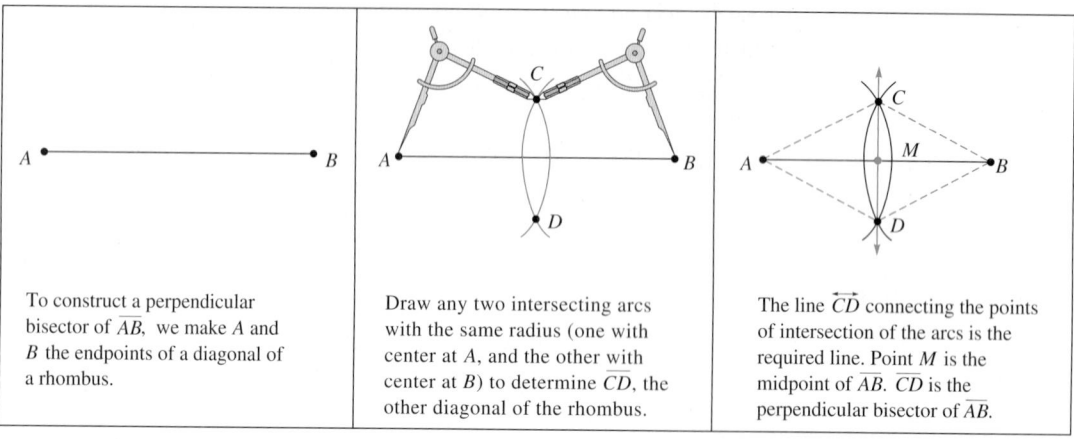

To construct a perpendicular bisector of $\overline{AB}$, we make A and B the endpoints of a diagonal of a rhombus.	Draw any two intersecting arcs with the same radius (one with center at A, and the other with center at B) to determine $\overleftrightarrow{CD}$, the other diagonal of the rhombus.	The line $\overleftrightarrow{CD}$ connecting the points of intersection of the arcs is the required line. Point M is the midpoint of $\overline{AB}$. $\overleftrightarrow{CD}$ is the perpendicular bisector of $\overline{AB}$.

Figure 44   Constructing a perpendicular bisector of a segment (rhombus method)

Constructing a perpendicular to a line ℓ at a point M on ℓ is based on the fact that the diagonals of a rhombus are perpendicular bisectors of each other. Observe in Figure 44 that $\overleftrightarrow{CD}$ is a perpendicular to $\overline{AB}$ through M. Thus, we construct a rhombus whose diagonals intersect at point M, as in Figure 45.

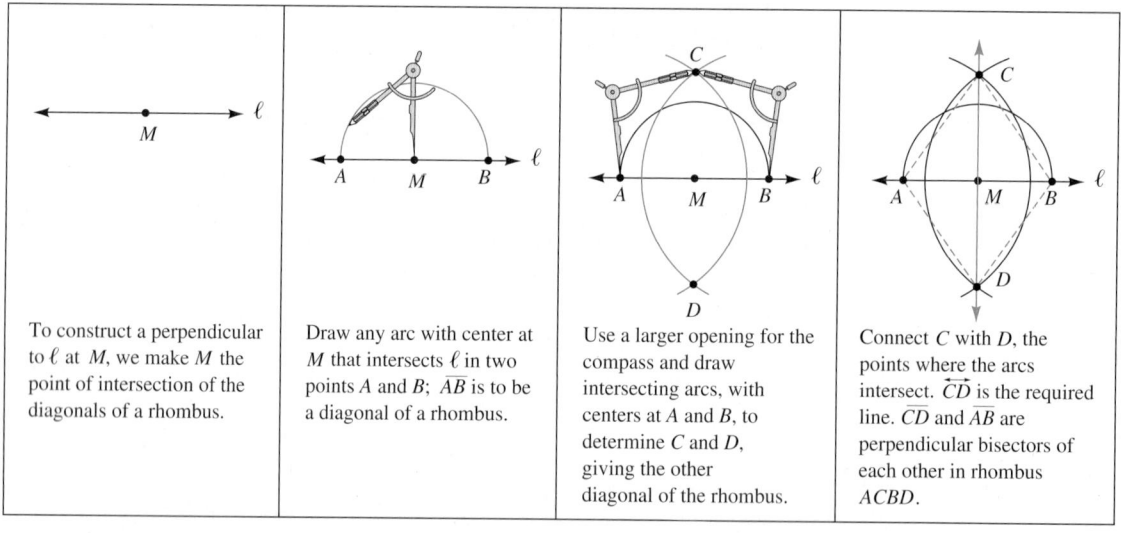

To construct a perpendicular to ℓ at M, we make M the point of intersection of the diagonals of a rhombus.	Draw any arc with center at M that intersects ℓ in two points A and B; $\overline{AB}$ is to be a diagonal of a rhombus.	Use a larger opening for the compass and draw intersecting arcs, with centers at A and B, to determine C and D, giving the other diagonal of the rhombus.	Connect C with D, the points where the arcs intersect. $\overleftrightarrow{CD}$ is the required line. $\overleftrightarrow{CD}$ and $\overline{AB}$ are perpendicular bisectors of each other in rhombus $ACBD$.

Figure 45   Constructing a perpendicular to a line from a point on the line (rhombus method)

Perpendicularity constructions can also be completed by means of paperfolding or by using a Mira. To use paperfolding to construct a perpendicular to a given line ℓ at a point P on the line, we fold the line onto itself, as shown in Figure 46(a). The fold line is perpendicular to ℓ. To perform the construction with a Mira, we place the Mira with the drawing edge on P, as shown in Figure 46(b), so that ℓ is reflected onto itself. The line along the drawing edge is the required perpendicular.

An altitude of a triangle was defined in Section 12-1. Constructing perpendiculars is useful in locating altitudes of a triangle. The construction of altitudes is described in Example 10.

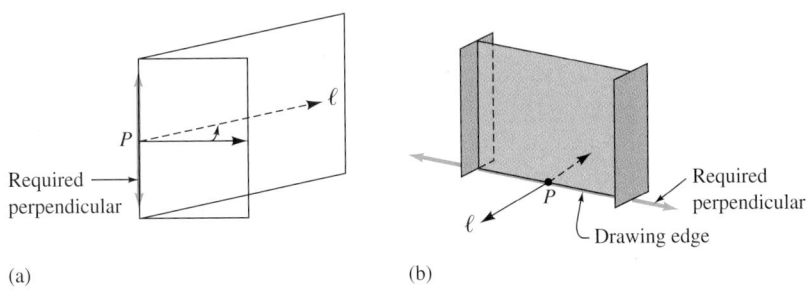

Figure 46

Example 10

For each part of Figure 47, given triangle *ABC*, construct the altitude from vertex *A*.

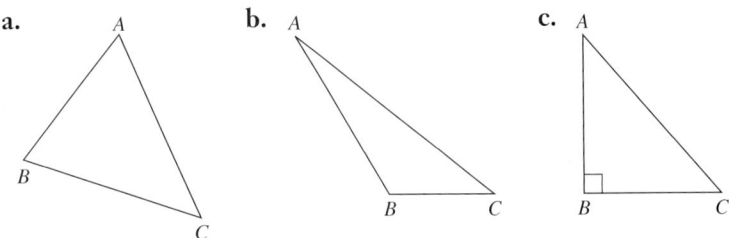

Figure 47

Solution

a. An altitude is the segment perpendicular from a vertex to the line containing the opposite side of a triangle, so we need to construct a perpendicular from point *A* to the line containing $\overline{BC}$. Such a construction is shown in Figure 48. $\overline{AD}$ is the required altitude.

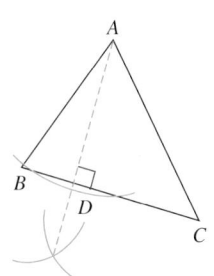

Figure 48

b. The construction of the altitude from vertex *A* is shown in Figure 49. Notice that the required altitude $\overline{AD}$ does not intersect the interior of $\triangle ABC$.

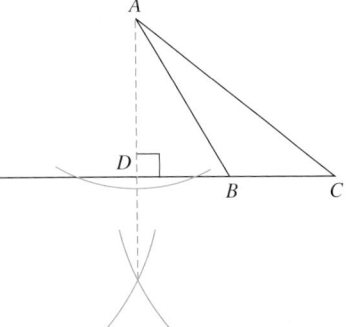

Figure 49

c. Triangle *ABC* is a right triangle. The altitude from vertex *A* is the side $\overline{AB}$. No construction is required.

Properties of Angle Bisectors

To investigate properties of an angle bisector, recall that we define the distance from a point to a line as the length of the perpendicular segment from the point to the line. Consider the angle bisector in Figure 50. It seems that any point P on the angle bisector is equidistant from the sides of the angle; that is, $PD = PE$.

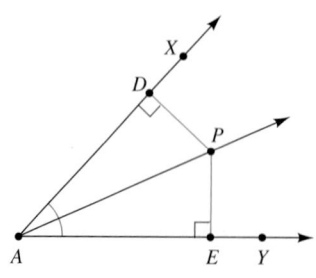

Figure 50

To justify this, we find two congruent triangles that have $\overline{PD}$ and $\overline{PE}$ as corresponding sides. The only triangles pictured are $\triangle ADP$ and $\triangle AEP$. Because $\overrightarrow{AP}$ is the angle bisector, $\angle DAP \cong \angle EAP$. Also, $\angle PDA$ and $\angle PEA$ are right angles and are thus congruent. $\overline{AP}$ is congruent to itself, so $\triangle PDA \cong \triangle PEA$ by AAS. Thus, $\overline{PD} \cong \overline{PE}$ because they are corresponding parts of congruent triangles PDA and PEA. Consequently, we have proved the first part of the following theorem.

Theorem 12-10

  a. Any point P on an angle bisector is equidistant from the sides of the angle.

  b. Any point in the interior of an angle that is equidistant from the sides of the angle is on the angle bisector of the angle.

Both parts of Theorem 12-10 can be stated as follows: A point in the interior of an angle is on an angle bisector of an angle if, and only if, it is equidistant from the sides of the angle. The angle bisector is on the line of symmetry of the angle.

We have proved only part (a) of Theorem 12-10. In Now Try This 7 you are asked to investigate the proof of part (b).

▶ **NOW TRY THIS 7**

NTT 7: Answers can be found in Answers at the back of the book.

Prove that if a point is in the interior of an angle and is equidistant from the sides of the angle, the point must be on the angle bisector of that angle.

Constructing the Incircle of a Triangle

The intersection of any two angle bisectors of a triangle is the **incenter** of the triangle. In Figure 51, P is the intersection of the angle bisectors of $\angle A$ and of $\angle B$. We will show that the third angle bisector, the bisector of $\angle C$, also goes through P, which implies that the three angle bisectors are concurrent (intersect in a single point). From P we construct the perpendiculars to the three sides of the triangle, $\overline{PN}, \overline{PK},$ and $\overline{PM}$. Because P is on the angle bisector of $\angle A$, from Theorem 12-10(a) we know that

$$PN = PK.$$

Similarly, because P is on the angle bisector of $\angle B$, we know that

$$PK = PM.$$

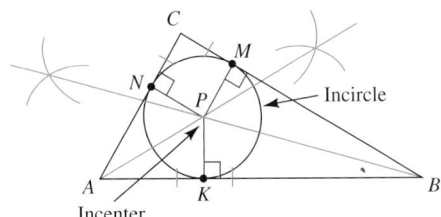

Figure 51

Now from (1) and (2) we conclude that $PN = PM$. But this means that P is equidistant from the sides of $\angle C$. Thus, by Theorem 12-10(b), P is on the angle bisector of $\angle C$. We have proved the following theorem.

Theorem 12-11

The angle bisectors of a triangle are concurrent, and the three distances from the point of intersection to the sides of the triangle are equal.

If in Figure 51 we draw a circle with center P and radius PM (or PK or PN), the circle seems to fit exactly inside the triangle. In fact each line segment "touches" the circle at one point only. The sides of the triangle are **tangent** to the circle. *A line is tangent to a circle if it intersects the circle in one, and only one, point.* It is possible to show that a line perpendicular to a radius at the endpoint of the radius that is not the center is tangent to the circle. Thus, the sides of $\triangle ABC$ in Figure 51 are tangent to the circle. Such a circle is **inscribed** in the triangle. The center of the inscribed circle, the **incircle,** is the **incenter** of the triangle.

To find the radius of the inscribed circle, it is sufficient to construct from the incenter just one perpendicular (to one of the sides). The point of intersection of the perpendicular with the corresponding side when connected with P determines the radius.

▶ **NOW TRY THIS 8**

NTT 8: Answer can be found in Answers at the back of the book.

Use any tools to investigate whether a circle can be inscribed in a square.

Assessment 12-3A

1. Draw a line ℓ and point P not on ℓ. Use a compass and a straightedge to construct a line m through P parallel to ℓ, using each of the following figures.
   a. Corresponding angles   Construction
   b. A rhombus   Construction

2. Draw a line ℓ and a point P, but not on ℓ. Construct a line through P parallel to ℓ using a property of alternate interior angles.

$P \bullet$

   Construction

3. Copy $\angle A$ shown below and bisect it.   Construction

A

4. In the figure below, $\overrightarrow{AC}$ is the angle bisector of $\angle BAC$. Solve for x.   25

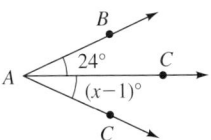

5. In the figure below, $\overrightarrow{BC}$ bisects $\angle ABD$.

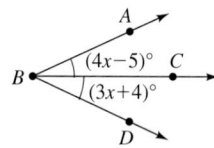

a. Solve for x.   9
b. Find the measure of $\angle ABD$.   62°

6. Construction companies avoid vandalism at night by hanging expensive pieces of equipment from the boom of a crane, as shown in the following figure:

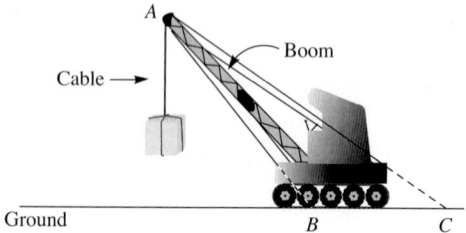

a. If you consider a triangle with two vertices A and B as marked in the figure and the intersection of a line through the cable holding the equipment and the ground as the third vertex, what type of triangle is formed?   Right triangle
b. If you consider the triangle formed by points A, B, and C, describe where the altitude containing vertex A of the triangle is.   *

7. Construct the perpendicular bisectors of each of the sides of the following triangles.

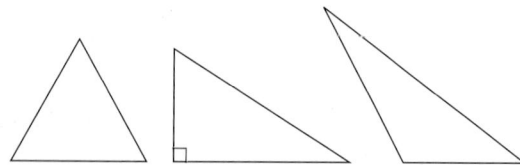

a. Make a conjecture about the perpendicular bisectors of the sides of an acute triangle.   *
b. Make a conjecture about the perpendicular bisectors of the sides of a right triangle.   *
c. Make a conjecture about the perpendicular bisectors of the sides of an obtuse triangle.   *
d. For each of the three triangles, construct the circle that circumscribes the triangle.   Construction

8. a. Given the following triangle ABC, construct a point P that is equidistant from the three vertices of the triangle. Explain why your construction is correct.   *

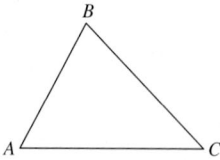

b. Repeat part (a) for the following obtuse triangle: Same as part (a).

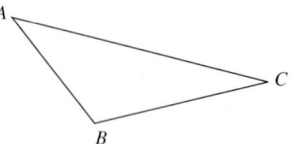

9. For which of the following figures is it possible to construct a circle that is inscribed in the figure (each side of the figure must be tangent to the circle)? If it is possible to find such a circle, draw the figure and construct the inscribed circle using only a straightedge and a compass; if not, explain how you decided that it is impossible to find an inscribed circle.
a. A rectangle   *
b. A rhombus   *
c. A regular hexagon   *

10. Given $\overline{AB}$ in the following figure, construct a square with $\overline{AB}$ as a side.   Construction

11. a. Given A, B, and C as vertices, construct a parallelogram $ABCD$.   Construction

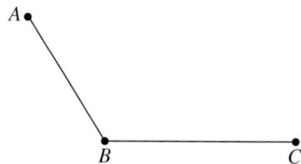

b. Suppose you are "charged" 10¢ each time you use your straightedge to draw a line segment and 10¢ each time you use your compass to draw an arc. What is the cheapest way to construct the parallelogram in part (a)?   40¢

12. Construct two segments $\overline{AB}$ and $\overline{CD}$ that are perpendicular bisectors of each other. Draw $\overline{AC}$, $\overline{CB}$, $\overline{BD}$, and $\overline{DA}$. What type of quadrilateral is $ACBD$? Explain why.   *

13. Given $\overline{AB}$, construct an isosceles triangle with altitude $\overline{AB}$ and apex B.   Construction

14. In right triangle ABC, point O is the incenter, $CD = 2''$, $AC = 8''$, $AB = 10''$. Find OD.   2″

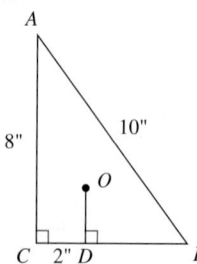

15. Describe how to construct the incircle of a regular pentagon.   *

16. In the parallelogram *ABCD* shown, find *EF*.   3″

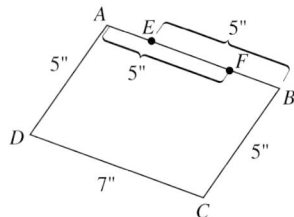

17. **a.** Show that any parallelogram can be dissected (cut apart) to form two non-isosceles trapezoids.   *
    b. Show that any two congruent trapezoids can always be put together to form a parallelogram.   *

18. Some car jacks are constructed like a collapsed rhombus. When used to raise a car, the rhombus is easily seen.

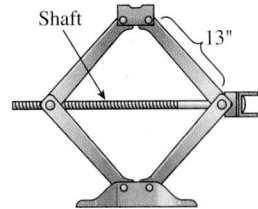

If the sides of the rhombus are 13″, what is the minimum length of the shaft?   As close to 26 in. as the jack can close.

19. Determine if it is possible to construct each of the following. If the construction is not possible, explain why.
    a. A square, given one side   Possible
    b. A rectangle, given one diagonal   *

c. A triangle with two obtuse angles   *
d. A parallelogram with exactly three right angles   *

20. Use compass and straightedge to construct angles with each of the following measures.
    a. 30°   *
    b. 45°   *
    c. 75°   *

21. Construct $\overline{AB}$ close to the bottom of a blank page. Use a compass and a straightedge to construct the perpendicular bisector of $\overline{AB}$. You are not allowed to put any marks below $\overline{AB}$.   Construction

22. Draw a convex quadrilateral similar to the one shown below and construct each of the following points, if possible. If it is not possible, explain why. Describe each construction in words and explain why it produces the required point.

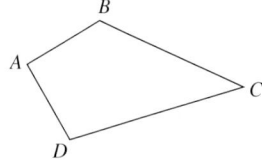

a. The point that is equidistant from $\overline{AB}$ and $\overline{AD}$ and also from points *B* and *C*   *
b. The point that is equidistant from $\overline{AB}$, $\overline{AD}$, and $\overline{BC}$ *

23. Construct a circle. Then construct an equilateral triangle inscribed in that circle. Describe the main steps in your construction and explain why your construction produces an equilateral triangle.   *

Assessment 12-3B

1. Draw a figure like the one below, then describe how to construct line *m* through *P* parallel to ℓ, using each of the following figures.
   a. Perpendicular lines   *
   b. A quadrilateral whose diagonals bisect each other. (*Hint*: Connect *P* with any point *Q* on ℓ. Through the midpoint *M* of $\overline{PQ}$ draw any line intersecting ℓ at *Q′*.)   *

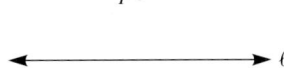

2. Draw a line ℓ and a point *P*, but not on ℓ. Construct a line through *P* parallel to ℓ using a property of alternate exterior angles.   Construction

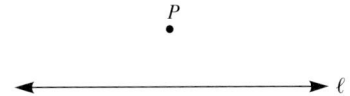

3. Copy line segment $\overline{AB}$ shown below and bisect it.   Construction

A •————————————• B

4. In the figure, $\overrightarrow{OP}$ is the perpendicular bisector of $\overline{MN}$.

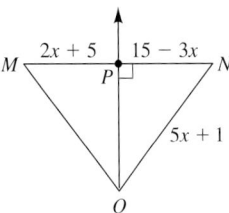

a. Solve for *x*.   2
b. Find the measure of $\overline{MO}$.   11

5. In the figure below, $\overrightarrow{AC}$ is the angle bisector of ∠*BAD*.

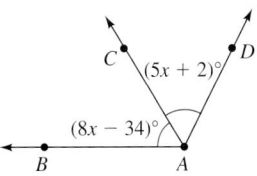

a. Solve for *x*.   12
b. Find the measure of ∠*BAD*.   124°

6. Construct an obtuse triangle and the three altitudes. Mark the point where the lines that contain the altitudes are concurrent.   Construction

7. Construct an obtuse triangle and the perpendicular bisectors of two of its sides. Then construct the circle that circumscribes the triangle.   Construction

8. Draw a large obtuse triangle and construct the circle inscribed in the triangle. Why is the center of the circle equidistant from the sides of the triangle?   *

9. Is it possible to inscribe a circle in every convex kite? Why or why not?   *

10. Given $\overline{AB}$ in the following figure, describe how to construct a square with $\overline{AB}$ as a diagonal.   *

11. Suppose you are "charged" 10¢ each time you use your straightedge to draw a line segment and 10¢ each time you use your compass to draw an arc. Determine the cheapest way to construct an equilateral triangle.   50¢

12. Construct a rectangle $ABCD$ such that $\overline{AC} \cong \overline{EF}$.   *

13. Given points E and B, construct a square $ABCD$ such that B is a vertex and E is the point of intersection of the two diagonals. Explain your construction.   *

14. In the isosceles right triangle shown, O is the incenter; the radius of the inscribed circle is r. Find AX. r

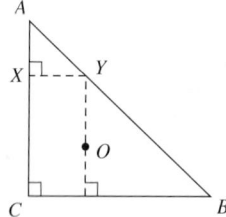

15. Describe how to construct the incircle of a regular decagon.   *

16. In the parallelogram shown, find x in terms of a and b.

$x = 2a - b$

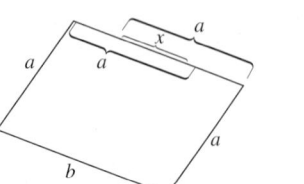

17. Explain why any rectangle can be dissected into two congruent trapezoids in many different ways.   *

18. In the following concave quadrilateral $APBQ$, $\overline{PQ}$ and $\overline{AB}$ are the diagonals; $\overline{AP} \cong \overline{BP}$, $\overline{AQ} \cong \overline{BQ}$, and $\overline{PQ}$ has been extended until it intersects $\overline{AB}$ at C.

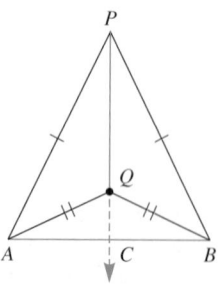

a. Make a conjecture concerning $\overleftrightarrow{PQ}$ and $\overline{AB}$.   *

b. Justify your conjecture in part (a).   *

c. Make conjectures concerning the relationships between $\overrightarrow{PQ}$ and $\angle APB$ and between $\overrightarrow{QC}$ and $\angle AQB$.   *

d. Justify your conjectures in (c).   *

19. Using any tools, determine if it is possible to construct a unique figure for each of the following. If the construction is not possible, explain why.

a. A parallelogram, given two of its adjacent sides   *

b. A rhombus, given its diagonals   *

c. A parallelogram given a side and all the angles   *

20. Using only a compass and a straightedge, construct angles with each of the following measures:

a. 15°   *

b. 105°   *

c. 120°   *

21. Draw a line ℓ and a point P not on the line and use the sliding triangle method to construct a perpendicular to ℓ through P using a straightedge and a right triangle.   *

22. Draw a convex quadrilateral similar to the one shown below and construct each of the following points, if possible. If it is not possible, explain why. Describe each construction in words and explain why it produces the required point.

a. The point that is equidistant from A, B, and C *

b. The point that is equidistant from A, B, C, and D *

c. The point that is equidistant from the four sides   *

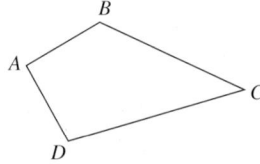

23. Given a circle, find an equilateral triangle for which the circle is the incircle. Describe the main steps in your construction and explain why your construction produces an equilateral triangle.   *

Mathematical Connections 12-3

Answers to Mathematical Connections can be found in the Answers section at the back of the book.

Reasoning

1. Draw a line ℓ and a point P not on ℓ. Construct a line m through P perpendicular to ℓ. Draw a point Q, but not on lines ℓ or m. Construct a line n through Q perpendicular to m. Are lines ℓ and n parallel? Justify your answer.

2. In the figure below, $AC = 30$. Explain why or why not B is the midpoint of $\overline{AC}$.

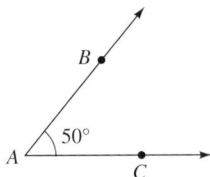

3. In the figure, $m(\angle A) = 50°$. Explain how to construct a $20°$ angle using this figure.

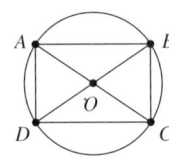

4. **a.** Construct a circle O and draw two diameters. Label them $\overline{AC}$ and $\overline{BD}$. Then draw $ABCD$ as shown below. Prove that $ABCD$ is a rectangle.

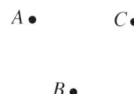

   b. Describe how to construct two rectangles whose diagonals are congruent, but the rectangles are not congruent.

5. Place three dots, A, B, and C, on a piece of paper as shown below to represent three cities. Show how to find the location to build an airport that is the same distance from each of the cities.

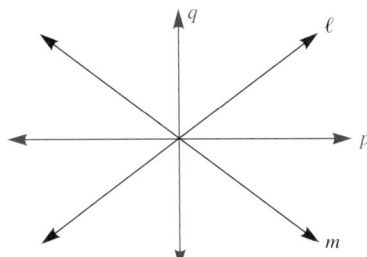

6. Lines ℓ and m intersect as shown to form two vertical angles. Lines p and q bisect the vertical angles. Explain why p and q are perpendicular.

7. Given an angle and a roll of tape, describe how you might construct the bisector of the angle.

8. If two pieces of tape of the same width cross each other, what type of parallelogram is $ABCD$? Justify your answer.

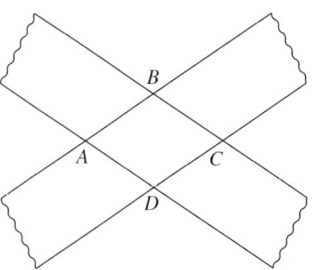

9. $ABCD$ is a parallelogram. The diagonals divide the parallelogram into four triangles with incenters at E, F, G, and H. Prove that $EFGH$ is a rhombus.

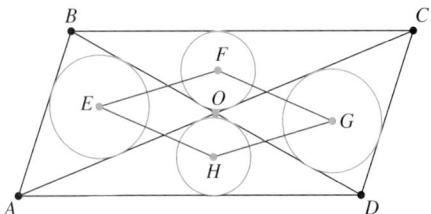

Open-Ended

10. Write a letter from you, a curriculum developer, to parents explaining whether or not the geometry curriculum in grades 5–8 should include construction problems that use only a compass and straightedge.

11. Patty paper constructions are accomplished using the waxed paper that is sometimes applied between hamburger patties by commercial meat companies. Research patty paper constructions and organize a presentation on them.

12. Given a circle and using any tools construct a pentagon for which the circle is an incircle. Describe the main steps of your construction.

Cooperative Learning

13. In your group, perform the paperfolding construction shown and answer the questions that follow. Let P and Q be two opposite vertices of a rectangular piece of paper, as shown in (i). Fold P onto Q so that a crease is formed. This results in (ii), where A and B are the endpoints of the crease. Next crease again so that point A folds onto point B. This results in (iii). Next, unfold to obtain two creases, as in (iv).

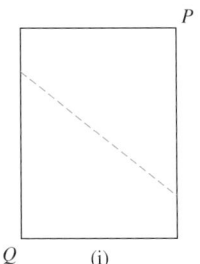
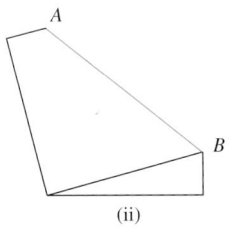

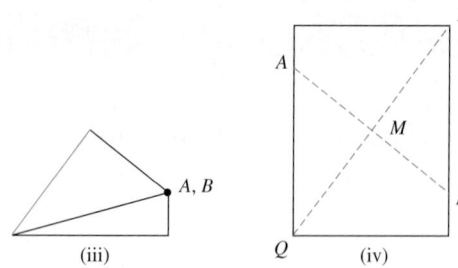

(iii)   (iv)

a. Individually write an explanation of why every point on $\overline{AB}$ is equidistant from the endpoints of $\overline{PQ}$. Compare the explanations in your group and prepare one explanation to be presented to the class.
b. Discuss in your group whether $APBQ$ is a rhombus.
14. Each member of the group should cut out a large acute scalene triangle. Make each one different. For each triangle fold the triangle to form the perpendicular bisectors of the sides. The fold for the perpendicular bisector of $\overline{AC}$ is shown below.

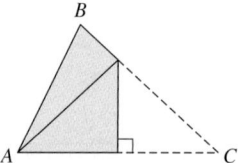

a. Do the three perpendicular bisectors meet at a common point for each triangle?
b. For each triangle, label the vertices as A, B, and C and the common intersection point P. Measure AP, BP, and CP. What do you observe?
c. What changes in this experiment would you have to make for different kinds of triangles?
15. In your group, discuss how you would do the compass and straightedge constructions in this chapter using (a) paperfolding (b) a MIRA.

Connecting Mathematics to the Classroom

16. A student asks if a line can be bisected. How do you respond?
17. In the figure $\overline{DE} \cong \overline{FE}$. A student claims that E is the midpoint of $\overline{DF}$. How do you respond?

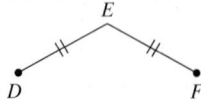

18. In the figure below, a student claims that $GD = GF$. Is she correct? Why?

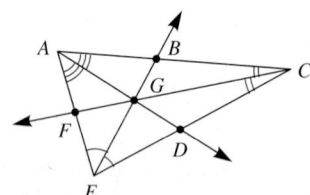

19. A student wants to know if you can bisect a given angle drawn on a large sheet of paper using only an unmarked ruler. How do you respond?

20. Gail is asked to draw a triangle and to construct its incircle. She finds the point O where two angle bisectors intersect and point D where the angle bisector $\overrightarrow{BO}$ intersects the opposite side and draws the circle with center O and radius OD. The teacher marks the construction wrong. Gail wants to know why. How do you respond?

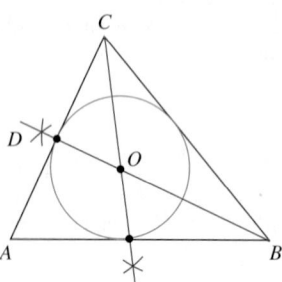

GeoGebra Activities

21. Use inductive reasoning to answer the following.
a. Draw all the altitudes of a triangle. Make conjectures about the lines containing the altitudes of each of the following types of triangles: acute, right, and obtuse.
b. Draw an angle and its angle bisector. Pick a point on the angle bisector and calculate the distance from the point to each side of the angle.
c. Move the point to different positions on the angle bisector. What do you notice about the distances?
22. Use GeoGebra Assessment Exercise 1 to inscribe a circle in a given triangle.

Review Problems

23. In the following figure, $\overrightarrow{AB} \parallel \overrightarrow{ED}$ and $\overline{BC} \cong \overline{CE}$. Explain why $DE = AB$.

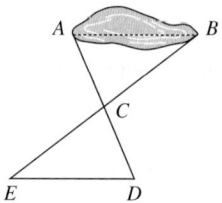

24. Draw $\triangle ABC$. Then construct $\triangle PQR$ congruent to $\triangle ABC$ using each of the following combinations.
a. Two sides of $\triangle ABC$ and an angle included between these sides
b. The three sides of $\triangle ABC$
c. Two angles and a side included between these angles
25. Given two right triangles, $\triangle ABC$ and $\triangle DEF$, with right angles at $\angle B$ and $\angle E$ if $\angle A$ and $\angle D$ are congruent and $\overline{AC}$ and $\overline{DF}$ are congruent, what can you conclude about the two triangles. Why?
26. Find the value of x.

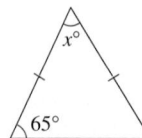

12-4 Similar Triangles and Other Similar Figures

12-4 Objectives

The student will be able to understand and explain

- Similar figures.
- Theorems for determining similarity for triangles.
- Properties of proportion for similar triangles.
- Midsegments of triangles and quadrilaterals.
- Indirect measurements using similar triangles.

Activity Manual

Use *Pattern Block Similarity* to introduce the concept of similarity.

Activity Manual

Use *Similar Triangles* to develop the concept of similar triangles.

When a germ is examined under a microscope or when a slide is projected on a screen, the shapes in each case usually remain the same, but the sizes are altered. Informally, such figures are similar. **Similar figures** have the same shape but not necessarily the same size. It seems that in any enlargement or reduction of polygons the resulting figure is similar to the original; that is, the corresponding angle measures remain the same and the corresponding sides are proportional. In general, we have the following definitions of similar triangles and similar polygons.

Definition of Similar Triangles

$\triangle ABC$ is similar to $\triangle DEF$, written $\triangle ABC \sim \triangle DEF$, if, and only if, the corresponding interior angles are congruent and the lengths of the corresponding sides are proportional; that is, $\angle A \cong \angle D$, $\angle B \cong \angle E$, $\angle C \cong \angle F$, and $\dfrac{AB}{DE} = \dfrac{AC}{DF} = \dfrac{BC}{EF}$. The common ratio of lengths is the **scale factor**.

Definition of Similar Polygons

Two polygons with the same number of vertices are similar if there is a one-to-one correspondence between the vertices of one and the vertices of the other such that the corresponding interior angles are congruent and the corresponding sides are proportional.

In similarity as with congruence of triangles, we do not need all the conditions in the definition to conclude that the triangles are similar. In fact, the following conditions suffice to conclude that the triangles are similar: SSS, SAS, and AA. We state these conditions in the following theorems, which could be proved in more advanced geometry texts.

Theorem 12-12: Side, Side, Side (SSS) Similarity

If the lengths of corresponding sides of two triangles are proportional, then the triangles are similar.

Theorem 12-13: Side, Angle, Side (SAS) Similarity

If in two triangles two sides of one triangle are proportional to their corresponding sides in the other triangle and the included angles are congruent, then the triangles are similar.

Theorem 12-14: Angle, Angle (AA) Similarity

If two angles of one triangle are congruent, respectively, to two angles of a second triangle, then the triangles are similar.

We refer to these theorems as SSS similarity, SAS similarity, and AA similarity. Conditions like SSSS or AAAA are not valid for quadrilaterals (Why?). See the student page shown on page 736 for an example.

School Book Page — Similar Figures

7-4 Similar Figures

✓ Check Skills You'll Need

1. **Vocabulary Review** How can you tell whether a relationship is *proportional*?

2. Does the table show a proportional relationship? Explain.

x	y
4	16
6	24
8	32

GO for Help
Lesson 3-3

© CONTENT STANDARD
8.G.4

What You'll Learn

To identify similar figures and to use proportions to find missing measurements in similar figures

🔊 **New Vocabulary** similar figures, similar polygons

Why Learn This?

Sometimes you want an image to be larger or smaller than the original.

Similar figures have the same shape but not necessarily the same size. The ratios of the lengths of corresponding sides in similar figures are proportional.

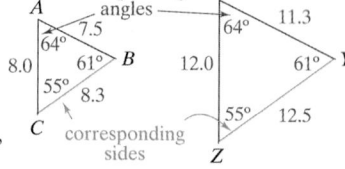

The symbol ~ means "is similar to."

If two polygons are **similar polygons,** then corresponding angles are congruent and the lengths of corresponding sides are in proportion. Recall that in a proportion, the *cross products* are equal. In the diagram above, $\triangle ABC \sim \triangle XYZ$.

EXAMPLE Identifying Similar Polygons

① Is rectangle *LMNO* similar to rectangle *HIJK*? Explain.

$\angle L \cong \angle H \quad \angle M \cong \angle I \quad \angle N \cong \angle J \quad \angle O \cong \angle K$

$\dfrac{MN}{IJ} \stackrel{?}{=} \dfrac{LM}{HI}$ ← Write a proportion.

$\dfrac{4}{3} \stackrel{?}{=} \dfrac{10}{8}$ ← Substitute.

$4 \cdot 8 \stackrel{?}{=} 3 \cdot 10$ ← Write the cross products.

$32 \neq 30$ ← Simplify.

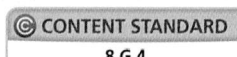

The corresponding angles are congruent, but the corresponding sides are not in proportion. So the rectangles are *not* similar.

✓ Quick Check

1. Rectangle *EFGH* has side lengths of 18 and 27. Rectangle *LMNO* has side lengths of 36 and 54. Are the rectangles similar? Explain.

In what follows, we give examples in which the similarity conditions are used.

Example 11

Given the pairs of similar triangles in Figure 52, find a one-to-one correspondence among the vertices of the triangles such that the corresponding angles are congruent. Then write the proportions for the corresponding sides that follow from the definition.

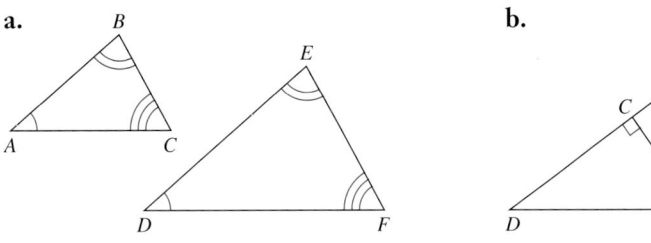

Figure 52

Solution

a. $\triangle ABC \sim \triangle DEF$

$$\frac{AB}{DE} = \frac{BC}{EF} = \frac{AC}{DF}$$

b. $\triangle ABD \sim \triangle ECD$

$$\frac{AB}{EC} = \frac{BD}{CD} = \frac{AD}{ED}$$

Example 12

For each part of Figure 53, find a pair of similar triangles.

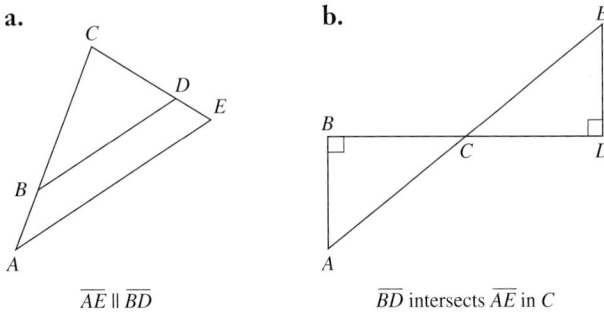

$\overline{AE} \parallel \overline{BD}$ $\overline{BD}$ intersects $\overline{AE}$ in C

Figure 53

Solution

a. Because $\overline{AE} \parallel \overline{BD}$, congruent corresponding angles are formed by a transversal cutting the parallel segments. Thus, $\angle CBD \cong \angle CAE$ and $\angle CDB \cong \angle CEA$. Thus, $\triangle CBD \sim \triangle CAE$ by AA similarity.

b. $\angle B \cong \angle D$ because both are right angles. Also, $\angle ACB \cong \angle ECD$ because they are vertical angles. Thus, $\triangle ACB \sim \triangle ECD$ by AA similarity.

▶ NOW TRY THIS 9

NTT 9: Answers can be found in Answers at the back of the book.

Are all right triangles in which the hypotenuse is twice as long as one of the legs similar? Explain your answer.

Example 13

a. In Figure 54 show that $\triangle ABC \sim \triangle EDC$ and then solve for x.

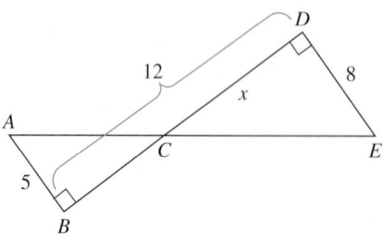

Figure 54

b. Explain whether the triangles in Figure 55 are necessarily similar.

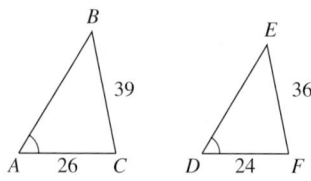

Figure 55

Solution

a. $\triangle ABC \sim \triangle EDC$ by AA similarity because $\angle B$ and $\angle D$ are right angles and $\angle ACB \cong \angle ECD$ are vertical angles.

$$\frac{AB}{ED} = \frac{AC}{EC} = \frac{BC}{DC}$$

Now, $AB = 5, ED = 8, CD = x,$ and $BC = 12 - x$. Thus,

$$\frac{5}{8} = \frac{12 - x}{x}$$

$$5x = 8(12 - x)$$

$$5x = 96 - 8x$$

$$13x = 96$$

$$x = \frac{96}{13}.$$

b. No, the triangles are not similar. The congruent angles are not included between the proportional sides.

Properties of Proportion

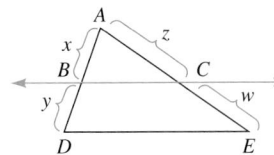

Figure 56

Similar triangles give rise to various properties that involve proportions. For example, in Figure 56 if $\overline{BC} \parallel \overline{DE}$, then $\dfrac{AB}{BD} = \dfrac{AC}{CE}$. This can be justified as follows: $\overline{BC} \parallel \overline{DE}$, so $\triangle ADE \sim \triangle ABC$ (Why?). Consequently, $\dfrac{AD}{AB} = \dfrac{AE}{AC}$, which may be written as follows.

$$\frac{x+y}{x} = \frac{z+w}{z}$$

$$\frac{x}{x} + \frac{y}{x} = \frac{z}{z} + \frac{w}{z}$$

$$1 + \frac{y}{x} = 1 + \frac{w}{z}$$

$$\frac{y}{x} = \frac{w}{z}$$

$$\frac{x}{y} = \frac{z}{w}$$

This result is summarized in the following theorem.

Activity Manual

Use *Side Splitter Theorem* to explore similar triangles and Theorem 12-15 using geometry drawing software.

Theorem 12-15
If a line parallel to one side of a triangle intersects the other sides, then it divides those sides into proportional segments.

Example 14

In Figure 57, given $\overline{DE} \parallel \overline{CB}$, find $\overline{AD}$.

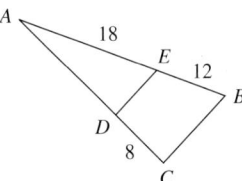

Figure 57

Solution   From Theorem 12-15, we have

$$\frac{AD}{8} = \frac{18}{12}$$

$$12AD = 8 \cdot 18$$

$$AD = \frac{144}{12} = 12.$$

The converse of Theorem 12-15 is also true; that is, if in Figure 56 we know that $\dfrac{AB}{BD} = \dfrac{AC}{CE}$, then we conclude that $\overline{BC} \parallel \overline{DE}$.

We can prove the converse using the SAS similarity condition. We reverse the steps in the proof of Theorem 12-15. From $\dfrac{x}{y} = \dfrac{z}{w}$ we get $\dfrac{x+y}{x} = \dfrac{z+w}{z}$ and hence $\dfrac{AD}{AB} = \dfrac{AE}{AC}$. Using this proportion and the fact that $\triangle ABC$ and $\triangle ADE$ share $\angle A$, we conclude by SAS similarity that $\triangle ABC \sim \triangle ADE$. Consequently, $\angle ABC \cong \angle ADE$, and therefore $\overline{BC} \parallel \overline{DE}$. We summarize this result in the following theorem.

Theorem 12-16

If a line divides two sides of a triangle into proportional segments, then the line is parallel to the third side.

Similarly, if lines parallel to $\overline{DE}$ intersect $\triangle ADE$, as shown in Figure 58, so that $a = b = c = d$, it can be shown that $e = f = g = h$. This result is stated in Theorem 12-17.

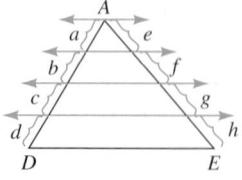

Figure 58

Theorem 12-17

If parallel lines cut off congruent segments on one transversal, then they cut off congruent segments on any transversal.

Theorem 12-17 can be used to divide a given segment into any number of congruent parts. For example, using only a compass and a straightedge, we can divide segment $\overline{AB}$ in Figure 59 into three congruent parts by making the construction resemble Figure 58.

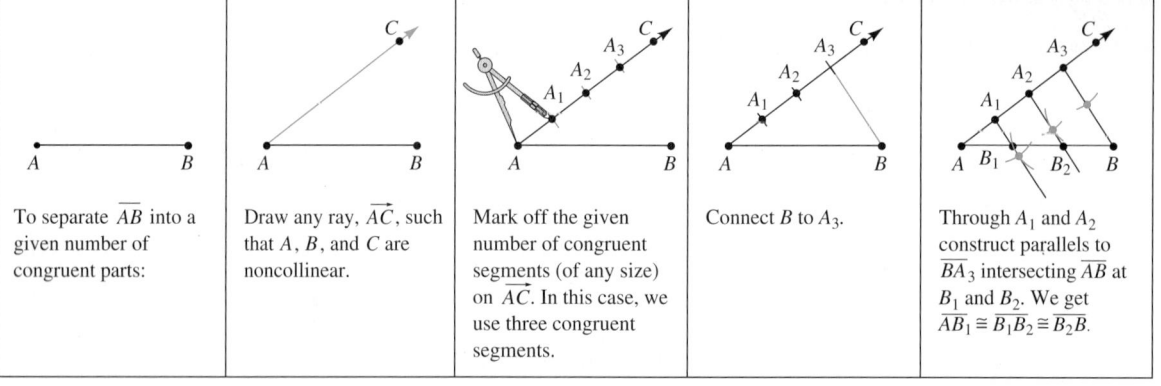

To separate $\overline{AB}$ into a given number of congruent parts:	Draw any ray, $\overrightarrow{AC}$, such that A, B, and C are noncollinear.	Mark off the given number of congruent segments (of any size) on $\overrightarrow{AC}$. In this case, we use three congruent segments.	Connect B to A_3.	Through A_1 and A_2 construct parallels to $\overline{BA_3}$ intersecting $\overline{AB}$ at B_1 and B_2. We get $\overline{AB_1} \cong \overline{B_1B_2} \cong \overline{B_2B}$.

Figure 59   Separating a segment into congruent parts

Note that in Figure 59 after connecting B with A_3 it is only necessary to construct $\overline{A_2B_2}$. We can then use a compass to mark off point B_1 such that $B_1B_2 = BB_2$, as in Figure 60.

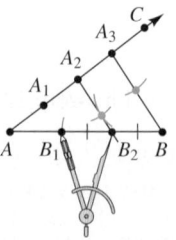

Figure 60

Midsegments of Triangles

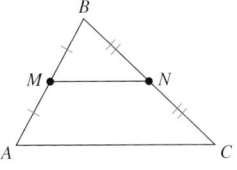

Figure 61

The segment connecting the midpoints of two sides of a triangle is a **midsegment**. In Figure 61, M and N are midpoints of $\overline{AB}$ and $\overline{BC}$, respectively, and $\overline{MN}$ is a midsegment. We have $\dfrac{BM}{AM} = \dfrac{BN}{CN} = 1$ and therefore by Theorem 12-16, $\overline{MN} \| \overline{AC}$. Consequently, by SAS similarity $\triangle MBN \sim \triangle ABC$.

Therefore,

$$\frac{MN}{AC} = \frac{MB}{AB} = \frac{MB}{2MB} = \frac{1}{2}.$$

Consequently, we have the following theorem.

> **Theorem 12-18:   The Midsegment Theorem**
>
> The midsegment joining the midpoints of two sides of a triangle is parallel to and is half as long as the third side.

The following theorem follows from Theorem 12-17.

> **Theorem 12-19**
>
> If a line bisects one side of a triangle and is parallel to a second side, then it bisects the third side, and therefore is a midsegment.

Example 15

In the quadrilateral $ABCD$ in Figure 62, M, N, P, and Q are the midpoints of the sides.

  a. What kind of quadrilateral is $MNPQ$?
  b. For what kind of quadrilateral $ABCD$ will $MNPQ$ be a rhombus?

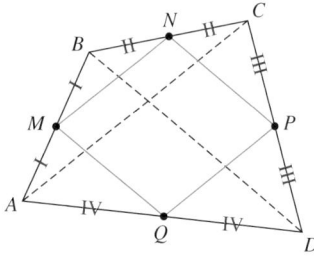

Figure 62

Solution

  a. $MNPQ$ appears to be a parallelogram. To prove this conjecture, observe that $\overline{NP}$ is a midsegment in $\triangle BCD$, and consequently $\overline{NP} \| \overline{BD}$ and $NP = \dfrac{1}{2}BD$. Similarly, in $\triangle ABD$, $\overline{MQ}$ is a midsegment, and therefore $\overline{MQ} \| \overline{BD}$. Consequently, $\overline{MQ} \| \overline{NP}$. In a similar way we could show that $\overline{MN} \| \overline{QP}$ (consider midsegments in $\triangle ABC$ and in $\triangle ADC$), and therefore by the definition of a parallelogram, $MNPQ$, is a parallelogram.

  b. Because $MQ = \dfrac{1}{2}BD$, $MN = \dfrac{1}{2}AC$, and $MNPQ$ is a parallelogram, $MNPQ$ will be a rhombus if, and only if, $MQ = MN$, or equivalently if, and only if, $BD = AC$. Thus, $MNPQ$ is a rhombus if, and only if, the diagonals of $ABCD$ are congruent.

A triangle has three medians. A **median** is a segment connecting a vertex to the midpoint of the opposite side. A careful drawing of the three medians shown in Figure 63 suggests that the three medians are concurrent, which they are. The point of intersection, G, is the **center of gravity**, or the **centroid**, of the triangle.

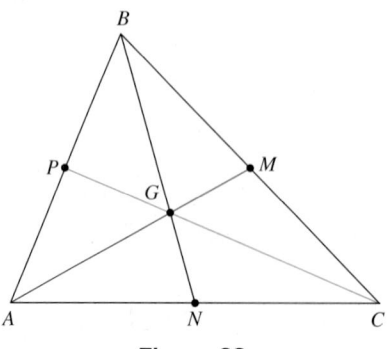

Figure 63

If a triangular piece of somewhat-thick, uniform material such as wood or metal is placed on an object such as a pencil tip at its centroid, it will balance. In the next example, we prove an interesting property of the centroid.

Example 16

Show that the centroid of a triangle divides each median into two segments with lengths in the ratio $1:2$.

Solution   In Figure 64, we have two medians of $\triangle ABC$ and their point of intersection G. We prove that $AG = 2MG$ and $BG = 2NG$. The fact that M and N are midpoints of two sides suggests constructing $\overline{MN}$, the midsegment. Theorem 12-18, the Midsegment Theorem tells us that $\overline{MN} \| \overline{AB}$ and $MN = \frac{1}{2}AB$. The fact that $\overline{MN} \| \overline{AB}$ implies that the comparably marked angles are congruent because they are alternate interior angles formed by a transversal of the parallel lines. Thus, $\triangle ABG \sim \triangle MNG$ by AA similarity. Using the fact that $AB = 2MN$ we have

$$\frac{BG}{NG} = \frac{AG}{MG} = \frac{AB}{MN} = 2.$$

Thus, $BG = 2NG$ and $AG = 2MG$.

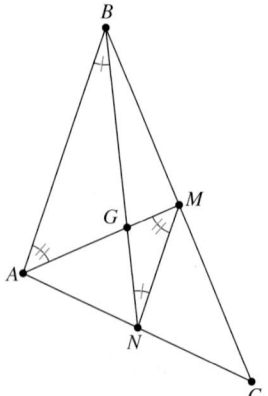

Figure 64

Indirect Measurements

Similar triangles have long been used to make indirect measurements. Thales of Miletus (ca. 600 BCE) is believed to have determined the height of the Great Pyramid of Egypt by using ratios involving shadows, similar to those pictured in Figure 65. The sun is so far away that it should make approximately congruent angles at B and B'. Because the angles at C and C' are right angles, $\triangle ABC \sim \triangle A'B'C'$. Hence,

$$\frac{AC}{A'C'} = \frac{BC}{B'C'}.$$

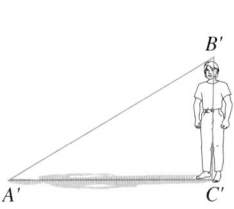
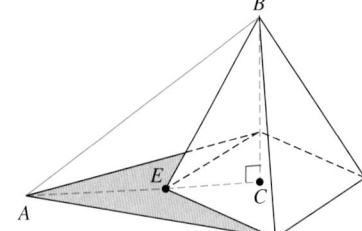

Figure 65

And because $AC = AE + EC$, the following proportion is obtained by substituting $AE + EC$ for AC in the previous proportion.

$$\frac{AE + EC}{A'C'} = \frac{BC}{B'C'}$$

The person's height and shadow can be measured. Also, the length AE of the shadow of the pyramid can be measured, and EC is half the length of the diagonal of the base. Each term of the proportion except the height of the pyramid is then known. Thus, the height BC of the pyramid can be found by solving the proportion.

Example 17

On a sunny day, a tall tree casts a 40-m shadow, as shown in Figure 66. At the same time, a meter-stick held vertically casts a 2.5-m shadow. How tall is the tree?

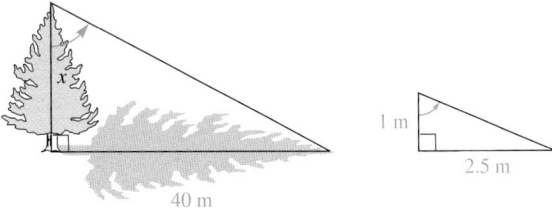

Figure 66

Solution   In Figure 66, the triangles are similar by AA similarity because the tree and the stick both meet the ground at right angles and the angles formed by the sun's rays are congruent because the shadows are measured at the same time. Let x be the height of the tree.

$$\frac{x}{40} = \frac{1}{2.5}$$

$$2.5x = 40$$

$$x = 16$$

The tree is 16 m tall.

Assessment 12-4A

1. If a shoelace represents the Nile river, and the scale is 1 cm : 110 km, what is the length of the Nile river if the shoelace is 61 cm long?   6710 km
2. The Washington Monument is 555 ft tall. If you were to draw the monument on paper with a scale 1 in.: 100 ft, how tall would the structure be in your drawing?   5.55 in.
3. Are the rectangles below similar? Tell why or why not.   *

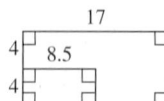

4. In rhombuses $ABCD$ and $A_1B_1C_1D_1$, $\angle BAD \cong \angle B_1A_1D_1$. Are the rhombuses similar? Why or why not?   *
5. Which of the following figures are always similar? Why?
   a. Any two equilateral triangles   Yes, AAA similarity.
   b. Any two squares   *
   c. Any two rectangles   *
   d. Any two rectangles in which one side is twice as long as the other.   *
6. Use grid paper to draw figures that have sides three times as large as the ones in the following figure and that are colored similarly.   *

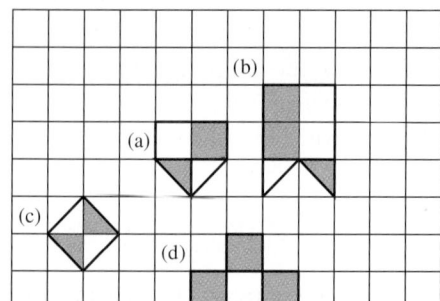

7. a. Which of the following pairs of triangles are similar? If the triangles are similar, explain why and state the correspondence.

   i.
   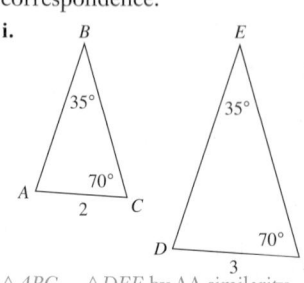
   $\triangle ABC \sim \triangle DEF$ by AA similarity

   ii.
   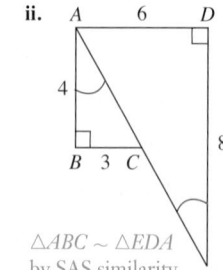
   $\triangle ABC \sim \triangle EDA$ by SAS similarity or AA similarity

   iii.
   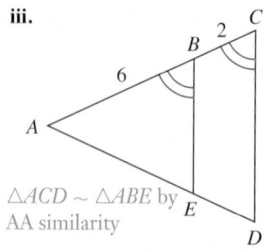
   $\triangle ACD \sim \triangle ABE$ by AA similarity

   iv.
   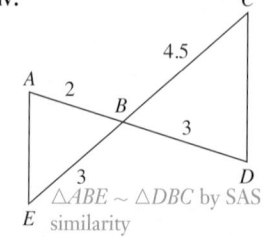
   $\triangle ABE \sim \triangle DBC$ by SAS similarity

b. For each pair of similar triangles in part (a), find the scale factor of the sides of the triangles.   *
8. In the following figures, find the measure of the sides marked x.
   a.
   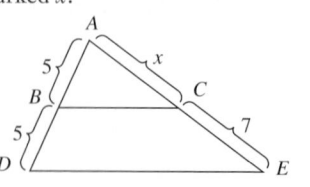
   $\triangle ABC \sim \triangle ADE$

   b.
   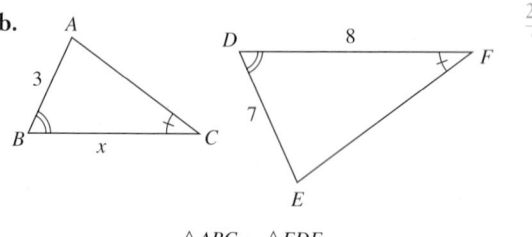
   $\triangle ABC \sim \triangle EDF$

9. Find the value of x and y. $x = 14, y = 18$
   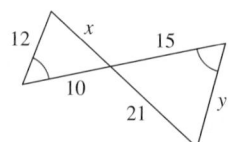

10. In the figure $\overline{AB} \parallel \overline{CD}$. Complete each proportion.
    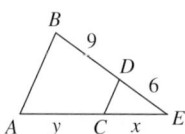

    a. $\dfrac{y}{x} = \dfrac{\frac{9}{6} = \frac{3}{2}}{}$

    b. $\dfrac{x}{x + y} = \dfrac{\frac{6}{15} = \frac{2}{5}}{}$

    c. $\dfrac{6}{x} = \dfrac{\frac{9}{y}}{}$

11. Draw a segment $\overline{AB}$ and then use a compass and a straightedge to separate $\overline{AB}$ into five congruent pieces.   Construction
12. Given segments of length a, b, and c as shown, construct a segment of length x so that $\dfrac{a}{b} = \dfrac{c}{x}$.   *

    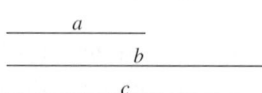

13. A photocopy of a polygon was reduced by 80% and then the copy was again reduced by 80%.
    a. Is the second photocopy similar to the original? Explain.   *
    b. What is the ratio of the corresponding sides of the second photocopy to the original?   0.64:1
14. Sketch two hexagons with corresponding sides proportional, but so that they are not similar. (Consider a regular hexagon and a hexagon with all sides congruent but not all angles congruent.)   Answers vary.

---

* Answers can be found in the Answers section at the back of the book.

15. If you copy a page on a machine at 75%, you should get a similar copy of the page. What is the corresponding setting to obtain the original from the copy?   *

16. Samantha wants to know how far above the ground the top of a leaning flagpole is. At high noon, when the sun is almost directly overhead, the shadow cast by the pole is 7 ft long. Samantha holds a plumb bob with a string 3 ft long up to the flagpole and determines that the point of the plumb bob touches the ground 13 in. from the base of the flagpole. How far above the ground is the top of the pole?   About 19 ft 5 in. or 233 in.

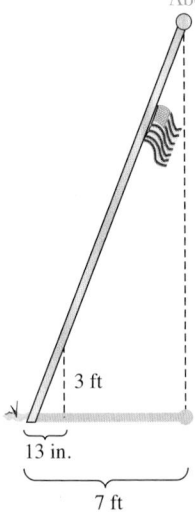

3 ft

13 in.

7 ft

17. In the following figure, find the distance *AB* across the pond using the similar triangles shown.   15 m

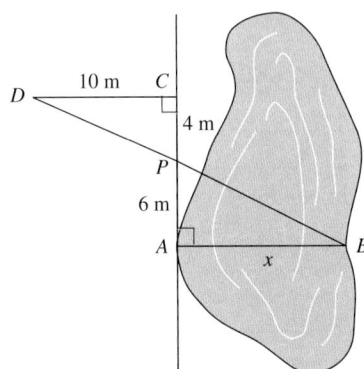

10 m   *C*

D

4 m

P

6 m

A

x   *B*

18. In the diagram below, $\overline{AB} \parallel \overline{DE} \parallel \overline{FG}$. *F* is one fourth the distance from *C* to *A*, and *G* is one fourth the distance from *C* to *B*. *AB* = 3, *AC* = 4, and *BC* = 4.5. Find the following.
   a. *CF*   1   b. *CG*   1.125   c. *FG*   0.75

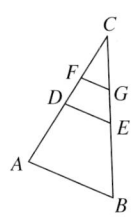

19. Given $\overline{BC} \parallel \overline{ED}$ and $\overline{AB} \parallel \overline{DC}$, prove △*ABC* ~ △*CDE*.   *

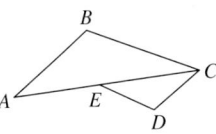

20. a. Examine several examples of similar polygons and make a conjecture concerning the ratio of their perimeters.   *
   b. Prove your conjecture in part (a).   *

21. The midpoints of the sides of a scalene triangle have been connected as shown.

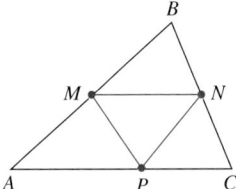

   a. Prove that the four smaller triangles are congruent.   *
   b. Is each of the smaller triangles similar to the original triangle? Why or why not?   *

22. The midpoints *M*, *N*, *P*, *Q* of the sides of a quadrilateral *ABCD* have been connected and an interior quadrilateral is obtained. We have shown that *MNPQ* is a parallelogram. What is the most you can say about the kind of parallelogram *MNPQ* is if *ABCD* is
   a. a rhombus?   Rectangle
   b. a kite?   Rectangle
   c. an isosceles trapezoid?   Rhombus
   d. a quadrilateral that is neither a rhombus nor a kite but whose diagonals are perpendicular to each other?   Rectangle

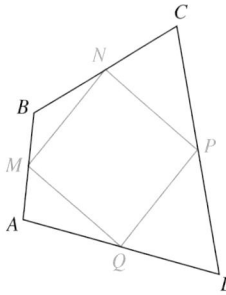

23. If you took cross sections of a typical ice cream cone parallel to the circular opening where the ice cream is usually placed, explain whether the cross sections would be similar.   *

24. Segments are drawn on a map connecting three newly planned cities, *A*, *B*, and *C*. On the map, *AB* = 4.2 cm, *BC* = 10.1 cm, *AC* = 12.2 cm. If in reality the straight-line distance from *A* to *B* is 512 mi, how far is it from *B* to *C* and from *A* to *C*?   *BC* ≈ 1231 mi, *AC* ≈ 1487 mi

Assessment 12-4B

1. School pictures come in 8 in. by 10 in., 5 in., by 7 in., and wallet size $2\frac{1}{4}$ in. by $3\frac{1}{4}$ in. Are any of these sizes similar to each other? Why?   *

2. When completed, the Crazy Horse Monument in South Dakota will be 563 ft high. The monument is based on a 16-foot-tall scale model of the structure. What is the scale used in the construction?   *

3. Are the quadrilaterals below similar? Tell why or why not.

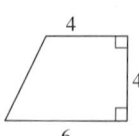 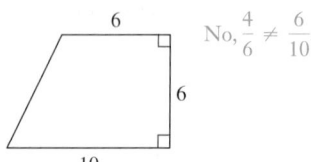   No, $\frac{4}{6} \neq \frac{6}{10}$.

4. Consider parallelograms $ABCD$ and $A_1B_1C_1D_1$ in which $\angle BAD \cong \angle B_1A_1D_1$. Explain whether or not the parallelograms are similar.   *

5. Which of the following figures are always similar?
   a. Any two rectangles in which the diagonal in one is twice as long as in the other.   No
   b. Any two rhombuses   No
   c. Any two circles   Yes
   d. Any two regular polygons   No
   e. Any two regular polygons with the same number of sides   Yes

6. On a piece of grid paper, draw similar but not congruent isosceles triangles.   *

7. Which of the following pairs of triangles are similar? If they are similar, explain why. Find the scale factor that is less than 1 and state the correspondence.

   a. 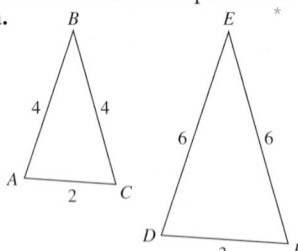   b.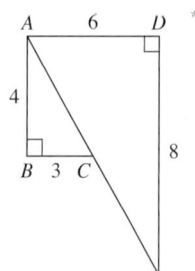

   c. 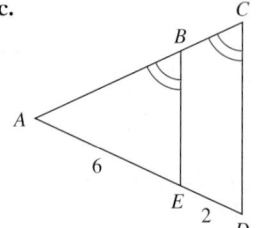   d.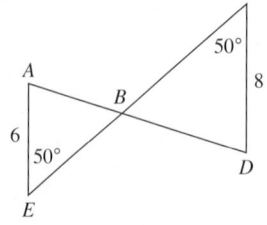

8. In the following figures, prove that the triangles in each part are similar and find the measure of the sides marked with x or y.   *

   a.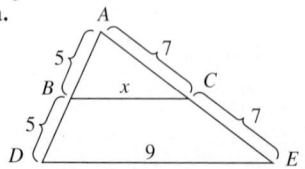

9. Find the value of x and y. $x = 4.5, y = 10$

   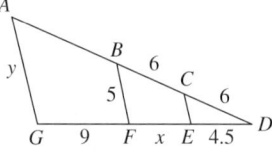

   $\overline{AG} \parallel \overline{BF} \parallel \overline{CE}$

10. a. Show that $\triangle ABC \sim \triangle DBE$.
    b. Find CE.   *

    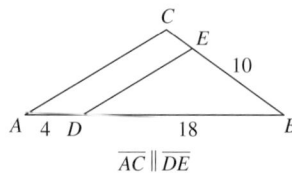

    $\overline{AC} \parallel \overline{DE}$

11. Draw a segment $\overline{AB}$ and then use a compass and a straightedge to separate $\overline{AB}$ into three congruent pieces.   Construction

12. Given segments of length a, b, and c as shown, construct a segment of length x so that $\dfrac{a}{b} = \dfrac{x}{c}$.   *

    a
    b
    c

13. Triangle ABC is similar to triangle DEF with a side of triangle ABC that is 75% of its corresponding side in triangle DEF. Also, triangle GHI is similar to triangle DEF with a side of triangle GHI that is 32% of its corresponding side in triangle DEF.
    a. Are triangles ABC and GHI similar to each other? Why or why not?   Yes, AA similarity or SAS similarity
    b. What is the ratio of corresponding sides of triangles ABC and GHI?   *

14. Sketch two pentagons with corresponding sides proportional but so that they are not similar.   *

15. If you copy a document on a machine, you should get a similar copy. Suppose you want to reduce a document to $\dfrac{1}{6}$ of its original size, and you first reduce it by 25%. By what percent do you need to reduce the copy to obtain the desirable size?   Approximately 77.8%

b.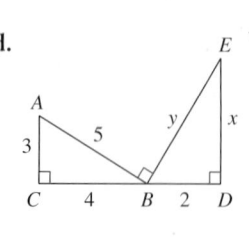

c.   d. (figures c and d)

16. To find the height of a tree, a group of Girl Scouts devised the following method. A girl walks toward the tree along its shadow until the shadow of the top of her head coincides with the shadow of the top of the tree. If the girl is 150 cm tall, her distance to the foot of the tree is 15 m, and the length of her shadow is 3 m, how tall is the tree?   9 m

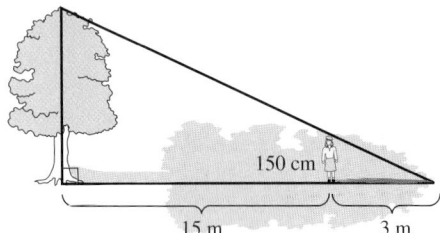

17. To find the height of a pole, Elka lays a mirror on the level ground 20 ft from the base of the pole. She moves back away from the mirror until she can exactly see the top of the pole. If she backed away 5.5 ft and her eyes are 5 ft above the ground, how tall is the flag pole?   About 18 ft

18. In the diagram below, $\overline{AB} \parallel \overline{DE} \parallel \overline{FG}$. D is the midpoint of $\overline{AC}$ and E is the midpoint of $\overline{CB}$. $AB = 3, AC = 4$, and $BC = 4.5$. Find the following.
  a. CD 2   **b.** CE 2.25   **c.** DE 1.5

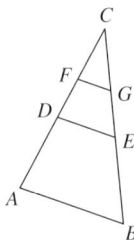

19. In the following figure, identify similar triangles and find DE and EA. $\triangle ABC \sim \triangle ADE, DE = \frac{12}{5}, EA = \frac{16}{5}$

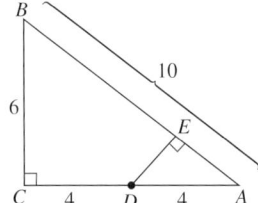

20. a. Examine several similar triangles and write a conjecture concerning the ratio of their corresponding heights.   *
  b. Prove your conjecture in part (a).   *

21. a. In the figure, $ABCD$ is a trapezoid. M is the midpoint of $\overline{AB}$. Through M, a line parallel to the bases has been drawn, intersecting $\overline{CD}$ at N. (i) Explain why N must be the midpoint of $\overline{CD}$, and (ii) express MN in terms of a and b, the lengths of the parallel sides of the trapezoid.   *

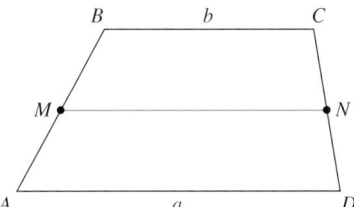

b. Denote MN by c. Use your answer to part (a) to show that b, c, and a form an arithmetic sequence.   *
c. In the trapezoid $ABCD$, the lengths of the bases are a and b as shown. Side $\overline{AB}$ has been divided into 9 congruent segments. Through the endpoints of the segments, lines parallel to $\overline{AD}$ have been drawn. In this way, 8 new segments connecting the sides $\overline{AB}$ and $\overline{CD}$ have been created. Show that the sequence of 10 terms, starting with b, proceeding with the lengths of the parallel segments, and ending with a, is an arithmetic sequence and find the sum of the sequence in terms of a and b.   *

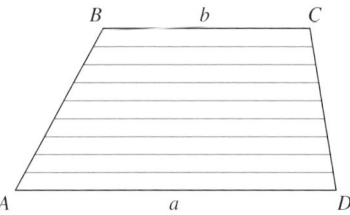

22. $ABCD$ is a convex quadrilateral and M, N, P, Q are the midpoints of its sides as shown. The diagonals $\overline{BD}$ and $\overline{AC}$ intersect at T, $\overline{NP}$ intersects $\overline{AC}$ at S, and $\overline{BD}$ intersects $\overline{MN}$ at V.
  a. Prove that $NSTV$ is a parallelogram.   *
  b. Complete the following statements and prove them.   *
    i. $MNPQ$ is a rectangle if, and only if, $\overline{AC}$ and $\overline{BD}$ are _____.
    ii. $MNPQ$ is a square if, and only if, $\overline{AC}$ and $\overline{BD}$ are _____.

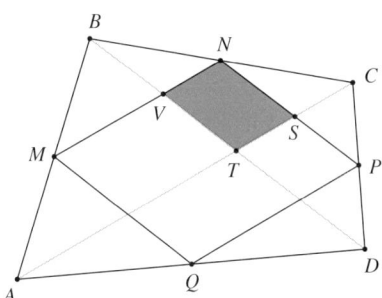

23. Are all semicircles (diameters not included) similar to each other?   Yes, all semicircles have the same shape.
24. Below is a partial map of New York City. All shown numbered streets are parallel. On Fifth Ave the distance between E 24th and E 33rd is about 2600 ft, whereas the distance between these two streets on Broadway is about 2800 ft. If the distance between E 30th and E 33rd is about 1120 ft on Broadway, what is the distance between these two streets on Fifth Ave?   1040 ft

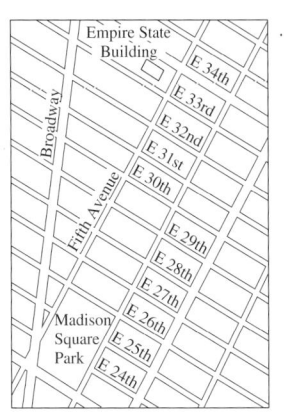

Mathematical Connections 12-4

Answers to Mathematical Connections can be found in the Answers section at the back of the book.

Reasoning

1. Do you think any two cubes are similar? Why or why not?
2. Write a description of what it takes for two prisms to be similar.
3. If two isosceles triangles have non-base angles of 40°, are they similar? Justify your answer.
4. If two right triangles have hypotenuses that are the same length, are the two triangles similar? Explain.
5. Suppose $\triangle TRI \sim \triangle RIT$, what do you know about $\triangle TRI$?
6. Assuming the lines on an ordinary piece of notebook paper are parallel and equidistant, describe a method for using the paper to divide a piece of licorice evenly among 2, 3, 4, or 5 children. Explain why it works.
7. In the following right triangle $ABC, \overline{CD} \perp \overline{AB}$:

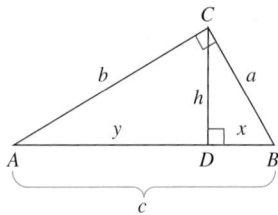

   a. Find three pairs of similar triangles. Justify your answers.
   b. Write the corresponding proportions for each set of similar triangles.
   c. Use part (b) and the figure to show that $a^2 = xc$. Also argue that $b^2 = yc$.
   d. Use part (c) to show that $a^2 + b^2 = c^2$. State this result in words using the legs and hypotenuse of a right triangle.
   e. Use part (b) to show that $h^2 = xy$.
   f. Show that x, h, and y form a geometric sequence.

8. A **golden triangle** is an isosceles triangle in which the apex angle measures 36°. If a circular arc centered at B and passing through C is drawn as shown below, prove that $\triangle BCD$ is also a golden triangle.

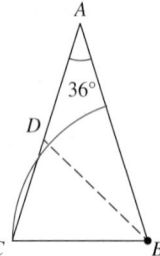

9. A **golden rectangle** is a rectangle in which the ratio of its length to its width is the golden ratio $\dfrac{1 + \sqrt{5}}{2}$. If you cut a square away from the golden rectangle as shown below, you obtain a square and a rectangle.

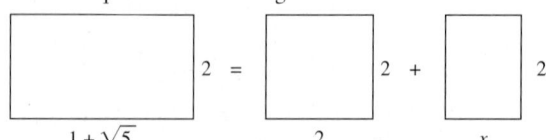

   a. Solve for x.
   b. Show that the smaller rectangle is also a golden rectangle, and that it is similar to the original rectangle.

Open-Ended

10. If two figures are similar but not congruent, how are they alike, and how are they different?
11. How are the SSS and SAS similarity theorems like SSS and SAS theorems for congruent triangles? How are they different?
12. Build two similar towers out of blocks.
    a. What is the ratio of the heights of the towers?
    b. What is the ratio of the perimeters of the bases of the towers?
13. On a sunny day, go outside and measure the heights of objects and their accompanying shadows. Use the data gathered by an entire class and plot graphs. Plot all data points on the same graph, with shadow lengths on the vertical axis and object heights on the horizontal axis. What do you observe? Why?

Cooperative Learning

14. Work with your group and choose one of the methods discussed in this section to estimate the height or distance of an object in the vicinity of the school. Tell which method you chose, and explain how you arrived at your estimate. Try another technique and compare your estimates.
15. A building was to be built on a triangular piece of property. The architect was given the approximate measurements of the angles of the triangular lot as 54°, 39°, and 87° and the lengths of two of the sides as 100 m and 80 m. When the architect began the design on drafting paper, she drew a triangle to scale with the corresponding measures and found that the lot was considerably smaller than she had been led to believe. It appeared that the proposed building would not fit. The surveyor was called. He confirmed each of the measurements and could not see a problem with the size. Neither the architect nor surveyor could understand the reason for the other's opinion.
    a. Have one person in your group play the part of the architect and explain why she felt she was correct.
    b. Have one person in the group explain the reason for the miscommunication.
    c. Have the group suggest a way to provide an accurate description of the lot.

Connecting Mathematics to the Classroom

16. Al writes that $\triangle ABC \sim \triangle TRI$. Betty writes that $\triangle ABC \sim \triangle RIT$. Who is correct and why?

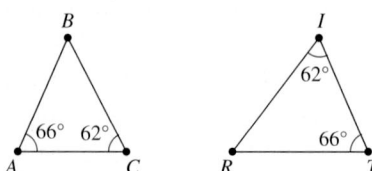

17. Bob says that if each right triangle has an acute angle with the same measure, the triangles are similar. How do you respond?

18. A student claims that if one angle in an isosceles triangle is congruent to an angle in another isosceles triangle, then the triangles are similar. How do you respond?

19. A student asks if, for the same n, all convex n-gons with all angles congruent are similar. How do you respond?

20. A student argues that in the following figure triangles ABC and DBE are similar because $\overline{DE}$ divides the sides proportionally. One side is divided in the ratio $\frac{2}{4}$, while the other is divided in the ratio $\frac{3}{6}$. How do you respond?

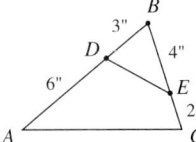

21. A student asks whether there is an ASA similarity condition for triangles. How do you respond?

GeoGebra Activities

22. Use GeoGebra Lab 7 activities 1–6 to:
    a. show that a line parallel to one side of a triangle and intersecting the other sides divides those sides into proportional segments.
    b. investigate properties of a midsegment of a triangle.

23. Use GeoGebra Lab 8 activities 1–9 to investigate properties of a midpoint quadrilateral.

24. Use GeoGebra Assessment A-IV exercise 12 to construct the indicated figure.

Review Problems

25. Given the following base of an isosceles triangle and the altitude to that base, construct the triangle:

    _____
                Base

    _____
                Altitude

26. Given the following length of a side of an equilateral triangle, construct an altitude of the equilateral triangle.

    _____

27. Describe how to construct an isosceles 45°-45°-90° triangle when given the length of the hypotenuse.

28. Use a compass and a straightedge to draw a pair of obtuse vertical angles and the angle bisector of one of these angles. Extend the angle bisector. Does the extended angle bisector bisect the other vertical angle? Justify your answer.

29. Describe a minimal set of conditions that can be used to argue that two quadrilaterals are congruent.

National Assessments

National Assessment of Educational Progress (NAEP) Questions

The figure below shows two right angles. The length of AE is x and the length of DE is 40.

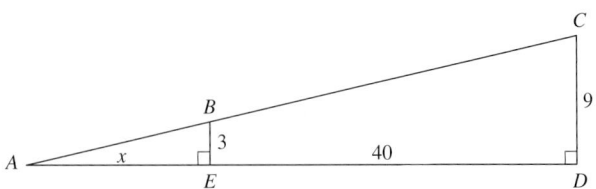

Show all of the steps that lead to finding the value of x. Your last step should give the value of x.

NAEP, Grade 8, 2007

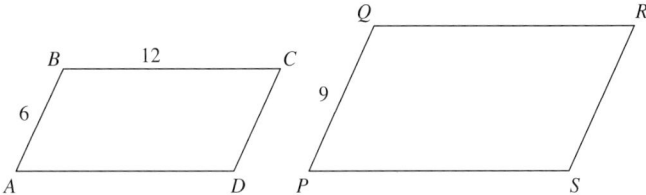

Parallelograms $ABCD$ and $PQRS$ above are similar. What is the length of side QR?
A. 4.5
B. 9
C. 12
D. 15
E. 18

NAEP, Grade 8, 2011

Hint for the Solution to the Preliminary Problem

Use Theorem 12-15 to help solve this problem.

Chapter 12 Summary

KEY CONCEPTS	DEFINITIONS, DESCRIPTIONS, AND THEOREMS
Section 12-1	
Similar figures (p. 691)	Objects that have the same shape but not necessarily the same size; the symbol ~ denotes *is similar to*.
Congruent figures (p. 692)	Objects that have the same shape and size; the symbol ≅ denotes *is congruent to*. *Congruent line segments*—line segments that have the same length. $\overline{AB} \cong \overline{CD}$ if, and only if, $AB = CD$. *Congruent angles*—angles that have the same measure. $\qquad \angle ABC \cong \angle DEF$ if, and only if, $m(\angle ABC) = m(\angle DEF)$. *Congruent triangles*—triangles that have corresponding congruent parts. $\qquad \triangle ABC \cong \triangle DEF$ if, and only if, $\angle A \cong \angle D, \angle B \cong \angle E, \angle C \cong \angle F,$ $\qquad \overline{AB} \cong \overline{DE}, \overline{BC} \cong \overline{EF},$ and $\overline{AC} \cong \overline{DF}.$
Triangle congruence theorems (p. 695)	*Theorem:* Side, Side, Side (SSS) Congruence $\qquad$ If the three sides of one triangle are congruent, respectively, to the three sides of a second triangle, then the triangles are congruent. *Theorem:* Side, Angle, Side (SAS) Congruence $\qquad$ If two sides and the included angle of one triangle are congruent, respectively, to two sides and the included angle of another triangle, then the two triangles are congruent. *Theorem:* Hypotenuse-Leg (HL) Congruence $\qquad$ If the hypotenuse and a leg of one right triangle are congruent, respectively, to the hypotenuse and a leg of another right triangle, then the triangles are congruent.
Perpendicular bisector (p. 700)	*Perpendicular bisector*—a line that is perpendicular to a segment and bisects it. *Theorem:* (a) Any point equidistant from the endpoints of a segment is on the perpendicular bisector of the segment. (b) Any point on the perpendicular bisector of a segment is equidistant from the endpoints of the segment.
Angle bisector (p. 700)	A ray that separates an angle into two congruent angles.
Isosceles triangle theorem (p. 700)	*Theorem:* (a) The angles opposite the congruent sides are congruent. (Base angles of an isosceles triangle are congruent.) (b) The angle bisector of an angle formed by two congruent sides in an isosceles triangle is the perpendicular bisector of the third side of the triangle.
Altitude of a triangle (p. 701)	The perpendicular segment from a vertex of the triangle to the line containing the opposite side of the triangle.

Section 12-1

Circumscribed figures (p. 702)

A circle is *circumscribed* about a given triangle if every vertex of the triangle is on the circle.

> The *circumcenter* (where the perpendicular bisectors of the sides of the triangle meet) is the center of the circumscribing circle.

A circle is *circumscribed* about a given quadrilateral if its center is equidistant from every vertex of the quadrilateral. It is not possible to construct a circumscribed circle about every quadrilateral because the perpendicular bisectors of the sides of an arbitrary quadrilateral do not always meet at a single point.

Theorem:
(a) If a circle can be circumscribed about a convex quadrilateral, then the sum of the measures of a pair of opposite angle of the quadrilateral is 180°; that is, the angles are supplementary.
(b) If the sum of the measures of a pair of opposite angles of a convex quadrilateral is 180°, then a circle can be circumscribed about the quadrilateral.

Geometric constructions (p. 692)

• Construct a line segment congruent to a given line segment.
• Construct a triangle congruent to a given triangle.
• Construct an angle congruent to a given angle.
• Construct a perpendicular bisector of a given segment.
• Construct a circle circumscribed about a triangle.

Section 12-2

Additional congruence theorems (p. 711)

Theorem: Angle, Side, Angle (ASA) Congruence
If two angles and the included side of one triangle are congruent, respectively, to two angles and the included side of another triangle, then the triangles are congruent.

Theorem: Angle, Angle, Side (AAS) Congruence
If two angles and a side opposite one of these two angles of a triangle are congruent to two corresponding angles and the corresponding side of another triangle, then the two triangles are congruent.

Theorem: The opposite sides and the opposite angles of a parallelogram are congruent.

Quadrilateral theorems (p. 714)

Trapezoid
Consecutive angles between parallel sides are supplementary.

Isosceles trapezoid
Each pair of base angles are congruent.
A pair of opposite sides are congruent.
If a trapezoid has congruent diagonals, it is isosceles.

Parallelogram
A parallelogram is a trapezoid in which each pair of opposite sides are parallel.
Opposite sides are congruent.
Opposite angles are congruent.
Diagonals bisect each other.
A quadrilateral in which the diagonals bisect each other is a parallelogram.

Rectangle
A rectangle has all the properties of a parallelogram.
All the angles of a rectangle are right angles.
A quadrilateral in which all the angles are right angles is a rectangle.
The diagonals of a rectangle are congruent and bisect each other.
A quadrilateral in which the diagonals are congruent and bisect each other is a rectangle.

Section 12-2

	Kite
	Lines containing the diagonals are perpendicular to each other.
	A line containing one diagonal is a bisector of the other diagonal.
	One diagonal bisects nonconsecutive angles.
	A quadrilateral in which the line containing one diagonal is the perpendicular bisector of the other diagonal is a kite.

Rhombus

A rhombus has all the properties of a parallelogram and a kite.

A quadrilateral in which all the sides are congruent is a rhombus.

The diagonals of a rhombus are perpendicular to and bisect each other. Each diagonal bisects opposite angles.

A quadrilateral in which the diagonals are perpendicular to and bisect each other is a rhombus.

Square

A square has all the properties of a parallelogram, a rectangle, and a rhombus.

A rhombus with a right angle is a square.

Quadrilateral congruence (p. 716) — SASAS is one congruence condition for quadrilaterals.

Section 12-3

Additional geometric constructions (p. 723)

- Construct a line parallel to a given line.
- Construct an angle bisector.
- Construct a line perpendicular to a given line from a point not on the line.
- Construct the perpendicular bisector of a line segment.
- Construct a line perpendicular to a given line from a point on the line.

Angle bisector theorems (p. 728)

Theorem:
(a) Any point on an angle bisector is equidistant from the sides of the angle.
(b) Any point in the interior of an angle that is equidistant from the sides of the angle is on the angle bisector of the angle.

Theorem: The angle bisectors of a triangle are concurrent, and the three distances from the point of intersection to the sides are equal.

Incircle of a triangle (p. 728)

A circle that is inscribed in a triangle. The sides of the triangle are *tangent* to the incircle.

Incenter—the intersection of any two angle bisectors of a triangle; the center of the inscribed circle of the triangle.

Section 12-4

Similar triangles (p. 735)

$\triangle ABC$ is similar to $\triangle DEF$, written $\triangle ABC \sim \triangle DEF$, if, and only if, the corresponding interior angles are congruent and the lengths of the corresponding sides are proportional; that is, $\angle A \cong \angle D$, $\angle B \cong \angle E$, $\angle C \cong \angle F$, and $\frac{AB}{DE} = \frac{AC}{DF} = \frac{BC}{EF}$.

Similar polygons (p. 735)

Two polygons with the same number of vertices are similar if there is a one-to-one correspondence between the vertices of one and the vertices of the other such that the corresponding interior angles are congruent and corresponding sides are proportional.

Section 12-4

Triangle similarity theorems (p. 735)	*Theorem:* Side, Side, Side (SSS) Similarity If the lengths of corresponding sides of two triangles are proportional, then the triangles are similar. *Theorem:* Side, Angle, Side (SAS) Similarity Given two triangles, if two sides are proportional and the angles included between those sides are congruent, then the two triangles are similar. *Theorem:* Angle, Angle (AA) Similarity If two angles of one triangle are congruent, respectively, to two angles of another triangles, then the triangles are similar.
Proportion theorems (p. 739)	*Theorem:* If a line parallel to one side of a triangle intersects the other sides, then it divides those sides into proportional segments. *Theorem:* If a line divides two sides of a triangle into proportional segments, then the line is parallel to the third side. *Theorem:* If parallel lines cut off congruent segments on one transversal, then they cut off congruent segments on any transversal. (Note: This theorem can be used to divide a given segment into any number of congruent parts.)
Midsegment (p. 741)	The segment connecting the midpoints of two sides of a triangle. *Theorem:* The midsegment joining the midpoints of two sides of a triangle is parallel to and is half as long as the third side. *Theorem:* If a line bisects one side of a triangle and is parallel to a second side, then it bisects the third side and therefore is a midsegment.
Median of a triangle (p. 742)	A segment connecting a vertex of a triangle to the midpoint of the opposite side.
Centroid of a triangle (p. 742)	The point where all three medians are concurrent. The centroid is often called the *center of gravity*.
Indirect measurements (p. 743)	Similar triangles can be used to make indirect measurements.

Chapter 12 Review

1. Each of the following figures contains at least one pair of congruent triangles. Identify them and tell why they are congruent.

   a.

   △*ADB* ≅ △*CDB* by SAS;
   △*ABC* ≅ △*CBA* by ASA
   or SSS

   b.

   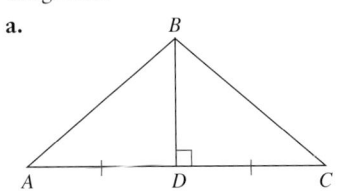

   AC = BD

   △*GAC* ≅ △*EDB* by
   SAS

   c.

   △*ABC* ≅ △*EDC* by AAS

   d.

   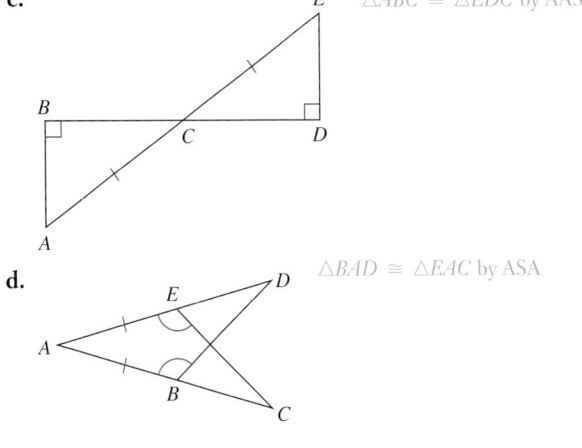

   △*BAD* ≅ △*EAC* by ASA

e. 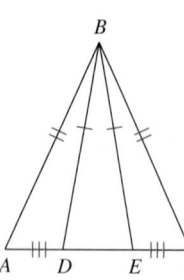 $\triangle ABD \cong \triangle CBD$ by ASA or SAS; $\triangle ABC \cong \triangle CBA$ by ASA

f. $\triangle ABD \cong \triangle CBD$ by SAS; $\triangle ABC \cong \triangle CBA$ by SAS

g. 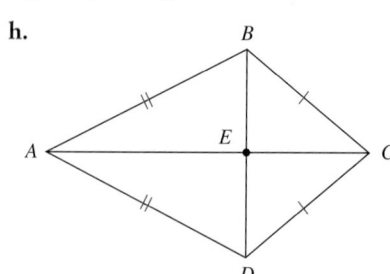 $\triangle ABD \cong \triangle CBE$ by SSS; $\triangle ABE \cong \triangle CBD$ by SSS; $\triangle ABC \cong \triangle CBA$ by SAS; $\triangle DBE \cong \triangle EBD$ by SAS

h. 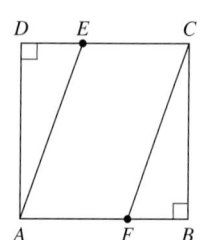 $\triangle ABC \cong \triangle ADC$ by SSS; $\triangle ABE \cong \triangle ADE$ by SSS or SAS; $\triangle EBC \cong \triangle EDC$ by SSS or SAS

2. In the following figure, $ABCD$ is a square and $\overline{DE} \cong \overline{BF}$. What kind of figure is $AECF$? Justify your answer.   *
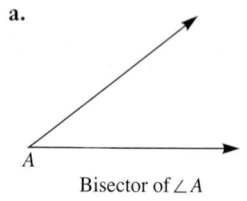

3. Construct each of the following by (1) using a compass and straightedge and (2) paperfolding.   Constructions

a.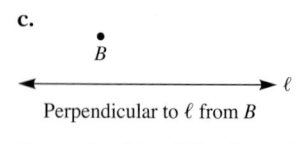
Bisector of $\angle A$

b.
Perpendicular to ℓ at B

c.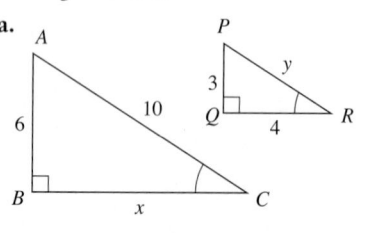
Perpendicular to ℓ from B

d.
Parallel to ℓ through P

4. For each of the following pairs of similar triangles, find the missing measures.

a. $x = 8, y = 5$

b. 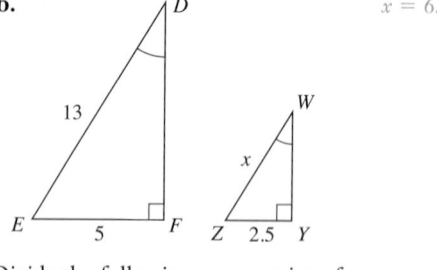 $x = 6.5$

5. Divide the following segment into four congruent parts.   Construction
_____

6. If $ABCD$ is a trapezoid, $\overline{EF} \parallel \overline{AD}$, and $\overline{AC}$ is a diagonal, what is the relationship between $\dfrac{a}{b}$ and $\dfrac{c}{d}$? $\dfrac{a}{b} = \dfrac{c}{d}$

7. Given the following figure, construct a circle so that A and B are on the circle and has its center on ℓ.   *
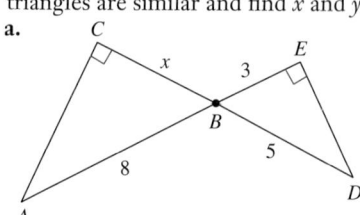

8. For each of the following figures, show that appropriate triangles are similar and find x and y.

a. 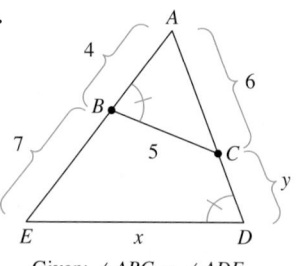 $\triangle ACB \sim \triangle DEB$ by AA similarity; $x = \dfrac{24}{5}$

b. $\triangle AED \sim \triangle ACB$ by AA similarity; $y = \dfrac{4}{3}, x = \dfrac{55}{6}$

Given: $\angle ABC \cong \angle ADE$

9. In the figure below, $\overline{DE} \parallel \overline{CB}$. Find AD.   15
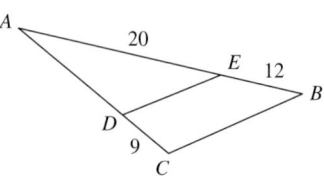

10. Given that $\ell \parallel m$, construct a line equidistant from ℓ and m.   Construction
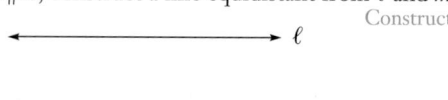

11. A swimming pool is shown with a rectangular-shaped patio surrounding it.

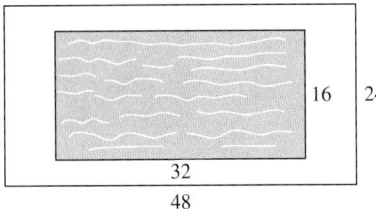

    a. Show that the rectangular patio is similar to the rectangular pool. *

    b. What is the scale factor of the patio to the pool? $\frac{3}{2}$

    c. What is the ratio of the perimeters of the patio and the pool? $\frac{144}{96} = \frac{3}{2}$

12. A student says that $\triangle ABE \cong \triangle ACD$ because the corresponding angles are congruent. How do you respond? *

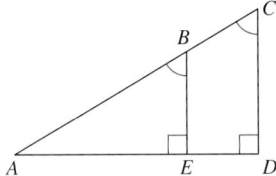

13. Given $\triangle ABC \cong \triangle TRI$, find the measures of

    a. $\angle T$ 70°   **b.** $\angle C$ 62°   **c.** $\angle B$ 48°

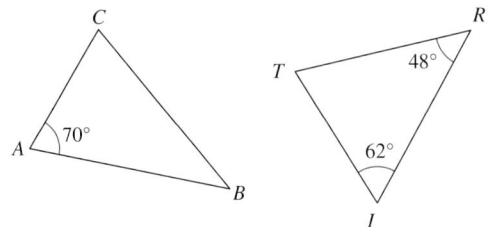

14. Given $\triangle ABC$, find the lengths of the three sides. 11, 11, 6

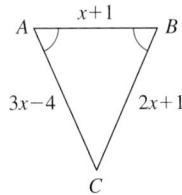

15. A person 2 m tall casts a shadow 1 m long when a building has a 6 m shadow. How high is the building? 12 m

16. Which of the following polygons can be inscribed in a circle? Assume (i) is not a square. Polygons (ii) and (iii)

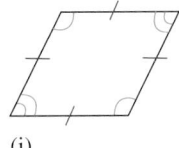 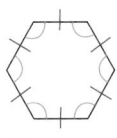 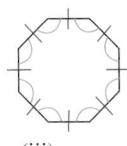

(i)   (ii)   (iii)

17. Determine the vertical height of the playground slide shown in the following figure. 6 m

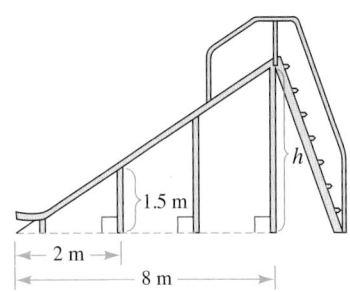

18. Find the distance d across the river sketched. $\frac{256}{5} = 51.2$ m

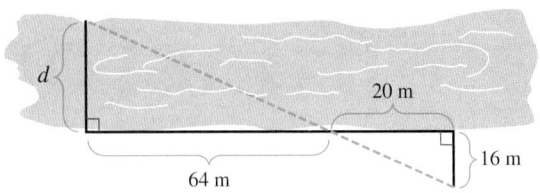

19. A regular hexagon $ABCDEF$ can be divided into two congruent trapezoids by drawing $\overline{AD}$.

    a. What is the relation of $\overline{AD}$ to the circumcircle of the regular hexagon? It is a diameter.

    b. Prove that $\angle ABD$ is a right angle. *

20. Is the following statement always true? If not, what condition on the diagonals could we add to make a true statement? *

    A quadrilateral whose diagonals are congruent and perpendicular is a square.

21. Why are two congruent triangles $\triangle ABC$ and $\triangle A'B'C'$ similar? *

22. $ABCD$ is a trapezoid with $\overline{BC} \parallel \overline{AD}$. Points M and N are midpoints of the diagonals. Line $\overleftrightarrow{CN}$ intersects $\overline{AD}$ at E.

    a. Prove that $\triangle BCN \cong \triangle DEN$. *

    b. Prove that $\overline{MN}$ is a midsegment of $\triangle ACE$. *

    c. If $AD = a, BC = b$, express MN in terms of a and b. Justify your answer. *

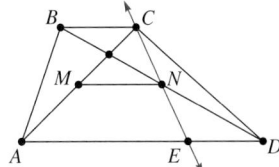

23. Given that $\angle 1 \cong \angle 2$ and $\angle 3 \cong \angle 4$, prove $\triangle BCE \cong \triangle DCE$. *

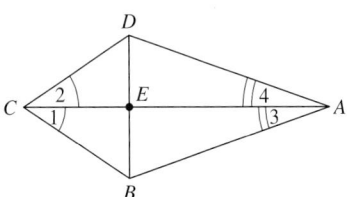

Chapter

13

Congruence and Similarity with Transformations

13-1 Translations and Rotations

13-2 Reflections and Glide Reflections

13-3 Dilations

13-4 Tessellations of the Plane

Preliminary Problem

Two farm houses, *H* and *T*, are located away from a road, as shown. A telephone company wants to construct underground lines from point *X* at the edge of the road so that the sum of the lengths of the cables connecting the houses (*H* and *T*) to *X* is as small as possible. Where should point *X* be located?

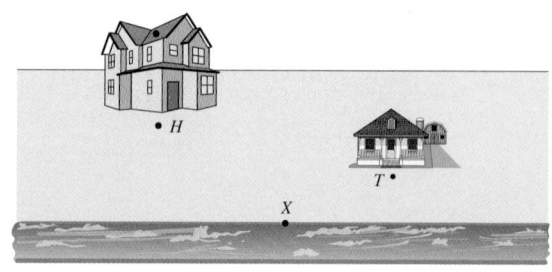

If needed, see Hint on page 807.

Euclid envisioned moving one geometric figure in a plane and placing it on top of another to determine whether the two figures were congruent. Intuitively, we know this can be done by making a tracing of one figure, then sliding, turning, or flipping the tracing, or using some combination of these motions, to place it atop the other figure. Additionally, similarities (and/or scaling) can be accomplished through a combination of these motions and dilations (size-altering transformations introduced in this chapter). This chapter also relates motions to symmetry and to tessellations.

CCSS *Common Core Standards* lists the following student expectations.

In grade 4: Identify line-symmetric figures and draw lines of symmetry (p. 32)

In grade 8:

- Verify experimentally the properties of rotations, reflections, and translations:

    Lines are taken to lines, and line segments to line segments of the same length.

    Angles are taken to angles of the same measure.

    Parallel lines are taken to parallel lines.

- Understand that a two-dimensional figure is congruent to another if the second can be obtained from the first by a sequence of rotations, reflections, and translations; given two congruent figures, describe a sequence that exhibits the congruence between them.
- Describe the effect of dilations, translations, rotations, and reflections on two-dimensional figures using coordinates.
- Understand that a two-dimensional figure is similar to another if the second can be obtained from the first by a sequence of rotations, reflections, translations, and dilations; given two similar two-dimensional figures, describe a sequence that exhibits the similarity between them. (pp. 55–56)

13-1 Translations and Rotations

13-1 Objectives

Students will be able to understand and explain

- Transformation of the plane.
- An isometry and its properties.
- Translations, rotations and their constructions.
- Coordinate representation of translations.
- Rotational symmetries.
- The relationship between slopes of two nonvertical perpendicular lines.

Think about a rug that completely covers a floor. If a long pin were stuck through the rug, it pairs a point on the rug with a corresponding point on the floor below. There is a one-to-one correspondence between the points of the rug and the points of the floor. If the rug were flipped over, and placed back on the floor so that it still covered the floor completely, then another one-to-one correspondence could be established between the points of the rug and the points of the floor. Similarly, a one-to-one correspondence between a plane and itself can be established so that there is a **transformation** from the plane to itself with each point from the original plane having an **image** point in the "transformed" plane and vice versa. Any transformation of the plane that preserves distance is an **isometry** (or **rigid motion**). Preserving distance means that given any two points P and Q in the original plane, the distance PQ between them is the same as the distance $P'Q'$ between their respective images P' and Q'. Isometries also preserve geometric shapes and relations including parallelism and perpendicularity. In this section, we examine two types of isometries: translations and rotations.

In his 1872 inaugural address at the University of Erlangen, Germany, Felix Klein (1849–1925), described geometry as the study of properties of figures that do not change under a particular set of transformations. Specifically, Euclidean geometry was described as the study of such properties of figures as area and length, which remain unchanged under a set of distance-preserving transformations.

Translations

Figure 1(a) shows a two-dimensional representation of a child moving down a slide without twisting or turning. This type of motion is a **translation**, or **slide**. In Figure 1(a), the child (**preimage** or **original**) at the top of the slide moves a certain distance in a certain direction, indicated by a **slide arrow**, along a **slide line** to obtain the **image** at the bottom of the slide. In Figure 1(b) the translation is determined by the **slide arrow**, or **vector**, from M to N. The vector determines the image of any point in a plane in the following way: The image of point A in the plane is the point A' obtained by sliding A along a line parallel to slide line $\overleftrightarrow{MN}$ in the direction from M to N by the distance MN indicated by the slide arrow. Hence in Figure 1(b) $AA' = MN = d$ and $\overleftrightarrow{MN}$ is parallel to $\overleftrightarrow{AA'}$. Under the translation, a figure changes neither its shape nor its size. In fact, a translation preserves both length and angle size, and thus congruence of figures.

In Figure 1(b) $\overline{AB}$ is slid, or translated, by the slide arrow from M to N along slide line ℓ making $\overline{AB} \cong \overline{A'B'}$ and $AA' = BB' = MN = d$. Thus, quadrilateral $AA'B'B$ is a parallelogram, and $\overline{AB} \parallel \overline{A'B'}$. This illustrates that under a translation, the image of a segment is a congruent segment parallel to the original (preimage).

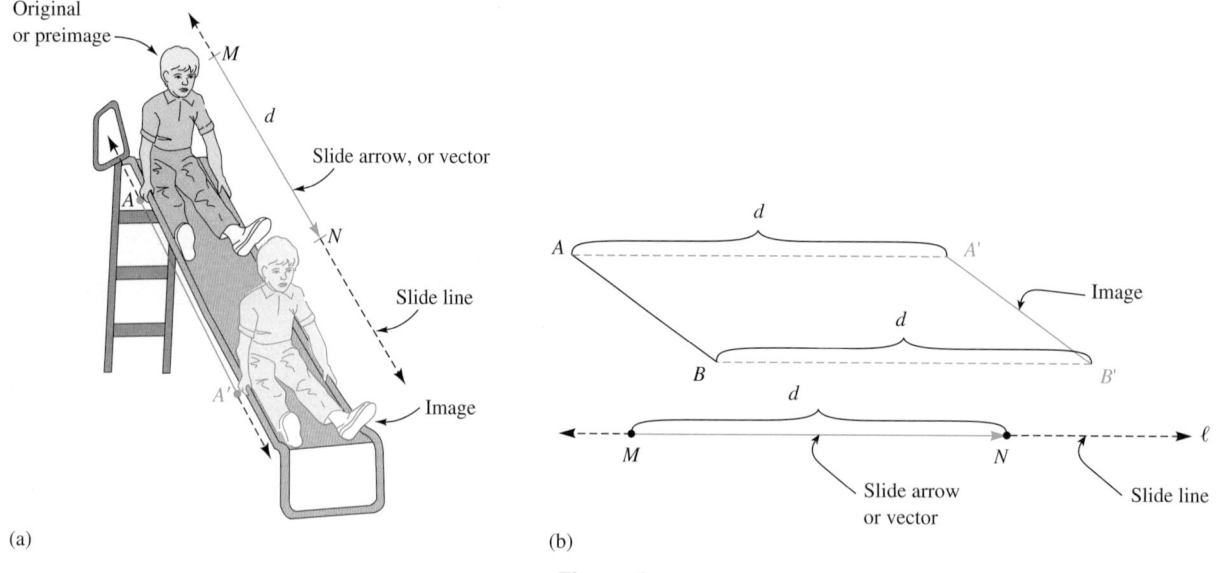

Figure 1

A definition of a translation follows.

Definition of a Translation

A **translation** by a slide arrow $\overrightarrow{MN}$ is a transformation of the plane to itself such that every point P in the plane has an image P' so that $PP' = MN$, $\overline{PP'} \parallel \overline{MN}$, and the direction from P to P' is the same as from M to N.

Notice that we use the same notation for a slide arrow as we used for a ray. It should be clear from the context which is which.

Constructions of Translations

Using tracing paper is a natural way to construct a "motion." The image of a figure under a translation constructed with tracing paper is seen in Figure 2.

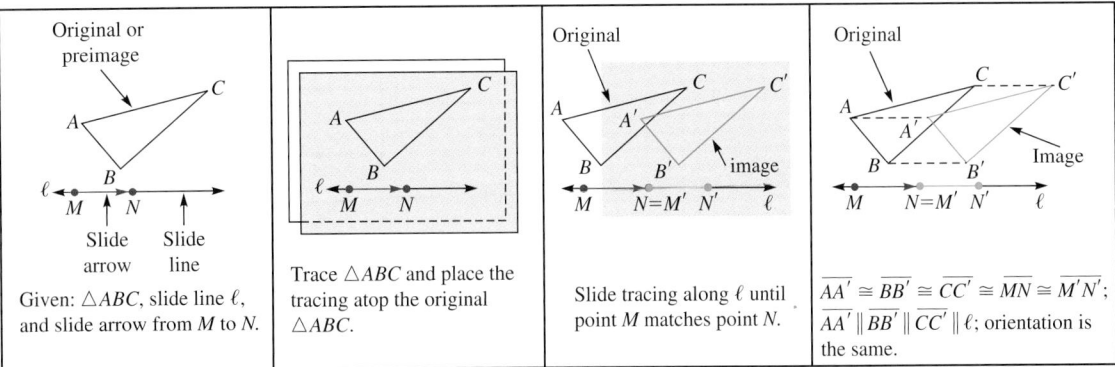

Figure 2 Construction of translation with tracing paper

Traditionally, most constructions in geometry have been accomplished with a compass and a straightedge. We leave the traditional construction as an activity in Now Try This 1.

To construct the image of an object under a translation, we first need to know how to construct the image A' of a single point A. In Figure 2, by definition of translation, $MN = AA'$ and $\overleftrightarrow{MN}$ is parallel to $\overleftrightarrow{AA'}$. Because a quadrilateral with a pair of opposite sides parallel and congruent is a parallelogram, $MAA'N$ is a parallelogram. To construct the translation image A' of a point A in Figure 3 with a compass and straightedge, we need only to construct a parallelogram $MAA'N$ so that $\overrightarrow{AA'}$ is in the same direction as $\overrightarrow{MN}$. One way to accomplish this is to use the fact that a quadrilateral with opposite sides congruent is a parallelogram.

▶ **NOW TRY THIS 1**

In Figure 3 use a compass and straightedge to construct the following:

a. The image of A under a translation that takes M to N.
b. The image of A under a translation that takes N to M.

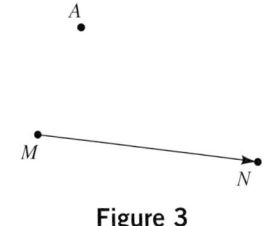

Figure 3

To find the image of a triangle under a translation, it suffices to find the images of the three vertices of the triangle and to connect these images with segments to form the triangle's image.

It is possible to use a geoboard, dot paper, or a grid to find an image of a segment. Example 1 uses dot paper.

Example 1

Find the image of $\overline{AB}$ under the translation from X to X' pictured on the dot paper in Figure 4.

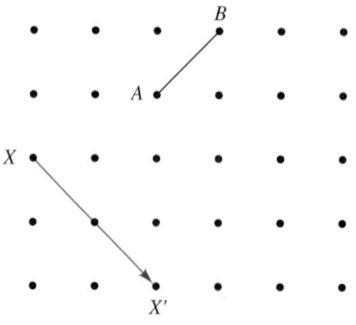

Figure 4

Solution X', the image of X under the translation, could be obtained by shifting X down 2 units vertically and then horizontally to the right 2 units, as shown in Figure 5. This shifting determines the slide arrow from X to X'. Therefore, the image of points A and B on the dot paper can be obtained by shifting each point first down 2 units and then to the right 2 units. Thus, $\overline{A'B'}$, the image of $\overline{AB}$, is found as in Figure 5.

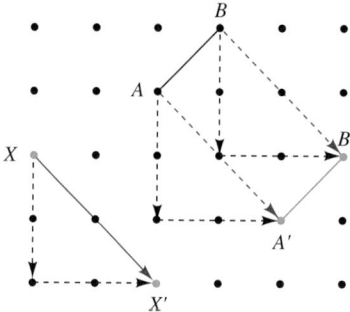

Figure 5

Coordinate Representation of Translations

CCSS In many applications of mathematics and as recommended in the grade 8 *Common Core Standards* (p. 56), it is necessary to use translations in a coordinate system. In Figure 6, $\triangle A'B'C'$ is the image of $\triangle ABC$ under the translation defined by the slide arrow from O to O', where O is the origin and O' has coordinates $(5, {}^-2)$. Point O' is the image of point O under the given translation. The point $O'(5, {}^-2)$ can be obtained by moving O horizontally to the right 5 units and then down 2 units. As each point in triangle ABC is translated in the direction from O to O' by the distance OO', we obtain the image of any point by moving it horizontally to the right 5 units and then vertically down 2 units. In Figure 6 the images A', B', and C' for points A, B, and C are shown. Table 1 shows how the coordinates of the image vertices A', B', and C' in Figure 6 are obtained from the coordinates of A, B, and C.

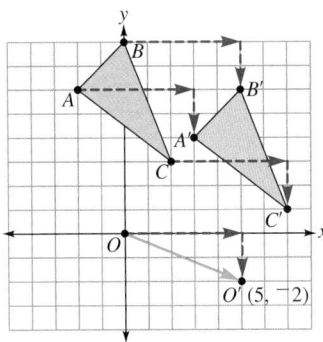

Point (x, y)	Image Point (x + 5, y − 2)
$A(^-2, 6)$	$A'(3, 4)$
$B(0, 8)$	$B'(5, 6)$
$C(2, 3)$	$C'(7, 1)$

Table 1

Figure 6

This discussion suggests that a translation is described by showing how the coordinates of any point (x, y) change. The translation in Table 1 can be written symbolically as $(x, y) \rightarrow (x + 5, y - 2)$, where "$\rightarrow$" denotes "moves to." In this notation, $(x + 5, y - 2)$ is the image of (x, y). If T is the function representing this translation and the plane is the domain, then the image of the point with coordinates (x, y) is $T(x, y) = (x + 5, y - 2)$. Thus, a translation is defined in terms of a coordinate system as follows:

Definition of a Translation in a Coordinate System

A **translation** is a function from the plane to the plane such that the image of the point with coordinates (x, y) is $(x + a, y + b)$, where a and b are real numbers.

Example 2

Find the coordinates of the image of the vertices of quadrilateral $ABCD$ in Figure 7 under the translations in parts (a) through (c). Draw the image in each case.

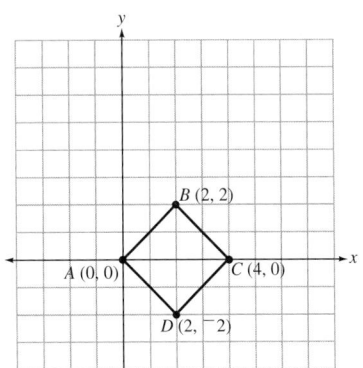

Figure 7

  a. $(x, y) \rightarrow (x - 2, y + 4)$
  b. A translation determined by the slide arrow from $A(0, 0)$ to $A'(^-2, 4)$
  c. A translation determined by the slide arrow from $S(4, ^-3)$ to $S'(2, 1)$

Solution

  a. Because $(x, y) \rightarrow (x - 2, y + 4)$, the images A', B', C', and D' of the corresponding points A, B, C, and D can be found as follows:

$$A(0, 0) \rightarrow A'(0 - 2, 0 + 4), \text{ or } A'(^-2, 4)$$
$$B(2, 2) \rightarrow B'(2 - 2, 2 + 4), \text{ or } B'(0, 6)$$
$$C(4, 0) \rightarrow C'(4 - 2, 0 + 4), \text{ or } C'(2, 4)$$
$$D(2, ^-2) \rightarrow D'(2 - 2, ^-2 + 4), \text{ or } D'(0, 2)$$

The square $ABCD$ and its image $A'B'C'D'$ are shown in Figure 8.

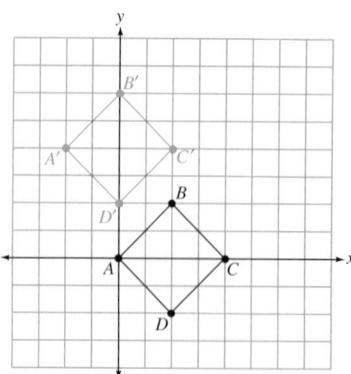

Figure 8

    b. This is the same translation as in part (a) and hence the image of $ABCD$ is $A'B'C'D'$ as in part (a).

    c. The translation from $S(4, ^-3)$ to $S'(2, 1)$ moves $S(4, ^-3)$ left 2 units to $(2, ^-3)$ and then vertically up 4 units to $S'(2, 1)$. Thus, any point (x, y) moves to a point with coordinates $(x - 2, y + 4)$. This is the same translation as in part (a), so the image of $ABCD$ is $A'B'C'D'$.

Translations are useful in determining **frieze patterns** (an infinite strip with a repeating pattern) such as those appearing in wallpaper designs. An example is seen in Figure 9.

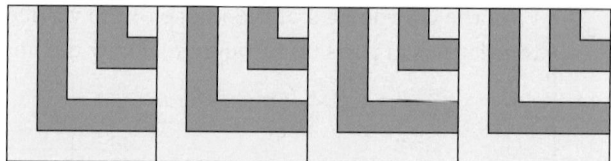

Figure 9

▶ NOW TRY THIS 2

NTT 2: Answers can be found in Answers at the back of the book.

In the wallpaper pattern of Figure 9, describe a translation that could be used to construct the wallpaper.

Figure 10

Rotations

A **rotation**, or **turn**, is another kind of isometry. Figure 10 illustrates congruent figures that resulted from a rotation about point O. The image of the letter **F** under a 30° counterclockwise rotation with center O is shown in green.

    A rotation can be constructed by using tracing paper, as in Figure 11, where point O is the **turn center** and α is the **turn angle**, which gives the direction and the amount of the turn illustrated by the **turn arrow**.

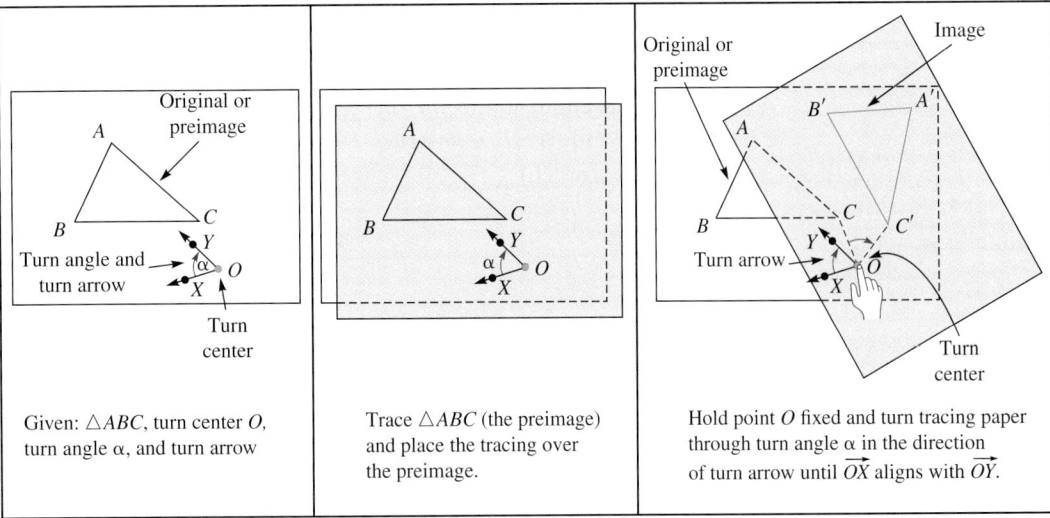

Figure 11 Construction of a rotation using tracing paper

To determine a rotation, we must know three pieces of data: the turn center; the direction of the turn, either clockwise (a negative measure) or counterclockwise (a positive measure); and the amount of the turn measured in degrees.

This discussion leads to the following definition.

Definition of a Rotation

A **rotation** is a transformation of the plane determined by holding one point—the center—fixed and rotating the plane about this point by a certain angle clockwise or counterclockwise.

To construct an image of a figure under a rotation as in Figure 11, observe that every point on the tracing paper construction except the center moves along a circle as shown in Figure 12. The angle formed by any point (not the turn center), the center of the rotation O, and the image of the point is congruent to the angle of the turn.

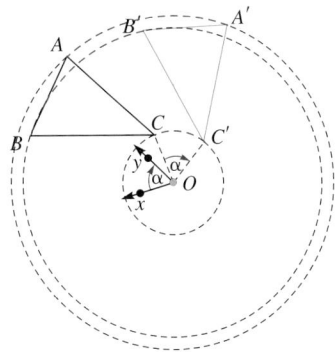

Concentric circles with radii OA, OB, and OC.
$\angle BOB' \cong \angle AOA' \cong \angle COC' \cong \angle XOY$.
Orientation is the same.

Figure 12

▶ **NOW TRY THIS 3**

Use a compass and a straightedge to construct the image of point P under a rotation with center O through the angle and in the direction given in Figure 13. (*Hint*: P' must be on a circle with center O and radius OP. Construct $\angle POP'$ congruent to α by first constructing a triangle with angle α and vertex A.)

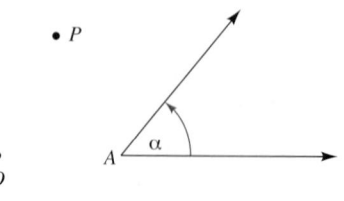

Figure 13

A rotation is an isometry, so the image of a figure under a rotation is congruent to the original figure. It can be shown that *under any isometry, the image of a line is a line, the image of a circle is a circle, and the images of parallel lines are parallel lines.*

For certain angles, like 90°, rotations may be constructed on a geoboard or dot paper, as demonstrated in Example 3.

Example 3

In Figure 14, find the image of $\triangle ABC$ under the rotation shown with center O.

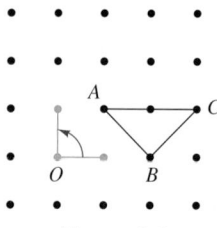

Figure 14

Solution $\triangle A'B'C'$, the image of $\triangle ABC$, is shown in Figure 15. The image of A is A' because $\angle A'OA$ is a right angle and $OA = OA'$. Similarly, B' is the image of B. To find the location of C', we can use the fact that rotation is an isometry and hence $\triangle A'B'C' \cong \triangle ABC$. Thus, $\angle B \cong \angle B'$. The location of point C' shown makes $\angle B \cong \angle B'$ and $C'B' = CB$ (Why?). The direction of the rotation is counterclockwise as specified.

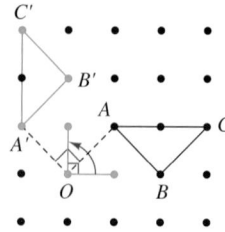

Figure 15

A rotation of 360° about a point moves any point and hence any figure onto itself. Such a transformation is an **identity transformation**. Any point may be the center of such a rotation.

A rotation of 180° about a point is a **half-turn**. Because a half-turn is a rotation, it has all the properties of rotations. Additionally, as suggested in Figure 16(b), *a line (or line segment) is parallel* *to its image under a half-turn.* (Why?) Figure 16 shows some shapes and their images under a half-turn about point O.

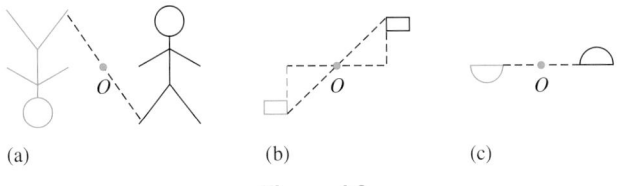

(a)   (b)   (c)

Figure 16

The half-screw in Figure 17(a) has a head that shows a practical example of a half-turn in hardware. To "lock" the screw, the head is turned $180°$ as shown in Figure 17(b).

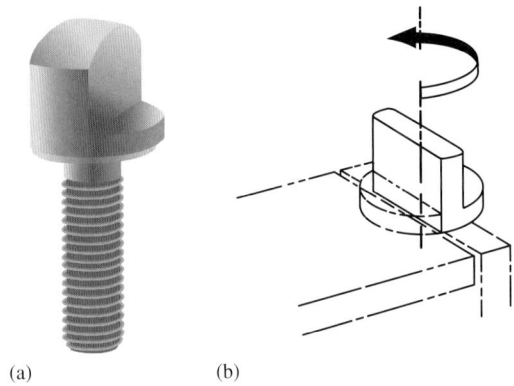

(a)   (b)

Figure 17

Applications of Rotations

One way to describe a figure with *turn symmetry* is to see if there is a center and turn angle(s) that will take the original figure to itself as an image. For example, Figure 18 shows a star that has several turn symmetries.

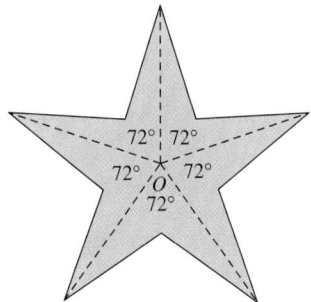

72°│72°
72° ⭐ 72°
    ╱O╲
    72°

Figure 18

The center, O, of the turn symmetries is the center of the circle that circumscribes the star. As marked, the turn symmetries of $72°$, $144°$, $216°$, and $288°$ are turn angles of rotations centered at O. Observe that if a figure has turn symmetry of $72°$, it also has turn symmetries of multiples of $72°$.

▶ **NOW TRY THIS 4**

NTT 4: Answer can be found in Answers at the back of the book.

  a. Draw a figure with point symmetry (see Chapter 11).
  b. Explain whether the figure drawn in part (a) is its own image under a half-turn.
  c. Given any line ℓ and a point P on the line, what is the image of ℓ under a half-turn about P?
  d. Given any line ℓ and a point P not on ℓ, describe how to construct the image of ℓ through a half-turn about P.

Slopes of Perpendicular Lines via Rotations

Transformations can be used to investigate various mathematical relationships. For example, they can be used to determine the relationship between the slopes of two perpendicular lines, neither of which is vertical.

First consider a special case in which the lines contain the origin. Suppose the two perpendicular lines are as pictured in Figure 19 with one point, B, of ℓ_1 having coordinates (a, b). The coordinates of point B determine the coordinates of point $A(a, 0)$, and triangle OAB is formed. If the plane containing the lines is rotated 90° counterclockwise about center O, then $\ell_2 = \ell_1'$, the image of ℓ_1 is ℓ_2. The image of triangle OAB is triangle $OA'B'$. Because the rotation takes a triangle to a congruent triangle, $\triangle OAB \cong \triangle OA'B'$. Thus, A' has coordinates $(0, a)$ and B' has coordinates $(^-b, a)$. (Why?)

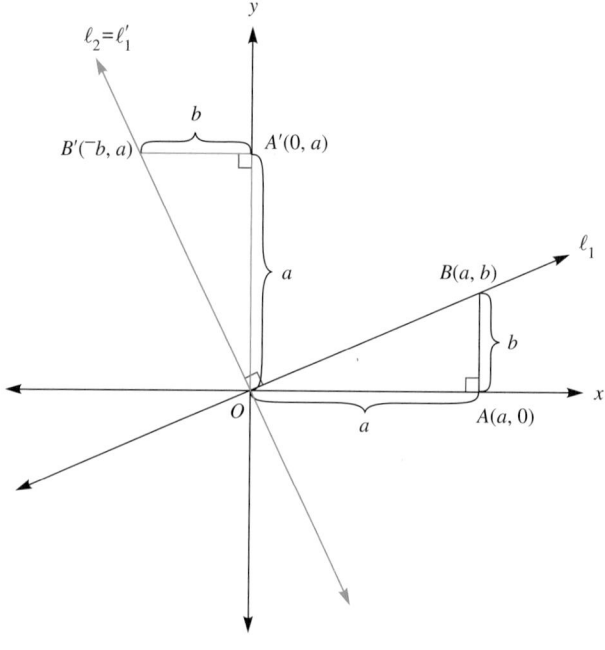

Figure 19

Now consider the slopes of ℓ_1 and ℓ_2. To find the slope of ℓ_1 we use the points $(0, 0)$ and $B(a, b)$ to find $\dfrac{b - 0}{a - 0} = \dfrac{b}{a}$. Similarly to find the slope of ℓ_2 we use $B'(^-b, a)$ and $(0, 0)$ and find $\dfrac{a - 0}{^-b - 0} = \dfrac{^-a}{b}$. Since the slope of ℓ_1 is $\dfrac{b}{a}$ and the slope of ℓ_2 is $\dfrac{a}{^-b}$, the slopes are negative reciprocals of each other and their product is $^-1$.

If two nonvertical perpendicular lines, ℓ and m, do not intersect at the origin, then two lines parallel to ℓ and m respectively can be found that do pass through the origin. Because nonvertical parallel lines have equal slopes, the relationship between the slopes, m_1 and m_2, of the perpendicular lines is the same as the relationship between the slopes of the perpendicular lines through the origin; that is, $m_1 m_2 = ^-1$.

It is also possible to prove the converse statement; that is, if the slopes of two lines satisfy the condition $m_1 m_2 = ^-1$, then the lines are perpendicular. We summarize these results in the following theorem.

Theorem 13-1:   Slopes of Perpendicular Lines

Two nonvertical lines are perpendicular if, and only if, their slopes m_1 and m_2 satisfy the condition $m_1 m_2 = ^-1$. Every vertical line has no slope but is perpendicular to every line with slope 0.

Example 4

Find the equation of line ℓ through point $(^-1, 2)$ and perpendicular to the line with equation $y = 3x + 5$.

Solution If m is the slope of ℓ, as in Figure 20, then the equation of line ℓ is $y = mx + b$.

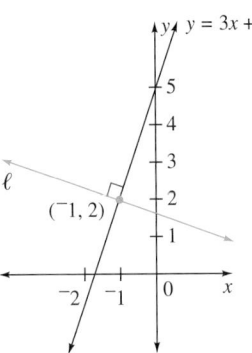

Figure 20

Because the line $y = 3x + 5$ has slope 3 and is perpendicular to ℓ, we have $3m = ^-1$; therefore, $m = \dfrac{^-1}{3}$. Consequently, the equation of ℓ is

$$y = \frac{^-1}{3}x + b.$$

Because the point $(^-1, 2)$ is on ℓ, we can substitute $x = ^-1, y = 2$ in $y = \dfrac{^-1}{3}x + b$ and solve for b as follows:

$$2 = \frac{^-1}{3}(^-1) + b$$

$$\frac{5}{3} = b$$

Consequently, the equation of ℓ is

$$y = \frac{^-1}{3}x + \frac{5}{3}.$$

Assessment 13-1A

1. For each of the following, find the image of the given quadrilateral under a translation from A to B.

   a.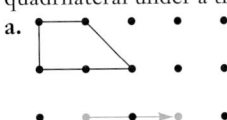

   b.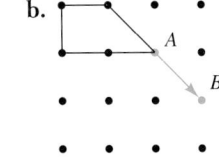

2. Construct the image of $\overline{BC}$ under the translation pictured in the figure by using the following.

   a. Tracing paper *
   b. Compass and straightedge *

   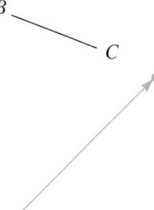

3. Find the coordinates of the image for each of the following points under the translation defined by $(x, y) \rightarrow (x + 3, y - 4)$.
   a. $(0, 0)$ $(3, ^-4)$ **b.** $(^-3, 4)$ $(0, 0)$ **c.** $(^-6, ^-9)$ $(^-3, ^-13)$

4. Find the coordinates of the points whose images under the translation $(x, y) \rightarrow (x - 3, y + 4)$ are the following.
   a. $(0, 0)$ $(3, ^-4)$ **b.** $(^-3, 4)$ $(0, 0)$ **c.** $(^-6, ^-9)$ $(^-3, ^-13)$

5. Consider the translation $(x, y) \rightarrow (x + 3, y - 4)$. In each of the following, draw the image of the figure under the translation and find the coordinates of the images of the labeled points:
   a.

   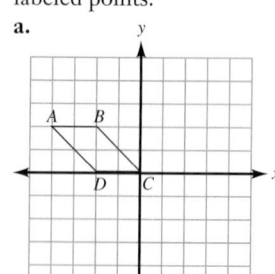

   b.

   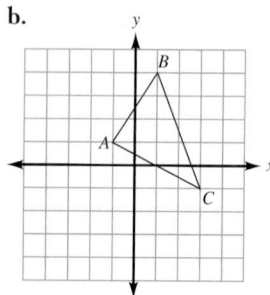

6. Consider the translation $(x, y) \rightarrow (x + 3, y - 4)$. In the following, draw the figure whose image is shown. *

   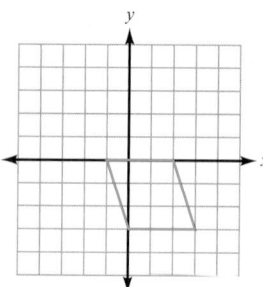

7. Find the image of the following quadrilateral under a 90° counterclockwise rotation about O. *

   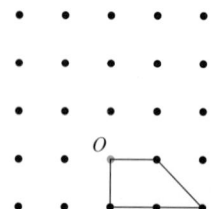

8. If ℓ is a line whose equation is $y = 2x - 1$, find the equation of the image of ℓ under each of the following translations.
   a. $(x, y) \rightarrow (x, y - 2)$ $y = 2x - 3$
   b. $(x, y) \rightarrow (x + 3, y)$ $y = 2x - 7$

9. If $y = ^-2x + 3$ is the image of line k under the translation $(x, y) \rightarrow (x + 3, y - 2)$, find the equation of k. $y = ^-2x - 1$

10. Find the image of line ℓ under a half-turn about point O as shown. *

    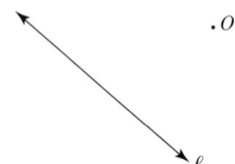

11. The image of $\overline{AB}$ under a rotation is given in the following figure. Find $\overline{AB}$. *

    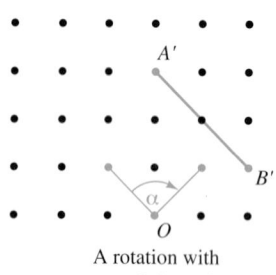

    A rotation with
    center O through α

12. The image of NOON is still NOON after a certain half-turn. List some other words that have the same property. What letters can such words contain? *

13. **a.** Draw a line ℓ and any two points A and B so that $\overline{AB}$ is parallel to line ℓ. Find the image of ℓ under a translation from A to B.   The line itself.
    b. Draw a line ℓ and any two points A and B so that $\overline{AB}$ is not parallel to ℓ. Construct ℓ', the image of ℓ under the translation from A to B.   Answers vary.
    c. How are ℓ and ℓ' in part (b) related? Why? *
    d. What is the image of $\angle ABC$ under 10 successive rotations about B if $m(\angle ABC) = 36°$. $\angle ABC$

14. Use any tools to construct P', the image of P when it is rotated about O, as shown in the figure, for angles with the following measures and direction:
    a. 45° counterclockwise *   **b.** 60° clockwise *
    c. 105° counterclockwise *

    • P

    •O

15. For each of the following points, find the coordinates of the image point under a half-turn about the origin.
    a. $(4, 0)$ $(^-4, 0)$
    b. $(2, 4)$ $(^-2, ^-4)$
    c. $(^-2, ^-4)$ $(2, 4)$
    d. (a, b) $(^-a, ^-b)$

16. For the following figure, find the image of the figure under a half-turn about O. *

17. Draw any line and label it ℓ. Use tracing paper to find ℓ', the image of ℓ under each of the following rotations. In each case, describe how ℓ' is related to ℓ.
    a. Half-turn about point O on ℓ $\ell = \ell$
    b. A 90° turn counterclockwise about point O not on ℓ $\ell' \perp \ell$

18. a. Find the final image of △ABC by performing two rotations in succession each with center O, one by angle α and one by angle β, in the directions shown in the figure. *

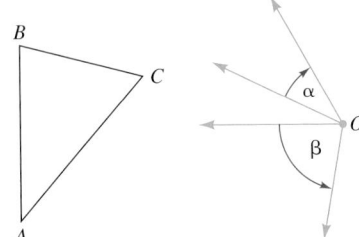

b. Is the order of the rotations important?   No
c. Could the result have been accomplished in one rotation? *

19. a. Use a drawing similar to Figure 19 to find the images of the following points under a 90° rotation counterclockwise about the origin:
  i. (2, 3) (⁻3, 2)   **ii.** (⁻1, 2) (⁻2, ⁻1)
  iii. (m, n) in terms of m and n   (⁻n, m)
b. Show that under a half-turn with the origin as center, the image of a point with coordinates (a, b) has coordinates (⁻a, ⁻b). *
c. Use what you found in part (a) to get the image of P(a, b) under rotation clockwise by 90° about the origin. (*Hint*: Rotate first as in part (a), then apply a half-turn about the origin.)   (b, ⁻a)

20. Find the equation of the line through (1, 0) and perpendicular to the given line.
a. $y = x + 2$ $y = ⁻x + 1$
b. $y = ⁻2x + 3$ $y = \frac{1}{2}x - \frac{1}{2}$
c. $x = ⁻4$ $y = 0$
d. $y = ⁻3$ $x = 1$

21. The following figure is a rhombus with sides of length a and one of the vertices at (h, k).

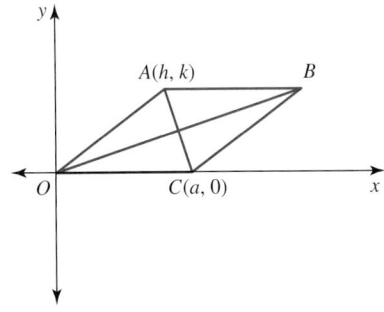

a. Find the coordinates of B in terms of a, h, and k. *
b. Prove that the diagonals of a rhombus are perpendicular to each other. *
c. Describe the turn symmetries of the rhombus. *

22. Use slide arrows $\overrightarrow{AB}$, $\overrightarrow{CD}$, and △PQR like the ones shown and answer the following.
a. Construct △P'Q'R', the image of △PQR under translation by $\overrightarrow{AB}$, and △P"Q"R" as the image of △P'Q'R' under translation by $\overrightarrow{CD}$.   Construction
b. Construct a single slide arrow that corresponds to the translation that takes △PQR directly to △P"Q"R". Explain how you constructed that slide arrow. *

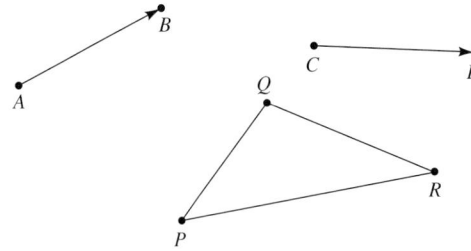

23. Describe the turn symmetries, if any, of the following figures.
a. Square *   **b.** Regular pentagon *
c. Regular n-gon *
d. Circle *
e. Isosceles triangle with exactly two congruent sides *

24. Which of the following figures have-half turn symmetries? If a figure has a half-turn symmetry, identify the turn center and tell why the figure has the symmetry.
a. Rectangle *   **b.** Parallelogram *
c. Kite that is not a rhombus   No half-turn symmetry
d. Non-regular pentagon with all sides congruent *

25. Construct a circle with center O and choose any point P on the circle. Answer the following.
a. Construct the image of the circle under a half-turn with turn center P. *
b. How are the two circles related? Why? *

26. Construct a circle with center O and a chord $\overline{AB}$ the same length as the radius. Then construct A' and B', the corresponding images of A and B under a half-turn with turn center O. Then construct O', the image of O under translation by slide arrow $\overrightarrow{BA}$, and finally construct P, the image of O under translation by $\overrightarrow{AB}$. What kind of polygon is ABPA'B'O'?   Regular hexagon

Assessment 13-1B

1. Under a translation from X to X', find the figure whose image is given in each of the following.
a. *   **b.** *

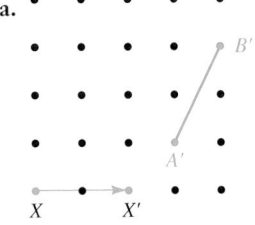

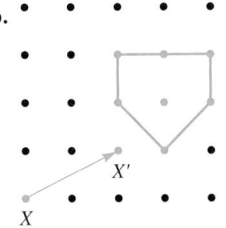

2. Construct $\overline{BC}$ whose image $\overline{B'C'}$ under the translation by $\overrightarrow{PQ}$ pictured in the figure by using the following.
a. Tracing paper *
b. Compass and straightedge *

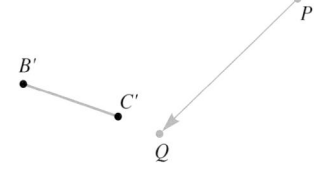

3. Find the coordinates of the image for each of the following points under the translation defined by $(x,y) \rightarrow (x + 3, y - 4)$.
   a. $(7, 14)$ $(10, 10)$
   b. $(^-3, ^-5)$ $(0, ^-9)$
   c. (h, k) $(h + 3, k - 4)$

4. Find the coordinates of the points whose images under the translation $(x,y) \rightarrow (x - 3, y + 4)$ are the following.
   a. $(7, 14)$ $(10, 10)$
   b. $(^-7, ^-10)$ $(^-4, ^-14)$
   c. (h, k) $(h + 3, k - 4)$

5. Consider the translation $(x,y) \rightarrow (x + 3, y - 4)$. On each of the following, draw the image of the figure under the translation, and find the coordinates of the images of the labeled points.
   a. 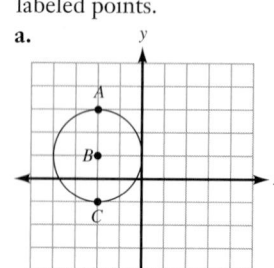   b.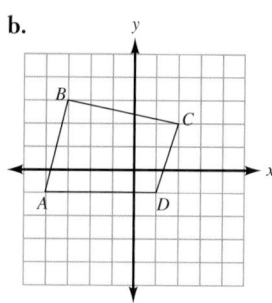

6. Consider the translation $(x,y) \rightarrow (x + 3, y - 4)$. On the following coordinate system draw the figure whose image is shown. *

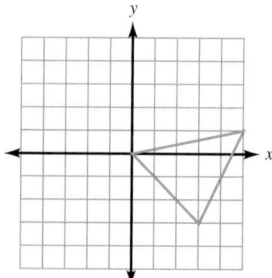

7. Find the figure whose image was obtained through a 90° clockwise rotation about point O and is shown below. *

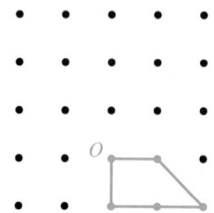

8. If ℓ is a line whose equation is $y = 2x - 1$, find the equation of the image of ℓ under each of the following translations.
   a. $(x,y) \rightarrow (x - 3, y + 2)$ $y = 2x + 7$
   b. $(x,y) \rightarrow (x - 5, y - 4)$ $y = 2x + 5$

9. If P' is the image of point P ($P' \neq P$) under a half-turn about O, what can be said about points P', P, and O? Why? *

10. Use a compass and a straightedge to find the preimage of ℓ under a half-turn about point O as shown. *

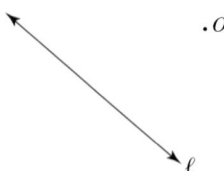

11. The image of $\overline{AB}$ under a half-turn through O is given in the following figure. Find $\overline{AB}$. *

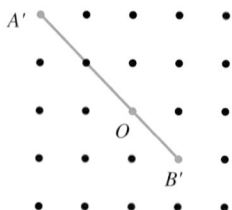

12. The image of MOW is still MOW after a certain half-turn. Explain whether MOM has this property. *

13. a. Refer to the following figure and use paper folding or any other method to show that if P' is the image of P under rotation about point O by a given angle, then O is on the perpendicular bisector of $\overline{PP'}$. *

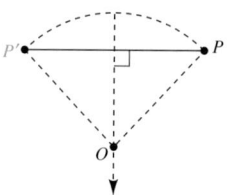

   b. $\triangle A'B'C'$ shown in the following figure was obtained by rotating $\triangle ABC$ about a certain point O. Explain how to find the point O and the angle of rotation. *

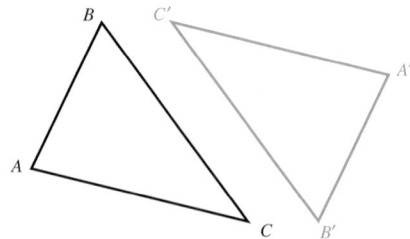

   c. Triangles ABC and $A'B'C'$ shown are congruent. Trace them and explain why it is impossible to find a rotation under which $\triangle A'B'C'$ is the image of $\triangle ABC$. *

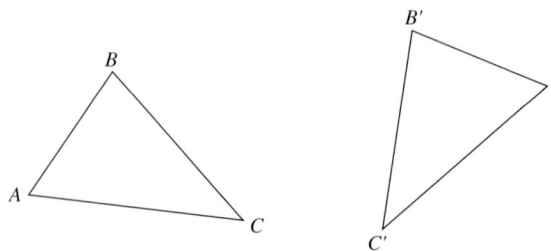

14. Construct P', the image of P under rotation about O (as shown in the figure), for angles with the following measures and direction. *
  a. 30° counterclockwise
  b. 30° clockwise
  c. 60° clockwise

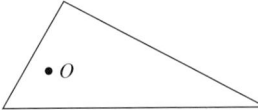

15. For each of the following points, find the coordinates of the image point under a half-turn about the origin:
  a. $(0, 3)$ $(0, ^-3)$
  b. $(^-2, 5)$ $(2, ^-5)$
  c. $(^-a, ^-b)$ (a, b)
16. For the following figure, find the image of the figure under a half-turn about O. *

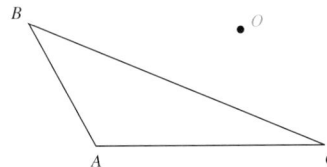

17. Draw any line and label it ℓ. Use tracing paper to find ℓ', the image of ℓ under each of the following rotations. In each case, describe in words how ℓ' is related to ℓ.
  a. Half-turn about point O, not on ℓ *
  b. A 60° turn counterclockwise about point O, not on ℓ *
18. When $\triangle ABC$ in the following figure is rotated about point O by 360°, each of the vertices traces a path. *

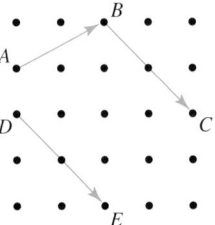

  a. What geometric figure does each vertex trace?   A circle
  b. Identify all points O for which two vertices trace an identical path. Justify your answer. *
  c. Given any $\triangle ABC$, is there a point O such that the three vertices trace an identical path? If so, describe how to find such a point. *
19. Find the equation of the image of the line $y = 3x - 1$ under the following transformations.
  a. Half-turn about the origin $y = 3x + 1$
  b. A 90° counterclockwise rotation about the origin $y = \frac{^-1}{3}x + \frac{1}{3}$
20. Find the equation of the line through $(^-1, ^-3)$ and perpendicular to the given line.
  a. $y = 2x + 1$ $y = ^-\frac{1}{2}x - \frac{7}{2}$
  b. $y = ^-2x + 3$ $y = \frac{1}{2}x - \frac{5}{2}$
  c. $x = ^-4$ $y = ^-3$
  d. $y = ^-3$ $x = ^-1$

21. The following figure shows $\overline{AB}$, one side of a rhombus. Describe how to use a half-turn about O to find the coordinates of the other two vertices of the rhombus. *

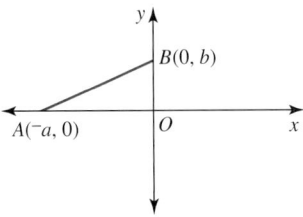

22. a. A translation from A to B is followed by a translation from B to C, as shown. Can the same result be accomplished by a single translation? If so, what is that translation?   A translation from A to C
  b. Find a single translation equivalent to a translation from A to B followed by a translation from D to E. *
  c. Suppose the order of the translations in part (b) is reversed; that is, a translation from D to E is followed by a translation from A to B. Is the result different from the one in part (b)?   No

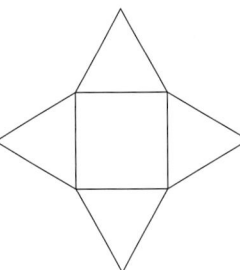

23. Describe all the turn symmetries in each of the following figures, identifying the turn center and turn angle in degrees clockwise or counterclockwise.
  a. Right isosceles triangle   None
  b. Equilateral triangle *
  c. A square with equilateral triangles on its sides as shown *

  d. Half a circle with its diameter   None

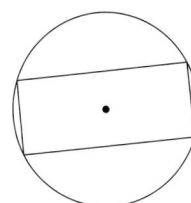

  e. Circle with an inscribed rectangle that is not a square *

24. Sketch a figure that has a half-turn symmetry but is neither a polygon nor a circle.   Answers vary.

25. Construct a circle with center O and choose any point P on the circle. Construct the image of the circle under a translation by $\overrightarrow{OP}$. How are the circle and its image related?   *

26. The accompanying figure consists of congruent squares with diagonals as shown. Imagine that the drawing extends indefinitely in both directions horizontally with the same

pattern of squares. What is the image of the infinite figure under translation by the slide arrow $\overrightarrow{AB}$?   *

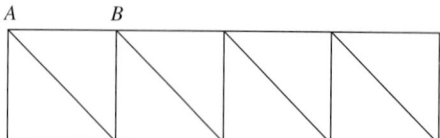

Mathematical Connections 13-1

Reasoning

1. If we are given two congruent nonparallel segments, show that it is always possible to find a translation followed by a rotation so that the image of one segment will be the other segment.

2. Given two parallel lines, explain how to transform one onto the other using the following.
  a. A rotation. Describe a center and an angle of rotation.
  b. A translation. Describe all possible translations.

3. Given any point with coordinates (h, k), what are the coordinates of the image of the point under half-turn about $A(1, 0)$?

4. For each of the following figures, trace the figure on tracing paper, rotate the tracing by $180°$ about the given point O, sketch the image, and then make a conjecture about the kind of figure that is formed by the union of the original figure and its image. In each case, explain why you think your conjecture is true.

a.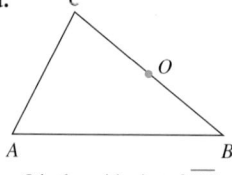
O is the midpoint of $\overline{BC}$.

b.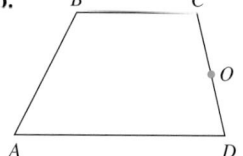
$ABCD$ is a trapezoid and O is the midpoint of $\overline{CD}$.

c.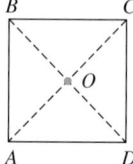
$ABCD$ is a square and O is the intersection of its diagonals.

5. When a line is rotated about a point O, by angle α, the image of the line can be found by rotating any two points on the line. A different way is to drop the perpendicular from O to ℓ. If P is the point where the perpendicular intersects ℓ, we find P' the image of P under rotation by α about O and construct

k the perpendicular line to $\overline{OP'}$ at P'. Explain why k is the image of ℓ.

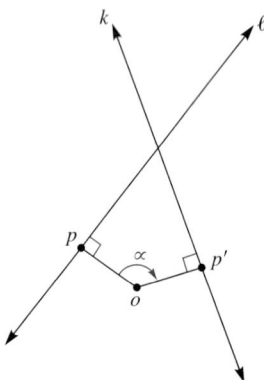

6. Justify each of the following.
  a. When a line is rotated by $90°$ clockwise or counter-clockwise, its image is perpendicular to the line.
  b. When a line is rotated by angle α ($\alpha \neq 180°$) about any point in the plane, then one of the angles formed by the line and its image is also α.

7. ABC is a triangle with a right angle at C. Squares are constructed on one leg and the hypotenuse. Line $\overleftrightarrow{CN}$ is perpendicular to $\overline{AB}$ and $\overline{FG}$. Use the concept of rotation and the result in problem 6 to explain why $\overline{CF}$ and $\overline{EB}$ are congruent and perpendicular.

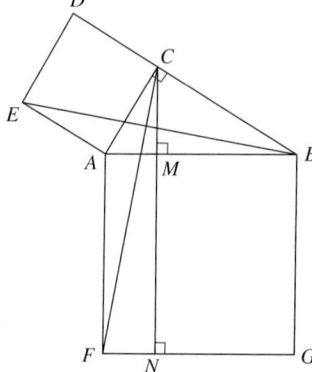

8. Square *ABCD* is divided into four congruent squares by segments connecting the midpoints *G, E, H, J* of the sides of the square.
   a. Use a rotation about *O* and the result of problem 6 to prove that $\overline{BH}$ and $\overline{AE}$ are congruent and perpendicular.
   b. Use slopes to show that $\overline{BH}$ and $\overline{AE}$ are perpendicular.

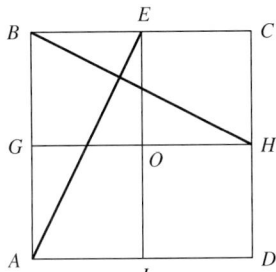

Open-Ended

9. A drawing of a cube, shown in the following figure, can be created by drawing a square *ABCD*, finding its image under a translation defined by the slide arrow from *A* to *A'* so that $AA' = AB$, and connecting the points *A, B, C,* and *D* with their corresponding images.

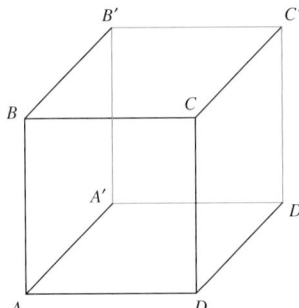

   Draw several other perspective geometric figures using translations. In each case, name the figures and indicate the slide arrow that defines the translation.

10. Wall stenciling has been used to obtain an effect similar to that of wallpapering. The stencil pattern in the following figure can be used to create a border on a wall.

   Measure the length of a wall of a room and design your own stencil pattern to create a border. Cut the pattern from a sheet of plastic or cardboard. Define the translation that will accomplish creating an appropriate border for the wall.

11. The following pattern can be created by rotating figure *A* about *O* clockwise by the indicated angle, then rotating the image *B* about *O* by the same angle, and then rotating the image *C* about *O* by the same angle, and so on until one of the images coincides with the original figure *A*.

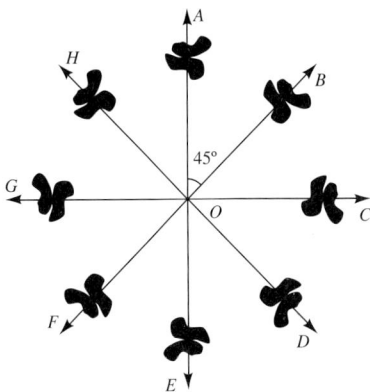

   Make several designs with different numbers of congruent figures around a circle in which the image of each figure under the same rotation is the next figure and so that one of the images coincides with the original figure.

Cooperative Learning

12. Mark a point *A* on a sheet of paper and set a straightedge through *A* as shown in the following figure. Find a circular shape (a jar lid is a good choice) and mark point *P* on the edge of the shape. Place the shape on the straightedge so that *P* coincides with *A*. Consider the path traced by *P* as the circle rolls so that its edge stays in contact with the straightedge all the time and until *P* comes in contact with the straightedge again at point *B*. (The drawing is not to scale.)

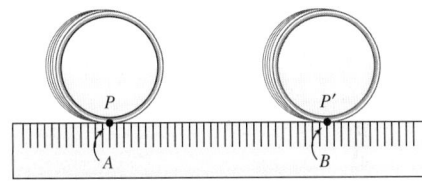

   a. Have one member of your group roll the circular shape and another draw the path traced by *P* as accurately as possible.
   b. Discuss how to check if the path traced by point *P* is an arc of a circle.
   c. Find the length of $\overline{AB}$.

Connecting Mathematics to the Classroom

13. A student asks if every translation on a grid can be accomplished by a translation along a vertical direction followed by a translation along a horizontal direction. How do you respond?
14. A student asks why, in a half-turn, the direction is never specified. How do you respond?
15. Noah claims that he can construct the two touching circles (they have exactly one point in common) shown in the figure in two different ways; by choosing a point *P* on the circle with center *O* and finding its image under a half-turn about *P* or by translating the circle with center *O* by $\overrightarrow{OP}$. Consequently, he says that the image of any figure under half-turn can also be achieved by a translation. How do you respond?

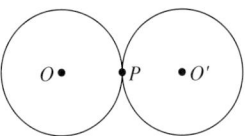

16. Alicia is interested in construction problems and would like to accomplish the following construction.

    Given ∠BAC and point P in the interior of the angle, construct X on $\overrightarrow{AB}$ and Y on $\overrightarrow{AC}$ so that $\overline{XY}$ goes through P in such a way that P is the midpoint of $\overline{XY}$.

    Alicia says that her idea is to pick several points on $\overrightarrow{AC}$, find their images under a half turn about P, and the point whose image will fall on $\overrightarrow{AB}$ is the required point X and its preimage will be Y. Alicia's teacher said that the idea is great, but she pointed out that perhaps none of the images of the chosen points will fall on $\overrightarrow{AB}$, and therefore one should find the images of all the points on $\overrightarrow{AC}$. How would you help Alicia?

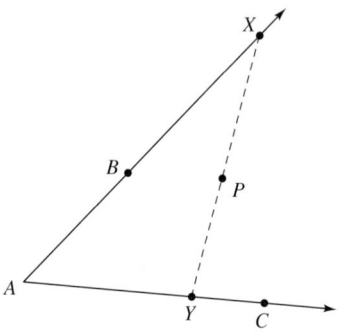

GeoGebra Activities

17. Use GeoGebra Lab 11 activities 6–8 to investigate the following properties of translations.
    - A figure and its image are congruent.
    - The image of a line is a line parallel to it.

18. Use GeoGebra Lab 11 activities 9–11 to investigate properties of rotations.
19. Use GeoGebra to draw an equilateral triangle and two altitudes of the triangle. Let O be the point at which the altitudes intersect. Rotate the triangle by 120° about O in any direction. Make a conjecture based on this experiment. Do you think your conjecture may be true for some triangles that are not equilateral?

National Assessments

National Assessment of Educational Progress (NAEP) Question

When the figure above is rotated 90° clockwise, which of the following is the resulting figure?

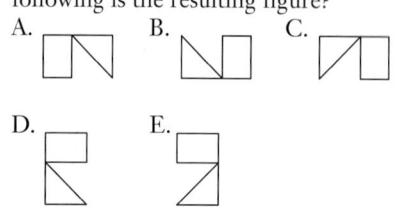

NAEP, Grade 8, 2011

13-2 Reflections and Glide Reflections

Reflections

Another isometry is a **reflection**, or **flip**. One example of a reflection often encountered in our daily lives is a mirror image. Figure 21 shows a figure with its mirror image.

Mirror

Figure 21

We obtain reflections in a line in various ways. Consider the half tree shown in Figure 22(a). Folding the paper along the **reflecting line** and drawing the image gives the **mirror image**, or **image**, of the half tree. In Figure 22(b), the paper is shown unfolded. Another way to simulate a reflection in a line involves using a Mira, as illustrated in Figure 22(c).

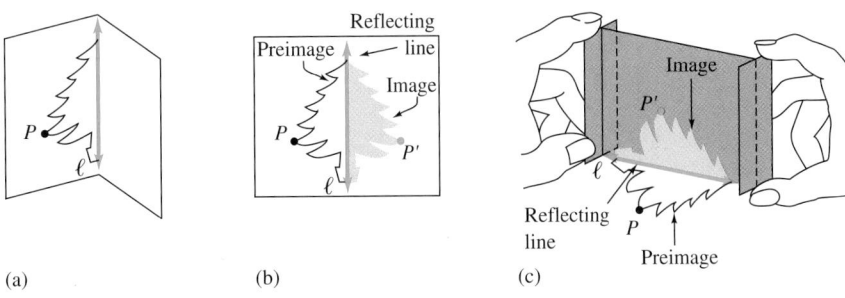

Figure 22

In Figure 23(a), the image of P under a reflection in line ℓ is P'. $\overline{PP'}$ is both perpendicular to and bisected by ℓ, or equivalently, ℓ is the perpendicular bisector of $\overline{PP'}$. In Figure 23(b), P is its own image under the reflection in line ℓ. If ℓ were a mirror, then P' would be the mirror image of P.

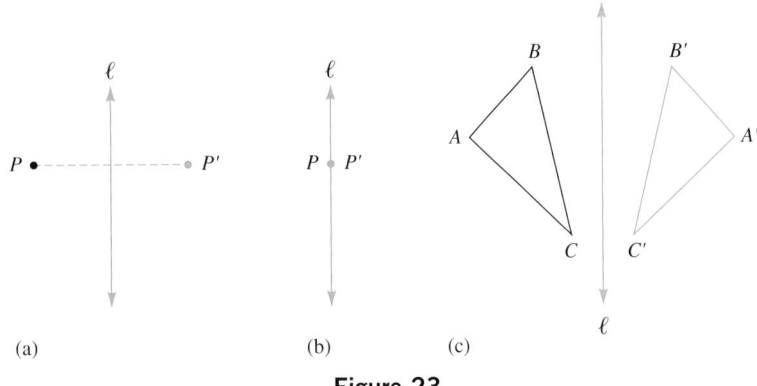

Figure 23

This leads us to the following definition of a reflection.

Definition of Reflection

A **reflection** in line ℓ is a function from the plane to the plane that pairs each point P not on ℓ with a point P' in such a way that ℓ is the perpendicular bisector of $\overline{PP'}$. If P is on ℓ, then $P' = P$.

In Figure 23(c), we see another property of a reflection. In the original triangle ABC, if we walk clockwise around the vertices, starting at vertex A, we see the vertices in the order A-B-C. However, in the reflection image of triangle ABC, if we start at A' (the image of A) and walk clockwise, we see the vertices in the order: A'-C'-B'. Thus a reflection does something that neither a translation nor a rotation does; it reverses the **orientation** of the original figure.

There are many methods of constructing a reflection image. We illustrated reflection constructions with paper folding and a Mira. Next, we illustrate the construction of the image of a figure under a reflection in a line with tracing paper.

Constructing a Reflection by Using Tracing Paper

Aligning the reference point in Figure 24 ensures that no translating occurs along the reflecting line when the reflection is performed. If we wish the image to be on the paper with the original, we may indent the tracing paper or acetate sheet to mark the images of the original vertices.

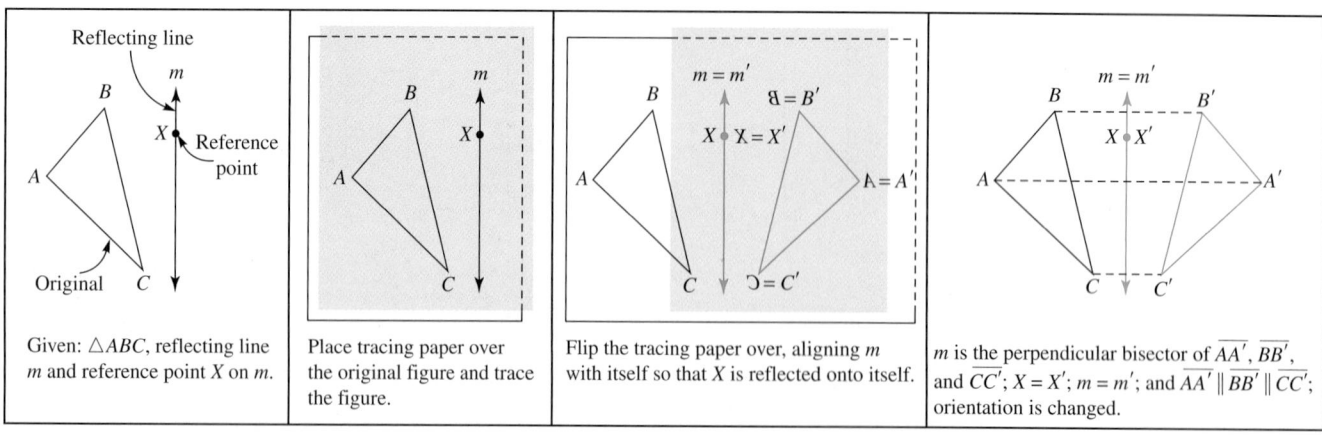

Given: △ABC, reflecting line *m* and reference point *X* on *m*. | Place tracing paper over the original figure and trace the figure. | Flip the tracing paper over, aligning *m* with itself so that *X* is reflected onto itself. | *m* is the perpendicular bisector of $\overline{AA'}$, $\overline{BB'}$, and $\overline{CC'}$; $X = X'$; $m = m'$; and $\overline{AA'} \parallel \overline{BB'} \parallel \overline{CC'}$; orientation is changed.

Figure 24   Construction of a reflection using tracing paper

As with other motions, a reflection may be constructed with a compass and straightedge as explored in Now Try This 5.

▶ **NOW TRY THIS 5**

NTT 5: Construct a perpendicular from *P* to line *m*. Find *P'* so that line *m* is the perpendicular bisector of $\overline{PP'}$. Points *P* and *P'* are the endpoints of a diagonal of a rhombus. The other diagonal lies along line *m*.

Use the definition of a reflection in a line to construct the image *P'* of point *P* in Figure 25 under reflection in line *m*. *Hint:* Construct the perpendicular to *m* through *P*.

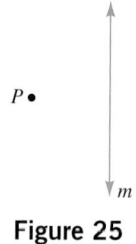

Figure 25

Some students have more difficulty applying motions to geometric figures, such as lines, than to points. Example 5 deals with a reflection of a line.

Example 5

Describe how to construct the image of line ℓ under a reflection in line *m* in Figure 26.

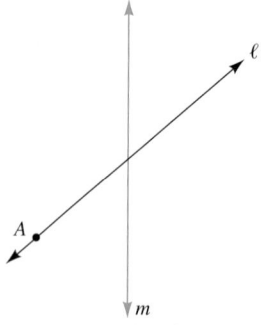

Figure 26

Solution   Under any isometry, the image of a line is a line. Thus, to determine the image of line ℓ, it is sufficient to choose any two points on the line and find their images. The images determine the line that is the image of line ℓ. We choose two points whose images are easy to find. Point *X*, the intersection of ℓ and *m*, is its own image. If we choose point *A* and use the method in

Now Try This 5, we construct A', the image of A, shown in Figure 27, and determine ℓ', the image of ℓ.

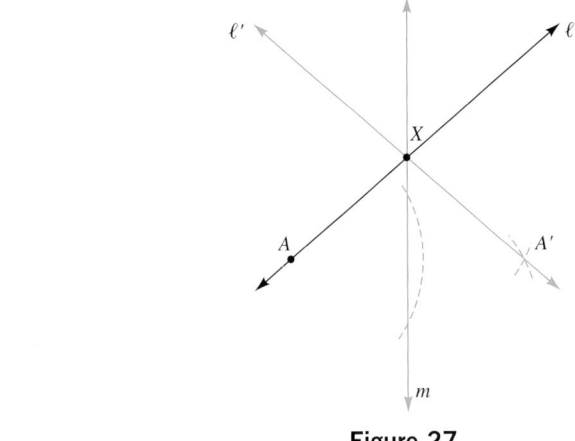

Figure 27

Constructing a Reflection on Dot Paper or a Geoboard

On dot paper or a geoboard, the images of figures under a reflection can sometimes be found by inspection, as seen in Example 6.

Example 6

In Figure 28, find the image of $\triangle ABC$ under a reflection in line m.

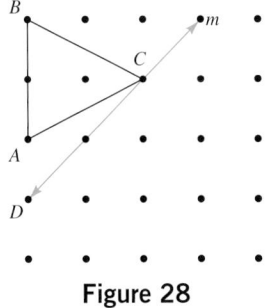

Figure 28

Solution   The image $A'B'C'$ is given in Figure 29. Note that C is the image of itself and the images of the vertices A and B are A' and B' such that m is the perpendicular bisector of $\overline{AA'}$ and $\overline{BB'}$.

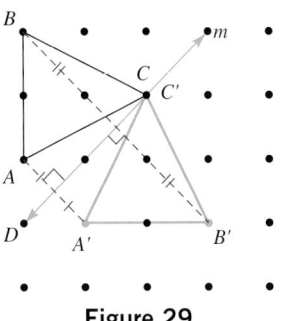

Figure 29

NTT 6: Answers can be found in Answers at the back of the book.

▶ **NOW TRY THIS 6**

Trace △*ABC* and △*A'B'C'* from Figure 29 on a sheet of paper (without tracing line *m*). Find the line of reflection using paper folding.

Reflections, rotations, translations, and glide reflections (introduced on page 780) appear in the school curriculum, as shown in the following partial student page.

School Book Page

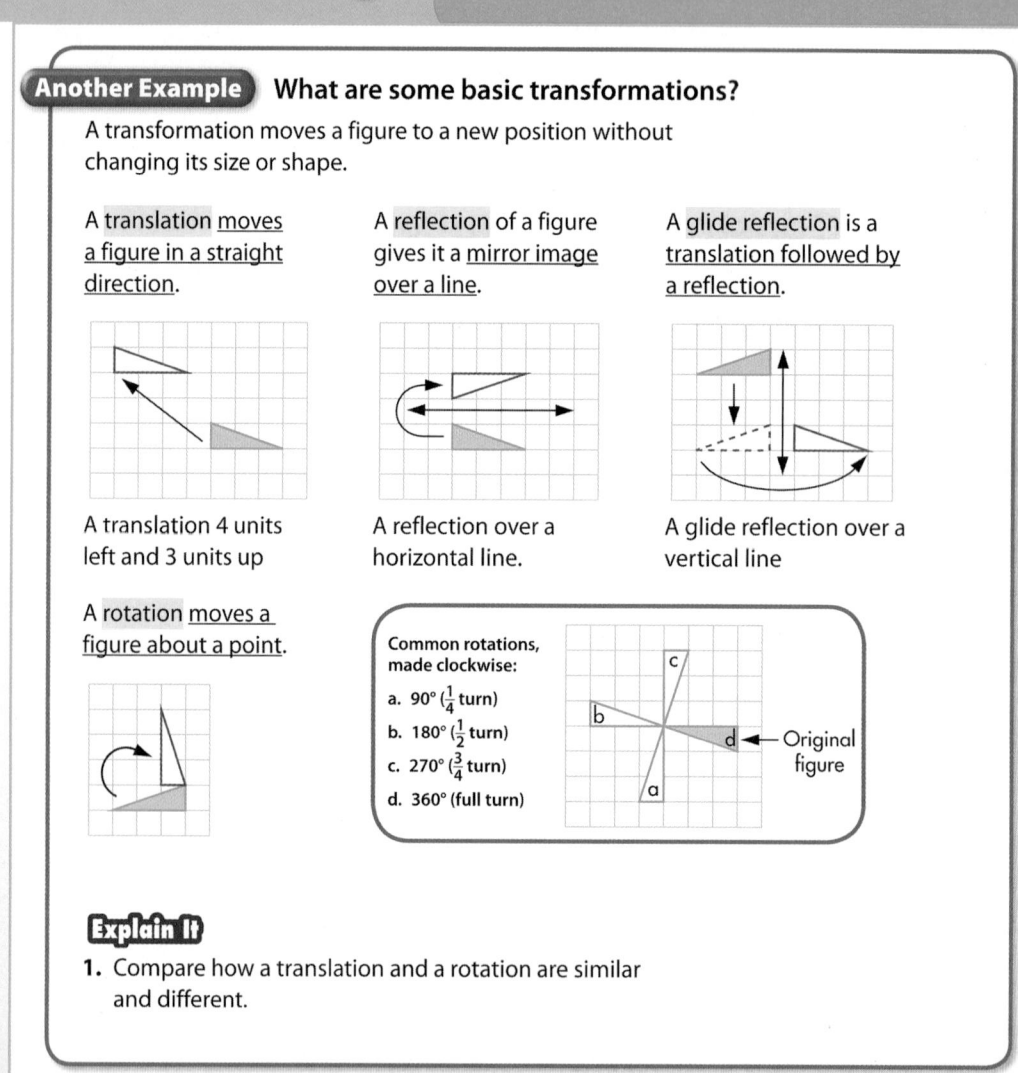

Another Example   **What are some basic transformations?**

A transformation moves a figure to a new position without changing its size or shape.

A translation moves a figure in a straight direction.

A reflection of a figure gives it a mirror image over a line.

A glide reflection is a translation followed by a reflection.

A translation 4 units left and 3 units up

A reflection over a horizontal line.

A glide reflection over a vertical line

A rotation moves a figure about a point.

Common rotations, made clockwise:
a. 90° ($\frac{1}{4}$ turn)
b. 180° ($\frac{1}{2}$ turn)
c. 270° ($\frac{3}{4}$ turn)
d. 360° (full turn)

← Original figure

Explain It

1. Compare how a translation and a rotation are similar and different.

Reflections in a Coordinate Grid

For some reflecting lines, like the x-axis, the y-axis and the line $y = x$, it is easy to find the coordinates of the image, given the coordinates of the point. In Figure 30, the line $y = x$ bisects the angle between the x-axis and the y-axis. The image of $A(1, 4)$ is the point $A'(4, 1)$. Also the image of $B(^-3, 0)$ is $B'(0, ^-3)$.

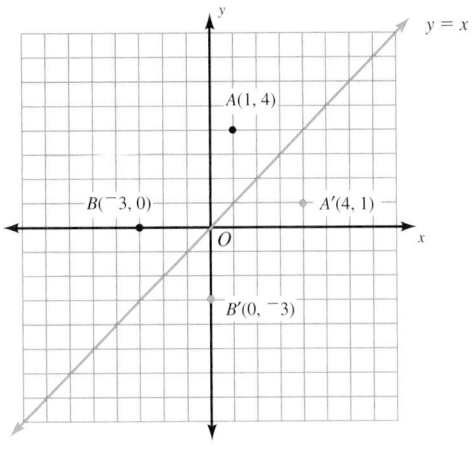

Figure 30

A reflection of a point with coordinates (a, b) in the line $y = x$ is generalized in Now Try This 7.

▶ **NOW TRY THIS 7**

NTT 7: Answers can be found in Answers at the back of the book.

Show that in general the image of $P(a, b)$ under reflection in the line $y = x$ is the point $P'(b, a)$, that is that the reflection in the line $y = x$ interchanges the coordinates of the point.

Applications of Reflections

One natural application of reflections is in finding lines of symmetry of figures. *A line of symmetry of a figure is a reflecting line that can be used to make a figure its own image under the reflection* as in Figure 31(a) and (b). Consider Figure 31(a) where various lines of symmetry (or reflecting lines) can be found. (How many are there?)

(a)

(b)

Figure 31

Another application is seen when a ray of light bounces off a mirror or a billiard ball bounces off the rail of a billiard table. The **angle of incidence**, the angle formed by the incoming ray in

Figure 32 and a line perpendicular to the mirror, is congruent to the **angle of reflection**, the angle between the reflected ray and the line perpendicular to the mirror.

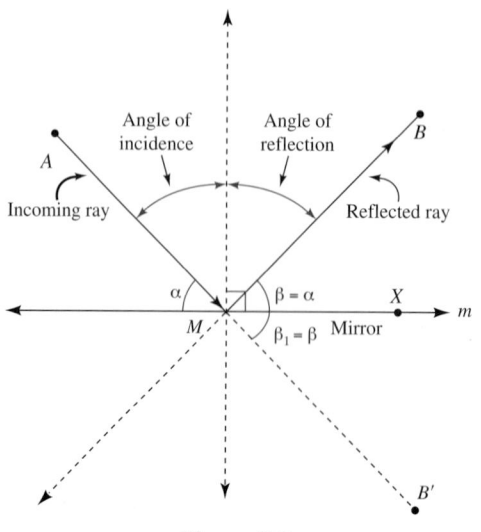

Figure 32

Because the angle of incidence is congruent to the angle of reflection, the respective complements of these angles must be congruent. If the measures of these complements are α and β, as indicated in Figure 32, then $\alpha = \beta$. Figure 32 shows B', the image of B under reflection in m, and hence $\angle XMB'$ is the image of $\angle XMB$. Notice that β, the measure of $\angle XMB$, must equal β_1, the measure of $\angle XMB'$, because reflection preserves angle measurement. Because $\alpha = \beta$ and $\beta = \beta_1$, we have $\alpha = \beta_1$. For that reason, points $A, M,$ and B' are collinear. We can show that these facts imply *Fermat's Principle:* Light follows the path of shortest distance; that is, the path A-M-B that light travels is the shortest among all the paths connecting A with a point in the mirror to B.

▶ **NOW TRY THIS 8**

NTT 8: Answers can be found in Answers at the back of the book.

Trace Figure 32 and mark on the mirror m a point P other than M. Prove that $AM + MB < AP + PB$. Show that $MB = MB'$ and $BP = B'P$, and then use the Triangle Inequality applied to $\triangle APB'$, and that $A, M,$ and B' are collinear.

Glide Reflections

Another basic isometry is a **glide reflection**. An example of a glide reflection is shown in the footprints of Figure 33. We consider the footprint labeled F_1 to have been translated to footprint F_2

Activity Manual

Use *Glide Reflections* to explore glide reflections and their properties.

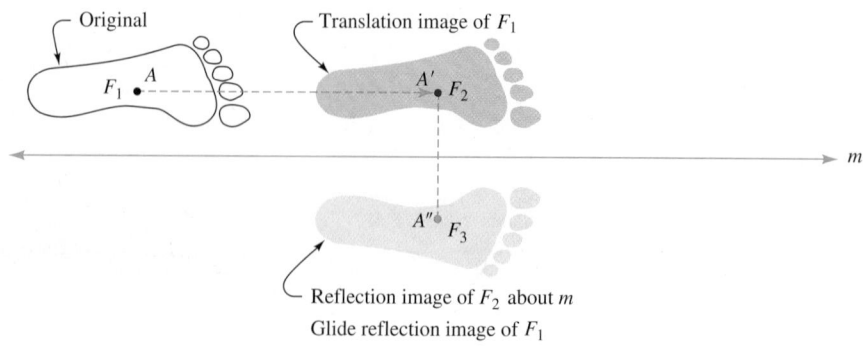

Figure 33

and then reflected over line m (parallel to the direction of the translation) to yield F_3, the image of F_2. F_3 is the final image of F_1. Point A is translated to point A' and then point A' is reflected over line m (parallel to the direction of the translation) to point A''. Thus, A'' is the image of A in a glide reflection. The illustration in Figure 33 leads us to the following definition.

Definition of Glide Reflection

A **glide reflection** is a transformation composed of a translation, followed by a reflection in a line parallel to the slide arrow.

Because a glide reflection is not equal to a translation, rotation or a reflection it is a new isometry. Given two congruent polygons it is possible to show that one can be transformed to the other by a sequence of isometries. In fact, it can be shown that for such polygons it is possible to transform one to the other by using a single isometry, that is by one translation, one rotation, one reflection or by one glide reflection.

Because constructing a glide reflection involves constructing a translation and a reflection, the task of constructing a glide reflection is not a new problem. An example is seen in Figure 34.

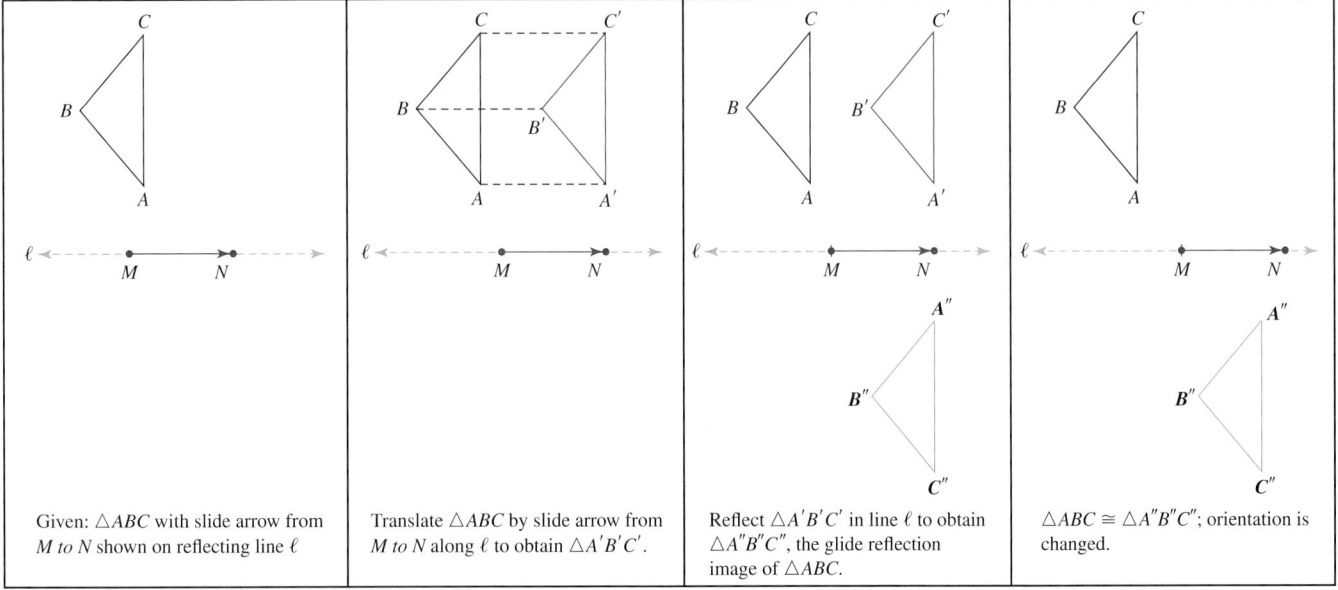

Given: $\triangle ABC$ with slide arrow from M to N shown on reflecting line ℓ	Translate $\triangle ABC$ by slide arrow from M to N along ℓ to obtain $\triangle A'B'C'$.	Reflect $\triangle A'B'C'$ in line ℓ to obtain $\triangle A''B''C''$, the glide reflection image of $\triangle ABC$.	$\triangle ABC \cong \triangle A''B''C''$; orientation is changed.

Figure 34 Construction of a glide reflection

Congruence via Isometries

We have seen that under an isometry, the image of a triangle is a congruent triangle. Given two congruent polygons, it is possible to show that one can be transformed to the other by using a sequence of isometries.

Definition of Congruent Figures via Isometries

Two geometric figures are **congruent** if, and only if, one is an image of the other under a single isometry or under a composition of isometries.

Example 7 shows one illustration of this approach to congruence.

Example 7

ABCD in Figure 35 is a rectangle. Describe a sequence of isometries to show the following.

a. $\triangle ADC \cong \triangle CBA$ **b.** $\triangle ADC \cong \triangle BCD$ **c.** $\triangle ADC \cong \triangle DAB$

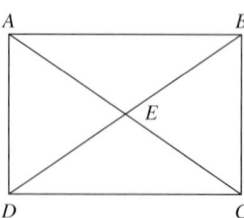

Figure 35

Solution   Answers vary.
a. A half-turn of $\triangle ADC$ with center *E* is one such transformation.
b. A reflection in a line passing through *E* and parallel to $\overline{AD}$ is one such transformation.
c. A reflection of $\triangle ADC$ in a line passing through *E* and parallel to $\overline{DC}$ is one such transformation.

Assessment 13-2A

1. Describe how to find the image of the given quadrilateral in a reflection in ℓ.   *

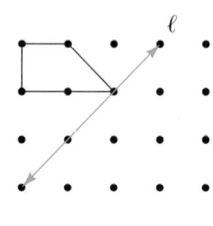

2. Determine which of the following figures have a reflecting line (or line of symmetry) such that the image of the figure under the reflection is the figure itself. In each case, find as many such reflecting lines as possible.
   a. Circle   The lines containing the diameters
   b. Segment   *
   c. Line   Any line perpendicular to the given line or the line itself
   d. Square   *
   e. Scalene triangle   None
   f. Equilateral triangle   Perpendicular bisector of each side
   g. Trapezoid whose base angles are not congruent   None
   h. Kite   *
   i. Regular hexagon   *
3. Determine the final result when $\triangle ABC$ is reflected in line ℓ and then the image is reflected again in ℓ.   The original figure

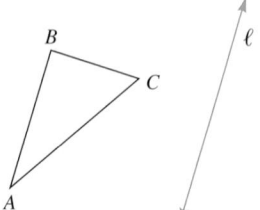

4. Draw a line and then draw a circle whose center is not on the line. Find the image of the circle under a reflection in the line.   *
5. **a.** Refer to the following figure and suppose lines ℓ and m are parallel and $\triangle ABC$ is reflected in ℓ to obtain $\triangle A'B'C'$ and then $\triangle A'B'C'$ is reflected in m to obtain $\triangle A''B''C''$. Determine whether the same final image is obtained if $\triangle ABC$ is reflected first in m and then its image is reflected in ℓ.   *

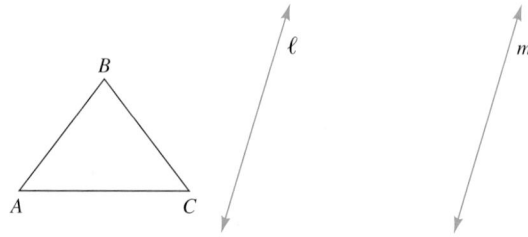

   b. Conjecture what single transformation will take $\triangle ABC$ directly to $\triangle A''B''C''$. Check your conjecture using tracing paper.   *
6. Use a Mira, if available, to investigate exercise 5.   *
7. Given $\triangle ABC$ and its reflection image $\triangle A'B'C'$, find the line of reflection.   *

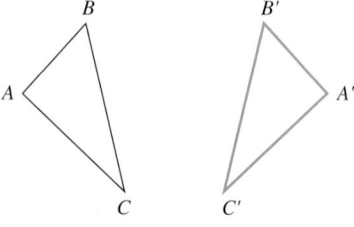

8. **a.** The word TOT is its own image when it is reflected through a vertical line through O, as shown in the following figure. List some other words that are their own images when reflected similarly.   *

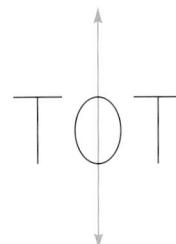

b. The image of BOOK is still BOOK when it is reflected through a horizontal line. List some other words that have the same property. Which uppercase letters can you use?   *

c. With an appropriate font, the image of 1881 is 1881 after reflection in either a horizontal or vertical line, as shown in the following figure. What some other natural numbers less than 2000 have this property?   *

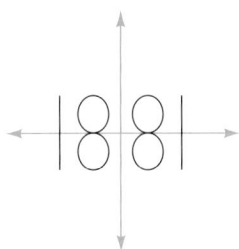

9. Find the equation of the image of the line with equation $y = 2x + 1$ when it is reflected in each of the following.
   a. x-axis $y = ^-2x - 1$
   b. y-axis $y = ^-2x + 1$
   c. $y = x$ $y = \frac{1}{2}x - \frac{1}{2}$
10. A glide reflection is determined by a translation parallel to a given line followed by a reflection in that line.
    a. Determine whether the same final image is obtained if the reflection is followed by the translation.   *
    b. Use your answer in (a) to determine whether the reflection and translation involved in the glide reflection commute.   *
11. Decide whether a reflection, a translation, a rotation, or a glide reflection will transform figure 1 into each of the other numbered figures (there may be more than one answer).   *

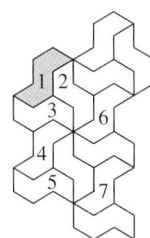

12. Given points $A(3, 4), B(2, ^-6)$, and $C(^-2, 5)$, find the coordinates of the images of these points under each of the following transformations.
    a. Reflection in the x-axis $A'(3, ^-4), B'(2, 6), C'(^-2, ^-5)$
    b. Reflection in the line $y = x$ $A'(4, 3), B'(^-6, 2), C'(5, ^-2)$

13. **a.** Conjecture what the image of a point with coordinates (x, y) will be under each of the transformations in exercise 12.   (i) $(x, ^-y)$ (ii) (y, x)
    b. Suppose a point P with coordinates (x, y) is reflected in the x-axis and then its image P' is reflected in the y-axis to obtain P''. What are the coordinates of P'' in terms of x and y?   *
14. Find the equations of the images of the following lines when reflected in the x-axis.
    a. $y = ^-x + 3$ $y = x - 3$
    b. $y = 0$ $y = 0$
15. Find the equation of the images of the following lines when the reflection line is the y-axis.
    a. $y = ^-x + 3$ $y = x + 3$
    b. $y = 0$ $y = 0$
16. **a.** The two circles "touch" each other at point P; that is, the tangent to one circle at P is also the tangent to the other circle. Find the line of reflection such that the image of the smaller circle will be in the interior of the larger circle, but still "touching" the larger circle.   *

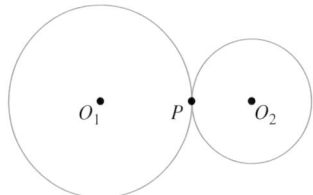

    b. Name a line of symmetry for the figure. $\overleftrightarrow{O_1 O_2}$
17. Two congruent circles with centers O_1 and O_2 intersect at points A and B.

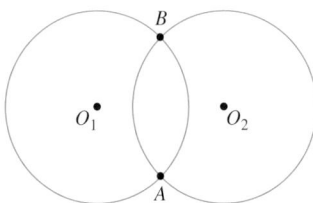

    a. In what line of reflection will the image of the circle with center O_1 be the circle with center O_2? $\overleftrightarrow{AB}$
    b. Can the circle with center O_1 be transformed into the circle with center O_2 by a translation? If so, describe the translation.   Yes, a translation taking O_1 to O_2.
18. Graph each of the following pairs of lines and for each construct the corresponding line of reflection so that the image of one line in the pair will be the second line. For each, identify the line of reflection.
    a. $y = ^-x$ and $y = x$ $x = 0$ or $y = 0$
    b. $y = 2x$ and $y = ^-2x$ $x = 0$ or $y = 0$
19. Point P' is the image of P (not shown) under a glide reflection determined by the slide arrow $\overrightarrow{AB}$ and line ℓ parallel to $\overleftrightarrow{AB}$.

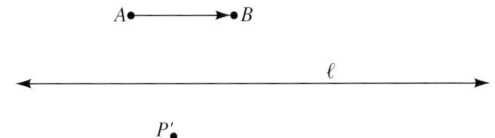

a. Describe the transformation that takes P' back to P. *
b. Construct any $\triangle DEF$ and find its image $\triangle D'E'F'$ under the glide reflection described earlier in the question. Then apply the same glide reflection to $\triangle D'E'F'$ to find its image $\triangle D''E''F''$. What seems to be a single transformation under which the image of $\triangle DEF$ will be $\triangle D''E''F''$? *

20. Consider the glide reflection determined by the slide arrow $\overrightarrow{OA}$, where O is the origin and $A(2, 0)$, and the line of reflection is the x-axis. Answer the following.
a. Find the image of any point (x, y) under this glide reflection in terms of x and y. $(x, y) \rightarrow (x + 2, {}^{-}y)$
b. If $(3, 5)$ is the image of a point P under the glide reflection, find the coordinates of P. $(1, {}^{-}5)$

Assessment 13-2B

1. Find the image of the given quadrilateral in a reflection in ℓ. *

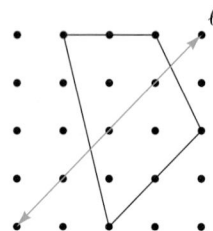

2. Determine which of the following figures have line of symmetry such that the image of the figure under the reflection is the figure itself. In each case, find as many reflecting lines as possible.
a. Arc *
b. Ray *
c. Two perpendicular lines *
d. Rectangle *
e. Isosceles triangle *
f. Isosceles trapezoid *
g. Rhombus *
h. Regular n-gon *

3. Determine the final result when $\triangle ABC$ is reflected in line ℓ and then the image is reflected again in ℓ. *

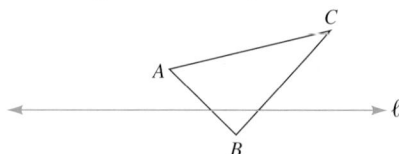

4. Sketch the image of the figure below through a reflection in line ℓ.

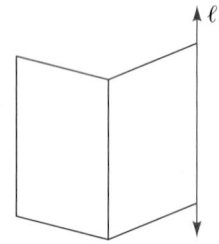

5. a. For the following figure, construct the image of $\triangle ABC$ if $\triangle ABC$ is reflected in ℓ to obtain $\triangle A'B'C'$ and then $\triangle A'B'C'$ is reflected in m to obtain $\triangle A''B''C''$ (ℓ and m intersect at O). *

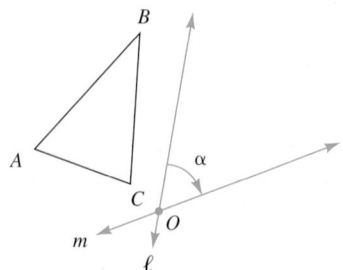

b. Conjecture what single transformation will take $\triangle ABC$ directly to $\triangle A''B''C''$. Check your conjecture using tracing paper.   Rotation about O by 2α clockwise
c. Answer the questions in (a) and in (b) for the case in which ℓ and m are perpendicular. *

6. Use a Mira, if available, to investigate exercises 4 and 5. *

7. a. Construct a "stylized" bow tie by using a reflection of the triangle below. *

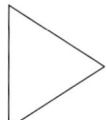

b. Tell which reflecting line was used in part (a) and why. *
c. Is there more than one reflecting line that could have been used in part (a)? If so, where are others? *

8. Draw a reflecting line to show that the name OTTO can be its own image under a reflection. *

9. Describe the set of all lines that are their own images when reflected in each of the following.
a. x-axis   The x-axis and all lines perpendicular to the x-axis
b. y-axis   The y-axis and all lines perpendicular to the y-axis
c. $y = x$ The line $y = x$ and all lines perpendicular to it

10. a. Copy the congruent triangles below on a piece of paper. Find as many reflecting lines as needed to take $\triangle XYZ$ to $\triangle X'Y'Z'$ using successive reflections. *

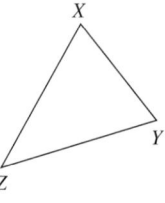

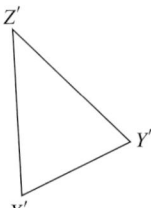

b. Explain why the isometry in part (a) cannot be a translation, a rotation, or a reflection. *

11. **a.** In the Pharlemina's Favorite quilt pattern below, describe a motion that will take part (a) green to part (b) blue. *

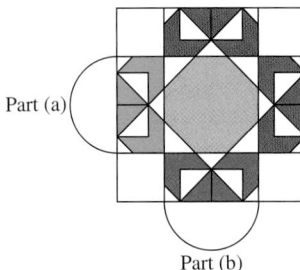

Part (a)

Part (b)

b. Follow the directions in (a) for the Dutchman's Puzzle quilt pattern shown. *

Part (a)   Part (b)

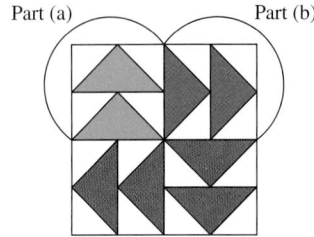

12. Given points $A(3, 4)$, $B(2, ^-6)$, and $C(^-2, 5)$, find the coordinates of the images of these points under each of the following transformations.
    a. Reflection in the y-axis $A'(^-3, 4), B'(^-2, ^-6), C'(2, 5)$
    b. Reflection in the line $y = ^-x$ $A'(^-4, ^-3), B'(6, ^-2), C'(^-5, 2)$
13. Conjecture what the image of a point with coordinates (x, y) will be under each of the transformations in exercise 12. *
14. Find the equations of the images of the following lines when reflected in the x-axis.
    a. $y = 3x$ $y = ^-3x$
    b. $y = ^-x$ $y = x$
    c. $x = 0$ $x = 0$
15. Find the equation of the images of the lines in exercise 14 when the reflection line is the y-axis. *
16. In which line will the two intersecting circles reflect onto themselves; that is, the image of the circles will be the same two circles? $\overleftrightarrow{O_1O_2}$

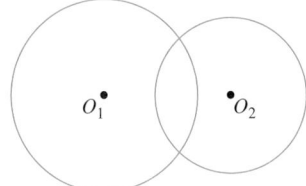

17. Construct a square and a circle of an appropriate size so that it will be possible to transform the circle by a reflection into the square such that the image of the circle will be tangent to all sides of the square. Identify the line of reflection. *

18. Graph each of the following pairs of lines and for each construct the corresponding line of reflection so that the image of one line in the pair will be the second line. For each, identify the line of reflection.
    a. $x = 0$ and $y = 0$ $y = x$ or $y = ^-x$
    b. $x = ^-2$ and $x = 3$ $x = \frac{1}{2}$
19. If $\overline{P'Q'}$ is the image of $\overline{PQ}$ (not shown) under a glide reflection determined by the slide arrow $\overrightarrow{AB}$ and $\overleftrightarrow{AB}$, answer the following.

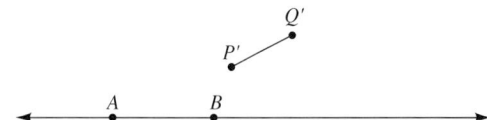

    a. Describe the transformation that takes $\overline{P'Q'}$ to $\overline{PQ}$. *
    b. Construct any quadrilateral $DEFG$ and find its image $D'E'F'G'$ under the glide reflection described earlier. Then apply the same glide reflection to $D'E'F'G'$ and find its image $D''E''F''G''$. What is a single transformation under which the image of $DEFG$ will be $D''E''F''G''$? *
20. Consider the glide reflection determined by the slide arrow $\overrightarrow{OA}$, where O is the origin and $A(0, 2)$, and the line of reflection is the y-axis.
    a. Find the image of any point (x, y) under this glide reflection in terms of x and y. $(x, y) \rightarrow (x, y + 2)$
    b. If $(3, 5)$ is the image of a point P under the glide reflection, find the coordinates of P. $(^-3, 3)$
21. A *fixed point* of a transformation is a point whose image is the point itself. List all the fixed points of the following transformations.
    a. Reflection in line ℓ All points on ℓ The point O
    b. Rotations by a given angle and direction about point O
    c. Translation with slide arrow from A to B; $A \neq B$ None
    d. Glide reflection determined by a translation with slide arrow from A to B followed by a reflection in line ℓ parallel to line AB; $A \neq B$ None

---

Mathematical Connections 13-2

Answers to Mathematical Connections can be found in the Answers section at the back of the book.

Reasoning

1. **a.** Draw an isosceles triangle ABC and then construct a line such that the image of $\triangle ABC$ when reflected in the line is $\triangle ABC$. Explain why the line you constructed has the required property.
   b. For what kind of triangles is it possible to find more than one line with the property in (a)? Justify your answer.

   c. Given a scalene triangle ABC, is it possible to find a line ℓ such that when $\triangle ABC$ is reflected in ℓ, its image is itself?
   d. Draw a circle with center O and a line with the property that the image of the circle, when reflected in the line, is the original circle. Identify all such lines. Justify your answer.

2. When a billiard ball bounces off a side of a pool table, assume the angle of incidence is congruent to the angle of reflection. In the following figure showing a scale drawing of a billiard table, a cue ball is at point A. Show how a player should aim to hit two sides of the table and then the ball at B. Justify your solution.

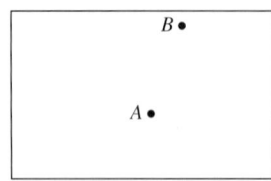

3. In $\triangle ABC$, M and N are midpoints of two sides as shown. Point A' is the intersection of the altitude to $\overline{CB}$ with $\overline{CB}$. Points D and E are the points of intersection of the perpendiculars from M and N respectively to $\overline{CB}$.
   a. Why A' is the reflection of A in $\overleftrightarrow{MN}$?
   b. Why is A' the reflection of C in $\overleftrightarrow{MD}$ and also the reflection of B in $\overleftrightarrow{NE}$?
   c. Explain why $\angle MA'N \cong \angle A$, $\angle MA'C \cong \angle C$, and $\angle NA'E \cong \angle B$.
   d. What property of angles in the triangle follows from part (c)? Why?

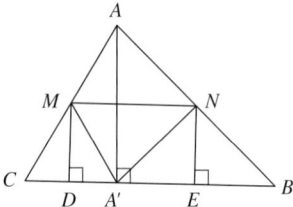

4. Use the fact that a rectangle has a reflection symmetry in either line connecting the midpoints of its sides to prove that the diagonals of a rectangle are congruent.

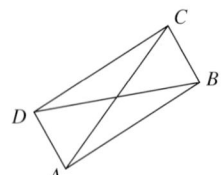

5. Use the following drawing to explain how a periscope works:

6. $\triangle A'B'C'$ is the image of $\triangle ABC$ under glide reflection determined by the slide arrow $\overrightarrow{DE}$ and the reflecting line $\overleftrightarrow{DE}$.

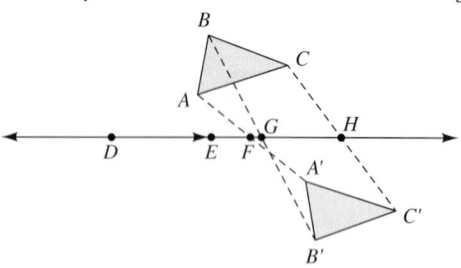

   a. Check that the intersections of $\overline{AA'}$, $\overline{BB'}$, and $\overline{CC'}$, with the line of reflection are the midpoints of these segments.
   b. Prove that if P is any point and P' is its image under the glide reflection, then the midpoint of $\overline{PP'}$ is on the line of reflection. (Use the theorem from Chapter 12 saying that if a line bisects one side of a triangle and is parallel to a second side, then it bisects the third side.)
   c. If it is given that $\triangle A'B'C'$ is the image of $\triangle ABC$ under a glide reflection, but neither the line of reflection nor the slide arrow is known, explain how to construct the line of reflection and the slide arrow.

7. Andrea, a civil engineer, was asked to make a plan for the shortest possible path connecting a landmark P and two roads on $\overrightarrow{AB}$ and $\overrightarrow{AC}$. She needed to find point X on $\overrightarrow{AB}$ and point Y on $\overrightarrow{AC}$ so that the perimeter of $\triangle PXY$ is as short as possible. She wanted to explain her approach to her teenage daughter. Andrea first drew arbitrary points X' on $\overrightarrow{AB}$ and Y' on $\overrightarrow{AC}$ and then $\triangle X'PY'$ for one possible path along the sides of the triangle, but not necessarily the shortest. Then she found P', the reflection of P in $\overrightarrow{AB}$ and P'' the reflection of P in $\overrightarrow{AC}$, and claimed that the perimeter of the triangle equals the length of the path $P'X'Y'P''$. She then connected P' with P'' by a straight line and found the intersection points X and Y with $\overrightarrow{AB}$ and $\overrightarrow{AC}$, respectively, claiming that the path along the sides of $\triangle XPY$ is the required shortest path.

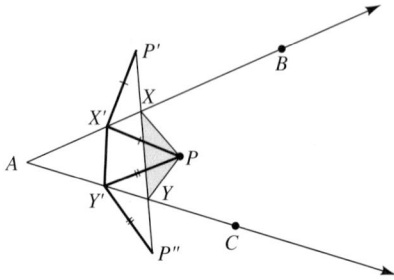

   Answer the following.
   a. Why the perimeter of $\triangle X'PY'$ is equal to the length of the path $P'X'Y'P''$?
   b. Why the length of the path $P'XPYP''$ is equal to $P'P''$?
   c. Why the perimeter of $\triangle XPY$ shorter than the perimeter of $\triangle X'PY'$? Did Andrea find the shortest possible path? Explain.

Open-Ended

8. In the following figure representing a miniature golf course hole, explain how to aim the ball so that it gets in the hole, if it is to bounce off
   a. one wall only.   b. two walls.

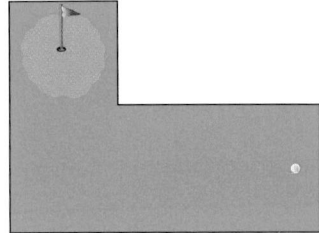

9. Design several wall stencil patterns using a reflection. In each case, explain how you would use the stencil in practice.
10. Design wall stencil patterns using a glide reflection.

Cooperative Learning

11. In the following figure representing a pool table, ball B is sent on a path that makes a 45° angle with the table wall, as shown. It bounces off the wall 5 times and returns to its original position.

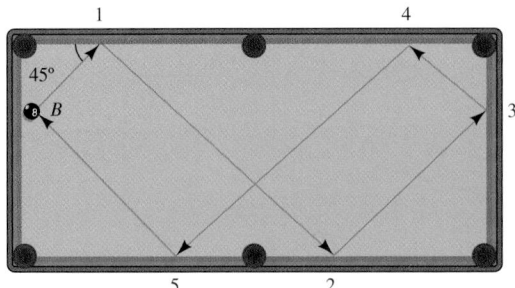

   a. Have each member of your group use graph paper to construct rectangular models of different-sized pool tables. Simulate the experiment using any tools (such as a straightedge, compass, and protractor) by choosing different positions for ball B.
   b. Share the results of your experiments with the rest of the group and together conjecture for which dimensions of the pool table and for what positions of B the experiment described in the problem will work.

Connecting Mathematics to the Classroom

12. A student asks, "If I have a point and its image, is that enough to determine whether the image was found using a translation, reflection, rotation, or glide reflection?" How do you respond?
13. Another student asks a question similar to question 12 but is concerned about a segment and its image. How do you respond to this student?
14. Sammi said that in the drawing below the image A' of point A under a reflection in line ℓ can also be found by a rotation through α shown with center O. Therefore, every reflection is actually a rotation. How do you respond?

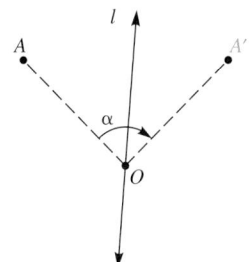

15. Gloria claims that Sammi's example in problem 14 is not a good one because only one point is used. She drew two examples of figures in which one is the image of the other under reflection in the y-axis as well as under a half-turn with center A. In the second example, the image of the two upper circles under reflection in line j are the two lower circles. However, the lower circles are also the image of the upper circles under a half-turn about N. Therefore, Gloria claims that the image of every figure under reflection can also be obtained by rotation. How do you respond?

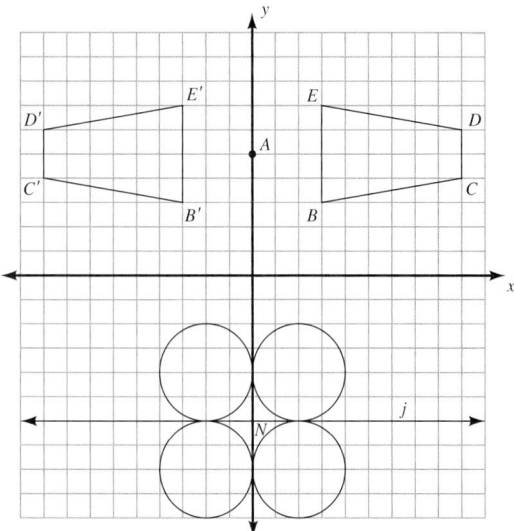

GeoGebra Activities

16. Use GeoGebra Lab 11 activities 1–5 to investigate properties of reflections.
17. Use GeoGebra Lab 12, activity 1 to investigate glide reflections.
18. a. Use GeoGebra to draw $\triangle ABC$ and three lines m, n, and p that intersect in a single point, as shown below. Reflect $\triangle ABC$ in line m to obtain its image $\triangle A'B'C'$. Then reflect $\triangle A'B'C'$ in line n to obtain $\triangle A''B''C''$. Finally, reflect $\triangle A''B''C''$ in line p to obtain the final image $\triangle A'''B'''C'''$.

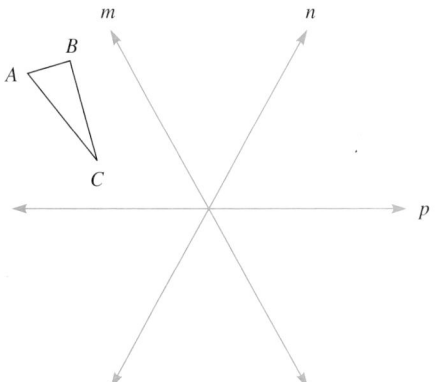

   b. Find a single line q that could be used to reflect the original $\triangle ABC$ onto the final image.

Review Problems

19. Which single digits are their own images under a rotation by an angle whose measure is less than 360°?
20. What is the image of a point (a, b) under a half-turn about the origin?

21. Find all possible rotations that transform a circle onto itself.

22. Explain how an isometry can be used to construct a rectangle whose area is equal to that of the parallelogram *ABCD* in the following figure:

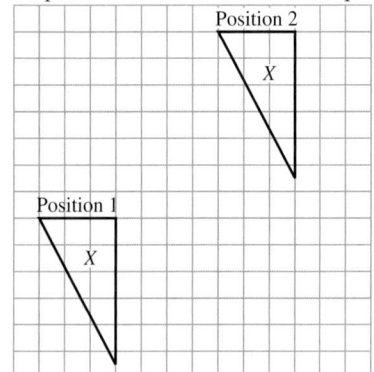

National Assessments

National Assessment of Educational Progress (NAEP) Questions

You will need the piece labeled *X* to answer this question.

Which word best describe how to move the piece labeled *X* from position 1 to position 2?

A. Flip
B. Fold
C. Slide
D. Turn

NAEP, Grade 4, 2009

Tony flips the figure over the dotted line. Which picture shows the result of the flip?

A. 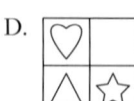   B.

C.   D.

NAEP, Grade 4, 2011

Which of the following figures shows the reflection of triangle of *ABC* over line *PQ*?

A. 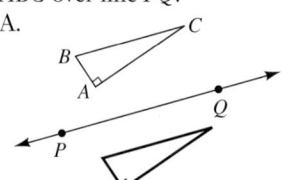   B.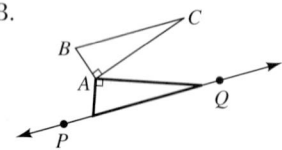

C. 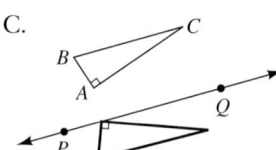   D.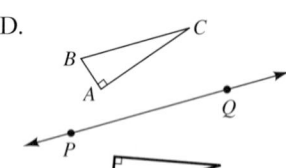

E.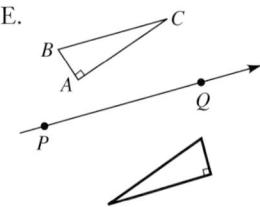

NAEP, Grade 8, 2011

13-3 Dilations

13-3 Objectives

Students will be able to understand and explain

• A dilation and its construction.

• An application of dilations.

Isometries preserve distance. Consequently, the image of a figure under an isometry is a figure congruent to the original. A different type of transformation may happen when a slide of △*ABC* is projected on a screen to obtain △*A'B'C'*. All objects on the slide are often enlarged on the screen by the same factor. Figure 36 shows an example of such a transformation, a **dilation** or a **size transformation**. The point *O* is the *center* of the dilation and 2 is the *scale factor*. Points *O*, *A*, and *A'* are collinear and *OA'* = 2*OA*; also, *O*, *C*, and *C'* are collinear and *OC'* = 2*OC*. Similarly, *O*, *B*, and *B'* are collinear and *OB'* = 2*OB*. It can be shown that △*A'B'C'* is similar to △*ABC* and that each side of △*A'B'C'* is twice as long as the corresponding sides of △*ABC*.

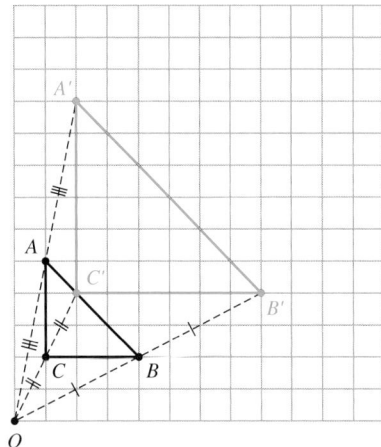

Figure 36

In general, we have the following definition and theorem.

Activity Manual

Use *Dilations* to introduce dilations and explore their properties.

> ## Definition of Dilation
>
> A **dilation** from the plane to the plane with center O and scale factor $r > 0$ is a transformation that assigns to each point A in the plane the point A' such that $O, A,$ and A' are collinear, O is not between A and A', and $OA' = rOA$. O is its own image.

> ## Theorem 13-2
>
> Under a dilation, the image of a polygon is a similar polygon.

It is possible to define a dilation when the scale factor is negative except that O *must be between A and A'.*

Figure 37 shows a construction of a dilation with center O and scale factor of $\frac{1}{2}$. This construction refers to compass and straightedge constructions in Chapter 12.

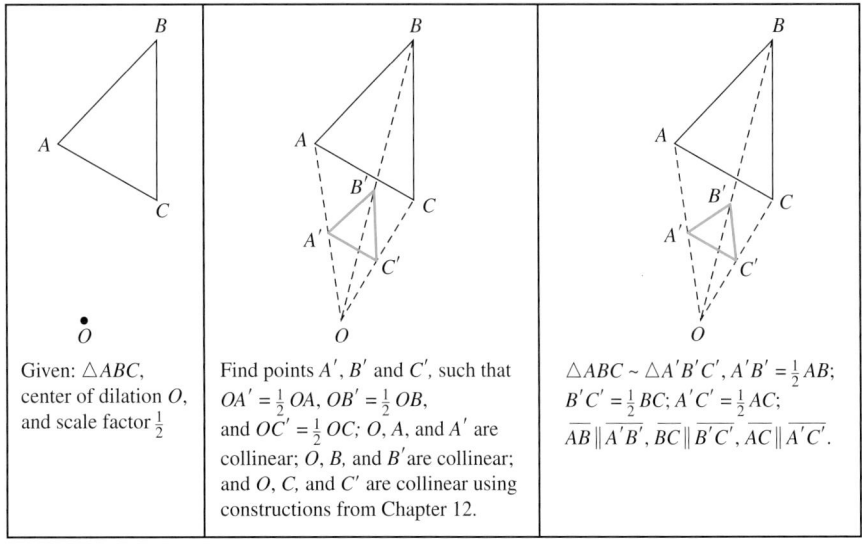

Given: $\triangle ABC$, center of dilation O, and scale factor $\frac{1}{2}$

Find points A', B' and C', such that $OA' = \frac{1}{2} OA$, $OB' = \frac{1}{2} OB$, and $OC' = \frac{1}{2} OC$; O, A, and A' are collinear; O, B, and B' are collinear; and O, C, and C' are collinear using constructions from Chapter 12.

$\triangle ABC \sim \triangle A'B'C'$, $A'B' = \frac{1}{2} AB$; $B'C' = \frac{1}{2} BC$; $A'C' = \frac{1}{2} AC$; $\overline{AB} \| \overline{A'B'}$, $\overline{BC} \| \overline{B'C'}$, $\overline{AC} \| \overline{A'C'}$.

Figure 37   Construction of a dilation with center O and scale factor $\frac{1}{2}$

Example 8

a. In Figure 38(a), find the image of point P under a dilation with center O and scale factor $\frac{2}{3}$.

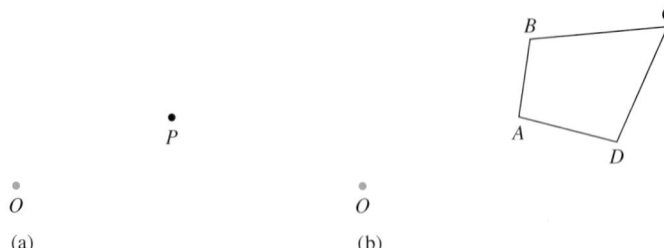

(a)   (b)

Figure 38

b. Find the image of the quadrilateral $ABCD$ in Figure 38(b) under the dilation with center O and scale factor $\frac{2}{3}$.

Solution

a. In Figure 39(a), we connect O with P and divide $\overline{OP}$ into three congruent parts. The point P' is the image of P because $OP' = \frac{2}{3}\,OP$.

b. We find the image of each of the vertices as in part (a) and connect the images to obtain the quadrilateral $A'B'C'D'$, shown in Figure 39(b).

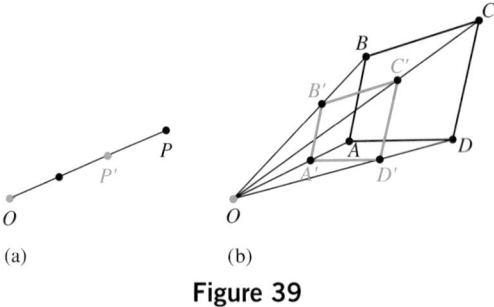

(a)   (b)

Figure 39

In Figure 39(b), the sides of the quadrilateral $A'B'C'D'$ are all parallel to the corresponding sides of the original quadrilateral, and the angles of the quadrilateral $A'B'C'D'$ are congruent to the corresponding angles of quadrilateral $ABCD$. Also, each side in the quadrilateral $A'B'C'D'$ is $\frac{2}{3}$ as long as the corresponding side of quadrilateral $ABCD$. These properties are true for any dilation and are summarized in the following theorem.

Theorem 13-3

A dilation with center O and scale factor $r > 0$ has the following properties:

a. The image of a line segment is a line segment parallel to the original segment and r times as long.

b. The image of an angle is an angle congruent to the original angle.

Example 9

Show that $\triangle ABC$ in Figure 40 is the image of $\triangle ADE$ under a dilation. Identify the center of the dilation and the scale factor.

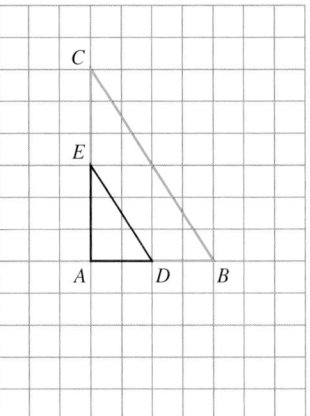

Figure 40

Solution   Because $\dfrac{AB}{AD} = \dfrac{AC}{AE} = 2$, we choose A as the center of the dilation and 2 as the scale factor. Notice that under this transformation, the image of A is A itself. The image of D is B, and the image of E is C.

From Theorem 13-2, we know that the image of a polygon under a dilation is a similar polygon. However, for any two similar polygons it is not always possible to find a dilation such that the image of one polygon under the dilation is the other polygon. But, given two similar polygons, we can "move" one polygon to a place such that it will be the image of the other under a dilation. Example 10 shows such an instance.

Example 10

Show that $\triangle ABC$ in Figure 41 is the image of $\triangle APQ$ under a succession of isometries followed by a dilation.

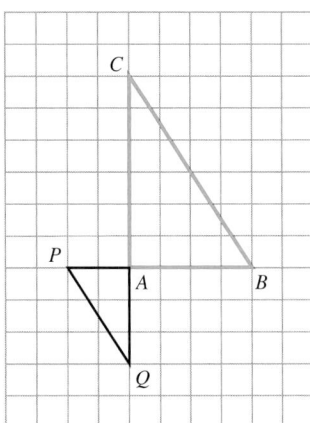

Figure 41

Solution   We use the strategy of *looking at a related problem*. In Example 9, the common vertex served as the center of the dilation. Here, we first rotate $\triangle APQ$ using a half-turn about A to obtain $\triangle AP'Q'$, as shown in Figure 42.

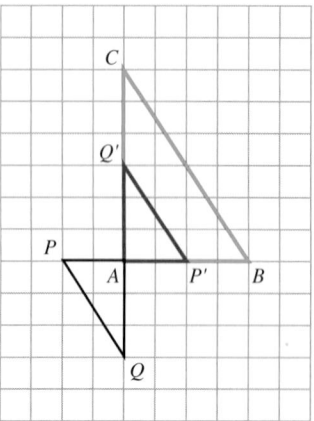

Figure 42

Now C is the image of Q' under a dilation with center at A and scale factor 2. Also, B is the image of P', and A is the image of itself under this transformation. Thus, $\triangle ABC$ can be obtained from $\triangle APQ$ by first finding the image of $\triangle APQ$ under a half-turn about A and then applying a dilation with center A and scale factor 2 to that image.

Earlier it was noted that a dilation could be defined using a negative scale factor. If so, a dilation with A as the center, and scale factor $^-2$ could be used to achieve the desired result.

Examples 9 and 10 are a basis for a definition of similar figures via isometries and dilations.

> **Definition of Similar Figures via Isometries and Dilations**
>
> Two figures are **similar** if, and only if, it is possible to transform one onto the other by an isometry (or a sequence of isometries) followed by a dilation.

Applications of Dilations

One way to make an object appear three-dimensional is to use a **perspective drawing**. For example, to make a letter appear three-dimensional we can use a dilation with an appropriate center O and a scale factor to create a three-dimensional effect, as shown in Figure 43 for the letter C.

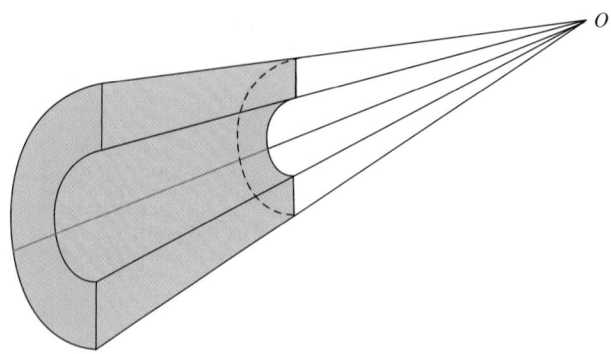

Figure 43

When a picture of an object is taken with an antique box camera in Figure 44(a) with the pinhole lens at O, the object appears upside down on the negative. The picture of the object on the negative can be interpreted as an image under composition of a half-turn and a dilation. Figure 44(b) illustrates the image of an arrow from A to B under a composition of a half-turn followed by a dilation with scale factor $\frac{1}{2}$.

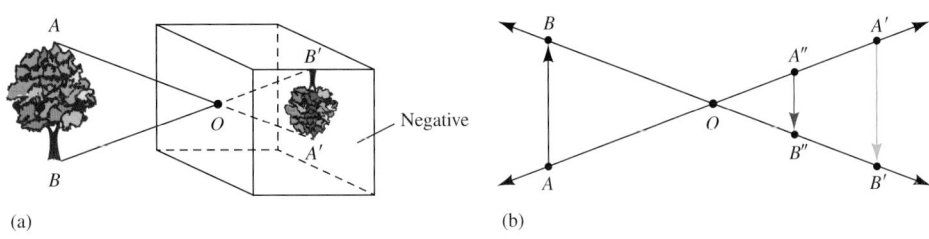

Figure 44

In Figure 44(b) the image A' of A under the half-turn with center O is found on the ray opposite $\overrightarrow{OA}$ so that $OA' = OA$. The point B', the image of B under the half-turn, is found similarly on the ray opposite $\overrightarrow{OB}$. The images of A' and B' under the dilation are A'' and B'', respectively. Consequently, the image of the arrow from A to B under the composition of the half-turn followed by the dilation is the arrow from A'' to B''.

A geometric construction application of dilations is shown in Example 11.

Example 11

Inscribe a square in the semicircle and its given diameter in Figure 45 so that two of the vertices of the square are on the semicircle and two are on the diameter $\overline{AB}$.

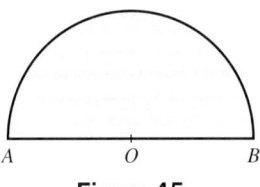

Figure 45

Solution The required square $XYZW$ is seen in Figure 46. It appears to be symmetrical about line n, the perpendicular bisector of $\overline{AB}$.

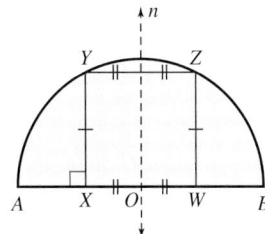

Figure 46

To solve the problem, we use the strategy of using a *related simpler problem*. It is easier to construct a square whose base lies on $\overline{AB}$ so that n is its perpendicular bisector and the other two vertices lie anywhere in the interior of the semicircular region as in Figure 47.

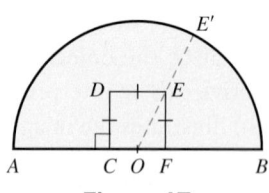

Figure 47

Such a square is *CDEF*. We know that under a dilation with center *O* with any scale factor, the image *C'D'E'F'* of square *CDEF* is also a square. From the definition of a dilation, we know that *O*, *E*, and *E'* are collinear. If we use any dilation with a positive scale factor, the image *E'* of *E* will still be on $\overrightarrow{OE}$. Under an appropriate dilation, the image of *E* will also be on the semicircle. Thus we find the exact image of *E* by drawing a ray with endpoint *O* and containing *E*. The intersection of the ray and the semicircle is the desired *E'*. Similarly the image *D'* of *D* can be found to determine the desired square as seen in Figure 48. Next we drop perpendiculars from *D'* and *E'* to $\overline{AB}$ to determine *C'* and *F'*. *C'D'E'F'* is the desired square.

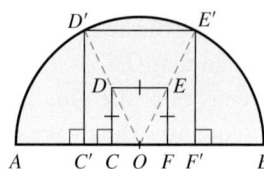

Figure 48

Assessment 13-3A

1. In the following figures, describe a sequence of isometries followed by a dilation so that the larger triangle is the final image of the smaller one.   *

   a.   **b.**

   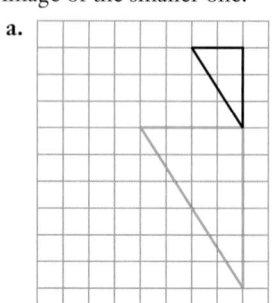

2. In the following drawing, find the image of △*ABC* under the dilation with center *O* and scale factor $\frac{1}{2}$.   *

   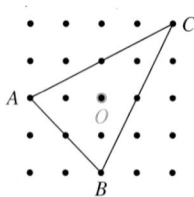

3. In each of the following drawings, find transformations that will take △*ABC* to its image, △*A'B'C'*, which is similar.
   a. *B'C'* = 2 *BC*   *

   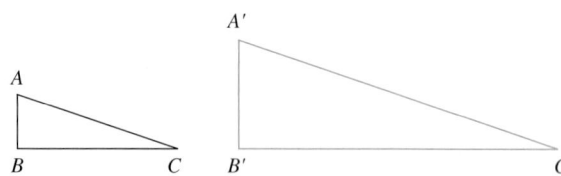

   b. *A'*, *B'*, and *C'* are the respective midpoints of $\overline{BC}, \overline{AC},$ and $\overline{AB}$.

   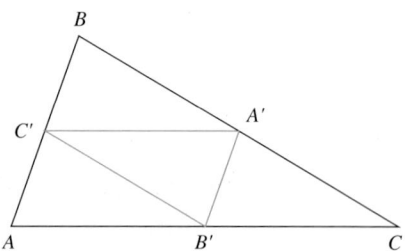

4. In the following figure, the smaller triangle is the image of the larger under a dilation centered at point O. Find the scale factor and the length of x and y as pictured.   *

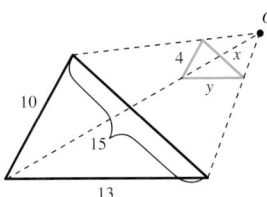

5. $\overline{A'B'}$ is the image of a candle $\overline{AB}$ produced by a box camera. Given the measurements in the figure, find the height of the candle.   12 cm

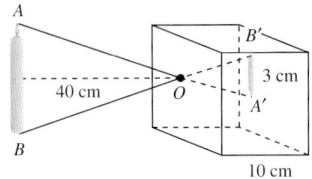

6. Find the coordinates of the images of $A(2, 3)$, and $B(^-2, 3)$ under the following transformations. Assume that all dilations are centered at the origin.
   a. A dilation with a scale factor 3 followed by a dilation with a scale factor 2   (12, 18), (^-12, 18)
   b. A dilation with a scale factor 2 followed by a dilation with a scale factor 3   Same as in (a)
7. If a dilation with center O and scale factor r takes a quadrilateral $ABCD$ to $A'B'C'D'$, what dilation will take $A'B'C'D'$ back to $ABCD$?   *
8. a. Explain why in a coordinate system a dilation with center at the origin and scale factor $r > 0$ is given by $(x, y) \rightarrow (rx, ry)$.   *

b. The transformation $(x, y) \rightarrow (^-2x, ^-2y)$ can be achieved by a dilation followed by an isometry. Find that dilation and the isometry.   *
c. Find the equations of the images of each of the following lines under the dilation in part (a) with the given scale factor r.

   i. $y = 2x, r = \dfrac{1}{2}$ $y = 2x$

   ii. $y = 2x, r = 2$ $y = 2x$

   iii. $y = 2x + 1, r = \dfrac{1}{3}$ $y = 2x + \dfrac{1}{3}$

   iv. $y = ^-x - 1, r = 3$ $y = ^-x - 3$

9. What sequence of transformations will transform a circle with center O_1 and radius 2 onto a circle with center O_2 and radius 3?   *
10. Consider a dilation on a number line where the center of the transformation has 0 as its coordinate and the scale factor is 3. Describe the set of images of the points whose coordinates are integers.   *
11. In the following figure, the smaller pentagon is the image of the larger under a dilation centered at point O. Find the scale factor and the length of x and y as pictured.   *

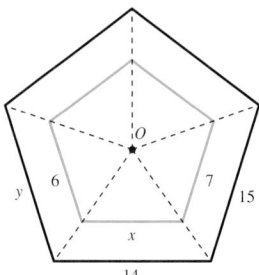

12. If a 2″ × 3″ photograph is enlarged to a 4″ × 6″ photograph, Describe how to represent this by a dilation.   *

Assessment 13-3B

1. In the following figures, describe a sequence of isometries followed by a dilation so that the larger triangle is the final image of the smaller one.   *

   a. 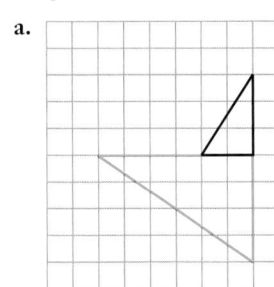   b.

2. Find the image of $\triangle ABC$ under the dilation with center O and scale factor $\dfrac{1}{2}$.   *

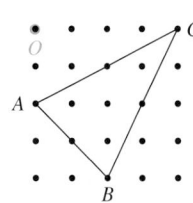

3. In each of the following drawings, find transformations that will take $\triangle ABC$ to its image, $\triangle A'B'C'$, which is similar.
   a. $AB = 2\, A'B'$ *

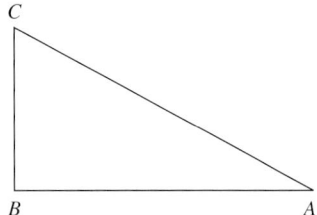
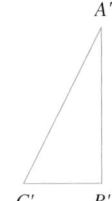

b. $\overline{AB} \parallel \overline{A'B'}$; points A, C, and A' are collinear; points B, C', and B' are collinear; $AB = \dfrac{2}{3}A'B'$ *

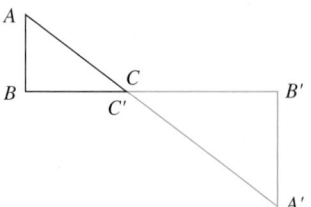

4. The following describes a dilation with center O and image of the segment of length 4 in blue. Find the scale factor and the lengths designated by x and y. $x = 12; y = 10$; scale factor 3

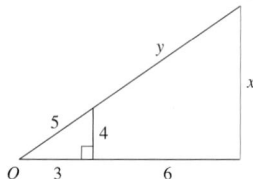

5. The following describes a dilation with center O and image in blue. Find the scale factor and the lengths designated by x and y. $x = 5; y = 4$; scale factor 2

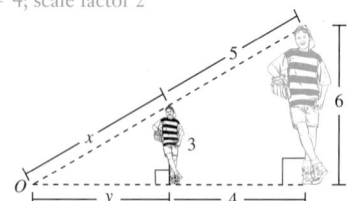

6. Find the coordinates of the images of $A(2, 3)$ and $B(^-2, 3)$ under the following transformations. Assume that all dilations are centered at the origin.
   a. A dilation with scale factor 2 followed by a translation with a slide arrow from $(2, 1)$ to $(3, 4)$ $(5, 9), (^-3, 9)$
   b. A translation with a slide arrow from $(2, 1)$ to $(3, 4)$ followed by a dilation with scale factor 2 $(6, 12), (^-2, 12)$
   c. What can you conclude from your answers to parts (a) and (b) concerning the order in which the transformations are performed? *

7. What dilation will transform a circle with center at the origin and radius 4 onto a circle with the same center and radius 3? *
8. What sequence of transformations will transform a circle with center O_1, and radius $\frac{1}{2}$ onto a circle with center O_2 and radius 3? *
9. Sketch the image of the Octagon Quilt pattern with the center of the pattern as the center of a dilation with a scale factor of 2. *

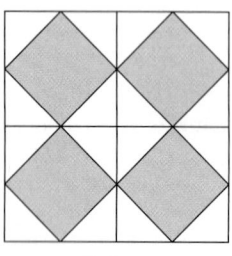

Octagon

10. Copy the following figure onto grid paper and determine the center and the scale factor of the dilation. *

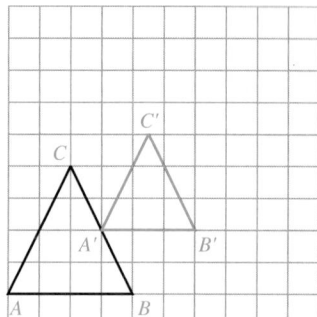

11. What dilation will undo a size transformation with center O and scale factor $\dfrac{3}{4}$?   Dilation with center O and scale factor $\dfrac{4}{3}$
12. Gina claims that she enlarged a $2'' \times 3''$ photograph to a $4\frac{1}{2}'' \times 6\frac{1}{2}''$ photograph. Explain whether or not this is possible. *

Mathematical Connections 13-3

Answers to Mathematical Connections can be found in the Answers section at the back of the book.

Reasoning

1. Which of the following properties do not change under a dilation? Explain how you can be sure of your answers.
   a. Distance between points
   b. Angle measure
   c. Parallelism; that is, if two lines are parallel to each other, then their images are parallel to each other.
2. Explain why under the transformation given by $(x, y) \rightarrow (3x, {}^-3y)$ the image of any figure will be similar to the original figure.
3. **a.** Consider two consecutive dilations, each with center O and scale factors $\dfrac{1}{2}$ and $\dfrac{1}{3}$, respectively. Suppose the

image of figure F under the first transformation is F' and the image of F' under the second transformation is F''. What single transformation will map F directly onto F''? Explain why.
   b. What would be the answer to (a) if the scale factors were r_1 and r_2?
4. **a.** Is the image of a circle with center O under a dilation with center O always a circle? Explain why or why not.
   b. Assume that under a dilation with scale factor r, the image of a segment of length a is a segment of length ra. Answer part (a) of this question in case the center of the dilation is not at the center of the circle.

5. a. Describe an isometry or a sequence of isometries followed by a dilation such that the larger triangle is the final image of the smaller one.
   b. Describe a dilation with center *A* followed by one or two isometries that take the smaller triangle onto the larger.

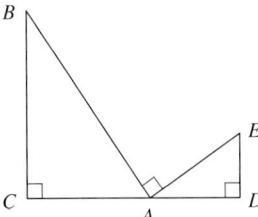

6. Construct an arbitrary triangle. Use an approach similar to the one in the solution of Example 11 (p. 793) to inscribe a square in the triangle as shown.

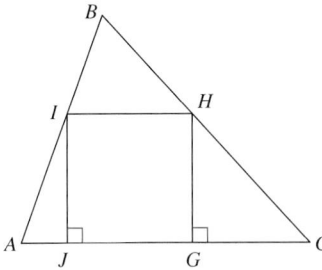

7. Draw any two circles of different size and describe a translation followed by a dilation that will transform the smaller circle onto the larger.
8. Tyto drew a triangle and found its image under dilation with center *O*. The original triangle was accidentally erased. Can Tyto reconstruct the erased triangle if he does not remember the scale factor of his dilation? Justify your answer.

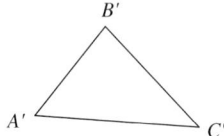

Open-Ended

9. Describe several real-life situations other than the ones discussed in this section in which dilations occur.
10. Use a dilation and isometries to draw a figure that has rotational and line symmetries.

Cooperative Learning

11. Have members of your group draw several figures and find their images under a dilation with a scale factor of 3 and center of your choice.
   a. How does the perimeter of each image compare to the perimeter of the original figure? Compare your answers.
   b. Make a conjecture concerning the relationship between the perimeter of each image and the perimeter of the original figure under a dilation with a scale factor *r*.
   c. Discuss your findings and come up with a group conjecture.

Connecting Mathematics to the Classroom

12. A student asks, "If I have two triangles that are not similar, is it possible to transform one to the other by a sequence of isometries followed by a dilation?" How do you respond?
13. A student says that a coordinate grid under a dilation with the center at the origin and scale factor 2 does not change the grid. The image is still a coordinate grid. How do you respond?

Review Problems

14. Describe a transformation that would "undo" each of the following.
   a. A translation determined by slide arrow from *M* to *N*
   b. A rotation of 75° with center *O* in a clockwise direction
   c. A rotation of 45° with center *A* in a counterclockwise direction
   d. A glide reflection that is the composition of a reflection in line *m* and a translation that takes *A* to *B*, where $\overleftrightarrow{AB} \parallel m$
   e. A reflection in line *n*
15. In the following coordinate plane, find the coordinates of the images of each of the given points in the transformation that is the composition of a reflection in line *m* followed by a reflection in line *n*.

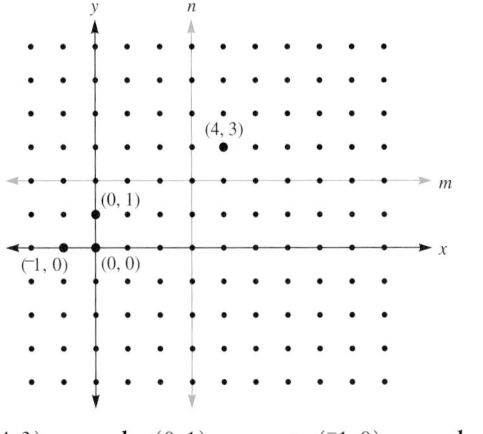

   a. $(4, 3)$ **b.** $(0, 1)$ **c.** $(^-1, 0)$ **d.** $(0, 0)$
16. Find each of the following.
   a. Reflection image of an angle in the line containing its angle bisector
   b. Reflection image of a square in the line containing one of its diagonals
17. Zuni art contains figures similar to the one partially drawn below. Use the pictured reflecting line ℓ to complete this image.

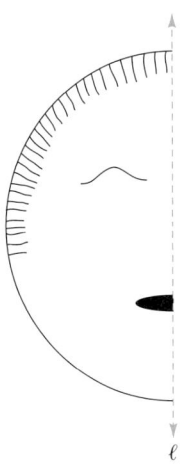

13-4 Tessellations of the Plane

In this section we use concepts from motion geometry to study *tessellations* of the plane. A **tessellation** of a plane is the filling of the plane with repetitions of congruent figures in such a way that no figures overlap and there are no gaps. Similarly, one can tessellate space. The tiling of a floor and various mosaics are examples of tessellations. Maurits C. Escher was a master of tessellations. Many of his drawings have fascinated mathematicians for decades. His *Study of Regular Division of the Plane with Reptiles* (pen, ink, and watercolor), 1939 shape as shown in Figure 49, is a tessellation of the plane by a lizardlike

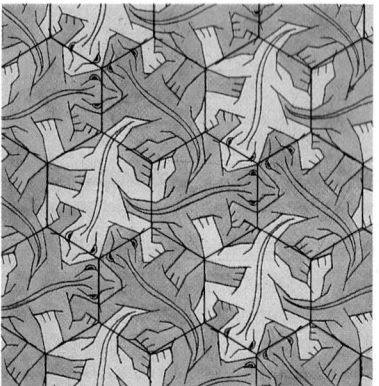

Study of Regular Division of the Plane with Reptiles (1939), M.C. Escher. Copyright © 2011 The M.C. Escher Company, Holland. All rights reserved. www.mcescher.com

Figure 49

At the heart of the tessellation in Figure 49, we see a regular hexagon. But perhaps the simplest tessellation of the plane can be achieved with squares. Figure 50 shows two different tessellations of the plane with squares.

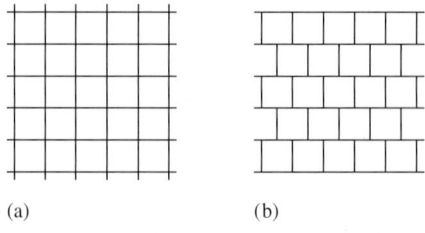

(a)   (b)

Figure 50

Tessellations with Regular Polygons

A **regular tessellation** is constructed with congruent regular polygons joined edge to edge. It is appealing and interesting because of its simplicity. Notice that the tessellation in Figure 50(b) is not a regular tessellation. Figure 51 shows portions of tessellations with equilateral triangles (a) and with regular hexagons (b).

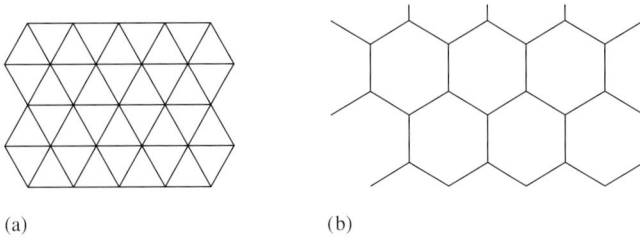

(a)   (b)

Figure 51

To determine other regular polygons that tessellate the plane, we investigate the possible size of the interior angle of a tessellating polygon. If n is the number of sides of a regular polygon, then because the sum of the measures of the exterior angles of the regular polygon is 360°, the measure of a single exterior angle of the polygon is $\dfrac{360°}{n}$. Hence, the measure of an interior angle is $180° - \dfrac{360°}{n}$ because an exterior angle is the supplement of an interior angle. Table 2 gives some values of n, the type of regular polygon related to each, and the angle measure of an interior angle found by using the expression $180° - \dfrac{360°}{n}$.

If a regular polygon tessellates the plane, the sum of the congruent angles of the polygons around every vertex must be 360°. If we divide 360° by each of the angle measures in the table, only 60°, 90°, and 120° divide 360°; hence of the listed regular polygons, only an equilateral triangle, a square, and a regular hexagon can tessellate the plane.

Can other regular polygons tessellate the plane? Notice that $\dfrac{360}{120} = 3$. Hence, 360 divided by a number greater than 120 is less than 3. However, the number of polygons coming together at each vertex cannot be less than 3. Because a polygon with more than six sides has an interior angle greater than 120°, it actually is not necessary to consider polygons with more than six sides. Consequently, no regular polygon with more than six sides can tessellate the plane.

Table 2

Number of Sides (n)	Regular Polygon	Measure of Interior Angle
3	Triangle	60°
4	Square	90°
5	Pentagon	108°
6	Hexagon	120°
7	Heptagon	$128\dfrac{4}{7}$
8	Octagon	135°
9	Nonagon	140°
10	Decagon	144°

The partial student page shown on page 800 introduces a connection between mathematics, art, and nature through tessellations.

School Book Page

Practice

For **1** through **4**, use each polygon to draw a tessellation.

1. hexagon

2. square

3. right triangle

4. equilateral triangle

For **5** through **8**, determine whether each shape tessellates.
If so, trace the figure and draw the tessellation.

5.

6.

7.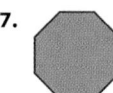

8.

Tessellations can also be seen in everyday life and in nature.
For **9** through **11**, describe the transformation used to tessellate
the shapes.

9.

10.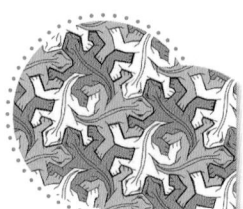

11.

Historical Note

Marjorie Rice

Mathematicians thought they had found all irregular pentagons that tessellate the plane. In 1975, Marjorie Rice (1923–), with no formal training in mathematics, discovered a new type of tessellating pentagon. She went on to discover four more by 1977. Her interest was piqued by reading an article in *Scientific American* by Martin Gardner (1914–2010). Two of the pentagons she found are shown below. The problem of how many types of pentagons tessellate remains unsolved.

Type 9 discovered in February 1976

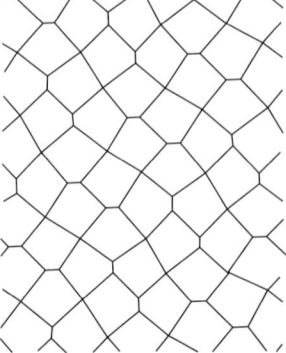

Type 13 discovered in December 1977

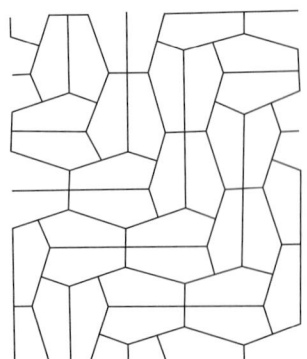

Tessellating with Other Shapes

Next, we consider tessellating the plane with arbitrary convex quadrilaterals. We investigate the problem, with the help of paper or cardboard quadrilaterals. Figure 52 shows an arbitrary convex quadrilateral and a way to tessellate the plane with the quadrilateral. Successive half-turns of the quadrilateral about the midpoints P, Q', and R'' of its sides produces four congruent quadrilaterals around a common vertex. Notice that the sum of the measures of the angles around vertex A is $a + b + c + d$. This is the sum of the measures of the interior angles of the quadrilateral, or $360°$. Hence, four congruent quadrilaterals fit around vertex A. This process can be repeated so

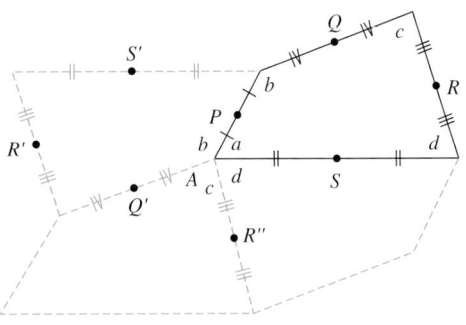

Figure 52

that four congruent quadrilaterals fit around each vertex of the original quadrilateral and its images. Thus, *any convex quadrilateral tessellates a plane*.

As we saw earlier in this section, a regular pentagon does not tessellate the plane. However, some irregular pentagons do. One is shown in Figure 53, along with a tessellation of the plane by the pentagon.

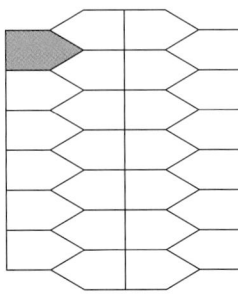

Figure 53

Creating Tessellations with Translations

What other types of designs can be made that tessellate a plane? The plane geometry and motions studied earlier provide some clues on how to design shapes that work. In Figure 54(a), triangle ABE is removed from the left of parallelogram $ABCD$ and slid to the right, forming the rectangle $BB'E'E$ of Figure 54(b). This notion can be used to create a tessellating shape.

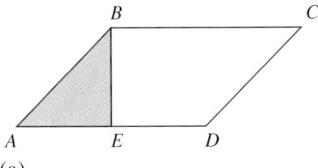
(a)

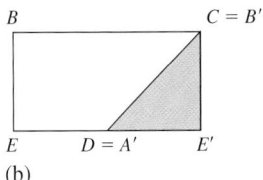
(b)

Figure 54

Consider any polygon that tessellates a plane, such as rectangle *ABCD* in Figure 55(a). On the left side of the figure draw any shape in the interior of the rectangle, as in Figure 55(b). Cut this shape from the rectangle and slide it to the right by the slide that takes *A* to *B*, as shown in Figure 55(c). The resulting shape will tessellate the plane. (Why?)

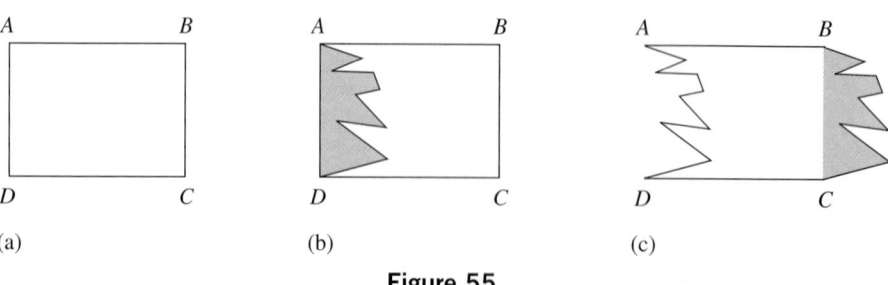

Figure 55

Creating Tessellations with Rotations

A second method of forming a tessellation involves a series of rotations of parts of a figure. In Figure 56(a), we start with an equilateral triangle *ABC*, choose the midpoint *O* of one side of the triangle, and cut out a shape, being careful not to cut away more than half of the interior of angle *B*. We then rotate the shape 180° clockwise around point *O* as in Figure 56(b). If we continue this process on the other two sides, then we obtain a shape that can be rotated around point *A* to tessellate the plane. Complete the tessellating shape and tessellate the plane with it in Now Try This 9.

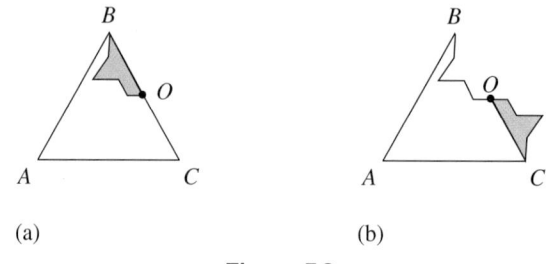

Figure 56

▶ NOW TRY THIS 9

NTT 9: Continue to create the shapes and rotate them to form the tessellation.

Continue the drawing of the tessellating shape in Figure 56. Cut out the shape and use it to tessellate the plane.

The partial student page shown on page 803 shows a grade 6 tessellation construction involving rotations.

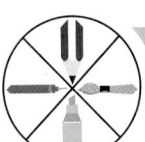

School Book Page Extensions

PRACTICE

C Extensions

20. Follow these steps to change a square into a shape that tessellates the plane.

a. Cut out a square piece of paper about 8 cm on a side. Label the sides and vertices as shown.

b. Draw and cut any shape out of side 1. Do <u>not</u> cut off a corner.

c. Rotate the piece about point *A* and tape it to side 2. Be sure to tape the piece the same distance from point *A* as it was before you cut it.

d. Similarly, cut into side 3, rotate the piece about point *B*, and tape the piece to side 4.

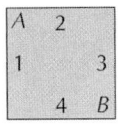 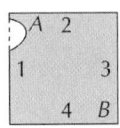 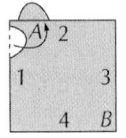 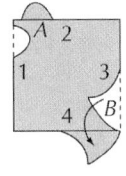

e. Repeat the process a few more times, cutting into any <u>unaltered</u> part of the square except a corner. Remember this plan:

- Rotate pieces from side 1 onto side 2, and from side 2 onto side 1. (Be sure to tape the piece the same distance from *A*.)

- Rotate pieces from side 3 onto side 4, and from side 4 onto side 3. (Be sure to tape the piece the same distance from *B*.)

f. Add artistic details and draw the tessellation.

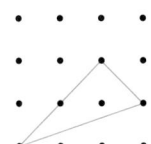

Assessment 13-4A

1. On dot paper, draw a tessellation of the plane using the following figure. *

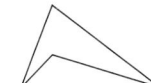

2. a. Tessellate the plane with the following quadrilateral. *

b. Is it possible to tessellate the plane with any quadrilateral? Why or why not? *

3. On dot paper use the following pentomino to make a tessellation of the plane, if possible. *

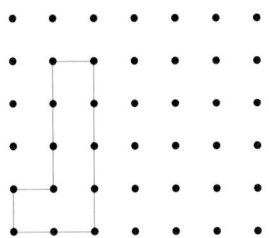

4. There are many ways to tessellate the plane by using combinations of regular polygons. An example follows.

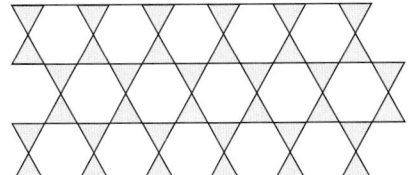

Produce other such tessellations using only equilateral triangles, squares, and regular hexagons. *

5. The shaded figure in the Card Trick quilt pattern is formed from four ell-shaped figures. Explain whether the outlined figure will tessellate a plane. *

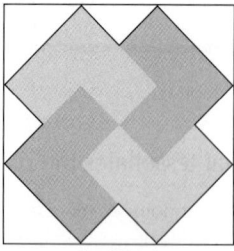

Card Trick

6. To determine whether a shape created using a glide reflection will tessellate the plane, complete the following.
   a. Start with a rectangle. Determine some shape that you might use with a slide to form a tessellating shape. Slide it as shown. Determine the horizontal line of symmetry of the rectangle, and reflect as shown.   Construction

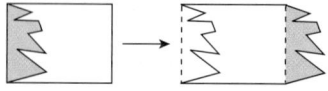 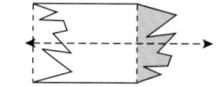

   b. Explain why the described series of motions is a glide reflection.   It combines a translation and a reflection
   c. Determine whether the final shape will tessellate the plane.   It will tessellate the plane.
7. The **dual of a regular tessellation** is the tessellation obtained by connecting the centers of the polygons in the original tessellation if their sides intersect in more than one point. The dual of the tessellation of equilateral triangles is

the tessellation of regular hexagons, shown in color in the following figure:

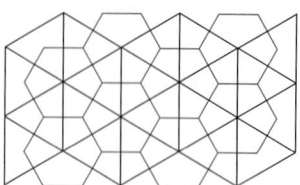

Describe and show the dual of each of the following:
   a. The regular tessellation of squares shown in Figure 50(a)   *
   b. A tessellation of regular hexagons   *
8. A sidewalk is made of tiles of the type shown in the following figure:

Each tile is made of three regular hexagons with some sides removed. Draw a partial tessellation composed of seven such figures. *
9. A portion of a Pieced Star Quilt pattern is shown below. Will this hexagon tessellate a plane? Justify your answer. *

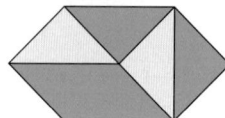

Assessment 13-4B

1. On dot paper, draw a tessellation of the plane using the following figure. *

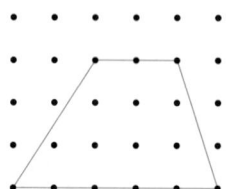

2. a. Tessellate the plane with the following right triangle. *

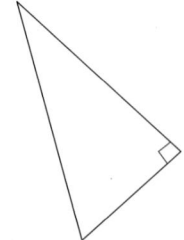

   b. Is it possible to tessellate a plane with any triangle? Why or why not? *
3. On dot paper, use each of the following pentominoes, one at a time, to make a tessellation of the plane, if possible: *

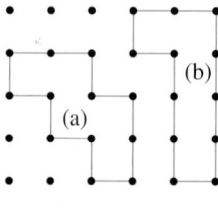

4. Produce a tessellation of a plane using a combination of regular octagons and squares. *

5. A "bow-tie" figure is formed by right triangles (white) near the center of the Brown Goose quilt pattern. Explain whether this bow-tie figure will tessellate a plane.   *

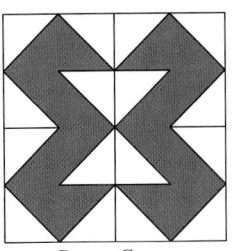

Brown Goose

6. a. Create a figure that will tessellate a plane by reflections alone.   *

   b. Create a figure that will not tessellate a plane by reflections alone.   Answers vary.

7. The partial student page below shows "student work." Answer questions 17 and 18.   *

School Book Page   Math and Art

The Dutch artist M. C. Escher (1898 to 1972) is renowned for his interesting tessellations. Inspired by Escher's tessellating shapes of fish and lizards, Jon and Miguel created the art below.

17. What transformation would move fish *A* to fish *B*?

18. What transformation would move lizard *C* to lizard *D*? lizard *C* to lizard *E*?

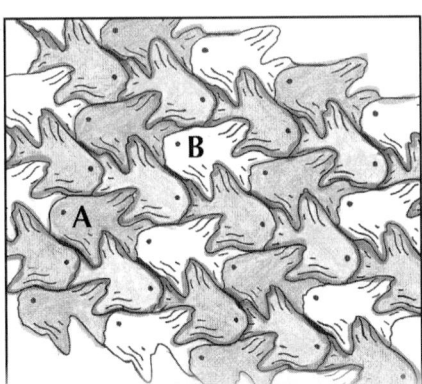

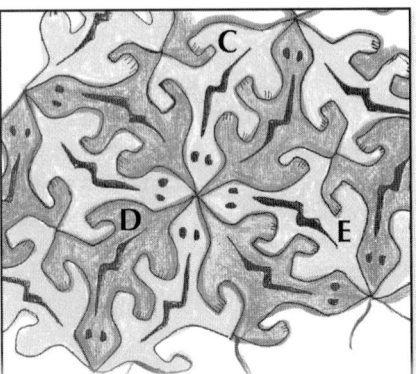

Source: p. 518; From SCOTT FORESMAN-ADDISON WESLEY MATHEMATICS. Copyright © 2008 Pearson Education, Inc., or its affiliates. Used by permission. All Rights Reserved.

8. A concrete tile similar to that shown below is used to construct a sound barrier wall for an interstate highway in Washington, DC. Sketch a tessellation using the figure to show that a wall could be built of the tiles.   *

9. Explain whether the "arrow" below will tessellate a plane.   *

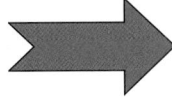

Mathematical Connections 13-4

Answers to Mathematical Connections can be found in the Answers section at the back of the book.

Reasoning

1. The following figure is a partial tessellation of the plane with the trapezoid *ABCD*.

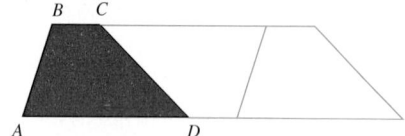

   a. Tessellate the plane with a triangle and show how the tessellation can be used to find the relationship between the length of the segment connecting the midpoints of the two sides of a triangle and the length of the third side (the Midsegment Theorem of Chapter 12).

   b. Explain how the tessellation can be used to find a relationship between the midsegment of the trapezoid and the bases.

2. Explain in your own words why only three types of regular polygons tessellate the plane.

3. The following figure shows how to tessellate the plane with irregular pentagons. Explain how the pentagons can be constructed.

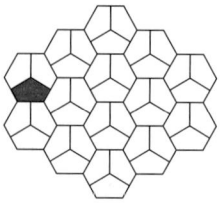

4. Construct a kite that is not a rhombus and rotate the kite by 180° about the midpoint of one of its sides so that the kite and its image make a hexagon.

   a. Explain why the opposite sides of the hexagon are parallel.

   b. Use the hexagon from part (a) to tessellate the plane. What isometry can be used for this purpose?

Open-Ended

5. There are endless numbers of figures that tessellate a plane. In the following drawing, the shaded figure is shown to tessellate the plane.

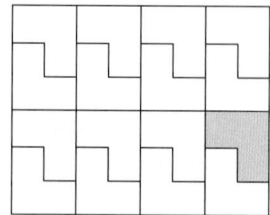

   Design several different polygons and show how each can tessellate the plane. What transformations are used in each of your designs? Explain how they are used to tessellate the plane.

6. Examine different quilt patterns or floor coverings and make a sketch of those you found that tessellate a plane.

7. A cube will tessellate space but a sphere will not. List several other solids that will tessellate space and several that will not.

8. List several figures other than rectangles that tessellate the plane using translations.

9. Sketch a figure that tessellates the plane using translations and half-turns.

10. Construct a dodecagon (12-sided polygon) and show how to tessellate the plane with it.

Cooperative Learning

11. Each member of a group is to find a drawing by M. C. Escher that does not appear in this text and in which the concept of tessellation is used. Each person then shows the other members of the group, in detail, how he or she thinks Escher created the tessellation.

12. a. Convince the members of your group that the following figure containing six equilateral triangles tessellates the plane.

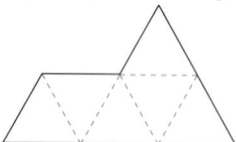

   b. As a group, find different figures that contain six equilateral triangles. How many such figures can you find? Discuss the meaning of "different."

   c. Find some of the figures in (b) that are rep-tiles. (A rep-tile is a figure whose copies can be used to form a larger figure similar to itself.) Convince other members of your group that your figures are rep-tiles and that they tessellate the plane.

13. Trace each of the following pentomino shapes and cut out several copies of each. Each member of a small group should pick a shape, decide if it tessellates the plane, and convince other members of the group that it does or does not tessellate. The group should report the answers with figures or an argument why a shape does not tessellate.

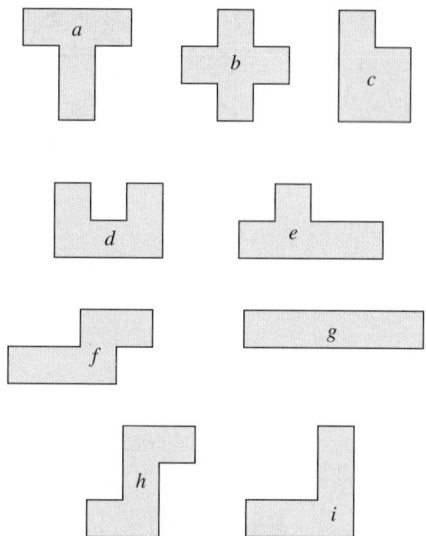

14. In your group, create as many congruent quadrilaterals with different side lengths cut out of paper as needed and put them together to show how they will tessellate the plane. Draw your tessellations on paper. What single isometry can be used for this purpose?

Connecting Mathematics to the Classroom

15. Isaiah says that the bricks used in a classroom wall construction form a tessellation. How do you respond?

16. A student asks if the image seen through a kaleidoscope tessellates a plane. How do you respond?

17. Jillian wants to know why a regular pentagon will not tessellate the plane. How do you respond?

Review Questions

18. Find the image of the figure below in each of the following.
    a. A translation from M to N
    b. A 90° rotation counterclockwise through M

19. With the quilt patterns below, define isometries that will take each pattern to itself.

a.

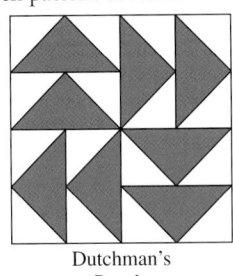

Dutchman's Puzzle

b.

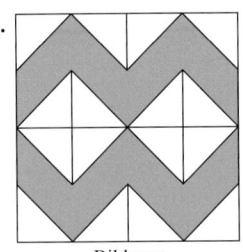

Ribbons

20. Determine whether the figure below could be its own image under some isometry. If so, which one?

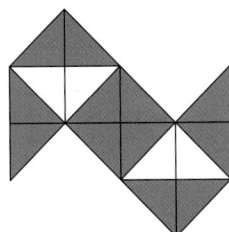

21. A quadrilateral has vertices at $(a, 0), (0, a), (^-a, 0)$, and $(0, ^-a)$, where $a > 0$.
    a. What kind of quadrilateral is it?
    b. Find the image of each vertex under the reflection in the line $y = x$.

22. Prove that under a dilation with center O and scale factor r, the image of $\overline{AB}$ is a parallel segment $\overline{A'B'}$.

23. What dilation, if any, allows a line with equation $y = kx$, $k > 0, k \neq 1$, to be the image of the line with equation $y = x$?

National Assessments

National Assessment of Educational Progress (NAEP) Question

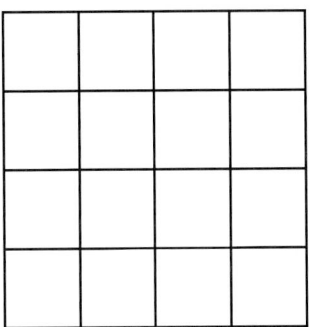

Identical puzzle pieces have been put together to form the large square shown above. Which of the following could be the shape of each puzzle piece?

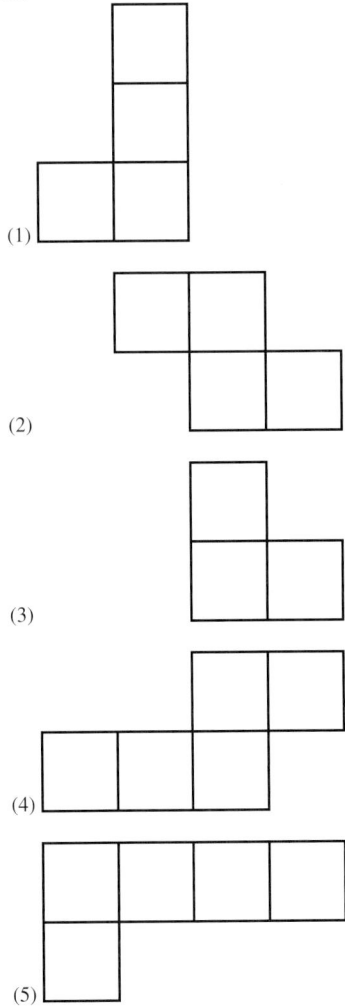

NAEP, 2009, Grade 8

Hint for Solving the Preliminary Problem

Reflect T in the line representing the road.

Chapter 13 Summary

KEY CONCEPTS	DEFINITIONS, DESCRIPTIONS, AND THEOREMS
Section 13-1	
Transformation (p. 757)	Any function from the plane to itself that is a one-to-one correspondence. Each *original* point in the plane has an *image* point in the "transformed" plane and vice versa.
Isometry (p. 757)	A transformation that preserves distance. *Isometry properties:* • Preserves congruence, angle measure, and parallelism. • The image of a line is a line. • The image of a circle is a circle. • The images of parallel lines are parallel lines.
Translation (p. 758)	A translation by a slide arrow from M to N ($\overrightarrow{MN}$) is a transformation of the plane to itself such that every point P has an image P' such that $PP' = MN$, $\overline{PP'} \parallel \overline{MN}$, and the direction from P to P' is the same as from M to N.
Translation in a coordinate system (p. 760)	A transformation that moves every point (x, y) in the plane to the point $(x + a, y + b)$, where a and b are real numbers.
Rotation (p. 762)	A transformation of the plane determined by holding one point, the center, fixed and rotating the plane about this point by a given angle measure clockwise or counterclockwise.
Identity transformation (p. 764)	A transformation that moves every point onto itself. A rotation of 360° about any point is an identity transformation.
Half-turn (p. 764)	A rotation of 180° about any center.
Turn symmetry (p. 765)	A figure has turn symmetry if there is a *turn center* and *turn angle* (whose measure is not a multiple of 360°) that will take the original to itself as an image.
Slopes of perpendicular lines (p. 766)	*Theorem:* Two nonvertical lines are perpendicular if, and only if, their slopes m_1 and m_2 satisfy the condition $m_1 m_2 = {}^-1$. Every vertical line has no slope but is perpendicular to every line with slope 0.
Section 13-2	
Reflection in a line ℓ (p. 774)	A transformation from the plane to the plane that pairs each point P not on ℓ with a point P' in such a way that ℓ is the perpendicular bisector of $\overline{PP'}$. If P is on ℓ, then $P' = P$.
Orientation (p. 775)	Reflections and glide reflections reverse the orientation of the original figure. Translations and rotations keep the orientation the same.
Relationship between angle of incidence and angle of reflection (p. 780)	In a reflection, the *angle of incidence* is congruent to the *angle of reflection*.
Glide reflection (p. 781)	A transformation composed of a translation followed by a reflection in a line parallel to the slide arrow.
Congruence via isometries (p. 781)	Two geometric figures are congruent if, and only if, one is an image of the other under a single isometry or under a composition of isometries.

Section 13-3

Dilation (p. 789)	A transformation from the plane to the plane, with center O and scale factor $r > 0$, that assigns to each point A in the plane the point A' such that O, A, and A' are collinear, O is not between A and A', and $OA' = rOA$. Point O is its own image.
Dilation properties (p. 789)	*Theorem:* A dilation with center O and scale factor $r > 0$ has the following properties: • The image of a line segment is a line segment parallel to the original segment and r times as long. • The image of an angle is an angle congruent to the original angle. • The image of a triangle is a similar triangle, and the image of a polygon is a similar polygon.
Similar figures (p. 792)	Two figures are similar if, and only if, one is the image of the other under an isometry (or a sequence of isometries) followed by a dilation.

Section 13-4

Tessellation (p. 798)	The filling of the plane with repetitions of congruent figures in such a way that no figures overlap and there are no gaps.
Regular tessellation (p. 798)	A tessellation using congruent regular polygons joined edge to edge.

Chapter 13 Review

1. Complete each of the following motions.

a. A reflection in ℓ

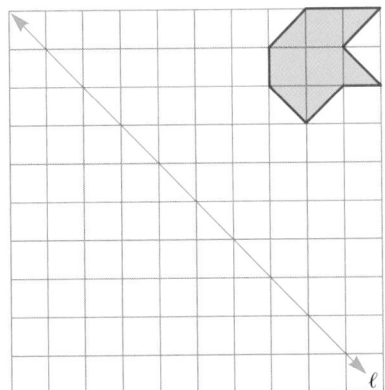

b. A rotation in O through the given arc

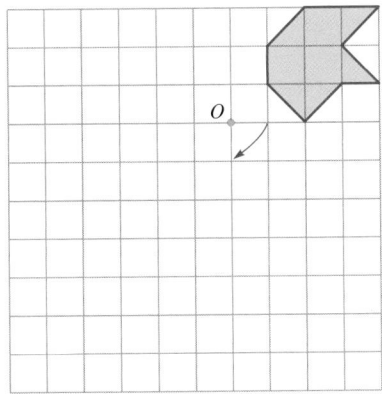

c. A translation, as pictured

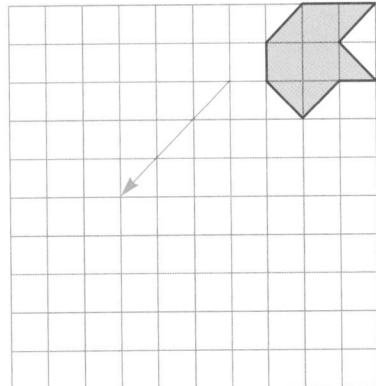

2. For each of the following figures, construct the image of $\triangle ABC$.   Constructions

a. Through a reflection in ℓ

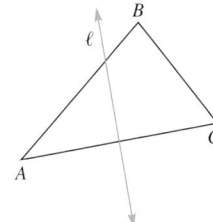

b. Through the given rotation in O

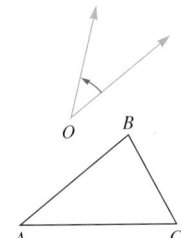

c. By the translation arrow pictured

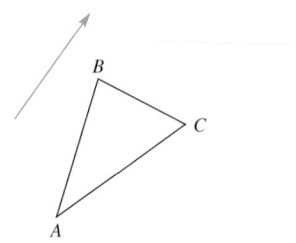

3. Determine any reflections or rotations, that take the following figures to themselves.

a.

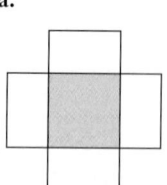

b.

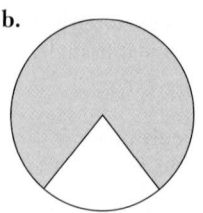

c.

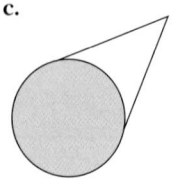

d.

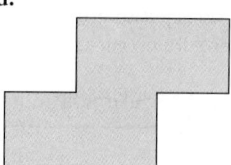

e.

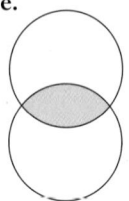

f.

4. In the following figure, $\triangle A'B'C'$ is the image of $\triangle ABC$ under a dilation.

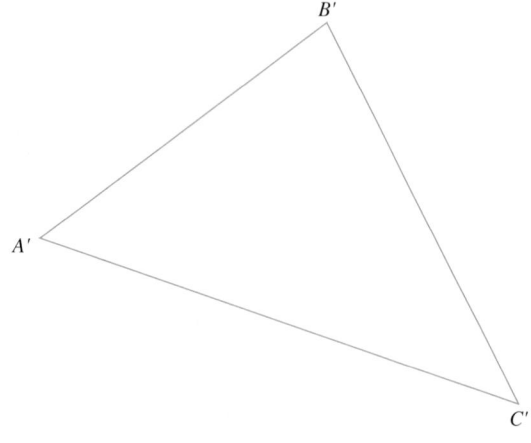

Locate points A, B, and C such that A' is the center of the dilation and $BC = \dfrac{1}{2}B'C'$. $A = A'$, B is the midpoint of $\overline{A'B'}$, and C is the midpoint of $\overline{A'C'}$.

5. Given that $STAR$ in the figure shown is a parallelogram, describe a sequence of isometries to show the following.
  a. $\triangle STA \cong \triangle ARS$ In each case half-turn about $\overline{X}$.
  b. $\triangle TSR \cong \triangle RAT$

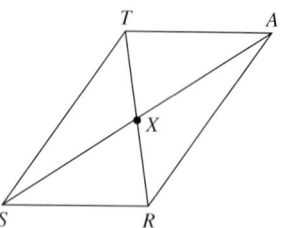

6. Given that $BEAUTY$ in the figure shown is a regular hexagon, describe a sequence of isometries that will transform the following. Answers vary.   Clockwise rotation by 120° about
  a. $BEAU$ onto $AUTY$ the center of the hexagon
  b. $BEAU$ onto $YTUA$ A reflection in the perpendicular bisector of $\overline{BY}$

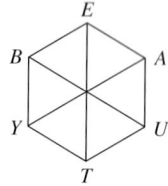

7. Given that $\triangle SNO \cong \triangle SWO$ in the following figure, describe an isometry that will transform $\triangle SNO$ onto $\triangle SWO$.   Reflection in $\overleftrightarrow{SO}$

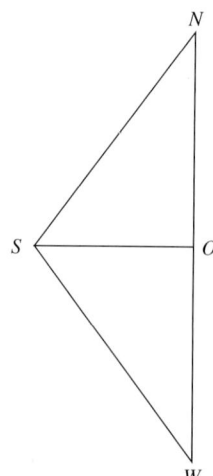

8. Show that $\triangle SER$ in the following figure is the image of $\triangle HOR$ under a succession of isometries with a dilation.   *

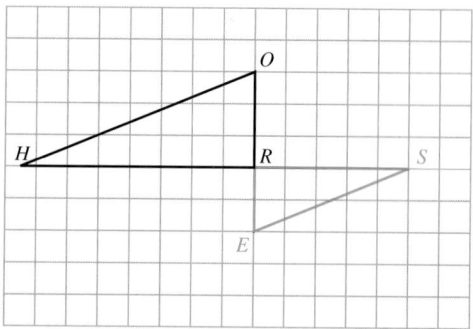

9. Show that △*TAB* in the following figure is the image of △*PIG* under a succession of isometries with a dilation.　*

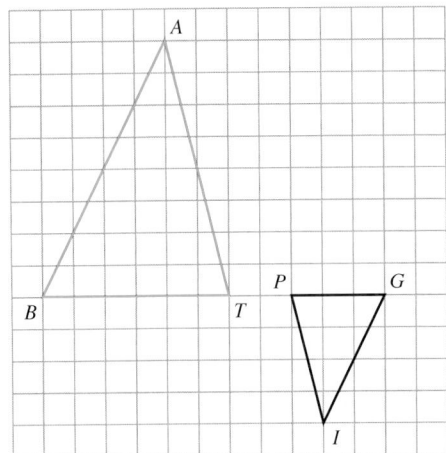

10. The triangle *A'B'C'* with *A'*(0, 7.91), *B'*(⁻5, ⁻4.93), *C'*(4.83, 0) is the image of triangle *ABC* under the translation $(x, y) \rightarrow (x + 3, y - 5)$. *A*(⁻3, 12.91), *B*(⁻8, 0.07),
    a. Find the coordinates of *A*, *B*, and *C*. *C*(1.83, 5)
    b. Under what translation will the image of △*A'B'C'* be △*ABC*? Under the translation $(x, y) \rightarrow (x - 3, y + 5)$

11. If a translation determined by $(x, y) \rightarrow (x + 3, y - 2)$ is followed by another translation determined by $(x, y) \rightarrow (x - 3, y + 2)$, describe a single transformation that would achieve the same thing. *

12. Suppose △*A"B"C"* with *A"*(0, 0), *B"*(1, 5), *C"*(⁻2, 7) is the image of △*ABC* under the translation $(x, y) \rightarrow (x + 2, y - 1)$ followed by the translation $(x, y) \rightarrow (x + 1, y + 3)$. *A*(⁻3, ⁻2),
    a. Find the coordinates of *A*, *B*, and *C*. *B*(⁻2, 3), *C*(⁻5, 5)
    b. Under what single transformation will the image of △*ABC* be △*A"B"C"*? $(x, y) \rightarrow (x + 3, y + 2)$

13. Write each of the following as a single transformation.
    a. i. A translation from *A* to *B* followed by a translation from *B* to *C* Translation from *A* to *C*.
       ii. A translation from *B* to *C* followed by a translation from *A* to *B* Translation from *A* to *C*.
    b. A rotation about *O* by 90° counterclockwise, followed by a rotation about *O* by 30° clockwise *
    c. i. A dilation with center *O* and scale factor 3 followed by a dilation with center *O* and scale factor 2 *
       ii. The dilations in part (i) in reverse order *

14. Given the line $y = 2x + 3$ and the point *P*(⁻1, 3), find the equation of the line through *P* perpendicular to the given line. $y = \frac{-1}{2}x + \frac{5}{2}$

15. Find the equation of the image of the line $y = ⁻x + 3$ under each of the following transformations.
    a. The translation $(x, y) \rightarrow (x + 2, y - 3)$ $y = ⁻x + 2$
    b. Reflection in the *x*-axis $y = x - 3$
    c. Reflection in the *y*-axis $y = x + 3$
    d. Reflection in the line $y = x$ $y = ⁻x + 3$
    e. Half-turn about the origin $y = ⁻x - 3$
    f. Dilation with center at the origin and scale factor 2 $y = ⁻x + 6$

16. a. Consider the translation $(x, y) \rightarrow (x + 3, y - 5)$. The image of (1, 2) is (4, ⁻3). What translation takes (4, ⁻3) to (1, 2)? $(x, y) \rightarrow (x - 3, y + 5)$
    b. What is the net result of following the translation $(x, y) \rightarrow (x + h, y + k)$ by the translation $(x, y) \rightarrow (x - h, y - k)$? The identity transformation $(x, y) \rightarrow (x, y)$

17. Explain why a regular octagon cannot tessellate the plane. *
18. For each of the following cases, find the image of the given figure using a compass and straightedge.
    a. Find images of the vertices.

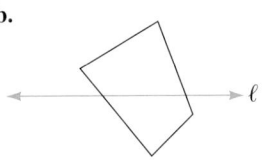

    Reflection about ℓ

    b.

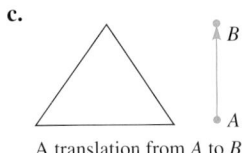

    Reflection about ℓ

    c.

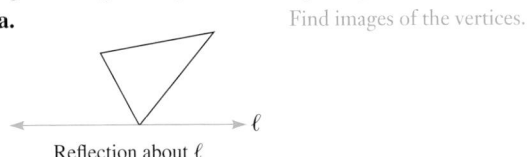

    A translation from *A* to *B*

19. Determine whether the following shapes tessellate the plane. *
    a.   b.   c.

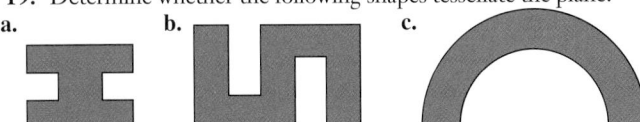

20. Three vertices of a rhombus are at *O*(0, 0), *A*(3, 4), *C*(*a*, 0). Answer the following.
    a. Find all possible coordinates of point *C* (use the Pythagorean Theorem). *
    b. Find all possible coordinates for the fourth vertex *B* using a translation. *
    c. Indicate the translations used in part (b). *
    d. Verify that the diagonals of each of the rhombi you found in part (b) are perpendicular to each other. *

21. Construct the image of a circle under dilation in point *A*, where *A* is on the circle and the scale factor is $\frac{1}{2}$. *

22. On a 1-m equilateral-triangle "pool table," a ball is hit at a 60° angle along a segment parallel to a side of the table and 10 cm from one pocket as shown. Find the length of the path as it travels around the table until it returns to where it started or falls into one of the pockets. *

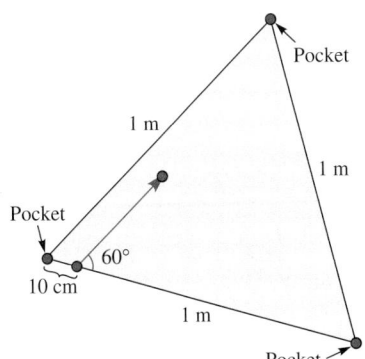

Chapter

14

Area, Pythagorean Theorem, and Volume

Preliminary Problem

In an Environmental Protection Agency clean-up site, contaminated dirt covers an area of 1.5 acres and the top 16 in. must be removed. If a truck hauls about 10 yd^3 in each load, how many truckloads will be needed to remove the contaminated dirt?

If needed, see Hint on page 893.

The *Common Core Standards* recommend that students begin the study of linear measure in grade 2 (p. 20), measure liquid volumes and masses in grade 3 as well as study perimeters and beginning areas (p. 25), study conversions of measures and use area formulas in grade 4 as well as measures within a system (p. 31), study properties of volumes and use volume formulas for prisms in grade 5 (p. 37), solve real-world problems involving area, surface area, and volume in grade 6 (p. 44), work with area and circumference of circles and continue work with volumes in grade 7 (p. 50), and apply the Pythagorean Theorem and study volumes of cylinders, cones, and spheres in grade 8 (p. 56). All of these topics are discussed in this chapter.

In this chapter, we use both the English and the metric systems of measurement for length, area, volume, mass, and temperature with the philosophy that students should learn to think within a system.

14-1 Linear Measure

14-1 Objectives

Students will be able to understand and explain

- The English system of linear measures.
- The metric system of linear measures.
- Conversion among measures.
- Dimensional analysis.
- Perimeter and circumference.
- Ratios of linear measures of similar figures.

NTT 1: Answers vary. One would expect answers to be different due to different hand sizes.

In the grade 4 *Common Core Standards*, we find that students are expected to "solve problems involving measurement and conversion of measurements from a larger unit to a smaller unit" (p. 31).

In the United States, two measurement systems are used regularly: the English system and the metric system. In the *Common Core Standards*, as early as grade 2, we find that students should be able to "estimate lengths using units of inches, feet, centimeters, and meters" (p. 20). This work with both systems carries on in other grades, and we believe that students should develop proficiency as well as develop benchmarks for measuring in both systems.

To measure a segment, we first decide on a unit of measure. Early attempts at measurement lacked a standard unit and used fingers, hands, arms, and feet as units of measure. "Hands" are still used to measure the heights of horses. These early crude measurements were refined eventually and standardized by the English.

▶ **NOW TRY THIS 1**

a. Estimate the length of this textbook page using paper clips.
b. Measure the textbook page in paper clips.
c. How close was your estimate to the measure?
d. Repeat parts (a–c) using your *hands*.
e. Estimate and then measure the width of a desk in hands.
f. In part (e), explain whether all students should obtain the same answer.

The English System

Originally, in the English system, a yard was the distance from the tip of the nose to the end of an outstretched arm of an adult person, and a foot was the length of a human foot. In 1893, the United States defined the yard and other units in terms of metric units. Some units of length in the English system and relationships among them are summarized in Table 1.

Table 1	
Unit	**Equivalent in Other Units**
yard (yd)	3 ft
foot (ft)	12 in.
mile (mi)	1760 yd, or 5280 ft

Converting Units of Measure

To convert from one unit of length to another, different processes can be used. For example, to convert 5.25 mi to yards we use the facts that 1 mi $= 5280$ ft and 1 ft $= \dfrac{1}{3}$ yd.

$$5.25 \text{ mi} = 5.25(5280) \text{ ft} = 5.25(5280)\left(\frac{1}{3}\right) \text{yd} = 9240 \text{ yd}$$

Likewise, to convert 432 in. to yards we use the facts that 1 ft $= \dfrac{1}{3}$ yd and 1 in. $= \dfrac{1}{12}$ ft.

$$432 \text{ in.} = 432\left(\frac{1}{12}\right) \text{ft} = 432\left(\frac{1}{12}\right)\left(\frac{1}{3}\right) \text{yd} = 12 \text{ yd}$$

Dimensional Analysis (Unit Analysis)

In the sciences, one technique for converting units of measure is **dimensional analysis**. This process works with *unit ratios* (ratios equivalent to 1) treated as fractions. Since 1 yd $= 3$ ft, we have $\dfrac{1 \text{ yd}}{3 \text{ ft}} = 1$ and $\dfrac{3 \text{ ft}}{1 \text{ yd}} = 1$. Similarly $\dfrac{5280 \text{ ft}}{1 \text{ mi}} = 1$. Ratios such as $\dfrac{1 \text{ yd}}{3 \text{ ft}}, \dfrac{3 \text{ ft}}{1 \text{ yd}}$, and $\dfrac{5280 \text{ ft}}{1 \text{ mi}}$ are unit ratios. Therefore, to convert 5.25 mi to yards, we do the following.

$$5.25 \text{ mi} = 5.25 \text{ mi} \cdot \frac{5280 \text{ ft}}{1 \text{ mi}} \cdot \frac{1 \text{ yd}}{3 \text{ ft}} = 9240 \text{ yd}$$

Example 1

If a cheetah is clocked at 60 miles per hour (mph), what is its speed in feet per second?

Solution

$$60\frac{\text{mi}}{\text{hr}} = \frac{60 \text{ mi}}{1 \text{ hr}} \cdot \frac{5280 \text{ ft}}{1 \text{ mi}} \cdot \frac{1 \text{ hr}}{60 \text{ min}} \cdot \frac{1 \text{ min}}{60 \text{ sec}} = 88\frac{\text{ft}}{\text{sec}}$$

Historical Note

The yard was defined in 1832 as the distance between the 27th and 63rd inches on a certain brass bar made by Troughton of London. In 1856, the yard was redefined in terms of the British Bronze Yard No. 11 (which was 0.00087 in. longer than the Troughton yard). In 1893, the yard was redefined in terms of the international meter as $\dfrac{3600}{3937}$ of a meter using an 1866 U.S. law making the practice of the metric system permissible. In 1960, the meter was redefined in terms of the wavelength of light from krypton-86 and still later in terms of the distance light travels in $\dfrac{1}{299,792,458}$ sec. Effective July 1, 1959, the yard is defined in terms of the international yard based on the international definition of a meter, and the inch is 2.54 cm.

Note that treating ratios as fractions in Example 2 allows us to use multiplication principles.

Complete each of the following conversions.

a. 219 ft = _____ yd
b. 8432 yd = _____ mi
c. 0.2 mi = _____ ft
d. 64 in. = _____ yd

Solution

a. Because 1 ft $= \frac{1}{3}$ yd, 219 ft $= 219\left(\frac{1}{3}\text{yd}\right) = 73$ yd.

Alternatively, 219 ft $= 219\text{ ft}\left(\frac{1\text{ yd}}{3\text{ ft}}\right) = 73$ yd.

b. Because 1 yd $= \frac{1}{1760}$ mi, 8432 yd $= 8432\left(\frac{1}{1760}\text{mi}\right) \approx 4.79$ mi.

Alternatively, 8432 yd $= 8432\text{ yd}\left(\frac{3\text{ ft}}{1\text{ yd}}\right)\left(\frac{1\text{ mi}}{5280\text{ ft}}\right) \approx 4.79$ mi.

c. 1 mi $= 5280$ ft. Hence, 0.2 mi $= 0.2(5280\text{ ft}) = 1056$ ft.

Alternatively, 0.2 mi $= 0.2\text{ mi} \cdot \frac{5280\text{ ft}}{1\text{ mi}} = 1056$ ft.

d. We have 1 yd $= 3$ ft and 1 ft $= 12$ in. Hence, 1 yd $= 3$ ft $= 3(12\text{ in.}) = 36$ in. Thus,

1 in. $= \frac{1}{36}$ yd; therefore, 64 in. $= 64\left(\frac{1}{36}\text{yd}\right) = \frac{16}{9}$ yd ≈ 1.78 yd. Alternatively, 64 in. $=$

64 in. $\left(\frac{1\text{ ft}}{12\text{ in.}}\right)\left(\frac{1\text{ yd}}{3\text{ ft}}\right) = \frac{16}{9}$ yd ≈ 1.78 yd.

The Metric System

The United States is the only major industrial nation in the world that uses the English system. However, the use of the **metric system** in the United States has been adopted in the scientific community and in many industries.

Different units of length in the metric system are obtained by multiplying a base unit by a power of 10. Table 2 gives some of the prefixes for these units, their symbols, and the multiplication factors.

Historical Note

The metric system, a decimal system, was proposed by Gabriel Mouton in 1670 in France. Only in 1790 did the French Academy of Sciences bring groups together to develop the system. At that time in France, there were 13 distinct measures for the *foot* ranging from 10.6 in. to 13.4 in. Recognizing the need for a standard base unit of linear measurement, the Academy chose $\frac{1}{10,000,000}$ of the distance from the equator to the North Pole on a meridian through Paris as the base unit of length and called it the *meter (m)*, from the Greek word *metron*, meaning "to measure."

The U.S. Congress included encouragement for U.S. industrial metrication in 1988 by designating the metric system as the preferred system of weights and measures and by requiring each federal agency to be metric by the end of fiscal year 1992. Since 2009, all products sold in Europe (with limited exceptions) are required to have only metric units on their labels. ●

Table 2

Prefix	Symbol	Factor	
kilo	k	1000	(one thousand)
*hecto	h	100	(one hundred)
*deka	da	10	(ten)
*deci	d	0.1	(one tenth)
centi	c	0.01	(one hundredth)
milli	m	0.001	(one thousandth)

*Not commonly used

Metric prefixes, combined with the base unit **meter**, name different units of length. Table 3 gives units, the symbol for each, and their relationship to the meter.

Table 3

Unit	Symbol	Relationship to Base Unit	
kilometer	km	1000	m
*hectometer	hm	100	m
*dekameter	dam	10	m
meter	**m**	**base unit**	
*decimeter	dm	0.1	m
centimeter	cm	0.01	m
millimeter	mm	0.001	m

*Not commonly used

Other metric prefixes are used for greater and lesser quantities, for example, *mega* (1,000,000) and *micro* (0.000001). The symbols for mega and micro are M and μ, respectively.

Benchmarks used for estimations for a meter, a decimeter, a centimeter, and a millimeter are shown in Figure 1. The kilometer is commonly used for measuring longer distances: 1 km = 1000 m. Nine football fields, including end zones, laid end to end are approximately 1 km long.

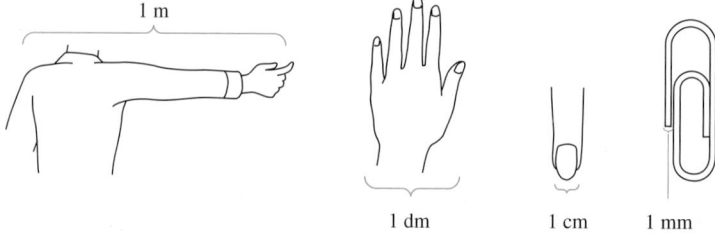

Figure 1

Conversions among metric lengths are accomplished by multiplying or dividing by powers of 10. As with converting dollars to cents or cents to dollars, we move the decimal point to the left or right, depending on the units. For example,

$$0.123 \text{ km} = 1.23 \text{ hm} = 12.3 \text{ dam} = 123 \text{ m} = 1230 \text{ dm} = 12{,}300 \text{ cm} = 123{,}000 \text{ mm}.$$

It is possible to convert units by using the chart in Figure 2. We count the number of steps from one unit to the other and move the decimal point that many steps in the same direction.

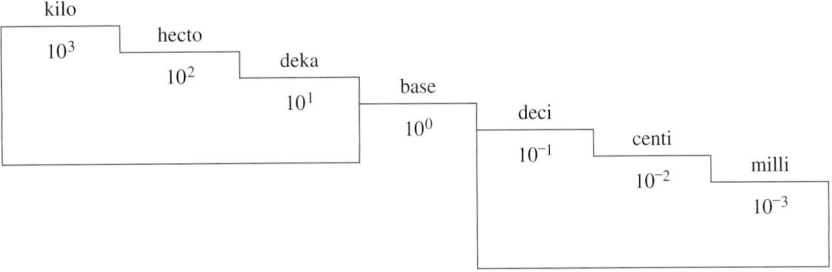

Figure 2

Example 3

Complete each of the following conversions.

a. 1.4 km = _____ m
b. 285 mm = _____ m
c. 0.03 km = _____ cm

Solution

a. Because 1 km = 1000 m, to change kilometers to meters, we multiply by 1000. Hence, 1.4 km = 1.4(1000 m) = 1400 m.

$$\text{Alternatively, } 1.4 \text{ km} = 1.4 \text{ km} \cdot \frac{1000 \text{ m}}{1 \text{ km}} = 1400 \text{ m}.$$

b. Because 1 mm = 0.001 m, to change from millimeters to meters, we multiply by 0.001. Thus, 285 mm = 285(0.001 m) = 0.285 m.

$$\text{Alternatively, } 285 \text{ mm} = 285 \text{ mm} \cdot \frac{1 \text{ m}}{1000 \text{ mm}} = 0.285 \text{ m}.$$

c. To change kilometers to centimeters, we first multiply by 1000 to convert kilometers to meters and then multiply by 100 to convert meters to centimeters. Therefore, we move the decimal point five places to the right to obtain 0.03 km = 3000 cm. An alternative approach is to use Figure 2. To go from kilo to centi on the steps, we move five places to the right, so we need to move the decimal point in 0.03 five places to the right, resulting in 3000.

Linear units of length or distance may be measured with rulers. Figure 3 shows part of a centimeter ruler.

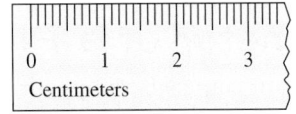

Figure 3

When drawings are given, we assume that the listed measurements are accurate. When actually measuring real-world objects, such accuracy is usually impossible. Measuring distances in the real world frequently results in errors. Thus, many industries rely on portable calibration units to test measuring instruments used in constructing parts. Calibration helps assure that all parts fit together. To calibrate measuring instruments, industrial technicians establish the greatest possible error (GPE) allowable in order to obtain the final fit. The **greatest possible error (GPE)** of a measurement is one-half the unit used. For example, if the width of a piece of board is measured as 5 cm, the actual width must be between 4.5 cm and 5.5 cm. Therefore, the GPE for this measurement is 0.5 cm.

Distance Properties

The expression "the shortest distance between two points is a straight line" is actually misleading. (Why?) A correct statement is "the shortest among all the paths in a plane connecting two points A and B is the segment $\overline{AB}$." (The length of $\overline{AB}$ is denoted by AB.) This and other basic properties of distance are listed below.

Properties of Distance

1. The distance between any two points A and B is greater than or equal to 0, written $AB \geq 0$.
2. The distance between any two points A and B is the same as the distance between B and A, written $AB = BA$.
3. For any three points A, B, and C, the distance between A and B plus the distance between B and C is greater than or equal to the distance between A and C, written $AB + BC \geq AC$.

In the special case where A, B, and C are collinear and B is between A and C, as in Figure 4(a), we have $AB + BC = AC$. Otherwise, if A, B, and C are not collinear, as in Figure 4(b), then they form the vertices of a triangle and $AB + BC > AC$. This inequality leads to the **Triangle Inequality**.

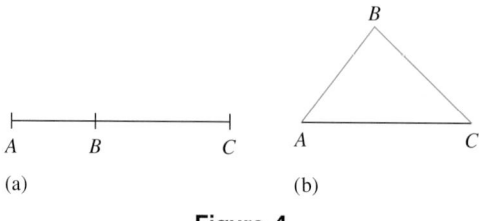

(a)   (b)

Figure 4

Theorem 14-1:   Triangle Inequality
The sum of the lengths of any two sides of a triangle is greater than the length of the third side.

Perimeter of a Plane Figure

In common language, the **perimeter** of a two-dimensional figure is the distance around the figure and has linear measure, as seen in Example 4.

Example 4

Find the perimeter of each shape in Figure 5.

a.
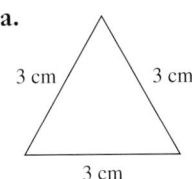

b.
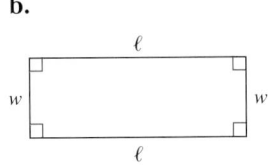

c.
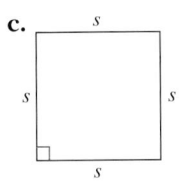

d.
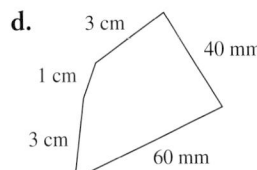

Figure 5

Solution

a. The perimeter is $3(3) = 9$ cm.

b. The perimeter is $2w + 2\ell$.

c. The perimeter is $4s$.

d. Because 40 mm = 4 cm and 60 mm = 6 cm, the perimeter is $1 + 3 + 4 + 6 + 3 = 17$ cm, or 170 mm.

When letters are used for distances, as in Example 4(b) and (c), we do not usually attach dimensions to an answer. If the perimeter is $4s$, we actually mean that it is $4s$ units of length.

Problem Solving Roping a Square

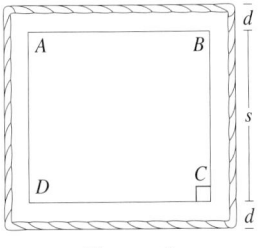

Figure 6

Given a square $ABCD$ with sides of length s, stretch a thin rope tightly around the square. Take the rope off, add 100 ft to it, and put the extended rope back around the square so that it is evenly spaced and the new rope makes a square around the original square, as in Figure 6. Find d, the distance between the squares.

Understanding the Problem We are to determine the distance between a square and a new square formed by adding 100 ft of rope to a rope that was stretched around the original square. Figure 6 shows the situation if the length of the side of the original square is s and the unknown distance is d.

Devising a Plan We can *write an equation* to model the problem. The perimeter of the new square is $4s + 100$. Another way to represent this perimeter is $4(s + 2d)$. Therefore, we have $4s + 100 = 4(s + 2d)$. We must solve this equation for d.

Carrying Out the Plan We solve the equation as shown.

$$4s + 100 = 4(s + 2d)$$
$$4s + 100 = 4s + 8d$$
$$100 = 8d$$
$$12.5 = d$$

Therefore, the distance between the squares is 12.5 ft.

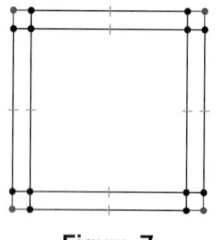

Figure 7

Looking Back A different way to think about the problem is to consider the individual parts that must sum to 100. The perimeter of the original square does not change in Figure 7, but the eight red segments sum to 100 ft so one red segment has length $\frac{100}{8}$, or 12.5 ft. The answer is the same regardless of the size of the original square. The distance is always 12.5 ft. This problem can be extended to figures other than squares.

Circumference of a Circle

A circle was defined as the set of all points in a plane that are the same distance from a given point, the center. The perimeter of a circle is its **circumference**. Ancient Greeks discovered that if they divided the circumference of any circle by the length of its diameter, they always obtained approximately the same number. It can be proven that the ratio of circumference C to diameter d is always the same for all circles. It is symbolized as π (**pi**). For most practical purposes, π is approximated by $\frac{22}{7}$, $3\frac{1}{7}$, or 3.14. These values are not exact values of π.

The relationship $\frac{C}{d} = \pi$ is used for finding the circumference of a circle and normally is written
$C = \pi d$ or $C = 2\pi r$ because the length of the diameter d is twice the length of the radius r of the circle. The exact circumference of a circle with diameter 6 cm is 6π cm, and an approximation might be
$6\pi \approx 6 \cdot 3.14 = 18.84$ cm.

The student page shown on page 821 shows two approaches to finding the circumference of a circle.

▶ NOW TRY THIS 2

To approximate the value of π, we need string, a marked ruler, and several different-sized round cans or jars. Pick a can and wrap the string tightly around the base of the can. Use a pen to mark a point on the string where the beginning of the string meets the string again. Unwrap the string and measure the length from the starting end to the marked point. Next, determine the diameter of the can by tracing the bottom of the can on a piece of paper. Fold the circle onto itself to find a line of symmetry. The chord determined by the line is a diameter of the circle. Measure the diameter and determine the ratio of the circumference to the diameter. Use the same units in all measurements. Repeat the experiment with at least three cans and find the average of the corresponding ratios.

In class, record all diameters and corresponding circumferences in columns A and B in a spreadsheet. Plot the graph of this data, with circumference on the vertical axis and diameter on the horizontal axis. What do we observe? Find a trend (fitted) line for the data. What is the slope of this line?

(**Historical Note**)

$\pi = 3.14159\,26535\,89793\,23846\,26433\,83279\,50288\,41971\,69399\,37510\,58209\ldots$

Archimedes (b. 287–212 BCE) approximated π by the inequality $3\frac{10}{71} < \pi < 3\frac{10}{70}$; a Chinese astronomer thought that $\pi = \frac{355}{113}$; German mathematician Ludolph van Ceulen (1540–1610) calculated π to 35 decimal places; and Leonhard Euler adopted the symbol π in 1737. In 1761, Johann Lambert, an Alsatian mathematician, proved that π is an irrational number. Alexander Yee and Shigern Kondo produced 12.1 trillion digits of π in 2013.   ●

School Book Page · Circumference

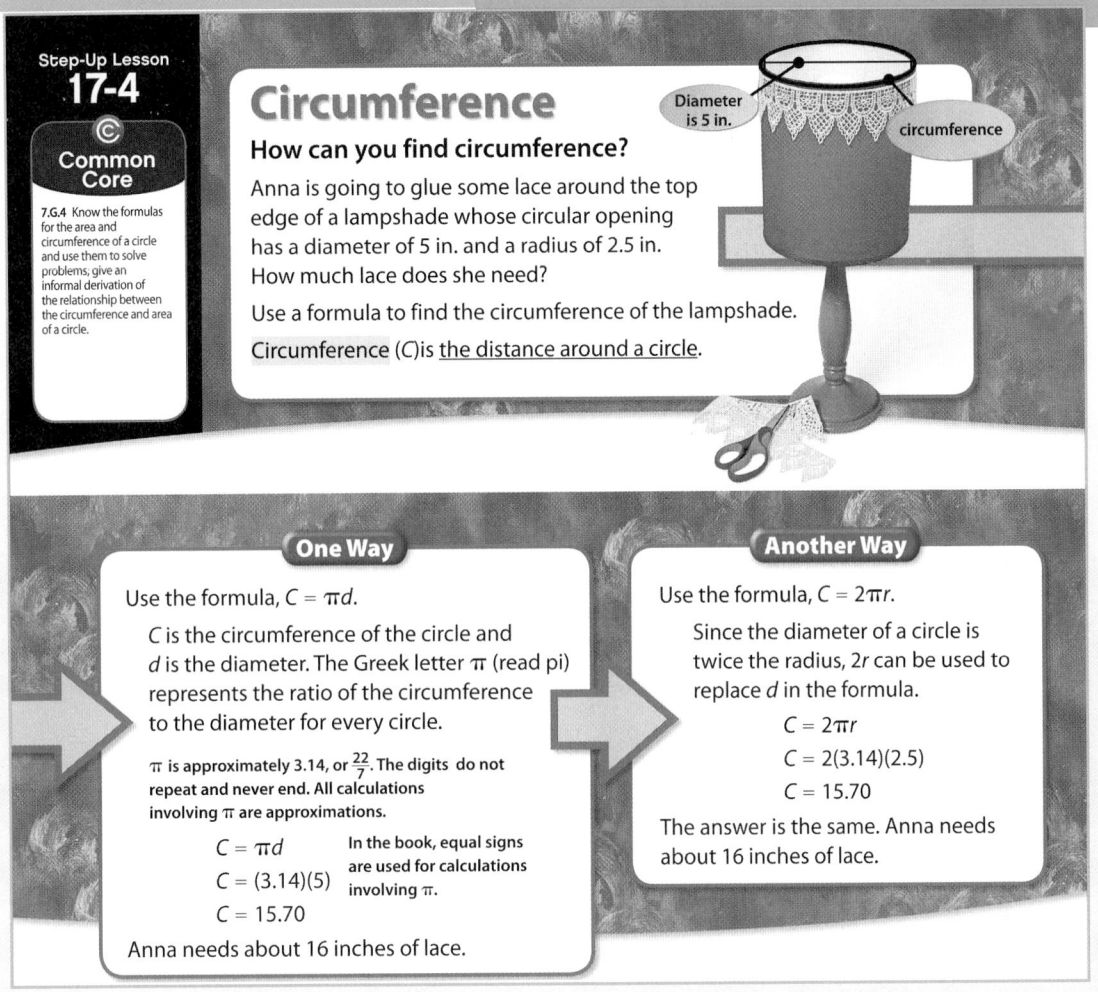

Step-Up Lesson 17-4

Common Core

7.G.4 Know the formulas for the area and circumference of a circle and use them to solve problems; give an informal derivation of the relationship between the circumference and area of a circle.

Circumference

How can you find circumference?

Anna is going to glue some lace around the top edge of a lampshade whose circular opening has a diameter of 5 in. and a radius of 2.5 in. How much lace does she need?

Diameter is 5 in.

circumference

Use a formula to find the circumference of the lampshade.

Circumference (*C*)is <u>the distance around a circle</u>.

One Way

Use the formula, $C = \pi d$.

C is the circumference of the circle and *d* is the diameter. The Greek letter π (read pi) represents the ratio of the circumference to the diameter for every circle.

π is approximately 3.14, or $\frac{22}{7}$. The digits do not repeat and never end. All calculations involving π are approximations.

$C = \pi d$
$C = (3.14)(5)$
$C = 15.70$

In the book, equal signs are used for calculations involving π.

Anna needs about 16 inches of lace.

Another Way

Use the formula, $C = 2\pi r$.

Since the diameter of a circle is twice the radius, $2r$ can be used to replace *d* in the formula.

$C = 2\pi r$
$C = 2(3.14)(2.5)$
$C = 15.70$

The answer is the same. Anna needs about 16 inches of lace.

Source: pp. 438–439; From enVisionMATH Common Core (Grade 6). Copyright © 2012 Pearson Education, Inc., or its affiliates. Used by permission. All Rights Reserved.

Arc Length

Earlier in the book, an arc was associated with a central angle and its degree measure. An arc length can be measured as part of the circumference of the circle containing the arc. Arc length depends on the radius of the circle and the central angle determining the arc. The length of an arc whose central angle measures $\theta°$ can be developed as in Figure 8 by using proportional reasoning. Since a circle has $360°$, an angle of $\theta°$ determines $\frac{\theta}{360}$ of a circle. Because the circumference of a circle is $2\pi r$, an arc of $\theta°$ has length $\left(\frac{\theta}{360}\right)(2\pi r)$, or $\frac{\pi r \theta}{180}$ unit lengths (depending on the unit for *r*).

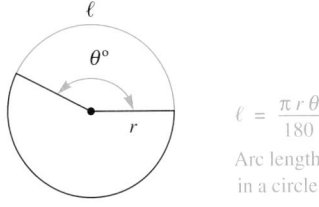

$\ell = \dfrac{\pi r \theta}{180}$

Arc length in a circle

Figure 8

Example 5

Find each of the following measures.

   a. The circumference of a circle whose radius is 2 m.
   b. The radius of a circle whose circumference is 15π m.
   c. The length of a 25° arc of a circle whose radius is 10 cm.
   d. The radius of an arc whose central angle is 87° and whose arc length is 154 cm.

Solution

   a. $C = 2\pi(2) = 4\pi$; thus the circumference is 4π m, or approximately 12.57 m.

   b. $C = 2\pi r$ implies $15\pi = 2\pi r$. Hence, $r = \dfrac{15}{2}$, and the radius is 7.5 m.

   c. The arc length is $\dfrac{\pi r\theta}{180} = \dfrac{\pi(10)(25)}{180}$ cm $= \dfrac{25\pi}{18}$ cm, or approximately 4.36 cm.

   d. The arc length ℓ is $\dfrac{\pi r\theta}{180}$, so $154 = \dfrac{\pi r(87)}{180}$. Thus, $r = \dfrac{27{,}720}{87\pi} \approx 101$ cm.

Comparing Linear Measurements of Similar Figures

Two planar figures are similar if they have the same shape but not necessarily the same size. As discussed in Chapter 12, the ratio of the corresponding side lengths is the *scale factor*, which we refer to as k. In Figure 9, $\triangle ABC \sim \triangle A_1B_1C_1$ with scale factor k; that is $\dfrac{a}{a_1} = \dfrac{b}{b_1} = \dfrac{c}{c_1} = k$.

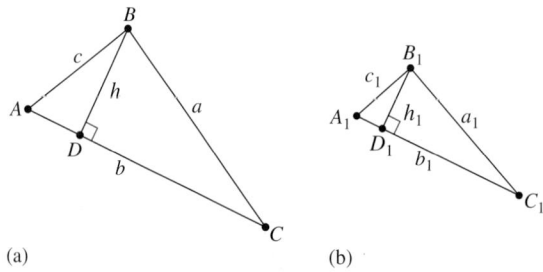

(a)   (b)

Figure 9

Because $\triangle ABD \sim \triangle A_1B_1D_1$ (why?), we have $\dfrac{h}{h_1} = \dfrac{c}{c_1} = k$. Therefore the heights of the two similar triangles also have the same scale factor, k. This is true in general and is summarized in Theorem 14-2.

Theorem 14-2

If the scale factor of two similar figures is k, then the ratio of any corresponding *linear measurements* of two similar figures, such as length, width, height, perimeter, diagonal, diameter, and slant height is k.

Assessment 14-1A

1. Use the following picture of a ruler to find each of the lengths in centimeters.

   a. *AB* 1 cm
   b. *DE* 1 cm
   c. *CJ* 8 cm
   d. *EF* 0.5 cm
   e. *IJ* 0.7 cm
   f. *AF* 5 cm
   g. *IC* 7.3 cm
   h. *GB* 5.2 cm

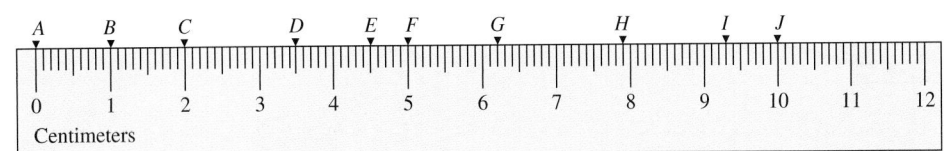

2. Estimate and then measure each of the following in terms of the units listed. *Answers vary.*
   a. The length of your desktop in cubits (elbow to outstretched fingers)
   b. The length of this page in pencil lengths
   c. The width of this book in pencil widths

3. Complete each of the following.
   a. 100 in. = _____ yd $2\frac{7}{9}$
   b. 400 yd = __14,400__ in.
   c. 300 ft = __100__ yd
   d. 372 in. = __31__ ft

4. Draw segments that you estimate to be of the given lengths. Use a metric ruler to check the estimates. *Answers vary.*
   a. 10 mm   **b.** 100 mm   **c.** 1 cm   **d.** 10 cm

5. Estimate the length of the following segment and then measure it:

   Express the measurement in each of the following units.
   a. Millimeters *Approximately 81 mm*
   b. Centimeters *Approximately 8.1 cm*

6. Choose an appropriate metric unit and estimate each of the following measures (check your estimates). *Answers vary.*
   a. The length of a pencil *Centimeters*
   b. The diameter of a nickel *Centimeters or millimeters*
   c. The width of the top of a desk *Centimeters or meters*

7. Repeat exercise 6 using English measures. *

8. Complete the following table. *

Item	m	cm	mm
a. Length of a piece of paper		35	
b. Height of a woman	1.63		
c. Width of a filmstrip			35
d. Length of a cigarette			100
e. Length of two meter-sticks laid end to end	2		

9. If the U.S. money system used metric prefixes and the base unit was a dollar, give metric names to each of the following amounts.
   a. Dime *   **b.** Penny *   **c.** $10 bill *
   d. $100 bill *   **e.** $1000 bill *

10. For each of the following, place a decimal point in the number to make the sentence reasonable.
    a. A stack of 10 dimes is 1350 mm high. *13.50*
    b. The desk is 770 m high. *0.770*
    c. The distance from one side of a street to the other is 100 m. *10.0*
    d. A dollar bill is 155 cm long. *15.5*

11. List the following in decreasing order: 8 cm, 5218 mm, 245 cm, 91 mm, 6 m, 700 mm. *

12. Draw a circle as accurately as possible whose circumference is 4 in. *Answers vary.*

13. **a.** What is the length of a semicircle of a circle whose radius is 1 unit? *π units*
    b. What is the length of a semicircle of a circle whose radius is $\frac{1}{2}$ unit? *$\frac{\pi}{2}$ units*

14. Guess the perimeter in centimeters of each of the following figures and then check the estimates using a ruler. *

    a.
    b.

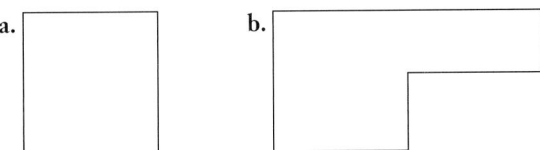

15. Complete each of the following.
    a. 10 mm = __1__ cm
    b. 262 m = __0.262__ km
    c. 3 km = __3000__ m
    d. 30 mm = __0.03__ m

16. Draw a triangle *ABC*. Measure the length of each of its sides in millimeters. For each of the following, tell which is greater and by how much.
    a. *AB* + *BC* or *AC* *AB + BC > AC*
    b. *BC* + *CA* or *AB* *BC + CA > AB*
    c. *AB* + *CA* or *BC* *AB + CA > BC*

17. Can the following be the lengths of the sides of a triangle?
    a. 23 cm, 50 cm, 60 cm *Yes*
    b. 10 cm, 40 cm, 50 cm *No*

18. If two sides of a triangle have lengths 31 cm and 85 cm, and the measure of the third side must be a whole number of centimeters,
    a. what is the longest the third side can be? *115 cm*
    b. what is the shortest the third side can be? *55 cm*

19. Take an $8\frac{1}{2} \times 11$-in. piece of paper, fold it as shown in the following figure, and then cut the folded paper along the diagonal as shown.   Answers vary.

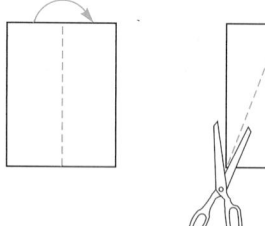

a. Rearrange the two smaller pieces to form a triangle with the minimum perimeter.   Perimeter is approximately 32.1 in.

b. Arrange the two smaller pieces to form a triangle with the maximum perimeter.   Perimeter is approximately 45.6 in.

20. For each of the following circumferences, find the radius of the circle.

a. 12π cm   6 cm

b. 6 m $\frac{3}{\pi}$ m

21. For each of the following, if a circle has the dimensions given, determine its circumference.

a. 6 cm diameter 6π cm

b. $\frac{2}{\pi}$ cm radius   4 cm

22. What happens to the circumference of a circle if the length of the radius is doubled?   The circumference will double.

23. Jets can exceed the speed of sound. A *Mach number* describes the speed of such planes. Mach 2 is twice the speed of sound. The speed of sound in air is approximately 344 m/sec.

a. If the speed of a plane is described as Mach 3, what is its speed in meters per second?   1032 m/sec

b. Describe the speed of 5000 km/hr as a Mach number.   *

24. Give the greatest possible error for each of the following measurements.

a. 23 m   0.5 m

b. 3.6 cm   0.05 cm

c. 3.12 m   0.005 m or 5 mm

25. a. Find the length of a 36° arc of a circle whose radius is 6 cm. $\frac{6\pi}{5}$ cm

b. Explain why you think that the arc in part (a) is longer or shorter in terms of centimeters if the radius had been 8 cm.   *

c. Find the arc length when the radius is increased to 8 cm.   The arc length is $\frac{8\pi}{5}$ cm.

26. Find the radius of the circle containing an 80° arc whose length is 14π m. $\frac{63}{2}$ m

27. Suppose you have three concentric circles and are looking at the arc lengths of a 60° angle of each. If the radii of the circles have ratio $2:3:4$, what is the ratio of the arc lengths? $2:3:4$

Assessment 14-1B

1. Use the following picture of a ruler to find each of the lengths in inches.

a. *AB* 1 in.	**e.** *IJ* $\frac{1}{2}$ in.
b. *DE* $\frac{3}{4}$ in.	**f.** *AF* 4 in.
c. *CJ* 4 in.	**g.** *IC* $3\frac{1}{2}$ in.
d. *EF* $\frac{3}{4}$ in.	**h.** *GB* $3\frac{5}{8}$ in.

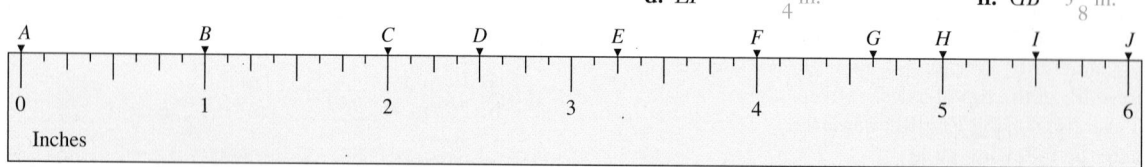

2. Estimate and then measure each of the following in terms of the units listed.   Answers vary.

a. The length of your desktop in mathematics book lengths

b. The length of this page in paper dollar widths

c. The width of this page in paper dollar lengths

3. Convert each of the following to the indicated unit.

a. 100 in. = _____ ft $8\frac{1}{3}$

b. 400 yd = __1200__ ft

c. 300 ft = __3600__ in.

d. 372 in. = _____ yd $10\frac{1}{3}$

4. Draw segments that you estimate to be of the following lengths. Use a metric ruler to check the estimates.   *

a. 0.01 m   **b.** 15 cm   **c.** 35 mm   **d.** 150 mm

5. Estimate the length of the following segment and then measure it.   Answers vary.

Express the measurement in each of the following units.

a. Millimeters   40 mm

b. Centimeters   4 cm

6. Choose an appropriate metric unit and estimate each of the following measures (check your estimates).   Answers vary.

a. The thickness of the top of a desk   Centimeters

b. The length of this page of paper   Centimeters

c. The height of a door   Meters or centimeters

7. Repeat exercise 6 using English measures.   *

8. Complete the following table.   *

Item	m	cm	mm
a. Width of a piece of paper		20	
b. Height of a woman	1.52		
c. Length of a pencil			90
d. Length of a baseball bat	1.1		

9. If eggs were sold in the United States using metric prefixes, and the base unit was a carton of 10 eggs, tell the number of eggs in each of the following containers.

a. Decicarton   1   **b.** Dekacarton   100

c. Hectocarton   1000   **d.** Kilocarton   10,000

10. For each of the following, place a decimal point in the number to make the sentence reasonable.
    a. The basketball player is 1950 cm tall. 195.0
    b. A new piece of chalk is about 8100 cm long. 8.100
    c. The speed limit in town is 400 km/hr. 40.0
11. List the following in decreasing order: 8 m, 5218 cm, 245 cm, 91 m, 6 m, 925 mm. 91 m; 5218 cm; 8 m; 6 m; 245 cm; 925 mm
12. Draw each of the following as accurately as possible.
    a. A triangle whose perimeter is 4 in. Answers vary.
    b. A 4-sided figure whose perimeter is 8 cm.
13. The following figure is a circle whose radius is 2 cm. The diameters of the two semicircular regions inside the large circle are also 2 cm long. Compute the length of the curve that separates the shaded and white regions. 2π cm

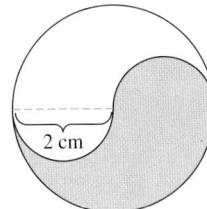

14. Guess the perimeter in centimeters of each of the following figures and then check the estimates using a ruler. *

    a. 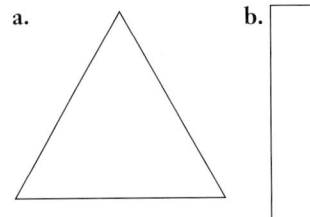   b.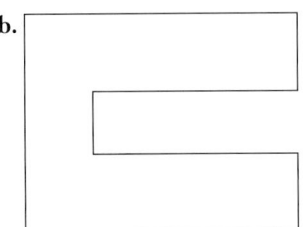

15. Complete each of the following conversions.
    a. 35 m = ___3500___ cm
    b. 359 mm = ___0.359___ m
    c. 647 mm = ___64.7___ cm
    d. 0.1 cm = ___1___ mm
16. Explain in your own words why the Triangle Inequality must be true. *
17. Can the following be the lengths of the sides of a triangle?
    a. 20 cm, 40 cm, 50 cm Yes
    b. 20 cm, 40 cm, 60 cm No
    c. 41 cm, 250 mm, 12 cm No
18. If two sides of a triangle have lengths 21 cm and 75 cm, and the measure of the third side must be a whole number of centimeters,
    a. what is the longest the third side can be? 95 cm
    b. what is the shortest the third side can be? 55 cm
19. The following figure made of 6 unit squares has a perimeter of 12 units. The figure is made in such a way that each square must share at least one complete side with another square.

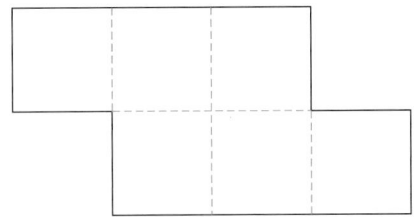

a. Add more squares to the figure above so that the perimeter of the new figure is 18. *
b. Consider any figure made of squares where each square must share at least one complete side with another square, what is the minimum number of squares required to build a figure of perimeter 18? 8
c. Under the same condition as part (b), what is the maximum number of squares possible to build a figure of perimeter 18? 20
20. For each of the following circumferences, find the radius of the circle. $\frac{0.335}{\pi}$ m
    a. 0.67 m
    b. 92π cm 46 cm
21. For each of the following, if a circle has the dimensions given, determine its circumference.
    a. 3-cm radius 6π cm
    b. 6π-cm diameter $6\pi^2$ cm
22. How does the radius of a circle change if the circumference is doubled? The radius is doubled.
23. Astronomers use a light-year to measure distance. A light-year is the distance light travels in 1 yr. The speed of light is approximately 300,000 km/sec.
    a. How long is 1 light-year in kilometers? *
    b. The nearest star (other than the sun) is Alpha Centauri. It is 4.34 light-years from Earth. How far is that in kilometers? About $4.1 \cdot 10^{13}$ km
    c. How long will it take a rocket traveling 60,000 km/hr to reach Alpha Centauri? About $6.8 \cdot 10^8$ hr or about 78,000 yr
24. Give the greatest possible error for each of the following measures.
    a. 136 m 0.5 m
    b. 3.5 ft 0.05 ft
    c. 3.62 cm 0.005 cm
25. a. Find the length of a 48° arc of a circle whose radius is 6 cm. $\frac{8\pi}{5}$ cm
    b. Explain why you think that the arc in part (a) is longer or shorter if the radius were 8 cm. *
    c. Find the arc length when the radius is increased to 8 cm. The arc length is $\frac{32}{15}\pi$ cm.
26. Find the radius of the circle containing 60° arc whose length is 12π m. 36 m
27. Suppose you have five concentric circles and are looking at the arc lengths of a 60° angle of each. If the radii or the circles have ratio 3:4:5, what is the ratio of the arc lengths? The arc lengths are in the same ratio, 3:4:5.

Mathematical Connections 14-1

Answers to Mathematical Connections can be found in the Answers section at the back of the book.

Reasoning

1. There has been considerable debate about whether the United States should change to the metric system.
   a. Based on your experiences with linear measure, what do you see as the advantages of changing?
   b. Which system do you think would be easier for children to learn? Why?
   c. What things will probably not change if the United States adopts the metric system?

2. In track, the second lane from the inside of the track is longer than the inside lane. Use this information to explain why, in running events that require a complete lap of the track, runners are lined up at the starting blocks as shown in the following figure and run counterclockwise.

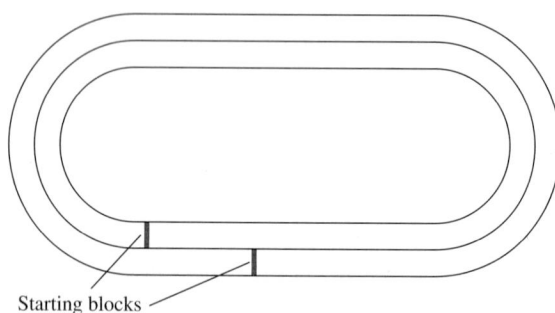

Starting blocks

3. To obtain an upper and lower bound for the circumference of a circle, a square is inscribed in the circle and a square is circumscribed about the circle. The perimeters of the squares become the bounds.

   a. Suppose the radius of the circle is $\frac{r}{2}$. Find the perimeters described.
   b. Use the perimeters found in part (a) to give upper and lower bounds for the value of π.

4. If one measured an object in both inches and centimeters, which measure do you expect to be more accurate and why?

Open-Ended

5. Observe that it is possible to build a triangle with toothpicks that has sides of 3, 4, and 5 toothpicks, as shown, and answer the questions that follow.

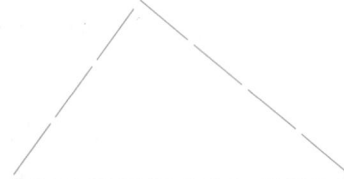

   a. Find two other triples of toothpicks that can be used as sides of a triangle and two other triples that cannot be used to create a triangle.
   b. Describe how to tell whether a given triple of numbers a, b, c can be used to construct a triangle with sides of a, b, and c toothpicks.

6. Research shoe sizes and write a paragraph with a rationale for standardizing shoe sizes.

Cooperative Learning

7. a. Help each person in the group find his or her height in centimeters.
   b. Help each person in the group find the length of his or her outstretched arms (horizontal) from fingertip to fingertip in centimeters.
   c. Compare the difference between the two measurements in parts (a) and (b). Compare the results of the group members and make a conjecture about the relationship between the two measurements.
   d. Compare your group's results with other groups to determine if they have similar findings.

8. Jerry wants to design a gold chain 60 cm long made of thin gold wire circles, each of which is the same size. He wants to use the least amount of wire and wonders what the radius of each circle should be.

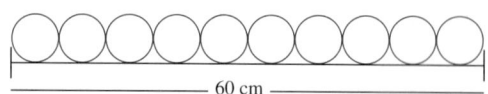

60 cm

   a. Each member of the group should choose a specific number of circles and find the length of wire needed to make a 60-cm chain with the chosen number of circles.
   b. Compare your results and make a conjecture based on the results.
   c. Justify your conjecture.

Connecting Mathematics to the Classroom

9. A student claims that the circumference of a semicircle is the same as that of a circle from which the semicircle was taken because one has to measure the "outer part" and the "inner part." How do you respond?

10. A student has a tennis ball can with a flat top and bottom containing three tightly fitting tennis balls. To the student's surprise, the circumference of the top of the can is longer than the height of the can. The student wants to know if this fact can be explained without performing any measurements. How do you respond?

11. A student asks why $\frac{22}{7}$ cannot always be used as the value of π. How do you respond?

12. A student imagines a wire stretched around Earth. She says that if the wire is cut, its length is increased by 20 m, and it is restretched around Earth, then the tallest person alive could walk under it. Do you agree with her? Why or why not?

National Assessments

National Assessment of Educational Progress (NAEP) Questions

Which of these units would be the best to use to measure the length of a school building?

A. Millimeters
B. Centimeters
C. Meters
D. Kilometers

NAEP, Grade 4, 2007

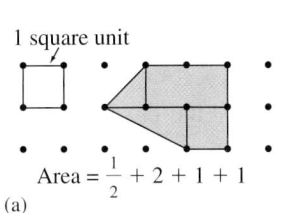

12 inches

Fred's Rope

Susan's Rope

If Fred's rope is 12 inches long, about how long is Susan's rope?

A. 16 inches
B. 20 inches
C. 24 inches
D. 30 inches

NAEP, Grade 4, 2007

14-2 Areas of Polygons and Circles

14-2 Objectives

Students will be able to understand and explain

- Areas of rectangles, parallelograms, triangles, kites, trapezoids, regular polygons, circles, and sectors of circles.

- Conversion of area units.

- Ratio of area measures of similar figures.

CCSS In the grade 3 *Common Core Standards*, we find that students should "apply the area and perimeter formulas for rectangles in real-world and mathematical problems" (p. 31). We also find in the grade 6 *Common Core Standards* that students should "find the area of right triangles, other triangles, special quadrilaterals, and polygons by composing into rectangles or decomposing into triangles and other shapes" (p. 44).

In this section, we quantify area using same-sized square units and develop formulas for the areas of various polygons. Technically, we find the areas of regions determined by shapes; for example, we use the vernacular *"find the area of a triangle"* instead of *"find the area of the region determined by a triangle."*

Area is *measured using square units and the area of a region is the number of nonoverlapping square units that covers the region.* A square measuring 1 ft on a side has an area of 1 square foot, denoted 1 ft^2. A square measuring 1 cm on a side has an area of 1 square centimeter, denoted 1 cm^2.

Students sometimes confuse an area of 5 cm^2 with the area of a square 5 cm on each side. The area of a square 5 cm on each side is $(5 \text{ cm})^2 = 25 \text{ cm}^2$. Five squares, each 1 cm by 1 cm, have the area of 5 cm^2. Thus, $5 \text{ cm}^2 \neq (5 \text{ cm})^2$.

Areas on a Geoboard

Addition Method

✋ Activity Manual

Use *Areas of Polygons* to develop the concept of area through the composition and decomposition of non-overlapping parts of figures on a geoboard.

In teaching the concept of area, intuitive activities precede the development of formulas. Many intuitive activities can be accomplished using a *geoboard* or *dot paper*. A square unit is defined in the upper left corner of the dot paper in Figure 10(a). The area of the shaded pentagon can be found by finding the sum of the areas of smaller pieces. Finding the area in this way uses the *addition method*. The region in Figure 10(b) has been decomposed into smaller pieces in Figure 10(c). What is the area of this shape?

1 square unit

$$\text{Area} = \frac{1}{2} + 2 + 1 + 1$$

(a)

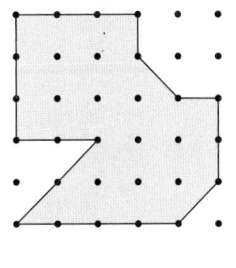

(b)

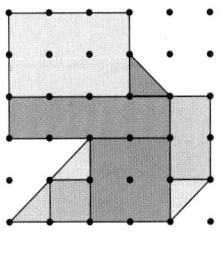

(c)

Figure 10

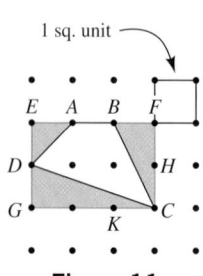

1 sq. unit

Figure 11

Rectangle Method

Another method of finding the area of shapes on the dot paper is the *rectangle method*. To find the area of quadrilateral *ABCD* in Figure 11, we construct the rectangle *EFCG* around the quadrilateral and then subtract the areas of the shaded triangles *EAD*, *BFC*, and *DGC* from the area of *EFCG*. The area of rectangle *EFCG* can be counted to be 6 square units. The area of $\triangle EAD$ is $\frac{1}{2}$ square unit, and the area of $\triangle BFC$ is half the area of rectangle *BFCK*, or $\frac{1}{2}$ of $2 = 1$ square unit. Similarly, the area of $\triangle DGC$ is half the area of rectangle *DHCG*; that is, $\frac{1}{2} \cdot 3 = \frac{3}{2}$ square units. Consequently, the area of *ABCD* is $6 - \left(\frac{1}{2} + 1 + \frac{3}{2}\right) = 3$ square units.

Example 6

Using a geoboard, find the area of each of the shaded regions of Figure 12.

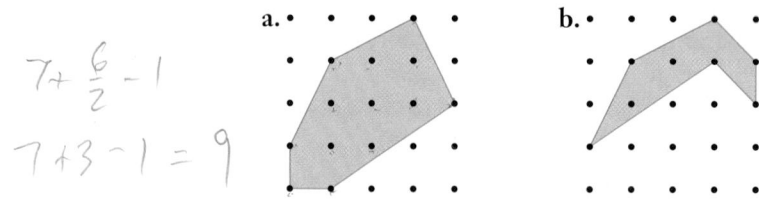

a.   b.

$7 + \frac{6}{2} - 1$

$7 + 3 - 1 = 9$

Figure 12

Solution

a. We construct a rectangle around the hexagon and then subtract the areas of regions *a*, *b*, *c*, *d*, and *e* from the area of this rectangle, as shown in Figure 13. Therefore, the area of the hexagon is $16 - (3 + 1 + 1 + 1 + 1) = 9$ square units. The addition method could also be used in this problem.

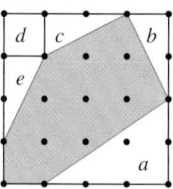

Figure 13

b. The area of the hexagon equals the area of the surrounding rectangle shown in Figure 14 minus the sum of the areas of figures *a*, *b*, *c*, *d*, *e*, *f*, and *g*. Thus, the area of the hexagon is

$$12 - \left(3 + 1 + \frac{1}{2} + \frac{1}{2} + 1 + 1 + 1\right) = 4 \text{ square units.}$$

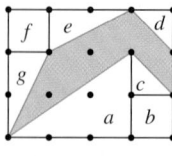

Figure 14

Converting Units of Area

The price of carpet for a house is quoted in terms of dollars per square yard, for example, $12.50/yd². The most commonly used units of area in the English system are the square inch (in.²), the square foot (ft²), the square yard (yd²), the square mile (mi²), and for land measure, the acre. In the metric system, the most commonly used units are the square millimeter (mm²), the square centimeter (cm²), the square meter (m²), the square kilometer (km²), and for land measure, the hectare (ha). It is often necessary to convert from one area measure to another within a system.

To determine how many 1-cm squares are in 1 m², look at Figure 15(a). There are 100 cm in 1 m, so each side of the square meter has a measure of 100 cm. Thus, it takes 100 rows of 100 1-cm squares each to fill a square meter; that is, $100 \cdot 100 = 10{,}000$ 1-cm squares. Because the area of each centimeter square is $1 \text{ cm} \cdot 1 \text{ cm} = 1 \text{ cm}^2$, there are 10,000 cm² in 1 m². In general, *the area A of a square that is s units on a side is s^2 square units*, as shown in Figure 15(b).

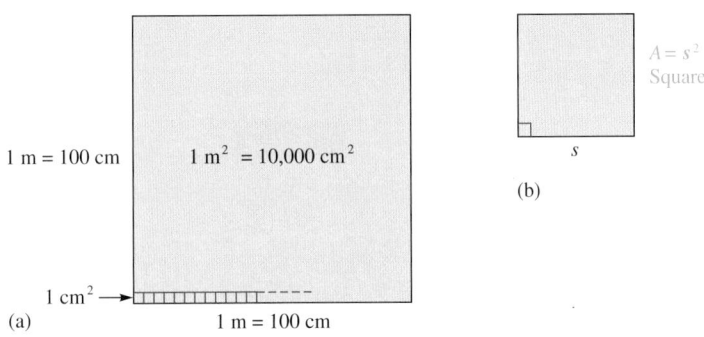

Figure 15

Other metric conversions of area measure can be developed similarly. For example, Figure 16(a) shows that $1 \text{ m}^2 = 10{,}000 \text{ cm}^2 = 1{,}000{,}000 \text{ mm}^2$. Likewise, Figure 16(b) shows that $1 \text{ m}^2 = 0.000001 \text{ km}^2$. Similarly, $1 \text{ cm}^2 = 100 \text{ mm}^2$ and $1 \text{ km}^2 = 1{,}000{,}000 \text{ m}^2$.

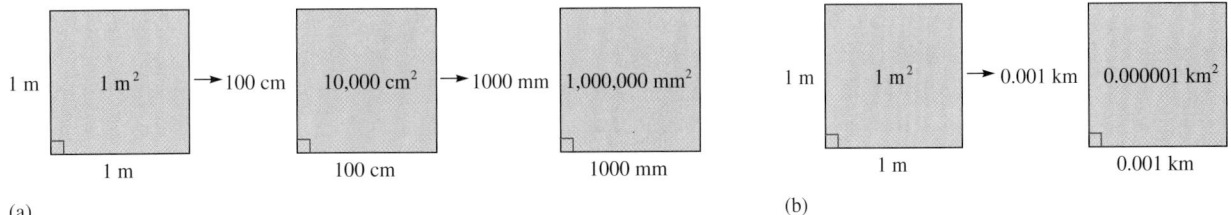

Figure 16

Table 4 shows symbols for metric units of area and their relationship to the square meter.

Table 4		
Unit	**Symbol**	**Relationship to Square Meter**
square kilometer	km²	1,000,000 m²
*square hectometer	hm²	10,000 m²
*square dekameter	dam²	100 m²
square meter	**m²**	**1 m²**
*square decimeter	dm²	0.01 m²
square centimeter	cm²	0.0001 m²
square millimeter	mm²	0.000001 m²

*Not commonly used

Example 7

Complete each of the following conversions.

  a. $5 \text{ cm}^2 =$ _____ mm^2
  b. $124{,}000{,}000 \text{ m}^2 =$ _____ km^2

Solution

  a. $1 \text{ cm}^2 = 100 \text{ mm}^2$ implies $5 \text{ cm}^2 = 5 \cdot 1 \text{ cm}^2 = 5 \cdot 100 \text{ mm}^2 = 500 \text{ mm}^2$.
  b. $1 \text{ m}^2 = 0.000001 \text{ km}^2$ implies $124{,}000{,}000 \text{ m}^2 = 124{,}000{,}000 \cdot 1 \text{ m}^2$
                $= 124{,}000{,}000 \cdot 0.000001 \text{ km}^2 = 124 \text{ km}^2$.

Based on the relationship among units of length in the English system, it is possible to convert among English units of area. For example, because $1 \text{ yd} = 3 \text{ ft}$, it follows that $1 \text{ yd}^2 = (1 \text{ yd})^2 = 1 \text{ yd} \cdot 1 \text{ yd} = 3 \text{ ft} \cdot 3 \text{ ft} = 9 \text{ ft}^2$. Similarly, because $1 \text{ ft} = 12 \text{ in.}$, $1 \text{ ft}^2 = (1 \text{ ft})^2 = 1 \text{ ft} \cdot 1 \text{ ft} = 12 \text{ in.} \cdot 12 \text{ in.} = 144 \text{ in.}^2$. Table 5 summarizes various relationships among units of area in the English system.

Table 5

Unit of Area	Equivalent in Other Units
1 ft^2	$\dfrac{1}{9} \text{ yd}^2$, or 144 in.^2
1 yd^2	9 ft^2, or 1296 in.^2
1 mi^2	$3{,}097{,}600 \text{ yd}^2$, or $27{,}878{,}400 \text{ ft}^2$

Land Measure

The concept of area is widely used in land measure. *The common unit of land measure in the English system is the **acre**.* Historically, an acre was the amount of land a man with one horse could plow in one day. There are 4840 yd^2 in 1 acre. *For very large land measures in the English system, the **square mile** (mi^2), or 640 acres, is used.*

*In the metric system, small land areas are measured in terms of a square unit 10 m on a side, called an **are** (pronounced "air") and denoted by **a**. Thus, $1 \text{ a} = 10 \text{ m} \cdot 10 \text{ m} = 100 \text{ m}^2$. Larger land areas are measured in **hectares**.* A hectare is 100 a. A hectare, denoted by **ha**, is the amount of land whose area is $10{,}000 \text{ m}^2$. It follows that 1 ha is the area of a square that is 100 m on a side. Therefore, $1 \text{ ha} = 1 \text{ hm}^2$. *For very large land measures, the **square kilometer**, denoted by km^2, is used.* One square kilometer is the area of a square with a side $1 \text{ km} = 1000 \text{ m}$ long. Land area measures are summarized in Table 6.

Table 6

	Unit of Area	Equivalent in Other Units
Metric	1 a	100 m^2
	1 ha	100 a, or $10{,}000 \text{ m}^2$, or 1 hm^2
	1 km^2	$1{,}000{,}000 \text{ m}^2$ or 100 ha
English	1 acre	4840 yd^2
	1 mi^2	640 acres

Example 8

a. A square field has a side of 400 m. Find the area of the field in hectares.
b. A square field has a side of 400 yd. Find the area of the field in acres.

Solution

a. $A = (400\,\text{m})^2 = 160{,}000\,\text{m}^2 = 160{,}000\,\cancel{\text{m}^2}\left(\dfrac{1\,\text{ha}}{10{,}000\,\cancel{\text{m}^2}}\right) = 16\,\text{ha}$

b. $A = (400\,\text{yd})^2 = 160{,}000\,\text{yd}^2 = 160{,}000\,\cancel{\text{yd}^2}\left(\dfrac{1\,\text{acre}}{4840\,\cancel{\text{yd}^2}}\right) \approx 33.1\,\text{acres}$

Area of a Rectangle

CCSS In the grade 3 *Common Core Standards*, we see that students should "find the area of a rectangle with whole-number side lengths by tiling it and show that the area is the same as would be found by multiplying the side lengths." (p. 25)

Suppose the square in Figure 17(a) represents 1 square unit. Then, we can tile the rectangle *ABCD* as seen in Figure 17(b). It contains $3 \cdot 4 = 12$ square units.

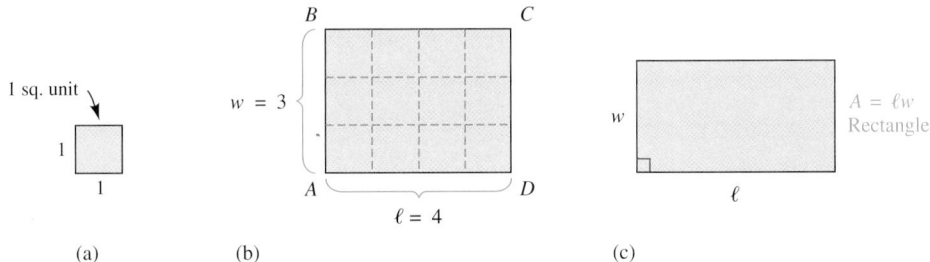

(a)   (b)   (c)

Figure 17

If the unit in Figure 17(a) is 1 cm², then the area of rectangle *ABCD* is 12 cm². In general, *the area A of any rectangle can be found by multiplying the lengths of two adjacent sides ℓ and w, or $A = \ell w$, as given in Figure 17(c).*

Example 9

Find the area of each rectangle in Figure 18.

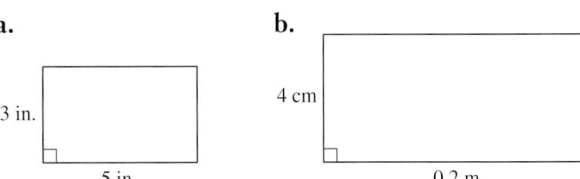

Figure 18

Solution

a. $A = (3\,\text{in.})(5\,\text{in.}) = 15\,\text{in.}^2$

b. First, write the lengths of the sides in the same unit of length. Because 0.2 m = 20 cm, $A = (4\,\text{cm})(20\,\text{cm}) = 80\,\text{cm}^2$. Alternatively, 4 cm = 0.04 m, so $A = (0.04\,\text{m})(0.2\,\text{m}) = 0.008\,\text{m}^2$.

▶ **NOW TRY THIS 3**

NTT 3: Approximately
100 cm²

Estimate the area in square centimeters of a dollar bill. Measure and calculate how close the estimate is to the actual area.

Area of a Parallelogram

The area of a parallelogram can be found by *reducing the problem to one that we already know how to solve*, in this case, finding the area of a rectangle. One important strategy for deriving the formula for the area of a parallelogram is by decomposing it. In decomposition, we cut a figure with unknown area into a number of pieces. By reassembling these pieces we obtain a figure whose area we know how to find.

Informally, to find the area of the parallelogram in Figure 19(a), we cut the shaded right triangular piece of the parallelogram and translate it to obtain the rectangle in Figure 19(b). Because the shaded areas are congruent, the area of the parallelogram in Figure 19(a) is the same as the area of the rectangle in Figure 19(b); that is, *the area A of the parallelogram is the length of its base b times the corresponding height h, or $A = bh$.*

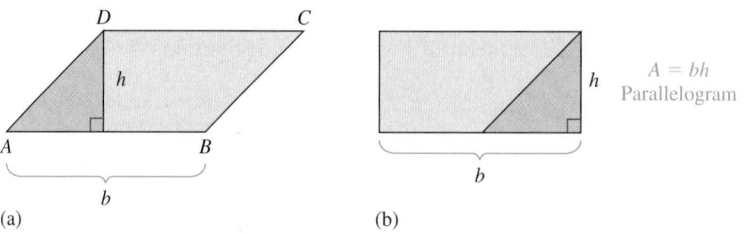

(a)   (b)

Figure 19

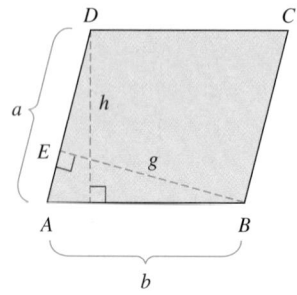

Figure 20

In general, any side of a parallelogram can be designated as a **base**. Each base has a corresponding base in a parallel line. For each set of bases, the **height** or **altitude** is the perpendicular distance between the bases and is always the length of a segment perpendicular to the lines containing the bases. The area of parallelogram $ABCD$ in Figure 20 is given by $A = bh$, that is, the length of the base times the corresponding height. Similarly EB, or g, is the height that corresponds to the bases $\overline{AD}$ and $\overline{BC}$, each of which has measure a. Consequently, the area of the parallelogram $ABCD$ is ag. Therefore, $A = ag = bh$.

Area of a Triangle

The formula for the area of a triangle can be derived from the formula for the area of a parallelogram. To explore this, suppose $\triangle BAC$ in Figure 21(a) has base of length b and height h. Let $\triangle ABC'$ be the image of $\triangle BAC$ when $\triangle BAC$ is rotated 180° about M, the midpoint of $\overline{AB}$, as in Figure 21(b). Proving that quadrilateral $BCAC'$ is a parallelogram is left as an exercise. Parallelogram $BCAC'$ has area bh and is constructed of congruent triangles BAC and ABC'. So the area of $\triangle ABC$ is $\frac{1}{2}bh$. In general, *the area of a triangle is equal to half the product of the length of a side and the height to that side.*

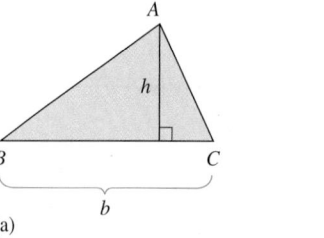
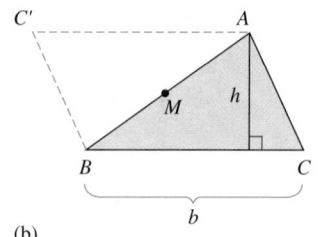

(a)   (b)

Figure 21

In Figure 22, $\overline{BC}$ is a base of $\triangle ABC$, and the corresponding height h_1, or AE, is the distance from the opposite vertex A to the line containing $\overline{BC}$. Similarly, $\overline{AC}$ can be chosen as a base. Then h_2, or BG, the distance from the opposite vertex B to the line containing $\overline{AC}$, is the corresponding height. If $\overline{AB}$ is chosen as a base, then the corresponding height is h_3, or CF. Thus, the area of $\triangle ABC$ is

$$\text{Area}(\triangle ABC) = \frac{bh_1}{2} = \frac{ah_2}{2} = \frac{ch_3}{2}.$$

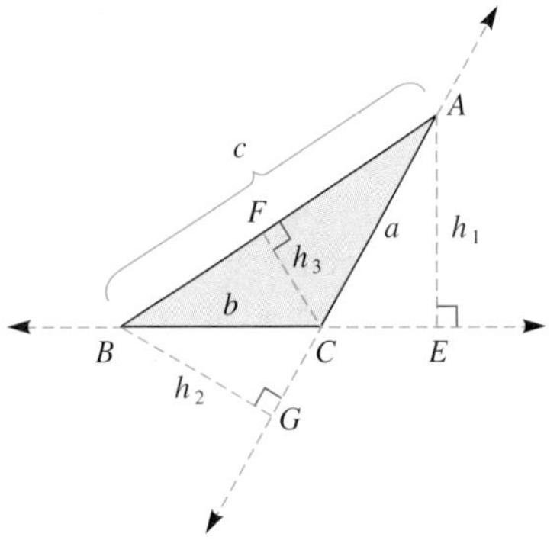

Figure 22

▶ **NOW TRY THIS 4**

NTT 4: Answer can be found in Answers at the back of the book.

To derive the formula for the area of a triangle from the formula for the area of a rectangle, cut out any triangle as in Figure 23(a); fold a perpendicular to the base with measurement b and containing point B to find the height h; and fold the altitude in half as shown in Figure 23(b). Next fold along the colored segments in the trapezoid in Figure 23(c) to obtain the rectangle in Figure 23(d).

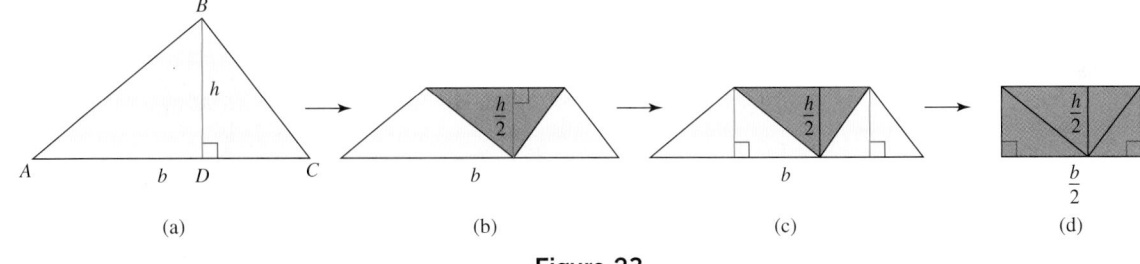

Figure 23

a. What is the area of the rectangle in Figure 23(d)?
b. How can the formula for the area of a triangle be developed from your answer in part (a)?

Example 10

In Figure 24, $\ell \parallel \overleftrightarrow{AB}$. How are the areas of $\triangle ABP$, $\triangle ABQ$, $\triangle ABR$, $\triangle ABS$, $\triangle ABT$, and $\triangle ABU$ related? Explain your answer.

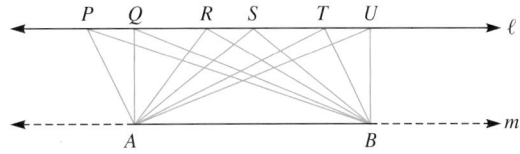

Figure 24

Solution   In Figure 24, *AB* is the length of the base of each of the triangles drawn. The perpendicular distance between two parallel lines is a constant; else the lines would intersect. (Why?) Thus, if $\overline{QA}$ is perpendicular to lines ℓ and *m*, then *QA* is the length of an altitude of each of the triangles.

Because the triangles all have base *AB*, the area of each triangle is equal to $\left(\dfrac{1}{2}\right)(AB)(QA)$.

Problem Solving   Fence Problem

Two fields, marked I and II in Figure 25, are divided by a common border consisting of two sections of fence as shown. The owners want to replace the sections of fence with a single straight fence so that the areas of the new regions are the same as the old areas. In other words, each owner should have the same amount of land as before the border was changed. Where should the new "straight" fence be placed?

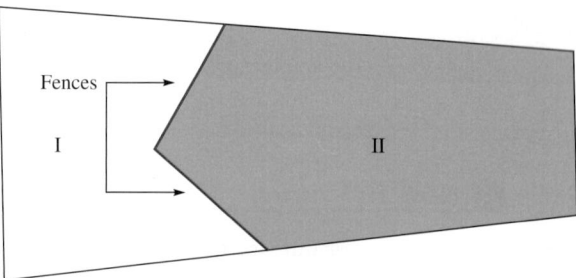

Figure 25

Solution   The owner of region II owns the region enclosed by △*ABC* as shown in Figure 26. The area of △*ABC* equals the area of any triangle with $\overline{AC}$ as a base and vertex on $\overleftrightarrow{ED}$ parallel to the base $\overline{AC}$. Thus, if point *B* "moves" along $\overline{ED}$, we get a variety of triangles whose areas are the same as the area of △*ABC*. If we choose △*ADC*, the area of region II does not change and the new border $\overline{CD}$ is straight. (Making the border become $\overline{AE}$ is another possibility.)

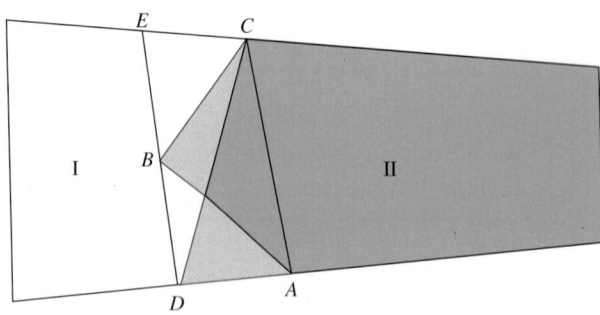

Figure 26

Example 11

Find the areas of the figures in Figure 27. Assume the quadrilaterals *ABCD* in (a) and (b) are parallelograms. (Figures are not drawn to scale.)

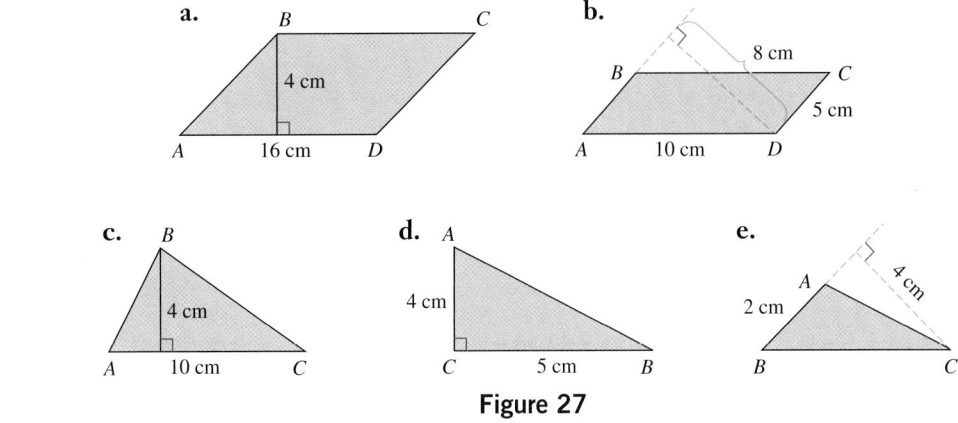

Figure 27

Solution

a. $A = bh = (16\,\text{cm})(4\,\text{cm}) = 64\,\text{cm}^2$

b. $A = bh = (5\,\text{cm})(8\,\text{cm}) = 40\,\text{cm}^2$

c. $A = \dfrac{1}{2}bh = \dfrac{1}{2}(10\,\text{cm})(4\,\text{cm}) = 20\,\text{cm}^2$

d. $A = \dfrac{1}{2}bh = \dfrac{1}{2}(5\,\text{cm})(4\,\text{cm}) = 10\,\text{cm}^2$

e. $A = \dfrac{1}{2}bh = \dfrac{1}{2}(2\,\text{cm})(4\,\text{cm}) = 4\,\text{cm}^2$

Area of a Kite

The area of a kite can be found by relating it to the area of a rectangle. Consider the kite shown in Figure 28(a), where d_1 and d_2 are the lengths of the diagonals. If the kite is decomposed and reassembled as shown in Figure 28(b), then a rectangle is formed with length d_1 and width $d_2/2$. The rectangle in Figure 28(b) has area $\dfrac{1}{2}(d_1 d_2)$. Therefore, the area of a kite is equal to half the product of the lengths of its diagonals. Partitioning the kite into triangles and finding the areas of the triangles can also be used to find the area of a kite.

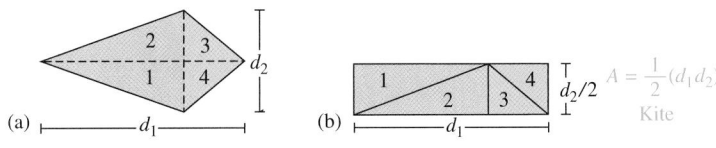

Figure 28

Since rhombuses and squares are kites, the area formula for kites can be used to find the areas of rhombuses and squares. (How?)

We found the area of a kite using the lengths of the two diagonals in Figure 28(a). The same formula works for any quadrilateral whose diagonals are perpendicular to each other, as in Figure 29. (Why?)

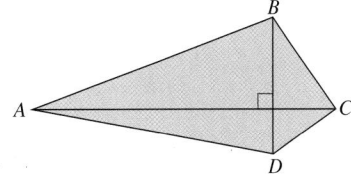

Figure 29

Area of a Trapezoid

Areas of general polygons can be found by decomposing the polygons into triangles, finding the areas of the triangles, and summing those areas. In Figure 30(a), trapezoid $ABCD$ has bases b_1 and b_2 and height h. By connecting points B and D, as in Figure 30(b), we create two triangles: one with base of length AB and height DE and the other with base of length CD and height BF. Because $\overline{DE} \cong \overline{BF}$, each has length h. Thus, the areas of triangles ADB and DCB are $\frac{1}{2}b_1h$ and $\frac{1}{2}b_2h$, respectively. Hence, the area of trapezoid $ABCD$ is $\frac{1}{2}b_1h + \frac{1}{2}b_2h = \frac{1}{2}h(b_1 + b_2)$; that is, *the area of a trapezoid is equal to half the height times the sum of the lengths of the bases.*

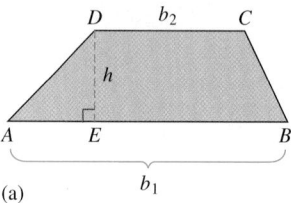

(a)

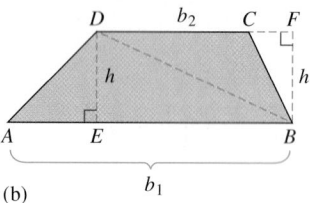

$A = \frac{1}{2}h(b_1 + b_2)$

Trapezoid

(b)

Figure 30

Example 12

Find the areas of the trapezoids in Figure 31.

a.

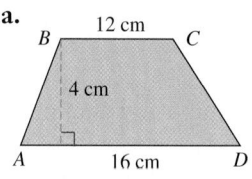

b.

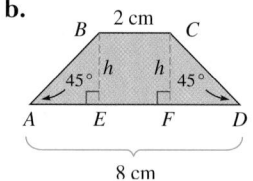

Figure 31

Solution

a. $A = \frac{1}{2}h(b_1 + b_2) = \frac{1}{2}(4\text{ cm})(12\text{ cm} + 16\text{ cm}) = 56\text{ cm}^2$

b. To find the area of trapezoid $ABCD$, we use the strategy of *determining a subgoal* to find the height h. In Figure 31(b), $BE = CF = h$. Also, $\overline{BE}$ is a side of $\triangle ABE$, which has angles with measures of 45° and 90°. Consequently, the third angle in triangle ABE has measure $180° - (45° + 90°) = 45°$. Therefore, $\triangle ABE$ is isosceles and $AE = BE = h$. Similarly, it follows that $FD = h$. Because $AD = 8\text{ cm} = h + EF + h$, we could find h if we knew the value of EF. From Figure 31(b), $EF = BC = 2\text{ cm}$ because $BCFE$ is a rectangle (Why?) and opposite sides of a rectangle are congruent. Now $h + EF + h = h + 2 + h = 8\text{ cm}$. Thus, $h = 3\text{ cm}$ and the area of the trapezoid is $A = \frac{1}{2}(3\text{ cm})(2\text{ cm} + 8\text{ cm}) = 15\text{ cm}^2$.

Area of a Regular Polygon

The area of a triangle can be used to find the area of any regular polygon. This is illustrated *using a simpler case* strategy involving a regular hexagon in Figure 32(a). The hexagon can be decomposed into six congruent triangles with side s and height a as shown in Figure 32(a). The height of such a triangle of a regular polygon is the **apothem**, denoted a. The area of each triangle is $\frac{1}{2}as$.

Because 6 triangles make up the hexagon, the area of the hexagon is $6\left(\frac{1}{2}as\right) = \frac{1}{2}a(6s)$. However, $6s$ is the perimeter p of the hexagon, so the area of the hexagon is $\frac{1}{2}ap$. The same process can be used to develop the formula for the area of any regular polygon; that is, *the area of any regular polygon is $\frac{1}{2}ap$, where a is the apothem(height of one of the triangles involved) and p is the perimeter of the polygon*, as shown in Figure 32(b).

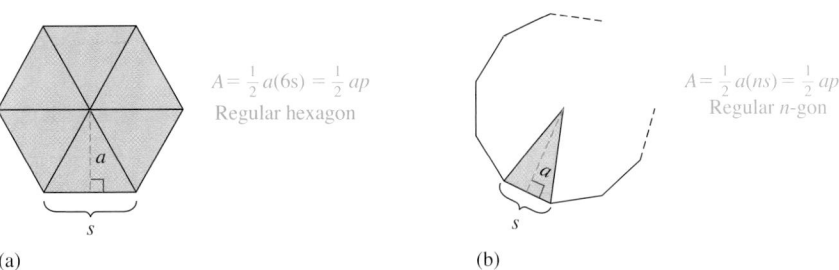

$A = \frac{1}{2}a(6s) = \frac{1}{2}ap$
Regular hexagon

$A = \frac{1}{2}a(ns) = \frac{1}{2}ap$
Regular *n*-gon

(a)   (b)

Figure 32

Area of a Circle

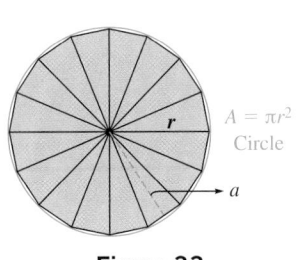

$A = \pi r^2$
Circle

Figure 33

We use the strategy of *examining a related problem* to find the area of a circle. The area of a regular polygon inscribed in a circle, as in Figure 33, approximates the area of the circle, and we know that *the area of any regular n-gon is $\frac{1}{2}ap$, where a is the height of a triangle of the n-gon and p is the perimeter*. If the number of sides n is made very large, then the perimeter and the area of the n-gon are close to those of the circle. Also, the apothem a gets closer and closer to the radius r of the circle, and the perimeter p approaches the circumference $2\pi r$. Because the area of the circle is approximately equal to the area of the n-gon, $\frac{1}{2}ap \approx \frac{1}{2}r(2\pi r) = \pi r^2$. In fact, *the area of the circle is precisely πr^2*.

A different approach is seen in the accompanying student page shown on page 838.

Area of a Sector

A **sector** of a circle is a piece-of-pie-shaped region of the circle determined by a central angle of the circle. The area of a sector depends on the radius of the circle and the measure of the central angle determining the sector. If the angle has a measure of 90°, as in Figure 34(a), the area of the sector is one-fourth the area of the circle, or $\frac{90}{360}\pi r^2$. The area of a sector with central angle of 1° is $\frac{1}{360}$ of the area of the circle, and *a sector with central angle $\theta°$ has area $\frac{\theta}{360}$ of the area of the circle*, or $\frac{\theta}{360}(\pi r^2)$, as shown in Figure 34(b).

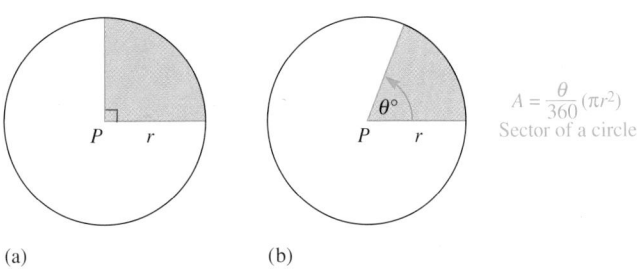

$A = \frac{\theta}{360}(\pi r^2)$
Sector of a circle

(a)   (b)

Figure 34

School Book Page   Area of a Circle

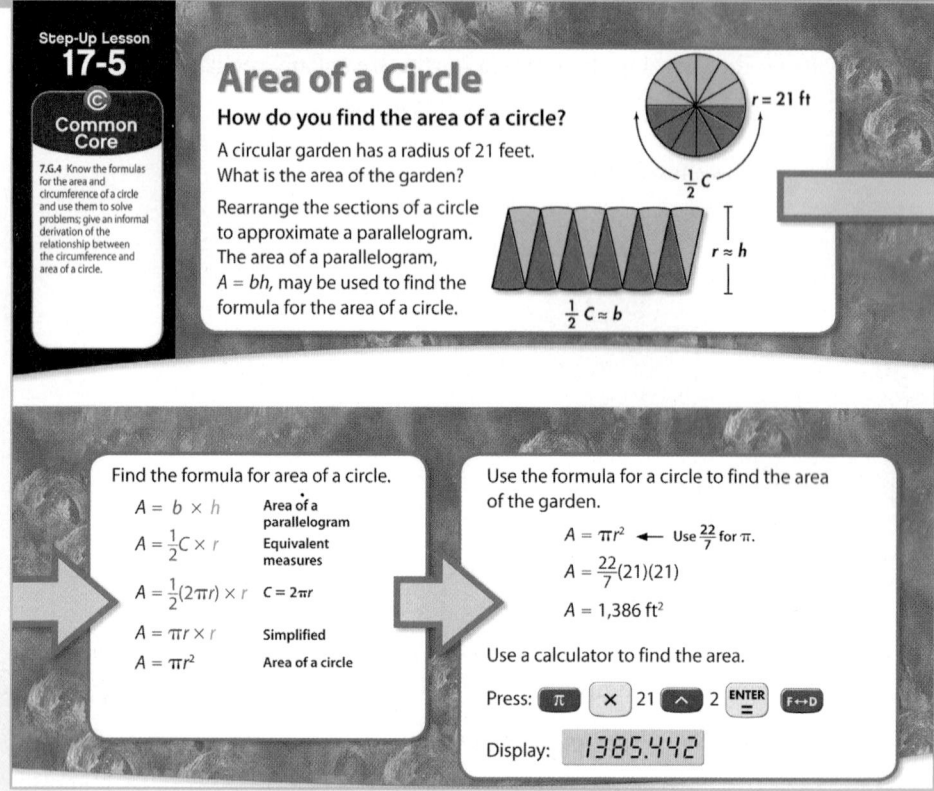

Finding the Areas of Other Shapes

Knowing how to find the areas of simple figures, such as squares, rectangles, parallelograms, triangles, trapezoids, and circles, can be used to find the areas of irregular-shaped figures by decomposing them into familiar shapes. Examine the student page shown on page 839 for two different methods of finding the area of an irregular shape.

Comparing Areas of Similar Figures

Next, in Figure 35, we find the areas of the two similar triangles with scale factor k and find the scale factor for the two areas.

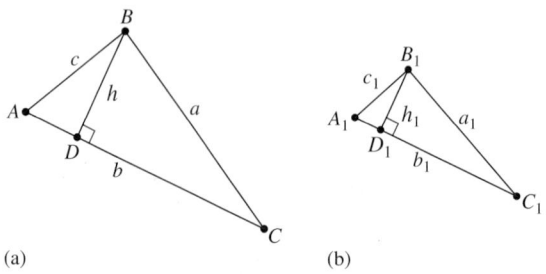

(a)   (b)

Figure 35

School Book Page · Finding Areas

You can find the area of any figure by separating it into familiar figures.

● More Than One Way

Anna and Ryan are helping their friends build a large wooden deck. What is the area of the deck?

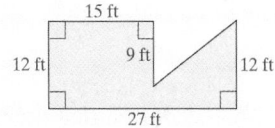

Anna's Method

I'll subtract the area of the triangle from the area of the rectangle.

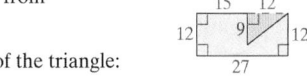

Area of the rectangle:

$A = bh$
$\quad = (27)(12) = 324$

Area of the triangle:

$A = \frac{1}{2}bh$
$\quad = \frac{1}{2}(12)(9) = 54$

Now I'll subtract the area of the triangle from the area of the rectangle.

$A = 324 - 54 = 270$

The area of the deck is 270 ft².

Ryan's Method

I'll add the areas of the rectangle and the trapezoid.

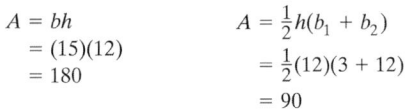

Area of the rectangle:

$A = bh$
$\quad = (15)(12)$
$\quad = 180$

Area of the trapezoid:

$A = \frac{1}{2}h(b_1 + b_2)$
$\quad = \frac{1}{2}(12)(3 + 12)$
$\quad = 90$

Now I'll add the two areas together.

$A = 180 + 90 = 270$

The area of the deck is 270 ft².

Choose a Method

Find the area of the figure.

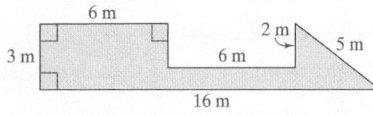

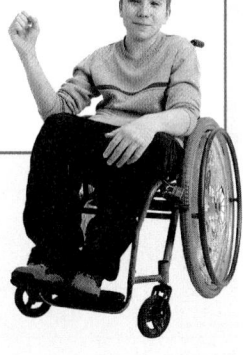

$$\frac{Area(\triangle ABC)}{Area(\triangle A_1B_1C_1)} = \frac{\frac{1}{2}bh}{\frac{1}{2}b_1h_1} = \frac{b}{b_1} \cdot \frac{h}{h_1} = k \cdot k = k^2$$

We have proved the following theorem.

Theorem 14-3

For similar triangles with scale factor k, the ratio of their areas is k^2.

Because any two similar polygons can be subdivided into nonoverlapping similar triangles, the analogous theorem for similar polygons holds.

Theorem 14-4
For similar polygons with scale factor k, the ratio of their areas is k^2.

Example 13

Is it true that the viewing area of a 35-inch flat screen is about twice the viewing area of a 25-inch flat screen? Recall that flat screens are measured diagonally.

Solution   Because we are dealing with areas of similar polygons, their areas are in the ratio of $35^2 : 25^2 = 1225 : 625 = 1.96 : 1$. Therefore the viewing area of the 35-inch flat screen is almost twice that of a 25-inch flat screen.

Assessment 14-2A

1. Estimate the area of your desktop in terms of a piece of notebook paper as your unit of area. Then measure the area of your desktop with the paper and compare it to your estimate.   Answers vary.
2. Choose the most appropriate metric units (cm², m², or km²) and English units (in.², yd², or mi²) for measuring the area of each of the following.   Answers vary.
   a. Sheet of notebook paper   cm²; in.²
   b. Quarter   cm² or mm²; in.²
   c. Desktop   m² or cm²; yd² or in.²
   d. Classroom floor   m²; yd²
3. Estimate and then measure the area of each of the following using cm² or m².   Answers vary.
   a. A door
   b. A desktop
4. Complete the following conversion table.   *

	Item	m²	cm²	mm²
a.	Area of a sheet of paper		588	
b.	Area of a cross section of a crayon			192
c.	Area of a desktop	1.5		
d.	Area of a dollar bill		100	

5. Complete the following conversions.
   a. 4000 ft² = _____ yd² $444\frac{4}{9}$
   b. 10^6 yd² = _Approx. 0.32_ mi²
   c. 10 mi² = _6400_ acres
   d. 3 acres = _130,680_ ft²

6. Find the areas of each of the following figures if the distance between two adjacent dots in a row or a column is 1 unit.   *

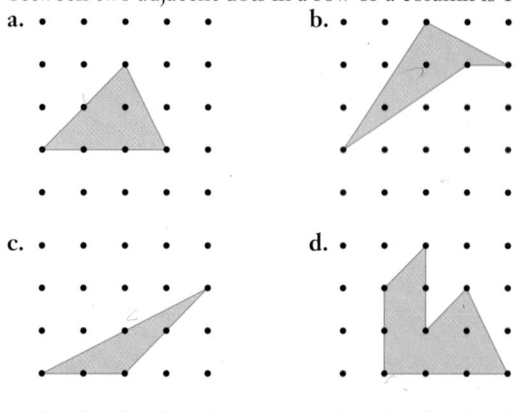

7. Complete each of the following sentences.
   a. A football field (with endzones included) is about 49 m × 100 m, or _4900_ m².
   b. About _98_ a are in two football fields with endzones.
   c. About _0.98_ ha are in two football fields with endzones.
8. Find the area of △ABC in each of the following drawings.   *
   a.   20 cm²   b.   7.5 m²

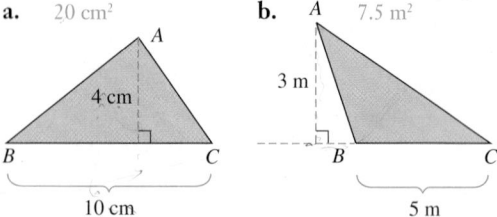

9. If a triangle is inscribed in a circle so that one of the triangle's sides is a diameter of the circle, what is the greatest area that the triangle can have in terms of the radius, r, of the circle? r^2

10. Two different squares have sides in the ratio $a : b$.
    a. Are the squares similar? Why? Yes; all squares are similar.
    b. What is the ratio of the areas of the squares? $a^2 : b^2$
11. Find the area of each of the following quadrilaterals. *
    a. Square 9 cm²

    3 cm

    b. Rectangle 96 cm²

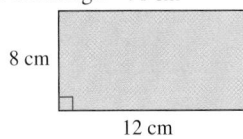

    8 cm
    12 cm

    c. Parallelogram 20 cm²

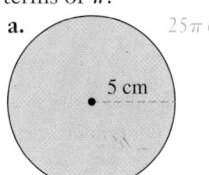

    5 cm   4 cm
    5 cm

    d. Trapezoid 84 cm²
    10 cm

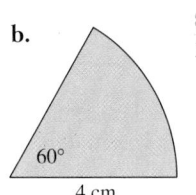

    √65 cm   7 cm
    14 cm

12. a. A rectangular piece of land is 1300 m × 1500 m. *
       i. What is the area in square kilometers? 1.95 km²
       ii. What is the area in hectares? 195 ha
    b. A rectangular piece of land is 1300 yd × 1500 yd.
       i. What is the area in square miles? Approx. 0.63 mi²
       ii. What is the area in acres? Approx. 403 acres
    c. Explain which measuring system you would rather use to solve problems like those in parts a and b. *
13. For a parallelogram whose sides are 6 cm and 10 cm, which of the following is true?
    a. The data are insufficient to enable us to determine the area. True
    b. The area has to be 60 cm². False
    c. The area is greater than 60 cm². False
    d. The area is less than 60 cm². *
14. If the diagonals of a rhombus are 12 cm and 5 cm long, find the area of the rhombus. 30 cm²
15. Find the cost of carpeting the following rectangular rooms.
    a. Dimensions: 6.5 m × 4.5 m; cost = \$13.85/m² \$405.11
    b. Dimensions: 15 ft × 11 ft; cost = \$30/yd² \$550
16. Find the area of each of the following. Leave your answers in terms of π.
    a. 25π cm²   b. $\frac{8}{3}\pi$ cm²

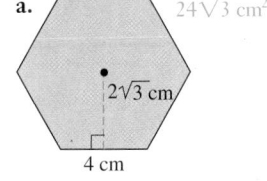

    5 cm

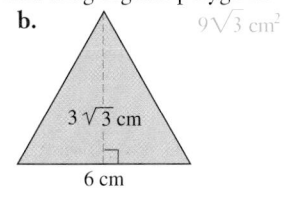

    60°
    4 cm

17. Joe uses stick-on square carpet tiles to cover his 3 m × 4 m bathroom floor. If each tile is 10 cm on a side, how many tiles does he need? 1200 tiles
18. Find the area of each of the following regular polygons.
    a. 24√3 cm²   b. 9√3 cm²

2√3 cm
4 cm

3√3 cm
6 cm

19. a. If a circle has a circumference of 8π cm, what is its area? *
    b. If a circle of radius r and a square with a side of length s have equal areas, express r in terms of s. $r = \frac{s}{\sqrt{\pi}}$

20. Find the area of each of the following shaded regions in parts (a)–(d). Assume all arcs are circular with centers marked. Leave all answers in terms of π.
    a. 2π cm²   b. $\left(\frac{\pi}{2} + 1\right)$ cm²

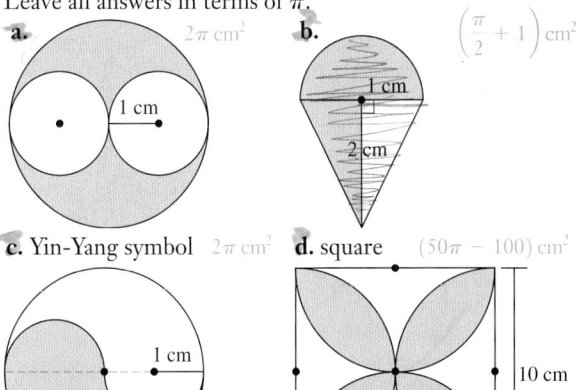

    1 cm

    1 cm
    2 cm

    c. Yin-Yang symbol 2π cm²   d. square $(50\pi - 100)$ cm²

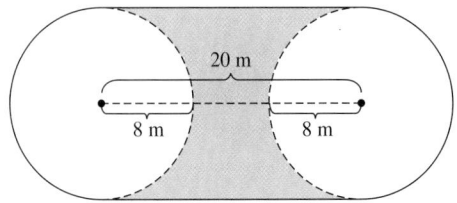

    1 cm

    10 cm

    e. In parts (a)–(d), what is the ratio of the white portion to the shaded region in each case? *
21. A circular flower bed is 6 m in diameter and has a circular sidewalk around it 1 m wide. Find the area of the sidewalk in square meters. 7π m²
22. a. If the area of a square is 144 cm², what is its perimeter? 48 cm
    b. If the perimeter of a square is 32 cm, what is its area? 64 cm²
23. a. What happens to the area of a square when the length of each side is doubled? The area is quadrupled.
    b. If the ratio of the sides of two squares is 1 to 5, what is the ratio of their areas? 1:25
24. Find the shaded area in the following figure. $(320 - 64\pi)$ m²

    20 m
    8 m   8 m

25. If the total area of a circular flower bed and its surrounding circular sidewalk of width 0.5 m is 148π m², what is the radius of the flower bed? $\left(2\sqrt{37} - \frac{1}{2}\right)$ m
26. Rheba wanted a piece of red circular glass inset into her right triangular window. If the window had sides with measures of 3 ft, 4 ft, and 5 ft, and the glass was to be an inscribed circle as shown, what is the radius of the circular glass? 1 ft

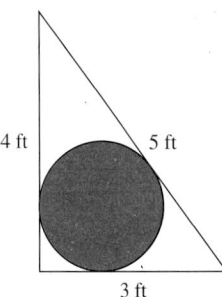

    4 ft   5 ft

    3 ft

27. Heron's formula can be used to find the area of a triangle if the lengths of the three sides are known. If the lengths of the three sides are a, b, and c units and the semiperimeter
    $$s = \frac{a + b + c}{2},$$ then the area of the triangle is given by

$\sqrt{s(s-a)(s-b)(s-c)}$. Use Heron's formula to find the areas of the right triangles with the sides given.
   a. 3 cm, 4 cm, 5 cm   6 cm²   **b.** 5 cm, 12 cm, 13 cm   30 cm²
28. The radius of Earth is approximately 6378 km. What is the approximate area of a cross section of Earth that contains the center of Earth?   Approximately 128,000,000 km²
29. The radius of a sector is 1 m.
   a. Find the area of a 1° sector of the circle. $\frac{\pi}{360}$ m²
   b. What is the area of the circle containing the sector? π m²
   c. If 360 of the 1° sectors of the circle are placed as the drawing on the student page shown on page 838 to approximate a parallelogram, what is the approximate area of the parallelogram? π m²
   d. What is the difference of the areas in parts (b) and (c) as a percentage of the area of the entire circle?   0
30. Find the area of the shaded portion of circle O. 3π cm²

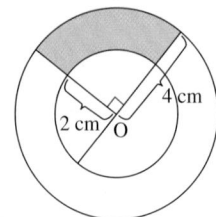

31. Find the areas of the shaded quilt patterns below if one side of each square is 6 cm.   *
   a.   **b.**

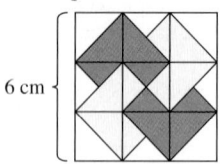 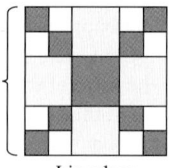

   Card trick   Lineolum

   c.   **d.**

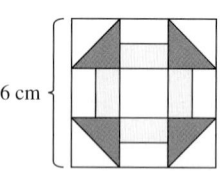 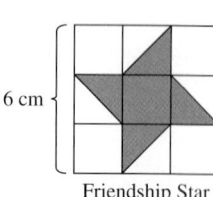

   6 cm   6 cm

   Churn dash   Friendship Star

32. Find the area of the white staircase in the following drawing.   *

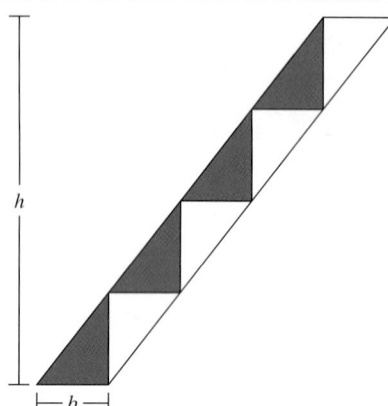

33. The area of a rectangle is 24 cm².
   a. Write an equation for the area in terms of its length x and its width y. $xy = 24$
   b. Explain whether you think the graph of the equation in part (a) lies along a line.   *
34. What is the length of the side of a square with the same area as that of a trapezoid whose bases have lengths 15 cm and 35 cm and whose altitude is 20 cm? $10\sqrt{5}$ cm
35. Find the area of the circumscribed circle of a regular hexagon of side 4 cm. 16π cm²

Assessment 14-2B

1. Estimate the area of your desktop in terms of your hand as your unit of area. Then measure the area of your desktop with your hand and compare it to your estimate.   Answers vary.
2. Choose the most appropriate metric units (cm², m², or km²) and English units (in.², yd², or mi²) for measuring the area of each of the following.   Answers vary.
   a. A parallel parking space   m², yd²
   b. An airport runway   km², mi² or m², yd²
   c. Your mathematics book cover   cm², in.²
3. Estimate and then measure the area of each of the following using cm², m², or km².   Answers vary. For example,
   a. A chair seat   1400 cm²
   b. A whiteboard or chalkboard   3 m²
4. Complete the following conversion table.

	m²	cm²	mm²
a.	52	520,000	52,000,000
b.	0.000105	1.05	105
c.	0.0086	86	8600
d.	0.01	100	10,000
e.	8.2	82,000	8,200,000

5. Complete the following conversions.
   a. 99 ft² = _____ yd²   11
   b. 10^6 yd² = _____ ft²   9,000,000
   c. 6.5 mi² = _____ acres   4160
   d. 3 acres = _____ yd²   14,520
6. Find the areas of each of the following figures if the distance between two adjacent dots in a row or a column is 1 unit.   *

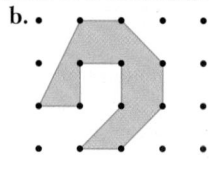

   a.   **b.**

7. If all vertices of a polygon are points on square-dot paper, the polygon is a **lattice polygon**. In 1899, Georg Pick discovered a surprising theorem involving I, the number of dots *inside* the polygon, and B, the number of dots that lie *on* the polygon. The theorem states that the area of any lattice polygon is $I + \frac{1}{2}B - 1$. Check that this is true for the polygons in exercise 6.   They check; that is, $I + \frac{1}{2}B - 1 = A$.

8. Find the area of △ABC in each of the following drawings. (Drawings are not to scale.)
   a. 900 cm² or 0.09 m²

   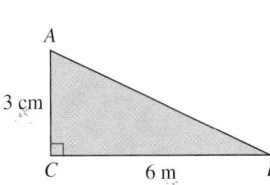

   b. 39 cm²

   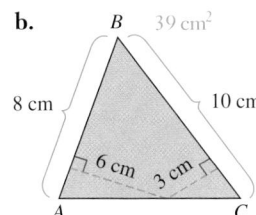

9. If a triangle and a square have one side in common, where could the third vertex of the triangle lie if the area of the triangle is exactly equal to area of the square? *

10. a. If triangle ABC is similar to triangle DEF and $\frac{AB}{DE} = \frac{2}{3}$, what is the ratio of the heights of the triangles? $\frac{2}{3}$
    b. What is the ratio of the areas of the two triangles in part (a)? $\frac{4}{9}$

11. Find the area of each of the following quadrilaterals:
    a. Square   81 cm²

    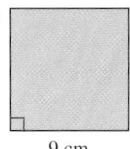

    9 cm

    b. Trapezoid   8 cm   105 cm²

    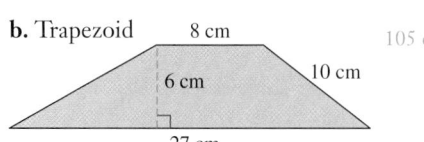

    27 cm

12. a. A rectangular piece of land is 1.2 km by 900 m.
    i. What is the area in square kilometers?   1.08 km²
    ii. What is the area in hectares?   108 ha
    b. A rectangular piece of land is 1.2 mi by 900 yd.
    i. What is the area in square miles?   About 0.61 mi²
    ii. What is the area in acres?   About 393 acres

13. a. If the area of a rectangle remains constant but its perimeter increases, how has the shape of the rectangle changed? *
    b. If the perimeter of a rectangle remains constant but its area increases, how does the shape of the rectangle change? *

14. If the diagonals of a rhombus are 1.2 m and 40 cm long, find the area of the rhombus in square meters.   0.24 m²

15. A rectangular plot of land is to be seeded with grass. If the plot is 22 m × 28 m and a 1-kg bag of seed is needed for 85 m² of land, how many bags of seed must you buy?   8

16. Find the area of each of the following regions. Leave your answers in terms of π.
    a. $\frac{9\pi}{2}$ cm²   b.   20 cm   100 cm²

    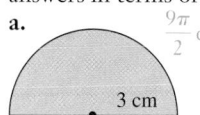

    3 cm

    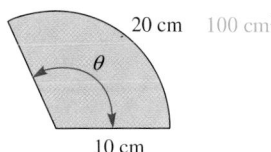

    θ

    10 cm

17. A rectangular field is 64 m × 25 m. Shawn wants to fence a square field that has the same area as the rectangular field. How long are the sides of the square field?   40 m

18. Find the area of the following figures.
    a.   156 cm²   b.   270 m²

    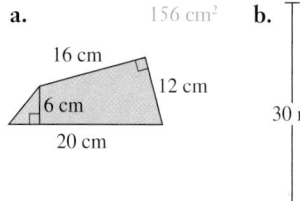

    16 cm
    6 cm   12 cm
    20 cm

    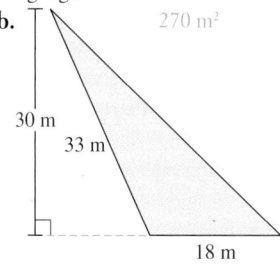

    30 m   33 m   18 m

19. Suppose the largest square peg possible is placed in a circular hole as shown in the following figure and that the largest circular peg possible is placed in a square hole. In which case is there a smaller percentage of space not occupied? *

    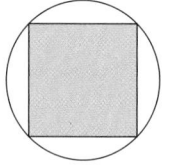
    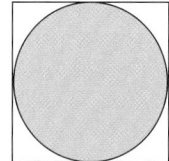

20. Find the area of each of the following shaded parts in (a)–(c). Assume all arcs are circular. Leave all answers in terms of π. *
    a.   b.   c.

    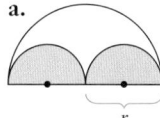   r
    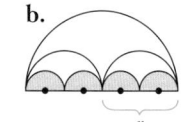   r
    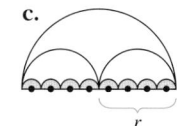   r

    d. In parts (a)–(c), what is the ratio of the white portion to the shaded region in each case?

21. For a dartboard, Joan is trying to determine how the area of the outside shaded region compares with the sum of the areas of the three inside shaded regions so that she can determine payoffs. How do they compare? *

    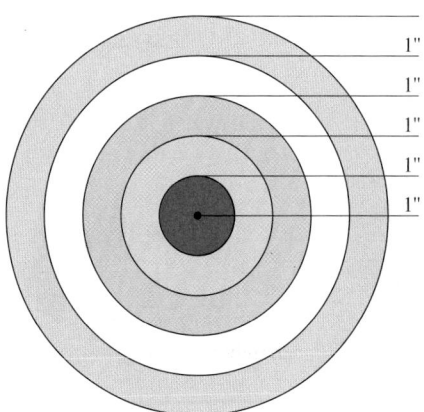

    1"
    1"
    1"
    1"
    1"

22. If the area of a square is 169 in.², what is its perimeter?   52 in.²

23. a. What happens to the area of a circle if its diameter is doubled?   The area is quadrupled.

b. What happens to the area of a circle if its radius is increased by 10%?   *

c. What happens to the area of a circle if its circumference is tripled?   The area is increased by a factor of 9.

24. Quadrilateral *MATH* has been dissected into squares. The area of the red square is 64 square units and the area of the blue square is 81 square units. Determine the dimensions and the area of quadrilateral *MATH*.   *

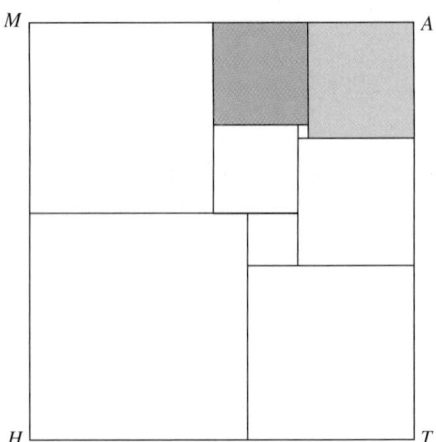

25. Explain how to use geometric shapes to find an equivalent algebraic expression not involving parentheses for $(a + b)(c + d)$.   *

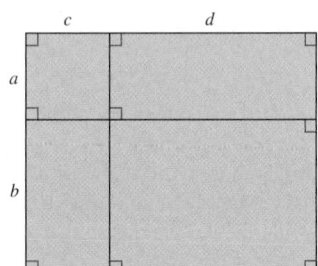

26. The rectangle on the right was apparently formed by decomposing the square on the left along the dotted lines and reassembling the pieces as pictured.

a. What is the area of the square on the left?   *

b. What is the area of the rectangle on the right?   *

c. How do you explain the discrepancy between the areas?   *

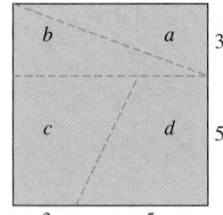
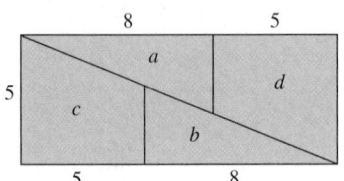

27. A store has wrapping paper on sale. One package is 3 rolls of $2\frac{1}{2}$ ft × 8 ft for $6.00. Another package is 5 rolls of $2\frac{1}{2}$ ft × 6 ft for $8.00. Which is the better buy per square foot?   *

28. Squares *A* and *B* are congruent. One vertex of *B* is at the center of square *A*. What is the ratio of the shaded area to the area of square *A*?   1 : 4

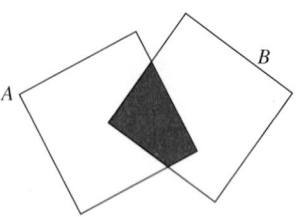

29. Given △*ABC* with parallel lines dividing $\overline{AB}$ into three congruent segments as shown, how does the area of △*BDE* compare with the area of △*ABC*?   *

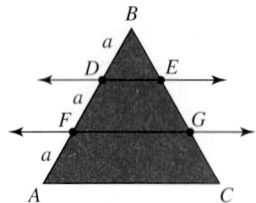

30. Use exercise 29 and compare the following areas.

a. Triangle *DBE* and trapezoid *DEGF*   *

b. Triangle *DBE* and trapezoid *FGCA*   *

c. Trapezoids *DEGF* and *FGCA*   *

d. Trapezoid *DEGF* and triangle *ABC*   *

e. Trapezoid *FGCA* and triangle *ABC*   *

f. Triangle *ABC* and trapezoid *DECA*   *

31. If the total area of a circular flower bed and its surrounding circular sidewalk of width 1 m is 148π m² what is the radius of the flower bed? $\left(2\sqrt{37} - 1\right)$ m

32. The diameter of Earth is approximately 12,756 km. What is the approximate area of a cross section of Earth that contains the center of Earth?   Approximately 128,000,000 km²

33. The radius of a sector is 2 m.

a. Find the area of a 1° sector of the circle. $\frac{\pi}{90}$ m²

b. What is the area of the circle containing the sector? 4π m²

c. If 360 of the 1° sectors of the circle are placed as the drawing on the student page shown on page 838 to approximate a parallelogram, what is the approximate area of the parallelogram? 4π m²

d. What is the difference of the areas in parts (b) and (c) as a percentage of the area of the entire circle?   0

34. Find the area of the shaded portion of circle *O*. 10π cm²

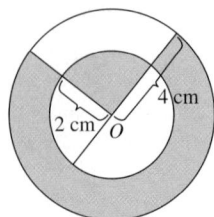

35. Find the areas of the shaded quilt patterns below if one side of each square is 6 cm.

a.

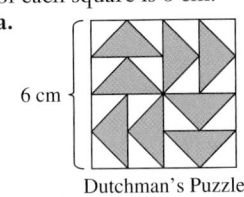

6 cm

Dutchman's Puzzle

8 cm²

b.

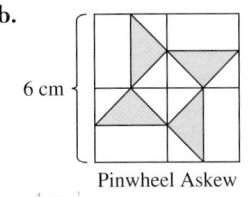

6 cm

Pinwheel Askew

4 cm²

c.

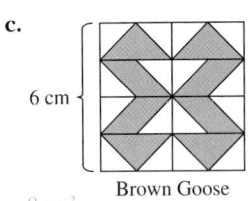

6 cm

Brown Goose

8 cm²

d.

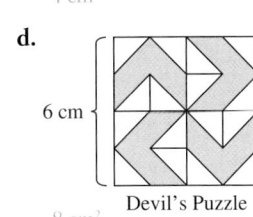

6 cm

Devil's Puzzle

8 cm²

36. The area of a rectangle is 36 cm².
   a. Write an equation for the area in terms of its length x and its width y. $xy = 36$
   b. Explain in geometric terms whether you think the graph of the equation in part (a) lies along a line. *

37. What is the length of the side of a square with the same area as that of a trapezoid whose bases have lengths 12 cm and 36 cm and whose altitude is 12 cm? $12\sqrt{2}$ cm

38. Find the area of the circumscribed circle of a regular hexagon of side 6 cm. 36π cm²

Mathematical Connections 14-2

Answers to Mathematical Connections can be found in the Answers section at the back of the book.

Reasoning

1. Suppose a triangle has sides of lengths 6 in., 11 in., and 13 in. Explain how you can find the area of this triangle when the height is not given.

2. John claimed he had a garden twice as large as Al's rectangular-shaped garden that measured 15 ft by 30 ft. When they visited John's rectangular-shaped garden, they found it measured 18 ft by 50 ft. Al claimed that it could not be twice as large since neither the length nor the width were twice as large. Who was correct and why?

3. a. If a 10-in. (diameter) pizza costs $10, how much should a 20-in. pizza cost? Explain the assumptions made to obtain the answer.
   b. If the ratio between the diameters of two pizzas is 1: k, what should the ratio be between the prices? Explain the assumptions made to obtain the answer.

4. Explain how a rotation in the following drawing can be used to determine a formula for the area of $\triangle ABC$.

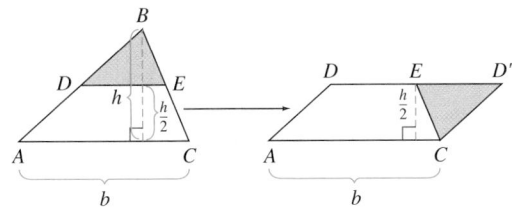

5. The area of a parallelogram can be found by using the concept of a half-turn. Consider the parallelogram $ABCD$, and let M and N be the midpoints of $\overline{AB}$ and $\overline{CD}$, respectively. Rotate the shaded triangle with vertex M about M by 180° clockwise and rotate the shaded triangle with vertex N about N by 180° clockwise. What kind of figure do you obtain? Now complete the argument to find the area of the parallelogram.

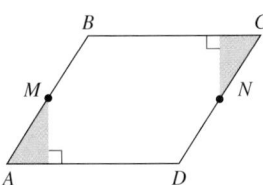

6. If the length of a rectangle is increased by 10% and the width of the rectangle is decreased by 10%, is the area changed? If so, does it increase or decrease and by what percent? Explain your answer.

7. Cut out a trapezoid $ABCD$ as shown. Copy and rotate $ABCD$ 180° about M, the midpoint of $\overline{CB}$. Use the total figure obtained to derive the formula for the area of a trapezoid.

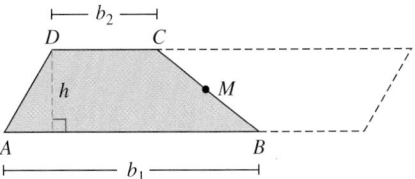

Open-Ended

8. a. Estimate the area in square centimeters that your handprint will cover.
   b. Trace the outline of your hand on square-centimeter grid paper and use the outline to obtain an estimate for the area. Explain how you arrived at your estimate.

9. a. Give dimensions of a square and a rectangle that have the same perimeter but such that the square has the greater area.
   b. Give dimensions of a square and a rectangle that have equal area but such that the rectangle has greater perimeter.

10. **a.** Draw a circle of radius 4 cm and divide it into eight equal-sized sectors.
    b. Cut out the eight equal-sized sectors and rearrange the sectors to form a parallelogram-shaped figure such as the one on the student page shown on page 838.
    c. The area of a parallelogram is found by multiplying the length of its base b by the height h, or $A = bh$. Use your figure to explain why this formula can be written as $A = \frac{1}{2}Cr$ to find the area of a circle, where C is the circumference and r is the radius of the circle.

Cooperative Learning

11. Use five 1×1 squares to build the cross shape shown and discuss the questions that follow.

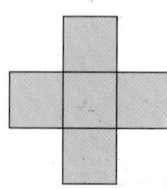

    a. What is the area of this shape?
    b. What is the perimeter of this shape?
    c. Add squares to the shape so that each added square shares a complete edge with at least one other square.
      i. What is the minimum number of squares that can be added so that the shape has a perimeter of 18?
      ii. What is the maximum number?
      iii. What is the maximum area the new shape could have and still have a perimeter of 18?
    d. Using the five squares, have members of the group start with shapes different from the original cross shape and answer the questions in part (c). Discuss your results.
    e. Explore shapes that are made up of more than five squares.
12. As a group, work on the following activities.
    a. On a 5 dot $\times$ 5 dot geoboard, make $\triangle DEF$ as shown.

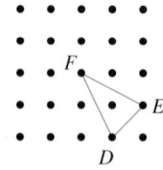

    Keep the rubber band around D and E fixed and move the vertex F to all the possible locations so that the triangles formed will have the same area as the area of $\triangle DEF$. How do the locations for the third vertex relate to $\overline{DE}$?
    b. On a 5 dot $\times$ 5 dot geoboard, construct, if possible, squares of areas 1, 2, 3, 4, 5, 6, and 7 square units.
    c. On a 5 dot $\times$ 5 dot geoboard, construct triangles that have areas $\frac{1}{2}$, 1, $1\frac{1}{2}$, 2, ..., until the maximum-sized triangle is reached.

Connecting Mathematics to the Classroom

13. On a field trip, Glenda, a sixth-grade student, was looking at a huge dinosaur footprint and wondering about its area.

Glenda said all you have to do is place a string around the border of the print and then take the string off and form it into a square and compute the area of the square. How would you help her?
14. A student asks, "Can I find the area of an angle?" How do you respond?
15. A student claims that because *are* and *hectare* are measures of area, we should say "square are" and "square hectare." How do you respond?
16. Larry and Gary are discussing whose garden has the most area to plant flowers. Larry claims that all they have to do is walk around the two gardens to get the perimeter and the one with the greatest perimeter has the greatest area. How would you help these students?
17. Jimmy claims that to find the area of a parallelogram he just has to multiply length times width. In the figure he multiplies $(25 \text{ in.})(20 \text{ in.}) = 500 \text{ in.}^2$. What would you tell him?

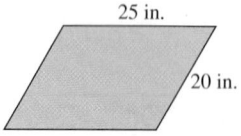

18. A student wants to know if it is possible to find the perimeters of the following figures if their areas are known. How do you respond?
    a. Square
    b. Rectangle
    c. Rhombus
    d. Circle

GeoGebra Activities

19. Use *GeoGebra Lab 9* to investigate how to motivate the formulas for finding areas of rectangles, parallelograms, and trapezoids.

Review Problems

20. A glass table top is essentially square but has rounded circular corners. Find its perimeter.

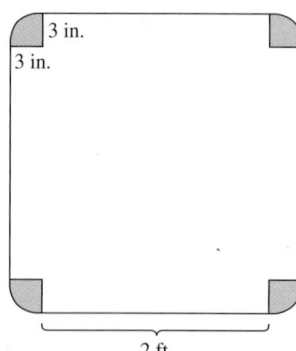

21. **a.** The earth has a circumference of approximately 39,750 km. With this circumference, what is its radius?
    b. Use the measurement in part (a) to estimate the length of an arc from the North Pole to the equator.
22. Compare the perimeter of a regular hexagon to the circumference of its circumscribed circle.

23. Two similar triangles have their sides in the ratio 1:3.
    a. What is the ratio of their perimeters?
    b. If the perimeter of the "larger" triangle is 36π cm, what is the perimeter of the smaller triangle?
24. If a 60° sector of a circle has radius 6 cm, what is the perimeter of the sector?
25. Convert the following measures as indicated.
    a. 2 m = _____ cm
    b. 2 in. = _____ ft
    c. 250 cm = _____ km
    d. 2500 yd = _____ mi

National Assessments

National Assessment of Educational Progress (NAEP) Questions

Mark's room is 12 feet wide and 15 feet long. Mark wants to cover the floor with carpet. How many square feet of carpet does he need?

Answer: _____ square feet

The carpet costs $2.60 per square foot. How much will the carpet cost?

Answer: $_____

NAEP, Grade 4, 2007

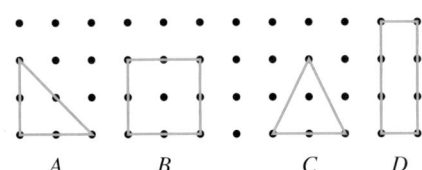

Which figure has the greatest area?
A. *A*   B. *B*   C. *C*   D. *D*

NAEP, Grade 4, 2009

How many square tiles, 5 inches on a side, does it take to cover a rectangular area that is 50 inches wide and 100 inches long?

NAEP, Grade 8, 2009

One side of a rectangle is 14 meters. The perimeter of the rectangle is 44 meters. What is the area of this rectangle?
A. 22 square meters   B. 64 square meters
C. 112 square meters   D. 121 square meters
E. 196 square meters

NAEP, Grade 8, 2013

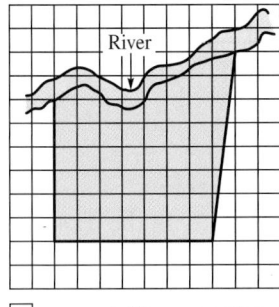

▢ represents 25 square meters

On the scale drawing above, the shaded area represents a piece of property along the river. Which of the following measurements is the best estimate of the area of the property?
A. 750 square meters
B. 850 square meters
C. 900 square meters
D. 1,050 square meters
E. 1,200 square meters

NAEP, Grade 8, 2011

14-3 The Pythagorean Theorem, Distance Formula, and Equation of a Circle

14-3 Objectives

Students will be able to understand and explain

- Pythagorean theorem and its converse.

- Measures of sides in special right triangles.

- Distance formula.

- Equation of a circle.

Surveyors often have to calculate distances that cannot be measured directly, such as distances across water, as illustrated in Figure 36.

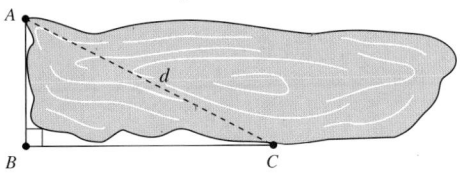

Figure 36

To measure the distance from point *A* to point *C*, they could use one of the most remarkable and useful theorems in mathematics: the **Pythagorean theorem**. This theorem is illustrated in Figure 37.

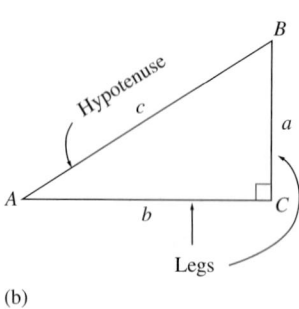

(a)

(b)

Figure 37

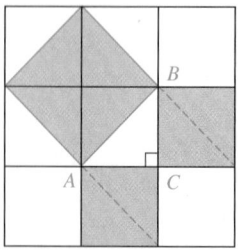

Figure 38

In the triangle in Figure 37(a) and in triangle *ABC* in Figure 37(b), the side opposite the right angle is the **hypotenuse**. The other two sides are **legs**. Interpreted in terms of area, the *Pythagorean theorem states that the area of a square with the hypotenuse of a right triangle as a side is equal to the sum of the areas of the squares with the legs as sides.*

Because the Pythagoreans affirmed geometric results on the basis of special cases, mathematical historians believe it is possible they may have discovered the theorem by looking at a floor tiling like the one illustrated in Figure 38. Each square can be divided by its diagonal into two congruent isosceles right triangles, so we see that the shaded square constructed with $\overline{AB}$ as a side consists of four triangles, each congruent to $\triangle ABC$. Similarly, each of the shaded squares with legs $\overline{BC}$ and $\overline{AC}$ as sides consists of two triangles congruent to $\triangle ABC$. Thus, the area of the larger square is equal to the sum of the areas of the two smaller squares. The theorem is true in general and is stated below.

Activity Manual
─────────────
Use *Pythagorean Puzzles* to introduce the Pythagorean theorem.

Theorem 14-5: Pythagorean Theorem

If a right triangle has legs of lengths *a* and *b* and hypotenuse of length *c*, then $c^2 = a^2 + b^2$.

There are hundreds of known proofs for the Pythagorean theorem. The classic book *The Pythagorean Proposition*, by Elisha Loomis*, contains many of these proofs. Some proofs involve the strategy of *drawing diagrams* with a square area c^2 equal to the sum of the areas a^2 and b^2 of two other squares. One such proof is given in Figure 39. In Figure 39(a), the measures of the legs of a right triangle *ABC* are *a* and *b* and the measure of the hypotenuse is *c*. We draw a square with sides of length $a + b$ and subdivide it, as shown in Figure 39(b). In Figure 39(c), another square with side of length $a + b$ is drawn and each of its sides is divided into two segments of length *a* and *b*, as shown.

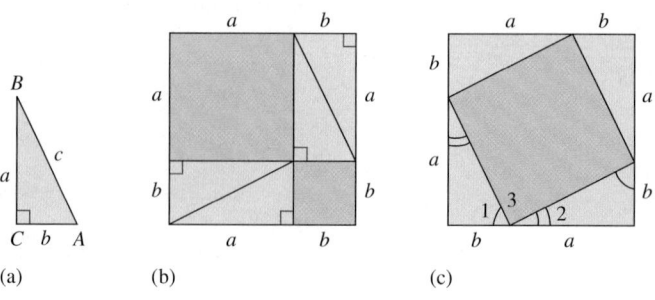

(a)   (b)   (c)

Figure 39

───────────

*Loomis, Elisha S. *The Pythagorean Proposition*. Reston, VA: National Council of Teachers of Mathematics, 1968.

Each cream-colored triangle is congruent to $\triangle ABC$ (Why?). Consequently, each triangle has hypotenuse c and the same area, $\frac{1}{2}ab$. Thus, the length of each side of the blue quadrilateral in Figure 39(c) is c and so the figure is a rhombus. Because the triangles are right triangles, their acute angles are complementary. Hence $m(\angle 1) + m(\angle 2) = 90°$ so $m(\angle 3) = 90°$. Therefore, the blue quadrilateral is a square whose area is c^2. To complete the proof, we consider the four triangles in Figure 39(b) and (c). Because the areas of the sets of four triangles in both Figure 39(b) and (c) are equal, the sum of the areas of the two shaded squares in Figure 39(b) equals the area of the shaded square in Figure 39(c); that is, $a^2 + b^2 = c^2$.

 The grade 8 *Common Core Standards* indicate that students should be able to "apply the Pythagorean Theorem to determine unknown side lengths in right triangles in real-world and mathematical problems in two and three dimensions" (p. 56). Examples are given next.

a. Find the value of x in Figure 40.

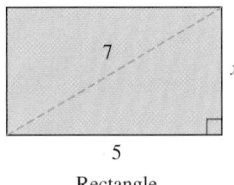

Rectangle

Figure 40

b. The size of a rectangular flat screen television is given as the length of the diagonal of the screen. If the length of the screen shown in Figure 41 is 34.5 in. and the width is 24 in., what is the diagonal length?

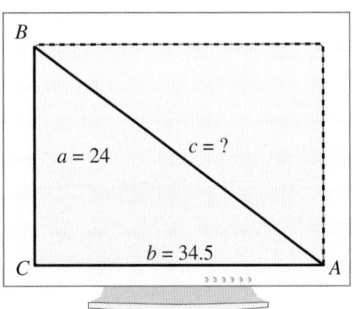

Figure 41

Solution

a. In the rectangle, the diagonal partitions the rectangle into two right triangles, each with 5 units and width x units as lengths of legs. Thus, we have the following:

$$5^2 + x^2 = 7^2$$
$$25 + x^2 = 49$$
$$x^2 = 24$$
$$x = \sqrt{24} \approx 4.9 \text{ units}$$

b. A right triangle is formed with the diagonal as the hypotenuse and the legs of measure 24 in. and 34.5 in. The Pythagorean theorem can be used to find the length of the diagonal.

$$c^2 = 24^2 + 34.5^2$$
$$c^2 = 576 + 1190.25$$
$$c^2 = 1766.25$$
$$c \approx 42 \text{ in.}$$

Because all the measurements are inches, the diagonal has approximate length 42 in.

Example 15

A pole $\overline{BD}$, 28 ft high, is perpendicular to the ground. Two wires $\overline{BC}$ and $\overline{BA}$, each 35 ft long, are attached to the top of the pole and to stakes A and C on the ground, as shown in Figure 42. If points A, D, and C are collinear, how far are the stakes A and C from each other?

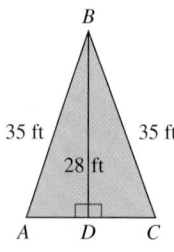

Figure 42

Solution Because a point equidistant from the endpoints of a segment must be on the perpendicular bisector of the segment, it follows that $AD = DC$. Therefore, AC is twice as long as DC. Our *subgoal* is to find DC. We may find DC by applying the Pythagorean theorem in triangle BDC.

$$28^2 + (DC)^2 = 35^2$$
$$(DC)^2 = 35^2 - 28^2$$
$$DC = \sqrt{441} = 21 \text{ ft}$$
$$AC = 2DC = 42 \text{ ft}$$

Example 16

How tall is the Great Pyramid of Cheops, a right square pyramid, if the base has a side length of 771 ft and the slant height (height of $\triangle EAB$) is 620 ft as in Figure 43?

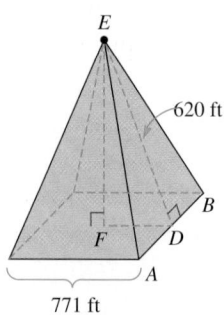

Figure 43

Solution In Figure 43, $\overline{EF}$ is a leg of a right triangle formed by $\overline{FD}, \overline{EF}$, and $\overline{ED}$. Because the pyramid is a right regular pyramid, $\overline{EF}$ intersects the base at its center. Thus, $DF = \left(\dfrac{1}{2}\right)AB = \left(\dfrac{1}{2}\right)771 = 385.5$ ft. Now ED, the slant height, has length 620 ft, and we apply the Pythagorean theorem as follows.

$$(EF)^2 + (DF)^2 = (ED)^2$$
$$(EF)^2 + (385.5)^2 = (620)^2$$
$$(EF)^2 = 235{,}789.75$$
$$EF \approx 485.6 \text{ ft}$$

Thus, the Great Pyramid is approximately 486 ft tall.

Special Right Triangles

An isosceles right triangle has two legs of equal length and two 45° angles. Any such triangle is called a **45°-45°-90° right triangle**. Drawing a diagonal of a square forms two of these triangles, as shown in Figure 44(a).

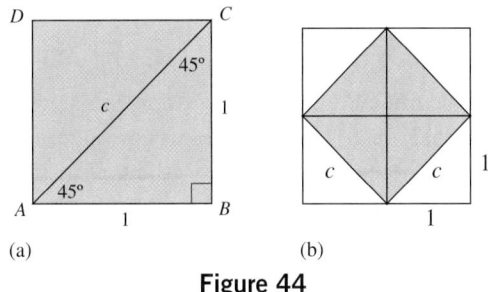

(a)   (b)

Figure 44

In Figure 44(b), we see several 45°-45°-90° triangles. Each side of the shaded square is the hypotenuse of a 45°-45°-90° triangle. The area of the shaded square is 2 square units. (Why?) Therefore, $c^2 = 2$ and $c = \sqrt{2}$. Another way to see that $c = \sqrt{2}$ is to apply the Pythagorean theorem to one of the nonshaded triangles. Because $c^2 = 1^2 + 1^2 = 2$, then $c = \sqrt{2}$.

In one isosceles right triangle in Figure 44, each leg is 1 unit long and the hypotenuse is $\sqrt{2}$ units long. This is generalized when the isosceles right triangle has a leg of length a, as follows.

Theorem 14-6:   45°-45°-90° Triangle Relationships

In an isosceles right triangle with the length of each leg a, the hypotenuse has length $a\sqrt{2}$.

Figure 45(a) shows that in terms of area a 30°-60°-90° triangle is half of an equilateral triangle. When the equilateral triangle has side 2 units long, then in the 30°-60°-90° triangle, the leg opposite the 30° angle is 1 unit long and the leg opposite the 60° angle has a length of $\sqrt{3}$ units. (Why?)

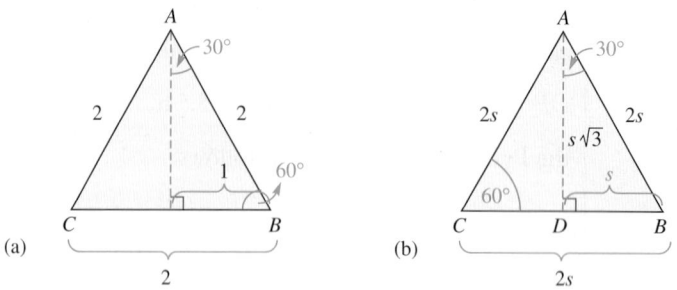

Figure 45

This example may also be generalized using the triangle in Figure 45(b). When the side of the equilateral triangle ABC is $2s$, then in triangle ABD, the side opposite the 30° angle, $\overline{BD}$, is s units long, and AD may be found using the Pythagorean theorem to have a length of $s\sqrt{3}$ units. This discussion is summarized in the following theorem.

Theorem 14-7: 30°-60°-90° Triangle Relationships

In a 30°-60°-90° triangle, the length of the hypotenuse is twice the length of the leg opposite the 30° angle, and the leg length opposite the 60° angle is $\sqrt{3}$ times the length of the shorter leg.

Converse of the Pythagorean Theorem

CCSS The grade 8 *Common Core Standards* state that students should be able to "explain a proof of the Pythagorean Theorem and its converse" (p. 56).

The converse of the Pythagorean theorem provided a useful way for early surveyors—in particular, the Egyptian rope stretchers—to determine right angles. Figure 46(a) shows a knotted rope with 12 equally spaced knots. Figure 46(b) shows how the rope might be held to form a triangle with sides of lengths 3, 4, and 5. The triangle formed is a right triangle and contains a 90° angle. Note that $5^2 = 3^2 + 4^2$.

Activity Manual

Use *Right or Not?* to reinforce the Pythagorean theorem and its converse.

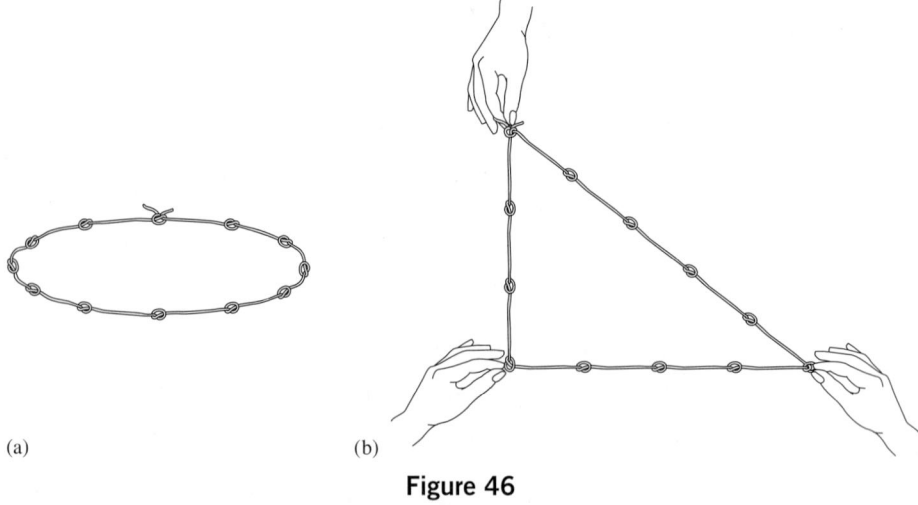

Figure 46

Given a triangle with sides of lengths a, b, and c such that $a^2 + b^2 = c^2$ as shown in Figure 47(a), must the triangle be a right triangle?

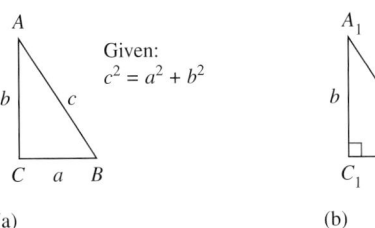

Figure 47

To investigate this question, we construct a right triangle with two sides a and b, as shown in Figure 47(b). By the Pythagorean theorem, $(A_1B_1)^2 = a^2 + b^2$. Therefore, $(A_1B_1)^2 = c^2$ and $A_1B_1 = c$. By the side-side-side (SSS) property, $\triangle ABC \cong \triangle A_1B_1C_1$ and hence $m(\angle C) = 90°$. Therefore, we have the converse of the Pythagorean theorem.

Theorem 14-8:   Converse of the Pythagorean Theorem

If $\triangle ABC$ is a triangle with sides of lengths a, b, and c such that $a^2 + b^2 = c^2$, then $\triangle ABC$ is a right triangle with the right angle opposite the side of length c.

Example 17

Determine whether the following can be the lengths of the sides of a right triangle.

a. $51, 68, 85$ b. $2, 3, \sqrt{13}$ c. $3, 4, 7$

Solution
a. $51^2 + 68^2 = 7225 = 85^2$, so 51, 68, and 85 can be the lengths of the sides of a right triangle.
b. $2^2 + 3^2 = 4 + 9 = 13 = (\sqrt{13})^2$, so 2, 3, and $\sqrt{13}$ can be the lengths of the sides of a right triangle.
c. $3^2 + 4^2 \neq 7^2$, so the measures cannot be the lengths of the sides of a right triangle. In fact, since $3 + 4 = 7$, segments with these lengths do not form a triangle.

▶ **NOW TRY THIS 5**

NTT 5: Answers can be found in Answers at the back of the book.

a. Draw three segments that can be used to form the sides of a right triangle.
b. Multiply the lengths of the three segments in part (a) by a fixed number and determine whether the resulting three lengths can be sides of a right triangle. Explain why or why not.
c. Using three new numbers, repeat the experiment in parts (a) and (b). Form a conjecture based on your experiments.

The Distance Formula: An Application of the Pythagorean Theorem

CCSS The grade 8 *Common Core Standards* state that students should be able to "apply the Pythagorean Theorem to find the distance between two points in a coordinate system" (p. 56).

Given the coordinates of two points A and B, we can find the distance AB. We first consider the special case in which the two points are on one of the axes. For example, in

Figure 48(a), $A(2, 0)$ and $B(5, 0)$ are on the x-axis. The distance between these two points is 3 units:

$$AB = OB - OA = 5 - 2 = 3$$

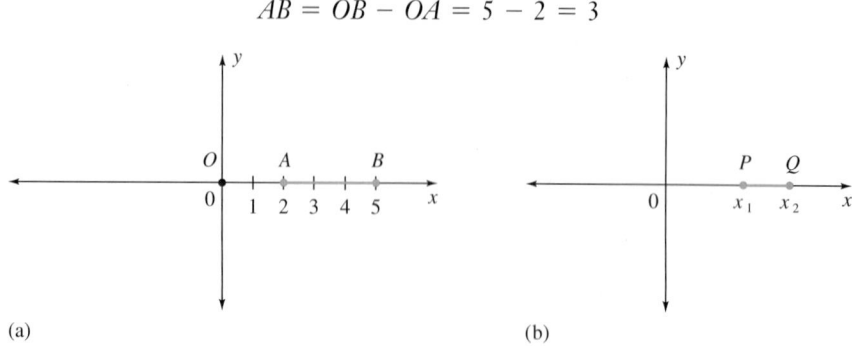

(a)   (b)

Figure 48

In general, if two points P and Q are on the x-axis, as in Figure 48(b), with x-coordinates x_1 and x_2, respectively, and $x_2 > x_1$, then $PQ = x_2 - x_1$. In fact, *the distance between two points on the x-axis is always the absolute value of the difference between the x-coordinates of the points.* (Why?) A similar result holds for any two points on the y-axis.

Figure 49 shows two points in the plane: $C(2, 5)$ and $D(6, 8)$. The distance between C and D can be found by using the strategy of *looking at a related problem*. We draw perpendiculars from the points to the x-axis and to the y-axis, as shown in Figure 49. The segments intersect at point E forming right triangle CDE. The lengths of the legs of triangle CDE are found by using horizontal and vertical distances and properties of rectangles.

$$CE = |6 - 2| = 4$$
$$DE = |8 - 5| = 3$$

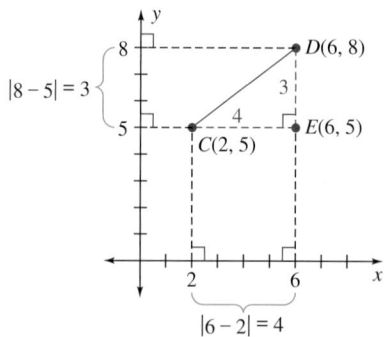

Figure 49

The distance between C and D can be found by applying the Pythagorean theorem to the triangle.

$$CD^2 = DE^2 + CE^2$$
$$= 3^2 + 4^2$$
$$= 25$$
$$CD = \sqrt{25} = 5$$

The method can be generalized to find a formula for the distance between any two points $A(x_1, y_1)$ and $B(x_2, y_2)$. Construct a right triangle with $\overline{AB}$ as its hypotenuse by drawing segments through A parallel to the x-axis and through B parallel to the y-axis, as shown in Figure 50. The lines containing the segments intersect at point C, forming right triangle ABC. Now, we apply the Pythagorean theorem.

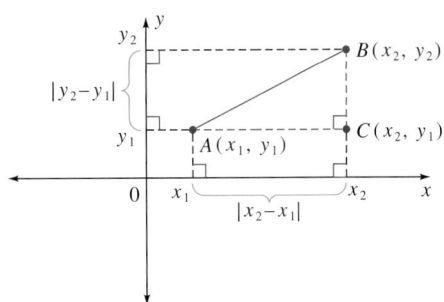

Figure 50

In Figure 50, we see that $AC = |x_2 - x_1|$ and $BC = |y_2 - y_1|$. By the Pythagorean theorem, $(AB)^2 = |x_2 - x_1|^2 + |y_2 - y_1|^2$, and consequently $AB = \sqrt{|x_2 - x_1|^2 + |y_2 - y_1|^2}$. Because $|x_2 - x_1|^2 = (x_2 - x_1)^2$ and $|y_2 - y_1|^2 = (y_2 - y_1)^2$, $AB = \sqrt{(x_2 - x_1)^2 + (y_2 - y_1)^2}$. This result is the **distance formula**.

> **Theorem 14-9: Distance Formula**
>
> The distance between the points $A(x_1, y_1)$ and $B(x_2, y_2)$ is given by
> $$AB = \sqrt{(x_2 - x_1)^2 + (y_2 - y_1)^2}.$$

▶ **NOW TRY THIS 6**

NTT 6: Answers can be found in Answers at the back of the book.

Does it make any difference in the distance formula if $x_1 - x_2$ and $y_1 - y_2$ are used instead of $x_2 - x_1$ and $y_2 - y_1$, respectively?

Example 18

a. Show that $A(7, 4)$, $B(^-2, 1)$, and $C(10, ^-5)$ are the vertices of an isosceles triangle.
b. Show that $\triangle ABC$ in (a) is a right triangle.

Solution
a. Using the distance formula, we find the lengths of the sides.

$$AB = \sqrt{(^-2 - 7)^2 + (1 - 4)^2} = \sqrt{(^-9)^2 + (^-3)^2} = \sqrt{90} = 3\sqrt{10}$$
$$BC = \sqrt{[10 - (^-2)]^2 + (^-5 - 1)^2} = \sqrt{12^2 + (^-6)^2} = \sqrt{180} = 6\sqrt{5}$$
$$AC = \sqrt{(10 - 7)^2 + (^-5 - 4)^2} = \sqrt{3^2 + (^-9)^2} = \sqrt{90} = 3\sqrt{10}$$

Thus, $AB = AC$, and so the triangle is isosceles.
b. Because $(\sqrt{90})^2 + (\sqrt{90})^2 = (\sqrt{180})^2$, $\triangle ABC$ is a right triangle with $\overline{BC}$ as hypotenuse and $\overline{AB}$ and $\overline{AC}$ as legs.

Example 19

Determine whether the points $A(0, 5)$, $B(1, 2)$, and $C(2, ^-1)$ are collinear.

Solution It is hard to tell by graphing the points whether the points are collinear (on the same line). If they are not collinear, they would be the vertices of a triangle, and hence the sum of the lengths of any two sides is greater than the length of the third (triangle inequality). Using the distance formula, we find the lengths of the sides.

$$AB = \sqrt{(0 - 1)^2 + (5 - 2)^2} = \sqrt{1 + 9} = \sqrt{10}$$
$$BC = \sqrt{(2 - 1)^2 + (^-1 - 2)^2} = \sqrt{1 + 9} = \sqrt{10}$$
$$AC = \sqrt{(0 - 2)^2 + [5 - (^-1)]^2} = \sqrt{4 + 36} = \sqrt{40} = 2\sqrt{10}$$

Thus, $AB + BC = 2\sqrt{10} = AC$, and consequently, A, B, and C are collinear.

An alternative solution is to show that the slopes of each of the segments that can be formed are the same.

Using the Distance Formula to Develop the Equation of a Circle

Recall that a *circle* is the set of all points in a given plane equidistant from a given point, the center. Let (x, y) be any point on a circle with the center at the origin, $(0, 0)$, as shown in Figure 51(a). Any point on the circle, if and only if, it is the same distance from the center and this distance is the *radius, r*.

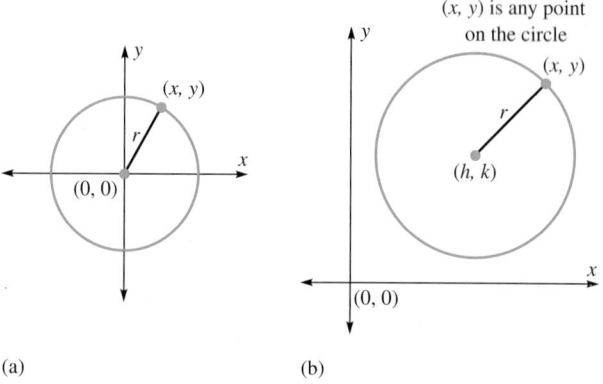

(a)   (b)

Figure 51

From the distance formula, we have $r = \sqrt{(x - 0)^2 + (y - 0)^2} = \sqrt{x^2 + y^2}$. An equivalent form can be obtained by squaring both sides, and we have $r^2 = x^2 + y^2$, which is the equation of a circle in standard form with center at $(0, 0)$.

Theorem 14-10: Equation of the Circle with Center at the Origin

An equation of the circle with the center at the origin and radius r is $x^2 + y^2 = r^2$.

If the center is at (h, k) and r is the radius as shown in Figure 51(b), then we use the distance formula to obtain the following.

$$\sqrt{(x - h)^2 + (y - k)^2} = r \quad \text{or} \quad (x - h)^2 + (y - k)^2 = r^2$$

Thus, we have:

Theorem 14-11: Equation of the Circle with Center at (h, k)

An equation of the circle with center (h, k) and radius r is $(x - h)^2 + (y - k)^2 = r^2$.

Example 20

a. Find an equation of the circle with its center at $(2, {}^-5)$ and radius of 3.
b. Given the equation of a circle $(x - 3)^2 + (y + 4)^2 = 3$, find the radius and the center.

Solution

a. Let $(h, k) = (2, {}^-5)$ and $r = 3$; then using $(x - h)^2 + (y - k)^2 = r^2$ we have $(x - 2)^2 + (y + 5)^2 = 9$.

b. Rewriting $(x - 3)^2 + (y + 4)^2 = 3$ as $(x - 3)^2 + [y - ({}^-4)]^2 = (\sqrt{3})^2$ and using $(x - h)^2 + (y - k)^2 = r^2$, we have $r^2 = (\sqrt{3})^2$ and $(h, k) = (3, {}^-4)$. Therefore, the radius is $\sqrt{3}$ and the center is at $(3, {}^-4)$.

Assessment 14-3A

1. Find the length of the following segments. Assume that the horizontal and vertical distances between neighboring dots is 1 unit.

a.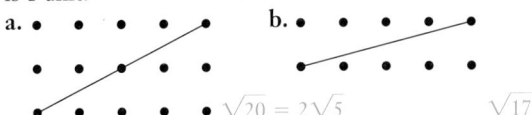

b.

$\sqrt{20} = 2\sqrt{5}$ 　　　　　 $\sqrt{17}$

2. Use the Pythagorean theorem to find x and y in each of the following:

a.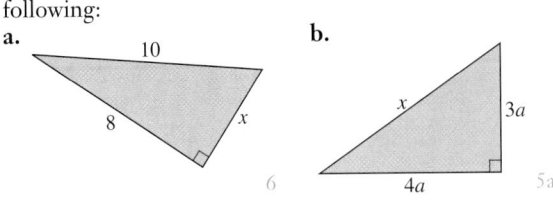
10, 8, 6, x

b.
x, $3a$, $4a$, $5a$

c.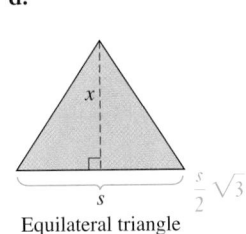
13, x, 13, 12, 5

d.
x, s, $\frac{s}{2}\sqrt{3}$
Equilateral triangle

e.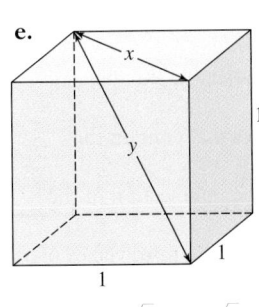
x, y, 1, 1, 1
$x = \sqrt{2}; y = \sqrt{3}$

f.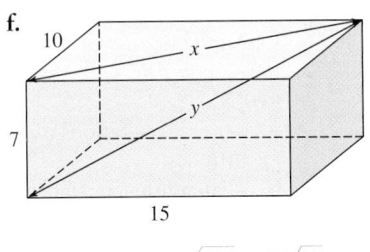
10, x, y, 7, 15
$x = \sqrt{325} = 5\sqrt{13}; y = \sqrt{374}$

3. On a 5 dot × 5 dot geoboard, construct segments of the following lengths.
a. $\sqrt{13}$ *
b. $\sqrt{5}$ *

4. Find a square on a 4 dot × 4 dot geoboard that has an area of 2 square units and a perimeter of $4\sqrt{2}$ units. *

5. What is the greatest perimeter of any isosceles triangle on a 5 dot × 5 dot geoboard? $8 + 4\sqrt{2}$ units

6. If the hypotenuse of a right triangle is 30 cm long and one leg is twice as long as the other, how long are the legs of the triangle? $6\sqrt{5}$ cm, $12\sqrt{5}$ cm

7. For each of the following, determine whether the given numbers represent lengths of the sides of a right triangle.
a. 10, 24, 16   No
b. 16, 34, 30   Yes
c. $\sqrt{2}, \sqrt{2}, 2$ Yes

8. What is the longest line segment that can be drawn in the interior of a right rectangular prism that is 12 cm wide, 15 cm long, and 9 cm high? $\sqrt{450} = 15\sqrt{2}$ cm

9. Starting from point A, a boat sails due south for 6 mi, then due east for 5 mi, and then due south for 4 mi. How far is the boat from A? $\sqrt{125} = 5\sqrt{5}$ mi

10. A 15-ft ladder is leaning against a wall and the wall is perpendicular to the ground. The base of the ladder is 3 ft from the wall. How high above the ground is the top of the ladder? $6\sqrt{6}$ ft

11. In the following figure, two poles are 25 m and 15 m high. A cable 14 m long joins the tops of the poles. Find the distance between the poles. $4\sqrt{6}$ m

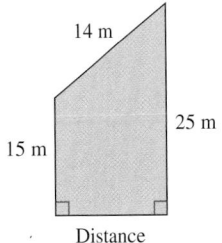
14 m, 25 m, 15 m, Distance

12. Find the area of each of the following figures.

a.

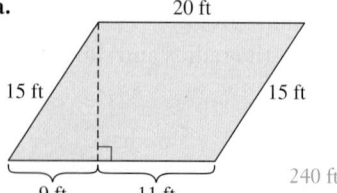

20 ft

15 ft   15 ft

9 ft   11 ft

240 ft²

b.

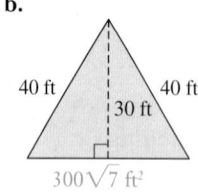

40 ft   40 ft

30 ft

300 √7 ft²

13. Find the area of each rhombus given below.

a. 16√21 cm²   **b.** 16√6 cm²

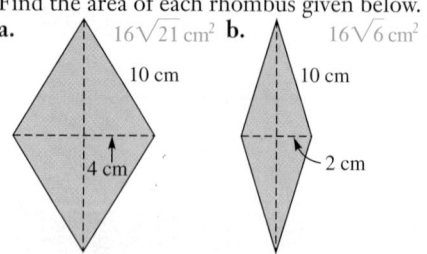

10 cm   10 cm

4 cm   2 cm

14. For each of the following, solve for the unknowns.

a.

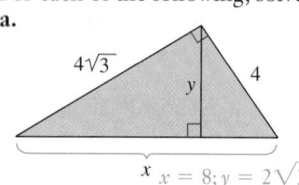

4√3   4

y

x   x = 8; y = 2√3

b.

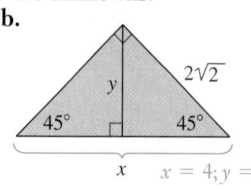

2√2

y

45°   45°

x   x = 4; y = 2

15. A company wants to lay a string of buoys across a lake. To find the length of the lake, they made the following measurements. What is the length of the lake?

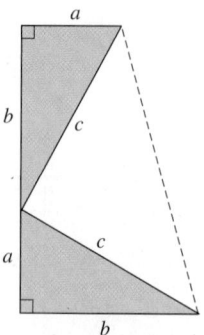

180 ft   30√11, or approximately 99.5 ft

150 ft

16. Before James Garfield was elected president of the United States, he discovered a proof of the Pythagorean theorem. He formed a trapezoid like the one that follows and found the area of the trapezoid in two ways. Use the drawing to complete the proof.   *

a

b   c

a   c

b

17. Use the following figure to prove the Pythagorean theorem by first proving that the quadrilateral with side c is a square. Then, compute the area of the square with side $a + b$ in two ways: as $(a + b)^2$ and as the sum of the areas of the four triangles and the square with side c.   *

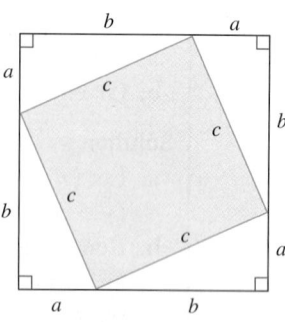

b   a

a   c

c   b

c

b   c

a

a   b

18. Equilateral triangles have been drawn on the sides of a right triangle as shown.

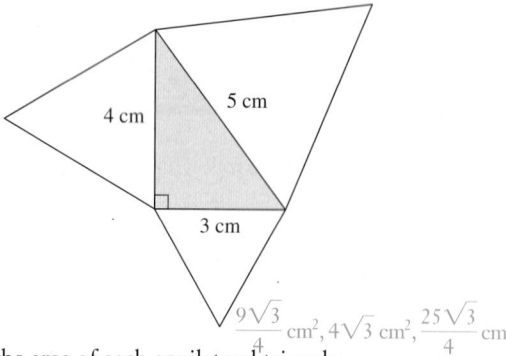

4 cm   5 cm

3 cm

$\frac{9\sqrt{3}}{4}$ cm², 4√3 cm², $\frac{25\sqrt{3}}{4}$ cm²

a. Find the area of each equilateral triangle.

b. How are the areas of the equilateral triangles related?   *

19. Find the distances between the centers of the circles shown. (*Hint:* Connect the centers of the circles.)   13

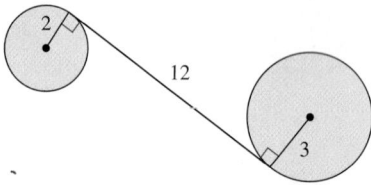

2   12   3

20. For each of the following pairs of points, find the length of $\overline{AB}$.

a. $A(0, 3), B(0, 7)$ 4

b. $A(0, 3), B(4, 0)$ 5

c. $A(^-1, 2), B(3, ^-4)$ 2√13

d. $A(4, ^-5), B\left(\frac{1}{2}, \frac{^-7}{4}\right)$ $\frac{\sqrt{365}}{4}$

21. If the length of the hypotenuse in a 30°-60°-90° triangle is $\frac{c}{2}$ units, what is the length of the side opposite the 60° angle? Explain your answer.   *

22. In triangle ABC with vertices at $A(0, 0), B(6, 0)$, and $C(0, 8)$,

a. write the equations of the lines that contain the altitudes. $x = 0; y = \frac{3x}{4}; y = 0$

b. what are the coordinates of the intersection of the altitudes? $(0, 0)$

23. a. Find the possible coordinates of the third vertex of an isosceles right triangle such that endpoints of one leg has coordinates $(0, 0)$ and $(8, 8)$ and the hypotenuse lies on the x-axis. $(16, 0)$

b. What are the lengths of the sides of the triangle in part (a)? $8\sqrt{2}, 8\sqrt{2},$ and 16

c. Show that the sides of the triangle satisfy the Pythagorean theorem. $(8\sqrt{2})^2 + (8\sqrt{2})^2 = 128 + 128 = 256 = 16^2$

24. Find an equation of the circle with the given center and radius.
   a. Center at $(^-3, 4)$, radius $= 4$ $\quad (x + 3)^2 + (y - 4)^2 = 16$
   b. Center at $(^-3, ^-2)$, radius $= \sqrt{2}$ $\quad (x + 3)^2 + (y + 2)^2 = 2$

25. Give the center and radius in each of the following circles.
   a. $x^2 + y^2 = 16$ $\quad (0, 0), 4$
   b. $(x - 3)^2 + (y - 2)^2 = 100$ $\quad (3, 2), 10$
   c. $(x + 2)^2 + (y - 3)^2 = 5$ $\quad (^-2, 3), \sqrt{5}$
   d. $x^2 + (y + 3)^2 = 9$ $\quad (0, ^-3), 3$

26. A boat starts at point A, moves 3 km due north, then 2 km due east, then 1 km due south, and then 4 km due east to point B. Find the distance AB. $\quad \sqrt{40} = 2\sqrt{10}$ km

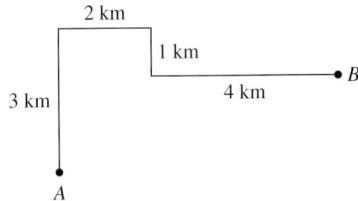

27. A farmer has a square plot of land. An irrigation system can be installed with the option of one large circular sprinkler, or nine small sprinklers as shown. The farmer wants to know which plan will provide water to the greater percentage of land in the field, regardless of the cost and the watering pattern. What advice would you give? *

a. 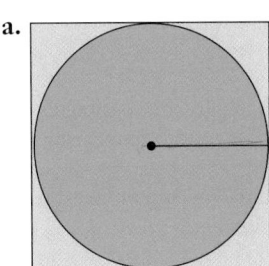 **b.**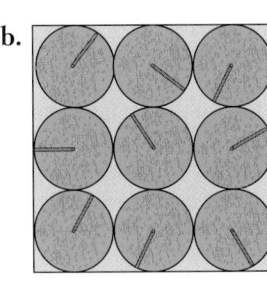

28. A baseball diamond is a square with side length 90 ft.
   a. What is the distance from first base to third base? *
   b. A player caught a ball halfway between first and second. How far was the player from third base? *
   c. How far was the player in part (b) from home base? *

29. The diagonals of a rhombus are 8 in. and 12 in. How long are the sides? $\sqrt{52} = 2\sqrt{13}$, or approximately 7.2 in.

30. The sides of a right triangle have lengths 3, 4, and 5 cm respectively. Show that the lengths of the sides of every similar triangle satisfy the Pythagorean theorem. *

31. In the figure shown, triangle ABC is a right triangle with right angle C and semicircles are drawn with centers at E, O, and P. Show that the area of the shaded portion is equal to the area of the right triangle. *

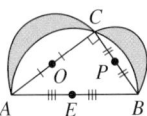

Assessment 14-3B

1. Find the length of the following segments. Assume that the horizontal and vertical distances between neighboring dots is 1 unit.

a. 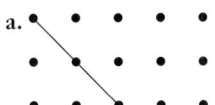 **b.**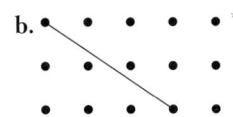

2. Use the Pythagorean theorem to find x in each of the following:

a. $\quad 9$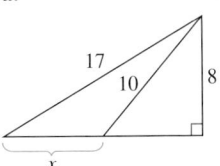

b. Right rectangular prism $\quad 13$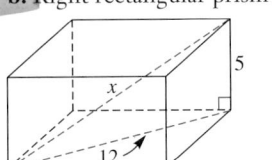

c. Right square pyramid $\quad 2\sqrt{2}$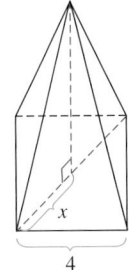

d. Right circular cone $\quad 3\sqrt{5}$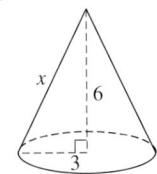

e. Cube $\quad 3\sqrt{3}$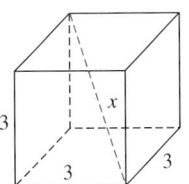

f.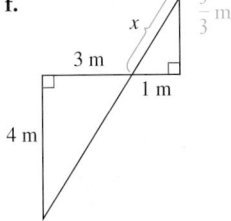

3. On a 5 dot × 5 dot geoboard, construct segments of the following lengths.
   a. $\sqrt{10}$ *
   b. $\sqrt{17}$ *

4. On a 4 dot × 4 dot geoboard, the greatest perimeter of any square is 12 units. Find a polygon on the geoboard with a greater perimeter. *

5. If possible, draw a square with the given number of square units on a 5 dot × 5 dot geoboard grid.
   a. 5 *
   b. 7   Not possible
   c. 8 *
   d. 14   Not possible
   e. 15   Not possible

6. A door is 6 ft 6 in. tall and 36 in. wide. Can a piece of plywood that is 7 ft by 8 ft be carried through the door?   Yes

7. For each of the following, determine whether the given numbers represent lengths of the sides of a right triangle.
   a. $\frac{3}{2}, \frac{4}{2}, \frac{5}{2}$ Yes
   b. $\sqrt{2}, \sqrt{3}, \sqrt{5}$ Yes
   c. 18, 24, 30   Yes

8. What is the longest piece of straight dry spaghetti that will fit in a cylindrical can that has a radius of 2 in. and height of 10 in.?   *

9. A cellphone tower C is located 3 mi from the interstate highway h. The tower has a range of 6.1 mi in all directions. If the interstate is along a straight line, how many miles of highway are in the range of this tower?   Approximately 10.6 mi

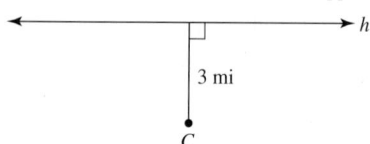

10. An access ramp enters a building 1 m above ground level and starts 3 m from the building. How long is the ramp?   *

11. To make a home plate for a neighborhood baseball park, we can cut the plate from a square, as shown in the following figure.

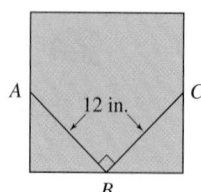

   If A, B, and C are midpoints of the sides of the square, what is the length of the side of the square to the nearest tenth of an inch? $12\sqrt{2}$ in. or approximately 16.97 in., so 17 in.

12. Find the area of each of the following triangles.
   a. *
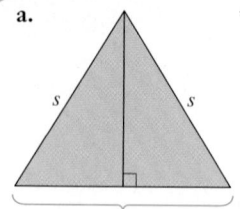
   b. *
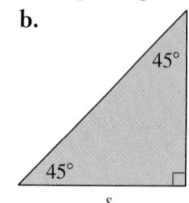

13. The following two rhombuses have perimeters that are equal. Use the properties of a rhombus to find the area of each rhombus.
   a. *
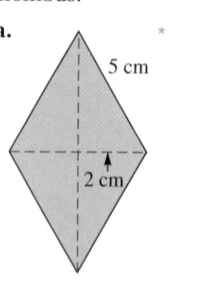
   b. *
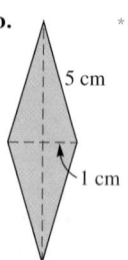

14. A builder needs to calculate the dimensions of a regular hexagonal window. Assuming the height CD of the window is 1.3 m, find the width AB (O is the midpoint of $\overline{AB}$) in the following figure. $\frac{2.6}{\sqrt{3}}$ m, or approximately 1.5 m

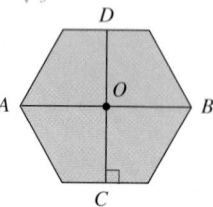

15. On a baseball field (90-ft square), if a player standing on third base throws on a straight line to a player on first base, how far is the ball thrown? $90\sqrt{2}$, or approximately 127 ft

16. Use the following drawing to prove the Pythagorean theorem by using corresponding parts of similar triangles $\triangle ACD$, $\triangle CBD$, and $\triangle ABC$. Lengths of sides are indicated by a, b, c, x, and y. (*Hint:* Show that $b^2 = cx$ and $a^2 = cy$.) *

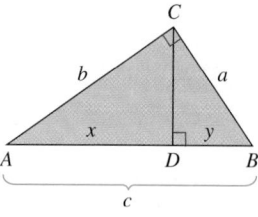

17. Show how the following figure could be used to prove the Pythagorean theorem. *

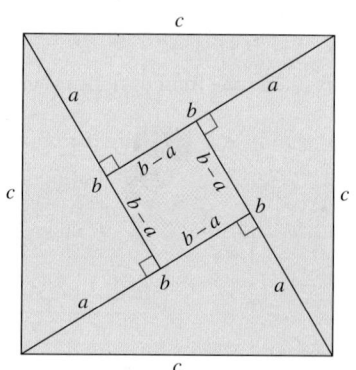

18. Semicircles are constructed on right triangle ABC with $\overline{AB}$, $\overline{BC}$, and $\overline{AC}$ as diameters, as shown below.

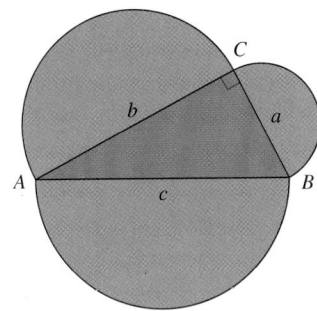

Is the area of the semicircle on the hypotenuse equal to the sum of the areas of the semicircles on the legs? Why?   *

19. Find the perimeter of the triangle with vertices at $A(0, 0)$, $B(^-4, ^-3)$, and $C(^-5, 0)$. $10 + \sqrt{10}$

20. Show that the triangle whose vertices are $A(^-2, ^-5)$, $B(1, ^-1)$, and $C(5, 2)$ is isosceles.   *

21. Triangle ABC has vertices at $A(0, 0)$, $B(6, 0)$, and $C(0, 8)$.
    a. Write the equations of the perpendicular bisectors of each of the sides of the triangle. $x = 3; y = 4; y = \frac{3}{4}x + \frac{7}{4}$
    b. What are the coordinates of the intersection of the perpendicular bisectors? $(3, 4)$
    c. What is the radius of the circumcircle for the triangle?   5
    d. What are the coordinates of the center of the circumcircle? $(3, 4)$

22. In an equilateral triangle with one vertex at the origin and one with coordinates $(8, 0)$, find the possible coordinates of the third vertex. $(4, 4\sqrt{3})$ or $(4, ^-4\sqrt{3})$

23. Find the equation of the circle with the given center and radius.
    a. Center at $(0, 0)$ and $r = \sqrt{5}$ $x^2 + y^2 = 5$
    b. Center at $(^-6, ^-7)$ and $r = 6$ $(x + 6)^2 + (y + 7)^2 = 36$

24. Give the center and radius for each circle.
    a. $(x - 3)^2 + (y + 2)^2 = 9$ $(3, ^-2), 3$
    b. $3x^2 + 3y^2 = 9$ $(0, 0), \sqrt{3}$

25. Find the area between two concentric (same center) circles whose equations are given below.
$$(x + 4)^2 + (y - 8)^2 = 9$$
and
$$(x + 4)^2 + (y - 8)^2 = 64 \quad 55\pi \text{ sq. units}$$

26. The distance from point A to the center of a circle with radius r is d. Express the length of the tangent segment $\overline{AP}$ in terms of r and d. $\sqrt{d^2 - r^2}$

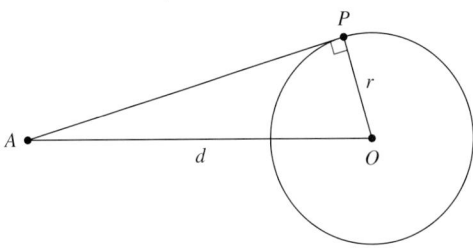

27. A baseball diamond is a square with side 90 ft.
    a. What is the distance from second base to home?   *
    b. A player caught a ball halfway between second and third. How far was the player from first base?   *
    c. How far was the player in part (b) from home?   *

28. The diagonals of a rhombus are 6 in. and 10 in. How long are the sides? $\sqrt{34}$ in.

29. The sides of a right triangle have lengths 5, 12, and 13 cm respectively. Show that the sides of any similar triangle satisfy the Pythagorean theorem.   *

30. Use the figure shown to show that the area of the square $CDOE$ is equal to half the area of square $BFAO$.   *

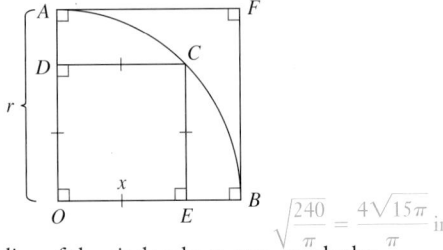

31. What is the radius of the circle whose area equals the area of a trapezoid with bases 15 in. and 25 in. and altitude 12 in.? $\sqrt{\frac{240}{\pi}} = \frac{4\sqrt{15\pi}}{\pi}$ in.

32. In the following figure, quadrilateral $ABCD$ is a parallelogram and P is any point on $\overline{AC}$. Prove that the area of $\triangle BCP$ is equal to the area of $\triangle DPC$.   *

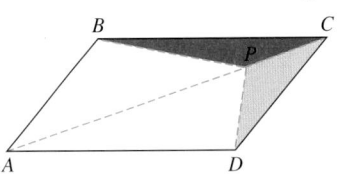

Mathematical Connections 14-3

Answers to Mathematical Connections can be found in the Answers section at the back of the book.

Reasoning

1. Given a square, describe how to use a compass and a straightedge to construct a square whose area is
   a. twice the area of the given square.
   b. half the area of the given square.

2. Explain how you would find the distance XY across the lake shown below, and then find XY.

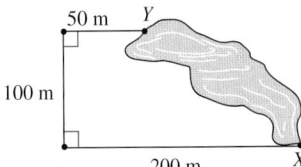

3. The sum of the squares of the lengths of all the sides of a right triangle is 200. Explain how to find the length of the hypotenuse and then find its length.
4. Explain how to construct a line segment of length $\sqrt{13}$ cm.
5. A **Pythagorean triple** is a sequence of three natural numbers a, b, and c that satisfy the relationship $a^2 + b^2 = c^2$. The least three numbers that form a Pythagorean triple are 3-4-5. Another triple is 5-12-13 because $5^2 + 12^2 = 13^2$.
   a. Find two other Pythagorean triples.
   b. Does doubling each number in a Pythagorean triple result in a new Pythagorean triple? Why or why not?
   c. Does adding a fixed number to each number in a Pythagorean triple result in a new Pythagorean triple? Why or why not?
   d. Suppose $a = 2uv$, $b = u^2 - v^2$, and $c = u^2 + v^2$, where u and v are natural numbers with $u > v$. Determine whether a-b-c is a Pythagorean triple.
6. Explain how to adapt the formula for a circle to describe the
   a. interior of the circle.
   b. exterior of the circle.

Open-Ended

7. Draw several kinds of triangles including a right triangle. Draw a square on each of the sides of the triangles. Compute the areas of the squares and use this information to investigate whether the Pythagorean theorem works for only right triangles. Use a geometry utility if available.
8. The lane of a rural highway may be only 9 ft wide. If a one-lane roundabout is to be built on the rural highway, decide the radius of the roundabout and explain your reasoning.

Cooperative Learning

9. Have each person in the group use a 1-m string to make a different right triangle. Measure each side to the nearest centimeter. Use these measurements to see how closely the your measurements come to satisfying the Pythagorean theorem.

Connecting Mathematics to the Classroom

10. As part of the discussion of the Pythagorean theorem, squares were constructed on each side of a right triangle. A student asks, "If different similar figures are constructed on each side of the triangle, does the same type of relationship still hold?" How do you reply?
11. Amy says that the equation of the circle she just drew is $(x - 3)^2 + (y + 2)^2 = {}^-16$. How do you respond?
12. One leg of a right triangle is 3 cm and the hypotenuse is 5 cm. Joni found the length of the other leg by evaluating $\sqrt{3^2 + 5^2}$. What error did she make?
13. June wants to know where all the points that satisfy the relation $x^2 + y^2 < 1$ are located. How do you respond?
14. Sarah says, "My father just bought carpet by the yard. Why did the clerk not talk about square yards of carpet?" How do you respond?
15. Jerald mentioned that his grandfather's land deed talked about square rods. He wants to know the meaning. What do you say?

GeoGebra Activities

16. Use *GeoGebra Lab 13* to investigate the Pythagorean theorem.

17. Use *GeoGebra* to determine the relationship between the length of the hypotenuse of a 45°-45°-90° triangle and the length of a leg.
   a. Construct a 45°-45°-90° triangle, label the vertices as in the figure below, and measure the lengths of the sides. Record the data for your triangle (triangle1) in the following table and compute the ratio:

	AC	CB	AB	AB/CB
Triangle 1				
Triangle 2				
Triangle 3				
Triangle 4				

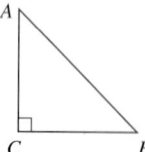

   b. Repeat (a) for three other triangles.
   c. Make a conjecture about the relationship between the length of the hypotenuse and the length of a leg for these triangles.
   d. Given a 30°-60°-90° triangle, determine the relationships between the lengths of the hypotenuse and the shorter leg and the relationships between the lengths of the longer and shorter legs.

Review Problems

18. Arrange the following in decreasing order: 3.2 m², 322 cm², 0.032 km², 3020 mm².
19. Find the area of each of the following figures.
   a.

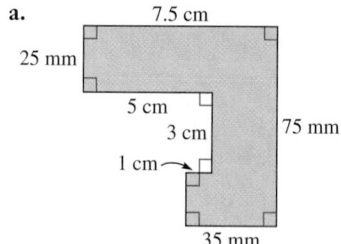

   b.

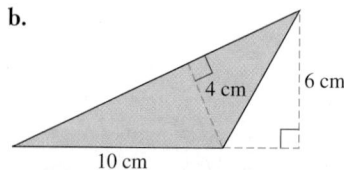

   c. Trapezoid

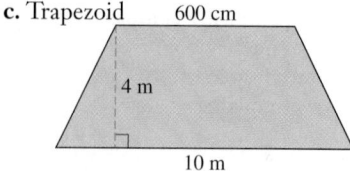

20. Complete the following table, which concerns circles:

	Radius	Diameter	Circumference	Area
a.	5 cm			
b.		24 cm		
c.				17π m^2
d.			20π cm	

21. A 10-m wire is wrapped around a circular region. If the wire fits exactly, what is the area of the region?

22. If Mary bought ribbon at $3.49 per yard and Samuel bought the same ribbon at $3.76 per meter, who got the better buy? Why?

23. What is the circumference of a U.S. penny to the nearest centimeter?

National Assessments

National Assessment of Educational Progress (NAEP) Questions

The endpoints of a line segment are the points with coordinates (2, 1) and (8, 9). What are the coordinates of the midpoint of this line segment?

A. $\left(2, 3\frac{1}{2}\right)$

B. $(3, 4)$

C. $(5, 5)$

D. $\left(4\frac{1}{2}, 5\frac{1}{2}\right)$

E. $(10, 10)$

NAEP Grade 8, 2005

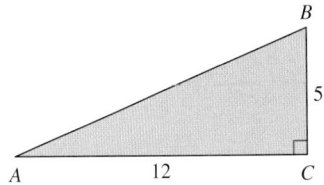

In the right triangle above, what is the length of $\overline{AB}$?

A. 8.5

B. 12

C. 13

D. 17

E. 30

NAEP, Grade 8, 2009

14-4 Surface Areas

14-4 Objective

Students will be able to understand and explain

- Surface areas of right prisms, right circular cylinders, right regular pyramids, right circular cones, and spheres.

Painting houses, buying roofing, seal-coating driveways, and buying carpet are among the common applications that involve computing areas. In many real-world problems, we must find the surface areas of such three-dimensional figures as prisms, cylinders, pyramids, cones, and spheres. Formulas for finding these areas are usually based on finding the area of two-dimensional pieces of the three-dimensional figures.

In the grade 6 *Common Core Standards*, we find that students "should represent three-dimensional figures using nets made up of rectangles and triangles [as in Chapter 11], and use the nets to find the surface area of these figures." Further, they should "apply these techniques in the context of solving real-world and mathematical problems." (p. 45)

Surface Area of Right Prisms

Consider the cereal box shown in Figure 52(a). Ignore any unseen flaps for gluing the box together. To find the amount of cardboard necessary to make the box, we cut the box along the edges and make it lie flat, as shown in Figure 52(b). When we do this we obtain a *net* for the box. The box is composed of a series of rectangular regions. We find the area of each rectangle and sum those areas to find the surface area of the box.

(a)

(b)

Figure 52

Example 21

a. Find the surface area of the box in Figure 52.
b. Could the box be made from a rectangular piece of cardboard 21 in. by 15 in.? If not, what size rectangle is needed?

Solution

a. The surface area of the box is $2(8 \cdot 11) + 2(2.5 \cdot 11) + 2(2.5 \cdot 8) = 271$ in.^{2}.
b. The box could be made with a piece of rectangular cardboard 21 in. by 15 in. by cutting and pasting parts.

A similar process can be used for many three-dimensional figures. For example, the surface area of the cube in Figure 53(a) is the sum of the areas of the faces of the cube. A net for a cube is shown in Figure 53(b). Because each of the six faces is a square of area 16 cm^2, the surface area is $6(16 \text{ cm}^2) = 96$ cm^2. In general, for a cube whose edge has length e units as in Figure 53(c), the surface area is $6e^2$.

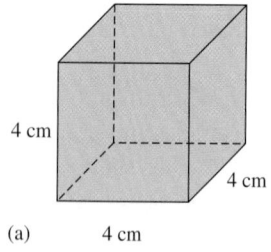

(a)   4 cm

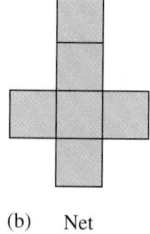

(b)   Net

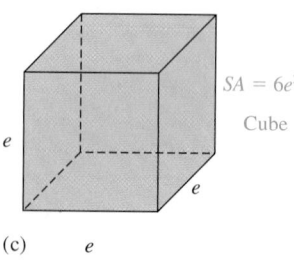

$SA = 6e^2$

Cube

(c) e

Figure 53

To find the surface area of a right prism, like the cereal box in Figure 52(a), we find the sum of the areas of the rectangles that make up the lateral faces and the areas of the top and bottom. The sum of the areas of the lateral faces is the **lateral surface area (LSA)**. The **surface area (SA)** is the sum of the lateral surface area and the area of the bases.

Figure 54 shows a right pentagonal prism with a net for the prism. If B stands for the area of each of the prism's bases, the surface area of the prism could be computed as $SA = ph + 2B$, where p is the perimeter of the base of the prism and h is the height. This formula holds for all right prisms.

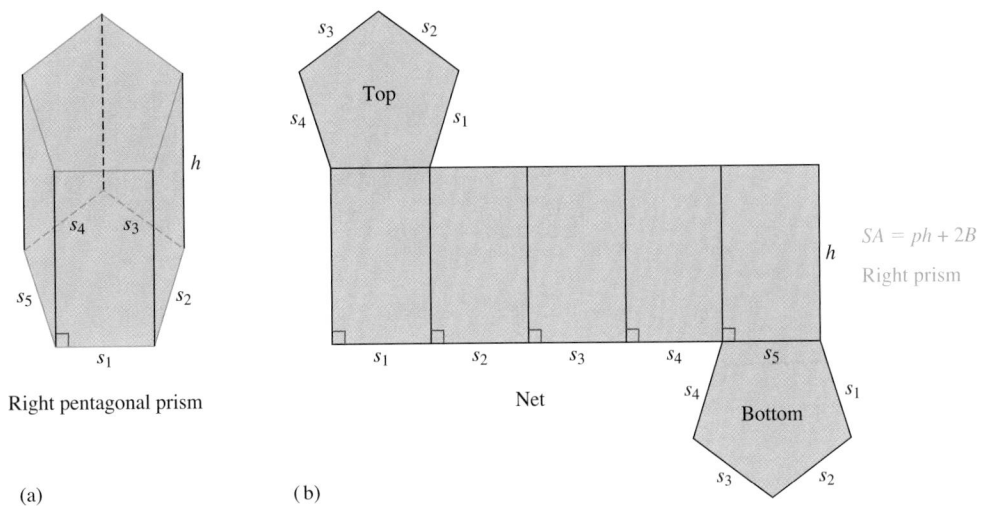

Right pentagonal prism
(a)

Net
(b)

$SA = ph + 2B$
Right prism

Figure 54

Example 22

Find the surface area of each right prism in Figure 55.

a. Right triangular prism   **b.** Right rectangular prism

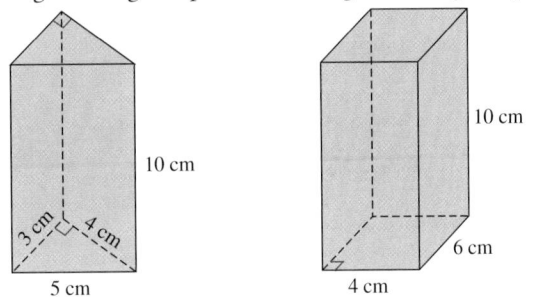

Figure 55

Solution

a. Each base is a right triangle. The area of the bases is $2\left(\frac{1}{2}(3 \cdot 4)\right) = 12 \text{ cm}^2$. The area of the three lateral faces is $4 \cdot 10 + 3 \cdot 10 + 5 \cdot 10$, or 120 cm^2. Thus, the surface area is $12 \text{ cm}^2 + 120 \text{ cm}^2 = 132 \text{ cm}^2$.

b. The area of the bases is $2(4 \cdot 6) = 48 \text{ cm}^2$. The lateral surface area is $2(10 \cdot 6) + 2(10 \cdot 4) = 200 \text{ cm}^2$. Thus, the surface area is 248 cm^2.

Note that in Example 22 we could have used the surface area formula developed in Figure 54. For example, in part (a) $P = 3 + 4 + 5 = 12$ cm and the area of a base is 6 cm^2, so $SA = ph + 2B = 12 \cdot 10 + 12 = 120 + 12 = 132 \text{ cm}^2$.

Surface Area of a Cylinder

As the number of sides of a right regular prism increases as in Figure 56, the figure approaches the shape of a right circular cylinder.

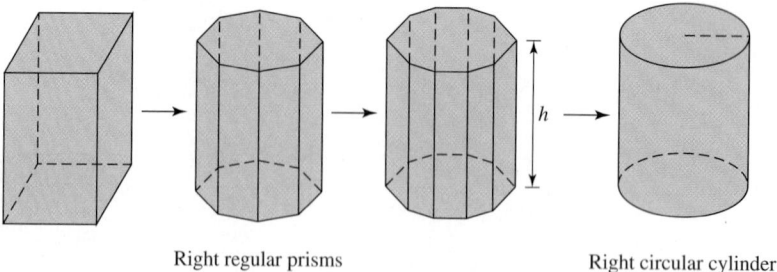

Right regular prisms   Right circular cylinder

Figure 56

To find the surface area of the right circular cylinder shown in Figure 57, we cut off the bases and slice the lateral surface open by cutting along any line perpendicular to the bases. Such a slice is shown as a dashed segment in Figure 57(a). Then we unroll the cylinder to form a rectangle, as shown in Figure 57(b). To find the total surface area, we find the area of the rectangle and the areas of the top and bottom circles. The length of the rectangle is the circumference of the circular base $2\pi r$, and its width is the height of the cylinder h. Hence, the area of the rectangle is $2\pi r h$. The area of each base is πr^2. *The surface area of a right circular cylinder is the sum of the areas of the two circular bases and the lateral surface area; that is, $SA = 2\pi r^2 + 2\pi r h$.*

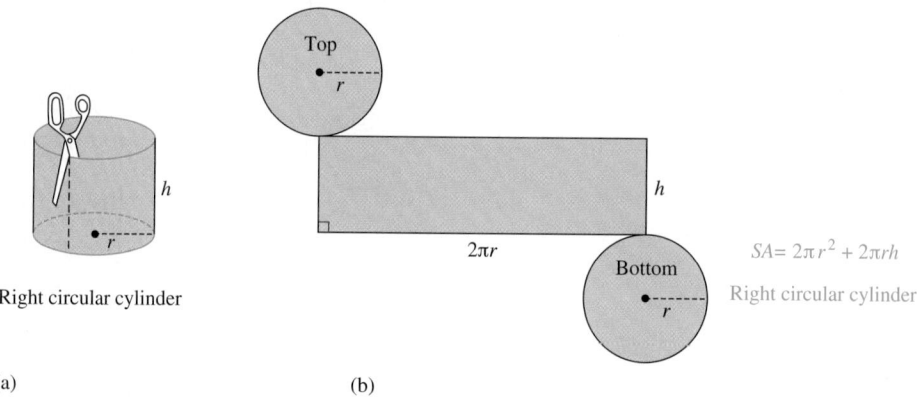

Right circular cylinder

$2\pi r$

$SA = 2\pi r^2 + 2\pi r h$

Right circular cylinder

(a)   (b)

Figure 57

Surface Area of a Pyramid

The surface area of a pyramid is the sum of the lateral surface area of the pyramid and the area of the base. A **right regular pyramid** is a pyramid such that the segments connecting the apex to each vertex of the base are congruent and the base is a regular polygon. The lateral faces of the right regular pyramid pictured in Figure 58(a) are congruent isosceles triangles. Each triangular face has an altitude of length ℓ, the *slant height*. Because the pyramid is right regular, each side of the base has the same length b. To find the lateral surface area of a right regular pyramid, we need to find the area of one face, $\frac{1}{2}b\ell$, and multiply it by n, the number of faces. Adding the lateral surface area $n\left(\frac{1}{2}b\ell\right)$ to the area of the base B gives the surface area, $SA = n\left(\frac{1}{2}b\ell\right) + B$. This formula can be simplified because nb is the perimeter, p, of the base. *Thus, the surface area of a right regular pyramid is given by $SA = \frac{1}{2}p\ell + B$, as shown in Figure 58(b).*

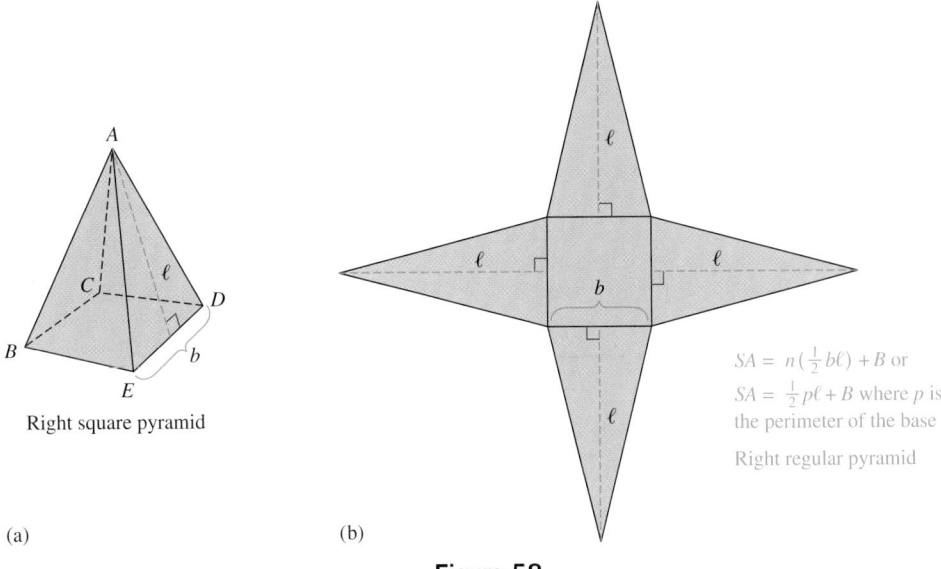

$SA = n\left(\frac{1}{2}b\ell\right) + B$ or

$SA = \frac{1}{2}p\ell + B$ where p is the perimeter of the base

Right regular pyramid

(a)   (b)

Figure 58

Example 23

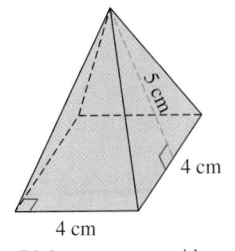

Right square pyramid

Figure 59

Find the surface area of the right square pyramid in Figure 59.

Solution   The surface area consists of the area of the square base plus the area of the four triangular faces. Hence, the surface area is

$$4\,\text{cm} \cdot 4\,\text{cm} + 4\left(\frac{1}{2} \cdot 4\,\text{cm} \cdot 5\,\text{cm}\right) = 16\,\text{cm}^2 + 40\,\text{cm}^2$$
$$= 56\,\text{cm}^2.$$

Example 24

The Great Pyramid of Cheops is a right square pyramid with a height of 148 m and a square base with perimeter of 940 m. The altitude of each triangular face is 189 m. The basic shape of the Transamerica Building in San Francisco is a right square pyramid that has a height of 260 m and a square base with a perimeter of 140 m. The altitude of each triangular face is 261 m. How do the lateral surface areas of the two structures compare?

Solution   The length of one side of the square base of the Great Pyramid is $\dfrac{940}{4} = 235$ m.

Likewise, the length of one side of the square base of the Transamerica Building is $\dfrac{140}{4} = 35$ m.

The lateral surface area (*LSA*) of the two are computed as follows:

$$(\text{Great Pyramid})\ LSA = 4\left(\frac{1}{2} \cdot 235 \cdot 189\right) = 88{,}830\,\text{m}^2$$

$$(\text{Transamerica})\ LSA = 4\left(\frac{1}{2} \cdot 35 \cdot 261\right) = 18{,}270\,\text{m}^2$$

Therefore, the lateral surface area of the Great Pyramid is approximately $\dfrac{88{,}830}{18{,}270} \approx 4.9$ times as great as that of the Transamerica Building.

Surface Area of a Cone

As the number of sides of a right regular pyramid increases, as shown in Figure 60, the figure approaches the shape of a right circular cone.

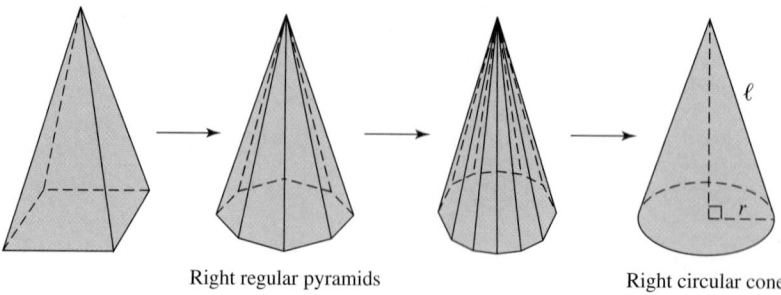

Right regular pyramids   Right circular cone

Figure 60

It is possible to find a formula for the surface area of a right circular cone by approximating the cone with a pyramid with many sides. We could inscribe in the circular base of the cone a regular polygon with many sides and use it as the base of a right regular pyramid. The lateral surface area of the pyramid is close to the lateral surface area of the cone. The greater the number of faces of the pyramid, the closer the surface area of the pyramid is to that of the cone.

In Figure 61(a), the lateral surface of the pyramid is $\frac{1}{2}ph$, where p is the perimeter of the base and h is the height of each triangle. With many sides in the pyramid, the perimeter of its base is close to the perimeter of the circle, $2\pi r$. The height of each triangle of the pyramid is close to the slant height ℓ, a segment that connects the apex of the cone with a point on the circular base.

Consequently, it is reasonable that the lateral surface area of the cone becomes $\frac{1}{2} \cdot 2\pi r \cdot \ell$, or $\pi r\ell$.

To find the total surface area of the cone, we add πr^2, the area of the base. Thus, *the surface area of a right circular cone is given by* $SA = \pi r^2 + \pi r\ell$, as shown in Figure 61(b).

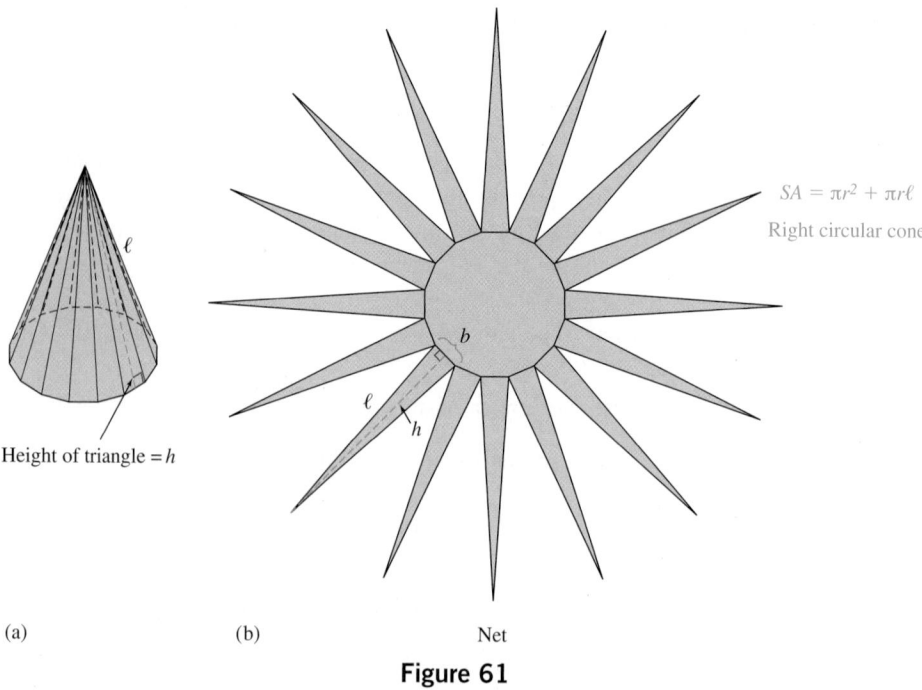

$SA = \pi r^2 + \pi r\ell$

Right circular cone

Height of triangle $= h$

(a)   (b)   Net

Figure 61

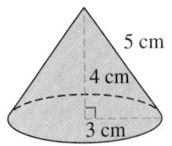

Example 25

Right circular cone

Figure 62

Find the surface area of the cone in Figure 62.

Solution The base of the cone is a circle with radius 3 cm and area $\pi(3 \text{ cm})^2 = 9\pi \text{ cm}^2$. The lateral surface has area $\pi(3 \text{ cm})(5 \text{ cm}) = 15\pi \text{ cm}^2$. Thus, we have the following surface area.

$$SA = \pi(3 \text{ cm})^2 + \pi(3 \text{ cm})(5 \text{ cm})$$
$$= 9\pi \text{ cm}^2 + 15\pi \text{ cm}^2$$
$$= 24\pi \text{ cm}^2$$

Surface Area of a Sphere

A **great circle** of a sphere is a circle on the sphere whose radius is equal to the radius of the sphere. A great circle is the intersection of a plane through the center of the sphere and the sphere. Because there are infinitely many different planes through the center, there are infinitely many great circles on a sphere. However, they are all congruent. Finding a formula for the surface area of a sphere is not easy using only elementary mathematics, but it is typically done using calculus. It can be shown that the surface area of a sphere is 4 times the area of a great circle of the sphere. Therefore, *the surface area of a sphere is given by $SA = 4\pi r^2$*, as shown in Figure 63.

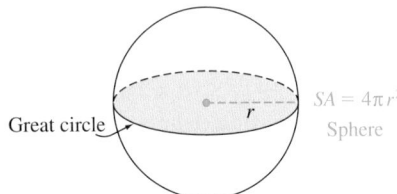

Figure 63

Assessment 14-4A

1. Which of these nets could be folded along the dotted segments to form a cube? *

   a. 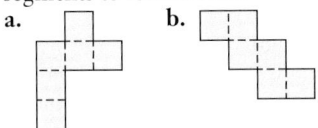   b.

   c. 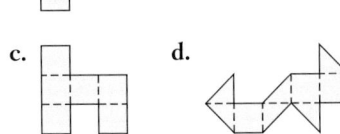   d.

2. Find the surface area of each of the following figures. *

   a. Cube

   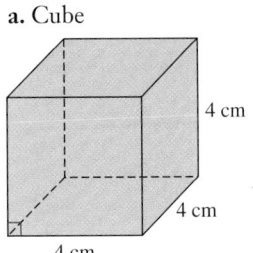

   b. Right circular cylinder

   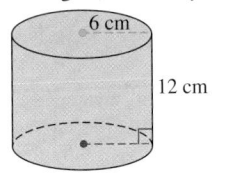

   c. Right rectangular prism

   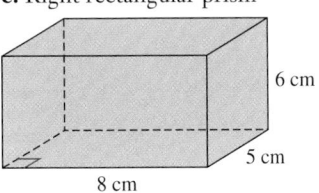

   d. Sphere

   e. Right circular cone

   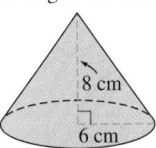

3. How many liters of paint must you buy to paint the walls of a rectangular prism-shaped room that is 6 m × 4 m with a ceiling height of 2.5 m if 1 L of paint covers 20 m²? (Assume there are no doors or windows and paint comes in 1-L cans.)   2.5 L, so buy 3 L

---

* Answers can be found in the Answers section at the back of the book.

4. The napkin ring pictured in the following figure is to be re-silvered. How many square millimeters must be covered? 2688π mm^2

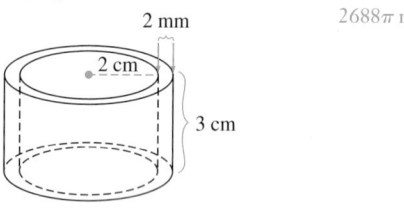

5. Assume the radius of Earth is 6370 km and Earth is a sphere. What is its surface area?   162,307,600π km^2
6. Two cubes have sides of length 4 cm and 6 cm, respectively. What is the ratio of their surface areas?   4:9
7. The base of a right pyramid is a regular hexagon with sides of length 12 m. The altitude of the pyramid is 9 m. Find the total surface area of the pyramid. $\left(108\sqrt{21} + 216\sqrt{3}\right)$ m^2
8. A soup can has a $2\frac{5}{8}$ in. diameter and is 4 in. tall. What is the area of the paper that will be used to make the label for the can if the paper covers the entire lateral surface area?   *
9. The top of a right rectangular box has an area of 88 cm^2. The sides have areas 32 cm^2 and 44 cm^2. What are the dimensions of the box? $\ell = 11$ cm, $w = 8$ cm, $h = 4$ cm
10. How does the lateral surface area of a right circular cone change if
    a. the slant height is tripled but the radius of the base remains the same?   The lateral surface area is multiplied by 3.
    b. the radius of the base is tripled but the slant height remains the same?   The lateral surface area is multiplied by 3.
    c. the slant height and the radius of the base are multiplied by 3?   The lateral surface area is multiplied by 9.
11. Find the surface area of a right square pyramid if the area of the base is 100 cm^2 and the height of the pyramid is 20 cm. $\left(100 + 100\sqrt{17}\right)$ cm^2
12. The sector shown in the following figure is rolled into a cone shape so that the dashed edges just touch. Find the following.

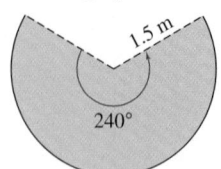

    a. The lateral surface area of the cone. 1.5π m^2
    b. The total surface area of the cone (Include the base.). 2.5π m^2
13. As seen in exercise 12, a sector of a circle can be used to construct a right circular cone. The length of the arc of the sector becomes the circumference of the circular base of the cone.

    a. If the length of the arc is 6π, what is the radius of the base of the cone that can be constructed?   3 units
    b. In part (a), the radius of the sector is 5 units; what is the slant height of the cone that can be constructed?   5 units
    c. Using the information in parts (a) and (b), what is the height of the cone that can be constructed?   4 units
    d. Using the information in parts (a)–(c), what is the angle measure for the original sector?   216°
14. If the cardboard tube of a toilet paper roll has diameter of 2.5 in. and is 4 in. tall, what is the lateral surface area of the outside of the cardboard roll? 10π in.^{2}
15. If two right circular cones are similar with radii of the bases in the ratio 1:2, what is the ratio of their surface areas?   1:4
16. Water covers approximately 70% of Earth's surface. Assume Earth is a sphere with diameter about 13,000 km. What amount of Earth's surface is covered with water?   *
17. If two cubes have total surface areas of 64 in.^{2} and 36 in.^{2}, what is the ratio of the lengths of their edges?   4:3
18. The total surface area of a cube is 10,648 cm^2. What is the length of each of the following items?
    a. One of the edges   *
    b. A diagonal that is not a diagonal of a face   *
19. Find the total surface area of the following stand, which was cut from a right circular cone: $\left(6400\pi\sqrt{2} + 13,600\pi\right)$ cm^2

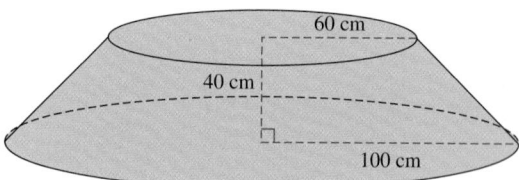

20. Find the numerical difference in the surface area of a square pyramid, with height of 10 cm and base side of 10 cm, and the inscribed right circular cone whose height is 10 cm, and whose base is inscribed in the square base of the pyramid. $100 + 100\sqrt{5} - \left(25\pi\sqrt{5} + 25\pi\right) \approx 69.44$ cm^2
21. A honeycomb is the basis of some window treatments. In one such treatment, the ends are open and the structure is a hexagonal prism without bases. What is the surface area (inside and outside) of one 4-cm (length of one side of the hexagon) cell if the window treatment is 48 cm wide?   2304 cm^2
22. A building had 54 rectangular plate glass windows that were all 4 ft by 8 ft by $\frac{1}{4}$ in. What is the total surface area of the glass including edges?   3483 ft^2

Assessment 14-4B

1. Which of the following nets could be folded to form a rectangular prism?   *

   a. 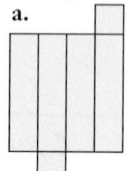   b. 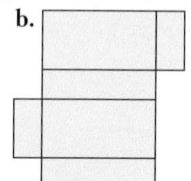   c.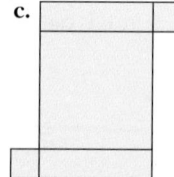

2. Find the surface area of each of the following.
   a. Right square pyramid   *

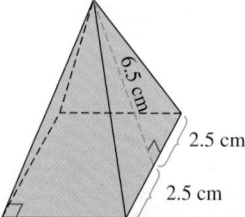

b. Right circular cylinder topped with hemisphere

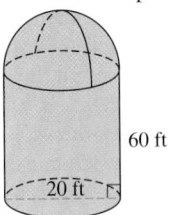

60 ft

20 ft

c. Right circular cone topped with hemisphere

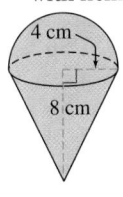

4 cm

8 cm

3. How many liters of paint must you buy to paint the walls of a rectangular prism-shaped room that is 8 m × 5 m with a ceiling height of 2.5 m if 1 L of paint covers 20 m²? (Assume there are no doors or windows and paint is sold in 1-L cans.)

4. Suppose one right circular cylinder has radius 2 m and height 6 m and another has radius 6 m and height 2 m.
 a. Which cylinder has the greater lateral surface area?
 b. Which cylinder has the greater total surface area?

5. What happens to the surface area of a sphere if the radius is
 a. doubled?   The surface area is multiplied by 4.
 b. tripled?   The surface area is multiplied by 9.

6. How does the surface area of a right rectangular box (including top and bottom) change if
 a. each dimension is doubled?
 b. each dimension is tripled?
 c. each dimension is multiplied by a factor of k?

7. Approximately how much material is needed to make the tent illustrated in the following figure (both ends and the bottom as well as the sides should be included)?

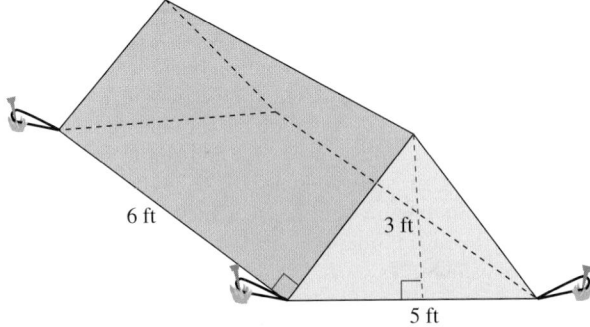

6 ft

3 ft

5 ft

8. A square piece of paper 10 cm on a side is rolled to form the lateral surface area of a right circular cylinder and then a top and bottom are added. What is the surface area of the cylinder? $100 + \frac{50}{\pi}$, or approximately 116 cm²

9. A structure is composed of unit cubes with at least one face of each cube connected to the face of another cube, as shown in the following figure.

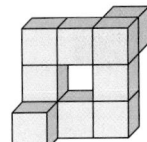

 a. If one cube is added, what is the maximum surface area the structure can have?   44
 b. If one cube is added, what is the minimum surface area the structure can have?   38
 c. Is it possible to design a structure so that one can add a cube and yet add nothing to the surface area of the structure? Explain your answer.

10. How does the lateral surface area of a right circular cylinder change if
 a. the radius of the base is doubled?   It is doubled.
 b. the height of the cylinder is doubled?   It is doubled.

11. Find the surface area of a right square pyramid if the area of the base is 169 cm² and the slant height of the pyramid is 13 cm.

12. The region in each of the following figures revolves about the indicated axis. For each case, a three-dimensional figure is obtained. Find the surface area of each.
 a.

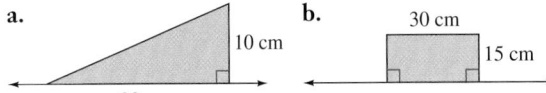

10 cm

20 cm

 b.

30 cm

15 cm

 c.

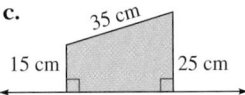

35 cm

15 cm

25 cm

13. A right square pyramid and a right circular cone are inscribed in a cube as shown. Find the
 a. surface area of the pyramid.
 b. surface area of the cone.

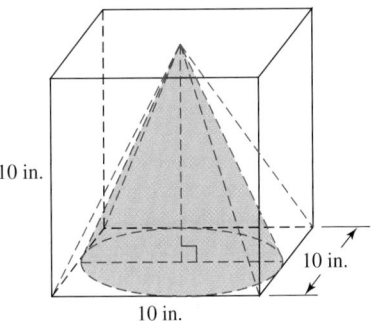

10 in.

10 in.

10 in.

14. A gas storage tank is in the shape of a right circular cylinder that has a radius of the base of 3 ft and a height of 8 ft. The farmer wants to paint the tank including both bases but only has 1 gallon of paint. If 1 gallon of paint will cover 350 ft², will the farmer have enough paint to complete the job? Explain.

15. If two right circular cones are similar with radii of the bases in the ratio of 2:3, what is the ratio of their surface areas? $\frac{4}{9}$

16. The diameter of Jupiter is about 11 times as great as the diameter of Earth. How do the surface areas compare?

17. If two cubes have edges of 2 ft and 4 ft, what is the ratio of their surface areas?   1:4

18. Find the surface area of the figure formed by removing a square prism section of the cube as shown below.   990 ft²

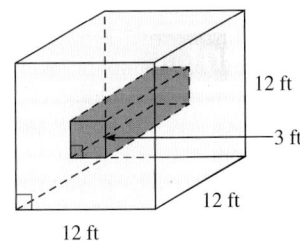

12 ft

3 ft

12 ft

12 ft

12 ft

19. In the figure shown, a right circular cylinder is inscribed in a right circular cone. Find the lateral surface area of the cylinder if the height of the cone is 40 cm, the height of the cylinder is 30 cm, and the radius of the base of the cone is 25 cm. 375π cm^2

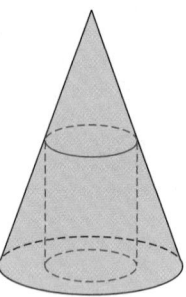

20. Find the numerical difference in the surface area of a right circular cylinder that has its base inscribed in the base of a rectangular prism with square base of side 10 cm and both have heights 10 cm and the surface area of the right circular cylinder that has its base circumscribed about the base of the rectangular prism with square base and the same height. $100\pi\sqrt{2} - 50\pi$, or approximately 287 cm^2

21. A honeycomb is the basis of some window treatments. In one such treatment, the ends are open and the structure is a hexagonal prism without bases. What is the surface area (inside and outside) of one 5 cm (length of one side of the hexagon) cell of the window treatment for a window that is 60 cm wide?   3600 cm^2

22. The Pyramid in Memphis, Tennessee, is 321 ft tall and has a square base with sides of 591 ft. The sides of the building are made of reflective glass. What is the surface area of the reflective glass?   About 515,711 ft^2

Mathematical Connections 14-4

Answers to Mathematical Connections can be found in the Answers section at the back of the book.

Reasoning

1. Tennis balls are packed tightly three to a can that is shaped like a cylinder.
   a. Estimate how the surface area of the balls compares to the lateral surface area of the can. Explain how you arrived at your estimate.
   b. See how close your estimate in part (a) was by actually computing the actual surface area of the balls and the lateral surface area of the can.

2. Which has the greater effect on the surface area of a right circular cylinder, doubling the radius or doubling the height?

3. In the drawing below, cube B was cut from a larger cube of surface area 216 cm^2 resulting in Figure A. The surface area of cube B is 24 cm^2. What effect did removing cube B from cube A have on the surface area? Explain.

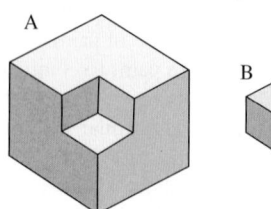
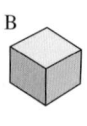

4. The lateral surface area of a right circular cone is given by the formula $\pi r \ell$ where r is the radius of the base and ℓ is the slant height. The area of the base of a circular cone is found using $A = \pi r^2$ where r is the radius of the circle making the base. If the area of the base and the lateral surface area are to be the same, what must be true? Prove your answer.

5. The diameter of a golf ball cannot be less than the diameter of a sphere with measure 42.67 mm.
   a. What is the surface area of a smooth golf ball with diameter 42.67 mm?
   b. A dimpled golf ball has to have symmetrical dimples. Explain whether a dimpled golf ball has greater surface area than a smooth one.

Open-Ended

6. One method of estimating body surface area in burn victims uses the fact that 100 handprints will approximately cover the whole body.

   a. What percentage of the body surface area is the surface area of two handprints?
   b. Estimate the percentage of the body surface area of one arm. Explain how you arrived at your estimate.
   c. Estimate your body surface area in square centimeters. Explain how you arrived at your estimate.
   d. Find the area of the flat part of your desk. How does the area of the desk compare with the surface area of your body?

7. Draw a net for a right prism that has surface area 80 cm^2.

Cooperative Learning

8. **a.** Shawn used small cubes to build a bigger cube that was solid and was three cubes long on each side. He then painted all the faces of the new, large cube red. He dropped the newly painted cube and all the little cubes came apart. He noticed that some cubes had only one face painted, some had two faces painted, and so on. Describe the number of cubes with 0, 1, 2, 3, 4, 5, or 6 faces painted. Have each member of the group choose a different number of faces and then combine your data to see if it makes sense. Look for any patterns that occur.
   b. What would the answers be if the large cube was four small cubes long on a side?
   c. Make a conjecture about how to count the cubes with different number of painted faces if the large cube were n small cubes long on a side.

9. As a group, work through the following activity to motivate the formula for the surface area of a sphere.
   a. Take an orange that is as close to spherical as you can find and determine its radius. (This will be approximate.)
   b. Take a compass and draw four disjoint circles that have the same radius as your orange.
   c. Peel the orange, breaking the skin into small pieces, and see how many circles can be filled with the pieces. Leave as little space as possible between pieces.
   d. Based on your experiment, how many circular areas ($A = \pi r^2$) can be covered by the surface (skin) of your spherical orange?
   e. How does this compare to the formula for the surface area of a sphere of the same radius?

Connecting Mathematics to the Classroom

10. A student wonders if she triples each measurement of a cereal box, will she need three times as much cardboard to make the new box. How would you help her decide?

11. Jodi says that if you double the radius of a right circular cone and divide the slant height by 2, then the surface area of the cone stays the same since the 2s cancel each other out. How do you respond?

12. Abi used the formula $SA = \pi r(r + \ell)$, where r is the radius and ℓ is the slant height, to find the surface area of a right circular cone. Is she correct? What do you tell her?

13. Jan says that if you double each of the dimensions of a rectangular box, it will take twice as much wrapping paper to wrap it. How do you respond?

14. Reba says that if she takes a block of modeling clay and makes different shapes with it, the surface area always remains the same regardless of the shape she makes. How do you respond?

Review Problems

15. Complete each of the following conversions.
  a. $10 \, \text{m}^2 = \underline{\quad} \, \text{cm}^2$ **b.** $13,680 \, \text{cm}^2 = \underline{\quad} \, \text{m}^2$
  c. $5 \, \text{cm}^2 = \underline{\quad} \, \text{mm}^2$ **d.** $2 \, \text{km}^2 = \underline{\quad} \, \text{m}^2$
  e. $10^6 \, \text{m}^2 = \underline{\quad} \, \text{km}^2$ **f.** $10^{12} \, \text{mm}^2 = \underline{\quad} \, \text{m}^2$

16. The sides of a rectangle are 10 cm and 20 cm long. Find the length of a diagonal of the rectangle.

17. The length of the side of a rhombus is 30 cm. If the length of one diagonal is 40 cm, find the length of the other diagonal.

18. Find the perimeters and the areas of the following figures.
  a.

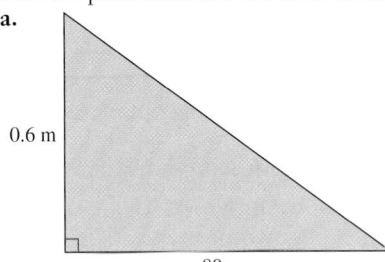

  b. Trapezoid

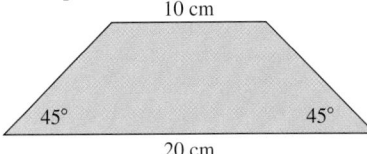

19. In the following, the length of the diagonal $\overline{AC}$ of rhombus $ABCD$ is 40 cm; $AE = 24$ cm. Find the length of a side of the rhombus and the length of the diagonal $\overline{BD}$.

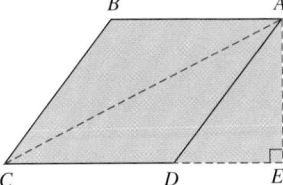

20. Find the length of the diagonal of a cube whose side is 1 unit long.

21. A manufacturer of paper cups wants to produce paper cups in the form of truncated cones 16 cm high, with one circular base of radius 11 cm and the other of radius 7 cm, as shown. When the base of such a cup is removed and the cup is slit and flattened, the flattened region looks like a part of a circular ring. To design a pattern to make the cup, the manufacturer needs the data required to construct the flattened region. Find these data.

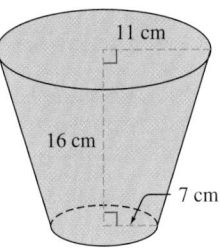

22. Convert the following measures.
  a. $150 \, \text{m} = \underline{\quad} \, \text{km}$ **b.** $0.002 \, \text{cm} = \underline{\quad} \, \text{mm}$
  c. $1.44 \, \text{yd}^2 = \underline{\quad} \, \text{in.}^2$ **d.** $1 \, \text{in.} = \underline{\quad} \, \text{cm}$

National Assessments

National Assessment of Educational Progress (NAEP) Questions

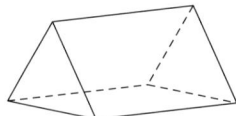

Which of the following can be folded to form the preceding prism?

A.

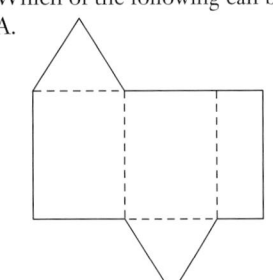

B.

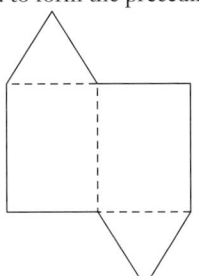

C.

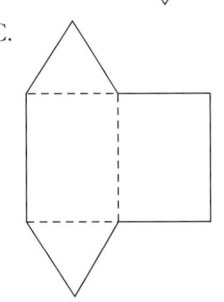

D.

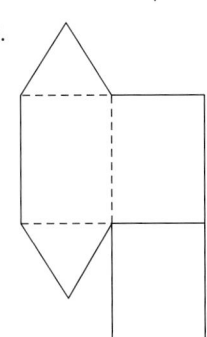

E.

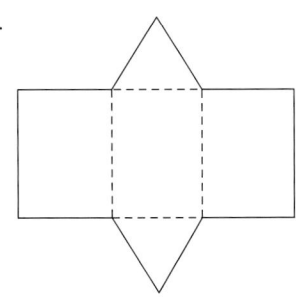

NAEP, Grade 8, 2005

14-5 Volume, Mass, and Temperature

In Section 14-4, we investigated surface areas of various-shaped containers. In this section, we explore how much containers will hold. Whereas surface area is the number of square units covering a three-dimensional figure, volume describes how much space a three-dimensional figure contains. The unit of measure for volume must be a shape that tessellates space. Cubes tessellate space; that is, they can be stacked so that they leave no gaps and fill space. Standard units of volume are based on cubes and are *cubic units*. A cubic unit is the amount of space enclosed within a cube that measures 1 unit on a side. The distinction between surface area and volume is demonstrated in Figure 64.

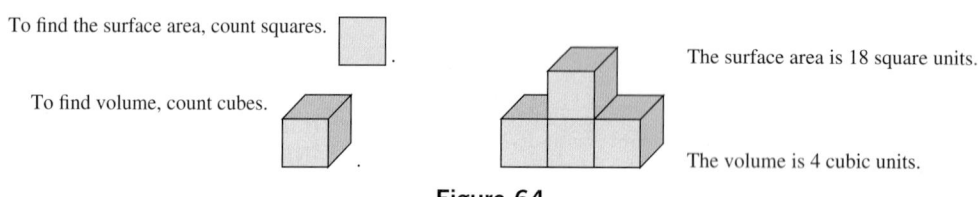

Figure 64

Volume of Right Rectangular Prisms

In the grade 5 *Common Core Standards*, we see that students:

Find the volume of a right rectangular prism with whole-number side lengths by packing it with unit cubes, and show that the volume is the same as would be found by multiplying the edge lengths, equivalently by multiplying the height by the area of the base. (p. 37)

Use *Volume of a Rectangular Solid* to help develop the formula for finding the volume of a rectangular prism.

The volume of a right rectangular prism can be found by determining how many cubes are needed to build it as a solid. To find the volume, count how many cubes cover the base and then how many layers of these cubes are used to fill the prism. As shown in Figure 65(a), there are $8 \cdot 4 = 32$, cubes required to cover the base and there are five such layers. The volume of the rectangular prism is $(8 \cdot 4)5 = 160$ cubic units. For any right rectangular prism with dimensions ℓ, w, and h measured in the same linear units, the volume of the prism is given by the area of the base, ℓw, times the height, h, or $V = \ell w h$, as shown in Figure 65(b).

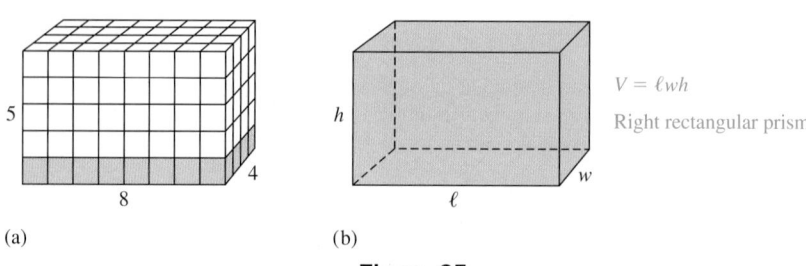

Figure 65

Converting Metric Measures of Volume

The most commonly used metric units of volume are the **cubic centimeter** and the **cubic meter**. A cubic centimeter is the volume of a cube whose length, width, and height are each 1 cm. One cubic centimeter is denoted 1 cm³. Similarly, a cubic meter is the volume of a cube whose length, width, and height are each 1 m. One cubic meter is denoted 1 m^3. Other metric units of volume are symbolized similarly.

Figure 66 shows that since $1 \text{ dm} = 10 \text{ cm}$, $1 \text{ dm}^3 = (10 \text{ cm})(10 \text{ cm})(10 \text{ cm}) = 1000 \text{ cm}^3$. Figure 67 shows that $1 \text{ m}^3 = 1,000,000 \text{ cm}^3$ and that $1 \text{ dm}^3 = 0.001 \text{ m}^3$. *Each metric unit of length is* 10 *times as great as the next smaller unit. Each metric unit of area is* 100 *times as great as the next smaller unit. Each metric unit of volume is* 1000 *times as great as the next smaller unit.* For example:

$$1 \text{ cm} = 10 \text{ mm}$$
$$1 \text{ cm}^2 = 100 \text{ mm}^2$$
$$1 \text{ cm}^3 = 1000 \text{ mm}^3$$

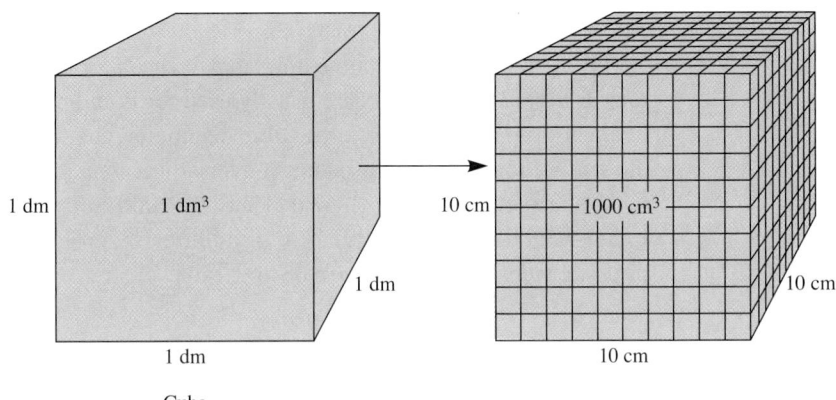

Figure 66

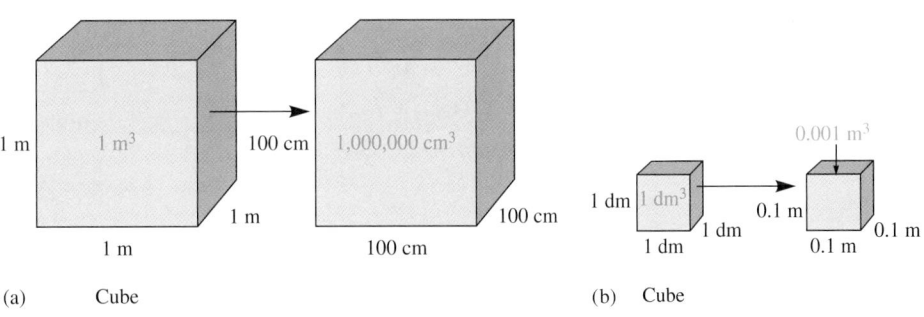

Figure 67

Because $1 \text{ cm} = 0.01 \text{ m}$, then $1 \text{ cm}^3 = (0.01 \cdot 0.01 \cdot 0.01) \text{ m}^3 = 0.000001 \text{ m}^3$. To convert from cubic centimeters to cubic meters, we move the decimal point six places to the left.

▶ **NOW TRY THIS 7**

NTT 7: Answers can be found in Answers at the back of the book.

a. Describe how many places to move the decimal point and in what direction in a metric area conversion if you know how many places and the direction to move in the corresponding length conversion.

b. Describe how many places to move the decimal point and in what direction in a metric volume conversion if you know how many places and the direction to move in the corresponding length conversion.

Example 26

Complete each of the following conversions:

   a. $5 \, \text{m}^3 = $ _____ cm^3
   b. $12{,}300 \, \text{mm}^3 = $ _____ cm^3

Solution

   a. $1 \, \text{m} = 100 \, \text{cm}$, so $1 \, \text{m}^3 = (100 \, \text{cm})(100 \, \text{cm})(100 \, \text{cm}) = 1{,}000{,}000 \, \text{cm}^3$.
      Thus, $5 \, \text{m}^3 = (5)(1{,}000{,}000 \, \text{cm}^3) = 5{,}000{,}000 \, \text{cm}^3$.
   b. $1 \, \text{mm} = 0.1 \, \text{cm}$, so $1 \, \text{mm}^3 = (0.1 \, \text{cm})(0.1 \, \text{cm})(0.1 \, \text{cm}) = 0.001 \, \text{cm}^3$.
      Thus, $12{,}300 \, \text{mm}^3 = 12{,}300(0.001 \, \text{cm}^3) = 12.3 \, \text{cm}^3$.

In the metric system, cubic units may be used for either dry or liquid measure, although units such as liters and milliliters are usually used for liquid measures. By definition, a **liter**, symbolized L, equals, or is the capacity of, a cubic decimeter; that is, $1 \, \text{L} = 1 \, \text{dm}^3$. In the United States, L is the symbol for liter, but this is not universally accepted.

Because $1 \, \text{L} = 1 \, \text{dm}^3$ and $1 \, \text{dm}^3 = 1000 \, \text{cm}^3$, it follows that $1 \, \text{L} = 1000 \, \text{cm}^3$ and $1 \, \text{cm}^3 = 0.001 \, \text{L}$. Also, $0.001 \, \text{L} = 1 \, \text{milliliter} = 1 \, \text{mL}$. Hence, $1 \, \text{cm}^3 = 1 \, \text{mL}$. These relationships are summarized in Figure 68 and Table 7.

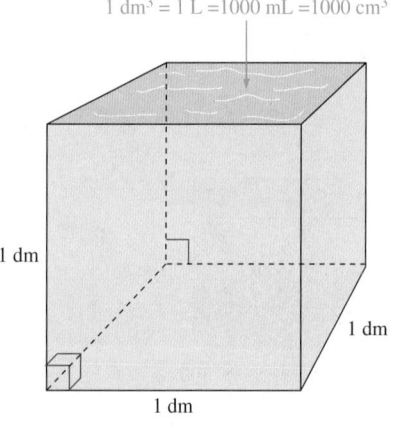

Cube

Figure 68

Table 7		
Unit	**Symbol**	**Relation to Liter**
kiloliter	kL	1000 L
*hectoliter	hL	100 L
*dekaliter	daL	10 L
liter	**L**	**1 L**
*deciliter	dL	0.1 L
centiliter	cL	0.01 L
milliliter	mL	0.001 L

*Not commonly used

Example 27

Complete the following conversions.

   a. $27 \, \text{L} = $ _____ mL
   b. $362 \, \text{mL} = $ _____ L
   c. $3 \, \text{mL} = $ _____ cm^3
   d. $3 \, \text{m}^3 = $ _____ L

Solution

   a. $1 \, \text{L} = 1000 \, \text{mL}$, so $27 \, \text{L} = 27 \cdot 1000 \, \text{mL} = 27{,}000 \, \text{mL}$. Alternatively,
   $$27 \, \text{L} = 27 \, \cancel{\text{L}} \cdot \frac{1000 \, \text{mL}}{1 \, \cancel{\text{L}}} = 27{,}000 \, \text{mL}.$$
   b. $1 \, \text{mL} = 0.001 \, \text{L}$, so $362 \, \text{mL} = 362(0.001 \, \text{L}) = 0.362 \, \text{L}$.
   c. $1 \, \text{mL} = 1 \, \text{cm}^3$, so $3 \, \text{mL} = 3 \, \text{cm}^3$.
   d. $1 \, \text{m}^3 = 1000 \, \text{dm}^3$ and $1 \, \text{dm}^3 = 1 \, \text{L}$, so $1 \, \text{m}^3 = 1000 \, \text{L}$ and $3 \, \text{m}^3 = 3000 \, \text{L}$.
      Alternatively, $3 \, \text{m}^3 = 3 \, \cancel{\text{m}^3} \cdot \frac{1000 \, \cancel{\text{dm}^3}}{1 \, \cancel{\text{m}^3}} \cdot \frac{1 \, \text{L}}{1 \, \cancel{\text{dm}^3}} = 3000 \, \text{L}.$

Converting English Measures of Volume

Basic units of volume in the English system are the cubic foot (1 ft^3), the cubic yard (1 yd^3), and the cubic inch (1 in.^3). In the United States, for liquid measure, 1 gallon $(\text{gal}) = 231 \text{ in.}^3$, which is about 3.8 L, and 1 quart $(\text{qt}) = \dfrac{1}{4} \text{gal}$, or about 58 in.^{3}.

Relationships among the one-dimensional units enable us to convert from one unit of volume to another, as shown in the following example.

Example 28

Convert each of the following measurements.

a. $45 \text{ yd}^3 = $ _____ ft^3
b. $4320 \text{ in.}^3 = $ _____ yd^3
c. $10 \text{ gal} = $ _____ ft^3
d. $3 \text{ ft}^3 = $ _____ yd^3

Solution

a. Because $1 \text{ yd}^3 = (3 \text{ ft})^3 = 27 \text{ ft}^3$, $45 \text{ yd}^3 = 45 \cdot 27 \text{ ft}^3 = 1215 \text{ ft}^3$.

b. Because $1 \text{ in.} = \dfrac{1}{36} \text{ yd}$, $1 \text{ in.}^3 = \left(\dfrac{1}{36}\right)^3 \text{yd}^3$. Consequently,

$$4320 \text{ in.}^3 = 4320\left(\frac{1}{36}\right)^3 \text{yd}^3 \approx 0.0926 \text{ yd}^3, \text{ or approximately } 0.1 \text{ yd}^3.$$

c. Because $1 \text{ gal} = 231 \text{ in.}^3$ and $1 \text{ in.}^3 = \left(\dfrac{1}{12}\right)^3 \text{ft}^3$,

$$10 \text{ gal} = 2310 \text{ in.}^3 = 2310\left(\frac{1}{12}\right)^3 \text{ft}^3 \approx 1.337 \text{ ft}^3, \text{ or approximately } 1.3 \text{ ft}^3.$$

Alternatively, $10 \text{ gal} = 10 \text{ gal} \cdot \dfrac{231 \text{ in.}^3}{1 \text{ gal}} \cdot \dfrac{\left(\dfrac{1}{12}\right)^3 \text{ft}^3}{1 \text{ in.}^3} \approx 1.3 \text{ ft}^3$

d. From (a), $1 \text{ ft}^3 = \dfrac{1}{27} \text{ yd}^3$. Hence, $3 \text{ ft}^3 = 3 \cdot \dfrac{1}{27} \text{ yd}^3 = \dfrac{1}{9} \text{ yd}^3 \approx 0.1 \text{ yd}^3$.

Volumes of Prisms and Cylinders

We have shown that the volume of a right rectangular prism, as shown in Figure 69, involves multiplying the area of the base times the height. If we denote the area of the base by B and the height by h, then $V = Bh$.

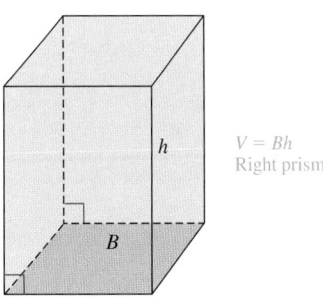

$V = Bh$
Right prism

Figure 69

Formulas for the volumes of many three-dimensional figures can be derived using the volume of a right prism. In Figure 70(a), a rectangular solid box has been sliced into thin layers. If the layers are shifted to form the solids in Figure 70(b) and (c), the volume of each of the three solids is the same as the volume of the original solid. This idea is the basis for **Cavalieri's Principle**.

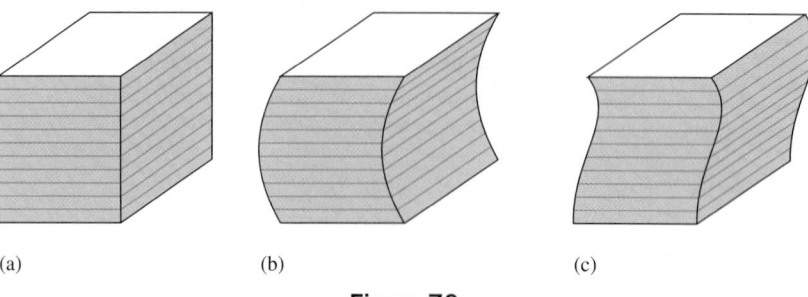

(a)   (b)   (c)

Figure 70

Cavalieri's Principle

Two solids each with a base in the same plane have equal volumes if every plane parallel to the bases intersects the solids in cross sections of equal area.

▶ **NOW TRY THIS 8**

a. The two right prisms in Figure 71 have the same height. How do their volumes compare? Explain why.

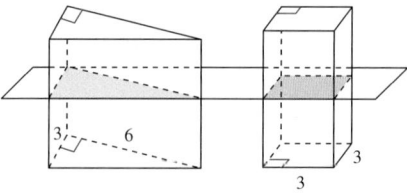

Figure 71

b. Consider the right prism and right circular cylinder in Figure 72(a) and (c) as stacks of papers. If the papers are shifted as shown in Figure 72(b) and (d), an oblique prism and an oblique cylinder, respectively, are formed.
  (i) Explain how the volume of the oblique prism is related to the volume of the right prism.
  (ii) Explain how the volume of the oblique cylinder is related to the volume of the right cylinder.

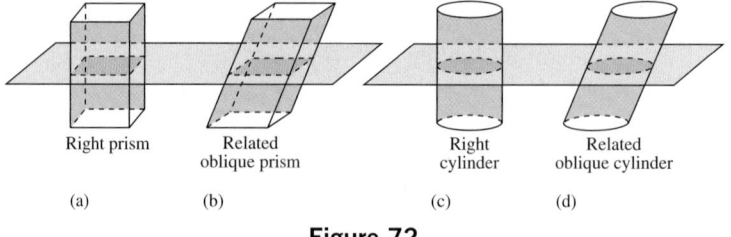

Right prism   Related   Right   Related
                oblique prism   cylinder   oblique cylinder

(a)   (b)   (c)   (d)

Figure 72

‿ **Historical Note** ‿

Bonaventura Cavalieri (1598–1647), an Italian mathematician and disciple of Galileo, contributed to the development of geometry, trigonometry, and algebra in the Renaissance. After reading Euclid's *Elements*, he was inspired to study mathematics. In 1629, Cavalieri became a professor at Bologna and held that post until his death. Cavalieri is best known for his principle concerning the volumes of solids.

Any oblique prism can be thought of as a stack of thin cards, all shaped like the base of the solid. The oblique stack can be straightened to form a right prism with the same volume. These prisms have the same height h and base area B so *the volume of any prism is given by $V = Bh$.*

The volume of a cylinder can be approximated using prisms with increasing numbers of sides in their bases. The volume of each prism is the product of the area of the base and the height. Similarly, the **volume V of a cylinder** is the product of the area of the base B and the height h. If the base is a circle of radius r, and the height of the cylinder is h, then $V = Bh = \pi r^2 h$.

Example 29

Find the volume of each figure in Figure 73.

a. Oblique prism

b. Right circular cylinder

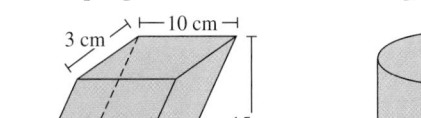
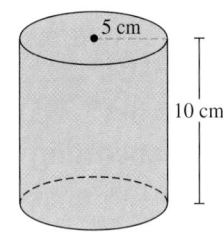

Figure 73

Solution
a. $V = Bh = (10\text{ cm} \cdot 3\text{ cm})15\text{ cm} = 450\text{ cm}^3$
b. $V = \pi r^2 h = \pi(5\text{ cm})^2 10\text{ cm} = 250\pi\text{ cm}^3$

Volumes of Pyramids and Cones

Figure 74(a) shows a right prism and a right pyramid with congruent bases and equal heights; h marks the perpendicular distance between the bases of the prism and cylinder and the perpendicular distance between the apexes and bases in the pyramid and cone; it is the height in each case.

How are the volumes of the containers in Figure 74 related? Students may explore the relationship by filling the pyramid with water, sand, or rice and pouring the contents into the prism. They should find that it takes three full pyramids to fill the prism and thus, the volume of the pyramid is equal to one-third the volume of the prism.

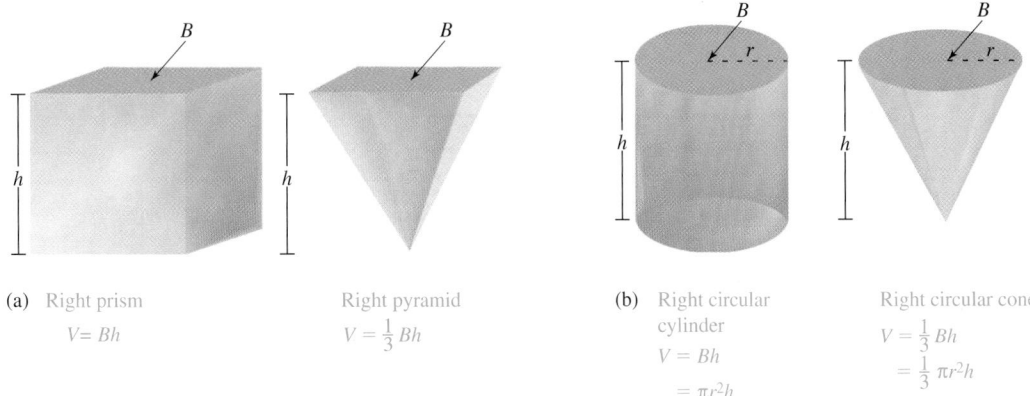

(a) Right prism
$V = Bh$

Right pyramid
$V = \frac{1}{3}Bh$

(b) Right circular cylinder
$V = Bh$
$= \pi r^2 h$

Right circular cone
$V = \frac{1}{3}Bh$
$= \frac{1}{3}\pi r^2 h$

Figure 74

This relationship between prisms and pyramids with congruent bases and heights, respectively, is true in general; that is, *for a pyramid $V = \dfrac{1}{3}Bh$, where B is the area of the base and h is the* *height.* The same relationship holds between the volume of a cone and the volume of a cylinder, where they have congruent bases and equal heights, as shown in Figure 74(b). Therefore, *the volume of a right circular cone is given by* $V = \frac{1}{3}Bh$, *or* $V = \frac{1}{3}\pi r^2 h$.

This relationship between the volume of a pyramid and the volume of a prism with congruent bases and congruent heights, as well as that of comparable cones and cylinders, are explored on the student page shown below.

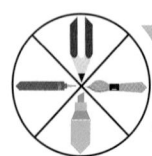

School Book Page   Generating Formulas for Volume

8-10b **Activity Lab**   **Hands On**

Generating Formulas for Volume

In this activity, you will relate the volume of a pyramid to the volume of a prism.

ACTIVITY

Step 1 Using poster board, draw and cut out four congruent isosceles triangles like the one below.

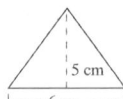

Step 2 Tape the edges of the four triangles to form a pyramid without a base. What is the area of the missing base?

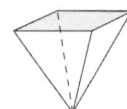

Step 3 Using poster board, draw and cut out four congruent rectangles and one square like the one below.

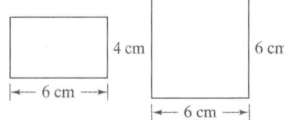

Step 4 Tape the edges of the polygons to form a prism without a base. Compare the areas of the missing base of the prism and the missing base of the pyramid.

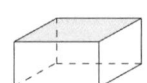

Step 5 Place the pyramid and the prism side by side. What do you notice about their heights?

Step 6 Fill the pyramid with rice. Pour the rice from the pyramid into the prism. Repeat until the prism is full.

Exercises

1. **a.** How many pyramids full of rice did you need to fill the prism?
   b. How does the volume of the pyramid compare to the volume of the prism?
   c. Make a conjecture about the formula for volume of a pyramid.

2. **Reasoning** To fill a cylinder with base area B and height h, you need 3 cones as shown at the right. Make a conjecture about the formula for volume of a cone.

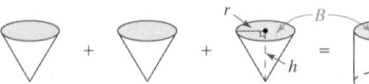

426   **Activity Lab**   Generating Formulas for Volume

Another way to determine the volume of a pyramid in terms of a prism is to start with a cube and draw three diagonals from one vertex to the nonadjacent vertices of one of the opposite faces as shown in Figure 75(a). We can see that there are three pyramids formed inside the cube, as shown in Figure 75(b).

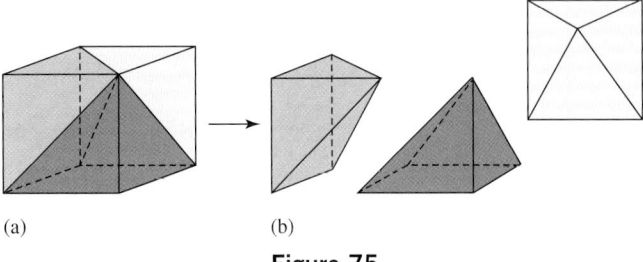

(a) (b)

Figure 75

The three pyramids are identical in size and shape, do not overlap, and their union is the whole cube. Therefore, each of these pyramids has a volume one-third that of the cube. Once again we see that for a pyramid $V = \dfrac{1}{3}Bh$, where B is the area of the base and h is the height.

This can be demonstrated by building three paper models of the pyramids and fitting them together into a prism. A net that can be enlarged and used for the construction is given in Figure 76.

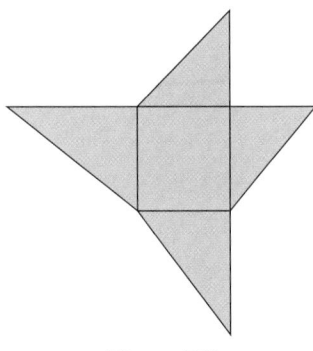

Figure 76

Example 30

Find the volume of each in Figure 77.

a. Right square pyramid

b. Right circular cone

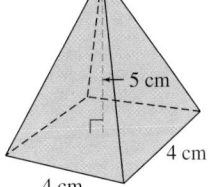

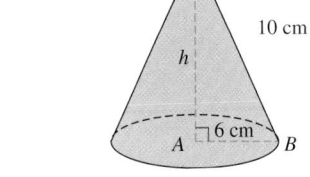

Figure 77

Solution

a. The figure is a pyramid with a square base, whose area is $4\,\text{cm} \cdot 4\,\text{cm}$ and whose height is $5\,\text{cm}$. Hence, $V = \dfrac{1}{3}Bh = \dfrac{1}{3}(4\,\text{cm} \cdot 4\,\text{cm})(5\,\text{cm}) = \dfrac{80}{3}\,\text{cm}^3$.

b. The base of the cone is a circle of radius $6\,\text{cm}$. Because the volume of the cone is given by $V = \dfrac{1}{3}\pi r^2 h$, we need to know the height. In the right triangle OAB, $OA = h$ and by the Pythagorean theorem, $h^2 + 6^2 = 10^2$. Hence, $h^2 = 100 - 36 = 64$, and $h = 8\,\text{cm}$. Thus, $V = \dfrac{1}{3}\pi r^2 h = \dfrac{1}{3}\pi(6\,\text{cm})^2(8\,\text{cm}) = 96\pi\,\text{cm}^3$.

Example 31

Figure 78 is a net for a pyramid. If each triangle is equilateral, find the volume of the pyramid.

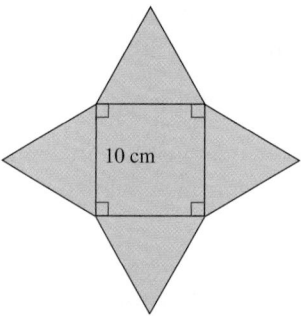

10 cm

Figure 78

Solution   The pyramid obtained from the folded model is shown in Figure 79.

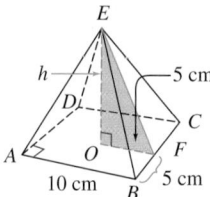

Figure 79

The volume of the pyramid is $V = \dfrac{1}{3}Bh = \dfrac{1}{3} \cdot 10^2 h$. We must find h. Observe that h is a leg in the right triangle EOF, where F is the midpoint of $\overline{CB}$. We know that $OF = 5\,\text{cm}$. If we knew EF, we could find h by applying the Pythagorean theorem to $\triangle EOF$. $\overline{EF}$ is a leg in the right triangle EBF. ($\overline{EF}$ is the perpendicular bisector of $\overline{BC}$ in the equilateral triangle BEC.) In the right triangle EBF, we have $(EB)^2 = (BF)^2 + (EF)^2$. Because $EB = 10\,\text{cm}$ and $BF = 5\,\text{cm}$, it follows that $10^2 = 5^2 + (EF)^2$, or $EF = \sqrt{75}\,\text{cm}$. In $\triangle EOF$, we have $h^2 + 5^2 = (EF)^2$, or $h^2 + 25 = 75$. Thus, $h = \sqrt{50}\,\text{cm}$ and $V = \dfrac{1}{3} \cdot 10^2 \cdot \sqrt{50} = \left(\dfrac{100}{3}\right)\sqrt{50}\,\text{cm}^3 \approx 236\,\text{cm}^3$.

Volume of a Sphere

To find the volume of a sphere, imagine that a sphere is composed of a great number of right regular congruent pyramids such that the apexes are at the center of the sphere and the vertices of the base lie on the sphere, as shown in Figure 80. If the pyramids have very small bases, then the height of each pyramid is nearly the radius r. Hence, the volume of each pyramid is $\dfrac{1}{3}Bh$ or

$\frac{1}{3}Br$, where B is the area of the base. If there are n pyramids each with base area B, then the total volume of the pyramids is $V = \frac{1}{3}nBr$. Because nB is the total surface area of all the bases of the pyramids and because the sum of the areas of all the bases of the pyramids is very close to the surface area of the sphere, $4\pi r^2$, the volume of the sphere is given by $V = \frac{1}{3}(4\pi r^2)r = \frac{4}{3}\pi r^3$.

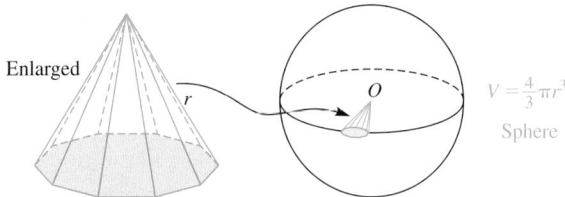

Enlarged

$V = \frac{4}{3}\pi r^3$

Sphere

Figure 80

Example 32

Find the volume of a sphere whose radius is 6 cm.

Solution $V = \frac{4}{3}\pi(6\,\text{cm})^3 = \frac{4}{3}\pi(216\,\text{cm}^3) = 288\pi\,\text{cm}^3$

Comparing Volumes of Similar Figures

Next we investigate the ratio of the volumes of two three-dimensional figures. Consider the two similar rectangular prisms shown in Figure 81 with scale factor 3. They have the same shape but not the same size.

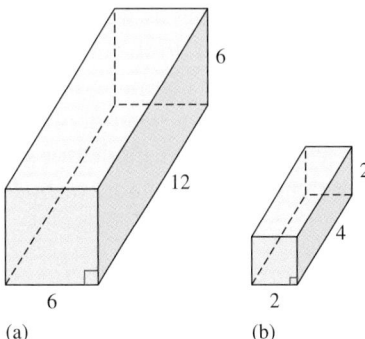

(a)   (b)

Figure 81

The surface areas and volumes of the two rectangular prisms in Figure 81 are

$SA_{(a)} = 2(6 \cdot 6) + 2(6 \cdot 12) + 2(6 \cdot 12) = 360\,\text{cm}$ $SA_{(b)} = 2(2 \cdot 2) + 2(4 \cdot 2) + 2(4 \cdot 2) = 40\,\text{cm}^2$
$V_{(a)} = Bh = 36 \cdot 12 = 432\,\text{cm}^2.$ $V_{(b)} = Bh = 4 \cdot 4 = 16\,\text{cm}^2.$

The ratios of the surface areas and the volumes for the two prisms are given below.

$$\frac{SA_{(a)}}{SA_{(b)}} = \frac{360}{40} = 9 = 3^2 \qquad \frac{V_{(a)}}{V_{(b)}} = \frac{432}{16} = 27 = 3^3$$

This example suggests that if two similar prisms have scale factor k, the ratio of their surface areas is k^2 and the ratio of their volumes is k^3. This is true in general for similar three-dimensional figures and is summarized in Theorem 14-12.

> ### Theorem 14-12: Similarity Principle of Measurement
>
> If the scale factor of two similar figures is k, then the ratio of their areas or surface areas is k^2 and the ratio of their volumes is k^3.

Example 33

   a. How does the surface area of a sphere 10 in. in diameter compare with the surface area of a sphere 5 in. in diameter?
   b. How do the volumes of the spheres in part (a) compare?

Solution
   a. Any two spheres are similar. The ratio of the diameters is $10:5$ or 2. By Theorem 14-12, the ratio of the surface areas of the spheres is $2^2 = 4$. Therefore the 10-in. sphere has 4 times the surface area of the 5-in. sphere.
   b. By Theorem 14-12 the ratio of the volumes is $2^3 = 8$. Therefore the volume of the 10-in. sphere is 8 times that of the 5-in. sphere.

Problem Solving   **Volume Comparisons: Cylinders and Boxes**

A metal can manufacturer has a large quantity of rectangular metal sheets 20 cm $\times$ 30 cm. Without cutting the sheets, the manufacturer wants to make cylindrical pipes with circular cross sections from some of the sheets and box-shaped pipes with square cross sections from the other sheets. The volume of the box-shaped pipes is to be greater than the volume of the cylindrical pipes. Is this possible? If so, how would the pipes be made and what are their volumes?

Understanding the Problem We are to use 20 cm $\times$ 30 cm rectangular sheets of metal to make some cylindrical pipes as well as some box-shaped pipes with square cross sections that have a greater volume than do the cylindrical pipes. We need to determine if this is possible and if so, design the pipes and compute the volumes.

  Figure 82 shows a sheet of metal and two sections of pipe made from it, one cylindrical and the other box-shaped. A model for such pipes can be designed from a piece of paper by bending it into a right circular cylinder or by folding it into a right square prism, as shown in the figure.

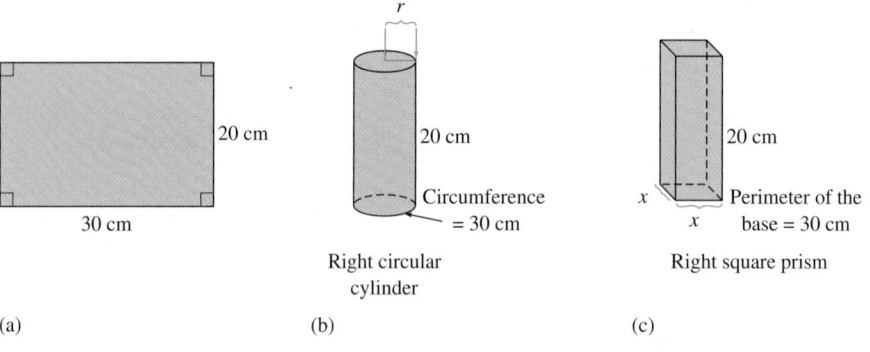

(a)   (b)   (c)

Right circular cylinder

Right square prism

Figure 82

Devising a Plan If we compute the volume of the cylinder in Figure 82(b) and the volume of the prism in Figure 82(c), we determine which is greater. If the prism has a greater volume, the solution of the problem will be complete. Otherwise, we look for other ways to design the pipes before concluding that a solution is impossible.

To compute the volume of the cylinder, we use the area of the circular base πr^2. To find r, we note that the circumference of the circle, $2\pi r$, is 30 cm. Thus, $r = \dfrac{30}{2\pi}$, and the area of the circle is $\pi r^2 = \pi \left(\dfrac{30}{2\pi}\right)^2 = \dfrac{900\pi}{4\pi^2} = \dfrac{225}{\pi}$.

With the given information, we also find the area of the base of the rectangular box. Because the perimeter of the base of the prism is $4x$, we have $4x = 30$, or $x = 7.5$ cm. Thus, the area of the square base is $x^2 = (7.5)^2 = 56.25$ cm^2.

Carrying Out the Plan Denoting the volume of the cylindrical pipe by V_1 and the volume of the box-shaped pipe by V_2, we have $V_1 = \left(\dfrac{225}{\pi}\right)20 \approx 1432$ cm^3. For the volume of the box-shaped pipe, we have $V_2 = 56.25 \cdot 20 = 1125$ cm^3. In the first design for the pipes, the volume of the cylindrical pipe is greater than the volume of the box-shaped pipe. This is not the required outcome.

Rather than bend the rectangular sheet of metal along the 30 cm side, we could bend it along the 20 cm side to obtain either pipe, as shown in Figure 83. Denoting the radius of the cylindrical pipe by r, the side of the box-shaped pipe by y, and their volumes by V_3 and V_4, respectively, we have $V_3 = \pi r^2 \cdot 30 = \pi \left[\dfrac{20}{(2\pi)}\right]^2 30 = \dfrac{(10^2 \cdot 30)}{\pi} \approx 955$ cm^3. Also, $V_4 = y^2 30 = \left(\dfrac{20}{4}\right)^2 30 = 25 \cdot 30 = 750$ cm^3. Because $V_2 = 1125$ cm^3 and $V_3 \approx 955$ cm^3, we see that the volume of the box-shaped pipe with an altitude of 20 cm is greater than the volume of the cylindrical pipe with an altitude of 30 cm.

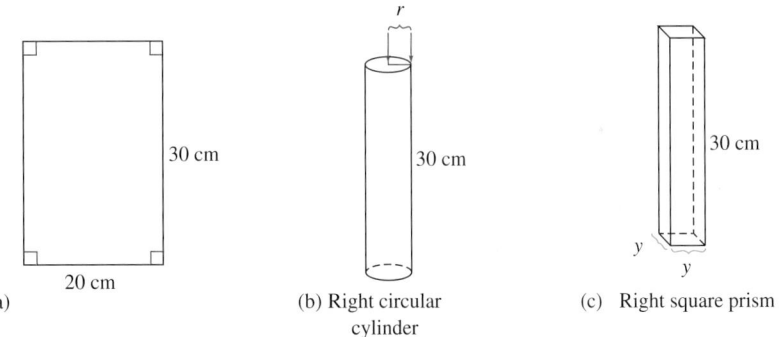

(a) 20 cm

(b) Right circular cylinder 30 cm

(c) Right square prism 30 cm

Figure 83

Looking Back We could ask for the volumes of other three-dimensional objects that can be obtained by bending the rectangular sheets of metal. Also, because the lateral surface areas of the four types of pipes were the same but their volumes were different, we might want to investigate whether there are other cylinders and prisms that have the same lateral surface area and the same volume. Is it possible to find a circular cylinder with lateral surface area of 600 cm^2 and smallest possible volume? Similarly, is there a circular cylinder with the given surface area and greatest possible volume?

Mass

Three centuries ago, Isaac Newton pointed out that the word *weight* is used for what is really mass. **Mass** is a quantity of matter, as opposed to **weight**, which is a force exerted by gravitational pull. When astronauts are in orbit above Earth, their weights have changed even though their masses remain the same. In common language on Earth, *weight* and *mass* are used interchangeably. In the English system, weight is measured in avoirdupois units such as tons, pounds, and ounces. One pound (lb) equals 16 ounces (oz) and 2000 lb equals 1 English ton.

In the metric system, a fundamental unit for mass is the **gram**, denoted g. An ordinary paper clip or a thumbtack each has a mass of about 1 g and weighs 1 g on Earth. As with other base metric units, prefixes are added to *gram* to obtain other units. For example, a kilogram (kg) is 1000 g. Two standard loaves of bread have a mass of about 1 kg. A person's mass is measured in kilograms. A newborn baby has a mass of about 3 kg. Another unit of mass is the *metric ton* (t), which is equal to 1000 kg. The metric ton is used to record the masses of objects such as cars and trucks. A small car has a mass of about 1 t. *Mega* (1,000,000) and *micro* (0.000001) are other prefixes used with gram.

Table 8 lists metric units of mass. Conversions that involve metric units of mass are handled in the same way as conversions that involve metric units of length.

Table 8

Unit	Symbol	Relationship to Gram
ton (metric)	t	1,000,000 g
kilogram	kg	1000 g
*hectogram	hg	100 g
*dekagram	dag	10 g
gram	**g**	**1 g**
*decigram	dg	0.1 g
*centigram	cg	0.01 g
milligram	mg	0.001 g

*Not commonly used

Example 34

Complete each of the following conversions.

a. 34 g = _____ kg   **b.** 6836 kg = _____ t

Solution

a. 34 g = 34(0.001 kg) = 0.034 kg   **b.** 6836 kg = 6836(0.001 t) − 6.836 t

Relationships Among Metric Units of Volume, Capacity, and Mass

The relationships among the units of volume, capacity, and mass in the metric system is illustrated in Figure 84.

1 cm³ (1 mL) of water   1 g

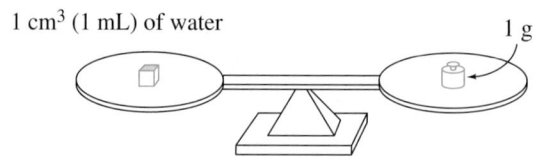

1 dm³ (1 L) of water

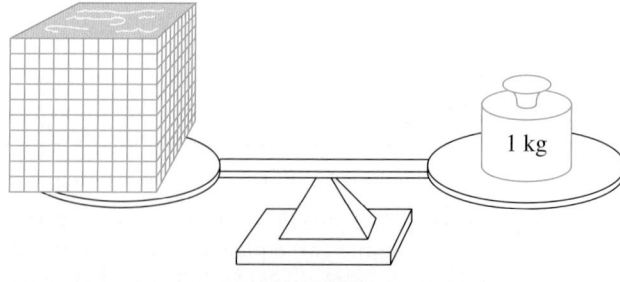

Figure 84

| **Example 35** | A waterbed measures 180 cm × 210 cm × 20 cm.

a. Approximately how many liters of water can it hold?
b. What is its mass in kilograms when it is full of water?

Solution

a. The volume of the waterbed (which is close to a rectangular prism) is approximated by multiplying the length ℓ times the width w times the height h.

$$V = \ell w h$$
$$= 180 \text{ cm} \cdot 210 \text{ cm} \cdot 20 \text{ cm}$$
$$= 756{,}000 \text{ cm}^3 = 756{,}000 \text{ mL}$$

Because 1 mL = 0.001 L, the volume is 756 L.

b. Because 1 L of water has a mass of 1 kg, 756 L of water has a mass of 756 kg, which is 0.756 t.

To see one advantage of the metric system, suppose the bed in Example 35 is 6 ft × 7 ft × 9 in. Try to approximate the volume in gallons and the weight of the water in pounds.

Temperature

For normal temperature measurements in the metric system, the base unit is the **degree Celsius**, named for Anders Celsius, a Swedish scientist. The Celsius scale has 100 equal divisions between 0 degrees Celsius (0°C), the freezing point of water, and 100 degrees Celsius (100°C), the boiling point of water, as seen in Figure 85. The **kelvin (K)** temperature scale is an extension of the degree Celsius scale down to *absolute zero*, a hypothetical temperature characterized by a complete absence of heat energy. The freezing point of water on this scale is 273.15 kelvin. In the English system, the Fahrenheit scale has 180 equal divisions between 32°F, the freezing point of water, and 212°F, the boiling point of water.

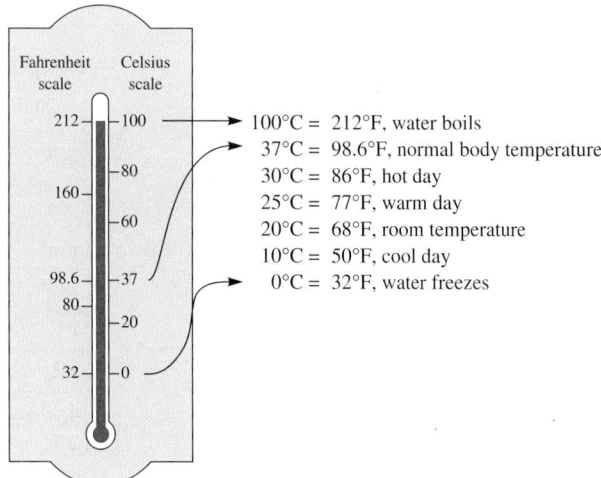

Figure 85

Figure 85 gives other temperature comparisons of the two scales and further illustrates the relationship between them. Because the Celsius scale has 100 divisions between the freezing point and the boiling point of water, whereas the Fahrenheit scale has 180 divisions, the relationship between the scales is 100 to 180, or 5 to 9. For every 5 degrees on the Celsius scale, there are 9 degrees on the Fahrenheit scale, and for each degree on the Fahrenheit scale, there is $\frac{5}{9}$ degree on the Celsius scale. Because the ratio between the number of degrees above freezing on the

Celsius scale and the number of degrees above freezing on the Fahrenheit scale remains the same and equals $\frac{5}{9}$, we may convert temperature from one system to the other.

For example, suppose we want to convert 50° on the Fahrenheit scale to the corresponding number on the Celsius scale. On the Fahrenheit scale, 50° is 50 − 32, or 18°, above freezing, but on the Celsius scale, it is $\frac{5}{9} \cdot 18 = 10°$ above freezing. Because the freezing temperature on the Celsius scale is 0°, 10° above freezing is 10° Celsius. Thus, 50°F = 10°C. In general, F degrees is $F - 32$ above freezing on the Fahrenheit scale, but only $\frac{5}{9}(F - 32)$ above freezing on the Celsius scale. Thus, we have the relation $C = \frac{5}{9}(F - 32)$. If we solve the equation for F, we obtain $F = \frac{9}{5}C + 32$.

▶ **NOW TRY THIS 9**

Does it ever happen that the temperature measured in Celsius degrees is the same if it is measured in Fahrenheit degrees? If so, when? Yes; when it is ⁻40°C, it is ⁻40°F.

Assessment 14-5A

1. Complete each of the following conversions.
   a. 8 m³ = ___8000___ dm³
   b. 675,000 m³ = ___0.000675___ km³
   c. 7000 mm³ = ___7___ cm³
   d. 400 in.³ = _____ yd³ $\frac{25}{2916}$, or about 0.00857
   e. 0.2 ft³ = ___345.6___ in.³
2. If a faucet is dripping at the rate of 15 drops/min and there are 20 drops/mL, how many liters of water are wasted in a 30-day month? 32.4 L
3. The Great Pyramid of Cheops has a square base of 771 ft on a side and a height of 486 ft. How many rooms 35 ft × 20 ft × 8 ft would be needed to have a volume equivalent to that of the Great Pyramid? Approximately 17,197 rooms
4. Find the volume of each of the following figures.

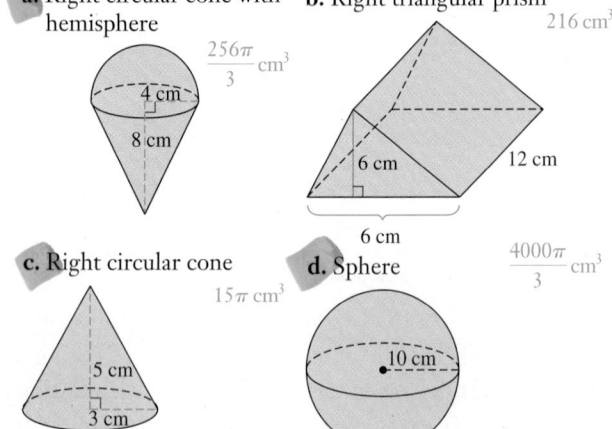

a. Right circular cone with hemisphere $\frac{256\pi}{3}$ cm³
b. Right triangular prism 216 cm³
c. Right circular cone 15π cm³
d. Sphere $\frac{4000\pi}{3}$ cm³

e. Right circular cylinder with hemispherical top $\frac{20,000\pi}{3}$ ft³

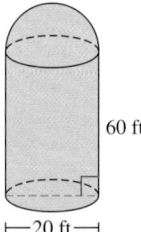

5. Complete the following table.

	a.	b.	c.	d.	e.	f.
cm³	2000	500	1500	5000	750	4800
dm³	2	0.5	1.5	5	0.750	4.8
L	2	0.5	1.5	5	0.750	4.8
mL	2000	500	1500	5000	750	4800

6. Place a decimal point in each of the following sentences to make it accurate.
   a. A paper cup holds about 2000 mL. 200.0
   b. A regular soft-drink bottle holds about 320 L. 0.320
   c. A quart milk container holds about 10 L. 1.0
   d. A teaspoonful of cough syrup is about 500 mL. 5.00
7. Two cubes have sides of lengths 4 cm and 6 cm, respectively. What is the ratio of their volumes? 8:27
8. What happens to the volume of a sphere if the radius is doubled? It is multiplied by 8.

* Answers can be found in the Answers section at the back of the book.

9. Complete the following table for right rectangular prisms with the given dimensions.

	a.	b.	c.	d.
Length	20 cm	10 cm	2 dm	15 cm
Width	10 cm	2 dm	1 dm	2 dm
Height	10 cm	3 dm	2 dm	2.5 dm
Volume (cm³)	2000	6000	4000	7500
Volume (dm³)	2	6	4	7.5
Volume (L)	2	6	4	7.5

10. Earth's diameter is approximately 4 times the Moon's and both bodies are spheres. What is the ratio of their volumes? 64:1

11. An Olympic-sized pool in the shape of a right rectangular prism is 50 m × 25 m. If it is 2 m deep throughout, how many liters of water does it hold? 2,500,000 L

12. A standard drinking straw is 25 cm long and 4 mm in diameter. How much liquid can be held in the straw at one time? π mL

13. a. What happens to the volume of an aquarium that is in the shape of a right rectangular prism if the length, width, and height are all doubled? It is multiplied by 8.
    b. What happens to the volume of the aquarium if all the measurements are tripled. It is multiplied by 27.
    c. When you multiply each linear dimension of the aquarium by a positive value *n*, what happens to the volume? It is multiplied by n^3.

14. The Great Pyramid of Cheops is a right square pyramid with height of 148 m and a square base with a perimeter of 940 m. The Transamerica Building in San Francisco has the basic shape of a right square pyramid that has a square base with a perimeter of 140 m and a height of 260 m. Which one has the greater volume and by how many times as great? *

15. A right circular cone-shaped paper water cup has a height of 8 cm and a radius of 4 cm. If the cup is filled with water to half its height, what portion of the volume of the cup is filled with water? $\frac{1}{8}$ of the cone is filled.

16. If each edge of a cube is increased by 30%, by what percent does the volume increase? *

17. A tennis ball can in the shape of a right circular cylinder holds three tennis balls snugly. If the radius of a tennis ball is 3.5 cm, what percentage of the can is not occupied by tennis balls? *

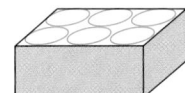
18. A box is packed with six soda cans, as in the following figure. What percentage of the volume of the interior of the box is not occupied by the cans? About 21%

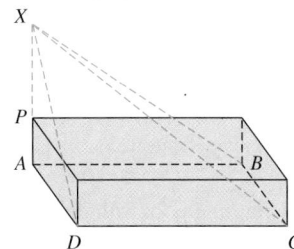

19. A right rectangular prism with base *ABCD* at the bottom is shown in the following figure.

Suppose *X* is drawn so that $AX = 3AP$, where *AP* is the height of the prism, and *X* is connected to *A*, *B*, *C*, and *D* to form a pyramid. How do the volumes of the pyramid and the prism compare? They are equal.

20. An engineer is to design a square-based pyramid whose volume is to be 100 m³.
    a. Find the dimensions (the length of a side of the square and the altitude) of one such pyramid. *
    b. How many (noncongruent) such pyramids are possible? Why? *

21. For each of the following objects, select the most appropriate metric unit of measure (gram, kilogram, or metric ton).
    a. Car Metric ton
    b. Adult Kilogram
    c. Can of frozen orange juice Gram
    d. Elephant Metric ton

22. For each of the following sentences, choose the correct unit (milligram, gram, or kilogram) to make it reasonable.
    a. A staple has a mass of about 340 _____. Milligram
    b. A professional football player has a mass of about 110 _____. Kilogram
    c. A vitamin tablet has a mass of about 1100 _____. Milligram

23. Complete each of the following conversions.
    a. 15,000 g = ____15____ kg
    b. 0.036 kg = ____36____ g
    c. 4320 mg = ____4.320____ g
    d. 0.03 t = ____30____ kg
    e. 25 oz = ____1.5625____ lb (16 oz = 1 lb)

24. A paper dollar has a mass of approximately 1 g. Is it possible to lift $1,000,000 in the following denominations?
    a. $1 bills No
    b. $10 bills Possibly
    c. $100 bills Yes
    d. $1000 bills Yes
    e. $10,000 bills Yes

25. A fish tank, which is a right rectangular prism, is 40 cm × 20 cm × 20 cm. If it is filled with water, what is the mass of the water? 16 kg

26. Convert each of the following from degrees Fahrenheit to the nearest integer degree Celsius.
    a. 10°F −12°C
    b. 30°F −1°C
    c. 212°F 100°C

27. Answer each of the following questions.
    a. The thermometer reads 20°C. Can you go snow skiing? No
    b. Your body temperature is 39°C. Are you ill? Yes
    c. The temperature reads 35°C. Should you go water skiing? Yes
    d. It's 30°C in the room. Are you comfortable, hot, or cold? Hot

28. a. Given any rectangle, describe ways to decompose the rectangle into two regions of equal area. *
    b. Given any right rectangular prism, describe how to decompose it into two solids with the same surface area. *

29. Kelvin is often used in the measure of the color temperature of light sources. For example, the sun has an effective temperature of 5778 K. What is this temperature in degree Celsius? About 5505 °C

30. If the weight of a $100 bill is 1 gram, how many $100 bills are there in 1 pound?   About 455

31. The heaviest freshwater fish caught in the United States is an alligator gar weighing 279 lb, and the heaviest freshwater fish caught in Vietnam is a 646-lb catfish. What fractional parts of an English ton are each of these fish?   0.1359 and 0.323, respectively

32. For printmaking, paper is sold by weight. For example, 500 sheets of some paper weighs 300 lb with a sheet size being 22″ by 30″. What is the weight of the paper in grams per square meter?   About 640 g/m²

33. A bathroom floor is to be tiled with 12-in. square tiles. The typical grout size is $\frac{1}{8}$ in. How many tiles are needed to cover a bathroom floor that is 8 ft by 12ft?   96 tiles

34. If a recipe calls for $\frac{1}{2}$ lb of chicken per person and you bought the chicken in kilograms, how much chicken is needed for 5 people?   About 1.1 kg

Assessment 14-5B

1. Complete each of the following conversions.
   a. 500 cm³ = _____ m³   0.0005
   b. 3 m³ = _____ cm³   3,000,000
   c. 0.002 m³ = _____ cm³   2000
   d. 25 yd³ = _____ ft³   675
   e. 1200 in.³ = _____ ft³ $\frac{25}{36}$, or approximately 0.694

2. Jeremy has a fish tank that has a 40 cm by 70 cm rectangular base. The water is 25 cm deep. When he drops rocks into the tank, the water goes up by 2 cm. What is the volume in liters of the rocks?   5.6 L

3. Maggie is planning to build a new one-story house with floor area of 2000 ft². She is thinking about putting in a 9-ft ceiling instead of an 8-ft ceiling. If she does this, how many more cubic feet of space will she have to heat and cool?   2000 ft³

4. Find the volume of each of the following.

   a. Right rectangular prism

   3 cm, 5 cm, 8 cm
   120 cm³

   b. Right square pyramid

   5 cm, 5 cm, 5 cm $\frac{125}{3}$ cm³

   c. Right circular cylinder

   12 cm, 6 cm
   432π cm³

   d.

   17 ft, 8 ft, 15 ft, 40 ft, 30 ft
   22,800 ft³

   e.

   6 ft, 8 ft, 10 ft, 20 ft, 50 ft, 60 ft
   76,200 ft³

5. Complete the following chart.   *

	a.	b.	c.	d.	e.	f.
cm³		200			202	6500
dm³	6					
L				3		
mL			1200			

6. Place a decimal point in each of the following sentences to make them accurate.
   a. A rectangular block that is 20 cm × 10 cm × 10 cm would displace 20,000 mL of water.   2000
   b. A box with a volume of 5600 cm³ would hold 5600 L.   5.6
   c. Jerry used 20,000 L of water to fill his young son's wading pool.   200
   d. An eye dropper holds about 600 mL.   6

7. a. If two cubes have sides in the ratio 2 : 5, what is the ratio of their volumes?   8 : 125
   b. If two similar cones have heights in the ratio $a:b$, what is the ratio of their volumes? $a^3 : b^3$

8. What happens to the volume of a sphere if the radius is tripled?   It is multiplied by 27.

9. Complete the following chart for right rectangular prisms with the given dimensions.   *

	a.	b.	c.	d.
Length	5 cm	8 cm	2 dm	15 cm
Width	10 cm	6 dm	1 dm	2 dm
Height	20 cm	4 dm		
Volume (cm³)				
Volume (dm³)				12
Volume (L)			10	

10. Two spherical cantaloupes of the same kind are sold at a fruit and vegetable stand. The circumference of one is 60 cm and that of the other is 50 cm. The larger melon is $1\frac{1}{2}$ times as expensive as the smaller. Which melon is the better buy and why?   *

11. A rectangular swimming pool with dimensions 10 m × 25 m is being built. The pool has a shallower end that is uniform in depth and a deep end that drops off as shown in the following figure. What is the volume of this pool in cubic meters?   600 m³

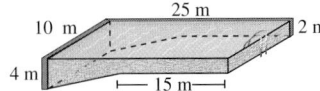

12. Determine how many liters a right circular cylindrical tank holds if it is 6 m long and 13 m in diameter.   About 796,000

13. Determine the volume of silver needed to make the napkin ring in the following figure out of solid silver. Give your answer in cubic millimeters.   1680π mm³, or approximately 5300 mm³

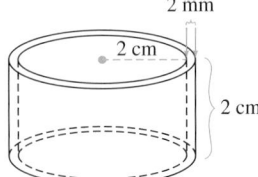

14. A theater decides to change the shape of its popcorn container from a regular box to a right regular pyramid, as shown in the following figure, and charge only half as much.

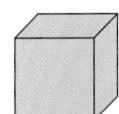 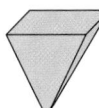

If the containers are the same height and the tops are the same size, is this a bargain for the customer? Explain.   *

15. A right circular cylindrical can is to hold approximately 1 L of water. What should be the height of the can if the radius is 12 cm?   *

16. One freezer measures 1.5 ft × 1.5 ft × 5 ft and sells for $350. Another freezer measures 2 ft × 2 ft × 4 ft and sells for $400. Which freezer is the better buy in terms of dollars per cubic foot?   The 2 ft × 2 ft × 4 ft freezer is the better buy at $25/ft³.

17. A heavy metal sphere with radius 10 cm is dropped into a right circular cylinder with base radius of 10 cm. If the original cylinder has water in it that is 20 cm high, how high is the water after the sphere is placed in it?   33.3 cm

18. A box contains a can (right circular cylinder) as in the accompanying figure. What percentage of the volume of the box does the can occupy?   Approximately 78.5%

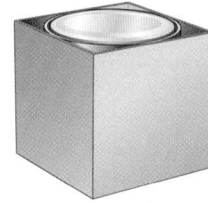

19. Half of the air is let out of a spherical balloon. If the balloon remains in the shape of a sphere, how does the radius of the smaller balloon compare to the original radius?   *

20. A square sheet of cardboard measuring *y* cm on a side is to be used to produce an open-top box when the maker cuts off a small square *x* cm × *x* cm from each corner and bends up the sides. Find the volume of the box if *y* = 200 and *x* = 20.   512,000 cm³

21. For each of the following objects, select the appropriate metric unit of measure (gram, kilogram, or metric ton).

    a. Jar of mustard   Gram
    b. Bag of peanuts   Gram
    c. Army tank   Metric ton
    d. Cat   Kilogram

22. For each of the following sentences, choose the correct unit (milligram, gram, or kilogram) to make it reasonable.

    a. A dime has a mass of 2 ___Gram___.
    b. The recipe said to add 4 ___Gram___ of salt.
    c. One strand of hair has a mass of 2 _____.   Milligram

23. Complete each of the following conversions.

    a. 8000 kg = ___8___ t
    b. 72 g = ___0.072___ kg
    c. 5.750 kg = ___5750___ g
    d. 2.6 lb = ___41.6___ oz (16 oz = 1 lb)
    e. 3.8 lb = ___60.8___ oz (16 oz = 1 lb)

24. A paper clip has a mass of about 1 g. Is it possible to lift

    a. 1000 paper clips?   1 kg, yes
    b. 100,000 paper clips?   100 kg = 220 lb; possible

25. a. Rainfall is usually measured in linear measure. Suppose St. Louis received 2 cm of rain on a given day. If a certain lot in St. Louis has measure 1 ha, how many liters of rainfall fell on the lot?   200,000 L

    b. What is the mass of the water that fell on the lot?   *

26. Convert each of the following from degrees Fahrenheit to the nearest integer degree Celsius.

    a. 0°F   ⁻18°C
    b. 100°F   38°C
    c. ⁻40°F   ⁻40°C

27. Answer each of the following questions.

    a. The thermometer reads 26°C. Will the outdoor ice rink be open?   No
    b. It is 40°C. Will you need a sweater at the outdoor concert?   No
    c. Your bath water is 16°C. Will you have a hot, warm, or chilly bath?   Chilly

28. a. Given any square, describe ways to decompose the square into two regions of equal area.   *

    b. Given any cube, describe how to decompose it into two solids with the same surface area.   *

29. Kelvin is often used in the measure of the color temperature of light sources. For example, the star Betelgeuse has an effective temperature of 3200 K. What is this temperature in degree Celsius?   2926.8°C

30. If the weight of a $1000 bill is 1 gram, how many $1000 bills are there in 1 pound?   About 455

31. The heaviest freshwater fish caught in the United States is an alligator gar weighing 279 lb, and the heaviest freshwater fish caught in Vietnam is a 646 lb catfish. How much does each weigh in kilograms?   About 127 and 293, respectively

32. For printmaking, paper is sold by weight. For example, 500 sheets of some paper weighs 140 lb with a sheet size being 22″ by 30″. What is the weight in of the paper in grams per square meter?   About 299 g/m²

33. A bathroom floor is to be tiled with 12-in. square tiles. The typical grout size is $\frac{1}{8}$ in. How many tiles are needed to cover a bathroom floor that is 6 ft by 8 ft?   95 tiles

34. If a recipe calls for 0.25 kg of chicken per person and you bought the chicken in pounds, how much chicken is needed for 5 people?   About 2.75 lb

Mathematical Connections 14-5

Reasoning

1. **a.** Which will increase the volume of a right circular cylinder more: doubling its height or doubling its radius? Explain.
   b. Is your answer the same for a right circular cone? Why?
2. Explain how you would find the volume of an irregular shape.
3. Read the following problems (i) and (ii):
   (i) A tank in the shape of a cube 5 ft 3 in. on a side is filled with water. Find the volume in cubic feet, the capacity in gallons, and the weight of the water in pounds.
   (ii) A tank in the shape of a cube 2 m on a side is filled with water. Find the volume in cubic meters, the capacity in liters, and the mass of the water in kilograms.
   Discuss which problem is easier to work and why.
4. A furniture company gives an estimate for moving based upon the size of the rooms in an apartment. Write a rationale for why this is feasible. What assumptions are being made?
5. A cylinder, a cone, and a sphere have the same radius and same height, as shown.

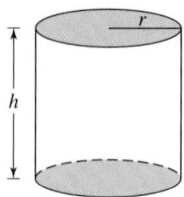 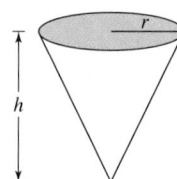 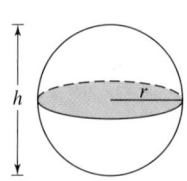

   a. Find the volume of each figure in terms of r.
   b. Use your answer to part (a) to show that the volumes are in the ratio $3:1:2$.
6. Two stacks of pennies shown are of the same height.

   a. Explain which has the greater surface area and why.
   b. Explain which has the greater volume and why.

Open-Ended

7. A right circular cylinder has a 4-in. diameter, is 6 in. high, and is completely full of water. Design a right rectangular prism that will hold almost exactly the same amount of water.
8. Circular-shaped cookies are to be packaged 48 to a box. Each cookie is approximately 1 cm thick and has a diameter of 6 cm. Design a box that will hold this volume of cookies and has the least amount of surface area.
9. Design a cylinder that will hold 1 L of juice. Give the dimensions of your cylinder and tell why you designed the shape as you did.
10. Explore Internet sources to determine if it is possible for two objects to have the same surface area, volume, and different weights.

Cooperative Learning

11. **a.** Find many different types of cans that are in the shape of a cylinder. Measure the height and diameter of each can.
    b. Compute the surface area and volume for each can.
    c. Based on the information collected, make a recommendation for designing an "ideal" can.
12. Bergmann's rule states that typically species of larger size are found in colder environments, and species of smaller size are found in warmer regions giving those in colder climates lower surface area to volume ratio. As a group, research Bergmann's rule and discuss what you found to report to the class.

Connecting Mathematics to the Classroom

13. A student asks whether the volume of a prism can ever have the same numerical value as its surface area. How do you answer?
14. A student says the volume of the cube shown below is 5 cm.[3] What is wrong with this interpretation?

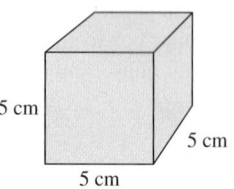

15. A student claims that it does not make any difference if his temperature is 2 degrees above normal Fahrenheit or 2 degrees above normal Celsius because in either case he is only 2 degrees above normal. How do you respond?
16. Andrea claims that if she doubles the length and width of the base of a rectangular prism and triples the height, she has increased the volume by a factor $2 \cdot 2 \cdot 3 = 12$. What would you tell her?
17. Jamie had $6.00 to spend on popcorn at a movie theater. She had to choose between buying two small right cylindrical containers at $3.00 each or one large right cylindrical container for $6.00. She noticed that the containers were about the same height and that the diameter of the large container looked about twice as long as the diameter of the small container. She bought two small containers and then asked in math class the next day if she made the right choice to get the most popcorn for her money. How would you help her?
18. A student asks if all cubes are similar and all spheres are similar. How do you respond?

Review Problems

19. Find the perimeter and the area of the following figures. Leave answers as exact values.

a.

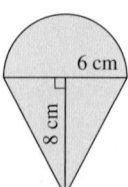

b. The shaded portion only

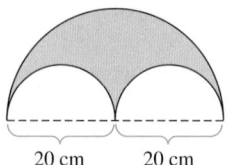

20. Complete the following conversions.
  a. $350 \text{ mm} = \underline{\hspace{1.5cm}} \text{ cm}$
  b. $1600 \text{ cm}^2 = \underline{\hspace{1.5cm}} \text{ m}^2$
  c. $0.4 \text{ m}^2 = \underline{\hspace{1.5cm}} \text{ mm}^2$
  d. $5.2 \text{ cm}^2 = \underline{\hspace{1.5cm}} \text{ m}^2$
21. Determine whether each of the following is a right triangle.

  a.

  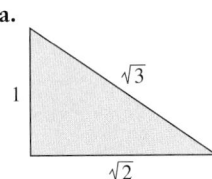

  b.

  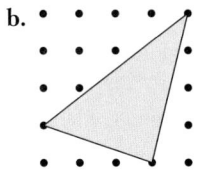

22. Find the surface area of each of the following. Leave answers as exact values.

  a. Right circular cone **b.** Right triangular prism

  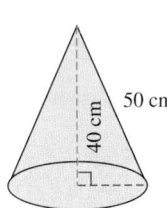
  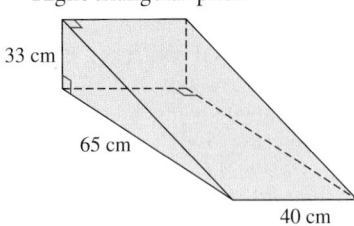

23. What is the length of a non-face diagonal of a 6-in. cube?
24. Why does a diagonal of the type described in exercise 23 have to be longer than the diagonal of a face of the cube?

National Assessments

National Assessment of Educational Progress (NAEP) Questions

How many 200-milliliter servings can be poured from a pitcher that contains 2 liters of juice?
A. 20
B. 15
C. 10
D. 5
E. 1
NAEP, Grade 8, 2007

Which unit would be best to measure the amount of liquid in a spoonful of lemon juice?
A. Milliliters
B. Liters
C. Millimeters
D. Meters
NAEP, Grade 4, 2011

Which of the following is a unit of volume?
A. Acre
B. Gram
C. Liter
D. Meter
E. Ton
NAEP, Grade 8, 2011

Hint for Solving the Preliminary Problem

Consider the number of square yards that 1.5 acres would cover. Then find the volume of a rectangular prism with that base and with a height of 16 in. Finally, determine how many truck loads need to be hauled away.

Chapter 14 Summary

KEY CONCEPTS	DEFINITIONS, DESCRIPTIONS, AND THEOREMS
Section 14-1	
Linear measurement systems (p. 813)	*English system*—commonly used units of length are inch (in.), foot (ft), yard (yd), and mile (mi). *Metric system*—commonly used units of length are meter (m), kilometer (km), centimeter (cm), and millimeter (mm).
Unit ratio (p. 814)	Any ratio that is equivalent to 1. For example, $\frac{12 \text{ in.}}{1 \text{ ft}}$ is a unit ratio.
Dimensional analysis (p. 814)	A process for converting units of measure using unit ratios treated as fractions.
Distance properties (p. 818)	• The distance between any two points A and B is greater than or equal to 0, written $AB \geq 0$. • The distance between any two points A and B is the same as the distance between B and A, written $AB = BA$. • For any three points A, B, and C, the distance between A and B plus the distance between B and C is greater than or equal to the distance between A and C, written $AB + BC \geq AC$.
Triangle Inequality (p. 818)	*Theorem:* The sum of the lengths of any two sides of a triangle is greater than the length of the third side.
Perimeter (p. 818)	The distance around a two-dimensional figure. The *circumference C* of a circle with radius r and diameter d is the perimeter of the circle and is given by $C = \pi d = 2\pi r$.
Arc length (p. 821)	The length of an arc whose central angle measures $\theta°$ is $\frac{\pi \theta r}{180}$.
Linear measure of similar figures (p. 822)	*Theorem:* If the scale factor of two similar figures is k, then the ratio of any corresponding linear measurements of the two similar figures, such as length, width, height, perimeter, diagonal, diameter, and slant height is k.
Section 14-2	
Area (p. 827)	The number of nonoverlapping square units covering a region. *Area* is measured in square units.
Finding area (p. 827)	The area of a region can be found using a *geoboard* or *dot paper*: • *Addition method* • *Rectangle method*
Units of measure for area (p. 829)	*English units*—commonly used units are square inch (in.²), square foot (ft²), and square mile (mi²). *Metric units*—commonly used units are square meter (m²), square kilometer (km²), square centimeter (cm²), and square millimeter (mm²). *English units of land measure*—acre and square mile (mi²). *Metric units of land measure*—are (a), hectare, (ha), and square kilometer (km²).

Section 14-2

Area formulas (p. 831)

Rectangle
$A = lw$, where l is the length and w is the width.

Square
$A = s^2$, where s is the length of a side.

Parallelogram
$A = bh$, where b is the length of the base and h is the height to that base.

Triangle
$A = \frac{1}{2}bh$, where b is the length of the base and h is the height to that base.

Kite
$A = \frac{1}{2}d_1d_2$, where d_1 and d_2 are the lengths of the diagonals.

Regular polygon
$A = \frac{1}{2}ap$, where a is the apothem and p is the perimeter.

Circle
$A = \pi r^2$, where r is the radius.

Sector
$A = \frac{\theta}{360}\pi r^2$, where θ is the degree measure of the central angle forming the sector and r is the radius of the circle containing the sector.

Area measure for similar figures (p. 839)

Theorem: For similar triangles with scale factor k, the ratio of their areas is k^2.

Theorem: For similar polygons with scale factor k, the ratio of their areas is k^2.

Section 14-3

Pythagorean Theorem (p. 848)

If a right triangle has legs of lengths a and b and hypotenuse of length c, then $c^2 = a^2 + b^2$; that is, the square of the length of the hypotenuse is equal to the sum of the squares of the lengths of the legs.

Converse of the Pythagorean Theorem: If $\triangle ABC$ has sides of lengths a, b, and c such that $a^2 + b^2 = c^2$, then $\triangle ABC$ is a right triangle with the right angle opposite the side of length c.

Special triangles (p. 851)

Theorem: In a 30°-60°-90° triangle, the length of the hypotenuse is 2 times the length of the leg opposite the 30° angle, and the length of the leg opposite the 60° angle is $\sqrt{3}$ times the length of the shorter leg.

Theorem: In a 45°-45°-90° triangle, the length of the hypotenuse is $\sqrt{2}$ times the length of a leg.

Distance formula (p. 853)

Theorem: The distance between the point $A(x_1, y_1)$ and $B(x_2, y_2)$ is $AB = \sqrt{(x_2 - x_1)^2 + (y_2 - y_1)^2}$.

Equation of a circle (p. 856)

Circle with center at the origin.

Theorem: An equation of the circle with center at the origin and radius r is $x^2 + y^2 = r^2$.

Circle with center at (h, k).

Theorem: An equation of the circle with center (h, k) and radius r is $(x - h)^2 + (y - k)^2 = r^2$.

Section 14-4

Lateral surface area (LSA) (p. 864)	The sum of the areas of the lateral faces.
Surface area (SA) (p. 864)	The sum of the lateral surface area and the area of the base(s). *Cube* $SA = 6e^2$, where e is the length of an edge. *Right Prism* $SA = 2B + ph$, where B is the area of the base, p is the perimeter of the base, and h is the height of the prism. *Right circular cylinder* $SA = 2\pi r^2 + 2\pi rh$, where r is the radius of the base and h is the height of the cylinder. *Right regular pyramid* $SA = B + \frac{1}{2}pl$, where B is the area of the base, p is the perimeter of the base, and l is the slant height. *Right circular cone* $SA = \pi r^2 + \pi rl$, where r is the radius of the base and l is the slant height. *Sphere* $SA = 4\pi r^2$, where r is the radius of the sphere.

Section 14-5

Volume (p. 874)	The amount of space a three-dimensional figure contains. *Volume* is measured in cubic units.
Units of measure for volume (p. 874)	*English units*—commonly used units are cubic inch (in.³), cubic foot (ft³), and cubic yard (yd³). *Metric units*—commonly used units are cubic meter (m³), cubic decimeter (dm³), and cubic centimeter (cm³). *Metric units for capacity*—typical units are liter (L), kiloliter, (kL), centiliter (cL), and milliliter (mL). *English units for capacity*—gallon (gal.), quart (qt.), pint (pt.), and cup (c).
Volume formulas (p. 877)	*Prism* $V = lwh$ for rectangular base or $V = Bh$, where l is the length, w is the width, and h is the height; B is the area of the base. *Cube* $V = e^3$, where e is the length of an edge. *Circular cylinder* $V = \pi r^2 h$, where r is the radius of the base and h is the height of the cylinder. *Pyramid* $V = \frac{1}{3}Bh$, where B is the area of the base and h is the height of the pyramid. *Circular cone* $V = \frac{1}{3}\pi r^2 h$, where r is the radius of the base and h is the height of the cone. *Sphere* $V = \frac{4}{3}\pi r^3$, where r is the radius of the sphere.
Cavalieri's Principle (p. 878)	Two solids with a base in the same plane have equal volumes if every plane parallel to the bases intersects the solids in cross sections of equal area.

Section 14-5

Similarity Principle of Measurement (p. 884)	*Theorem:* If the scale factor of two similar figures is k, then the ratio of their areas or surface areas is k^2 and the ratio of their volumes is k^3.
Mass (p. 885)	A quantity of matter.
Units of measure for mass (p. 886)	The base unit in the metric system for mass is the gram (g), with the metric ton (t), kilogram (kg), and milligram (mg) as commonly used measures. 1 L of water has a mass of 1 kg and 1 mL of water has a mass of 1 g.
Units of measure for temperature (p. 887)	*English unit*—the common unit is the degree Fahrenheit *Metric unit*—the common unit is the degree Celsius (with kelvin as an alternative scientific unit)
Basic referents for temperature (p. 887)	*English system* • 212°F—the boiling point of water • 32°F—the freezing point of water • 98.6°F—normal body temperature • 68°F—comfortable room temperature *Metric system* • 100°C—the boiling point of water • 0°C—the freezing point of water • 37°C—normal body temperature • 20°C—comfortable room temperature *Conversion formulas* • $C = \dfrac{5}{9}(F - 32)$ • $F = \dfrac{9}{5}C + 32$

Chapter 14 Review

1. Complete the following conversions.
   a. 50 ft = _____ yd   *
   b. 947 yd = _____ mi   *
   c. 0.75 mi = _____ ft   3960
   d. 349 in. = _____ yd $9\frac{25}{36}$, or approximately 9.694
   e. 5 km = _____ m   5000
   f. 165 cm = _____ m   1.65
   g. 52 cm = _____ mm   520
   h. 125 m = _____ km   0.125

2. Given three segments of length $p, q,$ and r where $p > q$, determine if it is possible to construct a triangle with sides of length $p, q,$ and r in each of the following cases. Justify your answers.
   a. $p - q > r$ Not possible; $p > q + r$
   b. $p - q = r$ Not possible; $p = q + r$

3. The diagonal of a rectangle has measure 1.3 m, and a side of the rectangle has measure 120 cm. Find the perimeter of the rectangle.   340 cm

4. The circumference of a circle is 3 m. What is its radius?   *
5. Sarah reports the radius of a circle as 6 cm and its circumference as 36π cm. Explain whether she is correct.   *
6. Determine the area of the shaded region on each of the following geoboards if the unit of measure is 1 cm².
   a.
   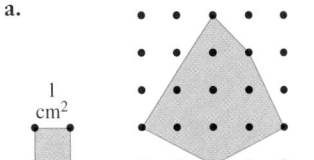
   a. 8.5 cm²
   b. 6.5 cm²
   c. 7 cm²
   b.
   c.
   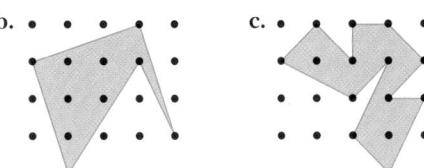

7. Explain how the formula for the area of a trapezoid can be found by using the following figures. *

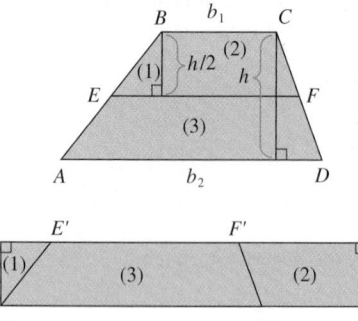

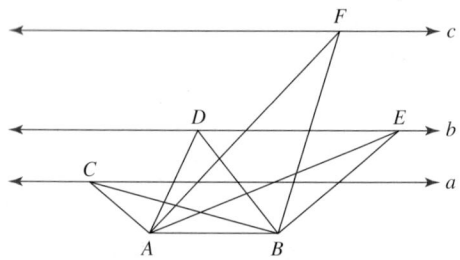

8. Lines *a*, *b*, and *c* are parallel to the line containing side $\overline{AB}$ of the triangles shown.

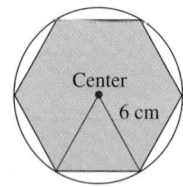

List the triangles in order of size of their areas from least to greatest. Explain why your order is correct. *

9. Use the figure shown to find each of the following areas.
   a. The area of the regular hexagon $54\sqrt{3}$ cm²
   b. The area of the circle 36π cm²

10. Find the area of each shaded region in the following figures.
   a. 12π cm²

   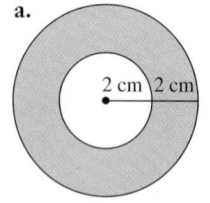

   b. $(12 + 4.5\pi)$ cm²

   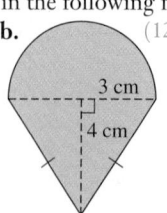

   c. Parallelogram 24 cm²

   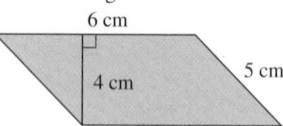

   d. Sector 4π cm²

   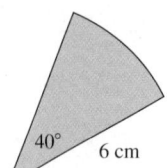

e. 64.5 cm² **f.** 178.5 m²

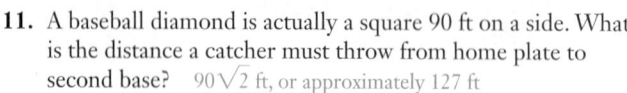

11. A baseball diamond is actually a square 90 ft on a side. What is the distance a catcher must throw from home plate to second base? $90\sqrt{2}$ ft, or approximately 127 ft

12. Find the length of segment *AG* in the spiral shown. 3

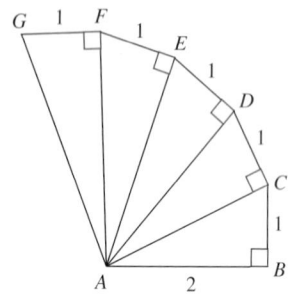

13. Determine whether each group of measures represent sides of a right triangle.
   a. 5 cm, 12 cm, 13 cm Yes
   b. 40 cm, 60 cm, 104 cm No

14. Find the surface area of the following box (include the top and bottom). 5400 cm²

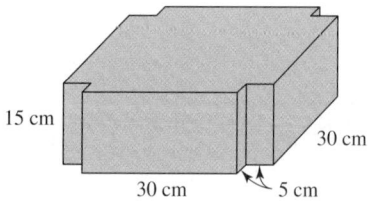

15. Find the surface area and volume of each of the following figures.
   a. Right square pyramid * **b.** Right circular cone *

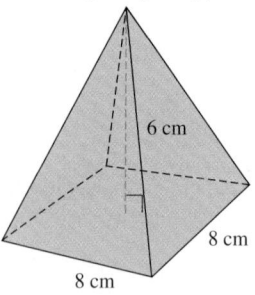

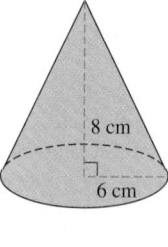

c. Sphere

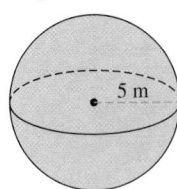

5 m

d. Right circular cylinder   *

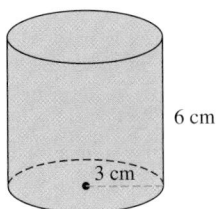

6 cm

3 cm

e. Right rectangular prism   *

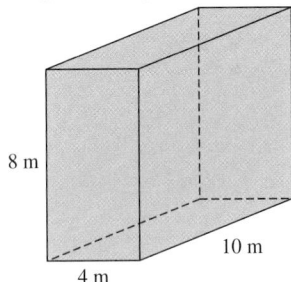

8 m

10 m

4 m

16. Find the lateral surface area of the following right circular cone. $65\pi\ \mathrm{m}^2$

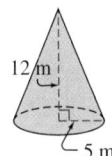

12 m

5 m

17. Doug's Dog Food Company wants to impress the public with the magnitude of the company's growth. Sales of Doug's Dog Food doubled from 2012 to 2014, so the company is displaying the following graph, which shows the radius of the base and the height of the 2014 can to be double those of the 2012 can. What does the graph really show with respect to the company's growth? Explain your answer.   *

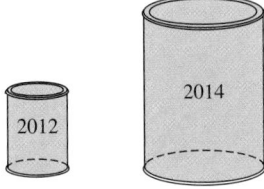

2014

2012

18. Find the area of the kite shown in the following figure. $252\ \mathrm{cm}^2$

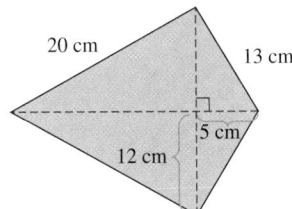

20 cm

13 cm

5 cm

12 cm

19. The diagonal of a rectangle has measure 1.3 m, and a side of the rectangle has measure 120 cm. Find the area of the rectangle. $6000\ \mathrm{cm}^2$

20. Find the area of a triangle that has side lengths of 3 m, 3 m, and 2 m. $2\sqrt{2}\ \mathrm{m}^2$

21. A poster is to contain 0.25 m² of printed matter, with margins of 12 cm at top and bottom and 6 cm at each side. Find the width of the poster if its height is 74 cm.   62 cm

22. A right circular cylinder of height 10 cm and a right circular cone share a circular base and have the same volume. What is the height of the cone?   30 cm

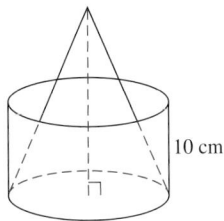

10 cm

23. On a 5 × 5 geoboard paper,
   a. draw a polygon whose perimeter is greater than 16.   *
   b. draw a polygon with least perimeter. What is the perimeter?   *
   c. draw a polygon with greatest area.*

24. What is the length of the diagonal of an $8\frac{1}{2} \times 11$ in. piece of paper?   Approximately 13.9 in.

25. a. Find an equation of the circle with center at $(3, {}^-4)$ and a radius of 5. $(x - 3)^2 + (y + 4)^2 = 25$
   b. Given that the equation of a circle is $36 = (x - 5)^2 + (y + 3)^2$, find the radius and the center. $6, (5, {}^-3)$

26. Complete each of the following with the appropriate metric unit.
   a. A very heavy object has mass that is measured in ___Metric tons___.
   b. A cube whose length, width, and height are each 1 cm has a volume of ___1 cm³___.
   c. If the cube in (b) is filled with water, the mass of the water is ___1 g___.
   d. 1 L = ___1___ dm³
   e. If a car uses 1 L of gas to go 12 km, the amount of gas needed to go 300 km is ___25___ L.
   f. 20 ha = ___2000___ a
   g. 51.8 L = ___51,800___ cm³
   h. 10 km² = ___10,000,000___ m²
   i. 50 L = ___50,000___ mL
   j. 5830 mL = ___5.83___ L
   k. 25 m³ = ___25,000___ dm³
   l. 75 dm³ = ___75,000___ mL
   m. 52,813 g = ___52.813___ kg
   n. 4800 kg ___4.8___ t

27. a. A tank that is a right rectangular prism is 1 m × 2 m × 3 m. If the tank is filled with water, what is the mass of the water in kilograms?   6000 kg
   b. Suppose the tank in (a) is exactly half full of water and then a heavy metal sphere of radius 30 cm is put into the tank. How high is the water now if the height of the tank is 3 m?   Approximately 1.6 m

28. For each of the following sentences, fill in the correct unit to make it reasonable.
   a. Anna filled the gas tank with 80 _____ L _____.
   b. A man has a mass of about 82 _____ kg _____.
   c. The textbook has a mass of 978 _____ g _____.
   d. A nickel has a mass of 5 _____ g _____.
   e. A typical adult cat has a mass of about 4 _____ kg _____.
   f. A compact car has a mass of about 1.5 _____ t _____.
   g. The amount of coffee in the cup is 180 _____ mL _____.

29. Decide if each of the following situations is likely or unlikely.
   a. Carrie's bath water has a temperature of 15°C.   Unlikely
   b. Anne found 26°C too warm and so lowered the thermostat to 21°C.   Likely
   c. Jim is drinking water that has a temperature of ⁻5°C.   Unlikely
   d. The water in the teakettle has a temperature of 120°C.   Unlikely
   e. The outside temperature dropped to 5°C, and ice appeared on the lake.   Unlikely

30. Complete each of the following conversions.
   a. 2 dm^3 of water has a mass of _____ 2000 _____ g.
   b. 1 L of water has a mass of _____ 1000 _____ g.
   c. 3 cm^3 of water has a mass of _____ 3 _____ g.
   d. 4.2 mL of water has a mass of _____ 0.0042 _____ kg.
   e. 0.2 L of water has a volume of _____ 0.0002 _____ m^3

31. Two similar spheres have radii 4 cm and 6 cm, respectively. If they can be filled with water, what is the ratio of the capacities of the two spheres?   8:27

32. If the volumes of two silos that are similar right circular cylinders are in the ratio 2:3, in what ratio do you expect the radii of the two silos to be? $\sqrt[3]{2} : \sqrt[3]{3}$

Credits

Text Credits

Chapter 1

2 Excerpts from Standards for Mathematical Practice. Copyright by Common Core State Standards Initiative. Used by permission of Common Core State Standards Initiative. **3** Excerpt from Standards for Mathematical Practice. Copyright by Common Core State Standards Initiative. Used by permission of Common Core State Standards Initiative. **5** Excerpt from CCSS.Math.Practice.MP1 and MP3, Standards for Mathematical Practice. Copyright by Common Core State Standards Initiative. Used by permission of Common Core State Standards Initiative. **7** Excerpt from CCSS.Math.Practice.MP1 and MP.4, Standards for Mathematical Practice. Copyright by Common Core State Standards Initiative. Used by permission of Common Core State Standards Initiative. Randall Inners Charles, enVisionMATH, Grade 4 © 2012. Printed and Electronically reproduced by permission of Pearson Education, Inc., Upper Saddle River, New Jersey. **11** Randall Inners Charles, MATHEMATICS Common Core, Course 1, © 2013. Printed and Electronically reproduced by permission of Pearson Education, Inc., Upper Saddle River, New Jersey. Randall Inners Charles, enVisionMATH, Grade 4 © 2012. Printed and Electronically reproduced by permission of Pearson Education, Inc., Upper Saddle River, New Jersey. **15** MATHEMATICS Common Core, Course 1, © 2013. Printed and Electronically reproduced by permission of Pearson Education, Inc., Upper Saddle River, New Jersey. **17** Excerpt from Standards for Mathematical Practice. Copyright by Common Core State Standards Initiative. Used by permission of Common Core State Standards Initiative.

Chapter 2

40 Excerpt from CCSS.Math.Practice.MP3: Construct Viable Arguments and Critique the Reasoning of Others, Standards for Mathematical Practice. Copyright by Common Core State Standards Initiative. Used by permission of Common Core State Standards Initiative. **53** Excerpt from CCSS.Math.Practice.MP2, Standards for Mathematical Practice. Copyright by Common Core State Standards Initiative. Used by permission of Common Core State Standards Initiative. **67** Excerpt from Grade 1, Measurement and Data, Standards for Mathematical Practice. Copyright by Common Core State Standards Initiative. Used by permission of Common Core State Standards Initiative. **72** Randall Inners Charles, enVisionMATH, Grade 4 © 2012. Printed and Electronically reproduced by permission of Pearson Education, Inc., Upper Saddle River, New Jersey.

Chapter 3

85 Excerpt from Toward Greater Focus and Coherence, Common Core Standards for Mathematics. Copyright by Common Core State Standards Initiative. Used by permission of Common Core State Standards Initiative. **100** Excerpt from Grade 1, Operations and Algebraic Thinking, Standards for Mathematical Practice. Copyright by Common Core State Standards Initiative. Used by permission of Common Core State Standards Initiative. **102** Excerpt from Grade K, Counting and Cardinality, Standards for Mathematical Practice. Copyright by Common Core State Standards Initiative. Used by permission of Common Core State Standards Initiative. **103** Excerpt from Grade 1, Standards for Mathematical Practice. Copyright by Common Core State Standards Initiative. Used by permission of Common Core State Standards Initiative. **105** enVisionMATH Common Core, Grade 3, ©2012. Printed and Electronically reproduced by permission of Pearson Education, Inc., Upper Saddle River, New Jersey. **108** enVisionMATH Common Core, Grade 3, ©2012. Printed and Electronically reproduced by permission of Pearson Education, Inc., Upper Saddle River, New Jersey. **114** Excerpts from Grade 3, Standards for Mathematical Practice, Common Core State Standards for Mathematics. Copyright by Common Core State Standards Initiative. Used by permission of Common Core State Standards Initiative. **115** enVisionMATH Common Core, Grade 3, ©2012. Printed and Electronically reproduced by permission of Pearson Education, Inc., Upper Saddle River, New Jersey. **118** Excerpt from Grade 3, Operations and Algebraic Thinking, Common Core State Standards for Mathematics. Copyright by Common Core State Standards Initiative. Used by permission of Common Core State Standards Initiative. **121** Excerpt from Grade 3, Operations and Algebraic Thinking, Common Core State Standards for Mathematics. Copyright by Common Core State Standards Initiative. Used by permission of Common Core State Standards Initiative. **125** enVisionMATH Common Core, Grade 4, ©2012. Printed and Electronically reproduced by permission of Pearson Education, Inc., Upper Saddle River, New Jersey. **130** Excerpts from Grade 2, Number and Operations in Base Ten, Common Core State Standards for Mathematics. Copyright by Common Core State Standards Initiative. Used by permission of Common Core State Standards Initiative. **131** Excerpt from Grade 4, Number and Operations in Base Ten, Common Core State Standards for Mathematics. Copyright by Common Core State Standards Initiative. Used by permission of Common Core State Standards Initiative. **132** Randall Inners Charles, SCOTT FORESMAN-ADDISON WESLEY MATHEMATICS, Vol 3, © 2008. Printed and Electronically reproduced by permission of Pearson Education, Inc., Upper Saddle River, New Jersey. **137** enVisionMATH Common Core, Grade 3, © 2012. Printed and Electronically reproduced by permission of Pearson Education, Inc., Upper Saddle River, New Jersey. **143** Randall Inners Charles, SCOTT FORESMAN-ADDISON WESLEY MATHEMATICS, Vol 3, © 2008. Printed and Electronically reproduced by permission of Pearson Education, Inc., Upper Saddle River, New Jersey. **150** Excerpt from Grade 4, Standards for Mathematical Practice, Common Core State Standards for Mathematics. Copyright by Common Core State Standards Initiative. Used by permission of Common Core State Standards Initiative.

Chapter 4

175 Excerpt from Grade 2, Operations & Algebraic Thinking, Standards for Mathematical Practice. Copyright by Common Core State Standards Initiative. Used by permission of Common Core State Standards Initiative. **184** Randall Inners Charles, enVisionMATH, Grade 6 Common Core, © 2012. Printed and Electronically reproduced by permission of Pearson Education, Inc., Upper Saddle River, New Jersey. **189** Excerpt from Grade 4, Operations and Algebraic Thinking, Standards for Mathematical Practice. Used by permission of Common Core State Standards Initiative. **192** Randall Inners Charles, enVisionMATH, Grade 6 Common Core, 2012. Printed and Electronically reproduced by permission of Pearson Education, Inc., Upper Saddle River, New Jersey. **196** enVisionMATH, Grade 6 Common Core, 2012. Printed and Electronically reproduced by permission of Pearson Education, Inc., Upper Saddle River, New Jersey. **202** Excerpt from Grade 6, The Number System, Standards for Mathematical Practice. Copyright by Common Core State Standards Initiative. Used by permission of Common Core State Standards Initiative. **205** MATHEMATICS Common Core, Course 1, © 2013. Printed and Electronically reproduced by permission of Pearson Education, Inc., Upper Saddle River, New Jersey.

Chapter 5

219 Excerpt from Grade 6, The Number System, Standards for Mathematical Practice. Copyright by Common Core State Standards Initiative. Used by permission of Common Core State Standards Initiative. **220** Excerpt from Grade 6, The Number System, Standards for Mathematical Practice. Copyright by Common Core State Standards Initiative. Used by permission of Common Core State Standards Initiative. **222** MATHEMATICS Common Core, Course 2, © 2013. Printed and Electronically reproduced by permission of Pearson Education, Inc., Upper Saddle River, New Jersey. **225** Excerpt from Grade 6, The Number System, Standards for Mathematical Practice. Copyright by Common Core State Standards Initiative. Used by permission of Common Core State Standards Initiative. **226** Excerpt from Grade 7, The Number System, Standards for Mathematical Practice. Copyright by Common Core State Standards Initiative. Used by permission of Common Core State Standards Initiative. **227** MATHEMATICS Common Core, Course 2, © 2013. Printed and Electronically reproduced by permission of Pearson Education, Inc., Upper Saddle River, New Jersey. **232** MATHEMATICS Common Core, Course 2, © 2013. Printed and Electronically reproduced by permission of Pearson Education, Inc., Upper Saddle River, New Jersey. **240** Excerpt from Grade 7, The Number System, Standards for Mathematical Practice. Copyright by Common Core State Standards Initiative. Used by permission of Common Core State Standards Initiative. **241** MATHEMATICS Common Core, Course 2, © 2013. Printed and Electronically reproduced by permission of Pearson Education, Inc., Upper Saddle River, New Jersey. **244** Excerpts from Standards for Mathematical Practice. Copyright by Common Core State Standards Initiative. Used by permission of Common Core State Standards Initiative.

Chapter 6

258 Excerpt from Grade 3, Standards for Mathematical Practice. Copyright by Common Core State Standards Initiative. Used by permission of Common Core State Standards Initiative. Excerpt from Grade 3, Number and Operations—Fractions, Standards for Mathematical Practice. Copyright by Common Core State Standards Initiative. Used by permission of Common Core State Standards Initiative. **260** Excerpts from Grade 3, Number and Operations—Fractions, Standards for Mathematical Practice. Copyright by Common Core State Standards Initiative. Used by permission of Common Core State Standards Initiative. **261** Excerpt from Grade 4, Number and Operations—Fractions, Standards for Mathematical Practice. Copyright by Common Core State Standards Initiative. Used by permission of Common Core State Standards Initiative. **262** Randall Inners Charles, enVisionMATH, Grade 6 Common Core, © 2012. Printed and Electronically reproduced by permission of Pearson Education, Inc., Upper Saddle River, New Jersey. **266** Excerpt from Grade 4, Number and Operations—Fractions, Standards for Mathematical Practice. Copyright by Common Core State Standards Initiative. Used by permission of Common Core State Standards Initiative. **275** Excerpt from Grade 5, Number and Operations—Fractions, Standards for Mathematical Practice. Copyright by Common Core State Standards Initiative. Used by permission of Common Core State Standards Initiative. **279** enVisionMATH, Grade 6 Common Core, © 2012. Printed and Electronically reproduced by permission of Pearson Education, Inc., Upper Saddle River, New Jersey. **283** Excerpt from Grade 5, Number and Operations—Fractions, Standards for Mathematical Practice. Copyright by Common Core State Standards Initiative. Used by permission of Common Core State Standards Initiative. **284** Randall Inners Charles, enVisionMATH, Grade 6 Common Core, © 2012. Printed and Electronically reproduced by permission of Pearson Education, Inc., Upper Saddle River, New Jersey. **292** Randall Inners Charles, enVisionMATH, Grade 6 Common Core, © 2013. Printed and Electronically reproduced by permission of Pearson Education, Inc., Upper Saddle River, New Jersey. **296** Excerpt from Grade 6, The Number System, Standards for

Mathematical Practice. Copyright by Common Core State Standards Initiative. Used by permission of Common Core State Standards Initiative. **298** MATHEMATICS Common Core, Course 1, © 2013. Printed and Electronically reproduced by permission of Pearson Education, Inc., Upper Saddle River, New Jersey. **311** Excerpt from Grade 7, Ratios and Proportional Relationships, Standards for Mathematical Practice. Copyright by Common Core State Standards Initiative. Used by permission of Common Core State Standards Initiative. **317** Excerpt from Grade 6, Ratios and Proportional Relationships, Standards for Mathematical Practice. Copyright by Common Core State Standards Initiative. Used by permission of Common Core State Standards Initiative. **322** Excerpt from Gulliver's Travels by Jonathan Swift. Published by Plain Label Books, © 2011.

Chapter 7

330 Excerpt from Grade 4, Number and Operations—Fractions, Standards for Mathematical Practice. Copyright by Common Core State Standards Initiative. Used by permission of Common Core State Standards Initiative. Excerpt from Grade 5, Number and Operations in Base Ten, Standards for Mathematical Practice. Copyright by Common Core State Standards Initiative. Used by permission of Common Core State Standards Initiative. **334** enVisionMATH Common Core, Grade 3, © 2012. Printed and Electronically reproduced by permission of Pearson Education, Inc., Upper Saddle River, New Jersey. **337** Excerpt from Grade 4, Number and Operations—Fractions, Standards for Mathematical Practice. Copyright by Common Core State Standards Initiative. Used by permission of Common Core State Standards Initiative. **340** Excerpt from Grade 5, Number and Operations in Base Ten, Standards for Mathematical Practice. Copyright by Common Core State Standards Initiative. Used by permission of Common Core State Standards Initiative. **343** enVisionMATH, Grade 5 © 2012. Printed and Electronically reproduced by permission of Pearson Education, Inc., Upper Saddle River, New Jersey. **347** enVisionMATH, Grade 5 © 2012. Printed and Electronically reproduced by permission of Pearson Education, Inc., Upper Saddle River, New Jersey. **348** Excerpt from Grade 5, Standards for Mathematical Practice. Copyright by Common Core State Standards Initiative. Used by permission of Common Core State Standards Initiative. **357** Excerpt from Grade 7, The Number System. Copyright by Common Core State Standards Initiative. Used by permission of Common Core State Standards Initiative. **361** MATHEMATICS Common Core, Course 3, © 2013. Printed and Electronically reproduced by permission of Pearson Education, Inc., Upper Saddle River, New Jersey. **366** Excerpt from Grade 7, Standards for Mathematical Practice. Copyright by Common Core State Standards Initiative. Used by permission of Common Core State Standards Initiative. **368** Excerpt from Grade 6, Ratios and Proportional Relationships, Standards for Mathematical Practice. Copyright by Common Core State Standards Initiative. Used by permission of Common Core State Standards Initiative. **370** MATHEMATICS Common Core, Course 2, © 2013. Printed and Electronically reproduced by permission of Pearson Education, Inc., Upper Saddle River, New Jersey. **374** Excerpt from Grade 7, Standards for Mathematical Practice. Copyright by Common Core State Standards Initiative. Used by permission of Common Core State Standards Initiative.

Chapter 8

388 Excerpt from Grade 8, The Number System, Standards For Mathematics. Copyright by Common Core State Standards Initiative. Used by permission of Common Core State Standards Initiative. Excerpt from Grade 8, Standards For Mathematics. Copyright by Common Core State Standards Initiative. Used by permission of Common Core State Standards Initiative. **400** Excerpt from Grade 8, Operations and Algebraic Thinking, Standards For Mathematics. Copyright by Common Core State Standards Initiative. Used by permission of Common Core State Standards Initiative. Excerpt from Grade 6, Expressions and Equations, Standards For Mathematics. Copyright by Common Core State Standards Initiative. Used by permission of Common Core State Standards

Initiative.   **402** enVisionMATH Common Core, Grade 4, © 2012. Printed and Electronically reproduced by permission of Pearson Education, Inc., Upper Saddle River, New Jersey.   **415** MATHEMATICS Common Core, Course 1, © 2013. Printed and Electronically reproduced by permission of Pearson Education, Inc., Upper Saddle River, New Jersey.   **421** Excerpt from Grade 8, Standards For Mathematics. Copyright by Common Core State Standards Initiative. Used by permission of Common Core State Standards Initiative.   **422** MATHEMATICS Common Core, Course 1, © 2013. Printed and Electronically reproduced by permission of Pearson Education, Inc., Upper Saddle River, New Jersey. **452** MATHEMATICS Common Core, Course 3, © 2013. Printed and Electronically reproduced by permission of Pearson Education, Inc., Upper Saddle River, New Jersey.

Chapter 9

469 Excerpt from Grade 7, Statistics and Probability, Standards For Mathematics. Copyright by Common Core State Standards Initiative. Used by permission of Common Core State Standards Initiative.   **470** Excerpt from Grade 7, Statistics and Probability, Standards For Mathematics. Copyright by Common Core State Standards Initiative. Used by permission of Common Core State Standards Initiative.   **472** Excerpt from Grade 7, Statistics and Probability, Standards For Mathematics. Copyright by Common Core State Standards Initiative. Used by permission of Common Core State Standards Initiative.   **477** MATHEMATICS Common Core, Course 2, © 2013. Printed and Electronically reproduced by permission of Pearson Education, Inc., Upper Saddle River, New Jersey. **484** Excerpt from Grade 7, Statistics and Probability, Standards For Mathematics. Copyright by Common Core State Standards Initiative. Used by permission of Common Core State Standards Initiative.   **506** Excerpt from Grade 7, Statistics and Probability, Standards For Mathematics. Copyright by Common Core State Standards Initiative. Used by permission of Common Core State Standards Initiative.   **509** MATHEMATICS Common Core, Course 2, © 2013. Printed and Electronically reproduced by permission of Pearson Education, Inc., Upper Saddle River, New Jersey.

Chapter 10

537 Excerpt from Grade 6, Statistics and Probability, Standards For Mathematics. Copyright by Common Core State Standards Initiative. Used by permission of Common Core State Standards Initiative. **538** MATHEMATICS Common Core, Course 2, © 2013. Printed and Electronically reproduced by permission of Pearson Education, Inc., Upper Saddle River, New Jersey.   **539** Excerpt from Grade 7, Statistics and Probability, Standards For Mathematics. Copyright by Common Core State Standards Initiative. Used by permission of Common Core State Standards Initiative.   **540** MATHEMATICS Common Core, Course 2, © 2013. Printed and Electronically reproduced by permission of Pearson Education, Inc., Upper Saddle River, New Jersey.   **546** Excerpt from Guidelines for Assessment and Instruction in Statistics Education (GAISE) Report: A PreK–12 Curriculum Framework. Published by American Statistical Association, © 2005.   **553** MATHEMATICS Common Core, Course 2, © 2009. Printed and Electronically reproduced by permission of Pearson Education, Inc., Upper Saddle River, New Jersey.   **565** enVisionMATH, Grade 6 © 2012. Printed and Electronically reproduced by permission of Pearson Education, Inc., Upper Saddle River, New Jersey.   **567** Excerpt from Grade 8, Statistics and Probability, Standards For Mathematics. Copyright by Common Core State Standards Initiative. Used by permission of Common Core State Standards Initiative.   **568** MATHEMATICS Common Core, Grade 3, ©2013. Printed and Electronically reproduced by permission of Pearson Education, Inc., Upper Saddle River, New Jersey.   **577** Excerpt from Grade 6, Statistics and Probability, Standards For Mathematics. Copyright by Common Core State Standards Initiative. Used by permission of Common Core State Standards Initiative.   **582** Excerpt from Grade 6, Statistics and Probability, Standards For Mathematics. Copyright by Common Core State Standards Initiative. Used by permission of Common Core State Standards Initiative.   **584** MATHEMATICS Common Core, Course 1, © 2013. Printed and Electronically reproduced by permission of Pearson Education, Inc., Upper Saddle River, New Jersey.

607 Excerpt from How to Lie with Statistics by Darrell Huff and Irving Geis. Published by W.W Norton and Company, © 1993.

Chapter 11

640 Excerpt from Grade 4, Standards For Mathematics. Copyright by Common Core State Standards Initiative. Used by permission of Common Core State Standards Initiative.   **646** enVisionMATH Common Core, Grade 5, © 2012. Printed and Electronically reproduced by permission of Pearson Education, Inc., Upper Saddle River, New Jersey.   **647** Excerpt from Grade 4, Geometry, Standards for Mathematics. Copyright by Common Core State Standards Initiative. Used by permission of Common Core State Standards Initiative.   **650** enVisionMATH Common Core, Grade 6, © 2012. Printed and Electronically reproduced by permission of Pearson Education, Inc., Upper Saddle River, New Jersey.   **656** Excerpt from Grade 7, Geometry, Standards for Mathematics. Copyright by Common Core State Standards Initiative. Used by permission of Common Core State Standards Initiative.   **670** Excerpt from Kindergarten Common Core Standards, Standards for Mathematics. Copyright by Common Core State Standards Initiative. Used by permission of Common Core State Standards Initiative.

Chapter 12

691 Excerpt from Grade 7, Geometry, Standards for Mathematics. Copyright by Common Core State Standards Initiative. Used by permission of Common Core State Standards Initiative.   **694** MATHEMATICS Common Core, Course 3, © 2013. Printed and Electronically reproduced by permission of Pearson Education, Inc., Upper Saddle River, New Jersey.   **736** MATHEMATICS Common Core, Course 3, © 2013. Printed and Electronically reproduced by permission of Pearson Education, Inc., Upper Saddle River, New Jersey.

Chapter 13

757 Excerpt from Grade 4 Geometry, Standards for Mathematics. Copyright by Common Core State Standards Initiative. Used by permission of Common Core State Standards Initiative.   **778** enVisionMATH Common Core, Grade 6, © 2012. Printed and Electronically reproduced by permission of Pearson Education, Inc., Upper Saddle River, New Jersey.   **800** enVisionMATH Common Core, Grade 6, © 2012. Printed and Electronically reproduced by permission of Pearson Education, Inc., Upper Saddle River, New Jersey.   **803** Randall Inners Charles, SCOTT FORESMAN-ADDISON WESLEY MATHEMATICS, Vol 3, © 2008. Printed and Electronically reproduced by permission of Pearson Education, Inc., Upper Saddle River, New Jersey.   **805** Randall Inners Charles, SCOTT FORESMAN-ADDISON WESLEY MATHEMATICS, Vol 3, © 2008. Printed and Electronically reproduced by permission of Pearson Education, Inc., Upper Saddle River, New Jersey.

Chapter 14

813 Excerpt from Grade 2 and 4 Measurement and Data, Standards for Mathematics. Copyright by Common Core State Standards Initiative. Used by permission of Common Core State Standards Initiative.   **821** enVisionMATH Common Core, Grade 6, ©2012. Printed and Electronically reproduced by permission of Pearson Education, Inc., Upper Saddle River, New Jersey.   **827** Excerpt from Grade 4 Measurement and Data, Standards for Mathematics. Copyright by Common Core State Standards Initiative. Used by permission of Common Core State Standards Initiative. Excerpt from Grade 6 Geometry, Standards for Mathematics. Copyright by Common Core State Standards Initiative. Used by permission of Common Core State Standards Initiative.   **831** Excerpt from Grade 3 Measurement and Data, Standards for Mathematics. Copyright by Common Core State Standards Initiative. Used by permission of Common Core State Standards Initiative.   **838** enVisionMATH Common Core, Grade 6, © 2012. Printed and Electronically reproduced by permission of Pearson Education, Inc., Upper Saddle River, New Jersey.   **839** MATHEMATICS Common Core, Course 2, © 2013. Printed and Electronically reproduced

Image Credits

Chapter 1

1 Sebastian Duda/Shutterstock **4** AP Images **5** Pearson Education **25** Pearson Education

Chapter 2

39 Norman Pogson/Shutterstock/Assetlibrary **43** Pearson Education **53** Pearson Education

Chapter 3

84 Maskot/Getty Images **88** Johnny Lott **89** Kmiragaya/Fotolia **114** Pearson Education **116** left, Discovod/Fotolia; right, Robcartorres/Fotolia **132** AJT/Shutterstock **143** left, Neil Robinson/Getty Images; right, Pearson Education **156** Pearson Education

Chapter 4

174 Srdjan Draskovic/Alamy **176** Pearson Education **184** Orphan Work **195** Pearson Education **196** Pearson Education **198** Pearson Education **205** top, Microimages/Fotolia ; bottom, Jupiter Images/Thinkstock

Chapter 5

218 Lisa F. Young/Shutterstock **219** Pearson Education **220** Pearson Education **241** Comstock/Thinkstock

Chapter 6

257 Gary Fiedtkou/GLT Products **295** Pearson Education

Chapter 7

329 TAGSTOCK2/Fotolia **330** Pearson Education **334** Vladislav Gajic/Fotolia, LLC

Chapter 8

387 Elenathewise/Fotolia **388** Pearson Education **390** Orphan Work **395** Pearson Education **401** top, middle, and bottom, Pearson Education **414** Pearson Education **422** Pearson Education

Chapter 9

468 Image Source/Getty Images **469** Pearson Education **471** Pearson Education **492** BitStrip cartoon **508** BitStrip cartoon **525** BitStrip cartoon

Chapter 10

536 Fuse/Getty Images **537** Pearson Education **538** Stockbyte/Thinkstock **548** Alfred Eisenstaedt/Time Life Pictures/Getty Images **594** Pearson Education

Chapter 11

620 WavebreakmediaMicro/Fotolia **622** Pearson Education **631** John Henshall/Alamy **673** Antonio Abrignani/Shutterstock **675** Pearson Education

Chapter 12

691 M.C. Escher's "Symmetry Work 22" ©2014 The M.C. Escher Company—The Netherlands. All rights reserved. **694** Pearson Education **695** Antonio Abrignani/Shutterstock **696** Mushakesa/Shutterstock **703** VonSteck/iStockphoto

Chapter 13

756 MaxyM/Shutterstock **758** Gianni Dagli Orti/The Art Archive/Alamy **779** Pichugin Dmitry/Shuttestock **798** M.C. Escher's " Study of Regular Division of the Plane with Reptiles (1939)" ©2014 The M.C. Escher Company—The Netherlands. All rights reserved. **800** Majorie Rice

Chapter 14

812 Dmitry Kalinovsky/Shutterstock **815** Jean-Loup /Charrnet/Photo Researchers, Inc./Science Source **820** Pearson Education **878** Pearson Education **880** Prentice Hall/Pearson Education

Answers to Problems

Answers to all exercises not shown as annotations.

CHAPTER 1

Assessment 1-1A

2. Building a staircase as seen in (a) gives a visual graphic of the sum $1 + 2 + \ldots + n$. Copying the staircase as in (b) and placing it as shown demonstrates that an array that is n units high and $n + 1$ units long is produced. There are $n(n + 1)$ units in (b), which is twice the number desired. So the sum $1 + 2 + \ldots + n$ must be $n(n + 1)/2$. Gauss's sum when $n = 100$ would be $100(100 + 1)/2$ or 5050. **7.** E is greater by 49. **8.** Dandy, Cory, Alabama, Bubba **10.** $a = 42; b = 32; c = 37; d = 2$
13. Choose Box B and pull out a fruit. If you pull an apple then Box B must contain only apples (why?). Because Box A is mislabeled it can't be "Oranges," but it can't be "Apples" either (why?). So, it is "Oranges and Apples." Thus, Box C is "Oranges." If an orange is pulled the reasoning is similar.

Assessment 1-1B

2. a. There are 50 sums of 101 as shown by the arcs, so the total is $50 \cdot 101$ or 5050. **b.** A diagram similar to the one in part 2 (a) would illustrate how the numbers can be paired to form 100 sums of 202. Since the last term is odd, the middle term, 101, is left unpaired. So, the sum of the first 201 natural numbers is $100 \cdot 202 + 101 = 20,301$. **4.** Answers vary. For example:
$1 + 10, 2 + 4 + 5, 2 + 9, 3 + 8, 4 + 7, 5 + 6, 1 + 1 + 9,$
$2 + 1 + 8, 3 + 1 + 7, 4 + 1 + 6, 5 + 1 + 5, 4 + 4 + 3$
5. If there are at least two colors of socks in the drawer then of any three chosen, two must be the same color. **7.** Q is greater by 97.
10. Answers vary. For example:

17	7	9
3	11	19
13	15	5

11. Put 4 marbles in each tray of the scale. Take the heavier 4 and place 2 in each tray. Take the heavier 2 and place 1 in each tray. The heavier marble will be obvious. **13. a.** Two possibilities: (1) 3 quarters, 4 dimes, and 4 pennies; (2) 1 quarter, 9 dimes, and 4 pennies. **b.** A solution consisting of the least number of coins requires the most use of the quarters. Since 4 quarters cannot be used, use 3. Now, four dimes can be used and no more.

Mathematical Connections 1-1

Reasoning

1. There are two magic squares; strategies vary.

26	21	28
27	25	23
22	29	24

27	20	25
22	24	26
23	28	21

2. Each domino must cover 1 black and 1 red square. Hence, 31 dominoes would cover 31 red and 31 black squares. This is impossible because the board has 30 red and 32 black squares.
3. a. 45 **b.** Answers vary. **c.** $\dfrac{n(n - 1)}{2}$

4. a. The first player selects one object from the larger pile, leaving the second player facing a (1, 1)-configuration, which is a loss for him or her. In the (1,100)-game, the first player can take 99 objects from the larger pile to win. **b.** If $a > 1$, the first player can win by taking $a - 1$ objects from the larger pile. **c.** The first player will lose any (a, a)-game. This is because the second player can play by mirroring the first player's move in the other pile. Either the second player has won at this point (by taking all of the remaining objects in one pile) or the first player faces a (b, b)-configuration, where $b < a$. Eventually, the first player will face the (1, 1)-game and lose. **d.** From part (c), we know that the first player to face a (k, k)-configuration will lose the game. The first player of the game therefore can win any (a, b)-game where $a \neq b$, by selecting as many objects as it is necessary to even up the piles ($a - b$ or $b - a$ objects). **5. a.** 7 **b.** $2^{64} - 1$ seconds, or approximately 585 billion years. The number of moves is $2^n - 1$ for n coins. This can be solved using the strategy of examining a simpler problem. If there is one coin, 1 move is necessary. If there are two coins, 3 moves are necessary. For three coins, the number of moves is 7. For four coins, the number of moves is 15.

Open-Ended

6. Answers vary. For example, any of the investigation problems in this section are examples of problems that could be approached with the strategy discussed. **7.** Answers vary. For example, if the average distance between adjacent people was 1.8 m, then it would take approximately 22,000,000 people.

Cooperative Learning

8. a. Play second and make sure that the sum showing when you hand the calculator to your opponent is a multiple of 3. **b.** Play first and press 4. After that, make sure that each time you hand the calculator to your opponent it displays 1 less than a multiple of 5. **c.** Play first and press 3. After that, make sure that each time you hand the calculator to your opponent it displays 3 more than a multiple of 10. **d.** Play second. Make sure the calculator displays a multiple of 3 each time you hand it to your opponent. **e.** Play second. Make sure the calculator displays a multiple of 4 each time you hand it to your opponent. **f.** Play first and subtract 3. Then make sure the calculator displays a multiple of 10 each time.

Connecting Mathematics to the Classroom

9. Answers vary. For example, it is in the last step where students examine whether the answer is reasonable and whether it checks given the original conditions in the problem. Many times, students discover wrong answers at this point since they may have never bothered to check whether the answer they obtained makes sense. It is also at this step that students reflect on the mathematics used and determine whether there might be different ways of solving the problem. Also at this stage students reflect on any connections to other problems or generalizations.   **10.** Answers vary. For example, intelligent guesses will help students systematically zero in on the exact answer because successive guesses can be based on the results given by the previous guesses. This is not possible with random guessing.   **11.** Answers vary. For example, if these nine numbers are to be used in a magic square, then the sum in each of the three columns must be the same and must be a natural number. The natural number must be 1/3 of the sum of all nine numbers. However, $1 + 3 + 4 + 5 + 6 + 7 + 8 + 9 + 10 = 53$ and $53/3 = 17\frac{2}{3}$, which is not a natural number. Therefore, these numbers cannot be used for a magic square.

Assessment 1-2A

2. e. arithmetic; $193 + 10 \cdot 2^{30}, 193 + 11 \cdot 2^{30}, 193 + 12 \cdot 2^{30}$
3. a. $397; 4n - 3$ **b.** $5020; 50n + 20$ **c.** $3^{99}; 3^{n-1}$
d. $100^{199}; 10^{2n-1}$ **e.** $193 + 106 \cdot 2^{30}; 193 + (n + 6) \cdot 2^{30}$ **10. c.** 15, 17, 21, 27, 35, 45   **14. a.** Answers vary. For example, if $n = 5$, then $\dfrac{5 + 5}{5} \neq 5 + 1$.   **b.** Answers vary. For example, if $n = 2$, then $(2 + 4)^2 \neq 2^2 + 4^2$.   **20. a.** 5 (the fifth Fibonacci term) **b.** 8 (the sixth Fibonacci term)   **c.** 13 (the seventh Fibonacci term)   **d.** $F_1 + F_2 + F_3 + \ldots + F_n = F_{n+2} - 1$ **e.** The sum of the first $n - 2$ terms of the Fibonacci sequence is one less than the nth term.

Assessment 1-2B

1. c. 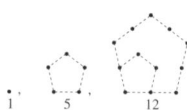   **2. a.** Arithmetic; $18, 22, 26$ **b.** Arithmetic; 39, 52, 65   **c.** Geometric; $4^4, 4^5, 4^6$ **d.** Geometric; $2^{14}, 2^{18}, 2^{22}$
e. Arithmetic; $100 + 10 \cdot 2^{50}, 100 + 12 \cdot 2^{50}, 100 + 14 \cdot 2^{50}$
3. a. $398; 4n - 2$ **b.** $99 \cdot 13; (n - 1)^{13}$ **c.** $4^{100}; 4^n$
d. $2^{398}; 2^{4n-2}$ **e.** $100 + 202 \cdot 2^{50}; 100 + 2(n + 1)2^{50}$
5. a. The sum of the first n odd natural numbers is n^2.
10. a. $3, 6, 12, 21, 33, 48$ **c.** $4, 7, 13, 22, 34, 49$ **13. a.** $4, 9, 14, 19, 24$ **b.** $4, 10, 16, 22, 28$ **c.** $6, 11, 16, 21, 26$ **d.** $0, 3, 8, 15, 24$ **14. a.** Answers vary. For example, let $n = 6$; then $\dfrac{3 + 6}{3} = \dfrac{9}{3} = 3 \neq 6$.   **b.** Answers vary. For example, let $n = 4$; then $(4 - 2)^2 = 2^2 = 4 \neq 4^2 - 4$.   **c.** $2, 1, 7$ **20. a.** $F_1 + F_3 = 1 + 2 = 3$ and $F_4 = 3$ **b.** $F_1 + F_3 + F_5 = 8 = F_6$ **c.** $F_1 + F_3 + F_5 + F_7 = 21 = F_8$
d. $F_1 + F_3 + F_5 + \ldots + F_{2k-1} = F_{2k}$

Mathematical Connections 1-2

Reasoning

1. a. Yes. The difference between terms in the new sequence is the same as in the old sequence because a fixed number was added to each number in the sequence.   **b.** Yes. If the fixed number is k, the difference between terms of the second sequence is k times the difference between terms of the first sequence.   **c.** Yes. The difference of the new sequence is the sum of the original differences.

2. Because the population is increasing, the ratio of the geometric sequence is greater than 1. Because the terms of such a geometric sequence increase faster than the terms of any arithmetic sequence, it is possible to show that given any increasing geometric sequence and any arithmetic sequence, for some n the nth term of the geometric sequence will be greater than the corresponding term of the arithmetic sequence.   **3. a.** Abby studied for 13.5 hours. Dan studied for 11.25 hours.   **b.** Week 17
4. Since a, b, and c form an arithmetic sequence, $b - a = c - b$. Hence, $2b = a + c$ or $b = \dfrac{a + c}{2}$.   **5.** For any x, the sequence $x, 2x, 3x$ are the first three terms in a Fibonacci-type sequence and in an arithmetic sequence.   **6. a.** n^2 **b.** If in the nth figure the four corner white tiles are not counted then we see that there are $4n$ white tiles around the $n \times n$ shaded square. Adding the corner tiles, we get the total $4n + 4$ white tiles. Another way is to count all the tiles and subtract the number of the shaded ones, that is, $(n + 2)^2 - n^2$, which also equals $4n + 4$.

Open-Ended

7. Answers vary. For example, two more patterns follow:

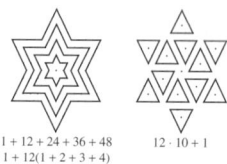

$1 + 12 + 24 + 36 + 48$
$1 + 12(1 + 2 + 3 + 4)$ $12 \cdot 10 + 1$

8. Answers vary. For example, the following is an array of pentagonal numbers:

The pattern for the number of dots is $1, 5, 12, 22, 35, 51, \ldots$ The number of additional dots for each pentagon forms an arithmetic sequence with first term 1 and second difference 3. For the 100th pentagonal number, we would have $1 + 4 + 7 + 10 + 13 + 16 + \ldots + 298$ dots, where $298 = 1 + (100 - 1)3$. Therefore, the 100th pentagonal number is $(100/2)(1 + 298) = 14,950$.   **9.** Answers will vary.   **10.** Answers vary.

Cooperative Learning

11. a. Answers vary. For example, each number other than 1 is the sum of the two numbers to the top right and top left. There is right-left symmetry. The natural numbers show up along two diagonals.   **b.** $1, 2, 4, 8, 16, \ldots$, or $2^0, 2^1, 2^2, 2^3, 2^4, \ldots$
c. $2^{15} = 32,768$ **d.** 2^{n-1} **12. a.** 81   **b.** 40   **c.** 3^{n-1}

Connecting Mathematics to the Classroom

13. Answers vary. For example, Joey could be told that he has noticed a pattern that works for many numbers but he must be careful in generalizing his observation to all numbers. He should be encouraged to look at more numbers to see if he can find a *counterexample* to his claim. If he starts investigating, he will find that 14 ends in 4 but is not divisible by 4. 34 is another number that ends in 4 but is not divisible by 4. These counterexamples prove that Joey's conjecture is false.   **14.** Al and Betty should be told that both answers could be correct as long as each person's rule works for all the given terms. Al is thinking of a geometric sequence in which each term is multiplied by 2 to get the next term. Betty is thinking of a different sequence. She starts with

2, then adds 2 to get the 2nd term, then adds 4 to get the next term, then 6, then 8, then 10, and so on. Betty's first difference is the arithmetic sequence 2, 4, 6, ... **15.** The sequence is both arithmetic and geometric (add 0 or multiply by 1 to obtain the terms of the sequence). The only other sequences that are both arithmetic and geometric are of the form $c, c, c, c, \ldots$ for some real number c. **16.** The student is wrong. For example, if we follow the student's procedure for the sequence 35, 40, 45, we get $\dfrac{45 - 35}{5} = 2$, rather than 3. The student would be correct if she said to add 1 to the quotient.

Review Problems

17. 90 **18.** 7 **19.** We need one 12-person tent and a combination of tents to hold 14 people. There are 10 ways: 662, 653, 6332, 62222, 5522, 5333, 53222, 33332, 332222, and 2222222.

Chapter 1 Review

3. The question "What makes you come so soon?" is asked when the scholar arrives two hours later than usual. This makes no sense *unless* the "ten o'clock" is at night. **5. a.** $3n + 2$ if the sequence is arithmetic with difference of 3. **b.** 3^n if the sequence is geometric with ratio 3. **c.** $2^{n+1} - 1$ **6.** 1, 4, 7, 10, 13 **7. a.** 10,100 **b.** 10,201 **8. b.** False; for example, 19 is odd and it ends in 9. **c.** True; the sum of any two even numbers, $2m$ and $2n$, is even because $2m + 2n = 2(m + n)$

9. Answers vary.

16	3	2	13
5	10	11	8
9	6	7	12
4	15	14	1

21. $n - m + 1$, answers vary.

22. Answers vary. For example, fill the 4-cup pot and empty it into the 7-cup pot. Repeat. There is now 1 cup in the 4-cup pot. Empty the 7-cup pot and pour the 1 cup into the 7-cup pot. Fill the 4-cup pot and empty it into the 7-cup pot. It will now contain 5 cups. **24. a.** A possible pattern is that each successive figure is constructed by adjoining another pentagon to the previous figure. **25. a.** The circled terms will constitute an arithmetic sequence because the common difference will be twice the difference in the original sequence. **b.** The new sequence will be a geometric sequence because the ratio will be the square of the ratio of the original sequence. **26.** If the sequence is $a_1, a_2, a_3, a_4, \ldots$ to find the first term we substitute $n = 1$ and get $1^2 - 1$ or 0, so $a_1 = 0$. For $n = 2$, we get $2^2 - 2$ or 2. Thus, $a_1 + a_2 = 2$; hence $a_2 = 2$. For $n = 3, a_1 + a_2 + a_3 = 3^2 - 3 = 6$. Substituting for a_1 and a_2, we get $a_3 = 6 - 2 = 4$. For $n = 4, a_1 + a_2 + a_3 + a_4 = 4^2 - 4 = 12$. Substituting for $a_1, a_2,$ and a_3, we get $0 + 2 + 4 + a_4 = 12$. Hence, $a_4 = 6$.

27. a. 7, 20 **b.** 13, 150 **c.** $\dfrac{a - b}{2}, \dfrac{a + b}{2}$

Answers to Now Try This

1. In Figure 1, we have $1 + 100 = 101$. To obtain each successive pair from the previous one, we add 1 and subtract 1 and hence the sum does not change. Gauss's approach for the sum of squares does not work because the sums change; for example,

$1^2 + 100^2 \neq 2^2 + 99^2$. **2.** First approach:
$25 + 26 + 27 + \ldots + 120 = (1 + 2 + 3 + \ldots + 25 + 26 + 27 + \ldots + 120) - (1 + 2 + 3 + \ldots + 24) = \dfrac{(1 + 120) \cdot 120}{2} - \dfrac{(1 + 24) \cdot 24}{2} = 121 \cdot 60 - 25 \cdot 12 = 6960$

Second approach:
There are $120 - 24$ or 96 terms in the sum. Hence, using Gauss's approach, the sum equals $\dfrac{(25 + 120) \cdot 96}{2}$ or 6960.

3. The first person played with 15 people; the second played with 14 because his game with the first person was already counted and so one. Thus, the total number of games played is $15 + 14 + 13 + \ldots + 1$, which using Gauss's approach is $\left(\dfrac{15 + 1}{2}\right) \cdot 15$ or 120. **5. a.** Answers vary. For example, the next three terms could be △, △, ○.
b. The pattern could be one circle, two triangles, one circle, two triangles, and so on. **6. a.** Inductive reasoning **b.** The next several numbers also work. **c.** If $x = 11$, then $11^2 + 11 + 11$ is not prime because it is divisible by 11. **7.** The following diagram shows the number of paths from A to every vertex and finally to B.

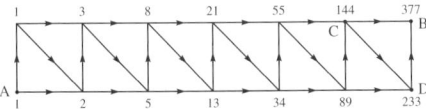

The pattern follows the Fibonacci sequence. Notice that to get to point B, we need to pass either through point C or through point D. To every path through C, there is only one way to get to point B without passing through D, that is, 144 possible paths. Thus, the number of paths to B is $144 + 233$ or 377. This reasoning applies to every vertex other than the first two vertices.
9. $10 \cdot 11$ or 110; $n(n + 1)$

Answer to the Preliminary Problem

Jill takes $1 + 2 + 3 + \ldots 10$, or 55 coins from the 10 boxes. If all the coins were genuine, the 55 coins would weigh $55 \cdot 2$ oz. or 110 oz. If the first box contained all the fake coins, the weight of all the coins would be $110 - 1$, or 109 oz. If the second box contained all the fake coins, the weight of all the coins would be $110 - 2$ or 108 oz. Thus, if all the 55 coins weigh 104 oz., Jill would write $104 = 110 - 6$ and she would know that the sixth box contains the fake coins. In general, if the coins weigh $110 - n$ oz., then the nth box contains the counterfeit coins.

CHAPTER 2

Assessment 2-1A

2. Answers vary. **a.** There exists a natural number n such that $n + 8 = 11$. **b.** There exists a natural number n such that $n^2 = 4$. **c.** For all natural numbers $n, n + 3 = 3 + n$. **d.** For all natural numbers $n, 5n + 4n = 9n$. **3.** Answers vary. **a.** For every natural number $n, n + 8 = 11$. **b.** Every natural number n satisfies $n^2 = 4$. **c.** There is no natural number n such that $n + 3 = 3 + n$. **d.** There is no natural number n such that $5n + 4n = 9n$.

6. a.

p	$\sim p$	$\sim(\sim p)$
T	F	T
F	T	F

b.

p	$\sim p$	$p \vee \sim p$	$p \wedge \sim p$
T	F	T	F
F	T	T	F

7. a.

p	q	$p \to q$	$\sim p$	$\sim p \vee q$
T	T	T	F	T
T	F	F	F	T
F	T	T	T	T
F	F	T	T	T

b. $(p \to q) \equiv (\sim p \vee q)$ **c.** If $2 + 3 = 5$, then $4 + 6 = 10$.
10. Answers vary. **a.** $2 + 3 \neq 5$ or $4 + 7 \neq 10$ **b.** The president of the United States in 2013 was Barack Obama. **c.** With every seat filled, the Supreme Court of the United States does not have 12 justices. **d.** A triangle has three sides of the same length and the triangle does not have two sides of the same length. **e.** A triangle has two sides of the same length and the triangle does not have three sides of the same length.
12. Dr. No is a male spy who is neither poor nor tall.
14. a. Converse: If a triangle has no two sides of the same length, then it is a scalene triangle. Inverse: If a triangle is not scalene, then it has two sides of the same length. Contrapositive: If a triangle has two sides of the same length, then the triangle is not scalene. **b.** Converse: If an angle is a right angle, then it is not acute. Inverse: If an angle is acute, then it is not a right angle. Contrapositive: If an angle is not a right angle, then it is an acute angle. **c.** Converse: If Mary is not a citizen of Cuba, then she is a U.S. citizen. Inverse: If Mary is not a U.S. citizen, then she is a citizen of Cuba. Contrapositive: If Mary is a citizen of Cuba, then she is not a citizen of the United States. **d.** Converse: If a number is not a natural number, then it is a whole number. Inverse: If a number is not a whole number, then it is a natural number. Contrapositive: If a number is a natural number, then it is not a whole number.
15. The statements are negations of each other.

p	q	$\sim q$	$p \wedge \sim q$	$\sim(p \wedge \sim q)$	$p \to q$	$\sim(p \to q)$
T	T	F	F	T	T	F
T	F	T	T	F	F	T
F	T	F	F	T	T	F
F	F	T	F	T	T	F

16. Answers vary. If a number is not a multiple of 4, then it is not a multiple of 8.
18.

p	q	r	$p \to q$	$q \to r$	$p \to r$	$(p \to q) \wedge (q \to r)$	$[(p \to q) \wedge (q \to r)] \to (p \to r)$
T	T	T	T	T	T	T	T
T	T	F	T	F	F	F	T
T	F	T	F	T	T	F	T
T	F	F	F	T	F	F	T
F	T	T	T	T	T	T	T
F	T	F	T	F	T	F	T
F	F	T	T	T	T	T	T
F	F	F	T	T	T	T	T

19. It is possible that some teachers with IQs of 145 or more are in Mensa if there is one person in the overlap of the circles representing IQs of 145 or more and those in Mensa because all considered are teachers. **20. a.** Some Beta Club students make A's. **b.** If I study for the final, then I will look for a teaching job. **c.** There exist triangles that are isosceles. **21. a.** If a figure is a square, then it is a rectangle. **b.** If a number is an integer, then it is a rational number. **c.** If a polygon has exactly three sides, then it is a triangle.

Assessment 2-1B

2. Answers vary. **a.** For all $n, n + 0 = n$. **b.** No natural number n exists such that $n + 1 = n + 2$. **c.** There exists a natural number n such that $3(n + 2) = 12$. **d.** There exists a natural number n such that $n^3 = 8$. **3.** Answers vary. **a.** There is no natural number n such that $n + 0 = n$. **b.** There exists at least one natural number n such that $n + 1 = n + 2$. **c.** For all natural numbers $n, 3(n + 2) = 12$. **d.** For all natural numbers $n, n^3 = 8$. **4. b.** All cats have nine lives. **c.** There exists a square that is not a rectangle. **9.** Answers vary. **a.** $4 + 6 \neq 10$ and $2 + 3 \neq 5$ **b.** A National Football League team must have 11 or fewer players on the field a game is in progress. **c.** The first president of the United States was not George Washington. **d.** A quadrilateral has three sides of the same length and the quadrilateral does not have four sides of the same length. **e.** A rectangle has four sides of the same length and it does not have three sides of the same length. **11.** Ms. Makeover is a married blond with straight hair. **13. a.** Converse: If $x^2 = 9$, then $x = 3$. Inverse: If $x \neq 3$, then $x^2 \neq 9$. Contrapositive: If $x^2 \neq 9$, then $x \neq 3$. **b.** Converse: If classes are canceled, then it snowed. Inverse: If it does not snow, then classes are not canceled. Contrapositive: If classes are not canceled, then it did not snow. **15. c.** Seven is a natural number but not because of the argument here; the argument is not valid. **16. a.** Helen is in Kappa Mu Epsilon. **17. a.** If a number is a natural number, then it is a real number. **b.** If a figure is a circle, then it is a closed figure. **18. b.** I am not going and she is not going.

Mathematical Connections 2-1

Reasoning

1. The truth value of neither questions nor commands can be determined. As a result, they are not considered mathematical statements. **2.** Answers vary. There are several ways to negate such a statement but one has to make sure that "all" are addressed. One form of the negation is "All A's are not B's." **3. a.** For a disjunction to be true, at least one of the statements forming the disjunction must be true. **b.** An implication is always true unless the conclusion is false and the hypothesis is true.
4. a. If there is no nail, then there is no shoe.
  If there is no shoe, then there is no horse.
  If there is no horse, there is no rider.
  If there is no rider, then the battle is lost.
  If the battle is lost, the war is lost.
  Therefore, if there is no nail, then the war is lost.
b. Yes, this follows from the repeated use of the chain rule.

5. When a comma or a semicolon is used in an e-mail address (depending on the server), the logical meaning is "and" so that all addresses will receive the e-mail. **6.** When both a statement and its converse are true, then the other forms of the statement (inverse and contrapositive) are true. The statement and its contrapositive have the same truth value, as do the converse and its contrapositive (the inverse of the original statement).

Open-Ended

7. Answers vary. An example could be seen when the statements p is "I bought a car" and q is "I take you on a date." As long as the promise is kept, the implication "If I bought a car, I will take you on a date" is considered true.

Case	p	q	Translation of symbols	Result
1	T	T	I bought a car; I take you on a date.	Promise Kept
2	T	F	I bought a car; I did not take you on a date.	Promise Broken
3	F	T	I did not buy a car; I take you on a date.	Promise Kept
4	F	F	I did not buy a car; I did not take you on a date.	Promise Kept

8. Yes. Consider the truth table below: A tautology $(p \leftrightarrow q)$ is true as long as the truth values for each of p and q are the same. Consider the following table that considers all the cases.

p	q	$\sim p$	$\sim q$	$\sim p \leftrightarrow \sim q$
T	T	F	F	T
F	F	T	T	T

Cooperative Learning

9. Answers vary. Statements (a) and (b) are false. Statement (c) causes the problem. If statement (c) is also false, then that makes statement (c) a true assertion, which is a contradiction. On the other hand, if statement (c) is true, then it wrongly asserts that it is false. **10.** Answers vary.

Connecting Mathematics to the Classroom

11. Answers vary. For example, a truth table could be used to show the possibilities. That approach may not satisfy the student, even though it is the mathematical way to do it. An example might satisfy the student, though it would not be a complete mathematical explanation. For example, consider the following:

All whole numbers are natural numbers [*This is a false hypothesis.*]
7 is a whole number.
Conclusion: 7 is a natural number.
The conclusion is true, and the argument seems valid.

12. Answers vary. For example, Mr. Johnson would have lied had he allowed no one to go to recess. He did not do that by restricting one child from going.

Assessment 2-2A

1. Answers vary. **a.** $\{a, s, e, m, n, t\}$ **b.** $\{20, 21, 22, 23, 24, \ldots\}$ **2. a.** $P = \{p, q, r, s\}$ **4. b.** $n(n-1)(n-2)\ldots 3 \cdot 2 \cdot 1 = n!$ The "first" element can be paired with n choices, leaving $n - 1$ elements for the "second" pairing and so forth. The Fundamental Counting Theorem says that the choices can be multiplied to find the total number of correspondences. **8.** $\overline{A}$ is the set of all college students with at least one grade that is not an A, that is, those college students who do not have a straight-A average. **9. b.** There is no limit on how many elements set C could have. **10. b.** Answers vary. For example, the sets are equal. **16. b.** No. A may equal B. **d.** No. Consider $A = \{1\}$ and $B = \{1, 2\}$. **17. a.** Let $A = \{1, 2, 3, \ldots, 100\}$ and $B = \{1, 2, 3\}$. Then $n(A) = 100$ and $n(B) = 3$. $B \subset A$. **b.** $n(\varnothing) = 0$. Let $A = \{1, 2, 3\}$, which implies that $n(A) = 3$. $\varnothing \subset A$, which implies that there is at least one more element in A than in $\varnothing$. Thus $0 < 3$. **19.** Answers vary. The set of natural numbers and the set of whole numbers **20.** There is a one-to-one correspondence between the two sets such that each even natural number $2n$ is paired with $2n - 1$.

21.

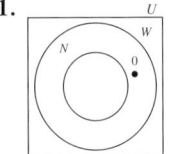

22.

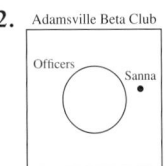

23. Answers vary. The only members of the Adamsville Beta Club are the officers.

Assessment 2-2B

1. Answers vary. **a.** $\{a, l, g, e, b, r\}$ **b.** $\{1, 2, 3, 4, 5, 6, 7, 8, 9\}$ **2. a.** $Q = \{q, r, s\}$ **4. b.** $(n-1)(n-2)(n-3) \cdot \ldots \cdot 1$. There are $n - 1$ choices with which to pair the "first" element, $n - 2$ choices with which to pair the "second" element, and so forth. The Fundamental Counting Principle then says that the product of the choices gives the total number of ways that the one-to-one correspondence can happen. **8.** $\overline{G}$ is the set of all women who did not graduate from Georgia State University. **9. a.** The empty set is a subset of every set; if $A = \varnothing$, then $n(A) = 0$. **b.** Yes. B can be the empty set if, and only if, $A = \varnothing = B$. **15. a.** No; for example, $A = \{1\}$ and $B = \{1, 2\}$; $A \subseteq B$, but $A \neq B$. **b.** No; $A \subset B$ implies B has at least one element that A does not have. **c.** No; they must be equivalent but they do not have to be equal, for example, $A = \{1\}$ and $B = \{2\}$. **16. a.** $0 = n(\varnothing)$; let $A = \{1, 2\}$; then $n(A) = 2$. Now $\varnothing \subset A$, because every element of $\varnothing$ (of which there are none) is an element of A and there is at least one element in A that is not in $\varnothing$. **b.** Let $A = \{1, 2, 3, \ldots, 99\}$ and $B = \{1, 2, 3, \ldots, 100\}$. Since $A \subset B, n(A) < n(B)$. So $99 < 100$. **19.** For every natural number n, let it be paired with $n - 1$. The pairing is a one-to-one correspondence between the set of natural numbers and the set of whole numbers.

20.

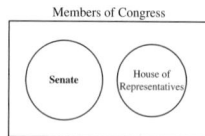

21. Answers vary. The only swimmers in the 100-m butterfly race are from the Maryville Swim Team.

22.

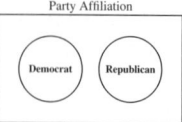

23. Answers vary. For example, A is not equivalent to B.
24. a. Answers vary. Let A be the set of all natural numbers not equal to 1 with N as the universal set. Then $\overline{A} = \{1\}$ is finite. **b.** Answers vary. Let A be the set of the even natural numbers with N as the universal set. $\overline{A}$ is the set of odd natural numbers, which is infinite.

Mathematical Connections 2-2

Reasoning

1. A set is well defined if any object can be classified as belonging to the set or not belonging to the set. For example, the set of U.S. presidents is well defined, but the set of rich U.S. presidents is not well defined because "rich" is a matter of opinion. **2. a.** This set is not well defined, since we do not know what is meant by "wealthy." **b.** This set is not well defined, since we do not know what is meant by "great." **c.** This set is well defined. Given a number, we can easily tell if it is a natural number greater than 100. **d.** This set is well defined. We could list them all. **e.** This set is well-defined; it is the empty set. **3.** Suppose set A is not empty. Then A contains at least one element. There is no element in $\varnothing$ to be paired with the element in set A. Thus there can be no one-to-one correspondence between $\varnothing$ and any set with an element. **4.** $\{\varnothing\}$ has exactly one element, namely $\varnothing$. Therefore $\varnothing \in \{\varnothing\}$. $\varnothing$ is a subset of every set. **5.** To show that $A \not\subseteq B$, we must be able to find at least one element of set A that does not belong to set B. **6.** If two sets are not finite, then the cardinal number of one set can be equal to the cardinal number of the other set, even though one is a proper subset of the other. In this case, the sets are infinite. "Less than" is only defined using finite sets. We note that infinities can be compared but not at this level for the most part. **7.** If A and B are finite sets, we say that $n(A) \leq n(B)$ in case A is a (not necessarily proper) subset of B.

Open-Ended

8. Answers vary. **a.** Let $A = \{1, 2, 3, 4, 5\}$; $B = \{1, 2, 3, 4, 5, 6, 7, 8, 9\}$; and $U = \{1, 2, 3, \ldots, 20\}$, $\overline{A} = \{6, 7, 8, \ldots, 20\}$ and $\overline{B} = \{10, 11, 12, \ldots, 20\}$ **b.** $\overline{B} \subset \overline{A}$
c.

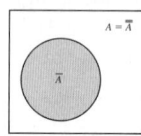

$\overline{B}$ contains only the shaded region. $\overline{A}$ contains all the area outside the circle labeled A. The dot in set B is in $\overline{A}$ but not in $\overline{B}$.
9. The simplest symbol for the white region is A.

10. We can use a one-to-one correspondence between the given set and a finite set with n elements as shown below:

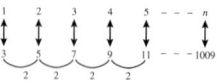

The pattern is an "add 2" pattern with the first term 3. A formula for the nth term of such a pattern is $2n + 1$. Thus, $2n + 1 = 1009$, so $n = 504$, and there are 504 elements in the given set.
11. Answers vary. The Venn diagram below depicts one way to show the information.

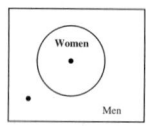

If $m = n(\text{Men})$ and $w = n(\text{Women})$, then $m \geq 1, n \geq 1$, $m + n = 100$. Other number sentences may be written as well but vary on symbolism and first identified unknowns.

Cooperative Learning

12. Answers vary on how the work is done, but the number of arrangements is 24.

Connecting Mathematics to the Classroom

13. If $A \subseteq B$, then every element in A is an element of B. Since $B \subseteq C$, every element in B is an element of C. Thus every element of A is an element in C and $A \subseteq C$. **14.** Answers vary. Exactly the assumptions that the student is making are unknown, but possibly the student thinks that either A or B must be the universal set. **15.** As a teacher, a response should be that yes, infinite sets can be compared as illustrated by a mathematician, Georg Cantor, around the turn of the twentieth century. It was groundbreaking work at the time. Perhaps the easiest example is that the number of natural numbers and the number of even natural numbers are the same.

Review Problems

16. a. False **b.** False **c.** True **d.** True **e.** False   **17. a.** False **b.** True **c.** False **d.** True **e.** False
18.

p	q	$\sim q$	$p \vee \sim q$
T	T	F	T
T	F	T	T
F	T	F	F
F	F	T	T

Assessment 2-3A

3. b. False. Let $A = \{a, b, c\}$ and $B = \{a, b\}$. Then $A - B = \{c\}$ but $B - A = \varnothing$. **c.** False. Let $U = \{a, b, c\}, A = \{a\}$, and $B = \{b\}$. Then $A \cap B = \varnothing$ and $\overline{A \cap B} = U$. $\overline{A} = \{b, c\}$, $\overline{B} = \{a, c\}$, and $\overline{A} \cap \overline{B} = \{c\}$. Thus $\overline{A \cap B} \neq \overline{A} \cap \overline{B}$. **d.** False. Let $A = \{a, b\}$; $B = \{b\}$. $A \cup B = \{a, b\}$, $(A \cup B) - A = \varnothing \neq B$. **e.** False. Let $A = \{1, 2, 3\}, B = \{3, 4, 5\}$. Then $(A - B) \cup A = \{1, 2, 3\}$, but $(A - B) \cup (B - A) = \{1, 2\} \cup \{4, 5\} = \{1, 2, 4, 5\}$.

5. a. 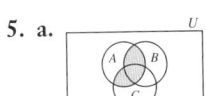 **b.** 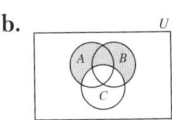 **c.**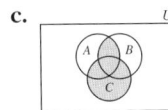

8. Yes; by definition, $A - B$ is the set of all elements in A that are not in B. If $A - B$ is the empty set, then this means that there are no elements in A that are not in B, which makes A a subset of B.

10. a. 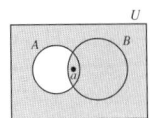 **b.** Answers vary. $B - (A \cap B)$

11. a. False $A \cup (B \cap C) \neq (A \cup B) \cap C$

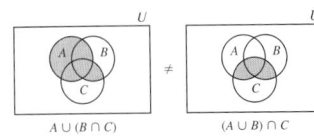

b. False $A - (B - C) \neq (A - B) - C$

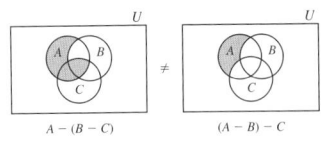

12. a. Yes. Let $A = \{1, 2, 3\}$ and $B = \{3, 4, 5\}$. $A \cap B = \{3\}$ and $A \cup B = \{1, 2, 3, 4, 5\}$. In this example $A \cap B \subseteq A \cup B$, and it is true in general. **b.** Yes. Consider the following Venn diagram: $\overline{A - B}$ is shaded; $a \in \overline{A - B}$ and in A.

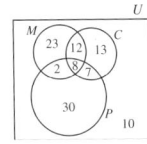

13. a. i. 5 **ii.** 2 **iii.** 2 **iv.** 3 **b. i.** $n + m$ **ii.** m **iii.** m **iv.** N
15. a. 319.2 million **b.** 148.0 million **16. a.** The set of college basketball players more than 200 cm tall **b.** The set of humans who are not college students or who are college students less than or equal to 200 cm tall **c.** The set of humans who are college basketball players or who are college students taller than 200 cm **d.** The set of all humans who are not college basketball players and who are not college students taller than 200 cm **e.** The set of all college students taller than 200 cm who are not basketball players **f.** The set of all college basketball players less than or equal to 200 cm tall **21.** Suppose M is the set of students taking mathematics, C is the set of students taking chemistry, and P is the set of students taking physics. The given information determines the numbers in the Venn diagram's regions below.

The total of all students is seen to be 105, which contradicts John's data that reported 100 students. Thus, on the basis of this report, John should not be hired for the job.
22. Steelers versus Jets, Bills versus Redskins, Cowboys versus Giants, Vikings versus Packers

23. a.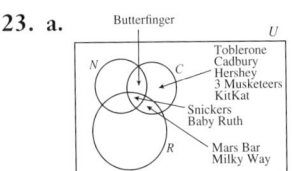

b. iii. Chocolate; Nuts/Peanut butter **iv.** Answers vary.
25. The families are the following: Tom, Jane, and Mary; and Abby, Harry, and Dick. **27. b.** $C = \{1, 2\}, D = \{1, 2, 3\}$

Assessment 2-3B

2. a. No. Let $A = \{a\}$ and $B = \{a, b\}$. $A - B = \varnothing \neq B - A$.
c. No. Let $B = \{a\}$ and $A = \{a, b\}$. $B - A = \varnothing \neq B \cup A$.
3. a. False. Let $A = \{1, 2\}, B = \{2\}$. Then $A - B = \{1\}$, but $A - \varnothing = \{1, 2\}$. **b.** False. Let $U = \{1, 2, 3\}, A = \{1, 2\}$, $B = \{2, 3\}$. Then $A \cup B = \{1, 2, 3\}$ and $\overline{A} = \{3\}$ and $\overline{B} = \{1\}$, making $\overline{A} \cup \overline{B} = \{1, 3\}$ and $\overline{A \cup B} = \varnothing$. **c.** False. Let $A = \{1, 2\}, B = \{2, 3\}$, and $C = \{1, 2, 4\}$. Now $A \cap (B \cup C) = \{1, 2\}$ but $(A \cap B) \cup C = \{1, 2, 4\}$. **d.** False. Let $A = \{1, 2\}, B = \{2, 3\}$. Now $(A - B) \cap A = \{1\}$ but $A = \{1, 2\}$. **e.** False. Let $A = \{1, 2, 3\}, B = \{1, 2, 4\}$, and $C = \{1, 2, 3, 4\}$. Now $A - (B \cap C) = \{3\}$ but $(A - B) \cap (A - C) = \varnothing$.
5. a. **b.** **c.** **d.**
9. a. **b.** Answers vary. For example, $\overline{A} \cap \overline{B}$.

10. a. 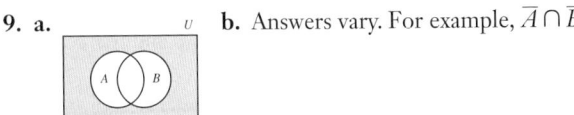 **b.**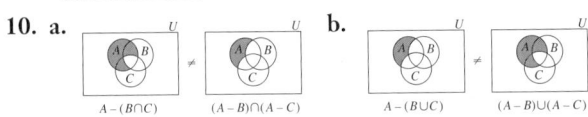

11. The set of persons fitting the description with blond hair, green eyes, and a beard is a subset of persons fitting the description with blond hair and green eyes. One expects the subset to have no more than the same number of elements. With a general populations, it would be expected to have fewer elements.
13. a. 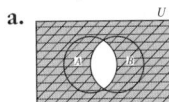 $\overline{A \cap B}$ is gray. $\overline{A}$ has diagonal lines.

$\overline{B}$ has horizontal lines. $\overline{A} \cup \overline{B}$ is gray. $\overline{A \cap B} = \overline{A} \cup \overline{B}$.
b. Answers vary. Let $U = \{1, 2, 3, 4, 5, 6, 7, 8, 9, 10\}$, $A = \{1, 2, 3, 4, 5\}$, and $B = \{3, 4, 5, 6\}$. Now $A \cap B = \{3, 4, 5\}, \overline{A} = \{6, 7, 8, 9, 10\}$ and $\overline{B} = \{1, 2, 7, 8, 9, 10\}$. Then we have $\overline{A \cap B} = \{1, 2, 6, 7, 8, 9, 10\}$ and $\overline{A} \cup \overline{B} = \{1, 2, 6, 7, 8, 9, 10\}$.
14. a. The set of all Paxson eighth graders who are members of the band but not the choir **b.** The set of all Paxson eighth graders who are members of both the band and the choir **c.** The set of all Paxson eighth graders who are members of the choir but not the band **d.** The set of all Paxson eighth graders who are members of neither the band nor the choir.
15. **16.**

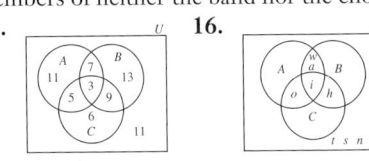

17. d. These are students at Hellgate who took algebra but neither biology nor chemistry. **e.** These are students at Hellgate who took both biology and chemistry but not algebra. **f.** Answers vary. $(C \cap B) - A$ or $(C \cap B) \cap \overline{A}$ **g.** Answers vary. $C \cap \overline{B}$ or $C - B$ **h.** Answers vary. $C - (A \cup B)$ or $C \cap \overline{A \cup B}$ **18.** The editor is correct. Sorting the data using a Venn diagram, the total number of people interviewed is 550, not 600. **21. a.** About 146.4 million **b.** About 171.2 million **23. a.** False because these are ordered pairs and order is important. **b.** False because the left side is an ordered pair and the right side is a set.

Mathematical Connections 2-3

Reasoning

1. a. This is not true. If $a \in A \cup B$, this means that a is an element of either A or B. There is nothing in this definition to make a an element of both A and B, which would have to happen for $a \in A \cap B$. **b.** No. For example, let $A = \{1, 2, 3, 4\}, B = \{4, 5, 6\}$, and $C\{3, 5, 6\}$. $A \cup B = A \cup C = \{1, 2, 3, 4, 5, 6\}$ but $B \neq C$. **c.** No. For example, let $A = \{1, 2, 3, 4\}, B = \{3, 5, 6, 7\}$, and $C = \{3, 5, 6\}$. $A \cap B = A \cap C = \{3\}$ but $B \neq C$. **2.** Answers vary. The complements of two sets are equal, if, and only if, the sets are equal. **3.** No. Suppose $A = \{1\}$ and $B = \{2\}$. Then $A \times B = \{(1, 2)\} \neq \{(2, 1)\} = B \times A$. **4.** No; suppose $A = \{1, 2, 3, 4, 5\}$ and $B = \{6, 7\}$. Then $n(A - B) = n(\{1, 2, 3, 4, 5\}) = 5$. However, $n(A) - n(B) = 5 - 2 = 3$ and $5 \neq 3$. **5.** This could happen if there were 110 students taking algebra but not biology and there were 90 students taking biology but not algebra.

Open-Ended

6. Answers vary. Two typical search items would be *mathematics* and *biology*. When those are entered into a search engine, they are treated as *mathematics and biology*. This is comparable to the intersection of two sets when the items found must be in both categories. **7.** Answers vary.

Cooperative Learning

8. a. $A \cup B$ is the set of all blocks that are green, large, or both green and large. $B \cup A$ is the set of all blocks that are large, green, or both large and green. The two sets are equal. **b.** $\overline{A \cap B}$ is the set of all blocks that are not both large and green. $\overline{A} \cap \overline{B}$ is the set of all the small blocks that are not green. The sets are not equal. **c.** $\overline{A \cap B}$ is the set of all blocks that are not both green and large. $\overline{A} \cup \overline{B}$ is the set of all blocks that are not green or are not large. The sets are equal. **d.** $A - B$ is the set of green blocks that are not large. $A \cap \overline{B}$ is the set of green blocks that are not large. The sets are equal. **9.** Answers vary. Typically in an exercise like this, students are looking at an intersection of sets trying to find the one individual with all the given characteristics.

Connecting Mathematics to the Classroom

10. Answers vary. The student is incorrectly thinking that all the elements in each set must be listed in the union of the two sets. However, mathematical convention lists each element exactly once in a set. **11.** The Cartesian product consists of all pairs in which the first component comes from the first set and the second component comes from the second

set. In a one-to-one correspondence, each element of the first set appears exactly once, as does each element of the second set. **12.** Answers vary. Addition is not an appropriate operation on sets. However, if the sets are disjoint, finite sets, then $n(A) + n(B) = n(A \cup B)$. **13.** Answers vary. To use set notation to explain the relation $\leq$, one should use the cardinal number of two sets, one that is a subset, not necessarily proper, of the other.

Review Problems

14. The contrapositive of the contrapositive of a statement is the statement itself. **15. a.** Mary will change the lunch menu. **b.** Samuel stays after school. **c.** The lake is not frozen. **16.** Answers vary. The region paired with the set interpretation of $p - q$ could be where p is true and q is false. The region paired with the set interpretation of $q - p$ could be where q is true but p is false. The region paired with the set interpretation of p *intersection* q could be the region where both p and q are true. Finally the region paired with the set interpretation of the intersection of the complements of p and q could represent the region where both are false. All cases are covered. **17. a.** Answers vary. For example, $\{x \mid 3 < x < 10 \text{ and } x \in N\}$ **b.** $\{15, 30, 45\}$ **18. a.** 6 **b.** 6 **19. a.** 8 **b.** 8 **c.** 12 **d.** 4 **e.** 16, 16 **20.** Answers vary. **21.** 60

Chapter 2 Review

1. Answers vary. Statement: $2 + 5 = 7$. Not a statement: He has red hair. **2.** In (i), every student made an A, B, or C on the final exam, whereas in (ii), at least one student made a C or better. **4. c.** Bach wrote some non-classical music. **5.** Converse: If someone will read a tweet, the whole world is tweeting. Inverse: If the whole world is not tweeting, no one will read a tweet. Contrapositive: If no one will read a tweet, the whole world is not tweeting.

6.

p	q	$\sim p$	$\sim q$	$\sim p \to q$	$\sim q \to p$
T	T	F	F	T	T
T	F	F	T	T	T
F	T	T	F	T	T
F	F	T	T	F	F

7. a.

p	q	$\sim q$	$p \vee \sim q$	$p \vee q$	$(p \vee \sim q) \wedge (p \vee q)$
T	T	F	T	T	T
T	F	T	T	T	T
F	T	F	F	T	F
F	F	T	T	F	F

b.

p	q	$\sim q$	$p \vee \sim q$	$(p \vee \sim q) \wedge \sim q$	$[(p \vee \sim q) \wedge \sim q] \to p$
T	T	F	T	F	T
T	F	T	T	T	T
F	T	F	F	F	T
F	F	T	T	T	F

8. a. Alfinia loves Mom and apple pie. **b.** The Washington Monument will eventually crack. **c.** Josef passed the math for elementary teachers course.

9. Answers vary. Pass → Dance; Dance → ~Sit; Sit; Conclusion: ~Pass; Valid: Transitivity and Modus Tollens   **10.** Valid: Modus Tollens.   **12.** $\varnothing$, $\{m\}$, $\{a\}$, $\{t\}$, $\{h\}$, $\{m,a\}$, $\{m,t\}$, $\{m,h\}$, $\{a,t\}$, $\{a,h\}$, $\{t,h\}$, $\{m,a,t\}$, $\{m,a,h\}$, $\{m,t,h\}$, $\{a,t,h\}$, $\{m,a,t,h\}$

14. a. 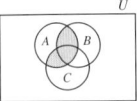   **b.**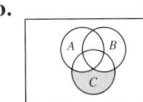

16. a. Answers will vary, for example, $t \leftrightarrow e$, $h \leftrightarrow n$, $e \leftrightarrow d$.
17. It is not true that $A \cap (B \cup C) = (A \cap B) \cup C$ for all A, B, and C, as shown in the following diagrams.

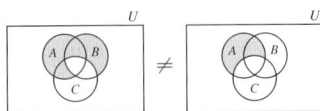

18. a. False, $U = \{1,2,3,4\}$, $A = \{1,2\}$, $B = \{1,2,3\}$, $\overline{A} = \{3,4\}$, $\overline{B} = \{4\}$, $\overline{A} \not\subseteq \overline{B}$.   **19. a.** False, $U = \{1,2,3,4\}$, $A = \{1,2,3\}$, $B = \{2,3,4\}$, $C = \{2,3\}$, $A - B = A - C$, $B \neq C$.   **b.** True   **21. a.** False. Consider the sets $\{a\}$ and $\{2\}$.   **b.** False. It is not a proper subset of itself.   **c.** False. Consider the sets $\{t,h,e\}$ and $\{e,n,d\}$. They have the same number of elements, but they are not equal.   **d.** False. This can be placed into one-to-one correspondence with the set of natural numbers.   **e.** False. The set $\{5,10,15,20,\ldots\}$ is a proper subset of the natural numbers and is equivalent to the natural numbers, since there is a one-to-one correspondence between the two sets.   **f.** False. Let $B = \{1,2,3\}$ and A be the set of natural numbers.   **h.** False. Let $A = \{1,2,3\}$ and $B = \{a,b,c\}$.   **22. a.** Because $A \cup B$ is the union of disjoint sets, $A - B$, $B - A$, and $A \cap B$, the equation is true.   **b.** True, because $A - B$ and B are disjoint as well as $B - A$ and A; also, $A \cup B = (A - B) \cup B = (B - A) \cup A$.

26.

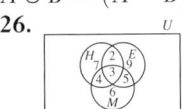

27. Answers vary.   **a.** $B \cup (C \cap A)$ **b.** $B - C$ or $B \cap \overline{C}$
29. a. Let $A = \{1,2,3,\ldots,13\}$ and $B = \{1,2,3\}$; then B is a proper subset of A. Therefore, B has fewer elements than A, so $n(B)$ is less than $n(A)$; thus, $3 < 13$.   **b.** Let $A = \{1,2,3,\ldots,12\}$ and $B = \{1,2,3,\ldots,9\}$. B is a proper subset of A, so A has more elements than B; thus $n(A)$ is greater than $n(B)$ and $12 > 9$.

Answers to Now Try This

1. a.

p	q	$\sim p$	$\sim q$	$p \vee q$	$\sim(p \vee q)$	$\sim p \wedge \sim q$
T	T	F	F	T	F	F
T	F	F	T	T	F	F
F	T	T	F	T	F	F
F	F	T	T	F	T	T

b. Answers vary, For example suppose p is the statement "I go to the movies" and q is the statement "I drive a car." De Morgan's second law of logic might be interpreted as "It is not the case

that I go to the movies or I drive a car" has the same meaning as "I do not go to the movies and I do not drive a car."   **2.** A biconditional is true when both statements have the same truth value.

p	q	$p \leftrightarrow q$
T	T	T
T	F	F
F	T	F
F	F	T

3. a. and **b.** Represent the correspondence as

$$1 \leftrightarrow A$$
$$2 \leftrightarrow B \quad \text{as} \quad \begin{matrix} 1\,2\,3\,4 \\ A\,B\,C\,D \end{matrix}$$
$$3 \leftrightarrow C$$
$$4 \leftrightarrow D$$

The 24 one-to-one correspondences are

1 2 3 4	1 2 3 4	1 2 3 4	1 2 3 4
A B C D	B A C D	C A B D	D A B C
A B D C	B A D C	C A D B	D A C B
A C B D	B C A D	C B A D	D B A C
A C D B	B C D A	C B D A	D B C A
A D B C	B D A C	C D A B	D C A B
A D C B	B D C A	C D B A	D C B A

c. We notice that $24 = 4 \cdot 3 \cdot 2 = 4 \cdot 3 \cdot 2 \cdot 1$. We also notice that we had four choices for people to swim in lane 1. After making a choice, we see that we had three choices for the swimmer in lane 2, leaving us with two choices for lane 3 and, finally, one choice for lane 4. Extrapolating from this, we conjecture that there are $5 \cdot 4 \cdot 3 \cdot 2 \cdot 1 = 120$ distinct one-to-one correspondences between a pair of five-element sets.   **5.** Suppose there is a greatest natural number β. If this is the case, then there must be a finite set with β elements in it. Now consider this finite set with one additional element inserted in it. Now there is a set with $\beta + 1$ elements and $\beta + 1$ is greater than β. This is a contradiction and there can be no greatest natural number and hence the set of natural numbers is not finite.   **6. a.** 31   **b.** $2^n - 1$, the number of subsets that a set has is 2^n as discussed in the section. Thus the number of proper subsets is 1 less.   **7.** It is always true that $A \cap (B \cap C) = (A \cap B) \cap C$. The following figure gives Venn diagrams of each side of this equation. Because the Venn diagrams result in the same set, the equation is always true.

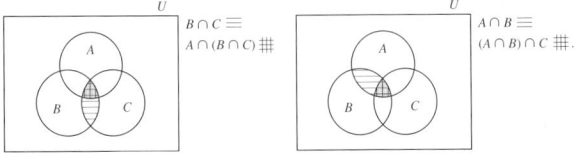

Similarly, it is always true that $A \cup (B \cup C) = (A \cup B) \cup C$. The following Venn diagrams justify this statement.

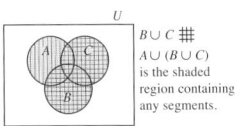
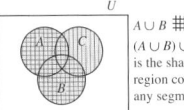

However, in general, $A - (B - C) \neq (A - B) - C$. To see this, consider the following counterexample:

$$A = \{1, 2, 3, 4, 5\}$$
$$B = \{1, 2, 3\}$$
$$C = \{3, 4\}$$

Then $A - (B - C) = A - \{1, 2\} = \{3, 4, 5\}$, but $(A - B) - C = \{4, 5\} - C = \{5\}$. Thus for the preceding choice of A, B, and C, we have that $A - (B - C) \neq (A - B) - C$.
8. Yes, see the Venn diagram for an argument of set equality. The property is the Distributive Property of Set Union over Set Intersection.

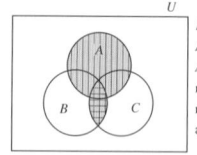 $B \cap C$ ▦
A ▥
$A \cup (B \cap C)$ is represented by regions containing a segment.

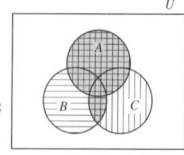 $A \cup B$ ≡
$A \cup C$ ▥
$(A \cup B) \cap (A \cup C)$ ▦.

Answer to the Preliminary Problem

The information given in the problem can be placed in the following Venn diagram where we know that 5 individuals were not invited. The rest of the numbers of elements in the regions are identified with variables.

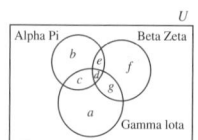

Using the problem information we have the following:
1. $c = 9 - d$
2. $g = 5 - d$
3. $e = 10 - d$
4. $a + c + d + g = 12$ or $a + 9 - d + d + 5 - d = 12$ or $a + 14 - d = 12$, which implies $a = d - 2$
5. $d + e + f + g = 21$ or $d + 10 - d + 5 - d + f = 21$ or $15 - d + f = 21$ or $f - d = 6$, which implies $f = d + 6$
6. $b + b + a + e = 20$ or $b + 9 - d + d + 10 - d = 20$ or $b + 19 - d = 20$ or $b - d = 1$, which implies $b = 1 + d$

Additionally we have $a + b + c + d + e + f + g + 5 = 37$. Combining all information into the equation 6, we have the following:

$$d - 2 + 1 + d + 9 - d + d + 10 - d + d + 6 + 5 - d + 5 = 37$$
$$d + 34 = 37$$
$$d = 3$$

Thus 3 coeds were invited to join all three groups, and $10 - 3 = 7$ were invited to join Alpha Pi and Beta Zeta but not Gamma Iota.

CHAPTER 3

Assessment 3-1A

1. a. Fifty-six million, two hundred eighty-three thousand, nine hundred fourteen. **b.** Five billion, three hundred sixty-five million, two hundred ninety-five thousand, two hundred thirty-four.
5. a. □, □ △, △ □ ○ **b.** □□, △ □ ○, □□ △ △
9. a. MCML; MCMXLVIII. **b.** ≪ ≪▾▾; ≪ ≺
c. ⌂99⌐; ⌂9∩∩∩∩∩∩∩∩∩∩∩∩IIIIIIIII **d.** ⦙⦙⦙⦙ ; ⦙⦙⦙⦙⦙

15. a. $(1, 10, 11, 100, 101, 110, 111, 1000, 1001,$ $1010, 1011, 1100, 1101, 1110, 1111)_{two}$
b. $(1, 2, 3, 10, 11, 12, 13, 20, 21, 22, 23, 30, 31, 32, 33)_{four}$
17. $2032_{four} = (2 \cdot 10^3 + 0 \cdot 10^2 + 3 \cdot 10^1 + 2 \cdot 1)_{four}$
$= 2 \cdot 4^3 + 0 \cdot 4^2 + 3 \cdot 4 + 2 \cdot 1 = 142$
22.

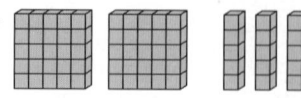

23. a. 4 quarters, 0 nickels, and 3 pennies. **b.** 73¢, in the fewest number of coins is 2 quarters, 4 nickels, and 3 pennies, so $73 = 243_{five}$. **28.** $a \cdot 6^3 + b \cdot 6^2 + c \cdot 6^1 + d \cdot 1$ **32.** 1 prize of $625, 2 prizes of $125, 1 prize of $25 **36.** Answers vary; some possibilities might be: **a.** Subtract a number with a 2 in the thousands place and a 2 in the tens place, or 2020. **b.** Subtract a number with a 5 in the tens place, or 50.

Assessment 3-1B

1. a. Two hundred fifty-three million, two hundred forty-three thousand, eight hundred ten **b.** Sixty-two billion, three hundred fifty-five million, two hundred eighty-eight thousand, four hundred thirty-two. **8. a.** $\overline{\text{MDCXXIV}}$. DC is greater than CD.
b. 30,456. The 3 in 30,456 represents 30,000 while the 3 in 3456 represents only 3000. **c.** ≺ ▾▾. The space indicates that ≺ is multiplied by 60; the ≺ without the space represents just 10. **d.** 999 represents 300. The other figure represents 211.
e. ⌣, represents $2 \cdot 20$. The other figure represents 13.

12. a. ∩∩∩∩∩∩IIIIIIII; LXXVIII **b.** 999 999 I; ⫶ **c.** ≺▾▾▾▾▾▾▾▾ ≺≺≺ ▾; ⫶
13. $47; 1 \cdot 27 + 2 \cdot 9 + 1 \cdot 2 = 47$
17. $(2 \cdot 10^3 + 0 \cdot 10^2 + 2 \cdot 10^1 + 2 \cdot 1)_{three}$
$= 2 \cdot 3^3 + 0 \cdot 3^2 + 2 \cdot 3 + 2$
$= 62$
23. 1 gross, 11 dozen, and 1 unit **24. a.** $EET9E_{twelve}$: EE_{twelve} is greater than $E0_{twelve}$. **b.** 1011011_{two}; any seven-digit number is greater than any six-digit number. **c.** 51000_{six}; 1000_{six} is greater than 0555_{six}. **36.** Answers vary.

Mathematical Connections 3-1

Reasoning

1. Answers vary. A number is an abstraction that, whereas a numeral is a written symbol such as 2 or 3 represent the abstract concept of a number. **2.** Answers vary. Place value is based on powers of the base. In the Hindu-Arabic system place value is based on powers of 10. Place value assigns a value to a digit based on its placement in a numeral. To find the value of a numeral we multiply the place value of a digit by its face value. For example in the numeral 3524, the 3 has place value thousands (10^3) and face value 3. **3.** Answers vary. Zero is a place holder in the Hindu-Arabic system. It is used to differentiate between numbers like 54 and 504. If zero were nothing, then we could eliminate it without changing our number system. **4. a.** Answers vary. The Egyptian system has no zero symbol and no place value. It is cumbersome to compute with this system and hard to work with large numbers. **b.** The Babylonian system has too few symbols to be useful. Also the use of the spacing to indicate place value makes the system unusable unless the numbers can be read in context. **c.** The Roman system is fairly complicated. It has no place value. It has no zero symbol. Large numbers are difficult to write. Computation is not easy. **5. a.** Answers vary. We name our numbers in groups of three digits. Thus the grouping in threes is natural. For example, 323,243. It helps with readability. It has been proposed with the metric system to drop the commas and simply use spaces instead. **b.** Answers vary.   **6. (a)** If each symbol in the Roman numeral has a value that is greater than or equal to the symbol to its immediate right, then the value of the numeral is found by adding the values of the symbols. For example, CXXIII has value $100 + 10 + 10 + 1 + 1 + 1 = 123$. **(b)** The only symbols whose value can be subtracted from the value of the symbol to the right are I, X, and C. The value of the symbol to be subtracted must be no less than one-tenth of the value of the symbol to its right, for example, CMIX has value $(1000 - 100) + (10 - 1) = 909$. **(c)** If a bar is placed above a number, its value is multiplied by 1000. For example, $\overline{V}$ represents 5000.

Open-Ended

7. Answers vary.   **8.** Four weights (1, 2, 4, and 8) are needed to check weights from 1 to 15; five weights (1, 2, 4, 8, and 16) are needed to check weights from 1 to 31; six weights (1, 2, 4, 8, 16, and 32) are needed to check weights 1 to 63, and so on.

Cooperative Learning

9. a. and **b.** Answers vary. Most students will probably emulate one of the systems studied in the section.

Connecting Mathematics to the Classroom

10. Answers vary. For example, years 1 to 100 were the first century, years 101 to 200 were the second century, and so on. So years 2001 to 2099 are the 21st century.   **11.** Answers vary. The technique that Allie used works with an additive system such as the Egyptian systerm, it works with smaller numbers in the Babylonian system, but it will not work in general with a system that has place value. This would be comparable to adding $41 + 41$ in the Hindu-Arabic system and getting 4411. Consider problems like $97 + 89$ and see what Allie would do. Convert the Babylonian numerals to Hindu-Arabic numerals and compare answers.   **12.** Answers vary. The two 3s have the same face value but have different place values.   **13.** A base-ten system uses place value and face value. The Roman system uses the additive, subtractive, and multiplicative properties and does not use place value.   **14.** In theory, it is correct. However, Romans reserved the bar for numbers greater than 4000. Because M is a special symbol for 1000, it is preferable to write MI for 1001 rather than $\overline{II}$. Because the Romans did not write $\overline{I}$, by definition it is not correct.

Assessment 3-2A

1. 13 and 4   **4.** Let $A = \{1, 2\}, B = \{2, 3\}$, so $A \cup B = \{1, 2, 3\}$. Then $n(A) = 2, n(B) = 2$. But $n(A) + n(B) = 4 \neq 3 = n(A \cup B)$.   **7.** Answers vary. A possible answer is 4, 6, 8, 5, 7, 9   **8.** 0, 1   **9. a.** 1, commutative property of addition **b.** 7, commutative property of addition **c.** 0, additive identity **d.** 7, associative and commutative properties of addition   **10. b.** Associative property of addition **c.** Commutative property of addition **f.** Associative property of addition **g.** Closure property of addition   **11.** No. If $k = 0$ and $a = b = 0$, then $a = b + k$ which implies $a < b$, which would imply that $0 < 0$, which is a contradiction.   **12. i.** For any whole numbers a and b, $a < b$ if, and only if, there exists a natural number k such that $b - k = a$ (or equivalently, if, and only if, $b - a$ is a natural number). **ii.** For any whole numbers a and b, $a > b$ if,

and only if, there exists a natural number k such that $a - k = b$ (or equivalently, if, and only if, $a - b$ is a natural number).

14.

8	3	4
1	5	9
6	7	2

or

8	1	6
3	5	7
4	9	2

17. a. Kent is shortest; Vera is tallest. **b.** Answers vary, as long as the players' heights increase in the order Kent, Mischa, Sally, Vera

19. a. Take-away:

Take-away
5 x's.
$8 - 5 = 3$
3 x's left

b. Missing addend: $\square + 5 = 8$ implies $\square = 3$
c. Comparison: difference is 3
d. Number line: $8 - 5 = 3$ **20.** Answers vary.

21. a. i. 1 **ii.** 1 **iii.** 1 **b.** Subtract 10 and add 1.
22. a. $5 + 6 = 11; 11 - 6 = 5; 11 - 5 = 6$
b.

$6 + 5 = 11$
$5 + 6 = 11$
$11 - 6 = 5$
$11 - 5 = 6$

24. a. $x + (y + z) = (x + y) + z$ (associative property of addition)
$= z + (x + y)$ (commutative property of addition)
b. $x + (y + z) = (y + z) + x$ (commutative property of addition)
$= y + (z + x)$ (associative property of addition)
$= y + (x + z)$ (commutative property of addition)

26. $a - (b + c)$ or $a - b - c$ **27.** Yes in both cases. A multiple of 5 plus a multiple of 5 is always a multiple of 5.

Assessment 3-2B

7. a. Answers vary. For example, $A = \{2, 5, 7, 8, 9, 10, 11, 12, 13, 14, \ldots\}$ **b.** The set must contain the rest of the whole numbers greater than 1.   **8.** All even numbers greater than or equal to 2.   **9. a.** 4, commutative property of addition **b.** 5, commutative property of addition **c.** 0, identity property of addition **d.** 4, associative property of addition   **10. c.** Commutative property of addition **d.** Associative property of addition
12. $a \geq b$ if, and only if, $a - b$ is a whole number. Alternative: $a \geq b$ if, and only if, $a - b = k$, for some whole number k.

14.

6	7	2
1	5	9
8	3	4

16. b. If the domino is horizontal and the sum of the dots in the right square plus the sum of the dots in the left square is known, and the domino is then turned 180°, the sum is the same.

17. a, b, c, e, d **19. a.** Take-away:

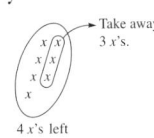

Take away
3 x's.
4 x's left

b. Missing addend: $\square + 3 = 7$ implies $\square = 4$.

c. Comparison: Difference is 4

d. Number line:

```
    7 − 3 = 4      3
  |←——————|←————|
  |←——————————————|
         7
  ┼─┼─┼─┼─┼─┼─┼─→
  0 1 2 3 4 5 6 7
```

21. a. $11 + 7 = 7 + 11 = 7 + (7 + 4) = (7 + 7) + 4 = 14 + 4 = 18$ **b.** $24 + 28 = 24 + (24 + 4) = (24 + 24) + 4 = 48 + 4 = 52$ **c.** $35 + 37 = 35 + (35 + 2) = (35 + 35) + 2 = 70 + 2 = 72$ **22. a.** $5 + 11 = 16$; $16 - 5 = 11$; $16 - 11 = 5$

b.

```
           11 + 5 = 16
      |←————11————|←—5—|
  ┼─┼─┼─┼─┼─┼─┼─┼─┼─┼─┼─┼─┼─┼─┼─┼→   11 + 5 = 16
  0 1 2 3 4 5 6 7 8 9 10111213141516
           5 + 11 = 16
      |←—5—|←————11————|
  ┼─┼─┼─┼─┼─┼─┼─┼─┼─┼─┼─┼─┼─┼─┼─┼→   5 + 11 = 16
  0 1 2 3 4 5 6 7 8 9 10111213141516
           16 − 5 = 11
      |←————————16————————|
      |←————11————|←—5—|
  ┼─┼─┼─┼─┼─┼─┼─┼─┼─┼─┼─┼─┼─┼─┼─┼→   16 − 5 = 11
  0 1 2 3 4 5 6 7 8 9 10111213141516
       16 − 11 = 5
      |←—5—|←————11————|
      |←————————16————————|
  ┼─┼─┼─┼─┼─┼─┼─┼─┼─┼─┼─┼─┼─┼─┼─┼→   16 − 11 = 5
  0 1 2 3 4 5 6 7 8 9 10111213141516
```

23. a. $a \leq b$ **b.** $a \geq 3$ and $b \geq a - 3$

24. a. $a + (b + c) = (a + b) + c$ (associative property of addition)

$\qquad\qquad = c + (a + b)$ (commutative property of addition)

b. $a + (b + c) = a + (c + b)$ (commutative property of addition)

$\qquad\qquad = (c + b) + a$ (commutative property of addition)

27. Yes, a multiple of 7 plus a multiple of 7 is always a multiple of 7.

Mathematical Connections 3-2

Reasoning

1. No; sets A (students taking algebra) and B (students taking biology) do not have to be disjoint. For example, suppose there are 11 students taking both algebra and biology. This implies the following Venn diagram:

```
   ┌─────────────────┐
   │  A        B      │
   │ (11(11)19)       │
   └─────────────────┘
```

From this Venn diagram we see that $n(A \cup B) = 41$ and there are not necessarily 52 students taking algebra or biology. **2.** The student is using the associative property to think of $9 + (1 + 6)$ as $(9 + 1) + 6$, which is $10 + 6$. She then uses place value to write this as 16. **3.** Answers vary. For example, **(i)** if $a > b$ then $a = b + k$ for some counting number k. Then $a + c = b + c + k$ and therefore $a + c > b + c$. **(ii)** If Adam has a dollars and Bob has b dollars and Adam has more money than Bob and each gets c additional dollars, Adam will still have more than Bob.
4. a. Suppose we have a blocks, and we want to take away b blocks and then take away c more blocks. This is the same as starting with a blocks, taking away c blocks, and then taking away b blocks. **b.** Suppose you have a dollars in your checking account and you spent b dollars in one grocery store and c dollars in another grocery store. Then your balance can be calculated as $a - b - c$ or by finding how much was spent on groceries altogether and subtracting that amount from a; that is, $a - (b + c)$. **c.** Suppose you have two checking accounts with a dollars in one and b dollars in the other. If you spend c dollars your balance in the combined account is $(a + b) - c$. If $b \geq c$ and you write a check of c dollars from the second account, your total balance will be $a + (b - c)$. However, the total balance will be as before. **d.** Notice that $a + b - c = (a + b) - c$ and $a - c + b = (a - c) + b$. The explanation is similar to the one given in part (c) except that the check is written now from the first account. **5.** Answers vary. It is very useful to have students learn more than one method to model addition and subtraction if the methods are to generalize to sets of numbers other than whole numbers. The missing addend approach is useful for all sets of numbers in solving subtraction problems. The method of counting to compute additions is not effective with sets of fractions or real numbers. **6.** Answers vary. For example, you need estimations or mental math to tell if a calculator is correct. You need basic facts to make estimations. **7. a.** When you put 9 and 4 next to each other, it is equal to the same length as 13. **b.** If you put 9 and 4 together on top of 4 and 9 together, they both equal 13. **c.** Take the length 9 away from 13 and the length left is equal to 4. **d.** Take the length 4 away from 13 and the length left is equal to 9. **8.** Answers vary. Subtraction and addition are inverses of each other; that is, they "undo" each other. For example, if we start with 8 objects and subtract 3, then add 3, we are right back where we started. **9.** Yes, the nonempty set $\{0\}$ is closed under subtraction since $0 - 0 = 0$. It is the only such subset.

10.

1	2	3
8	9	4
7	6	5

Explantions vary.

Open-Ended

11. Answers vary. Colored rods may be used to teach addition to students using the principle of counting on. Choose the rod representing the greater number and make a train of rods using unit rods until the second number is added. The total train represents the sum. **12.** Answers vary. For example, let $A = \{a, b\}$ and $B = \{a, b, c, d\}$. Then $4 - 2 = n(B - A) = n(\{c, d\}) = 2$. **13. a.** Answers vary. For example, on Friday 25 tickets to the play were sold. On Saturday, 8 more tickets were sold. How many tickets were sold altogether? **b.** Answers vary. For example, Tom traveled 25 mi on the first day of his trip. On the second day he traveled 8 miles. How many miles did he travel in the first two days of his trip? **c.** Answers vary. For example, the following diagram can be used:

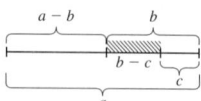

Cooperative Learning

14. a. The table shows that if you add any two single-digit whole numbers, your answer is also a whole number. **b.** The table shows that if you add any two single-digit whole numbers, then the order is not important; that is, if $a \in W$ and $b \in W$, $a + b = b + a$. Each row of answers has a corresponding column of identical answers. **c.** The first row and first column show that if you add any number to the identity, 0, you get the identical number. **d.** The properties reduce the number of facts to be remembered. For example, the 19 facts in the first row and column can be learned by just knowing that 0 is the additive identity. The commutative property also reduces the number of facts; for example, if you know $9 + 2$, then you know $2 + 9$. **15. a.** Yes, if any two elements of $\{a, b, c, d\}$ are chosen and the operation Δ is performed, the result belongs to the original set. **b.** Yes, for any elements x and y belonging to $\{a, b, c, d\}$, we have $x \Delta y = y \Delta x$. **c.** Yes, a **d.** For any elements x, y, z belonging to $\{a, b, c, d\}$, we have $x \Delta (y \Delta z) = (x \Delta y) \Delta z$. **16.** Answers vary.

Connecting Mathematics to the Classroom

17. It should be noted that 0 would be the identity for subtraction if, and only if, $0 - a = a$ and $a - 0 = a$ for all a were true which it is not. **18.** Answers vary. For example, the take-away model or the missing-addend model do not work for all types of subtraction problems. The model that is appropriate in this case is the *comparison* model. The pencils Karly has can be matched to some of the pencils that Sam has and then the answer is the number of Sam's pencils remaining. **19.** Answers vary. For example, the examples that the student is showing are all true, but producing examples that work is not proof that the claim is true in general. All that is needed is to produce one *counterexample* to show that the claim is not true. If we consider $5 - 8$, we can see that there is no whole number that satisfies this subtraction. If the set were closed under subtraction, then if any two elements were picked and one subtracted from the other, the answer would have to be a whole number. In the case of $5 - 8$, this does not happen. **20.** Answers vary. For example, John is correct in that he can get the same answer by adding up or adding down. He is using the fact that if a, b, and c are whole numbers, then $(a + b) + c = (c + b) + a$. The commutative and associative properties can be used to justify the steps given below.

$$a + b + c = (a + b) + c = c + (a + b)$$
$$= c + (b + a) = (c + b) + a$$

21. Answers vary. You can discuss the difference between 0 and *nothing* emphasizing that 0 is a number that tells "how many." Computations $2 - 1, 2 - 2$ might be addressed first and the need for a single answer to problems. A number line might be used to show that in $2 - 4$ you end up moving 2 units past 0 on the number line in the negative direction, and so there is a need for numbers to represent these points. The missing addend approach might be used. For example, $5 - 2 = x$ if, and only if, $5 = x + 2$. So $2 - 4 = x$ if and only if $2 = 4 + x$. We can see that 0 does not work as an answer. **22.** Answers vary. When you turn the numbers around you are looking at a different problem. For example, if you start out with 4 cookies and give a cookie to each of two friends, this is very different than starting out with 2 cookies and trying to give a cookie to each of 4 friends. **23.** In the first case we have $8 - (3 + 2)$, and in the second case we have $8 - (2 + 3)$. This is the commutative property of addition. The commutative property of subtraction does not hold; for example, $8 - 3 \neq 3 - 8$. **24.** You can show she in not correct by doing a physical example. Suppose Jane and Mark each have 5 pencils. After Jane gave Mark two pencils she now has 3 pencils and Mark has 7 pencils for a difference of 4 pencils. Jane is decreasing her total by 2 pencils and Mark is increasing his total by two pencils so the difference is $2 + 2 = 4$ pencils.

Review Problems

25. $5 \cdot 10^3 + 2 \cdot 10^2 + 8 \cdot 10 + 0 \cdot 1$ **26.** 1410 **27. a.** 1594 **b.** 11 **c.** 23 **28.** 10111_{twelve}

Assessment 3-3A

1. a. 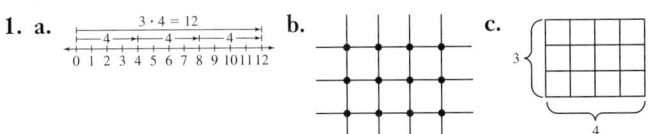 **b.** **c.**

d.
$$A = \{a, b, c\}$$
$$B = \{x, y, z, w\}$$
$$A \times B = \{(a, x), (a, y), (a, z), (a, w), (b, x), (b, y),$$
$$(b, z) (b, w), (c, x), (c, y), (c, z), (c, w)\}$$
$$n(A) = 3, n(B) = 4$$
$$n(A \times B) = 3 \cdot 4 = 12$$

2. a. $\{(a, x), (a, y), (a, z), (b, x), (b, y), (b, z)\}$
6. a. No; $2 + 3 = 5$ and 5 does not belong to the set. **b.** Yes. There will be no numbers in the set that will multiply to give a product of 5. **12. f.** Distributive property of multiplication over addition **14. a.** Distributive property of multiplication over addition **b.** $32 \cdot 12 = 32(10 + 2) = 320 + 64 = 384$
16. a. $(a + b)^2 = (a + b)(a + b) = a(a + b) + b(a + b)$
$$= a^2 + ab + ba + b^2 = a^2 + 2ab + b^2$$

b. The area of a square with sides $a + b$ can be expressed as $(a + b) \cdot (a + b)$, and also as the sum of areas of the four regions: two squares, $a \cdot a$ and $b \cdot b$, and two rectangles $a \cdot b$ and $b \cdot a$. Thus:
$$(a + b)^2 = a \cdot a + a \cdot b + b \cdot a + b \cdot b$$
$$= a^2 + 2ab + b^2.$$

17. The question is really to show that the area of the large square minus the area of the small square is the same as the area of the four rectangles. The area of the large square is $(a + b)^2$. The area of the small square is $(a - b)^2$. The difference between the two areas is the four shaded rectangles, each with area ab; the total area of the four is $4ab$. Therefore $(a + b)^2 - (a - b)^2 = 4ab$.
18. a. $51^2 = (50 + 1)(50 + 1) = 50^2 + 2 \cdot 50 \cdot 1 + 1^2$
$$= 2500 + 100 + 1 = 2601$$
b. $102^2 = (100 + 2)(100 + 2) = 100^2 + 2 \cdot 100 \cdot 2 + 2^2$
$$= 10,000 + 400 + 4 = 10,404$$

19. a. $(ab)c = c(ab)$ (commutative property of multiplication)
$$= (ca)b \text{ (associative property of multiplication)}$$
b. $(a + b)c = c(a + b)$ (commutative property of multiplication)
$$= c(b + a) \text{ (commutative property of addition)}$$
23. $72/8 = 9; 72/9 = 8; 8 \cdot 9 = 72; 9 \cdot 8 = 72$ **24.** The process always results in the original number.
Step 1: "Think of a number." Name this number x.
Step 2: $5x$
Step 3: $5x + 5$
Step 4: $\dfrac{5x + 5}{5} = x + 1$
Step 5: $x + 1 - 1 = x$
25. Answers vary, for example: **a.** There is no associative property of division; e.g., $(8 \div 4) \div 2 \neq 8 \div (4 \div 2)$. **b.** There is no distributive property of division; e.g., $8 \div (2 + 2) \neq (8 \div 2) + (8 \div 2)$. **26.** Answers vary. For example, suppose there are two bags of marbles containing a marbles in one and b marbles in the other. It is desired to divide the marbles equally among c boys. Then the number of marbles that each boy receives can be found in two different ways: **(i)** Put all the marbles in one bag. There will be $a + b$ marbles, and each boy will receive $(a + b) \div c$ marbles.

(ii) Divide the marbles in the first bag first and then the second. Each boy would receive $(a \div c) + (b \div c)$ marbles. Another way to show this is to let $a \div c = x$ and $b \div c = y$. Then $a = cx$ and $b = cy$. So $a + b = cx + cy = c(x + y)$. By the definition of division: $(x + y) = (a + b) \div c$. Substituting for x and y: $(a \div c) + (b \div c) = (a + b) \div c$.

28. Answers vary. One possibility is:

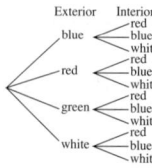

This results in $4 \cdot 3 = 12$ color schemes. **34.** Yes, for example, 3 # $2 = 3 + 2 + 4 = 9$ and 2 # $3 = 2 + 3 + 4 = 9$. In general, if, $a, b \in W$ then $a \# b = a + b + 4 = b + a + 4 = b \# a$
35. a. 625 **b.** n^2 **c.** 32

Assessment 3-3B

1. a.

$$\xleftarrow{\quad 5 \cdot 3 \quad}$$
0 1 2 3 4 5 6 7 8 9 10 11 12 13 14 15

b.

c.

d. $A = \{a, b, c, d, e\}$
$B = \{x, y, z\}$
$A \times B = \{(a, x), (a, y), (a, z), (b, x), (b, y), (b, z), (c, x),$
$(c, y), (c, z), (d, x), (d, y), (d, z), (e, x),$
$(e, y), (e, z)\}$
$n(A) = 5, n(B) = 3, n(A \times B) = 5 \cdot 3 = 15$
2. a. $A \times B = \{(a, x), (a, y), (a, z), (b, x), (b, y), (b, z),$
$(c, x), (c, y), (c, z), (d, x), (d, y), (d, z)\}$
b. 12 **c.** $4 \cdot 3 = 12$ **6. a.** No, $1 + 1 = 2$ **b.** Yes, the product of two whole numbers greater than 1 is greater than one and still a whole number. Also, any whole number times 0 is 0 which belongs to this set. **12. e.** Distributive properly of multiplication over addition **f.** Distributive property of multiplication over addition **13. a.** Commutative property of multiplication **b.** Distributive property of multiplication over addition **14. a.** Distributive property of multiplication over addition.
b. $8 \cdot 34 = 8(30 + 4) = 8 \cdot 30 + 8 \cdot 4 = 240 + 32 = 272$
15. a. $15(10 - 2) = 15 \cdot 10 - 15 \cdot 2$
$= 150 - 30 = 120$
b. $30(9 - 2) = 30 \cdot 9 - 30 \cdot 2$
$= 270 - 60 = 210$
16. The area of the shaded region is $a(b - c)$, but it can also be expressed as the area of the large rectangle minus the area of the small rectangle. **17.** The first two figures on the left illustrates a^2, viewed as the area of the large square, minus b^2, viewed as the area of the small square on the bottom right. The figure on the right illustrates how the pieces can be rearranged to form a rectangle with height $a + b$ and length $a - b$.
18. a. $19 \cdot 21 = 21 \cdot 19 = (20 + 1)(20 - 1) =$
$20^2 - 1 = 400 - 1 = 399$
b. $25 \cdot 15 = (20 + 5)(20 - 5) = 20^2 - 5^2 =$
$400 - 25 = 375$
c. $99 \cdot 101 = 101 \cdot 99 = (100 + 1)(100 - 1) =$
$100^2 - 1^2 = 10000 - 1 = 9999$
d. $101^2 - 99^2 = (101 + 99)(101 - 99) =$
$(200)(2) = 400$

19. a. $(ab)c = (ba)c$ (commutative property of multiplication
$= b(ac)$ associative property of multiplication)
b. $a(b + c) = ab + ac$ (distributive property of
multiplication over addition)
$= ac + ab$ (commutative property of addition)
20. a. Answers vary. $y(x - 1)$. **b.** $(x + 1)(y - 1)$
c. $ab^2(ab - 1)$ **23.** $30/6 = 5$; $30/5 = 6$; $5 \cdot 6 = 30$;
$6 \cdot 5 = 30$ **24. (a)** The original number is returned. **(b)** Yes,
$x \to 2x \to 2x + 2 \to x + 1 \to x$. **25.** Answers vary, for
example: **a.** There is no commutative property in division;
e.g., $(8 \div 4) \neq (4 \div 8)$. **b.** There is no commutative
property in subtraction; e.g., $8 - 4 \neq 4 - 8$. **26.** Write
$(a - b) \div c = d$, where d is a whole number. This can be
written as a multiplication problem $a - b = cd$. Similarly,
$b \div c$ can be written as a multiplication problem $b = ck$.
Combining this, we have $a - b = cd \Rightarrow a = cd + b \Rightarrow a =$
$cd + ck \Rightarrow a = c(d + k) \Rightarrow a \div c = d + k$. Recall that
$b \div c = k$. So, $a \div c = d + k \Rightarrow a \div c - k = d \Rightarrow$
$a \div c - b \div c = d = (a - b) \div c$.
34. Yes, for example, 3#5 $= 0 = $5#3; 3#4 $= 0 = $4#3;
4#3 $= 0 = $3#4; 2#4 $= 1 = $4#2.

Mathematical Connections 3-3

Reasoning

1. Answers vary. For example, a number is odd if, and only if, it has the form $2k + 1$ for some whole number k. Hence the product of two odd numbers can be written as $(2k + 1)(2m + 1) =$ $2(2km + k + m) + 1$, an odd number. **2.** 0 is not the identity for multiplication because if it were, then any number times 0 must be that number. The result in every case is 0, not the number multiplied by 0. **3.** Answers vary. For example, you might think of $9 \cdot 7$ as $7 \cdot 9$ and see if that helps. You might think of $9 \cdot 7$ as $9 \cdot 6 + 9$ or $54 + 9 = 63$ or $9 \cdot 7 = 9 \cdot 5 + 9 \cdot 2 =$ $45 + 18 = 63$. Also $9 \cdot 7 = (10 - 1)7 = 70 - 7 = 63$.
4. No, this is not the case when $x = 0$. **5.** Yes, this is the case when x is either 0 or 1. **6.** Let x and y be the whole numbers. Then $x = 0$ and $y = 0$, or $x = 2$ and $y = 2$.
7. Answers vary. Division with remainder 0 and multiplication are related. Division is the inverse of multiplication and vice versa; that is, these operations "undo" each other. For example, $(15 \div 3) \cdot 3 = 15$ and $(15 \cdot 3) \div 3 = 15$. **8.** You could factor out 37 and then perform the easy addition and multiplication; $37 \cdot 52 + 37 \cdot 48 = 37(52 + 48) = 37(100) = 3700$.

Open-Ended

9. Answers vary. **10.** Answers vary. For example, a taxi driver charges \$3 for entering a cab and \$2 per minute for 6 minutes. (The prices here are unrealistic, but this is the type of problem students may suggest.)

Cooperative Learning

11. a. Answers vary. **b.** Answers vary. We know that if $a \div b = c$, then $a = bc$, where a, b, and c are whole numbers and $b \neq 0$. Therefore, to find $35 \div 5$ we look in the table and go down to the 5 row, then over to 35, and then to find the other factor we go up to 7. Therefore, $35 \div 5 = 7$. **c.** The only way for a product of two numbers to be odd is if the two factors are odd. If the odd number is not in the first row nor in the first column, the eight products surrounding it all involve an even factor and hence are even. If the odd number is in the first row or first column the reasoning is similar.   **12. a.** Yes **b.** 18 and 19 **c.** Even **d.** Some reach 1, but it is not known if it terminates for all numbers.

Connecting Mathematics to the Classroom

13. The argument is not valid. By definition of division, $0 \div 0 = x$ if, and only if, $0 = 0 \cdot x$ has a unique solution. But the last equation is true for all whole numbers x. Because the equation has no unique solution, $0 \div 0$ is not meaningful.   **14.** You could encourage Sue to substitute numbers for a and b to see if her claim is true. For example, if $a = 2$ and $b = 4$, then $3(2 \cdot 4) = 3 \cdot 8 = 24$ and $(3 \cdot 2)(3 \cdot 4) = 6 \cdot 12 = 72$. Therefore, we have a counterexample to show Sue's claim is false. At this point the correct associative and distributive properties could be demonstrated.   **15.** This is true as long as $b \neq 0$. By definition of division, $(ab) \div b = x$ if, and only if, $ab = xb$ has a unique solution. If $b \neq 0$, the unique solution is a.   **16.** Since $1 \div a$ is not defined in the set of whole numbers, $1 \div a \neq a$ and therefore 1 is not the identity for division.   **17.** Have Amy consider whether the sets $\varnothing$, $\{0\}$, $\{1\}$, $\{0, 1\}$ are closed under multiplication.   **18.** By the distributive property of multiplication over addition $a(b + c) = ab + ac \neq a + bc$. A counterexample could be used, for example, $3 + 9 \cdot 7 = 3 + 63 = 66$ and $3(9 + 7) = 3 \cdot 16 = 48$.

Review Problems

19. Answers vary; an example would be $\{2, 6, 10, 14, \ldots\}$.
20. No. For example, $5 - 2 \neq 2 - 5$.   **21.** In base two there are only two digits, 0 and 1. The base-ten number 2 is represented by 10_{two}.   **22.** 10000_{three}

Assessment 3-4A

2.

3. a.
$$\begin{array}{r} 7\,\boxed{6}\,\boxed{2} \\ +\ 8\,\boxed{5}\,\boxed{3} \\ \hline 1\ 6\ 1\ 5 \end{array}$$

b.
$$\begin{array}{r} \boxed{2}\,6\,\boxed{7} \\ +\ \boxed{3}\,5\,\boxed{8} \\ \hline 6\ 2\ 5 \end{array}$$

4.
$$\begin{array}{r} \boxed{3}\,\boxed{4}\,\boxed{2}\,\boxed{8} \\ +\ \boxed{5}\,\boxed{6}\,\boxed{3}\,\boxed{1} \\ \hline 9\ 0\ 5\ 9 \end{array}$$

5. b.
$$\begin{array}{r} 321 \\ -\ 38 \end{array} \Rightarrow \begin{array}{r} 321 + 2 \\ -(38 + 2) \end{array} \Rightarrow \begin{array}{r} 323 \\ -\ 40 \end{array}$$
$$\Rightarrow \begin{array}{r} 323 + 60 \\ -(40 + 60) \end{array} \Rightarrow \begin{array}{r} 383 \\ -\ 100 \\ \hline 283 \end{array}$$

6. a. i.
$$\begin{array}{r} 6\ 8\ 7 \\ +\ 5\ 4\ 9 \\ \hline 1\ 6 \\ 1\ 2 \\ 1\ 1 \\ \hline 1\ 2\ 3\ 6 \end{array}$$

ii.
$$\begin{array}{r} 3\ 5\ 9 \\ +\ 6\ 7\ 3 \\ \hline 1\ 2 \\ 1\ 2 \\ 9 \\ \hline 1\ 0\ 3\ 2 \end{array}$$

b. The algorithm works because the placement of partial sums under their addends accounts for place value.   **7.** Answers vary; some possibilities are: **a.** $8 + 5 = 13$ and 13 was written with no regrouping, $2 + 7 = 9$ and 9 was simply placed in front of the 13.   **b.** $8 + 5 = 13$, but instead of writing 3 and regrouping with the 1, the 1 was written, and the 3 was regrouped.
c. Only the absolute difference in the units $(9 - 5 = 4)$, tens $(5 - 0 = 5)$, and the hundreds $(3 - 2 = 1)$ was recorded, without taking into account the signs of the numbers.   **d.** Three hundreds was regrouped as 2 hundreds and 10 tens, but 10 tens was not regrouped as $9 \cdot 10 + 15$ in order to obtain $15 - 9 = 6$ in the ones place.   **8.** By dinner time Tom had consumed $90 + 120 + 119 + 185 + 110 + 570 = 1194$ calories. Subtracting 1194 from 1500 gives $1500 - 1194 = 306$. Tom may have fish or salad, but not both. (He may have tea with either.)
9. Step 1 $\rightarrow$ Expanded form;
Step 2 $\rightarrow$ Commutative and associative properties of addition;
Step 3 $\rightarrow$ Distributive property of multiplication over addition;
Step 4 $\rightarrow$ Closure property of addition, one digit addition facts;
Step 5 $\rightarrow$ Expanded form condensed.
10. a.
$$\begin{aligned} 66 + 23 &= (6 \cdot 10 + 6) + (2 \cdot 10 + 3) \\ &= (6 \cdot 10 + 2 \cdot 10) + (6 + 3) \\ &= (6 + 2) \cdot 10 + (6 + 3) \\ &= 8 \cdot 10 + 9 \\ &= 89 \end{aligned}$$
b.
$$\begin{aligned} 124 + 235 &= (1 \cdot 100 + 2 \cdot 10 + 4) \\ &\quad + (2 \cdot 100 + 3 \cdot 10 + 5) \\ &= (1 \cdot 100 + 2 \cdot 100) \\ &\quad + (2 \cdot 10 + 3 \cdot 10) + (4 + 5) \\ &= (1 + 2) \cdot 100 + (2 + 3) \cdot 10 \\ &\quad + (4 + 5) \\ &= 3 \cdot 100 + 5 \cdot 10 + 9 \\ &= 359 \end{aligned}$$

11. a.
$$\begin{array}{r} 4\ 3\ 5\ 8 \\ +\ 3\ 8\ 6\ 4 \\ \hline 8\ 2\ 2\ 2 \end{array}$$

b.
$$\begin{array}{r} 4\ 9\ 2\ 3 \\ +\ 9\ 8\ 9\ 7 \\ \hline 1\ 4\ 8\ 2\ 0 \end{array}$$

13.

+	0	1	2	3	4	5	6	7
0	0	1	2	3	4	5	6	7
1	1	2	3	4	5	6	7	10
2	2	3	4	5	6	7	10	11
3	3	4	5	6	7	10	11	12
4	4	5	6	7	10	11	12	13
5	5	6	7	10	11	12	13	14
6	6	7	10	11	12	13	14	15
7	7	10	11	12	13	14	15	16

a. 474_{eight}

b. 667_{eight}

16. a.
$$\begin{array}{r} 4\ 3\ 2 \\ 9\ 7\ 6 \\ +\ 1\ 4\ 1\ 8 \\ \hline 2\ 8\ 2\ 6 \end{array}$$

b.
$$\begin{array}{r} 3\ 3\ 2 \ _{\text{five}} \\ 1\ 3\ 0 \ _{\text{five}} \\ 2\ 2 \ _{\text{five}} \\ 4\ 3\ 0 \ _{\text{five}} \\ 2\ 3 \ _{\text{five}} \\ +\ 1\ 2\ 0 \ _{\text{five}} \\ \hline 3\ 1\ 0 \ _{\text{five}} \end{array}$$

17. There is no numeral 5 in base five; $2_{\text{five}} + 3_{\text{five}} = 10_{\text{five}}$; $22_{\text{five}} + 33_{\text{five}} = 110_{\text{five}}$.

20. a.

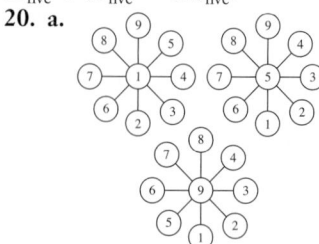

21. a. $93 + 39 = 132; 132 + 231 = 363$, which is a palindrome.
b. $588 + 885 = 1473; 1473 + 3741 = 5214; 5214 + 4125 = 9339$, which is a palindrome. **c.** $2003 + 3002 = 5005$, which is a palindrome.

23. a. Answers vary. Possibilities include compatible numbers.

$$
\begin{array}{r}
475 \longrightarrow 1000 \\
49 \diagdown \\
+ 525 \diagup \quad + 49 \\
\hline
1049
\end{array}
$$

b. Answers vary. Possibilities include breaking up and bridging.

$$
\begin{aligned}
375 - 76 &= 375 - 75 - 1 \\
&= 300 - 1 = 299
\end{aligned}
$$

c. Answers vary. Possibilities include compatible numbers.

$$
\begin{array}{r}
230 \longrightarrow 300 \\
60 \diagdown 60 \\
70 \\
44 \longrightarrow 50 \\
+ 6 \diagup + \\
\hline
410
\end{array}
$$

24. a. $567 + 30 = 597; 597 + 8 = 605$
b. $418 + 200 = 618; 618 + 10 = 628$; $628 + 5 = 633$

25. Answers vary.
 a. $85 - 49 \Rightarrow (85 + 1) - (49 + 1) = 86 - 50 = 36$
 b. $87 + 33 \Rightarrow (87 + 3) + (33 - 3) = 90 + 30 = 120$
 c. $143 - 97 = (143 + 3) - (97 + 3) = 146 - 100 = 46$
 d. $58 + 39 \Rightarrow (58 + 2) + (39 - 2) = 60 + 37 = 97$

26. a. $28 + 2 = 30; 30 + 20 = 50; 50 + 3 = 53$
   Therefore, $2 + 20 + 3 = 25$ is the difference.
 b. $47 + 3 = 50; 50 + 10 = 60; 60 + 3 = 63$
   Therefore, $3 + 10 + 3 = 16$ is the difference.

28. Answers vary. **c.** $2000 + 3000 + 6000 + 1000 = 12,000$

29. a. $2 + 3 + 5 + 0 = 10 \Rightarrow 10,000$
   $10,000 + 2200 \,(\text{adjust}) = 12,200$
 b. $2 + 4 + 9 + 3 + 4 = 22 \Rightarrow 2200$
   $2200 + 290 \,(\text{adjust}) = 2490$

30. a. (i) No. The numbers are not clustered. **(ii)** Yes. The numbers are clustered around 500. **b.** Estimates may vary. **31. a.** The range is $100 + 600 = 700$ to $200 + 700 = 900$. Then $700 < (145 + 678) < 900$. **b.** The range is $200 + 0 = 200$ to $300 + 100 = 400$. Then $200 < (278 + 36) < 400$.

32. Answers vary; e.g., $3300 - 100 - 300 - 400 - 500 = 2000$.
33. a. False. **b.** False. **c.** False. **d.** True. **34.** Answers vary. The clustering strategy yields $6 \cdot (\text{about } 70,000) \approx 420,000$ in attendance.

Assessment 3-4B

1. a.
$$
\begin{array}{r}
3\,8\,3 \\
-1\,5\,9 \\
\hline
2\,2\,4
\end{array}
$$
b.
$$
\begin{array}{r}
1\,3\,2\,9\,6 \\
-8\,3\,0\,9 \\
\hline
4\,9\,8\,7
\end{array}
$$

2. Base-ten blocks:

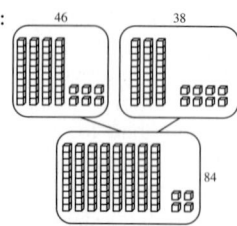

3. a.
$$
\begin{array}{r}
\boxed{8}\,\boxed{7}\,\boxed{6} \\
-\boxed{2}\,\boxed{3}\,\boxed{5} \\
\hline
6\ 4\ 1
\end{array}
$$
b.
$$
\begin{array}{r}
\boxed{6}\,\boxed{2}\,\boxed{3} \\
-\boxed{5}\,\boxed{8}\,\boxed{7} \\
\hline
3\ 6
\end{array}
$$

4.
$$
\begin{array}{r}
5\,3\,8\,4 \\
+\ 6\,3\,4\,5 \\
\hline
1\,1\,7\,2\,9
\end{array}
$$

5. a. $86 \Rightarrow 86 + 2 \Rightarrow 88$
$\quad -38 \quad -(38 + 2) \quad -40$
$\quad\quad\quad\quad\quad\quad\quad\quad\quad\quad\quad 48$

b. $582 \Rightarrow 582 + 6 \Rightarrow 588$
$\quad -44 \quad -(44 + 6) \quad -50$
$\quad\quad\quad\quad\quad\quad\quad\quad\quad\quad\quad 538$

6. a.
$$
\begin{array}{r}
9\,8\,7 \\
+\,3\,5\,6 \\
\hline
1\ 3 \\
1\ 3 \\
1\ 2 \\
\hline
1\ 3\ 4\ 3
\end{array}
$$
b.
$$
\begin{array}{r}
4\,1\,5 \\
+\,7\,9 \\
\hline
1\ 4 \\
8 \\
4 \\
\hline
4\ 9\ 4
\end{array}
$$

7. Answers vary, for example: **a.** A tens digit was not regrouped as 1 ten when the sum of the units digits was more than 9. **b.** Partial sums are not in the correct place value position. **c.** The units minuend is subtracted from the units subtrahend. **d.** One tens value should have been traded from the 5 in the minuend's ten position. **8.** 1 hour 34 minutes 15 seconds cooking time. He must start at 2:25:45 P.M.

9. Step 1 → Expanded form;
   Step 2 → Commutative and associative properties of addition;
   Step 3 → Distributive property of multiplication over addition;
   Step 4 → Closure property of addition, one digit addition facts;
   Step 5 → Expanded form condensed.

10. a.
$$
\begin{aligned}
46 + 32 &= (4 \cdot 10 + 6) + (3 \cdot 10 + 2) \\
&= (4 \cdot 10 + 3 \cdot 10) + (6 + 2) \\
&= (4 + 3) \cdot 10 + (6 + 2) \\
&= 7 \cdot 10 + 8 \\
&= 78
\end{aligned}
$$
b.
$$
\begin{aligned}
3214 + 783 &= (3 \cdot 10^3 + 2 \cdot 10^2 + 1 \cdot 10 + 4) \\
&\quad + (7 \cdot 10^2 + 8 \cdot 10 + 3) \\
&= (3 \cdot 10^3) + (2 + 7) \cdot 10^2 \\
&\quad + (1 + 8) \cdot 10 + (4 + 3) \\
&= 3 \cdot 10^3 + 9 \cdot 10^2 + 9 \cdot 10 + 7 \\
&= 3997
\end{aligned}
$$

11. a.
$$
\begin{array}{r}
2\ 3\ 4\ 5 \\
+\ 8\ 8\ 8\ 8 \\
\hline
\cancel{1}\ \cancel{1}\ \cancel{1}\ \cancel{1} \\
1\ 1\ 2\ 3\ 3
\end{array}
$$
b.
$$
\begin{array}{r}
8\ 7\ 1\ 3 \\
+\ 4\ 2\ 1\ 4 \\
\hline
\cancel{1}\ \cancel{1}\ \cancel{1}\ \cancel{1} \\
1\ 2\ 9\ 2\ 7
\end{array}
$$

13.

+	0	1	2	3	4	5
0	0	1	2	3	4	5
1	1	2	3	4	5	10
2	2	3	4	5	10	11
3	3	4	5	10	11	12
4	4	5	10	11	12	13
5	5	10	11	12	13	14

a. 43_{six} **b.** 154_{six}

16. a.

$$\begin{array}{r} 5\ \overset{1}{3}\ \overset{2}{7} \\ 3\ 1\ \cancel{8}_5 \\ +\ ^{1}2\ \cancel{3}_2\ \cancel{4}_0\ \cancel{5}_0 \\ \hline 3\ 2\ 0\ 0 \end{array}$$

b.

$$\begin{array}{r} ^{2}\cancel{4}_0\ 1_{\ six} \\ 3\ 2_{\ six} \\ 2\ 2_{\ six} \\ \cancel{4}_3\ \cancel{3}_2\ _{six} \\ 2\ 2_{\ six} \\ +\ \cancel{5}_4\ \cancel{4}_2\ _{six} \\ \hline 3\ 4\ 2_{\ six} \end{array}$$

17. There is no numeral 6 in base six. $23_{six} + 43_{six} = 110_{six}$.

20. a.

23. Step 1 → Associative property of addition;
Step 2 → Commutative property of addition;
Step 3 → Associative property of addition;
Step 4 → Closure property of whole-number addition.

24. a. $997 - 30 = 967; 967 - 2 = 965$ **b.** $560 + 100 = 660;$
$660 + 30 = 690; 690 + 6 = 696$

25. Answers vary.
  a. $75 - 38 \Rightarrow (75 + 2) - (38 + 2) = 77 - 40 = 37$
  b. $57 + 35 \Rightarrow (57 + 3) + (35 - 3) = 60 + 32 = 92$
  c. $137 - 29 \Rightarrow (137 + 1) - (29 + 1) = 138 - 30 = 108$
  d. $78 + 49 \Rightarrow (78 + 2) + (49 - 2) = 80 + 47 = 127$

26. a. $63 + 7 = 70; 70 + 4 = 74$
    Therefore, $7 + 4 = 11$ is the difference.
  b. $57 + 3 = 60; 60 + 10 = 70; 70 + 3 = 73$
    Therefore, $3 + 10 + 3 = 16$ is the difference.

29. a. $2 + 5 + 4 + 0 = 11 \Rightarrow 11,000$
    $11,000 + 1700 \text{ (adjust)} = 12,700$
  b. $3 + 5 + 6 + 2 = 16 \Rightarrow 1600$
    $1600 + 200 \text{ (adjust)} = 1800$

30. a. (i) No, the numbers are not clustered. **(ii)** Yes, the numbers are clustered around 2000, so $5 \cdot 2,000 = 10,000$. **b.** Estimates vary. **31.** Estimates may vary: **a.** The range is $100 + 700 = 800$ to $200 + 800 = 1000$. Then $800 < (123 + 780) < 1000$. **b.** The range is $400 + 200 = 600$ to $500 + 300 = 800$. Then $600 < (482 + 246) < 800$. **32.** Answers vary. For example, $65 + 45$ is about 100 and $190 + 212$ is about 400, so $100 + 400 + 420 = 920$. Then 1237 is about 1220 and $1220 - 920 = 300$. Therefore an estimate is about 300.

33. a. Yes. Rounding, Josh plans to write checks for about $40, $30, $60, and $250, or about $380. Since the check amounts were rounded up, he will have enough. **b.** Yes, $981 + $1140 is greater than $900 + $1100 = $2000. **c.** Alberto. He received 10 more votes than Juan from the first district, but only 1 less from the second.

34. Answers vary. Possibilities include:

Rounding	71,000
	65,000
	68,000
	73,000
	85,000
+	70,000
	432,000

Trading off
Observe that the high attendance on Friday can be distributed among the other day's attendance for approximately 72,000 visitors per day. $72,000 \times 6 = 432,000$.

Mathematical Connections 3-4

Reasoning

1. Answers vary. This approach emphasizes the meaning of place value of the digits and may be easier for young children than the standard algorithm. It can also serve as a transition to the standard algorithm.   **2.** Answers vary. As in problem 1, this approach may serve as a transition from a concrete base-ten blocks approach to the standard algorithm.   **3.** Answers vary. For example, the "scratch marks" represent the normal "carries" and is just a way to keep track of them.   **4. a.** You first subtract 200, leaving 385. Then subtract 100, leaving 285. At this point, we have subtracted $100 - 77 = 23$ too much, so we add $23 + 285$ to obtain 308.
4. b. $787 - 398 = 787 - 300 - 98$
$\qquad\qquad = 487 - 98$
$\qquad\qquad = 487 - 100 + 2$
$\qquad\qquad = 387 + 2$
$\qquad\qquad = 389$

5. Answers vary. The terms *regroup* and *trade* match more closely the physical actions done with manipulatives.   **6.** Answers vary. The front-end estimation is almost always less than the exact sum because each of the estimates is usually less than the actual values being added. The only case where this is not true is when each of the front-end numbers that is used is followed by zeroes. In this case, the estimate would equal the exact sum.   **7.** Answers vary. For example, students might suggest that mental computation mathematics and estimation are necessary every day in order to determine quickly whether their bills at various businesses are being computed correctly. Mental math and estimation help students to know whether the answers that appear on the calculator are reasonable. The *Common Core Standards* makes several points about the importance of mental math and estimation.   **8.** The estimate is always too high. If we increase x by an amount p and decrease y by an amount q, then the estimate is $(x + p) - (y - q)$. This can be rewritten as $(x - y) + (p + q)$. This shows that the estimate is always $(p + q)$ greater than the difference $(x - y)$.

Open-Ended

9. Students are encouraged to seek mathematics education articles to answer this question.   **10.** Answers vary. For example, an estimate is sufficient, when you are determining the amount of a tip for a waiter in a restaurant.   **11.** Answers vary. For example, **a.** an estimate for $230 + 520 + 640 + 170 + 160$ using front-end estimation is $1500 + 200$ (adjustment) $= 1700$. This is the same result as the one obtained by rounding and adding. **b.** An estimate for $210 + 520 + 640 + 130 + 100$ is 1600 using front-end estimation and 1500 using rounding.

Cooperative Learning

12. Answers vary. For example, the topic of constructivism might be discussed along with whether a student will understand and remember an algorithm that he or she has developed. There is also merit in finally developing an algorithm that is efficient; students will welcome it more after they have struggled developing their own. Some discussion might involve research that claims that providing opportunities for students to develop, use, and discuss invented algorithms helps to enhance number and operation sense. Other discussions might include the argument that exposing students to various algorithms only confuses them and students only need the standard algorithms. There are excellent articles on this topic in NCTM's 1998 *Yearbook, The Teaching and Learning of Algorithms in School Mathematics.*   **13.** Answers vary.   **14.** Play the game.

Connecting Mathematics to the Classroom

15. Answers vary. For example, you could talk about how adding 1 and subtracting 1 has the effect of adding 0 to the problem, which produces an equivalent problem. The reason for changing the original problem to the new problem is that the numbers are easier to compute. You could tell her that her technique works well and discuss how it works.   **16.** Answers vary. For example, you might ask her to explain her algorithm with different problems, making sure to choose computations where regrouping is necessary. She should understand that what she is really doing is the following: $97 - 28 = (90 + 7) - (20 + 8) = (90 - 20) + (7 - 8) = 70 + (-1) = 69$.
17. Answers vary. Joe is wrong. The teacher could ask Joe to perform the computation with base-ten blocks.   **18.** Answers vary. We could point out that Jill's $4 - 2$ is actually $400 - 200 = 200$, and $200 + 3 = 203$ not 23.   **19.** Betsy is confused on what you should add to check a subtraction. She should try smaller numbers to get a feeling for what needs to be done, for example, $9 - 5 = 4$. To check we add $4 + 5$ to see that we get back to 9. Number lines or colored rods could be used to show that $9 - 5 = 4$ and that $4 + 5$ gets her back to the length of 9.   **20.** Even though the answer is correct, the use of the equal sign is not correct, and this should not be allowed. The student wrote $7 + 2 = 9 + 3$, which is obviously incorrect even though the student knew that what he wanted to do was add 3 to the sum of $7 + 2$. The correct use of the equal sign must be emphasized.   **21.** The first thing Richie should do in rounding is to determine between which two consecutive tens the number lies. In this case they are 2560 and 2570. Next he should determine to which number 2568 is closer. In this case 2568 is closer to 2570, and so 2570 is the proper rounding. It should be pointed out that Richie's answer of 2578 is not between 2560 and 2570.   **22.** When rounding to the nearest hundred Ashley should determine between which two consecutive hundreds the

number lies. In this case they are 300 and 400. Because 345 is closer to 300, the proper rounding is to 300. She rounded to tens first and then to hundreds.   **23.** In this case one thousand is exchanged for 10 hundreds, leaving 4 thousands. Then one hundred is exchanged for 10 tens, leaving 9 hundreds. Then one hundred is exchanged for 10 tens, leaving 9 hundreds. Then one ten is exchanged for 10 ones, leaving 9 tens and a total of 14 ones. With these exchanges Pauli can perform the indicated subtraction.   **24.** Molly has a good idea and almost has it right. Point out that she needs to add 2 at the end instead of subtract 2. The reasons for this should be explained. For example,

$$
\begin{aligned}
261 - 48 &= 261 - (50 - 2) \\
&= 261 - 50 + 2 \\
&= (261 - 50) + 2 \\
&= 211 + 2 \\
&= 213.
\end{aligned}
$$

25. Answers vary. For example, the rounding strategy may not always be the easiest or fastest way to do an estimation. The clustering strategy is much faster if all the numbers are roughly grouped around a particular value. Depending upon the values of the numbers, strategies like using compatible numbers make the estimation process much easier. Front-end estimation is quick and easy and in many cases can lead to a better estimate.   **26.** By using the calculator first, she is not learning the estimation skills that are so useful in making decisions. One important use of estimation is to determine whether an answer is reasonable. For example, if the problem is $492 \cdot 63$, by estimating, the student would know that the answer should be approximately 30,000. If she gets an answer such as 17,712 $(492 \cdot 36)$ or 59,346 $(942 \cdot 63)$, she would know that there was an error in computation. Maybe she transposed two digits.

Review Problems

27. 1410   **28. a.** 1594 **b.** 11 **c.** 23   **29.** No. For example $2 + 3 = 5 \notin \{1, 2, 3\}$ **30.** For example, $(2 + 3) + 4 = 2 + (3 + 4)$ **31. a.** 10 **b.** 14 **c.** All whole numbers

Assessment 3-5A

2. a. 2^{100} is greater. $2^{80} + 2^{80} = 2^{80}(1 + 1) = 2^{80} \cdot 2 = 2^{81} < 2^{100}$
b. 2^{102} is greatest. $2^{102} = 2^2 \cdot 2^{100} > 3 \cdot 2^{100} > 4 \cdot 2^{99} = 2^{101}$
3.

$$3 \cdot 42 \rightarrow \cdots \rightarrow \cdots \rightarrow 126$$

4. a. The following partial products are obtained through the distributive property of multiplication over addition. The parenthetical computations below illustrate the corresponding base-ten-block notions from the model:

2 2	**b.** 1 5
× 1 3	× 2 1
6 (3 × 2)	5 (1 × 5)
6 0 (3 × 20)	1 0 (1 × 10)
2 0 (10 × 2)	1 0 0 (20 × 5)
2 0 0 (10 × 20)	2 0 0 (20 × 10)
2 8 6	3 1 5

Which is illustrated by:

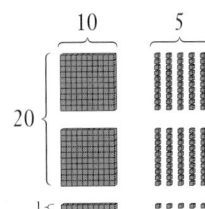

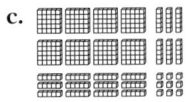**c.** To find $43_{\text{five}} \cdot 23_{\text{five}}$ count the number of flats, longs, and ones. There are $4 \cdot 2$ flats, $2 \cdot 3 + 3 \cdot 4$ longs, and $3 \cdot 3$ units. 5 units = 1 long, 5 longs = 1 flat, and 5 flats = 1 block; thus $43_{\text{five}} \cdot 23_{\text{five}} = 2$ blocks, 1 flat, 4 longs, and 4 units, or 2144_{five}.

6. a. $728 \times 94 = 68{,}432$: **b.** $306 \times 24 = 7344$:

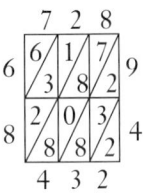 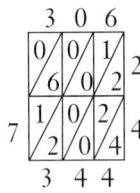

7. In millions of liters: 168,000; 40,000; 6400; 48,750; 11,500; 1500; 360 **8. a.** In base two, two is 10_{two}. Consider a three-digit number in base two: $abc_{\text{two}} \cdot 10_{\text{two}} = (a \cdot 10^2_{\text{two}} + b \cdot 10_{\text{two}} + c \cdot 1_{\text{two}}) \cdot 10_{\text{two}} = a \cdot 10^3_{\text{two}} + b \cdot 10^2_{\text{two}} + c \cdot 10_{\text{two}} + 0 \cdot 1_{\text{two}} = abc0_{\text{two}}$. So multiplying abc_{two} by 10_{two} appended a 0 in the "ones" place. **b.** In base two, 4 can be expressed as $10_{\text{two}} \cdot 10_{\text{two}}$. Thus, given what we learned in (a), multiplying by 4 in base two appends a base-two numeral by 00 by appending the original number by 0 twice. **c.** $110_{\text{two}} \cdot 11_{\text{two}} = 110_{\text{two}}(10_{\text{two}} + 1_{\text{two}})$
$= 110_{\text{two}} \cdot 10_{\text{two}} + 110_{\text{two}} \cdot 1_{\text{two}}$
$= 1100_{\text{two}} + 110_{\text{two}}$
$= 10010_{\text{two}}$

9.

	Halves		Doubles	
	→ 17	×	63	
Halve 17	8		126	Double 63
Halve 8	4		252	Double 126
Halve 4	2		504	Double 252
Halve 2	→ 1		1008	Double 504

The numbers in the doubles column paired with odd numbers in the halves column are 63 and 1008; $63 + 1008 = 17 \times 63 = 1071$.

13. a. Repeated subtraction
$$8)\overline{623}$$
$$\underline{560} \quad 70 \text{ eights}$$
$$63$$
$$\underline{56} \quad 7 \text{ eights}$$
$$7 \quad 77 \text{ R7}$$

Standard algorithm
$$77 \text{ R7}$$
$$8)\overline{623}$$
$$\underline{560}$$
$$63$$
$$\underline{56}$$
$$7$$

b. Repeated subtraction
$$36)\overline{298}$$
$$\underline{288} \quad 8 \text{ 36's}$$
$$10 \quad 8 \text{ R10}$$

Standard algorithm
$$8 \text{ R10}$$
$$36)\overline{298}$$
$$\underline{288}$$
$$10$$

c. Repeated subtraction
$$391)\overline{4001}$$
$$\underline{3910} \quad 10 \text{ 391's}$$
$$91 \quad 10 \text{ remainder } 91$$

Standard algorithm
$$10 \text{ R91}$$
$$391)\overline{4001}$$
$$\underline{3910}$$
$$91$$

16. a. Answers vary. One such is $36 \cdot 84 = 3024$ and $63 \cdot 48 = 3024$. **b.** Let the digits be $a, b, c,$ and d. Then $(10a + b) \cdot (10c + d) = (10b + a) \cdot (10d + c) \Rightarrow 100ac + 10bc + 10ad + bd = 100bd + 10bc + 10ad + ac \Rightarrow 99ac = 99bd \Rightarrow ac = bd$. So if $a \cdot c = b \cdot d$ then the products will always be the same when the digits are reversed (e.g., in part (a) above, $a \cdot c = b \cdot d \Rightarrow 3 \cdot 8 = 6 \cdot 4$). **19.** Answers vary. **a.** 5 was multiplied by 6 to obtain 30. The 3 was regrouped, then 3 was multiplied by 2 to obtain 6. The regrouping was added to obtain 9 which was recorded in the tens place. **b.** When 1 was brought down the quotient of 0 was not recorded.

20. $56 \cdot 10$
$= (5 \cdot 10 + 6) \cdot 10$ (expanded form)
$= (5 \cdot 10) \cdot 10 + 6 \cdot 10$ (distributive property of multiplication over addition)
$= 5(10 \cdot 10) + 6 \cdot 10$ (associative property of multiplication)
$= 5 \cdot 10^2 + 6 \cdot 10$ (definition of a^n)
$= 5 \cdot 10^2 + 6 \cdot 10 + 0 \cdot 1$ (additive identity and multiplication property of 0)
$= 560$ (place value)

21. c. Arithmetic, because each subsequent term is the result of adding 4 to the previous term. **23.** $323_{\text{five}} \cdot 42_{\text{five}} = 30221_{\text{five}}$:

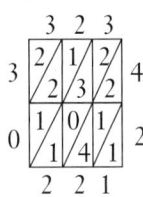

24. $32_a = 23_b \Rightarrow 3a + 2 = 2b + 3 \Rightarrow b = \frac{3a - 1}{2}$. The least value of a $(a > 1)$ for b to be whole is $a = 3 \Rightarrow a = 3$ and $b = 4$. But 23_{three} is not possible because there is no digit 3 in base three. The least possible solution is $a = 5$ and $b = 7$, or $32_{\text{five}} = 23_{\text{seven}} = 17$.

25. a.
$$768$$
$$\underline{\times \quad 8}$$
$$6104$$

b.
$$678$$
$$\underline{\times \quad 3}$$
$$2034$$

28. Estimates vary. The range is from $30 \cdot 20 = 600$ to $40 \cdot 30 = 1200$. Rounding, $38 \approx 35$ or 40 and $23 \approx 20$ or 25. Thus estimates are about $35 \cdot 20 = 700$ seats, or $40 \cdot 25 = 1000$ seats. 700 would be low (rounded down) and 1000 would be high (rounded up). **29.** Answers vary. **a.** Different; one factor is the same in each and the other is 4 times larger. **b.** Same; 22 was divided by 2 to obtain 11 while 32 was multiplied by 2 to obtain 64. The result is to multiply the original computation by $\frac{2}{2} = 1$, which does not change it. **c.** Same; 13 was multiplied by 3 and 33 was divided by 3. Thus the original computation was multiplied by 1. **30.** Answers vary. Note that in parts (b) through (d), a larger divisor produces a lower quotient when the dividend stays the same, and a larger dividend produces a higher quotient when the divisor stays the same. **a.** High; $299 \cdot 300 < 300 \cdot 300$. **b.** Low; $6001 \div 299 > 6000 \div 300$. **c.** Low; $6000 \div 299 > 6000 \div 300$. **d.** Low; $10 \cdot 99 = 990 < 999 \Rightarrow 999 \div 99 > 10$. **31.** Answers vary. One strategy to find $(n5)^2$ is to write $n(n + 1)$ and append 25 (because 5^2 is always 25); e.g., $65^2 = 6 \cdot 7$ and append 25 to give 4225 and

$75^2 = 7 \cdot 8$ and append 25 to give 5625. **32.** Answers vary; for example, $612 \cdot 73$.

Assessment 3-5B

2. a. They are the same because
$2^{20} + 2^{20} = 2^{20}(1 + 1) = 2^{20} \cdot 2 = 2^{21}$.
b. $3^{31} < 9 \cdot 3^{30} < 3 \cdot 3^{32}$ because $9 \cdot 3^{30} = 3^2 \cdot 3^{30} = 3^{32}$ and $3 \cdot 3^{32} = 3^{33}$.

3.

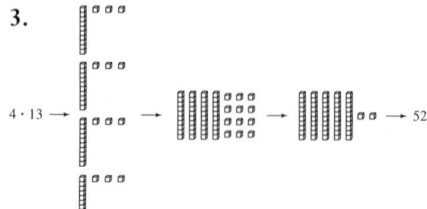

$4 \cdot 13 \rightarrow$  $\rightarrow$ 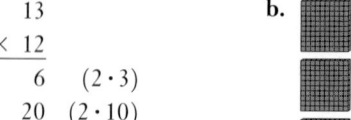 $\rightarrow 52$

4. a.

$$\begin{array}{r} 13 \\ \times\ 12 \\ \hline 6 \quad (2 \cdot 3) \\ 20 \quad (2 \cdot 10) \\ 30 \quad (10 \cdot 3) \\ 100 \quad (10 \cdot 10) \\ \hline 156 \end{array}$$

b.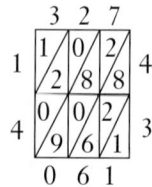

c. 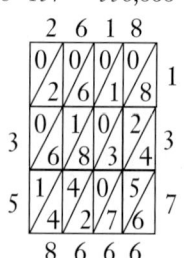 There are $2 \cdot 1$ blocks, $(2 \cdot 4 + 3 \cdot 1)$ longs, and $4 \cdot 3$ units $= 2$ blocks $+ (2$ blocks $+ 1$ long$) + (2$ longs $+ 2$ units$) = 4$ blocks $+ 3$ longs $+ 2$ units $= 432_{\text{five}}$.

6. a. $327 \cdot 43 = 14{,}061$ **b.** $2618 \cdot 137 = 358{,}666$

8. a. Use a three-digit number in base five, abc_{five}: $abc_{\text{five}} \cdot 10_{\text{five}} = (a \cdot 10^2 + b \cdot 10^1 + c \cdot 10^0)_{\text{five}} \cdot 10_{\text{five}} = (a \cdot 10^3 + b \cdot 10^2 + c \cdot 10^1)_{\text{five}} = abc0_{\text{five}}$ so multiplying by 10_{five} appended a 0 in the ones place **b.** Multiplying by 100_{five} is the same as multiplying twice by 10_{five} (i.e., $10_{\text{five}} \cdot 10_{\text{five}} = 100_{\text{five}}$). Since a zero is appended each time a number is multiplied by 10_{five}, multiplication by 100_{five} will result in annexation of two zeros (this is true for multiplying by 100 in any base, not just base-five).
c. $14_{\text{five}} \cdot 23_{\text{five}} = (10 + 4)_{\text{five}} \cdot 23_{\text{five}} = (10 \cdot 23 + 4 \cdot 23)_{\text{five}} = (230 + 202)_{\text{five}} = 432_{\text{five}}$ Observe that in base-five notation
$$4_{\text{five}} \cdot 23_{\text{five}} = [4 \cdot (2 \cdot 10 + 3)]_{\text{five}}$$
$$= (130 + 22)_{\text{five}} = 202_{\text{five}}.$$

9.

	Halves		Doubles	
	$\rightarrow$ 31	$\times$	⟨69⟩	
Halve 31	$\rightarrow$ 15		⟨138⟩	Double 69
Halve 15	$\rightarrow$ 7		⟨276⟩	Double 138
Halve 7	$\rightarrow$ 3		⟨552⟩	Double 276
Halve 3	$\rightarrow$ 1		⟨1104⟩	Double 552

$$\begin{array}{r} 69 \\ 138 \\ 276 \\ 552 \\ 1104 \\ \hline 2139 \end{array}$$
which is the product of 31×69.

13. a. Repeated subtraction

$$7)\overline{3\ 9\ 2}$$
$$\begin{array}{r} 3\ 5\ 0 \quad 50\ \text{sevens} \\ \hline 4\ 2 \\ 4\ 2 \quad \underline{6}\ \text{sevens} \\ \hline 0 \quad 56\ \text{R0} \end{array}$$

Standard algorithm
$$\begin{array}{r} 5\ 6\ \text{R0} \\ 7)\overline{3\ 9\ 2} \\ 3\ 5 \\ \hline 4\ 2 \\ 4\ 2 \\ \hline 0 \end{array}$$

b. Repeated subtraction

$$3\ 7)\overline{9\ 2\ 5}$$
$$\begin{array}{r} 7\ 4\ 0 \quad 20\ 37\text{'s} \\ \hline 1\ 8\ 5 \\ 1\ 8\ 5 \quad \underline{5}\ 37\text{'s} \\ \hline 0 \quad 25\ \text{R0} \end{array}$$

Standard algorithm
$$\begin{array}{r} 2\ 5\ \text{R0} \\ 3\ 7)\overline{9\ 2\ 5} \\ 7\ 4 \\ \hline 1\ 8\ 5 \\ 1\ 8\ 5 \\ \hline 0 \end{array}$$

c. Repeated subtraction

$$4\ 2\ 3)\overline{5\ 0\ 0\ 2}$$
$$\begin{array}{r} -\ 4\ 2\ 3\ 0 \quad 10 \quad 423\text{'s} \\ \hline 7\ 7\ 2 \\ -\ 4\ 2\ 3 \quad \underline{1} \quad 423 \\ \hline 3\ 4\ 9 \quad 11\ \text{R3}\ 4\ 9 \end{array}$$

Standard algorithm
$$\begin{array}{r} 1\ 1\ \text{R349} \\ 4\ 2\ 3)\overline{5\ 0\ 0\ 2} \\ 4\ 2\ 3 \\ \hline 7\ 7\ 2 \\ 4\ 2\ 3 \\ \hline 3\ 4\ 9 \end{array}$$

17. 8, 2, and 24 respectively **18.** $175 **19. a.** Regrouping was not used. Place value was not observed. **b.** 4 was multiplied by 6 to obtain 24. The 2 was regrouped; then 6 and 3 were added instead of multiplied and the 2 was added to obtain 11.

20.
$35 \cdot 100 = (3 \cdot 10 + 5) \cdot 100$	(expanded form)
$= (3 \cdot 10 + 5) \cdot 10^2$	(definition of a^n)
$= (3 \cdot 10) \cdot 10^2 + 5 \cdot 10^2$	(distributive property of multiplication over addition)
$= 3(10 \cdot 10^2) + 5 \cdot 10^2$	(associative property of multiplication)
$= 3 \cdot 10^3 + 5 \cdot 10^2$	($a^n \cdot a^m = a^{n+m}$)
$= 3 \cdot 10^3 + 5 \cdot 10^2 + 0 \cdot 10 + 0 \cdot 1$	(additive identity and multiplication property of 0)
$= 3500$	(place value)

21. c. This is an arithmetic sequence with $a_1 = 1$ and $d = 4$.
23. $423_{\text{five}} \cdot 23_{\text{five}} = 21334_{\text{five}}$:

25. a.

$$
\begin{array}{r}
7\ 6\ 2 \\
\times\ 8\ 3 \\
\hline
6\ 3\ 2\ 4\ 6
\end{array}
$$

b.

$$
\begin{array}{r}
3\ 7\ 8 \\
\times\ 2\ 6 \\
\hline
9\ 8\ 2\ 8
\end{array}
$$

27. Answers vary. $6 \cdot 65 = 6(60 + 5)$
$$= 6 \cdot 60 + 6 \cdot 5 = 360 + 30$$
$$= 390$$

28. Answers vary; for example $6 \cdot 3540$ is about $6 \cdot 3500 = 3(2 \cdot 3500) = 3 \cdot 7000 = 21,000$.

29. Answers vary: **a.** Different. The products are quite different. The number 22 is $\frac{1}{4}$ the number 88. **b.** Same; 93 was divided by 3 to obtain 31 and 15 was multiplied by 3 to obtain 45. **c.** Different; $20 \cdot 17 = 17 \cdot 20$; $12 < 17$ and $18 < 20$. **30. a.** High; $398 \cdot 500 < 400 \cdot 500$. **b.** Low; $8001 \div 398 > 8001 \div 400 > 8000 \div 400$. **c.** Low; $10,000 \div 999 > 10,000 \div 1000$. **d.** High; $1999 \div 201 < 2000 \div 200$. **31.** Answers vary. One strategy to mentally find $ab \cdot 99$, where ab represents the number $10a + b$, would be to write $(ab - 1)$ as the first two digits and then append the digits obtained from $100 - ab$. For example, to find $12 \cdot 99$ the first two digits are $12 - 1 = 11$ and the second two digits are $100 - 12 = 88$, or $12 \cdot 99 = 1188$. Another method is to show $ab \cdot 99$ as $ab(100 - 1) = 100ab - ab$. **32.** Answers vary, for example, $34 \cdot 82$.

Mathematical Connections 3-5

Reasoning

1. Because $345 \cdot 678 = 345 \cdot (6 \cdot 10^2 + 7 \cdot 10 + 8)$, one explanation could be as follows. Using the distributive property of multiplication over addition, first multiply 345 by 6 and the result by 10^2; then multiply 345 by 7 and the result by 10; then multiply 345 by 8. Add all the numbers previously obtained. **2.** Answers vary. If the number is ab, then the value is $10a + b$, the product is $1000a + 100b + 10a + b$, or $abab$. **3.** The result is always 4. Let the original number be x. The calculation appears as follows:

$$[(2x)3 + 24] \div 6 - x = 4$$

4. Answers vary. Some students may find one algorithm easier to understand or to use than others and therefore it will be easier for him or her to remember or to reproduce. **5.** Answers vary. NCTM suggests that the traditional algorithm for division be considered toward the end of grades 3–5 as one efficient way to calculate. Students should be able to justify the procedure. However, NCTM recommends that students consolidate and practice a small number of strategies for division and be able to use them fluently. Long division can be practiced by working on context problems and not necessarily just drill problems. If a student can demonstrate that he or she can handle division problems, there is no need to continue to practice them in excess. Division can then receive less emphasis. **6. a.** We are asking how many 43s are in 5283. To answer this we first answer how many 43s are in 5200. The answer 1 hundred is the result of regrouping five thousand, two hundred as 52 hundreds. Therefore there are one hundred 43s, so we place a 1 in the hundreds place in the quotient. **b.** We are regrouping 9 hundreds and 8 tens as 98 tens. **c.** We are regrouping 12 tens and 3 ones as 123. **d.** The R37 indicates a remainder of 37; that is, there are 122 43s in 5283 with 37 remaining. **7. a.** In this problem there are 100_{five} groups of 31_{five} in 4000_{five} with 400_{five} left over. The 4 represents the 400_{five}.

b.

$$
\begin{array}{r}
1\ 1\ 1\ \text{R}30_{\text{five}} \\
31_{\text{five}}\overline{)4\ 0\ 2\ 1_{\text{five}}} \\
-3\ 1 \\
\hline
4\ 2 \\
-3\ 1 \\
\hline
1\ 1\ 1 \\
-3\ 1 \\
\hline
3\ 0
\end{array}
$$

Open-Ended

8. Answers vary. The recommendation should be to try to complete a proof that the algorithm would work on a general set of numbers. If the student does not have the capacity to complete that task, one method of trial and error is to try a great number of cases. This is not a proof, and that should be emphasized, but it might produce a counterexample. **9.** Answers vary. She used the distributive property of multiplication over addition:
$49 \cdot 51 + 49 \cdot 49 = 49(51 + 49) = 4900$
$98 \cdot 37 + 2 \cdot 37 = (98 + 2) \cdot 37 = 3700$
$99 \cdot 37 + 37 = (99 + 1) \cdot 37 = 3700$.
Additional examples vary; for example,
$101 \cdot 37 - 37 = 101 \cdot 37 - 1 \cdot 37 = (101 - 1)37 = 3700$.

Cooperative Learning

10. Arguments vary depending upon groups. Some will argue that addition should be followed by subtraction, because they are inverses of each other. Others will argue that addition should be followed by multiplication, because multiplication is repeated addition. This would also postpone subtraction until students are more ready for it. **11. a.** Answers vary; for example, $19,875 \cdot 44$ is greater because $19,876 \cdot 43 = 19,875 \cdot 43 + 43$ and $19,875 \cdot 44 = 19,875 \cdot 43 + 19,875$ and $19,875 > 43$. **b.** Answers vary. **12. a.** A COMPUTER **b.** Answers vary. **c. (i)** When the person tells his age by listing cards$_n$ he is giving the base-two representation for his age. The number can then be determined by adding the numbers in the upper left-hand corners of the named cards. In this case, $16 + 4 + 2 = 22$. **(ii)** Card F would have 32 in the upper-left corner. Each of the numbers 1 through 63 could be written in base two, so you can tell where to place them on the cards.

Connecting Mathematics to the Classroom

13. If the repeated subtraction algorithm is done with large multiples of the divisor, the repeated subtraction can be quite efficient. However, if a student uses repeated subtraction by subtracting small multiples of the divisor, the process can be very time consuming. **14.** Evidently the student does not understand the process of long division. The repeated subtraction method should help in understanding the mistake.

$$
\begin{array}{r}
6\overline{)36} \\
-6\quad 1\ \text{six} \\
\hline
30 \\
-30\quad 5\ \text{sixes} \\
\hline
6\ \text{sixes}
\end{array}
$$

Instead of adding 1 and 5, the student wrote 15. **15.** We see on the calculator that 593 divided by 36 is $16.47\overline{2}$. This tells us there are 16 sets of 36 in 593 with some remain-

ing. To determine how many remain, we could multiply
$16 \cdot 36 = 576$ and subtract 576 from 593 to obtain a remainder of 17. Another way to think about it is to use the division algorithm; that is, $a = bq + r$. Solving for r, we have
$r = a - bq = 593 - 36 \cdot 16 = 17$.   **16.** If the number has
three digits with the units digit 0, we have $ab0 \div 10 = ab$
since $ab \cdot 10 = ab0$. This will not work if the 0 digit is not
the units digit.   **17. a.** The first equation is true because
$39 + 41 = 39 + (1 + 40) = (39 + 1) + 40 = 40 + 40$.
Similarly, $39 \cdot 41 = (40 - 1)(40 + 1) = 40^2 - 1^2$, but
$40^2 - 1 \neq 40^2$. **b.** Yes, this pattern continues because the numbers being considered are in the form $(a - 1)(a + 1)$, which is
equal to $a^2 - 1$. All the answers vary.   **18.** Howard may be used
to solving problems in the form $30 \div 5 = x$ rather $x \div 5 = 6$;
that is, he is used to seeing the blank come last. He needs more
work with the division/multiplication relationship; that is,
$x \div 5 = 6$ can be thought of as $x = 5 \cdot 6$.   **19. a.** The
student is ignoring the remainder in each division. For example,
the student is thinking of $6 \div 4$ as 1 and not $6 \div 4 = 1R2$.
b. The student is ignoring the 0 and is treating it as if it has
no value. The student should be asked to estimate the value of
$906 \div 5$, which is close to $1000 \div 5$ or 200. The student will then
see that the value cannot be 19.   **20.** Answers vary. **a.** The
student multiplied the ones $(5 \cdot 8 = 40$ or 40 ones$)$ and the
4 over the 6 represents the 4 tens from regrouping 40 as
$4 \cdot 10 + 0$. **b.** The student multiplied and added the tens
$(5 \cdot 6 \text{ tens} + 4 \text{ tens} = 34 \text{ tens})$. The 3 in the hundreds place
represents the regrouping of 34 tens as 3 hundreds, 4 tens.
21. a. The student multiplied the ones $(4_{\text{five}} \cdot 4_{\text{five}} = 31_{\text{five}}$
or 31_{five} ones$)$ and the 3 over the 3 represents the 3 fives from
the regrouping of 31_{five} as $3 \cdot 10_{\text{five}} + 1_{\text{five}}$.

Review Problems

22. For example, $3 + 0 = 0 + 3 = 0$.
23. a. $(a + b + 2)x$ **b.** $(3 + x)(a + b)$ **24.** 6979 mi
25. a. $36 = 4 \cdot 9$ **b.** $112 = 2x$ **c.** $48 = x \cdot 6$ or $48 = 6x$
d. $x = 7 \cdot 17$

Chapter 3 Review

7. a. 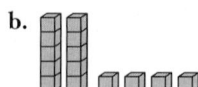 **b.**

10. Answers vary. One example would be selling pencils by units,
dozens, and gross; i.e., using base twelve.   **11.** Answers vary.
a. The Egyptian system had seven symbols. It was a tally system
and a grouping system, and it used the additive property. It did
not have a symbol for zero, which was not important inasmuch
as they did not use place value. **b.** The Babylonian system used
only two symbols. It was a place value system (base 60) and was
additive within the positions. It lacked a symbol for zero until
around 300 BCE **c.** The Roman system used seven symbols.
It was additive, subtractive, and multiplicative. It did not have a
symbol for zero. **d.** The Hindu-Arabic system uses ten symbols. It uses place value involving base ten and has a symbol
for zero.   **13. b.** $E0T018_{\text{twelve}}$ **15. a.** Distributive property
of multiplication over addition **b.** Commutative property of
addition **c.** Identity property of multiplication **d.** Distributive
property of multiplication over addition **e.** Commutative
property of multiplication **f.** Associative property of
multiplication   **16. a.** $13 = 3 + 10$. Since 10 is a natural
number, $3 < 13$. **b.** $12 = 3 + 9$. Since 3 is a natural number,

$12 > 9$.   **18. d.** $(x + 5)(3 + y)$
25. a. Let n be the original number. Then
$$\frac{2[2(n + 17) - 4] + 20}{4} - 20 =$$
$$\frac{4(n + 17) - 8 + 20}{4} - 20 =$$
$$\frac{4n + 80}{4} - 20 = n + 20 - 20 = n.$$

b. Answers vary. For example, if n is the original number:
$4(n + 18) - 7 = 4n + 65$. Then two more steps might be:

$4n + 65 - 65$ (subtract 65); $\dfrac{4n}{4}$ (divide by 4). **c.** Answers vary;
use the techniques of parts (a) and (b).

26. Scratch:

$$
\begin{array}{r}
^1 3 \ \ 1 \ 6 \\
7_1 \ 1 \ 2 \\
+ \ \ 9_1 \ 1 \\
\hline
1 \ 1 \ 1 \ 9
\end{array}
$$

Traditional:

$$
\begin{array}{r}
1 \\
3 \ 3 \ 1 \ 6 \\
7 \ 1 \ 2 \\
+ \ \ 9 \ 1 \\
\hline
1 \ 1 \ 1 \ 9
\end{array}
$$

27. Traditional:

$$
\begin{array}{r}
6 \ 1 \ 3 \\
\times \ \ 9 \ 8 \\
\hline
4 \ 9 \ 0 \ 4 \\
5 \ 5 \ 1 \ 7 \\
\hline
6 \ 0 \ 0 \ 7 \ 4
\end{array}
$$

Lattice:

$$
\begin{array}{c}
6 \quad 1 \quad 3 \\
6 \; \begin{array}{|c|c|c|} \hline 5/0 & 0/2 & 2/7 \\ \hline 4/9 & 9/7 & 7 \\ \hline \end{array} \; 9 \\
0 \; \begin{array}{|c|c|c|} \hline 4/0 & 0/2 & 2 \\ \hline 8/8 & 8/4 & 8 \\ \hline \end{array} \; 8 \\
0 \quad 7 \quad 4
\end{array}
$$

28. a. Repeated subtraction:

$$
\begin{array}{r}
9 \ 1 \ 2 \ )\overline{4 \ 8 \ 0 \ 3} \\
- \ 4 \ 5 \ 6 \ 0 \quad 5 \ 912\text{s} \\
\hline
2 \ 4 \ 3 \quad 5 \ 912\text{s} \Rightarrow 5 \ R243
\end{array}
$$

Traditional:

$$
\begin{array}{r}
5 \ R243 \\
9 \ 1 \ 2 \ )\overline{4 \ 8 \ 0 \ 3} \\
- \ 4 \ 5 \ 6 \ 0 \\
\hline
2 \ 4 \ 3
\end{array}
$$

b. Repeated subtraction:

$$
\begin{array}{r}
1 \ 1 \ )\overline{1 \ 0 \ 1 \ 1} \\
- \ 9 \ 9 \ 0 \quad 90 \ 11\text{'s} \\
\hline
2 \ 1 \\
- \ 1 \ 1 \quad 1 \ 11 \quad \Rightarrow 91 \ R10 \\
\hline
1 \ 0 \quad 91 \ 11\text{'s}
\end{array}
$$

Traditional:

$$
\begin{array}{r}
9 \ 1 \ RI0 \\
1 \ 1 \ )\overline{1 \ 0 \ 1 \ 1} \\
- \ 9 \ 9 \ 0 \\
\hline
2 \ 1 \\
- \ 1 \ 1 \\
\hline
1 \ 0
\end{array}
$$

c. Repeated subtraction:

$$
\begin{array}{r}
2 \ 3_{\text{five}} \ )\overline{3 \ 3 \ 1 \ 2_{\text{five}}} \\
- \ 2 \ 3 \ 0 \ 0 \quad (100 \ 23\text{s})_{\text{five}} \\
\hline
1 \ 0 \ 1 \ 2 \\
- \ 1 \ 0 \ 1 \ 0 \quad (20 \ 23\text{s})_{\text{five}} \\
\hline
2 \quad (120 \ 23\text{s})_{\text{five}}
\end{array}
$$

$\Rightarrow 120_{\text{five}} \ R \ 2_{\text{five}}$
Traditional:

$$
\begin{array}{r}
1 \ 2 \ 0_{\text{five}} \quad R2_{\text{five}} \\
2 \ 3_{\text{five}} \ )\overline{3 \ 3 \ 1 \ 2_{\text{five}}} \\
2 \ 3 \\
\hline
1 \ 0 \ 1 \\
1 \ 0 \ 1 \\
\hline
0 \ 2_{\text{five}}
\end{array}
$$

$\Rightarrow 120_{\text{five}} \ R \ 2_{\text{five}}$

d. Repeated subtraction:

$$
\begin{array}{r}
1 \ 1_{\text{two}} \ )\overline{1 \ 0 \ 1 \ 1_{\text{two}}} \\
1 \ 1 \ 0 \quad (10 \ 11\text{s})_{\text{two}} \\
\hline
1 \ 0 \ 1 \\
1 \ 1 \quad (1 \ 11)_{\text{two}} \\
\hline
1 \ 0_{\text{two}} \quad (11 \ 11\text{s})_{\text{two}}
\end{array}
$$

$\Rightarrow 11_{\text{two}} \ R \ 10_{\text{two}}$
Traditional:

$$
\begin{array}{r}
1 \ 1_{\text{two}} \ R10_{\text{two}} \\
1 \ 1_{\text{two}} \ )\overline{1 \ 0 \ 1 \ 1_{\text{two}}} \\
- \ 1 \ 1 \\
\hline
1 \ 0 \ 1 \\
- \ 1 \ 1 \\
\hline
1 \ 0_{\text{two}}
\end{array}
$$

$\Rightarrow 11_{\text{two}} \ R \ 10_{\text{two}}$

29. a. If $4803 \div 912 = 5$ remainder 243, then $912 \cdot 5 + 243 = 4803$.
b. If $1011 \div 11 = 91$ remainder 10, then $11 \cdot 91 + 10 = 1011$.
c. If $(3312 \div 23)_{five} = (120 \text{ remainder } 2)_{five}$, then
$(23 \cdot 120)_{five} + 2_{five} = 3312_{five}$ **d.** If $(1011 \div 11)_{two} = (11 \text{ remainder } 10)_{two}$, then $(11 \cdot 11)_{two} + 10_{two} = 1011_{two}$.
30. c. $8 \cdot 481 \cdot 73 \cdot 125 = (481 \cdot 73) \cdot 1000 = 35,113,000$
d. $374 \cdot 200 \cdot 893 \cdot 50 = (374 \cdot 893) \cdot 10,000 = 3,339,820,000$
36. $44_{five} \cdot 34_{five} = (4 \cdot 10_{five} + 4) \cdot 34_{five}$
$= 4 \cdot 34_{five} \cdot 10_{five} + 4 \cdot 34_{five}$
$= 3010_{five} + 301_{five}$
$= 3311_{five}$
37. $4_{five}\overline{)4\,3\,4}_{five}$
$\underline{-4\,0\,0}_{five}\quad (100 \cdot 4)_{five}$
$3\,4_{five}$
$\underline{-3\,1}_{five}\quad (4 \cdot 4)_{five}$
3_{five}

Thus, $434_{five} = 104_{five} \cdot 4_{five} + 3_{five}$ **38.** Answers vary. For example: **a.** $(26 + 24) + (37 - 7) = 50 + 30 = 80$
b. $(7 \cdot 9) \cdot (4 \cdot 25) = 63 \cdot 100 = 6300$ **39.** Methods vary.
For example: **a.** $63 \cdot 7 = (7 \cdot 60) + (7 \cdot 3) = 420 + 21 = 441$
(front-end multiplying) **b.** $85 - 49 = (85 + 1) - (49 + 1) = 86 - 50 = 36$ (trading off) **c.** $(18 \cdot 5) \cdot 2 = 18 \cdot (5 \cdot 2) = 18 \cdot 10 = 180$ (using compatible numbers) **d.** $2436 \div 6 = (2400 \div 6) + (36 \div 6) = 400 + 6 = 406$ (breaking up the dividend) **40.** Answers vary; for example: **(a)** Front-end: $5 + 3 + 2 + 4 + 9 = 23$; place value 2300; adjustments $40 + 100 + 60 + 0 + 100 = 300$; adjusted sum $= 2300 + 300 = 2600$. **(b)** Rounding: $500 + 400 + 300 + 400 + 1000 = 2600$. **41.** The addends cluster around 2400, so one would estimate the sum to be $4 \cdot 2400 = 9600$.
42. a. $999 \cdot 47 + 47 = 47(999 + 1) = 47 \cdot 1000 = 47,000$
b. $43 \cdot 59 + 41 \cdot 43 = 43 \cdot (59 + 41) = 43 \cdot 100 = 4300$
c. $1003 \cdot 79 - 3 \cdot 79 = 79 \cdot (1003 - 3) = 79 \cdot 1000 = 79,000$
d. $1001 \cdot 113 - 113 = 113 \cdot (1001 - 1) = 113 \cdot 1000 = 113,000$
e. $101 \cdot 35 = (100 + 1)35 = 100 \cdot 35 + 1 \cdot 35 = 3500 + 35 = 3535$ **f.** $98 \cdot 35 = (100 - 2)35 = 100 \cdot 35 - 2 \cdot 35 = 3500 - 70 = 3430$ **43. a.** $(3x^3 + 4x^2 + 7x + 8) + (5x^2 + 2x + 1) = 3x^3 + 9x^2 + 9x + 9$
c. Answers vary; for example,
$34 \cdot 10^2 = (3 \cdot 10 + 4) \cdot 10^2$
$= 3 \cdot 10^3 + 4 \cdot 10^2 + 0 \cdot 10 + 0 \cdot 1$
$= 3400;$
$(3x + 4)x^2 = 3x^3 + 4x^2$
44. Suppose $a, b \in B$. Then $a = 5j$ and $b = 5k$, where $j, k \in W$. Therefore $a + b = 5j + 5k = 5(j + k)$, where $(j + k) \in W$. Therefore $a + b \in B$ and B is closed under addition.

Answers to Now Try This

1. a. 3 blocks 12 flats 11 longs 17 units
$= 3$ blocks; 1 block 2 flats; 10 longs 1 long; 10 units 7 units
$= 4$ blocks; 2 flats; 1 flat 1 long; 1 long 7 units
$= 4$ blocks 3 flats 2 longs 7 units
$= 4327$
b. $3282 = 3 \cdot 10^3 + 2 \cdot 10^2 + 8 \cdot 10 + 2 \cdot 1$
2. a. ⚱︎𓏴𓏴𓏴𓍢𓎟𓎟999∩∩ΙΙ **b.** 203,034 **c.** Answers vary. For example, writing large numbers is very cumbersome as the system is additive and does not use place value. Performing operations

involving addition, subtraction, multiplication, and division is complicated because of the way that numbers are represented.
3. a. ▼▼▼ ≪▼▼▼▼▼ ≪▼ **b.** $2 \cdot 60^2 + 11 \cdot 60 + 1 \cdot 1 = 7861$
c. Answers vary. The Hindu-Arabic system has a symbol for 0, and this is very important in a system that uses place value. Because it uses base sixty, the Babylonian system requires the use of many symbols to write numbers such as 59.
6. For example, if the sets of elements are $\{a, b, c, d\}$ and $\{a, c, d\}$, then the union of the sets of elements is $\{a, b, c, d\}$. The union has only 4 elements while the original sets have 4 and 3, respectively. The sum of 4 and 3 is 7, not 4, the number of elements in the set union. **7.** Answers vary; for example, students are used to starting with 1 when they count, so they sometimes start with 1 on the number line. It should be stressed that we are working with whole numbers and the first whole number is 0. Next, to represent 3 on a number line an arrow (vector) of length 3 units must be used.
8. a. Closed an even number plus an even number is always even. **b.** Not closed, for example, $1 + 3 = 4$ and $4 \notin F$. **c.** Not closed, for example, $2 + 2 = 4$ and $4 \notin G$.
9. a. Use disjoint sets A and B such that $n(A) = 3$ and $n(B) = 5$. Then $n(A) + n(B) = n(A \cup B)$, $n(B) + n(A) = n(B \cup A)$. Because $A \cup B = B \cup A$, $n(A) + n(B) = n(B) + n(A)$. **b.**

c. Answers vary. **10.** Let $B \subseteq A$. If $n(A) = a$ and $n(B) = b$, then $a - b = n(A - B)$. For example, we can model the subtraction $4 - 1 = 3$ as follows: $A = \{a, b, d, e\}$ and $B = \{a\}$, $A - B = \{b, d, e\}$, $n(A) = 4, n(B) = 1$, $n(A - B) = 3$. **11.** Answers vary. **a.** **b.**

$7 + 8 = 15$ $7 + 4 = 11$
$8 + 7 = 15$ $4 + 7 = 11$
$15 - 7 = 8$ $11 - 4 = 7$
$15 - 8 = 7$ $11 - 7 = 4$

12. a. The set of whole numbers is not closed under subtraction; for example, $2 - 5$ is not a whole number. **b.** Subtraction is not associative for whole numbers; for example, $9 - (7 - 2) \neq (9 - 7) - 2$. **c.** Subtraction is not commutative for whole numbers; for example, $3 - 2 = 1$, but $2 - 3$ is not a whole number. **d.** There is no identity for whole-number subtraction; for example, $5 - 0 = 5 \neq 0 - 5$.
14. a. The set of whole numbers is not closed under division; for example, $8 \div 5$ is not a whole number. Likewise, $8 \div 2 \neq 2 \div 8$ and $(8 \div 4) \div 2 \neq 8 \div (4 \div 2)$ show it is neither commutative nor associative. **b.** 1 is not the identity for whole-number division because $n \div 1 = 1$ for all whole numbers n, but $1 \div n \neq n$ except when $n = 1$.
15. (i) The method is valid because subtracting and adding the same number is zero and does not change the original sum, i.e., $x + y - y + z = x + z$, **(ii)** Answers vary. For example,
$97 + 69 = (97 + 3) + (69 - 3)$
$= 100 + 66$
$= 166$.

16. a.

+	0_{two}	1_{two}
0_{two}	0_{two}	1_{two}
1_{two}	1_{two}	10_{two}

b. (i)

$$\begin{array}{r} 1111_{two} \\ + 111_{two} \\ \hline 10110_{two} \end{array}$$

(ii)

$$\begin{array}{r} 1101_{two} \\ - 111_{two} \\ \hline 110_{two} \end{array}$$

19. The base-ten representation of 726 is

If 1 flat is traded for 10 longs then 6 equal-sized piles can be formed. Therefore, $726 \div 6 = 121$. Answers vary for preferred technique. **20.** Answers vary. For example, **a.** To estimate $4525 \cdot 9$, we know $4525 \cdot 10 = 45,250$, and since we have only 9 sets of 4525, we can take away approximately 5000 from our estimate, and we have 40,250. **b.** To estimate $3625 \div 42$, we know the answer will be close to $3600 \div 40$, or 90.

Answer to Preliminary Problem

There are many ways to solve this problem. Consider rows and columns with only two symbols, for example,

Row 1 $2\square + \Delta = 35$
Column 2 $2\square + 2\Delta = 50$

We see an addition of one Δ adds 15 to the sum. Therefore, $\Delta = 15$. Then substitute $\Delta = 15$ in $2\square + \Delta = 35$ and we have $2\square + 15 = 35$ or $2\square = 20$ and $\square = 10$. Now $\bigcirc + 2\square = 32$ so $\bigcirc + 20 = 32$ and $\bigcirc = 12$. Therefore, $\bigcirc = 12$, $\Delta = 15$, and $\square = 10$. These answers can be checked by substitution in the original table.

CHAPTER 4

Assessment 4-1A

4. c. Yes; $8 \mid 1216$. **7. b.** $19 \mid 3800$ and $19 \mid 19$ **8. a.** True. Because $13 \mid 390,000$ and $13 \mid 26$; 13 divides the sum. **b.** True. Because $13 \mid 260,000$ and $13 \nmid 33$; 13 does not divide the sum. **c.** False. Because $17 \mid 34,000$ and $17 \nmid 15$; 17 does not divide the sum. **d.** True. Because $17 \mid 34,000$ and $17 \mid 51$; 17 divides the sum. **e.** False. Because $19 \mid 19,000$ and $19 \nmid 31$; 19 does not divide the sum. **f.** True. Because $31 \mid 93$; $31 \mid 93 \cdot 93^{10}$.
15. a. $(7 + 2 + 4 + 2 + 8 + 1) + 5$. Since the sum in the parentheses is divisible by 3, the remainder is found when 5 is divided by 3. The remainder is 2. **b.** A four-digit number in base ten can be written as $(a \cdot 999 + b \cdot 99 + c \cdot 9) + (a + b + c + d)$. Because the number in the first parentheses is divisible by 3, it leaves remainder 0 upon division by 3. So the remainder when $abcd$ is divided by 3 is the same as when $a + b + c + d$ is divided by 3. **c.** Yes, because $a \cdot 999 + b \cdot 99 + c \cdot 9$ also leaves remainder 0 upon division by 9 (see part (b)). **16.** 1, 3, 5, 9, and 15 divide n. 1 divides every number. Because $n = 45 \cdot d, d \in W$, then $n = (3 \cdot 15)d$ which implies n is divisible by 3 and 15. Also, $n = (5 \cdot 9)d$ which implies n is divisible by 5 and 9.
17. The last four digits represent a number divisible by 16.
18. a. $12,343 + 4546 + 56 = 16,945$; $4 + 1 + 2 = 7$ has a remainder of 7 when divided by 9, as does $1 + 6 + 9 + 4 + 5 = 25$. **b.** $987 + 456 + 8765 = 10,208$; $6 + 6 + 8 = 20$ has a remainder of 2 when divided by 9, as does $1 + 0 + 2 + 0 + 8 = 11$. **c.** $1003 - 46 = 957$; $4 - 1 = 3$ has a remainder of 3 when divided by 9, as does $9 + 5 + 7 = 21$.
d. $345 \cdot 56 = 19,320$; $3 \cdot 2 = 6$ has a remainder of 6 when divided

by 9, as does $1 + 9 + 3 + 2 + 0 = 15$. **e.** No. For example, $56 \div 4 = 14$; when divided by 9, $1 + 4$ does not have the same remainder as $2 \div 4$. **19. b.** Yes. Because
$$abccba = (a \cdot 10^5 + a) + (b \cdot 10^4 + b \cdot 10) + c \cdot 10^3 + c \cdot 10^2$$
$$= a \cdot 100,001 + b \cdot 10,001 + c \cdot 1100$$
$$= 11(a \cdot 9091 + b \cdot 910 + c \cdot 100)$$
20. $a \cdot 10^4 + b \cdot 10^3 + c \cdot 10^2 + d \cdot 10 + e$
$= a(9999 + 1) + b(999 + 1) + c(99 + 1) + d(9 + 1) + e$
$= (9999a + 999b + 99c + 9d) + (a + b + c + d + e)$ Because $(9999a + 999b + 99c + 9d)$ is divisible by 9, it follows that if $9 \mid (a + b + c + d + e)$, then $9 \mid (a \cdot 10^4 + b \cdot 10^3 + c \cdot 10^2 + d \cdot 10 + e)$.

Assessment 4-1B

6. a. True; 5 is a factor of $2 \cdot 3 \cdot 5 \cdot 7$. **b.** False; $5 \mid 2 \cdot 3 \cdot 5 \cdot 7$ and $5 \nmid 1$, so $5 \nmid [(2 \cdot 3 \cdot 5 \cdot 7) + 1]$. **c.** True; $6 \mid (2 \cdot 3) \cdot 2^2 \cdot 3 \cdot 17^4$ because $6 \mid (2 \cdot 3)$. **d.** True; $7 \mid 4200$ but $7 \nmid 22$ so $7 \nmid 4222$.
7. c. Because $2 \cdot 4 \cdot 6 = 2 \cdot 2^2 \cdot 2 \cdot 3 = 2^4 \cdot 6, 2^4 \mid (2 \cdot 4 \cdot 6 \cdot 8 \cdot 17^{10})$. Because $2^4 \nmid 1, 2^4 \nmid (2 \cdot 4 \cdot 6 \cdot 8 \cdot 17^{10})$. **d.** $2^4 \mid (10^4 + 6^4)$ because $2^4 \mid (2^4 \cdot 5^4)$ and $2^4 \mid (2^4 \cdot 3^4)$. **8. a.** False. Because $12 \mid 24,000$ and $12 \nmid 13$; 12 does not divide the sum. **b.** True. Because $12 \mid 24,000$ and $12 \mid 36$; 12 divides the sum. **c.** False. Because $19 \mid 38,000$ and $19 \nmid 37$; 19 does not divide the sum. **d.** True. Because $19 \mid 3,800,000$ and $19 \nmid 18$; 19 does not divide the sum. **e.** False. Because $23 \mid 23,000$ and $23 \mid 23$; 23 divides the sum. **f.** True. Because $23 \mid 46$; $23 \mid 46 \cdot 46^9$. **10. a.** No, $12 \mid 24,000$ and $12 \nmid 13$, so $12 \nmid 24,013$. **b.** Yes, $12 \mid 24,000$ and $12 \mid 36$, so $12 \mid 24,036$. **c.** Yes, $17 \mid 17,000$ and $17 \mid 34$, so $17 \mid 17,034$.
d. Yes, $3 \mid 3(2 \cdot 5 \cdot 7)$. **e.** No, $6 \mid (2 \cdot 3 \cdot 5 \cdot 7)$ and $6 \nmid 1$, so $6 \nmid (2 \cdot 3 \cdot 5 \cdot 7) + 1$. **12. a.** True **b.** False
13. b. 4 TDs with extra points and 4 FGs or 1 TD with extra points and 11 FGs **c.** 5 **14. a.** True
b. True **c.** False **d.** True **15. f.** The remainder when n is divided by 9 seems to be equal to the remainder when the sum of the digits of n is divided by 9. **16.** 1, 2, 4, 7, 14 divide n. 1 divides every number. Because $n = 28 \cdot d$, for some $d \in W$, then $n = (2 \cdot 14)d$ which implies n is divisible by 2 and 14. And, $n = (4 \cdot 7)d$ which implies n is divisible by 4 and 7.
17. A number is divisible by 25 if, and only if, the last two digits are 00, 25, 50, or 75. **18. a.** $99 + 28 = 227$; $0 + 1 = 1$ has a remainder of 1 when divided by 9, but $2 + 2 + 7 = 11$ has a remainder of 2 upon division by 9. **b.** $11,199 - 21 = 11,168$; $3 - 3 = 0$ has a remainder of 0 when divided by 9, but $1 + 1 + 1 + 6 + 8 = 17$ has a remainder of 8 upon division by 9. **c.** $99 \cdot 26 = 2575$; $0 \cdot 8 = 0$ has a remainder of 0 when divided by 9, but $2 + 5 + 7 + 5 = 19$ has a remainder of 1 upon division by 9. **19. a. i** $11 \mid [(4 + 5) - (5 + 4)]$, so $11 \mid 4554$
ii. $11 \mid [(9 + 3) - (3 + 9)]$, so $11 \mid 9339$
iii. $11 \mid [(2 + 0) - (0 + 2)]$, so $11 \mid 2002$
iv. $11 \mid [(2 + 2) - (2 + 2)]$, so $11 \mid 2222$ **20.** The proof is analogous to the proof of Theorem 4-8 for four digits. Just replace 3 by 9.

Mathematical Connections 4-1

Reasoning

1. a. We are given that n^2 is odd and must show that n is odd. Assume, to the contrary, that n is even. Then $n = 2k$, for some $k \in W$. But then $n^2 = (2k)^2 = 4k^2 = 2(2k^2)$. This means that n^2 is even, contradicting the conditions of the problem. Because the assumption that n was even led to a contradiction, n must be odd.

b. We are given that n^2 is even and must show that n is even. Assume, to the contrary, that n is odd. Then $n = 2k + 1$, for some $k \in W$. But then $n^2 = (2k + 1)^2 = 4k^2 + 4k + 1 = 2(2k^2 + 2k) + 1$. This means that n^2 is odd, contradicting the conditions of the problem. Because the assumption that n was odd led to a contradiction, n must be even. **2.** Yes; $18.95 is divisible by 5¢. **3. a.** No; in some cases the calculator rounds the answers. Try the following on an 8-digit calculator: $79,012,351 \div 2,469,136$ or $79,012,353 \div 2,469,136$. One or both will produce the answer 32. **b.** No; $d \nmid n$ because the display implies that n is not a multiple of d. **4. a.** Yes; $4 \mid 52,832$ **b.** Yes; $2 \mid 52,834$ and $2 \mid 324,514$ so $4 \mid (52,834 \cdot 324,514)$ **5. a.** No; if it is not divisible by 5, then it does not end in 0 or 5 therefore it is not divisible by 10. **b.** Yes; all odd multiples of 5 are not divisible by 10, but are divisible by 5. **6.** In the sum of the digits we can write each digit times 3 then factor out a 3, which makes the sum divisible by 3, and therefore the number is divisible by 3. For example, $777,555,222$ has a sum of the digits $7 + 7 + 7 + 5 + 5 + 5 + 2 + 2 + 2 = 3 \cdot 7 + 3 \cdot 5 + 3 \cdot 2 = 3 \cdot (7 + 5 + 2)$ and $3 \mid 3 \cdot (7 + 5 + 2)$ so $3 \mid 777,555,222$. **7.** 243; yes. Consider any number n of the form $abcabc$. Then we have the following:
$n = a \cdot 10^5 + b \cdot 10^4 + c \cdot 10^3 + a \cdot 10^2 + b \cdot 10^1 + c$
$= a \cdot (10^5 + 10^2) + b \cdot (10^4 + 10^1) + c \cdot (10^3 + 1)$
$= a \cdot (100,100) + b \cdot (10,010) + c \cdot (1001)$
$= a \cdot (1001 \cdot 100) + b \cdot (1001 \cdot 10) + c \cdot (1001 \cdot 1)$
$= (1001)(100a + 10b + c)$
$= (7 \cdot 11 \cdot 13)(100a + 10b + c)$
Therefore, if you divide by 1001, the quotient is abc.
8. 10-digit: 3,816,547,290; 9-digit: 381,654,729 **9.** 4, 6, 8 in any order ($4 + 6 + 8 = 18$ is divisible by 3 and 9 and all digits have to be even to be divisible by 2)

Open-Ended

10. a. No; there is no winning combination. **b.** Answers vary. For example, since many of these multiples of 3 sum to 99 ($33 + 66, 45 + 51 + 3$, etc.), the company could place at most 1000 cards with the number 1 on the card. This would ensure that there are at most 1000 winners. Other numbers could also be used. **11. a.** You can use counters and divide them into two groups. If no counters are left, then the number is even. If one counter is left, then the number is odd. **b.** You can arrange tiles in rows of three and if there are no tiles left over then the number is divisible by 3, but if there is a row with 1 or 2 counters then the number is not divisible by 3. **c.** Similar to (b) but use your tiles in rows of nine. If all counters fit into rows of nine, the number is divisible by 9. Each row of nine can then be divided into 3 groups of 3 tiles, showing that if $9 \mid a$, then $3 \mid a$.

Cooperative Learning

12. The sum of n consecutive numbers is divisible by n if, and only if, n is odd. **13.** Use base-ten blocks and use them similar to divisibility by 2 in the section to show divisibility by 3.

Connecting Mathematics to the Classroom

14. Use counters to show why 10 is even. When we divide 10 counters into two groups there are no counters left over. When a number is divided into two equal groups and nothing is leftover, then the number is even, so 10 is even. **15.** She is right. If each of the last two digits is divisible by 4 then the

number formed by the last two digits is divisible by 4 and hence the original number is divisible by 4. **16.** It has been shown that any four-digit number n can be written in the form $n = a \cdot 10^3 + b \cdot 10^2 + c \cdot 10 + d = (a \cdot 999 + b \cdot 99 + c \cdot 9) + (a + b + c + d)$. The test for divisibility by some number g will depend on the sum of the digits $a + b + c + d$ if, and only if, $g \mid (a \cdot 999 + b \cdot 99 + c \cdot 9)$ regardless of the values of a, b, and c. Since the only numbers greater than 1 that divide 9, 99, and 999 are 3 and 9, the test for divisibility by dividing the sum of the digits by the number works only for 3 and 9 and not for 6. **17.** It is true that a number is divisible by 21 if, and only if, it is divisible by 3 and by 7. However, the general statement is false. For example, 12 is divisible by 4 and by 6, but not by $4 \cdot 6$, or 24. One part of the statement is true, that is, "if a number is divisible by $a \cdot b$, then it is divisible by a and b." The statement "if a number is divisible by a and by b, it is divisible by ab" is true if a and b have no primes in common. This follows from the Fundamental Theorem of Arithmetic, which will be introduced in Section 4-2. **18.** You could review division into zero and show that we can divide 2 into zero. Brian might be confusing this with division by zero if he thinks we can't divide zero into two equal piles.

Assessment 4-2A

1. a.
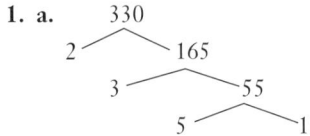

2. a. $2^3 \cdot 3^2 \cdot 7$ **b.** $3^2 \cdot 5^2 \cdot 11$ **c.** $2 \cdot 3^2 \cdot 5^4$ **8. a.** The Fundamental Theorem of Arithmetic states that n can be written as a product of primes in one and only one way. Since $2 \mid n$ and $3 \mid n$ and 2 and 3 are both prime, they must be included in the unique factorization: $2 \cdot 3 \cdot p_1 \cdot \ldots \cdot p_m = n$; $(2 \cdot 3)(p_1 \cdot p_2 \cdot \ldots \cdot p_m) = n$; therefore, $6 \mid n$. **b.** Yes. If $a \mid n$, there exists a whole number c such that $ca = n$. If $b \mid n$, there exists a whole number d such that $db = n$. Therefore $(ca)(db) = n^2 \Rightarrow (dc)(ab) = n^2 \Rightarrow ab \mid n^2$. **10.** 25 is not a prime factor. $2^3 \cdot 3^2 \cdot 5^6$ is the prime factorization. **11.** No, because $8^z = 2^{3z}$, which is its prime factorization. Because of the uniqueness of prime factorization, 2^{3z} cannot have a 5 to a non-zero power in its prime factorization. **12.** If $32n = 2^6 \cdot 3^5 \cdot 5^4 \cdot 7^3 \cdot 11^7$, then $n = 2 \cdot 3^5 \cdot 5^4 \cdot 7^3 \cdot 11^{11} = (3^4 \cdot 5^3 \cdot 7^2 \cdot 11) \cdot (2 \cdot 3 \cdot 5 \cdot 7 \cdot 11^6)$. Thus, $2 \cdot 3 \cdot 5 \cdot 7 \cdot 11^6$ is a factor of n. **13.** Yes; because $7^5 \cdot 11^3 = (7^4 \cdot 11^3) \cdot 7$, $7^4 \cdot 11^3$ is a factor $7^5 \cdot 11^3$. **14. a.** 1 by 48, 2 by 24, 3 by 16, 4 by 12 **b.** 1 by 47 **15. a.** 1, 2, 3, 5, 6, 10, 15, or 30 rows **b.** 1, 2, 4, 7, 14, or 28 rows **c.** 1 or 23 rows **d.** 1, 2, 3, 4, 5, 6, 8, 10, 12, 15, 20, 24, 30, 40, 60, or 120 rows **20.** (3, 5), (5, 7), (11, 13), (17, 19), (29, 31), (41, 43), (59, 61), (71, 73), (101, 103), (107, 109), (137, 139), (149, 151), (179, 181), (191, 193), (197, 199)

Assessment 4-2B

1. a.
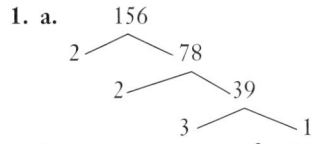

2. b. $2 \cdot 5 \cdot 7 \cdot 43$ **c.** $2 \cdot 5^2 \cdot 191$ **5. g.** Not prime **h.** Not prime **8.** If $4 \mid n$, then 2^2 is in the prime factorization of n. If $9 \mid n$, then 3^2 is in the prime factorization of n. Because 2^2 and 3^2

have no primes in common, by the Fundamental Theorem of Arithmetic, $2^2 \cdot 3^2$ must appear in the prime factorization of n. Therefore, $2^2 \cdot 3^2 \mid n$, or $36 \mid n$.   **10.** 9 is not a prime factor. $2^2 \cdot 3^4 \cdot 5^3$ is the prime factorization.   **11.** No, because 5^z has no factors of either 2 or 3.   **12.** If $2n = 2^6 \cdot 3^5 \cdot 5^4 \cdot 7^3 \cdot 11^7$, then $n = 2^5 \cdot 3^5 \cdot 5^4 \cdot 7^3 \cdot 11^6 = (2^4 \cdot 3^4 \cdot 5^3 \cdot 7^2 \cdot 11^5) \cdot (2 \cdot 3 \cdot 5 \cdot 7 \cdot 11)$. Thus, $2 \cdot 3 \cdot 5 \cdot 7 \cdot 11$ is a factor of n.   **13.** No, because no whole number times $3^2 \cdot 2^4$ will give $3^3 \cdot 2^2$ **14. a.** 1 by 24, 2 by 12, 3 by 8.   **b.** 1 array: 1 by 43.   **15. a.** 1 by 15, 3 by 5.   **b.** 1 by 24, 2 by 12, 3 by 8, 4 by 6.   **c.** 1 by 17.   **d.** 1 by 200, 2 by 100, 4 by 50, 5 by 40, 8 by 25, 10 by 20.   **19.** 11 red, 2 green, 23 blue   **20. c.** $23, 29, 31, 37, 53, 59, 71, 73, 79$ **d.** Answers vary. For example, 233.   **21. a. i.** Abundant   **ii.** Deficient   **iii.** Neither

Mathematical Connections 4-2

Reasoning

1. In any set of three consecutive numbers, there is one number that is divisible by 3 and at least one of the other two numbers is divisible by 2. Therefore, the product will be divisible by 2 and by 3 and so it is divisible by 6.   **2.** In any set of four consecutive numbers, there are one or two numbers divisible by 3, a number divisible by 4, and a number divisible by 2 but not 4. Therefore, the product of the four consecutive numbers will have 2, 4, and 3 as distinct factors and so the product is divisible by $2 \cdot 3 \cdot 4 = 24$.   **3.** The multiples of 4, 8, and 10 were crossed out with the multiples of 2. The multiples of 6 were crossed out when multiples of 2 and 3 were crossed out. The multiples of 9 were crossed out when the multiples of 3 were crossed out. All composite numbers less than 100 must have some factors less than or equal to 10 and these are all accounted for. Therefore, the remaining numbers that have not been crossed out are prime.   **4.** Let $a = 2 \cdot 3 \cdot 5 \cdot 7$ and $b = 11 \cdot 13 \cdot 17 \cdot 19$. Then each prime p less than or equal to 19 appears in the prime factorization of a or of b but not in both. If p is in the prime factorization of a, then $p \mid a$ but $p \nmid b$ and hence $p \nmid (a + b)$. A similar argument holds if p is in the prime factorization of b.   **5.** In Theorem 4-16 it states that if n is a whole number greater than 1 and not divisible by any prime p such that $p^2 \leq n$, then n is prime. The possible primes p such that $p^2 \leq 353$ are 2, 3, 5, 7, 11, 13, and 17. Because $2 \nmid 353, 3 \nmid 353, 5 \nmid 353, 7 \nmid 353, 11 \nmid 353, 13 \nmid 353$, and $17 \nmid 353$, the number 353 is prime.   **6.** Suppose n is composite and d is its least positive divisor other than 1. We need to show that d is prime. If not, then some prime less than d will divide d and hence will divide n which contradicts the fact that d is the least divisor of n.   **7. a.** When n is divided by a prime number in the list the remainder is 1.   **b.** Since $n > 1$, some prime appears in the prime factorization of n and hence it divides n.   **c.** Yes, the argument assures us that for each prime we can find a greater prime.   **8.** The students must have had the first 23 prime numbers for the numbers of tiles; that is 2, 3, 5, 7, 11, 13, 17, 19, 23, 29, 31, 37, 41, 43, 53, 59, 61, 67, 71, 73, 79, 83 tiles. Therefore, the number of tiles is the sum of the first 23 prime numbers, which is 874 tiles.   **9. a.** It has factors other than 1 and itself.   **b.** Because $(3 \cdot 4 \cdot 5 \cdot 6 \cdot 7 \cdot 8) + 2 = 2[(3 \cdot 2 \cdot 5 \cdot 6 \cdot 7 \cdot 8) + 1]$ and $2 \mid 2[(3 \cdot 2 \cdot 5 \cdot 6 \cdot 7 \cdot 8) + 1], (3 \cdot 4 \cdot 5 \cdot 6 \cdot 7 \cdot 8) + 2$ is composite.   **c.** Because $(3 \cdot 5 \cdot 7 \cdot 11 \cdot 13) + 5 = 5[(3 \cdot 1 \cdot 7 \cdot 11 \cdot 13) + 1]$ and $5 \mid 5[(3 \cdot 1 \cdot 7 \cdot 11 \cdot 13) + 1], (3 \cdot 5 \cdot 7 \cdot 11 \cdot 13) + 5$ is composite.   **d.** Because $(1 \cdot 2 \cdot 3 \cdot 4 \cdot 5 \cdot 6 \cdot 7 \cdot 8 \cdot 9 \cdot 10) + 7 = 7[(1 \cdot 2 \cdot 3 \cdot 4 \cdot 5 \cdot 6 \cdot 7 \cdot 8 \cdot 9 \cdot 10) + 1]$ and

$7 \mid 7[(1 \cdot 2 \cdot 3 \cdot 4 \cdot 5 \cdot 6 \cdot 7 \cdot 8 \cdot 9 \cdot 10) + 1]$, $10! + 7$ is composite.   **10.** 139 marbles   **11.** 3, 3, 8

Open-Ended

12. a. In the interval 0–99.   **i.** 25   **ii.** 21   **b.** The unique longest string in 100–199 is 114 through 126, of length 13.   **c. i.** 8   **ii.** 7   **d.** Answers vary.

Cooperative Learning

13. The people who won free admission and had their hats on at the end of the contest were 1st, 4th, 9th, 25th, 36th, 49th, 64th, 81st, and 100th in line. A possible strategy would be to start with a simpler problem of 50 people and making a chart to see who will win free admission.   **14.** Answers vary.

Connecting Mathematics to the Classroom

15. No. The method works for 3 and 4 because they have no common prime factors, but the method does not work for 2 and 6 because they have a common prime factor. A counterexample of 18 can be used to explain this to the students.   **16.** 25 ants can make 2 queues of 12 and have a remainder of 1, or 3 queues of 8 with a remainder of 1, or 4 queues of 6 with a remainder of 1, or 5 queues of 5 with a remainder of zero. Modeling this story with tiles can help students find the remainders and the solution.   **17.** As long as you factor to all prime factors the end result will be the same.   **18.** Bob has almost the right idea but it needs a little work. It should be pointed out that if a number is not divisible by 2 and 3, then it couldn't be divisible by 6, so there is no need to check 6. Also, if a number is not divisible by 2, then it can't be divisible by 4 or 8, so there is no need to check 4 and 8. Next, if a number is not divisible by 5, then it can't be divisible by 10, so there is no need to check 10. Thus, we have cut Bob's list to 2, 3, and 5, which are all primes. The Sieve of Eratosthenes can be used to motivate these concepts. Next, we need to explore what happens when the number to be checked is large and show that just checking 2, 3, and 5 is not adequate. For example, just checking for divisibility by 2, 3, and 5 is not enough to check whether 169 is prime. We can use the sieve to show that if we are trying to determine if a whole number n is prime, we only have to check primes p such that $p^2 \leq n$.   **19.** Not true: one counterexample is 11.   **20.** There are infinitely many primes, but there's no pattern that allows us to find the next prime so it is more complicated than knowing there are infinitely many numbers.   **21.** 1 is not prime because it does not have two distinct divisors; it only has one.

Review Problems

22. a. True   **b.** True   **c.** True   **23. a.** 2, 3, 6   **b.** 2, 3, 5, 6, 9, 10   **24.** If $15 \mid n, (3 \cdot 5) \mid n$ so $3 \mid n$.

Assessment 4-3A

1. $GCD(6, 8) = 2$ (1 red); $LCM(6, 8) = 24$ (4 dark green, 3 brown)   **2. a.** $GCD(18, 12) = 6, LCM(18, 12) = 36$ **b.** $GCD(20, 36) = 4, LCM(20, 36) = 180$ **c.** $GCD(8, 24, 64) = 8, LCM(8, 24, 64) = 192$ **d.** $GCD(7, 9) = 1, LCM(7, 9) = 63$ **3. a.** $GCD(132, 504) = 12, LCM(132, 504) = 5544$

b. $GCD(65, 1690) = 65$, $LCM(65, 1690) = 1690$
c. $GCD(96, 900, 630) = 6$, $LCM(96, 900, 630) = 50,400$
d. $GCD(108, 360) = 36$, $LCM(108, 360) = 1080$
4. a. $GCD(220, 2924) = 4$ **b.** $GCD(14,595, 10,856) = 1$
5. a. $LCM(24, 36) = 72$ **b.** $LCM(72, 90, 96) = 1440$
c. $LCM(90, 105, 315) = 630$
d. $LCM(9^{100}, 25^{100}) = 9^{100} \cdot 25^{100}$
8. b. $GCD(a, a) = a$ $LCM(a, a) = a$
c. $GCD(a^2, a) = a$, $LCM(a^2, a) = a^2$
d. $GCD(a, b) = a$ $LCM(a, b) = b$
11. The only prime factor of 4 is 2 and $97, 219, 988, 751$ is odd. Consequently, 1 is their only common divisor and they are relatively prime.
12. a. 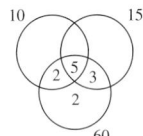 **b.**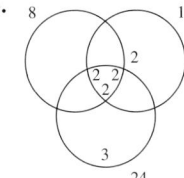

13. Answers vary. For example, $(1, 48), (3, 48), (24, 48)$.
17. 5 packages **18.** They should pass the starting point after $LCM(12, 18, 16) = 144$ min. **19.** 6 in each bag

Assessment 4-3B

1. $GCD(4, 10) = 2$ (1 red); $LCM(4, 10) = 20$ (5 purple, 2 orange) **2. a.** $GCD(12, 30) = 6$; $LCM(12, 30) = 60$
b. $GCD(18, 58) = 2$; $LCM(18, 58) = 522$
c. $GCD(6, 18, 24) = 6$; $LCM(6, 18, 24) = 72$
d. $GCD(36, 13) = 1$; $LCM(36, 13) = 468$
3. a. $GCD(11, 19) = 1$; $LCM(11, 19) = 209$
b. $GCD(140, 320) = 20$; $LCM(140, 320) = 2240$
c. $GCD(800, 75, 450) = 25$; $LCM(800, 75, 450) = 7200$
d. $GCD(103, 320) = 1$; $LCM(103, 320) = 32960$
11. $11 \nmid 181,345,913$
12. a. 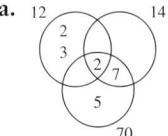 **b.**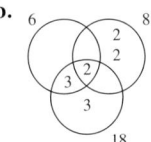

13. Answers vary. For example, $(1, 60), (2, 60), (30, 60)$.
16. 120th customer **18.** After 450 minutes, or 7.5 hrs at 2:30 P.M.

Mathematical Connections 4-3

Reasoning

1. No, the set of common multiples is infinite, and therefore there could be no GCM. **2.** No. $GCD(2, 4, 10) = 2$ $LCM(2, 4, 10) = 20$. GCD times LCM is 40 but $2 \cdot 4 \cdot 10 = 80$. **3.** No. Let $a = 2 \cdot 3$, $b = 3 \cdot 5$, $c = 5 \cdot 7$. Then $GCD(a, b, c) = 1$, but $GCD(a, b) = 3$, and $GCD(b, c) = 5$.
4. Yes. The hypothesis implies that 2 is a common divisor of a, b, and c. If a number greater than 2 divided a, b, and c, then in particular that number would have to divide a and b, which is impossible because $GCD(a, b) = 2$. Thus, $GCD(a, b, c) = 2$.
5. Yes. The LCM equals the product of the numbers if, and only if, the numbers have no prime factors in common. Because $GCD(a, b) \cdot LCM(a, b) = ab$ if, and only if, $GCD(a, b) = 1$; that is a and b have no factors in common. **6.** No. Answers vary: one way is to notice that $LCM(a, b) = \dfrac{ab}{GCD(a, b)}$. **7.** True.

Answers vary. For example, $m = 6$, and $n = 9$; then $GCD(6, 9) = 3$ and $LCM(6, 9) = 18$. $GCD(15, 18) = 3$.

Open-Ended

8. Answers vary. For example, $LCM(8, 12) = 24 < 96$; $LCM(6, 15) = 30 < 90$; $LCM(10, 25) = 50 < 250$.
9. a. $GCD(2a, 2b) = 2$ if $GCD(a, b) = 1$
b. $GCD(6a, 6b) = 6$ if $GCD(a, b) = 1$
c. $GCD(91a, 91b) = 91$ if $GCD(a, b) = 1$
10. For example, 1500 teeth and 72 teeth; 750 teeth and 36 teeth; 375 teeth and 18 teeth; smallest number of teeth is 6 teeth.

Cooperative Learning

11. a. Answers vary **b.** Answers vary.

Connecting Mathematics to the Classroom

12. Answers vary. Most teachers will use an example such as 6. The divisors are $\{1, 2, 3, 6\}$, whereas the multiples of 6 are $\{6, 12, 18, 24, 30, 36, \ldots\}$. **13.** She's incorrect. $GCD(a, 0) = a$ for $a \neq 0$. **14.** Using the prime factorization method for finding the LCM you can tell Aiko that he can multiply the numbers together if there are no common factors in their prime factorization. If there are common factors, then we use the prime factor with the highest exponent. **15.** There are 3333 multiples of 3 and 2000 multiples of 5, but you need to subtract multiples of 15 which have been double counted: $(3333 + 2000) - 666 = 4667$.

Review Problems

16. a. 7 **b.** 6 **c.** 9 **17. a.** $2^3 \cdot 3^7$ **b.** $3^2 \cdot 5 \cdot 727$ **c.** $2^{10} \cdot 3^9$
18. Not prime; $3 \mid 2223$ **19.** Answers vary. For example, 2^5.
20. 120 **21.** 53

Chapter 4 Review

4. b. Let n be a whole number then $n + (n + 1) + (n + 2) + (n + 3) + (n + 4) = 5n + 10 = 5(n + 2)$. Thus, the sum is divisible by 5. **5.** Check divisibility by 3 and 8, $24 \nmid 4152$. **6.** Answers vary. For example, 16. To obtain five divisors we raise a prime to the $(5 - 1)$ power. **7.** 1, 2, 3, 4, 6, 8, 9, 12, 16, 18, 24, 36, 48, 72, 144
8. $n = a \cdot 10^2 + b \cdot 10 + c$
$\quad = a \cdot (99 + 1) + b \cdot (9 + 1) + c$
$\quad = 99 \cdot a + 9 \cdot b + a + b + c$
Since $9 \mid 99a$ and $9 \mid 9b$, then $9 \mid [(99 \cdot a + 9 \cdot b) + (a + b + c)]$ if, and only if, $9 \mid (a + b + c)$. **9.** If 1009 is prime, $17 \nmid 1009$. We know $17 \mid 17$, so $17 \nmid (1009 + 17)$.
11. a. Because $(7 \cdot 11 \cdot 13 \cdot 17) + 17 = 17[(7 \cdot 11 \cdot 13) + 1]$ and $17 \mid 17[(7 \cdot 11 \cdot 13) + 1]$, $(7 \cdot 11 \cdot 13 \cdot 17) + 17$ is composite. **b.** Because $(1 \cdot 2 \cdot 3 \cdot 4 \cdot 5 \cdot 6 \cdot 7 \cdot 8 \cdot 9 \cdot 10) + k$ can be factored as in part (a) for the given values of k, $10! + k$ is composite. **12.** We first show that among any three consecutive odd whole numbers, there is always one that is divisible by 3. For that purpose, suppose that the first whole number in the triplet is not divisible by 3. Then by the division algorithm, that whole number can be written in the form $3n + 1$ or $3n + 2$ for some whole number n. Then the three consecutive odd whole numbers are $3n + 1, 3n + 3, 3n + 5$ or $3n + 2, 3n + 4, 3n + 6$. In the first triplet $3n + 3$ is divisible

by 3, and in the second $3n + 6$ is divisible by 3. This implies that if the first odd whole number is greater than 3 and not divisible 3, then the second or the third must be divisible by 3, and hence cannot be prime. **18.** No, they are the same if the numbers are equal. **19.** $LCM(a, b, c) = LCM(m, c)$, where $m = LCM(a, b). LCM(a, b) = \dfrac{ab}{GCD(a, b)}$ and $LCM(m, c) = \dfrac{mc}{GCD(m, c)}$. Each of these GCDs can be found using the Euclidean algorithm. **20.** We know that $GCD(a, b) \cdot LCM(a, b) = ab$. Because $GCD(a, b) = 1$, then $LCM(a, b) = ab$. **22.** 71 lattes. Because $9869 = 71 \cdot 139$ and 71 as well as 139 are prime, she sold 71 lattes at \$1.39 each.

Answers to Now Try This

1. If $5 \nmid a$ and $5 \nmid b$ then $5 \nmid (a + b)$ is not always true. For example, $5 \nmid 8$ and $5 \nmid 12$, but $5 \mid (8 + 12)$. The statement is sometimes true for example $5 \nmid 7$ and $5 \nmid 12$ and $5 \nmid (7 + 12)$. **3. a.** There will never be other entries in column 1 because 1 is the only number with one factor. Other numbers have at least the number itself and 1. **b.** $49, 121, 169$ **c.** 81 **d.** 64 **e.** The square numbers have an odd number of factors. Factors occur in pairs; for example, for 16 we have 1 and 16, 2 and 8, and 4 and 4. When we list the factors, we list only the distinct factors, so 4 is not listed twice, thereby making the number of factors of 16 an odd number. Similar reasoning holds for all square numbers. **f.** Answers vary. For example, only square numbers are listed in column 3; 2 is the only even number that will ever be in column 2, and column 2 contains prime numbers. **6. a.** The leftmost area contains the factors of 24 that are not factors of 40. The center (intersection) area is the factors of both 24 and 40. The rightmost area represents the factors of 40 that are not factors of 24. **b.** 8

c.

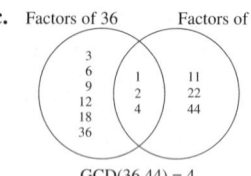

Factors of 36   Factors of 44

GCD(36,44) = 4

7.

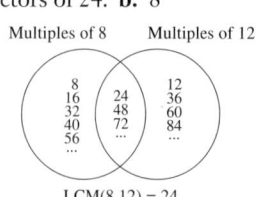

Multiples of 8   Multiples of 12

LCM(8,12) = 24

Answer to the Preliminary Problem

$LCM(23, 28, 33) = 21,252$ days after peak all three cycles will be at their peak again.

CHAPTER 5

Assessment 5-1A

1. f. $^{-}(a + b)$ or $^{-}a + ^{-}b$

4. a.

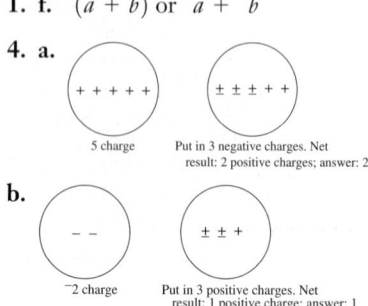

5 charge   Put in 3 negative charges. Net result: 2 positive charges; answer: 2

b.

−2 charge   Put in 3 positive charges. Net result: 1 positive charge; answer: 1

c.

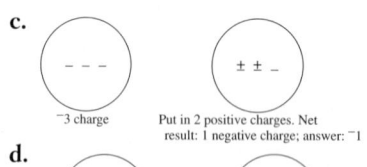

−3 charge   Put in 2 positive charges. Net result: 1 negative charge; answer: ⁻1

d.

−3 charge   Put in 2 negative charges. Net result: 5 negative charges; answer: ⁻5

5. a.

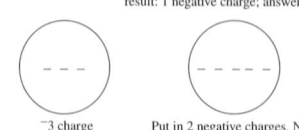

b.

c.

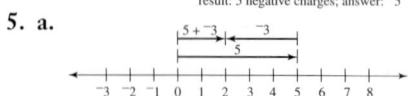

d.

6. a. $7 + ^{-}13 = ^{-}(|^{-}13| - |7|)$
$= ^{-}(13 - 7)$
$= ^{-}(6)$
$= ^{-}6$

b. $^{-}7 + ^{-}13 = ^{-}(|^{-}7| + |^{-}13|)$
$= ^{-}(7 + 13) = ^{-}(20)$
$= ^{-}20$

8. a. $^{-}2 + \_ = 3$, so $\_ = 5$.
b. $2 + \_ = ^{-}3$, so $\_ = ^{-}5$. **c.** $^{-}2 + \_ = ^{-}3$, so $\_ = ^{-}1$.
9. c. $35,000 + ^{-}1000 = 34,000$ leaving an altitude of $34,000'$
10. a. $^{-}45 + ^{-}55 + ^{-}165 + ^{-}35 + ^{-}100 + 75 + 25 + 400$
11. a.

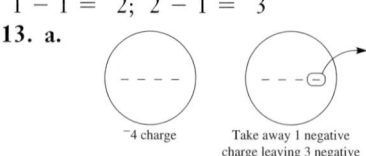

b.

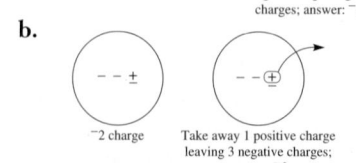

12. a. $^{-}4 - 2 = ^{-}6$; $^{-}4 - 1 = ^{-}5$; $^{-}4 - 0 = ^{-}4$; $^{-}4 - ^{-}1 = ^{-}3$
b. $3 - 1 = 2$; $2 - 1 = 1$; $1 - 1 = 0$; $0 - 1 = ^{-}1$;
$^{-}1 - 1 = ^{-}2$; $^{-}2 - 1 = ^{-}3$
13. a.

−4 charge   Take away 1 negative charge leaving 3 negative charges; answer: ⁻3

b.

−2 charge   Take away 1 positive charge leaving 3 negative charges; answer: ⁻3

15. b. $200 - 220$; $200 + ^{-}220$; $^{-}20$
16. a. $3 - (2 - 4x) = 3 + ^{-}(2 + ^{-}(4x)) = 3 + (^{-}2 + 4x) = (3 + ^{-}2) + 4x = 1 + 4x$
b. $x - (^{-}x - y) = x + ^{-}(^{-}x + ^{-}y) = x + (x + y) = (x + x) + y = 2x + y$
17. Let a, b, and c be any integers. We have

$a - b + c = a + \,^-b + c$ Theorem 5-4
$= a + \,^-(b + \,^-c)$ Theorem 5-3 and Theorem 5-4
$= a - (b - c)$ Theorem 5-4

The equation is true for all integers.
22. Answers vary. Take the opposite of the sum of the first 100 positive numbers, or 5050. The result is $^-5050$.   **24.** Answers vary. If the east coast time is 0, then the Pacific time is $^-3$.
25. $55 + 10 + \,^-7 + \,^-13 = 45$
26. $1 + 0 + \,^-2 + 2 + \,^-1 + \,^-3 = \,^-3$; he is 3 under par for these holes.

Assessment 5-1B

4. a.
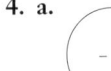 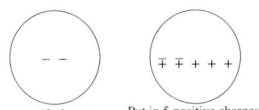

$^-2$ charge   Put in 5 positive charges. Net result: 3 positive charges; answer: 3

b.

$^-5$ charge   Put in 2 positive charges. Net result: 3 negative charges; answer: $^-3$

c.
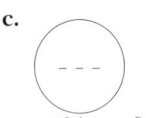

$^-3$ charge   Put in 3 negative charges. Net result: 6 negative charges; answer: $^-6$

d.
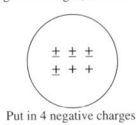

6 charge   Put in 4 negative charges. Net result: 2 positive charges; answer: 2

5. a.
```
        5
    ⌐2  ⌐2 + 5⌐
⌐3 ⌐2 ⌐1 0 1 2 3 4 5 6 7 8
```

b.
```
    2  ⌐5 + 2
      ⌐5⌐
⌐6 ⌐5 ⌐4 ⌐3 ⌐2 ⌐1 0 1 2 3 4 5
```

c.
```
    ⌐3 + ⌐3
   ⌐3  ⌐3
⌐7 ⌐6 ⌐5 ⌐4 ⌐3 ⌐2 ⌐1 0 1 2 3 4 5 6 7
```

d.
```
      6 + ⌐4  ⌐4
          6
⌐7 ⌐6 ⌐5 ⌐4 ⌐3 ⌐2 ⌐1 0 1 2 3 4 5 6 7
```

6. a. $5 + \,^-31 = \,^-(|\,^-31| - |\,5\,|)$
$= \,^-(31 - 5)$
$= \,^-26$
b. $^-5 + \,^-31 = \,^-(|\,^-5\,| + |\,^-31|)$
$= \,^-(5 + 31)$
$= \,^-36$
7. a. $^-3 - 5 = \,^-3 + \,^-5 = \,^-8$ **b.** $5 - (\,^-3) = 5 + 3 = 8$
8. a. $^-3 - 5 = x$ if, and only if, $^-3 = 5 + x$. Thus, $x = \,^-8$.
b. $5 - (\,^-3) = x$ if, and only if, $5 = \,^-3 + x$. Thus, $x = 8$.
c. $^-2 - \,^-3 = x$ if, and only if, $^-2 = x + \,^-3$. Thus, $x = 1$.
11. a.
```
      2  ⌐⌐3 - ⌐2
    ⌐3
⌐4 ⌐3 ⌐2 ⌐1 0 1 2 3 4 5 6 7
```
b.
```
      ⌐4 - 3
    ⌐3  ⌐4
⌐10 ⌐9 ⌐8 ⌐7 ⌐6 ⌐5 ⌐4 ⌐3 ⌐2 ⌐1 0 1 2
```

12. a. $^-2 - 1 = \,^-3$ **b.** $3 - 2 = 1$
$^-2 - 0 = \,^-2$ $2 - 2 = 0$
$^-2 - \,^-1 = \,^-1$ $1 - 2 = \,^-1$
$^-2 - \,^-2 = 0$ $0 - 2 = \,^-2$
$^-2 - \,^-3 = 1$ $^-1 - 2 = \,^-3$
        $^-2 - 2 = \,^-4$
        $^-3 - 2 = \,^-5$

13. a.
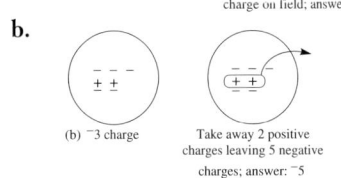

(a) $^-2$ charge   Take away 3 negative charges leaving 1 positive charge on field; answer: 1

b.

(b) $^-3$ charge   Take away 2 positive charges leaving 5 negative charges; answer: $^-5$

16. a. $4x - 2 - 3x = 4x + \,^-2 + \,^-3x = 4x + \,^-3x + \,^-2 = x + \,^-2 = x - 2$ **b.** $4x - (2 - 3x) = 4x + \,^-(2 + \,^-3x) = 4x + \,^-2 + \,^-(\,^-3x) = 4x + 3x + \,^-2 = 7x + \,^-2 = 7x - 2$
17. a. $^-x - y = \,^-x + \,^-y = \,^-y + \,^-x = \,^-y - x$ **b.** No. Because $^-x - y = \,^-x + \,^-y$ and $^-y - x = \,^-y + \,^-x$, the property in part (a) is just the commutative property of addition.
25. Answers vary. If x represents the amount of memory used $x + \,^-3.6 - \,^-7.2 = x + 3.6$ MB; she gained an extra 3.6 MB of memory.   **26. b.** All integers except 0   **d.** $x < 1$
28. $y = \begin{cases} x - 6 & \text{if } x \geq 6 \\ ^-x + 6 & \text{if } x < 6 \end{cases}$ **30. b.** False; let $x = \,^-1$.

Mathematical Connections 5-1

Reasoning

1. Answers vary. He could have driven 12 mi in either direction from milepost 68. Therefore, his location could be either at the $68 - 12 = 56$ milepost or at the $68 + 12 = 80$ milepost.
2. Answers vary. The logic is flowed. However, by definition of subtraction $(a - b) + b = a$. Also using the associative property of addition and the definition of an additive inverse, we have:
$(a + \,^-b) + b = a + \,^-b + b$
$= a + 0$
$= a$
Hence, $(a + \,^-b) + b = a + \,^-b + b$. Adding ^-b to both sides of the last equation, we obtain $a - b = a + \,^-b$.   **3.** Two numbers are additive inverses if, and only if, their sum is 0. We have:
$(b - a) + (a - b) = b + \,^-a + a + \,^-b$
$= b + 0 + \,^-b$
$= b + \,^-b$
$= 0$
4. No; if $x < 0$, then ^-x is positive.   **5.** Answers vary. Students may substitute different integers for a and b, plot them on a number line, and show that in each case the distance between the points is $|a - b|$. They should give at least three examples: when both integers are positive, one is positive and the other negative, and both are negative. A more general approach is as follows: If $a > b > 0$, then $AB = OA - OB = a - b = |a - b|$.

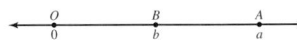

If $a > 0$ and $b < 0$, then $AB = OA + OB = a + {}^-b = a - b = |a - b|$.

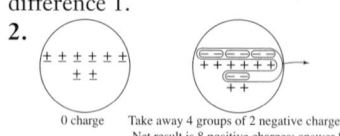

If $a < b < 0$, then $AB = OA - OB = {}^-a - {}^-b = {}^-a + b = b - a = |a - b|$.

6. Answers vary. $a < b$ if, and only if, there exists a positive integer c such that $a + c = b$. ${}^-8 < {}^-7$ because ${}^-8 + 1 = {}^-7$.

Open-Ended

7. Answers vary. For example, suppose Alice was figuring how much money she spent yesterday. She had one bill for $50, another bill for $85 arrived in the mail, and then she returned some books for a $30 credit.   **8.** Answers vary. For example, the floors above the ground could be numbered as usual, $1, 2, 3, \ldots, n$, the zero or ground floor could be called G, and the floors below ground could be called $1B, 2B, \ldots, mB$. The system could be modeled on a vertical number line with G replacing 0 and $1B, 2B, \ldots, mB$ replacing the negative integers.
9. a. 4 **b.** Yes. Let x be our number and let a be the answer. Then,

$$
\begin{aligned}
{}^-[{}^-(x - 10) + {}^-3] &= a \\
{}^-[{}^-(x + {}^-10) + {}^-3] &= a \\
{}^-({}^-x + 10 + {}^-3) &= a \\
{}^-({}^-x + 7) &= a \\
x + {}^-7 &= a \\
x &= a + 7.
\end{aligned}
$$

c. Answers vary. **10.** Answers vary.

Cooperative Learning

11. Answers vary. **12.** Answers vary.

Connecting Mathematics to the Classroom

13. The algorithm is correct, and the student should be congratulated for finding it. One way to encourage such creative behavior is to name and refer to the procedure after the student who invented it, for example, "David's subtraction method." In fourth grade the technique is explained by using a money model. Suppose you have $4 in one checking account and $80 in another, for a total of $84. You spent $27 by withdrawing $7 from the first account and $20 from the second. The first checking account is overdrawn by $3; that is, the balance is ${}^-\$3$. The balance in the second account is $60. After transferring $3 from the second account to the first, the balance in the first account is $0 and in the second $57. The algorithm will always work.
14. The student does not complete the argument in detail. Indeed $a - b = a + {}^-b$. However, $b - a = b + {}^-a$. In general, $a + {}^-b \neq b + {}^-a$. For example, $5 + {}^-2 \neq 2 + {}^-5$. The algorithm will not always work.   **15.** Answers vary. The picture is supposed to illustrate that an integer and its opposite are mirror images of each other. Because a could be negative, the picture is correct. For example, possible values for a and ${}^-a$ are $a = {}^-1, {}^-a = 1$, and $a = {}^-7, {}^-a = 7$. At this point, the teacher could remind the students that the "$-$" sign in ${}^-a$ does not mean that ${}^-a$ is negative. If a is positive, ${}^-a$ is negative, but if a is negative, ${}^-a$ is positive.   **16.** $123 - 45 - 67 + 89 = 100$
17. Because distance is always 0 or a positive number, and absolute value has the same properties, there is a natural connection between the two concepts. Distance is always either positive *or* 0.

Assessment 5-2A

1. $3({}^-1) = {}^-3; 2({}^-1) = {}^-2; 1({}^-1) = {}^-1; 0({}^-1) = 0; {}^-1({}^-1) = 1$; by continuing the pattern of an arithmetic sequence with fixed difference 1.
2.

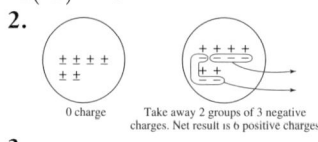

0 charge   Take away 4 groups of 2 negative charges. Net result is 8 positive charges; answer 8

3.

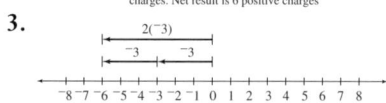

9. a. $4x \div 4 = a$ if and only if $4x = 4a$ if and only if $x = a$. Thus, $4x \div 4 = x$ **b.** ${}^-xy \div y = a$ if and only if ${}^-xy = ya = ay$ if and only if $a = {}^-x$. [This can only happen if $y \neq 0$.]. Thus, ${}^-xy \div y = x$. **17. a.** Commutative property of multiplication
c. Associative property of multiplication **d.** Distributive property of multiplication over addition
23. $(a - b)^2 = (a + {}^-b)(a + {}^-b) = a(a + {}^-b) + {}^-b(a + {}^-b)$
$= a^2 + (a)({}^-b) + ({}^-b)a + ({}^-b)({}^-b)$
$= a^2 + {}^-(ab) + {}^-(ba) + b^2$
$= a^2 + {}^-(ab) + {}^-(ab) + b^2 = a^2 - 2ab + b^2$
24. c. $2^7, {}^-2^8, r = {}^-2$; nth term is $2({}^-2)^{n-1}$ or ${}^-({}^-2)^n$
26. ${}^-5(6) + 3(8) = {}^-30 + 24 = {}^-6$; the net result is a descent of 6 ft.

Assessment 5-2B

1. $3({}^-2) = {}^-6; 2({}^-2) = {}^-4; 1({}^-2) = {}^-2; 0({}^-2) = 0; {}^-1({}^-2) = 2$; ${}^-2({}^-2) = 4$
2.

0 charge   Take away 2 groups of 3 negative charges. Net result is 6 positive charges

3.

5. a. $4({}^-20) = {}^-80$; 80 fewer sophomores **b.** $({}^-5)({}^-20) = 100$; 100 more sophomores **c.** $(n)({}^-20) = {}^-20n$, or $20n$ fewer sophomores **d.** $({}^-n)({}^-20) = 20n$ more sophomores
6. a. The quotient is not defined in the set of integers because there is no integer to multiply times ${}^-10$ to obtain 143.
8. c. 0; there are no division statements because division by 0 is not defined. **11. a.** $4({}^-11) = {}^-44$; 44 yd were lost
15. c. Distributive property of multiplication over addition
21. $(a - 1)^2 = (a + {}^-1)(a + {}^-1) = (a + {}^-1)(a) + (a + {}^-1)({}^-1)$
$= a^2 + {}^-1a + a({}^-1) + ({}^-1)({}^-1) = a^2 + {}^-a + {}^-a + 1$
$= a^2 + {}^-2a + 1 = a^2 - 2a + 1$
24. ${}^-54, {}^-27, {}^-18, {}^-9, {}^-6, {}^-3, {}^-2, {}^-1, 1, 2, 3, 6, 9, 18, 27, 54$
26. ${}^-4(6) + 2(8) = {}^-24 + 16 = {}^-8$; it descends 8 ft after 14 minutes **27.** $8 + (n - 1)(8 + {}^-6) = 8 + (n - 1)2 = 8 + 2n - 2 = 6 + 2n$

Mathematical Connections 5-2

Reasoning

1. The product cannot be found using the difference-of-squares formula. However, ${}^-x - y = {}^-1(x + y)$
so that $({}^-x - y)(x + y) = {}^-1(x + y)(x + y)$
$= {}^-1(x + y)^2 = {}^-1(x^2 + 2xy + y^2) = {}^-x^2 - 2xy - y^2$.

2. $(a - b)^2 = (a + {}^{-}b)^2$ Definition of subtraction $= a^2 + 2a({}^{-}b) + ({}^{-}b)^2$ Distributive property of multiplication over addition $= a^2 - 2ab + b^2$ since $({}^{-}b)^2 = b^2$ **3.** Because ab is an integer, $({}^{-}1)(ab) = {}^{-}ab$ by Theorem 5-7. $({}^{-}1)(ab) = ({}^{-}1a)b$ by the associative property of multiplication and $({}^{-}1a)b = ({}^{-}a)b$ by Theorem 5-6. The argument is valid. **4.** The "proof" starts with what we are trying to prove and the whole "proof" is based on the assumption that the statement is true. A proof could be built starting with the last line and building up. **5.** If $x < y$ then $y - x$ is positive, but this difference does not count the number of integers between the two numbers. The number of integers between x and y is $y - x - 1$. **6.** ${}^{-}500$ is less than 7 as indicated by being on the left of 7 on a traditional number line. Additionally we know that if ${}^{-}500 + n = 7$, then $n = 507$. Thus, one has to add a positive integer to ${}^{-}500$ to obtain 7. Thus, ${}^{-}500 < 7$. **7.** Answers vary. **a.** The argument is logical if we assume that $({}^{-}1)({}^{-}1)$ is either 1 or ${}^{-}1$. That assumption, however, has a flaw; $({}^{-}1)({}^{-}1)$ could be an integer other than 1 or ${}^{-}1$. **b.** Yes; for example, if we assume that $({}^{-}a)({}^{-}b)$ is either ab or ${}^{-}(ab)$, we could show in a similar way that ${}^{-}(ab)$ causes a contradiction.

Open-ended

8. Answers vary. For example, if the student answered only one problem and missed it, he or she would score ${}^{-}1$. If the student answered 5 correct and missed more than 20, he or she would receive a negative score. Any values of x and y such that $4x < y$ would result in a negative score, where x is the number of correct and y is the number of incorrect answers. **9.** Answers vary. **10.** Answers vary. For example, $1 = 4^4/4^4$, $2 = (4 \cdot 4)/(4 + 4)$, $3 = 4 - (4/4)^4$, $4 = [(4 - 4)/4] + 4$, $5 = 4 + 4^{(4-4)}$, $6 = 4 + [(4 + 4)/4]$, $7 = (44/4) - 4$, $8 = [(4 + 4)/4]4$, $9 = 4 + 4 + 4/4$, $10 = (44 - 4)/4$. **11.** In the division algorithm, $a = bn + q$ where $0 \le q < b$. If the last condition $0 \le q < b$ is not met, then one can continue increasing n by 1 until $a = bn + bx + q$ and $0 \le q < b$ is met. Then $a = b(n + x) + q$ and in the division algorithm n is replaced with $n + x$.

Cooperative Learning

12. Answers vary. **13.** Answers vary.

Connecting Mathematics to the Classroom

14. The student is correct that a debt of $5 is greater than a debt of $2. However, what this means is that on a number line ${}^{-}5$ its farther to the left than ${}^{-}2$. The fact that ${}^{-}5$ is farther to the left than ${}^{-}2$ on a number line implies that ${}^{-}5 < {}^{-}2$. **15.** The student does not fully understand the order of operations. The teacher should emphasize that in order to avoid ambiguity, mathematicians agree that multiplication is performed before addition or subtraction. A few simpler examples like $10 - 2 \cdot 3$ should be helpful. **16.** The procedure can be justified as follows. Since for all integers c, ${}^{-}c = ({}^{-}1)c$, the effect of forming the opposite of an algebraic expression is the same as multiplying the expression by ${}^{-}1$. However, in the expression $x - (2x - 3)$, the "$-$" is used to denote subtraction, not simply finding the opposite. If the expression is first rewritten as $x + {}^{-}(2x + {}^{-}3)$, then it is the case that ${}^{-}(2x + {}^{-}3) = {}^{-}1(2x + {}^{-}3)$, or ${}^{-}2x + 3$. Now the expression can be rewritten as $x + {}^{-}2x + 3$, which a student might obtain from the father's rule. **17.** One response to Mariana is to review the *Common Core Standards* where absolute value is involved. The approach is not the typical theoretical approach to absolute value but a "softer" approach. This may not convince her and the next best thing would be to demonstrate the approach with middle school students.

Review Problems

18.

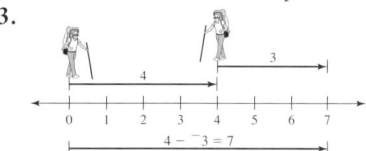

19. a. 5 **b.** ${}^{-}7$ **c.** 0 **20. a.** 14 **b.** 21 **c.** ${}^{-}4$ **d.** 22 **21. a.** 7 **b.** None **c.** All integers other than 7. **22.** Yes

Chapter 5 Review

3. c. All integers $x \ne 0$ **f.** All integer values **4.** $2({}^{-}3) = {}^{-}6$; $1({}^{-}3) = {}^{-}3$; $0({}^{-}3) = 0$; and if the pattern continues, we have ${}^{-}1({}^{-}3) = 3$; ${}^{-}2({}^{-}3) = 6$ and so on. **8. b.** False; let $x = 1$ and $y = {}^{-}1$ and the statement is not true. **9. b.** $3 - (4 - 5) \ne (3 - 4) - 5$ **d.** $8 \div (4 - 2) \ne (8 \div 4) - (8 \div 2)$ **10. g.** $x \ge 4$ or $x \le {}^{-}4$; that is, $\{\ldots, {}^{-}6, {}^{-}5, {}^{-}4, 4, 5, 6, \ldots\}$ **12. a.** Geometric, ratio ${}^{-}1$ **b.** Geometric, ratio ${}^{-}2$ **c.** Arithmetic, difference ${}^{-}3$ **14. a.** 7 **b.** 1029 **c.** 1911 **18.** Oregon, Nevada, Iowa, California, Arizona, Ohio, West Virginia, Alabama **19. c.** Answers vary, but the expectation is that the elevation would be quite high (Mauna Kea). **20. a.** Answers vary. One difference is 274 ft. **b.** Answers vary. **21.** Answers vary but the depth is 3963 m below sea level or ${}^{-}3963$ m. **23. a.** Answers vary. For example, number engaged is positive; number of casualties is negative. **24.** Answers vary. ${}^{-}2$ could mean two floors below ground level **27.** Use $(100 - 4)(100 + 4) = 10,000 - 16 = 9984$.

Answers to Now Try This

1. The sum of two negative integers is always negative. Consider number line models for example.

3.

4. a. Yes; because subtraction can be defined in terms of addition and the set of integers is closed under addition, then the set of integers is closed under subtraction. **b.** None of these properties hold for subtraction in the set of integers: $a - b \ne b - a$ (if $a \ne b$), $(a - b) - c \ne a - (b - c)$ (if $c \ne 0$), and $a - 0 \ne 0 - a$ if $a \ne 0$.

Answer to the Preliminary Problem

The table below shows the differences in the scores of each pair of students.

Ordered Pair (a, b)	Difference $a - b$
$(20, 17)$	$20 - 17 = 3$
$(15, 18)$	$15 - 18 = {}^{-}3$
$(21, 19)$	$21 - 19 = 2$
$(17, 22)$	$17 - 22 = {}^{-}5$
$(18, 18)$	$18 - 18 = 0$
$(19, 15)$	$19 - 15 = 4$
$(16, 14)$	$16 - 14 = 2$
$(20, 18)$	$20 - 18 = 2$
$(21, 20)$	$21 - 20 = 1$
$(18, 25)$	$18 - 25 = {}^{-}7$

There are fewer negative differences than positive differences so that would be a case for saying the experiment worked. However, the sum of all the differences is

$$3 + {}^-3 + 2 + {}^-5 + 0 + 4 + 2 + 2 + 1 + {}^-7 = {}^-1.$$

Because the sum of all the differences is negative, it would be very difficult to make a case for the experiment being a success.

CHAPTER 6
Assessment 6-1A

4. a. $\frac{2}{3}$ **b.** $\frac{4}{6} = \frac{2}{3}$ **c.** $\frac{6}{9} = \frac{2}{3}$ **d.** $\frac{8}{12} = \frac{2}{3}$. The diagrams

illustrate the Fundamental Law of Fractions. **8. a.** $\frac{4}{43}$ **b.** $\frac{17}{43}$

d. $\frac{39}{43}$ **15.** Answers vary. 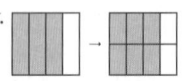 **17. a.**

26. n cannot be 0; otherwise there would $\frac{0}{0}$ in the theorem.

22. a. $\frac{6}{16} = \frac{3}{8}$; $\frac{6}{32,000} = \frac{3}{16,000}$ **b.** $\frac{10}{100} = \frac{1}{10}$ **c.** $\frac{15}{60} = \frac{1}{4}$

d. $\frac{8}{24} = \frac{1}{3}$ **27.** $n = \frac{n}{1}$ for all integers n, so every integer can be

written as a fraction. **28.** Drawing is only a representation, not

to scale.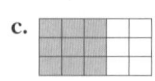

Assessment 6-1B

4. Answers vary. **a.** 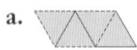 **b.**

c.   **d.** 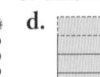 **e.** 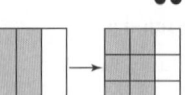 **f.**

5. Answers vary. **a.** No, the parts do not have to be equal.
b. Yes, because the square can be divided into 8 such shaded triangles of equal area. **c.** Yes, because the circle can be divided into 8 such shaded parts of equal area. **6.** Answers vary.
a. **b.** **c.** **d.**

15. Answers vary. 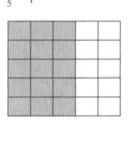 **21. a.** $\frac{12}{16} = \frac{3}{4}$

b. $\frac{5}{100} = \frac{1}{20}$ **c.** $\frac{25}{60} = \frac{5}{12}$ **d.** $\frac{16}{24} = \frac{2}{3}$ **24.** $n = \frac{n}{1}$, where n is an

integer. Because the set of integers is infinite, so is this representation.

29. a. Area of $a = \frac{1}{4}$ **b.** Area of $a = 1$

Area of $b = \frac{1}{4}$ Area of $b = 1$

Area of $c = \frac{1}{16}$ Area of $c = \frac{1}{4}$

Area of $d = \frac{1}{8}$ Area of $d = \frac{1}{2}$

Area of $e = \frac{1}{16}$ Area of $e = \frac{1}{4}$

Area of $f = \frac{1}{8}$ Area of $f = \frac{1}{2}$

Area of $g = \frac{1}{8}$ Area of $g = \frac{1}{2}$

Mathematical Connections 6-1
Reasoning

1. Answers vary. The fractions are using different bases with one being \$1 and the other being 1 hour, or 60 minutes. The fractions are each $\frac{1}{4}$ and are equivalent, but in context with the different bases, they represent different quantities. **2.** Not necessarily. The classes may have different numbers of students. If one has 21 students and the other 24, then in the first there are 7 girls and in the second 8 girls. **3.** The new fraction is equal to $\frac{1}{2}$.

$$\frac{ar_1}{br_1} + \frac{ar_2}{br_2} + \frac{ar_3}{br_3} + \ldots + \frac{ar_n}{br_n} = \frac{ar_1 + ar_2 + ar_3 + \ldots + ar_n}{br_1 + br_2 + br_3 + \ldots + br_n}$$
$$= \frac{a(r_1 + r_2 + r_3 + \ldots + r_n)}{b(r_1 + r_2 + r_3 + \ldots + r_n)} = \frac{a}{b}$$

4. 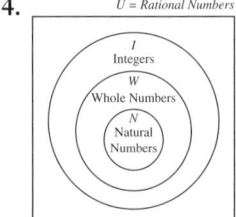 $N \subset W \subset I \subset U$

Open-Ended

5. Answers vary. **6.** Answers vary.
7. Answers vary depending upon the windows chosen.

Cooperative Learning

8. Answers vary. **9.** Answers vary.

Connecting Mathematics to the Classroom

10. $\frac{0}{6}$ is not in simplest form. A fraction $\frac{a}{b}$ is in simplest form

if and only if $\mathrm{GCD}(a, b) = 1$; however, $\mathrm{GCD}(0, 6) = 6$. The

simplest form is $\frac{0}{6} = 0$. **11.** The first student's approach is

correct. What the second student has done is to treat the problem

as if it had been $\left(\frac{1}{5}\right)\left(\frac{5}{3}\right) = \frac{1}{3}$, when in reality, the problem is

$\frac{15}{53}$. One cancels factors, not digits. **12.** According to Theorem 6-4,

there is another rational number between any two given

rational numbers. $\frac{9999}{10000}$ is one rational number between $\frac{999}{1000}$

and 1. **13.** Answers vary. The student was probably thinking that more pieces meant more pizza. A pizza (or circle) could be cut into 6 pieces, then each piece could be cut into 2 pieces; This shows the amount of pizza did not change from these last cuts, only the number of pieces changed. **14.** Answers vary; for

example, she could show $\frac{3}{4}$ of the faces by picking 3 of the 4 large

faces and 3 of the 4 small faces. **15.** Answers vary. **a.** Suppose

the rational numbers are $\frac{2}{16}$ and $\frac{1}{4}$. In this case, $\frac{1}{4} > \frac{2}{16}$ and Iris is incorrect   **b.** Suppose the rational numbers are $\frac{2}{3}$ and $\frac{1}{2}$. In this case, $\left(\frac{2}{3}\right) > \left(\frac{1}{2}\right)$ and Shirley is incorrect.   **16.** The whole in this case is the 3 sets of 5 dots. Since 2 sets are shaded, $\frac{2}{3}$ of the whole is shaded, and Steve is not correct. If each individual dot was considered, then there are 15 dots in the whole and 10 are shaded. Therefore, $\frac{10}{15} = \frac{2}{3}$ of the dots are shaded.

17. If you write each fraction over a common denominator, it is easier to compare them. Thus we have $\frac{3}{8} = \frac{9}{24}$ and $\frac{2}{3} = \frac{16}{24}$. Because $\frac{16}{24} > \frac{9}{24}$, then $\frac{2}{3} > \frac{3}{8}$.

18. Because the fraction of students passing in each class was $\frac{4}{5}$, the argument could be made that they did equally well on the test.

Assessment 6-2A

4. b. $\frac{1}{6}$, low   **d.** $\frac{1}{2}$, high   **6.**

About 0: $\frac{1}{10}$, $\frac{1}{100}$ About $\frac{1}{2}$: $\frac{4}{7}$, $\frac{8}{12}$, $\frac{2}{5}$, $\frac{9}{18}$ About 1: $\frac{7}{8}$, $\frac{13}{10}$

15. Answers vary. **a.** $\frac{1}{2} + \frac{3}{4} \in Q$ **b.** $\frac{1}{2} + \frac{3}{4} = \frac{3}{4} + \frac{1}{2}$
c. $\left(\frac{1}{2} + \frac{1}{3}\right) + \frac{1}{4} = \frac{1}{2} + \left(\frac{1}{3} + \frac{1}{4}\right)$ **16.** $1, \frac{7}{6}, \frac{8}{6}, \frac{9}{6}, \frac{10}{6}, \frac{11}{6}, 2$
17. b. $\frac{1}{n} = \frac{1}{n+1} + \frac{1}{n(n+1)}$

Assessment 6-2B

6.

About 0: $\frac{7}{800}$, $\frac{1}{100}$, $\frac{1}{30}$ About $\frac{1}{2}$: $\frac{36}{70}$, $\frac{19}{36}$ About 1: $\frac{14}{16}$

12. d. Not necessarily, the total number of dollars might have been greater in 2012 than in 2014, but the fraction of the total dollars was greater in 2014.   **16.** $1, \frac{7}{5}, \frac{9}{5}, \frac{11}{5}, \frac{13}{5}, 3$

19. d. No, $\frac{1}{2} + \frac{1}{2^2} + \frac{1}{2^3} + \cdots + \frac{1}{2^n} = \frac{2^n - 1}{2^n}$, so the numerator will always be less than the denominator.

20. Answers vary. **a.** About $\frac{1}{736}$ **b.** About $\frac{1}{2}$ **c.** About $\frac{2}{127}$

22. $\frac{303}{360} = \frac{101}{120}$ **23.** $\frac{7}{100}$

Mathematical Connections 6-2

Reasoning

1. Answers vary. For example, $\frac{1}{3} + \frac{1}{4}$ or $\frac{1}{12}$ does not represent the amount received since the fractions did not come from the same size "whole."   **2. a.** No, but it is easier to write in simplest terms if we do choose a least common denominator.   **b.** No. For example, $\frac{1}{3} + \frac{1}{6} = \frac{3}{6}$, which is not in simplest form.   **3.** Answers vary.
$5\frac{3}{4} = \frac{5}{1} + \frac{3}{4} = \frac{5 \cdot 4 + 1 \cdot 3}{1 \cdot 4} = \frac{5 \cdot 4 + 3}{4}$ **4.** No, Kara spent $\frac{1}{3}$

of $\frac{1}{2}$ of her allowance on Sunday, so she has
$\frac{1}{2} - \frac{1}{3} \cdot \frac{1}{2} = \frac{3}{6} - \frac{1}{6} = \frac{2}{6}$, or $\frac{1}{3}$, of her allowance left.

5. Answers vary. For example, $3\frac{3}{4} + 5\frac{1}{3} = \frac{15}{4} + \frac{16}{3} = \frac{45 + 64}{12} = \frac{109}{12} = 9\frac{1}{12}$ or $3\frac{3}{4} + 5\frac{1}{3} = (3 + 5) + \left(\frac{3}{4} + \frac{1}{3}\right) = 8\frac{13}{12} = 9\frac{1}{12}$. In the second method, the numbers are smaller to work with.   **6. a.** Yes. If $a, b, c,$ and d are integers, $b \neq 0, d \neq 0$, then $\frac{a}{b} - \frac{c}{d} = \frac{ad - bc}{bd}$ is a rational number.

b. No; for example, $\frac{1}{2} - \frac{1}{4} \neq \frac{1}{4} - \frac{1}{2}$.

c. No; for example, $\frac{1}{2} - \left(\frac{1}{4} - \frac{1}{8}\right) \neq \left(\frac{1}{2} - \frac{1}{4}\right) - \frac{1}{8}$.

d. No. If there is an identity for subtraction, it must be 0, since only for 0 does $\frac{a}{b} - 0 = \frac{a}{b}$. However, in general, $0 - \frac{a}{b} \neq \frac{a}{b} - 0$, and hence there is no identity.   **e.** No; since there is no identity, an inverse cannot be defined.

Open-Ended

7. Answers vary. For example, Mike ate a third of a pizza, leaving $\frac{2}{3}$ of the pizza for Ann. Ann gave $\frac{1}{4}$ of the entire pizza to her little brother. What fraction of the pizza was left for Ann?

8. a. Answers vary, for example, $\frac{2}{3}$ and $\frac{1}{3} \cdot \frac{b - a}{b}$.

b. Answers vary, for example, $\frac{2}{7}, \frac{4}{7},$ and $\frac{1}{7}$.   **c.** Answers vary, for example, $\frac{9}{8}$ and $\frac{1}{7}$.   **9.** Answers vary.

a. i. $\frac{1}{3} = \frac{1}{4} + \frac{1}{12}; \frac{1}{3} = \frac{1}{6} + \frac{1}{6}$
ii. $\frac{1}{7} = \frac{1}{8} + \frac{1}{56}; \frac{1}{7} = \frac{1}{14} + \frac{1}{14}$
b. $\frac{1}{n} - \frac{1}{n+1} = \frac{(n+1) - n}{n(n+1)} = \frac{1}{n(n+1)}$
c. Rewriting part (b) as a sum gives $\frac{1}{n} = \frac{1}{n+1} + \frac{1}{n(n+1)}$.
d. Answers vary. $\frac{1}{17} = \frac{1}{18} + \frac{1}{17(18)} = \frac{1}{18} + \frac{1}{306}$

Cooperative Learning

10. Answers vary. Depending on the people interviewed, students may hear an answer like the following from a teacher, "I use fractions in determining total grades for my classes. For example, if a paper is $\frac{1}{2}$ of the grade and a test is another $\frac{1}{3}$ of the grade, I need to know what fractional part of the grade is yet to be determined.

Connecting Mathematics to the Classroom

11. Answers vary. Kendra's picture shows that $\frac{1}{3}$ of the 3-square whole combined with $\frac{3}{4}$ of the 4-square whole gives $\frac{4}{7}$ of a

7-square whole. To do what Kendra is trying to do, she would need to use the same size whole rather than 3 different wholes. When $\frac{1}{3} + \frac{3}{4}$ are added, the same whole must be used.
12. Answers vary. For example, the teacher is thinking each rectangle, which is divided into 4 equal parts, represents a whole divided into fourths, so the picture is $2\frac{3}{4}$. Ken is thinking the three rectangles represent the whole and 11 of 12 parts are shaded.
13. Answers vary. Jill is confusing this with adding fractions with common denominators. If $a, b,$ and c are positive integers, then $\frac{a}{b+c} < \frac{a}{b}$, but $\frac{a}{b} + \frac{a}{c} > \frac{a}{b}$. A numerical example such as $\frac{1}{2} + \frac{1}{3} \neq \frac{1}{5}$ is sufficient to disprove Jill's claim. **14. a.** Like digits are being cancelled. **b.** Numerators and denominators are both being added. **c.** Numerators and denominators of fractional portions are both being subtracted.

Review Problems

15. a. $\frac{2}{3}$ **b.** $\frac{13}{17}$ **c.** $\frac{25}{49}$ **d.** a where $a \neq {}^-1$ **e.** Simplified
f. $a + b$ where $a \neq b$ **16. a.** Equal **b.** Not equal **c.** Equal
d. Not equal **17.** It is possible because the fraction $\frac{27}{103}$ is equal to $\frac{54}{206}$, meaning that there would be 54 bones in both hands.
18. There are infinitely many nonzero integers n, such that $\frac{3}{5} = \frac{3n}{5n}$.
19. $\frac{2}{5}$ **20.** $\frac{-1}{10} = \frac{-10}{100}$ and $\frac{-10}{100} < \frac{-1}{100}$ because $\frac{-10}{100} + \frac{9}{100} = \frac{-1}{100}$, and $\frac{9}{100}$ is a positive number. Thus, $\frac{-1}{100}$ is farther to the right on a number line (and greater than) $\frac{-1}{10}$.

Assessment 6-3A

1. Answers vary. **a.** $\frac{1}{4} \cdot \frac{1}{3} = \frac{1}{12}$ **b.** $\frac{2}{4} \cdot \frac{3}{5} = \frac{6}{20}$

2. Answers vary. **a.** 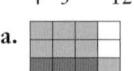 **b.**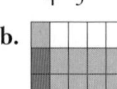

19. a., b., c., e., and **f.** are false; counterexamples vary.
d. True; $ab \neq 0$; use Theorem 6-19a. **22. d.** $\left(\frac{4}{5}\right)^{10}$
23. Answers vary. $2\left(\frac{a}{b}\right) = \frac{a}{b} + \frac{a}{b} < \frac{a}{b} + \frac{c}{d}$ because $\frac{a}{b} < \frac{c}{d}$. Thus, $2\left(\frac{a}{b}\right) < \frac{a}{b} + \frac{c}{d}, \frac{a}{b} < \frac{1}{2}\left(\frac{a}{b} + \frac{c}{d}\right)$. Also, $\frac{1}{2}\left(\frac{a}{b} + \frac{a}{b}\right) < \frac{1}{2}\left(\frac{a}{b} + \frac{c}{d}\right) < \frac{1}{2}\left(\frac{c}{d} + \frac{c}{d}\right) = \frac{1}{2}\left(\frac{2c}{d}\right) = \frac{c}{d}$. Thus, $\frac{a}{b} < \frac{1}{2}\left(\frac{a}{b} + \frac{c}{d}\right) < \frac{c}{d}$.
24. b. No; this only describes the fraction of students, not the total number of either males or females. **25.** Answers vary. **a.** About $\frac{1}{11}$ **b.** About $\frac{1}{6}$

Assessment 6-3B

1. a. $\frac{2}{3} \cdot \frac{1}{2} = \frac{2}{6} = \frac{1}{3}$ **b.** $\frac{1}{3} \cdot \frac{1}{2} = \frac{1}{6}$ **2. a.** 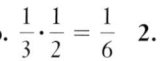 **b.**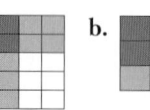

4. b. Answers vary. $\frac{y^2 - x^2}{xy}$ **6. d.** $\frac{-3}{2}$ or ${}^-1\frac{1}{2}$
19. a., c., e. are false; counterexamples vary.
b. True since $(ab)^{-m} = \frac{1}{(ab)^m} = \frac{1}{a^m b^m} = \frac{1}{a^m} \cdot \frac{1}{b^m}$. **d.** True since $2(a^{-1} + b^{-1})^{-1} = 2 \cdot \frac{1}{a^{-1} + b^{-1}} = 2 \cdot \frac{1}{\frac{1}{a} + \frac{1}{b}} = 2 \cdot \frac{1}{\frac{a+b}{ab}} = 2\frac{ab}{a+b} = \frac{2ab}{a+b}$.
f. True since $\left(\frac{a}{b}\right)^{-1} = \frac{1}{\frac{a}{b}} = \frac{b}{a}$. **20. a.** No integer solution
26. Answers vary. **a.** About $\frac{3}{67}$ **b.** About $\frac{2}{7}$ **29.** $\frac{1}{10}$ for stocks and $\frac{3}{20}$ for bonds

Mathematical Connections 6-3
Reasoning
1. Never less than n. $0 < \frac{a}{b} < 1$ implies $0 < 1 < \frac{b}{a}$.
The last inequality implies $0 < n < n\left(\frac{b}{a}\right)$. Therefore $n \div \left(\frac{a}{b}\right) = n\left(\frac{b}{a}\right) > n$. **2.** B is the closest. Because both C and D are positive and less than 1, their product is less then either.
3. The second number must be the reciprocal of the first and must be a positive number less than 1.

Open-Ended
4. Answers vary. **5.** Answers depend on the class. **6.** Answers depend on the class.

Cooperative Learning
7. The answers depend on the size of the bricks and the size of the joints. In all likelihood, the measurements will be made in fractions of inches for the size of the joints. The size of the bricks may be done in inches. An alternative is to measure in centimeters. All measurements are approximate and some rounding or estimation may occur. **8.** Answers vary depending on the state and year chosen. **9.** Answers depend on the group demographics.

Connecting Mathematics to the Classroom
10. Answers vary. For example, Bente is probably thinking of $12\frac{1}{4} \div 3\frac{3}{4}$ as $\frac{12 + \frac{1}{4}}{3 + \frac{3}{4}} = \frac{12}{3} + \frac{\frac{1}{4}}{\frac{3}{4}}$. In general, $\frac{a+b}{c+d} \neq \frac{a}{c} + \frac{b}{d}$, and so this will not work. The correct answer is determined by $12\frac{1}{4} \div 3\frac{3}{4} = \frac{49}{4} \div \frac{15}{4} = \frac{49}{15} = 3\frac{4}{15}$. **11.** Answers vary.

For example, $\frac{1}{2}$ of a number x is equivalent to $\frac{1}{2} \cdot x$ or $\frac{x}{2}$, whereas

dividing a number x by $\frac{1}{2}$ is equivalent to $\dfrac{x}{\frac{1}{2}} = \frac{x}{1} \cdot \frac{2}{1} = \frac{2x}{1} = 2x$.

Therefore, they are not the same.   **12.** Answers vary.
For example, yes she is correct, since
$$\frac{3}{4} \cdot \frac{2}{5} = \frac{3 \cdot 2}{4 \cdot 5} = \frac{3 \cdot 2}{5 \cdot 4} = \frac{3}{5} \cdot \frac{2}{4} = \frac{3}{5} \cdot \frac{1}{2} = \frac{3 \cdot 1}{5 \cdot 2} = \frac{3}{10}.$$
13. Answers vary. He is right. If a is divided by 2, we get
$\frac{a}{2} = \left(\frac{1}{2}\right)a$.   **14. a.** If instead of fractions, the question involved whole numbers, Jim would likely have an easier time. If 2 packages of sugar fill $\frac{1}{2}$ c, then 1 packet would fill $\frac{1}{2} \div 2c$, or $\frac{1}{4}$ c.

If instead of 2 packages we have $\frac{3}{4}$ of a package, we would fill $\frac{1}{2} \div \frac{3}{4} = \frac{1}{2} \cdot \frac{4}{3} = \frac{2}{3}$ of a cup. Another approach is to set up an equation: if x is the number of cups of sugar in one package of sugar, then in $\frac{3}{4}$ of a package there are $\frac{3}{4} x$ c, which is given to be $\frac{1}{2}$ c. So $\frac{3}{4}x = \frac{1}{2}, \frac{4}{3} \cdot \frac{3}{4}x = \frac{4}{3} \cdot \frac{1}{2}, x = \frac{2}{3}$ c.   **b.** Because in 2 c there are 4 half cups, we would need $\frac{3}{4} \cdot 4$, or 3 packages of sugar.   **c.** One loaf will require $\frac{1}{3} \div 2 = \frac{1}{6}$ of a cup. Hence three loaves will require $3 \cdot \frac{1}{6} = \frac{1}{2}$ of a cup.   **d.** 1 c of sugar will make $1 \div \frac{3}{4}$, or $\frac{4}{3} = 1\frac{1}{3}$ gal. Hence 2 c will make $2 \cdot 1\frac{1}{3} = 2\frac{2}{3}$ gal.   **e.** 17 dolls, with $1\frac{1}{8}$ in. of ribbon left over.   **15.** The student is correct when dividing a positive number by a number greater than 1. However, when the division is by a number between 0 and 1, the opposite happens. Recall that 12 divided by 4 means "How many 4's are there in 12?" $12 \div 4 = 3$ because $12 = 4 \cdot 3$. $5 \div \frac{1}{2}$ means "How many $\frac{1}{2}$s are there in 5?" $5 \div \frac{1}{2} = 10$ because $5 = \frac{1}{2} \cdot 10$.
16. The student is wrong unless $n = 0$ or $p = m$. The Fundamental Law of Fractions holds only for multiplication. For example, $\frac{7 + 3}{2 + 3} \neq \frac{7}{2}$.   **17.** Jillian is correct if a fractional answer is needed.

Review Problems
18. a. $\frac{25}{16}$ or $1\frac{9}{16}$ **b.** $\frac{25}{18}$ or $1\frac{7}{18}$ **c.** $\frac{5}{216}$ **d.** $\frac{259}{30}$ or $8\frac{19}{30}$ **e.** $\frac{37}{24}$ or $1\frac{13}{24}$ **f.** $\frac{^-39}{4}$ or $^-9\frac{3}{4}$ **19.** 120   **20. a.** $\frac{3x^2 + y^3}{x^2 y^2}$ **b.** $\frac{az - by}{xy^2 z}$ **c.** $\frac{2ab - b^2}{a^2 - b^2}$ **21. a.** This is not correct.   **b.** This is not correct   **c.** This is correct as long as $a \neq 0$.

3. a. 2:5. Because the ratio is 2:3, there are $2x$ boys and $3x$ girls; hence, the ratio of boys to all students is $\frac{2x}{2x + 3x} = \frac{2}{5}$.
13. Answers vary. $\frac{36\,oz}{12¢} = \frac{48\,oz}{16¢}; \frac{12¢}{16¢} = \frac{36\,oz}{48\,oz}; \frac{16¢}{12¢} = \frac{48\,oz}{36\,oz}$
20. The ratio between the mass of the gold in the ring and the mass of the ring is $\frac{18}{24}$. If x is the number of ounces of pure gold in the ring which weighs 4 oz, we have $\frac{18}{24} = \frac{x}{4}$. Hence, $x = \frac{(18 \cdot 4)}{24}$, or 3 oz. Consequently, the price of the gold in the ring is $3 \cdot \$1800$ or $\$5400$.   **22. b.** Let $\frac{a}{b} = \frac{c}{d} = \frac{e}{f} = r$.
Then, $a = br, c = dr, e = fr$.
So, $a + c + e = br + dr + fr$
$a + c + e = r(b + d + f)$
$\dfrac{a + c + e}{b + d + f} = r$.
23. As seen in the drawing, $\frac{1}{2}$ of stick A is $\frac{2}{3}$ of stick B, and stick B is 18 cm shorter than stick A.

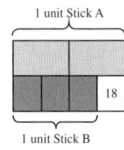

We have the following: Stick B is $3 \cdot 18$ unit sections while stick A is $4 \cdot 18$ unit sections. Thus, the lengths of the sticks are A, 72 cm, and B, 54 cm.

10. a.

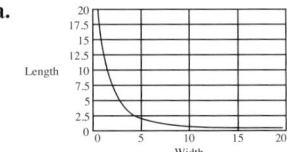

11. Answers vary. For example,

x	4	8	12	16
y	20	40	60	80

17. a. 50:13

Reasoning
1. a. 525 cm   **b.** For the first set, $\dfrac{\text{footprint length}}{\text{thighbone length}} = \frac{40}{100} = \frac{20}{50}$; that is, a 50-cm thighbone would correspond to a 20-cm footprint. Thus, it is not likely that the 50-cm thighbone is from the animal that left the 30-cm footprint. $\left(\text{Notice that } \frac{20}{50} \neq \frac{30}{50}.\right)$
2. No, the ratio of the prices is equal to the ratio of the areas and not to the ratio of the diameters.   **3. a.** $\frac{a}{b} = \frac{c}{d}$ implies

$\frac{a}{b} + 1 = \frac{c}{d} + 1$, which implies $\frac{a+b}{b} = \frac{c+d}{d}$. **b.** By inverting $\frac{b}{a} = \frac{d}{c}$ and by part (a), $\frac{b+a}{a} = \frac{d+c}{c}$. Then inverting again gives $\frac{a}{a+b} = \frac{c}{d+c}$. **c.** $\frac{a}{b} = \frac{c}{d}$ implies $\frac{a}{b} - 1 = \frac{c}{d} - 1$, which implies $\frac{a-b}{b} = \frac{c-d}{d}$. From part (a) and this last result, we have $\frac{a-b}{b} \div \frac{a+b}{b} = \frac{c-d}{d} \div \frac{c+d}{d}$, which implies $\frac{a-b}{a+b} = \frac{c-d}{c+d}$. **d.** $\frac{a}{b} = \frac{c}{d}$ if, and only if, $ad = bc$. Also, $\frac{d}{c-d} = \frac{b}{a-b}$, if and only if, $d(a-b) = b(c-d)$, $ad - bd = bc - bd$, $ad = bc$.
4. Yes, she is correct. One way for her to tell this is to realize that since $15 \cdot 7 \neq 15 \cdot 8$, then $15/7 \neq 15/8$. **5.** No, the dimensions don't vary proportionately because $4/6 \neq 5/7$ and $4/6 \neq 8/10$ and $\frac{5}{7} \neq \frac{8}{10}$. This can be seen by cross multiplication or just by reducing all three fractions to simplest terms—$\frac{2}{3}, \frac{5}{7}$, and $\frac{4}{5}$—and noticing that no two are equal. **6.** No, they can't form a proportion because for this to happen it would be necessary for $ab = ab + b^2$ and this cannot happen when $b \neq 0$.
7. Answers vary; for example, let m be the number of adult men living in the condo and w be the number of adult women. The number of married men is equal to the number of married women, so $\frac{2}{3}m = \frac{3}{4}w$. The ratio of married people to the total adult population is

$$\frac{\frac{2m}{3} + \frac{3w}{4}}{m+w} = \frac{\frac{2m}{3} + \frac{2m}{3}}{m+w} = \frac{\frac{4m}{3}}{m+w}.$$

Because $\frac{2m}{3} = \frac{3w}{4}, w = \frac{8m}{9}$. Thus,

$$\frac{\frac{4m}{3}}{m+w} = \frac{\frac{4m}{3}}{m+\frac{8m}{9}} = \frac{\frac{4m}{3}}{\frac{17m}{9}} = \frac{12}{17},$$ which is the desired ratio.

Open-Ended
8. Answers vary, but the discussion should include the fact that two equal ratios form a proportion. **9.** Answers vary depending on the current numbers. The filibuster rules will have to be checked on a government website. **10.** Check a website on fertilizers. The ratio will be explained there. **11.** Answers vary. For example, the rectangle that is the most pleasing to the eye has its sides in the golden ratio, which is approximately 1.618:1.

Cooperative Learning
12. Answers vary.

Connecting Mathematics to the Classroom
13. Mary has not paid attention to matching the units of the corresponding parts of the proportion. **14.** Yes, she is correct. Because each ratio is equal to the same number, they must equal each other and hence form a proportion. **15.** The way Al set up

the proportion assumes the tree is 15 ft tall. The correct proportion comparing the object to its shadow is

$$\frac{5\,\text{ft}}{\frac{3}{2}\,\text{ft}} = \frac{x}{15\,\text{ft}}, \quad \text{so } x = 50\,\text{ft}.$$

16. Collect data on the ratio of arm length to nose length by measuring the arms and noses of other students in her class. Find the average ratio, then use it to find the expected length of the nose of the Statue of Liberty. **17.** Google "Singapore math curriculum, bar models."

Review Problems
18. The numerator is 6 and the denominator is 1. **19.** $\frac{3}{4}$ is a proper fraction because the numerator and denominator are both positive with the numerator less than the denominator.
20. Any integer can be written as a rational number with the integer as the numerator and the denominator 1.
21. The statement is not true in general; for example, $\frac{25}{35} \neq \frac{2}{3}$ because $75 \neq 70$. **22.** At 6:00, the hands on the clock form a straight line, but the second hand is on 12. After that, the hands form a straight line approximately every 1 hr, 5 min, and 27 sec. So after 6:00, the minute and hour hands form a straight line at 7:05:27, 8:10:55, 9:16:22, 10:21:49, 11:27:16, 12:32:44, 1:38:11, 2:43:38, 3:49:05, and 4:54:33. **23.** No **24.** $99 \cdot 96 < 98 \cdot 97$ so $\frac{99}{98} < \frac{97}{96}$. **25. a.** $\frac{1}{6}$ of a day **b.** $\frac{ab}{a+b}$ hours. In 1 hr Amal can finish $\frac{1}{a}$ of the job, while Sharif can finish $\frac{1}{b}$ of the job in 1 hr. If they work together, they can finish $\frac{1}{a} + \frac{1}{b}$ of the job in 1 hr. If it takes them x hr to finish the job working together, then $x\left(\frac{1}{a} + \frac{1}{b}\right) = 1$ or $\left(\frac{a+b}{ab}\right)x = 1$. Hence, $x = \frac{ab}{a+b}$.

Chapter 6 Review
1. c.

2. Answers vary; for example, $\frac{10}{12}, \frac{15}{18}, \frac{20}{24}$.
6. $-2\frac{1}{3}, -1\frac{7}{8}, 0, \left(\frac{71}{140}\right)^{300}, \frac{69}{140}, \frac{1}{2}, \frac{71}{140}, \left(\frac{74}{73}\right)^{300}$
7. Yes. By the definition of multiplication and the commutative and associative laws of multiplication, we can do the following:
$$\frac{4}{5} \cdot \frac{7}{8} \cdot \frac{5}{14} = \frac{4 \cdot 7 \cdot 5}{5 \cdot 8 \cdot 14}$$
$$= \frac{4 \cdot 7 \cdot 5}{8 \cdot 14 \cdot 5}$$
$$= \frac{4}{8} \cdot \frac{7}{14} \cdot \frac{5}{5}.$$

8. Answers vary. **a.** 24, because $\frac{1}{3}(8 \cdot 9)$ is equal to $\left(\frac{1}{3} \cdot 9\right) \cdot 8 = 3 \cdot 8 = 24$. **b.** 66, because $36 \cdot 1\frac{5}{6}$ is equal to

$36 \cdot \dfrac{11}{6} = 6 \cdot 11 = 66$.   **12.** Answers vary. For example, $\dfrac{76}{100}$ and $\dfrac{78}{100}$.   **17.** It is not reasonable to say that the university won $\dfrac{3}{4} + \dfrac{5}{8}$, or $\dfrac{11}{8}$, of its basketball games. The correct fraction cannot be determined without additional information but it is between $\dfrac{5}{8}$ and $\dfrac{3}{4}$.   **22.** $\dfrac{^-12}{10}$ is greater than $\dfrac{^-11}{9}$ because $^-12 \cdot 9 > ^-11 \cdot 10$. Alternatively, $\dfrac{^-12}{10} - \dfrac{^-11}{9} = \dfrac{^-108}{90} - \dfrac{^-110}{90} = \dfrac{2}{90}$, which is positive; therefore $-\dfrac{12}{10} > \dfrac{^-11}{9}$.   **26.** Answers vary. For example, the problem is to find how many $\dfrac{1}{2}$-yd pieces of ribbon there are in $1\dfrac{3}{4}$ yd. There are 3 pieces of length $\dfrac{1}{2}$ yd with $\dfrac{1}{4}$ yd left over. This $\dfrac{1}{4}$ yd is $\dfrac{1}{2}$ of a $\dfrac{1}{2}$-yd piece. Therefore, there are 3 pieces of $\dfrac{1}{2}$-yd ribbon and 1 piece that is $\dfrac{1}{2}$ of the $\dfrac{1}{2}$-yd piece or $3\dfrac{1}{2}$ of the $\dfrac{1}{2}$-yd pieces. Thus, "3 pieces and $\dfrac{1}{4}$ yd left" and "$3\dfrac{1}{2}$ pieces" are correct answers.   **32.** The ratio of hydrogen to the total is $1:9$. Therefore, $\dfrac{1}{9} = \dfrac{x}{16}$ implies $x = 1\dfrac{7}{9}$ oz.   **33.** No, the ratio depends on how many chips came from each plant.
40. The ratio of professors of other political persuasions to liberals is $1:7$ to $1:9$.   **42.** The cup that has 1 oz cream   **44.** No, the will is impossible because the fractions of cats to be shared do not add to 1. If the woman had x cats then the number of cats her will directs to be distributed is $\dfrac{1}{2}x + \dfrac{1}{3}x + \dfrac{1}{9}x = \dfrac{17}{18}x$, but the sum should be $1x$, or $\left(\dfrac{18}{18}\right)x$.

Answers to Now Try This

1. Consider two rational numbers $\dfrac{a}{b}$ and $\dfrac{c}{d}$, where $\dfrac{a}{b} < \dfrac{c}{d}$. By the denseness property of rational numbers we can find a rational number x_1 between the two fractions. Since $\dfrac{a}{b} < x_1$, there is a rational number x_2 between $\dfrac{a}{b}$ and x_1. We next can find a rational number x_3 between $\dfrac{a}{b}$ and x_2 and so on. This process can be repeated indefinitely, and hence we obtain infinitely many rational numbers $x_1, x_2, x_3, \ldots$ between $\dfrac{a}{b}$ and $\dfrac{c}{d}$.   **2.** Because $\dfrac{a}{b} < \dfrac{c}{d}$ with $b > 0$ and $d > 0$, Theorem 6-3 implies $ad < bc$. Adding ab to each side of the inequality, we now have $ab + ad < ab + bc$. Thus, by factoring $a(b + d) < b(a + c)$.   **3.** $\dfrac{3}{4}$ is greater than $\dfrac{1}{2}, \dfrac{1}{2} + \dfrac{1}{2} = 1$, so $\dfrac{3}{4} + \dfrac{1}{2} > 1$. $\dfrac{4}{6}$ is less than 1, so it cannot be the correct answer for $\dfrac{3}{4} + \dfrac{1}{2}$.   **4.** Answers vary. For example, consider the following. If Caleb has $10.00, how many chocolate bars can he buy if   **a.** the price of one bar is $2.00?   **b.** the price

of one bar is $\$\dfrac{1}{2}$? For (a) the answer is $10 \div 2$ or 5. For (b) the answer is $10 \div \dfrac{1}{2}$, which is the same as finding the number of $\dfrac{1}{2}$ s in 10. Since there are two halves in 1, in 10 there are 20. Hence Caleb can buy 20 bars.

5. $\dfrac{a}{b} \div \dfrac{c}{d} = \dfrac{\dfrac{a}{c}}{\dfrac{b}{d}} = \dfrac{\dfrac{a}{c} \cdot \dfrac{d}{b}}{\dfrac{b}{d} \cdot \dfrac{d}{b}} = \dfrac{\dfrac{a}{c} \cdot \dfrac{d}{b}}{1} = \dfrac{ad}{bc} = \dfrac{a}{b} \div \dfrac{c}{d}$

Answer to Preliminary Problem

The area of the holes is $\dfrac{1}{4} + \dfrac{1}{7} = \dfrac{11}{28}$ of the whole washer. Thus the area of the rubber in the finished product is $1 - \dfrac{11}{28} = \dfrac{17}{28}$ of the whole washer. If the area of the original piece of rubber is $1\dfrac{3}{8}$, then the area of the finished washer is $\left(\dfrac{17}{28}\right)\left(1\dfrac{3}{8}\right) = \left(\dfrac{17}{28}\right)\left(\dfrac{11}{8}\right) = \dfrac{187}{224}$ in.^{2} or about $\dfrac{5}{6}$ in.^{2}

CHAPTER 7

Assessment 7-1A

1. a. $0 \cdot 10^0 + 0 \cdot 10^{^-1} + 2 \cdot 10^{^-2} + 3 \cdot 10^{^-3}$
b. $2 \cdot 10^2 + 0 \cdot 10^1 + 6 \cdot 10^0 + 0 \cdot 10^{^-1} + 6 \cdot 10^{^-2}$
c. $3 \cdot 10^2 + 1 \cdot 10^1 + 2 \cdot 10^0 + 0 \cdot 10^{^-1} + 1 \cdot 10^{^-2} + 0 \cdot 10^{^-3} + 3 \cdot 10^{^-4}$ **d.** $0 \cdot 10^0 + 0 \cdot 10^{^-1} + 0 \cdot 10^{^-2} + 0 \cdot 10^{^-3} + 1 \cdot 10^{^-4} + 3 \cdot 10^{^-5} + 2 \cdot 10^{^-6}$ **5. a.** $\dfrac{109}{250}$ **b.** $\dfrac{629}{25}$
c. $\dfrac{^-316{,}027}{1000}$ **d.** $\dfrac{140{,}951}{5000}$ **e.** $\dfrac{^-43}{10}$ **f.** $\dfrac{^-6201}{100}$ **6.** A rational number in simplest form can be written as a terminating decimal if, and only if, the prime factorization of the denominator contains no primes other than 2 or 5.   **a.** Terminating   **b.** Terminating   **c.** Terminating   **d.** Terminating   **e.** Not terminating   **f.** Terminating   **7. a.** 0.8   **b.** 3.05   **c.** 0.5   **d.** 0.03125   **e.** Not possible   **f.** 0.2128   **8.** One hour is 60 minutes, so 7 minutes would be $\dfrac{7}{60}$ of an hour. This is not a terminating decimal because $\dfrac{7}{60}$ is in simplest form and 3 is a factor of the denominator.   **9.** Answers vary. Many values between 0 and 100 are composed of whole-number powers of 2 and 5, thus dividing 100 and being capable of being expressed as a two-digit decimal. These numbers include the coin designations of 1, 5, 10, 25, and 50 cents, but there are others which could have been used, such as 2¢ or 20¢.   **10. a.** 13.492, 13.49199, 13.4919, 13.49183   **b.** $-1.4053, -1.45, -1.453, -1.493$ **12.** There are 32 of 100 squares shaded, representing $\dfrac{32}{100}$ of the whole grid $= 0.32$ of the grid.

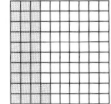

14. Answers vary. A decimal carried to the ten-thousandths place would have four digits to the right of the decimal point, and a number between 8.3400 and 8.3410 might be 8.3401, or 8.3405. **15. a.** Answers vary. One method could be to find the difference, no matter how slight, between the two decimal numbers and add some fraction of that to the lesser. **b.** Part (a) is a recursive process; no matter how small the difference between the terminating decimals, that difference can be divided. **16.** A meaning could be as follows: $3 \cdot 6^0 + 1 \cdot 6^1 + 4 \cdot 6^2 + 5 \cdot 6^3$ in base ten. In base six, 10_{six} would be used instead of 6.

Assessment 7-1B

1. a. $0 \cdot 10^0 + 0 \cdot 10^{-1} + 4 \cdot 10^{-2} + 5 \cdot 10^{-3}$
b. $1 \cdot 10^2 + 0 \cdot 10^1 + 3 \cdot 10^0 + 0 \cdot 10^{-1} + 3 \cdot 10^{-2}$
c. $2 \cdot 10^2 + 4 \cdot 10^1 + 5 \cdot 10^0 + 6 \cdot 10^{-1} + 7 \cdot 10^{-2} + 0 \cdot 10^{-3} + 1 \cdot 10^{-4}$ **d.** $0 \cdot 10^0 + 0 \cdot 10^{-1} + 0 \cdot 10^{-2} + 0 \cdot 10^{-3} + 3 \cdot 10^{-4} + 4 \cdot 10^{-5}$ **5. a.** $\frac{708}{25}$ **b.** $\frac{42{,}717}{1250}$ **c.** $\frac{-683}{25}$

7. a. 0.5 **b.** 0.015625 **c.** 0.2192 **d.** Not terminating **e.** 0.12 **f.** 0.4 **8.** All parts of an hour having a reduced fraction without 3 as a factor in the denominator; i.e., having a numerator divisible by 3: 0, 3, 6, 9, 12, 15, 18, 21, 24, 27, 30, 33, 36, 39, 42, 45, 48, 51, 54, 57 **9. d.** three thousand fourteen ten-thousandths **10. a.** 24.94189, 24.9419, 24.94199, 24.942 **b.** ‾34.2519, ‾34.251, ‾34.25, ‾34.205 **12.** There are 23 of 100 squares shaded, representing $\frac{23}{100}$ of the whole grid = 0.23 of the grid.

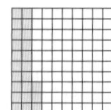

14. Answers vary. Write the decimals as 8.3450 and 8.3456; a decimal between them could be 8.34553. **15.** Answers vary but just as there are infinitely many rational numbers of the form $\frac{a}{b}$, where $a, b \in I$, this argument can be extended to terminating decimals. For example between 0.0625 and 0.125 $\left(\text{representing } \frac{1}{16} \text{ and } \frac{1}{8}\right)$, we know that $\frac{1}{8} = \frac{2}{16} = \frac{4}{32}$ and $\frac{1}{16} = \frac{2}{32}$, so $\frac{3}{32}$, or 0.09375, is between 0.0625 and 0.125. The process can continue and all are terminating decimals.
16. One meaning in base ten could be $0 \cdot 7^0 + 0 \cdot 7^1 + 0 \cdot 7^2 + 3 \cdot 7^3 + 3 \cdot 7^4 + 4 \cdot 7^5$. In base seven, 10_{seven} replaces 7.
18. $\frac{1}{16} = 0.0625; \frac{2}{16} = 0.125;$

$\frac{3}{16} = 0.1875; \frac{4}{16} = 0.25; \frac{5}{16} = 0.3125; \frac{6}{16} = 0.375;$

$\frac{7}{16} = 0.4375; \frac{8}{16} = 0.5; \frac{9}{16} = 0.5625; \frac{10}{16} = 0.625;$

$\frac{11}{16} = 0.6875; \frac{12}{16} = 0.75; \frac{13}{16} = 0.8125; \frac{14}{16} = 0.875;$

$\frac{15}{16} = 0.9375; \frac{16}{16} = 1$

Mathematical Connections 7-1

Reasoning
1. a. 3 ① 2 ② 5 ③ 6 ④ **b.** 0 ① 0 ② 3 ③ 2 ④
2. 0.018 L **3.** One day cannot be expressed as a terminating decimal because $\frac{1}{365}$ cannot be written as a terminating decimal.
4. There is no greatest terminating decimal less than 1 because the unit segment with endpoints 0 and 1 can be divided into smaller and smaller segments $\left(\text{whose lengths are powers of } \frac{1}{10}\right)$ and the smaller segments can be counted from the left, always letting another number be between any supposedly "closest" number and 1. **5.** The true meaning would be $\frac{5}{100}$¢, or \$0.0005, per copy and not the real intended price of 5¢ per copy.
6. Answers vary. For example, you could use 2 blocks to represent the units, 3 flats to represent the tenths, 4 longs to represent the hundredths, and 5 cubes to represent the thousandths.
7. Answers vary. For example, a fraction can be written as a terminating decimal if it can be written as a fraction with a denominator that is a power of 10. The denominator can be written as a power of 10 if it contains only factors of 2 and 5. Other factors may appear in the denominator if the fraction is not in simplest form. For example, in $\frac{28}{35}$ the denominator of 35 has a factor of 7, but in its simplest form, $\frac{4}{5}$, there is no factor of 7.

8. $0.340 = 3 \cdot 10^{-1} + 4 \cdot 10^{-2} + 0 \cdot 10^{-3} = 0.34$ **9. a.** $\frac{1}{5}$ is a number less than 1 and 2 is greater than 1 so it must be incorrect.
b. $\frac{2}{3}$ as a decimal is not terminating; 0.6 is terminating, so they can't be equal.

Open-Ended
10. Answers vary. **11.** Answers vary.

Cooperative Learning
12. Answers vary depending on the objects chosen. For example, if a 5 × 5 flat is used to represent 1, then a 1 × 5 long would represent 0.1, and a 1 × 1 cube would represent 0.01.
13. Stevin did not invent the system; he invented the notation for the system. **14. a.** In the first box because 9 is the greatest of the numbers. **b.** In the last box because it is the least of the numbers. **c.** (i) Yes, if 8 or 9 is drawn, (ii) No **d.** Carl

Connecting Mathematics to the Classroom
15. Answers vary. The student is mistaken. $0.86 = \frac{86}{100};$ $0.9 = \frac{90}{100}$ and $\frac{90}{100} > \frac{86}{100}$, so 0.9 > 0.86. **16.** Answers vary. One argument frequently made is that advanced mathematics needs concepts of rational numbers. Another is that the measurement system in the United States still uses fractions. Most importantly to understand decimals, we need to understand fractions. Also, fractions are used in everyday life even in countries that use the metric system.
17. Answers vary. $0.304 = \frac{304}{100}, 0.34 = 0.340 = \frac{340}{100}.$

Because $340 \neq 304$, the decimals are not equal. **18.** Answers vary. The second sequence is the term-by-term sum of the first sequence and the arithmetic sequence $1, 1, 1, \ldots$. Because $\dfrac{1.01}{1.1} \neq \dfrac{1.001}{1.01}$ it is not a geometric sequence. In general a sum of a geometric sequence and an arithmetic sequence is neither geometric nor arithmetic.

Assessment 7-2A

1.

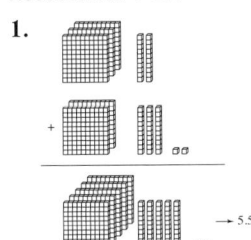

→ 5.52

2. a. $\dfrac{86}{10} + \dfrac{231}{10} + \dfrac{92}{100} = \dfrac{860}{100} + \dfrac{2310}{100} + \dfrac{92}{100} = \dfrac{3262}{100} = 32.62$

b. $\dfrac{232}{100} + \dfrac{21008}{1000} = \dfrac{2320}{1000} + \dfrac{21008}{1000} = \dfrac{23328}{1000} = 23.328$

3. a. $\dfrac{5}{10} \cdot \dfrac{6}{10} = \dfrac{30}{100} = 0.30$ **b.** $\dfrac{203}{1} \cdot \dfrac{3}{100} = \dfrac{609}{100} = 6.09$

c. $\dfrac{3}{1000} \cdot \dfrac{6}{1000} = \dfrac{18}{1,000,000} = 0.000018$ **4.** Answers vary.

a. 2989.536; 934.23 has 2 decimal places, and 3.2 has 1 decimal place so we move $2 + 1 = 3$ decimal places in the answer. **b.** The product is about $900 \cdot 3 = 2700$, so the decimal point is placed as 2989.536. **13.** Approximately \$28.58 Canadian **15.** Approximately 8.64 L **18.** A finite geometric sequence is one with a constant ratio between terms and a finite number of terms. 0.2222 can be expressed as a sum:
$\dfrac{2}{10} + \dfrac{2}{100} + \dfrac{2}{1000} + \dfrac{2}{10,000}$; note that the denominators are powers of ten. Thus to make it a geometric sequence with constant ratio $\dfrac{1}{10}$, it could be written as
$\dfrac{2}{10} + \left(\dfrac{2}{10}\right)\left(\dfrac{1}{10}\right) + \left(\dfrac{2}{10}\right)\left(\dfrac{1}{10}\right)^2 + \left(\dfrac{2}{10}\right)\left(\dfrac{1}{10}\right)^3$.

19. ⟵—┼—┼————┼—┼—⟶ **22.** 153.45 cm
   (b) 0 0.5 (a) 1

24. a. Approximately 13 or 14 **25. a.** Approximately 18.6 **c.** Approximately 121 **37.** Answers vary. For example,
$40 \cdot \$8 + 40 \cdot \left(\dfrac{1}{4}\right)\$ = \$320 + \$10 = \$330$.

40. a. $2 \cdot 1 + 0.25 = 2.25 = 1.5^2$
   $3 \cdot 2 + 0.25 = 6.25 = 2.5^2$
A conjecture is that the next two are: $4 \cdot 3 + 0.25 = (3.5)^2$ and $5 \cdot 4 + 0.25 = (4.5)^2$. **b.** Answers vary. Since $1.5 = 2 - 0.5, 2.5 = 3 - 0.5, 3.5 = 4 - 0.5$, and $4.5 = 5 - 0.5$, we conjecture that for each natural numbers, $n(n-1) + 0.25 = (n - .5)^2$. This is true since $(n - .5)^2 = (n - .5)(n - .5) = n^2 - .5n - .5n + .25 = n^2 - n + .25 = n(n-1) + .25$.

Assessment 7-2B

1.

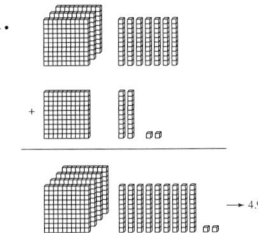

→ 4.92

2. a. $\dfrac{53}{10} + \dfrac{132}{10} + \dfrac{86}{100} = \dfrac{530}{100} + \dfrac{1320}{100} + \dfrac{86}{100} = \dfrac{1936}{100} = 19.36$

b. $\dfrac{542}{100} + \dfrac{32005}{1000} = \dfrac{5420}{1000} + \dfrac{32005}{1000} = \dfrac{37425}{1000} = 37.425$

3. a. $\dfrac{3}{10} \cdot \dfrac{8}{10} = \dfrac{24}{100} = 0.24$ **b.** $\dfrac{502}{1} \cdot \dfrac{4}{100} = \dfrac{2008}{100} = 20.08$

c. $\dfrac{4}{1000} \cdot \dfrac{6}{100} = \dfrac{24}{100,000} = 0.00024$ **4.** Answers vary.

a. 3780.341; 564.23 has 2 decimal places, and 6.7 has 1 decimal place, so we move the decimal point $2 + 1 = 3$ places. **b.** The product is about $600 \cdot 7 = 4,200$, so the decimal point is placed as 3780.341.
17. $0.3333333 = 0.3 + 0.03 + 0.003 + \cdots + 0.0000003$ or
$\dfrac{3}{10} + \dfrac{3}{10}\left(\dfrac{1}{10}\right) + \dfrac{3}{10}\left(\dfrac{1}{10}\right)^2 + \cdots + \dfrac{3}{10}\left(\dfrac{1}{10}\right)^6$.
This is the finite sum of a geometric sequence with
$a_1 = 0.3, n = 7, a_7 = 0.0000003$, and $r = \dfrac{0.03}{0.3} = \dfrac{1}{10} = 0.1$.
18. ⟵┼—┼————┼——⟶ **23. a.** Answers vary around 62
   (b) 0 0.5 (a) 1
or 63. **28. c.** 3,000,000,000 **32.** Answers vary, for example, 10.3 because $9 \cdot 10 = 90$ and $9 \cdot 0.3$ is greater than 2 and less than 4. **36.** Answers vary, for example, $40 \cdot \$6 + 40 \cdot (1/4)\$ = \$240 + \$10 = \$250$.

Mathematical Connections 7-2

Reasoning

1. 0.03. We know that 0.76 and 0.75 differ by 0.01 so $0.76 \cdot 3$ and $0.75 \cdot 3$ differ by $3 \cdot 0.01$ or 0.03. **2.** Answers vary. For example, the multiplication of decimals is exactly like the multiplication of whole numbers if the decimal points are ignored. The difference occurs when the decimal point is placed to obtain the final answer. **3.** Answers vary. For example, many of the estimation techniques that work for whole-number division also work for decimal division. The long division algorithm is more efficient when good estimates are used. Also, estimates are important to determine whether an answer obtained by long division is reasonable. Estimation techniques can also be used to place the decimal point in the quotient when decimals are divided. **4.** Answers vary. For example, which form is easier depends on the numbers to be multiplied or divided. In most cases, it is probably easier to work with decimals because the algorithms work just as they do for whole numbers except for the placement of the final decimal point, which in turn is very easy. However, when infinite repeating decimals are involved, it is much easier to work with fractions as will be seen in the next section. **5.** Answers vary. For example, lining up the decimal points acts like using place value.

6. Yes. Suppose the decimals are x and y. Because terminating decimals are rational numbers, inequalities for decimals have the same properties as inequalities among rationals. If $0 < x < 1$, multiply both sides of the inequality by y to get $0 \cdot y < xy < 1 \cdot y$ or $0 < xy < y$. Similarly $0 < xy < x$. **7.** $0.07 + 0.08 = 0.15$, which is 1 tenth and 5 hundredths. The 1 above the 6 represents the 1 tenth when we regroup.

Open-Ended

8. Answers vary depending on the articles chosen. **9.** Answers vary. For example, the calculator could be used to explore the result of placing the decimal point when multiplying by a power of 10 or of placing the decimal point when multiplying two decimals. **10.** Answers vary.

Cooperative Learning

11. Answers vary depending on groups. For example, students need to understand place value, expanded form, basic arithmetic facts, and whole-number arithmetic algorithms. They also need to understand what a decimal point does and how place value is used with decimals. **12.** Answers vary.

Connecting Mathematics to the Classroom

13. Answers vary. To show that the answer is correct, the computation might be done using fractions and showing how the fraction computation does the same thing that the rule does. For example,

$$0.125 \cdot 0.08 = \frac{125}{1000} \cdot \frac{8}{100} = \frac{1000}{100,000} = \frac{1}{100} = 0.01$$

A calculator could also be used to show this method results in the same answer as obtained on the calculator.
14. Answers vary. For example, using place value $0.3 = 3 \cdot (1/10)$ and $0.30 = 3 \cdot (1/10) + 0 \cdot (1/100) = 3 \cdot (1/10) + 0$. Because adding 0 does not change the value of the number, the two numbers represent the same amount. **15.** Answers vary. For example, Fred should be told that this is an excellent way to determine where to place the decimal point. He should be encouraged to try this technique to gain confidence that it works and increase his skills. Products should be computed in other ways to show that his method is correct and just a different way of doing the computation. **16.** In the second method, the student did not use the distributive property correctly. Notice that $\left(8 + \frac{1}{2}\right)\left(6 + \frac{1}{2}\right) = \left(8 + \frac{1}{2}\right)6 + \left(8 + \frac{1}{2}\right)\left(\frac{1}{2}\right)$. Because $\left(8 + \frac{1}{2}\right)6 = 8 \cdot 6 + \left(\frac{1}{2}\right)6 = 48 + 3$, the 3 is missing in the student's second computation. Adding 3 to the student's answer here results in the correct answer of $55\frac{1}{4}$. **17.** It is evident what happens when 0.5 is raised to large powers. Because $\left(\frac{1}{2}\right)^{10} = \frac{1}{1024}$ and $\frac{1}{2^{20}} = \left[\left(\frac{1}{2}\right)^{10}\right]^2 = \frac{1}{1,048,576}$, therefore $\frac{1}{2}$ raised to a positive integer gets quickly close to 0. In fact, any number between 0 and 1 when raised to a sufficiently large exponent will get as close to 0 as we wish. Using the $\boxed{x^2}$ key repeatedly, we get: 0.998001, 0.996005996, 0.99202794407, 0.98411944182, 0.96849107576, ..., 0.3589714782, ..., which

are approximate values of $0.999^2, 0.999^4, 0.999^8, 0.999^{16}, \ldots,$ 0.999^{1024}. We see that the 10th term in the sequence is less than 0.5 and hence further squaring should quickly result in numbers closer and closer to 0. **18. a.** The calculator does not carry the decimals out far enough to compare the two numbers.
b. $\dfrac{9444}{9445} - \dfrac{9443}{9444} > 0. \qquad \dfrac{9444^2 - 9443 \cdot 9445}{9444 \cdot 9445} > 0.$
The last inequality is true if, and only if, the numerator of the fraction is positive. Using a calculator we find that $9444^2 - 9443 \cdot 9445 = 1$ and hence that

$$\frac{9444}{9445} > \frac{9443}{9444}$$

We can also show $9444^2 - 9443 \cdot 9445 = 1$ without a calculator. Let $a = 9444$. Then $9444^2 - 9443 \cdot 9445 = a^2 - (a - 1)(a + 1) = a^2 - (a^2 - 1) = a^2 - a^2 + 1 = 1$. It is possible to determine which fraction is greater with fewer calculations, as follows:

$$\frac{9443}{9444} = \frac{9444 - 1}{9444} = 1 - \frac{1}{9444}$$

$$\frac{9444}{9445} = \frac{9445 - 1}{9445} = 1 - \frac{1}{9445}$$

Because $\dfrac{1}{9445} < \dfrac{1}{9444}, \dfrac{^-1}{9445} > \dfrac{^-1}{9444}$ and hence,

$1 - \dfrac{1}{9445} > 1 - \dfrac{1}{9444}$. Yet another approach is to multiply each decimal equivalent by 10. Because $\dfrac{9444}{9445} \cdot 10$ is displayed as 9.998412, and $\dfrac{9443}{9444} \cdot 10$ as 9.9989411, the first fraction is the greater one. However, this approach will not work to show that $\dfrac{94444}{94445} > \dfrac{94443}{94444}$.

Review Problems

19. $14.0479 = 1 \cdot 10^1 + 4 \cdot 10^0 + 0 \cdot 10^{-1} + 4 \cdot 10^{-2} + 7 \cdot 10^{-3} + 9 \cdot 10^{-4}$ **20. a.** Not a terminating decimal **b.** Is a terminating decimal **21.** Yes; for example, $\dfrac{13}{26} = \dfrac{1}{2} = 0.5$. **22.** 0.625. The decimal terminates because $\dfrac{35}{56} = \dfrac{5}{8}$ in simplest form and $8 = 2^3$.

Assessment 7-3A

1. No, the fraction is in simplest form, and the denominator contains factors other than 2's and 5's. **2. a.** No, the only difference is that the repeating block of 7's is indicated in different ways.
7. b. $\dfrac{61}{99}$ **f.** $\dfrac{^-2}{90}$ **9.** $^-1.454 > ^-1.45\overline{4} > ^-1.\overline{454} > ^-1.\overline{454} = ^-1.\overline{45}$ **10.** Answers vary. $\dfrac{6}{7} = 0.\overline{857142}, \dfrac{7}{8} = 0.875, \dfrac{8}{9} = 0.\overline{8}$
12. The repeating decimal part is determined by the 7 in the denominator of $3\dfrac{1}{7} = \dfrac{22}{7}$. The denominator, 7, has a prime factor other than 2 or 5 and so it cannot terminate. **14.** Yes, zeros can be repeated or 9s could be repeated. For example, $0.5 = 0.5000\ldots = 0.49999\ldots$ **17. a.** Answers vary. For example, 0.751, 0.752, 0.753. **b.** Answers vary. For example, 0.334, 0.335, 0.336. **19. b.** $\dfrac{1}{9999}$

Assessment 7-3B

1. No, the fraction is in simplest form and the denominator has factors other than 2's and 5's.   **2. a.** No, the 6's repeat after the 34 in all three cases.   **6. h.** $0.\overline{210526315789473684}$

12. Answers vary. The denominator in $\frac{1}{13}$ cannot be written in the form $2^n \cdot 5^m$, where n and m are whole numbers. The fraction cannot represent a terminating decimal. It must repeat. The maximum possible length of the repetend is 12 but in fact it has period only 6. **13.** $1.35\overline{775}$. The answer is a rational number, and there are four digits in the repetend.   **15. b.** Answers vary; for example, 203.768, 203.769, and 203.7691.

19. a. i. $\frac{2}{9}$ **ii.** $\frac{2}{90}$ or $\frac{1}{45}$ **iii.** $\frac{2}{900}$ or $\frac{1}{450}$ **b.** $\frac{2}{9000}$ or $\frac{1}{4500}$

Mathematical Connections 7-3

Reasoning

1. a. Mathematically the cost is $66\frac{2}{3}$¢ but realistically, the cost is 67¢. **b.** 67¢ **c.** The cost is rounded up. **d.** Most cash registers do not allow repeating decimals, so grocery stores do not use them. **e.** See part (d).   **2.** Yes. Zeros can be appended to any finite decimal to make it an infinite decimal. Also every finite decimal can be converted into an infinite decimal by using a repetend of 9. **3.** Answers vary. For example, it is easier to compute addition of fractions when there is a common denominator, as in $\frac{1}{7} + \frac{5}{7}$. When nonrepeating decimals are involved, it becomes hard to do additions because of lining up the digits using place value. When denominators are different and terminating decimals are obtained, it is easier to use decimals, as in $\frac{2}{5} + \frac{1}{4} = 0.40 + 0.25 = 0.65$.

4. $\frac{1}{11} = 0.\overline{09}$, $\frac{1}{111} = 0.\overline{009}$, $\frac{1}{1111} = 0.\overline{0009}$, so we would expect that $\frac{1}{11111} = 0.\overline{00009}$. When the divisions are performed longhand, we can see that for each successive number of 1s in the denominator, it takes one more place before a remainder of 1 occurs, and we have the initial division repeated.

Open-Ended

5. a. They each have six-digit repetends using each of the digits 1, 2, 4, 5, 7, 8 exactly once in the same cyclic order. **b.** Answers vary. For example, the patterns of the digits are cyclic; that is, they repeat in the same order. **c.** For example, $\frac{x}{17}$, where x is a natural number. The patterns of the digits repeat in cyclic order in the repetends. **6. a. i.** $0.\overline{6}$ **ii.** 1; 1 is the simplest form because it requires the fewest symbols. **iii.** $1.\overline{06}$ **b.** Because there is no right-hand end to start with, it is difficult to see how the traditional algorithm could be easily adapted into an algorithm in this context. **c.** A repeating decimal can be written as a rational number in the form $\frac{a}{b}$, where $b \neq 0$. The fractions can be multiplied and the product can be converted to a decimal. **7. a.** Answers vary. If we enter the numbers with several digits, the calculator may produce a clearly identifiable repeating decimal. For example, if we multiply 3.444444444... by 2.575575757... the calculator will display the answer 8.872053872053.... **b.** See part (a). **8.** Most would prefer $\frac{7}{3}$ as

a solution. However when melons are priced at 3 for $7, we might prefer to know that they are $2.333... each and hence actually $2.34 each. Thus the answer depends on the context.

Cooperative Learning

9. Answers vary.

Connecting Mathematics to the Classroom

10. Answers vary. A calculator is a tool that may aid in the computation of decimals. It can help by furnishing estimates for answers. This has to do with the value of the calculator as a tool. The value of repeating decimals is a different question. One major white-collar crime dealt with rounding off fractions of pennies and depositing that money in a bank account. These fractions could have been the result of using repeating decimals and rounding. Depending upon the context, the result of not using such decimals could lead to serious errors.   **11.** Yes, because every rational number can be written as a repeating decimal. For example, $0.45 = 0.44\overline{9}$. However the sum of two decimals that cannot be written as terminating decimals can still be a terminating decimal; for example $\frac{1}{11} + \frac{1}{110} = \frac{1}{10}$.   **12.** Because $0.3333 \neq \frac{1}{3}$ the answer is incorrect. However, it is a good approximation. **13.** Bob has the right idea. Terminating decimal can be written with repetend 0 as in $\frac{1}{5} = 0.2 = 0.200000$. But Bob should also consider a number like $2 = 1.999999...$ that has a repetend of 9.   **14.** If the goal is to get an approximation, then Joe is correct. Using his method $2 \cdot 0.142857142 = 0.285714284$, which is a good approximation of $\frac{2}{7}$. However, it is not accurate as $\frac{2}{7} \neq 0.285714285714$. This difference occurs from truncating the actual value of $\frac{1}{7}$. It might be easier to see with smaller numbers. For example, if Joe truncates $\frac{1}{6}$ to 0.16 then multiplies 0.16 by 2 to obtain the value of $\frac{2}{6}$ he would obtain 0.32. However, $\frac{2}{6} = \frac{1}{3} = 0.3333...$ and we can see what happens when we truncate the value. **15.** The repeating decimals $0.\overline{4}$ and $0.\overline{44}$ are equal and are just written in different ways. This can be seen by converting each to rational number form and simplifying:
$0.\overline{4} = \frac{4}{9} = \frac{44}{99} = 0.\overline{44}$.

Review Problems

16. $22,761.95 **17.** Approximately $2.35 \cdot 10^{13}$ **18.** 0.077. The rule says that the decimal point should be placed four digits from the right of the product of 22 and 35. This product is 770, and therefore the answer is 0.0770, which equals 0.077. **19.** Answers vary. For example, **a.** 3.024 **b.** ⁻3.024 **c.** 134.8 **d.** 0.00713

Assessment 7-4A

2.

6.
$\frac{60}{100} = \frac{x}{125}$, $x = 75$

18. $\frac{325}{500}; \frac{325}{500} = \frac{650}{1000} = \frac{65}{100} = 65\%$, while $\frac{600}{1000} = \frac{60}{100} = 60\%$.
19. b. 10 items. You get two more items for the same price.   **22.** The apprentice earns $700, the journeyman $1400, and the master $2100.   **25. a.** The report is essentially true.   **26.** No. Since 56% is more then double 25%, $950 should be more than double $500, but it is not.

32. *Interest Rate per Period*   **c.** $\frac{10}{12}\%$ or $8\frac{1}{3}\%$ **d.** $\frac{12}{365}\%$

Assessment 7-4B

2.

6.

$\frac{60}{100} = \frac{x}{150}, x = 90$

11. b. $1\frac{1}{2}$ in.   **12.** $17\frac{11}{17}\%$ or approximately 18%.

13. $18\frac{37}{91}\%$ or approximately 18%.   **16.** $\left(\frac{9}{34}\right)\%$ or

approximately 0.26%.   **30. c.** $30 \cdot 1.2 = 36$, this works since $30 + 0.20 \cdot 30 = 1 \cdot 30 + 0.20 \cdot 30 = (1 + 0.20)30 = 1.2 \cdot 30$.

31. *Interest Rate per Period*   **d.** $\frac{18}{365}\%$

38.

	A1's Investment	Betty's Investment
Year 1	1061.83	1070
Year 2	1127.49	1140
Year 3	1197.20	1210
Year 4	1271.22	1280
Year 5	1349.83	1350
Year 6	1433.29	1420

Mathematical Connections 7-4

Reasoning
1. Answers vary. For example, 10% of 850 is 85 and 1% of 850 is 8.5, so 11% of 850 is 93.5.   **2.** No, $0.4\% = \frac{0.4}{100} = 0.004$ and $0.004 \neq 0.4$.   **3.** It means that not only did you meet 100% of your savings goal, you surpassed it by 25%. If your savings goal was $100, then you saved $100 plus an extra $25.   **4.** Yes, 4% of $98 = \frac{4}{100} \cdot 98 = \frac{4 \cdot 98}{100 \cdot 1} = \frac{98 \cdot 4}{100 \cdot 1} = \frac{98}{100} \cdot \frac{4}{1} = 98\%$ of 4.   **5. a.** Greater, because if 25% of x is 55, then x must be 4 times as great as 55, or 220.   **b.** Less, because if 150% of x is 55, then x is only $\frac{2}{3}$ of 55, or $36\frac{2}{3}$.
6. Yes; for example, 35% of 100 = 35 is greater than 55% of 50 = 27.5.   **7.** The *whole* in each part is different, so 50% of the greater quantity is greater than 50% of the lesser quantity. To be equal, we would have to have the same size whole initially.
8. Answers vary. For example, a price can increase 150%. If an

item is bought for $100, it can be sold for $250, an increase of $150, or 150% of the original price. The price can't decrease 150%, because 100% is the entire amount. A price cannot be less than 0.   **9.** Let x be the amount invested. The first stock will be worth $(1.15x)0.85$ after 2 yr. The second stock will be worth $(0.85x)1.15$. Because each of these equals $(1.15 \cdot 0.85)x$ (commutative and associative properties of multiplication), the investments are equally good.   **10.** Let a be the original value of the house. Because it depreciated 10% each year for the first 3 yr, using compound depreciation, the price after 3 yr is $a(1 - 0.10)^3$, or $a \cdot 0.9^3$. Because of compound appreciation, after another 3 yr, the value of the house is $a \cdot 0.9^3 \cdot 1.1^3$, or $a(0.9^3 \cdot 1.1^3)$, which equals approximately $a \cdot 0.9703$. Because $0.9703a < a$, the value of the house had decreased after 6 yr. The value of the house decreased by approximately 3%.   **11.** If we want our money doubled, then $2 = 1(1 + 0.02)^n$, or $2 = 1.02^n$. By trial and error, we can find that 1.02^{35} is approximately 2, so it would take about 35 yr to double an investment at 2% compounded annually.   **12.** No, the percentages cannot be added because each time the percent is of a different quantity. After 5 yr, the car would have depreciated approximately 67%.   **13.** This is impossible because greater than 50% of the boys and 50% of the girls wanted a prom.   **14.** Yes, if the class has twice as many boys as girls.   **15.** Let x be the percent that Abe paid on his bill. Then $75x = 56.25$, and $x = 75\%$. So Abe received a 25% discount. Let y be the percent that Barb paid. Then $52y = 31.20$, and $y = 60\%$ and so her discount was 40%. Barb saved the greater percentage off the original price.   **16.** Dan is correct in that the sales tax is only going up by 1 percentage point. Stan is correct since increasing the sales tax by 1% over 5% is increasing it by $\frac{1}{5} = 0.20$ or 20%.

Open-Ended
17. Answers vary.   **18.** Answers vary.   **19.** Answers vary. For example,   **a.** 115 is 37% of what number?   **b.** a is $p\%$ of what number?   **20. a.** Answers vary.   **b.** Let a be an initial cost of an item that depreciates at a rate of $p\%$ each period of time. If n is the number of periods and $C(n)$ is the value (as a function of n) after n periods, then $C(n) = a\left(1 - \frac{p}{100}\right)^n$ **21.** Answers vary.

Cooperative Learning
22. Answers vary.   **23.** Answers vary.   **24.** Answers vary.

Connecting Mathematics to the Classroom
25. Jamal needs to understand that in order to compare percents the whole must be the same. Ask him to calculate the number of girls if Washington had 300 students (48% of 300 = 144), and Jefferson had 200 students (52% of 200 = 104). In this case, Washington School had more girls.   **26.** Prices can increase 120%; for example, a shirt that cost $10 can increase in cost to $22 for a 120% increase. However, in an election 100% of the votes is all that is possible.   **27.** $3\frac{1}{4}\% = 3\% + \frac{1}{4}\% = \frac{3}{100} + \frac{\left(\frac{1}{4}\right)}{100} = 0.03 + 0.0025 = 0.0325$. Knowing that $\frac{1}{4} = 0.25$, the student incorrectly wrote $\frac{1}{4}\% = 0.25$, not 0.25%.   **28.** Let s denote

the amount of salary. After a $p\%$ increase, the new salary is $s\left(1 + \dfrac{p}{100}\right)$. When this amount is decreased by $q\%$, the result is $s\left(1 + \dfrac{p}{100}\right)\left(1 - \dfrac{q}{100}\right)$. Similarly, if the initial salary is first decreased by $q\%$ and then the new amount is raised by $p\%$, the final salary is $s\left(1 - \dfrac{q}{100}\right)\left(1 + \dfrac{p}{100}\right)$. Because the two expressions are equal by the commutative property of multiplication, the student is right. **29.** No, she is not correct. Men make 25¢ more for every 75¢ that women make, so men make $\dfrac{25}{75} = 33\dfrac{1}{3}\%$ more than women. **30.** Because the formula for compound interest is $A = P(1 + r)^n$ and $P = d$ dollars and $r = 1$, then we have $A = d(1 + 1)^n = d \cdot 2^n$. Thus, the student is correct.

Review Problems

31. a. 21.6 lb **b.** 48 lb **32. a.** $\dfrac{418}{25}$ **b.** $\dfrac{3}{1000}$ **c.** $\dfrac{^-507}{100}$

d. $\dfrac{123}{1000}$ **33. a.** $4.\overline{9}$ **b.** $5.0\overline{9}$ **c.** $0.4\overline{9}$ **34.** $\dfrac{3}{12,500}$

35. $\dfrac{8}{33}$ **36. a.** 208,000 **b.** 0.00038

Chapter 7 Review

1. b. $D(0.09), E(0.15)$

3. A fraction in simplest from, $\dfrac{a}{b}$, can be written as a terminating decimal if, and only if, the prime factorization of the denominator contains no primes other than 2 or 5. **5. a.** $\dfrac{4}{7} = 0.\overline{571428}$ **b.** $\dfrac{1}{8} = 0.125$

c. $\dfrac{2}{3} = 0.\overline{6}$ **d.** $\dfrac{5}{8} = 0.625$ **6. a.** $0.28 = \dfrac{7}{25}$

b. $^-6.07 = \dfrac{^-607}{100}$ **c.** $0.\overline{3} = \dfrac{1}{3}$ **d.** $2.0\overline{8} = \dfrac{94}{45}$

9. $1.451\overline{9}, 1.45\overline{19}, 1.45\overline{19}, 1.4519, 0.13\overline{401}, ^-0.134, ^-0.13\overline{401}$.
11. a. Answers vary. 0.105, 0.104, 0.103, 0.102, 0.101
b. Answers vary; 0.0005, 0.001, 0.002, 0.004 **19.** A discount of $d\%$ means the customer pays $1 - \dfrac{d}{100}$ for the purchase. Discounts of 5%, 10%, and 20% mean the customer pays 0.95, 0.90, and 0.80, respectively, of cost. Their product, 0.684, is the same in any order; therefore, there is no difference. **22.** Answers vary. If the dress was originally priced at $100, 60% off would result in a sale price of $40. Then the additional 40% off coupon would result in a final price of $24. The reasoning could be applied to the actual list price of the dress. A percentage has to be a percentage of something, in this case her 40% coupon gives her 40% off the already discounted price, not 40% off the list price before the 60% discount. **23.** The store is losing on the item (9%).

Answers to Now Try This

2. a. Answers vary.

b. i. $3.6 \cdot 1000 = 3.6 \cdot 10^3 = \left(3 + \dfrac{6}{10}\right)10^3 =$

$3 \cdot 10^3 + \dfrac{6}{10} \cdot 10^3 = 3 \cdot 10^3 + 6 \cdot 10^2 = 3 \cdot 10^3 + 6 \cdot 10^2 +$

$0 \cdot 10^1 + 0 \cdot 1 = 3600$. Thus, we see that multiplication by 1000 results in moving the decimal point three places to the right. **ii.** In general, multiplication by 10^n, where n is a positive integer, results in moving the decimal point n places to the right. **3.** Answers vary. For example, using the front digits the first estimate is $2 + $0 + $6 + $4 + $5 = $17. Next, we adjust the estimate. Because $0.89 + $0.13 is about $1.00 and $0.75 + $0.05 is $0.80 and $0.80 + $0.39 is about $1.20, the adjustment is $2.20, and the estimate is $19.20.

Answer to the Preliminary Problem

The new copy will be 6.75 cm by 13.5 cm. The one-stage setting should be $(1.5)(1.5) = 2.25$ or 225%. If a specific number such as 100 is used, then 150% of 100 = 150. We ask, "what percent of 150 is 100?" Solving $\dfrac{100}{150} = \dfrac{x}{100}$ gives $x = 66\dfrac{2}{3}$; $66\dfrac{2}{3}\%$.

CHAPTER 8
Assessment 8-1A

1. Answers vary $0.232232223\ldots$ **8. b.** Answers vary. Three such numbers are: $0.546010010001\ldots, 0.547010010001\ldots,$ and $0.548010010001\ldots$ Then $0.\overline{54} < 0.546010010001\ldots < 0.547010010001\ldots < 00.548010010001\ldots < 0.\overline{55}$ **c.** Answers vary. $\dfrac{\sqrt{3}}{4}, \dfrac{\pi}{7},$ and $\dfrac{\sqrt{2}}{3}$ are three such irrational numbers.
9. Answers vary. For example, between any two rational numbers we could find three irrational numbers. Because there are infinitely many disjoint intervals bounded by rational numbers, there must be infinitely many irrational numbers.
13. e. All real numbers greater than zero
16. a. $5\sqrt[3]{2}, 5\sqrt[3]{4}$ **b.** $2^{3/4}, 2^{1/2}, 2^{1/4}$ or $^-2^{3/4}, 2^{1/2}, 2^{-1/4}$
c. There are two possible geometric sequences.
$\dfrac{5\sqrt{15}}{3}, 5, \sqrt{15}, 3$ $\dfrac{^-5\sqrt{15}}{3}, 5, ^-\sqrt{15}, 3$
d. There are two possible geometric sequences.
$\dfrac{2\sqrt{6}}{3}, ^-2, \sqrt{6}, ^-3$ $\dfrac{^-2\sqrt{6}}{3}, ^-2, ^-\sqrt{6}, ^-3$
21. $4^3 = 64$
$4.6^3 \approx 97.3$
$4.7^3 \approx 103.8$
$5^3 = 125$
So, an integer approximation of $\sqrt[3]{103}$ is 5.

Assessment 8-1B

1. Answers vary. **8. a.** Answers vary. For example,
$3 + \dfrac{\sqrt{2}}{3}, 3 + \dfrac{\sqrt{2}}{4}, 3 + \dfrac{\sqrt{2}}{5}$ **b.** Answers vary. Three such numbers are: $0.562010010001\ldots, 0.563010010001\ldots,$ and $0.564010010001\ldots$ **c.** Answers vary. The approach described in part (b) will produce three such irrational numbers.
9. $1 + \dfrac{\sqrt{2}}{n}$ for $n > 2$. **10. e.** $\overline{S} = Q$, where Q is the set of rational numbers. **16. a.** $4\sqrt[3]{2}, 4\sqrt[3]{4}$ **b.** $\sqrt[3]{2}, \sqrt[3]{4}$
c. $4, 2\sqrt{2}$ **d.** There are two possible geometric sequences.
$\dfrac{\sqrt{2}}{2}, 1, \sqrt{2}, 2$ $^-\dfrac{\sqrt{2}}{2}, 1, ^-\sqrt{2}, 2$

21. $12^3 = 1728$
$12.6^3 \approx 2000.4$
$12.7^3 \approx 2048.4$
$13^3 = 2197$
So, an integer approximation of $\sqrt[3]{2001}$ is 13.

Mathematical Connections 8-1

Reasoning

1. Assume on the contrary that $\sqrt[3]{2}$ is rational. Then $\sqrt[3]{2} = \dfrac{a}{b}$, where a and b are positive integers. Then $2 = \dfrac{a^3}{b^3}$ and $2b^3 = a^3$, which by the fact given in the problem implies that 2 appears as a factor on the right side of the equation a number of times that is a multiple of 3; on the left-hand side, there is one more 2 than a multiple of 3. This contradicts the uniqueness in the Fundamental Theorem of Arithmetic.   **2.** The value of $\sqrt{3}$ on a calculator is approximate because $\sqrt{3}$ is an irrational number and a non-terminating and nonrepeating decimal.   **3.** False, for example, $\sqrt{64 + 36} \neq \sqrt{64} + \sqrt{36}$. The values of a and b for which it is true are $a = 0$ and b any real number or $b = 0$ and a any real number.

$$\sqrt{a + b} = \sqrt{a} + \sqrt{b} \text{ if, and only if,}$$
$$(\sqrt{a + b})^2 = (\sqrt{a} + \sqrt{b})^2$$
$$a + b = a + b + 2\sqrt{a}\sqrt{b}$$
$$2\sqrt{ab} = 0$$
$$a = 0 \quad \text{or} \quad b = 0$$

4. Since π is irrational, its decimal expansion does not repeat. Therefore $\pi \neq \dfrac{22}{7}$.   **5. a.** Assume on the contrary that $\sqrt{p}$ is rational. Then $\sqrt{p} = \dfrac{a}{b}$. Then $p = \dfrac{a^2}{b^2}$ and $p \cdot b^2 = a^2$, which implies that p appears as a factor on the right side of the equation an even number of times; on the left-hand side, it appears an odd number of times. This contradicts the Fundamental Theorem of Arithmetic.
b. $\sqrt{\dfrac{7}{2}} = \dfrac{a}{b}$
$\dfrac{7}{2} = \dfrac{a^2}{b^2}$
$7b^2 = 2a^2$, which by the assumption in part (a) implies that 2 appears on the right side of the equation an odd number of times; on the left hand side, it appears an even number of times. This contradicts the Fundamental Theorem of Arithmetic.
6. $\left(\dfrac{4}{25}\right)^{-1/3} = \left(\dfrac{25}{4}\right)^{1/3}$, and $\left(\dfrac{4}{25}\right)^{-1/4} = \left(\dfrac{25}{4}\right)^{1/4}$.
Using the fact that for numbers $x > 1$, the bigger the exponent, the bigger is x raised to that exponent, we get:
$\left(\dfrac{25}{4}\right)^{1/4} < \left(\dfrac{25}{4}\right)^{1/3}$, Therefore
$\left(\dfrac{4}{25}\right)^{-1/4} < \left(\dfrac{4}{25}\right)^{-1/3} = \left(\dfrac{25}{4}\right)^{1/3}$.

7. a. Since the algebra is correctly applied, the conclusion that follows is $\dfrac{3}{\sqrt{5}} - \dfrac{2}{\sqrt{3}} > 0 \Rightarrow \dfrac{2}{\sqrt{3}} < \dfrac{3}{\sqrt{5}}$.

b. $\dfrac{6}{\sqrt{7}} - \dfrac{5}{\sqrt{6}} = \dfrac{6\sqrt{6} - 5\sqrt{7}}{\sqrt{42}} = \dfrac{\sqrt{216} - \sqrt{175}}{\sqrt{42}} > 0$.
This proves that $\dfrac{5}{\sqrt{6}} < \dfrac{6}{\sqrt{7}}$.

Open-Ended

8. Answers vary. For example: **a.** $1, 2, 3, 4, 5, \dots$
b. $\sqrt{2}, \sqrt{3}, \sqrt{5}, \sqrt{7}, \dots$ or $\pi, \pi + 1, \pi + 2, \pi + 3, \dots$
9. a. Answers vary. For example, $\dfrac{6}{15}\sqrt{2}, \dfrac{7}{16}\sqrt{2}$, and $\dfrac{8}{17}\sqrt{2}$ are three such irrational numbers.   **b.** Answers vary. For example $\left(\dfrac{n}{n + 1}\right)\dfrac{3}{7}\sqrt{2}$ for $n \geq 5$

Cooperative Learning

10. Answers vary.   **a.** When a number between 0 and 1 is raised to larger and larger exponents, the results approach 0.
b. Answers vary.   **c.** Answers vary.   **11.** $3.7^{2.4} = 3.7^{\frac{24}{10}} = 3.7^{\frac{12}{5}} = \sqrt[5]{3.7^{12}}$

Connecting Mathematics to the Classroom

12. To be a rational number a number must be able to be written in the form $\dfrac{a}{b}$ with both a and b integers and $b \neq 0$. However $\sqrt{2}$ is not an integer. There is no Distributive Property of Exponentiation over Addition, as the student is trying to use.   **13.** Using the Distributive Property of Multiplication over Addition, we can show that $(x + y)^2 = x^2 + y^2 + 2xy$. Hence, $(\sqrt{a} + \sqrt{b})^2 = (\sqrt{a})^2 + (\sqrt{b})^2 + 2\sqrt{a}\sqrt{b} = a + b + 2\sqrt{ab}$. Thus, $2\sqrt{ab}$ is missing from the student's answer.

14. Answers vary. $\sqrt{\sqrt{\sqrt{2}}} = \left(\left(2^{\frac{1}{2}}\right)^{\frac{1}{2}}\right)^{\frac{1}{2}} = 2^{\frac{1}{8}} = \sqrt[8]{2}$

15. The equation $x^2 = 2$ has two solutions: $\sqrt{2}$ and $-\sqrt{2}$, which is compactly written as $\pm\sqrt{2}$, but can be misleading. If $\sqrt{2}$ had two values, there wouldn't be a need to use the "$\pm$" notation infront of it.   **16.** If $a > 0$ the inequality is equivalent to each of the following: $(\sqrt[3]{a})^6 < (\sqrt{a})^6, a^2 < a^3, 1 < \dfrac{a^3}{a^2} = a$. Hence $\sqrt[3]{a} < \sqrt{a}$ if and only if $a > 1$.   **17.** $^-x > 0$ for $x = ^-9$, which is the solution   **18.** $\sqrt{a}\sqrt{b} = \sqrt{ab}$ only if $\sqrt{a}$ and $\sqrt{b}$ are real numbers. However, $\sqrt{^-1}$ is not a real number.

Assessment 8-2A

4. d. $q \cdot 2^n$ **f.** $4s + 15{,}000$ dollars
11. c. $\sqrt{3} + 198.5; (\sqrt{3} + 0.5) + 2(n - 1)$
13. $d = \dfrac{\sqrt{3} - \sqrt{2}}{100}; a_1 = \sqrt{2} - \left(\dfrac{99}{100}\right)(\sqrt{3} - \sqrt{2})$
17. a. $\sqrt{2}, \sqrt{3}, \sqrt{2} + \sqrt{3}, \sqrt{2} + 2\sqrt{3}, 2\sqrt{2} + 3\sqrt{3}, 3\sqrt{2} + 5\sqrt{3}, 5\sqrt{2} + 8\sqrt{3}, 8\sqrt{2} + 13\sqrt{3}, 13\sqrt{2} + 21\sqrt{3}, 21\sqrt{2} + 34\sqrt{3}$
b. i. $L_7 = 5\sqrt{2} + 8\sqrt{3} = F_5\sqrt{2} + F_6\sqrt{3}$
ii. $L_8 = F_6\sqrt{2} + F_7\sqrt{3}$
$L_9 = F_7\sqrt{2} + F_8\sqrt{3}$
$L_{10} = F_8\sqrt{2} + F_9\sqrt{3}$

Assessment 8-2B

2. a. $\dfrac{4(n+25)-60}{4}+5$ **8. a.** $P=dt$ dollars

d. $C=300+4n$ dollars   **10.** David: $d+10$, Matt: $2d-10$
11. b. $1-197\sqrt{2}; (1+\sqrt{2})-2\sqrt{2}(n-1)$
c. $199\sqrt{3}+100x; (x+\sqrt{3})+(x+2\sqrt{3})(n-1)$

13. $r=\sqrt[10]{4}=\sqrt[5]{2}; a_1=\dfrac{25}{2\sqrt[5]{2^4}}$ **17. g.** The sum of the first

n terms is 2 less than the two terms later in the sequence.   **h.** If the
nth term is F_n then, $F_1+F_2+F_3+\ldots+F_n=F_{n+2}-2$.

Mathematical Connections 8-2

Reasoning

1. Answers vary. Both students are correct. The first expression is
based on the first term and the second expression is based on the
middle term.   **b.** Yes   **c.** Yes, because the sum can be written as
$(x-2d)+(x-d)+x+(x+d)+(x+2d)=5x$.
2. a. If the seven consecutive terms of an arithmetic sequence
are 0, 12, 24, 36, 48, 60, 72, then their arithmetic average is
$\dfrac{0+12+24+36+48+60+72}{7}=36$, which is the

middle term.   **b.** Let $a_1,a_2,a_3,a_4,a_5,a_6,a_7$ be seven consecutive
terms of an arithmetic sequence and d the common difference.
Then:
$$a_2=a_1+d$$
$$a_3=a_2+d=a_1+2d$$
$$\vdots$$
$$a_7=a_6+d=a_1+6d$$
Their arithmetic average is
$$\dfrac{a_1+(a_1+d)+(a_1+2d)+\ldots+(a_1+6d)}{7}=$$
$\dfrac{7a_1+21d}{7}=a_1+3d$, which is the fourth term, i.e., the

middle term.   **3.** If the number is x and the answer a, then
$\dfrac{4x+16}{2}-7=a$, $2x+1=a$, and therefore $x=\dfrac{a-1}{2}$.
Thus, the teacher subtracted 1 from each answer and divided the
difference by 2.

Open-Ended

4. Answers vary.
5. Answers vary. Let $a_n=0.999^n$. Then
$a_1=0.999$, $a_2\doteq0.998$, $a_3\doteq0.997$ but $a_{5000}\doteq0.0067$.

Cooperative Learning

6. Answers vary

Connecting Mathematics to the Classroom

7. The student thinks about the distributive property of multiplication over addition and thinks that a similar property of
multiplication over multiplication is true. A counterexample
shows that this is wrong.   **8.** Yes; for example in $\{A\,|\,A\subset W\}$,
A is a variable set, any set that is a proper subset of W, the set of
whole numbers.   **9.** The student is right. The first statement
is the commutative property of set union, and the second of
set intersection.   **10.** Answers vary. $5n+4=5(n-1)+9$,
which has the form $a_1+(n-1)d$. Hence, it is an arithmetic sequence with $d=5$ and $a_1=9$. Notice that

$5\cdot3^{\frac{n}{2}}=5\cdot(\sqrt{3})^n=5\cdot(\sqrt{3})^{1+(n-1)}=5\cdot\sqrt{3}\cdot(\sqrt{3})^{n-1}$ and
hence has the form $a_1\cdot r^{n-1}$. Consequently, this is the nth term of
a geometric sequence with ratio $\sqrt{3}$ and first term $5\cdot\sqrt{3}$.

Review Problems

11. Answers vary. For example, rational numbers may be

1.411, 1.412; irrational numbers may be $1.41+\dfrac{0.001}{\sqrt{2}}$, and

$1.41+\dfrac{0.001}{\sqrt{3}}$.   **12. a.** Irrational   **b.** Irrational

c. Rational   **d.** Rational   **e.** Rational   **f.** Irrational   **13. a.** $\dfrac{9}{4}$

b. Not real   **c.** $-\dfrac{27}{8}$ **14. a.** $^-25$ **b.** $\{x\,|\,x\le0\}$ **c.** $^-25$

15. $n=3$

Assessment 8-3A

5. Let x be the amount the youngest receives. Then
$x+3x+x+14,000=486,000$, or $5x=472,000$.
Youngest received \$94,400.00; oldest \$283,200.00; middle
\$108,400.00.   **7.** Let x be the number of nickels. Then $67-x$ is
the number of dimes. So $10(67-x)+5x=420$, $x=50$. Thus,
50 nickels and 17 dimes.

Assessment 8-3B

1. a. $\square$, since $\triangle=2\bigcirc$ and $\square=4\bigcirc$ **b.** $\bigcirc$ because if
$2\triangle=\square$, then $\triangle<\square$. If $2\bigcirc=\triangle$, then $\bigcirc<\triangle$. Therefore,
$\bigcirc<\triangle<\square$.   **5.** The eldest will receive \$984,000, the middle
siblings will receive \$344,000 apiece, and the youngest sibling will
receive \$328,000.   **7.** 40

Mathematical Connections 8-3

Reasoning

1. Both are correct. For the first student, x is the first of the three
consecutive whole numbers. The second chose x to be the second
of the three consecutive whole numbers.
2. Answers vary. For example:

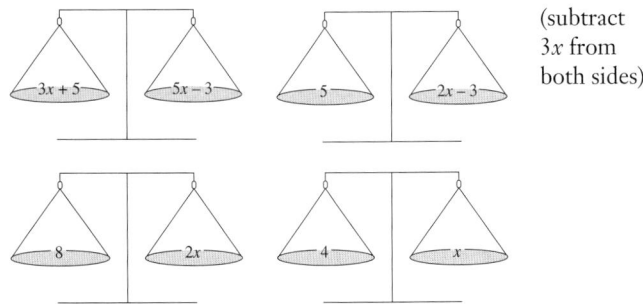

(subtract $3x$ from both sides)

(add 3 to each side)   (divide each side by 2)
3. $\sqrt{5281}\doteq72.67$ ft   **4. a.** 7 hours and

12 minutes   **b.** $\dfrac{ab}{a+b}$ hours

Open-Ended

5. Answers vary.   **a.** $-\left(\dfrac{x^2}{2}-4\right)=4-\dfrac{x^2}{2}$ **b.** $x^2+12=8$
c. $x^2=0$ **6. a.** Answers vary; for example, $x^2-3=0$
b. Answers vary; for example, $x^3-2=0$

Cooperative Learning

7. Answers vary.   **8.** Answers vary.

Connecting Mathematics to the Classroom

9. $x = 0$ is a solution. The student is wrong because we cannot divide by x if $x = 0$.   **10.** Equations can be set up with one unknown as follows. If Jillian delivers x papers, then Abby delivers $2x$ and Brandy $2x + 50$. Thus, $x + 2x + 2x + 50 = 550, 5x = 500$, and hence $x = 100$. Jillian delivers 100 papers, Abby 200, and Brandy 250.   **11.** Because there might be an error setting up the equation and hence the equation might not be a true modeling of the problem   **12.** He misused the equality sign. What he wrote implies that $4x + 5 = 40$, which is not true.

Review Problems

13. $x = 3y$ **14.** $10n$ **15.** Answers vary. If Jack has x CDs then Julie has $2x$ and Tyto $6x$.   **16. a.** $P = 90 + 3d$ dollars **b.** $15d$ dollars   **17. a.** If the middle term is x and the difference is d, then the terms are $x - d, x, x + d$. Their sum is $3x$.   **b.** If the middle term is x and the ratio is r then the terms are $\dfrac{x}{r}, x, rx$.

Their product is x^3. Thus, the product of any three consecutive terms in a geometric sequence is the middle term to the third power.   **18.** $\dfrac{\sqrt{5}}{32}$ **19.** $\dfrac{\sqrt[6]{5}}{\sqrt[3]{12}}$

Assessment 8-4A

3. a. Answers will vary. For example:

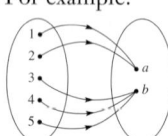

4. a.

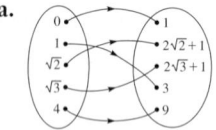

b. $(0, 1), (1, 3), (\sqrt{2}, 2\sqrt{2} + 1), (\sqrt{3}, 2\sqrt{3} + 1), (4, 9)$

c.

x	$f(x)$
0	1
1	3
$\sqrt{2}$	$2\sqrt{2} + 1$
$\sqrt{3}$	$2\sqrt{3} + 1$
4	9

d.

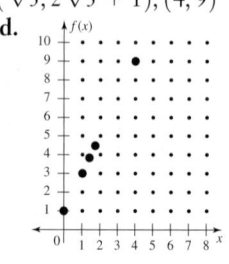

5. c. Not a function because $(4, {}^-2)$ and $(4, 2)$ both satisfy the relation, but inputs can have only one associated output.

6. a. i.

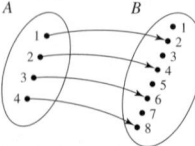

ii.

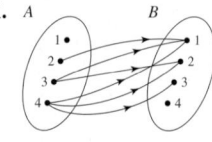

b. Part (i) is a function from A to B. For each element in A, there is a unique element in B. The range of the function is $\{2, 4, 6, 8\}$.

7.

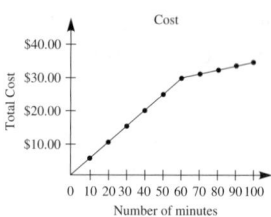

8. Answers vary. **a.** $L(n) = 2n + (n - 1)$, or $3n - 1$ **b.** $L(n) = n^2 + 1$

9. a.

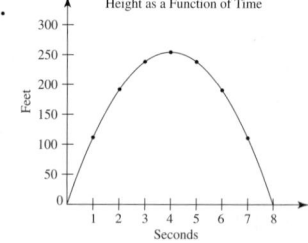

Notice that because we can't really depict 100 dots on the graphs a dot is drawn only for a multiple of 10 minutes.   **b.** That the company charges for each part of a minute at the rate of $0.50 per minute   **c.** The two segments represent different charges per minute. The one representing the higher cost is steeper. **d.** $C(t) = 0.50t$ if $0 \le t \le 60, C(t) = 30 + 0.10(t - 60)$ if $t > 60$ **13. a. (a)** 7   **(b)** 35   **(c)** $7(\sqrt{10} - 5)$ **(d)** $^-35$ **(e)** $\dfrac{^-245}{8}$ **(f)** $7(n - 5)$ **16. a.** $\sqrt{2}$ or $^-\sqrt{2}$

17. b. $\{(1, 9), (2, 8), (3, 7), (4, 6), (5, 5), (6, 4), (7, 3), (8, 2), (9, 1)\}$ **c.** The domain is $R^+ \times R^+$, and the range is R^+. **18. e.** Segments are used because the data are continuous rather than discrete. For example, there are a number of cars at 5:20 A.M. **19. a.** $H(2) = 192; H(6) = 192; H(3) = 240; H(5) = 240$. Some of the heights correspond to the ball going up, some to the ball coming down.

b.

At $t = 4$ sec, the ball's height is $H(4) = 256$ ft above the ground. **20.** $S(n) = (n + 1)^2 + (n + 2)n$ or $2n^2 + 4n + 1$ **22.** (a), (c), (d), (e), (h) are functions. (b) does not represent a function; if x, the input, is any given real number, then y is not unique, as it could be any real number y such that $y > x - 2$.   **f.** Not a function; if $x = 1$ then $y = 1$ or $^-1$.   **g.** Not a function; if $x = 0, y = 1$ or $^-1$.   **24. a.** Boys: B, H; girls: A, C, D, G, I, J, E, F **b.** $\{(A, B), (A, C), (A, D), (C, A), (C, B), (C, D), (D, A), (D, B), (D, C), (F, G), (G, F), (I, J), (J, I), (E, H)\}$ **26. b.** Reflexive,

symmetric, and transitive (and so an equivalence relation)
c. Reflexive, symmetric, and transitive (and so an equivalence relation)   **d.** Reflexive, symmetric, and transitive (and so an equivalence relation)

Assessment 8-4B

1. a. Multiply the input by $^-3$.   **2. a.** This is not a function since nothing is paired with 2.   **b.** This is not a function, since the input 1 is paired with several outputs.   **c.** Function   **d.** Not a function because $(2, b)$ and $(2, c)$ both satisfy the relation, but inputs can have only one associated output.   **3. a.** Answers vary. For example:

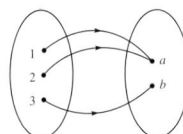

4. a.

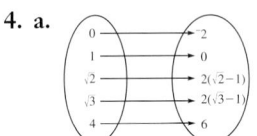

b. $\{(0, ^-2), (1, 0), (\sqrt{2}, 2(\sqrt{2} - 1)), (\sqrt{3}, 2(\sqrt{3} - 1)), (4, 6)\}$
c.

x	$f(x)$
0	$^-2$
1	0
$\sqrt{2}$	$2(\sqrt{2} - 1)$
$\sqrt{3}$	$2(\sqrt{3} - 1)$
4	6

d.

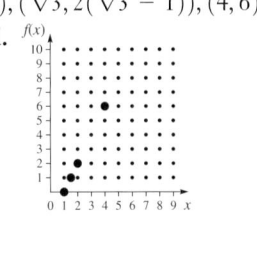

5. b. This is not a function, since, for example, $f(3) = 0$ because 3 is in R and $f(3) = 1$ because 3 is in $\{3, 4, 5, 6, \ldots\}$.
d. Not a function because $(2, 2)$ and $(2, ^-2)$ both satisfy the relation, but inputs can have only one associated output in a function.
8. Answers vary.   **a.** $L(n) = n(n + 1)$ **b.** $L(n) = 2^n$
9. a. Cost per minute for the sixth minute of the call in the first and the total cost for a 6 min call in the second   **b.** That the cost per minute is always the same regardless of the length of the conversation and that the company charges for each fraction of a minute   **c.** $c = 0.45$ for the first graph and $c = 0.45t$ for the second graph   **13. a.** (a) 34   **(b)** $7\sqrt{3} - 1$ **(c)** 69   **(d)** $7a - 1$
(e) $\dfrac{43}{6}$ **14. c.** All real numbers.   **17.**   **a.** $10; 6; 6; 4\sqrt{3}; 2x + 2y$
b. $\{(1, 9), (2, 8), (3, 7), (4, 6), (5, 5), (6, 4), (7, 3), (8, 2), (9, 1)\}$
c. No, because outputs are single numbers
18. b. and **c.**

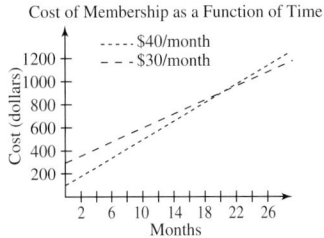

Cost of Membership as a Function of Time

19. a.

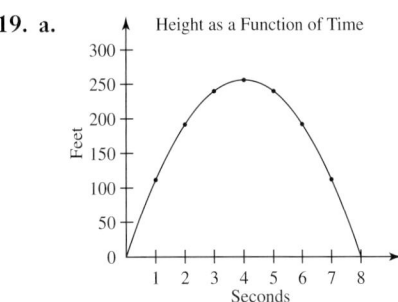

Height as a Function of Time

At $t = 4$ sec, the ball's height is $H(4) = 256$ ft above the ground.
b. $t = 1$ and $t = 7$ **21.**   **a.** $(1 + 2 + 3 + \ldots + n) + n$,
or $\dfrac{n(n + 1)}{2} + n$ **b.** $n + 2 + 2n$, or $3n + 2$ **22.** Only (b), (g) and (f) do not represent a function. (b) If x, the input, is any given real number, then y is not unique, as it could be any real number y such that $y < 20 - x$. (g) If $x = \sqrt{2}$ then $y = 1$ or $^-1$ (f) If $x = 1$ then $y = 1$ or $^-1$ **23.** All are functions except part (e), because for each input there is a single output. Domains are sets of real numbers. Part (e) has, for example, two outputs for the single input 1.   **24. a.** Only (i), (iii), and (iv) have the symmetric property; if $x = a$ and $y = b$ satisfies the relation, so does $x = b$ and $y = a$. In part (ii) and part (v), $a - b = 100$, and $b = a^2$ do not imply $b - a = 100$ or $a = b^2$ respectively. These parts do not have the symmetric property.   **b.** They are all functions.   **25. a.** A, C, D, I, J, G are girls; B, F are boys.   **b.** $\{(A, B), (A, D), (C, B), (C, A), (D, A), (A, C), (C, D), (D, C), (D, B), (G, F), (I, J), (J, I)\}$ **c.** No, because (A, B) and (A, D) are different ordered pairs with the same first component.   **26. b.** Relation but not a function   **c.** Relation but not a function   **27. a.** Reflexive, symmetric, and transitive; an equivalence relation   **d.** Reflexive, symmetric, and transitive; an equivalence relation.

Mathematical Connections 8-4

Reasoning

1. Yes; each element of A is paired with exactly one element of B.
2. Yes, answers vary.   **3. a.** This is not a function, since a faculty member may teach more than one class.   **b.** This is a function (assuming only one teacher per class).   **c.** This is not a function, since not every senator is paired with a committee. (Not every senator is the chairperson of a committee.)   **4. a.** f is a function with inputs that are subsets of S. For each subset A of S, there is a unique output—the complement of A. If $A = S$, then $\overline{A} = \varnothing$. Hence, for the input S, the output is the empty set and vice versa. The domain is the set of all the subsets of S. The range is the same.   **b.** Because the set of 20 elements has 2^{20} subsets, this is the number of elements in the domain as well as in the range because each subset has a complement.   **c.** Yes; for each output there is a unique input (if B is the output, $\overline{B}$ is the input).
5. a. $2^{3.14} = 2^{\frac{314}{100}} = \sqrt[100]{2^{314}}$ **b.** $\sqrt{3}$ can be approximated as closely as we wish by a rational number, $\dfrac{m}{n}$, where m and n are natural numbers. As m/n gets closer and closer to $\sqrt{3}$, the values of $2^{\frac{m}{n}}$ defined as $\sqrt[n]{2^m}$, where $\dfrac{m}{n}$ is in simplest form, get closer and closer to a particular real number, approximately 3.322;

that number is $2^{\sqrt{3}}$.   **c.** All real numbers as explained in part (b).
d. All real numbers greater than 0 because 2^x is always positive.
6. If P represents the initial investment, r the interest rate per
time period (such as annually), and n the number of time periods. Then the balance B is a function of $P, r,$ and n where:
$B(P, r, n) = P(1 + r)^n$.   **7.** No, justifications vary.

Open-Ended

8. Answers vary.   **9.** Answers vary.   **10.** Answers vary.
11. Answers vary.   **12.** Answers vary.
13. Answers vary. Three such functions can be
$f(x) = 2x$
$g(x) = \sqrt{x}$
$h(x) = {}^-x$
a. $h(g(f(1))) = {}^-\sqrt{2}$ **b.** $h(g(f(\sqrt{3}))) = {}^-\sqrt{2\sqrt{3}}$
c. $h(g(f(n))) = {}^-\sqrt{2n}$

Cooperative Learning

14. a. $\{2\}$
b.

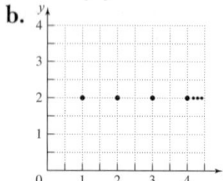

c. $f(x) = 2$ **d.** $\dfrac{4x + 8}{4} - x = 2$ **e.** Answers vary.
f. Answers vary.   **15.** Answers vary.   **16.** Answers vary.
One example is $a = 1$ and $b = 3$ and $f(x) = x^2$. Then
$f(a + b) = f(1 + 3) = f(4) = 4^2 = 16$. However
$f(a) + f(b) = f(1) + f(3) = 1^2 + 3^2 = 10$ and therefore
$f(a + b) \neq f(a) + f(b)$. It should be pointed out that $f(x)$ is
"f of x", not $f \cdot x$.

Connecting Mathematics to the Classroom

17. The student is wrong; the ordered pair (x, y) is considered
a single input.   **18.** It is a function. Each input has exactly one
output.   **19.** One way is to show that for a given output y there is
a unique input. If $y = 3x + 5$ and y is an output, then the unique
input is $\dfrac{y - 5}{3}$, a real number if y is a real number.   **20.** If the
domain does not include the numbers between two inputs, the
points corresponding to the two inputs should not be connected.
21. The first set represents a function because for each
x there is a unique y. The second is not a function because
for example if $x = 4$ there are two values of y; 2 or $^-2$.

Review Problems

22. a. $\dfrac{2\sqrt{2}}{1 + \sqrt{2}}$ **b.** $\dfrac{12}{3 - 2\sqrt{2}}$ **c.** $1 \pm \sqrt{2}$ **d.** $\dfrac{3}{2}$ **e.** $\{x \mid x \geq 1\}$
f. $\{x \mid x \leq 1\}$ **23.** 4 hr   **24. a.** Answers vary. For example, 1.8,
1.85   **b.** Answers vary. For example, $\dfrac{11 + 3^{-1/2}}{13}, \dfrac{11 + 2^{-1/2}}{13}$
25. Answers vary. For example, $\sqrt{3} + {}^-\sqrt{3} = 0$, a rational
number.

Assessment 8-5A

1. a. and **b.** The graph of $y = mx + 3$ contains the point
$(0, 3)$ and is parallel to the line $y = mx$. Similarly, the graph of

$y = mx - 3$ contains the point $(0, {}^-3)$ and is parallel to $y = mx$.

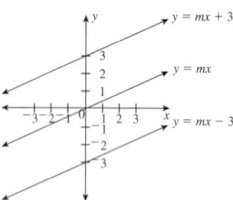

c. and **d.**

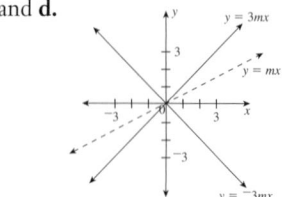

2. a.

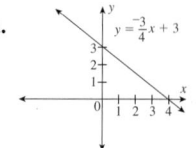

b.

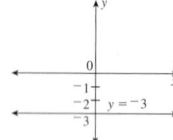

c.

3.

	x-intercept	y-intercept
a.	4	3
b.	None	$^-3$
c.	2	$^-30$

4. a. Using $(0, 32)$ and $(100, 212)$, the slope is
$(212 - 32)/(100 - 0) = \dfrac{9}{5}$. So $F = \left(\dfrac{9}{5}\right)C + b$.
Substitute in the point $(0, 32)$. Thus, $b = 32$, and the equation is
$F = \left(\dfrac{9}{5}\right)C + 32$.   **b.** $C = \dfrac{5}{9}(F - 32)$

5. a. $y = \left(\dfrac{1}{3}\right)x$; slope $\dfrac{1}{3}$, y-intercept 0

b. $y = {}^-x + 3$; slope $^-1$, y-intercept 3

c. $y = \left(\dfrac{1}{3}\right)x$; slope $\dfrac{1}{3}$, y-intercept 0

6. b. $y = \left(\dfrac{1}{2}\right)x$ **8. b.** $x > 0, y < 0$; x and y are real numbers.

11. d. Slope does not exist.   **12. a.** $y = \dfrac{1}{3}x + \dfrac{5}{3}$ **b.** $y = 2$
c. $y = x$ **d.** $x = \sqrt{5}$ **13.** Answers vary, depending on
estimates from the fitted line; for example: **a.** From the fitted line, estimate point coordinates of $(50, 8)$ and $(60, 18)$; the
slope is $\dfrac{10}{10} = 1$. Use the point $(50, 8)$ and substitute $T = 50$
and $C = 8$ into $C = 1T + b$ (i.e., an equation of the form
$y = mx + b$), so $8 = 1(50) + b; b = {}^-42$; the equation is then
$C = T - 42$.   **15. a.** The lines have the same x-intercept, $^-3$.
b. The lines have the same x-intercept, 1.   **c.** The lines have the
same slope, $^-2$.   **d.** The lines have the same slope, $^-1$.

16. a.

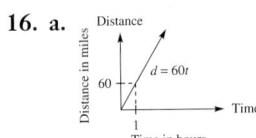

17. c. Infinitely many solutions of the form $\left(x, \dfrac{2}{3}x + \dfrac{1}{3}\right)$

Assessment 8-5B

1. a. and **b.** The graph of $y = mx$ contains the point $(0, 0)$ and is parallel to the line $y = mx + 5$. The graph of $y = mx - 5$ contains the point $(0, {}^-5)$ and is parallel to the line $y = mx$.

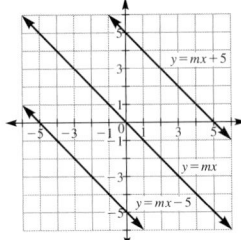

c. and **d.**

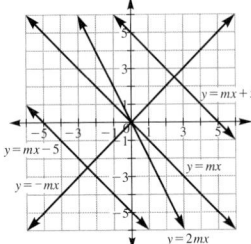

2. a.   **b.**   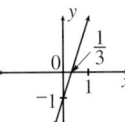   **c.**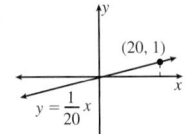

3. a. x-intercept 2, no y-intercept   **b.** x-intercept $\dfrac{1}{3}$;
y-intercept ${}^-1$ **c.** x-intercept 0, y-intercept 0
5. b. $y = \dfrac{3}{4}x + \dfrac{7}{4}$; slope $\dfrac{3}{4}$; y-intercept $\dfrac{7}{4}$
8. b. $y = x$, x any real number
9. a.

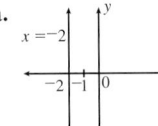

c. Answers vary. The equation of d_1 is $y = \dfrac{3}{2}x$. The equation of d_2
is $y = \dfrac{{}^-3x}{2} + 6$.   **10. a.** $y = {}^-2$ **b.** $x = {}^-4$ **12. a.** $y = \dfrac{1}{9}x + \dfrac{13}{9}$
b. $x = {}^-3$ **c.** $y = 20{,}000x - 19{,}990$ **d.** $y = \sqrt{5}$
14. The coordinates of A, B, and C are $(1, 0)$, $(2, {}^-2)$, and $(9, 5)$, respectively.   **15. a.** The lines have the same x-intercept, 3.
b. The lines have the same x-intercept, 3.   **c.** The lines have the same slope; 1   **d.** All are non-vertical lines through the point $(1, 1)$.

16. a.

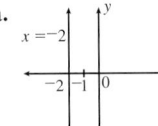

17. a. No solution   **b.** Infinitely many solutions of the form $\left(x, \dfrac{2}{3}x - \dfrac{1}{6}\right)$ where x is any real number.   **c.** Unique solution of $(2, 0)$ **d.** Infinitely many solutions of the form $\left(x, \dfrac{3}{2}x + \dfrac{1}{2}\right)$ where x is any real number.   **18.** $\left(\dfrac{16}{3}, \dfrac{8}{3}\right)$ is the common intersection point of lines containing the segments: $y = 8x - 40$; $y = \dfrac{{}^-4}{7}x + \dfrac{40}{7}$, $y = \dfrac{1}{2}x$.

Mathematical Connections 8-5

Reasoning

1. No (unless $r = 1$), because the slopes between two successive points are not the same.   **2.** Answers vary. Explanation 1: If two distinct lines have the same slope m, then the equations are $y = mx + b$ and $y = mx + c$ for some real numbers b and c (with $b \neq c$). To show that the lines are parallel, it is sufficient to show that the lines do not intersect; that is, that the system of equations has no solution. Indeed, if we try to solve the equations, we get $mx + b = mx + c$. Because $b \neq c$, this equation has no solution. Explanation 2: With $y = mx + b$ and $y = mx + c$, each is a vertical shift of the same line, $y = mx$.
3. a. $\left(\dfrac{a - b}{m - n}, m\left(\dfrac{a - b}{m - n}\right) + b\right)$ **b.** As long as $m \neq n$ the lines
will have different slopes and thus intersect in a single point.
4. The lines intersect at a common point.   **5. a.** $x + y = 2$ or $x + y = {}^-2$. Hence the graph consists of the two parallel lines $y = {}^-x + 2$ or $y = {}^-x - 2$

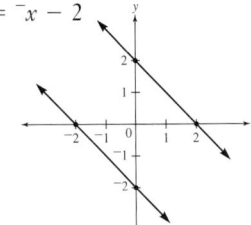

b. $x + y = 1$ or $x + y = {}^-1$. Hence the graph consists of the two parallel lines $y = {}^-x + 1$ or $y = {}^-x - 1$. The graph is similar to the one in part (a) except that one of the lines contains the points $(1, 0)$ and $(0, 1)$ and the other the points $({}^-1, 0)$ and $(0, {}^-1)$.
c. $x = 1$ or $x = {}^-1$. Thus the graph consists of two vertical lines one through $(1, 0)$, and the other through $({}^-1, 0)$

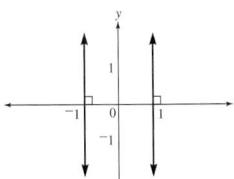

d. $y = 1$ or $y = {}^-1$. Thus the graph consist of two horizontal lines one through $(0, 1)$, and the other through $(0, {}^-1)$.

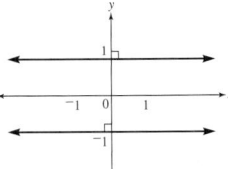

6. Because the coordinates can be irrational numbers, so can the ratio that is the slope. For example, the slope of the line through the points $(2, \sqrt{2})$ and $(1, 0)$ is $\dfrac{\sqrt{2} - 0}{2 - 1}$ or $\sqrt{2}$.

Open-Ended

7. Answers vary. **8. a.** Answers vary. **b.** Answers vary.

Cooperative Learning

9. Answers vary. **10. a.** All have the solution $x = {}^-1, y = 2$.
b. Same as in part (a). **c.** Answers may vary. If a, b, c are consecutive terms in an arithmetic sequence, then $x = {}^-1, y = 2$ satisfy equation $ax + by = c$ because $a({}^-1) + b \cdot 2 = c$ is equivalent to $b - a = c - b$.

Connecting Mathematics to the Classroom

11. The slope of a vertical line is undefined because division by 0 is impossible. When a line is closer and closer to being a vertical line, the absolute value of the slope is getting bigger and bigger.
12. Jonah needs to be reminded about order of operations; $5 - 5x \neq (5 - 5)x$. **13.** A line with undefined slope is perpendicular to the x-axis. Two lines perpendicular to another line are parallel. **14.** The system will have infinitely-many solutions because one equation will be a constant multiple of the other and therefore they will represent the same line.

In the case of the given equations, $\dfrac{2}{{}^-4} = \dfrac{{}^-3}{6} = \dfrac{{}^-5}{10} = \dfrac{{}^-1}{2}$

and hence $2 = ({}^-4)\left(\dfrac{{}^-1}{2}\right), {}^-3 = 6\left(\dfrac{{}^-1}{2}\right), {}^-5 = 10\left(\dfrac{{}^-1}{2}\right)$.

Substituting into the first equation we get

$0 = 2x - 3y - 5 = ({}^-4)\left(-\dfrac{1}{2}\right)x + 6\left(-\dfrac{1}{2}\right)y + 10\left(-\dfrac{1}{2}\right)$.

Dividing by $-\dfrac{1}{2}$, we get ${}^-4x + 6y + 10 = 0$, which is the second equation. Thus, the equations represent the same line.

Review Problems

15. a. $\sqrt{0.\overline{9}} = 1$ **b.** $x^2 + y^2 = 36$ **c.** 1 **16.** 2.45
17. a. $x = \dfrac{2}{4\sqrt{2}} = \dfrac{\sqrt{2}}{4}$ **b.** 9 or ${}^-9$ **c.** $x < \dfrac{{}^-\sqrt{7}}{3}$

18. a. $2\sqrt{7}$ **b.** $7 - \sqrt{7}$ **c.** ${}^-5\sqrt{7}$ **19.** $x = \dfrac{12 + \sqrt{2}}{3}$
20. a. $\{x \mid x \in R \text{ and } x \geq {}^-1\}$ **b.** $\{x \mid x \in R \text{ and } x \leq 0\}$

Chapter 8 Review

6. b. $\dfrac{1}{\sqrt[4]{4}}, \dfrac{1}{\sqrt[4]{16}}, \dfrac{1}{\sqrt[4]{64}}$ or $\dfrac{{}^-1}{\sqrt[4]{4}}, \dfrac{1}{\sqrt[4]{16}}, \dfrac{{}^-1}{\sqrt[4]{64}}$

14. a. If n is the original number, then each of the following lines shows the result of performing the instruction:

$$n$$
$$n + 17$$
$$2(n + 17) = 2n + 34$$
$$2n + 30$$
$$4n + 60$$
$$4n + 80$$
$$n + 20$$
$$n$$

b. Answers will vary. For example, the next two lines could be subtract 65 and then divide by 4.
20. c. $\{x \mid x \geq 0, x \text{ any real number}\}$ **21. a.** This is not a function, since one student can have two majors. **b.** This is a function. The range is the subset of the natural numbers that includes the number of pages in each book in the library. **c.** This is a

function. The range is $\{6, 8, 10, 12, \ldots\}$. **d.** This is a function. The range is $\{0, 1\}$. **e.** This is a function. The range is N.
22. a. $C(x) = 200 + 55(x - 1)$

b.

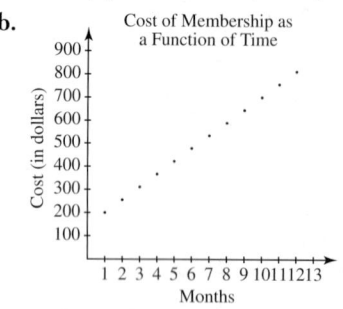

Cost of Membership as a Function of Time

c. In the ninth month, the cost exceeds \$600. **d.** In the 107th month **25. b.** The graph consists of points on the line $y = 4x + 2$ for $x = 1, 2, 3, 4, 5, 6$

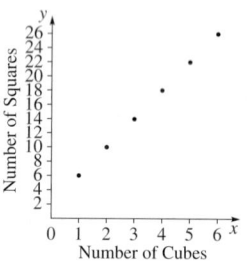

c. $y = 4x + 2$ **d.** The graph does not contain all the points on the line, and hence is not a straight line. The points lie along a line.
26. a.

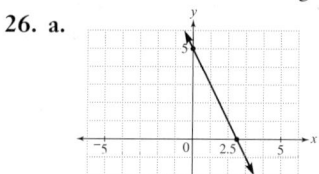

b. 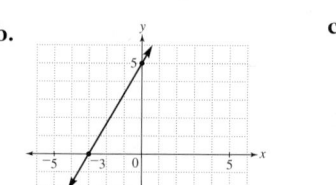 **c.**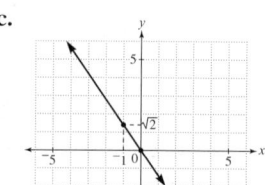

27. a. Line $\overleftrightarrow{CD}$ has equation $4x + 3y - 12 = 0$. **b.** $\left(0, \dfrac{8}{7}\right)$

Answers to Now Try This

1. a. Let g_k be the kth approximation. Then if $g_1 = 4$ then
$g_2 = \dfrac{1}{2}\left(\dfrac{13}{4} + 4\right) \doteq 3.625$, $g_3 = \dfrac{1}{2}\left(\dfrac{13}{3.625} + 3.625\right) \doteq 3.605$.
Because $g_4 \doteq 3.605$, 3.605 is accurate to 3 decimal places.
b. The algorithm for finding $\sqrt{a}$ is given by the recursive formula $g_{n+1} = \dfrac{1}{2}\left(\dfrac{a}{g_n} + g_n\right)$, where g_1 is the initial guess.
2. a. The approach works as shown.
$$\sqrt{\sqrt{\sqrt{a}}} = \left(\left(a^{1/2}\right)^{1/2}\right)^{1/2} = \left(a^{1/4}\right)^{1/2}$$
$$= a^{1/8}$$
$$= \sqrt[8]{a}$$

b. For $n = 2^k$, where k is a positive integer. As shown in part (a),

by repeatedly applying the square-root function we get $\sqrt[2^k]{a}$.
3. For a number like $8^{0.\overline{3}}$, one meaning is $8^{1/3}$ or $\sqrt[3]{8}$. Any repeating or terminating decimal can be converted to a number in $\dfrac{a}{b}$ form where a, b are integers, and $b \neq 0$. For a number like $8^{0.101001\cdots}$, one interpretation is as $8^{\left(\frac{1}{10}+\frac{0}{100}+\frac{1}{1000}+\frac{0}{10000}+\frac{0}{100000}+\frac{1}{1000000}+\cdots\right)}$ or $8^{\frac{1}{10}}\cdot 8^{0}\cdot 8^{\frac{1}{1000}}\cdot 8^{0}\cdot 8^{0}\cdot 8^{\frac{1}{1000000}}\cdots$. Each part could be evaluated and an approximation of the total value could be obtained.
5. a. After 10 hours, there are $2\cdot 3^{10} = 118{,}098$ bacteria, and after n hours, there are $2\cdot 3^n$ bacteria.   **b.** After 10 hours, there are $2 + 10\cdot 3 = 32$ bacteria, and after n hours, there are $2 + 3n$ bacteria. We see that after 10 hours each term of the geometric sequence is greater than the corresponding term of the arithmetic sequence. In general when $r > 1$ and the first term is positive, the terms of a geometric sequence eventually increase faster than the corresponding terms of any arithmetic sequence.   **6. a.** $\square = 3, \triangle = 9$ **b.** $\square = 4, \triangle = 2$
7. If Bob delivered b papers then Abby delivered $3b$ papers and Connie $3b + 13$ papers.
$$b + 3b + 3b + 13 = 496$$
$$b = 69$$
$$a = 3b = 207$$
$$c = 3b + 13 = 220$$
8. a. It is a function from the set of natural numbers to $\{0, 1\}$, because for each natural number there is a unique output in $\{0, 1\}$.   **b.** It is a function from the set of natural numbers to $\{0, 1\}$, because for each natural number there is a unique output in $\{0, 1\}$.   **9. a.** Girls: A, C, D, F, G, I; boys: B, J **b.** E and H
10. a. If $m = 0$, the line is the x-axis.   **b.** As m increases from 0, the slope is positive and the graph of the line becomes steeper as m becomes larger.   **c.** As m decreases from 0, the slope is negative and the graph of the line becomes steeper as the absolute value of m becomes larger.   **11.** If there were no restriction on the domain, a_n is replaced by y, and n is replaced by x, the equation becomes $y = a_1 + (x - 1)d$ or $y = dx + (a_1 - d)$. The slope of this line is d and the y-intercept is $a_1 - d$.   **12. a.** All the points on a horizontal line have the same y-coordinate. Thus, two points on a horizontal line have the form (x_1, y_1) and (x_2, y_2), where $y_2 = y_1$. The slope is $\dfrac{y_2 - y_1}{x_2 - x_1} = \dfrac{0}{x_2 - x_1} = 0$.
b. For any vertical line, $x_2 = x_1$ and therefore $x_2 - x_1 = 0$. If we attempted to find the slope, we would have to divide by 0, which is impossible. Hence, the slope of a vertical line is not defined.
13. a. The graphs are lines that intersect at $x = 4$ and $y = 3$.
b. The lines are parallel and not equal and hence the system has no solution. Algebraic approach: Assuming that there is a solution x and y, we multiply the first equation by 2 and add it side-by-side to the second. Therefore, x and y must satisfy $0\cdot x + 0\cdot y = 5$. However, no x and y satisfies this equation (a solution would imply $0 = 5$). This contradicts our assumption that the original system has a solution.   **c.** The equations represent the same line. If we divide both sides of the second equation by $^-2$ we get the first equation. Hence there are infinitely many solution: x is any real number and $y = 2x - 1$.

Answer to the Preliminary Problem

a. If the length of the sheet of paper is l and the width is w, then the ratio of length to width is $\dfrac{l}{w}$. The ratio of length to width of the half sheet is $\dfrac{w}{l/2} = \dfrac{2w}{l}$. Because the ratios need to be equal, we have:
$$\frac{l}{w} = \frac{2w}{l}$$
$$\frac{l^2}{w^2} = 2$$
$$\left(\frac{l}{w}\right)^2 = 2, \frac{l}{w} = \sqrt{2}.$$

b. When two sheets are joined along their lengths, the ratio of the length of the longer side to the shorter is $\dfrac{2w}{l}$. We have seen in part (a) that $\dfrac{l}{w} = \dfrac{2w}{l}$. Hence $\dfrac{2w}{l} = \sqrt{2}$.

CHAPTER 9
Assessment 9-1A

2. The probability is not likely because there is only one whole number 0 in the sample space that is not a natural number.   **8. a.** Answers vary, for example, choose one cell of the grid at random.

b. 70%, $P(\text{No rain}) = 1 - P(\text{Rain}) = 1 - 0.30 = 0.70$
16. No, she is not correct. The probability of drawing a white ball from box #1 is $\dfrac{3}{4} = \dfrac{6}{8}$. The probability of drawing a white ball from box #2 is $\dfrac{5}{8}$. Thus, the probability of drawing a white ball from box #1 is greater.   **17.** The probability is $\dfrac{1}{2}$ because it is a fair coin. The coin has no memory, so the probability of the event of a head on the 16th toss is the same as the probability of the event of a head on any toss regardless of this history.

Assessment 9-1B

1. c. No. This is an experiment with chance elements in it, and it likely will not happen that we get exactly the predicted number of successes on any given set of trials of the experiment.   **d.** Yes, if there are a large number of trials.   **3.** There are 435 members of the House of Representative and 100 senators. The probability that the congressperson drawn is a member of the House of Representatives is $\dfrac{435}{535}$ which is greater than the probability this congressperson is a senator, $\dfrac{100}{535}$.
8. Answers vary.

a. 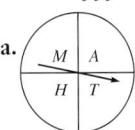   **b.**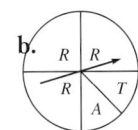

14. a. Not possible. Suppose x white, x black, and x red balls are added to the box. Then the probability of the event of drawing a black ball is $\dfrac{3 + x}{(5 + x) + (3 + x) + (2 + x)} = \dfrac{3 + x}{10 + 3x}$.
There is no x for which this ratio is $\dfrac{1}{3}$, because $\dfrac{3 + x}{10 + 3x} = \dfrac{1}{3}$ is

equivalent to $9 + 3x = 10 + 3x$, which has no solution.   **b.** Yes, add five balls of each color. Reason: the solution of the equation $\frac{3 + x}{10 + 3x} = 0.32$ is $x = 5$.   **15.** The spinner is not a good tool.

$P(\text{boy}) = P(\text{odd number}) = \frac{4}{7} \neq \frac{1}{2}$.

18. $P(\text{vowel}) = \frac{12}{50} = \frac{6}{25}; P(\text{consonant}) = \frac{38}{50} = \frac{19}{25}$, so I am more likely to choose a state whose name starts with a consonant.

21. $\frac{1}{6} - \frac{16}{100} = \frac{50}{300} - \frac{48}{300} = \frac{2}{300} = \frac{1}{150}$

Mathematical Connections 9-1

Reasoning

1. No; 0 and 1 are not the lead digits of any normal phone number.   **2.** All probabilities are less than or equal to 1 and greater than or equal to 0. If events A and B are mutually exclusive, $P(A \cup B) = P(A) + P(B) = 0.8 + 0.9 = 1.7$, which is impossible. Therefore, events A and B are not mutually exclusive.   **3.** Bobbie's reasoning is not correct. The outcomes of making a basket or missing it may not be equally likely; for most players, they would not be equally likely. To calculate her experimental probability of the event of making a free throw, divide the number of shots made by the number attempted.   **4.** Answers vary. E is the letter most used in the English language.   **5.** The probability that a 6 would appear 1000 times in a row with a fair die is so close to 0 that we can conclude this is not a fair die.

Open-Ended

6. a. $\frac{1}{4}$ **b.** Answers vary.   **c.** Answers vary. For example, when people pick a number, their choices are not random. They may have a favorite number or they may choose to avoid the extreme values. **d.** Answers vary.   **7.** Answers vary depending on the book selected.   **8.** Answers vary. For example, batting averages can be interpreted as experimental probabilities that a hitter will get a hit, or a free-throw shooting percentage can be interpreted as experimental probability that a basketball player will make a free throw. Insurance companies use experimental probabilities to determine rates.   **9.** Answers vary. For example, event A is an impossible event such as rolling a 10 on a single roll of a standard die. Event B has low probability, such as the chance of rain being 20%. Event C is marked at approximately 0.5, so this might be something like obtaining a head when tossing a fair coin one time. Event D has a high probability of happening, but it is not certain (for example, tossing a number less than 6 on a toss of a standard die). Event E has probability 1, so it has to happen (for example, tossing either a head or a tail on the toss of a fair coin). Event F has probability greater than 1, but this cannot happen, so no event is possible.

Cooperative Learning

10. a. Answers vary.   **b.** Answers vary.   **c.** The theoretical probabilities for the differences are $P(0) = \frac{6}{36} = \frac{1}{6}; P(1) = \frac{5}{18};$
$P(2) = \frac{2}{9}; P(3) = \frac{1}{6}; P(4) = \frac{1}{9}; P(5) = \frac{1}{18}; P(6) = 0.$
d. Using the probabilities from part (c), the 18 markers should be distributed from left to right as 3, 5, 4, 3, 2, 1.   **11. a.** Answers vary.   **b.** The person who receives 4 times the value of the number

on the die wins when 1, 2, and 3 are tossed. The person who receives the square of the number showing wins when a 5 or 6 is tossed. When a 4 is tossed, the game is a draw. The person who receives 4 times the value of the die has a greater chance of winning, and therefore the game is not fair.   **12. a.** Answers vary. **b.** Answers vary.   **c.** Answers vary.

Connecting Mathematics to the Classroom

13. A fair coin has "no memory." Hence the probability of a tail on each toss is $\frac{1}{2}$ regardless of how many tails have appeared in previous tosses.   **14.** If the four regions corresponding to the colors were determined by equal-sized angles, the events of the spinner's landing on each of the regions would be equally likely, and the student would be correct. However, since the four angles are not the same sizes, the events are not equally likely, and the student is wrong.   **15.** Tossing three heads on the first three tosses of a coin does not imply the coin is unfair. Only when a fair coin is tossed a much greater number of times can we expect to get approximately equal numbers of tails and heads. The probability of getting the same outcome is three tosses is $\frac{1}{4}$, not all that unlikely. It would be premature to conclude that the coin is unfair on this evidence.   **16.** For an experiment with sample space S with equally likely outcomes, the probability of an event A is defined by $P(A) = \frac{n(A)}{n(S)}$. Because $n(S)$ is never negative and $n(A)$ is never negative, $P(A)$ can never be negative.   **17.** The probability of an event is the ratio and does not necessarily reflect the number of elements in the event or in the sample space. For example, if $n(S) = 20$ and $n(A) = 12$, then $P(A) = \frac{12}{20}$, which could also be reported as $P(A) = \frac{3}{5}$.   **18.** Joe's conjecture is incorrect. Each of the numbers 1 through 4 has approximate probability $\frac{1}{4}$ of occurring because each angle where the arrow is located seems to measure 90 degrees and the spinner has the same chance of landing in any of the regions.   **19.** No, because the areas of the different sectors of the dartboard are unequal, we would not expect the probabilities to be equal.   **20.** Mari needs to be asked to think about the number of pages with words beginning with each letter. Because those numbers of pages are not equal, the probabilities cannot be equal.

Assessment 9-2A

1. a.

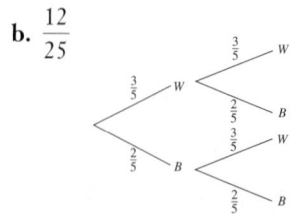

The probability of the event that two balls are of different colors is $\frac{3}{5} \cdot \frac{2}{4} + \frac{2}{5} \cdot \frac{3}{4} = \frac{3}{5}.$

b. $\frac{12}{25}$

8. a. The first spinner. If you choose the first spinner, you win if, and only if, the spinning combinations are as follows:

Outcome on spinner *A*	Outcome on spinner *B*
4	3
6	3 or 5
8	3 or 5

The probability of this happening is $\frac{1}{3} \cdot \frac{1}{3} + \frac{1}{3} \cdot \frac{2}{3} + \frac{1}{3} \cdot \frac{2}{3} = \frac{5}{9}$.

If you choose spinner *B*, the probability of winning is only $\frac{4}{9}$.

b. Answers vary. One choice is as follows:

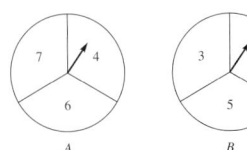

If you choose *A*, the probability of winning is $\frac{5}{9}$. If you choose *B*,

the probability of winning is only $\frac{4}{9}$.

14. a.

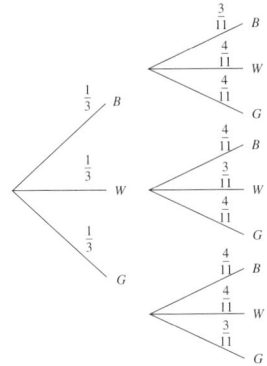

b. $\frac{3}{11}$ **c.** $\frac{1}{11}$ **18.** Billie-Bobby-Billie.   **19.** Answers vary. For example, 18 blue marbles may be added.   **22. b.** $\frac{2}{5}$

Assessment 9-2B

1. a. $\{(1, 1), (1, 2), (1, 3), (2, 1), (2, 2), (2, 3)\}$

4. a. Box 1, with probability $\frac{1}{3}$; Box 2 has probability $\frac{1}{5}$.

11. b. $P(\text{Region } A) = \frac{1}{25}$; $P(\text{Region } B) = \frac{3}{25}$;

$P(\text{Region } C) = \frac{1}{5}$; $P(\text{Region } D) = \frac{7}{25}$; $P(\text{Region } E) = \frac{9}{25}$

17. Each room has probability $\frac{1}{2}$ of being chosen. Hence, it does not matter where the car is placed.   **18.** She should serve the first one hard, and then it does not matter what she does on the second serve.

Mathematical Connections 9-2

Reasoning

1. If the die is fair, the probability of the event that Jim will roll a 3 on the next roll is $\frac{1}{6}$, which is the same probability of rolling any

one of the other numbers. The results of the rolls are independent. **2.** Answers vary. If treated as independent events, finding a suspect with blond hair and blue eyes has greater probability. The probability of the event red car introduces another number that is less than 1 (and still positive) into the product. When you multiply *a*, the probability that you have for blond hair and blue eyes by a number less than 1 and greater than 0, the probability becomes smaller. **3.** Put the red ball into one of the boxes and the three white balls into the other box. In this case the probability of the event of getting the red ball is $\left(\frac{1}{2}\right)1 + \left(\frac{1}{2}\right)0 = \frac{1}{2}$. In the three other arrangements, the probability of getting the red ball is smaller. **4.** Scenario (2) has greater probability, $\frac{1}{2}$. **5.** The probabilities could be equal if event *B* in $P(B|A)$ is the empty set; in that case both probabilities are 0.

Open-Ended

6. Answers vary. The game could be as simple as player *A* wins if the sum of the digits is even and player *B* wins if the sum of the digits is odd. **7.** One possibility is that one die has the numbers 0, 0, 0, 3, 3, 3 and the other die has the numbers 1, 2, 3, 7, 8, 9. The probability of each outcome is $\frac{1}{12}$. **8.** Answers vary, but $\frac{3}{5}$ of the area of the board must be labeled in a certain way. **9.** Answers vary.

Cooperative Learning

10. a. Answers vary. **b.** Answers vary.
c.

x	1	2	3	4
1	1	2	3	4
2	2	4	6	8
3	3	6	9	12
4	4	8	12	16

d. Yes, each player has probability $\frac{1}{2}$ of winning. **11.** Answers vary. For example, one player wins with products 1, 2, 3, 4, 5, 6, 8, 10 and the other player wins with products 9, 12, 15, 16, 18, 20, 24, 25, 30, 36. Then each player has probability $\frac{1}{2}$ of winning.

12. If the first player chooses *TT* and the second *HT*, then the first player wins the game if, and only if, tails appears on the first and second flips. The probability of this happening is $\frac{1}{4}$. The probabilities of winning the game for other choices are summarized below:

		First Player's Choice			
		HH	*HT*	*TH*	*TT*
	HH	—	0.50	0.75	0.50
Second Player's Choice	*HT*	0.50	—	0.50	0.25
	TH	0.25	0.50	—	0.50
	TT	0.50	0.75	0.50	—

Of the 12 possibilities, only 8 result in choices with equally likely probabilities of winning; that is, 8 fair and 4 not. Therefore, the game is not fair.   **13. a.** The game is not fair. You should choose spinner *A*.   **b.** The game is not fair. You should choose spinner *C*. It has a winning probability of $\frac{35}{99}$.   **14.** No matter which die the other player chooses, you can always choose one that will beat it $\frac{2}{3}$ of the time. Therefore, the strategy for playing this game is to go second and make your choice of die based on the information in the following table.

First Person's Choice	Second Person's Choice	Probability of Second Choice Winning
A	*D*	$\frac{2}{3}$
B	*A*	$\frac{2}{3}$
C	*B*	$\frac{2}{3}$
D	*C*	$\frac{2}{3}$

Connecting Mathematics to the Classroom

15. The sample space for this event is not $\{HH, HT, TT\}$ but rather $\{HH, HT, TH, TT\}$. Consequently the probability of *HH* is $\frac{1}{4}$. The student can think of the experiment as having 3 different outcomes but the outcomes are not equally likely.   **16.** Independence refers to whether one event affects another. A second outcome does not depend upon the first. For example, if you get a head on the first flip of a coin, the probability of the event of getting a head on the second flip is not changed. The term *mutually exclusive* is used to describe events that cannot occur simultaneously. For example, when you flip three coins, then the events "two or more heads" and "two or more tails" are mutually exclusive.   **17.** The student is not correct. The confusion probably lies in the fact that the student thinks that probabilities are additive. The student does not understand the Multiplication Rule for Probabilities. A tree diagram for the experiment could possibly help. A partial tree diagram is

$$\xrightarrow{\frac{1}{6}}5 \xrightarrow{\frac{1}{6}}5$$

Thus, $P(5, 5) = \left(\frac{1}{6}\right)\left(\frac{1}{6}\right) = \frac{1}{36}$.   **18.** One multiplies probabilities when events are independent and we are finding the probability of their intersection. Adding probabilities occurs when events are mutually exclusive and we are finding the probability of their union.   **19.** The sample space for the outcomes of the experiment is $\{BB, BW, WB, WW\}$. The probability of the event of two blacks is $\frac{1}{4}$, not $\frac{1}{2}$.   **20.** Alva's reasoning is not correct. If she chooses bag A, her chances of getting a red ball are $\frac{1}{5}$. If she chooses bag B, her chances of getting a red ball are $\frac{3}{16}$. Because $\frac{1}{5} > \frac{3}{16}$, she should choose bag A.

Review Problems

21. a. v **b.** iii **c.** ii **d.** i **e.** iv **22. a.** $\frac{1}{30}$ **b.** 0 **c.** $\frac{19}{30}$ **23.** $\frac{1}{3}$ **24. a.** $\frac{9}{19}$ **b.** $\frac{1}{19}$ **c.** $\frac{13}{19}$ **d.** $\frac{10}{19}$ **25.** 10 times

Assessment 9-3A

1. Answers vary; likely this would not work because the outcomes are not equally likely.   **2.** Answers vary. For example, let the digits 1 and 2 represent diamonds, digits 3 and 4 represent hearts, digits 5 and 6 represent spades, and 7 and 8 represent clubs. If 0 or 9 appear, then disregard these digits. Read the random digits in pairs to simulate two draws; repeat many times to estimate the probability.   **3. a.** Let 1, 2, 3, 4, 5, and 6 represent the numbers on the die and ignore the numbers 0, 7, 8, 9.   **b.** Number the persons 01, 02, 03, . . . , 18, 19, 20. Go to the random-digit table and mark off groups of two. The three persons chosen are the first three whose numbers appear. Skip over pairs of digits that exceed 20 or represent a person already chosen.   **c.** Answers vary. Represent red by the numbers 0, 1, 2, 3, 4; green by the numbers 5, 6, 7; yellow by the number 8; and white by the number 9.   **4.** Mark off 30 blocks of three digits in a random-digit table. Disregard 000 or any numbers that are greater than 500. Also disregard duplicates. These are the numbers of the 30 students who will be chosen for the trip.   **5.** To simulate Monday, let the digits 1 through 8 represent rain and 0 and 9 represent no rain. If rain occurred on Monday, repeat the same process for Tuesday. If it did not rain on Monday, let the digits 1 through 7 represent rain and 0, 8, and 9 represent dry. Repeat a similar process for the rest of the week.   **6.** Answers vary. For example, mark off blocks of two digits and let the digits 00, 01, 02, . . . , 13, 14 represent contracting the disease and 15 to 99 represent no disease. Mark off blocks of six digits to represent the three children. If at least one of the numbers of successive pairs within your 6-digit block representation of the family is in the range 00 to 14, then this represents a child in the three-child family having strep. Repeat many times to estimate the probability.   **9. b.** Answers vary. For example, let the digits 0, 1, 2, 3, 4 represent a victory by team A and the digits 5, 6, 7, 8, 9 represent a victory by team B. Then go to the random-digit table, pick a starting place, and count the number of digits (games) it takes for one of the teams to win. Repeat this experiment a number of times for four games and for seven games and use the definition of probability to compute the experimental probability.   **10.** One way to simulate the problem is to use a random-digit table repeatedly. Because Carmen's probability of making any basket is 80%, we could use the occurrence of a 0, 1, 2, 3, 4, 5, 6, or 7 to simulate making the basket and the occurrence of an 8 or a 9 to simulate missing the basket. Another way to simulate the problem is to construct a spinner with 80% of the spinner devoted to making a basket and 20% of the spinner devoted to missing the basket. This could be done by constructing the spinner with 80% of the 360 degrees (that is, 288 degrees) devoted to making the basket and 72 degrees devoted to missing the basket.   **30.** Answers vary. Let the two-digit numbers 00, 01, 02, 03, . . . , 57 represent the 58 consonants. Choose a random place to start the random digit table. Read the numbers in pairs. If one of the pairs listed above appears in reading the table, a consonant is found. Here *y* is counted as a consonant.

Assessment 9-3B

1. Answers will vary. Let red represent a boy and blue represent a girl.   **2.** Answers will vary. One possibility is to use digits 0, 1, 2, 3, 4, 5 to represent rain.   **3.** Answers will vary. Consider the people to be numbered as 00, 01, 02, 03, . . . , 09, 10, 11, . . . , 24. Then go to a random-digit table. Choose a starting point. Look at sets of numbers from the starting point in pairs. For example, if you see 97 85 80 56 42 88 04 76 89 60 . . . , the first pair that represents a person is 04. Then continue in this manner until the desired four people are found. Skip over all repeats.
4. Answers will vary. Mimic the solution to exercise 3. Number people with triples 000, 001, 002, . . . , 199 and use the process described, only now using triples instead of pairs.   **5.** Answers will vary. Use a random-digit table and look at pairs of digits where every odd digit represents tails and every even digit represents heads. For example, 83 represents a head and a tail while 71 represents two tails. Look at 25 such pairs to determine the experimental probability.   **8.** With 100 questions, each student could expect to be asked about 14 times.   **9.** Answers vary. For the simulation you choose 5 numbers from 12 possibilities. Two-digit numbers between 00 and 11 could be selected from a random number table with each number 00, 01, 02, . . . , 11 representing one of the signs. The probability should be around 0.65.   **10.** Answers vary. Use a random number table and read the numbers in groups of two. A number less than 45 represents a type-O donor.   **a.** Around 0.73   **b.** Around 8.9   **11. b.** The ratio of the probability of drawing a black card to the probability of drawing a non-black card   **12. c.** 1023 to 1   **23. c.** To lose about a nickel per play   **24.** $E = \frac{1}{6}(10) + \frac{5}{6}(-2) = 0$; therefore, you should come out about even if you play a long time.
30. Answers vary. Let the two-digit numbers 00, 01, 02, 03, . . . , 41 represent the 42 vowels. Choose a random place to start the random-digit table. Read the numbers in pairs. If one of the pairs listed above appears in reading the table, a vowel is found.

Mathematical Connections 9-3

Reasoning

1. Answers will vary. One possibility is to see Kanold, C. "Teaching Probability Theory Modeling Real Problems." *Mathematics Teacher* 85 (April 1994): 232–235.   **a.** Should be about 2   **b.** 1:1
2. Answers vary. One way is to turn left when an even number is rolled, turn right when the number 1 is rolled, and move straight when 3 or 5 is rolled.   **3.** 25 cents because $P(HH) = \frac{1}{4}$ so $E = \left(\frac{1}{4}\right)(\$1) = \$.25$.

Open-Ended

4. Answers vary; one could use a random-digit table with blocks of two digits, or a spinner could be designed with 12 sections representing the different months. The spinner could be spun 5 times to represent the birthdays of five people. We could then keep track of how many times at least two people have the same birthday. Repeat to estimate the probability.   **5.** Answers vary. For example, use a random-digit table. Let the digits 1–8 represent a win and the digits 0 and 9 represent losses. Mark off blocks of three. If only the digits 1–8 appear, then this represents three wins in a row.   **6.** Let the 10 ducks be represented by the digits 0, 1, 2, 3, . . . , 8, 9. Then pick a starting point in the table and

mark off 10 digits to simulate which ducks the hunters shoot at. Count how many of the digits 0 through 9 are not in the 10 digits; this represents the ducks that escaped. Do this experiment many times and take the average to determine an answer. See how close your simulation comes to the theoretical average of 3.5 ducks.
7. Answers vary. For example, a person pays $1.00 to play the game; he/she wins $2.00 if coins match and nothing if they don't match.   **8.** Answers vary. The premium would have to cost more than $\left(\frac{47}{100,000}\right)(50,000) = \$23.50$.   **9.** Answers vary. One possibility is a game involving a spinner with five sectors of equal area numbered 1 through 5. You pay $2.00 for playing the game. If the spinner lands on regions 1 or 2, you win $5.00. The expected winnings in this game are $5 \cdot \frac{2}{5} - 2$, or 0.

Cooperative Learning

10. a.–c. Answers vary.   **d.** The probability of the event of two boys and two girls is $\frac{3}{8}$.   **11. a.** Answers vary.   **b.** Answers vary.
c. 15   **d.** $\frac{1}{1024}$ **12. a.–c.** Answers vary.   **13.** Answers vary.
14. a. i. Use RANDINT(1, 6)   **ii.** Use RANDINT(1, 6) + RANDINT(1, 6)   **b. i.–ii.** Answers vary.   **c.** Answers vary.   **15.** Games and rules will vary, as will the odds and expected values of the game.

Connecting Mathematics to the Classroom

16. Answers vary. Maximilian could be correct, but students should be asked to explain how their simulations were designed and carried out.   **17.** Answers vary. Suppose the odds in favor of winning a game are 1:2. Even when the outcomes are equally likely, it does not mean that out of every three games the player will win one game. It only means that if a large number of games are played, the ratio between the number of wins and the number of losses is close to $\frac{1}{2}$. However, the answer is partially correct because the ratio of wins to losses is $\frac{P(W)}{1 - P(W)} = \frac{a}{b}$, $P(W) = \frac{a}{a + b}$.   **18.** The probability of the event occurring is $\frac{3}{7}$ and not $\frac{3}{4}$. The student likely is confusing odds and probability.

19. Answers vary. The probability is $\frac{1}{3}$ that an individual does not vote. Maria expects $48 - \frac{1}{3} \cdot 48$, or 32 to vote. Since she is guaranteed 24 votes and $24 > (51\%)(32)$, she could be confident of winning.
   Another way to consider the situation is to consider that 32 are expected to vote, BUT perhaps $\frac{1}{3}$ of 24, or 8, that she expected to vote for her might not. In that situation, she is guaranteed $24 - 8$, or 16, votes but needs $51\%(32)$, or 17. She is missing 1 vote. Her ground is certainly less safe in this scenario.

Review Problems

20. No, one person will win about $\frac{3}{8}$ of the games and the other about $\frac{5}{8}$ of the games.   **21. a.** $\frac{1}{4}$ **b.** $\frac{1}{52}$ **c.** $\frac{12}{13}$ **d.** $\frac{3}{4}$ **e.** $\frac{1}{2}$

f. $\frac{1}{52}$ **g.** $\frac{4}{13}$ **h.** 1 **22. a.** $\frac{15}{19}$ **b.** $\frac{56}{361}$ **c.** $\frac{28}{171}$ **23.** $\frac{8}{27}$
24. Answers vary. **a.** $\{1, 2, 3, 4\}$ **b.** $\{\text{Red, Blue}\}$ **c.** $\{(1,$ Red), (1, Blue), (2, Red), (2, Blue), (3, Red), (3, Blue), (4, Red), (4, Blue)$\}$ **d.** $\{(\text{Blue}, 1), (\text{Blue}, 2), (\text{Blue}, 3), (\text{Blue}, 4), (\text{Blue}, 5), (\text{Blue}, 6), (\text{Red}, 1), (\text{Red}, 2), (\text{Red}, 3), (\text{Red}, 4), (\text{Red}, 5), (\text{Red}, 6)\}$ **e.** $\{(1, 1), (1, 2), (1, 3), (1, 4), (2, 1), (2, 2), (2, 3), (2, 4), (3, 1), (3, 2), (3, 3), (3, 4), (4, 1), (4, 2), (4, 3), (4, 4)\}$ **f.** $\{(\text{Red, Red}), (\text{Red, Blue}), (\text{Blue, Red}), (\text{Blue, Blue})\}$ **25.** The blue section must have angle measure 300 degrees; the red has angle measure 60 degrees. **26.** $\frac{25}{676}$

Assessment 9-4A

14. a. $\frac{9}{133}$ **15. c.** About 0.995 **d.** About 0.001

Assessment 9-4B

17. 2,598,956 : 4 or 649,739 : 1

Mathematical Connections 9-4

Reasoning

1. Answers vary. For example, the Fundamental Counting Principle (FCP) says that to find the number of ways of making several decisions in a row, multiply the number of choices that can be made for each decision. The FCP can be used to find the number of permutations. A permutation is an arrangement of things in a definite order. A combination is a selection of things in which the order is not important. We could find the number of combinations by using the FCP and then dividing by the number of ways in which the things chosen for the permutation can be arranged.
2. There are 10 choices for the number on the first reel, 10 choices for the number on the second reel, and 10 choices for the number on the third reel. By the Fundamental Counting Principle, there are $10 \cdot 10 \cdot 10$, or 1000, choices for the combination of the lock. **3. a.** $7! \cdot 3!$. If the family is considered a unit and each of the remaining people also a unit, we have 7 units. There are 7! ways to arrange the 7 units. For each of the 7! ways, the family unit can be arranged in 3! ways and hence the number of seating arrangements is $7! \cdot 3!$ or 30,240. **b.** $10! - 7! \cdot 3!$ or 3,598,560. We need to subtract the answer in part (a) from the number of all possible seating arrangements. **4.** 3840. Consider each couple as a unit. The five units can be arranged in 5! ways. For each of the 5! arrangements, each of the five couples can be arranged in 2 ways. Consequently there are $5! \cdot 2^5$ arrangements. **5.** Answers vary. Typically the number of permutations is greater than the number of combinations, but that is not always the case. Consider n objects chosen 1 at a time.

Open-Ended

6. a. 1,000,000 **b.** Answers vary. For example, you would first find the population of California and then experiment with using letters in the license plates. This would help because the choice is for 26 letters in a slot rather than 10 numbers. **7.** Answers vary.

Cooperative Learning

8. a. Answers vary. The first and last numbers in every row are 1. Every other number is obtained by adding the numbers immediately above. The next two rows are 1, 7, 21, 35, 35, 21, 7, 1 and 1, 8, 28, 56, 70, 56, 28, 8, 1. **b.** Answers vary. For example, the

diagonal 1, 3, 6, 10, 15 are triangular numbers. **c.** The sums of the numbers in the rows are 1, 2, 4, 8, 16, 32, 64. The sum in row 10 is $2^{10} = 1024$. **d.** Yes, a similar relationship holds in all the rows for the entries in Pascal's triangle. **e.** The entries are given by ${}_nC_r$, where n is the row number and r is the position in the row, with the count starting at $r = 0$ for the leftmost entry. For example, the first three entries in row 6 are ${}_6C_0, {}_6C_1, {}_6C_2$.
9. Answers vary.

Connecting Mathematics to the Classroom

10. The student is confused about choosing four objects none at a time. There is one way to choose no objects. Therefore, we say ${}_4P_0 = 1$. **11.** We define 0! as 1 because it fits the formula for combinations. It is also consistent with the rest of mathematics. To define $\frac{1}{0}$ as 1 would cause many inconsistencies. If $\frac{1}{0} = 1$ and $\frac{1}{1} = 1$, then $\frac{1}{0} = \frac{1}{1}$, which should imply that $0 = 1$. This is not true. **12.** If the principle is used properly, one can compute the number of permutations. That does not imply that they are not needed. It is a concept that comes up a lot, so having a name for it and formulas to help with computations are useful.

Review

13. a. $\frac{33}{221}$ **b.** $\frac{26}{51}$ **14.** $\frac{1}{12}$ **15.** $E = \$0$ so the game is fair.
16. a. No **b.** The expected payoff is $\frac{1}{38} \cdot \$36.00$, or approximately 95¢. Therefore, you can expect to lose on the average about 5¢ a game if you play it a large number of times.
17. We first find the probability that all 40 children have different birthdays and then subtract the result from 1. We get

$$1 - \left(\frac{365 - 1}{365}\right)\left(\frac{365 - 2}{365}\right) \cdots \left(\frac{365 - 39}{365}\right) \approx 0.89$$

Thus, the probability that the friend wins the bet is approximately 0.89, or 89%. For 50 people, the probability rises to approximately 97%.

Chapter 9 Review

1. a. $\{HHH, HHT, HTH, HTT, TTT, TTH, THH, THT\}$
2. a. $\{\text{Monday, Tuesday, Wednesday, Thursday, Friday, Saturday, Sunday}\}$ **3.** Answers vary. There are 800 blue ones, 125 red ones, and 75 that are neither blue nor red. **6. a.** $\frac{1}{4}$
d. $\frac{12}{13}$ **7. a.** $\frac{64}{729}$ **11.** 4 to 48 or 1 to 12 **15.** $33\frac{1}{3}$ cents, so if 34 cents is charged the game is not fair. **16.** The expected value is $1.50. The expected net winnings are $-\$0.50$. **27.** Answers vary. For example, **a.** Randomly select digits 0–5 from a random-digit table; discard digits 6–9. **b.** Mark off two-digit numbers in a random digit table. Discard any other than 01–12. Select the months represented in the first three non-repeated numbers.
c. Let random digits 0–2 represent red; digits 3–5 represent white; digits 6–8 represent blue; discard any 9s. **28.** These events are not equally likely. If each probability is computed, we have
$$P(3H) = \frac{1}{8}, P(2H) = \frac{3}{8}, P(1H) = \frac{3}{8}, \text{ and } P(0H) = \frac{1}{8}.$$ **29. a.** $\frac{1}{8}$

36. a. 0.9999 **b.** 0.99999603 **37.** $\frac{3}{8}$

Answers to Now Try This

1. a. 1   **b.** Yes, they all sum to 1. 1 is the sum of the probabilities of all the different elements in any sample space.   **c.** $\frac{1}{4}$; red represents 90 degrees of the 360 degrees where the spinner is located.
4. a. Yes   **b.** Answers vary. With replacement: any game with the same number of white and black marbles. Without replacement: 3 black and 6 white or 3 white and 6 black, 6 black and 10 white or 6 white and 10 black marbles.   **c.** Without replacement: the white and black marbles need to be two consecutive triangular numbers; that is, $1 + 2 + \ldots + n$ and $1 + 2 + 3 + \ldots + n + n + 1$ (this is easier to discover using combinations introduced in Section 9-4).   **5. a.** Answers vary.
b. $\frac{3}{8}$ **c.** No, simulations will not always result in the same probability as the theoretical probability. However, if the experiment is repeated a great number of times, the simulated probability should approach the theoretical probability.   **6. b.** There is one way to toss a head and one way of not tossing a head, so the odds in favor are $1:1$.   **c.** There are 4 ways to draw an ace and 48 ways of not drawing an ace, so the odds in favor are $4:48$ or $1:12$.   **d.** There are 13 ways of drawing a heart and 39 ways of not drawing a heart, so the odds in favor are $13:39$ or $1:3$.
8. Answers vary.   **a.** We get an error message because 100! and 98! are too large for the calculator to handle.
b. $\dfrac{100!}{98!} = \dfrac{100 \cdot 99 \cdot 98!}{98!} = 9900$

Answer to the Preliminary Problems

Whenever any person entering the bus chooses a seat at random with both the seats assigned to the first person or to the 50th person are open, the probability is $\frac{1}{2}$ that one of those seats is chosen. At some point, one of these two seats has to be taken. If the seat chosen is the one assigned to the first person, then all the remaining people including the 50th person gets the correct seat. If the seat chosen is the one assigned to the 50th person, then the 50th person cannot get the correct seat but must choose the seat assigned to the first person. In any case, the probability that the 50th person gets the correct seat is $\frac{1}{2}$.

CHAPTER 10

Assessment 10-1A

1. Answers vary. Among the questions that the class will have to determine are the following:
- Do you count the houses all around the block or only on the side where your house is?
- Do you count the houses across the street from you? Are they considered on your block?
- What happens if you are in a new part of town where the blocks aren't developed yet?

Data to be collected will be determined by the question asked but likely will be a frequency count in the second grade. The frequency count could be shown in a bar graph and interpretations could be made about the graph.   **2.** Answers vary. First and foremost will be the question of what it means to be active.

Other questions to consider might include the following:
- Does this mean that they do the same type of activities but one group does it more than the other?
- Does this mean that one group sleeps more than the other? In middle school, there will be choices of both adults and sixth-grade students. Depending on understanding, a randomization might be made but likely not on a big scale. Convenient samples might be a class and its adult caregivers where answers to the question chosen could be obtained. If randomization is done, then it will likely be confined to the school itself. One unanswered question is, "What is an adult?" Is this term understood in the same way by all who do the study?

3. Among the questions the class must determine are: i. What is the definition of "classroom"? Are auditoriums, laboratories, libraries, and hallways to be counted in the definition? ii. How will the temperature be measured, that is, what instrument, level of sensitivity, and scale? iii. How often will the temperature be taken and at what time of day? iv. Is there a temperature baseline?   **4.** The sample in   **(i)** is more likely to be random and is more likely to provide better input to answer the question. The sample in   **(ii)** would most likely sample students at only one grade level and they would be likely to have similar tastes.   **5. b.** The question is biased because it uses words such as "refreshing," "ice-cold," and "hot," suggesting the person should like soda.   **c.** The question is fair because it does not make any assumptions about the subjects or contain any persuasive words.   **6.** Answers vary.   **a.** Elementary students might blindfold the adults and simply hand them two different cans to see if the adults could tell the difference.   **b.** Middle grade students might pour the liquids in unmarked cups, use a series of taste tests to eliminate random guessing, and so on.   **7.** A major question is, "What does it mean to visit a country?" Does this mean that your airline landed in the country; that you spent a night there; that you spent an extended vacation there? If a country has now separated into different countries as the USSR did, do you count each part that was visited when the country was the USSR, or do you not count a visit to the new countries at all because your visit was before they became separate countries?   **8.** A strong criticism of the prediction is that the sample of owners who had telephones and automobiles was not likely to be representative of voters in 1936.   **9.** This type of representation is likely not to be indicative of the class at all. Representative samples of comments would be more "fair" and would give a better picture of the class.   **10.** Whether or not the outlined sampling methods draw a representative sample depends in part on the study.   **a.** In general, not representative because the students could have all ridden the same bus, hence come from the same general location; or, these students constitute the "early risers."   **b.** In general, not representative because the students might inadvertently sort themselves by height, class, or by groups of acquaintances.   **c.** In general, not representative because the sample fails to account for the students who are not interested in sports, or can't attend for one reason or another. Also, there is no mention of how to choose the 50 students.   **d.** The responses in the drop box will be from those students for whom going to the drop box wasn't inconvenient or from those students who felt passionately about the topic of the questionnaire.   **11.** Second-grade students are likely to make many observations which cannot be determined from the graph but from their knowledge of each other. An example is "Alfie was the only one to wear dress shoes today." Reasonable interpretations are that on Tuesday the most popular shoes worn are tennis shoes and Crocs. A different interpretation is that on Tuesdays the most popular shoes are those with softer soles. **12. a.** Population: fans of the team to whom the stadium belongs. Sample: the 50 fans. In general, the survey method is representative. **b.** Population: students at a particular school. Sample: the first 75 students to pass through the main gate. Not representative because it doesn't account for the tardy students who may live farther away than most students (which is the reason they are not among the first to arrive). Also, the sample may neglect students entering school grounds from other entryways different from the main gate. **c.** Population: Households in town. Sample: The students at school. Not representative since it does not account for the childless households. **d.** Assume that the number of students at each grade level is the same. Population: Students at school. Sample: Groups of 5 students from each grade. The survey method is representative.

Assessment 10-1B

1. Among the questions the class must determine are: i. What defines a pet? What do you count as a pet? ii. Do you count the animals that live under the same roof as a student even though an animal belongs to a sibling or parent? iii. Do you count wild animals that may visit a residence regularly? iv. Do you count the pets that may have died in the past month? v. Which grades are of interest in the study? vi. How many students will be surveyed in each grade?

Data to be collected will be determined by the questions asked, but in the second grade will likely be a frequency count.

The frequency count could be displayed using a bar graph. Any interpretations or analysis will be based on the graph. **2.** Answers vary. A logical question is, "Could this sensitive question be asked?" If it is decided that the question could be asked about laziness, then the next question is likely to be what it means to be lazy and could the determination of laziness be done in such a way that the word *laziness* does not have to be used. Additional questions involve what population and sample to use and what is an adult. Other questions might be as follows:

- Does this mean that the people asked do the same type of activities but one group does them less than the other?
- Does this mean that one group sleeps more than the other?

3. Answers vary. You might ask the students what they think it means to be affluent? Is there a better word so that people with whom you talk understand the word better? Do you want a governmental definition of what it means to be affluent? Where could one be found? Where could you find a baseline of "normal" so that you would know what affluent means and what it means to be less than affluent? In a typical school, would one expect the students on one floor to be more affluent than those on a different floor? This is the type of question that a teacher might choose to discourage a class from asking in the school in order not to embarrass some students. But it is a typical question that a class might want to consider. **4. (i)** is more likely to be random **5. c.** The question is biased because it unfairly juxtaposes the sciences and sports; moreover, it makes it seem that the sciences are underfunded which may not be the case. **d.** The question is fair because it does not make any assumptions about the subjects or use any persuasive words. **6.** Answers vary. A major decision is what types of chocolate could be used. Does this mean a light chocolate versus a dark chocolate, milk chocolate versus other

kinds, and so on? All students might find it necessary to blindfold any adults in the test so that they cannot see the chocolates and tell a difference that way. An additional question is, "What is an adult?" Middle-school students might want to try to choose adults at random for the test and would have to consider how to randomize them. **a.** Elementary students might blindfold the adults and simply hand them two different types of chocolate to see if the adults could tell the difference. **b.** Middle-grade students might rewrap pieces of chocolate in brown paper, use a series of taste tests to eliminate random guessing, and so on. **7.** Among the questions the class must determine are: i. What is a "sporting event"? School-related? Do practice games or scrimmages count? Do games in which a student participated count? Should those events that are cancelled, forfeited, or postponed part way through count? What about those in which a student leaves out of his or her own discretion? ii. What kind of sports should be included or excluded? Classify as winter or summer? With professional leagues or can they be without? Physical or mental? Should non-traditional sports such as X-games, chess tournaments, daredevil shows, vehicle racing (car, boat, bike), and so on count? **8.** There are many factors that could have affected the game. The strength of the schedule, playing the game in a different stadium, different fans, and level of preparedness could all be examined. **9.** This type of representation is likely not to be indicative of the class at all. Each choice is "good" or better. There are no negative choices. **10. a.** The sample probably would not be representative. In most elementary schools, the younger students eat first, so the sample would not be unbiased. **b.** Representative because a random choice was made. **c.** Assuming that number of students in each are the same the sample is representative. **d.** Unless the teachers are asked to provide a random list of their students, the sample won't be representative of the students at the school because teachers are inclined to name their best or most outgoing students first. **11.** It is reasonable for students to talk about the most popular types of shoes worn and the least popular. They likely will begin to identify different people's shoes, but that is added information that they might already know that has nothing to do with the graph. It is important that they recognize what the graph says and what they are adding to the conversation from outside knowledge. **12. a.** Population: students at a particular school. Sample: the 50 students interviewed. The sample will not be representative because it doesn't account for those students who are not in the habit of recycling at school or those who happen not to have anything to recycle on that given day. **b.** Population: all faculty and staff at a particular school. The sample is a census—everyone in the population—so it is representative by default. **c.** Population: presumably males attending a particular school. Sample: the 50 students interviewed. The sample is not representative, it takes into account only those males who work or study at the school library in the afternoon. **d.** Population: the cars in your city. Sample: the cars observed and noted down during the several days of the study. The sample is not representative because it deals with cars that are from one residential district.

Mathematical Connections 10-1

Reasoning

1. The U.S. Library of Congress since it has textbooks from all publishers. **2.** Answers vary. One discussion might be why it is important for students to begin discussing data at an early age. The *Statistics Framework* might also help.

Open-Ended

3. Answers vary according to grade level and sophistication.   **4.** Answers vary depending on the level. In early grades, students may simply take a common page from a book and count. As students become older and more sophisticated with data, they could choose a text at random and choose a page at random and then determine how to find an average length of word to describe what they found.

Cooperative Learning

5. Answers vary.   **6.** A proprietary system(s) of gathering information on U.S. audience size and makeup for television shows. In short, there are two primary ways this is accomplished, using statistical models and the newest technology.   **7.** Answers vary.

Connecting Mathematics to the Classroom

8. The answer is "Yes." A manufacturer should be able to ensure with some degree of accuracy that the product is the "same" all the time. In order to do that, tools should be calibrated with small allowances for error.   **9.** An exit poll attempts to determine who or what voters in an election cast their ballot for as soon as they leave their polling station. Since the responses are provided by people, they are prone to error.   **10.** Answers vary.
11. Answers vary.

Assessment 10-2A

2.

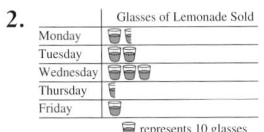

3.

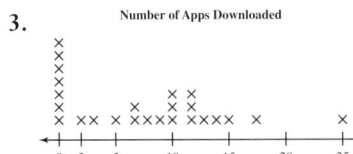

4. a. 72, 74, 81, 81, 82, 85, 87, 88, 92, 94, 97, 98, 103, 123, 125

5.

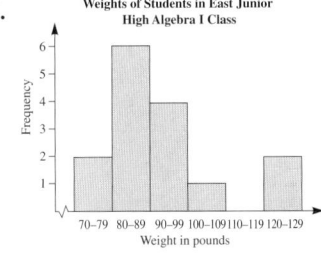

6. Answers vary. **a.** A dot plot will have 6 columns, one for each outcome 1 through 6.   **b.** A bar graph will have 6 bars, one for each outcome 1 through 6. The vertical axis will be scaled to show frequencies of each.

8. a. Ages of HKM Employees

```
1 | 889
2 | 0111333334566679
3 | 224447
4 | 1115568            3 | 4 represents
5 | 2248               34 years old
6 | 233
```

b. There are more employees in their 40s.

9.

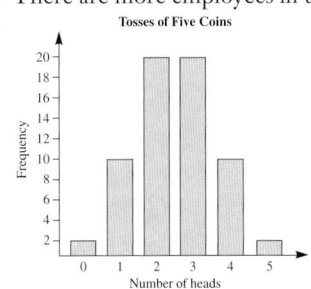

10. Percentages are approximate.

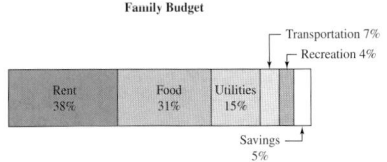

11.

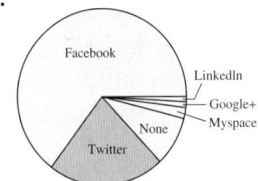

15. a. Answers vary. A graph of this type might be suspect. To have a survey where there are more people in their 70s–90s might mean the people are in a home for the aging. Also to have more people in their 90s than 80s reading might make one suspicious. Without more information, one cannot tell.   **b.** From this flawed "survey", one would suspect that people in their 70s read the most, but the graph only depicts the number of readers of mysteries.
16. a. 1 | 3 represents $130
Amounts Paid for Textbooks

```
1 | 36
2 | 244556
3 | 2445556
4 | 244556
5 | 3444
```

b.

Amounts	Frequency
100–149	1
150–199	1
200–249	3
250–299	3
300–349	3
350–399	4
400–449	3
450–449	3
500–549	4

c.

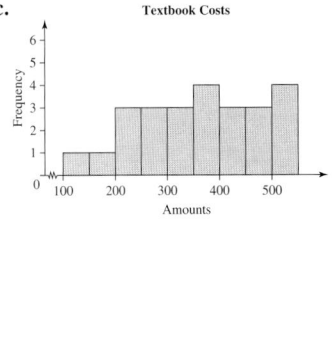

18. Measures are approximate: savings 0.8 cm; rent 2.4 cm; food 0.9 cm; auto payment 2.2 cm; tuition 1.7 cm.

Assessment 10-2B

2.

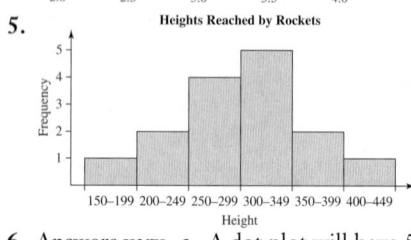

Sales of Hardware in the United States, 2010

Hardware	
Computers	■ ■ ■ ■ ■ ■
Smart phones	■ ■ ■ ■ ❘
Digital video recorders	■
Digital cameras	■
Camcorders	■ ❘
Portable media/MP3 players	■ ❘

Each ■ represents $5 million.

3.

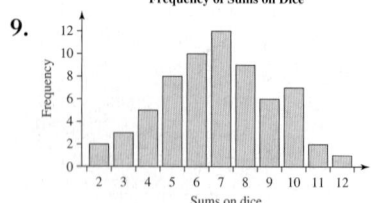

5.

Heights Reached by Rockets

(Frequency bar chart with Height on x-axis: 150–199, 200–249, 250–299, 300–349, 350–399, 400–449; Frequency on y-axis 1–5)

6. Answers vary. **a.** A dot plot will have 5 columns, one for each outcome 0–4. **b.** A bar graph will have 5 bars, one for each outcome 0–4. The vertical axis will be scaled to show frequencies of each. **8. a. Car Thefts**

```
1 |
2 |
3 | 5
4 | 89
5 | 023356
6 | 25669     8 | 2 represents
7 | 22885     82 car thefts
8 | 2
```

9.

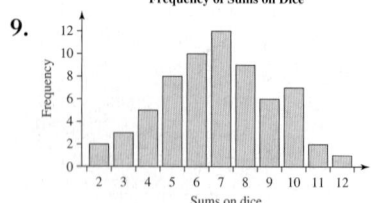

Frequency of Sums on Dice

(Bar graph with Sums on dice on x-axis: 2–12; Frequency on y-axis 0–12)

10.

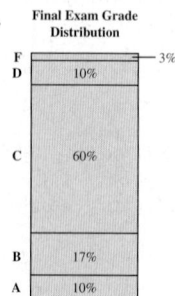

Final Exam Grade Distribution

F 3%
D 10%
C 60%
B 17%
A 10%

11.

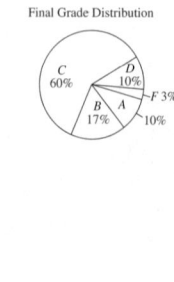

Final Grade Distribution

C 60%, D 10%, F 3%, A 10%, B 17%

12. c. Africa is $\frac{2}{3}$ the size of Asia. **f.** Approximately 59 million mi^2

15. a.

× Children of U.S. Presidents

(Line plot with x-axis 0–15)

b.

Number of Children	Tally	Frequency
0	⊥⊥⊥⊥❘	6
1	❘❘	2
2	⊥⊥⊥⊥ ⊥⊥⊥⊥	10
3	⊥⊥⊥⊥	5
4	⊥⊥⊥⊥ ❘❘❘	8
5	❘❘❘❘	4
6	❘❘❘❘	4
7	❘	1
8	❘	1
9		0
10	❘	1
11		0
12		0
13		0
14		0
15	❘	1

16. a. The greatest profit was in the 4th quarter and the greatest loss was in the 3rd quarter. **b.** Profit; they made a profit in 3 of the 4 quarters and each of these profits was greater than the 3rd quarter loss. **c.** Yes, the income is over $60,000 in the 2nd, 3rd, and 4th quarters and for each of these quarters, the expenses are greater than $60,000.

17. a.

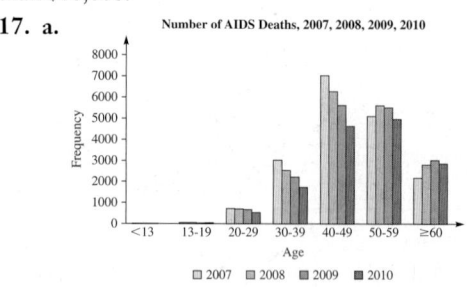

Number of AIDS Deaths, 2007, 2008, 2009, 2010

(Bar graph with Age on x-axis: <13, 13-19, 20-29, 30-39, 40-49, 50-59, ≥60; Frequency on y-axis 0–8000)

☐ 2007 ☐ 2008 ☐ 2009 ■ 2010

b. Answers vary. For example, the total number of deaths from AIDS decreased from 2007 to 2008. The deaths ages for ≥60 increased for two years and then decreased.

Mathematical Connections 10-2

Reasoning

1. a. Answers vary. For example, in a pictograph, we can observe change over time and make comparisons between similar situations. In a circle graph, it is hard to make these observations. **b.** Answers vary. For example, circle graphs are used when comparing parts to a whole. Circle graphs allow for visual comparisons of fractional parts. Bar graphs can't handle these comparisons as well.   **c.** Answers vary. For example, in a stem and leaf plot, we can see the same shape and information as in a histogram but no data points are lost in the display as they may be in a histogram, especially when intervals are used.   **2.** Answers vary. For example, if only percentages are shown on the circle graph, then the circle graph would not change. If data are shown, the numbers in the graph change but not the shape of the graph.   **3.** Answers vary. For example, the percents are of a whole and the circle represents the complete whole, or 100%. Because of rounding, it may happen that the sum of the percents is close to 100% but not exactly 100%   **4.** Answers vary. For example, the budget for 1 year is usually represented with a circle graph because a circle graph allows for a visual comparison of the relative sizes of fractional parts, which is what the graph of the federal budget is attempting to show.   **5. a.** Answers vary. For example, a different graph may be more appropriate since we have continuous data changing over time. A line graph is given though students see this in the next section.

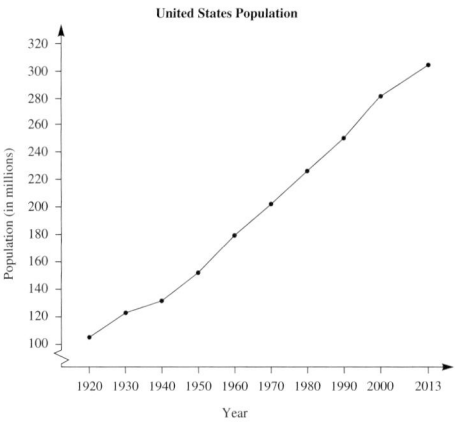

United States Population

b. The data fall into distinct categories and are not continuous, so we use a bar graph.

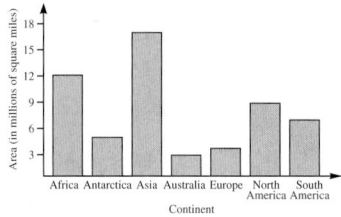

6. Answers vary. For example, the percentage share of large cars sold decreased 5.5% from 1990 to 2015.   **7.** Answers vary. For example, one conclusion that could be drawn is that by year 3, students were carrying a fraction of the weight they were carrying two years prior. Side-by-side circle graphs or a triple-bar chart can be used to effectively display the data. Note that year 2 sophomores were year 1 freshman. So color-coding individual classes may be something to consider.

Open-Ended

8. Answers vary.   **9.** Answers vary.
10. a.

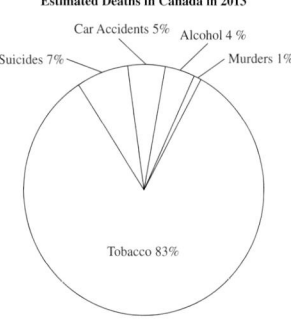

Estimated Deaths in Canada in 2013

Estimated Death Causes in Canada in 2013

Note: The data here are from the cigarette package and does not depict all Canadian deaths.

b. Answers vary.

Cooperative Learning

11. Answers vary. A circle graph might be a logical choice with the total graph representing 100% of their working time and sectors representing teaching, service, and research.   **12.** Answers vary. Expectations of word length on future pages depend on the first page chosen.

Connecting Mathematics to the Classroom

13. A stem and leaf plot does not have to be constructed with small numbers at the top. An advantage to constructing one in this way is that one can rotate the plot 90° counterclockwise to obtain a histogram.   **14.** Aliene's graph is acceptable though it may be difficult for some to read and needs a title.   **15.** A number like 3.14 can be represented as 3|14 where the unit of the leaf is in hundredths.

Review Problems

16. a. Fair **b.** Biased **c.** Fair **d.** Biased **e.** Biased **f.** Fair
17. (i) With this kind of sampling, the owners should expect only those patrons who are strongly opinionated (especially those involved in a rare incident) to mail in the card. While this will certainly provide the owners with some feedback, overall it may not be enough to get at the underlying issue or issues.   **(ii)** The owners should expect the same limited results as in the sampling method in part (i). There is little motivation for patrons to go through with the survey.   **(iii)** This is kind of sampling is unbiased. Patrons conveniently complete the questionnaire while still in the restaurant guaranteeing honest, precise responses while it's still fresh on their minds. Patrons are also well-motivated.   **(iv)** In general, this kind of sampling will be biased. Patrons may not be willing to be dissenting while face-to-face with the interviewer.

Assessment 10-3A

1. b. Approximately $14,000   **2. a.** About 1802   **c.** 1810–1820, because the slope of the line is steeper in this region

5.

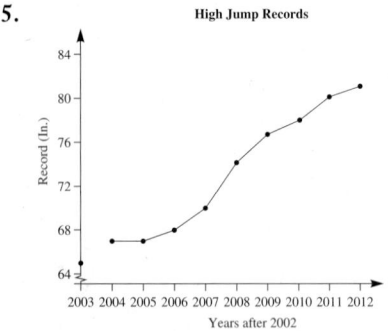

High Jump Records

6. c. About 22 years old

7. a.

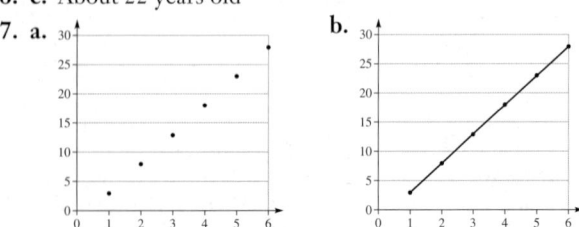

b.

8. a. i. Negative   **ii.** Answers vary.

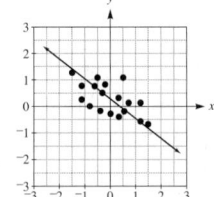

10. Answers vary.

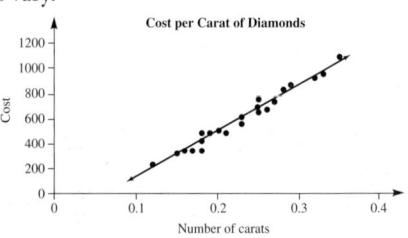

Cost per Carat of Diamonds

Using ordered data and drawing a trend line, an estimate for 0.5 carat is about $1700, but it is unwise to estimate outside the given range of data.

Assessment 10-3B

2. a. The number of workers per beneficiary will drop with only 1.9 workers/beneficiary in 2050. This shows that funding for social security will have problems in the future.   **3. b.** Between 2000–01 and 2001–02   **c.** The trend is positive with the number of men and women participating in NCAA sports increasing.
4. a. In both grades, the total number of spelling errors decreases with time. The 7th graders on the whole commit more errors than the 8th graders.   **c.** Seventh graders may make anywhere between 10 and 15 errors. The 8th graders may commit anywhere between 0–5 errors.   **5.** What happens to the temperature of ice when heated may not be intuitive at first as the temperature does not simply go up smoothly. You should have noticed two horizontal segments in your graph. This graph of temperature versus time is commonly known as the heating curve.

When the ice is heated, the temperature rises until it gets to 32°F. At this point, time is needed for the ice to change states

(melt), so the temperature stays the same at 32°F. Then the temperature again rises until it reaches the boiling point, when time is needed for the liquid water to boil. The temperature stays the same at 212°F until the state changes to gas.
6. a. Negative association

7. a

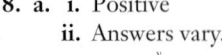
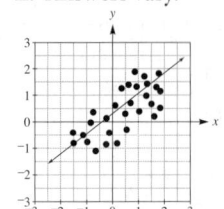

b.

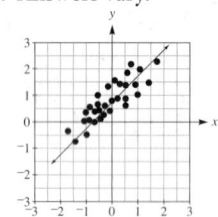

c. $y = {}^-3x + 23$
8. a. i. Positive
  ii. Answers vary.

b. i. Positive
  ii. Answers vary.

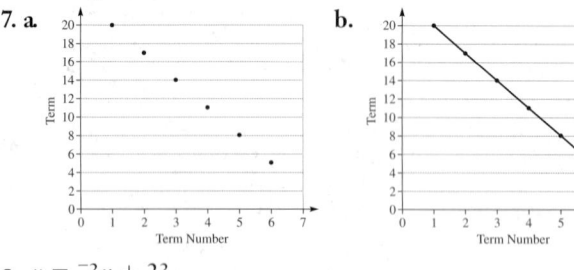

10. a.

Eggs Laid by Fleas

b. Likely around 400 because the number of eggs for the last few days are close.   **12.** There seems to be a positive linear association.   **13.** Answers vary. If $0 \le x \le 100$ the data is almost constant.

Mathematical Connections 10-3

Reasoning

1. Answers vary. Two variables are associated if measured changes in one variable causes change in the other.

Cooperative Learning

2. Answers vary depending upon books chosen.
3. Answers vary.

Open-Ended

4. Answers vary.   **5.** Answers vary.

Connecting Mathematics to the Classroom

6. Jacquie is incorrect. A scatterplot gives a good visual relationship between two variables. It shows if the relationship is close to a linear one, and if there is a positive, negative or no association. It also may show presence of outliers.   **7.** Merle has a valid point, but we need to understand the graph construction.

Review Problems

8. The sum of the percents is greater than 100%, so the data have an error.   **9.** If the miscellaneous category were only 10%, the stacked bar graph follows:

Smith Expenses

Misc. 10%
Gas 13%
Utilities 5%
Food 20%
Rent 32%
Taxes 20%

10. a. Mark McGwire home runs by season

```
0 | 399
1 |
2 | 249
3 | 223499
4 | 29
5 | 28
6 | 5          5 | 2 represents
7 | 0          52 home runs
```

b. There are 3 possible low outliers and a gap from 9 to 22. Most scores are in the 30s.   **11. a.** 21   **b.** ‾0.11   **c.** 31.89 **d.** 64.85   **12.** There is a negative association.   **13.** The data has a very slight positive, but strong linear association. The data are almost constant.   **14. a.** Negative association   **b.** Positive association   **c.** Positive association

Assessment 10-4A

1. b. Mean = 13.94; median = 12.5; mode = 12.5 **c.** Mean = 0; median = 0.05; mode = (none) **2. a.** Answers vary. An example is 1, 2, 3, 4, 5, 6, 6. **b.** Answers vary. An example is 1, 1, 1, 5, 9, 9, 9.

3. a. iii. Bi-modal: 75 and 88.   **6.** $\dfrac{100m + 50n}{m + n}$

11. a. Answers vary. The median of $32,000 reported with the interquartile range of $16,000 would be one appropriate set of choices.   **b.** Based on the answer in (a), we know that at least 50% of the salaries are at least within $16,000 of $32,000.   **15. a.** A—$25, B—$50   **d.** Answers vary. There is more variation at Theater B; also there are higher prices at Theater B.

16.

```
  20  30  40  50  60  70  80  90
```

*

17. a.

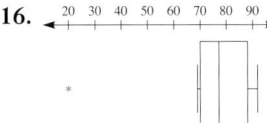

Heights of 8 Tallest Buildings in St. Louis and Los Angeles

St. Louis

Los Angeles

```
300   400   500   600   700   800   900   1000
                    Feet
```

b. Answers vary. For example, in the buildings listed, Los Angeles has the tallest buildings, and about 75% of the tallest buildings in Los Angeles are taller than the tallest listed building in St. Louis. **19. g.** Approximately 9.04   **23.** $6.75 is one standard deviation below the mean; $8.25 is one standard deviation above the mean. 68% of the area under the normal curve lies within 1 standard deviation from the mean. Therefore, the probability of having a wage between $6.75 and $8.25 is 0.68.   **24.** 90; two standard deviations above the mean is $79 + 2 \cdot 5.5 = 90$. Thus at least 90 will earn an A.   **27.** Jill would have the higher standing since Jack would be at the 65th percentile.

Assessment 10-4B

1. a. Mean = 84.4; median = 83; mode = 83 **c.** Mean = ‾0.05; median = ‾2.15; mode = (none) **d.** Mean = 12.82; median = 11.99; mode = (none) **3.** (b) Answers vary. For example, 70, 80, 80, 80, 80, 90. **5. d.** The mean in (b) is equal to the mean in (a) plus 10 yr. The mean in (c) is equal to the mean in (a) plus 20 yr or the mean in (b) plus 10 yr.   **6.** $\dfrac{h(100) + (n - h)50}{n}$

7. b. 0.60(TP) + 0.25(HW) + 0.15(FE) is the current scheme, where TP represents the term paper grade, HW represents homework average grade, and FE represents the final exam score for an individual. The percentages could be generalized with $x\%$ for the term paper, $y\%$ for the homework average, and $[100 - (x + y)]\%$ for the final exam grade as follows: $x\%(TP) + y\%(HW) + [100 - (x + y)]\%(FE)$. **9. a.** balance beam—Olga (9.575); uneven bars—Lisa (9.85); floor—Lisa (9.925)   **12. b.** The mean and median of an arithmetic sequence are the same. They are both equal to the average of the first and last terms of the sequence.   **13. b.** No, the range might be affected by extreme values.   **15. b.** About 21   **c.** The ranges are about the same with women slightly greater.   **d.** Men in this sample first marry about 2.7 years later than women. The spread in ages of first marriage for men and women is about the same. In this sample about 75% of the men first marry later than 75% of the women.

16.

```
  15  20  25  30  35  40
```

17. a.

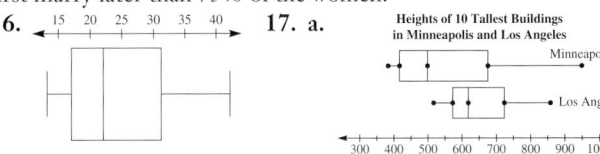

Heights of 10 Tallest Buildings in Minneapolis and Los Angeles

Minneapolis

Los Angeles

```
300  400  500  600  700  800  900  1000
                  Feet
```

c. Answers vary. For example, Minneapolis has more spread in its 10 tallest buildings and has taller buildings than Los Angeles. However, all of the tallest buildings in Los Angeles are higher than 50% of the tallest buildings in Minneapolis. All of the tallest buildings in Los Angeles are between 516 ft and 858 ft inclusive. The highest building in the two groups is located in Minneapolis and is 950 ft tall.

Mathematical Connections 10-4

Reasoning

1. Mode, answers vary.   **2.** The answers must be the mode. One cannot compute the mean and median on non-numerical data without a numerical coding.   **3.** The government probably uses the mean of data collected over a period of years. **4. a.** Mean = 90, median = 90, mode = 90.   **b.** Median or mode   **c.** Mean   **5. a.** For example, 10, 30, 70, and 90   **b.** Choose four numbers whose mean is 50.   **c.** The mean of the new numbers is 50.   **6.** Answers vary.   **a.** Suppose the scores were 100, 100, 50, 50. The mean is 75.   **b.** Suppose the scores were 100, 100, 100, and 50. The mean is 87.5 and so her reasoning is not valid.   **7.** No. To find the average speed we divide the distance traveled by the time it takes to drive it. The first part of the trip took $\frac{5}{30}$, or $\frac{1}{6}$, of an hour. The second part of the trip took $\frac{5}{50}$, or $\frac{1}{10}$, of an hour. Therefore, to find the average speed we compute $\dfrac{10}{\frac{1}{6} + \frac{1}{10}}$ to obtain 37.5 mph.   **8.** Answers vary. The mode could be an extreme value

in a data set (for example, the least value) and not represent the center at all.   **9.** Answers vary. A set of data that contains wait time might be appropriate if the times were determined during peak periods of the events. In that case, the mean absolute deviation or standard deviation would be appropriate for this numerical data.   **10. a.** Answers vary. For example, 3, 4, 5 and 12, 14, 16 have means 4 and 14, respectively.   **b.** If $a_1, a_2, \ldots, a_n$ are the first n terms in an arithmetic sequence then using the formula for the sum, (developed in Chapter 8) we have $\dfrac{a_1 + a_2 + a_3 + \cdots + a_n}{n} = \left(\dfrac{a_1 + a_n}{2}\right)n \div n = \dfrac{a_1 + a_n}{2}.$
11. Justifications vary.   **a.** The mean is multiplied by that constant. We illustrate the reason for three numbers x_1, x_2, x_3. If $\bar{x} = \dfrac{x_1 + x_2 + x_3}{3}$ and the constant is c then the new mean is $\dfrac{cx_1 + cx_2 + cx_3}{3} = c\left(\dfrac{x_1 + x_2 + x_3}{3}\right) = c\bar{x}$ **b.** The standard deviation is multiplied by the absolute value of that constant, if $s = \sqrt{(x_1 - \bar{x})^2 + (x_2 - \bar{x})^2 + (x_3 - \bar{x})^2}$, then the new standard deviation is

$$\sqrt{\dfrac{(cx_1 - c\bar{x})^2 + (cx_2 - c\bar{x})^2 + (cx_3 - c\bar{x})^2}{3}}$$
$$= \sqrt{c^2\left(\dfrac{(x_1 - \bar{x})^2 + (x_2 - x)^2 + (x_3 - \bar{x})^2}{3}\right)}$$
$$= |c|s.$$

12. The larger standard deviation implies that the data have more variability. The data are spread out more.   **13. a.** Shoe sizes of students   **b.** Exam scores; heights will be bimodal   **c.** SAT scores

Open-Ended
14. Answers vary depending on student choice.

Cooperative Learning
15. Answers vary.   **16.** Both the mean and median of each data set will increase by 5, decrease by 5, and increase five-fold, respectively.

Connecting Mathematics to the Classroom
17. The new mean is $\dfrac{9(10,000) + 20,000}{10} = 11,000.$
Consequently, the new mean has increased by $1000. The median

and mode may change in special cases.   **18.** The mean of two whole numbers is either a whole number or a whole number plus 0.5. If $\dfrac{a + b}{2} = 3.8$, then $a + b = 7.6$, which is not possible if a and b are whole numbers.   **19.** Since the median is 90, at least half of the class had grades of 90 or more. Since Tom scored 80, he did not do better than half of the class.   **20.** In a grouped frequency table, the precise values, of the raw data are not displayed, and hence it is impossible to conclude from the table which value occurs most often. Consequently, it is impossible to find the exact mode from the information given in a grouped frequency table. In this situation, the mode is usually given as a class interval.   **21.** If the mean is less than the median, then one can be certain that there were more scores above the mean than below it. The low scores tend to be further from the mean than the high scores.   **22.** No, it is not possible to have a standard deviation of ⁻5. By definition, the standard deviation is the principal square root of the variance.   **23.** Mel did not really miss the cutoff by a single point. She would have had to increase her score on each of the 10 tests by a single point to reach an average of 90 or increase her total score for the 10 tests by 10 points to reach an average of 90.

Review Problems
24. Approximately, midsize—173°, large—25°, luxury—61°, small—101°   **25. a.** Everest, approximately 8500 m
b. Aconcagua, Everest, McKinley
26. a. History Test Scores

5	5
6	48
7	2334679
8	0255567889
9	00346

7 | 2 represents a score of 72

b. History Test Scores

Classes	Tally	Frequency
55–59	|	1
60–64	|	1
65–69	|	1
70–74	||||	4
75–79	|||	3
80–84	||	2
85–89	ⵣⵣⵣⵣⵣ |||	8
90–94	||||	4
95–99	|	1

c.

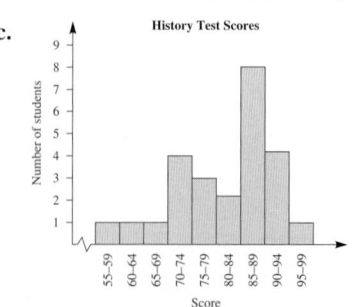

History Test Scores

d. Approximately 115°

Assessment 10-5A

This entire assessment is subject to varying answers. Each of the following are representative possibilities.   **1. a.** The ad should not be trusted without knowing more about the type of average in question, how it was obtained, and how likely it would be for someone to attain those average earnings.   **b.** The results obtained from the questionnaires will suffer from a type of response bias where the respondents ignore the latter part of it.   **c.** There is no mention of the size of the sample or the manner in which the sample was obtained. It is entirely possible that the sample contained only four dentists, who may have also been "cherry-picked" on top of it all.   **d.** The survey will not be representative of all viewers at home. Only those viewers with mobile phones and passionate enough to send in their opinions will get counted.   **e.** The question is biased as it contains persuasive words such as "much-needed."   **2.** One possibility is that the temperature is always 82°F or close to it.   **3.** It could very well be that most of the pickups sold in the last 10 yr were actually sold during the last 2 yr. In such a case, most of the pickups have been on the road for only 2 years, and therefore the given information would not substantiate, that the average life of a pickup is around 10 years.   **4.** The horizontal axis does not have uniformly sized intervals and both the horizontal axis and the graph are not labeled.   **5.** The three-dimensional drawing distorts the graph. The result of doubling the radius and the height of the can is to increase the volume by a factor of 8.   **6.** One would need more information; for example, do men drive more than women?   **7.** No, because the mean can be affected by a few high salaries.   **8.** The first graph shows a steep increase in the price of the LCD TV over the six months, which the advertising agency may want to show for the benefit of the store.   **9. a.** This bar graph would have perhaps 20 accidents as the baseline and some larger number (e.g., 50 as its maximum). Then 24 in 2011 would be 4 units above the baseline while 38 in 2015 would appear as 4.5 times or 350% taller than 24 of 2011, when in fact it is just 58% higher.   **b.** This bar graph would have zero accidents as its baseline and some larger number (e.g., 100) as its maximum value. The effect would be to show values from 24 to 38 as lying a line with a small positive slope   **10.** An example is 1, 1, 1, 1, 20, 30, 40, 50.   **11.** A median might be misleading, depending on the number of data points given. Also the mean would not be sufficient. A report of the mean, median, and standard deviation would be the most helpful.   **12.** The student is incorrect and, in addition, is misusing percentages. She mixes percentages of "effectiveness" with percentages of times taking the drug.   **13.** Answers vary.   **a.** You probably would not have a representative sample. This is a *convenience sample*.   **b.** You probably would not. The students eating in the cafeteria could likely be a biased sample.   **c.** Assign students numbers from 1 to n, where there are n students. Choose your sample using random-number selection methods. Make sure your sample is big enough.   **14.** The data are indicators of passenger complaints and not an overall airline rating. Larger airlines may have more complaints. The numbers are not percentages. The number of complaints might depend on how many flights each airline has per day.   **15.** Answers vary. You might conclude that the less you spend the better your students perform on the SAT exam in verbal and math scores.

Assessment 10-5B

1. a. Without knowing sales figures for the last 15 years, this claim cannot be substantiated. It may be that 95% of the manufacturer's cycles sold in the United States were sold in the last year.   **b.** "Up to" is quite indefinite (6 mpg is "up to" 30 mpg). The conditions under which 30 mpg may have been realized are not stated (the car may have been rolling downhill).   **c.** "Some" is indefinite (means 1 or more); moreover, here is no mention of a reference for the study.   **f.** Most accidents occur in the home because a majority of time is spent in the home. This is an example of carrying an argument to a deceptive extreme.   **2.** He is assuming that there are no deep holes in the river where he crosses.
3. We don't know who was surveyed, how many were surveyed, or how the question was phrased. Was the question biased?   **4.** There is no title and no label on the horizontal axis. The vertical axis does not have uniform spacing.
5. The three-dimensional graph distorts the data and makes it appear that many more cars were sold in 2015 than in the other years when in fact the number of cars sold in 2013 and 2015 were approximately the same. There is no scale on the vertical axis.   **6.** When the radius of a circle is doubled, the area is quadrupled, which is misleading since the number of majors has only doubled.   **7.** She could have taken a different number of quizzes during the first part of the quarter than the second part.
8. There are no labels for vertical axis, so we cannot compare actual sales. Also, there is no scale on the vertical axis.
9. a. Answers vary. The survey depicts that teachers are generally happy with their mathematics textbooks. The articles (given without data) lead one to infer that national experts in mathematics are unhappy with textbooks that teachers use.   **b.** Answers vary. The survey and articles do not agree. One tendency is to react that the teachers are in the classroom and are more knowledgeable about texts being used.   **10.** A student would need to know the highest possible score that a person could make. Also the scores of other students would be important along with the teacher's expectations.   **11.** Answers vary.   **a.** At grades K–4, homework of less than 1 hr (60 min) could be justified because 75% of the teachers surveyed assign homework that takes this long on the average. Perhaps 0–30 minutes for homework would be more appropriate at this grade level because almost 50% of the surveyed teachers assign this amount. It is less easy to justify a specific amount for grades 5–8, but 71% of teachers surveyed use the range from 31 to 120 min of homework.   **b.** A potential misuse at grades 5–8 might have one report that of the teachers who assign at least 91 min of homework, approximately half of those assign at least 2 hr of homework. It would be very difficult to justify at least 2 hr of homework at the K–4 level using these data.   **12.** No, for example, in the data set 2, 7, 7, 7, 8, 11 the mean and the median are equal to 7.   **13.** An example is 1, 2, 3, 50, 50, 50.   **14.** The region may be like the Netherlands where dikes keep out the water where the land is below sea level.   **15.** Comparable demographics of the sample and the population is a must.   **16. a.** As a reporter, one might use the first headline because it grabs the attention—even based on the same data.   **c.** If the headlines are based on the same data set as indicated, the second headline is the most informative.

17. a. $\frac{647}{649}$, or about 99.7%   **b.** $\frac{622}{649}$, or about 95.8%

c. For the lung cancer group, the probability is $\frac{647}{1269}$, or about 51%. For the control group, it is $\frac{2}{29}$, or about 7%. **d.** The evidence is not conclusive. **18.** You could not automatically conclude correctly that the population of the West Coast has increased since 1790. However, based on the westward movement of the mean center of population, there would be strong suspicion that that was the case. **19.** Though the fish and dairy departments have the same monthly figures, the graphic for the fish department is longer and gives the impression that the fish department is the highest grossing department. **20.** By starting the vertical scale at 300, rather than 0, the artist of the first graphic can give the impression that figures are dramatically rising. In the second graphic, the same artist can make it seem that the same figures are increasing but slowly and steadily.

Mathematical Connections 10-5

Open Ended

1. Answers vary. In general, a graph can be made to look "steeper" or more "shallow" by changing the scale on the vertical axis. **2.** Answers vary.

Review Problems

3. a. About 74.17 **b.** 75 **c.** 65 **d.** About 237.97 **e.** About 15.43 **f.** 13 **4.** About 27.74 **5.** About 76.7 **6.** Men's Olympic 100 m Run Times 1896–2008

```
 9 | 6778899
10 | 0001123334568888
11 | 00                10 | 0 represents
12 | 0                 10.0 sec.
```

7.

Women's Olympic 100 m Swim Time 1960–2012

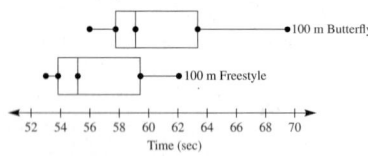

From examining the box plot, we can see that the times on the 100-m butterfly are much greater (relatively speaking) than the times on the 100-m freestyle.

Chapter 10 Review

1. i. If the average is reported as 2.41 children, the mean is being used. The mode would not have a decimal number, and the median would be either a whole number or one ending in .5. **ii.** If the average is 2.5, then either the mean or the median might have been used. **3. a.** Mean = 30, median = 30, mode = 10. **b.** Mean = 5, median = 5, modes = 3, 5, 6. **c.** Mean = 150, median = 150, mode = 100,200 (bi-modal) **d.** Mean = 13.01, median = 12.15, mode (none) **4. a.** Range = 50, variance ≈ 371.4, standard deviation ≈ 19.3, mean absolute deviation ≈ 17.14, IQR = 40. **b.** Range = 8, variance = 5.2, standard deviation = 2.28, mean absolute deviation = 1.8, IQR = 3.

5. a.

Ms Rider's Class Masses in Kilograms

```
        ×
  × × × × × 
  × × × ×  × ×  ×  ×  ×  × × ×
  +--+--+--+--+--+--+--+--+--+--+--+
  39 40 41 42 43 44 45 46 47 48 49
```

b. Ms Rider's Class Masses in Kilograms

```
3 | 99
4 | 001122223345678999      4|0 represents 40 kg
```

c. Ms Rider's Class Masses in Kilograms

Mass	Tally	Frequency
39	||	2
40	||	2
41	||	2
42	||||	4
43	||	2
44	|	1
45	|	1
46	|	1
47	|	1
48	|	1
49	|||	$\frac{3}{20}$

d.

Ms Rider's Class Masses in Kilograms

```
Frequency
7
6
5
4
3
2
1
    39 40 41 42 43 44 45 46 47 48 49
         Mass (kilograms)
```

6. a. Test Grades

Classes	Tally	Frequency
61–70	⊬|	6
71–80	⊬⊬|	11
81–90	⊬||	7
91–100	⊬|	6

b.

Grade Distribution

```
Number of students
12
11
10
 9
 8
 7
 6
 5
 4
 3
 2
 1
    61–70 71–80 81–90 91–100
          Test grades
```

7.

Wegetem Expenditures

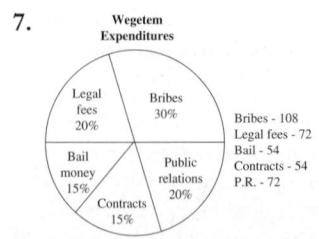

Bribes - 108
Legal fees - 72
Bail - 54
Contracts - 54
P.R. - 72

8. The graph is missing a title and axis labels. The bars are not of equal width.

10.

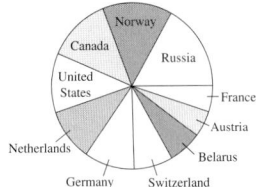

Gold medal counts, 2014 Winter Olympics

11. a. Life Expectancies of Males and Females

Females		Males
	67	1446
	68	28
	69	156
	70	0049
	71	02235578
	72	01145
	73	1689
7	74	123599
9310	75	14
86	76	
88532	77	
9999854332211	78	
99655443210	79	
42	80	
7 | 74 | represents 74.7 years old		| 67 | 1 represents 67.1 years old

b.

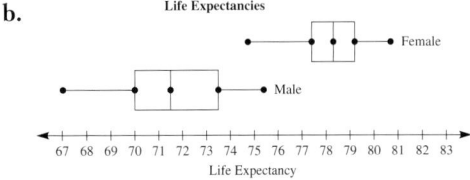

12. Larry was correct because his average was $3.2\overline{6}$, while Marc's was $2.7\overline{3}$.

14. c.

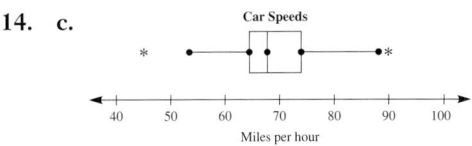

e. About 50% of people checked drove between 65 and 75 mph.   **16. a.** Collette is more consistent. There is less deviation from the mean in her scoring.   **c.** Collette scored more than might have been expected.   **19.** The bars would be approximately the same height in a vertical bar graph.
20. b. It is nearly impossible for this to happen.
c. Since the company claims a person can lose up to 6 lbs, any average loss from 0 to 6 is legitimate.   **21.** The bar graph is more appropriate. Line graphs are used to show change over time. The line graph indicates there are values between the colors, which is not true.   **22.** No reportable single number would be meaningful for such a pool.   **23.** Answers vary. A reasonable way to make the claim is to pull boxes at random after they are packed

and weigh the contents. If more than 98% of the boxes' contents have weights within 1 g of 138 g, the claim is reasonable. The choices of 98% and 1 g are arbitrary but reasonable choices to test this claim.   **24. a.** Answers vary. Perhaps to be with those of comparable age a typical senior might choose the first.   **25.** The areas representing the two categories appear roughly the same size.   **26.** Answers vary. **a.** One way would be to leave the television on, even if no one is watching.   **b.** They show very popular shows during "ratings sweeps" periods.   **27.** Answers vary. For example, graphs may show area or volume instead of relative size; another is to select a horizontal baseline that will support the point being made.   **32.** The March 31 Goal is portrayed almost 3 times greater than the number as of March 27, which it is not.   **33.** The first person has the calculator and picks a large random number. The first person then records the number, adds his salary to it, and passes the calculator to the second person. That person adds his salary and passes it to the next person. This continues for all five people. When the calculator is returned to the first person, he subtracts the random number that was used and divides by 5 to obtain the mean salary.

Answers to Now Try This

2. Ages of Presidents at Death

4	69	
5	36778	
6	003344567778	4|9 represents
7	0112347889	49 years old
8	01358	
9	0033	

3. It appears that the fifth-period class did better. We can see that there are more scores grouped toward the bottom, which is where the higher grades are located.
4. a. 2.

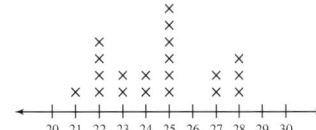

Number of Students in Math Classes

Part (a) of question 4 continued (answer to Quick Check 3).

Age	Tally	Frequency
20–29	||||||||	8
30–39	||||	4
40–49	|||	3
50–59	||	2
60–69	||	2
70–79	|	1

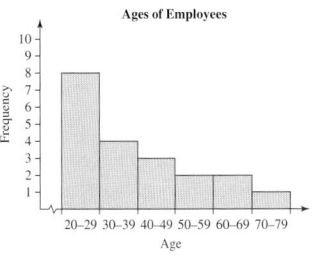

Ages of Employees

b. Yes, the interval 0–1 should be represented on the graph or a break shown as in part (a) above. **5.** Answers vary with the number of terms.

a.

# of Term	Value of Term
1	⁻10
2	⁻6
3	⁻2
4	2

b.

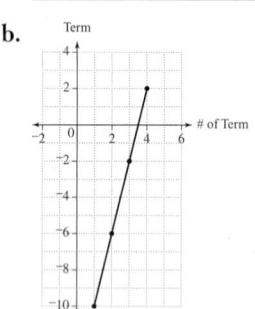

c. $y = 4x - 14$, where x is a natural number **6. a.** $y = 212.5x$
b. 425 cal **c.** $y = 112.5x$ **d.** 450 cal **e.** About 1190 cal
f. From 0 to 1 hr it will go from 0 to about 112, then from 1 hr to 4 hr it will go from 112 to about 750. **7. a.** A histogram is more appropriate to compare numbers of data that are grouped into numerical intervals. With the line graph there appears to be a frequency for *Times per month* such as 4.5, etc. **b.** Connecting the dots is visually okay, but is mathematically meaningless.
c. i. A circle graph is appropriate for showing the division of a whole into parts. **ii.** A line graph is appropriate for showing how data values change over time. **8. a.** Answers vary. For example, all the puppies could weigh 7 lb. Then $\frac{6 \cdot 7}{6} = 7$ lb.
Another possibility is 4, 6, 6, 7, 8, 9, 9. The mean for these weights is also 7. **b.** If all the scores were equal, then the mean is equal to the high score and also the low score. Otherwise, this is not possible. **c.** 5 **9.** Answers vary. For example, one set of data is 92, 94, 94, 94, 96, in which the mean, median, and mode are all 94. **10. a.** The average of 2.58 could only be a mean. To be a mode it would have to be a whole number. To be a median it would have to be a whole number or a whole number plus $\frac{1}{2}$.

b. The average of 2.5 could be a mean or a median. It could not be a mode since the mode for the number of children must be a whole number. **11.** The completed table follows:

	Overall Mean	Mean for Females	Mean for Males	Percent Females
Ramirez	218	230	205	52
Jonsey	221	224	199	88

The percentage of males in Ms. Jonsey's class is 100% − 88%, or 12%. Also the mean for Ms. Jonsey's class is determined as follows:

$$(88\%)(224) + 12\%(\text{Mean for males}) = 221$$

Solving, we find that the mean for males in Ms. Jonsey's class is 199.
For the entry for Mr. Ramirez's class, we know that the percentages of males and females must sum to 100%. If F is the percentage of females, then the percentage of males in that class must be $1.00 - F$. Further, we know that the overall mean is determined as follows:

$$(F)(230) + (1.00 - F)(205) = 218$$

Solving for F, we find that $F = 52\%$.
Finally, we observe that the means for both females and males were higher in Mr. Ramirez's class, but the overall mean is higher in Ms. Jonsey's class. **13.** Because there is no base for the percentages given, arguments are difficult to make. Assuming the base is the set of all parents, consider the following: **a.** The argument cannot be made because we do not know even if the other 82% answered this part of the survey. **b.** The argument cannot be made. The statement may be the result of considering test/learning to be two equal parts that make 18%. Hence, half of 18% is 9%. **c.** The argument cannot be made. **d.** This argument cannot be made. Possibly it could be made for 11%. **e.** The argument cannot be made. The indicated 9% does not tell us about the other 91% of parents.

Answer to the Preliminary Problem

If $g_1, g_2, \ldots, g_n$ are the ages of the n guests and c is Calvin's age, then the mean a of the $n + 1$ people's ages (n guests and Calvin) is: $a = \dfrac{g_1 + g_2 + , \ldots , + g_n + c}{n + 1}$. Hence $c = a(n + 1) - (g_1 + g_2 + , \ldots , + g_n)$. Since the guests' ages were announced, Calvin's age can be computed by multiplying the mean by the number of people at the party and subtracting the sum of the ages of all the guests.

CHAPTER 11

Assessment 11-1A

2. [S P U] **3. c.** False; they intersect in a line, the empty set, or a plane (if the two planes are the same plane). **e.** False, see $\overleftrightarrow{FA} \cup \overleftrightarrow{GH}$ in exercise 1. **5. a.** $\overleftrightarrow{AB}$ and $\overleftrightarrow{FH}, \overleftrightarrow{AD}$ and $\overleftrightarrow{GH}, \overleftrightarrow{BC}$ and $\overleftrightarrow{DH}, \overleftrightarrow{AE}$ and $\overleftrightarrow{BD}$, etc. **e.** $\overleftrightarrow{FH}$ is the line of interaction of the two planes. $\overline{DH}$ is perpendicular to plane FGH because it is perpendicular to $\overline{HG}$ and $\overline{EH}$ in that plane. Thus, $\overline{DH}$ is perpendicular to any line through H in the plane FGH which implies $\overline{DH} \perp \overline{FH}$. If a line ℓ through H is constructed in the plane FGH and perpendicular to $\overline{FH}, \overline{DH}$ will be perpendicular to ℓ. Then one of the dihedral angles created by the two planes BDH and FHG measures 90°. Thus, the planes are perpendicular because a dihedral angle measures 90°. **6. d.** Answers vary. $\overleftrightarrow{AC}$ and $\overleftrightarrow{BE}$ or $\overleftrightarrow{AB}$ and $\overleftrightarrow{CE}$. **8.** Answers vary. **a.** Edges of a room; vertical and horizontal parts of a window frame; some intersecting crossroads. **b.** Some branches in a tree; clock hands at 7:30; angle on a yield sign. **c.** The top of a coat hanger; clock hands at 7:15. **12. a.** $m(\angle AOB) = 22.5°; m(\angle COD) = 67.5°$
b. $m(\angle BOC) = 31.25°; m(\angle AOB) = 58.75°$ **c.** Assume that if the position of $\overrightarrow{OE}$ is changed, the other rays will be adjusted so that all x's are congruent and all y's are congruent. $3x$ and $3y$ will have different values, and thus, x and y will have different values. $3x + 3y$, though, will remain $180° \Rightarrow 3(x + y) = 180° \Rightarrow x + y = 60° \Rightarrow m(\angle BOC) = 60°$.

14. a.

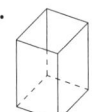
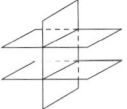

15. Perspectives vary; e.g.,

a.   **b.**   **c.**

16. Answers vary; e.g., **a.** A real-world example would be a paddle wheel:

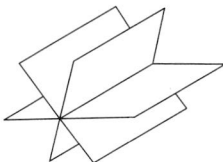

b. A real-world example would be the intersection of floor and two adjacent walls of a house:

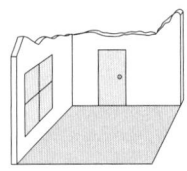

c. A real-world example would be a field irrigated with a central pivot:

Field Irrigates with a Central Pivot

Assessment 11-1B

2. 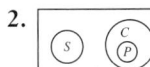 **3. a.** False; they could be skew.

b. False; the line can pass through and intersect at 1 point.
c. False; the end points differ. **e.** False; the definition requires skew lines cannot be contained in the same plane. **4.** Each point can serve as a vertex for 3 angles whose measures are less than 180°. For example:

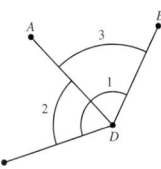

There are 4 possible vertices times 3 angles for each vertex, and thus, 12 distinct angles. **5. b.** Answers vary, for example ABF and BCD, or ADH and CDH. **c.** Answers vary, $\overline{AE}, \overline{BF}, \overline{CG},$ and $\overline{DH}$ **6. e.** None of the lines in the drawing are parallel.
f. Answers vary, for example, the plane determined by B, E, and D.

12. a. $m(\angle DOC) = 25\frac{5}{7}° \approx 25.71°$

$m(\angle BOA) = 34\frac{2}{7}° \approx 34.29°$

13. c. $_nC_3 = \dfrac{n(n-1)(n-2)}{6}$ **15.** Answers vary.

a. 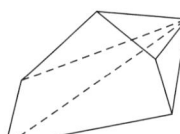   **b.**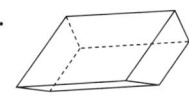

Mathematical Connections 11-1

Reasoning

1. a. 1, a line segment has 2 endpoints and 2 points determine a line. **b.** An infinite number. There are an infinite number of points on a line and any point not on the segment can be the endpoint of a ray containing the segment. **c.** An infinite number of planes can pass through a given line. **d.** No, if collinear they can be contained in an infinite number of planes. If noncollinear, exactly one plane contains them. **2.** A line has an infinite number of points. Pick two distinct points A and B on the line and the given point C not on the line. Now we have 3 noncollinear points that determine a unique plane. The same is true for any two distinct points that are chosen on the line. **3. a.** Parallel lines and skew lines are similar in that they do not intersect. However, a line is parallel to itself and therefore a line does intersect itself.
b. Parallel lines and skew lines are different in that parallel lines are coplanar, and skew lines are not coplanar. **4.** No, by convention the middle letter is the vertex and points A and C are points on the rays other than B. **5.** Points A, B, and C are collinear. If two distinct planes intersect, the intersection is a line. If points A, B, and C are in common, then they must lie on the line of intersection. **6. a.** Answers vary. **b.** The fire is located near the intersection of the two bearing lines. **c.** Answers vary.
7. No; if all four points are collinear, then one line is determined; if only three are collinear, then four lines are determined; if no three are collinear, then six lines are determined. **8.** Yes; through P in plane α, draw a line k perpendicular to $\overleftrightarrow{AB}$. By definition, since n is perpendicular to α it is perpendicular to every line in α through P. Thus, n and k are perpendicular, which implies that planes α and β are perpendicular. **9.** Yes, 2:27:16

Open-Ended

10. Answers vary. **a.** If the points on the three rays were labeled B, C, and D as shown, then you can't name any angle A because it is not clear whether you are referring to $\angle BAC$, $\angle CAD$, or $\angle BAD$.

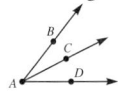

b. $\angle BAD$ and $\angle BAC$ in the given figure.

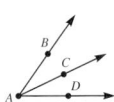

11. Answers vary. **12.** Answers vary.

Cooperative Learning

13. a. Answers vary. An angle of 20° can be drawn by tracing a 50° angle and a 30° angle, as shown in the following figure. Another 20° angle adjacent to the first 20° angle can be drawn in a similar way, thus, creating a 40° angle.

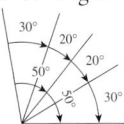

b. Yes; answers vary. **c.** All positive multiples of 10°; once a 10° angle is determined, using the 40° angle from (a) and the given 30° angle, the other multiples can be determined.

Connecting Mathematics to the Classroom

14. The segments have to lie on parallel lines. If the lines containing the segments were drawn, there would be an intersection point, and the lines would not be parallel.   **15.** Two points determine a line, so only two points are used to name the line.
16. Two segments are equal if they represent the same set of points. Both $\overline{AB}$ and $\overline{BA}$ represent the same set of points, so they are equal.   **17.** From the Denseness Property, we know that for any two real numbers, there is a real number between them. Because points of a line and the set of real numbers can be put in a one-to-one correspondence, we can always find a point between any two points. Since this is true for any two points, we see that there are an infinite number of points in a segment.   **18.** It is a matter of definition. Two distinct lines are parallel if they do not intersect and are in the same plane. Lines that do not intersect in exactly one points, and do not lie in a single plane are skew lines.   **19.** The measure of an angle has nothing to do with the fact that rays cannot be measured. The measure of an angle is a measure of the angle's opening. In degrees, the measure is based on constructing a circle with its center at the vertex of the angle and dividing the circle into 360 congruent parts. The number of parts in the arc that the angle intercepts is the measure of the given angle in degrees. The number of parts in the intercepted arc is the same regardless of the size of the circle (or protractor).   **20.** Extending the rays does not change the angle measure or the angle's opening. The angle measure is a measure of the opening, not the length of the rays.   **21.** The student is incorrect. While the degree is the basic unit of angle measure, it can be further subdivided. This in itself would prove that the student is incorrect. However, many geometry books also consider a Protractor Postulate, which puts all the rays in a half-plane emanating from a point in a one-to-one correspondence with the real numbers greater than 0° and less than 180°. This would allow infinitely many rays emanating from one point.   **22.** Since half-lines have no endpoints, the two half-lines have no common endpoint.

Assessment 11-2A

6. a. Possible; three sides of different lengths with one obtuse (i.e., greater than 90°) angle.

b. Possible; three sides of different lengths with a right angle.

c. Impossible. An equilateral triangle has three 60° angles.
d. Impossible. An equilateral triangle has three 60° angles.
e. Possible; two sides of equal length forming an obtuse angle.

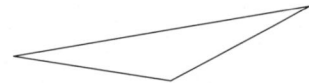

8. a. 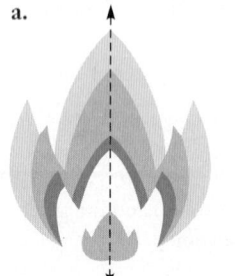   **b.**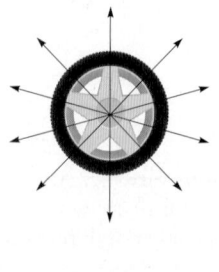

10. (i) Line symmetry: *a* and *b*; (ii) Turn symmetry: *a*; (iii) Point symmetry: *a*

11. a. 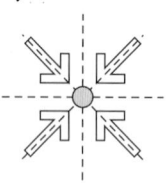   **b.**

12. Answers vary.

a.    **b.**

c. The letter **N** has 180° rotational symmetry and no line of symmetry.   **14. a.** 0, vertical and horizontal line symmetry; 3, horizontal line symmetry. Depending on how it is written the digit "1" might have line and point symmetry.   **b.** 0 and 1 depending on how they are drawn.   **15. a.** 180°   **b.** 40°, 80°, 120°, 160°, 200°, 240°, 280°, 320°

Assessment 11-2B

4. Both (b) and (d) are convex. In both (a) and (c) points can be found so that line segments connecting these points lie partially outside the figures.

a.   **c.**

Thus, (a) and (c) are concave. This is not possible for (b) and (d), so (b) and (d) are convex.

6. a.    **b.**

c. Not possible. A scalene triangle has no congruent sides and an equiangular triangle is an equilateral triangle, which has three congruent sides.   **d.** Equilateral triangles are equiangular triangles.

e. The triangle in (d) is one example.

8. a.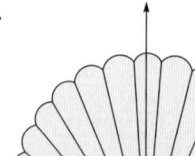

b.

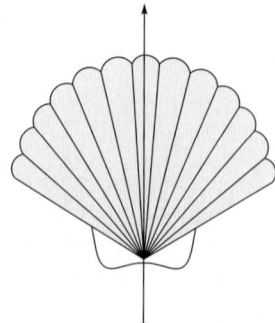

11. a. 4 lines of symmetry; 90°, 180°, and 270° turn symmetry; and point symmetry   **b.** Point symmetry and 180° turn symmetry (It also has 90° rotation symmetry if you ignore color.)   **c.** Point symmetry; 90°, 180°, and 270° turn symmetry   **d.** 4 lines of symmetry; 90°, 180°, and 270° turn symmetry; and point symmetry
14. a. 8, vertical and horizontal line symmetry   **b.** 8, point symmetry

Mathematical Connections 11-2

Reasoning

1. a. Answers vary. An $8\frac{1}{2}$ by 11-in. piece of rectangular paper requires only one fold. Fold the bottom left corner up until the bottom side meets the right side. The bottom side now measures a side on the right congruent to the bottom side. Cut off the top portion of the rectangle that is not covered by the fold.   **b.** Folding the square along one diagonal and then along the other creates congruent angles. Each is $\frac{360°}{4} = 90°$. The paper folding implies that the diagonals bisect each other. Unfolding and then folding the square so that opposite sides fall onto each other shows that the diagonals are congruent.   **2.** No, a concave polygon "bends in"; that is, at least one angle is greater than 180° and some are less than 180° or the figure could not close. Therefore, the figure is not equiangular and so it is not regular.   **3.** According to the definition in this text, isosceles triangles have at least two congruent sides. Equilateral triangles have three congruent sides; therefore, they have at least two congruent sides and are isosceles.
4. a. True   **b.** False, consider the figure shown in part (d).
c. False, if the diagonal lies outside then the polygon is concave.
d. False, consider the following figure.

Open-ended

5.

Polygon	Triangle	Quadrilateral	Pentagon
Concave	not possible		
Convex			
Regular			
Equilateral only	not possible		
Equiangular only	not possible		

6. Answers vary.

Cooperative Learning

7. Answers vary.

8.

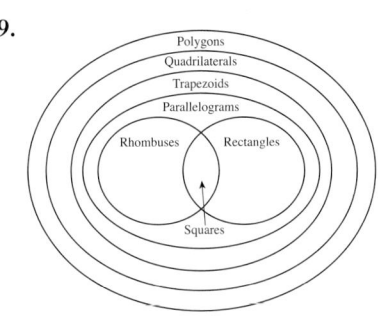

9.

10. a. No, the figure will always have sides the same length because the length of each side is the length of the cut.   **b.** No, the length of each side will be the length of the cut.   **c.** Yes, cut off the corner so that it is in the shape of an isosceles triangle.
11. a. (i) All but the green triangle and the yellow hexagon (ii) The orange square and the two non-square rhombuses, blue and light orange (iii) The square and the two non-square rhombuses (iv) The green triangle, orange square, and yellow hexagon.   **b.** The interior angle of the triangle is $\frac{360°}{6} = 60°$; the interior angle of the square is $\frac{360°}{4} = 90°$; the interior angle of the hexagon is $\frac{360°}{3} = 120°$; if the two trapezoids are placed together to form a hexagon, then the obtuse angles are 120° and the acute angles are 60°; if the 3 blue rhombuses are placed together, then the interior angle is $\frac{360°}{3} = 120°$; if the other rhombus is placed with the blue rhombus and square as shown, then the interior obtuse angle measures $360° - 90° - 120° = 150°$, so the acute angle is 30°.   **c.** Answers vary.

Connecting Mathematics to the Classroom

12. A regular polygon is a polygon in which all the angles are congruent and all the sides are congruent. In general neither condition implies the other, and hence neither is sufficient to describe a regular polygon. For example, a rhombus that is not a square has all sides congruent, but all its angles are not congruent. A rectangle that is not a square has all its angles congruent, but not all its sides congruent. Neither a rhombus nor a rectangle is a regular polygon unless it is a square.   **13.** Since an angle is a set of points determined by two rays with the same endpoint, to say that two angles are equal implies that the two sets of points determining the angles are equal. The only way this can happen is if the two angles are actually the same angle. To say that two angles are congruent is to say that the angles have the same size or measure.   **14.** To be regular, all sides must be congruent but also all angles must be congruent. All angles are not congruent unless the rhombus is a square.   **15.** This statement is correct. A rectangle is a parallelogram with four right angles. A square is a parallelogram with four right angles so a square is a rectangle. A square must be a parallelogram with right angles and all sides congruent. Not all rectangles satisfy the condition of all sides congruent, so only some rectangles are squares.   **16.** It is agreed that when naming polygons the order of the letters represent consecutive vertices (either clockwise or counterclockwise). A and C are not consecutive vertices.   **17.** This is not correct, as not only are four congruent sides needed for a square but also four right angles. The student could be shown a picture of a non-square rhombus and then asked whether this satisfies his definition and whether it is a square.   **18.** They are both correct. A rhombus with four congruent angles is a rhombus with four congruent sides and four congruent angles; it is a square. A rectangle with sides the same length has four right angles; it satisfies the definition of a square.

GeoGebra Activities

19. See online appendix.

Review Problems

20. a. 45   **b.** $\dfrac{n(n-1)}{2}$ **21.** $\varnothing$, 1 point, 2 points, ray, and possibly a line of the angle is a straight angle and the line is collinear with it.   **22. a.** False; a ray has one endpoint.   **b.** True   **c.** False; by definition skew lines cannot be contained in single plane.   **d.** False; $\overrightarrow{MN}$ has endpoint M and extends in the direction of point N; $\overrightarrow{NM}$ has endpoint N and extends in the direction of point M.   **e.** True   **f.** False; their intersection is a line.

Assessment 11-3A

8. Answers vary.   **a.** Yes. A pair of corresponding angles are 50° each (note that the supplementary angles formed by lines n and ℓ are 130° and 50°).   **b.** Yes. A pair of corresponding angles are 70° each (note that the supplementary angles formed by lines n and ℓ are 110° and 70°).   **c.** Yes. A pair of alternate interior angles are 40° each.   **d.** Yes. A pair of corresponding angles are 90° each.   **e.** Yes. The marked angles are alternate exterior angles.   **f.** Yes. Extend $\overline{AC}$ and label as follows:

Because x is the measure of an exterior angle in $\triangle BCD$, $x = z + w$. But $x = y + z$ so $z + w = z + y$ implying $w = y$. Because $\angle w$ and $\angle y$ are alternate interior angles, $m \parallel n$.
19. b. The measure of the exterior angle equals the sum of the measures of the nonadjacent interior angles. Since $\angle 1$ and $\angle C$ are supplementary, $m(\angle 1) + m(\angle C) = 180°$. Since the sum of the measures of the interior angles of a triangle is 180°, $m(\angle A) + m(\angle B) + m(\angle C) = 180°$. Therefore, $m(\angle 1) = m(\angle A) + m(\angle B)$.

20. $m(\angle x) = \dfrac{180°}{11} \approx 13.8°$

$m(\angle y) = \dfrac{360°}{13} \approx 27.7°$

$m(\angle z) = \dfrac{720°}{13} \approx 55.4°$

$m(\angle w) = \dfrac{1080°}{13} \approx 83.1°$

21. $m(\angle 1) = 120°, m(\angle 2) = 130°, m(\angle 3) = 50°$, $m(\angle 4) = 120°, m(\angle 5) = 60°, m(\angle 6) = 50°, m(\angle 7) = 130°$, $m(\angle 8) = 60°, m(\angle 9) = 70°, m(\angle 10) = 50°, m(\angle 11) = 50°$, $m(\angle 12) = 60°$

Assessment 11-3B

1. Answers vary. Vertical angles are created by intersecting lines and are the pair of angles whose sides are two pairs of opposite rays. Vertical dihedral angles are created by two distinct intersecting planes and are the pair of dihedral angles whose sides are two pairs of opposite half-planes.   **3. a.** Complementary, 70°; supplementary, 160°; vertical, 20°   **b.** Complementary, $(80 - x)°$; supplementary, $(170 - x)°$; vertical, $(10 + x)°$ **8. a.** Label the angle supplementary to y as x_1.

Then $m(\angle x_1) + m(\angle y) = 180°$ because the angles are supplementary, and since $m(\angle x) + m(\angle y) = 180°$ it follows that $m(\angle x_1) = m(\angle x)$. Since $\angle x_1$ and $\angle x$ are corresponding angles, then $k \parallel \ell$.   **b.** Extend the 30° ray from line l to line k; a triangle is formed. The interior angles are 20°, 30° (alternate interior angles), and 130° (total of 180° interior angles). $\angle x$ and the 130° angle are supplementary, thus, $m(\angle x) = 50°$.
c. Extend the 135° ray from line k to line l; a triangle is formed. The interior angles are 45° (supplement of 135°), 40° (supplement of 140°), and 95° (total of 180° interior angles). The 95° angle and $\angle x$ are supplements, thus, $m(\angle x) = 85°$.
14. a. $m(\angle x) = 36°; m(\angle y) = 108°$ **b.** $m(\angle x) = 120°$
c. $m(\angle x) = 93°\,20'; m(\angle y) = 104°; m(\angle z) = 114°\,40';$ $m(\angle u) = 125°\,20'; m(\angle v) = 136°; m(\angle w) = 146°40'$
19. Because the sum of the interior angles is 360°, $\angle A$ and $\angle D$ are supplementary. Also, $\angle D$ and $\angle C$ are supplementary. If we extend $\overline{AD}$ to form an alternate interior angle to $\angle C$, we see that these angles are congruent, and thus, $\overline{BC}$ is parallel to $\overline{AD}$. (Similarly, $\overline{AB}$ is parallel to $\overline{DC}$.) Thus, $ABCD$ is a parallelogram.
21. $m(\angle 1) = 70°, m(\angle 2) = 110°, m(\angle 3) = 70°$, $m(\angle 4) = 70°, m(\angle 5) = 70°$
22. $m(\angle 1) = m(\angle 2)$ (vertical angles)
$m(\angle 2) = m(\angle 3)$ (given)
$m(\angle 3) = m(\angle 4)$ (vertical angles)
Therefore, $m(\angle 1) = m(\angle 2) = m(\angle 3) = m(\angle 4)$ and so $m(\angle 1) = m(\angle 4)$.

Mathematical Connections 11-3

Reasoning

1. a. No. Two or more obtuse angles will produce a sum of more than 180°.   **b.** Yes. For example, each angle may have measure 60°.   **c.** No. It may have an obtuse or right angle as well.   **d.** No. If two angles are supplementary the sum of their measures is 180°. The third angle will produce a sum greater that 180°.   **2.** No. It is not possible. The sum of all the measures of the angles in $\triangle ABC$ must equal 180°, but $m(\angle ABC) + m(\angle ACB) + m(\angle BAC) = 90° + 90° + m(\angle BAC) > 180°$. Hence, the situation shown in the diagram is not possible.   **3.** Answers vary. No. The measures of the exterior angles corresponding to the given angles are 120°, 100°, 90°, and 45°; the sum of these is 355°. The measures

of the exterior angles of a convex polygon is 360°, so this cannot happen.   **4. a.** Yes   **b.** No. The sum of the measures of the interior angles of a polygon must be a multiple of 180°, and 1400° is not a multiple of 180°.   **c.** Yes   **5.** $m(\angle 4) = m(\angle 1) + m(\angle 2)$. We know that $m(\angle 1) + m(\angle 2) + m(\angle 3) = 180°$. We know also $m(\angle 3) + m(\angle 4) = 180°$. Therefore $m(\angle 1) + m(\angle 2) + m(\angle 3) = m(\angle 3) + m(\angle 4)$. Subtracting $m(\angle 3)$ from both sides, we have $m(\angle 4) = m(\angle 1) + m(\angle 2)$.   **6. a.** Five triangles will be constructed in which the sum of the angles of each triangle is 180°. The sum of the measures of the angles of all the triangles equals $5 \cdot 180°$, from which we subtract 360° (the sum of all the measures of the angles of the triangles with vertex P). Thus, $5 \cdot 180° - 360° = 540°$.   **b.** Here, n triangles are constructed, so we have $n \cdot 180°$ from which we subtract 360° (the sum of all the measures of the angles of the triangles with vertex P). Thus, we obtain $n \cdot 180° - 360°$ or $(n - 2) \cdot 180°$.   **7. a.** Fold the isosceles triangle so that the congruent sides match up. The two angles will fall on top of each other.   **b.** Fold the triangle so that the two congruent angles fall on top of each other. The two sides will match up.   **c.** Choose a vertex and fold the triangle at that vertex so that the other two vertices fall on top of each other. Two angles of the triangle should fall on top of each other. Repeat at a second vertex.   **d.** Fold the trapezoid so that its congruent sides fall on top of each other and check that the base angles fall on top of each other as well.   **8. a.** Divide the quadrilateral into two triangles: ABC and ACD. The sum of the measures of the interior angles of each triangle is 180°, so the sum of the measures of the interior angles of the quadrilateral is $2 \cdot 180°$, or 360°.   **b.** The formula is also true for concave polygons.   **c.** Any concave pentagon can be divided into three triangles, and a concave hexagon can be divided into four triangles. In general, any concave n-gon can be divided into $(n - 2)$ triangles, so that the sum of the measures of the angles of the triangles is the sum of the measures of the interior angles of the n-gon.   **9.** No. Regular hexagons fit because the measure of each vertex angle is 120°, three hexagons fit to form 360°, and the plane can be filled. For a regular pentagon, the measure of each vertex angle is 108°, so pentagons cannot be placed together to form 360° (360° is not divisible by 108°) and the plane cannot be filled.   **10.** Yes. Because the sum of the measures of the marked angles is 360° and opposite angles are congruent we get $2m(\angle 2) + 2m(\angle 1) = 360°$ or $m(\angle 1) + m(\angle 2) = 180°$. From problem 8(a) of Assessment 11-3B, we $a \parallel b$.   **11.** $m(\angle DCB) + m(\angle ABC) = 180° - [(m(\angle 3) + m(\angle 4)] + 180° - [(m(2) + m(1)]$
$= 360° - (2m(\angle 3) + 2m(\angle 2))$
$= 360° - 2(m(\angle 3) + m(\angle 2))$
$= 360° - 2 \cdot 90° = 180°$
Thus, by the result in problem 8(a) of Assessment 11-3B, the rays $\overrightarrow{CD}$ and $\overrightarrow{AB}$ are parallel.

Open-Ended

12. Answers vary, for example, 127°, 129°, 131°, 133°, 137°, 139°, 141°, 143°; their sum must equal 1080°.   **13.** Answers vary; you should get a multiple of 360°.   **14.** For an n-gon, the sum of the interior angles should be $(n - 2)180°$.

Cooperative Learning

15. a. If $m(\angle A) = \alpha$ and $m(\angle B) = \beta$, then
$m(\angle D) = 180° - \left(\dfrac{\alpha}{2} + \dfrac{\beta}{2}\right).$

b. If $m(\angle C)$ is always the same, no matter what the measures of $\angle A$ and $\angle B$ are, then $m(\angle D)$ is always the same.   **c.** Answers vary. The following is a possible solution. From (a):
$m(\angle D) = 180° - \left(\dfrac{\alpha + \beta}{2}\right) = \dfrac{360° - (\alpha + \beta)}{2}$. Because
$\alpha + \beta = 180° - m(\angle C)$, we get the following:
$m(\angle D) = \dfrac{360° - (180° - m(\angle C))}{2}$
$= \dfrac{360° - 180° + m(\angle C)}{2} = 90° + \dfrac{1}{2}m(\angle C)$
Because the answer for $m(\angle D)$ depends only on $m(\angle C)$, the conjecture is justified.   **16. a.** Because congruent supplementary angles are formed.   **b.** The theorem concerning the sum of the measures of the angles of a triangle.   **c.** When $\angle A$ and $\angle C$ are folded, congruent supplementary angles are formed and, hence, each is a right angle. When B is folded along $\overline{BB'}$, the crease $\overline{DE}$ formed is perpendicular to $\overline{BB'}$ (again because congruent supplementary angles are formed); consequently, $\overline{DE} \parallel \overline{GF}$. Thus, $\angle D$ and $\angle E$ are also right angles.
d. $GF = GB' + B'F = \dfrac{1}{2}AB' + \dfrac{1}{2}B'C =$
$\dfrac{1}{2}(AB' + B'C) = \dfrac{1}{2}AC$; hence, $GF = \dfrac{1}{2}AC$.

Connecting Mathematics to the Classroom

17. The only possible figures are acute triangles. To see why, let an n-gon ($n \geq 4$) have the property that each angle is acute. Then all the exterior angles would be obtuse. A quadrilateral would have more than $90° \cdot 4$, or 360°, as the sum of the measures of the exterior angles and for $n > 4$ the polygon would have more than $90° \cdot 4$ or 360° as the sum of the measures of its exterior angles, which is not possible.   **18.** Such a polygon would have to have four right exterior angles which already add up to 360°. If such a decagon existed, it would have the sum of measures of exterior angles greater than 360°, which is impossible. Therefore, such a decagon does not exist.   **19.** No, the sum of the measures of the three angles would be greater than 180°.

Review problems

20. a. All angles must be right angles and all diagonals are the same length.   **b.** All sides are the same length and all angles are right angles.   **c.** Impossible. All squares are parallelograms.   **21. a.** (i) Two sets of parallel sides: A, B, C, D, E, F, G. (ii) One set of parallel sides: I, J. (iii) No parallel sides: H.   **b.** (i) Four right angles: D, F, G. (ii) Two right angles: I. (iii) No right angles: A, B, C, E, H, J.   **c.** (i) Four congruent sides: B, C, F, G. (ii) Two pairs of congruent sides: A, D, E, H. (iii) One pair of congruent sides: J. (iv) No congruent sides: I.   **22.** The symbol reads the same forward, backwards, and upside down, reflected about a vertical line, and turned 180°.
23. Answers vary. **a.** The figure has 180° turn symmetry but no line symmetry.

b. The figure has point symmetry, 90° turn symmetry, and vertical and horizontal line symmetry.

24. a. (i) Four line symmetries, the diagonals and horizontal and vertical lines through the center. (ii) No lines of symmetry.
b. (i) 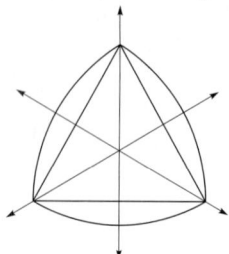 (ii) No lines of symmetry.

Switzerland

25. a. Turn symmetries of 90°, 180° (also called point symmetry), and 270° about the center of the square. **b.** Point symmetry about the center of the square. **26. a.** None.
b. 3, one through each vertex and the midpoint of its opposite side.

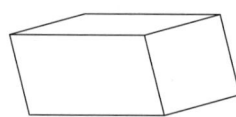

Assessment 11-4A

1. a. Answers vary. Quadrilateral pyramid; possibly square pyramid **b.** Quadrilateral prism; possibly trapezoidal or right trapezoidal prism **c.** Pentagonal pyramid **2. a.** (i) 6 (ii) 14 glued together **b.** (i) 24 (ii) 92 glued together **7. b.** False. No pyramid is a prism; a pyramid has one base, and a prism two bases. **d.** False. They lie in parallel planes. **e.** False. A prism must have two bases that lie in parallel planes. **8.** Answers vary, but all are possible; for example, **a.** An oblique square prism. Some faces are not bounded by rectangles.

b. An oblique square pyramid. The base is a square but a vertical line segment from the vertex does not intersect the base at its center.

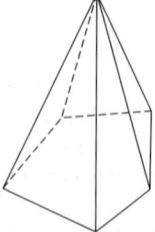

9. a. top, ○; side, △; front, △ **b.** top, ○; side, ○; front, ○
10.

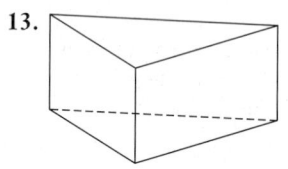

11. a. Right regular hexagonal pyramid. **b.** Right square pyramid. **c.** Cube. **d.** Right square prism **e.** Right regular hexagonal prism. **12. a.** No, one face is missing. **b.** Yes

13. 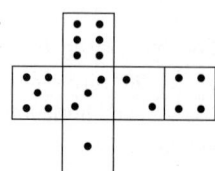 **14. b.**

17. a. Triangle **b.** Rectangle **18. a.** There will be three pairs of parallel faces, determined by any three pairs of opposite sides of the hexagonal base.

Assessment 11-4B

1. a. Triangular prism **b.** Quadrilateral pyramid **c.** Cylinder
2. a. (i) 7 (ii) 16 glued together **b.** (i) 28 (ii) 106 glued together
3. c. Regions formed by △BCE, △ADF, quadrilaterals DCEF, ABEF, ABCD **7. a.** False. The base can be any simple closed curve. **c.** False. They are parallelograms; if they were rectangles it would be a right prism. **8.** Answers vary; for example: **a.** Prism and pyramid (respectively) with a triangle as base:

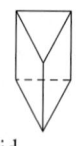

b. Prism and pyramid (respectively) with a pentagon as base:

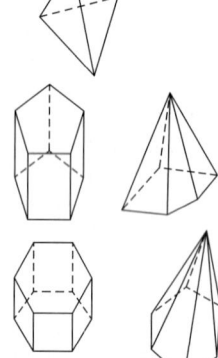

c. Prism and pyramid (respectively) with a regular hexagon as base:

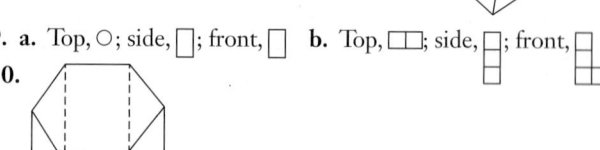

9. a. Top, ○; side, ▢; front, ▢ **b.** Top, ▭; side, ▢; front,
10.

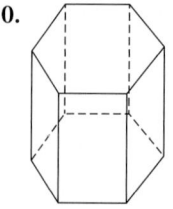

12. a. No; the faces don't match. **b.** No; there are two bottoms and no top.

13. Answers vary.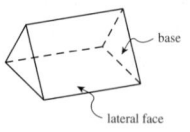

14. b. No; 17 is not a multiple of 3.
d. No; 23 is not a multiple of 2.
15. a. Truncated right circular cone:

b. Sphere:

c. Two right circular cones joined at their bases:

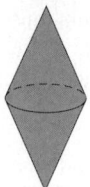

d. Inverted right circular cone:

17. a. The intersection is a pentagon:

Pentagon

b. The intersection is a circle:

Circle

c. The intersection is an ellipse (or oval):

Ellipse or oval

19. a. (i) A pyramid has $n + 1$ faces. (ii) A prism has $n + 2$ faces.
b. (i) A pyramid has $n + 1$ vertices. (ii) A prism has $2n$ vertices.
c. (i) A pyramid has $2n$ edges. (ii) A prism has $3n$ edges.
d. (i) Pyramids: $(n + 1) + (n + 1) - 2n = 2$ (ii) Prisms: $(n + 2) + 2n - 3n = 2$

Mathematical Connections 11-4

Reasoning

1. Three. Each pair of parallel faces could be considered bases.
2. Answers vary. For example, a cone is approximated by a many-sided pyramid and a cylinder is approximated by a many-sided prism. **3.** Both could be drawings of a quadrilateral pyramid. In (a), we are directly above the pyramid, and in (b), we are directly below the pyramid. **4.** An octagonal pyramid. To obtain 9 vertices you would need 8 on the base plus the apex. **5.** Answers vary. If the lateral faces are rectangles we have a right prism. If some lateral faces are parallelograms that are not rectangles, we have an oblique prism. **6.** 3. If there are 2 faces, then the shape is v-shaped and not closed, so we do not have a closed surface. If we have 3 faces then an intersection is possible to form a closed surface. **7.** Answers vary. **8. a.** A rectangle, $\overline{AD}$ is perpendicular to $\overline{AB}$ and to $\overline{AE}$ and therefore perpendicular to the plane *AEHB*. Since $\overline{MN} \| \overline{AD}$, $\overline{MN}$ is perpendicular to plane *AEHB*. Thus, $\overline{MN}$ is perpendicular to every line through M in that plane. So $\overline{MN} \perp \overline{MH}$ and $\angle NMH$ is a right angle, Similarly, the other angles of quadrilateral *MHGN* are right angles **b.** No

Open-Ended

9. Answers vary.

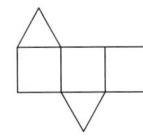 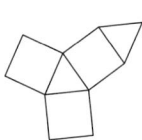

10. Answers vary. A sphere has infinitely many planes of symmetry.

Cooperative Learning

11. Answers vary. **12.** Answers vary. **13.** Answers vary.
14. a. Parallelogram, rectangle, square, scalene triangle, isosceles triangle that is not equilateral, equilateral triangle, pentagon, hexagon, a square and its interior, trapezoid that is not a parallelogram and a parallelogram that is neither a rhombus nor a rectangle, rhombus that is not a square, and line segment if the 3 points are on an edge. **b.** Triangle, quadrilateral, line segment, triangle and its interior.

Connecting Mathematics to the Classroom

15. In a sphere the surface does not consist of polygonal regions, so it cannot be a polyhedron. **16.** Trevor is only counting the vertices, faces, and edges in a two-dimensional drawing. He should be given a real cube and asked to count the vertices, faces, and edges. He should also be shown how to draw a three-dimensional cube by drawing each base and showing the vertices, faces, and edges using dashed segments for the hidden edges. **17.** Bonnie is assuming the surface the prism is lying on is the base. This is not the case as the bases must be two congruent polygonal faces that lie in parallel planes. **18.** No, it is not a regular polyhedron as it is made up of two different regular polygons, namely pentagons and hexagons. This assumes that the soccer ball is not a sphere in which case the answer is no as the surface would not consist of polygonal regions. **19.** There are two different nets shown below (assuming that the faces are indistinguishable).

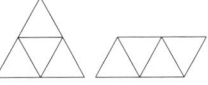

Review Problems

20. 161° 46′ 18″ **21.** Answers vary. **a.** $\overline{AB}$ **b.** $\overrightarrow{AC}$ **c.** $\overleftrightarrow{BC}$ **d.** $\overline{CD}$ **22.** No. Adjacent angles share a common side, and vertical angles do not. **23.** Answers vary. For example, the letter A. **24.** 35 **25.** 162° **26.** 110°

Chapter 11 Review

4. a. The measure of one of the dihedral angles formed by planes α and γ is $m(\angle APS) = 90°$, as given. The measure of one of the dihedral angles formed by planes β and γ is $m(\angle BPQ) = 90°$, since it is given that $\overline{PQ} \perp \overline{AB}$. **b.** $\overline{AB}$ is perpendicular to $\overline{PQ}$ and $\overline{PS}$ in plane γ.
5. Answers vary.
a. A simple closed curve:

b. A closed curve that is not simple:

c. A concave hexagon:

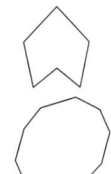

d. A convex decagon:

e. Draw a regular pentagon *ABCDE*. Draw line *CE* and reflect $\overline{CD}$ and $\overline{DE}$ about the line *CD*. The will create an equilateral pentagon that is not equiangular. An alternate way is to place an equilateral triangle on top of a square and erase the common edge. **f.** Draw a rectangle that is not a square. **6. a.** No. The sum of the measures of two obtuse angles is greater than 180°, which is the sum of the measures of all the angles of any triangle. **b.** No. The sum of the measures of the four angles in a parallelogram must be 360°. If all the angles are acute, the sum would be less than 360°. **16. b.** The measure of all the angles with vertices at P is 360°. If there are n triangles, then there is a total of $n \cdot 180°$ minus the 360° surrounding P, or $n \cdot 180° - 360° = (n - 2) \cdot 180°$. **c.** Answers vary.

One way would be to connect B with E and connect A with F. There will then be two quadrilateral and one triangle, given an angle sum of $2 \cdot 360° + 180° = 900°$. **17. a.** Alternate interior angles are congruent by construction. $\overleftrightarrow{AB} \parallel \overleftrightarrow{BC}$ by Theorem 11-2. **b.** Corresponding angles are congruent. **c.** $m(\angle B) + m(\angle C) + m(\angle BAC) = m(\angle BAD) + m(\angle DAE) + m(\angle BAC) = 180°$ **18.** If $a = b$, or $b = c$, or $a = c$, the proof is automatic. If none of these are true, we proceed as follows. Given three parallel lines with line l intersecting them:

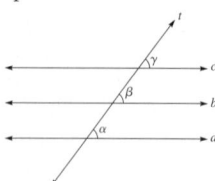

$a \parallel b$ implies $\alpha = \beta$. Next $b \parallel c$ implies $\beta = \gamma$. Thus, $\alpha = \gamma$ which implies $a \parallel c$ by congruent corresponding angles. **19.** Correct. If it is assumed that a rectangle has four right angles for a total angle measurement of $360°$ and that a diagonal divides it into two congruent triangles, then the sum of the measures in each right triangle is $180°$.

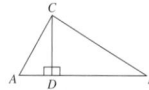

Thus, the sum of the measures of the angles in $\triangle ACD$ and $\triangle BCD$ is $2 \cdot 180° = 360°$. In this sum all the angles of the original triangle are included as well as the two right angles at D, so the sum of the measures of the angles in the original triangle is $360° - 2 \cdot 90° = 180°$. **20.** One approach would be to draw a line c through A parallel to a and then prove it to be parallel to b. If $c \parallel a$, then $\alpha_1 = z$ (corresponding angles). Since $x = \alpha_1 + \beta_1$ and $x = \alpha_1 + \beta_1 = y + z$ then $\beta_1 = \gamma$ which implies $c \parallel b$. By transitivity, $a \parallel b$.

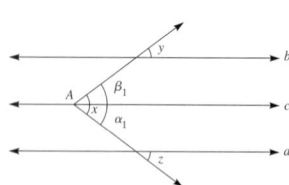

21. a. $\angle 3$ and $\angle 4$ are supplements of congruent angles. **b.** $m(\angle 3) = 180° - m(\angle 1)$ and $m(\angle 4) = 180° - m(\angle 2)$. If $m(\angle 1) < m(\angle 2)$ then $^-m(\angle 1) > ^-m(\angle 2)$. $180° - m(\angle 1) > 180° - m(\angle 2) \Rightarrow m(\angle 3) > m(\angle 4)$.
23. Answers vary. Three planes that intersect in a point:

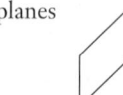

24. a. A triangle requires three points. The order of the points is not important; thus, the number of possible triangles is the number of combination of 10 points taken 3 at a time, or $_{10}C_3 = \dfrac{10!}{(10 - 3)!3!} = 120$.

b. $_nC_3 = \dfrac{n!}{(n - 3)!3!} = \dfrac{n(n - 1)(n - 2)}{6}$.

25. a. 18 **b.** 25 does not divide $360°$; such a regular polygon does not exist.

c. Does not exist; the sum is always $360°$. **d.** Does not exist; the equation $\dfrac{n(n - 3)}{2} = 4860$ has no natural number solution.

27. a. Line and turn **b.** Line, turn, and point **c.** Line.

28. a. 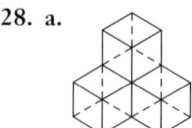 **b.** 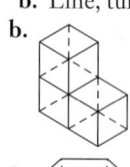 **c.**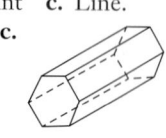

d. 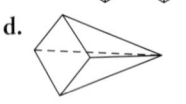 **e.** 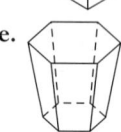 **f.**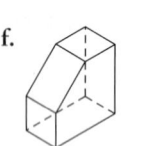

31. Answers vary. There are several possibilities.

a. 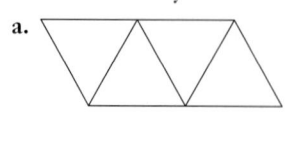 **b.**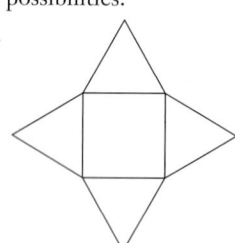

c. 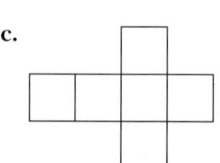 **d.**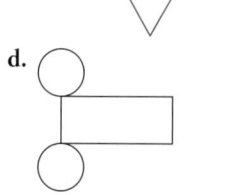

32. Answers vary. **a.** One possibility is:

b. Eight different nets. That is, the bottom square may be placed in any of eight positions. **33. d.** $5 + 5 - 8 = 2$
e. $12 + 8 - 18 = 2$ **f.** $10 + 7 - 15 = 2$

Answers to Now Try This

1. a. They do not have to be. Consider any point D such that $AD + DB > AB$. Point A, B, and D cannot be collinear. **b.** No, the points must be collinear. **c. i.** $\overleftrightarrow{AB}$ **ii.** $\overline{AB}$ **iii.** $\overleftrightarrow{AB}$ **iv.** $\overrightarrow{AB}$
v. $\overset{\circ\;\;\circ}{AB}$ **vi.** $\overset{\circ\;\;\circ}{AB}$ **3. a.** No. If skew lines had a point in common, there would be a single plane that contains the lines which would contradict the definition of skew lines. **b.** Skew lines cannot be parallel. By definition, parallel lines are in the same plane. Skew lines are not. **c.** Lines n and o are parallel; each of lines m, n, o, and ℓ is parallel to itself; lines n, m, and l are skew as are lines o and m. **4.** $8.42° = 8° + 0.42(60) = 8°25.2' = 8°25' + (0.2)(60) = 8°25'12''$ **5. a.** By folding a crease onto itself, we have created two angles that are both supplementary and congruent. They must have measure $90°$, making the creases perpendicular. **b.** Construction **c.** One obtains a $45°$ angle by bisecting a $90°$ angle. The $135°$ angle is $90° + 45°$. The $22°30'$ angle is obtained by bisecting the $45°$ angle. **d.** The least angle measures $90°$. **e.** The least angle measures $45°$. **f.** The least angle measures $\dfrac{360°}{2^n}$. **6. a.** It is possible for a line intersecting a plane to be perpendicular to only one line in the plane. Drawings will vary. **b.** It is not possible for a line intersecting a plane to be

perpendicular to two distinct lines lying in the plane and not be perpendicular to the plane.   **c.** Yes. If a line intersects a plane in point P and is perpendicular to two lines in the plane through P, then it is perpendicular to every line in the plane through P.   **d.** ℓ is perpendicular to α.   **8.** One approach to this problem is to start shading the area surrounding point X. If we stay between the lines, we should be able to decide whether the shaded area is inside or outside the curve. The shaded part of the following figure indicates that point X is located outside the curve.

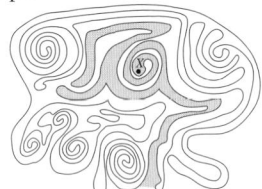

9. Answers vary.

a.

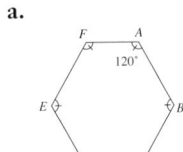

b.

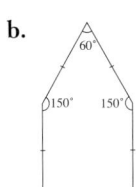

12. a. The sum of the measures of the interior and exterior angles is $n \cdot 180°$. Therefore, the sum of the measures of the interior angles is $n \cdot 180° - 360°$ or $(n - 2)180°$.   **b.** $\dfrac{(n - 2) \cdot 180°}{n}$ or $180° - \dfrac{360°}{n}$

13. Euler's formula is $V + F - E = 2; 8 + 6 - 12 = 2;$ $10 + 7 - 15 = 2; 12 + 8 - 18 = 2$

Answer to the Preliminary Problem

Walking around the star can solve the problem, but a simpler approach is to notice that by extending the sides of a regular pentagon we can obtain the vertices of the star. The sum of the measures of the interior angles of the pentagon is $3 \cdot 180°$, so the measure of each interior angle of the pentagon is $\dfrac{3 \cdot 180°}{5} = 108°$. We can choose any side of the pentagon and the isosceles triangle formed adjacent to the side to find that the base angles of the isosceles triangles each measure $72°$ (supplementary angles). From this we deduce that the measure of each shaded angle is $180° - 2 \cdot 72° = 36°$.

CHAPTER 12

Assessment 12-1A

1. a. True; CPCTC.   **b.** False; these are not corresponding angles.   **c.** False, these are not corresponding parts.
3. $\triangle ABD \cong \triangle CDB; \angle A \cong \angle C, \angle D \cong \angle B, \angle B \cong \angle D,$ $\overline{AB} \cong \overline{CD}, \overline{AD} \cong \overline{CB}, \overline{BD} \cong \overline{DB}$ **6.** We know that $\overline{AC} \cong \overline{EC}$ and $\overline{BC} \cong \overline{DC}$. $\angle ACB \cong \angle ECD$ because of vertical angles. Therefore, $\triangle ACB \cong \triangle ECD$ by SAS. Hence, $\angle DEC \cong \angle BAC$ by CPCTC and $\overline{AB} \parallel \overline{DE}$ since they have congruent alternate interior angles.   **8.** We know $\overline{AB} \cong \overline{BC}$ and $\overline{AD} \cong \overline{CD}$. Also, $\overline{BD} \cong \overline{BD}$. Therefore, $\triangle ABD \cong \triangle CBD$ by SSS and $\angle ABD \cong \angle CBD$ by CPCTC.   **9.** It is not possible if the

three points are collinear. If the three points are not collinear, then the point is the center of the circumcircle around the triangle determined by the three points.   **11. b.** The side of greatest length is opposite the angle of greatest measure.   **12.** $\triangle ADB \cong \triangle CBD$ by HL because $\overline{AB} \cong \overline{CD}, \overline{DB} \cong \overline{BD}$, and $\angle ADB$ and $\angle CBD$ are right angles. Thus, $\angle ABD \cong \angle CDB$. Because these angles are alternate interior angles created by lines $\overleftrightarrow{AB}, \overleftrightarrow{DC}$, and the transversal $\overline{BD}$, it follows that $\overline{AB} \parallel \overline{DC}$. Also $\overline{BC} \parallel \overline{AD}$ because $\angle ADB \cong \angle CBD$ (alternate interior angles). Therefore, $ABCD$ is a parallelogram since opposite sides are parallel.   **13.** Answers vary.   **a.** Construct a triangle congruent to $\triangle CAB$ or an isosceles triangle congruent to any isosceles triangle with vertex angle at A.   **b.** First construct a segment $\overline{AB}$ of length 4 cm and then find point C as the intersection of circles centered at A and B with respective radii of 2 cm and 3 cm.   **f.** One way is to use a protractor to draw the $75°$ angle and then mark the 6 cm and 7 cm sides on the sides of the angle.   **g.** Use a protractor to draw the $40°$ angle and mark its vertex as A. Then on one of the sides mark point B such that $AB = 7$ cm. Then let C be the intersection of the other side of the angle with a circle centered at B with radius 6 cm. Two triangles are possible.   **h.** Either proceed as in part (g) or construct a triangle with two sides of 6 cm each and included angle of $100°$.   **i.** Construct a right angle and then mark on its sides legs of 4 cm and 8 cm. Join the endpoints of these segments for the remaining side.   **j.** (b) Yes, by SSS; (c) Yes, by SSS; (d) There is no triangle because $4 + 5 < 10$; (e) Yes, by SSS; (f) Yes, by SAS; (g) The triangle is not unique; (h) Yes, by SAS; (i) Yes, by SAS.   **14.** Construct a right isosceles triangle and the perpendicular bisector of the hypotenuse.   **15. a.** Construct an angle congruent to $\angle A$. Construct an angle congruent to $\angle B$ with the same vertex as the first construction and sharing a side with that triangle and the other side in its exterior.   **b.** Construct an angle with vertex B congruent to $\angle A$ such that one side is a side of $\angle B$ and the other side is in the exterior of $\angle B$.   **16.** No, if a triangle is equilateral all the angles measure $60°$.   **17. a.** Construction. The triangles $\triangle ABO, \triangle BCO, \triangle CDO$, and $\angle DAO$ are congruent (SAS) isosceles right triangles. Therefore, the congruent angles in each triangle measure $45°$. Consequently all the angles in $ABCD$ are $90°$, and all the sides are congruent.   **b.** Because the arcs BE and EC each measures $45°$, the chords $\overset{\frown}{BE}$ and $\overset{\frown}{EC}$ are congruent. Bisecting each of the right central angles, we get the vertices of the regular octagon.   **c.** Answers vary. Construct F such that $CF = BE$. Then extend $\overline{OE}$ to intersect the circle at G. Next extend $\overline{OF}$ to intersect the circle at H. Now connect $E, C,$ F, D, G, A, H, B to obtain a regular octagon.   **18.** Answers vary. Fold the square in half so that one pair of opposite sides fall on each other. Unfold and repeat for the other pair of opposite sides. Where the two folds intersect is the required center. The segment connecting the center to one of the vertices of the square is the radius.   **19.** Point C can be found as the intersection of the line and the perpendicular bisector of $\overline{AB}$.   **20.** The center of the circle is the intersection of the perpendicular bisectors of any two adjacent sides of the square. The radius of the circle is the distance from the center to any of the vertices of the square. Alternatively the center can be found as the intersection of the diagonals.   **22. a.** Construct point C as the intersection of two circles with centers at A and B and radius AB.   **b.** Any of the angles of the triangle in part (a) will measure $60°$.   **c.** Any of the exterior angles in part (a) will measure $120°$.   **23. b.** From part (a), $\angle A \cong \angle B$ by CPCTC.

Assessment 12-1B

1. a. True, CPCTC   **b.** True, CPCTC   **c.** False, these are not corresponding parts   **3.** $\triangle ABC \cong \triangle DEC$; $\angle A \cong \angle D$, $\angle B \cong \angle E$, $\angle BCA \cong \angle ECD$, $\overline{AB} \cong \overline{DE}$, $\overline{BC} \cong \overline{EC}$, $\overline{CA} \cong \overline{CD}$ **5.** Draw $\overline{BD}$. We know that $\overline{AB} \cong \overline{CD}$, $\overline{AD} \cong \overline{BC}$, and $\overline{BD} \cong \overline{BD}$. Therefore, $\triangle ABD \cong \triangle CDB$ by SSS and $\angle ABD \cong \angle CDB$ by CPCTC. Hence, $\overline{AB} \parallel \overline{CD}$ because we have congruent alternate interior angles. $\angle ADB \cong \angle CBD$ by CPCTC and therefore, $\overline{AD} \parallel \overline{BC}$ because we have congruent alternate interior angles.   **10.** No; for example, consider the 4 vertices of a parallelogram that is not a rectangle. The perpendicular bisectors of the 4 sides are not concurrent.   **11.** No. Answers vary. If four such points A, B, C, D existed in the plane, any three would have to be the vertices of an equilateral triangle. Then D would be equidistant from the vertices of the equilateral $\triangle ABC$ and hence the center of the circle that circumscribes $\triangle ABC$. Because the three triangles with the common vertex D are congruent, $m(\angle ADB) = 120°$ and hence $AD \neq AB$ and the four points cannot be equidistant from each other.

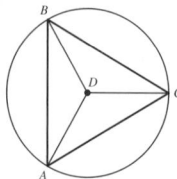

12. b. The side opposite the greatest angle is longer than the side opposite the smallest angle.   **c.** The hypotenuse is longer than any of the legs. This is so because in a right triangle one angle measures 90° and the other angles are acute. The hypotenuse is the side opposite the greatest angle.   **13. a.** The lengths must be the same because they are corresponding parts of congruent triangles.   **b.** You cannot make the same claim if the plane containing the stakes is not perpendicular to the antenna.   **14.** Construct an equilateral triangle and then the perpendicular bisector of a side.   **16. a.** By HL. Alternatively by ASA because the angles in each triangle measure 30°, 60°, 90°.   **b.** Let a be the length of each of the sides of the equilateral triangle $\triangle ABC$. Because $BD = DA, BD = \dfrac{a}{2}$. Thus in $\triangle BCD$, $\overline{BD}$ is opposite the 30° angle and $BD = \dfrac{a}{2} = \dfrac{BC}{2}$.

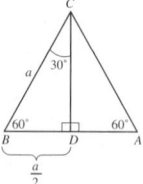

17. a. The 12-gon is regualr because it has congruent interior angles. The arcs BG and GC each measure 30°. Because $12 \cdot 30° = 360°$, 12 congruent 30° arcs can be constructed. The corresponding 12 chords are congruent to form a 12-gon.   **b.** Connect O with each of the vertices. Each angle with vertex O is $\dfrac{360°}{6}$, or 60°. Because each triangle like $\triangle BCO$ is isosceles, its base angles are congruent and hence each measures $\dfrac{(180° - 60°)}{2}$, or 60°. Thus each triangle is equilateral and therefore each side of the hexagon is congruent to the radius.   **18. a.** F is

the midpoint of both diagonals ($\triangle ABC \cong \triangle ADC$ by SSS and $\angle CAB \cong \angle CAD$ by CPCTC and $\triangle BAF \cong \triangle DAF$ by SAS implies $\overline{BF} \cong \overline{DF}$, so F is a midpoint; a similar argument will show $\overline{AF} \cong \overline{CF}$).   **19.** Answers vary. Pick any three points A, B, and C on the circle and construct the perpendicular bisectors of $\overline{AB}$ and $\overline{AC}$. The intersection of the perpendicular bisectors is the center.   **20.** The center of the circle is the intersection of the perpendicular bisectors of any two adjacent sides of the rectangle. The radius of the circle is the distance from the center to any of the vertices of the rectangle. Alternatively the center can be found as the intersection of the diagonals.   **21. a.** Not possible unless the rhombus is a square.   **b.** Possible. Answers vary. The center O of the circle is the intersection of any two perpendicular bisectors of two adjacent sides. Alternatively the center is the intersection of two segments joining opposite vertices. The radius is the segment from O to any of the vertices.   **22. b.** Use Theorem 12-5(b) to bisect a 60° angle and take the supplement of the resulting 30° angle.   **23. a.** The three sides are congruent in any order; that is, $\triangle ABC \cong \triangle ABC$, $\triangle ABC \cong \triangle BAC$, $\triangle ABC \cong \triangle CAB$, $\triangle ABC \cong \triangle ACB$, $\triangle ABC \cong \triangle BCA$, $\triangle ABC \cong \triangle CBA$.   **b.** If the rectangle is $ABCD$, then $ABCD \cong ABCD$, $ABCD \cong BADC$, $ABCD \cong DCBA$, $ABCD \cong CDAB$.   **24. b.** The center is on the hypotenuse.   **c.** Because the center of the circle is on the hypotenuse, the radius is half the length of the hypotenuse.

Mathematical Connections 12-1

Reasoning

1. $GHEF$ **2.** No, because 5 cm + 4 cm < 12 cm no triangle can be formed.   **3.** The third side must be less than 24 cm and greater than 4 cm.   **4. a.** $\overline{CD}$ and $\overline{CE}$ **b.** $\angle CAB$ and $\angle CBA$ **c.** No, no congruence criteria are satisfied.   **d.** Yes, SAS   **5.** P is not on the circle because of the definition of a circle.   **6.** Let $\angle A$ be the vertex angle formed by two congruent sides. Both parts of Theorem 12-5 can be proved by drawing the angle bisector of $\angle A$ and proving that the two triangles created are congruent by SAS.   **7. a.** $\triangle ABC \cong \triangle ADC$ by SSS. Hence, $\angle BAC \cong \angle DAC$ and $\angle BCA \cong \angle DCA$ by CPCTC. Therefore, $\overleftrightarrow{AC}$ bisects $\angle A$ and $\angle C$.   **b.** The angles formed are right angles. By part (a), $\angle BAM \cong \angle DAM$. Hence, $\triangle ABM \cong \triangle ADM$ by SAS. $\angle BMA \cong \angle DMA$ by CPCTC. Since $\angle BMA$ and $\angle DMA$ are adjacent congruent angles, each must be a right angle. Since vertical angles formed are congruent, all four angles formed by the diagonals are right angles.   **c.** By part (a) and SAS, $\triangle BAM \cong \triangle DAM$. Hence, $\overline{BM} \cong \overline{MD}$ by CPCTC.   **8. a.** If point C lies in the interior of $\triangle ABD$, part (a) is consistent.   **b.** For part (b) to hold, the diagonals must be extended in order to meet. By extending and allowing one diagonal to be outside the figure, the result holds.   **c.** See parts (b) and (a). With these conditions, the result is true.   **9.** No. If the diagonals of a rectangle are perpendicular it is a square. If they are not perpendicular, the rectangle is not a square. In each case the diagonals can be 19 in. long.   **10.** $\overline{CB} \cong \overline{CD}$ since each is 2 units long. $\overline{AB} \cong \overline{AD}$ because they can be viewed as hypotenuses of two congruent right triangles with legs 1 and 3 units long.   **11.** The construction will work by moving the drafting triangle as before until the other leg passes through the given point.   **12. a.** Following the directions in the problem after points A and B are constructed, we construct points C and D so that $AC = BD = r$, where r is the radius of the circle. We next construct point E so that $CE = r$. If we now draw an arc with center D and radius r, we find that the arc intersects the circle at the existing point E. Thus only six points are determined.

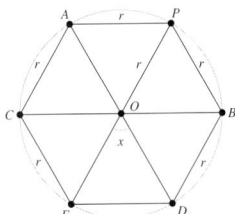

b. The figure is a regular hexagon. To see why, notice that the fact that the arc with center D and radius r intersects the circle at the existing point E is an experimental observation. However, rather than drawing that arc, we can just connect E with D and prove that $ED = r$. From the above construction it follows that the five triangles: $\triangle OBP$, $\triangle OPA$, $\triangle OAC$, $\triangle OCE$, and $\triangle OBD$ are equilateral and therefore all their angles measure 60°. Consequently $x = m(\angle EOD) = 360° - 5 \cdot 60° = 60°$. Because $\triangle OED$ is isosceles, $m(\angle OED) = m(\angle ODE)$ and therefore each of these angles measures $\dfrac{(180° - 60°)}{2}$ or 60°. Thus $\triangle EOD$ is equilateral and therefore $ED = r$. Because the angles at the vertices of the hexagon are each 60° + 60°, or 120°, we obtain a regular hexagon.

Open-Ended

13. Constructions vary.   **14.** Constructions vary.   **15.** Answers vary. For example, draw radius $\overline{OB}$. Now we have two isosceles triangles, $\triangle ABO$ and $\triangle OCB$ as shown below (the sides are congruent because they are radii). The base angles in each triangle are congruent. The measures, x, of the base angles of $\triangle ABO$ are equal. Similarly the measures, y, of the base angles of $\triangle OCB$ are equal. The sum of the measures of the angles in $\triangle ACB$ is 180°. Therefore, $x + x + y + y = 2x + 2y = 2(x + y) = 180°$ and $x + y = 90°$. Since the $m(\angle B) = x + y = 90°$, we have a right angle, and the proof of Thales' Theorem is complete.

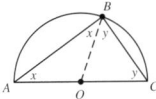

16. a. Answers vary. Some objects are tins of food and floor tiles. **b.** Answers vary. Photographs and their enlargements, an original and its projected image in an overhead projector, and a slide and its image are possible examples.   **17.** Answers vary. One possible pattern is a square stamp-block quilt, which is a quilt constructed entirely of squares.   **18. a.** $\triangle AFB \cong \triangle CED$ by SAS because $\overline{AF} \cong \overline{CE}$, $\overline{FB} \cong \overline{ED}$, and $\angle F \cong \angle E$ (each is a right angle). Hence, $\overline{AB} \cong \overline{CD}$ (corresponding parts in congruent triangles). **b.** Because $\triangle AFB$ is a right triangle, we have $m(\angle A) + m(\angle B) = 90°$. The congruence of triangles in part (a) implies that $\angle A \cong \angle C$. Hence, $m(\angle C) + m(\angle B) = 90°$. This implies that $\angle G$ in $\triangle BCG$ is a right angle and hence that $\overline{AB}$ and $\overline{CD}$ are perpendicular. **19. a.** The right angle is the greatest angle in a right triangle. **b.** The distance is the length of the perpendicular segment from the point to the line. Any other segment will be a hypotenuse of a right triangle in which the perpendicular segment is a leg and hence shorter than the hypotenuse.

Cooperative Learning

20. Answers vary.

Connecting Mathematics to the Classroom

21. For two figures to be congruent, they must be the same shape and the same size. All squares are the same shape but not the same size. A tracing of a small square can be placed on top of a large square to show that they are not congruent.   **22.** In the triangles, there are two sides and an angle in one triangle congruent to two sides and an angle of the other. However, in order to use SAS the angle must be the included angle between the two sides in each triangle. In these triangles, the angles are not the included angles. **23.** The symbol $\cong$ is used only for congruent objects. Because AB and CD designate lengths of segments and not the segments themselves, it is not true that $AB \cong CD$. Notice that if segments are congruent, then they are of the same length; hence it is correct to write $AB = CD$.   **24.** Perhaps the "best" definition relies on transformational geometry, discussed in Chapter 13. Two figures can be defined to be congruent if, and only if, one figure can be mapped onto the other by successively applying translation, reflection, rotation, or glide reflection.   **25.** She is correct; if $AC = BC$ all corresponding parts are congruently SSS.

GeoGebra Activities

26. See online appendix.   **27.** See online appendix.   **28.** See online appendix.   **29.** See online appendix.

Assessment 12-2A

2. a. No, by ASA, the triangle is unique. **b.** No, by AAS, the triangle is unique. **c.** Yes, the sides can be of any length.   **4.** When the parallel ruler is open at any setting, the distance $BC = BC$; it is given that $AB = DC$ and $AC = BD$, so $\triangle ABC \cong \triangle DCB$ by SSS. Hence, $\angle ABC \cong \angle DCB$ by CPCTC. Because these are alternate interior angles formed by lines $\overleftrightarrow{AB}$ and $\overleftrightarrow{CD}$ with transversal line $\overleftrightarrow{BC}$, $AB \parallel DC$.   **5. a.** $\triangle ABD \cong \triangle CBD$ by ASA **b.** There is not enough information for congruence.   **6.** $\angle C \cong \angle F$ is needed to have congruence by ASA or $\overline{AB} \cong \overline{DE}$ to use SAS. **8.** We know that $\overline{AB} \cong \overline{DE}$, $\overline{BC} \cong \overline{EF}$, and $\angle ABC \cong \angle DEF$. Therefore, $\triangle ABC \cong \triangle DEF$ by SAS and $\angle BAC \cong \angle EDF$ by CPCTC.   **9.** $\overline{BD} \cong \overline{BC}$, $\angle ABD \cong \angle EBC$ (vertical angles), and $\angle A \cong \angle E$ (alternate interior angles of parallel lines). Therefore, $\triangle ABD \cong \triangle EBC$ by AAS.   **12.** An isosceles trapezoid is formed, and the angles formed with each base are congruent. The congruent angles are sometimes referred to as the base angles of the isosceles trapezoid. Other pairs of angles are supplementary. **13. d.** False. A trapezoid may have only one pair of opposite sides parallel.   **14. b.** No. If the quadrilateral has three right angles, then the fourth must also be a right angle because the sum of the measures of the four angles is 360°.   **c.** No; any parallelogram with a pair of right angles must have right angles as its other pair and hence it must be a rectangle.   **15.** Because $AB = BC$, B is equidistant from A and C. By Theorem 12-4, point B is on the perpendicular bisector of $\overline{AC}$. Similarly, D is on the perpendicular bisector of $\overline{AC}$. Because two points determine a unique line, $\overleftrightarrow{BD}$ is the perpendicular bisector of $\overline{AC}$.   **18.** Answers vary. Either the arcs or the central angles must have the same measure (radii are the same since the sectors are part of the same circle). An alternative condition is that the segments joining endpoints of each arc are congruent.   **19. a.** Kite. $\overline{DX} \cong \overline{AX}$; $\angle D$ and

∠*A* are right angles; $\overline{DP} \cong \overline{AQ}$. Thus, △*PDX* ≅ △*QAX* by SAS. Hence, $\overline{PX} \cong \overline{QX}$ by CPCTC. $\overline{DC} \cong \overline{BA}$ as opposite sides of a rectangle. $\overline{PD} \cong \overline{QA}$. Hence, $\overline{CP} \cong \overline{BQ}$. $\overline{CY} \cong \overline{BY}$, given, and ∠*C* and ∠*B* are right angles. Therefore, △*CYP* ≅ △*BYQ* by SAS, so $\overline{QY} \cong \overline{PY}$ and *PXQY* is a kite.   **b.** The answer does not change. However, when *P* and *Q* are midpoints of $\overline{DC}$ and $\overline{AB}$, respectively, *PXQY* is a rhombus.   **20.** Make one of the quadrilaterals a square and the other a rectangle.   **21.** Construct the first kite by constructing a segment to become a diagonal and then construct two isosceles triangles with the segment as a common base. Construct the second kite starting with a segment not congruent to the first and construct two isosceles triangles with that segment as their common base but the sides congruent to the corresponding sides of the isosceles triangles in the first construction.   **23. b.** The corresponding lengths of the two perpendicular sides of the rectangles must be equal.   **c.** Answers vary; one solution is that two corresponding adjacent sides must have equal lengths and the included angle of one must be congruent to the other.   **24. a.** If in the accompanying figure $\overline{AD} \| \overline{BC}$ and $\overline{AD} \cong \overline{BC}$, then the pairs of alternate interior angles are congruent. That is, ∠*OBC* ≅ ∠*ADO* and ∠*BCO* ≅ ∠*DAO*. Thus, △*CBO* ≅ △*ADO* by ASA. Consequently, $\overline{BO} \cong \overline{OD}$ and $\overline{AO} \cong \overline{OC}$ (by CPCTC). Now △*ABO* ≅ △*DCO* by SAS as the angles at *O* are vertical. Hence, ∠*BAO* ≅ ∠*DCO*. These angles are alternate interior angles created by $\overline{AB}$, $\overline{CD}$, and the transversal $\overleftrightarrow{AC}$. Thus, $\overline{AB} \| \overline{CD}$ and by definition *ABCD* is a parallelogram ($\overline{BC} \| \overline{AD}$) is given).   **b.** In this figure, *AO* = *OC* and *BO* = *OD*. In addition, ∠*BOC* ≅ ∠*DOA* are vertical angles. Thus by SAS, △*BOC* ≅ △*DOA*. Consequently, ∠*ADO* ≅ ∠*CBO*. Because these are alternate interior angles created by lines $\overleftrightarrow{BC}, \overleftrightarrow{AD}$, and transversal $\overleftrightarrow{BD}$, $\overline{BC} \| \overline{AD}$. From the congruence of the triangles, it also follows that $\overline{BC} \cong \overline{DA}$. Thus, *ABCD* is a quadrilateral with pair of opposite sides parallel and congruent and therefore a parallelogram. (Use part (a).)

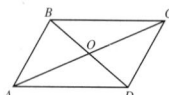

25. Answers vary; for example, the polygons must have the same number of sides with one pair of sides congruent. All regular polygons with the same number of sides are similar, so if they have the same number of sides with one pair congruent, they are congruent.

Assessment 12-2B

1. b. Infinitely many are possible.   **2.** (a) No; by ASA, the triangle is unique. (b) Yes; AAA determines a unique shape, but not size.   **3. b.** No; AAA does not ensure congruence.   **4.** Because the angles at *A* and at *C* are corresponding congruent angles (they are right angles), it follows that $\overline{AB} \| \overline{CD}$. We have △*ABD* ≅ △*DCA* by SAS since $\overline{AB} \cong \overline{BC}$ (given), $\overline{AD} \cong \overline{DA}$, and ∠*BAD* ≅ ∠*CDA* (alternate interior angles created by the parallels $\overline{AB}$ and $\overline{CD}$ and transversal $\overline{AD}$). Hence by CPCTC, ∠*ADB* ≅ ∠*DAC*, which implies that *k* ∥ *l*.

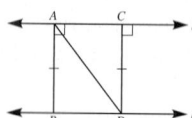

5. a. △*ADC* ≅ △*ABC* by ASA   **b.** Not enough information for congruence.   **6.** If $\overline{AB} \cong \overline{DE}$, we have congruence by

ASA or since ∠*BCA* must be congruent to ∠*ECD* (third angles in the triangle), then to use AAS we need $\overline{BC} \cong \overline{EC}$ or $\overline{AC} \cong \overline{DC}$.   **7.** *m*(∠1) = 120°, *m*(∠2) = 60°, *m*(∠3) = 60°, *m*(∠4) = 60°, *m*(∠5) = 30°   **8.** ∠*P* ≅ *R*, ∠*PQS* ≅ ∠*RSQ* (alternate interior angles of parallel lines), $\overline{SQ} \cong \overline{QS}$ (reflexive property), and so △*PSQ* ≅ △*RQS* by AAS. Therefore, $\overline{PQ} \cong \overline{RS}$ by CPCTC.   **9.** Because △*ISO* is isosceles, the base angles must be congruent and sum to 180° − 110° = 70°. Therefore, each base angle in △*ISO* measures 35°. Since △*ANG* is isosceles, each base angle has the same measure and so *m*(∠*G*) = 35°, and hence the measure of ∠*N* is 110°. Therefore, △*TRI* ≅ △*ANG* by SAS. Other angles and sides could have also been used to complete the proof.   **12.** Construct $\overline{CE}$ such that $\overline{CE} \| \overline{AB}$. Thus, *ABCE* is a parallelogram and consequently $\overline{AB} \cong \overline{CE}$, which makes △*DEC* isosceles. This implies that ∠*x* ≅ ∠*D*. Because ∠*x* ≅ ∠*D* (corresponding angles created by the parallels $\overline{AB}$ and $\overline{CE}$) and ∠*x* ≅ ∠*A* we have ∠*A* ≅ ∠*D*.

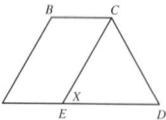

13. a. False, a square is a rectangle and a rhombus.   **c.** True (in fact, all squares are trapezoids).

14. a. Answers vary.

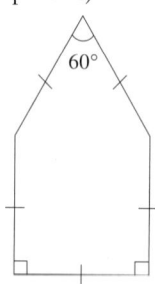

b. No, because the sum of the measures of four acute angles totals less than 360°.   **c.** Yes. To construct such a kite, construct a right triangle in which no angle measures 45° and reflect it along the hypotenuse as shown below.

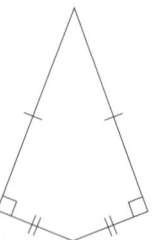

18. Answers vary. For example, two isosceles trapezoids *AEFD* and *ABCD*, where $\overline{EF} \| \overline{AD}$ as shown.

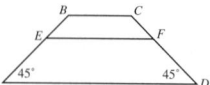

19. a. Because the diagonals bisect each other we know from 24(b) in Assessment 12-2A, that the quadrilateral is a parallelogram and that opposite sides are congruent. We need to prove that one of the angles of the quadrilateral is a right angle. In the figure below, because the diagonals are congruent, we know by SSS that △*ABD* ≅ △*DCA*.

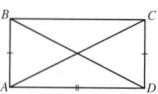

The fact $\triangle ABC \cong \triangle DCA$ follows from SSS by observing that $\overline{AB} \cong \overline{DC}$ (opposite sides of a parallelogram), $\overline{AD} = \overline{DA}$, and $\overline{BD} = \overline{CA}$ (given). Thus, $\angle BAD \cong \angle CDA$. These angles are also supplementary since $\overline{AB} \parallel \overline{CD}$. Thus, each must be a right angle. **b.** Construct two congruent line segments that bisect each other. The endpoints of these line segments will be the vertices of a rectangle. **c.** If the angles created by the diagonals are not congruent, the corresponding sides of the two rectangles will not be congruent. **20. b.** Suppose $ADCB$ in part (a) is a parallelogram. By SAS, $\triangle EDH \cong \triangle GBF$, thus $\overline{EH} \cong \overline{GF}$. Similarly, $\triangle EAF \cong \triangle GCH$ so $\overline{EF} \cong \overline{GH}$. If opposite sides of a quadrilateral are congruent, it is a parallelogram.

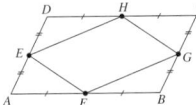

21. a. Answers vary. Two adjacent sides of one must be congruent to the corresponding adjacent sides of the other. **b.** Possibilities include: (i) The sides and one angle are congruent to the corresponding parts in the other kite, or (ii) corresponding diagonals are congruent. **c.** Answers vary. The vertex (where the congruent sides intersect) angles are congruent, and one of the two congruent sides in one triangle is congruent to the corresponding side in the other. **22. a.** $\angle ABD \cong \angle CDB$ and $\angle ADB \cong \angle CBD$ (alternate interior angles with respect to parallel lines) $\overline{BD} \cong \overline{DB}$. Then $\triangle ABD \cong \triangle CDB$ (by ASA). Therefore, $\angle BAD \cong \angle DCB$ (CPCTC). Similarly, $\angle ABC \cong \angle CDA$. **b.** Because $\triangle ABD \cong \triangle CDB$, we have $\overline{AB} \cong \overline{CD}$ and $\overline{AD} \cong \overline{CB}$ (CPCTC). **c.** $\angle BAC \cong \angle DCA$ and $\angle ABD \cong \angle CDB$ (alternate interior angles), and $\overline{AB} \cong \overline{DC}$ [from part (b)]. Then $\triangle BAF \cong \triangle DCF$, so $\overline{AF} \cong \overline{CF}$ and $\overline{BF} \cong \overline{DF}$ (CPCTC). **d.** In $\triangle ABD, m(\angle BAD) + m(\angle ABD) + m(\angle ADB) = 180°$. From part (a), $\angle CBD \cong \angle ADB$. Substitution yields $m(\angle BAD) + m(\angle ABD) + m(\angle CBD) = 180°$. Since $m(\angle ABC) = m(\angle ABD) + m(\angle CBD)$, then $m(\angle BAD) + m(\angle ABC) = 180°$. $\angle ABC$ and $\angle BAD$, therefore they are supplementary. **23.** Answers vary. Two rhombuses are congruent if a side of one is congruent to a side of the other and an angle of one is congruent to an angle of the other. To see this, note that in a rhombus all four sides are congruent. Therefore, showing that the two rhombuses have one pair of congruent sides is sufficient to conclude all the sides are congruent.

Mathematical Connections 12-2

Reasoning

1. a. Yes, if you know four parts then you have enough to use one of SSS, SAS, ASA, or AAS. **b.** No, for example, AAA is not enough to establish congruence. **2.** SSS, SAS, ASA, AAS, and HL (for right triangles) **3.** Show $\triangle ABC \cong \triangle EDC$ by ASA and then $\overline{AB} \cong \overline{DE}$ by CPCTC. The bridge is 92 m long. **4.** Each of the fabric triangles is congruent to the others by SAS. **5. a.** $\angle GHE$ **b.** $\overline{GH}$ **c.** Draw diagonals $\overline{BD}$ and $\overline{FH}$, then $\triangle BCD \cong \triangle FGH$ by SAS. **6.** The triangle formed by Stan's head, Stan's feet, and the opposite bank is congruent to the triangle formed by Stan's head, Stan's feet, and the spot just obscured by the bill of his cap. These triangles are congruent by ASA since the angle at Stan's feet is 90° in both triangles, Stan's height is the same in both triangles, and the angle formed by the bill of his cap is the same in both triangles. The distance across the river is approximately equal to the distance he paced off because these distances are corresponding parts of congruent triangles.

7. One way is to make both legs of the ironing board the same length and fasten them together with a hinge at their midpoints. If one of these legs is attached to the board at a fixed spot and the other leg can be attached at various spots, then the height of the ironing board can be adjusted. Since the legs form the diagonals of a rectangle, the board will always be parallel to the floor. (It can be shown that a quadrilateral whose diagonals are the same length and bisect each other is a rectangle. (See Exercise 19(a) in Section 12-2B.) In most commercially available ironing boards, the legs are designed to form the diagonals of a trapezoid. **8.** Given $\angle BAC$, construct a circle with center A and any radius. Let D and E be the points where the circle intersects the sides of the angle. Next construct the perpendicular bisector of $\overline{DE}$. **9.** No, because the congruent sides are not corresponding sides. **10. a.** The distances are equal. **b.** The distances from every point on the angle bisector of an angle to the sides of the angle are equal. **c.** $\triangle APC \cong \triangle APB$ by AAS; hence $\overline{PC} \cong \overline{PB}$. **d.** If a point P in the interior of an angle is equidistant from the sides of an angle, then it is on the angle bisector of the angle. To prove this statement, we assume that $\overline{PC} \cong \overline{PB}$ and prove that $\overline{AP}$ bisects $\angle A$. We have $\triangle APC \cong \triangle APB$ by HL. Thus, $\angle CAP \cong \angle PAB$ by CPCTC **11. a.** Yes **b.** No, for example, neither 4 angles nor 4 sides determine congruence.

Open-Ended

12. Answers vary. Possible questions and answers concerning figures with vertices on the nails (or dots of the dot paper) are: **a.** How many noncongruent right isosceles triangles are possible? Answer: 5 **b.** How many noncongruent isosceles trapezoids that are not rectangles are there? Answer: 6 **c.** How many noncongruent squares are there? Answer: 5

Cooperative Learning

13. a. Answers vary. In many secondary-school and middle-school geometry books, kites are not defined. For many of these books, a trapezoid is a quadrilateral with exactly one set of parallel sides. **b.** Answers vary. **c.** The definition used in this text allows a structure among the quadrilaterals that does not exist with the definition in part (a), namely, the subset relationships among the quadrilaterals. The one in this text does cause some difficulty in the definition of an isosceles trapezoid. Therefore it is defined in terms of its base angles, not its sides.

Connecting Mathematics to the Classroom

14. The student is wrong. $\angle 1 \cong \angle 2$ implies that $\overline{AD}$ and $\overline{BC}$ are parallel, but does not imply that the other two sides are parallel. **15.** The symbol $=$ is used for identical objects. Two triangles are equal if they represent the same set of points. Congruent triangles are not necessarily identical because their positions may be different. **16.** The SSS congruency condition assures that triangles are rigid and hence contribute to supporting the structure. **17.** Extend the shorter side and construct the perpendicular from a vertex not on the side to the line containing the side. **18.** This is true because the distance from A or from A' to the line $\overleftrightarrow{BC}$ is the distance between the two parallel lines. **19.** $\triangle ABC \cong \triangle EDC$ by SAS, so $\angle B \cong \angle D$. But in the picture the angles are not congruent, so the figure must not be accurate.

GeoGebra Activities

20. See online appendix.

Review Problems

21. The triangles that are congruent to triangle △*ABC* are triangles △*BCD*, △*CDE*, △*DEA*, and △*EAB*, as well as triangles △*CBA*, △*DCB*, △*EDC*, △*AED*, and △*BAE*. They are all congruent by SAS.   **22.** Construction   **23.** Construction   **24. a.** Yes, SAS   **b.** Yes, SSS   **c.** Yes, HL

Assessment 12-3A

6. b. The altitude is the extension of the cable from vertex *A* to the ground.   **7. a.** The perpendicular bisectors of the sides of an acute triangle meet inside the triangle.   **b.** The perpendicular bisectors of the sides of a right triangle meet at the midpoint of the hypotenuse.   **c.** The perpendicular bisectors of the sides of an obtuse triangle meet outside the triangle.   **8. a.** The point is equidistant from all vertices because it is on all three perpendicular bisectors. Being at the intersection of two of the perpendicular bisectors forces the point to be equidistant from all three vertices.   **9. a.** If the rectangle is not a square, it is impossible to construct an inscribed circle. The angle bisectors of a rectangle do not intersect in a single point.   **b.** Possible. The center of the circle is the intersection of the diagonals (which are also the angle bisectors of the vertices), and the radius of the circle is the distance from the center to any of the sides.   **c.** Possible. The intersection of the three longest diagonals is the center of the circle.   **12.** The figure is a rhombus. The diagonals bisect each other, so the figure is a parallelogram. Because in addition the diagonals are perpendicular to each other, it is a rhombus.   **15.** The center is where the angle bisectors of the angles meet (the incenter). The radius is the perpendicular distance from the incenter to a side.   **17.** Answers vary.   **a.** If the parallelogram is not a rectangle, cut along an altitude whose foot lies on the opposite side of the parallelogram. If the parallelogram is a rectangle, cut along any line through the point where the diagonals meet such that the line is not a diagonal and is not parallel to any side.   **b.** Make a copy of a given trapezoid *ABCD* and put it upside down next to $\overline{CD}$ as shown. More precisely, extend $\overline{BC}$ so that $\overline{CE} = a$ and extend $\overline{AD}$ so that $DF = b$. Because $\overline{BE} \| \overline{AF}$ and $BE = AF$ (the length of each is $a + b$), *ABEF* is a parallelogram.

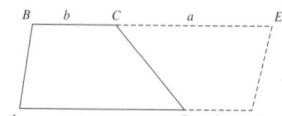

19. b. Infinitely many noncongruent rectangles can be constructed. The endpoints of two segments bisecting each other and congruent to the given diagonal determine a rectangle, but since the segments may intersect at any angle, there are infinitely many such rectangles.   **c.** Not possible because the sum of the measurements of the angles would be greater than 180°.   **d.** There is no parallelogram because the fourth angle must also be a right angle.   **20. a.** Construct an equilateral triangle and bisect one of its angles.   **b.** Bisect a 30° angle, then add the 30° and 15° angles or bisect a right angle.   **c.** Combine 60° and 15° angles or combine 45° and 30° angles.   **22. a.** The point is determined by the intersection of the angle bisector of ∠*A* and the perpendicular bisector of $\overline{BC}$. Because the point is on the angle bisectors of ∠*BAD*, it is equidistant from its sides. Because it is on the perpendicular bisector of $\overline{BC}$, it is equidistant from *B* and *C*.   **b.** The point is determined by the intersection of the angle bisectors of ∠*A* and ∠*B*.   **23.** Answers vary. One way is to construct six 60° central angles with common vertex at the center *O*. Then construct ⎸ree 120° central angles with vertex *O*. The sides of these angles

intersect the circle at points *A*, *B*, and *C*, which are vertices of an equilateral triangle. △*ABC* is equilateral because △*AOB*, △*BOC*, and △*AOC* are congruent (by SAS). Another approach is to construct a regular inscribed hexagon and then choose any vertex of the hexagon and two other nonconsecutive vertices.

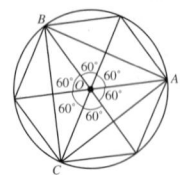

Assessment 12-3B

1. a. Construct line *n* through *P* perpendicular to ℓ, then a line through *P* perpendicular to *n*.   **b.** Through *P* draw any line intersecting ℓ. Let *Q* be the point of intersection. Find the midpoint *M* of $\overline{PQ}$. Through *M* draw any line intersecting ℓ at *Q'*. Find *P'* so that *M* is the midpoint of $\overline{P'Q'}$. Then $\overleftrightarrow{P'P}$ is the required line.   **8.** Construction. The center of the circle is on each angle bisector, therefore equidistant from the sides of each angle, that is, from the sides of the triangle.   **9.** Yes, because the angle bisectors are concurrent. One of the diagonals is on the angle bisectors of opposite angles. The other angle bisectors intersect on that diagonal.   **10.** Answers vary. One way is to construct the perpendicular bisector *n* of $\overline{AB}$ and label *M* its point of intersection with $\overline{AB}$. Next find two points *C* and *D* on *n* such that $MC = MD = MA$. The required square is *ACBD*.   **12.** Construction. Use the fact that the diagonals of a rectangle are congruent and bisect each other.   **13.** Construction. Draw $\overline{BE}$. Extend $\overline{BE}$ to a point *D* such that $BE = ED$. Now $\overline{BD}$ is one diagonal of the square. Next construct a perpendicular to $\overline{BD}$ at *E*. Then find points *A* and *C* such that $BE = AE = CE$. *ABCD* is the desired square.   **15.** The center is the intersection of any two angle bisectors or any two of the longest diagonals. The radius is the distance from the incenter to a side.   **17.** The following figure shows two such congruent trapezoids. For different values of *a* we get different trapezoids.

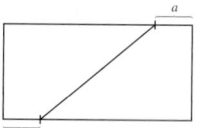

18. a. $\overleftrightarrow{PQ}$ is the perpendicular bisector $\overline{AB}$.   **b.** *Q* is on the perpendicular bisector of $\overline{AB}$ because $\overline{AQ} \cong \overline{QB}$; similarly, *P* is on the perpendicular bisector of $\overline{AB}$. There is unique line through two points so the perpendicular bisector is $\overleftrightarrow{PQ}$.   **c.** $\overrightarrow{PQ}$ is the angle bisector of ∠*APB*; $\overrightarrow{QC}$ is the angle bisector of ∠*AQB*.   **d.** Because $\overrightarrow{PC}$ and $\overrightarrow{QC}$ are on perpendicular bisectors of the bases of isosceles triangles △*APB* and △*AQB*, each is an angle bisector.   **19. a.** Without the angle between the sides, there are infinitely many parallelograms that could be constructed from the two given sides.   **b.** Possible. Construct two perpendicular segments bisecting each other and congruent to the given diagonals.   **c.** There is no unique parallelogram because the other pair of congruent sides can be of any length.   **20.** Answers vary.   **a.** Bisect a 60° angle from an equilateral triangle and then bisect it again.   **b.** $105° = 90° + 15°$; thus construct adjacent angles of 90° and 15°.   **c.** $120° = 180° - 60°$; thus a 120° angle is a supplement of a 60° angle.   **21.** Make the edge of the straightedge coincide with ℓ; let one of the legs of the right triangle slide along the leg of the straightedge until the other leg goes through *P*. The line along the leg containing *P* is the required perpendicular.   **22. a.** The point is determined by the intersection of the perpendicular bisectors of $\overline{AB}$ and $\overline{BC}$.   **b.** Not possible. If such a point existed, it would have to be on the perpendicular bisectors of all the sides, but because the perpendicular bisectors of the four sides of a quadrilateral do not necessarily intersect in a single point (this is the case for the given quadrilateral), such a point does not exist.   **c.** This is possible only if the angle bisectors are concurrent, which is not the case for a general quadrilateral.   **23.** Answers vary. Referring to the figure and answer to exercise 23 in Assessment 12-3A, construct an equilateral triangle ABC inscribed in the circle. Next construct tangents to the circle at points A, B, and C. The points of intersection of the tangents are the vertices of a required triangle. To prove that the triangle is equilateral, let D be the intersection of the perpendiculars at A and B, then the quadrilateral $AOBD$, where O is the center of the circle, has two right angles at A and B and a 120° angle at O. Hence the angle at D measures $360° - (90° + 90° + 120°)$ or 60°. Similarly the other angles measure 60° and hence the triangle is equilateral.

Mathematical Connections 12-3

Reasoning

1. Lines ℓ and n are parallel because congruent corresponding angles (right angles) are formed.   **2.** No. If B were the midpoint, then $(3x + 5) + (5x + 1) = 30$. Solving for x we have $x = 3$. If $x = 3$, then the two parts would have measures 14 and 16, which cannot happen if B is the midpoint.   **3.** Answers vary. Construct a perpendicular to $\overleftrightarrow{AC}$ at A. The new angle formed is the complement of $\angle A$ and has measure 40°. If we bisect this 40° angle, we have a 20° angle.   **4. a.** The diagonals of $ABCD$ are congruent and bisect each other, so the figure is a rectangle.   **b.** Construct a rectangle $ABCD$ as in part (a). To construct a rectangle that is not congruent to $ABCD$, choose different diameters that intersect at different angles than the diameters in $ABCD$.   **5.** Connect the three dots to form a triangle. Construct the perpendicular bisectors of the three sides of the triangle. The point where they meet will be the site of the airport.   **6.** In the figure below, $m(\angle 1) + m(\angle 2) + m(\angle 3) + m(\angle 4) = 180°$ (straight angle). Because $m(\angle 1) = m(\angle 2)$ and $m(\angle 3) = m(\angle 4)$, we have

$$m(\angle 2) + m(\angle 3) = \frac{180°}{2} = 90°$$ and therefore lines p and q are perpendicular.

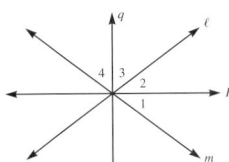

7. Answers vary. Given $\angle BAC$, place one strip of the tape so that an edge of the tape is along $\overline{AB}$ and another strip of the tape so that one of its edges is along $\overline{AC}$, as shown. Two edges of the strips of tape intersect in the interior of the angle at D. Connect A with D. $\overline{AD}$ is the angle bisector. Because the diagonals of a rhombus bisect its angles, this construction can be justified by showing that $AEDF$ is a rhombus. (E and F are the points of intersection of the tops of the tape pieces and their bottoms.) $AEDF$ is a parallelogram. It remains to be shown that $\overline{AF} \cong \overline{AE}$. For that purpose, we show that $\triangle FAG \cong \triangle EAH$. We have $\overline{FG} \cong \overline{EH}$ because the

two strips of tape have the same width. $\angle A \cong \angle A$, and the angles at H and G are right angles. Thus, the triangles are congruent by AAS.

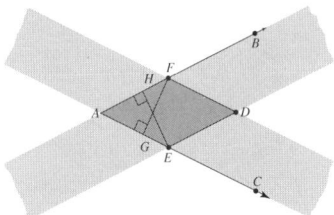

8. Rhombus. For proof, see the solution to problem 7.   **9.** Notice that the vertices E, F, G, H are on the angle bisectors of the four angles each with vertex at O. Because each pair of vertical angles at O are congruent, the triples F, O, H and G, O, E, are collinear. Since $\overrightarrow{OF}$ and $\overrightarrow{OG}$ bisect adjacent supplementary angles, $m(\angle FOG) = 90°$. Similarly, $m(\angle GOH) = 90°$. Because $\triangle ABO \cong \triangle CDO$ and $\triangle BCO \cong \triangle DAO$, it follows that $OF = OH$ and $OG = OE$. Consequently, $\overline{FH}$ and $\overline{GE}$ are perpendicular bisectors of each other, which makes $EFGH$ a rhombus.

Open-Ended

10. Answers vary. Most students will probably lobby to have other tools included as construction tools.   **11.** Answers vary.   **12.** Answers vary. Construct a circle with center O. Use a protractor or a Geometry Utility (GSP or GeoGebra) to construct five 72° central angles that are adjacent, each to the next, with vertices at O. At the intersections of the angles with the circle, construct tangents to the circle. The five tangents intersect at points that are the vertices of the required pentagon. (The construction can be achieved with only compass and straightedge but is beyond the scope of this text.)

Cooperative Learning

13. a. Answers vary. When we unfold the paper, we get two creases, $\overline{AB}$ and $\overline{PQ}$, each of which is a perpendicular bisector of the other. This is so because M is the midpoint of each segment and all the angles formed at M are right angles (two congruent angles are formed at M whose measures add up to 180°, and hence each must measure 90°). Every point on the perpendicular bisector of $\overline{PQ}$ is equidistant from the endpoints P and Q (Theorem 12-3).   **b.** Because A and B are on the perpendicular bisectors of $\overline{PQ}$, $AP = AQ$ and $PB = BQ$. Because Q is on the perpendicular bisector of $\overline{AB}$, $AQ = QB$. Hence $AP = AQ = QB = PB$. A quadrilateral with all sides congruent is a rhombus.   **14. a.** Yes   **b.** The measures are the same.   **c.** Answers vary.   **15.** Answers vary. Some are discussed in the text.

Connecting Mathematics to the Classroom

16. Answers vary. One might argue that if you choose any point P on a line and let A and B be points such that P is between A and B, then P bisects the line because the two half-lines $\overrightarrow{PA}$ and $\overrightarrow{PB}$ are congruent.   **17.** E is not on $\overline{DF}$. Therefore it is not a midpoint.   **18.** No. Perpendiculars must be constructed from the incenter to the sides in order for the segments to have equal measure.   **19.** The width of the ruler can be used to find points in the interior of the angle at a distance from a side that is the width of the ruler. When this is done at both sides of the angle, the point P where the edges intersect is on the angle bisector because it is the same distance from the sides of the angle. $\overleftrightarrow{AP}$ is the angle bisector.

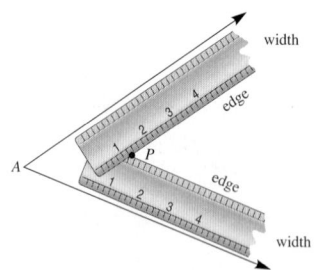

20. $\overline{OD}$ is the radius if, and only if, it is perpendicular to $\overline{AC}$. If $AB \neq BC$, then $\overline{OD}$ is not perpendicular to $\overline{AC}$.

GeoGebra Activities

21. a. In an acute triangle, the altitudes are concurrent at a point in the interior of the triangle and in a right triangle at the vertex of the right angle. In an obtuse triangle, the lines containing the altitudes are concurrent at a point in the exterior of the triangle. **b.** Answers vary, but the distances are equal. **c.** The distances from every point on the angle bisector to the sides of the angle are equal. **22.** See online appendix.

Review Problems

23. $\triangle ABC \cong \triangle DEC$ by ASA ($\overline{BC} \cong \overline{EC}$, $\angle ACB \cong \angle DCE$ as vertical angles, and $\angle B \cong \angle E$ as alternate interior angles formed by the parallels $\overline{AB}$ and $\overline{ED}$ and the transversal $\overleftrightarrow{EB}$). $\overline{AB} \cong \overline{DE}$ by CPCTC. **24.** Constructions **25.** Because $\angle B \cong \angle E$ and $\angle A \cong \angle D$, then $\angle C \cong \angle F$. Then because $\overline{AC} \cong \overline{DF}$, we have $\triangle ABC \cong \triangle DEF$ by SAS. **26.** 50°

Assessment 12-4A

3. Yes. Corresponding angles are congruent and sides are proportional. **4.** Yes, they are similar. It is given that $\angle BAD \cong \angle B_1A_1D_1$. Because the pairs $\angle ABC$ and $\angle BAD$ as well as $\angle A_1B_1C_1$ and $\angle B_1A_1D_1$ are supplementary, it follows that $\angle ABC \cong \angle A_1B_1C_1$. Thus the rhombi have congruent corresponding angles. Because in a rhombus adjacent sides are congruent, $\dfrac{AD}{AB} = 1 = \dfrac{A_1D_1}{A_1B_1}$. This implies $\dfrac{AD}{A_1D_1} = \dfrac{AB}{A_1B_1}$ and therefore ratios of corresponding sides are proportional.
5. b. Yes; sides are proportional and angles are congruent. **c.** No; two rectangles that are not squares are similar if, and only if, the corresponding sides are proportional. **d.** Always similar because the ratio of the corresponding longer sides equals the ratio of the corresponding shorter sides and the angles are congruent. **6.** Make all dimensions three times as long; for example, in part (c) each side would be three diagonal units long. One possible solution set is shown here:

a. 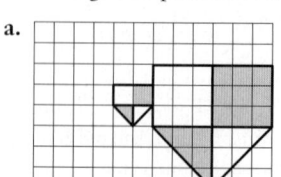 **b.**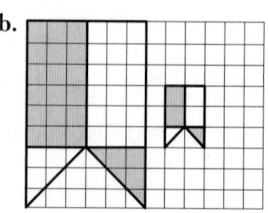

c. 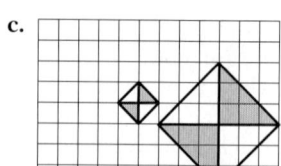 **d.**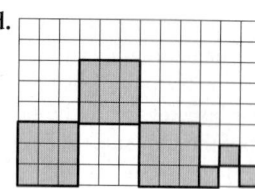

7. b. i. $\dfrac{2}{3}$ **ii.** $\dfrac{1}{2}$ **iii.** $\dfrac{4}{3}$ **iv.** $\dfrac{2}{3}$ or the reciprocals **12.** Construction as follows:

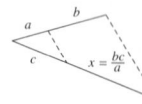

13. a. Yes, because the angles stay the same, and the ratios of corresponding sides are proportional. **15.** $133\dfrac{1}{3}\%$, but most copy machines will not allow this setting. **19.** $\angle BCA \cong \angle DEC$ (alternate interior angles), $\angle A \cong \angle ECD$ (alternate interior angles), $\triangle ABC \sim \triangle CDE$ (AA similarity). **20. a.** The ratio of the perimeters is the same as the ratio of the sides. **b.** If a, b, c, d are the sides of one quadrilateral and a_1, b_1, c_1, d_1 the corresponding sides of a similar quadrilateral then

$$\frac{a}{a_1} = \frac{b}{b_1} = \frac{c}{c_1} = \frac{d}{d_1} = r \text{ (the scale factor).}$$

Now, $\dfrac{a + b + c + d}{a_1 + b_1 + c_1 + d_1} = \dfrac{a_1r + b_1r + c_1r + d_1r}{a_1 + b_1 + c_1 + d_1}$

$$= \frac{(a_1 + b_1 + c_1 + d_1)r}{a_1 + b_1 + c_1 + d_1} = r.$$

Hence the ratio of the perimeters is r. An analogous proof works for any two similar n-gons. **21. a.** From the Midsegment Theorem, we know that each midsegment is half the measure of the opposite side of $\triangle ABC$. Thus the sides of each of the smaller triangles are half as long as the corresponding sides of $\triangle ABC$. Hence by SSS they are congruent to each other. **b.** Yes; the ratio of the corresponding sides is $\dfrac{1}{2}$, and therefore by SSS similarity the triangles are similar. **23.** They are circles, so have exactly the same shape, and hence are similar.

Assessment 12-4B

1. No. The corresponding sides are not proportional.

2. $1 : 35\dfrac{3}{16}$ or $1 : 35.1875$ **4.** They are not necessarily similar. As a counterexample, consider a square and a non-square rectangle.
5. e. Yes **6.** Answers vary. For example, $1 \times 1, 2 \times 2, 3 \times 3$ right isosceles triangles are all similar. **7. a.** $\triangle ABC \sim \triangle DEF$ by SSS similarity since $\dfrac{4}{6} = \dfrac{4}{6} = \dfrac{2}{3}$; scale factor $\dfrac{2}{3}$ **b.** $\triangle ABC \sim \triangle EDA$ by SAS similarity since $\dfrac{3}{6} = \dfrac{4}{8}$ and each has an included right angle; scale factor $\dfrac{1}{2}$ **c.** $\triangle ABE \sim \triangle ACD$ by AA similarity; scale factor $\dfrac{6}{6 + 2}$ or $\dfrac{3}{4}$ **d.** $\triangle ABE \sim \triangle DBC$ by AA similarity;

scale factor $\frac{6}{8}$ or $\frac{3}{4}$ **8. a.** $\triangle ABC \sim \triangle ADE$ by SAS

similarity because $\frac{5}{5+5} = \frac{7}{7+7} = \frac{1}{2}$; $x = 4.5$

b. $\triangle ABC \sim \triangle EDF$ by AA similarity; $x = \frac{20}{3}$

c. $\triangle QPT \sim \triangle RPS$ by SAS similarity since $\frac{3.2}{7.2} = \frac{4}{9}$; $x = \frac{27}{4}$

d. $\triangle ABC \sim \triangle BED$ by AA similarity since each has a right angle and $m(\angle CBA) = 90° - m(\angle DBE)$ and in $\triangle BDE$, $m(\angle E) = 90° - m(\angle DBE)$, so $m(\angle CBA) = m(\angle E)$; $x = \frac{8}{3}, y = \frac{10}{3}$ **10. a.** Both triangles share $\angle B$. In addition $\angle C \cong \angle E$ because they are corresponding angles. Thus $\triangle ABC \sim \triangle DBE$ by AA similarity.   **b.** $2\frac{2}{9}$

12. Let segments b and a be on a side of an arbitrary angle as shown. On the other side of the angle mark point D so that $DA = c$. Connect B with D, and through C draw $\overline{CE} \| \overline{BD}$. Then $DE = x$.

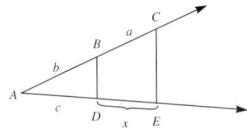

13. b. $\frac{75}{32}$ **14.** Make one pentagon regular and the other with two right angles that looks like a house and has congruent sides.   **20. a.** The ratio of corresponding heights is the same as the ratio of corresponding sides.   **b.** Suppose $\triangle ABC \sim \triangle A_1B_1C_1$; then $\triangle ABD \sim \triangle A_1B_1D_1$ (see figure) by AA similarity. Hence $\frac{BD}{B_1D_1} = \frac{AB}{A_1B_1}$. A similar argument works if the altitudes are not in the interior of the triangles.

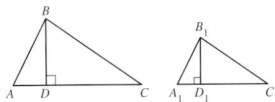

21. a. Answers vary. (i) Connect B with D and apply Theorem 12-16 to triangles ABD and BCD.

(ii) $MN = \frac{1}{2}a + \frac{1}{2}b = \frac{1}{2}(a+b)$.   **b.** From part (a),

$c = \frac{1}{2}(a+b)$ or $2c = a+b$.

$$c + c = a + b$$
$$c + c - b = a$$
$$c - b = a - c$$

This shows that b, c, and a form an arithmetic sequence having difference $c - b$, which is to $a - c$.   **c.** Part (b) proved that the lengths of any 3 consecutive segments form an arithmetic sequence, so the lengths of all 10 segments form an arithmetic sequence. Use the formula for the sum of an arithmetic sequence to find $S_{10} = \frac{10}{2}(b_1 + b_{10}) = 5(a+b)$.

22. a. Because $\overline{NP}$ and $\overline{MN}$ are midsegments, $\overline{NP} \| \overline{BD}$ and $\overline{MN} \| \overline{AC}$. Thus, $NSTV$ is a parallelogram.   **b. i.** Perpendicular. Then, and only then, the parallelogram will have a right angle and therefore be a rectangle.   **ii.** Perpendicular and congruent. Then,

and only then, $MN = NP$ (each is half as long as a diagonal) and $\overline{MN}$ and $\overline{NP}$ will be perpendicular.

Mathematical Connections 12-4

Reasoning

1. Any two cubes are similar because they have the same shape.   **2.** Answers vary. For example, the two prisms must be the same shape but not necessarily the same size. The prisms are similar if their bases are similar and all lengths of corresponding sides are proportional.   **3.** Yes, each has a non-base angle of 40° and since they are isosceles each must have congruent base angles of $\frac{(180° - 40°)}{2} = 70°$. Now the triangles are similar by AA similarity.   **4.** No, consider one right triangle to be a 3-4-5 triangle and the other triangle to be an isosceles right triangle with hypotenuse equal to 5.   **5.** All three angles are congruent so the triangle must be equilateral.   **6.** Lay the licorice diagonally on the paper so that it spans a number of spaces equal to the number of children. (See the figure.) Cut on the lines. Equidistant parallel lines will divide any transversal into congruent segments.

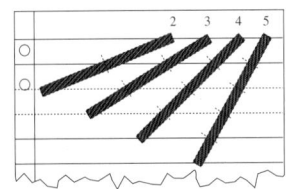

7. a. (i) $\triangle ABC \sim \triangle ACD$ by AA similarity because $\angle ACB$ and $\angle ADC$ are right angles and $\angle A$ is common to both. (ii) $\triangle ABC \sim \triangle CBD$ by AA similarity because $\angle ACB$ and $\angle CDB$ are right angles and $\angle B$ is common to both. (iii) Using (i) and (ii) $\triangle ACD \sim \triangle CBD$ by the transitive property of the similarity relation.   **b.** (i) $\frac{AB}{AC} = \frac{BC}{CD} = \frac{AC}{AD}$ (ii) $\frac{AB}{CB} = \frac{BC}{BD} = \frac{AC}{CD}$ (iii) $\frac{AC}{CB} = \frac{AD}{CD} = \frac{CD}{BD}$ **c.** From part (b): $\frac{a}{x} = \frac{c}{a}$; so $a^2 = cx$. Similarly, $\frac{b}{y} = \frac{c}{b}$; so $b^2 = yc$.

d. From part (c): $a^2 + b^2 = cx + cy$
$$= c(x + y)$$
$$= c \cdot c$$
$$= c^2$$

In a right triangle, the square of the hypotenuse is equal to the sum of the squares of the legs.   **e.** $\triangle ADC \sim \triangle CDB$ implies $\frac{AD}{CD} = \frac{DC}{DB}$ or $\frac{y}{h} = \frac{h}{x}$. Hence, $h^2 = xy$.   **f.** From (e), $\frac{h}{x} = \frac{y}{h}$ and hence x, h, y are in a geometric sequence.   **8.** Since $m(\angle A) = 36°$, $m(\angle C) + m(\angle B) = 144°$, and $m(\angle C) = m(\angle B) = 72°$. Since $\triangle BCD$ is isosceles, $m(\angle CDB) = 72°$. Hence, $m(\angle DBC) = 180° - 144° = 36°$, and therefore $\triangle BCD$ is a golden triangle.   **9. a.** $x = \sqrt{5} - 1 \approx 1.236$
b. The smaller rectangle is a golden rectangle if, and only if, $\frac{2}{\sqrt{5} - 1} = \frac{1 + \sqrt{5}}{2}$. This is true if $4 = (\sqrt{5} - 1)(\sqrt{5} + 1)$ which is true if $4 = 5 - 1$. Since $4 = 4$, the smaller rectangle is a golden rectangle and because the ratios of the side lengths are all $\frac{1 + \sqrt{5}}{2}$, it is similar to the original rectangle.

Open-Ended

10. Answers vary. For example, the figures have the same shape but not the same size. The corresponding angles are congruent and the corresponding sides are not equal in measure. The sides are proportional.   **11.** Answers vary. For example, both the SSS theorems relate the lengths of the sides in one triangle to the lengths of the sides in the other triangle. The congruence theorem requires the sides to be congruent, and the similarity theorem requires the sides to be proportional. Both SAS theorems relate congruent angles and the sides forming these angles. The congruence theorem requires the corresponding sides to be congruent, and the similarity theorem requires the corresponding sides to be proportional.   **12. a.** Answers vary depending upon the construction.   **b.** The perimeters of the bases should be in the same ratio as the heights in part (a).   **13.** Points lie along the same line because similar triangles are formed. The line goes through the origin.

Cooperative Learning

14. Answers vary.   **15. a.** Answers vary.   **b.** The following are two different-size triangles with the given data. The given measures of the angles were only approximate; such triangles with these exact measures do not exist. The triangles are similar but not congruent. (The ratio of the corresponding sides is $\frac{80}{100}$, or $\frac{4}{5}$.) Hence, the surveyor and the architect could both have been correct in their conclusions.

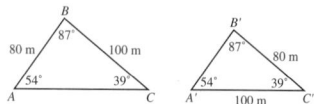

c. Answers vary.

Connecting Mathematics to the Classroom

16. Al is correct. When Betty listed the similarity statement for the triangles, she did not list the corresponding vertices in the correct order for each triangle.   **17.** Bob is correct and you should discuss why he is correct. Each right triangle has a right angle and these are congruent. In addition, there are two congruent acute angles so the triangles are similar by AA similarity.   **18.** The student is not correct and should be encouraged to try to find a counterexample. For example, suppose one triangle has angle measures of 40°, 70°, and 70° and another triangle has angle measures of 40°, 40°, and 100°. Two angles are congruent, but the triangles are not similar.   **19.** No, they are not necessarily similar. For example, a rectangle that is not a square and a square have all angles congruent but are not similar.   **20.** The student is incorrect. The corresponding sides are not proportional.   **21.** No, such a condition is not meaningful since at least two sides in one triangle and corresponding sides in the other are needed for a proportion. But ASA similarity would not be needed even if it made sense, because having two corresponding angles congruent already guarantees similarity.

GeoGebra Activities

22. See online appendix.   **23.** See online appendix.   **24.** See online appendix.

Review Problems

25. Construction. For example, start with the given base and construct the perpendicular bisector of the base. The vertex of the required triangle must be on that perpendicular bisector. Starting at the point where the perpendicular bisector intersects the base, mark on the perpendicular bisector a segment congruent to the given altitude. The endpoint of the segment not on the base is the vertex of the required isosceles triangle.   **26.** Construction. For example, construct an equilateral triangle with the given side, then construct the perpendicular from any vertex to the opposite side.   **27.** Answers vary. Students may suggest that angles of measure 45° be constructed with the endpoints of the hypotenuse as vertices of the 45° angles and the hypotenuse as one of the sides of the angles. Both angles need to be constructed on the same side of the hypotenuse.   **28.** Because vertical angles are congruent, referring to the figure we have $x = x_1$ and $y = y_1$. Since $x = y$, we get $x_1 = y_1$.   **29.** SASAS or ASASA

Chapter 12 Review

2. Parallelogram; $\triangle ADE \cong \triangle CBF$ by SAS, so $\angle DEA \cong \angle CFB$; $\angle DEA \cong \angle EAF$ (alternate interior angles between the parallels $\overline{DC}$ and $\overline{AB}$ and the transversal $\overline{AE}$), so $\angle EAF \cong \angle CFB$; and therefore $\overline{AE} \| FC$, $\overline{EC} \| \overline{AF}$ (parallel sides of the square); two pairs of parallel opposite sides implies a parallelogram.   **7.** Find point O, the intersection of the perpendicular bisector of $\overline{AB}$ and line ℓ. The required circle has center O and radius QA.

11. a. $\frac{48}{32} = \frac{24}{16} = \frac{3}{2}$, so the rectangles are similar.

12. The triangles are the same shape, but they cannot be congruent since they are not the same size. The student is confusing congruence and similarity. Examples of both congruence and similarity should be given.   **19. b.** Answers vary. $\overline{AD}$ and $\overline{BE}$ are diameters that bisect each other (at the center). Hence $ABDE$ is a rectangle and so $\angle ABD$ is a right angle.   **20.** No. The statement is true if, and only if, the diagonals bisect each other.

21. Congruent triangles have two corresponding angles that are congruent. This makes them similar by AA similarity.

22. a. $\triangle BCN \cong \triangle DEN$ by ASA because $BN = ND$ (given), $\angle CBN \cong \angle EDN$ (alternate interior angles created by the parallels $\overline{BC}$ and $\overline{AD}$) and transversal $\overline{BD}$, and the angles with vertex N are vertical angles.   **b.** From the congruence in part (a), it follows that $CN = EN$, and $AM = CM$ (given).

c. Because $\overline{MN}$ is a midsegment in $\triangle ACE$, $MN = \frac{1}{2}AE$.

Now $AE = AD - ED = AD - BC$ because $ED = BC$ (from the congruence in part (a)). Thus $AE = a - b$, and therefore $MN = \frac{1}{2}AE = \frac{1}{2}(a - b)$.   **23.** $\angle 1 \cong \angle 2, \angle 3 \cong \angle 4$ (given), $\overline{AC} \cong \overline{AC}$, (reflexive), $\triangle ABC \cong \triangle ADC$ by ASA. Therefore $\overline{BC} \cong \overline{DC}$ by CPCTC. $\overline{CE} \cong \overline{CE}$ (reflexive) and therefore $\triangle BCE \cong \triangle DCE$ by SAS.

Answers to Now Try This

1. a. $\angle A \cong \angle D, \angle B \cong \angle E, \angle C \cong \angle F, \overline{AB} \cong \overline{DE}, \overline{BC} \cong \overline{EF}$, $\overline{AC} \cong \overline{DF}$. **b.** $\triangle ABC \cong \triangle DEF, \triangle ACB \cong \triangle DFE$, $\triangle BAC \cong \triangle EDF, \triangle BCA \cong \triangle EFD, \triangle CAB \cong \triangle FDE, \triangle CBA \cong \triangle FED$. **2.** Construct a circle with center at P and any radius. Mark A and B as the points of intersection of the arc with ℓ. Now construct the perpendicular bisector of $\overline{AB}$. **4.** Answers vary for **(a)** and **(b)**, for example, the opposite angles are not supplementary. **5.** Yes. If $ABCD$ is a quadrilateral whose diagonals intersect at M, then congruent vertical angles with vertex at M are formed. Because the diagonals bisect each other, it follows from SAS that $\triangle AMD \cong \triangle CMB$. Hence, $\angle MAD \cong \angle MCB$ and therefore $\overline{BC}$ is parallel to $\overline{AD}$. In a similar way, we can show that $\overline{AB}$ is parallel to $\overline{DC}$ and hence $ABCD$ is a parallelogram. **6. a.** One way to accomplish the construction is to place the hypotenuse of the triangle on the given line and to place the ruler so that one of the legs of the triangle will be on the ruler. Now, keeping the ruler fixed, slide the triangle so that the side of the triangle on the ruler touches the ruler all the time. Slide the triangle on the ruler until the given point is on the hypotenuse. The line containing the hypotenuse is parallel to the given line. **b.** The angles formed by the hypotenuses and the ruler are congruent. Because they are corresponding angles, the hypotenuses are parallel. **7.** In Figure 12-50, if $PD = PE$ then by HL (Theorem 12-3), $\triangle APD \cong \triangle APE$ and hence $\angle PAD \cong \angle PAE$. **8.** Construct the diagonals of the square. Use the intersection of the diagonals as the center of the inscribed circle. The radius is the perpendicular distance from the center to any side. **9.** Using the result that the median to the hypotenuse in a right triangle is half as long as the hypotenuse (Example 9), we can prove that one of the angles in all such triangles is $60°$. Thus, all the triangles are similar by AA similarity.

Answer to the Preliminary Problem

The distance along Ocean Drive bordering the lots is $40\,\text{m} + 34\,\text{m} + 30\,\text{m} = 104\,\text{m}$. Let $x, y,$ and z be the ocean frontage for lots $A, B,$ and C respectively. Using Theorem 12-15 we can set up the following proportions:

Lot A: $\dfrac{104}{130} = \dfrac{40}{x}$ and $x = 50\,\text{m}$.

Lot B: $\dfrac{104}{130} = \dfrac{34}{y}$ and $y = 42.5\,\text{m}$.

Lot C: $\dfrac{104}{130} = \dfrac{30}{z}$ and $z = 37.5\,\text{m}$.

Therefore Lot A has the most ocean frontage and hence the highest selling price.

CHAPTER 13

Assessment 13-1A

1. a. 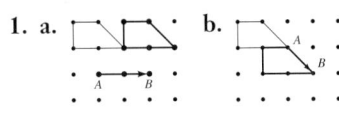 **b.**

2. a. Construction **b.** Construct the images B' and C' of B and C respectively. $\overline{B'C'}$ is the required image.

5. a. 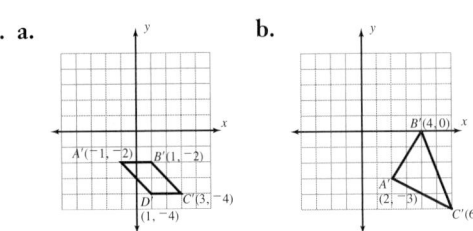 **b.**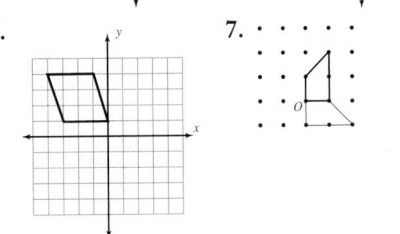

6. 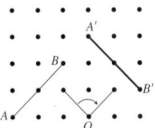 **7.**

10. Choose any two points P and Q on ℓ, and construct their images P' and Q'. $\overrightarrow{P'Q'}$ is the desired image. **11.** *Hint:* Reverse the rotation (to the counterclockwise direction) to locate $\overline{AB}$, that is, the preimage.

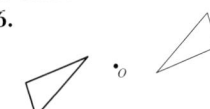

12. Answers vary, but H, I, N, O, S, X, or Z could appear in such rotational words. Examples include SOS. Variations could use M and W in rotational images, for example, MOW.
13. c. ℓ and ℓ' are parallel. If P and Q are any points on ℓ and P' and Q' their respective images, then from the definition of a translation $\overline{PP'}$ and $\overline{QQ'}$ are parallel and congruent to $\overline{AB}$. Hence, $\overline{PP'}$ and $\overline{QQ'}$ are parallel and congruent. Thus, $PP'Q'Q$ is a parallelogram and therefore $\ell' \parallel \ell$. **14.** *Hint:* An angle whose measure is $45°$ can be constructed by bisecting a right angle. An angle whose measure is $60°$ can be constructed by first constructing an equilateral triangle. These angles can be used to complete the construction.
16.

18. a. *Hint:* First rotate $\triangle ABC$ by angle α to obtain $\triangle A'B'C'$, and then rotate $\triangle A'B'C'$ by angle β to obtain $\triangle A''B''C''$. **c.** Yes, by rotation about O by angle $|\alpha - \beta|$ in the direction of the larger of α and β. **19. b.** The image of the point with coordinates (a, b) under a half-turn with the origin as center must be on a circle with center at $(0, 0)$ and passing through (a, b). It must also be on the line connecting $(0, 0)$ with (a, b). The equation of that line is $y = \dfrac{b}{a}x$. The only point that satisfies this equation and is at the same distance from the origin as (a, b) is $(^-a, ^-b)$. **21. a.** $B(h + a, k)$. **b.** Applying the Pythagorean Theorem in the triangle with hypotenuse $OA = a$ and legs of length h and k we get $h^2 + k^2 = a^2$. Then the product of the slopes of $\overline{OB}$ and $\overline{AC}$ is

$$\frac{k}{h + a} \cdot \frac{k}{h - a} = \frac{k^2}{h^2 - a^2} = \frac{k^2}{^-k^2} = ^-1.$$

c. There is a turn symmetry of $180°$ about the point of intersection of the two diagonals. **22. b.** Through B construct $\overrightarrow{BE}$ so that $\overrightarrow{BE} \parallel \overline{CD}, BE = CD,$ and $\overrightarrow{BE}$ points in the same direction as

$\overrightarrow{CD}$. Then $\overrightarrow{AE}$ is a slide arrow that corresponds to the required translation. **23. a.** Rotation by 90° or a multiple of 90° about the point of intersection of the diagonals. **b.** Rotation by 72° or a multiple of 72° about O, where O is the point of intersection of the perpendicular bisectors of the sides. **c.** Rotation by $\dfrac{360°}{n}$ and multiples of $\dfrac{360°}{n}$ about O, where O is the intersection of the perpendicular bisectors of the sides. **d.** Rotation about the center by any turn angle. **e.** No rotational symmetries **24. a.** *Hint:* Half-turn about the point of intersection of the diagonals. A rectangle has half-turn symmetry because the diagonals bisect each other. **b.** Same as (a) **25. a.** *Hint:* Find the image of the center and construct the circle with that image as the center and the same radius. **b.** The circles have a single point in common.

Assessment 13-1B

1. Reverse the translation so that the image completes a slide from X' to X (to its preimage). Then check by carrying out the given motion in the "forward" direction; that is, see if $\overline{AB}$ goes to $\overline{A'B'}$.
a. **b.**

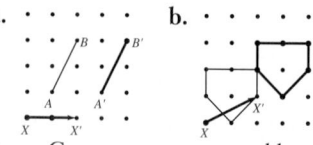

2. a. Construct as suggested by the following. Trace $\overline{B'C'}$ and the line containing the slide arrow on the tracing paper and label the trace of B' as B and the trace of C' as C. Mark on the original paper and on the tracing paper the initial point of the arrow by P and the head of the arrow by Q. Slide the tracing paper along the line $\overleftrightarrow{PQ}$ so that Q will fall on P. Trace $\overline{BC}$. The segment $\overline{BC}$ is the preimage of $\overline{B'C'}$ under the translation. **b.** *Hint:* Construct the images of B' and C' under the translation by slide arrow $\overrightarrow{QP}$.
5. a. **b.**

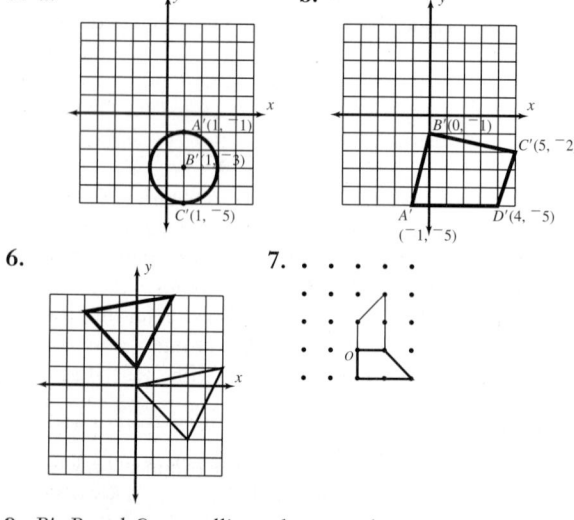

6. **7.**

9. P', P, and O are collinear because the measure of angle POP' must be 180°, and $OP = OP'$. **10.** Choose points P and Q on ℓ. Construct P' ($P' \neq P$) on $\overleftrightarrow{OP}$ such that $OP = OP'$. Similarly find Q'. $\overleftrightarrow{P'Q'}$ is the desired preimage. **11.** Locate $\overline{AB}$, the preimage, by completing a half turn through O.

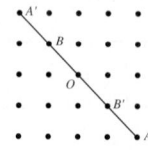

12. MOM does not have this property. There is no half-turn that will make MOM be the image of MOM. **13. a.** When the figure is creased and folded along the perpendicular through O to $\overline{PP'}$, the point P falls on P'. This shows that the perpendicular also bisects $\overline{PP'}$. Alternatively, by the definition of rotation, $PO = P'O$. This implies that O is equidistant from P and P', and hence, it is on the perpendicular bisector of $\overline{PP'}$. **b.** From (a), O is on the perpendicular bisector of $\overline{AA'}$ and $\overline{BB'}$ as well as $\overline{CC'}$. Consequently, O can be found by finding the point at which any two of the perpendicular bisectors intersect. $\angle AOA'$ is the angle of rotation which is 180°. **c.** The perpendicular bisectors of the segments $\overline{AA'}$, $\overline{BB'}$, and $\overline{CC'}$ are not concurrent. **14.** Construction method, vary. *Hint:* An angle whose measure is 30° can be constructed by first constructing an equilateral triangle and then bisecting one of its angles. **16.**

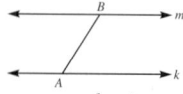

17. a. $\ell' \neq \ell$ and $\ell' \parallel \ell$ **b.** ℓ' and ℓ intersect at a 60° angle. **18. b.** The vertices A and B trace an identical path if, and only if, $OA = OB$; that is, if and only if, O is on the perpendicular bisector of $\overline{AB}$. Thus all points O for which two vertices trace an identical path are the points on the perpendicular bisectors of the sides of the triangle. **c.** Yes, the intersection of the perpendicular bisectors of the sides (center of the circumscribed circle) **21.** O must be the midpoint of the segments $\overline{AA'}$ and $\overline{BB'}$. A' must lie on the x-axis and have coordinates $(a, 0)$; B' must lie on the y-axis and have coordinates $(0, ^-b)$. **22. b.** A translation from A to C **23. b.** Turn symmetry about the intersection of perpendicular bisectors by 60° or a multiple of 60° in either direction **c.** Turn symmetry by 90° or a multiple of 90° about the intersection of the diagonals in either direction **e.** Half-turn about the center of the circle **25.** The circles have the same radius and only one point P in common. **26.** Translating the figure by $\overrightarrow{AB}$ or by $\overrightarrow{BA}$ results in the same figure.

Mathematical Connections 13-1

Reasoning

1. If the congruent segments are $\overline{AB}$ and $\overline{CD}$, find $\overline{C'D'}$, the image of $\overline{CD}$ under the translation from C to A. Then rotate $\overline{C'D'}$ about A by $\angle BAD'$ in an appropriate direction to make the image of D' be B. **2.** Answers vary. **a.** Apply a half-turn about any point on the line that is halfway between the given lines. Alternatively, the center can be determined by the midpoint of a segment whose endpoints are on the lines. **b.** If $k \parallel m$, A is any point on k and B is on m, then the image of k under the translation by $\overrightarrow{AB}$ is m.

3. $(2 - h, ^-k)$ One way to see why, is to notice that the y-coordinate of the image point is ^-k. Substituting $y = ^-k$ in the equation of the line through $(1, 0)$ and (h, k) we get $x = 2 - h$. **4. a.** A parallelogram with one diagonal; under a half-turn, the image of a line is parallel to the line. Thus, $\overline{AB} \parallel \overline{CD}$ and $\overline{AC} \parallel \overline{DB}$; therefore, $ABDC$ is a parallelogram.

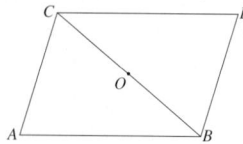

b. A parallelogram with an extra segment; the image of $\overline{AB}$ is $\overline{FE}$ and thus $\overline{AB} \parallel \overline{EF}$. Consequently, $\overline{BF} \parallel \overline{AE}$ and $ABFE$ is a parallelogram.

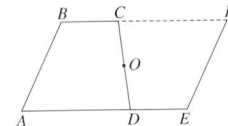

c. A square; because the image of A is C and the image of B is D, the image of $ABCD$ is $CDAB$. **5.** Since P is on ℓ, its image P' is on ℓ'. Rotation preserves angle measure. Because the image of $\overline{OP}$ is $\overline{OP'}$ and $\overline{OP}$ is perpendicular to ℓ, the image of ℓ must be perpendicular to $\overline{OP'}$. Since the line k is perpendicular to ℓ, by uniqueness of perpendicular to $\overline{OP'}$ at P', k must be the image of ℓ. **6. a.** *Hint:* Use the figure below for $\alpha = 90°$. Then $x = 90°$ and $y = 90°$. **b.** Because $OPQP'$ has two right angles we have $x + \alpha = 180°$. Also $x + y = 180°$, and hence $y = \alpha$.

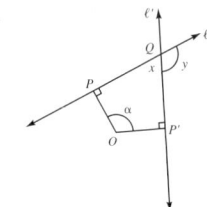

7. Rotate $\triangle CAF$ by $90°$ counterclockwise about A. The image of C is E, the image of F is B, and the image of A is A. Hence the image of $\overline{CF}$ is $\overline{EB}$. Because a rotation preserves distance $CF = EB$. From problem 6 we know that the angle between $\overline{CF}$ and its image equals the angle of rotation, which is $90°$. Thus, the segments are perpendicular. **8. a.** Rotate $\overline{BH}$ about O by $90°$ counterclockwise. The image of H is E since the angles at O are $90°$. The image of B is A because $\angle BOA$ is a right angle. Hence the image of $\overline{BH}$ is $\overline{EA}$. Consequently, the segments are congruent and by the same argument as in the answer to problem 7, they are perpendicular. **b.** We can create a coordinate system with $\overleftrightarrow{AD}$ as the x-axis, and $\overleftrightarrow{AB}$ as the y-axis and the origin at A. If BE is a unit then $A(0,0)$, $E(1,2)$ $B(0,2)$ and $H(2,1)$. Hence $m_{AE} = \dfrac{2-0}{1-0} = 2$, and $m_{BH} = \dfrac{1-2}{2-0} = \dfrac{^-1}{2}$. Since the product of the slopes is $^-1$, the segments are perpendicular.

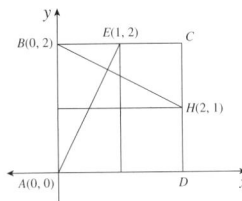

Open-Ended
9. Answers vary. **10.** Answers vary. **11.** Answers vary. If the rotation is by $30°$, there will be $\dfrac{360}{30}$, or 12 images.

Cooperative Learning
12. a. The path will look like the one shown in the following figure. Such a path traced by P on the circle is called a *cycloid*.

b. The path is not an arc of a circle. The perpendicular bisectors of all the chords (segments connecting two points on the arc)

do not intersect in a single point. **c.** The length of $\overline{AB}$ is the circumference of the circle.

Connecting Mathematics to the Classroom
13. Yes, the student is correct because the two described components could be constructed as components of the given translation. An analogy is the vertical and horizontal component of a vector. **14.** The result of a $180°$ rotation clockwise or counterclockwise is the same, so no direction is needed. **15.** This is true for circles but not for all figures. For example, the image of $\triangle ABC$ with a right angle at C, under half turn about C, cannot be obtained by a translation. **16.** Alicia needs to find the image of all the points on $\overrightarrow{AC}$, which means that she needs to find the image of $\overrightarrow{AC}$ under a half-turn in P. The image of a "good" point on $\overrightarrow{AC}$ must be on $\overrightarrow{AB}$ and on the image of $\overrightarrow{AC}$. Thus X is the intersection of $\overrightarrow{AB}$ with the image of $\overrightarrow{AC}$. Point Y can be found as the preimage of X under half-turn about P or by simply intersecting $\overleftrightarrow{XP}$ with $\overrightarrow{AC}$.

GeoGebra Activities
17. **(6)** Construction **(7) (a)** Congruent **(b)** Yes **(c)** No **(8) (a)** The segments are congruent. **(b)** Measurements **(c)** Yes **18.** 9–11 Constructions;
• The object and its rotation image have the same orientation.
• The object and image are congruent and the object and its image are the same figure.
19. An equilateral triangle has $120°$ rotational symmetry. Other triangles do not have this property.

Assessment 13-2A

1. *Construction. Hint:* Locate the images of vertices directly across (perpendicular to) ℓ on the geoboard. **2. b.** Perpendicular bisector of the segment or the line containing the segment **d.** Perpendicular bisectors of the sides and lines containing the diagonals **h.** If the kite is not a rhombus, the line containing the diagonal determined by vertices of the noncongruent angles is a line of symmetry. If a rhombus then each line containing a diagonal is a line of symmetry **i.** Perpendicular bisectors of parallel sides and three lines containing diameters determined by vertices on the circumscribed circle **4.** The image is a circle congruent to the original circle with a different center. **5. a.** The final images are congruent but in different locations, and hence not the same. **b.** A translation by a slide arrow from P to R is determined as follows: Let P be any point on ℓ and Q on m such that $\overrightarrow{PQ} \perp \ell$. Point R is on $\overrightarrow{PQ}$ such that $PQ = QR$. **6.** Constructions vary, but final image is a translation of the original. **7.** Answers vary. The line of reflection is the perpendicular bisector of $\overline{BB'}$. **8. a.** Examples include MOM, WOW, TOOT, and HAH. **b.** Examples include BOX, HIKE, CODE, etc. B, C, D, E, H, I, K (depending on the font), O, and X may be used. **c.** 1, 8, 11, 88, 101, 111, 181, 808, 818, 888, 1001, 1111, 1881 **10. a.** The images are the same. **b.** They commute. **11.** None of the images has a reverse orientation, so there are no reflections or glide reflections involved. Thus,

1 to 2 is a rotation.
1 to 3 is a rotation.
1 to 4 is a translation down.
1 to 5 is a rotation (with an exterior point as the center of rotation).
1 to 6 is a translation.
1 to 7 is a translation.

13. b. $(^-x, ^-y)$; the following figure:

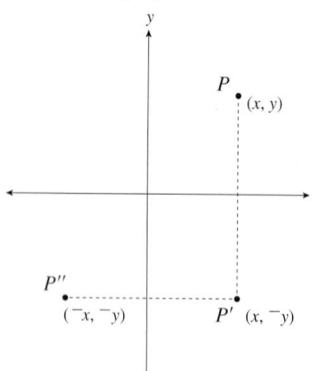

16. a. The line through P perpendicular to $\overleftrightarrow{O_1O_2}$ or the perpendicular bisector of QQ', where Q and Q' are the points of intersection other than P of $\overleftrightarrow{O_1O_2}$, with circle O_2 and circle O_1, respectively   **19. a.** Glide reflection determined by slide arrow $\overrightarrow{BA}$ and line ℓ.   **b.** Translation by a $\overrightarrow{AC}$, where A, B, and C are collinear and B is the midpoint of $\overline{AC}$.

Assessment 13-2B

1. Locate the images of the vertices directly across (perpendicular to) ℓ on the geoboard.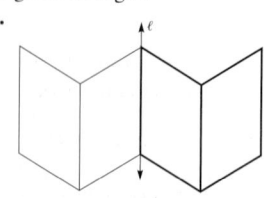

2. a. The perpendicular bisector of the chord connecting the endpoints of the arc   **b.** The line containing the ray   **c.** The lines bisecting the vertical angles formed by the perpendicular lines; and the lines themselves   **d.** Perpendicular bisectors of pairs of parallel sides; and diagonals if a square   **e.** If not equilateral, perpendicular bisector of the side that is not congruent to the other two; if equilateral, the perpendicular bisectors of each side   **f.** Perpendicular bisector of parallel sides if there is exactly one pair of parallel sides and they are not congruent   **g.** The lines containing the diagonals and lines bisecting parallel sides if a square   **h.** There will be n reflecting lines in all. If n is even, the lines contain the perpendicular bisectors of the parallel sides or the lines containing the diameters of the circumscribed circle containing the vertices. If n is odd, the lines are the ones containing the perpendicular bisectors of the sides.   **3.** The image is the original triangle.

4.

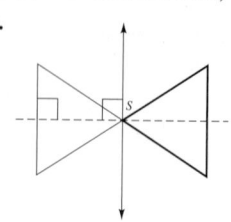

5. a. Constructions vary, but the final image is a rotation of this original.   **c.** Construction; a half-turn about O **6.** Construction

7. a.

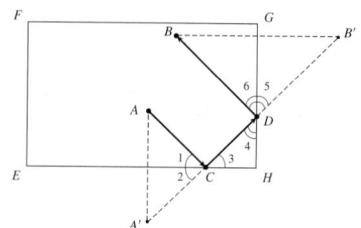

b. The answer in part (a) uses a line perpendicular to an altitude of the original triangle and contains the vertex of that altitude. Depending on the type of triangle, the "bow-tie" may be skewed, but the two "bases" are parallel.   **c.** There are three reflecting lines possible. Two (other than the one used in part (a) could be similarly found at the other vertices.   **8.** The reflecting line is shown below.

10. a. Answers may vary but no more than 3 are needed.   **b.** It cannot be a translation or rotation because the orientation is reversed. It cannot be a reflection because there is no single reflecting line; the perpendicular bisectors of $\overline{YY'}$ and $\overline{ZZ'}$ are not the same.   **11. a.** Answers vary. Part (a) could be moved to part (b) by a reflection in the line through the common point of the parts and containing a diagonal of the large square. Also a rotation about the center of the large square by 90° counterclockwise can be used.   **b.** Answers vary. A rotation of 90° clockwise about the center of the large square will work.   **13. a.** $(^-x, y)$ **b.** $(^-y, ^-x)$ **15. a.** $y = ^-3x$ **b.** $y = x$ **c.** $x = 0$ **17.** The diameter of the circle must be congruent to the side of the square. The line of reflection is the perpendicular bisector of the segment connecting the center of the circle with the point of intersection of the diagonals of the square.   **19. a.** Glide reflection determined by slide arrow $\overrightarrow{BA}$ and line $\overleftrightarrow{AB}$ **b.** Translation by a $\overrightarrow{AC}$, where A, B, and C are collinear and B is the midpoint of $\overline{AC}$.

Mathematical Connections 13-2

Reasoning

1. a. If $\overline{AB} \cong \overline{BC}$, then the perpendicular bisector of $\overline{AC}$ is the required line. The image of B is B, the image of A is C, and the image of C is A. Hence the image of $\triangle ABC$ is $\triangle CBA$.   **b.** Equilateral triangles; each side could be considered a base.   **c.** No   **d.** All lines containing diameters will satisfy this situation. Diameters divide a circle into two congruent semicircles.   **2.** Answers vary. Find A', the image of A under reflection in $\overline{EH}$, and B', the image of B under reflection in $\overline{GH}$. Mark the intersections of $\overline{A'B'}$ with $\overline{EH}$ and $\overline{GH}$, respectively, by C and D. The player should aim the ball at A toward the point C. The ball will hit C, bounce off D, then bounce off and hit B. To justify the answer, we need to show that the path A–C–D–B is such that $\angle 1 \cong \angle 3$ and $\angle 4 \cong \angle 6$. Notice that $\angle 1 \cong \angle 2$ and $\angle 6 \cong \angle 5$ because the image of an angle under reflection is congruent to the original angle. Also, $\angle 2 \cong \angle 3$ and $\angle 4 \cong \angle 5$, as each pair constitutes vertical angles. Consequently, $\angle 1 \cong \angle 3$ and $\angle 4 \cong \angle 6$.

3. a. By the midsegment theorem $\overline{MN}\parallel\overline{BC}$. Hence $\overline{MN}$ bisects the altitude of $\triangle ABC$ from A to $\overline{BC}$ and is perpendicular to $\overline{MN}$. **b.** Since $\overline{AA'}$ is perpendicular to $\overline{BC}$, $\overline{MD}$ is a $\overleftrightarrow{MD}$, its image is A'. Similar argument holds when B is reflected in $\overleftrightarrow{NE}$. **c.** Reflections are isometries that preserve angle measure. **d.** The sum of the measures of the interior angles in a triangle is 180°. The reason is that the angles at A' add up to a straight angle. **4.** Let M be the midpoint of $\overline{AB}$ and N the midpoint of $\overline{DC}$. The image of $\overline{AC}$ under reflection in $\overleftrightarrow{MN}$ is $\overline{BD}$ because the image of A is B and the image of C is D. **5.** The angle of incidence is the same as the angle of reflection. With the mirrors tilted 45°, the object's image reflects to 90° down the tube and then 90° to the eyepiece. The two reflections "counteract" each other, leaving the image upright. **6. a.** This can be checked with geometry utility or manually. **b.** Because the angles at Q and M are right angles, $\overline{MN}\parallel\overline{PQ}$. By the midsegment theorem, since M is the midpoint of $\overline{QP'}$, N is the midpoint of $\overline{PP'}$ (see figure below). **c.** Connect A with A' and B with B'. Mark the respective midpoints as F and H. Then $\overleftrightarrow{FH}$ is the line of reflection. Next construct A_1 the image of A in the line of reflection. $\overrightarrow{A_1A'}$ is the slide arrow.

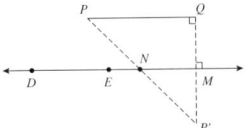

7. a. $X'P = X'P'$ and $Y'P = Y'P''$ because a reflection preserves distance. **b.** $XP = XP'$ and $YP = YP''$ because a reflection preserves distance. P', X, Y and P'' are collinear by construction. **c.** From part (b) it follows that the perimeter of $\triangle PXY$ equals $P'P''$. Similarly the perimeter of $\triangle X'PY'$ equals $P'X' + X'Y' + Y'P''$. Because the shortest path connecting P' with P'' is $\overline{P'P''}$, $P'P'' < P'X' + X'Y' + Y'P''$. Hence the perimeter of $\triangle PXY$ is less than the perimeter of $\triangle X'PY'$.

Open-Ended

8. Answers vary. **a.** Reflect P, the location of the ball in $\overline{AB}$. The intersection of $\overline{P'Q}$ with $\overline{AB}$ is the point at which the ball should be aimed.

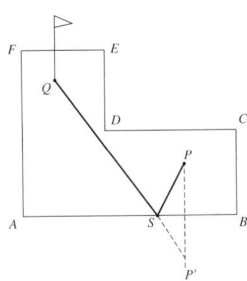

b. Reflect P in $\overline{CB}$ and Q in $\overline{AB}$. Connect the images P' and Q' by a straight line. The intersection of $\overline{P'Q'}$ with $\overline{BC}$ is the point at which the ball should be aimed. **9.** Answers vary. **10.** Answers vary.

Cooperative Learning

11. a. Constructions will vary. **b.** The experiment will work for rectangular tables in which the length is twice the width and for any position of B.

Connecting Mathematics to the Classroom

12. No, with a single point and its image, any of the described motions could work. **13.** Having only a segment and its image

is not enough to determine the transformation. **14.** Sammi is incorrect. To determine if the motions are equivalent, one has to consider the entire plane. The orientations are different and therefore the isometries cannot be equal. **15.** The figures drawn have additional reflection symmetries in lines perpendicular to the y-axis through A and through N, respectively. Figures that don't have such lines of symmetry will not have a half-turn symmetry. A scalene triangle is an example.

GeoGebra Activities

16. (5) (a) The measure of an angle and the measure of its reflected angle are equal. **(b)** The length of a segment and the length of its reflected segment are equal. **(c)** A polygon and its reflection are congruent. **(d)** The orientations of an object and its reflection are opposite. **(e)** The reflecting line contains the midpoint of each segment joining a point and its reflection. **17. (1) (i)** It might be called a "slide" reflection because it is a composition of a "slide" and a reflection. Glide is used instead of "slide." **(j)** They lie on the reflecting line. **18. a.** Construction **b.** The line desired, q, is such that the angle formed by lines m and n in that order is the same as the angle formed by the lines q and p in that order.

Review Problems

19. Depending on how they are drawn: 0, 1, and 8 **20.** $(^-a, ^-b)$
21. A rotation by any angle about the center of the circle will result in the same circle. **22.** Construct $\overline{BE}$ perpendicular to $\overline{AD}$, as shown. Next translate $\triangle ABE$ by the slide arrow from B to C. The image of $\triangle ABE$ is $\triangle DCE'$. The rectangle $BCE'E$ is the required rectangle.

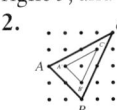

Assessment 13-3A

1. Answers vary. **a.** Slide the smaller triangle down 3 units (translation). Then complete a dilation with scale factor 2 using the top-right vertex as the center. **b.** Slide the smaller triangle right 5, and up 1. Then complete the dilation as in (a).
2.

(figure)

3. Answers vary. **a.** Translation taking B to B' followed by a dilation with center B' (and scale factor 2) **b.** Dilation with scale factor $\frac{1}{2}$ and center A followed by a half-turn with the midpoint of $\overline{C'B'}$ as center. **4.** $x = 6; y = 5.2$; scale factor $\frac{2}{5}$

7. Dilation with center O and scale factor $\frac{1}{r}$

8. a. Answers vary. A possible explanation follows:

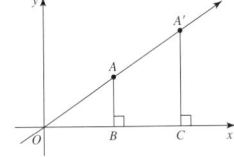

Let $A'(x', y')$ be the image of $A(x, y)$ under the dilation. From the definition of a dilation, we have $\frac{OA'}{OA} = r$. Since $\triangle OA'C \sim \triangle OAB$, $\frac{OC}{OB} = r$, which implies that $\frac{x'}{x} = r$ and hence $x' = rx$. Similarly, $y' = ry$.   **b.** Answers vary; the dilation with center at the origin and scale factor 2 followed by a half-turn about the origin.   **9.** Answers vary; a translation taking O_1 to O_2 followed by a dilation with center at O_2 and scale factor $\frac{3}{2}$.

10. The set of images of the set of integers on a number line is the set of points where coordinates are multiples of 3, that is, $\{\ldots, {}^-6, {}^-3, 0, 3, 6, 9, \ldots\}$.   **11.** $x = \frac{98}{15}$; $y = \frac{90}{7}$; scale factor $= \frac{7}{15}$ **12.** The enlargement of a $2'' \times 3''$ photograph to a $4'' \times 6''$ photograph can be achieved by a dilation with scale factor 2 and any center.

Assessment 13-3B

1. Answers vary.   **a.** Rotate the smaller triangle 90° counterclockwise with the lower-right vertex of the smaller triangle as the center of rotation. Then complete a dilation with scale factor 2 using the same point as center.   **b.** Assume the lower-left corner of the grid has coordinates $(0, 0)$. Translate the smaller triangle using $(x, y) \to (x - 5, y - 1)$. Next use a dilation with $(1, 2)$ as center and scale factor 2.

2.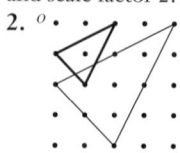

3. Answers vary.   **a.** Rotate the larger triangle 90° counterclockwise using center B; translate to take B to B'; then complete a dilation with scale factor $\frac{1}{2}$ and center B'.   **b.** Half-turn about C followed by a dilation with center C and scale factor $\frac{3}{2}$.

6. c. Answers depend on the order.   **7.** Dilation with center at the origin and scale factor $\frac{3}{4}$ **8.** Answers vary; a translation taking O_1 to O_2 followed by a dilation with center O_2 and scale factor 6.

9.

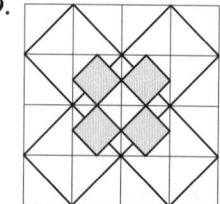

10. The scale factor $= \frac{A'B'}{AB} = \frac{3}{4}$. The center must be the intersection of $\overrightarrow{BB'}$ and $\overrightarrow{CC'}$ **12.** This is not possible because $\frac{4.5}{2} \neq \frac{6.5}{3}$.

Mathematical Connections 13-3

Reasoning

1. a. It does change unless the scale factor is 1. For example, consider the segment whose endpoints are $(0, 0)$ and $(1, 1)$, which

has length $\sqrt{2}$. Under the dilation with center at $(0, 0)$ and scale factor 2, the image of the segment is a segment whose endpoints are $(0, 0)$ and $(2, 2)$. That segment has length $2\sqrt{2}$.   **b.** It does not change. Under a dilation, the image of a triangle is a similar triangle and the corresponding angles of two similar triangles are congruent.   **c.** It does not change. Given two parallel lines, draw a transversal that intersects each line. Because the lines are parallel, the corresponding angles are congruent. From (b), the images of the angles will also be congruent and hence the image lines will be parallel.   **2.** The transformation can be achieved by a reflection followed by a dilation. Indeed $(x, y) \to (x, {}^-y)$; a reflection in the x-axis followed by $(x, {}^-y) \to (3x, {}^-3y)$; a dilation with center at the origin and scale factor 3, take (x, y) to $(3x, {}^-3y)$. Thus, the image of any figure will be similar to the figure.   **3. a.** A single dilation with center O and scale factor $\frac{1}{2} \cdot \frac{1}{3}$ or $\frac{1}{6}$. Let P be any point and P' its image under the first dilation and P'' the image of P' under the second dilation. Then $\frac{OP'}{OP} = \frac{1}{2}$ and $\frac{OP''}{OP'} = \frac{1}{3}$. Consequently, $\left(\frac{OP'}{OP}\right) \cdot \left(\frac{OP''}{OP'}\right) = \frac{1}{2} \cdot \frac{1}{3}$, or $\frac{OP''}{OP} = \frac{1}{6}$. Thus, P' can be obtained from P by a dilation with center O and scale factor $\frac{1}{2} \cdot \frac{1}{3}$ or $\frac{1}{6}$.   **b.** Dilation with center O and scale factor $r_1 r_2$ **4. a.** Yes. Suppose the dilation with center O has a scale factor r. The image of any point P on the circle with radius x is P' such that $\frac{OP'}{OP} = r$. Thus, $OP' = r(OP)$ or $OP' = rx$. This means that the image of every point on the circle is at the same distance rx from O and hence on a circle with radius rx.   **b.** Let C be the center of the circle with radius x and let P be any point on the circle. Let C' and P' be the respective images of C and P under a dilation with center O and scale factor r. Because the image of $\overline{CP}$ is $\overline{C'P'}$, it follows that $C'P' = rCP = rx$. This means that all the images of points on the circle are at the same distance rx from the point C'. Hence, the image of the circle is a circle with center C' and radius rx.   **5. a.** Answers vary. One possibility is to rotate $\triangle AED$ about A by 90° counterclockwise and get the image as $\triangle AE'D'$. Then find the image $AE'D''$ of $\triangle AE'D'$ under a half-turn in m, the midpoint of $\overline{AE}$. Finally apply the dilation with center A and scale factor $\frac{CA}{D''A}$

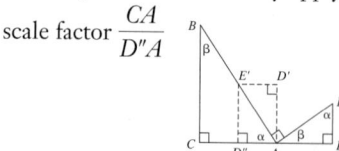

b. Answers vary. For example, dilation with center A and scale factor AB, followed by a rotation by 90° counterclockwise $\overline{AE}$ about A, followed by a half-turn about the midpoint of $\overline{AB}$.   **6.** Construct a square like the one shown. Construct $\overrightarrow{AD}$. The intersection of $\overrightarrow{AD}$ with $\overline{BC}$ is vertex H of the required square. Construct the other vertices by drawing lines parallel and perpendicular to $\overline{AC}$.

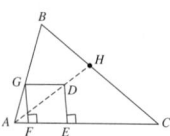

7. Let the center of the smaller circle be O and its radius r. The center of the second circle m and radius R. Translate the smaller circle by slide arrow $\overrightarrow{OM}$ and then apply the dilation with center m and scale factor $\dfrac{R}{r}$. The image of the smaller circle will be the larger one. **8.** The original triangle cannot be uniquely determined because the scale factor is not known. There are infinitely many possible preimages of $\triangle A'B'C'$. We can choose point A anywhere on $\overrightarrow{OA'}$, construct through A a line parallel to $\overrightarrow{A'B'}$, and mark B as the intersection of that parallel with $\overrightarrow{OB'}$. Similarly, point C is determined as the intersection of $\overrightarrow{OC'}$ with a line through B parallel to $\overrightarrow{B'C'}$. The dilation with center O and scale factor $\dfrac{OB'}{OB}$ will take $\triangle ABC$ onto $\triangle A'B'C'$.

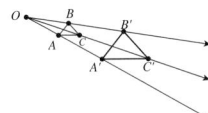

Open-Ended

9. Answers vary; for example, a 50% reduction in size when making a photocopy. **10.** Answers vary.

Cooperative Learning

11. a. If p is the perimeter of the figure and p' the perimeter of the image, then $p' = 3p$. **b.** $p' = rp$ **c.** Answers vary.

Connecting Mathematics to the Classroom

12. If two triangles are not similar, then they do not have the same shape and never would, even if the size is changed. It is not possible to transform one onto the other using isometries and a dilation.
13. The student is incorrect. In the original grid, a square might have area 1 sq. unit but in the image grid, that same square has area 4 sq. units. The student is correct that the image is a grid, but it is not the same size.

Review Problems

14. a. The translation determined by slide arrow from N to M **b.** A counterclockwise rotation of $75°$ about O **c.** A clockwise rotation of $45°$ about A **d.** A reflection in m and translation from B to A **e.** A second reflection in n **15. a.** $(4,3)$ reflects about m to $(4,1)$; $(4,1)$ reflects about n to $(2,1)$.
b. $(0,1) \rightarrow (0,3) \rightarrow (6,3)$ **c.** $(^-1,0) \rightarrow (^-1,4) \rightarrow (7,4)$
d. $(0,0) \rightarrow (0,4) \rightarrow (6,4)$ **16. a.** The angle itself
b. The square itself **17.**

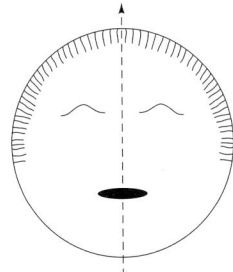

Assessment 13-4A

1. Answers vary.

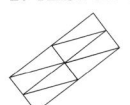

2. a. *Hint:* Perform half-turns about the midpoints of all sides.
b. Yes. Successive $180°$ turns of a quadrilateral about the midpoints of its sides will produce four congruent quadrilaterals around a common vertex, with each of the quadrilateral's angles being represented at each vertex.
3. Answers vary.

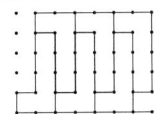

4. Answers vary. *Hint:* Consider figures like a pentagon formed by combining a square and an equilateral triangle. **5.** The shape will tessellate a plane as seen below:

7. a. The dual is another tessellation of squares (congruent to those given). **b.** The tessellation of equilateral triangles; it is illustrated in the statement of the problem.
8. Answers vary.

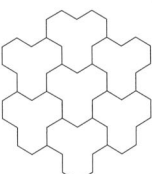

9. The hexagon will tessellate the plane as shown:

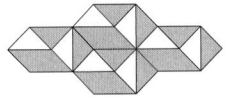

Assessment 13-4B

1. Answers vary.

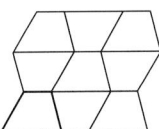

2. Answers vary. **a.**

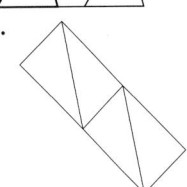

b. Yes; any triangle and one congruent to it can form a parallelogram and any parallelogram tessellates a plane.
3. Answers vary. Experimentation by cutting out shapes and moving them about is one way to learn about these types of problems.
a. 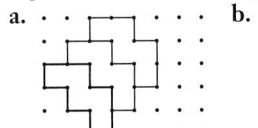 **b.**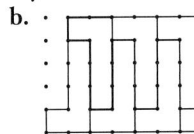

4. Answers vary.

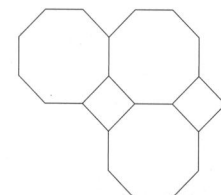

5. The bow-tie figure can tessellate the plane as shown:

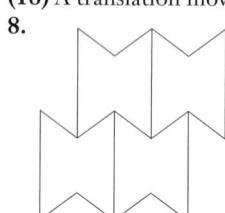

6. Answers vary.   **7.** **(17)** A translation moves *A* to *B*.
(18) A translation moves *C* to *D*; a rotation moves *C* to *E*.
8.

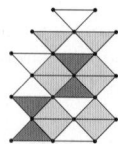

9. The arrow cannot tessellate the plane; the "head" fits the "tail," but there are gaps elsewhere.

Mathematical Connections 13-4

Reasoning

1. a. To tessellate the plane with $\triangle ABC$, we find $\triangle A'CB$—the image of $\triangle ABC$ under a half-turn about *M*, the midpoint of $\overline{BC}$. If *N* is the midpoint of $\overline{AB}$, then the image of *N* is *N'*. It can be shown that *N*, *M*, and *N'* are collinear and hence that $ANN'C$ is a parallelogram. Because the image of $\overline{NM}$ is $\overline{MN'}$, it follows that $NM = MN'$. Hence, $NM = \frac{1}{2}NN' = \frac{1}{2}AC$. Thus, $NM = \frac{1}{2}AC$. Also $\overline{NM} \parallel \overline{AC}$. **b.** The image of *ABCD* under a half-turn about *M* (the midpoint of *CD*) is the trapezoid *FEDC*. Because the trapezoids are congruent, *ABFE* is a parallelogram. If *N* is the midpoint of $\overline{AB}$, then its image *N'* is the midpoint of $\overline{EF}$. It can be shown that *N*, *M*, *N'* are collinear. Because *NBFN'* is a parallelogram ($\overline{BN}$ and $\overline{FN'}$ are congruent and parallel), $NN' = BF = a + b$. Since $NM = N'M$, $NM = \frac{a + b}{2}$.

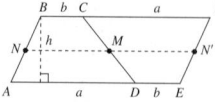

2. See page 799.   **3.** First tessellate the plane with regular hexagons and then divide each hexagon into congruent pentagons by three segments connecting the center of a hexagon to the midpoint of every other side. The segments inside one hexagon should not have points in common with segments inside a neighboring hexagon. Actually, one could draw the *Y*-shape segments in one hexagon and then apply a translation, taking the center of one hexagon to the center of a neighboring one.   **4. a.** Under a half-turn the image of a line is a parallel line.   **b.** Answers vary. For example, half-turns.

2. See page 799.

5. Answers vary. In the given design, the tessellation can be obtained by half-turns followed by translations.   **6.** Answers vary.
7. Answers vary. For example, a right rectangular prism will tesselate space, but a cylinder or a tetrahedron will not.   **8.** Answers vary. For example, we can cut out part of a square from the square

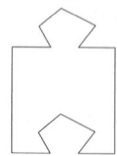

9. Answers vary. For example, an equilateral triangle using half-turns in a midpoint of a side and translation by a vector parallel to a side and congruent to the side.   **10.** Answers vary. For example,

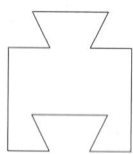

Cooperative Learning

11. Answers vary.   **12. a.** Two such figures can be put together to form a parallelogram. Because parallelograms tessellate the plane, the original figure tessellates the plane.   **b.** There are 12 such figures. Two figures are different if they are not similar.
c. Answers vary. For example the following figure is a rep-tile:

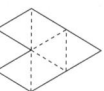

13. All will tessellate. Answers vary.   **14.** See page 800.

14. See page 800.

Connecting Mathematics to the Classroom

15. Isaiah is basically correct. The mortar joints may alter the appearance, but this is comparable to a rectangle tiling a plane.
16. Answers vary. Whether the image tessellates a plane depends on the kaleidoscope.   **17.** Each interior angle of a regular pentagon is 108°. If one puts three pentagons around a vertex, one gets 324°. What is left over is 36° and cannot be an angle of another pentagon.

Review Questions

18. a.   **b.**

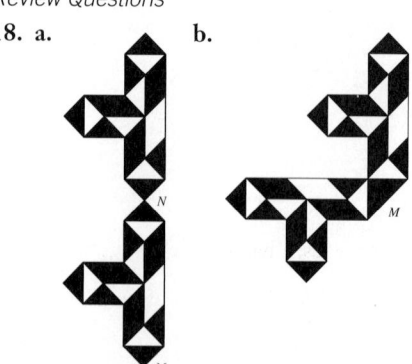

19. a. 90°, 180°, 270° rotation about center   **b.** 180° rotation about the center (half-turn about that center); reflections across vertical and horizontal lines through the center

20. 180° rotation about the center of the dark-colored square   **21. a.** It is a square.   **b.** The respective images are $(0, a), (a, 0), (0, \bar{a}), (\bar{a}, 0)$.   **22.** If O is on $\overleftrightarrow{AB}$, then $\overleftrightarrow{A'B'}$ is on $\overleftrightarrow{AB}$ and the segments are parallel. If O is not on $\overleftrightarrow{AB}$ as shown, then $OA' = rOA$, $OB' = rOB$, and $\angle O \cong \angle O$, making $\triangle OAB \sim \triangle OA'B'$. Thus, $\angle OA'B' \cong \angle OAB$. These are corresponding angles of $\overleftrightarrow{AB}$ and $\overleftrightarrow{A'B'}$ when cut by transversal $\overleftrightarrow{OA}$. Thus $\overleftrightarrow{AB} \parallel \overleftrightarrow{A'B'}$, implying $\overline{AB} \parallel \overline{A'B'}$.

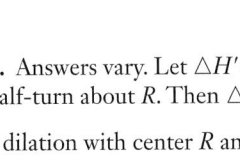

23. Such dilation does not exist because the image of a line is a parallel line (problem 22) but the lines intersect at $(0, 0)$.

Chapter 13 Review

1. a. 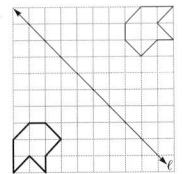   **b.** 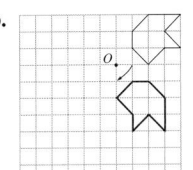   **c.**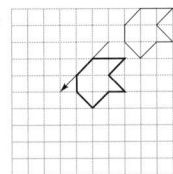

3. a. 4 reflections through dashed lines as shown; also rotations of 90°, 180°, and 270° about a center at the intersection of the dashed lines.

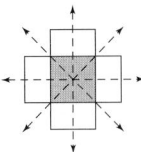

b. One reflection in the dashed line shown

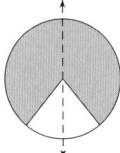

c. One reflection in the dashed line shown

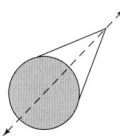

d. A half-turn about center O

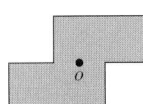

e. Two reflections in dashed lines; a half-turn about center O

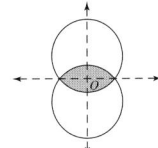

f. Two reflections in dashed lines; a half-turn about center O

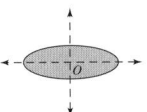

8. Answers vary. Let $\triangle H'O'R'$ be the image of $\triangle HOR$ under a half-turn about R. Then $\triangle SER$ is the image of $\triangle H'O'R'$ under a dilation with center R and scale factor $\frac{2}{3}$. Thus, $\triangle SER$ is the image of $\triangle HOR$ under the half-turn about R followed by the dilation described above.   **9.** Answers vary. Rotate $\triangle PIG$ 180° (half-turn) about the midpoint of $\overline{PT}$, then perform a dilation with scale factor 2 and center $P'(= T)$.   **11.** $(x, y) \rightarrow (x, y)$. It is the identity transformation with every point its own image.
13. b. A rotation about O by 60° counterclockwise.
c. i. and ii. A dilation with center O and scale factor 6.
17. An interior angle of a regular octagon has measure 135°. Two together have measure 270°; three together have measure more than 360°. Octagons cannot fit together at a point without overlapping or leaving a gap.   **19. a.** It will tessellate.   **b.** It will tessellate.   **c.** It will not tessellate.   **20. a.** $(\bar{5}, 0), (6, 0)$, or $\left(\frac{25}{6}, 0\right)$ **b.** $(\bar{2}, 4), (3, \bar{4})$, or $\left(\frac{\bar{7}}{6}, 4\right)$ **c.** Answers vary.
$(x, y) \rightarrow (x + a, y); (x, y) \rightarrow (x - a, y); (x, y) \rightarrow (x - 3, y - 4)$
d. The product of the slopes of respective diagonals is $\bar{1}$.
21. Find the image O' of the center of the circle O under the dilation with center A and scale factor $\frac{1}{2}$. Then construct the circle with center O' and radius $\frac{1}{2}$ of the radius of the circle.   **22.** As the path is traced, the length of $XY + YZ$ is the same as the length AC. We know this because of 60° angles formed as the ball bounces at Y making $\angle BYZ$ have a measure of 60°. (*Hint:* Remember congruent angles of incidence and angles of reflection.) Thus $AXYZ$ is a parallelogram making $\overline{AX} \cong \overline{ZY}$ and $\overline{XY} \cong \overline{AZ}$. Thus $XY + YZ = AX + AZ$.

Also $\triangle BYZ$ is equilateral so $\overline{BZ} \cong \overline{ZY}$. Thus $XY + YZ = AZ + ZB$ or AB. Hence $XY + YZ = 1$ m. Similarly $ZW + WP = BC = 1$ m, and $PQ + QX = AC = 1$ m. Thus the length of the path is $3(1 \text{ m}) = 3$ m. The perimeter of $\triangle ABC$ is also 3 m, so the ball travels a length equal to the perimeter.

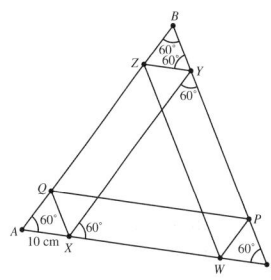

Answers to Now Try This

1. a. One way to do this is to connect A and M. Then construct point C so that $AC = MN$ and $NC = AM$. Then C is the required image of A.   **b.** Connect A and N.

Find point D so that $AD = MN$ and $DM = AN$. Then D is the image of A under the translation that takes N to M. **2.** Use repeatedly a translation defined by the slide arrow from the lower left corner of a square to the lower right corner. **4. a.** Answers will vary. **b.** A figure with point symmetry is its own image under a half-turn. **c.** ℓ is its own image ℓ'. **d.** Connect P to any point X on ℓ. Find the point X' on $\overrightarrow{XP}$ so that $\overline{XP} \cong \overline{X'P}$. Construct ℓ' through X' parallel to ℓ. ℓ' is the desired image. **6.** Find the line such that the figure folds onto the image. The fold line is the reflecting line. **7.** The accompanying figure suggests the reason why the image of $P(a, b)$ is $P'(b, a)$. The line $y = x$ bisects the right angle in the first quadrant formed by the x- and y-axes. Let P' be the reflection image of P in the line $y = x$. Hence $\triangle OPB \cong \triangle OP'B'$. Thus $OB = OB' = b$ and $PB = P'B' = a$. The coordinates of P' are (b, a).

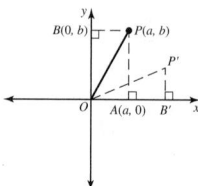

8. $MB = MB'$ and $BP = B'P$. Points A, P, and B' make a triangle. Therefore, they are not all on the same line and by the Triangle Inequality we know that $AP + PB'$ must be longer than AB'. A, M, and B' are collinear. Therefore, $AM + MB < AP + PB$.

Answer to the Preliminary Problem

Let H represent one house, X the roadside spot and T the other house. Let T' be the reflection of T in the road r as shown below. The intersection of $\overline{HT'}$ and r determines the point on the road at which X should be placed.

CHAPTER 14

Assessment 14-1A

7. Answers vary. **a.** Inches **b.** Inches **c.** Feet
8. a. 0.35; 350 **b.** 163; 1630 **c.** 0.035; 3.5 **d.** 0.1; 10
e. 200; 2000 **9. a.** Decidollar **b.** Centidollar **c.** Dekadollar
d. Hectodollar **e.** Kilodollar **11.** 6m; 5218 mm; 245 cm;
700 mm; 91 mm; 8 cm **14.** Answers vary. **a.** Approximately
7 cm **b.** Approximately 11 cm **23. b.** About Mach 4
25. b. The arc has to be longer because 8 cm is greater than
6 cm, and the radius is in the numerator of the fraction in the
computation.

Assessment 14-1B

4. Answers vary. **7.** Answers vary. **a.** Inches **b.** Inches
c. Feet **8. a.** 0.2; 200 **b.** 152; 1520 **c.** 0.09; 9 **d.** 110; 1100
14. Answers vary. **a.** 9 cm **b.** 17 cm **16.** Answers vary.
19. a. Answers vary. For example, add 4 squares to the right end
of the top row. **23. a.** About $9.5 \cdot 10^{12}$ km

25. b. It is shorter because the ratio of the radii is $3:4$, so the arc lengths must be in the same ratio.

Mathematical Connections 14-1

Reasoning

1. Answers vary. **a.** The metric system is a base-ten system and works "almost like" our money system. Conversions are much easier because of the decimal relationship between certain units of measure. **b.** Metric relationships are easier to remember. Also, because it is a base-ten system, conversions are easier. **c.** Original property descriptions and some building materials will probably not change. **2.** The outer curve has a greater radius and a correspondingly greater distance to run. To compensate for the extra distance, the runner in the outer lane is given an apparent head start. **3. a.** The square inscribed in the circle has perimeter $2r\sqrt{2}$. The square circumscribed about the circle has perimeter $4r$. **b.** $2.8 \approx 2\sqrt{2} < \pi < 4$ **4.** Answers vary. Possibly the centimeter measurement would be more accurate because the unit of measure is smaller.

Open-ended

5. a. Answers vary. For example: 1-1-1 and 2-2-1 work; 2-3-6 and 1-2-3 do not work. **b.** Using the Triangle Inequality, a triangle can be constructed if, and only if, $a + b > c$ and $a + c > b$ and $b + c > a$. **6.** Answers vary.

Cooperative Learning

7. a. Answers vary. **b.** Answers vary. **c.** Answers vary. Student should conjecture that the length of the outstretched arm is about the same as a person's height **d.** Answers vary. They should all agree with the conjecture in part (c). **8. a.** Answers vary. **b.** Regardless of the radius of each circle, the amount of wire needed is the same. **c.** Let the radius of each circle be r cm. The circumference of each circle is $2\pi r$. The number of circles is $\dfrac{60}{2r}$. (Why?) Hence the amount of wire, which is the total circumference of all the circles is $\left(\dfrac{60}{2r}\right)(2\pi r) = 60\pi$ cm. Because this number does not depend on the value of r, the amount of wire needed for the chain is the same regardless of the radius of each circle.

Connecting Mathematics to the Classroom

9. Though the question may seem confusing, some students may think that the circumference measures both the "outside" and "inside" of the curve instead of the curve itself. One typically discusses the length of the semicircle. **10.** The height is $3d$, where d is the diameter of a tennis ball. The perimeter of the can is πd or about $3.14d$, which is greater then $3d$. **11.** $\dfrac{22}{7}$ is an approximation. If more accuracy is needed, this approximation may not be accurate enough. **12.** The teacher should agree with her. This may not seem accurate but the height of the wire above Earth would be over 3 m.

Assessment 14-2A

4. a. 0.0588; 58,800 **b.** 0.000192; 1.92 **c.** 15,000; 1,500,000
d. 0.01; 10,000 **6. a.** 3 sq. units **b.** 3 sq. units **c.** 2 sq. units
d. 5 sq. units **12. c.** Answers vary. For example, the metric

system is easier because you only have to move the decimal point to convert units within the system.   **13. d.** Cannot tell because the height is unknown. The area is less than or equal to 60 cm².

19. a. 16π cm²   **20. e.** $1:1; 1:\left(\dfrac{\pi}{2}+1\right); 1:1; 1:(\pi-2):(4-\pi)$

31. a. 24 cm²   **b.** 28 cm²   **c.** 16 cm²   **d.** 12 cm²

32. $\dfrac{bh}{2}$ square units   **33. b.** Answers vary. The graph does not lie along a line but rather along a curve known as a hyperbola.

Assessment 14-2B

6. a. 6 sq. units   **b.** 4.5 sq. units   **9.** Answers vary. One possibility is to have vertex C on line ℓ parallel to $\overline{AB}$.

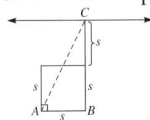

13. a. The shape of the rectangle becomes less like a square; that is, it becomes elongated.   **b.** The shape of the rectangle becomes more like a square. The maximum area for minimum perimeters for a rectangle is when you have a square.   **19.** The circle in the square has less wasted space.   **20. a.** $\dfrac{\pi r^2}{4}$ **b.** $\dfrac{\pi r^2}{8}$ **c.** $\dfrac{\pi r^2}{16}$

d. $1:1; 3:1; 7:1$ **21.** The area of the outside shaded portion is the same as the sum of the areas of the three inside shaded regions, 9π in.²   **23. b.** The area is 1.21 times as great or the area is increased by 21%.   **24.** $MA = 32$ units and $AT = 33$ units; area 1056 sq. units.

25.

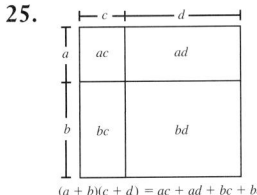

26. Although the pieces look like they should fit together, they do not really fit. To see this, assume the pieces do fit. We then obtain the following figure:

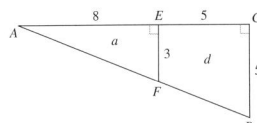

Since $\triangle AEF \sim \triangle ACB$, we have $\dfrac{8}{13} = \dfrac{3}{5}$, which is a contradiction. This implies that pieces like those in the figure cannot fit together to form a triangle. In order for the pieces to fit together, the measure of $\overline{EF}$ must satisfy $\dfrac{8}{13} = \dfrac{EF}{5}$; hence, $EF = \dfrac{40}{13} = 3\dfrac{1}{13}$.

Since $3\dfrac{1}{13}$ is close to 3, the discrepancy is so small that the pieces appear to fit.   **27.** The first is a better buy.   **29.** Triangle BDE has $\dfrac{1}{9}$ the area of triangle ABC.   **30. a.** $\dfrac{1}{3}$ **b.** $\dfrac{1}{5}$ **c.** $\dfrac{3}{5}$

d. $\dfrac{1}{3}$ **e.** $\dfrac{5}{9}$ **f.** $\dfrac{9}{8}$ **36. b.** Answers vary. The graph does not lie along a line but rather along a curve known as a hyperbola.

Mathematical Connections 14-2

Reasoning

1. Answers vary. The triangle may be drawn on graph paper and its area estimated. Students may look up Heron of Alexandria to find the formula $A = \sqrt{s(s-a)(s-b)(s-c)}$, where s is one-half of the perimeter of the triangle with sides a, b, and c. In this case, the area is $\sqrt{15(15-6)(15-11)(15-13)}$, or $\sqrt{1080}$, approximately 32.9 in.²   **2.** John is correct if they were thinking about area. John's garden has area 900 ft² and Al's garden has area 450 ft², so John has twice the area that Al has for a garden.
3. a. The area of the 10-in. pizza is 25π in.² The area of the 20-in. pizza is 100π in.² Because the area of the 20-in. pizza is 4 times as great, this pizza might cost 4 times as much, or $40. However, this is not the case because other factors are considered rather than just the area of the pizza.   **b.** If the price is based only on the area of pizza, then the ratio between prices should be $1:k^2$.   **4.** Rotate the shaded region 180° about point E. The area of the triangle is the same as the area of the parallelogram that is formed. The area of the parallelogram is $\left(\dfrac{h}{2}\right)b$.   **5.** After the rotations, a rectangle is formed. The area of the rectangle is length times width, which in the case of the parallelogram is the same as the base times the height.   **6.** The original area is lw. The new area is $(1.1 \cdot l)(0.9w) = 0.99\,(lw)$. Therefore, the area is decreased by a factor of 0.01 or 1%.   **7.** The new figure is a parallelogram with base $b_1 + b_2$ and height h, where b_1 and b_2 are the bases of the original trapezoid. The area of the parallelogram is $A = h(b_1 + b_2)$. Because this is twice the area of the original trapezoid, we divide by 2 yielding the formula for the area of the original trapezoid.

Open-ended

8. a. Answers vary depending on the size of the hand.
b. Answers vary. For example, many people will trace their hands on square-centimeter paper and then count the number of squares that are entirely contained in the outline. Next, they count the number of squares that are partially contained in the hand outline and multiply this number by $\dfrac{1}{2}$. The final estimate is the sum of the two numbers.   **9. a.** Answers vary; for example, a square that is 4 cm on a side and a rectangle that is 7 cm × 1 cm.
b. Answers vary. For example, a square that is 4 cm on a side and a rectangle that is 8 cm × 2 cm.   **10. a.** Construction
b. Construction   **c.** The length is approximately equal to half the circumference. The height is approximately equal to the radius r. Therefore $A = \dfrac{1}{2}Cr$. As the circle is cut into more and more sectors and put back together, the shape becomes more and more like a parallelogram.

Cooperative Learning

11. a. 5 sq. units   **b.** 12 units   **c. i.** 3 **ii.** 15 **iii.** 20
d. Answers vary depending on the chosen shape.   **e.** Answers depend on the chosen shape.   **12.** Answers vary.

Connecting Mathematics to the Classroom

13. Answers vary. For example, you could show her that with a given length of string you could enclose many different areas. For example, with a 16-in. string you could have a 4 in. × 4 in. square with area 16 in.². But you could also have a 1 in. × 7 in. rectangle with area 7 in.². If you formed a circle, you would have area over 20 in.². **14.** No. An angle is a union of two rays. The student probably means the area of the interior of an angle. However, because the area of the interior of an angle is infinite, it does not have a measurable area. **15.** We use square centimeters or square inches to indicate the area of a square 1 cm or 1 in. on a side. However, we cannot have a square with 1 *are* or 1 *hectare* on a side because *are* and *hectare* are not linear measures. The area of a square 10 m on a side is 1 a, and 1 ha is the area of a square 100 m on a side. **16.** The area of a garden does not depend on the perimeter of the garden. For example, a garden that is 2 m by 6 m has a perimeter of 16 m and an area of 12 m². A garden that is 4 m by 4 m also has a perimeter of 16 m but has an area of 16 m². **17.** If the parallelogram is also a rectangle, then what Jimmy says is correct, but if it is not a rectangle, the area becomes smaller as the marked angle becomes greater, as seen in the following figures. He needs to multiply the base times the height of the parallelogram to find the area.

18. a. Yes, because if $A = s^2$, then $s = \sqrt{A}$ and $p = 4s = 4\sqrt{A}$.
b. No, for example, if $A = 20$, then the sides could be 4 and 5 and $P = 18$; or the sides could be 2 and 10 and $P = 24$.
c. No, for example, if $A = 20$, then the side could be 5, the height 4 and $P = 4 \cdot 5 = 20$; or the side could be 10, and height 2, and $P = 4 \cdot 10 = 40$. **d.** Yes. $P = 2\pi\sqrt{\dfrac{A}{\pi}} = 2\sqrt{A\pi}$.

GeoGebra Activities

19. See Appendix answers.

Review Problems

20. $\left(8 + \dfrac{\pi}{2}\right)$ ft, or approximately 9.57 ft **21. a.** Approximately 6326 km **b.** 9937.5 km **22.** $(2\pi - 6)r$, or approximately $0.28r$, is the difference. **23. a.** 1:3 **b.** 12π cm **24.** $(12 + 2\pi)$ cm **25. a.** 200 **b.** $\dfrac{1}{6}$ **c.** 0.0025 **d.** About 1.42

Assessment 14-3A

3. Answers vary. **a.** Make a right triangle with legs of length 2 and 3, and then the hypotenuse has the required length. **b.** Make a right triangle with legs of length 1 and 2, and then the hypotenuse has the required length.
4. Answers vary, for example,

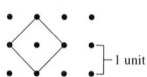

16. The area of the trapezoid is equal to the sum of the areas of the three triangles. Thus,

$$\frac{1}{2}(a + b)(a + b) = \frac{1}{2}ab + \frac{1}{2}ab + \frac{1}{2}c^2$$

$$\frac{1}{2}(a^2 + 2ab + b^2) = ab + \frac{1}{2}c^2$$

$$\frac{a^2}{2} + ab + \frac{b^2}{2} = ab + \frac{c^2}{2}.$$

Subtracting ab from both sides and multiplying both sides by 2, we have $a^2 + b^2 = c^2$. The angle formed by the two sides of length c has measure 90°. (Why?) **17.** That the small quadrilateral is a square that is found on pages 848–849. The area of the large square is equal to the sum of the area of the small square and the areas of the four right triangles. Therefore, $(a + b)^2 = c^2 + 4\left(\dfrac{ab}{2}\right)$. Thus, $a^2 + 2ab + b^2 = c^2 + 2ab$, which in turn implies that $c^2 = a^2 + b^2$.
18. b. The area of the largest triangle is equal to the sum of the areas of the other two triangles. **21.** $\dfrac{c\sqrt{3}}{4}$ using the 30°-60°-90° triangle relationship **27.** Both sprinkler systems cover the same percentage of the square field and it does not matter which system is used if the only selection criterion is the amount of land covered by the system. **28. a.** $90\sqrt{2}$ ft, or approximately 127 ft **b.** $\sqrt{10125} = 45\sqrt{5}$, or approximately 101 ft **c.** $\sqrt{10125} = 45\sqrt{5}$, or approximately 101 ft **30.** Any similar triangle will have sides of lengths $3k, 4k$, and $5k$, and $(3k)^2 + (4k)^2 = (5k)^2$.
31. The area is $\dfrac{1}{2}AC \cdot BC + \dfrac{1}{2}\left(\pi\left(\dfrac{1}{2}AC\right)^2 + \pi\left(\dfrac{1}{2}BC\right)^2\right) - \dfrac{1}{2}\pi\left(\left(\dfrac{1}{2}AB\right)^2\right) = \dfrac{1}{2}AC \cdot BC + \dfrac{1}{8}\pi(AC^2 + BC^2 - AB^2) = \dfrac{1}{2}AC \cdot BC$.

Assessment 14-3B

1. a. $\sqrt{8}$, or approximately 2.8 units **b.** $\sqrt{13}$, or approximately 3.6 units **3.** Answers vary. **a.** Make a right triangle with legs of length 1 and 3, and then the hypotenuse has the required length. **b.** Make a right triangle with legs of length 1 and 4, and then the hypotenuse has the required length. **4.** Answers vary. The perimeter of the figure shown is $13 + 2\sqrt{2} + \sqrt{5}$, which is certainly greater than 12.

5. a. **c.**

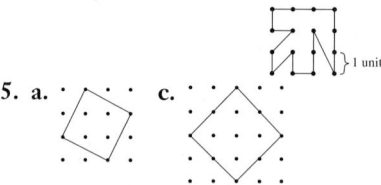

8. The longest piece of straight spaghetti will be $\sqrt{116} = 2\sqrt{29}$, or approximately 10.8 in. **10.** $\sqrt{10}$, or approximately 3.2 m
12. a. $\dfrac{s^2\sqrt{3}}{4}$ **b.** $\dfrac{s^2}{2}$ **13. a.** $4\sqrt{21}$ cm² **b.** $2\sqrt{24}$ cm²

or $4\sqrt{6}$ cm² **16.** $\triangle ACD \sim \triangle ABC$; $\dfrac{AC}{AB} = \dfrac{AD}{AC}$ implies

$\dfrac{b}{c} = \dfrac{x}{b}$, which implies $b^2 = cx$; $\triangle CBD \sim \triangle ABC$;

$\dfrac{AB}{CB} = \dfrac{CB}{DB}$ implies $\dfrac{c}{a} = \dfrac{a}{y}$, which implies

$a^2 = cx$; $a^2 + b^2 = cx + cy = c(x + y) = cc = c^2$.

17. It can be shown that the outside quadrilateral is a square of area c^2. The inside quadrilateral is a square with area $(b - a)^2$,

or $b^2 - 2ab + a^2$. Each of the four right triangles has area $\dfrac{ab}{2}$.

Therefore,

$$c^2 = (b^2 - 2ab + a^2) + 4\left(\dfrac{ab}{2}\right)$$
$$= b^2 - 2ab + a^2 + 2ab$$
$$= b^2 + a^2.$$

Therefore, $c^2 = a^2 + b^2$.

18. Yes; the areas are $\dfrac{\pi b^2}{8}, \dfrac{\pi a^2}{8}$, and $\dfrac{\pi c^2}{8}$ but $b^2 + a^2 = c^2$, so

$\dfrac{\pi b^2}{8} + \dfrac{\pi a^2}{8} = \dfrac{\pi c^2}{8}$.   **20.** The side lengths are $5, 7\sqrt{2}$,

and 5, so the triangle is isosceles.   **27. a.** $90\sqrt{2}$ ft, or approximately 127 ft   **b.** $\sqrt{10125}$, or approximately 101 ft
c. $\sqrt{10125} = 45\sqrt{5}$, or approximately 101 ft   **29.** Any similar triangle will have sides of lengths $5k, 12k$, and $13k$, and $(5k)^2 + (12k)^2 = (13k)^2$.   **30.** $OC = x\sqrt{2}$, so $OB = x\sqrt{2}$; the areas of the respective squares are x^2 and $2x^2$.   **32.** Draw altitudes $\overline{BE}$ and $\overline{DF}$ of triangles BCP and DCP, respectively. $\triangle ABE \cong \triangle CDF$ by AAS. Thus, $\overline{BE} \cong \overline{DF}$. Because $\overline{CP}$ is a base of $\triangle BCP$ and $\triangle DCP$, and because the heights are the same, the areas must be equal.

Mathematical Connections 14-3

Reasoning

1. Answers vary.   **a.** Let the length of the side of the square be s. Draw the diagonal of the square and make the new square have side lengths equal to the diagonal. Then the area is $\left(\sqrt{2}s\right)^2 = 2s^2$.   **b.** Make the lengths of the sides of the new

square $\dfrac{1}{2}$ the length of the diagonal, or $\left(\dfrac{\sqrt{2}s}{2}\right)$; then the area

of the new square is $\left(\dfrac{\sqrt{2}s}{2}\right)^2 = \dfrac{s^2}{2}$.   **2.** Draw a perpendicular

segment from Y to the segment representing 200 m. Draw segment $\overline{XY}$. A right triangle is formed with side lengths 100 m and 150 m. Using the Pythagorean theorem, we find that $XY = \sqrt{100^2 + 150^2} = \sqrt{32,500} \approx 180$ m.   **3.** If a and b represent the lengths of the legs and c represents the length of the hypotenuse in the right triangle, then $c^2 = a^2 + b^2$. We are given that $c^2 + a^2 + b^2 = 200$. Substituting, we have $c^2 + c^2 = 200$ and $2c^2 = 200$ and $c^2 = 100$. Solving for c, we have $c = 10$.
4. Answers vary. Because $13 = 2^2 + 3^2$, we can construct a right triangle with legs 2 cm and 3 cm.   **5. a.** Answers vary. For example, 6-8-10, 7-24-25, and 12-16-20.   **b.** Yes; we know that if a-b-c is a Pythagorean triple, then $a^2 + b^2 = c^2$. This implies that $4(a^2 + b^2) = 4c^2$, and that $(2a)^2 + (2b)^2 = (2c)^2$.
c. No. For example, consider adding 2 to 3-4-5, which results in 5-6-7, not a Pythagorean triple.

d. $a^2 + b^2 = (2uv)^2 + (u^2 - v^2)^2$
$\qquad = 4u^2v^2 + u^4 - 2u^2v^2 + v^4$
$\qquad = u^4 + 2u^2v^2 + v^4$
$\qquad = (u^2 + v^2)^2$
$\qquad = c^2$

Therefore a-b-c is a Pythagorean triple.   **6. a.** For the interior of the circle, the inequality should be $(x - h)^2 + (y - k)^2 < r^2$.
b. For the exterior of the circle, the inequality should be $(x - h)^2 + (y - k)^2 > r^2$.

Open-ended

7. Answers vary depending on the triangles drawn, but the Pythagorean theorem works only for the right triangles.
8. Answers vary.

Cooperative Learning

9. Answers vary depending on the triangles formed.

Connecting Mathematics to the Classroom

10. Yes, the same type of relationship does hold. For a proof and discussion, see G. Polya, *Mathematics and Plausible Reasoning*, Vol. 1 (Princeton, N.J.: Princeton University Press, 1954, pp. 15–17). Several examples were given in the Assessment sections.   **11.** This can't be the equation of a circle because of the $^{-}16$ value. The radius squared is always a positive number.
12. If x is the length of the missing leg, then $3^2 + x^2 = 5^2$. Therefore, $x^2 = 5^2 - 3^2$ and $x = \sqrt{5^2 - 3^2}$, not $\sqrt{3^2 + 5^2}$.
13. The points lie in the interior of the circle with center at $(0, 0)$ and having radius equal to 1.   **14.** What Sarah describes is what may happen, but is a misuse of measures for area. The clerk should have talked about square yards of carpet.   **15.** A square rod is the area of a square with sides one rod in length, where a rod is a unit of length equal to 16.5 feet.

GeoGebra Activities

16. See Appendix answers.   **17.** See Appendix answers.

Review Problems

18. 0.032 km^2, 3.2 m^2, 322 cm^2, 3020 mm^2 **19. a.** 33.25 cm^2
b. 30 cm^2 **c.** 32 m^2 **20. a.** 10 cm, 10π cm, 25π cm^2
b. 12 cm, 24π cm, $144\,\pi$ cm^2 **c.** $\sqrt{17}$ m, $2\sqrt{17}$ m, $2\pi\sqrt{17}$ m
d. 10 cm, 20 cm, 100π cm^2 **21.** $\dfrac{25}{\pi}$ m^2 **22.** Samuel got the

better buy by \$0.05 per yd.   **23.** 6 cm

Assessment 14-4A

1. a. No   **b.** Yes   **c.** No   **d.** Yes   **2. a.** 96 cm^2 **b.** 216π cm^2
c. 236 cm^2 **d.** 64π cm^2 **e.** 96π cm^2 **8.** 10.5π in.^{2}, or approximately 33 in.^{2} **16.** $118,300,000\pi$ km^2, or approximately

$370,000,000$ km^2 **18. a.** $\sqrt{\dfrac{10648}{6}}$, or approximately 42 cm

b. Approximately $42\sqrt{2} \approx 58.8$ cm

Assessment 14-4B

1. a. Yes   **b.** Yes   **c.** No   **2. a.** 90 cm^2 **b.** 1500π ft^2
c. $\left(32\pi + 16\pi\sqrt{5}\right)$ cm^2 **3.** 3.25 L, so buy 4 L
4. a. They have equal lateral surface areas.   **b.** The one with radius 6 m   **6. a.** The surface area is multiplied by 4.
b. The surface area is multiplied by 9.   **c.** The surface area is multiplied by k^2.   **7.** $45 + 6\sqrt{61}$, or approximately 92 ft^2

9. c. Yes; for example, place five cubes in the shape of a C. Then adding a cube to the center of the C would add no surface area.
11. 507 cm² **12. a.** The figure will be a right circular cone, $100\pi\left(1 + \sqrt{5}\right)$ cm². **b.** The figure will be a right circular cylinder, 1350π cm². **c.** The figure will be a truncated right cone with large end radius 25 cm and small end with radius 15 cm, surface area 2250 cm². **13. a.** $100\left(1 + \sqrt{5}\right)$ in.², or approximately 323.6 in.² **b.** $25\pi\left(1 + \sqrt{5}\right)$, or approximately 254.2 in.² **14.** Yes; SA $= 66\pi$ ft², or approximately 207 ft², so he will have enough paint. **16.** The surface area of Jupiter is 121 times as great as that of Earth.

Mathematical Connections 14-4

Reasoning

1. a. Estimates vary. **b.** The height of the can is $3d$ or $6r$, where d is the diameter of the ball. The circumference of the can is $2\pi r$. Therefore, the LSA is $(2\pi r)6r = 12\pi r^2$. The surface area of three balls is $3(4\pi r^2) = 12\pi r^2$. Therefore, the surface area of the three balls is the same as the lateral surface area of the can.
2. Doubling the radius **3.** No effect as 12 cm² were lost and 12 cm² were gained. **4.** $r = \ell$ because if $\pi r^2 = \pi r \ell$ then $r = \ell$. **5. a.** About 5720 mm² **b.** Answers vary depending on the ball.

Open-Ended

6. a. 2% **b.** Answers vary. **c.** Estimates vary depending on the size of the person and the desk. **d.** Answers vary.
7. Answers vary. For example, draw a net for a right rectangular prism that is 4 cm × 4 cm × 3 cm.

Cooperative Learning

8. a.

Number of Faces Painted	Number of Pieces
6	0
5	0
4	0
3	8
2	12
1	6
0	1

b.

Number of Faces Painted	Number of Pieces
6	0
5	0
4	0
3	8
2	24
1	24
0	8

c. There could never be more than three faces painted. The number of pieces with three faces painted is always 8. The number of

pieces with two faces painted is always a multiple of 12. The number of pieces with two faces painted is $12(n - 2)$. The number of pieces with one face painted is the number of pieces in the center square of each face. The length of the square is $(n - 2)$, so there are $(n - 2)^2$ pieces on each of the six faces. Therefore, there are $6(n - 2)^2$ pieces. The number of pieces with no faces painted is the number of interior cubes, which is a cube whose edge length is 2 less than the edge length of the original cube, or $(n - 2)^3$.
9. The peeling of an orange can be used to demonstrate the formula for the surface area of a sphere, $SA = 4\pi r^2$.

Connecting Mathematics to the Classroom

10. She would need 9 times as much cardboard. If each measurement is tripled, then the area of each face is increased by a factor of 9; that is, $A_1 = \ell w$ and $A_2 = (3\ell)(3w) = 9\ell w = 9A_1$. Because this is true for all faces, the surface area is multiplied by 9.
11. Jodi is incorrect. Because the surface area of a cone is $SA = \pi r^2 + \pi r \ell$, if she doubles the radius and halves the slant height she will have $SA = \pi(2r)^2 + \pi(2r)\dfrac{\ell}{2}$, which reduces to $SA = 4\pi r^2 + \pi r \ell$, which is not the same as the original surface area. **12.** Abi is correct. She is using the factored form of the formula for surface area of a cone. She should use the distributive property of multiplication over addition to confirm that the two forms are equivalent. **13.** Jan is incorrect. You could point out that if you double each side of a rectangle, you increase the area by a factor of 4. For example, $A_1 = \ell \cdot w$ and $A_2 = (2\ell)(2w) = 4(\ell \cdot w) = 4A_1$. You might also just look at a cube with side s. Then $SA = 6s^2$. If you double each side, then you have $SA = 6(2s)^2 = 6 \cdot 4s^2 = 4(6s^2)$, which is 4 times as great as the original surface area. **14.** She is not correct. For example, the surface area can be made as large as one wants by making a thinner and thinner pancake shape.

Review

15. a. 100,000 **b.** 1.3680 **c.** 500 **d.** 2,000,000 **e.** 1 **f.** 1,000,000 **16.** $10\sqrt{5}$ cm **17.** $20\sqrt{5}$ cm
18. a. 240 cm, 2400 cm² **b.** $\left(10\sqrt{2} + 30\right)$ cm, 75 cm²
19. Length of each side is 25 cm; diagonal is 30 cm long.
20. $\sqrt{3}$ units **21.** The cone and the flattened region obtained by slitting the cone along a slant height are shown.

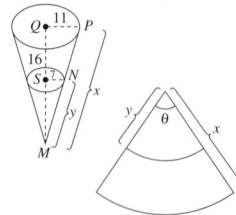

To construct the flattened ring we need to find $x, y,$ and θ.
Because $\triangle MQP \sim \triangle MSN$, we have $\dfrac{16 + MS}{MS} = \dfrac{11}{7}$. Hence, $MS = 28$ cm. In $\triangle MSN$, we have $28^2 + 7^2 = y^2$, or $y \approx 28.86$. In $\triangle PQM$: $x^2 = 11^2 + 44^2$, or $x \approx 45.35$ cm. To find θ, we roll the sector with radius y and central angle θ into the cone whose base is 7 cm and whose slant height is y. Hence, $2\pi y \cdot \dfrac{\theta}{360} = 2\pi \cdot 7$, or $\theta \approx \dfrac{7 \cdot 360}{28.86} \approx 87°19'$.
22. a. 0.15 **b.** 0.02 **c.** 1866.24 **d.** 2.54

Assessment 14-5A

14. The Great Pyramid has the greater volume. It is approximately 25.7 times as great.   **16.** It is multiplied by 2.197; 119.7% increase.   **17.** $66\frac{2}{3}$% occupied by the balls, so $33\frac{1}{3}$% occupied outside the balls.   **20. a.** Answers vary. For example, a square base with sides 5 m and a height of 12 m.   **b.** Infinitely many. Because $V = 100 = \dfrac{a^2 h}{3}$, where a is a side of the square base, then $300 = a^2 h$. This equation has infinitely many solutions.
28. Answers vary.   **a.** Draw any segment through the intersection point of the two diagonals that has endpoints on the parallel sides. There are infinitely many ways to do this.   **b.** Consider any plane through the intersection line that contains the point of intersection of the two diagonal planes.

Assessment 14-5B

5. a. 6000, 6, 6000   **b.** 0.2, 0.2, 200   **c.** 1200, 1.2, 1.2
d. 3000, 3, 3000   **e.** 0.202, 0.202, 202   **f.** 6.5, 6.5, 6500
9. a. 1000, 1, 1   **b.** 19,200, 19.2, 19.2   **c.** 50 cm, 10,000, 10
d. 40 cm, 12,000, 12   **10.** The larger melon is the better buy. The volume of the larger melon is 1.728 times the volume of the smaller melon, but the larger melon is 1.5 times as expensive.
14. No; it is only $\frac{1}{3}$ of the volume for $\frac{1}{2}$ the price.   **15.** $\dfrac{125}{18\pi}$, or approximately 2.2 cm   **19.** $\sqrt[3]{\frac{1}{2}}$, or approximately 0.8 times the original radius   **25. b.** 200,000 kg, or 200 t   **28.** Answers vary.
a. Draw any segment through the intersection point of the two diagonals that has endpoints on the parallel sides. There are infinitely many ways to do this.   **b.** Use the plane determined by 2 parallel diagonals in opposite faces.

Mathematical Connections 14-5

Reasoning

1. a. Doubling the height will only double the volume. Doubling the radius will multiply the volume by 4. This happens because the value of the radius is squared when volume is computed.
b. Yes. Doubling the height doubles the volume; doubling the radius multiplies the volume by 4.   **2.** Answers vary. For example, fill the shape with sand and dump the sand into a container that can be used to measure the sand.   **3.** The metric problem is much easier to work because the conversions are much easier. They just involve moving the decimal point. The relationships among length, volume, capacity, and mass are much easier than in the English system.   **4.** Answers vary. An assumption is that comparable-sized rooms hold a comparable amount of furniture.
5. a. We know that the height of each figure is $2r$ because the height of the sphere is $2r$. The volume of the cylinder is $\pi r^2 2r = 2\pi r^3$. The volume of the cone is $\frac{1}{3}\pi r^2 \cdot 2r = \frac{2}{3}\pi r^3$. The volume of the sphere is $\frac{4}{3}\pi r^3$.   **b.** Using a common denominator of 3, the three formulas are $\frac{6}{3}\pi r^3$, $\frac{2}{3}\pi r^3$, and $\frac{4}{3}\pi r^3$. The ratio is 6:2:4, which simplifies to 3:1:2.   **6. a.** The stack on the right has the greater surface area because the surface area on the left is only a part of that showing on the right. Each shifted coin adds additional surface area.   **b.** The volumes are the same using Cavalieri's principle.

Open-Ended

7. Answers vary, but should have volumes close to 24π or 75.4 in.^{3}; for example, a rectangular prism that is 6 in. long, 4 in. wide, and 3.14 in. high.   **8.** If the cookies are stood up so that the 6-cm diameter is toward the front of the box, then the minimum surface area is obtained by having two cookies across (12 cm), two cookies high (12 cm), and 12 cookies deep (12 cm).   **9.** Answers vary, but the volume must be 1000 cm^3. Some students will worry about shelf space while others will worry about what shape is easiest to hold.   **10.** Answers vary. For example, consider the same size cube of water and mercury. The mercury has the greater weight.

Cooperative Learning

11. a.–c. Answers vary.   **12.** Answers vary. There are people who dispute Bergmann's rule.

Connecting Mathematics to the Classroom

13. Consider a cube with side s cm. We need $s^3 = 6s^2$. This happens when $s = 6$. The volume is 216 cm^3 and its surface area is 216 cm^2.   **14.** The given box has a volume of 125 cm^3 and not 5 cm^3. The student most likely thinks 5 cm^3 means $(5 \text{ cm})^3$.
15. For each degree change in Celsius, there is a $\frac{9}{5}$ degree change in Fahrenheit. When a person's temperature is 2 degrees above normal Celsius, it is $\left(\frac{9}{5}\right)^2$ or 3.6 degrees above normal Fahrenheit. Therefore, being 2 degrees above normal Celsius could be more serious than being 2 degrees above normal Fahrenheit.   **16.** The volume of the original rectangular prism is given by $V_1 = \ell w h$. The volume of the new prism is $V_2 = (2\ell)(2w)(3h) = 2 \cdot 2 \cdot 3\,(\ell w h) = 12\ell w h = 12\,V_1$. Therefore, Andrea is correct.   **17.** Suppose the volume of each of the small containers is $\pi r^2 h$. Then the total volume is $2(\pi r^2 h)$ for two containers. The volume of the large container is $\pi (2r)^2 h = \pi 4r^2 h = 4\pi r^2 h$. Therefore, the volume of the large container is twice that of the two small containers combined.
18. Two figures are similar if they have the same shape, but may be different in size. Therefore, all cubes are similar and all spheres are similar.

Review Problems

19. a. $20 + 6\pi$ cm; $48 + 18\pi$ cm^2 **b.** 40π cm; 100π cm^2
20. a. 35   **b.** 0.16   **c.** 400,000   **d.** 0.00052   **21. a.** Yes
b. No   **22. a.** 2400π cm^2 **b.** $\left(6065 + 40\sqrt{5314}\right)$ cm^2
23. $6\sqrt{3}$ in.   **24.** The diagonal from exercise 23 is the hypotenuse of a right triangle containing the diagonal of a face as a leg.

Chapter 14 Review

1. a. $16\frac{2}{3}$ **b.** $\dfrac{947}{1760}$, or approximately 0.538   **4.** $\dfrac{1.5}{\pi}$ m
5. She is incorrect. A circle with radius 6 cm has circumference 12π cm. She may be confusing area and circumference.
7. The pieces of the trapezoid are rearranged to form a rectangle with width $\frac{h}{2}$ and length $(b_2 + b_1)$. The area is $A = \dfrac{h(b_1 + b_2)}{2}$, which is the area of the initial trapezoid.
8. Area($\triangle ABC$) < Area($\triangle ABD$) = Area($\triangle ABE$) < Area($\triangle ABF$). All the triangles have the same base, so the ordering is just by height and $\triangle ABD$ and $\triangle ABE$ have the same height.

15. a. $SA = \left(64 + 32\sqrt{13}\right)$ cm^2; $V = 128$ cm^3

b. $SA = 96\pi$ cm^2; $V = 96\pi$ cm^3

c. $SA = 100\pi$ m^2; $V = \dfrac{500\pi}{3}$ cm^3

d. $SA = 54\pi$ cm^2; $V = 54\pi$ cm^3

e. $SA = 304$ m^2; $V = 320$ cm^3 **17.** The graph on the right has 8 times the volume of the figure on the left, rather than double as it should be.

23. a. Answers vary.   **b.** Answers vary.

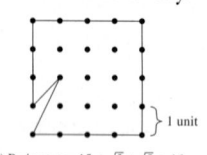

(a) Perimeter $= 15 + \sqrt{2} + \sqrt{5} > 16$

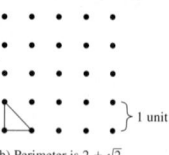

(b) Perimeter is $2 + \sqrt{2}$

c.

(c) Area $= 16$ units^2

Answers to Now Try This

4. a. $\dfrac{b}{2} \cdot \dfrac{h}{2} = \dfrac{bh}{4}$ **b.** The triangle was twice as large as the folded rectangle, so multiply by 2. Thus, the area of the triangle is $2 \cdot \dfrac{bh}{4} = \dfrac{1}{2}bh$.   **5. a.** You could build the triangle and then measure the angles to see whether there was a right angle. If the angle is a right angle, then the triangle is a right triangle. You could measure the three sides and use the Pythagorean theorem and its converse to see whether a right triangle is formed. **b.** If the three lengths of a right triangle are multiplied by a fixed number, then the resulting lengths determine a right triangle; for example, if the right triangle lengths are 3-4-5, and the fixed number is 5, then 15-20-25 is a right triangle.   **c.** If the three lengths of a right triangle are multiplied by a fixed number, then the resulting numbers determine a right triangle.
6. It makes no difference in the distance formula if $(x_1 - x_2)$ and $(y_1 - y_2)$ are used instead of $(x_2 - x_1)$ and $(y_2 - y_1)$, respectively. Because both quantities in the formula are squared, the result is the same whether the difference is positive or negative.
7. a. Move the decimal point twice as many places as in a linear conversion and in the same direction. For example, the area of a square that is 1 m on each side is 1 m^2; 1 m $= 10$ dm; and 1 m$^2 = 100$ dm^2.   **b.** Move the decimal point 3 times as many places as in a linear conversion and in the same direction; 1 m$^3 = 1000$ dm^3.

Answer to the Preliminary Problem

It would require 1.5 ~~acres~~ $\cdot \dfrac{4840 \text{ yd}^2}{1 \text{ acre}} \cdot 16 \text{ in.} \cdot \dfrac{1 \text{ yd}}{36 \text{ in.}} \cdot \dfrac{1 \text{ load}}{10 \text{ yd}^3} \approx 323$ loads. Thus, it would require 323 loads.

Index

Glossary of Symbols

Symbol	Meaning
$=$	is equal to
a_n	nth term of a sequence
a^n	a to the nth power
S_n	sum of the first n terms of a sequence
$p \vee q$	p or q
$\sim p$	negation of p or not p
$p \wedge q$	p and q
$p \equiv q$	p is logically equivalent to q
$p \rightarrow q$	p implies q
$p \leftrightarrow q$	p implies q and q implies p; or p if, and only if, q
4_{five}	4 base five
$E2T_{\text{twelve}}$	base ten meaning $11 \cdot 12^2 + 2 \cdot 12^1 + 10 \cdot 1$
$\{a, b, c\}$	set containing elements a, b, and c
$\{x \mid \ldots\}$	set builder notaion
$\in$	is an element of
$\notin$	is not an element of
$\varnothing$ or $\{\ \}$	empty set
$\subset$	is a proper subset of
$\subseteq$	is a subset of
$A \cup B$	union of sets A and B
$A \cap B$	intersection of sets A and B
U	universal set
$\overline{A}$	the complement of set A
$B - A$	set difference or complement of A relative to B
$A \sim B$	A is equivalent to B
$A \times B$	Cartesian product of sets A and B
$n(S)$	cardinal number of set S
$>$	is greater than
$<$	is less than
$\geq$	is greater than or equal to
$\leq$	is less than or equal to
$f(x)$	f of x, or output of f at x
(a, b)	ordered pair
$g \circ f$	composition of f with g
$(g \circ f)(x)$	$g(f(x))$

Symbol	Meaning
^-a	opposite of a or the additive inverse of a
$\lvert a \rvert$	absolute value of a
$a \mid b$	a divides b
$a \nmid b$	a does not divide b
$\sqrt{}$	principal square root
GCD	greater common divisor
LCM	least common multiple
$\dfrac{a}{b}$	fraction "a over b" or ratio, $a \div b$ with $b \neq 0$
$5\dfrac{3}{4}$	mixed number $5 + \dfrac{3}{4}$
a^0	$1, a \neq 0$
a^{-n}	$\dfrac{1}{a^n}, a \neq 0$
$\doteq$	is approximately equal
$\approx$	is approximately equal
$0.\overline{18}$	repeating decimal $0.18181818\ldots$
$\sqrt[n]{}$	the nth root
$a^{\frac{1}{n}}$	a to the $\dfrac{1}{n}$ power; or nth root of a
$a^{\frac{m}{n}}$	$\sqrt[n]{a^m}$
$\%$	percent
$P(E)$	probability of an event E
$P(\overline{A})$	probability of the complement of A
$n!$	n factorial which is equal to $n(n-1)(n-2) \cdot \ldots \cdot 3 \cdot 2 \cdot 1$ for $n \geq 1$
$0!$	zero factorial which equals 1
$_nP_r$	number of permutations of n objects chosen r at a time
$_nC_r$	number of combinations of n objects chosen r at a time
$P(B \mid A)$	conditional probability that event B occurs given that event A has occurred
E	mathematical expectation
$\overline{x}$	the arithmetic mean
MAD	mean absolute deviation